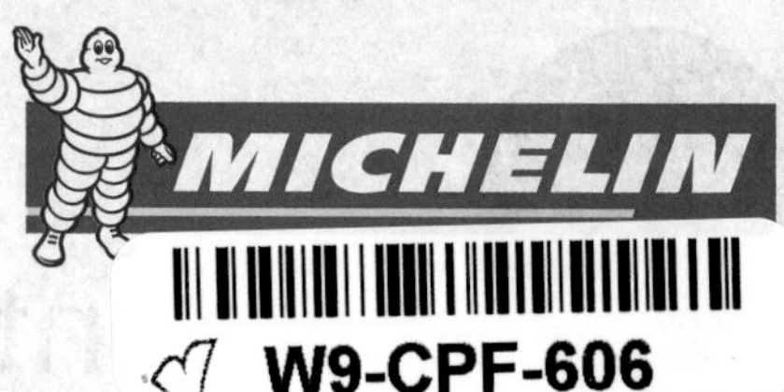

Great Britain & Ireland

the MICHELIN guide

2015

HOTELS & RESTAURANTS

Contents

MICHELIN

Dear reader

We are delighted to present the 2015 edition of the Michelin guide to Great Britain and Ireland – a guide to the best places to eat and stay in England, Wales, Scotland, Northern Ireland and the Republic of Ireland.

The guide caters for every type of visitor, from business traveller to families on holiday, and lists the best establishments across all categories of comfort and price – from lively bistros and intimate townhouses to celebrated restaurants and luxurious hotels. So, whether you're visiting for work or pleasure, you'll find something that's right for you.

All of the establishments in the guide have been selected by our team of famous Michelin inspectors, who are the eyes and ears of our readers. They always pay their own bills and their anonymity is key to ensuring that they receive the same treatment as any other guest.

Each year, they search for new establishments to add – and only the best make it through! The 'best of the best' are then recognised with awards.

Our famous one ✿, two ✿✿ and three ✿✿✿ stars identify establishments serving the highest quality cuisine – taking into account the quality of ingredients, the mastery of techniques and flavours, the levels of creativity and, of course, consistency.

Consult the MICHELIN guide at: **www.ViaMichelin.com**
and write to us at: **themichelinguide-gbirl@uk.michelin.com**

As you flick through this year's Michelin guide you'll notice more colour and greater clarity: we wanted the 2015 edition to be more enjoyable to read and to make your search for establishments easier and faster! This is because our commitment, for over a century, has been to help you make the best choices when it comes to your travels.

Stars are not our only awards; look out too for the Bib Gourmands and Bib Hotels, which highlight establishments offering good food and good accommodation at moderate prices.

Michelin Travel Partner is committed to remaining at the forefront of the culinary world and to meeting the needs of our readers. Please don't hesitate to contact us – we'd love to hear your opinions on the establishments listed within these pages, as well as those you feel could be of interest for future editions.

We hope you enjoy your dining and hotel experiences – happy travelling with the 2015 edition of the Michelin guide!

Food Collection - Photononstop

A Culinary History

Britain hasn't always been known for its vibrant culinary scene – indeed, the food of the 'masses' started out dull and dreary, with meals driven by need rather than desire. So how did we get to where we are today? Well, it took quite a few centuries…

There's no place like Rome

The Romans kick-started things with their prolific road building, opening up the country and allowing goods to be transported more easily, country-wide. The Vikings brought with them new smoking and drying techniques for preserving fish, and the Saxons, who were excellent farmers, cultivated a wide variety of herbs – used not only for flavouring but to bulk-out stews. They also made butter, cheese and mead (a drink made from fermented honey); with the lack of sugar to sweeten things, honey was very important, and bees were kept in every village. The Normans introduced saffron, nutmeg, pepper, ginger and sugar – ingredients used in the likes of plum pudding, hot cross buns and Christmas cake. They also encouraged the drinking

Manchester House

of wine. Meat was a luxury reserved for those with money, so the poor were left with bread, cheese and eggs as their staple diet.

Emilio Ereza/easyFotostock/Age Fotostock

The Middle Ages saw the wealthy eating beef, mutton, pork and venison, along with a great variety of birds, including blackbirds, greenfinches, herons and swans; and when the church decreed that meat couldn't be eaten on certain days, they turned to fish. Breakfast was eaten in private; lunch and dinner, in the great hall; and on special occasions they held huge feasts and banquets with lavish spectacles, musicians and entertainment. The poor, meanwhile, were stuck with their simple, monotonous fare: for lunch, cheese and coarse, dark bread made from barley or rye; and in the evening, pottage, a type of stew made by boiling grain, vegetables and, on occasion, some rabbit – if they could catch one.

Sugar and spice...

Things really began to take off in Tudor times, with spices being brought back from the Far East, and sugar from the Caribbean. Potatoes and turkeys were introduced from north America; the latter were bred almost exclusively in Norfolk, then driven to London in flocks of 500 or more and fattened up for several days before being sold. The poor baked bread, salted meat, preserved vegetables, made pickles and conserves, and even brewed their own beer. As the water was so dirty, the children drank milk, the adults drank ale, cider or perry, and the rich drank wine.

Joanna Wnuk/Zoonar GmbH RM/Age Fotostock

Little changed until the rise of the British Empire, when new drinks such as tea, coffee and chocolate appeared, and coffee houses started to spring up – places where professionals could meet to read the newspaper and 'talk shop'. More herbs and spices were brought back, this time from India, and exotic fruits such as bananas and pineapples came onto the scene. Despite improvements in farming, the poor continued to eat bread, butter, cheese, potatoes and bacon; butcher's meat remained a luxury.

Import-ant times

Advancements continued to pick up pace in Victorian times. The advent of the railways and steamships made it possible to import cheap grain from North America, and refrigeration units allowed meat to be brought in from Argentina and Australia. The first fish and chip shops opened in the 1860s and the first convenience food in tins and jars went on sale. The price of sugar also began to drop and sweets such as peanut brittle, liquorice allsorts and chocolate bars came into being.

In the early 20C, the cost of food fell dramatically: in 1914 it accounted for up to 60% of a working class family's income and by 1937, just 35%. Then, as things were beginning to look up, the war intervened and staple food items such as meat, sugar, butter, eggs and tea were rationed until long after the war had ended.

The late 20C saw a surge in technological and scientific advancements, and the creation of affordable fridges, freezers and microwave ovens meant that food could be stored for longer and cooked more easily. In an increasingly time-pressured world, convenience and time-saving became key, increasing the popularity of the 'ready meal' and takeaway outlets.

Pierre Lapin/Cephas/Photononstop

As immigration increased, so too did the number of restaurants serving cuisine from different nations. What started as a handful of Indian and Chinese restaurants, has now moved on in the 21C to cover everything from Thai to Turkish, Jamaican to Japanese.

Not only has the range of dining establishments increased but, with the opening up of European borders and the ease of travel and transport, many supermarkets have also started to stock a range of foreign products, from pierogi to paneer.

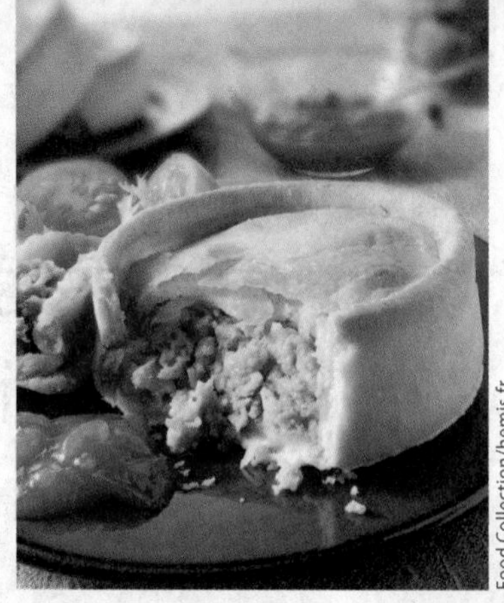

Food Collection/hemis.fr

The British Aisles

Supermarkets may now offer an endless choice of products but at the same time, an increased interest in health and wellbeing has sparked a trend for using seasonal ingredients from small, local producers – with a focus on reducing food miles. With increasing concerns about the origins of produce and the methods used in mass-production, many people are now turning back to the traditional 'farmers' market' or opting for 'organic' alternatives, where the consumer can trace the product back to its source or be assured of a natural, ethical or sustainable production method.

This can be seen in a true British institution – the pub. Take the traditional Sunday roast, one of the country's favourite meals; some chewy meat and microwaved veg won't cut it anymore – consumers now want to see top quality seasonal ingredients on their plate, sourced from the nearby farmer or the local allotment, and freshly prepared in the kitchen. And chefs are rising to the challenge: exploring new ways of using British ingredients, and reviving and reinventing traditional regional recipes.

In the past Britain may have lagged behind its European neighbours, due, in part, to its having a largely industrial economy. But what is in no doubt today, is that it's certainly making up for lost time. It may not have such a clear culinary identity as say, France or Italy, but it now offers greater choice and diversity by providing chefs with the freedom and confidence to take inspiration from wherever they wish and bring together flavours from across the globe.

The MICHELIN guide's commitments

Whether they are in Japan, the USA, China or Europe, our inspectors apply the same criteria to judge the quality of each and every hotel and restaurant that they visit. The Michelin guide commands a worldwide reputation thanks to the commitments we make to our readers – and we reiterate these below:

Anonymous inspections

Our inspectors make regular and anonymous visits to hotels and restaurants to gauge the quality of products and services offered to an ordinary customer. They settle their own bill and may then introduce themselves and ask for more information about the establishment. Our readers' comments are also a valuable source of information, which we can follow up with a visit of our own.

Independence

To remain totally objective for our readers, the selection is made with complete independence. Entry into the guide is free. All decisions are discussed with the Editor and our highest awards are considered at a European level.

Experienced in quality!

Selection and choice

The guide offers a selection of the best hotels and restaurants in every category of comfort and price. This is only possible because all the inspectors rigorously apply the same methods.

Annual updates

All the practical information, classifications and awards are revised and updated every year to give the most reliable information possible.

Consistency

The criteria for the classifications are the same in every country covered by the MICHELIN guide.

THE SOLE INTENTION OF MICHELIN IS TO MAKE YOUR TRAVELS SAFE AND ENJOYABLE

How to use this guide

LOCATING THE TOWN

Locate the town on the regional map at the begining of the guide (map number and coordinates).

Related Michelin publications: road map and tourist guide which cover the area.

HOTELS

From 🏨🏨🏨🏨🏨 to 🏨, ⌂.
In red: the most pleasant.

RESTAURANTS AND PUBS

From XXXXX to X, 🍺.
In red: the most pleasant.

STARS

✿✿✿ Exceptional cuisine.
✿✿ Excellent cooking.
✿ Very good cooking.

GOOD FOOD & ACCOMMODATION AT MODERATE PRICES

☺ Bib Gourmand.
🏨 Bib Hotel.

NEW ESTABLISHMENT IN THE GUIDE

CAMBRIDGE
Cambs – Pop. 117 717 – See regional map n°**12**A
▶London 55 mi – Coventry 88 mi – Ipswich 54
Michelin road map 504-U27 – Michelin Green G

Hotel Gloria
Whitehouse lane, Huntington Rd, CB3 OL
Northwest: 1,5 m by A1307 – ✆ (01223) 27
52 rm – 🚹£136 🚻£168/255 – ☕£7.50
Rest The Melrose – Menu £16 (lunch)
Built as a private house in 1852, now wit
porary rooms include state of the ar
and terrace.

XXX ✿ **Alexander House** (Johns)
Midsummer Common, CB4 1HA – ✆
– www.alexanderhouse.com – Clo
1 week spring, Sunday and Mond
Menu £30/50 (dinner only)
A river Cam idyll. Chic conservat
with blissful views over the rive
➜ Salad of smoked eel, pig's
and pistachios and asparagu
bois and mint.

XX ☺ **The Roasted Pepper**
35 Chesterton Rd, CB4 3AX –
– www.roastedpepper.co.
Menu £25 (dinner only) (b
Personally run Victorian t
dishes with mild Asian in

ENGLAND

at Histon
North: 3 mi on B104 – ✉ Ca

🏨 **Blue House** Ⓝ
44 High St, CB3 7HV
–Closed 2 weeks Ch
22 rm – 🚹£38 🚻
Red-brick 18C liste
overlooks meado
preserves. Imma

CANTERBURY
Kent – Pop. 47 123 (i
▶London 59 mi – B
Michelin Road ma

🏨 **Felix Ha**
Conifer D
✆ (087

ster 74 mi – Norwich 61 mi
AT BRITAIN

Townplan: Zd

w.hotelgloria.com

5/35
nd stylish public areas. The contem-
Sleek restaurant overlooks garden

Townplan: Ya

9 245
s Christmas, 2 weeks August,

room with smart first floor bar and terrace

apple purée. Braised turbot with peanuts
ni of apricot, Strawberry sorbet, fraises des

Townplan: Yc

351872
Christmas-New Year and Sunday
ential)
with smartly clad tables. Classic French and Italian
erved at reasonable prices.

t
262164 – www.bluehousefarm.com
w Year

e on a working farm... with beautiful blue windows; house
rden room for breakfast, including home-made bread and
ns.

) – See regional map n°9D2
6 mi – Dover 15 mi – Maidstone 28 mi – Margate 17 mi
– Michelin Green Guide GREAT BRITAIN

Townplan: Xc

BG, East: 0,75 m off Portsmouth Rd (A325)
– www.felixhall.com
£210 – £6.50
ing essential) (dinner only) £19/28
rved wooden staircase leads to the bedrooms; some are
ture, others are bright and modern. 19C restau-

nplan: Ze

LOCATING THE ESTABLISHMENT

Locate the establishment on the town plan within the guide's pages (coordinates & establishment letter).

PRICES

DESCRIPTION OF THE ESTABLISHMENT

FACILITIES AND SERVICES

See next pages.

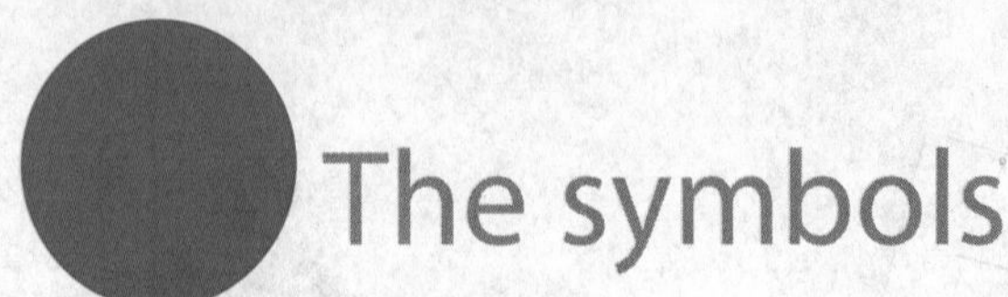

The symbols

CATEGORIES OF COMFORT

Within each category, establishments are listed in order of preference.

...	Hotels, classified by their comfort, from 5 to 1
	Other accommodation (guesthouses, farmhouses and private homes)
XXXXX ... X	Restaurants, classified by their comfort, from 5 to 1
	Pubs serving good food
without rest	Hotel with no restaurant
with rm	Restaurant with rooms

AWARDS

THE BEST CUISINE

- Exceptional cuisine, worth a special journey
- Excellent cooking, worth a detour
- Very good cooking in its category

GOOD FOOD AND ACCOMMODATION AT MODERATE PRICES

Bib Gourmand
Good cooking at moderate prices: less than £28 / €40 for a starter, main course and dessert

Bib Hotel
Good accommodation at moderate prices: under £90 / €115 for a room for 2 people, including breakfast

IN RED: THE MOST PLEASANT!

- Particularly pleasant accommodation
- Particularly pleasant restaurants and pubs

OTHER SPECIAL FEATURES

- Peaceful establishment
- Great view
- Particularly interesting wine list
- Notable cocktail list
- Vegetarian menu
- Restaurant offering lower priced pre and/or post theatre menus.
- Open for breakfast
- Small plates

SMOKING

In Great Britain and the Republic of Ireland the law prohibits smoking in all pubs, restaurants and hotel public areas.

New establishment in the guide

FACILITIES & SERVICES

30 rm	Number of rooms
	Garden or park · Terrace
	Open-air / indoor swimming pool
Spa	Sauna · Wellness centre
	Tennis · Exercise room
18	Golf course and number of holes
	Fishing available to hotel guests (charge may be made)
A/C	Air conditioning (in all or part of the establishment)
	Wi-fi access
	Lift (elevator) · Wheelchair access
	Special facilities for children
	Private dining rooms · Equipped conference rooms
P P	Car park · Enclosed car park · Garage
	No dogs allowed
	Credit cards not accepted
	Postal address
	Nearest Underground station (in London)

PRICES

HOTELS

Many hotels offer a special rate for a stay of two or more nights which comprises dinner, room and breakfast, usually for a minimum of two people. Please enquire with the hotel for rates.

£50/90 €90/170	Lowest / highest price for a single room
£100/120 €120/280	Lowest / highest price for a double room
£100/120 €120/280	Bed & breakfast rate
£5 €12	Breakfast price where not included in rate

Prices are given in £ sterling, except for the Republic of Ireland where euros are quoted.

All accommodation prices include both service and V.A.T. All restaurant prices include V.A.T. Service is also included when an **s** appears after the prices.

RESTAURANTS

Menu £13/28 Menu €25/45	Fixed price menu. Lowest / highest price
Carte £20/35 Carte €35/70	À la carte menu. Lowest / highest price
s	Service included

Town plan key

- Hotels
- Restaurants

SIGHTS

	Place of interest
	Interesting place of worship

ROADS

M 1	Motorway
	Numbered junctions: complete, limited
	Dual carriageway with motorway characteristics
	Main traffic artery
A 2	Primary route (GB) and National route (IRL)
	One-way street • Unsuitable for traffic or street subject to restrictions
	Pedestrian street • Tramway
Piccadilly P	Shopping street • Car park • Park and Ride
	Gateway • Street passing under arch • Tunnel
15'5	Low headroom (16'6" max.) on major through routes
	Station and railway
	Funicular • Cable-car
B	Lever bridge • Car ferry

VARIOUS SIGNS

	Tourist Information Centre
	Church/Place of worship • Mosque • Synagogue
	Communications tower or mast • Ruins
	Garden, park, wood • Cemetery
	Stadium • Racecourse • Golf course
	Golf course (with restrictions for visitors) • Skating rink
	Outdoor or indoor swimming pool
	View • Panorama
	Monument • Fountain • Hospital • Covered market
	Pleasure boat harbour • Lighthouse
	Airport • Underground station • Coach station
	Ferry services: passengers and cars
	Main post office
	Public buildings located by letter:
C H J	County Council Offices • Town Hall • Law Courts
M T U	Museum • Theatre • University, College
POL.	Police (in large towns police headquarters)

LONDON

BRENT WEMBLEY	Borough • Area
	Borough boundary
	Congestion Zone • Charge applies Monday-Friday 07.00-18.00
	Underground station

2015... *The news!*

Stars...

ENGLAND

Helmsley / Harome	Star Inn
Kenilworth	Cross at Kenilworth
Port Isaac	Outlaw's Fish Kitchen
Sparkwell	Treby Arms

➜ LONDON

Camden/ Bloomsbury	Kitchen Table at Bubbledogs
City of London	City Social
City of Westminster/ Mayfair	Fera at Claridge's
City of Westminster/ Mayfair	Gymkhana
City of Westminster/ Soho	Barrafina
Hackney/ Shoreditch	Clove Club

SCOTLAND

Eriska (Isle of)	Isle of Eriska
Skye (Isle of)/ Colbost	Three Chimneys & The House Over-By

WALES

Machynlleth	Ynyshir Hall
Monmouth / Whitebrook	Crown at Whitebrook

All of the starred establishments 2015
are at the end of the guide, on page 1044.

... and Bib Gourmand

ENGLAND	
Brighton	64°
Cirencester	Made by Bob
Clyst Hydon	Five Bells Inn
Derby	Ibérico World Tapas
Gerrards Cross	Three Oaks
Maidenhead	Crown
Mells	Talbot Inn
St Ives / Halsetown	Halsetown Inn
Tavistock	Cornish Arms
York	Le Langhe
→ LONDON	
Bromley/ Petts Wood	Indian Essence
Camden/ Bloomsbury	Barnyard
City of Westminster/ Soho	Palomar
City of Westminster/ Soho	Polpetto
Hackney/ Dalston	Rotorino
Islington/ Barnsbury	Roots at N1
Islington/ Islington	Yipin China
Wandsworth/ Putney	Bibo
Wandsworth/ Southfields	Earl Spencer
SCOTLAND	
Edinburgh	Passorn
Glasgow	The Gannet
Glasgow	Ox and Finch
NORTHERN IRELAND	
Belfast	Bar + Grill at James Street South
Belfast	Deanes at Queens
Lisbane	Old Schoolhouse Inn
REPUBLIC OF IRELAND	
Dublin	Etto

Starred establishments 2015

The colour corresponds to the establishment with the most stars in this location.

London This location has at least one 3 star restaurant ✱✱✱

Dublin This location has at least one 2 star restaurant ✱✱

Edinburgh This location has at least one 1 star restaurant ✱

All of the starred establishments 2015 are at the end of the guide, on page 1044.

SHETLAND ISLANDS
ORKNEY ISLANDS
Nairn
SCOTLAND
Auchterarder
Peat Inn
Elie
Balloch
Edinburgh
Leith
Summerhouse
Ambleside
Harome
Cartmel
Pateley Bridge
Oldstead
Ilkley
South Dalton
Langho
ENGLAND
Birkenhead
Sheffield
Chester
Baslow
Llandrillo
Nottingham
Morston
Hunstanton
Machynlleth
Montgomery
Hambleton
Birmingham
Ludlow
Kenilworth
Titley
Winchcombe
WALES
Eldersfield
Upper Slaughter
Cambridge
Llanddewi Skirrid
Cheltenham
Murcott
Woburn
Whitebrook
Great Milton
Malmesbury
Castle Combe
Marlow
Sprigg's Alley
London
Bristol
Little Bedwyn
Chew Magna
Colerne
Shinfield
Seasalter
Bath
Ripley
East Chisenbury
Bray
Biddenden
Bagshot
Knowstone
Winchester
Cranbrook
Petersfield
Bodiam
Chagford
Dorchester
Beaulieu
Royal Tunbridge Wells
Horsham
Torquay
Cuckfield
Lower Beeding

Bib Gourmand 2015

• Places with at least one Bib Gourmand establishment.

All of the Bib Gourmand establishments 2015 are at the end of the guide, on page 1046

SCOTLAND
Glasgow
Edinburgh
Peebles
Newcastle-upon-Tyne
North Shields
Durham
Hurworth-on-Tees
Masham
Thornton
York
Drighlington
Ramsbottom
Ripponden
Bury
ENGLAND
Chester
Nottingham
Derby
Stathern
Gedney Dyke
Thorpe Market
Ingham
Kibworth Beauchamp
Wymondham
Stamford
WALES
Bruntingthorpe
Keyston
Stanton
East Haddon
Belbroughton
Bury St. Edmunds
Bourton on the Hill
Aldeburgh
Brecon
Tewkesbury
Cheltenham
Hitchin
Cirencester
Wootton
Kelvedon
Upper South Wraxall
Britwell Salome
Hunsdon
Oxford
Long Ashton
Tetbury
London
Maidenhead
Wrington
Bristol
Cookham
GerrardsCross
Ramsgate
Wells
Mells
Preston Candover
Bruton
Longstock
West Hoathly
Clyst Hydon
Donhead-St-Andrew
Romsey
Droxford
Brighton
Hastings and St Leonards
Rockbeare
Christchurch

PLACE WITH AT LEAST...

- ● one hotel or a restaurant
- ✿ one starred establishment
- 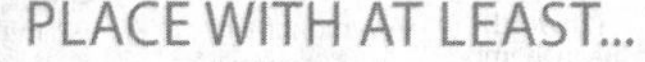 one Bib Gourmand restaurant
- XX one particularly pleasant restaurant or pub
- ⌂ one particularly pleasant hotel or guesthouse

Regional maps

Maps showing listed towns

Great Britain & Ireland in 39 maps

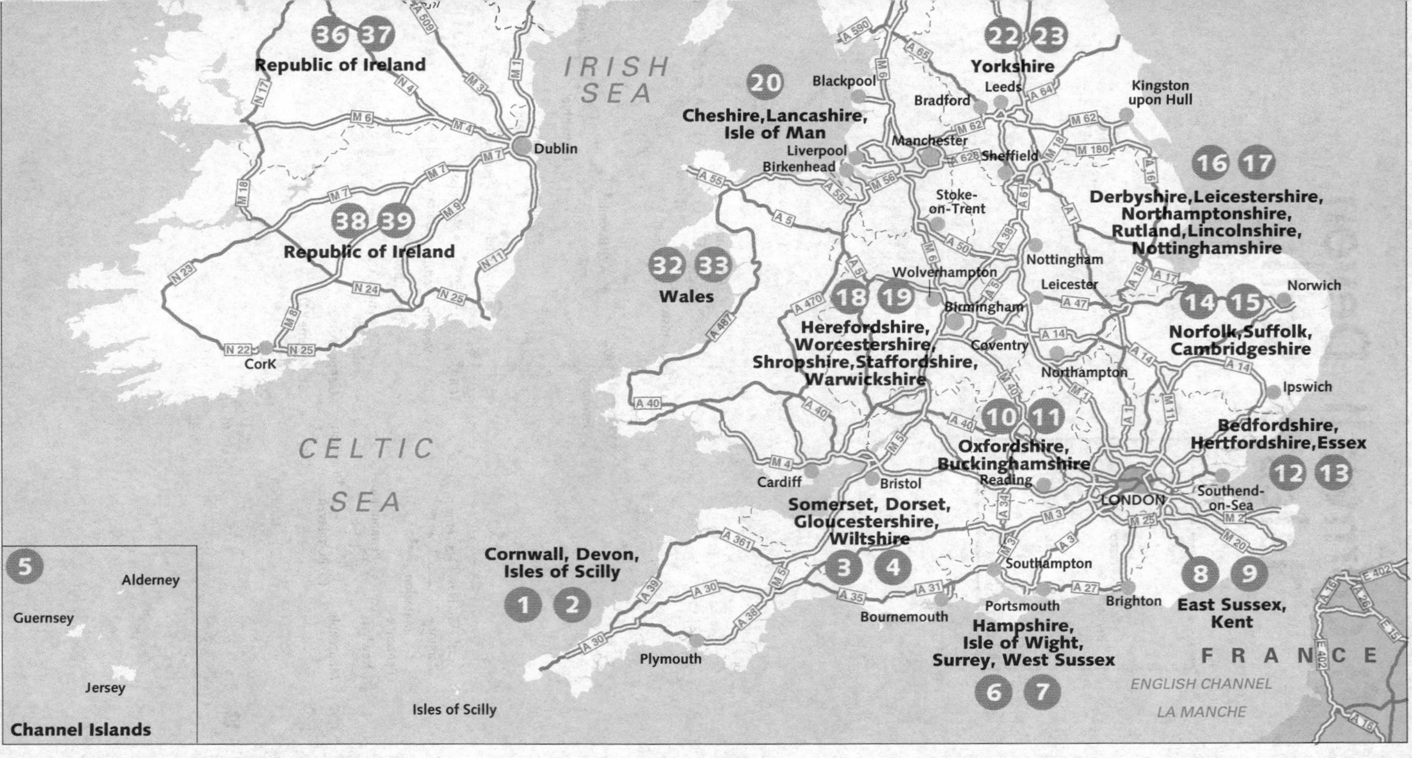

36 37 Republic of Ireland
38 39 Republic of Ireland
IRISH SEA
CELTIC SEA
Dublin
CorK
20 Cheshire, Lancashire, Isle of Man
22 23 Yorkshire
16 17 Derbyshire, Leicestershire, Northamptonshire, Rutland, Lincolnshire, Nottinghamshire
32 33 Wales
18 19 Herefordshire, Worcestershire, Shropshire, Staffordshire, Warwickshire
14 15 Norfolk, Suffolk, Cambridgeshire
10 11 Oxfordshire, Buckinghamshire
12 13 Bedfordshire, Hertfordshire, Essex
3 4 Somerset, Dorset, Gloucestershire, Wiltshire
1 2 Cornwall, Devon, Isles of Scilly
8 9 East Sussex, Kent
6 7 Hampshire, Isle of Wight, Surrey, West Sussex
5 Channel Islands
Alderney
Guernsey
Jersey
Isles of Scilly
Blackpool
Bradford
Leeds
Kingston upon Hull
Liverpool
Birkenhead
Manchester
Sheffield
Stoke-on-Trent
Nottingham
Wolverhampton
Leicester
Norwich
Birmingham
Coventry
Northampton
Ipswich
Cardiff
Bristol
Reading
LONDON
Southend-on-Sea
Southampton
Portsmouth
Brighton
Bournemouth
Plymouth
FRANCE
ENGLISH CHANNEL
LA MANCHE

1 Cornwall, Devon, Isles of Scilly

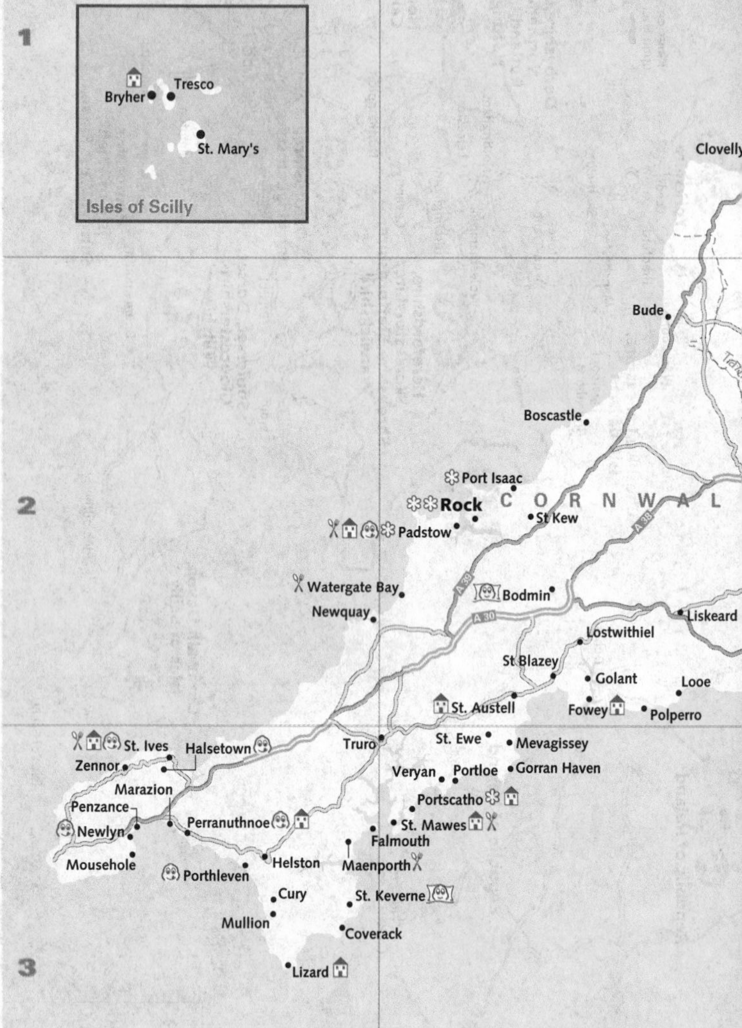

A
B
1
2
3
BRIST
Isles of Scilly
Bryher
Tresco
St. Mary's
Clovelly
Bude
Boscastle
Port Isaac
Rock
CORNWAL
St Kew
Padstow
Watergate Bay
Newquay
Bodmin
A 30
A 39
A 38
Liskeard
Lostwithiel
St Blazey
Golant
Looe
St. Austell
Fowey
Polperro
St. Ives
Halsetown
Zennor
Truro
St. Ewe
Mevagissey
Veryan
Portloe
Gorran Haven
Marazion
Penzance
Portscatho
Newlyn
Perranuthnoe
St. Mawes
Falmouth
Mousehole
Porthleven
Helston
Maenporth
Cury
St. Keverne
Mullion
Coverack
Lizard

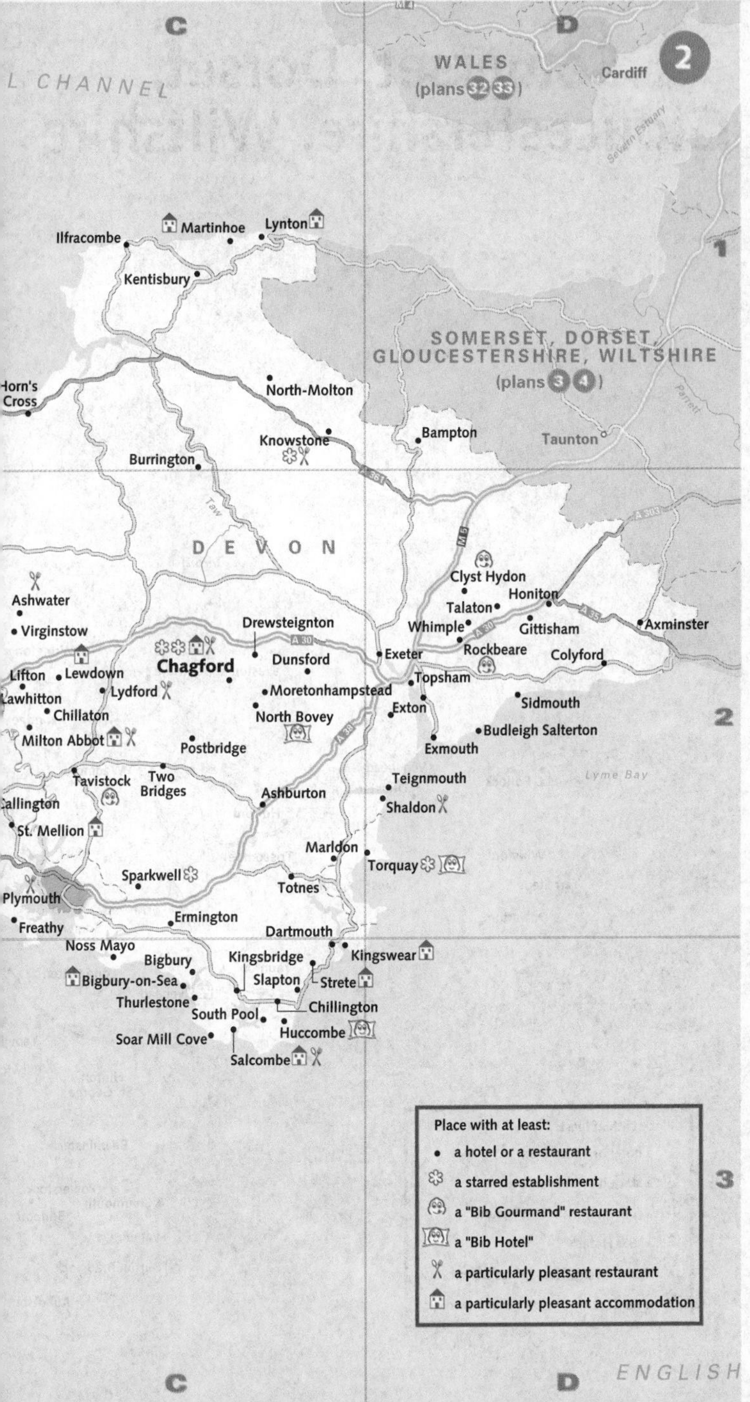
C
D
2
L CHANNEL
WALES
(plans 32 33)
Cardiff
Severn Estuary
Martinhoe
Lynton
Ilfracombe
Kentisbury
1
SOMERSET, DORSET,
GLOUCESTERSHIRE, WILTSHIRE
(plans 3 4)
Horn's Cross
North-Molton
Knowstone
Bampton
Taunton
Burrington
A 361
A 303
DEVON
M 5
Clyst Hydon
Honiton
Talaton
Ashwater
Virginstow
Drewsteignton
Whimple
Gittisham
Axminster
A 35
A 30
Chagford
Dunsford
Exeter
Rockbeare
Colyford
Lifton
Lewdown
Lydford
Topsham
Moretonhampstead
Lawhitton
Chillaton
North Bovey
Exton
Sidmouth
2
Milton Abbot
Postbridge
Budleigh Salterton
Exmouth
A 38
Tavistock
Two Bridges
Teignmouth
Lyme Bay
Callington
Ashburton
Shaldon
St. Mellion
Marldon
Torquay
Sparkwell
Totnes
Plymouth
Ermington
Freathy
Dartmouth
Noss Mayo
Kingswear
Bigbury
Kingsbridge
Bigbury-on-Sea
Slapton
Strete
Thurlestone
Chillington
South Pool
Huccombe
Soar Mill Cove
Salcombe
Place with at least:
a hotel or a restaurant
a starred establishment
a "Bib Gourmand" restaurant
a "Bib Hotel"
a particularly pleasant restaurant
a particularly pleasant accommodation
3
ENGLISH
C
D

3 Somerset, Dorset, Gloucestershire, Wiltshire

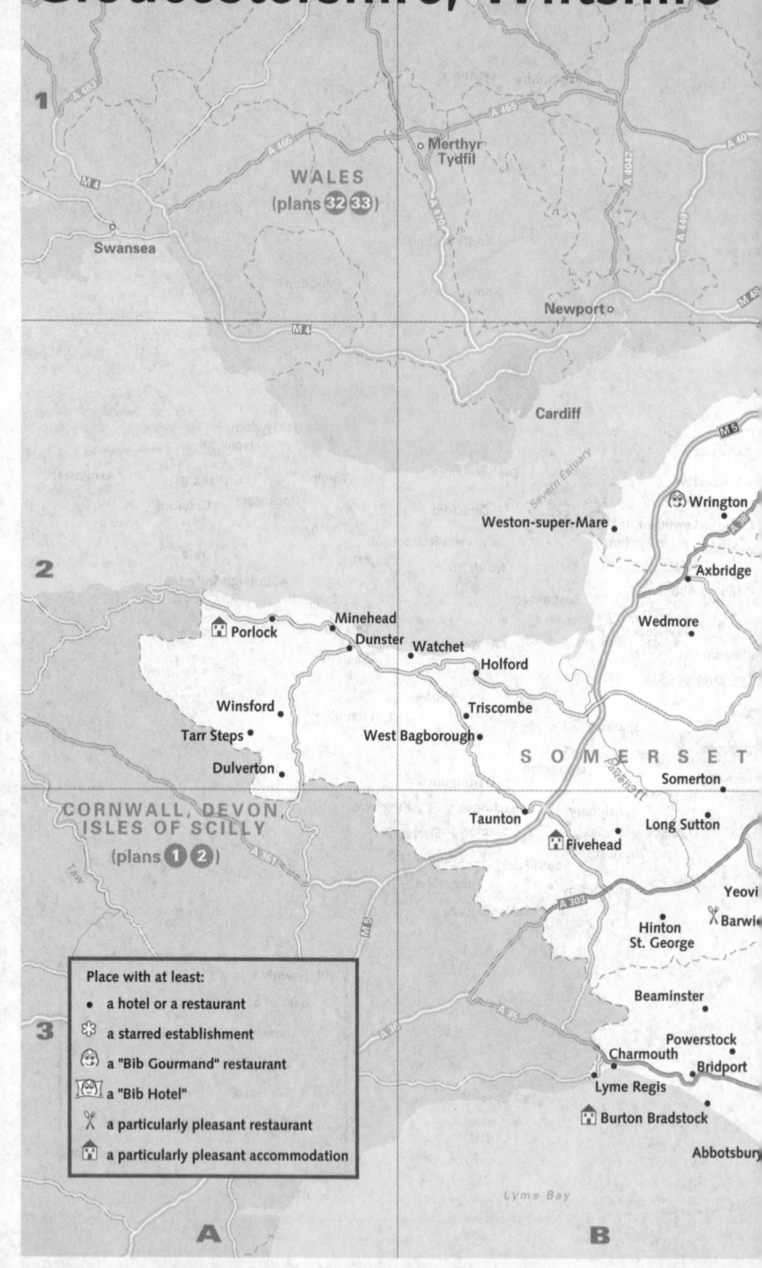

4
C
D
HEREFORDSHIRE, WORCESTERSHIRE, SHROPSHIRE, STAFFORDSHIRE, WARWICKSHIRE
(plans 18 19)
Tewkesbury
Chipping Campden
Broad Campden
Blockley
Bourton on the Hill
Moreton-in-Marsh
Winchcombe
Stow-on-the-Wold
Lower Swell
Daylesford
Cheltenham
Upper Slaughter
Lower Slaughter
Nether Westcote
GLOUCESTERSHIRE
Bourton-on-the-Water
1
Cowley
Cockleford
Arlingham
Northleach
Clearwell
Painswick
Bibury
Barnsley
Stroud
Sapperton
R. Wye
Southrop
Thames
Nailsworth
Cirencester
Tetbury
Thornbury
Westonbirt
Cricklade
OXFORDSHIRE, BUCKINGHAMSHIRE
(plans 10 11)
Malmesbury
Purton
Bristol
Foxham
Castle Combe
Long Ashton
Colerne
Ramsbury
Monkton Farleigh
Corsham
Calne
Marlborough
Chew Magna
Bath
Upper South Wraxall
Holt
Broughton Gifford
Hunstrete
Little Bedwyn
Newbury
Bradford-on-Avon
Avon
Devizes
2
Ston Easton
Norton St. Philip
WILTSHIRE
Holcombe
Edington
East Chisenbury
Avon
Mells
Wells
Shepton Mallet
Frome
Warminster
Shrewton
Batcombe
Bruton
Little Langford
Lovington
Fonthill Bishop
Teffont Evias
HAMPSHIRE, ISLE OF WIGHT, SURREY, WEST SUSSEX
(plans 6 7)
Gillingham
Tisbury
Salisbury
Corton Denham
West Hatch
Rimpton
Buckhorn Weston
Shaftesbury
Donhead-St-Andrew
Trent
Sherborne
Fontmell Magna
Tollard Royal
Nomansland
Farnham
DORSET
Evershot
Blandford Forum
Southampton
Cerne Abbas
Wimborne Minster
3
Maiden Newton
Bournemouth
Dorchester
Poole
Highcliffe
Wareham
Christchurch
West Lulworth
Studland
Isle of Wight
Corfe Castle
C
D
M 50
M 5
A 40
A 417
A 48
M 4
A 36
A 303
A 34
A 31
A 35
A 36
M 27
M 3
A 49

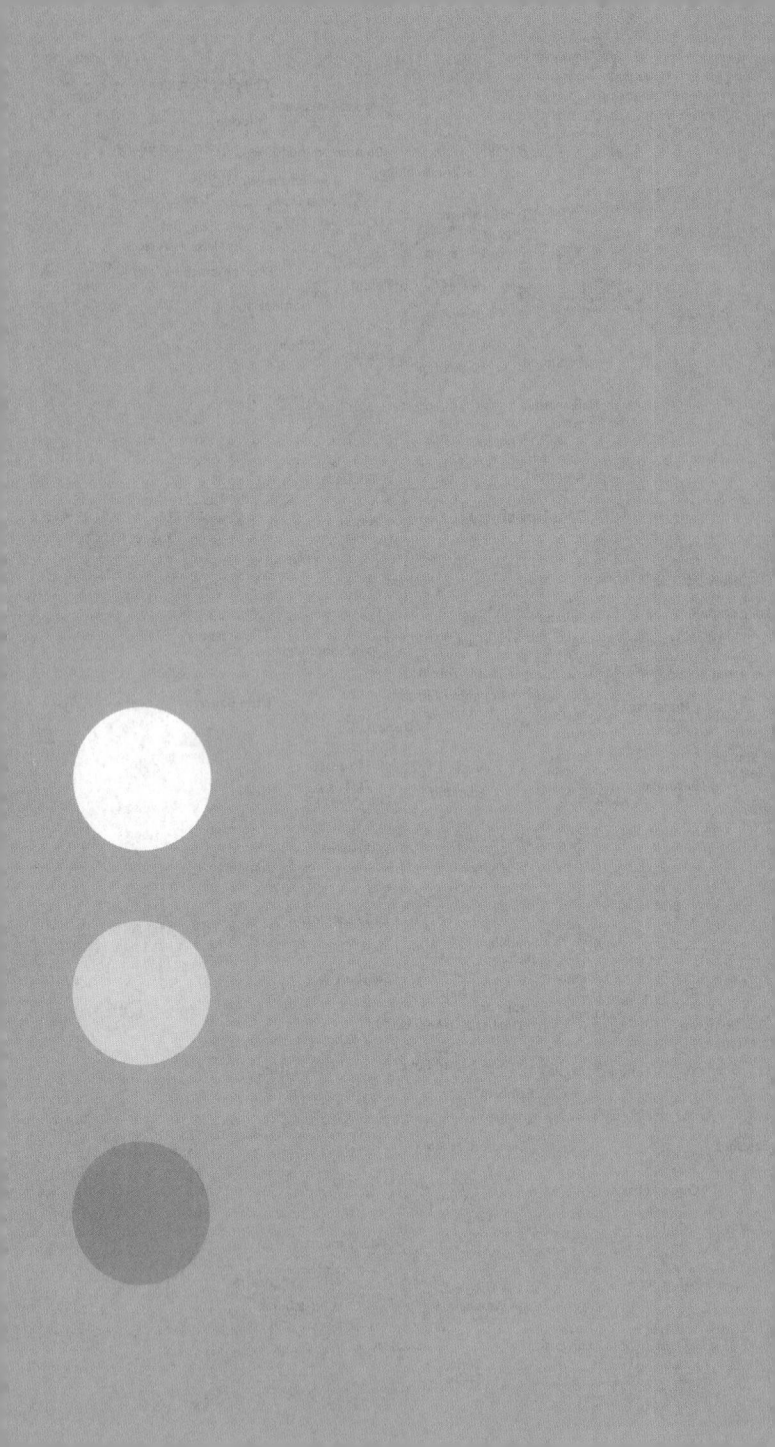

Channel Islands 5

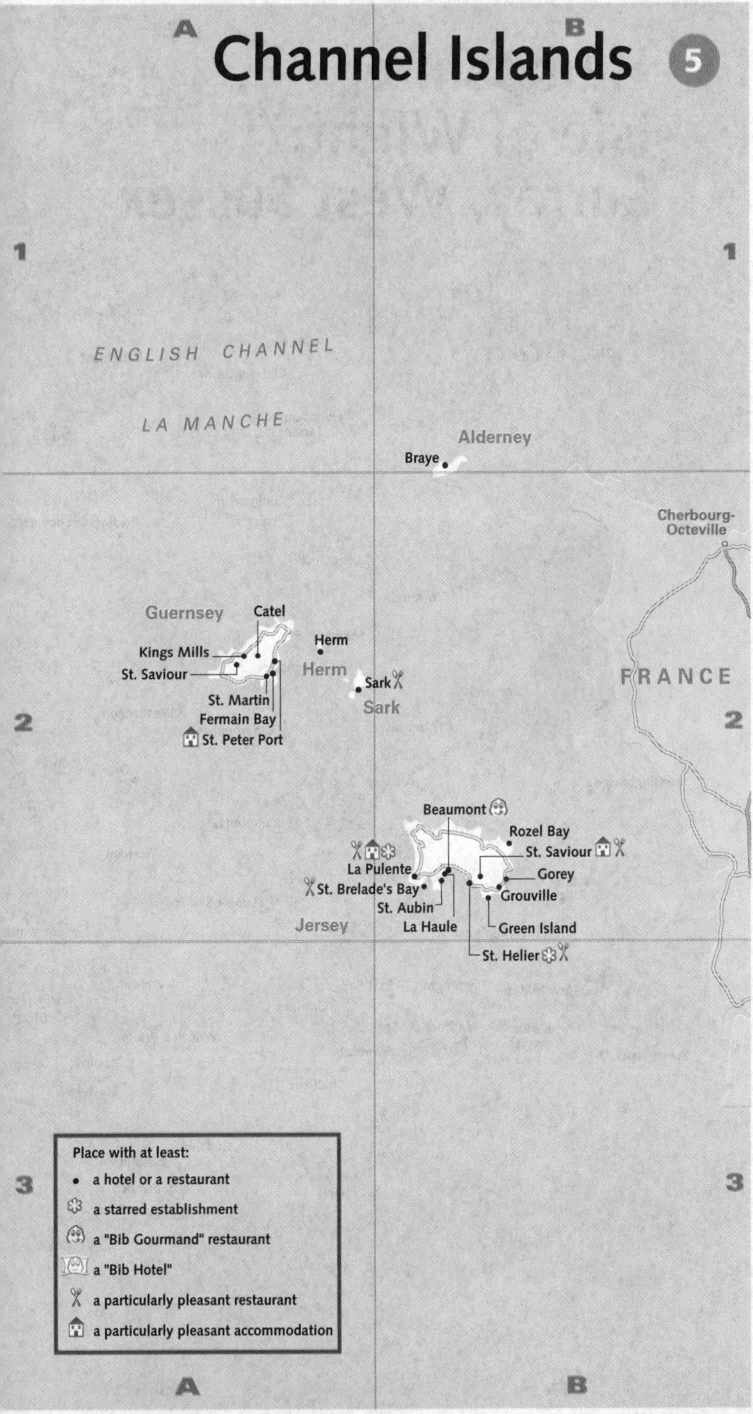

A B

1 1

ENGLISH CHANNEL

LA MANCHE

Alderney

Braye

Cherbourg-Octeville

Guernsey

Catel

Kings Mills

St. Saviour

St. Martin

Fermain Bay

St. Peter Port

Herm

Herm

Sark

Sark

FRANCE

2 2

Beaumont

Rozel Bay

St. Saviour

La Pulente

Gorey

St. Brelade's Bay

Grouville

St. Aubin

Jersey

La Haule

Green Island

St. Helier

Place with at least:

- a hotel or a restaurant
- a starred establishment
- a "Bib Gourmand" restaurant
- a "Bib Hotel"
- a particularly pleasant restaurant
- a particularly pleasant accommodation

3 3

A B

6 Hampshire, Isle of Wight, Surrey, West Sussex

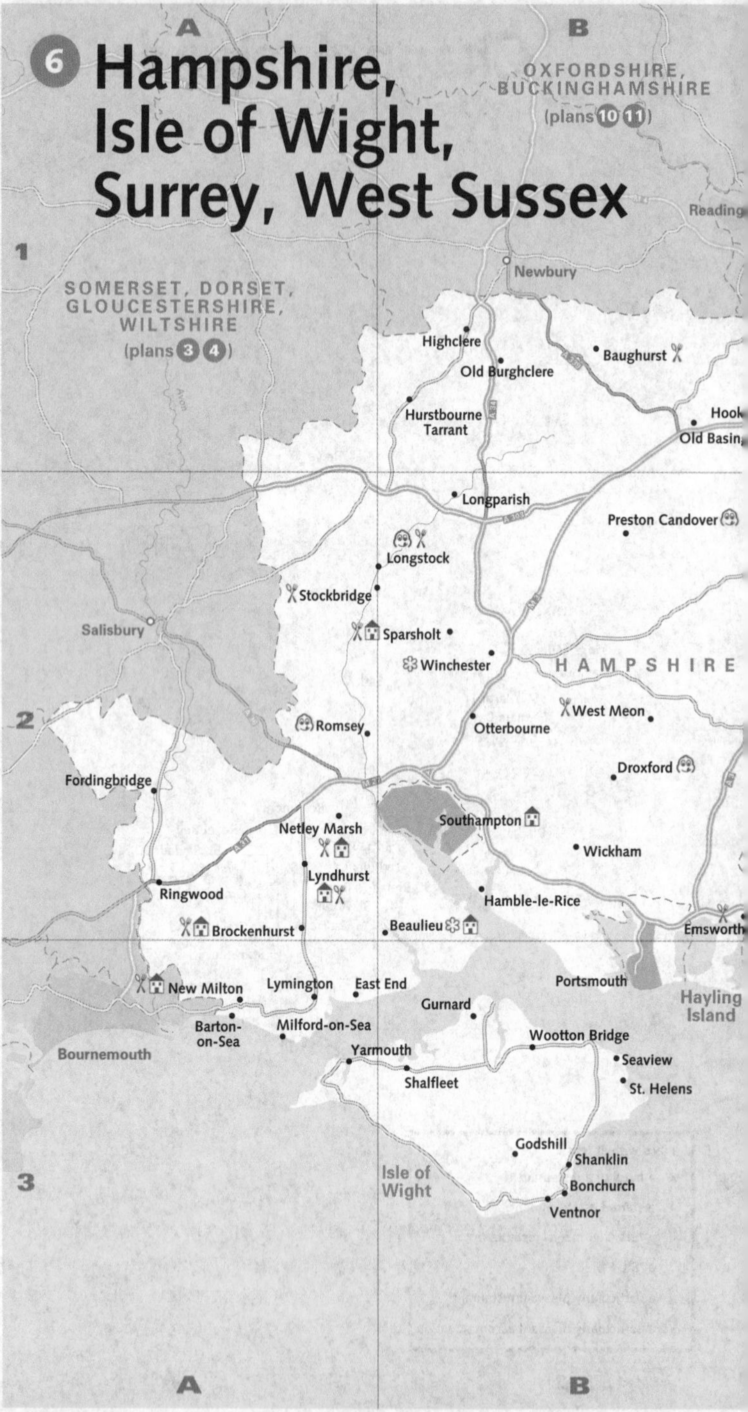

A B

OXFORDSHIRE, BUCKINGHAMSHIRE (plans 10 11)

Reading

1

Newbury

SOMERSET, DORSET, GLOUCESTERSHIRE, WILTSHIRE (plans 3 4)

Highclere

Baughurst

Old Burghclere

Hurstbourne Tarrant

Hook

Old Basing

Longparish

Preston Candover

Longstock

Stockbridge

Salisbury

Sparsholt

Winchester

HAMPSHIRE

2

West Meon

Romsey

Otterbourne

Droxford

Fordingbridge

Southampton

Netley Marsh

Wickham

Lyndhurst

Ringwood

Hamble-le-Rice

Brockenhurst

Beaulieu

Emsworth

New Milton

Lymington

East End

Portsmouth

Hayling Island

Gurnard

Barton-on-Sea

Milford-on-Sea

Wootton Bridge

Bournemouth

Yarmouth

Seaview

Shalfleet

St. Helens

Godshill

Shanklin

3

Isle of Wight

Bonchurch

Ventnor

A B

C
D
7
OXFORDSHIRE, BUCKINGHAMSHIRE
(plans 10 11)
LONDON
M 1
M 40
M 4
M 3
M 25
M 23
A 3
A 27
Egham
Laleham
Sunbury-on-Thames
BEDFORDSHIRE, HERTFORDSHIRE, ESSEX
(plans 12 13)
1
Bagshot
Windlesham
Weybridge
West End
Chobham
Stoke D'Abernon
Epsom
Woking
Farnborough
Ripley
Crookham Village
Dogmersfield
Redhill
Guildford
Dorking
Reigate
Farnham
Abinger Common
Lower Froyle
Tilford
Godalming
Horley
SURREY
Thursley
Cranleigh
Forest Green
Bordon
Chiddingfold
Turners Hill
East Grinstead
Horsham
West Hoathly
Liss
Lurgashall
Rogate
Henley
Lower Beeding
Horsted Keynes
2
Cuckfield
Petersfield
Petworth
Midhurst
Haywards Heath
Ditchling
WEST SUSSEX
EAST SUSSEX, KENT
Charlton
Henfield
Hurstpierpoint
Amberley
(plans 8 9)
Arundel
Chichester
West Wittering
Sidlesham
Littlehampton
Brighton
East Wittering
Place with at least:
a hotel or a restaurant
a starred establishment
a "Bib Gourmand" restaurant
a "Bib Hotel"
a particularly pleasant restaurant
a particularly pleasant accommodation
3
C
D

8 East Sussex, Kent

C
D
9
BEDFORDSHIRE
HERTFORDSHIRE, ESSEX
(plans 12 13)
Southend-on-Sea
1
Rainham
Sittingbourne
Seasalter
Whitstable
Herne Bay
Margate
Broadstairs
Ramsgate
Minster
A 299
Faversham
Milstead
M 2
Doddington
Hollingbourne
Canterbury
Sandwich
Leeds
Stalisfield
KENT
A 2
A 258
Deal
Ashford
Brabourne
Alkham
Dover
Biddenden
M 20
2
Folkestone
A 259
Stone in Oxney
New Romney
Rye
Winchelsea
Icklesham
Place with at least:
a hotel or a restaurant
a starred establishment
a "Bib Gourmand" restaurant
a "Bib Hotel"
a particularly pleasant restaurant
a particularly pleasant accommodation
3
C
D

10 Oxfordshire, Buckinghamshire

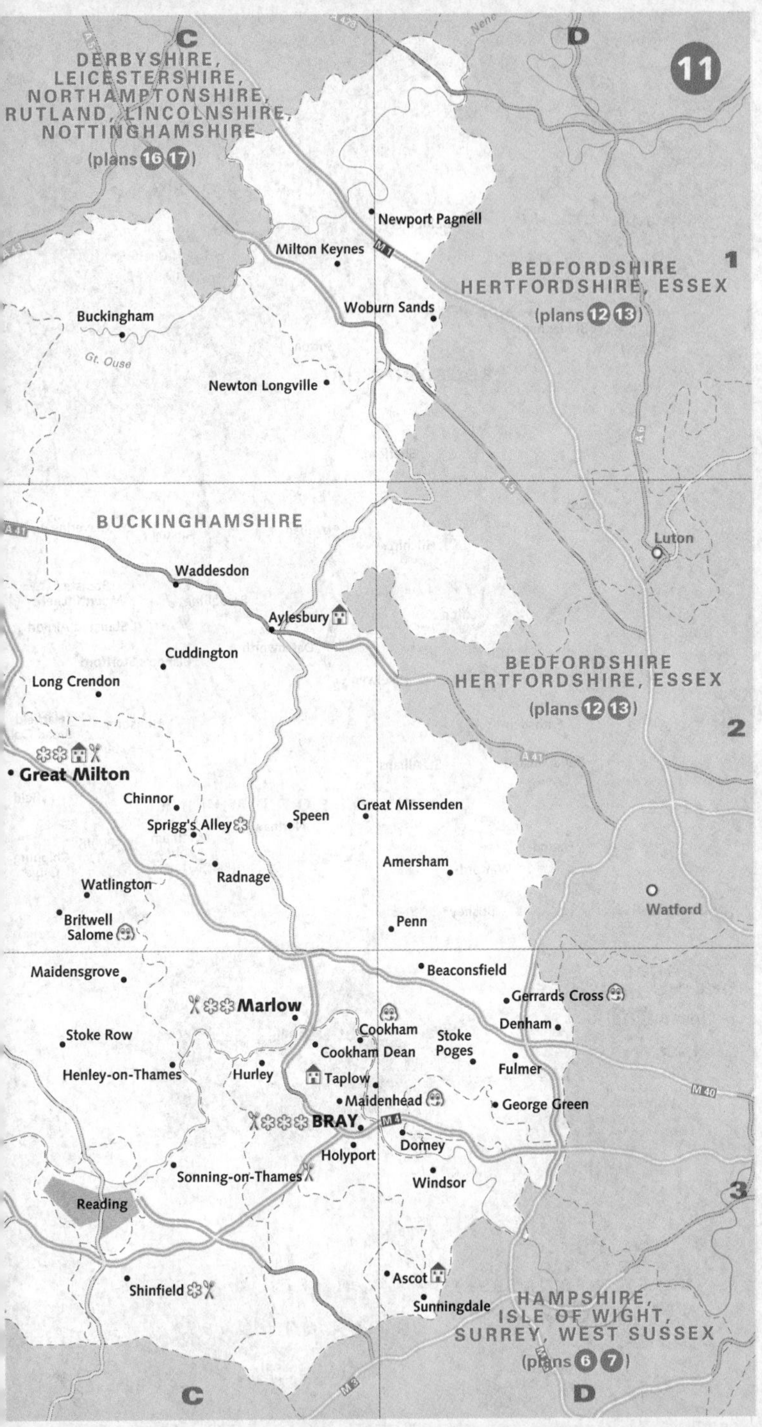

C
D
11
DERBYSHIRE, LEICESTERSHIRE, NORTHAMPTONSHIRE, RUTLAND, LINCOLNSHIRE, NOTTINGHAMSHIRE
(plans 16 17)
Nene
A 428
A 5
A 43
Newport Pagnell
M 1
Milton Keynes
1
BEDFORDSHIRE HERTFORDSHIRE, ESSEX
(plans 12 13)
Woburn Sands
Buckingham
Gt. Ouse
Newton Longville
A 6
BUCKINGHAMSHIRE
A 41
Luton
Waddesdon
Aylesbury
Cuddington
BEDFORDSHIRE HERTFORDSHIRE, ESSEX
(plans 12 13)
Long Crendon
2
Great Milton
A 41
Chinnor
Great Missenden
Sprigg's Alley
Speen
Amersham
Radnage
Watlington
Watford
Britwell Salome
Penn
Maidensgrove
Beaconsfield
Gerrards Cross
Marlow
Denham
Cookham
Stoke Row
Stoke Poges
Cookham Dean
Fulmer
Henley-on-Thames
Hurley
Taplow
M 40
Maidenhead
George Green
BRAY
M 4
Dorney
Holyport
Windsor
Sonning-on-Thames
3
Reading
Ascot
Shinfield
Sunningdale
HAMPSHIRE, ISLE OF WIGHT, SURREY, WEST SUSSEX
(plans 6 7)
M 3
C
D

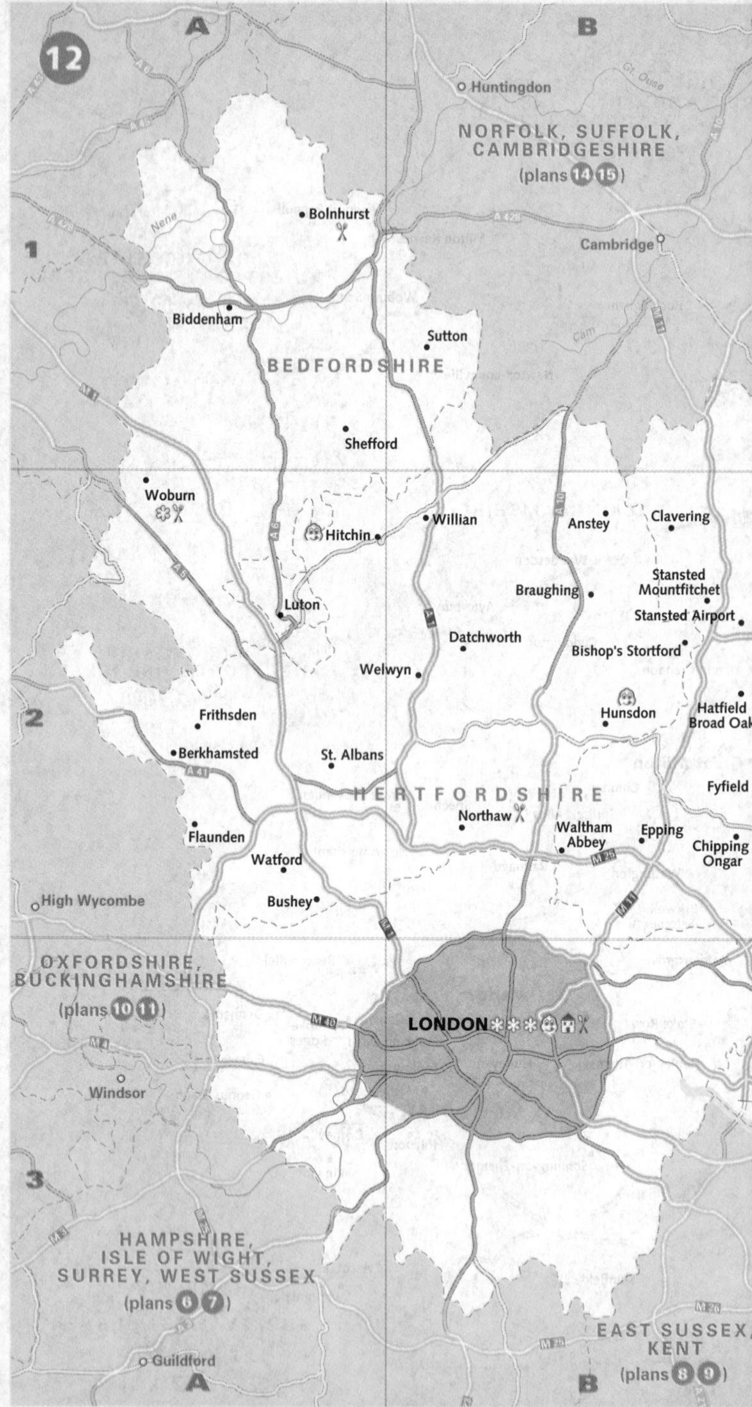

12
A
B
Huntingdon
NORFOLK, SUFFOLK, CAMBRIDGESHIRE
(plans 14 15)
Bolnhurst
Cambridge
1
Biddenham
Sutton
BEDFORDSHIRE
Shefford
Woburn
Hitchin
Willian
Anstey
Clavering
Stansted Mountfitchet
Braughing
Luton
Stansted Airport
Datchworth
Bishop's Stortford
Welwyn
Hunsdon
2
Frithsden
Hatfield Broad Oak
Berkhamsted
St. Albans
HERTFORDSHIRE
Fyfield
Northaw
Waltham Abbey
Epping
Flaunden
Chipping Ongar
Watford
High Wycombe
Bushey
OXFORDSHIRE, BUCKINGHAMSHIRE
(plans 10 11)
LONDON
Windsor
3
HAMPSHIRE, ISLE OF WIGHT, SURREY, WEST SUSSEX
(plans 6 7)
EAST SUSSEX, KENT
(plans 8 9)
Guildford
A
B

Bedfordshire, Hertfordshire, Essex

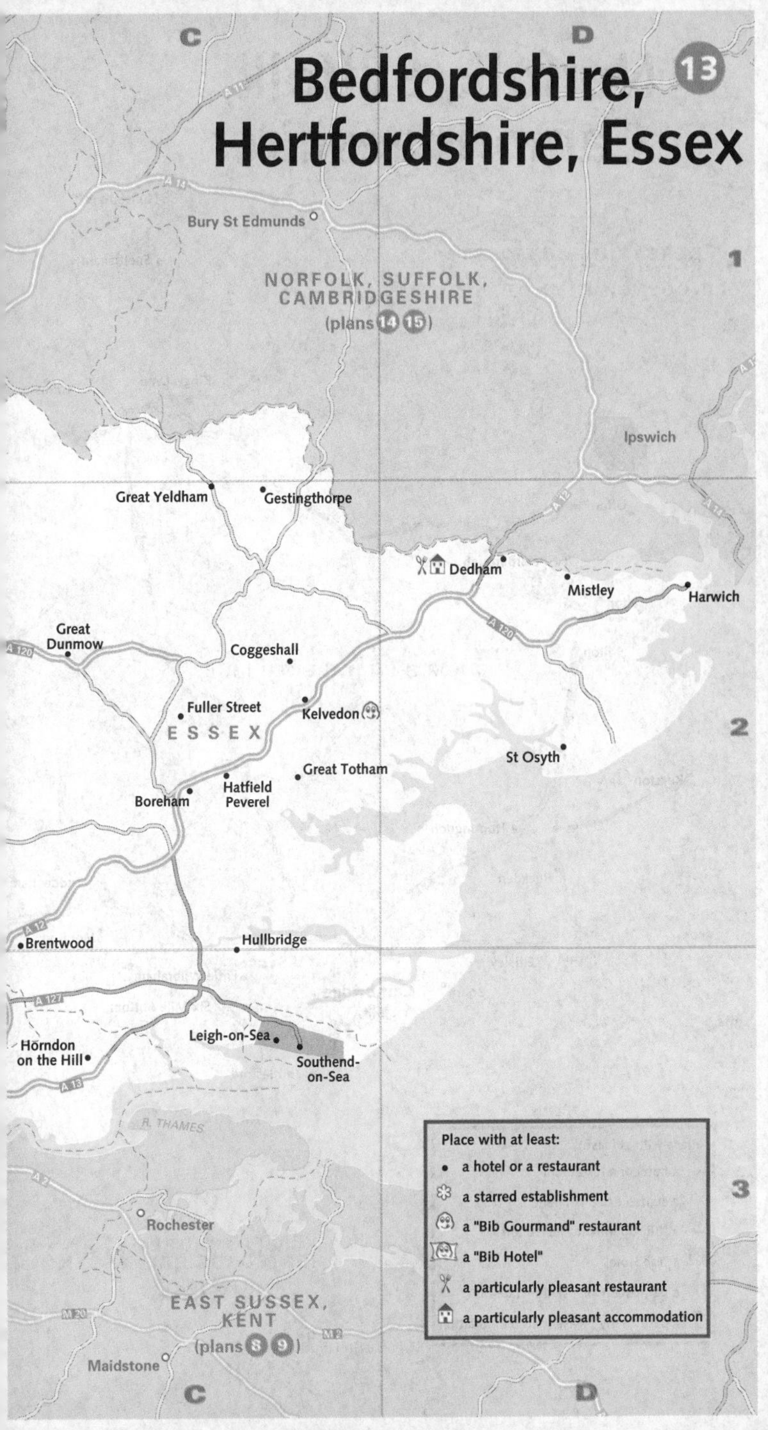

14 Norfolk, Suffolk, Cambridgeshire

A B

1 DERBYSHIRE, LEICESTERSHIRE, NORTHAMPTONSHIRE, RUTLAND, LINCOLNSHIRE, NOTTINGHAMSHIRE

(plans 16 17)

Spalding

The Wash

Hunstanton

Snettisham

King's Lynn

Grimston

A 17

A 47

Welland

Stamford

Ufford

Nene

Great Ouse

A 10

Peterborough

Elton

Stilton

CAMBRIDGESHIRE

A 1(M)

A 605

2

Keyston

Ely

Gt. Ouse

Huntingdon

A 11

Buckden

Tuddenham

A 14

Moulton

A 428

Eltisley

Bourn

Cambridge

Little Wilbraham

Six Mile Bottom

Cam

M 11

Whittlesford

Place with at least:

- a hotel or a restaurant
- a starred establishment
- a "Bib Gourmand" restaurant
- a "Bib Hotel"
- a particularly pleasant restaurant
- a particularly pleasant accommodation

3

A 10

BEDFORDSHIRE, HERTFORDSHIRE, ESSEX

(plans 12 13)

A 120

Bishop's Stortford

A B

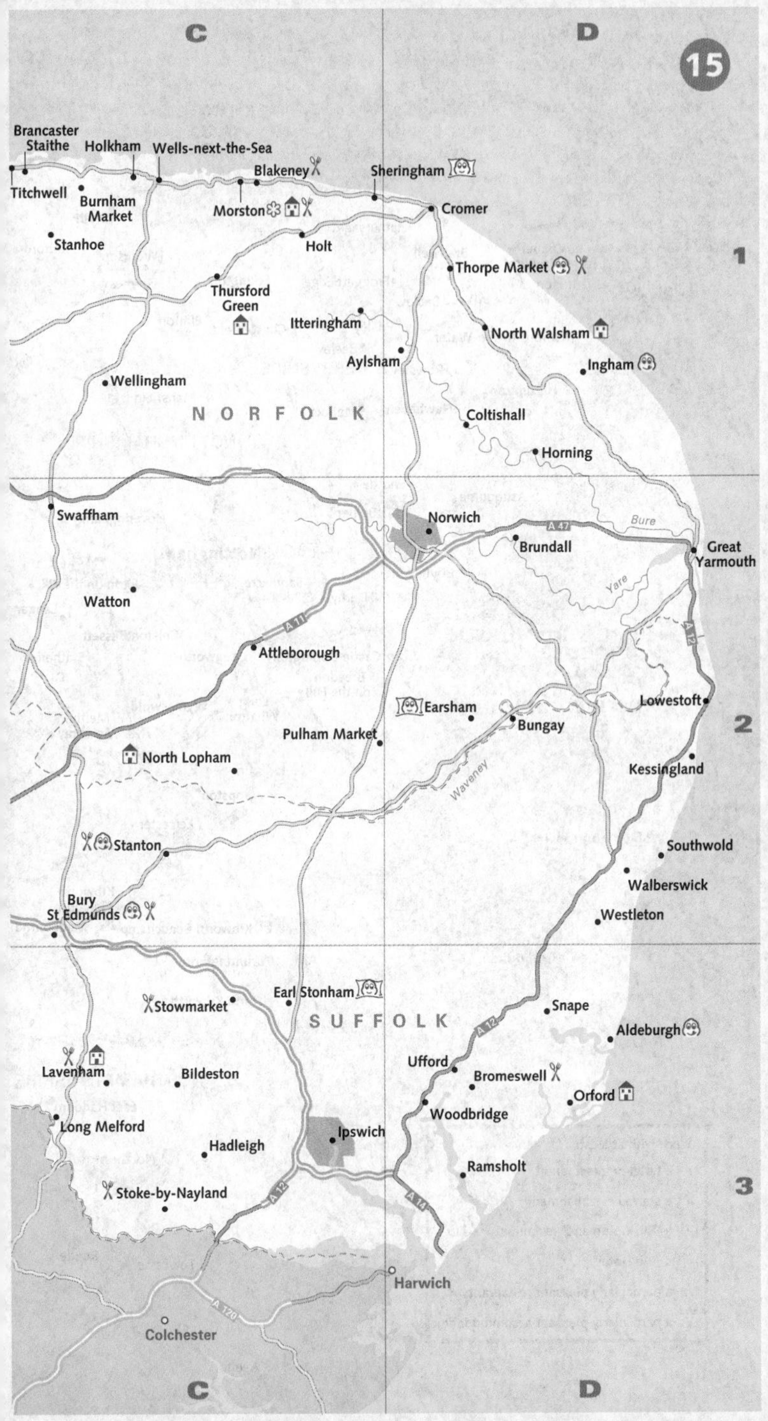

C
D
15
Brancaster Staithe
Holkham
Wells-next-the-Sea
Blakeney
Sheringham
Titchwell
Burnham Market
Morston
Cromer
Stanhoe
Holt
1
Thorpe Market
Thursford Green
Itteringham
North Walsham
Aylsham
Ingham
Wellingham
NORFOLK
Coltishall
Horning
Swaffham
Norwich
A 47
Bure
Brundall
Great Yarmouth
Yare
Watton
A 11
A 12
Attleborough
Earsham
Lowestoft
Bungay
2
Pulham Market
North Lopham
Kessingland
Waveney
Stanton
Southwold
Walberswick
Bury St Edmunds
Westleton
Earl Stonham
Stowmarket
SUFFOLK
Snape
A 12
Aldeburgh
Ufford
Lavenham
Bildeston
Bromeswell
Orford
Woodbridge
Long Melford
Ipswich
Hadleigh
Ramsholt
A 12
3
A 14
Stoke-by-Nayland
Harwich
A 120
Colchester
C
D

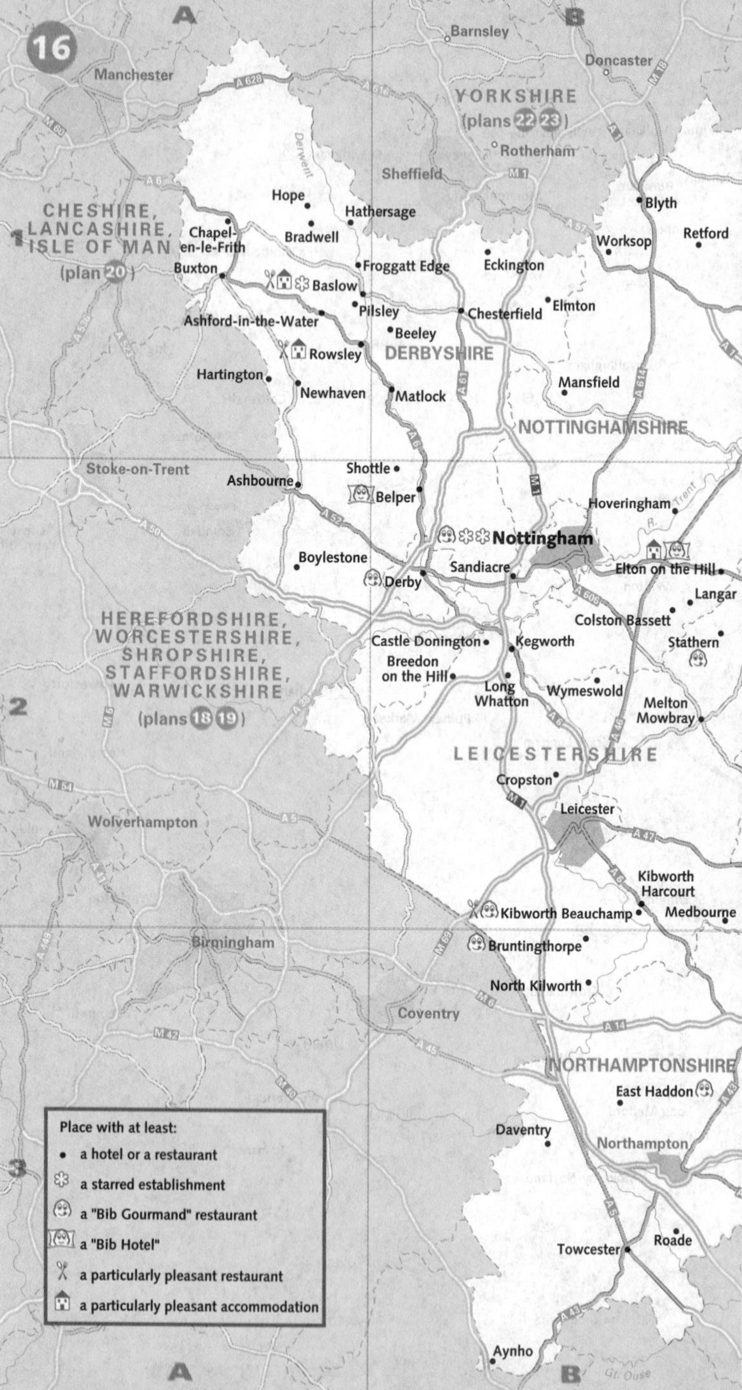

16
A
B
1
2
3
Manchester
Barnsley
Doncaster
YORKSHIRE
(plans 22 23)
Rotherham
Sheffield
CHESHIRE,
LANCASHIRE,
ISLE OF MAN
(plan 20)
Hope
Hathersage
Bradwell
Chapel-en-le-Frith
Buxton
Froggatt Edge
Eckington
Baslow
Pilsley
Ashford-in-the-Water
Chesterfield
Elmton
Beeley
Rowsley
DERBYSHIRE
Hartington
Newhaven
Matlock
Mansfield
Blyth
Retford
Worksop
NOTTINGHAMSHIRE
Stoke-on-Trent
Shottle
Ashbourne
Belper
Hoveringham
Nottingham
Boylestone
Sandiacre
Derby
Elton on the Hill
Langar
Colston Bassett
Stathern
HEREFORDSHIRE,
WORCESTERSHIRE,
SHROPSHIRE,
STAFFORDSHIRE,
WARWICKSHIRE
(plans 18 19)
Castle Donington
Kegworth
Breedon on the Hill
Long Whatton
Wymeswold
Melton Mowbray
LEICESTERSHIRE
Cropston
Leicester
Wolverhampton
Kibworth Harcourt
Kibworth Beauchamp
Medbourne
Bruntingthorpe
Birmingham
North Kilworth
Coventry
NORTHAMPTONSHIRE
East Haddon
Daventry
Northampton
Roade
Towcester
Aynho
Place with at least:
a hotel or a restaurant
a starred establishment
a "Bib Gourmand" restaurant
a "Bib Hotel"
a particularly pleasant restaurant
a particularly pleasant accommodation

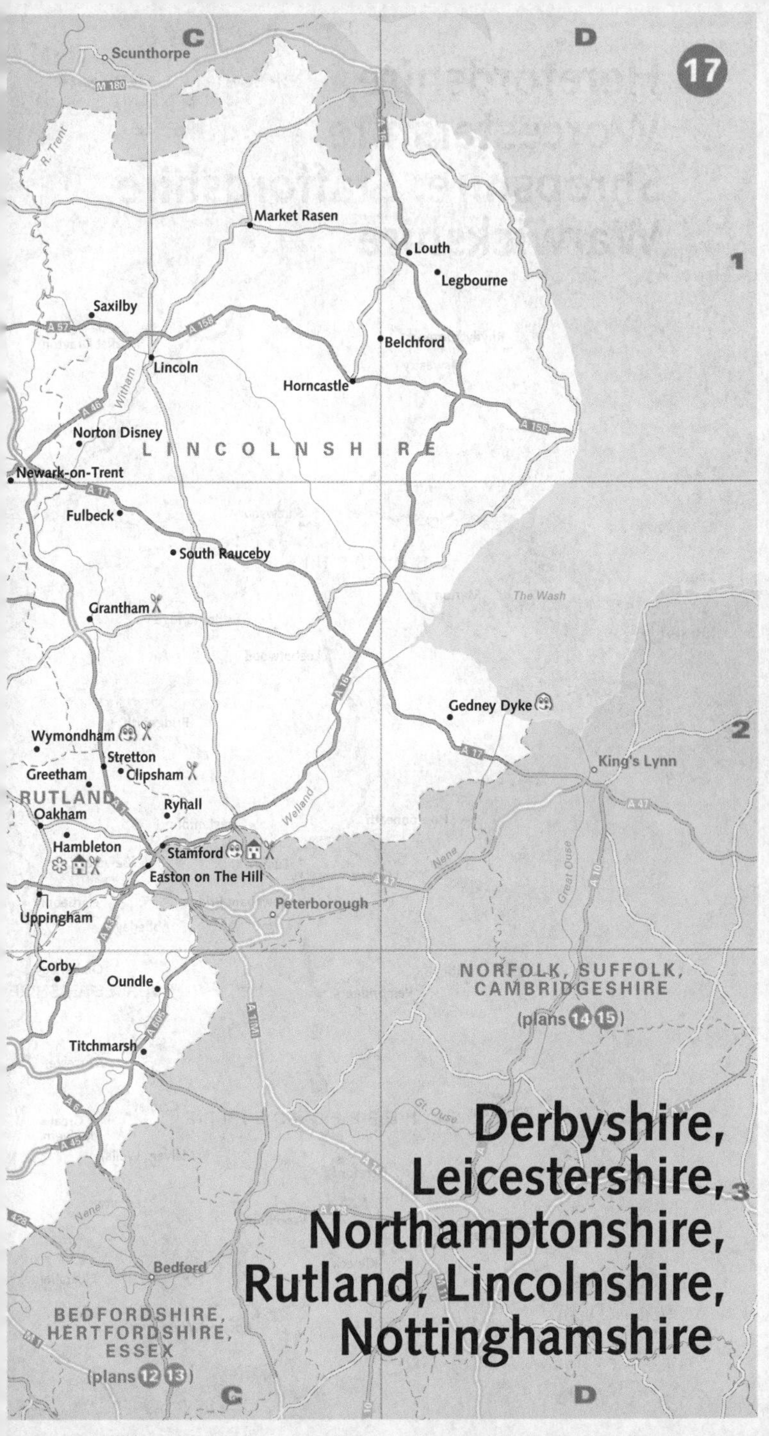

Derbyshire, Leicestershire, Northamptonshire, Rutland, Lincolnshire, Nottinghamshire

18 Herefordshire, Worcestershire, Shropshire, Staffordshire, Warwickshire

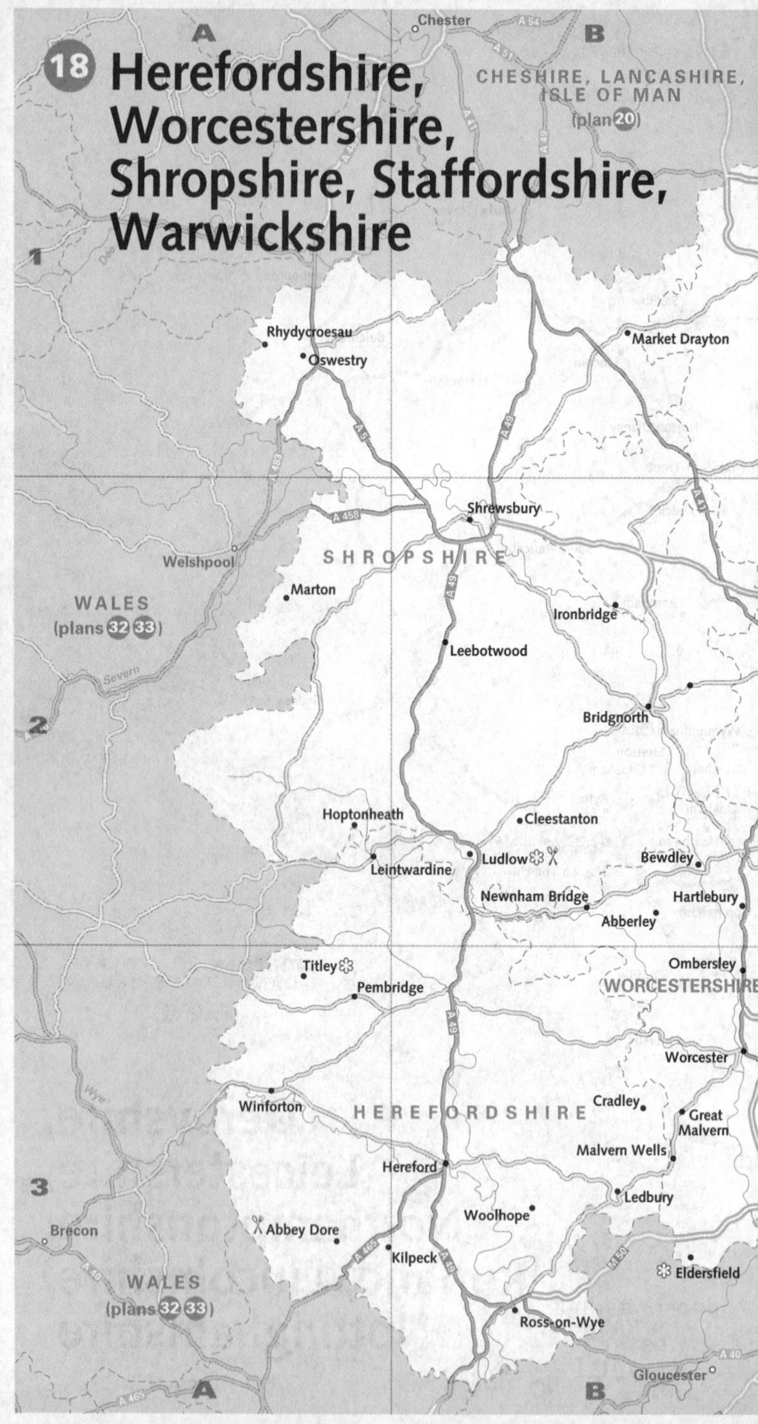

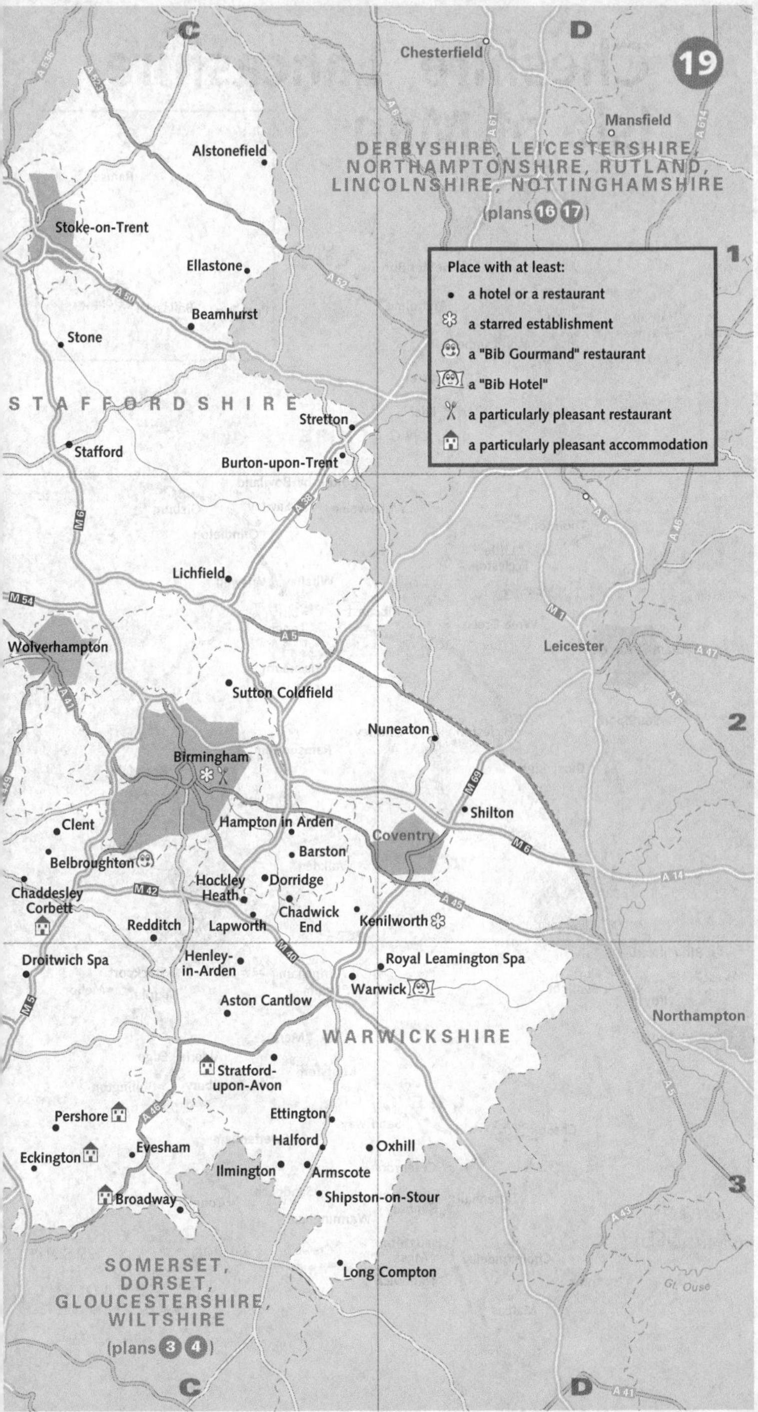
C
D
19
Chesterfield
Mansfield
DERBYSHIRE, LEICESTERSHIRE, NORTHAMPTONSHIRE, RUTLAND, LINCOLNSHIRE, NOTTINGHAMSHIRE
(plans 16 17)
Alstonefield
Stoke-on-Trent
Ellastone
Beamhurst
Stone
STAFFORDSHIRE
Stretton
Stafford
Burton-upon-Trent
1
Place with at least:
a hotel or a restaurant
a starred establishment
a "Bib Gourmand" restaurant
a "Bib Hotel"
a particularly pleasant restaurant
a particularly pleasant accommodation
Lichfield
Wolverhampton
Leicester
Sutton Coldfield
Nuneaton
2
Birmingham
Shilton
Clent
Hampton in Arden
Coventry
Belbroughton
Barston
Chaddesley Corbett
Hockley Heath
Dorridge
Chadwick End
Kenilworth
Redditch
Lapworth
Droitwich Spa
Henley-in-Arden
Royal Leamington Spa
Warwick
Aston Cantlow
Northampton
WARWICKSHIRE
Stratford-upon-Avon
Pershore
Ettington
Evesham
Halford
Oxhill
Eckington
Ilmington
Armscote
3
Broadway
Shipston-on-Stour
Long Compton
SOMERSET, DORSET, GLOUCESTERSHIRE, WILTSHIRE
(plans 3 4)
C
D

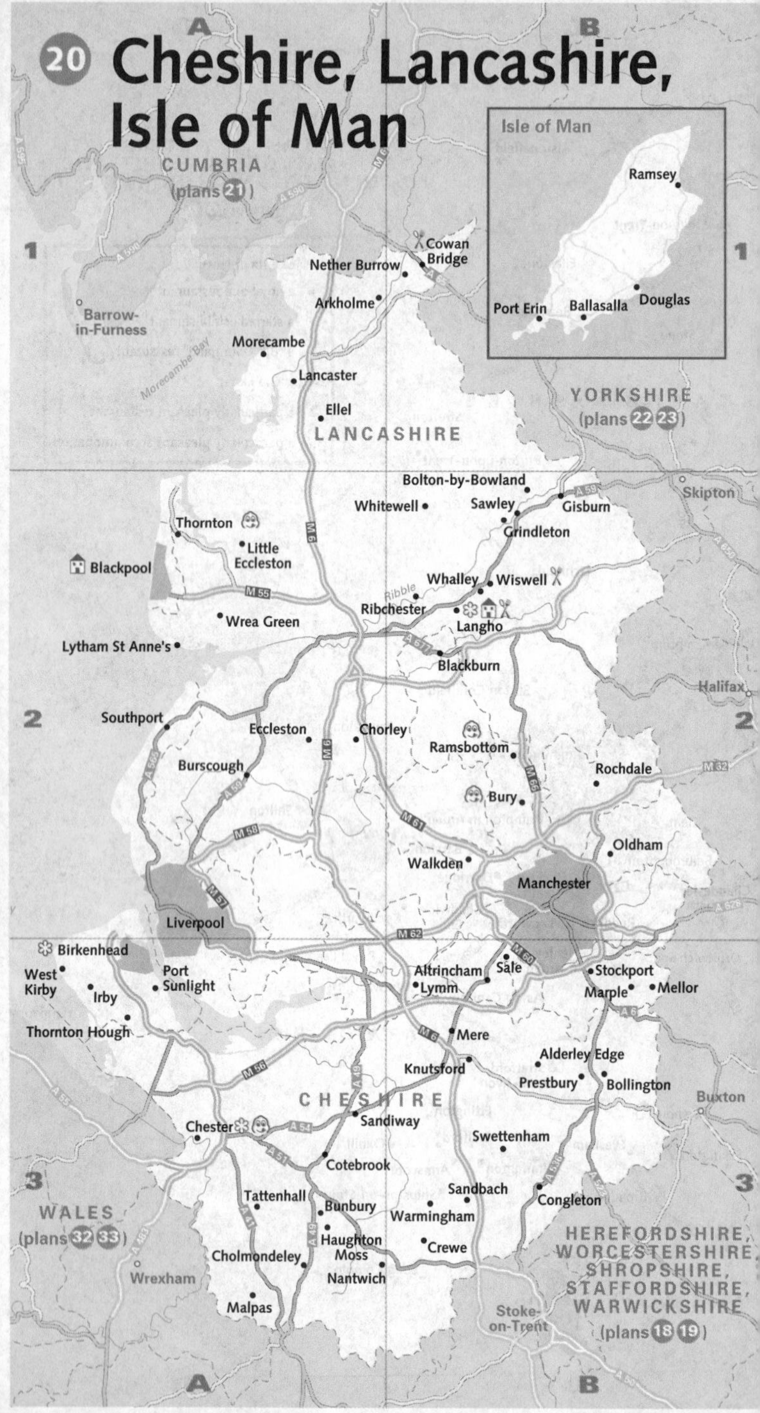
20 Cheshire, Lancashire, Isle of Man
A
B
1
2
3
CUMBRIA
(plans 21)
Isle of Man
Ramsey
Douglas
Port Erin
Ballasalla
Barrow-in-Furness
Morecambe Bay
Cowan Bridge
Nether Burrow
Arkholme
Morecambe
Lancaster
Ellel
LANCASHIRE
YORKSHIRE
(plans 22 23)
Bolton-by-Bowland
Whitewell
Sawley
Gisburn
Grindleton
Skipton
Thornton
Little Eccleston
Blackpool
Whalley
Wiswell
Ribble
Ribchester
Langho
Wrea Green
Lytham St Anne's
Blackburn
Halifax
Southport
Eccleston
Chorley
Ramsbottom
Burscough
Rochdale
Bury
Oldham
Walkden
Manchester
Liverpool
Birkenhead
West Kirby
Irby
Port Sunlight
Thornton Hough
Altrincham
Sale
Lymm
Stockport
Marple
Mellor
Mere
Knutsford
Alderley Edge
Prestbury
Bollington
Buxton
CHESHIRE
Chester
Sandiway
Swettenham
Cotebrook
Sandbach
Congleton
Tattenhall
Bunbury
Warmingham
Haughton Moss
Crewe
Cholmondeley
Nantwich
Malpas
WALES
(plans 32 33)
Wrexham
Stoke-on-Trent
HEREFORDSHIRE, WORCESTERSHIRE, SHROPSHIRE, STAFFORDSHIRE, WARWICKSHIRE
(plans 18 19)
M 6
M 55
M 58
M 61
M 65
M 62
M 60
M 57
M 56
M 62
A 59
A 590
A 65
A 671
A 565
A 59
A 6
A 54
A 51
A 49
A 41
A 536
A 523
A 55
A 483
A 628
A 650

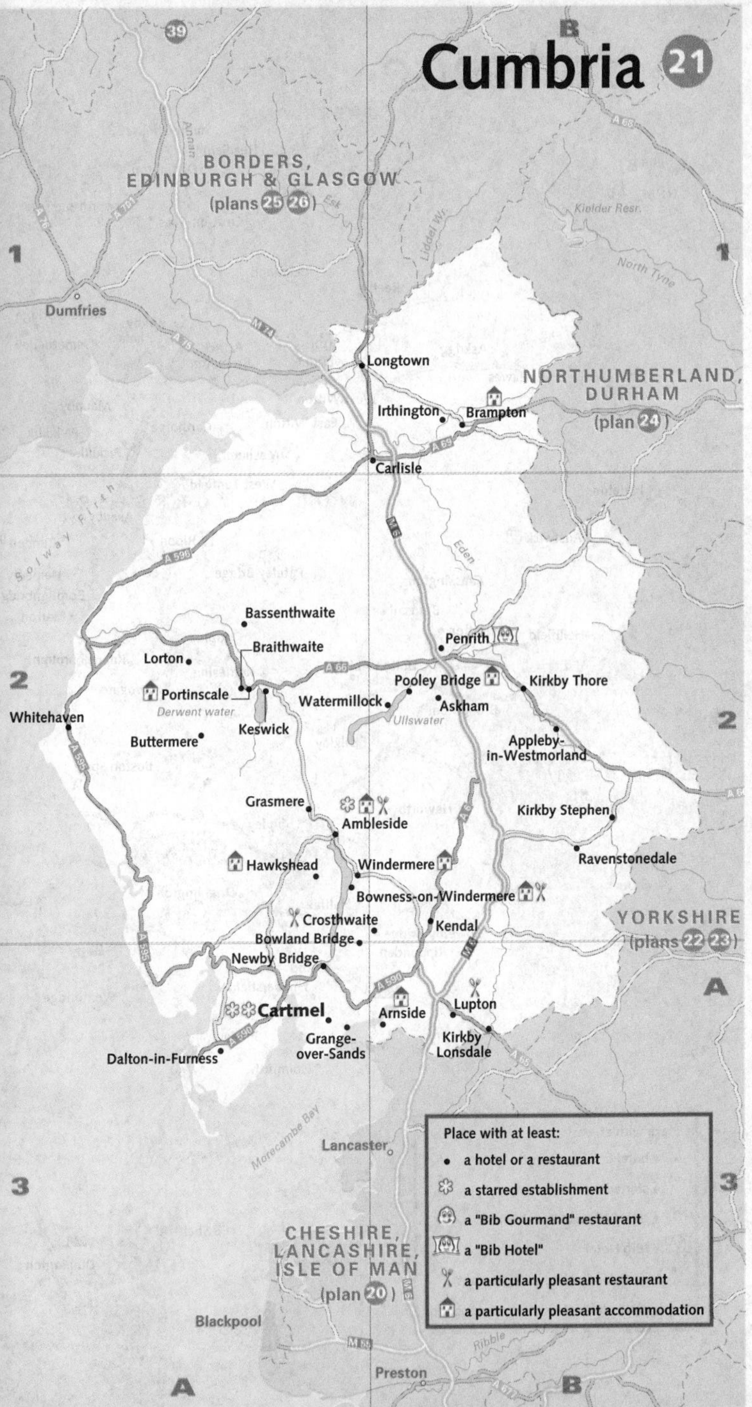
Cumbria 21
39
B
BORDERS, EDINBURGH & GLASGOW (plans 25 26)
Kielder Resr.
North Tyne
1
Dumfries
Longtown
NORTHUMBERLAND, DURHAM (plan 24)
Irthington
Brampton
Carlisle
Solway Firth
Eden
Bassenthwaite
Braithwaite
Penrith
Lorton
Portinscale
Pooley Bridge
Kirkby Thore
2
Watermillock
Askham
Whitehaven
Derwent water
Keswick
Ullswater
Buttermere
Appleby-in-Westmorland
Grasmere
Ambleside
Kirkby Stephen
Hawkshead
Windermere
Ravenstonedale
Bowness-on-Windermere
Crosthwaite
YORKSHIRE (plans 22 23)
Kendal
Bowland Bridge
Newby Bridge
A
Lupton
Cartmel
Arnside
Grange-over-Sands
Kirkby Lonsdale
Dalton-in-Furness
Morecambe Bay
Lancaster
3
CHESHIRE, LANCASHIRE, ISLE OF MAN (plan 20)
Blackpool
Ribble
Preston
A
B
Place with at least:
a hotel or a restaurant
a starred establishment
a "Bib Gourmand" restaurant
a "Bib Hotel"
a particularly pleasant restaurant
a particularly pleasant accommodation

22 Yorkshire

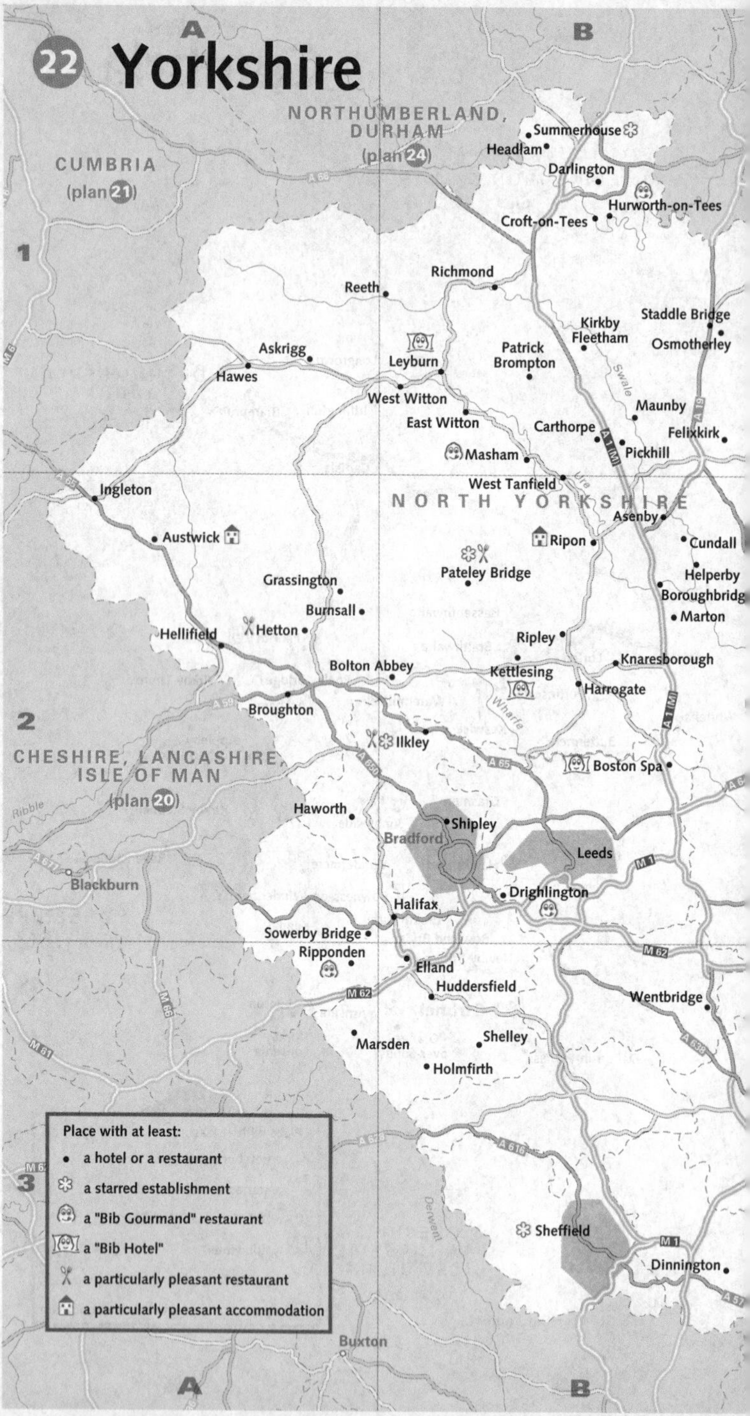

A B

NORTHUMBERLAND, DURHAM (plan 24)

CUMBRIA (plan 21)

CHESHIRE, LANCASHIRE, ISLE OF MAN (plan 20)

NORTH YORKSHIRE

1 2 3

Summerhouse, Headlam, Darlington, Hurworth-on-Tees, Croft-on-Tees, Richmond, Reeth, Kirkby Fleetham, Staddle Bridge, Osmotherley, Askrigg, Hawes, Leyburn, Patrick Brompton, West Witton, East Witton, Maunby, Carthorpe, Felixkirk, Pickhill, Masham, West Tanfield, Ingleton, Asenby, Austwick, Ripon, Cundall, Pateley Bridge, Helperby, Grassington, Boroughbridge, Burnsall, Marton, Hetton, Hellifield, Ripley, Knaresborough, Bolton Abbey, Kettlesing, Harrogate, Broughton, Ilkley, Boston Spa, Haworth, Shipley, Bradford, Leeds, Blackburn, Drighlington, Halifax, Sowerby Bridge, Ripponden, Elland, Huddersfield, Wentbridge, Marsden, Shelley, Holmfirth, Sheffield, Dinnington, Buxton

Place with at least:

- a hotel or a restaurant
- a starred establishment
- a "Bib Gourmand" restaurant
- a "Bib Hotel"
- a particularly pleasant restaurant
- a particularly pleasant accommodation

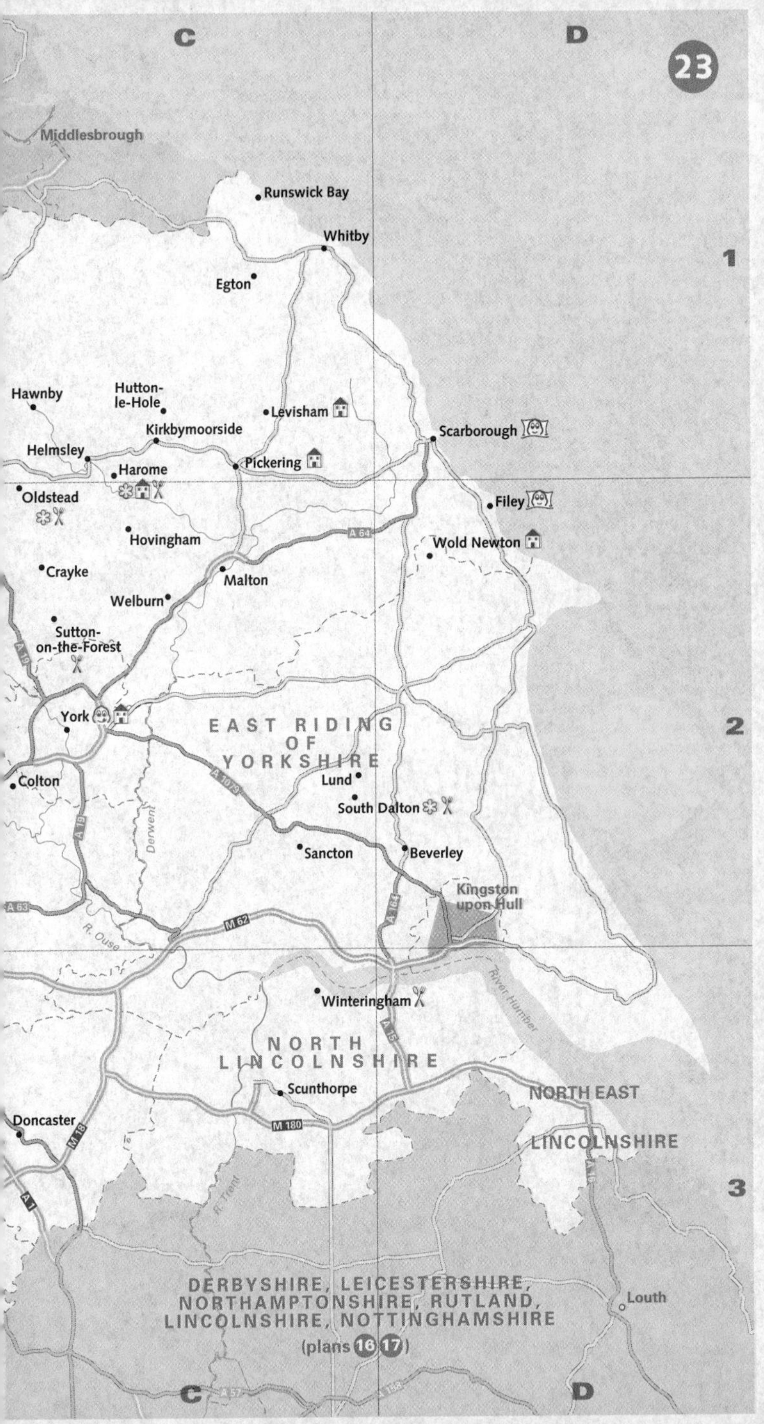

C
D
23
Middlesbrough
Runswick Bay
Whitby
1
Egton
Hawnby
Hutton-le-Hole
Levisham
Kirkbymoorside
Scarborough
Helmsley
Pickering
Harome
Oldstead
Filey
A 64
Hovingham
Wold Newton
Crayke
Malton
Welburn
Sutton-on-the-Forest
A 19
York
EAST RIDING OF YORKSHIRE
2
Colton
Lund
A 1079
South Dalton
A 19
Derwent
Sancton
Beverley
Kingston upon Hull
A 63
A 164
M 62
R. Ouse
River Humber
Winteringham
A 15
NORTH LINCOLNSHIRE
Scunthorpe
NORTH EAST
Doncaster
M 180
M 18
LINCOLNSHIRE
A 16
A 1
R. Trent
3
DERBYSHIRE, LEICESTERSHIRE,
NORTHAMPTONSHIRE, RUTLAND,
LINCOLNSHIRE, NOTTINGHAMSHIRE
(plans 16 17)
Louth
C
A 57
A 158
D

Northumberland, Durham

Place with at least:

- a hotel or a restaurant
- a starred establishment
- a "Bib Gourmand" restaurant
- a "Bib Hotel"
- a particularly pleasant restaurant
- a particularly pleasant accommodation

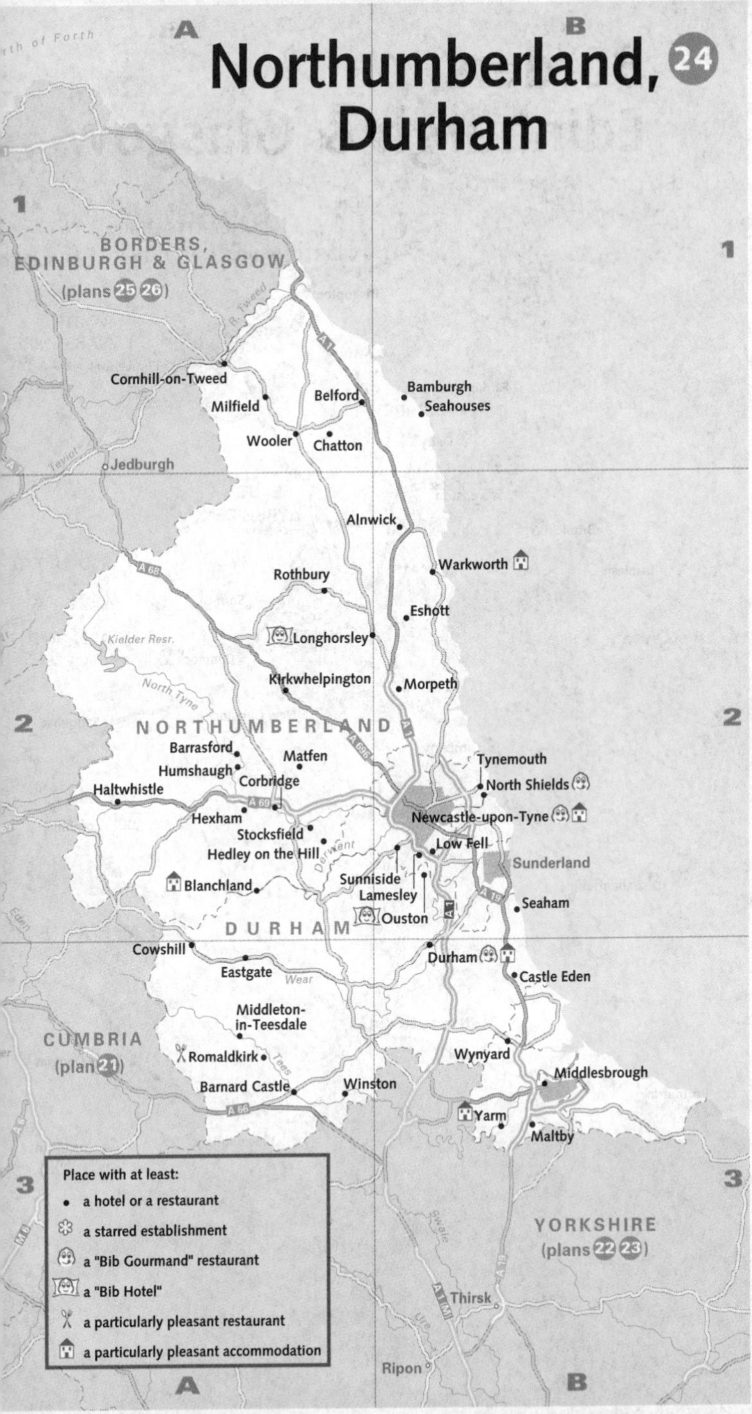

25 Borders, Edinburgh & Glasgow

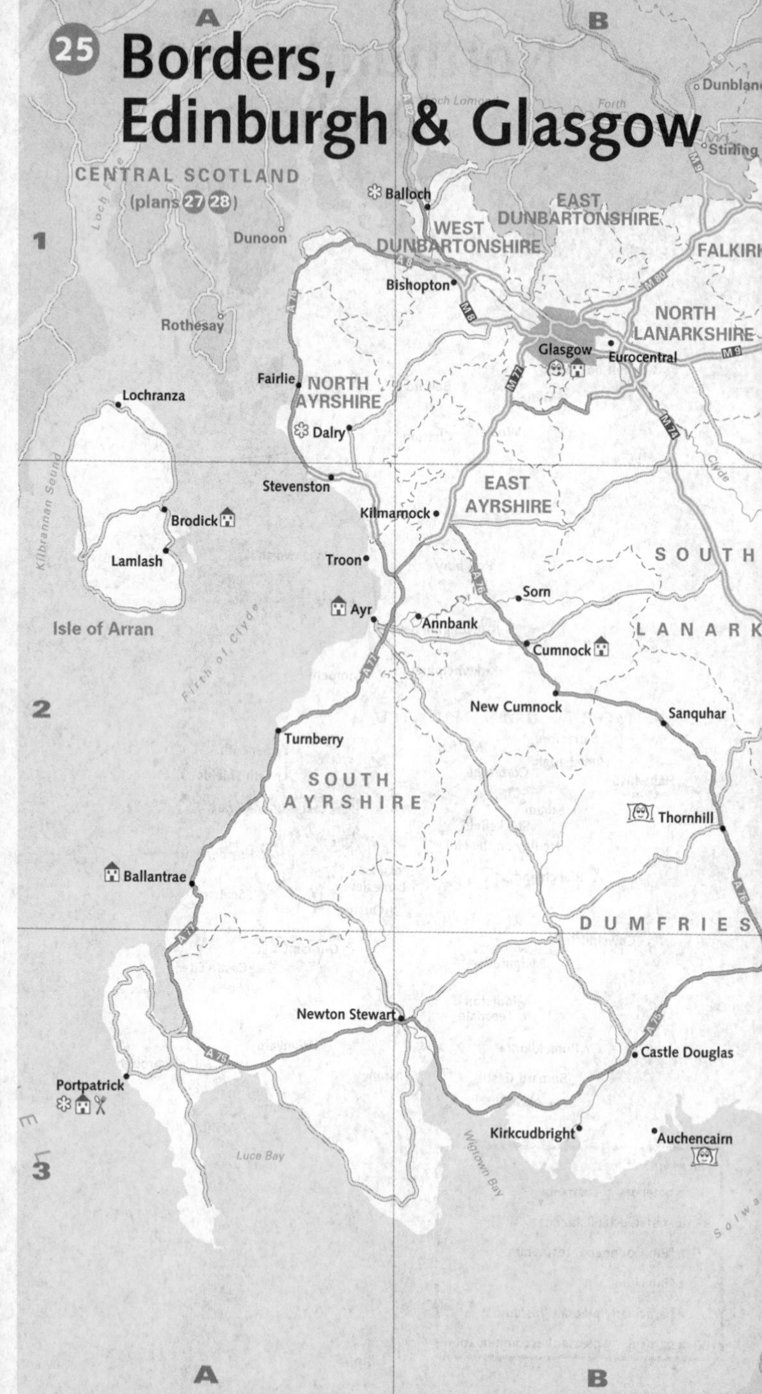

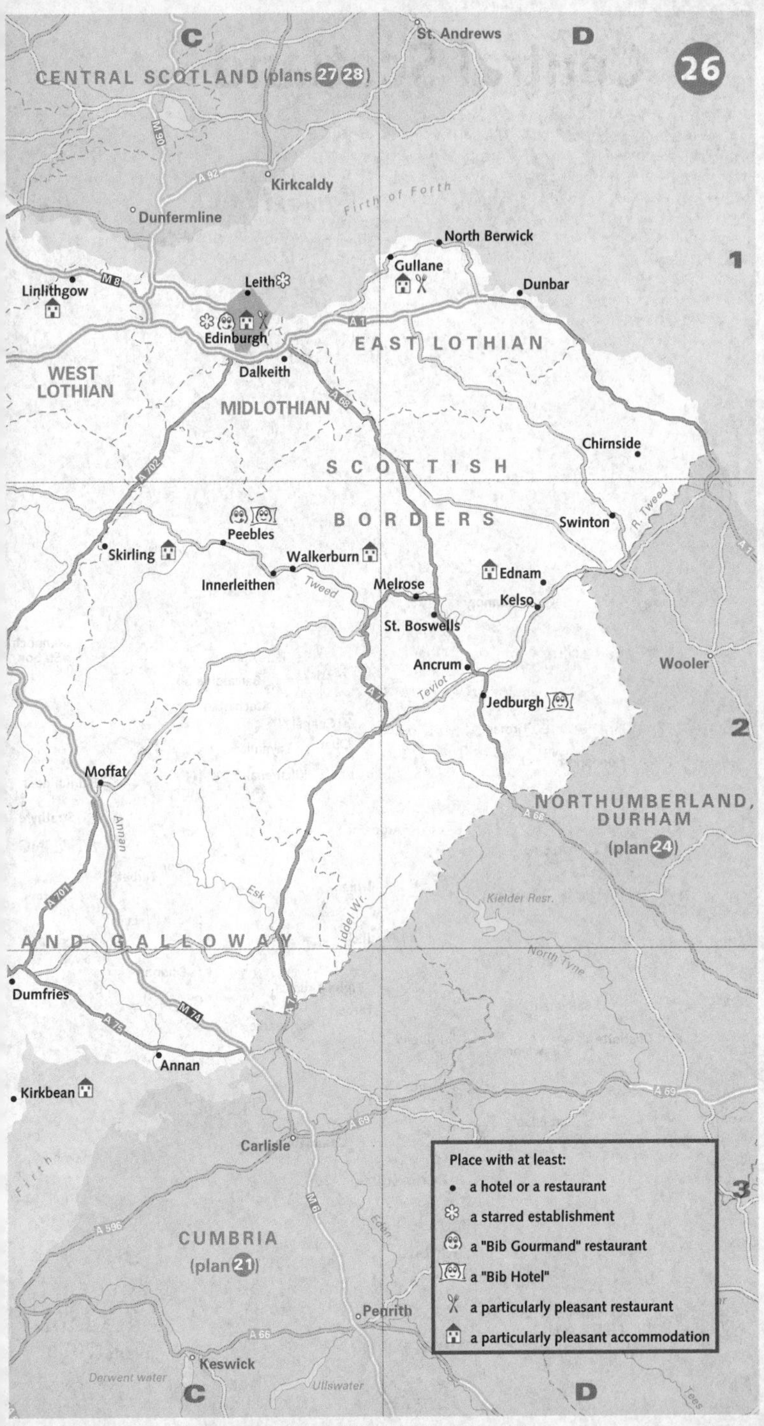

C
D
26
CENTRAL SCOTLAND (plans 27 28)
St. Andrews
Kirkcaldy
Firth of Forth
Dunfermline
North Berwick
Gullane
Dunbar
1
Linlithgow
Leith
Edinburgh
EAST LOTHIAN
WEST LOTHIAN
Dalkeith
MIDLOTHIAN
Chirnside
SCOTTISH
BORDERS
Swinton
R. Tweed
Peebles
Skirling
Walkerburn
Ednam
Innerleithen
Tweed
Melrose
Kelso
St. Boswells
Ancrum
Wooler
Teviot
Jedburgh
2
Moffat
Annan
NORTHUMBERLAND, DURHAM
(plan 24)
Kielder Resr.
Esk
Liddel Wr.
AND GALLOWAY
North Tyne
Dumfries
Annan
Kirkbean
Carlisle
Eden
CUMBRIA
(plan 21)
Penrith
Keswick
Derwent water
Ullswater
Tees
3
Place with at least:
• a hotel or a restaurant
a starred establishment
a "Bib Gourmand" restaurant
a "Bib Hotel"
a particularly pleasant restaurant
a particularly pleasant accommodation

27 Central Scotland

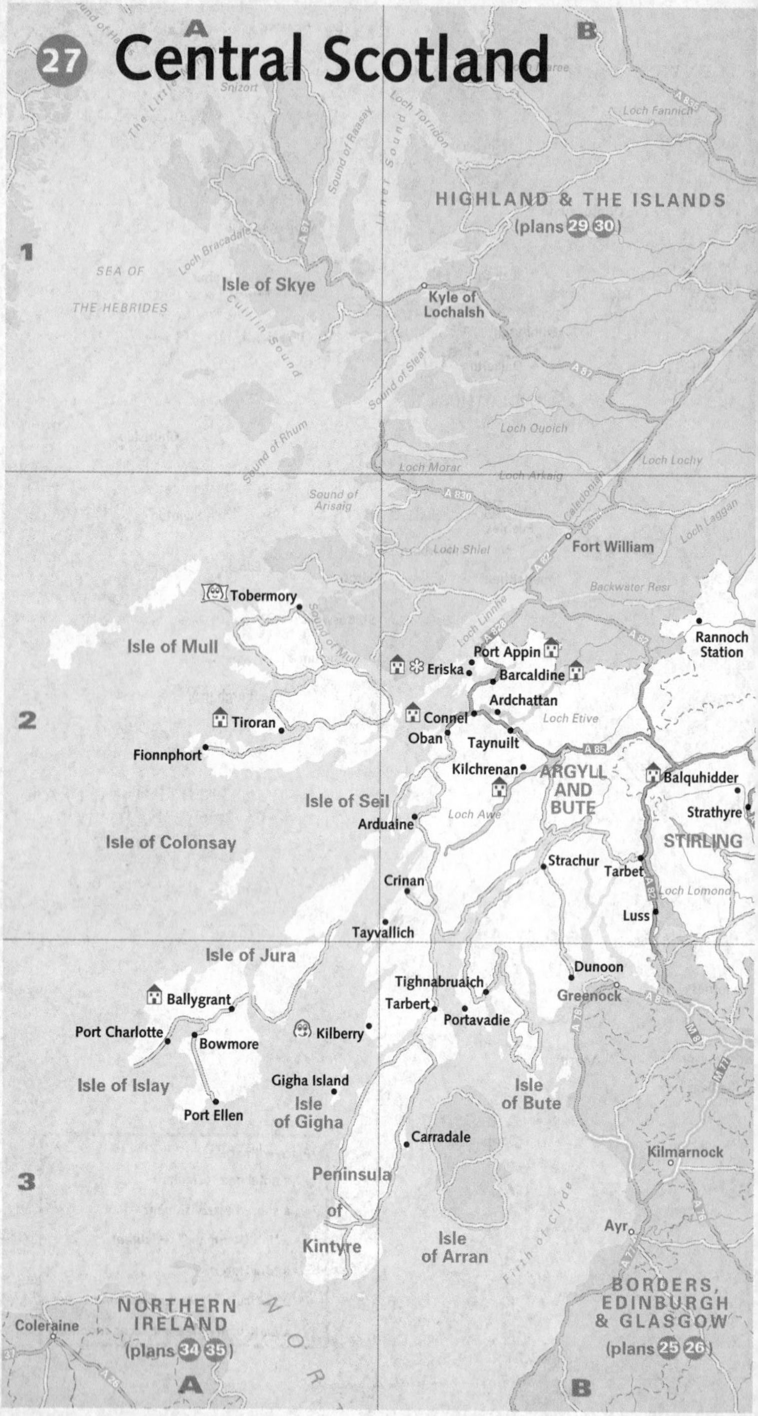

A B

HIGHLAND & THE ISLANDS (plans 29 30)

1

SEA OF THE HEBRIDES

Isle of Skye

Kyle of Lochalsh

Loch Bracadale

Sound of Raasay

Inner Sound

Loch Torridon

Loch Fannich

A 835

A 87

Cuillin Sound

Sound of Sleat

Sound of Rhum

Loch Quoich

Loch Morar

Loch Arkaig

Loch Lochy

Sound of Arisaig

A 830

Caledonian Canal

Loch Laggan

Loch Shiel

Fort William

A 82

Backwater Resr

Tobermory

Sound of Mull

Loch Linnhe

A 828

Isle of Mull

Rannoch Station

Port Appin

Eriska

Barcaldine

Ardchattan

2

Tiroran

Connel

Loch Etive

Oban

Taynuilt

Fionnphort

A 85

Kilchrenan

ARGYLL AND BUTE

Balquhidder

Strathyre

Isle of Seil

Loch Awe

Arduaine

Isle of Colonsay

STIRLING

Strachur

Tarbet

Crinan

Loch Lomond

Luss

Tayvallich

Isle of Jura

Dunoon

Tighnabruaich

Greenock

Ballygrant

Tarbert

Portavadie

Port Charlotte

Kilberry

Bowmore

Isle of Islay

Gigha Island

Isle of Bute

Isle of Gigha

Port Ellen

Carradale

Kilmarnock

3

Peninsula of Kintyre

Isle of Arran

Firth of Clyde

Ayr

A 77

NORTHERN IRELAND (plans 34 35)

Coleraine

BORDERS, EDINBURGH & GLASGOW (plans 25 26)

A B

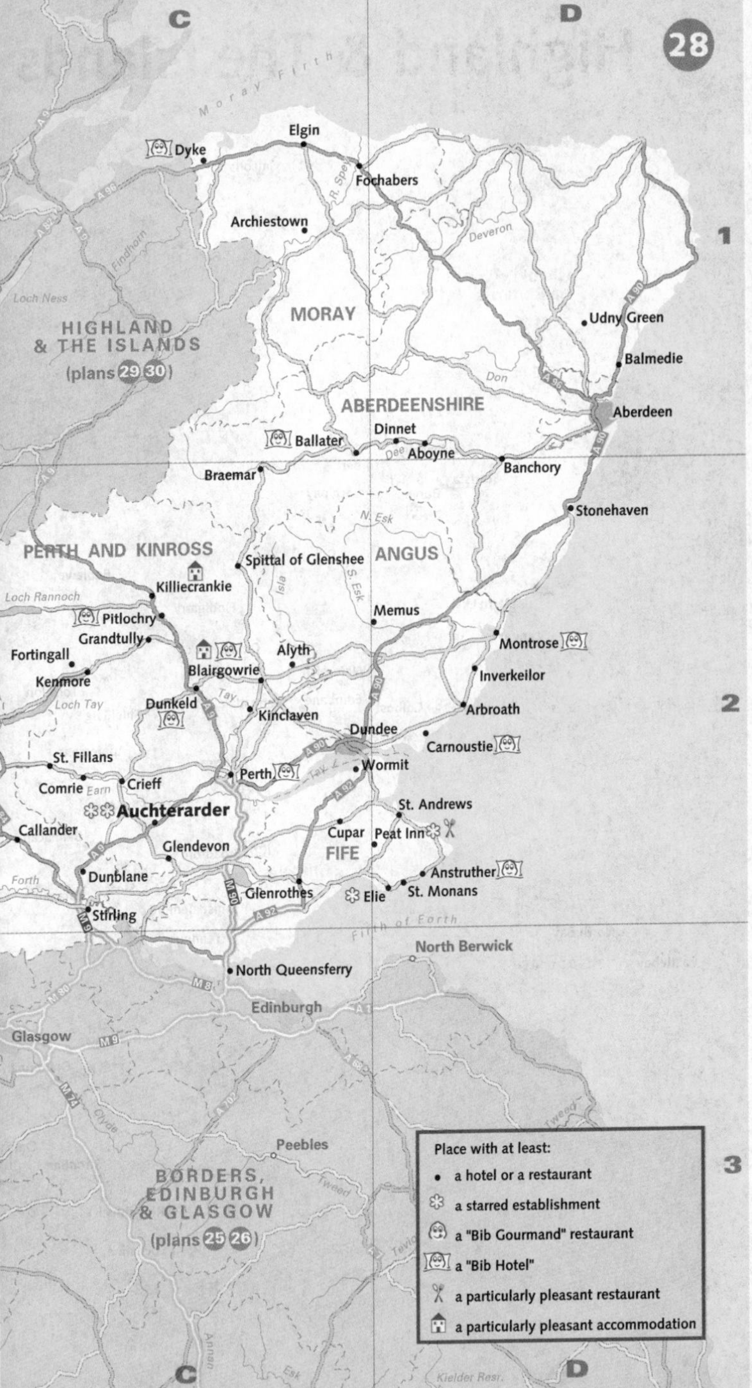
28
C
D
1
2
3
Moray Firth
Elgin
Dyke
Fochabers
Archiestown
Deveron
MORAY
Udny Green
Balmedie
HIGHLAND
& THE ISLANDS
(plans 29 30)
Loch Ness
Don
ABERDEENSHIRE
Aberdeen
Ballater
Dinnet
Aboyne
Banchory
Braemar
Stonehaven
N. Esk
PERTH AND KINROSS
Spittal of Glenshee
ANGUS
Killiecrankie
Loch Rannoch
Pitlochry
Memus
Grandtully
Montrose
Fortingall
Alyth
Blairgowrie
Inverkeilor
Kenmore
Loch Tay
Dunkeld
Kinclaven
Arbroath
Dundee
Carnoustie
St. Fillans
Perth
Wormit
Comrie
Crieff
St. Andrews
Auchterarder
Callander
Cupar
Peat Inn
Glendevon
FIFE
Dunblane
Anstruther
Glenrothes
Elie
St. Monans
Stirling
Firth of Forth
North Berwick
North Queensferry
Edinburgh
Glasgow
Peebles
BORDERS,
EDINBURGH
& GLASGOW
(plans 25 26)
Place with at least:
a hotel or a restaurant
a starred establishment
a "Bib Gourmand" restaurant
a "Bib Hotel"
a particularly pleasant restaurant
a particularly pleasant accommodation

29 Highland & The Islands

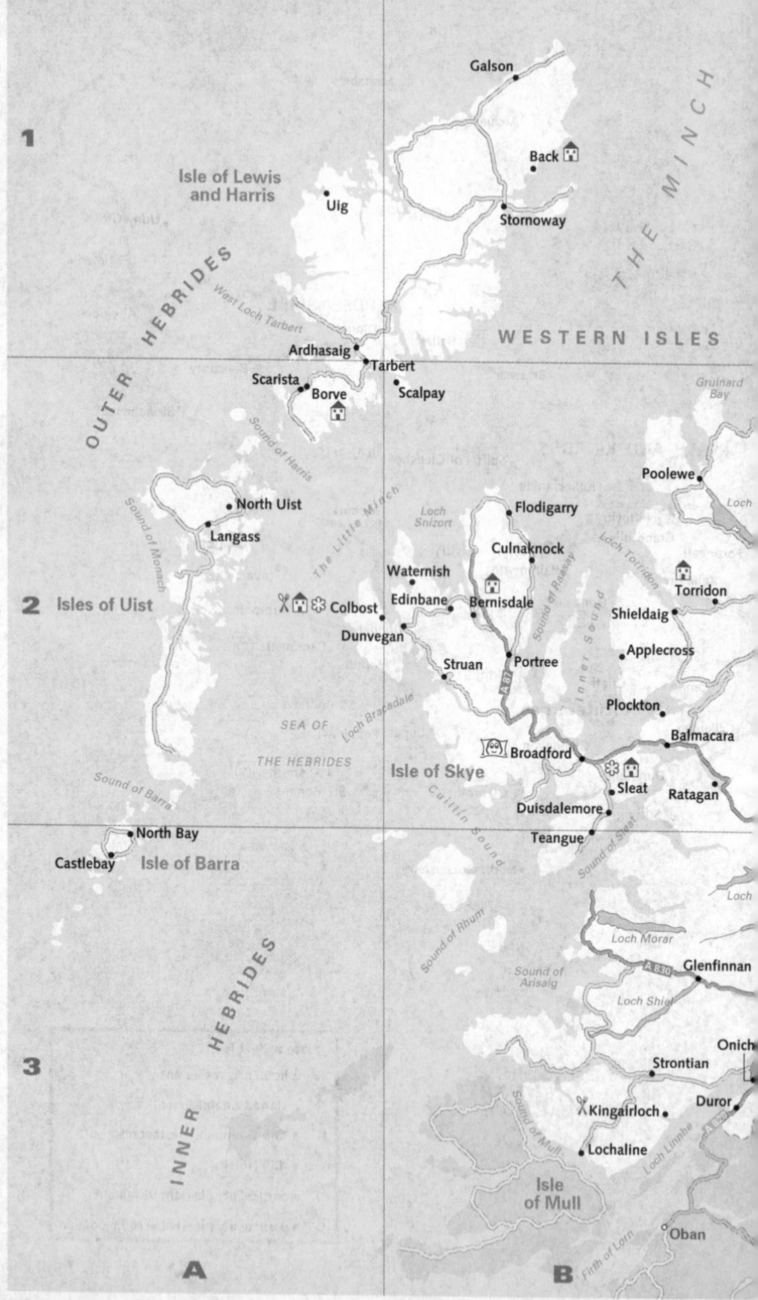
A
B
1
2
3
Galson
Back
Isle of Lewis and Harris
Uig
Stornoway
THE MINCH
OUTER HEBRIDES
West Loch Tarbert
WESTERN ISLES
Ardhasaig
Tarbert
Scarista
Borve
Scalpay
Sound of Harris
Gruinard Bay
Poolewe
Loch
North Uist
Langass
Sound of Monach
The Little Minch
Loch Snizort
Flodigarry
Culnaknock
Loch Torridon
Waternish
Torridon
Isles of Uist
Colbost
Edinbane
Bernisdale
Sound of Raasay
Shieldaig
Dunvegan
Inner Sound
Applecross
Struan
Portree
A 87
Plockton
Loch Bracadale
SEA OF THE HEBRIDES
Balmacara
Broadford
Isle of Skye
Sleat
Ratagan
Sound of Barra
Cuillin Sound
Duisdalemore
North Bay
Teangue
Castlebay
Isle of Barra
Sound of Sleat
Loch
Loch Morar
Sound of Rhum
Sound of Arisaig
A 830
Glenfinnan
Loch Shiel
INNER HEBRIDES
Onich
Strontian
Kingairloch
Duror
Sound of Mull
Lochaline
Loch Linnhe
A 828
Isle of Mull
Oban
Firth of Lorn

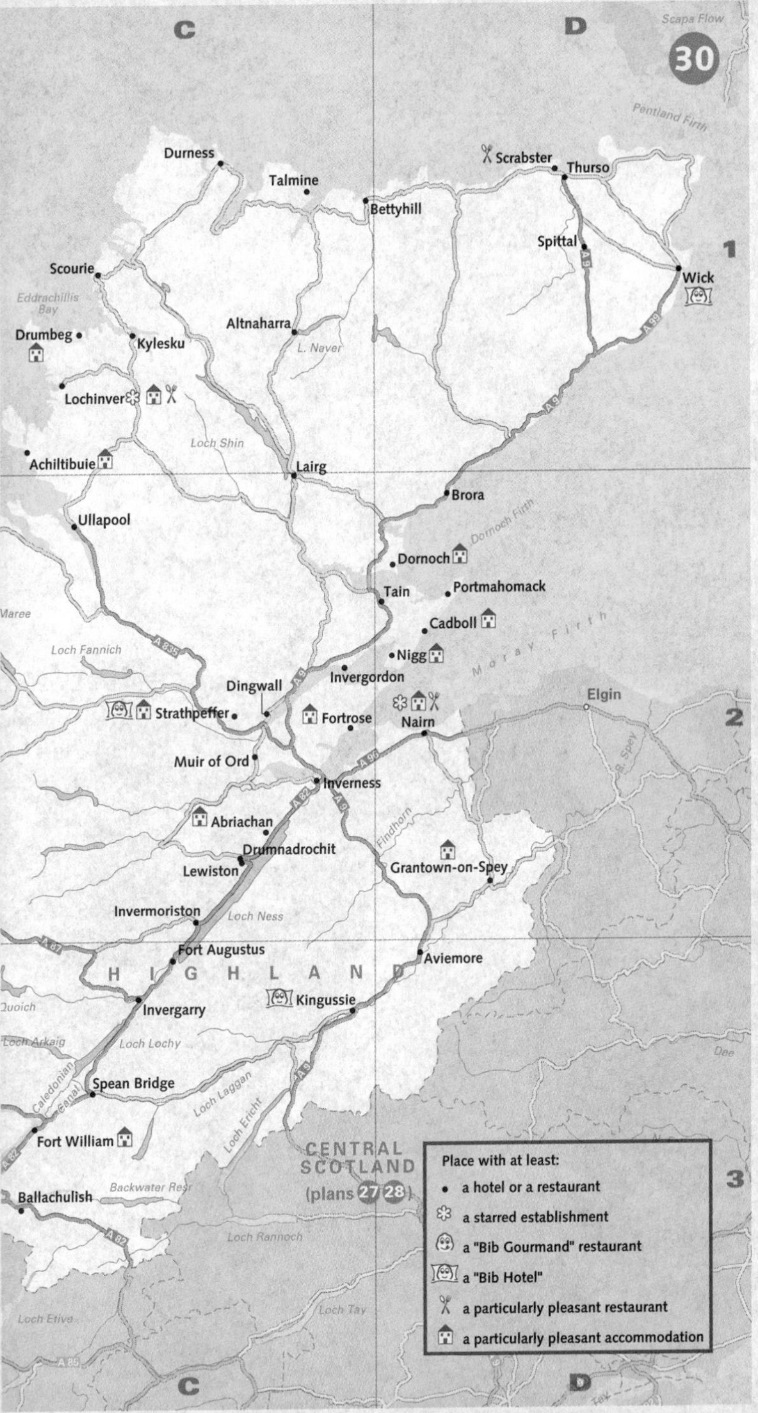
C
D
30
Scapa Flow
Pentland Firth
Durness
Talmine
Scrabster
Thurso
Bettyhill
Spittal
1
Scourie
Wick
Eddrachillis Bay
Altnaharra
Drumbeg
Kylesku
L. Naver
Lochinver
Loch Shin
Achiltibuie
Lairg
Brora
Ullapool
Dornoch Firth
Dornoch
Tain
Portmahomack
Maree
Cadboll
Moray Firth
Loch Fannich
Nigg
Invergordon
Dingwall
Elgin
Strathpeffer
Fortrose
Nairn
2
Muir of Ord
R. Spey
Inverness
Abriachan
Findhorn
Drumnadrochit
Lewiston
Grantown-on-Spey
Invermoriston
Loch Ness
Fort Augustus
Aviemore
HIGHLAND
Kingussie
Quoich
Invergarry
Loch Arkaig
Loch Lochy
Dee
Caledonian Canal
Spean Bridge
Loch Laggan
Loch Ericht
Fort William
CENTRAL SCOTLAND
(plans 27 28)
3
Ballachulish
Backwater Resr
Loch Rannoch
Loch Etive
Loch Tay
Tay
A 9
A 99
A 835
A 96
A 82
A 87
A 86
A 85
Place with at least:
a hotel or a restaurant
a starred establishment
a "Bib Gourmand" restaurant
a "Bib Hotel"
a particularly pleasant restaurant
a particularly pleasant accommodation

Shetland & Orkney 31

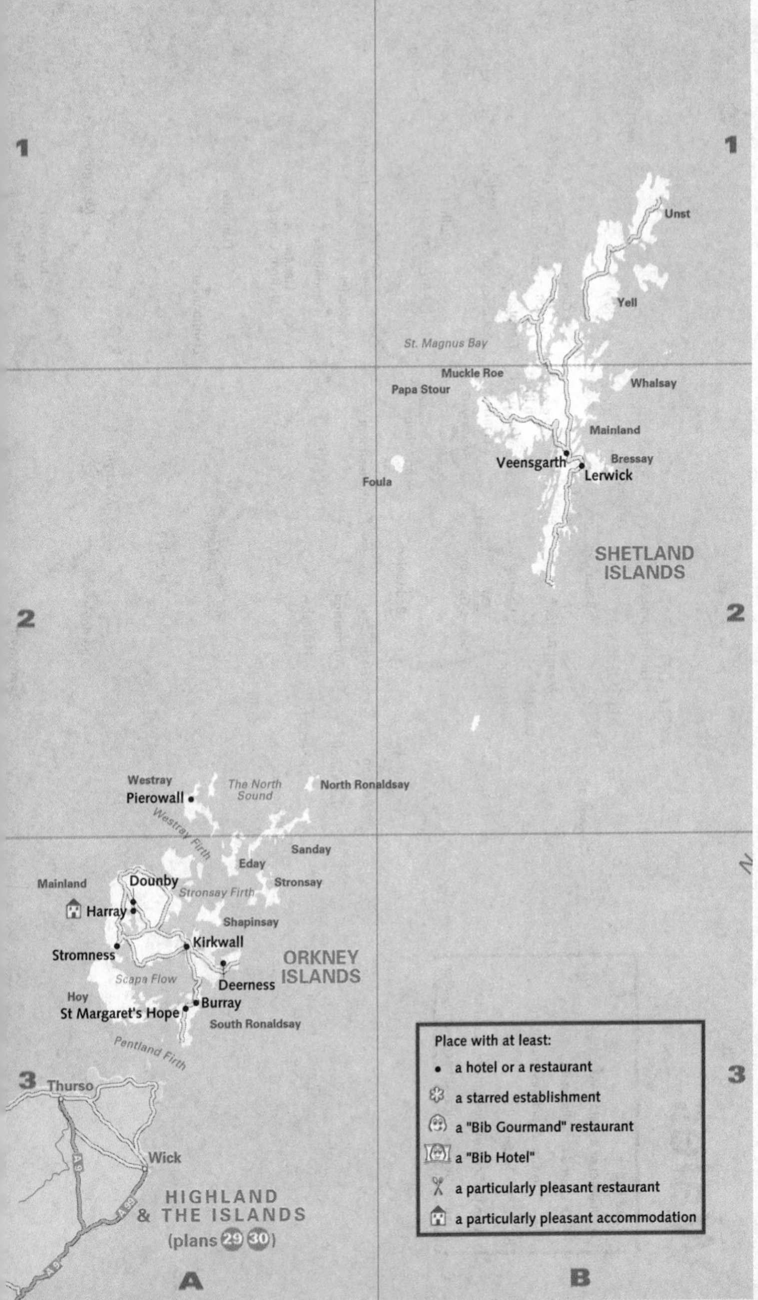

Wales

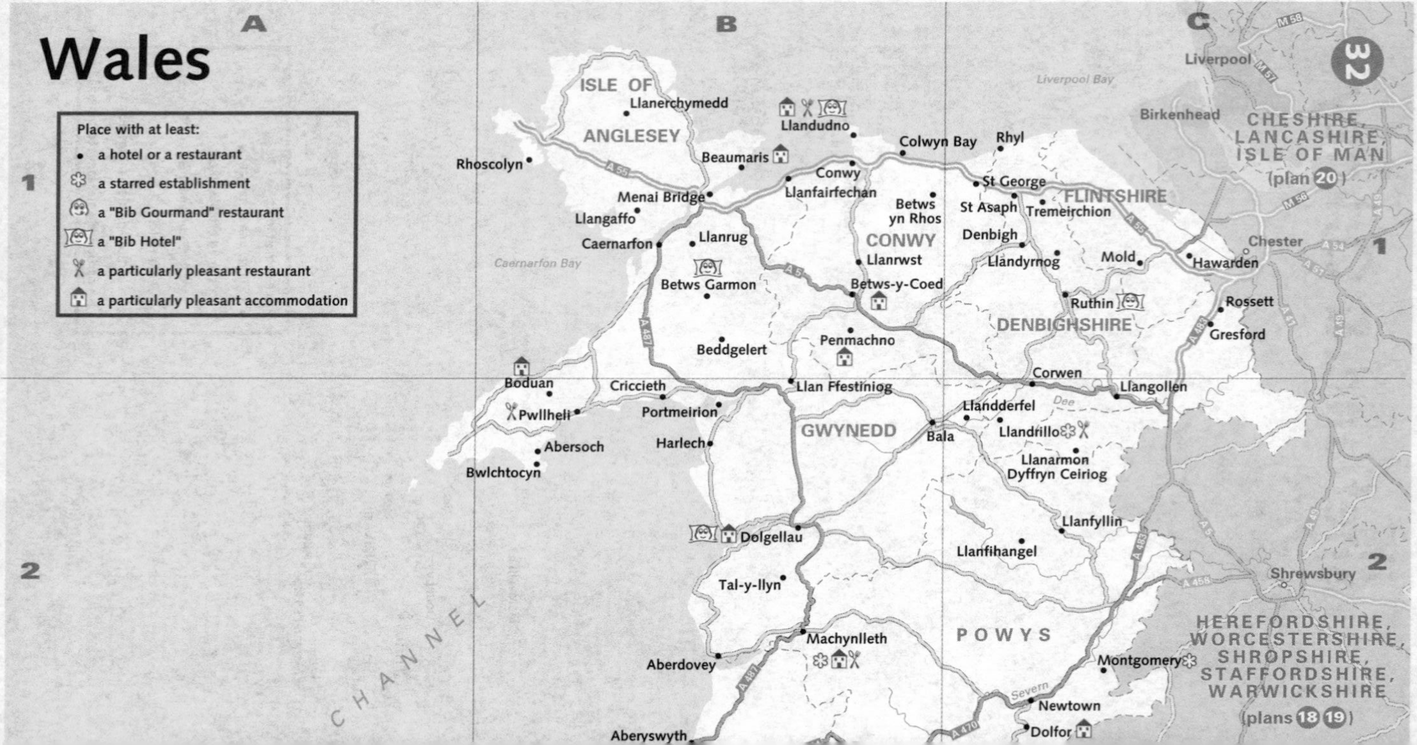

Place with at least:

- a hotel or a restaurant
- ✿ a starred establishment
- a "Bib Gourmand" restaurant
- a "Bib Hotel"
- a particularly pleasant restaurant
- a particularly pleasant accommodation

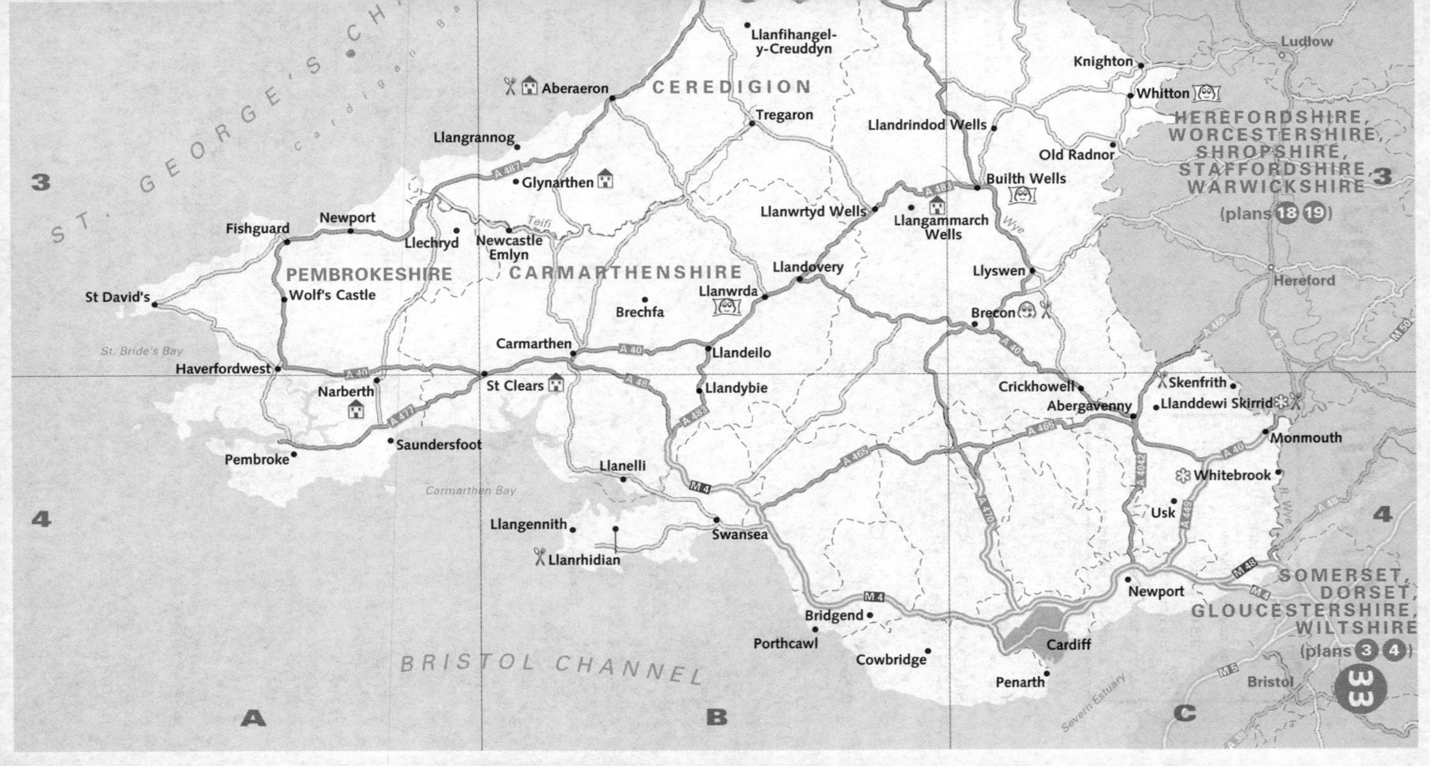

ST GEORGE'S CHANNEL
Cardigan Bay
CEREDIGION
PEMBROKESHIRE
CARMARTHENSHIRE
HEREFORDSHIRE, WORCESTERSHIRE, SHROPSHIRE, STAFFORDSHIRE, WARWICKSHIRE
(plans 18 19)
SOMERSET, DORSET, GLOUCESTERSHIRE, WILTSHIRE
(plans 3 4)
BRISTOL CHANNEL
St. Bride's Bay
Carmarthen Bay
Severn Estuary
Teifi
Wye
R. Wye
Ludlow
Knighton
Whitton
Old Radnor
Llanfihangel-y-Creuddyn
Aberaeron
Tregaron
Llandrindod Wells
Llangrannog
Glynarthen
Builth Wells
Llanwrtyd Wells
Llangammarch Wells
Fishguard
Newport
Llechryd
Newcastle Emlyn
Llandovery
Llyswen
Hereford
St David's
Wolf's Castle
Llanwrda
Brechfa
Brecon
Carmarthen
Llandeilo
Haverfordwest
Narberth
St Clears
Llandybie
Crickhowell
Skenfrith
Abergavenny
Llanddewi Skirrid
Monmouth
Pembroke
Saundersfoot
Llanelli
Whitebrook
Usk
Llangennith
Llanrhidian
Swansea
Newport
Bridgend
Porthcawl
Cowbridge
Cardiff
Penarth
Bristol
A 487
A 40
A 48
A 477
A 483
A 465
A 470
A 4042
A 449
A 49
A 38
M 4
M 48
M 5
M 50
3
4
A
B
C
33

34 Northern Ireland

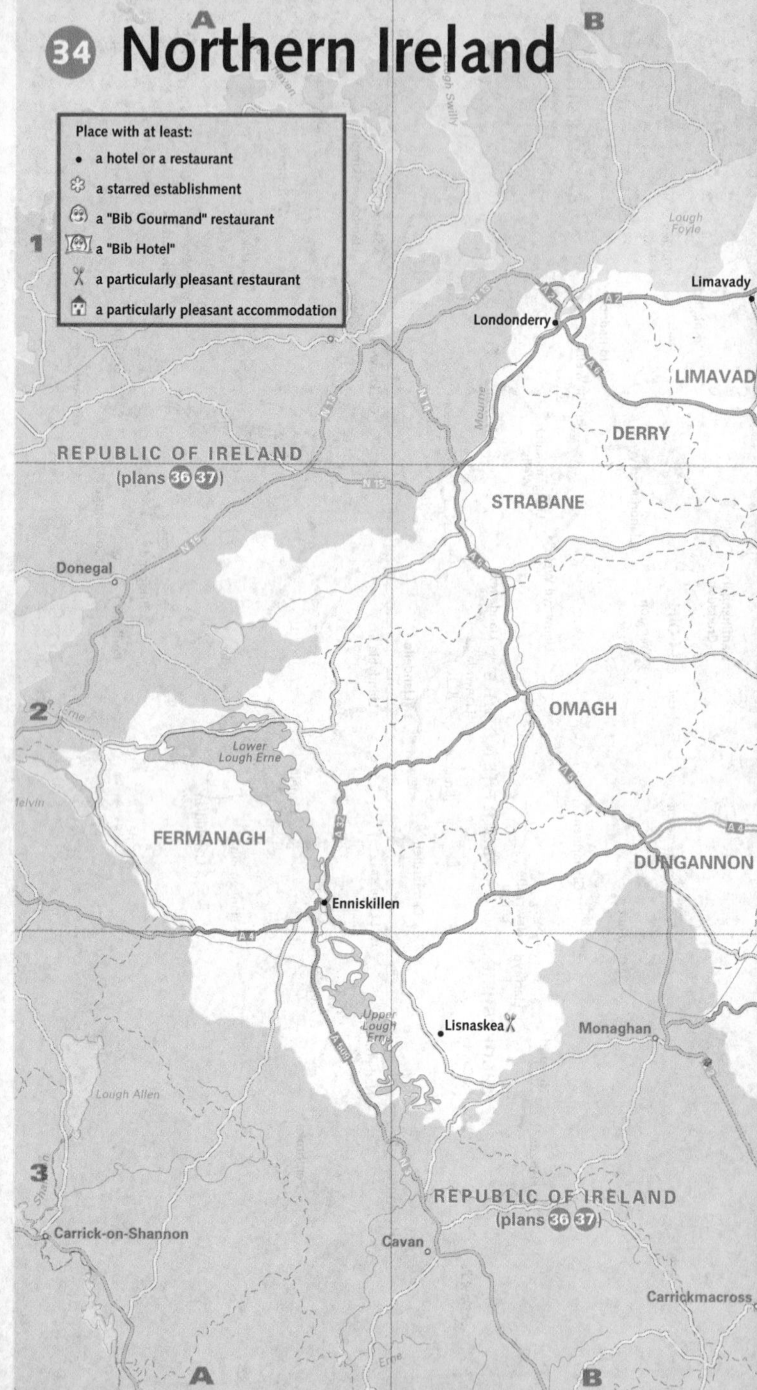

C
D
CENTRAL SCOTLAND
(plans 27 28)
35
Ballintoy
Portstewart
Portrush
Bushmills
NORTH CHANNEL
Coleraine
MOYLE
1
A 37
A 26
BALLYMONEY
Bann
Ballymena
MAGHERAFELT
Larne
A 26
A 8
Mounthill
Magherafelt
M 22
Ballyclare
COOKSTOWN
M 2
Newtownabbey
ANTRIM
Belfast Lough
2
Bangor
Holywood
Crumlin
A 2
Donaghadee
Lough Neagh
Belfast
Newtownards
Dungannon
M 1
M 1
Comber
Lisbane
CRAIGAVON
Killinchy
Hillsborough
A 24
Strangford Lough
A 3
A 1
Armagh
DOWN
BANBRIDGE
Bann
Dundrum
Newcastle
Dundrum Bay
NEWRY AND MOURNE
3
A 1
Warrenpoint
Carlingford Lough
N 1
Dundalk
Dundalk bay
M 1
C
D

36 Republic of Ireland

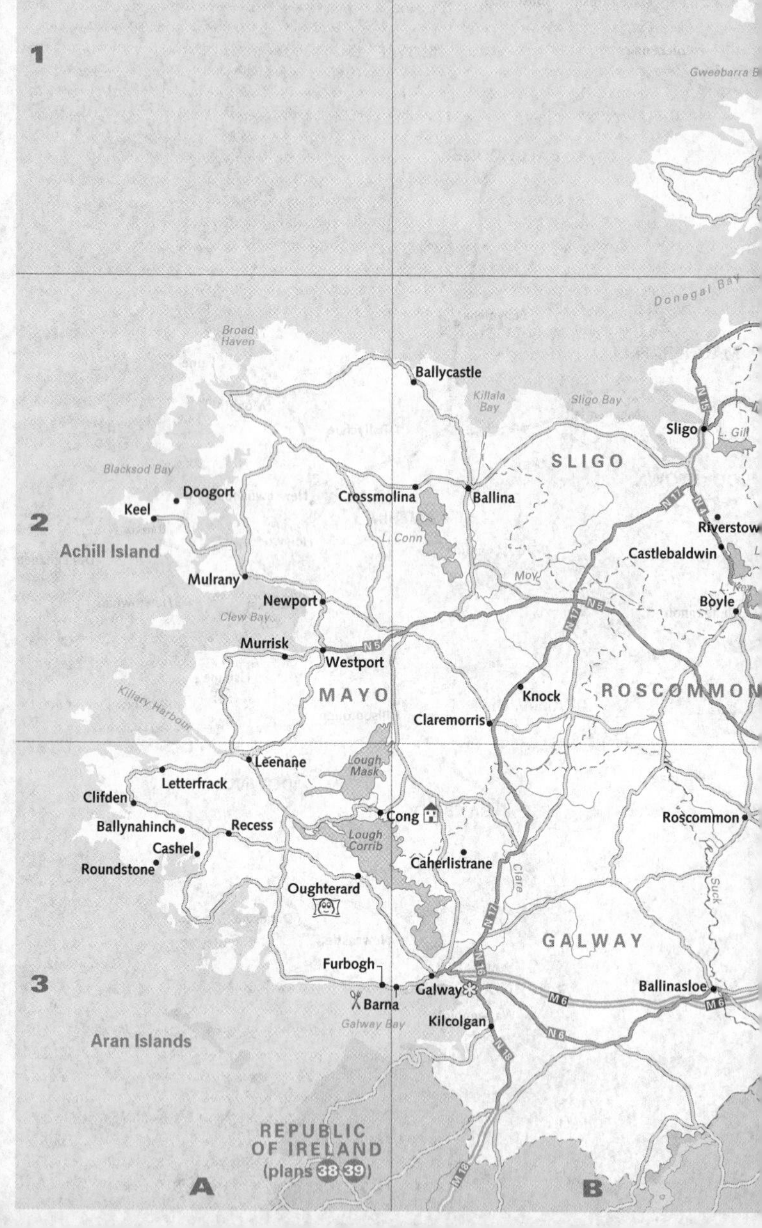

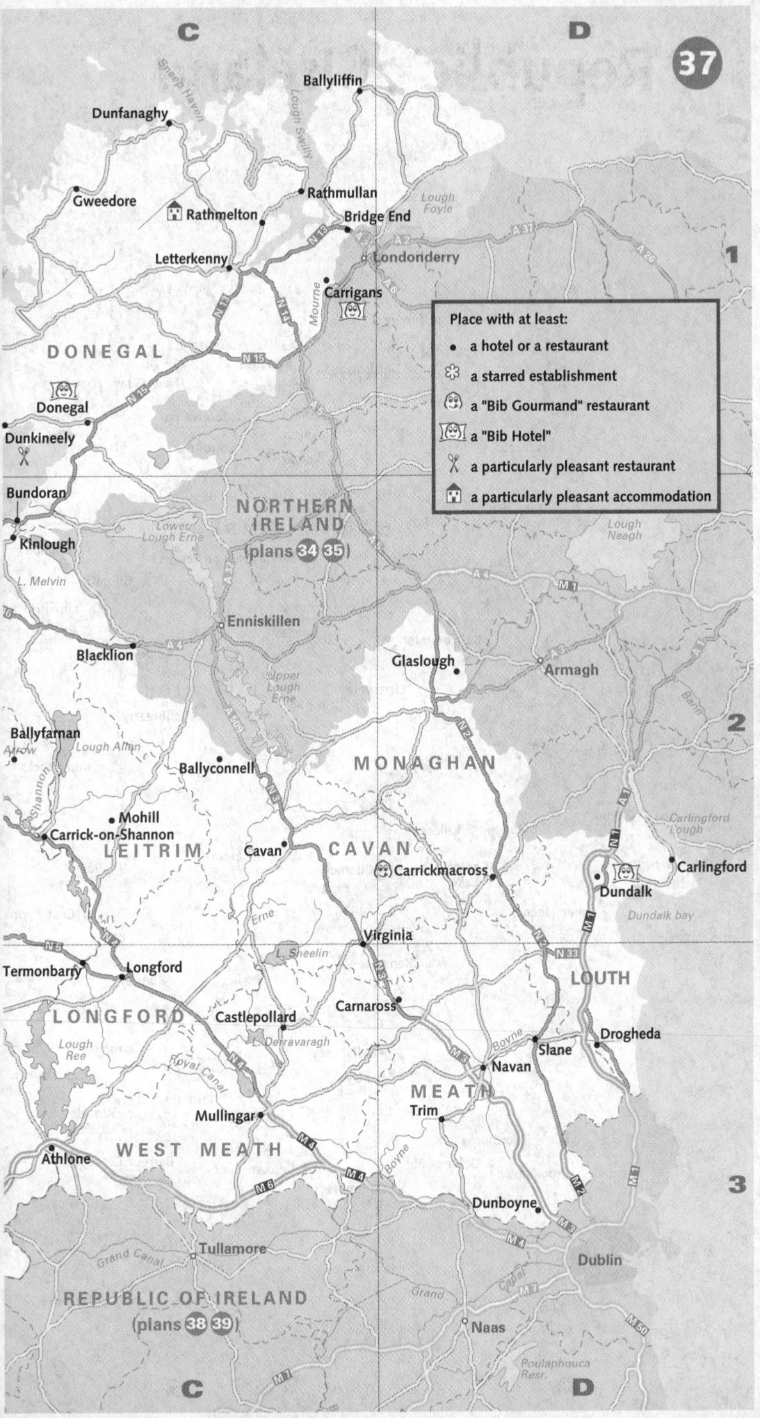
C
D
Place with at least:
a hotel or a restaurant
a starred establishment
a "Bib Gourmand" restaurant
a "Bib Hotel"
a particularly pleasant restaurant
a particularly pleasant accommodation
Ballyliffin
Dunfanaghy
Rathmullan
Gweedore
Rathmelton
Bridge End
Letterkenny
Londonderry
Carrigans
DONEGAL
Donegal
Dunkineely
Bundoran
Kinlough
NORTHERN IRELAND
(plans 34 35)
Enniskillen
Blacklion
Glaslough
Armagh
Ballyfarnan
Ballyconnell
MONAGHAN
Mohill
Carrick-on-Shannon
LEITRIM
Cavan
CAVAN
Carrickmacross
Carlingford
Dundalk
Virginia
Termonbarry
Longford
LOUTH
Carnaross
LONGFORD
Castlepollard
Drogheda
Slane
Navan
MEATH
Trim
Mullingar
Athlone
WEST MEATH
Dunboyne
Tullamore
Dublin
REPUBLIC OF IRELAND
(plans 38 39)
Naas
1
2
3

38 Republic of Ireland

A B

REPUBLIC OF IRELAND (plans 36 37)

Clifden
Lough Mask
Lough Corrib
Galway
Galway Bay
M 6
N 6
N 17
N 18
Clare

1

Inishmore
Aran Islands
Inishmaan
Inisheer
Ballyvaughan
Fanore
New Quay
Doolin
Lisdoonvarna
Liscannor
Lahinch
Corrofin
M 18
Spanish Point
CLARE
Doonbeg
Killaloe
Newmarket on Fergus
Bunratty
River Shannon
N 18
Limerick
M 7
Mouth of the Shannon
Ballybunnion
M 20
N 24
Adare
N 21
Listowel
LIMERICK
Ballingarry
Maigue
Tralee Bay

2

Castlegregory
Tralee
Kilmallock
N 21
N 23
N 22
Dingle
Cromane
Killorglin
Dingle Bay
Kanturk
Valencia Island
Caragh Lake
Killarney
Mallow
Blackwater
Castlelyons
Cahersiveen
KERRY
CORK
Portmagee
N 20
M 8
Kenmare
Blarney
Fota Island
Cork
N 22
N 25
Lee
N 28
Cobh
Carrigaline
Ballylickey
Bandon
Crosshaven
Bantry
Bantry Bay
Bandon
Kilbrittain
Durrus
Kinsale
Clonakilty
Dunmanus Bay
Toormore
Barrells Cross
Goleen
Crookhaven
Castletownshend

3

Baltimore
Roaringwater Bay

C E L T I

A B

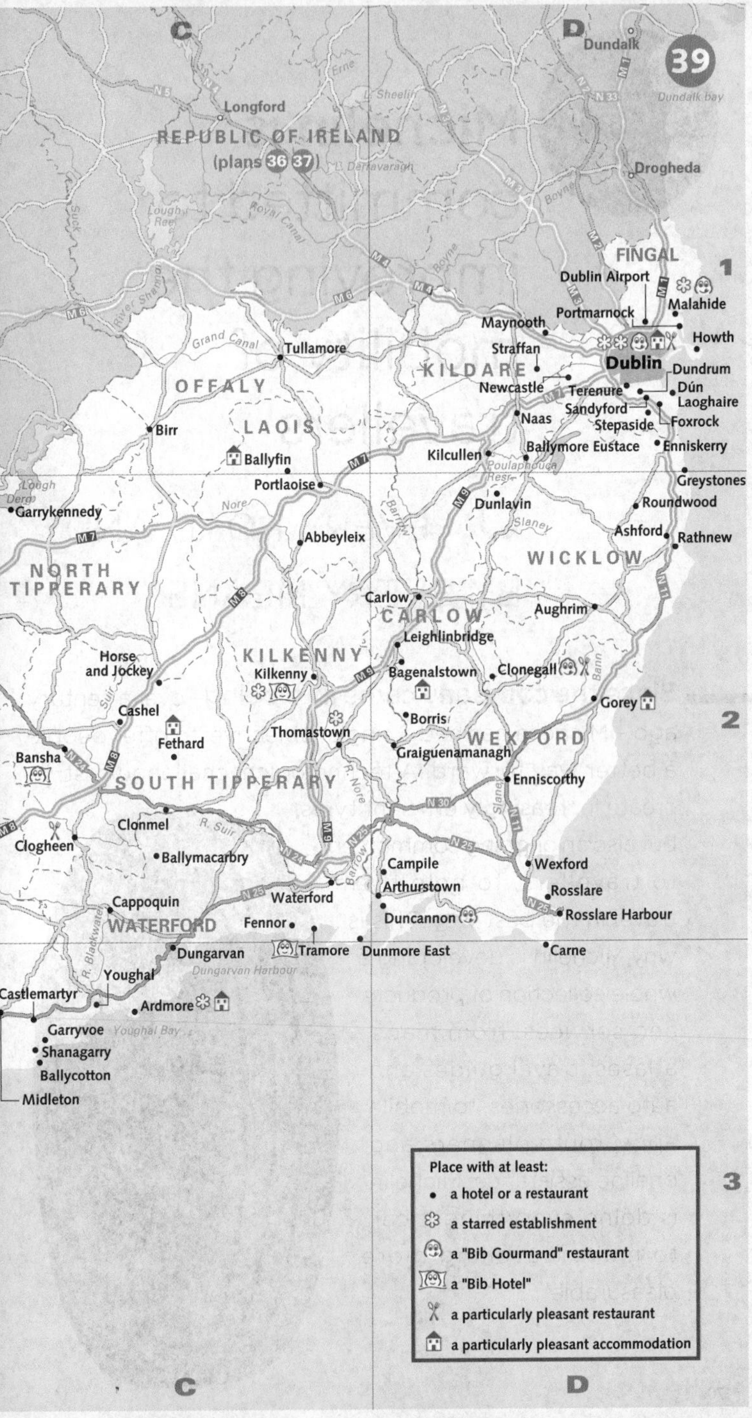

C
D
39
Dundalk
Dundalk bay
Longford
REPUBLIC OF IRELAND
(plans 36 37)
Drogheda
FINGAL
1
Dublin Airport
Malahide
Portmarnock
Maynooth
Howth
Straffan
Dublin
Tullamore
KILDARE
Dundrum
OFFALY
Newcastle
Terenure
Dún Laoghaire
Sandyford
Naas
Stepaside
Foxrock
Birr
LAOIS
Ballymore Eustace
Enniskerry
Ballyfin
Kilcullen
Portlaoise
Greystones
Garrykennedy
Dunlavin
Roundwood
Abbeyleix
Ashford
Rathnew
WICKLOW
NORTH TIPPERARY
Carlow
CARLOW
Aughrim
Leighlinbridge
KILKENNY
Horse and Jockey
Kilkenny
Bagenalstown
Clonegall
Gorey
Cashel
2
Borris
Fethard
Thomastown
WEXFORD
Bansha
Graiguenamanagh
SOUTH TIPPERARY
Enniscorthy
Clonmel
Clogheen
Campile
Wexford
Ballymacarbry
Arthurstown
Rosslare
Waterford
Cappoquin
Duncannon
Rosslare Harbour
WATERFORD
Fennor
Dungarvan
Tramore
Dunmore East
Carne
Dungarvan Harbour
Youghal
Castlemartyr
Ardmore
Garryvoe
Youghal Bay
Shanagarry
Ballycotton
Midleton
Place with at least:
a hotel or a restaurant
a starred establishment
a "Bib Gourmand" restaurant
a "Bib Hotel"
a particularly pleasant restaurant
a particularly pleasant accommodation
3
C
D

Michelin is committed to improving the mobility of travellers

On every road and by every means

Since the company came into being - over a century ago - Michelin has had a single objective: to offer people a better way forward. A technological challenge first, to create increasingly efficient tyres, but also an ongoing commitment to travellers, to help them travel in the best way. This is why Michelin is developing a whole collection of products and services: from maps, atlases, travel guides and auto accessories, to mobile apps, route planners and oneline assistance: Michelin is doing everything it can to make travelling more pleasurable!

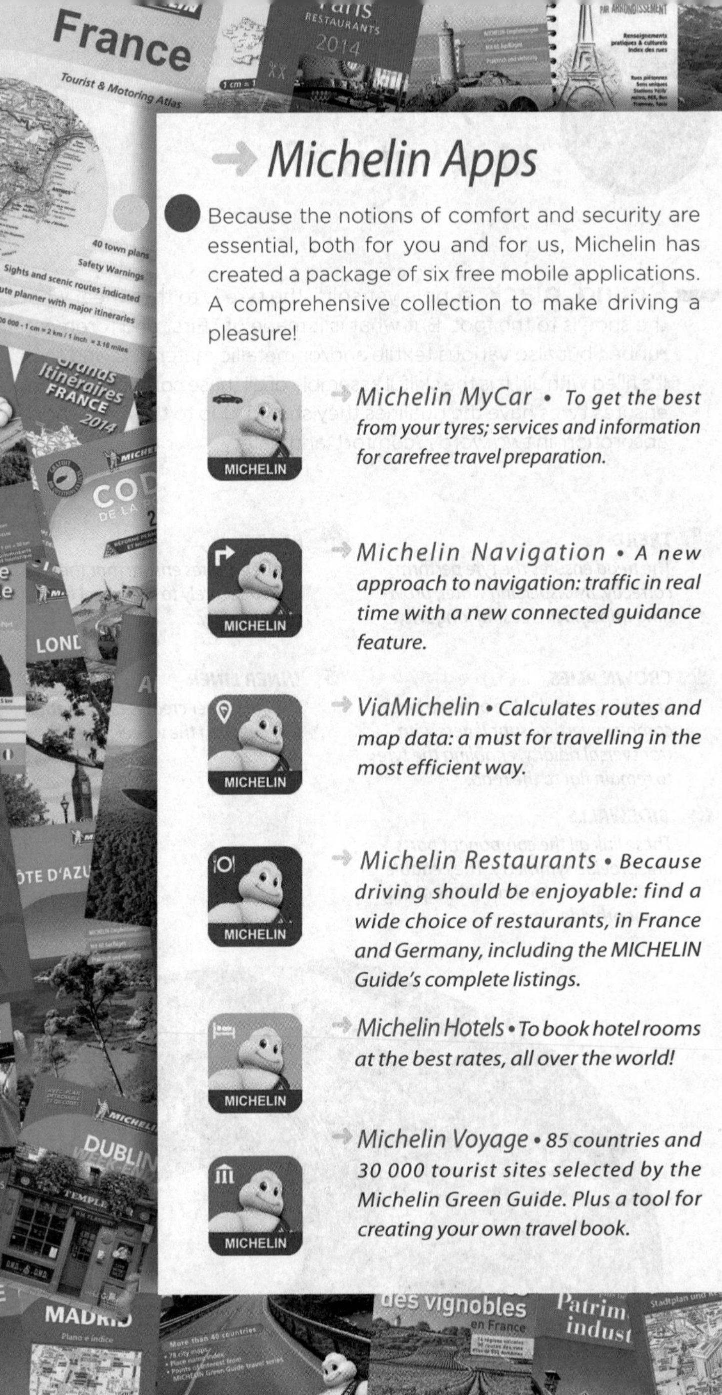

Michelin Apps

Because the notions of comfort and security are essential, both for you and for us, Michelin has created a package of six free mobile applications. A comprehensive collection to make driving a pleasure!

Michelin MyCar • *To get the best from your tyres; services and information for carefree travel preparation.*

Michelin Navigation • *A new approach to navigation: traffic in real time with a new connected guidance feature.*

ViaMichelin • *Calculates routes and map data: a must for travelling in the most efficient way.*

Michelin Restaurants • *Because driving should be enjoyable: find a wide choice of restaurants, in France and Germany, including the MICHELIN Guide's complete listings.*

Michelin Hotels • *To book hotel rooms at the best rates, all over the world!*

Michelin Voyage • *85 countries and 30 000 tourist sites selected by the Michelin Green Guide. Plus a tool for creating your own travel book.*

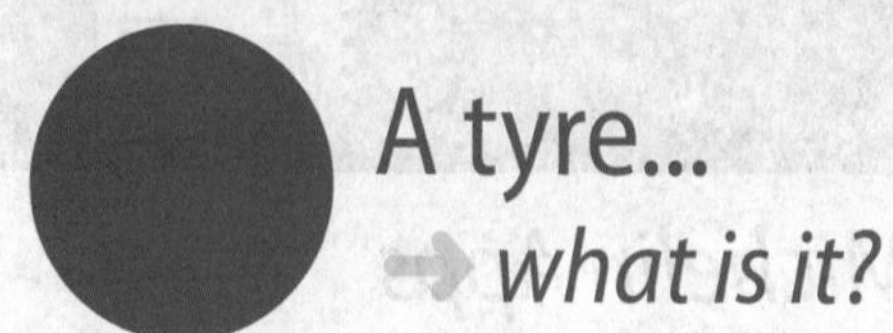

A tyre...
→ *what is it?*

Round, black, supple yet solid, the tyre is to the wheel what the shoe is to the foot. But what is it made of? First and foremost, rubber, but also various textile and/or metallic materials... and then it's filled with air! It is the skilful assembly of all these components that ensures tyres have the qualities they should: grip to the road, shock absorption, in two words: 'comfort' and 'safety'.

1 ***TREAD***
The tread ensures the tyre performs correctly, by dispersing water, providing grip and increasing longevity.

2 ***CROWN PLIES***
This reinforced double or triple belt combines vertical suppleness with transversal rigidity, enabling the tyre to remain flat to the road.

3 ***SIDEWALLS***
These link all the component parts and provide symmetry. They enable the tyre to absorb shock, thus giving a smooth ride.

4 ***BEADS***
The bead wires ensure that the tyre is fixed securely to the wheel to ensure safety.

5 ***INNER LINER***
The inner liner creates an airtight seal between the wheel rim and the tyre.

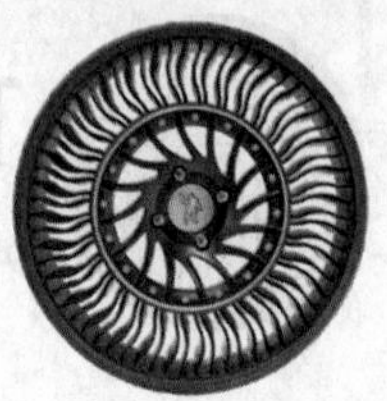

Michelin

→ *innovation in movement*

Created and patented by Michelin in 1946, the belted radial-ply tyre revolutionised the world of tyres. But Michelin did not stop there: over the years other new and original solutions came out, confirming Michelin's position as a leader in research and innovation.

→ *the right pressure!*

One of Michelin's priorities is safer mobility. In short, innovating for a better way forward. This is the challenge for researchers, who are working to perfect tyres capable of shorter braking distances and offering the best possible traction to the road. And so, to support motorists, Michelin organises road safety awareness campaigns all over the world: «Fill up with air» initiatives remind everyone that the right tyre pressure is a crucial factor in safety and fuel economy.

The Michelin strategy:
→ *multi-performance tyres*

Michelin is synonymous with safety, fuel saving and the capacity to cover thousands of miles. A MICHELIN tyre is the embodiment of all these things – thanks to our engineers, who work with the very latest technology.

Their challenge: to equip every tyre – whatever the vehicle (car, truck, tractor, bulldozer, plane, motorbike, bicycle or train!) – with the best possible combination of qualities, for optimal overall performance.

Slowing down wear, reducing energy expenditure (and therefore CO_2 emissions), improving safety through enhanced road handling and braking: there are so many qualities in just one tyre – that's Michelin Total Performance.

Every day, **Michelin** is working towards sustainable mobility

OVER TIME, WHILE RESPECTING THE PLANET

Sustainable mobility
→ *is clean mobility... and mobility for everyone*

Sustainable mobility means enabling people to get around in a way that is cleaner, safer, more economical and more accessible to everyone, wherever they might live. Every day, Michelin's 113 000 employees worldwide are innovating:

- by creating tyres and services that meet society's new needs,
- by raising young people's awareness of road safety,
- by inventing new transport solutions that consume less energy and emit less CO_2.

→ *Michelin Challenge Bibendum*

Sustainable mobility means allowing the transport of goods and people to continue, while promoting responsible economic, social and societal development. Faced with the increasing scarcity of raw materials and global warming, Michelin is standing up for the environment and public health. Michelin regularly organises 'Michelin Challenge Bibendum', the only event in the world which focuses on sustainable road travel.

Towns

from A to Z

Foundry

Great Britain

England

Channel Islands • Isle of Man

ABBERLEY

Worcestershire – Pop. 654 – ✉ Worcester – See Regional map n°**18-B2**
London 137 mi – Birmingham 27 mi – Worcester 13 mi
Michelin Road map 503-M27 and 504-M27

The Elms

Stockton Rd ✉ WR6 6AT – West : 0.75 mi on A 443 – ✆ (01299) 896 666 – www.theelmshotel.co.uk
23 rm – £ 75/140 £ 120/220
Rest *The Brookes* – Menu £ 21/39 – *(booking essential at lunch)*
Rest *Garden Café* – Carte £ 23/34 – *(lunch only)*
An impressive Queen Anne manor house where modern colours and fabrics blend with traditional furnishings. Bedrooms are split between the house and the old stables, and most have pleasant country views. There are plenty of facilities for families, including the Garden Café, which is child-friendly and set within the pleasant spa. Formal Brookes serves a classic menu.

ABBEY DORE

Herefordshire – See Regional map n°**18-A3**
London 170 mi – Gloucester 39 mi – Hereford 15 mi
Michelin Road map 503-L28

Toi et Moi

Holling Grange ✉ HR2 0JJ – Northwest : 1.5 mi on Ewyas Harold Common rd – ✆ (01981) 240 244 – www.toietmoi.co.uk – Closed January-March and Sunday-Wednesday
Menu £ 30/40 – *(booking essential)*
It's not just the views that set this charming little hillside restaurant apart. The spacious, Scandinavian lodge style building is simply but stylishly furnished; the atmosphere is delightfully relaxed; and the monthly French menu is refreshingly honest. Cooking is precise and flavours are pronounced.

ENGLAND

ABBOTSBURY

Dorset – Pop. 481 – See Regional map n°**3-B3**
London 146 mi – Bournemouth 44 mi – Exeter 50 mi – Weymouth 10 mi
Michelin Road map 503-M32 and 504-M32 – Michelin Green Guide GREAT BRITAIN

Abbey House without rest

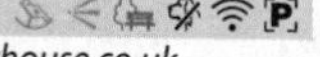

Church St ✉ DT3 4JJ – ✆ (01305) 871 330 – www.theabbeyhouse.co.uk
5 rm – £ 75/100 £ 75/110
Characterful guesthouse-cum-tea-shop in a stunning location beside the ruins of a 15C abbey. Well-kept, classical bedrooms; one has a half-tester and one runs almost the length of the building. Unique Benedictine watermill in the gardens.

ABBOTS RIPTON → See Huntingdon

Cambridgeshire – Michelin Road map 504-T26/27

ABINGDON

Oxfordshire – Pop. 38 262 – See Regional map n°**10-B2**
London 64 mi – Oxford 6 mi – Reading 25 mi
Michelin Road map 503-Q28 and 504-Q28 – Michelin Green Guide GREAT BRITAIN

Rafters without rest

Abingdon Rd, Marcham ✉ OX13 6NU – West : 3 mi on A 415 – ✆ (01865) 391 298 – www.bnb-rafters.co.uk
4 rm – £ 57/115 £ 109/139
An unassuming exterior conceals a stylish, modern hotel. Smart bedrooms have a Scandic feel and excellent facilities; one even has a water bed! The friendly owner serves homemade bread and local bacon and sausages at breakfast.

ABINGER COMMON

Surrey – See Regional map n°**7-D2**
London 32 mi – Croydon 26 mi – Barnet 62 mi – Ealing 44 mi
Michelin Road map 504-S30

Abinger Hatch

Abinger Ln ✉ RH5 6HZ – ✆ (01306) 730 737 – www.theabingerhatch.com
Carte £ 20/27
Set in prime walking country, this attractive 18C inn has been lovingly restored and oozes country gentility. The bar is the best spot to enjoy the flavoursome country cooking and the outside kitchen is a hit in warmer months.

ALDEBURGH

Suffolk – Pop. 2 341 – See Regional map n°**15-D3**
London 97 mi – Ipswich 24 mi – Norwich 41 mi
Michelin Road map 504-Y27

Wentworth

rm,

Wentworth Rd ✉ IP15 5BD – ✆ (01728) 452 312
– www.wentworth-aldeburgh.com
35 rm (dinner included) – £ 89/118 £ 143/285
Rest – Menu £ 14 (weekdays)/26
The friendly, engaging team know all the regulars at this family-run seaside hotel. The conservatory and large front terrace are popular spots. Extremely comfortable bedrooms come with a copy of locally set 'Orlando the Marmalade Cat'. The formal dining room serves a traditional daily menu.

Brudenell

The Parade ✉ IP15 5BU – ✆ (01728) 452 071 – www.brudenellhotel.co.uk
44 rm – £ 105/126 £ 147/352 **Rest** – Carte £ 21/39
Contemporary hotel right on the beachfront, with a relaxed ambience and superb sea views; take it all in from the large terrace. New England style bedrooms come with modern bathrooms and up-to-date facilities. The informal, split-level bar-cum-restaurant offers an accessible menu of modern classics.

White Lion N

rm,

Market Cross Pl ✉ IP15 5BJ – ✆ (01728) 452 720 – www.whitelion.co.uk
38 rm – £ 75/120 £ 120/275 **Rest** – Menu £ 16 – Carte £ 22/41
Don't be fooled by the worn exterior; inside it's smart and modern, with stylish bedrooms and several open-plan lounges, which provide the ideal spot for afternoon tea. The large brasserie serves an all-purpose daytime menu and a more structured evening selection; traditional fish dishes feature highly.

Lighthouse

AC

77 High St ✉ IP15 5AU – ✆ (01728) 453 377 – www.lighthouserestaurant.co.uk
– Closed lunch 1 January and lunch 26 December
Menu £ 10 – Carte £ 22/35 – *(booking essential)*
Popular, long-standing, split-level eatery with bright yellow décor, amiable service and a laid-back feel. Menus change constantly, featuring fish from the boats 200m away and local, seasonal meats and vegetables. Cooking is rustic and flavoursome, and dishes arrive generously proportioned.

Aldeburgh Market Cafe

170-172 High St ✉ IP15 5EY – ✆ (01728) 452 520
– www.thealdeburghmarket.co.uk – Closed 25 December
Carte £ 16/33
Set in a shop brimming with local veg and fresh seafood; the best tables are in the bay window, with views across the street. Well-priced, flavoursome cooking and friendly service. Arrive early to try one of the tasty breakfasts.

ALDERLEY EDGE

Cheshire East – Pop. 5 280 – See Regional map n°**20-B3**

London 187 mi – Chester 34 mi – Manchester 14 mi – Stoke-on-Trent 25 mi

Michelin Road map 502-N24 and 503

Alderley Edge

Macclesfield Rd ✉ SK9 7BJ – ☎ (01625) 583 033 – www.alderleyedgehotel.com

50 rm – †£ 100/400 ††£ 135/400 – 1 suite

Rest *The Brasserie* Rest *Alderley* – see restaurant listing

Well-run, early Victorian country house in an affluent village. Smart landscaped gardens; compact, fairly formal interior with modern, leather-furnished guest areas and stylish bedrooms. Good service from dedicated staff.

Alderley – Alderley Edge Hotel

Macclesfield Rd ✉ SK9 7BJ – ☎ (01625) 583 033 – www.alderleyedgehotel.com – Closed Sunday dinner to non residents

Menu £ 23/70 – Carte approx. £ 47

Smart, formal conservatory restaurant with a long-standing reputation. Modern British dishes display some interesting combinations. Good value lunch and daily evening menus. Excellent wine list with some fine vintage burgundies and clarets.

The Brasserie – Alderley Edge Hotel

Macclesfield Rd ✉ SK9 7BJ – ☎ (01625) 583 033 – www.alderleyedgehotel.com – Closed Sunday

Carte £ 21/33

Informal, French-style brasserie with mirrored walls and leather banquettes, on the ground floor of a well-run, busy hotel. Retro British dishes like prawn and crayfish cocktail, scampi in a basket and jam roly poly are given a modern twist.

Wizard Inn

Macclesfield Rd ✉ SK10 4UB – Southeast : 1.25 mi on B 5087 – ☎ (01625) 584 000 – www.ainscoughs.co.uk – Closed 25 December

Menu £ 20 (weekday dinner)/35 – Carte £ 20/46

Characterful, dog-friendly pub with flagged floors, old beams and open fires; set next to the Alderley Edge escarpment. The wide-ranging menu offers traditional pub favourites, retro British classics, and fish and meat platters.

ALDFIELD → See Ripon

North Yorkshire – Michelin Road map 502-P21

ALFRISTON

East Sussex – Pop. 829 – ✉ Polegate – See Regional map n°**8-A3**

London 66 mi – Eastbourne 9 mi – Lewes 10 mi – Newhaven 8 mi

Michelin Road map 504-U31

Wingrove House with rm

High St ✉ BN26 5TD – ☎ (01323) 870 276 – www.wingrovehousealfriston.com – Closed 25 December

7 rm – †£ 100/175 ††£ 100/175

Menu £ 29 – *(dinner only and lunch Saturday and Sunday)*

This imposing colonial-style building conceals a spacious brasserie and a comfy lounge. It's personally run and has a relaxed, informal feel. Menus change quarterly and offer appealing, unfussy dishes with a modern British style. Bedrooms are stylish and understated; two have access to the heated balcony.

ALKHAM

Kent – Pop. 351 – See Regional map n°**9-D2**

London 72 mi – Birmingham 198 mi – Liverpool 291 mi – Leeds 264 mi

Michelin Road map 504-X30

Alkham Court without rest
Meggett Ln ✉ CT15 7DG – Southwest : 1 mi by Alkham Valley Rd – ☎ (01303) 892 056 – www.alkhamcourt.co.uk
4 rm – †£ 100/120 ††£ 135/170
Set on a hill and surrounded by mature grounds, a delightful guesthouse with a hot tub, a sauna and a livery yard for over 20 horses. Homely, well-equipped bedrooms have stylish bathrooms. The large conservatory offers lovely views.

XX **Marquis** with rm
Alkham Valley Rd ✉ CT15 7DF – ☎ (01304) 873 410 – www.themarquisatalkham.co.uk – Closed Monday lunch
10 rm – †£ 69/139 ††£ 99/229 Menu £ 39 – Carte £ 32/46
Fashionable former pub with smart bar, stylish dining room and relaxed atmosphere. Accomplished cooking features classical combinations with original touches; portions are generous and presentation is modern. 'Foraging' and 'tasting' menus available. Chic, sexy bedrooms boast luxurious bathrooms.

ALNWICK

Northumberland – Pop. 8 116 – See Regional map n°**24**-B2
London 320 mi – Edinburgh 86 mi – Newcastle upon Tyne 34 mi
Michelin Road map 501-O17 and 502-O17 – Michelin Green Guide GREAT BRITAIN

Greycroft without rest
Croft Pl ✉ NE66 1XU – via Prudhoe St – ☎ (01665) 602 127 – www.greycroft.co.uk – Closed Christmas and New Year
6 rm – †£ 65/70 ††£ 95/135
Late 19C house by Alnwick Castle and Gardens. Individually decorated bedrooms have good facilities and homely touches; the bright conservatory breakfast room overlooks a walled garden. The welcoming owners will recommend local sights.

Aln House without rest
South Rd ✉ NE66 2NZ – Southeast : 0.75 mi by B 6346 on Newcastle rd – ☎ (01665) 602 265 – www.alnhouse.co.uk – Closed 23-31 December
6 rm – †£ 70/95 ††£ 90/105
Bay windowed, semi-detached Edwardian house with mature front and rear gardens; run by friendly, welcoming owners. Homely lounge and neatly laid breakfast room. Well-kept, individually decorated bedrooms have feature walls and bright décor.

at North Charlton North: 6.75 mi by A1 ✉ Alnwick

North Charlton Farm without rest
✉ NE67 5HP – ☎ (01665) 579 443 – www.northcharltonfarm.co.uk – Closed Christmas
3 rm – †£ 55 ††£ 80
Attractive house on working farm with agricultural museum. Offers traditional accommodation. Each bedroom is individually decorated and has countryside views.

at Chathill North: 8.75 mi by A1 off B6347

Doxford Hall H. and Spa rm,
✉ NE67 5DN – ☎ (01665) 589 700 – www.doxfordhall.com
30 rm – †£ 98/153 ††£ 125/245 – 1 suite
Rest *George Runciman* – Menu £ 25/30 (lunch) – Carte £ 30/50
Extended Georgian house with immaculately kept, formal gardens; a popular venue for weddings. Numerous comfy lounges and a smart spa. Bedrooms mix modern facilities and antique furniture; those in the original house are spacious and contemporary. Traditional menus in the formal, wood-panelled dining room.

ENGLAND

ALSTONEFIELD

Staffordshire – Pop. 274 – See Regional map n°**19-C1**

London 157 mi – Birmingham 66 mi – Liverpool 77 mi – Leeds 88 mi

Michelin Road map 504-O24

The George

DE6 2FX – (01335) 310 205 – www.thegeorgeatalstonefield.com – Closed 25 December

Carte £ 22/49

Simply furnished, 18C pub on the village green, with a roaring fire and a relaxed, cosy atmosphere; it has been in the same family for three generations. Daily changing menus offer well-priced, down-to-earth dishes.

ALTRINCHAM

Greater Manchester – Pop. 52 419 – See Regional map n°**20-B3**

London 191 mi – Chester 30 mi – Liverpool 30 mi – Manchester 8 mi

Michelin Road map 502-N23 and 503

Ash Farm without rest

Park Ln, Little Bollington WA14 4TJ – Southwest : 3.25 mi by A 56 – (0161) 929 92 90 – www.ashfarm.co.uk – Closed 22 December-2 January

5 rm – £ 49/69 £ 81/96

Red-brick, 18C former farmhouse with a pine-furnished breakfast room and a comfy lounge with a wood-burning stove. Some bedrooms are furnished in a traditional country house style; others are more modern. Large garden. Friendly owners.

ENGLAND

ALVESTON → See Stratford-upon-Avon

Warwickshire – Michelin Road map 504-O/P27

AMBERLEY

West Sussex – Pop. 586 – Arundel – See Regional map n°**7-C2**

London 56 mi – Brighton 24 mi – Portsmouth 31 mi

Michelin Road map 504-S31 – Michelin Green Guide GREAT BRITAIN

Amberley Castle

BN18 9LT Southwest : 0.5 mi on B 2139 – (01798) 831 992 – www.amberleycastle.co.uk

19 rm – £ 265/615 £ 265/615 – 6 suites

Rest *Queen's Room* – see restaurant listing

Stunning 12C castle displaying original stonework, battlements and evidence of a moat. The charming grounds consist of lovely gardens, lakes and a croquet lawn, and are matched inside by a characterful array of rooms. Sumptuous bedrooms have a palpable sense of history; those in the main castle are the best.

Queen's Room – Amberley Castle Hotel

BN18 9LT Southwest : 0.5 mi on B 2139 – (01798) 831 992 – www.amberleycastle.co.uk

Menu £ 26/65 – *(booking essential)*

Within the walls of a stunning 12C castle is this elegant dining room with a barrel-vaulted ceiling, lancet windows and an open fire. Ambitious modern dishes arrive artfully presented. Henry VIII's wives all visited, hence its name.

AMBLESIDE

Cumbria – Pop. 2 529 – See Regional map n°**21-A2**

London 276 mi – Birmingham 162 mi – Liverpool 93 mi – Leeds 121 mi

Michelin Road map 502-L20 – Michelin Green Guide GREAT BRITAIN

The Samling

Ambleside Rd LA23 1LR – South : 1.5 mi on A 591 – (015394) 31 922 – www.thesamlinghotel.co.uk

11 rm – £ 280/560 £ 300/690 – 2 suites

Rest *The Samling* ✿ – see restaurant listing

Located in a stunning position on the fellside and looking southwards along Lake Windermere; take in the fantastic view from the outdoor hot tub. Bedrooms are highly individual and range from classical and characterful to bold and eye-catching; some are duplex suites. Service is strong and structured.

AMBLESIDE

Street	Grid	No.
Borrans Rd	BY	2
Cheapside	AZ	4
Church St	AZ	6
Compston St	AZ	8
Kelsick Rd	AZ	12
King St	AZ	13
Lake Rd	AZ	
Market Pl.	AZ	14
North Rd	AZ	17
Old Lake Rd	AZ	20
St Mary's Lane	AZ	22
Smithy Brow	AZ	23

GRASMERE

Street	Grid	No.
Broadgate	BZ	3
Easedale Rd	BZ	10
Swan Lane	AY	24

BUILT UP AREA

KESWICK A 591
Sour Milk Gill
Rothay
B 5287
GRASMERE
TOWN END
RYDAL
Rydal Beck
Rydal Mount
B 5343
CHAPEL STILE
A 591
Scandale Beck
Great Langdale Beck
ELTERWATER
Loughrigg Tarn
AMBLESIDE
SKELWITH BRIDGE
CLAPPERSGATE
A 593
WATERHEAD
Brathay
B 5286
CONISTON A 593
WINDERMERE A 591
ENGLAND

A 591
POL.
Rydal Road
Kirkstone Road
Fair View Rd
Stock Ghyll
Stock Ghyll Lane
Park
Millans
Compston Rd
Vicarage Road
Lower Gale Road
Rothay Road
Wansfell Rd
Lake Road
AMBLESIDE
A 593
A 591

B 5287
GRASMERE
College St.
Rothay
Red Bank Road
Stock Lane
B 5287

Nanny Brow without rest
Clappersgate ✉ *LA22 9NF – Southwest : 1.25 mi on A 593 – ✆ (015394) 33 232 – www.nannybrow.co.uk* Town plan: BY**v**
13 rm ☕ – 🚹£ 115/265 🚹🚹£ 130/280
Charming Arts and Crafts house with views of the River Brathay and the Langdale Fells. Spacious, antique-furnished bedrooms sit above an elegant lounge. Original stained glass, wood panelling and impressive fireplaces feature.

Riverside without rest
Under Loughrigg ✉ *LA22 9LJ – ✆ (015394) 32 395 – www.riverside-at-ambleside.co.uk – Closed 7 December-24 January* Town plan: BY**s**
6 rm ☕ – 🚹£ 75/110 🚹🚹£ 110/130
A homely slate house in a peaceful riverside location; run by delightful owners. The steep, mature garden is filled with rhododendrons. Bedroom 2 has a four-poster, a whirlpool bath and water views. Breakfast is locally sourced.

Red Bank without rest
Wansfell Rd ✉ *LA22 0EG – ✆ (015394) 34 637 – www.red-bank.co.uk* Town plan: AZ**r**
3 rm ☕ – 🚹£ 60/90 🚹🚹£ 60/90
Well-maintained guesthouse close to the centre of town; a former doctor's surgery. Small seating area with wood burning stove; breakfast room overlooks the garden. 3 colour-themed bedrooms with compact, modern bathrooms. Tea on arrival.

The Samling
Ambleside Rd ✉ *LA23 1LR – South : 1.5 mi on A 591 – ✆ (015394) 31 922 – www.thesamlinghotel.co.uk*
Menu £ 45/85 – *(booking essential)*
Small hotel restaurant in an old farmhouse, which looks out over its 66 acre grounds and down Lake Windermere. The concise, interesting menu offers dishes with a classical base and a modern, innovative touch. Cooking is well-executed and has a Scandic edge; a little bit of theatre is added along the way.
→ Salmon, baby beetroot, liquorice & grapefruit. Suckling pig with wild garlic, morels & asparagus. Sloe gin crème brûlée, lemon verbena foam, damson ice cream & blackberries.

Log House Ⓝ with rm
Lake Rd ✉ *LA22 0DN – ✆ (015394) 31 077 – www.loghouse.co.uk – Closed 15-26 January* Town plan: BY**h**
3 rm ☕ – 🚹£ 90/100 🚹🚹£ 90/100
Menu £ 24/30 – Carte approx. £ 33 – *(Closed Monday and Tuesday)*
Keenly run restaurant with an intimate feel; set in a log house brought over from Norway by Alfred Heaton Cooper. Classical cooking uses Lakeland meats and fish from Fleetwood. Hearty main courses are followed by proper puddings.

Old Stamp House Ⓝ
Church St ✉ *LA22 0BU – ✆ (015394) 32 775 – www.oldstamphouse.com – Closed Christmas, 3-25 January, Sunday and Monday* Town plan: AZ**h**
Menu £ 23 (lunch) – Carte £ 29/40
Named after William Wordsworth, the 'Distributor of Stamps' for Westmorland from 1813-1843. A solid stone floor and exposed beams set the scene for an intimate experience. Cooking is modern, complex and champions Cumbrian produce.

Drunken Duck Inn with rm
Barngates ✉ *LA22 0NG – Southwest : 3 mi by A 593 and B 5286 on Tarn Hows rd – ✆ (01539) 436 347 – www.drunkenduckinn.co.uk – Closed 25 December*
17 rm ☕ – 🚹£ 79/244 🚹🚹£ 105/325 Carte £ 23/38 – *(booking essential)*
Attractive pub in the heart of the beautiful Lakeland countryside, with a characterful, fire-lit bar and two, more formal dining rooms. Simple lunches are followed by elaborate dinners with prices to match; cooking is generous and service, attentive. Ales are brewed on-site. Boutique, country house bedrooms – some with patios – have large squashy beds and country views.

ENGLAND

AMERSHAM (Old Town)

Buckinghamshire – Pop. 23 086 – See Regional map n°**11**-D2
London 34 mi – Birmingham 109 mi – Liverpool 203 mi – Leeds 189 mi
Michelin Road map 504-S29

Artichoke

9 Market Sq ✉ HP7 0DF – ✆ (01494) 726 611 – www.artichokerestaurant.co.uk – Closed 2 weeks late August, 1 week Easter, 1 week Christmas, Sunday and Monday
Menu £ 22 (weekday lunch)/68 – Carte lunch £ 39/47 – *(booking essential at dinner)*
16C red-brick house in a picturesque town. A narrow beamed room with cream-painted walls and polished tables leads through to a more modern extension complete with a semi-open kitchen. Ambitious modern dishes arrive nicely presented.

Gilbey's

1 Market Sq ✉ HP7 0DF – ✆ (01494) 727 242 – www.gilbeygroup.com – Closed 24-30 December
Menu £ 20 (weekdays)/26 – Carte £ 31/47 – *(booking essential)*
Part of a 17C school; a busy, long-standing neighbourhood restaurant consisting of three rustic rooms and a delightful terrace. It's rooted in tradition, from the furnishings to the food. Homemade jams feature for afternoon tea.

AMPLEFORTH → See Helmsley

North Yorkshire – Michelin Road map 502-Q21

ANSTEY

Hertfordshire – See Regional map n°**12**-B2
London 38 mi – Croydon 71 mi – Barnet 35 mi – Ealing 47 mi
Michelin Road map 504-Q25

Anstey Grove Barn without rest

✉ SG9 0BJ East : 0.5 mi on Meesden rd – ✆ (01763) 848 828 – www.ansteygrovebarn.co.uk
6 rm – †£ 60/100 ††£ 80/100, £ 10
Converted barn at the centre of what was a working pig farm; fronted by a pleasant rose and herb garden. Large, open-plan lounge and communal breakfast area. Bedrooms are light and airy; one has a four-poster and a roll-top bath.

APPLEBY-IN-WESTMORLAND

Cumbria – Pop. 2 862 – See Regional map n°**21**-B2
London 285 mi – Carlisle 33 mi – Kendal 24 mi – Middlesbrough 58 mi
Michelin Road map 502-M20

Appleby Manor Country House

Roman Rd ✉ CA16 6JB – East : 1 mi by B 6542 and Station Rd – ✆ (017683) 51 571 – www.applebymanor.co.uk – Closed Christmas
31 rm – †£ 85/170 ††£ 160/240
Rest – Carte £ 27/41 **s**
Rest *Bistro 1871* – Carte £ 18/34
A family-run Victorian gentleman's residence with mature gardens and spacious, traditional guest areas. Bedrooms are in various extensions: those in the original house are the most characterful; 'Deluxe' have whirlpool baths and TVs in the bathrooms. The formal two-roomed restaurant offers classical menus, while the smart bistro serves lighter, pub-style dishes.

Tufton Arms

Market Sq ✉ CA16 6XA – ✆ (017683) 51 593 – www.tuftonarmshotel.co.uk – Closed 24-27 December
22 rm – †£ 85/125 ††£ 140/220 **Rest** – Carte £ 19/37
16C coaching inn, in an old market town; a popular place for fishing and shooting parties. Guest areas include two traditional lounges and a bar; chic bedrooms are a complete contrast with their bold, contemporary furnishings. The classical, cane-furnished restaurant offers an easy-going menu.

ARKHOLME

Lancashire – See Regional map n°**20-A1**
London 254 mi – Birmingham 140 mi – Liverpool 71 mi – Leeds 99 mi
Michelin Road map 502-M21

Red Well Inn

LA6 1BQ Southwest : 3 mi on B 6254 – (015242) 21 240 – www.redwellinn.net
Carte £ 23/47 – *(booking advisable)*
An attractive 16C stone inn with a rustic bar and a more formal dining room. The son cooks while his parents look after the front of house. Menus offer something for everyone, from a homemade scotch egg with HP sauce to a classic fish pie.

ARLINGHAM

Gloucestershire – Pop. 459 – Gloucester – See Regional map n°**4-C1**
London 120 mi – Birmingham 69 mi – Bristol 34 mi – Gloucester 16 mi
Michelin Road map 503-M28 and 504-M28

XX **Old Passage Inn** with rm

rest,

Passage Rd GL2 7JR – West : 0.75 mi – (01452) 740 547 – www.theoldpassage.com – Closed 25-26 December, Sunday dinner and Monday and dinner Tuesday-Wednesday January-February
2 rm – £ 60/130 £ 80/130
Menu £ 15 (weekday lunch)/68 – Carte £ 35/71
Sit out on the terrace or beside the window, surrounded by colourful art, and watch the famous Severn bore travel up the estuary. Extensive seafood menus offer everything from a fish pie to a fruit de mer platter or lobster direct from their saltwater tank. Simply furnished modern bedrooms share the view.

ARMSCOTE

Warwickshire – See Regional map n°**19-C3**
London 98 mi – Birmingham 45 mi – Liverpool 139 mi – Leeds 145 mi
Michelin Road map 504-P27

Fuzzy Duck with rm

rest,

Ilmington Rd CV37 8DD – (01608) 682 635 – www.fuzzyduckarmscote.com – Closed 1 week January and Monday
4 rm – £ 110/160 £ 110/160 Carte £ 19/46 – *(booking advisable)*
Siblings Adrian and Tania – also owners of the Baylis and Harding toiletries company – have taken this place from a boarded up boozer to a modern, fashionably attired dining pub. Seasonal British dishes – including plenty of pub classics – show respect for the local ingredients. Stylish boutique bedrooms.

ARNSIDE

Cumbria – Pop. 2 334 – See Regional map n°**21-A3**
London 257 mi – Liverpool 74 mi – Manchester 69 mi – Bradford 97 mi
Michelin Road map 502-L21

Number 43

43 The Promenade LA5 0AA – (01524) 762 761 – www.no43.org.uk
6 rm – £ 95/145 £ 125/185 **Rest** – Menu £ 20
Stylishly converted Victorian townhouse boasting superb views over the estuary and fells. Contemporary bedrooms have smart bathrooms, quality furnishings, good facilities and plenty of extras. The comfortable open-plan lounge and dining room offers light meat and cheese sharing platters in the evening. Start the day with breakfast on the glass-enclosed terrace.

ARUNDEL

West Sussex – Pop. 3 285 – See Regional map n°**7-C2**
London 58 mi – Brighton 21 mi – Southampton 41 mi – Worthing 9 mi
Michelin Road map 504-S31 – Michelin Green Guide GREAT BRITAIN

Town House with rm

65 High St ✉ BN18 9AJ – ✆ (01903) 883 847 – www.thetownhouse.co.uk – Closed 2 weeks Easter, 2 weeks October, 25-26 December, 1-2 January, Sunday and Monday

4 rm – †£ 75/95 ††£ 95/130 Menu £ 20/30

Early 17C house displaying original sugar glass windows and an impressively ornate Renaissance ceiling with gilded walnut panelling, taken from a Medici palace in Florence. Smartly laid, intimate dining room. Confidently executed, tried-and-tested dishes with a classical base. Quirky, well-equipped bedrooms.

at Burpham Northeast: 3 mi by A27 ✉ Arundel

The George at Burpham

Main St ✉ BN18 9RR – ✆ (01903) 883 131 – www.georgeatburpham.co.uk

Menu £ 21 – Carte £ 20/42

A local consortium headed by three local businessmen saved this pub from closure and it's since been given a smart new look, to which beams, fires and a smugglers' wheel add character. The seasonal menu is full of tasty, popular classics.

ASCOT

Windsor and Maidenhead – Pop. 15 761 – See Regional map n°**11**-D3

London 37 mi – Birmingham 119 mi – Liverpool 213 mi – Leeds 214 mi

Michelin Road map 504-R29

ENGLAND

Coworth Park

London Rd ✉ SL5 7SE – East : 2.75 mi on A 329 – ✆ (01344) 876 600 – www.coworthpark.com

70 rm – †£ 325/660 ††£ 325/660 – 21 suites

Rest *Coworth Park* Rest *Barn* – see restaurant listing

18C property set in 246 acres, with its own championship polo pitches and a superb spa with a living roof of herbs and flowers. Guest areas are stylish and contemporary. Beautiful bedrooms feature bespoke furniture, marble bathrooms and excellent facilities; those in main house are the largest.

Coworth Park – Coworth Park Hotel

London Rd ✉ SL5 7SE – East : 2.75 mi on A 329 – ✆ (01344) 876 600 – www.coworthpark.com – Closed Sunday dinner and Monday

Menu £ 25/40 – Carte approx. £ 65

Bright, elegant restaurant in a beautiful mansion house, with stylish tableware, an eye-catching centrepiece and a lovely terrace offering views over the manicured gardens. The cooking is accomplished and service is professional.

Ascot Grill

6 Hermitage Par, High St ✉ SL5 7HE – ✆ (01344) 622 285 – www.ascotgrill.co.uk – Closed 25-26 December, first week January and Sunday

Menu £ 19 (lunch) – Carte £ 23/58

Neighbourhood restaurant with a slick, minimalistic interior featuring leather, silk and velvet; full-length windows open onto a pleasant pavement terrace. Wide-ranging modern grill menu offers steak and seafood. Good value lunches.

Barn – Coworth Park Hotel

London Rd ✉ SL5 7SE – East : 2.75 mi on A 329 – ✆ (01344) 876 600 – www.coworthpark.com

Menu £ 25 (weekday lunch)/35 – Carte £ 31/55

A buzzy, informal alternative to this 18C mansion's fine dining restaurant. The rustic room's floor-to-ceiling windows let in plenty of light and offer views over the fields. The menu features old favourites like steak and chips.

ASENBY

North Yorkshire – See Regional map n°**22-B2**

London 220 mi – Harrogate 21 mi – York 28 mi

Crab Manor

Dishforth Rd ✉ YO7 3QL – ✆ (01845) 577 286 – www.crabandlobster.co.uk

17 rm – †£ 110/170 ††£ 160/240 – 3 suites

Rest *Crab and Lobster* – see restaurant listing

Quirky, well-run hotel in extensive grounds. Stylish bedrooms are split between a Georgian manor house and Scandinavian log cabins, and are themed around famous hotels of the world; all have access to private or shared hot tubs.

Crab and Lobster – Crab Manor Hotel

Dishforth Rd ✉ YO7 3QL – ✆ (01845) 577 286 – www.crabandlobster.com

Menu £ 17 (lunch) – Carte £ 34/68

Charming thatched pub with a characterful, quirky interior packed full of memorabilia. The extensive menu features traditional British favourites and, satisfyingly, plenty of seafood dishes, from fish soup to whole lobster.

ASHBOURNE

Derbyshire – Pop. 8 377 – See Regional map n°**16-A2**

London 141 mi – Birmingham 45 mi – Manchester 46 mi – Sheffield 52 mi

Michelin Road map 502-O24 and 503 – Michelin Green Guide GREAT BRITAIN

Callow Hall

Mapleton Rd ✉ DE6 2AA – West : 0.75 mi by Union St (off Market Pl) – ✆ (01335) 300 900 – www.callowhall.co.uk

16 rm – †£ 110/195 ††£ 160/245 – 1 suite

Rest – Menu £ 25/40 – Carte £ 33/46

Traditional Victorian country house in 30 acres of gardens, fields and woodland. Individually styled bedrooms boast original features, spacious bathrooms, and traditional fabrics and furnishings. Seasonal menus showcase local produce in classically based dishes with the occasional modern touch.

at Shirley Southeast: 5 mi by A515 and off A52

Saracen's Head

Church Ln ✉ DE6 3AS – ✆ (01335) 360 330 – www.saracens-head-shirley.co.uk

Carte £ 20/40

A rustic, open-plan dining pub set in the shadow of the village church, in a remote, picturesque village. Menus are chalked on blackboards above the open fire and offer an eclectic mix, including some pub favourites in satisfying portions.

ASHBURTON

Devon – Pop. 3 346 – See Regional map n°**2-C2**

London 192 mi – Birmingham 187 mi – Liverpool 269 mi – Leeds 299 mi

Michelin Road map 503-I32 – Michelin Green Guide GREAT BRITAIN

Agaric with rm

30 North St ✉ TQ13 7QD – ✆ (01364) 654 478 – www.agaricrestaurant.co.uk – Closed first 2 weeks August, 2 weeks Christmas, Sunday-Tuesday and Saturday lunch

4 rm – †£ 58/90 ††£ 120/140

Menu £ 16 (weekday lunch) – Carte £ 29/42 – *(booking essential)*

Rustic neighbourhood restaurant with a small bar, exposed stone walls, a wood-burning stove and shelves and dressers filled with homemade preserves, chutneys and sauces. Good-sized, classically based menus feature Cornish fish and local beef. For the simple bedrooms, check in at the adjoining cookery shop.

ASHFORD

Kent – Pop. 67 528 – See Regional map n°**9-C2**

London 56 mi – Canterbury 14 mi – Dover 24 mi – Hastings 30 mi

Michelin Road map 504-W30

Eastwell Manor

Eastwell Park, Boughton Lees ✉ TN25 4HR – North : 3 mi by A 28 on A 251 – ✆ (01233) 213 000 – www.eastwellmanor.co.uk

42 rm ☕ – 🛉£ 140/230 🛉🛉£ 140/230 – 22 suites

Rest *Manor* – Menu £ 35 – Carte £ 33/54

Rest *Pavilion* – ✆ (01233) 213 100 – Carte £ 18/35

Impressive manor house with Tudor origins, surrounded by beautifully manicured gardens and extensive parkland. Rebuilt in 1926 following a fire but some superb plaster ceilings and stone fireplaces remain. Characterful guest areas and luxurious bedrooms. Sizeable spa and golf course. Choice of wood-panelled restaurant complete with pianist or more casual brasserie and terrace.

ASHFORD-IN-THE-WATER

Derbyshire – See Regional map n°**16**-A1

▶London 164 mi – Birmingham 87 mi – Leeds 72 mi

Michelin Road map 502-O24

Riverside House

Fennel St ✉ DE45 1QF – ✆ (01629) 814 275 – www.riversidehousehotel.co.uk

14 rm ☕ – 🛉£ 120/155 🛉🛉£ 145/195

Rest *Riverside Room* – Menu £ 12 (weekday lunch)/45

Charming former hunting lodge with gardens running down to the river. Comfy, individually styled bedrooms are named after flowers and birds: one is a four-poster and some have French doors opening onto garden terraces. Classical dining takes place over four different rooms. It has a homely feel throughout.

River Cottage without rest

Buxton Rd ✉ DE45 1QP – ✆ (01629) 813 327 – www.rivercottageashford.co.uk – Closed December and January

4 rm ☕ – 🛉£ 89/125 🛉🛉£ 100/125

Traditional stone cottage by the River Wye, with delightful gardens and two terraces. Bedrooms mix modern and antique furnishings and mattresses are handmade. Locally sourced ingredients and homemade preserves feature at breakfast.

ASHWATER

Devon – See Regional map n°**2**-C2

▶London 217 mi – Plymouth 36 mi – Torbay 62 mi – Exeter 42 mi

Michelin Road map 503-H31

Blagdon Manor with rm

✉ EX21 5DF Northwest : 2 mi by Holsworthy rd on Blagdon rd – ✆ (01409) 211 224 – www.blagdon.com – Closed January, Monday, Tuesday and lunch Wednesday

6 rm ☕ – 🛉£ 90/120 🛉🛉£ 145/250

Menu £ 35 (weekday dinner)/40 – *(booking essential)*

Former farmhouse with delightful gardens; set in a peaceful rural location and proudly run by a husband and wife team. Comfortable restaurant with lovely countryside views and a large flagged terrace for summer dining. Unfussy, seasonal cooking; dishes are classically based, with a modern touch. Immaculately kept, well-equipped bedrooms, with stylish modern bathrooms.

ASKHAM → See Penrith

Cumbria – Michelin Road map 502-M20

ASKRIGG

North Yorkshire – Pop. 1 002 – ✉ Leyburn – See Regional map n°**22**-A1

▶London 251 mi – Kendal 32 mi – Leeds 70 mi – Newcastle upon Tyne 70 mi

Michelin Road map 502-N21

ENGLAND

Yorebridge House

Bainbridge ✉ DL8 3EE – West : 1 mi – ✆ (01969) 652 060 – www.yorebridgehouse.com
13 rm – †£ 175/225 ††£ 200/285 – 3 suites
Rest – Menu £ 23/45 – Carte £ 32/40 – *(closed lunch in winter) (booking essential)*
Stylishly restored former school in a lovely Dales setting, with a snug bar and a lounge offering great views. Bold, modern bedrooms are themed after the owner's travels; those in the annexe have riverside patios and hot tubs. The brasserie offers modern British dishes crafted from top local ingredients.

Skeldale House Ⓝ without rest

Market Pl ✉ DL8 3HG – ✆ (01969) 650 746 – www.skeldalehouse.co.uk – Closed January and Christmas
5 rm – †£ 80/100 ††£ 80/100
You might recognise the handsome façade from 'All Creatures Great and Small'. Many 1860s features remain – including an impressive staircase – and the bright, spacious bedrooms are in keeping, with their period furnishings and brass beds.

ASTON CANTLOW

Warwickshire – Pop. 1 843 – See Regional map n°**19**-C3
London 104 mi – Birmingham 30 mi – Leicester 46 mi – Coventry 22 mi
Michelin Road map 503-O27 and 504-O27 – Michelin Green Guide GREAT BRITAIN

ENGLAND

King's Head

21 Bearley Rd ✉ B95 6HY – ✆ (01789) 488 242 – www.thekh.co.uk
Carte £ 18/44
Characterful black and white timbered inn, covered in ivy and set in a picturesque village. Rustic, open-fired bar and country chic restaurant. Menu of pub favourites and British classics with some modern twists; local game is a feature.

ASTON TIRROLD

Oxfordshire – See Regional map n°**10**-B3
London 58 mi – Reading 16 mi – Streatley 4 mi

Sweet Olive at The Chequers Inn

Baker St ✉ OX11 9DD – ✆ (01235) 851 272 – www.sweet-olive.com – Closed 3 weeks July, 2 weeks February, Sunday dinner and Wednesday
Carte £ 30/48 – *(booking essential)*
A charming red-brick Victorian pub at the heart of the village: cosy, welcoming and popular with the locals. The Gallic owners offer a French-influenced menu of tasty, seasonal dishes and an interesting selection of fine wines.

ATCHAM → See Shrewsbury

Shropshire – Michelin Road map 503-L25 and 504-L25

ATTLEBOROUGH

Norfolk – Pop. 10 549 – See Regional map n°**15**-C2
London 101 mi – Norwich 19 mi – Ipswich 42 mi – Peterborough 87 mi
Michelin Road map 504-X26

Mulberry Tree with rm

Station Rd ✉ NR17 2AS – ✆ (01953) 452 124 – www.the-mulberry-tree.co.uk – Closed Christmas and Sunday dinner
7 rm – †£ 79 ††£ 107 Carte £ 20/38
Contemporary bar-cum-restaurant in an imposing brick-built property, with a pleasant terrace and even a bowling green. The bar menu is popular at lunchtime, while the modern à la carte offers attractively presented, globally influenced dishes. Bedrooms are stylish and very comfortable.

AUSTWICK

North Yorkshire – Pop. 463 – See Regional map n°**22-A2**
London 259 mi – Kendal 28 mi – Lancaster 20 mi – Leeds 46 mi
Michelin Road map 502-M21

Traddock

LA2 8BY – (015242) 51 224 – www.thetraddock.co.uk
12 rm – £ 85/115 £ 95/200 **Rest** – Carte £ 25/38 – *(booking essential)*
Unusually named after a horse trading paddock; a Georgian country house with Victorian additions – once a private residence. Traditional interior with bright, airy lounges. Bedrooms boast feature beds, rural views and roll-top baths. Formal dining room serves local produce in modern versions of old classics.

Austwick Hall without rest

LA2 8BS – (015242) 51 794 – www.austwickhall.co.uk
4 rm – £ 110/140 £ 125/155
Characterful house in a delightful village on the edge of the dales, surrounded by tiered gardens and woodland. Spacious, antique-furnished bedrooms; the Blue Room has a roll-top bath which offers views down the garden. Nothing is too much trouble for the friendly owners. Tea is served on arrival.

Wood View without rest

The Green LA2 8BB – (015242) 51 190 – www.woodviewbandb.com
– Restricted opening in winter
5 rm – £ 48/67 £ 78/86
18C stone farmhouse by the village green, with an open-fired lounge and a cosy, low-ceilinged breakfast room with exposed beams. Simple, well-kept bedrooms have a mix of furnishings. There's even a bike store out back for cyclists.

ENGLAND

AXBRIDGE

Somerset – Pop. 2 057 – See Regional map n°**3-B2**
London 142 mi – Bristol 17 mi – Taunton 27 mi – Weston-Super-Mare 11 mi
Michelin Road map 503-L30

Oak House with rm

The Square BS26 2AP – (01934) 732 444 – www.theoakhousesomerset.com
– Closed 1-7 January, Monday and Tuesday
9 rm – £ 79/129 £ 79/129 Carte £ 24/40 – *(bar lunch)*
Oak-beamed 17C house overlooking the square, with a relaxed, rustic feel. One menu displays classic dishes with subtle modern touches; the other offers more originality. Cooking is well-judged with good ingredients, clear flavours and some flair. Enthusiastic young team. Comfortable, good value bedrooms.

AXMINSTER

Devon – Pop. 5 761 – See Regional map n°**2-D2**
London 156 mi – Exeter 27 mi – Lyme Regis 5 mi – Taunton 22 mi
Michelin Road map 503-L31

River Cottage Canteen

Trinity Sq EX13 5AN – (01297) 631 715 – www.rivercottage.net/axminster
– Closed 25-26 December and dinner Sunday and Monday
Menu £ 13/20 – Carte £ 24/34
Busy restaurant, deli and coffee shop owned by Hugh Fearnley-Whittingstall. Simple, industrial-style room with mismatched furniture. Blackboards change twice-daily, offering gutsy, flavoursome country cooking and showcasing local produce.

AYLESBURY

Buckinghamshire – Pop. 71 977 – See Regional map n°**11-C2**
London 46 mi – Birmingham 72 mi – Northampton 37 mi – Oxford 22 mi
Michelin Road map 504-R28 – Michelin Green Guide GREAT BRITAIN

Hartwell House
Oxford Rd ✉ HP17 8NR – Southwest : 2 mi on A 418 – ✆ (01296) 747 444 – www.hartwell-house.com
46 rm – 🛉£ 175 🛉🛉£ 270/700 – 10 suites
Rest – Menu £ 25 (weekdays)/62 – *(closed lunch 31 December)*
Erstwhile residency of Louis XVIII, exiled King of France; now owned by the National Trust. Impressive palatial house in 90 acres of parkland, boasting luxurious lounges, ornate furnishings, an intimate spa and magnificent, antique-filled bedrooms. Afternoon tea is a speciality. Formal restaurant offers good value lunches and traditional country house cooking.

AYLESFORD

Kent – See Regional map n°**8-B1**
London 37 mi – Maidstone 3 mi – Royal Tunbridge Wells 19 mi
Michelin Road map 504-V30

Hengist Ⓝ
7-9 High St ✉ ME20 7AX – ✆ (01622) 885 800 – www.hengistrestaurant.co.uk – Closed 25-26 December, Sunday dinner and Monday
Menu £ 20 – Carte £ 29/36
Pass through the rustic ground floor of this characterful 16C timbered house and head up to the boldly decorated dining rooms. Good-sized menus offer ambitious modern British dishes. In summer, sit on the terrace, beside the stream.

AYLSHAM

Norfolk – Pop. 6 016 – See Regional map n°**15-D1**
London 128 mi – Norwich 13 mi – Ipswich 57 mi – Stevenage 105 mi
Michelin Road map 504-X25

Old Pump House without rest
2 Holman Rd ✉ NR11 6BY – ✆ (01263) 733 789 – www.theoldpumphouse.com – Closed Christmas
5 rm – 🛉£ 80/98 🛉🛉£ 98/120
This tastefully furnished Georgian house is named after the old village water pump which stands in the square outside. Spacious bedrooms have period furnishings and the open-plan lounge and breakfast room overlooks the lovely garden.

AYNHO

Northamptonshire – Pop. 651 – See Regional map n°**16-B3**
London 73 mi – Birmingham 66 mi – Leicester 62 mi – Coventry 48 mi
Michelin Road map 504-Q28

Cartwright rest,
1-5 Croughton Rd ✉ OX17 3BE – ✆ (01869) 811 885 – www.oxfordshire-hotels.co.uk
21 rm – 🛉£ 120/160 🛉🛉£ 130/170
Rest – Menu £ 18 (weekday lunch) – Carte £ 23/32
Cotswold stone former coaching inn dating back to the 16C. Spacious modern bedrooms are split between the main house and the courtyard; the former are more characterful, with some timbered ceilings and original fireplaces. Brasserie restaurant serves a traditional menu; the grills and cheeseboard are popular.

AYOT GREEN → See Welwyn

Hertfordshire

BABBACOMBE → See Torquay

Torbay – Michelin Road map 503-J32

BAGSHOT

Surrey – Pop. 5 430 – See Regional map n°**7-C1**
London 37 mi – Reading 17 mi – Southampton 49 mi
Michelin Road map 504-R29

Pennyhill Park

London Rd ✉ *GU19 5EU – Southwest : 1 mi on A 30 –* ☎ *(01276) 471 774 – www.exclusivehotels.co.uk*

123 rm – †£ 225/365 ††£ 225/365 – 11 suites

Rest ***Michael Wignall at The Latymer*** ✿✿ – see restaurant listing

Rest ***Brasserie*** – Menu £ 30 – Carte £ 35/57 – *(buffet lunch)*

Impressive 19C manor house in 123 acres, boasting one of Europe's best spas. Both the guest areas and bedrooms are spacious, with period furnishings and modern touches; feature bathrooms come with rain showers or glass baths. Dine in the elegant restaurant or the stylish brasserie which opens onto the garden.

Michael Wignall at The Latymer – Pennyhill Park Hotel

London Rd ✉ *GU19 5EU – Southwest : 1 mi on A30 –* ☎ *(01276) 486 156 – www.exclusivehotels.co.uk – Closed 1-16 January, Sunday, Monday, lunch Tuesday and Saturday*

Menu £ 38/88 – *(booking essential)*

Elegant hotel dining room with oak-clad walls, a glass-enclosed chef's table and top quality place settings. Precise, confident cooking uses only the best ingredients. Flavours are clearly defined yet have a delicate edge and innovative combinations marry seamlessly. Fri and Sat they only serve tasting menus.

→ Mackerel with edamame, English 'wasabi' and crab. John Dory, jerk salsify and smoked sweetcorn. Lemon curd, soft meringue and lemon thyme ice cream.

BALLASALLA

→ See Man (Isle of)

– Michelin Road map 502-F21

BAMBURGH

Northumberland – Pop. 279 – See Regional map n°**24**-B1

▶London 337 mi – Edinburgh 77 mi – Newcastle upon Tyne 51 mi

Michelin Road map 501-O17 and 502-O17 – Michelin Green Guide GREAT BRITAIN

Lord Crewe Arms

Front St ✉ *NE69 7BL –* ☎ *(01668) 214 243 – www.lordcrewe.co.uk – Closed 6 January-7 February*

17 rm – †£ 98/135 ††£ 98/145

Rest ***Wynding Inn*** – Carte £ 19/43

Smart 17C former coaching inn, privately owned and superbly set in the shadow of a famous Norman castle. Comfy, cosy bedrooms have a modern feel, yet are in keeping with the age of the building. Characterful stone-walled bar and New England style restaurant serve brasserie dishes. Efficient service.

at Waren Mill West: 2.75 mi on B1342 ✉ Belford

Waren House

✉ *NE70 7EE –* ☎ *(01668) 214 581 – www.warenhousehotel.co.uk*

15 rm – †£ 70/95 ††£ 110/150 – 3 suites

Rest – Menu £ 42 – *(dinner only)*

Personally run, antique-furnished country house set in beautiful, tranquil gardens. Bedrooms – some named after the owners' family members – mix classic and modern styles: some have four-posters and coastal views. Formal dining room boasts an ornate ceiling; traditional menus showcase local ingredients.

BAMPTON

Devon – Pop. 1 260 – See Regional map n°**2**-D1

▶London 189 mi – Exeter 18 mi – Minehead 21 mi – Taunton 15 mi

Michelin Road map 503-J31

Swan with rm

Station Rd ✉ *EX16 9NG –* ☎ *(01398) 332 248 – www.theswan.co – Closed 25 December and Monday*

3 rm – †£ 65 ††£ 85 Carte £ 20/33

Laid-back, modernised, open-plan pub whose history can be traced back to 1450, when it provided accommodation for craftsmen working on the local church. Unfussy pub dishes arrive neatly presented on wooden boards and showcase local produce. Smart, modern bedrooms are found on the 2nd floor.

ENGLAND

BARNARD CASTLE

Durham – Pop. 7 040 – See Regional map n°**24-A3**

London 258 mi – Carlisle 63 mi – Leeds 68 mi – Middlesbrough 31 mi

Michelin Road map 502-O20 – Michelin Green Guide GREAT BRITAIN

Homelands

85 Galgate ✉ DL12 8ES – ✆ (01833) 638 757 – www.homelandsguesthouse.co.uk

5 rm – †£ 50/55 ††£ 80/85 **Rest** – Menu £ 10

Victorian terraced house just a short drive from Raby Castle. Pastel-coloured lounge filled with books and photos. Compact, individually furnished bedrooms; the largest and most peaceful is at the end of the long mature garden. Simple, home-cooked dinners of local produce, by arrangement.

at Greta Bridge Southeast: 4.5 mi off A66 ✉ Barnard Castle

Morritt

✉ DL12 9SE – ✆ (01833) 627 232 – www.themorritt.co.uk

26 rm – †£ 75/140 ††£ 80/179 – 1 suite

Rest *Gilroy's* – see restaurant listing

Rest *Bistro/Bar* – Carte £ 29/41

Attractive 19C inn on the site of an old Roman fort. The characterful interior cleverly blends the old and the new, with lovely parquet floors, antiques and feature bedsteads, offset by contemporary décor. Superb spa with a car garage theme. All-day snacks in the bar-bistro; modern menu in the restaurant.

Gilroy's – Morritt Hotel

✉ DL12 9SE – ✆ (01833) 627 232 – www.themorritt.co.uk

Menu £ 39

Smart hotel dining room with a lovely parquet floor, wood-panelling and bold splashes of colour here and there. Dishes are modern, attractively presented and employ some complex techniques. Start with a drink by the fire in the cosy lounge.

ENGLAND

at Hutton Magna Southeast: 7.25 mi by A66

Oak Tree Inn

✉ DL11 7HH – ✆ (01833) 627 371 – www.theoaktreehutton.co.uk
– Closed 24-27 and 31 December, 1 January and Monday

Carte £ 30/43 – *(dinner only) (booking essential)*

Small but charming whitewashed pub with six tables flanked by green settles and a bench table for drinkers. It's run by a husband and wife team; he cooks, while she serves. Cooking is hearty and flavoursome with a rustic British style.

at Romaldkirk Northwest: 6 mi by A67 on B6277 ✉ Barnard Castle

Rose and Crown with rm

✉ DL12 9EB – ✆ (01833) 650 213 – www.rose-and-crown.co.uk

14 rm – †£ 95/150 ††£ 115/200 Carte £ 22/40 **s**

Delightful Georgian inn overlooking three village greens, with a wonderfully characterful bar, a wood-panelled dining room and a brasserie. Reassuringly familiar menus list all the classics; they even serve afternoon tea. Individually decorated, well-equipped bedrooms – some are in a peaceful annexe.

BARNSLEY → See Cirencester

Gloucestershire – Michelin Road map 503-O28 and 504-O28

BARRASFORD

Northumberland – See Regional map n°**24-A2**

London 309 mi – Newcastle upon Tyne 29 mi – Sunderland 42 mi – Middlesbrough 66 mi

Barrasford Arms with rm

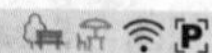

✉ NE48 4AA – ✆ (01434) 681 237 – www.barrasfordarms.co.uk
– Closed 25-26 December, Sunday dinner, Monday lunch and bank holidays

7 rm – †£ 50/67 ††£ 60/87 Carte £ 23/36

Personally run, 19C stone inn, close to Kielder Water and Hadrian's Wall. It has a traditional, homely atmosphere, with cosy fires and regular competitions for the locals. Pub classics are served at lunch, followed by more refined dishes at dinner. Bedrooms are modern, comfortable and sensibly priced.

BARSTON

West Midlands – See Regional map n°**19-C2**

London 110 mi – Birmingham 17 mi – Coventry 11 mi

Michelin Road map 504-O26

Malt Shovel

Barston Lane ✉ B92 0JP – West : 0.75 mi – ✆ (01675) 443 223 – www.themaltshovelatbarston.com – Closed Sunday dinner

Carte £ 24/39

The Mediterranean colour scheme gives a sunny feel all year round; an impression enhanced by the cheery, long-serving staff. The menu offers plenty of pub classics but the Malt Shovel is also well known for its fish.

BARTON-ON-SEA

Hampshire – See Regional map n°**6-A3**

London 108 mi – Bournemouth 11 mi – Southampton 24 mi – Winchester 35 mi

Michelin Road map 503-P31 and 504-P31

Pebble Beach with rm

rest,

Marine Dr ✉ BH25 7DZ – ✆ (01425) 627 777 – www.pebblebeach-uk.com

4 rm – £ 70 £ 90/100 Carte £ 27/45

Head straight for the terrace of this large split-level restaurant to be rewarded with impressive views over the Solent to the Isle of Wight. Inside, the open kitchen takes pride of place and the fish tank gives a clue as to the menu. Good-sized bedrooms are smart and well-kept; the Penthouse has great views.

BARWICK

→ See Yeovil

Somerset – Michelin Road map 503-M31 and 504-M31

BASLOW

Derbyshire – Pop. 1 178 – ✉ Bakewell – See Regional map n°**16-A1**

London 158 mi – Birmingham 70 mi – Manchester 35 mi – Sheffield 14 mi

Michelin Road map 502-P24 and 503 – Michelin Green Guide GREAT BRITAIN

Cavendish

Church Ln ✉ DE45 1SP – on A 619 – ✆ (01246) 582 311 – www.cavendish-hotel.net

24 rm – £ 147/177 £ 189/219, £ 19 – 1 suite

Rest *The Gallery* – see restaurant listing

Rest *Garden Room* – Carte £ 26/43

Elegant hotel on the Chatsworth Estate, boasting lovely parkland views. Bedrooms have a contemporary country house style and some of the furniture and paintings are from nearby Chatsworth House. The Garden Room offers an extensive menu along with afternoon teas; the formal restaurant serves classic fare.

Fischer's at Baslow Hall with rm

Calver Rd ✉ DE45 1RR – on A 623 – ✆ (01246) 583 259 – www.fischers-baslowhall.co.uk – Closed 25-26 and 31 December

10 rm – £ 100/145 £ 150/250 – 1 suite

Menu £ 21 (weekday lunch)/80 – *(booking essential)*

Fine Edwardian manor house with a country house feel, impressive formal grounds and a walled vegetable garden. The two dining rooms with their ornate ceilings and quality furnishings offer an array of interesting, modern, flavoursome dishes, prepared using skilful, labour intensive techniques. Service is professional. Charming bedrooms; the garden rooms are the largest.

→ Pan-fried langoustines, satay sauce and shellfish reduction. Fore rib of beef with caramelised onions, grilled asparagus and Parmentier potatoes. Yorkshire rhubarb crumble soufflé, rhubarb schnapps and clotted cream.

XXX **The Gallery** – Cavendish Hotel
Church Ln ✉ DE45 1SP – on A 619 – ✆ (01246) 582 311 – www.cavendish-hotel.net
Menu £ 35/45
Striking restaurant in an elegant hotel, which features a stylish mix of contemporary décor and antique furnishings. Dishes have a traditional base but techniques and presentation are modern. Service is detailed yet personable.

X **Rowley's**
Church St ✉ DE45 1RY – ✆ (01246) 583 880 – www.rowleysrestaurant.co.uk – Closed Sunday dinner and Monday except bank holidays
Menu £ 20 (lunch and early dinner) – Carte £ 23/39 – *(booking advisable)*
Stone-built former blacksmith's; now a contemporary bar-restaurant with a small terrace and friendly service. Dine in the buzzy ground floor bar or more intimate upstairs rooms. Hearty, satisfying dishes have classic French roots.

BASSENTHWAITE

Cumbria – Pop. 433 – See Regional map n°**21-A2**
London 300 mi – Carlisle 24 mi – Keswick 7 mi
Michelin Road map 501-K19 and 502-K19

Pheasant
✉ CA13 9YE Southwest : 3.25 mi by B 5291 on Wythop Mill Rd – ✆ (017687) 76 234 – www.the-pheasant.co.uk – Closed 24-25 December
15 rm – †£ 95/115 ††£ 120/200
Rest *Bistro* – Menu £ 20 (lunch) – Carte £ 20/31
Characterful 16C coaching inn with comfy lounges and welcoming open fires. Bedrooms are spacious and retain a classic look appropriate to the building's age; some have lovely country outlooks. Have drinks amongst polished brass in the bar then make for the rustic oak-furnished bistro or more formal restaurant.

Overwater Hall

✉ CA7 1HH Northeast : 2.5 mi by A 591, Uldale rd on Overwater rd – ✆ (017687) 76 566 – www.overwaterhall.co.uk – Closed 2-16 January
11 rm – †£ 75/150 ††£ 100/200 **Rest** – Menu £ 45 – *(dinner only)*
Castellated Georgian manor house built in 1811, set in 18 acres of mature gardens. Three good-sized lounges, one with a bar. Large, boldly patterned bedrooms come with rich fabrics, homemade fruit liqueurs and spacious, good quality bathrooms. Formal dining room offers a traditional country house menu.

BATCOMBE

Somerset – Pop. 439 – ✉ Shepton Mallet – See Regional map n°**4-C2**
London 130 mi – Bournemouth 50 mi – Bristol 24 mi – Salisbury 40 mi
Michelin Road map 503-M30

Three Horseshoes Inn with rm
✉ BA4 6HE – ✆ (01749) 850 359 – www.thethreehorseshoesinn.com – Closed 25 December
3 rm – †£ 60/75 ††£ 70/85 Carte £ 18/35
Enthusiastically run former blacksmith's workshop, hidden in a small hamlet off the beaten track, with a characterful beamed interior and a large inglenook fireplace. Menus cover all bases from pork pies and pub classics to more sophisticated dishes. Excellent cheeses. Comfortable, simply furnished bedrooms.

BATH

Bath and North East Somerset – Pop. 94 782 – See Regional map n°**4-C2**

London 119 mi – Bristol 13 mi – Southampton 63 mi – Taunton 49 mi

Michelin Road map 503-M29 and 504-M29 – Michelin Green Guide GREAT BRITAIN

© T. Mathews/Loop Images/age fotostock

Hotels

ENGLAND

Royal Crescent

16 Royal Cres ✉ BA1 2LS – ✆ (01225) 823 333 – www.royalcrescent.co.uk Town plan: AV**a**

45 rm – †£ 239/370 ††£ 265/395 – 12 suites

Rest *Dower House* – see restaurant listing

Smartly refurbished, Grade I listed building at the centre of the famous sweeping terrace. Ornate plasterwork, pastel shades and gilt-framed portraits evoke feelings of the Georgian era. Wood and stone feature in the lovely spa.

Bath Spa

Sydney Rd ✉ BA2 6JF – ✆ (0844) 879 91 06 – www.macdonaldhotels.co.uk/bathspa Town plan: Y**z**

rm,

129 rm – †£ 149/320 ††£ 165/360 – 11 suites

Rest *Vellore* – Menu £ 45 – *(dinner only)*

Charming Georgian mansion in landscaped gardens, with characterful period lounges and an excellent spa. Bedrooms are spacious and some have four-posters; the suites come with 24-hour butler service. The formal restaurant features impressive Corinthian columns, while the lounge-bar offers all-day dining.

Bath Priory – Bath Priory Hotel

Weston Rd ✉ BA1 2XT – ✆ (01225) 331 922 – www.thebathpriory.co.uk Town plan: Y**c**

33 rm – †£ 300/680 ††£ 320/700 – 6 suites

Rest *Bath Priory* ✿ – see restaurant listing

Charming Georgian and Victorian property in a smart residential area near Royal Victoria Park. It has a comfy country house feel, with an array of elegant, antique-filled guest areas and luxurious bedrooms which blend the traditional with the modern. A chic spa and excellent service complete the picture.

Homewood Park

Abbey Ln, Hinton Charterhouse ✉ BA2 7TB – Southeast : 7.5 mi on A 36 – ✆ (01225) 723 731 – www.homewoodpark.co.uk

21 rm – †£ 109/274 ††£ 120/285 – 2 suites

Rest *Tides* – Menu £ 25/35 – Carte £ 27/46

18C country house with mature gardens, a fashionable interior and a superb spa and beauty facility. Charming guest areas – many boasting open fires – have a modern country house feel; bedrooms are contemporary and have bold colour schemes. The stylish dining room serves a menu of modern classics.

Queensberry

Russel St ✉ *BA1 2QF* – ✆ *(01225) 447 928* – *www.thequeensberry.co.uk* Town plan: AV**x**

29 rm – †£ 100/195 ††£ 125/255, ☕ £ 18

Rest *Olive Tree* – see restaurant listing

A series of Georgian townhouses in one of the oldest parts of the city, run by a friendly, well-versed team. Guest areas include a charming wood-panelled lounge and a chic bar with an extensive array of unusual spirits. Funky, individually designed bedrooms have smart designer touches and a host of extras.

Francis

rm,

Queen Sq ✉ *BA1 2HH* – ✆ *(01225) 424 105* – *www.francishotel.com* Town plan: AV**c**

98 rm – †£ 149/239 ††£ 169/259, ☕ £ 20

Rest *Brasserie Blanc* – ✆ (01225) 303 860 – Menu £ 15/17 – Carte £ 20/40

Seven Grade I listed townhouses built between 1728 and 1736 by John Wood the Elder, overlooking the picturesque Queen Square. Contemporary interior with boldly coloured furnishings and a funky boutique style. Buzzy, brightly furnished restaurant; the lengthy menu offers satisfying French brasserie classics.

Dukes without rest

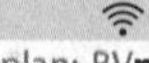

Great Pulteney St ✉ *BA2 4DN* – ✆ *(01225) 787 960* – *www.dukesbath.co.uk* – *Closed 23-30 December* Town plan: BV**n**

17 rm ☕ – †£ 90/195 ††£ 90/195 – 4 suites

Two Grade I listed Palladian-style townhouses, built in 1789, with a friendly, informal feel. Bedrooms are named after famous Dukes and have period themes. If you've skipped dinner, they offer a late night cheeseboard and port.

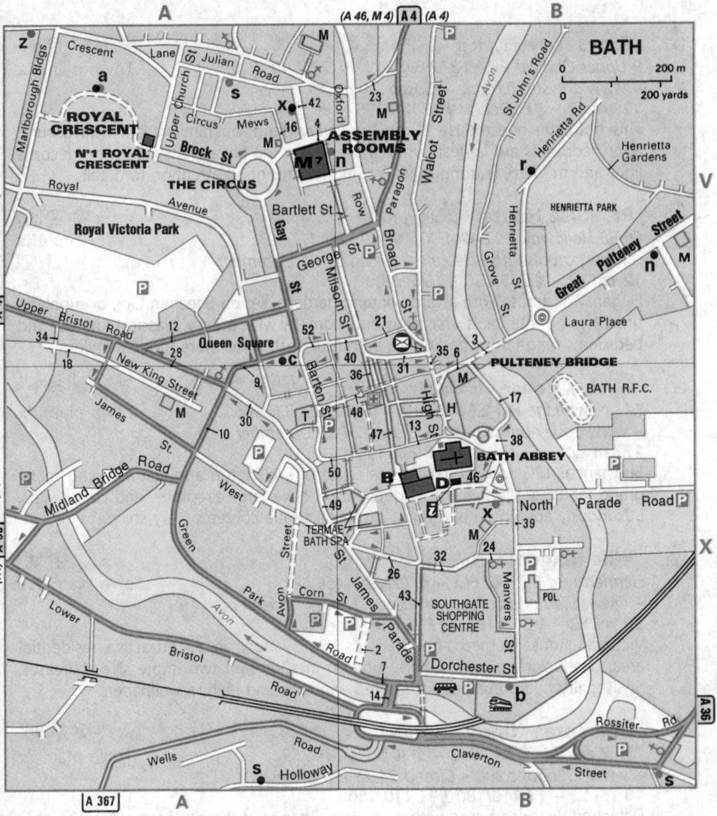

ENGLAND

BATH

Street	Grid	No.
Ambury	BX	2
Argyle St	BV	3
Bennett St	AV	4
Bridge St	BVX	6
Broad Quay	BX	7
Chapel Row	AVX	9
Charles St	AX	10
Charlotte St	AV	12
Cheap St	BX	13
Churchill Bridge	BX	14
Circus Pl	AV	16
Gay St	AV	
Grand Parade	BX	17
Great Stanhope St	AV	18
Green St	BV	21
Guinea Lane	BV	23
Henry St	BX	24
Lower Borough Walls	BX	26
Milsom St	ABV	
Monmouth Pl	AVX	28
Monmouth St	AX	30
New Bond St	BV	31
New Orchard St	BX	32
Nile St	AV	34
Northgate St	BVX	35
Old Bond St	BX	36
Orange Grove	BX	38
Pierrepont St	BX	39
Quiet St	BV	40
Russel St	AV	42
Southgate Shopping Centre	BX	
Southgate St	BX	43
Terrace Walk	BX	46
Union St	BX	47
Upper Borough Walls	BX	48
Westgate Buildings	AX	49
Westgate St	ABX	50
Wood St	AV	52
York St	BX	53

Dorian House without rest

1 Upper Oldfield Pk ✉ BA2 3JX – ✆ (01225) 426 336 Town plan: Z**u**

– www.dorianhouse.co.uk – Closed 24-25 December

13 rm – 🚹£ 65/175 🚹🚹£ 109/175

Charming 19C townhouse featuring original stained glass and musical memorabilia. Individually decorated bedrooms offer a high level of comfort; 4 have four-posters. The delightful conservatory breakfast room overlooks the garden.

Take note of the classification: you should not expect the same level of service in a X or 🏠 as in a XXXXX or 🏠🏠🏠.

Grays without rest
9 Upper Oldfield Pk ✉ BA2 3JX – ✆ (01225) 403 020 Town plan: Z**x**
– www.graysbath.co.uk – Closed 24-26 December
12 rm – £ 80/175 ££ 100/195
This boutique guesthouse is run by a very hands-on family team. The ground floor bedrooms are largest, while those at the top have a cosy feel. The décor is light and modern, featuring family antiques and good attention to detail.

Paradise House without rest
86-88 Holloway ✉ BA2 4PX – ✆ (01225) 317 723 Town plan: AX**s**
– www.paradise-house.co.uk – Closed 24-25 December
12 rm – £ 65/130 ££ 69/200
Elegant 18C house with award-winning gardens, set on Beechen Cliff, overlooking the city. The interior is charming and homely, with a cosy, classical lounge, and bedrooms range from traditional, with four-posters, to more modern styles.

Apsley House without rest
141 Newbridge Hill ✉ BA1 3PT – ✆ (01225) 336 966 Town plan: Y**x**
– www.apsley-house.co.uk – Closed 24-26 December
12 rm – £ 80/180 ££ 90/215
Substantial 18C house built for the Duke of Wellington and still retaining many grand features. High-ceilinged guest areas have large fireplaces and chandeliers. Luxuriously appointed bedrooms display a subtle contemporary style.

Villa Magdala without rest
Henrietta Rd ✉ BA2 6LX – ✆ (01225) 466 329 Town plan: BV**r**
– www.villamagdala.co.uk – Closed 1 week Christmas
20 rm – £ 69/185 ££ 79/195
Victorian house named after Napier's 1868 victory, in an attractive residential area, overlooking a park. Smart, modern interior with two impressive staircases. Stylish, airy bedrooms have shuttered windows and feature wallpapers.

ENGLAND

One Three Nine without rest
139 Wells Rd ✉ BA2 3AL – ✆ (01225) 314 769 Town plan: Z**r**
– www.139bath.co.uk – Closed 24-25 December
10 rm – £ 110/180 ££ 110/180
Detached Victorian house within walking distance of the city centre. A contemporary black and white sitting room and chic breakfast room set the tone. Sizeable bedrooms are equally stylish; some have four-poster beds and spa baths.

Brindleys without rest
14 Pulteney Gdns ✉ BA2 4HG – ✆ (01225) 310 444 Town plan: Z**a**
– www.brindleysbath.co.uk – Closed 24-26 December
6 rm – £ 80/160 ££ 100/180
Victorian house tucked away in a residential street and concealing a surprisingly chic interior. Cosy lounge and neatly laid breakfast room. Tastefully decorated bedrooms in colour themes ranging from lavender to monochrome.

Hill House without rest
25 Belvedere ✉ BA1 5ED – ✆ (01225) 920 520 Town plan: Y**a**
– www.hillhousebath.co.uk
6 rm – £ 80/105 ££ 110/140
A former hotel, pub and wine merchant's, this Georgian townhouse retains much of its original character, but with all the comfort expected by the modern traveller. Good-sized, contemporary bedrooms; those at the rear have city views.

Prices quoted after the symbol refer to the lowest rate for a single room in low season, followed by the highest rate in high season.
The same principle applies to the symbol for a double room.

Restaurants

XXX **Bath Priory** – Bath Priory Hotel

Weston Rd ✉ *BA1 2XT* – ✆ *(01225) 331 922* Town plan: Y**c**
– *www.thebathpriory.co.uk*
Menu £ 28/75 – Carte approx. £ 80 – *(closed 2 weeks January)*
Elegant hotel restaurant made up of several areas: a smart cocktail bar; an airy dining room overlooking the gardens; and a contemporary orangery and terrace. Cooking is refined and accomplished, delivering robust flavours in interesting, classically based dishes. A superb wine list accompanies.
→ Seared scallops, cauliflower and hazelnut couscous. Lamb with braised onion, peas, smoked garlic, charred lettuce and lamb jus. Hot pistachio soufflé, pistachio ice cream.

XXX **Dower House** – Royal Crescent Hotel

16 Royal Cres ✉ *BA1 2LS* – ✆ *(01225) 823 333* Town plan: AV**a**
– *www.royalcrescent.co.uk*
Menu £ 23 (weekday lunch)/38 – Carte approx. £ 55
Across the garden of a smart hotel is this elegant restaurant with gold and blue hues and a feature wall of hand-stitched silk. Dishes are modern and very visual; desserts are a highlight. 'Wine walls' display their finest bottles.

XX **Olive Tree** – Queensberry Hotel

Russel St ✉ *BA1 2QF* – ✆ *(01225) 447 928* Town plan: AV**x**
– *www.olivetreebath.co.uk*
Carte £ 38/55 – *(dinner only and lunch Friday-Sunday)*
Stylish, well-run restaurant in the basement of a boutique hotel, with a small bar and three dining rooms – all on different levels. The contemporary décor and artwork are matched by highly ambitious, original cooking in a modern vein.

XX **Allium Brasserie**

Abbey Hotel, 1 North Par ✉ *BA1 1LF* – ✆ *(01225) 461 603* – *www.abbeyhotelbath.co.uk* Town plan: BX**x**
Menu £ 18 (lunch and early dinner)/23 – Carte £ 38/45 – *(booking advisable)*
In a grand Georgian terrace is this distinctly modern hotel restaurant, with high ceilings, purple and white décor and vivid contemporary art. Keenly priced, all-day menu. Confident, modern brasserie cooking is skilful and highly original, with influences ranging from Britain to Asia and the Mediterranean.

XX **Menu Gordon Jones**

2 Wellsway ✉ *BA2 3AQ* – ✆ *(01225) 480 871* Town plan: Z**e**
– *www.menugordonjones.co.uk* – *Closed 2 weeks July, 2 weeks Christmas-New Year, Sunday and Monday*
Menu £ 45/55 – *(booking essential) (set menu only)*
Tiny restaurant comprising just 8 tables and an open kitchen. Daily 'surprise' menus are guided by the latest ingredients available; the chef cooks alone. Dishes are well-balanced, with interesting texture and flavour combinations.

XX **Mint Room**

Lower Bristol Rd ✉ *BA2 3EB* – ✆ *(01225) 446 656* Town plan: Z**b**
– *www.themintroom.co.uk*
Carte £ 20/27
Smart, spacious Indian restaurant with a distinctly modern, glitzy style. The experienced chef offers an impressive collection of appealing, well-presented dishes which display original and contemporary twists. Knowledgeable service.

X **Graze**

Unit 5, 9 Brunel Sq ✉ *BA1 1SX* – ✆ *(01225) 429 392* Town plan: BX**b**
– *www.bathales.com* – *Closed 25 December*
Menu £ 13 (weekday lunch) – Carte £ 19/42
Buzzy, modern, industrial-style restaurant next to Bath Spa Station, in the Vaults development; its terrace is a must for railway enthusiasts. The grill menu features steak cooked in the Josper oven. Superb ales from their own brewery.

ENGLAND

Casanis

4 Saville Row ✉ BA1 2QP – ✆ (01225) 780 055 Town plan: A/BV**n**
– www.casanis.co.uk – Closed 2 weeks January, 1 week July-August, 25-26 December, Sunday and Monday
Menu £ 18 – Carte £ 25/38 – *(booking essential)*
Sweet Gallic bistro tucked away in the shadow of the Assembly Rooms; run by a French chef and his charming wife. Small, cosy interior and lovely rear courtyard. Authentic, tasty cooking with a focus on classics from the south west.

Marlborough Tavern

35 Marlborough Buildings ✉ BA1 2LY – ✆ (01225) 423 731 – www.marlborough-tavern.com – Closed 25 December Town plan: AV**z**
Menu £ 15 (lunch) – Carte £ 24/39
18C pub on the edge of Victoria Park, close to the Royal Crescent. Chic, fashionable interior with boldly patterned wallpapers and contemporary art. Carefully sourced ingredients feature in pub classics and interesting specials.

Chequers

50 Rivers St ✉ BA1 2QA – ✆ (01225) 360 017 Town plan: AV**s**
– www.thechequersbath.com – Closed 25 December
Carte £ 29/43
Set in a smart residential street amid elegant Georgian terraces, with a brightly painted, simply furnished bar. Cooking is sophisticated and presentation, elaborate; lunch is good value and desserts offer something a little different.

White Hart

Widcombe Hill ✉ BA2 6AA – ✆ (01225) 338 053 Town plan: BX**s**
– www.whitehartbath.co.uk – Closed 25-26 December, Sunday dinner and bank holidays
Menu £ 13 (weekday lunch) – Carte £ 24/34 – *(booking essential at dinner)*
Appealing pub on south east edge of the city centre, with a local following and a neighbourhood feel. Generous portions of hearty cooking; smaller tapas plates are also popular.

Hare & Hounds

Lansdown Rd ✉ BA1 5TJ – ✆ (01225) 482 682 Town plan: Y**s**
– www.hareandhoundsbath.com
Carte £ 22/32
A huge pub, more suited to a celebration with friends than a romantic dinner for two. Its hillside location affords superb views and its gardens and terrace come into their own in summer. Menus offer modern versions of classic dishes.

at Box Northeast: 4.75 mi on A4 -(Y)✉ Bath

The Northey with rm

Bath Rd ✉ SN13 8AE – ✆ (01225) 742 333 – www.ohhcompany.co.uk – Closed 25-26 December
5 rm – †£ 89/160 ††£ 89/160 Carte £ 26/50
Traditional-looking, family-run coaching inn with an open-plan interior, a large dining room and a vast bar. Appealing monthly menus feature unfussy, seasonal British cooking. Seafood dishes – particularly the mussels – are a strength. Smart, contemporary bedrooms have bathrooms to match.

at Colerne Northeast: 6.5 mi by A4 -(Y)- Batheaston rd and Bannerdown Rd✉ Chippenham

Lucknam Park

✉ SN14 8AZ North : 0.5 mi on Marshfield rd – ✆ (01225) 742 777 – www.lucknampark.co.uk
42 rm – †£ 360 ††£ 360, £ 25 – 5 suites
Rest *The Park* ✻ **Rest *Brasserie*** – see restaurant listing
Grand Palladian mansion with a mile-long tree-lined drive, rich, elegant décor, luxurious furnishings and sumptuous fabrics. Extremely comfortable, classically furnished bedrooms. Top class facilities include an impressive modern spa and well-being centre, a renowned equestrian centre and a cookery school.

ENGLAND

XXXX **The Park** – Lucknam Park Hotel

✿ ✉ *SN14 8AZ North : 0.5 mi on Marshfield rd – ✆ (01225) 742 777 – www.lucknampark.co.uk – Closed Sunday dinner and Monday*

Menu £ 75 (weekdays)/105 – *(dinner only and Sunday lunch) (booking essential)*

An aperitif in the elegant library of this impressive mansion is a fine prelude to a formal dinner in the opulent dining room. Service is professional and the kitchen, knowledgeable. Classical menus display modern European influences, with dishes expertly crafted from top quality produce; some from the estate.

→ Poached langoustine with potato mousse and gribiche dressing. Fillet of beef, braised oxtail, celeriac fondant and horseradish. Croustillant of pineapple; rum and raisin parfait.

XX **Brasserie** – Lucknam Park Hotel

✉ *SN14 8AZ North : 0.5 mi on Marshfield rd – ✆ (01225) 742 777 – www.lucknampark.co.uk*

Menu £ 21 (lunch) – Carte £ 25/45

Stylish brasserie in a beautiful courtyard setting in Lucknam Park's state-of-the-art spa, with a spacious bar-lounge and an airy, open-plan dining room with full-length windows. Precise, modern cooking in well-judged combinations; many healthy options are available. Barbecues on the charming terrace in summer.

at Monkton Combe Southeast: 4.5 mi by A36 -(Y)✉ Bath

Wheelwrights Arms with rm

Church Ln ✉ BA2 7HB – ✆ (01225) 722 287 – www.wheelwrightsarms.co.uk – Closed dinner 25-26 December and 1 January

7 rm – †£ 85/95 ††£ 125/150

Menu £ 13 (weekday lunch) – Carte £ 23/34 **s**

Two charming 18C buildings in a sleepy little village, displaying exposed stone walls, parquet floors and open fires. Concise menu of traditional dishes. Sunday lunch is prime rib of beef carved at the table. Set in the old carpenter's workshop, individually designed bedrooms are warm and welcoming.

at Combe Hay Southwest: 5 mi by A367✉ Bath

Wheatsheaf with rm

✉ BA2 7EG – ✆ (01225) 833 504 – www.wheatsheafcombehay.com – Closed 1 week January, 24-25 December, Sunday dinner and Monday except bank holidays

3 rm – †£ 120/150 ††£ 120/150

Menu £ 14 (weekday lunch) – Carte £ 23/40

It began life as a farmhouse in 1576 but now boasts chic, über-modern styling typified by pink flocked wallpaper and vivid artwork; and a relaxed atmosphere helped on its way by open fires, comfy low sofas and the pub's resident spaniels. Flavourful, seasonal food is presented in a contemporary style. Bedrooms have a spacious, modern feel; Buttercup is the largest.

BAUGHURST

Hampshire – See Regional map n°**6-B1**

London 61 mi – Camberley 28 mi – Farnborough 27 mi

Wellington Arms with rm

Baughurst Rd ✉ RG26 5LP – Southwest : 0.5 mi – ✆ (0118) 982 01 10 – www.thewellingtonarms.com – Closed Sunday dinner

3 rm – †£ 95/200 ††£ 95/200

Menu £ 19 (weekday lunch) – Carte £ 21/43 – *(booking essential)*

Smart, cream pub with its own sheep, pigs, chickens, bees, herb beds and vegetable gardens! Produce is strictly local and home-grown/reared/made. The concise menu features 6 dishes per course, which are replaced as produce runs out; cooking is generous and satisfying. Smart, rustic bedrooms come with sheepskin rugs and big, comfy beds; the best is the 'Apartment'.

BEACONSFIELD

Buckinghamshire – Pop. 13 797 – See Regional map n°**11-D3**
London 26 mi – Aylesbury 19 mi – Oxford 32 mi – Croydon 37 mi
Michelin Road map 504-S29

Crazy Bear

75 Wycombe End ✉ HP9 1LX – ✆ (01494) 673 086 – www.crazybeargroup.co.uk
25 rm – †£ 190/490 ††£ 190/490
Rest *Thai* – see restaurant listing
Rest *English* – Menu £ 15 (lunch) – Carte £ 32/49 – *(booking advisable)*
Discreet, unique hotel with sumptuous, over-the-top styling and idiosyncratic furnishings. 10 moody, masculine bedrooms blend original features with rich fabrics; 7 slightly less flamboyant bedrooms are located over the road. The lavishly styled 'English' restaurant offers extensive menus and uses produce from their farm shop, while sexy 'Thai' serves Asian cuisine.

Thai – Crazy Bear Hotel

73 Wycombe End ✉ HP9 1LX – ✆ (01494) 673 086 – www.crazybeargroup.co.uk – Closed Monday
Carte £ 26/46 – *(booking essential)*
Part of the Crazy Bear but in a separate building: it's extravagant, sexy and atmospheric, with chandeliers, flock wallpaper, snakeskin handrails and studded leather chairs. Thai dishes dominate, but influences are drawn from all over Asia.

at Seer Green Northeast: 2.5 mi by A355 ✉ Buckinghamshire

Jolly Cricketers

24 Chalfont Rd ✉ HP9 2YG – ✆ (01494) 676 308 – www.thejollycricketers.co.uk
Carte £ 22/40 – *(closed Sunday dinner) (booking advisable)*
Charming Victorian pub filled with a host of cricketing memorabilia; even the menu is divided into 'Openers, Main Play and Lower Order'. Warming open fire and friendly staff. Appealing cooking pleasingly balances a selection of classics with more modern choices.

at Wooburn Common Southwest: 3.5 mi by A40 ✉ Beaconsfield

Chequers Inn

Kiln Ln ✉ HP10 0JQ – Southwest : 1 mi on Bourne End rd – ✆ (01628) 529 575 – www.chequers-inn.com
17 rm – †£ 85/100 ††£ 90/140, £ 10
Rest – Menu £ 14 (weekday lunch)/28 – Carte £ 28/42 – *(closed dinner 25 December and 1 January)*
Attractive 17C former inn, which has been family-owned and run since 1975. Good-sized bedrooms have flowery feature walls and old pine furnishings collected from antique shops. Enjoy drinks in the spacious, leather-furnished lounge, snacks in the cosy beamed bar or more ambitious dishes in the restaurant.

BEAMHURST

Staffordshire – See Regional map n°**19-C1**
London 147 mi – Birmingham 44 mi – Liverpool 74 mi – Bristol 125 mi

Gilmore at Strine's Farm

✉ ST14 5DZ On A 522. – ✆ (01889) 507 100 – www.restaurantgilmore.com – Closed 1 week Easter, 1 week January, 1 week July-August, 1 week October-November, Monday, Tuesday and dinner Sunday
Menu £ 25/40 – *(dinner only and lunch Thursday, Friday and Sunday) (booking essential)*
Converted farmhouse with three beamed rooms; the one by the kitchen with the quarry tiled flooring is the most popular. Homely décor and personal touches throughout. Traditionally based cooking makes use of local produce.

BEAMINSTER

Dorset – Pop. 2 957 – See Regional map n°**3-B3**
London 154 mi – Exeter 45 mi – Taunton 30 mi – Weymouth 29 mi
Michelin Road map 503-L31

BridgeHouse

3 Prout Bridge ✉ DT8 3AY – ✆ (01308) 862 200 – www.bridge-house.co.uk
13 rm – †£ 95/115 ††£ 125/200
Rest *Beaminster Brasserie* – see restaurant listing
Hugely characterful 13C priests' house. Relax by an inglenook fireplace in one of the traditional flag-floored lounges. Bedrooms in the main house are spacious and have original features; those in the 'CoachHouse' are more modern.

XX **Beaminster Brasserie** – BridgeHouse Hotel

3 Prout Bridge ✉ DT8 3AY – ✆ (01308) 862 200 – www.bridge-house.co.uk
Carte £ 32/46
Start with a fireside drink in the bar of this charming hotel, then head for the Georgian dining room, the conservatory or the covered terrace. Menus showcase local produce and dishes are fresh, vibrant and attractively presented.

BEARSTED

Kent – See Regional map n°**8-B2**
London 39 mi – Dover 40 mi – Royal Tunbridge Wells 22 mi
Michelin Road map 504-V30

XX **Fish On The Green** 

Church Ln ✉ ME14 4EJ – ✆ (01622) 738 300 – www.fishonthegreen.com – Closed 25 December-mid January, Sunday dinner and Monday
Menu £ 19 (lunch) – Carte £ 31/48
Tucked away on a corner of the green is this simply decorated restaurant with a pleasant terrace. Professional cooking focuses on fresh, tasty local seafood. The lunch menu is good value and service is polite and knowledgeable.

BEAULIEU

Hampshire – Pop. 726 – ✉ Brockenhurst – See Regional map n°**6-B2**
London 102 mi – Bournemouth 24 mi – Southampton 13 mi – Winchester 23 mi
Michelin Road map 503-P31 and 504-P31 – Michelin Green Guide GREAT BRITAIN

Montagu Arms

Palace Ln ✉ SO42 7ZL – ✆ (01590) 612 324 – www.montaguarmshotel.co.uk
18 rm – †£ 122/149 ††£ 143/198 – 4 suites
Rest *The Terrace* ✿ **Rest *Monty's Inn*** – see restaurant listing
With its characterful parquet floors and old wood panelling, this charming 18C inn has a timeless elegance. Traditional country house bedrooms marry antique furniture with modern facilities, and service is discreet and personalised. The wicker-furnished conservatory and terrace overlook the lovely gardens.

XXX ✿ **The Terrace** – Montagu Arms Hotel

Palace Ln ✉ SO42 7ZL – ✆ (01590) 612 324 – www.montaguarmshotel.co.uk – Closed Tuesday lunch and Monday
Menu £ 23 (weekday lunch)/70
This elegant dining room is found at the heart of an alluring 18C inn; head to the terrace for views across the lovely gardens. Service is polite and efficient, and only top quality produce is used in the refined, precisely prepared dishes. Cooking has a classical base and modern touches.
→ Spiced scallops with cauliflower purée, apple, coriander and cumin velouté. Roast duck breast, smoked bacon, chicory and creamed potatoes. Seville orange soufflé with Sichuan spiced chocolate ice cream.

X **Monty's Inn** – Montagu Arms Hotel

Palace Ln ✉ SO42 7ZL – ✆ (01590) 612 324 – www.montaguarmshotel.co.uk
Carte £ 24/38
Set within a large red-brick inn in a delightful village, this laid-back bar-restaurant is the perfect spot for a pint and a home-cooked classic. The eggs are from their own chickens and meats are free range and from nearby farms.

BEAUMONT

→ See Channel Islands (Jersey)
Saint Peter – Michelin Road map 503-P33

BEELEY

Derbyshire – Pop. 165 – See Regional map n°**16**-B1

London 160 mi – Derby 26 mi – Matlock 5 mi

Devonshire Arms with rm

Devonshire Sq ✉ DE4 2NR – ✆ (01629) 733 259 – www.devonshirebeeley.co.uk

14 rm – †£ 99/129 ††£ 99/189 Carte £ 28/49 – *(booking advisable)*

A stone inn with a characterful, beamed bar and a bright, modern brasserie with views of the village and stream. Extensive menu offers traditional dishes with a twist; game is a speciality in season. Cosy, country-chic bedrooms in the inn and next door; those in the house opposite are more modern.

BELBROUGHTON

Worcestershire – Pop. 1 272 – See Regional map n°**19**-C2

London 122 mi – Sheffield 108 mi – Kingston upon Hull 156 mi – Derby 64 mi

Michelin Road map 504-N26

The Queens

Queens Hill ✉ DY9 0DU – ✆ (01562) 730 276
– www.thequeensbelbroughton.co.uk – Closed 25 December

Menu £ 19 (weekdays) – Carte £ 23/36 – *(closed Sunday dinner) (bookings advisable at dinner)*

This 16C pub might have been refurbished but its traditional look and feel remains – a conscious effort by the owners to respect the locals' preferences. Refined, attractive dishes range from hearty pub favourites to flavoursome classics.

ENGLAND

BELCHFORD

Lincolnshire ✉ Horncastle – See Regional map n°**17**-C1

London 169 mi – Horncastle 5 mi – Lincoln 28 mi

Michelin Road map 502-T24

Blue Bell Inn

1 Main Rd ✉ LN9 6LQ – ✆ (01507) 533 602 – www.bluebellbelchford.co.uk
– Closed 12-26 January

Carte £ 20/34

Welcoming pub in a tiny village in the Lincolnshire Wolds. Traditional bar with a copper-topped counter and sofas leads to a bright red dining room. Menus cover all bases, offering honest, home-cooked dishes which are big on flavour.

BELFORD

Northumberland – Pop. 1 258 – See Regional map n°**24**-A1

London 335 mi – Edinburgh 71 mi – Newcastle upon Tyne 49 mi

Michelin Road map 501-O17 and 502-O17

Market Cross

1 Church St ✉ NE70 7LS – ✆ (01668) 213 013 – www.marketcrossbelford.co.uk
– Closed 23-27 December

4 rm – †£ 60/100 ††£ 80/110 **Rest** – Menu £ 19

200 year old stone townhouse close to the medieval cross in the market square; run by friendly, welcoming owners. Bright modern bedrooms come in neutral hues and feature Nespresso machines and complimentary sherry and Lindisfarne Mead. Local produce features at breakfast; dinner is by arrangement.

BELPER

Derbyshire – Pop. 23 417 – See Regional map n°**16**-B2

London 141 mi – Birmingham 59 mi – Leicester 40 mi – Manchester 55 mi

Michelin Road map 502-P24 and 503

Chevin Green Farm Ⓝ without rest 

Chevin Rd ✉ DE56 2UN – West : 2 mi by A 517 and Farnah Green Rd – ✆ (01773) 822 328 – www.chevingreenfarm.org.uk

5 rm ☕ – †£ 55/70 ††£ 80/95

Chevin Green has been in the family since 1929, when it was a working farm; the outbuildings are now homes, and the residents' families supply fresh produce to the farmhouse. The delightful owners have a passion for tea, so you'll find a great selection, alongside tea-themed artwork, ornaments and furnishings.

BENENDEN

Kent – Pop. 787 – See Regional map n°**8-B2**

London 55 mi – Hastings 23 mi – Royal Tunbridge Wells 19 mi

Michelin Road map 504-V30

Ramsden Farm without rest

Dingleden Ln ✉ TN17 4JT – Southeast : 1 mi by B 2086 – ✆ (01580) 240 203 – www.ramsdenfarmcottage.co.uk

3 rm ☕ – †£ 85/100 ††£ 90/110

Attractive clapperboard house with modern styling, a refreshingly relaxed air and fine countryside views. Spacious, up-to-date bedrooms; luxurious, modern bathrooms with underfloor heating.

BEPTON → See Midhurst

West Sussex

BERKHAMSTED

Hertfordshire – Pop. 20 641 – See Regional map n°**12-A2**

London 34 mi – Aylesbury 14 mi – St Albans 11 mi

Michelin Road map 504-S28 – Michelin Green Guide GREAT BRITAIN

The Gatsby

97 High St ✉ HP4 2DG – ✆ (01442) 870 403 – www.thegatsby.net – Closed 25-26 December

Menu £ 15 (lunch) – Carte £ 31/47

Charming cinema built in 1938 and sympathetically converted to incorporate a trendy art deco bar and glamorous restaurant. Dine among elegant columns and ornate plasterwork. Menus offer detailed, classically based dishes with modern twists.

Old Mill Ⓝ

London Rd ✉ HP4 2NB – ✆ (01442) 879 590 – www.theoldmillberkhamsted.co.uk – Closed 25 December

Menu £ 12 (lunch and early dinner) – Carte £ 23/59

An imposing red-brick building on the Grand Union Canal; its still-turning waterwheel a testament to its industrial past. All-encompassing menus move with seasons, with deli boards and grass-fed, dry-aged steaks a feature.

BERWICK

East Sussex – See Regional map n°**8-A3**

London 65 mi – Eastbourne 9 mi – Brighton and Hove 17 mi

Restaurant at the English Wine Centre with rm 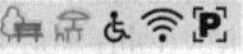

Alfriston Rd ✉ BN26 5QS – ✆ (01323) 870 164 – www.englishwine.co.uk – Closed last 2 weeks February, Christmas-New Year and Monday

5 rm ☕ – †£ 75/120 ††£ 135/175

Carte £ 25/32 – *(lunch only and dinner Friday-Saturday) (booking essential)*

A collection of delightful 16C and 17C barns; one houses a shop selling over 140 English wines and this pretty, intimate restaurant, where the sweet-natured staff serve traditional English dishes with a modern touch. Stylish bedrooms are situated in another building and have views over the South Downs.

ENGLAND

BEVERLEY

East Riding of Yorkshire – Pop. 30 587 – ✉ Kingston-Upon-Hull
– See Regional map n°**23-D2**
London 188 mi – Kingston-upon-Hull 8 mi – Leeds 52 mi – York 29 mi
Michelin Road map 502-S22 – Michelin Green Guide GREAT BRITAIN

XX **Whites** with rm
12a North Bar Without ✉ HU17 7AB – ✆ (01482) 866 121
– www.whitesrestaurant.co.uk – Closed 1 week Christmas, 1 week August, Sunday and Monday
4 rm – £ 95 £ 95
Menu £ 25 (weekdays)/50 – *(dinner only and Saturday lunch) (booking advisable)*
Small restaurant by the old city walls, its plain décor contrasting nicely with black wood tables and eye-catching glass art. Good value weekday set menu uses lesser-known cuts; à la carte offers more ambitious, complex dishes. Smart, modern bedrooms, some with bespoke furniture; rooftop terrace breakfast.

at Tickton Northeast: 3.5 mi by A1035 ✉ Kingston-Upon-Hull

Tickton Grange
✉ HU17 9SH on A 1035 – ✆ (01964) 543 666
– www.beverleyticktongrange.co.uk
21 rm – £ 94/116 £ 120/150
Rest *Hide* – see restaurant listing
Warm, welcoming, family-run hotel in a Georgian house – a popular wedding venue. Spacious main sitting room with a grand piano looks out over immaculately kept gardens. Homely bedrooms; those in the converted cottage are more contemporary.

ENGLAND

XX **Hide** – Tickton Grange Hotel
✉ HU17 9SH on A 1035 – ✆ (01964) 543 666
– www.beverleyticktongrange.co.uk
Menu £ 20 – Carte £ 37/44
Formal hotel restaurant with elegant furnishings. Accomplished, original dishes are presented in a modern style; flavours are distinct and combinations, well-judged. Dishes are more technical than their concise descriptions imply.

at South Dalton Northwest: 5 mi by A164 and B1248 ✉ Beverley

Pipe and Glass Inn (James Mackenzie) with rm
West End ✉ HU17 7PN – ✆ (01430) 810 246 – www.pipeandglass.co.uk – Closed 2 weeks January, Sunday dinner and Monday except bank holidays
2 rm – £ 135 £ 170 Carte £ 22/52
Warm, bustling and inviting pub; very personally run by its experienced owners. Dishes are generously proportioned, carefully executed and flavourful, with judicious use of local, seasonal and traceable produce. Luxurious designer bedrooms boast the latest mod cons and have their own patios overlooking the estate woodland; breakfast is served in your room.
→ Scampi, white bean and black pudding crumble with wild garlic crust. Rump of lamb, spring vegetable and pearl barley 'hotchpotch', mutton belly fritter. Liquorice panna cotta, Yorkshire rhubarb, parkin crumb & East Yorkshire sugar cakes.

BEWDLEY

Worcestershire – Pop. 8 571 – See Regional map n°**18-B2**
London 130 mi – Birmingham 30 mi – Liverpool 91 mi – Bristol 77 mi
Michelin Road map 503-N26

Kateshill House without rest
Redhill ✉ DY12 2DR – South : 0.25 mi on B 4194 – ✆ (01299) 401 563
– www.kateshillhouse.co.uk
8 rm – £ 65/80 £ 85/110
This elegant Georgian manor house is surrounded by beautiful gardens; where you'll find a tree from the reign of King Henry VIII. Sumptuous, contemporary furnishings provide a subtle contrast to the house's original features.

BIBURY

Gloucestershire – Pop. 570 – ✉ Cirencester – See Regional map n°**4-D1**

▶London 86 mi – Gloucester 26 mi – Oxford 30 mi

Michelin Road map 503-O28 and 504-O28 – Michelin Green Guide GREAT BRITAIN

Bibury Court

✉ *GL7 5NT* – ✆ *(01285) 740 337* – *www.biburycourt.com*

19 rm – †£ 145 ††£ 295 – 1 suite

Rest *Origin* – see restaurant listing

Lose yourself in the waterside gardens of this beautiful, part-16C manor house. Listed oak panelling lines the drawing room walls and there's a 1930s fireplace in the bar. Bedrooms are a mix of classic and contemporary styles.

Swan

✉ *GL7 5NW* – ✆ *(01285) 740 695* – *www.cotswold-inns-hotels.co.uk/swan*

22 rm ☕ – †£ 150/210 ††£ 170/210 – 4 suites

Rest *Brasserie* – Menu £ 18/35 – Carte dinner £ 28/42

Set in a delightful village, this ivy-clad coaching inn has a trout stream running through the garden and a cosy, characterful interior. Bedrooms mix cottagey character with contemporary touches; the best are in the annexes. The brasserie has an unusual log wall and opens onto a lovely flag-stoned courtyard.

Cotteswold House without rest

Arlington, on B4425 ✉ *GL7 5ND* – ✆ *(01285) 740 609* – *www.cotteswoldhouse.net*

3 rm ☕ – †£ 65 ††£ 85

This pleasant guesthouse is set just outside picturesque Bibury and provides an ideal base for exploring the area. The Victorian façade conceals traditional, spotlessly kept bedrooms and the friendly owner offers a warm welcome.

Origin – Bibury Court Hotel

✉ *GL7 5NT* – ✆ *(01285) 740 337* – *www.biburycourt.com*

Carte £ 27/50 – *(bookings essential for non-residents)*

As the name implies, locally sourced and foraged ingredients are key at this sophisticated hotel restaurant. Cooking is modern and original, with an understated style. The oak leaf light and striking wall mural are talking points.

BIDBOROUGH

Kent – See Regional map n°**8-B2**

▶London 35 mi – Brighton 37 mi – Oxford 100 mi

Kentish Hare

95 Bidborough Ridge ✉ *TN3 0XB* – ✆ *(01892) 525 709* – *www.thekentishhare.com* – *Closed Sunday dinner and Monday except bank holidays*

Menu £ 22 – Carte £ 23/44

Saved from development by local residents Lord and Lady Mills of Olympic Committee fame and run by the Tanner brothers, this smart, modern pub features a hare theme, quirky wallpaper and an open kitchen. Tasty steaks from the Kamado grill.

BIDDENDEN

Kent – Pop. 1 303 – See Regional map n°**9-C2**

▶London 52 mi – Ashford 13 mi – Maidstone 16 mi

Michelin Road map 504-V30 – Michelin Green Guide GREAT BRITAIN

Barclay Farmhouse without rest

Woolpack Corner ✉ *TN27 8BQ* – *South : 0.5 mi by A 262 on Benenden rd* – ✆ *(01580) 292 626* – *www.barclayfarmhouse.co.uk*

3 rm ☕ – †£ 70/75 ††£ 85/90

A converted farmhouse and barn conversion in an acre of neat gardens, complete with a duck pond. Comfortable bedrooms feature French oak furniture and characterful beams; extra touches include chocolate truffles on your pillow.

West House (Graham Garrett)

28 High St ✉ TN27 8AH – ✆ (01580) 291 341 – www.thewesthouserestaurant.co.uk – Closed Christmas-New Year, Saturday lunch, Sunday dinner and Monday

Menu £ 25 (weekday lunch)/60

Characterful beamed restaurant with contemporary oil paintings and a wood-burning stove – one of a row of old weavers' cottages in a picturesque village. Original, modern dishes display global influences and the occasional playful touch; and top quality ingredients allow the natural flavours to shine through.

→ Cured foie gras, duck confit and pickled rhubarb. Pork shoulder, cheek and faggot with roast quince and sage oil. Milk mousse, caramelised white chocolate and honey ice cream.

The Three Chimneys

Hareplain Rd ✉ TN27 8LW – West : 1.5 mi by A 262 – ✆ (01580) 291 472 – www.thethreechimneys.co.uk – Closed 25 and dinner 31 December

Carte £ 24/37 – *(booking essential)*

Delightful pub with a charming terrace and garden, dating back to 1420 and boasting a roaring fire, dimly lit low-beamed rooms and an old world feel. Dishes are mainly British based; there are some tempting local wines, ciders and ales too.

BIDDENHAM

Bedford – See Regional map n°**12-A1**

London 50 mi – Cambridge 33 mi – Northampton 20 mi

Michelin Road map 504-S27

ENGLAND

Three Tuns (N)

57 Main Rd ✉ MK40 4BD – ✆ (01234) 354 847 – www.thethreetunsbiddenham.co.uk – Closed Sunday dinner

Menu £ 17 (weekday lunch) – Carte £ 24/41

Set in a leafy residential suburb; if you're lost, look up above the rooftops for the majestic Canadian redwood tree. It's part-16C and part-19C, with a lovely terrace. Cooking is classical, seasonal and everything is homemade.

BIGBURY

Devon – See Regional map n°**2-C3**

London 195 mi – Exeter 41 mi – Plymouth 22 mi

Michelin Road map 503-I33

Oyster Shack

Milburn Orchard Farm, Stakes Hill ✉ TQ7 4BE – East : 1 mi by Easton rd on Tidal rd – ✆ (01548) 810 876 – www.oystershack.co.uk – Closed 2 January-2 February and Sunday dinner in winter

Carte £ 22/40 – *(booking essential)*

Former oyster farm with a small oyster bar and lounge, and a large terrace. The brightly decorated room is hung with fishing nets and centred around a large fish tank. Cooking is fresh and unfussy, focusing on shellfish and the daily catch.

BIGBURY-ON-SEA

Devon – Pop. 220 – ✉ Kingsbridge – See Regional map n°**2-C3**

London 196 mi – Exeter 42 mi – Plymouth 23 mi

Michelin Road map 503-I33

Burgh Island

✉ TQ7 4BG South : 0.5 mi by hotel transport – ✆ (01548) 810 514 – www.burghisland.com – Closed 4-20 January

25 rm (dinner included) – †£ 310 ††£ 400/665 – 10 suites

Rest – Menu £ 55/70 – *(dinner only and Sunday lunch) (bookings essential for non-residents)*

Grade II listed house on its own island, accessed using the hotel's Land Rover (or tractor at high tide!). It has classic art deco styling throughout, from the guest areas to the individually designed bedrooms; some rooms have small balconies and most have excellent bay views. 1930s themed 'black tie' dinners take place in the ballroom; there's live music Weds and Sat.

Henley
Folly Hill ✉ TQ7 4AR – ✆ (01548) 810 240 – www.thehenleyhotel.co.uk – March-October
5 rm – ♦£ 90 ♦♦£ 120/150 **Rest** – – *(dinner only) (residents only)*
Charming hotel affording superb views over Burgh Island and towards Bolt Tail. Homely lounge and wicker-furnished conservatory. Comfortable bedrooms cross New England and English Country styles; Room 6 boasts the best views. Concise, unfussy menus feature locally sourced ingredients.

BILDESTON

Suffolk – See Regional map n°**15-C3**
London 85 mi – Bury St Edmunds 18 mi – Ipswich 15 mi
Michelin Road map 504-W27

Bildeston Crown
104 High St ✉ IP7 7EB – ✆ (01449) 740 510 – www.thebildestoncrown.com
12 rm – ♦£ 80/90 ♦♦£ 100/195
Rest – Menu £ 45 – Carte £ 26/37
Rest *Ingrams* – Menu £ 45/70 – Carte £ 26/37 – *(booking essential)*
Hugely characterful 15C wool merchant's, with a lovely rear courtyard. Stylish, modern interior with warm colours and open fires. Bedrooms vary from florally feminine to bright and bold; all are luxurious with designer furniture and chic bathrooms. Sumptuous, formal Ingrams serves creative modern dishes; the charming beamed dining room offers a more classical menu.

BIRKENHEAD

Merseyside – Pop. 142 968 – See Regional map n°**20-A3**
London 208 mi – Liverpool 3 mi – Manchester 37 mi – Stoke-on-Trent 52 mi
Michelin Road map 502-K23 and 503-K23

Fraiche (Marc Wilkinson)
11 Rose Mount, Oxton ✉ CH43 5SG – Southwest : 2.25 mi by A 552 and B 5151 – ✆ (0151) 652 29 14 – www.restaurantfraiche.com – Closed 25 December, 1-7 July, Sunday dinner, Monday and Tuesday
Menu £ 40 (lunch)/75 – *(dinner only and Sunday lunch) (booking essential)*
Stylish, sophisticated restaurant – seating just 10-12 diners – with striking glass friezes and intimate mood lighting. The passionate chef cooks alone and offers a modern six course menu which uses ingredients from around the globe. Dishes feature some unusual combinations and are impressively presented.
→ Salt-cooked scallop, smoked yoghurt and parsley purée. Treacle-cured venison loin, crisp roots and celeriac cream. Pineapple sorbet, coconut and minted mango salad.

ENGLAND

BIRMINGHAM

West Midlands – Pop. 1 085 810 – See Regional map n°**19**-C2
London 122 mi – Bristol 91 mi – Newcastle upon Tyne 207 mi
Michelin Road map 503-O26 and 504-O26 – Michelin Green Guide GREAT BRITAIN

© O. Protze/age fotostock

Hotels

ENGLAND

Hyatt Regency

rm,

2 Bridge St ✉ *B1 2JZ* – ✆ *(0121) 643 12 34 – www.birmingham.regency.hyatt.com* Town plan: **5**KZ**a**
325 rm – †£ 117/219 ††£ 117/219, ☕ £ 18 – 4 suites
Rest *Aria* – Menu £ 15/20 – Carte £ 21/51
An eye-catching, mirror-fronted, tower block hotel in a prime city centre location, with a covered link to the International Convention Centre. Spacious bedrooms have floor to ceiling windows and an excellent level of facilities. Aria restaurant, in the atrium, offers modern European menus.

Hotel Du Vin

25 Church St ✉ *B3 2NR* – ✆ *(0121) 200 0600 – www.hotelduvin.com* Town plan: **6**LY**e**
66 rm – †£ 99/159 ††£ 109/399, ☕ £ 17
Rest *Bistro* – Menu £ 20 (weekday lunch) – Carte £ 25/50
Characterful former eye hospital with a relaxed, boutique style. Richly hued bedrooms are named after wine companies and estates; one suite boasts an 8 foot bed, 2 roll-top baths and a gym. Kick-back in the small cellar pub or comfy champagne bar. The classical bistro has a lively buzz and a French menu.

Hotel La Tour

rm,

Albert St ✉ *B5 5JE* – ✆ *(0121) 718 8000 – www.hotel-latour.co.uk – Closed 24-25 December* Town plan: **6**MY**a**
174 rm – †£ 85/250 ††£ 85/250, ☕ £ 16
Rest *Aalto* – Carte £ 18/41
Striking modern building with a stylish lobby featuring state-of-the-art self-check-in terminals. With their media hubs and TV recording facilities, bedrooms are ideal for business travellers; the smart bathrooms are shower-only. There are extensive events facilities, and a chic café, bar and brasserie.

Malmaison

rm,

Mailbox, 1 Wharfside St ✉ *B1 1RD* – ✆ *(0121) 246 50 00 – www.malmaison.com* Town plan: **6**LZ**e**
189 rm – †£ 89/245 ††£ 89/245, ☕ £ 16 – 1 suite
Rest *Brasserie* – Menu £ 16 – Carte £ 21/48 – *(closed dinner 25 December)*
A smart new-build with dark, moody décor, set next to designer clothes and homeware shops, on the site of the old Royal Mail sorting office. Bedrooms are spacious and stylish; the Penny Black suite has a mini-cinema and a steam room. The bustling black brasserie serves an accessible British menu.

INDEX OF STREET NAMES IN BIRMINGHAM

ENGLAND

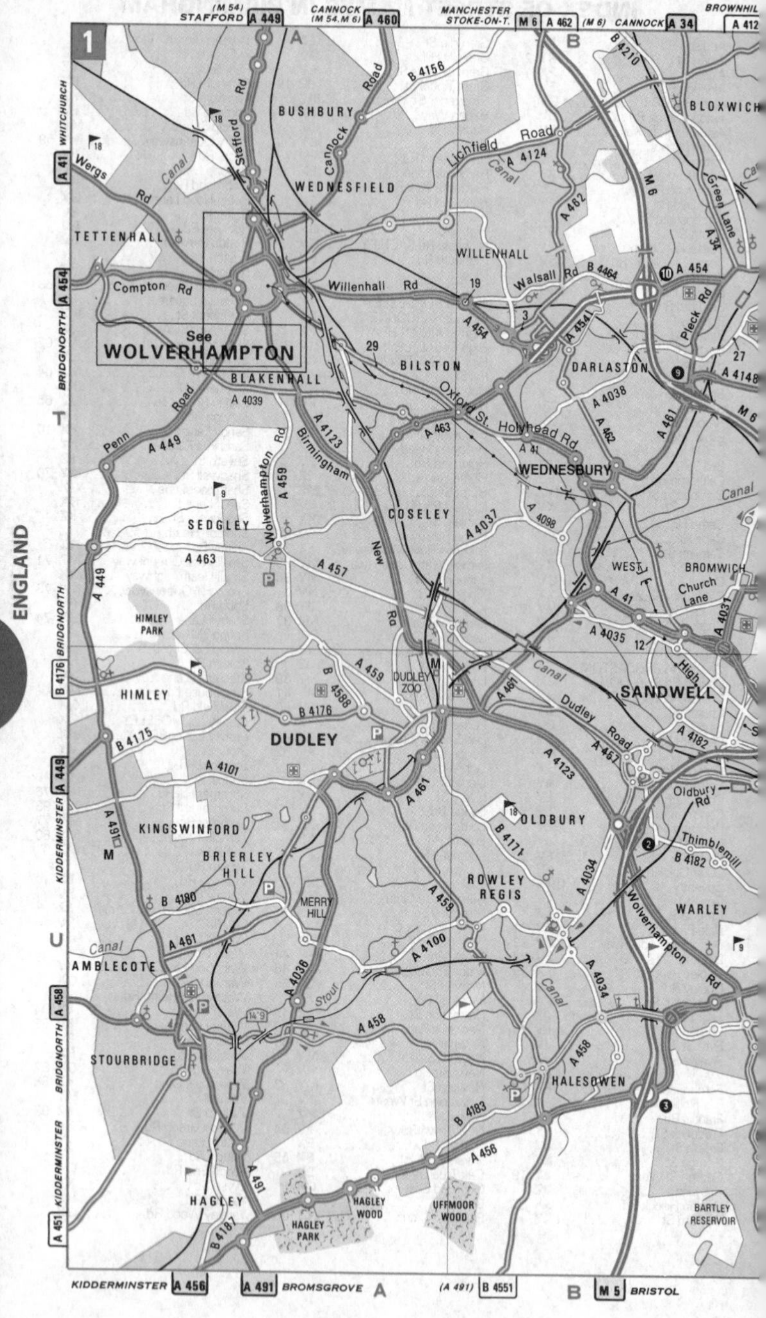

(M 54) STAFFORD A 449 — CANNOCK (M 54. M 6) A 460 — MANCHESTER STOKE-ON-T. M 6 A 462 (M 6) CANNOCK A 34 — BROWNHILLS A 412

1

WHITCHURCH A 41 — BRIDGNORTH A 454 — ENGLAND — BRIDGNORTH B 4176 — KIDDERMINSTER A 449 — BRIDGNORTH A 458 — KIDDERMINSTER A 451

BUSHBURY
WEDNESFIELD
TETTENHALL
Wergs Rd
Compton Rd
Stafford Rd
Cannock Road
Lichfield Road
Willenhall Rd
Walsall Rd
WILLENHALL
BLOXWICH
Green Lane
Pleck Rd
DARLASTON
See WOLVERHAMPTON
BLAKENHALL
BILSTON
Oxford St.
Holyhead Rd
WEDNESBURY
Penn Road
Birmingham
Wolverhampton Rd
New Rd
SEDGLEY
COSELEY
WEST BROMWICH
Church Lane
HIMLEY PARK
HIMLEY
DUDLEY
DUDLEY ZOO
SANDWELL
High
Dudley Road
Oldbury Rd
Thimblemill
KINGSWINFORD
BRIERLEY HILL
MERRY HILL
OLDBURY
ROWLEY REGIS
WARLEY
Wolverhampton Rd
AMBLECOTE
Canal
Stour
STOURBRIDGE
HALESOWEN
HAGLEY
HAGLEY WOOD
HAGLEY PARK
UFFMOOR WOOD
BARTLEY RESERVOIR

A 4124, A 462, A 454, B 4464, A 4541, A 4148, A 4038, A 4039, A 449, A 459, A 4123, A 463, A 41, A 4037, A 4098, A 457, A 4035, A 4031, A 4182, A 461, B 4588, A 4101, B 4175, A 491, B 4180, B 4171, A 4034, A 4100, A 4036, A 458, B 4183, A 456, B 4187, B 4182, M 6, B 4210, B 4156

KIDDERMINSTER A 456 — A 491 BROMSGROVE — (A 491) B 4551 — M 5 BRISTOL

BIRMINGHAM AND WOLVERHAMPTON

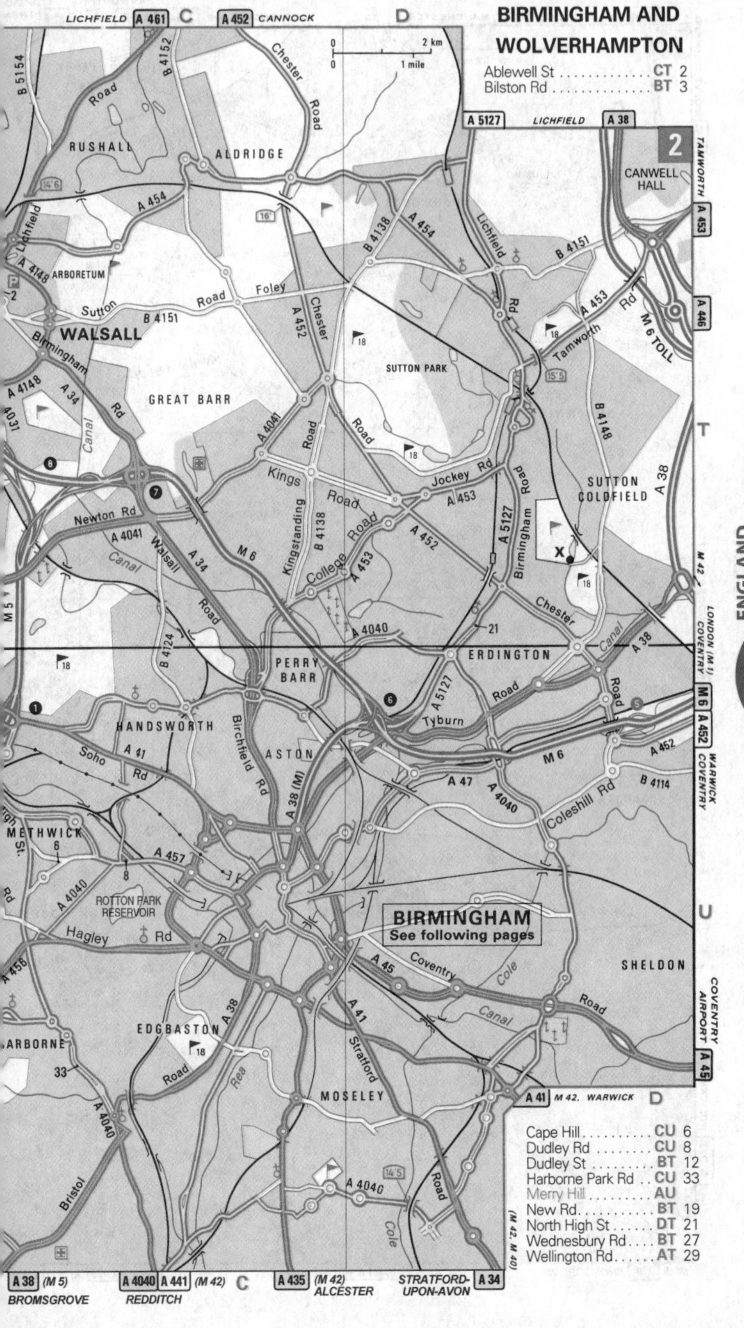

ENGLAND

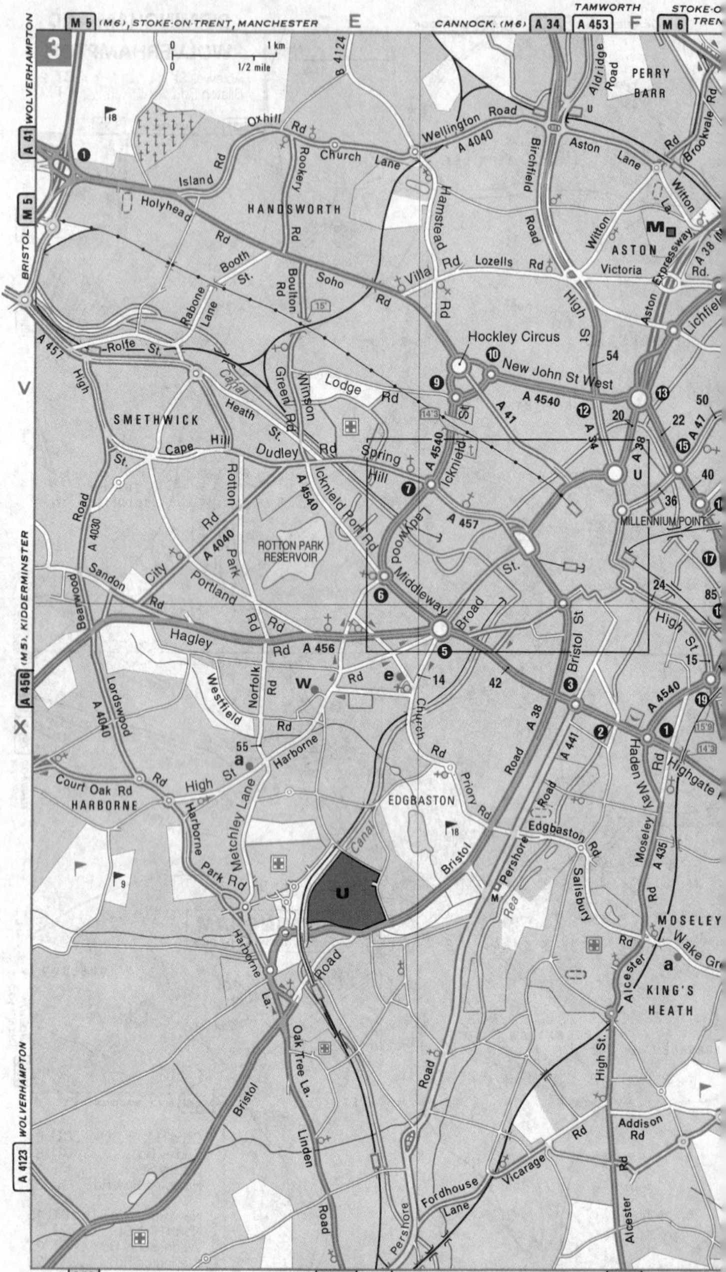

M 5 (M6), STOKE-ON-TRENT, MANCHESTER E CANNOCK. (M6) A 34 TAMWORTH A 453 F M 6 STOKE-ON-TRENT

3

WOLVERHAMPTON A 41

BRISTOL M 5

A 456 (M 5), KIDDERMINSTER

ENGLAND

A 4123 WOLVERHAMPTON

V

X

HANDSWORTH

PERRY BARR

ASTON

SMETHWICK

ROTTON PARK RESERVOIR

Hockley Circus

MILLENNIUM POINT

EDGBASTON

HARBORNE

MOSELEY

KING'S HEATH

Oxhill Rd

Church Lane

Wellington Road

A 4040

Aston Lane

Birchfield Road

Aldridge Road

Brookvale Rd

Witton La.

Witton Rd

Aston Expressway

Victoria Rd.

A 38 (M)

Lichfield

Island Rd

Holyhead Rd

Rookery Rd

Hamstead Rd

Lozells Rd

Villa Rd

Booth St.

Boulton Rd

Soho Rd

High St

Aston

Rabone Lane

Rolfe St.

Canal

A 457

High St.

Lodge Rd

Winson Green Rd

Heath St.

New John St West

A 4540

A 41

A 34

A 38

A 47

Cape Hill

Dudley Rd

Spring Hill

Icknield St

Icknield Port Rd

Ladywood Middleway

Rotton Park Rd

City Rd

Road A 4030

Sandon Rd

Portland Rd

Beardwood Rd

Hagley Rd A 456

Broad St.

Bristol St

Westfield Rd

Norfolk Rd

Lordswood Rd A 4040

Harborne Rd

Church Rd

Priory Rd

Bristol Road A 38

A 441

Haden Way

Highgate Rd

Court Oak Rd

High St

Metchley Lane

Harborne Park Rd

Edgbaston Rd

Pershore Road

Salisbury Rd

Moseley Rd A 435

Wake Green

Alcester Rd

Rea

Harborne La.

Oak Tree La.

Bristol Road

Linden Road

Pershore Road

Fordhouse Lane

Vicarage Rd

High St.

Addison Rd

Alcester Road

Road

Canal

1 2 3 5 6 7 9 10 12 13 15 17 19

14 15 20 22 24 36 40 42 50 54 55 85

(M 5) A 38 BROMSGROVE E REDDITCH A4040 A 441 REDDITCH F A 435 ALCESTER

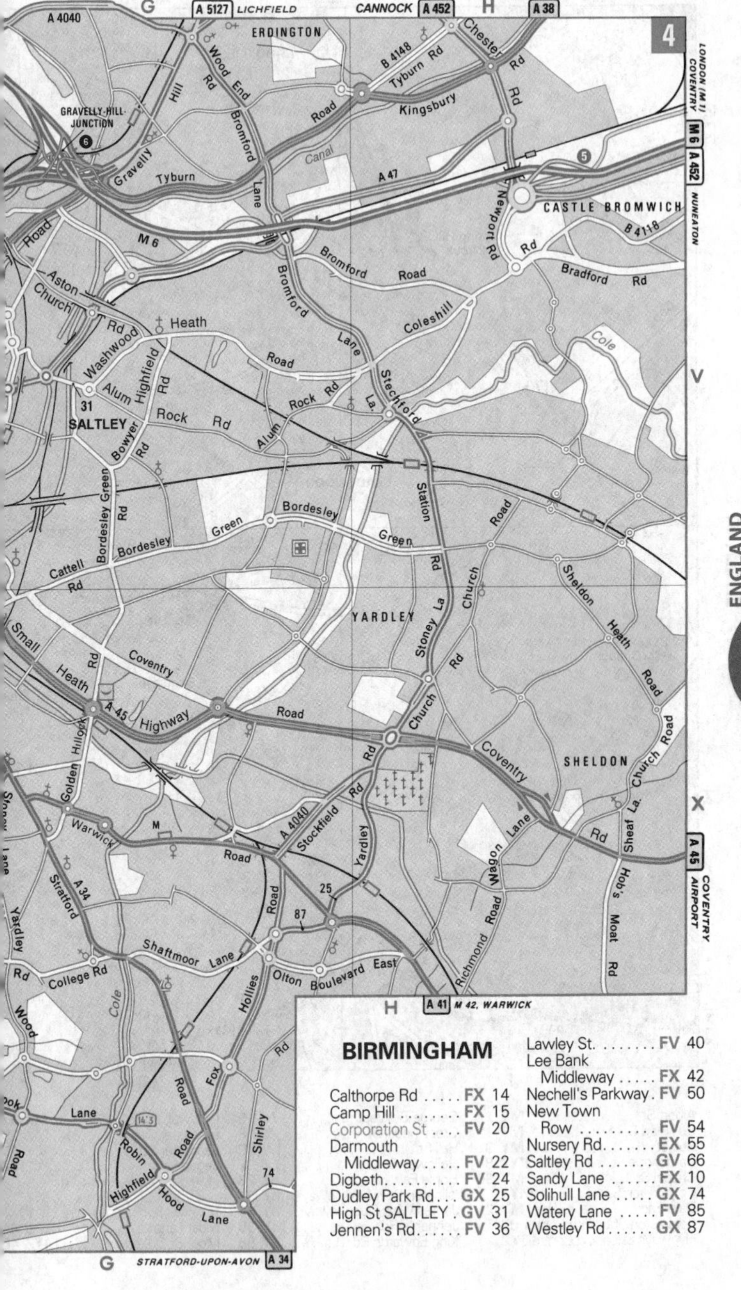

BIRMINGHAM

Calthorpe Rd	FX	14
Camp Hill	FX	15
Corporation St	FV	20
Darmouth Middleway	FV	22
Digbeth	FV	24
Dudley Park Rd	GX	25
High St SALTLEY	GV	31
Jennen's Rd	FV	36
Lawley St.	FV	40
Lee Bank Middleway	FX	42
Nechell's Parkway	FV	50
New Town Row	FV	54
Nursery Rd	EX	55
Saltley Rd	GV	66
Sandy Lane	FX	10
Solihull Lane	GX	74
Watery Lane	FV	85
Westley Rd	GX	87

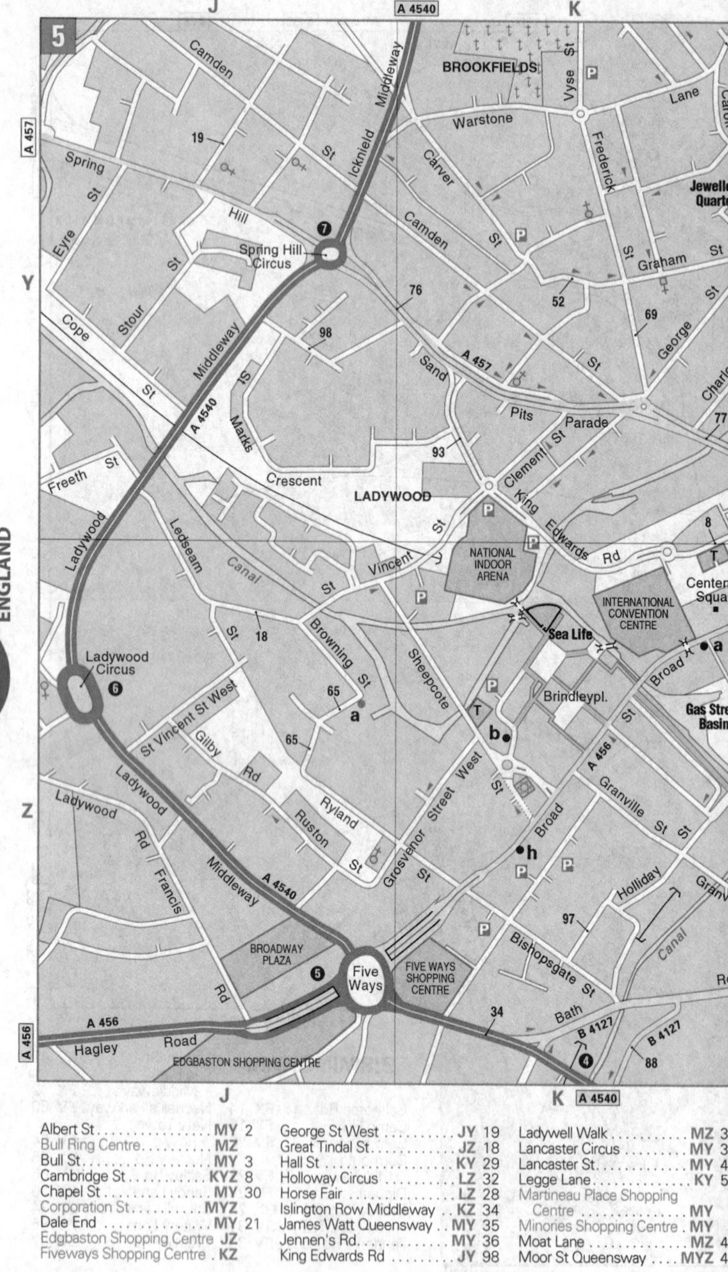

J
A 4540
K
5
Camden
Middleway
Icknield
BROOKFIELDS
Vyse
St
Lane
Warstone
Frederick
Carver
A 457
19
Spring
St
Hill
Eyre
Camden
St
Jewellery Quarter
Spring Hill Circus
7
St
Graham
St
Y
Stour
Cope
Middleway
76
52
69
George
St
98
Sand
A 457
St
St
Marks
A 4540
Pits
Parade
77
Freeth
St
Crescent
93
Clement
St
LADYWOOD
King
Edwards
Rd
Ladywood
Ledsam
Canal
St
Vincent
NATIONAL INDOOR ARENA
8
T
Centenary Square
INTERNATIONAL CONVENTION CENTRE
Sea Life
a
St
18
Browning
St
Sheepcote
Broad
Ladywood Circus
6
St Vincent St West
65
a
Brindleypl.
Gas Street Basin
Gilby
Rd
65
T
b
A 456
St
Granville
St
St
Z
Ladywood
Ladywood
Rd
Ryland
Ruston
Grosvenor
Street West
St
Broad
h
Francis
Middleway
A 4540
St
Grosvenor
St
Holliday
Granville
97
Canal
BROADWAY PLAZA
5
Five Ways
FIVE WAYS SHOPPING CENTRE
Bishopsgate
St
Rd
Row
34
Bath
B 4127
B 4127
A 456
Hagley
Road
A 456
EDGBASTON SHOPPING CENTRE
4
88
J
K
A 4540
ENGLAND

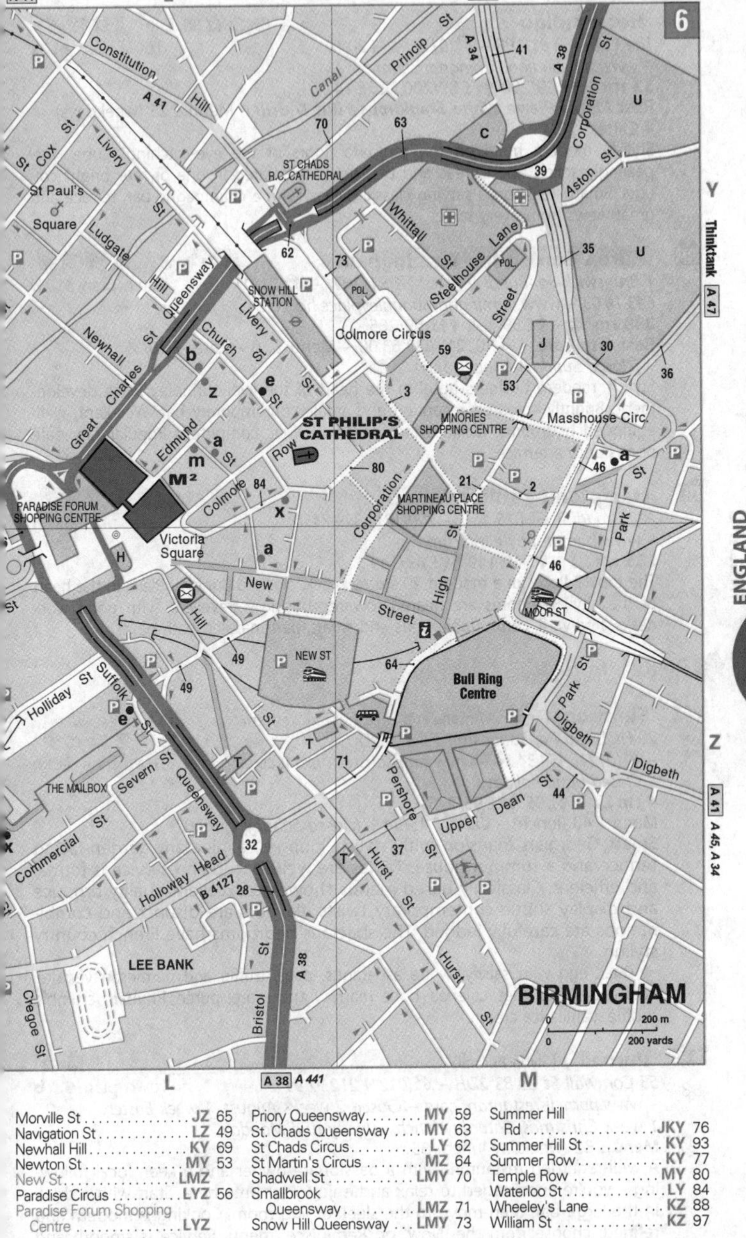

A 41
L
A 34
M
A 38 (M)
6
Constitution
Hill
A 41
Canal
Princip
St
A 34
41
A 38
St
Corporation
U
C
39
Aston
St
70
63
ST CHADS
R.C. CATHEDRAL
Cox
St
St
Livery
St Paul's
Square
Ludgate
Hill
Queensway
62
Whittall
St
Steelhouse
Lane
POL.
35
U
Y
Thinktank
A 47
73
POL.
SNOW HILL
STATION
Livery
St
Church
Colmore Circus
Street
J
Newhall
St
Charles
b
z
e
St
St
59
53
30
36
Great
ST PHILIP'S
CATHEDRAL
MINORIES
SHOPPING CENTRE
Masshouse Circ.
Edmund
a
m
St
Row
80
a
46
St
M²
Colmore
84
21
2
PARADISE FORUM
SHOPPING CENTRE
Corporation
MARTINEAU PLACE
SHOPPING CENTRE
Park
x
St
Victoria
Square
H
a
46
New
High
St
ENGLAND
Hill
Street
MOOR ST
49
NEW ST
64
Bull Ring
Centre
St
Park
49
Holliday
St
Suffolk
e
St
St
Digbeth
T
71
Z
T
Severn
St
Digbeth
THE MAILBOX
Queensway
Pershore
St
44
Dean
Upper
A 41
A 45, A 34
St
Commercial
32
37
St
T
Hurst
Holloway
Head
B 4127
28
St
LEE BANK
St
A 38
Hurst
St
BIRMINGHAM
Cregoe
St
Bristol
0
200 m
0
200 yards
L
A 38 A 441
M

Hotel Indigo
The Cube ✉ *B1 1PR* – ✆ *(0121) 643 20 10* Town plan: **6**LZ**x**
– *www.hotelindigobirmingham.com*
52 rm – †£ 89/200 ††£ 89/200, ☕ £ 14
Rest *Marco Pierre White Steakhouse Bar & Grill* – Menu £ 25 (weekdays) – Carte £ 28/45
Stylish, modern hotel on the top two floors of the eye-catching 'Cube'. Appealingly styled guest areas and bedrooms decorated in one of four bright colours. Smart steakhouse serving classic dishes, with a champagne bar, terrace and great views from every table.

Hilton Garden Inn Birmingham
1 Brunswick Sq, Brindley Place ✉ *B1 2HW* – ✆ *(0121) 643 10 03* – *www.birminghambrindleyplace.hgi.com* Town plan: **5**KZ**b**
238 rm ☕ – †£ 59/195 ††£ 69/205
Rest *City Café* – ✆ (0121) 633 63 00 – Menu £ 20 – Carte £ 20/35 – *(closed Sunday) (dinner only)*
Stylish, modern business hotel in the heart of the lively Brindley Place development. Brightly coloured reception and small, contemporary bar. Well-kept, well-equipped bedrooms; facilities include Apple iMac computers. Popular City Café opens onto a terrace.

Hampton by Hilton without rest
200 Broad St ✉ *B15 1SU* – ✆ *(0121) 329 7450* Town plan: **5**KZ**h**
– *www.hamptonbyhilton.com*
285 rm ☕ – †£ 49/149 ††£ 49/149
The top 17 floors of a modern 20 storey block, close to Brindley Place in the heart of the city. Bedrooms are geared towards business travellers, with good work desks, free wi-fi, comfortable beds and smart, part-marbled bathrooms.

ENGLAND

Restaurants

Simpsons (Andreas Antona and Luke Tipping) with rm
20 Highfield Rd, Edgbaston ✉ *B15 3DU*
– ✆ *(0121) 454 34 34* – *www.simpsonsrestaurant.co.uk* Town plan: **3**EX**e**
– *Closed bank holidays*
4 rm ☕ – †£ 95 ††£ 95/225
Menu £ 40 (lunch) – Carte £ 45/54 – *(closed Sunday dinner)*
Smart Georgian mansion with stylish lounges, a pleasant garden-facing terrace and a summer house. Tables are well-spaced and service is formal and efficient. Classically based menus showcase excellent quality produce and display subtle contemporary twists; flavours are distinct and combinations are carefully judged. The spacious bedrooms have French country styling.
→ Duck egg with salsify, white asparagus, peas, truffle and parmesan velouté. Beef cheek and fillet, celeriac, bone marrow and morel purée. Rhubarb crumble soufflé, vanilla ice cream.

Purnell's (Glynn Purnell)
55 Cornwall St ✉ *B3 2DH* – ✆ *(0121) 212 97 99* Town plan: **6**LY**b**
– *www.purnellsrestaurant.com* – *Closed 2 weeks August, 1 week Easter, 1 week Christmas, Saturday lunch, Sunday and Monday*
Menu £ 32 (weekday lunch)/85
A well-regarded restaurant with a passionate owner and a keen local following – you're encouraged to relax and enjoy your time here. Start with a drink in the large bar, then move to the sleek dining room. Cooking is modern and refined; choose from the 'Now' or 'Reminisce' menu. Service is smooth and friendly.
→ Confit Brixham brill, honey-pickled beetroot and smoked eel. Slow-cooked neck of lamb, wild garlic and goat's cheese royale. Frozen fennel cloud, grapefruit marmalade and liquorice cake.

XXX **Opus at Corwall Street**

54 Cornwall St ✉ B3 2DE – ✆ (0121) 200 2323 Town plan: **6**LY**z**
– www.opusrestaurant.co.uk – Closed 24 December-3 January, Saturday lunch, Sunday dinner and bank holidays
Menu £ 16 (weekdays) – Carte £ 24/44
Very large and popular restaurant with floor to ceiling windows; enjoy an aperitif in the cocktail bar before dining in the stylish main room or at the chef's table in the kitchen. Daily changing menu of modern brasserie dishes.

XX **adam's** (Adam Stokes)

21a Bennetts Hill ✉ B2 5QP – ✆ (0121) 643 3745 Town plan: **6**LZ**a**
– www.adamsrestaurant.co.uk – Closed Christmas-New Year, Sunday and Monday
Menu £ 32/80 – *(booking advisable)*
Smart restaurant with a huge feature photo of a Victorian columned hallway. At lunch there's a two-choice set menu; in the evening they offer a 5 and 9 course tasting selection with wine pairings. Cooking is intricate, original and attractively presented, and relies on top quality seasonal ingredients.
→ Asparagus with roasted lobster mayonnaise and wild garlic bread. Lamb, morels, radish and white sprouting broccoli. Dark chocolate, Earl Grey and malted barley.

XX **Turners** (Richard Turner)

69 High St, Harborne ✉ B17 9NS – ✆ (0121) 426 44 40 Town plan: **3**EX**a**
– www.turnersrestaurantbirmingham.co.uk – Closed Sunday, Monday and lunch Tuesday-Thursday
Menu £ 25 (lunch)/90 – *(booking essential)*
Busy neighbourhood restaurant in a suburban parade, smartly decorated with etched mirrors and velvet chairs; there are just 8 neatly set tables. Visually impressive, confidently crafted, flavoursome dishes use top quality seasonal ingredients. Cooking is classically based but has a modern touch.
→ Ceviche of Orkney scallop with fennel, cucumber, gazpacho and dill granita. Tasting of new season lamb with wild garlic, morels and asparagus. Variations of chocolate with miso, banana and lime.

XX **Carters of Moseley**

2c St Mary's Row, Wake Green Rd ✉ B13 9EZ Town plan: **3**FX**a**
– ✆ (0121) 449 8885 – www.cartersofmoseley.co.uk – Closed 10-26 August, 1-7 January, Monday and Tuesday
Menu £ 20/45 – *(booking advisable) (set menu only)*
Stylish neighbourhood restaurant with black ash tables and a large wine wall. Seasonal modern cooking features British ingredients in intensely flavoured, stimulating combinations. Afternoon tea – on Saturdays – is done very well.

XX **Loves**

The Glasshouse, Browning St ✉ B16 8FL – ✆ (0121) 454 51 51 – www.loves-restaurant.co.uk – Closed 2 weeks August, 1 week January, 1 week Easter and Sunday-Tuesday Town plan: **5**JZ**a**
Menu £ 30 (weekdays)/75 – *(dinner only and lunch Friday-Saturday)*
Spacious restaurant on the ground floor of an apartment block beside the canal basin, run by very welcoming owners. The husband creates original, modern dishes, while his clued-up wife makes recommendations from the interesting wine list.

XX **Waters on the Square** Ⓝ

Chad Sq., Hawthorne Rd, Edgbaston ✉ B15 3TQ Town plan: **3**EX**w**
– ✆ (0121) 454 54 36 – www.watersonthesquare.com – Closed Sunday dinner and Monday
Menu £ 15/28 – *(booking essential)*
Bright red chairs stand out again white walls at this unassuming neighbourhood restaurant. It's run by a well-regarded local chef and cooking is good value and classically based; dessert is a tasting plate of five mini treats.

ENGLAND

XX **Lasan**

3-4 Dakota Buildings, James St, St Pauls Sq ✉ B3 1SD Town plan: **5**KY**a**
– ✆ (0121) 212 36 64 – www.lasan.co.uk – Closed 25 December
Carte £ 26/46
An industrial-style restaurant in an old Jewellery Quarter art gallery. Original cooking takes authentic Indian flavours and delivers them in creative modern combinations; there are some particularly interesting vegetarian choices.

XX **Purnell's Bistro**

Ground Floor, Newater House, 11 Newhall St Town plan: **6**LY**a**
✉ B3 3NY – ✆ (0121) 200 1588 – www.purnellsbistro-gingers.com – Closed 25-30 December and Sunday dinner
Menu £ 20 – Carte £ 27/41
Glynn Purnell's newest venture is just around the corner from his eponymous restaurant. This simply styled, low-ceilinged bistro has a lively front bar and offers clever, modern cooking with original combinations. Friendly service.

XX **Asha's**

12-22 Newhall St ✉ B3 3LX – ✆ (0121) 200 27 67 Town plan: **6**LY**m**
– www.ashasuk.co.uk – Closed 26 December, 1 January and lunch Saturday-Sunday
Carte £ 22/68
A stylish, passionately run Indian restaurant with exotic décor; owned by renowned artiste/gourmet Asha Bhosle. Extensive menus cover most parts of the Subcontinent, with everything cooked to order. Tandoori kebabs are a speciality.

ENGLAND

XX **Fumo**

1 Waterloo St ✉ B2 5PG – ✆ (0121) 643 8979 Town plan: **6**LY**x**
– www.sancarlofumo.co.uk
Carte £ 18/35 – *(bookings not accepted)*
Set in a smart area; an elegant Italian restaurant with a 1930s edge and a lovely bar. Tables are closely set and waiters bustle around delivering good value 'cicchetti' – the tasty Venetian small plates are designed for sharing.

BISHOP'S STORTFORD

Hertfordshire – Pop. 37 838 – See Regional map n°**12**-B2
London 34 mi – Cambridge 27 mi – Chelmsford 19 mi – Colchester 33 mi
Michelin Road map 504-U28 – Michelin Green Guide GREAT BRITAIN

X **Lemon Tree**

14-16 Water Ln ✉ CM23 2JZ – ✆ (01279) 757 788 – www.lemontree.co.uk – Closed 25-27 December, 1 January and bank holidays
Menu £ 20 (weekday lunch) – Carte £ 22/42
Friendly little restaurant in a 200 year old house, hidden in the town centre. Characterful interior with a comfy bar-lounge and several beamed dining areas. Seasonal menus of unfussy, classical dishes; good value lunch selection.

BLACKAWTON → See Dartmouth

Devon – Michelin Road map 503-I32

BLACKBURN

Blackburn with Darwen – Pop. 117 963 – See Regional map n°**20**-B2
London 228 mi – Leeds 47 mi – Liverpool 39 mi – Manchester 24 mi
Michelin Road map 502-M22

Clog & Billycock

Billinge End Rd, Pleasington ✉ BB2 6QB – West : 2 mi by A 677 – ✆ (01254) 201 163 – www.theclogandbillycock.com – Closed 25 December
Carte £ 19/40
Spacious, modern, open-plan pub. Extensive menus offer plenty of choice and display a strong Lancastrian slant; cooking is rustic and generous. Most produce is sourced from within 25 miles.

at Langho North: 4.5 mi on A666 ✉ Whalley

Northcote

Northcote Rd ✉ BB6 8BE – North : 0.5 mi on A 59 at junction with A 666 – ☎ (01254) 240 555 – www.northcote.com
26 rm – †£ 218/268 ††£ 255/305 – 1 suite
Rest *Northcote* ✿ – see restaurant listing
This smart Victorian house sits on the edge of the Ribble Valley and is continually evolving and expanding. The individually designed bedrooms are spacious, stylish and sophisticated; all have queen or king-sized beds and some have garden terraces. Have afternoon tea beside the fire in the lounge.

Northcote (Nigel Haworth) – Northcote Hotel

Northcote Rd ✉ BB6 8BE – North : 0.5 mi on A 59 at junction with A 666 – ☎ (01254) 240 555 – www.northcote.com
Menu £ 28 (weekday lunch)/65 – Carte £ 54/80 (booking essential)
Elegant restaurant within a smart Victorian house. Refined, sophisticated cooking shows depth of flavour and a lightness of touch. Local and garden ingredients are the stars of the show. Watch the chefs in action from the glass-walled kitchen table or join them by taking part in one of the cookery classes.
→ Langoustine with Exmoor caviar, baby leeks and scorched leek oil. Milk-fed lamb 'roast and stew' with spring pod flowers. Pain perdu, toasted spelt and marmalade ice cream, onion caramel.

at Mellor Northwest: 3.25 mi by A677 ✉ Blackburn

Stanley House

rm,

✉ BB2 7NP Southwest : 0.75 mi by A 677 and Further Lane – ☎ (01254) 769 200 – www.stanleyhouse.co.uk
30 rm – †£ 155/250 ††£ 190/275
Rest *Grill on the Hill* – Carte £ 29/55 – *(closed Monday) (dinner only and Sunday lunch)*
Rest *Mr Fred's* – Carte £ 22/38
Attractive part-17C manor house boasting superb country views and a smart spa with four types of sauna. Bedrooms in the main house are elegant and feature original beams and mullioned windows; the 'Woodland Rooms' are more contemporary. The stylish 'Grill on the Hill' offers modern favourites and views over the garden to the coast; 'Mr Fred's' serves simpler fare.

ENGLAND

Millstone

Church Ln ✉ BB2 7JR – ☎ (01254) 813 333 – www.millstonehotel.co.uk
22 rm – †£ 65/125 ††£ 77/149 – 1 suite **Rest** – Carte £ 23/41
Characterful sandstone inn set in a charming Ribble Valley village. Bedrooms offer modern comforts and have a cottagey feel, while the dining room blends contemporary styling with traditional features. Classic dishes change with the seasons; the steak is a perennial favourite. Service is cheery.

BLACKPOOL

Blackpool – Pop. 147 663 – See Regional map n°**20-A2**
London 246 mi – Leeds 88 mi – Liverpool 56 mi – Manchester 51 mi
Michelin Road map 502-K22 – Michelin Green Guide GREAT BRITAIN

Number One South Beach

rm,

4 Harrowside West ✉ FY4 1NW – ☎ (01253) 343 900 Town plan: BZ**v**
– www.numberonehotels.com
13 rm – †£ 81/150 ††£ 125/155 – 1 suite
Rest – Carte £ 21/30 – *(dinner only and Sunday lunch)*
Modernised hotel close to the promenade, that's run with a passion and features bright, bold colour schemes. Striking, contemporary bedrooms – two with four-posters – come with smart bathrooms boasting whirlpool baths and TVs. Concise menus are largely made up of free range, organic and fair trade produce.

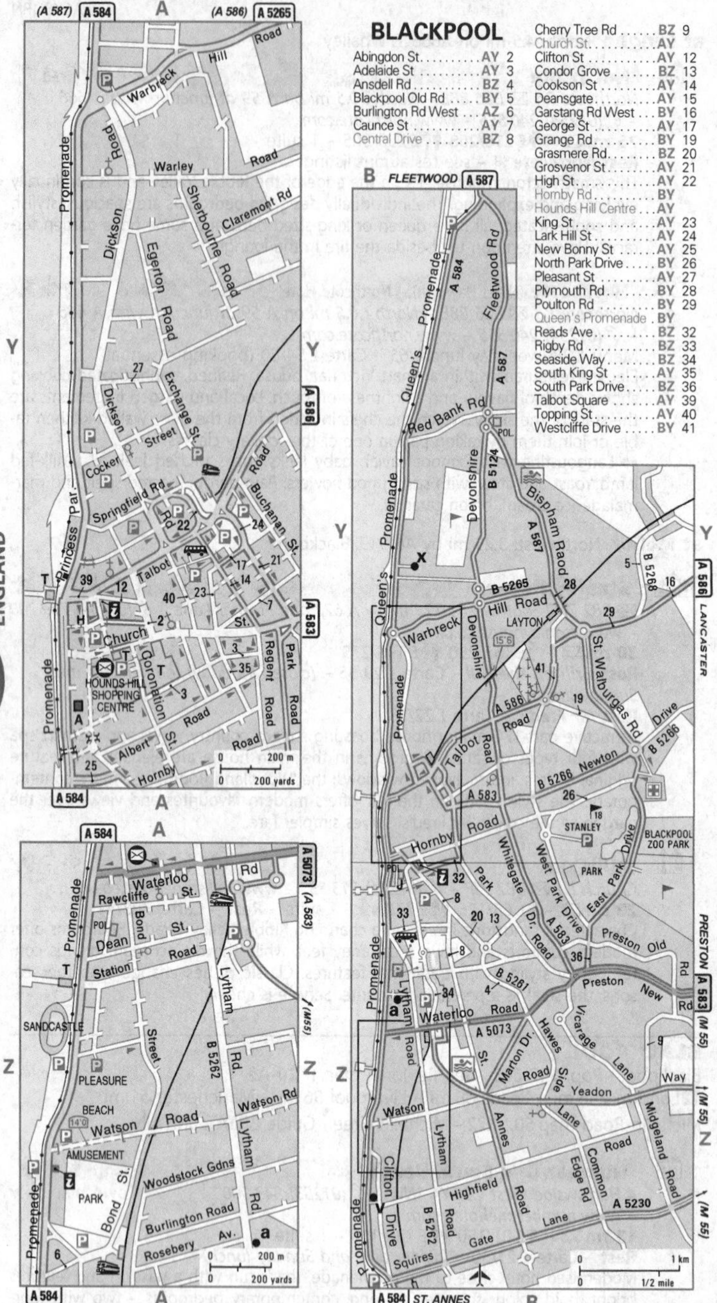

BLACKPOOL
Abingdon St. . . . . AY 2
Adelaide St . . . . AY 3
Ansdell Rd . . . . BZ 4
Blackpool Old Rd . . . . BY 5
Burlington Rd West . . . AZ 6
Caunce St . . . . AY 7
Central Drive . . . . BZ 8
Cherry Tree Rd . . . . . . BZ 9
Church St. . . . . AY
Clifton St . . . . AY 12
Condor Grove . . . . BZ 13
Cookson St . . . . AY 14
Deansgate . . . . AY 15
Garstang Rd West . . . . BY 16
George St . . . . AY 17
Grange Rd . . . . BY 19
Grasmere Rd . . . . BZ 20
Grosvenor St . . . . AY 21
High St . . . . AY 22
Hornby Rd . . . . BY
Hounds Hill Centre . . . AY
King St . . . . AY 23
Lark Hill St . . . . AY 24
New Bonny St . . . . AY 25
North Park Drive . . . . . BY 26
Pleasant St . . . . AY 27
Plymouth Rd . . . . BY 28
Poulton Rd . . . . BY 29
Queen's Promenade . . BY
Reads Ave . . . . BZ 32
Rigby Rd . . . . BZ 33
Seaside Way . . . . BZ 34
South King St . . . . AY 35
South Park Drive . . . . . BY 36
Talbot Square . . . . AY 39
Topping St . . . . AY 40
Westcliffe Drive . . . . . BY 41
ENGLAND
FLEETWOOD A 587
LANCASTER A 586
PRESTON A 583 (M 55)
A 584 ST. ANNES
HOUNDS HILL SHOPPING CENTRE
SANDCASTLE
PLEASURE BEACH
AMUSEMENT PARK
LAYTON
STANLEY PARK
BLACKPOOL ZOO PARK

Redstone without rest
9 Alexandra Rd ✉ FY1 6BU – ✆ (01253) 283 387 Town plan: BZ**a**
– www.theredstoneblackpool.co.uk – Closed 17-28 December
8 rm – †£ 80/110 ††£ 90/120
A very stylish, intimate hotel close to the famous Pleasure Beach. Small lounge and bijou basement bar. Smartly furnished bedrooms with good mod cons. Breakfast on soufflé omelette or Manx kippers next to a baby grand piano.

Number One St Lukes without rest
1 St Lukes Rd ✉ FY4 2EL – ✆ (01253) 343 901 Town plan: AZ**a**
– www.numberoneblackpool.com
3 rm – †£ 75/100 ††£ 100/130
Boutique guesthouse close to the promenade and Pleasure Beach; run by a very charming owner. Bedrooms are named after the town's piers: 'North' has an African feel and 'Central', a white four-poster and more feminine touch. They also have an outdoor hot tub and a mini pitch and putt green.

Langtrys without rest
36 King Edward Ave ✉ FY2 9TA – ✆ (01253) 352 031 Town plan: Y**x**
– www.langtrysblackpool.co.uk
6 rm – †£ 75/90 ††£ 110/130
Smart guesthouse in a peaceful residential area. Bedrooms have warm fabrics, modern facilities and extras such as robes, clothes brushes and small items travellers often forget. Bathrooms feature underfloor heating and one even has a TV.

at Thornton Northeast: 5.5 mi by A584 -(BY)- on B5412✉ Blackpool

Twelve
Marsh Mill, Fleetwood Rd North ✉ FY5 4JZ – ✆ (01253) 821 212
– www.twelve-restaurant.co.uk – Closed first 2 weeks January and Monday
Menu £ 18 (weekdays)/25 – Carte £ 30/44 – *(dinner only and Sunday lunch)*
Set beneath the sails of one of Europe's tallest working windmills is this passionately run cocktail bar and restaurant – which has an urban, industrial feel courtesy of brick walls, exposed pipework and grey beams. Good value menus offer modern dishes with the occasional innovative touch.

BLAKENEY

Norfolk – Pop. 801 – ✉ Holt – See Regional map n°**15-C1**
London 127 mi – King's Lynn 37 mi – Norwich 28 mi
Michelin Road map 504-X25

Blakeney
The Quay ✉ NR25 7NE – ✆ (01263) 740 797 – www.blakeneyhotel.co.uk
64 rm – †£ 93/129 ††£ 186/282
Rest – Menu £ 29 (dinner) – Carte lunch £ 21/29 – *(closed to non-residents 24-28, 31 December and 1 January)*
Traditional, privately owned hotel in a great quayside location, affording views over the estuary and salt marshes. Various comfy lounges and a bar with subtle modern touches. Individually designed bedrooms, some with balconies or sea views. Formal dining room offers a good outlook and a wide-ranging menu.

Blakeney House without rest
High St ✉ NR25 7NX – ✆ (01263) 740 561 – www.blakeneyhouse.com
9 rm – †£ 85/130 ††£ 100/175
This substantial Victorian house is tucked away in a peaceful spot close to Blakeney Quay. There's an elegant dining room offering a delicious breakfast menu and a lounge hung with dramatic modern art. Cosy bedrooms are currently being updated by the welcoming owner; one has a French theme.

ENGLAND

Wiveton Farm Café

✉ NR25 7TE West : 0.5 mi on A149 – ✆ (01263) 740 515 – www.wivetonhall.co.uk – Closed January-Easter

Carte approx. £ 26 – *(lunch only and dinner Thursday-Saturday)*

An extension of a farm shop, set down a dusty track and run by a smiley young team. Light breakfasts and tasty, salad-based lunches; weekends see more substantial breakfasts and 'Norfolk' tapas in the evenings. Unfussy preparation of local and farm produce. Glorious farm and coastal views from the terrace.

Moorings

High St ✉ NR25 7NA – ✆ (01263) 740 054 – www.blakeney-moorings.co.uk – Closed 3 weeks January, Tuesday-Thursday November-March, Sunday except bank holidays and Monday dinner

Menu £ 18 – Carte £ 25/38 – *(light lunch) (booking essential)*

Bright, relaxed village bistro just a stone's throw from the quay and run by an experienced couple. Light lunches and more substantial dinners featuring unfussy, seasonal dishes in classic combinations; tasty, homemade, old school puddings.

White Horse with rm

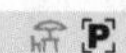

4 High St ✉ NR25 7AL – ✆ (01263) 740 574 – www.blakeneywhitehorse.co.uk – Closed 25 December

9 rm – †£ 55/80 ††£ 110/170 Carte £ 23/30 – *(booking advisable)*

Attractive brick and flint former coaching inn set by the harbour. The menu champions all things seasonal, local and British, so expect lobsters, crabs, Brancaster oysters and meat from Norfolk estates. Simply furnished bedrooms come in various shapes and sizes; one has a great view of the marshes.

at Cley next the Sea East: 1.5 mi on A149 ✉ Holt

Cley Windmill

The Quay ✉ NR25 7RP – ✆ (01263) 740 209 – www.cleywindmill.co.uk

9 rm – †£ 159/199 ††£ 159/199

Rest – Menu £ 33 – *(dinner only) (booking essential)*

With its views over the marshes and river, this restored 18C windmill is a birdwatcher's paradise. Snug, characterful bedrooms are split between the mill, the stables and the boatshed. The flagstoned dining room offers a set menu of homemade country dishes and the tea room opens in the summer months.

at Wiveton South: 1 mi by A149 on Wiveton Rd

Wiveton Bell with rm

Blakeney Rd ✉ NR25 7TL – ✆ (01263) 740 101 – www.wivetonbell.com

4 rm – †£ 95/130 ††£ 85/140 Carte £ 27/37 – *(booking essential)*

Modernised pub featuring beams, stripped floors and wood-burning stoves; with picnic tables out the front and a beautifully landscaped rear terrace. Seasonal menu offers pub classics, carefully crafted from quality local ingredients. Stylish, cosy bedrooms have smart bathrooms; continental breakfasts.

at Morston West: 1.5 mi on A149 ✉ Holt

Morston Hall

The Street ✉ NR25 7AA – ✆ (01263) 741 041 – www.morstonhall.com – Closed 1-25 January and 24-26 December

13 rm – †£ 120/240 ††£ 228/258

Rest *Morston Hall* ✿ – see restaurant listing

Attractive, personally run country house with manicured gardens, set in a small coastal hamlet. Comfortable guest areas feature antiques and paintings. Bedrooms are split between the main house and an annexe – the latter are larger and have subtle contemporary touches. Service is keen and friendly.

ENGLAND

Morston Hall (Galton Blackiston) – Morston Hall Hotel
The Street ✉ NR25 7AA – ✆ (01263) 741 041 – www.morstonhall.com
– Closed 1-25 January and 24-26 December
Menu £ 67 – *(dinner only and Sunday lunch) (booking essential) (set menu only)*
Set in an attractive country house surrounded by landscaped gardens: choose between a traditionally furnished room or a beautiful conservatory. The set 7 course daily menu (served at 8pm), offers well-balanced seasonal dishes. Cooking is classically based, sophisticated and exhibits a delicate, modern touch.
➜ Spelt-battered North Sea skate wing with lobster tartare. Norfolk Horn lamb, garden herb jus, buttery mashed potatoes and asparagus. Black fig millefeuille.

BLANCHLAND

Northumberland – See Regional map n°**24-A2**
London 286 mi – Newcastle upon Tyne 29 mi – Carlisle 50 mi
Michelin Road map 502-N22

Lord Crewe Arms Ⓝ
The Square ✉ DH8 9SP – ✆ (01434) 675 469
– www.lordcrewearmsblanchland.co.uk
21 rm – †£ 96/130 ††£ 140/160 – 3 suites
Rest *Bishop's Dining Room* – see restaurant listing
This 12C abbot's priory has also spent time as a hunting lodge and a lead miners' hostelry. Its hugely characterful guest areas don't disappoint; smell the chicken roasting over the open fire in the barrel-ceilinged bar. Bedrooms have a modern country charm and come with bespoke furnishings and walkers' packs.

Bishop's Dining Room Ⓝ – Lord Crewe Arms Hotel
The Square ✉ DH8 9SP – ✆ (01434) 675 469
– www.lordcrewearmsblanchland.co.uk
Carte £ 22/30
Bright, hunting-themed restaurant in a characterful hotel; the monks from the neighbouring abbey once dined here. Menus offer robust, flavoursome British dishes which feature kitchen garden, spit-roast and home-smoked produce.

ENGLAND

BLANDFORD FORUM

Dorset – Pop. 11 694 – See Regional map n°**4-C3**
London 124 mi – Bournemouth 17 mi – Dorchester 17 mi – Salisbury 24 mi
Michelin Road map 503-N31 and 504-N31

at Tarrant Launceston Northeast: 5.5 mi by A354

Launceston Farmhouse without rest
✉ DT11 8BY – ✆ (01258) 830 528 – www.launcestonfarm.co.uk
6 rm – †£ 70/125 ††£ 100/125
Charming guesthouse on a working cattle farm, which is the friendly owner's childhood home. Stylish bedrooms can be reached via a wrought iron spiral staircase and feature period furniture, modern bathrooms and homely extras.

at Farnham Northeast: 7.5 mi by A354 ✉ Blandford Forum

Farnham Farm House without rest
✉ DT11 8DG North : 1 mi by Shaftesbury rd – ✆ (01725) 516 254
– www.farnhamfarmhouse.co.uk – Closed 25-26 December
3 rm – †£ 70/80 ††£ 80/90
Welcoming farmhouse on a 300 acre working farm, complete with a swimming pool and a holistic therapy centre. Homely, immaculately kept bedrooms have country views. Enjoy tea and cake on arrival; the eggs are from their own hens.

BLEDINGTON ➜ See Stow-on-the-Wold

Gloucestershire – Michelin Road map 503-P28 and 504-P28

BLOCKLEY

Gloucestershire – Pop. 1 104 – ✉ Moreton-In-Marsh – See Regional map n°**4-D1**
London 91 mi – Birmingham 39 mi – Oxford 34 mi
Michelin Road map 503-O27 and 504-O27

Lower Brook House

Lower St ✉ GL56 9DS – ✆ (01386) 700 286 – www.lowerbrookhouse.com – Closed January and 16-27 December
6 rm – †£ 80/190 ††£ 80/190
Rest – Carte £ 15/26 – *(closed Sunday) (dinner only) (residents only)*
Behind the characterful 17C façade you'll find all you expect: exposed stone, old beams, original flagged floors and inglenook fireplaces. Pleasant bedrooms offer simple comforts. The concise supper menu can be taken in the restaurant, your room or in the cottage garden, with its dovecote and babbling brook.

BLYTH

Nottinghamshire – Pop. 968 – ✉ Worksop – See Regional map n°**16-B1**
London 166 mi – Doncaster 13 mi – Lincoln 30 mi – Nottingham 32 mi
Michelin Road map 502-Q23 and 503

White Swan at Blyth

High St ✉ S81 8EQ – ✆ (01909) 591 222 – www.whiteswanatblyth.co.uk
Carte £ 19/40
Very handy for travellers on the A1: look for the whitewashed walls and colourful window boxes. There are two choices menu-wise: an à la carte of ambitious, artfully presented creations, or the simple but tasty 'pub classics'.

ENGLAND

BODIAM

East Sussex – See Regional map n°**8-B2**
London 58 mi – Cranbrook 7 mi – Hastings 13 mi
Michelin Road map 504-V30 – Michelin Green Guide GREAT BRITAIN

Curlew

Junction Rd ✉ TN32 5UY – Northwest : 1.5 mi at junction with B 2244 – ✆ (01580) 861 394 – www.thecurlewrestaurant.co.uk – Closed 26 December, 1 January and Monday
Menu £ 20 (weekdays) – Carte £ 33/45
Smart, contemporary restaurant behind a white clapperboard pub façade, with funky cow print wallpaper and a Scandinavian feel. Menus offer precise, modern, well-considered combinations of first class ingredients. The wine lists promotes organic and biodynamic wines, and service is smooth and professional.
→ Scallops with celeriac, apple and sultana. Rump of lamb, asparagus and wild garlic. Salt-baked pineapple, lime, ginger and yoghurt.

BODMIN

Cornwall – Pop. 14 614 – See Regional map n°**1-B2**
London 270 mi – Newquay 18 mi – Plymouth 32 mi – Truro 23 mi
Michelin Road map 503-F32

Trehellas House

Washaway ✉ PL30 3AD – Northwest : 3 mi on A 389 – ✆ (01208) 72 700 – www.trehellashouse.co.uk
12 rm – †£ 35/60 ††£ 50/160
Rest – Carte £ 27/38 **s** – *(dinner only and Sunday lunch)*
Former posting inn, built by the Lordship of Pencarrow Manor to house officers from the local garrison. Cosy bedrooms with smart wood furnishings and understated décor. Popular restaurant offers extensive menu of local produce with venison a speciality. Good value 'steak and dessert' menu.

Bokiddick Farm without rest

Lanivet ✉ PL30 5HP – South : 5 mi by A 30 following signs for Lanhydrock and Bokiddick – ✆ (01208) 831 481 – www.bokiddickfarm.co.uk – Closed Christmas

3 rm – †£ 50/55 ††£ 80/90

A traditional farmhouse on a 180 acre working dairy farm – a warm welcome is guaranteed and they serve cream teas on arrival. Homely, spotlessly kept bedrooms come with super king sized beds and country views; the largest rooms are in the old barn. Hearty breakfasts are taken overlooking the garden.

BOLLINGTON

Cheshire East – Pop. 7 373 – ✉ Cheshire – See Regional map n°**20**-B3

London 178 mi – Birmingham 69 mi – Leeds 58 mi – Manchester 22 mi

Michelin Road map 502-N24

Oliver at Bollington Green

22 High St ✉ SK10 5PH – ✆ (01625) 575 058 – www.oliveratbollingtongreen.com – Closed Sunday dinner and Monday

Menu 20 – Carte £ 24/37 – *(light lunch) (bookings advisable at dinner)*

Bright neighbourhood restaurant opposite a tiny village green, run by an enthusiastic young couple. Light lunches and an interesting evening à la carte of refined, flavoursome dishes. The breads, ice-creams and chocolates are all homemade.

BOLNHURST

Bedford – See Regional map n°**12**-A1

London 64 mi – Bedford 8 mi – St Neots 7 mi

Plough at Bolnhurst

Kimbolton Rd ✉ MK44 2EX – South : 0.5 mi on B 660 – ✆ (01234) 376 274 – www.bolnhurst.com – Closed 2 weeks January, Sunday dinner and Monday

Menu £ 13 (weekday lunch)/20 – Carte £ 30/48

Charming whitewashed pub with a rustic bar, a modern restaurant, a lovely garden and a bustling atmosphere. Menus change with the seasons but always feature 28-day aged Aberdeenshire steaks, dishes containing Mediterranean ingredients like Sicilian black olives, and a great selection of wines and cheeses.

BOLTON ABBEY

North Yorkshire – Pop. 117 – ✉ Skipton – See Regional map n°**22**-B2

London 216 mi – Harrogate 18 mi – Leeds 23 mi – Skipton 6 mi

Michelin Road map 502-O22 – Michelin Green Guide GREAT BRITAIN

Devonshire Arms Country House

✉ BD23 6AJ – ✆ (01756) 710 441 – www.thedevonshirearms.co.uk

40 rm – †£ 145/225 ††£ 195/275 – 2 suites

Rest *Burlington* Rest *Brasserie* – see restaurant listing

A period coaching inn with a popular spa, set on the Duke and Duchess of Devonshire's 30,000 acre estate in the Yorkshire Dales. Comfy lounges display part of the owners' vast art collection and dogs are welcome too. Bedrooms in the wing are bright, modern and compact; those in the inn are more traditional.

Burlington – Devonshire Arms Country House Hotel

✉ BD23 6AJ – ✆ (01756) 710 441 – www.burlingtonrestaurant.co.uk – Closed Monday

Menu £ 65 – *(dinner only and Sunday lunch) (booking essential)*

Elegant, antique-filled hotel dining room hung with impressive oils; sit in the conservatory to overlook the Italian garden. Elaborate modern dishes utilise fine ingredients, with much coming from the kitchen garden and estate.

Brasserie – Devonshire Arms Country House Hotel

✉ BD23 6AJ – ✆ (01756) 718 105 – www.devonshirebrasserie.co.uk

Carte £ 25/42

Funky hotel brasserie with an attractive wine cellar; set opposite the kitchen garden. Sit on stripy banquettes in the bar or on red velour chairs in the dining room. The extensive à la carte offers satisfying brasserie classics.

ENGLAND

BOLTON-BY-BOWLAND

Lancashire – See Regional map n°**20**-B2

London 246 mi – Blackburn 17 mi – Skipton 15 mi

Michelin Road map 502-M/N22 – Michelin Green Guide GREAT BRITAIN

Middle Flass Lodge

Settle Rd ✉ BB7 4NY – North : 2.5 mi by Clitheroe rd on Settle rd – ✆ (01200) 447 259 – www.middleflasslodge.co.uk

7 rm – £ 50/55 £ 70/76 **Rest** – Menu £ 30

Friendly, welcoming owners in a delightfully located barn conversion. Plenty of beams add to rustic effect. Pleasantly decorated, comfy rooms with countryside outlook. Blackboard's eclectic menu boasts local, seasonal backbone.

BONCHURCH → See Wight (Isle of)

Isle of Wight – Michelin Road map 504-P32

BORDON

Hampshire – Pop. 16 035

London 54 mi – Croydon 57 mi – Barnet 67 mi – Ealing 49 mi

Michelin Road map 504-R30

Groomes

Frith End ✉ GU35 0QR – North : 2.75 mi by A 325 on Frith End Sand Pit rd – ✆ (01420) 489 858 – www.groomes.co.uk

7 rm – £ 90/130 £ 120/160

Rest – Menu £ 20 – *(dinner only) (residents only, set menu only)*

A former farmhouse set in 185 acres, which has been made 'green' by the installation of biomass boilers and solar panels. Spacious, modern bedrooms come with roll-top baths; it even has its own games room. Dining takes place at two communal tables – local produce features in dishes cooked on the Aga.

BOREHAM

Essex – See Regional map n°**13**-C2

London 42 mi – Colchester 20 mi – Cambridge 54 mi

Michelin Road map 504-V28

Lion Inn

Main Rd ✉ CM3 3JA – ✆ (01245) 394 900 – www.lioninnhotel.co.uk – Closed 25, 26 and 31 December

15 rm – £ 105/200 £ 105/200

Rest – Carte £ 18/30 – *(bookings not accepted)*

Keenly run, extended former pub with eco-friendly credentials and a French feel. Soundproofed bedrooms blend contemporary fabrics with reproduction furniture. Large open-plan lounge/brasserie with buzzy atmosphere; short menu of appealing, pub-style dishes.

BOROUGHBRIDGE

North Yorkshire – Pop. 3 610 – See Regional map n°**22**-B2

London 215 mi – Leeds 19 mi – Middlesbrough 36 mi – York 16 mi

Michelin Road map 502-P21

XX

thediningroom

20 St James's Sq ✉ YO51 9AR – ✆ (01423) 326 426 – www.thediningroomonline.co.uk – Closed 26 December, 1 January, Sunday dinner and Monday

Menu £ 20 – Carte £ 21/49 – *(dinner only and Sunday lunch) (booking essential)*

Characterful bow-fronted cottage concealing an opulent bar-lounge and an intimate beamed dining room. Wide-ranging menus offer boldly flavoured, Mediterranean-influenced dishes and chargrilled meats. In summer, head for the terrace.

XX **Grantham Arms** Ⓝ with rm 

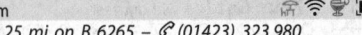

Milby ✉ YO51 9BW – North : 0.25 mi on B 6265 – ✆ (01423) 323 980 – www.granthamarms.co.uk

7 rm ☕ – 🚹£ 75/85 🚹🚹£ 85/100 Menu £ 20 – Carte £ 29/47

An intimate, glitzy restaurant with deep purple décor, chandeliers, an atmospheric cocktail bar and a 'gin bible' offering over 20 varieties. Modern cooking uses good texture and flavour combinations and everything is made on-site. Smart bedrooms have contemporary oak furnishings and Egyptian cotton linen.

at Roecliffe West: 1 mi

Crown Inn with rm 

✉ YO51 9LY – ✆ (01423) 322 300 – www.crowninnroecliffe.com

4 rm ☕ – 🚹£ 80/90 🚹🚹£ 100/120 Carte £ 25/39

14C inn in a delightful position by the village green. Menus offer pub classics alongside more ambitious dishes; if you can't decide on a dessert, try them all with the assiette of puddings. Well-appointed bedrooms come with feature beds, roll top baths and plenty of extra touches.

at Lower Dunsforth Southeast : 4.25 mi by B 6265

The Dunsforth Ⓝ 

Mary Ln ✉ YO26 9SA – ✆ (01423) 320 700 – www.thedunsforth.co.uk – Closed Sunday dinner and Monday

Menu £ 20 – Carte £ 28/48

A contemporary pub with a lively atmosphere in its fire-lit front rooms, and a smart restaurant for more intimate meals. Menus offer admirable choice and value for money; seasonality and freshness are key.

ENGLAND

BOSCASTLE

Cornwall – See Regional map n°**1-B2**

▶London 260 mi – Bude 14 mi – Exeter 59 mi – Plymouth 43 mi

Michelin Road map 503-F31 – Michelin Green Guide GREAT BRITAIN

Boscastle House without rest 

Tintagel Rd ✉ PL35 0AS – South : 0.75 mi on B 3263 – ✆ (01840) 250 654 – www.boscastlehouse.com – Closed 2 weeks Christmas

6 rm ☕ – 🚹£ 60/90 🚹🚹£ 102/140

Modern styling in a detached Victorian house with a calm, relaxing air. Bedrooms are light and spacious, with roll-top baths and walk-in showers. Hearty breakfasts with home-baked muffins and banana bread. Tea and cake on arrival.

Old Rectory without rest 

St Juliot ✉ PL35 0BT – Northeast : 2.5 mi by B 3263 – ✆ (01840) 250 225 – www.stjuliot.com – Closed Christmas

4 rm ☕ – 🚹£ 49/99 🚹🚹£ 70/110

Lovely house with Victorian walled garden. Characterful bedrooms: one with a wood-burning stove; another, a super king sized bed and whirlpool bath. Breakfasts include bacon and sausages from the owner's pigs. Thomas Hardy once stayed here.

BOSHAM → See Chichester

West Sussex – Michelin Road map 504-R31

BOSTON SPA

West Yorkshire – Pop. 4 662 – See Regional map n°**22-B2**

▶London 127 mi – Harrogate 12 mi – Leeds 12 mi – York 16 mi

Michelin Road map 502-P22

Four Gables without rest 

Oaks Ln ✉ LS23 6DS – West : 0.25 mi by A 659 – ☎ (01937) 845 592 – www.fourgables.co.uk – Closed Christmas-New Year
4 rm ☕ – †£ 52/72 ††£ 75/95
Grade II listed Arts and Crafts house hidden down a private road, yet only a short walk from town. Beautifully manicured garden and croquet lawn. Ornate plaster ceiling in lounge; quarry-floored breakfast room with homemade breads, jams and eggs from their own hens. Pretty, cosy bedrooms have good comforts.

BOUGHTON MONCHELSEA

Kent – Pop. 2 863 – See Regional map n°**8-B2**
▶London 40 mi – Maidstone 4 mi – Sevenoaks 23 mi

Mulberry Tree 
Hermitage Ln. ✉ ME17 4DA – South : 1.5 mi by Park Lane and East Hall Hill – ☎ (01622) 749 082 – www.themulberrytreekent.co.uk – Closed first 2 weeks January, Sunday dinner and Monday
Menu £ 18 (weekdays) – Carte £ 29/39
This rurally located restaurant has lovely gardens, a large paved terrace and a surprisingly stylish interior. Modern British menus feature confidently prepared, imaginatively presented dishes and ingredients are well-sourced.

ENGLAND

BOURN

Cambridgeshire – Pop. 669 – See Regional map n°**14-A3**
▶London 58 mi – Croydon 87 mi – Barnet 44 mi – Ealing 57 mi
Michelin Road map 504-T27

Willow Tree 
29 High St ✉ CB23 2SQ – ☎ (01954) 719 775 – www.thewillowtreebourn.com
Carte £ 13/46
Quirky pub with a life-sized cow model outside and gilt mirrors, chandeliers and Louis XV style furniture inside. Menus range from old pub classics to much more ambitious modern dishes; afternoon tea and a 'Deckchair' menu served May-Sept.

BOURNEMOUTH

Bournemouth – Pop. 187 503 – See Regional map n°**4-D3**
▶London 114 mi – Bristol 76 mi – Southampton 34 mi
Michelin Road map 503-O31 and 504-O31 – Michelin Green Guide GREAT BRITAIN

Bournemouth Highcliff Marriott rm, 
St Michael's Rd, West Cliff ✉ BH2 5DU – ☎ (01202) 557 702 – www.bournemouthhighcliffmarriott.co.uk Town plan: CZ**z**
160 rm ☕ – †£ 99/145 ††£ 149/225 – 3 suites
Rest *Highcliff Grill* – ☎ (01202) 200 800 – Carte £ 28/46 **s** – *(closed Sunday dinner) (dinner only and Sunday lunch)*
Set on the clifftop, this grand old seaside hotel has a funicular linking it directly to the beach. Smart guest areas and airy modern bedrooms; some with lovely sea views. Leisure club boasts a tennis court and indoor and outdoor pools. Stylish grill restaurant offers a modern steak and seafood based menu.

Miramar 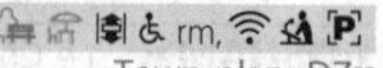
19 Grove Rd, East Overcliff ✉ BH1 3AL – ☎ (01202) 556 581 – www.miramar-bournemouth.com Town plan: DZ**u**
43 rm (dinner included) ☕ – †£ 30/180 ††£ 60/220
Rest – Menu £ 22 (weekday lunch)/32
Late Edwardian villa intended as a summer residence for the Austrian ambassador – until WW1 intervened. Close to town yet boasting peaceful, award winning gardens and superb sea views. Large, classical bedrooms; some with balconies. Traditional dinner menu and snacks in the bar or on the terrace.

Green House

4 Grove Rd ✉ BH1 3AX – ✆ (01202) 498 900 Town plan: DZ**n**
– www.thegreenhousehotel.com
32 rm – £ 129/149 £ 149/189
Rest *Arbor* – see restaurant listing
Bright, eco-friendly hotel, set in a small Victorian property and run by an enthusiastic team. Contemporary interior features reclaimed and eco-furnishings, including chairs made from old video game consoles and vegetable ink wallpapers.

Chocolate without rest

5 Durley Rd ✉ BH2 5JQ – ✆ (01202) 556 857 Town plan: CZ**a**
– www.thechocolateboutiquehotel.co.uk – Closed 2-27 December
15 rm – £ 65 £ 90/180
A unique, chocolate-themed hotel, owned by a chocolatier who runs regular workshops. Contemporary bedrooms come in browns and creams. The small lounge-bar features an automatic cocktail machine and they even serve 'choctails'.

Urban Beach

23 Argyll Rd ✉ BH5 1EB – ✆ (01202) 301 509 Town plan: DX**a**
– www.urbanbeach.co.uk
12 rm – £ 72 £ 97/180 **Rest** – Carte £ 16/40
A laid-back hotel with a large heated terrace; set close to the sea and the town. A beach shack style exterior conceals spacious designer bedrooms with stylish modern bathrooms. The small reception is located in the trendy bar-cum-bistro, which offers a large menu of steaks and modern classics.

ENGLAND

Edge

2 Studland Rd, (4th Floor), Alum Chine ✉ BH4 8JA Town plan: CX**s**
– ✆ (01202) 757 007 – www.edgerestaurant.co.uk
Menu £ 20 (lunch) – Carte £ 29/47 – *(booking essential)*
Stylish restaurant on the top levels of an apartment block, with floor to ceiling windows and excellent views over the town and Poole Bay. Seafood menus feature intricate modern dishes which are styled on classical combinations.

Arbor – Green House Hotel

4 Grove Rd ✉ BH1 3AX – ✆ (01202) 498 900 Town plan: DZ**n**
– www.arbor-restaurant.co.uk
Carte £ 21/37
Large restaurant in an eco-friendly hotel; it upholds a 'sustainable' ethos with FSC timber on the floors, low energy induction cookers in the kitchen and honey bees on the roof. Modern menus display innovative touches; produce is local.

Rock

Lansdeer Rd, Westbourne ✉ BH4 9EH – ✆ (01202) 765 696 – www.rockrestaurants.co.uk – Closed Sunday dinner Town plan: CX**x**
Menu £ 15 (lunch) – Carte £ 20/46
Grand 18C church with antique oak panelling and stunning stained glass; the open kitchen is in the old chancel. Modern British cooking is fresh and flavoursome; lighter options are available in the small outside area. Lunch is good value.

West Beach

Pier Approach ✉ BH2 5AA – ✆ (01202) 587 785 Town plan: DZ**c**
– www.west-beach.co.uk – Closed 25 December
Carte £ 19/47 – *(booking essential)*
Popular beachfront restaurant with a rustic interior, an open-plan kitchen and folding glass doors opening onto a decked terrace. Seafood-based menus feature some fish caught in front of the building; look out for the buoys where the nets lie. They also offer an express lunch menu and, in summer, takeaways.

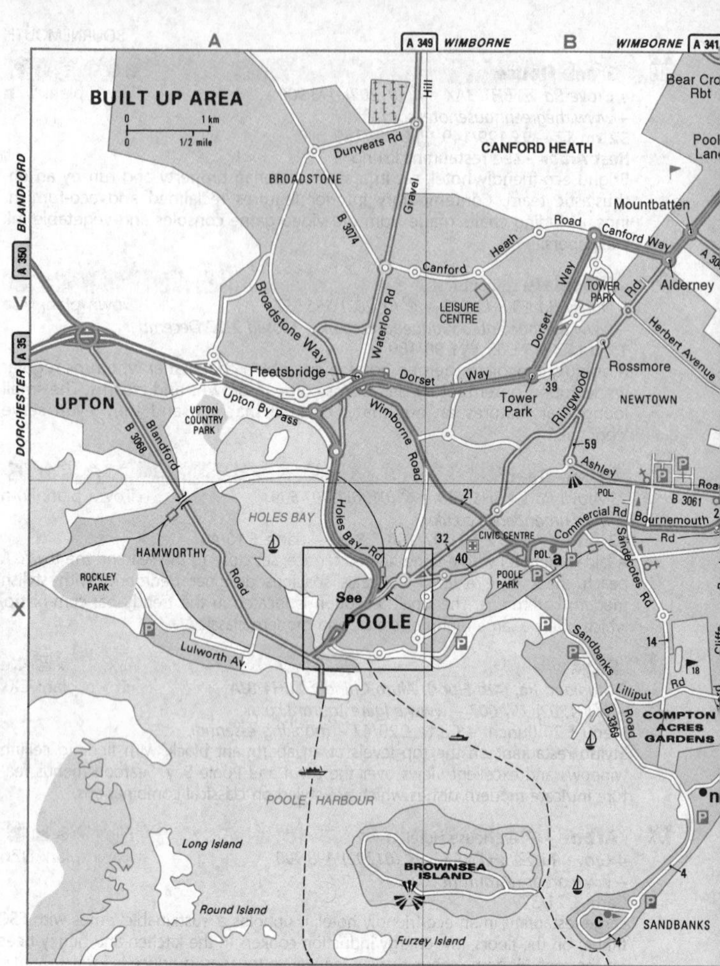

BOURNEMOUTH AND POOLE

Street	Grid	No.
Archway Rd	BX	2
Banks Rd	BX	4
Boscombe Overcliff Rd	EX	6
Boscombe Spa Rd	DX	7
Branksome Wood Rd	CY	9
Chessel Ave	EX	10
Clarendon Rd	CX	12
Commercial Rd	CY	13
Compton Ave	BX	14
Cranleigh Rd	EV	16
Durley Rd	CZ	17
Ensbury Park Rd	CV	19
Exeter Rd	CDZ	20
Fernside Rd	ABX	21
Fir Vale Rd	DY	23
Gervis Pl.	DY	24
Gloucester Rd	EV	26
Hampshire Centre	DV	
Hinton Rd	DZ	27
Lansdowne Rd	DY	30
Lansdowne (The)	DY	28
Leven Ave	CX	31
Longfleet Rd	BX	32
Madeira Rd	DY	34
Manor Rd	EY	35
Meyrick Rd	EYZ	36
Old Christchurch Rd	DY	
Old Wareham Rd	BV	39
Parkstone Rd	BX	40
Pinecliff Rd	CX	42
Post Office Rd	CY	43
Priory Rd	CZ	45
Queen's Rd	CX	46
Richmond Hill	CY	47
Richmond Park Rd	DV	48
Russell Cotes Rd	DZ	49
St Michael's Rd	CZ	51
St Paul's Rd	EY	52
St Peter's Rd	DY	53
St Stephen's Rd	CY	55
St Swithuns Rd South	EY	56
Seabourne Rd	EV	57
Seamoor Rd	CX	58
Sea View Rd	BV	59
Southbourne Grove	EX	61
Southbourne Overcliff Drive	EX	62
Sovereign Shopping Centre	EX	
Square (The)	CY	63
Suffolk Rd	CY	64
Surrey Rd	CX	66
Triangle (The)	CY	67
Upper Hinton Rd	DZ	68
Wessex Way	CX	70
Western Rd	CX	73
Westover Rd	DZ	75
West Cliff Promenade	CZ	71

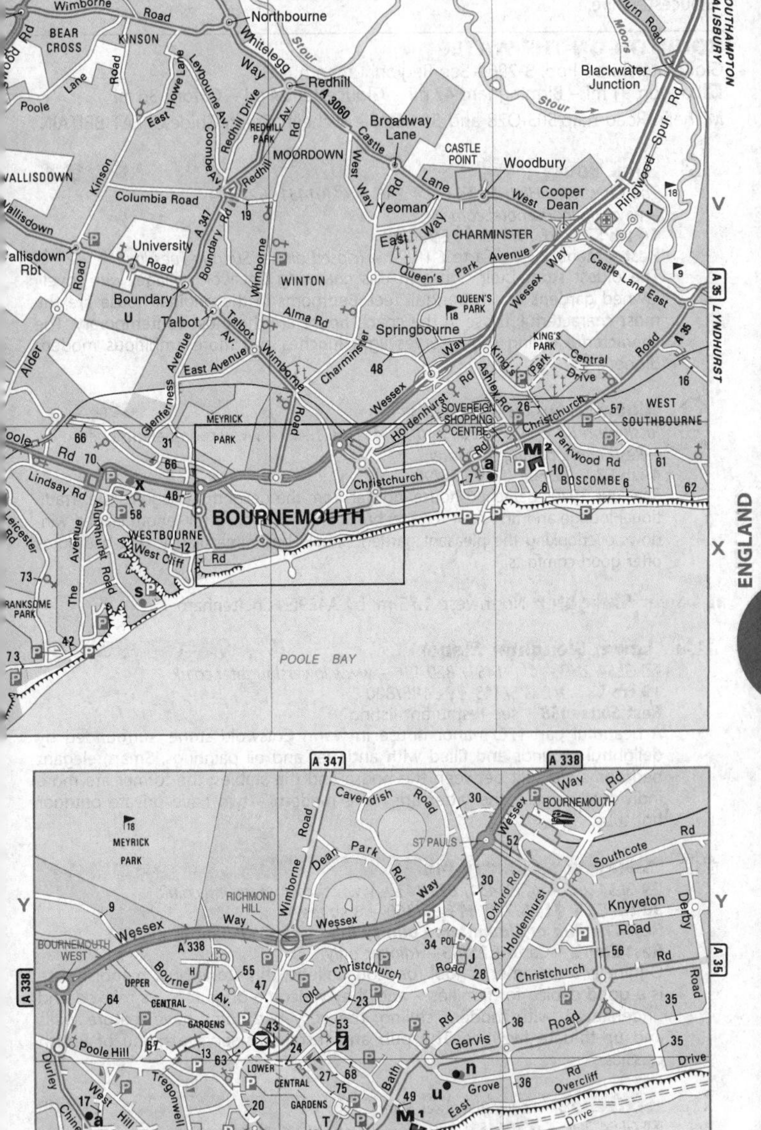
A 348 SOUTHAMPTON
C
A 347
FERNDOWN INTERNATIONAL AIRPORT
D
INTERNATIONAL AIRPORT
E
A 338
SOUTHAMPTON SALISBURY
Wimborne Road
BEAR CROSS
KINSON
Northbourne
Whitelegg Way
Stour
Redhill
A 3060
Poole Lane Road
Leybourne Av.
East Howe Lane
Redhill Drive
REDHILL PARK
Av.
Rd
Coombe Av.
Redhill
MOORDOWN
Castle
West Way
Broadway Lane
CASTLE POINT
Woodbury
Blackwater Junction
Moors
Hurn Road
Stour
Spur Rd
Ringwood
VALLISDOWN
Kinson
Columbia Road
A 347
Boundary Rd
19
Yeoman
Lane
West
Cooper Dean
J
18
V
Wallisdown
Wallisdown Rbt
University
Road
Boundary
U
Talbot
Wimborne
WINTON
East Way
CHARMINSTER
Queen's Park Avenue
Wessex Way
Castle Lane East
9
A 35
LYNDHURST
Alma Rd
Talbot Av.
QUEEN'S PARK
18
Springbourne
Alder
Glenferness Avenue
East Avenue
Wimborne Road
Charminster
48
Way
Rd
King's
KING'S PARK
Park
Central Drive
Road
A 35
16
Wessex
Holdenhurst
Ashley Rd
SOVEREIGN SHOPPING CENTRE
26
Christchurch
57
WEST SOUTHBOURNE
MEYRICK PARK
Poole Rd
66
31
66
70
Lindsay Rd
X
46
58
Alumhurst Road
The Avenue
Leicester Rd
WESTBOURNE
12
West Cliff Rd
S
73
BRANKSOME PARK
42
73
Christchurch
Rd
BOURNEMOUTH
a
M²
10
7
6
Parkwood Rd
BOSCOMBE
6
61
62
POOLE BAY
X
ENGLAND
A 347
A 338
Wimborne Road
Cavendish Road
30
Wessex Way Rd
BOURNEMOUTH
ST PAULS
52
Southcote Rd
Dean Park Rd
Way
30
Oxford Rd
Holdenhurst
18
MEYRICK PARK
Y
9
RICHMOND HILL
Wessex Way
Wessex
Knyveton Road
Derby Rd
Y
BOURNEMOUTH WEST
A 338
Bourne Av.
55
47
Old Christchurch Road
34
POL
J
28
Christchurch Road
56
Rd
A 35
A 338
UPPER CENTRAL GARDENS
64
23
Road
35
43
53
Rd
Gervis
36
Poole Hill
67
13
63
24
LOWER CENTRAL GARDENS
27
68
Bath
n
35
Drive
Durley Chine Rd.
West Hill
Tregonwell Rd
20
75
T
49
M¹
u
East
Grove
36
Rd
Overcliff
17
a
20
Drive
Z
45
Undercliff
Z
West Cliff Rd Rd
51
Z
INTERNATIONAL CENTRE
C
WATERFRONT COMPLEX
71
Promenade
T
West Undercliff
0 400 m
0 400 yards
C
D
E

BOURTON-ON-THE-HILL → See Moreton-in-Marsh

Gloucestershire

BOURTON-ON-THE-WATER

Gloucestershire – Pop. 3 296 – See Regional map n°**4**-D1

London 91 mi – Birmingham 47 mi – Gloucester 24 mi – Oxford 36 mi

Michelin Road map 503-O28 and 504-O28 – Michelin Green Guide GREAT BRITAIN

Dial House

The Chestnuts, High St ✉ GL54 2AN – ✆ (01451) 822 244 – www.dialhousehotel.com

14 rm – †£ 79/159 ††£ 99/249

Rest – Menu £ 35 – Carte £ 18/27 – *(closed dinner Sunday-Tuesday)*

The oldest stone-built house in this charming Cotswold village, with lovely lawned gardens and a tranquil feel. Bedrooms in the original house are the most characterful; those in the coach house are the most contemporary. The characterful dining room serves light lunches and more ambitious modern dinners.

Coombe House without rest

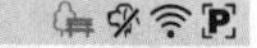

Rissington Rd ✉ GL54 2DT – ✆ (01451) 821 966 – www.coombehouse.net – Restricted opening in winter

4 rm – †£ 60/70 ††£ 75/90

Spacious 1920s detached house, not far from the delightful village centre. Traditional lounge and first floor terrace; breakfast room boasts full-length leaded windows overlooking the pleasant garden. Simple but immaculately kept bedrooms offer good comforts.

ENGLAND

at Lower Slaughter Northwest: 1.75 mi by A429 ✉ Cheltenham

Lower Slaughter Manor

✉ GL54 2HP – ✆ (01451) 820 456 – www.lowerslaughter.co.uk

19 rm – †£ 175/345 ††£ 185/800

Rest *Sixteen58* – see restaurant listing

A beautiful part-17C manor house in warm Cotswold stone, surrounded by delightful grounds and filled with antiques and oil paintings. Smart, elegant bedrooms are split between the house and the stables: the former are more individually styled; the latter are more modern – two have private outdoor hot tubs.

Slaughters Country Inn

✉ GL54 2HS – ✆ (01451) 822 143 – www.theslaughtersinn.co.uk

30 rm – †£ 85/230 ††£ 95/360 – 8 suites

Rest *The Pub at Slaughters Country Inn* – see restaurant listing

Rest *Eton's* – Carte £ 25/45 – *(dinner only)*

Originally a crammer school for Eton College, this stone-built manor house is a good choice for families – and they welcome dogs too! It's relaxed and understated, with modern styling; the cosy bedrooms have feature walls and up-to-date facilities. The pub and restaurant serve a menu of British classics.

XXX Sixteen58 – Lower Slaughter Manor

✉ GL54 2HP – ✆ (01451) 820 456 – www.lowerslaughter.co.uk

Menu £ 21 (weekday lunch)/85

Elegant dining room in a bright, airy extension of a fine manor house hotel, overlooking the lovely gardens. Immaculately laid tables have beautiful floral displays. Menus offer accomplished modern dishes with a classical base.

Good food at moderate prices? Look for the Bib Gourmand.

The Pub at Slaughters Country Inn
GL54 2HS – (01451) 822 143 – www.theslaughtersinn.co.uk
Carte £ 24/44
A trio of characterful rooms with wonky low ceilings and stone floors, within a hotel in a charming Cotswold village. The appealing menu offers hearty dishes and puddings that stray from the norm. Have afternoon tea on the terrace.

at Upper Slaughter Northwest: 2.5 mi by A429 Bourton-On-The-Water

Lords of the Manor
GL54 2JD – (01451) 820 243 – www.lordsofthemanor.com
24 rm – £ 199/495 £ 199/495 – 2 suites
Rest *Lords of the Manor* – see restaurant listing
Charming 17C former rectory in a pretty Cotswold village, with beautiful gardens, superb views and a real sense of tranquility. Two luxurious sitting rooms and a bar with a 'nature' colour theme. Bedrooms have a fittingly country house style and subtle contemporary touches. Staff are diligent and affable.

Lords of the Manor – Lords of the Manor Hotel
GL54 2JD – (01451) 820 243 – www.lordsofthemanor.com
Menu £ 69 – *(dinner only and Sunday lunch) (booking essential)*
Plush, formal dining room in a beautiful country house in a tranquil Cotswold village; enjoy an aperitif in the luxurious sitting rooms. Accomplished, understated dishes use well-judged, classical combinations and are executed using modern techniques. Service is professional and very personable.
→ Cornish crab, potato, cucumber and caviar. Poached and roast breast of pigeon, foie gras and mushroom ravioli. Apple millefeuille, clotted cream ice cream.

ENGLAND

BOWLAND BRIDGE

Cumbria – See Regional map n°**21-A2_3**
London 269 mi – Liverpool 86 mi – Preston 48 mi – Blackpool 60 mi

Hare and Hounds with rm
LA11 6NN – (015395) 68 333 – www.hareandhoundsbowlandbridge.co.uk – Closed 25 December
5 rm – £ 75/145 £ 125/165 Menu £ 13 – Carte £ 20/33
Charming, 17C Lakeland pub in a delightful village. Large front terrace leads through into a rustic, open-fired inner hung with old village photos and hop bines. Menus offer typical, hearty favourites and most produce is locally sourced. Bedrooms are well-equipped and elegant; some boast roll-top baths.

BOWNESS-ON-WINDERMERE → See Windermere

Cumbria – Michelin Road map 502-L20

BOX → See Bath

Wiltshire – Michelin Road map 503-N29 and 504-N29

BOYLESTONE

Derbyshire – See Regional map n°**16-A2**
London 142 mi – Derby 18 mi – Stoke on Trent 24 mi

Lighthouse N
New Rd DE6 5AA – behind Rose & Crown public house – (01335) 330 658 – www.the-lighthouse-restaurant.co.uk – Closed Sunday dinner and Monday-Wednesday
Carte £ 32/43 – *(dinner only and Sunday lunch)*
It may not be near the coast, but the Lighthouse does attract your attention. The self-taught chef prepares ambitious, complex dishes with good combinations of flavours and textures; the tasting menu, in particular, is a hit.

BRABOURNE

Kent – Pop. 1 442 – See Regional map n°**9-C2**

London 61 mi – Folkstone 17 mi – Canterbury 19 mi

Five Bells Inn with rm

TN25 5LP – (01303) 813 334 – www.fivebellsinnbrabourne.com

4 rm – £ 90/140 £ 100/140 Carte £ 21/41

Characterful 16C building: a glorious candlelit hotchpotch of exposed beams, hop bines, open fires, butcher's block tables and an appealing deli. The gutsy menu ranges from eggs Benedict to wood-fired pizzas and fish from the local boats. Service is chatty and welcoming, and the bedrooms, delightfully busy.

BRADFORD-ON-AVON

Wiltshire – Pop. 9 149 – See Regional map n°**4-C2**

London 118 mi – Bristol 24 mi – Salisbury 35 mi – Swindon 33 mi

Michelin Road map 503-N29 and 504-N29 – Michelin Green Guide GREAT BRITAIN

Woolley Grange

Woolley Green BA15 1TX – Northeast : 0.75 mi by B 3107 on Woolley St – (01225) 864 705 – www.woolleygrangehotel.co.uk

25 rm – £ 90/420 £ 120/560 – 6 suites

Rest – Menu £ 42 (dinner) – Carte £ 25/35

Fine Jacobean manor house that's geared towards families, with a crèche, a kids' club, a games room and outdoor activities. For adults, there's a chic spa and some lovely country views. Smart bedrooms come in many styles. Accomplished, classical cooking is served in the restaurant and more relaxed orangery.

Three Gables

St Margaret's St BA15 1DA – (01225) 781 666 – www.thethreegables.com – Closed 1-10 January, Sunday and Monday

Menu £ 16/30 – Carte £ 31/49

Personally and passionately run restaurant in a 350 year old house, with a lovely terrace and charming exposed stone and wattle and daub walls. Skilful, accomplished cooking; interesting, original dishes are based on classical combinations.

at Winsley West: 2 mi by A363 off B3108

Stillmeadow without rest

18 Bradford Rd BA15 2HW – (01225) 722 119 – www.stillmeadow.co.uk – Closed 23 December-2 January

4 rm – £ 90 £ 100

The name sums it up well, as it has a charming wildflower garden and is located on the edge of a small hamlet. Tasteful furnishings provide a good degree of luxury and comfort. Bedrooms are colour-themed and have thoughtful touches.

BRADWELL

Derbyshire – Pop. 1 416 – See Regional map n°**16-A1**

London 170 mi – Birmingham 99 mi – Liverpool 66 mi – Leeds 48 mi

Michelin Road map 504-O24

Samuel Fox Country Inn with rm

Stretfield Rd S33 9JT – (01433) 621 562 – www.samuelfox.co.uk – Closed 5-15 January

4 rm – £ 70/85 £ 100/130 Menu £ 20 (early dinner) – Carte £ 26/42

Attractive, light-stone building with a dramatic, hilly backdrop: named after the inventor of the steel-ribbed umbrella, born in the village. Classic dishes with modern touches; Spanish influences hint at the chef's time in Andalucia; try the 'secret supper' small plates on Fridays. Contemporary bedrooms.

BRAITHWAITE → See Keswick

Cumbria – Michelin Road map 502-K20

BRAMPFORD SPEKE → See Exeter

Devon

BRAMPTON

Cumbria – Pop. 4 229 – See Regional map n°**21-B1**

▶London 317 mi – Carlisle 9 mi – Newcastle upon Tyne 49 mi

Michelin Road map 501-L19 and 502-L19 – Michelin Green Guide GREAT BRITAIN

Farlam Hall

✉ *CA8 2NG Southeast : 2.75 mi on A 689 – ✆ (016977) 46 234 – www.farlamhall.co.uk – Closed 4-22 January and 25-30 December*

12 rm (dinner included) – †£ 120/150 ††£ 220/280

Rest – Menu £ 48 – *(dinner only) (booking essential)*

Well-run, family-owned Victorian country house, whose origins can be traced back to the 1600s. Bedrooms are furnished with antiques but also have Bose radios. The sumptuous formal dining room has romantic lake views, a traditional daily menu and attentive service. Enjoy afternoon tea in the comfy, curio-filled lounges, overlooking the immaculately kept ornamental gardens.

BRANCASTER STAITHE

Norfolk – See Regional map n°**15-C1**

▶London 131 mi – King's Lynn 25 mi – Boston 57 mi – East Dereham 27 mi

White Horse with rm

✉ *PE31 8BY – ✆ (01485) 210 262 – www.whitehorsebrancaster.co.uk*

15 rm – †£ 100/220 ††£ 100/220 Carte £ 25/35 – *(booking essential)*

The rear views over the marshes and Scolt Head Island really make this pub. Choose from old favourites, tapas-style dishes and a few more ambitious offerings on the bar menu; or seasonally changing dishes supplemented by daily specials on the à la carte. Smart, New England style bedrooms – some with terraces.

BRAUGHING

Hertfordshire – Pop. 854 – See Regional map n°**12-B2**

▶London 33 mi – Leeds 171 mi – Sheffield 153 mi – Manchester 200 mi

Golden Fleece

20 Green End ✉ SG11 2PG – ✆ (01920) 823 555 – www.goldenfleecebraughing.co.uk – Closed 25-26 December and Sunday dinner

Carte £ 21/37

Proudly run, part-16C pub with a spacious garden, a pretty terrace overlooking the village and striking period features including a vast inglenook fireplace. Tasty, comforting, country-style dishes; gluten and dairy free options.

BRAY

Windsor and Maidenhead – Pop. 8 121 – ✉ Maidenhead – See Regional map n°**11-C3**

▶London 30 mi – Oxford 36 mi – Bristol 93 mi

Michelin Road map 504-R29

see Maidenhead Plan

Waterside Inn (Alain Roux) with rm

Ferry Rd ✉ SL6 2AT – ✆ (01628) 620 691 – www.waterside-inn.co.uk – Closed 26 December-28 January Town plan: X**s**

11 rm – †£ 225/535 ††£ 225/535 – 2 suites

Menu £ 60 (weekday lunch)/155 – Carte £ 117/166 – *(closed Monday and Tuesday) (booking essential)*

An illustrious restaurant in a glorious spot on a bank of the Thames, with a relaxed, rustic dining room and a delightful terrace ideal for aperitifs. Service is charming and expertly structured. Carefully considered French menus reflect the seasons and use top quality luxury ingredients in perfectly judged, sophisticated combinations. Bedrooms are chic and sumptuous.

→ Tronçonnettes de homard poêlées minute au porto blanc. Filets de lapereau grillés, sauce à l'armagnac et aux marrons glacés. Soufflé chaud aux mirabelles.

ENGLAND

XXX **Fat Duck**

✿✿✿ *High St ✉ SL6 2AQ – ✆ (01628) 580 333* Town plan: X**e**
– www.thefatduck.co.uk – Closed January to mid-August , Sunday and Monday
Menu £ 195 – *(booking essential) (set menu only)*
Stylish restaurant in an old, low-beamed pub, owned by Heston Blumenthal. The 14 course menu lists intriguingly named creations such as the 'Sound of the Sea' or the Mad Hatter's Tea Party, which are presented in theatrical ways and stimulate the senses. Highly original dishes contain excellent contrasts of texture and taste.
→ Scallop with birch syrup and coral royale. Lamb with cucumber and caviar oil. Eggs in verjus, verjus in egg.

XX **Caldesi in Campagna**

Old Mill Ln ✉ SL6 2BG – ✆ (01628) 788 500 Town plan: X**x**
– www.caldesi.com – Closed Sunday dinner and Monday
Menu £ 20 (weekday lunch) – Carte £ 33/56
Sister of Café Caldesi in London, is this chic, sophisticated restaurant with a cosy conservatory and a lovely covered terrace – complete with a wood-fired oven. Flavoursome Italian dishes feature Tuscan and Sicilian specialities.

Hinds Head

✿ *High St ✉ SL6 2AB – ✆ (01628) 626 151* Town plan: X**e**
– www.hindsheadbray.com – Closed 25 December and Sunday dinner
Menu £ 18 (weekday lunch) – Carte £ 34/54 – *(booking essential)*
Listed 15C pub at the heart of a pretty village; its dark wood panelling and log fires giving it a characterful, almost medieval feel. Prime seasonal produce is used to create rich, satisfying dishes that are down-to-earth, fiercely British, carefully presented and big on flavour. Informed, engaging service.
→ Hash of snails. Veal sirloin, cabbage and soused onions. Caramelised butter loaf with apple and Pomona.

Royal Oak

✿ *Paley Street ✉ SL6 3JN – Southwest : 3.5 mi by A 308 and A 330 on B 3024 – ✆ (01628) 620 541 – www.theroyaloakpaleystreet.com – Closed Sunday dinner*
Menu £ 20 (weekday lunch) – Carte £ 25/52
A warm and welcoming beamed dining pub, with a smart extension and an elegantly manicured herb garden. The appealing menu champions seasonal British produce. Cooking is skilled, confident and sensibly avoids over-elaboration; fish and game are handled deftly. Formal service provides a sense of occasion.
→ Lasagne of wild rabbit with wood blewits. Peppered haunch of roe deer with creamed spinach and sauce poivrade. Banana soufflé with toffee ice cream.

Crown

High St ✉ SL6 2AH – ✆ (01628) 621 936 Town plan: X**a**
– www.thecrownatbray.com – Closed 25 December and Sunday dinner
Carte £ 26/44
Charmingly restored 16C building; formerly 2 cottages and a bike shop. Drinkers mingle with diners and the dark oak columns, low beams and roaring fires create a cosy atmosphere. Cooking is robust, flavoursome and British.

BRAYE → See Channel Islands (Alderney)
– Michelin Road map 503-Q33

BREEDON ON THE HILL

Leicestershire – Pop. 686 – ✉ Castle Donington – See Regional map n°**16-B2**
London 121 mi – Birmingham 35 mi – Sheffield 57 mi – Manchester 95 mi

Three Horseshoes Inn
44-46 Main St ✉ DE73 8AN – ✆ (01332) 695 129 – www.thehorseshoes.com – Closed 25-26 December, 1 January, Sunday dinner and Monday
Carte £ 20/40
Large, highly characterful, whitewashed pub with a pleasant terrace and numerous interlinking rooms featuring cosy fires and intimate corners. Blackboard menus display robust, classical dishes of flavoursome, seasonal produce.

BRENTWOOD

Essex – Pop. 52 586 – See Regional map n°**13**-C2
London 22 mi – Chelmsford 11 mi – Southend-on-Sea 21 mi
Michelin Road map 504-V29

Marygreen Manor
London Rd ✉ CM14 4NR – Southwest : 1.25 mi on A 1023 – ✆ (01277) 225 252 – www.marygreenmanor.co.uk
44 rm – †£ 75/160 ††£ 75/160, ☕ £ 15
Rest *Tudors* – Menu £ 18 (weekdays) – Carte £ 39/56
Tudor house with 15C origins; once owned by a servant of Catherine of Aragon. Charming open-fired rooms, ornate plaster ceilings and carved wood panelling. Bedrooms are split between the house and the courtyard; the former are more characterful. Formal restaurant offers elaborate, classically based dishes.

BRIDGNORTH

Shropshire – Pop. 12 315 – See Regional map n°**18**-B2
London 146 mi – Birmingham 26 mi – Shrewsbury 20 mi – Worcester 29 mi
Michelin Road map 502-M26 and 503 – Michelin Green Guide GREAT BRITAIN

Old Vicarage
Worfield ✉ WV15 5JZ – Northeast : 4 mi by A 454 – ✆ (01746) 716 497 – www.oldvicarageworfield.com
14 rm ☕ – †£ 65/110 ††£ 85/130
Rest *Orangery* – Menu £ 20 – Carte £ 22/39 – *(booking essential)*
Red-brick Edwardian vicarage in a quiet village; a popular place for weddings. From the lounge to the bedrooms it has a country house feel – many of the latter display impressive antiques; those in the coach house have spa baths. The smart restaurant has a tiled floor, a glass roof and pleasant garden views.

BRIDPORT

Dorset – Pop. 13 737 – See Regional map n°**3**-B3
London 150 mi – Exeter 38 mi – Taunton 33 mi – Weymouth 19 mi
Michelin Road map 503-L31

Roundham House without rest
Roundham Gdns, West Bay Rd ✉ DT6 4BD – South : 1 mi by B 3157 – ✆ (01308) 422 753 – www.roundhamhouse.co.uk – Closed November-May
8 rm ☕ – †£ 58 ††£ 94/98
Sizeable Edwardian house displaying rich colours and period furnishings. Comfy lounge; modern bedrooms with bold feature walls and good comforts. Elevated position offers pleasant country views.

Bull
34 East St ✉ DT6 3LF – ✆ (01308) 422 878 – www.thebullhotel.co.uk
19 rm ☕ – †£ 90/115 ††£ 100/265
Rest – Menu £ 14 (weekday lunch) – Carte £ 25/44
Stylishly refurbished, 16C coaching inn with a grand Victorian ballroom and a well-equipped games room. Chic bedrooms – upstairs and in a mews – are decorated with local auction house finds and artefacts from Parisian flea markets. Appealing classics in the bar; pizzas, pies and ciders in the former stables.

Riverside

West Bay ✉ DT6 4EZ – South : 1.75 mi by B 3157 – ☎ (01308) 422 011 – www.thefishrestaurant-westbay.co.uk – Closed 1 December-13 February, Sunday dinner and Monday except bank holidays
Menu £ 16/28 – Carte £ 19/53 – *(booking essential)*
Long-standing seafood restaurant with harbour views; accessed via a bridge. Good value daily menu offers extremely fresh, straightforward dishes crafted from local produce. Plenty of choice.

at Burton Bradstock Southeast: 2 mi by B3157

Norburton Hall without rest

Shipton Ln ✉ DT6 4NQ – North : 0.25 mi on Shipton Gorge rd – ☎ (01308) 897 007 – www.norburtonhall.com
3 rm – †£ 100/200 ††£ 125/220
Originally a 17C farmhouse; extended and turned into an Arts and Crafts gem in 1902. Woodwork, ornate carvings and period furniture abound. Comfortable bedrooms offer good quality bedding and modern bathrooms. 6 acres of mature grounds, with barbecue available. Charming owners.

BRIGHTON AND HOVE

Brighton and Hove – Pop. 229 700 – See Regional map n°**8-A3**
▶London 53 mi – Portsmouth 48 mi – Southampton 61 mi
Michelin Road map 504-T31 – Michelin Green Guide GREAT BRITAIN

Hotels

ENGLAND

Hotel du Vin

2-6 Ship St ✉ BN1 1AD – ✆ (01273) 718 588 – www.hotelduvin.com Town plan: CZ**a**
49 rm – †£ 105/250 ††£ 105/250, ☕ £ 17
Rest *Bistro* – Menu £ 17 – Carte £ 31/87 – *(booking essential)*
Made up of various different buildings; the oldest being a former wine merchant's. Kick-back in the cavernous, gothic-style bar-lounge or out on the terrace. Bedrooms are richly decorated and have superb monsoon showers. The relaxed brasserie, with its hidden courtyard, serves French bistro classics.

Drakes

43-44 Marine Par ✉ BN2 1PE – ✆ (01273) 696 934 – www.drakesofbrighton.com Town plan: CZ**u**
20 rm – †£ 115/145 ††£ 115/345, ☕ £ 13
Rest *Drakes* – see restaurant listing
A pair of 18C townhouses on the promenade, with a smart cocktail bar. Chic, well-equipped bedrooms have wooden feature walls and sea or city views – one even has a bath in the bay window! Minimum 2 night stay at weekends.

Myhotel Brighton without rest

17 Jubilee St ✉ BN1 1GE – ✆ (01273) 900 300 – www.myhotels.com Town plan: CY**z**
80 rm – †£ 70/80 ††£ 85/200, ☕ £ 10
Contemporary hotel in the heart of town – a hit with the younger crowd. It has a wacky designer interior with a funky bar and a modern bar-cum-breakfast room. Quirky, minimalist bedrooms come with the latest technological extras.

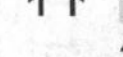

A Room with a View Ⓝ without rest

41 Marine Par. ✉ BN2 1PE – ✆ (01273) 682 885 – www.aroomwithaviewbrighton.com Town plan: CZ**u**
9 rm ☕ – †£ 55/59 ††£ 89/230
Snuggle into a Hungarian goose down duvet and, if your room is at the front of this Regency townhouse, enjoy the views out over the Channel. All have Nespresso machines and a soft drink mini-bar; Room 10 has a roof terrace.

BRIGHTON AND HOVE

Street	Grid	No.
Adelaide Crescent	AY	2
Brunswick Pl.	AY	3
Brunswick Square	AYZ	4
Carlton Terrace	AV	5
Chatham Pl.	BX	6
Churchill Square Shopping Centre	BYZ	
Denmark Rd	BY	7
Eastern Rd	CV	9
East St.	CZ	8
George St.	AV	10
Gladstone Terrace	CX	12
Gloucester Pl.	CY	13
Gloucester Rd	CY	14
Goldsmid Rd	BX	15
Grand Junction Rd	CZ	16
Hollingbury Park Ave	BV	17
Hollingdean Rd	CV	18
Hove St.	AV	19
London Rd	CX	
Marlborough Pl.	CY	21
Montpelier Pl.	BY	22
North St.	CZ	
Old Steine	CZ	23
Pavillon Parade	CZ	26
Richmond Pl.	CY	27
Richmond Terrace	CX	28
St George's Pl.	CY	30
St Peter's Pl.	CX	31
Terminus Rd	BCX	32
Upper Lewes Rd	CX	33
Warren Rd	CV	37
Waterloo Pl.	CX	39
Wellington Rd.	AV	40
Western Rd	ABY	
York Pl.	CY	42

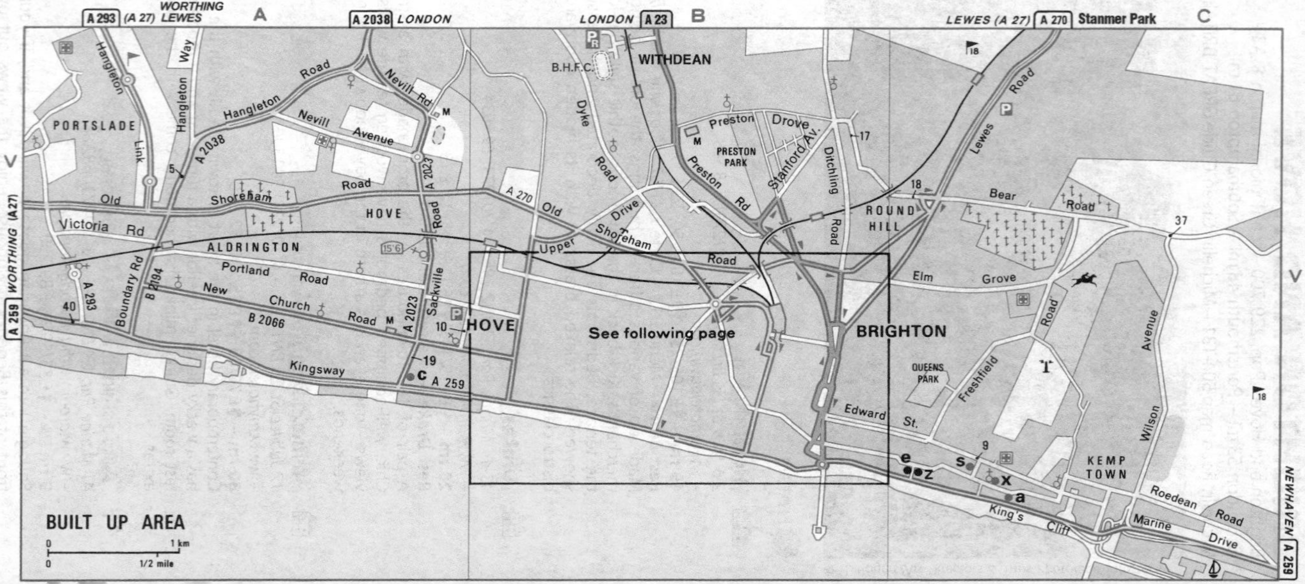

See following page

BUILT UP AREA

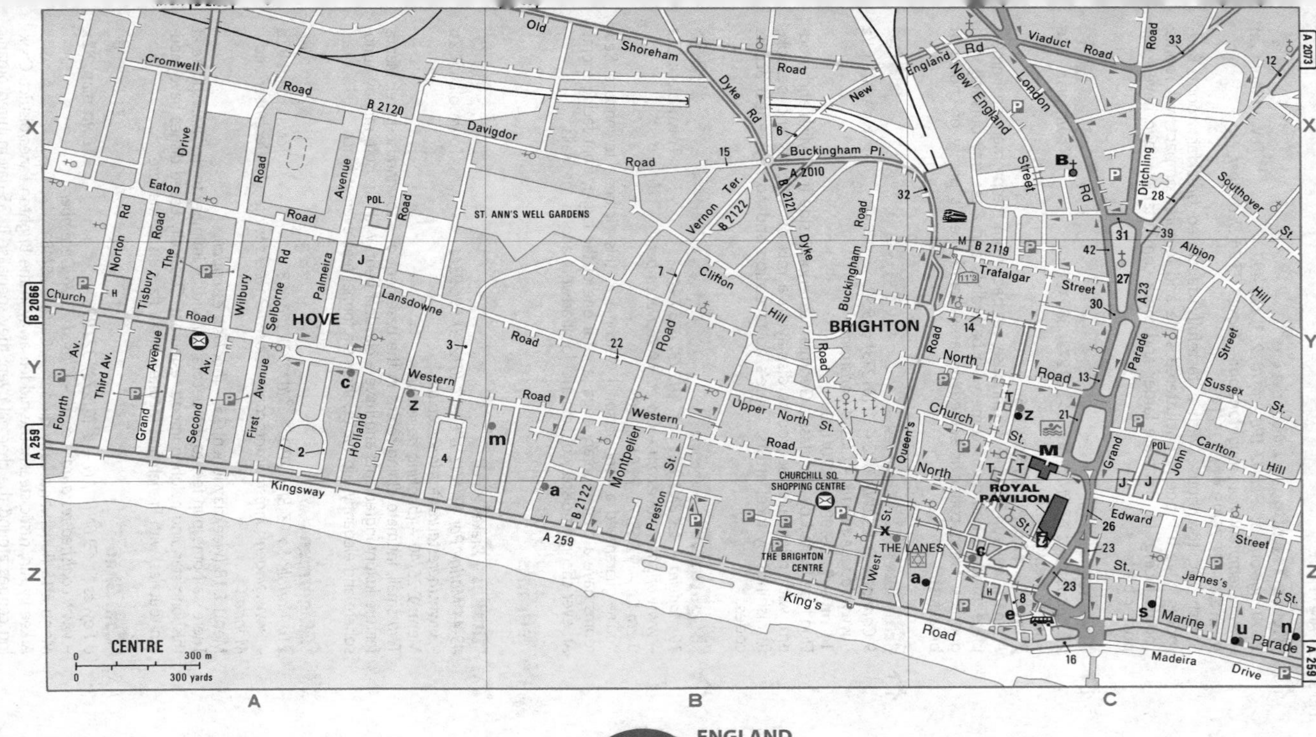

A 2073
A 259
B 2066
X
Y
Z
A
B
C
HOVE
BRIGHTON
ROYAL PAVILION
THE LANES
CHURCHILL SQ. SHOPPING CENTRE
THE BRIGHTON CENTRE
ST. ANN'S WELL GARDENS
POL.
Old Shoreham Road
Cromwell Road
B 2120
Davigdor Road
Dyke Rd
New England Rd
New England Street
London Rd
Viaduct Road
Ditching Road
Southover St.
Albion Hill
Buckingham Pl.
A 2010
B 2121
B 2122
Vernon Ter.
Dyke Road
Buckingham Road
B 2119
Trafalgar Street
A 23
Clifton Hill
North Road
Parade
Sussex Street
Sussex St.
Church St.
Grand Parade
John Street
Carlton Hill
Queen's Road
Upper North St.
Western Road
Montpelier Road
Preston St.
North St.
West St.
Edward Street
St. James's St.
Marine Parade
Madeira Drive
King's Road
A 259
Kingsway
Lansdowne Road
Holland Road
Palmeira Avenue
Selborne Rd
First Avenue
Wilbury Road
Second Av.
The Drive
Eaton Road
Tisbury Road
Grand Avenue
Norton Rd
Third Av.
Fourth Av.
Church Road
CENTRE
0
300 m
300 yards
ENGLAND

Kemp Townhouse without rest
21 Atlingworth St ✉ BN2 1PL – ☎ (01273) 681 400 Town plan: CZ**n**
– www.kemptownhousebrighton.com – Closed 25-26 December
9 rm ☕ – 🛉£ 75/95 🛉🛉£ 125/145
Stylish 19C townhouse with a tastefully decorated breakfast room. Bedrooms have a modern, uncluttered style and feature compact wet rooms; rooms facing the front are larger and more comfortable – two have four-poster beds.

Twenty One without rest
21 Charlotte St ✉ BN2 1AG – ☎ (01273) 686 450 Town plan: CV**e**
– www.thetwentyone.co.uk
7 rm ☕ – 🛉£ 65/95 🛉🛉£ 99/155
A smart, well-run Regency townhouse, set back from the promenade. Immaculate, modern bedrooms come with bathrobes and a tea tray bursting with goodies. Fresh coffee is served on arrival and there's plenty of choice at breakfast.

Fab Guest Ⓝ without rest
9 Charlotte St ✉ BN2 1AG – ☎ (01273) 625 505 Town plan: CV**z**
– www.fabguest.co.uk – Closed Christmas
14 rm – 🛉£ 59/90 🛉🛉£ 70/150
Don't be fooled by the classic Georgian exterior; inside it's stylish and modern, with minimalist bedrooms displaying a mix of antiques and bespoke furnishings by local artists. There's no reception and no keys – just access codes.

ENGLAND

brightonwave without rest
10 Madeira Pl ✉ BN2 1TN – ☎ (01273) 676 794 Town plan: CZ**s**
– www.brightonwave.com – Closed 14-26 December
8 rm ☕ – 🛉£ 65/75 🛉🛉£ 90/120
You're guaranteed a very personal welcome at this Victorian townhouse. Bedrooms have a contemporary edge: ask for one of the larger, front facing rooms. An ever-changing display of colourful local artwork adorns the walls.

Restaurants

Drakes – Drakes Hotel
43-44 Marine Par ✉ BN2 1PE – ☎ (01273) 696 934 Town plan: CZ**u**
– www.therestaurantatdrakes.co.uk
Menu £ 25/40 – *(booking advisable)*
Two small, intimate dining rooms in the basement of a townhouse hotel. Menus feature luxury ingredients and have a classical bent. With the soft, moody atmosphere and elegantly laid tables, there's a formal feel, even at lunch.

Gingerman
21a Norfolk Sq ✉ BN1 2PD – ☎ (01273) 326 688 Town plan: BZ**a**
– www.gingermanrestaurants.com – Closed 2 weeks winter, 25 December and Monday
Menu £ 18 (weekday lunch)/35 – *(booking essential)*
There's a homespun feel to the decoration and an intimacy to the atmosphere at this long-standing neighbourhood restaurant. Classically based dishes have modern touches, with French and Mediterranean flavours to the fore.

Coal Shed
8 Boyces St ✉ BN1 1AN – ☎ (01273) 322 998 Town plan: BZ**x**
– www.coalshed-restaurant.co.uk – Closed 25-26 December
Menu £ 15 (lunch and early dinner) – Carte £ 26/48
A keenly run, rustic steakhouse hidden away in the Brighton Lanes district. Cooking centres around the charcoal oven; they specialise in 35-day matured organic steaks but there's also a tasty selection of fresh fish dishes to try.

XX **24 St Georges**

24 St George's Rd ✉ BN2 1ED – ✆ (01273) 626 060 Town plan: CV**x**
– www.24stgeorges.co.uk – Closed 25-26 December, 1-2, 11-19 January, Sunday and Monday
Menu £ 22 (early dinner) – Carte £ 26/43 – *(dinner only and lunch Saturday and Sunday) (booking advisable)*
Shabby chic restaurant on the edge of Kemp Town, run by keen owners; its three adjoining rooms have a stylish, contemporary feel. Seasonal menus offer complex, technically skilled dishes. The staff are welcoming and knowledgeable.

XX **Graze**

42 Western Rd, Hove ✉ BN3 1JD – ✆ (01273) 823 707 Town plan: AY**z**
– www.graze-restaurant.co.uk – Closed 1-9 January
Menu £ 20 (lunch and early dinner)/55
Lively neighbourhood eatery with a quirky, informal feel and a great private dining room in the basement. Cooking is elaborate and adventurous. Good value midweek menu; the 7 course tasting menu must be ordered in advance at lunch.

X **Chilli Pickle**

17 Jubilee St ✉ BN1 1GE – ✆ (01273) 900 383 Town plan: CY**z**
– www.thechillipickle.com – Closed 25-26 December
Menu £ 24/28 – Carte £ 20/33
Simple restaurant with a relaxed, buzzy vibe and friendly, welcoming service. The passionate chef uses good quality ingredients to create oft-changing menus of thoughtfully prepared, authentic Indian dishes with delicate spicing. Beside the terrace they also have a cart selling street food style snacks.

ENGLAND

X **Terre à Terre**

71 East St ✉ BN1 1HQ – ✆ (01273) 729 051 Town plan: CZ**e**
– www.terreaterre.co.uk – Closed 25-26 December and Monday in winter
Menu £ 26/30 – Carte £ 26/33 – *(booking essential)*
Relaxed, friendly restaurant decorated in warm burgundy colours. Appealing menu of generous, tasty, original vegetarian dishes which include items from Japan, China and South America. Mini épicerie sells wine, pasta and chutney.

X **Sam's of Brighton**

1 Paston Pl ✉ BN2 1HA – ✆ (01273) 676 222 Town plan: CV**a**
– www.samsofbrighton.co.uk – Closed 25 December, Sunday dinner and Monday
Menu £ 15 (lunch and early dinner) – Carte £ 24/36
An established neighbourhood bistro where brown leather stands out against plain walls. The concise à la carte offers seasonal dishes and there's a good value set lunch and early evening menu. At weekends, they also serve brunch.

X **64°** N

53 Meeting House Ln. ✉ BN1 1HB – ✆ (01273) 770 115 Town plan: CZ**c**
– www.64degrees.co.uk – Closed 25 December and Sunday dinner
Carte £ 12/33 – *(booking essential)*
If you like things fun and fuss-free, then this intimate modern restaurant is the place for you! Menus are divided into four – 'Meat', 'Fish', 'Veg' and 'Dessert' – and each section also has four choices. Cooking is simple but well-textured and flavoursome; most of the dining takes place at the counter.

X **Little Fish Market** N

10 Upper Market St, Hove ✉ BN3 1AS – ✆ (01273) 722 213 – www.thelittlefishmarket.co.uk – Closed 1 week April, 1 week August, 1 week September, 1 week December, Sunday and Monday Town plan: BY**m**
Menu £ 46 – *(dinner only and Saturday lunch) (booking essential)*
Fish is the focus at this simple little restaurant – it's in a converted fishmonger's; it sits opposite the old Victorian fish market; and the menu offers refined, interesting seafood dishes. The owner cooks alone in the kitchen.

Ginger Dog

12 College Pl ✉ BN2 1HN – ✆ (01273) 620 990 Town plan: CV**s**
– www.gingermanrestaurants.com – Closed 25 December
Menu £ 13 (lunch) – Carte £ 25/37

Charming Victorian pub with a shabby-chic, canine-theme, a welcoming atmosphere and a relaxed feel. Fresh produce is to the fore; dishes are mostly British-based but with the odd nod to Italy. A ginger 'dog' biscuit is served with coffee.

Ginger Pig

3 Hove St, Hove ✉ BN3 2TR – ✆ (01273) 736 123 Town plan: AV**c**
– www.gingermanrestaurants.com – Closed 25 December
Menu £ 14 (weekday lunch) – Carte £ 24/35

Smart building by the seafront – formerly a hotel – boasting a mortar ship relief and a beautifully restored revolving door. Menus offer precise, flavoursome British dishes and vegetarians are well-catered for. Good value set lunch menu.

ENGLAND

BRISTOL

City of Bristol – Pop. 535 907 – See Regional map n°**4-C2**
London 121 mi – Birmingham 91 mi
Michelin Road map 503-M29 and 504-M29 – Michelin Green Guide GREAT BRITAIN

© I. Dagnall/age fotostock

Hotels

ENGLAND

Hotel du Vin

rm,
The Sugar House ✉ *BS1 2NU* – ✆ *(0844) 736 42 52* Town plan: CY**e**
– *www.hotelduvin.com*
40 rm – †£ 119/185 ††£ 119/325, ☕£ 17
Rest ***Bistro*** – Carte £ 26/44 – *(booking essential)*

Characterful 18C former sugar refinery with classical Hotel du Vin styling and a wine-theme running throughout. Dark-hued bedrooms and duplex suites boast Egyptian cotton linen – one room has twin roll-top baths. Cosy lounge-bar; French brasserie with a pleasant courtyard terrace for bistro classics.

Mercure Bristol Brigstow

rm,
5-7 Welsh Back ✉ *BS1 4SP* – ✆ *(0117) 929 10 30* Town plan: CY**n**
– *www.mercure.com*
116 rm – †£ 60/165 ††£ 68/195, ☕£ 17 – 1 suite
Rest ***Ellipse*** – Menu £ 18 **s** – Carte £ 21/41 **s**

Modern city centre hotel overlooking the River Avon. Stylishly furnished, curvaceous bedrooms have bold colour schemes and luxurious bathrooms, with a TV above the bath. Some have balconies; others, coffee machines and river views. Smart, contemporary Ellipse serves a menu of European classics.

Berwick Lodge Ⓝ

Berwick Dr ✉ *BS10 7TD – Northwest 5 mi by A 4018* Town plan: AV**w**
– ✆ *(0117) 958 1590 – www.berwicklodge.co.uk*
12 rm ☕ – †£ 85/95 ††£ 125/225
Rest – Menu £ 25 – Carte £ 36/42 – *(bookings essential for non-residents)*

A popular wedding and events venue, run by gregarious, hands-on owners. It's surrounded by 18 acres of grounds and offers views over Avonmouth and the Severn Bridge. Inside, original features combine with Eastern furnishings and mosaic tiles. The intimate restaurant has fine chandeliers and a modern menu.

Number 38 Clifton without rest

38 Upper Belgrave Rd ✉ *BS8 2XN* – ✆ *(01179) 466 905* Town plan: AX**a**
– *www.number38clifton.com*
9 rm ☕ – †£ 110/195 ††£ 125/210

Built in 1820, this substantial townhouse overlooks both the city and the Clifton Downs. Boutique bedrooms have coloured wood-panelled walls, Roberts radios and smart bathrooms with underfloor heating; the most luxurious are the loft suites, complete with copper baths. The rear terrace makes a great suntrap.

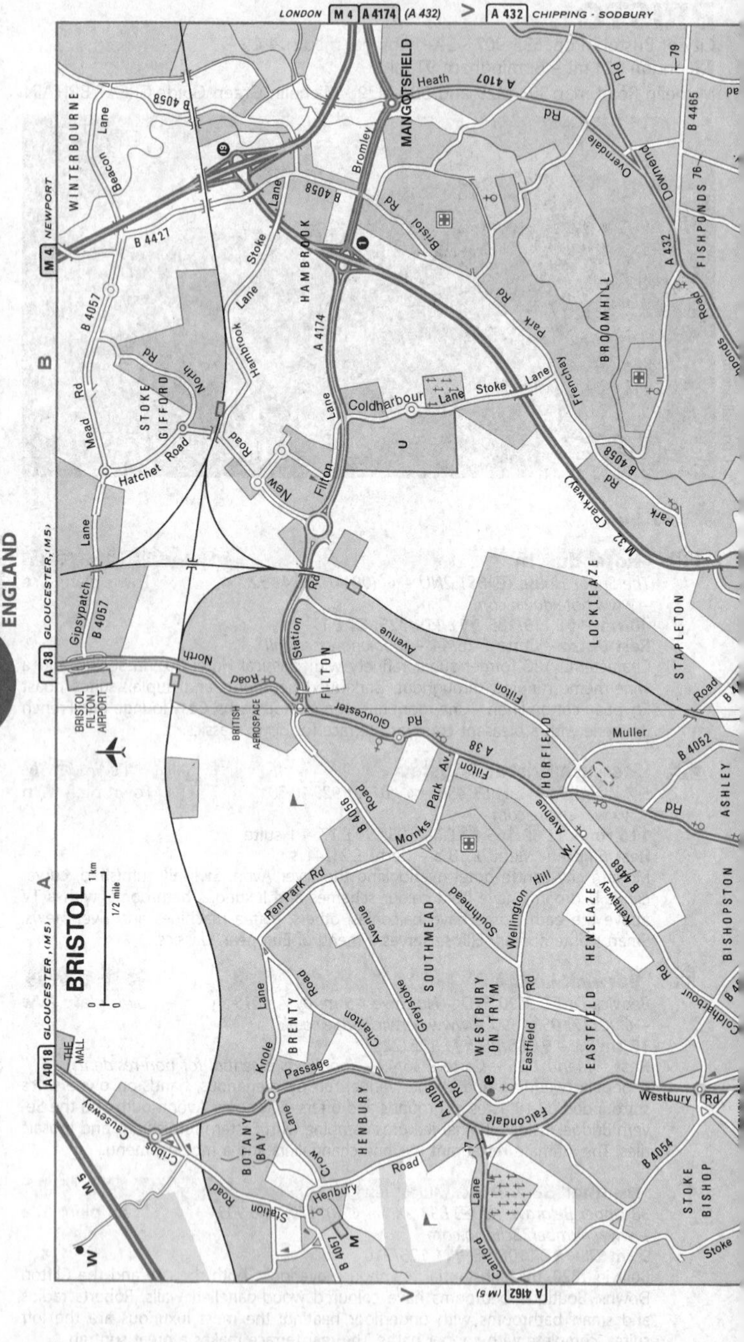

ENGLAND

A4018 GLOUCESTER, (M5) A

A 38 GLOUCESTER, (M5)

B

M 4 NEWPORT

BRISTOL

0 1 km
0 1/2 mile

BRISTOL FILTON AIRPORT
BRITISH AEROSPACE
THE MALL
WINTERBOURNE
STOKE GIFFORD
HAMBROOK
MANGOTSFIELD
BOTANY BAY
BRENTY
HENBURY
SOUTHMEAD
WESTBURY ON TRYM
FILTON
HORFIELD
LOCKLEAZE
BROOMHILL
EASTFIELD
HENLEAZE
STOKE BISHOP
BISHOPSTON
ASHLEY
STAPLETON
FISHPONDS

Gipsypatch Lane
B 4057
Mead Rd
Hatchet Road
North Rd
Beacon Lane
B 4427
B 4058
Hambrook Lane
Stoke Lane
New Road
Filton Lane
A 4174
Bromley Heath
Coldharbour Lane
Stoke Lane
Frenchay Park Rd
Bristol Rd
A 4107
Overndale Rd
Downend Road
A 432
B 4465
M 32 (Parkway)
Park Rd
North Road
Station Rd
Gloucester Rd
A 38
Filton Avenue
Filton Av.
Monks Park Av.
B 4056 Road
Pen Park Rd
Knole Lane
Passage
Charlton Road
Greystoke Avenue
Southmead Road
Wellington Hill W.
Kellaway Avenue
B 4468
Coldharbour Rd
Muller Road
B 4052
Rd
Cribbs Causeway
M 5
Station Road
Crow Lane
Henbury Road
B 4057
A 4018 Rd
Falcondale Rd
Canford Lane
Eastfield Rd
Westbury Rd
B 4054
Stoke
17
76
79
W
M
e
U

LONDON M 4 A 4174 (A 432) V

A 432 CHIPPING - SODBURY

A 4162 (M 5) V

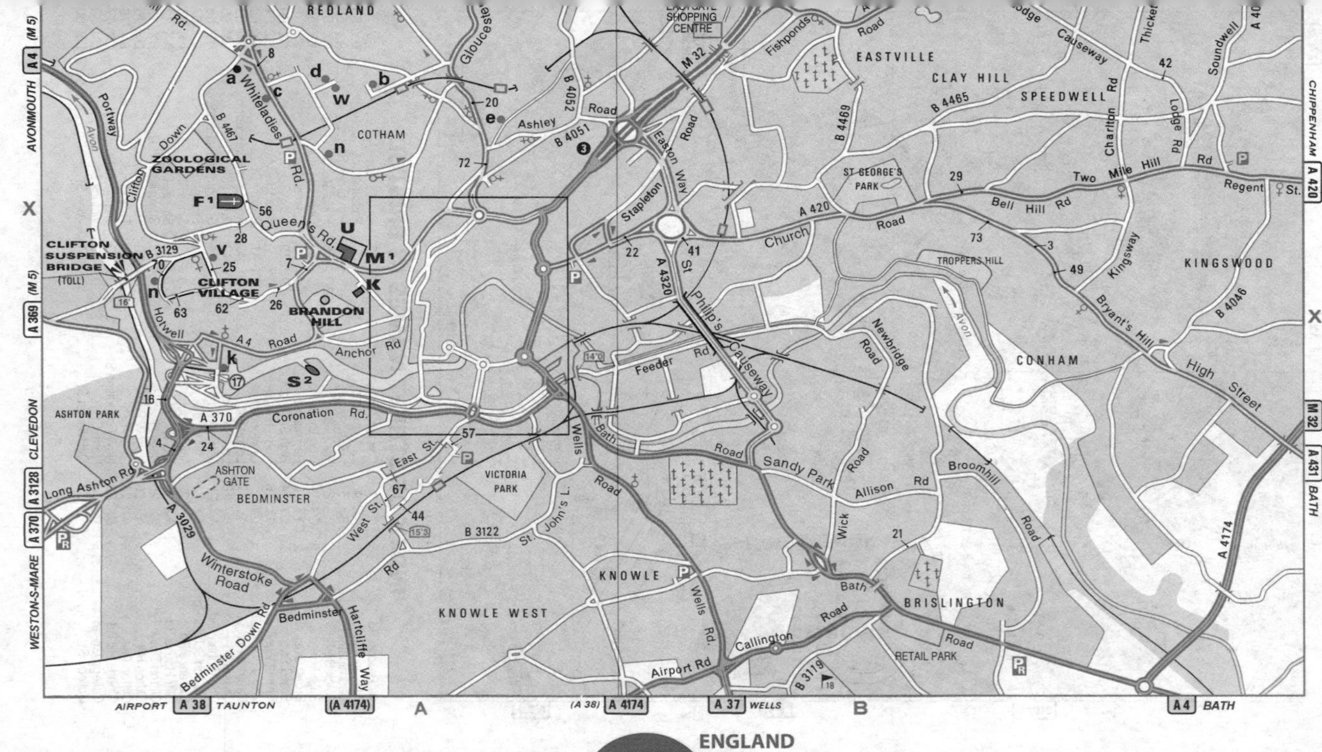

AVONMOUTH A 4 (M 5)
A 369 (M 5)
CLEVEDON A 3128
A 370 WESTON-S-MARE
REDLAND
Whiteladies Rd.
COTHAM
Gloucester
Ashley
B 4052
B 4051
Road
SHOPPING CENTRE
M 32
Fishponds
EASTVILLE
CLAY HILL
SPEEDWELL
B 4465
B 4469
Causeway
Charlton Rd
Lodge Rd
Soundwell
CHIPPENHAM A 420
Portway
Avon
Clifton Down
B 4467
ZOOLOGICAL GARDENS
Queen's Rd.
CLIFTON SUSPENSION BRIDGE (TOLL)
B 3129
CLIFTON VILLAGE
BRANDON HILL
Hotwell
A 4 Road
Anchor Rd
Easton Way
Stapleton
Road
ST GEORGE'S PARK
A 420
Church
Road
Two Mile Hill
Rd
Regent St.
Bell Hill Rd
TROPPERS HILL
Kingsway
KINGSWOOD
B 4046
Bryant's Hill
High Street
A 4320
St
Philip's Causeway
Feeder Rd
Newbridge Road
CONHAM
M 32
A 431 BATH
ASHTON PARK
A 370
Coronation Rd.
ASHTON GATE
BEDMINSTER
Long Ashton Rd
A 3029
Winterstoke Road
Bedminster Down Rd
Bedminster
Hartcliffe Way
East St.
West St.
VICTORIA PARK
B 3122
St. John's L.
Rd
KNOWLE WEST
Wells Road
Bath Road
Sandy Park Road
Wick Road
Allison Rd
Broomhill Road
KNOWLE
Wells Rd.
Bath Road
BRISLINGTON
Road
RETAIL PARK
Callington
Airport Rd
B 3119
A 4174
AIRPORT A 38 TAUNTON
(A 4174)
(A 38) A 4174
A 37 WELLS
A 4 BATH
ENGLAND

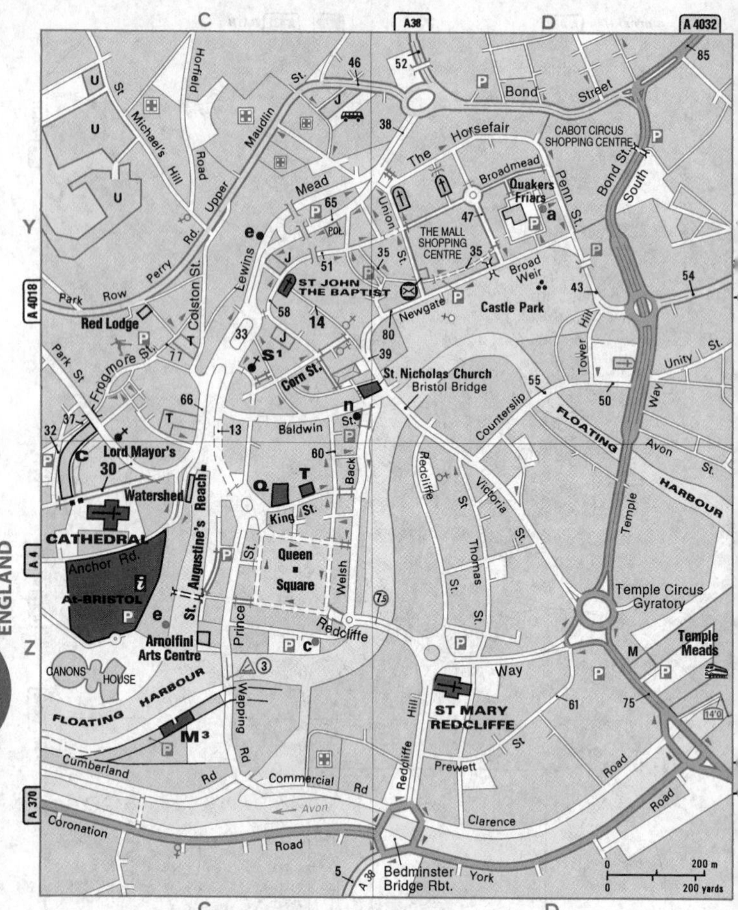

INDEX OF STREET NAMES IN BRISTOL

Restaurants

XXX **Second Floor at Harvey Nichols**

27 Philadelphia St, Quakers Friars, Cabot Circus Town plan: DY**a**
✉ BS1 3BZ – ✆ (0117) 916 8898 – www.harveynichols.com – Closed 25 December, 1 January, Easter Sunday, Sunday and Monday dinner
Menu £ 17 – Carte £ 30/38
A spacious and elegant light-filled restaurant with stylish gold décor. Good value lunch menu and concise à la carte offering original, modern dishes. Chic lounge bar for cocktails and light bites. Attentive service.

XX ✿ **Casamia** (Jonray and Peter Sanchez-Iglesias)

38 High St, Westbury-on-Trym ✉ BS9 3DZ – Northwest : 4 mi by A 4018 – ✆ (0117) 959 28 84 – www.casamiarestaurant.co.uk – Closed Sunday and Monday and Tuesday after bank holidays Town plan: AV**e**
Menu £ 38 (weekday lunch)/125 – *(booking essential) (set menu only)*
This understated, minimalist restaurant is passionately run by two brothers and a well-informed team. Like the details in the décor, the set 13 course menus change with the seasons (there's the option of 6 courses at lunch). Ambitious, skilful and highly innovative cooking uses modern techniques.
→ Spelt with parsley. Lamb, allium, mint and potatoes. Rhubarb and vanilla.

XX **Bordeaux Quay**

V Shed, Canons Way ✉ BS1 5UH – ✆ (0117) 943 12 00 – www.bordeaux-quay.co.uk – Closed 25-26 December Town plan: CZ**e**
Carte £ 22/38
Huge harbourside emporium which aims to be 100% organic. It houses a deli, a bakery, a bar and a laid-back brasserie. Above is a linen-laid restaurant offering adventurous Mediterranean-style cuisine, which opens at the weekend.

ENGLAND

XX **Rockfish Grill**

128 Whiteladies Rd ✉ BS8 2RS – ✆ (0117) 973 73 84 – www.rockfishgrill.co.uk – Closed 24 December-4 January, Sunday and Monday Town plan: AX**c**
Menu £ 15 (lunch) – Carte £ 24/46
Bringing a taste of the sea to the city. Pass the daily catch displayed on a marble slab (this was once a fishmonger's) on your way to the leather-furnished dining room. Simply prepared dishes are cooked in the Josper oven.

X ✿ **wilks** (James Wilkins)

1 Chandos Rd ✉ BS6 6PG – ✆ (0117) 973 79 99 – www.wilksrestaurant.co.uk – Closed 2 weeks January, 2 weeks August, Monday and Tuesday Town plan: AX**d**
Menu £ 23 (lunch and early dinner) – Carte £ 32/51 – *(booking essential)*
Appealing neighbourhood restaurant with a relaxed atmosphere and a simple, understated style. Menus are modern and highly original. Dishes are well-balanced and refreshingly lacking in over-adornment, displaying a lightness of touch and a real understanding of flavours. The set menu offers good value.
→ Wye Valley asparagus, ewes' curd, lemon & herb vinaigrette. Wild turbot, monk's beard, pancetta & Jersey Royal cream. Citrus meringue with lemon curd, mandarin & yuzu sorbet.

X **Flinty Red**

34 Cotham Hill ✉ BS6 6LA – ✆ (0117) 923 87 55 – www.flintyred.co.uk – Closed 1-7 January, 25-28 December, Monday lunch and Sunday Town plan: AX**n**
Menu £ 10 (lunch) – Carte £ 16/34 – *(booking essential)*
The combined effort of two couples; one pair are independent wine merchants, the other, chefs. Unfussy cooking relies on quality local produce and features some lesser-known cuts; dishes are largely Mediterranean but with some Asian influences. The rustic room is overseen by a friendly, knowledgeable team.

Riverstation

The Grove, Harbourside ✉ BS1 4RB – ☎ (0117) 914 44 34 – www.riverstation.co.uk – Closed 24-26 December
Town plan: CZ**c**

Menu £ 16/21 – Carte £ 26/35

Striking building where you can watch the canal boats passing by. The busy bar specialises in cocktails and offers a menu of Mediterranean and Asian inspired dishes. The upstairs restaurant and terrace serves modern European fare.

Wallfish Bistro

112 Princess Victoria St, Clifton Village ✉ BS8 4DB – ☎ (0117) 973 5435 – www.wallfishbistro.co.uk – Closed 24-31 December, Monday and Tuesday
Town plan: AX**n**

Menu £ 10 (weekday lunch) – Carte £ 22/43 – *(booking advisable)*

This friendly bistro is named after the West Country word for 'snail' and, satisfyingly, you'll find Herefordshire Wallfish on the menu. Careful, classical cooking focuses on good ingredients; fish from the day boats is popular.

Bell's Diner & Bar Rooms

1-3 York Rd, Montpelier ✉ BS6 5QB – ☎ (0117) 924 0357 – www.bellsdiner.com – Closed 24-26 December, 1 January, Sunday and lunch Monday
Town plan: AX**e**

Carte £ 21/39 – *(bookings advisable at dinner)*

A bustling city institution, which still retains evidence of its former grocer's shop days. Flavoursome, Mediterranean-style cooking shows a good understanding of ingredients; be sure to try the slow-cooked cauliflower in yoghurt.

ENGLAND

Moreish

6 Chandos Rd ✉ BS6 6PE – ☎ (0117) 970 60 78 – www.moreishrestaurant.co.uk – Closed 24-26 December and 1 January
Town plan: AX**w**

Menu £ 25 – Carte £ 22/29

Unassuming restaurant in a parade of shops; its name is a play on the chef's surname. The great value daily menu offers well-prepared, rustic dishes, from breakfast right through to dinner. Have drinks in the bar or on the small terrace.

Pump House

Merchants Rd ✉ BS8 4PZ – ☎ (0117) 927 2229 – www.the-pumphouse.com – Closed 25 December
Town plan: AX**k**

Carte £ 23/35

Victorian former pumping station for the adjacent docks; watch the boats go by from the terrace. Cavernous interior with rustic ground floor and smart mezzanine restaurant. Modern classics change with seasons; 5 and 8 course tasting menus.

Albion Public House and Dining Rooms

Boyces Ave, Clifton Village ✉ BS8 4AA – ☎ (0117) 973 35 22 – www.thealbionclifton.co.uk – Closed 25-26 December and dinner Sunday-Monday
Town plan: AX**v**

Carte £ 23/32 – *(booking essential)*

Trendy Grade II listed pub with a fun, friendly and informal feel and a canopy-covered terrace. Lunch sees sandwiches, 'brunch' dishes and traditional mains, while the evening à la carte offers satisfying seasonal cooking.

Kensington Arms

35-37 Stanley Rd ✉ BS6 6NP – ☎ (0117) 944 64 44 – www.thekensingtonarms.co.uk – Closed 25-26 December and Sunday dinner
Town plan: AX**b**

Carte £ 19/42

Charming, Victorian-style neighbourhood pub, with a traditional bar and an impressive, high-ceilinged dining room. Daily menus have a strong British and seasonal base; in winter you'll find hearty, nourishing dishes and proper puddings.

Take note of the classification: you should not expect the same level of service in a X or 🏠 as in a XXXXX or 🏠🏠🏠.

at Long Ashton Southwest: 2.5 mi by A370 off B3128

Bird in Hand

17 Weston Rd ✉ BS41 9LA – ☏ (01275) 395 222 – www.bird-in-hand.co.uk – Closed 25 December and Sunday dinner

Menu £ 14 – Carte £ 21/32 – *(booking essential at dinner)*

Tiny country pub with eclectic décor, including an antelope's head and a wall covered in pages from Mrs Beeton's Book of Household Management. Simple, super value set price lunch menu; the evening à la carte offers tasty, carefully cooked dishes which let local and foraged ingredients speak for themselves.

BRITWELL SALOME

Oxfordshire – Pop. 187 – See Regional map n°**11-C2**

London 75 mi – Oxford 21 mi – Reading 19 mi

Red Lion

✉ OX49 5LG – ☏ (01491) 613 140 – www.theredlionbritwellsalome.co.uk – Closed Sunday dinner, Monday and lunch Tuesday

Carte £ 23/38 – *(booking essential)*

A 'proper' pub next to the village cricket pitch, run by experienced owners. Well-executed dishes provide plenty of interest, from the tasty nibbles to the pie of the day. There's always plenty of pork, as whole beasts are delivered from the farm next door; the homemade black pudding scotch egg is a must-try.

BROAD CAMPDEN → See Chipping Campden

Gloucestershire

BROAD OAK

East Sussex – See Regional map n°**8-B3**

London 62 mi – Hastings 8 mi – Rye 7 mi

Michelin Road map 504-V31

Fairacres without rest

Udimore Rd ✉ TN31 6DG – on B 2089 – ☏ (01424) 883 236 – www.fairacresrye.co.uk – Closed Christmas-New Year

3 rm – †£ 70/110 ††£ 100/150

Three adjoining listed cottages in picture-postcard pink, with delightful gardens, a cosy beamed lounge and truly charming owners. Gloriously cluttered bedrooms display family knick-knacks and offer many thoughtful extras; the Garden Room has a balcony. Big breakfasts feature homemade bread and preserves.

BROADCLYST → See Exeter

Devon – Michelin Road map 503-J31

BROADSTAIRS

Kent – Pop. 23 632 – See Regional map n°**9-D1**

London 77 mi – Canterbury 18 mi – Ramsgate 2 mi

Michelin Road map 504-Y29

Belvidere Place without rest

Belvedere Rd ✉ CT10 1PF – ☏ (01843) 579 850 – www.belvidereplace.co.uk

5 rm – †£ 120 ††£ 150/170

Centrally located Georgian house with a charming owner, green credentials and an eclectic, individual style. Bohemian, shabby-chic lounge boasts a retro football table. Spacious bedrooms mix modern facilities with older antique furnishings.

Albariño

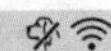

29 Albion St ✉ CT10 1LXG – ☏ (01843) 600 991 – www.albarinorestaurant.co.uk – Closed 25 December-2 January, 21 June-1 July and Sunday

Menu £ 20 (lunch) – Carte £ 13/28 – *(dinner only and Saturday lunch)*

Run by a husband and wife team and named after her favourite wine. Freshly prepared, full-flavoured tapas dishes; 3 per person will suffice – let the chef choose. Counter seating for 7. Good views of the Channel.

BROADWAY

Worcestershire – Pop. 2 496 – See Regional map n°**19-C3**
London 93 mi – Birmingham 36 mi – Cheltenham 15 mi – Oxford 38 mi
Michelin Road map 503-O27 and 504-O27 – Michelin Green Guide GREAT BRITAIN

Buckland Manor

Buckland ✉ WR12 7LY – Southwest : 2.25 mi by B 4632 – ☎ (01386) 852 626 – www.bucklandmanor.com
15 rm – £ 190/555 £ 210/575
Rest – Menu £ 26/65 – *(booking essential)*
With its 13C origins, beautiful gardens and peaceful hamlet setting, this is one of England's most charming country houses. The elegant interior comprises tastefully appointed country house bedrooms and traditionally furnished lounges featuring wood panelling and big open fires. The formal restaurant has garden views and offers classical cooking with modern touches.

Dormy House

Willersey Hill ✉ WR12 7LF – East : 4 mi by A 44 – ☎ (01386) 852 711 – www.dormyhouse.co.uk
40 rm – £ 160/480 £ 170/490 – 6 suites
Rest *Garden Room* – Menu £ 40
Rest *Potting Shed* – Carte £ 25/41
Behind the original farmhouse façade you'll find a funky, modern interior and a luxurious spa. The odd beam and fireplace remain but bold contemporary fabrics and designer furnishings feature now too. Wood and stone play a big part and the atmosphere is laid-back. The Potting Shed has a pub-like feel and the stylish restaurant offers a more sophisticated alternative.

ENGLAND

Lygon Arms

rm,

High St ✉ WR12 7DU – ☎ (01386) 852 255 – www.pumahotels.co.uk
78 rm – £ 90/200 £ 100/375 – 6 suites
Rest *Great Hall* – Menu £ 38 – Carte £ 33/48 – *(dinner only and Sunday lunch)*
Rest *Luke's* – Carte £ 23/35 – *(closed Monday-Tuesday)*
One of the most famous coaching inns in the country, with a hugely characterful interior of wood panelling, inglenook fireplaces and assorted comfy corners. Bedrooms vary in size and shape; those in the newer wing have a more contemporary style. Cosy Luke's serves modern British dishes; the impressive Great Hall has a 17C minstrels' gallery and a modern European menu.

Broadway

rest, rest,

The Green ✉ WR12 7AA – ☎ (01386) 852 401 – www.cotswold-inns-hotels.co.uk/broadway
19 rm – £ 150/170 £ 160/220
Rest *Tattersalls Brasserie* – Menu £ 15 – Carte £ 27/40
16C inn on the village green – once an abbots' retreat – with warmly decorated modern bedrooms and a horse racing theme. Relax in the timbered bar with its minstrels' gallery or have afternoon tea by the inglenook fireplace in the sitting room. The airy courtyard brasserie offers an extensive seasonal menu.

East House without rest

162 High St ✉ WR12 7AJ – ☎ (01386) 853 789 – www.easthouseuk.com
4 rm – £ 165/195 £ 165/195
Beautifully furnished, 18C former farmhouse in lovely mature gardens, with wood-burning stoves and a welcoming feel. Sumptuous beamed bedrooms mix antique furniture with modern technology; superb bathrooms have underfloor heating. The Jacobean Suite is the biggest room, with a four-poster and garden views.

Mill Hay House without rest

Snowshill Rd ✉ WR12 7JS – South : 0.5 mi – ☎ (01386) 852 498 – www.millhay.co.uk
3 rm – £ 145/210 £ 165/230
This lovely 17C house, tucked away on the edge of the village, comes with beautiful gardens overlooking a lake. With just three individually furnished bedrooms, the atmosphere is intimate, and guests are treated as family friends.

Windrush House without rest
Station Rd ✉ WR12 7DE – ☎ (01386) 853 577 – www.windrushhouse.com
5 rm – †£ 65/85 ††£ 80/100
Welcoming guesthouse in a pretty village. Individually decorated bedrooms have bold feature walls: some use Laura Ashley designs and have wrought iron beds; four-poster 'Snowshill' is the best. Homemade jams feature at breakfast.

Olive Branch without rest
78 High St ✉ WR12 7AJ – ☎ (01386) 853 440
– www.theolivebranch-broadway.com
8 rm – †£ 65/75 ††£ 98/125
Welcoming guesthouse run by an experienced husband and wife team. Pleasantly cluttered bedrooms with thoughtful extras; one has a small veranda. Rustic, characterful dining room with homemade cakes, breads and muesli at breakfast.

Russell's with rm
rest,
20 High St ✉ WR12 7DT – ☎ (01386) 853 555 – www.russellsofbroadway.co.uk
– Closed Sunday dinner except before bank holiday and bank holiday Mondays
7 rm – †£ 85/125 ††£ 115/300 Menu £ 14/27 – Carte £ 27/53
Attractive Cotswold stone house in the centre of the village, with a smart, modern, brasserie-style interior and both a front and rear terrace. Seasonal menus of modern dishes, with a well-priced set menu. Casual service. Stylish, modern bedrooms boast good facilities.

BROCKENHURST

Hampshire – Pop. 3 552 – See Regional map n°**6**-A2
London 99 mi – Bournemouth 17 mi – Southampton 14 mi – Winchester 27 mi
Michelin Road map 503-P31 and 504-P31 – Michelin Green Guide GREAT BRITAIN

ENGLAND

The Pig
Beaulieu Rd ✉ SO42 7QL – East : 1 mi on B 3055 – ☎ (01590) 622 354
– www.thepighotel.com
26 rm – †£ 139/269 ††£ 139/250
Rest *The Pig* – see restaurant listing
This smart manor house hotel follows a philosophy of removing barriers and bringing nature indoors. Characterful bedrooms are divided between the house and a stable block, and boast distressed wood floors, chunky furnishings and large squashy beds. The comfy lounges and dining room have a shabby-chic style.

New Park Manor
Lyndhurst Rd ✉ SO42 7QH – North : 1.5 mi on A 337 – ☎ (01590) 623 467
– www.newparkmanorhotel.co.uk
21 rm – †£ 115/195 ††£ 135/315 – 1 suite
Rest *The Stag* – Menu £ 39 – *(bar lunch)*
This elegantly proportioned former hunting lodge was built by Charles II on his return from France. Bedrooms fuse modern comforts with traditional features. Children are well-catered for with a crèche, a cinema and games rooms, while for adults there's an impressive spa. The restaurant offers relaxed dining.

Cloud
Meerut Rd ✉ SO42 7TD – ☎ (01590) 622 165 – www.cloudhotel.co.uk
– Closed 27 December-13 January
18 rm – †£ 119 ††£ 111/138
Rest *Encore* – Menu £ 17 (lunch) – Carte £ 16/30
Well-kept hotel made up of four cottages, set on the edge of a pretty New Forest village. It has a homely feel, from the cosy lounges to the immaculately kept bedrooms; a collection photos attest to the owner's past as a tiller girl. The theatrical-themed restaurant and conservatory offer traditional menus.

Cottage Lodge

Sway Rd ✉ S042 7SH – ☎ (01590) 622 296 – www.cottagelodge.co.uk – Closed 19-26 December

15 rm ☕ – †£ 50/110 ††£ 60/155

Rest *Fallen Tree* – Menu £ 21/26 – *(closed 1 week February, 1 week October-November and Wednesday) (dinner only) (booking essential)*

Cosy, low-ceilinged former forester's cottage in a charming village where New Forest ponies wander freely. Rustic furnishings include some four-poster beds made from local trees. Traditional, hearty dinners use organic produce. The building dates from 1650 and is part-constructed from a decommissioned ship.

Daisybank Cottage without rest

Sway Rd ✉ SO42 7SG – South : 0.5 mi on B 3055 – ☎ (01590) 622 086 – www.bedandbreakfast-newforest.co.uk

7 rm ☕ – †£ 90/120 ††£ 110/140

A charming Arts and Crafts house built in 1902. Modern bedrooms come with seating areas; one room opens onto an internal courtyard and another, onto a terrace. Aga-cooked breakfasts come in English, Irish and American versions.

The Pig – The Pig Hotel

Beaulieu Rd ✉ SO42 7QL – East : 1 mi on B 3055 – ☎ (01590) 622 354 – www.thepighotel.com

Menu £ 25/37

A delightful conservatory with plants dotted about, an eclectic collection of old tables and chairs, and a bustling atmosphere. The forager and kitchen gardener supply what's best and any ingredients they can't get themselves are sourced from within 25 miles. Cooking is unfussy, wholesome and British-based.

ENGLAND

BROMESWELL → See Woodbridge

Suffolk

BROUGHTON

North Yorkshire – See Regional map n°**22**-A2

London 228 mi – Sheffield 71 mi – Kingston upon Hull 94 mi – Derby 106 mi

Bull

✉ BD23 3AE – ☎ (01756) 792 065 – www.thebullatbroughton.com – Closed 25 December

Carte £ 19/40

Part of Ribble Valley Inns, a burgeoning pub company which proudly promotes local and very British ingredients and dishes. This solid, sizeable pub boasts log fires, beams and stone floors.

BROUGHTON GIFFORD

Wiltshire – See Regional map n°**4**-C2

London 109 mi – Bristol 31 mi – Cardiff 64 mi – Southampton 81 mi

The Fox

The Street ✉ SN12 8PN – ☎ (01225) 782 949 – www.thefox-broughtongifford.co.uk – Closed 26-27 December, 1-2 January, Sunday dinner and Monday

Menu £ 17 (weekday lunch) – Carte £ 27/47

Raising the profile of this pub, both locally and farther afield, has been a labour of love for its young owner. Cooking is simple, unfussy and fresh, and uses what's in the garden: salad leaves, fruits, chickens and pigs.

BRUNDALL

Norfolk – Pop. 4 019 – See Regional map n°**15**-D2

London 118 mi – Great Yarmouth 15 mi – Norwich 8 mi

Michelin Road map 504-Y26

Lavender House

39 The Street ✉ NR13 5AA – ✆ (01603) 712 215 – www.thelavenderhouse.co.uk – Closed 26 December-9 January, Sunday dinner and Monday-Wednesday
Menu £ 60 – *(dinner only and Sunday lunch) (booking advisable)*
Characterful thatched cottage with low beamed ceilings and inglenook fireplaces. Cooking has a rustic, north Italian style – good quality ingredients feature in gutsy dishes and flavours are clearly defined. They also run cookery courses.

BRUNTINGTHORPE

Leicestershire – See Regional map n°**16-B3**
London 96 mi – Leicester 10 mi – Market Harborough 15 mi
Michelin Green Guide GREAT BRITAIN

The Joiners

Church Walk ✉ LE17 5QH – ✆ (0116) 247 82 58 – www.thejoinersarms.co.uk – Closed Sunday dinner and Monday
Menu £ 17/22 – Carte £ 25/39 – *(booking essential)*
Neat and tidy whitewashed pub with a characterful low-beamed interior; run by an enthusiastic husband and wife team. Good value menus offer a mix of refined pub classics and brasserie-style dishes, cooked and presented in a straightforward manner. There's also a wide selection of wines by the glass.

BRUSHFORD → See Dulverton

Somerset – Michelin Road map 503-J30

BRUTON

Somerset – Pop. 2 984 – See Regional map n°**4-C2**
London 118 mi – Bristol 27 mi – Bournemouth 44 mi – Salisbury 35 mi
Michelin Road map 503-M30 and 504-M30

At The Chapel with rm

High St ✉ BA10 0AE – ✆ (01749) 814 070 – www.atthechapel.co.uk
8 rm – £ 100/250 £ 100/250 Carte £ 19/38 – *(booking advisable)*
Stylish, informal restaurant in a former 18C chapel, with a bakery to one side and a wine shop to the other. Well-priced, daily menus offer rustic, Mediterranean-influenced dishes; specialities include wood-fired breads, pizzas and cakes. Luxurious bedrooms have king-sized beds, 46" TVs and Egyptian cotton linen. Chic club lounge and cocktail bar opens at weekends.

BRYHER → See Scilly (Isles of)

– Michelin Road map 503-A/B34

BUCKDEN

Cambridgeshire – Pop. 2 385 – ✉ Huntingdon – See Regional map n°**14-A2**
London 65 mi – Bedford 15 mi – Cambridge 20 mi – Northampton 31 mi
Michelin Road map 504-T27

George

High St ✉ PE19 5XA – ✆ (01480) 812 300 – www.thegeorgebuckden.com
12 rm – £ 90/120 £ 90/120
Rest *Brasserie* – see restaurant listing
Delightfully restored, part black and white, part red-brick coaching inn. Original flag floors mix with modern furnishings, giving a stylish, understated feel. Tasteful, individually decorated bedrooms are named after famous Georges.

Brasserie – George Hotel

High St ✉ PE19 5XA – ✆ (01480) 812 300 – www.thegeorgebuckden.com
Menu £ 19 – Carte £ 29/41
Appealing, well-run brasserie in a stylish hotel, featuring a parquet floor, a glass skylight and a pleasant summer terrace. Monthly menus display a wide range of influences, from classic British dishes to those with a more global edge.

ENGLAND

BUCKHORN WESTON

Dorset – See Regional map n°**4**-**C3**

London 117 mi – Poole 36 mi – Bath 33 mi – Weymouth 37 mi

Stapleton Arms with rm

Church Hill ✉ SP8 5HS – ✆ (01963) 370 396 – www.thestapletonarms.com – Closed 25 December

4 rm – £ 70/90 £ 90/120 Carte £ 24/37

A welcoming, well-run pub with a homely, shabby-chic style. Menus showcase pub classics, with the occasional international influence, and snacks like pork pies can be wrapped up and taken home. Spacious bedrooms boast Egyptian cotton linen, smart bathrooms and a mix of modern and antique furnishings.

BUCKINGHAM

Buckinghamshire – Pop. 12 890 – See Regional map n°**11**-**C1**

London 64 mi – Birmingham 61 mi – Northampton 20 mi – Oxford 25 mi

Michelin Road map 503-Q27 and 504 – Michelin Green Guide GREAT BRITAIN

Villiers

rm, rest,

3 Castle St ✉ MK18 1BS – ✆ (01280) 822 444 – www.oxfordshire-hotels.co.uk

49 rm – £ 75/140 £ 90/160 – 4 suites

Rest *Villiers* – Menu £ 18 – Carte £ 23/37 – *(closed dinner 25 December)*

Proudly run hotel on a central street in a quaint market town. Bright, modern meeting rooms and a cosy lounge; the bar has a charming open fire. Bedrooms vary in style: all have modern facilities; some have original beams and some are duplex suites. The restaurant serves a mix of classical and modern dishes.

ENGLAND

BUCKLAND MARSH

Oxfordshire – Pop. 2 243 – See Regional map n°**10**-**A2**

London 76 mi – Faringdon 4 mi – Oxford 15 mi

Trout at Tadpole Bridge with rm

✉ SN7 8RF – ✆ (01367) 870 382 – www.troutinn.co.uk – Closed 25-26 December

6 rm – £ 85/100 £ 130/160 Carte £ 17/43

This pub's lawned gardens run down to the Thames; it has its own private moorings and an electric punt available for hire. Menus offer an appealing mix of British pub classics and Gallic influenced dishes, with plenty of fish and game in season. The spacious bedrooms are traditionally decorated.

BUDE

Cornwall – Pop. 5 091 – See Regional map n°**1**-**B2**

London 252 mi – Exeter 51 mi – Plymouth 50 mi – Truro 53 mi

Michelin Road map 503-G31 – Michelin Green Guide GREAT BRITAIN

Falcon

rest,

Breakwater Rd ✉ EX23 8SD – ✆ (01288) 352 005 – www.falconhotel.com – Closed 25 December

30 rm – £ 63/85 £ 125/145 – 1 suite

Rest – Carte £ 21/31 **s** – *(bar lunch Monday-Saturday)*

A formally run whitewashed hotel overlooking the Bude Canal; purportedly the oldest coaching house in North Cornwall. Homely, classically styled bedrooms have contemporary touches. The traditional restaurant and spacious bar are smartly dressed in red velour; look out for the old photos in the latter.

beach at bude without rest

Summerleaze Cres. ✉ EX23 8HL – ✆ (01288) 389 800 – www.thebeachatbude.co.uk – Closed 22 December-5 January

17 rm – £ 85/175 £ 95/185

Relaxed, spacious 'New England' style hotel with views over the Atlantic Ocean. Contemporary bedrooms have limed oak furnishings and all the latest mod cons. 'Deluxe' boast roll-top baths and a terrace or balcony; 'Premier' have sea views.

BUDLEIGH SALTERTON

Devon – Pop. 5 185 – See Regional map n°**2**-D2
London 182 mi – Exeter 16 mi – Plymouth 55 mi
Michelin Road map 503-K32

Heath Close

3 Lansdowne Rd ✉ EX9 6AH – West : 1 mi by B 3178 – ☎ (01395) 444 337 – www.heathclose.com

5 rm – †£ 85 ††£ 105 **Rest** – Carte £ 19/26

Smart detached house with a lovely rear garden. The open-plan lounge and dining room are stylish and modern. Good-sized bedrooms display personal touches and bathrooms have underfloor heating. The welcoming owners offer tea and cake on arrival and traditional home-cooked dinners on Friday and Saturday.

Rosehill (N) without rest

30 West Hill ✉ EX9 6BU – ☎ (01395) 444 031 – www.rosehillroomsandcookery.co.uk – Closed 25 December

4 rm – †£ 105/145 ††£ 105/145

After a tasty breakfast of French toast, eggs royale or smoked salmon, relax on the veranda, by the monkey puzzle tree. Bright, airy bedrooms come with king-sized beds and homemade treats. The owner also runs cookery courses.

Long Range without rest

5 Vales Rd ✉ EX9 6HS – by Raleigh Rd – ☎ (01395) 443 321 – www.thelongrangehotel.co.uk – Restricted opening in winter

9 rm – †£ 63/68 ††£ 100/138

Spotlessly kept guesthouse with a large garden, set on a quiet street. Choice of two lounges; one in a conservatory and complete with a small bar. Unfussy, brightly coloured bedrooms have good facilities; those to the rear can see the sea.

ENGLAND

BUNBURY

– Pop. 1 308 – ✉ Tarporley – See Regional map n°**20**-A3
London 183 mi – Birmingham 68 mi – Liverpool 39 mi – Sheffield 87 mi
Michelin Road map 502-M24

Yew Tree Inn

Long Ln, Spurstow ✉ CW6 9RD – ☎ (01829) 260 274 – www.theyewtreebunbury.com

Carte £ 20/40

Handsome, part red brick, part black and white timbered pub with a central bar and several smaller, rustic rooms. Extensive menus offer local and homemade produce. Regular themed events; try guest ales accompanied by British tapas on a Friday.

BUNGAY

Suffolk – Pop. 5 127 – See Regional map n°**15**-D2
London 108 mi – Beccles 6 mi – Ipswich 38 mi
Michelin Road map 504-Y26 – Michelin Green Guide GREAT BRITAIN

Castle Inn with rm

35 Earsham St ✉ NR35 1AF – ☎ (01986) 892 283 – www.thecastleinn.net – Closed 25 December, Sunday dinner and Monday in winter

4 rm – †£ 70/80 ††£ 90/100 Menu £ 19 (lunch) – Carte dinner £ 20/33

Sky-blue pub, formerly known as The White Lion, with an open-plan dining area and an intimate rear bar. Fresh, simple and seasonal country based cooking; the Innkeeper's platter of local produce is a perennial favourite. Tasty homemade cakes and cookies on display. Homely, comfortable bedrooms.

at Earsham Southwest: 3 mi by A144 and A143✉ Bungay

Earsham Park Farm without rest

Old Railway Rd ✉ NR35 2AQ – on A 143 – ✆ (01986) 892 180 – www.earsham-parkfarm.co.uk
3 rm – †£ 52/67 ††£ 82/105
Appealing red-brick farmhouse on a working farm. Country-style interior displays sculptures and stencilling by the charming owner. Individually styled bedrooms boast attractive furnishings. Extensive breakfasts include their own homemade bacon, sausages, preserves and muesli.

BURCOMBE

→ See Salisbury
Wiltshire

BURFORD

Oxfordshire – Pop. 1 171 – See Regional map n°**10**-A2
London 76 mi – Birmingham 55 mi – Gloucester 32 mi – Oxford 20 mi
Michelin Road map 503-P28 and 504

Bay Tree

Sheep St ✉ OX18 4LW – ✆ (01993) 822 791 – www.cotswold-inns-hotels.co.uk/baytree
21 rm – †£ 60/170 ††£ 80/190 – 3 suites
Rest – Menu £ 16/33 – Carte £ 25/39
Characterful, 16C, wisteria-clad house with low beamed ceilings and antique furnishings. Delightful bedrooms split between main house and adjacent cottage. Charming bar and lounges with vast stone fireplaces and a snack menu. Restaurant offers simple, modern dishes overlooking the beautiful landscaped garden.

Burford House

99 High St ✉ OX18 4QA – ✆ (01993) 823 151 – www.burfordhouse.co.uk – Closed 5-12 January
8 rm – †£ 95/180 ††£ 185/240
Rest *Centre Stage* – Menu £ 39 – *(closed dinner Sunday-Tuesday) (light lunch/dinner)*
The welcome is warm at this delightful 17C house, where comfortable bedrooms – including three four-posters – mix traditional styling with contemporary touches. A pair of cosy sitting rooms lead to the restaurant, which is decorated with framed posters from famous musicals and serves simple, modern dishes.

Bull with rm

105 High St ✉ OX18 4RG – ✆ (01993) 822 220 – www.bullatburford.co.uk
15 rm – †£ 65/120 ††£ 80/170 Menu £ 22 (lunch) – Carte £ 27/41
Sympathetically refurbished, 15C former inn on the high street; run with a hefty dose of Gallic charm. Characterful, open-fired reception and rustic, exposed stone walls. Tasty French cooking errs towards the classics, so expect terrines, smoked meats, and game in season. Cosy, characterful bedrooms.

Lamb Inn with rm

Sheep St ✉ OX18 4LR – ✆ (01993) 823 155 – www.cotswold-inns-hotels.co.uk/lamb
17 rm – †£ 155/265 ††£ 165/275 Menu £ 20/25 – Carte £ 25/46
Delightful collection of 15C weavers' cottages with a gloriously cosy feel. The elegant, candlelit dining room offers a tasting menu and an à la carte of classic dishes; a simpler menu is served in the bar and sitting rooms. Chatty service. Charming, individually furnished bedrooms; Rosie has a private garden.

Highway Inn with rm

117 High St ✉ OX18 4RG – ✆ (01993) 823 661 – www.thehighwayinn.co.uk – Closed 4-20 January and 24-26 December
10 rm – †£ 60/140 ††£ 90/140 Menu £ 15 – Carte £ 21/38
A family-run inn dating from 1480: full of charm and character, with beams, thick walls and an open fire. Cooking is simple, honest and traditionally based, with the emphasis on local produce. Individually designed bedrooms have a classical style and modern facilities; one has a four-poster bed.

at Swinbrook East: 2.75 mi by A40 ✉ Burford

Swan Inn with rm
✉ *OX18 4DY – ☎ (01993) 823 339 – www.theswanswinbrook.co.uk*
11 rm – £ 85/180 £ 100/180 Carte £ 19/38
Wisteria-clad, honey-coloured pub on the riverbank, boasting a lovely garden filled with fruit trees. The charming interior displays an open oak frame and exposed stone walls hung with old lithographs and handmade walking sticks. The daily menu showcases the latest local produce and features modern takes on older recipes. Well-appointed bedrooms have a luxurious feel.

BURNHAM MARKET

Norfolk – Pop. 877 – See Regional map n°**15-C1**
London 128 mi – Cambridge 71 mi – Norwich 36 mi
Michelin Road map 504-W25 – Michelin Green Guide GREAT BRITAIN

Hoste rest,
The Green ✉ *PE31 8HD – ☎ (01328) 738 777 – www.thehoste.com*
62 rm – £ 95/220 £ 115/240 – 6 suites
Rest – Carte £ 25/44 – *(booking advisable)*
Personally and passionately run inn, at the heart of a picturesque village. Stylish, luxurious bedrooms are split between the main building and two annexes, and there's a smart beauty and wellness spa in the wing. The extensive restaurant comprises an appealing bar, five dining rooms and a courtyard garden.

BURNSALL

North Yorkshire – Pop. 108 – ✉ Skipton – See Regional map n°**22-A2**
London 223 mi – Bradford 26 mi – Leeds 29 mi
Michelin Road map 502-O21

Devonshire Fell
✉ *BD23 6BT – ☎ (01756) 729 000 – www.devonshirefell.co.uk*
16 rm – £ 89/166 £ 139/249 **Rest** – Carte £ 24/46
Stone-built hotel – once a 19C gentleman's club for mill owners – set in a lovely hillside location and decorated with bold colours and striking, contemporary artwork. Spacious, modern bedrooms have dale views. Modern British menu served in the formal conservatory and funky, open-plan bar and bistro.

Red Lion with rm rest,
✉ *BD23 6BU – ☎ (01756) 720 204 – www.redlion.co.uk*
25 rm – £ 60/148 £ 83/158 Carte £ 21/41
Appealing stone inn on the riverbank with a cosy bar, laid-back lounge and a formally dressed dining room. Extensive menus offer pub favourites and local meat, fish and game, along with daily specials. Classic bedrooms have modern overtones; the annexe rooms are more contemporary.

BURPHAM → See Arundel

West Sussex – Michelin Road map 504-S30

BURRINGTON

Devon – Pop. 533 – See Regional map n°**2-C1**
London 260 mi – Barnstaple 14 mi – Exeter 28 mi – Taunton 50 mi
Michelin Road map 503-I31

Northcote Manor rm,
✉ *EX37 9LZ Northwest : 2 mi on A 377 – ☎ (01769) 560 501 – www.northcotemanor.co.uk*
16 rm – £ 120/180 £ 170/280 – 7 suites
Rest – Menu £ 23/45 – *(booking essential)*
Creeper-clad hall in the Torr Valley, dating from 1716. Fine fabrics and antiques feature in the elegant, individually styled rooms; well-judged attention to detail lends an air of idyllic calm. The country house restaurant features eye-catching murals.

ENGLAND

BURSCOUGH

Lancashire – See Regional map n°**20**-A2

London 215 mi – Liverpool 16 mi – Birmingham 101 mi

Michelin Road map 502-L23

Blue Mallard

Burscough Wharf, Liverpool Rd North ✉ L40 5RZ – ☎ (01704) 893 954 – www.thebluemallard.co.uk – Closed Monday dinner

Menu £ 14 (lunch and early dinner) – Carte £ 21/34

Beside the towpath you'll find a restored Victorian wharf filled with small artisan businesses and this unfussy first floor restaurant. Cooking is fresh, local and flavoursome, with a modern edge; the set menu offers great value.

BURTON BRADSTOCK → See Bridport

Dorset – Michelin Road map 503-L31

BURTON-UPON-TRENT

Staffordshire – Pop. 72 299 – See Regional map n°**19**-C1

London 128 mi – Birmingham 29 mi – Leicester 27 mi – Nottingham 27 mi

Michelin Road map 502-O25 and 503

99 Station Street

99 Station St ✉ DE14 1BT – ☎ (01283) 516 859 – www.99stationstreet.com – Closed Monday, Tuesday, Sunday dinner and Wednesday lunch

Menu £ 13 (lunch) – Carte £ 24/36

Amongst the vast brewing towers is this bright, boldly decorated neighbourhood restaurant, run by two experienced locals. They make everything on the premises daily and showcase regional ingredients; try the mature rare breed meats.

ENGLAND

BURY

Greater Manchester – Pop. 77 211 – See Regional map n°**20**-B2

London 211 mi – Leeds 45 mi – Liverpool 35 mi – Manchester 9 mi

Michelin Road map 502-N23 and 503

Waggon

131 Bury and Rochdale Old Rd, Birtle ✉ BL9 6UE – East : 2 mi on B 6222 – ☎ (01706) 622 955 – www.thewaggonatbirtle.co.uk – Closed 2 weeks summer, first week January, Monday and Tuesday

Menu £ 16 (lunch and early dinner) – Carte £ 20/41 – *(dinner only and lunch Thursday, Friday and Sunday)*

Unassuming former pub on a main road. The focus here is firmly on the food, which is well-cooked and well-priced. Classically based dishes change with the seasons; there's fresh fish daily, an excellent value midweek market menu and popular themed gourmet nights. A young team are guided by the charming owner.

BURY ST EDMUNDS

Suffolk – Pop. 41 113 – See Regional map n°**15**-C2

London 79 mi – Cambridge 27 mi – Ipswich 26 mi – Norwich 41 mi

Michelin Road map 504-W27 – Michelin Green Guide GREAT BRITAIN

Angel

3 Angel Hill ✉ IP33 1LT – ☎ (01284) 714 000 – www.theangel.co.uk

79 rm – †£ 95/185 ††£ 105/285 – 1 suite

Rest *Eaterie* – see restaurant listing

The creeper-clad Georgian façade hides a surprisingly stylish hotel. Relax in the atmospheric bar or smart lounges. Individually designed bedrooms offer either classic four-poster luxury or come with funky décor and iPod docks.

XX **Maison Bleue**

30-31 Churchgate St ✉ IP33 1RG – ✆ (01284) 760 623 – www.maisonbleue.co.uk – Closed 3 weeks January, 2 weeks summer, Sunday and Monday
Menu £ 19/34 – Carte £ 34/52
Passionately run neighbourhood restaurant in a converted 17C house, with a smart blue canopy, wooden panelling and impressive fish sculptures. Menus focus on seafood; cooking is modern in style but with classic influences and Gallic and Asian touches; you must try the excellent French cheeses.

X **Eaterie** – Angel Hotel

3 Angel Hill ✉ IP33 1LT – ✆ (01284) 714 000 – www.theangel.co.uk
Menu £ 18 (lunch) – Carte dinner £ 24/45
An airy two-roomed bistro in an attractive 15C coaching inn where Dickens once stayed. Impressive modern chandelier and display of the owner's contemporary art. Tasty, modern, British brasserie-style dishes use local produce.

X **Pea Porridge**

28-29 Cannon St ✉ IP33 1JR – ✆ (01284) 700 200 – www.peaporridge.co.uk – Closed 2 weeks summer, last week December, first week January, Sunday-Monday and lunch Tuesday
Menu £ 16 (weekdays) – Carte £ 25/36 – *(booking advisable)*
Run by an efficient team; a charming former bakery in two 19C cottages – keep an eye out for the old bread oven. Tasty country cooking is led by the seasons and has a strong Mediterranean bias. Biodynamic and organic old world wines feature. Its unusual name is a reference to the old town green.

at Ixworth Northeast: 7 mi by A143 ✉ Bury St Edmunds

XX **Theobalds**

68 High St ✉ IP31 2HJ – ✆ (01359) 231 707 – www.theobaldsrestaurant.co.uk – Closed 1 week early summer, Monday and dinner Sunday
Menu £ 28/34 – Carte approx. £ 37 – *(dinner only and lunch Friday and Sunday)*
Part-16C cottage in a charming village, with a cosy, fire-lit lounge and a beamed dining room. It's professionally run by a husband and wife and a jolly chef. Seasonal menus offer heartwarming, well-presented, traditional dishes.

at Whepstead South: 4.5 mi by A143 on B1066

White Horse 

Rede Rd ✉ IP29 4SS – ✆ (01284) 735 760 – www.whitehorsewhepstead.co.uk – Closed 1 week January, 25-26 December and Sunday dinner
Carte £ 23/33
Cheerfully run, 17C village pub; sit in a characterful beamed room, the brighter 'Gallery' displaying local artwork or a room opening onto the garden. The kitchen's strength is conventional dishes like fish and chips and homemade sausages.

at Horringer Southwest: 3 mi on A143 ✉ Bury St Edmunds

 **Ickworth**

✉ IP29 5QE – ✆ (01284) 735 350 – www.ickworthhotel.co.uk
39 rm – †£ 125/220 ††£ 175/275 – 12 suites
Rest *Frederick's* – Menu £ 42 **s** – *(dinner only)*
Rest *Conservatory* – Carte £ 18/41
Grand 200 year old mansion set in 1,800 acres: former home to the 7th Marquess of Bristol and now owned by the National Trust. The family-orientated hotel occupies the east wing and features huge, art-filled lounges, antique-furnished bedrooms and luxurious suites. Formal dining in Frederick's. Relaxed meals and high teas in the impressive former orangery.

BURYTHORPE → See Malton
North Yorkshire

BUSHEY

Hertfordshire – Pop. 25 328 – See Regional map n°**12-A2**
London 18 mi – Luton 21 mi – Watford 3 mi
Michelin Road map 504-S29

Plan: see Greater London (North-West) 1

XX **Alpine**

✉ *WD23 1JA – ✆ (020) 8950 2024* Town plan: BT**c**
– www.thealpinerestaurant.co.uk
Menu £ 21/24 – Carte £ 29/47
Long-standing family restaurant with low lighting, bold wallpaper and contemporary fabrics. Honest Italian menu displays influences from Sicily and Emilia-Romagna, ranging from family classics to more modern interpretations; homemade pasta.

BUTTERMERE

Cumbria – Pop. 139 – ✉ Cockermouth – See Regional map n°**21-A2**
London 306 mi – Carlisle 35 mi – Kendal 43 mi
Michelin Road map 502-K20

Wood House

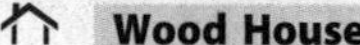

✉ *CA13 9XA Northwest : 0.5 mi on B 5289 – ✆ (017687) 70 208*
– www.wdhse.co.uk – March-October
3 rm – †£ 60/70 ††£ 120/140 **Rest** – Menu £ 29 **s**
Charming part-16C house with Victorian additions and lovely gardens, in a wonderfully serene lakeside setting. Welcoming owners, stunning views and no TVs to disturb the peace! Classical lounge and cosy dining room with communal antique table, silver cutlery and cut crystal glassware.

ENGLAND

BUXTON

Derbyshire – Pop. 22 115 – See Regional map n°**16-A1**
London 172 mi – Derby 38 mi – Manchester 25 mi – Stoke-on-Trent 24 mi
Michelin Road map 502-O24 and 503

Buxton's Victorian without rest

3A Broad Walk ✉ SK17 6JE – ✆ (01298) 78 759 – www.buxtonvictorian.co.uk
– Closed Christmas-New Year
4 rm – †£ 60/70 ††£ 86/104
Charming townhouse built in 1860 by the Duke of Devonshire, overlooking the boating lake and bandstand in the Pavilion Gardens. Traditional bedrooms are furnished with antiques and come with complimentary Buxton water and sherry.

CALLINGTON

Cornwall – Pop. 4 698 – See Regional map n°**2-C2**
London 237 mi – Exeter 53 mi – Plymouth 15 mi – Truro 46 mi
Michelin Road map 503-H32

Cadson Manor without rest

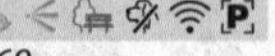

✉ *PL17 7HW Southwest : 2.75 mi by A 390 – ✆ (01579) 383 969*
– www.cadsonmanor.co.uk – Closed Christmas
4 rm – †£ 75 ††£ 115
Welcoming guesthouse on a 600 year old working farm, with views over an iron age settlement. Cosy, individually furnished bedrooms feature antiques, fresh flowers and a decanter of sherry. Rayburn-cooked breakfasts include weekly specials.

XX **Langmans**

3 Church St ✉ PL17 7RE – ✆ (01579) 384 933 – www.langmansrestaurant.co.uk
– Closed Sunday-Wednesday
Menu £ 40 – *(dinner only) (booking essential) (set menu only)*
Quaint, double-fronted shop conversion run by a husband and wife team. Pre-dinner drinks in the lounge are followed by a 6 course tasting menu in the formal rear dining room. Refined cooking with a good selection of Cornish cheeses.

CALNE

Wiltshire – Pop. 17 274 – See Regional map n°**4-C2**

London 91 mi – Bristol 33 mi – Southampton 63 mi – Swindon 17 mi

Michelin Road map 503-O29 and 504 – Michelin Green Guide THE WEST COUNTRY

Bowood

Derry Hill ✉ SN11 9PQ – West : 3 mi by A 4 on Derry Hill rd – ✆ (01249) 822 228 – www.bowood-hotel.co.uk

43 rm – †£ 140/310 ††£ 140/310

Rest *Shelburne* – Carte £ 27/50 – *(dinner only and Sunday lunch)*

Rest *Clubhouse Brasserie* – Carte £ 21/38

Smart, professionally run, purpose-built hotel in the grounds of Lord and Lady Lansdowne's Estate. Contemporary country house styling. Spacious bedrooms; some with balconies. Modern British cooking in formal Shelburne, with its attractive terrace. Brasserie menu served in the golf clubhouse.

at Compton Bassett Northeast: 4.5 mi by A4

White Horse Inn with rm

✉ SN11 8RG – ✆ (01249) 813 118 – www.whitehorse-comptonbassett.co.uk – Closed 2-9 January, Sunday dinner and Monday

8 rm – †£ 75/85 ††£ 85/95 Carte £ 25/40

A truly welcoming, 18C pub. The cosy bar has a wood burning stove and a jolly atmosphere and there's also a rustic dining room. All-encompassing menus offer everything from a croque monsieur to loin of venison from their own farm. Simply furnished, well-priced bedrooms are set across the large garden.

CAMBER → See Rye

East Sussex – Michelin Road map 504-W31

CAMBRIDGE

Cambridgeshire – Pop. 394 – See Regional map n°**14**-B3
London 55 mi – Coventry 88 mi – Ipswich 54 mi – Kingston-upon-Hull 137 mi
Michelin Road map 504-U27 – Michelin Green Guide GREAT BRITAIN

© Midsummer house

Hotels

ENGLAND

Hotel du Vin

rm,

15-19 Trumpington St ✉ CB2 1QA – ✆ (01223) 227 330 Town plan: Z**e**
– www.hotelduvin.com
41 rm – †£ 185/220 ††£ 205/255, ☐ £ 17
Rest *Bistro* – Menu £ 17 (weekdays) – Carte £ 27/50
Stylish hotel set over a row of 16C and 17C ex-university owned buildings. Original quarry tiled floors and wood-panelled walls feature, along with plenty of passages, nooks and crannies. Chic, modern bedrooms – one even has its own cinema. Clubby bar and an appealing brasserie with a Gallic-led menu.

Hotel Felix

Whitehouse Ln, Huntingdon Rd ✉ CB3 0LX – Northwest : 1.5 mi by A 1307 – ✆ (01223) 277 977 – www.hotelfelix.co.uk
52 rm ☐ – †£ 145/267 ††£ 250/314
Rest *Graffiti* – see restaurant listing
Set in 3 acres of gardens, a substantial Victorian mansion that was once a private house. Stylish, contemporary lounge and bar hung with modern art. Large, comfortable, boutique bedrooms with good mod cons; only four are in the main house.

Varsity H. & Spa

rm,

Thompson's Ln ✉ CB5 8AQ – ✆ (01223) 306 030 Town plan: Y**x**
– www.thevarsityhotel.co.uk
48 rm ☐ – †£ 149/395 ††£ 149/395 – 2 suites
Rest *River Bar Steakhouse & Grill* – Carte £ 27/46 **s** – *(dinner only and Saturday-Sunday lunch)*
Boutique hotel on banks of the River Cam. Smart spa, stylish roof terrace and tranquil lounge with complimentary drinks. Bedrooms have designer bathrooms; some boast coffee machines, fresh orchids and balconies. Informal restaurant set over two floors with a view of the Cam and a menu of steak and fish.

Can't choose between two similar establishments in the same town?
We list them in order of preference, within each category.

CAMBRIDGE

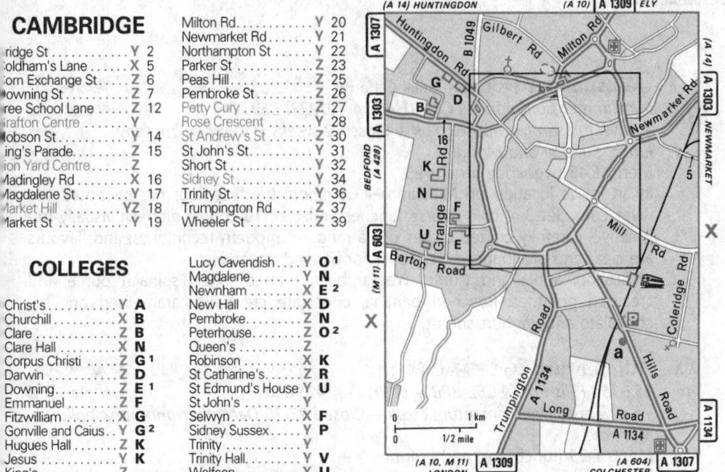

ridge St	Y	2
oldham's Lane	X	5
orn Exchange St	Z	6
owning St	Z	7
ree School Lane	Z	12
rafton Centre	Y	
obson St	Y	14
ing's Parade	Z	15
ion Yard Centre	Z	
ladingley Rd	X	16
lagdalene St	Y	17
larket Hill	YZ	18
larket St	Y	19
Milton Rd	Y	20
Newmarket Rd	Y	21
Northampton St	Y	22
Parker St	Z	23
Peas Hill	Z	25
Pembroke St	Z	26
Petty Cury	Z	27
Rose Crescent	Y	28
St Andrew's St	Z	30
St John's St	Y	31
Short St	Y	32
Sidney St	Y	34
Trinity St	Y	36
Trumpington Rd	Z	37
Wheeler St	Z	39

COLLEGES

Christ's	Y	A
Churchill	X	B
Clare	Y	B
Clare Hall	X	N
Corpus Christi	Z	G[1]
Darwin	Z	D
Downing	Z	E[1]
Emmanuel	Z	F
Fitzwilliam	X	G
Gonville and Caius	Y	G[2]
Hugues Hall	Z	K
Jesus	Y	K
King's	Z	
Lucy Cavendish	Y	O[1]
Magdalene	Y	N
Newnham	X	E[2]
New Hall	X	D
Pembroke	Z	N
Peterhouse	Z	O[2]
Queen's	Z	
Robinson	X	K
St Catharine's	Z	R
St Edmund's House	Y	U
St John's	Y	
Selwyn	X	F
Sidney Sussex	Y	P
Trinity	Y	
Trinity Hall	Y	V
Wolfson	X	U

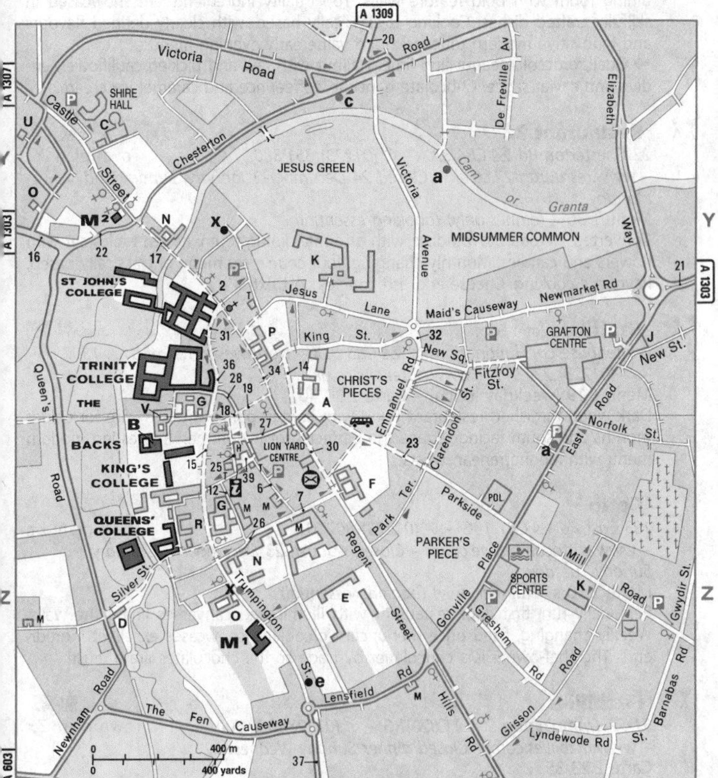

ENGLAND

Restaurants

Midsummer House (Daniel Clifford)

Midsummer Common ✉ CB4 1HA – ✆ (01223) 369 299 Town plan: Y**a**
– www.midsummerhouse.co.uk – Closed 2 weeks December, Tuesday lunch, Sunday and Monday
Menu £ 45 (weekday lunch)/95
In an idyllic location on Midsummer Common; the first floor bar overlooks the River Cam. Set 3, 4 or 5 course lunches and 6 or 10 course dinners: visually impressive, carefully crafted dishes use a range of modern techniques, and flavours are clear and pronounced. Service is formal and attentive.
→ Scallop, apple and truffle. Wagyu beef, braised oxtail, spinach purée and creamed potatoes. Poached banana, chocolate cremeux, caramelised brioche, chocolate and yoghurt sorbet.

Alimentum (Mark Poynton)

152-154 Hills Rd ✉ CB2 8PB – ✆ (01223) 413 000 Town plan: X**a**
– www.restaurantalimentum.co.uk – Closed 23-30 December and bank holiday Mondays
Menu £ 25 (lunch and early dinner)/49
Sleek, stylish restaurant with a spacious cocktail bar and a striking red & black dining room with bold feature walls. Top quality ingredients are showcased in skilfully crafted dishes. Cooking is classically based, with clearly defined flavours and innovative modern touches. Good value early evening menu.
→ Quail, broccoli, peanut and lime. Halibut with raw and pickled cauliflower, endive and caviar sauce. Chocolate ganache, toffee, rice and caramel ice cream.

ENGLAND

Restaurant 22

22 Chesterton Rd ✉ CB4 3AX – ✆ (01223) 351 880 Town plan: Y**c**
– www.restaurant22.co.uk – Closed 24 December-2 January, Sunday and Monday
Menu £ 36 – *(dinner only) (booking essential)*
Converted Victorian townhouse with a formal dining room; its ten tables set with flowers and candles. Monthly changing, four course set menu of classically based, flavourful cooking. Cheese and fish courses cost extra.

Graffiti – Hotel Felix

Whitehouse Ln, Huntingdon Rd ✉ CB3 0LX – Northwest : 1.5 mi by A 1307 – ✆ (01223) 277 977 – www.hotelfelix.co.uk
Menu £ 19 (weekday lunch) – Carte £ 30/40
Dark wood furnished restaurant hung with contemporary art. Cosy fire for colder months and south facing terrace the perfect spot in summer. Interesting modern menu with Mediterranean twists.

Cotto

183 East Rd ✉ CB1 1BG – ✆ (01223) 302 010 Town plan: Z**a**
– www.cottocambridge.co.uk – Closed August, 23 December-10 January, Sunday-Tuesday
Menu £ 50 **s** – *(dinner only) (booking essential)*
Personally run, first floor restaurant with illuminated canvasses lining the walls. Weekly changing, fixed price menu; classic cooking showcases excellent ingredients. The chef-owner is a chocolatier by trade so the chocolates are a must!

Fitzbillies

51-52 Trumpington St ✉ CB2 1RG – ✆ (01223) 352 500 Town plan: Z**x**
– www.fitzbillies.com – Closed dinner Sunday-Wednesday
Carte £ 23/35
1922 cake shop famed for its Chelsea buns; saved from closure and transformed into a stylish, modern eatery which retains its dark wood, art deco façade. Concise weekly menu offers simple, flavourful dishes. Excellent baked goods.

at Histon North: 3 mi on B1049 -(X)✉ Cambridge

XX **Phoenix**

20 The Green ✉ CB4 9JA – ✆ (01223) 233 766 – Closed 25-26 December
Menu £ 28 (lunch) – Carte £ 20/79
Smart Chinese restaurant within an old red-brick pub and overlooking the duck pond on the village green. The vast menu offers Cantonese, Malaysian and Thai dishes, along with plenty of Peking and Sichuan specialities. Friendly service.

at Horningsea Northeast: 4 mi by A1303 -(X)- and B1047 on Horningsea rd✉ Cambridge

Crown and Punchbowl with rm

High St ✉ CB25 9JG – ✆ (01223) 860 643 – www.thecrownandpunchbowl.com – Closed 26 December-1 January, dinner Sunday and bank holiday Monday
5 rm – †£ 80 ††£ 100 Carte £ 26/43
Homely dining pub with beams, open fires and chunky wood tables. Choose from the seasonal à la carte, daily specials or popular 'sausage board'. Cooking is sophisticated and ranges from a traditional blade of beef to more modern fish terrine. Relax on the terrace then head for one of the simple bedrooms.

at Madingley West: 4.5 mi by A1303 -(X)✉ Cambridge

Three Horseshoes

High St ✉ CB23 8AB – ✆ (01954) 210 221 – www.threehorseshoesmadingley.com
Carte £ 25/46 – *(booking advisable)*
Appealing thatched pub with a lively bar and more formal conservatory restaurant. Choose from the interesting bar menu or daily à la carte, which feature attractive modern dishes such as truffled mac and cheese or smoked eel with green tea.

at Little Wilbraham East: 7.25 mi by A1303 -(X)✉ Cambridge

Hole in the Wall

2 High St ✉ CB21 5JY – ✆ (01223) 812 282 – www.holeinthewallcambridge.com – Closed 2 weeks January, Sunday dinner, Monday and Tuesday lunch
Menu £ 16 (lunch) – Carte £ 24/44 – *(booking advisable)*
Charming 16C pub with a cosy, fire-lit, beamed bar. The regularly changing, seasonal menu offers European flavours presented in a modern fashion; dishes are prepared with zeal by the young chefs, one of whom was a past MasterChef finalist. Excellent value lunch menu. Heartwarming, classical desserts.

ENGLAND

CANTERBURY

Kent – Pop. 54 880 – See Regional map n°**9-D2**
London 59 mi – Brighton 76 mi – Dover 15 mi – Maidstone 28 mi
Michelin Road map 504-X30 – Michelin Green Guide GREAT BRITAIN

Abode Canterbury

30-33 High St ✉ CT1 2RX – ✆ (01227) 766 266 – www.michaelcaines.com Town plan: Y**a**
72 rm – †£ 95/500 ††£ 95/500, £ 12 – 1 suite
Rest *Michael Caines* – see restaurant listing
Centrally located former coaching inn; heavily beamed, yet with a stylish, boutique feel. Comfy champagne bar and atmospheric first floor lounge. Contemporary bedrooms come in 4 categories: 'Enviable' and 'Fabulous' are the most luxurious.

Magnolia House without rest

36 St Dunstan's Terr. ✉ CT2 8AX – ✆ (01227) 765 121 – www.magnoliahousecanterbury.co.uk – Closed 23-30 December Town plan: Y**s**
6 rm – †£ 50/55 ††£ 95/125
Whitewashed Georgian house on a quiet residential street close to town. The breakfast room overlooks an attractive walled garden. Smart, compact bedrooms are classically styled and come with fridges; one also has a four-poster bed.

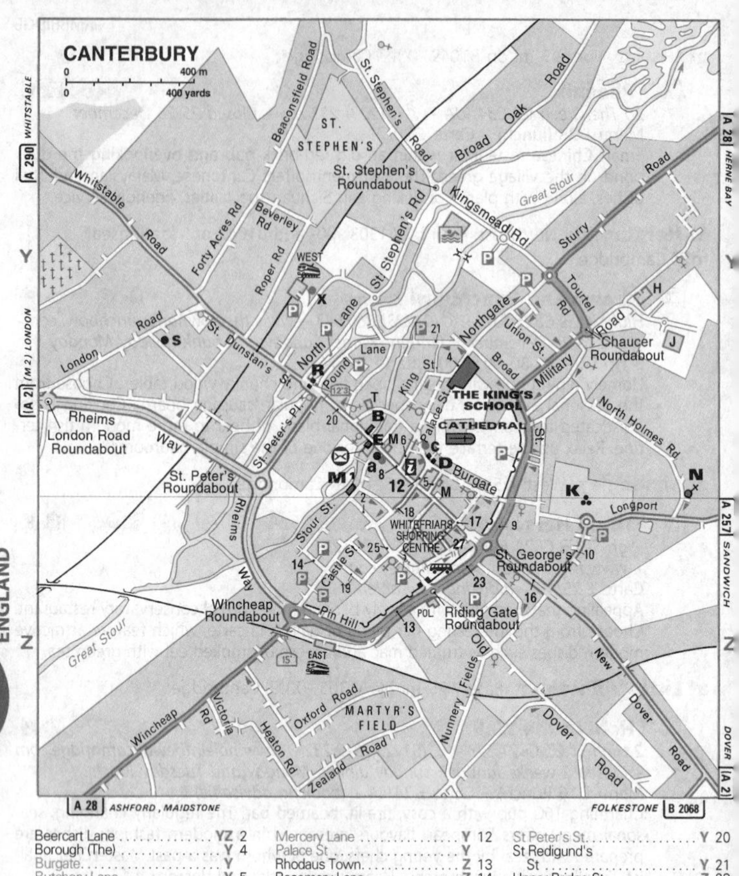

XX **Deesons**

25-27 Sun St ✉ CT1 2HX – ✆ (01227) 767 854 Town plan: Y**c**
– www.deesonsrestaurant.co.uk – Closed 25-26 December
Menu £ 14 (lunch) – Carte £ 27/42
Charming building in the shadow of the cathedral. The rustic interior consists of several different areas with old wood furnishings and funky modern wallpaper. Hearty British cooking uses ingredients from the owner's smallholding.

XX **Michael Caines** – Abode Canterbury Hotel

High St ✉ CT1 2RX – ✆ (01227) 826 684 Town plan: Y**a**
– www.michaelcaines.com – Closed Sunday dinner
Menu £ 18 (lunch) – Carte £ 30/41
Spacious, modern restaurant divided in two by a smart, glass-walled wine cellar. Accomplished, contemporary cooking is stylishly presented, with classic combinations of ingredients interpreted in a modern fashion. Private chef's table.

Goods Shed

Station Rd West, St Dunstans ✉ *CT2 8AN – ✆ (01227) 459 153 – www.thegoodsshed.net – Closed 25-26 December, 1-2 January, Sunday dinner and Monday* Town plan: Y**x**

Carte £ 26/42

Daily farmers' market and food hall in an early Victorian locomotive shed, selling an excellent variety of organic, free range and homemade produce. Hearty, rustic, daily changing dishes are served at scrubbed wooden tables.

at Lower Hardres South: 3 mi on B2068 -(Z)✉ Canterbury

Granville

Street End ✉ *CT4 7AL – ✆ (01227) 700 402 – www.thegranvillecanterbury.com – Closed 25 December, Sunday dinner and Monday*

Menu £ 18 (weekday lunch) – Carte £ 27/39

Sizeable, family-run pub with a Scandinavian-style, open-plan interior. The constantly evolving blackboard menu offers generous portions of unfussy, traditional dishes; veg is from their allotment.

CARBIS BAY → See St Ives

Cornwall – Michelin Road map 503-D33

CARLISLE

Cumbria – Pop. 75 306 – See Regional map n°**21**-B1

▶London 317 mi – Blackpool 95 mi – Edinburgh 101 mi – Glasgow 100 mi

Michelin Road map 501-L19 and 502 – Michelin Green Guide GREAT BRITAIN

ENGLAND

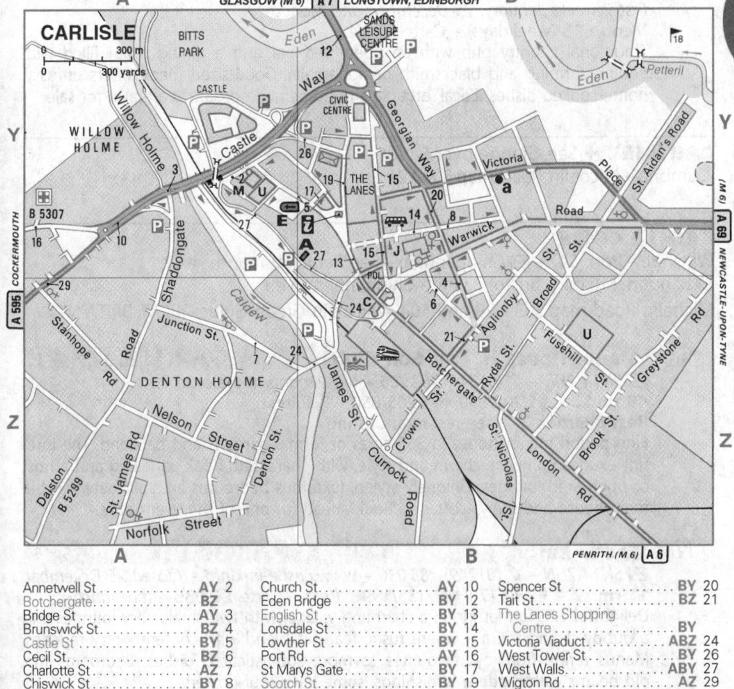

Annetwell St . . . AY 2
Botchergate . . . BZ
Bridge St . . . AY 3
Brunswick St . . . BZ 4
Castle St . . . BY 5
Cecil St . . . BZ 6
Charlotte St . . . AZ 7
Chiswick St . . . BY 8
Church St . . . AY 10
Eden Bridge . . . BY 12
English St . . . BY 13
Lonsdale St . . . BY 14
Lowther St . . . BY 15
Port Rd . . . AY 16
St Marys Gate . . . BY 17
Scotch St . . . BY 19
Spencer St . . . BY 20
Tait St . . . BZ 21
The Lanes Shopping Centre . . . BY
Victoria Viaduct . . . ABZ 24
West Tower St . . . BY 26
West Walls . . . ABY 27
Wigton Rd . . . AZ 29

Number Thirty One without rest
31 Howard Pl ✉ CA1 1HR – ✆ (01228) 597 080 Town plan: BY**a**
– www.number31.co.uk
4 rm – £ 65 £ 85
Terraced Victorian townhouse with bay windows, a sumptuous lounge filled with memorabilia and a plant-strewn terrace. Smart period style throughout. Warm, welcoming bedrooms are comfortably and individually furnished; 'Ruby' is the best.

at Warwick-on-Eden East: 4.5 mi by A69 -(BY)

Warwick Hall without rest
✉ CA4 8PG Northeast : 0.25 mi on A 69 – ✆ (01228) 561 546 – www.warwickhall.org
9 rm – £ 90/110 £ 128/135
Impressive sandstone house in a 270 acre riverside setting. The extremely spacious interior includes a charming lobby and an elegant drawing room. A sweeping stone staircase leads to period-furnished bedrooms – some with kitchens.

CARLYON BAY → See St Austell

Cornwall – Michelin Road map 503-F33

CARTHORPE

North Yorkshire – See Regional map n°**22-B1**
London 228 mi – Leeds 49 mi – Middlesbrough 40 mi – York 34 mi

ENGLAND

Fox and Hounds
✉ DL8 2LG – ✆ (01845) 567 433 – www.foxandhoundscarthorpe.co.uk – Closed first 2 weeks January, 25 December, and Monday
Menu £ 15 (weekdays) – Carte £ 21/42
Traditional country pub with an open-fired bar and a dining room filled with equine, farming and blacksmith paraphernalia. Good-sized menu offers unfussy, home-cooked dishes. Local, organic and homemade products are also for sale.

CARTMEL → See Grange-over-Sands

Cumbria – Michelin Road map 502-L21

CASTLE COMBE

Wiltshire – Pop. 347 – ✉ Chippenham – See Regional map n°**4-C2**
London 110 mi – Bristol 23 mi – Chippenham 6 mi
Michelin Road map 503-N29 and 504 – Michelin Green Guide GREAT BRITAIN

Manor House H. and Golf Club
✉ SN14 7HR – ✆ (01249) 782 206 – www.manorhouse.co.uk
48 rm – £ 205/850 £ 205/850 – 7 suites
Rest *Bybrook* – see restaurant listing
Fine period manor house in 365 acres of formal gardens and parkland. The interior exudes immense charm and style, with characterful oak panelling and a host of open-fired lounges. Uniquely styled, luxurious bedrooms are split between the main house and mews cottages. Book ahead for one of the event days.

Castle Inn
✉ SN14 7HN – ✆ (01249) 783 030 – www.castle-inn.info – Closed 25 December
11 rm – £ 80/170 £ 135/199 **Rest** – Carte £ 22/36 – *(bar lunch)*
Delightful 12C former inn in a charming village, with two small, cosy lounges and a pubby dining room – where rustic features blend with contemporary touches. Menus range from old favourites to more sophisticated dishes. Bedrooms mix old beams with modern furnishings; some have four-posters.

Bybrook – Manor House Hotel and Golf Club

✉ SN14 7HR – ☎ (01249) 782 206 – www.manorhouse.co.uk

Menu £ 25 (weekday lunch)/74 – *(closed Monday and Tuesday lunch)*

Spacious dining room within a charming 14C manor house, in 365 acres of formal gardens and parkland. Large, well-spaced tables are immaculately laid. Menus offer refined, carefully prepared dishes with a classical base and modern overtones, and feature local and kitchen garden produce. Smooth service.

→ Scallops with apple, walnut, cauliflower and pickled shallot. Slow-cooked rump of lamb, cauliflower couscous, golden raisins and chocolate. Burnt butter parfait, green apple sorbet, apple crisp.

CASTLE DONINGTON

Leicestershire – Pop. 6 416 – ✉ Derby – See Regional map n°**16**-**B2**

London 121 mi – Leeds 82 mi – Sheffield 52 mi – Manchester 96 mi

Michelin Road map 502-P25 and 503

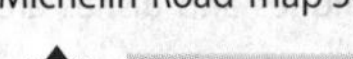

Radisson Blu East Midlands Airport

Herald Way, Pegasus Business Pk ✉ DE74 2TZ – Southeast : 4 mi by A 453 – ☎ (01509) 670 575 – www.radissonblu.com

218 rm – †£ 69/179 ††£ 69/179, ☕ £ 18 – 1 suite

Rest *Runway Brasserie* – Menu £ 26 – Carte £ 25/44 – *(bar lunch)*

An ultra-modern airport hotel with admirable green credentials and a well-equipped gym. Spacious bedrooms have feature walls, modern facilities and good soundproofing; some boast runway views. A European menu is served in the light, airy restaurant; watch the planes taking off and landing while you dine.

CASTLE EDEN

Durham – See Regional map n°**24**-**B3**

London 265 mi – Newcastle upon Tyne 28 mi – York 62 mi

Castle Eden Inn

Stockton Rd ✉ TS27 4SD – ☎ (01429) 835 137 – www.castleedeninn.com

Menu £ 18 (lunch) – Carte £ 22/46

A former coaching inn on what was once the main road to London: local gossip says that Dick Turpin was once tied up outside! The experienced owners offer a wide choice of dishes and the 'monthly specials' menu offers great value.

CATEL/CASTEL → See Channel Islands (Guernsey)

– Michelin Road map 503-P33

CERNE ABBAS

Dorset – See Regional map n°**4**-**C3**

London 132 mi – Bristol - 60 mi – Cardiff 115 mi – Southampton 58 mi

Michelin Road map 503-M31

New Inn with rm

14 Long St ✉ DT2 7JF – ☎ (01300) 341 274 – www.thenewinncerneabbas.co.uk – Closed 25-26 December

12 rm ☕ – †£ 80/155 ††£ 95/180 Carte £ 28/43

Sizeable 16C flint-faced pub set in picture postcard village, with exposed beams, a landscaped courtyard and a vast orchard garden. Freshly prepared, ably cooked dishes make good use of locally sourced produce. Bedrooms are stylish: some are in the main pub and others are in the converted stable block.

CHADDESLEY CORBETT

Worcestershire – Pop. 1 440 – See Regional map n°**18**-**B2**

London 123 mi – Birmingham 26 mi – Leicester 62 mi – Coventry 35 mi

Michelin Road map 503-N26 and 504

Brockencote Hall

✉ *DY10 4PY On A 448 – ✆ (01562) 777 876 – www.brockencotehall.com*
21 rm – £ 115/345 £ 135/365
Rest *The Chaddesley* – see restaurant listing
Professionally run 19C mansion with the feel of a French château; its long driveway leads past a lake and grazing cattle. Inside, period features blend well with contemporary country house furnishings and bold colour schemes. Bedrooms are spacious and well-equipped and some have pleasant park views.

The Chaddesley – Brockencote Hall Hotel

✉ *DY10 4PY On A 448 – ✆ (01562) 777 876 – www.brockencotehall.com*
Menu £ 30/60 **s**
Elegant restaurant in an impressive 19C mansion. Smartly laid tables overlook the gardens; in summer, head for the terrace. Accomplished cooking relies on classic combinations but uses modern techniques and dishes are nicely presented.

CHADWICK END

West Midlands – See Regional map n°**19-C2**
London 106 mi – Birmingham 13 mi – Leicester 40 mi – Stratford-upon-Avon 16 mi
Michelin Road map 503-O26 and 504

ENGLAND

Orange Tree

Warwick Rd ✉ B93 0BN – on A 4141 – ✆ (01564) 785 364 – www.lovelypubs.co.uk
Menu £ 14 – Carte £ 18/44 – *(booking advisable)*
This impressively smart pub has a unique style: cosy, rustic and contemporary by turns, with a bit of kitsch thrown in for good measure. Expect global influences alongside the more traditional pizza, pie or risotto.

CHAGFORD

Devon – Pop. 1 020 – See Regional map n°**2-C2**
London 218 mi – Exeter 17 mi – Plymouth 27 mi
Michelin Road map 503-I31 – Michelin Green Guide GREAT BRITAIN

Gidleigh Park

✉ *TQ13 8HH Northwest : 2 mi by Gidleigh Rd – ✆ (01647) 432 367 – www.gidleigh.co.uk – Closed 4-16 January*
23 rm – £ 325 £ 350 – 1 suite
Rest *Gidleigh Park* ✿✿ – see restaurant listing
Impressive black & white timbered Arts and Crafts house with lovely mature gardens and Teign Valley views. Luxurious lounges and drawing rooms have a classical country house feel but a contemporary edge. Wonderfully comfortable bedrooms echo this and come in an appealing mix of styles. Superb service.

Gidleigh Park (Michael Caines) – Gidleigh Park Hotel

✿✿

✉ *TQ13 8HH Northwest : 2 mi by Gidleigh Rd – ✆ (01647) 432 367 – www.gidleigh.co.uk – Closed 4-16 January*
Menu £ 44/140 – *(booking essential)*
Formal, three-roomed restaurant in a beautifully restored Edwardian house in 100 acres of parkland. Classical French menus showcase top quality local produce and vegetables from the kitchen garden in skilfully prepared combinations; the tasting menu features Michael Caines' signature dishes. Superb wine list.
→ Scallops, celeriac purée with a soy and truffle vinaigrette. Dartmoor lamb, boulangère potatoes and confit shoulder, fennel purée and a tapenade jus. Banana parfait, lime and butterscotch sauce, salted peanuts and lime sorbet.

at Sandypark Northeast: 2.25 mi on A382 ✉ Chagford

Mill End

✉ *TQ13 8JN On A 382 – ✆ (01647) 432 282 – www.millendhotel.com – Closed 5-21 January*
15 rm – £ 75/195 £ 90/210 – 1 suite
Rest – Menu £ 16 (lunch) – Carte £ 26/37
Whitewashed former mill off a quiet country road: once home to Frank Whittle, inventor of the jet engine. Comfy, cosy lounges with beams and open fires. Contemporary bedrooms have bold feature walls and colourful throws. Bright dining room offers classical dishes prepared using local produce.

Parford Well without rest

✉ *TQ13 8JW On Drewsteignton rd – ✆ (01647) 433 353 – www.parfordwell.co.uk – restricted opening in winter*
3 rm – £ 65/100 £ 85/105
Well-kept guesthouse with superb mature gardens. Homely lounge with a wood-burning stove, books and games. Two small breakfast rooms; one communal and one with a table for two. Individually decorated bedrooms offer pleasant country views.

at Easton Northeast: 1.5 mi on A382 ✉ Chagford

Easton Court without rest

Easton Cross ✉ TQ13 8JL – ✆ (01647) 433 469 – www.easton.co.uk
5 rm – £ 55/70 £ 70/85
This Devonshire Longhouse was once a regular haunt of writer Evelyn Waugh. Some of the spacious, simply styled bedrooms look out over the grounds. The sun rises over the hills in the summer, so breakfast in the garden is a must.

ENGLAND

CHANNEL TUNNEL ➜ See Folkestone

Kent – Michelin Road map 504-X30

CHANNEL ISLANDS

See Regional map n°**5**-B2

Michelin Road map 503-L/M33 – Michelin Green Guide GREAT BRITAIN

© Ormer by Shaun Rankin

ALDERNEY

Alderney – Pop. 2 400 – Michelin Road map 503-M33 – See Regional map n°**5**-B1

ENGLAND

BRAYE

Alderney

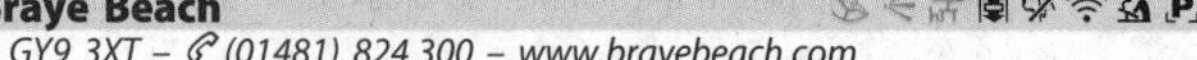

Braye Beach

✉ *GY9 3XT – ☎ (01481) 824 300 – www.brayebeach.com*

27 rm – †£ 90/180 ††£ 100/220 **Rest** – Menu £ 21/25

Stylish hotel on Braye beach, just a stone's throw from the harbour. The vaulted basement houses two lounges and a 19-seater cinema; above is a modern bar with a delightful terrace. Bedrooms are beech-furnished, and some have balconies and bay views. The formal restaurant showcases local island seafood.

GUERNSEY

Guernsey – Pop. 58 867 – Michelin Road map 503-L32 – See Regional map n°**5**-A2

CATEL/CASTEL

Cobo Bay rest,

Cobo Coast Rd ✉ GY5 7HB – ☎ (01481) 257 102 – www.cobobayhotel.com

34 rm – †£ 59/215 ††£ 99/215 **Rest** – Carte £ 27/57

Modern hotel set on the peaceful side of the island and well run by the 3rd generation of the family. Bright, stylish bedrooms come with fresh fruit, irons, safes and bathrobes – some have large balconies overlooking the sandy bay. Smart dining room; sit on the spacious terrace for lovely sunset views.

FERMAIN BAY

Fermain Valley rest,

Fermain Ln ✉ GY1 1ZZ – ☎ (01481) 235 666 – www.fermainvalley.com

45 rm – †£ 60/220 ††£ 125/235

Rest *Ocean* – see restaurant listing

Rest *Rock Garden Steakhouse* – Carte £ 24/54 – *(dinner only) (booking essential)*

Stylish hotel with beautiful gardens, hidden in a picturesque valley and affording pleasant bay views through the trees. Well-equipped bedrooms are widely dispersed; the 'Gold' rooms have balconies. Dine with a view in Ocean or from a steakhouse menu – accompanied by cocktails – in contemporary Rock Garden.

XX **Ocean** – Fermain Valley Hotel
Fermain Ln ✉ GY1 1ZZ – ☎ (01481) 235 666 – www.fermainvalley.com
Menu £ 18 (weekday lunch)/25 **s** – Carte £ 24/43 **s**
Informal hotel restaurant with a beautiful multi-level terrace and lovely sea views; a great spot for breakfast or afternoon tea. Menus champion seafood from local waters but there are choices 'from the field' and 'from the garden' too.

St Martin

St Peter Port 2 mi

Bella Luce
La Fosse ✉ GY4 6EB – ☎ (01481) 238 764 – www.bellalucehotel.com – April-December
23 rm – £ 99/162 £ 110/220
Rest *Bella Luce* – Menu £ 27 – Carte £ 24/47
Originally a Norman manor house; now a hotel with a cosy beamed bar, a cellar-like lounge and a stylish, intimate interior featuring voluptuous velvets. Opulent bedrooms have modern bathrooms and the pleasant gardens come with a pool. The restaurant offers an eclectic array of modern dishes.

La Barbarie
Saints Bay ✉ GY4 6ES – ☎ (01481) 235 217 – www.labarbariehotel.com – March-October
31 rm – £ 85/100 £ 90/150 – 1 suite
Rest – Menu £ 19 (weekday lunch)/25 – Carte £ 24/36
Attractive, stone-built former priory with an outdoor swimming pool and a cosy, cottagey style. Bedrooms are a mix of classical and modern styles; pay the extra for a spacious, newer room. Characterful bar and lounge with oak beams and an open fire. Traditional dining room features plenty of seafood dishes.

XX **Auberge**
Jerbourg Rd ✉ GY4 6BH – ☎ (01481) 238 485 – www.theauberge.gg – Closed 24 December-1 February and Sunday dinner
Menu £ 13 (weekdays)/23 – Carte £ 26/42 – *(booking essential)*
Long-standing restaurant in a great location. Simple interior with a bar and well-spaced tables; concertina doors open onto a lovely terrace, which offers views across to the other islands. Classical menu features plenty of island seafood.

St Peter Port

Michelin Green Guide GREAT BRITAIN

Old Government House H. & Spa rm,
St Ann's Pl ✉ GY1 2NU – ☎ (01481) 724 921 – www.theoghhotel.com
Town plan: Y**a**
62 rm – £ 193/218 £ 230/510 – 1 suite
Rest *The Curry Room at The Governors* – Menu £ 35
Rest *Brasserie* – ☎ (01481) 738 604 – Carte £ 30/40
Fine, classically furnished 18C building, with many of its original features restored, including a glorious ballroom. Individually styled bedrooms have padded walls, modern bathrooms and a personal touch. Relax in the well-equipped spa or outdoor pool. Authentic Indian cooking in The Curry Room. The smart yet informal brasserie has a delightful terrace.

Duke of Richmond rm,
Cambridge Pk. ✉ GY1 1UY – ☎ (01481) 726 221 – www.dukeofrichmond.com
Town plan: Y**s**
73 rm – £ 145/175 £ 145/175 – 1 suite
Rest *Leopard* – ☎ (01481) 740 866 – Carte £ 26/46 **s**
Contemporary hotel with a bright reception area and a stylish lounge ideal for afternoon tea. Smart, modern bedrooms; some with balconies. Relax in the secluded pool or on the patio overlooking the 19C Candie Gardens. A chic bar with leopard print furnishings leads to the restaurant and terrace.

ENGLAND

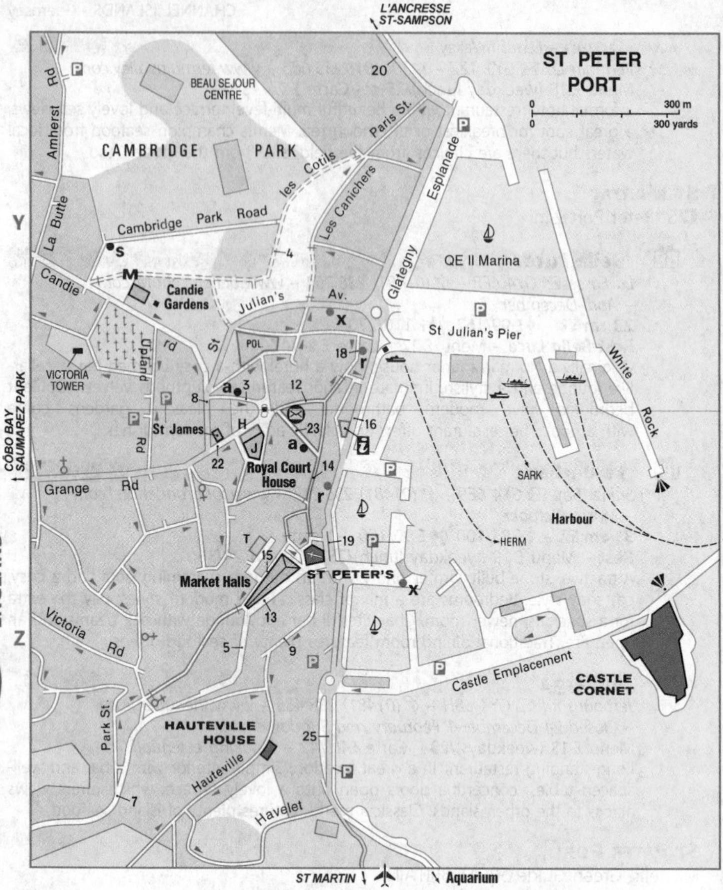

ST PETER PORT

Ann's Place . . . . . Y 3	Forest Lane . . . . . Y 12	Quay (The) . . . . . Z 19
Beauregard Lane . . . . . Y 4	Fountain Street . . . . . Z 13	St-George's Esplanade . . . . . Y 20
Bordage . . . . . Z 5	High Street . . . . . Z 14	St-James Street . . . . . Z 22
Charroterie . . . . . Z 7	Market Street . . . . . Z 15	Smith Street . . . . . Z 23
College Street . . . . . YZ 8	North Esplanade . . . . . YZ 16	South Esplanade . . . . . Z 25
Cornet Street . . . . . Z 9	Pollet . . . . . Y 18	

Duke of Normandie

Lefebvre St ✉ *GY1 2JP* – ✆ *(01481) 721 431* Town plan: Z**a**
– *www.dukeofnormandie.com*

37 rm ☕ – 🚹£ 49/70 🚹🚹£ 99/150 **Rest** – Carte £ 19/39 – *(dinner only)*

Superbly located in the centre of town, with a small private car park and access to a nearby leisure club. Modern, designer bedrooms display bright colours and have a comfy, cosy feel; some are set in the courtyard. The large bar is decorated with maritime memorabilia; the brasserie offers an accessible menu.

Is breakfast included? If it is, the cup symbol ☕ appears after the number of rooms.

XX **Nautique**

Quay Steps ✉ GY1 2LE – ✆ (01481) 721 714 Town plan: Z**r**
– www.lenautiquerestaurant.co.uk – Closed Saturday lunch and Sunday
Menu £ 16 (lunch) – Carte £ 29/57
Quayside former warehouse with a pleasant marina view and a characterful, nautically themed interior; ask for a window seat. Large menu of generously sized, classic dishes, with fish a feature.

XX **Pier 17**

Albert Pier ✉ GY1 1AD – ✆ (01481) 720 823 Town plan: Z**x**
– www.pier17restaurant.com – Closed 25-26 December and Sunday
Carte £ 25/37
Set at the end of a substantial stone pier in the centre of Guernsey harbour. The conservatory extension affords superb water views and the two terraces catch the last of the sun's rays. Tasty, traditionally based, seasonal dishes.

XX **Red**

61 Le Poulet ✉ GY1 1WL – ✆ (01481) 700 299 Town plan: Y**r**
– www.red.gg – Closed 25 December, Saturday lunch and Sunday
Menu £ 19 (lunch) – Carte £ 21/46 – *(booking essential)*
Harbourfront restaurant run by an experienced owner, with a large bar and formal cocktail lounge. Its name refers to red meat – with the large menu focusing on top quality Scottish chargrilled steaks – and red wines, which are a feature.

Swan Inn

St Julian's Ave ✉ GY1 1WA – ✆ (01481) 728 969 – Closed 25 December, Sunday in winter and bank holiday Mondays Town plan: Y**x**
Carte £ 19/32
Smart Victorian pub with a bottle-green façade, a traditional bar complete with a coal fire and a formal first floor dining room. The same menu is served throughout, offering plenty of choice, with hearty main courses and nursery puddings.

St Saviour

St Peter Port 4 mi

Farmhouse

Route des Bas Courtils ✉ GY7 9YF – ✆ (01481) 264 181 – www.thefarmhouse.gg
14 rm – £ 139/279 £ 139/279 **Rest** – Carte £ 23/48
Former farm restyled in a boutique vein. Stylish, sumptuous bedrooms come with hi-tech amenities and the bathrooms have heated floors. The pleasant garden features a pool, a terrace and a kitchen garden. Contemporary cooking has an international edge and uses the island's finest produce in eclectic ways.

Kings Mills

Fleur du Jardin with rm

Grand Moulins ✉ GY5 7JT – ✆ (01481) 257 996 – www.fleurdujardin.com – Closed dinner 25 December and 1 January
13 rm – £ 55/90 £ 65/120 – 2 suites Menu £ 13/16 – Carte £ 23/35
Attractive inn with a stylish terrace, lovely landscaped gardens and several charming, adjoining rustic rooms. The menu ranges from homemade burgers to sea bass and tasty island seafood specials. Stylish bedrooms have a New England theme, and there's even a heated outdoor pool.

HERM

Herm – Michelin Road map 503-M33 – See Regional map n°**5-A2**

White House

✉ GY1 3HR – ✆ (01481) 750 075 – www.herm.com – April-September
40 rm (dinner included) – £ 98/170 £ 190/300
Rest *Conservatory* – Menu £ 17/30 – Carte £ 43/48 – *(booking essential)*
Rest *Ship Inn* – Carte £ 19/35 – *(booking advisable)*
The only hotel on this tranquil, car-free island. Comfy, airy bedrooms are split between the house and various annexes; there are no clocks, TVs or radios. The open-fired lounge offers bay and island views; vast tropical gardens come with tennis courts and a pool. Traditional dining room offers plenty of seafood; popular pub-cum-brasserie serves more modern dishes.

JERSEY

C.I. – Pop. 85 150 – Michelin Road map 503-L33 – See Regional map n°**5-B2**

BEAUMONT

XX **Mark Jordan at the Beach**

La Plage, La Route de la Haule ✉ JE3 7YD – ✆ (01534) 780 180 – www.markjordanatthebeach.com – Closed 5-20 January

Menu £ 25/28 – Carte £ 28/58

Modern brasserie with a small lounge and bar; a paved terrace with bay views; and a dining room with heavy wood tables, modern seashore paintings and animal ornaments. Menus showcase island produce and fish from local waters. Cooking is refined but hearty, mixing tasty brasserie and restaurant style dishes.

GOREY

St Helier 4 mi

Michelin Green Guide GREAT BRITAIN

Moorings rest,

Gorey Pier ✉ JE3 6EW – ✆ (01534) 853 633 – www.themooringshotel.com

15 rm – £ 66/131 £ 82/163

Rest *Walker's* – see restaurant listing

Rest *Walker's Bistro* – Carte £ 26/43

Keenly run hotel below the ramparts of Mont Orgueil castle, overlooking the harbour. Leather-furnished first floor lounge. Modern bedrooms in cream, brown and purple colour schemes; some have small balconies. Formal restaurant or casual bistro and terrace for comfort dishes and seafood specials.

XX **Walker's** – Moorings Hotel

Gorey Pier ✉ JE3 6EW – ✆ (01534) 853 633 – www.themooringshotel.com

Menu £ 13/25 – Carte £ 35/54

Formal hotel restaurant with a modern lounge, harbour views and local artwork on display. Good value menus offer well-prepared, unashamedly traditional dishes in tried-and-tested combinations and feature the odd personal twist.

XX **Sumas**

Gorey Hill ✉ JE3 6ET – ✆ (01534) 853 291 – www.sumasrestaurant.com – Closed 23 December-20 January and Sunday dinner

Menu £ 23 (weekdays) – Carte £ 27/47 – *(booking essential)*

Well-known restaurant in a yellow-washed house, with a small heated terrace affording lovely views over the harbour. Modern European dishes feature island produce. The monthly changing lunch and midweek dinner menus represent good value.

X **Crab Shack Gorey**

La Route de la Cote ✉ JE3 6DR – ✆ (01534) 850 830 – www.jerseycrabshack.com – Closed 25-26 December and 1 January

Carte £ 18/33 – *(booking advisable)*

Laid-back, friendly restaurant with a decked terrace and superb views over the harbour. The pared-down, rustic interior is decorated with nautical memorabilia. Unfussy menus have a Mediterranean edge and focus on locally caught seafood.

Bass and Lobster

Gorey Coast Rd ✉ JE3 6EU – ✆ (01534) 859 590 – www.bassandlobster.com – Closed Sunday dinner and Monday

Menu £ 13/21 – Carte £ 27/40

Bright, modern 'foodhouse' close to the beach. Seasonal island produce; fresh, tasty seafood and shellfish dominate the menu. Fantastic oysters; good value lunches. Smooth, effective service.

ENGLAND

Green Island

Green Island

St Clement ✉ JE2 6LS – ✆ (01534) 857 787 – www.greenisland.je – Closed 23 December-1 March, Sunday dinner and Monday
Menu £ 17/24 – Carte £ 31/47 – *(booking essential)*
Friendly, personally run restaurant with a terrace and beachside kiosk; the southernmost restaurant in the British Isles. Mediterranean-influenced dishes and seafood specials showcase island produce. Flavours are bold and perfectly judged.

Grouville

St Helier 3 mi

Café Poste

La Rue de la ville es Renauds ✉ JE3 9FY – ✆ (01534) 859 696 – www.cafeposte.co.uk – Closed 11-27 November, Monday and Tuesday
Menu £ 17 – Carte £ 27/43
Popular all-day restaurant – formerly a post office – with a vast array of curios, a wood burning stove and a French country kitchen feel. The eclectic Mediterranean menu is supplemented by daily specials and a good value set selection.

La Haule

La Haule Manor without rest

St Aubin's Bay ✉ JE3 8BS – ✆ (01534) 741 426 – www.lahaulemanor.com – Closed December-February
16 rm – £ 97/189 £ 97/189
Attractive Georgian house overlooking the fort and bay, with a lovely terrace, a good-sized pool and neat lawned gardens. Stylish guest areas and spacious bedrooms mix modern and antique furnishings; those in the wing are the largest.

ENGLAND

La Pulente

St Helier 7 mi

Atlantic

Le Mont de la Pulente ✉ JE3 8HE – on B 35 – ✆ (01534) 744 101 – www.theatlantichotel.com – Closed 5 January-5 February
50 rm – £ 100/200 £ 150/550 – 1 suite
Rest *Ocean* ✿ – see restaurant listing
Stylish hotel with well-manicured grounds, set in a superb location overlooking St Ouen's Bay. Public areas are understated, with tiled floors, exposed brick, water features and a relaxed, intimate feel. Bedrooms are cool and fresh: some feature a patio; others, a balcony. Attentive, personable staff.

Ocean – Atlantic Hotel

✿

Le Mont de la Pulente ✉ JE3 8HE – on B 35 – ✆ (01534) 744 101 – www.theatlantichotel.com/dining – Closed 5 January-5 February
Menu £ 25/80 – *(booking essential)*
Elegant, well-run dining room with a fresh, understated feel, set in a stunning position overlooking St Ouen's Bay. Delicious, well-crafted dishes make use of fine ingredients from the island and display a real understanding of flavour. Smooth, professional service and a relaxed, friendly atmosphere.
→ Langoustine tails on a rock, oyster mayonnaise, Ebène caviar. Tasting of quail, roasted shallot purée, morels, Madeira jus. Toasted almond crème, apricot gel, apricot sorbet and crunchy hazelnuts.

Rozel Bay

St Helier 6 mi

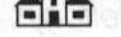

Chateau La Chaire

Rozel Valley ✉ JE3 6AJ – ✆ (01534) 863 354 – www.chateau-la-chaire.co.uk
14 rm – £ 105/180 £ 155/280 – 2 suites
Rest – Menu £ 30 (dinner) – Carte £ 35/40
Attractive 19C house surrounded by peaceful gardens and mature woodland. Traditionally styled guest areas and more modern, well-equipped bedrooms: 2nd floor rooms are cosy; 1st floor rooms are larger and some have balconies. Formal restaurant with a conservatory and terrace offers classics with a twist.

St Aubin

St Helier 4 mi

Somerville
rest,

Mont du Boulevard ✉ JE3 8AD – South : 0.75 mi via harbour – ✆ (01534) 741 226 – www.dolanhotels.com

59 rm – £ 67/130 £ 95/250

Rest *Tides* – Menu £ 22/32 – Carte £ 31/43

Imposing 19C, yellow-washed hotel affording excellent views over the village and bay. Smart, modern guest areas and a well-kept garden with a pleasant poolside terrace. Bright bedrooms vary in shape and size; go for one with a view. Large restaurant offers classical menus and a great outlook.

Panorama without rest

La Rue du Crocquet ✉ JE3 8BZ – ✆ (01534) 742 429 – www.panoramajersey.com – Closed November-early April

14 rm – £ 52/130 £ 108/175

Immaculate hotel with Georgian origins, colourful gardens and stunning views over the fort and bay. Traditional throughout, from the guest areas to the bedrooms. Afternoon tea in the conservatory on arrival; 1,400 teapots are on display.

St Brelade's Bay

St Helier 6 mi

Michelin Green Guide GREAT BRITAIN

ENGLAND

L'Horizon
rm, rest,

✉ JE3 8EF – ✆ (01534) 743 101 – www.handpickedhotels.co.uk/lhorizon

105 rm – £ 75/170 £ 145/295 – 6 suites

Rest *Grill Room* – Menu £ 47 – *(bar lunch Monday-Saturday)*

Long-standing hotel located right on the beachfront and boasting stunning views over the bay. Luxurious interior with extensive guest areas and subtle modern styling. Choose a deluxe bedroom, as they come with balconies and sea views. Stylish, formal restaurant; modern British menus focus on local seafood.

St Brelade's Bay

La Route de la Baie ✉ JE3 8EF – ✆ (01534) 746 141 – www.stbreladesbayhotel.com

74 rm – £ 93/145 £ 140/290 – 5 suites

Rest *Bay* – Menu £ 17/34 – Carte £ 28/42

Smart seafront hotel with charming tropical gardens and panoramic views across the bay. A modernised lounge and contemporary bedrooms fit well alongside original parquet floors and ornate plaster ceilings. Excellent health club. Formal restaurant offers impressive sea views and a classical menu.

Oyster Box

La Route de la Baie ✉ JE3 8EF – ✆ (01534) 850 888 – www.oysterbox.co.uk – Closed 25-26 December, 1 January, dinner Sunday-Monday October-April and Monday lunch

Carte £ 22/47 – *(booking essential)*

Glass-fronted eatery with pleasant heated terrace, set on the promenade and affording superb views over St Brelade's Bay. Stylish, airy interior hung with sail cloths and fishermen's floats. Laid-back, friendly service. Accessible seasonal menu features plenty of fish and shellfish; oysters are a speciality.

Crab Shack St Brelade's Bay

La Route de la Baie ✉ JE3 8EF – ✆ (01534) 850 855 – www.jerseycrabshack.com – Closed 25-26 December, 1 January and Monday dinner except bank holidays

Carte £ 18/33 – *(booking advisable)*

A scaled down version of next door Oyster Box, superbly sited on the beachfront; sit in a cosy booth or on a bench outside. Accessible modern dishes of prime island produce, with seafood a speciality. Relaxed, family-friendly atmosphere.

St Helier

Michelin Green Guide GREAT BRITAIN

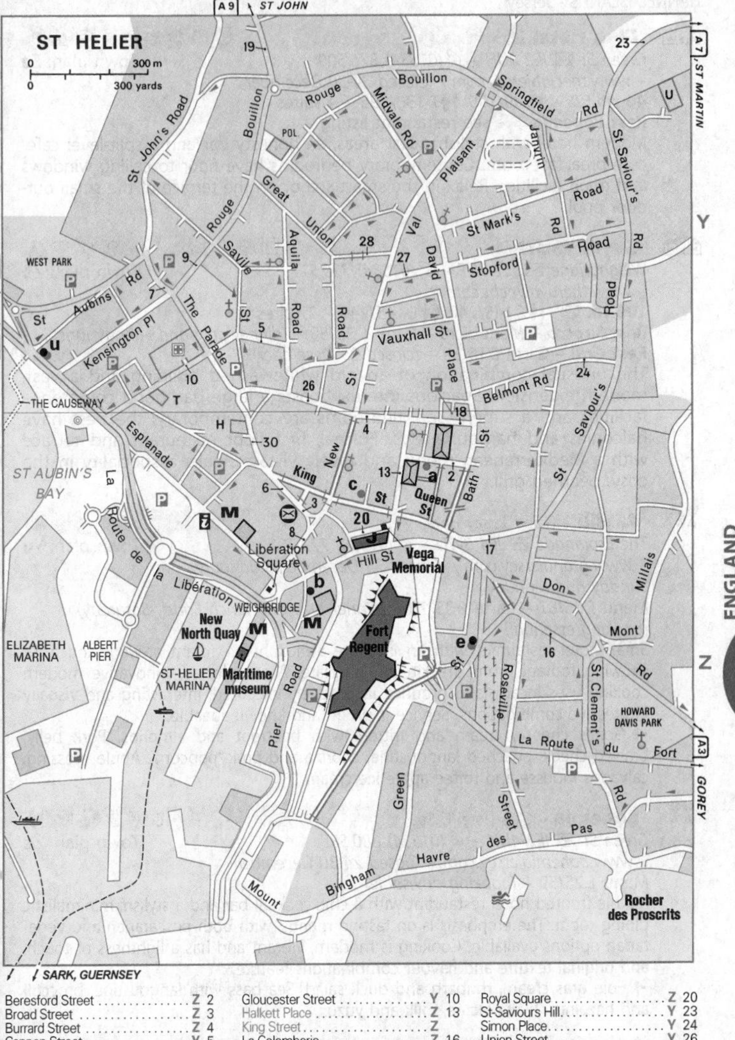

Beresford Street	Z	2	Gloucester Street	Y	10	Royal Square	Z	20
Broad Street	Z	3	Halkett Place	Z	13	St-Saviours Hill	Y	23
Burrard Street	Z	4	King Street	Z		Simon Place	Y	24
Cannon Street	Y	5	La Colomberie	Z	16	Union Street	Y	26
Charing Cross	Z	6	La Motte Street	Z	17	Victoria Street	Y	27
Cheapside	Y	7	Minden Place	Z	18	Windsor Road	Y	28
Conway Street	Z	8	Queen Street	Z		York Street	Y	30
Elizabeth Place	Y	9	Queen's Road	Y	19			

Grand Jersey

The Esplanade ✉ *JE2 3QA* – *(01534) 722 301* – *www.grandjersey.com* Town plan: Y**u**

117 rm – £ 109/295 £ 119/295 – 6 suites

Rest *Tassili* – see restaurant listing

Rest *Victoria's* – Menu £ 28 – Carte £ 25/41 – *(dinner only)*

Welcoming hotel with a large terrace, overlooking St Aubin's Bay. Stylish, modern interior with a chic champagne bar, well-equipped spa and corporate cinema. Contemporary bedrooms come in bold colours; some have balconies and sea views. Fine dining in sophisticated Tassili; brasserie menu in Victoria's.

Club Hotel & Spa

Green St ✉ JE2 4UH – ✆ (01534) 876 500 Town plan: Z**e**
– www.theclubjersey.com – Closed 24-30 December
46 rm – £ 99/195 £ 130/195 – 4 suites
Rest *Bohemia* ✿ – see restaurant listing
Modern hotel with stylish guest areas, an honesty bar and a split-level café-cum-breakfast-room. Contemporary bedrooms have floor to ceiling windows and good facilities. Relax in the smart spa or on the terrace of the small outdoor pool.

Royal Yacht

Weighbridge ✉ JE2 3NF – ✆ (01534) 720 511 Town plan: Z**b**
– www.theroyalyacht.com
109 rm – £ 145/240 £ 145/240 – 2 suites
Rest *Sirocco* – Menu £ 28 – Carte £ 33/50 – *(dinner only and Sunday lunch)*
Rest *Grill* – Carte £ 16/39 – *(closed 25 December)*
The unusual combination of an old whitewashed building and a vast, modern extension. Spacious interior boasts a large bar, good conference facilities and a superb spa. Bedrooms are contemporary; the best have balconies and harbour views. Formal, first floor restaurant and terrace with a Mediterranean menu and lovely vistas. Steaks a speciality in the cosy, beamed grill.

XXX ✿

Tassili – Grand Jersey Hotel

The Esplanade ✉ JE4 8WD – ✆ (01534) 722 301 Town plan: Y**u**
– www.grandjersey.com – Closed 25 December, 1 January, Sunday and Monday
Menu £ 25/87 – Carte £ 35/70 – *(dinner only and lunch Friday-Saturday) (booking essential)*
Small hotel restaurant with an intimate atmosphere, vibrant artwork and a TV showing footage from the kitchen hotplate. Accomplished, innovative modern cooking uses local island produce in precisely executed, interesting and visually impressive combinations. Service is proud and knowledgeable.
➜ Goat's cheese, cream and fritters with beetroot and almonds. Pork belly, braised cheek, poached langoustine, chorizo and pork 'popcorn'. Apple pressing, calvados mousse and toffee apple ice cream.

XX ✿

Bohemia – Club Hotel & Spa

Green St ✉ JE2 4UH – ✆ (01534) 880 588 Town plan: Z**e**
– www.bohemiajersey.com – Closed 24-30 December
Menu £ 25/59 – *(booking advisable)*
Marble-fronted hotel restaurant with a chic cocktail bar and a stylish, minimalistic dining room. The emphasis is on tasting menus, with both pescatarian and vegetarian options available. Cooking is modern, vibrant and has a lightness of touch, and original texture and flavour combinations feature.
➜ Foie gras cream, rhubarb and duck salad. Sea bass with langoustine, broccoli and hazelnut. Jivara lactée, milk and yuzu.

XX ✿

Ormer by Shaun Rankin

7-11 Don St ✉ JE2 4TQ – ✆ (01534) 725 100 Town plan: Z**o**
– www.ormerjersey.com – Closed 2 weeks Christmas-New Year and Sunday
Menu £ 24/75 – Carte £ 42/55 – *(booking advisable)*
This tasteful restaurant features attractive wood panelling and turquoise banquettes, and is named after a rare shellfish found in local waters. Cooking is refined and assured and uses only the very best seasonal island produce. Inside, it's intimate yet buzzy, and there's a pavement terrace for warmer days.
➜ Lobster ravioli, scallops, crab, ginger and coriander. Dover sole with charred leeks and sea vegetables. Apple soufflé with mascarpone ice cream.

Symbols shown in red indicate particularly charming establishments.

ENGLAND

Banjo with rm

8 Beresford St ✉ JE2 4WN – ✆ (01534) 850 890 Town plan: Z**a**
– www.banjojersey.com – Closed 25-26 December and Sunday
4 rm – †£ 70/130 ††£ 70/130, ☕ £ 10 Menu £ 17/20 (lunch) – Carte £ 25/44
Substantial former gentlemen's club with an ornate façade; the banjo belonging to the owner's great grandfather is displayed in a glass-fronted wine cellar. The appealing, wide-ranging menu features everything from brasserie classics to sushi. Stylish bedrooms have Nespresso machines and Bose sound systems.

ST SAVIOUR

▶St Helier 1 mi

Longueville Manor

Longueville Rd ✉ JE2 7WF – on A 3 – ✆ (01534) 725 501
– www.longuevillemanor.com – Closed 4-21 January
28 rm ☕ – †£ 100/450 ††£ 175/575 – 2 suites
Rest *Longueville Manor* – see restaurant listing
Iconic 13C manor house, which is very personally and professionally run. Comfortable, country house guest areas have a modern edge. Bedrooms come in either classic or contemporary styles and all are well-equipped. Relax in the lovely pool, on the charming terrace or in the 6 acres of delightful gardens.

Longueville Manor – Longueville Manor Hotel

Longueville Rd ✉ JE2 7WF – on A 3 – ✆ (01534) 725 501
– www.longuevillemanor.com – Closed 4-21 January
Menu £ 30/60 **s** – *(booking advisable)*
Set within a charming manor house; dine in the characterful 15C oak-panelled room, the brighter Garden Room or on the terrace. Daily menus champion island produce; seafood is a feature and many of the ingredients are foraged for or come from the impressive kitchen garden. Classical dishes have a modern edge.

SARK

Sark – Michelin Road map 503-L33 – See Regional map n°**5-A2**

Stocks

✉ GY10 1SD – ✆ (01481) 832 001 – www.stockshotel.com – Closed January-February
23 rm ☕ – †£ 239/259 ††£ 245/266 – 5 suites
Rest – Menu £ 27/35 **s** – Carte £ 31/50 **s**
Rest *Stocks Bistro* – Carte £ 25/41 – *(closed October-April)*
Set facing a wooded valley; a very personally run former farmhouse that's undergone a smart transformation. Immaculately kept, well-equipped, classical bedrooms. Small gym, arty island shop and fantastic wine cellar. Formal gardens have a split-level pool and jacuzzi. Eat in the panelled dining room, in the bistro or on the terrace; local island produce features.

Aval du Creux without rest

Harbour Hill ✉ GY10 1SB – ✆ (01481) 832 832 – www.avalducreux.com – Closed 6 October-December
26 rm ☕ – †£ 99/129 ††£ 158/270
Pretty hotel close to the harbour, with lovely gardens, a split-level swimming pool and a large terrace. Immaculately kept guest areas. Cosy, very comfortable bedrooms with bespoke furnishings, the latest mod cons and good extras.

Moinerie

✉ GY10 1SF – ✆ (01481) 832 832 – www.sarkislandhotels.com – Easter-October
14 rm ☕ – †£ 68/98 ††£ 119/170
Rest *Moinerie* – ✆ (01481) 832 989 – Menu £ 40 – Carte £ 26/41 – *(dinner only)*
Lovely hotel with a fantastic cobbled drive (the stones were brought in from France), and a cosy bar located in the former dower house. Elegant bedrooms feature fine soft furnishings; most are set around a courtyard and some are split-level. Eat in the large, baronial-style restaurant or delightful garden.

ENGLAND

La Sablonnerie with rm

Little Sark ✉ GY9 OSD – ✆ (01481) 832 061 – www.lasablonnerie.com – Closed mid October-mid April
22 rm ☕ – 🚹£ 50/108 🚹🚹£ 100/214 – 2 suites
Carte £ 25/47 – *(booking essential)*
Charming, whitewashed 16C former farmhouse with beautiful gardens. Cosy, beamed interior with a comfortable lounge for aperitifs. Regularly changing, five course menu offers a classic style of cooking using produce from their own farm. Prompt service. Neat, tidy bedrooms; Room 14, in the former stables, is the best.

CHAPEL ROW
West Berkshire – Pop. 637 – See Regional map n°**10-B3**
▶London 53 mi – Newbury 9 mi – Oxford 35 mi

Bladebone Inn

✉ RG7 6PD – ✆ (01189) 712 326 – www.thebladeboneinn.com
Menu £ 15 (weekday lunch) – Carte £ 25/39
Apparently named after the bone of a mammoth found on the riverbank. Snug, homely interior with open fires. Appealing menu ranges from 'posh' fish finger sandwiches to duck with cherry beer and almonds; they grow over 50 herbs.

CHAPEL-EN-LE-FRITH
Derbyshire – Pop. 6 598 – See Regional map n°**16-A1**
▶London 175 mi – Sheffield 27 mi – Manchester 21 mi – Stoke-on-Trent 34 mi
Michelin Road map 504-O24

ENGLAND

High Croft without rest
Manchester Rd ✉ SK23 9UH – West : 0.75 mi on B 5470 – ✆ (01298) 814 843 – www.highcroft-guesthouse.co.uk
4 rm ☕ – 🚹£ 65/75 🚹🚹£ 80/105
Immaculately kept Edwardian house with countryside views; Arts and Crafts features include wood panelling and stained glass windows. Comfortable lounge, elegant breakfast room and period-furnished bedrooms; the Atholl suite is the best.

CHARLTON
West Sussex – See Regional map n°**7-C2**
▶London 72 mi – Birmingham 165 mi – Leeds 258 mi – Sheffield 228 mi
Michelin Road map 504-R31

Fox Goes Free with rm
✉ PO18 0HU – ✆ (01243) 811 461 – www.thefoxgoesfree.com
5 rm ☕ – 🚹£ 65/175 🚹🚹£ 90/175
Carte £ 21/31 – *(closed dinner 26 December)*
Charming 17C flint pub with a superb garden and terrace and a lovely outlook. Original features include exposed stone walls, low beamed ceilings and brick floors. Dishes range from simple pub classics to more substantial local offerings; some are to share. Clean, unfussy bedrooms; a few with low beamed ceilings.

CHARMOUTH
Dorset – Pop. 1 352 – ✉ Bridport – See Regional map n°**3-B3**
▶London 157 mi – Dorchester 22 mi – Exeter 31 mi – Taunton 27 mi
Michelin Road map 503-L31

White House
2 Hillside, The Street ✉ DT6 6PJ – ✆ (01297) 560 411 – www.whitehousehotel.com – Restricted opening in winter
4 rm ☕ – 🚹£ 100/140 🚹🚹£ 120/180 **Rest** – Carte £ 25/44 – *(dinner only)*
Charming Regency house; personally run by a friendly couple. Spacious, comfy bedrooms retain some period features – one has a cast iron bed – and all have modern bathrooms, fresh flowers, iPod docks and seasonal fruit. The wood-furnished dining room offers concise modern menus of local produce.

Abbots House without rest

The Street ✉ DT6 6QF – ✆ (01297) 560 339 – www.abbotshouse.co.uk – Closed January and last 2 weeks December

4 rm ☕ – 🚹£ 110/130 🚹🚹£ 120/140

This cosy guesthouse dates back to 1480 and was originally an annexe of Forde Abbey. It has a beamed, wood-panelled lounge and a conservatory breakfast room overlooking a model railway in the garden. Bedrooms are bright and modern.

CHATHILL → See Alnwick

Northumberland

CHATTON

Northumberland – Pop. 438 – See Regional map n°**24-A1**

London 336 mi – Sunderland 63 mi – Newcastle upon Tyne 52 mi – South Shields 57 mi

Michelin Road map 502-017

Chatton Park House without rest

✉ NE66 5RA East : 1 mi on B 6348 – ✆ (01688) 215 507 – www.chattonpark.com – Closed 23 December-1 February

5 rm ☕ – 🚹£ 110/129 🚹🚹£ 110/199

Fine 1750s house set in 6 acres of formal gardens and mature grounds. Smart parquet-floored hallway and huge, open-fired sitting room. Spacious bedrooms blend modern décor with original features. Excellent breakfasts use local produce.

CHELTENHAM

Gloucestershire – Pop. 116 447 – See Regional map n°**4-C1**
London 99 mi – Birmingham 48 mi – Gloucester 9 mi
Michelin Road map 503-N28 and 504 – Michelin Green Guide GREAT BRITAIN

© Le Champignon Sauvage

Hotels

Ellenborough Park

Southam Rd ✉ GL52 3NJ – Northeast : 2.75 mi on B 4632 – ✆ (01242) 545 454 – www.ellenboroughpark.com Town plan: AX**a**
62 rm – £ 175 £ 230/375
Rest *The Beaufort* – see restaurant listing
Rest *Brasserie* – Carte £ 28/43 **s**
Part-15C timbered manor house, with stone annexes, an understated Indian-themed spa and large grounds stretching down to the racecourse. Beautifully furnished guest areas have an elegant, classical style. Nina Campbell designed bedrooms have superb bathrooms, the latest mod cons and plenty of extras. Dine in the sophisticated restaurant or informal brasserie.

Hotel du Vin

Parabola Rd ✉ GL50 3AQ – ✆ (01242) 588 450 – www.hotelduvin.com Town plan: BY**c**
49 rm – £ 115/185 £ 155/595 – 1 suite
Rest *Bistro* – Carte £ 27/78
Attractive Regency house in an affluent residential area. Inside it's chic and laid-back, with a leather-furnished bar and a comfy lounge. Some of the individually designed, well-equipped, wine-themed bedrooms have baths in the room. The French bistro features an eye-catching wine glass chandelier.

Montpellier Chapter

Bayshill Rd ✉ GL50 3AS – ✆ (01242) 527 788 – www.themontpellierchapterhotel.com Town plan: BX**r**
61 rm – £ 125/500 £ 125/500
Rest – Carte £ 30/46 – *(bookings advisable at dinner)*
Chic Regency townhouse, where stylish modern guest areas are hung with an impressive collection of contemporary art. Light wood furnished bedrooms come with Nespresso machines, complimentary mini bars and in-room info on an iPod touch. Dine on British dishes at marble-topped tables or on one of two terraces.

No 38 The Park (N) without rest

38 Eversham Rd ✉ GL52 2AH – ✆ (01242) 248 656 Town plan: CY**x**
14 rm – £ 125/240 £ 125/240
Behind the attractive Georgian façade is a very original, tastefully designed hotel with a relaxed atmosphere and supremely comfortable furnishings. Bedrooms come with coffee machines and vast walk-in showers or feature baths.

CHELTENHAM

Street	Grid	No.
Berkeley St	CYZ	4
Clarence St	CY	6
Crescent Terrace	BY	7
Deep St	AX	9
Dunalley St	CY	10
Henrietta St	CY	13
High St	BCY	
High St PRESTBURY	AX	14
Keynsham Rd	CZ	15
Knapp Rd	BY	16
Montpellier Ave	BZ	17
Montpellier Walk	BZ	18
North St	CY	20
Norwood Rd	BZ	21
Oriel Rd	CZ	22
Pittville St	CY	26
Portland St	CY	27
Promenade (The)	BZCY	28
Regent Arcade Shopping Centre	CY	
Regent St	CY	29
Rodney Rd	CY	30
Royal Well Rd	BCY	32
St James St	CY	33
St Johns Ave	CY	34
St Margaret's Rd	CY	35
Sandford Mill Rd	CZ	36
Sandford Terrace	CZ	37
Winchcombe St	CY	38

ENGLAND

Beaumont House without rest
56 Shurdington Rd ✉ GL53 0JE – ☎ (01242) 223 311 – www.bhhotel.co.uk Town plan: AX**u**
16 rm ☕ – †£ 72/199 ††£ 95/199
Your hosts here are warm and welcoming, just like the hotel. The lounge and breakfast room are comfortably and classically furnished, while the bedrooms are more contemporary; there are two themed rooms – Africa and Asia.

Wyastone Townhouse Ⓝ without rest
Parabola Rd ✉ GL50 3BG – ☎ (01242) 245 549 – www.wyastonehotel.co.uk – Closed 23 December-1 January Town plan: BY**a**
16 rm ☕ – †£ 80/98 ††£ 105/165
Nothing is too much trouble for the charming young owner of this attractive townhouse. Inside, contemporary décor blends with period features. Bedrooms – split between the house and the courtyard – are surprisingly spacious.

Butlers without rest
Western Rd ✉ GL50 3RN – ☎ (01242) 570 771 – www.butlers-hotel.co.uk Town plan: BY**v**
9 rm ☕ – †£ 75/88 ††£ 88/120
The bedrooms of this tastefully furnished Victorian townhouse are named after famous butlers – a theme which continues in the classical lounge and breakfast room. There's also an interesting collections of hats about the place!

ENGLAND

Hanover House without rest
65 St George's Rd ✉ GL50 3DU – ☎ (01242) 541 297 – www.hanoverhouse.org – Closed Christmas-New Year and Easter Town plan: BY**u**
4 rm ☕ – †£ 60/85 ††£ 100/120
Edward Elgar's wife once lived in this Victorian Italianate townhouse, hence the name of the bedrooms – Alice Elgar, Tennyson and Rossetti. It has a real family feel courtesy of its bright furnishings and warm, welcoming owners.

Georgian House without rest
77 Montpellier Terr ✉ GL50 1XA – ☎ (01242) 515 577 – www.georgianhouse.net – Closed 19 December-15 January Town plan: BZ**s**
3 rm ☕ – †£ 75/85 ††£ 90/115
The experienced owner of this terraced Georgian townhouse looks after his guests very personally – which is why so many come back time and again. The décor and furnishings respect the house's age; one of the rooms is a four-poster.

Detmore House Ⓝ without rest
London Rd, Charlton Kings ✉ GL52 6UT – ☎ (01242) 582 868 – www.detmorehouse.com Town plan: AX**s**
4 rm ☕ – †£ 65/95 ††£ 85/105
Peace and tranquillity reign at this 1840s country house, which is accessed via a private drive and offers pleasant rural views. Bedrooms are modern and comfortable – 'Oak' is the best. Breakfast is served at a fine oak table.

Restaurants

Le Champignon Sauvage (David Everitt-Matthias)
24-28 Suffolk Rd ✉ GL50 2AQ – ☎ (01242) 573 449 – www.lechampignonsauvage.co.uk – Closed 3 weeks June, 10 days Christmas, Sunday and Monday Town plan: BZ**a**
Menu £ 32 (weekdays)/59
The chef has cooked here passionately and proudly for over 25 years, creating dishes with classic French roots and a personal touch. Visually impressive and boldly flavoured, they often feature foraged ingredients such as dandelion or burdock. Tasting menu available evenings, Tues to Sat (order before 8.15pm).
→ Beef tartare and corned beef with wasabi mayonnaise and pickled shimeji mushrooms. Duck breast with parsnip cream and baby parsnips cooked with maple syrup and coffee. Chocolate delice with milk ice cream.

XXX **The Beaufort** – Ellenborough Park Hotel

Southam Rd ✉ GL52 3NJ – Northeast : 2.75 mi on B 4632 – ✆ (01242) 545 454 – www.ellenboroughpark.com – Closed Sunday dinner and Monday Town plan: AX**a**

Menu £ 45/70 **s** – *(dinner only and Sunday lunch)*

With its Tudor stone fireplaces, original oak wood panelling and stained glass windows, this characterful hotel restaurant lends itself to sophisticated dining. Cooking is modern and accomplished and relies on local ingredients.

XXX **Lumière**

Clarence Par ✉ GL50 3PA – ✆ (01242) 222 200 – www.lumiere.cc – Closed 2 weeks January, 2 weeks summer, Tuesday lunch, Sunday and Monday Town plan: BCY**z**

Menu £ 28/55 – *(booking essential)*

Friendly, personally run restaurant; its unassuming exterior concealing a long, stylish room decorated with mirrors. Seasonal dishes are modern and intricate with the occasional playful twist – desserts are often the highlight.

XX **Curry Corner**

133 Fairview Rd ✉ GL52 2EX – ✆ (01242) 528 449 – www.thecurrycorner.com – Closed 25 December, Friday lunch and Monday except bank holidays Town plan: CY**a**

Menu £ 25 – Carte £ 23/38

Long-standing, family-run restaurant in a smart Regency townhouse. Authentic, flavoursome dishes take their influences from across Bangladesh, India and Persia. Imported spices are ground and roasted every morning.

XX **Daffodil**

18-20 Suffolk Par ✉ GL50 2AE – ✆ (01242) 700 055 – www.thedaffodil.com – Closed 1-7 January, 26 December and Sunday Town plan: BZ**u**

Carte £ 20/46

Delightful 1920s art deco cinema, with original tiling still on display in the entrance. The kitchens are in the former screen area, the tables are in the old stalls, and the stylish lounge is up on the balcony. Classical brasserie dishes include steaks from the Josper grill. Service is slick and attentive.

XX **Prithvi** (N)

37 Bath Rd ✉ GL53 7HG – ✆ (01242) 226 229 – www.prithvirestaurant.com – Closed 21-27 December Town plan: CZ**s**

Menu £ 15 (lunch) – Carte £ 24/32 – *(booking essential at dinner)*

This smart Indian restaurant is a refreshing break from the norm, with its ambitious owner, designer décor, detailed service and refined cooking. Reinvented Indian and Bangladeshi dishes are presented in a sophisticated manner.

XX **Bhoomi** (N)

52 Suffolk Rd ✉ GL50 2AQ – ✆ (01242) 222 010 – www.bhoomi.co.uk – Closed 25-26 December, Monday and lunch Tuesday Town plan: BZ**b**

Carte £ 19/38

Its name means 'earth' in the Keralan dialect and the cooking focuses on southeast India (from where the young owner and chef originate). Preparation and presentation has been subtly modernised but the essence of each dish remains.

XX **Koloshi**

London Rd ✉ GL54 4HG – Southeast : 2.5 mi on A 40 – ✆ (01242) 516 400 – www.koloshi.co.uk – Closed 25-26 December and Monday

Menu £ 10/35 – Carte £ 21/31

Former pub, set by the reservoir; now a spacious Indian restaurant, its name meaning 'water carrying vessel' in Hindi. Visual, vibrant cooking is full of flavour; good vegetarian selection. Smartly attired staff provide professional service.

ENGLAND

131 The Promenade with rm

131 Promenade ✉ GL50 1NW – ✆ (01242) 822 939 Town plan: BZ**z**
– www.no131.com
11 rm – †£ 100/250 ††£ 100/250 Carte £ 23/48 – *(booking essential)*
The columned exterior of this fine 1820s building overlooks an attractive park. Inside, original features remain but it now has a cool, contemporary style, with impressive modern artwork featuring throughout. The menu lists well-prepared, unfussy classics, with steaks cooked on the Josper grill a feature at dinner. Bedrooms are individually and tastefully furnished.

Purslane

16 Rodney Rd ✉ GL50 1JJ – ✆ (01242) 321 639 Town plan: CY**p**
– www.purslane-restaurant.co.uk – Closed 18 January-4 February, 24 August-9 September, 24-29 December, Sunday and Monday
Menu £ 33
A stylishly minimalistic neighbourhood restaurant with relaxed, efficient service. Fresh seafood from Cornwall and Scotland is combined with good quality, locally sourced ingredients to produce interesting, original dishes.

The Tavern

5 Royal Well Pl ✉ GL50 3DN – ✆ (01242) 221 212 Town plan: BY**e**
– www.thetaverncheltenham.com – Closed 25-26 December
Menu £ 10 (weekday lunch) – Carte £ 13/41
Rustic, all-day eatery with a strong American theme, split over two floors and featuring large tables and bench seating suited to sharing. Stools set around the open kitchen make up the chef's table. Accessible menu offers the likes of sliders, chilli cheese dogs and steaks to share. Chatty service.

Svea

24 Rodney Rd ✉ GL50 1JJ – ✆ (01242) 238 134 Town plan: CY**s**
– www.sveacafe.co.uk – Closed Sunday-Monday and dinner Tuesday-Wednesday
Carte £ 25/33
A homely city centre café with pretty gingham-clothed tables, serving fresh, authentic Swedish cooking and monthly smorgasbords. As is tradition in Sweden, lunch is simpler, with light snacks, open sandwiches and homemade cakes.

Royal Oak

The Burgage, Prestbury ✉ GL52 3DL – ✆ (01242) 522 344 – www.royal-oak-prestbury.co.uk – Closed 25 December Town plan: AX**r**
Carte £ 22/39
This was once owned by batting legend Tom Graveney, hence the 'Pavilion' function room. Lunch offers tasty, satisfying dishes like kedgeree, while dinner steps things up a level. Sit in the cosy bar, dark wood dining room or heated garden.

at Shurdington Southwest: 3.75 mi on A46 -(AX)✉ Cheltenham

Greenway

✉ GL51 4UG – ✆ (01242) 862 352 – www.thegreenwayhotelandspa.com
19 rm – †£ 109/199 ††£ 149/199 – 1 suite
Rest *The Garden* – Menu £ 35/65
Rest *Brasserie* – Carte £ 22/44 – *(lunch only)*
16C ivy-clad manor house, set in 8 acres of peaceful grounds and offering pleasant views over the hills. Comfy drawing rooms and well-equipped bedrooms have a pleasant country house style. Enjoy a laid-back brasserie-style lunch on the terrace of the lovely spa. The oak-panelled restaurant offers classic dishes with modern overtones and overlooks the lily pond.

ENGLAND

at Piff's Elm Northwest: 4 mi on A4019 -(AX)

Gloucester Old Spot

Tewkesbury Rd ✉ *GL51 9SY – ✆ (01242) 680 321*
– www.thegloucesteroldspot.co.uk – Closed 25-26 December
Menu £ 13 (lunch) – Carte £ 21/41
Cosy, relaxing inn with a snug, quarry-tiled bar, a baronial dining room and open fires aplenty. Menus offer tasty, seasonal dishes, with rare breed pork a speciality. Nursery puddings. Cheery, welcoming staff.

CHELWOOD GATE

East Sussex – Pop. 600 – See Regional map n°**8-A2**
London 37 mi – Birmingham 163 mi – Leeds 246 mi – Sheffield 216 mi
Michelin Road map 504-U31

Red Lion

Lewes Rd ✉ *RH17 7DE – on A 275 – ✆ (01825) 740 265*
– www.redlionchelwoodgate.co.uk – Closed Sunday dinner
Carte £ 16/30
Set on the edge of Ashdown Forest, with a concise menu offering a mix of pub classics and French influenced dishes. The bright conservatory is the best place to dine and opens out onto a paved terrace and a lovely lawned garden.

CHESTER

Cheshire West and Chester – Pop. 86 011 – See Regional map n°**20-A3**
London 207 mi – Birkenhead 7 mi – Birmingham 91 mi – Liverpool 21 mi
Michelin Road map 502-L24 and 503 – Michelin Green Guide GREAT BRITAIN

Hotels

Chester Grosvenor

Eastgate ✉ CH1 1LT – ✆ (01244) 324 024 Town plan: B**a**
– www.chestergrosvenor.com – Closed 25-26 December
80 rm – ♦£ 155/305 ♦♦£ 185/305 – 6 suites
Rest *Simon Radley at Chester Grosvenor* ❀ **Rest *La Brasserie*** – see restaurant listing
19C hotel with a grand, black and white timbered façade, a stunning Rococo chocolate shop and a buzzy lounge serving all-day snacks. Stylish bedrooms blend traditional furnishings and modern fabrics; luxurious, marble-floored bathrooms.

DoubleTree by Hilton H. & Spa Chester

Warrington Rd ✉ CH2 3PD – Northeast : 2 mi on A 56
– ✆ (01244) 408 800 – www.doubletreechester.co.uk Town plan: A**s**
140 rm – ♦£ 112/203 ♦♦£ 125/226
Rest *Marco Pierre White Steakhouse Bar & Grill* – ✆ (01244) 408 830 – Carte £ 25/51
Rest *Brasserie* – Menu £ 20 **s** – Carte £ 23/33 **s**
Smart, stylish hotel offering sleek, spacious bedrooms with super king-sized beds, bright white décor and modern facilities. State-of-the-art conference facilities and superb spa with a well-equipped leisure club. Contemporary steakhouse in the 18C manor house; informal brasserie overlooks the courtyard.

Abode Chester

rm,

Grosvenor Rd ✉ CH1 2DJ – ✆ (01244) 347 000 Town plan: B**z**
– www.abodehotels.co.uk/chester
84 rm – ♦£ 79/165 ♦♦£ 79/490, £ 12
Rest *Michael Caines* – see restaurant listing
Rest *MC Café Bar & Grill* – Menu £ 19 – Carte £ 20/29 – *(closed Monday-Thursday) (dinner only)*
Contemporary hotel opposite the castle, just a short walk from the city. There are four categories of bedroom: 'Enviable' and 'Fabulous' are the best – ask for a room with a racecourse view. The ground floor café, bar and grill offers a brasserie menu; chic Michael Caines offers modern French fare.

Oddfellows

20 Lower Bridge St ✉ CH1 1RS – ✆ (01244) 895 700 Town plan: B**c**
– www.oddfellowschester.com – Closed 25 December
18 rm – ♦£ 90/325 ♦♦£ 99/354
Rest *The Garden by Simon Radley* – see restaurant listing
Originally an Oddfellows Hall built in 1676 to help the poor, but its name also suits its unique, quirky styling. Well-equipped, contemporary bedrooms include some duplex suites: one room has a circular bed; another, a double roll-top bath.

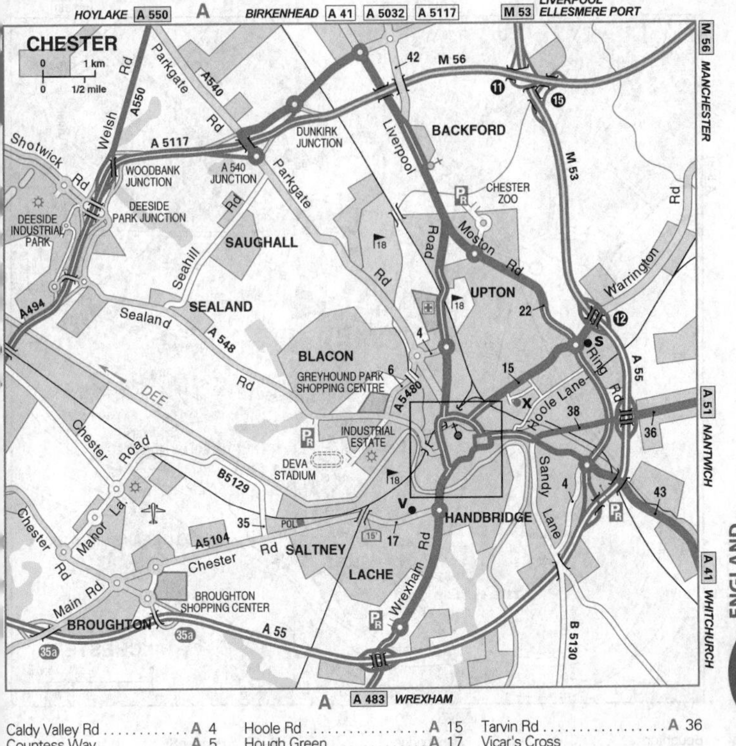

Caldy Valley Rd . . . . A 4
Countess Way . . . . A 5
Deva Link . . . . A 6
Greyhound Park Shopping Centre . . . . A
Hoole Rd . . . . A 15
Hough Green . . . . A 17
Long Lane . . . . A 22
Saltney Ferry Rd . . . . A 35
Tarvin Rd . . . . A 36
Vicar's Cross Rd . . . . A 38
Whitby Lane . . . . A 42
Whitchurch Rd . . . . A 43

Mitchell's of Chester without rest

28 Hough Grn ✉ CH4 8JQ – Southwest : 1 mi by A 483 on A 5104 – ✆ (01244) 679 004 – www.mitchellsofchester.com – Closed 23 December-2 January Town plan: A**v**

3 rm – †£ 45/98 ††£ 82/98

Proudly run Victorian house with homely bedrooms, thoughtful extras and smart, compact shower rooms; those on the first floor are the best. Classical lounge complete with a parrot. Spacious breakfast room; try the homemade preserves.

Restaurants

Simon Radley at Chester Grosvenor – Chester Grosvenor Hotel

Eastgate ✉ CH1 1LT – ✆ (01244) 324 024 – www.chestergrosvenor.com – Closed 25 December, Sunday (except at bank holidays when closed Tuesday) and Monday Town plan: B**a**

Menu £ 75/99 – *(dinner only)*

Elegant restaurant with a fresh, classic feel, a stylish cocktail lounge and an impressive wine cellar. Confident cooking shows respect for ingredients, bringing together clean, clear flavours in sophisticated dishes that display interesting, innovative touches. Formal and detailed service.

→ King scallop, crubeens, smoked eel, chicory and hazelnut. Duck breast, poached rhubarb, liver and gingerbread pain perdu. Chocolate cremeux with hazelnut praline and warm toffee.

ENGLAND

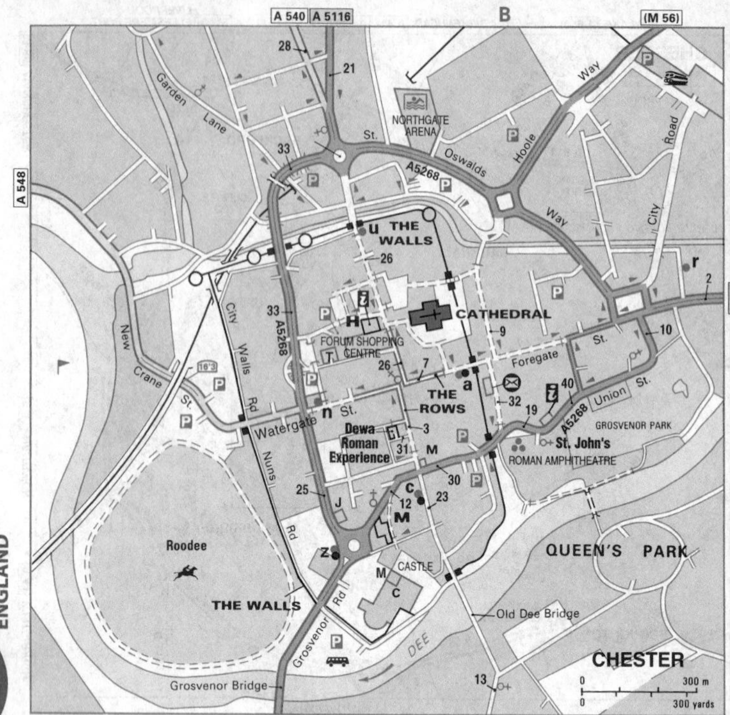

Boughton . . . . B 2
Bridge St . . . . B 3
Eastgate St . . . . B 7
Forum Shopping centre . . . . . B
Frodsham St . . . . B 9
Grosvenor Park Rd . . . . B 10
Grosvenor St . . . . B 12
Handbridge . . . . B 13
Little St John St. . . . . B 19
Liverpool Rd . . . . B 21
Lower Bridge St . . . . B 23
Nicholas St. . . . . B 25
Northgate St . . . . B 26
Parkgate Rd. . . . . B 28
Pepper St. . . . . B 30
Pierpoint Lane . . . . B 31
St John St . . . . B 32
St Martins Way . . . . B 33
Vicar's Lane . . . . B 40
Watergate St . . . . B

XX **Michael Caines** – Abode Chester Hotel

Grosvenor Rd ✉ CH1 2DJ – ✆ (01244) 405 820 Town plan: B**z**
– www.michaelcaines.com – Closed 1-4 January and Sunday dinner
Menu £ 15/23 – Carte £ 35/48

A stylish spot on the fifth floor of a hotel, where you can enjoy far-reaching views over the castle and racecourse. Menus combine a French base with a modern edge; the tasting menu best demonstrates the flavourful, artistic cooking.

XX **Upstairs at the Grill**

70 Watergate St ✉ CH1 2LA – ✆ (01244) 344 883 Town plan: B**n**
– www.upstairsatthegrill.co.uk – Closed 25 December and 1 January
Carte £ 27/51 – *(dinner only and lunch Friday-Sunday)*

Smart restaurant offering prime quality steaks – including porterhouse and bone-in fillet or rib-eye; the 5 week dry-aged cuts are from premium Welsh beef. Eat in the moody cocktail bar or downstairs amongst the cow paraphernalia.

XX **La Brasserie** – Chester Grosvenor Hotel

Eastgate ✉ CH1 1LT – ✆ (01244) 324 024 Town plan: B**a**
– www.chestergrosvenor.com – Closed 25-26 December
Carte £ 30/51

Parisian brasserie with a large, hand-painted glass skylight, mirrors, brass rails and colourful light fittings; sit on a leather banquette or in a booth. Refined British, French and Mediterranean dishes are cooked on the Josper grill.

The Garden by Simon Radley – Oddfellows Hotel

20 Lower Bridge St ✉ CH1 1RS – ✆ (01244) 895 700 Town plan: B**c**
– www.oddfellowschester.com – Closed 25 December
Carte £ 26/44 **s**
Set in an impressive Georgian hotel; have a drink in the quirky bar then head to the garden-themed restaurant with its bird motifs, flower displays, butterfly-filled glass boxes and large terrace. Unfussy, Mediterranean-influenced menus.

Joseph Benjamin

134-140 Northgate St ✉ CH1 2HT – ✆ (01244) 344 295 Town plan: B**u**
– www.josephbenjamin.co.uk – Closed 25 December-1 January and Monday
Carte £ 19/34 – *(lunch only and dinner Thursday-Saturday) (booking essential)*
This personally and passionately run bistro is named after its owners, Joe and Ben. The light, simple décor mirrors the style of cooking and the monthly menu offers tasty, well-judged dishes. They serve breakfast, lunch, coffee and home-made pastries and, from Thursday to Saturday, intimate candlelit dinners.

Sticky Walnut

11 Charles St ✉ CH2 3AZ – ✆ (01244) 400 400 Town plan: A**x**
– www.stickywalnut.com – Closed 25-26 December and Sunday dinner
Carte £ 18/33 – *(booking essential at dinner)*
Run by a confident young team, a quirky, slightly bohemian restaurant in a residential parade of shops. Concise menus feature quality ingredients in a mix of British, French and Italian dishes; the breads and pastas are all homemade.

Artichoke (N)

The Steam Mill, Steam Mill St ✉ CH3 5AN – ✆ (01244) Town plan: B**r**
329 229 – www.artichokechester.co.uk
Carte £ 22/35
Sit outside beside the canal towpath or inside the Victorian mill building, where you'll find original beams, bare brick walls and a contemporary cocktail bar. Cooking ranges from homemade cakes to seasonal 3 course meals.

Porta (N)

140 Northgate St ✉ CH1 2HT – ✆ n/a Town plan: B**u**
– www.portatapas.co.uk – Closed 25 December-1 January
Carte £ 8/20 – *(dinner only) (bookings not accepted)*
Close to the city wall, behind a narrow terrace, is this cosy, characterful little tapas bar. It has no phone number or reservation system, but it does offer generous, tasty dishes which are served by a friendly young team.

CHESTERFIELD

Derbyshire – Pop. 88 483 – See Regional map n°**16-B1**
London 149 mi – Birmingham 72 mi – Liverpool 77 mi – Manchester 44 mi
Michelin Road map 502-P24 – Michelin Green Guide GREAT BRITAIN

Casa

Lockoford Ln ✉ S41 7JB – North : 1 mi off A 61 – ✆ (01246) 245 999
– www.casahotels.com
100 rm – †£ 99/125 ††£ 109/140
Rest *Cocina* – see restaurant listing
Modern hotel with 11 state-of-the-art meeting rooms and a smart bar with a heated terrace. Sizeable bedrooms are furnished in autumnal colours and come with useful extras; some of the suites have balconies and outdoor hot tubs.

Non Solo Vino

417 Chatsworth Rd, Brampton ✉ S40 3AD – West : 1.25 mi on A 619
– ✆ (01246) 276 760 – www.nonsolovino.co.uk – Closed 10-17 August,
1-5 January and Monday
Menu £ 12 (lunch) – Carte £ 24/36
It began as a shop specialising in Italian wines and is now also a bright, contemporary restaurant. Adventurous, modern cooking features Italian classics with a twist; the tasting menu can be coupled with a wine tasting menu.

ENGLAND

Cocina – Casa Hotel

Lockoford Ln ✉ S41 7JB – North : 1 mi off A 61 – ✆ (01246) 245 999 – www.casahotels.com

Carte £ 21/46 – *(bar lunch/dinner)*

Stylish hotel restaurant with a well-stocked cocktail bar. Mediterranean menus have a strong Spanish influence; try the tapas or mature steaks from the Josper oven. The organic rare breed beef comes from the owners' 350 acre farm.

CHEW MAGNA

Bath and North East Somerset – Pop. 1 149 – See Regional map n°**4**-C2

London 128 mi – Bristol 9 mi – Cardiff 52 mi – Bournemouth 89 mi

Michelin Road map 503-M29 and 504

Pony & Trap (Josh Eggleton)

Knowle Hill, New Town ✉ BS40 8TQ – South : 1.25 mi on Bishop Sutton rd – ✆ (01275) 332 627 – www.theponyandtrap.co.uk – Closed Monday except December and bank holidays

Menu £ 50 – Carte £ 24/38 – *(booking essential)*

A cosy whitewashed pub with a characterful bar featuring church pews and an old range – and superb countryside views from the rustic dining room and terrace. Twice-daily menu of extremely fresh, seasonal produce, including locally sourced, hung and smoked meats and fish. Classical cooking with bold flavours.

➜ Smoked bone marrow, beef tartare, parsley & shallot salad. Lemon sole with monk's beard, brown shrimp, caper & lime butter. Treacle tart, burnt apple purée, mascarpone mousse and apple sorbet.

ENGLAND

CHICHESTER

West Sussex – Pop. 28 657 – See Regional map n°**7**-C2

London 69 mi – Brighton 31 mi – Portsmouth 18 mi – Southampton 30 mi

Michelin Road map 504-R31 – Michelin Green Guide GREAT BRITAIN

Goodwood rm, rm,

✉ PO18 0QB Northeast : 4 mi by A 285 and Lavant rd – ✆ (01243) 775 537 – www.goodwood.com

91 rm – £ 110/190 £ 110/190 – 5 suites

Rest *Richmond Arms* – Carte £ 30/58 – *(dinner only and Sunday lunch)*

Rest *Bar & Grill* – Carte £ 23/43

Refurbished hotel on the Goodwood Estate, with luxurious, English-style bedrooms in subtle, contemporary colour schemes; modern furniture and motor racing photos abound. Well-equipped spa. Smart Richmond Arms serves seasonal menu, with many ingredients from the estate. Informal Bar & Grill overlooks the golf course and offers modern classics.

Ship rest,

57 North St ✉ PO19 1NH – ✆ (01243) 778 000 – www.theshiphotel.net Town plan: BY**s**

37 rm – £ 92/125 £ 125/185

Rest *Murrays* – Menu £ 17/25 – Carte £ 20/41

Grade II listed former home to one of Nelson's men. Some impressive Georgian features remain, including a cantilevered wrought iron staircase. Stylish, up-to-date bedrooms and a spacious, contemporary bar. Airy brasserie offers modern European menu, with meat and game from the nearby estate.

Brasserie Blanc

Richmond House, The Square ✉ PO19 7SJ – ✆ (01243) 534 200 – www.brasserieblanc.com Town plan: BZ**z**

Menu £ 14/17 – Carte £ 16/40

Classically styled brasserie with a lovely terrace, tucked away in a modern flagstoned square. There's an impressive open kitchen and a display of artisan provisions for sale. Tasty, rustic French cooking uses local produce.

CHICHESTER

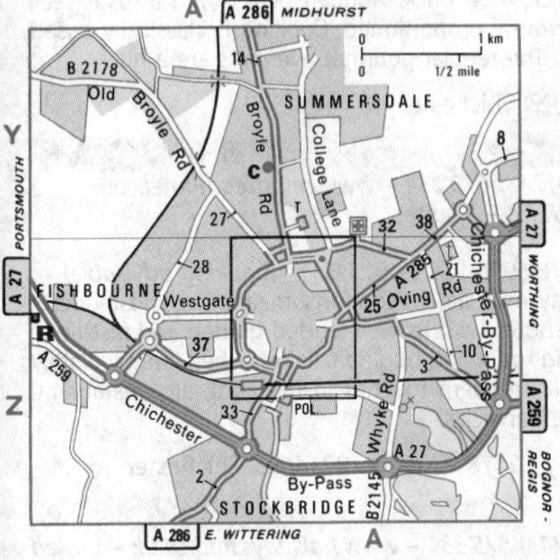

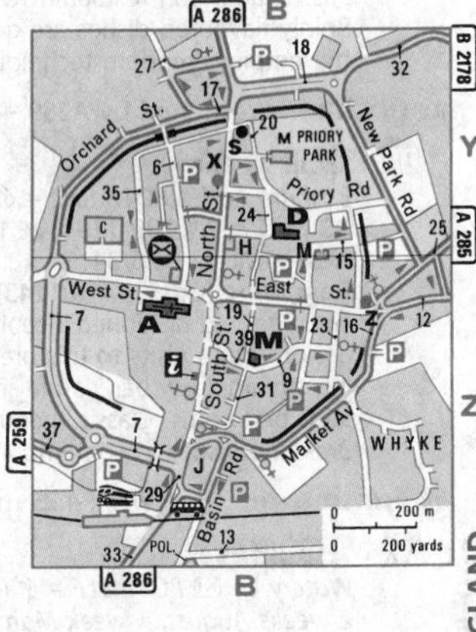

ENGLAND

Amelie and Friends

31 North St ✉ PO19 1LY – ✆ (01243) 771 444 Town plan: BY**x**
– www.amelieandfriends.com – Closed Sunday dinner and Monday-Wednesday dinner January-April
Carte £ 19/34
This simple, modern café sits within a grand Georgian building. Light, unfussy cooking relies on seasonal ingredients; at dinner, the menu features more ambitious combinations. A minimalist dining room leads to a heated terrace.

at Mid Lavant North: 2 mi on A286

Rooks Hill without rest

Lavant Rd ✉ PO18 0BQ – ✆ (01243) 528 400 – www.rookshill.co.uk
3 rm – †£ 85/115 ††£ 105/165
Grade II listed house with a pleasant view across to the Goodwood estate. Relax on the charming courtyard terrace or next to the wood burner in the cosy sitting room. Individually decorated bedrooms have contemporary touches.

Earl of March

✉ PO18 0BQ – ✆ (01243) 533 993 – www.theearlofmarch.com
Menu £ 20 (lunch and early dinner) **s** – Carte £ 28/42 **s**
18C inn with a perfect blend of country character and contemporary styling; its terrace offers amazing views of the South Downs. Good quality, seasonal produce is used in classic British dishes.

at East Lavant North: 2.5 mi off A286 -(AY)✉ Chichester

Royal Oak Inn with rm

Pook Ln ✉ PO18 0AX – ✆ (01243) 527 434 – www.royaloakeastlavant.co.uk
8 rm – †£ 95/185 ††£ 125/320 Carte £ 20/45 – *(closed 25 December)*
18C inn with a rustic, laid-back feel; arrive early for a spot by the fire. Cooking is fairly refined but steaks play an important role. There are interesting vegetarian options, a good cheese selection and plenty of wines by the glass. Spacious bedrooms are comfy and well-equipped; breakfast is a treat.

at Tangmere East: 2 mi by A27 -(AY)✉ Chichester

XX **Cassons**

Arundel Rd ✉ PO18 0DU – Northwest : 0.25 mi off A 27 (westbound) – ✆ (01243) 773 294 – www.cassonsrestaurant.co.uk – Closed 26-30 December, lunch Tuesday, Sunday dinner and Monday

Menu £ 28 (weekday dinner)/39 – Carte lunch £ 21/36

Passionately run restaurant with exposed brick, wooden beams and a rustic feel. Boldly flavoured dishes are generously proportioned. Cooking is classically based but employs modern techniques. The regular gourmet evenings are a hit.

at Bosham West: 4 mi by A259 -(AZ)✉ Chichester

Millstream rest,

Bosham Ln ✉ PO18 8HL – ✆ (01243) 573 234 – www.millstreamhotel.com

35 rm – £ 99/119 £ 159/229 – 3 suites

Rest – Menu £ 26/34

Rest *Marwick's* – ✆ (01243) 578 599 – Carte £ 21/31 – *(booking advisable)*

Genuine, old-fashioned hospitality and classic comforts mean that most guests are on return visits to this pretty hotel, with its well-tended garden and fast-flowing stream. Cosy bar, comfy sitting room and traditionally furnished, immaculately kept bedrooms. Classic menu with modern touches in the light, airy restaurant. Brasserie dishes in contemporary Marwick's.

at Funtington Northwest: 4.75 mi by B2178 -(AY)- on B2146✉ Chichester

ENGLAND

XX **Hallidays**

Watery Ln ✉ PO18 9LF – ✆ (01243) 575 331 – www.hallidays.info.co.uk – Closed 2 weeks August, 1 week March, 1 week Christmas-New Year, Saturday lunch, Sunday dinner, Monday and Tuesday

Menu £ 23/37 – Carte lunch £ 31/38

Charming thatched cottage with a low-beamed ceiling and a homely feel. The experienced chef knows about sourcing good, local ingredients and his menu changes weekly. Skilful, classical cooking.

at West Ashling Northwest: 4.5 mi by B2178 and B2146

Richmond Arms with rm

Mill Rd ✉ PO18 8EA – ✆ (01243) 572 046 – www.therichmondarms.co.uk – Closed Christmas-New Year, last week July, first week November, Sunday dinner, Monday and Tuesday

2 rm – £ 95/110 £ 110/125 Carte £ 28/45

Appealing, laid-back country pub opposite a duck pond in a lovely little village. The menu offers a broad mix, from freshly sliced hams and local steaks to game from the family estate in Anglesey; many dishes are cooked on the rotisserie or Japanese robata grill. Two luxurious bedrooms are found above.

CHIDDINGFOLD

Surrey – Pop. 2 211 – See Regional map n°**7-C2**

London 47 mi – Guildford 10 mi – Haslemere 5 mi

Michelin Road map 504-S30

Swan Inn with rm rest,

Petworth Rd ✉ GU8 4TY – ✆ (01428) 684 688 – www.theswaninnchiddingfold.com

10 rm – £ 100/180 £ 100/180 Carte £ 22/39

Elegant tile-hung pub with a 200 year old history and an up-to-date interior. The local Surrey set pop in for crab cakes or the 'terrine of the day' at lunch; the à la carte changes daily, depending on the latest local produce available. Bedrooms are cool and contemporary.

CHIEVELEY

West Berkshire – See Regional map n°**10-B3**

London 60 mi – Newbury 5 mi – Swindon 25 mi

Michelin Road map 503-Q29 and 504

XX **Crab at Chieveley** with rm — rest,

Wantage Rd ✉ RG20 8UE – West : 2.5mi by School Rd on B 4494 – ✆ (01635) 247 550 – www.crabatchieveley.com
14 rm – †£ 75/200 ††£ 75/200
Menu £ 20 (lunch and early dinner) – Carte £ 28/58
It might look like a normal thatched cottage from the outside and it does have low beams and plenty of rustic character inside too; but this seafood restaurant is a little different. Seafaring memorabilia adorns the restaurant and chic bedrooms are themed around world-famous resorts – some even have hot tubs.

CHILLATON → See Tavistock

Devon – Michelin Road map 503-H32

CHILLINGTON

Devon – See Regional map n°**2-C3**
London 217 mi – Plymouth 26 mi – Torbay 20 mi – Torquay 22 mi
Michelin Road map 503-I33

whitehouse without rest

✉ TQ7 2JX – ✆ (01548) 580 505 – www.whitehousedevon.com
6 rm – †£ 170/240 ††£ 190/260
Attractive Georgian house run in a relaxed manner. Stylish bedrooms feature bold décor and a mix of modern and retro furnishings; all feature heavy handmade beds and smart bathrooms. The breakfast room overlooks the gardens.

ENGLAND

CHINNOR

Oxfordshire – Pop. 5 473 – See Regional map n°**11-C2**
London 45 mi – Oxford 19 mi – Birmingham 88 mi
Michelin Road map 504-R28 – Michelin Green Guide GREAT BRITAIN

at Sprigg's Alley Southeast: 2.5 mi by Bledlow Ridge rd ✉ Chinnor

Sir Charles Napier

Sprigs Holly ✉ OX39 4BX – ✆ (01494) 483 011 – www.sircharlesnapier.co.uk – Closed 24-26 December, Sunday dinner and Monday except bank holidays
Menu £ 18 (weekdays) – Carte £ 38/58 – *(booking advisable)*
Attractive flint pub in a small hillside hamlet, with a hint of eccentricity in its décor. Relax on the pleasant terrace or in the delightful gardens in summer; and by candlelight beside the log fires in winter. Boldly flavoured French based dishes are prepared with skill and capture flavours to their full.
→ Double-baked smoked haddock and cheddar soufflé. Yuzu glazed duck with carrot and blood orange. Chocolate and peanut terrine with hazelnut and bitter orange ice cream.

CHIPPING CAMPDEN

Gloucestershire – Pop. 2 037 – See Regional map n°**4-D1**
London 93 mi – Birmingham 44 mi – Bristol 67 mi
Michelin Road map 503-O27 and 504 – Michelin Green Guide GREAT BRITAIN

Cotswold House H. and Spa

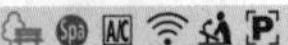

The Square ✉ GL55 6AN – ✆ (01386) 840 330 – www.cotswoldhouse.com
25 rm – †£ 100/520 ††£ 100/520 – 3 suites
Rest *Cotswold Grill* – see restaurant listing
Rest *Dining Room* – Menu £ 40 – Carte £ 26/43 – *(dinner only) (booking essential)*
A set of stylish Regency townhouses with lovely gardens, boldly decorated lounges hung with eclectic modern art, and a fine spiral staircase winding upwards towards luxurious modern bedrooms. Eat in the laid-back grill restaurant or the more formal dining room, surrounded by veneer panelling.

Noel Arms

High St ✉ GL55 6AT – ✆ (01386) 840 317 – www.bespokehotels.com/noelarmshotel
28 rm – £ 60/120 £ 70/150 **Rest** – Carte £ 24/35
Pick a characterful beamed bedroom in the main building (one has an ornate carved bed dating from 1657), or go for one with a touch more modernity in the newer extension. The wood-panelled bar might be traditional but the conservatory lounge and boldly coloured restaurant are more contemporary.

Kings

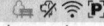

The Square ✉ GL55 6AW – ✆ (01386) 840 256 – www.kingscampden.co.uk
18 rm – £ 110/275 £ 130/305
Rest *Kings* – see restaurant listing
Beautiful Cotswold stone townhouse with a stylish boutique interior. Bedrooms in the main house mix antiques with modern facilities – some boast sleigh beds; rooms in the cottage at the end of the garden are more contemporary.

Seymour House without rest

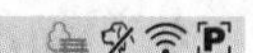

High St ✉ GL55 6AG – ✆ (01386) 840 064 – www.seymourhousebandb.co.uk – Closed Christmas-New Year
5 rm – £ 90/140 £ 120/140
Welcoming Cotswold stone house with early 18C origins, a lovely garden and a pretty breakfast terrace. It's tastefully furnished throughout, with a classical, understated style; fine furnishings, artwork and antiques feature.

Kings – Kings Hotel

The Square ✉ GL55 6AW – ✆ (01386) 840 256 – www.kingscampden.co.uk
Menu £ 16/33
An appealing, rustic restaurant in a stylish boutique townhouse. Exposed stone walls, wooden beams and a large inglenook fireplace feature. Modern British menus use top quality ingredients and dishes are refined and flavoursome.

Chef's Dozen

Island House, High St ✉ GL55 6AL – ✆ (01386) 840 598 – www.thechefsdozen.co.uk – Closed 4-13 January, 19-28 April, 25-26 December, Sunday, Monday and Tuesday lunch
Menu £ 19 (weekdays)/38 – *(booking advisable)*
This intimate restaurant and shady terrace sit close to the square and are run by a local chef with a passion for fine organic and wild ingredients. Dishes are modern, creative and attractive; this is inspired field-to-fork cooking.

Cotswold Grill – Cotswold House H. and Spa

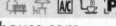

The Square ✉ GL55 6AN – ✆ (01386) 840 330 – www.cotswoldhouse.com
Carte £ 24/43
This relaxed, informal restaurant is found within a Regency townhouse hotel. Open all day, it serves breakfast and afternoon tea as well as an appealing, bistro-style menu of modern dishes including steaks, burgers and charcuterie.

Eight Bells Inn with rm

Church St ✉ GL55 6JG – ✆ (01386) 840 371 – www.eightbellsinn.co.uk – Closed 25 December
6 rm – £ 75/95 £ 95/140 Carte £ 24/36
Characterful country pub just off the historic high street in an old wool merchant's town. Cooking is traditionally British – homemade pies and winter casseroles fill you up, puddings are comforting and specials are just that, so arrive early. Traditionally furnished bedrooms; watch your head on the beams!

ENGLAND

at Mickleton North: 3.25 mi by B4035 and B4081 on B4632 ✉ Chipping Campden

Three Ways House

✉ *GL55 6SB – ✆ (01386) 438 429 – www.threewayshousehotel.com*
48 rm – †£ 88/130 ††£ 150 **Rest** – Menu £ 32/39 – Carte £ 22/34
This privately owned 1870s Cotswold hotel plays host to the famous 'Pudding Club' meetings – they do 'Pudding Breaks' and you can even stay in a pudding-themed room! Bedrooms are contemporary and individually designed; some have private patios. The formal, arcaded restaurant showcases local produce.

at Ebrington East: 2 mi by B4035

Ebrington Arms with rm

✉ *GL55 6NH – ✆ (01386) 593 223 – www.theebringtonarms.co.uk*
5 rm – †£ 104/150 ††£ 112/160 Carte £ 20/33
Proper village local with a beamed, flag-floored bar at its hub, set in a charming chocolate box village. Blackboard menu offers pub classics; the à la carte, a choice of more elaborate dishes. Bedrooms have country views; Room 3, with its four-poster bed and luxury bathroom, is best.

at Broad Campden South: 1.25 mi by B4081 ✉ Chipping Campden

Malt House

✉ *GL55 6UU – ✆ (01386) 840 295 – www.thecotswoldmalthouse.com*
8 rm – †£ 100/120 ††£ 120/170
Rest – Menu £ 30 – Carte £ 26/32 – *(dinner only)*
This attractive Cotswold stone guesthouse started life as a 16C malt house and two old cottages. Inside, characterful guest areas have exposed beams, inglenook fireplaces and Arts and Crafts furnishings; outside there's a lovely summerhouse, a croquet lawn and a wild flower meadow. Bedrooms are comfy and cosy. Breakfast and dinner feature fruit from the garden.

at Weston-sub-Edge Northwest : 3 mi. by B 4081 and B 4035 on B 4632

Seagrave Arms with rm

Friday St ✉ GL55 6QH – ✆ (01386) 840 192 – www.seagravearms.co.uk – Closed 1 week January and Monday except bank holidays
8 rm – †£ 75/90 ††£ 85/165 Menu £ 23 (weekday lunch) – Carte £ 26/34
A handsome building of Cotswold stone, with a cosy, fire-warmed bar and two traditional dining rooms. Attractively presented, modern dishes use well-judged combinations of ingredients from the local larder. Bedrooms are classic in style and the suite, with its spacious bathroom and roll-top bath, is the best.

CHIPPING NORTON

Oxfordshire – Pop. 5 719 – See Regional map n°**10**-**A1**
▶London 77 mi – Oxford 22 mi – Stow-on-the-Wold 9 mi
Michelin Road map 503-P28 and 504

Wild Thyme

10 New St ✉ OX7 5LJ – ✆ (01608) 645 060 – www.wildthymerestaurant.co.uk – Closed first week January, 1 week spring, Sunday and lunch Monday
Menu £ 19 (lunch) – Carte £ 27/48 – *(booking advisable)*
Friendly restaurant off the high street, with a tiny courtyard garden. Rustic tables; No. 10, in the window, is the best. Wholesome regional British cooking with Mediterranean influences. Local, artisan suppliers; tasty homemade breads.

CHIPPING ONGAR

Essex – Pop. 6 093 – See Regional map n°**12**-**B2**
▶London 28 mi – Birmingham 132 mi – Leeds 189 mi – Sheffield 163 mi
Michelin Road map 504-U28

XX **Smith's**

Fyfield Rd ✉ CM5 0AL – ✆ (01277) 365 578 – www.smithsrestaurants.com – Closed 25-26 December and Monday lunch
Menu £ 27/30 – Carte £ 30/60 – *(booking essential)*
Long-standing, locally acclaimed seafood restaurant with a buzzy atmosphere. The à la carte and extensive daily set menu offer dishes ranging from Cornish squid to Scottish smoked salmon. Lobster, cooked several ways, is a speciality.

CHIPSTEAD

Kent – See Regional map n°**8-B1**
London 27 mi – Maidstone 37 mi – Dartford 28 mi

George & Dragon

39 High St ✉ TN13 2RW – ✆ (01732) 779 019 – www.georgeanddragonchipstead.com
Carte £ 18/36
Superbly set, 450 year old inn with a beamed bar and a wonky-floored upstairs dining room. Delightful garden with terrace and children's play area. The menu is a roll call of seasonal English classics; herbs and salad are home-grown.

CHOBHAM

Surrey – Pop. 2 771 – See Regional map n°**7-C1**
London 32 mi – Birmingham 127 mi – Bristol 98 mi – Croydon 31 mi
Michelin Road map 504-S29

XXX **Stovell's**

125 Windsor Rd ✉ GU24 8QS – North : 0.75 mi on B 383 – ✆ (01276) 858 000 – www.stovells.com – Closed first 2 weeks January, last week August, 26-27 December, Saturday lunch, Sunday dinner and Monday
Menu £ 20/38 – *(booking essential)*
A keen husband and wife team run this elegant Tudor farmhouse, where old beams and contemporary furnishings sit side by side. Creative modern dishes feature meats cooked over apple wood and vine cuttings on the wood-fired grill.

ENGLAND

CHOLMONDELEY

Cheshire East – See Regional map n°**20-A3**
London 178 mi – Birmingham 65 mi – Leeds 86 mi – Sheffield 90 mi

Cholmondeley Arms with rm

Wrenbury Rd ✉ SY14 8HN – ✆ (01829) 720 300 – www.cholmondeleyarms.co.uk
6 rm – †£ 60/70 ††£ 80/100 Carte £ 19/33
The eponymous estate's old schoolhouse, with high, vaulted ceilings, large windows and roaring fires. Modern pub favourites might include calves' liver or homemade lamb faggots. Gin lovers will be in clover with more than 200 from which to choose. The 6 comfy bedrooms are in the Old Headmaster's House.

CHORLEY

Lancashire – Pop. 36 183 – See Regional map n°**20-A2**
London 222 mi – Blackpool 30 mi – Liverpool 33 mi – Manchester 26 mi
Michelin Road map 502-M23 and 504

XX **Red Cat**

Blackburn Rd, Whittle-Le-Woods ✉ PR6 8LL – Northeast : 2.5 mi on A 674 – ✆ (01257) 263 966 – www.theredcat.co.uk – Closed Sunday dinner, Monday and Tuesday
Menu £ 27 (lunch) – Carte £ 27/44
Restored pub with a series of cosy, rustic rooms displaying old beams, exposed stone and uneven floors. Menus showcase a wealth of local produce and range from a simple two course lunch to a more ambitious, interesting tasting selection.

CHORLTON-CUM-HARDY → See Manchester

Greater Manchester – Michelin Road map 502-N23 and 503

CHRISTCHURCH

Dorset – Pop. 54 210 – See Regional map n°**4-D3**
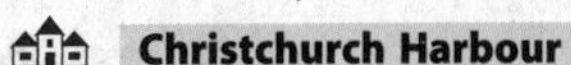London 111 mi – Bournemouth 6 mi – Salisbury 26 mi – Southampton 24 mi
Michelin Road map 503-O31 and 504 – Michelin Green Guide GREAT BRITAIN

Christchurch Harbour

95 Mudeford ✉ BH23 3NT – ✆ (01202) 483 434 – www.christchurch-harbour-hotel.co.uk
64 rm – ♦£ 90/250 ♦♦£ 99/395
Rest *Jetty* – see restaurant listing
Rest *Upper Deck* – Menu £ 16 (lunch) – Carte £ 25/47
Don't be fooled by the unassuming exterior; inside is a cool, chic hotel with a smart basement spa – its waterside location reflected in the modern, nautical-inspired décor. Some bedrooms have waterfront terraces or balconies. Both of the restaurants open onto delightful terraces with far-reaching views.

Captain's Club

Wick Ferry, Wick Ln ✉ BH23 1HU – ✆ (01202) 475 111 – www.captainsclubhotel.com
29 rm – ♦£ 179 ♦♦£ 249 – 12 suites **Rest** – Carte £ 23/38
Striking modern building with art deco and nautical influences, set in a lovely riverside spot – floor to ceiling windows offer fantastic views. Bedrooms are sleek and contemporary; some are three-roomed suites. The restaurant offers all-day menus. Relax in the stylish spa or out on the water in their boat.

Kings Arms

18 Castle St ✉ BH23 1DT – ✆ (01202) 588 933 – www.thekings-christchurch.co.uk
20 rm (dinner included) – ♦£ 68/119 ♦♦£ 75/169
Rest *Kings Arms* – see restaurant listing
This lovingly restored Georgian inn stands opposite the bowling green and castle ruins, and has been given a smart modern makeover. Guest areas have a chic yet characterful feel and the boutique-style bedrooms are well-appointed.

Druid House without rest

26 Sopers Ln ✉ BH23 1JE – ✆ (01202) 485 615 – www.druid-house.co.uk
9 rm – ♦£ 75/155 ♦♦£ 85/155
Hidden behind an unassuming exterior, a bright, well-kept house that's passionately run and great value for money. Bedrooms are bright and modern; some of those in the newer wing open out onto a small terrace. Excellent breakfasts include a buffet and hot specials such as muffins with poached eggs and bacon.

Splinters

12 Church St ✉ BH23 1BW – ✆ (01202) 483 454 – www.splinters.uk.com – Closed 1-13 January, Sunday and Monday
Menu £ 14/32 – Carte £ 21/39
A very traditional, family-run restaurant, named after the splinters the carpenters got when building the booths! Choose from several cosy, characterful rooms. Cooking is wholesome and classical, with rich, tasty sauces a feature.

Jetty – Christchurch Harbour Hotel

95 Mudeford ✉ BH23 3NT – East : 2 mi – ✆ (01202) 400 950 – www.thejetty.co.uk
Menu £ 18/30 – Carte £ 30/51
Set within the grounds of the Christchurch Harbour hotel, this contemporary, eco-friendly restaurant offers fantastic water views. Appealing menus reflect what's available locally, with fish from nearby waters and game from the forest.

Kings Arms – Kings Arms Hotel

18 Castle St ✉ BH23 1DT – ✆ (01202) 588 933 – www.thekings-christchurch.co.uk
Menu £ 15 (lunch and early dinner) – Carte £ 24/40
Smart, spacious hotel brasserie offering gutsy, no frills cooking that's packed with flavour. The Josper grill plays a big role, as does the good value £ 15 weekly menu, which is made up of produce sourced from within 15 miles. Friday is 'Fizz 'n' Chips' night and they also offer afternoon tea.

CHURCHILL

Oxfordshire – Pop. 502 – ✉ Chipping Norton – See Regional map n°**10-A1**
London 79 mi – Birmingham 46 mi – Cheltenham 29 mi – Oxford 23 mi
Michelin Road map 503-P28 and 504

Chequers

Church Rd ✉ OX7 6NJ – ✆ (01608) 659 393 – www.thechequerschurchill.com – Closed 25 December and dinner 26 December and 1 January
Menu £ 13 (lunch) – Carte £ 18/35
Welcoming sandstone pub in the heart of the village; it's a vital part of the community and the owners have got the formula just right. The bar is stocked with local ales; gutsy, traditional dishes include steaks cooked on the Josper grill.

CHURCH ENSTONE

Oxfordshire✉ Chipping Norton – See Regional map n°**10-B1**
London 72 mi – Banbury 13 mi – Oxford 38 mi

Crown Inn

Mill Ln ✉ OX7 4NN – ✆ (01608) 677 262 – www.crowninnenstone.co.uk – Closed 25-26 December, 1 January and Sunday dinner
Carte £ 19/33
17C inn set among pretty stone houses in a picturesque village. Sit in the slate-floored conservatory, the beamed dining room or the rustic bar. Meat, fruit and veg come from local farms; seafood is a speciality, as is the steak pie.

CIRENCESTER

ENGLAND

Gloucestershire – Pop. 16 325 – See Regional map n°**4-D1**
London 97 mi – Bristol 37 mi – Gloucester 19 mi – Oxford 37 mi
Michelin Road map 503-O28 and 504 – Michelin Green Guide GREAT BRITAIN

Fleece at Cirencester

Market Pl ✉ GL7 2NZ – ✆ (01285) 658 507 – www.thefleececirencester.co.uk
28 rm – †£ 85/180 ††£ 91/186
Rest *Fleece at Cirencester* – Carte £ 14/46
Charming, centrally located 18C coaching inn with an open-plan coffee shop and a cosy open-fired sitting room. Spacious modern bedrooms are individually furnished and well-kept; Rooms 1 and 4 are the best. The simple bistro dining room serves an accessible menu, with choices including deli boards and steaks.

No 12 without rest

12 Park St ✉ GL7 2BW – ✆ (01285) 640 232 – www.no12cirencester.co.uk
4 rm – †£ 100 ††£ 120
This 16C townhouse provides plenty of contrasts with its Georgian façade and modern interior. Large bedrooms blend stylish furnishings with original features. Local organic products are used at breakfast and there's a delightful garden.

Old Brewhouse without rest

7 London Rd ✉ GL7 2PU – ✆ (01285) 656 099 – www.theoldbrewhouse.com – Closed 24 December-2 January
10 rm – †£ 68/78 ††£ 80/94
17C former brewhouse in busy central spot, with a characterful cluttered interior and two stone-walled breakfast rooms. Choose between cottage-style bedrooms – most with wrought iron beds – or more modern rooms set around a small courtyard.

Made by Bob

The Corn Hall, 26 Market Pl ✉ GL7 2NY – ✆ (01285) 641 818 – www.foodmadebybob.com – Closed 25-26 December, 1 January and Sunday
Carte £ 23/36 – *(lunch only and dinner Thursday-Friday) (bookings not accepted)*
The name says it all: Bob makes most of the products himself – be it for the informal eatery or the crammed deli – and the rest of the ingredients are organic and locally sourced. Service is bright and breezy, and the flexible daily menus are appealing. If you can't find a seat, they also do takeaway.

Jesse's Bistro
14 Blackjack St ✉ GL7 2AA – ✆ (01285) 641 497 – www.jessesbistro.co.uk – Closed Monday dinner and Sunday
Carte £ 26/52
Rustic bistro where guests can interact with the team in the open-plan kitchen. Well-crafted, generously proportioned dishes feature fish from Cornwall and meats from their adjoining butcher's shop – many are cooked in the wood-fired oven.

at Barnsley Northeast: 4 mi by A429 on B4425 ✉ Cirencester

Barnsley House
✉ GL7 5EE – ✆ (01285) 740 000 – www.barnsleyhouse.com
18 rm – †£ 272/580 ††£ 290/590 – 8 suites
Rest *The Potager* – see restaurant listing
17C Cotswold manor house with a wonderfully relaxed vibe, set in the midst of beautiful gardens styled by Rosemary Verey. A very stylish interior blends original features with modern touches, from the open-fired lounges to the chic bedrooms; there's also a spa and even a cinema in the grounds.

The Potager – Barnsley House Hotel
✉ GL7 5EE – ✆ (01285) 740 000 – www.barnsleyhouse.com
Menu £ 26 (lunch) – Carte £ 29/51
Understated hotel restaurant with a pleasant garden outlook and a laid-back feel. Influencing more than just the name, the kitchen gardens inform what's on the menus each day. Unfussy cooking has Mediterranean overtones; don't miss the freshly baked breads with herb-infused oils and salsa verde.

Village Pub with rm
✉ GL7 5EF – ✆ (01285) 740 421 – www.thevillagepub.co.uk
6 rm – †£ 140/170 ††£ 140/170 Carte £ 25/40 – *(booking essential)*
A stylish and well-run pub with an interior straight out of any Country Homes magazine; it's got that cosy, open-fired, village pub vibe down to a tee. The appealing menu offers modern British dishes, with irresistible nibbles, locally sourced meats, charcuterie from Highgrove and comforting desserts. Individually decorated bedrooms; Number Six has a four-poster.

at Sapperton West: 5 mi by A419 ✉ Cirencester

The Bell
✉ GL7 6LE – ✆ (01285) 760 298 – www.bellsapperton.co.uk
Carte £ 20/39
Charming and characterful Cotswold pub with flagged floors, exposed stone, an abundance of beams and warming log fires. Menus offer the expected burger or fish and chips as well as dishes which allow the chef to show his repertoire.

CLANFIELD
Oxfordshire – Pop. 1 709 – See Regional map n°**10**-A2
London 75 mi – Oxford 24 mi – Ealing 68 mi – Coventry 56 mi
Michelin Road map 503-P28 and 504

Cotswold Plough
Bourton Rd ✉ OX18 2RB – on A 4095 – ✆ (01367) 810 222 – www.cotswoldploughhotel.com – Closed 24-27 December
11 rm – †£ 89/125 ††£ 115/175
Rest *Cotswold Plough* – see restaurant listing
16C wool merchant's house in the heart of a pretty village. Traditional, antique-furnished lounge and a characterful bar with two open fires and 52 types of gin. Spacious bedrooms display modern touches; 3 are four-posters.

Cotswold Plough – Cotswold Plough Hotel
Bourton Rd ✉ OX18 2RB – on A 4095 – ✆ (01367) 810 222 – www.cotswoldploughhotel.com – Closed 24-27 December
Carte £ 24/39
Three-roomed restaurant in a 16C stone-built hotel, with beamed ceilings, polished wood tables and a comfortingly traditional feel. Classically based menus feature steak and game in season. Service is relaxed and informal.

ENGLAND

CLAVERING

Essex – Pop. 882 – ✉ Saffron Walden – See Regional map n°**12-B2**
▶London 44 mi – Cambridge 25 mi – Colchester 44 mi – Luton 29 mi
Michelin Road map 504-U28

Cricketers with rm

✉ *CB11 4QT – ✆ (01799) 550 442 – www.thecricketers.co.uk – Closed 25-26 December*
20 rm – †£ 68 ††£ 95/120 Carte £ 21/37 – *(booking essential)*
Opposite the cricket pitch in a sleepy village; open fires, exposed beams and polished brass abound. Mainly Italian menu with global influences; tasty homemade pasta, wood-fired specialities and bread baked daily. Fruit, veg and herbs come from the owners' son, Jamie Oliver's, organic garden. Cosy bedrooms.

CLEARWELL

Gloucestershire – See Regional map n°**4-C1**
▶London 138 mi – Birmingham 85 mi – Bristol 31 mi – Cardiff 46 mi

Tudor Farmhouse

High St ✉ GL16 8JS – ✆ (01594) 833 046 – www.tudorfarmhousehotel.co.uk
23 rm – †£ 80/195 ††£ 95/210 – 1 suite
Rest – Menu £ 25 – Carte £ 28/41
A group of converted farm buildings in the heart of the Forest of Dean. Two cosy dining rooms serving carefully prepared, interesting dishes are found in the old farmhouse and, above them, characterful bedrooms with old beams and wonky floors. More modern bedrooms are housed in two of the outbuildings.

ENGLAND

CLEESTANTON → See Ludlow

Shropshire

CLENT

Worcestershire – See Regional map n°**19-C2**
▶London 127 mi – Birmingham 12 mi – Hagley 2 mi
Michelin Road map 504-N26 – Michelin Green Guide GREAT BRITAIN

Bell & Cross

Holy Cross ✉ DY9 9QL – Southwest : 0.5 mi – ✆ (01562) 730 319 – www.bellandcrossclent.co.uk – Closed 25 December and dinner 26 December and 1 January
Menu £ 17 (weekdays) – Carte £ 20/34
Charming pub with colourful window boxes and country views. Huge choice of dishes: lunch offers light bites and pub classics, while more substantial dishes appear on the à la carte. Influences range from Asia to the Med.

CLEY-NEXT-THE-SEA → See Blakeney

Norfolk – Michelin Road map 504-X25

CLIFTON → See Penrith

Cumbria – Michelin Road map 502-L20

CLIPSHAM

Rutland – See Regional map n°**17-C2**
▶London 101 mi – Leicester 35 mi – Coventry 72 mi – Nottingham 38 mi

Olive Branch & Beech House with rm

Main St ✉ LE15 7SH – ✆ (01780) 410 355 – www.theolivebranchpub.com
6 rm – †£ 98/115 ††£ 135/195
Menu £ 17/30 – Carte £ 28/49 – *(booking essential)*
Stone pub with delightful gardens and real rustic charm. Daily changing menu of classic dishes, with plenty of pasta and game; the provenance of ingredients is listed on the menu. Barn used for regular cookery exhibitions. Stylish bedrooms in the adjacent house include a host of extras.

CLOVELLY

Devon – Pop. 439 – ✉ Bideford – See Regional map n°**1**-**B1**
London 241 mi – Barnstaple 18 mi – Exeter 52 mi – Penzance 92 mi
Michelin Road map 503-G31 – Michelin Green Guide GREAT BRITAIN

Red Lion

The Quay ✉ EX39 5TF – ✆ (01237) 431 237 – www.clovelly.co.uk
17 rm – £ 84/121 £ 132/206 **Rest** – Menu £ 30 – *(dinner only)*
Traditional inn set in a wonderful location under the cliffs, right on the harbourfront. Good-sized, comfortable bedrooms all have sea views; the newest and largest rooms are in the converted sail loft. Classic dishes and a superb vista in the dining room; lighter snacks in the bar.

CLYST HYDON

Devon – See Regional map n°**2**-**D2**
London 188 mi – Bristol 74 mi – Exeter 12 mi
Michelin Road map 503-J31

Five Bells Inn

✉ EX15 2NT West : 0.5 mi on Clyst St Lawrence rd – ✆ (01884) 277 288 – www.fivebells.uk.com
Menu £ 15 (weekday lunch) – Carte £ 25/39 – *(bookings advisable at dinner)*
Pretty, thatched, Grade II listed pub, deep in the Devon countryside. Experienced chef uses the finest local ingredients in well-balanced dishes with real clarity of flavour. Blackboard of pub favourites and a more creative à la carte. Set lunch menu is excellent value for money. Smooth, friendly service.

COALPORT → See Ironbridge

Telford and Wrekin

COCKLEFORD

Gloucestershire ✉ Cheltenham – See Regional map n°**4**-**C1**
London 95 mi – Bristol 48 mi – Cheltenham 7 mi

The Green Dragon Inn with rm

✉ GL53 9NW – ✆ (01242) 870 271 – www.green-dragon-inn.co.uk – Closed dinner 25-26 December and 1 January
9 rm – £ 70/175 £ 95/175 Carte £ 23/35
Characterful stone pub with huge open fires and carved mice hidden in the woodwork – the hallmark of carpenter Robert 'Mouseman' Thompson. Hearty lunches, unusual starters and generous, meaty mains. Simple, modern bedrooms; one boasts a super king sized bed.

COGGESHALL

Essex – Pop. 3 919 – ✉ Colchester – See Regional map n°**13**-**C2**
London 49 mi – Braintree 6 mi – Chelmsford 16 mi – Colchester 9 mi
Michelin Road map 504-W28

Baumanns Brasserie

4-6 Stoneham St ✉ CO6 1TT – ✆ (01376) 561 453 – www.baumannsbrasserie.co.uk – Closed first 2 weeks January, Monday and Tuesday
Menu £ 18 (lunch) – Carte £ 30/49
Characterful 16C building on the market square; its walls packed with pictures and prints. Globally-influenced dishes are made up of lots of different ingredients. Service is warm and welcoming and it has a loyal local following.

at Pattiswick Northwest: 3 mi by A120 (Braintree Rd) ✉ Coggeshall

Compasses at Pattiswick

Compasses Rd ✉ CM77 8BG – ✆ (01376) 561 322 – www.thecompassesatpattiswick.co.uk
Carte £ 20/34
Remote pub with far-reaching views; make the most of these with a seat in the garden. Smart, spacious interior with open fires, chatty staff and a warm, relaxing feel. Wide-ranging menu of traditional English dishes and nursery puddings.

COLERNE → See Bath (Bath & North East Somerset)

Wiltshire – Michelin Road map 503-M29 and 504

COLSTON BASSETT

Nottinghamshire – Pop. 239 – ✉ Nottingham – See Regional map n°**16**-B2

London 129 mi – Leicester 23 mi – Lincoln 40 mi – Nottingham 15 mi

Michelin Road map 502-R25 and 504

The Martins Arms

School Ln ✉ NG12 3FD – ✆ (01949) 81 361 – www.themartinsarms.co.uk – Closed dinner 25 December and 1 January

Carte £ 22/52

Creeper-clad pub in a charming village, with a cosy, fire-lit bar and period furnished dining rooms. The menu has a meaty, masculine base, with a mix of classical and more modern dishes, and plenty of local game in season.

COLTISHALL

Norfolk – Pop. 2 310 – ✉ Norwich – See Regional map n°**15**-D1

London 125 mi – Norwich 8 mi – Ipswich 54 mi – Lowestoft 31 mi

Michelin Road map 504-Y25 – Michelin Green Guide GREAT BRITAIN

Norfolk Mead

Church Loke ✉ NR12 7DN – ✆ (01603) 737 531 – www.norfolkmead.co.uk

13 rm – †£ 125/175 ††£ 135/185

Rest – Menu £ 30 – *(dinner only and Sunday lunch)*

Former Georgian merchant's house in 8 acres of grounds, complete with an otter lake and a walled garden. Smart modern bedrooms come in neutral hues: one has a balcony; another, a courtyard; and many have rain showers. The stylish two-roomed bistro offers complex dishes and views over the meadow to the river.

COLTON

North Yorkshire – See Regional map n°**23**-C2

London 199 mi – Leeds 20 mi – York 10 mi

Ye Old Sun Inn with rm

Main St ✉ LS24 8EP – ✆ (01904) 744 261 – www.yeoldsuninn.co.uk – Closed 26 and dinner 31 December

3 rm – †£ 75/80 ††£ 85/95 Menu £ 20 – Carte £ 21/40

Rustic, family-run pub with warming open fires and a small deli. The owners are great ambassadors for local suppliers and seasonal produce, and give regular cookery demonstrations. Smart bedrooms are located in the house next door.

COLWALL → See Great Malvern

– Michelin Road map 501-M27

COLYFORD

Devon ✉ Colyton – See Regional map n°**2**-D2

London 168 mi – Exeter 21 mi – Taunton 30 mi – Torquay 46 mi

Michelin Road map 503-K31 – Michelin Green Guide GREAT BRITAIN

Swallows Eaves

rest,

Swan Hill Rd ✉ EX24 6QJ – ✆ (01297) 553 184 – www.swallowseaves.co.uk

7 rm – †£ 75/85 ††£ 95/135

Rest *Reeds* – Menu £ 24 – Carte lunch £ 22/26 – *(closed Sunday and Monday)*

Smart creamwashed house clad with wisteria, located in the heart of a pretty village. Bright bedrooms come with books, wi-fi and views over the gardens or the Axe Valley. Relax in the comfy lounge or out on the terrace. The light, airy restaurant serves traditional dishes of locally sourced produce.

COMBE HAY → See Bath

Bath and North East Somerset

COMPTON BASSETT → See Calne

Wiltshire – Michelin Road map 503-O29

CONDOVER → See Shrewsbury

Shropshire – Michelin Road map 503-L26

CONGLETON

Cheshire East – Pop. 26 178 – See Regional map n°**20-B3**

London 183 mi – Liverpool 50 mi – Manchester 25 mi – Sheffield 46 mi

Michelin Road map 502-N24 and 503 – Michelin Green Guide GREAT BRITAIN

XX **Pecks**

Newcastle Rd, Moreton ✉ CW12 4SB – South : 2.75 mi on A 34 – ✆ (01260) 275 161 – www.pecksrest.co.uk – Closed 25-30 December, Sunday dinner and Monday

Menu £ 23/48 – Carte lunch £ 27/52

Airy, modish restaurant with a unique style. A la carte lunches are followed by monthly changing 5 and 7 course set dinners at 8pm sharp. Traditional home-made dishes use good produce and arrive in generous portions.

CONSTANTINE BAY → See Padstow

Cornwall – Michelin Road map 503-E32

COOKHAM

Windsor and Maidenhead – Pop. 5 304 – ✉ Maidenhead – See Regional map n°**11-C3**

London 32 mi – High Wycombe 7 mi – Oxford 31 mi – Reading 16 mi

Michelin Road map 504-R29 – Michelin Green Guide GREAT BRITAIN

White Oak

Pound Ln ✉ SL6 9QE – ✆ (01628) 523 043 – www.thewhiteoak.co.uk – Closed dinner Sunday and bank holidays

Menu £ 14/25 – Carte £ 25/45

One could argue about whether this is a contemporary pub or a pubby restaurant, as it's set up quite formally, but what is in no doubt is the warmth of the welcome and the affection in which the place is held by its many regulars. Cooking is carefully executed and full of flavour. Great value 'Menu Auberge'.

COOKHAM DEAN

Windsor and Maidenhead – See Regional map n°**11-C3**

London 32 mi – High Wycombe 7 mi – Oxford 31 mi – Reading 16 mi

Michelin Green Guide GREAT BRITAIN

Sanctum on the Green rest,

The Old Cricket Common ✉ SL6 9NZ – ✆ (01628) 482 638 – www.sanctumonthegreen.com

9 rm – †£ 99/245 ††£ 99/245

Rest *Luke's Dining Room* – Carte £ 20/49

Hidden away on the side of the green, a part-timbered property with large decked terraces, lovely gardens and a heated outdoor pool. Contemporary furnishings contrast with old beams. Stylish, boutique bedrooms come in bold colours. Two lounges and an open-plan bar and dining area; tasty, classical cooking.

CORBRIDGE

Northumberland – Pop. 2 946 – See Regional map n°**24-A2**

London 300 mi – Hexham 3 mi – Newcastle upon Tyne 18 mi

Michelin Road map 501-N19 and 502 – Michelin Green Guide GREAT BRITAIN

Duke of Wellington with rm rest,

Newton ✉ NE43 7UL – East : 3.5 mi by A 69 – ✆ (01661) 844 446 – www.thedukeofwellingtoninn.co.uk

7 rm – †£ 70/90 ††£ 90/120 Menu £ 18 (weekdays) – Carte £ 22/36 **s**

Smart, modern pub looking out over the Tyne Valley: head for the dining area left of the bar. Wide-ranging menus include some local specialities – try the lamb or roe deer. Stylish, luxurious bedrooms are named after local rivers and come with underfloor heating and exposed beams.

CORBY

Northamptonshire – Pop. 54 927 – See Regional map n°**17**-C3
London 100 mi – Leicester 26 mi – Northampton 22 mi – Peterborough 24 mi
Michelin Road map 504-R26 – Michelin Green Guide GREAT BRITAIN

Hampton by Hilton without rest
Rockingham Leisure Park, Princewood Rd ✉ NN17 4AP – Northwest : 2.5 mi by Rockingham Rd off A 6116 – ✆ (01536) 211 001 – www.hamptonbyhilton.co.uk/corby
88 rm – †£ 49/109 ††£ 59/119
Smart hotel on a business park close to Rockingham Motor Speedway. Modern bedrooms have big comfy beds and are ideal for business travellers; contemporary bathrooms have large walk-in showers. There's a bar and snack shop but no restaurant.

CORFE CASTLE

Dorset – Pop. 1 355 – ✉ Wareham – See Regional map n°**4**-C3
London 129 mi – Bournemouth 18 mi – Weymouth 23 mi
Michelin Road map 503-N32 and 504 – Michelin Green Guide THE WEST COUNTRY

Mortons House
45 East St ✉ BH20 5EE – ✆ (01929) 480 988 – www.mortonshouse.co.uk
23 rm – †£ 85/100 ††£ 160 – 2 suites **Rest** – Carte £ 27/43
An Elizabethan manor house built in the shape of an "E" to honour the Queen. The castle ruins are close above it and a steam railway runs just below. Bedrooms are classical and well-kept; one has a Victorian bath and four are in an annexe. Have lunch in the bar or lounges and dinner in the panelled restaurant.

CORNHILL-ON-TWEED

Northumberland – Pop. 347 – See Regional map n°**24**-A1
London 345 mi – Edinburgh 49 mi – Newcastle upon Tyne 59 mi
Michelin Road map 501-N17 and 502 – Michelin Green Guide SCOTLAND

Tillmouth Park 
✉ TD12 4UU Northeast : 2.5 mi on A 698 – ✆ (01890) 882 255 – www.tillmouthpark.co.uk – Closed 2 January-2 April
14 rm – †£ 79/149 ††£ 175/245
Rest *Library* – Carte £ 23/37 – *(dinner only and Sunday lunch)*
Late Victorian country house in 15 acres; set in prime shooting and fishing country. Welcoming interior with characterful stained glass, grand staircases and traditional guest areas with lovely views. Spacious bedrooms; some four-posters. Wood-panelled restaurant for à la carte dinners and a set Sunday lunch.

Coach House
Crookham ✉ TD12 4TD – East : 4 mi on A 697 – ✆ (01890) 820 293 – www.coachhousecrookham.com
10 rm – †£ 45/70 ††£ 80/110
Rest – Menu £ 23 – *(dinner only) (bookings essential for non-residents)*
Keenly run hotel close to the Flodden battleground, consisting of a 1680s dower house and a collection of old farm buildings set around a courtyard. The stable block houses a lounge with an honesty bar and the largest, most modern bedrooms. The cosy breakfast-cum-dining room is in the original house.

CORSE LAWN → See Tewkesbury (Glos.)

Worcestershire

CORSHAM

Wiltshire – Pop. 13 432 – See Regional map n°**4**-C2
London 103 mi – Bristol 31 mi – Cardiff 64 mi – Plymouth 151 mi
Michelin Road map 504-N29

Methuen Arms with rm

2 High St ✉ SN13 0HB – ✆ (01249) 717 060 – www.themethuenarms.com
14 rm – †£ 85/115 ††£ 120/175 Menu £ 16/27 – Carte £ 27/45
17C coaching inn set in an attractive little town and named after the family who own Corsham Court. Eat in the 'Little Room' by the bar, the open-fired 'Nott Room' or the characterful restaurant. Good ingredients feature in tasty dishes – dinner steps things up a gear. Comfy, boutique-style bedrooms.

CORTON DENHAM

Somerset – Pop. 210 – ✉ Sherborne – See Regional map n°**4-C3**
London 123 mi – Bristol 36 mi – Cardiff 110 mi – Southampton 84 mi
Michelin Road map 504-M31

Queens Arms with rm

✉ DT9 4LR – ✆ (01963) 220 317 – www.thequeensarms.com
8 rm – †£ 80/130 ††£ 110/130
Menu £ 15 (weekday lunch) – Carte £ 26/44 – *(booking advisable)*
Relaxed, bohemian pub with open fires and a hotchpotch of tables that include a glass-topped cartwheel. One menu offers pub favourites; the other displays a more interesting array of dishes. Appealing selection of ciders, beers and whiskies. Bedrooms are modern, with good facilities – some have slipper baths.

COTEBROOK

Cheshire West and Chester – See Regional map n°**20-A3**
London 186 mi – Chester 13 mi – Manchester 33 mi

Fox and Barrel

Foxbank ✉ CW6 9DZ – ✆ (01829) 760 529 – www.foxandbarrel.co.uk – Closed dinner 25-26 December and 1 January
Carte £ 16/36
Well-run pub with wood-panelled walls, heaving bookshelves and a smart terrace. The constantly evolving menu offers originality and interest, with sensibly priced dishes arriving neatly presented and generously sized.

COVERACK

Cornwall – See Regional map n°**1-A3**
London 300 mi – Penzance 25 mi – Truro 27 mi
Michelin Road map 503-E33

Bay

North Corner ✉ TR12 6TF – ✆ (01326) 280 464 – www.thebayhotel.co.uk – Closed 1-22 December and 3 January-mid March
13 rm (dinner included) – †£ 85/190 ††£ 110/250
Rest – Menu £ 29/35 – *(dinner only) (bookings essential for non-residents)*
Imposing, family-run country house located in a pretty fishing village and boasting views over the bay. Homely lounge and bar. Spotless, modern bedrooms with a slight New England edge. Dining room and conservatory offer a classical daily menu and local seafood specials.

COWAN BRIDGE

Lancashire – See Regional map n°**20-B1**
London 263 mi – Carlisle 61 mi – Lancaster 18 mi
Michelin Road map 502-M21

XX **Hipping Hall** with rm

on A 65 ✉ LA6 2JJ – ✆ (01524) 271 187 – www.hippinghall.com – Closed 7-10 January
10 rm – †£ 120/315 ††£ 159/419
Menu £ 55/65 – *(dinner only and lunch Saturday-Sunday)*
Charming part-15/16C house – a former blacksmith's – named after the stepping (or 'hipping') stones over the beck by the old washhouse. The smart, airy restaurant has a superb beamed ceiling, a minstrel's gallery and an almost baronial feel. Well-executed modern dishes use top quality local ingredients. Sleek white bedrooms feature deep pile carpets and modern bathrooms.

ENGLAND

COWLEY

Gloucestershire – See Regional map n°**4-C1**
London 105 mi – Swindon 28 mi – Gloucester 14 mi – Cheltenham 6 mi
Michelin Road map 504-N28

Cowley Manor

GL53 9NL – (01242) 870 900 – www.cowleymanor.com
30 rm – £ 195/575 £ 195/575 – 8 suites
Rest – Carte £ 31/47 – *(bar lunch Monday-Saturday)*
Impressive Regency house in 55 acres, with beautiful formal gardens, a superb spa, and lake views from some of the bedrooms. Original features and retro furnishings mix with bold colours and modern fittings to create a laid-back, understated vibe. The carved wood panelling in the restaurant is a feature.

COWSHILL

Durham – See Regional map n°**24-A3**
London 295 mi – Newcastle upon Tyne 42 mi – Stanhope 10 mi – Wolsingham 16 mi
Michelin Road map 502-N19

Low Cornriggs Farm

Weardale DL13 1AQ – Northwest : 0.75 mi on A 689 – (01388) 537 600 – www.cornriggsfarm.co.uk – Closed 20 December-5 January
3 rm – £ 45 £ 68 **Rest** – Menu £ 20 s
Extended stone farmhouse dating back 300 years and offering lovely views over Weardale. Cosy flag-floored lounge with an open fire. Dine in the conservatory in summer or the beamed dining room in winter; steak pie is a speciality. Pine-furnished bedrooms have up-to-date facilities and neat, compact bathrooms.

CRADLEY → See Great Malvern

Herefordshire

CRANBROOK

Kent – Pop. 4 225 – See Regional map n°**8-B2**
London 53 mi – Hastings 19 mi – Maidstone 15 mi
Michelin Road map 504-V30 – Michelin Green Guide GREAT BRITAIN

Cloth Hall Oast without rest

Coursehorn Ln TN17 3NR – East : 1 mi by Tenterden rd – (01580) 712 220 – www.clothhalloast.co.uk – Closed Christmas
3 rm – £ 65/75 £ 90/125
Superbly restored oast house that was rebuilt in 2001. Antiques, family photos and fine artwork fill the drawing room. Bedrooms are well-equipped but retain some original character; one boasts a splendid four-poster bed. Communal breakfasts at an antique table set below restored rafters in the main hall.

Apicius (Tim Johnson)

23 Stone St TN17 3HE – (01580) 714 666 – www.restaurant-apicius.co.uk – Closed 2 weeks June-July, 2 weeks Christmas-New Year, Saturday lunch, Sunday dinner, Monday and Tuesday
Menu £ 28/43
Personally and passionately run restaurant in a pretty market town; its rustic walls filled with framed menus from the great and the good of the restaurant world. Skilfully prepared dishes use the best local ingredients in classic, tried-and-tested flavour combinations. The place has a warm, intimate feel.
→ Ham hock ballotine, seared foie gras, apple purée and pea velouté. Saddle of rabbit with baby spinach, roast garlic and tomatoes. Medjool date sponge, honey ice cream and toffee sauce.

CRANLEIGH

Surrey – Pop. 9 905 – See Regional map n°**7**-C2

London 40 mi – Birmingham 150 mi – Leeds 233 mi – Sheffield 203 mi

Restaurant 107

180 High St (1st Floor) GU6 8RG – (01483) 276 272 – www.restaurant107.co.uk – Closed Saturday lunch, Sunday dinner and Monday

Menu £ 18 – Carte £ 21/40

The very hands-on owner looked at 106 other places before deciding this light, airy first floor restaurant was the one for him. Like the subtly made-over room, the hearty, classically based dishes have a refined, modern edge.

CRAYKE

North Yorkshire York – See Regional map n°**23**-C2

London 217 mi – Birmingham 147 mi – Liverpool 114 mi – Sheffield 74 mi

Durham Ox with rm

Westway YO61 4TE – (01347) 821 506 – www.thedurhamox.com – Closed dinner 25 December

6 rm – †£ 100 ††£ 120/140

Menu £ 18 (weekday lunch) – Carte £ 20/40 – *(booking essential)*

Characterful, family-run pub dating back 300 years and set in a sleepy hamlet next to Crayke Castle. Menus change regularly and offer hearty dishes of fresh seafood, local meats and Crayke game, with 40-day dry-aged steaks a speciality. Bedrooms are set in old farm cottages; the suite features a jacuzzi.

CREWE

Cheshire East – Pop. 71 722 – See Regional map n°**20**-B3

London 174 mi – Birmingham 57 mi – Manchester 36 mi

Michelin Road map 502-M24

Crewe Hall

Weston Road CW1 6UZ – Southeast : 1.75 mi on A 5020 – (01270) 253 333 – www.qhotels.co.uk

117 rm – †£ 89/207 ††£ 101/219 – 4 suites

Rest *The Brasserie* – (01270) 259 319 – Menu £ 17 (lunch) – Carte £ 22/47 **s**

A tree-lined drive leads up to this impressive 19C mansion designed by Edward Barry. Dramatic Jacobean features provide plenty of character in the main house and lovely chapel, while bedrooms and events rooms in the extensions are stylish and contemporary. The modern brasserie offers a menu to match.

CRICKLADE

Wiltshire – See Regional map n°**4**-D1

London 89 mi – Birmingham 86 mi – Bristol 54 mi – Cardiff 87 mi

Michelin Road map 503-029

Red Lion with rm

74 High St SN6 6DD – (01793) 750 776 – www.theredlioncricklade.co.uk

5 rm – †£ 80/85 ††£ 80/85 Carte £ 20/40

Traditional 17C pub just off the Thames path with a low-beamed, characterful bar. Classical cooking makes good use of local produce; burgers are a speciality. They smoke some of their own meats and fish and brew and bottle their own beers. Comfortable, well-equipped bedrooms are in the old stables.

CROCKERTON → See Warminster

Wiltshire

CROFT-ON-TEES → See Darlington

North Yorkshire – Michelin Road map 502-P20

ENGLAND

CROMER

Norfolk – Pop. 7 949 – See Regional map n°**15-D1**
London 132 mi – Kings Lynn 43 mi – Norwich 23 mi
Michelin Road map 504-X25

No1 Cromer

1 New St ✉ NR27 9HP – ✆ (01263) 512 316 – www.no1cromer.com – Closed 25 December and Monday except June-September
Carte £ 19/27
This is fish and chips with a difference – looking out over the beach and pier and offering everything from fresh fish and battered local sausages to cockle popcorn and mushy pea fritters. Potatoes are from their farm and the variety changes throughout the year. Children's portions arrive in a beach bucket.

CROOKHAM VILLAGE

Hampshire – Pop. 3 648 – See Regional map n°**7-C1**
London 43 mi – Sheffield 191 mi – Kingston upon Hull 219 mi – Peterborough 115 mi
Michelin Road map 504-R30

Exchequer

Crondall Rd ✉ GU51 5SU – ✆ (01252) 615 336 – www.exchequercrookham.co.uk – Closed 25 December
Carte £ 20/39
Slick, modern pub with an inviting drinkers' area and a smart conservatory-style room. The menu offers mainly gutsy British staples but there's also a nod to the East; the blackboard best displays the kitchen's abilities. Service is keen.

ENGLAND

CROPSTON

Leicestershire – See Regional map n°**16-B2**
London 106 mi – Birmingham 49 mi – Sheffield 67 mi – Leicester 6 mi
Michelin Road map 502-Q25

Horseshoe Cottage Farm

Roecliffe Rd, Hallgates ✉ LE7 7HQ – Northwest : 1 mi on Woodhouse Eaves rd – ✆ (0116) 235 00 38 – www.horseshoecottagefarm.com
3 rm – †£ 65 ††£ 100 **Rest** – Menu £ 20
Well-run, extended farmhouse and outbuildings, beside Bradgate Country Park. Traditional bedrooms with beams, exposed stonework and coordinating fabrics. Small breakfast room and a larger, high-ceilinged drawing room, with a solid oak table where communal dinners are served; local and garden produce features.

CROSTHWAITE → See Kendal

Cumbria – Michelin Road map 502-L21

CRUDWELL → See Malmesbury

Wiltshire – Michelin Road map 503-N29 and 504

CUCKFIELD

West Sussex – Pop. 3 500 – See Regional map n°**7-D2**
London 37 mi – Croydon 27 mi – Barnet 51 mi – Ealing 48 mi
Michelin Road map 504-T30

Ockenden Manor

Ockenden Ln ✉ RH17 5LD – ✆ (01444) 416 111 – www.ockenden-manor.co.uk
28 rm – †£ 119/215 ††£ 249/395 – 3 suites
Rest *Ockenden Manor* ✿ – see restaurant listing
Part-Elizabethan manor house in 9 acres of parkland. Kick-back in the cosy panelled bar or beside the grand fireplace in the elegant drawing room. Stay in a characterful period bedroom or one of the modern rooms above the chic spa.

XXX **Ockenden Manor** – Ockenden Manor Hotel

Ockenden Ln ✉ RH17 5LD – ✆ (01444) 416 111 – www.ockenden-manor.co.uk
Menu £ 19 (weekday lunch)/75 – *(booking essential)*
Contemporary orangery dining room opening onto the manor house gardens and affording pleasant views over the South Downs. The passionate chef uses seasonal local produce to create appealing, original menus. Cooking is refined, flavours are well-balanced and dishes show good attention to detail.
→ Jersey Royal fricassee, chicken oysters, morels and English asparagus. Lamb saddle, breast, falafel and croquette with baba ganoush. Warm rhubarb clafoutis and ginger ice cream.

CUDDINGTON

Buckinghamshire – See Regional map n°**11**-C2
London 48 mi – Aylesbury 6 mi – Oxford 17 mi
Michelin Road map 503-M24 and 504 – Michelin Green Guide GREAT BRITAIN

Crown

Aylesbury Rd ✉ HP18 0BB – ✆ (01844) 292 222 – www.thecrowncuddington.co.uk – Closed Sunday dinner
Carte £ 21/33
Attractive thatched pub in a charming village, with traditional styling and a friendly, welcoming atmosphere. Seasonal menus display hearty comfort food in winter and lighter dishes in summer; the smoked haddock with Welsh rarebit is a hit.

CUNDALL

North Yorkshire – See Regional map n°**22**-B2
London 222 mi – Leeds 36 mi – York 29 mi

Cundall Lodge Farm without rest

✉ YO61 2RN Northwest : 0.5 mi on Asenby rd – ✆ (01423) 360 203 – www.cundall-lodgefarm.co.uk – Closed January and Christmas
3 rm – £ 55/65 £ 85/95
Grade II listed Georgian farmhouse on a working arable farm; its 150 acres include a stretch of the River Swale. Country bedrooms come with homemade shortbread and Roberts radios. The friendly owners have great local knowledge.

CURY → See Helston

Cornwall – Michelin Road map 503-E33

DALTON-IN-FURNESS

Cumbria – Pop. 7 827 – See Regional map n°**21**-A3
London 283 mi – Barrow-in-Furness 3 mi – Kendal 30 mi – Lancaster 41 mi
Michelin Road map 502-K21

Clarence House

Skelgate ✉ LA15 8BQ – ✆ (01229) 462 508 – www.clarencehouse-hotel.com – Closed 25-26 December
28 rm – £ 99/130 £ 130/210
Rest ***Clarence House*** – see restaurant listing
The majority of guests here are repeat customers – which says a lot about the way the family run it. Relax in the peaceful, mature gardens or in one of the plush sitting rooms. Some bedrooms come with jacuzzis or four-posters.

XX **Clarence House** – Clarence House Hotel

Skelgate ✉ LA15 8BQ – ✆ (01229) 462 508 – www.clarencehouse-hotel.co.uk – Closed 25-26 December
Menu £ 17/30 – Carte £ 28/48
This is a proper country house hotel restaurant with luxurious furnishings and willing service. Dishes are traditionally based but are modern in their execution. They use the finest Cumbrian meats, so steak is always a good bet.

DARGATE → See Faversham

Kent

ENGLAND

DARLEY ABBEY → See Derby

Derby – Michelin Road map 502-P25 and 503

DARLINGTON

Darlington – Pop. 92 363 – See Regional map n°**22-B1**
London 251 mi – Leeds 61 mi – Newcastle upon Tyne 35 mi
Michelin Road map 502-P20

Houndgate Townhouse

rest,

11 Houndgate ✉ DL1 5RF – ✆ (01325) 486 011 – www.houndgatetownhouse.co.uk
8 rm – †£ 80/135 ††£ 90/145
Rest – Menu £ 20 (weekdays) – Carte £ 27/34
This smart Georgian townhouse – formerly a registry office – is set on a quiet square in the heart of town. Inside, stylish colour schemes and contemporary furnishings create a boutique feel; bedroom two has a bath in the room. The bistro has comfy booths, a terrace and a menu of modern classics.

at Croft-on-Tees South: 4.5 mi on A167 ✉ Darlington

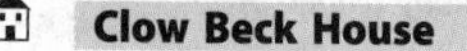

Clow Beck House

rm,

Monk End Farm ✉ DL2 2SP – West : 0.75 mi by A 167 off Barton rd – ✆ (01325) 721 075 – www.clowbeckhouse.co.uk – Closed 24 December-3 January
13 rm – †£ 85 ††£ 135
Rest – Carte £ 27/43 **s** – *(dinner only) (residents only)*
Collection of converted farm buildings not far from the River Tees. Welcoming owners and a homely interior. Immaculately kept, tastefully furnished bedrooms come with iPod docks, bathrobes and chocolates; the larger ones have dressing rooms. Home-cooked dinners, with a puzzle supplied while you wait.

ENGLAND

at Hurworth-on-Tees South: 5.5 mi by A167

Rockliffe Hall

✉ DL2 2DU – ✆ (01325) 729 999 – www.rockliffehall.com
61 rm – †£ 265/295 ††£ 210/440
Rest *The Orangery* – Carte £ 34/83 – *(dinner only)*
Rest *Brasserie* – Carte £ 20/49 **s** – *(closed dinner Sunday and Monday)*
Rest *Clubhouse Grill* – Carte £ 28/43 **s**
Impressive red-brick property in 376 acres of grounds, boasting a championship golf course and state-of-the-art leisure facilities. Grand guest areas and characterful bedrooms in the original Victorian house; modern bedrooms in the extensions. Ambitious restaurant menu; light, modern dishes in the airy brasserie; everything from sandwiches to Sunday lunch in the grill.

Bay Horse

45 The Green ✉ DL2 2AA – ✆ (01325) 720 663 – www.thebayhorsehurworth.com – Closed 25-26 December and Sunday dinner
Menu £ 14 (lunch)/25 (weekday dinner) – Carte £ 28/50
Smart village pub with pleasant terrace and gardens. Wide-ranging menu offers largely hearty classics; presentation ranges from simple and rustic to more modern and intricate.

at Summerhouse Northwest: 6.5 mi by A68 on B6279

Raby Hunt (James Close) with rm

✉ DL2 3UD – ✆ (01325) 374 237 – www.rabyhuntrestaurant.co.uk – Closed 1 week spring, 1 week autumn, 25-26 December, 1 January and Sunday to Tuesday
2 rm – †£ 125/150 ††£ 125/150 Menu £ 30/85 – *(booking essential)*
A former inn in a rural hamlet, where the Raby Castle hunt hounds were once kennelled; now a stylishly decorated, family-run restaurant with a small modern bar and an elegant dining room. The passionate, self-taught chef uses first class ingredients to create unfussy modern dishes with bold flavours and a confident touch. Bedrooms are comfortable and contemporary.
→ Smoked eel with duck liver parfait, beetroot and cherry. Red deer with ragu, celeriac and endive. Chocolate bar with salted caramel and popcorn ice cream.

at Headlam Northwest: 8 mi by A67 ✉ Gainford

Headlam Hall

✉ *DL2 3HA – ✆ (01325) 730 238 – www.headlamhall.co.uk – Closed 24-27 December*
39 rm – †£ 100/135 ††£ 125/165 – 4 suites
Rest – Menu £ 16 (weekday lunch) – Carte £ 25/40
Family owned and run manor house with delightful walled gardens, in a secluded countryside setting. Spacious antique-furnished sitting rooms. Well-equipped, traditionally styled bedrooms in the original house; others are more contemporary. Up-to-date leisure facilities. Bright restaurant offers classic dishes.

DARTMOUTH

Devon – Pop. 6 008 – See Regional map n°**2**-**C3**
London 236 mi – Exeter 36 mi – Plymouth 35 mi
Michelin Road map 503-J32 – Michelin Green Guide GREAT BRITAIN

Dart Marina

Sandquay Rd ✉ TQ6 9PH – ✆ (01803) 832 580 – www.dartmarina.com
51 rm – †£ 95/155 ††£ 140/300
Rest *River* – Menu £ 39 – *(dinner only and Sunday lunch)*
Once an old boat works and chandlery, now a relaxed, modern hotel with a small spa and leisure centre. Smart, contemporary bedrooms have lovely outlooks over either the river or the marina – many also boast balconies. The stylish, formal restaurant offers up-to-date versions of British classics.

Royal Castle

11 The Quay ✉ TQ6 9PS – ✆ (01803) 833 033 – www.royalcastle.co.uk
25 rm – †£ 110/120 ††£ 160/170 **Rest** – Menu £ 17/23 – Carte £ 26/41
Iconic 15C coaching inn consisting of two separate buildings joined by a smart glass atrium. Boldly coloured bedrooms offer good comforts – some have jacuzzi baths. Choice of two bars: one for drinkers and one serving all-day dishes. The restaurant offers modern takes on old classics and has great views.

Seahorse

5 South Embankment ✉ TQ6 9BH – ✆ (01803) 835 147 – www.seahorserestaurant.co.uk – Closed Monday and Sunday dinner
Menu £ 20 (lunch and early dinner) – Carte £ 31/52 – *(booking essential)*
Smart restaurant in a lovely spot on the embankment; sit outside looking over the estuary or inside, beside the glass-walled kitchen. Seafood orientated menus have a Mediterranean bias; whole fish cooked on the Josper grill are a hit.

Rockfish

8 South Embankment ✉ TQ6 9BH – ✆ (01803) 832 800 – www.rockfishdevon.co.uk – Closed 25 December
Carte £ 17/25 – *(bookings not accepted)*
Buzzy 'beach shack' style eatery run by a chatty team. Good old comfort dishes arrive in paper-lined baskets and rely on sustainable produce. Closely set tables have paper cloths proclaiming 'fish so fresh tomorrow's are still in the sea'.

at Kingswear East: via lower ferry ✉ Dartmouth

Nonsuch House

Church Hill ✉ TQ6 0BX – from lower ferry take first right onto Church Hill before Steam Packet Inn – ✆ (01803) 752 829 – www.nonsuch-house.co.uk – Closed January
4 rm – †£ 95/145 ††£ 120/180
Rest – Menu £ 38 **s** – *(closed Tuesday, Wednesday and Saturday) (dinner only) (residents only)*
Charming Edwardian house run by friendly hands-on owners; boasting lovely views over the castle, town and sea. Bright Mediterranean-style décor blends nicely with original features. Bedrooms are spacious and well-appointed and one has a small balcony. Tea and homemade cake on arrival; local, seasonal cooking and excellent views in the conservatory dining room.

ENGLAND

at Strete Southwest: 4.5 mi on A379 ✉ Dartmouth

Strete Barton House without rest 
Totnes Rd ✉ TQ6 0RU – ☎ (01803) 770 364 – www.stretebarton.co.uk – Closed 2 weeks January
6 rm – †£ 105/160 ††£ 105/160
Attractive part-16C manor house in a quiet village, with partial views over the rooftops to the sea. The contemporary interior has a personal style; bedrooms come with bold feature walls and modern facilities. Homemade cake is served on arrival and top quality local ingredients feature at breakfast.

Laughing Monk
Totnes Rd ✉ TQ6 0RN – ☎ (01803) 770 639 – www.thelaughingmonkdevon.co.uk – Closed December, January, Sunday and Monday
Menu £ 26 – Carte £ 30/45 – *(dinner only)*
Built in 1839 as the village schoolhouse; the original wooden floor and a huge stone fireplace remain. Tasty, traditional dishes feature meats from nearby farms and seafood from local waters; cooking is unfussy and uses classical pairings.

at Blackawton West: 5.5 mi by A3122

Normandy Arms with rm
Chapel St ✉ TQ9 7BN – ☎ (01803) 712 884 – www.thenormandyarms.co.uk – Closed January and Sunday-Monday in winter
3 rm – †£ 95/105 ††£ 95/105
Menu £ 30 (weekday dinner) – Carte £ 27/39 – *(dinner only and lunch in August)*
Pretty little pub with a cosy bar area and a dining room decorated with colourful artwork. Cooking keeps things simple, relying on careful preparation of good quality ingredients to keep flavours clear. Smart, unfussy bedrooms are named after cities in Normandy; the pub's name refers to the Normandy landings.

ENGLAND

DATCHWORTH

Hertfordshire – See Regional map n°**12**-B2
London 31 mi – Luton 15 mi – Stevenage 6 mi
Michelin Road map 504-T28

Coltsfoot Country Retreat 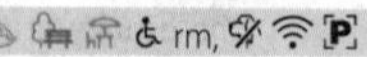
Coltsfoot Lane, Bulls Green ✉ SG3 6SB – South 0.75 mi by Bramfield Rd, turning at 'The Horns' – ☎ (01438) 212 800 – www.coltsfoot.com
15 rm – †£ 118/175 ††£ 138/199
Rest – Menu £ 27/33 – Carte £ 23/41 – *(closed Sunday) (dinner only) (booking essential)*
A former farmhouse dating back to the 16C; now a contemporary hotel and a popular wedding venue. Spacious bedrooms, some with terraces; Room 15 was where the prize bull was once kept. The bar and restaurant are in a converted barn and offer pleasant country views; menus are classical, with a modern twist.

Tilbury
1 Watton Rd ✉ SG3 6TB – ☎ (01483) 815 550 – www.thetilbury.co.uk – Closed Monday and Sunday dinner
Menu £ 18/21 – Carte £ 23/40
Charming 18C inn run by two brothers, set just off the village green. Something for everyone on a menu of two halves: classic dishes will please the traditionalists, while dishes like maple roasted guinea fowl showcase the kitchen's skills.

DAVENTRY

Northamptonshire – Pop. 23 879 – See Regional map n°**16**-B3
London 79 mi – Coventry 23 mi – Leicester 31 mi – Northampton 13 mi
Michelin Road map 504-Q27

Fawsley Hall

Fawsley ✉ NN11 3BA – South : 6.5 mi by A 45 off A 361 – ✆ (01327) 892 000 – www.fawsleyhall.com

56 rm ☕ – 🚹£ 125/245 🚹🚹£ 125/450 – 2 suites

Rest *The Brasserie* – see restaurant listing

Set in 2,000 peaceful acres, a luxurious Tudor manor house boasting Georgian and Victorian wings. Have afternoon tea in the grand hall or unwind in the exclusive leisure club and spa. Well-appointed bedrooms vary from wing to wing.

The Brasserie – Fawsley Hall Hotel

Fawsley ✉ NN11 3BA – South : 6.5 mi by A 45 off A 361 – ✆ (01327) 892 000 – www.fawsleyhall.com

Menu £ 32 – Carte £ 24/41

Situated in the heart of an impressive manor house, a smart yet informal dining room with an impressive stone fireplace and a courtyard terrace. The wide-ranging menu offers refined brasserie classics with modern twists. Friendly team.

at Staverton Southwest: 2.75 mi by A45 off A425 ✉ Daventry

Colledges House

Oakham Ln ✉ NN11 6JQ – off Glebe Ln – ✆ (01327) 702 737 – www.colledgeshouse.co.uk

4 rm ☕ – 🚹£ 68/70 🚹🚹£ 95/99 **Rest** – Menu £ 35

17C thatched cottage and barn conversion, run by a friendly, enthusiastic owner. The cosy lounge is filled with antiques and curios; the conservatory is a pleasant spot in summer. Traditional bedrooms have floral fabrics and good extras. Cordon bleu style dinners are taken communally at a solid oak table.

DAYLESFORD

→ See Stow-on-the-Wold

Gloucestershire – Michelin Road map 503-O28

DEAL

Kent – Pop. 30 555 – See Regional map n°**9-D2**

London 78 mi – Canterbury 19 mi – Dover 8 mi – Margate 16 mi

Michelin Road map 504-Y30

Dunkerley's

19 Beach St ✉ CT14 7AH – ✆ (01304) 375 016 – www.dunkerleys.co.uk

16 rm ☕ – 🚹£ 65/100 🚹🚹£ 90/150

Rest *Dunkerley's* – see restaurant listing

Very welcoming hotel in a good spot just off the main street, opposite the beach and pier. Bedrooms are a mix of styles: some are modern, some are more classical and some have feature wallpaper; four of them come with spa baths.

Number One without rest

1 Ranelagh Rd ✉ CT14 7BG – ✆ (01304) 364 459 – www.numberonebandb.co.uk

4 rm ☕ – 🚹£ 70/87 🚹🚹£ 77/97

Stylish guesthouse by the promenade, run by an enthusiastic owner. Bedrooms have bold wallpapers, fine bed linen and luxury bathrooms with tower showers. A delightful breakfast room hosts award-winning breakfasts of Kentish produce.

Dunkerley's – Dunkerley's Hotel

19 Beach St ✉ CT14 7AH – ✆ (01304) 375 016 – www.dunkerleys.co.uk – Closed Monday lunch

Menu £ 16/29

Traditional hotel restaurant with original stained glass windows, a terrace and views over the Channel. Cooking is hearty, with plenty of seafood on offer. Specials usually come from the day boats and there's a good range of wines.

ENGLAND

Victuals & Co

St Georges Passage ✉ *CT14 6TA – (01304) 374 389 – www.victualsandco.com – Closed Sunday dinner, Monday and Tuesday*
Menu £ 25 (weekday dinner) – Carte £ 22/42
Found down a narrow passageway, this enthusiastically run restaurant is named after the victuallers who supplied the local ships. Classic dishes are given modern twists; try some small plates followed by a tasting plate at lunch.

at Worth Northwest: 5 mi by A258

Solley Farm House without rest

The Street ✉ *CT14 0DG – (01304) 613 701 – www.solleyfarmhouse.co.uk*
3 rm – £ 95/105 £ 140/160
Attractive 300 year old house overlooking the duck pond and run by a charming owner. In the beamed lounge, a vast inglenook fireplace takes centre stage; colour-themed bedrooms come with great extras. Have breakfast on the terrace.

DEDDINGTON

Oxfordshire – Pop. 1 594 – See Regional map n°**10**-B1
London 72 mi – Birmingham 46 mi – Coventry 33 mi – Oxford 18 mi
Michelin Road map 503-Q28 and 504

Old Post House without rest

New St ✉ *OX15 0SP – on A 4260 – (01869) 338 978 – www.oldposthouse.co.uk*
3 rm – £ 65 £ 90
Charming 17C sandstone house with mullioned windows, a beautiful walled garden and an outdoor pool (for use by prior arrangement). Comfortable open-fired lounge and spacious, classically styled bedrooms. Tea and cake on arrival. Tasty Aga-cooked breakfasts, with homemade preserves for your toast.

ENGLAND

DEDHAM

Essex – Pop. 719 – ✉ Colchester – See Regional map n°**13**-D2
London 63 mi – Chelmsford 30 mi – Colchester 8 mi – Ipswich 12 mi
Michelin Road map 504-W28 – Michelin Green Guide GREAT BRITAIN

Maison Talbooth

Stratford Rd ✉ *CO7 6HN – West : 0.5 mi – (01206) 322 367 – www.milsomhotels.com*
12 rm – £ 170/220 £ 215/425
Rest ***Le Talbooth*** – see restaurant listing
Charming, part-Georgian house in rolling countryside, with a modern, country house feel and views over the river valley. Individually decorated bedrooms boast quality furnishings and come in a mix of classical and contemporary styles. Seek out the tennis court and lovely, year-round heated swimming pool.

Milsoms

rest,

Stratford Rd ✉ *CO7 6HW – West : 0.75 mi – (01206) 322 795 – www.milsomhotels.com*
15 rm – £ 130/205 £ 130/205 **Rest** – Carte £ 24/45
A late 19C country house with modern additions, overlooking Dedham Vale; its interior is stylish and contemporary, with comfortable and well-equipped 'New England' style bedrooms. All-day dining from an appealing menu in the airy bar-restaurant with its huge terrace.

Le Talbooth – Maison Talbooth Hotel

Gun Hill ✉ *CO7 6HN – West : 0.75 mi – (01206) 323 150 – www.milsomhotels.com – Closed Sunday dinner October-May*
Menu £ 31 (weekday lunch) – Carte £ 38/58
Delightful hotel restaurant with numerous private rooms and a lovely terrace, in an attractive riverside setting. To celebrate its 60th birthday, it was cleverly and subtly updated, with a zinc bar and stunning Italian chandeliers. Menus are light and modern, and are accompanied by a well-chosen wine list.

Sun Inn with rm
High St ✉ CO7 6DF – ✆ (01206) 323 351 – www.thesuninndedham.com – Closed 25-26 December
7 rm – ♦£ 85/140 ♦♦£ 130/160 Menu £ 19 (weekdays) – Carte £ 24/29
Brightly painted 15C pub in the heart of a picturesque village. Relaxed dining room and beautiful wooden bar stocked with real ales and homemade sausage rolls. Hearty, rustic Italian dishes – many available in two sizes – and a large selection of tasty antipasti. Snug bedrooms; two have a Scandic feel.

DENHAM

Buckinghamshire – Pop. 1 432 – See Regional map n°**11**-D3
London 20 mi – Buckingham 42 mi – Oxford 41 mi – Croydon 26 mi
Michelin Road map 504-S29 – Michelin Green Guide GREAT BRITAIN

Swan Inn
Village Rd ✉ UB9 5BH – ✆ (01895) 832 085 – www.swaninndenham.co.uk – Closed 25-26 December
Carte £ 21/36 – *(booking essential)*
Located in a picture postcard village; a wisteria-clad, red-brick Georgian pub with a pleasant terrace and mature gardens. Menus change with the seasons and offer plenty of interest – the side dishes are appealing and pudding is a must.

DERBY

Derby – Pop. 255 394 – See Regional map n°**16**-B2
London 132 mi – Birmingham 40 mi – Coventry 49 mi – Leicester 29 mi
Michelin Road map 502-P25 and 503 – Michelin Green Guide GREAT BRITAIN

Cathedral Quarter
16 St. Marys Gate ✉ DE1 3JR – ✆ (01332) 546 080 – www.cathedralquarterhotel.com Town plan: Y**x**
38 rm – ♦£ 110 ♦♦£ 130/200
Rest *Opulence* – Carte £ 26/34 – *(closed Sunday dinner and Monday) (dinner only and Sunday lunch)*
Boutique-style hotel retaining original Victorian features including mosaic floors, ornate ceilings and marble pillars. Bedrooms vary in size but all are furnished in a contemporary style. The first floor restaurant has wood panelling, an 8-seater chef's table and a menu of ambitious modern dishes.

Ibérico World Tapas Ⓝ
9-11 Bold Ln ✉ DE1 3NT – ✆ (01332) 345 456 – www.ibericotapas.com/derby – Closed Sunday Town plan: Y**s**
Menu £ 10/12 – Carte £ 15/36
It's all in the name: the main concept is Spanish, with plenty of tapas dishes and Spanish classics, but there's also a more global feel, courtesy of Mediterranean-style décor and some dishes with Asian origins. The imported hams are a must-try, and the lunch and early evening menus are excellent value.

at Darley Abbey North: 2.5 mi off A6 -(X)✉ Derby

Darleys
Darley Abbey Mill ✉ DE22 1DZ – ✆ (01332) 364 987 – www.darleys.com – Closed 25 December-15 January, Sunday dinner and bank holidays
Menu £ 23 (lunch) – Carte £ 35/41 – *(booking advisable)*
Popular weir-side restaurant, located in the old canteen of a 19C silk mill. Start with drinks in the modern bar-lounge or on the attractive terrace. Good value lunches are followed by more ambitious European dishes in the evening.

ENGLAND

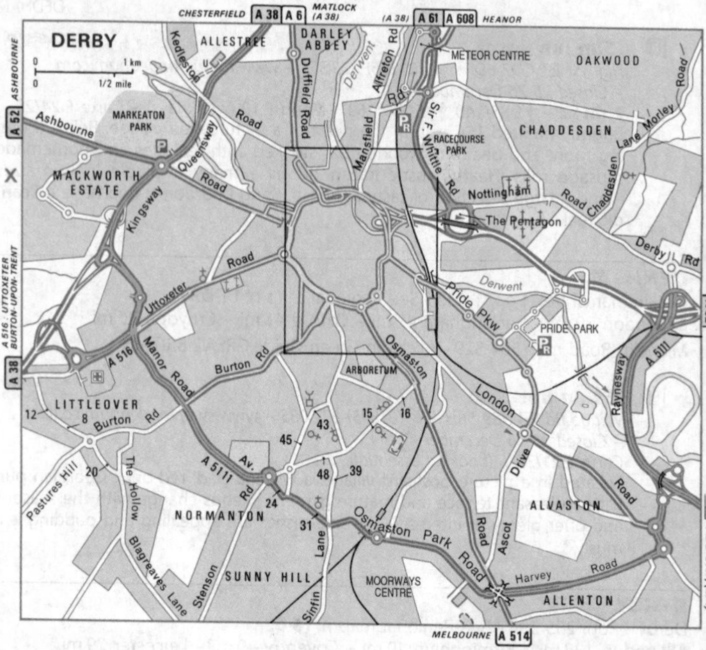

DERBY

CENTRE

Street	Grid	No.
Albert St	Z	2
Babington Lane	Z	3
Bold Lane	Y	4
Bradshaw Way	Z	5
Cathedral Rd	Y	7
Chain Lane	X	8
Charnwood St	Z	9
Corden Ave	X	12
Corn Market	Z	13
Corporation St	YZ	14
Dairy House Rd	X	15
Douglas St	X	16
Duffield Rd	Y	17
Eagle Shopping Centre	Z	
East St	Z	18
Full St	Y	19
Hillsway	X	20
Iron Gate	Y	22
Jury St	Y	23
Kenilworth Ave	X	24
King St	Y	25
Liversage St	Z	26
Market Pl.	YZ	27
Midland Rd	Z	28
Morledge	Z	29
Mount St	Z	30
Newdigate St	X	31
Normanton Rd	Z	33
Queen St	Y	34
Sacheveral St	Z	40
St Mary's Gate	Y	36
St Peter's St	Z	37
St Thomas Rd	X	39
Stafford St	Z	42
Stanhope St	X	43
Upper Dale Rd	X	45
Victoria St	Z	46
Walbrook Rd	X	48
Wardwick	Z	50

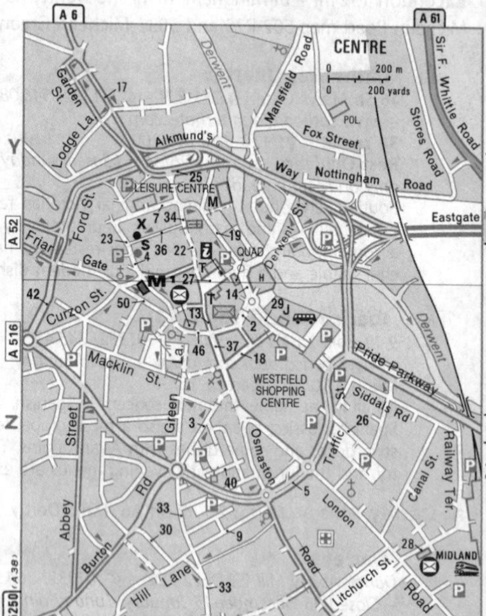

ENGLAND

DEVIZES

Wiltshire – Pop. 18 064 – See Regional map n°**4-C2**
London 98 mi – Bristol 38 mi – Salisbury 25 mi – Southampton 50 mi
Michelin Road map 503-O29 and 504 – Michelin Green Guide THE WEST COUNTRY

Blounts Court Farm without rest
Coxhill Ln, Potterne ✉ SN10 5PH – South : 2.25 mi by A 360 – ✆ (01380) 727 180 – www.blountscourtfarm.co.uk
3 rm – £ 50/56 £ 80/88
Delightfully run farmhouse set on a 150 acre working farm. The snug interior consists of a cosy lounge and a spacious breakfast room filled with clocks and curios; framed pastel artwork and country photos abound. Warm, comfy, well-kept bedrooms show good attention to detail.

at Rowde Northwest: 2 mi by A361 on A342✉ Devizes

George & Dragon with rm
High St ✉ SN10 2PN – ✆ (01380) 723 053 – www.thegeorgeanddragonrowde.co.uk – Closed Sunday dinner
3 rm – £ 85/95 £ 95/125 Menu £ 17 (weekdays)/20 – Carte £ 16/52
Rustic and cosy 16C coaching inn with open fires, solid stone floors and wooden beams. The oft-changing menu has a strong emphasis on seafood, with fish delivered daily from Cornwall. Old-world charm meets modern facilities in the individually designed bedrooms.

DIDSBURY → See Manchester

Greater Manchester – Michelin Road map 502-N23 and 503

DINNINGTON

South Yorkshire – Pop. 19 860 – See Regional map n°**22-B3**
London 40 mi – Birmingham 150 mi – Leeds 233 mi – Sheffield 203 mi
Michelin Road map 502-Q23

Throapham House without rest
Oldcotes Rd, Throapham ✉ S25 2QS – North : 1.5 mi by B 6060 on B 6463 – ✆ (01909) 562 208 – www.throapham-house.co.uk
3 rm – £ 65/85 £ 80/100
Comfy 19C house run by a friendly couple. Well-equipped, individually decorated bedrooms come with extra touches; Bradwell, with its beams, is the most characterful. Spacious first floor lounge. Homemade jams feature at breakfast.

DITCHLING

East Sussex – Pop. 1 476 – See Regional map n°**7-D2**
London 48 mi – Brighton and Hove 10 mi – Hastings 40 mi
Michelin Road map 504-T31

Tovey Lodge without rest
Underhill Ln ✉ BN6 8XE – South : 1 mi by B 2112 off Ditchling Beacon rd – ✆ (01273) 256 156 – www.toveylodge.co.uk – Closed January
5 rm – £ 65/155 £ 79/175
Well-appointed guesthouse with mature gardens and views over the South Downs. Smart bedrooms have modern facilities; Maple, with its balcony, is the best. Beyond the communal breakfast room you'll find a swimming pool and sauna.

DODDINGTON

Kent – See Regional map n°**9-C2**
London 50 mi – Maidstone 15 mi – Faversham 7 mi
Michelin Road map 504-W30

Old Vicarage without rest

Church Hill ✉ ME9 0BD – ✆ (01795) 886 136 – www.oldvicaragedoddington.co.uk – Closed 24 December-2 January
5 rm – †£ 60/72 ††£ 85/96
Grade II listed former vicarage with 16C origins, where wooden beams and exposed stone blend with modern furnishings. There's an impressive galleried hall and a striking antique dining table where the excellent breakfasts are taken. Good-sized bedrooms feature coffee machines and Bose sound systems.

DOGMERSFIELD

Hampshire – See Regional map n°**7**-C1
London 44 mi – Farnham 6 mi – Fleet 2 mi

Four Seasons

Dogmersfield Park, Chalky Ln ✉ RG27 8TD – ✆ (01252) 853 000 – www.fourseasons.com/hampshire
133 rm – †£ 265/285 ††£ 265/285, £ 25 – 22 suites
Rest *Seasons* – Menu £ 49/55 – *(closed Sunday dinner and Monday) (dinner only and Sunday lunch)*
Rest *Bistro* – Carte £ 26/49
An attractive part-Georgian house in 350 acres of parkland, where you can try your hand at all manner of outdoor pursuits. Luxurious bedrooms are well-equipped and come with marble bathrooms. A superb spa is found in the converted coach house. The contemporary restaurant offers classic dishes presented in a modern style, while the casual bistro offers steaks and grills.

ENGLAND

DONCASTER

South Yorkshire – Pop. 109 805 – See Regional map n°**23**-C3
London 173 mi – Kingston-upon-Hull 46 mi – Leeds 30 mi – Nottingham 46 mi
Michelin Road map 502-Q23 and 503

Mount Pleasant rm, rest,

Great North Rd ✉ DN11 0HW – Southeast : 6 mi on A 638 – ✆ (01302) 868 696 – www.mountpleasant.co.uk – Closed 24-25 December
68 rm – †£ 79/129 ††£ 89/199 – 2 suites
Rest *Garden* – Carte £ 22/46
Well-run hotel with luxurious, individually styled bedrooms – many with feature beds, jacuzzi baths and even saunas; try a room with a five-poster or glass bed. Good range of beauty treatments in the spa. Characterful bar and a formal restaurant with an impressive wall tapestry; extensive, classical menu.

DONHEAD-ST-ANDREW

Wiltshire – See Regional map n°**4**-C3
London 115 mi – Bournemouth 34 mi – Poole 32 mi – Bath 37 mi
Michelin Road map 503-N30 and 504

The Forester

Lower St ✉ SP7 9EE – ✆ (01747) 828 038 – www.theforesterdonheadstandrew.co.uk – Closed Sunday dinner
Menu £ 19/23 – Carte £ 24/38
Gloriously rustic, 13C thatched pub, hidden down narrow lanes in a delightful village. Exposed stone walls and vast open fires feature throughout. Seasonal menus showcase well-prepared, flavoursome dishes with a classical country base and a refined edge; they also offer a daily seafood selection.

DORCHESTER

Dorset – Pop. 19 060 – See Regional map n°**4**-C3
London 135 mi – Bournemouth 27 mi – Exeter 53 mi – Southampton 53 mi
Michelin Road map 503-M31 and 504 – Michelin Green Guide GREAT BRITAIN

Little Court without rest

5 Westleaze, Charminster ✉ DT2 9PZ – North : 1 mi by B3147, turning right at Loders garage – ✆ (01305) 261 576 – www.littlecourt.net

8 rm – †£ 69/119 ††£ 79/129

Lutyens-style house boasting Edwardian wood and brickwork, leaded windows and mature gardens with a pool and tennis court. Bedrooms display original features and modern furnishings; one has a four-poster bed.

Westwood House without rest

29 High St West ✉ DT1 1UP – ✆ (01305) 268 018 – www.westwoodhouse.co.uk – Closed 31 December-5 January

6 rm – †£ 60/75 ††£ 75/95

Georgian townhouse built in 1815 by Lord Illchester. Spotlessly kept bedrooms have bold colours, king-sized beds and fridges containing fresh milk. The sunny drawing room opens onto a conservatory where hearty breakfasts are served.

Sienna (Russell Brown)

36 High West St ✉ DT1 1UP – ✆ (01305) 250 022 – www.siennarestaurant.co.uk – Closed 2 weeks spring, 2 weeks autumn, Tuesday lunch, Sunday and Monday

Menu £ 26/65 – *(booking essential)*

This unassuming high street restaurant has just five tables, so you'll need to book ahead. Choose from the set or tasting menu – both showcase excellent quality local produce in superbly flavoured, accomplished dishes, which arrive in tried-and-tested combinations. Service is professional and friendly.

→ Potato gnocchi with wild garlic pesto. Venison saddle, ragout beignet, celeriac & pear. Bitter chocolate delice, crème fraîche ice cream, salted toffee sauce.

ENGLAND

Yalbury Cottage with rm

Lower Bockhampton ✉ DT2 8PZ – East : 3.75 mi by A 35 – ✆ (01305) 262 382 – www.yalburycottage.com – Closed Christmas-mid January

8 rm – †£ 70/85 ††£ 95/120

Menu £ 33/38 – *(dinner only and Sunday lunch and light lunch May-September)*

This proudly run restaurant is in an old thatched cottage and has a snug beamed interior. Cooking is gutsy and flavoursome, and produce is sourced from within 9 miles. In summer, try the English tapas, which features cured meats, cheese and bread baked in plant pots. Well-kept cottagey bedrooms are in a wing.

at Winterbourne Steepleton West: 4.75 mi by B3150 and A35 on B3159✉ Dorchester

Old Rectory without rest

✉ DT2 9LG – ✆ (01305) 889 468 – www.theoldrectorybandb.co.uk – Closed 1 week Christmas

4 rm – †£ 70 ††£ 80/110

A proudly run, attractive stone rectory in a pretty village. It's immaculately kept, from the comfy lounge and conservatory breakfast room to the homely bedrooms and smart bathrooms. Cross the brook to enter the mature gardens.

DORKING

Surrey – Pop. 17 098 – See Regional map n°**7-D2**

London 26 mi – Brighton 39 mi – Guildford 12 mi – Worthing 33 mi

Michelin Road map 504-T30

Two to Four

2-4 West St ✉ RH4 1BL – ✆ (01306) 889 923 – www.2to4.co.uk – Closed 25 December-early January, 1 week spring, 1 week summer, Sunday and Monday

Menu £ 19 (weekday lunch) – Carte £ 29/52

This 17C, Grade II listed property sports contemporary décor, although beams bear witness to its history and help give it a pleasant rustic feel. Friendly and informal; cosy in the evening. Menu is British at its core but with influences from all over; dishes are unfussy and well-presented.

DORNEY

Buckinghamshire – Pop. 278 – See Regional map n°**11-D3**

London 27 mi – Birmingham 111 mi – Bristol 97 mi – Croydon 35 mi

Palmer Arms

Village Rd ✉ SL4 6QW – ✆ (01628) 666 612 – www.thepalmerarms.com

Carte £ 21/41 – *(booking advisable)*

Run by a keen young couple; it's the food, not the furnishings, that matter here. Menus display a well-balanced mix of pub favourites and some more adventurous dishes. The private dining room offers far-reaching views.

DORRIDGE

West Midlands ✉ Birmingham – See Regional map n°**19-C2**

London 109 mi – Birmingham 11 mi – Warwick 11 mi

Michelin Road map 503-O26 and 504

Forest with rm

rest, rest,

25 Station Approach ✉ B93 8JA – ✆ (01564) 772 120 – www.forest-hotel.com – Closed 25 December and Sunday dinner

12 rm – †£ 85/99 ††£ 100/130 Menu £ 16 (weekdays) – Carte £ 22/38

Surprisingly stylish restaurant located opposite the railway station in a 19C hotel: choose the bar-lounge for unfussy classics or head to the dining room for ambitious dishes with interesting modern twists. Cooking is accomplished and well-judged. Comfortable, contemporary bedrooms complete the picture.

DOUGLAS → See Man (Isle of)

Douglas – Michelin Road map 502-G21

DOVER

Kent – Pop. 41 709 – See Regional map n°**9-D2**

London 76 mi – Eastbourne 68 mi – Maidstone 43 mi

Michelin Road map 504-Y30 – Michelin Green Guide GREAT BRITAIN

Wallett's Court Country House

West Cliffe, St Margaret's at Cliffe ✉ CT15 6EW – Northeast : 3.5 mi by A 258 on St Margaret's at Cliffe rd – ✆ (01304) 852 424 – www.wallettscourt.com

18 rm – †£ 95/205 ††£ 135/235 **Rest** – Menu £ 24/40

Family-run country house with 16C origins, in a peaceful setting. Guest areas are heavily beamed and bedrooms are traditional and characterful. The annexe rooms are more modern, with the converted grain store and Victorian bath house the most unusual. Classic menus are offered in the atmospheric restaurant.

DOWNTON → See Lymington

Hampshire – Michelin Road map 503-P31 and 504

DREWSTEIGNTON

Devon – Pop. 668 – See Regional map n°**2-C2**

London 190 mi – Plymouth 56 mi – Torbay 35 mi – Exeter 15 mi

Michelin Road map 503-I31

Old Inn with rm

✉ EX6 6QR – ✆ (01647) 281 276 – www.old-inn.co.uk – Closed Sunday-Tuesday

3 rm – †£ 70 ††£ 90/100

Menu £ 46 – *(dinner only and lunch Friday-Saturday) (booking essential)*

Olive green former pub in the centre of a lovely Devonshire village. It has two small, cosy dining rooms and a parquet-floored lounge with modern art for sale on the walls and a wood-burning stove in the large inglenook fireplace. A concise menu offers hearty, classical dishes. Bedrooms are simply furnished.

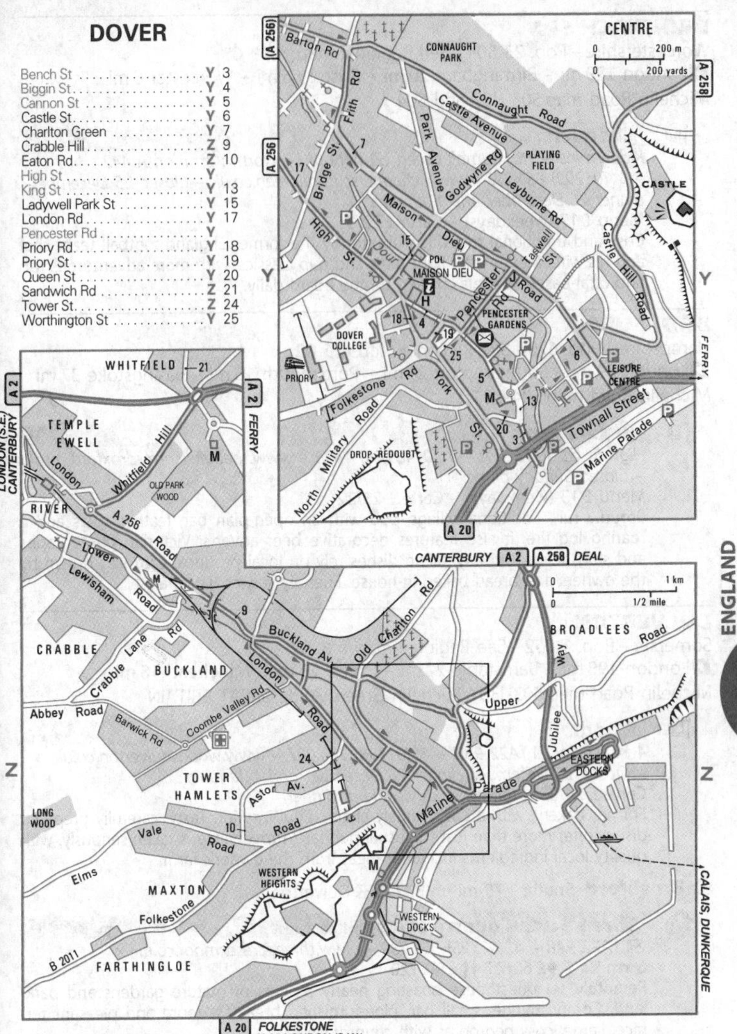

ENGLAND

DRIGHLINGTON

West Yorkshire – See Regional map n°**22**-B2
London 196 mi – Leeds 7 mi – Sheffield 41 mi – Manchester 35 mi
Michelin Road map 502-P22

Prashad

137 Whitehall Rd ✉ BD11 1AT – ✆ (0113) 285 20 37 – www.prashad.co.uk
– Closed 25 December and 1 January
Carte £ 17/32 – *(dinner only and lunch Friday-Sunday)*
Stylish former pub with a vibrant pink and blue colour scheme and wood panels from India fronting the bar; head upstairs to admire the huge picture of a Mumbai street scene. Authentic vegetarian dishes range from enticing street food to original creations with countrywide influences; be sure to try the dosas.

DROITWICH SPA

Worcestershire – Pop. 23 504 – See Regional map n°**19**-C3
London 129 mi – Birmingham 20 mi – Bristol 66 mi – Worcester 6 mi
Michelin Road map 503-N27 and 504

Chequers

Kidderminster Rd, Cutnall Green ✉ WR9 0PJ – North : 3 mi on A 442 – ✆ (01299) 851 292 – www.chequerscutnallgreen.co.uk – Closed 25 December, dinner 26 December and 1 January
Menu £ 17 (weekdays) – Carte £ 22/36
Cosy and traditional roadside pub, run by the former England football team chef and his wife. Menus offer light bites and pub classics, with more adventurous fish and offal-based specials chalked on the board daily.

DROXFORD

Hampshire – Pop. 675 – See Regional map n°**6**-B2
London 79 mi – Southampton 21 mi – Portsmouth 16 mi – Basingstoke 37 mi
Michelin Road map 504-Q31

Bakers Arms

High St ✉ SO32 3PA – ✆ (01489) 877 533 – www.thebakersarmsdroxford.com – Closed Sunday dinner
Menu £ 13 (weekdays) – Carte £ 23/32
Proudly run, traditional village pub with an open-plan bar, leather sofas and a roaring log fire; it also features decorative beer adverts, Victorian photographs and stag heads. Unfussy, filling dishes rely on local produce, with veg grown by the owners and bread baked in-house. Friendly service. Local ales.

ENGLAND

DULVERTON

Somerset – Pop. 1 052 – See Regional map n°**3**-A2
London 198 mi – Barnstaple 27 mi – Exeter 26 mi – Minehead 18 mi
Michelin Road map 503-J30 – Michelin Green Guide GREAT BRITAIN

Woods

4 Banks Sq ✉ TA22 9BU – ✆ (01398) 324 007 – www.woodsdulverton.co.uk – Closed 25 December, dinner 26 December and 1 January
Carte £ 24/33 – *(bookings advisable at dinner)*
Former bakery, with a cosy, hugely characterful interior. Tasty, carefully prepared dishes offer more than just the usual pub fare. Provenance is taken seriously, with quality local ingredients including meat from the owner's farm.

at Brushford South: 1.75 mi on B3222 ✉ Dulverton

Three Acres Country House without rest

✉ TA22 9AR – ✆ (01398) 323 730 – www.threeacresexmoor.co.uk
6 rm – †£ 60/75 ††£ 90/120
Remotely set guesthouse boasting nearly 3 acres of mature gardens and parkland. Comfy lounge, small bar, pine-furnished breakfast room and pleasant terrace. Large, cosy bedrooms with country views.

DUNSFORD

Devon – See Regional map n°**2**-C2
London 206 mi – Plymouth 40 mi – Exeter 8 mi
Michelin Road map 503-I31

Weeke Barton N

✉ EX6 7HH Southeast : 1.5 mi by B 3212 and Christow rd, turning right up unmarked road after river bridge – ✆ (01647) 253 505 – www.weekebarton.com – Closed Christmas and New Year
5 rm – †£ 100/120 ††£ 110/130 **Rest** – Menu £ 18
The owners of this 15C Devonshire longhouse are friendly and laid-back, and the place itself has a funky yet cosy feel. The interior combines old world character with stylish furnishings and bedrooms are modern and minimalistic. Rustic, home-cooked dishes feature in the communal dining room.

DUNSTER

Somerset – Pop. 408 – See Regional map n°**3**-A2
London 185 mi – Minehead 3 mi – Taunton 23 mi
Michelin Road map 503-J30 – Michelin Green Guide GREAT BRITAIN

Spears Cross N without rest

West St ✉ TA24 6SN – ✆ (01643) 821 439 – www.spearscross.co.uk
4 rm – †£ 70 ††£ 100/110
Built in 1460 and reputedly the oldest house in the street. Charming bedrooms feature traditional William Morris and Sanderson furnishings – one room has elm panelling. They also offer over 120 wines and malt whiskies for sale.

Exmoor House without rest

12 West St ✉ TA24 6SN – ✆ (01643) 821 268 – www.exmoorhousedunster.co.uk – Closed 2 January-27 February
6 rm – †£ 55/60 ††£ 75/87
Georgian terraced house in the centre of a historic town, run by warm, welcoming owners; look out for their year-round Christmas shop! The comfy lounge, spacious breakfast room and cosy bedrooms come in bright, contemporary tones.

DURHAM

Durham – Pop. 47 785 – See Regional map n°**24**-B3
London 267 mi – Leeds 77 mi – Middlesbrough 23 mi – Newcastle upon Tyne 20 mi
Michelin Road map 501-P19 and 502 – Michelin Green Guide GREAT BRITAIN

The Town House

34 Old Elvet ✉ DH1 3HN – ✆ (0191) 384 10 37 – www.thetownhousedurham.com Town plan: B**x**
11 rm – †£ 99/250 ††£ 99/250
Rest *The Town House* – see restaurant listing
Attractive Georgian townhouse with lavishly decorated rooms: the lounge has purple velvet furnishings and there's a mahogany bar. Sumptuous bedrooms vary from floor to floor but all have good extras and bathrooms with underfloor heating; some have baths in the room; those in the garden annexe have hot tubs.

Farnley Tower

The Avenue ✉ DH1 4DX – ✆ (0191) 375 00 11 – www.farnley-tower.co.uk – Closed 25 December and 1 January Town plan: A**c**
13 rm – †£ 55/75 ††£ 69/95
Rest *Restaurant DH1* – ✆ (0191) 384 66 55 – Menu £ 18 (weekdays)/38 – *(closed first week January, 24-26 December, Sunday and Monday) (dinner only)*
Spacious Victorian house hidden away in a quiet residential area overlooking the city; it's privately owned and has a relaxed air about it. Bedrooms vary in shape and size – those offering rooftop views are in demand. The dining room offers ambitious dishes in some unusual combinations.

Cathedral View Town House without rest

212 Lower Gilesgate ✉ DH1 1QN – ✆ (0191) 386 95 66 – www.cathedralview.com – Closed 20 December-6 January Town plan: B**n**
5 rm – †£ 80/100 ††£ 90/150
Cosy Georgian townhouse with a terraced garden. The breakfast room offers excellent cathedral views and an extensive menu with daily specials. Smart, modern bedrooms have bold feature walls, coordinating fabrics and good facilities.

Castle View without rest

4 Crossgate ✉ DH1 4PS – ✆ (0191) 386 88 52 – www.castle-view.co.uk – Closed 18 December-8 January Town plan: A**e**
5 rm – †£ 70/100 ††£ 100/120
Attractive Georgian townhouse beside a Norman castle on a steep cobbled hill; reputedly a former vicarage. Large bedrooms have modern monochrome colour schemes, good facilities and smart bathrooms. Have breakfast on the terrace in summer.

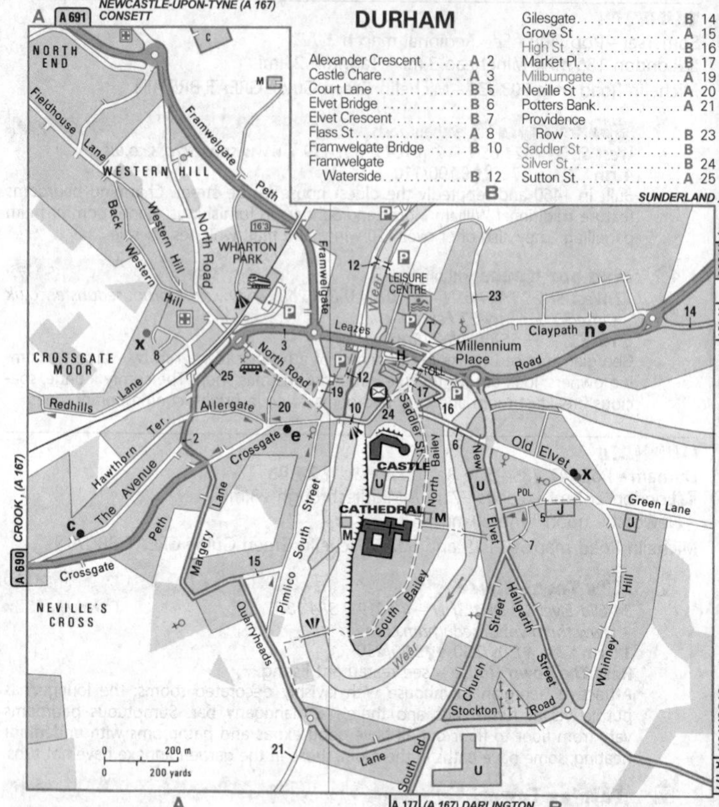

Bistro 21

Aykley Heads House, Aykley Heads ✉ *DH1 5TS – Northwest : 1.5 mi by A 691 and B 6532 –* ✆ *(0191) 384 43 54 – www.bistrotwentyone.co.uk – Closed Christmas, Sunday dinner and bank holiday Mondays*

Menu £ 19 (lunch and early dinner)/30 – Carte £ 22/35 – *(booking essential)*

Brightly painted restaurant with an internal courtyard and a herb garden. Formerly a manor house outbuilding, the rustic main room has high windows and French farmhouse styling; the bar is in a smaller vaulted room. Cooking is satisfying and filling, and centres around good old British classics.

Finbarr's

Waddington St, Flass Vale ✉ *DH1 4BG –* ✆ *(0191) 370 9999 – www.finbarrsrestaurant.co.uk – Closed 25-26 December* Town plan: A**x**

Menu £ 16 (lunch) – Carte £ 23/51 – *(booking advisable)*

Hidden away in a hotel just outside the city, a spacious restaurant with monochrome photos and well-spaced, smartly laid tables. Modern menus display international influences; the set menu provides good value. Smooth, professional service.

The Town House – The Town House Hotel

34 Old Elvet ✉ *DH1 3HN –* ✆ *(0191) 384 10 37 – www.gaddstownhouse.com – Closed Sunday dinner* Town plan: B**x**

Menu £ 15 (lunch) – Carte £ 20/41

Intimate hotel restaurant with a religious ceiling mural, a leopard print carpet and large purple chairs with gold tassels. Extensive menus are based around classic British dishes; steaks are a speciality and include chateaubriand for two.

EARL STONHAM

Suffolk – See Regional map n°**15-C3**

London 91 mi – Ipswich 12 mi – Colchester 33 mi – Clacton-on-Sea 38 mi

Michelin Road map 504-X27

Bays Farm without rest

Forward Grn ✉ IP14 5HU – Northwest : 1 mi by A1120 on Broad Green rd – ✆ (01449) 711 286 – www.baysfarmsuffolk.co.uk

4 rm – £ 70/115 £ 80/125

A delightful 17C farmhouse run by a charming host; surrounded by 3 acres of attractive gardens. There's a characterful lounge and a beamed dining room. Bedrooms are individually styled – the annexed 'Hayloft' is the most luxurious. Breakfast features local and garden produce, and homemade bread and jam.

Shepherd & Dog

✉ IP14 5HN Northwest : 0.5 mi on A 1120 – ✆ (01449) 711 685 – www.theshepherdanddog.com – Closed 1-14 January, Sunday dinner, Monday and Tuesday

Menu £ 11/28 – Carte £ 26/35

An unexpected find in sleepy Suffolk: relax in the lounge, enjoy traditional pub dishes in the bar or head to the snazzily named 'Eaterie', which serves modern cooking in a formal style to match its smart, contemporary décor.

EARSHAM → See Bungay

Norfolk – Michelin Road map 504-Y26

EAST CHILTINGTON → See Lewes

East Sussex

EAST CHISENBURY

Wiltshire – See Regional map n°**4-D2**

London 92 mi – Bristol 51 mi – Southampton 53 mi – Reading 51 mi

Red Lion Freehouse (Guy Manning) with rm

✉ SN9 6AQ – ✆ (01980) 671 124 – www.redlionfreehouse.com

5 rm – £ 130 £ 230

Menu £ 16 (weekday lunch) – Carte £ 30/50 – *(booking advisable)*

Delightful thatched pub off the beaten track, with simple country styling and a cosy, characterful feel. Daily menus focus on carefully sourced, seasonal ingredients and the down-to-earth dishes are stunning in their simplicity, precisely composed and packed with flavour. Set opposite, the smart, well-equipped bedrooms come with private terraces; all have river views.

→ Chisenbury nettle soup with crispy snails & wild garlic cream. Rib of Wiltshire beef for 2 with hand-cut chips & sauce béarnaise. Amalfi lemon tart with pine nut sablé and rosemary crème fraîche.

EAST CLANDON → See Guildford

Surrey

EAST END

Hampshire – See Regional map n°**6-A3**

London 100 mi – Bristol 85 mi – Southampton 21 mi

East End Arms with rm

Lymington Rd ✉ SO41 5SY – ✆ (01590) 626 223 – www.eastendarms.co.uk – Closed dinner Sunday and Monday

5 rm – £ 71 £ 99/120 Carte £ 23/41

Traditional country pub owned by John Illsley of Dire Straits. Shabby locals bar and classical pine-furnished dining room; great display of music-based photos. Concise menus of satisfying British dishes. Modern, cottage-style bedrooms provide a smart contrast.

EAST GARSTON

West Berkshire – See Regional map n°**10-B3**

London 69 mi – Bristol 58 mi – Hillingdon 56 mi – Ealing 63 mi

Queen's Arms with rm

Newbury St ✉ RG17 7ET – ✆ (01488) 648 757 – www.queensarmshotel.co.uk

8 rm – ♦£ 75/95 ♦♦£ 110/130 Carte £ 24/33

A proudly British inn nestled in the heart of racehorse country, with framed prints, a rustic bar and meaty, satisfying dishes – which range from warming braises to tasty local game. Country pursuits can be arranged and you might even spot a famous trainer or breeder in the bar. Modern bedrooms are kitted out by leading clothing and countrywear companies.

EAST GRINSTEAD

West Sussex – Pop. 29 084 – See Regional map n°**7-D2**

London 48 mi – Brighton 30 mi – Eastbourne 32 mi – Lewes 21 mi

Michelin Road map 504-T30

Gravetye Manor

Vowels Ln ✉ RH19 4LJ – Southwest : 4.5 mi by B 2110 taking second turn left towards West Hoathly – ✆ (01342) 810 567 – www.gravetyemanor.co.uk

17 rm – ♦£ 160/210 ♦♦£ 240/455 – 1 suite

Rest *Gravetye Manor* – see restaurant listing

A quintessential English country house set in a forest and surrounded by 35 acres of glorious gardens. Ornate Elizabethan ceilings and fireplaces dominate beautifully furnished lounges, which provide the perfect spot for afternoon tea. Bedrooms are luxurious and service is personalised and detailed.

ENGLAND

Gravetye Manor – Gravetye Manor Hotel

Vowels Ln ✉ RH19 4LJ – Southwest : 4.5 mi by B 2110 taking second turn left towards West Hoathly – ✆ (01342) 810 567 – www.gravetyemanor.co.uk

Menu £ 30/40 – Carte £ 58/68 – *(booking essential)*

Delightful country house dining room with wood-panelled walls and an intimate feel. Fresh flowers adorn the tables and ingredients from the walled garden are showcased. Accomplished cooking features classic dishes with subtle modern overtones; desserts are innovative. Service is professional yet personable.

EAST HADDON

Northamptonshire – See Regional map n°**16-B3**

London 76 mi – Birmingham 47 mi – Leicester 32 mi – Coventry 34 mi

Red Lion with rm

rest,

Main St ✉ NN6 8BU – ✆ (01604) 770 223 – www.redlioneasthaddon.co.uk – Closed 25 December

7 rm – ♦£ 80/95 ♦♦£ 95/110 Carte £ 22/38

Thatched honey-stone inn at the heart of an attractive village, boasting pretty gardens and a pleasing mix of exposed wood, brick and slate. Drinkers are welcome but it's the food that's the focus here: menus offer upgraded pub classics like mutton cottage pie, and they run a cookery school in the adjacent barn. Service is enthusiastic and bedrooms, warm and welcoming.

EAST HENDRED

Oxfordshire – See Regional map n°**10-B3**

London 70 mi – Oxford 18 mi – Swindon 30 mi

Michelin Road map 503-P29

Eyston Arms

High St ✉ OX12 8JY – ✆ (01235) 833 320 – www.eystonarms.co.uk – Closed 25 December and Sunday dinner

Carte £ 25/39

Set in a characterful, largely estate-owned village; a modern dining pub with scrubbed tables, tiled floors and exposed brickwork. Diverse menus offer popular antipasti boards, unfussy main dishes and desserts with a twist. Welcoming team.

EAST HOATHLY

East Sussex – Pop. 893 – See Regional map n°**8-B3**
London 60 mi – Brighton 16 mi – Eastbourne 13 mi – Hastings 25 mi
Michelin Road map 504-U31

Old Whyly

BN8 6EL Northwest : 0.5 mi, turning right by post box on right and then taking centre drive – (01825) 840 216 – www.oldwhyly.co.uk
4 rm – £ 85/110 £ 98/145 **Rest** – Menu £ 35
Charming red-brick house built in 1760, set in beautiful grounds and very personally run by its delightful owner. Guest areas mix the classic and the contemporary. Bedrooms are individually designed around a subtle theme: choose from Tulip, French or Chinese. The minimalist dining room offers a daily changing 3 course dinner, and homemade yoghurts and jams at breakfast.

EAST KENNETT → See Marlborough

Wiltshire

EAST LAVANT → See Chichester

West Sussex

EAST WITTERING

West Sussex – Pop. 5 647 – See Regional map n°**7-C3**
London 86 mi – Birmingham 178 mi – Leeds 272 mi – Sheffield 242 mi
Michelin Road map 504-R31

Samphire

57 Shore Rd PO20 8DY – (01243) 672 754 – www.samphireeastwittering.co.uk – Closed 2 weeks January, Christmas and Sunday
Menu £ 16 (lunch) – Carte £ 25/39
Modest, keenly run restaurant set 100 metres from the sea and featuring reclaimed wooden furniture. Fresh, locally caught seafood and fish – with a wide range of meat dishes too. Straightforward, tasty, good value cooking.

EAST WITTON

North Yorkshire Leyburn – See Regional map n°**22-B1**
London 238 mi – Leeds 45 mi – Middlesbrough 30 mi – York 39 mi
Michelin Road map 502-O21

Blue Lion with rm

rest,

DL8 4SN – (01969) 624 273 – www.thebluelion.co.uk
15 rm – £ 70/145 £ 94/145
Menu £ 19/29 – Carte £ 25/48 **s** – *(booking essential)*
Charming, characterful countryside pub. Daily-changing menu features a tasty mix of classic and modern dishes, all with seasonality and traceability at their core. Bedrooms – in the pub and outbuildings – are warm and cosy.

EASTBOURNE

East Sussex – Pop. 109 185 – See Regional map n°**8-B3**
London 68 mi – Brighton 25 mi – Dover 61 mi – Maidstone 49 mi
Michelin Road map 504-U31 – Michelin Green Guide GREAT BRITAIN

Grand

King Edward's Par. BN21 4EQ – (01323) 412 345 – www.grandeastbourne.com Town plan: Z**x**
152 rm – £ 200/570 £ 230/600 – 13 suites
Rest *Mirabelle* – see restaurant listing
Rest *Garden Restaurant* – Menu £ 23/39
Built in 1875 and offering all its name promises, the Grand retains many original features including ornate plasterwork, columned corridors and a Great Hall. The delightful gardens feature a superb outdoor pool and a sun terrace. Bedrooms are classical; pay the extra for a sea view. Dining is a formal affair.

ENGLAND

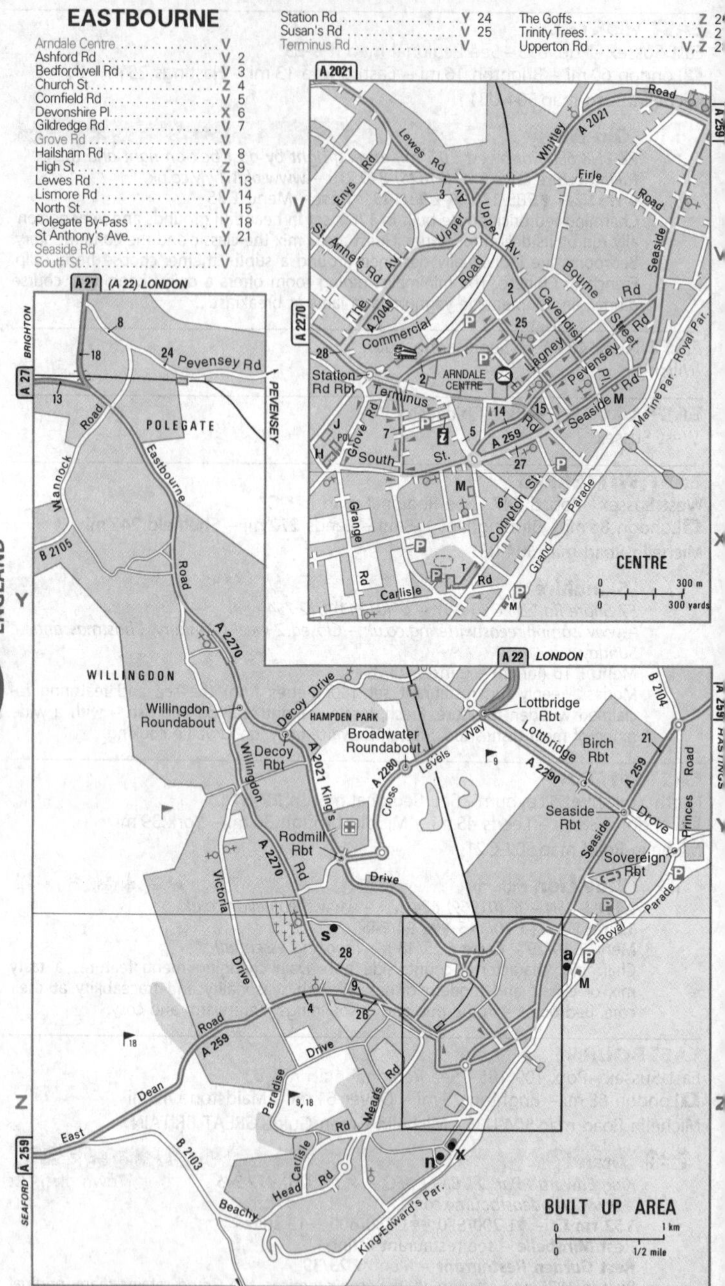

EASTBOURNE
Arndale Centre V
Ashford Rd ..... V 2
Bedfordwell Rd ..... V 3
Church St ..... Z 4
Cornfield Rd ..... V 5
Devonshire Pl. ..... X 6
Gildredge Rd ..... V 7
Grove Rd V
Hailsham Rd ..... Y 8
High St ..... Z 9
Lewes Rd ..... Y 13
Lismore Rd ..... V 14
North St ..... V 15
Polegate By-Pass ..... Y 18
St Anthony's Ave. ..... Y 21
Seaside Rd V
South St V
Station Rd ..... Y 24
Susan's Rd ..... V 25
Terminus Rd V
The Goffs ..... Z 2
Trinity Trees ..... V 2
Upperton Rd ..... V, Z 2
A 2021
Road
A 259
Whitley
A 2021
Lewes Rd
Enys Rd
Upper Av.
Upper Av.
Firle
Road
St Anne's Rd
The Av.
A 2040
Road
Bourne
Rd
Seaside
Cavendish
Commercial
Station Rd Rbt
Terminus
ARNDALE CENTRE
Langney
Street
Rd
Pevensey Pl.
Rd
Royal Par.
Marine Par.
Seaside
Grove Rd
South
St.
A 259
Rd
Compton St.
Grange Rd
Carlisle
Rd
Grand Parade
CENTRE
300 m
300 yards
A 2270
A 27
(A 22) LONDON
BRIGHTON
Pevensey Rd
PEVENSEY
POLEGATE
Road
Wannock
Eastbourne
B 2105
Road
A 2270
WILLINGDON
Willingdon Roundabout
ENGLAND
Decoy Drive
HAMPDEN PARK
Decoy Rbt
Broadwater Roundabout
A 22 LONDON
Lottbridge Rbt
Levels Way
Lottbridge
A 2290
A 2280
Cross
Willingdon
A 2021 King's
Rodmill Rbt
Drive
Birch Rbt
A 259
Seaside Rbt
Drove
Princes Road
B 2104
A 259 HASTINGS
Seaside
Sovereign Rbt
Royal Parade
Victoria Drive
A 2270
Rd
Road
A 259
Dean
East
Paradise
Drive
Meads
Rd
Carlisle
Rd
Head
B 2103
Beachy
King-Edward's Par.
SEAFORD
A 259
BUILT UP AREA
1 km
1/2 mile
BEACHY HEAD, SEVEN SISTERS

Waterside without rest
11-12 Royal Par ✉ BN22 7AR – ✆ (01323) 646 566 Town plan: Z**a**
– www.watersidehoteleastbourne.co.uk
19 rm ☕ – 🚹£ 65/150 🚹🚹£ 65/150
Modern seafront hotel with views of the beach and pier; take in the view from the boldly wallpapered cocktail bar. Bedrooms vary in size and have unusual feature walls; some of the baths are in the rooms and come with a view.

Ocklynge Manor Ⓝ without rest
Mill Rd ✉ BN21 2PG – ✆ (01323) 734 121 Town plan: Z**s**
– www.ocklyngemanor.co.uk
3 rm ☕ – 🚹£ 60/120 🚹🚹£ 100/120
Sit in the small summerhouse and admire the beautiful mature gardens of this charming, traditional guesthouse. Mabel Lucie Attwell – the illustrator of 'Peter Pan and Wendy' – once lived here. Homemade cake is served on arrival.

Brayscroft
13 South Cliff Ave ✉ BN20 7AH – ✆ (01323) 647 005 Town plan: Z**n**
– www.brayscrofthotel.co.uk
6 rm ☕ – 🚹£ 35/42 🚹🚹£ 75/90 **Rest** – Menu £ 15
Cosy Edwardian house located close to the seafront, gardens and pier. The traditional lounge and dining room display antiques and Italian artwork. Bedrooms are comfy and classically styled. Evening meals – by arrangement – are tailored to each guest and feature fresh, local, free range ingredients.

Southcroft
15 South Cliff Ave ✉ BN20 7AH – ✆ (01323) 729 071 Town plan: Z**n**
– www.southcrofthotel.com
6 rm ☕ – 🚹£ 40/55 🚹🚹£ 76/90 **Rest** – Menu £ 14
A terraced Edwardian guesthouse in a quiet residential area close to the promenade. The homely lounge is filled with books, games and lots of local information and the bedrooms are cosy and well-kept. Have your morning coffee out on the patio; home-cooked dinners are served by arrangement.

Mirabelle – Grand Hotel
King Edward's Par. ✉ BN21 4EQ – ✆ (01323) 412 345 Town plan: Z**x**
– www.grandeastbourne.com – Closed Sunday-Monday and Tuesday January-February
Menu £ 23/42 – *(booking essential)*
This traditional hotel restaurant features plush fabrics and tables laid with monogrammed silverware. The dress code is formal and the team are professional. Rich, well-executed cooking follows the seasons and has a modern touch.

EASTGATE

Durham – See Regional map n°**24-A3**
London 288 mi – Bishop Auckland 20 mi – Newcastle upon Tyne 35 mi – Stanhope 3 mi
Michelin Road map 502-N19

Horsley Hall
✉ DL13 2LJ Southeast : 1 mi by A 689 – ✆ (01388) 517 239
– www.horsleyhall.co.uk – Closed 22 December-8 January
7 rm ☕ – 🚹£ 80/95 🚹🚹£ 130/150
Rest – Menu £ 20/32 – *(closed Sunday lunch) (booking essential)*
An old ivy-clad hunting lodge with 14C origins, built for the Bishop of Durham. Impressive entrance hall and superb stained glass windows; lovely valley views from some rooms. Simple, cosy bedrooms – two with Edwardian bathrooms. The baronial-style dining room boasts an ornate ceiling; game is a speciality.

EASTON → See Chagford

Devon – Michelin Road map 503-I31

EASTON → See Wells

Somerset

ENGLAND

EASTON ON THE HILL

Northamptonshire – Pop. 1 015 – See Regional map n°**17**-C2

London 94 mi – Birmingham 75 mi – Leicester 30 mi – Coventry 61 mi

Exeter Arms with rm

21 Stamford Rd ✉ PE9 3NS – ✆ (01780) 756 321 – www.theexeterarms.net – Closed Sunday dinner

6 rm – †£ 70/100 ††£ 80/110 Carte £ 23/37

Sympathetically yet stylishly restored 18C inn adorned with copper pans, enamel signs and hop bines. Eat in the snug candlelit restaurant or stylish conservatory. Choose from tasty pizzas, 'home comforts' or the chef's signature dishes. Stylish, well-appointed bedrooms have smart, modern bathrooms.

EBRINGTON → See Chipping Campden

Gloucestershire – Michelin Road map 504-O27

ECCLESTON

Lancashire – Pop. 4 708 – See Regional map n°**20**-A2

London 219 mi – Birmingham 103 mi – Liverpool 29 mi – Preston 11 mi

Michelin Road map 502-L23

Parr Hall Farm without rest

Parr Ln. ✉ PR7 5SL – ✆ (01257) 451 917 – www.parrhallfarm.com

10 rm – †£ 45/50 ††£ 70/80

Welcoming, red-brick former farmhouse. Low-beamed, pine-furnished breakfast room. Bedrooms, located in the adjacent barn conversion, boast country style fabrics and modern bathrooms.

ENGLAND

ECKINGTON → See Pershore

Worcestershire – Michelin Road map 504-N27

ECKINGTON

Derbyshire – Pop. 16 684 – See Regional map n°**16**-B1

London 155 mi – Leeds 49 mi – Sheffield 10 mi – Manchester 58 mi

Michelin Road map 502-P24

Inn at Troway

Snowdon Ln, Troway ✉ S21 5RU – West : 3.5 mi by B 6052 on B 6056 – ✆ (01246) 417 666 – www.relaxeatanddrink.co.uk

Carte £ 19/33

Early Victorian pub in a picturesque location, with delightful countryside views. The wide-ranging menu offers hearty, satisfying dishes and there's a fine selection of local ales. Friendly, helpful team.

Devonshire Arms

Lightwood Ln, Middle Handley ✉ S21 5RN – Southwest : 2 mi by B 6052 on Middle Handley rd – ✆ (01246) 434 800 – www.devonshirearmsmiddlehandley.com – Closed Monday except bank holiday lunch and dinner Sunday

Carte £ 27/43

Smartly updated inn with several modern rooms and a small terrace. Fresh, seasonal ingredients are at the core of the hearty menu. They like to keep things local, with eggs coming from down the road and meat from the butcher who lives opposite.

EDINGTON

Wiltshire – See Regional map n°**4**-C2

London 105 mi – Bristol 43 mi – Cardiff 76 mi – Southampton 64 mi

Michelin Road map 503-N30

Three Daggers with rm
47 Westbury Rd ✉ BA13 4PG – ✆ (01380) 830 940 – www.threedaggers.co.uk
9 rm ☕ – 🚹£ 85/110 🚹🚹£ 100/165 Carte £ 20/39
Attractive pub with original wood beams and flagstones, and a large conservatory overlooking the garden. The accessible menu always features a homemade soup and a pie 'of the day', and the Huntsman's and Fisherman's sharing platters are extremely popular. Charming bedrooms feature bespoke oak furnishings.

EGHAM

Surrey – Pop. 25 996 – See Regional map n°**7-C1**
London 22 mi – Croydon 24 mi – Barnet 35 mi – Ealing 17 mi
Michelin Road map 504-S29

Great Fosters
Stroude Rd ✉ TW20 9UR – South : 1.25 mi by B 388 – ✆ (01784) 433 822 – www.greatfosters.co.uk
43 rm – 🚹£ 175/445 🚹🚹£ 175/445, ☕ £ 20 – 4 suites
Rest *Tudor Room* – see restaurant listing
Rest *Estate Grill* – Carte £ 33/69
Striking Elizabethan manor built as a hunting lodge for Henry VIII, boasting 50 acres of gardens and a beautiful parterre. The charming interior displays characterful original detailing. Bedrooms come with feature beds and a flamboyant touch; those in the annexes are more modern. The Estate Grill specialises in steaks from the Josper grill; fine dining in the Tudor Room.

XXX **Tudor Room** – Great Fosters Hotel
Stroude Rd ✉ TW20 9UR – South : 1.25 mi by B 388 – ✆ (01784) 433 822 – www.greatfosters.co.uk – Closed 2 weeks January, 2 weeks August, Saturday lunch, Sunday and Monday
Menu £ 30/60 – *(booking advisable)*
Intimate hotel restaurant with mullioned windows and burgundy décor – a large tapestry and gilt mirror hang on its walls. Cooking is assured, modern and creative. Influences come from across Europe and there's the odd Asian touch too.

EGTON

North Yorkshire – See Regional map n°**23-C1**
London 250 mi – Birmingham 180 mi – Leeds 72 mi – Sheffield 107 mi
Michelin Road map 502-S20

Wheatsheaf Inn
✉ YO21 1TZ – ✆ (01947) 895 271 – www.wheatsheafegton.com – Closed 25 December and Monday
Carte £ 20/34 – *(light lunch)*
Family-run, late 17C inn on the edge of the picturesque North Yorkshire Moors. Menu offers a real taste of Yorkshire with fresh, hearty dishes like lamb's kidneys, local steak, Whitby scampi and game from within 2 miles.

ELDERSFIELD

Worcestershire – See Regional map n°**18-B3**
London 124 mi – Birmingham 63 mi – Liverpool 145 mi – Bristol 52 mi

Butchers Arms (James Winter) 
Lime Street ✉ GL19 4NX – Southeast : 1 mi – ✆ (01452) 840 381 – www.thebutchersarms.net – Closed 1 week early January, 1 week late August, Sunday dinner, Monday, lunch Tuesday to Thursday and bank holidays
Carte £ 39/51 – *(booking essential)*
Small, traditional pub with part-oak flooring, original beams, hop bines and a wood burning stove. There are 25 spaces for diners and a few tables for local drinkers. The concise menu changes regularly and everything from the bread to the ice cream is homemade; cooking is clever and dishes, full of flavour.
→ Crispy pig's cheek with egg yolk ravioli and Bramley apples. Roast turbot, palourde clams, fried chorizo and buttered spinach. Dark chocolate fondant with honeycomb ice cream.

ELLAND

West Yorkshire – Pop. 15 625 – ✉ Halifax – See Regional map n°**22**-B3
London 204 mi – Bradford 12 mi – Burnley 29 mi – Leeds 17 mi
Michelin Road map 502-O22

La Cachette

31 Huddersfield Rd ✉ HX5 9AW – ☎ (01422) 378 833 – www.lacachette-elland.com – Closed 2 weeks August, 27 December-9 January, Sunday and bank holidays
Menu £ 15/24 – Carte £ 19/43
Long-standing, well-run bistro. Spacious bar and dining rooms display Gallic décor and memorabilia. Extensive choice from daily or weekly menus and specials. Classical, seasonal cooking displays international influences.

ELLASTONE

Staffordshire – See Regional map n°**19**-C1
London 148 mi – Birmingham 49 mi – Stoke-on-Trent 22 mi
Michelin Road map 502-O25

Duncombe Arms

Main Road ✉ DE6 2GZ – ☎ (01335) 324 275 – www.duncombearms.co.uk
Carte £ 23/47
A stylish dining pub owned by the Hon. Johnny Greenall – of the famous brewery family: his wife, Laura, is a descendant of the Duncombe family after which the pub is named. Food keeps to a core of classic pub dishes.

ENGLAND

ELLEL

Lancashire – See Regional map n°**20**-A1
London 240 mi – Leeds 85 mi – Sheffield 95 mi – Manchester 51 mi

Bay Horse Inn

Bay Horse Ln, Bay Horse ✉ LA2 0HR – South 1.5 mi by A 6 on Quernmore rd – ☎ (01524) 791 204 – www.bayhorseinn.com – Closed Monday except bank holiday lunch
Carte £ 22/39 **s**
Cosy, homely pub in a pleasant rural location, with a characterful interior and an attractive terrace. Seasonal, locally sourced produce is crafted into classic, tried-and-tested dishes. The Lancashire cheese board is a speciality.

ELMTON

Derbyshire – See Regional map n°**16**-B1
London 155 mi – Birmingham 78 mi – Leeds 51 mi – Sheffield 21 mi

Elm Tree

✉ S80 4LS – ☎ (01909) 721 261 – www.elmtreeelmton.co.uk – Closed Tuesday and Sunday dinner
Menu £ 11 (weekday lunch) – Carte £ 18/38
18C stone pub with a brightly lit bar, characterful beamed rooms, a wood-burning stove and a large garden. The good value menu offers pub classics presented in a modern manner, with most ingredients sourced from within 10 miles.

ELTISLEY

Cambridgeshire – See Regional map n°**14**-A3
London 62 mi – Croydon 73 mi – Barnet 49 mi – Ealing 61 mi
Michelin Road map 507-T27

Eltisley

2 The Green ✉ PE19 6TG – ☎ (01480) 880 308 – www.theeltisley.co.uk – Closed Monday in winter and Sunday dinner
Carte £ 22/36
Chic, stylish gastropub beside a village green. Simple, unfussy cooking relies on quality produce to speak for itself: meat is from nearby farms and veg, from their allotment. Everything from starters to desserts is homemade.

ELTON

Cambridgeshire – See Regional map n°**14-A2**

London 84 mi – Peterborough 11 mi – Bedford 40 mi – Kettering 24 mi

Michelin Road map 504-S26

Crown Inn with rm

8 Duck St ✉ PE8 6RQ – ✆ (01832) 280 232 – www.thecrowninn.org

8 rm – †£ 65/75 ††£ 95/150, ☕ £ 8 Menu £ 15 (weekdays) – Carte £ 25/38

17C honey-stone pub in a delightful country parish, with a thatched roof, a cosy inglenook fireplace in the bar and a laid-back feel. Extensive menus offer homely British dishes which arrive in generous portions. Bedrooms are smart and individually styled – some have feature beds or roll-top baths.

ELTON-ON-THE-HILL

Nottinghamshire – See Regional map n°**16-B2**

London 121 mi – Nottingham 15 mi – Lincoln 35 mi

The Grange (N) without rest

Sutton Ln. ✉ NG13 9LA – ✆ (07887) 952 181
– www.thegrangebedandbreakfastnotts.co.uk

3 rm ☕ – †£ 45/55 ††£ 75/79

What better way to start your holiday than in this charming Georgian farmhouse with a slice of homemade cake? The owners are lovely, the gardens are delightful and the country views are superb. Bedrooms are homely and come with good facilities and thoughtful touches; one is accessed via a spiral staircase.

ELY

Cambridgeshire – Pop. 19 090 – See Regional map n°**14-B2**

London 74 mi – Cambridge 16 mi – Norwich 60 mi

Michelin Road map 504-U26 – Michelin Green Guide GREAT BRITAIN

Poets House

St Mary's St ✉ CB7 4EY – ✆ (01353) 887 777 – www.poetshouse.com

21 rm ☕ – †£ 119/149 ††£ 119/149

Rest *Dining Room* – see restaurant listing

A series of 19C townhouses opposite the cathedral. Spacious, boutique bedrooms come with beautiful bathrooms and extras such as local vodka and gin. The modern bar overlooks the pretty walled garden and also offers afternoon tea.

Dining Room – Poets House Hotel

St Mary's St ✉ CB7 4EY – ✆ (01353) 887 777 – www.poetshouse.com

Menu £ 23 – Carte £ 30/47

Pretty hotel dining room which blends original features with contemporary décor. Ambitious modern dishes are attractively presented and full of flavour; there are plenty of vegetarian options too. Some tables have cathedral views.

at Sutton Gault West: 8 mi by A142 off B1381 ✉ Ely

Anchor Inn with rm

✉ CB6 2BD – ✆ (01353) 778 537 – www.anchor-inn-restaurant.co.uk

4 rm ☕ – †£ 60/155 ††£ 80/155

Menu £ 14 (weekday lunch) – Carte £ 23/42

Riverside pub dating back to 1650 and the creation of the Hundred Foot Wash. Tempting menu complemented by daily fish specials. For a pleasant river outlook head for the wood-panelled rooms to the front of the bar. Neat, pine-furnished bedrooms include two suites; one with river views.

at Little Thetford South: 2.75 mi by A10 ✉ Ely

Springfields without rest

Ely Rd ✉ CB6 3HJ – North : 0.5 mi on A 10 – ✆ (01353) 663 637
– www.smoothhound.co.uk/hotels/springfields – Closed Christmas-New Year

3 rm ☕ – †£ 60 ††£ 85

Delightfully run, curio-filled bungalow in pleasant gardens. Immaculately kept bedrooms have different coloured Toile de Jouy wallpapers and plenty of extra touches. Enjoy breakfast among the Cranberry Glass collection or in the courtyard.

EMSWORTH

Hampshire – Pop. 18 777 – See Regional map n°**6-B2**
London 75 mi – Brighton 37 mi – Portsmouth 10 mi – Southampton 22 mi
Michelin Road map 504-R31

XX **36 on the Quay** with rm — rest,

47 South St, The Quay ✉ PO10 7EG – ✆ (01243) 375 592 – www.36onthequay.co.uk – Closed first 2 weeks January, 1 week May, 1 week October and 24-26 December
7 rm – †£ 75/90 ††£ 100/120
Menu £ 24/58 – *(closed Sunday and Monday) (booking essential)*
Long-standing, intimate restaurant and conservatory bar-lounge in a quayside cottage with pleasant harbour views. Concise menus offer elaborate modern dishes in some unusual combinations and foraged ingredients feature highly. Stylish bedrooms have good comforts; be ready to order breakfast at check-in.

X **Fat Olives**

30 South St ✉ PO10 7EH – ✆ (01243) 377 914 – www.fatolives.co.uk – Closed 2 weeks late June, 1 week Christmas, 1 week spring, Sunday and Monday
Menu £ 21 (lunch) – Carte £ 29/43 – *(booking essential)*
This sweet 17C fisherman's cottage sits in a characterful coastal town, in a road leading down to the harbour. It's run by a charming couple and has a rustic modern feel, courtesy of locally crafted tables and upholstered chairs. Classic British dishes have a modern edge and rely on small local suppliers.

EPPING

– Pop. 10 289 – ✉ Essex – See Regional map n°**12-B2**
London 23 mi – Colchester 41 mi – Watford 31 mi – Birmingham 120 mi
Michelin Road map 504-U28

XX **Haywards** (N)

111 Bell Common ✉ CM16 4DZ – Southwest : 1 mi by B 1393 and Theydon Rd – ✆ (01992) 577 350 – www.haywardsrestaurant.co.uk – Closed 1-27 January, Monday, Tuesday, dinner Sunday and lunch Wednesday
Menu £ 25/35
This proudly run restaurant is the realisation of a couple's dream. A hammerbeam ceiling and cherry wood tables set the scene. Appealing dishes follow the seasons and flavours are well-balanced. Service is extremely welcoming.

EPSOM

Surrey – Pop. 31 474 – See Regional map n°**7-D1**
London 14 mi – Croydon 9 mi – Barnet 29 mi – Ealing 18 mi
Michelin Road map 504-T30

Chalk Lane

Chalk Ln ✉ KT18 7BB – Southwest : 0.5 mi by A 24 and Woodcote Rd – ✆ (01372) 721 179 – www.chalklanehotel.com
21 rm – †£ 87/105 ††£ 105/155
Rest – Carte £ 33/44 – *(dinner only and Sunday lunch)*
Personally run hotel in a residential area; comfortable and welcoming, with a charming, traditionally furnished interior to match its Victorian heritage. Individually styled bedrooms – one with a four-poster. More modern dining room serves a menu inspired by classic French cooking.

XXX **Le Raj**

211 Fir Tree Rd, Epsom Downs ✉ KT17 3LB – Southeast : 2 mi by B 289 and B 284 on B 291 – ✆ (01737) 371 371 – www.lerajrestaurant.co.uk
Carte £ 22/34
A local institution with a larger-than-life owner, a comfortable bar-lounge and a smart, wood-panelled restaurant. Waiters in bow ties and white gloves serve carefully prepared, well-presented, authentic Bangladeshi cooking.

ERMINGTON

Devon – See Regional map n°**2-C2**
London 216 mi – Plymouth 11 mi – Salcombe 15 mi
Michelin Road map 503-I32

XX **Plantation House** with rm

Totnes Rd ✉ PL21 9NS – Southwest : 0.5 mi on A 3121 – ✆ (01548) 831 100 – www.plantationhousehotel.co.uk

8 rm ☕ – 🚹£ 60/120 🚹🚹£ 125/230

Menu £ 36 **s** – *(dinner only) (bookings essential for non-residents)*

Georgian former rectory in a pleasant country spot, with a small drinks terrace, an open-fired lounge and two dining rooms: one formal, with black furnishings; one more relaxed, with polished wood tables. Interesting modern menus feature local produce. Stylish bedrooms come with fresh milk and homemade cake.

ESHOTT

→ See Morpeth

ETTINGTON

Warwickshire – Pop. 1 039 – See Regional map n°**19-C3**

London 95 mi – Birmingham 41 mi – Leicester 48 mi – Coventry 23 mi

Michelin Road map 504-P27

Chequers Inn

91 Banbury Rd ✉ CV37 7SR – ✆ (01789) 740 387 – www.the-chequers-ettington.co.uk – Closed Sunday dinner and Monday

Carte £ 21/35

Chandeliers, brushed velvet furniture and Regency chairs set at chequered tables mean this is not your typical pub. Menus display a broad international style; dishes range from British classics to others with a Mediterranean bent.

EVERSHOT

Dorset – Pop. 225 – ✉ Dorchester – See Regional map n°**4-C3**

London 149 mi – Bournemouth 39 mi – Dorchester 12 mi – Salisbury 53 mi

Michelin Road map 503-M31 and 504

Summer Lodge

9 Fore St ✉ DT2 0JR – ✆ (01935) 482 000 – www.summerlodgehotel.com

24 rm ☕ – 🚹£ 235/650 🚹🚹£ 235/650 – 4 suites

Rest – Menu £ 26/47 – Carte £ 52/61 – *(booking essential)*

Attractive former dower house in mature gardens, featuring a smart wellness centre, a pool and a tennis court. Plush, individually designed bedrooms come with marble bathrooms and the country house guest areas display heavy fabrics and antiques – the drawing room was designed by Thomas Hardy. The formal dining room offers classical cuisine and a superb wine list.

Acorn Inn

28 Fore St ✉ DT2 0JW – ✆ (01935) 83 228 – www.acorn-inn.co.uk

10 rm ☕ – 🚹£ 89/220 🚹🚹£ 99/220 **Rest** – Carte £ 20/44

Historic inn mentioned in 'Tess of the d'Urbervilles'. Individually styled bedrooms boast fabric-covered walls, good facilities and modern bathrooms. Guest areas include a characterful residents' lounge, a locals bar with a skittle alley and a classical restaurant.

Wooden Cabbage

East Chelborough ✉ DT2 0QA – West : 3.25 mi by Beaminter rd and Chelborough rd on East Chelborough rd – ✆ (01935) 83 362 – www.woodencabbage.co.uk – April-October

3 rm ☕ – 🚹£ 80/90 🚹🚹£ 110 **Rest** – Menu £ 40

Attractive former gamekeeper's cottage. Spacious guest areas include a cosy dining room used in winter and an airy conservatory used in summer. Pretty bedrooms boast good facilities and lovely countryside views. Meals (by arrangement) feature home-grown produce.

EVESHAM

Worcestershire – Pop. 23 576 – See Regional map n°**19-C3**

London 99 mi – Birmingham 30 mi – Cheltenham 16 mi

Michelin Road map 503-O27 and 504

ENGLAND

The Wood Norton 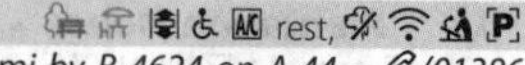

Worcester Rd ✉ WR11 4YB – Northwest : 2.5 mi by B 4624 on A 44 – ☎ (01386) 765 611 – www.thewoodnorton.com

50 rm – †£ 99/169 ††£ 85/169 – 2 suites

Rest – Menu £ 40 – *(bar lunch Monday-Saturday)*

Beautifully panelled country house in the shadow of the Malvern Hills; once a French duke's hunting lodge and then a BBC training centre. Bedrooms in the main house are characterful and those in the mews are more modern; all have unique photos from old BBC shows. The intimate restaurant overlooks the parterre.

EWHURST GREEN

East Sussex – See Regional map n°**8-B2**

London 61 mi – Eastbourne 24 mi – Royal Tunbridge Wells 22 mi

Prawles Court without rest

Shoreham Ln. ✉ TN32 5RG – Southwest : 1 mi – ☎ (01580) 830 136 – www.prawlescourt.com – Closed December and January, mid week November, February and March, (minimum 2 nights stay at weekends)

4 rm – †£ 115/125 ††£ 140/170

This lovely red-brick Arts and Crafts house is surrounded by 27 acres of beautiful gardens and grounds. It was designed by Nathaniel Lloyd and the guest areas retain a comfy, period style. Bedrooms are spacious and hugely impressive, featuring luxurious fabrics and furnishings, and a good range of facilities.

EXETER

Devon – Pop. 113 507 – See Regional map n°**2-D2**

London 201 mi – Bournemouth 83 mi – Bristol 83 mi – Plymouth 46 mi

Michelin Road map 503-J31 – Michelin Green Guide GREAT BRITAIN

ENGLAND

Abode Exeter

Cathedral Yard ✉ EX1 1HD – ☎ (01392) 319 955 – www.abodehotels.co.uk Town plan: Y**z**

52 rm – †£ 75/140 ††£ 75/375 – 1 suite

Rest ***Michael Caines*** – see restaurant listing

An attractive Georgian property in the shadow of the cathedral. The stylish interior features an all-day café, a pub and a chic cocktail bar. Some of the smart, boldly coloured bedrooms have roll-top baths with cathedral views

Magdalen Chapter

Magdalen St ✉ EX2 4HY – ☎ (01392) 281 000 – www.themagdalenchapter.com Town plan: Z**a**

59 rm – †£ 105/120 ††£ 140/250

Rest ***Magdalen Chapter*** – see restaurant listing

Converted Victorian eye hospital; now a stylish, modern hotel with a garden and a small spa tucked away to the rear. Chic, understated bedrooms come with mood lighting, espresso machines and iPads loaded with the hotel's information.

Southernhay House rest,

36 Southernhay East ✉ EX1 1NX – ☎ (01392) 435 324 – www.southernhayhouse.com Town plan: Z**x**

10 rm – †£ 150/240 ††£ 150/240

Rest – Carte £ 23/38 – *(closed Sunday dinner) (bookings essential for non-residents)*

Attractive Georgian townhouse with original ceiling roses and ornate coving. Smart, compact guest areas include a stylish lounge and a bar with bright blue furniture. Warmly decorated bedrooms have sumptuous beds, luxurious fabrics and chic bathrooms. Small dining room offers British-based menus.

Michael Caines – Abode Exeter Hotel

Cathedral Yard ✉ EX1 1HD – ☎ (01392) 223 638 – www.michaelcaines.com – Closed Sunday Town plan: Y**z**

Menu £ 18 (lunch) – Carte £ 36/57

Contemporary restaurant with well-spaced tables, set within a famous hotel; sit by the window for cathedral views. Modern British menus offer tasty, well-presented dishes comprising lots of different ingredients. Service is formal.

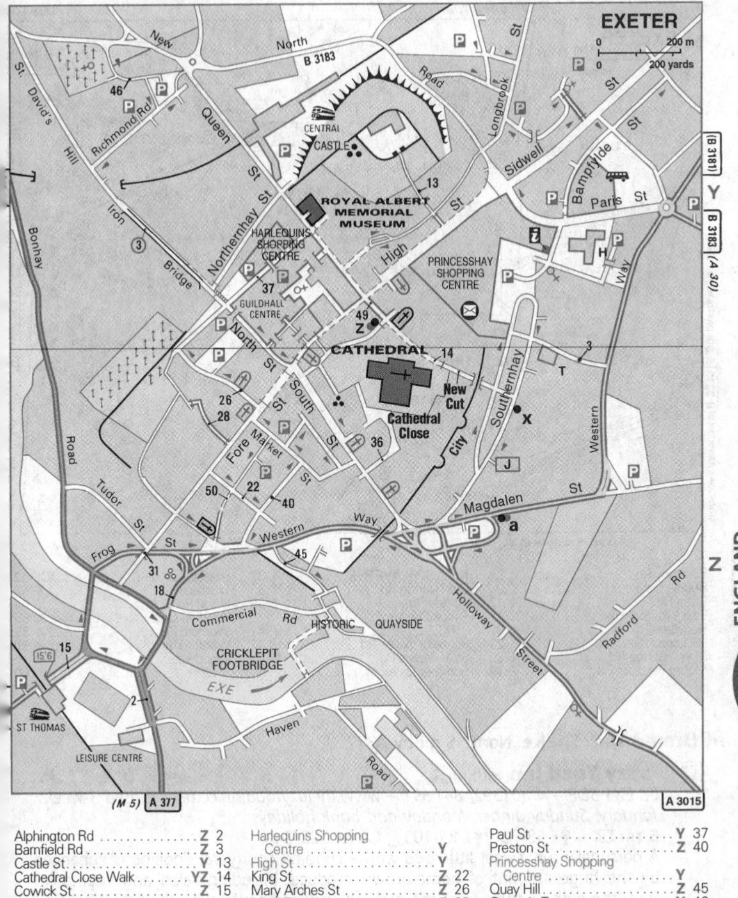

Alphington Rd . . . . Z 2
Barnfield Rd . . . . Z 3
Castle St . . . . Y 13
Cathedral Close Walk . . . . YZ 14
Cowick St . . . . Z 15
Edmund St . . . . Z 18
Fore St . . . . Z
Guildhall Shopping Centre . . . . . Y
Harlequins Shopping Centre . . . . Y
High St . . . . Y
King St . . . . Z 22
Mary Arches St . . . . Z 26
Mint (The) . . . . Z 28
New Bridge St . . . . Z 31
Palace Gate . . . . Z 36
Paul St . . . . Y 37
Preston St . . . . Z 40
Princesshay Shopping Centre . . . . Y
Quay Hill . . . . Z 45
Queen's Terrace . . . . Y 46
St Martin's Lane . . . . Y 49
Stepcote Hill . . . . Z 50

XX **Magdalen Chapter** – Magdalen Chapter Hotel

Magdalen St ✉ *EX2 4HY* – ✆ *(01392) 281 000* Town plan: Z**a**
– *www.themagdalenchapter.com*

Menu £ 20/34 – Carte £ 20/48

An impressive steel and glass extension to a 19C hotel, with a curved wood roof and overlooking a delightful terrace. The large menu of brasserie classics mixes British, French, Spanish and Italian influences. Produce is carefully sourced.

Rusty Bike

67 Howell Rd ✉ *EX4 4LZ* – ✆ *(01392) 214 440* Town plan: V**x**
– *www.rustybike-exeter.co.uk*

Carte £ 26/39 – *(dinner only and Sunday lunch)*

A bohemian pub which appeals to lovers of traditional British food. The daily changing menus feature hearty, masculine dishes. They butcher rare breeds of pig on-site, cure their own bresaola and smoke their own ham. Sit in the cosy snug.

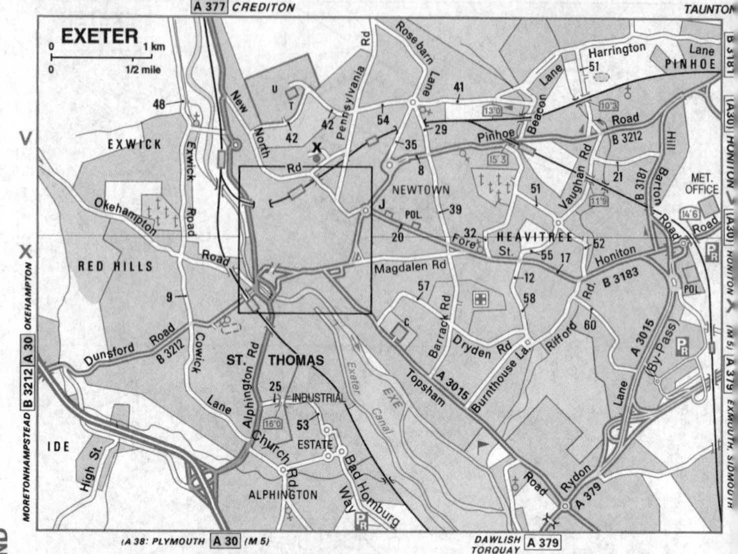

- Blackboy Rd. . . . . V 8
- Buddle Lane . . . . . X 9
- Butts Rd. . . . . X 12
- East Wonford Hill . . . . . X 17
- Heavitree Rd. . . . . VX 20
- Hill Lane . . . . . V 21
- Marsh Barton Rd. . . . . X 25
- Mount Pleasant Rd . . . . . V 29
- North St HEAVITREE . . . . . X 32
- Old Tiverton Rd . . . . . V 35
- Polsloe Rd . . . . . V 39
- Prince Charles Rd. . . . . V 41
- Prince of Wales Rd . . . . . V 42
- St Andrew's Rd. . . . . V 48
- Summer Lane . . . . . V 51
- Sweetbriar Lane. . . . . VX 52
- Trusham Rd. . . . . X 53
- Union Rd . . . . . V 54
- Whipton Lane . . . . . X 55
- Wonford Rd. . . . . X 57
- Wonford St . . . . . X 58
- Woodwater Lane . . . . . X 60

at Brampford Speke North: 5 mi by A377

Lazy Toad Inn with rm rest, P

EX5 5DP – (01392) 841 591 – www.thelazytoadinn.co.uk – Closed 3 weeks January, Sunday dinner, Monday and bank holidays

5 rm – £ 58/78 £ 85/105 Carte £ 23/34

A personally run, sweet little pub with a cobbled courtyard. Cooking is enhanced by the huge amount of home-grown produce, including salad and vegetables from the garden, fruits from the orchard and lambs raised on their smallholding. Individually styled bedrooms have king-sized beds and iPod docks.

at Broadclyst Northeast: 4.5 mi by B3212 on B3181

XX **The HH** P

EX5 3ET – (01392) 461 472 – www.the-hh.co.uk – Closed Christmas-New Year, Sunday and Monday

Menu £ 15 (weekday lunch) – Carte £ 30/49

Pleasant little restaurant which resembles a cottage. The interior blends the rustic and the contemporary, with its wooden beams, inglenook fireplace and modern décor. Interesting modern dishes are well presented and flavours are clear.

at Exeter Airport East: 5.5 mi by B3183 -(V)- A30 and B3184

Hampton by Hilton N P

EX5 2LJ East : 0.5 mi by Westcott rd – (01392) 348 348 – www.exterairport.hamptonbyhilton.com

120 rm – £ 65/125 £ 65/125

Rest *Marco's* – (01392) 348 111 – Carte £ 19/42

With its modern, open-plan business area and bar-lounge, the Hampton is ideal for corporate travellers. Bedrooms are well-soundproofed and come in raspberry, lemon or lime: all have work stations and spacious walk-in showers. Marco Pierre White's chic restaurant offers dishes from Italy and New York.

at Rockbeare East: 7.5 mi by B3183 -(V)- A30 and B3184 on B3174 ✉ Exeter

Jack in the Green

London Rd ✉ EX5 2EE – ✆ (01404) 822 240 – www.jackinthegreen.uk.com – Closed 25 December-3 January

Menu £ 25 – Carte £ 30/38

Green-painted pub with a warm, welcoming interior. Cooking is taken seriously and they are keen to support local producers. A vast array of menus feature both pub and restaurant style dishes, and you can mix and match between them; the 6 highlighted dishes make up the 'Totally Devon' set menu.

at Kenton Southeast: 7 mi by A3015 -(X)- on A379 ✉ Exeter

Rodean

The Triangle ✉ EX6 8LS – ✆ (01626) 890 195 – www.rodeanrestaurant.co.uk – Closed Sunday dinner and Monday

Menu £ 21 – Carte £ 32/41 – *(dinner only and Sunday lunch) (booking advisable)*

Family-run restaurant – once a butcher's shop – overlooking a tiny village green. Small bar-lounge and two traditional dining rooms with beams and dark wood panelling. Constantly evolving menus have a classical base and a personal touch.

EXETER AIRPORT → See Exeter

Devon – Michelin Road map 503-J31

EXMOUTH

Devon – Pop. 34 432 – See Regional map n°**2**-D2

London 175 mi – Cardiff 114 mi – Plymouth 52 mi – Torbay 30 mi

Michelin Road map 503-J32

Les Saveurs

9 Tower St ✉ EX8 1NT – ✆ (01395) 269 459 – www.lessaveurs.co.uk – Closed early January-mid February, Sunday and Monday

Carte £ 30/42 – *(dinner only)*

Traditional restaurant owned and run by a French chef and his family. Menus are unashamedly classical and feature dishes from their homeland; seafood features highly, most of which is caught by the chef himself. Don't miss the lemon tart.

EXTON

Devon – See Regional map n°**2**-D2

London 176 mi – Exmouth 4 mi – Topsham 3 mi

Michelin Road map 503-J30

Puffing Billy

Station Rd ✉ EX3 0PR – ✆ (01392) 877 888 – www.thepuffingbilly.co.uk

Menu £ 17 (weekdays) – Carte £ 20/33

Bright, modern, open-plan country dining pub with high vaulted ceilings, a semi-circular bar and a friendly, welcoming atmosphere. The eclectic menu offers tasty, globally influenced dishes, pub classics and local specialities.

FALMOUTH

Cornwall – Pop. 22 686 – See Regional map n°**1**-A3

London 308 mi – Penzance 26 mi – Plymouth 65 mi – Truro 11 mi

Michelin Road map 503-E33 – Michelin Green Guide GREAT BRITAIN

Greenbank

Harbourside ✉ TR11 2SR – ✆ (01326) 312 440 – www.greenbank-hotel.co.uk Town plan: A**a**

60 rm – †£ 50/105 ††£ 108/225

Rest *Harbourside* – Carte £ 25/45

17C harbourside coaching inn, where flagstone floors and a sweeping staircase contrast with bold modern colours and contemporary furnishings. Spacious bedrooms are decked out in light wood; the Master Suite has a balcony and a bath with harbour views. The all-day restaurant serves modern, seasonal fare.

ENGLAND

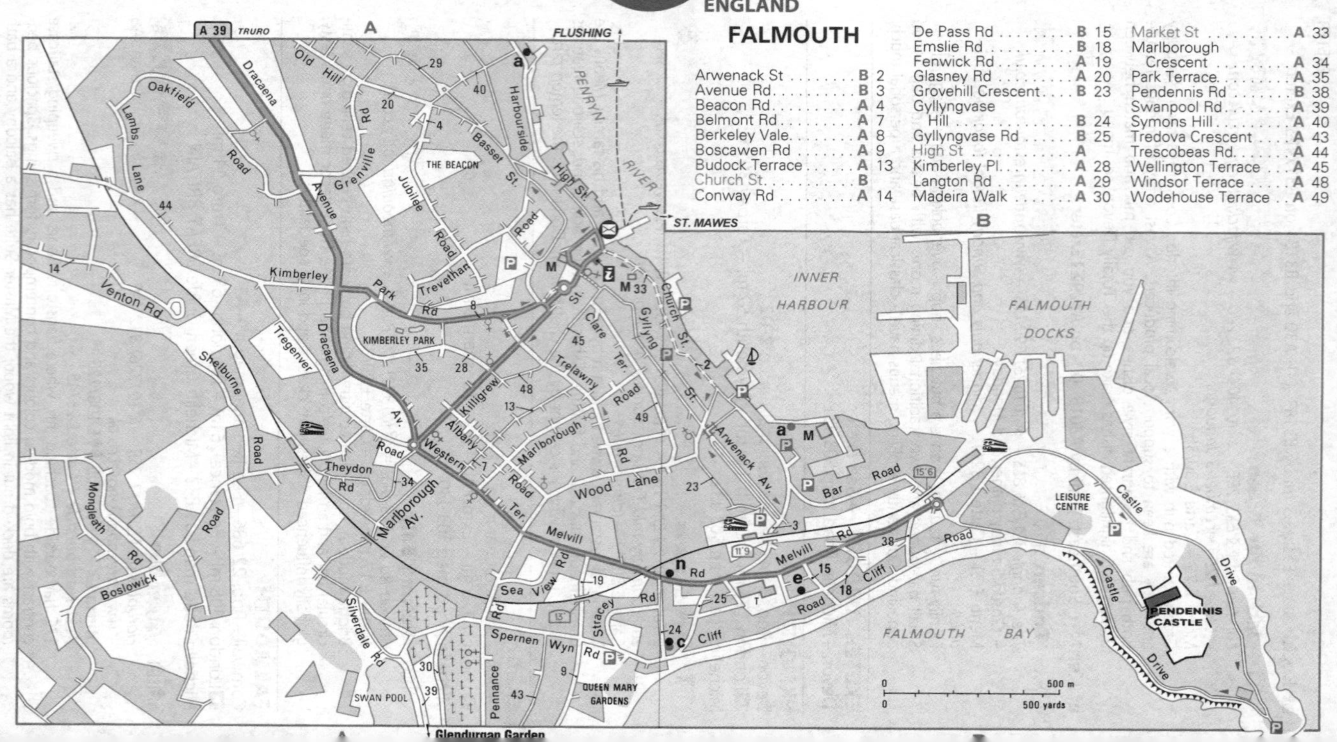
FALMOUTH
Arwenack St . . . . B 2
Avenue Rd. . . . . B 3
Beacon Rd. . . . . A 4
Belmont Rd . . . . A 7
Berkeley Vale. . . . . . . A 8
Boscawen Rd . . . . A 9
Budock Terrace . . . . . A 13
Church St. . . . . B
Conway Rd . . . . A 14
De Pass Rd . . . . B 15
Emslie Rd . . . . B 18
Fenwick Rd . . . . A 19
Glasney Rd . . . . A 20
Grovehill Crescent . . . B 23
Gyllyngvase Hill . . . . . B 24
Gyllyngvase Rd . . . . . B 25
High St . . . . A
Kimberley Pl. . . . . A 28
Langton Rd . . . . A 29
Madeira Walk . . . . A 30
Market St . . . . A 33
Marlborough Crescent . . A 34
Park Terrace. . . . . A 35
Pendennis Rd . . . . B 38
Swanpool Rd . . . . A 39
Symons Hill . . . . A 40
Tredova Crescent . . . . A 43
Trescobeas Rd. . . . . . . A 44
Wellington Terrace . . . A 45
Windsor Terrace . . . . . A 48
Wodehouse Terrace . . A 49
A
B
A 39 TRURO
FLUSHING
ST. MAWES
PENRYN RIVER
INNER HARBOUR
FALMOUTH DOCKS
FALMOUTH BAY
PENDENNIS CASTLE
LEISURE CENTRE
THE BEACON
KIMBERLEY PARK
QUEEN MARY GARDENS
SWAN POOL
Glendurgan Garden
Dracaena Avenue
Old Hill
Grenville Rd
Oakfield Road
Lambs Lane
Venton Rd
Kimberley Park Rd
Tregenver
Shelburne Road
Dracaena Av.
Jubilee Road
Trevethan Road
Basset St.
Harbourside
High St.
Killigrew St.
Clare Ter.
Trelawny Road
Church St.
Gyllyng St.
Arwenack Av.
Bar Road
Castle Drive
Albany Road
Marlborough Road
Wood Lane
Western Ter.
Melvill Rd
Theydon Rd
Marlborough Av.
Mongleath Rd
Boslowick Road
Silverdale Rd
Sea View Rd
Stracey Rd
Spernen Wyn Rd
Pennance
Cliff Road
500 m
500 yards

St Michael's H & Spa
Gyllyngvase Beach ✉ *TR11 4NB – ✆ (01326) 312 707* Town plan: B**c**
– www.stmichaelshotel.co.uk
61 rm – £ 89/249 ££ 178/340
Rest *Flying Fish* – see restaurant listing
Contemporary hotel with a nautical theme, from the reception desk 'boat' to the New England style bedrooms – some of which have balconies and sea views. Sea-blue décor, atmospheric lighting, friendly staff and a relaxed atmosphere.

Dolvean House without rest
50 Melvill Rd ✉ *TR11 4DQ – ✆ (01326) 313 658* Town plan: B**n**
– www.dolvean.co.uk – Closed first 2 weeks November and 22-28 December
10 rm – £ 41/46 ££ 80/100
Victorian house built in 1870; its homely lounge has lots of local guide books and magazines. Neat breakfast room. Good-sized bedrooms with thoughtful touches; Room 9, with a big bay window, is the best.

Chelsea House without rest
2 Emslie Rd ✉ *TR11 4BG – ✆ (01326) 212 230* Town plan: B**e**
– www.chelseahousehotel.com
9 rm – £ 40/45 ££ 60/95
Edwardian house in a quiet residential area close to the beaches. Pine-furnished breakfast room. Spacious, modern bedrooms, some with nautically themed décor and three with balconies; top floor rooms have the best views.

Flying Fish – St Michael's Hotel & Spa
Gyllyngvase Beach ✉ *TR11 4NB – ✆ (01326) 312 707* Town plan: B**c**
– www.stmichaelshotel.co.uk
Menu £ 35 (dinner) – Carte £ 27/44 – *(bookings essential for non-residents)*
Glass-fronted hotel restaurant overlooking the bay, with cool, azure-blue décor and stylish, atmospheric lighting. Deli dishes, sandwiches and salads at lunch; more elaborate, adventurous dinner dishes. Warm, friendly service.

Rick Stein's Fish
Discovery Quay ✉ *TR11 3XA – ✆ (01841) 532 700* Town plan: B**a**
– www.rickstein.com – Closed 24-26 December and Sunday-Monday in winter
Menu £ 13/20 – Carte £ 22/32 – *(booking advisable)*
With their own special beef dripping batter and fish chilli burgers to takeaway, this is more than your usual fish 'n' chips. Head inside and alongside your favourites you'll find the likes of dressed crab, fruits de mer and cod curry.

at Maenporth Beach South: 3.75 mi by Pennance Rd

Cove
Maenporth Beach ✉ *TR11 5HN – ✆ (01326) 251 136*
– www.thecovemaenporth.co.uk – Closed 25 December
Menu £ 25 – Carte £ 25/41
Bright, stylish restaurant in a smart glass-fronted building overlooking the beach, the cove and St Anthony's Head. The modern dining room is decorated in purple and there's a lovely split-level terrace with a retractable roof. Menus are contemporary, with a strong seafood base and some Asian influences.

FARINGDON

Oxfordshire – Pop. 7 121 – See Regional map n°**10-A2**
London 81 mi – Newbury 29 mi – Oxford 19 mi – Swindon 12 mi
Michelin Road map 503-P29

Restaurant 56 N
Sudbury House Hotel, 56 London St ✉ *SN7 7AA – ✆ (01367) 241 272*
– www.restaurant56.co.uk – Closed Sunday and Monday
Menu £ 30 (lunch) – Carte £ 47/57 – *(booking advisable)*
Georgian manor house found within the grounds of a hotel – its wood-panelling and red fabrics give it a smart, formal feel. Visually appealing dishes are crafted from top quality produce; classically based cooking has a modern edge.

ENGLAND

FARNBOROUGH

Hampshire – Pop. 65 034 – See Regional map n°**7-C1**
London 41 mi – Reading 17 mi – Southampton 44 mi – Winchester 33 mi
Michelin Road map 504-R30

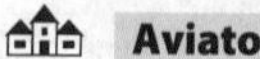

Aviator

Farnborough Rd ✉ GU14 6EL – Southwest : 1 mi on A 325 – ✆ (01252) 555 890 – www.aviatorbytag.com
169 rm – †£ 135/245 ††£ 135/245
Rest *Brasserie* – ✆ (01252) 555 895 – Menu £ 23 (lunch) **s** – Carte £ 28/50 **s**
Eye-catching modern hotel overlooking Farnborough Airport and boasting an unusual circular atrium, a smart first-floor lounge-bar and a small deli. Sleek, good-sized bedrooms feature light wood and modern facilities. The contemporary restaurant serves modern British dishes and steaks from the Josper grill.

FARNHAM → See Blandford Forum

Dorset – Michelin Road map 503-N31

FARNHAM

Surrey – Pop. 25 604 – See Regional map n°**7-C2**
London 45 mi – Reading 22 mi – Southampton 39 mi – Winchester 28 mi
Michelin Road map 504-R30

ENGLAND

Wheatsheaf Ⓝ

19 West St ✉ GU9 7DR – ✆ (01252) 717 135 – www.thewheatsheafatfarnham.co.uk – Closed 25 December
Carte £ 19/39
Meat is the speciality here, with tasty homemade burgers and steaks which use 21 day matured grassland beef from the local Surrey Farm. The smart, narrow dining room seems to stretch back for miles. Keen young staff know their stuff.

FARNINGHAM

Kent – See Regional map n°**8-B1**
London 22 mi – Dartford 7 mi – Maidstone 20 mi
Michelin Road map 504-U29

Beesfield Farm Ⓝ without rest

Beesfield Ln ✉ DA4 0LA – off A 225 – ✆ (01322) 863 900 – www.beesfieldfarm.co.uk – Closed December
4 rm – †£ 65/70 ††£ 80/90
Charming Kent longhouse surrounded by mature gardens, set on a 400 acre arable farm. The luxurious lounge is packed with photos, antiques and curios. Characterful beamed bedrooms are very individually styled and have country outlooks; one has its own sauna. Communal breakfasts feature honey from the farm.

FAVERSHAM

Kent – Pop. 19 829 – See Regional map n°**9-C1**
London 52 mi – Dover 26 mi – Maidstone 21 mi – Margate 25 mi
Michelin Road map 504-W30

XXX **Read's** with rm

Macknade Manor, Canterbury Rd ✉ ME13 8XE – East : 1 mi on A 2 – ✆ (01795) 535 344 – www.reads.com – Closed 2 weeks early September, 1 week early January, 25-26 December, Sunday and Monday
6 rm – †£ 125/185 ††£ 165/195 Menu £ 26/60
An elegant Georgian manor house in landscaped grounds, with traditional country house styling, antique furnishings and lovely oil paintings. Classically based dishes have subtle modern touches and make use of seasonal produce from the walled kitchen garden and the nearby quay. Comfortable bedrooms are full of period charm and thoughtful extras provide a sense of luxury.

at Dargate East: 6 mi by A2 off A299 ✉ Kent

The Dove

Plum Pudding Ln ✉ ME13 9HB – ✆ (01227) 751 360 – www.thedovedargate.co.uk – Closed first week January, Sunday dinner, Tuesday lunch and Monday
Carte £ 23/46 – *(booking advisable)*
Red-brick Victorian pub in the heart of a sleepy hamlet, on the aptly named Plum Pudding Lane. Open fires, wood floors and old black and white photos give it a cosy, rustic feel. Dishes would be equally at home in a restaurant.

at Oare Northwest: 2.5 mi by A2 off B2045 ✉ Kent

Three Mariners

2 Church Rd ✉ ME13 0QA – ✆ (01795) 533 633 – www.thethreemarinersoare.co.uk – Closed dinner 24-25 December
Menu £ 13/22 – Carte £ 25/39
Welcoming 500 year old pub set in a sleepy hamlet and boasting views across the marshes to the estuary. Constantly evolving menus offer an extensive range of British and Mediterranean-influenced dishes.

FELIXKIRK

North Yorkshire – See Regional map n°**22**-**B1**
London 228 mi – Harrogate 29 mi – Darlington 27 mi
Michelin Road map 502-Q21

Carpenter's Arms with rm

✉ YO7 2DP – ✆ (01845) 537 369 – www.thecarpentersarmsfelixkirk.com
10 rm – †£ 125/145 ††£ 125/175 Carte £ 22/41
A proper village pub with 18C origins, set in a village mentioned in the Domesday Book. Choose from blackboard specials or a wide-ranging menu of seasonal dishes, and be sure to save room for pudding. Stylishly appointed, well-equipped bedrooms overlook the Vale of Mowbray – as does the lovely terrace.

FERMAIN BAY

→ See Channel Islands (Guernsey) – Michelin Road map 503-L33

FERRENSBY

→ See Knaresborough
North Yorkshire

FILEY

North Yorkshire – Pop. 6 530 – See Regional map n°**23**-**D2**
London 240 mi – Leeds 66 mi – York 40 mi
Michelin Road map 502-T21

All Seasons (N) without rest

11 Rutland St ✉ YO14 9JA – ✆ (01723) 515 321 – www.allseasonsfiley.co.uk – Closed 24-26 December
6 rm – †£ 60/87 ††£ 80/97
This unassuming Victorian terraced house – just a stone's throw from the sea – conceals a smart, stylish interior, where no detail is forgotten. The cosy lounge is filled with magazines and local info, and bedrooms are bright, comfy and immaculately kept. You are welcomed with homemade cake and brownies.

FILKINS

Oxfordshire – Pop. 434 – See Regional map n°**10**-**A2**
London 78 mi – Birmingham 72 mi – Manchester 152 mi – Bristol 59 mi

Five Alls with rm

✉ GL7 3JQ – ✆ (01367) 860 875 – www.thefiveallsfilkins.co.uk – Closed 25 December and Sunday dinner
4 rm – †£ 90/110 ††£ 110/150 Menu £ 17/21 – Carte £ 27/41
Like its curious logo, this pub has it all: an open-fired bar where they serve snacks and takeaway burgers; a locals bar stocked with fine ales; three antique-furnished dining rooms; and a terrace and a garden with an Aunt Sally area. The menu is satisfyingly traditional and bedrooms are modern and cosy.

FIVEHEAD

Somerset – Pop. 609 – See Regional map n°**3-B3**

London 140 mi – Bristol 63 mi – Cardiff 84 mi – Bournemouth 77 mi

Michelin Road map 503-L30/31

Langford Fivehead

Lower Swell ✉ TA3 6PH – East : 0.5 mi by Westport rd on Swell rd – ☎ (01460) 282 020 – www.langfordfivehead.co.uk – Closed 2 January-3 February and 25-26 December

6 rm – †£ 185/290 ††£ 185/290

Rest – Menu £ 27/36 – *(closed Sunday dinner, Monday and lunch Tuesday) (bookings essential for non-residents)*

Beautiful 1453 country house on the Somerset Levels, surrounded by landscaped gardens – and very personally run. Tastefully furnished lounges have a classic English style and the luxurious bedrooms are furnished with antiques; one has a particularly impressive ceiling. Choose from a concise menu in the open-fired dining room; classic dishes have a subtle modern edge.

FLAUNDEN

Hertfordshire – Pop. 5 468 – See Regional map n°**12-A2**

London 35 mi – Reading 43 mi – Luton 23 mi – Milton Keynes 42 mi

Bricklayers Arms

Hogpits Bottom ✉ HP3 0PH – ☎ (01442) 833 322 – www.bricklayersarms.com – Closed 25 December

Menu £ 17 (weekdays) – Carte £ 24/46

Smart pub tucked away in a small hamlet. There are no snacks, just hearty, French-inspired dishes and old-school puddings. The wine list is a labour of love, featuring boutique Australian wines, and Sunday lunch is a real family affair.

ENGLAND

FLETCHING

East Sussex – Pop. 301 – See Regional map n°**8-A2**

London 45 mi – Brighton 20 mi – Eastbourne 24 mi – Maidstone 20 mi

Michelin Road map 504-U30/3

Griffin Inn with rm

✉ TN22 3SS – ☎ (01825) 722 890 – www.thegriffininn.co.uk – Closed 25 December

13 rm – †£ 70/145 ††£ 85/145

Menu £ 25 (weekday lunch) – Carte £ 26/46

Hugely characterful coaching inn, under the same ownership for over 30 years. There's a sizeable garden and a terrace with a wood-burning oven for summer BBQs. Menus feature British classics and some Mediterranean influences. Individually decorated bedrooms are accessed via narrow, sloping corridors.

FOLKESTONE

Kent – Pop. 51 337 – See Regional map n°**9-D2**

London 76 mi – Brighton 76 mi – Dover 8 mi – Maidstone 33 mi

Michelin Road map 504-X30 – Michelin Green Guide GREAT BRITAIN

Relish without rest

4 Augusta Gdns ✉ CT20 2RR – ☎ (01303) 850 952 Town plan: Z**n**
– www.hotelrelish.co.uk – Closed 21 December-2 January

10 rm – †£ 75/88 ††£ 98/150

A fine Regency house with a spacious, stylish interior. Contemporary bedrooms are named after their colour scheme or view – one has a four-poster bed. The smart lounge and breakfast room lead to a terrace overlooking the gardens.

XX Rocksalt with rm

rest, rest,

4-5 Fish Market ✉ CT19 6AA – ☎ (01303) 212 070 Town plan: Z**x**
– www.rocksaltfolkestone.co.uk – Closed Sunday dinner

4 rm – †£ 85/110 ††£ 85/110 Menu £ 22 (lunch) – Carte £ 27/57

Set within a stylish harbourfront eco-building affording lovely sea views. Smart cantilevered dining room with full-length windows opening onto a terrace; semi open air bar upstairs. Menus mix seafood and local meats; veg is from their farm. Nearby, bedrooms boast antique beds, Egyptian cotton linen and wet rooms.

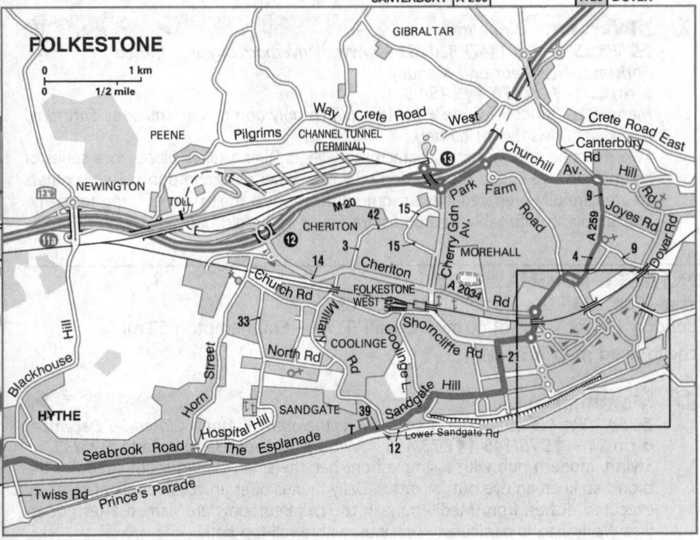

FOLKESTONE

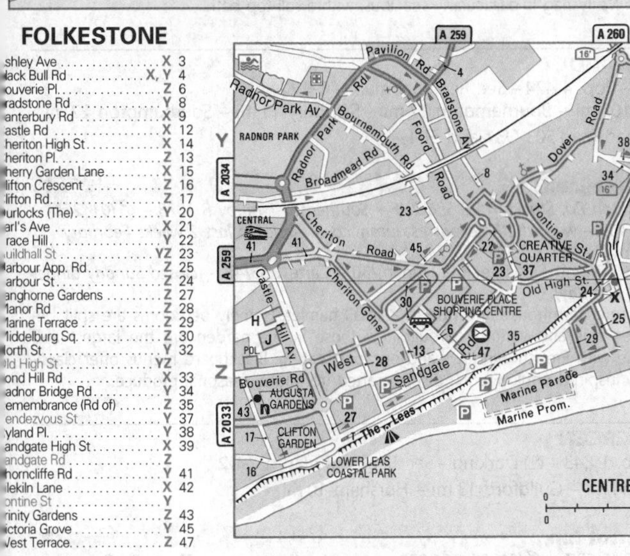

FOLKESTONE

shley Ave X 3
lack Bull Rd X, Y 4
ouverie Pl. Z 6
radstone Rd Y 8
anterbury Rd X 9
astle Rd X 12
heriton High St. X 14
heriton Pl. Z 13
herry Garden Lane X 15
lifton Crescent Z 16
lifton Rd. Z 17
urlocks (The) Y 20
arl's Ave X 21
race Hill Y 22
uildhall St YZ 23
arbour App. Rd. Z 25
arbour St. Z 24
anghorne Gardens Z 27
lanor Rd Z 28
larine Terrace Z 29
liddelburg Sq. Z 30
orth St. Y 32
ld High St. YZ
ond Hill Rd X 33
adnor Bridge Rd Y 34
emembrance (Rd of) Z 35
endezvous St Y 37
yland Pl. Y 38
andgate High St X 39
andgate Rd Z
horncliffe Rd Y 41
ilekiln Lane X 42
ontine St Y
rinity Gardens Z 43
ictoria Grove Y 45
Vest Terrace Z 47

If you are looking for particularly pleasant accommodation, book a hotel shown in red: 🏠, 🏠... 🏠🏠🏠.

FONTHILL BISHOP

Wiltshire – See Regional map n°4-C2

▶London 101 mi – Exeter 77 mi – Cheltenham 85 mi

Riverbarn Ⓝ with rm 

✉ *SP3 5SF – ✆ (01747) 820 232 – www.theriverbarn.org.uk – Closed Christmas-New Year and Monday*
3 rm – £ 60/70 £ 75/85
Menu £ 18 (lunch) – Carte £ 25/46 – *(lunch only and dinner Thursday-Saturday) (bookings advisable at dinner)*
Two riverside cottages in a characterful village. Dining takes places in a series of beamed, low-ceilinged rooms adorned with copper pans and prints. Two brothers create carefully prepared, flavoursome dishes, which their parents bring to the table. Simple, comfortable bedrooms are found in the old barn.

FONTMELL MAGNA

Dorset – Pop. 333 – See Regional map n°**4-C3**
London 115 mi – Bristol 60 mi – Cardiff 93 mi – Southampton 52 mi
Michelin Road map 503-N31

Fontmell with rm

✉ *SP7 0PA – ✆ (01747) 811 441 – www.thefontmell.com – Closed 26 December*
6 rm – £ 75/145 £ 75/155 Menu £ 16 (weekdays) – Carte £ 23/39
Stylish, modern pub with a simple front bar; the smart dining room straddles the brook, so keep an eye out for otters. Daily menus offer an eclectic mix of carefully executed dishes, from Mediterranean to Thai. Bedrooms are named after butterflies; Mallyshag is particularly spacious, with a roll-top bath.

ENGLAND

FORDINGBRIDGE

Hampshire – Pop. 4 474 – See Regional map n°**6-A2**
London 101 mi – Bournemouth 17 mi – Salisbury 11 mi – Southampton 22 mi
Michelin Road map 503-O31 and 504

Three Lions 

Stuckton Rd, Stuckton ✉ SP6 2HF – Southeast : 1 mi by B 3078 – ✆ (01425) 652 489 – www.thethreelionsrestaurant.co.uk – Closed last 2 weeks February
7 rm – £ 79 £ 125
Rest – Menu £ 24 (weekday lunch)/30 – Carte £ 35/48 – *(closed Sunday dinner and Monday)*
A former farmhouse and pub in a small hamlet. Homely bedrooms are split between this and various outbuildings; those in the garden are the largest and come with French windows and outdoor seating. Blackboard menus offer classically inspired Anglo-French dishes crafted from local seasonal produce.

FOREST GREEN

Surrey – Pop. 1 843 – ✉ Dorking – See Regional map n°**7-D2**
London 34 mi – Guildford 13 mi – Horsham 10 mi

Parrot Inn 

✉ *RH5 5RZ – ✆ (01306) 621 339 – www.theparrot.co.uk – Closed 25 December and Sunday dinner*
Carte £ 22/36
Traditional 17C pub set on the village green. Well-priced, generously proportioned dishes use produce from the pub's own farm. Homemade bread, cheese, cakes and preserves for sale.

FOREST ROW

East Sussex – Pop. 4 096 – See Regional map n°**8-A2**
London 35 mi – Brighton 26 mi – Eastbourne 30 mi – Maidstone 32 mi
Michelin Road map 504-U30

Ashdown Park

Colemans Hatch Rd, Wych Cross ✉ RH18 5JR – South : 3.25 mi by A 22 – ✆ (01342) 824 988 – www.ashdownpark.com
106 rm ☕ – 🚹£ 135/230 🚹🚹£ 135/230 – 3 suites
Rest *Anderida* – Menu £ 26/40 – Carte £ 37/54
Impressive Victorian building on the edge of Ashdown Forest. The spacious country house interior boasts grand staircases, impressive halls and open-fired lounges with parkland views. Elegant classical bedrooms feature antique furnishings. The traditional, formal restaurant has a pleasant estate outlook.

FOTHERINGHAY Northants ➜ See Oundle
– Michelin Road map 504-S26

FOWEY

Cornwall – Pop. 2 131 – See Regional map n°**1**-B2
▶London 277 mi – Newquay 24 mi – Plymouth 34 mi – Truro 22 mi
Michelin Road map 503-G32 – Michelin Green Guide GREAT BRITAIN

Fowey Hall

Hanson Dr ✉ PL23 1ET – West : 0.5 mi off A 3082 – ✆ (01726) 833 866 – www.foweyhallhotel.co.uk
36 rm ☕ – 🚹£ 140/350 🚹🚹£ 140/350 – 11 suites
Rest – Menu £ 42 (dinner) – Carte £ 31/46 **s**
Striking 19C manor house with an ornate, period-furnished lounge and a mix of traditional and modern bedrooms. Families are well-catered for and an informal feel pervades. Oak-panelled restaurant for adults; conservatory for those with children. Set menu has modern touches; less formal à la carte.

Old Quay House

28 Fore St ✉ PL23 1AQ – ✆ (01726) 833 302 – www.theoldquayhouse.com – Closed late November-early December
11 rm ☕ – 🚹£ 130/325 🚹🚹£ 150/325
Rest *Q* – see restaurant listing
19C former seamen's mission in a pretty harbour village; now a characterful boutique hotel with a friendly, laid-back feel. Bedrooms are individually decorated and have a contemporary, understated style; most have balconies and water views. Be sure to spend some time on the lovely terrace beside the river.

XX Q – Old Quay House Hotel

28 Fore St ✉ PL23 1AQ – ✆ (01726) 833 302 – www.theoldquayhouse.com – Closed late November-early December and lunch October-April
Menu £ 38 – Carte lunch £ 22/38
Light, bright hotel restaurant with wood framed mirrors, wicker furnishings and a glorious terrace with harbour views. Light lunches and more sophisticated dinners of modern, flavoursome dishes; fish is from Looe and shellfish, from Fowey.

X Bistro

24 Fore St. ✉ PL23 1AQ – ✆ (01726) 832 322 – www.thebistrofowey.com – Closed 2 weeks January and 2 weeks November
Menu £ 19 (weekdays)/25 – Carte £ 22/38
The ingredients might be Cornish but the tasty cooking takes its influences from across The Channel, with classic Gallic dishes the order of the day. Black & white photos fill the walls and there's even a display of old milk bottles!

ENGLAND

at Golant North: 3 mi by B3269 ✉ Fowey

Cormorant P

✉ *PL23 1LL – ✆ (01726) 833 426 – www.cormoranthotel.co.uk*
14 rm – ♀£ 70/235 ♀♀£ 80/235
Rest – Menu £ 33 – Carte £ 29/45 – *(bookings essential for non-residents)*
Well-run hotel in a superb waterside position. At only one room deep, all of its bedrooms overlook the estuary; the superior rooms boast balconies. Appealing seasonal menus feature local meats and seafood dishes. Light lunches offered in the formal restaurant or on the terrace.

FOXHAM

Wiltshire – See Regional map n°**4-C2**
London 94 mi – Bristol 28 mi – Cardiff 61 mi – Southampton 81 mi

Foxham Inn with rm — rest, P

✉ *SN15 4NQ – ✆ (01249) 740 665 – www.thefoxhaminn.co.uk – Closed 2 weeks early January and Monday*
2 rm – ♀£ 65/75 ♀♀£ 80/90 Carte £ 25/39 – *(booking advisable)*
Family-run pub in a sleepy Wiltshire village. A semi-covered terrace overlooks the fields and inside there's a cosy bar and a light, airy restaurant in a conservatory extension. Dishes are uniformly priced, and everything from the condiments to the ice creams is homemade. Bedrooms are warm and homely.

FREATHY

Cornwall – See Regional map n°**2-C2**
London 235 mi – Plymouth 9 mi – Tavistock 22 mi

The View P

✉ *PL10 1JY East : 1 mi – ✆ (01752) 822 345 – www.theview-restaurant.co.uk – Closed February, Monday and Tuesday*
Menu £ 16 (lunch) – Carte £ 28/37
Charming and informal converted café perched on a cliff, with coastal views. Relaxed daytime vibe; more atmospheric in the evening. Assured, confident, generous cooking and friendly service. Plenty of seafood and tasty homemade bread.

FRILSHAM → See Yattendon

West Berkshire

FRITHSDEN

Hertfordshire – See Regional map n°**12-A2**
London 33 mi – St Albans 11 mi – Aylesbury 16 mi

Alford Arms P

✉ *HP1 3DD – ✆ (01442) 864 480 – www.alfordarmsfrithsden.co.uk – Closed 25-26 December*
Carte £ 21/37
Attractive Victorian pub beside the village green. The traditional British menu follows the seasons closely, with salads and fish featuring in the summer and game and comfort dishes in the winter; have a look at the tempting specials board.

FROGGATT

Derbyshire – See Regional map n°**16-A1**
London 167 mi – Bakewell 6 mi – Sheffield 11 mi
Michelin Road map 502-P24 and 503

Chequers Inn with rm P

Hope Valley ✉ *S32 3ZJ – on A 625 – ✆ (01433) 630 231 – www.chequers-froggatt.com – Closed 25 December*
6 rm – ♀£ 85/115 ♀♀£ 85/115 Carte £ 25/33
Traditional 16C inn built right into the stone boulders of Froggatt Edge and boasting a direct path up to the peak. Cooking is unfussy, tasty and largely classical, with more imaginative specials on the blackboard. Comfortable bedrooms; Number One, to the rear, is the quietest.

FROME

Somerset – Pop. 26 203 – See Regional map n°**4-C2**

London 118 mi – Bristol 24 mi – Southampton 52 mi – Swindon 44 mi

Michelin Road map 503-M/N30 and 504

Babington House

Babington ✉ BA11 3RW – Northwest : 6.5 mi by A 362 on Vobster rd – ☎ (01373) 812 266 – www.babingtonhouse.co.uk

33 rm – †£ 360 ††£ 390/720, ☕ £ 16 – 11 suites

Rest *Orangery* – Carte £ 24/37

Behind this country house's classic Georgian façade is a cool, fashionable hotel with bold colour schemes and a bohemian feel. Kick-back in the luxurious lounges or relax in the beautiful spa with its superb fitness area and pool. Bedrooms are modern and understated. The newly built but classic-looking Orangery offers an accessible menu of Italian-influenced dishes.

FULBECK

Lincolnshire – See Regional map n°**17-C2**

London 123 mi – Birmingham 83 mi – Leeds 80 mi – Sheffield 54 mi

Hare & Hounds with rm

The Green ✉ NG32 3JJ – ☎ (01400) 273 322 – www.hareandhoundsfulbeck.com – Closed 25 December and Sunday dinner

8 rm ☕ – †£ 60 ††£ 80 Carte £ 19/36

Built in 1680 as a house, this charmingly decorated pub has been enthusiastically adopted by the locals. The ethos of 'simple pub classics done well' goes down a storm – the menus are refreshingly concise and local produce is to the fore. Smart, comfortable bedrooms in the old stables; popular jazz evenings.

ENGLAND

FULLER STREET

Essex – Pop. 50 – See Regional map n°**13-C2**

London 52 mi – Birmingham 141 mi – Leicester 112 mi – Coventry 123 mi

Michelin Road map 504-V28

Square & Compasses

✉ CM3 2BB – ☎ (01245) 361 477 – www.thesquareandcompasses.co.uk – Closed Sunday dinner

Carte £ 20/36 – *(booking essential)*

Charming little pub with low beams, wood burning stoves and character aplenty. Unfussy menus of freshly made pub classics and unashamedly traditional puddings; daily blackboards offer locally shot game and fish caught nearby. Friendly team.

FULMER

Buckinghamshire – Pop. 230 – See Regional map n°**11-D3**

London 21 mi – Croydon 49 mi – Barnet 30 mi – Ealing 13 mi

Michelin Road map 504

Black Horse with rm

Windmill Rd ✉ SL3 6HD – ☎ (01753) 663 183 – www.theblackhorsefulmer.co.uk – Closed 25 December

2 rm – †£ 100/210 ††£ 100/210 Menu £ 16 (weekday lunch) – Carte £ 21/42

Whitewashed village pub with thick walls, cosy alcoves, a wood-burning stove and a gem of a garden for sunny days. Stylish, formal dining area with delightful portraits; dishes include sharing boards, small plates and grills. Uniquely styled bedrooms with spacious, modern bathrooms.

FUNTINGTON → See Chichester

West Sussex – Michelin Road map 504-R31

FYFIELD

Essex – See Regional map n°**12**-B2

London 33 mi – Birmingham 134 mi – Croydon 44 mi – Leicester 111 mi

Queens Head

Queen St ✉ CM5 0RY – ✆ (01277) 899 231 – www.thequeensheadfyfield.co.uk – Closed 1-7 January, Sunday dinner and Monday

Menu £ 16 (lunch) – Carte £ 22/45

Characterful village pub with a pretty rear garden leading down to the river. The inviting interior features original 16C beams and fireplaces. Menus change every 2 months and offer a good choice of tasty, restaurant-style dishes.

FYFIELD → See Oxford

Oxfordshire

GEDNEY DYKE

Lincolnshire – Pop. 320 – See Regional map n°**17**-D2

London 112 mi – Birmingham 112 mi – Sheffield 91 mi – Cambridge 32 mi

Michelin Road map 504-U25

Chequers

Main St ✉ PE12 0AJ – ✆ (01406) 366 700 – www.the-chequers.co.uk – Closed Sunday dinner, Monday and Tuesday

Menu £ 20 (lunch) – Carte dinner £ 20/40

Formerly a pub, now a stylish modern bar and restaurant with a smart conservatory extension opening onto a pavement terrace. The chef is keen to use the wealth of produce on his doorstep. Preparation is precise and cooking is refined and flavoursome; the set menus represent particularly good value.

GEORGE GREEN

Buckinghamshire – Pop. 950 – See Regional map n°**11**-D3

London 56 mi – Croydon 49 mi – Barnet 78 mi – Ealing 60 mi

Pinewood

Wexham Park Ln, Uxbridge Rd ✉ SL3 6AP – on A 412 – ✆ (01753) 896 400 – www.pinewoodhotel.co.uk – Closed 24-28 December

49 rm – †£ 79/139 ††£ 89/159

Rest *Pinewood Brasserie* – Carte £ 19/36 **s**

Modern, purpose-built hotel in 4 acres; named after the nearby film studios and within easy reach of the M4, M25 and M40. Good-sized, well-equipped bedrooms are split between the house and an adjacent annexe. The simply decorated dining room serves a wide-ranging menu; go for a pizza from the wood-fired oven.

GERRARDS CROSS

Buckinghamshire – Pop. 20 633 – See Regional map n°**11**-D3

London 22 mi – Birmingham 106 mi – Bristol 112 mi – Cardiff 145 mi

Michelin Road map 504-S29

Three Oaks

Austenwood Ln ✉ SL9 8NL – Northwest : 0.75 mi by A 413 on Gold Hill rd – ✆ (01753) 899 016 – www.thethreeoaksgx.co.uk

Menu £ 15/19 – Carte £ 22/42

An appealing, well-run pub in a rural location, with several stylishly decorated rooms: dine in the brighter room overlooking the terrace and pretty garden. Cooking is tasty, satisfying and seasonal, and they offer a particularly good value set lunch menu. The bright young staff are eager to please.

GESTINGTHORPE

Essex – See Regional map n°**13**-C2

London 65 mi – Birmingham 133 mi – Liverpool 226 mi – Leeds 184 mi

Michelin Road map 504-V27

Pheasant with rm

✉ CO9 3AU South : 0.75 mi by Church St on Halstead rd – ✆ (01787) 465 010 – www.thepheasant.net – Closed first 2 weeks January

5 rm – †£ 85/125 ††£ 95/165 Carte £ 23/36

A true country inn centring around sustainability, where they grow vegetables and keep chickens and bees. Simple cooking offers traditional, heartwarming dishes and the inviting, low-beamed bar and takeaway fish & chips keep the locals happy. Modern bedrooms feature good quality bedding and country views.

GILLINGHAM

Dorset – Pop. 11 278 – See Regional map n°**4-C3**

London 116 mi – Bournemouth 34 mi – Bristol 46 mi – Southampton 52 mi

Michelin Road map 503-N30 and 504

Stock Hill Country House

Stock Hill ✉ SP8 5NR – West : 1.5 mi on B 3081 – ✆ (01747) 823 626 – www.stockhillhouse.co.uk

8 rm (dinner included) – †£ 105/145 ††£ 200/300

Rest – Menu £ 22/40 – *(booking essential)*

Personally-run Georgian country house with later extensions, set in attractive mature grounds. Classical lounges boast heavy fabrics and antiques. Spacious bedrooms – in the main house and stables – display a mix of cottagey and country house styles; all have good facilities. The formal two-roomed restaurant has its own kitchen garden and serves Austrian cuisine.

ENGLAND

GISBURN

Lancashire – See Regional map n°**20-B2**

London 242 mi – Bradford 28 mi – Skipton 12 mi

Michelin Road map 502-N22

Park House without rest

13 Church View ✉ BB7 4HG – ✆ (01200) 445 269 – www.parkhousegisburn.co.uk – Closed December and January

6 rm – †£ 55/85 ††£ 75/100

Imposing Victorian house with a classical open-fired drawing room and a small library leading to a hidden stepped garden. Bedrooms mix antique and more modern furnishings. Good breakfast selection; tea and homemade cake served on arrival.

La Locanda

Main St ✉ BB7 4HH – ✆ (01200) 445 303 – www.lalocanda.co.uk – Closed 25 December, 1 January, Tuesday lunch and Monday lunch except bank holidays

Menu £ 10/15 – Carte £ 17/39

Charming low-beamed, flag-floored cottage run by a keen couple. Comfy lounge serving Italian drinks, with the dining room above. Extensive menu of hearty homemade dishes; try the tasty pastas. Good quality local and imported produce.

GITTISHAM → See Honiton

Devon – Michelin Road map 503-K31

GLINTON → See Peterborough

Peterborough – Michelin Road map 504-T26

GODALMING

Surrey – Pop. 22 689 – See Regional map n°**7-C2**

London 39 mi – Guildford 5 mi – Southampton 48 mi

Michelin Road map 504-S30

La Luna 

10-14 Wharf St ✉ GU7 1NN – ✆ (01483) 414 155 – www.lalunarestaurant.co.uk – Closed Sunday and Monday
Menu £ 17 (lunch) – Carte £ 24/38
Contemporary Italian restaurant whose passionate owner looks after his guests with great enthusiasm. Classic Italian dishes use excellent ingredients. Particularly good selection of authentic antipasti and pasta.

at Lower Eashing West: 1.75 mi by A3100

Stag on the River with rm

Lower Eashing Rd ✉ GU7 2QG – ✆ (01483) 421 568 – www.stagontherivereashing.co.uk – Closed 25 December
7 rm – †£ 65/130 ††£ 65/130 Carte £ 22/39
Pretty 16C former mill with a smart, modern look; the terrace overlooks the old millstream. Hearty, traditional dishes and sharing plates; the 8hr roasted pork belly is a popular choice. Attractively appointed, modern bedrooms are named after local villages; Shackleford is the largest.

GODSHILL → See Wight (Isle of)
Isle of Wight – Michelin Road map 504-Q32

GOLANT Cornwall → See Fowey
– Michelin Road map 503-G32

GOLDSBOROUGH → See Whitby
North Yorkshire

GOREY → See Channel Islands (Jersey)
– Michelin Road map 503-P33

GORRAN HAVEN

Cornwall – See Regional map n°**1-B3**
London 260 mi – Plymouth 53 mi – Torbay 80 mi – Torquay 83 mi
Michelin Road map 503-F33

Llawnroc 

Chute Ln ✉ PL26 6NU – ✆ (01726) 843 461 – www.thellawnrochotel.co.uk – Closed 25-26 December and restricted opening in winter
18 rm – †£ 76/248 ††£ 95/310
Rest *Gwineas* – Carte £ 23/43
Unpretentious boutique hotel that's popular with families – enjoy tea on the terrific terrace. Boldly coloured, well-equipped bedrooms feature plenty of contemporary design touches; bathrooms have drench showers and Voya seaweed toiletries. Unfussy bistro dishes are served in the minimalistic restaurant.

GOUDHURST

Kent – Pop. 1 142 – See Regional map n°**8-B2**
London 47 mi – Ashford 22 mi – Maidstone 17 mi
Michelin Road map 504-V30

Goudhurst Inn

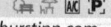

Cranbrook Rd ✉ TN17 1DX – ✆ (01580) 212 605 – www.thegoudhurstinn.com
Carte £ 22/43
An appealingly old-fashioned pub with a rustic bar, a small snug and a lovely rear terrace. Seasonal menus offer classic English dishes like steak and kidney pud or sausage and mash, alongside charcuterie boards and old school puddings.

The Vine

High St ✉ TN17 1AG – ✆ (01580) 211 753 – www.thevinegoudhurst.com
Menu £ 20 (weekday lunch) – Carte £ 26/40
When childhood friends acquired this part-17C pub, it was almost derelict and had squatters: now the cosy ground floor rooms have a rustic, shabby-chic feel, while the upstairs dining rooms are more formal. Traditional British dishes.

GRANGE-OVER-SANDS

Cumbria – Pop. 4 788 – See Regional map n°**21**-A3
London 268 mi – Kendal 13 mi – Lancaster 24 mi
Michelin Road map 502-L21 – Michelin Green Guide GREAT BRITAIN

Netherwood

rest,

Lindale Rd ✉ LA11 6ET – ✆ (015395) 32 552 – www.netherwood-hotel.co.uk
34 rm – £ 75/105 £ 120/180 **Rest** – Menu £ 19/34
Impressive castellated Victorian mansion on the hillside, affording lovely bay views. Traditional guest areas display wood panelling and original features. Bedrooms are simple and well-maintained; the most contemporary rooms are in the annexe. Formal dining comes with a great outlook.

Clare House

Park Rd ✉ LA11 7HQ – ✆ (015395) 33 026 – www.clarehousehotel.co.uk – Closed 15 December-30 March
18 rm (dinner included) – £ 72/77 £ 144/154
Rest – Menu £ 38 – *(booking essential) (bar lunch Monday-Saturday)*
Family-run Victorian house set in lovely gardens, overlooking Morecambe Bay. Two classical sitting rooms. Stylish, boldly coloured bedrooms in the main house and smaller, simpler rooms with balconies in the wing. The smart, modern dining room offers traditional daily menus.

at Cartmel Northwest: 3 mi ✉ Grange-Over-Sands

L'Enclume (Simon Rogan) with rm

rest,

Cavendish St ✉ LA11 6PZ – ✆ (015395) 36 362 – www.lenclume.co.uk
17 rm – £ 69/169 £ 99/239
Menu £ 45/120 – *(closed lunch Monday-Tuesday) (booking essential) (set menu only)*
Friendly, stone-built former smithy in an attractive village. Inventive, modern cooking uses top quality produce to create dishes with a pleasing lightness and a superb balance of flavours. Home-grown and foraged ingredients feature highly. Comfy, traditional bedrooms are spread about the village; breakfast is taken at Rogan and Company.
→ Cod 'yolk' with sage cream, pea shoots, salt and vinegar. Venison with charcoal oil, mustard and fennel. Sea buckthorn, sweet cheese and malt.

Rogan and Company

The Square ✉ LA11 6QD – ✆ (015395) 35 917 – www.roganandcompany.co.uk – Closed Sunday and lunch Monday
Menu £ 29/40
The informal cousin to L'Enclume, set in a converted cottage by a lovely stream. The open-plan interior has dark wood beams and a minimalist feel; watch the chefs in the large kitchen pass. Modern dishes rely on local, seasonal produce.

Pig & Whistle

✉ LA11 6PL – ✆ (01539) 536 482 – www.pigandwhistlecartmel.co.uk – Closed 25 December
Carte £ 23/35
Comfy, cosy local in a delightful village. It looks rather like a row of terraced cottages and with three tiny rooms, has an intimate feel. Reasonably priced, traditional pub menus: cooking is honest and careful with bold, defined flavours.

ENGLAND

GRANTHAM

Lincolnshire – Pop. 41 998 – See Regional map n°**17-C2**
London 113 mi – Leicester 31 mi – Lincoln 29 mi – Nottingham 24 mi
Michelin Road map 502-S25 and 504 – Michelin Green Guide GREAT BRITAIN

XX **Harry's Place**

17 High St, Great Gonerby ✉ NG31 8JS – Northwest : 2 mi on B 1174 – ✆ (01476) 561 780 – Closed 25 December-1 January, 1 week August, Sunday, Monday and bank holidays
Carte £ 57/67 – *(booking essential)*
Long-standing, intimate restaurant in a former farmhouse: it consists of just 3 tables and is personally run by a dedicated and delightful husband and wife team. Warm, welcoming feel, with fresh flowers, candles and antiques. Classically based menus offer 2 choices per course. Good cheese selection.

at Hough-on-the-Hill North: 6.75 mi by A607 ✉ Grantham

XX **Brownlow Arms** with rm — rest,

High Rd ✉ NG32 2AZ – ✆ (01400) 250 234 – www.thebrownlowarms.com – Closed Sunday dinner and Monday
7 rm – †£ 65/75 ††£ 98/110
Carte £ 29/45 – *(dinner only and Sunday lunch)*
Characterful former shooting lodge for the nearby Belton Estate, with wood-panelled walls and large open fireplaces. Lengthy menu and specials list offer classically based dishes with modern presentation. Lovely terrace and friendly service. Delightful bedrooms are furnished with contemporary fabrics and period pieces.

GRASMERE

ENGLAND

Cumbria ✉ Ambleside – See Regional map n°**21-A2**
London 282 mi – Carlisle 43 mi – Kendal 18 mi
Michelin Road map 502-K20 – Michelin Green Guide GREAT BRITAIN
Plan: see Ambleside

Rothay Garden — rm,

Broadgate ✉ LA22 9RJ – ✆ (015394) 35 334 – www.rothaygarden.com Town plan: AY**s**
30 rm – †£ 108/180 ††£ 135/280 **Rest** – Menu £ 40 **s** – *(dinner only)*
Slate-built Lakeland house with modern extensions, which include a spa and a copper-roofed conservatory restaurant with a lovely outlook and a classically based menu. Bedrooms are stylish and contemporary – many have king-sized beds and some have balconies or patios; the Loft Suites are the best.

Daffodil

Keswick Rd ✉ LA22 9PR – On A 591 – ✆ (015394) 63 550 – www.daffodilhotel.co.uk Town plan: AY**x**
78 rm – †£ 130/410 ††£ 140/420 – 2 suites **Rest** – Carte £ 28/41
Smart corporate hotel with lake and mountain views, set opposite the Wordsworth Museum. The small spa specialises in Rasul mud treatments. Bedrooms have multi-media panels, Molton Brown toiletries and king, super king or emperor sized beds. Light lunches, followed by hearty, traditional dishes in the evening.

Moss Grove Organic without rest

✉ LA22 9SW – ✆ (015394) 35 251 – www.mossgrove.com – Closed 24-25 December Town plan: BZ**s**
11 rm – †£ 84/164 ††£ 99/259
Laid-back house with a stylish interior featuring many reclaimed furnishings. Funky bedrooms boast large beds, Bose sound systems and whirlpool baths. Organic breakfasts include tasty veggie options; help yourself from the kitchen.

Grasmere

Broadgate ✉ LA22 9TA – ✆ (015394) 35 277 – www.grasmerehotel.co.uk – Restricted opening in winter Town plan: BZ**r**
11 rm – †£ 61/66 ††£ 112/142
Rest – Menu £ 26 **s** – *(dinner only) (booking essential)*
Small Victorian house close to the village centre, with the River Rothay running through the garden. The spacious lounge and bar are traditionally decorated; similarly styled bedrooms are named after writers and some have antique beds. The classically furnished dining room overlooks the garden.

Oak Bank

Broadgate ✉ LA22 9TA – ✆ (015394) 35 217 Town plan: BZ**x**
– www.lakedistricthotel.co.uk – Closed 2-22 January, 2-14 August, 20-26 December and 3-7 May
14 rm ☕ – 🚹£ 69/109 🚹🚹£ 69/164
Rest *Dining Room* – see restaurant listing
Passionately run Victorian house with a pretty rear garden. Relax beside the converted range in the sitting room or next to the open fire in the lounge-bar. Modern bedrooms have comfortable beds, bold fabrics and bright colours.

Dining Room – Oak Bank Hotel

Broadgate ✉ LA22 9TA – ✆ (015394) 35 217 Town plan: BZ**x**
– www.lakedistricthotel.co.uk – Closed 2-22 January, 2-14 August, 20-26 December and 3-7 May
Menu £ 25/38 – *(booking essential)*
Split-roomed hotel restaurant in a Victorian house, with a pleasant conservatory overlooking the garden. The concise daily menu features interesting modern dishes crafted from seasonal Lakeland produce; everything is made in-house.

GRASSINGTON

North Yorkshire – Pop. 1 126 – ✉ Skipton – See Regional map n°**22**-A2
London 240 mi – Bradford 30 mi – Burnley 28 mi – Leeds 37 mi
Michelin Road map 502-O21

Ashfield House

Summers Fold ✉ BD23 5AE – off Main St – ✆ (01756) 752 584 – www.ashfieldhouse.co.uk – Closed 23-26 December
8 rm ☕ – 🚹£ 63/90 🚹🚹£ 88/200
Rest – Menu £ 30/36 – *(closed Wednesday and Sunday) (dinner only) (booking essential)*
Bright, cheery hotel with a larger-than-life owner. Formerly three 1604 lead miner's cottages, its old beams and mullioned windows blend well with the Mediterranean colours. The cottage bedroom boasts a spiral staircase and terrace. Traditional menus feature local produce; vegetarian dishes are a speciality.

Grassington Lodge without rest

8 Wood Ln ✉ BD23 5LU – ✆ (01756) 752 518 – www.grassingtonlodge.co.uk – Closed 5 January-first week February
12 rm ☕ – 🚹£ 60/100 🚹🚹£ 75/100
Stone house close to the square, with a sleek breakfast room and two lounges; one offering complimentary sherry, the other with a large DVD collection and a laptop. Bedrooms are modern and unfussy; those in the eaves are the best.

Grassington House with rm

5 The Square ✉ BD23 5AQ – ✆ (01756) 752 406 – www.grassingtonhousehotel.co.uk – Closed 25 December
9 rm ☕ – 🚹£ 95 🚹🚹£ 110/130
Menu £ 17 (lunch and early dinner) – Carte £ 23/40
Georgian house with a large bar-lounge, two dining rooms and delightful service. Classical menus display Mediterranean touches and include their home-bred pork. Smart, modern bedrooms; No.6 has a roll-top bath in the room. Home-cured bacon or sausages are offered at breakfast and they host regular wine dinners.

GREAT DUNMOW

Essex – Pop. 7 749 – See Regional map n°**13**-C2
London 42 mi – Cambridge 27 mi – Chelmsford 13 mi – Colchester 24 mi
Michelin Road map 504-V28

Square 1

15 High St. ✉ CM6 1AB – ✆ (01371) 859 922 – www.square1restaurant.co.uk – Closed 25-26 December and Sunday dinner
Menu £ 15 (lunch) – Carte £ 25/37
Pretty little whitewashed building; once a 14C monastic reading room. Much original character remains in the form of exposed beams and low ceilings; which contrast with vibrant modern art. Unfussy monthly menu has Mediterranean leanings.

GREAT MALVERN

Worcestershire – Pop. 36 770 – See Regional map n°**18-B3**
London 127 mi – Birmingham 34 mi – Cardiff 66 mi – Gloucester 24 mi
Michelin Road map 503-N27 and 504

Cotford

51 Graham Rd ✉ WR14 2HU – ✆ (01684) 572 427 Town plan: B**s**
– www.cotfordhotel.co.uk
15 rm – £ 68/85 £ 125/140
Rest *L' Amuse Bouche* – see restaurant listing
The owners of this 1851 gothic-style house (built for the Bishop of Worcester), put a lot of effort into getting things right. It mixes the traditional and the contemporary and has stylish bedrooms and a chic black and pink bar.

L' Amuse Bouche – Cotford Hotel

51 Graham Rd ✉ WR14 2HU – ✆ (01684) 572 427 Town plan: B**s**
– www.cotfordhotel.co.uk
Carte £ 30/39 – *(dinner only and Sunday lunch)*
Start with an aperitif in the stylish bar or traditional lounge of this Gothic hotel, then head for the contemporary dining room overlooking the gardens. Boldly flavoured, classically based dishes have a subtle modern touch.

at Welland Southeast: 5 mi on B4208

The Inn at Welland

Hook Bank ✉ WR13 6LN – East : 1 mi on A 4104 Town plan: A**a**
– ✆ (01684) 592 317 – www.theinnatwelland.co.uk – Closed Sunday dinner and Monday
Carte £ 19/38
Light, open and stylish, with charming features and designer touches, its owners have turned this pub from wreck to 'by 'eck!' Pub classics and sandwiches sit alongside generously portioned modern British dishes on the menu.

at Malvern Wells South: 2 mi on A449 ✉ Malvern

Cottage in the Wood

rm,

Holywell Rd ✉ WR14 4LG – ✆ (01684) 588 860 Town plan: A**z**
– www.cottageinthewood.co.uk
30 rm – £ 79/121 £ 99/198
Rest *Outlook* – Carte £ 26/45 **s**
Three superbly set properties with far-reaching views across the vale. Bedrooms in the original cottage and Beech House are cosy and traditional; those in The Pinnacles are larger and some have balconies. The bright restaurant offers an extensive modern menu, over 700 wines and great views.

at Colwall Southwest: 3 mi on B4218 ✉ Great Malvern

Colwall Park

rest,

Walwyn Rd ✉ WR13 6QG – ✆ (01684) 540 000 Town plan: A**v**
– www.colwall.co.uk
22 rm – £ 80/135 £ 110/200 – 1 suite
Rest *Seasons* – Menu £ 19 (lunch) – Carte £ 25/37
Nestled in a leafy village in the Malvern Hills is this personally run Edwardian house with an attractive mock-Tudor façade. From the cosy lounges to the comfy bedrooms it has a traditional style but also displays modern touches. A brasserie menu is available in both the bar and high-ceilinged restaurant.

at Cradley West: 4 mi by B4219 and A4103

Old Rectory

✉ WR13 5LQ – ✆ (01886) 880 109 – www.oldrectorycradley.com
8 rm – £ 100 £ 130/150 **Rest** – Menu £ 38
Welcoming Georgian house in mature gardens; built in 1790 and set right next to the church. The place is packed with curios and antiques; many of the pictures were painted by the owner herself. Food plays a big role – jams are homemade, bacon is home-cured, meats are local and vegetables are from the garden.

GREAT MALVERN

Street	Square	No.
Albert Rd South	B	3
Blackmore Park Rd	A	5
Church St.	B	
Clerkenwell Crescent	B	6
Cockshot Rd	B	8
Court Rd	B	12
Croft Bank	A	13
Happy Valley off St Ann's Rd	B	15
Imperial Rd	B	16
Jubilee Drive	A	17
Lygon Bank	B	18
Madresfield Rd	B	20
Moorlands Rd	B	22
North Malvern Rd	B	23
Orchard Rd	B	24
Richmond Rd	B	25
Townsend Way	A	26
Upper Welland Rd	A	27
Walwyn Rd	A	29
Wells Rd.	A, B	30
Zetland Rd	B	31

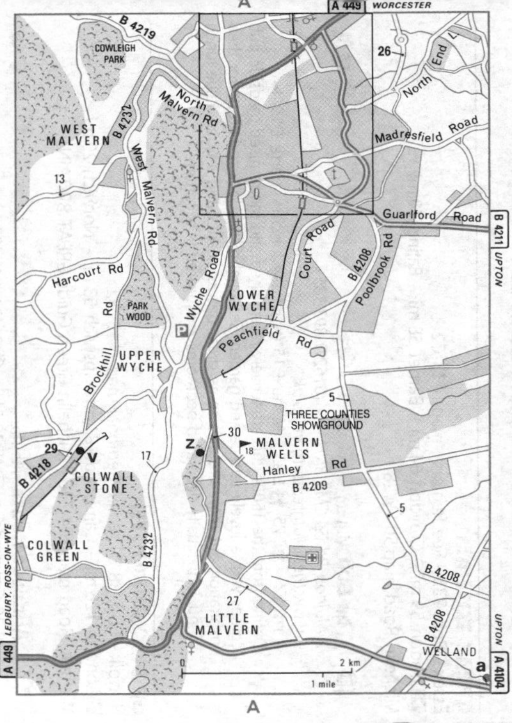

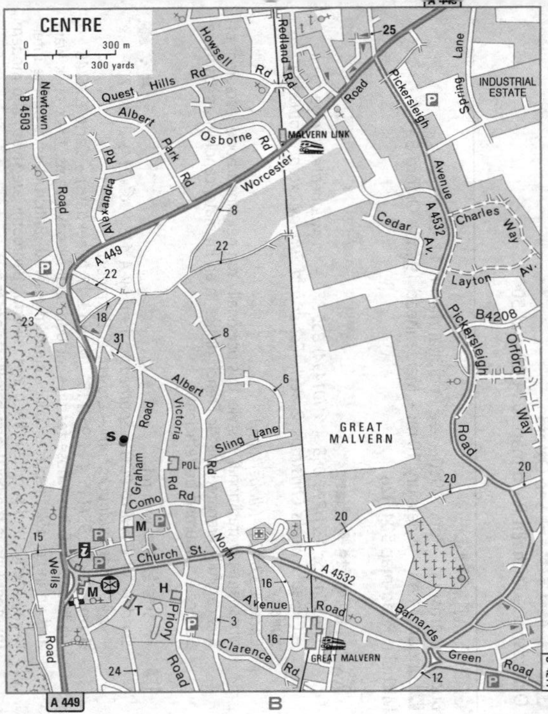

GREAT MILTON → See Oxford

Oxfordshire – Michelin Road map 503-Q28 and 504

GREAT MISSENDEN

Buckinghamshire – Pop. 7 980 – See Regional map n°**11**-C2

London 34 mi – Aylesbury 10 mi – Maidenhead 19 mi – Oxford 35 mi

Michelin Road map 504-R28

La Petite Auberge

107 High St ✉ HP16 0BB – ✆ (01494) 865 370 – www.lapetiteauberge.co.uk – Closed 2 weeks Christmas, 2 weeks Easter and Sunday except Mothering Sunday

Carte £ 32/43 – *(dinner only)*

Unashamedly traditional in style, this personally run neighbourhood restaurant offers carefully prepared, classic French dishes in an intimate, candlelit atmosphere. Service is unhurried but efficient.

Nags Head with rm

London Rd ✉ HP16 0DG – Southeast : 1 mi by A 413 – ✆ (01494) 862 200 – www.nagsheadbucks.com – Closed 25 December

5 rm – £ 95/115 £ 95/115 Menu £ 17 (weekdays) – Carte £ 25/48

Traditional 15C inn whose features include original oak beams, thick brick walls and an inglenook fireplace. Gallic charm mixes with British classics on the interesting menus and service is keen and cheerful. Bedrooms are stylish and modern (number One is the best), and breakfasts are tasty.

ENGLAND

GREAT TOTHAM

Essex – Pop. 735 – See Regional map n°**13**-C2

London 59 mi – Croydon 64 mi – Barnet 58 mi – Ealing 70 mi

Michelin Road map 504-W28

The Bull with rm

2 Maldon Rd ✉ CM9 8NH – ✆ (01621) 893 385 – www.thebullatgreattotham.co.uk

4 rm – £ 75 £ 85 Menu £ 15 (weekday lunch) – Carte £ 19/44

Dating from the 1500s, this attractively refurbished and modernised roadside pub comes with a lovely terrace and garden. Seasonal dishes look to Europe for their inspiration but there are also some great British classics and a good value lunch menu. Individually decorated bedrooms are located in a cottage.

GREAT YARMOUTH

Norfolk – Pop. 38 693 – See Regional map n°**15**-D2

London 126 mi – Cambridge 81 mi – Ipswich 53 mi – Norwich 20 mi

Michelin Road map 504-Z26 – Michelin Green Guide GREAT BRITAIN

Andover House with rm

28-30 Camperdown ✉ NR30 3JB – ✆ (01493) 843 490 – www.andoverhouse.co.uk

20 rm – £ 59/79 £ 69/99 – 4 suites Carte £ 22/38 **s** – *(dinner only)*

Modernised, listed Victorian property with a crisp, chic style and friendly, well-drilled service. Constantly evolving à la carte of modern, well-presented and accomplished dishes, with the occasional Asian touch. Simple, modern bedrooms; some with four-posters, some with large bay windows.

GREAT YELDHAM

Essex – Pop. 1 844 – See Regional map n°**13**-C2

London 64 mi – Birmingham 129 mi – Leeds 180 mi – Sheffield 154 mi

Michelin Road map 504-V27

XX **White Hart** with rm 
Poole St ✉ *CO9 4HJ – ✆ (01787) 237 250 – www.whitehartyeldham.co.uk – Closed dinner 25-26 December, Monday and lunch Tuesday*
13 rm ☕ – 🚹£ 70/80 🚹🚹£ 90/180 Carte £ 30/49 – *(booking advisable)*
Charming 16C inn with a characterful interior. The large, open-fired bar with its wonky floors and exposed beams serves unfussy favourites, while the elegant restaurant offers a refined, modern menu of skilfully prepared dishes which are full of flavour. Keenly priced bedrooms are cosy and well-maintained.

GREEN ISLAND → See Channel Islands (Jersey)
– Michelin Road map 503-P33

GREETHAM
Rutland – See Regional map n°**17**-**C2**
▶London 101 mi – Birmingham 86 mi – Liverpool 164 mi – Leeds 98 mi

Wheatsheaf Inn 
1 Stretton Rd ✉ *LE15 7NP – ✆ (01572) 812 325 – www.wheatsheaf-greetham.co.uk – Closed first 2 weeks January, Monday except bank holidays and Sunday dinner*
Carte £ 20/33
The aroma of fresh bread is the first thing you notice at this simple, family-friendly country pub. Robust modern cooking comes with hints of the Med; cheaper cuts keep prices sensible and desserts are a must. It's run by a charming couple.

GRETA BRIDGE → See Barnard Castle
Durham – Michelin Road map 502-O20

GRETTON → See Winchcombe
Gloucestershire

GRIMSTON → See King's Lynn
Norfolk – Michelin Road map 504-V25

GRINDLETON
Lancashire – Pop. 435 – See Regional map n°**20**-**B2**
▶London 238 mi – Birmingham 125 mi – Leeds 44 mi – Sheffield 85 mi
Michelin Road map 502-M22

Duke of York Inn 
Brow Top ✉ *BB7 4QR – ✆ (01200) 441 266 – www.dukeofyorkgrindleton.com – Closed 25 December, Monday except bank holidays and Tuesday following bank holidays*
Menu £ 17 (weekdays) – Carte £ 22/48
Ivy-clad pub in the heart of the Trough of Bowland, with views to Pendle Hill. Rustic bar and light, contemporary dining room. Excellent choice on seasonal menu, with plenty of regional dishes and fish. Good value daily set menu.

GRINSHILL → See Shrewsbury
Shropshire – Michelin Road map 503-L25

GROUVILLE → See Channel Islands (Jersey)
– Michelin Road map 503-M33

GUILDFORD
Surrey – Pop. 77 057 – See Regional map n°**7**-**C1**
▶London 33 mi – Brighton 43 mi – Reading 27 mi – Southampton 49 mi
Michelin Road map 504-S30 – Michelin Green Guide GREAT BRITAIN

ENGLAND

GUILDFORD

Bedford Rd . . . . Y 2
Bridge St . . . . Y 3
Castle St. . . . . Y 5
Chertsey St . . . . Y 6
Commercial Rd . . . . Y 8
Eastgate Gardens . . . . Y 9
Friary Bridge. . . . . Y 12
Friary Centre . . . . Y
High St. . . . . Y
Ladymead . . . . Z 13
Leapale Lane . . . . Y 15
Leapale Rd. . . . . Y 16
Leas Rd . . . . Y 17
Market St . . . . Y 18
Mary Rd . . . . Y 19
Middle Rd. . . . . Z 20
Millbrook . . . . Y 21
New Inn Lane . . . . Z 22
North St . . . . Y
One Tree Hill Rd. . . . . Z 24
Onslow St . . . . Y 25
Park St . . . . Y 27
Quarry St . . . . Y 28
Stoughton Rd. . . . . Z 30
Trood's Lane. . . . . Z 31
Tunsgate . . . . Y 33
Tunsgate Shopping Centre . . . . Y
Warwick's Bench . . . . Y 34
Woodbridge Rd . . . . Z 37

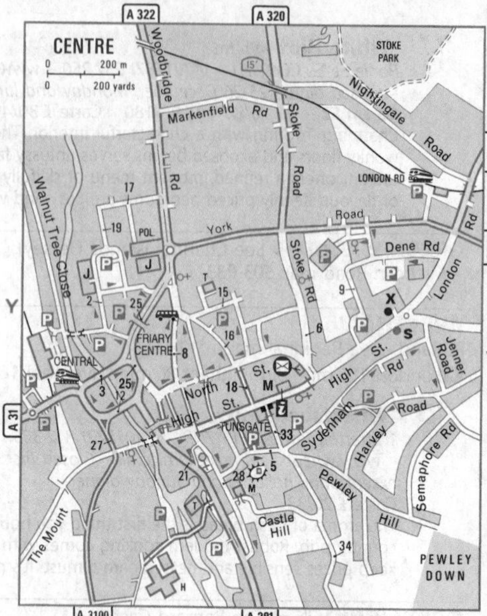

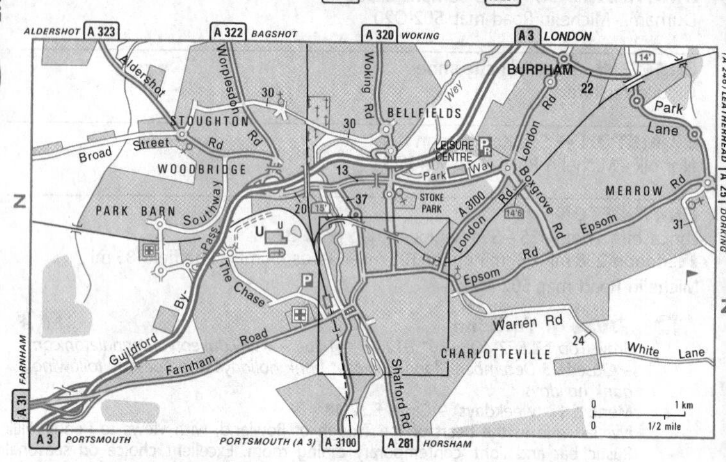

Radisson Blu Edwardian Guildford

3 Alexandra Terr, High St ✉ *GU1 3DA* – ✆ *(01483) 792 300*
– *www.radissonblu-edwardian.com/guildford* Town plan: Y**x**
183 rm – **†**£ 99/300 **††**£ 99/300
Rest *Scoff & Banter* – Menu £ 20 – Carte £ 19/37

Newly built hotel in the heart of the town; notable for its modern design and subtle theatrical theme. Well-soundproofed, contemporary bedrooms offer high levels of comfort and the latest technology. Curvaceous bar, theatre montages, and a menu of British classics with a modern edge in Scoff & Banter.

CAU

274 High St ✉ GU1 3JL – ✆ (01483) 459 777 Town plan: Ys
– www.caurestaurants.com – Closed 25-26 December and 1 January
Carte £ 19/28 – *(bookings advisable at dinner)*
The name stands for Carne Argentina Unica and beef reigns supreme; go for a steak, as it's what they do best. Staff are attentive, the atmosphere's lively, prices are reasonable and the surroundings, trendy and bright.

at East Clandon Northeast: 4.75 mi by A25 off A246

Queen's Head

The Street ✉ GU4 7RY – ✆ (01483) 222 332
– www.queensheadeastclandon.co.uk – Closed 25 December
Menu £ 18 (weekday lunch) – Carte £ 22/36
Charming 17C pub with a large garden where village celebrations are held. Four rooms feature open fires and bovine-themed pictures. Simple menu offers something for everyone, from sharing boards or ham hock to steak and ale pie or a roast.

at West Clandon Northeast: 4.75 mi by A25 and A246 on A247

Onslow Arms

The Street ✉ GU4 7TE – ✆ (01483) 222 447 – www.onslowarmsclandon.co.uk
Carte £ 23/41
Smartly refurbished pub, with old beams, copper artefacts and open fires giving a clue as to its true age. The same menu is served throughout, offering sharing platters, light bites and more sophisticated dishes in the evening.

at Shere East: 6.75 mi by A246 off A25 -(Z)✉ Guildford

Kinghams

Gomshall Ln ✉ GU5 9HE – ✆ (01483) 202 168
– www.kinghams-restaurant.co.uk – Closed 25 December-5 January, Sunday dinner and Monday
Menu £ 18 (weekdays) – Carte £ 32/41
Characterful 17C creeper-clad cottage with a cosy low-beamed interior and a pleasant terrace. Cooking has a classic foundation, with plenty of fish specials and game in season. The good value 2 course menu includes a side dish too.

GULVAL

➜ See Penzance
Cornwall – Michelin Road map 503-D33

GULWORTHY

➜ See Tavistock
Devon – Michelin Road map 503-H32

GURNARD

➜ See WIGHT (Isle of)

HADLEIGH

Suffolk – Pop. 8 150 – See Regional map n°**15-C3**
London 72 mi – Cambridge 49 mi – Colchester 17 mi – Ipswich 10 mi
Michelin Road map 504-W27

Edge Hall without rest

2 High St ✉ IP7 5AP – ✆ (01473) 822 458 – www.edgehall.co.uk – Closed 23-29 December
6 rm – †£ 55/65 ††£ 90/125
A lovely Queen Anne style house with a Georgian brick façade, dating from 1453 – supposedly the oldest house in the village. Bedrooms are spacious and furnished with antiques. The breakfast room overlooks the delightful garden.

HALFORD

Warwickshire – Pop. 301 – See Regional map n°**19-C3**
London 94 mi – Oxford 43 mi – Stratford-upon-Avon 8 mi
Michelin Road map 503-P27

ENGLAND

Old Manor House without rest 

Queens St ✉ CV36 5BT – ✆ (01789) 740 264 – www.oldmanor-halford.co.uk
3 rm ☕ – 🚹£ 65/100 🚹🚹£ 90/120
Characterful part-timbered house in a pleasant spot next to the River Stour. Well-appointed drawing room with garden views and an antique-furnished breakfast room with a large inglenook. Appealing period style bedrooms have rich fabrics.

HALFWAY BRIDGE → See Petworth

West Sussex – Michelin Road map 504-R31

HALIFAX

West Yorkshire – Pop. 88 134 – See Regional map n°**22**-B2
▶London 205 mi – Bradford 8 mi – Burnley 21 mi – Leeds 15 mi
Michelin Road map 502-O22

Holdsworth House 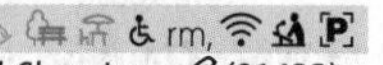

Holdsworth Rd ✉ HX2 9TG – North : 3 mi by A 629 and Shay Ln – ✆ (01422) 240 024 – www.holdsworthhouse.co.uk
39 rm ☕ – 🚹£ 85/95 🚹🚹£ 115/155 – 4 suites **Rest** – Carte £ 29/45
Attractive 17C property with beautiful gardens – including a parterre – within its old stone walls. Characterful interior displays original wood panelling and mullioned windows. Bedrooms are comfortable and contemporary. Three-roomed restaurant offers brasserie classics and some more refined, local dishes.

XX **Design House**

Dean Clough (Gate 5) ✉ HX3 5AX – ✆ (01422) 383 242 – www.designhouserestaurant.co.uk – Closed 26 December-8 January, Saturday lunch, Sunday and Monday
Menu £ 12/42
Long-standing restaurant in a converted mill complex, where a smart team offer a warm welcome. Bright artwork stands out against white tables in the low-ceilinged room. Cooking is modern and creative; the tasting menus are popular.

Shibden Mill Inn with rm

Shibden Mill Fold ✉ HX3 7UL – ✆ (01422) 365 840 – www.shibdenmillinn.com – Closed dinner 25-26 December and 1 January
11 rm ☕ – 🚹£ 95/162 🚹🚹£ 117/192
Menu £ 14 (lunch and early dinner) **s** – Carte £ 27/35 **s**
A former corn mill set in a tranquil, deep-sided valley, with beamed ceilings, welcoming fires and lots of cosy corners. Menus offer plenty of choice, with pub favourites alongside more ambitious dishes. Well-drilled staff. Comfy, individually furnished bedrooms; choose Room 14 if it's luxury you're after.

HALSETOWN → See St Ives

Cornwall – Michelin Road map 503-D33

HALTWHISTLE

Northumberland – Pop. 3 791 – See Regional map n°**24**-A2
▶London 335 mi – Carlisle 22 mi – Newcastle upon Tyne 37 mi
Michelin Road map 501-M19 and 502 – Michelin Green Guide GREAT BRITAIN

Centre of Britain 

Main St ✉ NE49 0BH – ✆ (01434) 322 422 – www.centre-of-britain.org.uk
12 rm ☕ – 🚹£ 59/79 🚹🚹£ 70/110 **Rest** – Menu £ 20 – *(dinner only)*
Yellow-painted former coaching inn in the town centre, with a pele tower dating from the 16C. Simple, well-kept bedrooms; those in the main house are larger and more characterful, while the cosy duplex chalet rooms are ideal for walkers, cyclists and guests with dogs. Traditional menus.

Ashcroft without rest
Lantys Lonnen ✉ *NE49 0DA* – ✆ *(01434) 320 213*
– www.ashcroftguesthouse.co.uk – Closed 25 December
9 rm – †£ 65/90 ††£ 80/110
Imposing Victorian house, formerly a vicarage, with beautifully kept gardens. Family run and attractively furnished throughout creating a welcoming atmosphere. Large bedrooms.

HAMBLE-LE-RICE

Hampshire – Pop. 4 695 – See Regional map n°**6-B2**
London 87 mi – Birmingham 149 mi – Leeds 243 mi – Sheffield 213 mi
Michelin Road map 503-Q31

Bugle
High St ✉ *SO31 4HA* – ✆ *(023) 8045 3000 – www.buglehamble.co.uk*
Carte £ 22/37 **s** – *(booking advisable)*
Set in a charming spot in a quaint little village, this grade II listed building is popular with the sailing community and has views over the marina. Menus offer soups, salads and sandwiches, small plates and traditional pub dishes.

HAMBLETON → See Oakham

Rutland

HAMPTON IN ARDEN

West Midlands – Pop. 1 678 – See Regional map n°**19-C2**
London 113 mi – Birmingham 15 mi – Coventry 11 mi
Michelin Road map 504-O26

Hampton Manor
Shadowbrook Ln ✉ *B92 0EN* – ✆ *(01675) 446 080 – www.hamptonmanor.eu*
15 rm – †£ 150/340 ††£ 150/340, £ 15 – 3 suites
Rest *Peel's* – see restaurant listing
Early Victorian manor house set in 45 acres; built for Sir Robert Peel's son. Contemporary décor blends with characterful original plasterwork and wooden panelling in the guest areas. Spacious, modern bedrooms have excellent bathrooms.

Peel's – Hampton Manor Hotel
Shadowbrook Ln ✉ *B92 0EN* – ✆ *(01675) 446 080 – www.hamptonmanor.eu*
– Closed Sunday and Monday
Menu £ 55/75 – Carte £ 36/58 – *(dinner only) (booking essential)*
An elegant dining room situated within an impressive manor house, with candlelit tables, beautiful plasterwork and hand-painted Chinoiserie wallpaper. Modern menus feature original, ambitious combinations. Service is attentive.

HAMPTON POYLE

Oxfordshire – Pop. 106 – See Regional map n°**10-B2**
London 68 mi – Birmingham 72 mi – Barnet 71 mi – Ealing 57 mi

Bell at Hampton Poyle with rm
11 Oxford Rd ✉ *OX5 2QD* – ✆ *(01865) 376 242*
– www.thebellathamptonpoyle.co.uk
9 rm – †£ 95/130 ††£ 120/155
Menu £ 10 (lunch and early dinner) – Carte £ 26/68
Almost Mediterranean in its style, with a very visual kitchen that includes a wood burning oven. Menu offers everything from meze and charcuterie boards to pub staples and seafood. They have the biggest gin selection in the world! Bright, fresh bedrooms are located above the bar and in a cottage.

HAROME → See Helmsley

North Yorkshire

ENGLAND

HARROGATE

North Yorkshire – Pop. 73 576 – See Regional map n°**22**-**B2**

London 211 mi – Bradford 18 mi – Leeds 15 mi – Newcastle upon Tyne 76 mi

Michelin Road map 502-P22 – Michelin Green Guide GREAT BRITAIN

Rudding Park

Rudding Park, Follifoot ✉ HG3 1JH – Southeast : 3.75 mi by A 661 – ✆ (01423) 871 350 – www.ruddingpark.com

90 rm – £ 130/175 £ 151/205 – 8 suites

Rest *Clocktower* – see restaurant listing

Grade I listed manor house in 250 acres. Sleek bedrooms are in a wing; the best boast media hubs, touch lighting and jacuzzis. Relax in the spa, the cinema or on one of the terraces. The old Victorian church is used for events.

Hotel du Vin

Prospect Pl ✉ HG1 1LB – ✆ (01423) 856 800 – www.hotelduvin.com Town plan: BZ**a**

48 rm – £ 95/165 £ 95/165, £ 17

Rest *Bistro* – Menu £ 15 (weekdays) – Carte £ 23/48

A smart hotel with a small basement spa, in a terrace of Georgian houses overlooking the green. The contemporary, boutique-style interior has wine-themed décor; the two attic bedrooms boast huge bathrooms with 'his and hers' roll-top baths. The stylish bistro has an open courtyard and a Gallic menu.

Ascot House

53 King's Rd ✉ HG1 5HJ – ✆ (01423) 531 005 – www.ascothouse.com Town plan: BY**z**

rest,

19 rm – £ 49/69 £ 69/105

Rest – Menu £ 25 – *(dinner only) (bookings essential for non-residents)*

Once home to W H Baxter, who invented the 'knapping' machine used in road-making. Original features include ornate plasterwork, coving and an impressive stained glass window. Floral fabrics and king-sized beds feature upstairs – No.22 has a turret. The traditional restaurant offers a classical menu.

Brookfield House without rest

5 Alexandra Rd ✉ HG1 5JS – ✆ (01423) 506 646 – www.brookfieldhousehotel.co.uk – Closed 2 weeks Christmas-New Year Town plan: BY**s**

6 rm – £ 65/95 £ 85/110

A well-run, three-storey Victorian townhouse on a quiet street. Modern bedrooms come in light hues: the first floor rooms are bright and airy, while the top floor rooms are cosy and intimate – all have fridges and ironing boards.

Bijou without rest

17 Ripon Rd ✉ HG1 2JL – ✆ (01423) 567 974 – www.thebijou.co.uk – Closed 24-27 December Town plan: AY**s**

10 rm – £ 50/69 £ 80/114

Well-run Victorian villa with an open-fired lounge. Funky bedrooms have minimalistic furnishings and thoughtful extras; those in the coach house are largest. Choose between an English or Italian breakfast and homemade waffles.

Van Zeller

8 Montpellier St ✉ HG1 2TQ – ✆ (01423) 508 762 – www.vanzellerrestaurants.co.uk – Closed 1 week January, Sunday and Monday Town plan: AZ**v**

Menu £ 35/50 – *(booking advisable)*

Smart shop conversion in a fashionable part of town, with two tables in the windows and the rest upstairs. Modern artwork hangs on cream walls. Well-executed dishes are elaborate and highly original; service is smooth and attentive.

Quantro

3 Royal Par ✉ HG1 2SZ – ✆ (01423) 503 034 – www.quantro.co.uk – Closed 25-26 December, 1 January and Sunday Town plan: AZ**a**

Menu £ 15 (lunch and early dinner) – Carte £ 28/38

A busy, buzzy brasserie with a keenly priced, internationally influenced menu which offers something for everyone. The sharing platters are a sure-fire hit and a choice of dish size on the à la carte suits the local workers.

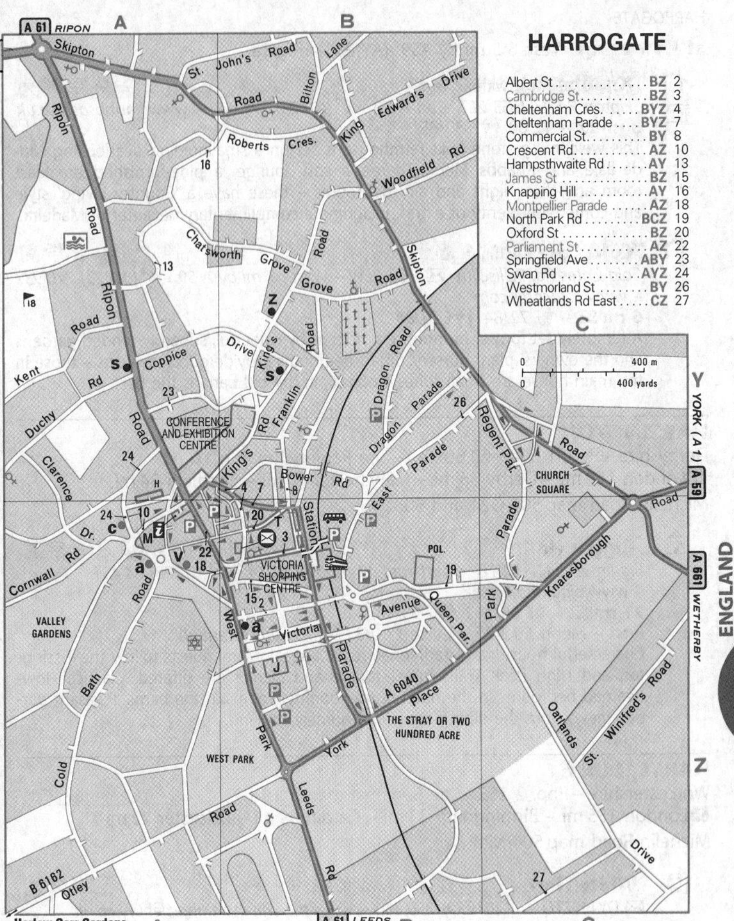

XX **Orchid**

28 Swan Rd ✉ *HG1 2SE – ✆ (01423) 560 425* Town plan: AZ**c**
– www.orchidrestaurant.co.uk – Closed 25-26 December and Saturday lunch
Menu £ 25/33 – Carte £ 16/35
Below the chic cocktail bar is a spacious room with etched glass screens, Asian artefacts and a TV screening live kitchen action. The extensive pan-Asian menu indicates the dishes' origins and spiciness; Sunday lunch is a buffet.

XX **Clocktower** – Rudding Park Hotel

Rudding Park, Follifoot ✉ *HG3 1JH – Southeast : 3.75 mi by A 661 – ✆ (01423) 871 350 – www.ruddingpark.co.uk*
Menu £ 39 **s** – Carte £ 39/57 **s**
Set in the old stables and named after the clock hanging above the door; a contemporary hotel dining room with an impressive pink chandelier. Menus offer an array of modern dishes; most ingredients are from within 20 miles.

at Kettlesing West: 6 5 mi by A59 -(AY)✉ Harrogate

Knabbs Ash without rest

Skipton Rd ✉ HG3 2LT – on A 59 – ☎ (01423) 771 040 – www.knabbsash.co.uk

3 rm ☕ – 🚹£ 60 🚹🚹£ 80/85

This welcoming stone-built farmhouse is set on a smallholding overlooking Nidderdale and Knabbs Moor. There's a cosy lounge, a pine-furnished breakfast room and three light and airy bedrooms – these have a 'Country Living' style and come with plenty of extras, including a complimentary decanter of Madeira.

Cold Cotes without rest

Cold Cotes Rd, Felliscliffe ✉ HG3 2LW – West : 1 mi by A 59 – ☎ (01423) 770 937 – www.coldcotes.com

6 rm ☕ – 🚹£ 72/84 🚹🚹£ 72/84

A remotely set former farmhouse bordered by colourful, superbly-tended gardens and the owners' plant nursery. Smart bedrooms provide good comforts – those in the main house are small suites; Room 6, in the old barn, is the best.

HARTINGTON

Derbyshire – Pop. 1 604 – ✉ Buxton – See Regional map n°**16**-A1

▶London 168 mi – Derby 36 mi – Manchester 40 mi – Sheffield 34 mi

Michelin Road map 502-O24 and 503

Biggin Hall

Biggin ✉ SK17 ODH – Southeast : 2 mi by B 5054 – ☎ (01298) 84 451 – www.bigginhall.co.uk

21 rm ☕ – 🚹£ 85/132 🚹🚹£ 95/142

Rest – Menu £ 12/25 – Carte £ 19/32 – *(booking essential)*

Characterful house with traditional, rustic appeal. Many guests follow the Tissington and High Peak Trails: bike storage and picnics are offered. Classical, low-beamed bedrooms in the main house; brighter rooms in the barns. Pleasant garden views from the dining room and homely cooking.

HARTLEBURY

Worcestershire – Pop. 2 253 – See Regional map n°**18**-B2

▶London 135 mi – Birmingham 33 mi – Cardiff 93 mi – Leicester 72 mi

Michelin Road map 504-N26

White Hart

✉ DY11 7TD – ☎ (01299) 250 286 – www.thewhitehartinhartlebury.co.uk – Closed 25 December and Sunday dinner

Menu £ 19 (lunch and early dinner) – Carte £ 20/37

Proudly run pub that's a proper village local. Carefully prepared, classically based dishes rely on quality produce; go for one of the specials from the board. Large garden with picnic benches; live music at their annual beer festival.

HARWICH

Essex – Pop. 19 738 – See Regional map n°**13**-D2

▶London 78 mi – Chelmsford 41 mi – Colchester 20 mi – Ipswich 23 mi

Michelin Road map 504-X28

Pier at Harwich

The Quay ✉ CO12 3HH – ☎ (01255) 241 212 – www.milsomhotels.com

14 rm ☕ – 🚹£ 120/230 🚹🚹£ 120/230

Rest *Harbourside* – see restaurant listing

Rest *Ha'Penny Pier* – Carte £ 22/41

Victorian hotel in a pleasant quayside spot – built to accommodate rail travellers waiting to board their cruise liners and an ideal place to stay if you're catching the ferry. Stylish, 'New England' style bedrooms; some boast port views. Smart seafood restaurant or casual all-day dining overlooking the pier.

ENGLAND

XX **Harbourside** – Pier at Harwich Hotel
The Quay ✉ CO12 3HH – ✆ (01255) 241 212 – www.milsomhotels.com – Closed Monday and Tuesday
Carte £ 32/53 **s**
Comfortable hotel dining room boasting crisp linen-laid tables and attractive port and North Sea views. Seafood-orientated menu offers everything from the traditional to the more contemporary.

HASTINGS and ST LEONARDS

East Sussex – Pop. 91 053 – See Regional map n°**8**-**B3**
London 65 mi – Brighton 37 mi – Folkestone 37 mi – Maidstone 34 mi
Michelin Road map 504-V31

Zanzibar

9 Eversfield Pl ✉ TN37 6BY – ✆ (01424) 460 109 – www.zanzibarhotel.co.uk Town plan: AZ**c**
8 rm – £ 99/235 £ 99/245
Rest *Pier Nine* – Menu £ 10 (weekday lunch) – Carte £ 26/42
An enthusiastically run Victorian seafront property with a stylish boutique interior. The lounge and bar lead to a delightful terrace and garden. Bedrooms are named and themed after places the owner has visited and have intimate lighting and good mod cons. Modern, seasonal menus also have global influences.

Hastings House without rest

9 Warrior Sq. ✉ TN37 6BA – ✆ (01424) 422 709 – www.hastingshouse.co.uk Town plan: AZ**u**
8 rm – £ 80/100 £ 89/150
Stylish, modern and very comfortable guesthouse just off the promenade; personally run by hospitable owners. Rooms 3, 5 and 7 are the best choice for their size and sea views.

Black Rock House without rest

10 Stanley Rd ✉ TN34 1UE – ✆ (01424) 438 448 – www.hastingsaccommodation.com Town plan: BZ**a**
5 rm – £ 85/95 £ 125/145
Smart Victorian villa hidden away in a residential area. The cool, contemporary interior has stripped wooden floors and stylish modern furnishings; individually designed bedrooms have good mod cons. Breakfasts showcase local produce.

XX Webbe's Rock-a-Nore

1 Rock-a-Nore ✉ TN34 3DW – ✆ (01424) 721 650 – www.webbesrestaurants.co.uk – Closed 24-26 December Town plan: BY**x**
Carte £ 25/44
Bright, modern seafood restaurant with an open kitchen, a marble-topped horseshoe bar, and a large terrace overlooking the Stade and its fishing huts. Straightforward cooking offers small plates and classics, dictated by the daily catch.

X St Clements

3 Mercatoria, St Leonards on Sea ✉ TN38 0EB – ✆ (01424) 200 355 – www.stclementsrestaurant.co.uk – Closed 25-26 December, 1 January, Sunday dinner and Monday Town plan: AZ**a**
Menu £ 14/24 – Carte £ 28/38
Pleasant neighbourhood restaurant with striking local artwork hung on plain walls. Comprehensive à la carte and concise, good value lunch and midweek menus. Tasty modern European cooking is unfussy with a rustic edge. Fresh fish from Hastings plays a key role.

ENGLAND

HASTINGS ST. LEONARDS

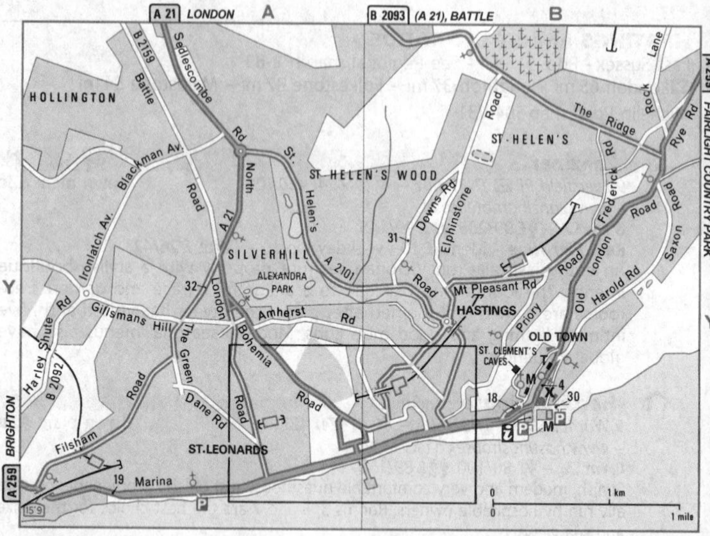

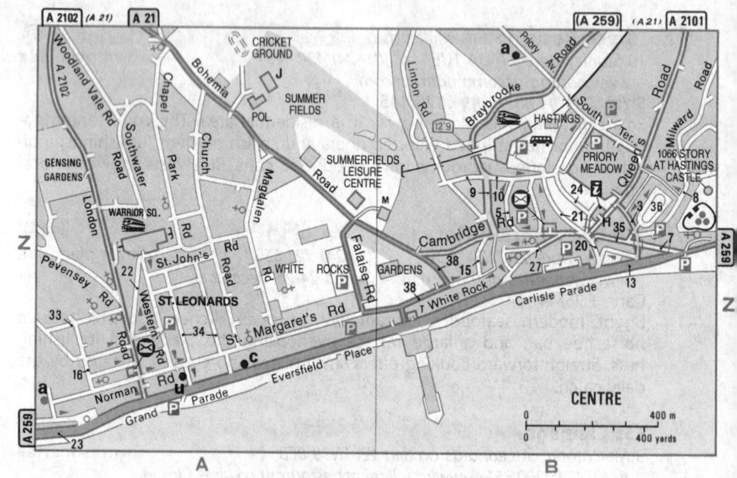

HATCH BEAUCHAMP → See Taunton

Somerset – Michelin Road map 503-K30

HATFIELD BROAD OAK

Essex – Pop. 916 – See Regional map n°**12-B2**
London 35 mi – Birmingham 128 mi – Liverpool 221 mi – Leeds 179 mi
Michelin Road map 504-U28

Duke's Head

High St ✉ CM22 7HH – ✆ (01279) 718 598 – www.thedukeshead.co.uk – Closed 25-26 December
Carte £ 22/36
17C pub with a large terrace and pleasant garden, run by an enthusiastic couple who support local clubs and host village events. Choose from a selection of well-crafted, generously sized dishes, or enjoy nibbles on a sofa by the fire.

HATFIELD PEVEREL

Essex – Pop. 3 251 – See Regional map n°**13-C2**
London 39 mi – Chelmsford 8 mi – Maldon 12 mi
Michelin Road map 504-V28 – Michelin Green Guide GREAT BRITAIN

Blue Strawberry Bistrot

The Street ✉ CM3 2DW – ✆ (01245) 381 333 – www.bluestrawberrybistrot.co.uk – Closed 26 December and Sunday dinner
Menu £ 15/20 (weekdays) – Carte £ 22/40
Attractive, creeper-clad, red-brick former coaching inn with a labyrinth of characterful, old-fashioned rooms and a well-equipped terrace. Traditional, keenly priced cooking is wholesome and satisfying. Polite service.

HATHERSAGE

Derbyshire – Pop. 2 018 – See Regional map n°**16-A1**
London 177 mi – Derby 39 mi – Manchester 34 mi – Sheffield 11 mi
Michelin Road map 502-P24 and 503

George

Main Rd ✉ S32 1BB – ✆ (01433) 650 436 – www.george-hotel.net
24 rm – †£ 105/174 ††£ 139/198
Rest *George's* – see restaurant listing
Eye-catching 14C coaching inn where modern furnishings blend nicely with traditional stone walls and exposed beams. Relax in the open-fired lounge or small cocktail bar. Smart, pastel-hued bedrooms are bright and contemporary.

George's – George Hotel

Main Rd ✉ S32 1BB – ✆ (01433) 650 436 – www.george-hotel.net
Menu £ 30/37
Formally laid restaurant decorated in subtle pastel shades and set within a 14C coaching inn. Extensive menus have a largely British base and dishes are classically grounded with modern touches. Cooking is refined and flavoursome.

HAUGHTON MOSS

Cheshire East – See Regional map n°**20-A3**
London 180 mi – Manchester 41 mi – Chester 17 mi

Nag's Head

Long Ln ✉ CW6 9RN – ✆ (01829) 260 265 – www.nagsheadhaughton.co.uk
Carte £ 22/40
Characterful timbered pub in a peaceful hamlet; sit at a table made from a shotgun or in the delightful garden overlooking the bowling green. Local produce features in regional specialities, pub classics and dishes from the charcoal grill.

HAWES

North Yorkshire – Pop. 887 – See Regional map n°**22-A1**
London 253 mi – Kendal 27 mi – Leeds 72 mi – Newcastle upon Tyne 76 mi
Michelin Road map 502-N21

Stone House

Sedbusk ✉ DL8 3PT – North : 1 mi by Muker rd – ✆ (01969) 667 571 – www.stonehousehotel.co.uk – Closed January and mid-week December
24 rm – ♦£ 73/195 ♦♦£ 124/195 – 2 suites
Rest – Menu £ 37 – *(light lunch)*
Characterful stone house built in 1908. Guest areas include a pleasant drawing room with an oak-panelled fireplace and a small billiard-room-cum-library. Bedrooms vary in size and décor; some have conservatories and are ideal for those with dogs. The traditional beamed dining room offers a classical menu.

HAWKSHEAD

Cumbria – Pop. 570 – ✉ Ambleside – See Regional map n°**21-A2**
London 283 mi – Carlisle 52 mi – Kendal 19 mi
Michelin Road map 502-L20 – Michelin Green Guide GREAT BRITAIN

West Vale without rest

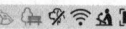

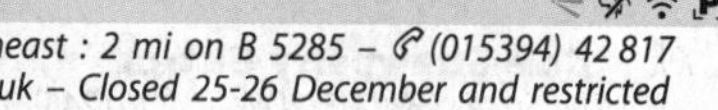

Far Sawrey ✉ LA22 0LQ – Southeast : 2 mi on B 5285 – ✆ (015394) 42 817 – www.westvalecountryhouse.co.uk – Closed 25-26 December and restricted opening 3 January-4 February
7 rm – ♦£ 90/105 ♦♦£ 90/170
Welcoming slate house boasting lovely countryside views; run by keen owners. Two comfy lounges and a smart country house style room for hearty breakfasts. Good-sized bedrooms with a warm, comfy, boutique style; 7 and 8, on the top floor, are the best. Tea and cake on arrival, and plenty of extra touches.

HAWNBY

North Yorkshire ✉ Helmsley – See Regional map n°**23-C1**
London 245 mi – Middlesbrough 27 mi – Newcastle upon Tyne 69 mi – York 30 mi
Michelin Road map 502-Q21

Laskill Country House

Easterside, Laskill ✉ YO62 5NB – Northeast : 2.25 mi by Osmotherley rd – ✆ (01439) 798 265 – www.laskillcountryhouse.co.uk – Closed 24-25 December
3 rm – ♦£ 45/65 ♦♦£ 90/120 **Rest** – Menu £ 25
Delightful manor-style house in popular shooting and walking area. Comfy lounge, small function suite and good-sized bedrooms with countryside views. Communal dining; wholesome home-cooked meals, with meat from the family's farms.

HAWORTH

West Yorkshire – Pop. 6 379 – ✉ Keighley – See Regional map n°**22-A2**
London 213 mi – Burnley 22 mi – Leeds 22 mi – Manchester 34 mi
Michelin Road map 502-O22 – Michelin Green Guide GREAT BRITAIN

Ashmount Country House

Mytholmes Ln ✉ BD22 8EZ – ✆ (01535) 645 726 – www.ashmounthaworth.co.uk
12 rm – ♦£ 55/125 ♦♦£ 95/245
Rest – Carte £ 23/42 – *(dinner only) (bookings essential for non-residents)*
Substantial Victorian house built by the Brontë sisters' physician. Luxurious bedrooms have state-of-the-art bathrooms – some with hot tubs. Original features include impressive stained glass paintings and an intricate plaster ceiling in the dining room; menus mix classics with more modern dishes.

Old Registry

2-6 Main St ✉ BD22 8DA – ✆ (01535) 646 503 – www.theoldregistryhaworth.co.uk – Closed 24-26 December
9 rm – †£ 80/120 ††£ 80/120
Rest – Menu £ 16 – Carte £ 22/31 – *(closed Sunday and Monday)*
Stone-built former registrar's office at the bottom of the village's cobbled main street. Individually decorated bedrooms feature rich fabrics and antiques; some have four-posters. Eat at simple wooden tables surrounded by Brontë memorabilia; local ingredients feature in traditionally based dishes.

HAYDON BRIDGE → See Hexham

Northumberland – Michelin Road map 501-N19 and 502

HAYLING ISLAND

Hampshire – Pop. 14 842 – See Regional map n°**6-B3**
London 77 mi – Brighton 45 mi – Southampton 28 mi
Michelin Road map 504-R31

Cockle Warren Cottage without rest

36 Seafront ✉ PO11 9HL – ✆ (023) 9246 4961 – www.cocklewarren.co.uk
6 rm – †£ 55/65 ††£ 70/85
Set just across from the beach, this welcoming guesthouse has a fish pond and fountain in the front courtyard and a lovely south-facing terrace and outdoor pool to the rear. Bedrooms are comfy and the owner is extremely welcoming.

HAYWARDS HEATH

West Sussex – Pop. 33 845 – See Regional map n°**7-D2**
London 39 mi – Croydon 30 mi – Barnet 53 mi – Ealing 50 mi
Michelin Road map 504-T31 – Michelin Green Guide GREAT BRITAIN

XX Jeremy's at Borde Hill

Borde Hill Gdns ✉ RH16 1XP – North : 1.75 mi by B 2028 and Balcombe Rd on Borde Hill Ln. – ✆ (01444) 441 102 – www.jeremysrestaurant.com – Closed 1-15 January, Monday except bank holidays and Sunday dinner
Menu £ 17 (weekdays) – Carte £ 32/44
Converted stable block with exposed rafters, contemporary sculptures, vivid artwork and delightful views towards the Victorian walled garden. Interesting, modern European dishes and a good value 'menu of the day'. Regular gourmet nights.

HEADLAM → See Darlington

Durham – Michelin Road map 502-O20

HEATHROW AIRPORT → See London

Greater London – Michelin Road map 504-S29

HEDLEY ON THE HILL

Northumberland – See Regional map n°**24-A2**
London 293 mi – Newcastle upon Tyne 16 mi – Sunderland 26 mi – South Shields 26 mi

Feathers Inn

✉ NE43 7SW – ✆ (01661) 843 607 – www.thefeathers.net – Closed first 2 weeks January, Monday except bank holidays and Sunday dinner
Carte £ 19/30
Traditional stone inn set on a steep hill in the heart of a rural village. Daily changing menu of hearty British classics, cooked using carefully sourced, regional produce, with meat and game to the fore. Relaxed, friendly atmosphere.

ENGLAND

HELLIFIELD

North Yorkshire – See Regional map n°**22**-A2
London 230 mi – Manchester 45 mi – Leeds 36 mi
Michelin Road map 502-N21

Hellifield Peel Castle without rest

Peel Grn ✉ BD23 4LD – ☎ (01729) 850 248 – www.peelcastle.co.uk – Closed 3 weeks January and Sunday-Tuesday
5 rm – †£ 135/185 ††£ 175/230
This 12C peel tower has been transformed from an old ruin into a boutique guesthouse. Smart, spacious bedrooms boast antique beds and striking modern bathrooms; go for the one with the roof terrace, which offers great rural views.

HELMSLEY

North Yorkshire – Pop. 1 515 – See Regional map n°**23**-C1
London 239 mi – Leeds 51 mi – Middlesbrough 28 mi – York 24 mi
Michelin Road map 502-Q21 – Michelin Green Guide GREAT BRITAIN

Black Swan

Market Pl ✉ YO62 5BJ – ☎ (01439) 770 466 – www.blackswan-helmsley.co.uk
45 rm – †£ 123/183 ††£ 135/195 – 1 suite
Rest *Gallery* – see restaurant listing
Set overlooking the historic marketplace, The Black Swan is one of the country's best known coaching inns. The charming interior features beamed lounges, a modern bar and a tea shop. Bedrooms are a mix of characterful and contemporary.

ENGLAND

Feversham Arms

1-8 High St ✉ YO62 5AG – ☎ (01439) 770 766 – www.fevershamarmshotel.com
33 rm – †£ 110/265 ††£ 120/430 – 20 suites
Rest *Feversham Arms* – see restaurant listing
19C former coaching inn with a lovely stone façade. Relax on the terrace beside the outdoor pool; the spa is superb and boasts a salt vapour room and an ice cave. Be sure to book one of the stylish newer bedrooms; many have stoves or fires.

No.54 without rest

54 Bondgate ✉ YO62 5EZ – ☎ (01439) 771 533 – www.no54.co.uk – Closed Christmas-New Year
3 rm – †£ 70/85 ††£ 100/130
Charming Victorian stone cottage located just off the main square. Simply decorated, cosy bedrooms are well-equipped and set around a rear courtyard. Friendly owner offers communal breakfasts of fresh, local produce.

Carlton Lodge without rest

Bondgate ✉ YO62 5EY – ☎ (01439) 770 557 – www.carlton-lodge.com – Closed January
8 rm – †£ 53/75 ††£ 85/105
Late 19C house on the edge of town, fronted by a colourful garden and run by charming owners. Spacious, simply appointed bedrooms are immaculately kept and have a homely feel. The tasty breakfast ingredients are locally sourced.

Feversham Arms – Feversham Arms Hotel

1-8 High St ✉ YO62 5AG – ☎ (01439) 770 766 – www.fevershamarmshotel.com
Carte £ 35/53 – *(bar lunch Monday-Saturday)*
Modern hotel restaurant with a pleasingly laid-back style. In summer, have lunch in the garden or on the poolside terrace. Dishes feature the latest local produce and cooking is refined and accurate; the tasting menu is worth a try.

Gallery – Black Swan Hotel

Market Pl ✉ YO62 5BJ – ☎ (01439) 770 466 – www.blackswan-helmsley.co.uk
Menu £ 30/55 – *(bar lunch Monday-Saturday)*
Bright modern restaurant within a historic 15C coaching inn; its walls filled with artwork for sale. At dinner, the plate becomes the canvas. Attractive, innovative dishes have the odd Asian influence; the tasting menu is a highlight.

at Nawton East: 3.25 mi on A170 ✉ York

Plumpton Court without rest

High St ✉ YO62 7TT – ✆ (01439) 771 223 – www.plumptoncourt.com – Restricted opening January-February

6 rm – †£ 60/65 ††£ 72/82

17C stone-built house with a small open-fired bar and a homely lounge. Comfy, cosy, simply furnished bedrooms with modern bathrooms. The cottage-style breakfast room offers local bacon and sausages. Relax in the secluded garden.

at Wombleton East: 4 mi by A170

Plough Inn

Main St ✉ YO62 7RW – ✆ (01751) 431 356 – www.theploughinnatwombleton.co.uk – Closed 25 December and Monday lunch

Carte £ 20/33

16C inn, popular with locals, serving tasty traditional dishes, including game in season. Prices are laudably low and service, friendly and relaxed. Sit in the hugely characterful restaurant, kept cosy by wood burners.

at Harome Southeast: 2.75 mi by A170 ✉ York

Pheasant

Mill St ✉ YO62 5JG – ✆ (01439) 771 241 – www.thepheasanthotel.com

16 rm – †£ 80/250 ††£ 120/320

Rest *Pheasant* – see restaurant listing

An attractive hotel in a picturesque hamlet, with a delightful duck pond and a mill stream close by. Beautiful, very comfortable lounges and spacious, well-furnished bedrooms; Rudland – running the width of the building and with views of the pond – is one of the best. Pleasant service. Excellent breakfasts.

Cross House Lodge

High St ✉ YO62 5JE – ✆ (01439) 770 397 – www.thestaratharome.co.uk

9 rm – †£ 150/260 ††£ 150/260

Rest *Star Inn* ✿ – see restaurant listing

These sympathetically converted farm buildings have a rustic ski-chalet style and ultra-stylish, individually decorated bedrooms; one boasts a snooker table; another, a bed suspended on ropes. Relax in the open-plan, split-level lounge; excellent breakfasts are taken in the dramatic beamed 'Wheelhouse'.

Pheasant – Pheasant Hotel

Mill St ✉ YO62 5JG – ✆ (01439) 771 241 – www.thepheasanthotel.com

Menu £ 29 – Carte £ 38/53

Elegant hotel dining room with both classical and contemporary touches – along with a less formal conservatory and a lovely terrace overlooking the village duck pond. Appealing menus of seasonal dishes with a classical base and a modern touch. Skilful, knowledgeable cooking; smooth, assured service.

Star Inn (Andrew Pern)

High St ✉ YO62 5JE – ✆ (01439) 770 397 – www.thestaratharome.co.uk – Closed Monday lunch except bank holidays

Menu £ 25 (weekdays) – Carte £ 32/55 – *(booking essential)*

14C thatched pub with a delightful terrace, a low-ceilinged bar and a brasserie-like restaurant with a chef's table. Dishes have assured flavours and a skilled, classical style; they use the very best of local produce, including veg from the kitchen garden and their own pigs and chickens. Attentive service.

→ Roe deer 'sausage' with pickled red cabbage purée, Pontefract cake and Pommery mustard seeds. Lemon sole with white crab crust, salt and pepper squid and bouillabaisse. Steamed butterscotch pear pudding with spice 'juice' and cinder toffee ice cream.

ENGLAND

at Ampleforth Southwest: 4.5 mi by A170 off B1257 ✉ Helmsley

Shallowdale House

✉ YO62 4DY West : 0.5 mi – ✆ (01439) 788 325 – www.shallowdalehouse.co.uk – Closed Christmas-New Year

3 rm ☕ – 🚹£ 95/110 🚹🚹£ 115/140 **Rest** – Menu £ 40

A remotely set, personally run house with a well-tended garden and stunning views of the Howardian Hills. Charming, antique-furnished interior, with an open-fired sitting room and good-sized bedrooms decorated in bright, Mediterranean tones. Four course set menu of home-cooked fare.

HELPERBY

North Yorkshire – See Regional map n°**22**-**B2**

London 220 mi – Leeds 36 mi – Sheffield 70 mi – Manchester 81 mi

Michelin Road map 502-Q21

Oak Tree Inn with rm

Raskelf Rd ✉ YO61 2PH – ✆ (01423) 789 189 – www.theoaktreehelperby.com

6 rm ☕ – 🚹£ 100/140 🚹🚹£ 100/140

Menu £ 15 (weekday lunch) – Carte £ 25/34

A pub of two halves, with a large bar, a tap room, two snugs and a smarter dining room. Menus offer hearty, generous dishes using ingredients from small local suppliers. Everything is homemade and combinations are familiar and comforting. Smart, modern bedrooms come with 'Yorkie' bars and jacuzzi baths.

ENGLAND

HELSTON

Cornwall – Pop. 11 311 – See Regional map n°**1**-**A3**

London 280 mi – Birmingham 275 mi – Croydon 288 mi – Barnet 293 mi

Michelin Road map 503-E33

at Trelowarren Southeast: 4 mi by A394 and A3083 on B3293 ✉ Helston

New Yard

Trelowarren Estate ✉ TR12 6AF – ✆ (01326) 221 595 – www.trelowarren.com – Closed October-May, Sunday dinner, Monday and Tuesday

Carte £ 21/44 – *(bookings advisable at dinner)*

Converted 17C stable building adjoining a craft gallery. Spacious, rustic room with timbered walls and doors opening onto the terrace. Seasonal menu uses quality Cornish produce; breads and ice creams are homemade. Friendly service.

at Cury South: 5 mi by A394 off A3083

Colvennor Farmhouse without rest

✉ TR12 7BJ – ✆ (01326) 241 208 – www.colvennorfarmhouse.com

3 rm ☕ – 🚹£ 50/55 🚹🚹£ 70/75

Part-17C farmhouse in a peaceful location, boasting a lovely mature garden and paddock to the rear. Homely lounge features a wood burning stove. Simple, wood-furnished bedrooms are of a reasonable size. Linen-laid breakfast room.

HEMINGFORD GREY → See Huntingdon

Cambridgeshire – Michelin Road map 504-T27

HENFIELD

West Sussex – Pop. 4 527 – See Regional map n°**7**-**D2**

London 47 mi – Brighton 10 mi – Worthing 11 mi

Michelin Road map 504-T31

Ginger Fox

Muddleswood Rd, Albourne ✉ BN6 9EA – Southwest : 3 mi on A 281 – ✆ (01273) 857 888 – www.gingermanrestaurants.com – Closed 25 December

Menu £ 15 (weekdays) – Carte £ 25/36

Spot the fox running across the thatched roof and you know you're in the right place. Monthly changing menu offers good value, flavourful dishes, with a popular vegetarian tasting plate. Desserts are a highlight, so save space.

HENLADE → See Taunton
Somerset

HENLEY → See Midhurst
West Sussex

HENLEY-IN-ARDEN
Warwickshire – Pop. 2 846 – See Regional map n°**19-C3**
London 104 mi – Birmingham 15 mi – Stratford-upon-Avon 8 mi – Warwick 8 mi
Michelin Road map 503-O27 and 504

Crabmill
Preston Bagot ✉ B95 5EE – East : 1 mi on A 4189 – ✆ (01926) 843 342 – www.thecrabmill.co.uk – Closed Sunday dinner
Menu £ 15 (weekdays) – Carte £ 22/40 – *(booking essential)*
Characterful timbered pub with a lawned garden, a peaceful terrace and various beamed snugs and lounges. The good-sized menu offers modern Mediterranean-influenced dishes; start with a tasty sharing plate before an interesting main course.

Bluebell
93 High St ✉ B95 5AT – ✆ (01564) 793 049 – www.bluebellhenley.co.uk
Menu £ 15/25 (weekdays) – Carte £ 25/41
Part-timbered pub on the high street, displaying an unusual mix of rustic character and formal elegance. The experienced chef uses the best local ingredients in honest, seasonal dishes and there's a wide range of wines, beers and cocktails.

ENGLAND

HENLEY-ON-THAMES
Oxfordshire – Pop. 11 494 – See Regional map n°**11-C3**
London 40 mi – Oxford 23 mi – Croydon 44 mi – Barnet 46 mi
Michelin Road map 504-R29

Hotel du Vin
rm, rm,
New St. ✉ RG9 2BP – ✆ (01491) 848 400 – www.hotelduvin.com
43 rm – †£ 130/300 ††£ 130/300, ☕ £ 17 – 2 suites
Rest *Bistro* – Carte £ 26/49
Characterful 1857 building that was formerly the Brakspear Brewery. Stylish bedrooms include airy doubles and duplex suites: one features two roll-top tubs and a great view of the church; others boast heated balconies and outdoor baths. Brasserie classics and a choice of over 700 wines in the bistro.

XX Shaun Dickens at The Boathouse Ⓝ
Station Rd ✉ RG9 1AZ – ✆ (01491) 577 937 – www.shaundickens.co.uk – Closed 2 weeks January, Sunday dinner and Monday
Menu £ 25 (lunch) – Carte £ 35/49
This modern restaurant is sure to please with its floor to ceiling glass doors and decked terrace overlooking the Thames. The young chef-owner offers an array of menus; attractively presented dishes centre around local ingredients.

X Luscombes at The Golden Ball

Lower Assendon ✉ RG9 6AH – Northwest : 0.75 mi by A 4130 on B 480 – ✆ (01491) 574 157 – www.luscombes.co.uk
Menu £ 13/25 – Carte £ 25/42
Pretty former pub – now a cosy, comfortable restaurant that's popular with the locals. Appealing menu of tasty, well-executed, modern classics; homemade preserves and afternoon tea are a feature. Friendly, attentive service.

Three Tuns
5 Market Pl ✉ RG9 2AA – ✆ (01491) 410 138 – www.threetunshenley.co.uk – Closed 25 December, Monday except bank holidays and Sunday dinner
Menu £ 10 (weekdays)/15 – Carte £ 25/40
Pretty, red-brick, town centre pub with a lively, open-fired front bar and a formal dining room for a more intimate meal. Seasonal, traditional dishes are well-presented, satisfying and full of flavour. Homemade bread. Friendly service.

at Stonor North: 4 mi by A4130 on B480

Quince Tree Café

✉ RG9 6HE – ✆ (01491) 639 039 – www.thequincetree.com
Carte £ 18/31 – *(lunch only) (bookings not accepted)*
Charming café with a green oak timber frame and floor to ceiling windows overlooking a herb garden and terrace. Pass through the deli to the modern dining room or up to the mezzanine. Open for breakfast and light Mediterranean lunches.

Quince Tree

✉ RG9 6HE – ✆ (01491) 639 039 – www.thequincetree.com – Closed 25 December, 1 January and Sunday dinner
Carte £ 24/40 – *(booking advisable)*
Delightfully set in a fold of the Chiltern Hills, with smart gardens and a sunny terrace. Sit in either the main room or the formal restaurant. Appealing dishes range from pub classics with a twist to more original modern dishes.

at Shiplake South: 2 mi on A4155

Plowden Arms

Reading Rd ✉ RG9 4BX – ✆ (01189) 402 794 – www.plowdenarmsshiplake.co.uk – Closed Mondays except bank holidays
Carte £ 21/39
An appealing pub with a delightful garden; inside, open fires, flickering candles and hop bines set the scene. The large blackboard offers tasty snacks and the interesting main menu features a number of Eliza Acton inspired dishes.

ENGLAND

at Shiplake Row South: 3.5 mi by A4155 on Binfield Heath rd

Orwells

Shiplake Row ✉ RG9 4DP – ✆ (01189) 403 673 – www.orwellsatshiplake.co.uk – Closed first 2 weeks January, first 2 weeks September, 1 week April, Sunday dinner, Tuesday and Monday except bank holidays
Carte £ 25/48
This 18C building may look like a rural inn but inside it has a more modern, formal feel. Creative cooking uses top produce and flavour combinations are superb. It's named after George Orwell, who spent his childhood in the area.

HEREFORD

Herefordshire – Pop. 60 415 – See Regional map n°**18-B3**
London 133 mi – Birmingham 51 mi – Cardiff 56 mi
Michelin Road map 503-L27 – Michelin Green Guide GREAT BRITAIN

Castle House

Castle St ✉ HR1 2NW – ✆ (01432) 356 321 – www.castlehse.co.uk Town plan: A**e**
24 rm – †£ 110/170 ††£ 150/230
Rest *Castle House* – see restaurant listing
This elegant Georgian house sits close to the cathedral. An impressive staircase leads to warmly furnished bedrooms of various sizes; some overlook the old castle moat. More contemporary rooms can be found in nearby 'Number 25'.

Brandon Lodge without rest

Ross Rd ✉ HR2 8BH – South : 1.25 mi on A 49 – ✆ (01432) 355 621 – www.brandonlodge.co.uk
10 rm – †£ 55/60 ††£ 70/80
Well-run, good value hotel with a welcoming owner. Bedrooms are split between the main house and the garden wing; the latter are more spacious, but all have good facilities. Neatly linen-laid breakfast room; comfy bar and lounge.

Somerville House without rest

12 Bodenham Rd ✉ HR1 2TS – ✆ (01432) 273 991 – www.somervillehouse.net Town plan: B**x**
12 rm – †£ 60/87 ††£ 77/112
Victorian villa with cathedral and hill views and an enclosed garden; home-grown apples, plums and pears are used to make their breakfast preserves. Spacious first floor rooms; those in the roof are smaller. Good facilities and a mini-bar.

HEREFORD

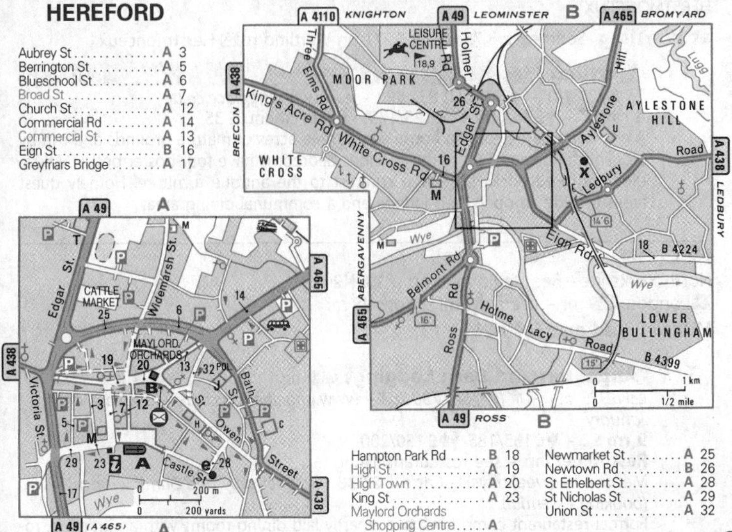

XX **Castle House** (N) – Castle House Hotel

Castle St ✉ *HR1 2NW* – ✆ *(01432) 356 321* – *www.castlehse.co.uk* — Town plan: A**e**

Carte £ 19/44

This elegant restaurant looks out over the hotel gardens and across the old moat of Hereford Castle. Classic dishes are reinvented in a modern manner and ingredients from Herefordshire feature highly. Menus offer plenty of choice.

HERNE BAY

Kent – Pop. 38 385 – See Regional map n°**9-D1**

London 65 mi – Maidenhead 33 mi – Dover 25 mi

Michelin Road map 504-X29

X **Le Petit Poisson**

Pier Approach, Central Par. ✉ *CT6 5JN* – ✆ *(01227) 361 199* – *www.lepetitpoisson.co.uk* – *Closed Sunday dinner and Monday except bank holidays when closed Tuesday*

Menu £ 12 (weekday lunch) – Carte £ 21/36

Head for the terrace of this whitewashed building opposite the pier. The split-level interior boasts flagged floors, exposed brick and eye-catching mosaic art. Constantly evolving blackboard menus offer tasty, unfussy seafood dishes.

HERSTMONCEUX

East Sussex – Pop. 1 130 – See Regional map n°**8-B3**

London 63 mi – Eastbourne 12 mi – Hastings 14 mi – Lewes 16 mi

Michelin Road map 504-U31

XXX **Sundial**

Gardner St ✉ *BN27 4LA* – ✆ *(01323) 832 217* – *www.sundialrestaurant.co.uk* – *Closed Sunday dinner and Monday*

Menu £ 27/42

With its original leaded windows and beamed ceiling, this characterful 16C cottage is a real hit with the locals. Service is structured and the room is formally laid. Rich, classic French dishes use luxurious seasonal ingredients.

at Wartling Southeast: 3.75 mi by A271 on Wartling rd ✉ Herstmonceux

Wartling Place

✉ *BN27 1RY – ✆ (01323) 832 590 – www.wartlingplace.co.uk*
4 rm – £ 85/100 £ 125/175 **Rest** – Menu £ 35
A charming part-Georgian house set in three acres of mature grounds and run by a delightful owner. Two of the spacious bedrooms have four-poster beds; DAB radios and iPod docks provide a contrast to the antique furniture. Homely guest areas include an open-fired lounge and a communal dining area.

HETTON

North Yorkshire – See Regional map n°**22**-N2
London 229 mi – Leeds 31 mi – York 48 mi
Michelin Road map 502-N21

Angel Inn and Barn Lodgings with rm

rest,

✉ *BD23 6LT – ✆ (01756) 730 263 – www.angelhetton.co.uk – Closed 4 days January*
9 rm – £ 135/185 £ 150/200
Rest *Angel Inn* – see restaurant listing
Menu £ 19 (weekdays) – Carte £ 27/38 – *(dinner only and Sunday lunch) (booking essential)*
Formal restaurant comprising two smartly laid dining rooms with an intimate, romantic feel; now something of a local institution and surprisingly busy considering its rural location. Classically based cooking displays a few modern touches. Attentive, professional team. Antique-furnished bedrooms in the 'Barn Lodgings'; more modern rooms in 'Sycamore Bank' cottage.

Angel Inn – Angel Inn and Barn Lodgings

✉ *BD23 6LT – ✆ (01756) 730 263 – www.angelhetton.co.uk – Closed 4 days January*
Carte £ 27/43 – *(booking essential)*
18C stone inn, its characterful interior featuring old beams, wood-burning stoves and log fires. Despite its rural location, it's a popular place, and the staff cope well with the numbers. Seasonally changing menus offer hearty dishes of local produce and even some Yorkshire tapas.

HEXHAM

Northumberland – Pop. 11 388 – See Regional map n°**24**-A2
London 304 mi – Carlisle 37 mi – Newcastle upon Tyne 21 mi
Michelin Road map 501-N19 and 502 – Michelin Green Guide GREAT BRITAIN

Bouchon

4-6 Gilesgate ✉ NE46 3NJ – ✆ (01434) 609 943 – www.bouchonbistrot.co.uk – Closed 24-26 December, Sunday and bank holidays
Menu £ 14 (weekday lunch) – Carte £ 22/37
Well-run French restaurant with a simply styled ground floor room and a more romantic first floor with opulent purple furnishings. Excellent value set price lunch menu and more ambitious à la carte. Classic French dishes use local produce.

Rat Inn 

Anick ✉ NE46 4LN – Northeast : 1.75 mi by A 6079 – ✆ (01434) 602 814 – www.theratinn.com – Closed 25 December, Monday except bank holidays and Sunday dinner
Carte £ 19/38
Traditional 18C drovers' inn with old wood beams and an open range. The daily changing blackboard menu features wholesome pub classics; the rib of beef for two is a must. The multi-levelled garden boasts arbours and Tyne Valley views.

at Slaley Southeast: 5.5 mi by B6306✉ Hexham

Slaley Hall
✉ *NE47 0BX Southeast : 2.25 mi – ✆ (01434) 673 350 – www.devere.co.uk*
141 rm – £ 99/180 £ 99/180 – 2 suites
Rest *Duke's Grill* – Carte £ 29/60 – *(dinner only)*
Rest *Hadrian's Brasserie* – Carte £ 26/53
Rest *Claret Jug* – Carte £ 23/46
Extended Edwardian manor house set in 1,000 acres and boasting two championship golf courses, a spa and extensive leisure facilities. Spacious, stylish guest areas. Largely classical bedrooms, with 'Double Deluxe' being more contemporary. Classical dishes served in formal, cosy Duke's; Brasserie menu in Hadrian's; British favourites offered in clubby Claret Jug.

at Haydon Bridge West: 7.5 mi on A69✉ Hexham

Langley Castle
Langley-on-Tyne ✉ NE47 5LU – South : 2 mi by Alston rd on A 686 – ✆ (01434) 688 888 – www.langleycastle.com
27 rm – £ 120/210 £ 155/279
Rest *Josephine's* – Menu £ 25/43 – Carte £ 35/47
Rest *Pavillion* – Carte £ 35/47
Impressive 14C castle in 12 acres; its charming guest areas feature stone walls, tapestries and heraldic shields. Superb hidden chapel. Characterful, comfy bedrooms have excellent bathrooms and some have four-posters or window seats; the Castle View rooms are more uniform in style. Classic dining in Josephine's. Grills to the fore in the modern glass extension, Pavillion.

ENGLAND

HEYTESBURY → See Warminster

Wiltshire – Michelin Road map 503-N30 and 504

HIGHCLERE

Hampshire – Pop. 2 409 – ✉ Newbury – See Regional map n°**6-B1**
London 69 mi – Newbury 5 mi – Reading 25 mi
Michelin Road map 503-P29

Yew Tree with rm
Hollington Cross, Andover Rd ✉ RG20 9SE – South : 1 mi on A 343 – ✆ (01635) 253 360 – www.theyewtree.co.uk
8 rm – £ 95/120 £ 95/120 Carte £ 23/41
Attractive 17C whitewashed inn, with a pretty terrace, a welcoming open-fired bar and three low-beamed dining rooms. Classically based dishes come in a choice of sizes and are given modern twists; the vegetarian dishes provide interest. Cosy bedrooms come with good mod cons and smart wet rooms.

HIGHCLIFFE

Dorset – See Regional map n°**4-D3**
London 112 mi – Bournemouth 10 mi – Salisbury 21 mi – Southampton 26 mi
Michelin Road map 503-O31 and 504

Lord Bute
179-185 Lymington Rd ✉ BH23 4JS – ✆ (01425) 278 884 – www.lordbute.co.uk
13 rm – £ 110/235 £ 110/235 – 2 suites
Rest – Menu £ 17/25 – Carte £ 30/47 – *(closed Sunday dinner and Monday)*
Some of the suites in this elegant hotel stand where the original 18C entrance lodges to Highcliffe Castle (home of Lord Bute), were once located. Bedrooms are well-appointed and decorated in a contemporary style. The smart restaurant and courtyard offer classical menus and host jazz and cabaret evenings.

HIGHER BURWARDSLEY → See Tattenhall

Cheshire West and Chester

HINTLESHAM → See Ipswich

Suffolk – Michelin Road map 504-X27

HINTON ST GEORGE

Somerset – See Regional map n°**3-B3**

London 138 mi – Taunton 21 mi – Weymouth 41 mi – Yeovil 13 mi

Lord Poulett Arms with rm

High St ✉ TA17 8SE – ✆ (01460) 73 149 – www.lordpoulettarms.com – Closed 25-26 December and 1 January

5 rm – †£ 65/150 ††£ 85/150 Carte £ 22/38

17C inn with a lavender-framed terrace, a boules pitch, an untamed garden and a country interior filled with hop bines and candles. A refreshing mix of classic and modern dishes; cooking is full of flavour and there's a fine selection of real ales. Smart, stylish bedrooms have Roberts radios instead of TVs.

HISTON → See Cambridge

Cambridgeshire – Michelin Road map 504-U27

HITCHIN

Hertfordshire – Pop. 34 266 – See Regional map n°**12-A2**

London 40 mi – Bedford 14 mi – Cambridge 26 mi – Luton 9 mi

Michelin Road map 504-T28

hermitage rd

20-21 Hermitage Rd ✉ SG5 1BT – ✆ (01462) 433 603 – www.hermitagerd.co.uk – Closed 25-26 December

Carte £ 21/31 – *(booking essential)*

Pass through the large cocktail bar to the vast, open-plan brasserie with its exposed brick walls, low-level booths and vibrant, buzzy atmosphere. An all-encompassing menu offers something for everyone; start with mussels or oysters – from their own beds – then move onto a grill or meat dish.

Radcliffe Arms

31 Walsworth Rd ✉ SG4 9ST – ✆ (01462) 456 111 – www.radcliffearms.com

Carte £ 21/42

True neighbourhood pub with central bar, gravity fed ales and a good spirit and wine selection. Tasty cooking focuses on well-presented, restaurant-style dishes. Breakfast is served from 8am.

HOCKLEY HEATH

West Midlands – Pop. 1 604 – ✉ Solihull – See Regional map n°**19-C2**

London 117 mi – Birmingham 11 mi – Coventry 17 mi

Michelin Road map 503-O26

Nuthurst Grange Country House

Nuthurst Grange Ln ✉ B94 5NL – South : 0.75 mi by A 3400 – ✆ (01564) 783 972 – www.nuthurst-grange.co.uk – Closed 24-26 December

19 rm – †£ 95/132 ††£ 143/165

Rest *Kingswood* – Menu £ 20/40 – *(closed Sunday dinner)*

With its lovely mature grounds and walled herb garden, this attractive part-Edwardian former farmhouse is a popular wedding venue. Spacious, country house style bedrooms are individually furnished; some have four-poster beds. The traditional dining room prepares classic dishes with a modern twist.

HOLCOMBE

Somerset – See Regional map n°**4-C2**

London 119 mi – Birmingham 106 mi – Leeds 228 mi – Sheffield 198 mi

Michelin Road map 503-M30

Holcombe Inn with rm

Stratton Rd ✉ BA3 5EB – West : 0.25 mi on Stratton-on-the-Fosse rd – ✆ (01761) 232 478 – www.holcombeinn.co.uk

8 rm – †£ 75/120 ††£ 100/120 Carte £ 26/49

Charming 17C inn set in the heart of the Somerset countryside, with a lovely south-facing garden and a peaceful air. Menus offer quite a range of dishes, from good old pub classics to more sophisticated offerings. Bedrooms are luxuriously appointed; some boast views over Downside Abbey.

HOLFORD

Somerset – Pop. 307 – ✉ Bridgwater – See Regional map n°**3-B2**
▶London 171 mi – Bristol 48 mi – Minehead 15 mi – Taunton 22 mi
Michelin Road map 503-K30 – Michelin Green Guide GREAT BRITAIN

Combe House

rest,

✉ TA5 1RZ Southwest : 0.75 by road next to Plough pub and Holford rd. – ☎ (01278) 741 382 – www.combehouse.co.uk
18 rm ☕ – 🚹£ 79/99 🚹🚹£ 89/159 **Rest** – Carte £ 20/35
Hidden up a narrow lane is this smart country house, with an old water wheel and mill alongside. It might be rustic outside but inside it's bright and modern. Bedrooms feature bold, contemporary fabrics and white furnishings, and there's a pleasant spa. The split-level restaurant offers modern classics.

HOLKHAM

Norfolk – See Regional map n°**15-C1**
▶London 124 mi – King's Lynn 32 mi – Norwich 39 mi
Michelin Road map 504-W25

Victoria

rm,

Park Rd ✉ NR23 1RG – ☎ (01328) 711 008 – www.holkham.co.uk/victoria
10 rm ☕ – 🚹£ 100/140 🚹🚹£ 120/240 **Rest** – Carte £ 23/48
Located close to the beach, at the gates of Holkham Hall, an extended flint inn with large lawned gardens and pleasant country views. A relaxed, modern style pervades and bedrooms have a stylish, homely feel. Dine on traditional British dishes while overlooking the marshes of the adjacent nature reserve.

ENGLAND

HOLLINGBOURNE

Kent – See Regional map n°**9-C2**
▶London 43 mi – Maidstone 7 mi – Faversham 23 mi
Michelin Road map 504-V30

The Windmill Ⓝ

32 Eyhorne St ✉ ME17 1TR – ☎ (01622) 889 000 – www.thewindmillbyrichardphillips.co.uk
Menu £ 15 (lunch) – Carte £ 26/45
This pub is as characterful as they come, with a giant inglenook and beams so low you have to watch your head. Hearty British dishes fittingly form the core of the menu, with bar snacks, comforting puddings and sharing roasts on Sundays.

HOLMFIRTH

West Yorkshire – Pop. 21 706 – See Regional map n°**22-B3**
▶London 187 mi – Leeds 35 mi – Sheffield 32 mi – Manchester 25 mi
Michelin Road map 502-O23

Sunnybank without rest

78 Upperthong Ln ✉ HD9 3BQ – Northwest : 0.5 mi by A 6024 – ☎ (01484) 684 065 – www.sunnybankguesthouse.co.uk
5 rm ☕ – 🚹£ 68/100 🚹🚹£ 78/110
Attractive Victorian house with lovely gardens, hidden away up a narrow road. Mix of period and modern furnishings, with a smart art deco piano in the lounge and original stained glass on the landing. Cosy bedrooms have a personal touch.

HOLT

Norfolk – Pop. 3 550 – See Regional map n°**15-C1**
▶London 124 mi – King's Lynn 34 mi – Norwich 22 mi
Michelin Road map 504-X25

Byfords

Shirehall Plain ✉ NR25 6BG – ☎ (01263) 711 400 – www.byfords.org.uk
17 rm ☕ – 🚹£ 120/130 🚹🚹£ 155/205 **Rest** – Carte £ 26/31
Grade II listed, 15C flint house. Stunning bedrooms come with feature beds, underfloor heating and plenty of extras. Numerous characterful rooms incorporate a deli, a café and a restaurant. Light meals are served during the day and more substantial dishes in the evening; it's a real hit with the locals.

HOLT

Wiltshire – Pop. 1 532 – See Regional map n°**4**-**C2**
London 110 mi – Salisbury 37 mi – Cheltenham 61 mi
Michelin Road map 503-N29

Tollgate Inn with rm

Ham Grn ✉ BA14 6PX – ✆ (01225) 782 326 – www.tollgateinn.co.uk – Closed Sunday dinner and Monday
4 rm – †£ 70/110 ††£ 90/110 Carte £ 20/39
The warm welcome and cheery, attentive staff at this village inn really set it apart. The menu keeps things simple, as befits a pub, with hearty, flavoursome dishes including steaks, fish of the day and a range of homemade pies. Cosy bedrooms have a homely style and charming personal touches.

HOLYPORT

Windsor and Maidenhead – See Regional map n°**11**-**C3**
London 30 mi – Birmingham 107 mi – Bristol 93 mi – Croydon 37 mi

Belgian Arms

Holyport St ✉ SL6 2JR – ✆ (01628) 634 468 – www.thebelgianarms.com – Closed Sunday dinner in winter and Monday dinner in summer
Carte £ 23/30
Pretty, wisteria-clad 17C inn tucked away by a pond, just off the village green. Gutsy pub dishes include tempting bar snacks and heartwarming desserts. It's a real locals' local, so there's always plenty going on.

ENGLAND

HONITON

Devon – Pop. 11 483 – See Regional map n°**2**-**D2**
London 186 mi – Exeter 17 mi – Southampton 93 mi – Taunton 18 mi
Michelin Road map 503-K31 – Michelin Green Guide THE WEST COUNTRY

Holt

178 High St ✉ EX14 1LA – ✆ (01404) 47 707 – www.theholt-honiton.com – Closed 25-26 December, 1 January, Sunday and Monday
Menu £ 11 (weekdays) – Carte £ 20/29
Rustic family-run pub providing a 'distinctive and sustainable taste of Devon'. Regularly changing menu of regional and homemade produce; local ales from the family brewery.

Railway with rm

rest,

Queen St ✉ EX14 1HE – ✆ (01404) 47 976 – www.therailwayhoniton.co.uk – Closed 25-26 December, Sunday and Monday
5 rm – †£ 85/95 ††£ 95/115 Carte £ 18/38
Smart, modern pub with a horseshoe bar, an open kitchen and a decked terrace. Authentic, affordable Mediterranean cooking features homemade pastas, brick-fired pizzas and well-cooked steaks. An eclectic wine list and an olive oil top-up service add to the fun, and comfortable bedrooms complete the picture.

at Gittisham Southwest: 3 mi by A30 ✉ Honiton

Combe House

✉ EX14 3AD – ✆ (01404) 540 400 – www.combehousedevon.com – Closed 2 weeks January
17 rm – †£ 190/440 ††£ 220/460 – 4 suites
Rest – Menu £ 36/54 – *(bookings essential for non-residents)*
Hugely impressive, listed Elizabethan mansion, set down a long drive and boasting wonderful country views. Characterful guest areas display original features and period furnishings. Imposing Great Hall; classical, country house bedrooms. Three dining rooms; menus feature produce from the superb gardens.

HOOK

Hampshire – Pop. 7 934 – ✉ Basingstoke – See Regional map n°**6**-**B1**
London 47 mi – Oxford 39 mi – Reading 13 mi – Southampton 31 mi
Michelin Road map 504-R30

Tylney Hall

Rotherwick ✉ RG27 9AZ – Northwest : 2.5 mi by A 30 and Newnham Rd on Ridge Ln – ✆ (01256) 764 881 – www.tylneyhall.com
112 rm ☕ – 🚹£ 158/290 🚹🚹£ 188/390 – 15 suites
Rest *Oak Room* – Menu £ 20 (lunch) – Carte £ 40/64 – *(booking essential)*
Impressively restored 19C mansion with a well-appointed spa and several sumptuous lounges. Country house style bedrooms boast good facilities – one even has a private conservatory. The formal panelled restaurant features classic menus and an evening pianist. The delightful gardens were designed by Jekyll.

Hogget

London Rd ✉ RG27 9JJ – (at the junction of A 30 and A 287) – ✆ (01256) 763 009 – www.thehogget.co.uk – Closed 25-26 December
Carte £ 18/33
Located at the junction of the A30 and A287. Wholesome, honest, flavourful cooking shows a real respect for the locally sourced ingredients, with sensibly priced dishes like pie and mash or slow-cooked lamb shank.

HOPE

Derbyshire ✉ Sheffield – See Regional map n°**16-A1**
London 180 mi – Derby 50 mi – Manchester 31 mi – Sheffield 15 mi
Michelin Road map 502-O23 and 503

Losehill House

Lose Hill Ln, Edale Rd ✉ S33 6AF – North : 1 mi by Edale Rd – ✆ (01433) 621 219 – www.losehillhouse.co.uk
23 rm ☕ – 🚹£ 150/225 🚹🚹£ 185/250 **Rest** – Menu £ 23/50
Peacefully located former walkers' hostel affording wonderful views up to Win Hill; in summer it's a popular wedding venue. It has an airy open-plan lounge-bar and bright modern bedrooms. Unwind in the spa or in the hot tub on the terrace. The formally laid restaurant offers classic dishes with a modern edge.

Underleigh House without rest

Losehill Ln, Hope Valley ✉ S33 6AF – North : 1 mi by Edale Rd – ✆ (01433) 621 372 – www.underleighhouse.co.uk – Closed Christmas-New Year and January
5 rm ☕ – 🚹£ 75/95 🚹🚹£ 95/115
Former Derbyshire longhouse and shippon with far-reaching views; the gregarious owner offers a friendly welcome. Traditional bedrooms, some opening onto the garden. Communal breakfasts include homemade preserves, bread and muesli.

HOPTON HEATH

Shropshire – See Regional map n°**18-A2**
London 162 mi – Birmingham 66 mi – Leeds 152 mi – Sheffield 131 mi

Hopton House without rest

✉ SY7 0QD on Clun rd – ✆ (01547) 530 885 – www.shropshirebreakfast.co.uk
3 rm ☕ – 🚹£ 90 🚹🚹£ 115/130
An unassuming former granary backed by a wild flower meadow and the Shropshire Hills. Stylish bedrooms come with sofas and double-ended baths. One room has a balcony; one has a terrace – and they all come with a freshly baked cake.

HORLEY

Surrey – Pop. 22 693 – See Regional map n°**7-D2**
London 27 mi – Brighton 26 mi – Royal Tunbridge Wells 22 mi
Michelin Road map 504-T30

Langshott Manor

Langshott ✉ RH6 9LN – North : 0.5 mi by A 23 turning right at Chequers H. onto Ladbroke Rd – ✆ (01293) 786 680 – www.alexanderhotels.com
22 rm – 🚹£ 99/199 🚹🚹£ 99/399, ☕ £ 17 – 1 suite
Rest *Mulberry* – see restaurant listing
Characterful 16C manor house set amidst roses, vines and ponds. The traditional exterior contrasts with contemporary furnishings; many of the bedrooms have fireplaces or four-posters and one has a balcony. Afternoon tea is a feature.

ENGLAND

XXX **Mulberry** – Langshott Manor Hotel

Langshott ✉ RH6 9LN – North : 0.5 mi by A 23 turning right at Chequers H. onto Ladbroke Rd – ✆ (01293) 786 680 – www.langshottmanor.com
Menu £ 15/50
Smart hotel dining room within a Part-Elizabethan manor house, which uses many herbs, fruits and vegetables from the gardens. It offers everything from breakfast to two tasting dinner menus. Dishes are modern and well-presented.

HORNCASTLE

Lincolnshire – Pop. 6 815 – See Regional map n°**17**-C1
London 143 mi – Lincoln 22 mi – Nottingham 62 mi
Michelin Road map 502-T24 and 504

XX **Magpies** with rm — rest, rest,

71-75 East St ✉ LN9 6AA – ✆ (01507) 527 004 – www.magpiesrestaurant.co.uk – Closed 26-30 December, 1-7 January, 6-15 April, 20-28 July, 19-27 October, Saturday lunch, Monday and Tuesday
3 rm – £ 70/80 £ 110/130 Menu £ 25/47
Three adjoining 18C cottages; now a cosy, family-run restaurant which hosts regular gourmet and wine dinners. Hearty, classically based dishes are attractively presented; don't miss the tasty homemade canapés and breads. Modern bedrooms have bold floral feature walls and impressive bathrooms.

HORNDON ON THE HILL

Thurrock – Pop. 1 596 – See Regional map n°**13**-C3
London 25 mi – Chelmsford 22 mi – Maidstone 34 mi – Southend-on-Sea 16 mi
Michelin Road map 504-V29

Bell Inn with rm

High Rd ✉ SS17 8LD – ✆ (01375) 642 463 – www.bell-inn.co.uk – Closed 25-26 December and bank holidays
27 rm – £ 65/140 £ 70/145 Menu £ 19 (dinner) – Carte £ 20/46
15C coaching inn, run by the same family for 70 years. Cooking is a step above your usual pub fare, displaying classically based dishes with some modern touches. Pub bedrooms are styled after Victorian mistresses; those in Hill House display thoughtful extras.

HORNING

Norfolk – See Regional map n°**15**-D1
London 121 mi – Great Yarmouth 16 mi – Norwich 11 mi
Michelin Road map 504-Y25

X **Bure River Cottage**

27 Lower St ✉ NR12 8AA – ✆ (01692) 631 421 – www.burerivercottagerestaurant.co.uk – Closed 25 December-13 February, Sunday and Monday
Carte £ 26/32 – *(dinner only) (booking advisable)*
Friendly restaurant tucked away in a lovely riverside village that's famed for its boating. Informal, L-shaped room with modern tables and chairs. Blackboard menu features fresh, carefully cooked fish and shellfish; much from Lowestoft.

HORNINGSEA → See Cambridge

Cambridgeshire

HORNINGSHAM → See Warminster

Wiltshire – Michelin Road map 504-N30

HORN'S CROSS

Devon ✉ Bideford – See Regional map n°**2**-C1
London 222 mi – Barnstaple 15 mi – Exeter 46 mi
Michelin Road map 503-H31 – Michelin Green Guide GREAT BRITAIN

ENGLAND

Roundhouse without rest

EX39 5DN West : 1 mi on A 39 – (01237) 451 687 – www.the-round-house.co.uk

3 rm – £ 50 £ 65

Spacious, welcoming guesthouse on the site of a 13C corn mill, with donkeys in the paddock, neat gardens and comfortable, homely guest areas. Immaculately kept bedrooms: ask for the round room (the largest) on the first floor.

HORRINGER → See Bury St Edmunds

Suffolk – Michelin Road map 504-W27

HORSHAM

West Sussex – Pop. 48 041 – See Regional map n°**7-D2**

London 39 mi – Brighton 23 mi – Guildford 20 mi – Lewes 25 mi

Michelin Road map 504-T30

Restaurant Tristan (Tristan Mason)

Stans Way, East St RH12 1HU – (01403) 255 688 – www.restauranttristan.co.uk – Closed 2 weeks late July-early August, 25-26 December, first week January, Sunday and Monday

Menu £ 18/65

16C property with a ground floor coffee shop and a heavily beamed upstairs restaurant. Well-presented, classic dishes are delivered with a modern touch; ingredients are excellent and flavours, distinct and well-matched. Service is enthusiastic and friendly and the atmosphere, refreshingly relaxed.

→ Scallops, Jerusalem artichoke and truffle. Guinea fowl, pearl barley and wild mushrooms. Green tea, milk and bergamot.

at Rowhook Northwest: 4 mi by A264 and A281 off A29 Horsham

Chequers Inn

RH12 3PY – (01403) 790 480 – www.thechequersrowhook.com – Closed 25 December and Sunday dinner

Carte £ 27/38

Part-15C inn with a charming open-fired, stone-floored bar and an unusual dining room extension. The chef-owner grows, forages for or shoots the majority of his produce. Classical menus.

HORSTED KEYNES

West Sussex – Pop. 1 180 – See Regional map n°**7-D2**

London 40 mi – Brighton 23 mi – Guildford 48 mi – Canterbury 75 mi

Michelin Road map 504-T30

Crown Inn with rm 

The Green RH17 7AW – (01825) 791 609 – www.thecrown-horstedkeynes.co.uk – Closed Sunday dinner

4 rm – £ 80/90 £ 90/110 Carte £ 25/45

With its beams and feature inglenook, the front bar of this pub is full of character, while the smart dining room houses a grand piano, played on Friday nights. Classical dishes form the core of the menu, with more ambitious, seasonal specials. Simple bedrooms have views of the green; one is a four-poster.

HOUGH-ON-THE-HILL → See Grantham

Lincolnshire

HOVERINGHAM

Nottinghamshire – Pop. 359 – See Regional map n°**16-B2**

London 135 mi – Birmingham 77 mi – Leeds 74 mi – Sheffield 57 mi

Reindeer Inn

Main St NG14 7JR – (01159) 663 629 – www.thereindeerinn.com – Closed Tuesday lunch, Sunday dinner and Monday

Menu £ 11/29 – Carte £ 29/38 – *(booking essential at lunch)*

Characterful country inn set next to a cricket pitch, with old beams, an open fire and a cosy, relaxed atmosphere. Well-priced menus offer mainly classical dishes. It's popular with the locals.

ENGLAND

HOVINGHAM

North Yorkshire ✉ York – See Regional map n°**23**-C2

London 235 mi – Leeds 47 mi – Middlesbrough 36 mi – York 25 mi

Michelin Road map 502-R21

Worsley Arms

High St ✉ YO62 4LA – ✆ (01653) 628 234 – www.worsleyarms.co.uk

20 rm – 🛉£ 70/95 🛉🛉£ 80/120

Rest – Carte £ 21/37 – *(dinner only and Sunday lunch)*

Characterful inn with cosy lounges and a large walled garden; dating back to 1841 and located in a delightful estate village. Homely bedrooms are split between the main building and a row of cottages on the green. Classic menus are served in the rustic bar at lunch and in the more formal dining room at dinner.

HUCCOMBE

Devon – See Regional map n°**2**-C3

London 217 mi – Bristol 121 mi – Cardiff 152 mi – Plymouth 30 mi

Huccombe House without rest

✉ TQ7 2EP – ✆ (01548) 580 669 – www.southdevonbandb.co.uk

3 rm – 🛉£ 70/80 🛉🛉£ 90

Converted Victorian school – the owner herself once went to school here! Pleasant lounge with high beamed ceilings and huge windows affording countryside views. Large bedrooms with sleigh beds made up with Egyptian cotton linen. Aga-cooked breakfasts at the communal table or on the patio.

HUDDERSFIELD

West Yorkshire – Pop. 162 949 – See Regional map n°**22**-B3

London 191 mi – Bradford 11 mi – Leeds 15 mi – Manchester 25 mi

Michelin Road map 502-O23 and 504

Eric's

73-75 Lidgets St, Lindley ✉ HD3 3JP – Northwest : 3.25 mi by A 629 and Birchencliffe Hill Rd. – ✆ (01484) 646 416 – www.ericsrestaurant.co.uk – Closed Monday except December and Sunday dinner

Menu £ 16 (weekdays)/24 – Carte £ 30/50 – *(bookings advisable at dinner)*

Contemporary neighbourhood restaurant offering seasonal menus of appealing modern dishes packed with bold, distinct flavours. Great value lunch and early evening menu. On selected Saturdays they host brunch or afternoon tea events.

HULLBRIDGE

Essex – Pop. 6 097 – See Regional map n°**13**-C2_3

London 40 mi – Croydon 46 mi – Barnet 50 mi – Ealing 63 mi

Anchor

Ferry Rd ✉ SS5 6ND – ✆ (01702) 230 777 – www.theanchorhullbridge.co.uk – Closed 25 December

Menu £ 14 (lunch and early dinner) – Carte £ 22/43

Modern, informal, open-plan restaurant with a pleasant terrace, a sleek bar and lots of windows to take in the river views. Wide-ranging, seasonal British menu; more adventurous specials at dinner.

HUMSHAUGH

Northumberland – See Regional map n°**24**-A2

London 290 mi – Birmingham 220 mi – Glasgow 132 mi

Michelin Road map 502-N18

Carraw without rest

Carraw Farm, Military Rd ✉ NE46 4DB – West : 5 mi on B 6318 – ✆ (01434) 689 857 – www.carraw.co.uk

4 rm – 🛉£ 60/65 🛉🛉£ 80/98

Converted farmhouse and barn on the foundations of Hadrian's Wall. Two bedrooms with exposed stone walls and beams, and two larger, more modern ones. Bright, pine-furnished breakfast room, lounge with local info and pleasant country views.

HUNSDON

Hertfordshire – See Regional map n°**12**-**B2**

London 26 mi – Bishop's Stortford 8 mi – Harlow 7 mi

Fox and Hounds

2 High St ✉ SG12 8NH – ✆ (01279) 843 999 – www.foxandhounds-hunsdon.co.uk – Closed 26 December, Sunday dinner and Monday

Menu £ 14 (weekdays) – Carte £ 24/40

Sizeable pub with a rustic interior, a large garden and a terrace. Concise menus offer tasty, unfussy dishes that display a clear understanding of flavours. Pastas are homemade, they smoke their own fish, and desserts are not to be missed; in summer, be sure to pay a visit to the popular outside seafood bar.

HUNSTANTON

Norfolk – Pop. 8 704 – See Regional map n°**14**-**B1**

London 120 mi – Cambridge 60 mi – Norwich 45 mi

Michelin Road map 502-V25 and 504

Lodge (N)

Old Hunstanton Rd ✉ PE36 6HX – Northeast : 1.5 mi on A 149 – ✆ (01485) 532 896 – www.thelodgehunstanton.co.uk – Closed January

16 rm – †£ 75/95 ††£ 120/140 **Rest** – Carte £ 19/42

After a long day at the beach head for this laid-back hotel and one of its modern, well-equipped, immaculately kept bedrooms. Dine in the large bar with its TV and pool table or head through to the more formal residents' dining room; the chef is Italian, so opt for a dish from his homeland.

The Neptune (Kevin Mangeolles) with rm

85 Old Hunstanton Rd, Old Hunstanton ✉ PE36 6HZ – Northeast : 1.5 mi on A 149 – ✆ (01485) 532 122 – www.theneptune.co.uk – Closed 3 weeks January, 2 weeks November, 26 December and Monday

5 rm – †£ 80/100 ††£ 100/140

Menu £ 34/70 – *(dinner only and Sunday lunch)*

Very personally run, attractive, red-brick former pub. New England style interior with a rattan-furnished bar and large nautical photographs in the dining room. The constantly evolving menu relies on the latest local produce to arrive at the door. Presentation is modern; service is relaxed and efficient. Comfy bedrooms have Nespresso machines and thoughtful extras.

→ Lobster salad, star anise mousse, pea purée and lobster croquettes. Loin and braised haunch of hare, celeriac tart and dauphine potatoes. Poached savarin, strawberries, lemon cream and mint ice cream.

at Thornham Northeast: 4.5 mi on A149

Orange Tree with rm

High St ✉ PE36 6LY – ✆ (01485) 512 213 – www.theorangetreethornham.co.uk

10 rm – †£ 79/130 ††£ 89/140 Carte £ 24/38 **s**

You're guaranteed a warm welcome at this 17C inn; even your dog will be offered a snack in the laid-back bar. An array of menus offer everything from pub classics to globally-influenced restaurant dishes, via some vegetarian choices and daily specials. Contemporary restaurant and compact, modern bedrooms.

HUNSTRETE

Bath and North East Somerset – See Regional map n°**4**-**C2**

London 124 mi – Bath 10 mi – Bournemouth 75 mi – Exeter 77 mi

Michelin Road map 503-M29

The Pig (N)

Hunstrete House ✉ BS39 4NS – ✆ (01761) 490 490 – www.thepighotel.com

29 rm – †£ 139/159 ††£ 189/209, £ 15 – 1 suite

Rest *The Pig* – see restaurant listing

Nestled in the Mendip Hills, with deer roaming around the parkland, this Grade II listed house is all about getting back to nature. It has a relaxed, friendly atmosphere and extremely comfortable bedrooms which feature handmade beds and fine linens; some are in converted sheds in the walled vegetable garden.

XX **The Pig** (N) – The Pig Hotel

Hunstrete House ✉ BS39 4NS – ✆ (01761) 490 490 – www.thepighotel.com
Carte £ 25/37 – *(booking advisable)*
This rustic hotel conservatory takes things back to nature with pots of fresh herbs placed on wooden tables and chimney pots filled with flowering shrubs. The extremely knowledgeable team serve dishes which showcase ingredients from their extensive gardens, along with produce sourced from within 25 miles.

HUNTINGDON

Cambridgeshire – Pop. 23 937 – See Regional map n°**14-A2**
London 69 mi – Bedford 21 mi – Cambridge 16 mi
Michelin Road map 504-T26

Old Bridge

1 High St ✉ PE29 3TQ – ✆ (01480) 424 300 – www.huntsbridge.com
24 rm – †£ 90/130 ††£ 120/230
Rest ***Terrace*** – see restaurant listing
Attractive 18C former bank next to the River Ouse; its bright, contemporary décor cleverly blended with the property's original features. Cosy, oak-panelled bar; individually styled, up-to-date bedrooms; and a superbly stocked wine shop.

XX **Terrace** – Old Bridge Hotel

1 High St ✉ PE29 3TQ – ✆ (01480) 424 300 – www.huntsbridge.com
Menu £ 17 (weekdays) – Carte £ 29/51 **s**
Light-filled conservatory restaurant with a pleasant terrace, serving an all-encompassing, daily changing menu of brasserie classics. The excellent wine list offers depth, variety and quality, with a fantastic selection by the glass.

ENGLAND

Abbots Ripton North: 6.5 mi by B1514 and A141 on B1090

Abbot's Elm with rm

Moat Ln ✉ PE28 2PA – ✆ (01487) 773 773 – www.theabbotselm.co.uk – Closed Sunday dinner
3 rm – †£ 60/70 ††£ 75/85 Menu £ 14 (weekday lunch) – Carte £ 19/39
A modern reconstruction of an attractive 17C pub. The bar offers light bites, hot plates and a 'menu du jour'; later in the week there's also a tasting menu and an à la carte of appealing, hearty dishes served in the formal dining room. Cosy bedrooms come with free wi-fi and fluffy bathrobes.

at Hemingford Grey Southeast: 5 mi by A1198 off A14 ✉ Huntingdon

The Cock

47 High St ✉ PE28 9BJ – ✆ (01480) 463 609 – www.cambscuisine.com
Menu £ 13 (weekday lunch) – Carte £ 22/37 – *(booking essential)*
Homely 17C country pub with a split-level bar and a spacious dining room; run by an experienced team. Tried-and-tested pub cooking offers good value lunches, extensive daily fish specials and a 'mix and match' sausage and mash board.

HURLEY

Windsor and Maidenhead – Pop. 1 712 – See Regional map n°**11-C3**
London 35 mi – Maidenhead 5 mi – Reading 18 mi

XX **Black Boys Inn** with rm

Henley Rd ✉ SL6 5NQ – Southwest : 1.5 mi on A 4130 – ✆ (01628) 824 212 – www.blackboysinn.co.uk – Closed Sunday dinner
7 rm – †£ 88/95 ††£ 88/120 Menu £ 13 (weekday lunch) – Carte £ 29/46
Rustic restaurant in a 16C former pub, with exposed beams and a wood burning stove. The experienced owners are avid Francophiles and the concise, traditional French menu reflects this. Polite service. Clean, unfussy bedrooms with thoughtful extras such as books.

HURSTBOURNE TARRANT

Hampshire – Pop. 676 – ✉ Andover – See Regional map n°**6-B1**
London 77 mi – Bristol 77 mi – Oxford 38 mi – Southampton 33 mi
Michelin Road map 503-P30 and 504

Esseborne Manor

✉ SP11 0ER Northeast : 1.5 mi on A 343 – ✆ (01264) 736 444 – www.esseborne-manor.co.uk

18 rm – £ 92/112 £ 112/180

Rest *Courtyard* – Menu £ 15/30 **s** – Carte £ 24/37 **s**

Set in attractive grounds, this Victorian country house is a popular wedding venue. Smart, classically decorated bedrooms are split between the house, a cottage and the courtyard; some have whirlpool baths, two have four-posters and one leads out into the herb garden. The restaurant serves modern classics.

HURSTPIERPOINT

– Pop. 12 730 – See Regional map n°**7-D2**
London 45 mi – Croydon 35 mi – Barnet 87 mi – Ealing 69 mi
Michelin Road map 504-T31

Fig Tree

120 High St ✉ BN6 9PX – ✆ (01273) 832 183 – www.figtreerestaurant.co.uk – Closed 2 weeks January, Tuesday lunch, Sunday dinner and Monday

Menu £ 19/23 – Carte £ 24/38

Attractive Victorian house in a pretty high street, personally run by a young couple: she looks after diners while he cooks. Carefully priced menus showcase local, seasonal ingredients. Loyal local following.

HURWORTH-ON-TEES → See Darlington

Darlington – Michelin Road map 502-P20

HUTTON-LE-HOLE

North Yorkshire – Pop. 162 – See Regional map n°**23-C1**
London 244 mi – Scarborough 27 mi – York 33 mi
Michelin Road map 502-R21

Burnley House without rest

✉ YO62 6UA – ✆ (01751) 417 548 – www.burnleyhouse.co.uk

8 rm – £ 56/68 £ 88/98

A cosy, welcoming guesthouse at the entrance to this picture postcard village on the edge of the moors. Small sitting room with a stone floor, coir carpet and wood-burning stove. Snug, bright bedrooms and a pretty garden.

HUTTON MAGNA → See Barnard Castle

Durham

ICKLESHAM

East Sussex – See Regional map n°**9-C3**
London 66 mi – Brighton 42 mi – Hastings 7 mi
Michelin Road map 504-V/W31

Manor Farm Oast without rest

Windmill Ln ✉ TN36 4WL – South : 0.5 mi – ✆ (01424) 813 787 – www.manorfarmoast.co.uk – Closed January and New Year

3 rm – £ 95 £ 105

Restored, extended oast house built in 1860 and surrounded by orchards and farmland. Original features remain both inside and out. The welcoming beamed lounge has an open fire; homely bedrooms feature large beds – one is completely round.

ENGLAND

IDEN GREEN

Kent – See Regional map n°**8-B2**
London 55 mi – Croydon 49 mi – Barnet 81 mi – Ealing 85 mi
Michelin Road map 504-V30

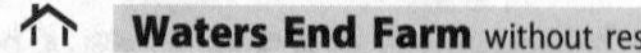

Waters End Farm without rest

Standen St ✉ TN17 4LA – Southeast : 1.25 mi – ☎ (01580) 850 731 – www.watersendfarm.co.uk – Closed September-April
5 rm – †£ 120/135 ††£ 120/135
Characterful part-timbered, part-brick house, in 43 peaceful acres. Bedrooms, in converted barns, boast heavy wood furniture and modern facilities. Eat beside the huge house mural in the breakfast room or out on the terrace in summer.

ILFRACOMBE

Devon – Pop. 11 184 – See Regional map n°**2-C1**
London 218 mi – Barnstaple 13 mi – Exeter 53 mi
Michelin Road map 503-H30 – Michelin Green Guide GREAT BRITAIN

Hamptons without rest

Excelsior Villas, Torrs Pk. ✉ EX34 8AZ – ☎ (01271) 864 246 – www.thehamptonshotel.com
6 rm – †£ 65/100 ††£ 75/125
Imposing Victorian villa with individual, bohemian style. Open-plan lounge and breakfast room with honesty bar and DVDs. Well-equipped, individually styled bedrooms are designed by the friendly owner; those to the front boast rooftop views.

Westwood without rest

Torrs Pk ✉ EX34 8AZ – ☎ (01271) 867 443 – www.west-wood.co.uk
5 rm – †£ 85/125 ††£ 85/125
Perched on the hillside overlooking the rooftops, this appealingly styled Victorian house offers warm décor and an eclectic mix of modern and retro furniture. Spacious bedrooms boast bold feature wallpaper; those to the front are the best.

Quay

11 The Quay ✉ EX34 9EQ – ☎ (01271) 868 090 – www.11thequay.co.uk – Closed 6-20 January
Carte £ 24/59
Wander down to the harbourside and this smart red building stands out; inside, it's the artwork of owner Damien Hirst which catches the eye. Well-priced, appealing menu of simple, flavoursome dishes, with local produce to the fore.

La Gendarmerie

63 Fore St ✉ EX34 9ED – ☎ (01271) 865 984 – www.lagendarmerie.co.uk – Closed November, Tuesday-Wednesday October-March and Monday
Menu £ 27 – *(dinner only) (booking advisable)*
Once a police station, now a simple little restaurant with exposed stone walls and an intimate feel; personally run by a husband and wife team. Concise, daily changing menu showcases market produce in precise, skilfully executed combinations.

ILKLEY

West Yorkshire – Pop. 14 809 – See Regional map n°**22-B2**
London 210 mi – Bradford 13 mi – Harrogate 17 mi – Leeds 16 mi
Michelin Road map 502-O22

Box Tree

37 Church St ✉ LS29 9DR – on A 65 – ☎ (01943) 608 484 – www.theboxtree.co.uk – Closed 26-30 December, 1-6 January, Sunday dinner and Monday
Menu £ 30/75 – *(dinner only and lunch Friday-Sunday)*
An iconic restaurant set in two charming sandstone cottages, with a plush, antique-furnished lounge and two luxurious dining rooms; it celebrated 50 years in 2012. Cooking is refined and skilful, with a classical French base, and dishes are light and delicate. Only the best ingredients are used.
→ Ravioli of caramelised calf's sweetbreads, morels and madeira jus. Rump of lamb, ratatouille, broccoli purée and chargrilled courgettes. Apricot soufflé with apricot coulis.

ILMINGTON

Warwickshire – See Regional map n°**19-C3**

London 91 mi – Birmingham 31 mi – Oxford 34 mi – Stratford-upon-Avon 9 mi

Michelin Road map 504-O27 – Michelin Green Guide GREAT BRITAIN

Folly Farm Cottage without rest

Back St ✉ CV36 4LJ – ☎ (01608) 682 425 – www.follyfarm.co.uk

3 rm – †£ 55/65 ††£ 64/88

Characterful barn conversion with lovely gardens. The cosy breakfast room has floral fabrics and a cottagey feel; try the 'Folly Challenge'! Traditional beamed bedrooms – one has a four-poster and all have homemade cake. Welcoming owners.

Howard Arms with rm

Lower Green ✉ CV36 4LT – ☎ (01608) 682 226 – www.howardarms.com

8 rm – †£ 60/150 ††£ 80/150 Carte £ 23/43

Delightful 17C Cotswold stone inn on a peaceful village green. Sit in the beamed bar with its inglenook fireplace, in the raised-level dining room or on the lovely terrace. Dishes are hearty and mainly British-based. Bedrooms are warm and cosy: some have antiques; those in the extension are more contemporary.

INGHAM

Norfolk – Pop. 376 – See Regional map n°**15-D1**

London 139 mi – Norwich 25 mi – Ipswich 65 mi – Lowestoft 30 mi

Michelin Road map 504-W27

Ingham Swan with rm

Sea Palling Rd ✉ NR12 9AB – ☎ (01692) 581 099 – www.theinghamswan.co.uk – Closed 25-26 December, Sunday dinner and Monday in winter

4 rm – †£ 75 ††£ 119

Menu £ 15/27 **s** – Carte £ 27/44 **s** – *(booking essential at dinner)*

This cosy, attractive, 14C pub sits in the shadow of an 11C church, and features a thatched roof and a rustic, beamed interior, with four smart, modern bedrooms in a converted outbuilding. Dishes can be quite complex, using plenty of ingredients, albeit in classic combinations, and formal service comes from a keen young team. Popular wine dinners and cookery classes.

ENGLAND

INGLETON

North Yorkshire – Pop. 1 641 – See Regional map n°**22-A2**

London 266 mi – Kendal 21 mi – Lancaster 18 mi – Leeds 53 mi

Michelin Road map 502-M21

Riverside Lodge

24 Main St ✉ LA6 3HJ – ☎ (015242) 41 359 – www.riversideingleton.co.uk – Closed 24-25 December

8 rm – †£ 45/49 ††£ 60/68 **Rest** – Menu £ 17 **s**

19C doctor's house with a homely interior and a snooker table and sauna hidden in the basement. Spacious, pine-furnished bedrooms have modern bathrooms. The conservatory dining room offers views over the Dales and the river. Breakfast features homemade preserves and muesli, along with a fish special.

IPSWICH

Suffolk – Pop. 144 957 – See Regional map n°**15-C3**

London 77 mi – Redbridge 64 mi – Romford 59 mi – Norwich 45 mi

Michelin Road map 504-X27 – Michelin Green Guide GREAT BRITAIN

Salthouse Harbour

1 Neptune Quay ✉ IP4 1AX – ☎ (01473) 226 789 – www.salthouseharbour.co.uk Town plan: X**a**

70 rm – †£ 135/185 ††£ 150/195

Rest *Eaterie* – see restaurant listing

Stylish former salt warehouse – its trendy lobby-lounge boasts floor to ceiling windows and great marina views. Modern boutique bedrooms have well-appointed bathrooms; some feature chaise longues, copper slipper baths or balconies.

IPSWICH

Argyle St . . . . X 2
Back Hamlet . . . . Z 3
Birkfield Drive . . . . Z 5
Bond St . . . . X 6
Bridgwater Rd . . . . Z 7
Buttermarket Centre . . . . X 9
Carr St . . . . X 10
Chevallier St . . . . Y 13
College St . . . . X 15
Corn Hill . . . . X 16
Dogs Head St . . . . X 18
Ellenbrook Rd . . . . Z 19
Falcon St . . . . X 21
Fore Hamlet . . . . Z 22
Franciscan Way . . . . X 24
Friars St . . . . X 25
Grey Friars Rd . . . . X 26
Grove Lane . . . . YZ 28
Handford Rd . . . . X, Y 30
Lloyds Ave . . . . X 31
Lower Orwell St . . . . X 32
Northgate St . . . . X 33
Orwell Pl . . . . X 34
Quadling St . . . . X 35
Queen St . . . . X 37
St Helen's St . . . . X, Y 39
St Margarets St . . . . X 40
St Nicholas St . . . . X 41
St Peter's St . . . . X 42
Salthouse St . . . . X 43
Silent St . . . . X 46
Tavern St X
Tower Ramparts Centre . . . . . X 47
Upper Orwell St . . . . X 49
Waterworks St . . . . X 51
Westgate St . . . . X 52
Wolsey St . . . . X 53
Yarmouth Rd . . . . Y 54

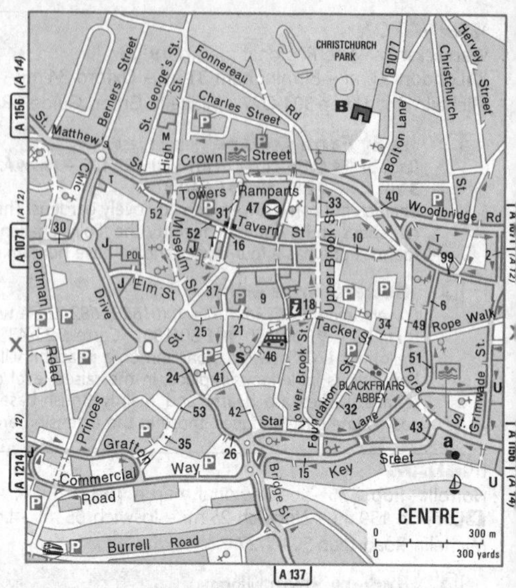

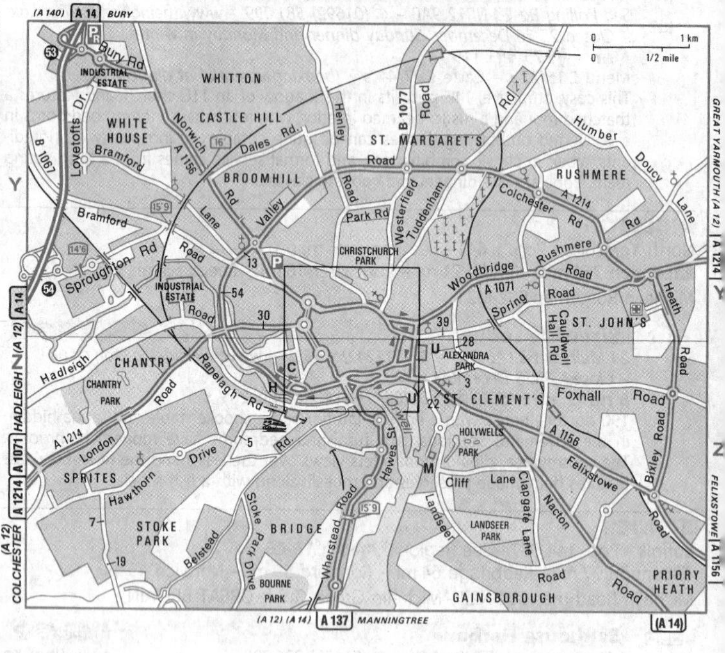

Kesgrave Hall

Hall Rd ✉ IP5 2PU – East : 4.75 mi by A 1214 on Bealings rd – ✆ (01473) 333 471 – www.kesgravehall.com
23 rm – †£ 135/310 ††£ 135/310 – 1 suite
Rest – Carte £ 24/43 – *(bookings not accepted)*
An impressive house built in 1812, with a delightful terrace overlooking large lawned gardens to a 38 acre wood. Stylish lounges have a relaxed, urban-chic feel. Luxurious bedrooms boast quality furnishings, modern facilities and stylish bathrooms. The busy brasserie offers a European menu.

Trongs

23 St Nicholas St ✉ IP1 1TW – ✆ (01473) 256 833 – Closed 3 weeks August and Sunday Town plan: X**s**
Carte £ 21/46
Brightly painted restaurant filled with flowers and candles. The owners are from Hanoi: the parents and one son cook – his brother runs front of house. The extensive menu specialises in vibrant dishes from northern China; try the spring rolls.

Eaterie – Salthouse Harbour Hotel

1 Neptune Quay ✉ IP4 1AX – ✆ (01473) 226 789 – www.salthouseharbour.co.uk Town plan: X**a**
Menu £ 18/22 (lunch) – Carte dinner £ 25/41
Modern hotel brasserie in an old salt warehouse, with a zinc-topped bar, gold pillars, modern art and padded booths. Tasty brasserie dishes and numerous specials focus largely on seafood. Eat on the terrace, overlooking the marina.

at Hintlesham West: 5 mi by A1214 on A1071 -(Y)✉ Ipswich

Hintlesham Hall

✉ IP8 3NS – ✆ (01473) 652 334 – www.hintleshamhall.com
33 rm – †£ 89/149 ††£ 119/169 – 3 suites
Rest – Menu £ 19/33 **s** – Carte £ 45/63
Impressive Georgian manor house with 16C roots; the original ornate plasterwork and gold leaf inlaid cornicing remain. Bedrooms in the main house are grand; the courtyard rooms are cosy – some have terraces. Dine in the impressive 'Salon' or wood-panelled 'Parlour'; fresh herbs come from the garden.

ENGLAND

IRBY

Merseyside – See Regional map n°**20-A3**
London 212 mi – Liverpool 12 mi – Manchester 46 mi – Stoke-on-Trent 56 mi
Michelin Road map 502-K23

Da Piero

5-7 Mill Hill Rd ✉ CH61 4UB – ✆ (0151) 648 73 73 – www.dapiero.co.uk – Closed 2 weeks August, 1 week January, Sunday and Monday
Carte £ 21/39 – *(dinner only) (booking essential)*
Family-owned and run restaurant with homely, understated décor and intimate, pleasant feel. Carefully prepared, classical Italian cooking, with lots of rustic Sicilian dishes.

IRONBRIDGE

Telford and Wrekin – Pop. 1 560 – See Regional map n°**18-B2**
London 135 mi – Birmingham 36 mi – Shrewsbury 18 mi
Michelin Road map 503-M26 and 504 – Michelin Green Guide GREAT BRITAIN

Library House without rest

11 Severn Bank ✉ TF8 7AN – ✆ (01952) 432 299 – www.libraryhouse.com
4 rm – †£ 75/85 ††£ 90/110
Attractive former library, just a stone's throw from the famous bridge. It has a farmhouse-style breakfast room and a homely lounge where books sit on the old library shelves. Tastefully furnished bedrooms are named after poets.

XX **Restaurant Severn**
33 High St. ✉ TF8 7AG – ✆ (01952) 432 233 – www.restaurantsevern.co.uk
– Closed 1 week January, 1 week August, Sunday, Monday and Tuesday
Menu £ 26/30 – *(dinner only) (booking essential)*
Traditional little restaurant with a loyal following; enter down a narrow side passage into a cosy low-beamed room. Classic dishes rely on seasonal local produce. It's run by a couple: she cooks starters and desserts; he cooks the mains.

at Coalport Southeast: 2 mi by B4373

Woodbridge Inn Ⓝ
✉ TF8 7JF – ✆ (01952) 882 054 – www.woodbridge-coalport.co.uk
Carte £ 22/45
Spacious, modernised pub in a superb spot on the banks of the River Severn. Inside, it's airy and open, yet with nooks and crannies galore. Menus list all the usual suspects but it's worth going off-piste occasionally.

IRTHINGTON

Cumbria – See Regional map n°**21**-**B1**
London 314 mi – Newcastle upon Tyne 54 mi – Sunderland 67 mi – Carlisle 8 mi

Golden Fleece Ⓝ with rm
Ruleholme ✉ CA6 4NF – Southeast : 1.5 mi by A 689 – ✆ (01228) 573 686
– www.thegoldenfleececumbria.co.uk – Closed 1-7 January
8 rm ☕ – †£ 65/75 ††£ 85/100 Carte £ 22/54
Located just off the A689 and handy for Carlisle Airport, Hadrian's Wall and Gretna Green. Dishes like twice-baked 3 cheese soufflé and pan-roasted Cumbrian lamb sit alongside tasty pub classics, juicy mature steaks and 'proper' puddings on something-for-everyone menus. Very comfortable bedrooms.

ENGLAND

ISLE OF MAN → See Man (Isle of)

I.O.M. – Michelin Road map 502-G21

ITTERINGHAM

Norfolk✉ Aylsham – See Regional map n°**15**-**C1**
London 126 mi – Cromer 11 mi – Norwich 17 mi
Michelin Road map 504-X25

Walpole Arms
The Common ✉ NR11 7AR – ✆ (01263) 587 258 – www.thewalpolearms.co.uk
– Closed 25 December and Sunday dinner in winter
Carte £ 20/39
Pretty 18C inn in a sleepy little village; its surprisingly modern interior designed in keeping with the building's age. Menus champion local, seasonal ingredients, with produce from their farm; rare breed beef is a speciality.

IXWORTH → See Bury St Edmunds

Suffolk – Michelin Road map 504-W27

KEGWORTH

Leicestershire – Pop. 3 601 – See Regional map n°**16**-**B2**
London 123 mi – Leicester 18 mi – Loughborough 6 mi – Nottingham 13 mi
Michelin Road map 502-Q25 and 503 – Michelin Green Guide GREAT BRITAIN

Kegworth House without rest
42 High St ✉ DE74 2DA – ✆ (01509) 672 575 – www.kegworthhouse.co.uk
– Closed Christmas and New Year
11 rm ☕ – †£ 87/150 ††£ 107/210
Charming, family-run, Georgian townhouse with many original features and a pleasant walled garden. Individually furnished bedrooms; Room 11, with its exposed beams and four-poster, is one of the best. Extensive buffet breakfasts.

KELVEDON

Essex – Pop. 4 717 – See Regional map n°**13-C2**
London 56 mi – Leicester 118 mi – Wandsworth 56 mi – Bromley 55 mi
Michelin Road map 504-W28

XX George & Dragon

Coggleshall Rd ✉ CO5 9PL – Northwest : 2 mi on B 1024 – ✆ (01376) 561 797 – www.georgeanddragonkelvedon.co.uk – Closed 25 December-2 January, Sunday and Monday

Carte £ 24/34

Clean, bright and welcoming former pub with a sleek, contemporary style, encompassing topiary planters, marble tiled floors, antique mirrors, and art deco pictures and statuettes. Simple, well-priced menu with locally caught fish specials. Pretty terrace. Hands-on owners.

KENDAL

Cumbria – Pop. 28 586 – See Regional map n°**21-B2**
London 270 mi – Bradford 64 mi – Burnley 63 mi – Carlisle 49 mi
Michelin Road map 502-L21 – Michelin Green Guide GREAT BRITAIN

Beech House without rest

40 Greenside ✉ LA9 4LD – (by All Hallows Ln) – ✆ (01539) 720 385 – www.beechhouse-kendal.co.uk – Closed 1 week Christmas

5 rm – †£ 60/75 ††£ 80/100

Pretty, three-storey Georgian house set just out of town. Modern, open-plan lounge with comfy sofas and communal breakfast tables. Bright, airy, pine-furnished bedrooms with up-to-date bathrooms. Welcoming owners.

XX Castle Dairy (N)

Wildman St ✉ LA9 6EN – ✆ (01539) 733 946 – www.castledairy.co.uk – Closed 25-30 December, Sunday and Monday

Menu £ 16/45 – Carte £ 22/47

This delightful Grade I listed building dates back to 1402 and there's a cobbled Roman road running through its centre. It's run by college apprentices, under the eye of an experienced chef. Cooking is skilled, modern and flavoursome.

X Newmoon

129 Highgate ✉ LA9 4EN – ✆ (01539) 729 254 – www.newmoonrestaurant.co.uk – Closed 1-7 January, 25-26 December, Sunday and Monday

Menu £ 14 – Carte £ 22/31 – *(booking advisable)*

Smart, high street restaurant with ground floor bar, intimate, beamed dining room and a loyal local following. The owner's Turkish heritage is reflected in the menu, which has a strong Mediterranean base; dishes are fresh and colourful.

X Sawadee Thai (N)

54 Stramongate ✉ LA9 4BD – ✆ (01539) 722 944 – www.thairestaurantkendal.co.uk – Closed 24-31 December and Monday

Menu £ 20 – Carte £ 13/32 – *(dinner only)*

The staff, dressed in authentic Thai silks, provide a very warm welcome at this smart neighbourhood restaurant. The appealing menu offers flavoursome dishes ranging from Tom Yam soup to Som Tam Thai salad and Geng Ba Jungle curry.

at Crosthwaite West: 5.25 mi by All Hallows Ln ✉ Kendal

Punch Bowl Inn with rm

✉ LA8 8HR – ✆ (01539) 568 237 – www.the-punchbowl.co.uk

9 rm – †£ 95/135 ††£ 105/185 Carte £ 23/37

Charming 17C inn set in the picturesque Lyth Valley, boasting antiques, cosy fires and exposed wood beams; dine either in the rustic bar or the more formal restaurant. Cooking has a classical base but also features some modern touches; dishes display a degree of complexity that you wouldn't usually find in a pub. Luxury bedrooms boast quality linens and roll-top baths.

ENGLAND

KENILWORTH

Warwickshire – Pop. 22 413 – See Regional map n°**19-C2**

London 102 mi – Birmingham 19 mi – Coventry 5 mi – Leicester 32 mi

Michelin Road map 503-P26 and 504 – Michelin Green Guide GREAT BRITAIN

Victoria Lodge without rest

180 Warwick Rd ✉ CV8 1HU – ✆ (01926) 512 020
– www.victorialodgekenilworth.co.uk – Closed 2 weeks Christmas-New Year

10 rm – †£ 52/68 ††£ 75/85

Keenly and proudly run red-brick house with a linen-laid breakfast room and a comfy lounge complete with a piano. Clean, well-maintained bedrooms; some with balconies or patios. Fresh milk and mineral water are in a fridge on the landing.

Beef

11 Warwick Rd ✉ CV8 1HD – ✆ (01926) 863 311 – www.beef-restaurant.com
– Closed last two weeks August, 1 January, 25-26 December and 31 December

Menu £ 17 (weekdays) – Carte £ 34/64

Rustic restaurant with exposed brickwork, slate floors and quirky cowhide banquettes. Menus offer robust, meaty dishes – Wagyu, dry-aged British, and grain-fed American beef feature highly, accompanied by beef dripping chips.

Cross at Kenilworth (N) (Adam Bennett)

16 New St ✉ CV8 2EZ – ✆ (01926) 853 840 – www.thecrosskenilworth.co.uk
– Closed Sunday dinner, Monday and bank holidays

Menu £ 25 (lunch) – Carte £ 30/45

Smartly furnished pub with eager, welcoming staff. Skilfully executed, classical cooking uses prime seasonal ingredients, and dishes not only look impressive but taste good too. Sit in the back room to watch the kitchen in action. The bright and airy room next door used to be a classroom.

→ Crispy duck egg, smoked haddock, leeks and Berkswell cheese. Monkfish with onion risotto, bacon and smoked sprout tops. Rhubarb trifle, gingerbread ice cream.

ENGLAND

KENTISBURY

Devon – See Regional map n°**2-C1**

London 220 mi – Exeter 58 mi – Barnstaple 10 mi

Michelin Road map 503-I30

Kentisbury Grange (N)

✉ EX31 4NL Southeast : 1 mi by B 3229 on A39 – ✆ (01271) 882 295
– www.kentisburygrange.co.uk

16 rm (dinner included) – †£ 195/330 ††£ 195/330

Rest *Coach House* – see restaurant listing

This Victorian country house might have a Grade II listing but inside it's been smartly refurbished with designer fabrics and furnishings; albeit in the colours of the original stained glass windows. Bedrooms are modern yet cosy.

Coach House (N) – Kentisbury Grange Hotel

✉ EX31 4NL Southeast : 1 mi by B 3229 on A39 – ✆ (01271) 882 295
– www.kentisburygrange.co.uk

Carte £ 25/38

This large hotel restaurant has a funky lounge under the eaves and an elegant dining room featuring booths and plush blue velvet chairs. The experienced chef prepares flavoursome modern dishes of local meats and south coast fish.

KENTON → See Exeter

Devon – Michelin Road map 503-J31

KERNE BRIDGE → See Ross-on-Wye

Herefordshire – Michelin Road map 503-M28 and 504

KESSINGLAND

Suffolk – Pop. 4 327 – See Regional map n°**15**-D2

London 126 mi – Norwich 28 mi – Ipswich 40 mi – Colchester 66 mi

Old Rectory

157 Church Rd ✉ NR33 7SQ – ☎ (01502) 742 188 – www.bandblowestoft.co.uk

3 rm – †£ 65/70 ††£ 90/110 **Rest** – Menu £ 25 **s**

1834 rectory with beautiful gardens, just a short walk from the beach. It retains plenty of original character, with individually furnished bedrooms boasting antique furniture and feature beds. A selection of dishes are offered at dinner; locally sourced produce includes vegetables from their own garden.

KESWICK

Cumbria – Pop. 4 984 – See Regional map n°**21**-A2

London 294 mi – Carlisle 31 mi – Kendal 30 mi

Michelin Road map 502-K20 – Michelin Green Guide GREAT BRITAIN

Lairbeck without rest

Vicarage Hill ✉ CA12 5QB – ☎ (017687) 73 373 Town plan: X**a**

– www.lairbeckhotel-keswick.co.uk – Closed Christmas-New Year

14 rm – †£ 55/59 ††£ 110/118

An attractive Victorian house in the suburbs – its mature garden boasting a huge Sequoia Redwood. Inside it has an original barley-twist staircase and a galleried landing. Bedrooms come in a mix of styles; some have lovely views.

Howe Keld without rest

5-7 The Heads ✉ CA12 5ES – ☎ (017687) 72 417 Town plan: Z**s**

– www.howekeld.co.uk

12 rm – †£ 55/95 ††£ 100/135

A comfortable, well-run guest house with boutique styling and strong eco-credentials. Contemporary bedrooms feature reclaimed wood furnishings. Good breakfasts with homemade granola, Cumbrian air-dried meats and home-baked bread.

Morrel's

34 Lake Rd ✉ CA12 5DQ – ☎ (017687) 72 666 Town plan: Z**x**

– www.morrels.co.uk – Closed Monday

Menu £ 18 – Carte £ 23/38 – *(dinner only)*

Popular local eatery with scrubbed wood flooring, etched glass dividers and a buzzy atmosphere. Seasonally changing dishes have subtle Mediterranean influences; some come in two sizes. Good value menus.

at Braithwaite West: 2 mi by A66 -(X)- on B5292✉ Keswick

Cottage in the Wood with rm

Magic Hill, Whinlatter Forest ✉ CA12 5TW – Northwest : 1.75 mi on B 5292 – ☎ (017687) 78 409 – www.thecottageinthewood.co.uk – Closed 4-23 January

10 rm – †£ 88 ††£ 110/215

Menu £ 21/45 **s** – *(closed Sunday, Monday and Tuesday lunch) (bookings essential for non-residents)*

A keenly run restaurant in a superb forest setting, with a lovely terrace and great views over the fells and valley below. Lunch offers robust dishes to satisfy walkers and dinner is more modern; many ingredients are foraged from the surrounding forest. Bedrooms are contemporary; some have whirlpool baths.

at Portinscale West: 1.5 mi by A66✉ Keswick

Swinside Lodge

Newlands ✉ CA12 5UE – South : 1.5 mi on Grange Rd Town plan: X**c**

– ☎ (017687) 72 948 – www.swinsidelodge-hotel.co.uk – Restricted opening January and December

7 rm (dinner included) – †£ 108/138 ††£ 172/240

Rest – Menu £ 45 **s** – *(dinner only) (bookings essential for non-residents)*

Whitewashed Georgian house in a countryside location, boasting lovely views over the fells. Local info in reception. Two small, traditional country house lounges filled with books and antiques, including an old jukebox. Comfortable bedrooms with homemade biscuits. Formal dining room has a house party atmosphere and offers a set 4 course menu.

KESWICK

Bank St	Z	2
Borrowdale Rd	Z	3
Brackenrigg Drive	Z	5
Brundholme Rd	X	6
Chestnut Hill	X	8
Church St	Z	10
Crosthwaite Rd	X	12
Derwent St	Z	13
High Hill	Z	14
Main St	Z	
Manor Brow	X	17
Market Square	Z	18
Museum Square	Z	19
Otley Rd	Z	20
Park Horse Yard	Z	21
Police Station Court	Z	22
Ratcliffe Pl.	Z	23
St Herbert St	Z	24
Standish St	Z	25
Station St	Z	26
The Crescent	Z	27
The Hawthorns	Y	29
The Headlands	Z	31
Tithebarn St	Z	32

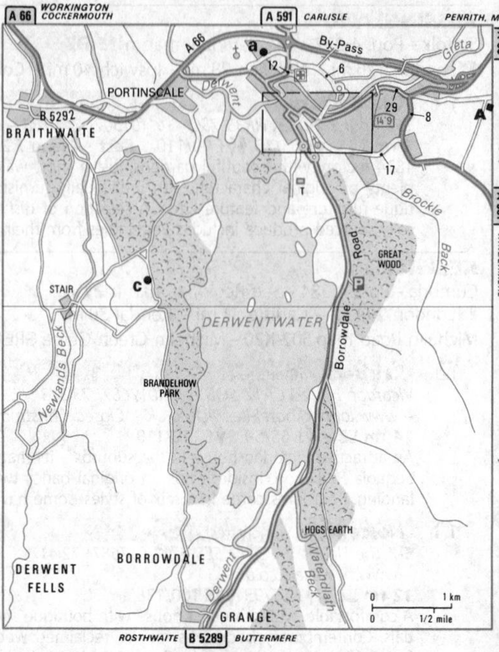

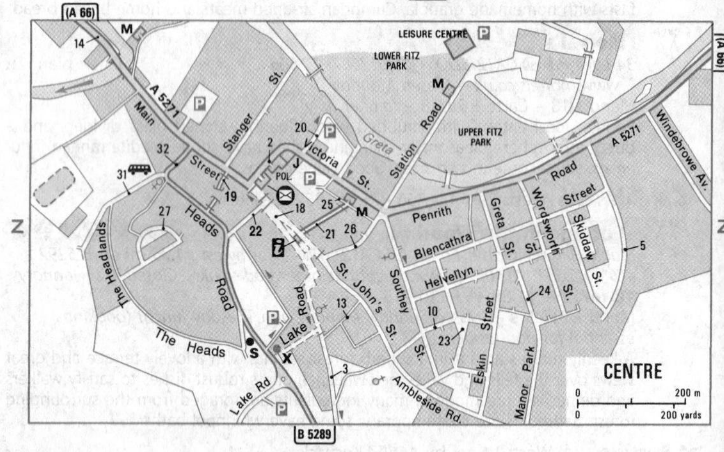

KETTLESING ➜ See Harrogate
North Yorkshire – Michelin Road map 502-P21

KEYSTON
Cambridgeshire – Pop. 257 – ✉ Huntingdon – See Regional map n°**14**-A2
▶London 75 mi – Cambridge 29 mi – Northampton 24 mi
Michelin Road map 504-S26

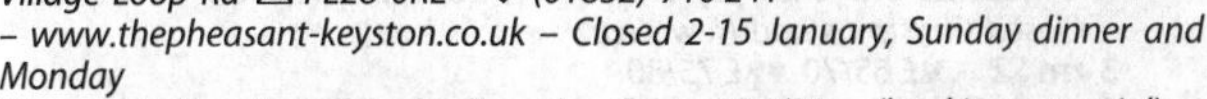

Pheasant

Village Loop Rd ✉ PE28 0RE – ✆ (01832) 710 241 – www.thepheasant-keyston.co.uk – Closed 2-15 January, Sunday dinner and Monday

Menu £ 16 (lunch and early dinner) – Carte £ 24/39 – *(booking essential)*

Hidden away in a sleepy hamlet, this is a big pub with enormous character; think exposed beams, hunting scenes, John Bull wallpaper and a stuffed albino pheasant. Wide-ranging seasonal menu includes a 'classic' section; excellent value set menu. Warm, attentive staff and delightful rear terrace.

KIBWORTH BEAUCHAMP

Leicestershire – Pop. 3 550 – ✉ Leicester – See Regional map n°**16**-B2

London 85 mi – Birmingham 49 mi – Leicester 6 mi – Northampton 17 mi

Michelin Road map 504-Q/R26

Lighthouse

9 Station St ✉ LE8 0LN – ✆ (0116) 279 62 60 – www.lighthousekibworth.co.uk – Closed 1 week Christmas-New Year, Sunday, Monday and bank holidays

Menu £ 15 (weekdays) – Carte £ 24/36 – *(dinner only) (booking essential)*

Deep blue painted building with a crisp white interior decorated with coastal pictures and other nautical knick-knacks; it might have a relaxed atmosphere but the tables are smartly laid. The appealing menu has its emphasis firmly on fresh seafood, offering everything from fish and chips to lobster.

KIBWORTH HARCOURT

Leicestershire – See Regional map n°**16**-B2

London 101 mi – Leicester 9 mi – Coventry 36 mi – Nottingham 41 mi

Michelin Road map 504-R26

Boboli

88 Main St ✉ LE8 0NQ – ✆ (0116) 279 33 03 – www.bobolirestaurant.co.uk – Closed 25-26 December and 1 January

Menu £ 14 (lunch) – Carte £ 19/47

Buzzy, laid-back restaurant with a sunny terrace; formerly a pub, it has a central bar and dining on three levels. Extensive selection of seasonally inspired dishes; flavours are bold and portions, large. Satisfyingly affordable wines.

KILPECK

Herefordshire – See Regional map n°**18**-A3

London 132 mi – Birmingham 71 mi – Liverpool 123 mi – Cardiff 47 mi

Michelin Road map 503-L28

Kilpeck Inn with rm

✉ HR2 9DN – ✆ (01981) 570 464 – www.kilpeckinn.com

4 rm – †£ 70/80 ††£ 70/120 Menu £ 13 (weekday lunch) – Carte £ 18/30

A popular pub which narrowly escaped being turned into private housing thanks to the villagers' valiantly fought 'Save Our Pub' campaign. Its spacious interior and bedrooms are smart, modern and characterful, with impressive green credentials. Menus offer locally sourced meats and old fashioned puddings.

KINGHAM

Oxfordshire – Pop. 547 – See Regional map n°**10**-A1

London 81 mi – Gloucester 32 mi – Oxford 25 mi – Cardiff 91 mi

Michelin Road map 503-P28 and 504

Mill House

✉ OX7 6UH – ✆ (01608) 658 188 – www.millhousehotel.co.uk

21 rm – †£ 107/152 ††£ 120/165 **Rest** – Menu £ 15/33

Privately run house in 10 acres of lawned gardens with a brook flowing through the grounds. Spacious lounge with comfortable armchairs and books. Comfortable, traditionally styled bedrooms. Modern décor suffuses restaurant.

ENGLAND

Moat End without rest
The Moat ✉ OX7 6XZ – by West St – ✆ (01608) 658 090 – www.moatend.co.uk – Closed Christmas and New Year
3 rm – †£ 65/70 ††£ 75/80
Stone-built barn conversion with ponies, hens and countryside views. Cosy sitting room with impressive wood-burning stove. Simple, neatly kept bedrooms. Communal breakfasts include fresh eggs, and bacon and sausages from a local butcher.

The Wild Rabbit Ⓝ with rm
Church St ✉ OX7 6YA – ✆ (01608) 658 389 – www.thewildrabbit.co.uk – Closed Monday
12 rm – †£ 95/225 ††£ 105/225 Carte £ 33/51 – *(booking advisable)*
A charming sandstone inn owned by the Bamford family, of Daylesford fame: its understated Cotswold makeover means flag floors, log fires, leather sofas and expanses of wood and stone. Rustic cooking is British at heart and full of flavour. Bedrooms are named after woodland animals and feature a preponderance of natural products; Rabbit is naturally the best.

Kingham Plough with rm
The Green ✉ OX7 6YD – ✆ (01608) 658 327 – www.thekinghamplough.co.uk – Closed 25 December
7 rm – †£ 80/110 ††£ 95/145 Carte £ 28/47
Rustic, laid-back pub and restaurant located on the green in an unspoilt Cotswold village. It's run by a friendly team and an experienced chef-owner. Menus mix modern, gutsy pub dishes with more ambitious offerings and evolve as new ingredients arrive. Comfy bedrooms await: numbers 2 and 4 are the best.

ENGLAND

KING'S LYNN

Norfolk – Pop. 46 093 – See Regional map n°**14-B1**
London 103 mi – Cambridge 45 mi – Leicester 75 mi – Norwich 44 mi
Michelin Road map 502-V25 and 504 – Michelin Green Guide GREAT BRITAIN

Bank House
King's Staithe Sq ✉ PE30 1RD – ✆ (01553) 660 492 – www.thebankhouse.co.uk
11 rm – †£ 80/120 ††£ 110/160 **Rest** – Carte £ 20/34
Grade II listed townhouse by the river – this is the place where Barclays Bank was founded! Cosy bedrooms come in various shapes and sizes: all have good facilities and excellent bathrooms; some have pleasant views. Dine from a modern European menu in the bar, the charming billiard room or the brasserie.

Market Bistro
11 Saturday Market Pl ✉ PE30 5DQ – ✆ (01553) 771 483 – www.marketbistro.co.uk – Closed 25-26 December, Sunday dinner and Monday
Menu £ 12 (weekday lunch) – Carte £ 19/39
17C beams and a fireplace remain but this relaxed bistro is more up-to-date than its exterior suggests. Fresh, unfussy cooking uses passionately sourced local produce and modern techniques. The chef's wife looks after the service.

at Grimston East: 6.25 mi by A148 ✉ King's Lynn

Congham Hall
Lynn Rd. ✉ PE32 1AH – ✆ (01485) 600 250 – www.conghamhallhotel.co.uk
26 rm – †£ 125/275 ††£ 125/275 – 2 suites
Rest *Congham Hall* – see restaurant listing
Part-Georgian country house in 30 acres of peaceful grounds. Guest areas include a snug bar and a spacious drawing room with a subtle modern style. Opt for a lovely Garden Room by the spa, overlooking the flower or herb gardens.

Congham Hall Ⓝ – Congham Hall Hotel
Lynn Rd. ✉ PE32 1AH – ✆ (01485) 600 250 – www.conghamhallhotel.co.uk
Carte £ 26/40
Start with a drink in the elegant hotel bar, then head for the spacious dining room with its super terrace and garden views. Appealing menus have something to please everyone, from good old classics to more modern fare.

KINGS MILLS → See Channel Islands (Guernsey)

KINGSBRIDGE

Devon – Pop. 6 116 – See Regional map n°**2**-C3

London 236 mi – Exeter 36 mi – Plymouth 24 mi – Torquay 21 mi

Michelin Road map 503-I33

 **Buckland-Tout-Saints**

Goveton ✉ TQ7 2DS – Northeast : 3 mi by A 381 – ✆ (01548) 853 055 – www.tout-saints.co.uk – Closed 2-16 January

16 rm – £ 119/175 £ 150/199 – 2 suites

Rest – Menu £ 18/35 – Carte dinner £ 38/50

Appealing Queen Anne mansion set in large, peaceful grounds. Traditional, antique-furnished interior with wood-panelling in many rooms. Bedrooms vary in shape and size; some have a classic country house feel and others are more contemporary. Choice of two dining rooms offering accomplished dishes.

KINGSTON BAGPUIZE → See Oxford

Oxfordshire – Michelin Road map 503-P28 and 504

KINGSWEAR → See Dartmouth

Devon – Michelin Road map 503-J32

KINTBURY

West Berkshire – Pop. 2 086 – See Regional map n°**10**-B3

London 65 mi – Birmingham 108 mi – Leicester 107 mi – Ealing 60 mi

Michelin Road map 504-P29

Dundas Arms with rm

53 Station Rd ✉ RG17 9UT – ✆ (01488) 658 263 – www.dundasarms.co.uk

8 rm – £ 80/100 £ 100/140 Menu £ 18 (lunch) – Carte £ 24/41

Enjoy pub classics and a pint of real ale in the garden of this 18C inn; set in a wonderful location between the Kennet River and the Kennet and Avon Canal. More adventurous dinner menu. Stylish, comfy bedrooms are fittingly named after birds or fish; the latter have their own private riverside terraces.

KIRKBY FLEETHAM

North Yorkshire – Pop. 556 – See Regional map n°**22**-B1

London 234 mi – Liverpool 124 mi – Leeds 53 mi – Sheffield 84 mi

Michelin Road map 502-P20

Black Horse Inn with rm

Lumley Ln ✉ DL7 0SH – ✆ (01609) 749 010 – www.blackhorsekirkbyfleetham.com

7 rm – £ 75/140 £ 75/160

Menu £ 15 (lunch and early dinner) – Carte £ 21/46 – *(booking advisable)*

Subtly modernised 18C pub with original beams, a smart new flagged floor, a candlelit bar and a rear dining room. Menus range from tasty sharing boards to flavoursome British classics that are a step above your usual pub fare. Stylish bedrooms come with good comforts and designer bathrooms.

KIRKBY LONSDALE

Cumbria – Pop. 1 843 – See Regional map n°**21**-B3

London 259 mi – Carlisle 62 mi – Kendal 13 mi – Lancaster 17 mi

Michelin Road map 502-M21

 **Royal**

Main St ✉ LA6 2AE – ✆ (01524) 271 966 – www.royalhotelkirkbylonsdale.co.uk

14 rm – £ 63/135 £ 85/180 **Rest** – Carte £ 22/42

Well-run Georgian hotel overlooking a characterful town square. The décor is a mix of modern and shabby-chic, and the owner has a keen eye for detail. Bedrooms are spacious; some have free-standing baths in the room. Snug, open-fired lounge and an all-day brasserie serving classics and wood-fired pizzas.

ENGLAND

Plato's

2 Mill Brow ✉ LA6 2AT – ✆ (01524) 274 180 – www.platoskirkbylonsdale.co.uk
8 rm ☕ – †£ 80/100 ††£ 92/160 **Rest** – Carte £ 20/40
Georgian-style townhouse once home to Plato Harrison wine merchants. Tastefully decorated bedrooms blend modern furnishings with period charm and come with thoughtful extras. The all-day coffee-shop-cum-café offers an extensive range of modern, international dishes ranging from tapas to tasting boards.

Sun Inn with rm

6 Market St ✉ LA6 2AU – ✆ (015242) 71 965 – www.sun-inn.info – Closed Monday lunch
11 rm ☕ – †£ 78/158 ††£ 108/178 Menu £ 30 (dinner) – Carte £ 26/38
17C inn with characterful beamed bar and more formal, smartly furnished restaurant, which comes into its own in the evening. Pub classics and tapas-style small plates at lunch; dinner is a more serious affair. Well-lit, modern bedrooms boast quality linen and thoughtful extras; delicious breakfasts.

at Lupton Northwest: 4.75 mi on A65

Plough with rm

Cow Brow ✉ LA6 1PJ – ✆ (015395) 67 700 – www.theploughatlupton.co.uk
6 rm ☕ – †£ 85/125 ††£ 115/195 Carte £ 22/35
A homely former coaching inn with exposed beams, antique tables, comfy sofas and open fires, set on the main road running from the Lake District to North Yorkshire. Choose from an appealing menu of traditional dishes. Smart, individually styled bedrooms with roll-top baths complete the picture.

ENGLAND

KIRKBY STEPHEN

Cumbria – Pop. 1 522 – See Regional map n°**21**-B2
London 296 mi – Carlisle 46 mi – Darlington 37 mi – Kendal 28 mi
Michelin Road map 502-M20

Augill Castle

✉ CA17 4DE Northeast : 4.25 mi by A 685 – ✆ (01768) 341 937 – www.stayinacastle.com
15 rm ☕ – †£ 140/200 ††£ 140/280
Rest – Menu £ 30 – *(dinner only) (booking essential) (residents only)*
A carefully restored, castellated folly filled with period furniture and antiques. There are three interconnecting sitting rooms with vast open fires and a dining room with an ornate plaster ceiling; traditional dishes are taken at a communal table. Many of the bedrooms have four-posters or roll-top baths.

KIRKBY THORE

Cumbria – Pop. 758 – See Regional map n°**21**-B2
London 275 mi – Preston 68 mi – Sunderland 68 mi – Newcastle upon Tyne 68 mi
Michelin Road map 502-M20

Bridge

✉ CA10 1UZ on A66 – ✆ (01768) 362 766 – www.thebridgebistro.co.uk – Closed dinner Sunday-Thursday
Carte £ 21/38
Remodelled village pub with a bright extension and a bistro feel. It's open all day and for dinner on Fri and Sat. Cooking has a likeable simplicity, with the odd Asian touch, and there's a tempting display of cakes on the counter.

KIRKBYMOORSIDE

North Yorkshire – Pop. 2 751 – See Regional map n°**23**-C1
London 244 mi – Leeds 61 mi – Scarborough 26 mi – York 33 mi
Michelin Road map 502-R21

Brickfields Farm without rest

Kirby Mills ✉ YO62 6NS – East : 0.75 mi by A 170 on Kirby Mills Industrial Estate rd – ✆ (01751) 433 074 – www.brickfieldsfarm.co.uk

8 rm – £ 60 £ 100/130

Red-brick former farmhouse set in 16 acres. Modern bedrooms have lovely bathrooms; some open onto terraces and one features a 17C four-poster marriage bed. Enjoy local meats and homemade preserves in the conservatory breakfast room.

Cornmill without rest

Kirby Mills ✉ YO62 6NP – East : 0.5 mi by A 170 – ✆ (01751) 432 000 – www.kirbymills.co.uk

5 rm – £ 55/78 £ 75/125

Charming 18C cornmill with a pleasant courtyard and gardens; look for the mill race running beneath the glass panel in the characterful breakfast room. The cosy lounge and elegant bedrooms are set in the old farmhouse and stables.

KIRKWHELPINGTON

Northumberland – Pop. 353 – ✉ Morpeth – See Regional map n°**24-A2**

London 305 mi – Carlisle 46 mi – Newcastle upon Tyne 20 mi

Michelin Road map 501-N/O18 and 502 – Michelin Green Guide GREAT BRITAIN

Shieldhall

Wallington ✉ NE61 4AQ – Southeast : 2.5 mi by A 696 on B 6342 – ✆ (01830) 540 387 – www.shieldhallguesthouse.co.uk – Closed Christmas-New Year

4 rm – £ 60/68 £ 80/98 **Rest** – Menu £ 30

Early 17C farmhouse and outbuildings, where Capability Brown's uncle once lived. Mix of rustic and country house guest areas; library-lounge has garden views. Individually styled bedrooms, with furniture handmade by the owner. Beamed, flag-floored dining room for classical British dishes and Aga-cooked breakfasts.

KIRTLINGTON

Oxfordshire – See Regional map n°**10-B2**

London 70 mi – Bicester 11 mi – Oxford 16 mi

Michelin Road map 503-Q28

Dashwood rm,

South Green, Heyford Rd ✉ OX5 3HJ – ✆ (01869) 352 707 – www.thedashwood.co.uk – Closed 25 December-3 January

12 rm – £ 80/110 £ 110/135, £ 13

Rest – Menu £ 13 (lunch and early dinner) – Carte £ 23/42 – *(closed Sunday and Monday lunch)*

Grade II listed former pub and barn, built in classic Cotswold stone; popular with visitors to Bicester Village. Clean, fresh, uncluttered bedrooms are decorated in a contemporary style; Room 1 is the best, with air con and a spacious bathroom. Modern European menu served in informal, ground floor restaurant.

KNARESBOROUGH

North Yorkshire – Pop. 15 484 – See Regional map n°**22-B2**

London 217 mi – Bradford 21 mi – Harrogate 3 mi – Leeds 18 mi

Michelin Road map 502-P21

Newton House without rest

5-7 York Pl ✉ HG5 0AD – ✆ (01423) 863 539 – www.newtonhouseyorkshire.com

12 rm – £ 60/95 £ 95/125

Listed Georgian townhouse with a spacious lounge, an honesty bar and traditional bedrooms complete with books, sweets and mini-bars. Breakfast is a highlight, with Aga-baked garden fruits, homemade granola and rare breed meats.

at Ferrensby Northeast: 3 mi on A6055

XX **General Tarleton Inn** with rm

Boroughbridge Rd ✉ HG5 0PZ – ✆ (01423) 340 284 – www.generaltarleton.co.uk
13 rm ☕ – †£ 75/137 ††£ 129/150
Menu £ 15 (lunch and early dinner) – Carte £ 25/41
18C coaching inn with a chic cocktail bar, a smart restaurant, a wicker-furnished conservatory and a large terrace. Menus offer a good range of hearty, classical dishes with a seasonal Yorkshire base. Bedrooms feature solid oak furnishings and come with home-baked biscuits; ask for one of the newer rooms.

KNOWSTONE

Devon ✉ South Molton – See Regional map n°**2-C1**
▶London 183 mi – Bristol 78 mi – Cardiff 109 mi – Plymouth 78 mi

Masons Arms (Mark Dodson)

✉ *EX36 4RY – ✆ (01398) 341 231 – www.masonsarmsdevon.co.uk – Closed first week January, 1 week mid February, 10 days August-September, Sunday dinner and Monday*
Menu £ 25 (lunch)/36 – Carte £ 36/48 – *(booking essential)*
Pretty 13C thatched inn set in Exmoor's foothills, with a cosy bar and a bright dining room featuring a celestial ceiling mural. The experienced owners offer sophisticated cooking of French and British classics, using first class local produce. Flavours are pronounced and assured, and service is friendly.
➜ Ham hock croquette, pea purée and mint butter sauce. Monkfish wrapped in prosciutto, salmon sausage and scallops, orange & balsamic sauce. White chocolate parfait, marmalade glaze.

ENGLAND

KNUTSFORD

Cheshire East – Pop. 13 191 – See Regional map n°**20-B3**
▶London 187 mi – Chester 25 mi – Liverpool 33 mi – Manchester 18 mi
Michelin Road map 502-M24 and 503

XX **Belle Epoque Brasserie** with rm

60 King St ✉ WA16 6DT – ✆ (01565) 633 060 – www.thebelleepoque.com – Closed Monday
7 rm ☕ – †£ 95 ††£ 115
Menu £ 15 (lunch and early dinner) – Carte £ 26/52
Long-standing restaurant with striking exterior features and an impressive art nouveau interior; look out for the lovely mosaic floor. Relaxed brasserie-style dining, featuring British classics, grills and a few more modern dishes. Bedrooms are stylish and contemporary.

at Mobberley Northeast: 2.5 mi by A537 on B5085 ✉ Knutsford

Hinton without rest

Town Ln ✉ WA16 7HH – on B 5085 – ✆ (01565) 873 484 – www.thehinton.co.uk
6 rm ☕ – †£ 45/48 ††£ 63/72
Welcoming creamwashed guesthouse on the main road through the village, with a homely, comfortable lounge and bright, well-kept bedrooms offering good facilities. Linen-clad breakfast room, or eat in the conservatory, overlooking the garden.

at Lower Peover Southwest: 3.25 mi by A50 on B5081

Bells of Peover

The Cobbles ✉ WA16 9PZ – ✆ (01565) 722 269 – www.thebellsofpeover.com
Menu £ 17 (lunch) – Carte £ 23/39
16C coaching inn down a narrow cobbled lane – whose regulars once included Generals Eisenhower and Patton. Cosy, open-fired bar and three tastefully decorated, contemporary dining rooms. The refined, balanced dishes are keenly priced.

LA PULENTE

➜ See Channel Islands (Jersey)
– Michelin Road map 503-P33

LA HAULE → See Channel Islands (Jersey)

– Michelin Road map 503-L33

LALEHAM

Surrey – See Regional map n°**7-C1**

London 20 mi – Bristol 110 mi – Cardiff 143 mi – Southampton 63 mi

Three Horseshoes

25 Shepperton Rd ✉ TW18 1SE – ✆ (01784) 455 014 – www.3horseshoeslaleham.co.uk – Closed 26 December

Carte £ 23/48

A pub with 17C origins but 21C sensibilities; take a seat in one of several smart rooms or in the pretty walled garden. The menu's got something for everyone from sandwiches and salads to meaty main courses, pub classics and sharing plates.

LAMESLEY

Tyne and Wear – See Regional map n°**24-B2**

London 273 mi – Sheffield 130 mi – Nottingham 153 mi – York 85 mi

Stables Lodge without rest

South Farm ✉ NE11 0ET – ✆ (0191) 492 17 56 – www.thestableslodge.co.uk

4 rm – †£ 69/95 ††£ 89/159

Converted stone barn and outbuildings with a comfy, characterful style. Rustic, open-plan guest areas with heavy wood furniture and warm fabrics and colours. Bedrooms are spacious and cosy with modern facilities; one has its own hot tub.

LANCASTER

Lancashire – Pop. 48 085 – See Regional map n°**20-A1**

London 252 mi – Blackpool 26 mi – Bradford 62 mi – Burnley 44 mi

Michelin Road map 502-L21 – Michelin Green Guide GREAT BRITAIN

Ashton

Wyresdale Rd ✉ LA1 3JJ – Southeast : 1.25 mi by A 6 on Clitheroe rd – ✆ (01524) 68 460 – www.theashtonlancaster.com

5 rm – †£ 100/120 ††£ 120/180 **Rest** – Menu £ 25 **s**

Georgian house in lawned gardens; personally run by friendly owner. Good-sized bedrooms are decorated in bold colours and feature a blend of modern and antique furniture. Small, informal dining room; home-cooked comfort food makes good use of local produce.

LANGAR

Nottinghamshire – See Regional map n°**16-B2**

London 132 mi – Boston 45 mi – Leicester 25 mi – Lincoln 37 mi

Michelin Road map 502-R25

Langar Hall

✉ NG13 9HG – ✆ (01949) 860 559 – www.langarhall.co.uk

12 rm – †£ 90/140 ††£ 110/199 – 1 suite

Rest – Menu £ 25 (lunch and early dinner) – Carte £ 26/51

Characterful Georgian manor surrounded by over 20 acres of pastoral land and ponds; its antique-furnished bedrooms named after those who've featured in the house's history. Dine by candlelight in the elegant, pillared dining room; classically based cooking features veg from the kitchen garden and local game.

LANGHO → See Blackburn

Lancashire – Michelin Road map 502-M22

LANGTHWAITE → See Reeth

North Yorkshire – Michelin Road map 502-O20

LAPWORTH

Warwickshire – Pop. 2 100 – See Regional map n°**19-C2**

London 108 mi – Birmingham 23 mi – Leicester 47 mi – Coventry 19 mi

Boot Inn

Old Warwick Rd ✉ *B94 6JU* – ✆ *(01564) 782 464* – *www.bootinnlapworth.co.uk*
Menu £ 15 (lunch and early dinner) – Carte £ 23/40 – *(booking essential)*
Large, buzzy red-brick pub close to the M40, boasting a large terrace, a traditional quarry-floored bar and a modern first floor restaurant. Dishes range from sandwiches, a picnic board and sharing plates to more sophisticated specials.

LASKILL → See Hawnby

North Yorkshire – Michelin Road map 502-Q21

LAVENHAM

Suffolk – Pop. 1 413 – ✉ Sudbury – See Regional map n°**15-C3**
London 66 mi – Cambridge 39 mi – Colchester 22 mi – Ipswich 19 mi
Michelin Road map 504-W27 – Michelin Green Guide GREAT BRITAIN

Swan

rest,

High St ✉ *CO10 9QA* – ✆ *(01787) 247 477* – *www.theswanatlavenham.co.uk*
45 rm – £ 105 £ 195/350 – 1 suite
Rest *Brasserie* – see restaurant listing
Rest *Gallery* – Menu £ 17/40 **s**
Characterful 15C coaching inn with delightful, timbered lounges and a superbly atmospheric bar. Beamed, individually decorated bedrooms have a subtle contemporary style. Eat in the smart brasserie or from a modern menu under a timbered roof and a minstrels' gallery – with piano accompaniment at weekends.

Lavenham Priory without rest

Water St ✉ *CO10 9RW* – ✆ *(01787) 247 404* – *www.lavenhampriory.co.uk*
– *Closed Christmas-New Year*
6 rm – £ 87/97 £ 120/203
Part-13C, Grade I listed priory in a historic town, with gorgeous gardens and a mini parterre. The characterful interior features an inglenook fireplace, Elizabethan murals, a Jacobean staircase and an atmospheric dining room. Heavily beamed bedrooms have feature beds and roll-top or slipper baths.

Great House with rm

Market Pl ✉ *CO10 9QZ* – ✆ *(01787) 247 431* – *www.greathouse.co.uk* – *Closed 3 weeks January, 2 weeks summer, Sunday dinner, Monday and lunch Tuesday*
3 rm – £ 95/125 £ 99/225, £ 12 – 2 suites
Menu £ 19/34 – Carte £ 39/50
Passionately run restaurant on the main square of an attractive town; its impressive Georgian façade concealing a timbered house with 14C origins. Choose between two dining rooms and a smart enclosed terrace. Concise menus offer ambitious dishes with worldwide influences and a French heart. Stylish, contemporary décor blends well with the old beams in the bedrooms.

Brasserie – Swan Hotel

High St ✉ *CO10 9QA* – ✆ *(01787) 247 477* – *www.theswanatlavenham.co.uk*
Carte £ 23/41
Smart hotel restaurant which blends modern furnishings with traditional elements of the historic inn in which it resides. In winter, sit by the fire; in summer, sit on the terrace overlooking the gardens. Classic bistro menu.

LAWHITTON

Cornwall – See Regional map n°**2-C2**
London 221 mi – Bristol 136 mi – Cardiff 156 mi – Plymouth 26 mi

Primrose Cottage without rest

✉ *PL15 9PE Southeast : 1.25 mi on B 3362* – ✆ *(01566) 773 645*
– *www.primrosecottagesuites.co.uk* – *Closed Christmas*
3 rm – £ 70/90 £ 90/130
Part-18C house with a friendly owner and lovely gardens leading down to the river. Good-sized bedrooms boast their own entrances, separate sitting rooms and afford great country views. Complimentary wine and homemade cakes; light suppers available in your room.

LEDBURY

Herefordshire – Pop. 8 862 – See Regional map n°**18-B3**
London 119 mi – Birmingham 53 mi – Bristol 58 mi
Michelin Road map 503-M27 and 504

Feathers

High St ✉ HR8 1DS – ✆ (01531) 635 266 – www.feathers-ledbury.co.uk
22 rm – £ 95/125 £ 145/245
Rest *Quills* – Menu £ 19 – Carte £ 29/41 – *(dinner only Friday-Saturday and lunch Sunday)*
Rest *Fuggles* – Menu £ 19 (weekday dinner) – Carte £ 29/40
Family-run, 16C black and white timbered coaching inn. Comfy bedrooms are a clever blend of old and new: those in the main inn are the most characterful, while the 'Superior' rooms are the most contemporary. Dine from modern seasonal menus in linen-clad Quills or beneath hop hung beams in informal Fuggles.

at Trumpet Northwest: 3.25 mi on A438 ✉ Ledbury

Verzon with rm

rest,

Hereford Rd ✉ HR8 2PZ – ✆ (01531) 670 381 – www.verzonhouse.com
8 rm – £ 80 £ 100/150 Menu £ 20 (weekday lunch) – Carte £ 26/44
Smartly restored Georgian manor house with a surprisingly stylish interior and a laid-back vibe. The chic restaurant offers a menu of precisely prepared, classic British dishes which show respect for fine local ingredients. Seductive modern bedrooms are named after cider apples; most have country views.

ENGLAND

LEEBOTWOOD

Shropshire – See Regional map n°**18-B2**
London 171 mi – Birmingham 55 mi – Shrewsbury 10 mi
Michelin Road map 503-L26

The Pound

✉ SY6 6ND – ✆ (01694) 751 477 – www.thepound.org.uk – Closed one week autumn, Sunday dinner and Monday
Carte £ 20/31
This 15C pub is not as characterful as its thatched exterior leads you to expect: inside, it's modern, with smartly laid tables and plenty of space. Precise, accomplished cooking, with some of the best fish and chips around!

LEEDS

Kent – See Regional map n°**9-C2**
London 41 mi – Ealing 53 mi – Stratford 41 mi – Bromley 33 mi
Michelin Road map 504-V30

Leeds Castle

✉ ME17 1PL – ✆ (01622) 767 823 – www.leeds-castle.co.uk – Closed 25 December
17 rm – £ 90/120 £ 120/200
Rest *Great British Kitchen* – Menu £ 25 – Carte £ 22/31 – *(dinner only)*
This unique accommodation is in the grounds of 900 year old Leeds Castle. Stay in smart, modern bedrooms in the old 1920s staff accommodation blocks or a more historic room in the Maiden's Tower (an old Tudor bake house beside the castle). The timbered café morphs into a candlelit restaurant in the evening.

LEEDS

West Yorkshire – Pop. 474 632 – See Regional map n°**22**-B2
London 204 mi – Liverpool 75 mi – Manchester 43 mi – Newcastle upon Tyne 95 mi
Michelin Road map 502-P22 – Michelin Green Guide GREAT BRITAIN

© Foundry

Hotels

Malmaison

1 Swinegate ✉ LS1 4AG – ☎ (0113) 398 10 00 – www.malmaison.com Town plan: GZ**n**
100 rm – †£ 139/159 ††£ 139/159, ☕ £ 15 – 1 suite
Rest – Menu £ 16/20 – Carte £ 19/39
Chic, boutique hotel in the former offices of the city's tram and bus department; hence the name of the stylish suite, 'Depot'. Generously sized bedrooms have warm colour schemes and good comforts. Smart, intimate guest areas include a relaxing bar and a modern take on a brasserie.

Doubletree by Hilton

2 Wharf Approach, Granary Wharf ✉ LS1 4BR – ☎ (0113) 241 10 00 – www.doubletree.com Town plan: FZ**c**
333 rm – †£ 69/149 ††£ 69/149, ☕ £ 17 – 6 suites
Rest *City Café* – Menu £ 20 – Carte £ 24/42
Modern business hotel overlooking the canal basin. Photos of the city's industrial landmarks hang on white walls; well-equipped bedrooms boast iMac TVs and panoramic city views. Relax on the quayside terrace or in the 13th floor sky lounge. The chic restaurant serves modern cuisine.

Quebecs without rest

9 Quebec St ✉ LS1 2HA – ☎ (0113) 244 89 89 – www.quebecshotel.co.uk – Closed 23-27 December Town plan: FZ**a**
43 rm – †£ 70/110 ††£ 80/265, ☕ £ 15 – 2 suites
Interesting 19C building; formerly a Liberal Club. Original features include wood-panelling, an oak staircase and stained glass windows depicting Yorkshire cities. Bedrooms blend the classic with the contemporary and offer good comforts.

New Ellington

23-25a York Pl ✉ LS1 2EY – ☎ (0113) 204 21 50 – www.thenewellington.com – Closed 23-27 December Town plan: FZ**x**
34 rm ☕ – †£ 85/195 ††£ 85/195 – 1 suite
Rest *Digby's* – Carte £ 22/44 – *(closed Sunday and bank holidays) (dinner only)*
Named after composer and bandleader Duke Ellington, and featuring themed prints and framed sheet music. Classical bedrooms are well-equipped, with fridges, Nespresso machines and numerous audio-visual connections; iPods and games consoles can be borrowed. Basement restaurant offers original modern menus.

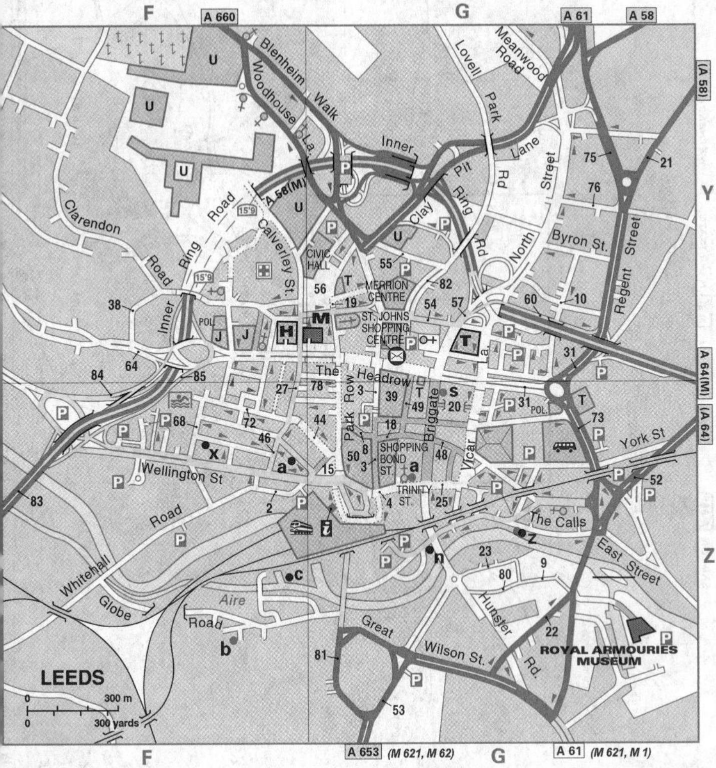

Street	Grid	No.
Aire St.	FZ	2
Albion St	GZ	3
Boar Lane	GZ	4
Bond St	GZ	8
Bowman Lane	GZ	9
Bridge St.	GY	10
Briggate	GZ	
City Square	GZ	15
Commercial St	GZ	18
Cookridge St.	GY	19
County Arcade	GZ	20
Cross Stamford St	GY	21
Crown Point Rd	GZ	22
Dock St	GZ	23
Duncan St	GZ	25
Eastgate	GZ	31
East Parade	FGZ	27
Hanover Way	FY	38
Headrow Centre	GZ	39
Headrow (The)	GY	
Infirmary St	GZ	44
King St	FZ	46
Kirkgate	GZ	48
Lands Lane	GZ	49
Leeds Shopping Plaza	GZ	50
Marsh Lane	GZ	52
Meadow Lane	GZ	53
Merrion Centre	GY	
Merrion St.	GY	54
Merrion Way	GY	55
Millennium Square	GY	56
New Briggate	GY	57
New York Rd.	GY	60
Park Lane	FY	64
Queen St	FZ	68
St John's Centre	GY	
St Paul's St.	FZ	72
St Peter's St	GZ	73
Sheepscar St South	GY	75
Skinner Lane	GY	76
South Parade	FGZ	78
Trinity St Shopping Centre	GZ	
Victoria Rd	GZ	81
Wade Lane	GY	82
Waterloo St	GZ	80
Wellington Rd	FZ	83
Westgate	FZ	85
West St	FZ	84

42 The Calls

42 The Calls ✉ *LS2 7EW – ✆ (0113) 244 00 99 – www.42thecalls.co.uk – Closed 3 days Christmas* Town plan: GZ**z**

38 rm – ♦£ 75/185 ♦♦£ 85/185, ☕ £ 15 – 3 suites

Rest *Brasserie Forty 4* – see restaurant listing

Converted 18C grain mill on the banks of the River Aire. Many of the well-equipped bedrooms display original beams, steel girders or industrial machinery; choose one with a river view. Comprehensive, award-winning breakfasts.

Is breakfast included? If it is, the cup symbol ☕ appears after the number of rooms.

ENGLAND

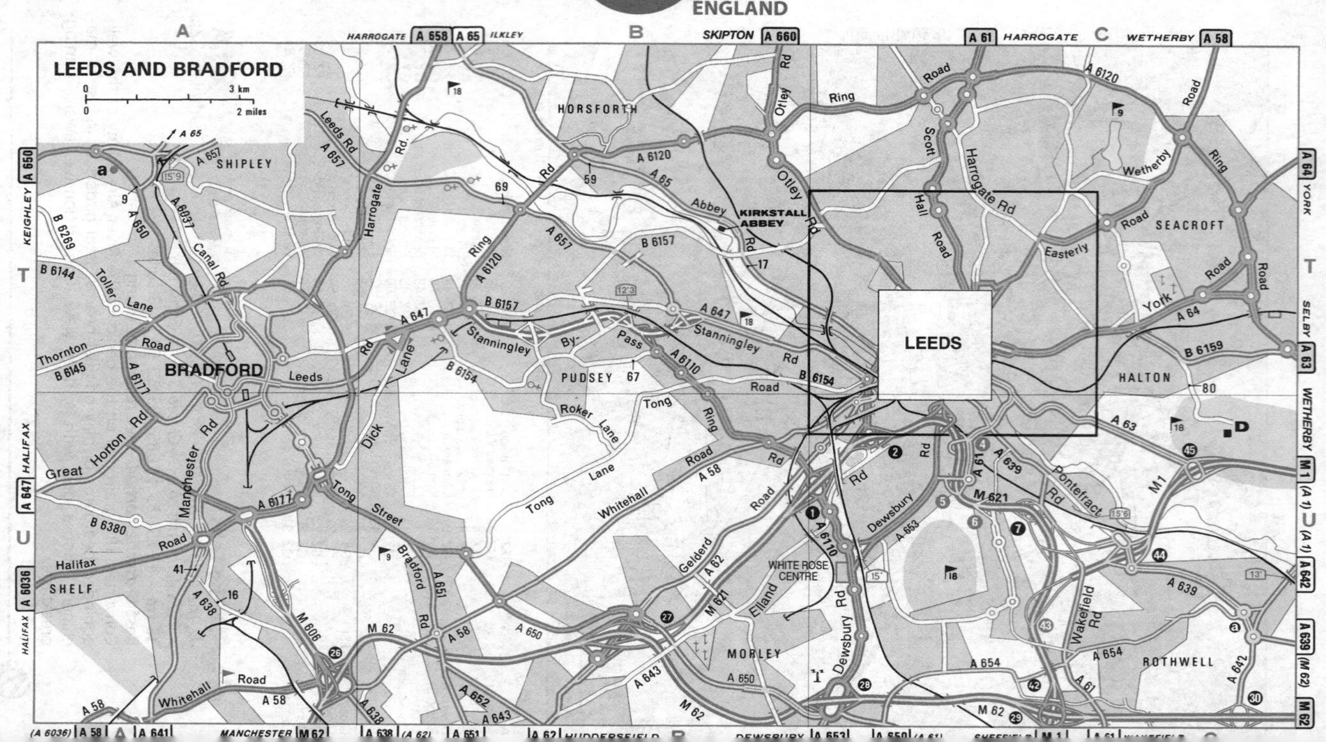
LEEDS AND BRADFORD
0 3 km
0 2 miles
HARROGATE A 658 A 65 ILKLEY
SKIPTON A 660
A 61 HARROGATE
WETHERBY A 58
A 64 YORK
SELBY A 63
WETHERBY M 1 (A 1)
(A 1) A 642
A 639 (M 62)
M 62
KEIGHLEY A 650
HALIFAX A 647
HALIFAX A 6036
(A 6036) A 58
A 641
MANCHESTER M 62
A 638 (A 62)
A 651
A 62 HUDDERSFIELD
DEWSBURY A 653
A 650 (A 61)
SHEFFIELD M 1
A 61 WAKEFIELD
LEEDS
BRADFORD
SHIPLEY
HORSFORTH
KIRKSTALL ABBEY
SEACROFT
HALTON
PUDSEY
MORLEY
ROTHWELL
SHELF
WHITE ROSE CENTRE
Harrogate Rd
Scott Hall Road
Ring Road
Otley Rd
Abbey Rd
Wetherby Road
Easterly Road
York Road
Stanningley By-Pass
Stanningley Rd
Ring Road
Tong Road
Roker Lane
Tong Lane
Whitehall Road
Gelderd Road
Elland Road
Dewsbury Rd
Pontefract Rd
Wakefield Rd
Leeds Rd
Canal Rd
Toller Lane
Thornton Road
Great Horton Rd
Manchester Rd
Halifax Road
Dick Lane
Tong Street
Bradford Rd
Whitehall Road

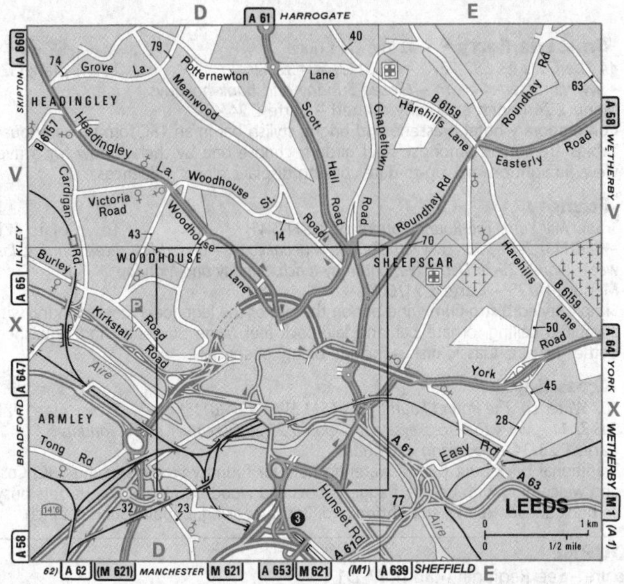

Restaurants

XX Fourth Floor at Harvey Nichols

107-111 Briggate ✉ LS1 6AZ – ✆ (0113) 204 80 00 Town plan: GZ**s**
– www.harveynichols.com – Closed 25 December, 1 January, Easter Sunday and dinner Sunday and Monday

Menu £ 20 (lunch and early dinner) – Carte £ 32/43 – *(booking essential at lunch)*

Bright, stylish dining room with rooftop views, metal fretwork screens and a Scandic feel; located on the top floor of a chic store. Watch the chefs prepare tasty, modern, globally influenced dishes. Pleasant service is from a smart team.

XX Crafthouse

Trinity Leeds (5th Floor), 70 Boar Ln ✉ LS1 6HW Town plan: GZ**a**
– ✆ (0113) 897 0444 – www.crafthouse-restaurant.co.uk – Closed 25 December

Menu £ 23 (lunch and early dinner) – Carte £ 26/71

Located in the Trinity shopping centre, with a wraparound terrace and rooftop views. It has a dark, moody, masculine feel; the open-plan kitchen and counter take centre stage. Menus offer European classics and meats from the Josper grill.

XX Angelica

Trinity Leeds (6th Floor), 70 Boar Ln ✉ LS1 6HW Town plan: GZ**a**
– ✆ (0113) 897 0099 – www.angelica-restaurant.co.uk – Closed 25 December

Carte £ 16/42

Set above its sister 'Crafthouse' and also boasting a terrace and skyline views. A large bar dominates the room and cocktails are a speciality. Cooking is simple, modern and global – sharing plates and seafood from the Raw Bar feature.

XX **Brasserie Forty 4** – 42 The Calls Hotel

44 The Calls ✉ LS2 7EW – ✆ (0113) 234 32 32 Town plan: GZ**z**
– www.brasserie44.com – Closed Sunday and bank holidays
Menu £ 24 (lunch and early dinner) – Carte £ 24/42
Contemporary hotel brasserie and bright, stylish bar in an 18C former warehouse. Tables are spread amongst steel girders; choose one by the window for a river view. Straightforward, up-to-date cooking displays global influences.

X **Foundry**

1 Saw Mill Yard, The Round Foundry ✉ LS11 5WH Town plan: FZ**b**
– ✆ (0113) 245 03 90 – www.thefoundrywinebar.co.uk – Closed first week January, last week August, 25-26 December, Saturday lunch, Sunday and Monday
Menu £ 14/25 – Carte £ 21/60
Simply styled bistro-cum-wine bar on the site of the legendary steel foundry, with a vaulted ceiling, ornate bar and laid-back feel. Wine box ends and 'squashed' bottles feature. Classic dishes include plenty of specials.

Cross Keys

107 Water Ln, The Round Foundry ✉ LS11 5WD – ✆ (0113) Town plan: FZ**b**
243 37 11 – www.the-crosskeys.com – Closed 25-26 December and 1 January
Carte £ 23/34 – *(booking essential)*
Traditional brick-built pub: a watering hole for foundry workers in the 19C. Cosy and welcoming with beams, flagged floors and wood-burning stoves. It gets busy, so book ahead. Hearty, straightforward, British cooking; popular Sunday lunch.

ENGLAND

LEGBOURNE

Lincolnshire – See Regional map n°**17**-**D1**
▶London 151 mi – Kingston upon Hull 48 mi – Nottingham 68 mi – Peterborough 66 mi

XX **Michael Bullamore at The Queens Head**

Station Rd ✉ LN11 8LL – ✆ (01507) 604 803 – www.thequeensheadlegbourne.co.uk – Closed 3 weeks Christmas-New Year, Sunday and Monday
Menu £ 30/45 – *(booking essential)*
Intimate former pub in a rural setting. Modern wallpaper and bright prints stand out against a lovely old tiled floor. The locally taught chef offers a tasting menu of creative modern dishes and herbs and salad are from the garden.

LEICESTER

Leicester – Pop. 443 760 – See Regional map n°**16**-B2
▶London 107 mi – Birmingham 43 mi – Coventry 24 mi – Nottingham 26 mi
Michelin Road map 502-Q26 and 503 – Michelin Green Guide GREAT BRITAIN

Leicester Marriott

Smith Way, Grove Park, Enderby ✉ LE19 1SW Town plan: AY**z**
– Southwest : 4 mi by A 5460 off A 563 at junction 21 of M1 – ✆ (0116) 282 01 00 – www.leicestermarriott.co.uk
227 rm – †£ 139/159 ††£ 159/169, ☕ £ 16 – 1 suite
Rest *Mixx* – Carte £ 24/38 – *(dinner only and Sunday lunch)*
Purpose-built hotel on a suburban business park. Stylish open-plan guest areas include an atrium lounge and informal café. Uniform bedrooms boast a good level of facilities. Smart executive lounge and excellent leisure club. East meets West in the restaurant; choose from the buffet or an eclectic à la carte.

Belmont

De Montfort St ✉ LE1 7GR – ✆ (0116) 254 47 73 Town plan: CY**c**
– www.belmonthotel.co.uk – Closed 24-25 December and 1 January
75 rm ☕ – †£ 69/99 ††£ 79/119 – 1 suite
Rest *Windows on New Walk* – Menu £ 18 (lunch) – Carte £ 25/39 – *(closed Saturday lunch and Sunday dinner)*
Friendly, family-run hotel in a city suburb, made up of a collection of houses – each with its own classical style. Spacious guest areas and a contemporary bar. Bedrooms vary in shape and size but all are modern and offer good facilities. Formal restaurant serves classical dishes with a Mediterranean edge.

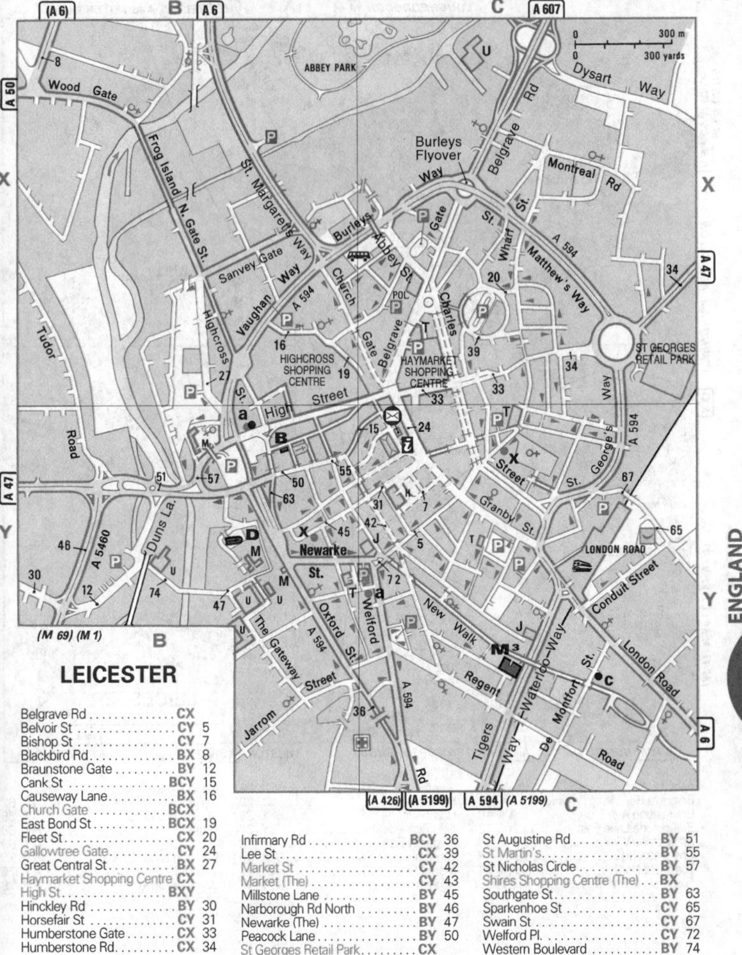

LEICESTER

Hotel Maiyango

13-21 St Nicholas Pl ✉ LE1 4LD – ✆ (0116) 251 88 98 Town plan: BY**a**
– www.maiyango.com – Closed 25-26 December
14 rm – †£ 79/200 ††£ 79/200, ☕ £ 8 – 1 suite
Rest *Maiyango* – see restaurant listing
Privately owned city centre hotel in a 150 year old shoe factory. Stylish interior with a trendy bar opening onto a terrace overlooking the rooftops. Spacious, individually designed bedrooms boast bespoke wood furniture and a colonial feel.

Chutney Ivy

41 Halford St ✉ LE1 1TR – ✆ (0116) 251 1889 Town plan: CY**x**
– www.chutneyivy.com – Closed 25-26 December,1 January, Saturday lunch and Sunday
Menu £ 9 (weekday lunch) – Carte £ 14/33
Keenly run former warehouse with a smart industrial feel; its floor-to-ceiling windows open onto the pavement. Mix of modern and classic dishes, with influences from Hyderabad, Goa and Bengal. Watch the chefs in the open kitchen.

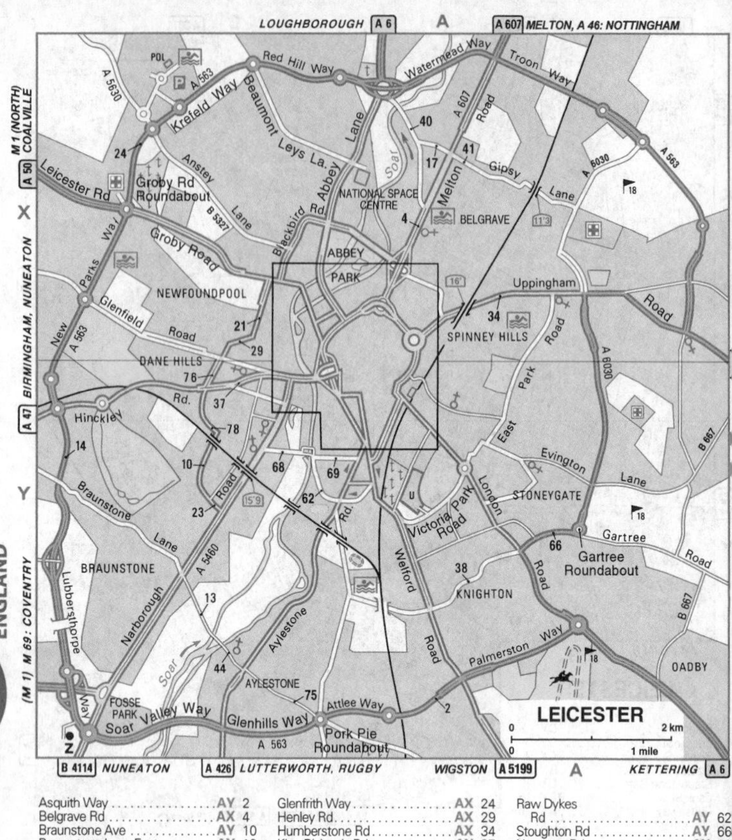

Asquith Way	AY	2	Glenfrith Way	AX	24	Raw Dykes Rd	AY	62
Belgrave Rd	AX	4	Henley Rd	AX	29	Stoughton Rd	AY	66
Braunstone Ave	AY	10	Humberstone Rd	AX	34	Upperton Rd	AY	68
Braunstone Lane East	AY	13	King Richards Rd	AY	37	Walnut St	AY	69
Braunstone Way	AY	14	Knighton Rd	AY	38	Wigston Lane	AY	75
Checketts Rd	AX	17	Loughborough Rd	AX	40	Woodville Rd	AY	76
Fosse Rd North	AX	21	Marfitt St	AX	41	Wyngate Drive	AY	78
Fullhurst Ave	AY	23	Middleton St	AY	44			

XX **Maiyango** - Hotel Maiyango

13-21 St Nicholas Pl ✉ LE1 4LD – ✆ (0116) 251 88 98 Town plan: BY**a**
– www.maiyango.com – Closed 25-26 December and lunch Sunday-Tuesday
Menu £ 30/45

Glass-fronted restaurant in a stylish hotel. Round dark wood booths and silk drapes create an Oriental feel and there's a relaxed, funky vibe. Refined cooking uses local farm and allotment produce, and is Mediterranean and Asian-led.

X **Boot Room**

27-29 Millstone Ln ✉ LE1 5JN – ✆ (0116) 262 25 55 Town plan: BY**x**
– www.thebootroomeaterie.co.uk – Closed 2 weeks January, 2 weeks summer, Sunday and Monday
Menu £ 11 (weekday lunch) – Carte £ 24/37

Set in an interesting, brick-built former shoe factory; the original cast iron girders and pillars still remain. Simple styling, friendly service and a warm, laid-back feel. Unfussy British cooking with some European and Asian influences.

Shivalli

21 Welford Rd ✉ LE2 7AD – ✆ (0116) 255 01 37 Town plan: CY**a**
– www.shivallirestaurant.com – Closed 25 December
Carte £ 11/18
Simple, part-panelled restaurant with Indian artefacts on the walls. Appealing South Indian, vegetarian menu with most dishes also suitable for vegans. Tasty, authentic cooking with honest flavours. Good value thalis and buffet lunches.

LEIGH-ON-SEA

Southend-on-Sea – See Regional map n°**13-C3**
London 37 mi – Brighton 85 mi – Dover 86 mi – Ipswich 57 mi
Michelin Road map 504-W29

Sandbank

1470 London Rd ✉ SS9 2UR – ✆ (01702) 719 000
– www.sandbankrestaurant.co.uk – Closed Sunday dinner and Monday
Menu £ 15/20 (weekdays) – Carte £ 30/40
Former bank in a parade of shops; now a spacious restaurant with a high ceiling, a classic black and white theme and a tropical fish tank in a dramatic feature wall. Wide-ranging menu of well-presented dishes with clear flavours.

LEINTWARDINE

Herefordshire ✉ Craven Arms – See Regional map n°**18-A2**
London 156 mi – Birmingham 55 mi – Hereford 24 mi – Worcester 40 mi
Michelin Road map 503-L26

The Lion with rm

rest,

✉ SY7 0JZ – ✆ (01547) 540 203 – www.thelionleintwardine.co.uk – Closed 25 December
8 rm – †£ 85/95 ††£ 105/125 Carte £ 25/46
18C, riverside inn set by an attractive medieval bridge and owned by a local mineral water producer. Casual, country style interior with a bar, a choice of dining areas, a terrace and a garden. Classic, satisfying dishes use local produce. Smart, modern bedrooms with good facilities; some have river views.

LEVISHAM → See Pickering

North Yorkshire – Michelin Road map 502-R21

LEWDOWN

Devon – See Regional map n°**2-C2**
London 238 mi – Exeter 37 mi – Plymouth 29 mi
Michelin Road map 503-H32

Lewtrenchard Manor

✉ EX20 4PN South : 0.75 mi by Lewtrenchard rd – ✆ (01566) 783 222
– www.lewtrenchard.co.uk
14 rm – †£ 120/200 ††£ 145/235 – 1 suite
Rest *Lewtrenchard Manor* – see restaurant listing
Hugely impressive Grade II listed Jacobean manor house in mature grounds. The characterful antique-furnished interior features huge fireplaces, ornate oak panelling, intricately designed ceilings and mullioned windows. Bedrooms are spacious and well-equipped; those in the coach house are the most modern.

Lewtrenchard Manor – Lewtrenchard Manor Hotel

✉ EX20 4PN South : 0.75 mi by Lewtrenchard rd – ✆ (01566) 783 222
– www.lewtrenchard.co.uk
Menu £ 20/50 – *(booking essential)*
Intimate wood-panelled dining room in a Jacobean manor house. Cooking is contrastingly modern yet refreshingly unadorned; flavoursome garden produce features. For a more unique experience book 'Purple Carrot' (the chef's table).

LEWES

East Sussex – Pop. 17 297 – See Regional map n°**8-A3**
London 53 mi – Brighton 8 mi – Hastings 29 mi – Maidstone 43 mi
Michelin Road map 504-U31 – Michelin Green Guide GREAT BRITAIN

Shelleys

High St ✉ BN7 1XS – ✆ (01273) 472 361 – www.the-shelleys.co.uk
19 rm – £ 130/160 ££ 160/190 – 1 suite **Rest** – Menu £ 15/33
Formerly an inn and before that, a private house dating back to 1577, owned by the great poet's family. Spacious, classically styled bedrooms include a four-poster room and a suite overlooking the lovely gardens. The intimate dining room, with its elegant chandeliers, overlooks the lawns.

Real Eating Company

18 Cliffe High St ✉ BN7 2AJ – ✆ (01273) 402 650 – www.real-eating.co.uk – Closed 25 December and Sunday dinner
Carte £ 20/43
Buzzy all-day restaurant offering cakes throughout the day in the café and an extensive menu of seasonal local produce in the rustic dining room. Cooking is honest and unfussy and features plenty of hearty British favourites.

at East Chiltington Northwest: 5.5 mi by A275 and B2116 off Novington Lane✉ Lewes

Jolly Sportsman

Chapel Ln ✉ BN7 3BA – ✆ (01273) 890 400 – www.thejollysportsman.com – Closed 25 December
Menu £ 15 (lunch) – Carte £ 26/41 – *(booking essential)*
An olive green, clapperboard pub, popular with the locals. Choose from interesting bar bites, good value set menus, a rustic, British-based à la carte and blackboard specials; many of the herbs and fruits are from their own polytunnel.

LEYBURN

North Yorkshire – Pop. 2 183 – See Regional map n°**22-B1**
London 251 mi – Darlington 25 mi – Kendal 43 mi – Leeds 53 mi
Michelin Road map 502-O21

Clyde House without rest

5 Railway St ✉ DL8 5AY – ✆ (01969) 623 941 – www.clydehouse.com – Closed 8-21 January
5 rm – £ 50/55 ££ 85/95
18C former coaching inn on the main market square, run by an experienced owner and immaculately kept throughout. Small, cosy sitting room and cottagey breakfast room. Smart, comfortable bedrooms with good quality soft furnishings, hair dryers and bathrobes. Extensive buffet and 'full Yorkshire' breakfasts.

Sandpiper Inn with rm

Market Pl ✉ DL8 5AT – ✆ (01969) 622 206 – www.sandpiperinn.co.uk – Closed Tuesday in winter and Monday
2 rm – £ 80/90 ££ 90/100 Carte £ 24/41 **s**
A friendly Yorkshire welcome is extended at this characterful, stone-built, part-16C pub just off the main square. Subtle, refined cooking offers a modern take on the classics and the skilled kitchen prides itself on the provenance of its ingredients. Two country-chic style bedrooms offer excellent comforts.

LICHFIELD

Staffordshire – Pop. 32 877 – See Regional map n°**19-C2**
London 128 mi – Birmingham 16 mi – Derby 23 mi
Michelin Road map 502-O25 and 503 – Michelin Green Guide GREAT BRITAIN

Netherstowe House

Netherstowe Ln ✉ WS13 6AY – Northeast : 1.75 mi following signs for A 51 and A 38, off Eastern Ave – ✆ (01543) 254 270 – www.netherstowehouse.com
17 rm (dinner included) – †£ 128 ††£ 185/215 – 8 suites
Rest – Menu £ 16/39
Rest *Steakhouse Brasserie* – Carte £ 28/45
Extensively restored 19C country house; professionally run by a family team. Period lounges and elegant, luxurious bedrooms come with antique furnishings and original fireplaces; modern apartments with kitchenettes are located in the grounds. The elegant, formal restaurant offers ambitious modern cooking; the atmospheric cellar brasserie specialises in local steaks.

St Johns House without rest

28 St John St ✉ WS13 6PB – ✆ (01543) 252 080 – www.stjohnshouse.co.uk – Closed 25-30 December
9 rm – †£ 70 ††£ 105/115
Impressive Regency townhouse fronted by large columns. Enter through a beautiful tiled hallway to a contemporary drawing room with ornate cornicing and chandeliers. Individually styled bedrooms have a modern, understated feel.

Wine House

27 Bird St ✉ WS13 6PW – ✆ (01543) 419 999 – www.thewinehouselichfield.co.uk
Menu £ 19 (lunch) – Carte £ 26/51
Smart red-brick restaurant with a loyal local following. There's an open-fired bar at one end and a dining room at the other; it takes its name from the impressive glass wine cellar. Classically based menus have the occasional modern twist.

at Wall South: 2.75 mi by A5127

The Trooper

Watling St ✉ WS14 0AN – ✆ (01543) 480 413 – www.thetrooperwall.co.uk
Carte £ 18/42
Open fires welcome you into the lounge, where you'll find locals sitting around a central bar; to the rear, an extension leads out onto a huge terrace and garden. Tasty, restaurant-style dishes, supplemented by pub classics at lunch.

ENGLAND

LIFTON

Devon – Pop. 1 180 – See Regional map n°**2-C2**
London 238 mi – Bude 24 mi – Exeter 37 mi – Launceston 4 mi
Michelin Road map 503-H32

Arundell Arms

Fore St ✉ PL16 0AA – ✆ (01566) 784 666 – www.arundellarms.com
25 rm – †£ 95/120 ††£ 180/200 **Rest** – Carte £ 33/48
Family-run roadside coaching inn with cosy, traditional bedrooms and access to 20 miles of private fishing on the River Tamar and its tributaries. The characterful lounge and bar serve a brasserie menu, while the restaurant – which overlooks the terrace and gardens – offers classical fare.

LINCOLN

Lincolnshire – Pop. 100 160 – See Regional map n°**17-C1**
London 140 mi – Leeds 73 mi – Nottingham 38 mi
Michelin Road map 502-S24 and 504 – Michelin Green Guide GREAT BRITAIN

Doubletree by Hilton Lincoln

Brayford Wharf North ✉ LN1 1YW – ✆ (01522) 565 180 – www.lincoln.doubletree.com Town plan: Z**a**
115 rm – †£ 85/165 ††£ 95/175 – 8 suites
Rest *Electric* – Menu £ 25 (weekday dinner) – Carte £ 26/40 – *(booking advisable)*
Modern corporate hotel on the site of the old City of Lincoln Electrical works. Minimalistic bedrooms have sleek, contemporary lines; suites overlook the marina. State-of-the-art conference rooms. Smart brasserie with floor to ceiling windows; the modern menu has British influences.

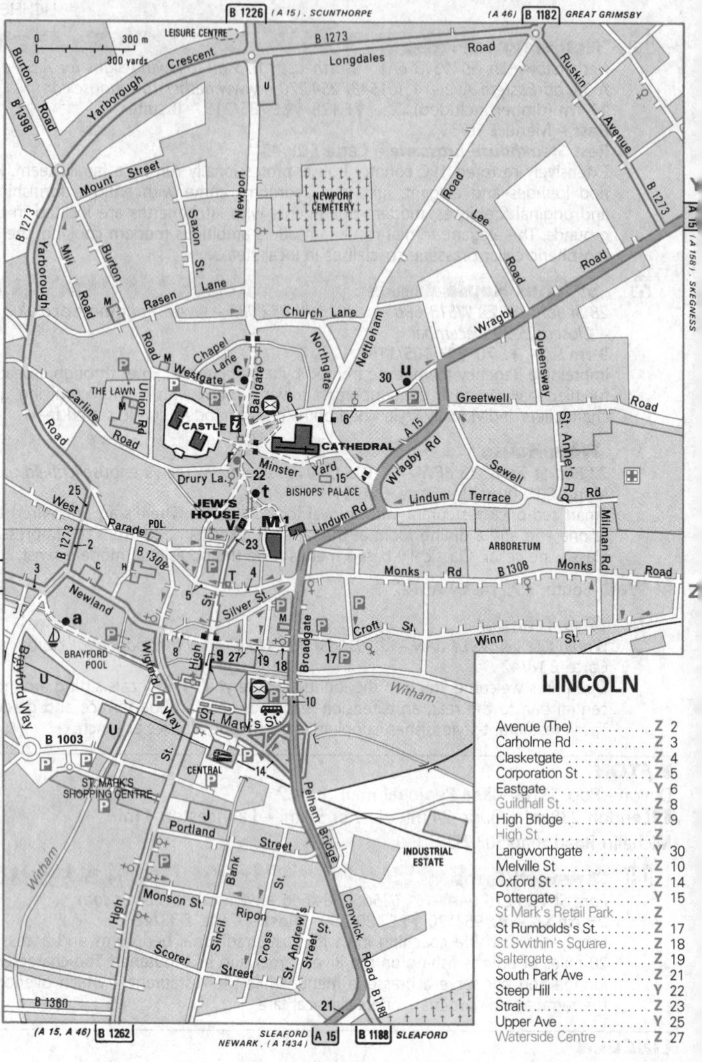

LINCOLN

Street	Zone	No.
Avenue (The)	Z	2
Carholme Rd	Z	3
Clasketgate	Z	4
Corporation St	Z	5
Eastgate	Y	6
Guildhall St	Z	8
High Bridge	Z	9
High St	Z	
Langworthgate	Y	30
Melville St	Z	10
Oxford St	Z	14
Pottergate	Y	15
St Mark's Retail Park	Z	
St Rumbolds's St	Z	17
St Swithin's Square	Z	18
Saltergate	Z	19
South Park Ave	Z	21
Steep Hill	Y	22
Strait	Z	23
Upper Ave	Y	25
Waterside Centre	Z	27

The Rest without rest

55A Steep Hill ✉ LN2 1LR – ✆ (01522) 247 888 Town plan: Y**t**
– www.theresthotellincoln.co.uk

10 rm ☕ – 🚹£ 89/119 🚹🚹£ 89/169

With direct access to the bedrooms from the street, guests can come and go freely at this laid-back hotel. Breakfast is served in the coffee shop-cum-bar. Chic bedrooms feature bespoke furnishings and bathrooms with heated floors.

The sun's out? Enjoy eating outside on the terrace:

Bail House without rest

34 Bailgate ✉ LN1 3AP – ☎ (01522) 541 000 Town plan: Y**c**
– www.bailhouse.co.uk
10 rm – †£ 69/159 ††£ 69/159, ☕ £ 7
Part-14C baronial hall with a Georgian façade and Victorian additions. Modern facilities mix with original features in the characterful bedrooms: one has an exposed Roman wall. Breakfast is served in the neighbouring restaurant.

St Clements Lodge without rest

21 Langworthgate ✉ LN2 4AD – ☎ (01522) 521 532 Town plan: Y**u**
– www.stclementslodge.co.uk
3 rm ☕ – †£ 60 ††£ 75/80
Cosy, Edwardian-style house close to the cathedral and castle (where you can view the Magna Carta). Cheerful owners offer good old-fashioned hospitality. Spacious, well-equipped bedrooms have pine furnishings and a homely feel.

Jews House

15 The Strait ✉ LN2 1JD – ☎ (01522) 524 851 Town plan: Y**v**
– www.jewshouserestaurant.co.uk – Closed 2 weeks January, 2 weeks July, 1 week October, Sunday and Monday
Menu £ 16 (lunch) – Carte £ 30/38
At the bottom of a steep cobbled hill is this cosy stone house dating from 1150; reputedly Europe's oldest surviving dwelling. Bold, ambitious dishes display an eclectic mix of influences – the tasting menu is a hit. Service is charming.

Wig & Mitre

✉ LN2 1LU – ☎ (01522) 535 190 – www.wigandmitre.com Town plan: Y**r**
– Closed 25 December
Menu £ 15 (lunch and early dinner) – Carte £ 21/33
Well-established pub with a cosy bar, period dining rooms and an airy beamed restaurant. Menus offer classical dishes with the odd Mediterranean or Asian influence, alongside daily specials, hearty breakfasts and over 20 wines by the glass.

ENGLAND

LISKEARD

Cornwall – Pop. 9 237 – See Regional map n°**1-B2**
London 261 mi – Exeter 59 mi – Plymouth 19 mi – Truro 37 mi
Michelin Road map 503-G32

Pencubitt Country House

Station Rd ✉ PL14 4EB – South : 0.5 mi by B 3254 on Lamellion rd – ☎ (01579) 342 694 – www.pencubitt.com – Closed January and February
9 rm ☕ – †£ 50/70 ††£ 70/120
Rest – Menu £ 24 – *(Closed Sunday and Monday) (dinner only) (residents only)*
Sympathetically restored Victorian property with delightful views over the gardens and countryside – take it all in from the veranda or the balcony in bedroom 3. Look out too, for the original windows and staircase in the lovely hall. They offer home-cooked dinners, cream teas and picnics, by arrangement.

LISS

Hampshire – Pop. 6 248 – See Regional map n°**7-C2**
London 53 mi – Bristol 104 mi – Cardiff 137 mi – Plymouth 184 mi
Michelin Road map 504-R30

Madhuban Tandoori

94 Station Rd ✉ GU33 7AQ – ☎ (01730) 893 363
– www.madhubanrestaurant.co.uk – Closed 25-26 December and Friday lunch
Carte £ 14/23
Smartly furnished restaurant owned by three enthusiastic brothers. The focus is on fresh north Indian dishes; most of which can be prepared to the desired heat – the menu provides a useful glossary of terms. They also sell their sauces.

LITTLE BEDWYN → See Marlborough

Wiltshire – Michelin Road map 503-P29 and 504

LITTLE COXWELL

Oxfordshire – Pop. 132 – See Regional map n°**10-A2**

London 79 mi – Sheffield 158 mi – Derby 120 mi – York 202 mi

Eagle Tavern with rm

SN7 7LW – (01367) 241 879 – www.eagletavern.co.uk – Closed Sunday dinner and Monday

6 rm – £ 60/70 £ 70/90 Menu £ 12 (weekday lunch) – Carte £ 18/33

Welcoming pub built in 1901 for the farmers of this sleepy hamlet; although it might look slightly different now, a convivial atmosphere still reigns. The self-taught chef cooks the kind of food he himself likes to eat and dishes range from the simple to the complex. Bedrooms are cosy and worth the money.

LITTLE ECCLESTON

Lancashire – See Regional map n°**20-A2**

London 238 mi – Liverpool - 55 mi – Leeds 83 mi – Manchester 51 mi

Cartford Inn with rm

Cartford Ln PR3 0YP – (01995) 670 166 – www.thecartfordinn.co.uk – Closed 25 December and Monday lunch except bank holidays

14 rm – £ 70/110 £ 100/200 Carte £ 21/38

Tiny 17C coaching inn next to the Pilling Marshes, with a series of cosy little rooms; one overlooking the river. Cooking is in the tried-and-tested vein, offering proper pub classics, with signature dishes under the heading of 'Cartford Favourites'. Choose between quirky or French farmhouse style bedrooms.

ENGLAND

LITTLE LANGFORD → See Salisbury

Wiltshire

LITTLE MARLOW → See Marlow

Buckinghamshire

LITTLE PETHERICK → See Padstow

Cornwall – Michelin Road map 503-F32

LITTLE THETFORD → See Ely

Cambridgeshire

LITTLE WILBRAHAM → See Cambridge

Cambridgeshire

LITTLETON → See Winchester

Hants. – Michelin Road map 503-P30 and 504

LITTLEHAMPTON

West Sussex – Pop. 55 706 – See Regional map n°**7-C3**

London 64 mi – Brighton 18 mi – Portsmouth 31 mi

Michelin Road map 504-S31

Bailiffscourt H. & Spa

Climping St, Climping BN17 5RW – West : 2.75 mi by A 259 – (01903) 723 511 – www.hshotels.co.uk

39 rm – £ 189/289 £ 219/559 **Rest** – Menu £ 19/50

Charming, reconstructed medieval manor in immaculately kept gardens. Bedrooms are split between the main house and the outbuildings; the newer rooms are in the grounds and are more suited to families. Beautiful spa facility. Classic country house cooking served in the formal dining room.

Amberley Court without rest

Crookthorn Ln, Climping BN17 5SN – West : 1.75 mi by B 2187 off A 259 – (01903) 725 131 – Closed mid-December to mid-January

3 rm – £ 55 £ 79/89

Sweet little thatched guesthouse with exposed beams and a homely feel, run by a very welcoming owner. Small breakfast room and open-fired seating area. One of the simple, immaculately kept bedrooms is situated in the grounds.

LIVERPOOL

Merseyside – Pop. 552 267 – See Regional map n°**20-A3**
▶London 219 mi – Birmingham 103 mi – Leeds 75 mi – Manchester 35 mi
Michelin Road map 502-L23 and 503-L23 – Michelin Green Guide GREAT BRITAIN

Hilton
3 Thomas Steers Way ✉ L1 8LW – ✆ (0151) 708 42 00 — Town plan: **3**CZ**x**
– www.hilton.co.uk/liverpool
214 rm – †£ 69/295 ††£ 91/339, ☕ £ 15 – 11 suites
Rest *Exchange* – Menu £ 15/35 – Carte £ 21/48
Spacious, light-filled hotel in a waterfront location, with the latest in modern styling and facilities. Floor to ceiling windows in the bedrooms. Trendy cocktail bar, good conference facilities and a well-equipped gym. Accessible menu of international dishes in Exchange.

Malmaison
7 William Jessop Way, Princes Dock ✉ L3 1QZ — Town plan: **3**CY**n**
– ✆ (0151) 229 50 00 – www.malmaison.com
130 rm – †£ 69/250 ††£ 69/250, ☕ £ 16 – 2 suites
Rest *Brasserie* – Menu £ 16 (lunch and early dinner) – Carte £ 23/36 – *(closed Saturday lunch)*
Contemporary hotel with a striking stone and black glass façade, overlooking the marina. Chic bedrooms are decorated in sensuous purple or orange tones and boast sunken baths; two are football-themed suites. Sexy, sophisticated bar and an industrial-style brasserie with pop art and a stylish chef's table.

Hope Street
40 Hope St ✉ L1 9DA – ✆ (0151) 709 30 00 — Town plan: **4**EZ**a**
– www.hopestreethotel.co.uk
89 rm ☕ – †£ 86/200 ††£ 96/210
Rest *London Carriage Works* – see restaurant listing
Minimalist, boutique hotel in two interlinking buildings: bedrooms in the former carriage works have a slightly rustic edge, while those in the old police station are more modern. The top floor suites offer stunning city skyline views.

Hard Days Night
Central Buildings, North John St ✉ L2 6RR – ✆ (0151) 236 19 64 – www.harddaysnighthotel.com – Closed 25 December — Town plan: **3**CY**b**
110 rm – †£ 90/275 ††£ 100/285, ☕ £ 16 – 2 suites
Rest *Blakes* – Menu £ 14 (lunch and early dinner) **s** – Carte dinner £ 28/53 **s**
Unique Beatles themed hotel – their story recounted in artwork from doorstep to rooftop – with contemporary bedrooms featuring original works, and suites styled around Lennon and McCartney. Blakes, named after the designer of the Sgt. Pepper album cover, features a modern brasserie menu.

Hotel Indigo
10 Chapel St ✉ L3 9AG – ✆ (0151) 559 0111 — Town plan: **3**CY**a**
– www.hotelindigoliverpool.com
151 rm – †£ 89/259 ††£ 89/259, ☕ £ 14
Rest *Marco Pierre White Steakhouse Bar & Grill* – ✆ (0151) 559 0555 – Menu £ 10/20 – Carte £ 27/45 – *(closed Saturday lunch)*
Smart, modern hotel on the site of a former cotton trading hall and seaman's mission; characterised by its use of vibrant colours. Compact bedrooms have powerful walk-in showers. Staff are smart and cheery. All-day snacks in the lounge; classic dishes in the brightly decorated restaurant.

Hampton by Hilton without rest
Kings Dock Mill, 7 Hurst St ✉ L1 8DA – ✆ (0871) 902 16 18 – www.liverpoolcitycentre.hamptonbyhilton.com — Town plan: **4**DZ**s**
151 rm ☕ – †£ 59/219 ††£ 59/219
Smart, well-priced hotel, a 10min walk from the city centre, offering good modern comforts. It's worth paying a little extra for the 6th floor rooms, which have great views across the river. Buffet breakfasts. Hands-on staff.

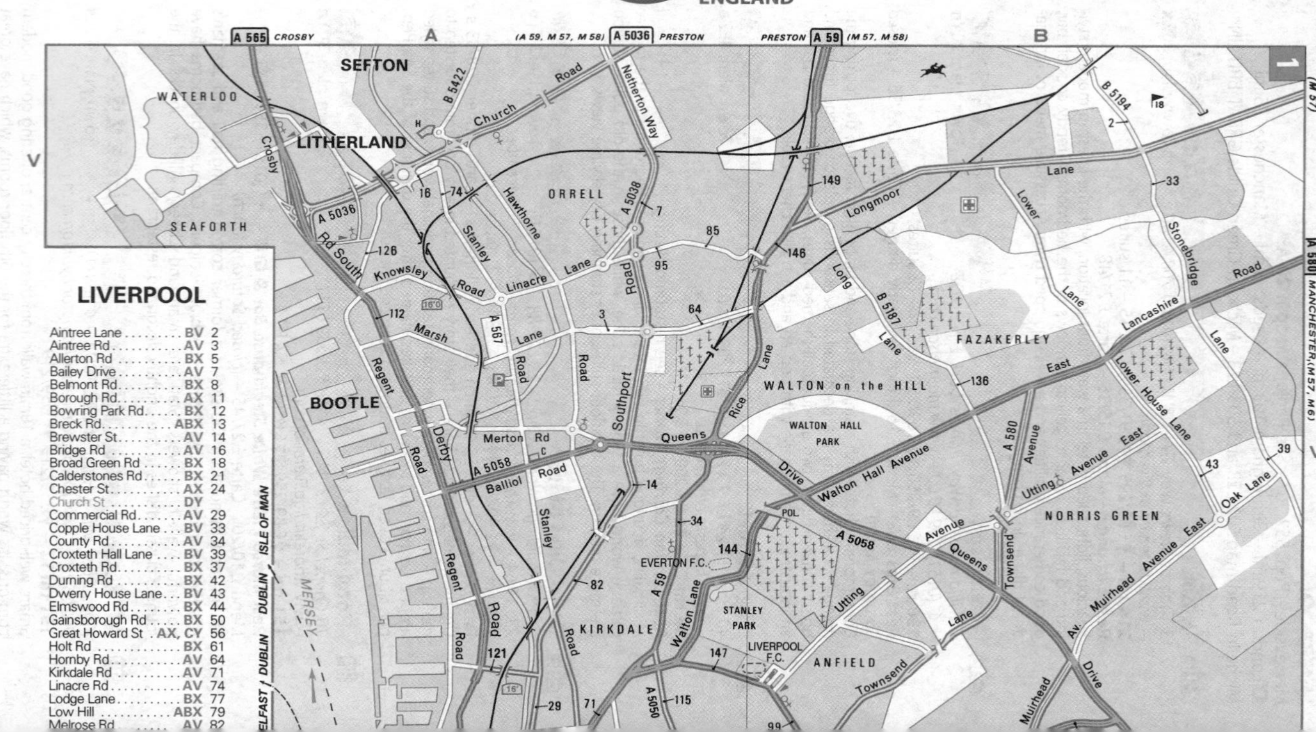

LIVERPOOL

Street	Grid	No.
Aintree Lane	BV	2
Aintree Rd	AV	3
Allerton Rd	BX	5
Bailey Drive	AV	7
Belmont Rd	BX	8
Borough Rd	AX	11
Bowring Park Rd	BX	12
Breck Rd	ABX	13
Brewster St	AV	14
Bridge Rd	AV	16
Broad Green Rd	BX	18
Calderstones Rd	BX	21
Chester St	AX	24
Church St	DY	
Commercial Rd	AV	29
Copple House Lane	BV	33
County Rd	AV	34
Croxteth Hall Lane	BV	39
Croxteth Rd	BX	37
Durning Rd	BX	42
Dwerry House Lane	BV	43
Elmswood Rd	BX	44
Gainsborough Rd	BX	50
Great Howard St	AX, CY	56
Holt Rd	BX	61
Hornby Rd	AV	64
Kirkdale Rd	AV	71
Linacre Rd	AV	74
Lodge Lane	BX	77
Low Hill	ABX	79
Melrose Rd	AV	82

ISLE OF MAN / DUBLIN
DUBLIN / BELFAST

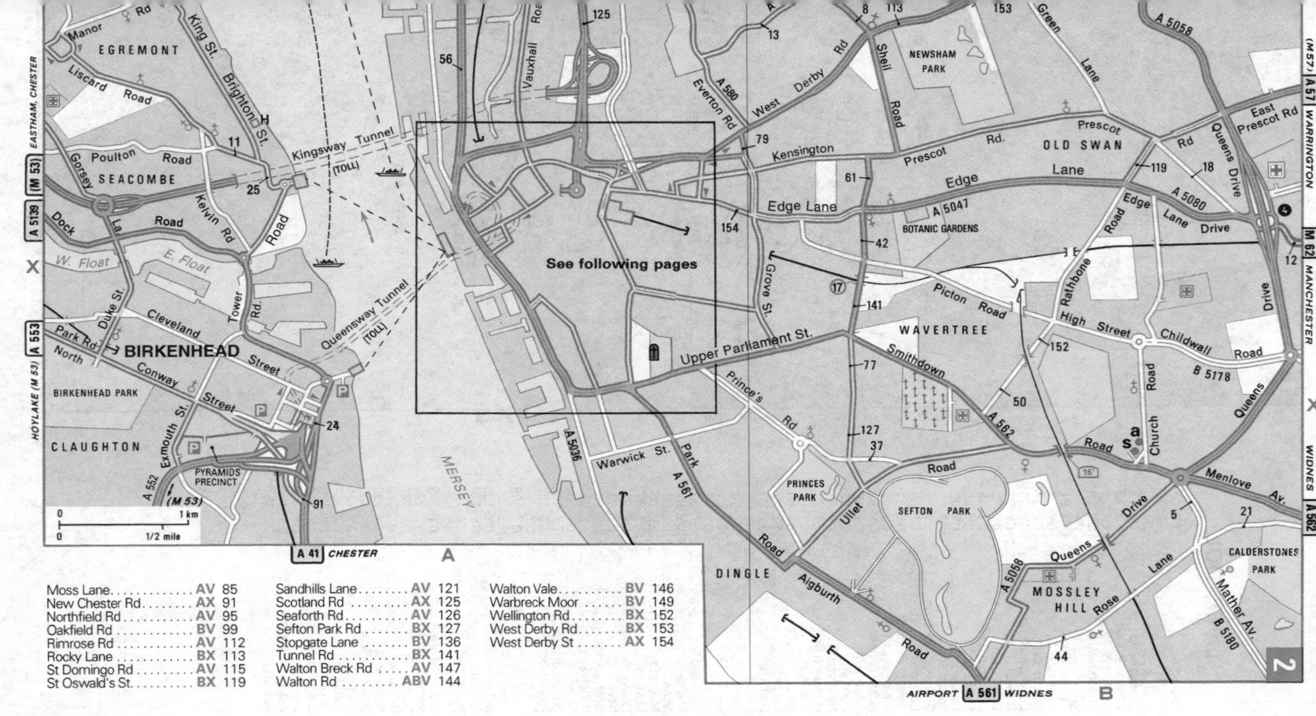

Street	Grid	No.
Moss Lane	AV	85
New Chester Rd	AX	91
Northfield Rd	AV	95
Oakfield Rd	BV	99
Rimrose Rd	AV	112
Rocky Lane	BX	113
St Domingo Rd	AV	115
St Oswald's St.	BX	119
Sandhills Lane	AV	121
Scotland Rd	AX	125
Seaforth Rd	AV	126
Sefton Park Rd	BX	127
Stopgate Lane	BV	136
Tunnel Rd	BX	141
Walton Breck Rd	AV	147
Walton Rd	ABV	144
Walton Vale	BV	146
Warbreck Moor	BV	149
Wellington Rd	BX	152
West Derby Rd	BX	153
West Derby St	AX	154

LIVERPOOL

Argyle St	DZ	6
Blackburne Pl.	EZ	10
Bold St.	DZ	
Brunswick Rd	EY	19
Canada Boulevard	CYZ	22
Canning Pl.	CZ	23
Churchill Way	DY	26
Church St	DY	
Clarence St.	EYZ	27
Clayton Square Shopping Centre	DY	
College Lane	DZ	28
Commutation Row	DY	30
Cook St	CY	32
Crosshall St.	DY	36
Daulby St.	EY	40
Erskine St	EY	45
Fontenoy St	DY	48
Forrest St	DZ	49
George's Dock Lane	CY	51
Grafton St	DZ	53
Great Charlotte St	DY	54
Great Howard St	CY	56
Hatton Garden	DY	57
Haymarket	DY	58
Hood St.	DY	62
Houghton St.	DY	65
Huskisson St.	EZ	66
James St.	CY	68
King Edward St.	CY	69
Knight St	EZ	72
Leece St	EZ	73
Lime St	DY	
Liver St	CZ	76
London Rd	DEY	
Lord St	CDY	
Mansfield St.	DEY	80
Mathew St.	CDY	81
Moss St.	EY	86
Mount St	EZ	88
Myrtle St	EZ	89
Newington St	DZ	92
New Quay	CY	93
North John St	CY	96
Norton St.	EY	97
Parker St	DY	103
Prescot St	EY	105
Prince's Rd	EZ	107
Queen Square	DY	
Ranelagh St	DY	108
Renshaw St	DEZ	
Richmond St.	DY	109
Roe St.	DY	114
St James Pl.	EZ	117
St John's Centre	DY	
St John's Lane	DY	118
School Lane	DYZ	122
Scotland Pl.	DY	123
Sefton St	DZ	129
Seymour St	EY	130
Skelhorne St	DY	133
Stanley St.	CDY	135
Suffolk St.	DZ	137
Tarleton St.	DY	139
Victoria St	DY	143
Water St	CY	150
William Brown St	DY	156
York St.	DZ	157

ENGLAND

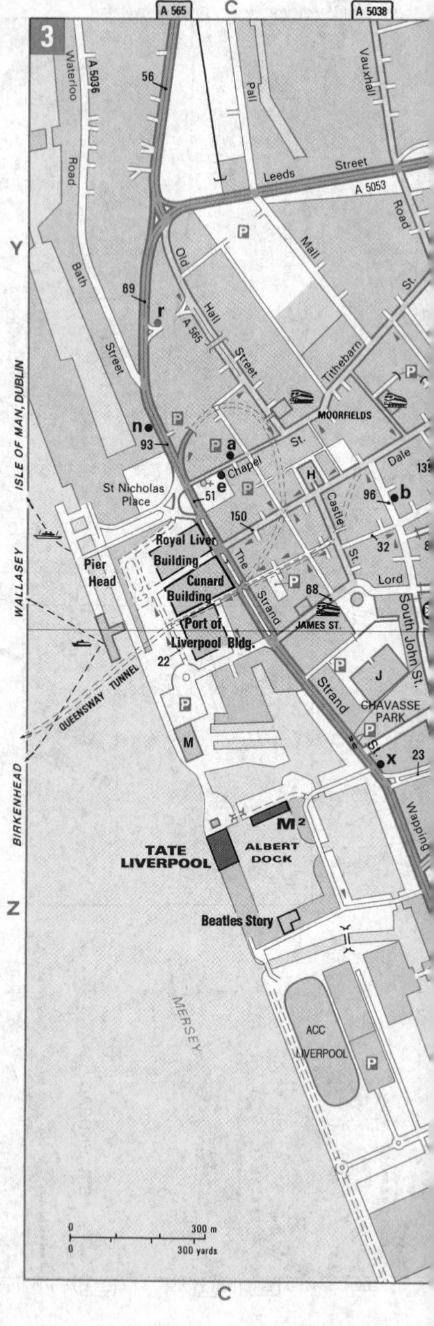

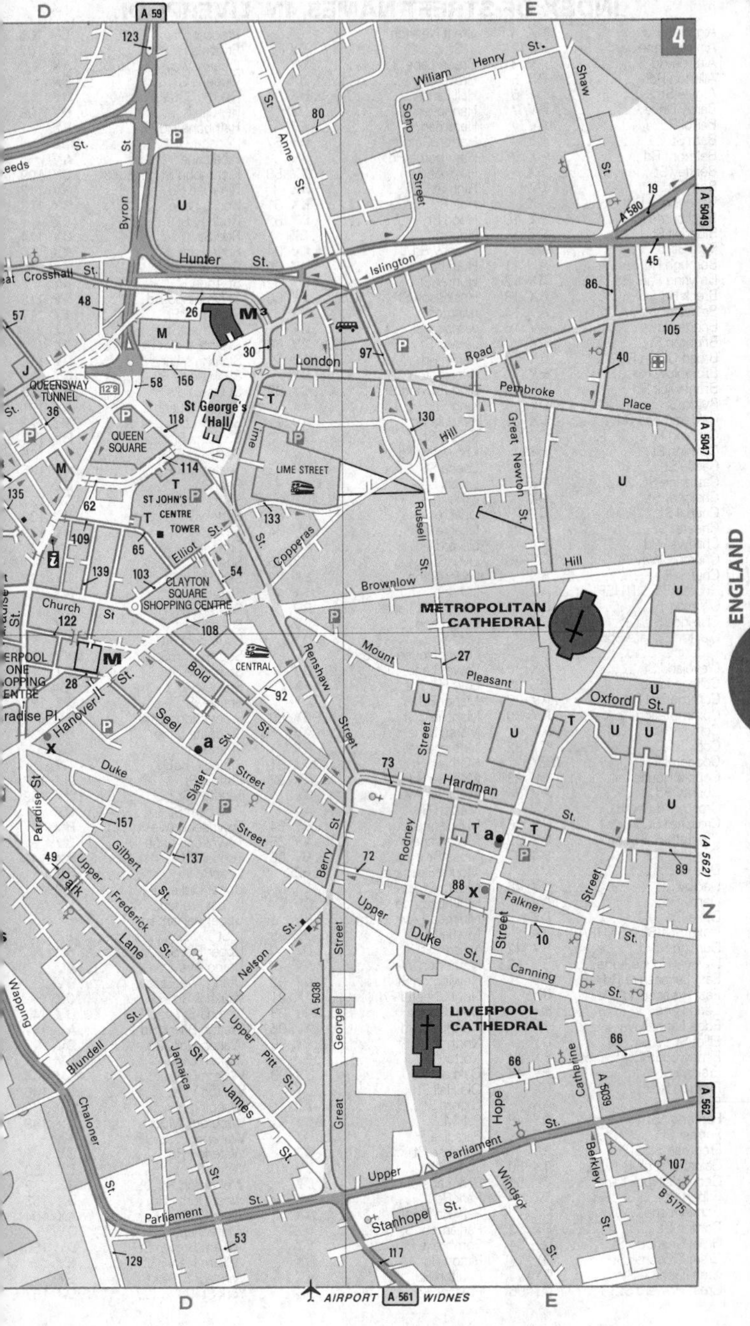
D
E
4
A 59
A 5049
A 580
A 5047
(A 562)
A 562
Y
N
ENGLAND
Leeds
St.
Byron
Hunter St.
Crosshall St.
Islington
William Henry St.
Shaw St.
Soho Street
Anne St.
London Road
Pembroke Place
QUEENSWAY TUNNEL
QUEEN SQUARE
St George's Hall
LIME STREET
Lime St.
ST JOHN'S CENTRE TOWER
Elliot St.
Copperas Hill
Great Newton St.
Russell St.
Hill
Brownlow Hill
CLAYTON SQUARE SHOPPING CENTRE
Church St
LIVERPOOL ONE SHOPPING CENTRE
Paradise Pl.
Paradise St
METROPOLITAN CATHEDRAL
Mount Pleasant
Oxford St.
CENTRAL
Renshaw Street
Bold St.
Hanover St.
Seel Street
Slater St.
Duke Street
Berry St.
Hardman St.
Rodney Street
Falkner St.
Gilbert St.
Upper Frederick St.
Park Lane
Upper Duke St.
Canning St.
Nelson St.
Wapping
Blundell St.
Jamaica St
Upper Pitt St.
James St.
A 5038
Great George Street
LIVERPOOL CATHEDRAL
Hope Street
Catharine
A 5039
Chaloner St.
Parliament St.
Upper Parliament St.
Stanhope St.
Windsor St.
Berkley St.
B 5175
AIRPORT
A 561
WIDNES
123
80
19
45
48
26
57
86
105
30
97
40
58
156
36
118
130
114
135
62
133
109
65
139
103
54
122
108
27
28
92
73
157
137
72
89
49
88
10
66
107
53
117
129
M³
M
J
T
P
U
X
a

INDEX OF STREET NAMES IN LIVERPOOL

ENGLAND

The Nadler without rest
29 Seel St ✉ L1 4AU – ✆ (0151) 705 2626 Town plan: **4**DZ**a**
– www.thenadler.com/liverpool
106 rm – †£ 49/159 ††£ 59/169, ☕ £ 6
Something a little different, this converted 19C mill has rooms ranging from small singles to spacious duplex suites; one with a decked courtyard. All have modern bathrooms and kitchenettes. Pre-order breakfast to be delivered to your room.

Racquet Club rest,
Hargreaves Buildings, 5 Chapel St ✉ L3 9AG Town plan: **3**CY**e**
– ✆ (0151) 236 66 76 – www.racquetclub.org – Closed first week January, 25 December and bank holidays
8 rm – †£ 80/140 ††£ 80/140, ☕ £ 12
Rest *Ziba* – Carte £ 24/39 **s** – *(closed Saturday lunch and Sunday)*
Ornate Victorian building, formerly a Shipping Agency office and then a gentleman's club, boasting a grand façade and a bohemian style. Bedrooms differ greatly both in layout and décor but most feature antique furniture and eclectic art. Airy restaurant; wide-ranging menu of British dishes.

Panoramic 34
West Tower (34th floor), Brook St ✉ L3 9PJ – ✆ (0151) 236 55 34 – www.panoramic34.com – Closed 25-26 December, 1 January and Monday Town plan: **3**CY**r**
Menu £ 22 (lunch) – Carte £ 29/46
On the 34th floor of the city's highest skyscraper you'll find this elegant restaurant with under-lit tables and fabulous 360° views. Ambitious dishes arrive swiftly and are attractively presented; the lunch menu offers good value.

London Carriage Works – Hope Street Hotel
40 Hope St ✉ L1 9DA – ✆ (0151) 705 22 22 Town plan: **4**EZ**a**
– www.thelondoncarriageworks.co.uk
Menu £ 18 (lunch and early dinner) – Carte £ 23/54
Start with a drink in the hotel's lounge-bar, then head to the spacious modern restaurant divided by large shards of glass. The set menu represents the best value, while the à la carte steps things up a gear; both rely on local produce.

60 Hope Street
60 Hope St ✉ L1 9BZ – ✆ (0151) 707 60 60 Town plan: **4**EZ**x**
– www.60hopestreet.com – Closed 26 December and 1 January
Menu £ 25 – Carte £ 28/58
An attractive Grade II listed Georgian house concealing a well-established modern brasserie with battleship grey walls and a smart basement wine bar. Menus feature interesting regional dishes; the set selection provides good value.

Spire
1 Church Rd ✉ L15 9EA – ✆ (0151) 734 50 40 Town plan: **2**BX**a**
– www.spirerestaurant.co.uk – Closed 1-7 January and lunch Saturday-Monday
Menu £ 12 (lunch and early dinner) – Carte £ 25/41
Simple neighbourhood restaurant set in the Penny Lane area of the city. Good value, understated menus offer regional and modern European dishes. Flavoursome cooking and friendly service.

Hanover Street Social
Casartelli Building, 16-20 Hanover St ✉ L1 4AA Town plan: **4**DZ**x**
– ✆ (0151) 709 87 84 – www.hanoverstreetsocial.co.uk – Closed 25 December
Menu £ 11 (weekday lunch) – Carte £ 20/31
Lively restaurant near the old docks, with a smart, rustic interior featuring a metal-topped cocktail bar and exposed bricks and air ducts. All-day menus offer something for everyone, from small plates and grills to charcuterie and oysters.

ENGLAND

X **Neon Jamón** N

12 Southdown Pl ✉ L15 9EH – ✆ (0151) 734 38 40 Town plan: **2**BX**s**
– www.neonjamon.com
Menu £ 7 (weekday lunch) – Carte £ 20/30 – *(bookings not accepted)*
In the bustling Penny Lane, you'll find this equally buzzy, informal tapas bar. Service is friendly and obliging, and dishes are carefully prepared and full of flavour. Sit at the counter or a table backed by bare brick walls.

LIZARD

Cornwall – See Regional map n°**1-A3**
London 326 mi – Penzance 24 mi – Truro 29 mi
Michelin Road map 503-E34 – Michelin Green Guide GREAT BRITAIN

Landewednack House

Church Cove ✉ TR12 7PQ – East : 1 mi by A 3083 – ✆ (01326) 290 877
– www.landewednackhouse.com
5 rm – †£ 55/110 ††£ 110/190 **Rest** – Menu £ 38 **s**
Charming part-17C rectory overlooking Church Cove; take in the view from the delightful gardens. Bedrooms are a mix of shapes and styles but all come with fireplaces and a decanter of sherry. The lovely dining room has a communal table laid with cut crystal glassware and menus are discussed with residents. It's the most southernmost guesthouse in mainland England.

ENGLAND

LONDON

England – Pop. 2 396 830 – See regional map n° **20**-A4
Birmingham 86 mi – Glasgow 221 mi – Leeds 43 mi
Michelin road map 502, 503, 504-N23 – Michelin Green guide GREAT BRITAIN

C. Parker/Axiom Photographic/age fotostock

Index of...

Maps & establishments

Alphabetical index of hotels

Alphabetical index of restaurants

LONDON

LONDON

Starred Restaurants

Bib Gourmand

Good food at moderate prices

Particularly pleasant hotels

Particularly pleasant restaurants

Restaurants by cuisine type

Argentinian

	page
Casa Malevo	489
Zoilo	512

Asian

	page
Bone Daddies	524
E and O	463
Eight over Eight	456
Flesh and Buns	426
Kopapa	425
Singapore Garden	429
Spice Market	520
XO	422
Zen Oriental	445

Austrian

	page
Fischer's	509

Basque

	page
Donostia	511

British creative

	page
Dairy	469
Fera at Claridge's	496

British modern

	page
Anchor and Hope	481
Berners Tavern	508
Bistro Union	469
Bluebird	456
Brown Dog	472
Chelsea Ram	459
Chiswell Street Dining Rooms	434
Corrigan's Mayfair	499
Dean Street Townhouse Restaurant	519
Dinner by Heston Blumenthal	492
Drapers Arms	452
Fox and Grapes	471
Great Queen Street	428
Hampshire Hog	443
Harwood Arms	442
Hereford Road	488
Hoi Polloi	439
Keeper's House	502
Linnea	473
London House	484
Lyle's	440
Magdalen	476
Malt House	442
Market	427
The National Dining Rooms	516
New Angel	488
1901	431
Olympic Café + Dining Room	472
Pantechnicon	491
Paradise by way of Kensal Green	421
Parlour	421
Peasant	451
Picture	511
Plum + Spilt Milk	468
Prince Arthur	438
Prince of Wales	486
Quo Vadis	518
Restaurant at St Paul's Cathedral	435
Rivington Grill (Greenwich)	437
Roast	479
Sands End	442
sixtyone	508
Tate Modern (Restaurant)	480
La Trompette	446
Victoria	472
Well	451
Wells	428

British traditional

	page
Beagle	438
Bedford and Strand	529
Bird of Smithfield	434
Boisdale of Belgravia	533
Boisdale of Bishopsgate	433
Boisdale of Canary Wharf	482
Builders Arms	459
Bull and Last	427
Butlers Wharf Chop House	477
Cadogan Arms	459
Camberwell Arms	478
Canton Arms	470
Crown	475
Dining Room at The Goring	531
Gilbert Scott	468
Grazing Goat	512
Great British	504

LONDON

Greek

Indian

Italian

Japanese

Korean

Lebanese

Mediterranean

Mexican

North-African

North-American

Peruvian

Polish

Spanish

Other world kitchens

Regional/country

Outside dining

Restaurants open late

Time of last orders in brackets

Restaurant		Page
Arbutus (23.30)	X✿	520
L'Atelier de Joël Robuchon (00.00)	XX✿	527
Balthazar (23.30)	XX	528
Bar Boulud (23.30)	XX	492
Bentley's (Oyster Bar) (23.45)	X	504
Boisdale of Belgravia (23.30)	XX	533
Brasserie Max (23.30)	XX	425
Brasserie Zédel (00.00)	XX☺	518
Le Caprice (23.30)	XX	514
Cecconi's (23.15)	XXX	499
Ceviche (23.30)	X	524
Chicken Shop (Kentish Town) (00.00)	X	429
China Tang (23.45)	XXXX	497
Chutney Mary (23.30)	XXX	455
Colbert (23.30)	XX	457
Delaunay (00.00)	XXX	527
Duck and Waffle (00.00)	XX	434
Floridita (23.30)	XX	519
Hakkasan Hanway Place (00.00)	XX✿	424
Hakkasan Mayfair (23.30)	XX✿	501
Haozhan (02.00)	XX	519
Hoi Polloi (01.00)	XX	439
The Ivy (00.00)	XXX	527
J. Sheekey (23.30)	XX	527
J. Sheekey Oyster Bar (23.30)	X	528
Malabar (23.30)	XX	462
Momo (23.15)	XX	501
Mr Chow (23.30)	XX	493
Nobu (02.15)	XX	502
Nobu Berkeley St (00.00)	XX	501
Palomar (23.30)	X☺	522
Plum Valley (23.15)	XX	519
Poissonnerie (23.30)	XX	456
Refuel (00.00)	XX	520
Roka (Bloomsbury) (23.30)	XX	424
Roka (Mayfair) (23.30)	XX	501
Shoryu (23.30)	X	516
Soho Kitchen and Bar (01.00)	X	524
Spuntino (01.00)	X	523
Wild Honey (23.30)	XX✿	500
The Wolseley (00.00)	XXX	514
Yauatcha (23.30)	XX✿	518

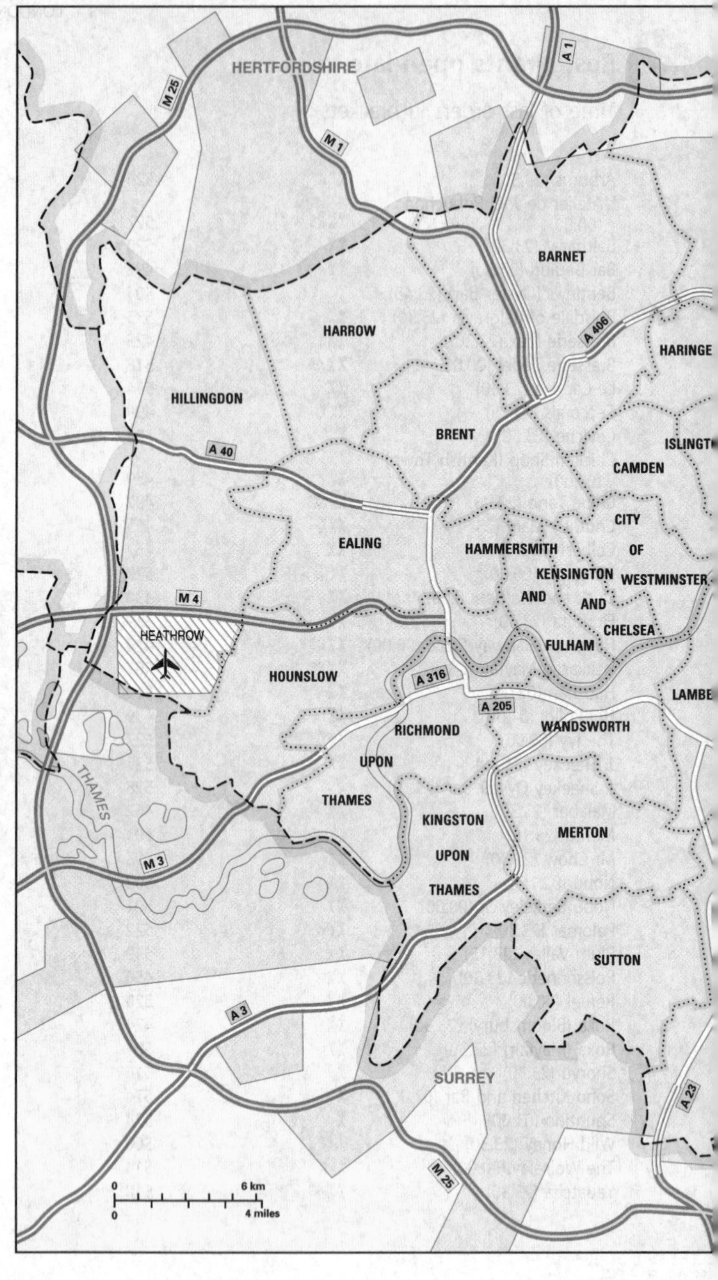
HERTFORDSHIRE
M 25
M 1
A 1
BARNET
A 406
HARROW
HARINGE
HILLINGDON
BRENT
A 40
ISLINGT
CAMDEN
CITY
OF
WESTMINSTER
EALING
HAMMERSMITH
AND
FULHAM
KENSINGTON
AND
CHELSEA
M 4
HEATHROW
HOUNSLOW
A 316
A 205
LAMBE
RICHMOND
UPON
THAMES
WANDSWORTH
THAMES
KINGSTON
UPON
THAMES
MERTON
M 3
SUTTON
A 3
SURREY
A 23
M 25
0
6 km
0
4 miles

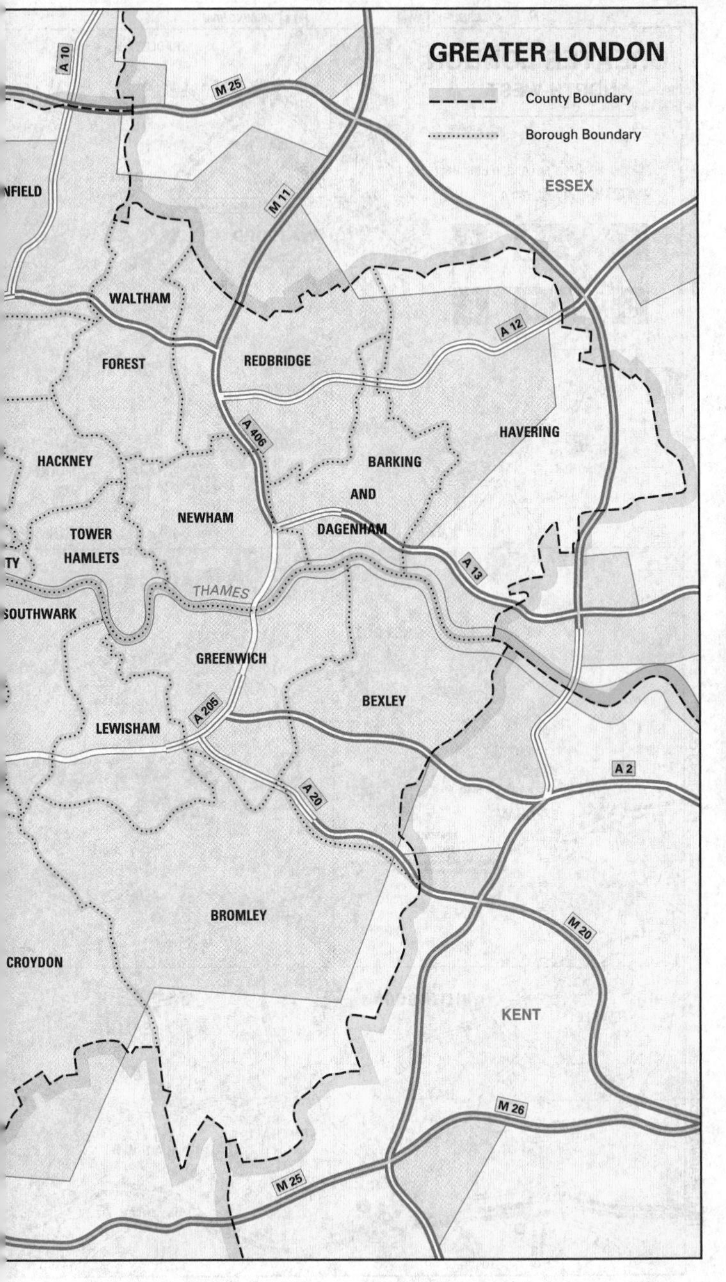
GREATER LONDON
County Boundary
Borough Boundary
ESSEX
NFIELD
WALTHAM
FOREST
REDBRIDGE
HAVERING
HACKNEY
BARKING
AND
DAGENHAM
NEWHAM
TOWER
HAMLETS
TY
THAMES
SOUTHWARK
GREENWICH
BEXLEY
LEWISHAM
BROMLEY
CROYDON
KENT
A 10
M 25
M 11
A 12
A 406
A 13
A 205
A 2
A 20
M 20
M 26
M 25

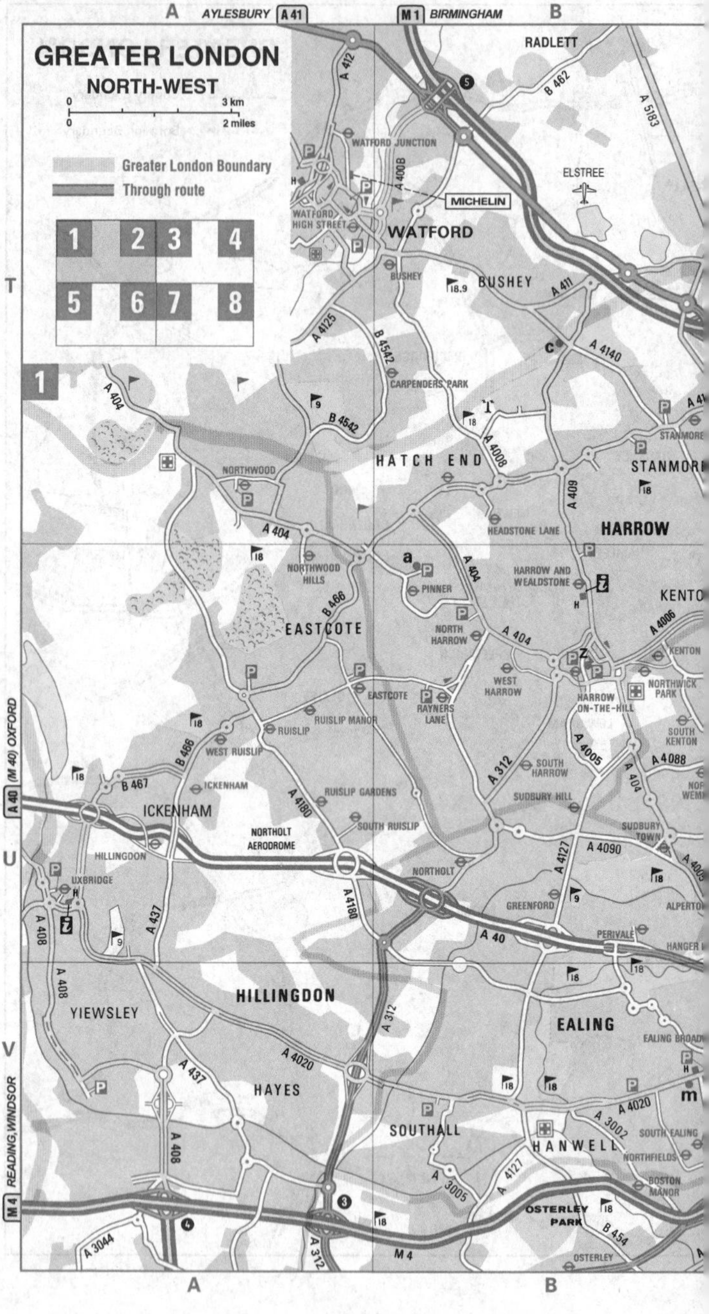
GREATER LONDON
NORTH-WEST
0 3 km
0 2 miles
Greater London Boundary
Through route
1 2 3 4
5 6 7 8
AYLESBURY A 41
M 1 BIRMINGHAM
A
B
T
U
V
RADLETT
WATFORD JUNCTION
ELSTREE
MICHELIN
WATFORD HIGH STREET
WATFORD
BUSHEY
CARPENDERS PARK
HATCH END
NORTHWOOD
STANMORE
HEADSTONE LANE
HARROW
NORTHWOOD HILLS
PINNER
HARROW AND WEALDSTONE
KENTON
EASTCOTE
NORTH HARROW
WEST HARROW
RAYNERS LANE
HARROW ON-THE-HILL
NORTHWICK PARK
RUISLIP MANOR
RUISLIP
WEST RUISLIP
SOUTH KENTON
SOUTH HARROW
ICKENHAM
RUISLIP GARDENS
SUDBURY HILL
SOUTH RUISLIP
NORTHOLT AERODROME
SUDBURY TOWN
HILLINGDON
NORTHOLT
UXBRIDGE
GREENFORD
ALPERTON
PERIVALE
HANGER LANE
HILLINGDON
YIEWSLEY
EALING
EALING BROADWAY
HAYES
SOUTHALL
HANWELL
SOUTH EALING
NORTHFIELDS
BOSTON MANOR
OSTERLEY PARK
OSTERLEY
A 40 (M 40) OXFORD
M 4 READING, WINDSOR
A 412
B 462
A 5183
A 4008
A 411
A 4125
B 4542
A 4140
A 404
A 409
A 4006
B 466
B 467
A 312
A 4005
A 4088
A 4180
A 4127
A 4090
A 437
A 408
A 40
A 4020
A 3002
A 3005
A 3044
B 454
M 4
LONDON

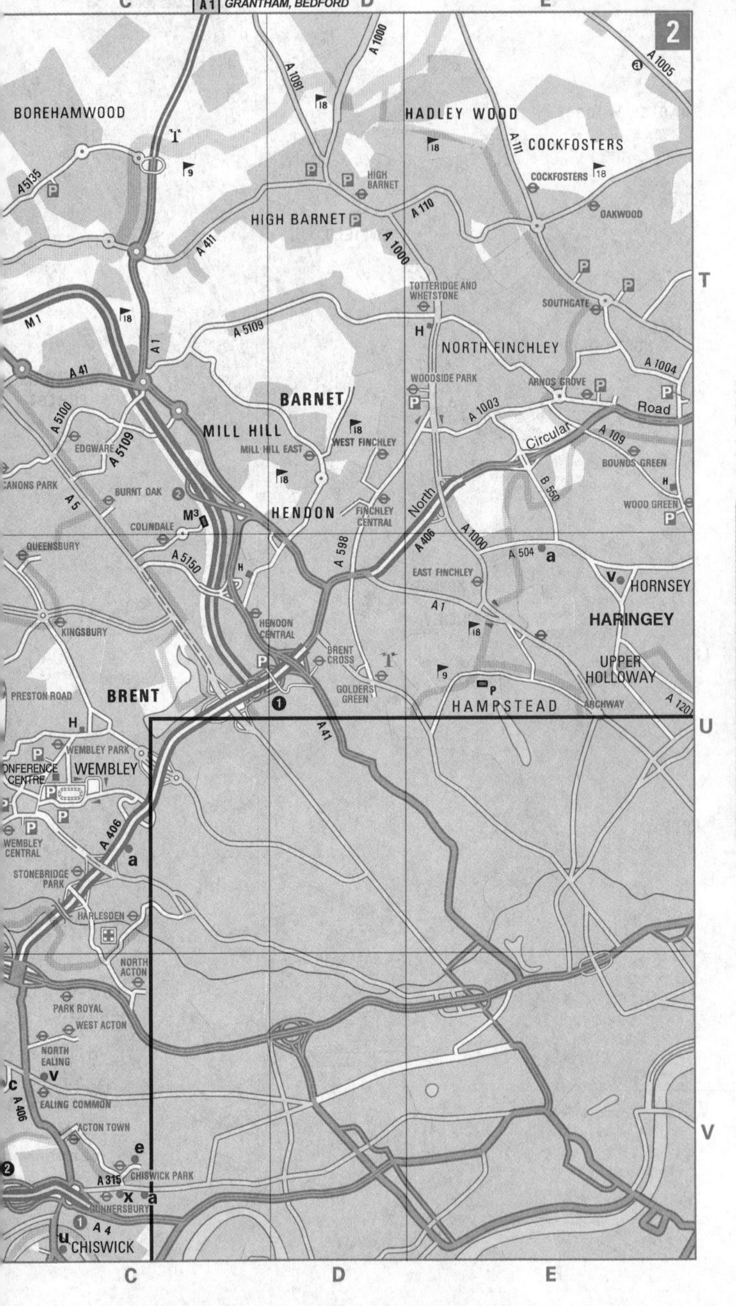
C
A 1 GRANTHAM, BEDFORD
D
E
2
BOREHAMWOOD
HADLEY WOOD
COCKFOSTERS
HIGH BARNET
SOUTHGATE
NORTH FINCHLEY
BARNET
MILL HILL
HENDON
EDGWARE
CANONS PARK
BURNT OAK
COLINDALE
QUEENSBURY
KINGSBURY
HENDON CENTRAL
BRENT CROSS
GOLDERS GREEN
HAMPSTEAD
EAST FINCHLEY
HORNSEY
HARINGEY
UPPER HOLLOWAY
ARCHWAY
WOOD GREEN
BOUNDS GREEN
ARNOS GROVE
WOODSIDE PARK
TOTTERIDGE AND WHETSTONE
OAKWOOD
WEST FINCHLEY
MILL HILL EAST
FINCHLEY CENTRAL
North Circular Road
PRESTON ROAD
BRENT
WEMBLEY PARK
WEMBLEY
WEMBLEY CENTRAL
STONEBRIDGE PARK
HARLESDEN
NORTH ACTON
PARK ROYAL
WEST ACTON
NORTH EALING
EALING COMMON
ACTON TOWN
CHISWICK PARK
GUNNERSBURY
CHISWICK
T
U
V
C
D
E

LONDON

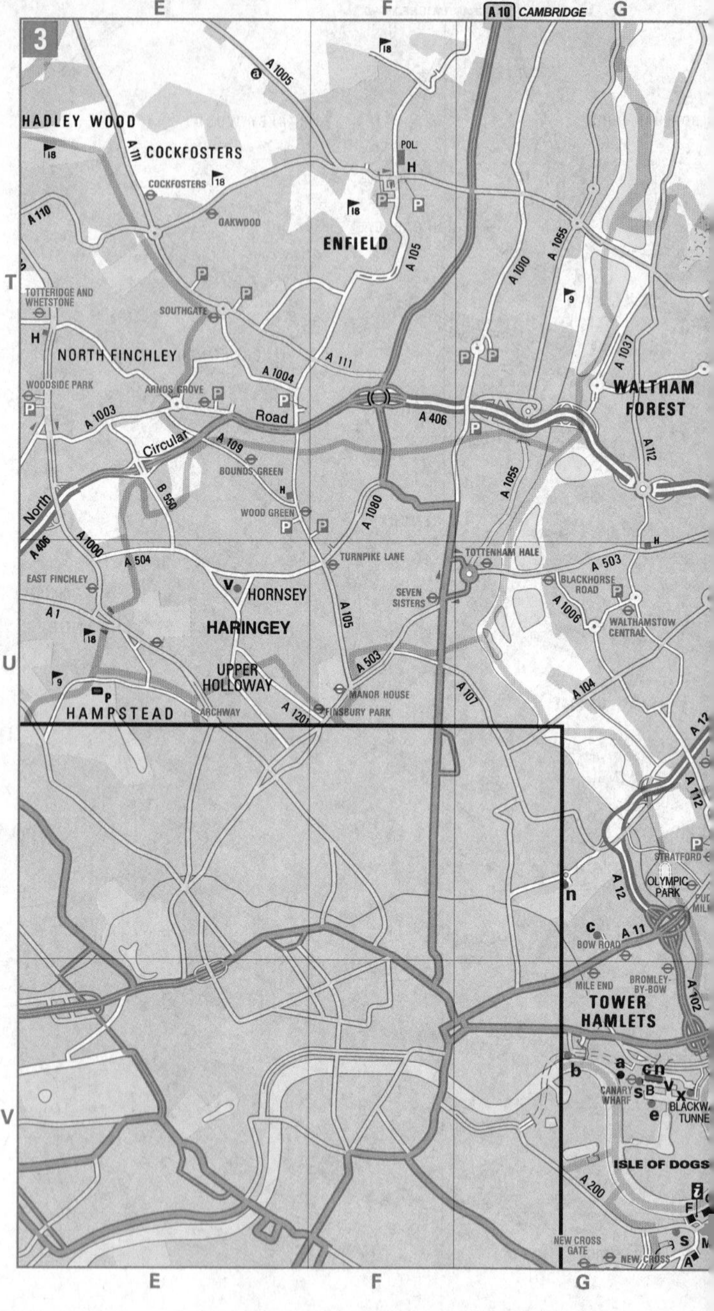

E
F
A 10 CAMBRIDGE
G
3
A 1005
HADLEY WOOD
A 111
COCKFOSTERS
COCKFOSTERS
POL.
H
A 110
OAKWOOD
ENFIELD
A 105
A 1010
A 1055
T
TOTTERIDGE AND WHETSTONE
SOUTHGATE
H
NORTH FINCHLEY
A 111
A 1004
A 1037
WOODSIDE PARK
ARNOS GROVE
WALTHAM FOREST
A 1003
Road
A 406
Circular
A 109
A 112
BOUNDS GREEN
North
B 550
A 1055
WOOD GREEN
A 1080
A 406
A 1000
A 504
TOTTENHAM HALE
TURNPIKE LANE
A 503
EAST FINCHLEY
HORNSEY
SEVEN SISTERS
BLACKHORSE ROAD
A 1006
A 1
HARINGEY
A 105
WALTHAMSTOW CENTRAL
U
UPPER HOLLOWAY
A 503
A 107
A 104
MANOR HOUSE
HAMPSTEAD
ARCHWAY
A 1201
FINSBURY PARK
A 112
STRATFORD
OLYMPIC PARK
A 12
n
c
BOW ROAD
A 11
MILE END
BROMLEY-BY-BOW
A 102
TOWER HAMLETS
a
b
c n
CANARY WHARF
s B
v
x
BLACKW
TUNNE
e
V
ISLE OF DOGS
A 200
NEW CROSS GATE
NEW CROSS
E
F
G
LONDON

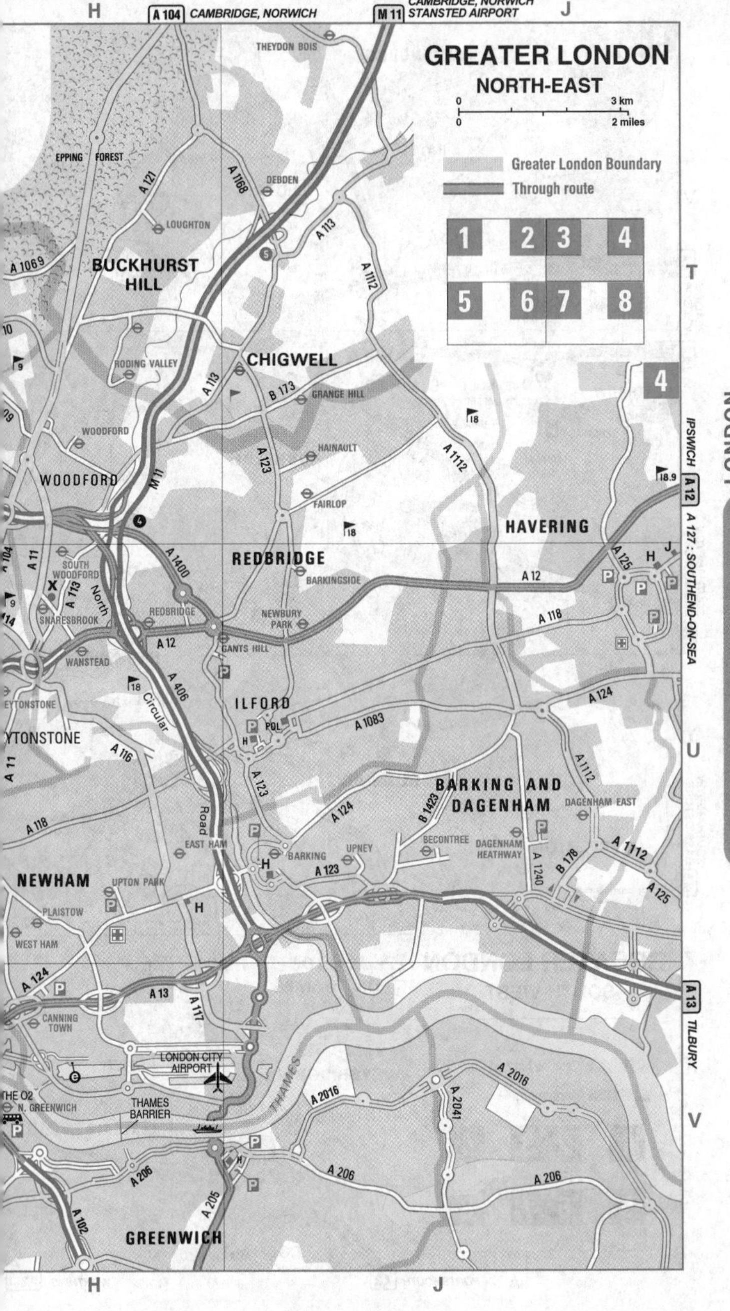

GREATER LONDON
NORTH-EAST
0 3 km
0 2 miles
Greater London Boundary
Through route
1 2 3 4
5 6 7 8
A 104 CAMBRIDGE, NORWICH
M 11 CAMBRIDGE, NORWICH STANSTED AIRPORT
THEYDON BOIS
EPPING FOREST
DEBDEN
LOUGHTON
BUCKHURST HILL
CHIGWELL
RODING VALLEY
GRANGE HILL
WOODFORD
HAINAULT
FAIRLOP
HAVERING
REDBRIDGE
SOUTH WOODFORD
BARKINGSIDE
SNARESBROOK
NEWBURY PARK
WANSTEAD
GANTS HILL
North Circular Road
ILFORD
LEYTONSTONE
BARKING AND DAGENHAM
DAGENHAM EAST
BECONTREE
DAGENHAM HEATHWAY
EAST HAM
BARKING
UPNEY
NEWHAM
UPTON PARK
PLAISTOW
WEST HAM
CANNING TOWN
LONDON CITY AIRPORT
THE O2
N. GREENWICH
THAMES BARRIER
THAMES
GREENWICH
IPSWICH A 12
A 127 : SOUTHEND-ON-SEA
A 13 TILBURY
LONDON

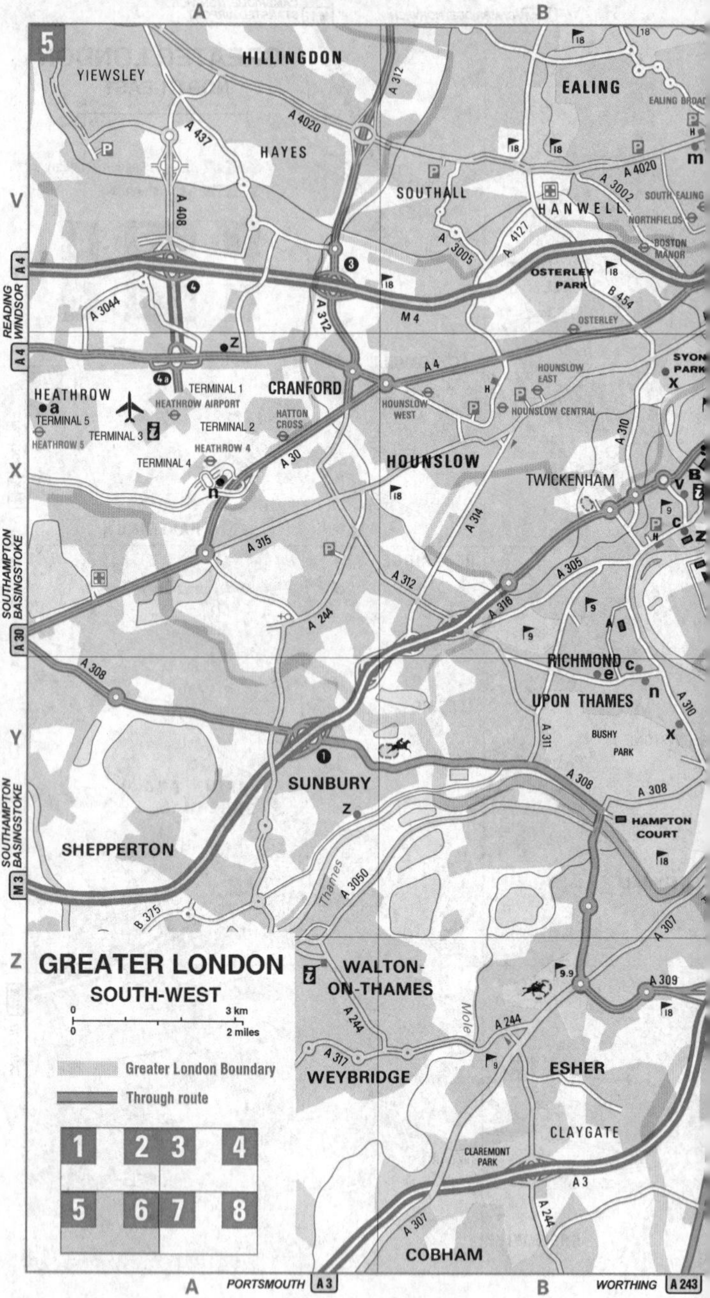

GREATER LONDON
SOUTH-WEST

0 3 km
0 2 miles

Greater London Boundary
Through route

1	2	3	4
5	6	7	8

5

LONDON

A B
V X Y Z

HILLINGDON
YIEWSLEY
HAYES
EALING
EALING BROADWAY
SOUTHALL
HANWELL
SOUTH EALING
NORTHFIELDS
BOSTON MANOR
OSTERLEY PARK
OSTERLEY
SYON PARK
HEATHROW
HEATHROW AIRPORT
TERMINAL 1
TERMINAL 2
TERMINAL 3
TERMINAL 4
TERMINAL 5
HEATHROW 4
HEATHROW 5
HATTON CROSS
CRANFORD
HOUNSLOW WEST
HOUNSLOW EAST
HOUNSLOW CENTRAL
HOUNSLOW
TWICKENHAM
RICHMOND UPON THAMES
BUSHY PARK
HAMPTON COURT
SUNBURY
SHEPPERTON
WALTON-ON-THAMES
WEYBRIDGE
ESHER
CLAYGATE
CLAREMONT PARK
COBHAM
Thames
Mole

READING WINDSOR A 4
SOUTHAMPTON BASINGSTOKE A 30
SOUTHAMPTON BASINGSTOKE M 3
PORTSMOUTH A 3
WORTHING A 243

M 4, A 4, A 30, A 312, A 4020, A 437, A 408, A 3044, A 3005, A 4127, A 3002, B 454, A 315, A 244, A 314, A 310, A 305, A 316, A 308, A 311, A 3050, B 375, A 307, A 309, A 317, A 3

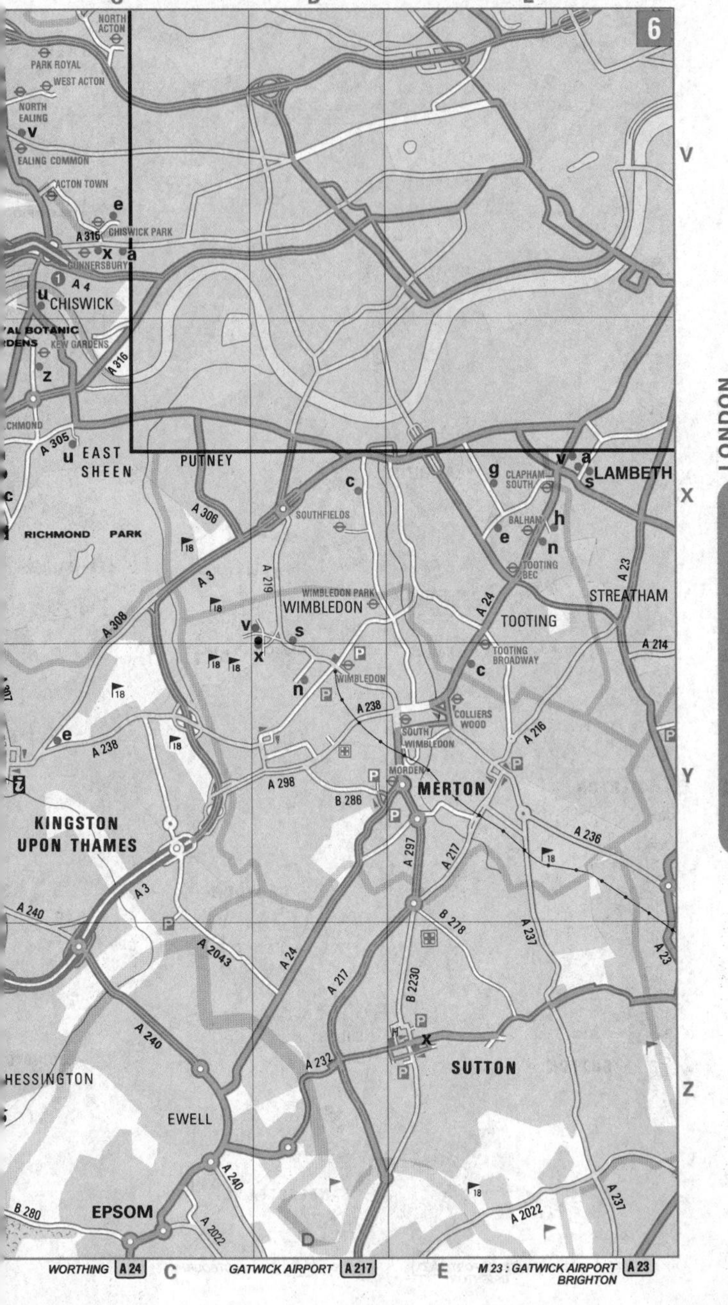

C
D
E
6
V
X
Y
Z
LONDON
NORTH ACTON
PARK ROYAL
WEST ACTON
NORTH EALING
EALING COMMON
ACTON TOWN
CHISWICK PARK
A 315
GUNNERSBURY
A 4
CHISWICK
KEW GARDENS
A 316
A 305
EAST SHEEN
PUTNEY
RICHMOND PARK
A 306
SOUTHFIELDS
CLAPHAM SOUTH
LAMBETH
BALHAM
TOOTING BEC
A 23
STREATHAM
A 3
A 219
WIMBLEDON PARK
WIMBLEDON
A 24
TOOTING
A 308
A 214
TOOTING BROADWAY
A 238
COLLIERS WOOD
SOUTH WIMBLEDON
A 216
MORDEN
A 298
MERTON
B 286
KINGSTON UPON THAMES
A 297
A 217
A 236
A 240
B 278
A 237
A 2043
B 2230
A 232
SUTTON
HESSINGTON
EWELL
B 280
EPSOM
A 2022
WORTHING A 24
GATWICK AIRPORT A 217
M 23 : GATWICK AIRPORT BRIGHTON A 23

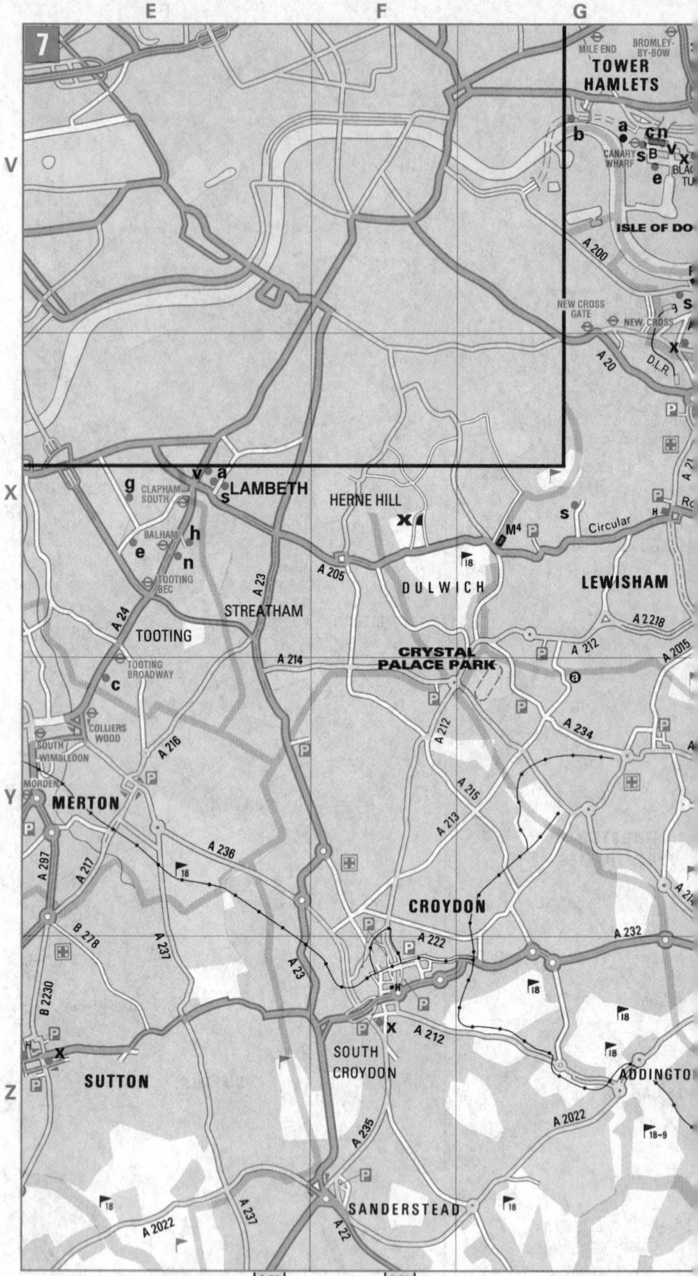

E F G

7

V
X
Y
Z

MILE END
BROMLEY-BY-BOW
TOWER HAMLETS
b a c n
CANARY WHARF
s B v x
e
ISLE OF DO
A 200
NEW CROSS GATE
NEW CROSS
s
x
A 20
D.L.R.

g CLAPHAM SOUTH
v a
s LAMBETH
HERNE HILL
x
s
M4
Circular
BALHAM h
e n
TOOTING BEC
A 205
18
DULWICH
LEWISHAM
A 23
A 24
STREATHAM
TOOTING
A 2218
CRYSTAL PALACE PARK
A 212
A 2015
A 214
TOOTING BROADWAY
c
a
COLLIERS WOOD
SOUTH WIMBLEDON
A 216
A 212
A 234
MORDEN
MERTON
A 215
A 213
A 236
A 297
A 217
18
CROYDON
B 278
A 237
A 222
A 232
A 23
18
18
B 2230
A 212
18
x
SOUTH CROYDON
x
SUTTON
ADDINGTON
A 2022
18-9
A 235
SANDERSTEAD
18
18
A 2022
A 237
A 22

E M 23 : GATWICK AIRPORT BRIGHTON A 23 F A 22 M 25, EASTBOURNE G

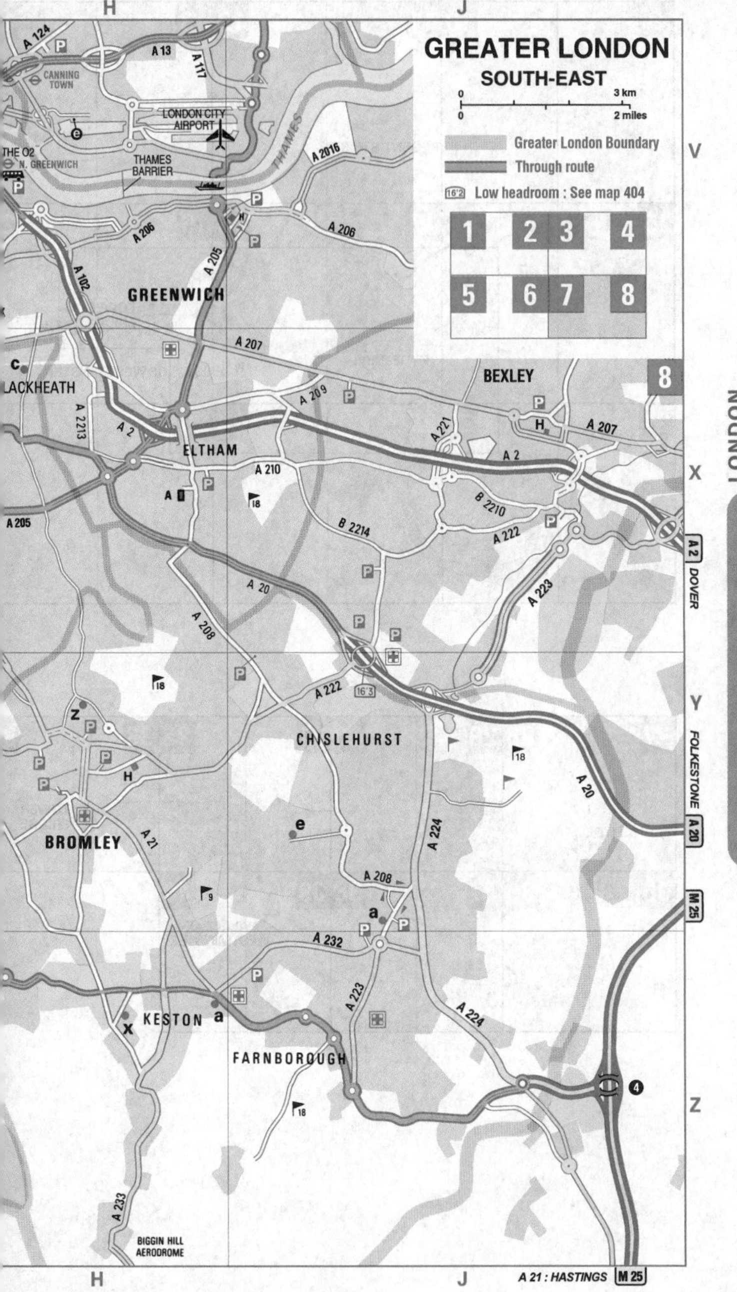
GREATER LONDON
SOUTH-EAST
0 3 km
0 2 miles
Greater London Boundary
Through route
Low headroom : See map 404
1 2 3 4
5 6 7 8
H
J
V
X
Y
Z
CANNING TOWN
LONDON CITY AIRPORT
THE O2
N. GREENWICH
THAMES BARRIER
THAMES
GREENWICH
LACKHEATH
ELTHAM
BEXLEY
CHISLEHURST
BROMLEY
KESTON
FARNBOROUGH
BIGGIN HILL AERODROME
A 124
A 13
A 117
A 2016
A 206
A 205
A 102
A 207
A 209
A 2213
A 2
A 221
A 210
B 2210
B 2214
A 222
A 223
A 20
A 208
A 21
A 224
A 232
A 233
A 2 DOVER
FOLKESTONE
A 20
M 25
A 21 : HASTINGS
M 25

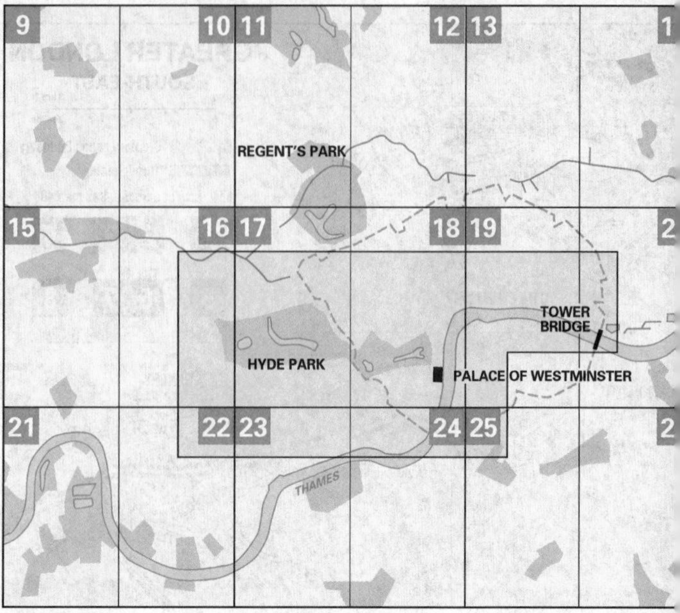

9
10
11
12
13
1
REGENT'S PARK
15
16
17
18
19
2
TOWER BRIDGE
HYDE PARK
PALACE OF WESTMINSTER
21
22
23
24
25
2
THAMES

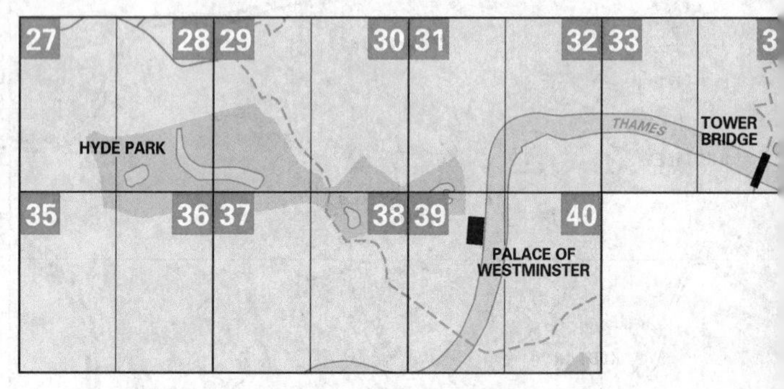

INDEX OF STREET NAMES IN LONDON CENTRE

PLAN 09

PLAN 10

PLAN 11

PLAN 12

LONDON

LONDON

Street	Plan	Grid	No.
Oxford Gardens	16	MZD	
Royal Crescent	16	MZE	371
St Ann's Rd	16	MZE	
St Mark's Rd	16	MZD	
Shirland Rd	16	NZD	
Sinclair Rd	16	MZE	
Sixth Ave	16	MZC	
Sutherland Ave	16	NZD	
Walterton Rd	16	NZD	347
Warwick Ave	16	OZD	
West Cross Route	16	MZE	

PLAN 17

Street	Plan	Grid	No.
Allsop Pl.	17	QZD	4
Blomfield Rd	17	OZD	
Broadley St	17	PZD	
Clifton Gardens	17	PZD	
Frampton St	17	PZD	
Hall Rd	17	PZC	
Lisson Grove	17	PZD	
Maida Ave	17	PZD	
North Carriage Drive	17	PZE	
Park Rd	17	QZD	
Rossmore Rd	17	QZD	
St John's Wood Rd	17	PZD	
Warrington Crescent	17	OZD	348

PLAN 18

Street	Plan	Grid	No.
Bernard St	18	SZD	25
Chester Rd	18	RZC	
Euston Rd	18	RZD	
Fitzroy Square	18	RZD	
Great Ormond St	18	SZD	
Guilford St	18	SZD	
Herbrand St	18	SZD	218
Hunter St	18	SZD	233
Judd St	18	SZC	
Park Crescent	18	RZD	28
Robert St	18	RZC	
Russell Square	18	SZD	
Sidmouth St	18	SZD	385
Tavistock Pl.	18	SZD	
Tavistock Square	18	SZD	409
Upper Woburn Pl.	18	SZD	432
Woburn Pl.	18	SZD	

PLAN 19

Street	Plan	Grid	No.
Bath St	19	VZC	
Beech St	19	VZD	
Borough Rd	19	UZE	
Bowling Green Lane	19	UZD	43
Bunhill Row	19	VZD	
Calthorpe St	19	TZD	65
Central St	19	VZC	
Chiswell St	19	VZD	
City Rd	19	VZC	
Clerkenwell Rd	19	UZD	474
Corporation Row	19	UZD	110
Dufferin St	19	VZD	141
Elephant and Castle Shopping Centre	19	UZF	
Falmouth Rd	19	VZE	
Fann St	19	VZD	166
Goswell Rd	19	UZC	
Great Dover St	19	VZE	
Harper Rd	19	VZE	
King's Cross Rd	19	TZC	
Lever St	19	VZC	
Lloyd Baker St	19	UZC	265
Long Lane SOUTHWARK	19	VZE	
Merrick Square	19	VZE	
Moreland St	19	VZC	293
Myddelton St	19	UZC	296
Newington Causeway	19	VZE	307
New Kent Rd	19	VZF	
Old St	19	VZD	
Paul St	19	VZD	
Percival St	19	UZD	
Pilgrimage St	19	VZE	349
Rosebery Ave	19	UZD	
St John St	19	UZC	
Suffolk St	19	VZE	
Tabard St	19	VZE	408
Trinity Church Square	19	VZE	
Trinity St	19	VZE	
Whitecross St	19	VZD	
Worship St	19	VZD	

PLAN 20

Street	Plan	Grid	No.
Abbey St	20	XZE	
Appold St	20	XZD	5
Back Church Rd	20	XZD	
Bermondsey St	20	XZE	
Bethnal Green Rd	20	XZD	
Bigland St	20	YZD	
Brady St	20	YZD	
Brick Lane	20	XZD	
Brunel Rd	20	YZE	
Cable St	20	YZD	
Cambridge Heath Rd	20	YZD	
Cannon Street Rd	20	YZD	
Cavell St	20	YZD	
Cephas St	20	YZD	
Cheshire St	20	XZD	
Christian St	20	YZD	
Clements Rd	20	YZE	
Club Row	20	XZD	
Commercial Rd	20	YZD	
Curtain Rd	20	XZD	126
Dock St	20	XZD	
Drummond Rd	20	YZE	
Fielgate St	20	XZD	
Globe Rd	20	YZC	
Grange Rd	20	XZE	
Great Eastern St	20	XZD	192
Highway (The)	20	YZE	
Jamaica Rd	20	XZE	
Jubilee St	20	YZD	
Lower Rd	20	YZE	
Luke St	20	XZD	
Mile End Rd	20	YZD	
New Rd	20	YZD	
Old Montague St	20	XZD	
Pages Walk	20	XZF	
Redman's Rd	20	YZD	
Roman Rd	20	YZC	
Rovel Rd	20	XZE	75
Salter Rd	20	YZE	
Sclater St	20	XZD	470
Shoreditch High St	20	XZD	384
Sidney St	20	YZD	
Spa Rd	20	XZE	
Stepney Way	20	YZD	
Surrey Quay's Rd	20	YZE	377
Tarling St	20	YZD	
Thomas Moore St	20	XZE	365
Turin St	20	XZC	
Vallance Rd	20	YZD	
Vaughan Way	20	XZE	
Wapping High St	20	YZE	
Wapping Lane	20	YZE	
Wapping Wall	20	YZE	
Whitechapel Rd	20	XZD	

PLAN 21

Street	Plan	Grid	No.
Banin St	21	LZF	
Barnes High St	21	KZH	404
Bath Rd	21	KZF	
Brook Green	21	LZF	
Burlington Lane	21	KZG	
Castelnau	21	LZG	
Chancellor's Rd	21	LZG	21
Chiswick High Rd	21	KZG	
Chiswick Lane	21	KZG	
Chiswick Mall	21	KZG	
Church Rd RICHMOND UPON THAMES	21	KZH	
Dailing Rd	21	LZF	13
Devonshire Rd	21	KZG	
Dorchester Grove	21	KZG	402
Dover House Rd	21	LZH	
Erpingham Rd	21	LZH	
Ferry Rd	21	KZG	
Glenthorne Rd	21	LZF	
Great West Rd	21	KZG	
Gwendolen Ave	21	LZH	
Hammersmith Bridge	21	LZG	
Hammersmith Bridge Rd	21	LZG	431
Hertford Ave	21	KZH	
Hotham Rd	21	LZH	
Howards Lane	21	LZH	
King St HAMMERSMITH	21	KZG	
Lonsdale Rd	21	KZG	
Lower Richmond Rd	21	LZH	
Mill Hill Rd	21	KZH	
Prebend Gardens	21	KZF	
Priory Lane	21	KZH	
Queen's Ride Lower	21	LZH	
Rainville Rd	21	LZG	
Rannoch Rd	21	LZG	
Rocks Lane	21	LZH	
Roehampton Lane	21	KZH	
Station Rd	21	KZH	
Stevenage Rd	21	LZG	
Suffolk Rd	21	KZG	
Talgarth Rd	21	LZG	
Terrace (The)	21	KZH	
Turnham Green Terrace	21	KZG	389
Upper Richmond Rd	21	LZH	
Upper Richmond Rd West	21	KZH	
Verdun Rd	21	KZG	
Vine Rd	21	KZH	
White Hart Lane	21	KZH	

PLAN 22

Street	Plan	Grid	No.
Armoury Way	22	NZH	7
Bagley's Lane	22	OZH	
Baron's Court Rd	22	MZG	
Bishops Rd	22	NZG	
Bishop's Park Rd.	22	MZH	
Broomhouse Lane	22	NZH	
Carnwath Rd	22	NZH	
Charlwood Rd	22	MZH	
Clancarty Rd	22	NZH	
Crabtree Lane	22	MZG	164
Dawes Rd	22	MZG	
Disraeli Rd	22	MZH	
Edith Rd	22	MZG	
Estcourt Rd	22	MZG	203
Fairfield St	22	OZH	165
Fawe Park Rd	22	MZH	
Filmer Rd	22	MZG	
Finlay St	22	MZH	
Fulham High St	22	MZH	172
Fulham Palace Rd	22	MZG	
Gliddon Rd	22	MZG	182
Greyhound Rd	22	MZG	
Gunterstone Rd	22	MZG	
Halford Rd	22	NZG	
Hammersmith Rd	22	MZG	
Harwood Rd	22	NZG	
Hugon Rd	22	NZH	
Hurlingham Rd	22	NZH	
Munster Rd	22	MZG	
Musard Rd	22	MZG	
New King's Rd	22	NZH	
Oakhill Rd	22	NZH	

PLAN 23

PLAN 24

PLAN 25

PLAN 26

Rotherhithe New Rd 26 YZG
Rye Lane 26 XZH
St George's Way 26 XZG
St James Rd 26 YZG
Shenley Rd 26 XZH
Southwark Park Rd 26 XZF
Stuart Rd 26 YZH
Summer Rd 26 XZG
Surrey Canal Rd 26 YZG
Trafalgar Ave 26 XZG
Verney Rd 26 YZG
Willowbrook Rd 26 XZG
Willow Walk 26 XZF
Yaldind Rd 26 XZF 369

PLAN 27

Artesian Rd 27 AAU
Aubrey Walk 27 AAV
Bark Pl. 27 ABU
Bayswater Rd 27 ABV
Bedford Gardens 27 AAV
Bishop's Bridge Rd 27 ABT
Bourne Terrace 27 ABT
Broad Walk (The) 27 ABV
Campden Grove 27 AAV
Campden Hill Rd 27 AAV
Campden Hill Square 27 AAV
Chepstow Crescent 27 AAU 84
Chepstow Pl. 27 AAU
Chepstow Rd 27 AAT
Chepstow Villas 27 AAU
Colville Rd 27 AAU
Colville Terrace 27 AAU
Dawson Pl. 27 AAU
Garway Rd 27 ABU
Gloucester Terrace 27 ABT
Great Western Rd 27 AAT
Harrow Rd 27 ABT
Hereford Rd 27 ABU
Holland Park Ave 27 AAV
Inverness Terrace 27 ABU
Kensington Church St 27 AAV
Kensington Gardens Square 27 ABU
Kensington Palace Gardens 27 ABV
Kensington Park Rd 27 AAU
Kensington Pl. 27 AAV
Ladbroke Rd 27 AAV
Ladbroke Square 27 AAV
Ledbury Rd 27 AAT
Leinster Square 27 ABU
Linden Gardens 27 AAU
Moscow Rd 27 ABU
Newton Rd 27 ABT
Notting Hill Gate 27 AAV
Orme Court 27 ABU 328
Ossington St 27 ABU
Palace Court 27 ABU
Palace Gardens Terrace 27 ABV
Palace Green 27 ABV
Pembridge Crescent 27 AAU
Pembridge Gardens 27 AAU
Pembridge Rd 27 AAU
Pembridge Square 27 AAU
Pembridge Villas 27 AAU
Porchester Gardens 27 ABU
Porchester Rd 27 ABT
Porchester Square 27 ABT 197
Portobello Rd 27 AAU
Queensborough Terrace 27 ABU
Queensway 27 ABU
St Luke's Rd 27 AAT
St Petersburgh Pl. 27 ABU
Sheffield Terrace 27 AAV
Talbot Rd 27 AAT
Tavistock Rd 27 AAT
Uxbridge St 27 AAV
Westbourne Gardens 27 ABT
Westbourne Grove 27 AAU
Westbourne Park Rd 27 AAT
Westbourne Park Villas 27 ABT

PLAN 28

Chilworth St 28 ACU
Church St 28 ADT
Cleveland Square 28 ACU
Cleveland Terrace 28 ACT
Craven Hill 28 ACU
Craven Rd 28 ACU
Craven Terrace 28 ACU
Devonshire Terrace 28 ACU 136
Eastbourne Terrace 28 ACT
Edgware Rd 28 ADT
Gloucester Square 28 ADU
Hyde Park Gardens 28 ADU
Lancaster Gate 28 ACU
Lancaster Terrace 28 ADU 257
Leinster Gardens 28 ACU
Leinster Terrace 28 ACU
London St 28 ADT
Norfolk Pl. 28 ADT
North Wharf Rd 28 ADT
Orsett Terrace 28 ACT
Porchester Terrace 28 ACU
Praed St 28 ADU
Queen Anne's Gate 28 ACU 94
Queen's Gardens 28 ACU
Radnor Pl. 28 ADT
Ring (The) 28 ADV
Sale Place 28 AET
South Wharf Rd 28 ADT
Spring St 28 ADU
Stanhope Terrace 28 ADU 158
Sussex Gardens 28 ADU
Sussex Pl. 28 ADU
Sussex Square 28 ADU
Westbourne Crescent 28 ADU 448
Westbourne St 28 ADU
Westbourne Terrace 28 ACT
Westbourne Terrace Rd 28 ACT 452

PLAN 29

Albion St 29 AFU
Aybrook St 29 AGT
Baker St 29 AGT
Bell St 29 AET
Blandford St 29 AGT
Bryanston Pl. 29 AFT
Bryanston Square 29 AFT 14
Bryanston St 29 AFU
Cambridge Square 29 AET 67
Chapel St 29 AET
Chiltern St 29 AGT
Clarendon Pl. 29 AEU 93
Connaught Square 29 AFU
Connaught St 29 AFU
Crawford Pl. 29 AFT
Crawford St 29 AFT
Culross St 29 AGU
Dorset St 29 AGT
Dunraven St 29 AGU 149
Enford St 29 AFT
George St 29 AFT
Gloucester Pl. 29 AGT
Granville Pl. 29 AGU 476
Great Cumberland Pl. 29 AFT
Green St 29 AGU
Harcourt St 29 AFT
Harrowby St 29 AFT
Hyde Park Square 29 AEU
Hyde Park St 29 AEU
Kendal St 29 AFU
Lees Pl. 29 AGU
Manchester Square 29 AGT 281
Manchester St 29 AGT
Marble Arch 29 AGU
Marylebone Rd 29 AFT
Montagu Pl. 29 AFT
Montagu Square 29 AGT 90
Mount St 29 AGV
Norfolk Crescent 29 AFT
North Audley St 29 AGU 314
North Row 29 AGU
Old Marylebone Rd 29 AFT
Orchard St 29 AGU
Oxford Square 29 AFU 332
Oxford St 29 AGU
Paddington St 29 AGT
Park Lane 29 AGU
Park St MAYFAIR 29 AGU
Portman Square 29 AGT
Portman St 29 AGU
Reeves Mews 29 AGV 103
Rotten Row 29 AEV
Serpentine Rd 29 AFV
Seymour St 29 AFU
Shouldham St 29 AFT
Southwick St 29 AET 156
Stanhope Pl. 29 AFU 400
Upper Berkeley St 29 AFU
Upper Brook St 29 AGU
Upper Grosvenor St 29 AGU
Upper Montagu St 29 AFT
Wigmore St 29 AGU
Woods Mews 29 AGU
York St 29 AFT

PLAN 30

Adam's Row 30 AHU
Albemarle St 30 AIU 225
Aldford St 30 AHV 2
Argyll St 30 AIU
Arlington St 30 AIV 6
Avery Row 30 AHU 12
Beak St 30 AIU
Berkeley Square 30 AHU
Berkeley St 30 AIV
Binney St 30 AHU
Bolton St 30 AIV
Brick St 30 AHV
Brook St 30 AHU
Brook's Mews 30 AHU
Bruton St 30 AIU
Burlington Arcade 30 AIV
Bury St 30 AIV
Carlos Pl. 30 AHU 35
Carnaby St 30 AIU
Cavendish Square 30 AHT
Chandos St 30 AIT 36
Charles St 30 AHV
Cleveland St 30 AIT
Clifford St 30 AIU 38
Conduit St 30 AIU
Cork St 30 AIU
Curzon St 30 AHV
Davies St 30 AHU
Deanery St 30 AHV 132
Devonshire St 30 AHT 48
Dover St 30 AIV
Duke St 30 AHU
Duke St ST. JAMES 30 AIV
Eastcastle St 30 AIT
Farm St MAYFAIR 30 AHV
Foley St 30 AIT
Gilbert St 30 AHU
Grafton St 30 AIU 62
Great Castle St 30 AIT 189
Great Marlborough St 30 AIU

LONDON

LONDON

PLAN 31

PLAN 32

Theobald's Rd 32 AMT
Tudor St 32 ANU
Upper Ground 32 AMV
Victoria Embankment 32 AMU
Waterloo Bridge 32 AMV
Waterloo Rd 32 ANV

PLAN 33

Aldersgate St 33 APT
Bankside 33 APV 291
Basinghall St 33 AQT
Blackfriars Bridge 33 AOU
Blackfriars Rd 33 AOV
Borough High St 33 AQV
Bow Lane 33 AQU
Cannon St 33 APU
Charterhouse Square 33 APT 475
Cheapside 33 AQU
Cowcross St 33 AOT 113
Ewer St 33 APV
Farringdon St 33 AOT
Finsbury Square 33 AQT 310
Fore St 33 AQT
Foster Lane 33 APT
Giltspur St 33 APT
Great Guilford St 33 APV
Great Suffolk St 33 APV
Gresham St 33 AQT
John St 33 APT 299
King Edward St 33 APT 247
King St CITY OF LONDON 33 AQU
Limeburner Lane 33 AOT 298
Little Britain 33 APT 264
London Wall 33 APT
Long Lane CITY 33 APT
Lothbury 33 AQT
Ludgate Hill 33 AOU
Millennium Bridge 33 APU
Montague St 33 APT 292
Moorgate 33 AQT
Moor Lane 33 AQT
Nelson Square 33 AOV
Newcomen St 33 AQV
Newgate St 33 APT
New Bridge St 33 AOU
New Change 33 APU
Old Bailey 33 AOT
Old Jewry 33 AQU
Park St SOUTHWARK 33 APV
Paternoster Square 33 APT
Poultry 33 AQU
Princes St 33 AQU
Queen St 33 AQU
Queen Street Pl 33 AQU 301
Queen Victoria St 33 APU
Redcross Way 33 AQV
Ropemaker St 33 AQT
St Martin's-le-Grand 33 APT 380
St Paul's Churchyard 33 APU
St Swithin's Lane 33 AQU 308
St Thomas St 33 AQV
Silk St 33 AQT
Southwark Bridge 33 AQV
Southwark Bridge Rd 33 APV
Southwark St 33 APV
Stoney St 33 AQV
Sumner St 33 APV 169
Union St 33 AOV
Upper Thames St 33 AQU
Walbrook Crescent 33 AQU 304
Warwick Lane 33 APT 294
West Smithfield 33 AOT
Wood St 33 AQT

PLAN 34

Aldgate High St 34 ASU
Bell Lane 34 AST
Bevis Marks 34 ART 34
Bishopsgate 34 ART
Blomfield St 34 ART
Braham St 34 ASU
Brick Lane 34 AST
Broadgate 34 ART
Brushfield St 34 AST
Byward St 34 ARU
Camomile St 34 ART 71
Commercial St 34 AST
Coopers Row 34 ASU 318
Cornhill 34 ARU 309
Crucifix Lane 34 ARV 125
Druid St 34 ARV
Duke St Hill 34 ARV
Duke's Pl 34 AST 145
Eastcheap 34 ARU
East Smithfield 34 ASU
Eldon St 34 ART
Fenchurch St 34 ARU
Finsbury Circus 34 ART
Fish Street Hill 34 ARU 319
Gainford St 34 ASV
Goodman's Yard 34 ASU
Goulston St 34 AST
Gracechurch St 34 ARU
Great Tower St 34 ARU
Harrow Pl 34 AST 317
Hay's Galleria Shopping Centre 34 ARV
Houndsditch 34 ART
King William St 34 ARU 250
Leadenhall St 34 ARU
Leman St 34 ASU
Liverpool St 34 ART
Lloyd's Ave 34 ASU
Lombard St 34 ARU 268
London Bridge 34 ARV
Lower Thames St 34 ARU
Mansell St 34 ASU
Mark Lane 34 ARU
Middlesex St 34 AST
Minories 34 ASU
New St 34 ART
Old Broad St 34 ART
Pepys St 34 ASU
Prescot St 34 ASU
Princelet St 34 AST
Princes St 34 AQU
Royal Mint Rd 34 ASU
St Botolph St 34 AST
St Mary Axe 34 ART
Shad Thames 34 ASV
Shorter St 34 ASU
Snows Fields 34 ARV 386
South Pl 34 ART 391
Spital Square 34 AST 399
Sun St 34 ART
Sun Street Passage 34 ART
Threadneedle St 34 ARU
Throgmorton Ave 34 ART
Throgmorton St 34 ART 418
Tooley St 34 ARV
Tower Bridge 34 ASV
Tower Bridge Approach 34 ASV
Tower Bridge Rd 34 ASV
Tower Hill 34 ASU
Wentworth St 34 AST
Weston St 34 ARV 188
Whitechapel High St 34 AST
Wilson St 34 ART
Wormwood St 34 ART 472

PLAN 35

Abingdon Rd 35 AAX
Argyll Rd 35 AAX
Barkston Gardens 35 ABY
Bolton Gardens 35 ABZ
Bramham Gardens 35 ABY
Campden Hill Rd 35 AAX
Collingham Gardens 35 ABY 99
Collingham Rd 35 ABY 101
Cornwall Gardens 35 ABY
Courtfield Gardens 35 ABY
Cromwell Crescent 35 AAY 119
Cromwell Rd 35 AAY
Eardley Crescent 35 AAZ 151
Earl's Court Gardens 35 ABY
Earl's Court Rd 35 AAY
Earl's Court Square 35 ABZ
Edwardes Square 35 AAY
Finborough Rd 35 ABZ
Holland St 35 AAX
Holland Walk 35 AAX
Hornton St 35 AAX
Ifield Rd 35 ABZ
Kensington Court 35 ABX 241
Kensington Court Pl 35 ABX 242
Kensington High St 35 AAX
Kensington Rd 35 ABX
Kensington Square 35 ABX
Kenway Rd 35 ABY
Knaresborough Pl 35 ABY
Lexham Gardens 35 ABY
Lillie Rd 35 AAZ
Logan Pl 35 AAY
Longridge Rd 35 AAY
Marloes Rd 35 ABX
Melbury Rd 35 AAX
Nevern Pl 35 AAY
Nevern Square 35 AAY
North End Rd 35 AAZ
Old Brompton Rd 35 ABZ
Pembrocke Gardens 35 AAY 342
Pembroke Rd 35 AAY
Penywern Rd 35 ABZ
Philbeach Gardens 35 AAZ
Phillimore Gardens 35 AAX
Redcliffe Gardens 35 ABZ
Redcliffe Square 35 ABZ
St Albans Grove 35 ABX
Scarsdale Villas 35 AAY
Seagrave Rd 35 AAZ
Templeton Pl 35 AAY 410
Trebovir Rd 35 AAZ
Warwick Gardens 35 AAY
Warwick Rd 35 AAY
Young St 35 ABX

PLAN 36

Ashburn Pl 36 ACY
Beaufort St 36 ADZ
Bina Gardens 36 ACY
Boltons (The) 36 ACZ
Bute St 36 ADY 59
Cale St 36 ADZ
Carlyle Square 36 ADZ
Cathcart Rd 36 ACZ
Chelsea Square 36 ADZ
Courtfield Rd 36 ACY
Cranley Gardens 36 ACZ
Cranley Pl 36 ADY 215
Cromwell Pl 36 ADY 120
De Vere Gardens 36 ACX
Dovehouse St 36 ADZ
Drayton Gardens 36 ACZ
Elm Park Gardens 36 ADZ
Elm Park Rd 36 ADZ
Elvaston Pl 36 ACX
Evelyn Gardens 36 ACZ
Exhibition Rd 36 ADX
Flower Walk 36 ACX
Foulis Terrace 36 ADZ 170
Fulham Rd 36 ADZ
Gilston Rd 36 ACZ
Glendower Pl 36 ADY 180

LONDON

Gloucester Rd 36 ACX
Grenville Pl. 36 ACY
Harcourt Terrace 36 ACZ 477
Harrington Gardens 36 ACY
Harrington Rd 36 ADY
Hollywood Rd 36 ACZ
Hyde Park Gate 36 ACX
Kensington Gore 36 ACX
King's Rd 36 ADZ
Launceston Pl. 36 ACX 259
Little Boltons (The) 36 ACZ
Manresa Rd 36 ADZ
Neville Terrace 36 ADZ 300
Old Church St 36 ADZ
Onslow Gardens 36 ADZ
Onslow Square 36 ADY
Palace Gate 36 ACX
Park Walk 36 ACZ
Pelham St 36 ADY
Prince Consort Rd 36 ADX
Prince's Gardens 36 ADX 356
Queensberry Pl. 36 ADY 360
Queen's Gate 36 ACX
Queen's Gate Gardens 36 ACY 198
Queen's Gate Pl. 36 ACY 363
Queen's Gate Terrace 36 ACX
Redcliffe Rd 36 ACZ
Roland Gardens 36 ACZ
South Parade 36 ADZ
Stanhope Gardens 36 ACY
Sumner Pl. 36 ADY
Sydney Pl. 36 ADY 405
Thurloe Pl. 36 ADY
Thurloe Square 36 ADY
Tregunter Rd 36 ACZ
Vale (The) 36 ADZ
Victoria Grove 36 ACX
Victoria Rd KENSINGTON 36 ACX
Wetherby Gardens 36 ACY

PLAN 37

Basil St 37 AFX
Beauchamp Pl. 37 AFX
Belgrave Square 37 AGX
Bourne St 37 AGY
Bray Pl. 37 AFY 45
Britten St 37 AEZ
Brompton Rd 37 AFX
Cadogan Gardens 37 AGY 23
Cadogan Gate 37 AGY 220
Cadogan Pl. 37 AGY
Cadogan Square 37 AGY
Cadogan St 37 AFY
Carriage Rd (The) 37 AFX
Chelsea Bridge Rd 37 AGZ
Chelsea Embankment 37 AGZ
Chelsea Manor St 37 AFZ
Cheltenham Terrace 37 AGZ
Chesham Pl. 37 AGX
Chesham St 37 AGY
Chester Row 37 AGY
Cheval Pl. 37 AFX
Christchurch St 37 AFZ
Draycott Ave 37 AFY
Draycott Pl. 37 AFY
Eaton Pl. 37 AGY
Egerton Gardens 37 AFY 160
Egerton Gardens Mews 37 AFY 162
Egerton Terrace 37 AFY 161
Elystan Pl. 37 AFZ
Elystan St 37 AEY
Ennismore Gardens 37 AEX
Flood St 37 AFZ
Franklin's Row 37 AGZ
Glebe Pl. 37 AEZ
Grosvenor Crescent 37 AGX
Hans Crescent 37 AFX
Hans Pl. 37 AFX
Hans Rd 37 AFX
Harriet St 37 AGX 214
Hasker St 37 AFY
Holbein Mews 37 AGZ 223
Holbein Pl. 37 AGY
Ixworth Pl. 37 AEY
Jubilee Pl. 37 AFZ
Knightsbridge 37 AFX
Lennox Gardens 37 AFY
Lennox Gardens Mews 37 AFY 263
Lower Sloane St 37 AGY
Lowndes Square 37 AGX
Lowndes St 37 AGX
Lyall St 37 AGY
Markham St 37 AFZ
Milner St 37 AFY
Montpelier Square 37 AFX
Montpelier St 37 AFX
Moore St 37 AFY
Mossop St 37 AFY
Oakley St 37 AEZ
Ormonde Gate 37 AGZ 329
Pimlico Rd 37 AGZ
Pont St 37 AFY
Radnor Walk 37 AFZ
Rawlings St 37 AFY
Redesdale St 37 AFZ 367
Royal Hospital Rd 37 AFZ
Rutland Gate 37 AEX
St Leonard's Terrace 37 AGZ
Shawfield St 37 AFZ
Sloane Ave 37 AFY
Sloane Square 37 AGY
Sloane St 37 AGX
Smith St 37 AFZ
South Terrace 37 AEY
Sydney St 37 AEZ
Symons St 37 AGY 407
Tedworth Square 37 AFZ
Tite St 37 AFZ
Trevor Pl. 37 AFX
Trevor Square 37 AFX
Walton St 37 AFY
West Halkin St 37 AGX
Whiteheads 37 AFY
William St 37 AGX 468
Wilton Pl. 37 AGX

PLAN 38

Alderney St 38 AIY
Belgrave Pl. 38 AHX
Belgrave Rd 38 AIY
Birdcage Walk 38 AIX
Bressenden Pl. 38 AIX
Buckingham Gate 38 AIX
Buckingham Palace Rd 38 AHY
Carlisle Pl. 38 AIY
Castle Lane 38 AIX
Chapel St BELGRAVIA 38 AHX
Charlwood St 38 AIZ
Chelsea Bridge 38 AHZ
Chester Square 38 AHY
Chester St 38 AHX
Churchill Gardens Rd 38 AIZ
Clarendon St 38 AIZ
Constitution Hill 38 AHX
Cumberland St 38 AIZ
Denbigh St 38 AIZ
Duke of Wellington Pl. 38 AHX 142
Eaton Square 38 AHY
Ebury Bridge 38 AHZ
Ebury Bridge Rd 38 AHZ
Ebury St 38 AHY
Eccleston Bridge 38 AHY 157
Eccleston Square 38 AIY
Eccleston St 38 AHY
Elizabeth St 38 AHY
Francis St 38 AIY
Gillingham St 38 AIY
Gloucester St 38 AIZ
Grosvenor Gardens 38 AHX
Grosvenor Pl. 38 AHX
Grosvenor Rd 38 AHZ
Guildhouse St 38 AIY 201
Halkin St 38 AHX
Hobart Pl. 38 AHX
Hudson's Pl. 38 AIY
Hugh St 38 AIY
Lower Belgrave St 38 AHY
Lower Grosvenor Pl. 38 AIX 274
Lupus St 38 AIZ
Palace St 38 AIX
St George's Drive 38 AIY
South Eaton Pl. 38 AHY
Sutherland St 38 AHZ
Terminus Pl. 38 AIY 412
Upper Belgrave St 38 AHX
Vauxhall Bridge Rd 38 AIY
Victoria St 38 AIX
Warwick Square 38 AIY
Warwick Way 38 AHZ
Wilton Rd 38 AIY
Wilton St 38 AHX

PLAN 39

Abingdon St 39 AKY
Albert Embankment 39 ALY
Artillery Row 39 AJX 8
Atterbury St 39 ALZ
Aylesford St 39 AKZ
Bessborough Gardens 39 AKZ
Bessborough St 39 AKZ 30
Bridge St 39 ALX
Broad Sanctuary 39 ALX 52
Caxton St 39 AJX
Chichester St 39 AJZ
Claverton St 39 AJZ
Dolphin Square 39 AJZ
Douglas St 39 AKY
Erasmus St 39 AKY
Glasshouse St LAMBETH 39 ALZ 108
Great College St 39 ALX
Great George St 39 AKX 193
Great Peter St 39 AKY
Great Smith St 39 AKX
Greencoat Pl. 39 AJY
Greycoat Pl. 39 AJY 200
Greycoat St 39 AJY
Horseferry Rd 39 AKY
Howick Pl. 39 AJY
John Islip St 39 AKZ
King Charles St 39 AKX
Lambeth Bridge 39 ALY
Marsham St 39 AKY
Millbank 39 ALZ
Monck St 39 AKY
Montpelier Walk 37 AFX
Moreton St 39 AJZ
Nine Elms Lane 39 AKZ
Old Pye St 39 AKX
Page St 39 AKY
Palmer St 39 AJX
Parlament Square 39 ALX
Parliament St 39 ALX
Parry St 39 ALZ 341
Petty France 39 AJX
Ponsonby Pl. 39 AKZ
Rampayne St 39 AKZ

Regency St . . . . 39 AKY
Rochester Row. . . . . 39 AJY
St Anne's St . . . . 39 AKX
St George's Square . 39 AJZ
South Lambeth Rd . . 39 ALZ 154
Storeys Gate . . . . 39 AKX
Tachbrook St. . . . . . . 39 AJY
Thirleby Rd . . . . 39 AJY 416
Thorney St. . . . . 39 ALY
Tinworth St . . . . 39 ALZ 129
Tothill St. . . . . 39 AKX
Tufton St . . . . 39 AKX
Vauxhall Bridge . . . . . 39 ALZ
Vincent Square . . . . . 39 AJY
Vincent St . . . . 39 AKY
Westminster Bridge . 39 ALX

PLAN 40

Baylis Rd . . . . 40 ANX
Black Prince Rd. . . . . 40 AMY
Braganza St. . . . . 40 AOZ
Brook Drive . . . . 40 ANY
Chester Way . . . . 40 ANY
Clayton St . . . . 40 ANZ
Cleaver St . . . . 40 ANZ
Cooks St . . . . 40 AOZ
Courtenay St . . . . 40 AMZ
Dante Rd . . . . 40 AOY
De Laune St . . . . 40 ANZ
Durham St. . . . . 40 AMZ 150
Fitzalan St . . . . 40 AMY
Garden Row . . . . 40 AOX 173
Harleyford Rd . . . . . . 40 AMZ
Hayles St. . . . . 40 AOY
Hercules Rd . . . . 40 AMX
Johnathan St. . . . . . . 40 AMZ
Juxon St . . . . 40 AMY
Kennington Lane . . . 40 AMZ
Kennington Oval . . . . 40 AMZ
Kennington Rd . . . . . 40 ANX
Kennington Park Rd 40 ANZ
Lambeth High St . . . 40 AMY
Lambeth Palace Rd . 40 AMX
Lambeth Rd . . . . 40 AMY
Lambeth Walk . . . . . 40 AMY
London Rd . . . . 40 AOX
Lower Marsh . . . . . . 40 AMX
Newburn St . . . . 40 AMZ
Pearman St . . . . 40 ANX
Ravensdon St . . . . . . 40 ANZ 219
Renfrew Rd . . . . 40 ANY
St George's Rd . . . . . 40 ANX
Sancroft St . . . . 40 AMZ
Stannary St . . . . 40 ANZ
Tyers St. . . . . 40 AMZ
Vauxhall St. . . . . 40 AMZ
Vauxhall Walk . . . . . . 40 AMZ
Walcot Square . . . . . 40 ANY
Walnut Tree Walk. . . 40 AMY
Webber St. . . . . 40 ANX
Westminster Bridge Rd . . . . 40 AMX
West Square . . . . 40 AOY
Wincoot St . . . . 40 ANY
York Rd . . . . 40 AMX

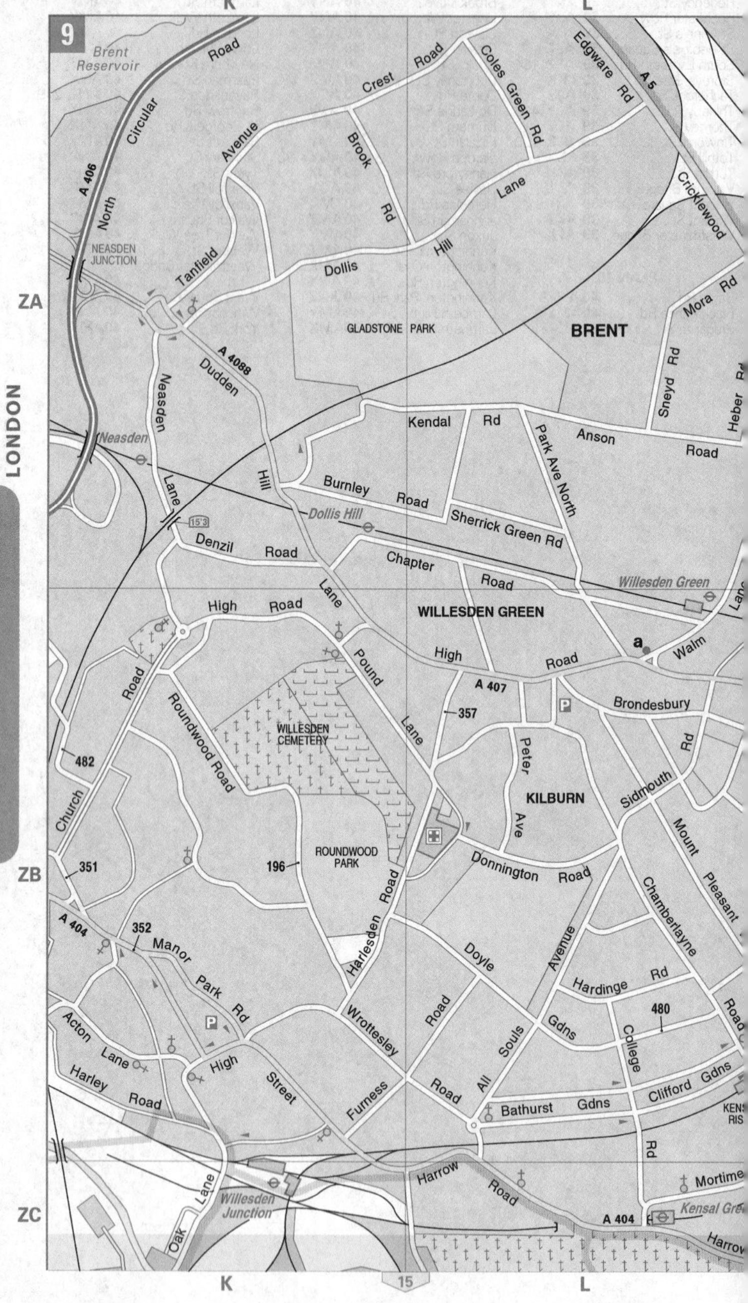

K
L
9
Brent Reservoir
North Circular Road
A 406
Crest Road
Coles Green Rd
Edgware Rd
A 5
Avenue
Brook Rd
Lane
Cricklewood
Tanfield
Dollis
Hill
NEASDEN JUNCTION
ZA
GLADSTONE PARK
BRENT
Mora Rd
Sneyd Rd
Heber Rd
A 4088
Dudden
Neasden
Lane
LONDON
Neasden
Kendal Rd
Park Ave North
Anson Road
Burnley Road
Dollis Hill
Sherrick Green Rd
Denzil Road
Chapter Road
Willesden Green
High Road
Lane
WILLESDEN GREEN
a
Walm
High Road
A 407
Pound
Brondesbury
Road
Roundwood Road
357
WILLESDEN CEMETERY
Lane
Peter Ave
Rd
482
KILBURN
Sidmouth
Church
Mount Pleasant
ROUNDWOOD PARK
196
Donnington Road
ZB
351
Harlesden Road
Chamberlayne
A 404
352
Manor Park Rd
Doyle
Avenue
Hardinge Rd
Acton Lane
Road
Gdns
480
College
Road
High Street
Wrottesley
All Souls
Clifford Gdns
Harley Road
Furness
Road
Bathurst Gdns
Rd
Harrow Road
Mortimer
Lane
Willesden Junction
Oak
ZC
A 404
Kensal Gre
Harrow
K
15
L

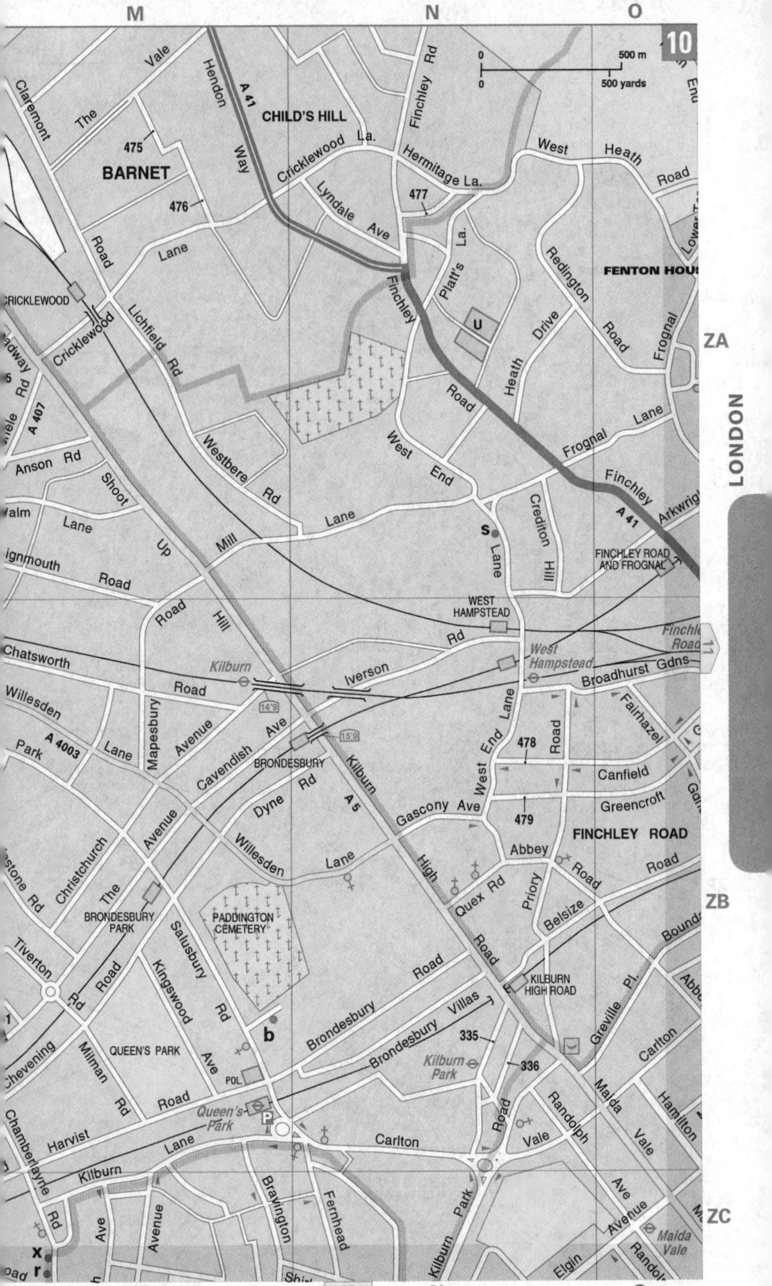

10

LONDON

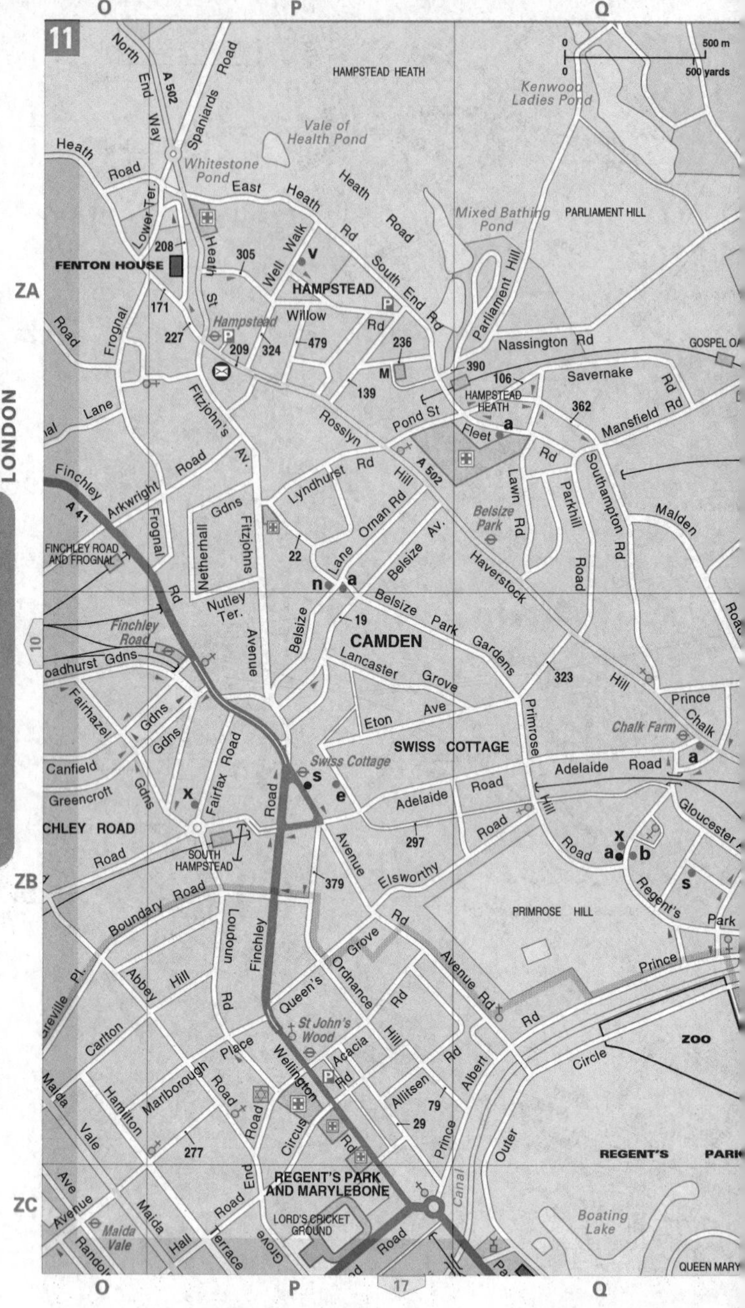
O
P
Q
11
0
500 m
0
500 yards
HAMPSTEAD HEATH
Kenwood Ladies Pond
North End Way
A 502
Spaniards Road
Vale of Health Pond
Heath Road
Whitestone Pond
East Heath Rd
Heath Road
Mixed Bathing Pond
PARLIAMENT HILL
Lower Ter.
208
305
Well Walk
FENTON HOUSE
Heath St
HAMPSTEAD
South End Rd
Parliament Hill
ZA
171
Hampstead
Willow Rd
227
209
324
479
236
Nassington Rd
GOSPEL OAK
Frognal
Road
390
M
106
HAMPSTEAD HEATH
Savernake Rd
139
362
Mansfield Rd
Lane
Fitzjohn's Av.
Rosslyn Hill
Pond St
Fleet Rd
a
LONDON
Finchley Rd
A 41
Road
Arkwright
Lyndhurst Rd
A 502
Lawn Rd
Parkhill Road
Southampton Rd
Malden
Frognal
Gdns
Fitzjohns
Netherhall
Belsize Park
Oman Rd
22
Belsize Av.
Haverstock
FINCHLEY ROAD AND FROGNAL
n
a
Lane
Nutley Ter.
Belsize
19
Belsize Park Gardens
Finchley Road
10
Avenue
CAMDEN
Lancaster Grove
323
Hill
Broadhurst Gdns
Fairhazel Gdns
Gdns
Eton Ave
Primrose
Prince
Chalk
Chalk Farm
Fairfax Road
SWISS COTTAGE
Swiss Cottage
s
Adelaide Road
a
Canfield
Gdns
x
e
Road
Adelaide
Road
Greencroft
Road
Hill
FINCHLEY ROAD
Avenue
297
Road
Road
x
a
b
Gloucester
Road
SOUTH HAMPSTEAD
ZB
379
Elsworthy
s
Boundary Road
Loudoun Rd
Finchley
Grove
Rd
Regent's Park
PRIMROSE HILL
Greville Pl.
Abbey Hill
Queen's
Ordnance
Avenue Rd
Prince
Rd
Rd
St John's Wood
Hill
Carlton
Place
Acacia Rd
Circle
ZOO
Wellington Rd
Rd
Albert
Marlborough
Road
Allitsen
79
Hamilton
Maida Vale
Road
Circus
Prince
Outer
29
277
REGENT'S PARK
REGENT'S PARK AND MARYLEBONE
Canal
Ave
Avenue
Maida Vale
Maida
End
Boating Lake
ZC
Road
LORD'S CRICKET GROUND
Hall
Terrace
Grove
Road
Randolph
QUEEN MARY
17

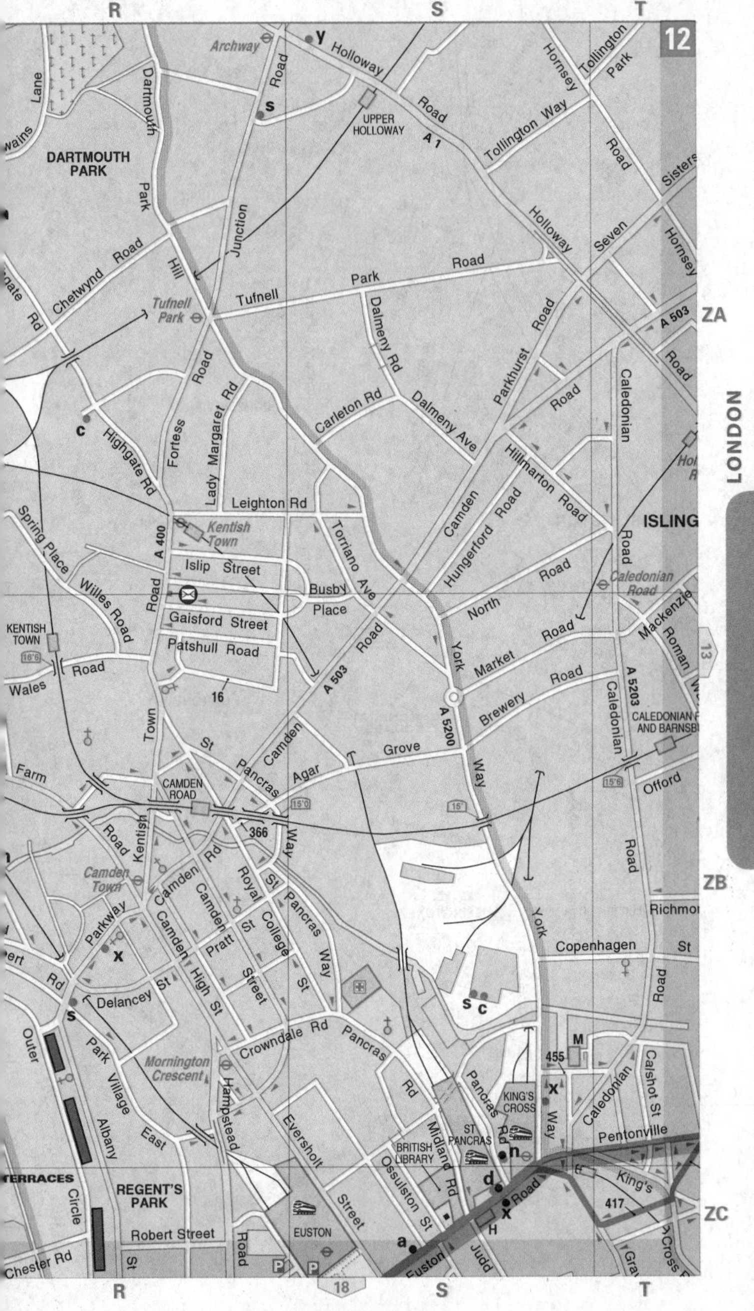

R
S
T
12
Archway
Holloway
Road
UPPER HOLLOWAY
A 1
Hornsey
Tollington
Park
Tollington Way
Lane
Dartmouth
DARTMOUTH PARK
Park
Hill
Junction
Road
Sisters
Seven
Holloway
Hornsey
Chetwynd
Tufnell
Park
Tufnell Park
Rd
Dalmeny Rd
Parkhurst
A 503
ZA
Fortress
Lady Margaret Rd
Carleton Rd
Dalmeny Ave
Caledonian
LONDON
Highgate Rd
c
s
y
Hillmarton Road
Camden
Hungerford Road
ISLING
Leighton Rd
Kentish Town
Torriano Ave
A 400
Spring Place
Islip Street
Busby Place
Caledonian Road
North
Willes Road
Gaisford Street
Mackenzie
Roman
Patshull Road
York
Market
13
KENTISH TOWN
Wales
16
A 503
Brewery
A 5203
CALEDONIAN R AND BARNSBU
A 5200
Town
St
Pancras
Camden
Agar
Grove
Way
Farm
CAMDEN ROAD
366
15'
15'0
15'6
16'6
Offord
Kentish
Camden Town
Rd
Royal
College
Parkway
Pratt
High St
ZB
Richmon
Copenhagen
St
x
Delancey
Street
Crowndale Rd
Pancras
Outer
Park Village East
Mornington Crescent
Hampstead
Eversholt
Albany
M
455
KING'S CROSS
Calshot St
Pentonville
Midland Rd
ST PANCRAS
BRITISH LIBRARY
Ossulston St
n
d
King's
417
ZC
TERRACES
REGENT'S PARK
Circle
Robert Street
EUSTON
a
H
Judd
Euston
Gra
Cross
Chester Rd
P
18

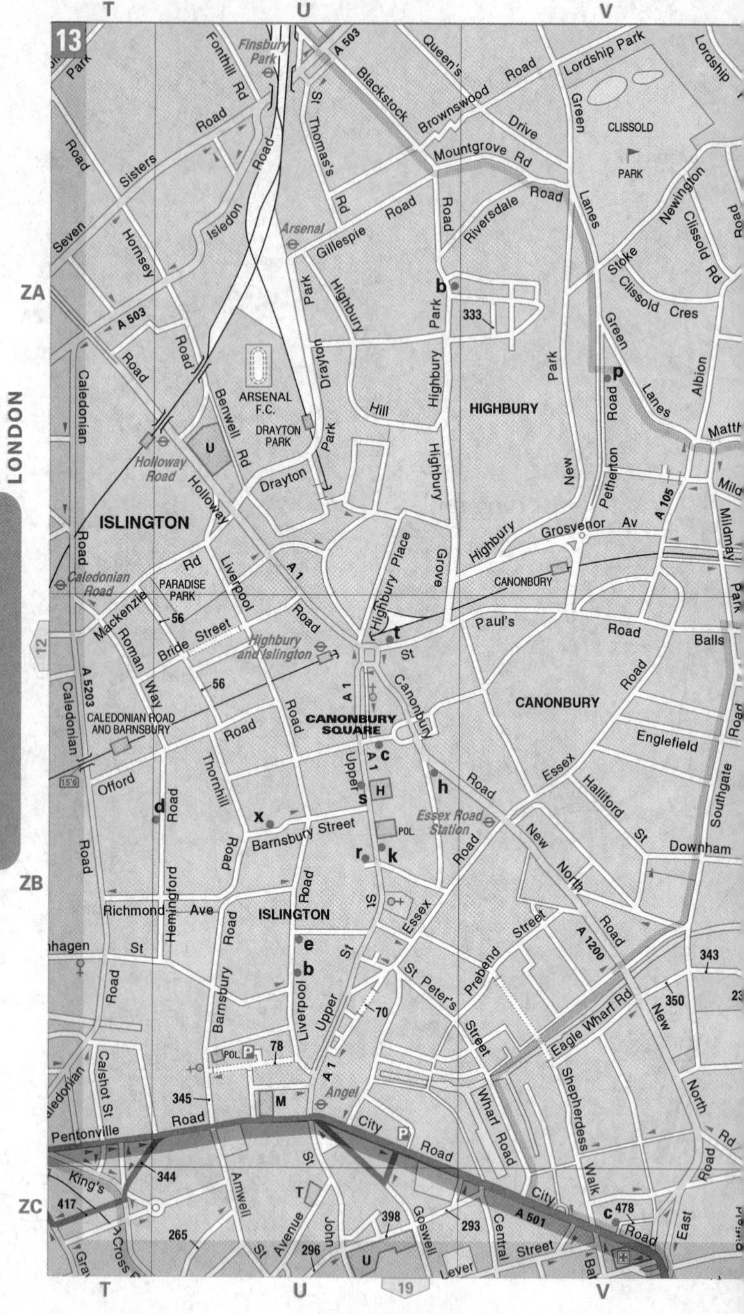
13
T
U
V
ZA
ZB
ZC
Finsbury Park
A 503
Queen's
Lordship Park
Lordship
Fonthill Rd
Blackstock
Road
Brownswood
St Thomas's
CLISSOLD
PARK
Green Lanes
Drive
Mountgrove Rd
Sisters
Road
Seven
Hornsey
Isledon
Arsenal
Gillespie
Rd
Riversdale
Road
Newington
Clissold Rd
Stoke
Clissold Cres
Park
Highbury
333
ARSENAL F.C.
DRAYTON PARK
Drayton
Hill
HIGHBURY
New
Petherton
Albion
Lanes
Holloway Road
Holloway
Benwell Rd
Caledonian
ISLINGTON
Caledonian Road
Mackenzie
Rd
PARADISE PARK
Liverpool
A 1
Highbury Place
Grove
Grosvenor Av
A 105
Mildmay
Matth
CANONBURY
Paul's
Balls
Roman Way
Bride Street
56
Highbury and Islington
St
A 5203
CALEDONIAN ROAD AND BARNSBURY
CANONBURY SQUARE
Canonbury
Englefield
Southgate
Offord
Thornhill
Upper
H
Essex
Essex Road Station
POL
Barnsbury Street
Halliford St
Downham
New North
Richmond Ave
Hemingford
ISLINGTON
Essex
Prebend Street
A 1200
nhagen St
St Peter's
343
350
Eagle Wharf Rd
Barnsbury
70
78
345
Calshot St
Pentonville
Angel
M
City Road
Wharf Road
Shepherdess Walk
North Rd
344
King's
417
Cross
265
Amwell
T
Avenue
John
296
398
Goswell
293
Central
A 501
City
Street
Lever
478
East
12
19
15'6

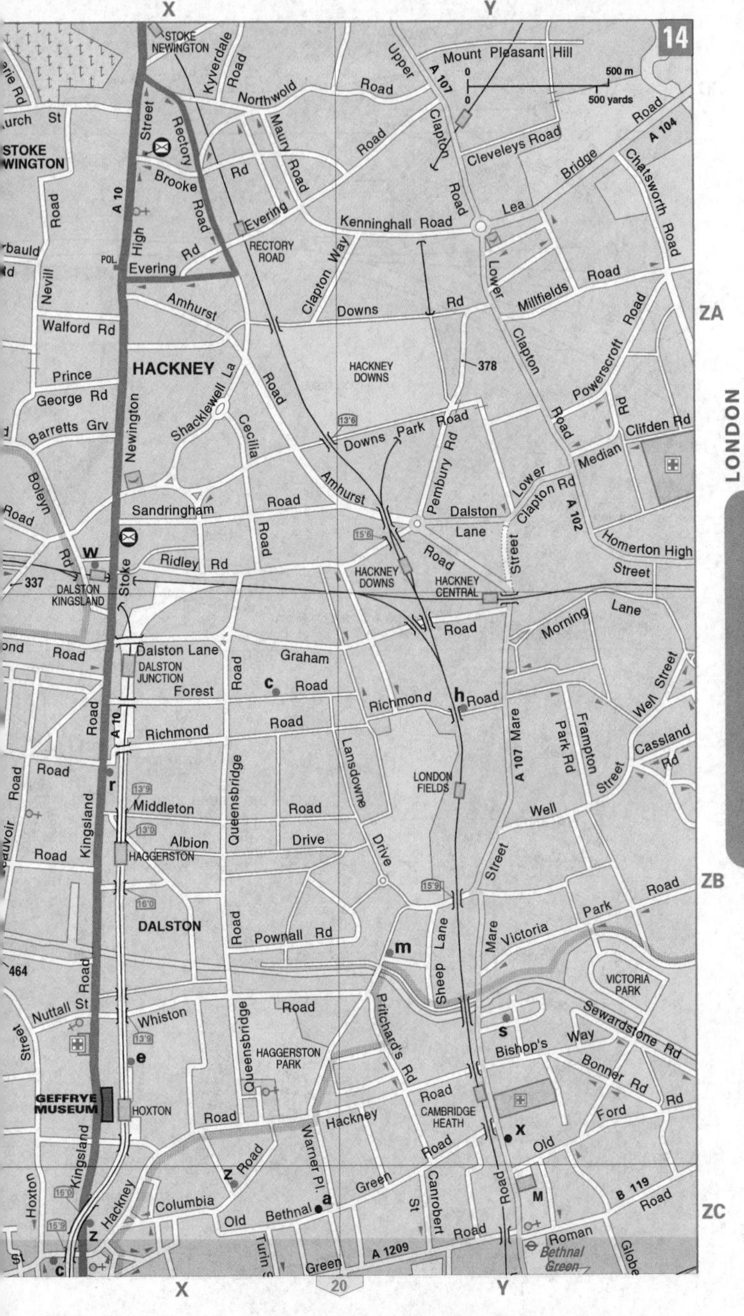

X
Y
14
STOKE NEWINGTON
HACKNEY
DALSTON
LONDON
ZA
ZB
ZC
20
500 m
500 yards
A 10
A 107
A 104
A 102
A 1209
B 119
Mount Pleasant Hill
Northwold Road
Upper Clapton Road
Cleveleys Road
Lea Bridge Road
Chatsworth Road
Kenninghall Road
Rectory Road
Evering Rd
Brooke Road
Stoke Newington High Street
Amhurst Road
Downs Rd
Millfields Road
Powerscroft Road
Clifden Rd
Median Rd
Lower Clapton Rd
HACKNEY DOWNS
Downs Park Road
Pembury Rd
Dalston Lane
Homerton High Street
Sandringham Road
Ridley Rd
DALSTON KINGSLAND
DALSTON JUNCTION
HACKNEY CENTRAL
Graham Road
Morning Lane
Well Street
Richmond Road
Mare Street
Cassland Rd
LONDON FIELDS
Lansdowne Drive
Queensbridge Road
Middleton Road
Albion Drive
HAGGERSTON
Victoria Park Road
VICTORIA PARK
Sewardstone Rd
Bishop's Way
Bonner Rd
Sheep Lane
Pritchard's Rd
HAGGERSTON PARK
GEFFRYE MUSEUM
HOXTON
CAMBRIDGE HEATH
Hackney Road
Old Bethnal Green Road
Columbia Road
Roman Road
Bethnal Green
Globe Road
Old Ford Rd
Kingsland Road
Whiston Road
Nuttall St
Pownall Rd
Walford Rd
Prince George Rd
Barretts Grv
Shacklewell La
Cecilia Road
Boleyn Road
Nevill Road
Frampton Park Rd
Canrobert St
Warner Pl.

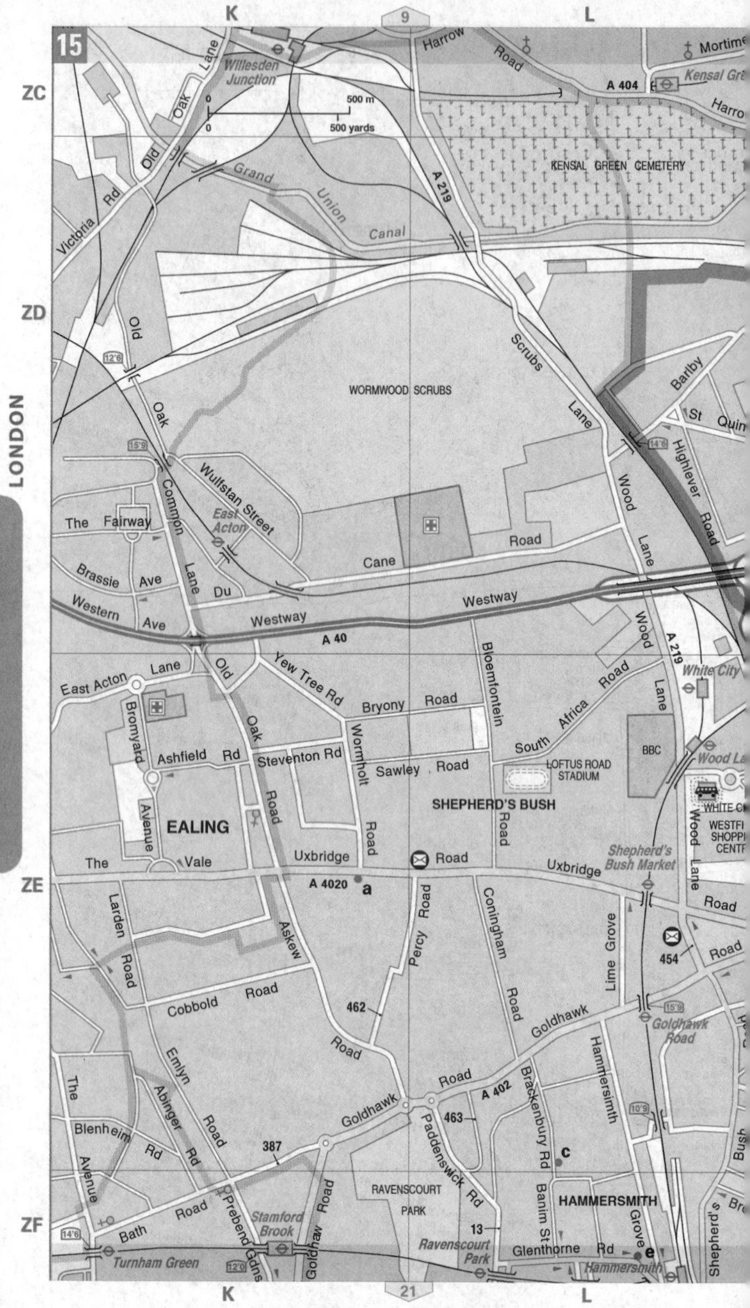
15
K
L
9
21
ZC
ZD
ZE
ZF
LONDON
Willesden Junction
Kensal Green
KENSAL GREEN CEMETERY
Grand Union Canal
WORMWOOD SCRUBS
East Acton
Westway
A 40
EALING
SHEPHERD'S BUSH
LOFTUS ROAD STADIUM
BBC
White City
Wood Lane
Shepherd's Bush Market
Goldhawk Road
RAVENSCOURT PARK
Ravenscourt Park
HAMMERSMITH
Hammersmith
Stamford Brook
Turnham Green
Uxbridge Road
A 4020
Goldhawk Road
A 402
Harrow Road
A 404
A 219
Scrubs Lane
Old Oak Common Lane
Wood Lane
Du Cane Road
Western Ave
East Acton Lane
Yew Tree Rd
Bloemfontein Road
South Africa Road
Askew Road
Percy Road
Coningham Road
Lime Grove
Brackenbury Rd
Paddenswick Rd
Prebend Gdns
Bath Road
500 m
500 yards

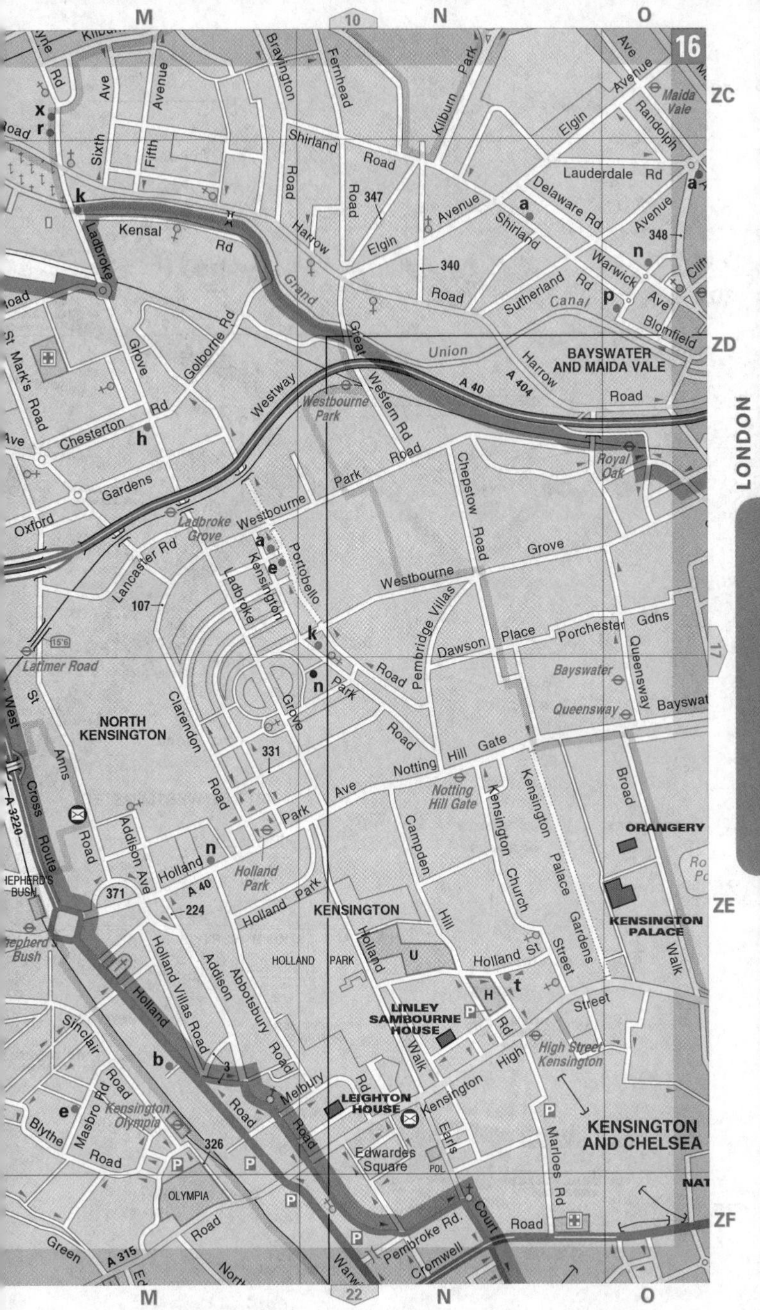

16
LONDON
BAYSWATER AND MAIDA VALE
NORTH KENSINGTON
KENSINGTON
HOLLAND PARK
KENSINGTON AND CHELSEA
KENSINGTON PALACE
ORANGERY
LINLEY SAMBOURNE HOUSE
LEIGHTON HOUSE
OLYMPIA
Grand Union Canal
Westway
A 40
A 404
A 3220
A 315
Westbourne Park
Royal Oak
Ladbroke Grove
Latimer Road
Bayswater
Queensway
Notting Hill Gate
Holland Park
Shepherd's Bush
High Street Kensington
Kensington Olympia
Maida Vale

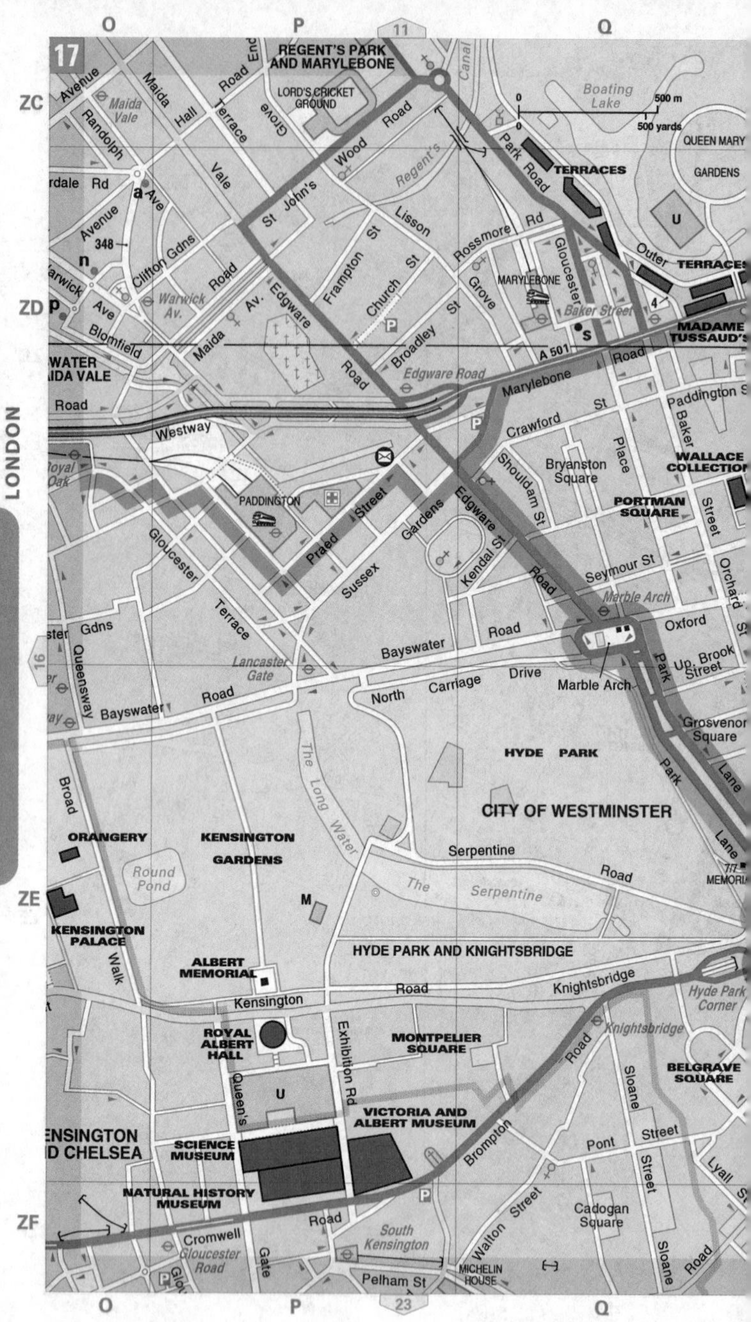
17
REGENT'S PARK AND MARYLEBONE
LORD'S CRICKET GROUND
HYDE PARK
CITY OF WESTMINSTER
KENSINGTON GARDENS
ORANGERY
KENSINGTON PALACE
ALBERT MEMORIAL
ROYAL ALBERT HALL
MONTPELIER SQUARE
VICTORIA AND ALBERT MUSEUM
SCIENCE MUSEUM
NATURAL HISTORY MUSEUM
HYDE PARK AND KNIGHTSBRIDGE
BELGRAVE SQUARE
PORTMAN SQUARE
WALLACE COLLECTION
MADAME TUSSAUD'S
QUEEN MARY GARDENS
PADDINGTON
MARYLEBONE
MICHELIN HOUSE
Marble Arch
The Serpentine
The Long Water
Round Pond
Boating Lake
LONDON

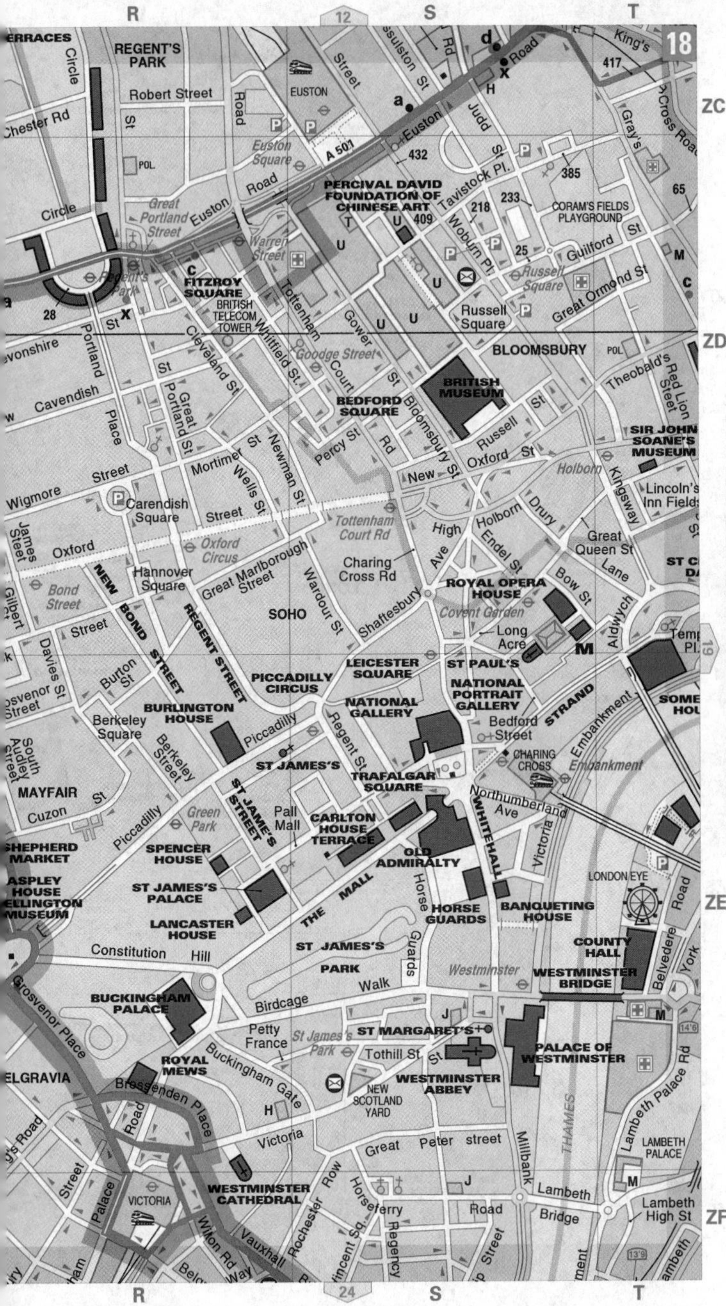

R 12 S T

18

ZC ZD ZE ZF

LONDON

ERRACES Circle REGENT'S PARK Robert Street St Chester Rd POL. Circle Great Portland Street Euston Road Euston Square Warren Street Regent's Park 28 X C FITZROY SQUARE BRITISH TELECOM TOWER

EUSTON Road P P A 501 Euston 432 a Street Ossulston St Rd d Road X H Judd St King's 417 Gray's Cross Road ZC

PERCIVAL DAVID FOUNDATION OF CHINESE ART 409 Tavistock Pl. 218 233 385 CORAM'S FIELDS PLAYGROUND 65 Woburn Pl. P P 25 Russell Square Guilford St M Great Ormond St C U U T U U U Russell Square P

Tottenham Whitfield St. Gower Goodge Street Court St Cleveland St St Devonshire Portland Place Cavendish Great Portland St

BLOOMSBURY POL Theobald's Red Lion Street ZD BRITISH MUSEUM BEDFORD SQUARE Bloomsbury St Rd Percy St Russell St SIR JOHN SOANE'S MUSEUM New Oxford St Holborn Kingsway Lincoln's Inn Fields

Wigmore Street P Cavendish Square Mortimer St Wells St Newman St Street James Street Oxford Oxford Circus Tottenham Court Rd High Holborn Drury Great Queen St Lane Endell St Ave Charing Cross Rd St

NEW BOND STREET Hannover Square Great Marlborough Street Wardour St SOHO Shaftesbury ROYAL OPERA HOUSE Covent Garden Bow St Long Acre Aldwych Temple Pl. 19 M ST CLEMENT DANES

Gilbert Bond Street Street Davies St Burton St Grosvenor Street REGENT STREET LEICESTER SQUARE ST PAUL'S PICCADILLY CIRCUS NATIONAL PORTRAIT GALLERY STRAND Embankment SOMERSET HOUSE BURLINGTON HOUSE NATIONAL GALLERY Berkeley Square Piccadilly Regent St Bedford Street Berkeley Street South Audley Street CHARING CROSS Embankment ST JAMES'S TRAFALGAR SQUARE

MAYFAIR St Curzon St ST JAMES'S STREET Pall Mall Green Park Northumberland Ave WHITEHALL Victoria CARLTON HOUSE TERRACE Piccadilly SHEPHERD MARKET SPENCER HOUSE OLD ADMIRALTY P APSLEY HOUSE WELLINGTON MUSEUM ST JAMES'S PALACE THE MALL Horse Guards LONDON EYE Road ZE HORSE GUARDS BANQUETING HOUSE LANCASTER HOUSE

Constitution Hill ST JAMES'S PARK COUNTY HALL Belvedere York Westminster WESTMINSTER BRIDGE Walk Grosvenor Place BUCKINGHAM PALACE Birdcage J M 14'6 Petty France St James's Park ST MARGARET'S Tothill St St PALACE OF WESTMINSTER ROYAL MEWS BELGRAVIA Buckingham Gate WESTMINSTER ABBEY Lambeth Palace Rd Bressenden Place NEW SCOTLAND YARD H THAMES Road Victoria Great Peter street Millbank LAMBETH PALACE King's Road Street Rochester Row Horseferry J M Lambeth Palace VICTORIA WESTMINSTER CATHEDRAL Road Bridge Lambeth High St ZF Vincent Sq. Regency Street Wilton Rd Vauxhall Bridge Way 13'9 Belgrave Embankment Lambeth

R 24 S T

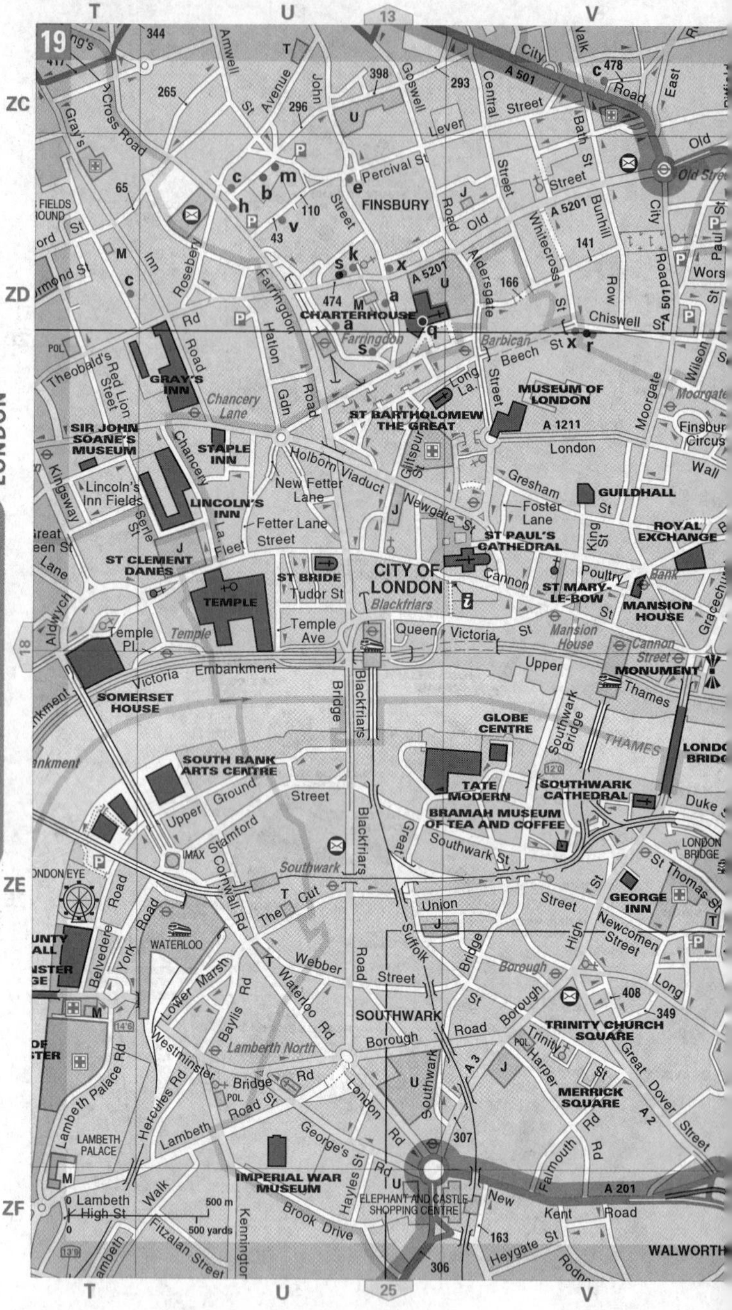

T U V

13

19

ZC

ZD

ZE

ZF

LONDON

FINSBURY
CHARTERHOUSE
GRAY'S INN
SIR JOHN SOANE'S MUSEUM
STAPLE INN
LINCOLN'S INN
ST CLEMENT DANES
TEMPLE
ST BRIDE
CITY OF LONDON
ST BARTHOLOMEW THE GREAT
MUSEUM OF LONDON
GUILDHALL
ST PAUL'S CATHEDRAL
ROYAL EXCHANGE
ST MARY-LE-BOW
MANSION HOUSE
MONUMENT
SOMERSET HOUSE
GLOBE CENTRE
SOUTH BANK ARTS CENTRE
TATE MODERN
SOUTHWARK CATHEDRAL
BRAMAH MUSEUM OF TEA AND COFFEE
GEORGE INN
WATERLOO
SOUTHWARK
TRINITY CHURCH SQUARE
MERRICK SQUARE
LAMBETH PALACE
IMPERIAL WAR MUSEUM
ELEPHANT AND CASTLE SHOPPING CENTRE
WALWORTH
THAMES

18

500 m
500 yards

T U V

25

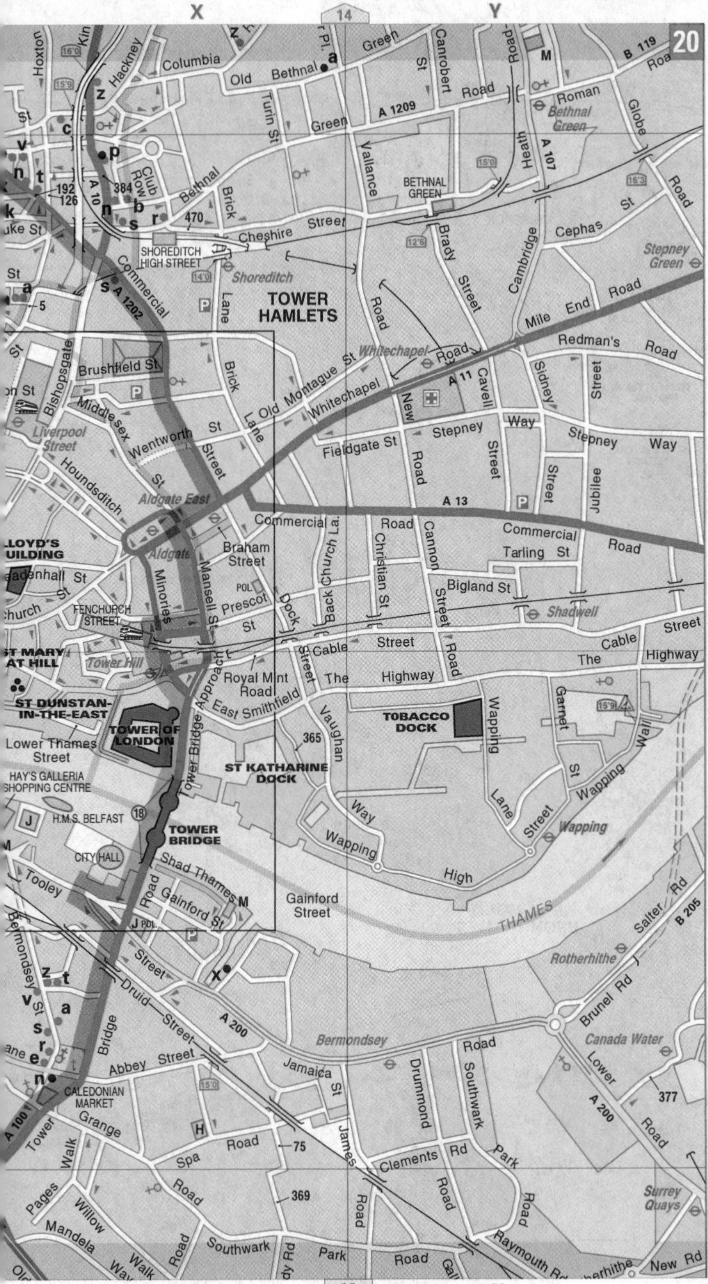

X Y
14
20
LONDON
ZC
ZD
ZE
ZF

Columbia
Old Bethnal Green
Bethnal Green
Hackney
Hoxton
Canrobert St
Road
A 1209
Roman
Bethnal Green
Globe Road
B 119
Turin St
Green
Vallance Road
BETHNAL GREEN
Heath
A 107
Club Row
A 10
384
192
126
470
Brick Lane
Cheshire Street
Brady Street
Cambridge
Cephas St
Stepney Green
SHOREDITCH HIGH STREET
Shoreditch
TOWER HAMLETS
Commercial
A 1202
Mile End Road
Redman's Road
Whitechapel
Road
A 11
Cavell
Sidney
Street
Bishopsgate
Brushfield St
Old Montague St
Whitechapel
New Road
Stepney Way
Stepney Way
Middlesex
Wentworth St
Street
Liverpool Street
Fieldgate St
Stepney Street
Street
Jubilee
Houndsditch
Aldgate East
A 13
Commercial
Road
Cannon
Commercial
Tarling St
Road
LLOYD'S BUILDING
Aldgate
Braham Street
Christian St
Leadenhall St
Minories
Mansell St
POL
Bigland St
Back Church La.
Street
Fenchurch
FENCHURCH STREET
Prescot St
Dock
Shadwell
Street
Cable
ST MARY AT HILL
Tower Hill
Cable Street
Street
Road
The Highway
The Highway
Royal Mint Road
Street
Tower Bridge Approach
East Smithfield
ST DUNSTAN-IN-THE-EAST
TOWER OF LONDON
Vaughan
TOBACCO DOCK
Wapping
Garnet
Wall
Lower Thames Street
365
ST KATHARINE DOCK
St
Wapping
HAY'S GALLERIA SHOPPING CENTRE
Way
Lane
Street
Wapping
H.M.S. BELFAST
18
TOWER BRIDGE
Wapping
CITY HALL
High
Shad Thames
Tooley
Road
Gainford St
Gainford Street
THAMES
Salter Rd
B 205
Bermondsey
Rotherhithe
Street
Druid
Street
Brunel Rd
A 200
Bermondsey
Canada Water
Bridge
Road
Abbey Street
Jamaica St
Drummond
Southwark
Lower
CALEDONIAN MARKET
A 200
377
A 100
Tower
Grange
Walk
Road
Spa
75
James
Clements Rd
Park
Road
Surrey Quays
Pages
Willow
Road
369
Road
Road
Road
Mandela Way
Walk
Road
Southwark Park Road
Raymouth Rd
New Rd
X Y
26

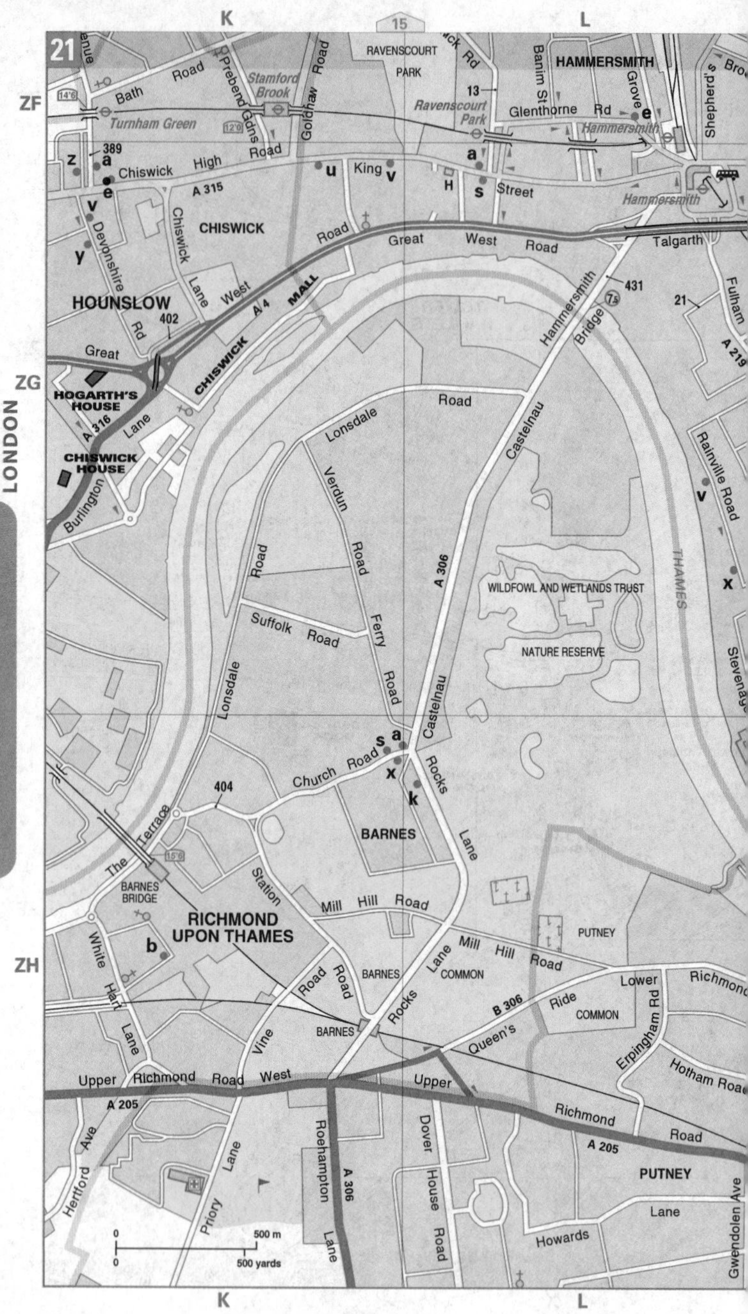
K
L
15
21
ZF
ZG
ZH
LONDON
RAVENSCOURT PARK
HAMMERSMITH
Stamford Brook
Turnham Green
Ravenscourt Park
Hammersmith
Bath Road
Prebend Gdns
Goldhawk Road
Banim St
Glenthorne Rd
Grove
Shepherd's
Chiswick High Road
King Street
A 315
CHISWICK
HOUNSLOW
Devonshire Rd
Chiswick Lane
Great West Road
Talgarth
CHISWICK MALL
A 4
Great Chertsey
HOGARTH'S HOUSE
CHISWICK HOUSE
A 316
Burlington Lane
Hammersmith Bridge
Fulham
A 219
Lonsdale Road
Verdun Road
Castelnau
A 306
Rainville Road
WILDFOWL AND WETLANDS TRUST
NATURE RESERVE
THAMES
Suffolk Road
Ferry Road
Lonsdale Road
Stevenage
Church Road
Rocks Lane
BARNES
The Terrace
BARNES BRIDGE
Station Road
Mill Hill Road
RICHMOND UPON THAMES
PUTNEY
White Hart Lane
Vine Road
BARNES COMMON
Lower Richmond
Erpingham Rd
B 306
Queen's Ride
COMMON
BARNES
Hotham Road
Upper Richmond Road West
Upper Richmond Road
A 205
Hertford Ave
Priory Lane
Roehampton Lane
Dover House Road
PUTNEY
Lane
Howards
Gwendolen Ave
500 m
500 yards

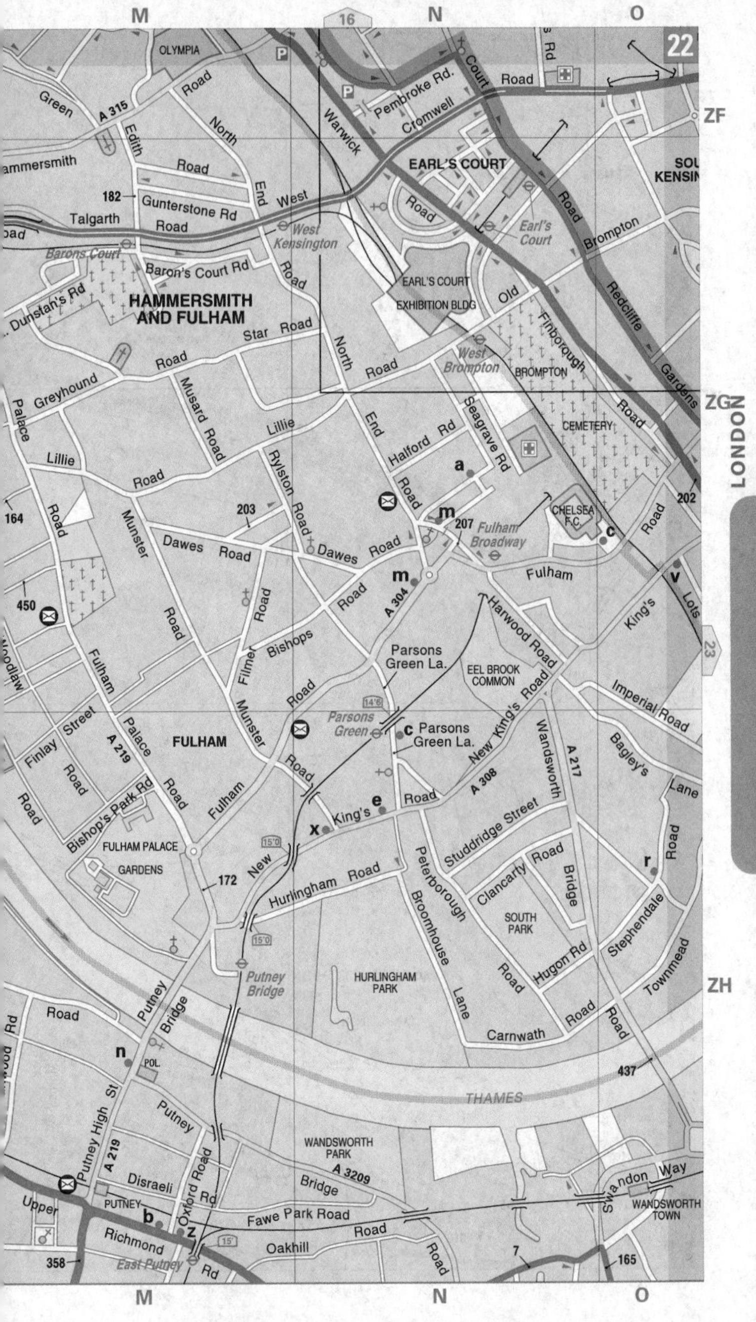

OLYMPIA
HAMMERSMITH AND FULHAM
EARL'S COURT
EARL'S COURT EXHIBITION BLDG
West Kensington
Earl's Court
West Brompton
BROMPTON CEMETERY
CHELSEA F.C.
Fulham Broadway
Parsons Green
EEL BROOK COMMON
FULHAM
FULHAM PALACE GARDENS
SOUTH PARK
HURLINGHAM PARK
Putney Bridge
THAMES
WANDSWORTH PARK
PUTNEY
WANDSWORTH TOWN
East Putney
Barons Court
LONDON

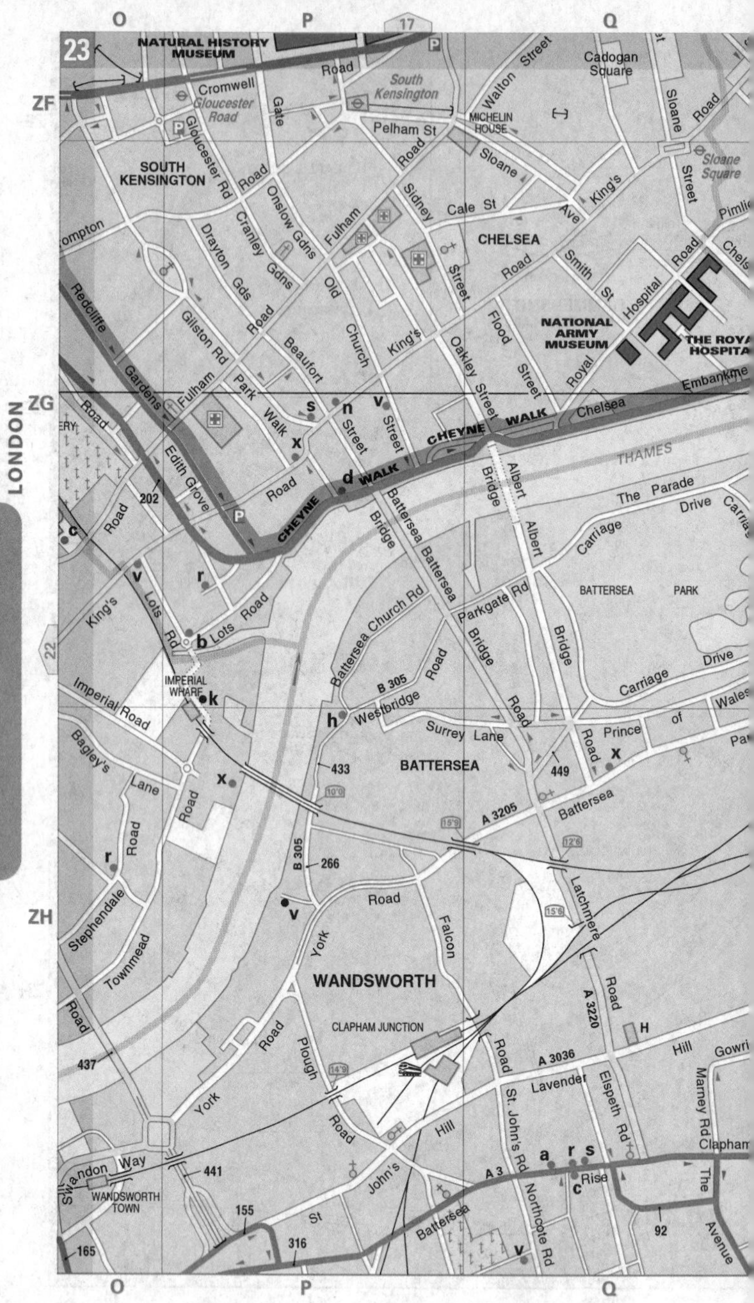

NATURAL HISTORY MUSEUM
SOUTH KENSINGTON
CHELSEA
NATIONAL ARMY MUSEUM
THE ROYAL HOSPITAL
MICHELIN HOUSE
Cadogan Square
Sloane Square
South Kensington
Gloucester Road
THAMES
BATTERSEA PARK
BATTERSEA
IMPERIAL WHARF
WANDSWORTH
CLAPHAM JUNCTION
WANDSWORTH TOWN
CHEYNE WALK
Cromwell Road
Pelham St
Sloane Avenue
King's Road
Fulham Road
Old Church Street
Oakley Street
Flood Street
Royal Hospital Road
Chelsea Embankment
Battersea Bridge
Albert Bridge
Battersea Church Rd
Parkgate Rd
Westbridge Road
Surrey Lane
Prince of Wales Drive
Carriage Drive
The Parade
Imperial Road
Lots Road
Edith Grove
Redcliffe Gardens
Latchmere Road
Falcon Road
York Road
Plough Road
Lavender Hill
St. John's Rd
Northcote Rd
Elspeth Rd
Battersea Rise
Clapham
Swandon Way
A 3205
A 3220
A 3036
A 3
B 305

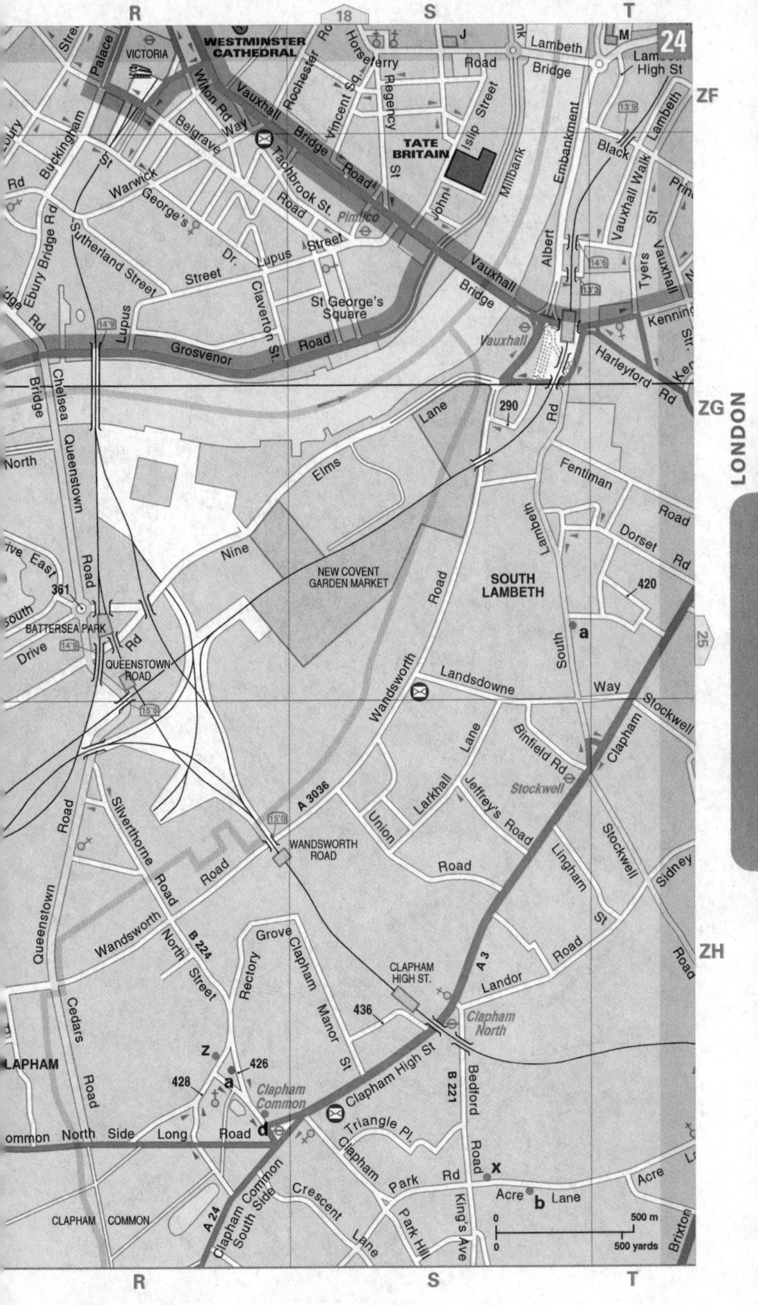

R
18
S
T
24
WESTMINSTER CATHEDRAL
VICTORIA
TATE BRITAIN
Pimlico
Vauxhall
ZF
ZG
ZH
LONDON
Lambeth Bridge
Lambeth High St
Vauxhall Bridge Road
Grosvenor Road
St George's Square
NEW COVENT GARDEN MARKET
SOUTH LAMBETH
BATTERSEA PARK
QUEENSTOWN ROAD
WANDSWORTH ROAD
CLAPHAM HIGH ST.
Stockwell
Clapham North
Clapham Common
LAPHAM
CLAPHAM COMMON
Wandsworth Road
Nine Elms Lane
Queenstown Road
Chelsea Bridge
Clapham High St
Bedford Road
Acre Lane
Landor Road
Stockwell Road
Clapham Park Rd
500 m
500 yards
25

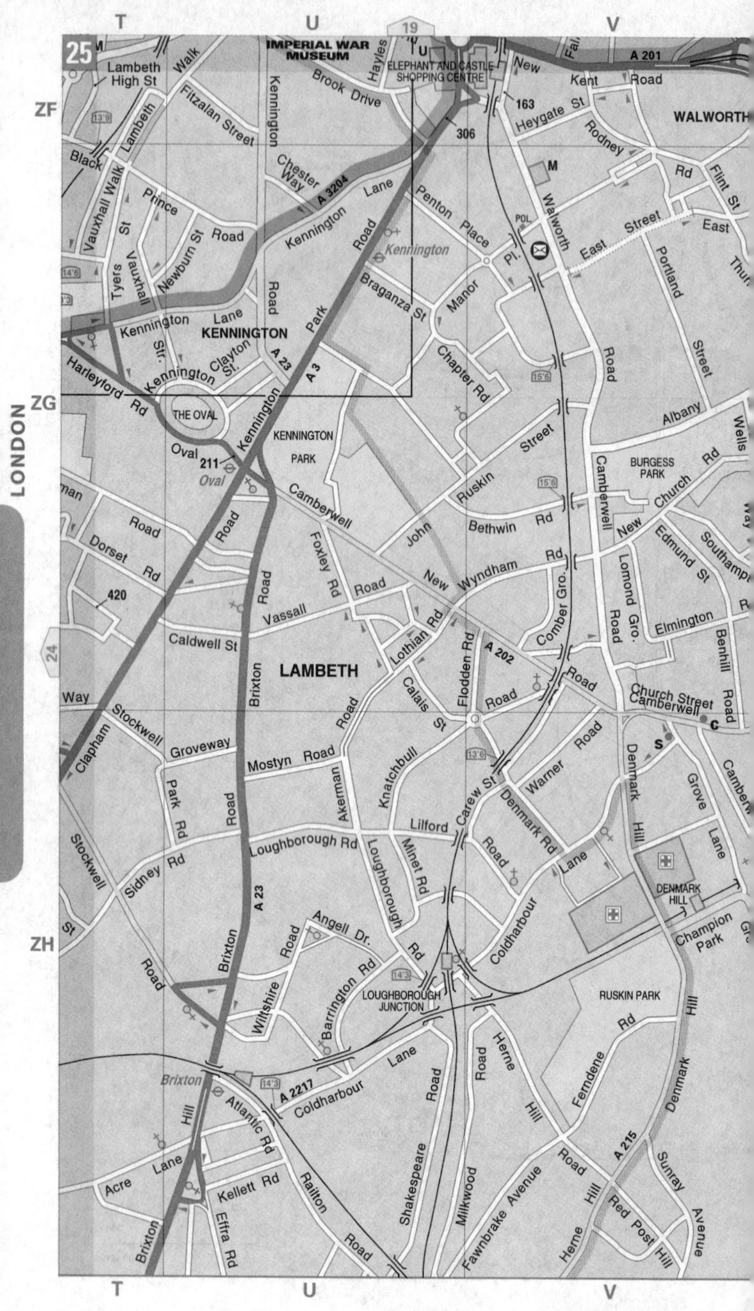
T
U
V
25
19
IMPERIAL WAR MUSEUM
ELEPHANT AND CASTLE SHOPPING CENTRE
A 201
WALWORTH
KENNINGTON
THE OVAL
KENNINGTON PARK
BURGESS PARK
LAMBETH
LOUGHBOROUGH JUNCTION
RUSKIN PARK
DENMARK HILL
ZF
ZG
ZH
24
A 3204
A 23
A 3
A 202
A 2217
A 215
Kennington
Oval
Brixton
Lambeth High St
Walk
Fitzalan Street
Kennington Road
Brook Drive
Hayles
New Kent Road
Heygate St
Rodney Rd
Flint St
East Street
Portland Street
Penton Place
Walworth Road
Kennington Lane
Chester Way
Black Prince Road
Vauxhall Walk
Tyers St
Vauxhall St
Newburn St
Kennington Park Road
Braganza St
Manor Pl.
Chapter Rd
Clayton St.
Harleyford Rd
Kennington Oval
Albany Road
Wells
Ruskin Street
Camberwell Road
Camberwell New Road
Bethwin Rd
John
New Church Rd
Edmund St
Dorset Rd
Foxley Rd
New Wyndham Rd
Lomond Gro.
Comber Gro.
Vassall Road
Caldwell St
Lothian Rd
Flodden Rd
Elmington
Benhill Road
Brixton Road
Calais St
Church Street
Camberwell
Stockwell
Groveway
Mostyn Road
Akerman Road
Knatchbull
Carew St
Warner Road
Denmark Hill
Grove Lane
Clapham
Park Rd
Lilford
Loughborough Rd
Loughborough Rd
Minet Rd
Denmark Rd
Coldharbour Lane
Sidney Rd
Angell Dr.
Wiltshire Road
Barrington Rd
Champion Park
Herne Hill
Ferndene Rd
Atlantic Rd
Coldharbour Lane
Shakespeare Road
Milkwood Road
Acre Lane
Kellett Rd
Railton Road
Effra Rd
Brixton Hill
Fawnbrake Avenue
Herne Hill Road
Red Post Hill
Sunray Avenue
306
163
211
420

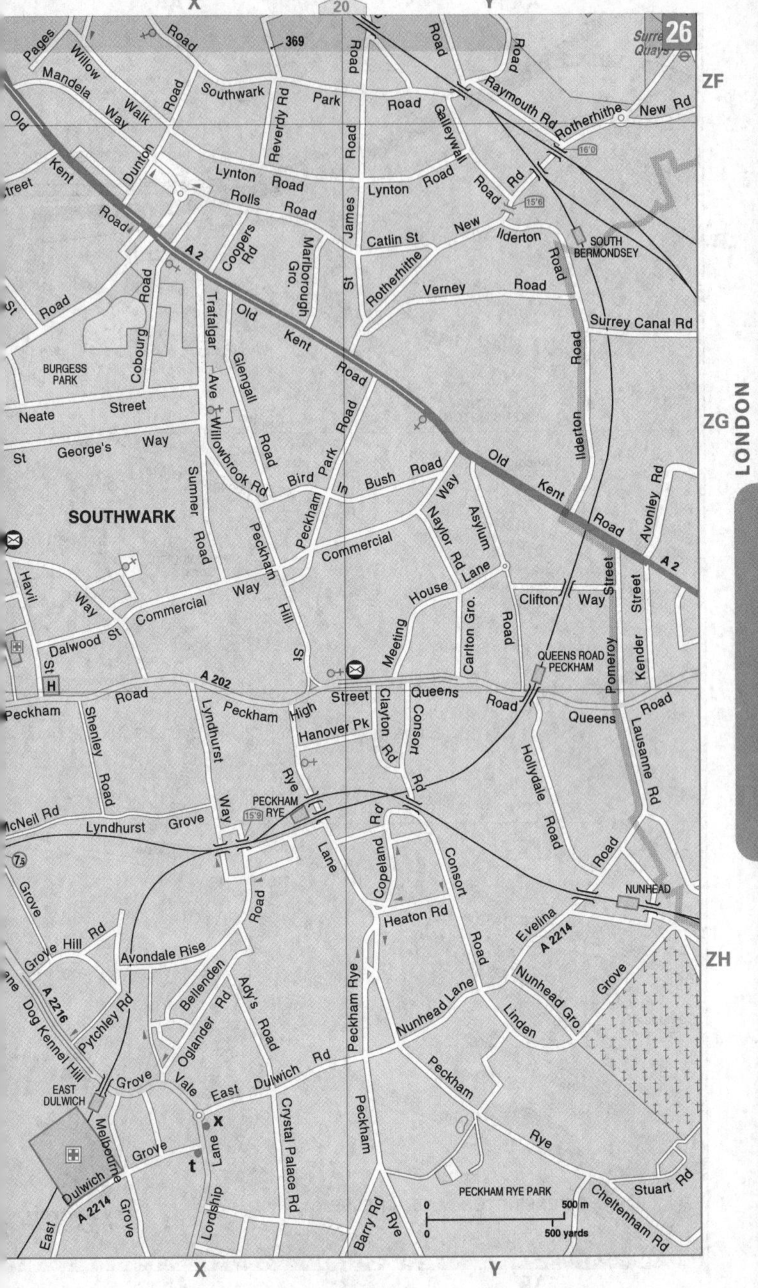

X
20
Y
26
Surrey Quays
ZF
ZG
ZH
LONDON
369
Pages Willow Walk
Mandela Way
Old Kent Road
Southwark Park Road
Reverdy Rd
Galleywall Road
Raymouth Rd
Rotherhithe New Rd
16'0
Dunton Road
Lynton Road
Rolls Road
St James Road
Catlin St
Rotherhithe New Road
Ilderton Road
15'6
SOUTH BERMONDSEY
Coopers Rd
Marlborough Gro.
A 2
Verney Road
Surrey Canal Rd
Cobourg Road
Trafalgar Ave
Glengall Road
BURGESS PARK
Neate Street
St George's Way
Willowbrook Rd
Bird In Bush Road
Peckham Park Road
Naylor Rd
Asylum Road
Avonley Rd
SOUTHWARK
Sumner Road
Peckham Hill St
Commercial Way
Havil St
Dalwood St
House Lane
Meeting House Lane
Carlton Gro.
Clifton Way
Pomeroy Street
Kender Street
QUEENS ROAD PECKHAM
A 202
Peckham Road
Peckham High Street
Queens Road
Shenley Road
Lyndhurst Way
Hanover Pk
Clayton Rd
Consort Rd
Hollydale Road
Lausanne Rd
Rye Lane
PECKHAM RYE
15'9
McNeil Rd
Lyndhurst Grove
Copeland Rd
Consort Road
NUNHEAD
Grove Hill Rd
Heaton Rd
Evelina Road
A 2214
Avondale Rise
Bellenden Rd
Ady's Road
Peckham Rye
Nunhead Lane
Nunhead Gro.
Linden Grove
A 2216
Dog Kennel Hill
Pytchley Rd
Oglander Rd
East Dulwich Rd
Grove Vale
EAST DULWICH
Crystal Palace Rd
Peckham Rye
Melbourne Grove
Dulwich Grove
Lordship Lane
X
t
PECKHAM RYE PARK
Barry Rd
Cheltenham Rd
Stuart Rd
A 2214
East
0
500 m
500 yards
X
Y

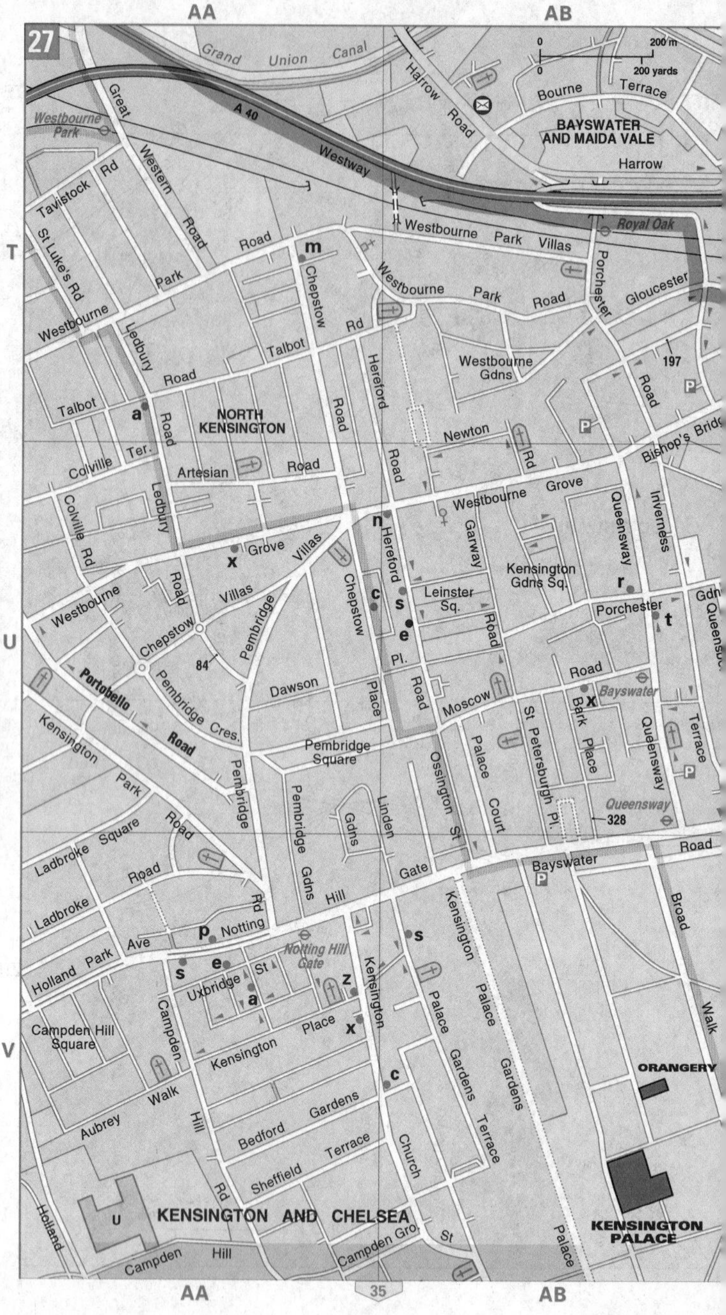

LONDON

27

AA AB

BAYSWATER AND MAIDA VALE

NORTH KENSINGTON

KENSINGTON AND CHELSEA

ORANGERY

KENSINGTON PALACE

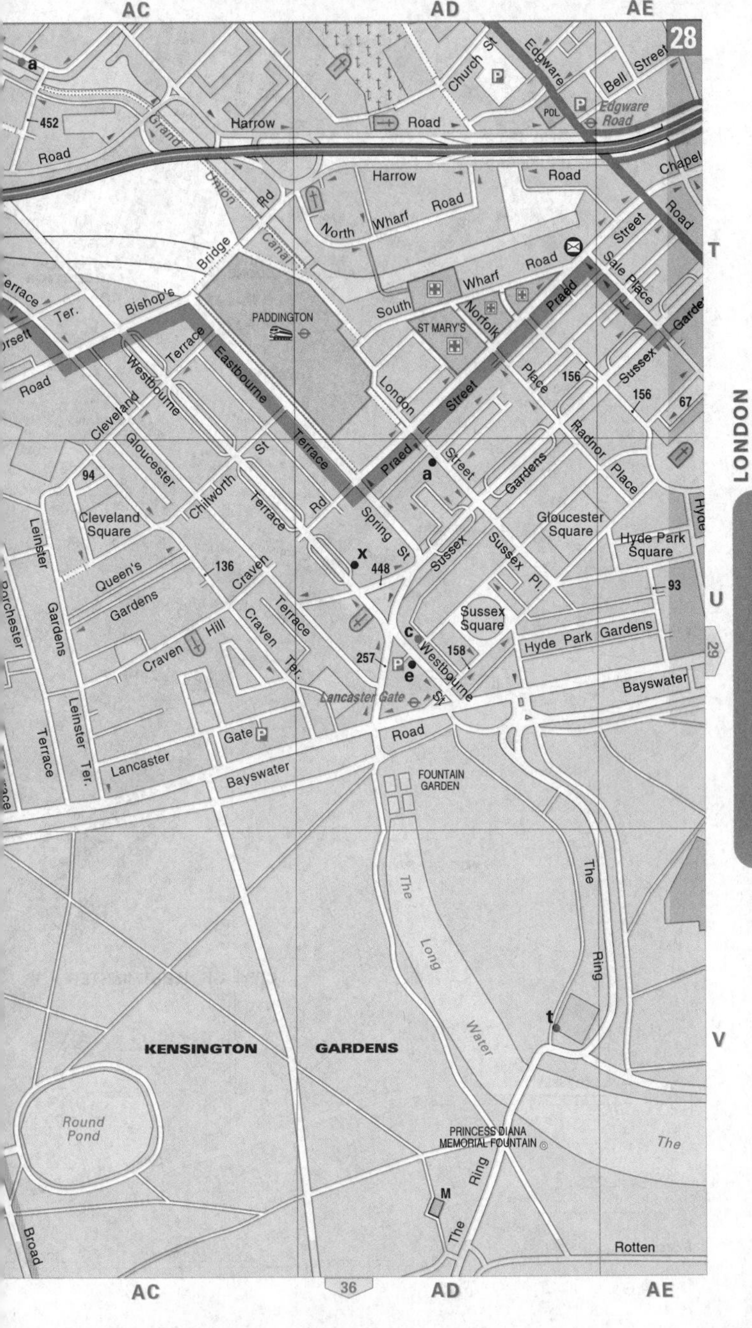

AC
AD
AE
28
LONDON
T
U
V
29
36
Edgware Road
Harrow Road
Church St
Bell Street
Grand Union Canal
North Wharf Road
South Wharf Road
Bishop's Bridge Rd
PADDINGTON
ST MARY'S
Norfolk Place
Praed Street
Sale Place
Sussex Gardens
London Street
Eastbourne Terrace
Westbourne Terrace
Cleveland Square
Gloucester Square
Hyde Park Square
Hyde Park Gardens
Sussex Square
Sussex Pl.
Radnor Place
Spring St
Chilworth St
Craven Terrace
Craven Hill
Queen's Gardens
Leinster Gardens
Leinster Ter.
Leinster Terrace
Lancaster Gate
Lancaster Terrace
Bayswater Road
Westbourne St
FOUNTAIN GARDEN
The Long Water
The Ring
KENSINGTON GARDENS
Round Pond
PRINCESS DIANA MEMORIAL FOUNTAIN
Rotten
Broad
Chapel

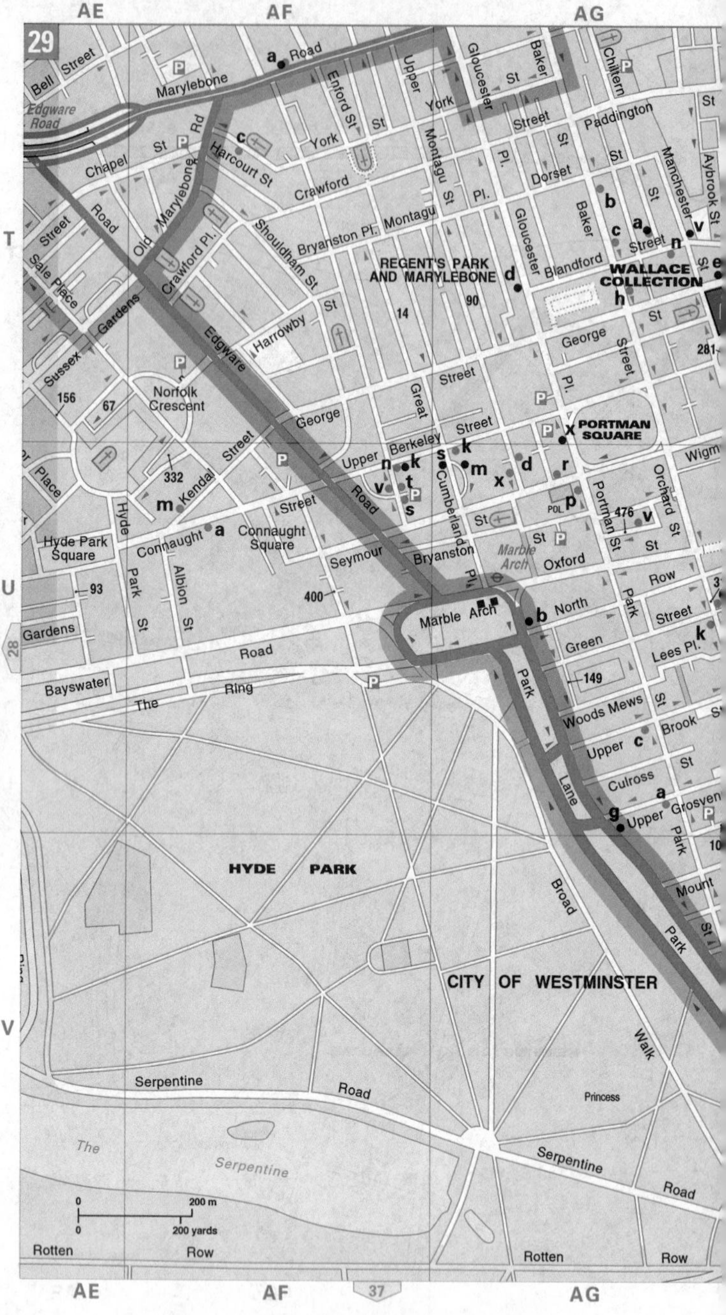

AE AF AG

29

Bell Street
Marylebone Road
Edgware Road
Enford St
Upper York St
Gloucester Pl.
Baker St
Chiltern St
Paddington St
York St
Chapel St
Old Marylebone Rd
Harcourt St
Crawford St
Montagu St
Dorset St
Aybrook St
Manchester St
Sale Place
Crawford Pl.
Shouldham St
Bryanston Pl.
Montagu Pl.
Blandford Street
T
REGENT'S PARK AND MARYLEBONE
WALLACE COLLECTION
90
14
Sussex Gardens
Harrowby St
George Street
Edgware Road
156
67
Norfolk Crescent
George Street
Great Cumberland Pl.
PORTMAN SQUARE
Upper Berkeley Street
332
Kendal Street
Portman St
Orchard St
476
Wigmore
Hyde Park Square
Hyde Park St
Albion St
Connaught Street
Connaught Square
Seymour Street
Bryanston St
Marble Arch
Oxford Street
U
93
400
Marble Arch
North Row
Park Street
Gardens
Bayswater Road
Green Street
Lees Pl.
The Ring
Park Lane
149
Woods Mews
Brook St
Upper Brook St
Culross St
Upper Grosvenor St
Park St
Mount St
Park Lane
HYDE PARK
Broad Walk
CITY OF WESTMINSTER
V
Serpentine Road
Princess
The Serpentine
Serpentine Road
0 200 m
0 200 yards
Rotten Row
AE AF 37 AG

LONDON

28

AH
AI
AJ
30
BRITISH TELECOM TOWER
Marylebone High St
Weymouth
Wimpole
Harley
Street
Portland
Great Portland St
Great Cavendish
New Cavendish Street
Cleveland
Charlotte
Goodge St
Foley St
Great Titchfield Street
Langham Place
Wells St
Newman St
Berner's
Welbeck
Queen Anne Street
Mortimer
Regent
Cavendish Sq.
Wigmore St
Henrietta Pl.
Holles St
Margaret
Oxford Circus
Oxford St
Eastcastle Street
Poland
Noel St
James St
Duke St
Vere St
Argyll
NEW BOND ST
Princes St
Great Marlborough St
Bond St
South Molton St
Hannover Sq.
Hanover St
Gilbert
Binney
Davies
Brook St
Maddox
Carnaby
Marshall
Broadwick
Lexington
Kingly St
Brook's Mews
MAYFAIR
George St
Saville Row
Golden Sq.
Beak
Grosvenor Square
Grosvenor Street
Conduit
Bruton Street
Cork St
Vigo St
REGENT ST
Adam's Row
Mount Row
South Audley St
Mount Street
Berkeley Square
BURLINGTON HOUSE
BURLINGTON ARCADE
OLD BOND ST
Sackville St
Farm Street
Hay's Mews
Dover Street
Albemarle Street
Berkeley St
PICCADILLY
JERMYN ST
PICCADILLY ARCADE
ST JAMES SQUARE
Hill St
Charles Street
Curzon St
Bolton Street
Bury St
Duke St
King St
ST JAMES'S ST
Curzon Street
Green Park
Queen's Walk
Pall Mall
SHEPHERD MARKET
Hertford St
Brick St
Old Park La.
QUEEN'S CHAPEL
SPENCER HOUSE
GREEN PARK
ST JAMES PALACE
LANCASTER HOUSE
T
U
V
31
38
LONDON

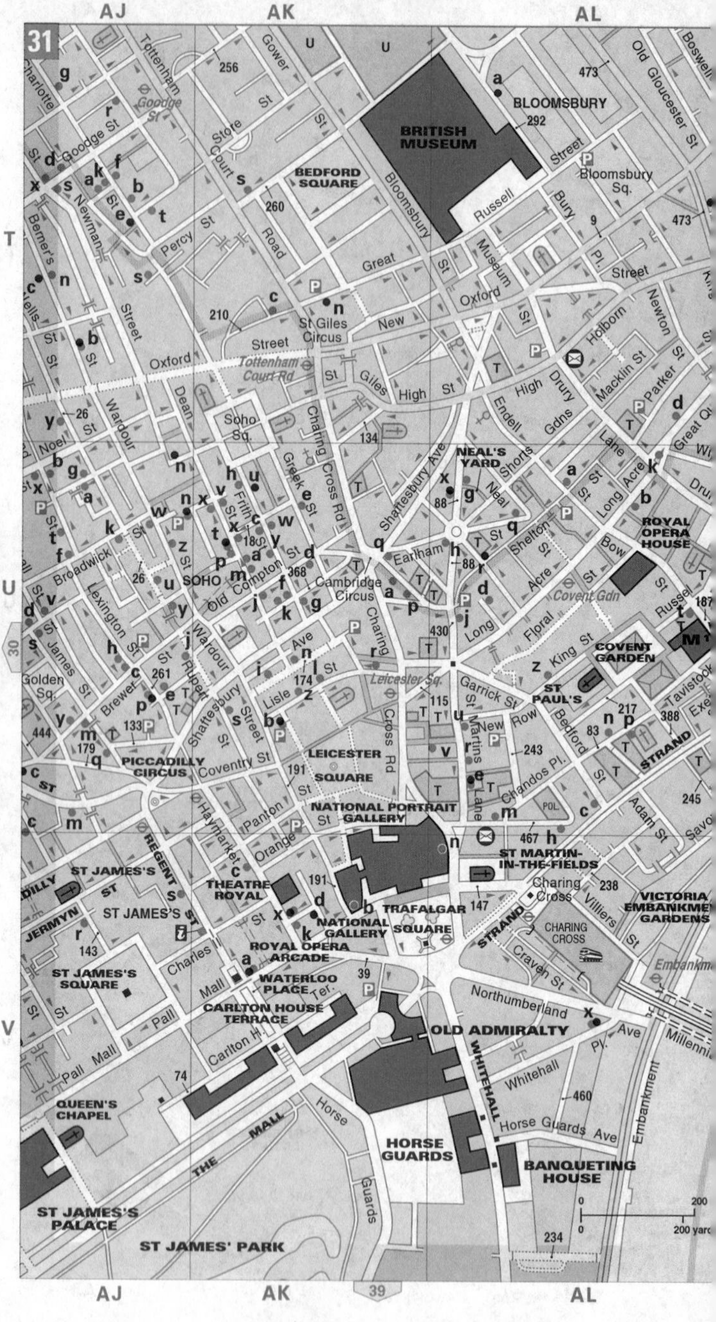

31

AJ AK AL

T

U

V

30

39

AM AN AO

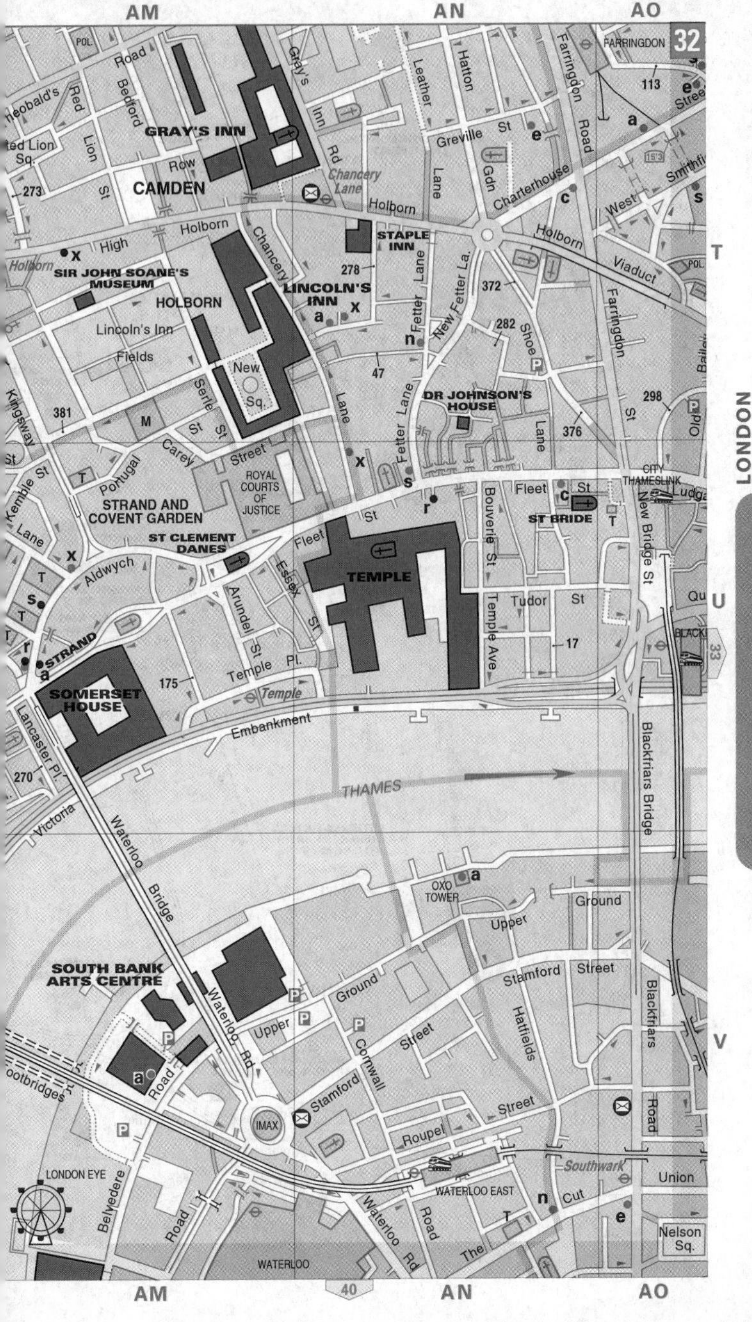

T U V

AM AN AO

40

LONDON

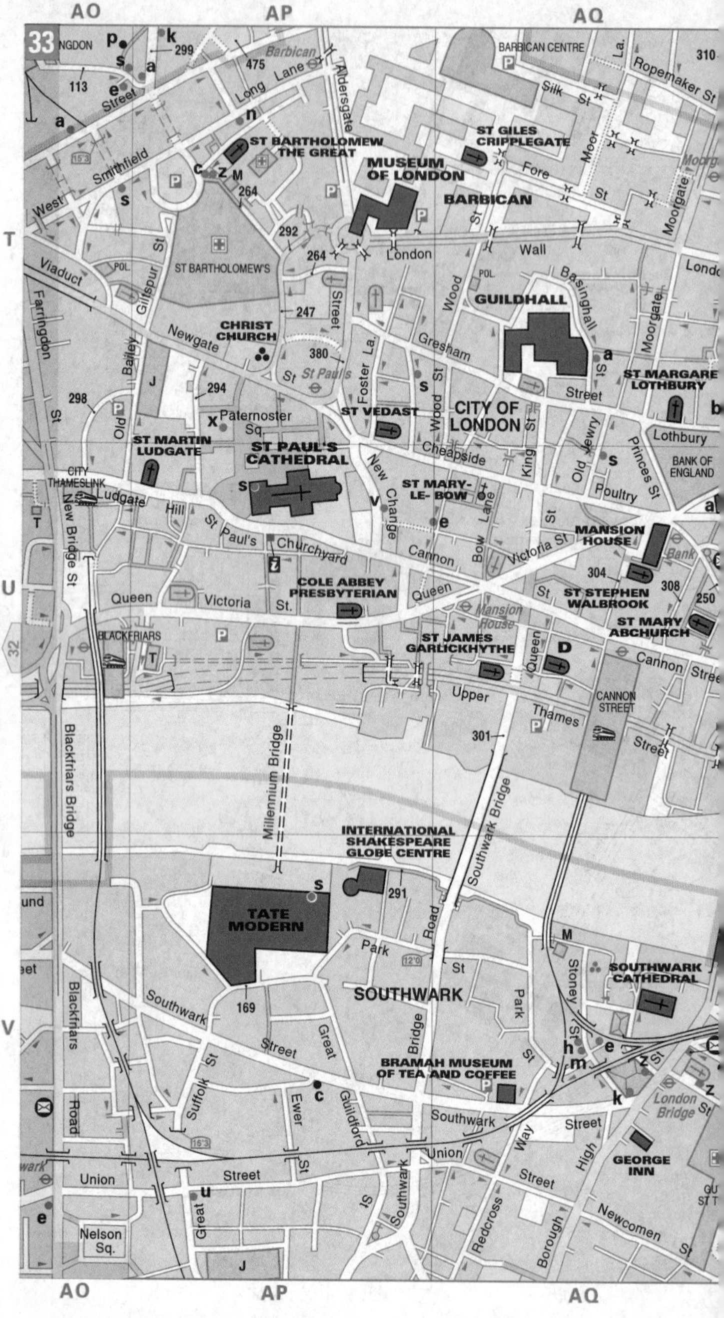

LONDON

33

ST BARTHOLOMEW THE GREAT

MUSEUM OF LONDON

BARBICAN

ST GILES CRIPPLEGATE

BARBICAN CENTRE

ST BARTHOLOMEW'S

CHRIST CHURCH

GUILDHALL

ST MARGARET LOTHBURY

ST VEDAST

CITY OF LONDON

ST MARTIN LUDGATE

ST PAUL'S CATHEDRAL

BANK OF ENGLAND

ST MARY-LE-BOW

MANSION HOUSE

COLE ABBEY PRESBYTERIAN

ST STEPHEN WALBROOK

ST MARY ABCHURCH

ST JAMES GARLICKHYTHE

CANNON STREET

BLACKFRIARS

CITY THAMESLINK

INTERNATIONAL SHAKESPEARE GLOBE CENTRE

TATE MODERN

SOUTHWARK

SOUTHWARK CATHEDRAL

BRAMAH MUSEUM OF TEA AND COFFEE

GEORGE INN

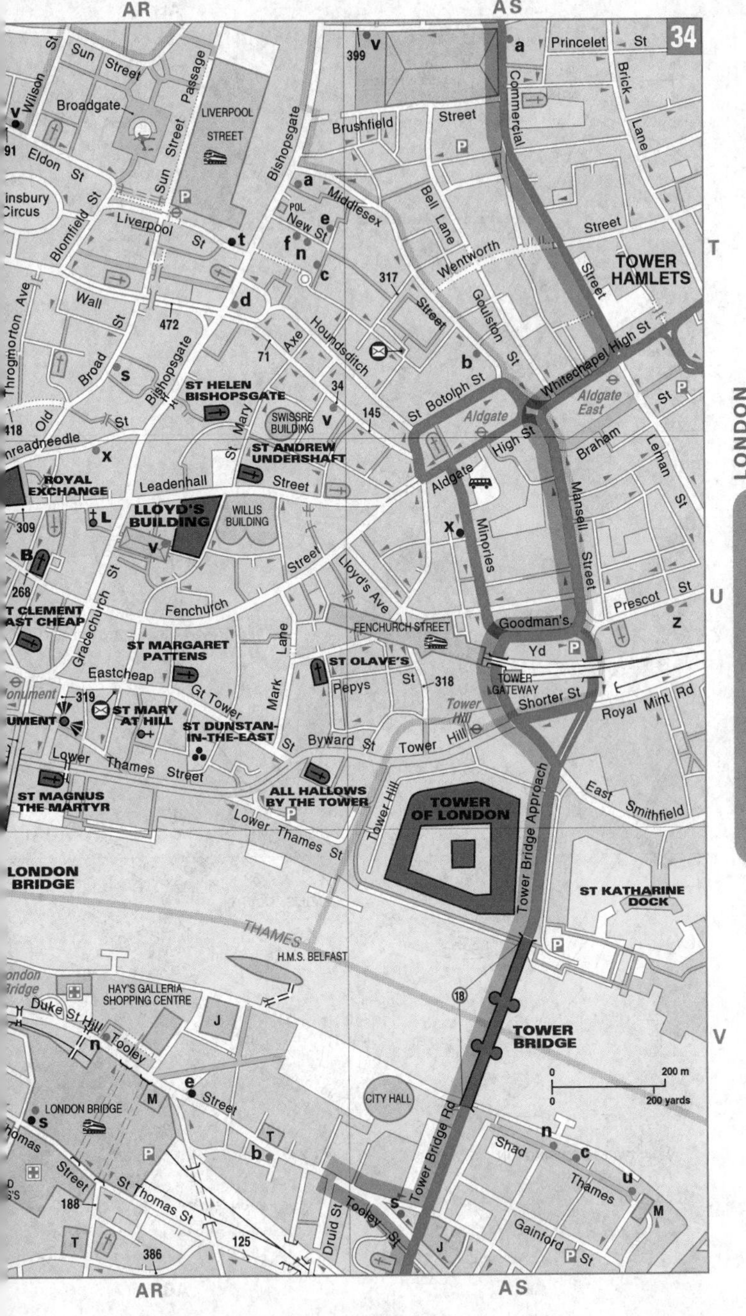
AR
AS
34
T
U
V
LONDON
TOWER HAMLETS
LIVERPOOL STREET
Broadgate
Bishopsgate
Brushfield Street
Commercial Street
Princelet St
Brick Lane
Middlesex Street
Bell Lane
Wentworth Street
Goulston St
Houndsditch
Whitechapel High St
Aldgate East
Aldgate High St
St Botolph St
ST HELEN BISHOPSGATE
SWISSRE BUILDING
ST ANDREW UNDERSHAFT
Leadenhall Street
ROYAL EXCHANGE
LLOYD'S BUILDING
WILLIS BUILDING
Fenchurch Street
Lloyd's Ave
Minories
Mansell Street
Leman St
Braham St
Prescot St
Goodman's Yd
FENCHURCH STREET
ST OLAVE'S
ST MARGARET PATTENS
ST MARY AT HILL
ST DUNSTAN-IN-THE-EAST
Eastcheap
Gt Tower St
Byward St
Tower Hill
TOWER GATEWAY
Shorter St
Royal Mint Rd
East Smithfield
ST MAGNUS THE MARTYR
ALL HALLOWS BY THE TOWER
Lower Thames Street
TOWER OF LONDON
Tower Bridge Approach
ST KATHARINE DOCK
LONDON BRIDGE
THAMES
H.M.S. BELFAST
HAY'S GALLERIA SHOPPING CENTRE
Duke St Hill
Tooley Street
CITY HALL
TOWER BRIDGE
0 200 m
0 200 yards
Tower Bridge Rd
Shad Thames
Gainford St
St Thomas St
Druid St
LONDON BRIDGE
Eldon St
Liverpool St
Blomfield St
Wall
Broad St
Throgmorton Ave
Old Broad St
Threadneedle
St Mary Axe
Gracechurch St
Mark Lane
Pepys St
ST CLEMENT EAST CHEAP
Sun Street
Sun Street Passage
Wilson St
Finsbury Circus
Thomas Street
Monument
MONUMENT

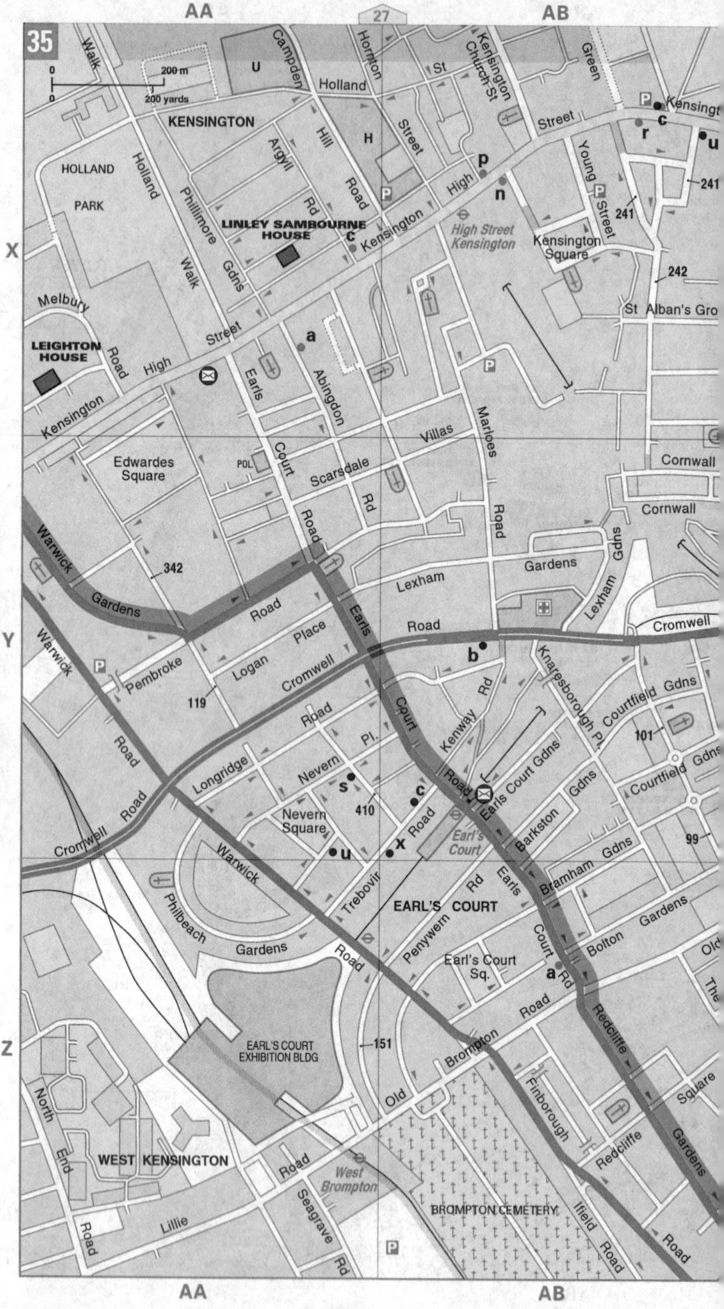

AA
27
AB
35
0 200 m
0 200 yards
KENSINGTON
HOLLAND PARK
LINLEY SAMBOURNE HOUSE
LEIGHTON HOUSE
High Street Kensington
Kensington Square
Edwardes Square
EARL'S COURT
Earl's Court
Earl's Court Sq.
Nevern Square
EARL'S COURT EXHIBITION BLDG
WEST KENSINGTON
West Brompton
BROMPTON CEMETERY
Walk
Holland Walk
Campden Hill Road
Holland St
Hornton Street
Kensington Church St
Green
Kensington High Street
Young Street
Argyll Rd
Phillimore Gdns
Phillimore Walk
Melbury Road
Earls Court Road
Abingdon Road
Villas
Marloes Road
Scarsdale Villas
POL
St Alban's Gro
Cornwall
Lexham Gardens
Lexham Gdns
Warwick Gardens
Warwick Road
Pembroke Road
Logan Place
Cromwell Road
Longridge Road
Nevern Pl.
Nevern Road
Kenway Rd
Knaresborough Pl.
Courtfield Gdns
Earls Court Gdns
Barkston Gdns
Bramham Gdns
Bolton Gardens
Trebovir Road
Penywern Rd
Philbeach Gardens
Old Brompton Road
Finborough Road
Redcliffe Gardens
Redcliffe Square
Ifield Road
North End Road
Lillie Road
Seagrave Rd
Old
The
U
H
P
X
Y
Z
a b c n p r s u x
101
119
151
241
242
342
410
99

AA
AB

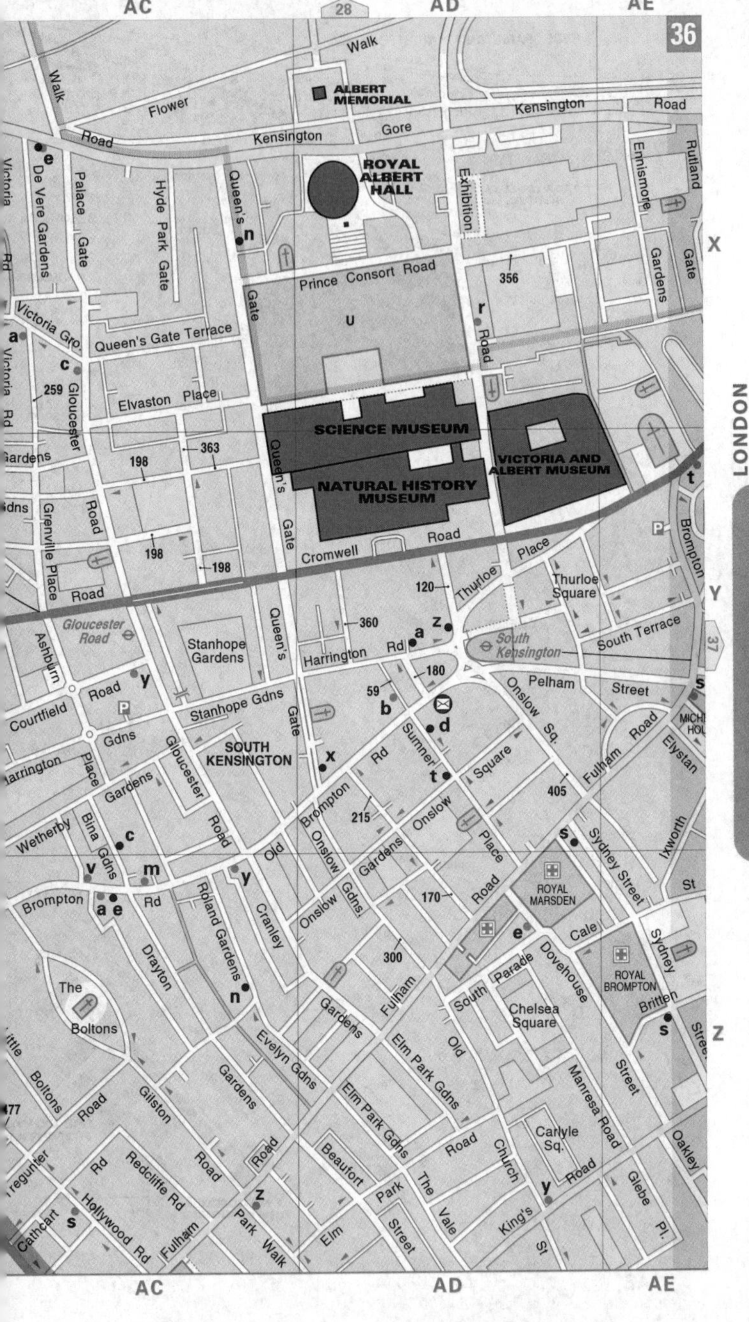
AC
AD
AE
28
36
LONDON
X
Y
Z
ALBERT MEMORIAL
ROYAL ALBERT HALL
SCIENCE MUSEUM
NATURAL HISTORY MUSEUM
VICTORIA AND ALBERT MUSEUM
SOUTH KENSINGTON
ROYAL MARSDEN
ROYAL BROMPTON
Kensington Road
Kensington Gore
Flower Walk
Prince Consort Road
Queen's Gate
Exhibition Road
Cromwell Road
Thurloe Place
Thurloe Square
South Terrace
Pelham Street
Onslow Sq.
Fulham Road
Brompton Road
Old Brompton Rd
Harrington Rd
Sumner Place
Onslow Gardens
Cranley Gardens
Roland Gardens
Drayton Gardens
Gloucester Road
Stanhope Gardens
Stanhope Gdns
Elvaston Place
Queen's Gate Terrace
Hyde Park Gate
Palace Gate
De Vere Gardens
Victoria Gro.
Courtfield Gdns
Wetherby Gardens
Bina Gdns
The Boltons
Redcliffe Rd
Hollywood Rd
Gilston Road
Evelyn Gdns
Elm Park Gdns
Beaufort Street
The Vale
Old Church Street
Carlyle Sq.
Chelsea Square
Dovehouse Street
Manresa Road
King's Road
Sydney Street
Ixworth Pl.
Elystan St
Britten Street
Glebe Pl.
Oakley Street
Ennismore Gardens
Rutland Gate
Park Walk
Gloucester Road
South Kensington
Ashburn Place
Grenville Place
Cale St
South Parade
356
363
198
259
120
360
180
59
215
405
170
300

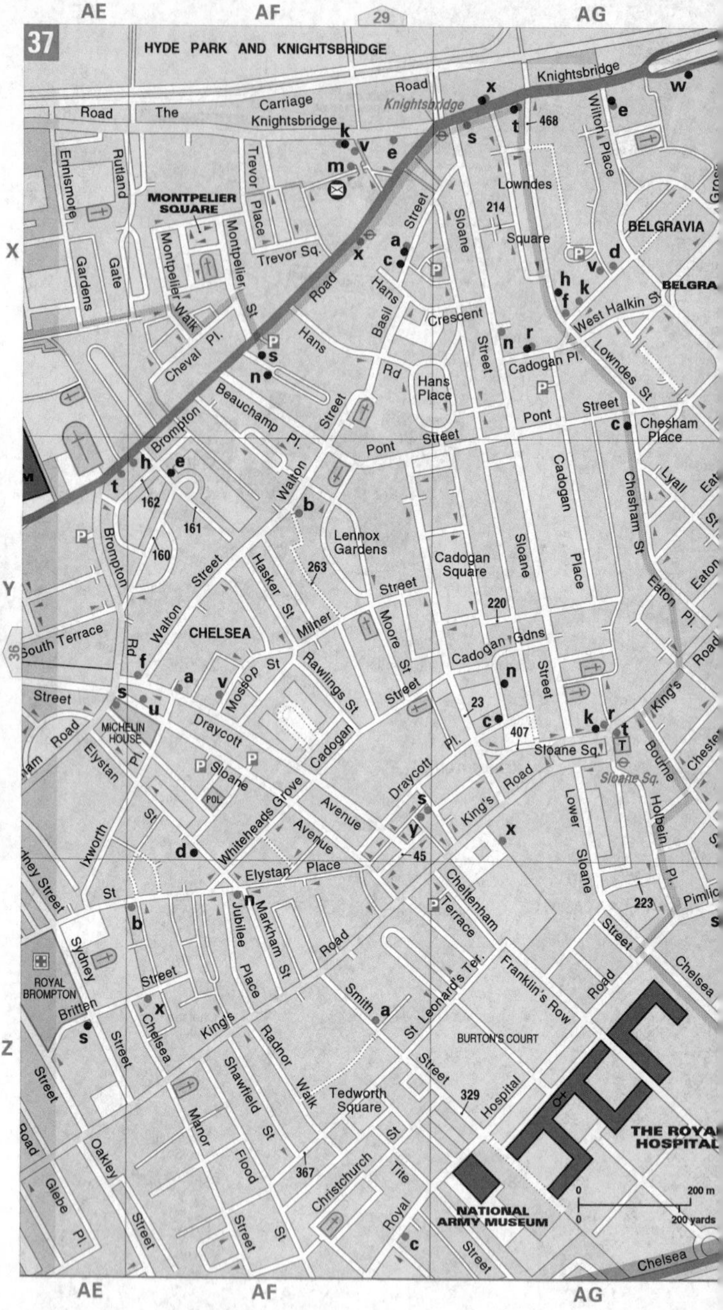

AE AF 29 AG

37 HYDE PARK AND KNIGHTSBRIDGE

Road The Carriage Road
Knightsbridge
Knightsbridge
Knightsbridge
Ennismore Gardens
Rutland Gate
MONTPELIER SQUARE
Montpelier Walk
Montpelier St
Trevor Place
Trevor Sq.
Brompton Road
Cheval Pl.
Hans Road
Basil Street
Hans Crescent
Sloane Street
Lowndes Square
214
468
Wilton Place
BELGRAVIA
BELGRA
West Halkin St
Cadogan Pl.
Lowndes St
Hans Rd
Hans Place
Pont Street
Chesham Place
Beauchamp Pl.
Walton Street
Lyall
Eaton
162
161
160
263
Lennox Gardens
Cadogan Square
Cadogan Place
Chesham St
Brompton Rd
CHELSEA
Hasker St
Milner Street
Moore St
220
Cadogan Gdns
Eaton Pl.
36 South Terrace
Street
Mossop St
Rawlings St
Sloane Street
King's Road
MICHELIN HOUSE
Elystan Pl.
Draycott Avenue
Cadogan Street
Draycott Pl.
23
407
Sloane Sq.
Sloane Sq.
Bourne St
Chester
Sloane Avenue
POL
Whiteheads Grove
King's Road
Lower Sloane Street
Holbein Pl.
Elystan St
Ixworth
45
Elystan Place
Cheltenham Terrace
223
Pimlico Road
Sydney Street
St
Jubilee Place
Markham St
Road
Chelsea
Sydney Street
ROYAL BROMPTON
Britten Street
Chelsea
Smith Street
St Leonard's Ter.
Franklin's Row
King's Road
BURTON'S COURT
Radnor Walk
Street
Shawfield St
Tedworth Square
329
Hospital Road
THE ROYAL HOSPITAL
Manor Street
Flood Street
367
Christchurch St
Tite St
Royal Hospital Road
Oakley Street
Glebe Pl.
Street
Road
NATIONAL ARMY MUSEUM
0 200 m
0 200 yards
Chelsea

X Y Z

AE AF AG

LONDON

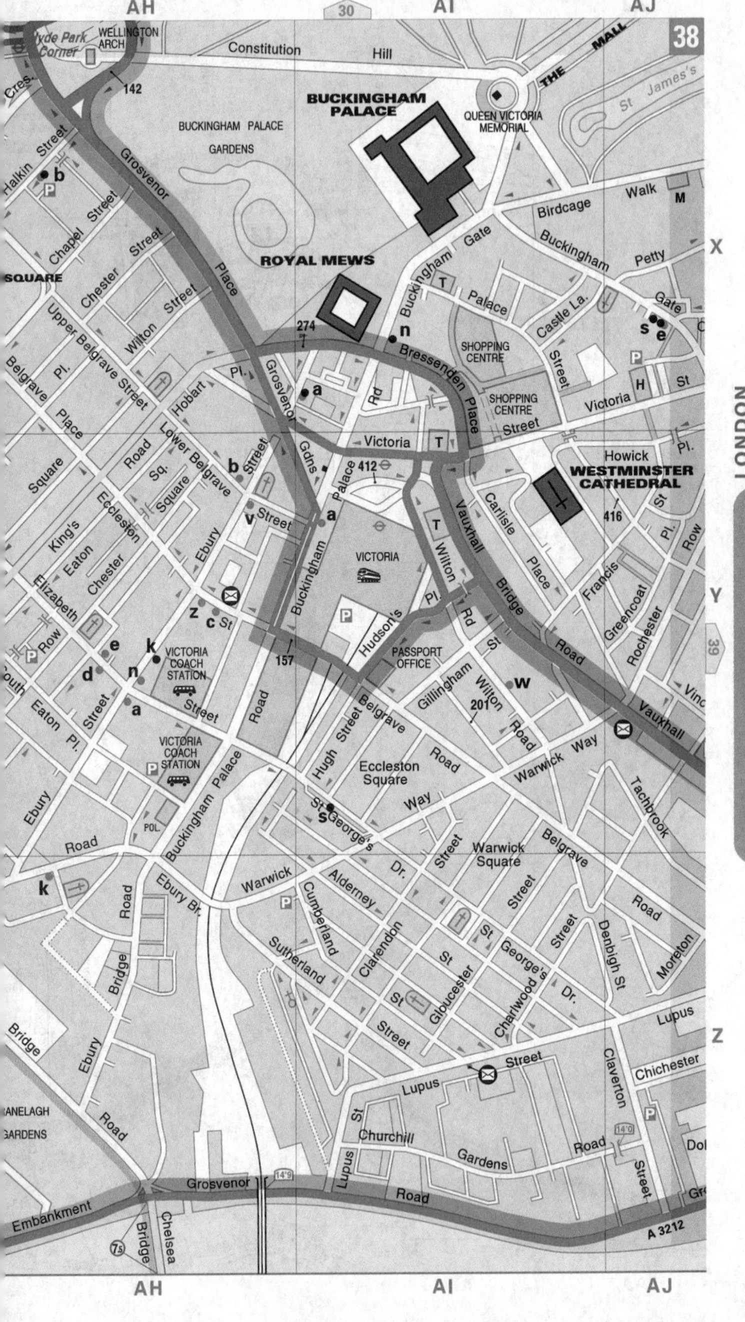

AH
30
AI
AJ
38
Hyde Park Corner
WELLINGTON ARCH
Constitution Hill
THE MALL
St James's
BUCKINGHAM PALACE
QUEEN VICTORIA MEMORIAL
BUCKINGHAM PALACE GARDENS
ROYAL MEWS
WESTMINSTER CATHEDRAL
VICTORIA
VICTORIA COACH STATION
PASSPORT OFFICE
SHOPPING CENTRE
Eccleston Square
Warwick Square
RANELAGH GARDENS
LONDON
X
Y
Z
39
A 3212
AH
AI
AJ

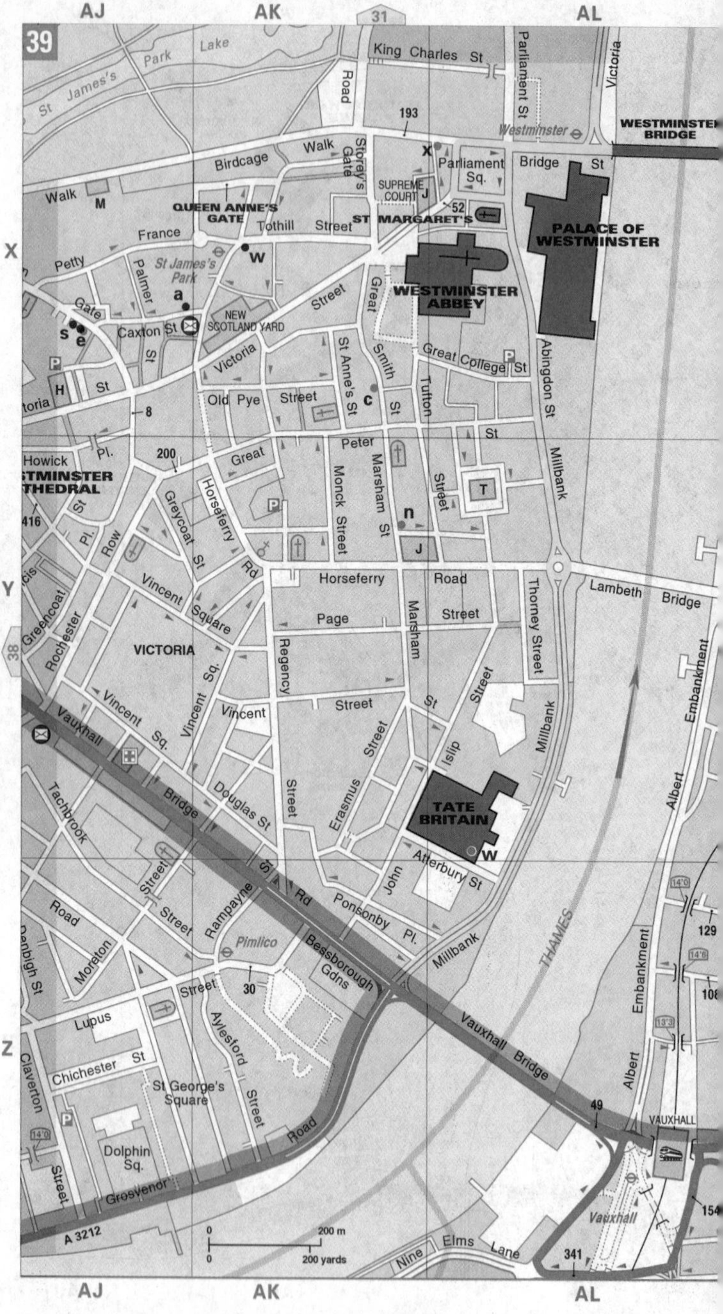
AJ
AK
AL
31
39
X
Y
Z
38
St James's Park Lake
King Charles St
Parliament St
Victoria
Road
193
Westminster
WESTMINSTER BRIDGE
Birdcage Walk
Storey's Gate
Parliament Sq.
Bridge St
M
SUPREME COURT
J
52
QUEEN ANNE'S GATE
Tothill Street
ST MARGARET'S
PALACE OF WESTMINSTER
France
Petty
Palmer
St James's Park
W
a
Gate
Caxton St
NEW SCOTLAND YARD
Great
Street
WESTMINSTER ABBEY
s
e
Victoria
St Anne's St
Smith
Great College St
Abingdon St
P
H
St
Victoria
Old Pye Street
c
Tufton
St
8
Peter
St
Howick
Pl.
200
WESTMINSTER CATHEDRAL
Great
Marsham St
Millbank
Greycoat
Horseferry
Monck Street
Street
T
416
Pl.
Row
n
J
Rd
Horseferry Road
Vincent Square
Lambeth Bridge
Greencoat
Rochester
Page Street
Marsham
Thorney Street
VICTORIA
Sq.
Regency
Street
Vincent Sq.
Vincent
Street
St
Vauxhall
Islip
Millbank
Embankment
Bridge
Douglas St
Street
Erasmus
TATE BRITAIN
Albert
Tachbrook
W
Atterbury St
John
St
Rd
Street
Ponsonby Pl.
14'0
Road
Street
Rampayne
Pimlico
Bessborough Gdns
Millbank
THAMES
129
Moreton
14'6
Denbigh St
Street
30
108
Embankment
Vauxhall Bridge
Lupus
13'3
Claverton
Chichester St
St George's Square
Aylesford
Street
Albert
49
VAUXHALL
Road
Dolphin Sq.
Street
14'0
Grosvenor
154
A 3212
Vauxhall
0
200 m
200 yards
Elms Lane
Nine
341

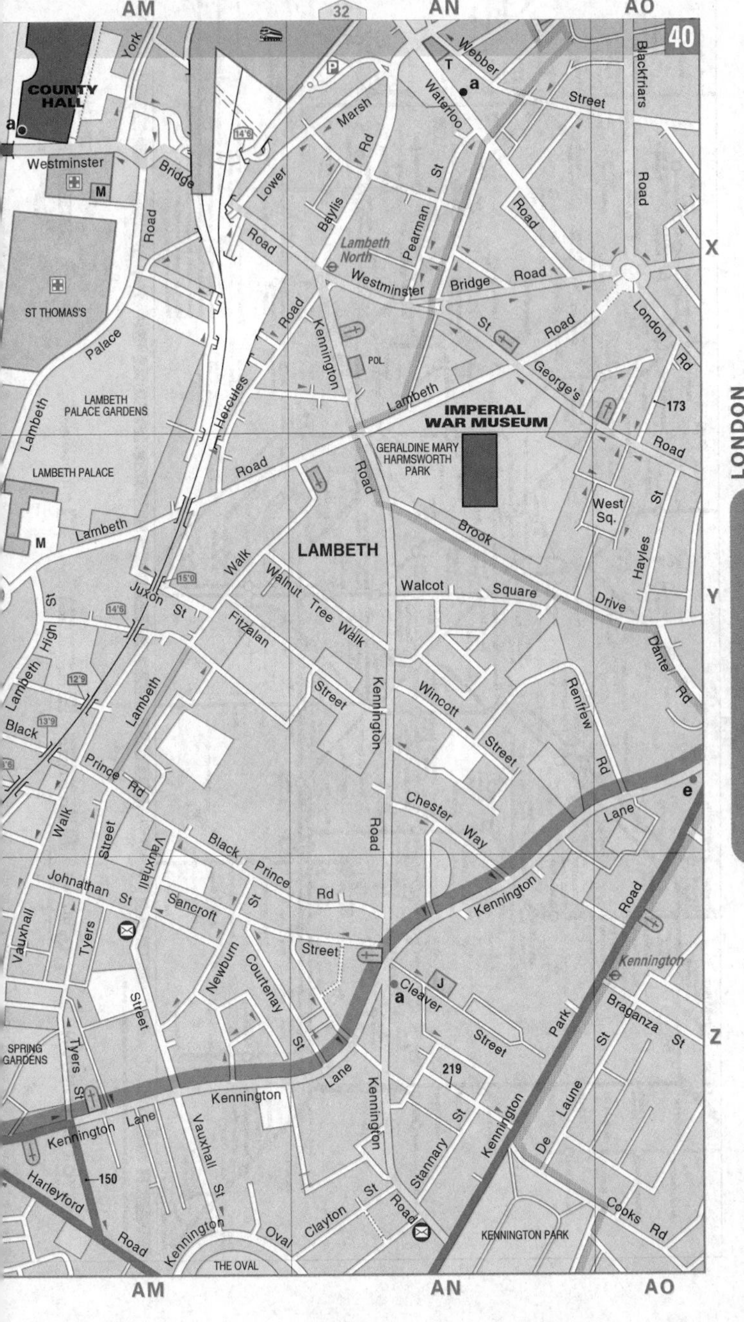

AM
32
AN
AO
40
COUNTY HALL
York
Webber
Waterloo
Street
Blackfriars
Marsh
Rd
Westminster
Bridge
Lower
Baylis
Pearman
St
Road
Lambeth North
Westminster
Bridge
Road
ST THOMAS'S
Palace
Kennington
Road
St
George's
London
Rd
POL.
Lambeth
Hercules
LAMBETH PALACE GARDENS
IMPERIAL WAR MUSEUM
GERALDINE MARY HARMSWORTH PARK
173
LAMBETH PALACE
West Sq.
Brook
Hayles
LAMBETH
Walk
Walnut Tree Walk
Walcot
Square
Drive
Juxon
Fitzalan
Street
Wincott
Dante
Rd
Renfrew
High
Black
Prince
Chester
Way
Lane
Johnathan St
Sancroft
Black Prince Rd
Vauxhall
Tyers
Newburn
Courtenay
Cleaver
Street
Kennington
Braganza St
Park
De Laune
SPRING GARDENS
219
Stannary
Kennington Lane
Harleyford
Road
Oval
Clayton
Cooks Rd
KENNINGTON PARK
THE OVAL
150
X
Y
Z
LONDON

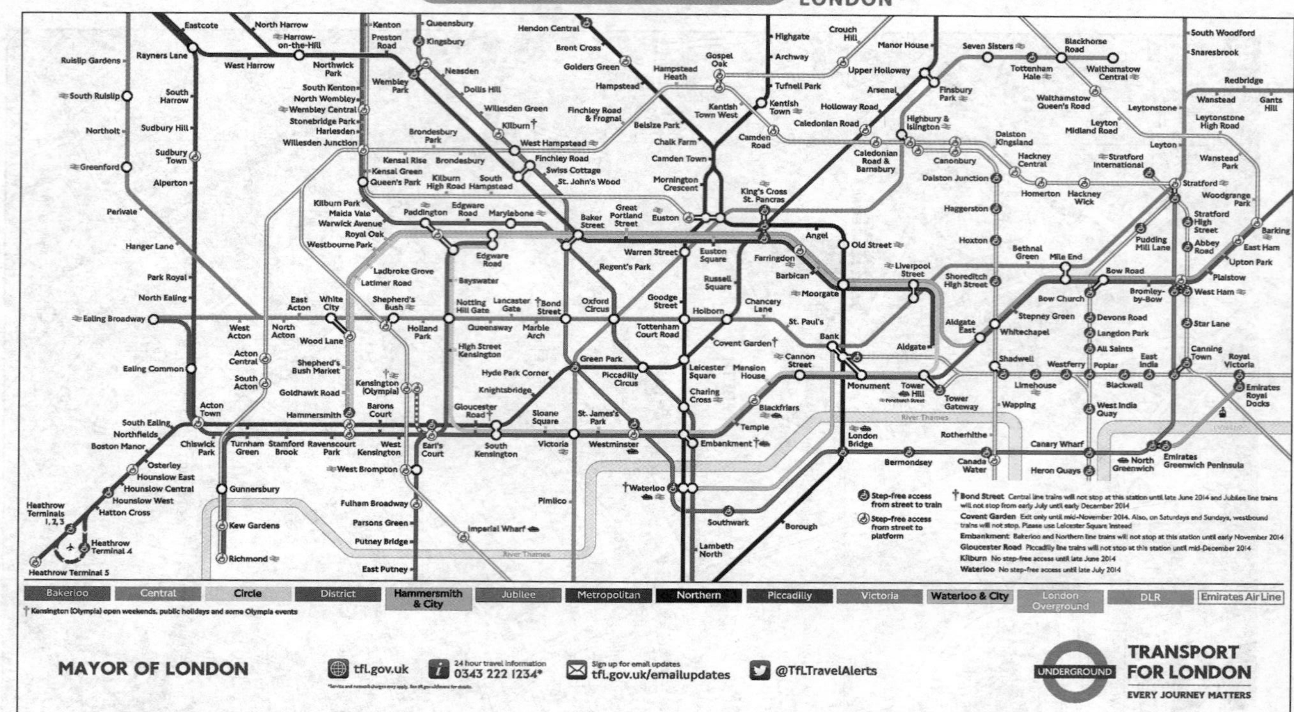

Bakerloo
Central
Circle
District
Hammersmith & City
Jubilee
Metropolitan
Northern
Piccadilly
Victoria
Waterloo & City
London Overground
DLR
Emirates Air Line
MAYOR OF LONDON
TRANSPORT FOR LONDON
EVERY JOURNEY MATTERS
UNDERGROUND
tfl.gov.uk
24 hour travel information 0343 222 1234*
Sign up for email updates tfl.gov.uk/emailupdates
@TfLTravelAlerts
Step-free access from street to train
Step-free access from street to platform
† Kensington (Olympia) open weekends, public holidays and some Olympia events
River Thames
Heathrow Terminals 1, 2, 3
Heathrow Terminal 5
Heathrow Terminal 4
Hatton Cross
Hounslow West
Hounslow Central
Hounslow East
Osterley
Boston Manor
Northfields
South Ealing
Ealing Broadway
Ealing Common
North Ealing
Park Royal
Hanger Lane
Perivale
Greenford
Northolt
South Ruislip
Ruislip Gardens
Rayners Lane
Eastcote
South Harrow
Sudbury Hill
Sudbury Town
Alperton
West Harrow
North Harrow
Harrow-on-the-Hill
Northwick Park
South Kenton
North Wembley
Wembley Central
Stonebridge Park
Harlesden
Willesden Junction
Kenton
Preston Road
Wembley Park
Queensbury
Kingsbury
Neasden
Dollis Hill
Willesden Green
Kilburn
Brondesbury Park
Brondesbury
Kensal Rise
Kensal Green
Queen's Park
Kilburn Park
Maida Vale
Warwick Avenue
Royal Oak
Westbourne Park
Kilburn High Road
South Hampstead
West Hampstead
Finchley Road
Swiss Cottage
St. John's Wood
Finchley Road & Frognal
Hampstead
Golders Green
Brent Cross
Hendon Central
Hampstead Heath
Belsize Park
Chalk Farm
Camden Town
Mornington Crescent
Gospel Oak
Kentish Town West
Kentish Town
Camden Road
Highgate
Archway
Tufnell Park
Caledonian Road
Holloway Road
Arsenal
Crouch Hill
Upper Holloway
Manor House
Finsbury Park
Highbury & Islington
Caledonian Road & Barnsbury
Canonbury
Dalston Junction
Dalston Kingsland
Haggerston
Hoxton
Shoreditch High Street
Seven Sisters
Tottenham Hale
Blackhorse Road
Walthamstow Central
Walthamstow Queen's Road
Hackney Central
Homerton
Hackney Wick
Leyton Midland Road
Leytonstone
Leyton
Stratford International
Stratford
Stratford High Street
Woodgrange Park
Wanstead Park
Leytonstone High Road
Wanstead
Redbridge
Gants Hill
South Woodford
Snaresbrook
Barking
East Ham
Upton Park
Plaistow
West Ham
Abbey Road
Pudding Mill Lane
Bromley-by-Bow
Bow Road
Mile End
Bethnal Green
Bow Church
Stepney Green
Whitechapel
Devons Road
Langdon Park
All Saints
Poplar
Westferry
Limehouse
Shadwell
Wapping
Star Lane
Canning Town
East India
Blackwall
West India Quay
Royal Victoria
Emirates Royal Docks
Emirates Greenwich Peninsula
North Greenwich
Canary Wharf
Heron Quays
Rotherhithe
Canada Water
Bermondsey
London Bridge
Borough
Southwark
Lambeth North
Waterloo
Embankment
Temple
Blackfriars
Mansion House
Cannon Street
Monument
Tower Hill
Tower Gateway
Aldgate
Aldgate East
Liverpool Street
Old Street
Moorgate
Bank
St. Paul's
Barbican
Farringdon
Chancery Lane
Angel
King's Cross St. Pancras
Euston
Euston Square
Russell Square
Holborn
Covent Garden
Leicester Square
Charing Cross
Goodge Street
Tottenham Court Road
Warren Street
Great Portland Street
Regent's Park
Oxford Circus
Piccadilly Circus
Green Park
Westminster
St. James's Park
Victoria
Pimlico
Sloane Square
Hyde Park Corner
Knightsbridge
South Kensington
Gloucester Road
High Street Kensington
Bond Street
Marble Arch
Baker Street
Marylebone
Edgware Road
Paddington
Lancaster Gate
Queensway
Bayswater
Notting Hill Gate
Holland Park
Ladbroke Grove
Latimer Road
Shepherd's Bush
Kensington (Olympia)
Earl's Court
West Kensington
Barons Court
West Brompton
Fulham Broadway
Parsons Green
Putney Bridge
East Putney
Imperial Wharf
Wood Lane
White City
East Acton
North Acton
West Acton
Shepherd's Bush Market
Goldhawk Road
Hammersmith
Ravenscourt Park
Stamford Brook
Turnham Green
Chiswick Park
Acton Town
Acton Central
South Acton
Gunnersbury
Kew Gardens
Richmond
† Bond Street Central line trains will not stop at this station until late June 2014 and Jubilee line trains will not stop from early July until early December 2014
Covent Garden Exit only until mid-November 2014. Also, on Saturdays and Sundays, westbound trains will not stop. Please use Leicester Square instead
Embankment Bakerloo and Northern line trains will not stop at this station until early November 2014
Gloucester Road Piccadilly line trains will not stop at this station until mid-December 2014
Kilburn No step-free access until late June 2014
Waterloo No step-free access until late July 2014
© Transport for London
Reg. user No. 14/2681/P
Version C 05 2014

LONDON
Boroughs and areas

Greater London is divided, for administrative purposes, into 32 boroughs plus **the City:** these sub-divide naturally into minor areas, usually grouped around former villages or quarters, which often maintain a distinctive character.

BRENT

Church End

Shayona
54-62 Meadow Garth ✉ NW10 8HD Town plan: **2**CU**a**
⊖ Stonebridge Park – ✆ (020) 8965 3365 – www.shayonarestaurants.com – Closed 23-24 October, 11-12 November and 25 December
• INDIAN • Menu £ 8 (weekday lunch) – Carte £ 14/20
Opposite the striking Swaminarayan Temple is this simple, sattvic restaurant: it's vegetarian and 'pure' so avoids onion or garlic. Expect curries from the north, dosas from the south and Mumbai street food. No alcohol so try a lassi.

Kensal Green

Paradise by way of Kensal Green
19 Kilburn Ln ✉ W10 4AE ⊖ Kensal Green. Town plan: **10**MZC**x**
– ✆ (020) 8969 0098 – www.theparadise.co.uk
• BRITISH MODERN • Menu £ 30 – Carte £ 24/41 – *(dinner only and lunch Saturday and Sunday)*
Less a pub, more a veritable fun palace. Music, comedy and film nights happen upstairs; the bar and restaurant are wonderfully quirky; staff are contagiously enthusiastic and the European themed food is prepared with genuine care.

Parlour Ⓝ
5 Regent St ✉ NW10 5LG ⊖ Kensal Green Town plan: **10**MZC**r**
– ✆ (020) 8969 2184 – www.parlourkensal.com – Closed 24 December-1 January
• BRITISH MODERN • Menu £ 10 (weekday lunch) – Carte £ 25/36
A fun, warmly run and slightly quirky neighbourhood hangout. The menu is a wonderfully unabashed mix of tradition, originality and reinvention. Don't miss the cow pie which even Dan, however Desperate, would struggle to finish.

Queen's Park

Ostuni Ⓝ
43-45 Lonsdale Rd ✉ NW6 6RA ⊖ Queen's Park Town plan: **10**MZB**b**
– ✆ (020) 7624 8035 – www.ostuniristorante.co.uk
• ITALIAN • Menu £ 20/40 – Carte £ 15/37
The cuisine of Puglia, the red hot heel in Italy's boot, is celebrated at this rustic local restaurant. Don't miss the olives, creamy burrata, fava bean purée, the sausages and bombette, or the orecchiette – the ear-shaped pasta.

Willesden Green

Sushi-Say
33B Walm Ln. ✉ NW2 5SH ⊖ Willesden Green Town plan: **9**LZB**a**
– ✆ (020) 8459 2971 – Closed 2 weeks August, 25-31 December, 1-2 January, Wednesday after bank holidays, Monday and Tuesday
• JAPANESE • Carte £ 18/38 – *(dinner only and lunch Saturday-Sunday)*
Very popular with the locals, attracted by sweet service and an extensive selection of Japanese food. Sit at the counter to watch the skill of the owner as he prepares the sushi.

BROMLEY

Keston

XX **Lujon**

6 Commonside ✉ BR2 6BP – ✆ (01689) 855 501 – www.lujon.co.uk – Closed Sunday dinner and Monday Town plan: **8**HZ**x**

• MODERN • Carte £ 22/50

Exotic name for a neat, contemporary restaurant in shades of grey, occupying a pleasant spot overlooking the Common. The European cooking is modern but the combinations of ingredients are reassuringly familiar.

Farnborough

XXX **Chapter One**

Farnborough Common, Locksbottom ✉ BR6 8NF – ✆ (01689) 854 848 – www.chaptersrestaurants.com – Closed 2-4 January Town plan: **8**HZ**a**

• MODERN • Menu £ 20/38 – Carte £ 28/39

Long-standing restaurant with many regulars, its stylish bar leading into an elegant, modern dining room. Wide-ranging menus offer keenly priced, carefully prepared modern European dishes; cooking is light and delicate, mixing classic and modern flavours. Assured service.

Orpington

XX **Xian**

324 High St. ✉ BR6 0NG – ✆ (01689) 871 881 – Closed 2 weeks April, 2 days late October, 25-26 December, Sunday lunch and Monday Town plan: **8**JY**a**

• CHINESE • Menu £ 10/20 – Carte £ 15/24

Stylish, modern dining room with banquette seating, bamboo matting on the walls and six super lithographs of the famous Terracotta Warriors of Xian. Appealing menu offers flavoursome, authentic Chinese dishes, with something for everyone.

Petts Wood

XX **Indian Essence** N

176-178 Petts Wood Rd ✉ BR5 1LG – ✆ (01689) 838 700 – www.indianessence.co.uk – Closed Monday lunch Town plan: **8**JY**e**

• INDIAN • Menu £ 19/25 (weekdays) – Carte £ 24/31

Atul Kochhar of Benares is one of the owners of this smart and contemporary Indian restaurant. Everything is made in-house, from the masala paste to the kulfi; dishes are vibrant and flavoursome and the prices are good.

Sundridge Park

XX **Cinnamon Culture**

46 Plaistow Ln ✉ BR1 3PA – ✆ (020) 8289 0322 – www.cinnamonculture.com – Closed 26 December Town plan: **8**HY**z**

• INDIAN • Menu £ 16 (lunch and early dinner) – Carte £ 23/38

Former Victorian pub transmogrified into a smart Indian restaurant where the cooking is undertaken with care. A plethora of menus include Tasting and Vegetarian options, as well as a monthly menu focusing on one region.

CAMDEN

Belsize Park

XX **XO**

29 Belsize Ln ✉ NW3 5AS ⊖ Belsize Park – ✆ (020) 7433 0888 – www.rickerrestaurants.com/xo – Closed 25-26 December, 1 January and bank holidays Town plan: **11**PZA**a**

• ASIAN • Menu £ 18 (lunch) – Carte £ 20/52

Busy bar behind which is a slick and stylish dining room. Vibrant atmosphere; popular with all the good-looking locals. Japanese, Korean, Thai and Chinese cooking; dishes are best shared.

XX **Hazara** Ⓝ

44 Belsize Ln ✉ NW3 5AR ⊖ Belsize Park Town plan: **11**PZA**n**
– ✆ (020) 7423 1147 – www.hazararestaurant.com – Closed 25-26 December and 1 January
• INDIAN • Carte £ 25/50 – *(dinner only and lunch Saturday-Sunday)*
At this keenly run, modern Indian restaurant, the adventurous diner will find specialities from all regions. Game and fish stand out – the owner goes personally to Smithfield and Billingsgate to ensure the quality of the produce.

X **Retsina**

48-50 Belsize Ln ✉ NW3 5AR ⊖ Belsize Park Town plan: **11**PZA**n**
– ✆ (020) 7431 5855 – www.retsina-london.com – Closed 25-26 December, 1 January, Monday lunch and bank holidays
• GREEK • Menu £ 19 (lunch) – Carte £ 22/36
Family-run restaurant whose unapologetically traditional menu offers all the Greek classics but the charcoal grill makes souvla, kebabs and cutlets the best choices. Simple, bright and airy room with a friendly atmosphere.

X **Tandis**

73 Haverstock Hill ✉ NW3 4SL ⊖ Chalk Farm Town plan: **11**QZB**x**
– ✆ (020) 7586 8079 – www.tandisrestaurant.com – Closed 25 December
• OTHER WORLD KITCHENS • Carte £ 18/28
Enticing Iranian food comes in the form of invigorating 'koresht' stews and succulent 'kababs', along with specialities such as 'sabzi polo' and 'kashke bademjaan'. Contemporary décor.

Bloomsbury

Covent Garden

10 Monmouth St ✉ WC2H 9HB ⊖ Covent Garden Town plan: **31**ALU**x**
– ✆ (020) 7806 1000 – www.firmdalehotels.com
58 rm – †£ 282/348 ††£ 342/420, ☕ £ 20 – 1 suite
Rest *Brasserie Max* – see restaurant listing
Popular with those of a theatrical bent. Boldly designed, stylish bedrooms, with technology discreetly concealed. Boasts a very comfortable first floor oak-panelled drawing room with its own honesty bar.

Montague on the Gardens

15 Montague St. ✉ WC1B 5BJ ⊖ Holborn Town plan: **31**ALT**a**
– ✆ (020) 7637 1001 – www.montaguehotel.com
112 rm – †£ 192/336 ††£ 216/360, ☕ £ 20 – 12 suites
Rest *Blue Door Bistro* – Menu £ 28 (lunch and early dinner) – Carte £ 26/58
A traditional but elegant British feel to this period townhouse; its clubby bar and conservatory overlook a secluded, private garden. Individually decorated bedrooms. Bistro divided between two small, pretty rooms.

Radisson Blu Edwardian Mercer Street

20 Mercer St ✉ WC2H 9HD ⊖ Covent Garden Town plan: **31**ALU**r**
– ✆ (020) 7836 4300 – www.radissonblu-edwardian.com
137 rm – †£ 180/450 ††£ 195/675, ☕ £ 23
Rest *The Dial* – Menu £ 15/20 – Carte £ 20/37
Radisson Edwardian spent considerable funds transforming their former Mountbatten hotel. The bedrooms come with a contemporary look and the relaxed restaurant blends in nicely with the theatreland neighbourhood.

Bloomsbury

16-22 Gt Russell St ✉ WC1B 3LR Town plan: **31**AKT**n**
⊖ Tottenham Court Road – ✆ (020) 7347 1000
– www.doylecollection.com/bloomsbury
153 rm – †£ 185/355 ††£ 185/355, ☕ £ 21
Rest *Landseer* – Menu £ 20 (dinner) – Carte £ 33/49
Neo-Georgian building by Edward Lutyens, built for the YWCA in 1929. Now boasts a smart, comfortable interior, from the lobby to the contemporary bedrooms. Restaurant with largely British menu and clubby bar.

DoubleTree by Hilton London - West End

92 Southampton Row ✉ *WC1B 4BH* ⊖ *Russell Square*
– ✆ *(020) 7242 2828 – www.doubletree3hilton.com* Town plan: **31**ALT**x**
216 rm – †£ 200/220 ††£ 239/280, ☕ £ 19 – 8 suites
Rest – Menu £ 25 – Carte £ 29/37
Now a corporate-minded hotel with a contemporary feel – the stained glass windows and original staircase are the only clues to the early 1900s origins of the building. Basement restaurant with a wide ranging menu including grills; or order snacks in the brighter bar just off the foyer.

Pied à Terre

34 Charlotte St ✉ *W1T 2NH* ⊖ *Goodge Street* Town plan: **31**AJT**f**
– ✆ *(020) 7636 1178 – www.pied-a-terre.co.uk – Closed last week December-5 January, Saturday lunch, Sunday and bank holidays*
• INNOVATIVE • Menu £ 28/65 – *(booking essential)*
David Moore's Pied à Terre celebrated its 21st birthday in 2012 and remains in rude health. Head Chef Marcus Eaves' cooking is bold and imaginative and the wine list offers over 700 bins, with considerable depth across all major regions. Each year a different artist is commissioned to decorate the room.
→ Roast breast, crispy leg and Kiev of quail, Douglas Fir purée and hazelnut vinaigrette. Monkfish with blackened spices, onion squash and mussels. Rhubarb and cardamom millefeuille, rhubarb sorbet.

Hakkasan Hanway Place

8 Hanway Pl. ✉ *W1T 1HD* Town plan: **31**AKT**c**
⊖ *Tottenham Court Road* – ✆ *(020) 7927 7000 – www.hakkasan.com – Closed 24-25 December*
• CHINESE • Menu £ 35/118 – Carte £ 34/91
There are now Hakkasans all over the world but this was the original. It has the sensual looks, air of exclusivity and glamorous atmosphere synonymous with the 'brand'. The exquisite Cantonese dishes are prepared with care and consistency by the large kitchen team; lunch dim sum is a highlight.
→ Dim sum platter. Roasted silver cod with champagne and honey. Jivara bomb.

Kitchen Table at Bubbledogs (James Knappett)

70 Charlotte St ✉ *W1T 4QG* ⊖ *Goodge Street* Town plan: **30**AJT**g**
– ✆ *(020) 7637 7770 – www.kitchentablelondon.co.uk – Closed 1-14 January, 18-25 April, 19 August-2 September, 23-27 December, Sunday and Monday*
• MODERN • Menu £ 78 – *(dinner only) (booking essential) (set menu only)*
Fight through the crowds enjoying a curious mix of hot dogs and champagne and head for the curtain – behind it is a counter for 19 diners. Chef-owner James prepares a no-choice menu of around 12 dishes. The produce is exemplary; the cooking has a clever creative edge, and the dishes have real depth.
→ Scallop with ginger mayonnaise and dried coral. Lamb sweetbreads, peas and girolles. Strawberry salad, young coconut jelly, yoghurt sorbet and tips of the Christmas tree.

Mon Plaisir

19-21 Monmouth St. ✉ *WC2H 9DD* Town plan: **31**ALU**g**
⊖ *Covent Garden* – ✆ *(020) 7836 7243 – www.monplaisir.co.uk – Closed Christmas-New Year, Sunday and bank holidays*
• FRENCH • Menu £ 13/25 – Carte £ 28/42
This proud French institution opened in the 1940s. Enjoy satisfyingly authentic classics in any of the four contrasting rooms, full of Gallic charm; apparently the bar was salvaged from a Lyonnais brothel.

Roka

37 Charlotte St ✉ *W1T 1RR* ⊖ *Goodge Street* Town plan: **31**AJT**k**
– ✆ *(020) 7580 6464 – www.rokarestaurant.com – Closed 25 December*
• JAPANESE • Carte £ 18/89
Bright, atmospheric interior of teak and oak; bustling and trendy feel. Contemporary touches added to Japanese dishes; try specialities from the on-view Robata grill. Capable and chatty service.

LONDON

Fino

33 Charlotte St ✉ W1T 1RR – (entrance on Rathbone St.) ⊖ Goodge Street – ✆ (020) 7813 8010 – www.finorestaurant.com – Closed Saturday lunch, Sunday and bank holidays Town plan: **31**AJT**a**

• SPANISH • Menu £ 18 (weekday lunch) – Carte £ 15/29

Seafood is handled especially well in this lively, quite smart and smoothly run basement tapas restaurant. Sensibly divided menu, with dishes designed for sharing. Youthful, helpful service.

Brasserie Max – Covent Garden Hotel

10 Monmouth St ✉ WC2H 9HB ⊖ Covent Garden – ✆ (020) 7806 1007 – www.firmdalehotels.com Town plan: **31**ALU**x**

• MEATS AND GRILLS • Menu £ 24 (lunch and early dinner) – Carte £ 34/65 – *(booking essential)*

It's not just shoppers and theatregoers who appreciate this stylish brasserie. Its international menu, grilled specialities, Sunday brunches and afternoon teas have widespread appeal.

Dabbous (Ollie Dabbous)

39 Whitfield St ✉ W1T 2SF ⊖ Goodge Street – ✆ (020) 7323 1544 – www.dabbous.co.uk – Closed 3 weeks Christmas-New Year, 2 weeks August, 1 week Easter, Sunday and Monday Town plan: **31**AJT**r**

• MODERN • Menu £ 28/59 – *(booking essential)*

One of the hottest tickets in town – the kitchen adopts the 'less is more' approach; the food comes with elegantly restrained finesse and a bewitching purity. Most have the 7-course menu with its stimulating and sublime combinations of ingredients. The ersatz industrial room has a simple elegance.

→ Speckled endive with gingerbread, mint and bergamot. Cod wrapped in wood shavings, honey and turnip dressing. Peach in its own juice.

Kopapa

32-34 Monmouth St ✉ WC2H 9HA ⊖ Covent Garden – ✆ (020) 7240 6076 – www.kopapa.co.uk – Closed 25-26 December Town plan: **31**ALU**h**

• ASIAN • Menu £ 22 (dinner) – Carte £ 30/42 – *(booking advisable)*

Kopapa, a Maori word for a gathering, is Peter Gordon's just-drop-in-anytime place. It's busy but fun, with breakfast morphing into all-day dining. Go for the 'fusion'-inspired dishes - they'll give your taste buds the best workout.

Gail's Kitchen

11-13 Bayley St ✉ WC1B 3HD ⊖ Goodge Street – ✆ (020) 7323 9694 – www.gailskitchen.co.uk – Closed 25 December Town plan: **31**AKT**s**

• MEDITERRANEAN • Carte £ 14/21

From the bakery people comes this engagingly run eatery that occupies a rather small space within the Myhotel. The enticing Mediterranean dishes are prepared with care and designed for sharing; the snacks are great too.

Drakes Tabanco Ⓝ

3 Windmill St ✉ W1T 2HY ⊖ Goodge Street – ✆ (020) 7637 9388 – www.drakestabanco.com – Closed Sunday and bank holidays Town plan: **31**AJT**t**

• SPANISH • Carte £ 20/34

Taking advantage of our newfound fondness for fino is this simple tabanco, from the people behind nearby Barrica and Copita. The small, Andalusian-inspired tapas menu uses imported produce from Spain alongside British ingredients.

Salt Yard

54 Goodge St. ✉ W1T 4NA ⊖ Goodge Street – ✆ (020) 7637 0657 – www.saltyard.co.uk – Closed 25-26 and dinner 24 and 31 December, 1 January and Sunday Town plan: **31**AJT**d**

• MEDITERRANEAN • Carte £ 13/32

Ground floor bar and buzzy basement restaurant specialising in good value plates of tasty Italian and Spanish dishes, ideal for sharing; charcuterie a speciality. Super wine list.

Honey & Co

25a Warren St ✉ W1T 5LZ ⊖ Warren Street Town plan: **18**RZD**c**
– ✆ (020) 7388 6175 – www.honeyandco.co.uk – Closed last week August, 25-26 December and Sunday
• OTHER WORLD KITCHENS • Menu £ 16/30 – Carte £ 22/29 – *(booking essential)*
The husband and wife team at this sweet little café were both Ottolenghi head chefs so expect cooking full of freshness and colour. Influences stretch beyond Israel to the wider Middle East. Open from 8am; packed at night.

Barrica

62 Goodge St ✉ W1T 4NE ⊖ Goodge Street Town plan: **31**AJT**x**
– ✆ (020) 7436 9448 – www.barrica.co.uk – Closed 25-26 December, 1 January, Sunday and bank holidays
• SPANISH • Menu £ 12/26 – *(booking essential)*
All the staff at this lively little tapas bar are Spanish, so perhaps it's national pride that makes them run it with a passion lacking in many of their competitors. When it comes to the food authenticity is high on the agenda.

Cigala

54 Lamb's Conduit St. ✉ WC1N 3LW Town plan: **19**TZD**a**
⊖ Russell Square – ✆ (020) 7405 1717 – www.cigala.co.uk – Closed 25-26 December, 1 January, Easter Sunday and Easter Monday
• SPANISH • Menu £ 18 (weekday lunch) – Carte £ 23/51 – *(booking essential)*
Longstanding Spanish restaurant, with a lively and convivial atmosphere, friendly and helpful service and an appealing and extensive menu of classics. The dried hams are a must and it's well worth waiting the 30 minutes for a paella.

Barnyard N

18 Charlotte St ✉ W1T 2LZ ⊖ Goodge Street Town plan: **31**AJT**b**
– ✆ (020) 7580 3842 – www.barnyard-london.com – Closed Sunday dinner
• REGIONAL/COUNTRY • Carte £ 20/25 – *(bookings not accepted)*
Dude food prepared with integrity draws the crowds to this fun little place co-owned by Ollie Dabbous. The food arrives all at once on enamel plates, and dishes are full of rustic, artery-hardening goodness yet are prepared with precision and care. Just be ready to queue, as it seats fewer than 50.

Tsunami

93 Charlotte St. ✉ W1T 4PY ⊖ Goodge Street Town plan: **30**AIT**a**
– ✆ (020) 7637 0050 – www.tsunamirestaurant.co.uk – Closed Christmas-New Year, Saturday lunch and Sunday
• JAPANESE • Carte £ 18/46 **s**
Sister to the original in Clapham. Sweet, pretty place, with lacquered walls, floral motif and moody lighting. Contemporary Japanese cuisine is carefully prepared and sensibly priced.

Flesh & Buns N

41 Earlham St ✉ WC2H 9LX ⊖ Leicester Square Town plan: **31**ALU**q**
– ✆ (020) 7632 9500 – www.fleshandbuns.com – Closed 24-25 December and 1 January
• ASIAN • Menu £ 20 (lunch and early dinner) – Carte £ 21/42 – *(booking advisable)*
A loud, fun basement next to the Donmar. There's plenty of Japanese dishes but star billing goes to the hirata bun – the soft Taiwanese-style steamed pillows of delight that sandwich your choice of meat or fish filling.

Ape & Bird N

142 Shaftesbury Ave ✉ WC2H 8HJ Town plan: **31**AKU**q**
⊖ Leicester Square – ✆ (020) 7836 3119 – www.apeandbird.com – (bookings not accepted dinner) Closed 25 December and 1 January
• MODERN • Carte £ 24/34
Simple, stripped back styling and a mural of famous Sohoians. Dishes are British, but their construction owes more to Italian principles: a few, top quality ingredients cooked with care to create plates full of flavour, aroma and appeal.

LONDON

Lady Ottoline

11a Northington St ✉ WC1N 2JF Town plan: **19**TZD**c**
⊖ Chancery Lane. – ✆ (020) 7831 0008 – www.theladyottoline.com
– Closed 24 December-2 January and bank holidays
• BRITISH TRADITIONAL • Menu £ 28 (lunch and early dinner) – Carte £ 24/35
Sister to Princess of Shoreditch, this large red-bricked Victorian pub is largely unchanged from when it was called The Kings Arms. Enjoy the same gutsy cooking in the busy bar or the Queen Anne style upstairs dining room.

CAMDEN TOWN

Market

43 Parkway ✉ NW1 7PN ⊖ Camden Town Town plan: **12**RZB**x**
– ✆ (020) 7267 9700 – www.marketrestaurant.co.uk – Closed 25 December-3 January, Sunday dinner and bank holidays
• BRITISH MODERN • Menu £ 10 (weekday lunch) – Carte £ 27/38 – *(booking essential)*
Market fresh produce used to create satisfying and refreshingly matter of fact British dishes, at excellent prices that entice plenty of passers-by. Appealing décor of exposed brick walls, old school chairs and zinc-topped tables.

Made Bar & Kitchen

Roundhouse, Chalk Farm Rd ✉ NW1 8EH Town plan: **11**QZB**a**
⊖ Chalk Farm – ✆ (020) 7424 8495 – www.roundhouse.org.uk/made
– Closed 25 December, 1-2 January, Sunday dinner and Monday
• OTHER WORLD KITCHENS • Carte £ 21/33
Attached to the Roundhouse is this large bar and dining room where the posters instil curiosity or nostalgia, depending on your age. What sets it apart is the food: small plates in vibrant, unusual and exciting combinations.

York & Albany with rm

127-129 Parkway ✉ NW1 7PS ⊖ Camden Town. Town plan: **12**RZB**s**
– ✆ (020) 7388 3344 – www.gordonramsay.com/yorkandalbany
• MODERN • **10 rm** – †£ 187/205 ††£ 187/330
Menu £ 24 (weekday lunch) – Carte £ 31/41 – *(booking essential)*
The same menu is now served throughout this handsome 1820s John Nash coaching inn; part of Gordon Ramsay's empire. There's everything on offer, from wood-fired pizzas to lamb shoulder or lemon sole. The ground floor has the buzz; the bedrooms have character.

DARTMOUTH PARK

Bull & Last

168 Highgate Rd ✉ NW5 1QS ⊖ Tufnell Park. Town plan: **12**RZA**a**
– ✆ (020) 7267 3641 – www.thebullandlast.co.uk – Closed 24-25 December
• BRITISH TRADITIONAL • Carte £ 23/42 – *(booking essential)*
A busy Victorian pub with plenty of charm and character; the upstairs is a little quieter. Cooking is muscular, satisfying and reflects the time of year; charcuterie is a speciality.

EUSTON

Pullman London St Pancras

100-110 Euston Rd ✉ NW1 2AJ ⊖ Euston Town plan: **18**SZC**a**
– ✆ (020) 7666 9000 – www.pullmanhotels.com
312 rm – †£ 220/460 ††£ 220/460, £ 20 – 2 suites
Rest *Golden Arrow* – Carte £ 33/81 – *(bar lunch Saturday, Sunday and bank holidays)*
Designed primarily for the business traveller, Pullman is a stylish and modern brand from the Accor group. The open- plan reception and chic lounge lead into a relaxed eatery offering the brasserie classics. State-of-the-art conference facilities include a theatre. Ideally located for Eurostar.

LONDON

Hampstead

Wells

30 Well Walk ✉ NW3 1BX ⊖ Hampstead. Town plan: **11**PZA**v**
– ✆ (020) 7794 3785 – www.thewellshampstead.co.uk
• BRITISH MODERN • Carte £ 25/35

Part country pub, part city sophisticate; busy ground floor, with more sedate upstairs restaurant. Cooking is hearty in flavour and sophisticated in look, with a pleasing British edge.

Hatton Garden

Bleeding Heart

Bleeding Heart Yard ✉ EC1N 8SJ – off Greville St. Town plan: **32**ANT**e**
⊖ Farringdon – ✆ (020) 7242 2056 – www.bleedingheart.co.uk
– Closed 24 December-1 January, Saturday, Sunday and bank holidays
• FRENCH • Menu £ 25 (lunch and early dinner) **s** – Carte £ 27/56 **s** – *(booking essential)*

Dickensian yard plays host to this atmospheric, candlelit restaurant; popular with those from The City. Classic French cuisine is the draw, with service that's formal but has personality. Wines from owners' New Zealand estate.

Holborn

Rosewood London

252 High Holborn ✉ WC1V 7EN Holborn Town plan: **32**AMT**x**
⊖ Holborn – ✆ (020) 7781 8888 – www.rosewoodhotels.com/london
306 rm – †£ 350/600 ††£ 350/600, ☕ £ 30 – 44 suites
Rest *Holborn Dining Room* – ✆ (0203) 747 8620 – Carte £ 25/40

A beautiful Edwardian building that was once the HQ of Pearl Assurance. The styling is very British and the bedrooms are uncluttered and smart. Cartoonist Gerald Scarfe's work adorns the walls of his eponymous bar. A classic brasserie with a menu of British favourites occupies the former banking hall.

Moti Mahal

45 Great Queen St. ✉ WC2B 5AA ⊖ Holborn Town plan: **31**ALU**k**
– ✆ (020) 7240 9329 – www.motimahal-uk.com – Closed 25-28 December, Saturday lunch, Sunday and bank holidays
• INDIAN • Menu £ 16/23 – Carte £ 27/43

The menu follows the path of the 16C Grand Trunk Road, stretching from Bengal through northern India to the mountains of the northwest frontier. The tandoor features heavily but there are also plenty of unfamiliar dishes to try.

Asadal

227 High Holborn ✉ WC1V 7DA ⊖ Holborn Town plan: **31**ALT**n**
– ✆ (020) 7430 9006 – www.asadal.co.uk – Closed 25-26 December, 1 January and Sunday lunch
• KOREAN • Carte £ 20/30

Sharing is the key in this busy basement, where you'll be oblivious to its unprepossessing location. Hotpots, dumplings and barbeques are the highlights from the easy-to-follow menu. Staff cope well with the evening rush.

Great Queen Street

32 Great Queen St ✉ WC2B 5AA ⊖ Holborn Town plan: **31**ALT**d**
– ✆ (020) 7242 0622 – www.greatqueenstreetrestaurant.co.uk
– Closed Christmas-New Year, Sunday dinner and bank holidays
• BRITISH MODERN • Menu £ 15 (weekday lunch) – Carte £ 19/37 – *(booking essential)*

The menu is a model of British understatement and is dictated by the seasons; the cooking, confident and satisfying with laudable prices and generous portions. Lively atmosphere and enthusiastic service.

Kentish Town

X **Chicken Shop**

79 Highgate Rd ✉ NW5 1TL ⊖ Kentish Town — Town plan: **12**RZA**c**
– ✆ (020) 3310 2020 – www.chickenshop.com
• MEATS AND GRILLS • Carte £ 16/21 – *(dinner only and lunch Saturday-Sunday) (bookings not accepted)*

Simply great chicken – marinated, steamed and finished over wood and charcoal – with a choice of sides and three desserts. It all happens in a noisy, mildly chaotic basement but it's great fun and good value. Be ready to queue.

Primrose Hill

XX **Odette's**

130 Regent's Park Rd. ✉ NW1 8XL ⊖ Chalk Farm — Town plan: **11**QZB**b**
– ✆ (020) 7586 8569 – www.odettesprimrosehill.com – *Closed 25-26 December and 1 January*
• MODERN • Menu £ 15 (weekday lunch) – Carte £ 30/40

A longstanding local favourite. Warm and inviting interior, with chatty yet organised service. Robust and quite elaborate cooking, with owner passionate about his Welsh roots. Good value lunch menu.

XX **Michael Nadra Primrose Hill**

42 Gloucester Ave ✉ NW1 8JD ⊖ Camden Town — Town plan: **12**RZB**m**
– ✆ (020) 7722 2800 – www.restaurant-michaelnadra.co.uk/primrose
– *Closed 24-28 December and 1 January*
• MODERN • Menu £ 20/55

Michael Nadra went north for his second branch and took over this unusual, modern building. The menu resembles his Chiswick operation, which means flavours from the Med but also the odd Asian note. The bar offers over 20 martinis.

X **L'Absinthe**

40 Chalcot Rd ✉ NW1 8LS ⊖ Chalk Farm — Town plan: **11**QZB**s**
– ✆ (020) 7483 4848 – www.labsinthe.co.uk – *Closed August and Christmas*
• FRENCH • Menu £ 10 (weekday lunch) – Carte £ 21/40

A classic French bistro offering a great atmosphere, a roll-call of favourites from cassoulet to duck confit, and a terrific wine list where only corkage is charged on the retail price. Ask for a table on the ground floor.

Swiss Cottage

XX **Bradley's**

25 Winchester Rd. ✉ NW3 3NR ⊖ Swiss Cottage — Town plan: **11**PZB**e**
– ✆ (020) 7722 3457 – www.bradleysnw3.co.uk – *Closed Sunday dinner*
• MODERN • Menu £ 16/28 – Carte £ 33/43

A stalwart of the local dining scene and ideal for visitors to the nearby Hampstead Theatre. The thoughtfully compiled and competitively priced set menus of mostly classical cooking draw in plenty of regulars.

XX **Singapore Garden**

83 Fairfax Rd. ✉ NW6 4DY ⊖ Swiss Cottage — Town plan: **11**PZB**x**
– ✆ (020) 7328 5314 – www.singaporegarden.co.uk – *Closed 24-28 December*
• ASIAN • Menu £ 20 (lunch) – Carte £ 23/49

A smart, bright and comfortable room, with endearingly enthusiastic service. Your best bet is to pick vibrant and zesty dishes from the list of Singaporean and Malaysian specialities.

West Hampstead

X **One Sixty** (N)

291 West End Ln. ✉ NW6 1RD — Town plan: **10**NZA**s**
⊖ West Hampstead – ✆ (020) 77949 786 – www.one-sixty.co.uk
– *Closed 24 December-2 January*
• NORTH-AMERICAN • Carte £ 19/33 – *(dinner only and lunch Saturday-Sunday)*

A fun, stripped back bar and restaurant, based on an American smokehouse. Meats are smoked in-house to a temperature of 160°f – hence the name. Eat with your fingers and explore the list of over 50 craft beers from around the world.

LONDON

Andaz Liverpool Street
40 Liverpool St. ✉ *EC2M 7QN* ⊖ *Liverpool Street* Town plan: **34**ART**t**
– ✆ (020) 7961 1234 – www.andaz.com
267 rm – †£ 144/402 ††£ 180/438, ☕ £ 18 – 3 suites
Rest ***1901*** – see restaurant listing
Rest ***Miyako*** – ✆ (020) 7618 7100 – Carte £ 16/42 – *(closed Christmas, Saturday, Sunday and bank holidays) (booking essential)*
Rest ***Eastway Brasserie*** – ✆ (020) 7618 7400 – Menu £ 20 – Carte £ 24/40
A contemporary and stylish interior hides behind the classic Victorian façade. Bright and spacious bedrooms boast state-of-the-art facilities. Various dining options include a brasserie specialising in grilled meats, a compact Japanese restaurant and a traditional pub.

Threadneedles
5 Threadneedle St. ✉ *EC2R 8AY* ⊖ *Bank* Town plan: **34**ARU**y**
– ✆ (020) 7657 8080 – www.hotelthreadneedles.co.uk
74 rm – †£ 355/450 ††£ 355/750, ☕ £ 23
Rest – Menu £ 24/28 – Carte £ 28/44
A converted bank, dating from 1856, with a smart, boutique feel and a stunning stained-glass cupola in the lounge. Bedrooms are very stylish and individual, featuring Egyptian cotton sheets, iPod docks and thoughtful extras. Spacious bar and restaurant; a striking backdrop to the classical menu.

LONDON

Apex Temple Court
1-2 Serjeant's Inn, Fleet St ✉ *EC4Y 1LL* Town plan: **32**ANU**r**
⊖ *Blackfriars – ✆ (020) 3004 4141 – www.apexhotels.co.uk*
184 rm – †£ 99/399 ††£ 99/399, ☕ £ 20
Rest ***Chambers*** – Menu £ 13 (dinner) – Carte £ 23/44
Smart, corporate hotel fashioned out of former law firm offices and tucked away in a courtyard. Chambers is a well-kept brasserie with a Mediterranean menu. Four grades of bedroom, but all are bright, light and a good size.

Montcalm London City at The Brewery
52 Chiswell St ✉ *EC1Y 4SA* ⊖ *Barbican – ✆ (020)* Town plan: **19**VZD**r**
7614 0100 – www.themontcalmlondoncity.co.uk
236 rm – †£ 168/350 ††£ 168/350, ☕ £ 25 – 11 suites
Rest ***Chiswell Street Dining Rooms*** – see restaurant listing
The majority of the contemporary rooms are in the original part of the Whitbread Brewery, built in 1714; ask for a quieter one overlooking the courtyard, or one of the 25 found in one of 4 restored Georgian townhouses across the road.

Hotel Indigo London - Tower Hill
142 Minories ✉ *EC3N 1LS* ⊖ *Aldgate – ✆ (020)* Town plan: **34**ASU**x**
7265 1014 – www.hotelindigo.com/lontowerhill
46 rm – †£ 155/395 ††£ 155/395, ☕ £ 9 **Rest** – Carte £ 21/35
Quieter than its city location would suggest, this business hotel comes with funky modern bedrooms equipped with iPod docks and coffee machines. Tower Bridge and Tower Hill suites have skyline views. Popular menu in Square Mile brasserie.

City Social Ⓝ
Tower 42, 25 Old Broad St (24th floor) Town plan: **34**ART**s**
✉ *EC2N 1HQ* ⊖ *Liverpool Street – ✆ (020) 7877 7703*
– www.citysociallondon.com – Closed Sunday
• MODERN • Carte £ 34/55
Jason Atherton took over in 2014 and made the place bigger and better looking with a darker, moodier feel. The City views are as impressive as ever, especially from tables 10 & 15. The flexible menu is largely European and the cooking manages to be both refined and robust at the same time.
➜ Pig's trotter and ham hock with black pudding, apple and Madeira. Braised Isle of Gigha halibut with chorizo & red pepper stew, crispy squid and fennel. White chocolate mousse, caramel hazelnuts and salted caramel ice cream.

XXX **Lutyens**

85 Fleet St. ✉ EC4Y 1AE ⊖ Blackfriars Town plan: **32**ANU**c**
– ✆ (020) 7583 8385 – www.lutyens-restaurant.com – Closed 1 week Christmas-New Year, Saturday, Sunday and bank holidays
• MODERN • Menu £ 22 (lunch and early dinner) – Carte £ 33/58
The unmistakable hand of Sir Terence Conran: timeless and understated good looks mixed with functionality, and an appealing Anglo-French menu with plenty of classics such as fruits de mer and game in season.

XXX **1901** – Andaz Liverpool Street Hotel

Liverpool St. ✉ EC2M 7QN ⊖ Liverpool Street Town plan: **34**ART**t**
– ✆ (020) 7618 7000 – www.andaz.com – Closed Christmas, Saturday lunch, Sunday and bank holidays
• BRITISH MODERN • Menu £ 30 – Carte £ 34/52
The crisp white decoration and judicious lighting highlight the immense Doric columns, the cornicing and the beautiful cupola above. The menu champions British produce and the cooking is modern and quite ambitious in its reach.

XX **Club Gascon** (Pascal Aussignac)

57 West Smithfield ✉ EC1A 9DS ⊖ Barbican Town plan: **33**APT**z**
– ✆ (020) 7600 6144 – www.clubgascon.com – Closed Christmas-New Year, Saturday lunch, Sunday and bank holidays
• FRENCH • Menu £ 25/60 – Carte £ 39/55 – *(booking essential)*
The gastronomy of Gascony and France's southwest are the starting points but the assured and intensely flavoured cooking also pushes at the boundaries. Marble and huge floral displays create suitably atmospheric surroundings.
➜ Razor clams with hay-infused emulsion and truffle vinaigrette. Cappuccino of black pudding, lobster and asparagus. Black olive 'millionaire'.

XX **Bread Street Kitchen**

10 Bread St ✉ EC4M 9AJ ⊖ St Paul's – ✆ (020) 3030 4050 – www.breadstreetkitchen.com – Closed 25-26 December Town plan: **33**AQU**e**
• MODERN • Carte £ 37/59 – *(booking advisable)*
Gordon Ramsay's take on NY loft-style dining comes with a large bar, thumping music, an open kitchen and enough zinc ducting to kit out a small industrial estate. For the food, think modern bistro dishes with an element of refinement.

XX **New St Grill**

16A New St ✉ EC2M 4TR ⊖ Liverpool Street Town plan: **34**ART**n**
– ✆ (020) 3503 0785 – www.newstreetgrill.com – Closed 23 December-7 January except dinner 31 December, Saturday lunch and Sunday dinner
• MEATS AND GRILLS • Menu £ 22 (lunch and early dinner) – Carte £ 28/58
D&D converted an 18C warehouse to satisfy our increasing appetite for red meat. They use Black Angus beef; grass-fed British and aged for 28 days, or corn-fed American, aged for 40 days. Start with a drink in the Old Bengal Bar.

XX **1701**

Bevis Marks Synagogue, Bevis Marks ✉ EC3A 5DQ Town plan: **34**ART**v**
⊖ Aldgate – ✆ (020) 7621 1701 – www.restaurant1701.co.uk – Closed Christmas, New Year, Saturday, Sunday and Jewish bank holidays
• INNOVATIVE • Menu £ 25 (weekday lunch) – Carte £ 35/51 – *(booking advisable)*
A bright, kosher restaurant housed in a modern extension to Bevis Marks Synagogue which was built in 1701. The palpably ambitious kitchen fuses together different elements of Jewish cuisine in a modern and original way.

XX **Sauterelle**

The Royal Exchange ✉ EC3V 3LR ⊖ Bank Town plan: **33**AQU**a**
– ✆ (020) 7618 2483 – www.royalexchange-grandcafe.co.uk – Closed Easter, Saturday, Sunday and bank holidays
• FRENCH • Menu £ 20 – Carte £ 34/59
Impressive location on the mezzanine floor of The Royal Exchange; ask for a table overlooking the Grand Café which was the original trading floor. A largely French-inspired contemporary menu makes good use of luxury ingredients.

XX **Sushisamba**

Heron Tower (38th and 39th Floor), 110 Bishopsgate ✉ EC2N 4AY ⊖ Liverpool Street – ✆ (020) 3640 7330 – www.sushisamba.com Town plan: **34**ART**d**

• JAPANESE • Carte £ 33/73 – *(booking essential)*

Stunning views, a great destination bar and a menu that blends Japanese, Peruvian and Brazilian influences – it may not come cheap but this US import is all about giving its young, fashionable fan base a fun night out.

XX **The Chancery**

9 Cursitor St ✉ EC4A 1LL ⊖ Chancery Lane – ✆ (020) 7831 4000 – www.thechancery.co.uk – Closed 23-30 December, 1 January, Saturday lunch, Sunday and bank holidays Town plan: **32**ANT**a**

• MODERN • Menu £ 29/35

An elegant restaurant that's so close to the law courts you'll assume your fellow diners are barristers, jurors, or the recently acquitted. The menu is appealing concise; dishes come with a classical backbone and bold flavours.

XX **Mint Leaf Lounge**

12 Angel Ct, Lothbury ✉ EC2R 7HB ⊖ Bank – ✆ (020) 7600 0992 – www.mintleaflounge.com – Closed 25-26 December, 1 January, Saturday, Sunday and bank holidays Town plan: **33**AQT**b**

• INDIAN • Menu £ 30 (lunch and early dinner) – Carte £ 27/43

A bigger, shinier bar but a smaller dining room than the St James's original – well, this is the City, after all. The Indian food has a subtle southern bias and the tandoor oven, chargrill and tawa plate are all used extensively.

XX **Vanilla Black**

17-18 Tooks Ct. ✉ EC4A 1LB ⊖ Chancery Lane – ✆ (020) 7242 2622 – www.vanillablack.co.uk – Closed 2 weeks Christmas and bank holidays Town plan: **32**ANT**x**

• INNOVATIVE • Menu £ 20/40

Proving that vegetarian food can be flavoursome, creative and satisfying, with a menu that is varied, imaginative and, at times, ambitious. This is a well-run, friendly restaurant with understated décor, run by a husband and wife.

XX **Cinnamon Kitchen**

9 Devonshire Sq ✉ EC2M 4YL ⊖ Liverpool Street – ✆ (020) 7626 5000 – www.cinnamon-kitchen.com – Closed Saturday lunch, Sunday and bank holidays Town plan: **34**ART**e**

• INDIAN • Menu £ 21 (lunch and early dinner) – Carte £ 24/52

Sister to The Cinnamon Club. Contemporary Indian cooking, with punchy flavours and arresting presentation. Sprightly service in large, modern surroundings. Watch the action from the Tandoor Bar.

XX **Kenza**

10 Devonshire Sq. ✉ EC2M 4YP ⊖ Liverpool Street – ✆ (020) 7929 5533 – www.kenza-restaurant.com – Closed 24-25 December, Saturday lunch and bank holidays Town plan: **34**ART**c**

• LEBANESE • Menu £ 15/30 – Carte £ 29/69

Exotic basement restaurant, with lamps, carvings, pumping music and nightly belly dancing. Lebanese and Moroccan cooking are the menu influences and the food is authentic and accurate.

XX **Cigalon**

115 Chancery Ln ✉ WC2A 1PP ⊖ Chancery Lane – ✆ (020) 7242 8373 – www.cigalon.co.uk – Closed Christmas and New Year, Saturday, Sunday and bank holidays Town plan: **32**ANU**x**

• FRENCH • Menu £ 15/27 – Carte £ 22/40

Pays homage to the food and wine of Provence, in an appropriately bright space that was a once an auction house. All the classics are here, from bouillabaisse to pieds et paquets. Busy bar in the cellar.

XX **The Mercer**

34 Threadneedle St ✉ EC2R 8AY ⊖ Bank Town plan: **34**ARU**x**
– ✆ (020) 7628 0001 – www.themercer.co.uk – Closed 25-26 December, Saturday, Sunday and bank holidays
• BRITISH TRADITIONAL • Carte £ 27/53
There's nothing like an old banking hall if you want a little grandeur and a feeling of space. The menu is from the John Bull wing of British cuisine: there are roasts and grills but the pies are the real favourites. Plenty of wines by the glass and some of the older Bordeaux vintages are well priced.

XX **Boisdale of Bishopsgate**

Swedeland Crt, 202 Bishopsgate ✉ EC2M 4NR Town plan: **34**ART**a**
⊖ Liverpool Street – ✆ (020) 7283 1763 – www.boisdale.co.uk – Closed Saturday lunch, Sunday and bank holidays
• BRITISH TRADITIONAL • Carte £ 29/59
It's champagne and oysters on the ground floor and Scottish hospitality and live jazz in the clubby, unapologetically masculine vaulted restaurant below. Enjoy smoked salmon, roast haggis and dry-aged, grass-fed Aberdeenshire beef.

XX **The White Swan**

108 Fetter Ln (1st floor) ✉ EC4A 1ES Town plan: **32**ANT**n**
⊖ Chancery Lane – ✆ (020) 7242 9696 – www.thewhiteswanlondon.com – Closed 25-26 December, Saturday, Sunday and bank holidays
• MODERN • Menu £ 29 (weekday lunch) – Carte £ 26/42
The classically educated kitchen uses British ingredients but also flavours from the Med. To reach this clubby, part-panelled first floor room – a haven of serenity – one must fight through the hordes of drinkers on the ground floor.

XX **Manicomio**

6 Gutter Ln ✉ EC2V 8AS ⊖ St Paul's – ✆ (020) Town plan: **33**APT**s**
7726 5010 – www.manicomio.co.uk – Closed 1 week Christmas, Saturday, Sunday and bank holidays
• ITALIAN • Menu £ 23 (weekday dinner) – Carte £ 28/51
They serve breakfast, cater for private parties, operate a café, provide takeaway, serve drinks and run a restaurant – all within this Norman Foster designed building. The regional Italian fare makes good use of quality ingredients.

XX **Luc's Brasserie**

17-22 Leadenhall Mkt ✉ EC3V 1LR ⊖ Bank Town plan: **34**ARU**v**
– ✆ (020) 7621 0666 – www.lucsbrasserie.com – Closed Christmas, New Year, Saturday, Sunday and bank holidays
• FRENCH • Menu £ 20 – Carte £ 25/65 – *(lunch only and dinner Tuesday-Thursday) (booking essential at lunch)*
A classic French brasserie looking down on the Victorian splendour of Leadenhall Market and run with impressive efficiency. The menu has all the French favourites you'll ever need, along with steaks in all sizes and chops aplenty.

XX **Bevismarks** (N)

3 Middlesex St ✉ E1 7AA ⊖ Aldgate – ✆ (020) Town plan: **34**AST**b**
7247 5474 – www.bevismarkstherestaurant.com – Closed Saturday and Sunday
• OTHER WORLD KITCHENS • Menu £ 19 (lunch) – Carte £ 31/47
A kosher restaurant, licensed by the Sephardi Kashrut Authority & Beth Din (Glatt), and previously based at Bevis Marks Synagogue. Influences are Ashkenazi and Sephardi but there are also Asian touches and 'modern British' dishes.

XX **Barbecoa**

20 New Change Passage ✉ EC4M 9AG Town plan: **33**APU**v**
⊖ St Paul's – ✆ (020) 3005 8555 – www.barbecoa.com – Closed 24-26 December and 1 January
• MEATS AND GRILLS • Carte £ 30/58 – *(booking essential)*
Set up by Jamie Oliver, to show us what barbecuing is all about. The prime meats, butchered in-house, are just great; go for the pulled pork shoulder with cornbread on the side. By dessert you may be willing to share.

LONDON

XX **Goodman City**

11 Old Jewry ✉ EC2R 8DU ⊖ Bank – ✆ (020) 7600 8220 – www.goodmanrestaurants.com – Closed Saturday, Sunday and bank holidays Town plan: **33**AQU**s**

• MEATS AND GRILLS • Menu £ 19 (lunch) – Carte £ 43/66

Machismo reigns at this archetypal steakhouse with corn-fed, wet-aged USDA steaks and grass-fed, dry-aged Irish and Scottish steaks. All are perfectly cooked on the Josper grill, although starters and sides aren't quite as good.

XX **Chiswell Street Dining Rooms** – Montcalm London City

56 Chiswell St ✉ EC1Y 4SA ⊖ Barbican – ✆ (020) 7614 0177 – www.chiswellstreetdining.com – Closed 25-26 December, 1 January, Saturday and Sunday Town plan: **19**VZD**r**

• BRITISH MODERN • Carte £ 29/55

The Martin brothers used their Botanist restaurant as the model for this corner of the old Whitbread Brewery. The cocktail bar comes alive at night. Makes good use of British produce, especially fish from nearby Billingsgate.

XX **Duck & Waffle**

Heron Tower (40th floor), 110 Bishopsgate ✉ EC2N 4AY ⊖ Liverpool Street – ✆ (020) 3640 7310 – www.duckandwaffle.com Town plan: **34**ART**d**

• MODERN • Carte £ 27/64 – *(booking essential)*

The UK's highest restaurant, on the 40th floor of Heron Tower, is a cheaper and less excitable alternative to Sushisamba one floor down. The menu is varied and offal is done well – try the crispy pig's ears. It's open 24 hours a day.

X **Bird of Smithfield**

26 Smithfield St ✉ EC1A 9LB ⊖ Farringdon – ✆ (020) 7559 5100 – www.birdofsmithfield.com – Closed Christmas, New Year, Sunday and bank holidays Town plan: **33**AOT**s**

• BRITISH TRADITIONAL • Carte £ 28/61 – *(booking essential)*

Feels like a private members' club but without the smugness. Five floors of fun include a cocktail bar, lounge, rooftop terrace and small, friendly restaurant. The appealing British menu makes good use of the country's larder.

X **Hawksmoor**

10-12 Basinghall St ✉ EC2V 5BQ ⊖ Bank – ✆ (020) 7397 8120 – www.thehawksmoor.com – Closed 24 December-2 January, Saturday, Sunday and bank holidays Town plan: **33**AQT**a**

• MEATS AND GRILLS • Carte £ 34/79 – *(booking essential)*

Fast and furious, busy and boisterous, this handsome room is the backdrop for another testosterone filled celebration of the serious business of beef eating. Nicely aged and rested Longhorn steaks take centre-stage.

X **Fish Market**

16B New St ✉ EC2M 4TR ⊖ Liverpool Street – ✆ (020) 3503 0790 – www.fishmarket-restaurant.co.uk – Closed 25-26 December,1 January, Sunday and bank holidays Town plan: **34**ART**f**

• FISH AND SEAFOOD • Menu £ 17/25 – Carte £ 24/52 – *(booking advisable)*

How to get to the seaside from Liverpool Street? Simply step into this bright fish restaurant, in an old warehouse of the East India Company, and you'll almost hear the seagulls. The menu is lengthy and the cooking style classic.

X **Chabrot**

62-63 Long Ln ✉ EC1A 9EJ ⊖ Barbican – ✆ (020) 7796 4550 – www.chabrot.com – Closed August, Christmas, Saturday and Sunday Town plan: **33**APT**n**

• FRENCH • Menu £ 15 (weekday lunch) – Carte £ 25/42

Relive that romantic weekend in Paris here at this reassuringly familiar Gallic bistrot and sister to the original branch in Knightsbridge. Classics like tête de veau, confit de canard and boudin noir are here in all their glory.

Cellar Gascon

59 West Smithfield ✉ EC1A 9DS ⊖ Barbican Town plan: **33**APT**c**
– ✆ (020) 7600 7561 – www.cellargascon.com – Closed Christmas-New Year, Saturday, Sunday and bank holidays

• FRENCH • Menu £ 9 (lunch) – Carte £ 15/24 – *(booking essential at lunch)*

It's not unlike a smart tapas bar and the monthly changing menu has plenty of treats: pâtés, rillettes, hams, cheeses and even some salads for the virtuous; but the Toulouse sausages and the Gascony pie stand out.

Vivat Bacchus

47 Farringdon St ✉ EC4A 4LL ⊖ Farringdon Town plan: **32**ANT**c**
– ✆ (020) 7353 2648 – www.vivatbacchus.co.uk – Closed Christmas and New Year, Saturday, Sunday and bank holidays

• MEATS AND GRILLS • Carte £ 22/47

Wine is the star at this bustling City spot: from 4 cellars come 500 labels and 15,000 bottles. The menu complements the wine: steaks, charcuterie, sharing platters and South African specialities feature along with great cheese.

Paternoster Chop House

Warwick Ct., Paternoster Sq. ✉ EC4M 7DX Town plan: **33**APT**x**
⊖ St Paul's – ✆ (020) 7029 9400 – www.paternosterchophouse.co.uk – Closed Christmas, Saturday and dinner Sunday

• BRITISH TRADITIONAL • Menu £ 23 (weekdays) – Carte £ 26/46

Appropriately British menu in a restaurant lying in the shadow of St Paul's Cathedral. Large, open room with full-length windows; busy bar attached. Kitchen uses thoughtfully sourced produce.

28°-50° Fetter Lane

140 Fetter Ln ✉ EC4A 1BT ⊖ Temple – ✆ (020) Town plan: **32**ANU**s**
7242 8877 – www.2850.co.uk – Closed Saturday, Sunday and bank holidays

• MODERN • Carte £ 27/40

From the owners of Texture comes this cellar wine bar and informal restaurant. The terrific wine list is thoughtfully compiled and the grills, cheeses, charcuterie and European dishes are designed to allow the wines to shine.

Restaurant at St Paul's Cathedral

St Paul's Churchyard ✉ EC4M 8AD ⊖ St Paul's Town plan: **33**APU**s**
– ✆ (020) 7248 1574 – www.restaurantatstpauls.co.uk – Closed 25-26 December, 1 January and Good Friday

• BRITISH MODERN • Menu £ 22/26 – *(lunch only) (booking advisable)*

Tucked away in a corner of the crypt of Sir Christopher Wren's 17C masterpiece, offering respite to tired tourists and weary worshippers. The monthly menu is reassuringly concise, seasonal and a celebration of all things British.

Jugged Hare

42 Chiswell St ✉ EC1Y 4SA ⊖ Barbican. – ✆ (020) Town plan: **19**VZD**x**
7614 0134 – www.thejuggedhare.com – Closed 25-26 December

• BRITISH TRADITIONAL • Menu £ 38 – Carte £ 29/59 – *(booking advisable)*

Vegetarians may feel ill at ease – and not just because of the taxidermy. The atmospheric dining room, with its open kitchen down one side, specialises in stout British dishes, with meats from the rotisserie a highlight.

CROYDON

South Croydon

Albert's Table

49b South End ✉ CR0 1BF – ✆ (020) 8680 2010 Town plan: **7**FZ**x**
– www.albertstable.co.uk – Closed Sunday dinner and Monday

• MODERN • Menu £ 23/35

The owner-chef has a notable pedigree and his surprisingly spacious restaurant, named after his grandfather, deserves success. Service is earnest and the accomplished, modern European cooking defined by its well-judged flavours.

EALING

ACTON GREEN

XX **Le Vacherin**

76-77 South Par ✉ W4 5LF ⊖ Chiswick Park Town plan: **6**CV**e**
– ✆ (020) 8742 2121 – www.levacherin.com – Closed Monday lunch
• FRENCH • Menu £ 19 (lunch) – Carte £ 28/48
Authentic feel to this comfortable brasserie, with its brown leather banquette seating, mirrors and belle époque prints. French classics from snails to duck confit; beef is a speciality.

Duke of Sussex

75 South Par ✉ W4 5LF ⊖ Chiswick Park. Town plan: **6**CV**e**
– ✆ (020) 8742 8801 – www.realpubs.co.uk
• MEDITERRANEAN • Carte £ 23/36
Bustling Victorian pub, whose striking dining room was once a variety theatre complete with proscenium arch. Stick to the Spanish dishes; stews and cured meats are the specialities. BYO on Mondays.

LONDON

EALING

X **Charlotte's Place**

16 St Matthew's Rd ✉ W5 3JT ⊖ Ealing Common Town plan: **2**CV**c**
– ✆ (020) 8567 7541 – www.charlottes.co.uk – Closed 26 December and 1 January
• MODERN • Menu £ 18/33
Warmly run neighbourhood restaurant opposite the Common; divided between bright ground floor room and cosier downstairs. Menu is an appealing mix of British and Mediterranean influences.

X **Kiraku**

8 Station Par, Uxbridge Rd. ✉ W5 3LD Town plan: **2**CV**v**
⊖ Ealing Common – ✆ (020) 8992 2848 – www.kiraku.co.uk
– Closed Christmas-New Year, Tuesday following bank holidays and Monday
• JAPANESE • Carte £ 15/37
The name of this cute little Japanese restaurant means 'relax and enjoy' - easy with such charming service. Extensive menu includes zensai, skewers, noodles, rice dishes and assorted sushi; ask if you want them in a particular order.

X **Atari-ya**

1 Station Par, Uxbridge Rd ✉ W5 3LD Town plan: **2**CV**v**
⊖ Ealing Common – ✆ (020) 8202 2789 – www.atariya.co.uk – Closed bank holiday Mondays
• JAPANESE • Carte £ 12/26
Atari-ya are importers and suppliers of fish and assorted Japanese ingredients and so are well-placed to run a few accessibly-priced sushi bars around the capital. Go for nigiri to fully appreciate the texture and flavour of the fish.

X **Kerbisher & Malt**

53 New Broadway ✉ W5 5AH ⊖ Ealing Broadway Town plan: **5**BV**m**
– ✆ (020) 8840 4418 – www.kerbisher.co.uk
• FISH AND CHIPS • Carte £ 12/20
The fish and chip shop reinvented... fresh, sustainably sourced fish is cooked to order in rapeseed oil; chips are made from British spuds and fried separately; and packaging is biodegradable. There's another branch in Hammersmith.

The Grove

The Green ✉ W5 5QX ⊖ Ealing Broadway. Town plan: **5**BV**g**
– ✆ (020) 8567 2439 – www.thegrovew5.co.uk
• MODERN • Menu £ 13 (weekday lunch) – Carte £ 22/36
A beast of a pub with an enormous front terrace; inside, it's half bar, half restaurant. The menus change monthly – lunch is standard issue, but at dinner the skilful kitchen uses British ingredients in dishes with a French edge.

GREENWICH

XX **Inside**
19 Greenwich South St ✉ SE10 8NW ⊖ Greenwich Town plan: **7**GX**x**
– ✆ (020) 8265 5060 – www.insiderestaurant.co.uk
– Closed 25-26 December, Sunday dinner and Monday
• MODERN • Menu £ 18/25 – Carte £ 26/39
Inside is tidy, comfortable and uncluttered, although it does take a few diners to generate an atmosphere. On offer is a well-priced set menu, with quite elaborate, largely European cooking.

X **Rivington Grill**
178 Greenwich High Rd ✉ SE10 8NN Town plan: **7**GV**s**
⊖ Greenwich (DLR) – ✆ (020) 8293 9270 – www.rivingtongreenwich.co.uk
– Closed 25-26 December
• BRITISH MODERN • Carte £ 20/40
Spread over two floors and part of the Picturehouse complex. The extensive menu doubles as a placemat and is comfortingly familiar: there are pies, chops, plenty of things 'on toast' and assorted meats cooked on the grill.

LONDON

HACKNEY

Dalston

X **Rotorino** N
434 Kingsland Rd ✉ E8 4AA ⊖ Dalston Junction Town plan: **14**XZA**w**
– ✆ (020) 7249 9081 – www.rotorino.com
– Closed 23 December-2 January
• ITALIAN • Carte £ 15/35 – *(dinner only and lunch Saturday-Sunday)*
You'll immediately warm to this stylish yet down to earth Italian. The staff are very welcoming and knowledgeable and the delicious Southern Italian specialities like caponata and gnudi are great value. Ask for one of the booths.

X **White Rabbit** N
15-16 Bradbury St ✉ N16 8JN Town plan: **14**XZB**r**
⊖ Dalston Kingsland – ✆ (020) 7682 0163 – www.whiterabbitdalston.com
• MODERN • Menu £ 18 (early dinner) – Carte £ 23/35 – *(dinner only and lunch Saturday-Sunday)*
Stripped down and sparse, with white walls, girders and bare concrete. Staff are a friendly bunch, the atmosphere is laid-back and the menu is all about small plates and sharing. Original cooking has Mediterranean and Asian influences.

Hackney

X **Lardo**
197-205 Richmond Rd ✉ E8 3NJ Town plan: **14**YZB**h**
⊖ Dalston Junction – ✆ (020) 8985 2683 – www.lardo.co.uk
• ITALIAN • Carte £ 17/30
Housed in the striking 1930s Arthaus building, this delightful Italian eatery may boast the ubiquitous faux industrial look but there's nothing bogus about the cooking – the small plates really hit the spot. Try the succulent home-cured meats and the terrific pizzas from the shiny wood-fired oven.

X **Market Cafe**
2 Broadway Mkt ✉ E8 4QG ⊖ Bethnal Green Town plan: **14**YZB**m**
– ✆ (020) 7249 9070 – www.market-cafe.co.uk
– Closed 25-26 December
• MODERN • Menu £ 20 (dinner) – Carte £ 21/32
This former pub by the canal appeals to local hipsters with its retro looks, youthful service team and Italian-influenced menu. Cooking is fresh and generous and uses some produce from the local market; homemade pasta a feature.

Prince Arthur

95 Forest Rd ✉ E8 3BH ⊖ Dalston Junction. Town plan: **14**XZB**c**
– ✆ (020) 7249 9996 – www.theprincearthurlondonfields.com
– Closed 25 December
• BRITISH MODERN • Menu £ 10 (weekdays) – Carte £ 25/41 – *(dinner only and lunch Saturday-Sunday)*
It may not be the most handsome pub around, but when it comes to good food and conviviality, this Prince does just fine. The menu changes every three months and delivers just the sort of stout, substantial dishes you want in a pub.

Hoxton

The Hoxton

81 Great Eastern St. ✉ EC2A 3HU ⊖ Old Street Town plan: **20**XZD**x**
– ✆ (020) 7550 1000 – www.hoxtonhotels.com
208 rm – £ 69/299 £ 69/299
Rest *Hoxton Grill* – ✆ (020) 7739 9111 – Menu £ 17 (weekday lunch)
– Carte £ 17/44
Industrial-styled urban lodge with a rakish, relaxed air – a hotel run for the convenience of its guests rather than the management. Bedrooms are compact but come with some nice touches. Youthful clientele and even younger staff. Open-plan restaurant with American menu and great cocktails.

Fifteen London

15 Westland Pl ✉ N1 7LP ⊖ Old Street – ✆ (020) Town plan: **13**VZC**c**
3375 1515 – www.fifteen.net – Closed 25-26 December and 1 January
• MODERN • Menu £ 19 (lunch) – Carte £ 27/41 – *(booking essential)*
Trainees at Jamie Oliver's charitable restaurant learn about cooking seasonal British food – dishes that have personality and are all about flavour. The same menu is served in the ground floor restaurant and the livelier cellar.

Beagle

397-400 Geffrye St ✉ E2 8HZ ⊖ Hoxton – ✆ (020) Town plan: **14**XZB**e**
7613 2967 – www.beaglelondon.co.uk – Closed lunch Monday-Tuesday
• BRITISH TRADITIONAL • Menu £ 15 (lunch and early dinner) – Carte £ 21/36
– (booking essential)
Occupying three vast converted railway arches: one houses the bar; one the dining room; and the third is the kitchen. The British menu, with touches of Italian, changes twice a day and its contents are determined by the seasons.

Shoreditch

Ace Hotel

100 Shoreditch High St ✉ E1 6JQ Town plan: **20**XZD**p**
⊖ Shoreditch High Street – ✆ (020) 7613 9800 – www.acehotel.com
265 rm – £ 215/395 £ 215/395, £ 15 – 3 suites
Rest *Hoi Polloi* – see restaurant listing
The first Ace hotel in Europe and what better location for this achingly trendy hotel than hipster-central itself – Shoreditch. Locals are welcomed in, the lobby has a DJ, urban-chic rooms have day-beds if you want friends over and the minibars offer everything from Curly Wurlys to champagne.

Boundary with rm

2-4 Boundary St ✉ E2 7DD Town plan: **20**XZD**b**
⊖ Shoreditch High Street – ✆ (020) 7729 1051 – www.theboundary.co.uk
– Closed Sunday dinner
• FRENCH • **17 rm** – £ 275/670 £ 275/670, £ 15
Menu £ 22 – Carte £ 34/58 – *(dinner only and Sunday lunch)*
Sir Terence Conran has taken a warehouse and created a 'caff' with a bakery and shop, a rooftop terrace and a stylish, good-looking French restaurant serving plenty of cross-Channel classics. Comfy and individual bedrooms.

XXX **L'Anima**

1 Snowden St. ✉ EC2A 2DQ ⊖ Liverpool Street Town plan: **20**XZD**a**
– ✆ (020) 7422 7000 – www.lanima.co.uk – Closed 25-26 December, Saturday lunch, Sunday and bank holidays
• ITALIAN • Carte £ 35/70 – *(booking essential)*

Very handsome room, with limestone and leather creating a sophisticated, glamorous environment. Appealing menu is a mix of Italian classics and less familiar dishes, with the emphasis firmly on flavour. Service is smooth and personable.

XX **HKK**

✿ *Broadgate West, 88 Worship St ✉ EC2A 2BE* Town plan: **20**XZD**h**
⊖ Liverpool Street – ✆ (020) 3535 1888 – www.hkklondon.com – Closed 25 December and Sunday
• CHINESE • Menu £ 29/98 – Carte lunch £ 26/62

From the Hakkasan group comes this most sophisticated of Cantonese restaurants. The room is elegant and graceful; the service smooth and assured. Expect the classic flavour combinations but delivered in a modern, refined way.

→ Cherry wood roasted Peking duck. Jasmine tea smoked Wagyu beef. Almond brûlée tart with wine poached plum.

XX **Merchants Tavern** Ⓝ

36 Charlotte Rd ✉ EC2A 3PG ⊖ Old Street Town plan: **20**XZD**t**
– ✆ (020) 7060 5335 – www.merchantstavern.co.uk – Closed 25-26 December and Monday
• BRITISH TRADITIONAL • Menu £ 18 (weekday lunch) – Carte £ 32/49

The 'pub' part – a Victorian warehouse – gives way to a large restaurant with the booths being the prized seats. The cooking is founded on the sublime pleasures of seasonal British cooking, in reassuringly familiar combinations.

XX **Eyre Brothers**

70 Leonard St ✉ EC2A 4QX Town plan: **20**XZD**k**
⊖ Shoreditch High Street – ✆ (020) 7613 5346 – www.eyrebrothers.co.uk – Closed 24 December-4 January, Saturday lunch, Sunday and bank holidays
• SPANISH • Menu £ 12 (lunch and early dinner) – Carte £ 25/51

Sleek, confidently run and celebrating all things Iberian by drawing on the brothers' memories of their childhood in Mozambique. Delicious hams; terrific meats cooked over lumpwood charcoal. If a larger group, pre-order paella or suckling pig.

XX **Hoi Polloi** Ⓝ – Ace Hotel

100 Shoreditch High St ✉ E1 6JQ Town plan: **14**XZD**p**
⊖ Shoreditch High Street – ✆ (020) 8880 6100 – www.hoi-polloi.co.uk
• BRITISH MODERN • Carte £ 22/48

The boys from Bistrotheque and Shrimpy's are behind this hip, modern brasserie. It's open from early morning to the wee small hours offering everything from shakes first thing to midnight burgers and soundly prepared British dishes.

X **Clove Club** (Isaac McHale)

✿ *380 Old St ✉ EC1V 9LT ⊖ Old Street – ✆ (020)* Town plan: **20**XZC**c**
7729 6496 – www.thecloveclub.com – Closed 2 weeks Christmas-New Year, August bank holiday, Monday lunch and Sunday
• MODERN • Menu £ 35/55 – *(bookings advisable at dinner) (set menu only)*

An unrelentingly sparse room at Shoreditch Town Hall is the chosen site for three friends who made their names in pop-ups. The set menu showcases expertly sourced produce in dishes that are full of originality, verve and flair – but where flavours are expertly judged and complementary.

→ Smoked wild pollan with caviar and crème fraîche. Salt-baked duck, gingerbread and turnip. Amalfi lemonade and Sarawak black pepper ice cream.

LONDON

Lyle's

Tea Building, 56 Shoreditch High St ✉ E1 6JJ Town plan: **14**XZD**s**
⊖ Shoreditch High Street – ✆ (020) 3011 5911 – www.lyleslondon.com – Closed Saturday lunch, Sunday and bank holidays
• BRITISH MODERN • Menu £ 39 (dinner) – Carte lunch £ 18/29 – *(set menu only at dinner)*
The young chef-owner is an acolyte of Fergus Henderson and delivers similarly unadulterated flavours from seasonal British produce, albeit from a set menu. This pared-down approach extends to a room that's high on functionality.

Casa Negra

54-56 Great Eastern St ✉ EC2A 3QR ⊖ Old Street Town plan: **20**XZD**n**
– ✆ (020) 7033 7360 – www.casanegra.co.uk – Closed Saturday lunch, Sunday and Monday
• MEXICAN • Carte £ 24/54 – *(booking essential at dinner)*
Will Ricker turned his former Great Eastern Dining Room into this lively Mexican bar and restaurant and, judging by the crowds, has another hit to go with his La Bodega Negra in Soho. Have cocktails and the braised beef rib.

LONDON

Andina

1 Redchurch St ✉ E2 7DJ Town plan: **20**XZD**n**
⊖ Shoreditch High Street – ✆ (020) 7920 6499 – www.andinalondon.com
• PERUVIAN • Menu £ 9 (weekday lunch) – Carte £ 11/30 – *(booking essential)*
Andina may be smaller and slightly more chaotic that its sister Ceviche, but this friendly picantería with live music is equally popular. The Peruvian specialities include great salads and skewers, and ceviche that packs a punch.

Rivington Grill

28-30 Rivington St ✉ EC2A 3DZ ⊖ Old Street Town plan: **20**XZD**e**
– ✆ (020) 7729 7053 – www.rivingtonshoreditch.co.uk – Closed 25-26 December
• BRITISH TRADITIONAL • Carte £ 22/42
Very appealing 'back to basics' British menu, with plenty of comforting classics including a section 'on toast'. This converted warehouse is popular with the local community of artists.

Tramshed

32 Rivington St ✉ EC2A 3LX ⊖ Old Street Town plan: **20**XZD**v**
– ✆ (020) 7749 0478 – www.chickenandsteak.co.uk – Closed 25-26 December
• MEATS AND GRILLS • Menu £ 10 (weekday lunch) – Carte £ 19/64
Mark Hix's impressive brasserie – complete with Damien Hirst tank – is found within a 1905 Grade II warehouse. It's all about chicken and beef: Swainson House Farm chickens and Glenarm steaks are accurately cooked and delicious.

Viet Grill

58 Kingsland Rd ✉ E2 8DP ⊖ Hoxton – ✆ (020) 7739 6686 – www.vietgrill.co.uk Town plan: **20**XZC**z**
• VIETNAMESE • Menu £ 10/23 – Carte £ 17/30
Owned by the team behind Cây Tre which means that service is charming and helpful and the Vietnamese food is fresh and authentic. Larger parties should consider ordering one of their 'feast' menus, which require 48 hours' notice.

Princess of Shoreditch

76-78 Paul St ✉ EC2A 4NE ⊖ Old Street Town plan: **19**VZD**a**
– ✆ (020) 7729 9270 – www.theprincessofshoreditch.com – Closed 24-26 December
• BRITISH TRADITIONAL • Menu £ 28 (lunch and early dinner) – Carte £ 24/34 – *(booking essential)*
There has been a pub on this corner site since 1742 but it is doubtful many of the previous incarnations were as busy or as pleasant as the Princess is today. The best dishes are those with a rustic edge, such as goose rillettes or chicken pie.

South Hackney

Empress
130 Lauriston Rd, Victoria Park ✉ E9 7LH Town plan: **3**GU**n**
⊖ Homerton. – ✆ (020) 8533 5123 – www.empresse9.co.uk – Closed 25 December and Monday lunch except bank holidays
• MEDITERRANEAN • Menu £ 20 (weekday dinner) – Carte £ 23/33
Sourdough is from the local baker; the butcher and fishmonger are within walking distance. Dishes like pearl barley and feta risotto demonstrate the kitchen's confidence and ability; prices are good and Sunday lunch a languid affair.

HAMMERSMITH and FULHAM

Fulham

Blue Elephant
The Boulevard, Imperial Wharf ✉ SW6 2UB Town plan: **23**PZH**x**
⊖ Imperial Wharf – ✆ (020) 7751 3111 – www.blueelephant.com – Closed 25-26 December, 1 January and Monday lunch
• THAI • Menu £ 38 (lunch and early dinner) – Carte £ 27/54 – *(booking advisable)*
Relocated from Fulham Road to these swankier and appropriately exotic premises, spread over two floors and with two great riverside terraces. The menu traverses Thailand; curries are a strength.

Tendido Cuatro
108-110 New Kings Rd ✉ SW6 4LY Town plan: **22**NZH**x**
⊖ Parsons Green – ✆ (020) 7371 5147 – www.cambiodetercio.co.uk – Closed 2 weeks Christmas
• SPANISH • Menu £ 30 (lunch and early dinner) – Carte £ 24/46
Along with tapas, the speciality is paella. Designed for a hungry two, they vary from seafood to quail and chorizo; vegetarian to cuttlefish ink. Vivid colours used with abandon deck out the busy room.

Kozu Ⓝ
58 New King's Rd ✉ SW6 4LS ⊖ Parsons Green Town plan: **22**NZH**e**
– ✆ (020) 7731 2520 – www.kozu.co.uk – Closed 24-26 December and Monday
• JAPANESE • Carte £ 31/54
After nearly 30 years, Mark Barnett retired his Mao Tai Chinese restaurant and in its place opened this fun, contemporary wine bar serving Japanese food. The menu mixes the modern with the classic, and the Nobu influences are obvious.

Manuka Kitchen
510 Fulham Rd ✉ SW6 5NJ Town plan: **22**NZG**m**
⊖ Fulham Broadway – ✆ (020) 7736 7588 – www.manukakitchen.com – Closed 16-30 August, 25-26 December, Sunday dinner and Monday
• MODERN • Menu £ 12 (weekday lunch) – Carte £ 22/29
The two young owners run their simple little restaurant with great enthusiasm and their prices are keen. Like the magical Manuka honey, the chef is from New Zealand; his menu is varied and his food is wholesome and full of flavour.

Claude's Kitchen
51 Parsons Green Ln ✉ SW6 4JA Town plan: **22**NZH**c**
⊖ Parsons Green. – ✆ (020) 7371 8517 – www.amusebouchelondon.com – Closed Sunday dinner
• MODERN • Carte £ 23/33 – *(dinner only and lunch Saturday-Sunday) (booking essential)*
Two operations in one converted pub: 'Amuse Bouche' is a well-priced champagne bar; upstairs is an intimate dining room with a weekly changing menu. The cooking is colourful and fresh, with the odd challenging flavour combination.

LONDON

Harwood Arms

Walham Grove ✉ SW6 1QP Town plan: **22**NZG**a**
⊖ Fulham Broadway. – ✆ (020) 7386 1847 – www.harwoodarms.com
– Closed 24-27 December, 1 January and Monday lunch
• BRITISH MODERN • Menu £ 25 (weekday lunch) – Carte £ 38/46 – *(booking essential)*

Its reputation may have spread like wildfire but this remains a proper, down-to-earth pub that just happens to serve really good food. The cooking is very seasonal, proudly British, full of flavour and doesn't seem out of place in this environment. Service is suitably relaxed and friendly.

→ Berkshire game faggots with celeriac, prune and pickled walnuts. Roast cod with Jersey Royals, purple sprouting broccoli and laverbread. Buttermilk pudding with English strawberries and toasted almonds.

Malt House with rm

rest,

17 Vanston Pl ✉ SW6 1AY ⊖ Fulham Broadway. Town plan: **22**NZG**m**
– ✆ (020) 7084 6888 – www.malthousefulham.co.uk – Closed 25 December
• BRITISH MODERN • **6 rm** – £ 125/150 £ 125/150 Carte £ 23/42

A smart Fulham pub with a friendly atmosphere helped along by the charming young staff. The menu is all-encompassing enough to satisfy both the traditionalist and the more adventurous eater. Six elegant bedrooms upstairs.

Sands End

135-137 Stephendale Rd ✉ SW6 2PR Town plan: **22**OZH**r**
⊖ Fulham Broadway. – ✆ (020) 7731 7823 – www.thesandsend.co.uk
– Closed 25 December
• BRITISH MODERN • Menu £ 11 (weekday lunch) – Carte £ 28/39
– (booking advisable)

Cosy, warm and welcoming little corner pub, offering appealing bar snacks and a thoughtfully put-together menu with a British bias. Game is handled deftly and ingredients are well-sourced.

Hammersmith

River Café (Ruth Rogers)

Thames Wharf, Rainville Rd ✉ W6 9HA Town plan: **21**LZG**v**
⊖ Barons Court – ✆ (020) 7386 4200 – www.rivercafe.co.uk
– Closed Christmas and New Year, Sunday dinner and bank holidays
• ITALIAN • Carte £ 57/87 – *(booking essential)*

It's all about the natural Italian flavours of the superlative ingredients. The on-view kitchen with its wood-fired oven dominates the stylish riverside room; the contagiously effervescent atmosphere is helped along by very charming service.

→ Wood roasted langoustines, chilli and oregano. Roast turbot tranche with an anchovy and rosemary sauce and broad beans. Panna cotta with champagne rhubarb.

Potli

319-321 King St ✉ W6 9NH ⊖ Ravenscourt Park Town plan: **21**KZF**v**
– ✆ (020) 8741 4328 – www.potli.co.uk
• INDIAN • Menu £ 20 (lunch and early dinner) – Carte £ 18/28

Named after a sort of spiced bouquet garni – apt, since spicing plays a big part at this smart, warmly run Indian restaurant. Food markets across India provide the ideas, with smaller dishes like 'Chicken 65' inspired by street food.

Indian Zing

236 King St. ✉ W6 0RF ⊖ Ravenscourt Park Town plan: **21**LZG**a**
– ✆ (020) 8748 5959 – www.indianzing.co.uk
• INDIAN • Menu £ 12/27 – Carte £ 20/41

Chef-owner Manoj Vasaikar seeks inspiration from across India. His cooking balances the traditional with the more contemporary and delivers many layers of flavour – the lamb dishes and breads are particularly good. The restaurant is always busy yet service remains courteous and unhurried.

LONDON

Brackenbury

129 - 131 Brackenbury Rd ✉ W6 0BQ Town plan: **15**LZE**c**
Ravenscourt Park – ☎ (020) 8741 4928 – www.brackenburyrestaurant.co.uk – Closed Christmas, Easter, Monday and dinner Sunday
• MEDITERRANEAN • Menu £ 22 (lunch) – Carte £ 28/36
A much loved neighbourhood restaurant reopened by Ossie Gray of The River Café. The kitchen looks to Italy, France and the Med for inspiration and doesn't waste time on presentation; dishes feel instinctive and flavours marry well.

Azou

375 King St ✉ W6 9NJ ⊖ Stamford Brook Town plan: **21**KZG**u**
– ☎ (020) 8563 7266 – www.azou.co.uk – Closed 1 January and 25 December
• NORTH-AFRICAN • Carte £ 20/38 – *(dinner only) (booking essential)*
Silks, lanterns and rugs add to the atmosphere of this personally run, North African restaurant. Most come for the excellent tajines, with triple steamed couscous. Much is designed for sharing.

Hampshire Hog

227 King St ✉ W6 9JT ⊖ Ravenscourt Park Town plan: **21**LZG**s**
– ☎ (020) 8748 3391 – www.thehampshirehog.com – Closed 24-25 December
• BRITISH MODERN • Menu £ 10/28 – Carte £ 24/43
For years the owners ran The Engineer in Primrose Hill. 'The Hog' is a sizeable pub with a great terrace and garden. It offers everything from breakfast, bar snacks and cocktails to an appealing seasonal menu in a roomy dining room.

Havelock Tavern

57 Masbro Rd, Brook Grn ✉ W14 0LS Town plan: **16**MZE**e**
⊖ Kensington Olympia. – ☎ (020) 7603 5374 – www.havelocktavern.com – Closed 25-26 December
• MEDITERRANEAN • Carte £ 19/29 **s**
Warm, friendly and atmospheric pub with easy-going service and pleasantly mixed clientele. Blackboard menu offers robust, satisfying pub food. Arrive early if you don't want to wait for a table.

Crabtree

4 Rainville Rd ✉ W6 9HA ⊖ Barons Court Town plan: **21**LZG**x**
– ☎ (020) 7385 3929 – www.thecrabtreew6.co.uk
• MODERN • Carte £ 25/38
With a beer garden seating over 80 and a separate dining room terrace, this Victorian pub makes great use of its riverside location. Parfaits and terrines are highlights but Veggies are also considered. Service is unhurried.

Dartmouth Castle

26 Glenthorne Rd ✉ W6 0LS ⊖ Hammersmith. Town plan: **21**LZF**e**
– ☎ (020) 8748 3614 – www.thedartmouthcastle.co.uk – Closed 24 December-5 January
• MEDITERRANEAN • Carte £ 19/30
The Mediterranean exerts quite an influence on the large menu at this popular, welcoming and traditional pub. Spread over two levels but the ground floor is the more atmospheric.

Shepherd's Bush

Princess Victoria

217 Uxbridge Rd ✉ W12 9DH ⊖ Shepherd's Bush. Town plan: **15**KZE**a**
– ☎ (020) 8749 5886 – www.princessvictoria.co.uk – Closed 24-27 December
• BRITISH TRADITIONAL • Menu £ 13 (weekday lunch) – Carte £ 21/45
Magnificent Victorian gin palace, with original plasterwork. The kitchen knows its butchery; pork board, homemade sausages and terrines all feature. Excellent wine list, with over 350 bottles.

LONDON

HARINGEY

Crouch End

X **Bistro Aix**

54 Topsfield Par, Tottenham Ln ✉ N8 8PT Town plan: **3**EU**v**
⊖ Crouch Hill – ✆ (020) 8340 6346 – www.bistroaix.co.uk – Closed 26 December and 1 January
• FRENCH • Menu £ 18 – Carte £ 26/50 – *(dinner only and lunch Friday-Sunday)*
Dressers, cabinets and contemporary artwork lend an authentic Gallic edge to this bustling bistro, a favourite with many of the locals. Traditionally prepared French classics are the highlights of an extensive menu.

HARROW

Harrow on the Hill

XX **Incanto**

41 High St. ✉ HA1 3HT ⊖ Harrow on the Hill Town plan: **1**BU**z**
– ✆ (020) 8426 6767 – www.incanto.co.uk – Closed 24-26 December, 1 January, Easter Sunday, Sunday dinner and Monday
• MODERN • Menu £ 18 (weekday lunch) – Carte £ 27/39
Within Grade II former post office; split-level restaurant to rear of well stocked deli. Well-paced service; Italian bias to the modern cooking from an ambitious kitchen. Notable wine list is predominantly Italian.

Pinner

XX **Friends**

11 High St ✉ HA5 5PJ ⊖ Pinner – ✆ (020) 8866 0286 – www.friendsrestaurant.co.uk – Closed 25-26 December, Sunday dinner, Monday and bank holidays Town plan: **1**BU**a**
• MODERN • Menu £ 25 (weekday lunch) – Carte £ 33/44
This characterful, low-beamed restaurant has been proudly and personally run for over 20 years – and has a history stretching back over 500 more. Cooking is classical and carefully done, and the service is well-paced and friendly.

HEATHROW AIRPORT

Sofitel

Terminal 5, Heathrow Airport ✉ TW6 2GD Town plan: **5**AX**a**
⊖ Heathrow Terminal 5 – ✆ (020) 8757 7777 – www.sofitel.com
605 rm – †£ 169/289 ††£ 169/289, ☕ £ 20 – 27 suites
Rest *La Belle Époque* – Menu £ 25 (weekday lunch) – Carte £ 37/56 – *(closed Saturday lunch, Sunday and bank holidays)*
Rest *Vivre* – Menu £ 29 – Carte £ 27/51 – *(dinner only)*
Smart and well-run contemporary hotel, designed around a series of atriums, with direct access to T5. Crisply decorated, comfortable bedrooms with luxurious bathrooms. Choice of restaurant: international or classic French cuisine.

Hilton London Heathrow Airport Terminal 5

Poyle Rd, Colnbrook ✉ SL3 OFF – West : 2.5 mi by A 3113 – ✆ (01753) 686 860 – www.hilton.com/heathrowterminal5 – Closed 25-26 December
&rm,
350 rm ☕ – †£ 179/299 ††£ 191/310 – 3 suites
Rest *Mr Todiwala's Kitchen* – see restaurant listing
Rest *Gallery* – Menu £ 29 – Carte £ 30/49
A feeling of light and space pervades this modern, corporate hotel. Soundproofed rooms are fitted to a good standard; the spa offers wide-ranging treatments. Open-plan Gallery for British comfort food.

Hilton London Heathrow Airport

Terminal 4 ✉ TW6 3AF ⊖ Heathrow Terminal 4 – ✆ (020) 8759 7755 – www.hilton.com/heathrow Town plan: **5**AX**n**

398 rm – †£ 92/255 ††£ 96/260, ☕ £ 21 – 5 suites

Rest *Zen Oriental* – see restaurant listing

Rest *Aromi* – Menu £ 23 (dinner) – Carte £ 26/48 – *(closed Saturday lunch and Sunday)*

Group hotel with a striking modern exterior and linked to Terminal 4 by a covered walkway. Good-sized bedrooms, with contemporary styled suites. Casual dining in Aromi which occupies part of the vast atrium.

London Heathrow Marriott

Bath Rd, Hayes ✉ UB3 5AN Town plan: **5**AX**z**
⊖ Heathrow Terminal 1,2,3 – ✆ (020) 8990 1100 – www.londonheathrowmarriott.co.uk

393 rm ☕ – †£ 129/260 ††£ 139/270 – 2 suites

Rest *Tuscany* – Carte £ 33/52 – *(closed Christmas-New Year, Easter and Sunday) (dinner only)*

Rest *Allie's American Grille* – Carte £ 26/58

Built at the end of 20C, this modern, comfortable hotel is centred around a large atrium, with comprehensive business facilities: there is an exclusive Executive floor. Italian cuisine in bright and convivial Tuscany. Grill favourites in Allie's.

Mr Todiwala's Kitchen – Hilton London Heathrow Airport Terminal 5 Hotel

Poyle Rd, Colnbrook ✉ SL3 OFF – West : 2.5 mi by A 3113 – ✆ (01753) 766 482 – www.hilton.com/heathrowterminal5 – Closed 25-26 December and Sunday

• INDIAN • Menu £ 20 – Carte £ 30/49 – *(dinner only and lunch Thursday-Saturday)*

Secreted within the Hilton is Cyrus Todiwala's appealingly stylish, fresh-looking restaurant. The choice ranges from street food to tandoor dishes, Goan classics to Parsee specialities; order the 'Kitchen menu' for the full experience.

Zen Oriental – Hilton London Heathrow Airport Hotel

Terminal 4 ✉ TW6 3AF ⊖ Heathrow Terminal 4 Town plan: **5**AX**n**
– ✆ (020) 8759 7755 – www.hilton.com/heathrow – Closed 25-26 December

• ASIAN • Carte £ 34/63 – *(booking essential at dinner)*

With its capable service and appealing menu of authentically executed classics, Zen Oriental has long been a favourite at the Hilton. Popular for business lunches; busy at dinner with hotel guests.

HOUNSLOW

BRENTFORD

Hilton London Syon Park

Park Rd ✉ TW8 8JF – ✆ (020) 7870 7777 – www.londonsyonpark.com Town plan: **5**BX**x**

137 rm – †£ 169/199 ††£ 169/199, ☕ £ 18 – 1 suite

Rest *Marco Pierre White Steakhouse Bar & Grill* – Carte £ 26/57 – *(bar lunch)*

A large, impressively decorated, purpose-built hotel in the grounds of Syon House – the London residence of the Duke of Northumberland. Most of the smart, stylish rooms have a terrace or balcony; ask for one overlooking the walled garden.

CHISWICK

High Road House

162 Chiswick High Rd ✉ W4 1PR Town plan: **21**KZG**e**
⊖ Turnham Green – ✆ (020) 8742 1717 – www.highroadhouse.co.uk

14 rm – †£ 116/215 ††£ 116/215, ☕ £ 22

Rest *High Road Brasserie* – see restaurant listing

Cool, sleek hotel and club, the latter a slick place to lounge around or play games. Light, bright bedrooms with crisp linen. A carefully appointed, fairly-priced destination.

LONDON

LONDON

La Trompette

5-7 Devonshire Rd ✉ W4 2EU ⊖ Turnham Green Town plan: **21**KZG**y**
– ✆ (020) 8747 1836 – www.latrompette.co.uk – Closed 24-26 December and 1 January
• BRITISH MODERN • Menu £ 28 (lunch and early dinner)/45 – (booking essential)
Chez Bruce's sister is a delightful neighbourhood restaurant that's now a little roomier. The service is charming and the food terrific. Dishes at lunch are quite simple but great value; the cooking at dinner is a tad more elaborate.
➜ Scallops with raisin, pomegranate, pine nut and coriander dressing. Caramelised suckling pig with creamed potato, sprouting broccoli, kale and roast carrot. Rhubarb crumble soufflé with rhubarb ripple ice cream.

Hedone (Mikael Jonsson)

301-303 Chiswick High Rd ✉ W4 4HH Town plan: **6**CV**x**
⊖ Chiswick Park – ✆ (020) 8747 0377 – www.hedonerestaurant.com – Closed two weeks in summer, two weeks Christmas-New Year, Sunday and Monday
• MODERN • Menu £ 45/95 – (dinner only and lunch Thursday-Saturday)
Mikael Jonsson, former lawyer turned chef, is not one for complacency so his restaurant continues to evolve. The content of his set menus is governed entirely by what ingredients are in their prime – and it is this passion for produce which underpins the superlative and very flavoursome cooking.
➜ Luberon asparagus, avocado, pistachio and wild primrose. Rack of salt marsh lamb with fresh peas, carrots and spinach. Warm chocolate, passion fruit jelly, powdered raspberry, Madagascan vanilla ice cream.

Michael Nadra

6-8 Elliott Rd ✉ W4 1PE ⊖ Turnham Green Town plan: **21**KZG**z**
– ✆ (020) 8742 0766 – www.restaurant-michaelnadra.co.uk
– Closed 24-26 December, 1 January and Sunday dinner
• MODERN • Menu £ 20/55
Hidden down a side street is this small, intimate place where the closely set tables add to the bonhomie. The cooking is influenced by the Mediterranean and the fish dishes stand out. Prices are fair and the service is warm.

Charlotte's Bistro

6 Turnham Green Terr ✉ W4 1QP Town plan: **21**KZG**a**
⊖ Turnham Green – ✆ (020) 8742 3590 – www.charlottes.co.uk
• MODERN • Menu £ 16/27 – Carte £ 25/33 – (booking advisable)
A pleasant, unpretentious bistro; run by a friendly team, with a well-priced menu of flavoursome, well prepared dishes of largely European provenance. Little sister to Charlotte's Place in Ealing.

Sam's Brasserie

11 Barley Mow Passage ✉ W4 4PH Town plan: **2**CV**a**
⊖ Turnham Green – ✆ (020) 8987 0555 – www.samsbrasserie.co.uk
– Closed 24-26 December
• MEDITERRANEAN • Menu £ 14 (lunch and early dinner) – Carte £ 25/41
A former Sanderson wallpaper mill, now a bustling, fun brasserie with Sir Peter Blake artwork adding to the hip feel. Appealing, modern menu; satisfying dishes deliver on flavour. Look out for regular Soul and Jazz evenings.

Vinoteca Ⓝ

18 Devonshire Rd ✉ W4 2HD ⊖ Turnham Green Town plan: **21**KZG**v**
– ✆ (020) 3701 8822 – www.vinoteca.co.uk – Closed 25 December
• MODERN • Carte £ 25/42
Dinner bookings are a must at this 4th outpost of the group. A short menu has strong Italian roots, with dishes relying on quality ingredients for fresh flavours. Sunday is a traditional roast; Monday night, wine is at shop prices.

High Road Brasserie – High Road House Hotel

162 Chiswick High Rd. ✉ W4 1PR Town plan: **21**KZG**e**
⊖ Turnham Green – ✆ (020) 8742 7474 – www.highroadhouse.co.uk
• FRENCH • Carte £ 20/36 – *(booking essential)*

Authentic brasserie, with mirrors, panelling and art deco lighting. Despite the high volume of customers, the classic dishes are prepared with care and staff cope well with being busy.

ISLINGTON

ARCHWAY

500

782 Holloway Rd ✉ N19 3JH ⊖ Archway Town plan: **12**SZA**y**
– ✆ (020) 7272 3406 – www.500restaurant.co.uk – Closed 2 weeks summer and 2 weeks Christmas-New Year
• ITALIAN • Carte £ 24/32 – *(dinner only and lunch Friday-Sunday) (booking essential)*

Small, fun and well-priced Italian that's always busy. Good pastas and bread; the veal chop and rabbit are specialities. The passion of the ebullient owner and keen chef are evident.

St John's Tavern

91 Junction Rd ✉ N19 5QU ⊖ Archway. – ✆ (020) 7272 1587 – www.stjohnstavern.com – Closed 25-26 December and 1 January Town plan: **12**RZA**s**
• MODERN • Carte £ 25/35 – *(dinner only and lunch Friday-Sunday) (booking advisable)*

Having undergone an English Heritage restoration, the pub is a beacon of hope on stubbornly unchanging Junction Road. Great bar snacks but head to the large, theatre-like dining room for robust English food with nods to the Med.

BARNSBURY

Roots at N1

115 Hemingford Rd ✉ N1 1BZ Town plan: **13**UZB**d**
⊖ Caledonian Road – ✆ (020) 7697 4488 – www.rootsatn1.com
– Closed 25-26 December and Monday
• INDIAN • Carte £ 26/35 – *(dinner only) (booking essential)*

A warm and welcoming Indian restaurant run with a palpable sense of pride by three friends who worked together at Benares. The menu is appealingly concise and combinations are original; tandoor cooked dishes are a highlight.

CANONBURY

Trullo

300-302 St Paul's Rd ✉ N1 2LH Town plan: **13**UZB**t**
⊖ Highbury & Islington – ✆ (020) 7226 2733 – www.trullorestaurant.com
– Closed Christmas-New Year and Sunday dinner
• ITALIAN • Menu £ 15 (lunch) – Carte £ 24/37 – *(booking essential)*

While the ground floor has kept its well-worn, homely feel, the basement has a new, all-American look, with exposed brick, industrial ducting and red banquettes. Rustic, well-priced dishes include house specialities cooked on the charcoal grill and great pasta, hand-rolled before each service.

Canonbury Kitchen

19 Canonbury Ln ✉ N1 2AS Town plan: **13**UZB**c**
⊖ Highbury & Islington – ✆ (020) 7226 9791 – www.canonburykitchen.com
– Closed Sunday dinner
• ITALIAN • Carte £ 23/36 – *(dinner only and lunch Saturday-Sunday)*

A bright, local Italian with seating for just 40; exposed brick walls and painted floorboards add to the fresh feel. The kitchen keeps things simple and the menu pricing is prudent.

Primeur N

116 Petherton Rd ✉ N5 2RT ⊖ Canonbury Town plan: **13**VZA**p**
– www.primeurn5.co.uk – Closed Christmas, Monday, dinner Sunday and lunch Tuesday-Thursday
• MODERN • Carte £ 20/31
Housed in a former garage, with huge concertina doors, communal and counter seating and a laid-back, quirky feel. The menu offers a mix of Mediterranean and classic British dishes, of which sharing is encouraged.

Smokehouse N

63-69 Canonbury Rd ✉ N1 2DG Town plan: **13**UZB**h**
⊖ Highbury & Islington. – ☎ (020) 7354 1144
– www.smokehouseislington.co.uk – Closed 24-26 December
• MODERN • Carte £ 26/37 – *(dinner only and lunch Saturday-Sunday) (booking advisable)*
You can smell the oak chips in the smoker as you approach this warm, modern pub. Meat is the mainstay – the peppered ox cheeks are a firm favourite – but whilst flavours are gutsy, the smoking and barbecuing is never overpowering.

Fancy a last minute break?
Check hotel websites to take advantage of price promotions.

Clerkenwell

Malmaison

18-21 Charterhouse Sq ✉ EC1M 6AH ⊖ Barbican Town plan: **19**UZD**q**
– ☎ (020) 7012 3700 – www.malmaison.com
97 rm – †£ 130/350 ††£ 130/360, ☐ £ 15
Rest *Stripbar & Steak* – Menu £ 20 (lunch) – Carte £ 23/41 – *(closed Saturday lunch)*
Striking early 20C red-brick building overlooking pleasant square. Stylish, comfy public areas. Bedrooms in vivid, bold colours, with plenty of extra touches. Modern brasserie with international menu; grilled meats a highlight.

The Rookery without rest

12 Peters Ln, Cowcross St ✉ EC1M 6DS Town plan: **33**AOT**p**
⊖ Farringdon – ☎ (020) 7336 0931 – www.rookeryhotel.com
33 rm – †£ 168/222 ††£ 210/312, ☐ £ 12
A row of charmingly restored 18C houses. Wood panelling, stone-flagged flooring, open fires and antique furniture. Highly individual bedrooms, with Victorian bathrooms.

Comptoir Gascon

61-63 Charterhouse St. ✉ EC1M 6HJ Town plan: **33**AOT**a**
⊖ Farringdon – ☎ (020) 7608 0851 – www.comptoirgascon.com
– Closed Christmas-New Year, Sunday, Monday and bank holidays
• FRENCH • Menu £ 15 (weekday lunch) – Carte £ 17/45 – *(booking essential)*
Buzzy restaurant; sister to Club Gascon. Rustic and satisfying specialities from the SW of France include wine, cheese, bread and especially duck. Further produce on display to take home.

Polpo Smithfield

3 Cowcross St ✉ EC1M 6DR ⊖ Farringdon. Town plan: **33**AOT**s**
– ☎ (020) 7250 0034 – www.polpo.co.uk – Closed Christmas, New Year and Sunday dinner
• ITALIAN • Carte £ 12/24
For his third Venetian-style bacaro, Russell Norman converted an old meat market storage facility; it has an elegantly battered feel. Head first for the Negroni bar downstairs; then over-order tasty, uncomplicated and very satisfying dishes to share. Bookings only taken up to 5.30pm.

St John

26 St John St ✉ EC1M 4AY ⊖ Farringdon Town plan: **33**APT**k**
– ✆ (020) 7251 0848 – www.stjohnrestaurant.com – Closed Christmas-New Year, Saturday lunch, Sunday dinner and bank holidays
• BRITISH TRADITIONAL • Carte £ 25/59 – *(booking essential)*

A glorious celebration of British fare and a champion of 'nose to tail eating'. Utilitarian surroundings and a refreshing lack of ceremony ensure the food is the focus; it's appealingly simple, full of flavour and very satisfying.

➜ Roast bone marrow & parsley salad. Roast Tamworth loin, turnips & trotter. Pear & sherry trifle.

Foxlow Ⓝ

69-73 St John St ✉ EC1M 4AN ⊖ Farringdon Town plan: **19**UZD**a**
– ✆ (020) 7014 8070 – www.foxlow.co.uk – Closed 24-31 December and Sunday dinner
• MEATS AND GRILLS • Carte £ 20/37

From the clever Hawksmoor people comes this fun and funky place where the staff ensure everyone's having a good time. There are steaks available but plenty of other choices with influences from Italy, Asia and the Middle East.

Hix Oyster and Chop House

36-37 Greenhill Rents ✉ EC1M 6BN ⊖ Farringdon Town plan: **33**AOT**e**
– ✆ (020) 7017 1930 – www.hixoysterandchophouse.co.uk – Closed 25-29 December, Saturday lunch, Sunday dinner and bank holidays
• BRITISH TRADITIONAL • Menu £ 20 (lunch and early dinner)
– Carte £ 27/54

Appropriately utilitarian surroundings put the focus on seasonal and often underused British ingredients. Cooking is satisfying and unfussy, with plenty of oysters and aged beef served on the bone.

Vinoteca

7 St John St. ✉ EC1M 4AA ⊖ Farringdon Town plan: **33**APT**a**
– ✆ (020) 7253 8786 – www.vinoteca.co.uk – Closed 25-26 December, 1 January, Sunday and bank holidays
• MODERN • Carte £ 24/32

This cosy and enthusiastically run 'bar and wine shop' is always busy and full of life. The thrilling wine list is constantly evolving and the classic European dishes, cured meats and cheeses are ideal accompaniments.

FINSBURY

South Place

3 South Pl ✉ EC2M 2AF ⊖ Moorgate – ✆ (020) 3503 0000 – www.southplacehotel.com – Closed 26-31 December Town plan: **34**ART**v**
80 rm – †£ 185/350 ††£ 185/350, ☕ £ 15 – 1 suite
Rest *Angler* ✿ – see restaurant listing
Rest *3 South Place* – ✆ (020) 3215 1270 – Menu £ 20 (dinner)
– Carte £ 26/42

Restaurant group D&D's first venture into the hotel business is a stylish affair; unsurprising as its interior was designed by Conran & Partners. Bedrooms are a treat for those with an eye for aesthetics and no detail has been forgotten. The ground floor hosts 3 South Place, a bustling bar and grill.

Zetter

St John's Sq., 86-88 Clerkenwell Rd. ✉ EC1M 5RJ Town plan: **19**UZD**s**
⊖ Farringdon – ✆ (020) 7324 4444 – www.thezetter.com
72 rm ☕ – †£ 115/235 ††£ 115/235
Rest *Bistrot Bruno Loubet* – see restaurant listing

A trendy and discreet converted 19C warehouse with well-equipped bedrooms that come with pleasant touches, such as Penguin paperbacks. The more idiosyncratic Zetter Townhouse across the square is used as an overflow.

XX ✿

Angler – South Place Hotel

3 South Pl ✉ *EC2M 2AF* ⊖ *Moorgate – ✆ (020) 3215 1260 – www.anglerrestaurant.com – Closed 26 December-1 January (except dinner 31 December), Saturday lunch and Sunday* Town plan: **34**ART**v**

• FISH AND SEAFOOD • Menu £ 25/65 – Carte £ 36/67 – *(booking advisable)*

The rooftop restaurant of D&D's South Place hotel is a bright, light and very comfortable space; its adjoining bar and terrace the perfect spot for a pre-prandial cocktail. The menu champions the best of British seafood and the freshness of the ingredients really shines through.

→ Yellow fin tuna tartare, lime and chilli. Angler and lobster pie, button mushrooms and mashed potato. Chocolate fondant, pistachio ice cream.

X

Quality Chop House

92-94 Farringdon Rd ✉ *EC1R 3EA* ⊖ *Farringdon – ✆ (020) 7278 1452 – www.thequalitychophouse.com – Closed Sunday dinner and bank holidays* Town plan: **19**UZD**h**

• BRITISH TRADITIONAL • Menu £ 10 (weekdays)/35 – Carte £ 22/44 – *(booking advisable)*

Back in the hands of owners who respect its history, this 'progressive working class caterer' is once again championing gusty British grub. It also has a terrific, concise wine list with plenty of gems. The Grade II listed room, with its trademark booths, has been an eating house since 1869.

X

Moro

34-36 Exmouth Mkt ✉ *EC1R 4QE* ⊖ *Farringdon – ✆ (020) 7833 8336 – www.moro.co.uk – Closed dinner 24 December-2 January, bank holidays and Sunday dinner* Town plan: **19**UZD**m**

• MEDITERRANEAN • Carte £ 30/40 – *(booking essential)*

It's the stuff of dreams – pack up your worldly goods, drive through Spain, Portugal, Morocco and the Sahara and then back in London open a restaurant and share your love of Moorish cuisine. The wood-fired oven and chargrill fill the air with wonderful aromas and food is vibrant and colourful.

X

Medcalf

40 Exmouth Mkt. ✉ *EC1R 4QE* ⊖ *Farringdon – ✆ (020) 7833 3533 – www.medcalfbar.co.uk – Closed 25 December-1 January, Sunday dinner and bank holidays* Town plan: **19**UZD**m**

• BRITISH TRADITIONAL • Menu £ 15 (weekday dinner) – Carte £ 23/32 – *(booking essential)*

When Albert Medcalf opened his butcher's in 1912 he probably never thought that a century later it would be home to a busy, hip restaurant. Good use is made of the same sort of quality British produce for which Albert was renowned.

X

The Modern Pantry

47-48 St John's Sq. ✉ *EC1V 4JJ* ⊖ *Farringdon – ✆ (020) 7553 9210 – www.themodernpantry.co.uk – Closed 25-26 December* Town plan: **19**UZD**k**

• OTHER WORLD KITCHENS • Menu £ 22 (weekday lunch)/45 – Carte £ 26/39 – *(booking advisable)*

Fusion cooking that uses complementary flavours to create vibrant, zesty dishes. The simple, crisp ground floor of this Georgian building has the buzz; upstairs is more intimate. Clued-up service.

X

Bistrot Bruno Loubet – Zetter Hotel

St John's Sq., 86-88 Clerkenwell Rd. ✉ *EC1M 5RJ* ⊖ *Farringdon – ✆ (020) 7324 4444 – www.bistrotbrunoloubet.com – Closed 24-26 December* Town plan: **19**UZD**s**

• FRENCH • Menu £ 20 (weekday lunch) – Carte £ 27/43 – *(booking advisable)*

The trendy Zetter hotel and Bruno Loubet's flavoursome French cooking are a good fit. The classic bistro dishes come with added sophistication; the bright room has plenty of buzz and the service is informed and unhurried.

Morito

32 Exmouth Mkt ✉ EC1R 4QE ⊖ Farringdon Town plan: **19**UZD**b**
– ✆ (020) 7278 7007 – www.morito.co.uk – Closed 24 December-2 January, bank holidays and Sunday dinner
• SPANISH • Carte £ 16/23 – *(bookings not accepted at dinner)*
From the owners of next door Moro comes this authentic and appealingly down to earth little tapas bar. Seven or eight dishes between two should suffice but over-ordering is easy and won't break the bank.

Caravan

11-13 Exmouth Market ✉ EC1R 4QD Town plan: **19**UZD**c**
⊖ Farringdon – ✆ (020) 7833 8115 – www.caravanonexmouth.co.uk – Closed Sunday
• OTHER WORLD KITCHENS • Carte £ 19/45 – *(booking advisable)*
A discernible Antipodean vibe pervades this casual eatery, from the laid-back charm of the service to the kitchen's confident combining of unusual flavours. Cooking is influenced by owner's travels – hence the name.

Clerkenwell Kitchen

27-31 Clerkenwell Cl ✉ EC1R 0AT ⊖ Farringdon Town plan: **19**UZD**v**
– ✆ (020) 7101 9959 – www.theclerkenwellkitchen.co.uk – Closed Christmas-New Year, Saturday, Sunday and bank holidays
• MODERN • Carte £ 17/23 – *(lunch only) (booking advisable)*
The owner of this simple, friendly, tucked away eatery worked with Hugh Fearnley-Whittingstall and is committed to sustainability. Daily changing, well-sourced produce; fresh, flavoursome cooking.

Peasant

240 St John St ✉ EC1V 4PH ⊖ Farringdon. Town plan: **19**UZD**e**
– ✆ (020) 7336 7726 – www.thepeasant.co.uk – Closed 25 December-1 January and bank holidays except Good Friday
• BRITISH MODERN • Menu £ 24 (weekday dinner) – Carte £ 15/28 – *(booking essential)*
This handsome Victorian pub was at the vanguard of the gastropub movement. Share a cheeseboard or meze in the bar or book in the upstairs restaurant for more sophisticated yet equally gutsy cooking.

Well

180 St John St ✉ EC1V 4JY ⊖ Farringdon. Town plan: **19**UZD**x**
– ✆ (020) 7251 9363 – www.downthewell.com – Closed 25-26 December
• BRITISH MODERN • Carte £ 23/41
This well-supported local pub from the Martin Brothers comes with the sort of food that is reassuringly familiar yet done well, and service that instils confidence. Eat on the ground floor, rather than in the less welcoming basement.

HIGHBURY

Au Lac

82 Highbury Park ✉ N5 2XE ⊖ Arsenal – ✆ (020) 7704 9187 – www.aulac.co.uk – Closed 24-26 December, 1-2 January and 1 week early August Town plan: **13**UZA**b**
• VIETNAMESE • Menu £ 14/18 – Carte £ 12/24 – *(dinner only and lunch Thursday-Friday)*
Sweet, longstanding Vietnamese restaurant run by two brothers. New dishes are regularly added to the already lengthy but authentic and keenly priced menu, whose dishes exhibit plenty of fresh and lively flavours.

ISLINGTON

Almeida

30 Almeida St. ✉ N1 1AD ⊖ Angel – ✆ (020) 7354 4777 – www.almeida-restaurant.com – Closed 26 December, 1 January, Sunday dinner and Monday lunch Town plan: **13**UZB**r**
• FRENCH • Menu £ 17 (lunch and early dinner) – Carte £ 24/47
A D&D restaurant opposite the award-winning theatre, so expect it to be very busy pre and post curtain-up. It's smoothly run and comfortable and the reliable cooking comes with a classical base and a Mediterranean bias.

LONDON

Ottolenghi

287 Upper St. ✉ N1 2TZ ⊖ Highbury & Islington Town plan: **13**UZB**k**
– ✆ (020) 7288 1454 – www.ottolenghi.co.uk – Closed 25-26 December, Sunday dinner and bank holidays

• MEDITERRANEAN • Menu £ 17 (lunch) – Carte dinner approx. £ 27 – *(booking essential)*

You've bought the book; now see how the dish is meant to taste at Yotam Ottolenghi's deli/restaurant. The freshness is palpable, with flavours from the Med, North Africa and Middle East. You'll never think of salad in the same way.

Yipin China

70-72 Liverpool Rd ✉ N1 0QD ⊖ Angel – ✆ (020) 7354 3388 – www.yipinchina.co.uk – Closed 25 December Town plan: **13**UZB**b**

• CHINESE • Carte £ 19/42

The menu at this modest little place features Hunanese, Cantonese and Sichuanese specialities, but it is the spicy, chilli-based dishes from Hunan province which use techniques like smoking and curing that really stand out.

Fish & Chip Shop

189 Upper St ✉ N1 1RQ Town plan: **13**UZB**s**
⊖ Highbury and Islington – ✆ (020) 3227 0979
– www.thefishandchipshop.uk.com – Closed Sunday

• FISH AND CHIPS • Carte £ 18/39 – *(booking essential at dinner)*

Not exactly your average chippy – there are cocktails, weekend brunches and starters like crab on toast. Butties are fun for a quick snack but most come for Camden Hells battered fish. They do takeaway and more shops are planned.

Drapers Arms

44 Barnsbury St ✉ N1 1ER Town plan: **13**UZB**x**
⊖ Highbury & Islington. – ✆ (020) 7619 0348 – www.thedrapersarms.com
– Closed 25-26 December

• BRITISH MODERN • Carte £ 22/33 – *(bookings advisable at dinner)*

Anyone unfamiliar with Britain's bounteous larder should get along to this down-to-earth Georgian pub to enjoy ingredients like lamb's tongues, smoked eel, blade steak and rabbit in dishes that are satisfying, gutsy and affordable.

Pig and Butcher

80 Liverpool Rd ✉ N1 0QD ⊖ Angel. – ✆ (020) 7226 8304 – www.thepigandbutcher.co.uk – Closed 25-27 December Town plan: **13**UZB**e**

• BRITISH TRADITIONAL • Carte £ 26/46 – *(dinner only and lunch Friday-Sunday) (booking advisable)*

Dating from the mid-19C, when cattle drovers taking livestock to Smithfield Market would stop for a swift one, and now fully restored. There's a strong British element to the daily menu; meat is butchered and smoked in-house.

KENSINGTON and CHELSEA (Royal Borough of)

CHELSEA

Jumeirah Carlton Tower

Cadogan Pl ✉ SW1X 9PY ⊖ Knightsbridge Town plan: **37**AGX**r**
– ✆ (020) 7235 1234 – www.jumeirahcarltontower.com

186 rm – †£ 330/775 ††£ 330/775, ☕ £ 39 – 30 suites

Rest ***Rib Room*** – see restaurant listing

Imposing international hotel overlooking a leafy square and just yards from all the swanky boutiques. Well-equipped rooftop health club has great views. Generously proportioned bedrooms boast every conceivable facility.

Chelsea Harbour
Chelsea Harbour ✉ *SW10 0XG* ⊖ *Imperial Wharf* Town plan: **23**PZG**k**
– ✆ *(020) 7823 3000* – *www.thechelseaharbourhotel.co.uk*
157 rm – †£ 220/300 ††£ 220/300, ☕ £ 24
Rest *Chelsea Riverside Brasserie* – Menu £ 32 (lunch and early dinner) – Carte £ 29/54
Formerly called Wyndham Grand. Modern hotel within an exclusive marina and retail development. Many of the large, well-appointed rooms have balconies for views across the Thames. Bright restaurant offers a wide-ranging menu.

Park Tower Knightsbridge
101 Knightsbridge ✉ *SW1X 7RN* ⊖ *Knightsbridge* Town plan: **37**AGX**t**
– ✆ *(020) 7235 8050* – *www.theparktowerknightsbridge.com*
258 rm – †£ 309/759 ††£ 309/759, ☕ £ 28 – 22 suites
Rest *One-O-One* – see restaurant listing
Built in the 1970s in a unique cylindrical shape. The well-equipped bedrooms are all identical in size. Top floor executive rooms come with commanding views of Hyde Park and The City.

LONDON

The Capital
22-24 Basil St. ✉ *SW3 1AT* ⊖ *Knightsbridge* Town plan: **37**AFX**a**
– ✆ *(020) 7589 5171* – *www.capitalhotel.co.uk*
49 rm – †£ 200/340 ††£ 250/430, ☕ £ 17 – 1 suite
Rest *Outlaw's at The Capital* ✿ – see restaurant listing
This fine, thoroughly British hotel has been under the same private ownership for over 40 years. Known for its discreet atmosphere, conscientious and attentive service and immaculately kept bedrooms courtesy of different designers.

Draycott
26 Cadogan Gdns ✉ *SW3 2RP* ⊖ *Sloane Square* Town plan: **37**AGY**c**
– ✆ *(020) 7730 6466* – *www.draycotthotel.com*
35 rm – †£ 186/199 ††£ 282/378, ☕ £ 22
Rest – Carte £ 33/56 – *(room service only)*
Charming 19C house with elegant sitting room overlooking tranquil garden for afternoon tea. Bedrooms are individually decorated in a country house style and are named after writers or actors.

Egerton House
17-19 Egerton Terr ✉ *SW3 2BX* Town plan: **37**AFY**e**
⊖ *South Kensington* – ✆ *(020) 7589 2412* – *www.egertonhousehotel.com*
28 rm ☕ – †£ 310/440 ††£ 325/455
Rest – Carte £ 35/55 – *(room service only)*
Compact but comfortable townhouse in a very good location, well-maintained throughout and owned by the Red Carnation group. High levels of personal service make the hotel stand out.

Knightsbridge
10 Beaufort Gdns ✉ *SW3 1PT* ⊖ *Knightsbridge* Town plan: **37**AFX**s**
– ✆ *(020) 7584 6300* – *www.knightsbridgehotel.com*
44 rm – †£ 234/252 ††£ 264/894, ☕ £ 19 **Rest** *(room service only)*
Charming and attractively furnished townhouse in a Victorian terrace, with a very stylish, discreet feel. Every bedroom is immaculately appointed and has a style all of its own; fine detailing throughout.

The Levin
28 Basil St. ✉ *SW3 1AS* ⊖ *Knightsbridge* Town plan: **37**AFX**c**
– ✆ *(020) 7589 6286* – *www.thelevinhotel.co.uk*
12 rm ☕ – †£ 240/399 ††£ 295/499
Rest *Le Metro* – Menu £ 14/16 – Carte £ 24/30
A discreet townhouse and sister to The Capital next door. Impressive façade, contemporary interior and comfortable bedrooms in subtle art deco style, with marvellous champagne mini bars. Simple dishes served all day down at Le Metro.

No.11 Cadogan Gardens

11 Cadogan Gdns ✉ *SW3 2RJ* ⊖ *Sloane Square* Town plan: **37**AGY**n**
– ✆ *(020) 7730 7000 – www.no11cadogangardens.com*
54 rm – †£ 270/450 ††£ 270/450, ☕ £ 22 – 5 suites
Rest *Tartufo* – Menu £ 35/45 – *(closed Sunday dinner)*
Townhouse hotel fashioned out of four red-brick houses and exuberantly dressed in bold colours and furnishings. Theatrically decorated bedrooms vary in size from cosy to spacious. Intimate basement Italian restaurant with accomplished and ambitious cooking.

Beaufort

rm,

33 Beaufort Gdns ✉ *SW3 1PP* ⊖ *Knightsbridge* Town plan: **37**AFX**n**
– ✆ *(020) 7584 5252 – www.thebeaufort.co.uk*
29 rm – †£ 168/228 ††£ 228/312, ☕ £ 15 **Rest** – – *(room service only)*
A vast collection of English floral watercolours adorn this 19C townhouse, set in a useful location. Modern and co-ordinated rooms. Tariff includes all drinks and afternoon tea.

Sydney House without rest

9-11 Sydney St. ✉ *SW3 6PU* ⊖ *South Kensington* Town plan: **36**ADY**s**
– ✆ *(020) 7376 7711 – www.sydneyhousechelsea.co.uk – Closed 25-29 December*
21 rm – †£ 125/255 ††£ 125/355, ☕ £ 15
Stylish and compact Georgian townhouse made brighter through plenty of mirrors and light wood. Thoughtfully designed bedrooms; Room 43 has its own terrace. Part of the Abode group.

The Sloane Square

rm,

7-12 Sloane Sq. ✉ *SW1W 8EG* ⊖ *Sloane Square* Town plan: **37**AGY**k**
– ✆ *(020) 7896 9988 – www.sloanesquarehotel.co.uk*
102 rm – †£ 210/265 ††£ 240/325, ☕ £ 15
Rest Côte – Menu £ 14 (lunch and early dinner) – Carte £ 20/33
Well-placed, red-brick hotel boasting bright, contemporary décor. Stylish, co-ordinated bedrooms, with laptops; library of DVDs and games available. Rooms at the back are slightly quieter.

Gordon Ramsay (Clare Smyth)

✿✿✿ *68-69 Royal Hospital Rd.* ✉ *SW3 4HP* Town plan: **37**AFZ**c**
⊖ *Sloane Square* – ✆ *(020) 7352 4441 – www.gordonramsay.com*
– Closed 23-27 December, Saturday and Sunday
• FRENCH • Menu £ 55/185 – *(booking essential)*
Attention to detail ensures that Gordon Ramsay's flagship restaurant still provides the consummate dining experience. Composed, reassuring and discreet service adds to the calmness of the room; Clare Smyth's cooking is poised, elegant and a little more daring.
→ Cheltenham beetroot with clementine, thyme, hazelnuts and smoked goat's curd. Turbot with seaweed, palourde clams, fennel and Romanesco. Smoked chocolate cigar with blood orange and cardamom ice cream.

Bibendum

Michelin House, 81 Fulham Rd. ✉ *SW3 6RD* Town plan: **37**AEY**s**
⊖ *South Kensington* – ✆ *(020) 7581 5817 – www.bibendum.co.uk*
– Closed dinner 24 December, 25-26 December and 1 January
• FRENCH • Menu £ 28 (weekdays)/36 – Carte £ 37/72
Located on the 1st floor of a London landmark – Michelin's former HQ, dating from 1911. French food comes with a British accent and there's fresh seafood served in the oyster bar below. It's maintained a loyal following for over 20 years.

Rib Room – Jumeirah Carlton Tower Hotel

Cadogan Pl ✉ *SW1X 9PY* ⊖ *Knightsbridge* Town plan: **37**AGX**r**
– ✆ *(020) 7858 7250 – www.theribroom.co.uk*
• MEATS AND GRILLS • Menu £ 28/58 – Carte £ 50/116
Rib of Aberdeen Angus, steaks and other classic British dishes attract a prosperous, international crowd; few of whom appear to have a beef with the prices at this swish veteran.

XXX **Five Fields**

8-9 Blacklands Terr ✉ SW3 2SP ⊖ Sloane Square Town plan: **37**AFY**s**
– ✆ (020) 7838 1082 – www.fivefieldsrestaurant.com – Closed first 2 weeks January, first 2 weeks August, Sunday and Monday
• MODERN • Menu £ 50 – *(dinner only)*
Expect some rather daring combinations on the plate, along with bold flavours; desserts have a unique identity all of their own. This formally run restaurant may be comparatively small but it comes with a warm, intimate feel.

XXX **Chutney Mary**

535 King's Rd. ✉ SW10 0SZ ⊖ Fulham Broadway Town plan: **22**OZG**v**
– ✆ (020) 7351 3113 – www.realindianfood.com
• INDIAN • Menu £ 26 – Carte £ 34/58 – *(dinner only and lunch Saturday-Sunday)*
Since 1990 it has offered a side order of sophistication along with regional specialities from across India. Wine pairings and cocktails also set it apart. The conservatory is slightly less hectic and away from the larger groups.

XXX **One-O-One** – Park Tower Knightsbridge Hotel

101 Knightsbridge ✉ SW1X 7RN ⊖ Knightsbridge Town plan: **37**AGX**t**
– ✆ (020) 7290 7101 – www.oneoonerestaurant.com
• FISH AND SEAFOOD • Menu £ 21 (lunch) – Carte £ 55/98
Smart ground floor restaurant; lacking a little in atmosphere but the seafood is good. Much of the excellent produce from Brittany and Norway; don't miss the King crab legs which are the stars of the show.

XXX **Baku**

164 Sloane St (1st Floor) ✉ SW1X 9QB Town plan: **37**AGX**n**
⊖ Knightsbridge – ✆ (020) 7235 5399 – www.bakulondon.com
• OTHER WORLD KITCHENS • Menu £ 17/27 – Carte £ 28/63
Named after the capital city, Baku offers diners the chance to try subtly lightened Azerbaijani cuisine in fairly opulent surroundings. Kebabs, tandir dishes, soups and plenty of sturgeon from the Caspian Sea feature.

XXX **Toto's** (N)

Walton House, Lennox Garden Mews ✉ SW3 2JH Town plan: **37**AFY**b**
– (Off Walton St) ⊖ South Kensington – ✆ (020) 7589 2062 – www.totosrestaurant.com
• ITALIAN • Menu £ 25 – Carte £ 39/54 – *(booking essential at dinner)*
A Chelsea institution returned in 2014, when new owners reopened this discreet Italian restaurant for grown-ups. The kitchen has made the food more contemporary without doing anything to alarm those with more traditional tastes.

XXX **Fifth Floor at Harvey Nichols**

109-125 Knightsbridge ✉ SW1X 7RJ Town plan: **37**AGX**s**
⊖ Knightsbridge – ✆ (020) 7235 5250 – www.harveynichols.com – Closed Christmas, Easter and Sunday dinner
• MODERN • Menu £ 22/32 – Carte £ 45/52
The room has had more makeovers than many of its glamorous customers but now the cooking has also changed. It's still largely European in its influences but dishes are elaborately constructed and considerably more sophisticated.

XX ✿ **Outlaw's at The Capital** – The Capital Hotel

22-24 Basil St. ✉ SW3 1AT ⊖ Knightsbridge Town plan: **37**AFX**a**
– ✆ (020) 7591 1202 – www.capitalhotel.co.uk – Closed Sunday
• FISH AND SEAFOOD • Menu £ 27 (lunch) – Carte £ 47/65 *– (booking essential)*
Chef Nathan Outlaw brings his award-winning formula up from Cornwall: great seafood where the quality of the fish shines through and the flavours harmonise perfectly. The well-structured wine list features the ever popular Levin Sauvignon Blanc from the owner's own estate in the Loire.
➜ Lobster risotto, orange, basil and lobster dressing. Turbot with crispy oysters, cabbage & bacon, oyster sauce. Quince and ginger cheesecake, quince and cider sorbet.

XX **Rasoi** (Vineet Bhatia)
10 Lincoln St ✉ SW3 2TS ⊖ Sloane Square Town plan: **37**AFY**y**
– ✆ (020) 7225 1881 – www.rasoirestaurant.co.uk – Closed 25-26 December, 1-2 January and Saturday lunch
• INDIAN • Menu £ 23/89 – Carte £ 65/86
With outposts in Geneva, Mauritius and Dubai, Vineet Bhatia proves that Indian food is as open to innovation and interpretation as any other cuisine. His exotically decorated dining room sits within an archetypical Chelsea townhouse.
➜ Smoked tandoori salmon, herb mash, cucumber and dill raita. Grilled duck, mushroom khichdi, peppercorn jus and sesame duck confit tikki. Chocolate cravings.

XX **Medlar**
438 King's Rd ✉ SW10 0LJ ⊖ South Kensington Town plan: **23**PZG**x**
– ✆ (020) 7349 1900 – www.medlarrestaurant.co.uk – Closed 24-26 December and 1 January
• MODERN • Menu £ 27 (weekday lunch)/45
A charming, comfortable and very popular restaurant with a real sense of neighbourhood, from two alumni of Chez Bruce. The service is engaging and unobtrusive; the cooking is quite elaborate and comes with a classical base.

XX **Le Colombier**
145 Dovehouse St. ✉ SW3 6LB Town plan: **36**ADZ**e**
⊖ South Kensington – ✆ (020) 7351 1155 – www.le-colombier-restaurant.co.uk
• FRENCH • Menu £ 20 (weekday lunch) – Carte £ 34/57
Proudly Gallic corner restaurant in an affluent residential area. Attractive enclosed terrace. Bright and cheerful surroundings and service; traditional French cooking.

XX **Racine**
239 Brompton Rd ✉ SW3 2EP Town plan: **37**AEY**t**
⊖ South Kensington – ✆ (020) 7584 4477 – www.racine-restaurant.com – Closed 25 December
• FRENCH • Menu £ 18/20 – Carte £ 30/53
An authentic feel to this French brasserie, with dark leather seats, wood floors and mirrors. The menu provides a roll-call of classic regional specialities, from steak tartare to fruits de mer.

XX **Poissonnerie**
82 Sloane Ave. ✉ SW3 3DZ ⊖ South Kensington Town plan: **37**AFY**u**
– ✆ (020) 7589 2457 – www.poissonnerie-chelsea.co.uk – Closed Easter and 25-26 December
• FISH AND SEAFOOD • Menu £ 28/35 – Carte £ 41/54
A stoically traditional institution for over 50 years. The owner still greets his immaculately groomed guests personally and the freshness of the fish in the classic seafood recipes is a given. The oysters are particularly good.

XX **Eight over Eight**
392 King's Rd ✉ SW3 5UZ ⊖ South Kensington Town plan: **23**PZG**s**
– ✆ (020) 7349 9934 – www.rickerrestaurants.com – Closed 25 December and 1 January
• ASIAN • Menu £ 35/50 – Carte £ 15/45
Reopened after a fire, with a slightly plusher feel; still as popular as ever with the fashionable crowds. Influences stretch across South East Asia and dishes are designed for sharing.

XX **Bluebird**
350 King's Rd. ✉ SW3 5UU ⊖ South Kensington Town plan: **23**PZG**n**
– ✆ (020) 7559 1000 – www.bluebird-restaurant.co.uk
• BRITISH MODERN • Menu £ 20 – Carte £ 21/62
Not just for a night out with friends – with a foodstore, cellar, bakery, café and courtyard there's enough here for a day out too. Big menu to match the big room: everything from British classics to steaks, salads and shellfish.

XX **Painted Heron**

112 Cheyne Walk ✉ SW10 0DJ Town plan: **23**PZG**d**
⊖ Fulham Broadway – ✆ (020) 7351 5232 – www.thepaintedheron.com – Closed Monday
• INDIAN • Menu £ 20/65 – Carte £ 26/37
Smart, well-supported and quite formally run Indian restaurant. Nooks and crannies create an intimate atmosphere; and there's a heated cigar terrace. Fish and game dishes are the highlights of the contemporary cooking.

XX **il trillo**

4 Hollywood Rd ✉ SW10 9HY ⊖ Earl's Court Town plan: **36**ACZ**s**
– ✆ (020) 3602 1759 – www.iltrillo.net – Closed 25-26 December
• ITALIAN • Menu £ 28 – Carte £ 25/54 – *(dinner only and lunch Saturday-Sunday)*
The Bertuccelli family have been making wine and running a restaurant in the Tuscan Hills for over 30 years. Two of the brothers now run this smart local which showcases the produce and wine from their region. Delightful courtyard.

XX **Colbert**

50-52 Sloane Sq ✉ SW1W 8AX ⊖ Sloane Square Town plan: **37**AGY**t**
– ✆ (020) 7730 2804 – www.colbertchelsea.com – Closed 25 December and dinner 24 December
• FRENCH • Carte £ 18/55 – *(booking advisable)*
With its posters, chessboard tiles and red leather seats, Colbert bears more than a passing resemblance to a Parisian pavement café. It's an all-day, every day operation with French classics from croque monsieur to steak Diane.

XX **Manicomio**

85 Duke of York Sq, King's Rd ✉ SW3 4LY Town plan: **37**AGY**x**
⊖ Sloane Square – ✆ (020) 7730 3366 – www.manicomio.co.uk – Closed 25 December-1 January
• ITALIAN • Menu £ 23 (lunch and early dinner) – Carte £ 29/49
Modern, busy Italian, popular with shoppers and visitors to the Saatchi Gallery; the simplest dishes are the best ones. The terrific terrace fills quickly. Next door is their café and deli.

XX **Marco**

Stamford Bridge, Fulham Rd. ✉ SW6 1HS Town plan: **22**OZG**c**
⊖ Fulham Broadway – ✆ (020) 7915 2929 – www.marcorestaurant.org – Closed Sunday and Monday
• FRENCH • Carte £ 24/44 – *(dinner only) (booking advisable)*
Marco Pierre White's brasserie at Chelsea Football Club offers an appealing range of classics, from British favourites to satisfying French and Italian fare; puddings are a highlight. Comfortable and well-run room.

XX **Good Earth**

233 Brompton Rd. ✉ SW3 2EP ⊖ Knightsbridge Town plan: **37**AFY**h**
– ✆ (020) 7584 3658 – www.goodearthgroup.co.uk – Closed 23-31 December
• CHINESE • Carte £ 23/46
The menu might appear predictable but this long-standing Chinese has always proved a reliable choice in this area. Although there's no particular geographical bias, the cooking is carefully executed and dishes are authentic.

XX **The Botanist**

7 Sloane Sq ✉ SW1W 8EE ⊖ Sloane Square Town plan: **37**AGY**r**
– ✆ (020) 7730 0077 – www.thebotanistonsloanesquare.com – Closed 25-26 December
• MODERN • Menu £ 21 (dinner) – Carte £ 29/54
Push through the busy bar to get to this stylish, comfortable restaurant. An extensive menu; the simplest dishes are usually the best ones. Open all day and useful for a bite before curtain-up at The Royal Court or Cadogan Hall.

XX **Joe's**

126 Draycott Ave ✉ SW3 3AH Town plan: **37**AFY**f**
⊖ South Kensington – ✆ (020) 7225 2217 – www.joseph.co.uk
– Closed 25 December and dinner Sunday-Monday
• MODERN • Carte £ 24/46

Joe's gives its glamorous customers what they want – Mediterranean influenced favourites and light, healthy dishes. The attractive room is framed by bookcases of wine and magazines, and the good looking staff really do seem to care.

X **Bo Lang** Ⓝ

100 Draycott Ave ✉ SW3 3AD Town plan: **37**AFY**a**
⊖ South Kensington – ✆ (020) 7823 7887 – www.bolangrestaurant.com
• CHINESE • Menu £ 22 (weekday lunch) – Carte £ 25/48

It's all about dim sum at this diminutive Hakkasan wannabe. The kitchen has a deft touch but stick to the more traditional combinations; come with friends for the cocktails and to mitigate the effects of some ambitious pricing.

X **Henry Root**

9 Park Walk ✉ SW10 0AJ ⊖ South Kensington Town plan: **36**ACZ**z**
– ✆ (020) 7352 7040 – www.thehenryroot.com – Closed 25-27 December
• FRENCH • Carte £ 20/37 – *(booking advisable)*

William Donaldson satirised many of the good and the great of his day through the letters of his alter ego, Henry Root. His name lives on in this cheery local spot, with its appealing menu that includes small plates and charcuterie.

X **Tom's Kitchen**

27 Cale St. ✉ SW3 3QP ⊖ South Kensington Town plan: **37**AFZ**b**
– ✆ (020) 7349 0202 – www.tomskitchen.co.uk – Closed 25-26 December
• MODERN • Carte £ 29/55

A converted pub, whose white tiles and mirrors help to give it an industrial feel. Appealing and wholesome dishes come in man-sized portions. The eponymous Tom is Tom Aikens.

X **Galvin Demoiselle**

Ground Floor Food Hall, Harrods, 87-135 Brompton Rd ✉ SW1X 7XL ⊖ Knightsbridge – ✆ (020) 7893 8590 Town plan: **37**AFX**x**
– www.galvinrestaurants.com – Closed 25 December and Sunday dinner
• FRENCH • Carte £ 34/46 – *(bookings not accepted)*

The Galvin brothers' café overlooks Harrods food hall. The light, French-accented menu is ideal for the busy shopper. You'll find a different soup each day, salads, charcuterie, cocottes and their popular baked lobster fishcake.

X **Geales**

1 Cale St ✉ SW3 3QT ⊖ South Kensington Town plan: **37**AFZ**n**
– ✆ (020) 7965 0555 – www.geales.com – Closed 22 December-3 January and Monday
• FISH AND SEAFOOD • Menu £ 13 (weekday lunch) – Carte £ 23/39

Fish and chips are the main draw at this cosy, warmly run and sweetly decorated spot. Other choices can include fish pie and soft shell crab tempura, along with wholesome, homemade puddings.

Admiral Codrington

17 Mossop St ✉ SW3 2LY ⊖ South Kensington. Town plan: **37**AFY**v**
– ✆ (020) 7581 0005 – www.theadmiralcodrington.com
– Closed 24-26 December
• MODERN • Carte £ 25/45

Busy front bar and a separate, rather smart restaurant with a retractable roof. Head for the more familiar dishes from the monthly-changing menu. Beef is big here and is aged in-house; burgers are very popular. A Chelsea institution.

Chelsea Ram
32 Burnaby St ✉ SW10 0PL ⊖ Fulham Broadway. Town plan: **23**PZG**r**
– ✆ (020) 7351 4008 – www.geronimo-inns.co.uk/thechelsearam
• BRITISH MODERN • Carte £ 22/29
A proper 'locals' pub; Thursday is steak night and Friday, fish night. Blackboard specials supplement the menu of sturdy pub classics and seasonal dishes. Dining tables wind around the bar, with quieter ones under a glass roof.

Cadogan Arms
298 King's Rd ✉ SW3 5UG ⊖ South Kensington. Town plan: **36**ADZ**y**
– ✆ (020) 7352 6500 – www.thecadoganarmschelsea.com
– Closed 25-26 December
• BRITISH TRADITIONAL • Carte £ 23/42 – *(bookings advisable at dinner)*
A Victorian corner pub, owned by the Martin brothers, and just as welcoming to drinkers as to diners. The best dishes are the filling, blokey and meaty ones. Original tiling and panelling add to the warmth; pool tables upstairs.

Builders Arms
13 Britten St ✉ SW3 3TY ⊖ South Kensington. Town plan: **37**AFZ**x**
– ✆ (020) 7349 9040 – www.geronimo-inns.co.uk
• BRITISH TRADITIONAL • Carte £ 26/40 – *(bookings not accepted)*
Smart looking and busy pub for the Chelsea set; drinkers are welcomed as much as diners. Cooking reveals the effort put into sourcing decent ingredients; rib of beef for two is a favourite. Thoughtfully compiled wine list.

LONDON

Pig's Ear
35 Old Church St ✉ SW3 5BS Town plan: **23**PZG**v**
⊖ South Kensington. – ✆ (020) 7352 2908 – www.thepigsear.info
• BRITISH TRADITIONAL • Carte £ 14/38
Honest pub, with rough-and-ready ground floor bar for lunch; more intimate, wood-panelled upstairs dining room for dinner. Robust, confident and satisfying cooking with a classical bent.

Phoenix
23 Smith St ✉ SW3 4EE ⊖ Sloane Square. Town plan: **37**AFZ**a**
– ✆ (020) 7730 9182 – www.geronimo-inns.co.uk/thepheonix – Closed dinner 25 December
• MODERN • Carte £ 15/42
Friendly, conscientiously run Chelsea local, where satisfying and carefully prepared pub classics are served in the roomy, civilised bar or in the warm, comfortable dining room at the back.

Lots Road Pub & Dining Room
114 Lots Rd ✉ SW10 0RJ ⊖ Fulham Broadway. Town plan: **23**PZG**b**
– ✆ (020) 7352 6645 – www.lotsroadpub.com – Closed 25 December
• BRITISH TRADITIONAL • Carte £ 22/35
It may be a little worn around the edges but when a kitchen occupies half the bar you know they take food seriously. The short menu may seem safe but uses good produce cooked with care and respect. Try the daily "season's eatings".

EARL'S COURT

K + K George
1-15 Templeton Pl ✉ SW5 9NB ⊖ Earl's Court Town plan: **35**AAY**s**
– ✆ (020) 7598 8700 – www.kkhotels.com
154 rm ☕ – 🚹£ 150/330 🚹🚹£ 150/375 **Rest** – Carte £ 21/36 **s**
Five converted 19C houses overlooking large rear garden. Scandinavian-style rooms with low beds, white walls and light wood furniture. Breakfast room has the garden view. Informal dining in the bar.

Twenty Nevern Square without rest
20 Nevern Sq. ✉ SW5 9PD ⊖ Earl's Court Town plan: **35**AAY**u**
– ✆ (020) 7565 9555 – www.twentynevernsquare.co.uk
20 rm ☕ – 🚹£ 80/200 🚹🚹£ 100/350
Privately owned townhouse overlooking an attractive Victorian garden square. It's decorated with original pieces of hand-carved Indonesian furniture; breakfast in a bright conservatory. Some bedrooms have their own terrace.

Mayflower without rest
26-28 Trebovir Rd. ✉ *SW5 9NJ* ⊖ *Earl's Court* Town plan: **35**ABY**x**
– ✆ *(020) 7370 0991* – *www.mayflowerhotel.co.uk*
47 rm – †£ 89/129 ††£ 119/350
Conveniently placed, friendly establishment with a secluded rear breakfast terrace and basement breakfast room. Individually styled bedrooms with Asian influence.

Amsterdam without rest
7-9 Trebovir Rd. ✉ *SW5 9LS* ⊖ *Earl's Court* Town plan: **35**ABY**c**
– ✆ *(020) 7370 2814* – *www.amsterdam-hotel.com*
19 rm – †£ 80/160 ††£ 100/260
Basement breakfast room and a small secluded garden. The brightly decorated bedrooms are light and airy. Some have smart wood floors; some boast their own balcony.

Garnier
314 Earl's Court Rd ✉ *SW5 9QB* ⊖ *Earl's Court* Town plan: **35**ABZ**a**
– ✆ *(020) 7370 4536* – *www.garnier-restaurant-london.co.uk*
• FRENCH • Menu £ 18 (lunch) – Carte £ 35/61
A wall of mirrors, rows of simply dressed tables and imperturbable service lend an authentic feel to this Gallic brasserie. The extensive menu of comforting French classics is such a good read, you'll find it hard to choose.

Can't choose between two similar establishments in the same town?
We list them in order of preference,
within each category.

KENSINGTON

Royal Garden
2-24 Kensington High St ✉ *W8 4PT* Town plan: **35**ABX**c**
⊖ *High Street Kensington* – ✆ *(020) 7937 8000* – *www.royalgardenhotel.co.uk*
394 rm – †£ 160/440 ††£ 210/490, £ 25 – 17 suites
Rest *Min Jiang* – see restaurant listing
Rest *Park Terrace* – Menu £ 17/38 – Carte approx. £ 33
A tall, modern hotel with many of its rooms enjoying enviable views over the adjacent Kensington Gardens. All the modern amenities and services, with well-drilled staff. Bright, spacious Park Terrace offers an international menu as well as afternoon tea for which you're accompanied by a pianist.

The Milestone
1-2 Kensington Ct ✉ *W8 5DL* Town plan: **35**ABX**u**
⊖ *High Street Kensington* – ✆ *(020) 7917 1000* – *www.milestonehotel.com*
62 rm – †£ 342/504 ††£ 342/504, £ 27 – 6 suites
Rest *Cheneston's* – Menu £ 30 (lunch and early dinner) – Carte £ 43/63 – *(bookings essential for non-residents)*
Elegant and enthusiastically run hotel with decorative Victorian façade and a very British feel. Charming oak-panelled sitting room is popular for afternoon tea; snug bar in former stables. Meticulously decorated bedrooms offer period detail. Ambitious cooking in discreet Cheneston's restaurant.

Baglioni
60 Hyde Park Gate ✉ *SW7 5BB* Town plan: **36**ACX**e**
⊖ *High Street Kensington* – ✆ *(020) 7368 5700* – *www.baglionihotels.com*
67 rm – †£ 300/500 ††£ 300/500, £ 30 – 15 suites
Rest *Brunello* – see restaurant listing
Opposite Kensington Palace and no escaping the fact that this is an Italian owned hotel. The interior is bold and ornate and there's a trendy basement bar. Stylish bedrooms have a masculine feel and boast impressive facilities.

XXX **Launceston Place**

✿ *1a Launceston Pl ✉ W8 5RL ⊖ Gloucester Road* Town plan: **36**ACX**a**
– ✆ (020) 7937 6912 – www.launcestonplace-restaurant.co.uk
– Closed 22-30 December, 1 January, Tuesday lunch and Monday
• MODERN • Menu £ 30 (weekday lunch)/70 – *(bookings advisable at dinner)*

Under the watchful eye of head chef Tim Allen, this longstanding neighbourhood restaurant continues to deliver food that is original and highly polished. Unsurprisingly for a Yorkshireman, his cooking also comes with guts and substance. Only a tasting menu is offered on Friday and Saturday nights.

→ Pigeon, hazelnut, crumbled frozen foie gras, chicory and pear. Suckling pig, loin and belly with black pudding and Braeburn apple, English brassicas. Yorkshire rhubarb, candied ginger tapioca, iced apple and galette of caramelised sourdough.

XXX **Min Jiang** – Royal Garden Hotel

2-24 Kensington High St (10th Floor) ✉ W8 4PT Town plan: **35**ABX**c**
⊖ High Street Kensington – ✆ (020) 7361 1988 – www.minjiang.co.uk
• CHINESE • Menu £ 40/80 – Carte £ 25/92

The cooking at this stylish 10th floor Chinese restaurant covers all provinces, but Cantonese and Sichuanese dominate. Wood-fired Beijing duck is a speciality. The room's good looks compete with the great views of Kensington Gardens.

XX **Kitchen W8**

✿ *11-13 Abingdon Rd ✉ W8 6AH* Town plan: **35**AAX**a**
⊖ High Street Kensington – ✆ (020) 7937 0120 – www.kitchenw8.com
– Closed 25-26 December and bank holidays
• MODERN • Menu £ 25 (lunch and early dinner)/60 – Carte £ 35/54

A joint venture between restaurateur Rebecca Mascarenhas and Philip Howard of The Square. Not as informal as the name suggests but still refreshingly free of pomp. The cooking has depth and personality and prices are quite restrained considering the quality of the produce and the kitchen's skill.

→ Smoked eel with Cornish mackerel, leek hearts and sweet mustard. Bresse pigeon with heritage beetroot, bulgur wheat, hazelnuts and bacon. Chocolate pavé with thyme salt caramel, banana and popcorn.

XX **Pavilion** Ⓝ

96 Kensington High St ✉ W8 4SG Town plan: **35**ABX**p**
⊖ High Street Kensington – ✆ (020) 7221 2000 – www.kensingtonpavilion.com
– Closed Christmas to New Year and Sunday dinner
• MODERN • Carte £ 27/59

Attractive and stylish room with a smart central bar and a separate marble counter in front of the open kitchen. An appealing contemporary menu comes with a certain originality and the produce is exemplary – especially the steaks.

XX **Brunello** – Baglioni Hotel

60 Hyde Park Gate ✉ SW7 5BB Town plan: **36**ACX**e**
⊖ High Street Kensington – ✆ (020) 7368 5900 – www.baglionihotels.com
• ITALIAN • Menu £ 23 (lunch) – Carte £ 39/64

Brunello now seems to have sensibly settled on a kitchen that is less about showiness and more about delivering recognisable Italian classics. This works because there's frankly more than enough drama in the exuberant decoration.

XX **Clarke's**

124 Kensington Church St ✉ W8 4BH Town plan: **27**ABV**c**
⊖ Notting Hill Gate – ✆ (020) 7221 9225 – www.sallyclarke.com
– Closed Christmas-New Year, Sunday and bank holidays
• MODERN • Menu £ 35 (dinner) – Carte £ 35/50 – *(booking advisable)*

Forever popular restaurant, serving a choice of dishes boasting trademark fresh, seasonal ingredients and Sally Clarke's famed lightness of touch. Has enjoyed a loyal local following for over 30 years.

LONDON

XX **Chakra**

157-159 Notting Hill Gate ✉ W11 3LF Town plan: **27**AAV**s**
⊖ Notting Hill Gate – ✆ (020) 7229 2115 – www.chakralondon.com – Closed 25-26 December and 1 January
• INDIAN • Menu £ 10/20 (lunch) – Carte £ 21/41 – *(booking advisable)*
The influences come from the Royal kitchens of the Maharajahs, particularly those from the North Western province of Lucknow. The spicing is more subtle than usual, the aroma fresher and the presentation more striking.

XX **Babylon**

The Roof Gardens, 99 Kensington High St Town plan: **35**ABX**n**
✉ W8 5SA – (entrance on Derry St) ⊖ High Street Kensington – ✆ (020) 7368 3993 – www.roofgardens.virgin.com – Closed 24-30 December, 1-2 January and Sunday dinner
• MODERN • Menu £ 23/48 – Carte £ 29/73
Found on the 7th floor and affording great views of the city skyline and an amazing 1.5 acres of rooftop garden. Stylish modern décor in keeping with the contemporary, British cooking.

XX **One Kensington** Ⓝ

1 Kensington High St ✉ W8 5NP Town plan: **35**ABX**r**
⊖ High Street Kensington – ✆ (020) 7795 6533 – www.one-kensington.com – Closed Monday lunch
• INTERNATIONAL • Menu £ 25/29 – Carte £ 34/51
This striking, Grade II listed Victorian former bank is now home to a partnership between Massimiliano Blasone and the people behind Tamarind – and the kitchen does everything from tagliolini to beef pie, veal schnitzel to Sunday roast. The cooking is perfectly competent but lacks identity.

XX **Yashin**

1A Argyll Rd. ✉ W8 7DB Town plan: **35**AAX**c**
⊖ High Street Kensington – ✆ (020) 7938 1536 – www.yashinsushi.com – Closed 24-25 and 31 December,1 January
• JAPANESE • Carte £ 24/95 – *(booking essential)*
Ask for a counter seat to watch the chefs prepare the sushi; choose 8, 11 or 15 pieces, to be served together. The quality of fish is clear; tiny garnishes and the odd bit of searing add originality.

XX **Cibo**

3 Russell Gdns ✉ W14 8EZ Town plan: **16**MZE**b**
⊖ Kensington Olympia – ✆ (020) 7371 6271 – www.ciborestaurant.net – Closed 1 week Christmas, Easter and bank holidays
• ITALIAN • Menu £ 20 (weekday lunch) – Carte £ 27/40
Long-standing neighbourhood Italian with local following. More space at the back of the room. Robust, satisfying cooking; the huge grilled shellfish and seafood platter a speciality.

XX **Malabar**

27 Uxbridge St. ✉ W8 7TQ ⊖ Notting Hill Gate Town plan: **27**AAV**e**
– ✆ (020) 7727 8800 – www.malabar-restaurant.co.uk – Closed 1 week Christmas
• INDIAN • Menu £ 18 (lunch and early dinner) **s** – Carte £ 16/31 **s** – *(buffet lunch Sunday)*
Opened in 1983 in a residential Notting Hill street, but keeps up its appearance, remaining fresh and good-looking. Balanced menu of carefully prepared and sensibly priced Indian dishes.

X **Terrace** Ⓝ

33c Holland St ✉ W8 4LX Town plan: **16**NZE**t**
⊖ High Street Kensington – ✆ (020) 7937 9252 – www.theterraceonhollandstreet.co.uk
• MODERN • Menu £ 18 (weekday lunch) – Carte £ 25/45
A sweet little neighbourhood restaurant, tucked away in a corner spot on a quiet residential street. The short menu changes daily and concentrates on seasonal, British-inspired dishes with classic combinations and bold flavours.

LONDON

X **Kensington Place**

201-209 Kensington Church St. ✉ W8 7LX Town plan: **27**AAV**z**
⊖ Notting Hill Gate – ✆ (020) 7727 3184 – www.kensingtonplace-restaurant.co.uk – Closed Sunday dinner, Monday lunch and bank holidays
• MODERN • Menu £ 25 (lunch) – Carte £ 24/39
An iconic restaurant which opened in 1987 as a big, boisterous, brasserie; these days a little less noisy but it remains well run. The menu offers a wide choice of modern European favourites, with the emphasis on very fresh fish.

X **The Shed**

122 Palace Gardens Terr. ✉ W8 4RT Town plan: **27**ABV**s**
⊖ Notting Hill Gate – ✆ (020) 7229 4024 – www.theshed-restaurant.com – Closed Monday lunch and Sunday
• BRITISH TRADITIONAL • Menu £ 25 (dinner) – Carte £ 18/30
It's more than just a shed but does have a higgledy-piggledy charm and a healthy dose of the outdoors. One brother cooks, one manages and the third runs the farm which supplies the produce for the earthy, satisfying dishes.

X **Mazi**

12-14 Hillgate St ✉ W8 7SR ⊖ Notting Hill Gate Town plan: **27**AAV**a**
– ✆ (020) 7229 3794 – www.mazi.co.uk – Closed 24-26 December and 1-2 January
• GREEK • Menu £ 13 (weekday lunch) – Carte £ 23/52
It's all about sharing at this simple, bright Greek restaurant where traditional recipes are given a modern twist to create vibrant, colourful and fresh tasting dishes. The garden terrace at the back is a charming spot in summer.

NORTH KENSINGTON

The Portobello without rest

22 Stanley Gdns. ✉ W11 2NG ⊖ Notting Hill Gate Town plan: **16**NZE**n**
– ✆ (020) 7727 2777 – www.portobellohotel.com – Closed 24-27 December
21 rm – †£ 125/175 ††£ 175/385
An attractive Victorian townhouse in an elegant terrace. Original and theatrical décor. Circular beds, half-testers, Victorian baths: no two bedrooms are the same.

XXX **Ledbury** (Brett Graham)

✿✿ *127 Ledbury Rd. ✉ W11 2AQ ⊖ Notting Hill Gate* Town plan: **27**AAT**a**
– ✆ (020) 7792 9090 – www.theledbury.com – Closed 25-26 December, August bank holiday and Monday and Tuesday lunch
• MODERN • Menu £ 45/110
Brett Graham's husbandry skills and close relationship with his suppliers ensure the quality of the produce shines through and flavour combinations linger long in the memory. This smart yet unshowy restaurant comes with smooth and engaging service. Only a tasting menu is served at dinner on weekends.
→ Flame-grilled fillet of mackerel, pickled cucumber, Celtic mustard and shiso. Roast breast and confit leg of pigeon with quince. Brown sugar tart with stem ginger ice cream.

XX **Edera**

148 Holland Park Ave. ✉ W11 4UE Town plan: **16**MZE**n**
⊖ Holland Park – ✆ (020) 7221 6090 – www.edera.co.uk
• ITALIAN • Carte £ 26/52
Warm and comfortable neighbourhood restaurant with plenty of local regulars and efficient, well-marshalled service. Robust cooking has a subtle Sardinian accent and comes in generous portions.

XX **E&O**

14 Blenheim Cres. ✉ W11 1NN Town plan: **16**MZD**a**
⊖ Ladbroke Grove – ✆ (020) 7229 5454 – www.rickerrestaurants.com – Closed 25 December
• ASIAN • Menu £ 20/59 – Carte £ 22/55
Mean, moody and cool and that's just the customers. Sophisticated, chic and noisy, thanks to contented groups of diners. Menus scour the Far East, with dishes designed for sharing.

LONDON

XX **Notting Hill Kitchen** Ⓝ

92 Kensington Park Rd ✉ W11 2PN Town plan: **16**NZD**k**
⊖ Notting Hill Gate – ✆ (020) 7313 9526 – www.nottinghillkitchen.co.uk – Closed 25-26 December, 1 January and Sunday dinner-Wednesday lunch
• MODERN • Menu £ 32 (weekday lunch) – Carte £ 36/56

The discreet terracotta tiles outside are the only clue that it's Iberian cooking happening inside these converted Edwardian townhouses. Go for the simpler rather than the more creative dishes – or stay in the bar for the tapas.

X **Dock Kitchen**

Portobello Dock, 342-344 Ladbroke Grove Town plan: **16**MZD**k**
✉ W10 5BU ⊖ Ladbroke Grove – ✆ (020) 8962 1610 – www.dockkitchen.co.uk – Closed Christmas, Sunday dinner and bank holidays
• MEDITERRANEAN • Menu £ 18/45 – Carte £ 30/44

What started as a 'pop-up' became a permanent feature in this open-plan former Victorian goods yard. The chef's peregrinations inform his cooking, which relies on simple, natural flavours.

X **Polpo Notting Hill** Ⓝ

126-128 Notting Hill Gate ✉ W11 3QG Town plan: **27**AAV**p**
⊖ Notting Hill Gate – ✆ (020) 7229 3283 – www.polpo.co.uk – Closed 25-26 December and 1 January
• ITALIAN • Carte £ 22/40

The fourth Polpo is Russell Norman's most commercially minded one but is shares the same appealing lack of pretence – and the no booking policy. It's about the whole package, from the shared plates to the appealing vibe.

X **Granger & Co**

175 Westbourne Grove ✉ W11 2SB ⊖ Bayswater Town plan: **27**AAU**x**
– ✆ (020) 7229 9111 – www.grangerandco.com – Closed August bank holiday weekend and 25-26 December
• MODERN • Carte £ 19/44 – *(bookings not accepted)*

When Bill Granger moved from sunny Sydney to cool Notting Hill he opened a local restaurant too. He's brought with him that delightful 'matey' service that only Aussies do, his breakfast time ricotta hotcakes and a fresh, zesty menu.

X **Electric Diner**

191 Portobello Rd ✉ W11 2ED Town plan: **16**MZD**e**
⊖ Ladbroke Grove – ✆ (0207) 8908 9696 – www.electricdiner.com – Closed 24-25 August and 25 December
• MEATS AND GRILLS • Carte £ 15/36 – *(bookings not accepted)*

Next to the iconic Electric Cinema is this loud, brash and fun all-day operation with an all-encompassing menu; the flavours are as big as the portions. The long counter and red leather booths add to the authentic diner feel.

Portobello House with rm

225 Ladbroke Grove ✉ W10 6HQ Town plan: **16**MZD**h**
⊖ Ladbroke Grove. – ✆ (020) 3181 0920 – www.portobellohouse.com – Closed 25 December
• MODERN • **12 rm** ☕ – †£ 110/160 ††£ 120/230 Carte £ 18/31

Whether it's a smart pub, bistro or hotel – or all three – may be up for discussion but what is indisputable is that this is a great addition to this end of Ladbroke Grove. The menu is a combination of British stoutness and Italian flair. The bedrooms are comfortable and contemporary.

South Kensington

The Pelham

15 Cromwell Pl ✉ SW7 2LA ⊖ South Kensington Town plan: **36**ADY**z**
– ✆ (020) 7589 8288 – www.thepelhamhotel.co.uk
51 rm – †£ 180/335 ††£ 260/480, ☕ £ 18 – 1 suite
Rest ***Bistro Fifteen*** – Menu £ 20 – Carte £ 21/40

Immaculately kept hotel, with willing staff and a discreet atmosphere. Decoratively it's a mix of English country house and city townhouse, with a panelled sitting room and library with honesty bar. Sweet and intimate basement restaurant with European menu.

Blakes rest,
33 Rowland Gdns ✉ SW7 3PF ⊖ Gloucester Road Town plan: **36**ACZ**n**
– ✆ (020) 7370 6701 – www.blakeshotels.com
47 rm – £ 215/300 £ 263/359 – 8 suites **Rest** – Carte £ 34/77
Behind the Victorian façade is one of London's first 'boutique' hotels. Dramatic, bold and eclectic décor, with oriental influences and antiques from around the world. Ambitious, Asian-influenced cooking in the intimate restaurant.

Kensington rm,
109-113 Queen's Gate ✉ SW7 5LR Town plan: **36**ADY**x**
⊖ South Kensington – ✆ (020) 7589 6300 – www.doylecollection.com
150 rm – £ 174/486 £ 186/654, £ 20 – 3 suites
Rest – Menu £ 25/35 – Carte £ 26/50
Grand façade to this well-placed, corporate hotel fashioned from several townhouses. Appealing superior rooms and studios; quite compact singles. Pleasant drawing room with fireplace; brasserie-style dining and popular afternoon tea.

Number Sixteen rm,
16 Sumner Pl. ✉ SW7 3EG ⊖ South Kensington Town plan: **36**ADY**d**
– ✆ (020) 7589 5232 – www.numbersixteenhotel.co.uk
41 rm – £ 209 £ 302, £ 20
Rest – Carte approx. £ 20 – *(room service only)*
Elegant and delightfully furnished 19C townhouses in smart neighbourhood. Discreet entrance, comfortable sitting room, charming breakfast terrace and pretty little garden at the back. Bedrooms in an English country house style.

Ampersand
10 Harrington Rd ✉ SW7 3ER Town plan: **36**ADY**a**
⊖ South Kensington. – ✆ (020) 7589 5895 – www.ampersandhotel.com
111 rm – £ 155/170 £ 174/216, £ 14 – 5 suites
Rest *Apero* – ✆ (020) 7591 4410 – Menu £ 12/30 – Carte £ 27/34
A bright, elegant converted Victorian hotel in London's cultural centre – the nearby museums inspire the bedroom decoration. Rooms aren't the largest but they're smart and well-lit. Basement restaurant has a Mediterranean menu.

The Cranley
10 Bina Gdns ✉ SW5 0LA ⊖ Gloucester Road Town plan: **36**ACY**c**
– ✆ (020) 7373 0123 – www.cranleyhotel.com
39 rm – £ 135/215 £ 155/235, £ 18 – 2 suites
Rest – – *(room service only)*
Delightful Regency townhouse combines charm and period details with modern comforts and technology. Individually styled bedrooms; some with four-posters. Breakfast served in bedrooms.

The Rockwell
181-183 Cromwell Rd. ✉ SW5 0SF ⊖ Earl's Court Town plan: **35**ABY**b**
– ✆ (020) 7244 2000 – www.therockwell.com
40 rm – £ 108/135 £ 150/180 **Rest** – Carte £ 32/49
Two Victorian houses with open, modern lobby and secluded, south-facing garden terrace. Bedrooms come in bold, warm colours; 'Garden Rooms' have their own patios. Small dining room offers easy menu of modern European staples.

The Gore
190 Queen's Gate ✉ SW7 5EX ⊖ Gloucester Road Town plan: **36**ACX**n**
– ✆ (020) 7584 6601 – www.gorehotel.com
50 rm – £ 126/246 £ 168/546, £ 15
Rest *Bistro 190* – Menu £ 17/27 – Carte £ 28/42 – *(closed 25-26 December) (booking essential)*
Idiosyncratic, hip Victorian house close to the Royal Albert Hall, whose charming lobby is covered with pictures and prints. Individually styled bedrooms have plenty of character and fun bathrooms. Bright and casual bistro.

LONDON

Aster House without rest

3 Sumner Pl. ✉ *SW7 3EE* ⊖ *South Kensington* Town plan: **36**ADY**t**
– ✆ (020) 7581 5888 – www.asterhouse.com
13 rm – £ 90/135 £ 120/295
An end of terrace Victorian house in a charming neighbourhood and great location for visiting museums. Pretty little rear garden; breakfast served in first floor conservatory. Ground floor bedrooms available.

Bombay Brasserie

Courtfield Rd. ✉ *SW7 4QH* ⊖ *Gloucester Road* Town plan: **36**ACY**y**
– ✆ (020) 7370 4040 – www.bombaybrasserielondon.com – Closed 25 December
• INDIAN • Menu £ 24 (lunch and early dinner) – Carte £ 29/52 – *(bookings advisable at dinner)*
Plush new look for this well-run, well-known and comfortable Indian restaurant; very smart bar and conservatory with a show kitchen. More creative dishes now sit alongside the more traditional.

L'Etranger

36 Gloucester Rd. ✉ *SW7 4QT* ⊖ *Gloucester Road* Town plan: **36**ACX**c**
– ✆ (020) 7584 1118 – www.etranger.co.uk
• INNOVATIVE • Menu £ 18/26 – Carte £ 35/61 – *(booking essential)*
Eclectic menu mixes French dishes with techniques and flavours from Japanese cooking. Impressive wine and sake lists. Moody and atmospheric room; ask for a corner table.

Cambio de Tercio

163 Old Brompton Rd. ✉ *SW5 0LJ* Town plan: **36**ACZ**a**
⊖ *Gloucester Road – ✆ (020) 7244 8970 – www.cambiodetercio.co.uk*
– Closed 2 weeks December and 2 weeks August
• SPANISH • Carte £ 30/60 **s**
A longstanding, ever-improving Spanish restaurant. Start with small dishes like the excellent El Bulli inspired omelette, then have the popular Pluma Iberica. There are super sherries and a wine list to prove there is life beyond Rioja.

Yashin Ocean House (N)

117-119 Old Brompton Rd ✉ *SW7 3RN* Town plan: **36**ACZ**y**
⊖ *Gloucester Road – ✆ (020) 7373 3990 – www.yashinocean.com*
– Closed 24-26 December, dinner 31 December and 1 January
• JAPANESE • Menu £ 20 (lunch) – Carte £ 25/58
The USP of this chic Japanese restaurant is 'head to tail' eating although, as there's nothing for carnivores, 'fin to scale' would be more precise. Stick with specialities like the whole dry-aged sea bream for the full umami hit.

Ognisko (N)

55 Prince's Gate, Exhibition Rd ✉ *SW7 2PN* Town plan: **36**ADX**r**
⊖ *South Kensington – ✆ (020) 7589 0101 – www.ogniskorestaurant.co.uk*
– Closed 24-26 December and 1 January
• POLISH • Menu £ 17 (lunch and early dinner) – Carte £ 24/36
Ognisko Polskie Club was founded in 1940 in this magnificent townhouse – its restaurant now open to the public. The gloriously traditional Polish menu celebrates cooking that is without pretence and truly from the heart.

Bangkok

9 Bute St ✉ *SW7 3EY* ⊖ *South Kensington* Town plan: **36**ADY**b**
– ✆ (020) 7584 8529 – www.bangkokrestaurant.co.uk
– Closed 24 December-2 January and Sunday
• THAI • Carte £ 24/40
For over 40 years Bangkok has been providing fresh, authentic and traditional Thai food for its many regulars. The surroundings are pleasantly modest, the prices down-to-earth and the atmosphere warm.

Tendido Cero

174 Old Brompton Rd. ✉ *SW5 0LJ* Town plan: **36**ACZ**v**
⊖ *Gloucester Road* – ✆ *(020) 7370 3685* – *www.cambiodetercio.co.uk*
– *Closed two weeks Christmas-New Year*
• SPANISH • Menu £ 23.15 – Carte £ 17/51
It's all about the vibe here at Abel Lusa's tapas bar, just across the road from his Cambio de Tercio restaurant. Colourful surroundings, well-drilled service and a menu of favourites all contribute to the fun and lively atmosphere.

Capote y Toros

157 Old Brompton Road ✉ *SW5 0LJ* Town plan: **36**ACZ**v**
⊖ *Gloucester Road* – ✆ *(020) 7373 0567* – *www.cambiodetercio.co.uk*
– *Closed two weeks Christmas, Sunday and Monday*
• SPANISH • Carte £ 15/39 – *(dinner only)*
Expect to queue at this compact and vividly coloured spot which celebrates sherry, tapas, ham... and bullfighting. Sherry is the star; those as yet unmoved by this most underappreciated of wines will be dazzled by the variety.

Margaux N

152 Old Brompton Rd ✉ *SW5 0BE* Town plan: **36**ACZ**m**
⊖ *Gloucester Road* – ✆ *(020) 7373 5753* – *www.barmargaux.co.uk*
– *Closed 1 week Christmas*
• MEDITERRANEAN • Menu £ 15 (weekday lunch) – Carte £ 30/56
Spain and Italy are the primary influences at this modern bistro. There are classics aplenty alongside more unusual dishes. The wine list provides a good choice of varietals and the ersatz industrial look is downtown Manhattan.

KING'S CROSS ST PANCRAS

St Pancras Renaissance

Euston Rd ✉ *NW1 2AR* ⊖ *King's Cross St Pancras* Town plan: **12**SZC**d**
– ✆ *(020) 7841 3540* – *www.stpancrasrenaissance.co.uk*
245 rm – †£ 390/450 ††£ 390/450, ☕ £ 19 – 10 suites
Rest *Gilbert Scott* – see restaurant listing
Rest *Booking Office* – ✆(020) 7841 3566 – Menu £ 25 (lunch) **s**
– Carte £ 33/53
This restored Gothic jewel was built in 1873 as the Midland Grand hotel and reopened in 2011 under the Marriott brand. A former taxi rank is now a spacious lobby and all-day dining is in the old booking office. Luxury suites in Chambers wing; Barlow wing bedrooms are a little more functional.

Great Northern H. London

Pancras Rd ✉ *N1C 4TB* ⊖ *Kings Cross St Pancras* Town plan: **12**SZB**n**
– ✆ *(020) 3388 0800* – *www.gnhlondon.com*
91 rm – †£ 288/450 ††£ 288/450, ☕ £ 15 – 1 suite
Rest *Plum + Spilt Milk* – see restaurant listing
Built as a railway hotel in 1854; reborn as a stylish townhouse. Connected to King's Cross' western concourse and just metres from Eurostar check-in. Bespoke furniture in each of the modern bedrooms, and a pantry on each floor.

Megaro

23-27 Euston Rd ✉ *WC1H 8AB* – *(entrance on Belgrove St)* ⊖ *King's Cross St Pancras* – ✆ *(020) 7843 2222* Town plan: **12**SZC**x**
– *www.hotelmegaro.co.uk*
49 rm – †£ 110/160 ††£ 110/160, ☕ £ 10
Rest *Karpo* – ✆(020) 7843 2221 – Carte £ 20/41
Contemporary hotel fashioned out of a converted bank. The rooms are unfussy and the bathrooms smart. Daily 'absinthe hour' in the basement bar; simple seasonal modern European menu. Pastries for breakfast from their on-site bakery.

XX **Gilbert Scott** – St Pancras Renaissance Hotel

Euston Rd ✉ NW1 2AR ⊖ King's Cross St Pancras Town plan: **12**SZC**d**
– *✆ (020) 7278 3888 – www.thegilbertscott.co.uk*
• BRITISH TRADITIONAL • Menu £ 21 (lunch and early dinner) – Carte £ 28/61
Run under the aegis of Marcus Wareing and named after the architect of this Gothic masterpiece, the restaurant has the look of a Grand Salon but the buzz of a brasserie. It celebrates the UK's many regional and historic specialities.

XX **Plum + Spilt Milk** – Great Northern Hotel London

Pancras Rd ✉ N1C 4TB ⊖ Kings Cross St Pancras Town plan: **12**SZB**n**
– *✆ (020) 3388 0818 – www.plumandspiltmilk.com*
• BRITISH MODERN • Menu £ 21 (lunch) – Carte £ 32/53
Bright brasserie in the Grade II listed Great Northern hotel; ideal for those who've just arrived, or are about to leave, by train. Classic British dishes like potted shrimps and 'pie of the day'. Start with a drink in the GNH bar.

X **Grain Store**

Granary Sq, 1-3 Stable St ✉ N1C 4AB Town plan: **12**SZB**s**
⊖ King's Cross St Pancras – ✆ (020) 7324 4466 – www.grainstore.com
– Closed 24-25 December, 1 January and Sunday dinner
• MODERN • Carte £ 22/32
Big, buzzy 'canteen' from Bruno Loubet and the Zetter hotel people. Eclectic, clever dishes – influenced by Bruno's experiences around the world – are packed with interesting flavours and textures; vegetables often take the lead role.

X **Caravan**

The Granary Building, 1 Granary Sq. ✉ N1C 4AA Town plan: **12**SZB**c**
⊖ King's Cross St Pancras – ✆ (020) 7101 7661 – www.caravankingscross.co.uk
– Closed Sunday dinner
• OTHER WORLD KITCHENS • Carte £ 19/45 – *(booking essential)*
This second Caravan pitched up near King's Cross in an old granary warehouse. The industrial-chic look is matched by a great atmosphere – crowds flock here for breakfast, brunch, great coffee, pizza and globally influenced dishes.

Fellow

24 York Way ✉ N1 9AA Town plan: **12**SZB**x**
⊖ King's Cross St Pancras. – ✆ (020) 7833 4395 – www.thefellow.co.uk
– Closed 25-27 December
• MODERN • Carte £ 25/37
Anonymous façade but moody and atmospheric inside, with a cool cocktail bar. The lean menu of European dishes uses well-sourced ingredients. Fish from Cornish day boats is a highlight; cheeses are British and puds worth a flutter.

KINGSTON UPON THAMES

Kingston-upon-Thames

XX **Roz ana**

6-8 Kingston Hill ✉ KT2 7NH – ✆ (020) 8546 6388 Town plan: **6**CY**e**
– www.roz-ana.com – Closed 24-27 December
• INDIAN • Menu £ 23/35 – Carte £ 15/37
It may have smart surroundings, a cocktail bar and pleasant service but it is the cooking that marks out this Indian restaurant. Expect vibrant and satisfying dishes from across India, from monkfish Ambat to Chennai prawn Biryani.

Surbiton

XX **The French Table**

85 Maple Rd ✉ KT6 4AW – ✆ (020) 8399 2365 Town plan: **6**CY**a**
– www.thefrenchtable.co.uk – Closed Sunday and Monday
• MEDITERRANEAN • Menu £ 20 (lunch) – Carte £ 36/54
Husband and wife team run this lively local. Expect zesty and satisfying French-Mediterranean cooking; learn how with Saturday morning cookery lessons. They also run the bakery next door.

Brixton

Upstairs

89b Acre Ln. ✉ *SW2 5TN* ⊖ *Clapham North* Town plan: **24**SZH**b**
– ✆ (020) 7733 8855 – www.upstairslondon.com – Closed 24 December-7 January, 5-14 April, 16 August-1 September, Sunday and Monday
• MODERN • Menu £ 29 – *(dinner only)*
Ring the bell on Branksome Road; a narrow staircase leads up to a converted flat and this speakeasy effect adds to the charm. The menu changes every five weeks and the chef showcases his technical ability with some original touches.

Boqueria

192 Acre Ln. ✉ *SW2 5UL* ⊖ *Clapham North* Town plan: **24**SZH**x**
– ✆ (020) 7733 4408 – www.boqueriatapas.com
• SPANISH • Carte £ 10/17 – *(dinner only and lunch Saturday-Sunday)*
Contemporary tapas bar, named after Barcelona's famous food market. Sit at the counter rather than in the unremarkable dining room. Highlights include the assorted cured hams and an excellent Crema Catalana.

Clapham Common

Trinity

4 The Polygon ✉ *SW4 0JG* ⊖ *Clapham Common* Town plan: **24**RZH**a**
– ✆ (020) 7622 1199 – www.trinityrestaurant.co.uk – Closed 23-29 December, Monday lunch and Sunday dinner
• INNOVATIVE • Menu £ 27 (weekday lunch) – Carte £ 30/53
Smartly decorated and smoothly run neighbourhood restaurant; ask for a table by the windows in summer. Sophisticated cooking displays some innovative combinations. Good value lunch menu.

Dairy (N)

15 The Pavement ✉ *SW4 0HY* Town plan: **24**RZH**d**
⊖ *Clapham Common – ✆ (020) 7622 4165 – www.the-dairy.co.uk – Closed Christmas, Sunday dinner, Monday and Tuesday lunch*
• BRITISH CREATIVE • Carte £ 20/25 – *(booking essential at dinner)*
The higgledy-piggledy, homemade look of this fun, lively restaurant adds to its charm. What you don't expect is such innovative cooking. The earthy, easy-to-eat food is driven by seasonality – some produce is grown on the roof.

Bistro Union

40 Abbeville Rd ✉ *SW4 9NG* ⊖ *Clapham Common* Town plan: **7**EX**s**
– ✆ (020) 7042 6400 – www.bistrounion.co.uk – Closed 24-28 December and Sunday dinner
• BRITISH MODERN • Carte £ 18/37 – *(booking advisable)*
'Comforting' is the word that comes to mind at this affordable, fun and bustling offspring of Trinity restaurant. The food evokes feelings of nostalgia while simultaneously being bang on-trend. Start with some of their great snacks.

Abbeville Kitchen

47 Abbeville Rd ✉ *SW4 9JX* ⊖ *Clapham Common* Town plan: **7**EX**a**
– ✆ (020) 8772 1110 – www.abbevillekitchen.com – Closed 25-26 December
• MEDITERRANEAN • Carte £ 20/31 – *(dinner only and lunch Friday-Sunday) (bookings advisable at dinner)*
The food is gutsy and wholesome, the choice is varied – it's not often one sees empanadas and braised goat on the same menu – and the prices are fair. The owner has a small boulangerie on this road so the bread's good too.

Rookery

69 Clapham Common South Side ✉ *SW4 9DA* Town plan: **7**EX**v**
⊖ *Clapham Common – ✆ (020) 8673 9162 – www.therookeryclapham.co.uk – Closed 25-26 December*
• BRITISH TRADITIONAL • Carte £ 20/34 – *(dinner only and lunch Saturday-Sunday)*
The on-trend Rookery shows that Soho doesn't have a monopoly on ersatz Brooklyn speakeasies. Come for the impressive selection of artisan beers and a short yet appealing menu; the kitchen delivers some punchy flavours.

Zumbura

36a Old Town ✉ SW4 0LB ⊖ Clapham Common Town plan: **24**RZH**z**
– *✆ (020) 7720 7902 – www.zumbura.com – Closed 1 January*
• INDIAN • Carte £ 13/28 – *(dinner only)*
Going from running a furniture business to opening a restaurant seems to be working for the three friends behind this modern Indian. It's all about small plates, which are fresh tasting, subtly spiced and surprisingly light.

Kennington

Kennington Tandoori

313 Kennington Rd ✉ SE11 4QE ⊖ Kennington Town plan: **40**ANZ**a**
– *✆ (020) 7735 9247 – www.kenningtontandoori.com – Closed 25 December*
• INDIAN • Menu £ 20 (lunch) – Carte £ 20/33 – *(booking advisable)*
Known as KT, the Hoque family's long-standing Indian restaurant was reinvigorated a couple of years ago when their son Kowsar took over. This stylish spot has a familiar menu of classics but what sets it apart is the skilled execution.

Lobster Pot

3 Kennington Ln. ✉ SE11 4RG ⊖ Kennington Town plan: **40**AOY**e**
– *✆ (020) 7582 5556 – www.lobsterpotrestaurant.co.uk*
– Closed 25 December-2 January, Sunday and Monday
• FRENCH • Carte £ 28/65
Family-run, with exuberant décor of fish tanks, portholes and even the sound of seagulls. Classic seafood menu with fruits de mer, plenty of oysters and daily specials. Good crêpes too.

Prices quoted after the symbol 🚹 refer to the lowest rate for a single room in low season, followed by the highest rate in high season.
The same principle applies to the symbol 🚹🚹 for a double room.

Southbank

London Marriott H. County Hall

Westminster Bridge Rd ✉ SE1 7PB ⊖ Westminster – ✆ (020) 7928 5200 – www.marriott.co.uk Town plan: **40**AMX**a**
200 rm – 🚹£ 350/550 🚹🚹£ 370/570, ☕ £ 22 – 5 suites
Rest *Gillray's* – ✆ (020) 7902 8000 – Carte £ 34/96
Occupying the historic County Hall building. Many of the spacious and comfortable bedrooms enjoy river and Parliament outlooks. Impressive leisure facilities. World famous views too from Gillray's, which specialises in steaks.

Skylon

1 Southbank Centre, Belvedere Rd ✉ SE1 8XX Town plan: **32**AMV**a**
⊖ Waterloo – ✆ (020) 7654 7800 – www.skylon-restaurant.co.uk
– Closed 25 December and Sunday dinner
• MODERN • Menu £ 29/48
Ask for a window table here at the Royal Festival Hall. Informal grill-style operation on one side, a more formal and expensive restaurant on the other, with a busy cocktail bar in the middle.

Stockwell

Canton Arms

177 South Lambeth Rd ✉ SW8 1XP ⊖ Stockwell. Town plan: **24**SZG**a**
– *✆ (020) 7582 8710 – www.cantonarms.com – Closed Christmas-New Year, Monday lunch, Sunday dinner and bank holidays*
• BRITISH TRADITIONAL • Carte £ 19/31 – *(bookings not accepted)*
An appreciative crowd of all ages come for the earthy, robust and seasonal British dishes which suit the relaxed environment of this pub so well. Staff are attentive and knowledgeable.

LEWISHAM

Blackheath

Chapters

43-45 Montpelier Vale ✉ SE3 0TJ – ✆ (020) 8333 2666 Town plan: **8**HX**c**
– www.chaptersrestaurants.com – Closed 2-3 January
• MODERN • Menu £ 15/18 – Carte £ 21/34
A classic, bustling brasserie that keeps the locals happy, by being open all day and offering everything from Mediterranean-influenced main courses to meats cooked over charcoal. There's also a kids' menu and wines by the pichet.

Forest Hill

Babur

119 Brockley Rise ✉ SE23 1JP ⊖ Honor Oak Park Town plan: **7**GX**s**
– ✆ (020) 8291 2400 – www.babur.info – Closed dinner 25 December-lunch 27 December
• INDIAN • Carte £ 25/32
Good looks and innovative cooking make this passionately run and long-established Indian restaurant stand out. Influences from the south and north west feature most and seafood is a highlight - look out for the 'Treasures of the Sea' menu.

MERTON

Wimbledon

Cannizaro House

West Side, Wimbledon Common ✉ SW19 4UE Town plan: **6**DXY**x**
⊖ Wimbledon – ✆ (020) 8879 1464 – www.cannizarohouse.com
46 rm ☕ – 🚹£ 155/525 🚹🚹£ 155/525 – 2 suites
Rest *Cannizaro House* – see restaurant listing
Part-Georgian mansion in charming spot overlooking Wimbledon Common. Modern bedrooms; funky suites; 'Sophia Johnson' has lovely balcony overlooking the park. Local artists' work decorates.

Cannizaro House – Cannizaro House Hotel

West Side, Wimbledon Common ✉ SW19 4UE Town plan: **6**DXY**x**
⊖ Wimbledon – ✆ (020) 8879 1464 – www.cannizarohouse.com
• MODERN • Menu £ 45
Choose between the elegant main room and the more intimate Loggia overlooking an Italian sunken garden. Expect carefully prepared and appealing British dishes with a modern edge. A slightly corporate feel but staff lighten the mood.

Lawn Bistro

67 High St. ✉ SW19 5EE ⊖ Wimbledon – ✆ (020) Town plan: **6**DXY**s**
8947 8278 – www.thelawnbistro.co.uk – Closed 18 August-2 September, Sunday dinner and Monday
• MODERN • Menu £ 15/25 – Carte £ 26/44
Casual yet nicely manicured, this attractively decorated bistro sits in the heart of the village. The modern European food is clean and well defined; menus are thoughtfully compiled and the kitchen even does its own butchery.

Light House

75-77 Ridgway ✉ SW19 4ST ⊖ Wimbledon Town plan: **6**DY**n**
– ✆ (020) 8944 6338 – www.lighthousewimbledon.com
– Closed 25-26 December, 1 January and Sunday dinner
• MEDITERRANEAN • Menu £ 15/24 – Carte £ 25/44
The robust and flavoursome Italian dishes provide the highlights of the menu. This large, well lit room attracts plenty of locals and the service remains calm and cheery.

Fox and Grapes with rm

rest,

9 Camp Rd ✉ SW19 4UN ⊖ Wimbledon. – ✆ (020) Town plan: **6**DX**v**
8619 1300 – www.foxandgrapeswimbledon.co.uk – Closed 25 December
• BRITISH MODERN • **3 rm** – 🚹£ 100/125 🚹🚹£ 100/125 Carte £ 20/46
Well-run pub right on the common and bigger than it looks from the outside. Carefully prepared modern pub classics and grills from the Josper oven are served in the cosy snug and vaulted bar. Three cosy bedrooms are available.

LONDON

REDBRIDGE

WANSTEAD

Provender
17 High St ✉ E11 2AA ⊖ Snaresbrook – ✆ (020) 8530 3050 – www.provenderlondon.co.uk Town plan: **4**HU**x**
• FRENCH • Menu £ 16 (weekdays) – Carte £ 20/41
A modern, busy and bustling neighbourhood bistro courtesy of experienced restaurateur Max Renzland. The well-priced French cooking is pleasingly rustic and satisfying, with great charcuterie, appealing salads and well-timed grills.

RICHMOND-UPON-THAMES

BARNES

Sonny's Kitchen
94 Church Rd ✉ SW13 0DQ – ✆ (020) 8748 0393 – www.sonnyskitchen.co.uk – Closed 25 December, 1 January and bank holiday Mondays Town plan: **21**KZH**x**
• MODERN • Menu £ 18/25 – Carte £ 26/44
Long-time owner Rebecca Mascarenhas has been joined by Phil Howard, chef of The Square, and they're rejuvenating this much-loved neighbourhood spot. Menus are all-encompassing; the atmosphere's great and the artwork interesting.

Indian Zilla
2-3 Rocks Ln. ✉ SW13 0DB – ✆ (020) 8878 3989 – www.indianzilla.co.uk – Closed 25 December Town plan: **21**LZH**k**
• INDIAN • Carte £ 20/38 – *(dinner only and lunch Saturday-Sunday)*
Bright, and contemporary restaurant with attentive, friendly service. Modern menu includes a few classics; the authentic, fully-flavoured dishes display a lightness of touch.

Olympic Café + Dining Room (N)
117-123 Church Rd ✉ SW13 9HL – ✆ (020) 8912 5161 – www.olympiccinema.co.uk Town plan: **21**KZH**s**
• BRITISH MODERN • Carte £ 16/41 – *(bookings advisable at dinner)*
An all-day brasserie housed in what was once the world's greatest recording studio – artists like the Stones and Led Zeppelin recorded seminal albums here. No 'Goat's Head Soup', instead an appealing selection of British comfort food.

Riva
169 Church Rd. ✉ SW13 9HR – ✆ (020) 8748 0434 – Closed 2 weeks August, Christmas-New Year, Saturday lunch and bank holidays Town plan: **21**LZH**a**
• ITALIAN • Carte £ 29/52
A restaurant built on customer loyalty; the regulars are showered with attention from the eponymous owner. Gutsy, no-nonsense dishes, full of flavour. Interesting all-Italian wine list.

Brown Dog
28 Cross St ✉ SW13 0AP ⊖ Barnes Bridge (Rail). – ✆ (020) 8392 2200 – www.thebrowndog.co.uk – Closed 25 December Town plan: **21**KZH**b**
• BRITISH MODERN • Carte £ 20/37
Pretty Victorian pub with a genuine neighbourhood feel; snug bar, intimate dining room and a look that combines the traditional with the modern. Concise, balanced menu delivers wholesome, commendably priced dishes.

EAST SHEEN

Victoria with rm
10 West Temple Sheen ✉ SW14 7RT ⊖ Mortlake (Rail). – ✆ (020) 8876 4238 – www.thevictoria.net Town plan: **6**CX**u**
• BRITISH MODERN • **7 rm** – †£ 120 ††£ 130
Menu £ 15 (lunch and early dinner) – Carte £ 23/44
Beautifully restored pub and a genuine local, playing its part in the community. The kitchen takes its sourcing seriously; eat in the bar or more formal conservatory overlooking the terrace. Recently refurbished bedrooms available.

Kew

XX The Glasshouse

14 Station Par. ✉ TW9 3PZ ⊖ Kew Gardens – ✆ (020) 8940 6777 – www.glasshouserestaurant.co.uk – Closed 24-26 December and 1 January Town plan: **6**CX**z**

• MODERN • Menu £ 28 (weekday lunch)/43

The Glasshouse is the very model of a modern neighbourhood restaurant and sits in the heart of lovely, villagey Kew. Food is confident yet unshowy – much like the locals – and comes with distinct Mediterranean flavours along with the occasional Asian hint. Service comes with the eagerness of youth.

→ Octopus terrine with Cornish mussels, aioli, confit red pepper, fennel and citrus dressing. Rump, pie and tongue of lamb with Lyonnaise onions, glazed salsify and rosemary jus. Coconut semifreddo with Alphonso mango and pineapple carpaccio.

XX Linnea (N)

12 Kew Grn. ✉ TW9 3BH ⊖ Kew Gardens – ✆ (020) 8940 5696 – www.linneakew.co.uk – Closed Christmas, Easter, 2 weeks August, Sunday and Monday Town plan: **6**CV**u**

• BRITISH MODERN • Carte £ 24/47

The chef-owner of this pared down yet elegant room is from Sweden – Linnea is his country's national flower. The monthly menu offers modern, unfussy dishes with Scandinavian techniques of pickling, curing and air-drying in evidence.

XX Kew Grill

10b Kew Grn. ✉ TW9 3BH ⊖ Kew Gardens – ✆ (020) 8948 4433 – www.awtrestaurants.com/kewgrill – Closed 25 December-4 January Town plan: **6**CV**u**

• MEATS AND GRILLS • Carte £ 27/54 – *(booking essential)*

It's all about steaks – Aberdeen Angus and hung for 35 days – at this long, narrow restaurant, tucked away down a side street. The look may be a tad faded but the service is warm and friendly and it's well supported by the locals.

Richmond

Petersham

rest,

Nightingale Ln ✉ TW10 6UZ ⊖ Richmond – ✆ (020) 8940 7471 – www.petershamhotel.co.uk – Closed 25-26 December Town plan: **6**CX**c**

58 rm – £ 75/130 £ 155/215 – 1 suite

Rest *Restaurant at The Petersham* – ✆ (020) 8939 1084 – Menu £ 23 (lunch and early dinner) – Carte £ 36/57

Extended over the years, a fine example of Victorian Gothic architecture, with Portland stone and self-supporting staircase. The most comfortable bedrooms overlook the Thames. Formal restaurant in which to enjoy a mix of classic and modern cooking; ask for a window table for terrific park and river views.

Bingham

61-63 Petersham Rd. ✉ TW10 6UT ⊖ Richmond – ✆ (020) 8940 0902 – www.thebingham.co.uk Town plan: **6**CX**c**

15 rm – £ 99/195 £ 110/210, £ 17

Rest *Bingham Restaurant* – see restaurant listing

A pair of conjoined and restored Georgian townhouses; a short walk from Richmond centre. Ask for a room overlooking the river and garden. Contemporary styled bedrooms; some with four-posters.

XX Bingham Restaurant – Bingham Hotel

61-63 Petersham Rd. ✉ TW1O 6UT ⊖ Richmond – ✆ (020) 8940 0902 – www.thebingham.co.uk – Closed Sunday dinner Town plan: **6**CX**c**

• MODERN • Menu £ 15 (weekday lunch) – Carte £ 43/56

Charming spot, especially if you've arrived on foot from along the river; dine on the balcony overlooking the garden or in the more traditional dining room. There's a modern style to the cooking and dishes are visually impressive.

LONDON

XX **Dysart Arms**

135 Petersham Rd ✉ TW10 7AA – ✆ (020) 8940 8005 Town plan: **6**CX**d**
– www.thedysartpetersham.co.uk – Closed Sunday dinner
• MODERN • Menu £ 19 (weekdays) – Carte £ 30/51 – *(booking advisable)*
A pub built in the 1900s as part of the Arts and Crafts movement but now run as quite a formal restaurant. The kitchen uses top-notch ingredients and adds subtle Asian tones to a classical base. Occasional musical recital suppers.

X **Petersham Nurseries Café**

Church Ln (off Petersham Rd) ✉ TW10 7AG – ✆ (020) 8940 5230 – www.petershamnurseries.com – Closed 25-26 December and Monday Town plan: **6**CX**x**
• MODERN • Carte £ 31/52 – *(lunch only) (booking advisable)*
On a summer's day there can be few more delightful spots for lunch, whether that's on the terrace or in the greenhouse. The kitchen uses the freshest seasonal produce in unfussy, flavoursome dishes that have a subtle Italian accent.

X **Matsuba**

10 Red Lion St ✉ TW9 1RW ⊖ Richmond – ✆ (020) 8605 3513 – Closed 25-26 December, 1 January and Sunday Town plan: **6**CX**n**
• JAPANESE • Carte £ 21/39
Family-run Japanese restaurant with just 11 tables; understated but well-kept appearance. Extensive menu offers wide range of Japanese dishes, along with bulgogi, a Korean barbecue dish.

X **Swagat**

86 Hill Rise ✉ TW10 6UB ⊖ Richmond – ✆ (020) 8940 7557 – www.swagatindiancuisine.co.uk – Closed 25-26 December Town plan: **6**CX**b**
• INDIAN • Menu £ 25 – Carte £ 18/31 – *(dinner only) (booking essential)*
A very likeable little Indian restaurant, run by two friends who met while training with Oberoi hotels in India. One partner organises the warm service; the other prepares dishes with a pleasing degree of lightness and subtlety.

TEDDINGTON

XX **Rétro Bistrot**

114-116 High St ✉ TW11 8JB – ✆ (0208) 977 22 39 – www.retrobistrot.co.uk – Closed first 2 weeks August, first 10 days January and Sunday dinner Town plan: **5**BY**n**
• FRENCH • Menu £ 13/23 – Carte £ 27/48
There's substance as well as style to this French bistrot. The classic bourgeois cuisine is prepared with innate skill; service is warm and effusive and the slick decoration conductive to merrymaking.

XX **Al Borgo**

3 Church Rd. ✉ TW11 8PF – ✆ (020) 8943 4456 – www.alborgo.co.uk – Closed 1-9 January, Sunday and bank holidays Town plan: **5**BY**e**
• ITALIAN • Menu £ 18 (weekdays) – Carte £ 25/45
A refreshingly unpretentious and keenly run Italian restaurant that exudes warmth and bonhomie. Homemade focaccia and pasta are the highlights. Look out too for seasonal offerings such as the black truffle menu.

X **Simply Thai**

196 Kingston Rd. ✉ TW11 9JD – ✆ (020) 8943 9747 – www.simplythai-restaurant.co.uk – Closed 25-26 December Town plan: **5**BY**x**
• THAI • Menu £ 16 – Carte £ 21/32 – *(dinner only)*
Extremely busy local Thai restaurant; the owner does all the cooking and her passion is clear. New creations sit alongside classics on the large menu. Prices are competitive; service can sometimes struggle to keep up.

King's Head

123 High St ✉ TW11 8HG ⊖ Teddington (Rail). Town plan: **5**BY**c**
– ✆ (020) 3166 2900 – www.whitebrasserie.com – Closed 25 December
• MODERN • Menu £ 12/14 – Carte £ 19/34
Britain has its pubs and France its brasseries; The King's Head does its bit for the entente cordiale by combining both. Have a drink in the front bar, then enjoy rustic classics in the rear brasserie.

Twickenham

A Cena

418 Richmond Rd. ✉ TW1 2EB ⊖ Richmond Town plan: **5**BX**e**
– ✆ (020) 8288 0108 – www.acena.co.uk – Closed Sunday dinner, Monday lunch and bank holidays
• ITALIAN • Carte £ 17/46
The menu at this bigger-than-you-first-think restaurant covers all parts of Italy but there's more of a northern bias in winter; pasta is a highlight. The owners may not be Italian but you can't fault their passion and enthusiasm.

Brula

43 Crown Rd., St Margarets ✉ TW1 3EJ – ✆ (020) 8892 0602 – www.brula.co.uk – Closed 26 December, Sunday dinner and Monday Town plan: **5**BX**v**
• FRENCH • Menu £ 15/20 – Carte £ 24/44 – *(booking essential)*
Traditional in look, with its mirrors and chandeliers but friendly service and popular with the locals. They come for the good value, well-crafted cooking, which is largely French but now comes with a few Spanish and Italian influences.

Crown Ⓝ

174 Richmond Rd, St Margarets ✉ TW1 2NH Town plan: **5**BX**c**
– ✆ (020) 8892 5896 – www.crowntwickenham.co.uk – Closed 26 December
• BRITISH TRADITIONAL • Carte £ 23/36
Relaxed, stylish pub with parquet floors and feature fireplaces; sit in the airy, elegant rear restaurant, with its high vaulted ceiling and garden view. Global, bound-to-please menus offer fresh, tasty, amply-sized dishes.

SOUTHWARK

Bermondsey

Shangri-La Ⓝ

The Shard, 31 St Thomas St ✉ SE1 1RX Town plan: **34**ARV**s**
⊖ London Bridge – ✆ (020) 7234 8000 – www.shangri-la.com/london
202 rm – 🚹£ 450/575 🚹🚹£ 450/575, ☕ £ 20 – 17 suites
Rest *Ting* – Menu £ 30 – Carte £ 42/67
When your hotel occupies floors 34-52 of The Shard, you know it's going to have the wow factor. The pool is London's highest and north-facing bedrooms have the best views. An East-meets-West theme includes the restaurant's menu and afternoon tea when you have a choice of traditional English or Asian.

Hilton London Tower Bridge

5 More London, Tooley St ✉ SE1 2BY Town plan: **34**ARV**e**
⊖ London Bridge – ✆ (020) 3002 4300 – www.towerbridge.hilton.com
245 rm – 🚹£ 129/529 🚹🚹£ 129/629, ☕ £ 20
Rest *The Larder* – Carte £ 27/48 – *(dinner only)*
Usefully located new-style Hilton hotel with boldly decorated open-plan lobby. Contemporary bedrooms boast well-designed features; 4 floors of executive rooms. The Larder has an international menu.

Bermondsey Square

Bermondsey Sq, Tower Bridge Rd ✉ SE1 3UN Town plan: **20**XZE**n**
⊖ London Bridge – ✆ (020) 7378 2450 – www.bermondseysquarehotel.co.uk
80 rm – 🚹£ 99/300 🚹🚹£ 99/300, ☕ £ 14
Rest *GB Grill & Bar* – Carte £ 19/40
Cleverly designed hotel in a regenerated square, with subtle '60s influences and a relaxed, hip feel. Well-equipped bedrooms, including stylish loft suites. British food and grilled meats in the open-plan GB Grill & Bar.

LONDON

London Bridge

8-18 London Bridge St ✉ *SE1 9SG* Town plan: **33**AQV**a**
⊖ *London Bridge – ✆ (020) 7855 2200 – www.londonbridgehotel.com*
138 rm – †£ 319 ††£ 319, ☕ £ 17 – 3 suites
Rest *Londinium* – Carte £ 28/43 – *(dinner only)*
In one of the oldest parts of London, independently owned with an ornate façade dating from 1915. Modern interior with classically decorated bedrooms and an impressive gym. Londinium for brasserie dining.

Le Pont de la Tour

36d Shad Thames, Butlers Wharf ✉ *SE1 2YE* Town plan: **34**ASV**c**
⊖ *London Bridge – ✆ (020) 7403 8403 – www.lepontdelatour.co.uk*
– Closed 26 December and 1 January
• FRENCH • Menu £ 15/25 – Carte £ 36/68
Providing, since 1991, seasonal French cooking, an urbane atmosphere and a wonderful riverside location, with views of Tower Bridge. Simpler dishes served in the livelier cocktail bar and grill.

Story (Tom Sellers)

201 Tooley St. ✉ *SE1 2UE* ⊖ *London Bridge* Town plan: **34**ASV**s**
– ✆ (020) 7183 2117 – www.restaurantstory.co.uk – Closed 2 weeks Christmas-New Year, 2 weeks August-September, Sunday and Monday
• MODERN • Menu £ 35 (weekday lunch)/80 – *(booking essential)*
Amazing what you can create out of an old public toilet on a traffic island. In what looks like a Nordic eco-lodge, Tom Sellers offers 6 or 10 courses of earthy yet delicate, playful yet easy to eat dishes; go for 10, as 6 is too few. With just 13 tables, getting a booking is another story.
→ Onion, apple and gin. Lamb, grilled salad and sheep's yoghurt. Almond and dill.

Magdalen

152 Tooley St. ✉ *SE1 2TU* ⊖ *London Bridge* Town plan: **34**ARV**b**
– ✆ (020) 7403 1342 – www.magdalenrestaurant.co.uk – Closed Sunday, Saturday lunch and bank holidays
• BRITISH MODERN • Menu £ 16 (weekday lunch) – Carte £ 28/41
The clever sourcing and confident British cooking will leave you satisfied. Add genial service, an affordable lunch menu and a food-friendly wine list and you have the favourite restaurant of many.

Hutong Ⓝ

Level 33, The Shard, 31 St Thomas St ✉ *SE1 9RY* Town plan: **34**ARV**s**
⊖ *London Bridge – ✆ (020) 3011 1257 – www.hutong.co.uk*
– Closed 25-26 December and 1 January
• CHINESE • Carte £ 23/50 – *(booking essential)*
You no longer need to fly to Hong Kong to get a view with your Peking duck. On the 33rd floor of The Shard – ask to sit in 'Beijing' – you'll find a menu focusing on the more northerly Chinese regions; specialities include de-boned lamb ribs, soft shell crab and roast duck. Prices are equally vertiginous.

Oblix

Level 32, The Shard, St Thomas St. ✉ *SE1 9RY* Town plan: **34**ARV**s**
⊖ *London Bridge – ✆ (020) 7268 6700 – www.oblixrestaurant.com*
• MEATS AND GRILLS • Carte £ 42/124
From the Zuma/Roka people comes this New York grill restaurant, where meat and fish from the rotisserie, grill and Josper oven are the stars of the show. Views are far-reaching and there's live music in the adjacent lounge bar.

Aqua Shard Ⓝ

Level 31, The Shard, 31 St Thomas St ✉ *SE1 9RY* Town plan: **34**ARV**s**
⊖ *London Bridge – ✆ (020) 3011 1256 – www.aquashard.co.uk*
– Closed 25 December and 1 January
• MODERN • Menu £ 26 (weekday lunch) – Carte £ 33/68
The Shard's most accessible restaurant covers all bases by serving breakfast, brunch, lunch, afternoon tea and dinner. If you don't mind queuing, you can even come just for a drink. The contemporary cooking makes good use of British ingredients and comes with a degree of finesse in flavour and looks.

Zucca

184 Bermondsey St ✉ SE1 3TQ ⊖ Borough – ✆ (020) 7378 6809 – www.zuccalondon.com – Closed 24 December-7 January, Sunday dinner and Monday Town plan: **20**XZE**s**

• ITALIAN • Carte £ 23/39 – *(booking essential at dinner)*

Bright and buzzy modern room, where the informed Italian cooking is driven by the fresh ingredients, the prices are more than generous and the service is sweet and responsive. The appealing antipasti is great for sharing.

Blueprint Café

Design Museum, Shad Thames, Butlers Wharf ✉ SE1 2YD ⊖ London Bridge – ✆ (020) 7378 7031 – www.blueprintcafe.co.uk – Closed 26-27 December, 1-4 January and Sunday dinner Town plan: **34**ASV**u**

• MODERN • Menu £ 15/20 – Carte £ 28/39

Large retractable windows make the most of the river views from this bright restaurant above the Design Museum. The first change of head chef in 16 years was seamless: the cooking remains light, seasonally pertinent and easy to eat.

Village East

171-173 Bermondsey St ✉ SE1 3UW ⊖ London Bridge – ✆ (0207) 357 60 82 – www.villageeast.co.uk – Closed 24-26 December Town plan: **20**XZE**a**

• MODERN • Menu £ 14/24 – Carte £ 19/45

Bar and counter dining are the focus of this trendy restaurant: choose one of the 'ringside seats' to observe the kitchen action. Modern dishes and Mediterranean-inspired plates, with great steaks and burgers.

Cantina Del Ponte

36c Shad Thames, Butlers Wharf ✉ SE1 2YE ⊖ London Bridge – ✆ (020) 7403 5403 – www.cantina.co.uk – Closed 24-26 December Town plan: **34**ASV**c**

• ITALIAN • Menu £ 13/23 – Carte £ 18/50

This Italian stalwart offers an appealing mix of classic dishes and reliable favourites from a sensibly priced menu, in pleasant faux-rustic surroundings. Its pleasant terrace takes advantage of its riverside setting.

Butlers Wharf Chop House

36e Shad Thames, Butlers Wharf ✉ SE1 2YE ⊖ London Bridge – ✆ (020) 7403 3403 – www.chophouse-restaurant.co.uk Town plan: **34**ASV**n**

• BRITISH TRADITIONAL • Carte £ 29/64

Grab a table on the terrace in summer and dine in the shadow of Tower Bridge. Rustic feel to the interior; noisy and fun. The menu focuses on traditional English ingredients and dishes; grilled meats a speciality.

Vivat Bacchus London Bridge

4 Hays Ln ✉ SE1 2HB ⊖ London Bridge – ✆ (020) 7234 0891 – www.vivatbacchus.co.uk – Closed Christmas-New Year, Saturday lunch, Sunday and bank holidays Town plan: **34**ARV**n**

• MEATS AND GRILLS • Carte £ 24/47

Wines from the South African owners' homeland feature strongly and are well-suited to the meat dishes – the strength here. Choose one of the sharing boards themed around various countries, like Italian hams or South African BBQ.

Pizarro

171-173 Bermondsey St ✉ SE1 3UW ⊖ Borough – ✆ (020) 7378 9455 – www.josepizarro.com – Closed 24-28 December Town plan: **20**XZE**r**

• MEDITERRANEAN • Carte £ 22/31

José Pizarro has a refreshingly simple way of naming his establishments: after José, his tapas bar, comes Pizarro, a larger restaurant a few doors down. Go for the small plates, like prawns with piquillo peppers and jamón.

Antico

214 Bermondsey St ✉ SE1 3TQ ⊖ London Bridge Town plan: **20**XZE**e**
– ✆ (020) 7407 4682 – www.antico-london.co.uk – Closed 25 December, 1 January and Monday
• ITALIAN • Menu £ 15 (lunch and early dinner) – Carte £ 23/34
Once an antiques warehouse – hence the name – Antico is fun, bright and breezy, with honest and straightforward Italian food; the homemade pasta is good. Check out the seasonal ragu, risotto and sorbet on the blackboard.

Casse Croûte

109 Bermondsey St ✉ SE1 3XB ⊖ London Bridge Town plan: **20**XZE**t**
– ✆ (020) 7407 2140 – www.cassecroute.co.uk – Closed Sunday dinner
• FRENCH • Carte £ 25/32 – *(booking essential)*
Squeeze into this tiny bistro and you'll find yourself transported to rural France. A blackboard menu offers three choices for each course but new dishes are added as others run out. The cooking is rustic, authentic and heartening.

José

104 Bermondsey St ✉ SE1 3UB ⊖ London Bridge Town plan: **20**XZE**v**
– ✆ (020) 7403 4902 – www.josepizarro.com – Closed 24-26 December and Sunday dinner
• SPANISH • Carte approx. £ 25
Standing up while eating tapas feels so right, especially at this small, fun bar that packs 'em in like boquerones. Five dishes each should suffice; go for the daily fish dishes from the blackboard. There's a great list of sherries too.

Garrison

99-101 Bermondsey St ✉ SE1 3XB Town plan: **20**XZE**z**
⊖ London Bridge. – ✆ (020) 7089 9355 – www.thegarrison.co.uk – Closed 25-26 December
• MEDITERRANEAN • Menu £ 12/16 – Carte £ 21/35 – *(booking essential at dinner)*
Known for its charming vintage look, booths and sweet-natured service, The Garrison boasts a warm, relaxed vibe. Open from breakfast until dinner, when a Mediterranean-led menu pulls in the crowd.

Camberwell

Crooked Well

16 Grove Ln ✉ SE5 8SY ⊖ Denmark Hill (Rail). Town plan: **25**VZH**s**
– ✆ (020) 7252 7798 – www.thecrookedwell.com – Closed Monday lunch
• MODERN • Menu £ 10 (weekday lunch) – Carte £ 21/39
Warmly run pub that manages to look both new and lived-in at the same time. The kitchen mixes things up by offering sturdy classics like rabbit and bacon pie alongside more playful dishes such as a deconstructed peach Melba.

Camberwell Arms

65 Camberwell Church St ✉ SE5 8TR Town plan: **25**VZH**c**
⊖ Denmark Hill – ✆ (020) 7358 4364 – www.thecamberwellarms.co.uk – Closed 27 December-2 January, Sunday dinner, Monday lunch, Tuesday lunch after bank holidays and bank holiday Mondays
• BRITISH TRADITIONAL • Carte £ 24/34 – *(bookings not accepted)*
The people behind the Anchor & Hope and Canton Arms bring their successful formula to SE5: well-informed staff, a no bookings policy, a daily menu supplemented by a blackboard and simple dishes with satisfying, punchy flavours.

East Dulwich

Toasted

38 Lordship Ln ✉ SE22 8HJ – ✆ (020) 8693 9250 Town plan: **26**XZH**t**
– www.toasteddulwich.co.uk – Closed Sunday dinner
• MODERN • Carte £ 18/42
A lively wine shop and eatery with a lived-in feel. Wine bought directly from French vineyards is stored in large tanks; there are also about 200 wines on the list. The menu is short, flavours are bold and combinations quite daring.

Palmerston
91 Lordship Ln ✉ SE22 8EP Town plan: **26**XZH**x**
⊖ East Dulwich (Rail). – ✆ (020) 8693 1629 – www.thepalmerston.co.uk
– Closed 25-26 December and 1 January
• MEDITERRANEAN • Menu £ 14 (weekday lunch) – Carte £ 28/64
A brightly run Victorian pub that has a comfortable, lived-in feel and lies at the heart of the local community. The cooking has a satisfying, gutsy edge with meat dishes, especially game, being the highlight.

SOUTHWARK

citizenM without rest
20 Lavington St ✉ SE1 0NZ ⊖ Southwark Town plan: **33**APV**c**
– ✆ (020) 3519 1680 – www.citizenm.com
192 rm – †£ 120/249 ††£ 120/249, ☐ £ 12
A new type of budget hotel with an eye for the aesthetic. Relaxing, open-plan lobby with sofas, books, tables, desks and a bar for snacks and drinks. Upstairs, the bedrooms may be pod-like but are well-lit and cleverly designed.

Hampton by Hilton
157 Waterloo Rd ✉ SE1 8XA ⊖ Waterloo Town plan: **40**ANX**a**
– ✆ (020) 7401 8080 – www.hilton.com/waterloo
297 rm ☐ – †£ 129/300 ††£ 129/300
Rest *Assado* – ✆ (020) 7870 3747 – Menu £ 10 (lunch) – Carte £ 18/27
A useful budget hotel from Hilton, near the Old Vic and Waterloo. Crisply decorated rooms and plenty of lounge space on the ground floor. Assado is a big, bright restaurant from Cyrus Todiwala fusing Indian and Portuguese cuisine.

Oxo Tower
Oxo Tower Wharf (8th floor), Barge House St Town plan: **32**ANV**a**
✉ SE1 9PH ⊖ Southwark – ✆ (020) 7803 3888 – www.harveynichols.com
– Closed 25 December and dinner 24 December
• MODERN • Menu £ 35 (early dinner) – Carte £ 42/75
Rest *Oxo Tower Brasserie* – see restaurant listing
Top of a converted iconic factory, providing stunning views of the Thames and beyond. Stylish, minimalist interior with huge windows. Expect quite ambitious, mostly European, cuisine.

Roast
The Floral Hall, Borough Mkt ✉ SE1 1TL Town plan: **33**AQV**e**
⊖ London Bridge – ✆ (0845) 034 73 00 – www.roast-restaurant.com
– Closed 25 December and 1 January
• BRITISH MODERN • Menu £ 30 (weekdays)/35 – Carte £ 30/60
– (booking essential)
Known for its British food and for promoting UK producers – not surprising considering the restaurant's in the heart of Borough Market. The 'dish of the day' is often a highlight; service is affable and there's live music at night.

Baltic
74 Blackfriars Rd ✉ SE1 8HA ⊖ Southwark Town plan: **33**AOV**e**
– ✆ (020) 7928 1111 – www.balticrestaurant.co.uk – Closed 24-26 December and Monday lunch
• OTHER WORLD KITCHENS • Menu £ 20/23 – Carte £ 25/36 – *(bookings advisable at dinner)*
In this converted 18C coach builder's works you'll find a big, bright restaurant specialising in Eastern European food – from Poland, Russia, Bulgaria, even Siberia. Dumplings and meat dishes stand out, as do the great vodkas.

Del Mercato

Park St ✉ SE1 9AD ⊖ London Bridge – ✆ (020) 7407 3651 – www.delmercato.co.uk – Closed 25-26 December, 1-2 January, Saturday lunch and Sunday Town plan: **33**AQV**z**

• ITALIAN • Menu £ 18/30 – Carte £ 27/38

Owned by Vinopolis and occupying 3,000 sq ft of space under railway arches. It comprises a bakery, an espresso bar, a trattoria that does a brisk trade in pizzas and homemade pasta, and a stylish upstairs restaurant with a skilful kitchen and a competitive set menu run alongside the à la carte.

Union Street Café

47 - 51 Great Suffolk Street ✉ SE1 0BS ⊖ London Bridge – ✆ (020) 7592 7977 – www.gordonramsay.com – Closed 25-26 December and 1 January Town plan: **33**APV**u**

• ITALIAN • Menu £ 25 (lunch and early dinner) – Carte £ 29/48

Occupying a former warehouse, this Gordon Ramsay restaurant has been busy since day one and comes with a New York feel, a faux industrial look and a basement bar. The Italian menu keeps things simple and stays true to the classics.

Rabot 1745

2-4 Bedal St, Borough Mkt ✉ SE1 9AL ⊖ London Bridge – ✆ (020) 7378 8226 – www.rabot1745.com – Closed 25-26 December, Sunday dinner and Monday Town plan: **33**AQV**z**

• MODERN • Menu £ 18 (weekday lunch) – Carte £ 29/49

Want something different? How about cocoa cuisine? Rabot 1745 is from the owners of Hotel Chocolat and is named after their estate in St Lucia. They take the naturally bitter, spicy flavours of the bean and use them subtly in classically based dishes. The chocolate mousse dessert is pretty good too!

Oxo Tower Brasserie

Oxo Tower Wharf (8th floor), Barge House St ✉ SE1 9PH ⊖ Southwark – ✆ (020) 7803 3888 – www.harveynichols.com – Closed 25 December and dinner 24 December Town plan: **32**ANV**a**

• MODERN • Menu £ 30 (lunch and early dinner) – Carte £ 35/59

Less formal but more fun than the next-door restaurant. Open-plan kitchen produces modern, colourful and easy-to-eat dishes with influences from the Med. Great views too from the bar.

Elliot's

12 Stoney St., Borough Market ✉ SE1 9AD ⊖ London Bridge – ✆ (020) 7403 7436 – www.elliotscafe.com – Closed Sunday and bank holidays Town plan: **33**AQV**h**

• MODERN • Carte £ 17/35 – *(booking advisable)*

Open from breakfast onwards, this busy and unpretentious café sources most of its ingredients from Borough Market, in which it stands. The appealing menu is concise and the cooking is earthy, pleasingly uncomplicated and very satisfying.

Tate Modern (Restaurant)

Tate Modern (6th floor), Bankside ✉ SE1 9TG ⊖ Southwark – ✆ (020) 7887 8888 – www.tate.org.uk – Closed 24-26 December Town plan: **33**APV**s**

• BRITISH MODERN • Menu £ 24 (lunch) – Carte £ 29/43 – *(lunch only and dinner Friday-Saturday)*

Ask for a front window table facing St Paul's at this big, bright restaurant on Level 6. The menu is seasonal and the influences largely British; the kitchen has a light touch and each dish comes with a suggested wine pairing.

Tapas Brindisa

18-20 Southwark St, Borough Market ✉ SE1 1TJ ⊖ London Bridge – ✆ (020) 7357 8880 – www.tapasbrindisa.com Town plan: **33**AQV**k**

• SPANISH • Carte £ 20/32 – *(bookings not accepted)*

A blueprint for many of the tapas bars that subsequently sprung up over London. It has an infectious energy and the well-priced, robust dishes include Galician-style hake and black rice with squid; do try the hand-carved Ibérico hams.

Wright Brothers

11 Stoney St., Borough Market ✉ *SE1 9AD* Town plan: **33**AQV**m**
⊖ *London Bridge – ✆ (020) 7403 9554 – www.thewrightbrothers.co.uk – Closed dinner 24 December-dinner 28 December, 1-2 January, Easter Sunday and bank holidays*
• FISH AND SEAFOOD • Carte £ 28/53 – *(booking advisable)*
Originally an oyster wholesaler; now offers a wide range of oysters along with porter, as well as fruits de mer, daily specials and assorted pies. It fills quickly and an air of contentment reigns.

Anchor & Hope

36 The Cut ✉ *SE1 8LP* ⊖ *Southwark. – ✆ (020) 7928 9898 – www.anchorandhopepub.co.uk – Closed Christmas-New Year, Sunday dinner, Monday lunch and bank holidays* Town plan: **32**ANV**n**
• BRITISH MODERN • Menu £ 15 (weekday lunch) – Carte £ 21/33 – *(bookings not accepted)*
As popular as ever thanks to its congenial feel and lived-in looks but mostly because of the appealingly seasonal menu and the gutsy, bold cooking that delivers on flavour. No reservations so be prepared to wait at the bar.

SUTTON

See Regional map n°**12-B1**

Sutton

Brasserie Vacherin

12 High St ✉ *SM1 1HN – ✆ (020) 8722 0180 – www.brasserievacherin.co.uk – Closed 25 December* Town plan: **7**EZ**x**
• FRENCH • Menu £ 18 (lunch and early dinner) – Carte £ 21/34
Relaxed, modern French brasserie with tiled walls, art nouveau posters and deep red banquettes. Good value midweek set price menu and à la carte of French classics. Diligent service.

TOWER HAMLETS

Bethnal Green

Town Hall

Patriot Sq ✉ *E2 9NF* ⊖ *Bethnal Green – ✆ (020) 7871 0460 – www.townhallhotel.com* Town plan: **14**YZB**x**
98 rm – †£ 160/355 ††£ 160/355, ☕ £ 15 – 1 suite
Rest *Corner Room* **Rest *Typing Room*** – see restaurant listing
Edwardian, former council offices converted into a hotel in 2010. Its period character is balanced with modernity, with individually decorated, understated bedrooms and frequently changing art.

Typing Room – Town Hall Hotel

Patriot Sq ✉ *E2 9NF* ⊖ *Bethnal Green – ✆ (020) 7871 0461 – www.typingroom.com – Closed Sunday dinner, Monday and Tuesday* Town plan: **14**YZB**x**
• MODERN • Menu £ 27 (lunch) – Carte £ 38/51
Jason Atherton has backed one of his protégés in a room once home to the town hall's typing pool. The open kitchen dominates the room and the cooking is clever and accomplished, with flavours that are distinct and complementary.

Brawn

49 Columbia Rd. ✉ *E2 7RG* ⊖ *Bethnal Green – ✆ (020) 7729 5692 – www.brawn.co – Closed Christmas-New Year, Sunday dinner, Monday lunch and bank holidays* Town plan: **20**XZD**z**
• MODERN • Carte £ 19/33
Unpretentious and simply kitted out baby sister to Terroirs; the name captures the essence of the cooking perfectly: it is rustic, muscular and makes very good use of pig. Great local atmosphere and polite, helpful service.

Corner Room – Town Hall Hotel

Patriot Sq ✉ E2 9NF ⊖ Bethnal Green – ✆ (020) 7871 0461 – www.cornerroom.co.uk Town plan: **14**YZB**x**

• INNOVATIVE • Menu £ 19 (lunch) – Carte £ 21/43

Hidden upstairs in the old town hall is this bright, intimate space – first have a drink in the little bar. The core ingredient of each dish is British and the assured cooking makes you feel you're getting a real taste of nature.

Bistrotheque

23-27 Wadeson St ✉ E2 9DR ⊖ Bethnal Green – ✆ (020) 8983 7900 – www.bistrotheque.com – Closed 24 and 26 December Town plan: **14**YZB**s**

• MODERN • Menu £ 18 (dinner) – Carte £ 21/48 – *(dinner only and lunch Saturday-Sunday) (booking advisable)*

When the exterior is as irredeemably bleak as this, you just know it's going to be painfully cool inside. This bustling space in a converted sweatshop is great fun; its menu is French-bistro in style. Live music at weekend brunch.

Bow

Morgan Arms

43 Morgan St ✉ E3 5AA ⊖ Bow Road. – ✆ (020) 8980 6389 – www.morganarmsbow.com – Closed 25 December Town plan: **3**GU**c**

• BRITISH TRADITIONAL • Carte £ 18/37

Characterful pub with mismatch of furniture and shabby-chic appeal. Constantly evolving menu offers robust cooking which occasionally uses some unfamiliar ingredients; simpler food is served in the lively bar.

Canary Wharf

Four Seasons

Westferry Circus ✉ E14 8RS ⊖ Canary Wharf – ✆ (020) 7510 1999 – www.fourseasons.com/canarywharf Town plan: **3**GV**a**

127 rm – †£ 210/405 ††£ 210/405, ☕ £ 27 – 14 suites

Rest *Quadrato* – ✆ (020) 7510 1858 – Carte £ 21/58

Professionally run international hotel geared mainly to the local corporate market. The deluxe rooms boast impressive views across the river. Spacious restaurant, with river-facing terrace and menu that covers all parts of Italy.

Plateau

Canada Place (4th floor), Canada Square ✉ E14 5ER ⊖ Canary Wharf – ✆ (020) 7715 7100 – www.plateaurestaurant.co.uk – Closed 25 December, 1 January and Sunday Town plan: **3**GV**n**

• MODERN • Menu £ 15/25 – Carte £ 29/60

Impressive open-plan space with dramatic glass walls and ceilings and striking 1950s influenced design. Rotisserie meats in the contemporary Bar & Grill; globally-influenced dishes in the more formal restaurant.

Roka Canary Wharf

4 Park Pavilion (1st Floor) ✉ E14 5FW ⊖ Canary Wharf – ✆ (020) 7636 5228 – www.rokarestaurant.com – Closed 25 December Town plan: **3**GV**v**

• JAPANESE • Carte £ 20/89 – *(booking essential)*

You'll be hit by a wall of sound at this large and perennially busy operation in the shadow of Canary Wharf Tower. The meats cooked on the robata grill are highlights of the Japanese menu.

Boisdale of Canary Wharf

Cabot Pl ✉ E14 4QT ⊖ Canary Wharf – ✆ (020) 7715 5818 – www.boisdale.co.uk – Closed bank holidays Town plan: **3**GV**s**

• BRITISH TRADITIONAL • Menu £ 18 – Carte £ 26/64 – *(booking advisable)*

It's the 1st floor for the relaxed, art deco inspired Oyster bar, with its crustacea, burgers and steaks. The grander 2nd floor has a stage for live jazz (a charge is made) and offers plenty of dishes of a Scottish persuasion.

XX **Goodman Canary Wharf**

Discovery Dock East, 3 South Quay ✉ E14 9RU Town plan: 3GV**e**
⊖ South Quay (DLR) – ✆ (020) 7531 0300 – www.goodmanrestaurants.com – Closed 25-26 December, 1 January, Saturday lunch, Sunday and bank holidays
• MEATS AND GRILLS • Carte £ 25/67 – *(booking advisable)*
Whether you like corn or grass fed Scottish fillet, rib on the bone or US strip loin, the delightful staff will explain the maturation process; you decide on the cut and weight. A lively brasserie with waterfront views.

XX **Iberica Canary Wharf**

Cabot Sq ✉ E14 4QQ ⊖ Canary Wharf – ✆ (020) 7636 8650 – www.ibericalondon.co.uk – Closed 24-25 December, 1 January and dinner on Sunday and bank holidays Town plan: 3GV**c**
• SPANISH • Carte £ 18/46
Lively, modern Spanish restaurant whose narrow shop front belies its vast interior; choose the bustle of the ground floor or the quieter mezzanine. The tapas is an appealing mix of the traditional and the more contemporary.

The Gun

27 Coldharbour ✉ E14 9NS ⊖ Blackwall (DLR). Town plan: 3GV**x**
– ✆ (020) 7515 5222 – www.thegundocklands.com – Closed 25-26 December
• BRITISH TRADITIONAL • Carte £ 28/54 – *(booking essential)*
Its popularity far outweighs its size but just head to the smart dining room at the far end or to the terrace overlooking the river. The broadly British dishes are the best things on the menu – appropriate for such a historic pub.

LONDON

LIMEHOUSE

Narrow

44 Narrow St ✉ E14 8DP ⊖ Limehouse (DLR). Town plan: 3GV**b**
– ✆ (020) 7592 7950 – www.gordonramsay.com
• BRITISH TRADITIONAL • Carte £ 31/42 – *(booking essential)*
Terrific river views from this Grade II listed former dockmaster's house; part of Gordon Ramsay's group. Sit in the conservatory and order British classics like Scotch egg, cottage pie, and bread and butter pudding.

SPITALFIELDS

XXX ✿ **Galvin La Chapelle**

35 Spital Sq ✉ E1 6DY ⊖ Liverpool Street Town plan: 34AST**v**
– ✆ (020) 7299 0400 – www.galvinrestaurants.com – Closed dinner 24-26 December and 1 January
• FRENCH • Menu £ 24 (lunch and early dinner)/29 – Carte £ 37/62
The Victorian splendour of St Botolph's Hall, with its vaulted ceiling, arched windows and marble pillars, lends itself perfectly to its role as a glamorous restaurant. The food is bourgeois French with a sophisticated edge and is bound to satisfy.
➜ Smoked eel, caramelised pineapple, Alsace bacon, parsley & horseradish. Tagine of pigeon, couscous, confit lemon & harissa sauce. Chilled Valrhona chocolate, banana and yoghurt ice cream.

XX **Les Trois Garcons**

1 Club Row ✉ E1 6JX ⊖ Shoreditch High Street Town plan: 20XZD**r**
– ✆ (020) 7613 1924 – www.lestroisgarcons.com – Closed 23 December-3 January and Sunday
• FRENCH • Carte £ 31/56 – *(dinner only and lunch Wednesday-Friday)*
Extraordinarily eccentric decoration, with stuffed animals, twinkling beads, velvet drapes, chandeliers and handbags hanging from the ceiling. By contrast, the French food is surprisingly traditional.

X **Hawksmoor**

157a Commercial St ✉ E1 6BJ Town plan: 20XZD**s**
⊖ Shoreditch High Street – ✆ (020) 7426 4850 – www.thehawksmoor.com – Closed 24-26 December and Sunday dinner
• MEATS AND GRILLS • Carte £ 27/75 – *(booking essential)*
Unremarkable surroundings and ordinary starters and puds but no matter: this is all about great British beef, hung for 35 days, from Longhorn cattle in the heart of the Yorkshire Moors.

X **Galvin Café a Vin**

35 Spital Sq (entrance on Bishops Sq) ✉ E1 6DY Town plan: **34**AST**v**
⊖ Liverpool Street – ✆ (020) 7299 0404 – www.galvinrestaurants.com
– Closed 24-26 December and 1 January
• FRENCH • Menu £ 17 (lunch and early dinner) – Carte £ 26/36
In the same building as La Chapelle is this simpler yet equally worthy operation from the Galvin brothers. The room may not have the grandeur of next door but it's fun and lively and offers classic French bistro food at good prices.

X **St John Bread and Wine**

94-96 Commercial St ✉ E1 6LZ ⊖ Shoreditch Town plan: **34**AST**a**
– ✆ (020) 7251 0848 – www.stjohnbreadandwine.com – Closed 25-26 December and 1 January
• BRITISH TRADITIONAL • Carte £ 19/30
Part-wine shop/bakery and local restaurant. Highly seasonal and appealing menu changes twice a day; cooking is British, uncomplicated and very satisfying. Try the less familiar dishes.

LONDON

WHITECHAPEL

XX **Cafe Spice Namaste**

16 Prescot St. ✉ E1 8AZ ⊖ Tower Hill – ✆ (020) 7488 9242 – www.cafespice.co.uk – Closed Saturday lunch, Sunday and bank holidays Town plan: **34**ASU**z**
• INDIAN • Menu £ 35 – Carte £ 22/33
Fresh, vibrant and fairly priced Indian cuisine from Cyrus Todiwala, served in a colourfully decorated room that was once a magistrate's court. Engaging service from an experienced team.

WANDSWORTH

BALHAM

X **Lamberts**

2 Station Par, Balham High Rd. ✉ SW12 9AZ Town plan: **6**EX**n**
⊖ Balham – ✆ (020) 8675 2233 – www.lambertsrestaurant.com
– Closed 25-26 December, 1 January, Sunday dinner and Monday
• BRITISH TRADITIONAL • Menu £ 15 (weekday lunch) – Carte £ 27/42
Locals come for the relaxed surroundings, hospitable service and tasty, seasonal food. Sunday lunch is very popular. The enthusiasm of the eponymous owner has rubbed off on his team.

X **Harrison's**

15-19 Bedford Hill ✉ SW12 9EX ⊖ Balham – ✆ (020) 8675 6900 – www.harrisonsbalham.co.uk – Closed 24-28 December Town plan: **6**EX**h**
• MODERN • Menu £ 17 (weekdays) – Carte £ 27/39
Lively, popular sister to Sam's Brasserie in Chiswick. Open all day, with an appealing list of favourites, from fishcakes to 'Harrison's burgers'. Weekend brunches; kids' menu; good value weekday set menus.

BATTERSEA

XX **London House** Ⓝ

7-9 Battersea Sq, Battersea Village ✉ SW11 3RA Town plan: **22**PZH**h**
⊖ Clapham Junction – ✆ (020) 7592 8545
– www.gordonramsay.com/londonhouse – Closed Monday except bank holidays
• BRITISH MODERN • Menu £ 28/35 – *(dinner only and lunch Friday-Sunday)*
One doesn't associate neighbourhood restaurants with Gordon Ramsay but London House looks set to succeed. It's comfortable and well run and the classically-based dishes come with modern touches and ingredients that marry well.

Chada

208-210 Battersea Park Rd. ✉ SW11 4ND Town plan: **23**QZH**x**
⊖ Clapham Junction – ✆ (020) 7622 2209 – www.chadathai.com – Closed Sunday and bank holidays
• THAI • Carte £ 17/34 – *(dinner only)*
Going strong after 20 years; its striking façade stands out in an otherwise unremarkable street. The welcome is warm, the service polite and the Thai food appealing and keenly priced.

Sinabro

28 Battersea Rd ✉ SW11 1EE Town plan: **23**QZH**r**
⊖ Clapham Junction – ✆ (0203) 302 3120 – www.sinabro.co.uk – Closed 1 week August, 25 December, 1 January and Monday
• MODERN • Menu £ 29
With its surfeit of stainless steel, this simple restaurant has the feel of a kitchen; choose a seat at the counter. Dishes have their heart in classic French cooking but are modern in their presentation. Charming service. Weekend brunches.

Soif

27 Battersea Rise ✉ SW11 1HG Town plan: **23**QZH**c**
⊖ Clapham Junction – ✆ (020) 7233 1112 – www.soif.co – Closed Christmas and New Year, Sunday dinner, Monday lunch and bank holidays
• FRENCH • Carte £ 22/32 – *(booking essential at dinner)*
Great food, an appealingly louche look and a thoughtful wine list – yes, it's another terrific eaterie from the team behind Terroirs and Brawn. The cooking is robust and satisfying; anything 'piggy' is done particularly well.

Entrée

2 Battersea Rise ✉ SW11 1ED Town plan: **23**QZH**s**
⊖ Clapham Junction – ✆ (020) 7223 5147 – www.entreebattersea.co.uk – Closed 24-28 December, Sunday dinner and Monday
• MODERN • Carte £ 27/45 – *(dinner only and lunch Saturday-Sunday)*
They've gone for a casual bistro look which, along with a basement bar and weekend pianist, hits the right note with locals. Sensibly priced menu mixes French classic and modern European dishes.

Lola Rojo

78 Northcote Rd ✉ SW11 6QL Town plan: **23**QZH**v**
⊖ Clapham Junction – ✆ (020) 7350 2262 – www.lolarojo.net – Closed 25-26 December and lunch 1 January
• SPANISH • Carte £ 14/37 – *(booking essential)*
Few spots on Northcote Road are as fun as this lively, if cramped, Spanish eatery. The owner-chef comes from Valencia so paella is a sure thing but other Catalan tapas specialities are also worth seeking out.

Rosita

124 Northcote Rd ✉ SW11 6QU Town plan: **6**EX**g**
⊖ Clapham Junction – ✆ (020) 7998 9093 – www.rositasherry.net – Closed 25-26 December, 1 January and Monday
• MEDITERRANEAN • Carte £ 15/26 – *(dinner only and lunch Friday-Sunday)*
From the owners of nearby Lola Roja comes this fun sherry and tapas bar. Dishes include flavoursome meats and seafood cooked by Josper grill. There are many sherries by the glass and suggested pairings with certain dishes.

Hana

60 Battersea Rise ✉ SW11 1EG Town plan: **23**QZH**a**
⊖ Clapham Junction – ✆ (020) 7228 2496 – www.hanakorean.co.uk – Closed 24-26 December
• KOREAN • Carte £ 16/26
A warm, sweet little Korean restaurant. Yang Yeum chicken and Pa Jeon pancake are popular starters; bibimbap rice dishes burst with flavour; seafood cooked on the barbeque is very good; and they do their own version of Bossam.

Battersea Heliport

Hotel Verta

Bridges Wharf ✉ SW11 3BE – ✆ (020) 7801 3500 Town plan: **23**PZH**v**
– www.hotelverta.co.uk
68 rm – †£ 120/200 ††£ 120/200, ☕ £ 15 – 2 suites **Rest** – Carte £ 27/44
Built in 2010, in a unique riverside location with a heliport. Well-equipped bedrooms; those without views are bigger than those with. Impressive spa facilities. International menu in the bistro and bar.

Putney

Enoteca Turi

28 Putney High St ✉ SW15 1SQ ⊖ Putney Bridge Town plan: **22**MZH**n**
– ✆ (020) 8785 4449 – www.enotecaturi.com – Closed 25-26 December, 1 January, Sunday and lunch bank holiday Mondays
• ITALIAN • Menu £ 19/34 – Carte £ 26/46
Giuseppe Turi's restaurant has been warming Putney hearts for nearly 25 years. The focus is on Northern Italy and dishes are full of flavour. The room has an appealing Mediterranean feel and there are no bad tables. Wine plays a big part here, with lesser known Italian producers to the fore.

LONDON

Bibo

146 Upper Richmond Rd ✉ SW15 2SW Town plan: **22**MZH**b**
⊖ East Putney – ✆ (020) 8780 0592 – www.biborestaurant.com
– Closed 25-26 December and bank holiday Mondays
• ITALIAN • Carte £ 24/31
Rebecca Mascarenhas is the neighbourhood restaurant expert and, with Bibo, she's hit the bullseye once again. This fun Italian comes with an appealing vibe, clued up service and well-priced food that's effortlessly easy to enjoy.

Prince of Wales

138 Upper Richmond Rd ✉ SW15 2SP Town plan: **22**MZH**z**
⊖ East Putney. – ✆ (020) 8788 1552 – www.princeofwalesputney.co.uk
– Closed 23 December-1 January and Monday lunch except bank holidays
• BRITISH MODERN • Carte £ 25/39
Idiosyncratic decoration and good food make this substantial Victorian pub stand out. The daily changing menu reads well and includes British specialities like Cornish sardines as well as Spanish delicacies; simpler menu in the bar.

Southfields

Earl Spencer

260-262 Merton Rd ✉ SW18 5JL ⊖ Southfields Town plan: **6**DX**c**
– ✆ (020) 8870 9244 – www.theearlspencer.com – Closed 25-26 December
• TRADITIONAL • Carte £ 23/30
A handsome Edwardian pub a baseline lob away from the All England Tennis Club. The cooking is fervently seasonal; flavours are assured and ingredients marry well. The only irritant is that one has to order everything at the bar.

Tooting

Chicken Shop

141 Tooting High St ✉ SW17 0SY Town plan: **6**EY**c**
⊖ Tooting Broadway – ✆ (020) 8767 5200 – www.chickenshop.com
• MEATS AND GRILLS • Carte £ 15/18 – *(bookings not accepted)*
Tooting has already taken to the second branch of Chicken Shop. The ingeniously simple idea is serving just whole, half or quarter chickens that are succulent and flavoursome, along with a few sides and a couple of puddings.

WANDSWORTH

Chez Bruce (Bruce Poole)

2 Bellevue Rd ✉ SW17 7EG ⊖ Tooting Bec – ☎ (020) 8672 0114 – www.chezbruce.co.uk – Closed 24-26 December and 1 January Town plan: **6**EX**e**

• FRENCH • Menu £ 28/45 – *(booking essential)*

Flavoursome, uncomplicated French cooking with hints of the Mediterranean prepared with innate skill; well-organised, personable service and an easy-going atmosphere - some of the reasons why Chez Bruce remains a favourite of so many.
→ Calf's brains with dressed Puy lentils, sauce gribiche and capocollo. Sea bass with morels, garlic leaves, crushed potatoes and asparagus. Lemon meringue ice cream sandwich with lemon curd, poppy seeds and raspberries.

WESTMINSTER (City of)

See Regional map n°**12**-B3

BAYSWATER AND MAIDA VALE

Lancaster London

Lancaster Terr ✉ W2 2TY ⊖ Lancaster Gate – ☎ (020) 7262 6737 – www.lancasterlondon.com Town plan: **28**ADU**e**

416 rm – †£ 129/429 ††£ 165/465, ☕ £ 16 – 22 suites

Rest *Island* – ☎ (020) 7551 6070 – Menu £ 13 (lunch and early dinner) – Carte £ 21/34

Rest *Nipa* – ☎ (020) 7551 6039 – Menu £ 35 – Carte £ 26/56 – *(dinner only)*

An imposing 1960s hotel overlooking Hyde Park, known for its extensive conference suites. Bedrooms are bright and well-equipped. Island has an accessible, Med-influenced menu, with steaks a highlight; Nipa is their longstanding Thai restaurant.

Hotel Indigo London - Paddington

16 London St ✉ W2 1HL ⊖ Paddington – ☎ (020) 7706 4444 – www.hotelindigo.com Town plan: **28**ADU**a**

64 rm – †£ 109/279 ††£ 129/379, ☕ £ 20

Rest *London Street Brasserie* – Carte £ 20/35

You'll find a smart, modern, corporate townhouse behind the imposing period façade. Bright bedrooms come with feature walls depicting scenes of the local area. All-day menu of steaks, pasta and brasserie classics.

Royal Park without rest

3 Westbourne Terr ✉ W2 3UL ⊖ Lancaster Gate – ☎ (020) 7479 6600 – www.theroyalpark.com Town plan: **28**ADU**x**

48 rm – †£ 203/419 ††£ 203/419, ☕ £ 14 – 3 suites

Three attractive 19C townhouses set back from the road, in a pleasant location near Hyde Park. Quiet lounges with period furnishings. Breakfast served in the well-appointed bedrooms.

New Linden without rest

59 Leinster Sq. ✉ W2 4PS ⊖ Bayswater – ☎ (020) 7221 4321 – www.newlinden.com Town plan: **27**ABU**e**

50 rm ☕ – †£ 110/120 ††£ 119/299

Smart four-storey white stucco façade. Basement breakfast room opens onto summer courtyard. Bedrooms are its strength: flat screen TVs and wooden floors; two split-level family rooms.

Le Café Anglais

8 Porchester Gdns ✉ W2 4BD ⊖ Bayswater – ☎ (020) 7221 1415 – www.lecafeanglais.co.uk – Closed 25-26 December, 1 January and 31 August Town plan: **27**ABU**r**

• MEDITERRANEAN • Menu £ 30 (weekday lunch) – Carte £ 25/54

Big, bustling and contemporary brasserie with art deco styling, within Whiteley's shopping centre. Large, appealing selection of classic brasserie food; the rotisserie is the centrepiece. More casual oyster bar by entrance.

XX **Angelus**

4 Bathurst St ✉ W2 2SD ⊖ Lancaster Gate Town plan: **28**ADU**c**
– ✆ (020) 7402 0083 – www.angelusrestaurant.co.uk – Closed 24 December-2 January
• FRENCH • Menu £ 22 (lunch) – Carte £ 38/64

Hospitable owner has created an attractive French brasserie within a 19C former pub, with a warm and inclusive feel. Satisfying and honest French cooking uses seasonal British ingredients.

XX **New Angel** Ⓝ

39 Chepstow Pl ✉ W2 4TS ⊖ Bayswater Town plan: **27**AAU**c**
– ✆ (020) 7221 7620 – www.thenewangel-nh.co.uk – Closed 25 December, Sunday dinner, Monday and bank holidays
• BRITISH MODERN • Menu £ 32/54

Many thought celebrated chef John Burton-Race had left London for good when he headed west over a decade ago. But now he's back in a converted pub which resembles a bistrot-deluxe. Despite the classical French nature to the cooking, there's a hint of modernity and a refinement to the flavours.

LONDON

XX **Marianne** Ⓝ

104A Chepstow Rd ✉ W2 5QS Town plan: **27**AAT**m**
⊖ Westbourne Park – ✆ (020) 3675 7750 – www.mariannerestaurant.com – Closed 22-24 August and Monday
• FRENCH • Menu £ 55 – *(dinner only and lunch Friday-Sunday) (booking essential)*

The eponymous Marianne was a finalist on MasterChef. Her restaurant is a sweet little place with just 6 tables. A concise daily menu lets her own cooking style come through – it's classically based but keeps things quite light.

XX **Shiori** Ⓝ

45 Moscow Rd ✉ W2 4AH ⊖ Bayswater Town plan: **27**ABU**x**
– ✆ (020) 7221 9790 – www.theshiori.com – Closed Sunday and Monday
• JAPANESE • Menu £ 70/95 – *(booking essential)*

Takashi & Hitomi Takagi's kaiseki restaurant brings a little of Kyoto to West London. The finest UK produce is supplemented by vegetables imported from Japan; the resulting dishes are beautifully presented, delicate, balanced and original. The small but immaculately dressed room seats just 16.

XX **Toa Kitchen** Ⓝ

100 Queensway ✉ W2 3RR ⊖ Bayswater Town plan: **27**ABU**t**
– ✆ (020) 7792 9767 – www.toakitchen.com – Closed 25 December
• CHINESE • Carte £ 14/54

There's an overwhelming number of Chinese restaurants on Queensway so search out Toa Kitchen and head for the "Chef's Specials" for good, authentic Cantonese dishes. Service from owner Mr Fung and his team is also a cut above average.

X **Hereford Road**

3 Hereford Rd ✉ W2 4AB ⊖ Bayswater – ✆ (020) 7727 1144 – www.herefordroad.org – Closed 24 December-3 January and 27-29 August Town plan: **27**ABU**s**
• BRITISH MODERN • Menu £ 14 (weekday lunch) – Carte £ 23/32 – *(booking essential)*

Converted butcher's shop specialising in tasty British dishes without frills, using first-rate, seasonal ingredients; offal a highlight. Booths for six people are the prized seats. Friendly and relaxed feel.

X **Assaggi**

39 Chepstow Pl, (1st Floor) ✉ W2 4TS Town plan: **27**AAU**c**
⊖ Bayswater – ✆ (020) 7792 5501 – Closed 2 weeks Christmas, Sunday and bank holidays
• ITALIAN • Carte £ 42/56 – *(booking essential)*

A warm welcome is guaranteed for all-comers at this simply decorated Italian restaurant above what was once a pub. Prices are driven by the superlative ingredients; preparations are straightforward to bring out natural flavours.

Kateh

5 Warwick Pl ✉ W9 2PX ⊖ Warwick Avenue Town plan: **28**ACT**a**
– ✆ (020) 7289 3393 – www.kateh.net – Closed 25-26 December
• MEDITERRANEAN • Carte £ 21/36 – *(dinner only and lunch Friday-Sunday) (booking essential)*

Booking is imperative if you want to join the locals who have already discovered what a little jewel they have in the form of this buzzy, busy Persian restaurant. Authentic stews, expert chargrilling and lovely pastries and teas.

Kurobuta Marble Arch (N)

17-20 Kendal St ✉ W2 2AW ⊖ Marble Arch Town plan: **29**AFU**m**
– ✆ (020) 3475 4158 – www.kurobuta-london.com
– Closed 25 December
• JAPANESE • Carte £ 40/60

The Aussie owner-chef's fun Japanese restaurant was influenced by izakaya. The robata grill provides the sticky BBQ pork belly for the pork buns; the black pepper soft shell crabs fly out of the kitchen; and the yuzu tart is good.

Casa Malevo

23 Connaught St ✉ W2 2AY ⊖ Marble Arch Town plan: **29**AFU**a**
– ✆ (020) 7402 1988 – www.casamalevo.com
– Closed 21-26 December
• ARGENTINIAN • Carte £ 21/45 – *(dinner only)*

Meat lovers should head for this warm, country style 'cocina Argentina'. Kick things off with empanadas or homemade chorizo then order a cut of premium Argentinian beef; the Malbec and bone marrow sauce hits the spot too.

El Pirata DeTapas

115 Westbourne Grove ✉ W2 4UP ⊖ Bayswater Town plan: **27**ABU**n**
– ✆ (020) 7727 5000 – www.elpiratadetapas.co.uk
– Closed 24-26 December, 24-25 August and 1 January
• SPANISH • Menu £ 10/25 – Carte £ 19/29

Contemporary yet warm Spanish restaurant with a genuine neighbourhood feel. Authentic flavours from a well-priced and appealing selection of tapas, ideal for sharing with friends.

Prince Alfred & Formosa Dining Room

5A Formosa St ✉ W9 1EE ⊖ Warwick Avenue. Town plan: **17**OZD**n**
– ✆ (020) 7286 3287 – www.theprincealfred.com
• MODERN • Carte £ 24/41

The Prince Alfred is a striking Victorian pub; sadly, the eating is done in the Formosa Dining Room extension but at least it's a lively room. Cooking has a rustic edge; steaks, pork belly and sticky toffee pudding are perennials.

Waterway

54 Formosa St ✉ W9 2JU ⊖ Warwick Avenue. Town plan: **17**OZD**p**
– ✆ (020) 7266 3557 – www.thewaterway.co.uk
• MODERN • Carte £ 23/39

Terrific decked terrace by the canal its most appealing feature. Contemporary interior with busy cocktail bar; menu in separate dining room mixes the classics with more ambitious dishes.

Truscott Arms (N)

55 Shirland Rd ✉ W9 2JD ⊖ Warwick Avenue Town plan: **16**NZD**a**
– ✆ (020) 7266 9198 – www.thetruscottarms.com
• MODERN • Menu £ 32 (dinner) – Carte £ 24/43

A Victorian pub resuscitated and restored by a husband and wife team. Local artwork and ornate ceiling in upstairs dining room. The kitchen displays ambition and uses modern techniques to produce quite elaborate dishes.

BELGRAVIA

Berkeley
Wilton Pl ✉ *SW1X 7RL* ⊖ *Knightsbridge* Town plan: **37**AGX**e**
– ✆ *(020) 7235 6000 – www.the-berkeley.co.uk*
210 rm – †£ 270/720 ††£ 330/840, ☕ £ 32 – 28 suites
Rest *Marcus* ✿✿ Rest *Koffmann's* – see restaurant listing
Discreet and very comfortable hotel with impressive rooftop pool and opulently decorated, immaculately kept bedrooms. Relax in the gilded, panelled Caramel Room or have a drink in the ice cool Blue Bar. Choice of two restaurants.

Halkin
5 Halkin St ✉ *SW1X 7DJ* ⊖ *Hyde Park Corner* Town plan: **38**AHX**b**
– ✆ *(020) 7333 1000 – www.comohotels.com/thehalkin*
41 rm – †£ 280/795 ††£ 280/795, ☕ £ 28 – 6 suites
Rest *Ametsa with Arzak Instruction* ✿ – see restaurant listing
Opened in 1991 as one of London's first boutique hotels and still looking sharp today. Thoughtfully conceived bedrooms with silk walls and marbled bathrooms; everything at the touch of a button. Abundant Armani-clad staff. Small, discreet bar.

The Wellesley
11 Knightsbridge ✉ *SW1X 7LY* Town plan: **37**AGX**w**
⊖ *Hyde Park Corner* – ✆ *(020) 7235 3535 – www.thewellesley.co.uk*
36 rm – †£ 450/550 ††£ 450/550, ☕ £ 34 – 14 suites
Rest – Menu £ 30 – Carte £ 59/111
Stylish, elegant townhouse inspired by the jazz age, on the site of the famous Pizza on the Park. Impressive cigar lounge and bar with a super selection of whiskies and cognacs. Smart bedrooms have full butler service; those facing Hyde Park the most prized. Modern Italian food in the discreet restaurant.

Belgraves
rm, rm,
20 Chesham Pl ✉ *SW1X 8HQ* ⊖ *Knightsbridge* Town plan: **37**AGX**c**
– ✆ *(020) 7858 0100 – www.thompsonhotels.com*
85 rm – †£ 359/599 ††£ 360/660, ☕ £ 20
Rest *Pont St* – ✆ (020) 3189 4850 – Carte £ 27/52
US group Thompson's first UK venture is an elegant and stylish boutique-style hotel with a hint of bohemia. Uncluttered, decently proportioned bedrooms come with oak flooring and lovely marble bathrooms. Light, Mediterranean-influenced dishes served in Pont St restaurant.

Jumeirah Lowndes
rm,
21 Lowndes St ✉ *SW1X 9ES* ⊖ *Knightsbridge* Town plan: **37**AGX**h**
– ✆ *(020) 7823 1234 – www.jumeirah.com*
87 rm – †£ 216/480 ††£ 216/480, ☕ £ 30 – 6 suites
Rest *Lowndes Bar & Kitchen* – Menu £ 20/40 – Carte £ 29/47
Compact yet friendly, modern corporate hotel within this exclusive residential area. Good levels of personal service offered. Close to the famous shops of Knightsbridge. Informal restaurant with appealing courtyard terrace.

Marcus – Berkeley Hotel
✿✿
Wilton Pl ✉ *SW1X 7RL* ⊖ *Knightsbridge* Town plan: **37**AGX**e**
– ✆ *(020) 7235 1200 – www.marcus-wareing.com – Closed Sunday*
• MODERN • Menu £ 38 (weekday lunch)/85
A reinvention for Marcus Wareing's flagship restaurant. The room is now lighter and less claustrophobic but is still elegant and comfortable. Service remains professional but is a little more engaging. The food is lighter, less elaborate and healthier and flavours are cleaner and more distinct.
➜ Foie gras, mango and granola. Beef fillet with potato, cabbage and short rib. Pineapple pain perdu, coconut and lime.

Pétrus

1 Kinnerton St ✉ SW1X 8EA ⊖ Knightsbridge — Town plan: **37**AGX**v**
– ✆ (020) 7592 1609 – www.gordonramsay.com/petrus
– Closed 25-26 December, 1 January and Sunday
• FRENCH • Menu £ 35/75

Elegant Gordon Ramsay restaurant, opened in 2010, in stylish tones of silver, oyster and – as a nod to the name – claret. Experienced team bring personality to the service. Elaborate French-based cooking uses top quality ingredients.

➜ Scallops with peas, lettuce, lardo di Colonnata and lemon thyme. Mutton cooked over charcoal, smoked aubergine and mint & sheep's yoghurt. Coconut soufflé with pineapple sorbet.

Ametsa with Arzak Instruction – Halkin Hotel

5 Halkin St ✉ SW1X 7DJ ⊖ Hyde Park Corner — Town plan: **38**AHX**b**
– ✆ (020) 7333 1234 – www.comohotels.com/thehalkin
– Closed 24-26 and 31 December, 1 January and lunch Sunday and Monday
• INNOVATIVE • Menu £ 28/145 – Carte £ 53/84

The father and daughter team from the celebrated Arzak restaurant in San Sebastián bring the Basque country to Belgravia. Traditional Basque flavours are presented in a modern way, with much originality and a little playfulness.

➜ Egg with squid noodles. Sea bass with leeks. Chocolate wooden board.

Amaya

Halkin Arcade, 19 Motcomb St ✉ SW1X 8JT — Town plan: **37**AGX**k**
⊖ Knightsbridge – ✆ (020) 7823 1166 – www.amaya.biz
• INDIAN • Menu £ 21/55 – Carte £ 34/64

Order a selection of small dishes from the tawa griddle, tandoor or sigri grill and finish with a curry or biryani. Dishes like lamb chops are aromatic and satisfying and the cooking is skilled and consistent. This busy Indian restaurant is bright, colourful and lively; ask for a table by the open kitchen.

➜ Rock oysters with coconut and ginger moilee sauce. Slow-roasted leg of baby lamb, cumin and garam masala. Blood orange brûlée.

Koffmann's – Berkeley Hotel

Wilton Pl ✉ SW1X 7RL ⊖ Knightsbridge — Town plan: **37**AGX**e**
– ✆ (020) 7235 1010 – www.the-berkeley.co.uk
• FRENCH • Menu £ 22/28 (weekdays) – Carte £ 45/68

Pierre Koffmann, one of London's most fêted chefs, was enticed out of retirement to open this comfortable, well run and spacious restaurant. Expect classic signature dishes and plenty of gutsy flavours true to his Gascon roots.

Zafferano

15 Lowndes St ✉ SW1X 9EY ⊖ Knightsbridge — Town plan: **37**AGX**f**
– ✆ (020) 7235 5800 – www.zafferanorestaurant.co.uk
• ITALIAN • Menu £ 23 (weekday lunch) – Carte £ 35/79
– (booking essential)

The immaculately coiffured regulars continue to support this ever-expanding, long-standing and capably run Italian restaurant. They come for the reassuringly familiar, if rather steeply priced dishes from all parts of Italy.

Pantechnicon

10 Motcomb St ✉ SW1X 8LA ⊖ Knightsbridge. — Town plan: **37**AGX**d**
– ✆ (020) 7730 6074 – www.thepantechnicon.com
– Closed 25 December
• BRITISH MODERN • Carte £ 29/50 – (booking advisable)

Urbane, enthusiastically run pub with a busy ground floor and altogether more formal upstairs dining room. Traditional dishes are given a modern twist; oysters and Scottish steaks are perennials.

LONDON

HYDE PARK AND KNIGHTSBRIDGE

Mandarin Oriental Hyde Park

66 Knightsbridge ✉ SW1X 7LA ⊖ Knightsbridge Town plan: **37**AGX**x**
– ✆ (020) 7235 2000 – www.mandarinoriental.com/london
194 rm – **†**£ 390/870 **††**£ 450/942, ☕ £ 26 – 25 suites
Rest *Dinner by Heston Blumenthal* ✿✿ **Rest *Bar Boulud*** – see restaurant listing
Built in 1889, this classic international hotel, with its striking façade, remains one of London's grandest. The luxurious bedrooms have a charming English country feel; many enjoy views of Hyde Park. Impressive service levels.

Bulgari

171 Knightsbridge ✉ SW7 1DW ⊖ Knightsbridge Town plan: **37**AFX**k**
– ✆ (020) 7151 1010 – www.bulgarihotels.com/london
85 rm – **†**£ 528/1128 **††**£ 528/1128, ☕ £ 24 – 7 suites
Rest *Rivea* – see restaurant listing
Impeccably tailored hotel, opened in 2012, makes stunning use of materials like silver, mahogany, silk and marble. Luxurious bedrooms with sensual curves, sumptuous bathrooms and a great spa – and there is substance behind the style. Down a sweeping staircase to the Alain Ducasse restaurant.

LONDON

Dinner by Heston Blumenthal – Mandarin Oriental Hyde Park Hotel

✿✿

66 Knightsbridge ✉ SW1X 7LA ⊖ Knightsbridge – ✆ (020) 7201 3833 – www.dinnerbyheston.com – Closed 2 days Christmas Town plan: **37**AGX**x**
• BRITISH MODERN • Menu £ 38 (weekday lunch) – Carte £ 63/75
Don't come expecting 'molecular gastronomy' – this is all about respect for, and a wonderful renewal of, British food, with just a little playfulness thrown in. Each one of the meticulously crafted and deceptively simple looking dishes comes with a date relating to its historical provenance.
➜ Scallops with cucumber ketchup, roasted cucumber heart and borage. Spiced pigeon, onion, ale and artichokes. Tipsy cake and spit-roast pineapple.

Rivea Ⓝ – Bulgari Hotel

171 Knightsbridge ✉ SW7 1DW ⊖ Knightsbridge Town plan: **37**AFX**k**
– ✆ (020) 7151 1025 – www.rivealondon.com
• MEDITERRANEAN • Menu £ 35 (lunch) – Carte £ 22/42
Alain Ducasse brings a taste of the Riviera to the Bulgari Hotel. The small plates of French and Italian specialities are bursting with flavour, colour and freshness. The theme is also reflected in the room's bright palette.

Bar Boulud – Mandarin Oriental Hyde Park Hotel

66 Knightsbridge ✉ SW1X 7LA ⊖ Knightsbridge Town plan: **37**AGX**x**
– ✆ (020) 7201 3899 – www.barboulud.com
• FRENCH • Menu £ 19 (lunch and early dinner) – Carte £ 23/53
Daniel Boulud's London outpost is fashionable, fun and frantic. His hometown is Lyon but he built his considerable reputation in New York, so charcuterie, sausages and burgers are the highlights.

The Magazine Ⓝ

Serpentine Sackler Gallery, West Carriage Dr. Town plan: **28**ADV**t**
Kensington Gardens ✉ W2 2AR ⊖ Lancaster Gate – ✆ (020) 7298 7552 – www.magazine-restaurant.co.uk – Closed Sunday dinner, Tuesday dinner and Monday
• MODERN • Carte £ 27/51
Designed by Zaha Hadid, the Serpentine Sackler Gallery comprises a restored 1805 gunpowder store and a modern tensile extension. The Magazine is a bright open space with an eclectic mix of modern European and Japanese cuisines.

XX **Zuma**

5 Raphael St ✉ SW7 1DL ⊖ Knightsbridge Town plan: **37**AFX**m**
– ✆ (020) 7584 1010 – www.zumarestaurant.com – Closed 25 December
• JAPANESE • Carte £ 26/70

Now a global brand but this was the original. The glamorous clientele come for the striking surroundings, bustling atmosphere and easy-to-share food. Go for the more modern dishes and those cooked on the robata grill.

XX **Mr Chow**

151 Knightsbridge ✉ SW1X 7PA ⊖ Knightsbridge Town plan: **37**AFX**e**
– ✆ (020) 7589 7347 – www.mrchow.com – Closed 1 January, 24-26 December, Easter Monday dinner and Monday lunch
• CHINESE • Menu £ 26/50 – Carte £ 39/63

Long-standing Chinese restaurant, opened in 1968. Smart clientele, stylish and comfortable surroundings and prompt service from Italian waiters. Carefully prepared and satisfying food.

X **Chabrot**

9 Knightsbridge Grn ✉ SW1X 7QL Town plan: **37**AFX**v**
⊖ Knightsbridge – ✆ (020) 7225 2238 – www.chabrot.co.uk – Closed 25 December and 1 January
• FRENCH • Carte £ 23/46

A warm, cosy and well-run French bistrot. The kitchen looks to the SW of France and Pays Basque for inspiration; dishes are authentic, hearty and tasty and many of the regulars plan their visit according to the plat du jour.

MAYFAIR

Dorchester

Park Ln. ✉ W1K 1QA ⊖ Hyde Park Corner Town plan: **30**AHV**a**
– ✆ (020) 7629 8888 – www.dorchestercollection.com
250 rm – 🚹£ 355 🚹🚹£ 415, ☕ £ 34 – 50 suites
Rest *Alain Ducasse at The Dorchester* ✿✿✿ **Rest *China Tang*** – see restaurant listing

Luxury hotel on a grand scale offering every possible facility. Striking marbled and pillared promenade provides one of the best backdrops to afternoon tea. Impressive spa and bedrooms quintessentially English in style. Exemplary levels of service.

Claridge's

Brook St ✉ W1K 4HR ⊖ Bond Street Town plan: **30**AHU**c**
– ✆ (020) 7629 8860 – www.claridges.co.uk
203 rm – 🚹£ 480/780 🚹🚹£ 540/900, ☕ £ 32 – 67 suites
Rest *Fera at Claridge's* ✿ – see restaurant listing
Rest *Foyer & Reading Room* – ✆ (020) 7107 8886 – Menu £ 35/45
– (closed Sunday) (booking essential)

Claridge's has a long, illustrious history dating back to 1812 and this iconic and very British hotel has been a favourite of the royal family over generations. Its most striking decorative feature is the art deco. The hotel also moves with the times: its restaurant was re-launched in 2014 as Fera.

Connaught

Carlos Pl. ✉ W1K 2AL ⊖ Bond Street Town plan: **30**AHU**e**
– ✆ (020) 7499 7070 – www.the-connaught.co.uk
121 rm ☕ – 🚹£ 400/840 🚹🚹£ 450/990 – 26 suites
Rest *Hélène Darroze at The Connaught* ✿✿ – see restaurant listing
Rest *Espelette* – ✆ (020) 3147 7100 – Carte £ 45/82

One of London's most famous hotels; restored and renovated but still retaining an elegant British feel. All the luxurious bedrooms come with large marble bathrooms and butler service. There's a choice of two stylish bars and Espelette is an all-day venue for classic French and British dishes.

Four Seasons

Hamilton Pl, Park Ln ✉ W1J 7DR Town plan: **30**AHV**v**
⊖ Hyde Park Corner – ✆ (020) 7499 0888 – www.fourseasons.com/london
193 rm – †£ 384 ††£ 384, ☕ £ 32 – 33 suites
Rest *Amaranto* – see restaurant listing
Reopened in 2011 after a huge refurbishment project and has raised the bar for luxury hotels. Striking lobby sets the scene; sumptuous bedrooms have a rich, contemporary look and boast every conceivable comfort. Great views from the stunning rooftop spa.

InterContinental

1 Hamilton Pl, Park Ln ✉ W1J 7QY Town plan: **30**AHV**k**
⊖ Hyde Park Corner – ✆ (020) 7409 3131 – www.london.intercontinental.com
447 rm – †£ 275/790 ††£ 275/790, ☕ £ 28 – 48 suites
Rest *Theo Randall* – see restaurant listing
Rest *Cookbook Café* – Carte £ 35/53
International hotel whose position facing the park is an impressive feature. Everything leads off from the large, open-plan lobby. English-style bedrooms with hi-tech equipment; luxurious suites. Casual, family-friendly Cookbook Café.

LONDON

London Hilton

22 Park Ln. ✉ W1K 1BE ⊖ Hyde Park Corner Town plan: **30**AHV**e**
– ✆ (020) 7493 8000 – www.hilton.co.uk/londonparklane
453 rm – †£ 322/869 ††£ 322/869, ☕ £ 20 – 56 suites
Rest *Galvin at Windows* ✿ – see restaurant listing
Rest *Podium* – ✆ (020) 7208 4022 – Menu £ 25 – Carte £ 38/65
Rest *Trader Vic's* – ✆ (020) 7208 4113 – Carte £ 39/112 – *(dinner only)*
The bedrooms at this 28 storey hotel, which celebrated 50 years in 2013, now come with a sharper and more contemporary edge. For Polynesian food and a Mai Tai, head to the iconic brand that is Trader Vic's; for casual, all-day dining, try Podium. Extensive banqueting and conference facilities.

Grosvenor House

Park Ln ✉ W1K 7TN ⊖ Marble Arch – ✆ (020) Town plan: **29**AGU**g**
7499 6363 – www.londongrosvenorhouse.co.uk
494 rm – †£ 258/550 ††£ 258/550, ☕ £ 29 – 52 suites
Rest *JW Steakhouse* – ✆ (020) 7399 8460 – Carte £ 30/89
A large, landmark property occupying a commanding position by Hyde Park. Uniform, comfortable but well proportioned bedrooms in classic Marriott styling. Busy banqueting department boasts the largest ballroom in Europe. JW Steakhouse is the place for beer, bourbon and beef.

45 Park Lane

45 Park Ln ✉ W1K 1PN ⊖ Hyde Park Corner Town plan: **30**AHV**r**
– ✆ (020) 7493 4545 – www.45parklane.com
46 rm – †£ 595/834 ††£ 595/834, ☕ £ 21 – 10 suites
Rest *Cut* – see restaurant listing
It was the original site of the Playboy Club and has been a car showroom but now 45 Park Lane has been reborn as The Dorchester's sister hotel. The bedrooms, all with views over Hyde Park, are wonderfully sensual and the marble bathrooms are beautiful.

Westbury

Bond St ✉ W1S 2YF ⊖ Bond Street – ✆ (020) Town plan: **30**AIU**z**
7629 7755 – www.westburymayfair.com
246 rm – †£ 335/599 ††£ 335/599, ☕ £ 26 – 13 suites
Rest *Alyn Williams at The Westbury* ✿ – see restaurant listing
Rest *Tsukiji* – ✆ (020) 8382 5066 – Menu £ 29/46 – Carte £ 27/59 – *(closed Christmas and Sunday) (booking advisable)*
Now as stylish as when it opened in the 1950s. Smart, comfortable bedrooms with terrific art deco inspired suites. Elegant, iconic Polo bar and bright, fresh sushi bar. All the designer brands outside the front door.

Brown's
Albemarle St ✉ *W1S 4BP* ⊖ *Green Park* Town plan: **30**AIV**d**
– ✆ *(020) 7493 6020 – www.roccofortehotels.com*
117 rm – †£ 420/905 ††£ 460/945, ☕ £ 32 – 12 suites
Rest ***Hix Mayfair*** – see restaurant listing
Opened in 1837 by James Brown, Lord Byron's butler. This urbane and very British hotel with an illustrious past offers a swish bar with Terence Donovan prints, bedrooms in neutral hues and a classic English sitting room for afternoon tea.

London Marriott H. Grosvenor Square
84-86 Duke St ✉ *W1K 6JP* ⊖ *Bond Street* Town plan: **30**AHU**s**
– ✆ *(020) 7493 1232 – www.marriottgrosvenorsquare.com*
237 rm – †£ 249/599 ††£ 249/599, ☕ £ 13 – 11 suites
Rest ***Maze Grill*** – see restaurant listing
A well-appointed international hotel that benefits from an excellent location in the heart of Mayfair. Bedrooms are specifically equipped for business travellers. Ask for a Balcony room: they have access to a private roof garden.

London Marriott H. Park Lane
140 Park Ln ✉ *W1K 7AA* ⊖ *Marble Arch* Town plan: **29**AGU**b**
– ✆ *(020) 7493 7000 – www.londonmarriottparklane.co.uk*
157 rm – †£ 480/650 ††£ 480/650, ☕ £ 13 – 9 suites
Rest ***Lanes of London*** – ✆ (020) 7647 5664 – Carte £ 19/40
International hotel located close to Hyde Park and Oxford Street. One of only two hotels on Park Lane with a pool. Smart, generously sized and well-equipped bedrooms. Lanes offers Indian, Lebanese, Vietnamese and British dishes.

Metropolitan
Old Park Ln ✉ *W1K 1LB* ⊖ *Hyde Park Corner* Town plan: **30**AHV**c**
– ✆ *(020) 7447 1000 – www.metropolitan.com/metropolitanlondon*
144 rm – †£ 318/534 ††£ 366/582, ☕ £ 28 – 3 suites
Rest ***Nobu*** – see restaurant listing
Minimalist interior and a voguish reputation have made this hotel and its Met Bar the favoured choice of pop stars and celebrities. Sleek design and fashionably attired staff set it apart.

Athenaeum
116 Piccadilly ✉ *W1J 7BJ* ⊖ *Hyde Park Corner* Town plan: **30**AHV**g**
– ✆ *(020) 7499 3464 – www.athenaeumhotel.com*
164 rm – †£ 225/440 ††£ 265/525, ☕ £ 23 – 28 suites
Rest – Menu £ 20/45 – Carte £ 38/59
Refurbished 1920s building opposite the park; its stylish bedrooms come in cool pastel shades and have floor to ceiling windows. Bright restaurant and a bar offering over 270 different whiskies. The hotel also organises events for kids.

Chesterfield
35 Charles St ✉ *W1J 5EB* ⊖ *Green Park* – ✆ *(020) 7491 2622 – www.chesterfieldmayfair.com* Town plan: **30**AHV**f**
107 rm – †£ 195/390 ††£ 220/540, ☕ £ 15 – 4 suites
Rest ***Butlers*** – Menu £ 24 – Carte £ 36/69 – *(closed lunch Saturday and Sunday)*
An assuredly English feel to this Georgian house. Discreet lobby leads to a clubby bar and wood panelled library. Individually decorated bedrooms, with some antique pieces. Intimate and pretty restaurant.

Alain Ducasse at The Dorchester – Dorchester Hotel
Park Ln ✉ *W1K 1QA* ⊖ *Hyde Park Corner* Town plan: **30**AHV**a**
– ✆ *(020) 7629 8866 – www.alainducasse-dorchester.com – Closed 10 August-2 September, 26-30 December, Saturday lunch, Sunday and Monday*
• FRENCH • Menu £ 55/90
Luxury and extravagance are the hallmarks of Alain Ducasse's London outpost. The dining room is elegant without being staid; food is modern and refined yet satisfying and balanced. Service is formal, thoughtful and well-organised.
→ Sauté of lobster, truffled chicken quenelles and pasta. Fillet of beef Rossini with Périgueux sauce. 'Baba like in Monte-Carlo'.

LONDON

Sketch (The Lecture Room & Library)

9 Conduit St (1st floor) ✉ W1S 2XG Town plan: **30**AIU**h**
⊖ Oxford Circus – ✆ (020) 7659 4500 – www.sketch.uk.com – Closed last 2 weeks August, Saturday lunch, Sunday and Monday
• FRENCH • Menu £ 35/95 – Carte £ 97/131 – *(booking essential)*
Mourad Mazouz and Pierre Gagnaire's 18C funhouse is awash with colour, energy and vim and the luxurious 'Lecture Room & Library' provides the ideal setting for the sophisticated French cooking. Relax and enjoy artfully presented, elaborate dishes that provide many varieties of flavours and textures.
→ Langoustine five ways. Rack of Querçy lamb, tamarind jus and braised fennel. Pierre Gagnaire's 'Grand Dessert'.

Hélène Darroze at The Connaught – Connaught Hotel

Carlos Pl. ✉ W1K 2AL ⊖ Bond Street – ✆ (020) 7107 8880 – www.the-connaught.co.uk – Closed 2 weeks August, Sunday and Monday Town plan: **30**AHU**e**
• FRENCH • Menu £ 30/92 – *(booking essential)*
A discreet mahogany-panelled room is the setting for Hélène Darroze's elegant yet dazzling cooking. It's largely informed by Landes and the SW of France but she's not shy of the occasional Asian or North African flavour. There's a surprise element to the dishes and service is professional and engaging.
→ Oyster 'fine de claire' with oscietra caviar and white beans. XXL scallop, tandoori spices, carrot, citrus and coriander. Baba Armagnac, rhubarb and galangal.

Le Gavroche (Michel Roux Jnr)

43 Upper Brook St ✉ W1K 7QR ⊖ Marble Arch – ✆ (020) 7408 0881 – www.le-gavroche.co.uk – Closed Christmas-January, Saturday lunch, Sunday and bank holidays Town plan: **29**AGU**c**
• FRENCH • Menu £ 55/124 – Carte £ 63/156 – *(booking essential)*
Classical, rich and indulgent French cuisine is the draw at Michel Roux's renowned London institution. The large, smart basement room has a clubby, masculine feel; service is formal and structured but also has charm.
→ Mousseline de homard au champagne et caviar. Râble de lapin et galette au parmesan. Soufflé aux fruits de la passion et glace Ivoire.

Square (Philip Howard)

6-10 Bruton St. ✉ W1J 6PU ⊖ Green Park – ✆ (020) 7495 7100 – www.squarerestaurant.com – Closed 24-26 December and Sunday lunch Town plan: **30**AIU**v**
• FRENCH • Menu £ 33/90
Confident and accomplished kitchen which understands the importance of sound techniques, prime ingredients and clarity of flavour. The room is comfortable and the buoyant atmosphere prevents things becoming too formal. Good cheeseboard and wine list, which is rooted in the Old World.
→ Foie gras with caramelised pineapple, pink grapefruit, honey and mead. Turbot with crushed Jersey Royals, pickled celery, mussels and clam. Brillat-Savarin cheesecake with Yorkshire rhubarb, blood orange and cardamom ice cream.

Fera at Claridge's (N) – Claridge's Hotel

Brook St ✉ W1K 4HR ⊖ Bond Street – ✆ (020) 7107 8888 – www.feraatclaridges.co.uk Town plan: **30**AHU**c**
• BRITISH CREATIVE • Menu £ 85/125 – *(booking advisable)*
Earth-father, forager supreme and gastronomic alchemist Simon Rogan brings his wonderfully natural, unforced style of cooking to the capital. The deftly balanced and cleverly textured dishes deliver multi-dimensional layers of flavours and the grand room has been transformed into a thing of beauty.
→ Prawns from Gairloch, pickled Alexanders, asparagus and shellfish butter. Goosnargh duck, yellow bean purée, leek and hyssop. Iced sorrel, nitro sweet cheese and apple.

XXXX **Alyn Williams at The Westbury** – Westbury Hotel

37 Conduit St ✉ W1S 2YF ⊖ Bond Street Town plan: **30**AIU**z**
– ✆ (020) 7183 6426 – www.alynwilliams.com – Closed first 2 weeks January, last 2 weeks August, Saturday lunch, Sunday and Monday
• MODERN • Menu £ 28 (weekday lunch)/58

Confident, cheery service ensures the atmosphere never strays into terminal seriousness; rosewood panelling and a striking wine display add warmth. The cooking is creative and even playful but however elaborately constructed the dish, the combinations of flavours and textures always work.

➜ Scallops with squid ink, fennel and pumpernickel. Wood pigeon, ramsons, morels and honey shallots. Iced coconut parfait, lime and peanuts.

XXXX **China Tang** – Dorchester Hotel

Park Ln ✉ W1K 1QA ⊖ Hyde Park Corner Town plan: **30**AHV**a**
– ✆ (020) 7629 9988 – www.chinatanglondon.co.uk – Closed 24-25 December
• CHINESE • Menu £ 28 (lunch) – Carte £ 28/79

Sir David Tang's atmospheric, art deco-inspired Chinese restaurant, downstairs at The Dorchester, is always abuzz with activity. Be sure to see the terrific bar, before sharing the traditional Cantonese specialities.

XXX **Greenhouse**

27a Hay's Mews ✉ W1J 5NY Town plan: **30**AHV**m**
⊖ Hyde Park Corner – ✆ (020) 7499 3331 – www.greenhouserestaurant.co.uk – Closed Saturday lunch, Sunday and bank holidays
• INNOVATIVE • Menu £ 35/120 – Carte £ 93/113

Chef Arnaud Bignon's cooking is confident, balanced and innovative and uses the best from Europe's larder; his dishes exude an exhilarating freshness. The breadth and depth of the wine list is astounding. This is a discreet, sleek and contemporary restaurant with well-judged service.

➜ Cornish crab, mint jelly, cauliflower, apple and curry. Lamb, miso, puntarella, mooli and onion. Orange, saffron, date and filo pastry.

XXX **Cut** – 45 Park Lane Hotel

45 Park Ln ✉ W1K 1PN ⊖ Hyde Park Corner Town plan: **30**AHV**r**
– ✆ (020) 7493 4545 – www.45parklane.com
• MEATS AND GRILLS • Menu £ 34 (weekday lunch) – Carte £ 41/129 – *(booking essential)*

The first European venture from Wolfgang Puck, the US-based Austrian celebrity chef, is this very slick, stylish and sexy room where glamorous people come to eat meat. The not-inexpensive steaks are cooked over hardwood and charcoal and finished off in a broiler.

XXX **Hibiscus** (Claude Bosi)

29 Maddox St ✉ W1S 2PA ⊖ Oxford Circus Town plan: **30**AIU**s**
– ✆ (020) 7629 2999 – www.hibiscusrestaurant.co.uk – Closed first week January, last week August, Monday except September to December, Sunday and bank holidays
• INNOVATIVE • Menu £ 35/105

Choose 3, 6 or 8 courses and be prepared for a surprise as the kitchen will choose the dishes. Claude Bosi's cooking is as innovative as ever; the combinations of flavours and textures are well-judged and dishes are underpinned by fine ingredients. The last revamp left the room brighter and lighter.

➜ Cardigan Bay prawn, chestnut mushrooms, smoked butter & Beluski caviar. Cornish sea bream, morels, coffee, tarragon oil & parmesan. Asparagus cream, black olives & lemon.

Prices quoted after the symbol 🚹 refer to the lowest rate for a single room in low season, followed by the highest rate in high season. The same principle applies to the symbol 🚹🚹 for a double room.

LONDON

XXX ✿ **Murano** (Angela Hartnett)

20 Queen St ✉ W1J 5PP ⊖ Green Park – ✆ (020) 7495 1127 – www.muranolondon.com – Closed Christmas and Sunday Town plan: **30**AHV**b**

• ITALIAN • Menu £ 25/95

Angela Hartnett's Italian influenced cooking exhibits an appealing lightness of touch, with assured combinations of flavours, borne out of confidence in the ingredients. This is a stylish, elegant room run by a well-organised, professional and friendly team who put their customers at ease.

➜ Scallop ceviche, spiced avocado purée, ginger and coriander cress. Cumbrian lamb, pea purée, goat's cheese dauphine. Caramelised pear tart, almond crumble and milk ice cream.

XXX ✿ **Galvin at Windows** – London Hilton Hotel

22 Park Ln (28th floor) ✉ W1K 1BE Town plan: **30**AHV**e**

⊖ Hyde Park Corner – ✆ (020) 7208 4021 – www.galvinatwindows.com – Closed Saturday lunch and Sunday dinner

• MODERN • Menu £ 29/68

The cleverly laid out room makes the most of the spectacular views across London from the 28th floor. Relaxed service takes the edge off the somewhat corporate atmosphere. The bold cooking uses superb ingredients and the classically based food comes with a pleasing degree of flair and innovation.

➜ Scallops, sea vegetables, caviar & lemongrass velouté. Rack of lamb with pea purée, spring vegetables, lamb Bolognese & mint jus. Hot lemon & milk chocolate soufflé, rosemary ice cream.

XXX ✿ **Benares** (Atul Kochhar)

12a Berkeley Square House ✉ W1J 6BS Town plan: **30**AIU**q**

⊖ Green Park – ✆ (020) 7629 8886 – www.benaresrestaurant.com – Closed 24-26 December and 1-2 January

• INDIAN • Menu £ 35/82 – Carte £ 44/73

Modern techniques are used to add contemporary touches to the classical base; the inventive Indian food here continues to evolve. The smart first-floor surroundings match the food in their sophistication. Popular and smart 'Chef's Table'.

➜ Chicken tikka pie, wild berry chutney. Rump of lamb, shoulder samosa and Calcutta style chickpeas. Masala chai soufflé, vanilla ice cream.

XXX ✿ **Tamarind**

20 Queen St. ✉ W1J 5PR ⊖ Green Park – ✆ (020) 7629 3561 – www.tamarindrestaurant.com – Closed 25-26 December, 1 January and Saturday lunch Town plan: **30**AHV**h**

• INDIAN • Menu £ 21/68 – Carte £ 35/65

Makes the best use of its basement location through smoked mirrors, gilded columns and a somewhat exclusive feel. The appealing and enjoyable Indian food is mostly traditionally based; kebabs and curries are the specialities, complemented by carefully judged vegetable dishes.

➜ Chickpeas, wheat crisps, yoghurt, blueberries and tamarind chutney. Chicken tikka, fresh tomato sauce with ginger and fenugreek. Tandoori grilled pineapple with rose ice cream.

XXX ✿ **Kai**

65 South Audley St ✉ W1K 2QU Town plan: **30**AHV**n**

⊖ Hyde Park Corner – ✆ (020) 7493 8988 – www.kaimayfair.co.uk – Closed 25-26 December and 1 January

• CHINESE • Carte £ 39/149 – *(booking essential)*

There are a few classics on the menu but Chef Alex Chow's strengths are his modern creations and re-workings of Chinese recipes. His dishes have real depth, use superb produce and are wonderfully balanced. The interior is unashamedly glitzy and the service team anticipate their customers' needs well.

➜ Lightly seared sirloin with soy vinaigrette, shallot oil and coriander. Sea bass with caramelised black vinegar syrup marinade. Durian soufflé, vanilla and salted caramel.

LONDON

XXX **Cecconi's**

5a Burlington Gdns ✉ W1S 3EP ⊖ Green Park Town plan: **30**AIU**d**
– ✆ (020) 7434 1500 – www.cecconis.com
• ITALIAN • Carte £ 40/49 – *(booking essential)*
Branches of this fashionable restaurant are now opening up around the world. Regulars pop in for a bite at the bar; the restaurant prepares the classic dishes with care. Open from breakfast onwards; popular for weekend brunches.

XXX **34**

34 Grosvenor Sq (entrance on South Audley St) Town plan: **30**AHU**b**
✉ W1K 2HD ⊖ Marble Arch – ✆ (020) 3350 3434 – www.34-restaurant.co.uk
– Closed 25-26 December, dinner 24 December and lunch 1 January
• MEATS AND GRILLS • Menu £ 28 (weekday dinner) – Carte £ 32/61
A wonderful mix of art deco style and Edwardian warmth makes it feel like a glamorous brasserie. A parrilla grill used for beef – a mix of Scottish dry-aged, US prime, organic Argentinian and Australian Wagyu – as well as fish and game.

XXX **Bentley's (Grill)**

11-15 Swallow St. ✉ W1B 4DG ⊖ Piccadilly Circus Town plan: **30**AJU**c**
– ✆ (020) 7734 4756 – www.bentleys.org – Closed 25 December and 1 January
• FISH AND SEAFOOD • Menu £ 29 (dinner) – Carte £ 34/60
Entrance into striking bar; panelled staircase to richly decorated restaurant. Carefully sourced seafood or meat dishes enhanced by clean, crisp cooking. Unruffled service.

XXX **Theo Randall** – Intercontinental Hotel

1 Hamilton Pl, Park Ln ✉ W1J 7QY Town plan: **30**AHV**k**
⊖ Hyde Park Corner – ✆ (020) 7318 8747 – www.theorandall.com
– Closed Christmas, Easter, Saturday lunch, Sunday dinner and bank holidays
• ITALIAN • Menu £ 27/33 – Carte £ 46/72
Expect simple, flavoursome and seasonal Italian dishes from the former head chef of the River Café. The pleasingly rustic nature of the food is somewhat at odds with the formal service and the corporate feel of the dining room.

XXX **Scott's**

20 Mount St ✉ W1K 2HE ⊖ Bond Street Town plan: **30**AHU**d**
– ✆ (020) 7495 7309 – www.scotts-restaurant.com – Closed 25-26 December
• FISH AND SEAFOOD • Carte £ 39/79
Stylish yet traditional and one of London's most fashionable addresses, so getting a table can be tricky. Oak panelling is juxtaposed with vibrant artwork from young British artists. Enticing choice of top quality fish and shellfish.

XXX **Corrigan's Mayfair**

28 Upper Grosvenor St. ✉ W1K 7EH Town plan: **29**AGU**a**
⊖ Marble Arch – ✆ (020) 7499 9943 – www.corrigansmayfair.com
– Closed 18-27 August, 25-30 December, Saturday lunch and bank holidays
• BRITISH MODERN • Menu £ 29 (lunch and early dinner) – Carte £ 45/71
Richard Corrigan's flagship celebrates British and Irish cooking, with game a speciality. The room is comfortable, clubby and quite glamorous and feels as though it has been around for years.

XXX **Sartoria**

20 Savile Row ✉ W1S 3PR ⊖ Green Park Town plan: **30**AIU**b**
– ✆ (020) 7534 7000 – www.sartoria-restaurant.co.uk – Closed 25 December, Saturday lunch, Sunday and bank holidays
• ITALIAN • Menu £ 25 – Carte £ 33/55
In the street renowned for English tailoring, a coolly sophisticated and stylish restaurant to suit those looking for classic Italian cooking with some modern touches thrown in. It also comes with confident service.

LONDON

XXX **Hix Mayfair** – Brown's Hotel

Albemarle St ✉ W1S 4BP ⊖ Green Park – ✆ (020) 7518 4004 – www.roccofortecollection.com Town plan: **30**AIV**d**

• BRITISH TRADITIONAL • Menu £ 33 – Carte £ 35/69

This wood-panelled dining room is lightened with the work of current British artists. Mark Hix's well-sourced menu of British classics will appeal to the hunter-gatherer in every man.

XXX **Amaranto** – Four Seasons Hotel

Hamilton Pl, Park Ln ✉ W1J 7DR ⊖ Hyde Park Corner – ✆ (020) 7499 0888 – www.fourseasons.com/london/dining Town plan: **30**AHV**v**

• ITALIAN • Menu £ 26 (weekday lunch) – Carte £ 30/72

It's all about flexibility as the Italian influenced menu is served in the stylish bar or the comfortable lounge, on the great terrace or in the restaurant decorated in the vivid colours of the amaranth plant.

XX ✿ **Wild Honey**

12 St George St. ✉ W1S 2FB ⊖ Oxford Circus – ✆ (020) 7758 9160 – www.wildhoneyrestaurant.co.uk – Closed 25-26 December and 1 January Town plan: **30**AIU**w**

• MODERN • Menu £ 29/75 (weekdays) – Carte £ 46/57

Skilled kitchen uses seasonal ingredients at their peak to create dishes full of flavour and free from ostentation. Attractive and comfortable oak-panelled room. Personable and unobtrusive service adds to the relaxed feel.

→ Scottish crab, guacamole and green mango. Rose veal with root vegetables, gnocchi and black truffles. Wild honey ice cream and honeycomb.

XX ✿ **Brasserie Chavot**

41 Conduit St ✉ W1S 2YQ ⊖ Bond Street – ✆ (020) 7183 6425 – www.brasseriechavot.com Town plan: **30**AIU**z**

• FRENCH • Carte £ 34/56

Mosaic flooring, smoked mirrors, red leather seats and sparkling chandeliers add style; a satisfied buzz and great service make it fun. Eric Chavot's ability is obvious in his hearteningly rustic, refreshingly unfussy and hugely enjoyable French classics.

→ Deep-fried soft shell crab. Filet de canette à l'orange. Ile flottante.

XX ✿ **Pollen Street Social** (Jason Atherton)

8-10 Pollen St ✉ W1S 1NQ ⊖ Oxford Circus – ✆ (020) 7290 7600 – www.pollenstreetsocial.com – Closed Sunday and bank holidays Town plan: **30**AIU**c**

• INNOVATIVE • Menu £ 30 (lunch) – Carte £ 52/69 – *(booking essential)*

Jason Atherton's cooking marries innovation and imagination with skilful technique and an innate understanding of good ingredients. Dishes are elaborately constructed but there are never too many flavours. The room is smoothly run but not overly formal. Try their terrific version of a Negroni.

→ Steak tartare, smoked beetroot, wild leaves and berry pearls. Pork belly and cheek with black pudding, Jersey Royals and pink apple purée. Chocolate marquise, praline, milk mousse and honey ice cream.

XX ✿ **Gymkhana** (N)

42 Albemarle St ✉ W1S 4JH ⊖ Green Park – ✆ (020) 3011 5900 – www.gymkhanalondon.com – Closed 22-28 December, 1-4 January and Sunday Town plan: **30**AIV**a**

• INDIAN • Menu £ 25 (lunch and early dinner)/65 – Carte £ 28/61 – *(booking essential)*

If you enjoyed Trishna then you'll love Karam Sethi's Gymkhana – that's if you can get a table. Inspired by Colonial India's gymkhana clubs, the interior is full of wonderful detail and plenty of wry touches; ask to sit downstairs. The North Indian dishes have a wonderful richness and depth of flavour.

→ Lasooni wild tiger prawns, red pepper chutney. Kid goat methi keema, salli and pao. Saffron and pistachio kulfi falooda.

XX **Hakkasan Mayfair**

17 Bruton St ✉ W1J 6QB ⊖ Green Park – ☎ (020) 7907 1888 – www.hakkasan.com – Closed 25 December Town plan: **30**AIU**l**

• CHINESE • Menu £ 35/130 – Carte £ 32/72 **s** – *(booking essential)*

Less a copy, more a sister to the original; a sister who's just as fun but lives in a nicer part of town. This one has a funky, more casual ground floor to go with the downstairs dining room. You can expect the same extensive choice of top quality, modern Cantonese cuisine; dim sum is a highlight.

→ Crispy duck salad with pomelo, pine nut and shallot. Roasted silver cod with champagne and honey. Apple Tatin.

XX **Umu**

14-16 Bruton Pl. ✉ W1J 6LX ⊖ Bond Street – ☎ (020) 7499 8881 – www.umurestaurant.com – Closed Christmas, New Year, Saturday lunch, Sunday and bank holidays Town plan: **30**AIU**k**

• JAPANESE • Menu £ 25/115 – Carte £ 56/124

Stylish, discreet interior using natural materials, with central sushi bar. Extensive choice of Japanese dishes; choose one of the seasonal kaiseki menus for the full experience. Over 160 different labels of sake.

→ Sashimi selection. Wild lobster with shichimi pepper. Japanese tiramisu with matcha green tea.

XX **Maze**

10-13 Grosvenor Sq ✉ W1K 6JP ⊖ Bond Street – ☎ (020) 7107 0000 – www.gordonramsay.com/maze Town plan: **30**AHU**z**

• MODERN • Menu £ 30 (lunch) – Carte £ 32/44

Choose a variety of small but expertly formed dishes at this sleek and stylish David Rockwell designed restaurant from the Gordon Ramsay stable. The cooking is contemporary and nicely balanced; four dishes per person should suffice.

→ Beef fillet tataki, wakame seaweed and pickled onion. Pigeon breast with consommé, wild garlic and pâté en croûte. Lemon meringue pie, blackberry sorbet.

XX **Hawksmoor**

5a Air St ✉ W1B 4EA ⊖ Piccadilly Circus – ☎ (020) 7406 3980 – www.thehawksmoor.com – Closed 24-26 December Town plan: **30**AIU**t**

• MEATS AND GRILLS • Menu £ 23 (lunch and early dinner) – Carte £ 35/74 – *(booking advisable)*

The best of the Hawksmoors is large, boisterous and has an appealing art deco feel. Expect top quality, 35-day aged Longhorn beef but also great seafood, much of which is charcoal grilled. The delightful staff are well organised.

XX **Momo**

25 Heddon St. ✉ W1B 4BH ⊖ Oxford Circus – ☎ (020) 7434 4040 – www.momoresto.com – Closed 24-25 December and 1 January Town plan: **30**AIU**n**

• NORTH-AFRICAN • Menu £ 20/52 – Carte £ 31/48

Lanterns, rugs, trinkets and music contribute to the authentic Moroccan atmosphere; come in a group to better appreciate it. The more traditional dishes are the kitchen's strength.

XX **Roka** Ⓝ

30 North Audley St ✉ W1K 6ZF ⊖ Bond Street – ☎ (020) 7305 5644 – www.rokarestaurant.com Town plan: **29**AGU**k**

• JAPANESE • Carte £ 30/89

London's third Roka ventures into the rarefied surroundings of Mayfair and the restaurant's seductive looks are a good fit. All the favourites from their modern Japanese repertoire are here, with the robata grill taking centre stage.

XX **Nobu Berkeley St**

15 Berkeley St. ✉ W1J 8DY ⊖ Green Park – ☎ (020) 7290 9222 – www.noburestaurants.com – Closed 25 December, 1 January and Sunday lunch Town plan: **30**AIV**b**

• JAPANESE • Menu £ 35/90 – Carte £ 28/93 – *(booking essential)*

This branch of the glamorous chain is more of a party animal than its elder sibling at The Metropolitan. Start with cocktails then head upstairs for Japanese food with South American influences; try dishes from the wood-fired oven.

LONDON

XX **Coya**

118 Piccadilly ✉ W1J 7NW ⊖ Hyde Park Corner Town plan: **30**AHV**d**
– ✆ (020) 7042 7118 – www.coyarestaurant.com – Closed 24-26 December and 1 January
• PERUVIAN • Menu £ 27 (lunch) – Carte £ 32/94 – *(booking advisable)*
From the people behind Zuma and Roka comes this lively, loud and enthusiastically run basement restaurant that celebrates all things Peruvian. Try their ceviche and their skewers, as well as their Pisco Sours in the fun bar.

XX **La Petite Maison**

54 Brooks Mews ✉ W1K 4EG ⊖ Bond Street Town plan: **30**AHU**m**
– ✆ (020) 7495 4774 – www.lpmlondon.co.uk – Closed Christmas-New Year
• FRENCH • Carte £ 31/62 **s** – *(booking essential)*
A little piece of southern France and Ligurian Italy in Mayfair. The slickly run sister to the Nice original has a buzzy, glamorous feel, with prices to match. Just reading the menus of Mediterranean dishes will improve your tan.

XX **Keeper's House** Ⓝ

Royal Academy of Arts, Burlington House, Piccadilly Town plan: **30**AIV**x**
✉ W1J 0BD ⊖ Green Park – ✆ (020) 7300 5881 – www.keepershouse.org.uk – Closed 25-26 December and Sunday
• BRITISH MODERN • Carte £ 35/53 – *(dinner only)*
Built in 1860 and fully restored, this house is part of the Royal Academy. Two intimate dining rooms are lined with green baize and hung with architectural casts. The emphasis is on seasonality, freshness and contrasts in textures.

XX **Sketch (The Gallery)**

9 Conduit St ✉ W1S 2XG ⊖ Oxford Circus Town plan: **30**AIU**h**
– ✆ (020) 7659 4500 – www.sketch.uk.com – Closed 25 December
• MODERN • Carte £ 34/74 – *(dinner only) (booking essential)*
The striking 'Gallery' has a new look from India Mahdavi and artwork from David Shrigley. At dinner the room transmogrifies from art gallery to fashionable restaurant, with a menu that mixes the classic, the modern and the esoteric.

XX **Nobu** – Metropolitan Hotel

19 Old Park Ln ✉ W1Y 1LB ⊖ Hyde Park Corner Town plan: **30**AHV**c**
– ✆ (020) 7447 4747 – www.noburestaurants.com
• JAPANESE • Menu £ 45 (lunch) – Carte £ 29/71 – *(booking essential)*
Nobu restaurants are now all over the world but this was Europe's first and opened in 1997. It retains a certain exclusivity and is buzzy and fun. The menu is an innovative blend of Japanese cuisine with South American influences.

XX **Maze Grill** – London Marriott Hotel Grosvenor Square

10-13 Grosvenor Sq ✉ W1K 6JP ⊖ Bond Street Town plan: **30**AHU**s**
– ✆ (020) 7495 2211 – www.gordonramsay.com/mazegrill
• MEATS AND GRILLS • Carte £ 27/82
An addendum to Maze, with a menu specialising in steaks, from Hereford grass-fed to Wagyu 9th grade; all appealingly served on wooden boards. Individually priced side dishes and sauces can push the bill up.

XX **Goodman**

26 Maddox St ✉ W1S 1QH ⊖ Oxford Circus Town plan: **30**AIU**u**
– ✆ (020) 7499 3776 – www.goodmanrestaurants.com – Closed Sunday and bank holidays
• MEATS AND GRILLS • Carte £ 27/73 – *(booking essential)*
A worthy attempt at recreating a New York steakhouse; all leather and wood and macho swagger. Beef is dry or wet aged in-house and comes with a choice of four sauces; rib-eye the speciality.

XX **Alloro**

19-20 Dover St ✉ W1S 4LU ⊖ Green Park Town plan: **30**AIV**r**
– ✆ (020) 7495 4768 – www.atozrestaurants.com/alloro – Closed 25 December, Saturday lunch and Sunday
• ITALIAN • Menu £ 36 (weekday lunch) – Carte £ 44/61 – *(booking essential)*
Confidently run and smartly dressed Italian with an appealing menu of easy-to-eat dishes; breads and pasta are made in-house. Great atmosphere, especially at busy lunchtimes. Boisterous adjacent baretto.

XX **Hush**

8 Lancashire Ct., Brook St. ✉ W1S 1EY Town plan: **30**AHU**v**
⊖ Bond Street – ✆ (020) 7659 1500 – www.hush.co.uk – Closed 25 December and 1 January
• MODERN • Carte £ 21/28 – *(booking essential)*
Appealing and all-purpose European brasserie-style menu served in a busy room with smart destination bar upstairs and plenty of private dining. Tucked away in a charming courtyard, with a pleasant summer terrace.

XX **Mews of Mayfair**

10-11 Lancashire Ct, Brook St ✉ W1S 1EY Town plan: **30**AHU**a**
– (1st floor) ⊖ Bond Street – ✆ (020) 7518 9388 – www.mewsofmayfair.com – Closed 25 December
• MODERN • Carte £ 21/68
This pretty restaurant, bright in summer and warm in winter, is on the first floor of a mews house, once used as storage rooms for Savile Row. Seasonal menus offer something for everyone.

XX **Sumosan**

26 Albemarle St. ✉ W1S 4HY ⊖ Green Park Town plan: **30**AIU**e**
– ✆ (020) 7495 5999 – www.sumosan.com – Closed lunch Saturday-Sunday and bank holidays
• JAPANESE • Menu £ 25 (weekday lunch) – Carte £ 19/104
Its modern Japanese food and stylish surroundings have been attracting a glamorous crowd for over a decade. The produce is of unimpeachable quality, there's plenty of choice and the kitchen knows how to make a dish look good.

XX **Veeraswamy**

Victory House, 99 Regent St ✉ W1B 4RS – (entrance on Swallow St.) ⊖ Piccadilly Circus – ✆ (020) 7734 1401 – www.realindianfood.com Town plan: **30**AIU**t**
• INDIAN • Menu £ 28 (weekday lunch) – Carte £ 34/64
May have opened back in 1926 but this Indian restaurant feels fresh and is awash with vibrant colours and always full of bustle. Skilled kitchen cleverly mixes the traditional with more contemporary creations.

XX **Kiku**

17 Half Moon St. ✉ W1J 7BE ⊖ Green Park Town plan: **30**AIV**g**
– ✆ (020) 7499 4208 – www.kikurestaurant.co.uk – Closed 25-27 December, 1 January, Sunday and lunch on bank holidays
• JAPANESE • Menu £ 22 (weekday lunch) – Carte £ 23/87
For over 35 years this earnestly run, authentically styled, family owned restaurant has been providing every style of Japanese cuisine to its homesick Japanese customers, from shabu shabu to sukiyaki, yakitori to teriyaki.

XX **Cafe at Sotheby's**

34-35 New Bond St. ✉ W1A 2AA ⊖ Bond Street Town plan: **30**AIU**y**
– ✆ (020) 7293 5077 – www.sothebys.com/cafe – Closed 3 weeks August, Christmas and New Year, Saturday, Sunday and bank holidays
• MODERN • Carte £ 32/42 **s** – *(lunch only) (booking essential)*
Occupying a cosy space just off the foyer of the famous auction house. The appealing lunch menu changes weekly; the lobster sandwich is a perennial favourite. Service is discreet.

LONDON

LONDON

Bentley's (Oyster Bar)

11-15 Swallow St ✉ W1B 4DG ⊖ Piccadilly Circus Town plan: **30**AJU**c**
– ✆ (020) 7734 4756 – www.bentleys.org – Closed 25 December and 1 December
• FISH AND SEAFOOD • Menu £ 29 (early dinner) – Carte £ 30/59
Sit at the counter to watch white-jacketed staff open oysters by the bucket load. Interesting seafood menus feature tasty fish pies; lots of daily specials on blackboard.

Le Boudin Blanc

5 Trebeck St ✉ W1J 7LT ⊖ Green Park Town plan: **30**AHV**q**
– ✆ (020) 7499 3292 – www.boudinblanc.co.uk – Closed Christmas
• FRENCH • Menu £ 15 – Carte £ 27/53
Appealing, lively French bistro in Shepherd Market, spread over two floors. Satisfying French classics and country cooking is the draw, along with authentic Gallic service. Good value lunch menu.

Little Social

5 Pollen St ✉ W1S 1NE ⊖ Oxford Circus Town plan: **30**AIU**r**
– ✆ (020) 7870 3730 – www.littlesocial.co.uk – Closed Sunday and bank holidays
• FRENCH • Menu £ 21 (lunch) – Carte £ 29/58 – *(booking essential)*
Jason Atherton's lively French bistro, opposite his Pollen Street Social restaurant, has a clubby feel and an appealing, deliberately worn look. Service is breezy and capable and the food is mostly classic with the odd modern twist.

Peyote (N)

13 Cork St ✉ W1S 3NS ⊖ Green Park – ✆ (020) 7409 1300 – www.peyoterestaurant.com – Closed Saturday lunch and Sunday Town plan: **30**AIU**m**
• MEXICAN • Carte £ 26/58 – *(booking essential)*
From the people behind Zuma and Roka comes a 'refined interpretation of Mexican cuisine' at this fun, glamorous spot. There's an exhilarating freshness to the well-judged dishes; don't miss the great guacamole or the cactus salad.

28°-50° Mayfair (N)

17-19 Maddox St ✉ W1S 2QH ⊖ Oxford Circus Town plan: **30**AIU**f**
– ✆ (020) 7495 1505 – www.2850.co.uk – Closed 25 December, 1 January and Sunday
• MODERN • Menu £ 19 (lunch) – Carte £ 26/44
The group's third wine-bar-restaurant is possibly their best and, as this is Mayfair, almost certainly their most profitable. Modern, unfussy dishes provide great accompaniment to the thoughtfully put-together wine list.

Great British

14 North Audley St ✉ W1K 6WE ⊖ Marble Arch Town plan: **29**AGU**e**
– ✆ (020) 7741 2233 – www.eatbrit.com – Closed 25 December, 1 January and Sunday dinner
• BRITISH TRADITIONAL • Menu £ 17 (dinner) – Carte £ 24/40
As the name suggests, it waves the Union Flag in this most British of London districts. Sausages come with bubble and squeak, fish and chips with curry sauce, and apple crumble with 'proper' custard. They do a great breakfast too.

Burger & Lobster

29 Clarges St ✉ W1J 7EF ⊖ Green Park. Town plan: **30**AIV**v**
– ✆ (020) 7409 1699 – www.burgerandlobster.com – Closed Sunday dinner and bank holidays
• MEATS AND GRILLS • Menu £ 20 – *(bookings not accepted)*
Choose a burger, a lobster or a lobster roll, with chips, salad and sauces, and mousse for dessert – an ingeniously simple idea. The lobsters are Canadian and the burgers 10oz. It's a well organised bunfight in an old pub.

Only Running Footman

5 Charles St ✉ W1J 5DF ⊖ Green Park. Town plan: **30**AHV**x**
– ✆ (020) 7499 2988 – www.therunningfootmanmayfair.com
• BRITISH TRADITIONAL • Menu £ 35 – Carte £ 20/49
The busy ground floor bar with its appealing menu of pub classics doesn't take bookings. By contrast, upstairs is formal and its menu more European and ambitious but the simpler dishes are still the best.

Regent's Park and Marylebone

The Landmark London

222 Marylebone Rd ✉ NW1 6JQ ⊖ Edgware Road Town plan: **29**AFT**a**
– ✆ (020) 7631 8000 – www.landmarklondon.co.uk
300 rm – †£ 252/780 ††£ 252/780, ☕ £ 29 – 9 suites
Rest *Winter Garden* – see restaurant listing
Imposing Victorian Gothic building with a vast glass-enclosed atrium, overlooked by many of the modern, well-equipped bedrooms. Choice of relaxed wood panelled cellar bar or more sophisticated Mirror bar.

The London Edition

10 Berners Street ✉ W1T 3NP Town plan: **31**AJT**b**
⊖ Tottenham Court Road – ✆ (020) 7781 0000
– www.edition-hotels.marriott.com/london
173 rm – †£ 315/395 ††£ 315/395, ☕ £ 20 – 9 suites
Rest *Berners Tavern* – see restaurant listing
Berners, a classic Edwardian hotel, strikingly reborn through a partnership between Ian Schrager and Marriott – the former's influence most apparent in the stylish lobby and bar. Slick, understated rooms; the best ones have balconies.

LONDON

Langham

1c Portland Pl., Regent St. ✉ W1B 1JA Town plan: **30**AIT**n**
⊖ Oxford Circus – ✆ (020) 7636 1000 – www.langhamhotels.com
380 rm – †£ 288/780 ††£ 288/780, ☕ £ 30 – 25 suites
Rest *Roux at The Landau* – see restaurant listing
Was one of Europe's first purpose-built grand hotels when it opened in 1865. Now back to its best, with its famous Palm Court for afternoon tea, a stylish Artesian bar and bedrooms that are not without personality and elegance.

Hyatt Regency London-The Churchill

rm, rm,
30 Portman Sq ✉ W1H 7BH ⊖ Marble Arch Town plan: **29**AGT**x**
– ✆ (020) 7486 5800 – www.london.churchill.hyatt.com
434 rm – †£ 240/600 ††£ 240/600, ☕ £ 28 – 47 suites
Rest *The Montagu* – ✆ (020) 7299 2037 – Menu £ 25 (lunch)/45
– Carte £ 26/58
Smart well-located property whose best bedrooms overlook the attractive square opposite. Elegant marbled lobby with plenty of staff. Well-appointed and refurbished bedrooms have the international traveller in mind. A British menu and afternoon tea served in The Montagu.

Chiltern Firehouse

1 Chiltern St ✉ W1U 7PA ⊖ Baker Street Town plan: **29**AGT**a**
– ✆ (020) 7073 7676 – www.chilternfirehouse.com
26 rm – †£ 480/900 ††£ 540/1020, ☕ £ 20 – 6 suites – ††£ 1500/4140
Rest *Chiltern Firehouse* – see restaurant listing
From Chateau Marmont in LA to The Mercer in New York, André Balazs' hotels are effortlessly cool. For his London entrance, he has sympathetically restored and extended a gothic Victorian fire station. The style comes with an easy elegance; it's an oasis of calm and hardly feels like a hotel at all.

Charlotte Street

15 Charlotte St ✉ W1T 1RJ ⊖ Goodge Street Town plan: **31**AJT**e**
– ✆ (020) 7806 2000 – www.charlottestreethotel.co.uk
52 rm – †£ 264/330 ††£ 360/492, ☕ £ 20 – 4 suites
Rest *Oscar* – ✆ (020) 7907 4005 – Menu £ 23/25 – Carte £ 31/60
Stylish interior designed with a charming, understated English feel. Impeccably kept and individually decorated bedrooms. Popular in-house screening room. Colourful restaurant whose terrace spills onto Charlotte Street; grilled meats a highlight.

Sanderson

50 Berners St ✉ W1T 3NG ⊖ Oxford Circus Town plan: **31**AJT**c**
– ✆ *(020) 7300 1400 – www.morganshotelgroup.com*
150 rm – †£ 234/538 ††£ 234/538, ☐ £ 18
Rest *Suka* – Carte £ 26/31
Designed by Philippe Starck and still attracting a suitably fashionable crowd. The Purple Bar is dark and moody; the Long Bar is bright and stylish. Pure white bedrooms with idiosyncratic design touches such as a framed picture... on the ceiling.

Montcalm

34-40 Great Cumberland Pl. ✉ W1H 7TW Town plan: **29**AGU**m**
⊖ Marble Arch – ✆ (020) 7402 4288 – www.montcalm.co.uk
126 rm – †£ 360 ††£ 360/720, ☐ £ 20 – 17 suites
Rest *Crescent* – ✆(020) 7958 3241 – Menu £ 20 – *(lunch only and Sunday dinner)*
Named after an 18C French general, the Montcalm forms part of a crescent of townhouses with a Georgian façade. A top-to-toe refurbishment has created smart, contemporary bedrooms in lively colours. Seasonal British dishes served in Crescent restaurant.

LONDON

Durrants

rest,

26-32 George St ✉ W1H 5BJ ⊖ Bond Street Town plan: **29**AGT**e**
– ✆ *(020) 7935 8131 – www.durrantshotel.co.uk*
92 rm – †£ 195 ††£ 250/350, ☐ £ 20 – 4 suites
Rest – ✆(020) 7935 8131 – Menu £ 20 (weekdays) – Carte £ 35/54
Traditional, privately owned hotel with friendly, long-standing staff. Bedrooms are now brighter in style but still retain a certain English character. Clubby dining room for mix of British classics and lighter, European dishes.

Dorset Square

39-40 Dorset Sq ✉ NW1 6QN ⊖ Marylebone Town plan: **17**QZD**s**
– ✆ *(020) 7723 7874 – www.dorsetsquarehotel.co.uk*
38 rm – †£ 198 ††£ 252, ☐ £ 15
Rest *Potting Shed* – Menu £ 17 (weekdays) – Carte £ 25/45
Having reacquired this Regency townhouse, Firmdale refurbished it fully before reopening it in 2012. It has a contemporary yet intimate feel and visiting MCC members will appreciate the cricketing theme, which even extends to the cocktails in their sweet little basement brasserie.

Marble Arch by Montcalm without rest

31 Great Cumberland Pl. ✉ W1H 7TA Town plan: **29**AGU**s**
⊖ Marble Arch – ✆ (020) 7258 0777 – www.themarblearch.co.uk
42 rm – †£ 173/204 ††£ 204/312, ☐ £ 20
Bedrooms at this 5-storey Georgian townhouse come with the same high standards of stylish, contemporary design as its parent hotel opposite, the Montcalm, but are just a little more compact.

Mandeville

rm,

Mandeville Pl ✉ W1U 2BE ⊖ Bond Street Town plan: **30**AHT**x**
– ✆ *(020) 7935 5599 – www.mandeville.co.uk*
142 rm ☐ – †£ 227/583 ††£ 249/608 – 2 suites
Rest *Reform Social & Grill* – Carte £ 25/55
Usefully located hotel with marbled reception leading into a very colourful and comfortable bar. Stylish rooms have flatscreen TVs and make good use of the space available. Modern British cuisine served in bright restaurant.

No. Ten Manchester Street

rm,

10 Manchester St ✉ W1U 4DG ⊖ Baker Street Town plan: **29**AGT**v**
– ✆ *(020) 7317 5900 – www.tenmanchesterstreethotel.com*
44 rm – †£ 195 ††£ 225, ☐ £ 20 – 9 suites
Rest – Menu £ 25/40 – Carte £ 35/67
Converted Edwardian house in an appealing, central location. Discreet entrance leads into stylish little lounge; semi-enclosed cigar bar also a feature. Neat and well-kept bedrooms.

Sumner without rest

54 Upper Berkeley St ✉ W1H 7QR ⊖ Marble Arch Town plan: **29**AFU**k**
– ✆ (020) 7723 2244 – www.thesumner.com
19 rm – 🛉£ 160/300 🛉🛉£ 160/300
Two Georgian terrace houses in central location. Comfy, stylish sitting room; basement breakfast room. Largest bedrooms, 101 and 201, benefit from having full-length windows.

Hart House without rest

51 Gloucester Pl ✉ W1U 8JF ⊖ Marble Arch Town plan: **29**AGT**d**
– ✆ (020) 7935 2288 – www.harthouse.co.uk
15 rm – 🛉£ 110/145 🛉🛉£ 150/190
Within an attractive Georgian terrace and run by the same family for over 35 years. Warm and welcoming service; well-kept, competitively priced bedrooms over three floors.

Locanda Locatelli

8 Seymour St. ✉ W1H 7JZ ⊖ Marble Arch Town plan: **29**AGU**r**
– ✆ (020) 7935 9088 – www.locandalocatelli.com – Closed 25-26 December and 1 January
• ITALIAN • Carte £ 35/63
Giorgio Locatelli's Italian restaurant may be into its second decade but still looks as dapper as ever. The service is smooth and the room was designed with conviviality in mind. The hugely appealing menu covers all regions; unfussy presentation and superb ingredients allow natural flavours to shine.
→ Ox tongue with green sauce. Fillet of sea bass with artichoke purée, tomato crust and vernaccia wine sauce. Chocolate and Gianduiotto liqueur fondant with milk ice cream.

Roux at The Landau – Langham Hotel

1c Portland Pl., Regent St. ✉ W1B 1JA Town plan: **30**AIT**n**
⊖ Oxford Circus – ✆ (020) 7636 1000 – www.langhamhotels.com
– Closed Saturday lunch and Sunday
• FRENCH • Menu £ 35 – Carte £ 43/95
Grand, oval-shaped hotel restaurant run under the aegis of the Roux organisation. Classical, French-influenced cooking is the order of the day, but a lighter style of cuisine using the occasional twist is also emerging.

Latium

21 Berners St. ✉ W1T 3LP ⊖ Oxford Circus Town plan: **31**AJT**n**
– ✆ (020) 7323 9123 – www.latiumrestaurant.com – Closed 25-26 December, 1 January, lunch Saturday- Sunday and bank holidays
• ITALIAN • Menu £ 23 (weekdays)/36
Bright and contemporary surroundings but with warm and welcoming service. Owner-chef from Lazio but dishes come from across Italy, often using British produce. Ravioli is the house speciality and the fassone beef is always good.

Orrery

55 Marylebone High St ✉ W1U 5RB Town plan: **18**RZD**a**
⊖ Regent's Park – ✆ (020) 7616 8000 – www.orrery-restaurant.co.uk
• MODERN • Menu £ 25 (weekday lunch)/65 – *(booking essential)*
These are actually converted stables from the 19C but, such is the elegance and style of the building, you'd never know. Featured is elaborate, modern European cooking; dishes are strong on presentation and come with the occasional twist.

Texture (Agnar Sverrisson)

34 Portman St ✉ W1H 7BY ⊖ Marble Arch Town plan: **29**AGU**p**
– ✆ (020) 7224 0028 – www.texture-restaurant.co.uk – Closed 5-18 August, 1 week Easter, Christmas, New Year, Sunday and Monday
• INNOVATIVE • Menu £ 25/107 – Carte £ 53/79
Technically skilled but light and invigorating cooking from Icelandic chef-owner, who uses ingredients from home. Bright restaurant with high ceiling and popular adjoining champagne bar. Pleasant service from keen staff, ready with a smile.
→ Chargrilled pigeon, sweetcorn, bacon popcorn and red wine essence. Lightly salted cod, smoked quinoa, sorrel and cauliflower. Skyr with Gariguette strawberries and ice cream.

LONDON

L'Autre Pied

5-7 Blandford St. ✉ W1U 3DB ⊖ Bond Street Town plan: **30**AHT**k**
– ✆ (020) 7486 9696 – www.lautrepied.co.uk – Closed 4 days Christmas, 1 January and Sunday dinner
• MODERN • Menu £ 23/70 – Carte £ 43/59
Chef Andy McFadden's dishes are visual and easy to eat and provide pleasing contrasts in textures; venison dishes are a particular speciality. This sibling of Pied à Terre has a more relaxed, neighbourhood atmosphere; ask for a table by the window to better enjoy the local 'village' feel.
→ Ceviche of scallops with crab and horseradish milk. Hogget, red pepper ketchup and violet artichokes. Valrhona cremeux, pistachio and tonka bean ice cream.

Berners Tavern – The London Edition Hotel

10 Berners St ✉ WIT 3NP Town plan: **31**AJT**b**
⊖ Tottenham Court Road – ✆ (020) 7908 7979 – www.bernerstavern.com
• BRITISH MODERN • Carte £ 28/61
What was once a hotel ballroom is now a very glamorous restaurant, with every inch of wall filled with gilt-framed pictures. Jason Atherton has put together an appealing, accessible menu and the cooking is satisfying and assured.

LONDON

Royal China Club

40-42 Baker St ✉ W1U 7AJ ⊖ Baker Street Town plan: **29**AGT**c**
– ✆ (020) 7486 3898 – www.royalchinagroup.co.uk – Closed 25-27 December
• CHINESE • Carte £ 23/71
'The Club' is the glittering bauble in the Royal China chain but along with the luxurious feel of the room comes an appealing sense of calm. Their lunchtime dim sum is very good; at dinner try their more unusual Cantonese dishes.

Galvin Bistrot de Luxe

66 Baker St. ✉ W1U 7DJ ⊖ Baker Street Town plan: **29**AGT**b**
– ✆ (020) 7935 4007 – www.galvinrestaurants.com – Closed dinner 24 December, 25-26 December and 1 January
• FRENCH • Menu £ 20 (lunch)/22 – Carte £ 33/56
Firmly established modern Gallic bistro with ceiling fans, globe lights and wood-panelled walls. Satisfying and precisely cooked classic French dishes from the Galvin brothers. The elegant basement cocktail bar adds to the comfy feel.

Chiltern Firehouse – Chiltern Firehouse Hotel

1 Chiltern St ✉ WIU 7PA ⊖ Baker Street Town plan: **29**AGT**a**
– ✆ (020) 7073 7676 – www.chilternfirehouse.com
• OTHER WORLD KITCHENS • Carte £ 36/61
How appropriate – the hottest ticket in town is a converted fire station. The room positively bursts with energy but what makes this celebrity hangout unusual is that the food is rather good. Nuno Mendes' menu is full of vibrant North and South American dishes that are big on flavour.

Beast

3 Chapel Pl ✉ W1G 0BG ⊖ Bond Street Town plan: **30**AHU**d**
– ✆ (020) 7495 1816 – www.beastrestaurant.co.uk
– Closed Sunday-Wednesday, Saturday lunch and bank holidays
• MEATS AND GRILLS • Menu £ 75 – *(booking essential) (set menu only)*
An underground banquet hall with three exceedingly long tables set for communal dining. The main event is a perfectly cooked hunk of rib eye steak and a large platter of succulent warm king crab. Bring a big appetite and a fat wallet.

sixtyone

61 Upper Berkeley St ✉ W1H 7PP ⊖ Marble Arch Town plan: **29**AGU**k**
– ✆ (020) 7958 3222 – www.sixtyonerestaurant.co.uk – Closed Sunday dinner
• BRITISH MODERN • Menu £ 15 (weekday lunch) – Carte £ 26/42
A joint venture between chef Arnaud Stevens and Searcy's, in a space leased from the Montcalm hotel. The room is stylish and slick; the modern cooking is elaborate and quite playful, although the best dishes are often the simplest.

XX **Zayna**

25 New Quebec St. ✉ W1H 7SF ⊖ Marble Arch Town plan: **29**AGU**x**
– ✆ (020) 7723 2229 – www.zaynarestaurant.co.uk
• INDIAN • Carte £ 20/37

The keen owner spent his early years in Kashmir and Punjab hence a menu of delicacies from Pakistan and north India. Choose your preferred cooking method such as tawa, pan or grill; only halal meat and free-range chicken are used.

XX **Archipelago**

53 Cleveland St ✉ W1T 4JJ ⊖ Goodge Street Town plan: **30**AIT**e**
– ✆ (020) 7383 3346 – www.archipelago-restaurant.co.uk – Closed 24-28 December, Saturday lunch, Sunday and bank holidays
• INNOVATIVE • Carte £ 27/43

New premises for this true one-off, but the same eccentric decoration that makes you feel you're in a bazaar. The exotic menu reads like an inventory at an omnivore's safari park; it could include crocodile, zebra and wildebeest.

XX **Winter Garden** – The Landmark London Hotel

222 Marylebone Rd ✉ NW1 6JQ ⊖ Edgware Road Town plan: **29**AFT**a**
– ✆ (020) 7631 8000 – www.landmarklondon.co.uk
• MEDITERRANEAN • Menu £ 30/40 – Carte £ 36/50

Dining options north of Marylebone Road can be limited, so the Winter Garden, in the vast atrium of the Landmark Hotel, is a useful spot for a business lunch. The kitchen has a lightness of touch and the confidence not to overcrowd a plate.

XX **Fischer's** (N)

50 Marylebone High St ✉ W1U 5HN Town plan: **30**AHT**b**
⊖ Baker Street – ✆ (020) 7466 5501 – www.fischers.co.uk
• AUSTRIAN • Carte £ 19/46

An Austrian café and konditorei that summons the spirit of old Vienna, from the owners of The Wolseley et al. Open all day; breakfast is a highlight – the viennoiserie are great. Schnitzels are also good – upgrade to a Holstein.

XX **The Providores**

109 Marylebone High St. ✉ W1U 4RX Town plan: **30**AHT**y**
⊖ Bond Street – ✆ (020) 7935 6175 – www.theprovidores.co.uk
– Closed 25-26 December
• INNOVATIVE • Carte £ 38/51

Packed ground floor for tapas; upstairs for innovative fusion cooking, with spices and ingredients from around the world, including Australasia. Starter-sized dishes at dinner allow for greater choice.

XX **Iberica Marylebone**

195 Great Portland St ✉ W1W 5PS Town plan: **18**RZD**x**
⊖ Great Portland Street – ✆ (020) 7636 8650 – www.ibericalondon.co.uk
– Closed 24-26 December, Sunday dinner and bank holidays
• SPANISH • Carte £ 18/46

Some prefer the intimacy of upstairs, others the bustle of the ground floor with its bar and deli. Along with an impressive array of Iberico hams are colourful dishes to share, such as glossy black rice with cuttlefish and prawns.

XX **Levant**

Jason Ct., 76 Wigmore St. ✉ W1U 2SJ Town plan: **30**AHT**c**
⊖ Bond Street – ✆ (020) 7224 1111 – www.levant.co.uk
– Closed 25-26 December
• LEBANESE • Menu £ 10 (lunch)/50 – Carte £ 23/71

Come in a group to best enjoy the Lebanese and Middle Eastern specialities; it's worth ordering one of the 'Feast' menus. Belly dancing, a low slung bar, lanterns and joss sticks add to the exotic feel of this basement restaurant.

XX **Royal China**

24-26 Baker St ✉ W1U 7AB ⊖ Baker Street Town plan: **29**AGT**h**
– ✆ (020) 7487 4688 – www.royalchinagroup.co.uk
• CHINESE • Menu £ 30/38 – Carte £ 18/74
Barbequed meats, assorted soups and stir-fries attract plenty of large groups to this smart and always bustling Cantonese restaurant. Over 40 different types of dim sum served during the day.

X ✿ **Lima**

31 Rathbone Pl ✉ W1T 1JH ⊖ Goodge Street Town plan: **31**AJT**s**
– ✆ (020) 3002 2640 – www.limalondon.com – Closed 23 December-3 January and Sunday
• PERUVIAN • Menu £ 20 (lunch and early dinner)/48 – Carte £ 38/52
Lima is one of those restaurants that just makes you feel good about life – and that's even without the Pisco Sours. The Peruvian food at this informal, fun place is the ideal antidote to our recessionary times: it's full of punchy, invigorating flavours and fantastically vivid colours.
➜ Sea bream, tiger's milk, ají limo pepper and cancha corn. Beef with wild black quinoa, Cuzco corn and pink molle pepper. Dulche de leche ice cream with beetroot emulsion and maca root crust.

X ✿ **Trishna** (Karam Sethi)

15-17 Blandford St. ✉ W1U 3DG ⊖ Baker Street Town plan: **29**AGT**r**
– ✆ (020) 7935 5624 – www.trishnalondon.com – Closed 24-28 December and 1-4 January
• INDIAN • Menu £ 19 (lunch)/60 – Carte £ 22/49
Double-fronted, modern Indian restaurant, refurbished in an elegant, understated style. The coast of southwest India provides many influences and the food is balanced, satisfying and executed with care; be sure to order the wondrously rich Dorset brown crab.
➜ Baby squid with turmeric, fennel seed, samphire, mango and ginger. Bream, green chilli, coriander and tandoor smoked tomato kachumber. Warm heritage carrot pudding, samosa and masala chai ice cream.

X **The Wallace**

Hertford House, Manchester Sq ✉ W1U 3BN Town plan: **29**AGT**k**
⊖ Bond Street – ✆ (020) 7563 9505
– www.peytonandbyrne.co.uk/the-wallace-restaurant/index.html
– Closed 24-26 December
• FRENCH • Menu £ 23/26 – Carte £ 31/44 – *(lunch only and dinner Friday-Saturday)*
Large glass-roofed courtyard on the ground floor of Hertford House, home to the splendid Wallace Collection. French-influenced menu, with fruits de mer section; terrines are the house speciality.

X **Caffé Caldesi**

118 Marylebone Ln. (1st floor) ✉ W1U 2QF Town plan: **30**AHT**s**
⊖ Bond Street – ✆ (020) 7487 0754 – www.caldesi.com
• ITALIAN • Menu £ 16 (weekday lunch) – Carte £ 23/54
Head upstairs at this converted corner pub for generously proportioned, big flavoured classics from across Italy - they do a very good pumpkin soufflé. The ground floor has a simpler and more accessibly priced menu.

X **Roti Chai** 

3 Portman Mews South ✉ W1H 6HS Town plan: **29**AGU**v**
⊖ Marble Arch – ✆ (020) 7408 0101 – www.rotichai.com – Closed 25 December
• INDIAN • Carte £ 15/31
Representing the new wave of modern, casual Indian restaurants, in appropriately vivid colours. The ground floor is for quick and easy pan-Indian street food; downstairs is swankier and offers a contemporary update of Indian home cooking.

Il Baretto

43 Blandford St. ✉ W1U 7HF ⊖ Baker Street Town plan: **29**AGT**n**
– ✆ (020) 7486 7340 – www.ilbaretto.co.uk
• ITALIAN • Menu £ 26 – Carte £ 35/83
The robata grill is the star of the show at this lively Italian restaurant. The extensive and variably priced menu offers something for everyone, from pizzas to succulent lamb chops. The basement setting adds to the 'local' feel.

28°-50° Marylebone

15-17 Marylebone Ln. ✉ W1U 2NE ⊖ Bond Street Town plan: **30**AHT**c**
– ✆ (020) 7486 7922 – www.2850.co.uk – Closed 25-26 and 31 December, 1 January and Sunday
• MODERN • Menu £ 16 (weekday lunch) – Carte £ 22/53
This second wine bar from the owners of Texture restaurant offers a great choice of wines by the glass and a terrific "Collectors' List". Most plump for the grilled meats from the coal burning oven. Service is as bright as the room.

Riding House Café

43-51 Great Titchfield St ✉ W1W 7PQ Town plan: **30**AIT**k**
⊖ Oxford Circus – ✆ (020) 7927 0840 – www.ridinghousecafe.co.uk – Closed 25-26 December
• MODERN • Menu £ 11/18 – Carte £ 17/40
It's less a café, more a large, quirkily designed, all-day New York style brasserie and cocktail bar. The 'small plates' have more zing than the main courses. The 'unbookable' side of the restaurant is the more fun part.

LONDON

Picture

110 Great Portland St. ✉ W1W 6PQ Town plan: **30**AIT**t**
⊖ Oxford Circus – ✆ (020) 7637 7892 – www.picturerestaurant.co.uk – Closed bank holidays and Sunday
• BRITISH MODERN • Carte £ 24/28
An ex Arbutus and Wild Honey triumvirate have created this cool, great-value restaurant. The look may be a little stark but the delightful staff add warmth. The small plates are vibrant and colourful, and the flavours are assured.

Donostia

10 Seymour Pl ✉ W1H 7ND ⊖ Marble Arch Town plan: **29**AFU**s**
– ✆ (020) 3620 1845 – www.donostia.co.uk – Closed Monday lunch
• BASQUE • Menu £ 36 – Carte £ 18/40
The two young owners were inspired by the food of San Sebastiàn to open this pintxos and tapas bar. Sit at the counter for Basque classics like cod with pil-pil sauce, chorizo from the native pig Kintoa and slow-cooked pig's cheeks.

Ergon (N)

16 Picton Pl ✉ WIU 1BP ⊖ Bond Street Town plan: **30**AHU**g**
– ✆ (020) 7486 9210 – www.ergonproducts.co.uk
• GREEK • Menu £ 10 (weekday lunch) – Carte £ 22/37
The London branch of this successful group in Greece is a bright eatery with a downstairs deli stocked with Hellenic produce. The menu is a blend of classic and modern Greek dishes designed for sharing; the wine list is all Greek too.

Vinoteca

15 Seymour Pl. ✉ W1H 5BD ⊖ Marble Arch Town plan: **29**AFU**v**
– ✆ (020) 7724 7288 – www.vinoteca.co.uk – Closed Christmas, bank holidays and Sunday dinner
• MODERN • Carte £ 25/40 – *(booking advisable)*
Follows the formula of the original: great fun, great wines, gutsy and wholesome food, enthusiastic staff and almost certainly a wait for a table. Influences from sunnier parts of Europe, along with some British dishes.

LONDON

Bonnie Gull

21a Foley St ✉ W1W 6DS ⊖ Goodge Street Town plan: **30**AITb
– ✆ (020) 7436 0921 – www.bonniegull.com
• FISH AND SEAFOOD • Carte £ 23/56 – *(booking essential)*

Sweet Bonnie Gull calls itself a 'seafood shack' – a reference perhaps to its modest beginnings as a pop-up. Start with an order from the raw bar then go for a classic like Cullen skink, a whole Devon cock crab or fish and chips.

Lockhart Ⓝ

22-24 Seymor Pl ✉ W1H 7NL ⊖ Marble Arch Town plan: **29**AFUt
– ✆ (020) 3011 5400 – www.lockhartlondon.com – Closed Sunday dinner and Monday
• OTHER WORLD KITCHENS • Carte £ 22/47

Owned by two Texan couples, this fun spot specialises in the fiery flavours of Texas, Louisiana and New Mexico. Start with a mezcal-based cocktail then tuck into a wonderfully smoky meat dish like the lip-smackingly good bbq chicken.

Yalla Yalla

12 Winsley St. ✉ W1W 8HQ ⊖ Oxford Circus Town plan: **30**AITv
– ✆ (020) 7637 4748 – www.yalla-yalla.co.uk – Closed 25-26 December, 1 January and Sunday
• LEBANESE • Carte £ 19/29

It's fun, loud and you can't book, but the name means "Hurry up!" so you won't wait long. This is Beirut street food, meant for sharing. Try homemade soujoc (spicy sausages), sawda djej (chicken livers) and a succulent lamb dish.

Dinings

22 Harcourt St. ✉ W1H 4HH ⊖ Edgware Road Town plan: **29**AFTc
– ✆ (020) 7723 0666 – www.dinings.co.uk – Closed Christmas and Sunday
• JAPANESE • Carte £ 16/76 – *(booking essential)*

It's hard not to be charmed by this sweet little Japanese place, with its ground floor counter and basement tables. Its strengths lie with the more creative, contemporary dishes; sharing is recommended but prices can be steep.

Zoilo

9 Duke St. ✉ W1U 3EG ⊖ Bond Street Town plan: **30**AHTz
– ✆ (020) 7486 9699 – www.zoilo.co.uk
• ARGENTINIAN • Menu £ 10 (weekdays) – Carte £ 14/46

It's all about sharing so grab a seat at the counter and discover Argentina's regional specialities. Don't miss chewy melted provoleta cheese, beetroot with goat's curd and garrapiñada (a Buenos Aires street snack), and escabeche.

Newman Street Tavern

48 Newman St ✉ W1T 1QQ ⊖ Goodge Street. Town plan: **30**AJTs
– ✆ (020) 3667 1445 – www.newmanstreettavern.co.uk – Closed 24 December, 1 January, Sunday dinner and bank holidays
• BRITISH TRADITIONAL • Menu £ 20 – Carte £ 24/42

The experienced team behind this Edwardian pub have created a warm, welcoming spot. The kitchen celebrates the best of British and the menu is instantly appealing. Eat in the busy bar or in the more sedate first floor dining room.

Grazing Goat with rm

6 New Quebec St ✉ W1H 7RQ ⊖ Marble Arch. Town plan: **29**AGUd
– ✆ (020) 7724 7243 – www.thegrazinggoat.co.uk
• BRITISH TRADITIONAL • **8 rm** – †£ 205 ††£ 240, ☕ £ 13
Carte £ 31/41 – *(booking essential at dinner)*

A smart city facsimile of a country pub; it's first-come-first-served in the bar but you can book in the upstairs dining room. Proper pub classics such as pies and Castle of Mey steaks are on offer. Bedrooms with Nordic style bathrooms.

Portman

51 Upper Berkeley St ✉ *W1H 7QW* Town plan: **29**AFU**n**
⊖ *Marble Arch.* – ✆ *(020) 7723 8996* – *www.theportmanmarylebone.com*
• MODERN • Menu £ 32/38 – Carte £ 20/48

The condemned on their way to Tyburn Tree gallows would take their last drink here. Now it's an urbane pub with a formal upstairs dining room. The ground floor is more fun for enjoying the down-to-earth menu.

St James's

Ritz

150 Piccadilly ✉ *W1J 9BR* ⊖ *Green Park* Town plan: **30**AIV**c**
– ✆ *(020) 7493 8181* – *www.theritzlondon.com*

134 rm – £ 315/865 £ 345/995, £ 35 – 45 suites

Rest *Ritz Restaurant* – see restaurant listing

World famous hotel, opened in 1906 as a fine example of Louis XVI architecture and decoration. Elegant Palm Court famed for its afternoon tea. Many of the lavishly appointed and luxurious rooms and suites overlook the park.

Haymarket

1 Suffolk Pl. ✉ *SW1Y 4HX* ⊖ *Piccadilly Circus* Town plan: **31**AKV**x**
– ✆ *(020) 7470 4000* – *www.haymarkethotel.com*

50 rm – £ 368 £ 368, £ 20 – 3 suites

Rest *Brumus* – see restaurant listing

Smart and spacious hotel in John Nash Regency building, with a stylish blend of modern and antique furnishings. Large, comfortable bedrooms in soothing colours. Impressive basement pool is often used for private parties.

Sofitel London St James

6 Waterloo Pl. ✉ *SW1Y 4AN* ⊖ *Piccadilly Circus* Town plan: **31**AKV**a**
– ✆ *(020) 7747 2200* – *www.sofitelstjames.com*

183 rm – £ 300/702 £ 300/702, £ 23 – 18 suites

Rest *Balcon* – see restaurant listing

Great location for this international hotel in a Grade II former bank. The triple-glazed bedrooms are immaculately kept; the spa is one of the best around. The bar is inspired by Coco Chanel; the lounge by an English rose garden.

Dukes

35 St James's Pl. ✉ *SW1A 1NY* ⊖ *Green Park* Town plan: **30**AIV**f**
– ✆ *(020) 7491 4840* – *www.dukeshotel.com*

90 rm – £ 234/250 £ 276/496, £ 24 – 6 suites

Rest *Thirty Six by Nigel Mendham* – Menu £ 32/60 – *(closed Sunday dinner and Monday lunch)*

The wonderfully located Dukes has been steadily updating its image over the last few years, despite being over a century old. Bedrooms are now fresh and uncluttered and the atmosphere less starchy. The basement restaurant offers a modern menu, with dishes that are original in look and elaborate in construction.

Stafford

16-18 St James's Pl. ✉ *SW1A 1NJ* ⊖ *Green Park* Town plan: **30**AIV**u**
– ✆ *(020) 7493 0111* – *www.kempinski.com/london*

105 rm – £ 336/700 £ 336/700, £ 25 – 15 suites

Rest *The Lyttelton* – Menu £ 20 (lunch) – Carte £ 45/115

Styles itself as a 'country house in the city'; its bedrooms are divided between the main house, converted 18C stables and a more modern mews. Legendary American bar a highlight; traditional British food served in the restaurant.

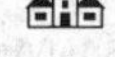

St James's Hotel and Club

7-8 Park Pl. ✉ *SW1A 1LS* ⊖ *Green Park* Town plan: **30**AIV**k**
– ✆ *(020) 7316 1600* – *www.stjameshotelandclub.com*

60 rm – £ 260/3000 £ 260/3000, £ 24 – 10 suites

Rest *Seven Park Place* ✿ – see restaurant listing

1890s house, formerly a private club in a wonderfully central yet quiet location. Modern, boutique-style interior with over 300 European works of art from the '20s to the '50s. Fine finish to the compact but well-equipped bedrooms.

LONDON

Cavendish

81 Jermyn St ✉ SW1Y 6JF ⊖ Piccadilly Circus Town plan: **30**AIV**p**
– ✆ (020) 7930 2111 – www.thecavendishlondon.com
230 rm – †£ 179/288 ††£ 179/288, ☐ £ 23 – 2 suites
Rest – Menu £ 21 (weekdays) – Carte £ 33/40 – *(closed 25 December and lunch Saturday-Sunday)*
There's been a hotel on this site since the 18C; this one was built in the '60s but is smart and contemporary inside. Great location, bistro-style dining with British menu and good views across London from the top 5 floors; a parking space for every room too!

Ritz Restaurant – Ritz Hotel

150 Piccadilly ✉ W1J 9BR ⊖ Green Park Town plan: **30**AIV**c**
– ✆ (020) 7493 8181 – www.theritzlondon.com
• BRITISH TRADITIONAL • Menu £ 49 (weekday lunch) **s** – Carte £ 69/79 **s**
Grand and lavish restaurant, with Louis XVI decoration, trompe l'oeil and ornate gilding. Delightful terrace over Green Park. Structured, formal service. Classic, traditional dishes are the highlight of the menu. Jacket and tie required.

Seven Park Place – St James's Hotel and Club

7-8 Park Pl ✉ SW1A 1LS ⊖ Green Park Town plan: **30**AIV**k**
– ✆ (020) 7316 1615 – www.stjameshotelandclub.com – Closed Sunday and Monday
• MODERN • Menu £ 26/72 – *(booking essential)*
William Drabble's cooking is all about the quality of the produce, much of which comes from the Lake District, and his confident cooking allows natural flavours to shine. This diminutive restaurant is concealed within the hotel and divided into two; ask for the warmer, gilded back room.
→ Poached lobster tail with cauliflower purée and lobster butter sauce. Assiette of lamb with onions and thyme. Banana parfait, set chocolate custard and honeycomb.

The Wolseley

160 Piccadilly ✉ W1J 9EB ⊖ Green Park Town plan: **30**AIV**q**
– ✆ (020) 7499 6996 – www.thewolseley.com – Closed dinner 24 December
• MODERN • Carte £ 24/72 – *(booking essential)*
This feels like a grand and glamorous European coffee house, with its pillars and high vaulted ceiling. Appealing menus offer everything from caviar to a hot dog. It's open from early until late and boasts a large celebrity following.

Balcon – Sofitel London St James Hotel

8 Pall Mall. ✉ SW1Y 5NG ⊖ Piccadilly Circus Town plan: **31**AKV**a**
– ✆ (020) 7389 7820 – www.thebalconlondon.com
• FRENCH • Menu £ 21/36 – Carte £ 33/49
A former banking hall with vast chandeliers and a grand brasserie look. It's open from breakfast onwards and the menu features French classics like snails and cassoulet; try the charcuterie from Wales and France.

Matsuri

15 Bury St. ✉ SW1Y 6AL ⊖ Green Park – ✆ (020) 7839 1101 – www.matsuri-restaurant.com – Closed 25 December and 1 January Town plan: **30**AIV**w**
• JAPANESE • Menu £ 40 (lunch) – Carte £ 32/118
Sweet natured service at this long-standing, traditional Japanese stalwart. Teppan-yaki is their speciality, with Scottish beef the highlight; sushi counter also available. Good value lunch menus and bento boxes.

Le Caprice

Arlington House, Arlington St. ✉ SW1A 1RJ Town plan: **30**AIV**h**
⊖ Green Park – ✆ (020) 7629 2239 – www.le-caprice.co.uk
– Closed 24-26 December
• MODERN • Menu £ 25 (dinner) – Carte £ 32/61
For over 30 years Le Caprice's effortlessly sophisticated atmosphere and surroundings have attracted a confident and urbane clientele. Perennials on their catch-all menu include their famous burger and rich salmon fishcake.

XX Sake No Hana

23 St James's St ✉ SW1A 1HA ⊖ Green Park Town plan: **30**AIV**n**
– ✆ (020) 7925 8988 – www.sakenohana.com – Closed 25 December and Sunday

• JAPANESE • Menu £ 29/65 – Carte £ 23/62

A modern Japanese restaurant within a Grade II listed '60s edifice – and proof that you can occasionally find good food at the end of an escalator. As with the great cocktails, the menu is best enjoyed when shared with a group.

XX Boulestin (N)

5 St James's St ✉ SW1A 1EF ⊖ Green Park Town plan: **30**AIV**s**
– ✆ (020) 7930 2030 – www.boulestin.com – Closed bank holidays and Sunday

• FRENCH • Menu £ 25 (dinner) – Carte £ 32/61

Nearly a century after Xavier Marcel Boulestin opened his eponymous restaurant showcasing 'Simple French Cooking for English homes', his spirit has been resurrected at this elegant brasserie, with a simpler bistro attached.

XX Café Murano (N)

33 St. James's St ✉ SW1A 1HD ⊖ Green Park Town plan: **30**AIV**m**
– ✆ (0203) 371 5559 – www.cafemurano.co.uk – Closed Sunday dinner

• ITALIAN • Menu £ 22 – Carte £ 25/53 – *(booking essential)*

Angela Hartnett and her chef have created an appealing and flexible menu of delicious North Italian delicacies – the lunch menu is very good value. It's certainly no ordinary café and its popularity means pre-booking is essential.

LONDON

XX Franco's

61 Jermyn St ✉ SW1Y 6LX ⊖ Green Park Town plan: **30**AIV**i**
– ✆ (020) 7499 2211 – www.francoslondon.com – Closed Sunday and bank holidays

• ITALIAN • Menu £ 20/26 – Carte £ 31/62 – *(booking essential)*

Open from breakfast until late, with café at the front leading into smart, clubby restaurant. Menu covers all parts of Italy and includes popular grill section and plenty of classics.

XX Avenue

7-9 St James's St. ✉ SW1A 1EE ⊖ Green Park Town plan: **30**AIV**y**
– ✆ (020) 7321 2111 – www.avenue-restaurant.co.uk – Closed Saturday lunch, Sunday dinner and bank holidays

• MODERN • Menu £ 24 (weekday lunch) – Carte dinner £ 27/52

Avenue has gone all American, with a new look from Russell Sage and a contemporary menu inspired by what's cooking in Manhattan. Wine is also made more of a feature; and, of course, the cocktails at the long, lively bar are great.

XX Mint Leaf

Suffolk Pl ✉ SW1Y 4HX ⊖ Piccadilly Circus Town plan: **31**AKV**k**
– ✆ (020) 7930 9020 – www.mintleafrestaurant.com – Closed 25-26 December, 1 January and lunch Saturday-Sunday

• INDIAN • Menu £ 30/38 – Carte £ 25/43

Cavernous and moodily lit basement restaurant incorporating trendy bar with lounge music and extensive cocktail list. Contemporary Indian cooking with curries the highlight.

XX Al Duca

4-5 Duke of York St ✉ SW1Y 6LA Town plan: **31**AJV**r**
⊖ Piccadilly Circus – ✆ (020) 7839 3090 – www.alduca-restaurant.co.uk – Closed Easter, 25 December, Sunday and bank holidays

• ITALIAN • Menu £ 20 – Carte approx. £ 41

Cooking which focuses on flavour continues to draw in the regulars at this warm and spirited Italian restaurant. Prices are keen when one considers the central location and service is brisk and confident.

LONDON

XX **Quaglino's**

16 Bury St ✉ SW1Y 6AJ ⊖ Green Park Town plan: **30**AIV**j**
– ✆ (020) 7930 6767 – www.quaglinos-restaurant.co.uk – Closed Christmas, Easter Monday and Sunday
• MODERN • Menu £ 20/25 – Carte £ 34/60
It may be synonymous with the early '90s but the old girl can still shake it on a weekend for those wanting a fun night out with a bit of glitz. The kitchen delivers on brasserie classics like pork belly and duck confit.

XX **Brumus** – Haymarket Hotel

1 Suffolk Pl ✉ SW1Y 4HX ⊖ Piccadilly Circus Town plan: **31**AKV**x**
– ✆ (020) 7470 4000 – www.haymarkethotel.com
• MODERN • Menu £ 20 – Carte £ 22/53
Pre-theatre dining is an altogether less frenzied activity when you can actually see the theatre from your table. This is a modern, elegant space with switched-on staff. Stick to the good value set menu or the 'dish of the day'.

X **Portrait**

National Portrait Gallery (3rd floor), St Martin's Pl. Town plan: **31**ALV**n**
✉ WC2H 0HE ⊖ Charing Cross – ✆ (020) 7312 2490 – www.searcys.co.uk – Closed 24-26 December
• MODERN • Menu £ 30 – Carte £ 32/47 – *(lunch only and dinner Thursday-Saturday) (booking essential)*
On the top floor of National Portrait Gallery with rooftop local landmark views: a charming spot for lunch. Modern British/European dishes; weekend brunch.

X **The National Dining Rooms**

Sainsbury Wing, The National Gallery, Trafalgar Sq Town plan: **31**AKV**b**
✉ WC2N 5DN ⊖ Charing Cross – ✆ (020) 7747 2525 – www.peytonandbyrne.co.uk – Closed 24-26 December and 1 January
• BRITISH MODERN • Menu £ 30 – Carte £ 24/35 – *(lunch only and Friday dinner)*
Set on the East Wing's first floor, you can tuck into cakes in the bakery or grab a prime corner table in the restaurant for great views and proudly seasonal British menus.

X **Shoryu**

9 Regent St. ✉ SW1Y 4LR ⊖ Piccadilly Circus Town plan: **31**AJV**s**
– www.shoryuramen.com – Closed 25 December and 1 January
• JAPANESE • Carte £ 17/35 – *(bookings not accepted)*
Owned by Japan Centre opposite and specialising in Hakata tonkotsu ramen. The base is a milky broth made from pork bones to which is added hosomen noodles, egg, and assorted toppings. Its restorative powers are worth queuing for. There are a two larger branches in Soho.

X **Chop Shop** (N)

66 Haymarket ✉ SW1Y 4RF ⊖ Piccadilly Circus Town plan: **31**AKV**c**
– ✆ (020) 7842 8501 – www.chopshopuk.com
• MEATS AND GRILLS • Menu £ 22 (weekday lunch) – Carte £ 20/48
Spread over two floors and with an ersatz industrial look, this lively spot could be in Manhattan's Meatpacking district. Start with a cocktail, then order 'jars', 'crocks' or 'planks' of mousses, meatballs and cheeses; then it's the main event – great steaks and chops.

Soho

Soho

4 Richmond Mews ✉ W1D 3DH Town plan: **31**AJU**n**
⊖ Tottenham Court Road – ✆ (020) 7559 3000 – www.sohohotel.com
91 rm – †£ 353/402 ††£ 353/402, ☕ £ 20 – 5 suites
Rest *Refuel* – see restaurant listing
Stylish and fashionable hotel that mirrors the vibrancy of the neighbourhood. Boasts two screening rooms, a comfortable drawing room and up-to-the-minute bedrooms; some vivid, others more muted but all with hi-tech extras.

Café Royal

68 Regent St ✉ *W1B 4DY* ⊖ *Piccadilly Circus* Town plan: **30**AJU**c**
– ✆ (020) 7406 3333 – www.hotelcaferoyal.com
159 rm – †£ 480/660 ††£ 480/660, ☕ £ 32 – 25 suites
Rest *Ten Room* – ✆ (020) 7406 3310 – Carte £ 23/56
The iconic Café Royal's colourful history goes back to 1865. It's been redeveloped into this luxury hotel, with cool, contemporary bedrooms and stunning bathrooms. The spa is amazing; the rococo Oscar Wilde Bar has been restored to its original splendour and Ten Room serves classic and modern British dishes.

Ham Yard Ⓝ

1 Ham Yard, ✉ *W1D 7DT* ⊖ *Piccadilly Circus* Town plan: **31**AJU**p**
– ✆ (020) 3642 2000 – www.firmdalehotels.com
89 rm – †£ 318 ††£ 318, ☕ £ 14 – 9 suites
Rest *Ham Yard* – see restaurant listing
Opened in 2014, this stylish hotel from the Firmdale group is set around a courtyard – a haven of tranquillity in the West End. Each of the rooms is different but all are supremely comfortable. There's also a great roof terrace, a theatre, a fully stocked library and bar... and even a bowling alley.

W London

10 Wardour St ✉ *W1D 6QF* ⊖ *Leicester Square* Town plan: **31**AKU**b**
– ✆ (0207) 758 10 00 – www.wlondon.co.uk
192 rm – †£ 324/647 ††£ 324/647, ☕ £ 27 – 15 suites
Rest *Spice Market* – see restaurant listing
An achingly trendy hotel bang in the heart of Leicester Square. A DJ plays in the lobby lounge at weekends; there's an over-subscribed bar with low slung tables and slick, über cool bedrooms in categories called 'Fantastic' or 'Spectacular'. Anyone over 40 will feel slightly bewildered.

Sanctum Soho

20 Warwick St. ✉ *W1B 5NF* ⊖ *Piccadilly Circus* Town plan: **30**AIU**g**
– ✆ (020) 7292 6100 – www.sanctumsoho.com
30 rm – †£ 210/360 ††£ 210/360, ☕ £ 15
Rest *No. 20* – Menu £ 25 (dinner) – Carte £ 21/60
Plenty of glitz and bling at this funky, self-styled rock 'n' roll hotel, with some innovative touches such as TVs behind mirrors. Rooftop lounge and hot tub. Relaxed and comfortable dining with plenty of classic dishes.

Dean Street Townhouse

69-71 Dean St. ✉ *W1D 3SE* Town plan: **31**AKU**t**
⊖ *Tottenham Court Road – ✆ (020) 7434 1775*
– www.deanstreettownhouse.com
39 rm – †£ 342/540 ††£ 384/540, ☕ £ 15
Rest *Dean Street Townhouse Restaurant* – see restaurant listing
In the heart of Soho and where bedrooms range from tiny to bigger; the latter have roll-top baths in the room. All are well designed and come with a good range of extras. Cosy ground floor lounge.

Nadler Soho without rest

10 Carlisle St ✉ *W1D 3BR* ⊖ *Tottenham Court Road* Town plan: AJU**n**
– ✆ (020) 3697 3697 – www.thenadler.com
78 rm – †£ 150/330 ††£ 150/330, ☕ £ 10 – 1 suite
On a quiet lane, but in the heart of Soho, is a townhouse with a concept: no bar nor restaurant, just comfortable, very well-equipped bedrooms, most of which have a small kitchenette. The smart receptionists double as concierge.

Hazlitt's

6 Frith St ✉ *W1D 3JA* ⊖ *Tottenham Court Road* Town plan: **31**AKU**u**
– ✆ (020) 7434 1771 – www.hazlittshotel.com
30 rm – †£ 199/222 ††£ 227/288, ☕ £ 12 **Rest** *(room service only)*
Three adjoining early 18C townhouses and former home of the eponymous essayist. Idiosyncratic bedrooms, many with antique furniture and Victorian baths; ask for one of the newer ones.

Quo Vadis
26-29 Dean St ✉ W1D 3LL Town plan: **31**AKU**v**
⊖ Tottenham Court Road – ✆ (020) 7437 9585 – www.quovadissoho.co.uk – Closed 25-26 December, 1 January and bank holidays
• BRITISH MODERN • Menu £ 18 – Carte £ 26/38
A stylish, elegant Soho institution dating from the 1920s and now owned by the Hart Brothers. First order some great 'bites' then choose from a menu of satisfying British dishes that includes a daily pie and braised dish along with grilled meats and assorted seafood.

Gauthier - Soho
21 Romilly St ✉ W1D 5AF ⊖ Leicester Square Town plan: **31**AKU**k**
– ✆ (020) 7494 3111 – www.gauthiersoho.co.uk – Closed Monday lunch, Sunday and bank holidays except Good Friday
• FRENCH • Menu £ 18 (lunch) – Carte £ 45/67
Tucked away from the mischief of Soho is this charming Georgian townhouse, with dining spread over three floors. Alex Gauthier offers assorted menus of his classically based cooking, with vegetarians particularly well looked after.

Red Fort
77 Dean St. ✉ W1D 3SH Town plan: **31**AKU**t**
⊖ Tottenham Court Road – ✆ (020) 7437 2525 – www.redfort.co.uk – Closed lunch Saturday-Sunday
• INDIAN • Menu £ 15 – Carte £ 31/59 – *(bookings advisable at dinner)*
A feature in Soho since 1983 but the last makeover gave it a stylish, contemporary look. Balanced Indian cooking uses much UK produce such as Herdwick lamb; look out for more unusual choices like rabbit.

Imperial China
White Bear Yard, 25a Lisle St ✉ WC2H 7BA Town plan: **31**AKU**l**
⊖ Leicester Square – ✆ (020) 7734 3388 – www.imperialchina-london.com – Closed 25 December
• CHINESE • Carte £ 19/51 – *(booking advisable)*
Sharp service and comfortable surroundings are not the only things that set this restaurant apart: the Cantonese cooking exudes freshness and vitality, whether that's the steamed dumplings or the XO minced pork with fine beans.

Yauatcha
15 Broadwick St ✉ W1F 0DL Town plan: **31**AJU**k**
⊖ Tottenham Court Road – ✆ (020) 7494 8888 – www.yauatcha.com – Closed 25 December
• CHINESE • Menu £ 29/55 – Carte £ 24/57
Refined, delicate and delicious dim sum; ideal for sharing in a group. Stylish surroundings spread over two floors: the lighter, brighter ground floor or the darker, more atmospheric basement. Afternoon teas also a speciality.
→ Scallop shui mai. Kung Pao chicken. Raspberry délice.

Brasserie Zédel
20 Sherwood St ✉ W1F 7ED ⊖ Piccadilly Circus Town plan: **31**AJU**q**
– ✆ (020) 7734 4888 – www.brasseriezedel.com – Closed 25 December
• FRENCH • Menu £ 12/20 – Carte £ 15/26 – *(booking advisable)*
A grand French brasserie, which is all about inclusivity and accessibility, in a bustling subterranean space restored to its original art deco glory. Expect a roll-call of classic French dishes and some very competitive prices.

Bob Bob Ricard
1 Upper James St ✉ W1F 9DF ⊖ Oxford Circus Town plan: **31**AJU**s**
– ✆ (020) 3145 1000 – www.bobbobricard.com – Closed Christmas, Easter and Sunday
• MODERN • Carte £ 32/80
Everyone needs a little glamour now and again and this place provides it. The room may be quite small but it sees itself as a grand salon – ask for a booth. The menu is all-encompassing – oysters and caviar to pies and burgers.

LONDON

XX **Ham Yard** Ⓝ – Ham Yard Hotel

1 Ham Yard, ✉ W1D 7DT ⊖ Piccadilly Circus Town plan: **31**AJU**p**
– ✆ (020) 3642 2000 – www.firmdalehotels.com
• MODERN • Carte £ 24/35

An exuberantly decorated restaurant; start with a cocktail – the bitters and syrups are homemade with herbs from the hotel's roof garden. The menu moves with the seasons and the kitchen has the confidence to keep dishes simple.

XX **Dean Street Townhouse Restaurant**

69-71 Dean St. ✉ W1D 3SE Town plan: **31**AKU**t**
⊖ Tottenham Court Road – ✆ (020) 7434 1775
– www.deanstreettownhouse.com
• BRITISH MODERN • Menu £ 20 – Carte £ 26/78 – *(booking essential)*

Georgian house now home to a fashionable and very busy bar and restaurant; the Parlour is the less hectic area. Appealingly classic British food includes some retro dishes and satisfying puddings.

XX **Aqua Kyoto**

240 Regent St. (5th floor) ✉ W1F 7EB – (entrance Town plan: **30**AIU**x**
on Argyll St.) ⊖ Oxford Circus – ✆ (020) 7478 0540 – www.aqua-london.com
– Closed 25 December and 1 January
• JAPANESE • Menu £ 20 (lunch) – Carte £ 26/88 **s**

The louder and more boisterous of the two large restaurants on the 5th floor of Aqua London. It's ideally suited to a night out with a group of friends as many of the contemporary Japanese dishes are designed for sharing.

XX **Floridita**

100 Wardour St ✉ W1F 0TN Town plan: **31**AJU**z**
⊖ Tottenham Court Road – ✆ (020) 7314 4000 – www.floriditalondon.com
– Closed Sunday, Monday and bank holidays
• OTHER WORLD KITCHENS • Menu £ 20/38 – *(dinner only)*

Mediterranean tapas on the ground floor; the huge downstairs for live music, dancing and Latin American specialities, from Cuban spice to Argentinean beef. Great cocktails and a party atmosphere.

XX **Vasco and Piero's Pavilion**

15 Poland St ✉ W1F 8QE ⊖ Oxford Circus Town plan: **31**AJU**b**
– ✆ (020) 7437 8774 – www.vascosfood.com – Closed Saturday lunch, Sunday and bank holidays
• ITALIAN • Carte £ 24/44 – *(booking essential at lunch)*

Regulars and tourists have been flocking to this institution for over 40 years; its longevity is down to a twice daily changing menu of Umbrian-influenced dishes rather than the matter-of-fact service or simple decoration.

XX **Plum Valley**

20 Gerrard St. ✉ W1D 6JQ ⊖ Leicester Square Town plan: **31**AKU**i**
– ✆ (020) 7494 4366 – Closed 23-24 December
• CHINESE • Menu £ 38 – Carte £ 19/37

Its striking black façade make this modern Chinese restaurant easy to spot in Chinatown. Mostly Cantonese cooking, with occasional forays into Vietnam and Thailand; dim sum is the strength.

XX **Haozhan**

8 Gerrard St ✉ W1D 5PJ ⊖ Leicester Square Town plan: **31**AKU**n**
– ✆ (020) 7434 3838 – www.haozhan.co.uk
– Closed 24-25 December
• CHINESE • Menu £ 15/48 – Carte £ 20/78

Interesting fusion-style dishes, with mostly Cantonese but other Asian influences too. Specialities like jasmine ribs or wasabi prawns reveal a freshness that marks this place out from the plethora of Chinatown mediocrity.

Refuel – Soho Hotel

4 Richmond Mews ✉ W1D 3DH Town plan: **31**AJU**n**
⊖ Tottenham Court Road – ☎ (020) 7559 3007 – www.sohohotel.com
• MODERN • Menu £ 21 – Carte £ 27/57
At the heart of the cool Soho hotel is their aptly named bar and restaurant. With a menu to suit all moods and wallets, from Dover sole to burgers, and a cocktail list to lift all spirits, it's a fun and bustling spot.

Spice Market – W London Hotel

10 Wardour St ✉ W1D 6QF ⊖ Leicester Square Town plan: **31**AKU**b**
– ☎ (0207) 758 10 00 – www.wlondon.co.uk
• ASIAN • Menu £ 48 – Carte £ 28/57
Over two floors and as strikingly decorated and as fun as Jean-Georges Vongerichten's original in Manhattan's Meatpacking district. Influences from across Asia in dishes designed for sharing; curries a highlight.

MASH

77 Brewer St ✉ W1F 9ZN ⊖ Piccadilly Circus Town plan: **30**AJU**m**
– ☎ (020) 7734 2608 – www.mashsteak.co.uk – Closed 23-25 December and Sunday lunch
• MEATS AND GRILLS • Menu £ 25 – Carte £ 48/76
A team from Copenhagen raised the old Titanic and restored the art deco to create this striking 'Modern American Steak House', offering Danish, Nebraskan and Uruguayan beef. A great bar and slick service add to the grown up feel.

Social Eating House

58 Poland St ✉ W1F 7NR ⊖ Oxford Circus Town plan: **30**AJU**t**
– ☎ (020) 7993 3251 – www.socialeatinghouse.com – Closed Christmas, Sunday and bank holidays
• MODERN • Menu £ 19 (lunch) – Carte £ 37/48
Jason Atherton creates a bit of Brooklyn in Soho. The bustle and din let you know instantly you're in the right place. The cooking would make Escoffier proud with its 'faites simple' approach; staff are unstuffy and always on the ball.
→ Smoked Shetland salmon, miso crème fraîche, BBQ cucumber and spring truffle. Charred côte de porc, heritage carrots, white polenta and spring cabbage. Coconut meringue, mango sorbet, calamansi and curry crumble.

Arbutus

63-64 Frith St. ✉ W1D 3JW Town plan: **31**AKU**h**
⊖ Tottenham Court Road – ☎ (020) 7734 4545 – www.arbutusrestaurant.co.uk – Closed 25-26 December and 1 January
• MODERN • Menu £ 18 (weekday lunch) – Carte £ 28/40 – *(booking advisable)*
A relaxed setting, enthusiastic service, a terrific wine list that doesn't break the bank, and wonderfully flavoursome cooking – what's not to like? The technically confident kitchen has an innate understanding of the 'less is more' principle along with an appreciation of what-goes-with-what.
→ Squid and mackerel 'burger' with razor clams. Slow-cooked short rib of Wagyu beef Indonesian style and mango salad. Chocolate soup, cardamom ice cream.

Barrafina

54 Frith St. ✉ W1D 3SL ⊖ Tottenham Court Road Town plan: **31**AKU**c**
– ☎ (020) 7813 8016 – www.barrafina.co.uk – Closed 25 December and 1 January
• SPANISH • Carte £ 17/28 – *(bookings not accepted)*
For proof that great food is about great sourcing, come to this terrific, warmly run tapas bar from the Hart brothers – but be prepared to queue for gaps at the counter. Wonderful, fresh ingredients and expert cooking allow natural flavours to shine – the seafood is particularly stunning.
→ Sardines a la plancha. Pluma Ibérica with confit potatoes. Crema Catalana.

Bocca di Lupo

12 Archer St ✉ WID 7BB ⊖ Piccadilly Circus Town plan: **31**AJU**e**
– ✆ (020) 7734 2223 – www.boccadilupo.com – Closed 24 December-1 January and 31 August
• ITALIAN • Carte £ 17/45 – *(booking essential)*
Atmosphere, food and service are all best when sitting at the marble counter, watching the chefs at work. Specialities from across Italy come in large or small sizes and are full of flavour and vitality. Try also their gelato shop opposite.

Dehesa

25 Ganton St ✉ W1F 9BP ⊖ Oxford Circus Town plan: **30**AIU**i**
– ✆ (020) 7494 4170 – www.dehesa.co.uk – Closed Christmas
• MEDITERRANEAN • Carte £ 19/29
Repeats the success of its sister restaurant, Salt Yard, by offering tasty, good value Spanish and Italian tapas. Unhurried atmosphere in appealing corner location. Terrific drinks list too.

Nopi

21-22 Warwick St. ✉ W1B 5NE ⊖ Piccadilly Circus Town plan: **30**AIU**g**
– ✆ (020) 7494 9584 – www.nopi-restaurant.com – Closed 25-26 December, 1 January, Sunday and bank holidays
• MEDITERRANEAN • Carte £ 30/44
The bright, clean look of Yotam Ottolenghi's charmingly run all-day restaurant matches the fresh, invigorating food. The sharing plates take in the Mediterranean, the Middle East and Asia and the veggie dishes stand out.

LONDON

Ember Yard Ⓝ

60 Berwick St ✉ W1F 8DX ⊖ Oxford Circus Town plan: **30**AJT**y**
– ✆ (020) 7439 8057 – www.emberyard.co.uk – Closed 25-26 December and 1 January
• MEDITERRANEAN • Carte approx. £ 35 – *(booking advisable)*
Those familiar with the Salt Yard Group will recognise the Spanish and Italian themed menus – but their 4th fun outlet comes with a focus on cooking over charcoal or wood. There's even a seductive smokiness to some of the cocktails.

Polpetto Ⓝ

11 Berwick St ✉ W1F 0PL Town plan: **31**AJU**u**
⊖ Tottenham Court Road – ✆ (020) 7439 8627 – www.polpetto.co.uk – Closed Sunday dinner
• ITALIAN • Carte £ 12/25 (bookings not accepted at dinner)
Re-opened by Russell Norman in bigger premises. The style of food is the perfect match for this relaxed environment: the small, seasonally inspired Italian dishes are uncomplicated, appealingly priced and deliver great flavours.

Polpo Soho

41 Beak St. ✉ W1F 9SB ⊖ Oxford Circus Town plan: **30**AJU**d**
– ✆ (020) 7734 4479 – www.polpo.co.uk – Closed dinner 24 December, 25-26 and 31 December, 1 January and Sunday dinner
• ITALIAN • Carte £ 12/24 – *(bookings not accepted at dinner)*
A fun and lively Venetian bacaro, with a stripped-down, faux-industrial look. The small plates, from arancini and prosciutto to fritto misto and Cotechino sausage, are so well priced that waiting for a table is worth it.

Copita

27 d'Arblay St ✉ W1F 8EP ⊖ Oxford Circus Town plan: **30**AJU**a**
– ✆ (020) 7287 7797 – www.copita.co.uk – Closed Sunday and bank holidays
• MEDITERRANEAN • Carte £ 17/29 – *(bookings not accepted)*
Perch on one of the high stools or stay standing and get stuck into the daily menu of small, colourful and tasty dishes. Staff add to the atmosphere and everything on the Spanish wine list comes by the glass or copita.

LONDON

Palomar ⓝ

34 Rupert St ✉ W1D 6DN ⊖ Piccadilly Circus Town plan: **31**AJU**s**
– ✆ (020) 7439 8777 – www.thepalomar.co.uk – Closed 25-26 December and Sunday dinner
• OTHER WORLD KITCHENS • Carte £ 19/38 – *(booking advisable)*
A hip slice of modern-day Jerusalem in the heart of theatreland, with a zinc kitchen counter running back to an intimate, wood-panelled dining room. Like the atmosphere, the contemporary Middle Eastern cooking is fresh and vibrant.

Mele e Pere

46 Brewer St ✉ W1F 9TF ⊖ Piccadilly Circus Town plan: **31**AJU**h**
– ✆ (020) 7096 2096 – www.meleepere.co.uk – Closed 25-26 December, 1 January and Easter
• ITALIAN • Menu £ 16 (dinner) – Carte £ 26/39
Head downstairs – the 'apples and pears'? – to a vaulted, if somewhat hard-edged room with an appealing Vermouth bar. The owner-chef has worked in some decent London kitchens but hails from Verona so expect gutsy Italian dishes.

Blanchette ⓝ

9 D'Arblay St ✉ W1F 8DR ⊖ Oxford Circus Town plan: **30**AJU**g**
– ✆ (020) 7439 8100 – www.blanchettesoho.co.uk – Closed Sunday dinner
• FRENCH • Carte £ 13/20 – *(booking essential)*
Run by three frères, Blanchette takes French bistro food and gives it the 'small plates' treatment. It's named after their mother – the ox cheek bourguignon is her recipe. Tiles and exposed brick add to the rustic look.

Wright Brothers Soho

13 Kingly St. ✉ W1B 5PW ⊖ Oxford Circus Town plan: **30**AIU**z**
– ✆ (020) 7434 3611 – www.thewrightbrothers.co.uk – Closed 24-28 December, 1-2 January, Easter Sunday and bank holidays
• FISH AND SEAFOOD • Menu £ 15 (weekday lunch) – Carte £ 28/59
A seafood restaurant with a utilitarian look; avoid downstairs which is meant to resemble a lobster pot. Oysters are a speciality; fish is from Cornwall; and the 'surfboards' are ideal for anyone wanting a quick one course lunch.

HIX

66-70 Brewer St. ✉ WIF 9UP ⊖ Piccadilly Circus Town plan: **30**AJU**y**
– ✆ (020) 7292 3518 – www.hixsoho.co.uk – Closed 25-26 December
• BRITISH TRADITIONAL • Menu £ 20 (weekday lunch)/28 – Carte £ 29/59
The exterior may hint at exclusivity but inside this big restaurant the atmosphere is fun, noisy and sociable. The room comes decorated with the works of eminent British artists. Expect classic British dishes and ingredients.

10 Greek Street

10 Greek St ✉ W1D 4DH Town plan: **31**AKU**e**
⊖ Tottenham Court Road – ✆ (020) 7734 4677 – www.10greekstreet.com – Closed Christmas, Easter and Sunday
• MODERN • Carte £ 23/37
With just 28 seats and a dozen at the counter, the challenge is getting a table at this modishly sparse-looking bistro (no bookings taken at dinner). The chef-owner's blackboard menu comes with Anglo, Med and Middle Eastern elements.

Cinnamon Soho

5 Kingly St ✉ W1B 5PF ⊖ Oxford Circus Town plan: **30**AIU**a**
– ✆ (020) 7437 1664 – www.cinnamonsoho.com – Closed 1 January
• INDIAN • Menu £ 10 (weekday lunch)/35 – Carte £ 21/33 – *(bookings not accepted)*
This Cinnamon outpost is altogether more fun than its two older siblings. It blends Indian flavours with traditional British dishes, so you can order Rogan Josh shepherd's pie, curried Cullen skink or Cumbrian lamb biryani.

Tapas Brindisa

46 Broadwick St. ✉ W1F 7AF ⊖ Oxford Circus Town plan: **31**AJU**f**
– ✆ (020) 7534 1690 – www.brindisatapaskitchens.com – Closed dinner 24-27 December
• SPANISH • Menu £ 20 (weekday lunch) – Carte £ 15/25 – *(bookings not accepted at dinner)*
Sister to the original Tapas Brindisa in Borough Market. Expect the same quality of tapas from these importers of Spanish produce and the same bustling atmosphere. Service is obliging but bookings are not taken.

Burger & Lobster

36 Dean St ✉ W1D 4PS ⊖ Leicester Square Town plan: **31**AKU**x**
– ✆ (020) 7432 4800 – www.burgerandlobster.com – Closed bank holidays
• MEATS AND GRILLS • Menu £ 25
A sizeable place, yet as busy as the first branch in Mayfair. Choose a lobster roll in a brioche bun, a 1½lb Maine or Canadian lobster, or a 280g burger of Irish or Nebraskan beef. Bookings only taken for parties of 6 or more.

Vinoteca

53-55 Beak St ✉ W1F 9SH ⊖ Oxford Circus Town plan: **30**AJU**v**
– ✆ (020) 3544 7411 – www.vinoteca.co.uk – Closed 24-26 December and 1 January
• MODERN • Carte £ 18/40 – *(booking advisable)*
The terrific wine list mixes the classic with the esoteric and emerging markets are also covered. The food isn't forgotten – cured meats and cheeses are a highlight and European dishes like bavette and risotto also hit the spot.

Antidote (N)

12A Newburgh St ✉ W1F 7RR ⊖ Oxford Circus Town plan: **30**AIU**j**
– ✆ (020) 7287 8488 – www.antidotewinebar.com – Closed Sunday
• MODERN • Carte £ 23/40 – *(booking advisable)*
On the ground floor is a wine bar serving cheese, charcuterie and 'small plates'. The keenly run upstairs restaurant offers fresh, vibrant and contemporary cuisine, with the kitchen under the guidance of Mikael Jonsson of Hedone.

Spuntino

61 Rupert St. ✉ W1D 7PW ⊖ Piccadilly Circus Town plan: **31**AJU**j**
– ✆ n/a – www.spuntino.co.uk – Closed dinner 24 December, 25-26, 31 December and 1 January
• NORTH-AMERICAN • Carte £ 16/23 – *(bookings not accepted)*
Influenced by Downtown New York, with its no-booking policy and industrial look. Sit at the counter and order classics like Mac 'n' cheese or mini burgers. The staff, who look like they could also fix your car, really add to the fun.

Bibigo

58-59 Great Marlborough St ✉ W1F 7JY Town plan: **30**AJU**x**
⊖ Oxford Circus – ✆ (020) 7042 5225 – www.bibigouk.com
• KOREAN • Menu £ 13 (lunch) – Carte £ 16/30
The enthusiastically run Bibigo represents Korea's largest food company's first foray into the UK market. Watch the kitchen send out dishes such as kimchi, Bossam (simmered pork belly) and hot stone galbi (chargrilled short ribs).

Imli Street

167-169 Wardour St ✉ W1F 8WR Town plan: **31**AJU**w**
⊖ Tottenham Court Road – ✆ (020) 7287 4243 – www.imlistreet.com – Closed 25-26 December and 1 January
• INDIAN • Menu £ 24 – Carte £ 19/43 – *(bookings not accepted)*
Imli has a brighter look these days and comes with a terrific cocktail bar – a great place to wait for a table. The sharing plates are mostly influenced by southern India, although there are also some Indo-Chinese dishes.

LONDON

Ceviche

17 Frith St ✉ *W1D 4RG* Town plan: **31**AKU**w**
⊖ Tottenham Court Road – ☎ (020) 7292 2040 – www.cevicheuk.com
• PERUVIAN • Carte £ 15/27

Based on a Lima Pisco bar, Ceviche is as loud as it is fun. First try the deliriously addictive drinks based on the Peruvian spirit Pisco, and then share some thinly sliced sea bass or octopus, along with anticuchos skewers.

Cây Tre

42-43 Dean St ✉ *W1D 4PZ* Town plan: **31**AKU**m**
⊖ Tottenham Court Road – ☎ (020) 7317 9118 – www.caytresoho.co.uk
• VIETNAMESE • Menu £ 23/29 – Carte £ 17/28 – *(booking advisable)*

Bright, sleek and bustling surroundings where Vietnamese standouts include Cha La Lot (spicy ground pork wrapped in betel leaves), slow-cooked Mekong catfish with a well-judged sweet and spicy sauce, and 6 versions of Pho (noodle soup).

Rosa's Carnaby Ⓝ

23a Ganton Street ✉ *W1F 9BW ⊖ Oxford Circus* Town plan: **30**AIU**u**
– ☎ (020) 7287 9617 – www.rosaslondon.com
• THAI • Menu £ 22 (lunch and early dinner) – Carte £ 17/31 – *(booking essential)*

A bright, bustling café celebrating traditional Thai flavours, with the occasional modern twist. Perch on low stools and rub elbows with your neighbours while the unfailingly polite staff cope capably with the rush of customers.

Rosa's Soho

48 Dean St ✉ *W1D 5BF ⊖ Leicester Square* Town plan: **31**AKU**j**
– ☎ (020) 7494 1638 – www.rosaslondon.com – Closed Easter and Christmas
• THAI • Menu £ 22/32 – Carte £ 17/31 – *(booking advisable)*

The worn-in, pared down look of this authentic Thai café adds to its intimate feel. Signature dishes include warm minced chicken salad and a sweet pumpkin red curry. Tom Yam soup comes with a lovely balance of sweet, sour and spice.

Bone Daddies

30-31 Peter St ✉ *W1F 0AR ⊖ Piccadilly Circus* Town plan: **31**AJU**y**
– ☎ (020) 7287 8581 – www.bonedaddiesramen.com – Closed 25 December
• ASIAN • Carte £ 18/29 – *(bookings not accepted)*

Maybe ramen is the new rock 'n' roll. The charismatic Aussie chef-owner feels that combinations are endless when it comes to these comforting bowls. Be ready to queue then share a table. It's a fun place, run by a hospitable bunch.

Soho Kitchen & Bar Ⓝ

19-21 Old Compton St. ✉ *W1D 5JJ* Town plan: **31**AKU**d**
⊖ Leicester Square – ☎ (020) 7734 5656 – www.sohodiner.com
• NORTH-AMERICAN • Carte £ 17/32

Most punters who pack out this appealing retro-style diner are here for the comforting American classics like mac & cheese, a hot dog or a burger. The buzz is great, the cocktails are on tap and it's open till the wee small hours.

Barshu

28 Frith St. ✉ *W1D 5LF ⊖ Leicester Square* Town plan: **31**AKU**g**
– ☎ (020) 7287 8822 – www.barshurestaurant.co.uk – Closed 24-25 December
• CHINESE • Carte £ 24/56 – *(booking advisable)*

The fiery and authentic flavours of China's Sichuan province are the draw here; help is at hand as the menu has pictures. It's decorated with carved wood and lanterns; downstairs is better for groups.

Ba Shan

24 Romilly St. ✉ *W1D 5AH ⊖ Leicester Square* Town plan: **31**AKU**f**
– ☎ (020) 7287 3266 – Closed 24-25 December
• CHINESE • Carte £ 15/37 – *(booking advisable)*

Whilst there are some Sichuan dishes, this bigger-than-it-looks Chinese restaurant excels in specialities from Hunan. That means plenty of heat but also pickling, curing and smoking; dishes arrive when ready so sharing is best.

Baozi Inn

25-26 Newport Court ✉ WC2H 7JS Town plan: **31**AKU**r**
⊖ Leicester Square – ✆ (020) 7287 6877 – Closed 24-25 December
• CHINESE • Carte approx. £ 14 – *(bookings not accepted)*
Buzzy, busy little place that's great for a quick bite, especially if you like pork buns, steaming bowls of noodles, a hit of Sichuan fire and plenty of beer or tea. You'll leave feeling surprisingly energised and rejuvenated.

Manchurian Legends

16 Lisle St ✉ WC2H 7BE ⊖ Leicester Square Town plan: **31**AKU**z**
– ✆ (020) 7287 6606 – www.manchurianlegends.com – Closed Christmas
• CHINESE • Menu £ 16/25 – Carte approx. £ 46
Try specialities from a less familiar region of China: Dongbei, the 'north east'. As winters there are long, stews and BBQ dishes are popular, as are pickled ingredients and chilli heat. Further warmth comes from the sweet natured staff.

Beijing Dumpling

23 Lisle St. ✉ WC2H 7BA ⊖ Leicester Square Town plan: **31**AKU**l**
– ✆ (0207) 287 68 88 – Closed 24-25 December
• CHINESE • Menu £ 16/20 – Carte £ 10/40
This relaxed little place serves freshly prepared dumplings of both Beijing and Shanghai styles. Although the range is not as comprehensive as the name suggests, they do stand out, especially varieties of the famed Siu Lung Bao.

Tonkotsu

63 Dean St ✉ W1D 4QG Town plan: **31**AKU**p**
⊖ Tottenham Court Road – ✆ (020) 7437 0071 – www.tonkotsu.co.uk
• JAPANESE • Carte £ 19/25 – *(bookings not accepted)*
Some things are worth queuing for. Good ramen is all about the base stock: 18 hours goes into its preparation here to ensure the bowls of soup and wheat-based noodles reach a depth of flavour that seems to nourish one's very soul.

Ducksoup

41 Dean St ✉ W1D 4PY ⊖ Leicester Square Town plan: **31**AKU**a**
– ✆ (020) 7287 4599 – www.ducksoupsoho.co.uk – Closed Christmas, Easter, Sunday dinner and bank holidays
• MODERN • Carte £ 19/35
It's compact, with bar seating; decoratively it's knowingly underwhelming; and the menu is handwritten each day – yes, every 'on-trend' box is ticked here. Dishes are all about the produce and are confidently unadorned.

Koya

49 Frith St ✉ W1D 4SG ⊖ Tottenham Court Road Town plan: **31**AKU**y**
– ✆ (020) 7434 4463 – www.koya.co.uk – Closed Christmas
• JAPANESE • Carte £ 10/29 – *(bookings not accepted)*
Come for authentic udon noodles, made with wheat kneaded by foot, at this sweetly run, simply adorned place. The dashi base stock is freshly made every day. Be respectful by slurping with abandon. Next door Koya Bar offers a similar menu to a simpler backdrop.

Pitt Cue Co.

1 Newburgh St ✉ W1F 7RB ⊖ Oxford Circus Town plan: **30**AIU**p**
– ✆ (020) 7287 5578 – www.pittcue.co.uk
• MEATS AND GRILLS • Carte £ 18/34 – *(bookings not accepted)*
The owners started out selling their American barbecue dishes from a van before finding this tiny spot. The ribs are smoked in-house for 6 hours before roasting; the pulled pork is excellent. It's messy, filling and fun; be ready to queue.

Strand and Covent Garden

Savoy

Strand ✉ *WC2R 0EU* ⊖ *Charing Cross* Town plan: **31**ALU**s**
– ✆ *(020) 7836 4343* – *www.fairmont.com/savoy*
268 rm – †£ 445 ††£ 445, ☕ £ 30 – 45 suites
Rest *Savoy Grill* – see restaurant listing
Rest *Kaspar's* – ✆ (020) 7420 2111 – Menu £ 28 (early dinner) – Carte £ 34/63
A legendary hotel renewed after a 3 year renovation; its luxurious bedrooms and stunning suites come in Edwardian or art deco styles. Have tea in the Thames Foyer, the hotel's heart, or drinks in the famous American Bar or the moodier Beaufort Bar. Along with the Savoy Grill is Kaspar's, an informal seafood bar and grill which replaced the River restaurant.

One Aldwych

1 Aldwych ✉ *WC2B 4RH* ⊖ *Temple* Town plan: **32**AMU**r**
– ✆ *(020) 7300 1000* – *www.onealdwych.com*
105 rm – †£ 306/564 ††£ 342/594, ☕ £ 26 – 12 suites
Rest *Axis* – see restaurant listing
Rest *Indigo* – Menu £ 25 – Carte £ 30/47 – *(closed lunch Saturday-Sunday)*
Former 19C bank, now a stylish hotel with lots of artwork; the lobby changes its look seasonally and doubles as a bar. Stylish, contemporary bedrooms with the latest mod cons; the deluxe rooms and suites are particularly desirable. Impressive leisure facilities. Light, accessible menu at Indigo.

ME London

336-337 Strand ✉ *WC2R 1HA* ⊖ *Temple* Town plan: **32**AMU**a**
– ✆ *(020) 7395 3400* – *www.melondonuk.com*
157 rm – †£ 300/600 ††£ 330/720, ☕ £ 25 – 16 suites
Rest *STK* – ✆ (020) 7395 3450 – Menu £ 30 – Carte £ 32/99
– *(closed 25-26 December and 1 January) (dinner only)*
Rest *Cucina Asellina* – ✆ (020) 7395 3445 – Menu £ 16/20 – Carte £ 25/49
Rest *Radio* – Carte £ 16/28 – *(closed 25-26 December)*
On the site of the Gaiety theatre and Marconi House, now a striking hotel designed by Fosters + Partners. Eye-catching pyramid shaped reception; bedrooms that are crisply decorated, cleverly lit and very comfortable. Steaks in the glitzy STK; Cucina Asellina offers a contemporary setting for Italian food; Radio has a simple menu and comes with a stunning rooftop bar.

Waldorf Hilton

Aldwych ✉ *WC2B 4DD* ⊖ *Temple* Town plan: **32**AMU**s**
– ✆ *(020) 7836 2400* – *www.hilton.co.uk/waldorf*
298 rm – †£ 259/329 ††£ 289/359, ☕ £ 23 – 12 suites
Rest *Homage* – Carte £ 28/60 – *(dinner only)*
Impressive curved and columned façade: an Edwardian landmark in a great location. Popular for afternoon tea; relaxed brasserie style dining. On-going refurbishment of bedrooms.

St Martins Lane

45 St Martin's Ln ✉ *WC2N 3HX* ⊖ *Charing Cross* Town plan: **31**ALU**e**
– ✆ *(020) 7300 5500* – *www.stmartinslane.com*
206 rm – †£ 222/479 ††£ 222/479, ☕ £ 26 – 2 suites
Rest *Asia de Cuba* – Menu £ 19/22 – Carte £ 48/85
The unmistakable hand of Philippe Starck is evident at this most contemporary of hotels. Unique and stylish, from the starkly modern lobby to the state-of-the-art bedrooms, which come in a blizzard of white.

Savoy Grill – Savoy Hotel

Strand ✉ *WC2R 0EU* ⊖ *Charing Cross* Town plan: **31**ALU**s**
– ✆ *(020) 7592 1600* – *www.gordonramsay.com/thesavoygrill*
• BRITISH TRADITIONAL • Menu £ 30 (lunch) – Carte £ 34/63
Archives were explored, designers briefed and much money spent, with the result that the Savoy Grill has returned to the traditions that made it famous. As befits the name, it is the charcoal grilling of meats that takes centre stage.

XXX **Delaunay**

55 Aldwych ✉ WC2B 4BB ⊖ Temple Town plan: **32**AMU**x**
– ✆ (020) 7499 8558 – www.thedelaunay.com – Closed 25 December and dinner 24 December
• MODERN • Carte £ 20/52 – *(booking essential)*
The Delaunay was inspired by the grand cafés of Europe but, despite sharing the same buzz and celebrity clientele as its sibling The Wolseley, is not just a mere replica. The all-day menu is more mittel-European, with great schnitzels and wieners.

XXX **The Ivy**

1-5 West St ✉ WC2H 9NQ ⊖ Leicester Square Town plan: **31**AKU**p**
– ✆ (020) 7836 4751 – www.the-ivy.co.uk – Closed 25 December
• BRITISH TRADITIONAL • Menu £ 27 – Carte £ 27/67
One of the original celebrity hang-out restaurants; still pulling them in. Appealing menu, from shepherd's pie to fishcakes and nursery puddings. Staff go about their business with alacrity.

XXX **Axis** – One Aldwych Hotel

1 Aldwych ✉ WC2B 4RH ⊖ Temple Town plan: **31**AMU**r**
– ✆ (020) 7300 0300 – www.onealdwych.com/axis – Closed early August-early September, Christmas-New Year and Monday
• MODERN • Menu £ 25 – Carte £ 30/41
A spiral marble staircase leading down to this impressively high-ceilinged restaurant adds to the expectation. The menu is a combination of British classics and lighter European choices.

XX ✿ **L'Atelier de Joël Robuchon**

13-15 West St. ✉ WC2H 9NE ⊖ Leicester Square Town plan: **31**AKU**a**
– ✆ (020) 7010 8600 – www.joelrobuchon.co.uk
– Closed 25-26 December, 1 January, and August bank holiday Monday
• FRENCH • Menu £ 129 – Carte £ 31/109
Creative, skilled and occasionally playful cooking; dishes may look delicate but pack a punch. Ground floor 'Atelier' comes with counter seating and chefs on view. More structured 'La Cuisine' upstairs and a cool bar above that.
→ Scallops with chicory salad and mustard dressing. Quail stuffed with foie gras and mashed potatoes. Orange rum baba, Tahitian vanilla cream.

XX **J. Sheekey**

28-34 St Martin's Ct. ✉ WC2 4AL Town plan: **31**ALU**v**
⊖ Leicester Square – ✆ (020) 7240 2565 – www.j-sheekey.co.uk
– Closed 25-26 December
• FISH AND SEAFOOD • Carte £ 32/69 – *(booking essential)*
Festooned with photographs of actors and linked to the theatrical world since opening in 1890. Wood panels and alcove tables add famed intimacy. Accomplished seafood cooking.

XX **Rules**

35 Maiden Ln ✉ WC2E 7LB ⊖ Leicester Square Town plan: **31**ALU**n**
– ✆ (020) 7836 5314 – www.rules.co.uk – Closed 25-26 December
• BRITISH TRADITIONAL • Carte £ 35/60 – *(booking essential)*
London's oldest restaurant boasts a fine collection of antique cartoons, drawings and paintings. Tradition continues in the menu, specialising in game from its own estate.

XX **Clos Maggiore**

33 King St ✉ WC2E 8JD ⊖ Leicester Square Town plan: **31**ALU**z**
– ✆ (020) 7379 9696 – www.closmaggiore.com – Closed 24-25 December
• FRENCH • Menu £ 18 (weekdays)/33 – Carte £ 32/58
One of London's most romantic restaurants – but be sure to ask for the enchanting conservatory with its retractable roof. The sophisticated French cooking is joined by a wine list of great depth. Good value and very popular pre/post theatre menus.

LONDON

LONDON

Les Deux Salons

40-42 William IV St ✉ WC2N 4DD Town plan: **31**ALU**m**
⊖ Charing Cross – ✆ (020) 7420 2050 – www.lesdeuxsalons.co.uk – Closed 25-26 December and 1 January
• FRENCH • Menu £ 13/23 – Carte £ 16/48

Authentic Parisian brasserie complete with smoked mirrors, globe lights and striking mosaic floor. Ground floor is the better salon for atmosphere. Appealing menu mixes French classics, chargrilled meats and the odd British interloper.

Balthazar

4-6 Russell St. ✉ WC2B 5HZ ⊖ Covent Garden Town plan: **31**ALU**t**
– ✆ (020) 3301 1155 – www.balthazarlondon.com – Closed 25 December
• FRENCH • Carte £ 26/62 – *(booking essential)*

Those who know the original Balthazar in Manhattan's SoHo district will find the London version of this classic brasserie uncannily familiar in looks, vibe and food. The Franglais menu keeps it simple and the cocktails are great.

Le Deuxième

65a Long Acre ✉ WC2E 9JH ⊖ Covent Garden Town plan: **31**ALU**b**
– ✆ (020) 7379 0033 – www.ledeuxieme.com – Closed 24-25 December
• MODERN • Menu £ 15/28 – Carte £ 27/41

Caters well for theatregoers: opens early, closes late. Buzzy eatery, simply decorated in white with subtle lighting. International menu but emphasis within Europe.

J. Sheekey Oyster Bar

33-34 St Martin's Ct. ✉ WC2 4AL Town plan: **31**ALU**v**
⊖ Leicester Square – ✆ (020) 7240 2565 – www.j-sheekey.co.uk – Closed 25-26 December
• FISH AND SEAFOOD • Carte £ 22/39

An addendum to J. Sheekey restaurant. Sit at the bar to watch the chefs prepare the same quality seafood as next door but at slightly lower prices; fish pie and fruits de mer are the popular choices. Open all day.

Hawksmoor

11 Langley St ✉ WC2H 9JG ⊖ Covent Garden Town plan: **31**ALU**f**
– ✆ (020) 7420 9390 – www.thehawksmoor.com – Closed 24-26 December
• MEATS AND GRILLS • Carte £ 27/79

Steaks from Longhorn cattle lovingly reared in North Yorkshire and dry-aged for at least 35 days are the stars of the show. Atmospheric, bustling basement restaurant in former brewery cellars.

Terroirs

5 William IV St ✉ WC2N 4DW ⊖ Charing Cross Town plan: **31**ALU**h**
– ✆ (020) 7036 0660 – www.terroirswinebar.com – Closed 25-26 December, 1 January, Sunday and bank holidays
• FRENCH • Menu £ 10 (lunch) – Carte £ 25/34

Eat in the ground floor bistro/wine bar or from a slightly different menu two floors below at 'Downstairs at Terroirs'. Flavoursome French cooking, with extra Italian and Spanish influences. Thoughtfully compiled wine list.

Opera Tavern

23 Catherine St. ✉ WC2B 5JS ⊖ Covent Garden Town plan: **31**ALU**y**
– ✆ (020) 7836 3680 – www.operatavern.co.uk – Closed 25-26 and 31 December, 1 January and Sunday dinner
• MEDITERRANEAN • Carte £ 12/30

Shares the same appealing concept of small plates of Spanish and Italian delicacies as its sisters, Salt Yard and Dehesa. All done in a smartly converted old boozer which dates from 1879; ground floor bar and upstairs dining room.

Polpo Covent Garden

6 Maiden Ln. ✉ WC2E 7NA ⊖ Leicester Square Town plan: **31**ALU**p**
– ✆ (020) 7836 8448 – www.polpo.co.uk – Closed 24-26 December
• ITALIAN • Carte £ 12/26 – *(bookings not taken at dinner)*

First Soho, now Covent Garden gets a fun Venetian bacaro. The small plates are surprisingly filling, with delights such as pizzette of white anchovy vying with fennel and almond salad, fritto misto competing with spaghettini and meatballs.

Green Man & French Horn

54 St Martin's Ln ✉ WC2N 4EA Westminster Town plan: **31**ALU**w**
⊖ Leicester Square – ✆ (020) 7836 2645 – www.greenmanfrenchhorn.co – Closed Christmas and New Year
• FRENCH • Carte £ 23/33
A small old pub so artfully transformed into a bustling French bistro/wine bar, it feels as though it's been here for years. The wine list and menu take their inspiration from the Loire River and Valley; the cooking is comforting and earthy and the wines from small organic and biodynamic growers.

Bedford & Strand

1a Bedford St ✉ WC2E 9HH ⊖ Charing Cross Town plan: **31**ALU**c**
– ✆ (020) 7836 3033 – www.bedford-strand.com – Closed 24 December-2 January, Sunday and bank holidays
• BRITISH TRADITIONAL • Menu £ 20 – Carte £ 21/41 – *(booking essential)*
It calls itself a 'wine room and bistro' which neatly sums up both the philosophy and the style of this usefully located basement: interesting wines, reassuringly familiar French and British dishes and relaxed surroundings.

Dishoom

12 Upper St Martin's Ln ✉ WC2H 9FB Town plan: **31**ALU**j**
⊖ Leicester Square – ✆ (020) 7420 9320 – www.dishoom.com – Closed 24 December dinner, 25-26 December and 1-2 January
• INDIAN • Menu £ 20/35 – Carte £ 10/26
A facsimile of a Bombay café, of the sort opened by Persian immigrants in the early 20C. Try baked roti rolls with chai, vada pav – Bombay's version of the chip butty; a curry or grilled meats. There's another branch in Shoreditch.

Suda

23 Slingsby Pl, St Martin's Courtyard ✉ WC2E 9AB Town plan: **31**ALU**d**
⊖ Covent Garden – ✆ (020) 7240 8010 – www.suda-thai.com – Closed 25 December and 1 January
• THAI • Menu £ 11/26 **s** – Carte £ 22/29
This shiny Thai restaurant in a new development may look like a branded chain but the quality of its food far exceeds one's expectations. Come in a group, sit upstairs, order cocktails and share plenty of dishes.

10 Cases

16 Endell St ✉ WC2H 9BD ⊖ Covent Garden Town plan: **31**ALU**a**
– ✆ (020) 7836 6801 – www.the10cases.co.uk – Closed Easter, Christmas-New Year and bank holidays
• FRENCH • Carte £ 23/46 – *(booking essential)*
Cosy and inviting little bistrot offering an unpretentious daily menu of 3 starters, 3 main courses and 3 desserts, along with a very reasonably priced wine list of 10 reds and 10 whites available by the glass, carafe or bottle.

Mishkin's

25 Catherine St ✉ WC2B 5JS ⊖ Covent Garden Town plan: **31**ALU**w**
– ✆ (020) 7240 2078 – www.mishkins.co.uk – Closed 24-26 December and 1-2 January
• NORTH-AMERICAN • Carte £ 14/24
The Jewish-American deli – but with cocktails – was the inspiration behind this fun spot from the Polpo people. Lox beigel, chopped liver and salt beef sit alongside nibbles like cod cheek popcorn; the Reuben sandwich hits the spot.

VICTORIA

Corinthia

Whitehall Pl. ✉ SW1A 2BD ⊖ Embankment Town plan: **31**ALV**x**
– ✆ (020) 7930 8181 – www.corinthia.com/london
294 rm – †£ 318/1140 ††£ 318/1140, ☕ £ 33 – 23 suites
Rest *Northall* Rest *Massimo* – see restaurant listing
The restored Victorian splendour of this grand, luxurious hotel cannot fail to impress. Tasteful and immaculately finished bedrooms are some of the largest in town; suites come with butlers. The stunning spa is over four floors.

LONDON

Goring

15 Beeston Pl ✉ SW1W 0JW ⊖ Victoria — Town plan: **38**AIX**a**
– ✆ (020) 7396 9000 – *www.thegoring.com*
69 rm – †£ 310/630 ††£ 310/1025, ☕ £ 32 – 8 suites
Rest *Dining Room at The Goring* – see restaurant listing
This very English, very charming and immaculately kept hotel is still owned and run by the Goring family who built it in 1910 – the fourth generation now at the helm. Many of the attractive bedrooms overlook a peaceful garden.

InterContinental London Westminster

22-28 Broadway ✉ SW1H 9JS ⊖ St James's Park — Town plan: **39**AKX**w**
– ✆ (020) 3301 8080 – *www.westminster.intercontinental.com*
256 rm – †£ 249/289 ††£ 249/289, ☕ £ 24 – 45 suites
Rest *Blue Boar Smokehouse* – ✆ (020) 3301 1400 – Carte £ 28/51
Its proximity to the seat of power is a recurring theme at this hotel which opened in 2013. Apart from its façade, little remains of the original 19C building. A cool, crisp reception area sets the tone; bedrooms are stylish and contemporary. The Smokehouse specialises in ribs, pulled pork and steaks.

St James' Court

45 Buckingham Gate ✉ SW1E 6BS — Town plan: **39**AJX**e**
⊖ St James's Park – ✆ (020) 7834 6655 – *www.tajhotels.com/stjamescourt*
318 rm – †£ 198/594 ††£ 198/594, ☕ £ 21 – 20 suites
Rest *Quilon* ✿ – see restaurant listing
Rest *Bank* – ✆ (020) 7630 6644 – Carte £ 27/61
– *(closed 25-26 December and 1 January)*
Rest *Bistro 51* – Menu £ 30 – Carte £ 28/44
Built in 1897 as serviced accommodation for visiting aristocrats. Behind the impressive Edwardian façade lies an equally elegant interior. Quietest bedrooms overlook a courtyard. Relaxed, bright Bistro 51 comes with an international menu; Bank offers brasserie classics in a conservatory.

51 Buckingham Gate without rest

51 Buckingham Gate ✉ SW1E 6AF — Town plan: **39**AJX**s**
⊖ St James's Park – ✆ (020) 7769 7766
– *www.taj51buckinghamgate.co.uk*
85 suites – ††£ 300/6300, ☕ £ 25
In the courtyard of the Crowne Plaza but offering greater levels of comfort and service. Contemporary in style, suites range from one to nine bedrooms. Butler service available. Restaurants located in adjacent hotel.

St Ermin's

2 Caxton St. ✉ SW1H 0QW ⊖ St James's Park — Town plan: **39**AJX**a**
– ✆ (020) 7222 7888 – *www.sterminshotel.co.uk*
331 rm – †£ 209/599 ††£ 209/599, ☕ £ 25 – 41 suites
Rest *Caxton Grill* – Carte £ 26/52 – *(closed lunch Saturday-Sunday)*
Built as an apartment block in 1897 but has spent most of its life as a hotel and is a favoured spot for many a politician. A comprehensive refurbishment restored many of its original features, including the stunning rococo lobby. The restaurant specialises in meat cooked on the Josper grill.

41 without rest

41 Buckingham Palace Rd. ✉ SW1W 0PS — Town plan: **38**AIX**n**
⊖ Victoria – ✆ (020) 7300 0041 – *www.41hotel.com*
28 rm ☕ – †£ 338 ††£ 338 – 6 suites
Smart, discreet addendum to The Rubens hotel next door. Attractively decorated and quiet lounge where breakfast is served; comfortable bedrooms boast fireplaces and plenty of extras. Light lunches and dinners for residents only.

The Rubens at The Palace

39 Buckingham Palace Rd ✉ SW1W 0PS — Town plan: **38**AIX**n**
Victoria – ✆ (020) 7834 6600 – www.rubenshotel.com
161 rm – †£ 149/259 ††£ 159/269, ☕ £ 20 – 1 suite
Rest *Library* – Menu £ 38 – Carte £ 31/80 – *(closed 25-30 December) (dinner only)*
Rest *Old Masters* – Menu £ 33 – *(closed lunch Saturday and Sunday)*
Rest *bbar* – ✆ (020) 7958 7000 – Carte £ 23/47 – *(closed Christmas, Easter, Sunday and bank holidays)*

Discreet, comfortable hotel in great location for tourists. Constant reinvestment ensures bright and contemporary bedrooms. Old Masters for a buffet-style carvery; 'fine dining' in cosy Library; South African themed bbar.

Eccleston Square

37 Eccleston Sq ✉ SW1V 1PB Victoria — Town plan: **38**AIY**s**
– ✆ (020) 3489 1001 – www.ecclestonsquarehotel.com
39 rm – †£ 210/310 ††£ 210/310, ☕ £ 15
Rest *Bistrot on the Square* – Menu £ 19 (weekday lunch) – Carte £ 24/32

Attractive townhouse in a smart square, with a crisp, contemporary interior. Bedrooms are decorated to a high standard and come full of assorted electronic gadgetry. Varied international menu in Bistrot; afternoon tea a feature.

Lord Milner without rest

111 Ebury St ✉ SW1W 9QU Victoria — Town plan: **38**AHY**k**
– ✆ (020) 7881 9880 – www.lordmilner.com
11 rm – †£ 100/125 ††£ 124/160, ☕ £ 8.50

A four storey terraced house, with individually decorated bedrooms, three with four-poster beds and all with smart marble bathrooms. Garden Suite is the best room; it has its own patio. Breakfast served in your bedroom.

Quilon – St James' Court Hotel

41 Buckingham Gate ✉ SW1E 6AF — Town plan: **39**AJX**e**
St James's Park – ✆ (020) 7821 1899 – www.quilon.co.uk
– *Closed 25 December*
• INDIAN • Menu £ 24/53 – Carte £ 28/55

An extensive 2012 makeover left this long-standing restaurant looking slick and contemporary. The elegant surroundings provide the perfect backdrop to chef Sriram Aylur's accomplished and light style of cooking, which focuses on India's southwest coast and mixes the modern with the traditional.

→ Chargrilled scallops. Braised lamb shank. Spiced, cold chocolate fondant.

Dining Room at The Goring – Goring Hotel

15 Beeston Pl ✉ SW1W 0JW Victoria — Town plan: **38**AIX**a**
– ✆ (020) 7396 9000 – www.thegoring.com – *Closed Saturday lunch*
• BRITISH TRADITIONAL • Menu £ 43 (weekday lunch)/53

A paean to all things British and the very model of discretion and decorum – the perfect spot for those who 'like things done properly'. The menu is an appealing mix of classics and lighter, more modern dishes.

Roux at Parliament Square

Royal Institution of Chartered Surveyors, Parliament Sq. ✉ SW1P 3AD Westminster – ✆ (020) 7334 3737 — Town plan: **39**ALX**x**
– *www.rouxatparliamentsquare.co.uk – Closed 22 December-5 January, Saturday, Sunday and bank holidays*
• MODERN • Menu £ 35 (weekday lunch) – Carte £ 38/62 – *(bookings advisable at lunch)*

Light floods through the Georgian windows of this comfortable restaurant within the offices of the Royal Institute of Chartered Surveyors. Carefully crafted, contemporary cuisine, with some interesting flavour combinations.

XXX **Northall** - Corinthia Hotel

Whitehall Pl. ✉ WC2N 5AE ⊖ Embankment Town plan: **31**ALV**x**
– ✆ (020) 7321 3100 – www.thenorthall.co.uk
• BRITISH TRADITIONAL • Menu £ 28/30 – Carte £ 26/75

The Corinthia Hotel's British restaurant champions our indigenous produce, and its menu is an appealing document. It occupies two rooms: head for the more modern one with its bar and booths, which is less formal than the other section.

XXX **The Cinnamon Club**

30-32 Great Smith St ✉ SW1P 3BU Town plan: **39**AKX**c**
⊖ St James's Park – ✆ (020) 7222 2555 – www.cinnamonclub.com – Closed bank holidays and Sunday
• INDIAN • Menu £ 24 (weekdays) – Carte £ 31/61

Tourists and locals, politicians and business types – this smart Indian restaurant housed in the listed former Westminster Library attracts all types. The fairly elaborate dishes arrive fully garnished and the spicing is quite subtle.

LONDON

XXX **Santini**

29 Ebury St ✉ SW1W 0NZ ⊖ Victoria – ✆ (020) Town plan: **38**AHY**v**
7730 4094 – www.santinirestaurant.com – Closed 23-26 December, 1 January and Easter
• ITALIAN • Menu £ 25 (dinner) – Carte £ 30/67

Santini has looked after its many immaculately coiffured regulars for 30 years. The not inexpensive menu of classic Italian dishes is broadly Venetian in style; the daily specials, pasta dishes and desserts are the standout courses.

XXX **Grand Imperial**

Grosvenor Hotel, 101 Buckingham Palace Rd Town plan: **38**AIY**a**
✉ SW1W 0SJ ⊖ Victoria – ✆ (020) 7821 8898
– www.grandimperiallondon.com – Closed 25-26 December
• CHINESE • Menu £ 18 (weekday lunch) – Carte £ 21/110

Grand it most certainly is, as this elegant restaurant is in the Grosvenor Hotel's former ballroom. It specialises in Cantonese cuisine, particularly the version found in Hong Kong; steaming and frying are used to great effect.

XX **Tinello**

87 Pimlico Rd ✉ SW1W 8PH ⊖ Sloane Square Town plan: **37**AGZ**s**
– ✆ (020) 7730 3663 – www.tinello.co.uk – Closed Sunday and bank holidays
• ITALIAN • Carte £ 24/52 – *(booking essential at dinner)*

The brothers Sali have created a warm, friendly, romantic and very popular Italian restaurant. Their native Tuscany informs the cooking, so expect dishes like ribollita, liver crostini, and pappardelle with wild boar ragout.

XX **Osteria Dell' Angolo**

47 Marsham St ✉ SW1P 3DR ⊖ St James's Park Town plan: **39**AKY**n**
– ✆ (020) 3268 1077 – www.osteriadellangolo.co.uk – Closed Easter, 17-31 August, 23-27 December, 1-7 January, Saturday lunch, Sunday and bank holidays
• ITALIAN • Menu £ 18 (weekday lunch) – Carte £ 30/42 – *(booking essential)*

At lunch, this Italian opposite the Home Office is full of bustle and men in suits; at dinner it's a little more relaxed. Staff are personable and the menu is reassuringly familiar; homemade pasta and seafood dishes are good.

XX **Rex Whistler** Ⓝ

Tate Britain, Millbank ✉ SW1P 4RG Victoria Town plan: **39**ALY**w**
⊖ Pimlico – ✆ (020) 7887 8825 – www.tate.org.uk – Closed 24-26 December
• BRITISH TRADITIONAL • Menu £ 29 – *(lunch only)*

The £ 45million renovation of Tate Britain included a freshening up of its restaurant and restoration of Whistler's mural, 'The Expedition in Pursuit of Rare Meats', which envelops the room. The monthly menu is stoutly British and the remarkably priced wine list has an unrivalled 'half bottle' selection.

XX **Il Convivio**

143 Ebury St ✉ SW1W 9QN ⊖ Sloane Square Town plan: **38**AHY**a**
– ✆ (020) 7730 4099 – www.ilconvivio.co.uk – Closed Christmas-New Year, Easter, Sunday and bank holidays
• ITALIAN • Menu £ 18 (lunch)/24 – Carte £ 29/51
Handsome Georgian townhouse with a retractable roof and Dante's poetry embossed on the walls. All of the pasta is made on the top floor; the squid ink spaghetti is a staple. Dishes are artfully presented and flavoursome.

XX **Massimo** – Corinthia Hotel

10 Northumberland Ave. ✉ WC2N 5AE Town plan: **31**ALV**x**
⊖ Embankment – ✆ (020) 7321 3156 – www.corinthia.com/london – Closed Sunday
• ITALIAN • Menu £ 30 – Carte £ 31/76
Opulent, visually impressive room with an oyster bar on one side. On offer are traditional dishes true to the regions of Italy; fish and seafood dishes stand out. Impressive private dining room comes with its own chef.

XX **Boisdale of Belgravia**

15 Eccleston St ✉ SW1W 9LX ⊖ Victoria Town plan: **38**AHY**c**
– ✆ (020) 7730 6922 – www.boisdale.co.uk – Closed 25 December, Saturday lunch, Sunday and bank holidays
• BRITISH TRADITIONAL • Menu £ 18 – Carte £ 24/69
A proudly Scottish restaurant with acres of tartan and a charmingly higgledy-piggledy layout. Stand-outs are the smoked salmon and the 28-day aged Aberdeenshire cuts of beef. Live nightly jazz.

XX **The Ebury Restaurant & Wine Bar**

139 Ebury St. ✉ SW1W 9QU ⊖ Victoria Town plan: **38**AHY**n**
– ✆ (020) 7730 5447 – www.eburyrestaurant.co.uk – Closed Christmas-New Year
• FRENCH • Menu £ 21/27 – Carte £ 28/54
Going strong for over 50 years and as likeable as ever. Some imaginative touches but generally quite classic cooking. Dairy and gluten free menus offered, along with a keenly-priced wine list.

X **A. Wong**

70 Wilton Rd ✉ SW1V 1DE ⊖ Victoria Town plan: **38**AIY**w**
– ✆ (020) 7828 8931 – www.awong.co.uk – Closed 23-27 December, 1-2 January, Sunday and Monday lunch
• CHINESE • Menu £ 14 – Carte £ 16/38 – *(booking essential)*
Andrew Wong transformed his mother's restaurant into a modern and lively Chinese restaurant. He's taken classics from across China and introduced the odd twist here and there, whilst keeping the original combinations intact.

X **Olivocarne**

61 Elizabeth St ✉ SW1W 9PP ⊖ Sloane Square Town plan: **38**AHY**d**
– ✆ (020) 7730 7997 – www.olivorestaurants.com
• ITALIAN • Carte £ 31/47
Just when you thought Mauro Sanno had this part of town sewn up he opens another restaurant. This one focuses on meat dishes, along with a selection of satisfying Sardinian specialities and is smarter and larger than his others.

X **Olivo**

21 Eccleston St ✉ SW1W 9LX ⊖ Victoria Town plan: **38**AHY**z**
– ✆ (020) 7730 2505 – www.olivorestaurants.com – Closed lunch Saturday-Sunday and bank holidays
• ITALIAN • Menu £ 25 (weekday lunch) – Carte £ 33/45 – *(booking essential)*
Carefully prepared, authentic Sardinian specialities are the highlight at this popular Italian restaurant. Simply decorated in blues and yellows, with an atmosphere of bonhomie.

Olivomare

10 Lower Belgrave St ✉ SW1W 0LJ ⊖ Victoria Town plan: **38**AHY**b**
– ✆ (020) 7730 9022 – www.olivorestaurants.com – Closed bank holidays
• FISH AND SEAFOOD • Carte £ 35/44

Expect understated and stylish piscatorial decoration and seafood with a Sardinian base. Fortnightly changing menu, with high quality produce, much of which is available in the deli next door.

Thomas Cubitt

44 Elizabeth St ✉ SW1W 9PA ⊖ Sloane Square. Town plan: **38**AHY**e**
– ✆ (020) 7730 6060 – www.thethomascubitt.co.uk
• MODERN • Carte £ 28/42 – *(booking essential)*

A pub of two halves: choose the busy ground floor bar with its accessible menu or upstairs for more ambitious, quite elaborate cooking with courteous service and a less frenetic environment.

The Orange with rm

37 Pimlico Rd ✉ SW1W 8NE ⊖ Sloane Square. Town plan: **38**AHZ**k**
– ✆ (020) 7881 9844 – www.theorange.co.uk
• MEDITERRANEAN • **4 rm** – †£ 205 ††£ 240, ☕ £ 15 Carte £ 28/42

The old Orange Brewery is as charming a pub as its stucco-fronted façade suggests. Try the fun bar or book a table in the more sedate upstairs room. The menu has a Mediterranean bias; spelt or wheat based pizzas are a speciality. Bedrooms are stylish and comfortable.

LONDON STANSTED AIRPORT

Essex ✉ Stansted Mountfitchet – See Regional map n°**12-B2**

▶London 37 mi – Cambridge 29 mi – Chelmsford 18 mi – Colchester 29 mi

Michelin Road map 504-U28

Radisson Blu H. London Stansted Airport

rm,

Waltham Close ✉ CM24 1PP – follow signs for short stay parking and car rental returns – ✆ (01279) 661 012 – www.stansted.radissonblu.com

494 rm – †£ 86/300 ††£ 86/300, ☕ £ 10 – 6 suites

Rest *New York Grill Bar* – Carte £ 26/63 – *(closed Christmas) (dinner only)*

Rest *Angels' Wine Tower Bar* – Menu £ 24 – Carte £ 19/37

Rest *Fillini* – Menu £ 23 – Carte £ 21/46 – *(dinner only)*

Spacious, modern hotel with great facilities and lots of parking, just a stone's throw from the terminal. Smart, well-equipped bedrooms come in 3 colour schemes. The vast atrium is dominated by a 40ft glass wine cellar, where 'Angels' fly up to get your bottle. Choose from snacks in the Tower Bar, Italian fare in Fillini or American steakhouse dishes in the Grill Bar.

LONG ASHTON → See Bristol

North Somerset – Michelin Road map 503-M29

LONG COMPTON

Warwickshire – Pop. 705 – ✉ Shipston-On-Stour – See Regional map n°**11-C2**

▶London 81 mi – Birmingham 53 mi – Liverpool 147 mi – Bristol 72 mi

Michelin Road map 504-Q/R28

Red Lion with rm

Main St ✉ CV36 5JS – ✆ (01608) 684 221 – www.redlion-longcompton.co.uk

5 rm ☕ – †£ 60 ††£ 90/140 Menu £ 14 (weekdays) – Carte £ 25/31

18C former coaching inn with flag floors, log fires and a warm, modern feel. Seasonal menu of tasty, home-cooked pub classics, with more adventurous daily specials. Keen service. Good-sized garden and children's play area. Stylish bedrooms have a contemporary, country-chic feel and a good level of facilities.

LONG CRENDON

Buckinghamshire – Pop. 2 335 – ✉ Aylesbury – See Regional map n°**11-C2**

▶London 50 mi – Aylesbury 11 mi – Oxford 15 mi – Birmingham 82 mi

Michelin Road map 504-Q/R28

Angel with rm

47 Bicester Rd ✉ HP18 9EE – ✆ (01844) 208 268 – www.angelrestaurant.co.uk – Closed 24-26 December, 1-2 January and Sunday dinner

4 rm ☕ – †£ 75 ††£ 110 Menu £ 15 (weekday lunch) – Carte £ 24/47

Sweet former pub with low ceilings and plenty of character. Large, leather-furnished bar and a collection of intimate dining rooms leading to an airy conservatory. Traditional, unfussy, British-based dishes are accompanied by a well-chosen wine list. Bedrooms are cosy and individually decorated.

Mole & Chicken with rm

Easington ✉ HP18 8EY – North 0.5 mi by Dorton rd – ✆ (01844) 208 387 – www.themoleandchicken.co.uk – Closed 25 December

5 rm ☕ – †£ 85 ††£ 110 Menu £ 16 (weekdays) – Carte £ 27/46

Charming pub built in 1831 as part of a local farm workers' estate, with wonky low ceilings, open fires and a large garden offering commanding country views. The slightly curious menu ranges from classics to dishes influenced by Asia and the Lebanon. Delightful modern bedrooms are in the adjoining house.

ENGLAND

LONG MELFORD

Suffolk – Pop. 2 898 – See Regional map n°**15-C3**

London 62 mi – Cambridge 34 mi – Colchester 18 mi – Ipswich 24 mi

Michelin Road map 504-W27 – Michelin Green Guide GREAT BRITAIN

Black Lion

Church Walk, The Green ✉ CO10 9DN – ✆ (01787) 312 356 – www.blacklionhotel.net

10 rm – †£ 102/136 ††£ 125/175 – 1 suite

Rest *Black Lion* – see restaurant listing

Whitewashed Georgian inn overlooking the green, with a cosy, classical interior. Bedrooms are individually decorated in rich colours and named after wines. After dinner, sink into a deep sofa by the open fire in the panelled bar.

Scutchers

Westgate St ✉ CO10 9DP – on A 1092 – ✆ (01787) 310 200 – www.scutchers.com – Closed 2 weeks Christmas and Sunday-Wednesday

Carte £ 32/47

This converted medieval hall house is now a smart, personally run restaurant. Cooking is skilful, classical and full of flavour; everything from the bread to the sorbet is homemade. The wine list features some top class producers.

Black Lion – Black Lion Hotel

Church Walk, The Green ✉ CO10 9DN – ✆ (01787) 312 356 – www.blacklionhotel.net

Menu £ 16 (weekdays) – Carte £ 29/38 – *(booking advisable)*

First you must choose which of the three intimate rooms to dine in at this Georgian inn; then there's the huge array of menus to decide between. Cooking is rooted in the traditional British vein and dishes are full of flavour.

LONG SUTTON

Somerset ✉ Langport – See Regional map n°**3-B3**

London 131 mi – Bristol 39 mi – Cardiff 83 mi – Bournemouth 64 mi

Michelin Road map 503-L30

Devonshire Arms with rm

✉ TA10 9LP – ✆ (01458) 241 271 – www.thedevonshirearms.com – Closed 25-26 December and 1 January

9 rm – †£ 85/140 ††£ 95/145 Carte £ 25/39

Spacious Grade II listed hunting lodge set on the village green. The interior is contemporary, with a relaxing, open-plan bar and formal dining room. Locally sourced produce is used in seasonal European dishes. Comfortable bedrooms boast excellent quality linen and toiletries.

LONG WHATTON

Leicestershire – Pop. 1 124 – See Regional map n°**16-B2**

London 120 mi – Birmingham 43 mi – Liverpool 101 mi – Leeds 84 mi

Royal Oak with rm

The Green ✉ LE12 5BD – ✆ (01509) 843 694 – www.theroyaloaklongwhatton.co.uk

7 rm – †£ 79/105 ††£ 79/105

Menu £ 16 (weekday dinner) – Carte £ 21/39

Smartly modernised pub in a sleepy village, with a spacious yet cosy bar, an intimate dining room and large grounds. Menus offer plenty of choice, from sharing platters and pub favourites to appealing main courses with a quirky touch. Well-equipped bedrooms are in an adjacent block; one has a whirlpool bath.

LONGHORSLEY → See Morpeth

Northumberland – Michelin Road map 501-O18

LONGPARISH

Hampshire – See Regional map n°**6-B2**

London 67 mi – Bristol 86 mi – Cardiff 119 mi – Plymouth 152 mi

Plough Inn

SP11 6PB – (01264) 720 358 – www.theploughinn.info – Closed Sunday dinner and Monday

Carte £ 30/47

A sweet pub with a wine cave, a cheese trolley and a laid-back feel; ask for a table in one of the bay windows. Pub classics on the bar menu; refined, elaborate dishes on the à la carte, with desserts a modern take on the traditional.

LONGSTOCK

Hampshire Stockbridge – See Regional map n°**6-B2**

London 74 mi – Bristol 77 mi – Cardiff 110 mi – Plymouth 148 mi

Michelin Road map 503-P30 and 504

Peat Spade Inn with rm

Village St SO20 6DR – (01264) 810 612 – www.peatspadeinn.co.uk – Closed 25 December

8 rm – £ 80/145 £ 80/145 Carte £ 22/33 – *(booking advisable)*

Charming 19C inn set in the heart of the Test Valley, with period furnishings, warming fires, welcoming candlelight and a country pursuits theme. Menus offer generous, classically based dishes with bold flavours and a refined style. Stylish bedrooms are split between the inn and annexe; the residents' lounge overlooks the garden and its sunken fire-pit.

LONGTOWN

Cumbria – See Regional map n°**21-A1**

London 326 mi – Carlisle 9 mi – Newcastle upon Tyne 61 mi

Michelin Road map 502-L18

Bessiestown Farm

Catlowdy CA6 5QP – Northeast : 8 mi by Netherby St on B 6318 – (01228) 577 219 – www.bessiestown.co.uk – Closed 25 December

5 rm – £ 59 £ 90 **Rest** – Menu £ 20

Converted farmhouse with spacious, comfortable bedrooms, set on a 150 acre sheep farm close to the English-Scottish border. The light, airy conservatory overlooks a windswept garden. Homemade bread and preserves feature at breakfast. 2 course dinners by arrangement in the bright dining room.

LOOE

Cornwall – Pop. 5 112 – See Regional map n°**1-B2**

London 264 mi – Plymouth 23 mi – Truro 39 mi

Michelin Road map 503-G32

Barclay House

St Martins Rd, East Looe PL13 1LP – East : 0.5 mi by A 387 on B 3253 – (01503) 262 929 – www.barclayhouse.co.uk

12 rm – £ 55/90 £ 80/170 – 1 suite

Rest *Barclay House* – see restaurant listing

Imposing, whitewashed Victorian house in an elevated position; sit on the terrace and take in the view. Guest areas mix the traditional and the modern. Room 7 has an attractive estuary vista and room 9 boasts a balcony and a whirlpool bath.

Beach House without rest

Marine Dr, Hannafore PL13 2DH – Southwest : 0.75 mi by Quay Rd – (01503) 262 598 – www.thebeachhouselooe.co.uk – Closed Christmas

5 rm – £ 65/75 £ 90/130

Detached house in a fantastic location, looking out to sea. Personally run, with immaculately kept bedrooms; Fistral, with its balcony and sea views, is the best. In-house beauty therapist; treatments by appointment.

XX **Barclay House** – Barclay House Hotel

St Martins Rd, East Looe ✉ PL13 1LP – East : 0.5 mi by A 387 on B 3253 – ✆ (01503) 262 929 – www.barclayhouse.co.uk – Closed Sunday

Menu £ 32/39 – *(dinner only)*

Modern restaurant in a hillside hotel; its impressive terrace offering extensive views of the estuary. Seasonal dishes feature seafood from the day boats. Choose from the à la carte or a 6 course tasting menu with matching wine flights.

X **Trawlers on the Quay**

The Quay, East Looe ✉ PL13 1AH – ✆ (01503) 263 593 – www.trawlers-restaurant.co.uk – Closed Monday and Tuesday in winter

Menu £ 10 – Carte £ 18/31

Bright, contemporary restaurant on the edge of the quay; ask for a window table for great views to West Looe. The menu focuses on seafood and ranges from light lunches up to the full three courses; ambitious, boldly flavoured cooking.

LORTON

Cumbria – See Regional map n°**21-A2**

London 302 mi – Carlisle 33 mi – Lancaster 71 mi

Michelin Road map 502-K20

Winder Hall Country House

✉ CA13 9UP On B 5289 – ✆ (01900) 85 107 – www.winderhall.co.uk – Closed January

7 rm – £ 95/125 £ 110/155

Rest ***Cedar Tree*** – Menu £ 25 – Carte £ 20/33 – *(booking essential)*

Part-Jacobean manor house dating back to 1663, with leaded mullion windows, a relaxed, easy-going feel, and a comfy, characterful lounge and bar. Bedrooms range from olde worlde to more contemporary. The hot tub boasts fell views. Home-cooked meals in the pleasant oak-panelled dining room.

New House Farm

✉ CA13 9UU South : 1.25 mi on B 5289 – ✆ (0784) 115 98 18 – www.newhouse-farm.com

5 rm – £ 50/90 £ 100/180 **Rest** – Menu £ 34

Part-17C former farmhouse complete with several beamed, open-fired lounges, a hot tub boasting fell views and a tea room in the old cow byres. Richly furnished bedrooms have king or super king sized beds and some feature double jacuzzis; the annexe rooms are the best. Meals are cooked on the Aga.

Old Vicarage

Church Ln ✉ CA13 9UN – North : 0.5 mi by B 5289 on Lorton Church rd – ✆ (01900) 85 656 – www.oldvicarage.co.uk – Restricted opening in winter

5 rm – £ 85/95 £ 100/140 **Rest** – Menu £ 35

Charming slate house with lovely gardens and a welcoming owner. Comfy lounge and traditional dining room with fell views and home-cooked dinners. Immaculately kept, sympathetically styled bedrooms; one with a roll-top bath, another with a four-poster – the Coach House rooms have exposed slate walls.

LOSTWITHIEL

Cornwall – Pop. 2 659 – See Regional map n°**1-B2**

London 244 mi – Bristol 148 mi – Cardiff 179 mi – Plymouth 32 mi

Michelin Road map 503-G32

XX **Asquiths**

19 North St ✉ PL22 0EF – ✆ (01208) 871 714 – www.asquithsrestaurant.co.uk – Closed first 2 weeks January, Sunday and Monday

Carte £ 25/32 – *(dinner only)*

Smartly converted shop with exposed stone walls hung with modern Cornish art, funky lampshades and contemporary styling. Confidently executed dishes feature some original flavour combinations. The atmosphere is relaxed and intimate.

LOUTH

Lincolnshire – Pop. 16 419 – See Regional map n°**17-D1**

▶London 156 mi – Boston 34 mi – Grimsby 17 mi – Lincoln 26 mi

Michelin Road map 502-T/U23

Brackenborough

rest,

Cordeaux Corner, Brackenborough ✉ LN11 0SZ – North : 2 mi by A 16 – ✆ (01507) 609 169 – www.oakridgehotels.co.uk

24 rm ☕ – †£ 92/117 ††£ 108/129 **Rest** – Carte £ 20/39

Contemporary hotel with a relaxed feel and a warm, personal style. Spacious, individually designed bedrooms have bold feature walls, Egyptian cotton linen and the latest mod cons; executive rooms come with jacuzzi baths. The bistro and conservatory lounge-bar serve grills and classics with a modern twist.

LOVINGTON

Somerset – See Regional map n°**4-C2**

▶London 126 mi – Bristol 30 mi – Taunton 33 mi

Michelin Road map 503-M30

Pilgrims with rm

rm,

✉ BA7 7PT – ✆ (01963) 240 597 – www.thepilgrimsatlovington.co.uk – Closed Sunday dinner, Monday and lunch Tuesday

5 rm ☕ – †£ 80/120 ††£ 95/120

Menu £ 22 (weekday lunch) – Carte £ 22/46

Cosy, hugely characterful restaurant with low-beamed ceilings, flagged floors and a roaring fire; run by a passionate husband and wife team. Well-prepared, classical dishes are made with quality local produce. Comfortable, contemporary bedrooms, luxurious bathrooms and substantial breakfasts.

LOW FELL

Tyne and Wear – See Regional map n°**24-B2**

▶London 272 mi – Newcastle upon Tyne 5 mi – Durham 15 mi

Eslington Villa

rest,

8 Station Rd ✉ NE9 6DR – West : 0.75 mi by Belle Vue Bank, turning left at T junction, right at roundabout then taking first turn right – ✆ (0191) 487 60 17 – www.eslingtonvilla.co.uk – Closed 25-26 December and 1 January

18 rm ☕ – †£ 85/95 ††£ 95/105 **Rest** – Menu £ 15/28

Comprising two red-brick Victorian houses in the city suburbs. It's well-run by its hand-on owners and has a relaxed atmosphere and a surprisingly large rear garden. Individually styled bedrooms have a contemporary edge. Dine from a traditional menu with modern twists in the dining room or conservatory.

LOW ROW → See Reeth

North Yorkshire – Michelin Road map 502-N20

LOWER BEEDING

West Sussex – See Regional map n°**7-D2**

▶London 40 mi – Brighton 20 mi – Guildford 25 mi – Southampton 67 mi

Michelin Road map 504-T30

South Lodge

Brighton Rd ✉ RH13 6PS – South : 1.5 mi by B 2110 on A 281 – ✆ (01403) 891 711 – www.exclusivehotels.co.uk

85 rm ☕ – †£ 165/350 ††£ 165/350 – 4 suites

Rest *The Pass* ✿ **Rest *Camellia*** – see restaurant listing

Intricate carved fireplaces and ornate ceilings are on display in this Victorian mansion, which affords superb South Downs views from its 93 acres. Bedrooms are beautifully appointed; those in the wing are larger with feature bathrooms.

XX ✿ **The Pass** – South Lodge Hotel

Brighton Rd ✉ RH13 6PS – South : 1.5 mi by B 2110 on A 281 – ✆ (01403) 891 711 – www.southlodgehotels.co.uk – Closed first 2 weeks January, Monday and Tuesday

Menu £ 35/95 – *(number of covers limited, pre-book)*

A unique hotel restaurant where every table is the chef's table! High level chairs and banquettes are arranged around a glass-walled kitchen, and TVs screening live kitchen action are mounted on the walls. Expect beautifully presented, intricate modern dishes in balanced, well-thought-out combinations.

→ Pork, apple and celeriac. Cod with aubergine and tomato. Rhubarb, liquorice, apple.

XX **Camellia** Ⓝ – South Lodge Hotel

Brighton Rd ✉ RH13 6PS – South : 1.5 mi by B 2110 on A 281 – ✆ (01403) 891 711 – www.exclusivehotels.co.uk

Menu £ 18/38 – Carte £ 46/58

Named after the tree which covers the front of the house, Camellia occupies three wood-panelled rooms with grand fireplaces and chandeliers. Refined modern dishes are light but boldly flavoured, and use produce from the walled garden.

Crabtree Ⓝ

Brighton Rd ✉ RH13 6PT – South : 1.5 mi by B 2110 on A 281 – ✆ (01403) 892 666 – www.crabtreesussex.com – Closed Sunday dinner

Menu £ 15 (weekday lunch) – Carte £ 25/36

A family-run affair with a cosy, lived-in feel, warming fires and cheery, helpful staff. Traditional English dishes come with a touch of refinement and plenty of flavour, and the wine list is well-priced and full of helpful information.

LOWER DUNSFORTH → See Boroughbridge

North Yorkshire – Michelin Road map 502-Q21

LOWER EASHING → See Godalming

Surrey

LOWER FROYLE

Hampshire – See Regional map n°**7**-C2

London 48 mi – Southampton 34 mi – Newbury 30 mi

The Anchor Inn with rm

✉ GU34 4NA – ✆ (01420) 23 261 – www.anchorinnatlowerfroyle.co.uk – Closed 25 December

5 rm – †£ 120/150 ††£ 120/150 Carte £ 25/46

Part-whitewashed, part-tile hung 14C inn in pretty countryside, boasting low beams, open fires and antiques aplenty. Good-sized menus offer classic pub dishes with a refined edge; cooking is hearty and flavoursome. Chic, wonderfully restful bedrooms are named after famous war poets. The courtyard garden is a suntrap, with uninterrupted countryside views.

LOWER HARDRES → See Canterbury

Kent – Michelin Road map 504-X30

LOWER ODDINGTON → See Stow-on-the-Wold

Gloucestershire

LOWER PEOVER → See Knutsford

Cheshire East

LOWER SLAUGHTER → See Bourton-on-the-Water

Gloucestershire – Michelin Road map 503 and 504-O28

LOWER SWELL → See Stow-on-the-Wold

Gloucestershire

LOWESTOFT

Suffolk – Pop. 70 945 – See Regional map n°**15**-D2
London 116 mi – Ipswich 43 mi – Norwich 30 mi
Michelin Road map 504-Z26 – Michelin Green Guide GREAT BRITAIN

Britten House without rest

21 Kirkley Cliff Rd ✉ NR33 0DB – ☎ (01502) 573 950 – www.brittenhouse.co.uk
10 rm – †£ 50/75 ††£ 65/95
Fine brick-built Victorian house overlooking the promenade; the birthplace of Benjamin Britten in 1913. Classically furnished bedrooms are named after composers; choose Mozart or Elgar, both of which have sea views.

LUDLOW

Shropshire – Pop. 10 515 – See Regional map n°**18**-B2
London 162 mi – Birmingham 39 mi – Hereford 24 mi
Michelin Road map 503-L26 – Michelin Green Guide GREAT BRITAIN

Fishmore Hall

✉ SY8 3DP North : 1.5 mi by B 4361 and Kidderminster rd on Fishmore Rd – ☎ (01584) 875 148 – www.fishmorehall.co.uk
15 rm – †£ 110/210 ††£ 150/250
Rest *Forelles* – see restaurant listing
Whitewashed Georgian mansion in half an acre of mature gardens, just out of town. Original features mix with modern fittings to create a boutique country house feel. Smart bedrooms have bold wallpapers, stylish bathrooms and good views.

Overton Grange

Old Hereford Rd ✉ SY8 4AD – South : 1.75 mi on B 4361 – ☎ (01584) 873 500 – www.overtongrangehotel.com – Closed 28 December-9 January
14 rm – †£ 95/145 ††£ 145/245
Rest – Menu £ 33/43 – *(booking essential)*
Well-maintained Edwardian country house where subtle modern touches sit alongside original features. Well-equipped bedrooms and smart bathrooms. Good-sized pool, sauna and 2 treatment rooms. Dining rooms offer immaculately laid tables and countryside views; cooking has a refined French base.

Dinham Hall

Dinham ✉ SY8 1EJ – ☎ (01584) 876 464 – www.dinhamhall.com Town plan: Z**b**
13 rm – †£ 125/245 ††£ 139/245
Rest *Elliott's* – Menu £ 20/35
18C former schoolhouse with a pretty walled garden, set overlooking the castle. Cosy guest areas are filled with antiques and ornaments. Comfy, traditionally styled bedrooms display original features and come with good mod cons. The bistro-style conservatory serves classic British dishes given a modern twist.

La Bécasse

17 Corve St ✉ SY8 1DA – ☎ (01584) 872 325 – www.labecasse.co.uk – Closed 25-30 December, Sunday and Monday Town plan: Y**a**
Menu £ 30/55
A fine 16C townhouse on a historic street, featuring old beams, oak panelling and sloping floors. Tables are crisply laid and service is formal and attentive. Well-prepared, classic French dishes display a light, modern touch.

Can't choose between two similar establishments in the same town? We list them in order of preference, within each category.

ENGLAND

LUDLOW

Bull Ring	Z	2
Castle Square	Z	4
Church St	Z	6
College St.	Z	8
Fishmore Rd	Y	10
Henley Rd	Y	12
High St	Z	14
King St	Z	16
Lower Raven Lane	Z	18
Market St	Z	20
Silk Mill	Z	22

Mr Underhill's at Dinham Weir (Chris Bradley) with rm

Dinham ✉ *SY8 1EH – ✆ (01584) 874 431 – www.mr-underhills.co.uk*
– Closed 2 weeks June, 1 week October, Christmas and New Year — Town plan: Z**f**

4 rm ☕ – 👤£ 195/300 👥£ 275/360

Menu £ 68 – *(closed Monday and Tuesday) (dinner only) (booking essential) (set menu only)*

Smart, comfortable restaurant in a stunning location by the weir. Traditionally based menus showcase superlative ingredients in skilfully and accurately prepared dishes, where natural flavours take the lead. Be sure to start your meal with drinks on the pretty terrace. Stylish bedrooms are all 'spa' suites and boast steam showers and garden views.

→ Brill, polenta chips, mushy peas and white ketchup. Slow-roasted venison with elderberries and braised venison cannelloni. Chocolate and hazelnut.

XX **Forelles** – Fishmore Hall Hotel

✉ SY8 3DP North : 1.5 mi by B 4361 and Kidderminster rd on Fishmore Rd – ✆ (01584) 875 148 – www.fishmorehall.co.uk

Menu £ 25/49

Attractive conservatory restaurant named after the pear tree outside, with lovely views over the hotel gardens. Attractively presented dishes use local produce and modern techniques, and feature good flavour and texture combinations.

X **French Pantry**

15 Tower St. ✉ SY8 1RL – ✆ (01584) 879 133 Town plan: Z**r**

– www.thefrenchpantry.co.uk – Closed 1-5 January and Sunday

Menu £ 25 (dinner) – Carte lunch £ 24/32 – *(booking essential)*

Pretty little café-cum-bistro on a paved side street, selling produce and wines imported from Parisian markets. Authentic French dishes are crafted from local and imported ingredients. Cooking is rustic, hearty and full of flavour.

X **Green Café**

Mill on the Green ✉ SY8 1EG – ✆ (01584) 879 872 Town plan: Z**f**

– www.thegreencafe.co.uk – Closed 23 December-13 February and Monday

Carte £ 16/25 – *(lunch only)*

Simple little eatery with delightful waterside terrace, set in a charming 14C watermill on the banks of the River Teme. Concise menu of unfussy, daily changing dishes that showcase British ingredients in simple, flavoursome combinations.

Charlton Arms Ⓝ with rm rest,

Ludford Bridge ✉ SY8 1PJ – ✆ (01584) 872 813 Town plan: Z**x**

– www.thecharltonarms.co.uk – Closed 25-26 December

9 rm – †£ 60/80 ††£ 80/120 Carte £ 22/33

Claude Bosi is arguably the man who put Ludlow on the map and this pub in a commanding position on the banks of the river Terne is owned by his brother Cedric and Cedric's wife, Amy. Menus have something for everyone and dishes are good value and full of flavour. Up-to-date bedrooms; most have river outlooks.

at Cleestanton Northeast: 5.5 mi by A4117 and B4364

Timberstone Ⓝ

✉ SY8 3EL – ✆ (01584) 823 519 – www.timberstoneludlow.co.uk

4 rm – †£ 60/95 ††£ 95 **Rest** – Menu £ 25

This pair of cosy 17C cottages offer a wonderfully peaceful atmosphere and lovely rural views. Beamed bedrooms come with stylish modern bathrooms; one room even has its own balcony. Dine around the large farmhouse table – there's always a good selection, which includes many organic or home-grown options.

LUND

East Riding of Yorkshire – See Regional map n°**23-C2**

London 213 mi – Leeds 61 mi – Sheffield 64 mi – Bradford 67 mi

Michelin Road map 502-S22

Wellington Inn

19 The Green ✉ YO25 9TE – ✆ (01377) 217 294 – www.thewellingtoninn.co.uk – Closed 25 December, 1 January and Monday

Carte £ 25/39

Well-run pub with beamed, open-fired bars and more formal, linen-laid dining rooms. Experienced kitchen uses quality ingredients in dishes that are generous, both in flavour and portion. Efficient service. Good selection of Yorkshire beers.

LUPTON → See Kirkby Lonsdale

Cumbria – Michelin Road map 502-L21

LURGASHALL

West Sussex – See Regional map n°**7-C2**

London 49 mi – Bristol 124 mi – Cardiff 157 mi – Plymouth 197 mi

Michelin Road map 504-S30

Barn at Roundhurst 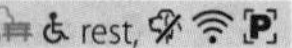

Lower Roundhurst Farm, Jobson's Ln ✉ GU27 3BY – Northwest : 3 mi by Haslemere rd – ✆ (01428) 642 535 – www.thebarnatroundhurst.com
6 rm ☕ – †£ 120/160 ††£ 130/200 **Rest** – Menu £ 40
Beautifully restored, mid-17C threshing barn, on a 250 acre organic farm in the South Downs. The spacious lounge features fresh flowers, sculptures and modern art. Meals use eggs and meats from the farm, along with other local ingredients. Bedrooms, in the old outbuildings, are stylish and modern, and come with home-made biscuits, iPod docks and luxurious bathrooms.

Noah's Ark Inn

The Green ✉ GU28 9ET – ✆ (01428) 707 346 – www.noahsarkinn.co.uk
Carte £ 22/37
Quintessentially English pub in a picturesque location right on the village green, overlooking the cricket pitch. Gloriously rustic interior with an inglenook and exposed beams. Wide-ranging menus; tasty, generously proportioned dishes.

LUTON

Luton – Pop. 211 228 – See Regional map n°**12-A2**
London 35 mi – Cambridge 36 mi – Ipswich 93 mi – Oxford 45 mi
Michelin Road map 504-S28 – Michelin Green Guide GREAT BRITAIN

Luton Hoo

The Mansion House ✉ LU1 3TQ – Southeast : 2.5 mi by A 505 on A 1081 – ✆ (01582) 734 437 – www.lutonhoo.com
135 rm ☕ – †£ 280/1100 ††£ 280/1100 – 9 suites
Rest *Wernher* – Menu £ 25/43 – *(closed Monday and Tuesday)*
Rest *Adam's Brasserie* – Carte £ 26/46 – *(closed Sunday dinner)*
Stunning 18C house in over 1,000 acres of gardens; some designed by Capability Brown. The main mansion boasts an impressive hallway, numerous beautifully furnished drawing rooms and classical, luxurious bedrooms. The marble-filled Wernher restaurant offers sophisticated modern cuisine. The old stable block houses the smart spa and the casual, contemporary brasserie.

ENGLAND

LYDDINGTON → See Uppingham

Rutland

LYDFORD

Devon – Pop. 1 734 – ✉ Okehampton – See Regional map n°**2-C2**
London 234 mi – Exeter 33 mi – Plymouth 25 mi
Michelin Road map 503-H32 – Michelin Green Guide GREAT BRITAIN

Dartmoor Inn with rm 

Moorside ✉ EX20 4AY – East : 1 mi on A 386 – ✆ (01822) 820 221 – www.dartmoorinn.com – Closed Sunday dinner and Monday lunch except bank holidays
4 rm ☕ – †£ 75/90 ††£ 100/135 Menu £ 17 (weekdays) – Carte £ 20/45
Rustic pub with a shabby-chic style; low ceilings add a cosy feel, while artwork provides a modern touch. Classic dishes are satisfying and full of flavour; there is an emphasis on local produce and Devon Ruby Red beef and dishes from the charcoal grill are the specialities. Spacious, elegant bedrooms.

LYME REGIS

Dorset – Pop. 4 712 – See Regional map n°**3-B3**
London 160 mi – Dorchester 25 mi – Exeter 31 mi – Taunton 27 mi
Michelin Road map 503-L31 – Michelin Green Guide GREAT BRITAIN

Alexandra

Pound St ✉ DT7 3HZ – ✆ (01297) 442 010 – www.hotelalexandra.co.uk – Closed 1-30 January
25 rm ☕ – †£ 90/235 ††£ 177/235 **Rest** – Carte £ 26/38
18C dower house with superb views over the Cobb and out to sea. There's a small terrace and a lookout tower (for hire) in the lovely gardens. The lounges and bedrooms are contemporary; No.12 has a large bay window to take in the views. Modern menus are served in the formal restaurant and conservatory.

Hix Townhouse without rest

1 Pound St ✉ *D17 3HZ – ✆ (01297) 442 499 – www.hixtownhouse.co.uk*
8 rm – £ 110/155 £ 120/165
Georgian townhouse with stylishly understated bedrooms designed around various themes, including hunting and sailing; two rooms have lounges and two have terraces. There's a communal kitchen and breakfast is delivered in a hamper.

Hix Oyster & Fish House

Lister Gdns, Cobb Rd ✉ *DT7 3JP – ✆ (01297) 446 910 – www.hixoysterandfishhouse.co.uk – Closed 25-26 December, Monday and dinner Sunday November-March*
Menu £ 21 (weekdays) – Carte £ 24/53 – *(booking essential)*
Modern, Scandic-style restaurant with a chef's table, a terrace and breathtaking views over Lyme Bay and the Cobb. Menus focus on the latest catch brought in by the day boats and dishes have a likeable simplicity. Service is charming.

LYMINGTON

Hampshire – Pop. 15 218 – See Regional map n°**6-A3**
London 103 mi – Bournemouth 18 mi – Southampton 19 mi – Winchester 32 mi
Michelin Road map 504-P31

Stanwell House

14-15 High St ✉ *SO41 9AA – ✆ (01590) 677 123 – www.stanwellhouse.com*
29 rm – £ 99/114 £ 109/140 – 1 suite
Rest *Bistro* – Menu £ 14/28 – Carte £ 30/38
Rest *Seafood at Stanwells* – Carte approx. £ 34 – *(dinner only) (booking essential)*
Attractive 18C house in the town centre, run by a friendly owner. Tastefully designed bedrooms are comfy and well-equipped; those in the original house are the most characterful and those in the extension are more contemporary. Dine in the smart seafood restaurant, the rustic bistro or the trendy wine bar.

Mill at Gordleton

Silver St, Hordle ✉ *SO41 6DJ – Northwest : 3.5 mi by A 337 off Sway Rd – ✆ (01590) 682 219 – www.themillatgordleton.co.uk – Closed 25 December*
8 rm – £ 100/125 £ 150/275 – 1 suite
Rest – Menu £ 16/29 – Carte £ 32/54
Charming, part-17C creeper-clad water mill with delightful terraces and colourful gardens. The comfy country house interior shows an eye for detail and bedrooms are extremely cosy. Have snacks in the bar or more substantial modern dishes in the restaurant; in summer, take afternoon tea by the river.

Elderflower with rm

4-5 Quay St ✉ *SO41 3AS – ✆ (01590) 676 908 – www.elderflowerrestaurant.co.uk – Closed 1-14 January, Sunday dinner, Monday and Tuesday*
3 rm – £ 79 £ 89 Menu £ 25 (weekday lunch) – Carte £ 33/50
Their motto is 'quintessentially British, with a sprinkling of French', and that's just what you'll find at this proudly run restaurant. Cooking is playful and imaginative, with elderflower always featuring somewhere on the menu. Bedrooms are simply appointed and the quay is just a stone's throw away.

at Downton West: 3 mi on A337 ✉ Lymington

Olde Barn without rest

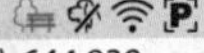

Christchurch Rd ✉ *SO41 0LA – East : 0.5 mi on A 337 – ✆ (01590) 644 939 – www.theoldebarn.co.uk*
3 rm – £ 50/70 £ 50/75
This attractively converted 17C barn houses a traditional lounge and a communal breakfast room. Homely, cottage-style bedrooms are spotlessly kept – they are located in a smart red-brick building which was once the dairy.

LYMM

Warrington – Pop. 11 608 – See Regional map n°**20-B3**
London 190 mi – Liverpool 26 mi – Leeds 62 mi – Sheffield 68 mi
Michelin Road map 502-M23

Church Green

Higher Ln ✉ WA13 0AP – on A 56 – ☎ (01925) 752 068 – www.thechurchgreen.co.uk – Closed 25 December
Carte £ 21/59 – *(booking essential)*
Double gable-fronted Victorian pub beside Lymm Dam, with a smart interior, an attractive terrace and a kitchen garden. Appealing menu includes 'pub classics' and 'steak house' sections: choose a cut, then add sauce, garnish and extras.

LYNDHURST

Hampshire – Pop. 2 347 – See Regional map n°**6-A2**
London 95 mi – Bournemouth 20 mi – Southampton 10 mi – Winchester 23 mi
Michelin Road map 503 and 504-P31 – Michelin Green Guide GREAT BRITAIN

Lime Wood

Beaulieu Rd ✉ SO43 7FZ – Southeast : 1 mi by A 35 on B 3056 – ☎ (023) 8028 7177 – www.limewoodhotel.co.uk
32 rm – †£ 255/315 ††£ 255/315, ☕ £ 19 – 14 suites
Rest *Hartnett Holder & Co* – see restaurant listing
Impressive Georgian mansion with a stunning spa topped by a herb garden roof. Stylish guest lounges have quality fabrics and furnishings; one is set around a courtyard and features a retractable glass roof. Beautifully furnished bedrooms boast luxurious marble-tiled bathrooms, and many have New Forest views.

ENGLAND

Hartnett Holder & Co – Lime Wood Hotel

Beaulieu Rd ✉ SO43 7FZ – Southeast : 1 mi by A 35 on B 3056 – ☎ (023) 8028 7177 – www.limewood.co.uk
Menu £ 20 (lunch) – Carte £ 19/77
Elegant restaurant in an impressive Georgian mansion, offering views out over the delightful grounds. A central bar divides the room into several different dining areas; sit on the sofas, at the bar counter or in leather tub chairs. The tempting, Italian-based menu features home-smoked charcuterie.

LYNMOUTH → See Lynton

Devon – Michelin Road map 503-I30

LYNTON

Devon – Pop. 1 157 – See Regional map n°**2-C1**
London 206 mi – Exeter 59 mi – Taunton 44 mi
Michelin Road map 503-I30 – Michelin Green Guide GREAT BRITAIN

Hewitt's - Villa Spaldi

North Walk ✉ EX35 6HJ – ☎ (01598) 752 293 – www.hewittshotel.com – Closed October-March
8 rm ☕ – †£ 80/120 ††£ 120/180
Rest – Menu £ 29 – *(dinner only) (booking essential)*
Splendid cliffside Arts and Crafts house in mature gardens. Antique-furnished bedrooms with up-to-date facilities, sea views and smart, modern bathrooms. Informal weekday meals in wood-panelled bar; fine dining on Friday and Saturday evenings. High tea, with its homemade scones and excellent tea selection, is a must and the terrace is a delightful spot for breakfast.

St Vincent

Market St, Castle Hill ✉ EX35 6JA – ☎ (01598) 752 720 – www.st-vincent-hotel.co.uk
7 rm ☕ – †£ 45 ††£ 75/85 **Rest** – Carte £ 16/20
Whitewashed, Grade II listed Georgian House in the village centre, 200m from the coastal path. Lovely fire-lit lounge with honesty bar and well-kept, uncluttered bedrooms with smart bathrooms. Simple home-cooked meals use local produce where possible. Tea and cakes – outside if sunny.

Castle Hill without rest

Castle Hill ✉ EX35 6JA – ☎ (01598) 752 291 – www.castlehill.biz

7 rm ☕ – 👤£ 50/75 👥£ 70/95

Stone-built house on the main street of this popular tourist village. Spacious, simply decorated bedrooms; 3 of the 7 have their own sitting area. Lounge with plenty of local info and a large fish tank. Friendly owners.

at Lynmouth East: 1 mi

Shelley's without rest

8 Watersmeet Rd ✉ EX35 6EP – ☎ (01598) 753 219 – www.shelleyshotel.co.uk – Closed November-February

11 rm ☕ – 👤£ 85/149 👥£ 85/149

A bright, keenly run hotel overlooking the sea; the eponymous poet honeymooned here in 1812. Traditionally styled guest areas include a homely lounge and a formally laid breakfast room with coastal views. Good-sized bedrooms.

Heatherville

Tors Park ✉ EX35 6NB – by Tors Rd bearing left at the fork – ☎ (01598) 752 327 – www.heatherville.co.uk – May-October

6 rm ☕ – 👤£ 80/125 👥£ 100/125 **Rest** – Menu £ 28

Large Victorian house on the side of the valley, with a lovely coastal outlook. Immaculately kept, decently sized bedrooms have warm, traditional décor and fabrics. Comfortable lounge, cosy bar and large, linen-laid dining room where home-cooked meals are served.

at Martinhoe West: 4.25 mi via Coast rd (toll) ✉ Barnstaple

Old Rectory

✉ EX31 4QT – ☎ (01598) 763 368 – www.oldrectoryhotel.co.uk – Closed November-March

11 rm (dinner included) ☕ – 👤£ 145/195 👥£ 160/210

Rest – Menu £ 35 – *(dinner only residents only)*

Built in the 19C for a rector of Martinhoe's 11C church, this quiet country retreat is in a charming spot, with a well-tended 3 acre garden and a cascading brook. Fresh, bright bedrooms are modern, yet retain period touches: Heddon and Paddock are two of the best. Comfortable dining room; simple home-cooking.

LYTHAM ST ANNE'S

Lancashire – Pop. 42 953 – See Regional map n°**20-A2**

London 237 mi – Blackpool 7 mi – Liverpool 44 mi – Preston 13 mi

Michelin Road map 502-L22

Rooms without rest

35 Church Rd, Lytham ✉ FY8 5LL – ☎ (01253) 736 000 – www.theroomslytham.com

5 rm ☕ – 👤£ 100/125 👥£ 125/180

Mid-Victorian terrace on the approach road into this delightful estuary town. Striking, contemporary bedrooms come with good mod cons. Room One (on the top floor) is the largest, with a stone bath as part of the room. Bounteous breakfasts.

at St Anne's

Grand

South Promenade ✉ FY8 1NB – ☎ (01253) 643 424 – www.the-grand.co.uk – Closed 24-26 December

54 rm ☕ – 👤£ 75/105 👥£ 85/220

Rest ***Cafe Grand*** – see restaurant listing

Keenly run by an experienced local hotelier: the most architecturally pleasing building on the promenade. Contemporary interior with Victorian stained glass windows and grand staircase in situ. Turret rooms have the best views.

Cafe Grand – Grand Hotel

South Promenade ✉ FY8 1NB – ☎ (01253) 643 409 – www.the-grand.co.uk – Closed 24-26 December

Carte £ 21/70

Contemporary hotel restaurant with a fun, friendly atmosphere and a circular bar counter off to one side. Menus offer an interesting mix of Mediterranean dishes and modern-classics, including tapas and dishes 'a la plancha'.

MADINGLEY → See Cambridge

Cambridgeshire – Michelin Road map 504-U27

MAENPORTH BEACH → See Falmouth

Cornwall

MAIDENCOMBE → See Torquay

Torbay – Michelin Road map 503-J32

MAIDENHEAD

Windsor and Maidenhead – Pop. 63 580 – See Regional map n°**11-C3**
London 33 mi – Oxford 32 mi – Reading 13 mi
Michelin Road map 504-R29

Fredrick's

Shoppenhangers Rd ✉ SL6 2PZ – (01628) 581 000 – www.fredricks-hotel.co.uk Town plan: X**c**
36 rm – £ 99/159 £ 109/179 – 1 suite
Rest *Fredrick's* – Menu £ 19/29 – Carte £ 24/62
It's hard to imagine that this smart red-brick hotel – with its stylish spa – was once an inn. It's classically styled, with a marble reception, a clubby bar and a formal restaurant serving modern French dishes. Bedrooms have panelled walls and bespoke wooden furnishings, and most overlook the gardens.

Boulters Riverside Brasserie

Boulters Lock Island ✉ SL6 8PE – (01628) 621 291 – www.boultersrestaurant.co.uk – Closed 26-30 December, Sunday dinner and Monday Town plan: V**x**
Menu £ 16 (weekday lunch) – Carte £ 27/41
Stylish modern eatery beside a lock, on a small island in the Thames. Full-length windows open onto the terrace; excellent river views. Hearty yet refined brasserie classics use quality produce.

Crown (N)

Burchett's Green ✉ SL6 6QZ – West : 4 mi by A 4, A 404 and Burchett's Green Rd – (01628) 824 079 – www.thecrownatburchettsgreen.com – Closed last 2 weeks of August, Christmas and Monday
Carte £ 22/30 – *(dinner only and Sunday lunch)*
Local drinkers fill the small bar, which leads to two intimate, open-fired dining rooms. The experienced chef-owner takes his cooking very seriously – the pub is closed on Mondays so he can visit his suppliers personally. Cooking is diverse; the appealing, flavoursome dishes are chalked on the board daily.

MAIDEN NEWTON

Dorset – See Regional map n°**4-C3**
London 144 mi – Bristol 93 mi – Cardiff 113 mi – Southampton 66 mi
Michelin Road map 503-M31 and 504

Le Petit Canard

Dorchester Rd ✉ DT2 0BE – (01300) 320 536 – www.le-petit-canard.co.uk – Closed 2 weeks January, Sunday dinner and Monday
Menu £ 29/34 – *(dinner only and Sunday lunch)*
This double-fronted former shop has a welcoming feel, with its cosy beamed interior and flickering candlelight. Run by a husband and wife team, it offers a seasonal menu of classic dishes; tasty duck and homemade bread feature.

MAIDENSGROVE

Oxfordshire – Pop. 1 572 – ✉ Henley-On-Thames – See Regional map n°**11-C3**
London 43 mi – Oxford 23 mi – Reading 15 mi

Five Horseshoes

✉ RG9 6EX – (01491) 641 282 – www.thefivehorseshoes.co.uk – Closed Monday except bank holidays
Menu £ 13 (weekday lunch) – Carte £ 22/41
Charming, part-17C inn; a walkers' paradise. The large garden and terrace afford delightful country views and there's a wood-fired oven for bespoke pizzas. Cooking is wholesome, with plenty of meaty dishes and a good value set selection.

ENGLAND

MAIDENHEAD

Street	Grid	No.
Bad Godesberg Way	Y	2
Belmont Park Ave	V	3
Blackamoor Lane	V	5
Boyn Hill Ave	Z	6
Braywick Rd	Z	7
Bridge St	Y	9
College Rd	V	13
Cookham Rd	Y	14
Crescent (The)	Y	15
Ferry Rd	X	17
Frascati Way	YZ	18
Furze Platt Rd	V	20
Grenfell Pl.	Z	21
Gringer Hill	V	22
Harrow Lane	V	24
High St	Y	
High St BRAY-ON-THAMES	X	25
King's Grove	Z	27
Linden Ave	V	28
Lower Cookham Rd	V	29
Manor Lane	X	31
Market St	Y	32
Nicholson's Walk Shopping Centre	YZ	
Norreys Drive	X	35
Oldfield Rd	V	36
Ray Mill Rd West	V	39
Ray St	V	38
St Ives Rd	Y	41
St Mark Rd	V	42
Stafferton Way	Z	43
Upper Bray Rd	X	45

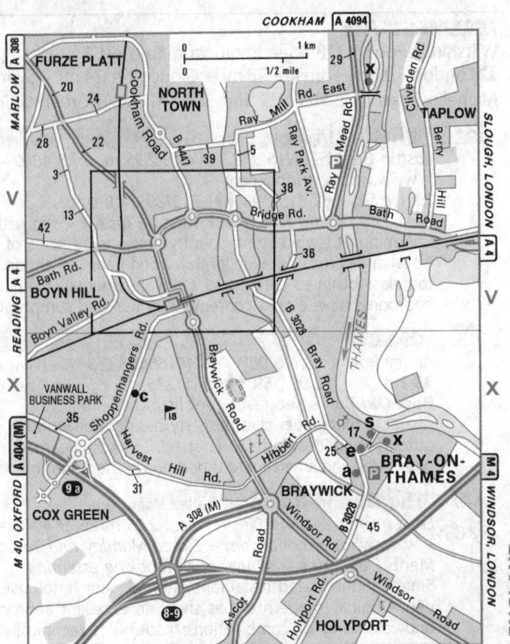

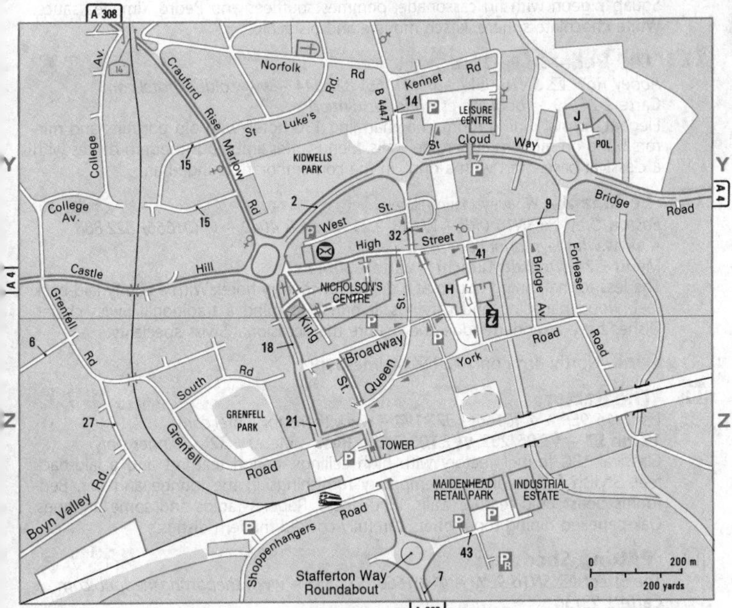

MALMESBURY

Wiltshire – Pop. 6 318 – See Regional map n°**4-C2**

London 108 mi – Bristol 28 mi – Gloucester 24 mi – Swindon 19 mi

Michelin Road map 503-N29 and 504 – Michelin Green Guide GREAT BRITAIN

Whatley Manor

Easton Grey ✉ *SN16 0RB – West : 2.25 mi on B 4040 –* ✆ *(01666) 822 888 – www.whatleymanor.com*

23 rm – ♦£ 315/895 ♦♦£ 315/895 – 8 suites

Rest *The Dining Room* ✿✿ **Rest *Le Mazot*** – see restaurant listing

Charming Cotswold stone country house in 12 acres of beautiful formal gardens. Guest areas include a delightful wood-panelled sitting room, a stunning spa, a top class business centre and a private cinema. Luxurious, individually decorated bedrooms have a chic, contemporary feel and sumptuous bathrooms.

Old Bell

Abbey Row ✉ *SN16 0BW –* ✆ *(01666) 822 344 – www.oldbellhotel.com*

33 rm – ♦£ 90/159 ♦♦£ 115/275

Rest *Old Bell* – see restaurant listing

Characterful creeper-clad property beside a beautiful abbey; built in 1220 and reputedly the oldest hotel in England. The cosy beamed interior has parquet floors, open fires and smart feature bedrooms; the uniform annexe rooms are simpler.

The Dining Room – Whatley Manor Hotel

✿✿

Easton Grey ✉ *SN16 0RB – West : 2.25 mi on B 4040 –* ✆ *(01666) 822 888 – www.whatleymanor.com – Closed Monday and Tuesday*

Menu £ 85/110 **s** – *(dinner only) (booking essential)*

Smart, sophisticated restaurant in an elegant hotel, overlooking the kitchen garden. Original, modern dishes show an excellent appreciation of ingredients and understanding of combinations; cooking is technically skilled and flavours are stunning. The team are attentive and the wine list, extensive.

→ Langoustine tails, confit chicken oysters, Swiss chard and cauliflower purée. Squab pigeon with fig cassonade, pommes soufflées and Pedro Ximenez sauce. White chocolate sphere, kirsch mousse and pistachio.

Old Bell – Old Bell Hotel

Abbey Row ✉ *SN16 0BW –* ✆ *(01666) 822 344 – www.oldbellhotel.com*

Carte £ 26/49 – *(booking essential at dinner)*

Elegant, formal dining room in a charming 13C hotel, with old portraits and mirrors hung on modern aubergine walls. Menus offer ambitious modern dishes with a classical base. Start with a drink in the contemporary lounge-bar.

Le Mazot – Whatley Manor Hotel

Easton Grey ✉ *SN16 0RB – West : 2.25 mi on B 4040 –* ✆ *(01666) 822 888 – www.whatleymanor.com*

Menu £ 24 (weekday lunch) – Carte £ 30/49 **s**

The less formal dining option at a delightful country hotel. With a comfy laid-back feel, wood panelling and carvings, it brings to mind a traditional Swiss chalet. Dishes have a modern edge and feature the occasional Swiss speciality.

at Crudwell North: 4 mi on A429 ✉ Malmesbury

The Rectory

✉ *SN16 9EP –* ✆ *(01666) 577 194 – www.therectoryhotel.com*

12 rm – ♦£ 95/205 ♦♦£ 105/205 **Rest** – Menu £ 32 – *(dinner only)*

Classical 18C former rectory with high ceilings, period features and a laid-back feel. Stylish fabrics and contemporary furnishings in the lounge and bar. Bedrooms boast bold feature walls, iPod docks, Roberts radios and some antiques. Oak-panelled dining room offers carefully cooked modern dishes.

Potting Shed Pub

The Street ✉ *SN16 9EW –* ✆ *(01666) 577 833 – www.thepottingshedpub.com*

Carte £ 23/36

Spacious, light-filled pub with contemporary décor, exposed beams and a relaxing feel. Monthly changing menus offer wholesome, satisfying dishes, with vegetables and herbs from their garden.

MALPAS

Cheshire West and Chester – Pop. 3 684 – See Regional map n°**20-A3**
London 177 mi – Birmingham 60 mi – Chester 15 mi – Shrewsbury 26 mi
Michelin Road map 502-L24

Tilston Lodge without rest

Tilston ✉ SY14 7DR – Northwest : 3 mi on Tilston Rd – ✆ (01829) 250 223
3 rm – £ 50/60 £ 80/100
Victorian hunting lodge with colourful gardens and welcoming owners. Classical bedrooms feature objets d'art and offer country views; two have four-posters. Spacious lounge and breakfast room. Juices are made from their home-grown apples.

MALTBY

Stockton-on-Tees – See Regional map n°**24-B3**
London 251 mi – Liverpool 141 mi – Leeds 69 mi – Sheffield 101 mi
Michelin Road map 502-Q23

Chadwicks Inn

High Ln ✉ TS8 0BG – ✆ (01642) 590 300 – www.chadwicksinnmaltby.co.uk – Closed 26 December, 1 January and Monday except bank holidays
Carte £ 28/41 – *(booking advisable)*
This pub dates back over 200 years and was a favourite haunt of the Spitfire pilots before their missions. The à la carte features ambitious, intricate dishes, supplemented by a simpler bistro menu. The live acoustic evenings are popular.

MALTON

North Yorkshire – Pop. 4 888 – See Regional map n°**23-C2**
London 234 mi – Pickering 9 mi – Scarborough 23 mi
Michelin Road map 502-R21 – Michelin Green Guide GREAT BRITAIN

Talbot

Yorkersgate ✉ YO17 7AJ – ✆ (01653) 639 096 – www.talbotmalton.co.uk
26 rm – £ 145/245 £ 145/245 – 2 suites
Rest *James Martin at the Talbot* – see restaurant listing
Early 17C hunting lodge owned by the Fitzwilliam Estate, featuring an impressive wooden staircase and country house guest areas filled with family artefacts and hung with portraits. Traditional bedrooms have smart marble bathrooms.

XX James Martin at the Talbot – Talbot Hotel

Yorkersgate ✉ YO17 7AJ – ✆ (01653) 639 096 – www.talbotmalton.co.uk
Menu £ 24 (lunch) – Carte £ 32/43 – *(booking advisable)*
Grand country house restaurant hung with an elegant chandelier and fine paintings. Concise menus use quality local and estate ingredients; classic combinations have a delicate touch and a subtle modern style. Service is amiable.

New Malton

2-4 Market Pl ✉ YO17 7LX – ✆ (01653) 693 998 – www.thenewmalton.co.uk – Closed 25-26 December and 1 January
Carte £ 20/28
18C stone pub with open fires, reclaimed furniture and photos of old town scenes. A good-sized menu offers hearty pub classics with the odd more adventurous dish thrown in; cooking is unfussy and flavoursome with an appealing Northern bias.

at Burythorpe South: 4.25 mi by Pocklington rd

Burythorpe House

✉ YO179LB – ✆ (01653) 658 200 – www.burythorpehouse.co.uk
13 rm – £ 85/130 £ 95/215
Rest – Menu £ 30 – *(dinner only and Sunday lunch)*
Victorian country house set in 1.5 acres. Lovely large drawing room with open fire and oil paintings. Spacious, uniquely furnished bedrooms come with a host of extras; some are classically styled, others, more modern. Traditional cooking served in oak-panelled dining rooms.

MALVERN WELLS → See Great Malvern

Worcestershire – Michelin Road map 503-N27

ENGLAND

MAN (Isle of)

I.O.M. – Pop. 80 058 – See Regional map n°**20-B1**
Michelin Road map 502-G21 – Michelin Green Guide GREAT BRITAIN

BALLASALLA

Abbey

Rushen Abbey, Mill Rd ✉ IM9 3DB – ☎ (01624) 822 393
– *www.theabbeyrestraurant.co.im – Closed Monday October-April*
Menu £ 30 – Carte £ 25/49
An appealing former pub that was once a judge's house and a jam factory. Inside it's a cosy mix of the old and new; outside, a delightful terrace overlooks the abbey gardens. Careful modern British cooking showcases homemade produce.

DOUGLAS

 **Claremont** 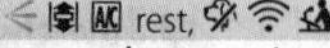

18-22 Loch Promenade ✉ IM1 2LX – ☎ (01624) 617 068 – www.claremont.im
56 rm – †£ 80/140 ††£ 110/190
Rest *Coast* – Menu £ 10 (weekday lunch) – Carte £ 18/36
Smart, modern hotel made up of several Victorian seaside properties. Bedrooms have good quality dark wood furnishings, Hungarian duck feather pillows, superb wet rooms, and state-of-the-art TV and audio equipment. The large brasserie-style restaurant serves modern dishes, which are presented by a cheery team.

 **Regency** 

Queens Promenade ✉ IM2 4NN – ☎ (01624) 680 680 – www.regency.im
38 rm – †£ 85/135 ††£ 160/190 – 4 suites
Rest *Stephen Dedman - A Restaurant* – see restaurant listing
Restored Victorian townhouse featuring wood panelling, stained glass and a substantial collection of seascape watercolours. Bedrooms are well-equipped for business travellers and mobile phones and iPads are available on loan.

 **Penta** without rest 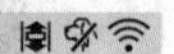

Queens Promenade ✉ IM9 4NE – ☎ (01624) 680 680 – www.regency.im
23 rm – †£ 50/100 ††£ 62/120
Good value hotel with bay views and a complimentary shuttle bus to the financial district from 8-9.30am. Large, functional bedrooms are well-maintained. Guests have access to all of the Regency's facilities, including the restaurant.

 **Inglewood** without rest 

26 Palace Terr, Queens Promenade ✉ IM2 4NF – ☎ (01624) 674 734
– www.inglewoodhotel-isleofman.com – Closed 16 October-3 November and Christmas-New Year
16 rm – †£ 55/99 ††£ 85/110
Modern hotel at the quieter end of the promenade; the front-facing rooms enjoy views over the bay. Spacious bedrooms have chunky, contemporary furnishings, leather armchairs and modern shower rooms. Well-stocked residents' bar.

 **Stephen Dedman - A Restaurant** – Regency Hotel 

Queens Promenade ✉ IM2 4NN – ☎ (01624) 680 680 – www.regency.im
Menu £ 28 – Carte £ 42/49 – *(dinner only)*
Traditional oak-panelled hotel restaurant displaying a collection of original island pictures. The menu of the day is rooted in the classics, while the à la carte offers original modern dishes which arrive artistically presented.

 **Portofino** Ⓝ 

Quay West ✉ IM1 5AG – ☎ (01624) 617 755 – www.portofino.im
– Closed 25 December, Saturday lunch and Sunday
Menu £ 20/28 – Carte £ 24/49
This proudly run restaurant is on the ground floor of a chic apartment block on the harbour's edge. Menus offer classical international dishes with lots of Italian choices and verbally presented specials. Tables are smartly laid.

ENGLAND

XX **JAR**

Admirals House, 11-12 Loch Promenade ✉ IM1 2LX – ✆ (01624) 663 553 – www.admiralhouse.com/jar-restaurant – Closed 25 December, 1 January and lunch Saturday-Sunday

Carte £ 29/45

With its smart cocktail bar and huge hand-painted modern murals, JAR is more than 'Just Another Restaurant'. Menus are centred around small plates and sharing. It's set on the promenade and has a pleasant coastal outlook.

XX **Macfarlane's**

24 Duke St ✉ IM1 2AY – ✆ (01624) 624 777 – www.macfarlanes.im – Closed 2 weeks early August, 1 week spring, 1 week Christmas-New Year, Sunday and Monday

Menu £ 15 (weekday lunch)/28 – Carte £ 24/58 – *(dinner only and lunch Thursday-Friday) (booking essential)*

Small restaurant in the heart of town, run by a personable couple. Sit in high-sided booths or on tall banquettes. Unfussy menus rely on fresh local produce; the blackboard specials have fresh fish and shellfish to the fore.

X **Tanroagan**

9 Ridgeway St ✉ IM1 1EW – ✆ (01624) 612 355 – www.tanroagan.co.uk – Closed 25-26 December and Sunday

Menu £ 19 (weekday lunch) – Carte £ 23/54

Friendly restaurant off the quayside, with seafaring décor and a cosy feel. Fish from the island's day boats are simply cooked, making the most of their natural flavours. Portions are hearty; bread, desserts and ice creams are homemade.

PORT ERIN

Rowany Cottier without rest

Spaldrick ✉ IM9 6PE – ✆ (01624) 832 287 – www.rowanycottier.com – April-October

5 rm – †£ 50/70 ††£ 84/92

Large, purpose-built house set close to Bradda Glen. Pleasant guest areas have views over Port Erin and the Calf of Man. Bedrooms are simple and well-kept. Locally sourced breakfasts feature homemade bread.

RAMSEY

River House without rest

✉ IM8 3DA North : 0.25 mi by A 9 turning left immediately after bridge – ✆ (01624) 816 412 – www.theriverhouse-iom.com

4 rm – †£ 60/95 ††£ 95/115

Attractive Georgian country house in an idyllic riverside setting; its bright, spacious interior filled with antique furnishings and objets d'art. Traditional bedrooms come with floral fabrics, knick-knacks and large baths.

ENGLAND

MANCHESTER

Greater Manchester – Pop. 510 746 – See Regional map n°**20-B2**

London 202 mi – Birmingham 86 mi – Glasgow 221 mi – Leeds 43 mi

Michelin Road map 502-N23 and 503-N23 – Michelin Green Guide GREAT BRITAIN

© Manchester House

Hotels

ENGLAND

Lowry rm,

50 Dearmans Pl, Chapel Wharf, Salford ✉ M3 5LH – ✆ (0161) 827 40 00 – www.roccofortehotels.com Town plan: CY**n**

165 rm – †£ 139/589 ††£ 139/589, ☕ £ 22 – 7 suites

Rest *River Bar & Grill* – ✆ (0161) 827 4041 – Menu £ 25 (weekday lunch) – Carte £ 28/54

Modern and hugely spacious, with excellent facilities, an impressive spa and a minimalist feel: art displays and exhibitions feature throughout. Stylish bedrooms with oversized windows; some have river views. The airy first floor restaurant serves a wide-ranging menu.

Radisson Edwardian rm,

Free Trade Hall, Peter St ✉ M2 5GP – ✆ (0161) 835 9929 – www.radissonedwardian.com/manchester Town plan: CZ**a**

263 rm ☕ – †£ 110/360 ††£ 110/360 – 4 suites

Rest *Opus One* – ✆ (0161) 835 8904 – Menu £ 25 (dinner) – Carte £ 27/40

Rest *Steak and Lobster at Alto* – ✆ (0161) 835 8903 – Menu £ 17 – Carte £ 26/29

This 14 floor hotel cleverly incorporates the façade of the former Free Trade Hall and has a great pool and spa. Bedrooms are contemporary – some have part-covered verandas; the Valentino Suite is the best and offers superb views. Sultry 'Opus One' is popular for afternoon tea, cocktails and seasonal modern dinners. Informal 'Steak and Lobster' serves an all-day menu.

Malmaison

Piccadilly ✉ M1 3AQ – ✆ (0161) 278 10 00 – www.malmaison-manchester.com Town plan: CZ**u**

167 rm – †£ 99/199 ††£ 99/199, ☕ £ 16 – 1 suite

Rest *Smoak Bar & Grill* – ✆ (0161) 278 10 01 – Carte £ 23/36

Old cotton warehouse and dolls hospital joined by a striking granite extension. Stylish bedrooms: some in dark, masculine shades; others in more subtle pastel hues. Uniquely designed suites include Man Utd and Man City themes. Smoak offers a menu inspired by American steakhouses.

Take note of the classification: you should not expect the same level of service in a X or 🏠 as in a XXXXX or 🏨.

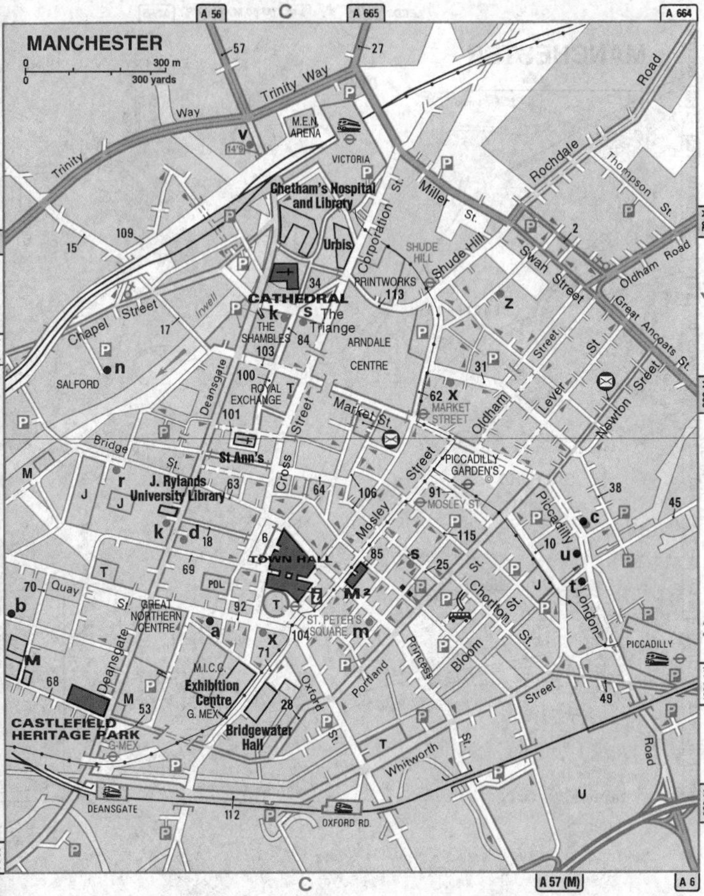

MANCHESTER

Street	Grid	No.
Addington St	CY	2
Albert Square	CZ	6
Aytoun St	CZ	10
Blackfriars Rd	CY	15
Blackfriars St	CY	17
Brazennoze St	CZ	18
Charlotte St	CZ	25
Cheetham Hill Rd	CY	27
Chepstow St	CZ	28
Church St	CY	31
Corn Exchange	CY	34
Dale St	CZ	38
Deansgate	CYZ	
Ducie St	CZ	45
Fairfield St	CZ	49
Great Bridgewater St	CZ	53
Great Ducie St	CY	57
Great Northern centre	CZ	
High St	CY	62
John Dalton St	CZ	63
King St	CZ	64
Liverpool Rd	CZ	68
Lloyd St	CZ	69
Lower Byrom St	CZ	70
Lower Mosley St	CZ	71
Mosley St	CZ	
New Cathedral St	CY	84
Nicholas St	CZ	85
Parker St	CZ	91
Peter St	CZ	92
Princess St	CZ	
St Ann's Square	CY	100
St Ann's St	CY	101
St Mary's Gate	CY	103
St Peter's Square	CZ	104
Shambles Shopping Centre (The)	CY	
Spring Gardens	CZ	106
Viaduct St	CY	109
Whitworth St West	CZ	112
Withy Grove	CY	113
York St	CZ	115

Abode

107 Piccadilly ✉ M1 2DB – ✆ (0161) 247 77 44 – www.abodehotels.co.uk

Town plan: CZ**c**

61 rm – †£ 69/170 ††£ 89/190, ☕ £ 12

Rest *Michael Caines* – see restaurant listing

This late Victorian former cotton merchant's HQ still has its iron columns and girders in situ. It has a boutique ambience with open-plan guest areas, modern bedrooms and stylish bathrooms; the 5th floor bedrooms are all suites.

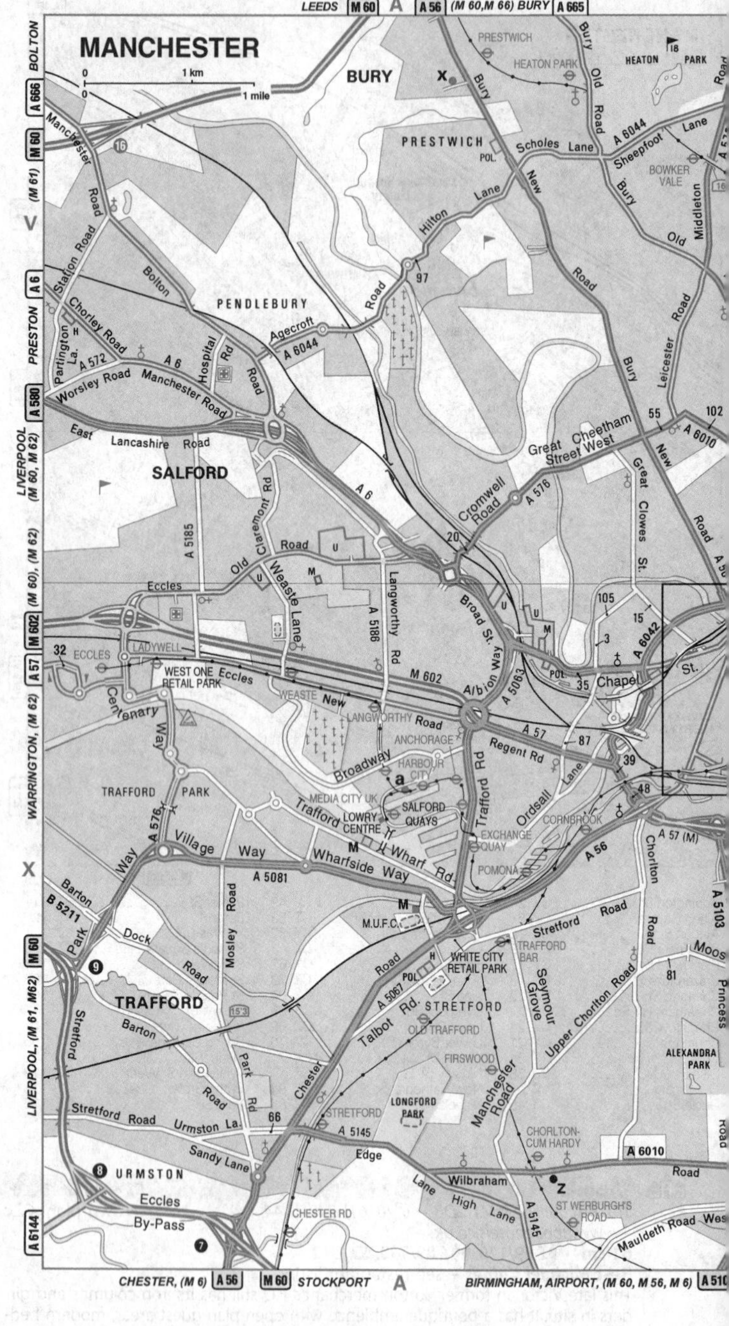
MANCHESTER
0 1 km
0 1 mile
LEEDS M 60 A A 56 (M 60, M 66) BURY A 665
BOLTON A 666 M 60 (M 61)
V
PRESTON A 6
LIVERPOOL (M 60, M 62) A 580
ENGLAND
(M 62) (M 60), M 602
A 57
WARRINGTON, (M 62)
X
M 60
LIVERPOOL, (M 61, M62)
A 6144
CHESTER, (M 6) A 56 M 60 STOCKPORT A BIRMINGHAM, AIRPORT, (M 60, M 56, M 6) A 510
BURY
PRESTWICH
HEATON PARK
HEATON PARK
PRESTWICH
POL.
Scholes Lane
Bury Old Road
Bury New Road
A 6044
Sheepfoot Lane
BOWKER VALE
Bury Old Road
Middleton Road
Hilton Lane
97
Manchester Road
Station Road
Bolton Road
PENDLEBURY
Agecroft Road
A 6044
Chorley Road
Partington La.
A 572
A 6
Worsley Road
Manchester Road
Hospital Rd
Road
East Lancashire Road
SALFORD
Claremont Rd
A 6
Cromwell Road
A 576
Great Cheetham Street West
55
102
A 6010
Leicester Road
Great Clowes St.
New Road
A 5185
Old Road
Weaste Lane
Langworthy Rd
A 5186
20
Broad St.
Eccles
ECCLES
32
LADYWELL
WEST ONE RETAIL PARK
Eccles New
WEASTE
M 602
Albion Way
A 5063
105
15
3
A 6042
Chapel St.
35
POL.
Centenary Way
LANGWORTHY Road
ANCHORAGE
A 57
Regent Rd
87
39
48
Broadway
HARBOUR CITY
a
TRAFFORD PARK
MEDIA CITY UK
SALFORD QUAYS
LOWRY CENTRE
Trafford Wharf Rd
Trafford Rd
Ordsall Lane
CORNBROOK
A 57 (M)
EXCHANGE QUAY
POMONA
A 56
Chorlton Road
A 5103
A 576
Village Way
A 5081
Wharfside Way
M
Barton
B 5211
Park
Dock Road
Mosley Road
M.U.F.C.
Stretford Road
TRAFFORD BAR
Seymour Grove
Moss
81
Princess
9
TRAFFORD
Road
WHITE CITY RETAIL PARK
A 5067
POL.
H
Talbot Rd.
STRETFORD
OLD TRAFFORD
Upper Chorlton Road
Stretford
Barton Road
Park Rd
Chester
FIRSWOOD
Manchester Road
ALEXANDRA PARK
LONGFORD PARK
Stretford Road
Urmston La.
66
STRETFORD
A 5145
CHORLTON-CUM HARDY
A 6010
Road
8 URMSTON
Sandy Lane
Edge Lane
Wilbraham Road
Z
High Lane
A 5145
ST WERBURGH'S ROAD
Mauldeth Road West
Eccles By-Pass
7
CHESTER RD

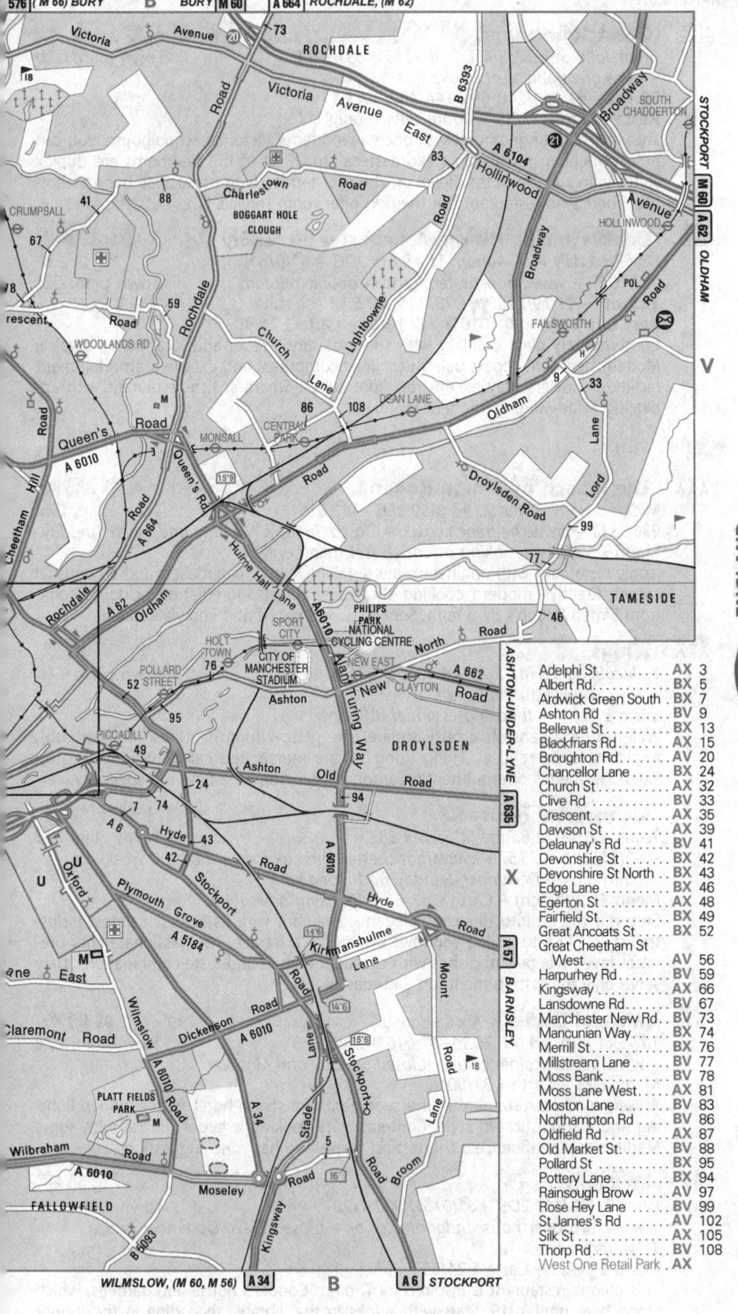
576 (M 66) BURY
B
BURY M 60
A 664 ROCHDALE, (M 62)
Victoria Avenue
ROCHDALE
Victoria Avenue East
B 6393
Broadway
SOUTH CHADDERTON
STOCKPORT M 60
A 6104
Hollinwood Avenue
HOLLINWOOD
A 62 OLDHAM
Charlestown Road
BOGGART HOLE CLOUGH
CRUMPSALL
Rochdale Road
Road
Broadway
Road
POL.
FAILSWORTH
Crescent
WOODLANDS RD
Church Lane
Lightbowne Road
V
DEAN LANE
Oldham
Lane
Queen's Road
MONSALL
CENTRAL PARK
Queen's Rd
A 6010
Road
Droylsden Road
Lord
Cheetham Hill Road
A 664
Hulme Hall Lane
TAMESIDE
Rochdale
A 62
Oldham
A6010
PHILIPS PARK
NATIONAL CYCLING CENTRE
SPORT CITY
HOLT TOWN
CITY OF MANCHESTER STADIUM
North Road
POLLARD STREET
NEW EAST
A 662
New Road
CLAYTON
Ashton
Alan Turing Way
ASHTON-UNDER-LYNE
PICCADILLY
DROYLSDEN
Ashton Old Road
A 635
A 6
Hyde Road
A 6010
X
U
Oxford
Plymouth Grove
Stockport
A 5184
Hyde Road
Kirkmanshulme Lane
A 57
BARNSLEY
Mount Road
Lane East
Wilmslow
Dickenson Road
A 6010
Claremont Road
Lane
Stockport Road
PLATT FIELDS PARK
A 6010
Road
A 34
Stade
Lane
Wilbraham Road
A 6010
Moseley Road
Broom Lane
FALLOWFIELD
B 5093
Kingsway
WILMSLOW, (M 60, M 56) A 34
B
A 6 STOCKPORT

ENGLAND

Great John Street

Great John St ✉ *M3 4FD* – *(0161) 831 3211* Town plan: CZ**b**
– *www.greatjohnstreet.co.uk*
30 rm – £ 144/240 £ 144/480, £ 17
Rest – Carte £ 17/35 – *(room service only)*
This stylish, boutique hotel was once a wonderful Victorian schoolhouse; you can hold a meeting in the old Headmaster's study! All of the bedrooms are duplex suites with roll-top baths. Relax on the roof terrace with its cocktail bar and hot-tub. There's no restaurant but they do offer room service.

Doubletree by Hilton Manchester Piccadilly

One Piccadilly Pl, 1 Auburn St ✉ *M1 3DG* – *(0161) 242 10 00* – *www.manchesterpiccadilly.doubletree.com* Town plan: CZ**t**
285 rm – £ 79/225 £ 79/225, £ 18 – 1 suite
Rest *City Café* – (0161) 242 10 20 – Carte £ 26/40
Contemporary glass building with spacious, airy interior and local art on display. Modern bedrooms boast pale hues, iMac computers and excellent entertainment facilities; showers only except top floor suites. Smart, stylish restaurant with appealing, wide-ranging, modern menu.

Restaurants

The French by Simon Rogan

Midland Hotel, Peter St. ✉ *M60 2DS* – *(0161) 236 3333* – *www.the-french.co.uk* – *Closed Sunday, Monday and lunch Tuesday* Town plan: CZ**x**
Menu £ 59/84 – *(booking essential) (set menu only)*
Iconic restaurant with original ornate detailing, crystal chandeliers and an unusual carpet. Creative modern cooking showcases British ingredients, including some from Simon Rogan's own farm. Service is well-paced and knowledgeable.

Wings

1 Lincoln Sq ✉ *M2 5LN* – *(0161) 834 90 00* Town plan: CZ**d**
– *www.wingsrestaurant.co.uk*
Carte £ 22/71 – *(booking essential at dinner)*
Well-run restaurant off a busy square. The narrow room features comfy booths, terracotta army replicas, Hong Kong skyline murals and celebrity-signed plates. Extensive menus offer authentic Cantonese dim sum; sea bass is a speciality.

Manchester House (N)

Tower 12, 18-22 Bridge St ✉ *M3 3BZ* Town plan: CZ**r**
– *(0161) 835 25 57* – *www.manchesterhouse.uk.com* – *Closed 2 weeks January, 25-26 December, Sunday and Monday*
Menu £ 23 (lunch) – Carte £ 47/66 – *(booking advisable)*
Step out the lift into this cool, elegant restaurant with its Scandic, almost industrial style. Floor to ceiling windows open onto a terrace. The passionate chef prepares inventive, playful dishes with excellent texture and taste combinations; they serve only the tasting menu on Saturday nights.

Michael Caines – Abode Hotel

107 Piccadilly ✉ *M1 2DB* – *(0161) 200 56 78* Town plan: CZ**c**
– *www.michaelcaines.co.uk* – *Closed Sunday and Monday*
Menu £ 25 – Carte £ 37/50
A lively modern restaurant in the basement of a stylish hotel, with subdued lighting and a sophisticated style. Contemporary cooking is largely British with some Mediterranean influences. The tasting menu also has wine suggestions.

Mr Cooper's (N)

Peter St ✉ *M60 2DS* – *(0161) 932 4128* Town plan: CZ**x**
– *www.mrcoopershouseandgarden.co.uk* – *Closed 25-26 December and 1 January*
Menu £ 19/23 – Carte £ 24/35
This unique restaurant is inspired by Thomas Cooper's house and gardens, which stood here until 1819. Start with drinks in the 'library', then dine in the indoor 'garden'. Dishes are modern and flavoursome with global influences.

ENGLAND

XX **Australasia**

1 The Avenue, Spinningfields ✉ M3 3AP Town plan: CZ**k**
– ✆ (0161) 831 0288 – www.australasia.uk.com – Closed 25-26 December and 1 January
Menu £ 11 (weekday lunch) – Carte £ 25/78
Fun, fashionable basement restaurant on the site of the old Manchester Evening News; come for cocktails, small plates, sushi, designer styling, DJs and a clubby vibe. Vibrant dishes have European/Pacific Rim/Asian influences. Helpful staff.

XX **63 Degrees**

20 Church St ✉ M4 1PN – ✆ (0161) 832 5438 Town plan: CY**x**
– www.63degrees.co.uk – Closed Sunday and Monday
Menu £ 18 (weekdays)/25 – Carte £ 31/61
Family-run restaurant near Arndale shopping centre. Elegant, contemporary lighting illuminates rustic stencilled walls. The cooking also mixes the classical with the modern, using traditional combinations and the latest techniques.

XX **Second Floor at Harvey Nichols**

21 New Cathedral St ✉ M1 1AD – ✆ (0161) 828 8898 Town plan: CY**k**
– www.harveynichols.com – Closed 25-28 December, 1 January and dinner Sunday-Monday
Menu £ 30/55
Smart restaurant with stylish colour-changing lighting and oversized windows offering views over Exchange Square and the cathedral. Elaborate modern European menus display interesting twists and dishes are attractively presented.

XX **Yang Sing**

34 Princess St ✉ M1 4JY – ✆ (0161) 236 22 00 Town plan: CZ**m**
– www.yang-sing.com – Closed 25 December
Menu £ 12 (weekday lunch)/30 – Carte £ 19/42
Family-run Chinese restaurant spread over 4 floors of an imposing Victorian building, with a '1930s Shanghai' basement room, a classic ground floor and private rooms above. Authentic Cantonese cooking features tasty dim sum at lunch.

XX **San Carlo Bottega** Ⓝ

Selfridges (2nd floor), 1 Exchange Square Central Town plan: CY**s**
✉ M3 1BD – ✆ (0161) 838 05 71 – www.sancarlobottega.co.uk – Closed 25 December
Carte £ 20/30
Take time out from shopping at Selfridges to relax in the elegant cocktail bar or long, brasserie-like dining room, which offers views across to the Cathedral. Tasty cicchetti dishes use fine Italian produce and arrive as they're ready.

X **Second Floor Brasserie at Harvey Nichols**

21 New Cathedral St ✉ M1 1AD – ✆ (0161) 828 88 98 Town plan: CY**k**
– www.harveynichols.com – Closed 25 December, 1 January, Easter Sunday and dinner Sunday-Monday
Carte £ 20/37
Relaxed bar and brasserie with colour-changing lighting and a buzzy atmosphere; it's popular with shoppers and they don't take bookings at lunch, so arrive in good time. Brunch is followed by a selection of modern British dishes.

X **Umezushi** Ⓝ

4 Mirabel St ✉ M3 1PJ – ✆ (0161) 832 18 52 Town plan: CY**v**
– www.umezushi.co.uk – Closed Christmas-New Year, Monday and the last Sunday of every month
Carte £ 14/70
A lovely little Japanese restaurant hidden under the railway arches, with a corrugated barrel ceiling, five light wood tables and counter seating for six. Tasty, unfussy dishes use good quality produce and arrive in no time.

ENGLAND

X **TNQ**

108 High St ✉ M4 1HQ – ✆ (0161) 832 71 15 Town plan: CY**z**
– www.tnq.co.uk – Closed 24-26 December and 1 January
Menu £ 17 (lunch) – Carte £ 23/40 – *(booking essential at dinner)*
Friendly neighbourhood restaurant with floor to ceiling windows and a homely feel. Keenly priced seasonal menus offer neatly presented classic dishes. The 3 course 'Love Lunch' is very popular, as are the monthly theme evenings.

X **Yuzu** Ⓝ

39 Faulkner St ✉ M1 4EE – ✆ (0161) 236 41 59 Town plan: CZ**s**
– www.yuzumanchester.co.uk – Closed Sunday and Monday
Carte £ 10/21 – *(bookings advisable at lunch)*
Climb the steps to the upper floor of this converted Victorian warehouse, where you'll find an open kitchen, a counter and four communal tables. The Japanese cooking is fresh, authentic and healthy; the dumplings are delicious.

at Didsbury South: 5.5 mi by A5103 -(AX)- on A5145✉ Manchester

Didsbury House 

Didsbury Pk ✉ M20 5LJ – South : 1.5 mi on A 5145 – ✆ (0161) 448 22 00
– www.didsburyhouse.com
27 rm – †£ 88/143 ††£ 88/143, ☕ £ 16 – 2 suites
Rest – Carte £ 19/37 **s** – *(room service only)*
Whitewashed Victorian villa – now a boutique townhouse – where original features include an impressive stained glass window. Bedrooms are stylish and well-appointed; some are duplex suites. There's no designated restaurant area but you can dine from an accessible menu in the bar, the lounges or your room.

ENGLAND

 **Eleven Didsbury Park** 

11 Didsbury Pk ✉ M20 5LH – South : 1.5 mi by A 5145 – ✆ (0161) 448 77 11
– www.elevendidsburypark.com
20 rm – †£ 88/143 ††£ 88/143, ☕ £ 16 – 1 suite
Rest – Carte £ 19/37 **s** – *(room service only)*
Chic, comfortable townhouse in a pleasant residential setting. Contemporary bedrooms have warm décor and good facilities; many come with a bath tub beside the bed. Have breakfast in a simply furnished room overlooking the delightful garden. The informal all-day menu is available as room service only.

at Salford Quays Southwest: 2.25 mi by A56 off A5063✉ Manchester

XX **Damson** Ⓝ

Orange Building, Media City ✉ M50 2HF – ✆ (0161) 751 70 20 – www.damsonrestaurant.co.uk – Closed Sunday dinner Town plan: AX**a**
Menu £ 17 – Carte £ 30/54
Enter into the futuristic MediaCityUK – home of the BBC – and head for this smart first floor restaurant on the quay. The elaborate à la carte menu offers refined, modern dishes and the full-length windows afford great water views.

at Chorlton-Cum-Hardy Southwest: 4 mi by A5103 -(AX)- on A6010✉ Manchester

 **Abbey Lodge** without rest 

501 Wilbraham Rd ✉ M21 0UJ – ✆ (0161) 862 92 66 Town plan: AX**z**
– www.abbey-lodge.co.uk
4 rm ☕ – †£ 50/60 ††£ 70/90
Red-brick Edwardian house in the city suburbs; a 'wishing table' provides a splash of colour on the stairwell. Warm, homely bedrooms offer good facilities; Rooms 3 and 4 are the largest. Continental-style buffet in your room.

at Prestwich Northwest: 5 mi on A56

XX **Aumbry**

2 Church Ln ✉ M25 1AJ – ✆ (0161) 798 58 41 Town plan: AV**x**
– www.aumbryrestaurant.co.uk – Closed 24-25 December, 1 January and Monday
Menu £ 60/75 – *(dinner only and lunch Friday-Sunday) (booking essential)*
Friendly neighbourhood restaurant of just 9 tables, set within a pretty little cottage. Well-presented dishes showcase local produce and offer good combinations of flavours; cooking blends heritage recipes with modern approaches.

MANSFIELD

Nottinghamshire – Pop. 77 551 – See Regional map n°**16-B1**
▶London 143 mi – Chesterfield 12 mi – Worksop 14 mi

Michelin Road map 502-Q24 and 503

XX **No.4 Wood Street**

4 Wood St ✉ NG18 1QA – ✆ (01623) 424 824 – www.4woodstreet.co.uk – Closed Sunday dinner, Monday and lunch Tuesday
Menu £ 12 (weekday lunch)/18 – Carte £ 23/32 – *(booking advisable)*
Modern restaurant on the first floor of a converted warehouse. Exposed stone walls and chunky wood furniture give it a rustic feel. Classical cooking has clearly defined flavours. Start with a speciality gin in the spacious lounge.

MARAZION

Cornwall – Pop. 1 294 – ✉ Penzance – See Regional map n°**1-A3**
▶London 318 mi – Penzance 3 mi – Truro 26 mi

Michelin Road map 503-D33

Mount Haven 

Turnpike Rd ✉ TR17 0DQ – East : 0.25 mi – ✆ (01736) 710 249 – www.mounthaven.co.uk – Closed January
18 rm – †£ 90/130 ††£ 130/240
Rest – Menu £ 14/19 – Carte £ 20/39 – *(bar lunch Monday-Saturday)*
Small hotel overlooking St Michael's Bay, with a spacious bar and a lounge featuring Indian fabrics and artefacts. Contemporary bedrooms come with good modern amenities and most have a balcony and a view. Bright, attractive dining room offers elaborate modern dishes with ambitious flavour combinations.

X **Ben's Cornish Kitchen** 

West End ✉ TR17 0EL – ✆ (01736) 719 200 – www.benscornishkitchen.com – Closed 25-26 December, 1 January, Monday lunch and Sunday
Menu £ 18 (lunch) – Carte dinner £ 24/43
Rustic family-run eatery; sit upstairs for views over the rooftops to St Michael's Mount. Unfussy lunches are followed by sophisticated dinners, which feature some interesting flavour combinations. They offer 25 wines by the glass.

at Perranuthnoe Southeast: 1.75 mi by A394✉ Penzance

Ednovean Farm without rest 

✉ TR20 9LZ – ✆ (01736) 711 883 – www.ednoveanfarm.co.uk – Closed Christmas
3 rm – †£ 90/130 ††£ 90/130
17C granite barn in a tranquil spot overlooking the bay and surrounded by 22 acres of sub-tropical gardens and paddocks. Individually styled bedrooms and locally produced toiletries; the Blue Room has a French bed, a roll-top bath and a terrace. Have a range-cooked breakfast at the oak table or a continental selection in your room. Complimentary sherry in the hall.

Victoria Inn with rm 

✉ *TR20 9NP – ✆ (01736) 710 309 – www.victoriainn-penzance.co.uk – Closed 25-26 December, 1 January, Monday in winter and Sunday dinner*

2 rm ☕ – 🚹£ 50/75 🚹🚹£ 75 Carte £ 23/37

Characterful, pink-washed pub in the heart of the village, with a cosy, homely feel, great local art and a suntrap rear terrace. Tasty, wholesome, carefully prepared pub classics showcase quality local produce, including plenty of seafood. Service is cheery, there's a great selection of local ales and you'll find two modest bedrooms situated directly above the pub.

MARGATE

Kent – Pop. 61 223 – See Regional map n°**9-D1**

▶London 74 mi – Canterbury 17 mi – Dover 21 mi – Maidstone 43 mi

Michelin Road map 504-Y29

Sands Ⓝ 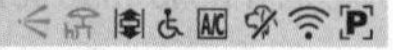

16 Marine Dr ✉ CT9 1DH – (entrance on High St) – ✆ (01843) 228 228 – www.sandshotelmargate.co.uk

20 rm ☕ – 🚹£ 99/220 🚹🚹£ 99/220

Rest *Bay @ Sands* – Menu £ 18 (weekday lunch) – Carte £ 23/45

Set between the high street and the sea – a smartly refurbished hotel, with extremely stylish bedrooms. Have a cocktail in the white leather furnished lounge-bar overlooking the beach before watching the sun go down from the roof terrace. The brasserie serves modern British dishes and also shares the view.

Reading Rooms without rest 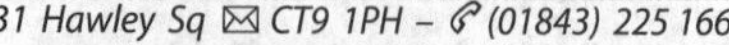

31 Hawley Sq ✉ CT9 1PH – ✆ (01843) 225 166 – www.thereadingroomsmargate.co.uk

3 rm ☕ – 🚹£ 95/150 🚹🚹£ 95/180

Passionately run guesthouse with stripped plaster, worn woodwork and a unique shabby-chic style. Eclectic bedrooms – one per floor – boast distressed furniture, super-comfy beds and huge bathrooms. Extensive breakfasts served in your room.

Ambrette Margate

44 King St ✉ CT9 1QE – ✆ (01843) 231 504 – www.theambrette.co.uk – Closed 25-26 December and Monday

Menu £ 20 (lunch) – Carte £ 21/35

Quirky restaurant with modest surroundings. The concise menu showcases Kentish produce in an original modern style; freshly prepared dishes offer well-balanced flavours and subtle Indian spicing – you won't find any curries here!

MARKET DRAYTON

Shropshire – Pop. 11 773 – See Regional map n°**18-B1**

▶London 159 mi – Nantwich 13 mi – Shrewsbury 21 mi

Michelin Road map 502-M25 and 503

Goldstone Hall 

Goldstone ✉ TF9 2NA – South : 4.5 mi by A 529 – ✆ (01630) 661 202 – www.goldstonehall.com

12 rm ☕ – 🚹£ 81/110 🚹🚹£ 140/170

Rest – Menu £ 30 (weekdays) **s** – Carte £ 28/61 **s**

Attractive red-brick house with numerous extensions, surrounded by 5 acres of peaceful grounds. Lovely panelled drawing room and characterful beamed seating area with small bar. Classically styled bedrooms have plenty of space and pleasant country views. Modern menus feature kitchen garden produce.

MARKET RASEN

Lincolnshire – Pop. 4 773 – See Regional map n°**17-C1**

▶London 158 mi – Nottingham 54 mi – Kingston upon Hull 37 mi – Sheffield 53 mi

Michelin Road map 504-T23

Advocate Arms with rm

2 Queen St ✉ LN8 3EH – ✆ (01673) 842 364 – www.advocatearms.co.uk – Closed Sunday dinner except in December

10 rm – †£ 55/90 ††£ 55/90, ☕£ 7 Carte £ 13/44

Former hotel close to the market square, with an original revolving door and a smart, modern interior divided by etched glass walls. Lunch sticks to good old pub classics and at dinner, mature local steaks are a speciality; they also serve breakfast and afternoon tea. Bedrooms are spacious and well-equipped.

MARLBOROUGH

Wiltshire – Pop. 8 092 – See Regional map n°**4-D2**

London 84 mi – Bristol 47 mi – Southampton 40 mi – Swindon 12 mi

Michelin Road map 503-O29 and 504 – Michelin Green Guide GREAT BRITAIN

Coles

27 Kingsbury Hill ✉ SN8 1JA – ✆ (01672) 515 004 – www.colesrestaurant.co.uk – Closed 25 December, Sunday and bank holidays except Good Friday

Menu £ 16 (lunch) – Carte £ 26/39

Cosy, buzzy bistro with a loyal local following. Two rooms feature an eclectic range of memorabilia – including architects' plans and vineyard maps. The menu is equally as diverse, with dishes ranging from fishcakes to monkfish 'ossobuco'.

at Little Bedwyn East: 9.5 mi by A4 ✉ Marlborough

Harrow at Little Bedwyn (Roger Jones)

✉ SN8 3JP – ✆ (01672) 870 871 – www.theharrowatlittlebedwyn.com – Closed 25 December-4 January and Sunday-Tuesday

Menu £ 40/75 – Carte approx. £ 55

Former pub with smartly laid tables and an intimate atmosphere. Flavourful, seasonal cooking is presented in a modern style, whilst still retaining a classical base; produce is top quality and fish plays an important role. The wine list is comprehensive and they also hold regular wine evenings.

→ Deep-fried lobster with spiced sea salt. Poached and roasted quail, fresh morels and asparagus. Selection of mini desserts.

at West Overton West: 4 mi on A4

Bell

Bath Rd ✉ SN8 1QD – ✆ (01672) 861 099 – www.thebellwestoverton.co.uk – Closed Sunday dinner and Monday except bank holidays

Carte £ 25/44

A simple, friendly pub, rescued from oblivion by a local couple, who hired an experienced pair to run it. The menu mixes pub classics with Mediterranean-influenced dishes; presentation is modern but not at the expense of flavour.

at East Kennett West: 5.25 mi by A4

Old Forge without rest

✉ SN8 4EY – ✆ (01672) 861 686 – www.theoldforge-avebury.co.uk – Closed 25-26 December

4 rm ☕ – †£ 65/75 ††£ 75/85

Converted former smithy with a relaxing, homely feel. Comfortable bedrooms have classic country house style; the family room has pleasant countryside views. Communal breakfast.

MARLDON

Devon – Pop. 1 906 – See Regional map n°**2-C2**

London 193 mi – Plymouth 30 mi – Torbay 3 mi – Exeter 23 mi

Michelin Road map 503-J32

ENGLAND

Church House Inn

Village Rd ✉ TQ3 1SL – ☎ (01803) 558 279 – www.churchhousemarldon.com – Closed dinner 25-26 December

Carte £ 23/36

Charming, well-run inn with wooden beams, open fires and original Georgian windows. Extensive choice on blackboard menus, with classically based dishes and some Mediterranean influences. Exotic theme nights and friendly, helpful service.

MARLOW

Buckinghamshire – Pop. 14 823 – See Regional map n°**11-C3**

London 35 mi – Aylesbury 22 mi – Oxford 29 mi – Reading 14 mi

Michelin Road map 504-R29

Danesfield House

Henley Rd ✉ SL7 2EY – Southwest : 2.5 mi on A 4155 – ☎ (01628) 891 010 – www.danesfieldhouse.co.uk

86 rm – †£ 139/264 ††£ 179/264 **Rest** – Carte £ 28/63

Stunning house built in Italian Renaissance style, with breathtaking views of the Thames and the Chilterns. Bedrooms at the front are the best; most are traditional and some have four-poster beds. Unwind in the characterful guest areas or the smart spa, then dine in the intimate formal restaurant or the charming orangery – the latter has a great garden outlook.

Compleat Angler

Marlow Bridge, Bisham Rd ✉ SL7 1RG – ☎ (0844) 879 91 28 – www.macdonald-hotels.co.uk/compleatangler

64 rm – †£ 130/290 ††£ 140/310 – 3 suites

Rest *Riverside* – ☎ (01628) 405 406 – Menu £ 25 (lunch) – Carte £ 40/55

Well-kept hotel in an idyllic spot on the Thames, with views of the weir and the characterful chain bridge. Comfy, corporate-style bedrooms blend classic furnishings with contemporary fabrics: some have balconies – opt for a Feature Room. The restaurant offers modern British cooking overlooking the river.

Vanilla Pod

31 West St ✉ SL7 2LS – ☎ (01628) 898 101 – www.thevanillapod.co.uk – Closed 24 December-8 January, Sunday, Monday and bank holidays

Menu £ 20/45 **s** – *(booking essential)*

Intimate, well-established restaurant – in T. S. Eliot's former home – with a plush interior and nicely spaced, smartly laid tables. Ambitious cooking has classical French foundations and displays original touches.

Hand and Flowers (Tom Kerridge) with rm

126 West St ✉ SL7 2BP – ☎ (01628) 482 277 – www.thehandandflowers.co.uk – Closed 24-26 December, 1 January and Sunday dinner

8 rm – †£ 140/190 ††£ 140/190

Menu £ 16 (weekday lunch) – Carte £ 43/64 – *(booking essential)*

A pretty little pub with low beams, flagged floors and a characterful lounge bar for pre and post-dinner drinks. Classic dishes display assured flavours, with quality ingredients marrying perfectly to turn the simple into the sublime. Dine without booking at the metal-topped bar counter. Beautifully furnished bedrooms are a stone's throw away; some have outdoor jacuzzis.

→ Smoked haddock omelette with parmesan. Slow-cooked duck breast with Savoy cabbage and duck fat chips. Hand & Flowers chocolate and ale cake with salted caramel and muscovado ice cream.

Royal Oak

Frieth Rd, Bovingdon Green ✉ SL7 2JF – West : 1.25 mi by A 4155 – ☎ (01628) 488 611 – www.royaloakmarlow.co.uk – Closed 25-26 December

Carte £ 21/37

Part-17C, country-chic pub with a herb garden, a petanque pitch and a pleasant terrace. Set close to the M40 and M4, it's an ideal London getaway. Cooking is British-led; wash down an ox cheek pasty with a pint of local Rebellion ale.

ENGLAND

at Little Marlow East: 3 mi on A4155

Queens Head
Pound Ln ✉ SL7 3SR – ✆ (01628) 482 927 – www.marlowslittlesecret.co.uk – Closed 25-26 December
Menu £ 30 – Carte £ 24/36
16C pub that's popular with walkers, with keen young partners at its helm and poised, friendly service. The refined à la carte changes regularly and features produce from local farms, forages and shoots; lunch also offers pub classics.

MARPLE

Greater Manchester – Pop. 18 241 – See Regional map n°**20**-B3
London 190 mi – Chesterfield 35 mi – Manchester 11 mi
Michelin Road map 502-N23 and 503

Springfield without rest
99 Station Rd ✉ SK6 6PA – ✆ (0161) 449 07 21 – www.springfieldhotelmarple.co.uk
8 rm – †£ 60/65 ††£ 65/85
Personally run, part-Victorian house with sympathetic extensions and pleasant rural views. Bright breakfast room; individually styled bedrooms. Useful for visits to the Peak District.

MARSDEN

West Yorkshire – Pop. 3 499 – ✉ Huddersfield – See Regional map n°**22**-A3
London 195 mi – Leeds 22 mi – Manchester 18 mi – Sheffield 30 mi
Michelin Road map 502-O23 and 504

Olive Branch with rm
Manchester Rd ✉ HD7 6LU – ✆ (01484) 844 487 – www.olivebranch.uk.com
3 rm – †£ 60/80 ††£ 80/110
Menu £ 20 – Carte £ 22/45 – *(dinner only and Sunday lunch)*
Characterful drovers' inn with stone floors, rustic walls, a secluded garden and pleasant views from its terrace. The classical, French-influenced menu is supplemented by fish specials and there's a good choice of wines by the glass. Bedrooms are modern, cosy and individually themed.

MARTINHOE → See Lynton

Devon

MARTON

Shropshire – See Regional map n°**18**-A2
London 181 mi – Leeds 133 mi – Sheffield 132 mi – Manchester 95 mi
Michelin Green Guide GREAT BRITAIN

Sun Inn
✉ SY21 8JP – ✆ (01938) 561 211 – www.suninn.org.uk – Closed Sunday dinner, Monday and lunch Tuesday
Carte £ 23/35
Welcoming country pub on the English-Welsh border, with a cosy bar and a brightly painted restaurant. The concise menu offers satisfying and comforting home-cooked dishes which include some great fish specials.

MARTON CUM GRAFTON

North Yorkshire – See Regional map n°**22**-B2
London 206 mi – Birmingham 136 mi – Liverpool 103 mi – Leeds 28 mi

Punch Bowl Inn
✉ YO51 9QY – ✆ (01423) 322 519 – www.thepunchbowlmartoncumgrafton.com
Carte £ 22/38
Delightful inn, part-dating from the 14C; arrive early in summer to bag a seat on the terrace. All-encompassing, seasonal menu includes a seafood platter and a 'Yorkshire board', with excellent fish and chips and rib-eye steak to die for.

ENGLAND

MASHAM

North Yorkshire – Pop. 1 205 – ✉ Ripon – See Regional map n°**22-B1**
London 231 mi – Leeds 38 mi – Middlesbrough 37 mi – York 32 mi
Michelin Road map 502-P21

Swinton Park

Swinton ✉ HG4 4JH – Southwest : 1 mi – ✆ (01765) 680 900 – www.swintonpark.com
31 rm – †£ 195/460 ††£ 195/460 – 4 suites
Rest *Samuels* – see restaurant listing
17C castle with Georgian and Victorian additions, set on a 22,000 acre estate. The grand interior features open fires, ornate plasterwork, oil portraits and antiques. Try your hand at shooting, fishing, riding, falconry or cooking.

Bank Villa

The Avenue ✉ HG4 4DB – on A 6108 – ✆ (01765) 689 605 – www.bankvilla.com
5 rm – †£ 45/65 ††£ 55/125 **Rest** – Menu £ 20 **s** – Carte £ 22/31
Stone-built Georgian villa with a lovely stepped garden; the welcoming owners look after their guests well. Relax in one of two cosy lounges or the conservatory. Comfy bedrooms have modern feature walls; those in the eaves are the most characterful. Unfussy dinners. Homemade yoghurt features at breakfast.

Samuels – Swinton Park Hotel

Swinton ✉ HG4 4JH – Southwest : 1 mi – ✆ (01765) 680 900 – www.swintonpark.com – Closed Monday lunch
Menu £ 27/65
Beautiful rococo-style dining room with an ornate gilt ceiling and park views; set within a castle. Well-spaced tables are adorned with lilies. Complex modern cooking uses produce from the huge kitchen gardens and local suppliers.

Vennell's

7 Silver St ✉ HG4 4DX – ✆ (01765) 689 000 – www.vennellsrestaurant.co.uk – Closed first 2 weeks January, 1 week Easter, 1 week August, Sunday dinner and Monday
Menu £ 28 **s** – *(dinner only and Sunday lunch) (booking essential)*
This endearing, personally run restaurant has stylish purple walls, boldly patterned chairs and a striking feature wall – at weekends, sit downstairs amongst the local art for a more intimate experience. Seasonal menus offer 4 choices per course; cooking is well-judged, flavourful and has a modern edge.

MATFEN

Northumberland – Pop. 500 – See Regional map n°**24-A2**
London 309 mi – Carlisle 42 mi – Newcastle upon Tyne 24 mi
Michelin Road map 501-O18 and 502

Matfen Hall

✉ NE20 0RH – ✆ (01661) 886 500 – www.matfenhall.com
53 rm – †£ 79/285 ††£ 79/285
Rest *Library* – Carte £ 33/51 – *(dinner only and Sunday lunch)*
Impressive 19C country mansion: popular as a wedding venue and for its golf course and spa. Spacious, traditional country house style bedrooms have good facilities; some boast four-posters and most offer rural views. Superb Great Hall and pleasant conservatory bar. Formal dining in the original library.

David Kennedy at Vallum

Military Rd ✉ NE18 0LL – Southeast : 3 mi by Newcastle rd on B 6318 – ✆ (01434) 672 406 – www.vallumfarm.co.uk – Closed 25-26 December, 1-2 January, Sunday dinner and Monday October-March
Menu £ 15 *(weekdays)* Carte-dinner £ 22/38
A converted milking shed with country views, in an artisan producers' collective. Classic British dishes are hearty and flavoursome, with a real emphasis on Northumbrian produce. Good value lunch and early evening menus. Friendly service.

MATFIELD

See Regional map n°**8-B2**

London 43 mi – Maidstone 15 mi – Royal Tunbridge Wells 6 mi

Wheelwrights Arms

The Green ✉ TN12 7JX – ✆ (01892) 722 129 – www.thewheelwrightsarmsmatfield.co.uk – Closed Sunday dinner and Monday

Carte £ 20/34

17C former Kentish farmhouse: outside it's all clapperboard and colourful flower baskets; inside it's rustic with low beamed ceilings crammed with hanging hops. Expect an abundance of local, seasonal produce in classic dishes.

MATLOCK

Derbyshire – Pop. 14 956 – See Regional map n°**16-B1**

London 150 mi – Sheffield 23 mi – Derby 19 mi

Michelin Road map 502-P24 – Michelin Green Guide GREAT BRITAIN

Stones

1C Dale Rd ✉ DE4 3LT – ✆ (01629) 56 061 – www.stones-restaurant.co.uk – Closed 25 December-2 January, Sunday, Monday and lunch Tuesday

Menu £ 17/30 – *(booking advisable)*

Negotiate the steep steps down to this small riverside restaurant and head for the front room with its floor to ceiling windows. Unfussy, modern British dishes are attractively presented and display the odd Mediterranean touch.

MAUNBY

North Yorkshire – See Regional map n°**22-B1**

London 228 mi – Leeds 40 mi – York 32 mi

Buck Inn

✉ YO7 4HD – ✆ (01845) 587 777 – www.thebuckinnmaunby.co.uk – Closed 26 December, 1 January, Sunday dinner and Monday

Menu £ 17 – Carte £ 23/36

Well run pub with a characterful beamed bar and light and airy dining rooms. Creative, modern dishes are well-constructed and tasty. The weekday lunch and early dinner 'Market Menu' offers particularly good bang for your buck.

MAWGAN PORTH → See Newquay

Cornwall – Michelin Road map 503-E32

MEDBOURNE

Leicestershire – See Regional map n°**16-B2**

London 93 mi – Corby 9 mi – Leicester 16 mi

Michelin Road map 504-R26

Homestead House without rest

Ashley Rd ✉ LE16 8DL – ✆ (01858) 565 724 – www.homesteadhouse.co.uk

3 rm – †£ 38 ††£ 60

Well-kept, detached house in an elevated position, with colourful flowerbeds set around an apple tree. Spacious lounge with leather sofas and an open fire. Traditional bedrooms offer good comforts; the two at the front have rural views.

MELLOR → See Blackburn

Lancashire

MELLOR

Greater Manchester – See Regional map n°**20-B3**

London 185 mi – Bristol 163 mi – Cardiff 184 mi – Plymouth 277 mi

Oddfellows

Moor End Rd ✉ SK6 5PT – ✆ (0161) 449 7826 – www.oddfellowsmellor.com – Closed Monday except bank holidays

Carte £ 19/38

A complete refurbishment has given Oddies – as it is known locally – a light, uncluttered feel; wood burning stoves add an element of cosiness. The appealing, daily changing menu offers 'British food with a modern twist'.

MELLS

Somerset – Pop. 2 222 – See Regional map n°**4**-C2

London 117 mi – Bath 16 mi – Frome 3 mi

Michelin Road map 504-M30

Talbot Inn with rm

Selwood St ✉ BA11 3PN – ✆ (01373) 812 254 – www.talbotinn.com

8 rm – †£ 95/150 ††£ 95/150 Carte £ 22/33

Characterful 15C coaching inn with a cobbled courtyard, a cosy sitting room with an open fire, a snug bar offering real ales and an elegant Grill Room to keep carnivores happy at weekends. Delightful bedrooms are well-priced and understated in style. Food is seasonal, modern and full of flavour; and staff may be casually attired, but their manner is anything but.

MELTON MOWBRAY

Leicestershire – Pop. 27 158 – See Regional map n°**16**-B2

London 113 mi – Leicester 15 mi – Northampton 45 mi – Nottingham 18 mi

Michelin Road map 502-R25 and 504

Stapleford Park

✉ LE14 2EF East : 5 mi by B 676 on Stapleford rd – ✆ (01572) 787 000 – www.staplefordpark.com

55 rm – †£ 140/250 ††£ 210/500 – 3 suites

Rest *Grinling Gibbons Dining Room* – Carte £ 36/55 – *(dinner only) (booking essential)*

Beautiful stately home in 500 acres of landscaped grounds, with grand drawing rooms, a lovely leather-furnished bar, exceedingly comfortable bedrooms and marble bathrooms. The extensive leisure facilities are a replica of those at Buckingham Palace! Ornate rococo dining room; mix of classic and modern dishes.

ENGLAND

MERE

Cheshire East – See Regional map n°**20**-B3

London 185 mi – Bristol 152 mi – Cardiff 173 mi – Plymouth 266 mi

Michelin Road map 502-M23

Mere

rm,

Chester Rd ✉ WA16 6LJ – on A 556 – ✆ (01565) 830 155 – www.themereresort.co.uk

81 rm – †£ 115/210 ††£ 125/220 – 10 suites

Rest *Browns* – Carte £ 29/44 – *(dinner only)*

Red-brick house set in 150 acres, complete with a lake and a championship golf course. Spacious guest areas include numerous meeting rooms and a smart spa. Contemporary bedrooms offer the latest mod cons. Snacks in the spa and golf club; bistro-style menu in the glass-roofed courtyard restaurant.

MEVAGISSEY

Cornwall – Pop. 2 117 – See Regional map n°**1**-B3

London 287 mi – Newquay 21 mi – Plymouth 44 mi – Truro 20 mi

Michelin Road map 503-F33 – Michelin Green Guide GREAT BRITAIN

Trevalsa Court

School Hill ✉ PL26 6TH – East : 0.5 mi – ✆ (01726) 842 468 – www.trevalsa-hotel.co.uk – Closed January and December

14 rm – †£ 60/105 ††£ 110/250 **Rest** – Carte £ 20/39 – *(dinner only)*

Charming Arts and Crafts style house which combines dark wood panelling and stone fireplaces with bright modern art and bold soft furnishings. Most of the well-appointed bedrooms have coastal views. The oak-panelled dining room looks onto the lovely terrace and garden and dishes showcase local produce.

MICKLETON → See Chipping Campden

Gloucestershire – Michelin Road map 503-O27

MID LAVANT → See Chichester

West Sussex – Michelin Road map 504-R31

MIDDLESBROUGH

Middlesbrough – Pop. 174 700 – See Regional map n°**24-B3**
London 246 mi – Leeds 66 mi – Newcastle upon Tyne 41 mi
Michelin Road map 502-Q20

Brasserie Hudson Quay

Windward Way ✉ TS2 1QG – East : 0.5 mi by A 66 – ☎ (01642) 261 166 – www.brasseriehudsonquay.com
Menu £ 17 (weekday lunch) – Carte £ 22/43
Be sure to grab a window seat so that you can look out over Hudson Quay's old docks. Lunch offers snacks and a good value menu that's popular with local office workers, while dinner offers sharing plates and brasserie classics.

MIDDLETON-IN-TEESDALE

Durham – Pop. 934 – See Regional map n°**24-A3**
London 260 mi – Carlisle 91 mi – Leeds 124 mi – Middlesbrough 70 mi
Michelin Road map 502-N20

Grove Lodge

Hude ✉ DL12 0QW – Northwest : 0.5 mi on B 6277 – ☎ (01833) 640 798 – www.grovelodgeteesdale.co.uk
6 rm – †£ 55 ††£ 82 **Rest** – Menu £ 16
Old Victorian shooting lodge, perched on a hillside overlooking the valley; a place to relax and escape from technology. Traditional lounges are furnished with antiques and heavy fabrics. Neat, up-to-date bedrooms; some have private bathrooms. Home-cooked dinners are served in the formally laid dining room.

MIDHURST

West Sussex – Pop. 4 914 – See Regional map n°**7-C2**
London 57 mi – Brighton 38 mi – Chichester 12 mi – Southampton 41 mi
Michelin Road map 504-R31

Spread Eagle

South St ✉ GU29 9NH – ☎ (01730) 816 911 – www.hshotels.co.uk
39 rm – †£ 79/229 ††£ 99/229 – 2 suites **Rest** – Carte £ 30/45
Part-15C coaching inn retaining plenty of its original character and decked out with antiques, tapestries and gleaming brass – although there's also a modern, well-equipped spa. Bedrooms are traditional. Dine next to an inglenook fireplace under wooden beams and look out for the Christmas puddings too!

at Henley North: 4.5 mi by A286

Duke of Cumberland Arms

✉ GU27 3HQ – ☎ (01428) 652 280 – www.dukeofcumberland.com – Closed 25-26 December and dinner Sunday-Monday
Carte £ 33/41
A hidden gem, with a delightfully low-beamed interior featuring a huge fireplace and flag floors; tiered gardens have babbling brooks, trout ponds and views over the Downs. Appealing, daily changing menu of carefully prepared, seasonal dishes; 2 courses at lunch and 3 at dinner. Charming service.

at Bepton Southwest: 2.5 mi by A286 on Bepton rd✉ Midhurst

Park House

✉ GU29 0JB – ☎ (01730) 819 000 – www.parkhousehotel.com – Closed 24-26 December
21 rm – †£ 135/300 ††£ 135/350 – 1 suite
Rest – Carte £ 38/44 – *(booking essential)*
Family-run country house with a light modern style and smart spa and leisure facilities. Spacious, homely bedrooms are split between this and South Downs Cottage; they come in neutral hues and most have views of the well-tended gardens and golf course. The stylish conservatory restaurant serves modern menus.

at Redford Northwest: 4 mi by A272 then following signs for Redford

 **Redford Cottage** without rest 

GU29 0QF – (01428) 741 242

3 rm  – †£ 75/95 ††£ 95

Hospitable owners welcome you to this charming 16C cottage, set in 3 acres of delightful gardens. Cosy beamed lounge with wood burner; traditionally furnished bedrooms. Aga-cooked breakfasts use local ingredients, with many home-made items.

MILFIELD

Northumberland – See Regional map n°**24-A1**

London 336 mi – Glasgow 118 mi – Edinburgh 72 mi – Aberdeen 204 mi

 **Red Lion Inn** with rm 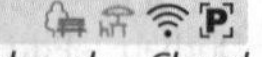

Main Rd NE71 6JD – (01668) 216 224 – www.redlionmilfield.co.uk – Closed 1 January and 25 December

2 rm – †£ 40 ††£ 70 Carte £ 16/30 – *(booking advisable)*

Set close to the Scottish border, this former coaching inn really is the heart of the village. It has a traditional look and feel, matched by a classical menu which makes good use of the larders of both Scotland and England – and you definitely won't leave hungry! Bedrooms are fittingly homely.

MILFORD-ON-SEA

Hampshire – Pop. 4 348 – Lymington – See Regional map n°**6-A3**

London 109 mi – Bournemouth 15 mi – Southampton 24 mi – Winchester 37 mi

Michelin Road map 503-P31 and 504

 **Verveine** 

98 High St SO41 0QE – (01590) 642 176 – www.verveine.co.uk – Closed Sunday and Monday

Menu £ 15 (lunch) – Carte £ 32/56

Bright, New England style restaurant fronted by a fishmonger's. Breads are baked twice-daily, veg is from the raised beds and smoking takes place on-site. The focus is on wonderfully fresh fish and cooking is accurate and original.

MILSTEAD

Kent – Pop. 264 – See Regional map n°**9-C1**

London 46 mi – Maidstone 29 mi – Canterbury 19 mi

 **Red Lion** 

Rawling St ME9 0RT – (01795) 830 279 – www.theredlionmilstead.co.uk – Closed Sunday and Monday

Carte £ 22/40 – *(booking advisable)*

Simple, cosy country pub, personally run by an experienced couple. Ever-changing blackboard menu offers French-influenced country cooking. Dishes are honest, wholesome and richly flavoured.

MILTON ABBOT → See Tavistock

Devon – Michelin Road map 503-H32

MILTON KEYNES

Milton Keynes – Pop. 171 750 – See Regional map n°**11-C1**

London 56 mi – Bedford 16 mi – Birmingham 72 mi – Northampton 18 mi

Michelin Road map 504-R27

XX **Brasserie Blanc** 

Chelsea House, 301 Avebury Blvd MK9 2GA Town plan: EZ**c**

– (01908) 546 590 – www.brasserieblanc.com – Closed 26 December and 1 January

Menu £ 12/17 – Carte £ 23/41 – *(booking essential)*

Bustling French brasserie and a small shop, set within a striking modern building and accessed via a revolving 1930s mahogany door. Friendly team and a lively, buzzy atmosphere. Menus focus on tasty, wholesome, classic brasserie dishes.

ENGLAND

X **Jamie's Italian**

3-5 Silbury Arcade ✉ *MK9 3AG – ✆ (01908) 769 011* Town plan: EY**a**
– www.jamiesitalian.com – Closed 26-26 December and Easter Sunday
Menu £ 12 (lunch) – Carte £ 14/32 – *(booking advisable)*
Busy, buzzy restaurant with a laid-back, family-friendly feel. The passionate team serve flavoursome, rustic Italian dishes; all of the pasta is made on-site. For a quieter time, head for the upstairs floor, which opens at the weekend.

MINEHEAD

Somerset – Pop. 11 981 – See Regional map n°**3-A2**
London 187 mi – Bristol 64 mi – Exeter 43 mi – Taunton 25 mi
Michelin Road map 503-J30 – Michelin Green Guide GREAT BRITAIN

Channel House

Church Path ✉ *TA24 5QG – off Northfield Dr – ✆ (01643) 703 229*
– www.channelhouse.co.uk – March-October
8 rm – †£ 83/101 ††£ 126/162 **Rest** – Menu £ 25 **s** – *(dinner only)*
Passionately run, detached Edwardian house in an elevated position, with the sea just visible through its mature gardens. Comfy lounge and a cosy bar. Immaculately kept bedrooms have a modern edge; Rooms 7 and 8 are the most comfortable. Traditional, daily changing dinner menu and comprehensive breakfasts.

Old Stables Ⓝ without rest

Northfield Rd ✉ *TA24 5QH – ✆ (07435) 964 882*
– www.theoldstablesminehead.co.uk
3 rm – †£ 50/70 ††£ 60/90
Once the stables of the Northfield Hotel; now a delightful guesthouse with a stylish yet homely feel, just minutes from the sea. The owner's monochrome photos hang on white walls. Try the homemade cakes and preserves at breakfast.

Glendower House without rest

30-32 Tregonwell Rd ✉ *TA24 5DU – ✆ (01643) 707 144*
– www.glendower-house.co.uk – Closed January
11 rm – †£ 40/60 ††£ 60/80
Well-run guesthouse, a few minutes' walk from the seafront. Traditionally furnished lounge. Individually decorated, immaculately kept bedrooms; those upstairs at the front are larger. Good breakfasts, with ingredients from local farms.

MINSTER

Kent – See Regional map n°**9-D1**
London 73 mi – Canterbury 14 mi – Dover 21 mi – Brighton 103 mi
Michelin Road map 504-X29

XX **Corner House** Ⓝ with rm

42 Station Rd ✉ *CT12 4BZ – ✆ (01843) 823 000*
– www.thecornerhouseminster.co.uk – Closed first 2 weeks January, Sunday dinner and Monday
2 rm – †£ 75/85 ††£ 75/85, £ 8
Menu £ 13 (weekday lunch) – Carte approx. £ 29
Pass the stone bar inset with a cart wheel, and the small lounge and terrace, to the characterful dining room with its low beamed ceiling and quarry tiled floor. Classic recipes use good quality produce; the dishes for two are a hit. Bedrooms have smart feature walls and modern facilities.

MINSTER LOVELL

Oxfordshire – Pop. 1 236 – See Regional map n°**10-A2**
London 74 mi – Birmingham 87 mi – Bristol 67 mi – Sheffield 151 mi
Michelin Road map 503-P28

Minster Mill without rest

✉ *OX29 0RN – ✆ (01993) 774 441 – www.oldswanandminstermill.com*
44 rm – †£ 145/355 ††£ 165/375
17C Cotswold stone mill set on the riverbank in a small hamlet. Comfy lounge and minstrels' gallery. Corporate-style bedrooms with contemporary furnishings; the best boast riverside terraces. Meals are at sister establishment, the Old Swan.

ENGLAND

HORIZONTAL ROADS

Bletcham Way (H10) CX
Chaffron Way (H7) .... BX, CV
Childs Way (H6) .... BX, CV
Dansteed Way (H4) .... ABV
Groveway (H9) CVX
Millers Way (H2) .... AV
Monks Way (H3) .... ABV
Portway (H5) .... BCV
Ridgeway (H1) .... AV
Standing Way (H8) .... BX, CV

MILTON KEYNES

Buckingham Rd .... BX
London Rd .... CUV
Manor Rd CX
Marsh End Rd .... CU
Newport Rd .... BV
Northampton Rd .... AU
Stoke Rd CX
Stratford Rd .... AV
Whaddon Way .... BX
Wolverton Rd .... BU

VERTICAL ROADS

Brickhill St (V10) .... BU, CX
Fulmer St (V3) .... ABX
Grafton St (V6) .... BVX
Great Monks St (V5) .... AV
Marlborough St (V8) .... BV, CX
Overstreet (V9) .... BV
Saxon St (V7) .... BVX
Snelshall St (V1) .... BX
Tattenhoe St (V2) .... ABX
Tongwell St (V11) CVX
Watling St (V4) .... AV, BX

ENGLAND

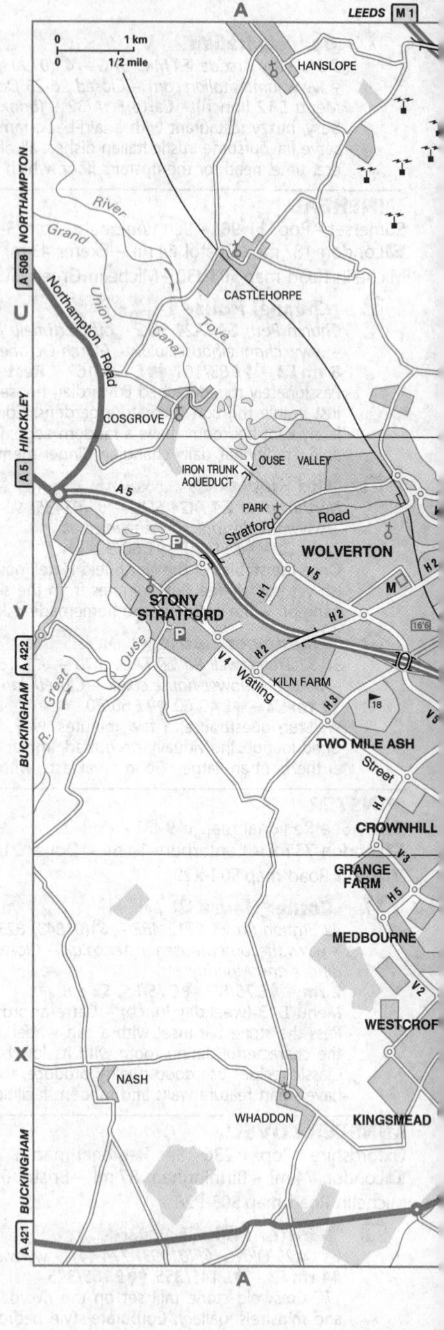

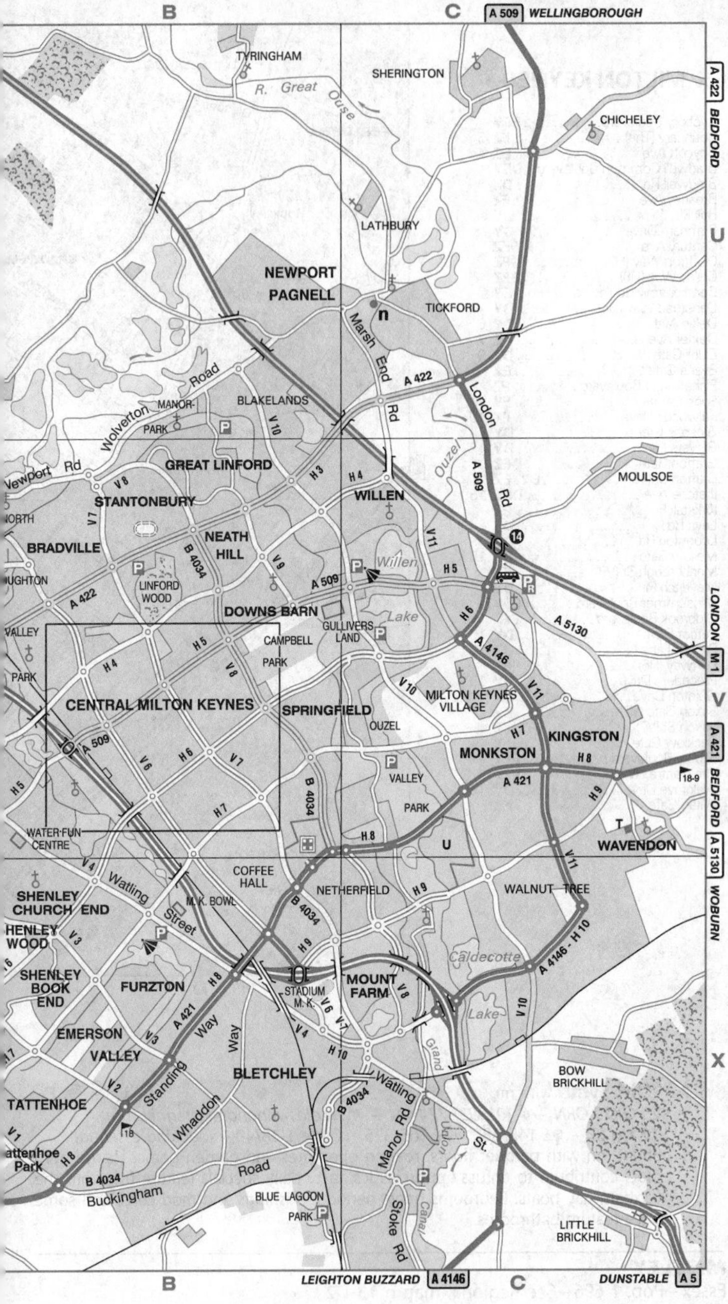

B C A 509 WELLINGBOROUGH

TYRINGHAM
SHERINGTON
R. Great Ouse
A 422 BEDFORD
CHICHELEY
LATHBURY
U
NEWPORT
PAGNELL
TICKFORD
n
Marsh End Rd
A 422
London Rd
A 509
Wolverton Road
MANOR-PARK
BLAKELANDS
V 10
Ouzel
Newport Rd
V 8
GREAT LINFORD
H 3
H 4
WILLEN
MOULSOE
STANTONBURY
V 7
NORTH
BRADVILLE
NEATH
HILL
B 4034
V 9
V 11
Willen
H 5
14
ENGLAND
LONDON M 1
OUGHTON
A 422
LINFORD
WOOD
A 509
DOWNS BARN
Lake
H 6
A 5130
VALLEY
GULLIVERS
LAND
CAMPBELL
PARK
H 5
H 4
V 8
A 4146
PARK
V 10
MILTON KEYNES
VILLAGE
V 11
V
CENTRAL MILTON KEYNES
SPRINGFIELD
OUZEL
KINGSTON
A 509
H 6
V 6
V 7
MONKSTON
H 7
H 8
A 421 BEDFORD
18-9
H 5
VALLEY
PARK
A 421
B 4034
H 7
H 9
WATER-FUN
CENTRE
H 8
U
T
WAVENDON
A 5130 WOBURN
V 4
COFFEE
HALL
V 11
Watling
NETHERFIELD
H 9
WALNUT TREE
SHENLEY
CHURCH END
M. K. BOWL
B 4034
Street
SHENLEY
WOOD
V 3
H 9
Caldecotte
A 4146 - H 10
SHENLEY
BROOK
END
FURZTON
H 8
STADIUM
M. K.
MOUNT
FARM
V 8
V 6
V 7
Lake
V 10
A 421
Way
Way
V 4
EMERSON
VALLEY
V 3
H 10
Grand
X
BLETCHLEY
Standing
Watling
BOW
BRICKHILL
TATTENHOE
V 2
Whaddon
B 4034
Manor Rd
V 1
18
St.
Tattenhoe
Park
H 8
Road
B 4034
Union
Buckingham
Canal
BLUE LAGOON
PARK
Stoke Rd
LITTLE
BRICKHILL
B
LEIGHTON BUZZARD A 4146
C
DUNSTABLE A 5

ENGLAND

MILTON KEYNES

Street	Grid	No.
Avebury Boulevard	EFY	
Boundary (The)	FZ	3
Boycott Ave	EZ	4
Bradwell Common Boulevard	DEY	
Bradwell Rd	DZ	
Brearley Ave	EFZ	
Brill Pl.	DY	
Burnham Drive	DY	
Century Ave	EFZ	
Chaffron Way (H7)	FZ	
Childs Way (H6)	EFZ	
Conniburrow Boulevard	EY	
Dansteed Way (H4)	DY	
Deltic Ave	DY	6
Dexter Ave	FZ	7
Elder Gate	DZ	9
Evans Gate	EZ	
Fishermead Boulevard	FZ	
Food Centre	FY	
Fulwoods Drive	FZ	10
Gibsons Green	DY	
Glovers Lane	DY	12
Grafton Gate	DEZ	
Grafton St (V6)	DY, EZ	
Ibstone Ave	DEY	13
Kirkstall Pl.	EZ	
Leys Rd	DZ	
Loughton Rd	DY	
Mallow Gate	EY	15
Marlborough St (V8)	FY	
Mayditch Pl.	DY	
Midsummer Boulevard	EFY	
Oldbrook Boulevard	EFZ	
Patriot Drive	DY	16
Pitcher Lane	DZ	
Portway (H5)	EFY	
Precedent Drive	DY	18
Quinton Drive	DY	
Saxon Gate (V7)	EY	
Saxon St (V7)	EY, FZ	
Secklow Gate	FY	
Silbury Boulevard	EFY	
The Centre : MK	EFY	
Walgrave Drive	DY	19
Witan Gate	EZ	

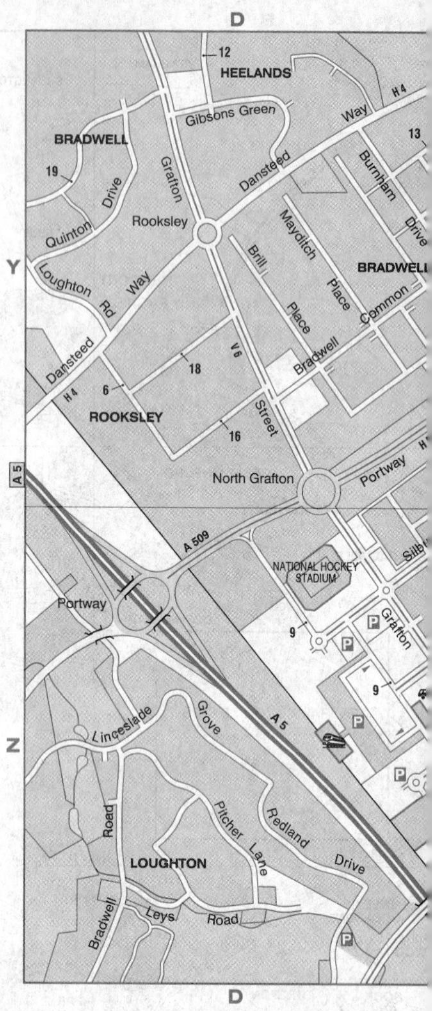

Old Swan with rm

✉ *OX29 ORN* – ✆ *(01993) 774 441* – *www.oldswanandminstermill.com*
16 rm – †£ 145/285 ††£ 165/375 Carte £ 28/40 – *(booking essential)*
Smart inn with parquet floors, roaring open fires and garden games. Large herb plots contribute to unfussy pub classics; tasty daily specials feature fish from the Brixham day boats. Bedrooms boast period furnishings and mod cons, and some have feature bathrooms.

MISTLEY

Essex – Pop. 1 696 – See Regional map n°**13**-D2
London 69 mi – Colchester 11 mi – Ipswich 14 mi
Michelin Road map 504-X28

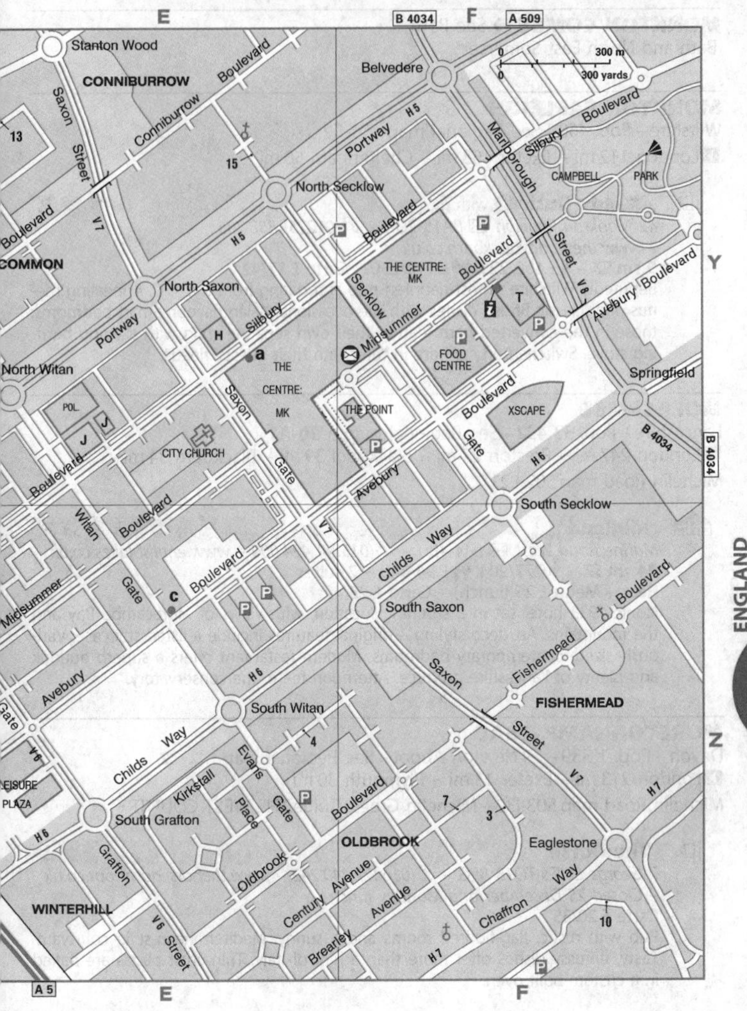

✕ **Mistley Thorn** with rm

High St ✉ *CO11 1HE* – ✆ *(01206) 392 821* – *www.mistleythorn.co.uk*

11 rm ☕ – 🚹£ 85/195 🚹🚹£ 100/195 Menu £ 15 (weekdays) – Carte £ 22/40

Simply decorated restaurant in a historic coastal town. The appealing menu offers something for everyone, from local mussels and oysters to steak, arancini or seafood stew; with fish a feature and American and Italian influences evident. Bright, comfortable bedrooms; some with river views.

MITTON → See Whalley

Lancashire – Michelin Road map 502-M22

MOBBERLEY → See Knutsford

Cheshire East – Michelin Road map 502-N24 and 503

MONKTON COMBE → See Bath

Bath and North East Somerset

MONKTON FARLEIGH

Wiltshire – Pop. 460 – See Regional map n°**4-C2**

London 112 mi – Exeter 103 mi – Cheltenham 58 mi

Muddy Duck Ⓝ with rm

42 Monkton Farleigh ✉ BA15 2QN – ✆ (01225) 858 705 – www.themuddyduckbath.co.uk

5 rm – £ 100/225 £ 110/250 Carte £ 17/42

Reputedly Wiltshire's most haunted pub and dating from the 17C. Appealing menus offer classic British dishes with the occasional Asian flavour. Smart bedrooms; those in the converted barn feature their own separate snug with a wood burning stove. Switched-on staff are in tune with their guests' needs.

MORECAMBE

Lancashire – Pop. 33 432 – See Regional map n°**20-A1**

London 247 mi – Preston 27 mi – Blackpool 39 mi – Blackburn 34 mi

Michelin Road map 502-L21

Midland

Marine Road West ✉ LA4 4BU – ✆ (01524) 424 000 – www.englishlakes.co.uk

44 rm – £ 77/204 £ 94/348 – 2 suites

Rest – Menu £ 25 (lunch) – Carte £ 25/42

Iconic 1933 hotel set in a stunning location, with views of Morecambe Bay and the mountains. Art deco styling – original features include a listed staircase. Variously sized, contemporary bedrooms. Modern restaurant offers a superb outlook and plenty of Lancashire produce. Afternoon tea in the conservatory.

ENGLAND

MORETONHAMPSTEAD

Devon – Pop. 1 339 – ✉ Newton Abbot – See Regional map n°**2-C2**

London 213 mi – Exeter 13 mi – Plymouth 30 mi

Michelin Road map 503-I32 – Michelin Green Guide THE WEST COUNTRY

The Horse 

7 George St ✉ TQ13 8PG – ✆ (01647) 440 242 – www.thehorsedartmoor.co.uk – Closed 25 December and Monday lunch

Carte £ 20/35

Pub with rustic, flag-floored rooms and a sunny, Mediterranean-style courtyard. Tasty, unfussy dishes offer more than a hint of Italy. Thin crust pizzas are baked in a custom-built oven.

MORETON-IN-MARSH

Gloucestershire – Pop. 3 493 – See Regional map n°**4-D1**

London 86 mi – Birmingham 40 mi – Gloucester 31 mi – Oxford 29 mi

Michelin Road map 503-O28 and 504 – Michelin Green Guide GREAT BRITAIN

Manor House rm,

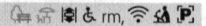

High St ✉ GL56 0LJ – ✆ (01608) 650 501 – www.cotswold-inns-hotels.co.uk/manor

35 rm – £ 79/138 £ 89/158 – 1 suite

Rest *Mulberry* – see restaurant listing

Rest *Beagle Brasserie* – Menu £ 15 (weekday lunch) – Carte £ 24/44

Part-16C manor house with a smart interior which mixes old beams and inglenook fireplaces with modern fabrics and contemporary art. Chic, stylish bedrooms boast bold décor and feature walls; those in the main house are the most characterful. Dine in the sophisticated restaurant or classical brasserie.

Old School without rest 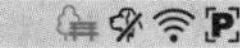
Little Compton ✉ GL56 0SL – East : 3.75 mi on A 44 – ✆ (01608) 674 588 – www.theoldschoolbedandbreakfast.com
4 rm – †£ 96/120 ††£ 120/140
Change pace at this laid-back, stone-built hotel – formerly a school – where you can relax in the gardens over a game of boules or croquet. The impressive upstairs lounge features an exposed A-frame ceiling and original ecclesiastical windows; bright, modern bedrooms offer a high level of facilities.

XXX **Mulberry** – Manor House Hotel
High St ✉ GL56 0LJ – ✆ (01608) 650 501 – www.cotswold-inns-hotels.co.uk/manor
Menu £ 39 – *(dinner only and Sunday lunch)*
Formal restaurant with an enclosed walled garden, set within a part-16C manor house. Cooking is modern and adventurous and features some challenging combinations – choose between a 4 course set menu and an 8 course tasting menu.

at Bourton-on-the-Hill West: 2 mi on A44 ✉ Moreton-In-Marsh

Horse & Groom with rm 
✉ GL56 9AQ – ✆ (01386) 700 413 – www.horseandgroom.info – Closed 25, 31 December and Sunday dinner except bank holidays
5 rm – †£ 80 ††£ 96/170 Carte £ 21/36 – *(booking essential)*
Grade II listed, honey-coloured, Cotswold stone pub on the main street of a pretty village, high on the hillside. Study the daily changing blackboard menu then order at the bar. The unfussy dishes are good value, fresh and flavoursome. Individually decorated bedrooms are stylish and contemporary – and breakfast is well worth getting up for.

MORPETH

Northumberland – Pop. 14 403 – See Regional map n°**24-B2**
▶London 301 mi – Edinburgh 93 mi – Newcastle upon Tyne 15 mi
Michelin Road map 501-O18 and 502

at Eshott North: 8.5 mi by A1 ✉ Morpeth

 **Eshott Hall** 
✉ NE65 9EN – ✆ (01670) 787 454 – www.eshotthall.co.uk – Closed 25-26 December
16 rm – †£ 90/175 ††£ 120/270 **Rest** – Carte £ 39/48
Attractive Georgian manor house in a quiet, rural location – yet only 5min from the A1. Classically stylish guest areas. Smart, modern bedrooms boast warm fabrics, antique furniture and good facilities. Formal dining room offers contemporary menus; local produce includes fruit and veg from the kitchen garden.

at Longhorsley Northwest: 6.5 mi by A192 on A697 ✉ Morpeth

Thistleyhaugh Farm 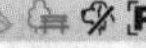

✉ NE65 8RG Northwest : 3.75 mi by A 697 and Todburn rd taking first right turn – ✆ (01665) 570 629 – www.thistleyhaugh.co.uk – Closed Christmas-1 February
5 rm – †£ 70/85 ††£ 90/100 **Rest** – Menu £ 25
Attractive Georgian farmhouse, set off the beaten track on a 750 acre organic farm, with the River Coquet flowing through its grounds. Cosy, open-fired lounge and antique-filled dining room. Spacious, comfortable bedrooms – most have luxurious bathrooms with feature baths. Communal dinners; home-cooking features beef and lamb from the farm. Charming owners.

MORSTON

→ See Blakeney
Norfolk

MOULSFORD

Oxfordshire – Pop. 601 – See Regional map n°**10-B3**
▶London 53 mi – Newbury 16 mi – Reading 13 mi

XX **Beetle & Wedge Boathouse** with rm 
Ferry Ln ✉ OX10 9JF – ✆ (01491) 651 381 – www.beetleandwedge.co.uk – Closed first week January
3 rm – £ 75 £ 90/100
Menu £ 20 (weekdays) – Carte £ 25/37 – *(booking essential)*
Former boathouse named after the beetle (mallet) and wedge (splitter) used in skiff making. It's in a wonderful Thameside location and has a charming terrace and oversized windows ideal for bird watching. Cooking is honest and robust and features dishes from the chargrill. Cosy bedrooms are in an annexe.

MOULTON

Suffolk – See Regional map n°**14**-**B2**
London 64 mi – Ipswich 42 mi – Cambridge 14 mi
Michelin Road map 504-V27

Packhorse Inn with rm 
Bridge St ✉ CB8 8SP – ✆ (01638) 751 818 – www.thepackhorseinn.com
8 rm – £ 85/175 £ 100/175 Carte £ 28/42
Smart modern pub set in a pretty village and named after its famous 15C packhorse bridge. 'Packhorse Favourites' like Suffolk rib-eye and chips are offered alongside more adventurous, artily presented dishes. Bedrooms are ultra-stylish with quality furnishings, roll top baths and welcome extras.

ENGLAND

MOUSEHOLE

Cornwall ✉ Penzance – See Regional map n°**1**-**A3**
London 321 mi – Penzance 3 mi – Truro 29 mi
Michelin Road map 503-D33 – Michelin Green Guide GREAT BRITAIN

X **Cornish Range** with rm
6 Chapel St ✉ TR19 6SB – ✆ (01736) 731 488 – www.cornishrange.co.uk – Closed 2 weeks January-February
3 rm – £ 65/110 £ 65/110
Menu £ 18 – Carte £ 21/33 – *(dinner only) (booking essential)*
Former pilchard processing cottage hidden away in a backstreet of an old fishing village; bright, modern artwork adorns the walls. Simple brunch and lunch menus, good value early evening selection and a seafood orientated à la carte. Good-sized, comfy bedrooms – one used to be artist Jack Pender's studio.

X **2 Fore Street** 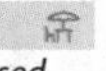
2 Fore St ✉ TR19 6PF – ✆ (01736) 731 164 – www.2forestreet.co.uk – Closed January and Monday in winter
Carte approx. £ 29 – *(booking essential at dinner)*
Friendly, harbourside café-cum-bistro with a delightful terrace and garden. All-day menus offer everything from coffee and cake to a full meal, with brunch a feature at weekends. Tasty, unfussy dishes are guided by the day's catch.

X **Old Coastguard** with rm 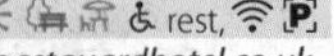
The Parade ✉ TR19 6PR – ✆ (01736) 731 222 – www.oldcoastguardhotel.co.uk – Closed 25 December and early January
14 rm – £ 90/150 £ 120/200
Menu £ 19 (weekday lunch) – Carte £ 22/32 **s**
Old coastguard's cottage in a small fishing village, with a laid-back, open-plan interior, a sub-tropical garden and views towards St Clement's Isle. Well-presented brasserie dishes display a Mediterranean edge; great wine selection. Individually styled bedrooms – some with balconies, most with sea views.

MULLION

Cornwall – Pop. 1 955 – ✉ Helston – See Regional map n°**1**-**A3**
London 287 mi – Birmingham 282 mi – Croydon 295 mi – Barnet 300 mi
Michelin Road map 503-E33

Polurrian Bay

✉ *TR12 7EN – ✆ (01326) 240 421 – www.polurrianhotel.com*
41 rm – £ 120/520 £ 120/520
Rest – Menu £ 35 – Carte £ 54/75 – *(dinner only)*
Imposing Victorian hotel with 12 acres of grounds, in a commanding clifftop position. Spacious, modern interior is geared towards families, with a crèche, games room and cinema. Most of the bright bedrooms boast views across Mount's Bay. Unfussy menus showcase seasonal, local produce.

MURCOTT

Oxfordshire – Pop. 1 293 – ✉ Kidlington – See Regional map n°**10-B2**
London 70 mi – Oxford 14 mi – Witney 20 mi

Nut Tree (Mike North)

Main St ✉ OX5 2RE – ✆ (01865) 331 253 Town plan: 10**B2**
– www.nuttreeinn.co.uk – Closed 27 December-2 January, Sunday dinner and Monday except bank holidays
Menu £ 18 (weekdays)/55 – Carte £ 32/53
Characterful thatched pub with a cosy bar and a smart restaurant. The appealing menus change constantly, relying on the latest seasonal ingredients to arrive at the door, and produce is organic, free range or wild wherever possible; they even rear rare breed pigs. Combinations are classical and satisfying.
→ Mosaic of ham hock, chicken and foie gras, sauce gribiche. Olive oil poached fillet of halibut, green herb risotto, cucumber and fennel salad. Dark chocolate ganache, white chocolate mousse and orange jelly.

NAILSWORTH

Gloucestershire – Pop. 7 728 – See Regional map n°**4-C1**
London 110 mi – Bristol 30 mi – Swindon 28 mi
Michelin Road map 503-N28 and 504

Wild Garlic with rm — rest,

3 Cossack Sq ✉ GL6 0DB – ✆ (01453) 832 615 – www.wild-garlic.co.uk – Closed first 2 weeks January, Wednesday lunch, Sunday dinner, Monday and Tuesday
3 rm – £ 75/100 £ 85/125 Carte £ 28/37
An attractive little restaurant in the heart of a market town. Two smart, contemporary, semi-panelled rooms feature bright food-themed photos and have a rustic feel. Monthly menus reflect the latest local ingredients available; there's also a popular tasting menu. Stylish, modern bedrooms are well-equipped.

mark@street

Market St ✉ GL6 0HL – ✆ (01453) 839 251 – www.marketstreetnailsworth.co.uk – Closed 2 weeks January, 1 week September, Sunday dinner and Monday
Carte £ 20/34
Small, friendly restaurant on a narrow street. Simple lunch menus are supplemented by brunch at the weekends. Candlelit dinners offer well-balanced, classical dishes presented in a modern way; the vegetables are from their allotment.

NANTWICH

Cheshire East – Pop. 17 226 – See Regional map n°**20-A3**
London 176 mi – Chester 20 mi – Liverpool 45 mi – Manchester 40 mi
Michelin Road map 502-M24 and 503

Rookery Hall

Worleston ✉ CW5 6DQ – North : 2.5 mi by A 51 on B 5074 – ✆ (0845) 072 75 33 – www.handpicked.co.uk/hotels/rookery-hall
70 rm – £ 95/270 £ 95/270 – 2 suites
Rest – Menu £ 37 – Carte £ 26/61 **s** – *(dinner only and Sunday lunch) (booking essential)*
19C property set in pleasant grounds, with considerable extensions and a smart, impressive spa. The main building offers characterful, country house bedrooms; more modern rooms are located in the purpose-built rear wing. The formal, two-roomed, wood-panelled dining room overlooks the gardens.

NAWTON → See Helmsley

ENGLAND

NETHER BURROW

Lancashire ✉ Kirkby Lonsdale – See Regional map n°**20-B1**

London 257 mi – Liverpool 73 mi – Leeds 101 mi – Manchester 68 mi

Highwayman

✉ LA6 2RJ – ✆ (01524) 273 338 – www.highwaymaninn.co.uk – Closed 25 December

Carte £ 19/40

Sizeable 18C coaching inn with open-fired, stone-floored bar and lovely terrace. A rustic, no-nonsense approach to food makes for well-crafted, flavourful dishes. Produce is local and seasonal, with Lancashire hotpot a perennial favourite.

NETHER WESTCOTE → See Stow-on-the-Wold

Gloucestershire

NETLEY MARSH → See Southampton

Hampshire – Michelin Road map 503-P31 and 504

NEW MILTON

Hampshire – Pop. 19 969 – See Regional map n°**6-A3**

London 106 mi – Bournemouth 12 mi – Southampton 21 mi – Winchester 34 mi

Michelin Road map 503-P31 and 504

Chewton Glen

Christchurch Rd ✉ BH25 6QS – West : 2 mi by A 337 and Ringwood Rd on Chewton Farm Rd – ✆ (01425) 275 341 – www.chewtonglen.com

70 rm – †£ 325/1595 ††£ 325/1595, ☕ £ 26 – 15 suites

Rest *Vetiver* – see restaurant listing

Professionally run country house with an impressive spa, set in 130 acres of New Forest parkland – try a host of outdoor pursuits, including croquet, archery and clay pigeon shooting. Luxurious bedrooms range from classic to contemporary; opt for one with a balcony or terrace, or try a unique Treehouse suite.

Vetiver – Chewton Glen Hotel

Christchurch Rd ✉ BH25 6QS – West : 2 mi by A 337 and Ringwood Rd on Chewton Farm Rd – ✆ (01425) 275 341 – www.chewtonglen.com

Menu £ 25 (weekday lunch) **s** – Carte £ 40/69 **s**

Stylish hotel restaurant comprising 5 impressive rooms, including one with wines displayed in illuminated cases. The seasonally inspired à la carte offers everything from fish and chips to oysters or caviar; from Friday-Sunday they also offer specials from the trolley. Some of the produce is from the garden.

NEW ROMNEY

Kent – See Regional map n°**9-C2**

London 71 mi – Brighton 60 mi – Folkestone 17 mi – Maidstone 36 mi

Michelin Road map 504-W31

Romney Bay House

Coast Rd, Littlestone ✉ TN28 8QY – East : 2.25 mi by B 2071 – ✆ (01797) 364 747 – www.romneybayhousehotel.co.uk – Closed 1 week Christmas and 1st week January

10 rm ☕ – †£ 70/95 ††£ 95/165

Rest – Menu £ 45 – *(closed Sunday, Monday and Thursday) (dinner only) (booking essential) (set menu only)*

Built by Sir Clough Williams-Ellis in the 1920s, for actress Hedda Hopper, and accessed via a private coast road. Open-fired drawing room with honesty bar; first floor lounge has a telescope and lovely views out to sea. Homely bedrooms. Conservatory dining room offers a daily, seafood-based menu.

NEWARK-ON-TRENT

Nottinghamshire – Pop. 37 084 – See Regional map n°**17-C1**

London 127 mi – Lincoln 16 mi – Nottingham 20 mi – Sheffield 42 mi

Michelin Road map 502-R24 and 504 – Michelin Green Guide GREAT BRITAIN

Grange

73 London Rd ✉ NG24 1RZ – South : 0.5 mi on Grantham rd (B 6326) – ☎ (01636) 703 399 – www.grangenewark.co.uk – Closed 22 December-6 January

19 rm ☕ – †£ 75/110 ††£ 95/165

Rest *Cutlers* – Carte £ 24/34 – *(closed Sunday dinner) (dinner only and Sunday lunch)*

Personally run hotel with a small terrace and award-winning gardens. The main house has mock Tudor gables, a Victorian-style bar and lounge, and a smart restaurant decorated with antique plates and cutlery. Individually styled bedrooms are split between this and a second house, and offer good comforts.

at Norwell North: 7.25 mi by A1

Willoughby House without rest

Main St ✉ NG23 6JN – ☎ (01636) 636 266 – www.willoughbyhousebandb.co.uk

3 rm ☕ – †£ 60/75 ††£ 85/105

Three-storey, red-brick Georgian farmhouse and converted stables. Chic, stylish interior with a small open-fired lounge and a deep scarlet breakfast room. Bedrooms feature quality furnishings and antiques, along with contemporary art and homemade flapjacks. The owner has an eye for detail.

NEWBIGGIN → See Penrith

Cumbria – Michelin Road map 502-L19

NEWBURY

West Berkshire – Pop. 38 762 – See Regional map n°**10-B3**

London 67 mi – Bristol 66 mi – Oxford 28 mi – Reading 17 mi

Michelin Road map 503-Q29 and 504

Plans pages 582, 583

ENGLAND

The Vineyard

Stockcross ✉ RG20 8JU – Northwest : 2 mi by A 4 on B 4000 – ☎ (01635) 528 770 – www.the-vineyard.co.uk Town plan: AV**b**

49 rm ☕ – †£ 214/362 ††£ 235/694 – 26 suites

Rest *The Vineyard* – see restaurant listing

Extended former hunting lodge with over 1,000 pieces of art and a striking fire and water feature. Some bedrooms have a country house style, while others are more contemporary; all boast smart marble bathrooms. The owner also has a vineyard in California, hence the stunning wine vault and the wine-themed bar.

Donnington Valley H. & Spa

Old Oxford Rd, Donnington ✉ RG14 3AG – North : 1.75 mi by A 4 off B 4494 – ☎ (01635) 551 199 – www.donningtonvalley.co.uk Town plan: AV**a**

111 rm ☕ – †£ 89/211 ††£ 89/226

Rest *Winepress* – see restaurant listing

Modern business-orientated hotel on the town outskirts, with large grounds and a golf course. Guest areas are spacious and stylishly furnished and there's a well-equipped gym and spa. Smart bedrooms offer a high level of facilities.

The Vineyard – Vineyard Hotel

Stockcross ✉ RG20 8JU – Northwest : 2 mi by A 4 on B 4000 – ☎ (01635) 528 770 – www.the-vineyard.co.uk Town plan: AV**b**

Menu £ 29 – Carte £ 46/58

Smartly dressed hotel restaurant split over two levels. Choose 4 or 5 dishes from the modern main menu or try one of the tasting menus accompanied by matching wines; some from their own Californian vineyard. Cooking is accomplished.

Winepress – Donnington Valley Hotel & Spa

Old Oxford Rd, Donnington ✉ RG14 3AG – North : 1.75 mi by A 4 off B 4494 – ☎ (01635) 551 199 – www.donningtonvalley.co.uk Town plan: AV**a**

Menu £ 28 (dinner) **s** – Carte £ 28/50 **s**

A split-level restaurant with an unusual pyramid roof, set within a business-led hotel. Lunch offers an accessible menu popular with local workers, while dinner offers more substantial classical dishes. The wine list is impressive.

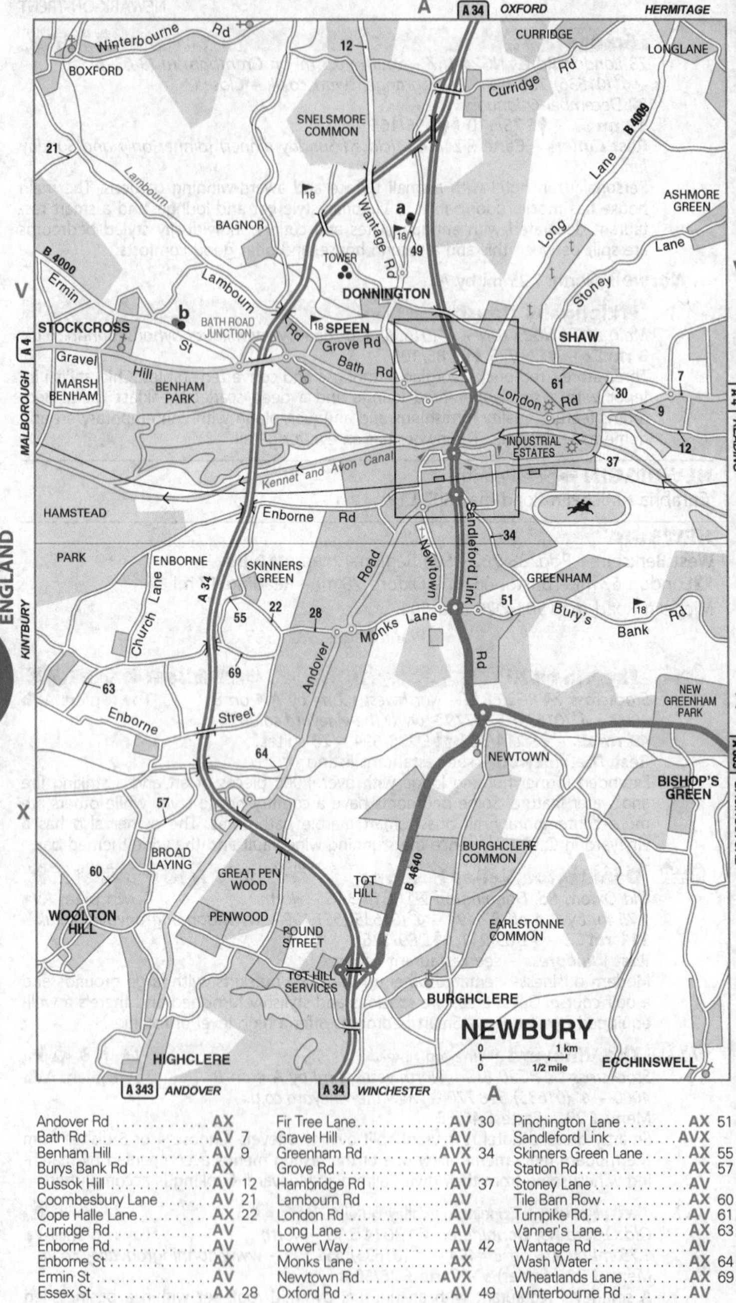

A
A 34
OXFORD
HERMITAGE
Winterbourne Rd
BOXFORD
12
CURRIDGE
LONGLANE
Curridge Rd
B 4009
SNELSMORE
COMMON
21
Lambourn
Lane
Long
ASHMORE
GREEN
18
a
BAGNOR
Wantage Rd
18
49
Lane
Long
B 4000
Ermin
TOWER
Lambourn
Stoney
V
DONNINGTON
b
BATH ROAD
JUNCTION
STOCKCROSS
18 SPEEN
SHAW
A 4
Rd
St
Grove Rd
Gravel
Bath Rd
MARSH
BENHAM
Hill
BENHAM
PARK
61
7
London
30
Rd
A 4
MALBOROUGH
9
READING
INDUSTRIAL
ESTATES
12
37
Kennet and Avon Canal
HAMSTEAD
Enborne Rd
Sandleford Link
34
Newtown
Road
PARK
ENBORNE
SKINNERS
GREEN
GREENHAM
ENGLAND
Church Lane
A 34
22
28
Monks Lane
51
Bury's
Bank Rd
18
KINTBURY
55
Rd
69
Andover
63
NEW
GREENHAM
PARK
Enborne
Street
A 339
64
NEWTOWN
BISHOP'S
GREEN
BASINGSTOKE
X
57
BURGHCLERE
COMMON
BROAD
LAYING
60
GREAT PEN
WOOD
TOT
HILL
B 4640
WOOLTON
HILL
PENWOOD
EARLSTONNE
COMMON
POUND
STREET
TOT HILL
SERVICES
BURGHCLERE
NEWBURY
0 1 km
0 1/2 mile
HIGHCLERE
ECCHINSWELL
A 343
ANDOVER
A 34
WINCHESTER
A

NEWBURY

Almond Ave .... BY 3
Andover Rd .... BZ 4
Bartholomew St .... BZ 6
Bone Lane .... BZ 10
Carnegie Rd.......... BZ 13
Castle Grove .... BY 15
Cheap St .... BZ 16
Chesterfield Rd .... BZ 18
Craven Rd .... BZ 24
Dolman Rd .... BY 25
Donnington Link .... BY 27
Greenham Hill .... BZ 31
Greenham Rd .... BZ 33
Hambridge Rd.......... BZ 36
Kennett Shopping Centre .... BZ
Kiln Rd.......... BY 40
Kings Rd .... BZ
London Rd.......... BY
Love Lane .... BY
Maple Crescent .... BY 43
Market St.......... BZ 45
Mill Lane .... BZ
Newtown Rd.......... BZ 48
New Rd .... BZ 46
Northbrook St.......... BYZ
Northcroft Lane.......... BZ
Old Bath Rd.......... BY
Oxford Rd .... BY
Park Way .... BYZ 50
Pound St .... BZ
Queens Rd .... BZ
Racecourse Rd .... BZ
Rockingham Rd .... BZ 52
St Johns Rd.......... BZ
Sandleford Link .... BZ 54
Shaw Hill.......... BY
Shaw Rd .... BY
Station Rd .... BZ
Strawberry Hill .... BY 58
Western Ave.......... BY
West St .... BZ 66
Wharf St .... BZ 67

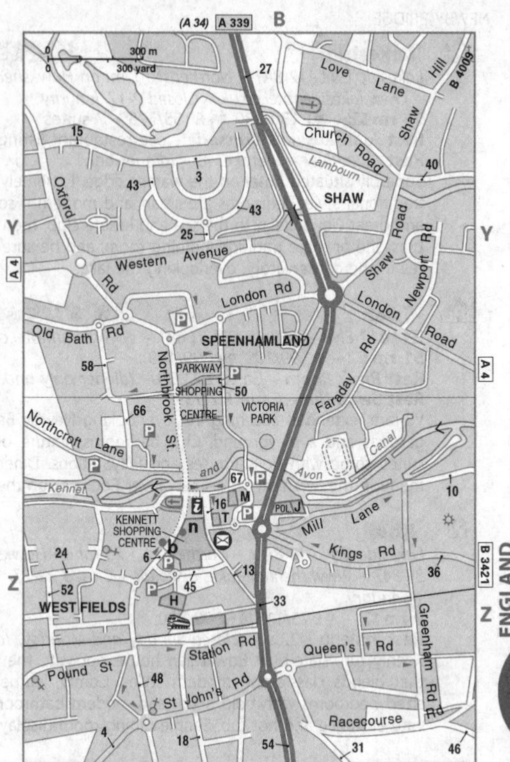

ENGLAND

Brebis

16 Bartholomew St ✉ RG14 5LL – ✆ (01635) 40 527 Town plan: BZ**b**
– www.brebis.co.uk – Closed 24 December-6 January, 14-28 January, 19 August-2 September and Sunday-Tuesday
Carte £ 14/34
Simplicity is key at this stylish little eatery. The floors are made from reclaimed wood, the service is friendly and the cooking keeps things straightforward. Tasty, carefully prepared French country dishes use good ingredients.

The Newbury

137 Bartholomew St ✉ RG14 5HB – ✆ (01635) 49 000 Town plan: BZ**n**
– www.thenewburypub.co.uk
Carte £ 22/45
Relaxed, trendy high street pub behind a traditional façade. Dishes range from pub classics to more adventurous offerings. There's brunch at weekends, an experienced team in charge and a lively buzz when it's busy.

NEWBY BRIDGE

Cumbria ✉ Ulverston – See Regional map n°**21**-A3
London 270 mi – Kendal 16 mi – Lancaster 27 mi
Michelin Road map 502-L21 – Michelin Green Guide GREAT BRITAIN

Lakeside

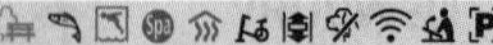

Lakeside ✉ LA12 8AT – Northeast : 1 mi on Hawkshead rd – ✆ (015395) 30 001 – www.lakesidehotel.co.uk – Closed 2-17 January
75 rm – £ 130/330 £ 155/375 – 7 suites
Rest *John Ruskin's Brasserie* – see restaurant listing
Rest *Lakeview* – Menu £ 48 – *(dinner only)*
Superbly situated hotel on the water's edge. Extremely comfy guest areas have a traditional style. Bedrooms are smart and modern – some have four-poster beds and great views. Relax in the spa and leisure club, then dine in the stylish modern brasserie or more traditional dining room; and be sure to find time for afternoon tea in the conservatory, overlooking the lake.

Swan

rm, rm,

✉ LA12 8NB – ✆ (015395) 31 681 – www.swanhotel.com
51 rm – £ 99/199 £ 99/199
Rest *River Room* – Carte £ 21/39 – *(dinner only and Sunday lunch)*
Rest *Swan Inn* – Carte £ 21/39
Vibrant, extended coaching inn overlooking Newby Bridge; set in 10 acres, with gardens and a playground. Chic bedrooms feature bold wallpapers; the family suites come with dolls houses and PlayStations. Dine from the same accessible menu in the Swan Inn, the smart River Room or on the waterside terrace.

Knoll

Lakeside ✉ LA12 8AU – Northeast : 1.25 mi on Hawkshead rd – ✆ (015395) 31 347 – www.theknoll-lakeside.co.uk – Closed 22-27, 31 December and 1 January
9 rm – £ 75/115 £ 99/230
Rest – Menu £ 22 **s** – *(closed Sunday and Monday) (dinner only)*
Keenly run, slate-built Edwardian house opposite the lake, with a smart interior that blends classic and modern styles. Comfy, leather-furnished lounge. Good-sized bedrooms with bold décor and modern bathrooms; 'The Retreat' has a private entrance and hot tub. Simple dining room displays heart-themed art.

ENGLAND

XX

John Ruskin's Brasserie – Lakeside Hotel

Lakeside ✉ LA12 8AT – Northeast : 1 mi on Hawkshead rd – ✆ (015395) 30 001 – www.lakesidehotel.co.uk – Closed 2-17 January
Carte £ 31/42 – *(dinner only)*
This stylish brasserie resides within in a superbly situated hotel on Lake Windermere's shore. The menu offers old favourites and brasserie classics. Have a drink in the conservatory or on the terrace to fully appreciate the view.

NEWCASTLE INTERNATIONAL AIRPORT → See Newcastle Upon Tyne

Tyne and Wear – Michelin Road map 502-O18

NEWCASTLE UPON TYNE

Tyne and Wear – Pop. 268 064 – See Regional map n°**24**-**B2**
London 276 mi – Edinburgh 105 mi – Leeds 95 mi
Michelin Road map 501-O19 and 502-O19 – Michelin Green Guide GREAT BRITAIN

Jesmond Dene House

Jesmond Dene Rd ✉ NE2 2EY – Northeast : 1.5 mi by B 1318 off A 189 – ✆ (0191) 212 30 00 – www.jesmonddenehouse.co.uk Town plan: BV**x**
40 rm – £ 125/250 £ 140/400
Rest *Jesmond Dene House* – see restaurant listing
Stone-built Arts and Crafts house in a peaceful city dene; originally owned by the Armstrong family. Characterful guest areas with wood panelling, local art and striking original fireplaces. Individually furnished bedrooms have bold feature walls, modern facilities and smart bathrooms with underfloor heating.

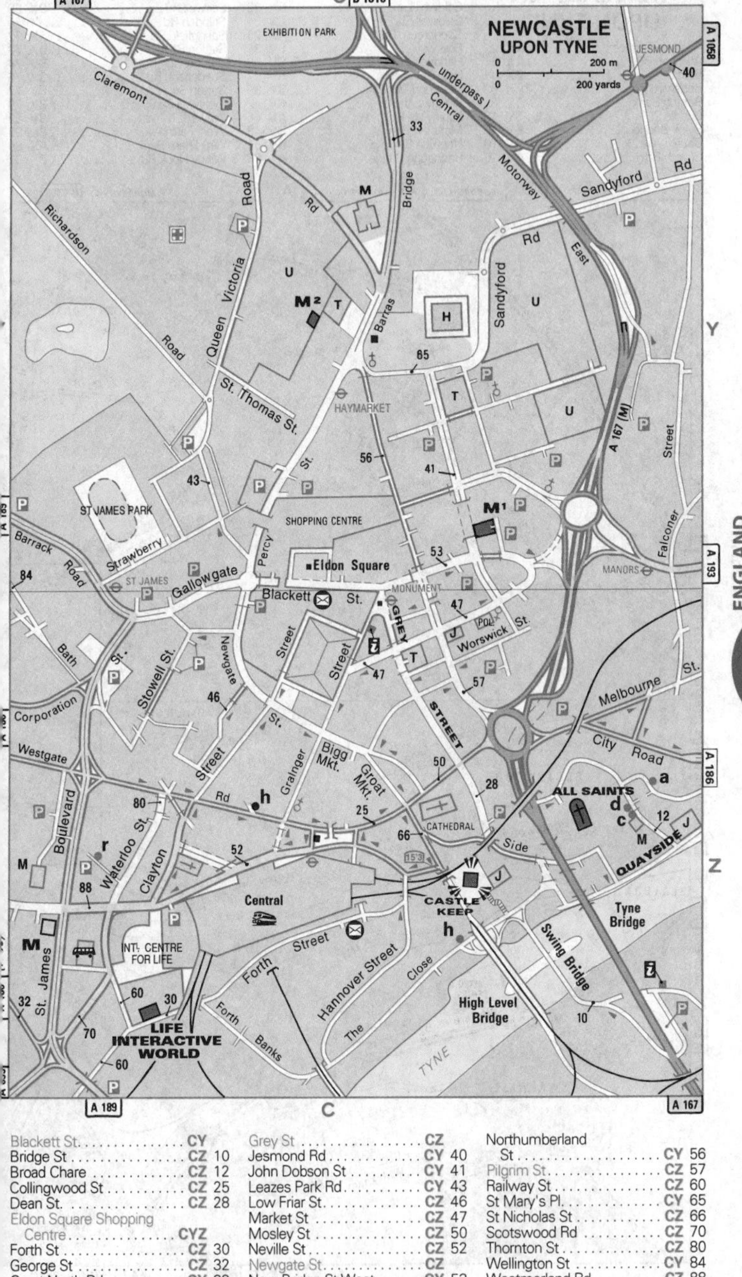
NEWCASTLE UPON TYNE
EXHIBITION PARK
Claremont
Central
Motorway
Sandyford
Rd
Richardson
Road
Queen Victoria
Road
Bridge
Barras
HAYMARKET
St. Thomas St.
ST JAMES PARK
SHOPPING CENTRE
Eldon Square
Blackett St.
Barrack Road
Gallowgate
Strawberry
ST JAMES
Percy
MONUMENT
GREY
STREET
Worswick St.
Melbourne St.
City Road
Falconer
MANORS
Bath
Stowell St.
Newgate
Corporation
Westgate
Boulevard
Waterloo St.
Clayton
Grainger
Bigg Mkt.
Groat Mkt.
CATHEDRAL
ALL SAINTS
QUAYSIDE
Side
CASTLE KEEP
Central
INT. CENTRE FOR LIFE
LIFE INTERACTIVE WORLD
Forth Street
Hannover Street
The Close
Forth Banks
High Level Bridge
Swing Bridge
Tyne Bridge
TYNE
St. James
JESMOND
ENGLAND
A 167
B 1318
A 1058
A 193
A 186
A 189
A 167 (M)

NEWCASTLE-UPON-TYNE

Adelaide Terrace . . . . . AX 2
Atkinson Rd . . . . . AX 3
Bath St . . . . . BX 4
Bensham Rd . . . . . AX 6
Benton Bank . . . . . BV 8
Buddle St . . . . . BV 13
Byker Bridge . . . . . BV 15
Church Ave . . . . . AV 16
Church Rd . . . . . AV 18
Clayton Rd . . . . . BV 21
Coldwell Lane . . . . . BX 22
Coldwell St . . . . . BX 24
Condercum Rd . . . . . AX 26
Fossway . . . . . BV 31
Haddrick's Mill Rd . . . . . BV 36
High St West . . . . . BV 37
Jesmond Dene Rd . . . . . BV 39
Killingworth Rd . . . . . BV 42
Lobley Hill Rd . . . . . AX 45
Matthew Bank . . . . . BV 49
Neptune Rd . . . . . BV 51
Redheugh Bridge . . . . . AX 62
Red Hall Drive . . . . . BV 61
Saltwell Rd . . . . . BX 69
Shipdon Rd . . . . . AX 71
Springfield Rd . . . . . AV 72
Station Rd . . . . . BX 73
Stephenson Rd . . . . . BV 74
Sunderland Rd . . . . . BX 76
Sutton St . . . . . BV 77
Swalwell Bank . . . . . ABX 79
Waverdale Ave . . . . . BV 83
West Farm Ave . . . . . BV 87
Whickham Bank . . . . . AX 89
Windy Nook Rd . . . . . BX 91

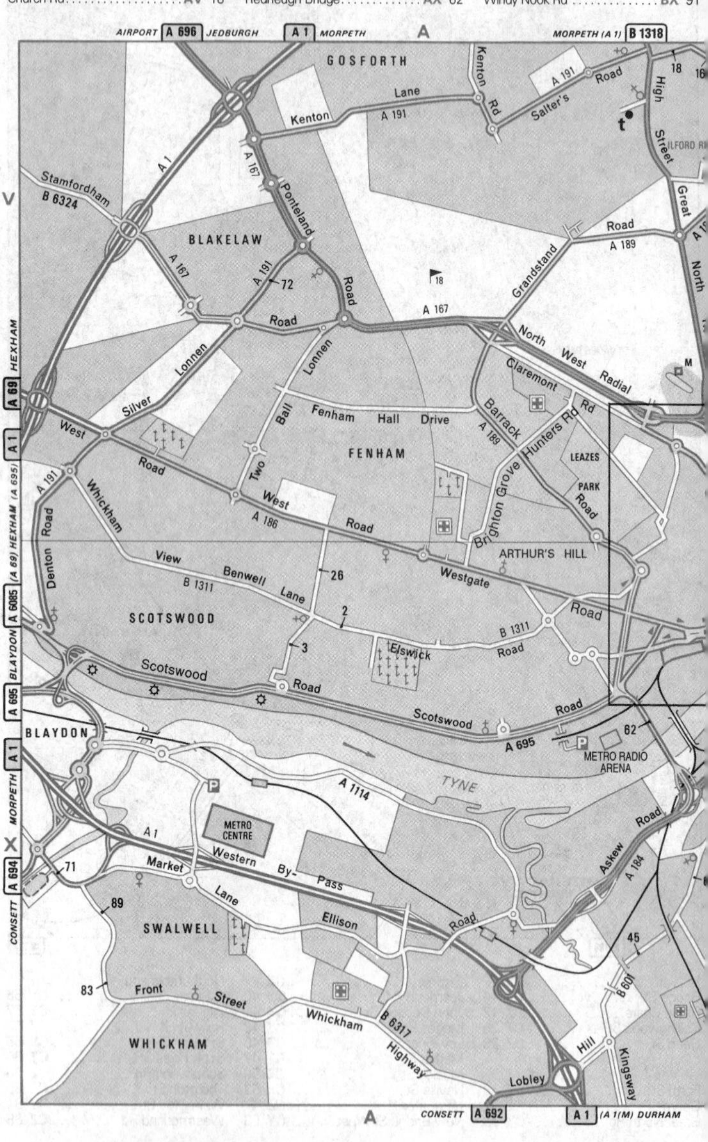

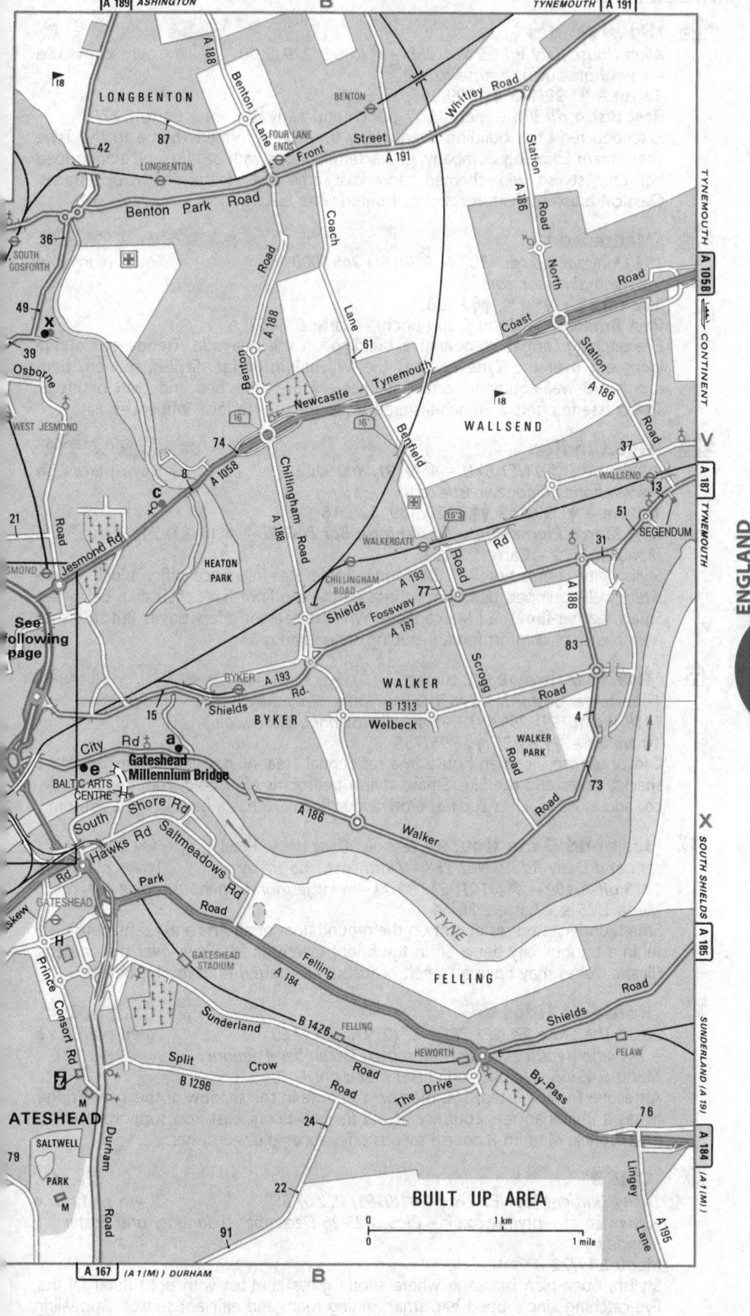

A 189 ASHINGTON
B
TYNEMOUTH A 191
LONGBENTON
A 188
Benton Lane
BENTON
Whitley Road
87
42
FOUR LANE ENDS
Front Street
A 191
LONGBENTON
Station Road
A 186
Benton Park Road
36
SOUTH GOSFORTH
Coach Lane
North Road
49
X
39
Osborne
Road
Benton
A 188
61
Coast Road
Station
A 186
Road
Newcastle - Tynemouth
16'
18
WALLSEND
WEST JESMOND
74
A 1058
Benfield
Chillingham
8
c
Road
A 188
37
WALLSEND
13
21
Road
15'3
51
SEGENDUM
Jesmond Rd
HEATON PARK
WALKERGATE
Rd
Road
31
SMOND
CHILLINGHAM ROAD
A 193
77
A 186
See following page
Shields
Fossway
A 187
83
Scrogg
BYKER
A 193
WALKER
15
Shields
Rd.
Road
B 1313
BYKER
Welbeck
4
City
Rd
a
WALKER PARK
e
Gateshead Millennium Bridge
Road
BALTIC ARTS CENTRE
73
South
Shore Rd
A 186
Road
X
Hawks Rd
Saltmeadows
Walker
Rd
Park
Rd
GATESHEAD
Road
TYNE
H
GATESHEAD STADIUM
Felling
A 184
FELLING
Prince Consort Rd
Road
Sunderland
Shields
B 1426
FELLING
HEWORTH
PELAW
Split
Crow
Road
B 1296
Road
The Drive
By-Pass
M
ATESHEAD
24
76
SALTWELL PARK
Durham
79
M
Road
22
BUILT UP AREA
Lingey Lane
0
1 km
0
1 mile
A 195
91
A 167 (A 1(M)) DURHAM
B
TYNEMOUTH A 1058
CONTINENT
V
A 187 TYNEMOUTH
ENGLAND
SOUTH SHIELDS A 185
SUNDERLAND (A 19)
A 184 (A 1(M))

Hotel du Vin

Allan House, City Rd ✉ NE1 2BE – ✆ (0191) 229 22 00 Town plan: BX**a**
– www.hotelduvin.com/newcastle
42 rm – †£ 99/145 ††£ 99/395, ☕ £ 17
Rest *Bistro du Vin* – Menu £ 17 (lunch and early dinner) – Carte £ 27/51
Extended red-brick building overlooking the river – formerly home to the Tyne Tees Steam Shipping Company. Characterful lounge with gas fire and zinc-topped bar. Chic, stylish, wine-themed bedrooms; some boast feature baths or terraces. Classical brasserie features a glass-fronted wine tasting room.

Malmaison

104 Quayside ✉ NE1 3DX – ✆ (0191) 245 5000 Town plan: BX**e**
– www.malmaison.com
122 rm ☕ – †£ 111 ††£ 123
Rest *Brasserie* – Menu £ 20 (lunch) – Carte £ 19/52
Eye-catching former co-operative building on the quayside. Trendy bar-lounge looks out over the Tyne towards the Millennium Bridge. Stylish, modern bedrooms are well-equipped; one suite has a four-poster bed and twin bathtubs. The brasserie offers a French-inspired bistro menu with local influences.

Hotel Indigo

2-8 Fenkle St ✉ NE1 5XU – ✆ (0191) 300 9222 Town plan: CZ**h**
– www.hotelindigonewcastle.co.uk
148 rm – †£ 99/169 ††£ 129/199, ☕ £ 16
Rest *Marco Pierre White Steakhouse Bar & Grill* – ✆ (0191) 211 2870 – Menu £ 15/29 – Carte £ 27/53
Stylish city centre hotel in the former Eagle Star Insurance office block. Good-sized, well-equipped bedrooms; those on the top floor have their own balconies. Smart, leather-furnished Marco Pierre White restaurant offers classic British dishes with plenty of comfort food, including steaks and grills.

ENGLAND

The Townhouse without rest

1 West Ave, Gosforth ✉ NE3 4ES – North : 2.5 mi by B 1318 – ✆ (0191) 285 6812 – www.thetownhousehotel.co.uk Town plan: AV**t**
10 rm ☕ – †£ 85/95 ††£ 95/135
End of terrace Victorian house in a residential area. All-day café serves breakfast, snacks, cakes and the like. Smart, stylish bedrooms offer bold, contemporary décor and extra touches such as iPod docks; Room 10 has a bath in the bedroom.

XXX **Jesmond Dene House** – Jesmond Dene House Hotel

Jesmond Dene Rd ✉ NE2 2EY – Northeast : 1.5 mi by B 1318 off A 189 – ✆ (0191) 212 30 00 – www.jesmonddenehouse.co.uk Town plan: BV**x**
Menu £ 25 **s** – Carte £ 26/64
Smart, understated restaurant on the ground floor of an Arts and Crafts house hotel in a tranquil city dene. Sit in the bright extension for views over the gardens. Classic dishes may have a French heart but are crafted from local produce.

XX **House of Tides** Ⓝ

28-30 The Close ✉ NE1 3RF – ✆ (0191) 230 37 20 Town plan: CZ**h**
– www.houseoftides.co.uk – Closed 20 December-4 January
Menu £ 45/65 – *(dinner only) (set menu only)*
Attractive Grade I listed, 16C merchant's house in the shadow of the Tyne Bridge. It has a utilitarian feel courtesy of old flagged floors, cast iron supports and exposed brick. Modern 8 course menus offer accomplished dishes.

XX **Café 21**

Trinity Gardens ✉ NE1 2HH – ✆ (0191) 222 07 55 Town plan: CZ**a**
– www.cafetwentyone.co.uk – Closed 25-26 December, 1 January and Easter Monday
Menu £ 17/22 – Carte £ 30/54
Stylish, open-plan brasserie where subtle greys contrast with bold floral fabrics. Eye-catching zinc-topped bar, smart dining room and efficient service. Appealing British and French classics, with a good value set lunch menu.

Peace & Loaf

217 Jesmond Rd, Jesmond ✉ NE2 1LA – ✆ (0191) 281 52 22 – www.peaceandloaf.co.uk – Closed 25-26 December and Sunday dinner Town plan: BV**c**

Menu £ 20 (lunch and early dinner) – Carte £ 27/39

Found in a smart suburban parade, this fashionable restaurant and bar is set over three levels and has a lively atmosphere. Attractively presented modern dishes are ambitious, complex and employ many different cooking techniques.

Caffé Vivo

29 Broad Chare ✉ NE1 3DQ – ✆ (0191) 232 13 31 – www.caffevivo.co.uk – Closed Sunday, Monday and bank holidays Town plan: CZ**d**

Menu £ 19 – Carte £ 16/40

In a quayside warehouse – with a theatre. Zinc ducting and steel pillars give it an industrial feel, while hams, salamis and oils add a touch of the Mediterranean. Simple, satisfying cooking of classic Italian dishes. Good value lunch menu.

Electric East

Waterloo Square, St James's Boulevard ✉ NE1 4DN – ✆ (0191) 221 10 00 – www.electric-east.co.uk – Closed 24-26 December, 1 January, bank holidays and Sunday Town plan: CZ**r**

Menu £ 12 (weekdays) – Carte £ 20/34 – *(dinner only and lunch Friday)*

Enter past the tuk tuk into a large bar, then on into a long, narrow room with heavy wood furnishings, lanterns and a simple, rustic, southeast Asian style. Extensive menus mix dishes from Vietnam, China and Japan. Polite, unfussy service.

Broad Chare

25 Broad Chare ✉ NE1 3DQ – ✆ (0191) 211 2144 – www.thebroadchare.co.uk – Closed 25 December and Sunday dinner Town plan: CZ**c**

Carte £ 22/35 – *(booking advisable)*

Owned by Terry Laybourne and next to its sister operation, Caffé Vivo. Sit in the snug ground floor bar or upstairs dining room. Choose from a snack menu of 'Geordie Tapas', an appealing 'on toast' selection, hearty daily specials and tasty nursery puddings. Over 40 ales, including some which are custom-made.

ENGLAND

at Newcastle International Airport Northwest: 6.75 mi by A167 off A696 -(AV)

✉ Newcastle Upon Tyne

Doubletree by Hilton Newcastle International Airport

Woolsington ✉ NE13 8BZ – ✆ (01661) 824 266 – www.doubletree-newcastle.com

179 rm – £ 60/220 £ 70/230

Rest *Fratello's* – Carte £ 16/36

A modern, V-shaped building: the closest hotel to the airport. Contemporary bedrooms and compact, well-equipped bathrooms are geared towards the modern business traveller; ask for a room with a runway view. Traditional pub menu in the bar; the restaurant with a terrace serves Mediterranean-influenced dishes.

NEWHAVEN

Derbyshire – See Regional map n°**16**-A1

London 159 mi – Leeds 84 mi – Manchester 38 mi – Derby 22 mi

The Smithy without rest

✉ SK17 0DT South : 1 mi on A 515 – ✆ (01298) 84 548 – www.thesmithybedandbreakfast.co.uk

4 rm – £ 50 £ 95

Friendly owners keep the blacksmith theme alive at this cosy guesthouse. Tools and the old forge are found in the rustic breakfast room; while the bedrooms come with wrought-iron beds and are named Anvil, Swage, Bellows and Forge.

NEWLYN

Cornwall – Pop. 3 536 – See Regional map n°**1**-A3

London 288 mi – Camborne 16 mi – Saint Austell 44 mi – Falmouth 29 mi

Michelin Road map 503-D33

Tolcarne Inn

Tolcarne Pl ✉ TR18 5PR – ✆ (01736) 363 074 – www.tolcarneinn.co.uk
Carte £ 21/35
Unassuming family-run pub beside the sea wall. Inside it's narrow and cosy, with 18C beams, a wood burning stove and a long bar. The experienced chef offers appealing, flavoursome dishes which centre around fresh, locally landed fish and shellfish. They host jazz nights every first and third Sunday.

NEWNHAM BRIDGE

Worcestershire – See Regional map n°**18-B2**
London 145 mi – Birmingham 36 mi – Worcester 20 mi
Michelin Road map 503-M27

Talbot Inn with rm

✉ WR15 8JF – ✆ (01584) 781 941 – www.talbotinnnewnhambridge.co.uk
7 rm – †£ 65/85 ††£ 85/115 Carte £ 22/30
Red-brick, 19C inn, originally built as a hunting lodge and once popular with hop pickers here for the harvest. Menus offer something for everyone; locally shot game in season is a speciality. Staff are friendly and efficient. Bedrooms provide contemporary comforts; ask for a room at the back.

NEWPORT PAGNELL

Milton Keynes – Pop. 15 118 – See Regional map n°**11-C1**
London 57 mi – Bedford 13 mi – Luton 21 mi – Northampton 15 mi
Michelin Road map 504-R27

Robinsons

18-20 St John St ✉ MK16 8HJ – ✆ (01908) 611 400 Town plan: CU**n**
– www.robinsonsrestaurant.co.uk – Closed bank holidays
Menu £ 18 (weekday lunch)/26 – Carte £ 35/50
Large, striking building with a fire-lit bar-lounge and a split-level dining room. Seasonal menus offer a mix of modern British and Mediterranean dishes; go for the good value set priced menu. The Tuesday steak nights are popular.

NEWQUAY

Cornwall – Pop. 20 189 – See Regional map n°**1-A2**
London 291 mi – Exeter 83 mi – Penzance 34 mi – Plymouth 48 mi
Michelin Road map 503-E32 – Michelin Green Guide GREAT BRITAIN

at Watergate Bay Northeast: 3 mi by A3059 on B3276 ✉ Newquay

Watergate Bay

On The Beach ✉ TR8 4AA – ✆ (01637) 860 543 – www.watergatebay.co.uk
69 rm – †£ 101/251 ††£ 135/335
Rest *Zacry's* – ✆ (01637) 861 231 – Carte £ 30/46 – *(dinner only)*
Rest *Beach Hut* – ✆ (01637) 860 877 – Carte £ 20/34
Long-standing seaside hotel where fresh, contemporary bedrooms range from standards to family suites; some have freestanding baths with sea outlooks. The beautiful infinity pool and hot tub share the view and there's direct beach access, beach changing rooms and even a surfboard store. Dine in the bar, the laid-back sandy-floored café or the smart modern bistro.

Fifteen Cornwall

On The Beach ✉ TR8 4AA – ✆ (01637) 861 000 – www.fifteencornwall.co.uk
Menu £ 28 (lunch) – Carte £ 24/56 – *(booking essential)*
Lively beachfront restaurant with fabulous bay views; a registered charity set up by Jamie Oliver to train local youngsters to be chefs. Unfussy Italian menus feature homemade pasta, steaks from the Josper grill and imported olives and oils – 80% of the produce is from Cornwall. They open for breakfast too.

ENGLAND

at Mawgan Porth Northeast: 6 mi by A3059 on B3276

Scarlet

Tredragon Rd ✉ TR8 4DQ – ✆ (01637) 861 800 – www.scarlethotel.co.uk – Closed 2-31 January

37 rm – †£ 175/445 ††£ 195/465

Rest *Scarlet* – see restaurant listing

Eco-centric, adults only hotel set high on a cliff and boasting stunning coastal views. Modern bar and lounges, and a great spa offering extensive treatments. Bedrooms range from 'Just Right' to 'Indulgent' and have unusual open-plan bathrooms and a cool, Scandic style – every room has a terrace and sea view.

Bedruthan

✉ TR8 4BU Northeast : 0.5 mi on B 3276 – ✆ (01637) 860 860 – www.bedruthan.com – Closed Christmas-February

89 rm – †£ 60/75 ††£ 150/300 – 10 suites

Rest *Herring* – Carte £ 18/30 – *(dinner only)*

Rest *Wild Café* – Carte £ 18/30

Unassuming hotel set in an elevated position overlooking the shore and boasting direct access to the beach. The interior is surprisingly contemporary and bedrooms are bright. Facilities and activities are family-orientated but the cocktail bar and lounge are set aside for adults. Interesting modern menus in Herring and accessible, family-focused dining in Wild Café.

XX

Scarlet – Scarlet Hotel

Tredragon Rd ✉ TR8 4DQ – ✆ (01637) 861 800 – www.scarlethotel.co.uk – Closed 2-31 January

Menu £ 23/43 – Carte £ 25/42 – *(bookings essential for non-residents)*

Contemporary hotel restaurant with huge windows offering stunning coastal views; start with a drink on the lovely terrace or in the chic bar. Concise daily menus promote small local suppliers; cooking is light, modern and seasonal.

NEWTON LONGVILLE

Buckinghamshire – Pop. 1 846 – See Regional map n°**11-C1**

London 52 mi – Birmingham 77 mi – Bristol 110 mi – Sheffield 126 mi

Michelin Road map 504-R28

Crooked Billet

2 Westbrook End ✉ MK17 0DF – ✆ (01908) 373 936 – www.thebillet.co.uk – Closed 25-26 December, Sunday dinner and Monday

Carte £ 21/39 – *(booking advisable)*

Charming 17C thatched pub with a smart yet informal interior, where a cheery bunch of locals prop up the bar. Modern, seasonal dishes are crafted from local produce.

NEWTON-ON-OUSE → See York

North Yorkshire – Michelin Road map 502-Q22

NOMANSLAND

Hampshire – See Regional map n°**4-D3**

London 96 mi – Bournemouth 26 mi – Salisbury 13 mi – Southampton 14 mi

Michelin Road map 503-P31 and 504

XX

Les Mirabelles

Forest Edge Rd ✉ SP5 2BN – ✆ (01794) 390 205 – www.lesmirabelles.co.uk – Closed 22 December-13 January, 1 week May, 1 week September, Sunday and Monday

Menu £ 19 (weekdays) – Carte £ 30/52

This bright, modern restaurant overlooks the common and is enthusiastically run by a welcoming Frenchman. The well-balanced menu features unfussy, classic Gallic dishes and the superb wine selection lists over 3,000 bins!

NORTH BOVEY

Devon – Pop. 254 – ✉ Newton Abbot – See Regional map n°**2**-C2

London 197 mi – Plymouth 41 mi – Torbay 23 mi – Exeter 15 mi

Michelin Road map 503-I32

Bovey Castle

✉ *TQ13 8RE Northwest : 2 mi by Postbridge rd, bearing left at fork just out of village – ✆ (01647) 445 000 – www.boveycastle.com*

64 rm – †£ 195/275 ††£ 195/275, ☕ £ 15 – 4 suites

Rest *Edwardian Grill* – Carte £ 34/64 – *(dinner only and Sunday lunch)*

Rest *Castle Bistro* – Carte £ 18/36

Impressive manor house within an extensive country estate, beautifully set in Dartmoor National Park. Relaxed, homely feel and a high degree of comfort throughout. Bedrooms come in pastel hues and with contemporary touches but retain a classic edge. Modern grill-style menu in formal Edwardian Grill or Mediterranean-influenced dishes in Castle Bistro.

Gate House without rest

✉ *TQ13 8RB just off village green, past "Ring of Bells" public house – ✆ (01647) 440 479 – www.gatehouseondartmoor.com – Closed 24-26 December*

3 rm ☕ – †£ 55/88 ††£ 80/88

Charming 15C medieval hall house in the heart of an attractive village, boasting a characterful thatched roof, a large oak door and a lovely country garden with a small pool. Homely lounge, cosy low-beamed breakfast room and simple, spotlessly kept bedrooms, some with moor views. Charming owners.

NORTH CHARLTON → See Alnwick

Northumberland – Michelin Road map 501-O17 and 502

NORTH KILWORTH

Leicestershire – See Regional map n°**16**-B3

London 95 mi – Leicester 20 mi – Market Harborough 9 mi

Michelin Road map 502-Q26

Kilworth House

Lutterworth Rd ✉ *LE17 6JE – West : 0.5 mi on A 4304 – ✆ (01858) 880 058 – www.kilworthhouse.co.uk*

44 rm ☕ – †£ 130/300 ††£ 130/300 – 3 suites

Rest *Wordsworth* – Menu £ 49 – *(dinner only and Sunday lunch)*

Rest *Orangery* – Menu £ 23/30 – Carte £ 28/40

Impressively restored and extended Victorian mansion in 38 acres of tranquil grounds, which feature a popular open-air theatre. Spacious, classical drawing rooms. Immaculately kept bedrooms with luxurious bathrooms; the largest are in the main house. Traditional menus in the ornate restaurant and light, brasserie-style dishes in the attractive orangery.

NORTH LOPHAM

Norfolk – See Regional map n°**15**-C2

London 98 mi – Norwich 34 mi – Ipswich 31 mi – Bury Saint Edmunds 20 mi

Michelin Road map 504-W26

Church Farm House

Church Rd ✉ *IP22 2LP – ✆ (01379) 687 270 – www.churchfarmhouse.org – Closed January-mid February*

3 rm ☕ – †£ 55/70 ††£ 110 **Rest** – Menu £ 30

Characterful thatched farmhouse in the shadow of the village church, with lovely gardens and a terrace for summer breakfasts. The comfy conservatory and spacious beamed lounge are filled with antiques and musical curios; bedrooms are traditional. The charming owners prepare homely meals of local produce.

NORTH MOLTON

Devon – Pop. 721 – See Regional map n°**2**-C1

London 192 mi – Cardiff 118 mi – Plymouth 87 mi – Swansea 153 mi

Michelin Road map 503-I30

Heasley House

Heasley Mill ✉ EX36 3LE – Northwest : 1.25 mi by Heasley Mill rd. – ☎ (01598) 740 213 – www.heasley-hotel.co.uk – Closed February-mid-March and 24 December-2 January

7 rm – †£ 110/170 ††£ 150/170

Rest – Menu £ 32 – *(dinner only) (booking essential) (residents only, set menu only)*

Former Georgian Dower House in a remote Devon village bordering Exmoor National Park. It has a clean, fresh style with whitewashed walls, rush matting and quirky modern artwork. Tea and cakes are served on arrival. Simple, wholesome cooking.

NORTH SHIELDS

Tyne and Wear – Pop. 39 042 – See Regional map n°**24**-B2

London 288 mi – Newcastle upon Tyne 9 mi – Sunderland 14 mi – Middlesbrough 39 mi

Michelin Road map 502-P18

Irvins Brasserie

The Richard Irvin Building, Union Quay ✉ NE30 1HJ – ☎ (0191) 296 32 38 – www.irvinsbrasserie.co.uk – Closed Monday

Menu £ 16 – Carte £ 22/37

Busy, informal restaurant in an old industrial building on the historic fish quay; brick walls and exposed pipes feature. The experienced chef has worked in a variety of places – menus are appealing and eclectic, with personal twists.

David Kennedy's River Cafe

51 Bell St, Fish Quay ✉ NE30 1HF – ☎ (0191) 296 61 68 – www.davidkennedysrivercafe.com – Closed 25-26 December, 1-2 January, Monday, Sunday dinner and lunch Tuesday-Wednesday

Menu £ 8 (lunch and early dinner) – Carte £ 18/31 – *(booking advisable)*

Laid-back restaurant run by a friendly local team, set above a pub in the North Shields fish quay. The daily changing à la carte offers unfussy, bistro-style dishes of fresh local produce, including fish from the market on the quayside. The 3 course set lunch and early dinner menu is a steal.

Staith House (N)

57 Low Lights ✉ NE30 1JA – ☎ (0191) 270 8441 – www.thestaithhouse.co.uk – Closed 25 December, 1 January and Sunday dinner

Menu £ 10 (lunch and early dinner) – Carte £ 18/41 – *(booking essential at dinner)*

There's a pleasing no-frills feel to this cosy quayside pub with its portholes and nautical charts. Bypass classics like burger and chips in favour of fish or shellfish straight from the sea; cooking is robust, tasty and well-priced.

NORTH WALSHAM

Norfolk – Pop. 12 463 – See Regional map n°**15**-D1

London 133 mi – Norwich 15 mi – Ipswich 61 mi – Lowestoft 34 mi

Michelin Road map 503-Y25 and 504 – Michelin Green Guide GREAT BRITAIN

Beechwood

20 Cromer Rd ✉ NR28 0HD – ☎ (01692) 403 231 – www.beechwood-hotel.co.uk

21 rm – †£ 88 ††£ 100/160

Rest – Menu £ 25/39 – *(dinner only and Sunday lunch)*

Attractive, creeper-clad, part-Georgian property, where the keen owners offer a warm welcome. The cosy interior displays original features and a host of memorabilia. Period bedrooms vary in size and comfort – many have feature beds and some have terraces onto the lovely gardens. A '10 Mile Menu' offers local ingredients in modern dishes with influences from the Med.

NORTHAW

Hertfordshire – See Regional map n°**12**-B2
London 22 mi – Birmingham 110 mi – Bristol 134 mi – Croydon 57 mi
Michelin Road map 504-T28

Sun at Northaw

1 Judges Hill ✉ EN6 4NL – ☎ (01707) 655 507 – www.thesunatnorthaw.co.uk – Closed Sunday dinner and Monday except bank holidays when closed Tuesday
Menu £ 13 (weekday lunch) – Carte £ 27/48
A restored, whitewashed, part-16C inn which sits by the village green; passionately run and contemporary in style, it's deceptively spacious, with a traditional edge. Hearty, unfussy, flavoursome cooking uses seasonal East of England produce, and beers and ciders are equally local. Friendly service.

NORTHLEACH

Gloucestershire – Pop. 1 854 – See Regional map n°**4**-D1
London 87 mi – Birmingham 73 mi – Bristol 54 mi – Coventry 47 mi

Wheatsheaf Inn with rm

West End ✉ GL50 3EZ – ☎ (01451) 860 244 – www.cotswoldswheatsheaf.com
14 rm – †£ 120/180 ††£ 120/180
Menu £ 15 (weekday lunch) – Carte £ 23/40
Smart, 17C coaching inn with a pretty tiered terrace and two traditional dining rooms, either side of the stone-floored, open-fired bar. The same menu is available throughout, offering classical dishes and something to suit every taste. Stylish, contemporary bedrooms have quirky touches and feature interesting French flea market finds; some have baths in the rooms.

ENGLAND

NORTON DISNEY

Lincolnshire – See Regional map n°**17**-C1
London 134 mi – Nottingham 30 mi – Lincoln 13 mi
Michelin Road map 502-R24

Brills Farm

Brills Hill ✉ LN6 9JN – West : 2 mi on Newark Rd – ☎ (01636) 892 311 – www.brillsfarm-bedandbreakfast.co.uk – Closed Christmas-New Year
3 rm – †£ 56 ††£ 92 **Rest** – Menu £ 30 – *(dinner only by reservation)*
Charming Georgian farmhouse in a commanding hilltop position on a 2,000 acre working farm. Elegant country bedrooms have period wallpapers, goose down duvets and lovely rural views. Tasty Aga-cooked dinners are served by arrangement (min. 6 people), at an antique table; the bacon is from their farm.

NORTON ST PHILIP

Somerset – Pop. 556 – ✉ Bath – See Regional map n°**4**-C2
London 113 mi – Bristol 22 mi – Southampton 55 mi – Swindon 40 mi
Michelin Road map 503-N30 and 504

The Plaine without rest

✉ BA2 7LT – ☎ (01373) 834 723 – www.theplaine.co.uk
3 rm – †£ 50/109 ††£ 60/130
Charming 17C stone cottages in a delightful village, on the site of the original market place. Snug, beamed interior with an airy breakfast room. Simple bedrooms feature fresh, colour-themed linens. Bubbly owner.

NORWELL → See Newark-on-Trent

Nottinghamshire

NORWICH

Norfolk – Pop. 186 682 – See Regional map n°**15**-D2
London 109 mi – Kingston-upon-Hull 148 mi – Leicester 117 mi
Michelin Road map 504-Y26 – Michelin Green Guide GREAT BRITAIN

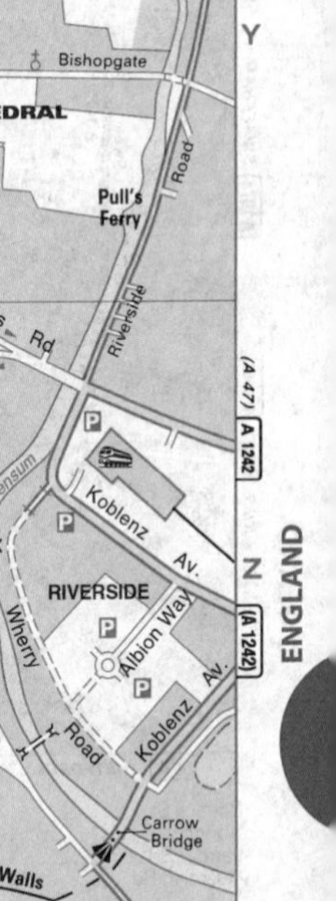

St Giles House

41-45 St Giles St ✉ NR2 1JR – ✆ (01603) 275 180 — Town plan: YZ**a**
– www.stgileshousehotel.com

24 rm ☕ – 🚹£ 120/210 🚹🚹£ 130/220 – 3 suites **Rest** – Carte £ 23/39

Stylish, centrally located hotel with an impressive façade, columns and wood panelling. Luxurious 'Deluxe' front suites; the rear bedrooms are quieter and more contemporary. The open-plan lounge, bar and dining room has a pleasant terrace and serves modern brasserie classics.

38 St Giles without rest

38 St Giles St ✉ NR2 1LL – ✆ (01603) 662 944 — Town plan: Z**x**
– www.38stgiles.co.uk – Closed 24-27 December

7 rm ☕ – 🚹£ 90 🚹🚹£ 130/160

City centre townhouse where boutique styling blends with original features. Elegant, uncluttered bedrooms boast high ceilings and wood panelling, along with silk curtains, handmade mattresses and quality linen. Excellent breakfasts.

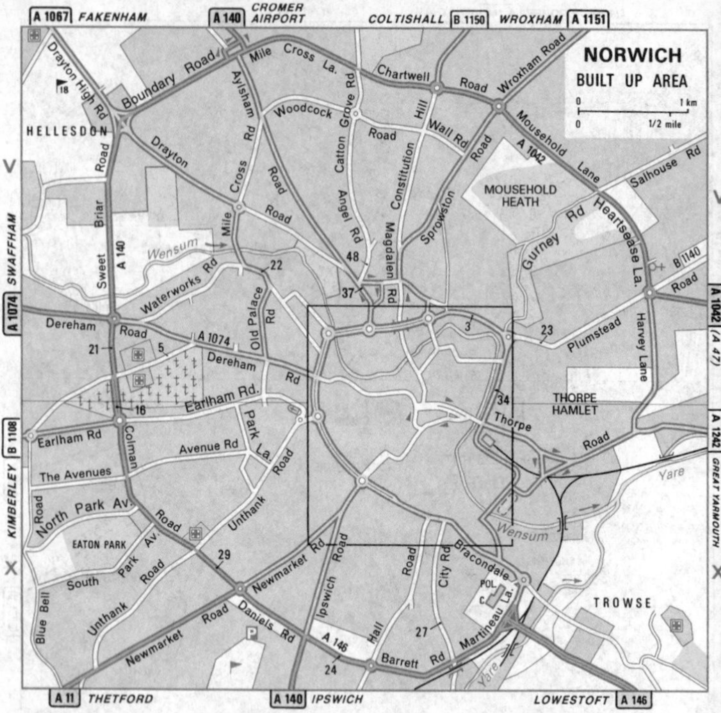

Barrack St	V	3	Heigham St	V	22	Mile End Rd	X	29
Bowthorpe Rd	V	5	Ketts Hill	V	23	Riverside Rd	V	34
Farrow Rd	V	16	Lakenham Rd	X	24	St Augustine's St	V	37
Guardian Rd	V	21	Long John Hill	X	27	Waterloo Rd	V	48

Catton Old Hall without rest 

Lodge Ln, Old Catton ✉ NR6 7HG – North : 3.5 mi by Catton Grove Rd off St Faiths Rd – ✆ (01603) 419 379 – www.catton-hall.co.uk
7 rm ☕ – 🚹£ 85/150 🚹🚹£ 85/150
Attractive, personally run, 17C merchant's house with a characterful interior. Individually designed bedrooms include 5 feature rooms; Anna Sewell, with exposed rafters and a vast four-poster, is the best.

Roger Hickman's

79 Upper St Giles St ✉ NR2 1AB – ✆ (01603) 633 522 Town plan: Z**c**
– www.rogerhickmansrestaurant.com – Closed 1 week August, 1 week Christmas, Sunday and Monday
Menu £ 23/60
Personally run restaurant in a historic part of the city, with soft hues, modern art and romantic corners. Service is attentive yet unobtrusive. Cooking is modern, intricate and displays respect for ingredients' natural flavours.

Bishop's

8-10 St Andrew's Hill ✉ NR2 1AD – ✆ (01603) 767 321 Town plan: Y**a**
– www.bishopsrestaurant.co.uk – Closed Sunday and Monday
Menu £ 15/34 – *(booking essential)*
Intimate restaurant of only eight tables, in a 15C building with a country-chic décor of floral prints, oval mirrors, crystal chandeliers and silk curtains. Simply presented, traditional dishes. Efficient service.

Tatlers
21 Tombland ✉ NR3 1RF – ✆ (01603) 766 670 Town plan: Y**c**
– www.tatlersrestaurant.co.uk – Closed 25 December and Sunday
Carte £ 24/33
Georgian merchant's house close to the cathedral, with high ceilings, bay windows and shabby-chic styling. Satisfying, flavourful bistro classics use the best of local ingredients; service is efficient and polite.

Reindeer
10 Dereham Rd ✉ NR2 4AY – ✆ (01603) 612 995 Town plan: Y**r**
– www.thereindeerpub.co.uk – Closed 25-26 December and Monday
Carte £ 19/35
Rustic neighbourhood pub with a keen local following. Plenty of space is kept aside for drinkers, who have 10 real ales to choose from. Straightforward, proudly British cooking employs lesser-used cuts and offers plenty of sharing dishes.

at Stoke Holy Cross South: 5.75 mi by A140 -(X)✉ Norwich

Wildebeest
82-86 Norwich Rd ✉ NR14 8QJ – ✆ (01508) 492 497 – www.animalinns.co.uk
Menu £ 15 (weekday lunch)/23 – Carte £ 25/42 – *(booking essential)*
Unusually decorated pub with African rugs, wooden wild animals and tree trunk tables. An array of menus offer modern British and European flavours. Wednesday steak nights feature cuts from their own herd of cattle. Smart, polite service.

ENGLAND

NOSS MAYO

Devon – See Regional map n°**2**-C3
London 217 mi – Plymouth 11 mi – Torbay 32 mi – Exeter 45 mi
Michelin Road map 503-H33

Ship Inn
✉ PL8 1EW – ✆ (01752) 872 387 – www.nossmayo.com
Carte £ 22/32
Large, busy, well-run pub with characterful, nautical décor and wonderful waterside views from its peaceful spot on the Yealm Estuary. Appealing menu of unfussy pub classics. Bright, friendly service. Keep an eye on the tide!

NOTTINGHAM

Nottingham – Pop. 289 301 – See Regional map n°**16**-B2
London 135 mi – Birmingham 50 mi – Leeds 74 mi – Leicester 27 mi
Michelin Road map 502-Q25 and 503 – Michelin Green Guide GREAT BRITAIN

Hart's
Standard Hill, Park Row ✉ NG1 6FN – ✆ (0115) 988 19 00 – www.hartsnottingham.co.uk Town plan: CZ**e**
32 rm – †£ 125/265 ††£ 125/265, ☕ £ 14 – 2 suites
Rest *Hart's* – see restaurant listing
Sophisticated, boutique-style hotel built on the ramparts of a medieval castle. Compact bedrooms have modern bathrooms and a high level of facilities; some open onto garden terraces. The small bar-lounge doubles as a breakfast room.

Restaurant Sat Bains with rm
Trentside,Lenton Ln ✉ NG7 2SA – ✆ (0115) 986 65 66 Town plan: AZ**n**
– www.restaurantsatbains.com – Closed 2 weeks August, 2 weeks late December-early January, 1 week April, Sunday and Monday
4 rm ☕ – †£ 115 ††£ 129 – 4 suites Menu £ 75/99
Smart, formal restaurant, with an intimate dining room, crisply laid tables and slick, knowledgeable service; incongruously located near a flyover. 7 and 10 course tasting menus feature refined, highly original dishes with playful twists. Lunch is served at the three kitchen tables. Bedrooms are modern.
→ Crab satay. Pressed lamb, pickled vegetables and mint gastrique. Aerated chocolate, cherry, salt and tobacco.

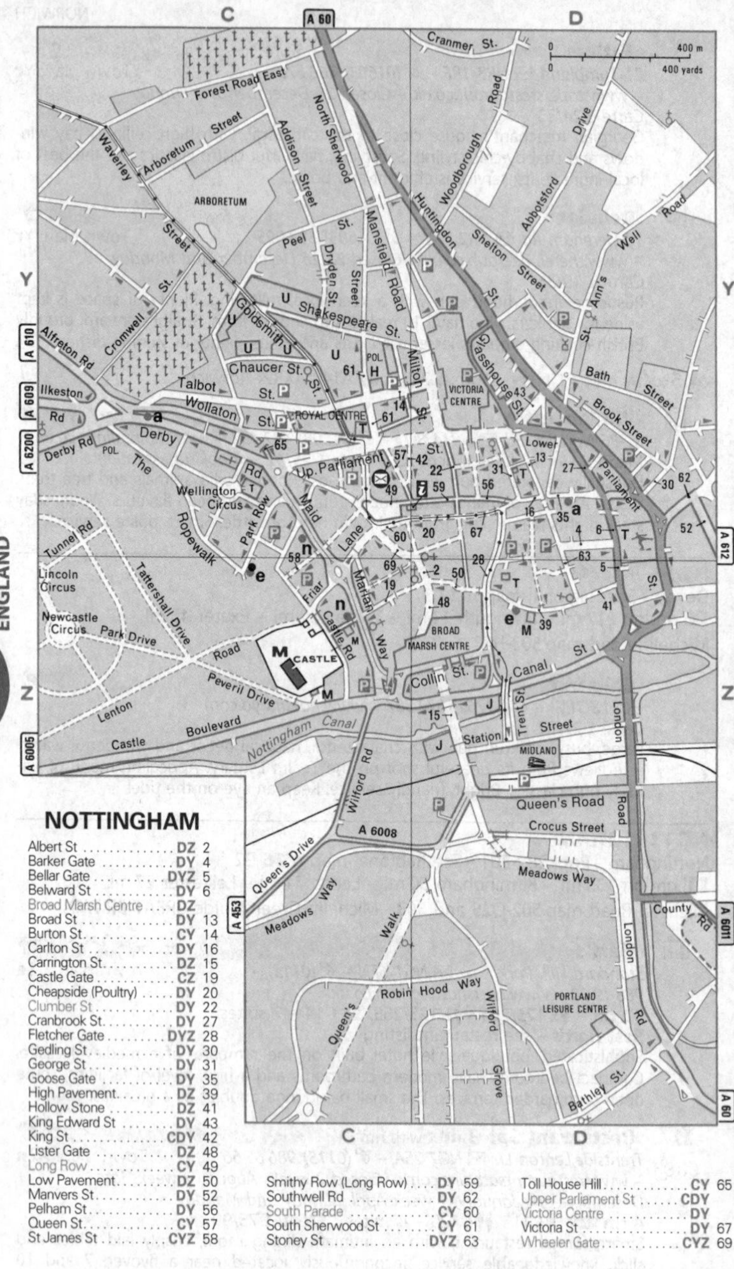

NOTTINGHAM

Street	Grid	No.
Albert St	DZ	2
Barker Gate	DY	4
Bellar Gate	DYZ	5
Belward St	DY	6
Broad Marsh Centre	DZ	
Broad St	DY	13
Burton St	CY	14
Carlton St	DY	16
Carrington St	DZ	15
Castle Gate	CZ	19
Cheapside (Poultry)	DY	20
Clumber St	DY	22
Cranbrook St	DY	27
Fletcher Gate	DYZ	28
Gedling St	DY	30
George St	DY	31
Goose Gate	DY	35
High Pavement	DZ	39
Hollow Stone	DZ	41
King Edward St	DY	43
King St	CDY	42
Lister Gate	DZ	48
Long Row	CY	49
Low Pavement	DZ	50
Manvers St	DY	52
Pelham St	DY	56
Queen St	CY	57
St James St	CYZ	58
Smithy Row (Long Row)	DY	59
Southwell Rd	DY	62
South Parade	CY	60
South Sherwood St	CY	61
Stoney St	DYZ	63
Toll House Hill	CY	65
Upper Parliament St	CDY	
Victoria Centre	DY	
Victoria St	DY	67
Wheeler Gate	CYZ	69

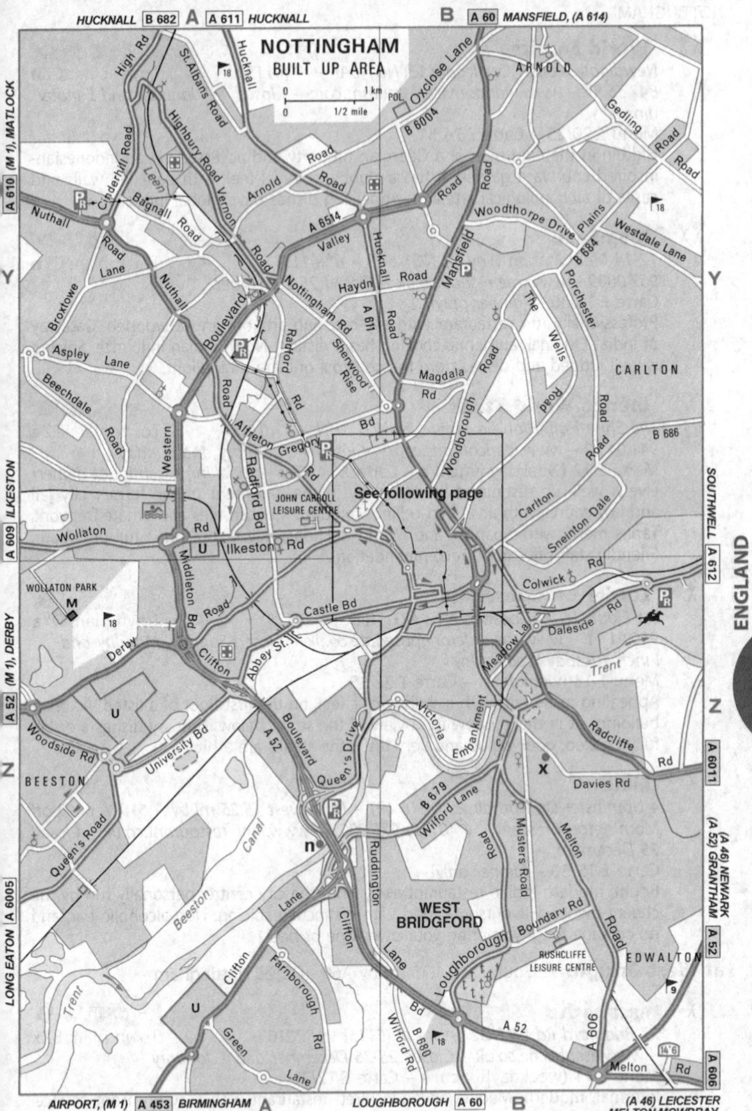

XX **Hart's** – Hart's Hotel

Standard Ct., Park Row ✉ NG1 6GN — Town plan: CZ**e**
– ✆ (0115) 988 19 00 – *www.hartsnottingham.co.uk – Closed 1 January and dinner 25-26 December*
Menu £ 19/24 – Carte £ 30/51

Contemporary restaurant in the A&E department of the old city hospital; ask to sit in one of the central booths. British brasserie dishes feature on the daily menu and cooking is flavourful and well-priced. Service is polite.

XX **World Service**

Newdigate House, Castlegate ✉ *NG1 6AF – ✆ (0115) 847 55 87 – www.worldservicerestaurant.com – Closed 1-7 January and Sunday dinner* Town plan: CZ**n**

Menu £ 20/25 – Carte £ 26/51

Hidden in the extension of a Georgian property and accessed via an Indonesian-inspired courtyard garden. It has a clubby, colonial feel, with panelled walls and cases of archaeological artefacts. Appealing dishes have global influences.

XX **MemSaab**

12-14 Maid Marian Way ✉ *NG1 6HS – ✆ (0115) 957 0009 – www.mem-saab.co.uk – Closed 25 December* Town plan: CY**n**

Carte £ 18/36 – *(dinner only)*

Professionally run restaurant with eye-catching artwork and a wooden 'Gateway of India'. Original, authentic cooking has a distinct North Indian influence. Spicing is well judged and dishes from the charcoal grill are a highlight.

X **Ibérico World Tapas**

The Shire Hall, High Pavement ✉ *NG1 1HN – ✆ (0115) 941 04 10 – www.ibericotapas.com – Closed 1-5 January and Sunday* Town plan: DZ**e**

Menu £ 12 (weekday lunch) **s** – Carte £ 14/23 **s** – *(booking essential at dinner)*

Lively, well-run restaurant hidden away in the basement of the former city jail and law courts, with a vaulted ceiling, colourful Moorish tiles and ornate fretwork. Tapas menu with 'Spanish' and 'World' sections; skilful cooking is full of flavour. Friendly staff offer good recommendations.

ENGLAND

X **Larder on Goosegate**

1st Floor, 16-22 Goosegate ✉ *NG1 1FE – ✆ (0115) 950 01 11 – www.thelarderongoosegate.co.uk – Closed Sunday, Monday and lunch Tuesday-Wednesday* Town plan: DY**a**

Menu £ 13 (weekdays) – Carte £ 22/35

Appealing restaurant with a shabby-chic feel, on the first floor of a listed Victorian building; sit in the window for a view of the street below. Unfussy dishes are skilfully cooked, good value and very tasty; the steaks are a hit.

X **Lime**

4 Upminster Dr, Nuthall ✉ *NG16 1PT – Northwest : 5.25 mi by A 610, A 6002 off Mornington Crescent – ✆ (0115) 975 0005 – www.lime-restaurant.co.uk – Closed 25 December*

Carte £ 15/30 – *(dinner only)*

Bright, modern Indian restaurant away from the city centre; personally run by the cheery owner. Flavoursome food with distinctive spicing. Non-alcoholic bar, and no corkage fee if you bring your own wine or beer.

at West Bridgford Southeast: 1.75 mi by A60 -(DZ)✉ Nottingham

X **escabeche**

27 Bridgford Rd ✉ *NG2 6AU – ✆ (0115) 981 7010 – www.escabeche.co.uk – Closed 25-26 December and 1 January* Town plan: BZ**x**

Menu £ 11 (weekday lunch) **s** – Carte £ 12/21

Informal, modern, Mediterranean-inspired restaurant with a sunny front terrace. The broad main menu lists vibrant, well-presented tapas dishes, offering a great variety of flavours. Excellent value set menu.

at Plumtree Southeast: 5.75 mi by A60 -(BZ)- off A606✉ Nottingham

XX **Perkins**

Old Railway Station, Station Rd ✉ *NG12 5NA – ✆ (0115) 937 36 95 – www.perkinsrestaurant.co.uk – Closed Sunday dinner*

Menu £ 17/19 – Carte £ 26/39 – *(booking advisable)*

Formerly a Victorian railway station, now a bright family-run brasserie; find a spot in the conservatory overlooking the railway line. Menus evolve daily and the modern British cooking features home-smoked fish, game and cheeses.

at Stapleford Southwest: 5.5 mi by A52 -(AZ)-

Crème

12 Toton Ln ✉ NG9 7HA – ✆ (0115) 939 74 22 – www.cremerestaurant.co.uk – Closed 25-26 and 31 December, Saturday lunch, Sunday dinner and Monday
Menu £ 18/21 – Carte £ 24/35 – *(booking advisable)*
Well-run neighbourhood restaurant with a spacious, comfortable lounge area and a stylish, modern, formally laid dining room. Seasonally changing, modern British menu; well-presented dishes are served by friendly staff.

at Sherwood Business Park Northwest: 10 mi by A611 -(AY)- off A608✉ Nottingham

Dakota

Lake View Dr ✉ NG15 0EA – ✆ (01623) 727 670 – www.dakotanottingham.co.uk
92 rm – †£ 79/119 ††£ 79/129, ☕ £ 14
Rest *Grill* – Carte £ 24/35
An eye-catching black glass cube in the heart of a business park by the M1. Spacious modern bedrooms have good facilities and walk-in showers; executive rooms have super king sized beds and extras such as bathrobes and chocolates. The roomy, laid-back restaurant offers an international grill-style menu.

NUNEATON

Warwickshire – Pop. 86 552 – See Regional map n°**19**-D2
▶London 102 mi – Birmingham 25 mi – Coventry 17 mi
Michelin Road map 503-P26

Leathermill Grange without rest

Leathermill Lane, Caldecote ✉ CV10 0RX – Northwest : 3.5 mi by B 4114 on B 4111 – ✆ (01827) 714 637 – www.leathermillgrange.co.uk – Closed 25 December-1 January
3 rm ☕ – †£ 60/80 ††£ 70/90
Red-brick Victorian farmhouse in a peaceful rural spot; the welcoming owners serve homemade cake on arrival. Traditional, pine-furnished bedrooms and a spacious Victoriana-style lounge with rich furnishings. Tasty, Aga-cooked breakfasts.

OAKHAM

Rutland – Pop. 10 922 – See Regional map n°**17**-C2
▶London 103 mi – Leicester 26 mi – Northampton 35 mi – Nottingham 28 mi
Michelin Road map 502-R25 and 504 – Michelin Green Guide GREAT BRITAIN

Barnsdale Lodge

The Avenue, Rutland Water ✉ LE15 8AH – East : 2.5 mi on A 606 – ✆ (01572) 724 678 – www.barnsdalelodge.co.uk
45 rm ☕ – †£ 80/95 ††£ 100/150
Rest – Menu £ 16 (weekday lunch) – Carte £ 24/43
Collection of interconnecting former farm buildings in neat, lawned gardens. Characterful guest areas with York stone flooring in the lounge and bar. Individually designed bedrooms boast good facilities and a country chic style. Classic dishes with Mediterranean influences in the dining room and conservatory.

at Hambleton East: 3 mi by A606✉ Oakham

Hambleton Hall

✉ LE15 8TH – ✆ (01572) 756 991 – www.hambletonhall.com
17 rm ☕ – †£ 195/440 ††£ 265/535 – 1 suite
Rest *Hambleton Hall* ✿ – see restaurant listing
Beautiful Victorian manor house in a peaceful location, with mature grounds sloping down to Rutland Water. Classical country house drawing rooms boast heavy drapes, open fires and antiques. Good-sized bedrooms are designed by the owner herself and come with a host of thoughtful extras. Service is engaging.

XXX **Hambleton Hall** – Hambleton Hall Hotel 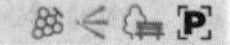

✉ *LE15 8TH – ✆ (01572) 756 991 – www.hambletonhall.com*
Menu £ 32/75
Traditional dining room in a lovely Victorian manor house, boasting superb views over Rutland Water. Intricate, highly technical cooking marries together a host of top quality seasonal ingredients. Classically based Gallic dishes display modern touches; the delicious bread is from their own artisan bakery.
→ Assiette of tomato with basil ice cream. Roast duck with tamarillo purée and a turmeric flavoured cassoulet. Pavé of white & dark chocolate with raspberries.

Finch's Arms with rm — rest,

Oakham Rd ✉ LE15 8TL – ✆ (01572) 756 575 – www.finchsarms.co.uk
10 rm – †£ 80/110 ††£ 100/130 Menu £ 14/20 – Carte £ 20/41
Quaint stone inn with a characterful bar, two very stylish dining rooms and a delightful terrace overlooking Rutland Water. Assured, seasonal dishes rely on local produce; desserts are satisfyingly old school and afternoon tea is also an option. Ultra-modern bedrooms complete the picture.

OARE → See Faversham
Kent – Michelin Road map 504-W30

OBORNE → See Sherborne
Dorset – Michelin Road map 503-M31 and 504

OFFCHURCH → See Royal Leamington Spa
Warwickshire

ENGLAND

OLD BASING
Hampshire – See Regional map n°**6**-B1
London 50 mi – Bristol 84 mi – Cardiff 117 mi – Plymouth 169 mi
Michelin Road map 503-Q30

Crown 

The Street ✉ RG24 7BW – ✆ (01256) 321 424 – www.thecrownoldbasing.com – Closed 1 January and Sunday dinner
Carte dinner £ 25/38
Popular with locals and with a likeable simplicity to its menus. Choices range from simple snacks to flavoursome, classic dishes like roast chicken. Everything is homemade, from the bread to the fudge that comes with your coffee.

OLD BURGHCLERE
Hampshire ✉ Newbury – See Regional map n°**6**-B1
London 77 mi – Bristol 76 mi – Newbury 10 mi – Reading 27 mi
Michelin Road map 504-Q29

XX **Dew Pond**

✉ RG20 9LH – ✆ (01635) 278 408 – www.dewpond.co.uk – Closed 2 weeks Christmas-New Year, Sunday and Monday
Menu £ 36 – *(dinner only)*
Long-standing, part-16C farmhouse with well-tended gardens leading down to a dew pond. Cooking is classic French and the dining rooms display local art for sale. Have an aperitif on the terrace, overlooking the real Watership Down.

OLDHAM
Greater Manchester – Pop. 96 555 – See Regional map n°**20**-B2
London 212 mi – Leeds 36 mi – Manchester 7 mi – Sheffield 38 mi
Michelin Road map 502-N23 and 504

White Hart Inn with rm
51 Stockport Rd, Lydgate ✉ *OL4 4JJ – ✆ (01457) 872 566 – www.thewhitehart.co.uk*
12 rm – †£ 95 ††£ 128 Carte £ 23/37
Extended stone inn overlooking Saddleworth Moor, with exposed beams and open fires. An array of menus includes a good value lunch and early evening selection, a 'brasserie' menu of classics and a 'restaurant' menu which shifts things up a gear. Individually styled bedrooms are named after noteworthy locals.

OLDSTEAD

North Yorkshire – See Regional map n°**23-C2**
London 235 mi – Leeds 54 mi – Sheffield 86 mi
Michelin Road map 502-Q21

Black Swan with rm
✉ *YO61 4BL – ✆ (01347) 868 387 – www.blackswanoldstead.co.uk – Closed lunch Monday-Wednesday*
4 rm – †£ 170/290 ††£ 170/290
Menu £ 28 (weekdays)/75 – Carte approx. £ 48
Owned by a family who've lived and farmed here for generations. Enjoy an aperitif in the characterful beamed bar, then head to the smart upstairs restaurant. Carefully presented, ambitious dishes use first rate ingredients; cooking is modern and highly skilled. Tasting menus with matching wines available. Antique-furnished bedrooms have luxurious bathrooms and private patios.
→ Sea trout, horseradish, nettles and spelt. Venison saddle and sausage with celeriac, hazelnut and blackberry. Carrot cake, walnut and mascarpone.

OMBERSLEY

Worcestershire – Pop. 623 – See Regional map n°**18-B3**
London 128 mi – Birmingham 25 mi – Coventry 41 mi
Michelin Road map 503-N27 and 504

Venture In
Main St ✉ *WR9 0EW – ✆ (01905) 620 552 – Closed 2 weeks August, 1 week March, 1 week June, 1 week Christmas, Monday and dinner Sunday*
Menu £ 26/45
Black and white timbered house with 15C origins, exposed beams and a large inglenook fireplace. The concise menu is supplemented by specials. Cooking is classically based but has modern overtones; the chef-owner adds personal twists.

ORFORD

Suffolk – Pop. 1 153 – ✉ Woodbridge – See Regional map n°**15-D3**
London 103 mi – Ipswich 22 mi – Norwich 52 mi
Michelin Road map 504-Y27

Crown and Castle
✉ *IP12 2LJ – ✆ (01394) 450 205 – www.crownandcastle.co.uk*
21 rm – †£ 118 ††£ 135/215 – 1 suite
Rest *Trinity* – see restaurant listing
Beside a castle in a sleepy village; a refreshingly well-run Tudor-style house, where the service is relaxed yet professional. Most of the modern, individually designed bedrooms are in chalets in the grounds – all have good quality furnishings; many have seating areas, terraces and distant sea views.

Trinity – Crown and Castle Hotel
✉ *IP12 2LJ – ✆ (01394) 450 205 – www.crownandcastle.co.uk*
Carte £ 29/40 – *(closed lunch 31 December) (booking essential at dinner)*
Have a drink in the hotel's funky bar before heading through to the relaxed dining room with red banquettes and eclectic art. Simple yet precise cooking relies on quality, seasonal ingredients. Service is friendly and efficient.

ENGLAND

OSMOTHERLEY

North Yorkshire – Pop. 668 – ✉ Northallerton – See Regional map n°**22**-B1
London 245 mi – Darlington 25 mi – Leeds 49 mi – Middlesbrough 20 mi
Michelin Road map 502-Q20

Golden Lion with rm

6 West End ✉ DL6 3AA – ✆ (01609) 883 526 – www.goldenlionosmotherley.co.uk – Closed 25 December, lunch Monday and Tuesday except bank holidays

7 rm – †£ 65/95 ††£ 95/100 Carte £ 20/39

18C stone inn set in a historic village in the North York Moors; make for the atmospheric bar which offers over 80 different whiskies. Cooking is traditional and satisfying, with filling dishes on the main menu and more ambitious weekly specials. Modern bedrooms have heavy oak furnishings and good facilities.

OSWESTRY

Shropshire – Pop. 16 660 – See Regional map n°**18**-A1
London 182 mi – Birmingham 66 mi – Chester 28 mi
Michelin Road map 502-K25 and 503

XX Sebastians N with rm

45 Willow St ✉ SY11 1AQ – ✆ (01691) 655 444 – www.sebastians-hotel.co.uk – Closed 25-26 December, 1 January, Sunday and Monday

5 rm – †£ 75 ††£ 85, £ 12 Menu £ 23/45 – *(dinner only)*

Housed in three characterful 17C cottages, Sebastians is a long-standing restaurant with an open fire, lots of beams and bags of charm. Cooking uses good ingredients and is classically based, and you'll be well looked after by the team. Many of the cosy, characterful bedrooms are set around a courtyard.

at Rhydycroesau West: 3.5 mi on B4580 ✉ Oswestry

Pen-Y-Dyffryn

✉ SY10 7JD – ✆ (01691) 653 700 – www.peny.co.uk – Closed 15 December-15 January

12 rm – †£ 75/95 ††£ 130/190

Rest – Menu £ 39 – *(dinner only) (booking essential)*

Early Victorian rectory in a peaceful countryside setting, with a pretty garden and lovely views. Classical guest areas feature antique furnishings; bedrooms have good facilities and contemporary fabrics – coach house rooms have their own terrace. Daily menus use local and organic produce.

OTTERBOURNE

Hampshire – Pop. 1 246 – See Regional map n°**6**-B2
London 72 mi – Birmingham 134 mi – Bristol 96 mi – Cardiff 129 mi
Michelin Road map 504-P30

White Horse

Main Rd ✉ SO21 2EQ – ✆ (01962) 712 830 – www.whitehorseotterbourne.co.uk

Carte £ 19/39

Smart pub with designer décor, vintage adverts and leather sofas; one side is for drinkers; the other, for diners. Wide-ranging menu with lovely local cheeses, artisan bread, Sunday roasts and afternoon teas. Friendly service.

OUNDLE

Northamptonshire – Pop. 5 735 – ✉ Peterborough – See Regional map n°**17**-C3
London 89 mi – Leicester 37 mi – Northampton 30 mi
Michelin Road map 504-S26

XX Oundle Mill with rm

rest,

Barnwell Rd ✉ PE8 5PB – South : 1 mi by West St and Mill Rd – ✆ (01832) 272 621 – www.oundlemill.co.uk – Closed Monday and Tuesday

2 rm – †£ 140/150 ††£ 200/250 Menu £ 15/23 – Carte £ 25/37

17C limestone watermill on the banks of the Nene. Interior fuses original features with strikingly modern new designs, including glass floors looking down to the water. Detailed modern British cooking; locally and ethically sourced produce. Well-appointed bedrooms boast low beams and original mill workings.

ENGLAND

at Fotheringhay North: 3.75 mi by A427 off A605

Castle Farm without rest
PE8 5HZ – (01832) 226 200 – www.castlefarm-guesthouse.co.uk
5 rm – £ 45/60 £ 80/100
Large 19C, wisteria-clad former farmhouse with lawned gardens leading down to the River Nene. Comfy lounge with deep sofas and a pleasant aspect. Spacious, traditionally styled bedrooms: two are in the wing; the best one is at the front.

Falcon Inn
PE8 5HZ – (01832) 226 254 – www.thefalcon-inn.co.uk
Menu £ 14 (weekdays) – Carte £ 21/34
Attractive stone inn with a neat garden and terrace. Good-sized menus feature unusual combinations and interesting modern takes on classic dishes. You'll find the regulars playing darts in the tap bar and diners in the conservatory.

OUSTON

Durham – See Regional map n°**24**-B2
London 197 mi – Cardiff 141 mi – Swansea 177 mi – Gloucester 241 mi

Low Urpeth Farm without rest
DH2 1BD North : 1 mi on Kibblesworth rd – (0191) 410 2901 – www.lowurpeth.co.uk
3 rm – £ 55/65 £ 78/85
A stone-built Victorian farmhouse on a working arable farm: a very welcoming place, full of warmth and run with pride. Cakes and biscuits are served on arrival in the traditional, antique-furnished lounge; breakfast features homemade bread and preserves, and the spacious, comfy bedrooms have country views.

ENGLAND

OXFORD

Oxfordshire – Pop. 159 994 – See Regional map n°**10-B2**
London 59 mi – Birmingham 63 mi – Brighton 105 mi – Bristol 73 mi
Michelin Road map 503-Q28 and 504 – Michelin Green Guide GREAT BRITAIN

© Belmond le Manoir aux Quat'Saisons

Hotels

ENGLAND

Randolph

Beaumont St. ✉ OX1 2LN – ✆ (0844) 879 91 32 Town plan: BY**n**
– www.macdonaldhotels.co.uk/randolph – Restricted opening Christmas
151 rm – †£ 159/299 ††£ 209/339, ☕ £ 20 – 9 suites
Rest *Randolph* – see restaurant listing

A grand old lady with her make-up firmly intact, this fine Victorian building offers immense charm and character. Delightful wrought iron stairway; plush period bedrooms. Afternoon tea in the drawing room with its Sir Osbert Lancaster oils.

Malmaison

rm,

Oxford Castle, 3 New Rd ✉ OX1 1AY – ✆ (01865) 268 400 – www.malmaison.com Town plan: BZ**a**
95 rm – †£ 120/240 ††£ 120/240, ☕ £ 16 – 3 suites
Rest *Brasserie* – Carte £ 25/55

Unique hotel in an old 13C prison not far from the castle. Pleasant rooftop terrace contrasts with moody interior: the most characterful bedrooms are in the old A Wing cells; feature rooms are in the Governor's House and House of Correction. Basement brasserie serves accessible menu, with steaks a speciality.

Old Bank

92-94 High St ✉ OX1 4BJ – ✆ (01865) 799 599 Town plan: BZ**s**
– www.oldbank-hotel.co.uk
42 rm – †£ 145/320 ††£ 145/320, ☕ £ 15 – 1 suite
Rest *Quod* – see restaurant listing

Warm, welcoming hotel in the heart of the city, with a smart neo-classical façade: once the area's first bank. Sleek, elegant bedrooms have modern furnishings and eclectic artwork; those higher up boast great views. Personable team.

Old Parsonage Ⓝ

1 Banbury Rd ✉ OX2 6NN – ✆ (01865) 310 210 Town plan: BY**p**
– www.oldparsonage-hotel.co.uk
35 rm – †£ 195 ††£ 195/375, ☕ £ 15
Rest – Menu £ 18 (lunch and early dinner) – Carte £ 25/44

This ivy-clad sandstone parsonage sits in the historic town centre and dates from the 1660s. Enter into the original house via a pretty terrace; inside it's chic and modern – bold greys and purples feature in the bedrooms, along with the latest mod cons. Appealing menus offer classic British comfort food.

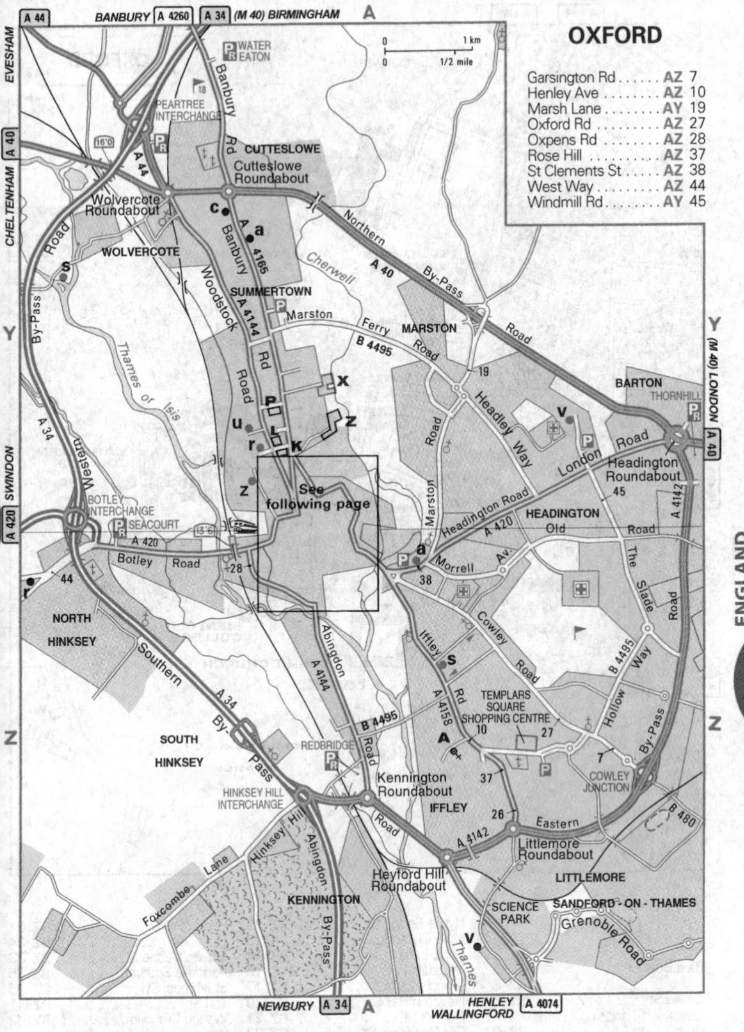

Remont without rest

367 Banbury Rd. ✉ OX2 7PL – ✆ (01865) 311 020 Town plan: AY**c**
– www.remont-oxford.co.uk – Closed 2 weeks Christmas

25 rm ☕ – 🛉£ 89/143 🛉🛉£ 89/143

Spacious, stylish hotel on the outskirts of the city. Immaculately kept, well-equipped, modern bedrooms have personality; the rear room is the quietest. The light, contemporary breakfast room overlooks the garden.

Burlington House without rest

374 Banbury Rd ✉ OX2 7PP – ✆ (01865) 513 513 Town plan: AY**a**
– www.burlington-house.co.uk – Closed 21 December-2 January

12 rm ☕ – 🛉£ 74/139 🛉🛉£ 98/159

Handsome former merchant's house dating from 1889. Smart lounge with guest info overlooks a Japanese courtyard garden. Individually styled, modern bedrooms feature vivid wallpaper. Homemade bread and fresh fruit and juices at breakfast.

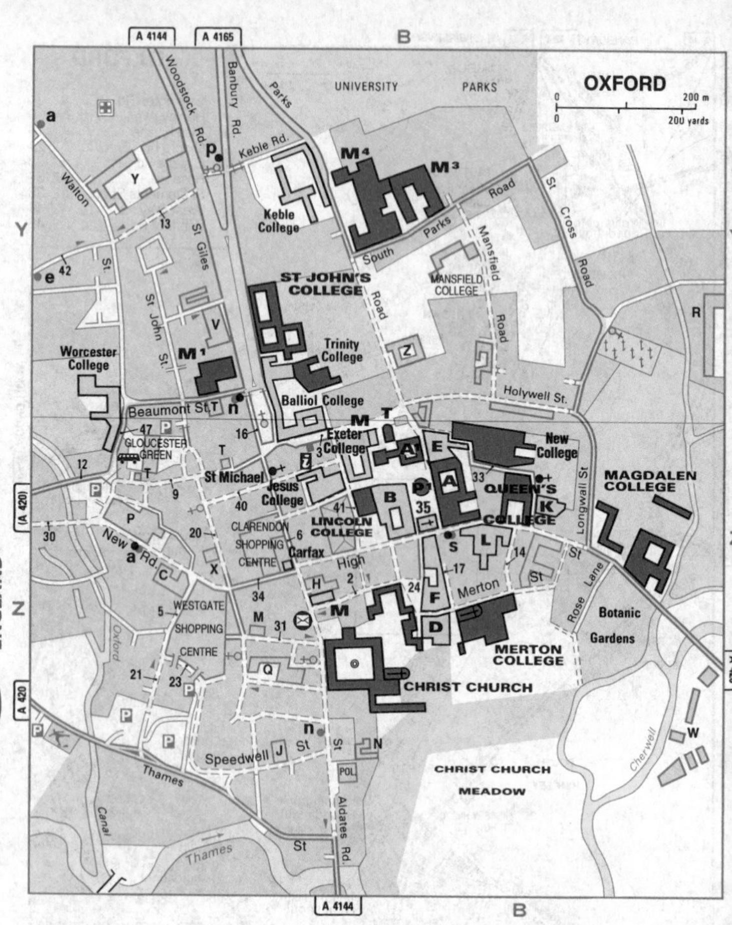

ENGLAND

OXFORD

Blue Boar St .... BY 2
Broad St .... BZ 3
Castle St .... BZ 5
Clarendon Shopping Centre BZ
Cornmarket St. .... BZ 6
George St .... BZ 9
High St. .... BZ
Hythe Bridge St .... BZ 12
Little Clarendon St .... BY 13
Logic Lane .... BZ 14
Magdalen St. .... BYZ 16
Magpie Lane .... BZ 17
New Inn Hall St. .... BZ 20
Norfolk St .... BZ 21
Old Greyfriars St .... BZ 23
Oriel Square .... BZ 24
Park End St .... BZ 30
Pembroke St. .... BZ 31
Queen St .... BZ 34
Queen's Lane .... BZ 33
Radcliffe Square .... BZ 35
St Michael St. .... BZ 40
Turl St. .... BZ 41
Walton Crescent. .... BY 42
Westgate Shopping Centre .... BZ
Worcester St. .... BZ 47

COLLEGES

All Souls .... BZ **A**
Balliol .... BY
Brasenose .... BZ **B**
Christ Church .... BZ
Corpus Christi .... BZ **D**
Exeter .... BZ
Hertford .... BZ **E**
Jesus .... BZ
Keble .... BY
Lady Margaret Hall .... AY **Z**
Linacre .... BZ **N**
Lincoln .... BZ
Magdalen .... BZ
Mansfield .... BY
Merton .... BZ
New .... BZ
Nuffield .... BZ **P**
Oriel .... BZ **F**
Pembroke .... BZ **Q**
Queen's .... BZ
St Anne's .... AY **K**
St Anthony's .... AY **L**
St Catherine's .... BY **R**
St Cross .... BY **V**
St Edmund Hall .... BZ **K**
St Hilda's .... BZ **W**
St Hugh's .... AY **P**
St John's .... BY
St Peter's .... BZ **X**
Sommerville .... BY **Y**
Trinity .... BY
University .... BZ **L**
Wadham .... BY **Z**
Wolfson .... AY **X**
Worcester .... BY

Restaurants

Randolph - Randolph Hotel
Beaumont St. ✉ OX1 2LN – ✆ (0844) 879 91 32 Town plan: BY**n**
– www.macdonaldhotels.co.uk – Closed Christmas
Menu £ 45 – Carte £ 35/50 – *(dinner only and lunch Saturday-Sunday)*
Set within an elegant Victorian hotel; an impressive, high-windowed, grand salon featuring University crests and exuding a formal feel. Classic menus offer dishes such as calves' liver or Dover sole, as well as some fine Scottish beef.

Shanghai 30's
82 St Aldates ✉ OX1 1RA – ✆ (01865) 242 230 Town plan: BZ**n**
– www.shanghai30s.com
Carte £ 15/34
Delightful, colonial-style restaurant in a characterful 15C building; the rooms are listed and feature wood panelling and ornate plaster ceilings. Menus offer a wide range of authentic Chinese dishes; don't miss the fiery Sichuan section.

Brasserie Blanc
71-72 Walton St. ✉ OX2 6AG – ✆ (01865) 510 999 Town plan: AY**z**
– www.brasserieblanc.com
Menu £ 17 (lunch) – Carte £ 20/39
A bustling brasserie with smartly laid tables; its walls filled with black and white photos of Raymond Blanc and his staff. French country cooking includes all the old favourites. Gluten free menu; children warmly welcomed.

Quod - Old Bank Hotel
92-94 High St ✉ OX1 4BJ – ✆ (01865) 799 599 Town plan: BZ**s**
– www.oldbank-hotel.co.uk
Menu £ 17 (weekday lunch) – Carte £ 21/40
Lively, Italian-influenced brasserie with a busy, buzzy vibe; set within a city centre hotel and once the banking hall of the area's very first bank. Accessible menu and twice-daily blackboard specials. Lovely decked terrace to the rear.

Branca
111 Walton St. ✉ OX2 6AJ – ✆ (01865) 556 111 Town plan: BY**a**
– www.branca.co.uk – Closed 24-25 December
Menu £ 13 (lunch and early dinner) – Carte £ 19/34
Bustling restaurant with a spacious, modern interior and French doors opening onto a courtyard terrace. The menu is a roll call of Italian classics; portions are generous and lunch deals, good value. Friendly young staff; adjoining deli.

Al Shami
25 Walton Cres ✉ OX1 2JG – ✆ (01865) 310 066 Town plan: BY**e**
– www.al-shami.co.uk
Carte £ 13/20
Smart, established neighbourhood restaurant serving well-priced, tasty Middle Eastern food. Beautiful, ornate ceiling in rear dining room. Lengthy menu offers wide range of authentic Lebanese dishes.

Fishers
36-37 St Clements ✉ OX4 1AB – ✆ (01865) 243 003 Town plan: AZ**a**
– www.fishers-restaurant.com – Closed 25-26 December and 1 January
Carte £ 22/41
Long-standing rustic seafood restaurant with a simple, nautical feel. There's something for everyone on the daily changing menu, from traditional fish and chips to roasted sea bass and tomatoes. Classic desserts; friendly service.

Magdalen Arms
243 Iffley Rd ✉ OX4 1SJ – ✆ (01865) 243 159 – Closed 24-26 December, 1 January, Monday lunch and bank holidays Town plan: AZ**s**
Carte £ 23/34
Buzzy pub that's a hit with the locals, boasting quirky standard lamps, eclectic 1920s posters, board games and a bar billiards table. Tasty, good value dishes change twice daily and are informed by the latest local, seasonal produce to arrive at the door. Try the delicious fresh juices and homemade lemonade.

Rickety Press

67 Cranham St ✉ *OX2 6DE – ☎ (01865) 424 581* Town plan: AY**r**
– www.thericketypress.com – Closed 25-27 December
Carte £ 17/38
Professionally run by three old school friends; a friendly, shabby-chic pub in a residential area, with a cosy bar, a conservatory and a large room filled with wooden pews. Monthly menus use vibrant, seasonal ingredients which provide plenty of flavour, such as Sandy Lane lamb and Cerne Abbas cheddar.

The Anchor

2 Hayfield Rd ✉ *OX2 6TT – ☎ (01865) 510 282* Town plan: AY**u**
– www.theanchoroxford.com
Carte £ 19/43
Not your typical pub, with subtle art deco styling and black and white dining room floor tiles. The main menu offers largely British classics with some Mediterranean influences as well as morning coffee and cakes and weekend brunches.

Black Boy

91 Old High St, Headington ✉ *OX3 9HT* Town plan: AY**v**
– ☎ (01865) 741 137 – www.theblackboy.uk.com – Closed 26 December and 1 January
Carte £ 21/42
Sizeable pub just off Headington village, serving sensibly priced pub classics with a French edge. Try the homemade breads, mix and match tapas dishes and the popular Sunday roasts. Tuesday is quiz night and Thursday is for jazz-lovers.

ENGLAND

at Sandford-on-Thames Southeast: 5 mi by A4158 ✉ Oxford

Oxford Thames Four Pillars

rm, rest,

Henley Rd ✉ *OX4 4GX – ☎ (01865) 334 444*
– www.four-pillars.co.uk/thames Town plan: AZ**v**
84 rm – †£ 99/250 ††£ 120/300
Rest *River Room* – Menu £ 20 – Carte £ 26/38
Extended sandstone cottages and a tithe barn set in 30 acres of peaceful parkland leading to the Thames. The bright College Hall bedrooms are the best; some have garden views and balconies. Great outlook over the river and gardens from the formal restaurant, which serves traditional dishes with a modern edge.

at Toot Baldon Southeast: 5.5 mi by B480 -(AZ) ✉ Oxford

Mole Inn

✉ *OX44 9NG – ☎ (01865) 340 001 – www.themoleinn.com – Closed 25 December*
Menu £ 20 – Carte £ 28/34 – *(booking advisable)*
Popular pub with a pleasant terrace, beautiful gardens and a warm, welcoming atmosphere. The appealing menu caters for all tastes and appetites; sourcing is taken seriously and dishes disappear from the menu as ingredients are used up.

at Great Milton Southeast: 12 mi by A40 off A329 -(AY) ✉ Oxford

Belmond Le Manoir aux Quat' Saisons

Church Rd ✉ *OX44 7PD – ☎ (01844) 278 881 – www.manoir.com*
32 rm – †£ 555/675 ††£ 555/675 – 16 suites – ††£ 855/1790
Rest *Belmond Le Manoir aux Quat' Saisons* ✿✿ – see restaurant listing
Majestic, part-15C country house offering the ultimate in guest services. Bedrooms are extremely comfortable – those in the Garden Wing are the most luxurious and have subtle themes. Relax by an open fire in the sumptuous sitting rooms or out on the delightful terrace overlooking the pristine gardens.

Belmond Le Manoir aux Quat' Saisons (Raymond Blanc)
Church Rd ✉ OX44 7PD – ✆ (01844) 278 881 – www.manoir.com
Menu £ 79/134 – Carte £ 116/124 – *(booking essential)*
Elegant beamed restaurant in a truly luxurious hotel; head for the large conservatory overlooking the lovely gardens. French-inspired cooking uses seasonal garden produce and dishes are prepared with skill, clarity and a lightness of touch. Choose from the monthly à la carte or one of two superb tasting menus.
→ Confit of salmon, cucumber, mouli and horseradish. Sea bass with langoustine, smoky mash and star anise. Exotic fruit raviole, kaffir lime and coconut jus.

at Kingston Bagpuize Southwest: 11.5 mi by A420(AZ) ✉ Oxford

Fallowfields
Faringdon Rd. ✉ OX13 5BH – ✆ (01865) 820 416 – www.fallowfields.com
10 rm – †£ 110/125 ††£ 125/190
Rest *Fallowfields* – see restaurant listing
18C manor house in 12 acres of gardens and parkland; they keep an array of animals, from chickens and ducks to pigs and cows. Spacious bedrooms come in a mix of traditional and more modern styles; the rear rooms have the best views.

Fallowfields – Fallowfields Hotel
Faringdon Rd. ✉ OX13 5BH – ✆ (01865) 820 416 – www.fallowfields.com
Menu £ 30/69 – Carte £ 50/66 – *(bookings advisable at dinner)*
Light, airy restaurant in an 18C manor house, overlooking the croquet lawn and paddocks. Elaborate modern cooking showcases produce from their garden, orchard and livestock. Every dish on the menu has a suggested wine pairing.

at Fyfield Southwest: 9.5 mi by A420(AZ) ✉ Abingdon

White Hart
Main Rd ✉ OX13 5LW – ✆ (01865) 390 585 – www.whitehart-fyfield.com – Closed Monday except bank holidays
Menu £ 20 (weekday lunch) – Carte £ 28/41
Intriguing 15C former chantry house with a cosy open-fired bar, an impressive flag-floored, vaulted dining room, and a pleasant terrace; along with a minstrels' gallery and a secret tunnel. The diverse range of dishes relies on produce from the vegetable plot; save room for one of the excellent desserts.

OXHILL

Warwickshire – Pop. 303 – See Regional map n°19-C3
London 90 mi – Banbury 11 mi – Birmingham 37 mi
Michelin Road map 503-P27 and 504

Oxbourne House without rest
✉ CV35 0RA – ✆ (01295) 688 202 – www.oxbournehouse.com
3 rm – †£ 50/75 ††£ 80/95
Large brick house in a quiet village, with a lovely mature garden and a tennis court. Elegant, antique-furnished lounge features a wood burning stove. Comfy, immaculately kept bedrooms offer good facilities and extras; one is split-level.

PADSTOW

Cornwall – Pop. 2 449 – See Regional map n°1-B2
London 288 mi – Exeter 78 mi – Plymouth 45 mi – Truro 23 mi
Michelin Road map 503-F32 – Michelin Green Guide GREAT BRITAIN

Metropole
Station Rd ✉ PL28 8DB – ✆ (01841) 532 486 – www.the-metropole.co.uk Town plan: BY**a**
58 rm – †£ 69/160 ††£ 69/279
Rest – Menu £ 33 – *(bar lunch Monday-Saturday)*
Grand 19C hotel perched on a cliff above the old railway station, just a short walk from town. Characterful, well-appointed guest areas. Bedrooms are a mix of traditional and contemporary styles; No.6 boasts great harbour and estuary views. Simply prepared lunches; more elaborate dinners.

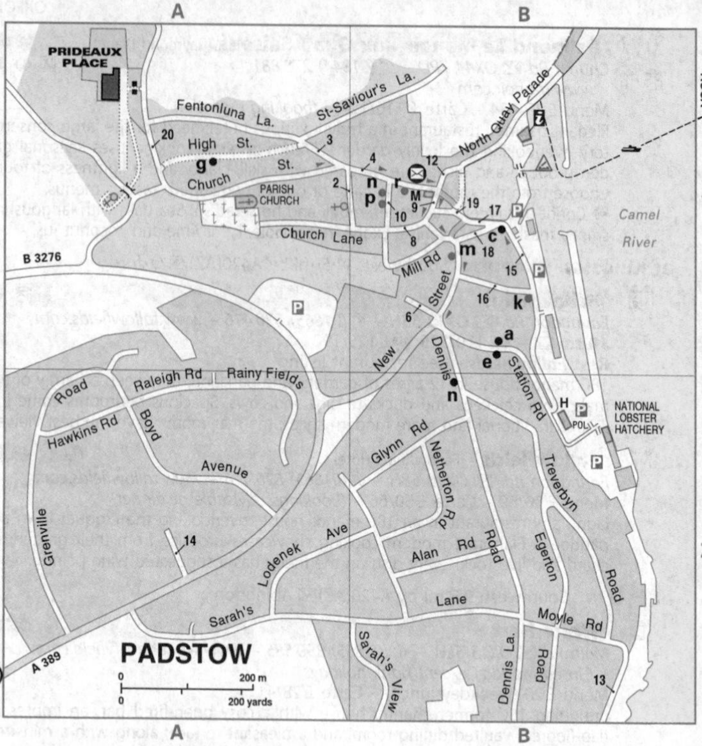

ENGLAND

PADSTOW

Barry's Lane	ABY 2	Middle St	BY 10	St Edmund's Lane	BY 16
Cross St	AY 3	Mill Square	BY 12	South Quay	BY 17
Duke St	BY 4	Porthilly View	BZ 13	Strand St	BY 18
Hill St	BY 6	Raleigh Close	AZ 14	The Strand	BY 19
Lanadwell St	BY 8	Riverside	BY 15	Tregirls Lane	AY 20
Market Pl	BY 9				

Old Custom House Inn rest,

South Quay ✉ PL28 8BL – ✆ (01841) 532 359 Town plan: BY**c**
– www.oldcustomhousepadstow.co.uk
21 rm – £ 140/195 £ 140/195
Rest *Pescadou* – Carte £ 27/42 **s** – *(booking essential)*

Well-run, slate hotel; formerly a grain store and an exciseman's house. Relax in the beauty studio or the ice cream parlour. Nautically themed bedrooms feature good mod cons – some have roll-top baths or harbour/estuary views. Traditional bar and open-plan seafood restaurant; watch the chefs at work.

Treverbyn House without rest

Station Rd ✉ PL28 8DA – ✆ (01841) 532 855 Town plan: BY**e**
– www.treverbynhouse.com – Closed 25 December-13 February
3 rm – £ 90/100 £ 95/125

Charming Edwardian house built for a wine merchant and run by a delightful owner. Comfy bedrooms feature interesting furniture from local sale rooms; one has a huge roll-top bath and all have harbour views – the Turret Room is the best. Have breakfast in your bedroom, the dining room or the garden.

Treann House without rest
24 Dennis Rd ✉ PL28 8DE – ✆ (01841) 533 855 Town plan: BZ**n**
– www.treannhouse.com – Closed January-March
3 rm ☕ – 🚹£ 95/120 🚹🚹£ 105/130
Edwardian house set in an elevated position, with first floor views over the Camel Estuary. Chic breakfast room, cool lounge and superb bedrooms which mix antiques with contemporary furnishings to create an understated, elegant style.

Woodlands Country House without rest
Treator ✉ PL28 8RU – West : 1.25 mi on B 3276 – ✆ (01841) 532 426
– www.woodlands-padstow.co.uk – Closed 20 December-1 February
8 rm ☕ – 🚹£ 74/97 🚹🚹£ 102/145
Characterful Victorian house with a great coastal outlook to the rear. Tastefully furnished lounge, breakfast room and honesty bar; pictures, books and objets d'art abound. Comfy, homely bedrooms; 'Beach' is the largest and the best. The homemade muesli and hot specials are a feature at breakfast.

Althea Library without rest
27 High St ✉ PL28 8BB – (access via 64 Church St.) Town plan: AY**g**
– ✆ (01841) 532 717 – www.althealibrary.co.uk – Closed 30 April-1 May and 22-26 December
3 rm ☕ – 🚹£ 76/80 🚹🚹£ 96/120
Grade II listed former Sunday school and library, just 5min from the harbour. Homely lounge and breakfast room; pine-furnished bedrooms. In summer, the aga-cooked breakfasts are served on the terrace, next to the pond and water feature.

Seafood with rm
AC rest,
Riverside ✉ PL28 8BY – ✆ (01841) 532 700 Town plan: BY**k**
– www.rickstein.com – Closed 24-26 December
16 rm ☕ – 🚹£ 150/285 🚹🚹£ 150/285
Menu £ 39 (lunch) – Carte £ 41/89 – *(booking essential)*
Stylish, laid-back, local institution – dominated by a large stainless steel topped bar. Daily menus showcase fresh fish and shellfish. Classic dishes sit alongside those influenced by Rick Stein's travels; perhaps Singapore chilli crab or Madras fish curry. New England style bedrooms boast good quality furnishings; some have terraces or balconies and estuary views.

Paul Ainsworth at No.6
6 Middle St ✉ PL28 8AP – ✆ (01841) 532 093 Town plan: BY**n**
– www.number6inpadstow.co.uk – Closed 13 January-4 February, 24-26 December, 1 May, Sunday and Monday
Menu £ 25 (lunch) – Carte £ 46/57
Delightful Georgian townhouse on a harbour backwater, with a relaxed air and friendly, enthusiastic service. Modern seasonal cooking displays originality and textures and flavours are refined; try the 'Trip to the Fairground' for dessert. The intimate ground floor is buzzier than the refined upstairs room.
→ Mackerel with celeriac remoulade, Parma ham and cucumber. Short ribs with onions, red chicory and horseradish. Bread and butter pudding, vanilla ice cream.

St Petroc's with rm
rm,
4 New St ✉ PL28 8EA – ✆ (01841) 532 700 Town plan: BY**m**
– www.rickstein.com – Closed 24-26 December
14 rm ☕ – 🚹£ 160/270 🚹🚹£ 160/270
Menu £ 22 (lunch) – Carte £ 30/46 – *(booking essential)*
Attractive house on a steep hill, with an oak-furnished bistro and a front and rear terrace. The menu offers a mix of simply prepared seafood, grills and old-fashioned classics. Smart, well-appointed bedrooms are split between the house and an annexe; relax in the small lounge or peaceful library.

ENGLAND

Rick Stein's Café with rm

10 Middle St ✉ *PL28 8AP* – *(01841) 532 700* Town plan: BY**p**
– *www.rickstein.com* – *Closed 24-26 December and 1 May*
3 rm – £ 110/150 £ 110/150
Menu £ 24 – Carte £ 25/33 – *(booking essential at dinner)*
Deceptively large café hidden behind a tiny shop front on a side street. Concise, seasonally changing menu of tasty, unfussy cooking with influences from Thailand, Morocco and the Med. Homemade bread and great value set menus. Comfy, simply furnished bedrooms; breakfast in the café or small courtyard garden.

Margot's

11 Duke St ✉ *PL28 8AB* – *(01841) 533 441* Town plan: BY**r**
– *www.margotsbistro.co.uk* – *Closed January, 24-31 December, Sunday and Monday*
Carte £ 26/37 – *(dinner only and lunch May-September) (booking essential)*
Small yellow and blue bistro with a relaxed atmosphere and a loyal local following. Daily menus feature the latest seasonal produce in classical bistro-style dishes; cooking is rustic and flavoursome. Dinner also offers a tasting menu.

at St Merryn West: 2.5 mi by A389 on B3276|✉ Padstow

Cornish Arms

Churchtown ✉ *PL28 8ND* – *(01841) 532 700* – *www.rickstein.com*
Carte £ 20/32 – *(bookings not accepted)*
Popular with locals – one of them was Rick Stein, who liked it so much, he now leases it! Nicely priced menu of pub classics, with seafood specials, Sunday roasts and nursery puddings. Cosy, beamed bar; light, airy dining room.

ENGLAND

at Constantine Bay West: 4 mi by B3276✉ Padstow

Treglos

rm, rest,

✉ *PL28 8JH* – *(01841) 520 727* – *www.tregloshotel.com*
– *Closed Christmas-February*
42 rm – £ 72/110 £ 144/220 – 4 suites
Rest – Menu £ 34 – *(bar lunch Monday-Saturday)*
Long-standing, family-owned hotel, with tiered lawns leading down to the beach. Guest areas are spacious and well-kept and there's a lovely pool and spa. Classically styled bedrooms exhibit modern touches and many have balconies and sea views. Dress smartly for dinner in the traditional, formal restaurant.

at Little Petherick South: 3 mi on A389✉ Wadebridge

Molesworth Manor without rest

✉ *PL27 7QT* – *(01841) 540 292* – *www.molesworthmanor.co.uk*
– *February-October*
9 rm – £ 80/90 £ 118/128
Part 16C and 17C former rectory set in mature gardens and run by affable owners. Elegant drawing room with honesty bar; spacious bedrooms boast period features, roll top baths and large walk in showers. Homemade preserves at breakfast.

PAINSWICK

Gloucestershire – Pop. 1 762 – See Regional map n°**4**-**C1**
London 107 mi – Bristol 35 mi – Cheltenham 10 mi
Michelin Road map 503-N28 and 504 – Michelin Green Guide GREAT BRITAIN

Cotswolds 88

Kemps Ln ✉ *GL6 6YB* – *(01452) 813 688* – *www.cotswolds88hotel.com*
– *Closed 2-16 January*
17 rm – £ 99/375 £ 110/395
Rest *Juniper* – see restaurant listing
Regency-style stone house with attractive gardens, in a delightful village. The interior couldn't be more of a contrast, with vivid colour schemes, vibrant furnishings and striking objets d'art. Each room is uniquely designed.

XX **Juniper** - Cotswolds 88 Hotel

Kemps Ln ✉ GL6 6YB – ☎ (01452) 813 688 – www.cotswolds88hotel.com – Closed 2-16 January

Menu £ 13 (weekday lunch)/50

Striking restaurant in a fine Regency hotel – its bold décor includes black and white carpets, electric-red wallpaper, faux snakeskin tables and vibrant red leather chairs. Creative, seasonal cooking showcases modern techniques.

PATELEY BRIDGE

North Yorkshire – Pop. 1 432 – ✉ Harrogate – See Regional map n°**22**-B2

London 225 mi – Leeds 28 mi – Middlesbrough 46 mi – York 32 mi

Michelin Road map 502-O21 – Michelin Green Guide GREAT BRITAIN

XXX ✿ **Yorke Arms** (Frances Atkins) with rm

rm, P

Ramsgill-in-Nidderdale ✉ HG3 5RL – Northwest : 5 mi by Low Wath Rd – ☎ (01423) 755 243 – www.yorke-arms.co.uk

16 rm – †£ 250 ††£ 345/430 – 4 suites

Menu £ 40 (weekday lunch)/85 – Carte £ 47/70 – *(closed Sunday dinner to non-residents)*

Charming, part-17C former shooting lodge overlooking the village green and run in a friendly, professional manner. Traditional, antique-furnished restaurant with a beamed ceiling and open fires. Measured and accomplished classical cooking demonstrates a good understanding of flavours; presentation is contemporary. Bedrooms have a subtle modern style and good comforts.

→ Scallops with cured wild salmon and pea purée. Chargrilled calves' liver, slow-cooked pork collar and red orange. Lychee soufflé, jasmine tea sorbet and almond pastry.

PATRICK BROMPTON

North Yorkshire ✉ Bedale – See Regional map n°**22**-B1

London 242 mi – Newcastle upon Tyne 58 mi – York 43 mi

Michelin Road map 502-P21

Elmfield House without rest

P

Arrathorne ✉ DL8 1NE – Northwest : 2.25 mi by A 684 on Richmond rd – ☎ (01677) 450 558 – www.elmfieldhouse.co.uk

4 rm – †£ 70/75 ††£ 82/89

Spacious guesthouse in a peaceful farmland setting, complete with livery stables, a fishing lake and a 14 acre forest. Bedrooms are warm and welcoming – two have four-poster beds. Relax in the vast conservatory or cottagey lounge.

Mill Close Farm without rest

P

✉ DL8 1JY Northeast : 1.25 mi by Hackforth rd. – ☎ (01677) 450 257 – www.millclose.co.uk – Closed January and December

3 rm – †£ 55/60 ††£ 85/100

Modernised farmhouse with a walled garden and a summerhouse. Bedrooms blend contemporary furnishings with traditional features and have an uncluttered, homely feel; two boast whirlpool baths.

PATTISWICK → See Coggeshall

Essex

PEMBRIDGE

Herefordshire – Pop. 489 – See Regional map n°**18**-A3

London 162 mi – Hereford 15 mi – Leominster 7 mi

Michelin Road map 503-L27

Old Rectory N without rest

P

Bridge St ✉ HR6 9EU – ☎ (01544) 387 968 – www.theoldrectorypembridge.co.uk

3 rm – †£ 80/110 ††£ 100/130

This meticulously restored Victorian rectory sits by the river, on the edge of a black & white timbered village. It's tastefully and luxuriously furnished, in a period style, and features fine furniture, antiques and rich fabrics.

PENN

Buckinghamshire – Pop. 3 779 – See Regional map n°**11-D2**
London 31 mi – High Wycombe 4 mi – Oxford 36 mi
Michelin Road map 504-R/S29

Old Queens Head

Hammersley Ln ✉ HP10 8EY – ☎ (01494) 813 371
– www.oldqueensheadpenn.co.uk – Closed 25-26 December
Carte £ 21/37
Smart country pub purchased in 1666 by one of the King's physicians; find a spot on the paved terrace or take in the view from the dining room. Big, hearty dishes are the order of the day; come on a Saturday for a laid-back brunch.

PENRITH

Cumbria – Pop. 15 181 – See Regional map n°**21-B2**
London 290 mi – Carlisle 24 mi – Kendal 31 mi – Lancaster 48 mi
Michelin Road map 501-L19 and 502

Brooklands without rest

2 Portland Pl ✉ CA11 7QN – ☎ (01768) 863 395
– www.brooklandsguesthouse.com – Closed Christmas and New Year
6 rm – †£ 40/70 ††£ 80/90
Victorian terraced house located close to the town centre, run by warm, welcoming owners. Traditional, antique-furnished hall and smart breakfast room with marble-topped tables. Homely, pine-furnished bedrooms boast good modern facilities; one has a four-poster.

ENGLAND

at Temple Sowerby East: 6.75 mi by A66 ✉ Penrith

Temple Sowerby House

✉ CA10 1RZ – ☎ (01768) 361 578 – www.templesowerby.com
– Closed Christmas
12 rm – †£ 99/110 ††£ 140/170
Rest – Menu £ 43 – *(dinner only) (booking essential)*
Attractive, red-brick Georgian mansion with spacious, classically styled guest areas. Traditional country house bedrooms boast antique furnishings and contemporary facilities. Enthusiastic owners. Ambitious, modern menus of local, seasonal produce served overlooking enclosed, lawned gardens.

at Clifton Southeast: 3 mi on A6

George and Dragon with rm

✉ CA10 2ER – ☎ (01768) 865 381 – www.georgeanddragonclifton.co.uk
– Closed 26 December
11 rm – †£ 79/119 ††£ 95/155 Menu £ 13/40 – Carte £ 26/38
Whitewashed coaching inn with a characterful 18C bar and modern, brasserie-style restaurant. Appealing dishes feature vegetables from the garden, game from the moors and organic meats from the Lowther Estate farms. Modern bedrooms showcase furniture and paintings from the family's collection.

at Askham South: 6 mi by A6

Askham Hall

✉ CA10 2PF – ☎ (01931) 712 350 – www.askhamhall.co.uk
– Closed Christmas-mid February
13 rm – †£ 138/308 ††£ 150/320
Rest *Garden Room Conservatory* – Menu £ 45 – *(dinner only)*
A fine, family-run castle on the edge of the Lowther Estate, dating from the 1300s and now stylishly and sympathetically refurbished. Spacious rooms are packed with period family furnishings. A 3 course menu reflects the seasons and features meat from the farm and vegetables from the superb kitchen garden.

at Newbiggin West: 3.5 mi by A66 ✉ Penrith

Old School

✉ CA11 0HT – ✆ (01768) 483 709 – www.theold-school.com – Closed 21 December-1 January

3 rm – †£ 40/55 ††£ 80/90 **Rest** – Menu £ 12/20

Grey-stone Victorian schoolhouse in a small village. Compact, traditionally styled guest areas. Classical bedrooms are named after the colour of their décor – red, green and blue – the latter is the largest and has the best outlook. Home-cooked meals eaten at a communal oak table.

PENSHURST

Kent – Pop. 708 – See Regional map n°**8-B2**

London 40 mi – Royal Tunbridge Wells 7 mi – Maidstone 22 mi

Michelin Road map 504-U30

Leicester Arms with rm

✉ TN11 8BT – ✆ (01892) 871 617 – www.theleicesterarmshotel.com

13 rm – †£ 99/119 ††£ 119/169 Carte £ 20/39

Sympathetically refurbished 16C former coaching inn offering evolving menu of rustic and satisfying pub classics. Sit in the garden room: a large bright space with a lovely rural view. Bedrooms are furnished in a contemporary style: ask for Room 8, which is the biggest, with the best outlook.

PENZANCE

Cornwall – Pop. 16 336 – See Regional map n°**1-A3**

London 319 mi – Exeter 113 mi – Plymouth 77 mi – Taunton 155 mi

Michelin Road map 503-D33 – Michelin Green Guide GREAT BRITAIN

Hotel Penzance without rest

Britons Hill ✉ TR18 3AE – ✆ (01736) 363 117 – www.hotelpenzance.com – Closed 2-12 January Town plan: Y**c**

25 rm – †£ 89/160 ††£ 150/205

Two adjoining Edwardian merchants' houses in a residential street, overlooking the bay. Relax in a period lounge or out on the terrace beside the pool. Bedrooms range from classic to modern in their styling and are well-equipped.

Abbey without rest

Abbey St ✉ TR18 4AR – ✆ (01736) 366 906 – www.theabbeyonline.co.uk – Closed 4 January-15 March and 20-28 December Town plan: Y**u**

8 rm – †£ 90/150 ††£ 130/200

17C townhouse in powder blue, with tranquil walled gardens and distant harbour views. It has a relaxed, slightly quirky atmosphere, plenty of shabby-chic charm, a lovely antique-filled sitting room and bright, well-kept bedrooms.

Chy-An-Mor without rest

15 Regent Terr ✉ TR18 4DW – ✆ (01736) 363 441 – www.chyanmor.co.uk – March-November Town plan: Y**e**

9 rm – †£ 41/46 ††£ 72/95

This fine Georgian townhouse overlooks the promenade; fittingly, its name means 'House of the Sea'. Bedrooms have lovely soft furnishings – two have 6ft cast iron beds. In the evening, twinkling garden lights welcome you home and at breakfast they offer homemade muffins, Scotch pancakes and granola sundaes.

Summer House

Cornwall Terr ✉ TR18 4HL – ✆ (01736) 363 744 – www.summerhouse-cornwall.com – Closed 3 October-24 March Town plan: Z**s**

5 rm – †£ 90/150 ††£ 120/150 **Rest** – Menu £ 30

Bright blue Regency townhouse with a Mediterranean-style terraced garden. Spacious yellow lounge has a light, airy feel. Contemporary bedrooms: many with a nautical theme; one with a small seating area. Pleasant dining room with a trompe l'oeil; light suppers during the week, more formal menu at the weekend.

ENGLAND

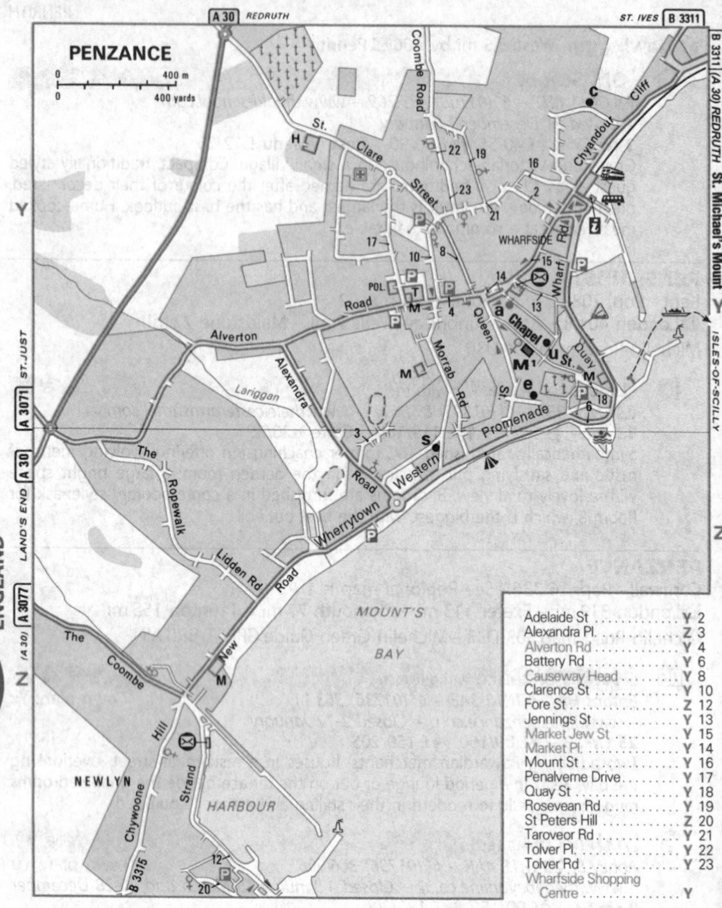

XX **Harris's**

46 New St ✉ *TR18 2LZ – ✆ (01736) 364 408* Town plan: Y**a**
– www.harrissrestaurant.co.uk – Closed 3 weeks winter, 25-26 December, Sunday and Monday except Monday dinner June-September
Carte £ 27/47

Long-standing, split-level restaurant with a spiral staircase and an unusual Welsh black metal plate ceiling; run by a keen husband and wife. Classical cooking uses seasonal Cornish produce; try the steamed lobster when it's in season.

at Gulval Northeast: 1.25 mi by A30

Coldstreamer with rm

✉ *TR18 3BB – ✆ (01736) 362 072 – www.coldstreamer-penzance.co.uk – Closed 25-26 December*
3 rm – †£ 65/75 ††£ 75/85 Carte £ 21/32

Dating from 1895, this striking pub sits opposite the church in the heart of Gulval. Its large bar is adorned with Coldstream Guards memorabilia; it has a bright dining room and fresh, well-appointed bedrooms. Concise menus feature local, seasonal produce in unfussy, traditional dishes. Good value lunches.

PERRANUTHNOE → See Marazion

PERRANUTHNOE → See Marazion

Cornwall – Michelin Road map 503-D33

PERSHORE

Worcestershire – Pop. 7 125 – See Regional map n°**19-C3**
London 106 mi – Birmingham 33 mi – Worcester 8 mi
Michelin Road map 503-N27 and 504

Barn without rest

Pensham Hill House, Pensham ✉ WR10 3HA – Southeast : 1 mi by B 4084 – ☎ (01386) 555 270 – www.pensham-barn.co.uk
3 rm – £ 55/60 £ 90/95
A hugely characterful series of outbuildings in a hillside location, run by a charming owner. There's a homely beamed lounge and three warmly decorated, well-equipped bedrooms: two share the lovely view and the third has a sauna. Communal breakfasts feature apple juice from the fruit trees in the garden.

Belle House

Bridge St ✉ WR10 1AJ – ☎ (01386) 555 055 – www.belle-house.co.uk – Closed first 2 weeks January, 25 December, Sunday and Monday
Menu £ 24/32 **s**
A pleasantly restored Georgian house in the centre of town, offering classically based cooking with modern touches; be sure to try the homemade bread. The well-stocked 'traiteur' selling freshly prepared takeaway dishes is a hit.

at Eckington Southwest: 4 mi by A4104 on B4080

Eckington Manor

rest,

Manor Farm, Hammock Rd ✉ WR10 3BH – (via Drakes Bridge Rd) – ☎ (01386) 751 600 – www.eckingtonmanor.co.uk
16 rm – £ 75/125 £ 85/195
Rest – Menu £ 18 (weekday lunch) – Carte £ 22/44 – *(closed Sunday and Monday)*
A series of characterful, converted barns and a 13C manor house, set on a 300 acre farm. The charming owner runs it with pride and welcomes guests with homemade cake. Bedrooms are stylish; some have a freestanding bath in the room and all have eye-catching bathrooms with underfloor heating. The restaurant offers country views and unfussy dishes of local ingredients.

PETERBOROUGH

Peterborough – Pop. 161 707 – See Regional map n°**14-A2**
London 85 mi – Cambridge 35 mi – Leicester 41 mi – Lincoln 51 mi
Michelin Road map 502-T26 and 504 – Michelin Green Guide GREAT BRITAIN

Clarkes

10 Queen St ✉ PE1 1PA – ☎ (01733) 892 681 – www.clarkespeterborough.co.uk – Closed first week January, Monday and dinner 25-26 December and Sunday Town plan: Y**x**
Menu £ 15 (weekday lunch)/40
Contemporary restaurant on a paved square in the heart of the city. It's a spacious, formally run place; enjoy a drink in the smart bar or, in summer, make for the pleasant private courtyard. Cooking complex, modern and seasonal.

Beehive

62 Albert Pl ✉ PE1 1DD – ☎ (01733) 310 600 – www.beehivepub.co.uk – Closed 1 January and Sunday dinner Town plan: Z**x**
Carte £ 21/40
Set just off the city centre ring road, with a smart modern interior, a zinc-topped bar and a mix of high stools, armchairs and banquettes. Dishes are well-presented, flavoursome and satisfying; the house pâté with chutney is a must-try.

ENGLAND

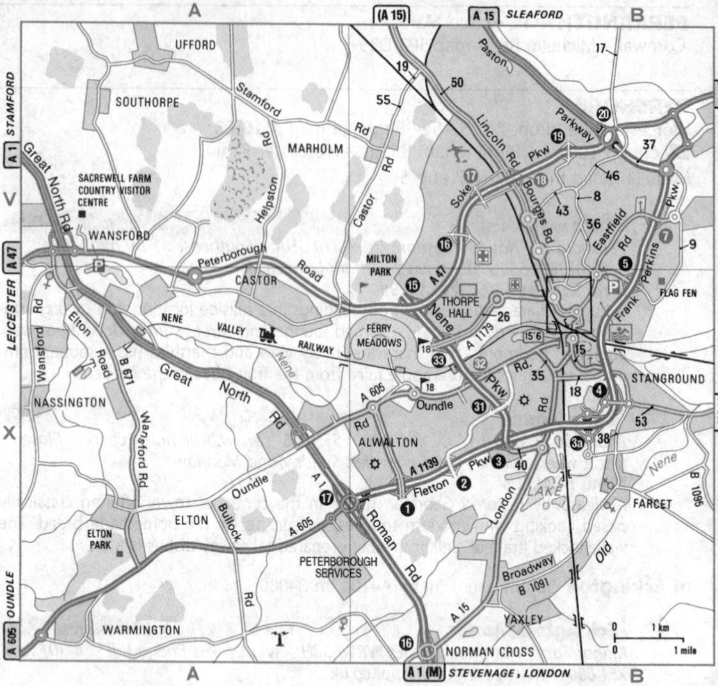

PETERBOROUGH

- Bridge St. . . . . Z
- Cattle Market Rd . . . . Y 2
- Church St . . . . YZ
- City Rd . . . . Y 3
- Cowgate . . . . Y 5
- Cross St. . . . . Z 6
- Dogsthorpe Rd . . . . BV 8
- Edgerley Drain Rd . . . . BV 9
- Embankment Rd . . . . Z 12
- Exchange St . . . . Y 13
- Fletton Ave . . . . BX 15
- Geneva St . . . . Y 16
- Guntons Rd . . . . BV 17
- High St . . . . BX 18
- Hurn Rd . . . . BV 19
- Longthorpe Parkway . . . . . . BX 26
- Long Causeway . . . . Y 25
- Market Way . . . . Y 28
- Midgate . . . . Y 29
- New Rd . . . . BX 35
- Park Rd . . . . BV 36
- Paston Parkway . . . . BV 37
- Peterborough Rd . . . . BX 38
- Phorpres Way . . . . BX 40
- Queensgate Shopping Centre . . . . Y
- Rivergate . . . . Z 42
- Rivergate Shopping Centre . . . . Z
- St Paul's Rd . . . . BV 43
- Thorpe Rd . . . . Y 45
- Welland Rd . . . . BV 46
- Wentworth St. . . . . Z 48
- Werrington Parkway . . . . . . BV 50
- Wheelyard . . . . Y 52
- Whittlesey Rd . . . . BX 53
- Woodcroft Rd . . . . BV 55

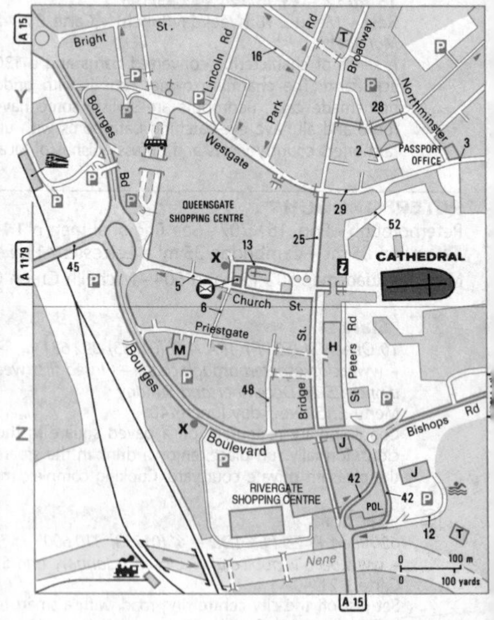

at Glinton North: 5 mi off A15

Blue Bell

10 High St ✉ PE6 7LS – ✆ (01733) 252 285 – www.thebluebellglinton.co.uk – Closed Sunday dinner
Carte £ 22/40
Welcoming 18C pub in a pretty village. A colourful flower display greets you at the front and there's a pleasant terrace hidden at the back. Lunch offers pub favourites and dinner has a more modern edge; be sure to save room for dessert.

PETERSFIELD

Hampshire – Pop. 14 974 – See Regional map n°**7**-C2
London 60 mi – Brighton 45 mi – Portsmouth 21 mi – Southampton 34 mi
Michelin Road map 504-R30

Langrish House

Langrish ✉ GU32 1RN – West : 3.5 mi by A 272 – ✆ (01730) 266 941 – www.langrishhouse.co.uk – Closed 27 December-12 January
13 rm – £ 98/108 £ 119/188
Rest – Menu £ 24 (lunch) – Carte £ 31/48
Mid-17C house surrounded by 15 acres of lovely gardens and grounds, and run by charming owners. Spacious country house lounges include one in the old Civil War cellars. Traditional bedrooms are individually themed and have good modern facilities. The tiny formal dining room offers contemporary cuisine.

JSW (Jake Watkins) with rm

rest,

20 Dragon St ✉ GU31 4JJ – ✆ (01730) 262 030 – www.jswrestaurant.com – Closed 2 weeks January, 2 weeks May and 2 weeks August
4 rm – £ 90/115 £ 105/130
Menu £ 23 (weekday lunch)/50 **s** – *(closed Sunday dinner to Tuesday)*
17C former coaching inn, in a pleasant town. The spacious beamed restaurant leads through to a wood-furnished terrace. Technically accomplished cooking is refined, flavoursome and relies on top quality ingredients: choose from an array of menus. Bedrooms are modern and have good facilities.
→ Scallops with cauliflower cheese and ceps. Texture of lamb with vinaigrette of summer vegetables. Vanilla cheesecake, ginger beer jelly and rhubarb.

Annie Jones

10 Lavant St ✉ GU32 3EW – ✆ (01730) 262 728 – www.anniejones.co.uk – Closed 25-26 and 31 December and Monday
Menu £ 18 (lunch and early dinner)/35 **s**
Relaxed neighbourhood restaurant on a busy street. Start with a drink on the terrace then make for the tapas bar to sample authentic, tasty small plates. The adjoining bistro has a bohemian feel and serves Mediterranean cuisine.

PETWORTH

West Sussex – Pop. 2 544 – See Regional map n°**7**-C2
London 54 mi – Brighton 31 mi – Portsmouth 33 mi
Michelin Road map 504-S31 – Michelin Green Guide GREAT BRITAIN

Old Railway Station without rest

✉ GU28 0JF South : 1.5 mi by A 285 – ✆ (01798) 342 346 – www.old-station.co.uk – Closed 23-26 December
10 rm – £ 58/150 £ 78/230
The perfect place for train enthusiasts: 8 of the 10 bedrooms are sited in genuine Pullman carriages; wonderfully restored, with impressive marquetry and sited at what was the platform of the station house. Check in at the ticket booth.

Leconfield

New St ✉ GU28 0AS – ✆ (01798) 345 111 – www.theleconfield.co.uk – Closed Sunday dinner and Monday
Menu £ 29 (weekdays) – Carte £ 39/53
Attractive, red-brick 19C building; inside it resembles a stylish brasserie – tastefully furnished, with a formal restaurant, a timbered first floor dining room and a cobbled courtyard terrace. Concise menu of refined, classic dishes.

ENGLAND

at Tillington West: 1 mi on A272

Horse Guards Inn with rm
Upperton Rd ✉ GU28 9AF – ✆ (01798) 342 332 – www.thehorseguardsinn.co.uk – Closed 25 December
3 rm – †£ 85/120 ††£ 95/140 Carte £ 21/37
In an elevated spot in the heart of a quiet village sits this pretty mid-17C inn; which is as charming on the inside as it is out. Local seafood stands out and some of the vegetables come from their own patch. Young, friendly service. Simple, rustic bedrooms, with a family room in the cottage next door.

at Halfway Bridge West: 3 mi on A272✉ Petworth

Halfway Bridge with rm
✉ GU28 9BP – ✆ (01798) 861 281 – www.halfwaybridge.co.uk
7 rm – †£ 85 ††£ 140/230 Carte £ 26/53
Charming 17C brick and flint pub; the open-fired bar is a great place to sit. Dishes are classically based but presented in a modern style – influences could come from Morocco, France or Italy, and puddings are nursery-style with a twist. The country-chic bedrooms are in the nearby converted stables.

PICKERING

North Yorkshire – Pop. 6 588 – See Regional map n°**23**-**C1**
London 237 mi – Middlesbrough 43 mi – Scarborough 19 mi – York 25 mi
Michelin Road map 502-R21

ENGLAND

White Swan Inn
Market Pl ✉ YO18 7AA – ✆ (01751) 472 288 – www.white-swan.co.uk
21 rm – †£ 119/149 ††£ 149/179 – 2 suites **Rest** – Carte £ 27/48
Well-run former coaching inn, with its cosy bar and lounges decorated in modern hues. Appealing bedrooms boast good mod cons and smart bathrooms; those in the outbuildings have heated stone floors and one even has a bath in the lounge. The brasserie-style restaurant specialises in meats and grills.

17 Burgate without rest
17 Burgate ✉ YO18 7AU – ✆ (01751) 473 463 – www.17burgate.co.uk – Restricted opening in spring and winter
5 rm – †£ 70/95 ††£ 75/110
Substantial 17C townhouse with colourful gardens, run by a charming, experienced couple. The lounge features a large inglenook fireplace and a comprehensive honesty bar; the breakfast room has Mackintosh-style chairs and offers a menu of local produce. Spacious modern bedrooms are individually styled.

Bramwood without rest
19 Hall Garth ✉ YO18 7AW – ✆ (01751) 474 066 – www.bramwoodguesthouse.co.uk – Closed Christmas
8 rm – †£ 43/48 ††£ 68/82
Friendly Georgian townhouse with a cosy, homely interior and pretty gardens complete with a pergola. Have breakfast in the large kitchen beside the china-filled dressers or in smarter dining room. Bedrooms are comfy and cottagey.

at Levisham Northeast: 6.5 mi by A169✉ Pickering

Moorlands Country House 
✉ YO18 7NL – ✆ (01751) 460 229 – www.moorlandslevisham.co.uk – May-October, minimum 2 night stay
4 rm – †£ 100/130 ††£ 140/160 **Rest** – Menu £ 25
19C restored vicarage in the heart of the national park, boasting superb views down the valley. Spacious, well-maintained interior with a classically decorated lounge and flowery wallpapers. Comfortable bedrooms boast rich colour schemes; one has a four-poster bed. Traditional three course dinners. Menu changes daily.

at Sinnington Northwest: 4 mi by A170 ✉ York

Fox and Hounds with rm

Main St ✉ YO62 6SQ – ✆ (01751) 431 577 – www.thefoxandhoundsinn.co.uk – Closed 25-27 December
10 rm – †£ 59/94 ††£ 60/170 Carte £ 24/44
Pretty 18C inn in a sleepy hamlet, with spacious, homely, individually decorated bedrooms: well-located for visiting the moors. Formal dining room, residents lounge and cosy bar with exposed beams and hanging hop bines. Big portions of proper, hearty, Yorkshire cooking. Service is a strength.

PICKHILL

North Yorkshire – Pop. 401 – ✉ Thirsk – See Regional map n°**22-B1**
London 229 mi – Leeds 41 mi – Middlesbrough 30 mi – York 34 mi
Michelin Road map 502-P21

Nags Head Country Inn with rm

✉ YO7 4JG – ✆ (01845) 567 391 – www.nagsheadpickhill.co.uk – Closed 25 December
12 rm – †£ 60/78 ††£ 80/97 Carte £ 14/33
Quirky pub close to the A1; it has a rustic open-fired bar filled with framed ties and a dining area hung with hunting scenes. Classic dishes are listed on blackboards, alongside local cheeses; game season is the best time to visit, as the owner likes to shoot. Cosy bedrooms are set in the pub and an annexe.

PIFF'S ELM → See Cheltenham

Gloucestershire

PILSLEY

Derbyshire – See Regional map n°**16-A1**
London 161 mi – Manchester 37 mi – Sheffield 22 mi – Nottingham 20 mi

Devonshire Arms with rm

rest,

✉ DE45 1UL – ✆ (01246) 583 258 – www.devonshirepilsley.co.uk
13 rm – †£ 75/105 ††£ 99/165 Carte £ 19/32 – *(booking advisable)*
Traditional pub dishes get a makeover on the menu sourced from the Chatsworth Estate; servings are generous and dishes, satisfyingly filling. The stylish, contemporary bedrooms were designed by the Duchess of Devonshire. Stock up in the nearby Chatsworth Farm shop before going home.

PLUMTREE → See Nottingham

Nottinghamshire

PLYMOUTH

Plymouth – Pop. 234 982 – See Regional map n°**2-C2**
London 242 mi – Bristol 124 mi – Southampton 161 mi
Michelin Road map 503-H32 – Michelin Green Guide GREAT BRITAIN

Tanners

Prysten House, Finewell St ✉ PL1 2AE – ✆ (01752) 252 001 – www.tannersrestaurant.com – Closed Christmas-New Year, Sunday and Monday
Town plan: BZ**n**
Menu £ 17/20 **s** – Carte £ 37/43 **s** – *(booking essential)*
Hugely characterful building with a modern lounge and decked courtyard; reputedly the oldest house in the city. Stone-faced walls, mullioned windows and an illuminated well feature. Interesting menus have modern touches and personal twists.

Rhodes @ The Dome

Hoe Rd ✉ PL1 2NZ – ✆ (01752) 266 600 – www.rhodesatthedome.co.uk
Town plan: BZ**d**
Menu £ 20 (lunch and early dinner) – Carte £ 21/39
Contemporary restaurant with a stunning panoramic view over Plymouth Sound; start off with a cocktail beneath the vast cupola. The menu offers unfussy, fairly priced brasserie classics; from a burger to a smoked salmon croque monsieur.

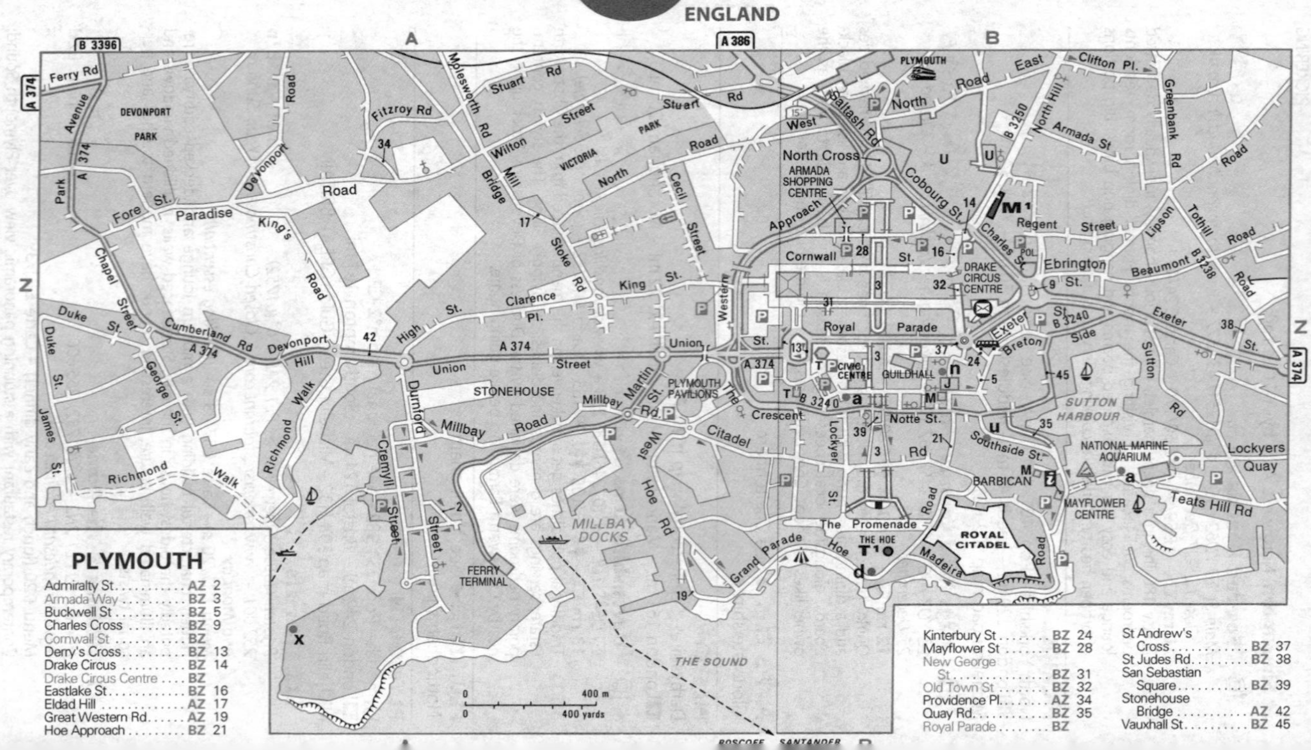
PLYMOUTH
Admiralty St . . . . AZ 2
Armada Way . . . . BZ 3
Buckwell St . . . . BZ 5
Charles Cross . . . . BZ 9
Cornwall St . . . . BZ
Derry's Cross . . . . BZ 13
Drake Circus . . . . BZ 14
Drake Circus Centre . . . . BZ
Eastlake St . . . . BZ 16
Eldad Hill . . . . AZ 17
Great Western Rd . . . . . . AZ 19
Hoe Approach . . . . BZ 21
Kinterbury St . . . . BZ 24
Mayflower St . . . . BZ 28
New George St . . . . BZ 31
Old Town St . . . . BZ 32
Providence Pl . . . . AZ 34
Quay Rd . . . . BZ 35
Royal Parade . . . . BZ
St Andrew's Cross . . . . . . BZ 37
St Judes Rd . . . . BZ 38
San Sebastian Square . . . . BZ 39
Stonehouse Bridge . . . . . . AZ 42
Vauxhall St . . . . BZ 45
DEVONPORT PARK
VICTORIA PARK
STONEHOUSE
North Cross
ARMADA SHOPPING CENTRE
DRAKE CIRCUS CENTRE
CIVIC CENTRE
GUILDHALL
PLYMOUTH PAVILIONS
SUTTON HARBOUR
NATIONAL MARINE AQUARIUM
BARBICAN
MAYFLOWER CENTRE
ROYAL CITADEL
THE HOE
MILLBAY DOCKS
FERRY TERMINAL
THE SOUND
ROSCOFF
SANTANDER
0 400 m
0 400 yards

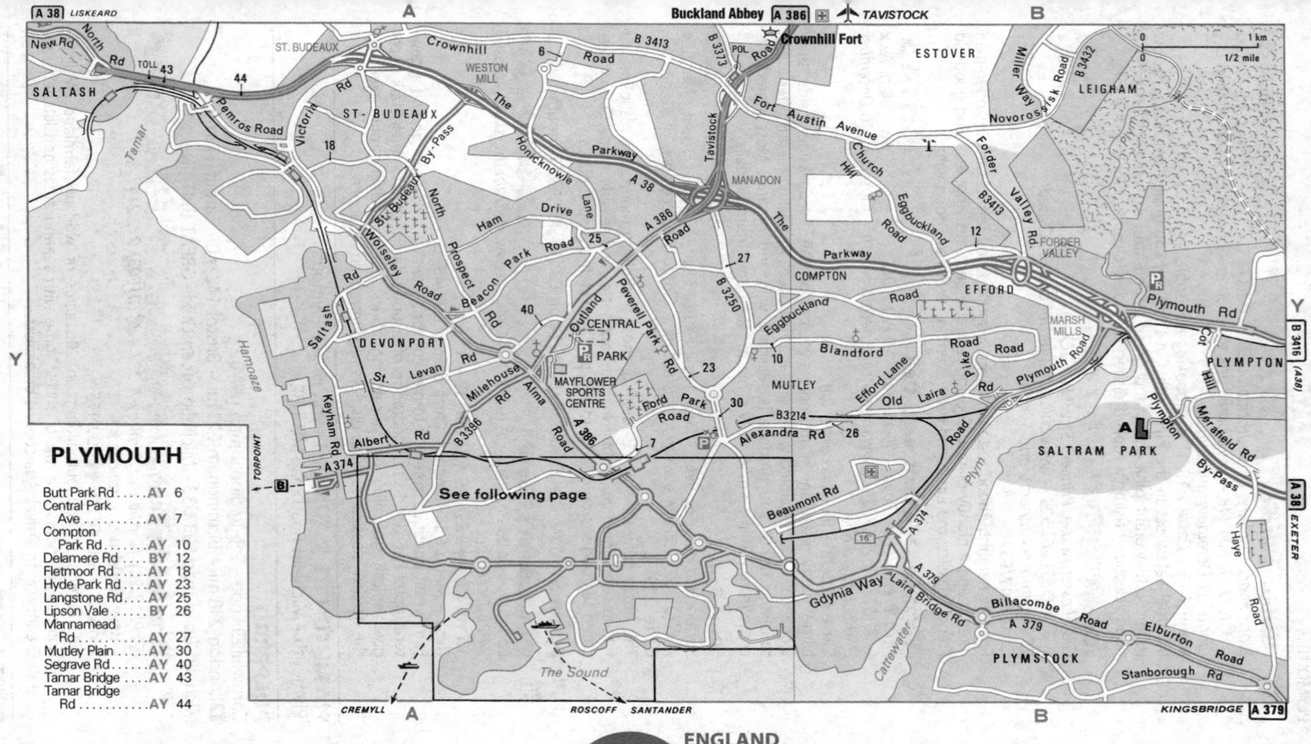
A 38 LISKEARD
Buckland Abbey
A 386
TAVISTOCK
Crownhill Fort
ESTOVER
LEIGHAM
SALTASH
ST. BUDEAUX
ST-BUDEAUX
WESTON MILL
MANADON
COMPTON
EFFORD
FORDER VALLEY
MARSH MILLS
PLYMPTON
B 3416 (A38)
A 38 EXETER
SALTRAM PARK
MUTLEY
DEVONPORT
CENTRAL PARK
MAYFLOWER SPORTS CENTRE
PLYMSTOCK
See following page
Hamoaze
The Sound
Tamar
Plym
Cattewater
TORPOINT
CREMYLL
ROSCOFF SANTANDER
KINGSBRIDGE A 379
ENGLAND
PLYMOUTH
Butt Park Rd ..... AY 6
Central Park Ave ..... AY 7
Compton Park Rd ..... AY 10
Delamere Rd ..... BY 12
Fletmoor Rd ..... AY 18
Hyde Park Rd ..... AY 23
Langstone Rd ..... AY 25
Lipson Vale ..... BY 26
Mannamead Rd ..... AY 27
Mutley Plain ..... AY 30
Segrave Rd ..... AY 40
Tamar Bridge ..... AY 43
Tamar Bridge Rd ..... AY 44

XX **Barbican Kitchen**

Black Friars Distillery, 60 Southside St ✉ PL1 2LQ Town plan: BZ**u**
– ✆ (01752) 604 448 – www.barbicankitchen.com – Closed 25-26 December, dinner 31 December and Sunday
Menu £ 15 – Carte £ 18/41 **s** – *(booking advisable)*
Informal eatery set in the Plymouth Gin Distillery, comprising two long, narrow rooms with vibrant pink chairs and green banquettes. Brasserie menus offer a good selection of simply cooked dishes, with classic comfort food to the fore.

XX **Chloe's**

Gill Akaster House, Princess St ✉ PL1 2EX Town plan: BZ**a**
– ✆ (01752) 201 523 – www.chloesrestaurant.co.uk – Closed 25 December-4 January and Sunday
Carte £ 17/53
Friendly neighbourhood restaurant with a small paved terrace, an airy, open-plan interior and a nightly pianist. Cooking is hearty and satisfying, featuring good old French classics; the lunch and early evening menus are good value.

X **River Cottage Canteen & Deli**

No 1 Brew House, Royal William Yard ✉ PL1 3QQ Town plan: AZ**x**
– ✆ (01752) 252 702 – www.rivercottage.net/plymouth – Closed 25-26 December and Sunday dinner
Carte £ 20/38 – *(booking essential)*
Large, buzzy restaurant in an impressive spot on the old dockside; inside, thick stone walls and reclaimed wood give it a rustic feel. Appealing menus offer gutsy, satisfying dishes and produce is seasonal, wild and organic. Most ingredients come from within 50 miles; buy some to take home from the deli.

X **Rockfish** N

Sutton Harbour, Cox Side, 3 Rope Walk ✉ PL4 OLB Town plan: BZ**r**
– ✆ (01752) 255 974 – www.rockfish.co.uk – Closed 25 December
Carte £ 19/35
This buzzy quayside shack is ideal for those in 'holiday mode'. The rustic interior features reclaimed wood, hull-shaped banquettes and seaside snaps. Simply prepared seafood sits on greaseproof paper, atop stainless steel plates.

at Plympton St Maurice East: 6 mi by A374 on B3416 -(BY)✉ Plymouth

St Elizabeth's House rest,

Longbrook St ✉ PL7 1NJ – ✆ (01752) 344 840 – www.stelizabeths.co.uk – Closed 24-26 December
15 rm – †£ 89/129 ††£ 99/139 – 1 suite
Rest – Menu £ 15 (lunch) – Carte dinner £ 24/45
Family-run boutique hotel – a former convent – with a stylish lounge and a pewter-topped bar. Good-sized bedrooms offer up-to-date facilities – their stark décor given splashes of colour by eye-catching fabrics. The smart dining room overlooks the garden; classical cooking displays Mediterranean influences.

PLYMPTON ST MAURICE Devon → See Plymouth
Plymouth – Michelin Road map 503-H32

POLPERRO
Cornwall ✉ Looe – See Regional map n°**1-B2**
London 238 mi – Birmingham 223 mi – Bristol 142 mi – Cardiff 173 mi
Michelin Road map 503-G33 – Michelin Green Guide GREAT BRITAIN

Trenderway Farm without rest 

✉ PL13 2LY Northeast : 2 mi by A 387 – ✆ (01503) 272 214 – www.trenderwayfarm.co.uk
7 rm – †£ 99/175 ††£ 99/175
16C farmhouse and outbuildings in 206 acres of working farmland. Well-appointed bedrooms in a mix of styles; some with seating areas and kitchenettes. Cream tea on arrival; Aga-cooked breakfasts.

PONTELAND → See Newcastle upon Tyne
Northumberland – Michelin Road map 501-O19 and 502

POOLE

Poole – Pop. 154 718 – See Regional map n°**4-C3**

London 116 mi – Bournemouth 4 mi – Dorchester 23 mi – Southampton 36 mi

Michelin Road map 503-O31 and 504 – Michelin Green Guide GREAT BRITAIN

Plan: see Bournemouth

Hotel du Vin
rm,

7-11 Thames St. ✉ *BH15 1JN* – ✆ *(0844) 748 92 65* – *www.hotelduvin.com* **Town plan:a**

38 rm – †£ 99/285 ††£ 99/395, £ 17

Rest *Bistro* – Menu £ 20 (lunch and early dinner) – Carte £ 22/40

A strikingly extended Queen Anne property in the old town. Smart guest areas have eye-catching wine-themed murals; stylish, modern bedrooms are named after wine or champagne houses – one boasts an 8ft bed and twin roll-top baths. Local produce features in classic French dishes and there's a 300 bin wine list.

Harbour Heights
rm,

Haven Rd, Sandbanks ✉ *BH13 7LW* – *Southeast : 3 mi by A 35 and B 3369* – ✆ *(01202) 707 272* – *www.harbourheights.com* Town plan: BX**n**

38 rm – †£ 99/174 ††£ 119/274

Rest *Harbar Bistro* – Menu £ 23/30 – Carte £ 31/82

1920s whitewashed hotel, perched on the hillside, overlooking Poole Bay and Brownsea Island; the modern lounge-bar boasts a superb three-tiered terrace which makes the most of the view. Contemporary bedrooms come with good mod cons and smart bathrooms. The open-plan restaurant serves a modern menu.

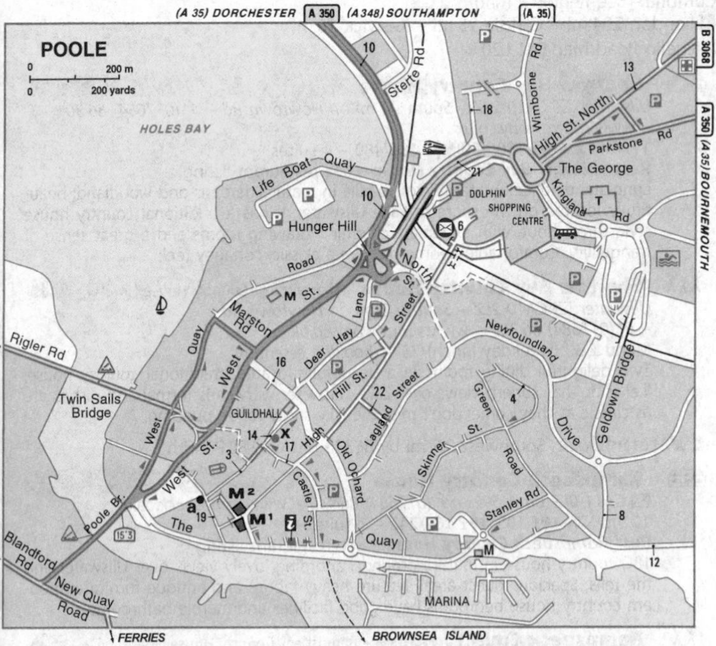

ENGLAND

Church St	3	Furnell Rd	8	New Orchard	16
Dolphin Quay Shopping Centre		High St		New St	17
Emerson Rd	4	Holes Bay Rd	10	Serpentine Rd	18
Falkland Square	6	Labrador Drive	12	Thames St	19
Fishermans Rd	7	Longfleet Rd	13	Towngate Bridge	21
		Market St	14	Westons Lane	22

Cafe Shore

10-14 Banks Rd, Sandbanks ✉ BH13 7QB – Southeast : 3.5 mi by A 35 and B 3369 – ✆ (01202) 707 271 – www.cafeshore.co.uk Town plan: BX**c**

Menu £ 15 (weekdays) – Carte £ 25/60

Stylish restaurant on the Sandbanks Peninsula, with a drinks terrace, a trendy lounge-bar and a softly lit dining room offering great views across the harbour. Extensive modern menus lean towards well-executed fresh fish dishes and steaks.

Isabel's

32 Station Rd, Lower Parkstone ✉ BH14 8UD – ✆ (01202) 747 885 – www.isabelsrestaurant.co.uk – Closed 25-26 December, 1 January, Sunday and Monday Town plan: BX**a**

Menu £ 25/35 – Carte £ 29/40 – *(dinner only) (booking essential)*

Lovingly run restaurant in a former chemist's shop, where the old shelving is still in situ. Grab a booth in the characterful red dining room or make for the basement room which opens onto the garden. Hearty French dishes feature.

Guildhall Tavern

15 Market St ✉ BH15 1NB – ✆ (01202) 671 717 – www.guildhalltavern.co.uk – Closed 25 December-4 January, 2 weeks July, 1 week April, Sunday and Monday **Town plan:x**

Menu £ 18 (weekday lunch) – Carte £ 29/47 – *(booking advisable)*

Proudly run restaurant opposite the Guildhall, with a bright, cheery interior and a nautical theme. Tasty, classical French dishes are generously proportioned and largely seafood-based. They also host monthly gourmet evenings.

ENGLAND

POOLEY BRIDGE

Cumbria – See Regional map n°**21**-B2

London 294 mi – Carlisle 25 mi – Keswick 16 mi

Michelin Road map 501-L20

Sharrow Bay Country House

Ullswater ✉ CA10 2LZ – South : 2 mi on Howtown Rd – ✆ (017684) 86 301 – www.sharrowbay.co.uk

17 rm – £ 180/480 £ 180/480 – 4 suites

Rest *Sharrow Bay Country House* – see restaurant listing

Long-standing, celebrated Victorian villa in mature gardens and woodland; beautifully located on the shore of Lake Ullswater. It has a traditional country house style throughout, with extremely charming drawing rooms and a great sense of tranquillity. Comfortable bedrooms have a classic, cottagey feel.

Sharrow Bay Country House – Sharrow Bay Country House Hotel

Ullswater ✉ CA10 2LZ – South : 2 mi on Howtown Rd – ✆ (017684) 86 301 – www.sharrowbay.co.uk

Menu £ 30 (weekday lunch)/75 – *(booking essential)*

Two delightful dining rooms in a beautifully located, traditional country house; 'Lakeside' has superb views over Lake Ullswater. Service is formal and dishes are as classic as they come; don't miss the icky sticky toffee pudding.

at Watermillock Southwest 2.5 mi by B5320 on A592✉ Penrith

Rampsbeck Country House

✉ CA11 0LP on A 592 – ✆ (017684) 86 442 – www.rampsbeck.co.uk

19 rm – £ 105 £ 160/242 – 1 suite

Rest *Rampsbeck Country House* – see restaurant listing

18C country house in mature grounds, affording lovely views over Ullswater and the fells. Spacious guest areas feature heavy fabrics and antique furniture; modern country house bedrooms have good facilities and marble bathrooms.

Rampsbeck Country House – Rampsbeck Country House Hotel

✉ CA11 0LP on A 592 – ✆ (017684) 86 442 – www.rampsbeck.co.uk

Menu £ 32/60 **s** – *(booking essential)*

Elegant hotel restaurant with good-sized tables and beautiful lake and fell views. The oft-changing menu showcases local produce; cooking is modern and follows the seasons. Take your canapés and coffee in one of the drawing rooms.

PORLOCK

Somerset – Pop. 1 395 – ✉ Minehead – See Regional map n°**3-A2**
London 190 mi – Bristol 67 mi – Exeter 46 mi – Taunton 28 mi
Michelin Road map 503-J30 – Michelin Green Guide THE WEST COUNTRY

Oaks

✉ TA24 8ES – ✆ (01643) 862 265 – www.oakshotel.co.uk – April-October
7 rm – †£ 110/150 ††£ 150/180
Rest – Menu £ 38 **s** – *(dinner only) (booking essential)*
Imposing Edwardian house boasting great views over the weir and Porlock Bay. Antique-filled entrance hall with beautiful parquet floor. Cake on arrival in snug lounge. Large, comfy bedrooms come with fresh fruit bowls, good mod cons and smart bathrooms. Dining room offers classical daily menu and views from every table.

Cross Lane House (N)

Allerford ✉ TA24 8HW – East : 1.25 mi on A 39 – ✆ (01643) 863 276 – www.crosslanehouse.com – Closed 3 January-12 February and 1 week mid November
4 rm – †£ 100/125 ††£ 110/175
Rest – Menu £ 29 – *(Closed Sunday dinner and Monday) (booking essential at dinner)*
A very stylishly restored farmhouse and outbuildings dating from 1584. Inside it cleverly blends the old with the new, and great attention has been paid to detail. Cake is served on arrival and afternoon tea is a feature. The intimate formal restaurant offers a concise menu of modern dishes.

PORT ERIN → See Man (Isle of)

Port Erin – Michelin Road map 502-F21

PORT SUNLIGHT

Merseyside – See Regional map n°**20-A3**
London 206 mi – Liverpool 6 mi – Bolton 42 mi – St Helens 20 mi
Michelin Road map 502-L23

Leverhulme

Lodge Ln, Central Rd ✉ CH62 5EZ – ✆ (0151) 644 66 55 – www.leverhulmehotel.co.uk
21 rm – †£ 210/510 ††£ 210/510
Rest *Twenty-eight Miles* – Carte £ 27/53
Attractive Edwardian building – originally the cottage hospital for a charming conservation village; now a boutique hotel where art deco features blend with contemporary styling. Well-equipped bedrooms and modern bathrooms. The restaurant serves tapas-style dishes; ingredients are sourced from within 28 miles.

PORT ISAAC

Cornwall – See Regional map n°**1-B2**
London 264 mi – Plymouth 50 mi – Newquay 24 mi
Michelin Road map 503-F32

Outlaw's Fish Kitchen (N)

1 Middle St ✉ PL29 3RH – ✆ (01208) 881 183 – www.outlaws.co.uk – Closed January, Sunday and Monday October-May
Carte approx. £ 35 – *(booking essential at dinner)*
This intimate 15C building has low ceilings and wonky walls and is found in the heart of this famous harbourside fishing village. The day boats guide the menu, which offers a delicious mix of old favourites and appealing small plates – 3 or 4 dishes should suffice. Cornish gins, beers and wines also feature.
→ Crab on toast. Crispy monkfish cheeks. Dark chocolate mousse, banana curd and salted peanuts.

PORTHLEVEN

Cornwall – Pop. 3 059 – See Regional map n°**1-A3**
London 284 mi – Helston 3 mi – Penzance 12 mi

Kota with rm
Harbour Head ✉ TR13 9JA – ✆ (01326) 562 407 – www.kotarestaurant.co.uk – Closed 1 January-10 February, 25-26 December, Sunday and Monday
2 rm – †£ 50/80 ††£ 65/90 Menu £ 22 – Carte £ 25/41 – *(dinner only)*
Welcoming 18C harbourside granary; its name meaning 'shellfish' in Maori. Cottagey interior with thick stone walls, a tiled floor and a mix of wood furnishings. Menus offer a mix of unfussy and more elaborate dishes, and display subtle Asian influences courtesy of the owner's Chinese and Malaysian background; many of the ingredients are foraged for. Simple bedrooms.

PORTINSCALE → See Keswick

Cumbria

PORTLOE

Cornwall – See Regional map n°**1-B3**
London 296 mi – Plymouth 51 mi – Truro 15 mi
Michelin Road map 503-F33

Lugger (N)
✉ TR2 5RD – ✆ (01872) 501 322 – www.luggerhotel.co.uk
23 rm – †£ 65/75 ††£ 99/255 **Rest** – Carte £ 29/47 – *(bar lunch)*
This 17C smugglers' inn sits in a picturesque fishing village and affords dramatic views over the rugged bay. It's snug and cosy throughout, with open fires, low ceilings and friendly, personal service. Have a drink on the terrace and dinner in the elegant dining room, which serves seafood fresh from the bay.

ENGLAND

PORTSCATHO

Cornwall ✉ Truro – See Regional map n°**1-B3**
London 298 mi – Plymouth 55 mi – Truro 16 mi
Michelin Road map 503-F33 – Michelin Green Guide GREAT BRITAIN

Driftwood
Rosevine ✉ TR2 5EW – North : 2 mi by A 3078 – ✆ (01872) 580 644 – www.driftwoodhotel.co.uk – Closed 8 December-5 February
15 rm – †£ 135/220 ††£ 160/300
Rest *Driftwood* ✿ – see restaurant listing
Charming clifftop hotel looking out over mature grounds, which stretch down to the shore and a private beach. Stylish, contemporary guest areas are decorated with pieces of driftwood. Smart bedrooms – in the main house and annexed cottages – have a good level of modern facilities; some have decked terraces.

Rosevine
Rosevine ✉ TR2 5EW – North : 2 mi by A 3078 – ✆ (01872) 580 206 – www.rosevine.co.uk – Closed mid November-early December and January
15 suites – ††£ 155/415, £ 10
Rest – Menu £ 24/32 – Carte £ 26/40 – *(closed Sunday dinner October-May) (bar lunch) (bookings essential for non-residents)*
Dramatically refurbished country house overlooking the sea, with modern guest areas and stylish bedrooms with kitchenettes. They cater strongly for families: children have their own lounge, they offer family high tea, and the large grounds have a pool and play area. The all-day brasserie uses local produce.

Driftwood – Driftwood Hotel
✿
Rosevine ✉ TR2 5EW – North : 2 mi by A 3078 – ✆ (01872) 580 644 – www.driftwoodhotel.co.uk – Closed 8 December-5 February
Menu £ 55/90 – *(dinner only) (booking essential)*
Bright, New England style restaurant in an attractive house in a peaceful clifftop setting; it's delightfully run by a friendly, efficient team and boasts superb views out to sea. Unfussy, modern, seasonally pertinent dishes display technical adroitness and feature excellent flavour and texture combinations.
→ Ballotine of lemon sole, shiitake mushroom, soy, ginger, radish & sea purslane. Beef sirloin and feather blade, potato crisp, garlic & spinach purée. Thunder and Lightning' tart, saffron jelly & ginger beer.

PORTSMOUTH and SOUTHSEA

Portsmouth – Pop. 238 137 – See Regional map n°**6**-B3

London 78 mi – Brighton 48 mi – Salisbury 44 mi – Southampton 21 mi

Michelin Road map 503-Q31 and 504 – Michelin Green Guide GREAT BRITAIN

Clarence without rest

Clarence Rd, Southsea ✉ PO5 2LQ – ✆ (023) 9287 6348 – www.theclarencehotel.co.uk – Closed 24 December-10 January Town plan: AZ**c**

8 rm – †£ 99/159 ††£ 99/245

Immaculately kept, bay windowed house, just a short walk from the sea. Bedrooms come in various sizes and feature contemporary décor, superb modern bathrooms and pleasing extra touches; some have a TV inset in the bathroom wall.

Retreat without rest

35 Grove Rd South, Southsea ✉ PO5 3QS – ✆ (023) 9235 3701 – www.theretreatguesthouse.co.uk Town plan: CZ**e**

4 rm – †£ 85 ††£ 110

Grade II listed Arts and Crafts house run by very friendly owners. It was built for the local mayor in 1889 and still has its original floors and stained glass windows. Rooms are spacious and understated and it has a relaxed air.

Restaurant 27

27a South Par, Southsea ✉ PO5 2JF – ✆ (023) 9287 6272 – www.restaurant27.com – Closed 25-26 December, Sunday dinner, Monday and Tuesday Town plan: AZ**x**

Menu £ 50 – *(dinner only and Sunday lunch) (booking advisable)*

This long-standing, elegant restaurant is professionally and passionately run by its owner-chef. Contemporary cooking has a slightly Scandic style; attractively presented dishes taste as good as they look and are full of flavour.

Brasserie Blanc

1 Gunwharf Quays ✉ PO1 3FR – ✆ (023) 9289 1320 – www.brasserieblanc.com Town plan: BY**x**

Menu £ 12/17 – Carte £ 21/40

Large bustling brasserie on the ground floor of the 'Lipstick' tower, complete with a bar, a small shop and a terrace. Watch the chefs prepare unfussy French classics in the open kitchen: the set menu is particularly good value.

POSTBRIDGE

Devon – See Regional map n°**2**-C2

London 207 mi – Exeter 21 mi – Plymouth 21 mi

Michelin Road map 503-I32

Lydgate House

✉ PL20 6TJ – ✆ (01822) 880 209 – www.lydgatehouse.co.uk – Closed January

7 rm – †£ 45/55 ††£ 85/120

Rest – Menu £ 28 – *(closed Sunday and Monday) (dinner only) (residents only)*

Personally run whitewashed house, set in a secluded spot high on the moors and accessed via a narrow track. Homely, cosy lounge and conservatory restaurant offering home-cooked local produce. Bedrooms are named after birds; many offer lovely views over the 36 acre grounds and the East Dart River.

POWERSTOCK

Dorset – See Regional map n°**3**-B3

London 144 mi – Bristol 92 mi – Cardiff 113 mi – Plymouth 87 mi

Michelin Road map 503-L31

Three Horseshoes Inn with rm

✉ DT6 3TF – ✆ (01308) 485 328 – www.threeshoesdorset.co.uk – Closed 25 December and Monday in winter

3 rm – †£ 70/80 ††£ 80/110 Carte £ 21/37

A cosy, traditional pub in a wonderful setting. Robust, gutsy dishes are packed with flavour and they make their own breads, pies, ice creams, chutneys and pickles; try the wild boar scotch egg or the veal and bone marrow burger. Spacious bedrooms; the two in the annexe have super views across the valley.

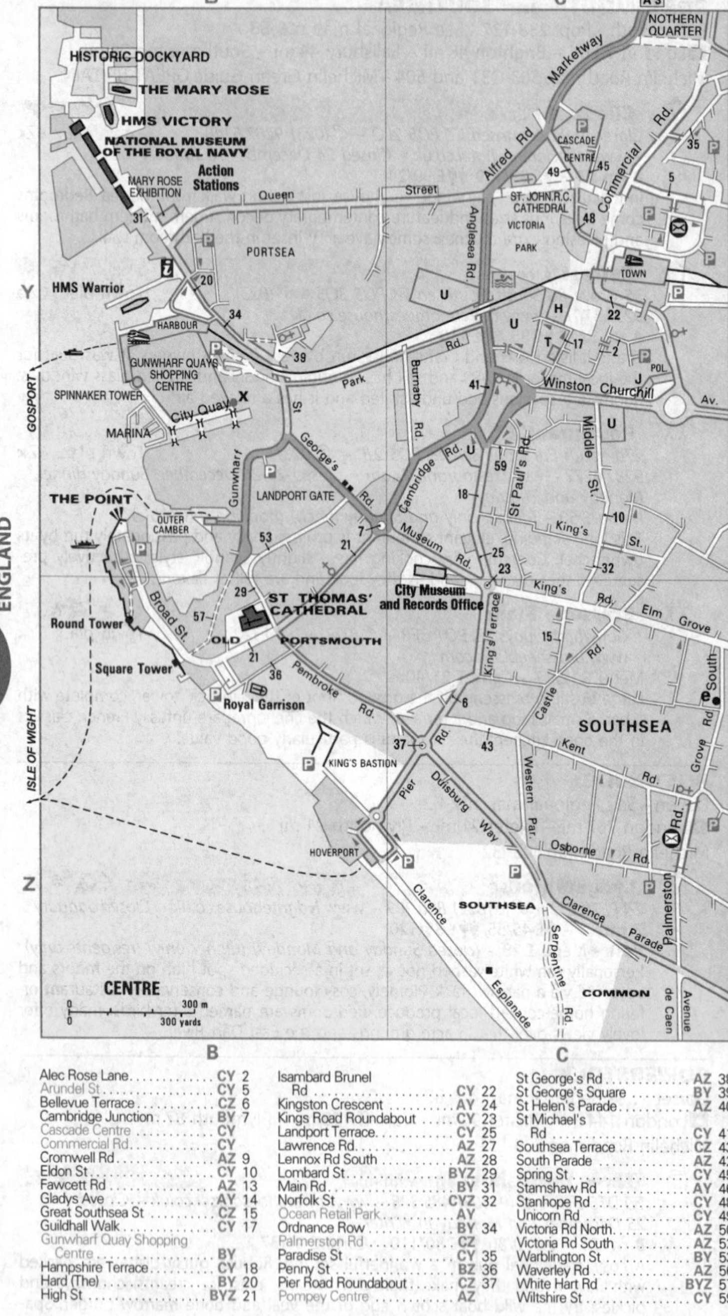

Alec Rose Lane .... CY 2
Arundel St .... CY 5
Bellevue Terrace .... CZ 6
Cambridge Junction .... BY 7
Cascade Centre .... CY
Commercial Rd .... CY
Cromwell Rd .... AZ 9
Eldon St .... CY 10
Fawcett Rd .... AZ 13
Gladys Ave .... AY 14
Great Southsea St .... CZ 15
Guildhall Walk .... CY 17
Gunwharf Quay Shopping Centre .... BY
Hampshire Terrace .... CY 18
Hard (The) .... BY 20
High St .... BYZ 21
Isambard Brunel Rd .... CY 22
Kingston Crescent .... AY 24
Kings Road Roundabout .... CY 23
Landport Terrace .... CY 25
Lawrence Rd .... AZ 27
Lennox Rd South .... AZ 28
Lombard St .... BYZ 29
Main Rd .... BY 31
Norfolk St .... CYZ 32
Ocean Retail Park .... AY
Ordnance Row .... BY 34
Palmerston Rd .... CZ
Paradise St .... CY 35
Penny St .... BZ 36
Pier Road Roundabout .... CZ 37
Pompey Centre .... AZ
St George's Rd .... AZ 38
St George's Square .... BY 39
St Helen's Parade .... AZ 40
St Michael's Rd .... CY 41
Southsea Terrace .... CZ 43
South Parade .... AZ 42
Spring St .... CY 45
Stamshaw Rd .... AY 46
Stanhope Rd .... CY 48
Unicorn Rd .... CY 49
Victoria Rd North .... AZ 50
Victoria Rd South .... AZ 52
Warblington St .... BY 53
Waverley Rd .... AZ 56
White Hart Rd .... BYZ 57
Wiltshire St .... CY 59

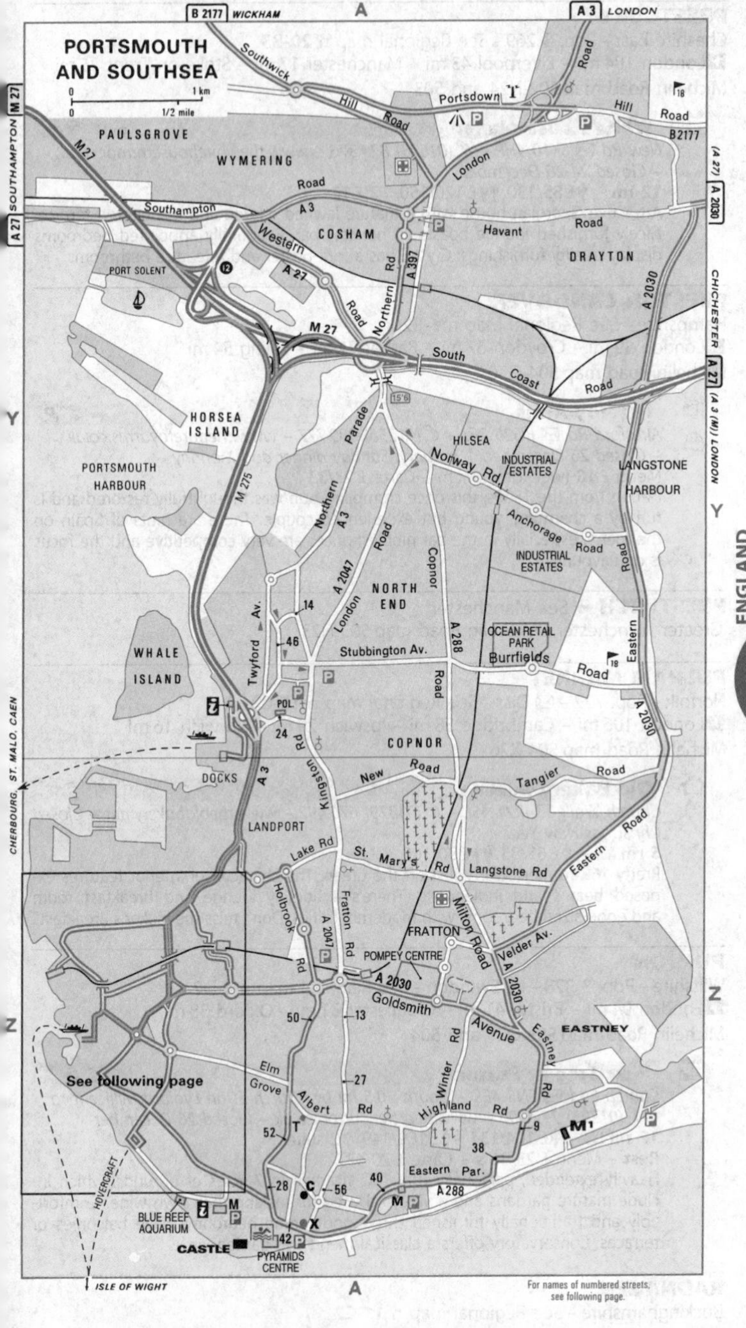
PORTSMOUTH AND SOUTHSEA
0 1 km
0 1/2 mile
B 2177 WICKHAM
A 3 LONDON
M 27 SOUTHAMPTON
A 27
A 27 (A 3 (M)) LONDON
A 2030 (A 27) CHICHESTER
CHERBOURG, ST. MALO, CAEN
ISLE OF WIGHT
HOVERCRAFT
PAULSGROVE
WYMERING
COSHAM
DRAYTON
PORT SOLENT
HORSEA ISLAND
PORTSMOUTH HARBOUR
WHALE ISLAND
HILSEA
INDUSTRIAL ESTATES
LANGSTONE HARBOUR
NORTH END
OCEAN RETAIL PARK
COPNOR
DOCKS
LANDPORT
FRATTON
POMPEY CENTRE
EASTNEY
BLUE REEF AQUARIUM
CASTLE
PYRAMIDS CENTRE
See following page
Southwick Hill Road
Portsdown Hill Road
London Road
Southampton Road
Western Road
Northern Rd
Havant Road
South Coast Road
Northern Parade
Norway Rd.
Anchorage Road
London Road
Copnor Road
Stubbington Av.
Burrfields Road
Eastern Road
Twyford Av.
Kingston Rd
New Road
Tangier Road
Lake Rd
St. Mary's Rd
Langstone Rd
Holbrook Rd
Fratton Rd
Milton Road
Velder Av.
Goldsmith Avenue
Eastney Rd
Elm Grove
Albert Rd
Winter Rd
Highland Rd
Eastern Par.
A 3
A 27
A 397
M 27
M 275
A 2047
A 288
A 2030
B2177
POL
For names of numbered streets, see following page.
ENGLAND
A
Y
Z

PRESTBURY

Cheshire East – Pop. 3 269 – See Regional map n°**20**-B3
London 184 mi – Liverpool 43 mi – Manchester 17 mi – Stoke-on-Trent 25 mi
Michelin Road map 502-N24 and 503

White House Manor without rest 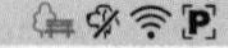

New Rd ✉ SK10 4HP – ✆ (01625) 829 376 – www.thewhitehousemanor.co.uk – Closed 24-26 December

12 rm – †£ 85/130 ††£ 120/150, ☕ £ 12

Attractive Georgian house with a mature lawned garden and a sheltered terrace. Nicely furnished lounge boasts an honesty bar. Beautifully appointed bedrooms display quality furnishings; Crystal has a four-poster and a feature bathroom.

PRESTON CANDOVER

Hampshire – See Regional map n°**6**-B2
London 59 mi – Croydon 67 mi – Barnet 72 mi – Ealing 54 mi
Michelin Road map 504-Q30

Purefoy Arms 

Alresford Rd ✉ RG25 2EJ – ✆ (01256) 389 777 – www.thepurefoyarms.co.uk – Closed 26 December, 1 January, Sunday dinner and Monday

Menu £ 18 (weekday lunch) – Carte £ 23/33

Dating from the 1860s, this once crumbling pub was thoughtfully restored and is run by a charming, young but experienced couple. There are hints of Spain on the menu, especially in the bar nibbles; prices are very competitive and the focus is on flavour.

ENGLAND

PRESTWICH → See Manchester

Greater Manchester – Michelin Road map 503-N23

PULHAM MARKET

Norfolk – Pop. 722 – ✉ Diss – See Regional map n°**15**-C2
London 106 mi – Cambridge 58 mi – Ipswich 29 mi – Norwich 16 mi
Michelin Road map 504-X26

Old Bakery without rest 

Church Walk ✉ IP21 4SL – ✆ (01379) 676 492 – www.theoldbakery.net – Closed Christmas-New Year

5 rm ☕ – †£ 65/85 ††£ 80/100

Pretty 16C former bakery just off the green. The characterful interior features exposed beams and inglenooks. There's a homely lounge and breakfast room and good-sized bedrooms with modern facilities. Don't miss the 'Baker's Breakfast'.

PURTON

Wiltshire – Pop. 3 328 – ✉ Swindon – See Regional map n°**4**-D2
London 94 mi – Bristol 41 mi – Gloucester 31 mi – Oxford 38 mi
Michelin Road map 503-O29 and 504

Pear Tree at Purton 

Church End ✉ SN5 4ED – South : 0.5 mi by Church St on Lydiard Millicent rd – ✆ (01793) 772 100 – www.peartreepurton.co.uk – Closed 26 December

17 rm ☕ – †£ 104/134 ††£ 109/149 – 2 suites

Rest – Menu £ 23/36 **s** – Carte £ 20/43

Heavily extended, personally run, 16C vicarage in 7 acres of grounds, which include mature gardens and a vineyard used for making their own wine. Comfortably and traditionally furnished throughout; some bedrooms have balconies or terraces. Conservatory offers a classical menu and garden views.

RADNAGE

Buckinghamshire – See Regional map n°**11**-C2
London 39 mi – Oxford 22 mi – Reading 31 mi

Three Horseshoes Inn with rm 

Bennett End ✉ HP14 4EB – North : 1.25 mi by Town End rd. – ✆ (01494) 483 273 – www.thethreehorseshoes.net – Closed Sunday dinner and Monday lunch except bank holidays

6 rm – †£ 80 ††£ 90/150 Menu £ 16 (weekdays) – Carte £ 29/40

Attractive 18C pub in a fantastic hillside location, with a lovely terrace boasting views over the duck pond. Classical dishes display French touches, with lighter offerings at lunch and a more formal à la carte and some tapas dishes at dinner. Bedrooms are contemporary and lavish; Molières is the best.

RAINHAM

Medway – See Regional map n°**9-C1**

London 14 mi – Basildon 16 mi – Dartford 9 mi

Michelin Road map 504-U29

XX **Barn**

507 Lower Rainham Rd ✉ ME8 7TN – North : 1.75 mi by Station Rd – ✆ (01634) 361 363 – www.thebarnrestaurant.co.uk – Closed 25-26 December, 1 January, Saturday lunch, Sunday dinner, Monday and bank holidays

Carte £ 33/42 **s** – *(dinner only and Sunday lunch)*

Black and white timbered barn transported from Essex and reconstructed on this site. It's heavily beamed throughout, with a rustic dining room and an upstairs lounge. The enthusiastic owner offers a menu of elaborate modern dishes.

RAMSBOTTOM

Greater Manchester – Pop. 17 872 – See Regional map n°**20-B2**

London 223 mi – Blackpool 39 mi – Burnley 12 mi – Leeds 46 mi

Michelin Road map 502-N23

XX **Sanmini's**

7 Carrbank Lodge, Ramsbottom Ln ✉ BL0 9DJ – ✆ (01706) 821 831 – www.sanminis.com – Closed Monday

Menu £ 30 – Carte £ 17/31 – *(dinner only and lunch Saturday-Sunday) (booking essential)*

Charming little restaurant in a Victorian gatehouse. Neatly presented south Indian dishes have gentle spicing and are made from scratch; the family are doctors, so the cooking's healthy too. They also offer their own label beer.

X **Hearth of the Ram**

13 Peel Brow ✉ BL0 0AA – ✆ (01706) 828 681 – www.hearthoftheram.com

Carte £ 17/32

Rustic former pub with characterful original features, a friendly team and a laid-back feel. The experienced chef offers a good value menu – choose from enticing pies and platters during the day and more sophisticated dishes in the evening. Cooking is classically based but has a light, modern touch.

RAMSBURY

Wiltshire – Pop. 1 540 – See Regional map n°**4-D2**

London 73 mi – Bristol 53 mi – Cardiff 86 mi – Plymouth 172 mi

Michelin Road map 503-P29

Bell with rm 

The Square ✉ SN8 2PE – ✆ (01672) 520 230 – www.thebellramsbury.com – Closed 25 December

9 rm – †£ 110/150 ††£ 110/150 Carte £ 24/37

Charming 16C pub with stylish, well-appointed bedrooms. Dine on pub favourites among hop-covered beams in the open-fired bar or sit on smart tartan banquettes in the crisply laid dining room and choose from more ambitious, accomplished dishes. You'll find the locals at the back in 'Café Bella'.

RAMSEY → See Man (Isle of)

Ramsey – Michelin Road map 502-G21

ENGLAND

RAMSGATE

Kent – Pop. 40 515 – See Regional map n°**9**-**D1**

London 77 mi – Canterbury 17 mi – Brighton 97 mi

Michelin Road map 504-Y30

XX **Age & Sons**

Charlotte Ct ✉ CT11 8HE – ✆ (01843) 851 515 – www.ageandsons.co.uk – Closed 1-14 January, Sunday dinner and Monday-Wednesday

Menu £ 13/16 (weekdays) – Carte £ 19/35

Attractively converted wine warehouse in a pedestrianised courtyard – the name stuck after the initial 'P' fell off the wine merchant's sign! Breakfast is offered on the ground floor; above is the formal 'Age' restaurant and below is the moody 'Son' bar. Interesting modern dishes are gutsy and flavourful.

RAMSHOLT

Suffolk – See Regional map n°**15**-**D3**

London 96 mi – Norwich 54 mi – Ipswich 17 mi – Colchester 38 mi

Ramsholt Arms N

Dock Rd ✉ IP12 3AB – ✆ (01394) 411 209 – www.theramsholtarms.com – Closed January and Monday-Wednesday November-March

Menu £ 10 – Carte £ 17/29

Honest, well-priced pub food and Suffolk ales in a great location. This striking inn is set against the spectacular backdrop of the River Deben; particularly magnificent at sunset and on summer days. Plenty of room on the terrace.

ENGLAND

RAVENSTONEDALE

Cumbria – Pop. 886 – See Regional map n°**21**-**B2**

London 272 mi – Bristol 247 mi – Cardiff 268 mi – Plymouth 361 mi

Michelin Road map 502-M20

King's Head with rm

✉ CA17 4NH – ✆ (01539) 623 050 – www.kings-head.com – Closed 25 December

6 rm – †£ 70/79 ††£ 85/98 Carte £ 20/37

Whitewashed inn consisting of four 17C cottages; its smart interior featuring polished timbers, a flagged floor and a wood-burning stove. Well-prepared, appealingly presented, tasty dishes; eat in the garden, with a view of the babbling beck. Comfortable, elegant bedrooms.

READING

Reading – Pop. 218 705 – See Regional map n°**11**-**C3**

London 43 mi – Oxford 29 mi – Bristol 78 mi

Michelin Road map 503-Q29 and 504

The Forbury rm, rest,

26 The Forbury ✉ RG1 3EJ – ✆ (0118) 952 77 70 – www.theforburyhotel.co.uk Town plan: Y**c**

23 rm – †£ 138/300 ††£ 138/300

Rest *Cerise* – Carte £ 30/44

An impressive former civic hall overlooking Forbury Square Gardens; now a smart townhouse hotel where contemporary designs meet with original features. Luxurious bedrooms come with Nespresso machines, fridges and Bang & Olufsen electronics. The chic basement bar and restaurant offer modern menus.

Holiday Inn

Wharfedale Rd, Winnersh Triangle ✉ RG41 5TS – Southeast : 4.5 mi by A 4 and A 3290 off Winnerish rd – ✆ (0118) 944 04 44 – www.hireadinghotel.com

174 rm – †£ 65/169 ††£ 65/224, £ 10

Rest *Caprice* – ✆ (0118) 944 42 18 – Menu £ 24 – Carte £ 29/40

Conveniently located for the M4, with spacious open-plan guest areas, smart function facilities and a well-equipped leisure club. Stylish, uniform bedrooms come with good facilities and compact, up-to-date bathrooms. Have snacks in the comfy lounge or classic dishes in the formal split-level restaurant.

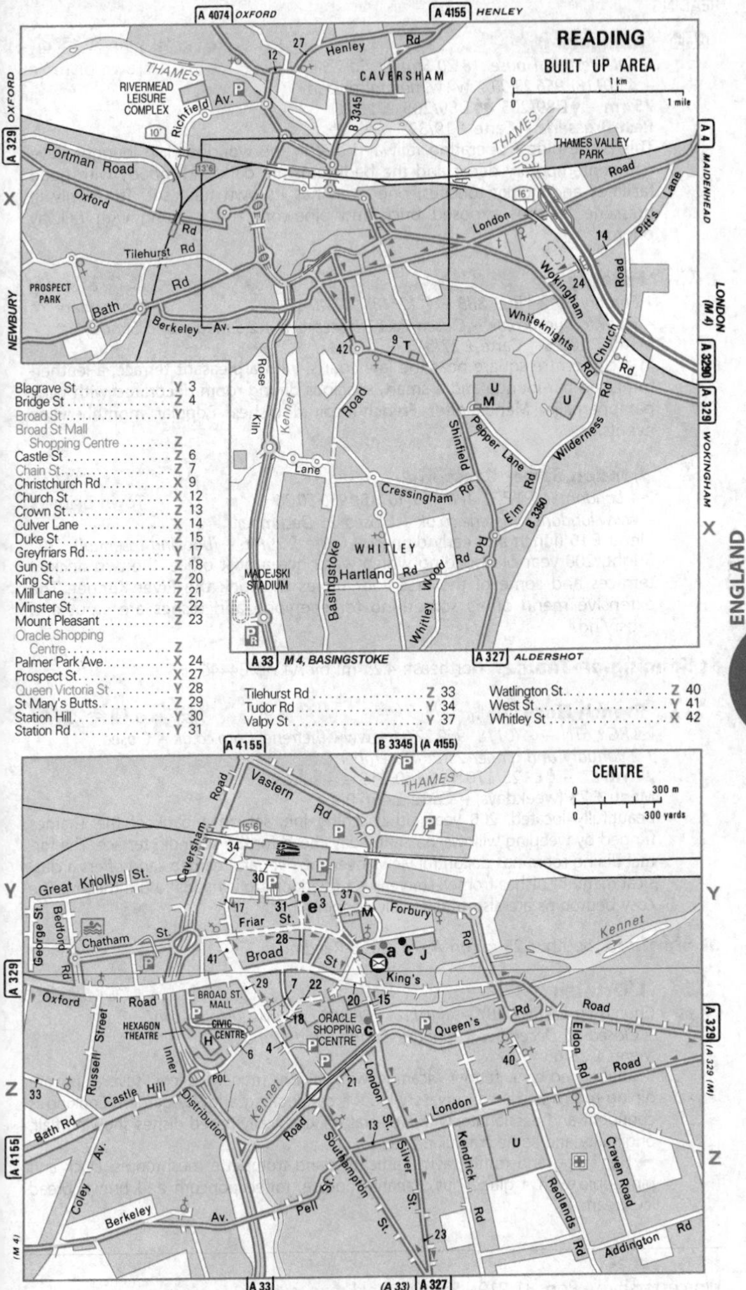
READING
BUILT UP AREA
0 1 km
0 1 mile
A 4074 OXFORD
A 4155 HENLEY
A 329 OXFORD
A 4 MAIDENHEAD
LONDON (M 4)
A 3290
A 329 WOKINGHAM
NEWBURY
A 33 M 4, BASINGSTOKE
A 327 ALDERSHOT
THAMES
CAVERSHAM
RIVERMEAD LEISURE COMPLEX
Richfield Av.
Henley Rd
B 3345
THAMES VALLEY PARK
Portman Road
Oxford Rd
Tilehurst Rd
PROSPECT PARK
Bath Rd
Berkeley Av.
London Road
Pitt's Lane
Wokingham Road
Whiteknights Rd
Church Rd
Rose Kiln Lane
Kennet
Basingstoke Road
Shinfield Rd
Pepper Lane
Wilderness Rd
Cressingham Rd
Elm Rd
B 3350
WHITLEY
Hartland Rd
Whitley Wood Rd
MADEJSKI STADIUM
Blagrave St Y 3
Bridge St Z 4
Broad St Y
Broad St Mall Shopping Centre Z
Castle St Z 6
Chain St Z 7
Christchurch Rd X 9
Church St X 12
Crown St Z 13
Culver Lane X 14
Duke St Z 15
Greyfriars Rd Y 17
Gun St Z 18
King St Z 20
Mill Lane Z 21
Minster St Z 22
Mount Pleasant Z 23
Oracle Shopping Centre Z
Palmer Park Ave X 24
Prospect St X 27
Queen Victoria St Y 28
St Mary's Butts Z 29
Station Hill Y 30
Station Rd Y 31
Tilehurst Rd Z 33
Tudor Rd Y 34
Valpy St Y 37
Watlington St Z 40
West St Y 41
Whitley St X 42
CENTRE
0 300 m
0 300 yards
A 4155
B 3345 (A 4155)
Vastern Rd
Caversham Road
Great Knollys St.
George St.
Bedford Rd
Chatham St.
Friar St.
Forbury Rd
Broad St
King's Rd
Queen's Rd
Kennet
A 329
A 329 (M)
Oxford Road
BROAD ST. MALL
HEXAGON THEATRE
CIVIC CENTRE
ORACLE SHOPPING CENTRE
Russell Street
Inner Distribution Road
POL.
Castle Hill
Bath Rd
Coley Av.
Berkeley Av.
Pell St.
Southampton St.
London St.
Silver St.
London Road
Kendrick Rd
Eldon Rd
Craven Road
Redlands Rd
Addington Rd
A 4155
(M 4)
A 33
(A 33) A 327
ENGLAND

Malmaison

Great Western House, 18-20 Station Rd ✉ RG1 1JX – ✆ (0118) 956 23 00 – www.malmaison.com
Town plan: Y**e**

75 rm – 🚹£ 89/205 🚹🚹£ 89/205, ☕ £ 16

Rest *Brasserie* – Carte £ 19/39

This is the oldest operating railway hotel in the world! Stylish lounges have rich contemporary décor and the bedrooms are dark and moody with good facilities and quirky touches; one even has its own train set. The dimly lit brasserie features exposed brick and pipework and is hung with railway photos.

Forbury's

1 Forbury Sq ✉ RG1 3BB – ✆ (0118) 957 40 44 – www.forburys.co.uk – Closed 26-27 December, 1-2 January and Sunday
Town plan: Y**a**

Menu £ 20/25 – Carte £ 27/51

In a city centre square near the law courts, with a pleasant terrace, a leather-furnished bar-lounge and a smart, spacious dining room decorated with wine paraphernalia. Menus offer French-inspired dishes. Popular monthly wine events.

London Street Brasserie

2-4 London St ✉ RG1 4PN – ✆ (0118) 950 50 36 – www.londonstbrasserie.co.uk – Closed 25 December
Town plan: Z**c**

Menu £ 16 (lunch and early dinner) – Carte £ 29/46 – *(booking essential)*

Bright, 200 year old building which was once a post office; the two decked terraces and some of the first floor tables overlook the River Kennet. The extensive menu offers something for everyone and dishes are stout and satisfying.

ENGLAND

at Sonning-on-Thames Northeast: 4.25 mi by A4 on B4446

French Horn with rm

✉ RG4 6TN – ✆ (0118) 969 22 04 – www.thefrenchhorn.co.uk – Closed 1-2 January and dinner 25-26 December

21 rm ☕ – 🚹£ 125/170 🚹🚹£ 160/215 – 4 suites

Menu £ 28 (weekdays) – Carte £ 46/70 **s**

Beautifully located, 200 year old coaching inn, set on a bank of the Thames fringed by weeping willows; on sunny days head for the splendid terrace. The formal dining room has delightful views over the river and gardens and offers a classical menu of dishes from yesteryear – a gueridon trolley adds to the theatre. The cosy bedrooms are also traditionally appointed.

at Shinfield South: 4.25 mi on A327 -(X)✉ Reading

L'Ortolan

Church Ln ✉ RG2 9BY – ✆ (0118) 988 8500 – www.lortolan.com – Closed 25 December-3 January, Sunday and Monday

Menu £ 28/65

Beautiful, red-brick former vicarage with stylish, modern décor, several private dining rooms and a conservatory-lounge overlooking a lovely garden. Cooking is confident and passionate, with well-crafted, classically based dishes showing flair, originality and some playful, artistic touches.

→ Hen's egg and truffle ravioli, artichoke and trompette mushrooms. Duck and pineapple with a ginger jus. Banana mousse, toffee popcorn and brown bread ice cream.

REDDITCH

Worcestershire – Pop. 81 919 – See Regional map n°**19**-C2

London 111 mi – Birmingham 15 mi

Michelin Road map 503-O27 and 504

Old Rectory

Ipsley Lane, Ipsley ✉ B98 0AP – Southeast : 2.5 mi by A 4023 off B 4497 – ✆ (01527) 523 000 – www.theoldrectory-hotel.co.uk – Closed 25-31 December
10 rm ☕ – 🚹£ 79/168 🚻£ 92/175
Rest – Menu £ 20/30 – *(closed Friday-Sunday)*
Part-Elizabethan, part-Georgian former rectory in well-tended gardens. Spacious guest areas have a cosy, country house feel. Bedrooms are split between the house and stables; the latter, with their exposed beams, are the most characterful. Dine in the bright conservatory restaurant overlooking the garden.

REDFORD → See Midhurst
West Sussex

REDHILL
Surrey – Pop. 34 498 – See Regional map n°**7-D2**
▶London 22 mi – Brighton 31 mi – Guildford 20 mi – Maidstone 34 mi
Michelin Road map 504-T30

The Pendleton in St Johns Ⓝ

26 St Johns ✉ RH1 6QF – South : 1 mi by A 23 and Pendleton Rd – ✆ (01737) 760 212 – www.thependleton.co.uk – Closed 25 December-2 January, Sunday dinner, Monday and Tuesday
Carte £ 25/39 – *(bookings advisable at dinner)*
It's got a new name and a smart new look, and it's very popular, so make sure you book. Seasonal French classics, with some Mediterranean and South American influences. Portions are generous and flavours, well-pronounced.

REETH
North Yorkshire – Pop. 724 – ✉ Richmond – See Regional map n°**22**-B1
▶London 253 mi – Leeds 53 mi – Middlesbrough 36 mi – Newcastle upon Tyne 61 mi
Michelin Road map 502-O20

Burgoyne

On The Green ✉ DL11 6SN – ✆ (01748) 884 292 – www.theburgoyne.co.uk – Restricted opening in January
10 rm ☕ – 🚹£ 78/123 🚻£ 95/220 – 1 suite
Rest – Menu £ 40 – *(dinner only) (booking essential)*
A late Georgian house with a cosy, comforting feel, set in a lovely spot overlooking the village green and the Yorkshire Dales. The two lounges are filled with antiques and vases of flowers. Bedrooms are individually styled and traditionally appointed. The elegant dining room offers an all-encompassing menu.

at Low Row West: 4 mi on B6270

Punch Bowl Inn with rm

✉ DL11 6PF – ✆ (01748) 886 233 – www.pbinn.co.uk – Closed 25 December
11 rm ☕ – 🚹£ 99/140 🚻£ 99/140 Carte £ 20/33
A traditional 17C stone-built inn with a contrastingly modern, shabby-chic interior. It's a popular stop-off for walkers, who can refuel on classic dishes like lamb shank or beef and red wine casserole. Supremely comfortable bedrooms are decorated in a fresh, modern style; all have views over Swaledale.

at Langthwaite Northwest: 3.25 mi on Langthwaite rd✉ Reeth

Charles Bathurst Inn with rm

✉ DL11 6EN – ✆ (0333) 700 07 79 – www.cbinn.co.uk – Closed 25 December
19 rm ☕ – 🚹£ 81/107 🚻£ 99/125 Carte £ 21/35
Characterful 18C hostelry set in a peaceful hillside village, with commanding rural views. Hearty British pub classics at lunch; more elaborate dishes in the evening from a menu inscribed on a mirror. Local beers include Black Sheep Ale. Bedrooms are spacious and comfortable.

ENGLAND

REIGATE

Surrey – Pop. 22 123 – See Regional map n°**7-D2**
London 26 mi – Brighton 33 mi – Guildford 20 mi – Maidstone 38 mi
Michelin Road map 504-T30

XX **Tony Tobin @ The Dining Room**
59a High St (1st Floor) ✉ RH2 9AE – ☎ (01737) 226 650 – www.tonytobinrestaurants.co.uk – Closed 23 December-4 January, Sunday, Monday and bank holidays
Menu £ 17/48
Chic, contemporary restaurant with a comfortable atmosphere and professional staff. Cooking demonstrates the chef's classical background whilst also incorporating some international influences. Most plump for the 5 course tasting menu.

X **Barbe**
71 Bell St ✉ RH2 7AN – ☎ (01737) 241 966 – www.labarbe.co.uk – Closed 26-28 December, 1 January, Saturday lunch, Sunday dinner and bank holiday Mondays
Menu £ 15/35
Long-standing French bistro with a cheery owner and huge local following. Two main dining areas strewn with Gallic memorabilia. Simply laid, tightly packed tables. Classical, bi-monthly menu.

RETFORD

Nottinghamshire – Pop. 22 023 – See Regional map n°**16-B1**
London 148 mi – Lincoln 23 mi – Nottingham 31 mi – Sheffield 27 mi
Michelin Road map 502-R24 and 503

Barns without rest
Morton Farm, Babworth ✉ DN22 8HA – Southwest : 2.25 mi by A 620 on B 6420 – ☎ (01777) 706 336 – www.thebarns.co.uk – Closed Christmas-New Year
6 rm – †£ 39/60 ††£ 64/75
18C barn with a pleasant garden and a traditionally styled interior. The oak-beamed breakfast room is furnished with old dressers and Regency-style tables and chairs. Country bedrooms have good rural outlooks; one has a four-poster.

RIBCHESTER

Lancashire – Pop. 888 – See Regional map n°**20-B2**
London 229 mi – Blackburn 7 mi – Manchester 41 mi
Michelin Road map 502-M22

XXX **Angels**
Fleet Street Ln ✉ PR3 3ZA – Northwest : 1.5 mi by B 6245 (Longridge Rd) – ☎ (01254) 820 212 – www.angelsribchester.co.uk – Closed Monday
Menu £ 20/45 – Carte £ 35/50 – *(dinner only and Sunday lunch)*
Smartly converted roadside pub with a cocktail bar and comfy lounge seating. Two formally dressed dining rooms, with a grand piano played on Friday evenings. Classic dishes with a modern edge; tasty, well-balanced and good value.

RICHMOND

North Yorkshire – Pop. 8 413 – See Regional map n°**22-B1**
London 243 mi – Leeds 53 mi – Middlesbrough 26 mi – Newcastle upon Tyne 44 mi
Michelin Road map 502-O20 – Michelin Green Guide GREAT BRITAIN

Easby Hall without rest
Easby ✉ DL10 7EU – Southeast : 2.5 mi by A 6108 off B 6271 – ☎ (01748) 826 066 – www.easbyhall.com
3 rm – †£ 120/150 ††£ 150/180
The views of the church, the abbey ruins and the hills are as stunning as this part-18C hall itself. There are two gardens, a kitchen garden, an orchard and a paddock – and even stables for your horse! Inside it's elegant and luxurious. Tea and scones or cocktails are served on arrival, depending on the time.

Millgate House without rest
3 Millgate ✉ DL10 4JN – ✆ (01748) 823 571 – www.millgatehouse.com
4 rm ☕ – 🚹£ 85/110 🚹🚹£ 110/145
Traditional Georgian guesthouse with a beautiful garden leading down to the river and a wonderful collection of silverware, grandfather clocks and antiques on display. Most rooms offer commanding views over the waterfall and castle.

Frenchgate with rm
59-61 Frenchgate ✉ DL10 7AE – ✆ (01748) 822 087 – www.thefrenchgate.co.uk
9 rm ☕ – 🚹£ 88/198 🚹🚹£ 118/250 Menu £ 18/39
Part-dating from the 17C, with two open-fired lounges filled with vivid art, a simply furnished dining room and a lovely terrace and walled garden. Modern, ambitious dishes. Immaculately kept, well-equipped bedrooms; breakfast features local bacon and sausages, and preserves made from berries picked nearby.

Richmond Grill + Brasserie Ⓝ
2-3 Trinity Sq. Market Pl. ✉ DL10 4HY – ✆ (01748) 822 602 – www.rgandb.co.uk – Closed Sunday dinner and Monday
Carte £ 24/47
This modern brasserie provides a complete contrast to the cobbled marketplace in which it stands. Bold wallpaper, lime green banquettes and grey chairs feature. Menus offer grills, sharing plates and modern takes on brasserie classics.

RIMPTON

Somerset – Pop. 235 – See Regional map n°**4-C3**
London 126 mi – Bath 50 mi – Bournemouth 44 mi – Exeter 57 mi

White Post Ⓝ with rm
✉ BA22 8AR – ✆ (01935) 851 525 – www.thewhitepost.com – Closed 1-14 January and Sunday dinner
3 rm ☕ – 🚹£ 80 🚹🚹£ 95 Carte £ 21/43
On the Dorset/Somerset border, with stunning views of the West Country. Plenty of pub classics alongside more imaginative creations and quirky touches like piggy nibbles and the Sunday roast board: surely every carnivore's dream dish? Bedrooms are simply furnished: ask for Dorset, which has the best views.

RINGWOOD

Hampshire – Pop. 13 943 – See Regional map n°**6-A2**
London 102 mi – Bournemouth 11 mi – Salisbury 17 mi – Southampton 20 mi
Michelin Road map 503-O31 and 504

Moortown Lodge without rest
244 Christchurch Rd ✉ BH24 3AS – South : 1 mi on B 3347 – ✆ (01425) 471 404 – www.moortownlodge.co.uk
7 rm ☕ – 🚹£ 75/98 🚹🚹£ 88/98
Welcoming Georgian hunting lodge built in 1760, set on a busy road at the edge of the forest. The large main room has fireside sofas and neatly laid breakfast tables. Well-kept bedrooms offer good comforts; some have feature beds.

RIPLEY

North Yorkshire – Pop. 193 – ✉ Harrogate – See Regional map n°**22-B2**
London 213 mi – Bradford 21 mi – Leeds 18 mi – Newcastle upon Tyne 79 mi
Michelin Road map 502-P21

Boar's Head
✉ HG3 3AY – ✆ (01423) 771 888 – www.boarsheadripley.co.uk
25 rm ☕ – 🚹£ 80/100 🚹🚹£ 100/125
Rest *Brasserie* – Menu £ 18/40 – Carte £ 20/31
18C creeper-clad coaching inn, set in an estate-owned village and reputedly furnished from the nearby castle's attics. Family portraits and knick-knacks fill the lounges. Comfy bedrooms are found in the inn, the courtyard and an adjacent house. The all-encompassing menu is served in various different rooms.

RIPLEY

Surrey – Pop. 2 041 – See Regional map n°**7-C1**
London 24 mi – Croydon 22 mi – Barnet 46 mi – Ealing 28 mi
Michelin Road map 504-S30

Broadway Barn without rest

High St ✉ GU23 6AQ – ✆ (01483) 223 200 – www.broadwaybarn.com
4 rm – †£ 95 ††£ 95
The name is misleading, as this charming red-brick Georgian building was formerly an antique shop. Inside it's smart and modern with spacious guest areas; bedrooms show good attention to detail and come with thoughtful extras.

Drake's (Steve Drake)

The Clock House, High St ✉ GU23 6AQ – ✆ (01483) 224 777 – www.drakesrestaurant.co.uk – Closed 2 weeks August, 1 week January, 1 week Christmas, Tuesday lunch, Sunday and Monday
Menu £ 28/60
Red-brick Georgian building with a large double-sided clock above the door and a drinks terrace overlooking a beautiful garden to the rear. The panelled bar leads to an elegant modern dining room. At dinner, choose between two set menus; cooking is creative, very visual and pushes the boundaries.
→ Red mullet, pear and saffron with buckwheat and lemongrass. Breast of veal, parsnip and bay purée, asparagus and sumac. Macerated strawberries, coconut, lime and pea & mint ice cream.

Anchor

High St ✉ GU23 6AE – ✆ (01483) 211 866 – www.ripleyanchor.co.uk – Closed Sunday dinner and Monday
Carte £ 24/41
A smart yet rustic pub with polished slate floors and on-trend grey walls; it is nowhere near water but it is near a famous 19C cycle route, which explains the bicycle theme. Classic dishes are carefully executed and bursting with flavour.

ENGLAND

RIPON

North Yorkshire – Pop. 16 363 – See Regional map n°**22-B2**
London 222 mi – Leeds 26 mi – Middlesbrough 35 mi – York 23 mi
Michelin Road map 502-P21 – Michelin Green Guide GREAT BRITAIN

Old Deanery

Minster Rd ✉ HG4 1QS – ✆ (01765) 600 003 – www.theolddeanery.co.uk
10 rm – †£ 85/110 ††£ 105/150
Rest – Menu £ 15 (weekday lunch) – Carte £ 23/39
Attractive former deanery opposite Ripon Cathedral. Inside, modern furnishings blend with older features; climb the 18C oak staircase to the comfy, up-to-date bedrooms – some have beams, Victorian-style baths and cathedral views. The large bar and three-roomed restaurant serve a menu of modern dishes.

Sharow Cross House

Dishforth Rd, Sharow ✉ HG4 5BQ – Northeast : 1.75 mi by A 61 on Sharow rd – ✆ (01765) 609 866 – www.sharowcrosshouse.co.uk – Closed 23 December-2 January
3 rm – †£ 70/80 ††£ 90/100 **Rest** – Menu £ 28
This fine Victorian villa was originally the country residence of a soap manufacturer from Bradford. The characterful interior is spacious and light-filled; homemade cake is served in the comfy lounge on arrival. Tastefully furnished bedrooms come with thoughtful extras and the master room has cathedral views. Choose dinner in advance from a series of seven set menus.

at Aldfield Southwest: 3.75 mi by B6265 ✉ Ripon

Bay Tree Farm without rest

✉ HG4 3BE – ✆ (01765) 620 394 – www.baytreefarm.co.uk
6 rm – †£ 60/80 ††£ 85/95
18C sandstone barn on a working beef farm, with a smartly furnished farmhouse interior and country views. The open-fired lounge is hung with farm implements and opens onto the garden. The welcoming owners always make time to talk.

RIPPONDEN

West Yorkshire – Pop. 4 665 – See Regional map n°**22-A3**
London 200 mi – Bristol 195 mi – Cardiff 216 mi – Plymouth 309 mi
Michelin Road map 502-O22

El Gato Negro

1 Oldham Rd ✉ HX6 4DN – ✆ (01422) 823 070 – www.elgatonegrotapas.com – Closed 2 weeks January, 2 weeks August, Sunday and Monday
Menu £ 35 – Carte £ 22/34 – *(dinner only and Saturday lunch) (booking essential)*
Laid-back former pub in a small valley town; the eye-catching modern exterior conceals two warm, rustic rooms with stone walls and open fires. Appealing Spanish menus feature refined, carefully prepared, authentic tapas dishes; the chef visits Spain regularly. Knowledgeable staff guide you through the menu.

ROADE

Northamptonshire – Pop. 2 312 – See Regional map n°**16-B3**
London 66 mi – Coventry 36 mi – Leicester 42 mi – Northampton 5 mi
Michelin Road map 504-R27

Roade House with rm

rest,

16 High St ✉ NN7 2NW – ✆ (01604) 863 372 – www.roadehousehotel.co.uk – Closed 26-30 December, Sunday dinner and bank holiday Mondays
10 rm – †£ 70/82 ††£ 82/90 Menu £ 21 (lunch) – Carte £ 28/42
Personally run, former village pub and schoolhouse, with an open-fired lounge and a simple, linen-laid dining room. The set lunch and à la carte dinner menus are crafted from local produce and offer classical cooking with modern touches. Pleasant bedrooms are furnished in pine.

ROCHDALE

Greater Manchester – Pop. 107 926 – See Regional map n°**20-B2**
London 224 mi – Blackpool 40 mi – Burnley 11 mi – Leeds 45 mi
Michelin Road map 502-N23

Peacock Room at The Crimble

Crimble Ln, Bamford ✉ OL11 4AD – West : 2 mi on B 6222 – ✆ (01706) 368 591 – www.thedeckersgroup.com – Closed Monday, Tuesday and lunch Saturday
Carte £ 25/41
A winding drive leads up to this landmark Victorian house. Bypass the pub and head for the restaurant, where you'll find a large mirror-ceilinged room with vast chandeliers. Constantly evolving modern menus rely on local produce.

Nutters

Edenfield Rd, Norden ✉ OL12 7TT – West : 3.5 mi on A 680 – ✆ (01706) 650 167 – www.nuttersrestaurant.com – Closed 5-6 January, 29-30 December and Monday
Menu £ 14 (weekday lunch) – Carte £ 27/41
Enthusiastically run restaurant in a beautiful old manor house – and a popular spot for afternoon tea. Appealing menus list modern British dishes with international influences. Can't decide? Go for the 6 course 'Surprise' menu.

ROCK

Cornwall – Pop. 4 593 – ✉ Wadebridge – See Regional map n°**1-B2**
London 266 mi – Newquay 24 mi – Tintagel 14 mi – Truro 32 mi
Michelin Road map 503-F32 – Michelin Green Guide GREAT BRITAIN

St Enodoc

✉ PL27 6LA – ✆ (01208) 863 394 – www.enodoc-hotel.co.uk – Closed late December-January
20 rm – †£ 155/265 ††£ 195/295 – 4 suites
Rest *Restaurant Nathan Outlaw* ✿✿ **Rest *Outlaw's*** – see restaurant listing
Beautifully located hotel boasting stunning bay views. It has a strong New England theme throughout, with pastel painted woodwork and stripy sofas. Comfy guest areas and modern, well-appointed bedrooms.

XXX ✿✿ **Restaurant Nathan Outlaw** – St Enodoc Hotel
✉ *PL27 6LA* – ✆ *(01208) 862 737* – *www.nathan-outlaw.com*
– Closed 21 December-30 January, Sunday and Monday
Menu £ 99 – *(dinner only) (booking essential) (set menu only)*
Highlight of the St Enodoc Hotel is this stylish, modern restaurant of just nine tables, with understated décor which puts the spotlight on the accomplished cooking. Top quality fresh fish is their focus and dishes are simple yet superbly crafted with delicate, defined flavours. Friendly, professional service.
→ Port Isaac crab and asparagus. Red mullet with Porthilly sauce. Raspberry and pistachio ice cream sandwich.

XX **Dining Room**
Pavilion Buildings, Rock Rd ✉ *PL27 6JS* – ✆ *(01208) 862 622*
– www.thediningroomrock.co.uk – Closed 2 weeks January-February, 2 weeks November, Monday except bank holidays and Tuesday
Carte £ 34/42 – *(dinner only) (booking essential)*
Immaculately kept, understated restaurant with modern seascapes on the walls; run by a friendly, family-led team. Flavoursome, classically based cooking features local seasonal produce. Everything is homemade, including the butter.

X **Outlaw's** – St Enodoc Hotel
✉ *PL27 6LA* – ✆ *(01208) 862 737* – *www.nathan-outlaw.com*
– Closed 21 December-30 January
Menu £ 25/45
All day, split-level restaurant and bar overlooking the Camel Estuary and opening out onto a lovely rear terrace. Menus feature light offerings and simply executed steak and seafood dishes; the use of local ingredients is key.

ENGLAND

at Trebetherick North: 1 mi by Trewint Lane

 **St Moritz** rm,
✉ *PL27 6SD* – ✆ *(01208) 862 242* – *www.stmoritzhotel.co.uk*
30 rm – †£ 90/267 ††£ 120/355 – 15 suites
Rest – Carte £ 29/43 – *(dinner only in winter)*
Rest ***Sea Side*** – Carte £ 21/32 – *(lunch only in winter)*
Art deco style hotel with a leisure club, indoor and outdoor swimming pools and a 6 room spa. Contemporary bedrooms have a minimalistic style and spacious bathrooms. Suites have an open plan lounge, a kitchen and balconies with estuary views. Modern brasserie serves a simple, flavoursome menu of unfussy dishes. Informal, poolside restaurant, Sea Side.

ROCKBEARE → See Exeter
Devon

ROECLIFFE → See Boroughbridge
North Yorkshire

ROGATE
West Sussex – Pop. 1 785 – ✉ Petersfield (hants.) – See Regional map n°**7-C2**
▶London 63 mi – Brighton 42 mi – Guildford 29 mi – Portsmouth 23 mi
Michelin Road map 504-R30

 **Mizzards Farm** without rest
✉ *GU31 5HS Southwest : 1 mi by Harting rd* – ✆ *(01730) 821 656*
– Closed Christmas and New Year
3 rm – †£ 60/70 ††£ 80/98
16C farmhouse boasting delightful gardens with a pond and sculptures. An impressive wooden staircase leads to 3 individually furnished bedrooms: two are classic and cosy, the third is rather more grand, with a sumptuous bathroom.

ROMALDKIRK → See Barnard Castle
Durham – Michelin Road map 502-N20

ROMSEY

Hampshire – Pop. 16 998 – See Regional map n°**6-A2**
London 82 mi – Bournemouth 28 mi – Salisbury 16 mi – Southampton 8 mi
Michelin Road map 503-P31 and 504 – Michelin Green Guide GREAT BRITAIN

White Horse

Market Pl ✉ SO51 8ZJ – ✆ (01794) 512 431 – www.thewhitehorseromsey.com
31 rm – †£ 85/95 ††£ 115/235, ☕ £ 15
Rest *Silks Brasserie* – Menu £ 15 (weekdays) – Carte £ 24/64
Smartly refurbished coaching inn; one of only 12 in the country to have continuously served as a hotel since the 14C – maybe even earlier! Guest areas feature beams, exposed brick and inglenook fireplaces. Well-equipped modern bedrooms include two duplex suites. The extensive brasserie menu suits all tastes.

Ranvilles Farm House without rest

Ower ✉ SO51 6AA – Southwest : 2 mi on A 3090 (southbound carriageway) – ✆ (023) 8081 4481 – www.ranvilles.com – Closed 25 December
5 rm ☕ – †£ 35/50 ††£ 70/85
Attractive, part-16C farmhouse in colourful grounds. The spacious beamed interior has a cottagey, country house feel and period pieces feature throughout – the comfy lounge boasts an antique breakfast table. Bedrooms are homely.

Three Tuns

58 Middlebridge St ✉ SO51 8HL – ✆ (01794) 512 639 – www.the3tunsromsey.co.uk – Closed 25-26 December
Carte £ 20/33
A delightful pub, dating back to the 1720s; it oozes charm, with a rustic beamed bar and a panelled dining room. The well-priced, 'proper' pub menu proudly lists local suppliers and dishes might include ham hock terrine or pot roast partridge. Service comes from a young, very hospitable team.

ENGLAND

ROSS-ON-WYE

Herefordshire – Pop. 10 582 – See Regional map n°**18-B3**
London 118 mi – Gloucester 15 mi – Birmingham 61 mi
Michelin Road map 503-M28 and 504 – Michelin Green Guide GREAT BRITAIN

Wilton Court

Wilton Ln, Wilton ✉ HR9 6AQ – West : 0.75 mi by B 4260 – ✆ (01989) 562 569 – www.wiltoncourthotel.com – Closed 2-15 January
10 rm ☕ – †£ 100/150 ††£ 135/175 **Rest** – Menu £ 17/33 – Carte £ 29/41
Attractive, part-Elizabethan house out of the town centre, on the banks of the River Wye. Traditionally styled, comfortable bedrooms have good facilities; those to the front have a river view. Tasty breakfasts with homemade preserves. Choice of two dining rooms; classic menus utilise local produce.

Bridge House without rest

Wilton ✉ HR9 6AA – West : 0.75 mi by B 4260 – ✆ (01989) 562 655 – www.bridgehouserossonwye.co.uk
6 rm ☕ – †£ 85 ††£ 105/125
You get a lot more than you bargained for at this 18C townhouse: original features combine with chic, stylish furnishings; there's a superb view of the town and the River Wye; and the ruins of Castle Wilton border the grounds.

at Walford South: 3 mi on B4234

Mill Race

✉ HR9 5QS – ✆ (01989) 562 891 – www.millrace.info
Carte £ 26/38
Contemporary village pub with an atmosphere of relaxed contentment. Their own farm provides much of the meat and a blackboard informs customers how far ingredients have travelled. Hearty, satisfying dishes with recommended wine matches.

at Kerne Bridge South: 3.75 mi on B4234✉ Ross-On-Wye

Lumleys without rest
✉ HR9 5QT – ✆ (01600) 890 040 – www.thelumleys.co.uk
3 rm – †£ 50/70 ††£ 70/80
Double-fronted brick house with colourful gardens; formerly the village pub, now a cosy, characterful guesthouse run with love and care. It has cluttered, homely bedrooms, a comfy first floor lounge and a drying room for walkers.

at Upton Bishop Northeast: 3 mi by A40 on B4221

Moody Cow Ⓝ with rm
✉ HR9 7TT – ✆ (01989) 780 470 – www.moodycowpub.co.uk – Closed 5-21 January, Sunday dinner and Monday
1 rm – †£ 65/88 ††£ 65/88, £ 11 Carte £ 24/41
A traditional country pub serving classic dishes to match the surroundings. What the food may lack in originality, it makes up for with quality ingredients, careful cooking and distinct flavours. Friendly owners run the place with a passion. One cosy bedroom is accessed via a spiral staircase.

ROTHBURY

Northumberland – Pop. 2 326 – ✉ Morpeth – See Regional map n°**24**-A2
London 311 mi – Edinburgh 84 mi – Newcastle upon Tyne 29 mi
Michelin Road map 501-O18 and 502 – Michelin Green Guide GREAT BRITAIN

Farm Cottage without rest
Thropton ✉ NE65 7NA – West : 2.25 mi on B 6341 – ✆ (01669) 620 831 – www.farmcottageguesthouse.co.uk – Closed 1 week Christmas
4 rm – †£ 60 ††£ 85/92
18C stone cottage run by friendly owners – one of them was born here! Cosy, open-fired lounge filled with curios and a small breakfast room overlooking the garden. Traditional, homely bedrooms; the one in the annexe is the most modern.

Thropton Demesne Farmhouse without rest
Thropton ✉ NE65 7LT – West : 2.5 mi on B 6341 – ✆ (01669) 620 196 – www.thropton demesne.co.uk – Closed January
3 rm – †£ 85 ††£ 85
Extended stone farmhouse with lovely valley views. Comfy lounge and conservatory; bright, well-kept bedrooms with good facilities – one has a private bathroom. Artwork is by the chatty owner. Homemade bread and marmalade at breakfast.

ROWDE → See Devizes

Wiltshire – Michelin Road map 503-N29 and 504

ROWHOOK → See Horsham

West Sussex

ROWSLEY

Derbyshire – Pop. 451 – ✉ Matlock – See Regional map n°**16**-A1
London 157 mi – Derby 23 mi – Manchester 40 mi – Nottingham 30 mi
Michelin Road map 502-P24 and 503 – Michelin Green Guide GREAT BRITAIN

Peacock 
Bakewell Rd ✉ DE4 2EB – ✆ (01629) 733 518 – www.thepeacockatrowsley.com – Closed first 2 weeks January and 24-26 December
15 rm – †£ 90/123 ††£ 170/270
Rest *Peacock* – see restaurant listing
Characterful 17C Dower House of the Duchess of Rutland, with gardens leading down to the river. Snug, open-fired sitting room and antique-furnished bedrooms with good facilities; one has a four-poster. The charming bar boasts exposed stone walls and old wood-panelling and serves a snack menu. It's run by a lovely team.

ENGLAND

East Lodge

Main St ✉ DE4 2EF – ✆ (01629) 734 474 – www.eastlodge.com
12 rm ☕ – 👤£ 90/295 👥£ 90/295
Rest *East Lodge* – see restaurant listing
17C hunting lodge in 10 acres of landscaped gardens with ponds and a fountain. Guest areas are elegant and well-appointed. Smart bedrooms, several with four-posters, have good views and state-of-the-art bathrooms – some with TVs.

Peacock – Peacock Hotel

Bakewell Rd ✉ DE4 2EB – ✆ (01629) 733 518 – www.thepeacockatrowsley.com – Closed first 2 weeks January, 24-26 December and Sunday dinner
Menu £ 18/30 – Carte dinner £ 48/62
Elegant hotel restaurant which mixes old stone mullioned windows, Mousey Thompson oak furnishings and antique oil paintings with modern lighting and contemporary art. Classical dishes at lunch; more complex, elaborate combinations featuring lots of ingredients in the evening. Attentive, formal service.

East Lodge – East Lodge Hotel

Main St ✉ DE4 2EF – ✆ (01629) 734 474 – www.eastlodge.com
Carte £ 27/50
Two formal traditionally furnished dining rooms in a country house hotel, serving classic dishes with a modern touch. Book a place at the chef's table to sample the 8 course tasting menu, which really showcases the kitchen's skills.

ENGLAND

ROYAL LEAMINGTON SPA

Warwickshire – Pop. 55 733 – See Regional map n°**19**-D3
▶London 99 mi – Birmingham 23 mi – Coventry 9 mi – Leicester 33 mi
Michelin Road map 503-P27 and 504

ROYAL LEAMINGTON SPA

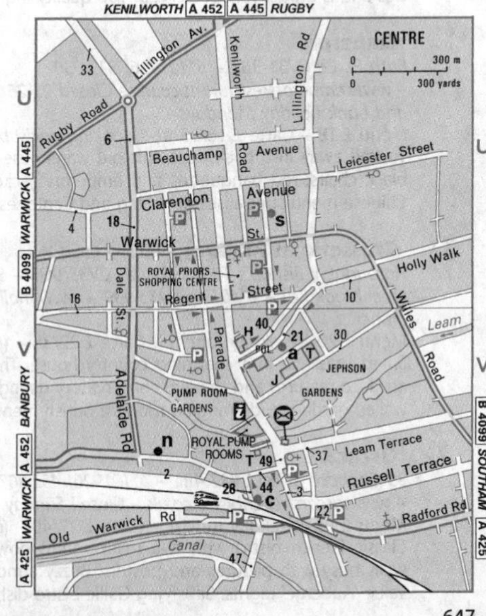

Mallory Court

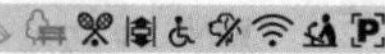

Harbury Ln, Bishop's Tachbrook ✉ CV33 9QB – South : 2.25 mi by B 4087 (Tachbrook Rd) – ✆ (01926) 330 214 – www.mallory.co.uk

31 rm – †£ 125/475 ††£ 155/525

Rest *Dining Room at Mallory* Rest *Brasserie at Mallory* – see restaurant listing

Part-Edwardian house in Lutyens' style, with lovely gardens. Classic lounges display fine antiques and quality furnishings. Fresh flowers and fruit feature in the bedrooms; those in the main house are in keeping with the building's age.

Adams without rest

22 Avenue Rd ✉ CV31 3PQ – ✆ (01926) 450 742 Town plan: V**n**

– www.adams-hotel.co.uk – Closed 23 December-2 January

12 rm – †£ 83/89 ††£ 85/99

Attractive detached Regency house with bay windows on either side. Bedrooms are classically styled and come with extra touches; the four at the rear are smaller but quieter. Smart bar-lounge with ornate cornicing. Extensive breakfasts.

XXX

Dining Room at Mallory – Mallory Court Hotel

Harbury Ln, Bishop's Tachbrook ✉ CV33 9QB – South : 2.25 mi by B 4087 (Tachbrook Rd) – ✆ (01926) 330 214 – www.mallory.co.uk – Closed Saturday lunch

Menu £ 33/65 – *(booking essential)*

Elegant wood-panelled dining room hidden within a lovely country house and looking out over its delightful grounds. Herbs, vegetables and soft fruits come from the kitchen garden. Cooking is modern; the simplest dishes are the best.

ENGLAND

XX

Restaurant 23

34 Hamilton Terr ✉ CV32 4LY – ✆ (01926) 422 422 Town plan: V**a**

– www.restaurant23.co.uk – Closed 25-26 December, 1 January and Sunday dinner and Monday

Menu £ 20/35 – Carte £ 42/56 – *(booking advisable)*

Smart restaurant with a chic cocktail bar and a stylish, elegant dining room, which is intimately candlelit at dinner. Modern cooking has classical European tendencies and is attractively presented. Top quality ingredients are the focus.

XX

Emperors

Bath Pl. ✉ CV31 3BP – ✆ (01926) 313 030 Town plan: V**i**

– www.emperorsrestaurant.co.uk – Closed 25-26 December, 1 January, Sunday and bank holiday Mondays

Menu £ 18 – Carte £ 16/35 **s** – *(booking advisable)*

Tucked away in a backstreet, this old warehouse is now a smart restaurant with black chairs, red banquettes and emperors' jackets on the walls. The extensive Chinese menu specialises in Peking and Cantonese dishes, especially seafood.

XX

Brasserie at Mallory – Mallory Court Hotel

Harbury Ln, Bishop's Tachbrook ✉ CV33 9QB – South : 2.25 mi by B 4087 (Tachbrook Rd) – ✆ (01926) 453 939 – www.mallory.co.uk – Closed Sunday dinner

Menu £ 20 (weekday lunch) – Carte £ 22/38 – *(booking essential)*

Smart brasserie in a charming country house. The bar-lounge has striking black art deco features and the airy conservatory dining room looks out over the pretty walled garden. Wide-ranging modern British menus follow the seasons.

X

Oscar's

39 Chandos St ✉ CV32 4RL – ✆ (01926) 452 807 Town plan: U**s**

– www.oscarsfrenchbistro.co.uk – Closed Sunday and Monday

Menu £ 13 (weekday lunch) – Carte £ 27/40 – *(booking essential)*

Classic French bistro with two rustic rooms downstairs and a third above; the walls busy with pictures and posters. Buzzy atmosphere, especially on the good value 'Auberge' nights. Satisfying Gallic bistro dishes and friendly service.

at Weston under Wetherley Northeast: 4.5 mi by A445 on B4453 ✉ Royal Leamington Spa

Wethele Manor without rest
✉ *CV33 9BZ – ✆ (01926) 831 772 – www.wethelemanor.com*
9 rm ☕ – †£ 65/75 ††£ 70/100
16C farmhouse on a 250 acre arable farm with a pond, an orchard and lamas! Classical bedrooms: some have antiques or four-posters; the family rooms are duplex. Comfy lounge in the old milking parlour; the timbered breakfast room has a well.

at Offchurch East: 3.5 mi by A425

Stag
Welsh Rd ✉ CV33 9AQ – ✆ (01926) 425 801 – www.thestagatoffchurch.com
Carte £ 23/42
16C thatched pub with a boldly coloured bar and two modern dining rooms. The extensive menu changes with the seasons, offering generous, classical dishes, alongside antipasti and charcuterie sharing plates. Service is efficient.

ROYAL TUNBRIDGE WELLS

Kent – Pop. 57 772 – See Regional map n°**8**-**B2**
▶London 36 mi – Brighton 33 mi – Folkestone 46 mi – Hastings 27 mi
Michelin Road map 504-U30 – Michelin Green Guide GREAT BRITAIN

ENGLAND

ROYAL TUNBRIDGE WELLS

Benhall Mill Rd . . . . **A** 3
Bishop's Down . . . . **A** 4
Calverley Rd . . . . **B**
Crescent Rd . . . . **B** 9
Fir Tree Rd . . . . **A** 10
Grosvenor Rd . . . . **B** 12
Hall's Hole Rd . . . . **A** 13
High Rocks Lane . . . . **A** 16
High St . . . . **B** 14
Hungershall Park Rd . . . . **A** 17
Lansdowne Rd . . . . **B** 18
Lower Green Rd . . . . **A** 20
Major York's Rd . . . . **A** 21
Monson Rd . . . . **B** 22
Mount Ephraim . . . . **A, B** 23
Mount Ephraim Rd . . . . **B** 24
Mount Pleasant Rd . . . . **B** 25
Pantiles (The) . . . . **B** 26
Prospect Rd . . . . **A** 27
Royal Victoria Pl. Shopping Centre . . . . **B**
Rusthall Rd . . . . **A** 28
St John's Rd . . . . **B** 29
Tea Garden Lane . . . . **A** 30
Vale Rd . . . . **B** 33
Victoria Rd . . . . **B** 34
Warwick Park . . . . **B** 35

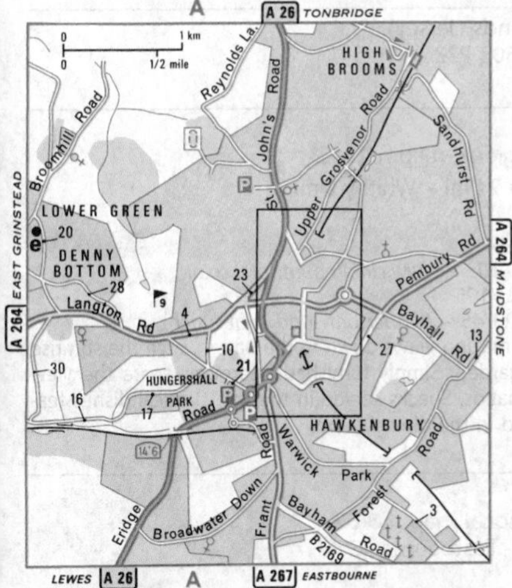

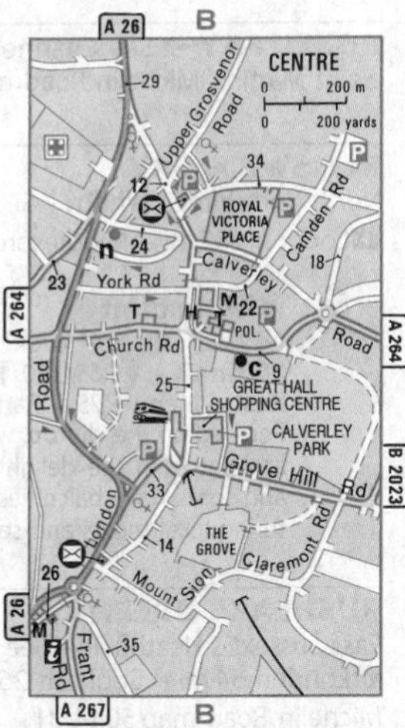

Hotel du Vin

 rest,

Crescent Rd ✉ TN1 2LY – ✆ (08447) 489 266 Town plan: B**c**
– www.hotelduvin.com
34 rm ☕ – 🚹£ 138/288 🚹🚹£ 151/352
Rest ***Bistro*** – Carte £ 28/52 – *(booking essential)*
Attractive Georgian property in the town centre, boasting southerly views over Calverley Park. It's wine-themed throughout, with a well-stocked clubby bar, two comfy lounges and contemporary bedrooms; some have emperor-sized beds and baths in the rooms. The rustic bistro and terrace serve French cuisine.

Danehurst without rest

41 Lower Green Rd, Rusthall ✉ TN4 8TW – West : 1.75 mi Town plan: A**e**
by A 264 – ✆ (01892) 527 739 – www.danehurst.net – Closed 20 December-2 January
4 rm ☕ – 🚹£ 75/110 🚹🚹£ 85/155
Quiet Edwardian house with a terrace and koi carp pond, set in a residential area and run by charming owners. It has top quality furnishings and displays good attention to detail. Tasty homemade bread and jam feature at breakfast.

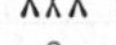

Thackeray's

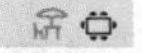

85 London Rd ✉ TN1 1EA – ✆ (01892) 511 921 Town plan: B**n**
– www.thackerays-restaurant.co.uk – Closed Sunday dinner and Monday
Menu £ 17/75 – Carte £ 46/52
Grade II listed clapperboard house; the oldest in town and once home to the author Thackeray. It has two stylish dining rooms and a delightful terrace; original features include lovely oak flooring. Exacting, skilful cooking has clear, well-defined flavours: classical dishes display modern elements.
➜ Saddle of rabbit, medjool dates and bread sauce. Monkfish tail with fennel pollen and avocado mousse. Rhubarb soufflé, tonka bean custard and nutmeg.

ENGLAND

at Speldhurst Northwest: 3.5 mi by A26 -(A)

George & Dragon

Speldhurst Hill ✉ TN3 0NN – ✆ (01892) 863 125 – www.speldhurst.com
Carte £ 21/45
Hugely characterful Wealden Hall house dating back to 1212 and boasting an impressive beamed ceiling and an unusual Queen's post. Generous cooking uses local, organic produce, offering pub classics alongside more elaborate dishes.

ROZEL BAY ➜ See Channel Islands (Jersey)
Saint Martin – Michelin Road map 503-P33

RUNSWICK BAY

North Yorkshire ✉ Whitby – See Regional map n°**23-C1**
▶ London 285 mi – Middlesbrough 24 mi – Whitby 9 mi

Cliffemount

✉ TS13 5HU – ✆ (01947) 840 103 – www.cliffemounthotel.co.uk
20 rm ☕ – 🚹£ 65/140 🚹🚹£ 75/195
Rest – Menu £ 25 – Carte £ 23/45 – *(dinner only and light lunch)*
Perched on the clifftop, with amazing views down to the bay – watch the sun rise and set from the delightful garden. Simply furnished bedrooms share the view and some have balconies or patios. Snacks served in the bar; classical dishes featuring local meats and seafood in the dining room.

RUSHLAKE GREEN

East Sussex ✉ Heathfield – See Regional map n°**8-B2**
▶ London 54 mi – Brighton 26 mi – Eastbourne 13 mi
Michelin Road map 504-U31

 **Stone House** 

✉ TN21 9QJ (Northeast corner of the green) – ✆ (01435) 830 553 – www.stonehousesussex.co.uk – Closed 23 December-2 January and 17 February-16 March

7 rm ☕ – †£ 113/280 ††£ 148/280 – 1 suite

Rest – Menu £ 33 **s** – Carte £ 22/32 **s** – *(dinner only and lunch mid-May-August) (booking essential) (residents only)*

Beautiful gardens lead up to this charming part-15C house, set in 1,000 acres of tranquil grounds. It's been in the family for 500 years and is very personally run. The traditional country house interior features original staircases, wood-panelling and antiques; some of the individually decorated bedrooms have four-poster beds. Classic menus use kitchen garden produce.

RYE

East Sussex – Pop. 3 708 – See Regional map n°**9-C2**

▶London 61 mi – Brighton 49 mi – Folkestone 27 mi – Maidstone 33 mi

Michelin Road map 504-W31 – Michelin Green Guide GREAT BRITAIN

 **George in Rye**  

98 High St. ✉ TN31 7JT – ✆ (01797) 222 114 – www.thegeorgeinrye.com

34 rm ☕ – †£ 115/135 ††£ 135/225 **Rest** – Carte £ 21/47

Charming, centrally located former coaching inn offering an attractive blend of the old and the new. Characterful beamed bar and cosy, wood-panelled lounge. Individually styled bedrooms with bold, modern colour schemes. Grill-based menu with steaks the highlight.

ENGLAND

Mermaid Inn 

Mermaid St. ✉ TN31 7EY – ✆ (01797) 223 065 – www.mermaidinn.com

31 rm ☕ – †£ 90/220 ††£ 150/220 **Rest** – Menu £ 30/39

One of England's oldest coaching inns, offering immense charm and character, from its heavy beams and carved wooden fireplaces to its tapestries, false stairways and priests' holes. Formal dining features mainly local fish and game. The owner has been looking after guests here for over three decades.

Jeake's House without rest

Mermaid St. ✉ TN31 7ET – ✆ (01797) 222 828 – www.jeakeshouse.com

11 rm ☕ – †£ 70/79 ††£ 90/140

Three 17C houses joined together over time, set down a cobbled lane. A former wool store and Quaker meeting place, it is set apart by its substantial charm. Characterful beamed rooms are warmly decorated and filled with antiques.

Oaklands without rest 

Udimore Rd ✉ TN31 6AB – Southwest : 1.25mi on B 2089 – ✆ (01797) 229 734 – www.oaklands-rye.co.uk – Closed January and February

3 rm ☕ – †£ 80/90 ††£ 95/120

Delightfully set Edwardian house with lovely gardens and town, coast and white cliff views. Guest areas feature souvenirs from the owner's travels – the breakfast table is an Omani front door. Immaculately kept bedrooms; 2 are four-posters.

Willow Tree House without rest 

113 Winchelsea Rd. ✉ TN31 7EL – South : 0.5 mi on A 259 – ✆ (01797) 227 820 – www.willow-tree-house.com

6 rm ☕ – †£ 85/105 ††£ 90/130

300 year old boathouse on the main road into town. Comfy bedrooms are decorated in warm colours and are tastefully furnished; those at the top have exposed beams. Substantial breakfasts are served in a conservatory-style room.

Webbe's at The Fish Café

17 Tower St. ✉ TN31 7AT – ✆ (01797) 222 226 – www.webbesrestaurants.co.uk – Closed 24 December-10 January
Menu £ 20 (weekday lunch) – Carte £ 23/34
Relaxed café in a former antiques warehouse and teddy bear factory, with terracotta-coloured brick walls, a small counter and a cookery school above. Extensive menus offer simply prepared seafood from the Rye and Hastings day boats.

Tuscan Kitchen

8 Lion St ✉ TN31 7LB – ✆ (01797) 223 269 – www.tuscankitchenrye.co.uk – Closed Monday and Tuesday
Carte £ 20/45 – *(dinner only and lunch Friday and Sunday) (booking advisable)*
Centrally located, with dark wood tables, studded leather chairs, Italian memorabilia and even a stuffed wild boar. Rustic, classical cooking with everything homemade. The olive oil comes from the family farm in Tuscany.

Ambrette

24 High St ✉ TN31 7JF – ✆ (01797) 222 043 – www.theambrette.co.uk – Closed Monday
Menu £ 20 (lunch) – Carte dinner £ 23/37
Set in a historic building with a fine Georgian façade and an elegant, formal interior: sister to the Margate restaurant of the same name. Skilful, modern, subtly flavoured interpretations of traditional Indian dishes.

ENGLAND

Ship Inn with rm

The Strand ✉ TN31 7DB – ✆ (01797) 222 233 – www.theshipinnrye.co.uk
10 rm – †£ 75/100 ††£ 85/125 Carte £ 23/35
16C former warehouse on the quayside; now a laid-back pub with quirky styling incorporating stuffed boars heads, fairy lights and retro posters. Concise daily menu of flavoursome pub favourites with a modern twist; steak is a popular choice. Compact bedrooms have eye-catching feature walls and bold styling.

at Camber Southeast: 4.25 mi by A259 ✉ Rye

Gallivant

New Lydd Rd. ✉ TN31 7RB – ✆ (01797) 225 057 – www.thegallivanthotel.com
20 rm – †£ 115/175 ††£ 115/175
Rest *Beach Bistro* – see restaurant listing
Laid-back hotel opposite Camber Sands, run by a friendly team. Relax in the shabby chic lounge or on the terrace. Bedrooms come in blues and whites, with distressed wood furniture and modern facilities; some have decked terraces.

Beach Bistro – Gallivant Hotel

New Lydd Rd. ✉ TN31 7RB – ✆ (01797) 225 057 – www.thegallivanthotel.com
Menu £ 20 (weekday lunch) – Carte £ 26/39
Informal hotel bistro with distressed wood furniture, white and blue hues and a pleasant covered terrace. Appealing all-day menus keep local seafood to the fore; refreshingly, the good value two-choice set menu is always available.

Don't expect guesthouses to provide the same level of service as a hotel. They are often characterised by a warm welcome and décor which reflects the owner's personality. Those shown in red are particularly pleasant.

RYHALL

Rutland – Pop. 1 459 – See Regional map n°**17**-C2
London 94 mi – Sheffield 81 mi – Kingston upon Hull 98 mi – Rotherham 78 mi
Michelin Road map 504-S25

Wicked Witch

Bridge St ✉ PE9 4HH – ✆ (01780) 763 649 – www.ryhallwitch.co.uk – Closed 1-8 January and Sunday dinner
Menu £ 15/26 – Carte £ 28/49
Former pub; now a glitzy, modern restaurant with a relaxed formality. Seasonal menus follow the décor's lead, offering modern dishes with an emphasis on presentation. Combinations are ambitious and original, with wide-ranging influences.

ST ALBANS

Hertfordshire – Pop. 82 146 – See Regional map n°**12**-A2
London 27 mi – Cambridge 41 mi – Luton 10 mi
Michelin Road map 504-T28 – Michelin Green Guide GREAT BRITAIN

St Michael's Manor

St Michael's Village, Fishpool St ✉ AL3 4RY – ✆ (01727) 864 444 – www.stmichaelsmanor.com Town plan: AY**d**
29 rm – £ 125 £ 145/207 – 1 suite
Rest *Lake* – see restaurant listing
Part-16C William and Mary manor house with well-kept gardens and lake views. Characterful guest areas display contemporary touches. Traditionally styled bedrooms are well-appointed; the annexe rooms are more modern – some have terraces.

Thompson @ Darcy's

2 Hatfield Rd ✉ AL1 3RP – ✆ (01727) 730 777 – www.thompsonatdarcys.co.uk Town plan: BY**t**
Menu £ 17/30 – Carte £ 29/48
Come on Sunday for 'lobster and steak night' or any day of the week for refined, tasty dishes with a modern edge. Three contemporary dining rooms feature bold artwork from the local gallery. Try the lesser-known wines by the glass.

Lake – St Michael's Manor Hotel

St Michael's Village, Fishpool St ✉ AL3 4RY – ✆ (01727) 864 444 – www.stmichaelsmanor.com Town plan: AY**d**
Menu £ 22 – Carte £ 36/46
Spacious, airy conservatory in a family owned manor house, which looks out over well-tended gardens and a lake. Daily changing dishes feature contemporary twists; the Lake Menu represents good value. Formal service from a chatty team.

ST ANNE'S → See Lytham St Anne's

Lancashire – Michelin Road map 502-K22

ST AUBIN → See Channel Islands (Jersey)

– Michelin Road map 503-P33

ST AUSTELL

Cornwall – Pop. 23 864 – See Regional map n°**1**-B2
London 281 mi – Newquay 16 mi – Plymouth 38 mi – Truro 14 mi
Michelin Road map 503-F32

ST ALBANS

Anchorage House

Nettles Corner, Boscundle ✉ PL25 3RH – East : 2.75 mi by A 390 – ✆ (01726) 814 071 – www.anchoragehouse.co.uk – 15 March-October

5 rm ☕ – 🚹£ 70/80 🚹🚹£ 90/130 **Rest** – Menu £ 25

Modern guesthouse owned by an ex-Canadian Naval Commander. Afternoon tea is served in the comfy lounge. Charming, antique-filled bedrooms boast modern fabrics, state-of-the-art bathrooms and plenty of extras. Facilities include an indoor pool, a gym, a sauna and a chill-out lounge. The conservatory dining room offers simple, home-cooked dishes. The owners are lovely.

Grange (N)

19 Southbourne Rd ✉ PL25 4RU – ✆ (01726) 73 351 – www.accommodationstaustell.co.uk – Closed Christmas

3 rm – 🚹£ 45/75 🚹🚹£ 55/125 **Rest** – Menu £ 15/25

A cheery owner welcomes you to this small but perfectly formed guesthouse. Bedrooms are bright and modern yet have a cosy, homely feel; one has a four-poster bed and a roll-top bath. The extensive breakfast menu features items from the local butcher's; dinners, by arrangement, feature old favourites.

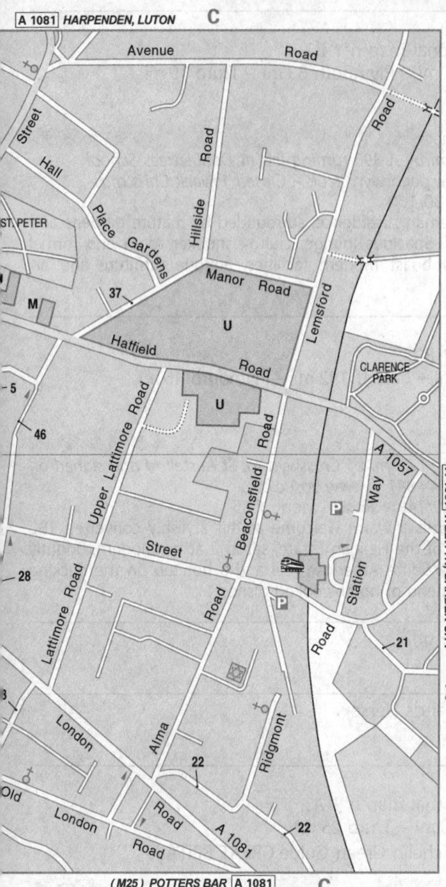

Abbey Mill Lane . . . AZ
Albert St. . . . BZ
Alma Rd . . . CZ
Avenue Rd . . . CY
Beaconsfield Rd . . . CYZ
Belmont Hill . . . BZ
Branch Rd . . . AY
Bricket Rd . . . BCYZ 5
Britton Ave . . . BY 6
Carlisle Ave . . . BCY 8
Catherine St . . . BY
Chequer St . . . BZ 10
Church Crescent . . . ABY 11
Cottonmill Lane . . . BCZ 13
Dalton St . . . BY 15
Drovers Way . . . BY 16
Etna Rd . . . BY 18
Fishpool St . . . AYZ
Folly Ave . . . BY 20
Folly Lane . . . ABY
Grange St . . . BY
Grimston Rd . . . CZ 21
Grosvenor Rd . . . CZ 22
Hall Pl. Gardens . . . CY
Hatfield Rd . . . CY
High St . . . BZ
Hillside Rd . . . CY
Holywell Hill . . . BZ
Lattimore Rd . . . CZ
Lemsford Rd . . . CY
London Rd . . . BCZ
Lower Dagnall St . . . BYZ 26
Maltings Shopping Centre . . . BZ
Manor Rd . . . CY
Market Pl. . . . BZ 29
Marlborough Rd . . . CZ 28
Mount Pleasant . . . AY
New England St . . . AY
Normandy Rd . . . BY
Old London Rd . . . CZ
Portland St . . . AY
Ridgemont Rd . . . CZ
Russell Ave . . . BY 35
St Peter's Rd . . . CY 37
St Peter's St . . . BCY
Sopwell Lane . . . BZ
Spencer St . . . BY 39
Spicer St College . . . BYZ 40
Station Way . . . CZ
Thorpe Rd . . . BZ 42
Upper Dagnall St . . . BYZ 44
Upper Lattimore Rd . . . CYZ
Upper Marlborough Rd . . . CYZ 46
Verulam Rd . . . ABY
Victoria St . . . BCZ
Watson's Walk . . . CZ 48
Welclose St . . . AYZ 49
Worley Rd . . . BY

at Carlyon Bay East: 2.5 mi by A3601 ✉ St Austell

Carlyon Bay
rest,

✉ *PL25 3RD – ✆ (01726) 812 304 – www.carlyonbay.com*
86 rm (dinner included) – £ 75/130 £ 130/410
Rest *Bay View* – Menu £ 22/38 – Carte £ 35/49
Rest *Taste* – Carte £ 25/43 – *(dinner only)*
Imposing 1920s hotel boasting original art deco features and superb bay views. Large, traditionally furnished guest areas. Modern bedrooms feature lightly hued fabrics: rear rooms are bright; front rooms have views. Aptly named Bay View serves unfussy classics. Taste offers grills and seafood, using the best Cornish produce.

Brett@Austell's
10 Beach Rd ✉ PL25 3PH – ✆ (01726) 813 888 – www.austells.co.uk
– Closed first 2 weeks January and Monday
Menu £ 28 – Carte £ 28/43 – *(dinner only and Sunday lunch)*
Keenly run neighbourhood restaurant with a brightly lit, mirror-filled interior. Modern, seasonal menus showcase local produce in elaborate, confidently executed dishes with original touches. Watch the chefs in the open-plan kitchen.

ST BLAZEY

Cornwall – Pop. 9 958 – See Regional map n°**1-B2**

London 276 mi – Newquay 21 mi – Plymouth 33 mi – Truro 19 mi

Michelin Road map 503-F32

Penarwyn House without rest

✉ PL24 2DS South : 0.75 mi by A 390 turning left at Doubletrees School – ✆ (01726) 814 224 – www.penarwyn.co.uk – Closed 1 week Christmas

3 rm – £ 70/105 £ 80/160

Whitewashed former gentleman's residence, surrounded by mature gardens and run by welcoming owners. Spacious lounge, clubby snooker room and formal breakfast room. Bedrooms boast modern facilities, antique furniture and art deco touches.

ST EWE

Cornwall – See Regional map n°**1-B3**

London 258 mi – Bristol 161 mi – Cardiff 192 mi – Plymouth 46 mi

Michelin Road map 503-F33

Lower Barn

rm,

Bosue ✉ PL26 6ET – North : 1.25 mi by Crosswyn rd, St Austell rd and signed off St. Mawes rd – ✆ (01726) 844 881 – www.bosue.co.uk

6 rm – £ 65/75 £ 80/140 **Rest** – Menu £ 35

The gregarious owner extends a warm welcome at this stylishly converted 18C granite barn; formerly part of the Heligan Estate, set in 2 acres. Modern, brightly furnished bedrooms have a South American feel and a hot tub on the decking overlooks the garden. Set menu of home-cooked dishes.

ENGLAND

ST HELENS → See Wight (Isle of)

– Michelin Road map 504-Q31

ST HELIER → See Channel Islands (Jersey)

– Michelin Road map 503-P33

ST IVES

Cornwall – Pop. 9 966 – See Regional map n°**1-A3**

London 319 mi – Penzance 10 mi – Truro 25 mi

Michelin Road map 503-D33 – Michelin Green Guide GREAT BRITAIN

Tide House N without rest

Skidden Hill ✉ TR26 2DU – ✆ (01736) 791 803 Town plan: Y**h**

– www.thetidehouse.co.uk – Closed 21-27 December and 3 January- 9 February

6 rm – £ 140/295 £ 140/295

It may have been built in 1540 but this intimate hotel is now smart and modern, with top quality furnishings and a nautical, New England feel. There's a snug for adults, a den for children and the breakfast room opens onto a deck.

No 27 N without rest

27 The Terrace ✉ TR26 2BP – ✆ (01736) 797 450 Town plan: Y**n**

– www.27theterrace.co.uk

9 rm – £ 60/120 £ 80/140

Unusually for St Ives, this smartly restored Georgian house has its own car park and a sun terrace… even more unusually, it has its own beach! Take in a view of the bay from the airy breakfast room. Bedrooms are modern and appealing.

Blue Hayes without rest

Trelyon Ave ✉ TR26 2AD – ✆ (01736) 797 129 Town plan: Y**u**

– www.bluehayes.co.uk – March-October

6 rm – £ 100/200 £ 170/250

Built in 1922 for Professor Whitnall, a surgeon friend of Edward III. Comfortable bedrooms: one with French doors onto a roof terrace; another with four-poster and balcony. Single course dinner available. Breakfast on the terrace in summer.

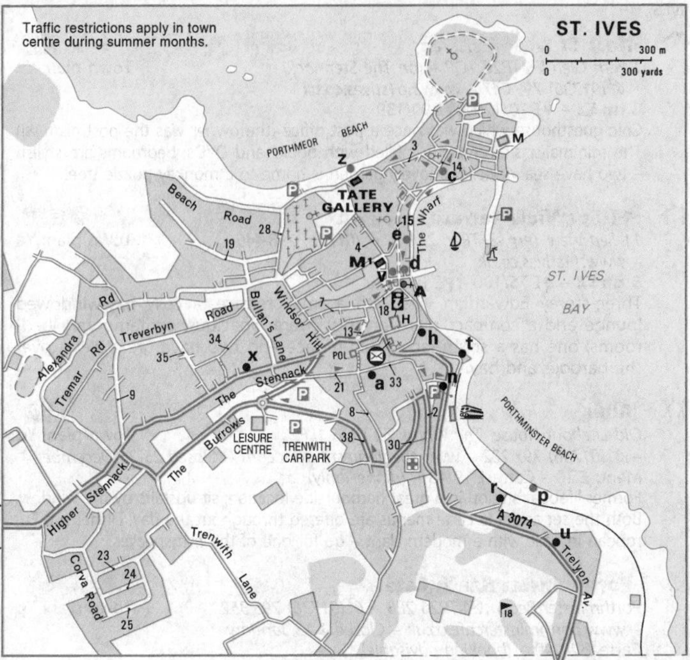

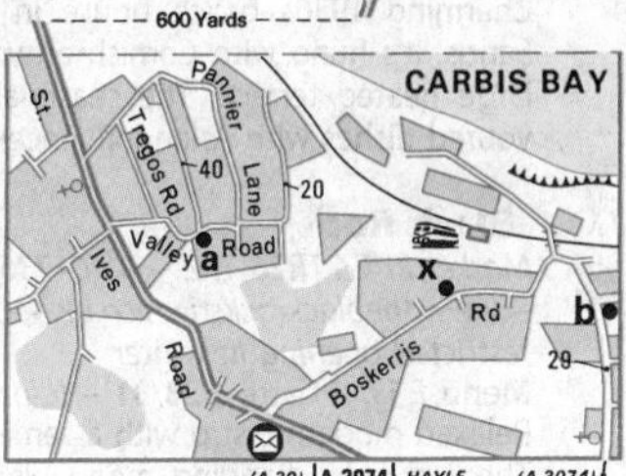

Traffic restrictions apply in town centre during summer months.

ST. IVES

CARBIS BAY

Albert Rd	Y 2	Porthia Crescent	Y 24
Back Rd West	Y 3	Porthia Rd	Y 25
Barnoon Hill	Y 4	Porthmeor Hill	Y 28
Bedford Rd	Y 7	Porthrepta Rd	Z 29
Bishop's Rd	Y 8	Talland Rd	Y 30
Carnellis Rd	Y 9	Tregenna Terrace	Y 33
Chapel St	Y 13	Trelawney Rd	Y 34
Fish St	Y 14	Trerice Rd	Y 35
Fore St	Y 15	Trewidden Rd	Y 38
High St	Y 18	Wheal Whidden	Z 40
Orange Lane	Y 19		
Parc Owles	Z 20		
Park Ave	Y 21		
Penwith Rd	Y 23		

ENGLAND

Primrose Valley without rest

Porthminster Beach ✉ *TR26 2ED – ✆ (01736) 794 939* Town plan: Y**r**
– www.primroseonline.co.uk – Closed 21-27 December
10 rm ☕ – 🚹£ 65/230 🚹🚹£ 75/240

Navigate the steep road up to this terraced Edwardian villa, where you'll find individually furnished bedrooms with good mod cons – Room 3 has a terrace with views over the lovely beach. Extensive breakfasts feature organic produce.

Trevose Harbour House Ⓝ without rest 

22 The Warren ✉ *TR26 2EA – ✆ (01736) 793 267* Town plan: Y**t**
– www.trevosehouse.co.uk – March-mid December
6 rm ☕ – 🚹£ 90/255 🚹🚹£ 140/265

The owners have decorated this elegant hotel themselves, so you'll find lots of knick-knacks and some unusual, personal touches. It's simple but stylish, with a mix of period and modern furnishings. The breakfasts are top notch.

No.1 St Ives without rest

1 Fern Glen ✉ TR26 1QP – (on The Stennack) Town plan: Y**x**
– ✆ (01736) 799 047 – www.no1stives.co.uk
4 rm – £ 70/120 £ 90/139
Chic guesthouse which was once a post office (the owner was the postmistress!) The minimalist sitting room is filled with books and DVDs; bedrooms are stylish – two have sea views. The lovely garden is home to a monkey puzzle tree.

11 Sea View Terrace without rest

11 Sea View Terr ✉ TR26 2DH – ✆ (01736) 798 440 Town plan: Y**a**
– www.11stives.co.uk
3 rm – £ 75/100 £ 100/140
Three-storey Edwardian villa with a small terrace, a cosy bay-windowed lounge and a compact rear breakfast room. Spacious, contemporary bedrooms; one has a south-facing sun-terrace and two have great views over the harbour and bay.

Alba

Old Lifeboat House, The Wharf ✉ TR26 1LF Town plan: Y**d**
– ✆ (01736) 797 222 – www.thealbarestaurant.com – Closed 25-26 December
Menu £ 20 – Carte £ 19/43 – *(dinner only)*
Former lifeboat station in a great harbourside location; sit upstairs by the window. Both the set and à la carte menus are offered throughout the day. Dishes are European in base with a modern slant – go for one of the fish specials.

Porthminster Beach Café 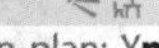

Porthminster Beach ✉ TR26 2EB – ✆ (01736) 795 352 Town plan: Y**p**
– www.porthminstercafe.co.uk – Closed 1-13 January
Carte £ 21/40 – *(booking advisable)*
Charming 1930s beach house in a superb location overlooking Porthminster Sands. It's hung with Cornish artwork, has a nautical style and leads out onto a large heated terrace. The seasonal seafood menu offers unfussy, vibrantly flavoured dishes with Asian influences. Service is relaxed and friendly.

Black Rock

Market Pl ✉ TR26 1RZ – ✆ (01736) 791 911 Town plan: Y**v**
– www.theblackrockstives.co.uk – Closed November-February, Sunday and restricted opening in winter
Menu £ 17 – Carte £ 23/31 – *(dinner only) (booking advisable)*
Relaxed modern bistro with a semi-open kitchen and a contemporary art display. The regularly changing menu places its emphasis on fresh local seafood and cooking is gutsy, rustic and big on flavour. The owner is a third generation fisherman and has lots of local contacts.

Alfresco N 

Beach House, The Wharf ✉ TR26 1LG Town plan: Y**e**
– ✆ (01736) 793 737 – www.alfresco-stives.co.uk – Closed 4 January-7 February and 25-26 December
Menu £ 16 – Carte £ 28/43
This open-fronted restaurant is a breath of fresh air. They serve coffee and cakes in the morning, followed by modern, tasty dishes at lunch and dinner. Local fish takes centre stage and their Exe mussel chowder is well-known.

seagrass

Fish St ✉ TR26 1LT – ✆ (01736) 793 763 Town plan: Y**c**
– www.seagrass-stives.com – Closed 1-2 January, dinner 25 December, Sunday and Monday November-April except bank holidays
Menu £ 17 – Carte £ 20/44 – *(dinner only) (booking advisable)*
Personally run with a reassuring efficiency, this first floor restaurant just off Harbour Beach puts Cornish produce centre stage, with a menu of classic dishes cooked in a modern style. Marble-topped bar; modern décor.

ENGLAND

Porthmeor Café Bar
Porthmeor Beach ✉ TR26 1JZ – ✆ (01736) 793 366 Town plan: Y**z**
– www.porthmeor-beach.co.uk – Closed November-March
Carte £ 16/36 – *(bookings not accepted at lunch) (booking essential at dinner)*
Simple beachfront café; a very popular spot, as all of the tables have a view. Service is friendly and the atmosphere, laid-back. They offer breakfast, fresh cakes, Mediterranean small plates and a few more substantial dishes too.

at Carbis Bay South: 1.75 mi on A3074✉ St Ives

Boskerris
Boskerris Rd ✉ TR26 2NQ – ✆ (01736) 795 295 Town plan: Z**x**
– www.boskerrishotel.co.uk – Closed mid-November-March
15 rm – †£ 98/265 ††£ 130/265
Rest – Carte £ 24/33 – *(closed Sunday) (dinner only) (residents only)*
Contemporary hotel with panoramic views of Carbis Bay and the coastline. Contemporary lounge-bar with French styling and doors onto the terrace. Uncluttered bedrooms have a cool, modern style; some have roll-top baths and iPod docks. Enthusiastic young owners. Concise menu of good, honest home-cooking.

Beachcroft without rest
Valley Rd ✉ TR26 2QS – ✆ (01736) 794 442 Town plan: Z**a**
– www.beachcroftstives.co.uk – Closed November-March except New Year
5 rm – †£ 130/150 ††£ 160/190
Set in an elevated position, with stunning views across the bay. Contemporary interior with subtle 1920s touches. Comfy, understated bedrooms have bespoke furnishings and luxurious bathrooms. Have your breakfast on the delightful terrace.

Headland House without rest
Headland Rd ✉ TR26 2NS – ✆ (01736) 796 647 Town plan: Z**b**
– www.headlandhousehotel.co.uk – March-October
7 rm – †£ 85/140 ††£ 95/155
Substantial house built in 1901, with a decked terrace, an attractive garden and a lovely conservatory breakfast room. Contemporary, New England style décor; cake is served every afternoon in the lounge. The sea is at the end of the road.

at Halsetown Southwest: 1.5 mi on B3311

Halsetown Inn
✉ TR26 3NA – ✆ (01736) 795 583 – www.hasletowninn.co.uk – Closed January and Sunday dinner
Menu £ 12 (weekday lunch) – Carte £ 20/33
Relaxed, slightly quirky pub, a short drive from St Ives; there are various little areas to sit in, as well as a lovely suntrap of a terrace. Tasty seasonal cooking, with strong Asian influences; Wednesday theme nights include Chinese or Thai. Excellent value set lunch menu and warm, friendly staff.

ST KEVERNE
Cornwall – Pop. 939 – See Regional map n°**1-A3**
London 302 mi – Penzance 26 mi – Truro 28 mi
Michelin Road map 503-E33

Old Temperance House without rest
The Square ✉ TR12 6NA – ✆ (01326) 280 986 – www.oldtemperancehouse.co.uk
4 rm – †£ 59 ††£ 85
Pretty pink-washed cottage framed by olive trees. The interior is contemporary and immaculately kept; bright bedrooms display thoughtful touches. Fresh fruit and produce from the local butcher features at breakfast.

Greenhouse
6 High St. ✉ TR12 6NN – ✆ (01326) 280 800 – www.tgor.co.uk – Closed last 2 weeks January
Carte £ 21/35 – *(dinner only and occasional Sunday lunch) (booking advisable)*
Simple eatery in a sleepy little village, where they sell their own bread and meringues. Daily blackboard menus are centred around local, organic and gluten free produce; cooking is unfussy and flavoursome. Seafood is a feature.

ENGLAND

ST KEW

Cornwall – See Regional map n°**1-B2**

London 265 mi – Newquay 20 mi – Liskeard 24 mi

St Kew Inn

PL30 3HB – (01208) 841 259 – www.stkewinn.co.uk

Carte £ 23/37

Characterful country pub in quintessentially English location. Wide-ranging menu of fresh, tasty dishes and St Austell beer in wooden casks. Attractive garden with picnic tables and heaters.

ST MARTIN → See Channel Islands (Guernsey)

– Michelin Road map 503-P33

ST MARY'S → See Scilly (Isles of)

– Michelin Road map 503-B34

ST MAWES

Cornwall Truro – See Regional map n°**1-B3**

London 299 mi – Plymouth 56 mi – Truro 18 mi

Michelin Road map 503-E33

Hotel Tresanton

27 Lower Castle Rd TR2 5DR – (01326) 270 055 – www.tresanton.com – Closed 2 weeks January

30 rm – £ 170/340 £ 190/370 – 4 suites

Rest *Restaurant Tresanton* – see restaurant listing

Collection of old fishermen's cottages and a former yacht club. Elegant, nautically themed guest areas include an intimate bar and a movie room. Understated bedrooms, some in cottages, have a high level of facilities and superb sea views. Lovely split-level terrace shares the outlook. Delightful team.

Idle Rocks

Harbourside TR2 5AN – (01326) 270 270 – www.idlerocks.com – Closed 5-29 January

20 rm – £ 150/350 £ 150/350

Rest *Idle Rocks* – Menu £ 21 (weekday lunch) – Carte £ 32/50

Boutique hotel on the water's edge, with fabulous views over the harbour and the estuary. The décor is personalised and local art is displayed throughout. Cosy, contemporary bedrooms have pleasing subtle touches and are well-equipped. The relaxed restaurant has bay views, a modern menu and a superb terrace.

Nearwater without rest

Polvarth Rd. TR2 5AY – East : 0.5 mi on A 3078 – (01326) 279 278 – www.nearwaterstmawes.co.uk – Closed Christmas

3 rm – £ 80/95 £ 90/120

Modern, purpose-built guesthouse with small lawned garden, set on the main road of a popular coastal town. Open-plan lounge and breakfast room with real fires and subtle nautical theme. Smart, New England style bedrooms offer good mod cons.

Restaurant Tresanton – Hotel Tresanton

27 Lower Castle Rd TR2 5DR – (01326) 270 055 – www.tresanton.com – Closed 2 weeks January

Menu £ 25 (weekday lunch) – Carte £ 33/58 – *(booking essential)*

Appealing hotel restaurant boasting a large terrace and superb bay views; popular for its Sunday BBQs and live jazz band. Bright interior with nautical theme and attractive mosaic flooring. Daily menus offer unfussy dishes crafted from quality local produce; seafood is a feature. Polite, efficient service.

Watch House

1 The Square TR2 5DJ – (01326) 270 038 – www.watchhousestmawes.co.uk – Closed 25-26 December and Monday-Tuesday except June-September

Carte £ 27/42

Old Customs and Excise watch house on the quayside, with a nautically styled interior, friendly service and harbour views. Light lunches and substantial dinners; unfussy cooking follows a Mediterranean theme – try the tasty fish specials.

ST MELLION

Cornwall – See Regional map n°**2**-C2

London 225 mi – Bristol 129 mi – Cardiff 160 mi – Plymouth 13 mi

Pentillie Castle rm,

✉ *PL12 6QD Southeast : 1 mi by A 388 on Cargreen rd – ✆ (01579) 350 044 – www.pentillie.co.uk*

9 rm – †£ 105/215 ††£ 120/235 **Rest** – Menu £ 28

17C house – later transformed into a castle – set in 2,000 acres overlooking the river. Classical guest areas include a dining room with a crystal chandelier; traditional menus require a minimum of 6 guests. Spacious, elegant bedrooms with antique furnishings, luxurious bathrooms and some great views.

ST MERRYN → See Padstow

Cornwall – Michelin Road map 503-F32

ST OSYTH

Essex – Pop. 2 118 – See Regional map n°**13**-D2

London 83 mi – Croydon 88 mi – Barnet 81 mi – Ealing 94 mi

Michelin Road map 504-X28

Park Hall without rest

Park Hall ✉ CO16 8HG – East : 1.5 mi on B 1027 – ✆ (01255) 820 922 – www.parkhall.info

3 rm – †£ 55/90 ††£ 60/180

14C antique-filled former monastery in 600 acres of arable farmland, with 5 acres of grounds, where peacocks roam free. Traditionally styled rooms come with many thoughtful extras.

ST PETER PORT → See Channel Islands (Guernsey)

– Michelin Road map 503-P33

ST SAVIOUR → See Channel Islands (Jersey)

– Michelin Road map 503-P33

ST SAVIOUR → See Channel Islands (Guernsey)

– Michelin Road map 503-P33

SALCOMBE

Devon – Pop. 1 893 – See Regional map n°**2**-C3

London 243 mi – Exeter 43 mi – Plymouth 27 mi – Torquay 28 mi

Michelin Road map 503-I33 – Michelin Green Guide GREAT BRITAIN

Salcombe Harbour N

Cliff Rd ✉ TQ8 8JH – ✆ (01548) 844 444 – www.salcombe-harbour-hotel.co.uk Town plan: Z**s**

50 rm – †£ 119/435 ††£ 129/445 – 1 suite

Rest *Jetty* – Carte £ 32/45

Take in views of the estuary from this contemporary seaside hotel, with its sleek, nautical edge. Stylish bedrooms come with Nespresso machines and tablets; many also have balconies. For relaxation there's a chic spa and even a cinema! The restaurant offers modern menus, with local seafood a feature.

South Sands

Bolt Head ✉ TQ8 8LL – Southwest : 1.25 mi – ✆ (01548) 845 900 – www.southsands.com Town plan: Z**x**

27 rm – †£ 190/375 ††£ 190/375 – 5 suites

Rest *Beachside* – see restaurant listing

Stylish hotel by the water's edge, with a subtle New England theme running throughout and South Sands views. Small, modern bar and lounges. Smart bedrooms have heavy wood furnishings and good facilities; opt for one with a balcony.

SALCOMBE

Allenhayes Rd . . . . Y 2
Bonaventure Rd. . . . . . Y 3
Buckley St . . . . Y 4
Camperdown Rd . . . . . Y 7
Church St . . . . Y 8
Coronation Rd . . . . . . Y 9
Devon Rd. . . . . Y 13
Fore St . . . . Y
Fortescue Rd . . . . Z 14
Grenville Rd . . . . Y 15
Herbert Rd . . . . Z 18
Knowle Rd . . . . Y 19
Moult Rd . . . . Z 20
Newton Rd. . . . . Y 23
Sandhills Rd . . . . Z 24
Shadycombe Rd . . . . . Y 25

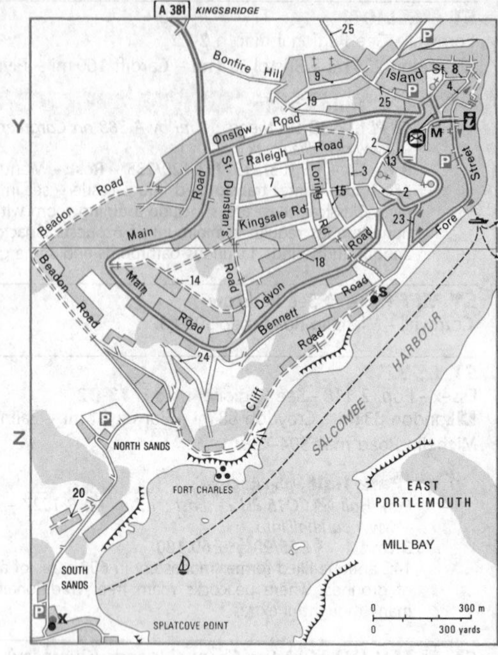

Beachside – South Sands Hotel

Bolt Head ✉ TQ8 8LL – Southwest : 1.25 mi – ✆ (01548) 845 900 – www.southsands.com Town plan: Z**x**

Menu £ 24 – Carte £ 27/68 – *(booking advisable)*

Large, airy, hotel restaurant with full-length windows opening onto a delightful decked terrace overlooking the bay. Modern, daily changing menus offer a good mix of unfussy, flavoursome dishes, with plenty of fresh seafood options.

at Soar Mill Cove Southwest: 4.25 mi by A381 -(Y)- via Malborough village✉ Salcombe

Soar Mill Cove

✉ TQ7 3DS – ✆ (01548) 561 566 – www.soarmillcove.co.uk – Closed 1 January-14 February

22 rm – †£ 119/180 ††£ 159/249 **Rest** – Carte £ 28/54

Family-run hotel built from local slate and stone; delightfully set above a secluded cove. Relax in the modern lounge or smart bar. Spacious bedrooms come in bright, contemporary styles; half have private patios and sea views. Blue-hued restaurant offers a modern menu and a lovely outlook from every table.

SALE

Greater Manchester – Pop. 134 022 – ✉ Manchester – See Regional map n°**20-B3**

London 212 mi – Liverpool 36 mi – Manchester 6 mi – Sheffield 43 mi

Michelin Road map 502-N23 and 503

Cornerstones without rest

230 Washway Rd ✉ M33 4RA – (on A 56) – ✆ (0161) 283 69 09 – www.cornerstonesguesthouse.com – Closed Christmas-New Year

9 rm – †£ 35/55 ††£ 60/65, £ 7

Substantial red-brick Victorian house with neat garden, in leafy suburban location. Slightly wacky interior with bohemian-style lounge and breakfast room. Bedrooms range from retro to modern.

SALFORD QUAYS ➜ See Manchester
Gtr Manchester

SALISBURY
Wiltshire – Pop. 44 748 – See Regional map n°4-D3
▶London 91 mi – Bournemouth 28 mi – Bristol 53 mi – Southampton 23 mi
Michelin Road map 503-O30 and 504 – Michelin Green Guide GREAT BRITAIN

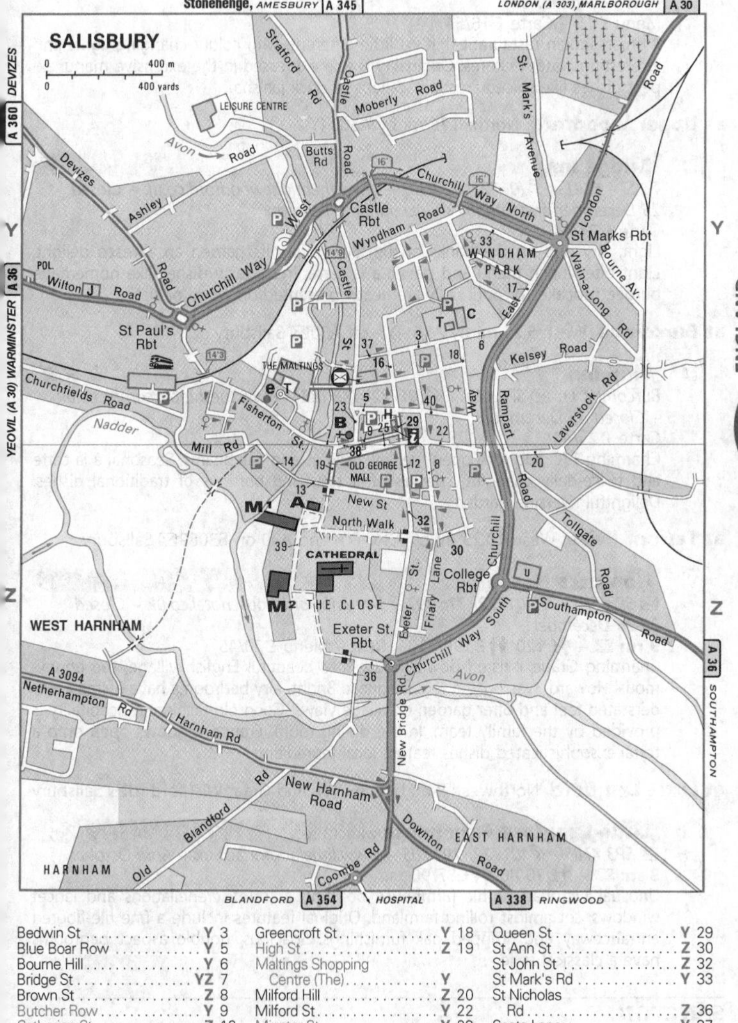

Bedwin St . . . . Y 3
Blue Boar Row . . . . Y 5
Bourne Hill . . . . Y 6
Bridge St . . . . YZ 7
Brown St . . . . Z 8
Butcher Row . . . . Y 9
Catherine St. . . . . Z 12
Crane Bridge Rd . . . . Z 14
Crane St . . . . Z 13
Endless St . . . . Y 16
Estcourt Rd . . . . Y 17
Greencroft St . . . . Y 18
High St . . . . Z 19
Maltings Shopping Centre (The) . . . . Y
Milford Hill . . . . Z 20
Milford St . . . . Y 22
Minster St . . . . Y 23
New Canal . . . . Z 25
Old George Mall Shopping Centre . . . . Z
Queen St . . . . Y 29
St Ann St . . . . Z 30
St John St . . . . Z 32
St Mark's Rd . . . . Y 33
St Nicholas Rd . . . . Z 36
Scots Lane . . . . Y 37
Silver St . . . . YZ 38
West Walk . . . . Z 39
Winchester St . . . . Y 40

Cricket Field House without rest

Wilton Rd ✉ SP2 9NS – West : 1.25 mi on A 36 – ✆ (01722) 322 595 – www.cricketfieldhouse.co.uk

15 rm ☕ – 🚹£ 65/95 🚹🚹£ 65/150

Family-run hotel overlooking the local cricket pitch. They offer a host of hot and cold dishes in the conservatory breakfast room. Comfy bedrooms are set around an internal courtyard; there's a min. 2 night weekend stay Apr-Oct.

Anokaa

60 Fisherton St ✉ SP2 7RB – ✆ (01722) 414 142 – www.anokaa.com Town plan: Y**e**

Menu £ 15 – Carte £ 18/54

A smart Indian restaurant that's a little different, with colour-changing lights and interesting water features. Originality is also expressed in the extensive menu: expect dishes like spiced crushed scallops or duck jaalsha.

at Upper Woodford North: 6.75 mi by A360-(Y)

Bridge Inn

✉ SP4 6NU – ✆ (01722) 782 323 – www.thebridgewoodford.co.uk – Closed 25 December and Sunday dinner January-February

Carte £ 23/44

Light, airy pub on the banks of the River Avon; its garden an alfresco delight. Light bites lunch menu and classic à la carte; fresh, tasty dishes like homemade burger, fishcakes or pork belly are neatly presented on wood or slate.

ENGLAND

at Burcombe West: 5.25 mi by A36 -(Y)- off A30✉ Salisbury

Ship Inn

Burcombe Ln ✉ SP2 0EJ – ✆ (01722) 743 182 – www.theshipburcombe.co.uk – Closed 25 December

Carte £ 23/44

Charming 17C pub with open fire, low ceilings and oak beams. Seasonal à la carte and twice-daily changing specials offer satisfying portions of traditional dishes. Delightful riverside garden.

at Teffont Evias West: 10.25 mi by A36 -(Y)- and A30 on B3089✉ Salisbury

Howard's House

✉ SP3 5RJ – ✆ (01722) 716 392 – www.howardshousehotel.co.uk – Closed 25-26 December

9 rm ☕ – 🚹£ 120 🚹🚹£ 190/210 **Rest** – Menu £ 20/45

Charming Grade II listed dower house in a beautiful English village; the eponymous 'Howard' was once a regular guest. Bright, airy bedrooms have a smart, understated feel and offer garden or village views. Good old-fashioned hospitality is provided by the family team. In the dining room, French windows open onto a terrace; sophisticated dishes feature local ingredients.

at Little Langford Northwest: 8 mi by A36 -(Y)- and Great Wishford rd✉ Salisbury

Little Langford Farmhouse without rest

✉ SP3 4NP – ✆ (01722) 790 205 – www.littlelangford.co.uk – April-October

3 rm ☕ – 🚹£ 70/80 🚹🚹£ 87/90

Unusual Victorian gothic farmhouse boasting a turret, crenellations and lancet windows; set amidst rolling farmland. Original features include a fine tile-floored entranceway and stripped oak furnishings. Spacious, double aspect bedrooms have a classical style.

SANCTON

East Riding of Yorkshire – Pop. 286 – See Regional map n°**23**-C2

London 194 mi – Croydon 205 mi – Ealing 193 mi – Wandsworth 199 mi

Michelin Road map 502-S22

Star

King St ✉ YO43 4QP – ✆ (01430) 827 269 – www.thestaratsancton.co.uk – Closed Monday
Menu £ 17 (weekday lunch) – Carte £ 25/46
Personally run pub in a small village, with a cosy bar and two smart dining rooms. Choose from hearty pub classics or boldly flavoured dishes which display a little more imagination. The menus proudly list the ingredients' local suppliers.

SANDBACH

Cheshire East – Pop. 17 976 – See Regional map n°**20**-**B3**
London 177 mi – Liverpool 44 mi – Manchester 28 mi – Stoke-on-Trent 16 mi
Michelin Road map 502 and 503

Old Hall

High St ✉ CW11 1AL – ✆ (01270) 758 170 – www.oldhall-sandbach.co.uk
Carte £ 20/40
Total restoration of this 17C black and white former manor house has created a smart new look, whilst retaining original features like oak panelling and timber beams. The daily menu focuses on keenly priced pub classics.

SANDFORD-ON-THAMES → See Oxford

Oxfordshire

SANDIACRE

Derbyshire – Pop. 9 600 – See Regional map n°**16**-**B2**
London 123 mi – Birmingham 46 mi – Leeds 75 mi – Sheffield 45 mi

XX La Rock

4 Bridge St ✉ NG10 5QT – ✆ (0115) 939 9833 – www.larockrestaurant.co.uk – Closed 26 December-mid-January, 2 weeks summer and Sunday dinner-Wednesday lunch
Carte £ 27/52
Charming, personally run restaurant with an airy feel – it was once a butcher's. Exposed brick walls and antler chandeliers feature. Cooking combines classical flavours with modern techniques; home-grown fruits are well utilised.

SANDIWAY

Cheshire West and Chester – Pop. 4 430 – ✉ Northwich – See Regional map n°**20**-**A3**
London 191 mi – Liverpool 34 mi – Manchester 22 mi – Stoke-on-Trent 26 mi
Michelin Road map 502-M24 and 503

Nunsmere Hall

Tarporley Rd ✉ CW8 2ES – Southwest : 1.5 mi A 556 on A 49 – ✆ (01606) 889 100 – www.nunsmere.co.uk
36 rm – †£ 85/305 ††£ 90/310, ☕ £ 20
Rest *Crystal* – see restaurant listing
Built in 1904 for Sir Aubrey Brocklebank, chairman of Cunard Line shipping. Attractive gardens and lovely terrace; several sumptuous lounges and a maritime-themed bar. Spacious, individually furnished bedrooms, some with modern touches.

XXX Crystal – Nunsmere Hall Hotel

Tarporley Rd ✉ CW8 2ES – Southwest : 1.5 mi by A 556 on A 49 – ✆ (01606) 889 100 – www.nunsmere.co.uk
Menu £ 23/35 – *(booking essential)*
Long, narrow hotel dining room with traditional styling and views over the terrace and garden. Simply prepared, classically based dishes have strong, gutsy flavours; be sure to try the homemade bread to start and chocolates to finish.

SANDSEND → See Whitby

North Yorkshire – Michelin Road map 502-R/S20

SANDWICH

Kent – Pop. 4 398 – See Regional map n°**9-D2**

London 72 mi – Canterbury 13 mi – Dover 12 mi

Michelin Road map 504-Y30 – Michelin Green Guide GREAT BRITAIN

Bell at Sandwich

The Quay ✉ CT13 9EF – ✆ (01304) 613 388 – www.bellhotelsandwich.co.uk

37 rm – £ 85/95 £ 85/110

Rest *Old Dining Room* – ✆ (01304) 626 992 – Carte £ 23/33 – *(bar lunch)*

Substantial Victorian property with a cool modern interior, located next to the River Stour. Kick-back in the bar, in one of the lounges or on the terrace. Stylish modern bedrooms come in cool pastel shades and some overlook the river. Dine from accessible menus in the restaurant or brasserie.

SANDYPARK → See Chagford

Devon – Michelin Road map 503-I31

SAPPERTON → See Cirencester

Gloucestershire

SAWDON → See Scarborough

North Yorkshire

SAWLEY

Lancashire – Pop. 237 – See Regional map n°**20-B2**

London 242 mi – Blackpool 39 mi – Leeds 44 mi – Liverpool 54 mi

Michelin Road map 502-M22

Spread Eagle with rm

✉ BB7 4NH – ✆ (01200) 441 202 – www.spreadeaglesawley.co.uk

7 rm – £ 70 £ 110/140

Menu £ 15 (lunch and early dinner) – Carte £ 25/32

Stylishly made-over, but still very much at the heart of the community. Gutsy, flavourful cooking, with a menu of pub favourites available in two sizes; plus platters, tapas-style nibbles and daily changing specials. Comfortable bedrooms feature smart, modern bathrooms.

SAXILBY

Lincolnshire – Pop. 3 992 – See Regional map n°**17-C1**

London 145 mi – Lincoln 7 mi – Newark-on-Trent 22 mi

Michelin Road map 502-S24

Canal View without rest

Lincoln Rd ✉ LN1 2NF – on A 57 – ✆ (01522) 704 475 – www.canal-view.co.uk

3 rm – £ 50/75 £ 70/80

Guests are welcomed to this pleasant guesthouse with a cup of tea and a slice of homemade cake. Neat bedrooms come with fridges, goose feather duvets and Egyptian cotton linen. As the name suggests, it has a view over the canal.

SCARBOROUGH

North Yorkshire – Pop. 61 749 – See Regional map n°**23-D1**

London 253 mi – Kingston-upon-Hull 47 mi – Leeds 67 mi – Middlesbrough 52 mi

Michelin Road map 502-S21 – Michelin Green Guide GREAT BRITAIN

Crown Spa

rest,

8-10 Esplanade ✉ YO11 2AG – ✆ (01723) 357 400 – www.crownspahotel.com Town plan: Z**n**

115 rm – £ 48/250 £ 59/250, £ 15 – 2 suites

Rest *Taste* – ✆ (01723) 357 439 – Menu £ 15/24 **s** – Carte £ 25/46 **s**

19C landmark hotel, in a prime position on the headland of a Victorian seaside town. Contemporary guest areas, superb leisure facilities and state-of-the-art meeting rooms. Smart bedrooms feature bespoke furnishings and the latest mod cons. Informal, bistro-style dining is split over four different rooms.

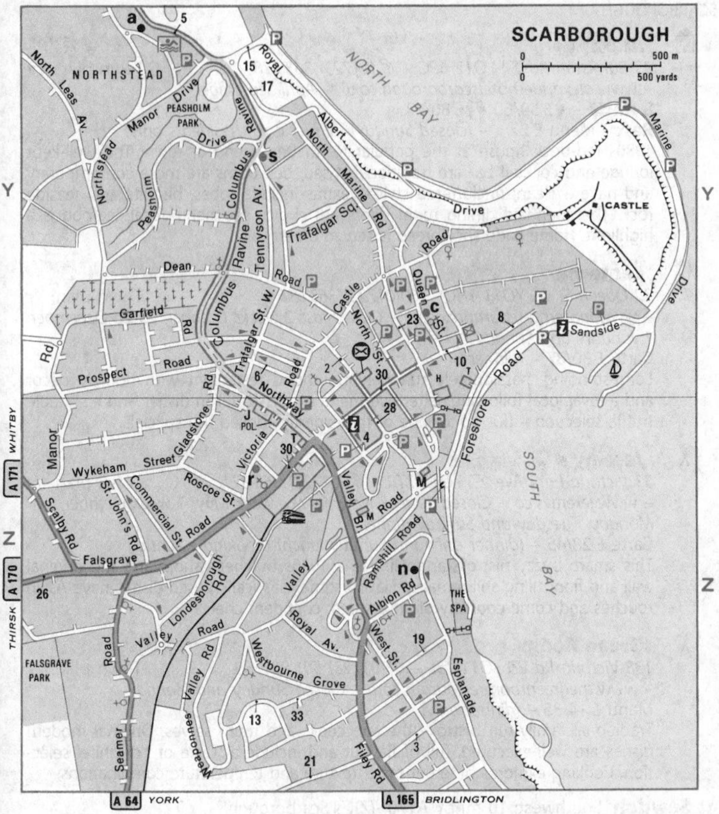

SCARBOROUGH

Aberdeen Walk . . . . Y 2	Falsgrave Rd . . . . Z	St Thomas St. . . . . Y 23
Avenue Victoria . . . . Z 3	Newborough . . . . Y 10	Stepney Rd . . . . Z 26
Brunswick Pavillon Shopping Centre . . . . Z 4	Oriel Crescent . . . . Z 13	Vernon Rd . . . . Z 28
Burniston Rd . . . . Y 5	Peasholm Gap . . . . Y 15	Victoria Rd . . . . YZ
Cambridge St . . . . Y 6	Peasholm Rd . . . . Y 17	Westborough . . . . YZ 30
Eastborough . . . . Y 8	Prince of Wales Terrace . . . . . Z 19	Westbourne Rd . . . . Z 33
	Queen Margaret's Rd . . . . Z 21	

Ox Pasture Hall

Lady Edith's Dr, Raincliffe Woods ✉ *YO12 5TD – West : 3.25 mi by A 171 following signs for Raincliffe Woods – ✆ (01723) 365 295 – www.oxpasturehallhotel.com*

32 rm ☕ – 🚹£ 85/140 🚹🚹£ 95/350

Rest *Courtyard* – Menu £ 20 (lunch) – Carte £ 28/45 **s**

Rest *Bistro* – Menu £ 15 (lunch) **s** – Carte £ 22/30 **s**

This charming creeper-clad farmhouse in set 17 acres of landscaped grounds and is a popular venue for weddings. Guest areas are stylish and contemporary. Bedrooms are well-equipped – those in the courtyard wing are the most modern and afford the best views. Dine from a modern menu in the formal restaurant or choose from hearty, unfussy dishes in the bistro.

When making a booking, check the category and price of the room.

Alexander

33 Burniston Rd ✉ YO12 6PG – ✆ (01723) 363 178 Town plan: Y**a**
– www.alexanderhotelscarborough.co.uk – April-September
8 rm – £ 50/60 £ 80/92
Rest – Menu £ 22 **s** – *(closed Sunday) (dinner only) (residents only)*
1930s red-brick house at the popular North Beach end of town. The well-kept lounge and cocktail bar are traditional styled; bedrooms are more contemporary and have a clean, uncluttered style – extras include robes, biscuits and seaside rock. The linen-laid dining room offers a 3 choice set menu; local seafood is a highlight. Homemade shortbread is served on arrival.

Lanterna

33 Queen St ✉ YO11 1HQ – ✆ (01723) 363 616 Town plan: Y**c**
– www.lanterna-ristorante.co.uk – Closed last 2 weeks October, 25-26 December, 1 January and Sunday
Carte £ 30/87 – *(dinner only)*
Long-standing, passionately run neighbourhood restaurant with homely décor and a loyal local following. Extensive menu of classic Italian dishes and a sizeable truffle selection – but go for one of the expertly cooked fish specials.

Jeremy's

33 Victoria Park Ave ✉ YO12 7TR – ✆ (01723) 363 871 Town plan: Y**s**
– www.jeremys.co – Closed 1 week New Year, 1 week May, 1 week October, Monday, Tuesday and Sunday dinner
Carte £ 28/45 – *(dinner only and Sunday lunch) (booking essential)*
This smart, buzzy bistro started life as a 1930s butcher's shop, and the original wall and floor tiling still remains. Flavoursome, classically based dishes have Asian touches and come courtesy of an assured, confident chef.

Green Room

138 Victoria Rd ✉ YO11 1SL – ✆ (01723) 501 801 Town plan: Z**r**
– www.thegreenroomrestaurant.com – Closed Sunday and Monday
Menu £ 14/35 – *(dinner only)*
Traditional family-run bistro – the son cooks and mum serves. Original modern dishes are well-executed, full of flavour and include a 'Taste of Yorkshire' selection. Cooking explores different taste, texture and temperature combinations.

at Sawdon Southwest: 10 mi by A170 -(Z)✉ Scarborough

Anvil Inn

Main St ✉ YO13 9DY – ✆ (01723) 859 896 – www.theanvilinnsawdon.co.uk – Closed 25-26 December, 1 January, Monday and Tuesday
Carte £ 25/39
Formerly a smithy, with bellows, tools, forge and anvil still in situ. Classical cooking features locally sourced produce and the odd international influence. Intimate restaurant.

SCILLY (Isles of)

Cornwall – See Regional map n°**1-A3**
London 295 mi – Camborne 23 mi – Saint Austell 52 mi – Falmouth 36 mi
Michelin Road map 503-A/B34 – Michelin Green Guide GREAT BRITAIN

BRYHER

Michelin Green Guide GREAT BRITAIN

Hell Bay

✉ TR23 0PR – ✆ (01720) 422 947 – www.hellbay.co.uk – March-October
25 rm (dinner included) – £ 169/400 £ 270/640 – 14 suites
Rest *Hell Bay* – see restaurant listing
Several charming, New England style buildings arranged around a central courtyard, with a contemporary, nautical-style interior displaying an impressive collection of modern art. Immaculately kept bedrooms come with plenty of thoughtful extras. Fabulous coastal location allows for far-reaching views.

Bank Cottage without rest
TR23 0PR – (01720) 422 612 – www.bank-cottage.com – May-October
4 rm – £ 58 £ 116
Friendly guesthouse with a well-tended, sub-tropical garden, a koi carp pond and even a rowing boat. Lounge boasts an honesty bar and artefacts from shipwrecks. Bedrooms are simple and compact – one has a roof terrace. Free use of kitchen.

Hell Bay – Hell Bay Hotel
TR23 0PR – (01720) 422 947 – www.hellbay.co.uk – March-October
Menu £ 43 (dinner) – Carte lunch £ 23/37 – *(booking essential)*
Hotel restaurant with a relaxed 'boat house' feel. Light, Mediterranean-influenced lunches in the bar, courtyard or terrace. Dinner steps things up a gear, with unfussy, modern dishes displaying fresh ingredients and clear flavours.

St Mary's

Cornwall – Pop. 1 607
Michelin Green Guide GREAT BRITAIN

Star Castle
The Garrison TR21 0JA – (01720) 422 317 – www.star-castle.co.uk – Closed 2 January-10 February
38 rm – £ 67/132 £ 134/346 – 4 suites
Rest *Castle Dining Room* – Carte £ 23/39 – *(dinner only)*
Rest *Conservatory* – Carte £ 23/39 – *(closed November-March) (dinner only)*
Elizabethan castle in the shape of an 8-pointed star. Well-appointed, classical bedrooms and brighter garden suites – some with harbour or island views. 17C staircase leads from the stone ramparts to the charming Dungeon bar. Fabulous fireplace and kitchen garden produce in the Dining Room. Seafood menus in the Conservatory.

Atlantic
Hugh St, Hugh Town TR21 0PL – (01720) 422 417 – www.atlantichotelscilly.co.uk – Closed November-February
25 rm (dinner included) – £ 75/110 £ 180/280
Rest – Menu 20 – *(bar lunch)*
Former Customs Office in a charming bay setting, affording lovely views across the harbour. Bedrooms – accessed through twisty passages – are well-equipped, and many share the view. Comfortable lounge and small bar. Wicker-furnished restaurant offers an accessible menu.

Evergreen Cottage without rest
Parade, Hugh Town TR21 0LP – (01720) 422 711 – www.evergreencottageguesthouse.co.uk – Closed 1 week February and Christmas-New Year
5 rm – £ 40 £ 80/82
300 year old captain's cottage in the heart of town, with colourful, welcoming window boxes. The interior is cosy, with a small, low-ceilinged lounge and breakfast room. The oak-furnished bedrooms are compact but spotlessly kept.

Tresco

Cornwall – Pop. 167 – New Grimsby
Michelin Green Guide GREAT BRITAIN

Sea Garden Cottages
Old Grimsby TR24 0QQ – (01720) 422 849 – www.tresco.co.uk – mid February-mid November
9 rm – £ 135/235 £ 135/235
Rest *The Ruin* – (01720) 424 849 – Carte £ 23/39 – *(booking essential)*
Smart aparthotel divided into New England style 'cottages': each has an open-plan kitchen and lounge and a first floor bedroom; all offer stunning views over St Martin's, Old Grimsby Quay and Blockhouse Point from their terraces and balconies. Relaxed, beachside restaurant serves a Mediterranean menu.

ENGLAND

New Inn 

New Grimsby ✉ TR24 0QQ – ☎ (01720) 422 849 – www.tresco.co.uk

16 rm – £ 70/150 £ 140/300

Rest – Carte £ 21/44 – *(booking essential)*

Stone-built inn boasting a large terrace, an appealing outdoor pool and pleasant coastal views. Bedrooms are bright, fresh and very comfy. Regular live music events attract guests from near and far. The hugely characterful bar and restaurant offer accessible menus.

SCUNTHORPE

North Lincolnshire – Pop. 79 977 – See Regional map n°**23**-**C3**

London 167 mi – Leeds 54 mi – Lincoln 30 mi – Sheffield 45 mi

Michelin Road map 502-S23

XXX **San Pietro** with rm 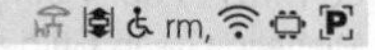

11 High St East ✉ DN15 6UH – ☎ (01724) 277 774 – www.sanpietro.uk.com – Closed first week January, 25-26 December, Monday lunch, Sunday dinner and bank holiday Mondays

14 rm – £ 99 £ 119/199 Menu £ 19/39

Smart restaurant with a chic bar-lounge, housed in a 19C listed windmill. Seasonal menus offer skilfully cooked dishes with Italian and Mediterranean influences; desserts are a highlight. Professional service comes from a smartly attired team. Nearby, stylish modern bedrooms complete the picture.

ENGLAND

SEAHAM

Durham – Pop. 22 373 – See Regional map n°**24**-B2

London 284 mi – Newcastle upon Tyne 17 mi – Leeds 84 mi

Michelin Road map 502-P/Q19

Seaham Hall Ⓝ 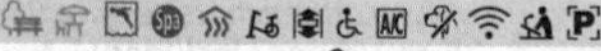

Lord Byron's Walk ✉ SR7 7AG – North : 1.5 mi by B 1287 – ☎ (0191) 516 14 00 – www.seaham-hall.com

20 rm – £ 225/785 £ 225/785 – 4 suites

Rest *Byron's* – Carte £ 21/53

Rest *Ozone* – Carte approx. £ 25

An imposing, part-18C mansion which combines grand original features with striking modern styling. Bedrooms are spacious and contemporary, and come with luxurious touches such as Nespresso machines. There's a chic lounge; a grill restaurant complete with velour booths and a zinc-topped bar; and a stylish Asian restaurant set within the impressively equipped spa.

SEAHOUSES

Northumberland – See Regional map n°**24**-B1

London 328 mi – Edinburgh 80 mi – Newcastle upon Tyne 46 mi

Michelin Road map 501-P17 and 502 – Michelin Green Guide GREAT BRITAIN

Olde Ship rm,

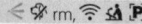

9 Main St ✉ NE68 7RD – ☎ (01665) 720 200 – www.seahouses.co.uk – March-November

17 rm – £ 47/94 £ 94/130

Rest – Carte £ 20/29 **s** – *(bar lunch Monday-Saturday)*

A long-standing, stone-built, family-run inn in a popular seaside town; full to bursting with nautical memorabilia. This cosy former farmhouse offers comfy, individually designed bedrooms; those in the annexe are bigger, with better views but less character. Formal dining room serves simple, traditional menu.

St Cuthbert's House without rest

192 Main St ✉ NE68 7UB – Southwest : 0.5 mi by Beadnell rd on North Sunderland rd – ☎ (01665) 720 456 – www.stcuthbertshouse.com – Restricted opening in winter

6 rm – †£ 75/110 ††£ 95/120

Former Georgian Presbyterian chapel, with comfortable modern bedrooms, a homely lounge and a wood-furnished breakfast room; large arched windows and many original features remain. The friendly, welcoming owners often host music nights.

SEASALTER → See Whitstable

Kent – Michelin Road map 504-X29

SEAVIEW → See Wight (Isle of)

Isle of Wight – Michelin Road map 503-Q31 and 504

SEER GREEN → See Beaconsfield

Buckinghamshire

SHAFTESBURY

Dorset – Pop. 7 314 – See Regional map n°**4-C3**

London 115 mi – Bournemouth 31 mi – Bristol 47 mi – Dorchester 29 mi

Michelin Road map 503-N30 and 504 – Michelin Green Guide GREAT BRITAIN

ENGLAND

Grosvenor Arms Ⓝ

High St ✉ SP7 8JA – ☎ (01747) 850 580 – www.thegrosvenorarms.co.uk

16 rm – †£ 125/200 ††£ 125/200

Rest *Grosvenor Arms* – see restaurant listing

A modern take on a classic coaching inn, with a Georgian-style façade and a stylish interior. Understated bedrooms have a boutique feel and come with espresso machines. Kick-back with a drink on the delightful courtyard terrace.

Fleur de Lys

Bleke St ✉ SP7 8AW – ☎ (01747) 853 717 – www.lafleurdelys.co.uk – Closed 2 weeks January

8 rm – †£ 85/125 ††£ 100/160

Rest – Menu £ 27/34 – *(closed lunch Monday-Tuesday and Sunday dinner)*

Keenly run, ivy-clad stone house in a lovely market town. Comfortable, well-kept bedrooms are named after grape varieties; each comes with its own laptop. Cosy lounge features a mahogany bar. Dine from traditional menus in the L-shaped restaurant or on the wood-furnished terrace.

Retreat without rest

47 Bell St ✉ SP7 8AE – ☎ (01747) 850 372 – www.the-retreat.co.uk – Closed 28 December-31 January

9 rm – †£ 55/60 ††£ 85/90

Pretty Georgian house on a narrow street in a delightful market town; built for a local doctor on the old site of a school for poor boys. Wood-furnished breakfast room and immaculately kept bedrooms with good facilities. Charming owner.

XX **Grosvenor Arms** Ⓝ

High St ✉ SP7 8JA – ☎ (01747) 850 580 – www.thegrosvenorarms.co.uk

Carte £ 25/44

Bright, contemporary brasserie in an updated coaching inn. Service is relaxed and attentive and the cooking is modern and refreshing. There's a selection of nibbles and tapas, homemade pizzas and clean, unfussy dishes in two sizes.

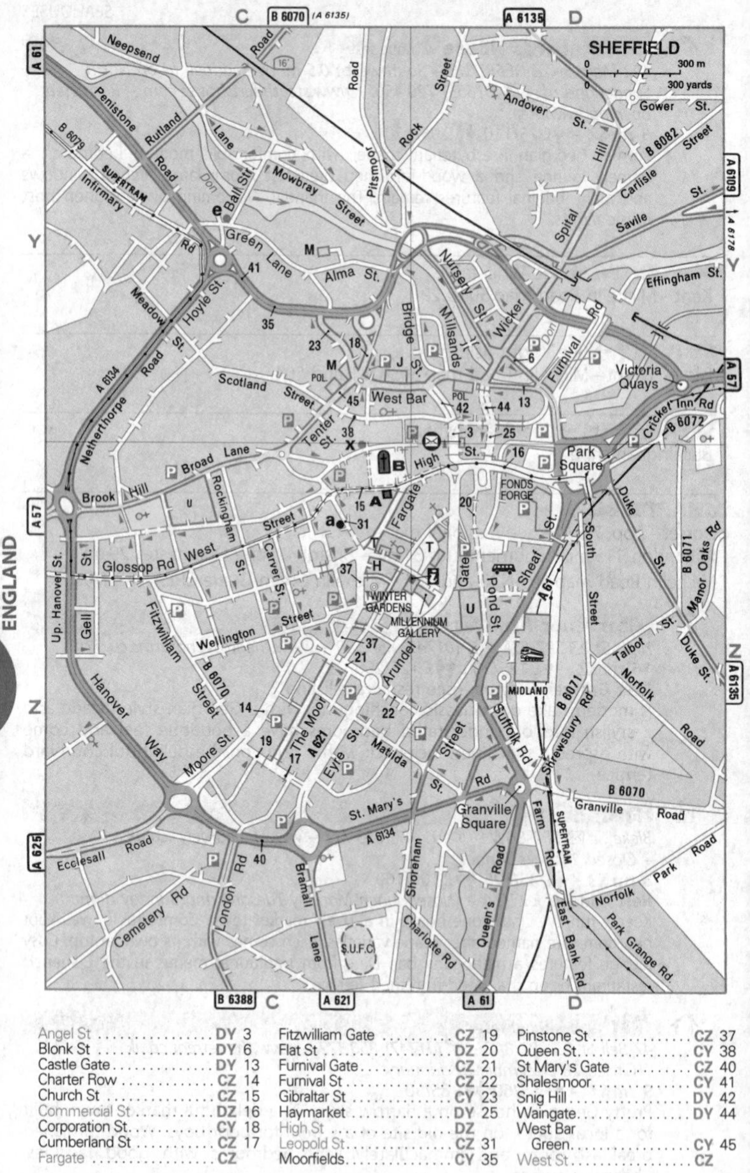

Angel St . . . . DY 3		Fitzwilliam Gate . . . . CZ 19		Pinstone St . . . . CZ 37			
Blonk St . . . . DY 6		Flat St . . . . DZ 20		Queen St. . . . . CY 38			
Castle Gate . . . . DY 13		Furnival Gate . . . . CZ 21		St Mary's Gate . . . . CZ 40			
Charter Row . . . . CZ 14		Furnival St . . . . CZ 22		Shalesmoor. . . . . CY 41			
Church St . . . . CZ 15		Gibraltar St . . . . CY 23		Snig Hill . . . . DY 42			
Commercial St . . . . DZ 16		Haymarket . . . . DY 25		Waingate. . . . . DY 44			
Corporation St. . . . . CY 18		High St . . . . DZ		West Bar Green. . . . . CY 45			
Cumberland St . . . . CZ 17		Leopold St. . . . . CZ 31		West St . . . . CZ			
Fargate . . . . CZ		Moorfields. . . . . CY 35					

SHALDON

Devon – Pop. 1 762 – See Regional map n°**2**-D2

London 188 mi – Exeter 16 mi – Torquay 7 mi – Paignton 13 mi

Michelin Road map 503-J32

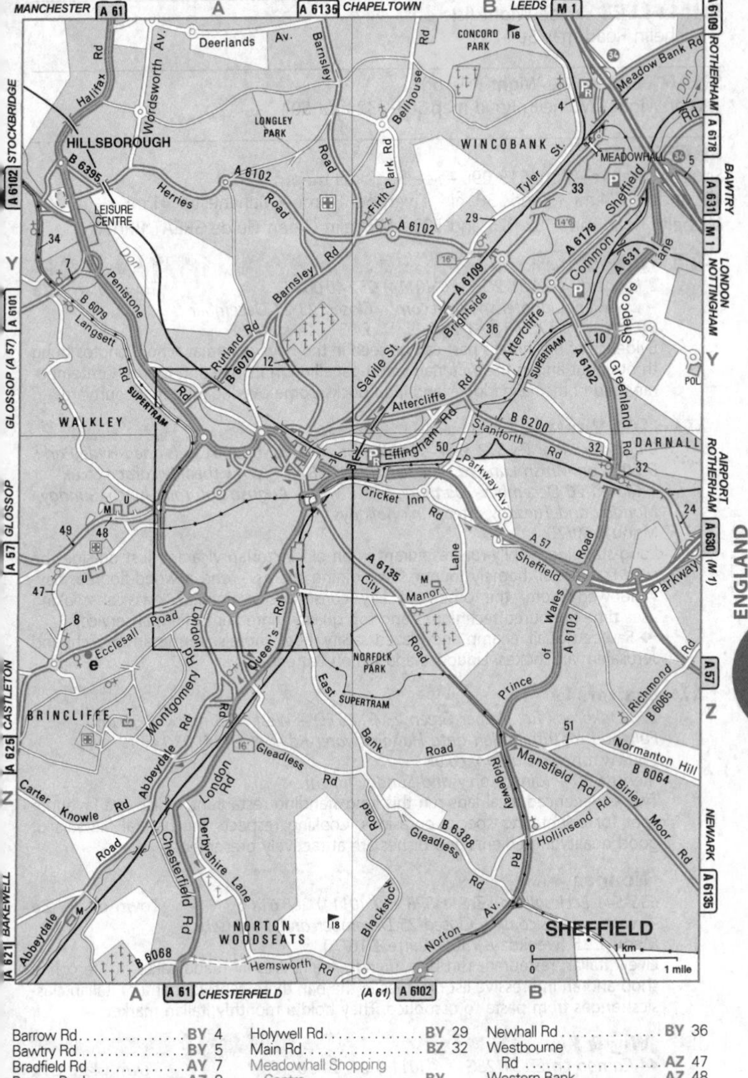

Barrow Rd	BY 4	Holywell Rd	BY 29	Newhall Rd	BY 36
Bawtry Rd	BY 5	Main Rd	BZ 32	Westbourne Rd	AZ 47
Bradfield Rd	AY 7	Meadowhall Shopping Centre	BY	Western Bank	AZ 48
Brocco Bank	AZ 8	Meadow Hall Rd	BY 33	Whitham Rd	AZ 49
Broughton Lane	BY 10	Middlewood Rd	AY 34	Woodbourn Rd	BYZ 50
Burngreave Rd	AY 12			Woodhouse Rd	BZ 51
Handsworth Rd	BZ 24				

ODE

21 Fore St ✉ TQ14 0DE – ✆ (01626) 873 977 – www.odetruefood.co.uk – Closed October 25-26 December, Sunday-Tuesday and bank holidays

Menu £ 35/40 – *(dinner only) (booking essential)*

Proudly run neighbourhood restaurant in a glass-fronted Georgian house on a narrow village street. It has a strong sustainable and organic ethos, sourcing recycled glassware, biodynamic wines and produce from small local suppliers and foragers. Simple dishes are precisely prepared and attractively presented.

SHALFLEET → See Wight (Isle of)
– Michelin Road map 504-P31

SHANKLIN → See Wight (Isle of)
Isle of Wight – Michelin Road map 503-Q32 and 504

SHEFFIELD
South Yorkshire – Pop. 518 090 – See Regional map n°**22**-B3
London 174 mi – Leeds 36 mi – Liverpool 80 mi – Manchester 41 mi
Michelin Road map 502-P23 and 503 – Michelin Green Guide GREAT BRITAIN

Leopold without rest
2 Leopold St ✉ S1 2GZ – ✆ (0114) 252 40 00 Town plan: CZ**a**
– www.leopoldhotelssheffield.com – Closed 23-27 December
90 rm – †£ 79/149 ††£ 79/249, ☕ £ 13 – 14 suites
Evidence of this hotel's past can be seen in the boys grammar school photos hung throughout and in the Victorian wood-panelling in its meeting rooms. Contemporary bedrooms have fridges and iPod docks; some overlook the rear courtyard.

XXX **Old Vicarage** (Tessa Bramley)
Ridgeway Moor ✉ S12 3XW – Southeast : 6.75 mi by A 6135 (signed Hyde Park), B 6054 on Marsh Lane rd. – ✆ (0114) 247 58 14 – www.theoldvicarage.co.uk – Closed 26 December-6 January, first 2 weeks August, Saturday lunch, Sunday, Monday and Tuesday after bank holidays
Menu £ 40/75
Long-standing, family-run restaurant in an old Victorian vicarage just outside the city. Traditional, homely lounge. Two dining rooms - one a wood-floored, bay-windowed room, the other, an airy conservatory. Refined, classical cooking uses time-honoured techniques and top quality ingredients. Formal service.
→ Sautéed quail, champ and glazed salsify. Beef, morels, parmesan gnocchi and Jerusalem artichokes. Liquorice and lemon Battenberg.

XX **Rafters** (N)
220 Oakbrook Rd, Nether Green ✉ S11 7ED – West : 2.5 mi by A 57 and Fulwood rd, turning left onto Hangingwater Rd – ✆ (0114) 230 48 19 – www.raftersrestaurant.co.uk
Menu £ 39 – *(dinner only and Sunday lunch)*
Two experienced local lads run this long-standing restaurant, which is a favourite spot for celebrating special occasions. Cooking respects the natural flavours of good quality ingredients and dishes are attractively presented.

X **Nonnas**
535-541 Ecclesall Rd ✉ S11 8PR – ✆ (0114) 268 61 66 Town plan: AZ**e**
– www.nonnas.co.uk – Closed 25 December and 1 January
Menu £ 25 (weekdays)/30 – Carte £ 16/70
Lively Italian restaurant run by a friendly team. Freshly made cakes in the coffee shop and an impressive list of wines in the bar; the extensive menu of Italian classics ranges from pasta to ossobuco. They hold a monthly Italian market.

Wig & Pen
44 Campo Ln ✉ S1 2EG – ✆ (0114) 272 21 50 Town plan: CY**x**
– www.the-wigandpen.co.uk – Closed 25-26 December and 1 January
Menu £ 17 (dinner) – Carte £ 19/29
Sister to the Milestone, but nearer to the heart of the city; its busy bar a magnet for office workers on their way home. Good value lunch menu of light dishes like fishcakes or risotto; more elaborate, ambitious dishes at dinner.

Milestone
84 Green Ln ✉ S3 8SE – ✆ (0114) 272 83 27 Town plan: CY**e**
– www.the-milestone.co.uk – Closed 25-26 December and 1 January
Menu £ 14 – Carte £ 17/38
Spacious 18C pub in a recently regenerated area of the city. The hearty gastro menu offers modern dishes with their emphasis firmly on seasonal, organic, locally sourced ingredients; presentation mixes the traditional and the contemporary.

ENGLAND

at Totley Southwest: 5.5 mi on A621 -(AZ)✉ South Yorkshire

Cricket Inn

Penny Ln ✉ S17 3AZ – (off Hillfoot Rd) – ✆ (0114) 236 52 56 – www.cricketinn.co.uk

Menu £ 15 (weekday lunch) – Carte £ 20/40

Hidden away next to the cricket pitch, with open fires and rustic wood floors. Wide-ranging, Yorkshire-based menu offers bar snacks through to grills and roasts. Hearty, wholesome cooking.

SHEFFORD

Central Bedfordshire – Pop. 5 954 – See Regional map n°**12-A1**

London 48 mi – Bedford 10 mi – Luton 16 mi – Northampton 37 mi

Michelin Road map 504-S27

Black Horse with rm

rest, rest,

Ireland ✉ SG17 5QL – Northwest : 1.5 mi by Northbridge St and B 658 on Ireland rd – ✆ (01462) 811 398 – www.blackhorseireland.com – Closed 25-26 December and 1 January

2 rm – †£ 75 ††£ 75 Menu £ 15 (weekday lunch) – Carte £ 24/41

It may look traditional from the outside, but inside this pub is as stylish and modern as you can get, with marble floors, a granite bar and hi-tech fittings. The eclectic menu offers generous dishes ranging from suet pies to confit of duck or sea bass. Set in the garden, bedrooms are comfy and cosy.

SHELLEY

West Yorkshire – See Regional map n°**22-B3**

London 185 mi – Bristol 197 mi – Cardiff 218 mi – Plymouth 311 mi

Michelin Road map 502-O23

Three Acres

rm, rest,

Roydhouse ✉ HD8 8LR – Northeast : 1.5 mi on Flockton rd – ✆ (01484) 602 606 – www.3acres.com – Closed 25-26 December and 1 January

17 rm – †£ 50/75 ††£ 75/125

Rest – Menu £ 40 – Carte £ 29/56 – *(booking essential)*

Well-established, traditional stone inn perched on top of the moors, with two smart meeting rooms and warmly decorated, modern bedrooms; those in the adjacent cottages are quieter and more contemporary. Busy bar and a maze of charmingly cluttered, low-beamed dining rooms; extensive, classical menu.

SHEPTON MALLET

Somerset – Pop. 10 369 – See Regional map n°**4-C2**

London 127 mi – Bristol 20 mi – Southampton 63 mi – Taunton 31 mi

Michelin Road map 503-M30 and 504

Charlton House

rm, rest,

✉ BA4 4PR East : 1 mi on A 361 – ✆ (08442) 483 830 – www.bannatyne.co.uk

28 rm – †£ 100/400 ††£ 100/400 **Rest** – Menu £ 20/35

Fine 17C house previously owned by Mulberry and now by Duncan Bannatyne: influences from both are evident. Smart boutique styling, with a touch of informality; individually furnished bedrooms feature luxurious bathrooms. Superb spa. Carefully prepared, modern European dishes served in conservatory.

SHERBORNE

Dorset – Pop. 9 523 – See Regional map n°**4-C3**

London 128 mi – Bournemouth 39 mi – Dorchester 19 mi – Salisbury 36 mi

Michelin Road map 503-M31 and 504 – Michelin Green Guide GREAT BRITAIN

The Green

3 The Green ✉ DT9 3HY – ✆ (01935) 813 821 – www.greenrestaurant.co.uk – Closed 25-26 December, Sunday and Monday

Menu £ 20 (weekdays) – Carte £ 26/46

Pretty Grade II listed stone property at the top of the hill, with a traditional bistro style, an inglenook fireplace and ecclesiastical panelling. Concise à la carte and a good value set lunch; classical, confident, satisfying cooking.

ENGLAND

at Oborne Northeast: 2 mi by A30 ✉ Sherborne

Grange

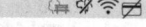

✉ *DT9 4LA – ✆ (01935) 813 463 – www.thegrangeatoborne.co.uk*
18 rm ☕ – †£ 88/109 ††£ 119/169 **Rest** – Menu £ 21/35
Family-run, stone-built country house in pretty village; dating back 200 years. Comfy guest areas overlook attractive mature gardens. Spacious bedrooms boast good facilities; some have balconies or patios. Menus showcase the latest local, seasonal ingredients.

SHERE → See Guildford
Surrey – Michelin Road map 504-S30

SHERINGHAM
Norfolk – Pop. 7 367 – See Regional map n°**15**-C1
London 136 mi – Cromer 5 mi – Norwich 27 mi
Michelin Road map 504-X25

Ashbourne House without rest

1 Nelson Rd ✉ NR26 8BT – ✆ (01263) 821 555
– www.ashbournehousesheringham.co.uk – Closed 21 December-3 January
4 rm ☕ – †£ 55/60 ††£ 75/80
Well-appointed guesthouse in an elevated position; its large, landscaped garden has access to the clifftop. Comfortable bedrooms: two with coastal views. Impressive fireplace in the wood-panelled breakfast room.

SHERWOOD BUSINESS PARK → See Nottingham
Nottinghamshire

SHILTON
Warwickshire ✉ Coventry – See Regional map n°**19**-D2
London 97 mi – Bristol 99 mi – Cardiff 131 mi – Plymouth 213 mi
Michelin Road map 503-P26 and 504

Barnacle Hall without rest
Shilton Ln. ✉ CV7 9LH – West : 1 mi by B 4029 following signs for garden centre
– ✆ (024) 7661 2629 – www.barnaclehall.co.uk – Closed 24 December-2 January
3 rm ☕ – †£ 40/50 ††£ 70/80
Welcoming farmhouse in mature gardens, on a 170 acre arable farm. Traditional, beamed interior with a comfy, fire-lit lounge and 16C origins; spacious bedrooms offer pleasant country views. Hearty, home-cooked, communal breakfasts.

SHINFIELD → See Reading
Wokingham – Michelin Road map 504-R29

SHIPLAKE → See Henley-on-Thames
Oxfordshire – Michelin Road map 504-R29

SHIPLAKE ROW → See Henley-on-Thames
Oxfordshire

SHIPLEY
West Yorkshire – Pop. 28 694 – See Regional map n°**22**-B2
London 216 mi – Bradford 4 mi – Leeds 12 mi
Michelin Road map 502-O22

Plan: see Leeds

Zaara's
34-38 Bradford Rd ✉ BD18 3NT – ✆ (01274) 588 114 Town plan: AT**a**
– www.zaaras.com – Closed 25 December and Monday except bank holidays
Menu £ 13 (weekdays) – Carte £ 14/21 – *(dinner only)*
Modern Indian restaurant with an intimate red colour scheme, a wooden feature wall and smart black furnishings. The owner and chefs specialise in dishes from their home region, Punjab; try the dry curries, homemade paneer or karahi dishes.

ENGLAND

SHIPSTON-ON-STOUR

Warwickshire – Pop. 5 038 – See Regional map n°**19-C3**

London 87 mi – Leeds 146 mi – Sheffield 116 mi – Manchester 139 mi

Michelin Road map 503-P27

George

8 High St ✉ CV36 4AJ – ✆ (01608) 661 453 – www.georgehotelshipston.com

15 rm – †£ 60/80 ††£ 65/90 **Rest** – Menu £ 11 (lunch) – Carte £ 24/35

Red-brick coaching inn at the centre of a busy market town, with a shabby-chic interior, a leather-furnished library and an open-fired bar. Modern, minimalistic bedrooms are named after foods and feature striking food-themed headboards. Seasonal Mediterranean and English based menus in the smart dining room.

SHIRLEY → See Ashbourne

Derbyshire – Michelin Road map 502-O26

SHOTTLE

Derbyshire – See Regional map n°**16-B2**

London 140 mi – Sheffield 33 mi – Derby 13 mi

Dannah Farm Country House without rest

Bowmans Ln. ✉ DE56 2DR – North : 0.25 mi by Alport rd – ✆ (01773) 550 273 – www.dannah.co.uk – Closed 24-26 December

8 rm – †£ 89/105 ††£ 185/285

18C stone farmhouse on 154 acre working farm owned by the Chatsworth Estate; its outbuildings converted into spacious, well-equipped bedrooms. Many rooms have spa baths and the Granary and Studio Suites have hot tubs and terraces.

ENGLAND

SHREWSBURY

Shropshire – Pop. 71 715 – See Regional map n°**18-B2**

London 164 mi – Birmingham 48 mi – Chester 43 mi – Derby 67 mi

Michelin Road map 502-L25 and 503 – Michelin Green Guide GREAT BRITAIN

Lion and Pheasant

49-50 Wyle Cop ✉ SY1 1XJ – ✆ (01743) 770 345 – www.lionandpheasant.co.uk – Closed 25-26 December **Town plan:s**

22 rm – †£ 79/109 ††£ 99/159

Rest ***Lion and Pheasant*** – see restaurant listing

A collection of adjoining 16C and 18C townhouses on a famous medieval street. Inside it's modern, quirky and understated. Chic bedrooms – designed by the owner's daughter – have a French boutique feel; the rear rooms are quieter.

Henry Tudor House Ⓝ

Barracks Passage, Wyle Cop ✉ SY1 1XA – ✆ (01743) 361 666 – www.henrytudorhouse.com – Closed 25-26 December and 1 January **Town plan:t**

Menu £ 13 (lunch) – Carte dinner £ 23/35

This impressive 15C timbered building is one of the oldest in town. Inside it's been subtly modernised and features a chic bar and a conservatory with unusual birdcage chandeliers. The atmospheric restaurant opens at weekends.

Lion and Pheasant Ⓝ – Lion and Pheasant Hotel

49-50 Wyle Cop ✉ SY1 1XJ – ✆ (01743) 770 345 – www.lionandpheasant.co.uk – Closed 25-26 December **Town plan:s**

Menu £ 15 (weekday lunch) – Carte £ 26/49

Head through the hotel's café-bar and up the stairs to this cosy beamed restaurant. Carefully prepared dishes rely on quality ingredients and have a subtle modern touch. Another more formally set room is also opened at weekends.

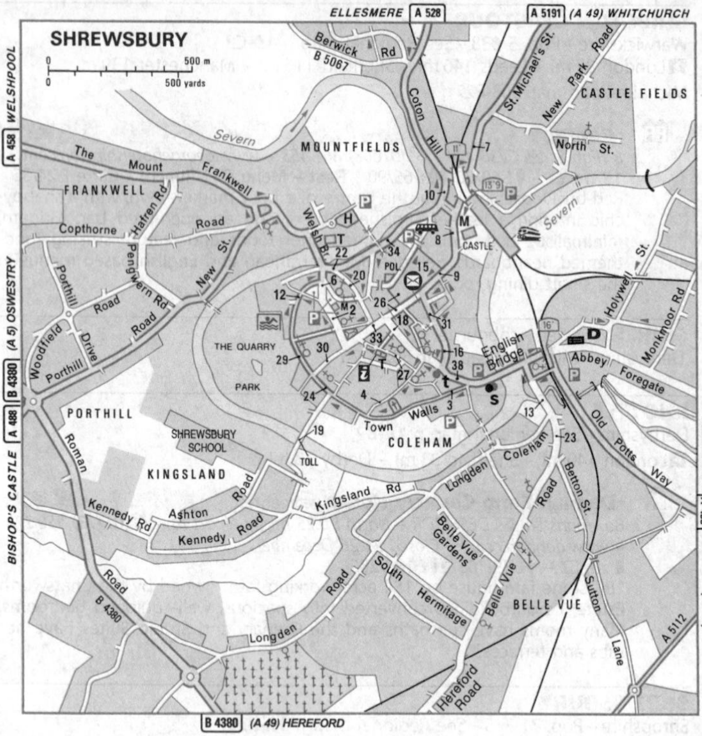

SHREWSBURY

Barker St	2	Coleham Head	13	Pride Hill	26
Beeches Lane	3	Darwin Centre	15	Princess St	27
Belmont	4	Dogpole	16	St Chad's Terrace	29
Bridge St	6	High St	18	St John's Hill	30
Castle Foregate	7	Kingsland Bridge	19	St Mary's St	31
Castle Gates	8	Mardol	20	Shoplatch	33
Castle St	9	Mardol Quay	22	Smithfield Rd	34
Chester St	10	Moreton Crescent	23	Wyle Cop	38
Claremont Bank	12	Murivance	24		

at Grinshill North: 7.5 mi by A49✉ Shrewsbury

Inn at Grinshill with rm

The High St ✉ SY4 3BL – ✆ (01939) 220 410 – www.theinnatgrinshill.co.uk – Closed first week January, Sunday dinner, Monday and Tuesday

6 rm ☕ – 🚹£ 90 🚹🚹£ 120 Carte £ 19/46 **s**

Family-owned and very personally run, this inn stands in the middle of a pretty Shropshire village and its food revolves around the seasons. A cosy bar plays host to walkers and locals while the contemporary restaurant has a view to the kitchen. Six pretty bedrooms are individually decorated and comfortable.

at Atcham Southeast: 3 mi by A5064 on B4380

Mytton and Mermaid

✉ SY5 6QG – ✆ (01743) 761 220 – www.myttonandmermaid.co.uk – Closed 25 December

16 rm ☕ – 🚹£ 65/85 🚹🚹£ 110/175

Rest ***Mytton and Mermaid*** – see restaurant listing

A popular riverside coaching inn with a pleasant terrace and lawned gardens; escape from the crowds in the cosy sitting room. Bedrooms in the main house are traditional – most have river views; more modern rooms are in the old stables.

Mytton and Mermaid – Mytton and Mermaid Hotel
✉ *SY5 6QG – ✆ (01743) 761 220 – www.myttonandmermaid.co.uk – Closed 25 December*
Carte £ 24/35
Choose between three dining areas at this 18C coaching inn: the bustling bistro, the dining room or the pleasant terrace. The same extensive menu is served throughout, offering tasty, classically based dishes and daily specials.

at Condover South: 5 mi by A49

Grove Farm House without rest
✉ *SY5 7BH South : 0.75 mi on Dorrington rd – ✆ (01743) 718 544 – www.grovefarmhouse.com*
4 rm – †£ 60/65 ††£ 85/90
The friendly owners of this 18C farmhouse have opened up their family home. Bedrooms are pleasantly furnished and come with well-equipped bathrooms and country views. Extensive breakfasts showcase local and homemade choices.

SHREWTON

Wiltshire – Pop. 1 723 – See Regional map n°**4-D2**
London 91 mi – Bristol 53 mi – Southampton 52 mi – Reading 69 mi
Michelin Road map 503-O30

Rollestone Manor
✉ *SP3 4HF Southeast : 0.5 mi on A 360 – ✆ (01980) 620 216 – www.rollestonemanor.com – Closed 24-26 December*
7 rm – †£ 70/87 ††£ 87/105
Rest – Carte £ 18/44 – *(dinner only) (bookings essential for non-residents)*
Grade II listed house on a main road just outside the village, on a part-working farm; once the home of Jane Seymour's family. Good-sized, antique-furnished bedrooms offer modern facilities; one even has a bath in the room, set on top of a plinth. The contemporary restaurant serves modern classics.

SHURDINGTON → See Cheltenham

Gloucestershire – Michelin Road map 503-N28 and 504

SIBFORD GOWER

Oxfordshire – See Regional map n°**10-B1**
London 82 mi – Oxford 28 mi – Cheltenham 40 mi

Wykham Arms
Temple Mill Rd ✉ OX15 5RX – ✆ (01295) 788 808 – www.wykhamarms.co.uk – Closed Monday except bank holidays
Carte £ 25/34
17C thatched pub with sand-coloured stone walls, set down narrow country lanes in a small village. Menus feature local produce and range from bar snacks and light bites to the full 3 courses. There's a good range of wines by the glass.

SIDFORD → See Sidmouth

Devon – Michelin Road map 503-K31

SIDLESHAM

West Sussex – See Regional map n°**7-C3**
London 84 mi – Bristol 137 mi – Cardiff 170 mi – Plymouth 187 mi
Michelin Road map 504-R31

Landseer House without rest
Cow Ln ✉ PO20 7LN – South : 1.5 mi by B 2145 and Keynor Ln – ✆ (01243) 641 525 – www.landseerhouse.co.uk
6 rm – †£ 80/150 ††£ 85/175
Tastefully furnished guesthouse, with numerous antiques and pleasant views of the surrounding wetlands. Contemporary bedrooms; go for Room 1 – the most luxurious. Those in the garden have their own terraces and kitchens.

ENGLAND

Crab & Lobster with rm

Mill Ln ✉ PO20 7NB – ✆ (01243) 641 233 – www.crab-lobster.co.uk
5 rm – £ 90/100 £ 155/275
Menu £ 22 (weekday lunch) – Carte £ 29/63 – *(booking advisable)*
Historic inn, in a wonderful setting on a nature reserve, with pretty gardens and a light, relaxed feel. Seasonal menu focuses on seafood. Very comfy bedrooms have a modern, minimalist style; one has its own garden and an open-fired stove.

SIDMOUTH

Devon – Pop. 12 569 – See Regional map n°**2-D2**
London 176 mi – Exeter 14 mi – Taunton 27 mi – Weymouth 45 mi
Michelin Road map 503-K31 – Michelin Green Guide GREAT BRITAIN

Riviera rest, rest,

The Esplanade ✉ EX10 8AY – ✆ (01395) 515 201 – www.hotelriviera.co.uk – Closed 2 January-12 February
26 rm (dinner included) – £ 109/188 £ 218/422
Rest – Menu £ 25/42 – Carte £ 30/55
Long-standing, family-run hotel with characterful Regency façade. Superbly kept classical guest areas; fresh flowers and friendly staff abound. Smart bedrooms in rich blues and gold, some with a view. Traditional menus have a modern edge. Cream teas a speciality.

ENGLAND

at Sidford North: 2 mi ✉ Sidmouth

XX **Salty Monk** with rm

Church St ✉ EX10 9QP – on A 3052 – ✆ (01395) 513 174 – www.saltymonk.co.uk – Closed January, 2 weeks November and Monday
6 rm – £ 85/150 £ 130/180
Menu £ 39 (dinner) – Carte £ 24/46 – *(dinner only and lunch Thursday-Sunday) (booking essential)*
Smart, proudly run restaurant in an old 16C salt house, featuring striking purple woodwork and a pleasant blend of the old and new. The Abbots Den offers a casual brasserie menu, while the Garden Room serves more elaborate modern dishes. Bedrooms have good extras and there's a gym and hot tub in the garden.

SINNINGTON → See Pickering

North Yorkshire – Michelin Road map 502-R21

SISSINGHURST

Kent – See Regional map n°**8-B2**
London 50 mi – Maidstone 13 mi – Ashford 18 mi
Michelin Road map 504-V30

The Milk House  with rm rest,

The Street ✉ TN17 2JG – ✆ (01580) 720 200 – www.themilkhouse.co.uk – Closed 25 December
4 rm – £ 95/120 £ 95/120 Carte £ 17/41
Set on a road originally known as Milk Street: turn right into the bar with its soft sofas, huge fire and Grazing Menu; turn left into the dining room for a seasonal menu of modern British dishes. Pub Classics and Children's menus available in either area. Upstairs bedrooms are smart and contemporary.

SITTINGBOURNE

Kent – Pop. 48 948 – See Regional map n°**9-C1**
London 44 mi – Canterbury 18 mi – Maidstone 15 mi – Sheerness 9 mi
Michelin Road map 504-W29

Hempstead House
London Rd, Bapchild ✉ ME9 9PP – East : 2 mi on A 2 – ✆ (01795) 428 020 – www.hempsteadhouse.co.uk
34 rm – †£ 85/115 ††£ 110/160
Rest *Lakes* – see restaurant listing
Privately run red-brick Victorian house in pleasant landscaped gardens. Classical bedrooms are found in the main house; more contemporary rooms are set above the luxurious spa. The wood-panelled lounges are cosy and characterful.

Lakes – Hempstead House Hotel
London Rd, Bapchild ✉ ME9 9PP – East : 2 mi on A 2 – ✆ (01795) 428 020 – www.hempsteadhouse.co.uk
Menu £ 28 – Carte £ 29/39 – *(residents only Sunday dinner)*
Set in the conservatory of a well-run Victorian hotel, this formal conservatory restaurant features Georgian columns, crystal chandeliers and smartly laid tables. Menus are classical. Start with a drink in the homely sitting rooms.

SIX MILE BOTTOM
Cambridgeshire – See Regional map n°**14-B3**
London 59 mi – Birmingham 106 mi – Norwich 55 mi – Cambridge 9 mi

Paddocks House
London Rd ✉ CB8 0UE – ✆ (01638) 593 222 – www.thehousecollection.com
13 rm – †£ 139/169 ††£ 139/169 – 1 suite
Rest *Dining Room* – Menu £ 23 – Carte £ 32/52
Black, grey and silver décor gives this stylish hotel a masculine feel, and horse-themed prints are a reminder that Newmarket is nearby. Spacious bedrooms boast excellent quality linens and all but one have a bath in the room; No.12 even has its own cinema! The intimate dining room offers modern classics.

SLALEY → See Hexham
Northumberland

SLAPTON
Devon – See Regional map n°**2-C3**
London 223 mi – Plymouth 30 mi – Torbay 26 mi – Exeter 50 mi
Michelin Road map 503-J33

Tower Inn with rm
Church Rd ✉ TQ7 2PN – ✆ (01548) 580 216 – www.thetowerinn.com – Closed first 2 weeks January and Sunday dinner in winter
3 rm – †£ 60/65 ††£ 75/85 Menu £ 20 (weekday dinner) – Carte £ 21/33
Charming pub overlooked by the ruins of a chantry tower (leave your car in the village and walk the narrow lane). Menus differ between services and offer pub food with a twist: maybe fish and chips in vodka batter at lunch or sea bass with crab dumplings in the evening. Simple bedrooms await.

SNAPE
Suffolk – Pop. 1 509 – See Regional map n°**15-D3**
London 113 mi – Ipswich 19 mi – Norwich 50 mi
Michelin Road map 504-Y27

Crown Inn with rm
Bridge Rd ✉ IP17 1SL – ✆ (01728) 688 324 – www.snape-crown.co.uk
2 rm – †£ 70/90 ††£ 70/90 Carte £ 20/30
The affable owners of this characterful 15C former smugglers' inn grow fruit and vegetables and raise various animals, which provide much of the meat for their constantly evolving menus; the rosettes in the bar come from showing their Gloucester Old Spot pigs. Rustic bedrooms have beams and sloping floors.

SNETTISHAM
Norfolk – Pop. 2 570 – See Regional map n°**14-B1**
London 113 mi – King's Lynn 13 mi – Norwich 44 mi
Michelin Road map 504-V25

ENGLAND

Rose and Crown with rm
Old Church Rd ✉ PE31 7LX – ✆ (01485) 541 382 – www.roseandcrownsnettisham.co.uk
16 rm ☕ – 👤£ 80/110 👥£ 100/130 Carte £ 20/33
14C pub featuring a warren of rooms with uneven floors and low beamed ceilings. Gutsy cooking uses locally sourced produce, with globally influenced dishes alongside trusty pub classics. Impressive children's adventure fort. Modern bedrooms are decorated in sunny colours, and offer a good level of facilities.

SOAR MILL COVE → See Salcombe
Devon – Michelin Road map 503-I33

SOMERTON
Somerset – Pop. 4 133 – See Regional map n°**3-B2**
London 138 mi – Bristol 32 mi – Taunton 17 mi
Michelin Road map 503-L30

Lynch Country House without rest
4 Behind Berry ✉ TA11 7PD – ✆ (01458) 272 316 – www.thelynchcountryhouse.co.uk
9 rm ☕ – 👤£ 70/95 👥£ 80/115
Personally run Regency house with mature grounds that incorporate some unusual plants and a lake frequented by a variety of wildfowl. Traditional country house interior with a conservatory breakfast room and individually decorated bedrooms.

White Hart Ⓝ with rm
Market Pl ✉ TA11 7LX – ✆ (01458) 272 273 – www.whitehartsomerton.com
8 rm ☕ – 👤£ 85/130 👥£ 85/130 Carte £ 21/34
A 16C inn on the village's main market square; its beautiful parquet-floored entrance leads to six characterful rooms, including 'the barn' where you can watch the chefs at work. Seasonal food centres around the wood burning oven. Cosy, modern bedrooms; Room 3, with a bath centre stage, is the best.

SONNING-ON-THAMES → See Reading
Wokingham – Michelin Road map 504-R29

SOUTH DALTON → See Beverley
East Riding of Yorkshire

SOUTH POOL
Devon – See Regional map n°**2-C3**
London 218 mi – Plymouth 26 mi – Torbay 25 mi – Exeter 46 mi

Millbrook Inn
✉ TQ7 2RW – ✆ (01548) 531 581 – www.millbrookinnsouthpool.co.uk
Menu £ 12 (weekday lunch) – Carte £ 24/49
Characterful, passionately run, shabby-chic pub squeezed between the houses on a narrow village street. Choice of cosy, low-beamed interior or two terraces. Cooking is traditional and hearty with Mediterranean influences.

SOUTH RAUCEBY
Lincolnshire – Pop. 335 – See Regional map n°**17-C2**
London 131 mi – Nottingham 40 mi – Leicester 54 mi
Michelin Road map 502-S24/2

Bustard Inn
44 Main St ✉ NG34 8QG – ✆ (01529) 488 250 – www.thebustardinn.co.uk – Closed 1 January, Sunday dinner and Monday except bank holidays
Menu £ 13 (weekday lunch) – Carte £ 22/46
Grade II listed inn set in a peaceful hamlet, with a light and airy flag-floored bar and a spacious, beamed restaurant. Good value lunch menu and a more ambitious à la carte offering modern-style, English dishes.

SOUTHAMPTON

Southampton – Pop. 253 651 – See Regional map n°**6-B2**
London 87 mi – Bristol 79 mi – Plymouth 161 mi
Michelin Road map 503-P31 and 504 – Michelin Green Guide GREAT BRITAIN

Pig in the Wall without rest

8 Western Esplanade ✉ *SO14 2AZ* – ✆ *(023) 8063 6900* Town plan: AZ**a**
– *www.thepighotel.co.uk*
12 rm – †£ 129/185 ††£ 129/185, ☕ £ 10
Delightfully run, early 19C property that's been lovingly restored. The rustic lounge-cum-deli serves superb breakfasts and light meals; for something more substantial they will chauffeur you to their sister restaurant. Smart, boutique bedrooms come with antiques, super-comfy beds and Egyptian cotton linen.

White Star Tavern, Dining and Rooms with rm

♿ rest, AC rest,
28 Oxford St ✉ *SO14 3DJ* – ✆ *(023) 8082 1990*
– *www.whitestartavern.co.uk* – *Closed 25-26 December* Town plan: AZ**x**
14 rm – †£ 105/145 ††£ 105/145, ☕ £ 9 Carte £ 19/40
Eye-catching black pub with vast windows and smart pavement terrace, set in the lively maritime district. Choice of all day tapas-style small plates or modern British à la carte of meaty dishes. Smart, modern bedrooms boast good facilities and extra touches.

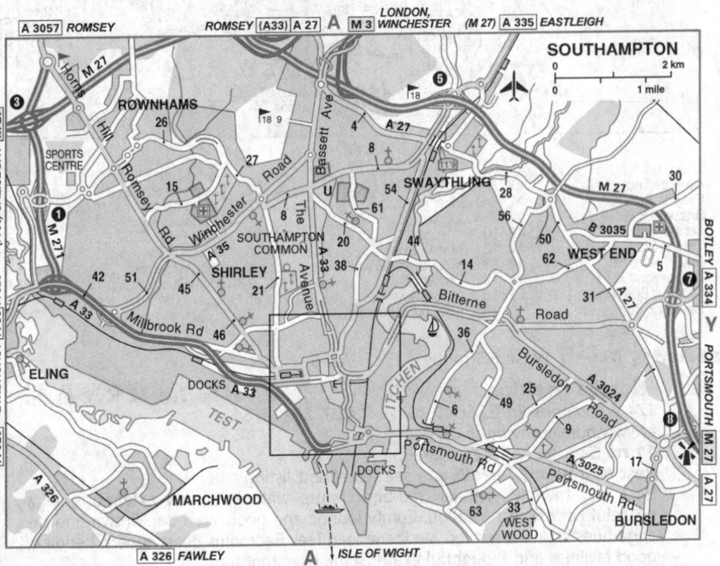

Basset Green Rd . . . AY 4	Kathleen Rd . . . AY 25	Shirley High Rd . . . AY 45
Botley Rd . . . AY 5	Lordswood Rd . . . AY 27	Shirley Rd . . . AY 46
Bridge Rd . . . AY 6	Lords Hill Way . . . AY 26	Spring Rd . . . AY 49
Burgess Rd . . . AY 8	Mansbridge Rd . . . AY 28	Swaything Rd . . . AY 50
Butts Rd . . . AY 9	Moorgreen Rd . . . AY 30	Tebourba Way . . . AY 51
Cobden Ave . . . AY 14	Moor Hill . . . AY 31	Thomas Lewis Way . . . AY 54
Coxford Rd . . . AY 15	Newtown Rd . . . AY 33	Townhill Way . . . AY 56
Hamble Lane . . . AY 17	Peartree Ave . . . AY 36	Welbeck Ave . . . AY 61
Highfield Lane . . . AY 20	Portswood Rd . . . AY 38	Westend Rd . . . AY 62
Hill Lane . . . AY 21	Redbridge Rd . . . AY 42	Weston Lane . . . AY 63
Kane's Hill . . . AY 24	St Denys Rd . . . AY 44	

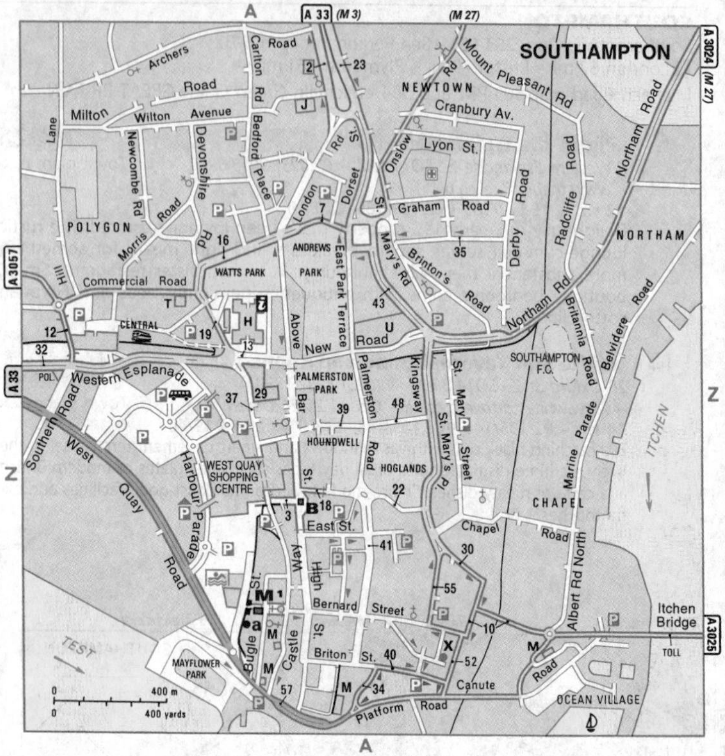

SOUTHAMPTON

Street	Grid	No.
Above Bar St	AZ	
Avenue (The)	AZ	2
Bargate St	AZ	3
Brunswick Pl.	AZ	7
Central Bridge	AZ	10
Central Station Bridge	AZ	12
Civic Centre Rd	AZ	13
Cumberland Pl.	AZ	16
Hanover Buildings	AZ	18
Havelock Rd	AZ	19
High St	AZ	
Houndwell Pl.	AZ	22
Inner Ave.	AZ	23
Marlands Shopping Centre	AZ	29
Marsh Lane	AZ	30
Mountbatten Way	AZ	32
Orchard Pl.	AZ	34
Oxford Ave	AZ	35
Portland Terrace	AZ	37
Pound Tree Rd	AZ	39
Queen's Terrace	AZ	40
Queen's Way	AZ	41
St Andrew's Rd	AZ	43
South Front	AZ	48
Terminus Terrace	AZ	52
Threefield Lane	AZ	55
Town Quay	AZ	57
West Quay Shopping Centre	AZ	

at Netley Marsh West: 6.5 mi by A33 off A336

Hotel TerraVina

174 Woodlands Rd ✉ SO40 7GL – ✆ (023) 8029 3784
– www.hotelterravina.co.uk

11 rm ☕ – 🚹£ 165 🚹🚹£ 165/265

Rest *Restaurant TerraVina* – see restaurant listing

Neat and friendly Victorian red-brick house with wood-clad extensions, in a peaceful New Forest location. Comfy lounge and good-sized bar. Brown and orange hues create a relaxed Mediterranean feel. Bedrooms boast superb bedding, good facilities and thoughtful extras; some have roof terraces.

Restaurant TerraVina – Hotel TerraVina

174 Woodlands Rd ✉ SO40 7GL – ✆ (023) 8029 3784
– www.hotelterravina.co.uk

Menu £ 27 (weekday lunch) – Carte £ 37/51

Modern hotel restaurant with an open-plan kitchen, a glass-fronted wine cave and a large covered terrace. Lunch sticks to the classics, while dinner introduces some imaginative modern dishes and a 6 course tasting menu. Service is attentive and the sommelier offers some original and well-judged wine pairings.

SOUTHEND-ON-SEA

Southend-on-Sea – Pop. 175 547 – See Regional map n°**13**-**C3**
London 39 mi – Cambridge 69 mi – Croydon 46 mi – Dover 85 mi
Michelin Road map 504-W29

Pier View without rest

5 Royal Terr. ✉ SS1 1DY – ✆ (01702) 437 900 – www.pierviewguesthouse.co.uk
8 rm – †£ 55/60 ††£ 80/140
Georgian townhouse in an elevated position overlooking the promenade, estuary and pier. Individually decorated bedrooms are very comfortable; a sea view room is a must. The first floor breakfast room still has its original cornicing.

SOUTHPORT

Merseyside – Pop. 91 703 – See Regional map n°**20**-A2
London 221 mi – Liverpool 25 mi – Manchester 38 mi – Preston 19 mi
Michelin Road map 502-K23

Vincent

98 Lord St. ✉ PR8 1JR – ✆ (01704) 883 800 – www.thevincenthotel.com
59 rm – †£ 93/208 ††£ 93/208, £ 10 – 2 suites
Rest *V-Café* – see restaurant listing
Striking glass, steel and stone hotel beside the gardens and bandstand. Stylish, boutique interior with chic bar, fitness room and spa. Sleek, modern bedrooms come in dark colours, boasting Nespresso machines and deep Japanese soaking tubs.

XX Warehouse (N)

30 West St ✉ PR8 1 QN – ✆ (01704) 544 662 – www.warehouserestaurant.co.uk – Closed Sunday and Monday
Menu £ 15 (lunch and early dinner) – Carte £ 29/42
Its old warehouse setting gives this laid-back neighbourhood restaurant a slightly industrial feel, courtesy of exposed brick walls and metalwork screens. Unfussy dishes rely on seasonal ingredients and arrive smartly presented.

X V-Café – Vincent Hotel

98 Lord St. ✉ PR8 1JR – ✆ (01704) 883 800 – www.thevincenthotel.com
Menu £ 14 (weekday dinner) – Carte £ 23/49
Relaxed café in a striking modern hotel, its glass façade overlooking the street. Open all-day and offering everything from sushi at the counter to 3 courses of globally influenced dishes.

X Bistrot Vérité

7 Liverpool Rd, Birkdale ✉ PR8 4AR – South : 1.5 mi by A 565 – ✆ (01704) 564 199 – www.bistrotverite.co.uk – Closed 1 week summer, 1 week winter, 25-26 December, 1 January, Sunday and Monday
Carte £ 21/42 – *(booking essential)*
Simple neighbourhood bistro with panelled walls and candles; sit on the red banquette which runs down one side. Gutsy, traditional French cooking, with desserts a speciality. Friendly, efficient service.

SOUTHROP

Gloucestershire – See Regional map n°**4**-**D1**
London 87 mi – Birmingham 77 mi – Bristol 60 mi – Sheffield 146 mi
Michelin Road map 503-O28 and 504

Swan

✉ GL7 3NU – ✆ (01367) 850 205 – www.theswanatsouthrop.co.uk
Carte £ 26/45
Delightful Virginia creeper clad inn set in a quintessential Cotswold village in the Leach Valley. With its characterful low-beamed rooms and charming service, it's popular with locals and visitors alike. Dishes are mainly British-based and feature garden produce; try the delicious homemade bread.

SOUTHWOLD

Suffolk – Pop. 1 098 – See Regional map n°**15**-D2
London 108 mi – Great Yarmouth 24 mi – Ipswich 35 mi – Norwich 34 mi
Michelin Road map 504-Z27

Swan

rm,

Market Pl. ✉ IP18 6EG – ✆ (01502) 722 186 – www.adnams.co.uk
42 rm – £ 115/125 £ 185/205 – 2 suites
Rest – Menu £ 20 (weekday lunch)/35 – Carte lunch £ 25/44
Attractive 17C coaching inn set in the town centre, close to the brewery. The cosy lounge and bar display subtle modern touches. Bedrooms are a mix: some are traditional, some are boldly coloured and some are charming. The grand dining room is hung with portraits and chandeliers and has a modern European menu.

Crown with rm

90 High St ✉ IP18 6DP – ✆ (01502) 722 275 – www.adnams.co.uk/hotels
14 rm – £ 135/140 £ 145/235 Carte £ 22/35
17C Georgian-fronted former coaching inn with appealing, relaxed style, buzzing atmosphere and nautically themed locals bar. Modern, seasonal menu served in all areas. Contemporary, individually styled bedrooms; those at the rear are the quietest.

SOWERBY BRIDGE

West Yorkshire – Pop. 4 601 – ✉ Halifax – See Regional map n°**22**-A2
London 211 mi – Bradford 10 mi – Burnley 35 mi – Manchester 32 mi
Michelin Road map 502-O22

ENGLAND

Gimbals

76 Wharf St ✉ HX6 2AF – ✆ (01422) 839 329 – www.gimbals.co.uk – Closed 25-27 December, 1-2 January, Sunday and Monday
Menu £ 17/25 – Carte £ 23/38 – *(dinner only)*
Personally and passionately run restaurant on the high street of a former mill town; look out for the eye-catching illuminated window display. Modern monthly menus have subtle Mediterranean influences and the desserts are a real highlight.

SPARKWELL

Devon – See Regional map n°**2**-C2
London 210 mi – Bristol 114 mi – Cardiff 145 mi – Plymouth 10 mi

Treby Arms (Anton Piotrowski)

✉ PL7 5DD – ✆ (01752) 837 363 – www.thetrebyarms.co.uk – Closed 25-26 December, 1 January and Monday
Menu £ 20 (lunch) – Carte £ 26/49 – *(booking essential)*
A row of whitewashed cottages converted into a pub: hidden in a tiny hamlet but very busy, so book ahead. Carefully prepared, visually appealing and boldly flavoured modern dishes often feature a playful twist to surprise and delight. The 6 or 8 course 'taster' menus best demonstrate the chef's talent.
→ Ham hock and foie gras terrine, burnt leek, quail egg and pineapple chutney. Duck breast with broccoli purée, pork crackling and duck heart. 'The man from Del Monte goes to the Treby'.

SPARSHOLT → See Winchester

Hampshire – Michelin Road map 503-P30 and 504-P30

SPEEN

Buckinghamshire ✉ Princes Risborough – See Regional map n°**11**-C2
London 41 mi – Aylesbury 15 mi – Oxford 33 mi – Reading 25 mi
Michelin Road map 504-R28

Old Plow

Flowers Bottom ✉ HP27 0PZ – West : 0.5 mi by Chapel Hill and Highwood Bottom – ✆ (01494) 488 300 – www.theoldplow.co.uk – Closed August, 1 week late May, Christmas, Sunday and Monday
Carte £ 28/46
Characterful roadside inn with low beams and open fires; sit in the dining room or more casual bistro. Classically based cooking features mature local steaks and seafood which arrives daily from Brixham. They celebrated 25 years in 2013.

SPELDHURST ➜ See Royal Tunbridge Wells

Kent – Michelin Road map 504-U30

SPRIGG'S ALLEY ➜ See Chinnor

Oxfordshire

ST BRELADE'S BAY ➜ See Channel Islands (Jersey)

– Michelin Road map 503-P33

STADDLEBRIDGE

North Yorkshire – See Regional map n°**22**-**B1**

London 236 mi – Leeds 48 mi – York 34 mi

Cleveland Tontine with rm

rm,

DL6 3JB *On southbound carriageway of A 19* – *(01609) 882 671 – www.theclevelandtontine.co.uk*

7 rm – £ 115/175 £ 130/190

Menu £ 18 – Carte £ 26/56 – *(booking essential)*

This established basement bistro is something of a local institution. Start with a drink in the champagne and cocktail bar then make for the characterful bistro or airy conservatory. Quirky modern bedrooms boast bold wallpapers and free-standing baths. Yorkshire meets France on the classically based menus.

STADHAMPTON

Oxfordshire – Pop. 702 – See Regional map n°**10**-**B2**

London 53 mi – Aylesbury 18 mi – Oxford 10 mi

Michelin Road map 503-Q28 and 504

Crazy Bear

Bear Ln *OX44 7UR* – *off Wallingford rd* – *(01865) 890 714 – www.crazybeargroup.co.uk*

16 rm – £ 100/180 £ 100/410

Rest *Thai* – see restaurant listing

Rest *English* – Menu £ 20 (lunch) – Carte £ 28/46

Wacky converted pub with a red London bus reception, a characterful bar, a smart glasshouse and even a Zen garden. Sumptuous, quirky bedrooms are spread about the place; some have padded walls and infinity baths. The flamboyant English restaurant with mirrored walls serves classic British and French dishes.

Thai – Crazy Bear Hotel

Bear Ln *OX44 7UR* – *off Wallingford rd* – *(01865) 890 714 – www.crazybeargroup.co.uk*

Menu £ 30 – Carte £ 19/45 – *(booking essential)*

Cosy hotel restaurant in an intimate basement room, with ornate silk hangings and just 8 polished brass tables. Flavoursome, authentic dishes are skilfully prepared by a Thai chef; the 8, 10 and 12 course set menus are popular.

STAFFORD

Staffordshire – Pop. 68 472 – See Regional map n°**19**-**C1**

London 142 mi – Birmingham 26 mi – Stoke-on-Trent 17 mi

Michelin Road map 502-N25 and 503

Moat House

Lower Penkridge Rd, Acton Trussell *ST17 0RJ* – *South : 3.75 mi by A 449 – (01785) 712 217 – www.moathouse.co.uk – Closed 25 December*

41 rm – £ 75/145 £ 95/200 – 1 suite

Rest *Orangery* – see restaurant listing

Rest *Old Farmhouse* – Carte £ 18/34

The original 15C farmhouse is now a classically styled pub and the sympathetically added extensions house a modern orangery restaurant and attractively furnished contemporary bedrooms. As its name suggests, it's surrounded by a moat; there's also a duck pond to the front and a canal to the rear.

The Swan (N)

46 Greengate St ✉ ST16 2JA – ✆ (01785) 258 142 – www.theswanstafford.co.uk – Closed 24-25 December

31 rm – †£ 65/90 ††£ 75/135

Rest *Brasserie* – Menu £ 12 (lunch and early dinner) – Carte £ 21/33

This 17C coaching inn is found among some impressive old buildings, including a neighbouring Jacobean townhouse. Inside it's stylish and contemporary with up-to-date bedrooms. The brasserie offers a large menu of modern classics and there's also a coffee shop and two bars which share a pleasant terrace.

Pillar

The Post House, 35 Greengate St, (1st floor) ✉ ST16 2HZ – ✆ (01785) 231 450 – www.pillarrestaurant.co.uk – Closed Sunday

Carte £ 18/41 – *(dinner only)*

Red-brick former post office with a modern ground floor bistro, an intimate cocktail bar and a trendy club. Smart, formal first floor dining room features eye-catching lampshades and an open kitchen. Classic cooking has a modern touch.

Orangery (N) – Moat House Hotel

Lower Penkridge Rd, Acton Trussell ✉ ST17 0RJ – South: 3.75 mi by A 449 – ✆ (01785) 712 217 – www.moathouse.co.uk – Closed 25 December

Menu £ 21 (lunch and early dinner) – Carte £ 32/49

Head to this attractive hotel conservatory for views over the leafy garden to barges passing by on the canal. Cooking is in a modern British vein and dishes are accomplished and well-judged. On Saturdays they offer a 'Gourmet' menu.

STALISFIELD

See Regional map n°**9-C2**

London 51 mi – Bristol 169 mi – Cardiff 202 mi – Plymouth 261 mi

Plough

Stalisfield ✉ ME13 0HY – ✆ (01795) 890 256 – www.theploughinnstalisfield.co.uk – Closed Monday except bank holidays

Menu £ 14/20 – Carte £ 26/33

Rurally set, 15C pub with thick walls, exposed beams, farming implements and hop bines. The usual suspects on the bar snack menu; more ambitious dishes on the à la carte. Nursery puddings and an impressive range of Kentish real ales.

STAMFORD

Lincolnshire – Pop. 22 574 – See Regional map n°**17-C2**

London 92 mi – Leicester 31 mi – Lincoln 50 mi – Nottingham 45 mi

Michelin Road map 502-S26 and 504 – Michelin Green Guide GREAT BRITAIN

George of Stamford

71 St Martins ✉ PE9 2LB – ✆ (01780) 750 750 – www.georgehotelofstamford.com

47 rm – †£ 95/115 ††£ 165/290 – 1 suite

Rest *The Oak Panelled Restaurant* – see restaurant listing

Rest *Garden Room* – Carte £ 26/43 – *(bookings not accepted)*

This characterful coaching inn dates back over 500 years and, despite its bedrooms having a surprisingly contemporary feel, still offers good old-fashioned hospitality. There are plenty of places to relax, with various bars, lounges and a walled garden. Dine in the laid-back Garden Room or more formal restaurant – both spill out into the lovely courtyard in summer.

William Cecil

High St, St Martins ✉ PE9 2LJ – ✆ (01780) 750 070 – www.thewilliamcecil.co.uk

28 rm – †£ 95/325 ††£ 110/375 – 1 suite

Rest – Carte £ 28/54 – *(bar lunch Monday-Saturday)*

Extended 17C cream-stone rectory, named after the 1st Baron Burghley, with access through the garden to the estate. Contemporary, shabby-chic, panelled interior. Colonial-style bedrooms feature wood carvings and pastoral scene wallpaper. Restaurant has intimate, Regency-style booths and a classical menu.

Crown

All Saints Pl. ✉ PE9 2AG – ✆ (01780) 763 136 – www.thecrownhotelstamford.co.uk
28 rm – £ 85/155 £ 95/165 **Rest** – Carte £ 23/37
Former coaching inn set in historic market town. Main house bedrooms have a funky, boutique style; those in the Town House are larger with a more classical feel. Dine in the modern cocktail bar, in one of the cosy lounges or in the quieter rear dining room.

The Oak Panelled Restaurant – George of Stamford Hotel

71 St Martins ✉ PE9 2LB – ✆ (01780) 750 750 – www.georgehotelofstamford.com
Menu £ 26 (weekday lunch) – Carte £ 34/52
Smart dress is required in this lovely oak-panelled dining room, which is found at the heart of an equally charming 16C coaching inn. Classical menus are largely British based with a few international influences. 'Carving', 'cheese' and 'sweet' trollies all feature and the wine list is top notch.

Jim's Yard

3 Ironmonger St ✉ PE9 1PL – off Broad St – ✆ (01780) 756 080 – www.jimsyard.biz – Closed last week July, first week August, 26 December-10 January, Sunday and Monday
Menu £ 15/20 – Carte £ 24/36
Two 18C houses with a covered courtyard, tucked away in the town centre. Choose between the small ground floor conservatory which opens onto the terrace or the more intimate beamed dining room up in the eaves. Daily menus of appealing classical dishes and great value lunches. Friendly team.

Bull & Swan with rm

St Martins ✉ PE9 2LJ – ✆ (01780) 766 412 – www.thebullandswan.co.uk
7 rm – £ 75/110 £ 95/140 Carte £ 22/44
Stone-built former hall house converted to an inn during the 1600s and still the only pub south of the river. Characterful beamed bar and smarter dining room. Menu ranges from sharing slates to regional classics and locally sourced steaks. Stylish bedrooms are named after members of a historic drinking club.

STANFORD DINGLEY

West Berkshire – Pop. 179 – See Regional map n°**10**-B3
London 52 mi – Sheffield 168 mi – Nottingham 130 mi – Bristol 69 mi

Bull Inn with rm

Cock Ln ✉ RG7 6LS – ✆ (01189) 744 582 – www.thebullinnstanforddingley.co.uk
5 rm – £ 60/69 £ 60/69, £ 12 Carte £ 17/43
Locals and their dogs gather in the rustic bar of this beamed 15C inn, while the garden plays host to alfresco diners, chickens and the annual village dog show. The experienced chef-owner offers a wide range of tasty dishes; 'beer tapas' allows you to sample local ales and bedrooms are cosy and great value.

STANHOE

Norfolk – Pop. 289 – See Regional map n°**15**-C1
London 124 mi – Norwich 36 mi – Kings Lynn 18 mi
Michelin Road map 504-W25

Duck Inn with rm

Burnham Rd ✉ PE31 8QD – ✆ (01485) 518 330 – www.duckinn.co.uk
2 rm – £ 75/85 £ 95/125 Carte £ 16/37
Local ales and bar bites like scotch quail's egg in the buzzy, slate-floored bar. Three dining rooms with a rustic, relaxed feel for open sandwiches, fresh fish dishes and thick, juicy local steaks. Fairy lights and ducks in the picket fence fringed garden. Bedrooms are cosy and well-kept.

ENGLAND

STANSTED MOUNTFITCHET

Essex – Pop. 6 669 – See Regional map n°**12-B2**
London 38 mi – Birmingham 125 mi – Croydon 59 mi – Barnet 37 mi
Michelin Road map 504-U28

Chimneys without rest

44 Lower St ✉ CM24 8LR – on B 1351 – ✆ (01279) 813 388 – www.chimneysguesthouse.co.uk
4 rm – †£ 58/67 ††£ 82
Charming 17C house with low-beamed ceilings, a cosy lounge and snug breakfast room. Bedrooms have a modern, cottagey style, displaying pine furnishings and homely touches. Tasty breakfast offerings might include Manx kippers or smoked haddock with poached eggs.

STANTON

Suffolk – Pop. 2 073 – See Regional map n°**15-C2**
London 88 mi – Cambridge 38 mi – Ipswich 40 mi – King's Lynn 38 mi
Michelin Road map 504-W27

Leaping Hare

Wyken Vineyards ✉ IP31 2DW – South : 1.25 mi by Wyken Rd – ✆ (01359) 250 287 – www.wykenvineyards.co.uk – Closed 25 December-5 January
Menu £ 19/26 – Carte £ 26/37 – *(lunch only and dinner Friday-Saturday) (booking essential)*
This beautiful 17C timber-framed barn sits at the centre of a 7 acre vineyard. Carefully judged cooking relies on well-sourced, seasonal ingredients; many from their own farm. Sit on the lovely terrace and try the interesting all-day light bites, or something from the accomplished, daily changing menu.

STAPLEFORD → See Nottingham

Nottinghamshire – Michelin Road map 504-Q25

STATHERN

Leicestershire ✉ Melton Mowbray – See Regional map n°**16-B2**
London 119 mi – Birmingham 69 mi – Sheffield 62 mi – Leicester 24 mi
Michelin Road map 502-R25

Red Lion Inn

2 Red Lion St ✉ LE14 4HS – ✆ (01949) 860 868 – www.theredlioninn.co.uk – Closed Sunday dinner and Monday
Menu £ 18 (weekdays) – Carte £ 22/41 – *(booking essential)*
Large, creamwashed village pub. Good value menus offer straightforward pub classics, alongside well-presented, refined restaurant-style dishes. Produce is sourced from their kitchen garden and local suppliers; the map on the back of the menu emphasis their proximity. Service is friendly and attentive.

STAVERTON → See Daventry

– Michelin Road map 504-Q27

STILTON

Cambridgeshire – Pop. 2 455 – ✉ Peterborough – See Regional map n°**14-A2**
London 76 mi – Cambridge 30 mi – Northampton 43 mi – Peterborough 6 mi
Michelin Road map 504-T26

Bell Inn

rm,

Great North Rd ✉ PE7 3RA – ✆ (01733) 241 066 – www.thebellstilton.co.uk – Closed 25 December
22 rm – †£ 80/88 ††£ 108/140
Rest *Galleried Restaurant* – Menu £ 25/30 – Carte £ 21/33 – *(closed Sunday dinner and bank holidays except 26 December and 1 January) (dinner only and Sunday lunch)*
Historic coaching inn with a characterful beamed lounge and bar; run by a hospitable, hands-on owner. Comfy bedrooms have a traditional feel: some feature four-posters; the newest are in the old smithy overlooking the garden. The first floor restaurant offers a seasonal menu with a strong classical base.

STOCKBRIDGE

Hampshire – Pop. 570 – See Regional map n°**6**-B2
London 75 mi – Salisbury 14 mi – Southampton 19 mi – Winchester 9 mi
Michelin Road map 503-P30 and 504

Greyhound on the Test with rm

31 High St ✉ SO20 6EY – ✆ (01264) 810 833 – www.thegreyhoundonthetest.co.uk – Closed 25 December
10 rm – £ 70/80 £ 110/180
Menu £ 19 (weekday lunch) – Carte £ 23/40 – *(booking advisable)*
Eye-catching pub with mustard-coloured walls, a red tiled roof and over a mile of River Test fishing rights to the rear. Low beams and wood burning stoves abound, and elegant décor gives it a French bistro feel. Menus offer an appealing range of well-presented, classically based, refined brasserie-style dishes. Homely bedrooms have large showers and quality bedding.

STOCKPORT

Greater Manchester – Pop. 105 878 – See Regional map n°**20**-B3
London 201 mi – Liverpool 42 mi – Leeds 50 mi – Sheffield 52 mi
Michelin Road map 502-N23

XX Damson

113 Heaton Moor Rd ✉ SK4 4HY – Northwest : 2.25 mi by A 6, Heaton Rd, A 5145 and Bank Hall Rd – ✆ (0161) 432 46 66 – www.damsonrestaurant.co.uk – Closed 26 December and 1 January
Menu £ 20 – Carte £ 28/54 – *(dinner only and lunch Friday and Sunday)*
Smart, modern, glass-fronted restaurant on a corner site, with a pavement terrace, damson walls, velvet chairs and rustic tables. Appealing menu of traditional dishes with modern touches. Attentive, formal service.

ENGLAND

STOCKSFIELD

London 279 mi – Liverpool 156 mi – Glasgow 140 mi – Manchester 146 mi

Locksley without rest

45 Meadowfield Rd ✉ NE43 7PY – Southeast : 2 mi by A 695 and New Ridley Road – ✆ (01661) 844 778 – www.locksleybedandbreakfast.co.uk – Closed 31 December
3 rm – £ 40 £ 65/70
Welcoming, immaculately kept house in a peaceful location: a good base for discovering the Tyne Valley. Homely lounge with a piano and a gas-fired stove. Spacious bedrooms have superb bathrooms; family and ground floor rooms are available.

STOKE BY NAYLAND

Suffolk – See Regional map n°**15**-C3
London 70 mi – Bury St Edmunds 24 mi – Cambridge 54 mi – Colchester 11 mi
Michelin Road map 504-W28

Crown with rm

✉ CO6 4SE – ✆ (01206) 262 001 – www.crowninn.net – Closed 25-26 December
11 rm – £ 95/150 £ 130/245 Carte £ 19/36
Smart, relaxed pub in a great spot overlooking the Box and Stour river valleys. Globally influenced menus feature produce from local farms and estates, with seafood from the east coast. Well-priced wine list with over 25 wines by the glass. Large, luxurious, superbly equipped bedrooms with king or super king sized beds; some have French windows and terraces.

STOKE D'ABERNON

Surrey – See Regional map n°**7**-D1
London 21 mi – Brighton 49 mi – Guildford 13 mi
Michelin Road map 504-S30

Old Plough
2 Station Rd ✉ KT11 3BN – ✆ (01932) 862 244 – www.oldploughcobham.co.uk – Closed 26th December
Carte £ 22/42
The fourth venture for this small pub group has a smart yet satisfyingly pubby feel. Sit in a comfy chair in the open-fired bar or at a chunky wood table in the restaurant, and choose from sharing plates or more sophisticated dishes.

STOKE HOLY CROSS → See Norwich
Norfolk – Michelin Road map 504-X26

STOKE POGES
Buckinghamshire – Pop. 3 962 – See Regional map n°**11**-D3
▶London 23 mi – Bristol 99 mi – Croydon 44 mi
Michelin Road map 504-S29

Stoke Park
Park Rd ✉ SL2 4PG – Southwest : 0.75 mi on B 416 – ✆ (01753) 717 171 – www.stokepark.com – Closed 24-26 December
49 rm – †£ 290/960 ††£ 290/960, ☕ £ 22 – 1 suite
Rest *Humphry's* – see restaurant listing
Grade I listed Palladian property – once home to the Penn family, who created England's first country club. Extensive sporting activities, impressive spa and characterful guest areas. Mix of chic and luxurious 'Feature' bedrooms.

ENGLAND

Stoke Place
rm,
Stoke Green ✉ SL2 4HT – South : 0.5 mi by B 416 – ✆ (01753) 534 790 – www.stokeplace.co.uk
39 rm ☕ – †£ 105/250 ††£ 195/390
Rest *Garden Room* – Menu £ 20/45
17C Queen Anne mansion, set by a large lake and surrounded by 22 acres of delightful gardens and parkland. Quirky guest areas display bold wallpapers and original furnishings. Bedrooms are uniquely styled; those in the garden are simpler.

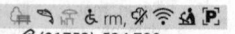

XXXX **Humphry's** – Stoke Park Hotel
Park Rd ✉ SL2 4PG – ✆ (01753) 717 171 – www.humphrysrestaurant.co.uk – Closed 24-26 December
Menu £ 29/65 – *(booking essential)*
Impressive hotel dining room named after 18C landscape gardener Humphry Repton, who designed the surrounding gardens; the lake and parkland views are superb. Classically based dishes are presented in a modern style. Service is professional.

STOKE ROW
Oxfordshire – Pop. 651 – See Regional map n°**11**-C3
▶London 45 mi – Henley-on-Thames 6 mi – Reading 10 mi

Cherry Tree Inn with rm
rest,
✉ RG9 5QA – ✆ (01491) 680 430 – www.thecherrytreeinn.co.uk – Closed 2 January
4 rm ☕ – †£ 65/95 ††£ 85/110 Carte £ 19/34
Cosy and relaxing 400 year old inn with four intimate dining areas. Classic pub dishes sit alongside more modern creations on the monthly changing à la carte and the seasonal, fish-based blackboard menu. Food is full of flavour and served by attentive staff. Stylish bedrooms are named after fruit trees.

STOKE-ON-TRENT
Stoke-on-Trent – Pop. 270 726 – See Regional map n°**19**-C1
▶London 162 – Birmingham 46 – Leicester 59 – Liverpool 58
Michelin Road map 502-N24 – Michelin Green Guide GREAT BRITAIN G.

STOKE-ON-TRENT NEWCASTLE-UNDER-LYME

Alexandra Rd . . . . U 3
Bedford Rd . . . . U 4
Brownhills Rd . . . . U 12
Church Lane . . . . U 19
Cobridge Rd . . . . U 21
Davenport St. . . . . U 23
Elder Rd . . . . U 24
Etruria Vale Rd . . . . U 27
Grove Rd. . . . . V 30
Hanley Rd . . . . U 31
Heron St . . . . V 34
Higherland. . . . . V 37
High St . . . . U 35
Manor St. . . . . V 44
Mayne St . . . . V 45
Moorland Rd. . . . . U 48
Porthill Rd . . . . U 59
Snow Hill . . . . U 63
Stoke Rd. . . . . U 68
Strand (The) . . . . V 69
Victoria Park Rd . . . . U 75
Victoria Pl. Link . . . . V 76
Watlands View . . . . U 77
Williamson St . . . . U 78
Wolstanton Link Rd . . . . U 80

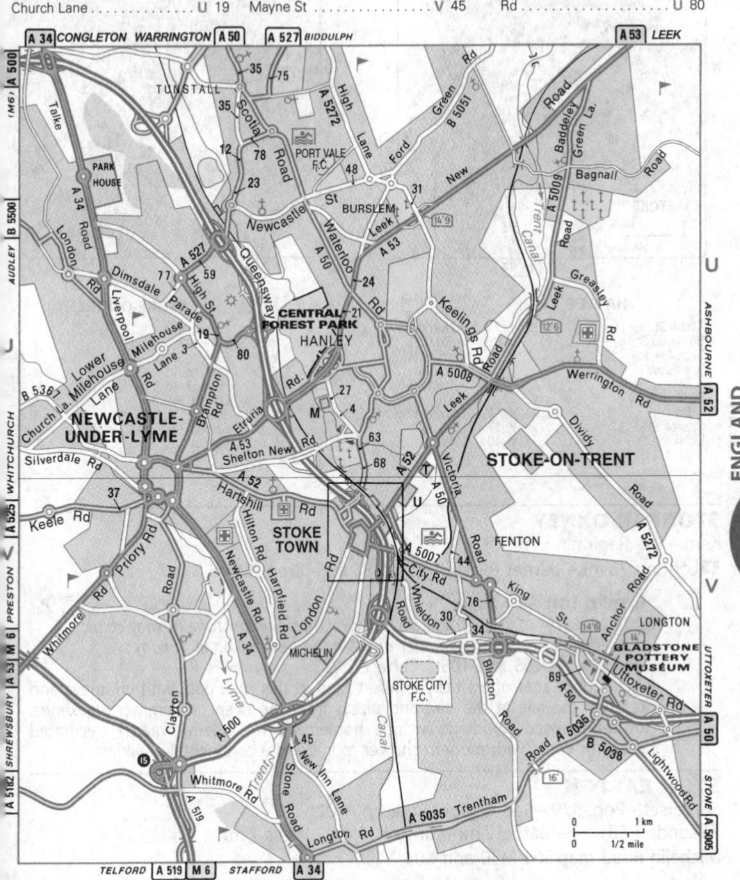

STONE

Staffordshire – Pop. 16 385 – See Regional map n°**19**-C1
London 151 mi – Birmingham 37 mi – Stoke-on-Trent 10 mi
Michelin Road map 502-N25

XX Cullens (N)

16-18 Radford St ✉ ST15 8DA – ☎ (01785) 818 925
– www.cullensrestaurant.co.uk – Closed 1-7 January
Menu £ 19/35
Cullens is run by an experienced young couple and is simply but comfortably furnished in a classic style. Fresh ingredients are carefully cooked in a subtle modern manner. Dishes are attractively presented and lunch is a steal.

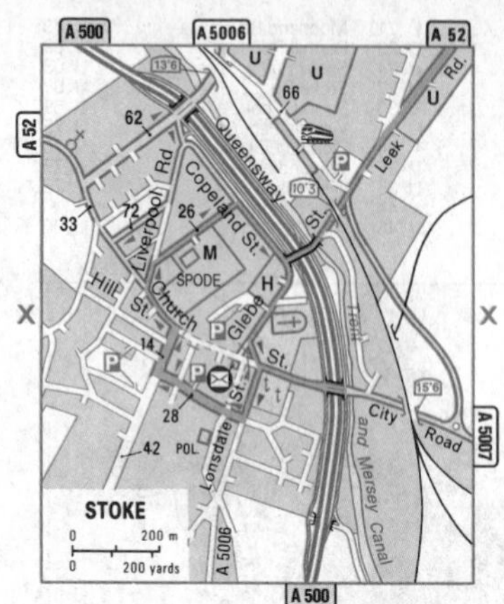

HANLEY

- Albion St . . . . . . Y 2
- Bethesda St . . . . . . Y 6
- Birch Terrace . . . . . . Y 7
- Botteslow St . . . . . . Y 10
- Bucknall New Rd . . . . . . Y 13
- Charles St . . . . . . Y 17
- Lichfield St . . . . . . Y 40
- New Hall St . . . . . . Y 49
- Old Hall St . . . . . . Y 52
- Parliament Row . . . . . . Y 55
- Percy St . . . . . . Y 56
- Piccadilly . . . . . . Y 58
- Potteries Shopping Centre . . . . . . Y
- Quadrant Rd . . . . . . Y 60
- Stafford St . . . . . . Y 65
- Vale Pl . . . . . . Y 70

STOKE-ON-TRENT

- Campbell Pl. . . . . . . X 14
- Church St X
- Elenora St . . . . . . X 26
- Fleming Rd . . . . . . X 28
- Hartshill Rd . . . . . . X 33
- London Rd . . . . . . X 42
- Shelton Old Rd . . . . . . X 62
- Station Rd . . . . . . X 66
- Vale St . . . . . . X 72

ENGLAND

STONE IN OXNEY

Kent – See Regional map n°**9-C2**

London 73 mi – Barnet 89 mi – Ealing 85 mi – Brent 86 mi

Crown Inn with rm

rest,

TN30 7JN – (01233) 758 302 – www.thecrowninnstoneinoxney.co.uk – Closed January, Sunday dinner and Monday except bank holidays

2 rm – £ 105 £ 105 Carte £ 20/33

A self-taught chef offers tasty comfort food in this rural pub, with chutneys and preserves for sale at the bar, and pizzas from the oven on summer weekends. Not-to-be-missed puddings include homemade ice cream. Smartly decorated bedrooms come with modern shower rooms and a continental breakfast.

STON EASTON

Somerset – Pop. 579 – See Regional map n°**4-C2**

London 131 mi – Bath 12 mi – Bristol 11 mi – Wells 7 mi

Michelin Road map 503-M30 and 504

Ston Easton Park

BA3 4DF – (01761) 241 631 – www.stoneaston.co.uk

22 rm – £ 130/166 £ 166/346 – 2 suites

Rest *Sorrel* – see restaurant listing

Striking aristocratic Palladian mansion in 36 acres of delightful grounds designed by Humphry Repton. Fine rooms of epic proportions are filled with antiques, curios and impressive floral arrangements. Many of the stylish, uniquely designed bedrooms have coronet or four-poster beds; one is set in a cottage.

Sorrel – Ston Easton Park Hotel

BA3 4DF – (01761) 241 631 – www.stoneaston.co.uk

Menu £ 23/50 – *(bookings essential for non-residents)*

Set in a striking Palladian mansion and surrounded by extensive formal gardens, this elegant, formal restaurant has high ceilings, panelled walls and crisp white linen on the tables. Classical menus showcase luxurious ingredients and produce from the Victorian kitchen garden. Service is professional.

STONOR → See Henley-on-Thames
Oxfordshire

STOWMARKET
Suffolk – Pop. 19 280 – See Regional map n°**15-C3**
London 95 mi – Ipswich 14 mi – Colchester 35 mi – Clacton-on-Sea 40 mi
Michelin Road map 504-W27

Buxhall Coach House
Buxhall Vale, Buxhall ✉ IP14 3DH – West : 3 mi by B 1115 and Rattlesden rd – ✆ (01449) 736 032 – www.buxhallcoachhouse.com – Closed February, Sunday dinner, Monday and Tuesday
Carte £ 25/50 – *(booking advisable)*
A realisation of a family dream: a homely, farmhouse-style restaurant run by a welcoming mother-daughter team. Pass the large, open-plan kitchen with its Aga, to the cosy dining room. Daily menus offer flavoursome Northern Italian dishes; good quality ingredients are cooked simply and with plenty of care.

STOW-ON-THE-WOLD
Gloucestershire – Pop. 2 042 – See Regional map n°**4-D1**
London 86 mi – Birmingham 44 mi – Gloucester 27 mi – Oxford 30 mi
Michelin Road map 503-O28 – Michelin Green Guide GREAT BRITAIN

Number Four at Stow

Fosseway ✉ GL54 1JX – South : 1.25 mi by A 429 on A 424 – ✆ (01451) 830 297 – www.hotelnumberfour.co.uk – Closed 23-30 December
18 rm – †£ 110/150 ††£ 120/180 – 3 suites
Rest *Cutlers* – Menu £ 15 (weekday lunch) – Carte £ 26/43 – *(closed Sunday dinner except bank holiday weekends)*
Contemporary, open-plan hotel; so named as it's the fourth this experienced family own. The comfy lounge boasts bold brushed velvet seating, while the bright, compact bedrooms feature smart leather headboards, cream furniture and modern facilities. The comfortable brasserie offers a classical menu.

Number Nine without rest

9 Park St ✉ GL54 1AQ – ✆ (01451) 870 333 – www.number-nine.info
3 rm – †£ 45/65 ††£ 75/85
Expect a warm welcome at this ivy-clad, 18C stone house, close to the historic town square. The cosy lounge and breakfast room boast exposed stone walls, open fireplaces and dark wood beams. A winding staircase leads up to the pleasant wood-furnished bedrooms, which come with plenty of extras.

Bell with rm

Park St ✉ GL54 1AJ – ✆ (01451) 870 916 – www.thebellatstow.com – Closed 5-8 May
5 rm – †£ 70/120 ††£ 70/120 Carte £ 22/33
Cotswold stone inn with welcoming open fires, at the centre of a delightful market town. Menus offer plenty of choice and portions are hearty; meat comes from the local butcher, the fish board changes daily and puddings are heartwarming. Comfortable bedrooms, some with country views, complete the picture.

at Lower Oddington East: 3 mi by A436 ✉ Stow-On-The-Wold

Fox Inn with rm

✉ GL56 0UR – ✆ (01451) 870 555 – www.foxinn.net
3 rm – †£ 75/100 ††£ 85/110 Carte £ 25/38 – *(booking essential)*
Creeper-clad, quintessentially English pub at the heart of a peaceful Cotswold village, with beamed ceilings, solid stone walls, flagged floors and plenty of cosy nooks and crannies. The menu focuses on carefully prepared, tasty British classics and the comfortable bedrooms are individually furnished.

at Daylesford East: 3.5 mi by A436 ✉ Stow-On-The-Wold

Café at Daylesford Organic with rm

✉ *GL56 0YG – ☎ (01608) 731 700 – www.daylesfordorganic.com – Closed 25-26 December and 1 January*
4 rm – †£ 330 ††£ 330/990, ☕ £ 20
Carte £ 18/31 – *(lunch only and dinner Friday-Saturday) (bookings not accepted)*
Stylish café attached to a farm shop; its rustic interior boasting an open charcoal grill and a wood-fired oven. Throughout the day, tuck into light dishes and small plates; at night, candle-lit suppers step things up a gear. Everything is organic, with much of the produce coming from the farm. Stay overnight in one of their rustic cottages and unwind in the lovely spa.

at Bledington Southeast: 4 mi by A436 on B4450

Kings Head Inn with rm

The Green ✉ OX7 6XQ – ☎ (01608) 658 365 – www.kingsheadinn.net – Closed 25 December
12 rm ☕ – †£ 75/100 ††£ 95/125 Carte £ 27/40
Charming 16C former cider house on a picturesque village green, bisected by a stream filled with bobbing ducks. Appealing bar snacks include pheasant in a basket; pub classics and some interesting modern dishes on the à la carte. Large bar with a vast inglenook fireplace. Cosy bedrooms.

ENGLAND

at Nether Westcote Southeast: 4.75 mi by A429 and A424

Feathered Nest with rm

✉ *OX7 6SD – ☎ (01993) 833 030 – www.thefeatherednestinn.co.uk – Closed 25 December, Sunday dinner and Monday except bank holidays*
4 rm ☕ – †£ 150/200 ††£ 190/250 Carte £ 38/52
This pub offers something for everyone with its laid-back bar, rustic snug, casual conservatory and formal dining room. Sit on quirky horse saddle stools and choose from the bar menu or sample more complex dishes at elegant antique tables; the wine list features over 200 bins. Comfy bedrooms boast antiques, quality linens and roll-top baths. The views are superb.

at Lower Swell West: 1.25 mi on B4068 ✉ Stow-On-The-Wold

Rectory Farmhouse without rest

✉ *GL54 1LH by Rectory Barns Rd – ☎ (01451) 832 351 – www.rectoryfarmhouse.yolasite.com – Closed Christmas-New Year*
3 rm ☕ – †£ 85/95 ††£ 104/110
Charming 17C stone-built farmhouse; to the rear, a terrace overlooks the lovely enclosed garden with its pond and water feature. Relax in the characterful beamed lounge; the cottagey bedrooms have good facilities and extras. Aga-cooked breakfasts are taken in the country kitchen, conservatory or garden.

STRATFORD-UPON-AVON

Warwickshire – Pop. 27 830 – See Regional map n°**19-C3**
▶ London 96 mi – Birmingham 23 mi – Coventry 18 mi – Leicester 44 mi
Michelin Road map 503-P27 and 504 – Michelin Green Guide GREAT BRITAIN

Welcombe H. Spa and Golf Club

Warwick Rd ✉ CV37 0NR – Northeast : 1.5 mi on A 439 – ☎ (01789) 295 252 – www.menzieshotels.co.uk
rest,
78 rm ☕ – †£ 110/150 ††£ 150/170 – 5 suites
Rest *Trevelyan* – Menu £ 30 – Carte £ 32/52
Imposing Jacobean-style house built in 1866, featuring a golf course and a superb spa and leisure club. Well-proportioned, wood panelled guest areas with marble fireplaces. Grand, well-equipped bedrooms; the best are in the main house. The bar and restaurant overlook an impressive parterre and water feature.

STRATFORD-UPON-AVON

Banbury Rd . . . . B 2
Bell Court Shopping Centre . . . . A 39
Benson Rd. . . . . B 3
Bridge Foot . . . . B 6
Bridge St . . . . B 8
Chapel Lane . . . . A 13
Chapel St. . . . . A 14
Church St . . . . A 16
Clopton Bridge . . . . B 18
College Lane . . . . A 19
Ely St . . . . A 22
Evesham Pl. . . . . A 24
Great William St . . . . A 25
Greenhill St . . . . A 27
Guild St . . . . A 28
Henley St. . . . . A 29
High St. . . . . A 31
Rother St. . . . . A 32
Scholars Lane . . . . A 33
Sheep St . . . . AB 35
Tiddington Rd . . . . B 38
Trinity St. . . . . A 40
Warwick Rd. . . . . B 42
Waterside . . . . B 43
Windsor St . . . . A 45
Wood St . . . . A 47

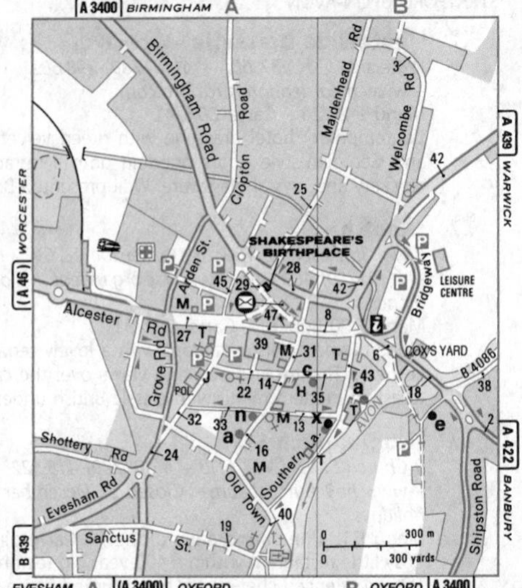

Ettington Park

Alderminster ✉ *CV37 8BU – Southeast : 6.5 mi on A 3400 –* ☎ *(01789) 450 123 – www.handpickedhotels.co.uk/ettingtonpark*

48 rm – †£ 134/232 ††£ 144/357

Rest *Oak Room* – Menu £ 40 **s** – Carte £ 51/58 **s** – *(bar lunch Monday-Saturday)*

Impressive neo-Gothic mansion surrounded by lovely gardens. Characterful guest areas have vaulted ceilings and ornate rococo plasterwork. 'Feature' bedrooms boast original fireplaces and four-posters; other rooms are more contemporary. The Oak Room – named after its smart panelling – offers a modern menu.

Arden

Waterside ✉ *CV37 6BA –* ☎ *(01789) 298 682* Town plan: B**x**
– www.theardenhotelstratford.com

45 rm – †£ 123/148 ††£ 145/405

Rest *Waterside Brasserie* – see restaurant listing

Set in a great location opposite the RSC theatre, with pretty gardens and a split-level terrace overlooking the river. Smart bar-lounge and a second plush lounge for afternoon tea. Twisty corridors lead to stylish modern bedrooms in green, cream and gold colour schemes; one has a roll-top bath in the room.

White Sails without rest

85 Evesham Rd ✉ *CV37 9BE – Southwest : 1 mi on B 439 –* ☎ *(01789) 550 469 – www.white-sails.co.uk – Closed Christmas-New Year*

4 rm – †£ 90/115 ††£ 105/130

Detached Edwardian house; look out for the 'Sail' signs. Leather-furnished lounge with local info, a Nespresso machine and a decanter of sherry. Smart bedrooms with superb bathrooms and good extras. Comprehensive buffet breakfasts.

Cherry Trees without rest

Swan's Nest Ln ✉ *CV37 7LS –* ☎ *(01789) 292 989* Town plan: B**e**
– www.cherrytrees-stratford.co.uk – Closed December and January

3 rm – †£ 95/110 ††£ 110/135

Unassuming guesthouse with a Japanese-style garden, located just over the River Avon. First floor breakfast room, where homemade bread and granola are served. Comfortable bedrooms come with plenty of extras; two have small conservatories.

XX **Waterside Brasserie** – Arden Hotel
Waterside ✉ CV37 6BA – ✆ (01789) 298 682 Town plan: B**x**
– www.theardenhotelstratford.com
Menu £ 19/24 – Carte £ 26/41
Contemporary hotel brasserie with green velvet chairs, deep purple banquettes and Georgian-style doors opening onto a terrace overlooking the river. Quality crockery and crystal glassware. Well-presented British brasserie classics.

XX **Rooftop**
Royal Shakespeare Theatre, Waterside ✉ CV37 6BB Town plan: B**a**
– ✆ (01789) 403 449 – www.rsc.org.uk/eat – Closed 25 December and Sunday dinner
Menu £ 20 (lunch) – Carte £ 21/31
Modern, open-plan restaurant with a lovely terrace, set on top of the Royal Shakespeare Theatre and boasting views over the canal basin, river and gardens. Interesting modern menu with classic British undertones; attractive presentation.

XX **No 9 Church St.**
9 Church St ✉ CV37 6HB – ✆ (01789) 415 522 Town plan: A**a**
– www.no9churchst.com – Closed 25 December-3 January, Sunday and bank holidays
Menu £ 18 (lunch and early dinner) – Carte dinner £ 23/49 **s**
Cosy little restaurant within a 400 year old townhouse, a little off the main streets. The experienced chef-owner has returned home to offer honest, flavoursome British cooking with a modern twist. Classical puddings and friendly service.

XX **Church Street Town House** with rm
16 Church St ✉ CV37 6HB – ✆ (01789) 262 222 Town plan: A**n**
– www.churchstreettownhouse.com
12 rm – †£ 110/200 ††£ 110/200
Menu £ 15 (lunch and early dinner) – Carte £ 22/37
Handsome, part-17C property opposite Shakespeare's old school. The bright, bold restaurant has an open kitchen and a zinc-topped bar. Appealing, wide-ranging menus have Mediterranean-influences and offer good value lunch and pre-theatre choices. Funky bedrooms display rich colours and silver furnishings.

X **Lambs**
12 Sheep St ✉ CV37 6EF – ✆ (01789) 292 554 Town plan: B**c**
– www.lambsrestaurant.co.uk – Closed 25-26 December and lunch Monday except bank holidays
Menu £ 14 – Carte £ 21/42
Attractive 16C house with an interesting history; dine on one of several intimate levels, surrounded by characterful beams and original features. The classic bistro menu lists simply, carefully prepared favourites and daily fish specials.

at Alveston East: 2 mi by B4086 -(B) ✉ Stratford-Upon-Avon

X **Baraset Barn**
1 Pimlico Ln ✉ CV37 7RJ – off B 4086 – ✆ (01789) 295 510
– www.barasetbarn.co.uk – Closed 1 January and Sunday dinner
Menu £ 14 (weekdays) – Carte £ 25/43
Modernised barn offering something for everyone, with its original features, contemporary furnishings and large terraces. The good-sized menu also caters for one and all, and includes a tasty rotisserie selection and daily fish specials.

STRETE → See Dartmouth
Devon

STRETTON
Staffordshire – See Regional map n°**19**-C1
London 134 mi – Bristol 126 mi – Cardiff 147 mi – Plymouth 240 mi
Michelin Road map 502-P25

ENGLAND

Dovecliff Hall

Dovecliff Rd ✉ *DE13 0DJ – ✆ (01283) 531 818 – www.dovecliffhallhotel.co.uk*
15 rm – †£ 55/85 ††£ 80/190
Rest – Menu £ 18 (weekday lunch) – Carte £ 28/41 – *(closed Sunday dinner)*
Imposing red-brick Georgian manor house in 7 acres of gardens, overlooking the River Dove. Characterful guest areas with antiques and drapes. Bedrooms combine traditional styling with modern facilities and all have pleasant country views. Menu of classics in the orangery restaurant.

STRETTON

Rutland – See Regional map n°**17-C2**
London 100 mi – Bristol 150 mi – Cardiff 177 mi – Plymouth 264 mi

Jackson Stops Inn

Rookery La ✉ *LE15 7RA – ✆ (01780) 410 237 – www.thejacksonstops.com – Closed Monday except bank holidays and Sunday dinner*
Menu £ 15 (lunch) – Carte £ 24/41
Lovely stone and thatch pub with several different areas – a small open-fired bar, a cosy barn and a restaurant. Dishes are rooted in tradition but display some interesting touches. Locally reared and smoked meats are a feature.

STROUD

Gloucestershire – Pop. 32 670 – See Regional map n°**4-C1**
London 113 mi – Bristol 30 mi – Gloucester 9 mi
Michelin Road map 503-N28 and 504

The Bear of Rodborough (N)

Rodborough Common ✉ *GL5 5DE – Southeast : 2 mi by A 419 on Butterow Hill rd – ✆ (01453) 878 522 – www.cotswold-inns-hotels.co.uk*
45 rm – †£ 80/95 ††£ 85/150
Rest *The Library* – Menu £ 32 – *(bar lunch Monday-Saturday)*
There's plenty of character to this 17C coaching inn, which stands on Rodborough Common and affords pleasant country views. The cosy beamed lounge and bar provide an atmospheric setting for a casual meal, while the library offers more formal modern cooking. Bedrooms are stylish and contemporary.

Bisley House (N)

Middle St ✉ *GL5 1DZ – ✆ (01453) 751 328 – www.bisleyhousecafe.co.uk – Closed Monday*
Carte £ 21/30
Stroud's oldest pub has been given a new lease of life and now sports a bright, modern look, with tiled floors, white walls – and not a beam or a horse brass in sight! The menu changes almost daily and cooking is simple, fresh and tasty.

STUDLAND

Dorset – Pop. 299 – See Regional map n°**4-C3**
London 135 mi – Bournemouth 25 mi – Southampton 53 mi – Weymouth 29 mi
Michelin Road map 503-O32 and 504

Pig on the Beach (N)

Manor Rd ✉ *BH19 3AU – ✆ (01929) 450 288 – www.thepighotel.com*
23 rm – †£ 155/175 ††£ 155/295, £ 15 **Rest** – Carte £ 27/44
The latest member of the 'Pig' collection is this mellow country house hotel, which has the same shabby-chic style as its sisters, along with far-reaching coastal views. Have a beauty treatment in the old sheep huts, then head to the Victorian greenhouse for tasty, unfussy dishes of local and garden produce.

Shell Bay

Ferry Rd ✉ *BH19 3BA – North : 3 mi or via car ferry from Sandbanks – ✆ (01929) 450 363 – www.shellbay.net – Closed October-February*
Carte £ 22/62 – *(booking essential)*
Simply furnished seafood restaurant with a decked terrace; superbly set on the waterfront and boasting views over the water to Brownsea Island – all tables have a view. The daily menu mixes the classical with the more adventurous.

SUMMERHOUSE → See Darlington
Darlington

SUNBURY ON THAMES
Surrey – Pop. 27 415 – See Regional map n°**7**-C1
London 16 mi – Croydon 38 mi – Barnet 44 mi – Ealing 10 mi
Michelin Road map 504-S29

Plan: see Greater London (South-West) 5

Indian Zest
21 Thames St ✉ TW16 5QF – ✆ (01932) 765 000 Town plan: BY**z**
– www.indianzest.co.uk – Closed dinner 25 December and lunch 26 December
Menu £ 11/32 – Carte £ 19/31
Pleasant restaurant with two small terraces, in a building dating back over 450 years. Pretty interior with black and white photos of Colonial India and a fine array of polo mallets. Large, interesting dishes originate from all over India.

SUNNINGDALE
Windsor and Maidenhead – See Regional map n°**11**-D3
London 33 mi – Croydon 39 mi – Barnet 46 mi – Ealing 22 mi
Michelin Road map 504-S29

Bluebells
Shrubbs Hill, London Rd ✉ SL5 0LE – Northeast : 0.75 mi on A 30 – ✆ (01344) 622 722 – www.bluebells-restaurant.com – Closed 1-12 January, 25-26 December, Sunday dinner and Monday
Menu £ 22/29 (lunch) – Carte dinner £ 35/61
The smart façade of this professionally run restaurant is matched by a sophisticated interior, where white leather furnishings stand out against dark green walls. Beautifully presented dishes are crafted using modern techniques.

ENGLAND

SUNNISIDE
Tyne and Wear – See Regional map n°**24**-B2
London 283 mi – Newcastle upon Tyne 6 mi – Sunderland 16 mi – Middlesbrough 41 mi

Hedley Hall without rest
Hedley Lane ✉ NE16 5EH – South : 2 mi by A 6076 – ✆ (01207) 231 835 – www.hedleyhall.com – Closed Christmas-New Year
4 rm – £ 65/75 ££ 95
Stone-built former farmhouse in a quiet location close to the Beamish Open Air Museum. Formal, linen-laid breakfast room and a comfy lounge with a large conservatory extension. Good-sized bedrooms offer pleasant countryside views.

SUTTON
Central Bedfordshire – See Regional map n°**12**-B1
London 47 mi – Cambridge 35 mi – Huntingdon 22 mi
Michelin Road map 504-T27

John O'Gaunt Inn

30 High St ✉ SG19 2NE – ✆ (01767) 260 377 – www.johnogauntsutton.co.uk – Closed Monday except bank holidays and Sunday dinner
Carte £ 26/38
Well-run by experienced owners, this is a cosy, honest village inn with a fire-warmed bar, a smart dining room and delightful gardens overlooking wheat fields. The tried-and-tested menu includes a classics section and some tasty steaks.

SUTTON COLDFIELD
West Midlands – Pop. 109 015 – See Regional map n°**19**-C2
London 124 mi – Birmingham 8 mi – Coventry 29 mi
Michelin Road map 503-O26 and 504

Plan: see Birmingham

The Belfry (N)

Lichfield Rd, Wishaw ✉ B76 9PR – East : 6 mi by A 453 on A 446 – ☎ (0844) 234 77 92 – www.thebelfry.co.uk

319 rm – †£ 110/250 ††£ 110/250 – 19 suites

Rest *Ryder Grill* – Carte £ 31/56 – *(dinner only)*

Rest *Sam's Clubhouse* – Carte £ 21/32

Home to the PGA, The Belfry comes with three championship golf courses, a superb golf academy and even bespoke light fittings made from clubs. Bedrooms are contemporary and there's an impressive spa and fitness facility. The stylish restaurant offers steaks and grills, while the clubhouse has a pubby style.

New Hall (N)

Walmley Rd ✉ B76 1QX – Southeast : 2.5 mi by A 5127 off Wylde Green Rd – ☎ (0845) 072 75 77 – www.handpickedhotels.co.uk Town plan: **2**DT**x**

59 rm – †£ 99/151 ††£ 109/161 – 5 suites

Rest *The Bridge* – Menu £ 45 – *(closed 23 December-31 January and Monday-Wednesday) (dinner only)*

Rest *Terrace Brasserie* – Carte £ 35/46

Despite its name, this is one of the oldest inhabited moated houses in England, dating back to the 13C. Mature, topiary-filled grounds give way to a characterful interior of wood panelling and stained glass; bedrooms are luxurious. Refined, elaborate dishes are offered in the elegant dining room, while the 'Terrace' serves an accessible menu with subtle modern twists.

SUTTON COURTENAY

Oxfordshire – Pop. 2 421 – See Regional map n°**10-B2**

London 72 mi – Bristol 77 mi – Coventry 70 mi

Michelin Road map 504-Q29

Fish

4 Appleford Rd ✉ OX14 4NQ – ☎ (01235) 848 242 – www.thefishatsuttoncourtenay.co.uk – Closed January, Monday except bank holidays and Sunday dinner

Menu £ 14 (weekdays) – Carte £ 25/47

A taste of France in Oxfordshire: expect French pictures, French music and charming Gallic service. Robust country cooking offers both French and British classics; ask for wine recommendations. Sit in the lovely garden or conservatory.

SUTTON GAULT → See Ely

Cambridgeshire – Michelin Road map 504-U26

SUTTON-ON-THE-FOREST

North Yorkshire – Pop. 539 – See Regional map n°**23-C2**

London 230 mi – Kingston-upon-Hull 50 mi – Leeds 52 mi – Scarborough 40 mi

Michelin Road map 502-P21

The Park (N)

Sutton Park ✉ YO61 1DP – ☎ (01347) 810 852 – www.theparkrestaurant.co.uk – Closed 24-26 December, 2 weeks January, 2 weeks summer, Sunday and Monday

Menu £ 48 – *(dinner only) (booking essential) (set menu only)*

A former sawmill in the grounds of Sutton Park house; which is a tea shop by day and a relaxed, intimate restaurant by night. Produce is from the kitchen garden and local estate. Modern cooking is skilled and well-balanced.

Rose & Crown

Main St ✉ YO61 1DP – ☎ (01347) 811 333 – www.theroseandcrownyork.co.uk – Closed first week January and Monday except bank holidays

Menu £ 18/28 (weekdays) **s** – Carte £ 25/37 **s** – *(booking essential)*

Welcoming pub in a beautiful village, surrounded by some delightful Georgian country houses. There's a rustic bar and an elegant restaurant which leads through to a conservatory and a superb terrace. Menus offer plenty of choice, from hearty, classically based dishes through to afternoon tea.

SWAFFHAM

Norfolk – Pop. 6 734 – See Regional map n°**15**-**C2**

London 97 mi – Cambridge 46 mi – King's Lynn 16 mi – Norwich 27 mi

Michelin Road map 504-W26 – Michelin Green Guide GREAT BRITAIN

Strattons

4 Ash Cl. ✉ PE37 7NH – ✆ (01760) 723 845 – www.strattonshotel.com – Closed 16-27 December

14 rm – £ 92/210 £ 155/230

Rest *Rustic* – Carte £ 27/35 – *(booking essential at lunch)*

Laid-back, eco-friendly hotel, in an eye-catching 17C villa with Victorian additions. Quirky, individually styled bedrooms are spread about the place; some are duplex or have terraces or courtyards. The rustic basement restaurant serves modern British dishes; on quieter days, breakfast is taken in their deli.

SWETTENHAM

Cheshire East – Pop. 248 – See Regional map n°**20**-**B3**

London 177 mi – Birmingham 63 mi – Liverpool 43 mi – Leeds 79 mi

Swettenham Arms

✉ CW12 2LF – ✆ (01477) 571 284 – www.swettenhamarms.co.uk – Closed dinner 25 December

Carte £ 18/42

Traditional pub with a beaten copper bar, open fires, horse brasses and a lavender meadow. Seasonal menus provide plenty of choice, from sharing platters and pub classics to carefully prepared, well-presented restaurant-style dishes.

ENGLAND

SWINBROOK → See Burford

Oxfordshire – Michelin Road map 503-P28 and 504

TALATON

Devon – See Regional map n°**2**-**D2**

London 165 mi – Bristol 76 mi – Exeter 14 mi

Michelin Road map 503-K31

Larkbeare Grange without rest

Larkbeare ✉ EX5 2RY – South : 1.5 mi by Fairmile rd – ✆ (01404) 822 069 – www.larkbeare.net

4 rm – £ 85/120 £ 110/190

A friendly, experienced couple run this well-kept house. Start the day with homemade yoghurt and preserves, and end it in the cosy lounge beside the woodburner. Bedrooms feature stripped pine furnishings and floral fabrics.

TANGMERE → See Chichester

West Sussex – Michelin Road map 504-R31

TAPLOW

Buckinghamshire – Pop. 518 – See Regional map n°**11**-**C3**

London 33 mi – Maidenhead 2 mi – Oxford 36 mi – Reading 12 mi

Michelin Road map 504-R29

Cliveden

✉ SL6 0JF North : 2 mi by Berry Hill – ✆ (01628) 668 561 – www.clivedenhouse.co.uk

39 rm – £ 252/492 £ 252/492 – 9 suites

Rest *André Garrett at Cliveden* – see restaurant listing

Stunning Grade I listed, 19C stately home in a superb location, boasting views over the formal parterre and National Trust gardens towards the Thames. The opulent interior boasts sumptuous antique-filled lounges and luxuriously appointed bedrooms. Unwind in the smart spa then take a picnic or afternoon tea hamper and kick-back in style on one of their vintage launches.

Taplow House

Berry Hill ✉ SL6 ODA – ✆ (01628) 670 056 – www.taplowhouse.com
32 rm – †£ 89/209 ††£ 99/229
Rest *Berry's* – Menu £ 29
Rest *Woofy's* – Carte £ 22/27
Georgian house built in 1751 – its expansive gardens boasting Europe's tallest tulip tree, which was reputedly planted by Elizabeth I. Characterful guest areas and well-equipped bedrooms cleverly blend modern and period furnishings. Formal, classical cooking in Berry's; snacks and steaks in Woofy's.

André Garrett at Cliveden – Cliveden Hotel

✉ SL6 0JF North : 2 mi by Berry Hill – ✆ (01628) 607 100 – www.clivedenhouse.co.uk/restaurant
Menu £ 28/65
A grand hotel dining room with views over the parterre garden. Classic recipes are brought up-to-date in refined, well-presented dishes where local and seasonal produce feature highly. These are accompanied by a superb wine list.

TARRANT LAUNCESTON → See Blandford Forum

Dorset

TARR STEPS

Somerset – See Regional map n°**3-A2**
London 191 mi – Taunton 31 mi – Tiverton 20 mi
Michelin Road map 503-J30

Tarr Farm Inn with rm

✉ TA22 9PY – ✆ (01643) 851 507 – www.tarrfarm.co.uk – Closed 1-13 February
9 rm – †£ 75/90 ††£ 100/150 Carte £ 24/37
Cosy, beamed pub in an idyllic riverside spot, overlooking a 1000 BC, stone-slab clapper bridge. If it's sunny, head for the garden for afternoon tea; if not, make for the narrow bar or cosy restaurant for everything from potted shrimps and sharing boards to Devon Ruby steak. Comfy, well-equipped bedrooms.

TATTENHALL

Cheshire West and Chester – Pop. 1 950 – See Regional map n°**20-A3**
London 200 mi – Birmingham 71 mi – Chester 10 mi – Liverpool 29 mi
Michelin Road map 502-L24 and 503

Higher Huxley Hall without rest

Red Lane ✉ CH3 9BZ – North : 2.25 mi on Huxley rd – ✆ (01829) 781 100 – www.huxleyhall.co.uk – Closed Christmas
4 rm – †£ 65/75 ††£ 90/100
Attractive, part-13C farmhouse boasting an original Elizabethan staircase and field and castle views. Classical, open-fired lounge and linen-laid breakfast room. Homely bedrooms with good facilities.

at Higher Burwardsley Southeast: 1 mi ✉ Tattenhall

Pheasant Inn with rm

✉ CH3 9PF – ✆ (01829) 770 434 – www.thepheasantinn.co.uk
12 rm – †£ 100/150 ††£ 110/160 Carte £ 20/42
Well-run, modern pub set atop a sandstone escarpment, with views across the Cheshire Plains. The menu focuses on simple pub classics, with no-nonsense cooking and clear, gutsy flavours. Spacious, beamed bedrooms in the main building; more modern rooms with views in the barn. Staff are keen to please.

TAUNTON

Somerset – Pop. 60 479 – See Regional map n°**3-B3**
London 168 mi – Bournemouth 69 mi – Bristol 50 mi – Exeter 37 mi
Michelin Road map 503-K30 – Michelin Green Guide GREAT BRITAIN

ENGLAND

TAUNTON

- Bath Pl. . . . . V 3
- Billetfield . . . . V 6
- Billet St. . . . . V 4
- Birch Grove . . . . U 7
- Bishop's Hull Rd . . . . AZ 9
- Bridge St . . . . U 12
- Bridge (The) . . . . U 10
- Burton Pl. . . . . V 13
- Cann St . . . . V 15
- Chritchard Parkway . . . BYZ 45
- Cleveland St . . . . U 16
- Comeytrowe Lane . . . . . AZ 18
- Corporation St . . . . V 19
- County Walk Shopping Centre V
- Duke St . . . . V 21
- East St V
- Fore St . . . . V 22
- Hamilton Rd . . . . BZ 24
- Hammet St . . . . V 25
- High St V
- Hurdle Way . . . . V 27
- Ilminster Rd. . . . . BZ 28
- Magdalene St . . . . V 30
- Middleway . . . . AZ 31
- North St . . . . V 33
- Obridge Viaduct . . . . BY 34
- Old Market Shopping Centre V
- Portland St. . . . . U 36
- Priory Ave . . . . U 37
- Shoreditch Rd . . . . BZ 39
- Shuttern . . . . V 40
- Silver St South . . . . V, Z 42
- Upper High St . . . . V 43
- Upper Wood St . . . . U 44
- Wellington New Rd . . . . AZ 46
- Wilton St . . . . V 48
- Winchester St . . . . U 49
- Wood St . . . . U 51

ENGLAND

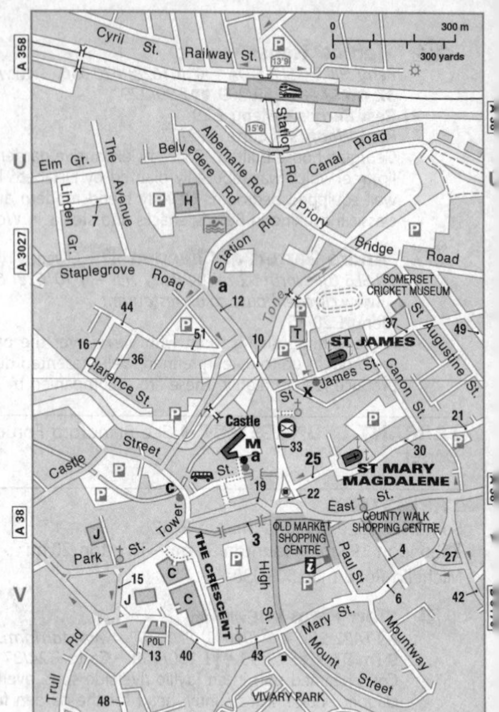

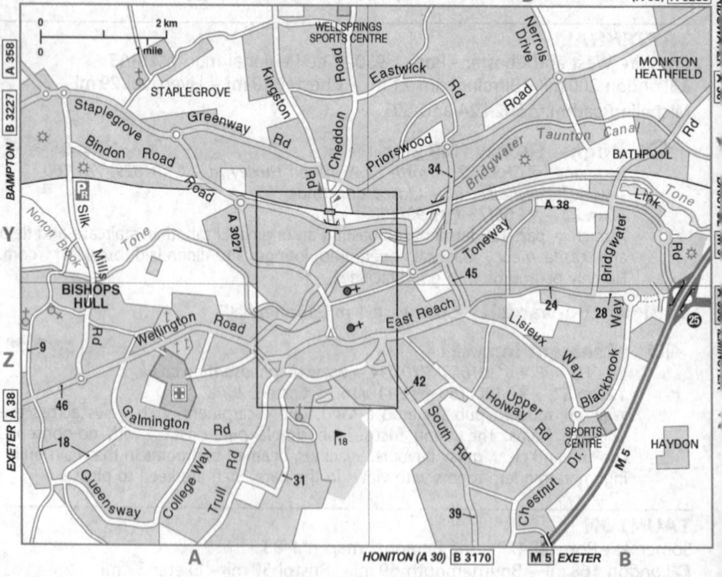

0 300 m
0 300 yards
A 358
Cyril St.
Railway St.
Station Rd
Albemarle Rd
Belvedere Rd
The Avenue
Elm Gr.
Linden Gr.
Canal Road
Priory Bridge Road
Station Rd
Staplegrove Road
A 3027
SOMERSET CRICKET MUSEUM
ST JAMES
St Augustine St.
James St.
Canon St.
Clarence St.
Castle
Castle Street
St.
North St
ST MARY MAGDALENE
East St.
Tower St.
Park St.
THE CRESCENT
High St.
OLD MARKET SHOPPING CENTRE
COUNTY WALK SHOPPING CENTRE
Paul St.
Mary St.
Mount Street
Mountway
Trull Rd
POL.
VIVARY PARK
A 38
U
V
A
B
(A 38) A 3259

0 2 km
0 1 mile
MINEHEAD A 358
BAMPTON B 3227
EXETER A 38
WELLSPRINGS SPORTS CENTRE
STAPLEGROVE
Staplegrove Road
Greenway
Bindon Road
Kingston Rd
Cheddon Rd
Eastwick Rd
Nerrols Drive
Road
MONKTON HEATHFIELD
Priorswood
Taunton Canal
Bridgwater
BATHPOOL
A 3027
A 38
Link
Tone
Norton Brook
Silk Mills
Toneway
Bridgwater Way
Bridgwater Rd
BISHOPS HULL
Rd
Wellington Road
East Reach
Lisieux Way
Galmington Rd
Queensway
College Way
Trull Rd
South Rd
Upper Holway Rd
Blackbrook
SPORTS CENTRE
HAYDON
Chestnut Dr.
M 5
Y
Z
A
B
HONITON (A 30) B 3170
M 5 EXETER

Castle

Castle Grn ✉ TA1 1NF – ✆ (01823) 272 671 Town plan: V**a**
– www.the-castle-hotel.com
44 rm – †£ 89/99 ††£ 99/129, ☕ £ 13
Rest *Castle Bow Bar & Grill* – see restaurant listing
Rest *Brazz* – ✆ (01823) 252 000 – Menu £ 10 – Carte £ 22/37
Part-12C, wisteria-clad Norman castle with impressive gardens, a keep and two wells. It's been run by the Chapman family for three generations and retains a fittingly traditional style. Well-kept, individually decorated bedrooms. Castle Bow serves modern dishes; relaxed Brazz offers brasserie classics.

Castle Bow Bar & Grill – Castle Hotel

Castle Grn ✉ TA1 1NF – ✆ (01823) 328 328 Town plan: V**a**
– www.castlebow.com – Closed Sunday dinner, Monday and Tuesday
Carte £ 30/46 – *(dinner only and Sunday lunch) (booking advisable)*
Elegant, art deco style restaurant in the old snooker room of a Norman castle. Regularly changing menus showcase top quality regional produce. Well-balanced dishes are classically based yet refined, and feature some playful modern touches.

Willow Tree

3 Tower Ln ✉ TA1 4AR – ✆ (01823) 352 835 Town plan: V**c**
– www.thewillowtreerestaurant.com – Closed January, August, Sunday, Monday and Thursday
Menu £ 28 (weekdays)/33 – *(dinner only) (booking essential)*
Intimate restaurant in a 17C townhouse, featuring exposed beams and a large inglenook fireplace. Daily menus evolve with the seasons and blend a robust classical base with artful, innovative ideas. Service is friendly and efficient.

Mint and Mustard

10 Station Rd ✉ TA1 1NH – ✆ (01823) 330 770 Town plan: U**a**
– www.mintandmustard.com – Closed 25-26 December and 1 January
Menu £ 28 – Carte £ 15/30
Smart glass doors lead to a teak-furnished lounge and a contemporary, split-level restaurant in shades of green and mustard. Thalis and curries at lunch; highly original, modern dishes at dinner. The Keralan specialities are a highlight.

Augustus

3 The Courtyard, St James St. ✉ TA1 1JR Town plan: V**x**
– ✆ (01823) 324 354 – www.augustustaunton.co.uk – Closed 23 December-2 January, Sunday and Monday
Carte £ 20/36 – *(booking essential)*
Simple little bistro set in a small courtyard and run by an experienced chef. Good-sized menu of hearty, unfussy dishes which mix French, British and some Asian influences – supplemented by blackboard specials. Bright and breezy service.

at Henlade East: 3.5 mi on A358 -(BZ)✉ Taunton

Mount Somerset

Lower Henlade ✉ TA3 5NB – South : 0.75 mi by Stoke Rd – ✆ (01823) 442 500
– www.mountsomersethotel.co.uk
19 rm ☕ – †£ 85/195 ††£ 100/270
Rest *Somerset Dining Room* – Menu £ 18 (weekday lunch)/55
– Carte £ 21/39 **s** – *(booking advisable)*
Fine Regency country house with well-tended formal gardens and lovely views. Contemporary décor blends with period features including a copula and a cantilevered staircase. Elegant bedrooms come with excellent feature bathrooms. The capacious dining room offers a mix of traditional and modern dishes.

ENGLAND

at Hatch Beauchamp Southeast: 6 mi by A358 -(BZ)⊠ Taunton

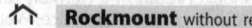

Farthings
Village Rd ⊠ TA3 6SG – ✆ (01823) 480 664 – www.farthingshotel.co.uk
12 rm – £ 110/155 £ 130/195
Rest – Carte £ 27/50 **s** – *(bookings essential for non-residents)*
Extended Georgian house in mature, well-tended gardens, with a small bar and a cosy, country house style lounge; many original features remain. Charming, antique-filled bedrooms – the master rooms are particularly comfortable. Two-roomed restaurant offers constantly evolving, classical menu.

TAVISTOCK
Devon – Pop. 12 280 – See Regional map n°**2**-C2
London 239 mi – Exeter 38 mi – Plymouth 16 mi
Michelin Road map 503-H32

Rockmount without rest
Drake Rd ⊠ PL19 0AX – ✆ (01822) 611 039 – www.rockmount-tavistock.com
5 rm – £ 45/60 £ 65/110
1920s house with a contrastingly contemporary interior, set beside the Tavistock viaduct and overlooking the town's rooftops. Individually furnished bedrooms are compact but come with plenty of extras. Breakfast is brought to your room.

Gorton's
19 Plymouth Rd ⊠ PL19 8AU – ✆ (01822) 617 581
– www.gortons-tavistock.co.uk – Closed 1 week January, 1 week April, 1 week June, 1 week October, 22-30 December, Sunday, Monday and lunch Tuesday
Menu £ 25 (weekday lunch)/42 – *(booking essential)*
Regulars at his previous place of work persuaded experienced restaurateur Peter Gorton to open this eponymous restaurant. An elegant and intimate establishment, it offers tasty classical cooking which uses quality local produce.

Cornish Arms
15 West St ⊠ PL19 8AN – ✆ (01822) 612 145
– www.thecornisharmstavistock.co.uk – Closed dinner 24 December
Carte £ 19/36
It might have been refurbished but the Cornish Arms is still a pleasingly traditional pub and its quarry-tiled bar is invariably filled with regulars playing darts and watching football. The ambitious, talented chef prepares a range of tasty classic and modern dishes, and attractive, sophisticated desserts.

at Gulworthy West: 3 mi on A390⊠ Tavistock

Horn of Plenty with rm
Gulworthy ⊠ PL19 8JD – Northwest : 1 mi by B 3362 – ✆ (01822) 832 528
– www.thehornofplenty.co.uk
16 rm – £ 85/185 £ 95/195 Menu £ 20/65
Extremely friendly restaurant in an attractive creeper-clad country house, which offers lovely moor and valley views; ask for a window table. The modern menu has wide-ranging influences – the tasting menu best showcases the chef's talent. Bedrooms are bright and modern and many have balconies or terraces.

at Milton Abbot Northwest: 6 mi on B3362⊠ Tavistock

Hotel Endsleigh
⊠ PL19 0PQ Southwest : 1 mi – ✆ (01822) 870 000 – www.hotelendsleigh.com
– Closed 2 weeks January
16 rm – £ 189/284 £ 210/315 – 3 suites
Rest ***Restaurant Endsleigh*** – see restaurant listing
Restored Regency lodge in an idyllic rural setting; spacious guest areas offer wonderful countryside views and have a warm, classical style with a contemporary edge. Comfortable, antique-furnished bedrooms boast an understated elegance; choose one overlooking the magnificent gardens.

Restaurant Endsleigh – Hotel Endsleigh

PL19 0PQ Southwest : 1 mi – (01822) 870 000 – www.hotelendsleigh.com – Closed 2 weeks January

Menu £ 28/40 – *(bookings essential for non-residents)*

Elegant, wood-panelled restaurant in a peacefully located hotel; ask for a window table for superb countryside views. Classic cooking with a modern edge; dishes are neatly presented and flavoursome, with local produce to the fore. Attentive service, with a pleasant degree of informality.

at Chillaton Northwest: 6.25 mi by Chillaton rd Tavistock

Tor Cottage without rest

PL16 0JE Southwest : 0.75 mi by Tavistock rd, turning right at bridle path – (01822) 860 248 – www.torcottage.co.uk – Closed mid-December-1 February (minimum 2 night stay)

5 rm – £ 98 £ 150/155

Remotely set cottage in 28 hillside acres, with peaceful gardens and a lovely outdoor pool. Bedrooms, most in converted outhouses, boast small kitchenettes and wood burning stoves. Breakfast is taken on the terrace or in the conservatory. Charming owner.

TEFFONT EVIAS → See Salisbury

Wiltshire

TEIGNMOUTH

Devon – Pop. 15 129 – See Regional map n°**2**-D2

London 216 mi – Exeter 16 mi – Torquay 8 mi

Michelin Road map 503-J32

Thomas Luny House without rest

Teign St TQ14 8EG – follow signs for the Quays, off the A 381 – (01626) 772 976 – www.thomas-luny-house.co.uk

4 rm – £ 60/75 £ 80/105

Classical house built in 1808 for maritime artist Thomas Luny. Inside it remains traditional, from the comfy guest areas to the spacious bedrooms. Good quality breakfasts include home-grown figs in season; cake is served on arrival.

TEMPLE SOWERBY → See Penrith

Cumbria – Michelin Road map 502-M20

TETBURY

Gloucestershire – Pop. 5 250 – See Regional map n°**4**-C1

London 113 mi – Bristol 27 mi – Gloucester 19 mi

Michelin Road map 503-N29 and 504 – Michelin Green Guide GREAT BRITAIN

Calcot Manor

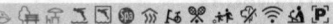

Calcot GL8 8YJ – West : 3.5 mi on A 4135 – (01666) 890 391 – www.calcotmanor.co.uk

35 rm – £ 262 £ 315 – 1 suite

Rest *Gumstool Inn* – see restaurant listing

Rest *Conservatory* – Menu £ 24 (lunch) – Carte £ 33/61 – *(booking essential)*

Impressive collection of converted farm buildings in a peaceful country setting, comprising ancient barns, old stables and a characterful farmhouse. Comfy lounges and stylish bedrooms have good mod cons; the outbuildings house a crèche, conference rooms and a superb spa complex. The laid-back conservatory offers classical dishes and there's a popular pub in the grounds.

ENGLAND

The Close
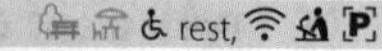

Long St ✉ GL8 8AQ – ✆ (01666) 502 272 – www.theclose-hotel.com
18 rm – †£ 150/190 ††£ 160/250
Rest *The Dining Room* – Menu £ 38 – *(dinner only)*
Rest *Brasserie* – Carte £ 27/43
The rear garden and courtyard of this 16C townhouse provide the perfect spot on a warm summer's day. Bold colours and contemporary furnishings blend well with the building's period features; look out for the superb cupola ceiling in the bar. Choose from a list of classics in the brasserie or a selection of refined, modern dishes in the more sophisticated restaurant.

Gumstool Inn – Calcot Manor Hotel

Calcot ✉ GL8 8YJ – West : 3.5 mi on A 4135 – ✆ (01666) 890 391 – www.calcotmanor.co.uk
Carte £ 22/36
Set in the grounds of 700 year old Calcot Manor; an attractive outbuilding which cleverly blends classic country style with a more modern edge. Wide-ranging British menus showcase the latest meats and fish to arrive at the door. A flexible format offers snacks, two sizes of starter and hearty main courses.

TEWKESBURY

Gloucestershire – Pop. 19 778 – See Regional map n°**4-C1**
London 108 mi – Birmingham 39 mi – Gloucester 11 mi
Michelin Road map 503-N28 and 504 – Michelin Green Guide GREAT BRITAIN

ENGLAND

Owens

73 Church St ✉ GL20 5RX – ✆ (01684) 292 703 – www.eatatowens.co.uk – Closed Sunday dinner and Monday
Carte £ 21/39
Simple, rustic restaurant with a characterful low-beamed interior, an open fire and just 10 tables; set in a charming 15C house in the shadows of Tewkesbury Abbey. Good value, seasonal menus offer French and British dishes. Cooking is clean, unfussy and flavoursome, and service is friendly and efficient.

at Corse Lawn Southwest: 6 mi by A38 and A438 on B4211 ✉ Gloucester

Corse Lawn House

✉ GL19 4LZ – ✆ (01452) 780 771 – www.corselawn.com – Closed 24-26 December
18 rm – †£ 75/95 ††£ 120/160 – 3 suites
Rest *Corse Lawn House* – Menu £ 34 **s** – Carte £ 28/40 **s**
Rest *Bistro* – Menu £ 22 **s** – Carte £ 28/40 **s**
Elegant Grade II listed Queen Anne house, just off the village green and fronted by a pond. The traditionally appointed interior features open fires and antiques; some of the spacious bedrooms have four-poster or half-tester beds. Dine from classical menus in the formal restaurant or characterful bistro-bar.

THORNBURY

South Gloucestershire – Pop. 11 687 – ✉ Bristol – See Regional map n°**4-C1**
London 128 mi – Bristol 12 mi – Gloucester 23 mi – Swindon 43 mi
Michelin Road map 503-M29 and 504

Thornbury Castle

Castle St ✉ BS35 1HH – ✆ (01454) 281 182 – www.thornburycastle.co.uk
26 rm – †£ 175/195 ††£ 185/285 – 3 suites
Rest *Tower* – see restaurant listing
Impressive 16C castle with a vineyard, hidden away in a surprisingly tranquil spot in the centre of town. The luxurious library has a high ceiling and an open fire. Baronial bedrooms feature old wooden beams and four-posters.

XX **Tower** – Thornbury Castle Hotel

Castle St ✉ BS35 1HH – ✆ (01454) 281 182 – www.thornburycastle.co.uk
Menu £ 15 (weekday lunch)/52
Sited in a tower within the main 16C part of Thornbury Castle; a small, partly wood-panelled, circular room decorated in deep red, with coats of arms and an impressive fireplace. Elegantly laid tables; elaborate, modern dishes.

THORNHAM → See Hunstanton
Norfolk – Michelin Road map 504-V25

THORNTON → See Blackpool
Lancashire – Michelin Road map 502-K22

THORNTON HOUGH
Merseyside ✉ Wirral – See Regional map n°**20**-A3
London 215 mi – Birkenhead 12 mi – Chester 17 mi – Liverpool 12 mi
Michelin Road map 502-K24

Thornton Hall

Neston Rd ✉ CH63 1JF – on B 5136 – ✆ (0151) 336 3938 – www.thorntonhallhotel.com
62 rm – †£ 79/179 ††£ 79/179, ☕ £ 15 – 1 suite
Rest *Lawns* – see restaurant listing
Extended manor house on the Wirral Peninsula. Wood panelling and stained glass feature in the main house, along with some luxurious bedrooms – the remainder are more contemporary, with balconies or terraces. Impressively equipped spa.

Mere Brook House without rest

Thornton Common Rd ✉ CH63 OLU – East : 1.5 mi by B 5136 – ✆ (07713) 189 949 – www.merebrookhouse.co.uk – Closed 20 December-2 January
8 rm ☕ – †£ 75/120 ††£ 90/130
Restored Victorian house with colourful gardens and beehives which provide their honey. Bedrooms mix modern fabrics with traditional furnishings; stay in the original house or the newer cottage which has its own lounge and pantry kitchen.

XX **Lawns** – Thornton Hall Hotel

Neston Rd ✉ CH63 1JF – on B 5136 – ✆ (0151) 336 3938 – www.lawnsrestaurant.com
Menu £ 22 (weekday lunch) – Carte £ 26/72
Grand hotel restaurant with oak-panelled walls, overlooking the lawns; formerly the house's billiard room. Chandeliers hang from the embossed leather ceiling. Elaborate modern cooking shows respect for local ingredients. Friendly service.

THORPE MARKET
Norfolk ✉ North Walsham – See Regional map n°**15**-D1
London 134 mi – Norwich 20 mi – Ipswich 63 mi – Lowestoft 39 mi
Michelin Road map 504-X25

Gunton Arms with rm

Gunton Park ✉ NR11 8TZ – South : 1 mi on A 149 – ✆ (01263) 832 010 – www.theguntonarms.co.uk – Closed 25 December
8 rm ☕ – †£ 85/175 ††£ 95/185 Carte £ 22/40 – *(booking advisable)*
Charming pub overlooking the Gunton Estate deer park. Enjoy a tasty homemade snack over a game of pool or darts in the flag-floored bar, or make for a gnarled wood table by the fireplace in the Elk Room. Dishes are fiercely seasonal; some are cooked over the fire. Elegant bedrooms have a country house feel.

THURLESTONE
Devon – See Regional map n°**2**-C3
London 214 mi – Plymouth 21 mi – Torbay 23 mi – Exeter 43 mi
Michelin Road map 503-I33

ENGLAND

Thurlestone rm, rest,

✉ *TQ7 3NN – (01548) 560 382 – www.thurlestone.co.uk – Closed 3-16 January*

65 rm – £ 80/140 £ 160/280 – 6 suites

Rest *Margaret Amelia* – Menu £ 40 – *(dinner only and Sunday lunch)*

Rest *Village Inn* – Carte £ 24/54

Long-standing, family-friendly hotel with a subtle contemporary style, superb sea views and plenty of activities. Have afternoon tea in the comfy drawing room or relax on the terrace overlooking the manicured grounds. Ask for a room with a view; some even come with children's beds. Refined, traditional dishes in Margaret Amelia and pub fare in the cosy Village Inn.

THURSFORD GREEN

Norfolk – See Regional map n°**15-C1**

London 120 mi – Fakenham 7 mi – Norwich 29 mi

Holly Lodge

The Street ✉ NR21 0AS – (01328) 878 465 – www.hollylodgeguesthouse.co.uk

3 rm – £ 70/100 £ 90/120 **Rest** – Menu £ 20

Remotely set 18C house with delightful gardens and a nice pond. Individually themed bedrooms are located in the old stable block and boast exposed beams, feature beds and numerous extra touches. Communal breakfasts, in the smart conservatory, use local and homemade produce. Home-cooked dinners offer a daily changing set menu.

ENGLAND

THURSLEY

Surrey – See Regional map n°**7-C2**

London 40 mi – Birmingham 144 mi – Bristol 115 mi – Ealing 43 mi

Three Horseshoes N

Dye House Rd ✉ GU8 6QD – (01252) 703 268 – www.threehorseshoesthursley.com – Closed Sunday dinner

Carte £ 21/43

No doubting this pub is at the heart of the community – the locals clubbed together to save it from developers. Hearty, traditional meals are high on flavour yet low on price. Real fires and fresh flowers give the place a homely feel.

TICEHURST

East Sussex – Pop. 1 705 – ✉ Wadhurst – See Regional map n°**8-B2**

London 49 mi – Brighton 44 mi – Folkestone 38 mi – Hastings 15 mi

Michelin Road map 504-V30

Bell with rm

High St ✉ TN5 7AS – (01580) 200 234 – www.thebellinticehurst.com

7 rm – £ 85/150 £ 95/190 Carte £ 27/40 – *(booking advisable)*

With top hats as lampshades, tubas in the loos and a dining room called 'the stable with a table', 'quirky' is this 16C coaching inn's middle name. Seasonal menus offer proper, tasty pub food, and rustic bedrooms – each with their own silver birch tree – share the pub's idiosyncratic charm.

TICKTON → See Beverley

East Riding of Yorkshire – Michelin Road map 502-S22

TILFORD

Surrey – See Regional map n°**7-C2**

London 43 mi – Bristol 101 mi – Cardiff 134 mi – Bournemouth 70 mi

Duke of Cambridge

Tilford Rd ✉ GU10 2DD – (01252) 792 236 – www.dukeofcambridgetilford.co.uk – Closed 25 December

Carte £ 21/36

18C pub in the heart of the forest, with a rustic, flag-floored bar, a cosy snug and an appealing heated terrace covered by an impressive oak-beamed roof. Menu offers everything from deli boards and pub classics to more adventurous dishes.

TILLINGTON → See Petworth

West Sussex – Michelin Road map 504-S31

TISBURY

Wiltshire – Pop. 2 178 – See Regional map n°**4-C3**

London 103 mi – Bristol 45 mi – Cardiff 87 mi – Torbay 98 mi

Michelin Road map 503-N30

Beckford Arms with rm

Fonthill Gifford ✉ SP3 6PX – Northwest : 2 mi by Greenwich Rd – ✆ (01747) 870 385 – www.beckfordarms.com – Closed 25 December

10 rm ☕ – †£ 95/120 ††£ 95/175 Carte £ 20/37 – *(booking essential)*

Charming 18C inn with a beamed dining room, a rustic bar and a lovely country house sitting room – where films are screened on Sundays. There's a delightful terrace and garden with hammocks, a petanque pitch and even a dog bath. Tasty, unfussy classics and country-style dishes. Tasteful bedrooms provide thoughtful comforts. Smart duplex suites, a 3min drive away.

TITCHMARSH

Northamptonshire – See Regional map n°**17-C3**

London 79 mi – Bristol 137 mi – Plymouth 255 mi – Bournemouth 161 mi

Michelin Road map 504-S26

Wheatsheaf

1 North St ✉ NN14 3DH – ✆ (01832) 732 203 – www.thewheatsheafattitchmarsh.co.uk – Closed Sunday dinner

Menu £ 19 (weekday lunch) – Carte £ 18/37

Remotely set, 17C honey-stone inn with a delightful bar, two smart dining rooms and a spacious garden and terrace. Wildlife photography brightens the walls. Proper pub cooking uses quality seasonal ingredients and everything is homemade.

TITCHWELL

Norfolk – Pop. 99 – See Regional map n°**15-C1**

London 128 mi – King's Lynn 25 mi – Boston 56 mi – Wisbech 36 mi

Michelin Road map 504-V25

Titchwell Manor

✉ PE31 8BB – ✆ (01485) 210 221 – www.titchwellmanor.com

27 rm ☕ – †£ 75/155 ††£ 75/275

Rest *The Conservatory* – see restaurant listing

This attractive brick farmhouse has a stylish interior, where bare floorboards and seaside photos feature. Bedrooms in the main house are classical, while those in the grounds are modern and colourful; all are smartly appointed.

Briarfields Ⓝ rm,

Main Street ✉ PE31 8BB – ✆ (01485) 210 742 – www.briarfieldshotelnorfolk.co.uk

23 rm ☕ – †£ 75/85 ††£ 110/155 **Rest** – Carte £ 22/38

In winter, sink into a sofa by the cosy fire; in summer, relax on the deck overlooking the salt marshes and the sea, or in the secluded courtyard, beside the pond. Bedrooms are modern and immaculately kept; some have patio doors.

The Conservatory Ⓝ – Titchwell Manor Hotel

✉ PE31 8BB – ✆ (01485) 210 221 – www.titchwellmanor.com

Menu £ 55 (dinner) – Carte £ 22/50 **s**

This appealing hotel restaurant provides plenty of choice. The trendy 'Eating Rooms' area offers a menu of comfort food and sea views from the terrace. The smart 'Conservatory' offers the same, alongside a more ambitious modern menu.

TITLEY

Herefordshire ✉ Kington – See Regional map n°**18-A3**

London 176 mi – Plymouth 196 mi – Torbay 175 mi – Exeter 159 mi

Michelin Road map 503-L27

Stagg Inn (Steve Reynolds) with rm

✉ HR5 3RL – ✆ (01544) 230 221 – www.thestagg.co.uk – Closed 2 weeks January-February, first 2 weeks November, 25-26 December, Monday and Tuesday

6 rm – £ 70/120 £ 100/140 Carte £ 31/42 – *(booking essential)*

Part-medieval, part-Victorian pub with a delightfully cosy interior. Cooking is fittingly straightforward, relying on classically based recipes, careful preparation and top quality produce. Menus are short, simple and to the point, while the dishes themselves are truly satisfying. Bedrooms in the pub are snug but can be noisy; opt for one in the former vicarage.

→ Wye Valley asparagus, slow-cooked egg and hazelnuts. Chicken with artichoke, purple sprouting broccoli and potato dauphinoise. Lemon tart, blackcurrant compote, cassis sorbet and candied lemon.

TOLLARD ROYAL

Wiltshire – See Regional map n°**4-C3**

London 118 mi – Bristol 63 mi – Southampton 40 mi – Portsmouth 59 mi

King John Inn with rm

✉ SP5 5PS – ✆ (01725) 516 207 – www.kingjohninn.co.uk – Closed 25 December

11 rm – £ 135/185 £ 140/195 Carte £ 30/55

Creeper-clad Victorian pub in a pretty village, with a smart, spacious, open-plan interior. Daily changing, classically based menus, with game a speciality. Contemporary bedrooms mix modern facilities with antique furniture; some are in the coach house opposite.

ENGLAND

TOOT BALDON → See Oxford

Oxfordshire

TOPSHAM

Devon – Pop. 3 730 – ✉ Exeter – See Regional map n°**2-D2**

London 175 mi – Torbay 26 mi – Exeter 4 mi – Torquay 24 mi

Michelin Road map 503-J31

Salutation Inn with rm

rest,

68 Fore St ✉ EX3 0HL – ✆ (01392) 873 060 – www.salutationtopsham.co.uk

6 rm – £ 113/150 £ 125/185

Menu £ 43/92 – *(light lunch) (booking essential at dinner)*

1720s coaching inn with a surprisingly contemporary interior. The glass-covered courtyard serves breakfast, light lunches and afternoon tea. The stylish dining room offers nicely balanced, weekly 5, 7 and 9 course set menus of well-judged modern cooking. Bedrooms are similarly up-to-date and understated.

La Petite Maison

35 Fore St ✉ EX3 0HR – ✆ (01392) 873 660 – www.lapetitemaison.co.uk – Closed 2 weeks autumn, 1 week April, 26-30 December, Sunday and Monday

Menu £ 34/40 – *(booking essential at lunch)*

Cosy two-roomed restaurant in a charming riverside village, with bright décor and eye-catching Peter Blake art. Seasonally evolving menus feature meat from the village butcher's and cheese from the nearby shop. Friendly, welcoming owners.

TORQUAY

Torbay – Pop. 49 094 – See Regional map n°**2-C-D2**

London 223 mi – Exeter 23 mi – Plymouth 32 mi

Michelin Road map 503-J32 – Michelin Green Guide GREAT BRITAIN

Marstan without rest

Meadfoot Sea Rd ✉ TQ1 2LQ – ✆ (01803) 292 837 – www.marstanhotel.co.uk – Closed November-February except 23 December-2 January

Town plan: CX**a**

9 rm – £ 55/120 £ 75/150

Keenly run Victorian villa in a quiet part of town, with an opulent lounge, a pool, a hot tub and a lovely suntrap terrace. Comfy bedrooms have antique furnishings and good facilities. Substantial breakfasts include homemade granola.

Somerville without rest
515 Babbacombe Rd. ✉ TQ1 1HJ – ✆ (01803) 294 755 Town plan: CX**u**
– www.somervillehotel.co.uk
9 rm – £ 60/95 £ 70/160
Comfortable hotel, an easy walk down the hill into town. Open-plan lounge and breakfast room filled with ornaments. Modern, slightly kitsch bedrooms with antique French furniture and good mod cons; Room 12 has direct access to the garden.

Kingston House without rest
75 Avenue Rd ✉ TQ2 5LL – ✆ (01803) 212 760 Town plan: BY**n**
– www.kingstonhousetorquay.co.uk – Closed 20 December-6 January
5 rm – £ 65/70 £ 80/90
This enthusiastically run Victorian guesthouse shows good attention to detail, with fresh flowers in the hall, homemade scones served beside the fireplace on arrival, and thoughtful touches such as locally made chocolates in the modern bedrooms. Sit on Lloyd Loom chairs at breakfast, overlooking the courtyard.

Room in the Elephant (Simon Hulstone)
3-4 Beacon Terr ✉ TQ1 2BH – (1st Floor) – ✆ (01803) 200 044 – www.elephantrestaurant.co.uk – Closed October-Easter, Sunday and Monday Town plan: CZ**e**
Menu £ 55/73 – *(dinner only) (set menu only)*
First floor restaurant in an elegant Georgian terrace overlooking Torbay, with a Colonial-style cocktail bar and a simply decorated dining room. The tasting menu offers appealing, classical combinations with no unnecessary elaboration. Ingredients are top notch – most come from their 94 acre farm near Brixham.
➜ Tartare of scallop, green tomato and sorrel granité. Deer with onion ash, haunch croquette, celeriac, garlic and capers. Chilled chocolate fondant, salted caramel ice cream, vanilla salt.

ENGLAND

Orange Tree
14-16 Parkhill Rd ✉ TQ1 2AL – ✆ (01803) 213 936 Town plan: CZ**u**
– www.orangetreerestaurant.co.uk – Closed 1 week January, 1 week February, 2 weeks October, 26-29 December, Sunday and Monday
Carte £ 27/44 – *(dinner only) (booking essential)*
Modern, split-level restaurant with a homely feel, set down a narrow town centre backstreet. The seasonally evolving menu is made up classically based, French-influenced dishes, which are carefully prepared and rely on fresh, local produce.

Brasserie
3-4 Beacon Terr ✉ TQ1 2BH – ✆ (01803) 200 044 Town plan: CZ**e**
– www.elephantrestaurant.co.uk – Closed 3 weeks January, Sunday and Monday
Menu £ 15 (weekday lunch) – Carte £ 26/44
Light, airy brasserie underneath 'Room in the Elephant', displaying an intriguing mix of nautical colours and Indian artefacts. Menus revolve around the seasons; cooking is fresh and simple. Good value wines and an upstairs cocktail bar.

On the Rocks
1 Abbey Cres. ✉ TQ2 5HB – ✆ (01803) 203 666 Town plan: CZ**r**
– www.ontherocks-torquay.co.uk – Closed 26 December and 1 January
Carte £ 19/35 – *(bookings advisable at dinner)*
Two local lads opened this lovely restaurant overlooking Torbay. It's modern and laid-back, with dining over two floors and furniture made from reclaimed scaffold boards. Appealing menus champion produce from the bay and the fields above.

Number 7
7 Beacon Terr. ✉ TQ1 2BH – ✆ (01803) 295 055 Town plan: CZ**e**
– www.no7-fish.com – Closed 2 weeks February, 1 week November, Christmas-New Year, Monday November-May and Sunday October-June
Carte £ 23/48 – *(dinner only and lunch Wednesday-Saturday) (booking advisable)*
Personally run bistro in a terrace of Regency houses. The walls are covered with fish-related photos and artefacts, as well as extensive blackboard menus of seafood fresh from the Brixham day boats; the simplest dishes are the best.

TORBAY
TORQUAY-PAIGNTON

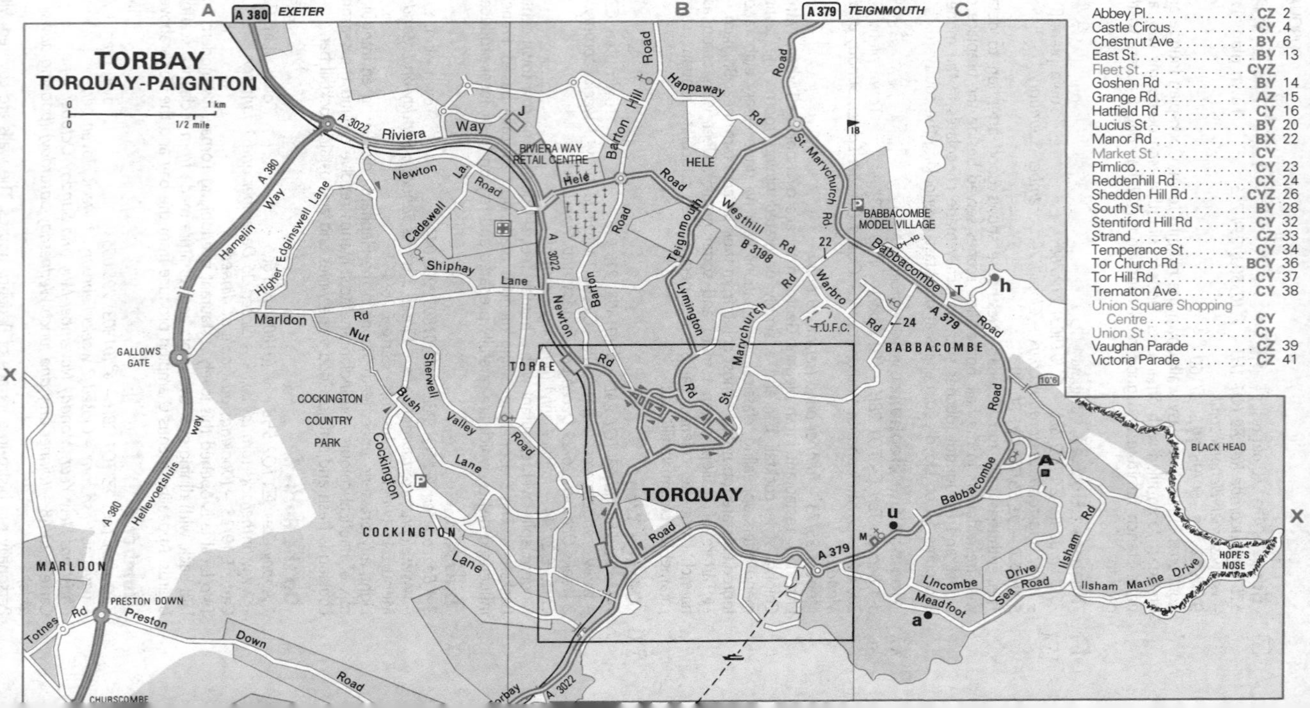

Street	Grid	No.
Abbey Pl.	CZ	2
Castle Circus	CY	4
Chestnut Ave	BY	6
East St.	BY	13
Fleet St	CYZ	
Goshen Rd	BY	14
Grange Rd.	AZ	15
Hatfield Rd	CY	16
Lucius St	BY	20
Manor Rd	BX	22
Market St	CY	
Pimlico	CY	23
Reddenhill Rd	CX	24
Shedden Hill Rd	CYZ	26
South St	BY	28
Stentiford Hill Rd	CY	32
Strand	CZ	33
Temperance St	CY	34
Tor Church Rd	BCY	36
Tor Hill Rd	CY	37
Trematon Ave	CY	38
Union Square Shopping Centre	CY	
Union St	CY	
Vaughan Parade	CZ	39
Victoria Parade	CZ	41

TORQUAY CENTRE

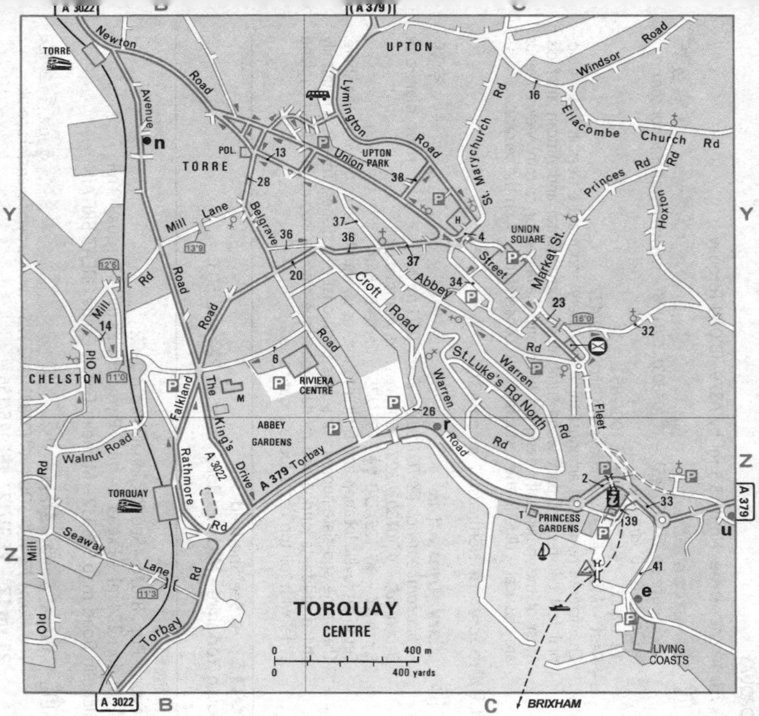

ENGLAND

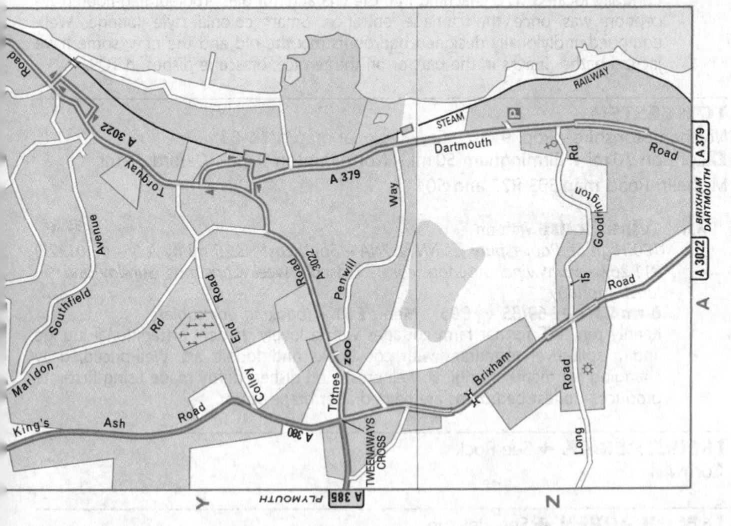

at Maidencombe North: 3.5 mi by A379 -(BX)✉ Torquay

Orestone Manor

Rockhouse Ln ✉ TQ1 4SX – ✆ (01803) 328 098 – www.orestonemanor.com – Closed 3-30 January

12 rm ☕ – †£ 80/200 ††£ 100/285

Rest – Menu £ 25 (weekdays) – Carte £ 29/42

Characterful house set amongst thick shrubbery and mature trees. It has a Colonial feel courtesy of dark wood furnishings and Oriental and African artefacts. Most of the individually designed bedrooms have sea or country views. Menus are classical – dine in the restaurant, the conservatory or on the terrace.

at Babbacombe Northeast: 2 mi on A379

Cary Arms with rm

Babbacombe Beach ✉ TQ1 3LX – East : 0.25 mi by Beach Rd. – ✆ (01803) 327 110 – www.caryarms.co.uk Town plan: CX**h**

8 rm ☕ – †£ 125/220 ††£ 155/275 Carte £ 25/34

Set in an idyllic location and built into the rocks, with terraces down to the shore. The stone and slate-floored bar serves traditional pub dishes. There's a nautically styled residents lounge and modern, boutique-chic bedrooms in a New England style, with roll-top baths looking out to sea.

TOTLEY ➜ See Sheffield

South Yorkshire – Michelin Road map 502-P24 and 503

ENGLAND

TOTNES

Devon – Pop. 8 076 – See Regional map n°**2**-C2

▶London 224 mi – Exeter 24 mi – Plymouth 23 mi – Torquay 9 mi

Michelin Road map 503-I32 – Michelin Green Guide GREAT BRITAIN

Royal Seven Stars 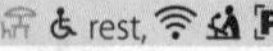

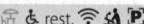

The Plains ✉ TQ9 5DD – ✆ (01803) 862 125 – www.royalsevenstars.co.uk

21 rm ☕ – †£ 91/122 ††£ 125/156

Rest *TQ9* – Carte £ 23/39 – *(bar lunch Monday-Saturday)*

Centrally located, 17C coaching inn; the characterful glass-roofed, flag-floored reception was once the carriage entrance. Smart colonial-style lounge. Well-equipped, individually designed bedrooms mix the old and the new; some have jacuzzi baths. Snacks in the bars or on the terrace; brasserie dishes in TQ9.

TOWCESTER

Northamptonshire – Pop. 9 057 – See Regional map n°**16**-B3

▶London 70 mi – Birmingham 50 mi – Northampton 9 mi – Oxford 36 mi

Michelin Road map 503-R27 and 504

XX **Vine House** with rm 

100 High St, Paulerspury ✉ NN12 7NA – Southeast : 3.25 mi by A 5 – ✆ (01327) 811 267 – www.vinehousehotel.com – Closed 1 week Christmas, Sunday and lunch Monday

6 rm ☕ – †£ 69/85 ††£ 95 Menu £ 31 – *(booking advisable)*

Keenly run, 17C former farm cottages with a lovely garden, a traditional lounge and a split-level restaurant with cookbooks and foodie art. Well-priced, daily changing set menu of original, well-presented dishes; deftly made using first-rate produce. Modest bedrooms are named after grape vines.

TREBETHERICK ➜ See Rock

Cornwall

TRELOWARREN ➜ See Helston

Cornwall

TRENT

Dorset – See Regional map n°**4-C3**
London 128 mi – Southampton 67 mi – Bristol 39 mi – Bournemouth 46 mi
Michelin Road map 503-M31

Rose & Crown with rm — rest,

DT9 4SL – (01935) 850 776 – www.roseandcrowntrent.co.uk
3 rm – £ 75/85 £ 85/110 Carte £ 20/36
Pretty 14C part-thatched pub, with plenty of rustic charm courtesy of an open-fired lounge and a bar complete with a grandfather clock. On sunny days head for the conservatory or lovely garden. Menus showcase West Country produce.

TRESCO

→ See Scilly (Isles of)
– Michelin Road map 503-B34

TRISCOMBE

Somerset – See Regional map n°**3-B2**
London 163 mi – Bristol 50 mi – Swansea 116 mi – Exeter 42 mi
Michelin Road map 503-K30

Blue Ball Inn with rm — rest,

TA4 3HE – (01984) 618 242 – www.blueballinn.info – Closed 25-26 December, dinner 1 January, Sunday dinner and Monday
3 rm – £ 55/90 £ 75/110 Carte £ 26/38
Characterful former barn in the Quantock Hills; rustic and cosy with exposed rafters and open fires. Lunchtime sandwiches and pub classics provide fuel for passing walkers; dinner sees well-presented, original, modern dishes. Lovely tiered garden and stylish, comfortable bedrooms in a pretty thatched cottage.

TRUMPET

→ See Ledbury
Herefordshire

TRURO

Cornwall – Pop. 20 332 – See Regional map n°**1-B3**
London 295 mi – Exeter 87 mi – Penzance 26 mi – Plymouth 52 mi
Michelin Road map 503-E33 – Michelin Green Guide GREAT BRITAIN

Mannings — rm, rest,

Lemon St TR1 2QB – (01872) 270 345 – www.manningshotels.co.uk – Closed Christmas
42 rm – £ 65/85 £ 85/129
Rest *Mannings* – (01872) 247 900 – Carte £ 20/42 – *(closed Sunday lunch)*
Imposing hotel located in the city centre, close to the cathedral. Boutique bedrooms are bright, modern and stylish; spacious apartment-style rooms, in the neighbouring mews, boast over-sized beds and galley kitchens. Chic cocktail bar. Stylish restaurant offers eclectic, all-day menu.

Tabb's

85 Kenwyn St TR1 3BZ – (01872) 262 110 – www.tabbs.co.uk – Closed 1 week January, 1 week October, Saturday lunch, Sunday and Monday
Menu £ 20 (lunch) – Carte £ 29/39
A series of lilac-painted rooms with matching chairs, in a small former pub. The appealing menu lists refined, classically based dishes where good quality produce shines through. Tasty tapas-style lunches offer three dishes for £ 12.

Bustophers

62 Lemon St TR1 2PN – (01872) 279 029 – www.bustophersbarbistro.co.uk – Closed Sunday dinner and Monday
Menu £ 15/20 – Carte £ 22/37
Busy, informal wine bar-bistro, just off the town centre, with a central bar and an open kitchen. Seasonal menus champion Cornish produce and offer a mix of modern and classic dishes, with some Mediterranean touches.

X **Saffron**

5 Quay St ✉ TR1 2HB – ✆ (01872) 263 771 – www.saffronrestauranttruro.co.uk – Closed 25-26 December, Monday dinner January-April, Sunday and bank holidays
Carte £ 20/43
Smart rustic restaurant in the city's heart, run by a charming owner. There's a snug bar to the front, a lovely open room behind and pots of fresh flowers throughout. A blackboard lists what's in season, which is reflected on the menu.

TUDDENHAM

Suffolk – Pop. 400 – See Regional map n°**14-B2**
London 76 mi – Birmingham 120 mi – Sheffield 152 mi – Croydon 96 mi
Michelin Road map 504-V27

XX **Tuddenham Mill** with rm

High St ✉ IP28 6SQ – ✆ (01638) 713 552 – www.tuddenhammill.co.uk
15 rm – †£ 185/395 ††£ 185/395
Menu £ 20 (lunch) – Carte dinner £ 26/40
Delightful 18C watermill overlooking the millpond; the old workings are still in situ in the stylish bar and there's a beamed restaurant with black furnishings above. Cooking features quality seasonal produce in unusual, innovative combinations. Some of the trendy bedrooms are in attractive outbuildings.

TURNERS HILL

ENGLAND

West Sussex – Pop. 885 – See Regional map n°**7-D2**
London 33 mi – Brighton 24 mi – Crawley 7 mi
Michelin Road map 504-T30

Alexander House

rm, rest,

East St ✉ RH10 4QD – East : 1 mi on B 2110 – ✆ (01342) 714 914 – www.alexanderhouse.co.uk
58 rm – †£ 155/305 ††£ 155/305, £ 20 – 2 suites
Rest *AG's* – see restaurant listing
Rest *Reflections* – Carte £ 28/53
Stunning 18C country house in extensive grounds, once owned by Percy Shelley's family. Bedrooms are spacious and well-equipped – some have four-poster beds, claw-foot baths or double showers. The superb spa has 25 treatment rooms and a Grecian pool. Dine in the contemporary brasserie or formal AG's.

XXX **AG's** N – Alexander House Hotel

East St ✉ RH10 4QD – East : 1 mi on B 2110 – ✆ (01342) 714 914 – www.alexanderhouse.co.uk – closed Monday
Carte £ 54/62 – *(dinner only and Sunday lunch) (booking essential)*
Have drinks in the smart champagne bar before dinner in the formal two-roomed restaurant of this fabulous 18C country house. Presentation and flavour combinations are modern and original and cooking follows the seasons closely.

TWO BRIDGES

Devon ✉ Yelverton – See Regional map n°**2-C2**
London 226 mi – Exeter 25 mi – Plymouth 17 mi
Michelin Road map 503-I32 – Michelin Green Guide GREAT BRITAIN

Prince Hall

✉ PL20 6SA East : 1 mi on B 3357 – ✆ (01822) 890 403 – www.princehall.co.uk
8 rm – †£ 60/190 ††£ 120/190
Rest – Menu 43 **s** – *(booking essential) (bar lunch Monday-Saturday)*
Remote former hunting lodge with a welcoming, shabby-chic interior and wide-ranging views. Dogs are welcome throughout, except for in the bright restaurant, where you'll find vibrantly flavoured dishes with Mediterranean influences. Homely bedrooms display subtle modern touches; some overlook the moor.

TYNEMOUTH

Tyne and Wear – Pop. 67 519 – See Regional map n°**24-B2**

London 290 mi – Newcastle upon Tyne 8 mi – Sunderland 7 mi

Michelin Road map 501-P18 and 502

Grand

14 Grand Par. ✉ *NE30 4ER* – ✆ *(0191) 293 6666 – www.grandhotel-uk.com*

46 rm – †£ 75/185 ††£ 85/195

Rest *Victoria* – Carte £ 23/31 – *(closed Sunday dinner)*

Victorian hotel with superb sea views: once the Duchess of Northumberland's holiday home. Impressive carved staircase and sizeable guest areas boasts ornate coving and pillars. Mix of simply furnished and more comfortable bedrooms; 222 has a four-poster and jacuzzi. Classical dining room with a menu to match.

Martineau without rest

57 Front St ✉ *NE30 4BX* – ✆ *(0191) 257 90 38 – www.martineau-house.co.uk – Closed 24-26 December*

4 rm – †£ 75/85 ††£ 95

Attractive 18C red-brick house named after Harriet Martineau. Cosy, individually furnished bedrooms come with thoughtful extras; two boast pleasant Tyne views. Superb communal breakfasts with a river and South Shields outlook.

UCKFIELD

East Sussex – Pop. 15 213 – See Regional map n°**8-A2**

London 45 mi – Brighton 17 mi – Eastbourne 20 mi – Maidstone 34 mi

Michelin Road map 504-U31

Horsted Place

Little Horsted ✉ *TN22 5TS – South : 2.5 mi by B 2102 and A 22 on A 26 –* ✆ *(01825) 750 581 – www.horstedplace.co.uk – Closed first week January*

20 rm – †£ 105/360 ††£ 105/360 – 5 suites

Rest – Menu £ 19 (weekday lunch) – Carte approx. £ 38 – *(closed Saturday lunch)*

Impressive country house in Victorian Gothic style. The tiled entrance hall leads to an impressive main gallery, where ornate sitting rooms are furnished with fine antiques. Individually styled bedrooms are well-equipped; most have great views over the parkland. The formal dining room offers a classical menu.

UFFORD

Suffolk – See Regional map n°**15-D3**

London 91 mi – Bristol 221 mi – Bournemouth 211 mi – Poole 215 mi

Michelin Road map 504-Y27

Ufford Crown

High St ✉ *IP13 6EL –* ✆ *(01394) 461 030 – www.theuffordcrown.com – Closed Tuesday*

Carte £ 21/40

Welcoming former coaching inn run by an enthusiastic husband and wife team. Daily menu of honest, flavoursome food includes a great grill section with lamb cutlets and sharing rib of beef. Portions are generous and service is keen.

UFFORD

Peterborough – Pop. 163 – See Regional map n°**14-A2**

London 90 mi – Leicester 38 mi – Coventry 69 mi – Nottingham 50 mi

White Hart with rm

rm,

Main St ✉ *PE9 3BH –* ✆ *(01780) 740 250 – www.whitehartufford.co.uk*

6 rm – †£ 75/110 ††£ 85/120 Carte £ 23/38

Delightful 17C inn with a super sun-trap of a terrace and garden. Eat in the cosy bar, rustic restaurant or lovely conservatory. Menus offer a broad range of dishes, with much of the meat coming from their own farm. Sweet, individually styled bedrooms; one is a four-poster and those outside allow dogs to stay.

UPPER SLAUGHTER → See Bourton-on-the-Water

Gloucestershire – Michelin Road map 503-O28

UPPER SOUTH WRAXALL

Wiltshire – See Regional map n°**4-C2**

London 201 mi – Birmingham 326 mi – Liverpool 419 mi – Leeds 393 mi

Longs Arms

BA15 2SB – (01225) 864 450 – www.thelongsarms.com – Closed 3 weeks January-February, Sunday dinner and Monday

Carte £ 23/42 – *(booking essential)*

Handsome, bay-windowed, Bath stone pub opposite a medieval church in a sleepy village. Traditional British dishes are full-flavoured, hearty and satisfying; everything is homemade and they smoke their own meats and fish. Dine in the characterful area in front of the bar. Warm, friendly service.

UPPER WOODFORD → See Salisbury

Wiltshire – Michelin Road map 503-O30

UPPINGHAM

Rutland – Pop. 4 745 – See Regional map n°**17-C2**

London 101 mi – Leicester 19 mi – Northampton 28 mi – Nottingham 35 mi

Michelin Road map 504-R26

Lake Isle with rm

rest,

16 High St East LE15 9PZ – (01572) 822 951 – www.lakeisle.co.uk – Closed 26 December-2 January, Sunday dinner and Monday lunch

12 rm – £ 60/85 £ 85/110 Carte £ 26/41 – *(light lunch)*

Pleasant town centre property accessed via a narrow passageway, with a small, characterful lounge and heavy wood furnishings. Light lunches and much more elaborate dinners with modern influences and the odd Asian touch. Bedrooms boast good facilities and extras: superior are the largest, with whirlpool baths.

ENGLAND

at Lyddington South: 2 mi by A6003 Uppingham

Marquess of Exeter with rm

52 Main St LE15 9LT – (01572) 822 477 – www.marquessexeter.co.uk – Closed 25 December

17 rm – £ 80/105 £ 100/135

Menu £ 16 (weekday lunch) – Carte £ 24/37

Attractive 16C thatched pub with a cosy bar, characterful exposed beams, inglenook fireplaces and a rustic dining room. The daily changing menu offers tasty, classical combinations of local, home-grown and home-reared produce. Comfortable bedrooms are located across the car park.

Old White Hart with rm

51 Main St LE15 9LR – (01572) 821 703 – www.oldwhitehart.co.uk – Closed 25 December and Sunday dinner in winter

10 rm – £ 65/70 £ 90/100 Carte £ 22/31

This pub offers all you'd expect from a traditional 17C coaching inn – and a lot more besides. It's got the chocolate box village setting, the open fires and the seasonal menu of hearty, classic dishes; but also gives you a relaxing ambience, charming service, a 10-piste petanque pitch and stylish bedrooms.

UPTON BISHOP → See Ross-on-Wye

Herefordshire

VENTNOR → See Wight (Isle of)

Isle of Wight – Michelin Road map 503-Q32 and 504

VERYAN

Cornwall – Pop. 877 – Truro – See Regional map n°**1-B3**

London 291 mi – St Austell 13 mi – Truro 13 mi

Michelin Road map 503-F33 – Michelin Green Guide THE WEST COUNTRY

Nare

Carne Beach ✉ TR2 5PF – Southwest : 1.25 mi – ✆ (01872) 501 111 – www.narehotel.co.uk

37 rm ☕ – †£ 143/276 ††£ 276/518 – 7 suites

Rest *Quarterdeck* – see restaurant listing

Rest *Dining Room* – Menu £ 50 – *(dinner only and Sunday lunch) (booking essential)*

Personally run, classic country house with a stunning bay outlook; take it in from the pool or hot tub. Most bedrooms have views and some have patios or balconies. Have afternoon tea in the drawing room, evening canapés in the bar, then choose from a traditional daily menu or more modern fare in Quarterdeck.

Quarterdeck – Nare Hotel

Carne Beach ✉ TR2 5PF – Southwest : 1.25 mi – ✆ (01872) 500 000 – www.narehotel.co.uk

Carte £ 27/44 – *(bookings essential for non-residents)*

Informal restaurant in a classic country house, with large black and white prints on the walls and a nautical theme. The menu offers a range of dishes, from omelette Arnold Bennett to lobster – the local Fowey Oysters are a hit.

VIRGINSTOW

Devon – See Regional map n°**2**-C2

London 227 mi – Bideford 25 mi – Exeter 41 mi – Launceston 11 mi

Michelin Road map 503-H31

Percy's

Coombeshead Estate ✉ EX21 5EA – Southwest : 1.75 mi on Tower Hill rd – ✆ (01409) 211 236 – www.percys.co.uk

7 rm ☕ – †£ 125/215 ††£ 140/230

Rest – Menu £ 40 – *(dinner only) (booking essential) (set menu only)*

Stone house in 130 acres of fields and woodland. The owners grow veg, breed racehorses, rear pigs and sheep, and sell wool, skins and produce. Spacious, comfy bedrooms in the former barn – some have jacuzzi baths. Set menu of traditional dishes in the formal dining room; ingredients are from the estate.

WADDESDON

Buckinghamshire – Pop. 1 797 – ✉ Aylesbury – See Regional map n°**11**-C2

London 51 mi – Aylesbury 5 mi – Northampton 32 mi – Oxford 31 mi

Michelin Road map 504-R28 – Michelin Green Guide GREAT BRITAIN

Five Arrows with rm

High St ✉ HP18 0JE – ✆ (01296) 651 727 – www.thefivearrows.co.uk

16 rm ☕ – †£ 75/100 ††£ 105/235

Menu £ 15 (weekday lunch) – Carte £ 25/38

Half-timbered Victorian building on the Rothschild Estate, with Elizabethan chimney stacks, attractive gabling and mullioned windows. Individually styled, antique-furnished bedrooms are split between the main house and courtyard. The traditional restaurant serves classical menus and local game in season.

WALBERSWICK

Suffolk – Pop. 380 – See Regional map n°**15**-D2

London 115 mi – Norwich 31 mi – Ipswich 31 mi – Lowestoft 16 mi

Michelin Road map 504-Y27

Anchor with rm

Main St ✉ IP18 6UA – ✆ (01502) 722 112 – www.anchoratwalberswick.com – Closed 25 December

10 rm ☕ – †£ 85/125 ††£ 100/150 Carte £ 23/39

Welcoming, relaxing pub in an Arts and Crafts building; its sizeable garden features a wood-fired oven and seaward views. Global flavours feature alongside British classics; try some home-baked bread. Excellent beers and wines. Impressive breakfasts. Choose a wood-clad chalet in the garden.

WALFORD → See Ross-on-Wye
Herefordshire

WALKDEN
Greater Manchester – Pop. 21 194 – See Regional map n°**20-B2**
London 205 mi – Birmingham 91 mi – Liverpool 30 mi – Sheffield 62 mi
Michelin Road map 502-M23

XX **Grenache** N

15 Bridgewater Rd ✉ M28 3JE – ✆ (0161) 799 8181 – www.grenacherestaurant.co.uk – Closed Sunday dinner-Tuesday
Carte £ 23/53 – *(dinner only and Sunday lunch)*
A gregarious owner and a passionate chef run this smart neighbourhood restaurant. Cooking is modern and seasonal with clean, clear flavours. The atmosphere is friendly and laid-back, and the young serving team are attentive.

WALL → See Lichfield
Staffordshire – Michelin Road map 504-O26

WALTHAM ABBEY
Essex – Pop. 18 743
London 17 mi – Croydon 26 mi – Barnet 13 mi – Ealing 21 mi
Michelin Road map 504-U28

XX **Parsons**

58 Sun St ✉ EN9 1EJ – ✆ (01992) 700 655 – www.parsonsrestaurant.com – Closed 1-5 January
Menu £ 17/28 – Carte £ 22/43
Large converted pub with an equally sizeable terrace; owned by an experienced chef and two master butchers. Good value menus of unfussy, well-known dishes. The plain walls are hung with bright pictures and there's good disabled access.

WAREHAM
Dorset – Pop. 5 496 – See Regional map n°**4-C3**
London 123 mi – Bournemouth 13 mi – Weymouth 19 mi
Michelin Road map 503-N31 and 504 – Michelin Green Guide GREAT BRITAIN

Priory rm,

Church Grn ✉ BH20 4ND – ✆ (01929) 551 666 – www.theprioryhotel.co.uk
18 rm – †£ 172/300 ††£ 215/375 – 2 suites
Rest – Menu £ 48 (dinner) – Carte £ 31/43
Delightfully located part-16C priory, which is proudly and personally run. Have afternoon tea on the terrace, overlooking the beautiful manicured gardens and on towards the river – here, peace and tranquility reign. The country house inspired bedrooms are charming; those in the 'Boathouse' are the most luxurious. Dress smartly for dinner in the formal candlelit cellar.

Gold Court House without rest

St John's Hill ✉ BH20 4LZ – ✆ (01929) 553 320 – www.goldcourthouse.co.uk – Closed 25 December-2 January
3 rm – †£ 60 ††£ 85
Charmingly run Georgian house in a small square off the high street; which stands on the foundations of a 13C goldsmith's house. It has a fire-lit lounge, a lovely breakfast room with garden views and traditional, restful bedrooms.

WAREN MILL → See Bamburgh
Northumberland – Michelin Road map 501-O17 and 502

WARKWORTH
Northumberland – See Regional map n°**24-B2**
London 316 mi – Alnwick 7 mi – Morpeth 24 mi
Michelin Road map 502-P17

Roxbro House without rest

5 Castle Terr ✉ NE65 0UP – ✆ (01665) 711 416 – www.roxbrohouse.co.uk – Closed 24-28 December

6 rm ☕ – 🚹£ 99 🚹🚹£ 99/120

'Elegant' and 'opulent' are suitable adjectives to describe these two houses in the shadow of Warkworth Castle, where boutique bedrooms mix modern facilities with antique furniture. Choose between two comfy lounges – one with an honesty bar; tasty breakfasts are served in a conservatory-style room.

WARMINGHAM

Cheshire East – See Regional map n°**20-B3**

▶ London 174 mi – Birmingham 61 mi – Manchester 33 mi – Bristol 143 mi

Bear's Paw with rm

School Ln ✉ CW11 3QN – ✆ (01270) 526 317 – www.thebearspaw.co.uk

17 rm ☕ – 🚹£ 100/155 🚹🚹£ 110/160 Carte £ 19/43

Handsome 19C inn with a spacious, wood-panelled bar and a huge array of local ales. The menu will please all appetites, with everything from nibbles, salads and deli boards to European dishes, pub favourites and steak you can cook yourself on a hot stone. Stylish, good value bedrooms.

WARMINSTER

Wiltshire – Pop. 17 490 – See Regional map n°**4-C2**

▶ London 111 mi – Bristol 29 mi – Exeter 74 mi – Southampton 47 mi

Michelin Road map 503-N30 and 504 – Michelin Green Guide GREAT BRITAIN

Bishopstrow H. and Spa

Boreham Rd ✉ BA12 9HH – Southeast : 1.5 mi on B 3414 – ✆ (01985) 212 312 – www.bishopstrow.co.uk

32 rm ☕ – 🚹£ 120/195 🚹🚹£ 155/230 – 4 suites

Rest *Mulberry* – Carte £ 26/43

It may look like a typical Georgian country house but both the drawing rooms and the bedrooms have a stylish, modern edge. There's a well-equipped spa and a stunning glass conservatory which overlooks the terrace to the manicured gardens. The elegant restaurant serves classic dishes with a modern edge.

Weymouth Arms with rm

12 Emwell St ✉ BA12 8JA – ✆ (01985) 216 995 – www.weymoutharms.co.uk – Closed Monday-Wednesday lunch

6 rm – 🚹£ 65/75 🚹🚹£ 75/85, ☕ £ 7 Carte £ 19/40

Grade II listed building with plenty of history. It's immensely characterful, with original wood panelling, antiques and lithographs, as well as two fireplaces originally intended for nearby Longleat House. Cooking is fresh and fittingly traditional. Cosy bedrooms have charming original fittings.

at Heytesbury Southeast: 3.75 mi by B3414 ✉ Warminster

Resting Post without rest

67 High St ✉ BA12 0ED – ✆ (01985) 840 204 – www.therestingpost.co.uk

3 rm ☕ – 🚹£ 50/60 🚹🚹£ 70/80

This attractive 17C listed cottage is the village's former post office; look out for the mail box on the wall outside. Neat, cosy bedrooms feature up-to-date bathrooms. Traditional English breakfasts are taken in the original shop.

Angel Inn

High St ✉ BA12 0ED – ✆ (01985) 840 330 – www.theangelatheytesbury.co.uk

Carte £ 20/41

Pretty, family-run, 16C pub with open fires and beams; it boasts a typically English feel, emphasised by the locals and their dogs. Flavoursome dishes come in generous portions and make use of fresh, regional produce.

at Crockerton South: 2 mi by A350

Bath Arms with rm — rest,

Clay St ✉ BA12 8AJ – on Shearwater rd – ✆ (01985) 212 262 – www.batharmscrockerton.co.uk – Closed dinner 25-26 December

2 rm – £ 80/110 £ 80/110 Carte £ 22/33

Down-to-earth pub; once part of the Longleat Estate. Daily changing menu features classic pub dishes, snacks and grills, along with a selection of daily specials; try the legendary 'sticky' beef with braised red cabbage. Two ultra-spacious, contemporary bedrooms, amusingly named 'Left' and 'Right'.

at Horningsham Southwest: 5 mi by A362✉ Wiltshire

Bath Arms with rm

Longleat ✉ BA12 7LY – ✆ (01985) 844 308 – www.batharms.co.uk

16 rm – £ 65/135 £ 75/145 Carte £ 21/39

Charming pub within the Longleat estate, with open fire in bar, grand dining room and delightful terrace. Appealing menus offer something for everyone; produce is locally sourced, much of it from the estate. Quirky, comfortable, individually themed bedrooms.

WARTLING → See Herstmonceux

East Sussex – Michelin Road map 504-V31

ENGLAND

WARWICK

Warwickshire – Pop. 31 345 – See Regional map n°**19-C3**

London 96 mi – Birmingham 20 mi – Coventry 11 mi – Leicester 34 mi

Michelin Road map 503-P27 and 504 – Michelin Green Guide GREAT BRITAIN

Charter House without rest

87 West St ✉ CV34 6AH – ✆ (01926) 496 965 – Closed 1 week Christmas Town plan: Y**c**

3 rm – £ 65/69 £ 85/95

Hugely characterful timbered house dating from 1480 and used as an officers' billet by Cromwell's troops in 1641; there is a tunnel connecting the house to the castle! The pretty breakfast room has a flag floor and wattle and daub walls. Well-appointed bedrooms feature heavy fabrics and come with good extras.

Park Cottage without rest

113 West St ✉ CV34 6AH – ✆ (01926) 410 319 – www.parkcottagewarwick.co.uk – Closed 23-31 December Town plan: Y**e**

7 rm – £ 60/75 £ 75/90

15C cross-wing house with wattle and daub walls; set within the grounds of Warwick Castle and originally belonging to the Earl – the 300 year old yew tree was used to make longbows. Cottagey breakfast room and spacious bedrooms with extras.

Saffron Gold

Unit 1, Westgate House, Market St ✉ CV34 4DE – ✆ (01926) 402 061 – www.saffrongoldwarwick.co.uk Town plan: Y**n**

Carte £ 16/38 – *(dinner only)*

Smoothly run by the friendly owner and his attentive team, a modern Indian restaurant with a split-level dining room adorned with contemporary art. Extensive menus offer interesting, authentic cooking, with Goan fish dishes a highlight.

Tailors

22 Market Pl ✉ CV34 4SL – ✆ (01926) 410 590 – www.tailorsrestaurant.co.uk – Closed Christmas, Sunday and Monday Town plan: Y**a**

Menu £ 20/40

As well as a tailor's, this has also formerly been a fishmonger's, a butcher's and a casino! Cosy interior with polished wood tables and a brick fireplace. Simple, good value lunches and ambitious dinners with unusual flavour combinations.

WARWICK-ROYAL LEAMINGTON SPA

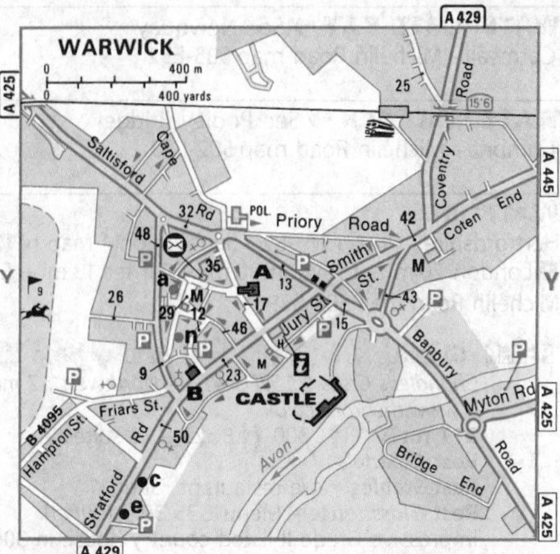

Birmingham Rd	Z	7
Bowling Green St	Y	9
Brook St	Y	12
Butts (The)	Y	13
Castle Hill	Y	15
Church St	Y	17
High St	Y	23
Jury St	Y	
Lakin Rd	Y	25
Linen St	Y	26
Market Pl	Y	29
Old Square	Y	35
Old Warwick Rd	Z	36
Radford Rd	Z	39
Rock (The)	Y	32
St John's Rd	Y	42
St Nicholas Church St	Y	43
Shires Retail Park	Z	
Smith St	Y	
Swan St	Y	46
Theatre St	Y	48
West St	Y	50

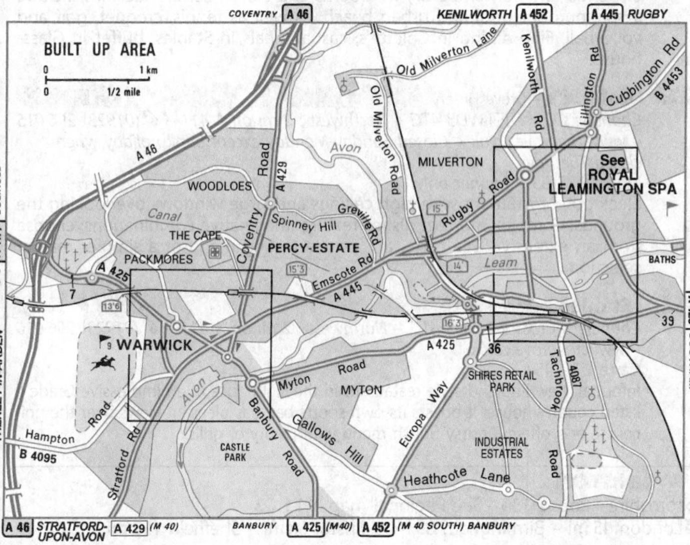

WARWICK-ON-EDEN

→ See Carlisle

Cumbria

WATCHET

Somerset – Pop. 3 581 – See Regional map n°3-B2
London 174 mi – Bristol 60 mi – Exeter 49 mi – Cardiff 86 mi
Michelin Road map 503-K30

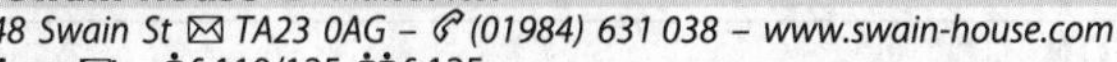

Swain House without rest

48 Swain St ✉ TA23 0AG – ✆ (01984) 631 038 – www.swain-house.com
4 rm – £ 110/125 £ 125
In the characterful high street of this coastal town, you'll find this super smart guesthouse with spacious bedrooms and a sleek yet cosy feel. Parts of famous paintings make up feature walls and all have roll-top baths and rain showers.

WATERGATE BAY → See Newquay
Cornwall – Michelin Road map 503-E32

WATERMILLOCK → See Pooley Bridge
Cumbria – Michelin Road map 502-L20

WATFORD
Hertfordshire – Pop. 131 982 – See Regional map n°**12**-A2
London 20 mi – Croydon 30 mi – Barnet 13 mi – Ealing 19 mi
Michelin Road map 504-S29

Grove
rm,

Chandler's Cross ✉ WD3 4TG – Northwest : 2 mi on A 411 – ✆ (01923) 807 807 – www.thegrove.co.uk
217 rm – ♦£ 300 ♦♦£ 325 – 12 suites
Rest *Colette's*
Rest *Stables* – see restaurant listing
Rest *Glasshouse* – Menu £ 35/39 – *(buffet)*
Impressive Grade II listed country house in 300 acres of pretty grounds. Mix of period and contemporary bedrooms and suites. Leisure facilities include a spa, outdoor pool and urban beach; as well as tennis, croquet, golf and volleyball. Fine dining in Colette's; casual meals in Stables; buffet in Glass-house.

Colette's – Grove Hotel
Chandler's Cross ✉ WD3 4TG – Northwest : 2 mi on A 411 – ✆ (01923) 296 015 – www.thegrove.co.uk – Closed Sunday-Monday except bank holiday when closed Tuesday
Menu £ 75/85 – *(dinner only)*
Sleek hotel restaurant with high ceilings and large windows overlooking the grounds. Complex modern dishes feature imaginative combinations; choose from an extensive à la carte, a 7 course tasting menu or a simpler market selection.

Stables – Grove Hotel
Chandler's Cross ✉ WD3 4TG – Northwest : 2 mi on A 411 – ✆ (01923) 296 010 – www.thegrove.co.uk
Carte £ 29/45
Informal, New England style restaurant in the clubhouse of an impressive Grade II listed country house. It boasts its own sports bar, has pleasant views over the golf course and offers a gutsy British menu with plenty of grills.

WATLINGTON
Oxfordshire – Pop. 2 139 – See Regional map n°**11**-C2
London 45 mi – Birmingham 89 mi – Bristol 88 mi – Sheffield 153 mi
Michelin Road map 504-Q29

Fat Fox Inn with rm

13 Shireburn St ✉ OX49 5BU – ✆ (01491) 613 040 – www.thefatfoxinn.co.uk – Closed dinner 25 December and 1 January
9 rm – ♦£ 60/109 ♦♦£ 70/119 Carte £ 16/36
In the heart of a busy market village; a 19C pub run with honesty and integrity by experienced owners. The menu reflects what they themselves like to eat, covering all bases from potted mackerel to pheasant pie. Fight the cats for a seat by the wood burning range, then settle in to one of the cosy bedrooms.

WATTON
Norfolk – Pop. 7 435 – See Regional map n°**15**-C2
London 95 mi – Norwich 22 mi – Swaffham 10 mi
Michelin Road map 504-W26

XX **Café at Brovey Lair** with rm rest,

Carbrooke Rd., Ovington ✉ IP25 6SD – Northeast : 1.75 mi by A 1075 – ✆ (01953) 882 706 – www.broveylair.com – Closed 25 December and 1 January

3 rm – †£ 120/135 ††£ 135/150

Menu £ 53 – *(booking essential 2 days in advance, lunch by arrangement) (set menu only)*

Dining here has more of a dinner party atmosphere than a restaurant feel. The spacious conservatory has an open kitchen with stool seating and a teppan-yaki grill. The no-choice set menu revolves around seafood and Asian flavours. Well-appointed bedrooms are situated beside the pool in lovely gardens.

WEDMORE

Somerset – Pop. 1 409 – See Regional map n°**3-B2**

London 155 mi – Bristol 23 mi – Cardiff 67 mi – Plymouth 100 mi

Michelin Road map 503-L30

Swan with rm rest,

Cheddar Rd ✉ BS28 4EQ – ✆ (01934) 710 337 – www.theswanwedmore.com – Closed 25 December

6 rm – †£ 85 ††£ 85/125 Carte £ 23/36 – *(booking essential)*

Spacious and airy former coaching inn with a bright, buzzy bar and comfy restaurant; the open plan kitchen and its appealing display of freshly baked bread links the two. Daily menus feature good quality, seasonal British ingredients in unfussy, flavoursome dishes. Stylish bedrooms complete the picture.

WELBURN

North Yorkshire – See Regional map n°**23-C2**

London 225 mi – Leeds 40 mi – York 14 mi

Michelin Road map 502-R21

Crown and Cushion N

✉ YO60 7DZ – ✆ (01653) 618 777 – www.thecrownandcushionwelburn.com

Menu £ 17 – Carte £ 26/40

Well run 18C pub two miles from Castle Howard. The menu champions local meats and the kitchen's pride and joy is its charcoal-fired rotisserie. Dishes are hearty; sandwiches are doorstops and puddings are of the nursery variety.

WELLAND → See Great Malvern

Worcestershire – Michelin Road map 503-N27

WELLINGHAM

Norfolk – See Regional map n°**15-C1**

London 120 mi – King's Lynn 29 mi – Norwich 28 mi

Michelin Road map 504-W25

Manor House Farm without rest

✉ PE32 2TH – ✆ (01328) 838 227 – www.manor-house-farm.co.uk

3 rm – †£ 75 ††£ 110/120

Attractive, wisteria-clad farmhouse with large gardens, set by a church in a beautifully peaceful spot. Spacious, airy bedrooms are located in the former stables. Home-grown and home-reared produce is served at breakfast.

WELLS

Somerset – Pop. 10 536 – See Regional map n°**4-C2**

London 132 mi – Bristol 20 mi – Southampton 68 mi – Taunton 28 mi

Michelin Road map 503-M30 and 504 – Michelin Green Guide GREAT BRITAIN

Swan

11 Sadler St ✉ BA5 2RX – ✆ (01749) 836 300 – www.swanhotelwells.co.uk
49 rm ☐ – †£ 100/112 ††£ 124/147 – 1 suite
Rest *15c A.D.* – Carte £ 29/46 – *(bar lunch Monday-Saturday)*
15C former coaching inn with a good outlook onto the famous cathedral; its charming interior has subtle, contemporary touches, particularly in the lounge and bar. Comfortable, stylish, well-equipped bedrooms and opulent 'Cathedral Suite'. Formal, wood-panelled restaurant serves classic dishes.

Beryl without rest

✉ BA5 3JP East : 1.25 mi by B 3139 off Hawkers Lane – ✆ (01749) 678 738 – www.beryl-wells.co.uk – Closed 23-30 December
13 rm ☐ – †£ 80/100 ††£ 100/160
Fine 19C country house in mature gardens, overlooking the town and run by a charming owner. Delightful, antique-filled drawing room. Individually styled bedrooms: some have four-posters; 'Master and Butterfly' is the best.

Stoberry House without rest

Stoberry Park ✉ BA5 3LD – Northeast : 0.5 mi by A 39 on College Rd – ✆ (01749) 672 906 – www.stoberryhouse.co.uk
5 rm ☐ – †£ 65/110 ††£ 85/145
18C coach house with a delightful walled garden, overlooking Glastonbury Tor. Large lounge with a baby grand piano and antique furniture. Breakfast is an event, with 7 homemade breads, a porridge menu and lots of cooked dishes. Immaculately kept bedrooms come with fresh flowers, chocolates and a pillow menu.

ENGLAND

Old Spot

12 Sadler St ✉ BA5 2SE – ✆ (01749) 689 099 – www.theoldspot.co.uk – Closed 1 week Christmas, Monday, Sunday dinner and Tuesday lunch
Menu £ 16/23 (lunch) – Carte dinner £ 24/40
Simple, understated restaurant with an airy feel. Framed menus hang on plain walls and it affords stunning cathedral views from the rear. Well-executed dishes rely on flavoursome English produce but have a classical French and Italian base. Preparation is unfussy and some lesser-used ingredients feature.

at Easton Northwest: 3 mi on A371 ✉ Wells

Beaconsfield Farm without rest

✉ BA5 1DU – ✆ (01749) 870 308 – www.beaconsfieldfarm.co.uk – Closed 23 December-2 January
3 rm ☐ – †£ 75/95 ††£ 85/115
A former farmhouse hidden away in the foothills of the Mendip Hills and run by a personable owner. The lounge and bedrooms have a modern feel, while the breakfast room, which overlooks the colourful garden, is more traditional.

WELLS-NEXT-THE-SEA

Norfolk – Pop. 2 165 – See Regional map n°**15**-C1
London 122 mi – Cromer 22 mi – Norwich 38 mi
Michelin Road map 504-W25

Crown

The Buttlands ✉ NR23 1EX – ✆ (01328) 710 209 – www.flyingkiwiinns.co.uk
12 rm ☐ – †£ 80/165 ††£ 100/185
Rest *Crown* – Carte £ 23/36
Characterful 16C former coaching inn located in the centre of town, overlooking the green. Individually styled bedrooms blend classical furniture with more modern décor and facilities. Dine from an accessible menu in the charming bar, orangery or dining room.

Machrimore without rest
Burnt St ✉ NR23 1HS – on A 149 – ✆ (01328) 711 653 – www.machrimore.co.uk
4 rm – ♦£ 65 ♦♦£ 84/88
Cross the delightful gardens with their illuminated water features to this collection of converted farm outbuildings. Bedrooms are well-equipped and come with quality furniture and private patios. Photos of old Wells feature throughout.

at Wighton Southeast: 2.5 mi by A149

Meadowview without rest
53 High St ✉ NR23 1PF – ✆ (01328) 821 527 – www.meadow-view.net
5 rm – ♦£ 90/100 ♦♦£ 95/110
Set in the centre of a peaceful village, this smart, modern guesthouse is the perfect place to unwind, as its neat garden boasts a hot tub and a comfy seating area overlooking a meadow. Breakfast is cooked on the Aga in the country kitchen.

WELWYN

Hertfordshire – Pop. 3 497 – See Regional map n°**12**-B2
London 31 mi – Bedford 31 mi – Cambridge 31 mi
Michelin Road map 504-T28

Tewin Bury Farm
✉ AL6 0JB Southeast : 3.5 mi by A 1000 on B 1000 – ✆ (01438) 717 793 – www.tewinbury.co.uk
29 rm – ♦£ 100/144 ♦♦£ 119/159
Rest *Williams'* – see restaurant listing
A collection of converted farm buildings on a 400 acre working farm, next to a nature reserve. Rustic interior with comfy oak-furnished bedrooms in various wings. The function room is in an impressive tithe barn beside the old mill race.

Williams' – Tewin Bury Farm Hotel
✉ AL6 0JB Southeast : 3.5 mi by A 1000 on B 1000 – ✆ (01438) 717 793 – www.tewinbury.co.uk
Menu £ 15 (weekday lunch) – Carte £ 27/40
Rustic hotel restaurant in an old timber chicken shed on a working farm. Modern interior with brick walls, an open kitchen, a smart bar and a large terrace. Well-executed, classical dishes display modern touches.

at Ayot Green Southwest: 2.5 mi by B197

Waggoners
Brickwall Close ✉ AL6 9AA – ✆ (01707) 324 241 – www.thewaggoners.co.uk
Menu £ 18 (weekday lunch) – Carte £ 27/61 – *(booking advisable)*
Charming 17C pub on the edge of the Brocket Hall Estate. Sit in the delightfully simple open-fired bar or very formal dining room. Choose from unfussy bar snacks or a much more ambitious French-based à la carte, with prices to match.

WENTBRIDGE

West Yorkshire ✉ Pontefract – See Regional map n°**22**-B3
London 183 mi – Leeds 19 mi – Nottingham 55 mi – Sheffield 28 mi
Michelin Road map 502-Q23 and 504

Wentbridge House
Old Great North Rd. ✉ WF8 3JJ – ✆ (01977) 620 444 – www.wentbridgehouse.co.uk
41 rm – ♦£ 85/185 ♦♦£ 125/225
Rest *Fleur de Lys* – Carte £ 26/57 – *(dinner only and Sunday lunch)*
Rest *Wentbridge Brasserie* – Menu £ 16 (weekday lunch) – Carte £ 24/52
Personally run, bay-windowed house, dating back to the 19C and surrounded by 20 acres of immaculate gardens. Bedrooms are a mix of characterful, wood-panelled period styles and spacious modern designs with up-to-date facilities. Classical menu in formal restaurant; smart brasserie serves more modern dishes.

ENGLAND

WEST ASHLING → See Chicester
West Sussex

WEST BAGBOROUGH
Somerset – See Regional map n°**3-B2**
London 161 mi – Bristol 57 mi – Cardiff 88 mi – Plymouth 82 mi
Michelin Road map 503-K30

Rising Sun Inn with rm
rest,
TA4 3EF – (01823) 432 575 – www.risingsuninn.info – Closed 25 December
2 rm – £ 65 £ 95 Carte £ 22/37
Traditional-looking pub in the Quantock Hills, with several little rooms, a pleasing mix of old tables and chairs, smart slate floors and bright modern art. Menus offer plenty of choice, from typical pub-style light bites to more hearty classics. Two contemporary bedrooms offer great views.

WEST BRIDGFORD → See Nottingham
Nottinghamshire – Michelin Road map 502-Q25

WEST CLANDON → See Guildford
Surrey

WEST DIDSBURY → See Manchester
Greater Manchester

ENGLAND

WEST END
Surrey – Pop. 4 135 – Guildford – See Regional map n°**7-C1**
London 37 mi – Bracknell 7 mi – Camberley 5 mi – Guildford 8 mi
Michelin Road map 504-S29

The Inn @ West End
42 Guildford Rd GU24 9PW – on A 322 – (01276) 858 652 – www.the-inn.co.uk
Menu £ 13/28 – Carte £ 26/50
A big-hearted pub offering genuine hospitality and a lively atmosphere. Wide-ranging menus offer generously proportioned, seasonal dishes with robust flavours and original touches. The wine shop specialises in European wines.

WEST HATCH
Wiltshire – See Regional map n°**4-C3**
London 104 mi – Birmingham 131 mi – Sheffield 225 mi – Leicester 162 mi

Pythouse Kitchen Garden Shop and Café
SP3 6PA – (01747) 870 444 – www.pythousekitchengarden.co.uk – Closed 25-26 December, 1 January and Tuesday
Carte approx. £ 22 – *(lunch only and dinner Friday-Saturday) (booking advisable)*
Simple, rustic café in a former potting shed, serving breakfast, coffee, lunch and afternoon tea; order in the well-stocked shop. Tasty, unfussy cooking uses seasonal produce from the charming 18C walled garden. Save room for some cake!

WEST HOATHLY
West Sussex – Pop. 709 – See Regional map n°**7-D2**
London 36 mi – Bristol 141 mi – Croydon 26 mi – Barnet 78 mi

Cat Inn with rm

Queen's Sq ✉ *RH19 4PP – ✆ (01342) 810 369 – www.catinn.co.uk*
– Closed 25 December and Sunday dinner
4 rm – £ 85/110 £ 120/160 Carte £ 22/36
Popular with the locals and very much a village pub, with beamed ceilings, pewter tankards, open fires and plenty of cosy corners. Carefully executed, good value cooking focuses on tasty pub classics like locally smoked ham, egg and chips or steak, mushroom and ale pie. Service is friendly and efficient – and four tastefully decorated bedrooms complete the picture.

WEST KIRBY

Merseyside – See Regional map n°**20-A3**
London 219 mi – Chester 19 mi – Liverpool 12 mi
Michelin Road map 502-K23 and 504 – Michelin Green Guide GREAT BRITAIN

Peel Hey

Frankby Rd, Frankby ✉ *CH48 1PP – East : 2.25 mi by A 540 on B 5139*
– ✆ (0151) 677 90 77 – www.peelhey.com
10 rm – £ 65/75 £ 85/115, £ 10
Rest – Menu £ 17/20 – *(dinner only and Sunday lunch)*
Personally run, detached 19C house with attractive bedrooms; those to the rear are quieter, with countryside views. Comfortable conservatory and pleasant lawned garden. Simple evening meals and Sunday lunch.

WEST LULWORTH

Dorset ✉ Wareham – See Regional map n°**4-C3**
London 129 mi – Bournemouth 21 mi – Dorchester 17 mi – Weymouth 19 mi
Michelin Road map 503-N32 and 504

Bishops

Lulworth Cove ✉ *BH20 5RQ – ✆ (01929) 400 552 – www.bishopscottage.co.uk*
5 rm – £ 100 £ 160 **Rest** – Carte £ 16/32
Attractive cottage part-dating from the 17C, set on the hillside in a pretty village and looking over the Jurassic Coast. Sizeable, very contemporary bedrooms with stylish bathrooms. Rustic bar with a wood-burning stove. Pre-book dinner in the dining room, which doubles as a vegetarian café during the day.

WEST MALLING

Kent – Pop. 2 266 – See Regional map n°**8-B1**
London 35 mi – Maidstone 7 mi – Royal Tunbridge Wells 14 mi
Michelin Road map 504-V30

Swan

35 Swan St. ✉ *ME19 6JU – ✆ (01732) 521 910 – www.theswanwestmalling.co.uk*
– Closed 1-2 January
Menu £ 18 (weekdays) – Carte £ 24/49 – *(booking essential)*
Informal 15C former coaching inn where original beams blend with stylish, contemporary furnishings. The nicely appointed bar and lounge are upstairs. Modern European menus offer flavoursome combinations; side dishes are required.

WEST MEON

Hampshire – See Regional map n°**6-B2**
London 74 mi – Southampton 27 mi – Portsmouth 21 mi – Basingstoke 32 mi
Michelin Road map 504-Q30

Thomas Lord

High St ✉ *GU32 1LN – ✆ (01730) 829 444 – www.thomaslord.co.uk – Closed 25 December*
Menu £ 16 – Carte £ 23/40
Early 19C pub named after the founder of Lord's Cricket Ground and featuring cricketing memorabilia; sit by the fire in the bar. Menus mix the classics with a few more modern dishes, and many of the ingredients come from the kitchen garden. Regular music evenings and a friendly, welcoming team.

ENGLAND

WEST OVERTON → See Marlborough

Wiltshire – Michelin Road map 503-O29

WEST TANFIELD

North Yorkshire – Pop. 293 – ✉ Ripon – See Regional map n°**22**-B2
London 237 mi – Darlington 29 mi – Leeds 32 mi – Middlesbrough 39 mi
Michelin Road map 502-P21

Old Coach House without rest

2 Stable Cottage, North Stainley ✉ HG4 3HT – Southeast : 1 mi on A 6108 – ✆ (07912) 632 296 – www.oldcoachhouse.info

8 rm – £ 60/70 £ 70/110

Smart 18C coach house nestled between the dales and the moors. Bedrooms differ in size but all have a bright modern style and are furnished by local craftsmen. The breakfast room overlooks the fountain in the courtyard garden.

WEST WITTERING

West Sussex – Pop. 875 – See Regional map n°**7**-C3
London 87 mi – Southampton 38 mi – Brighton and Hove 41 mi
Michelin Road map 504-R31

Beach House with rm

Rookwood Rd ✉ PO20 8LT – ✆ (01243) 514 800 – www.beachhse.co.uk

7 rm – £ 70/80 £ 95/150

Menu £ 10 (weekday lunch) – Carte £ 21/41 – *(closed Monday and Sunday-Thursday dinner November-May) (booking advisable)*

It might be 10 minutes' from the beach but the Beach House definitely has a seaside feel, with its large veranda, shuttered windows and scrubbed wooden tables. Tasty breakfasts, coffee and cakes morph into fresh, bistro-style dishes later in the day. Bedrooms are simple and modern, with comfy beds.

WEST WITTON

North Yorkshire ✉ Leyburn – See Regional map n°**22**-B1
London 241 mi – Kendal 39 mi – Leeds 60 mi – Newcastle upon Tyne 65 mi
Michelin Road map 502-O21

Wensleydale Heifer

✉ DL8 4LS – ✆ (01969) 622 322 – www.wensleydaleheifer.co.uk

13 rm – £ 70/170 £ 120/240

Rest – Menu £ 20 – Carte £ 31/56

Pretty, whitewashed former pub on the main street of the village. Quirky, themed bedrooms boast quality linen and the latest mod cons. Characterful lounge has a roaring fire. Dine in the fish bar or at clothed tables in the beamed restaurant; cooking has a strong seafood base.

WESTON-SUB-EDGE → See Chipping Campden

Gloucestershire

WESTON UNDER WETHERLEY → See Royal Leamington Spa

Warwickshire – Michelin Road map 503-P27

WESTONBIRT

Gloucestershire – See Regional map n°**4**-C1
London 104 mi – Bristol 24 mi – Cardiff 57 mi – Plymouth 144 mi
Michelin Road map 503-N29

Hare & Hounds

✉ *GL8 8QL On A 433 – ✆ (01666) 881 000 – www.cotswold-inns-hotels.co.uk – Closed 6 January*

42 rm – £ 93/150 £ 158/198 – 3 suites

Rest *Beaufort* – Menu £ 39/55 – *(dinner only and Sunday lunch)*

Rest *Jack Hare's* – Menu £ 16 (weekdays) – Carte £ 21/28

Attractive former farmhouse with lovely gardens, set between Highgrove House and the National Arboretum. The country house style interior features several lounges and a small library; bedrooms blend modern fabrics with period furniture – half are located in the old outbuildings. Formal Beaufort offers classical dishes with a modern edge, while Jack Hare's serves a pub-style menu and real ales.

WESTFIELD

East Sussex – Pop. 1 509 – See Regional map n°**8-B3**

London 66 mi – Brighton 38 mi – Folkestone 45 mi – Maidstone 30 mi

Michelin Road map 504-V31

Wild Mushroom

Woodgate House, Westfield Ln. ✉ TN35 4SB – Southwest : 0.5 mi on A 28 – ✆ (01424) 751 137 – www.webbesrestaurants.co.uk – Closed 1 week October, 1-10 January, 25-26 December, Sunday dinner, Monday and Tuesday

Menu 24 (lunch) – Carte £ 25/44 – *(booking essential)*

Keenly run restaurant in a 17C farmhouse, with a contemporary dining room and an intimate lounge-bar in the conservatory. Good value French menus feature well-presented, tried-and-tested combinations; a tasting menu is available.

WESTLETON

Suffolk – Pop. 349 – ✉ Saxmundham – See Regional map n°**15-D2**

London 97 mi – Cambridge 72 mi – Ipswich 28 mi – Norwich 31 mi

Michelin Road map 504-Y27

Westleton Crown with rm

The Street ✉ IP17 3AD – ✆ (01728) 648 777 – www.westletoncrown.co.uk

34 rm – £ 90/100 £ 95/215 Carte £ 28/42

Good-looking, 17C former coaching inn with an appealing terrace and garden, set in a pretty little village. Welcoming beamed bar with open fires; more modern conservatory. Seasonal menu, with special diets well-catered for. Uncluttered bedrooms are named after birds found on the adjacent RSPB nature reserve.

WESTON-SUPER-MARE

North Somerset – Pop. 83 641 – See Regional map n°**3-B2**

London 147 mi – Bristol 24 mi – Taunton 32 mi

Michelin Road map 503-K29

Duets

103 Upper Bristol Rd. ✉ BS22 8ND – ✆ (01934) 413 428 Town plan: BY**a**

– www.duets.co.uk – Closed 1 week spring, 1 week summer, 1 week winter, Sunday dinner, Monday and Tuesday

Menu £ 18/31 – Carte £ 31/38 – *(booking essential at lunch)*

A husband and wife team duet here, with him in the kitchen and her out front; there's also always a duet dish on the menu. Carefully prepared classical dishes follow the seasons. It's more modern inside than the exterior suggests.

Cove

Birnbeck Rd ✉ BS23 2BX – ✆ (01934) 418 217 Town plan: AY**e**

– www.the-cove.co.uk – Closed 25 December and Monday October-May

Menu £ 15/20

Stylish, modern restaurant on the promenade; every table has bay views. Light bites at lunch. More formal dinner menu offers carefully cooked European dishes with modern touches. Open for breakfast every day. Keen, helpful service.

ENGLAND

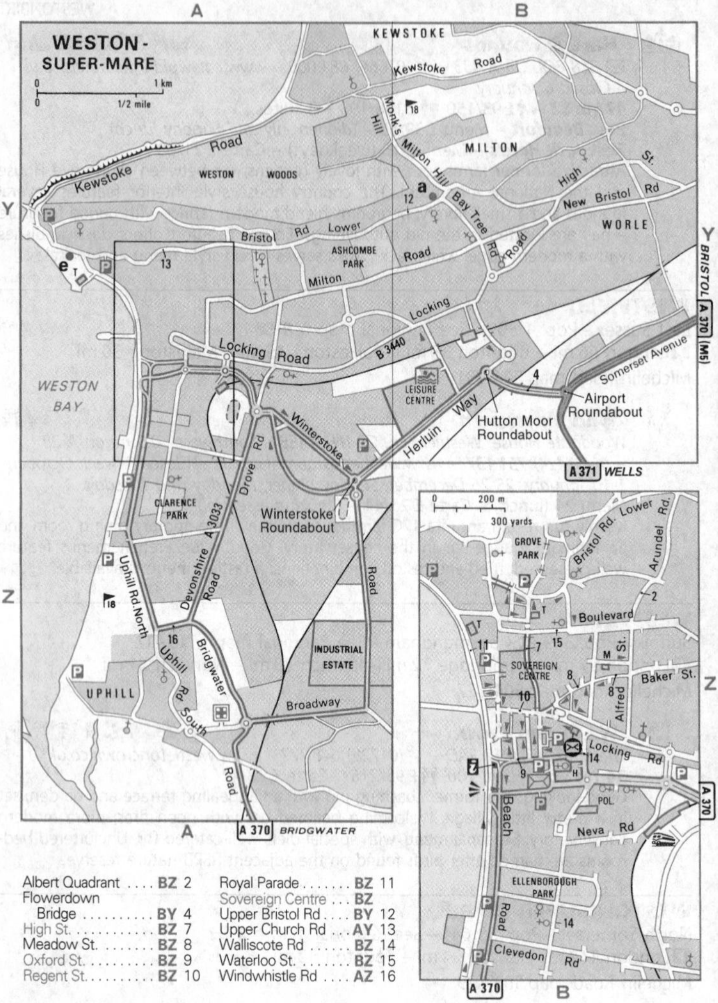

Street	Grid	No.
Albert Quadrant	BZ	2
Flowerdown Bridge	BY	4
High St.	BZ	7
Meadow St.	BZ	8
Oxford St.	BZ	9
Regent St.	BZ	10
Royal Parade	BZ	11
Sovereign Centre	BZ	
Upper Bristol Rd	BY	12
Upper Church Rd	AY	13
Walliscote Rd	BZ	14
Waterloo St.	BZ	15
Windwhistle Rd	AZ	16

WEYBRIDGE

Surrey – Pop. 29 837 – See Regional map n°7-C1
▶London 23 mi – Crawley 27 mi – Guildford 17 mi – Reading 33 mi
Michelin Road map 504-S29

 **Brooklands** 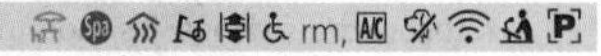

Brooklands Dr ✉ KT13 OSL – Southwest : 1.5 mi by B 374 and A 318 – ✆ (01932) 335 700 – www.brooklandshotelsurrey.com

120 rm – †£ 120/240 ††£ 120/240, ☕ £ 15.95 – 15 suites

Rest *1907* – Menu £ 35 – Carte £ 29/55 – *(closed dinner 25 and 26 December)*

Contemporary hotel with an art deco feel, situated next to Mercedes Benz World, on what was once Brooklands racetrack. Stylish, good-sized bedrooms. Great spa with outdoor hot tub. Chic, brasserie-style bar/restaurant serving well-presented modern dishes; head to the far end for a more intimate atmosphere.

WHALLEY

Lancashire – Pop. 3 230 – ✉ Blackburn – See Regional map n°**20-B2**
▶London 233 mi – Blackpool 32 mi – Burnley 12 mi – Manchester 28 mi
Michelin Road map 502-M22

Food by Breda Murphy

Abbots Ct, 41 Station Rd ✉ BB7 9RH – ☎ (01254) 823 446 – www.foodbybredamurphy.com – Closed 24 December-7 January, Sunday and Monday

Carte £ 23/33 – *(lunch only)*

Opposite the station, with a smart shop selling gadgets and books and a deli counter for takeaway meals, cakes and coffee. Bright, modern restaurant offers tasty, home-cooked lunches and charming service; open for dinner once a month.

at Mitton Northwest: 2.5 mi on B6246 ✉ Whalley

Three Fishes

Mitton Rd ✉ BB7 9PQ – ☎ (01254) 826 888 – www.thethreefishes.com – Closed 25 December

Carte £ 19/40

Spacious, modern country inn offering an extensive, seasonally changing menu which celebrates Lancastrian produce. Family-friendly, with a children's menu and a popular Sunday roast.

WHEPSTEAD → See Bury St Edmunds

Suffolk – Michelin Road map 504-W27

WHIMPLE

Devon – See Regional map n°**2-D2**
▶London 166 mi – Bristol 81 mi – Cardiff 112 mi – Plymouth 52 mi
Michelin Road map 503-J31

Woodhayes Country House without rest

Woodhayes Ln ✉ EX5 2TQ – ☎ (01404) 823 120 – www.woodhayescountryhouse.co.uk

6 rm – †£ 80/140 ††£ 80/180

18C yellow-washed house with mature grounds, in a peaceful village. Small comfy lounge, where tea and cake are served on arrival. Good-sized bedrooms with simple, neutral décor and modern facilities. Order breakfast the night before.

WHITBY

North Yorkshire – Pop. 13 213 – See Regional map n°**23-C1**
▶London 257 mi – Middlesbrough 31 mi – Scarborough 21 mi – York 45 mi
Michelin Road map 502-S20 – Michelin Green Guide GREAT BRITAIN

Raithwaite Hall

Sandsend Rd ✉ YO21 3ST – West : 2 mi on A 197 – ☎ (01947) 661 661 – www.raithwaiteestate.com

81 rm – †£ 135/200 ††£ 145/499 – 18 suites

Rest *Brace* – Menu £ 20/35 – Carte £ 25/51 – *(dinner only and Sunday lunch)*

Rest *Hunters* – ☎ (01947) 661 662 – Menu £ 30 – Carte £ 23/38

Modern resort hotel in 80 acres of delightful parkland, complete with a carp lake. Bedrooms are stylish and well-equipped; some have small terraces and some are duplex suites. Brace serves modern menus of fine local produce, while informal Hunters offers brasserie-style dishes. Kick-back in the smart spa.

Bagdale Hall

1 Bagdale ✉ YO21 1QL – ☎ (01947) 602 958 – www.bagdale.co.uk

16 rm – †£ 65/150 ††£ 70/250

Rest – Menu £ 21 – Carte £ 24/45 – *(closed Sunday) (dinner only)*

Charming Tudor manor house built in 1516, featuring carved wood fireplaces, mullioned windows and antique furnishings. Period bedrooms – some with four-posters – and smart bathrooms; more modern rooms in a rear wing. Spacious dining room with 19C Delft tiles from Holland and a traditional menu.

ENGLAND

Dillons of Whitby without rest

14 Chubb Hill Rd ✉ YO21 1JU – ✆ (01947) 600 290 – www.dillonsofwhitby.co.uk
5 rm – †£ 70/85 ††£ 75/120
Charming Victorian townhouse built for a sea captain, set opposite the beautiful Pannett Park. Immaculately kept bedrooms are individually themed and feature Egyptian cotton linens. Extensive breakfasts are something of an event.

Green's

13 Bridge St ✉ YO22 4BG – ✆ (01947) 600 284 – www.greensofwhitby.com – Closed 25-26 December and 1 January
Menu £ 10 (weekday lunch) – Carte £ 23/41 – *(booking essential)*
Established eatery near the quay. Lively bistro atmosphere downstairs and a more formal room above. Menus feature grills and local seafood: blackboards name the skipper and his daily catch; the mussels are particularly good.

at Sandsend Northwest: 3 mi on A174✉ Whitby

Estbek House with rm

East Row ✉ YO21 3SU – ✆ (01947) 893 424 – www.estbekhouse.co.uk – Closed January-9 February
5 rm – †£ 90/165 ††£ 100/200 Carte £ 35/60 – *(dinner only)*
Personally run Regency house close to the beach, with a lovely front terrace and elegant dining room. Basement bar overlooks the kitchens and doubles as a breakfast room. Menus offer unfussy dishes of sustainable wild fish from local waters. Smart bedrooms come with stylish bathrooms.

at Goldsborough Northwest: 6 mi by A174

Fox & Hounds

✉ YO21 3RX – ✆ (01947) 893 372 – www.foxandhoundsgoldsborough.co.uk – Closed Christmas and Sunday-Tuesday
Carte £ 31/49 – *(dinner only)*
Former village pub with a homely, cottagey style, set in tiny coastal hamlet. Constantly evolving menu features local produce and unfussy cooking, with an emphasis on fresh fish and seafood.

WHITEHAVEN

Cumbria – Pop. 23 986 – See Regional map n°**21**-A2
London 332 mi – Carlisle 39 mi – Keswick 28 mi – Penrith 47 mi
Michelin Road map 502-J20

Zest

Low Rd ✉ CA28 9HS – South : 0.5 mi on B 5345 (St Bees) – ✆ (01946) 692 848 – www.zestwhitehaven.com – Closed 25 December, 1 January and Sunday-Tuesday
Carte £ 20/36 – *(dinner only)*
An unassuming exterior conceals a stylish red-hued room with spotted chairs, stripy booths and a lively atmosphere. The extensive modern menu has an Asian edge and they are known for their excellent selection of Cumbrian steaks.

WHITEWELL

Lancashire – Pop. 5 617 – ✉ Clitheroe – See Regional map n°**20**-B2
London 281 mi – Lancaster 31 mi – Leeds 55 mi – Manchester 41 mi
Michelin Road map 502-M22

Inn at Whitewell with rm

rest,

Forest of Bowland ✉ BB7 3AT – ✆ (01200) 448 222 – www.innatwhitewell.com
23 rm – †£ 90/174 ††£ 125/248 Carte £ 28/42
14C creeper-clad inn, high on the banks of the River Hodder, with stunning valley views. Characterful bar and more formal restaurant. Classic menus of regionally inspired dishes. Spacious bedrooms; some traditional in style, with four-posters and antique baths.

ENGLAND

WHITSTABLE

Kent – Pop. 32 100 – See Regional map n°**9-C1**
London 68 mi – Dover 24 mi – Maidstone 37 mi – Margate 12 mi
Michelin Road map 504-X29

XX **East Coast Dining Room**

101 Tankerton Rd ✉ CT5 2AJ – East : 1 mi on B 2205 – ☎ (01227) 281 180 – www.eastcoastdiningroom.co.uk – Closed 1-20 January, Sunday dinner, Monday and Tuesday

Menu £ 13 (weekday lunch) – Carte £ 29/36

Find a spot on the terrace or head inside, where you'll find reupholstered chairs from the 1960s and 70s, along with pictures of designer chairs. Concise, modern British menus offer fresh, flavoursome dishes; fish is a strength.

X **JoJo's**

2 Herne Bay Rd ✉ CT5 2LQ – East : 1.75 mi by B 2205 – ☎ (01227) 274 591 – www.jojosrestaurant.co.uk – Closed Sunday dinner, Monday, Tuesday and lunch Wednesday

Carte £ 12/33

Unusually converted from a supermarket, this buzzy coffee shop, deli and restaurant offers good views over the Thames Estuary. The self-taught chef offers a large menu of Mediterranean and meze-style dishes and sharing boards.

X **Whitstable Oyster Company**

Royal Native Oyster Stores, Horsebridge ✉ CT5 1BU – ☎ (01227) 276 856 – www.whitstableoystercompany.com – Closed 25-26 December and lunch Monday-Thursday November-January

Carte £ 29/50 – *(booking essential)*

An old seafront oyster warehouse with a rough, rustic interior and a great informal atmosphere. Blackboards list simply prepared seafood dishes; from Sept-Dec try oysters from their own beds – the staircase leads to the seedling pool.

Pearson's Arms

The Horsebridge, Sea Wall ✉ CT5 1BT – ☎ (01227) 773 133 – www.pearsonsarmsbyrichardphillips.co.uk – Closed dinner Sunday, Monday and Tuesday

Menu £ 13 (weekday lunch) – Carte £ 19/37

Characterful refurbished pub in a great spot, with the Thames Estuary stretched out in front. Busy ground floor bar for nibbles like jellied eels; top floor dining room serves reassuringly familiar dishes, with Kentish produce to the fore.

at Seasalter Southwest: 2 mi by B2205 ✉ Whitstable

The Sportsman (Steve Harris)

Faversham Rd ✉ CT5 4BP – Southwest : 2 mi following coast rd – ☎ (01227) 273 370 – www.thesportsmanseasalter.co.uk – Closed 25-26 December, Sunday dinner and Monday

Menu £ 45/65 – Carte £ 35/45 – *(booking advisable)*

An unassuming-looking pub serving top class food: dishes feature just four or five complementary ingredients and are prepared with precision; flavours are extremely well-judged and presentation is original. The full tasting menu must be booked in advance; the 5 course option can be ordered on arrival.

→ Grilled slip sole and seaweed butter. Braised turbot with crab bisque. Lemon tart with meringue ice cream.

WHITTLESFORD

Cambridgeshire – See Regional map n°**14-B3**
London 50 mi – Cambridge 11 mi – Peterborough 46 mi
Michelin Road map 504-U27

XX **Tickell Arms**

1 North Rd ✉ CB22 4NZ – ☎ (01223) 833 025 – www.cambscuisine.com

Menu £ 19 (weekday lunch) – Carte £ 24/41

17C former pub named after a notorious, self-made squire – whose coat of arms still adorns the walls. Sit in the open-fired bar, rustic dining room or airy conservatory. Seasonal British and European cooking; good value midweek lunches.

ENGLAND

WICKHAM

Hampshire – Pop. 1 915 – See Regional map n°**6**-**B2**

London 74 mi – Portsmouth 12 mi – Southampton 11 mi – Winchester 16 mi

Michelin Road map 503-Q31 and 504-Q31

Old House

The Square ✉ PO17 5JG – ✆ (01329) 835 870 – www.oldhousehotel.co.uk – Closed 19-20 May

12 rm – £ 83 £ 110/190

Rest – Menu £ 17 (weekday lunch) – Carte £ 29/90 – *(closed Sunday dinner)*

Lovely creeper-clad Queen Anne townhouse, built in 1707. Bedrooms are characterful; some have original fireplaces and all have modern furnishings – with their tiled floors, those in the garden have a slightly Mediterranean feel. The small restaurant and airy conservatory offer modern takes on classic dishes.

WIGHT (Isle of)

Isle of Wight – Pop. 138 500 – See Regional map n°**6**-**A/B 3**

Michelin Road map 503-P/Q31 and 504 – Michelin Green Guide GREAT BRITAIN

Bonchurch

Pond Café

✉ PO38 1RG – ✆ (01983) 855 666 – www.thehambrough.com/the-pond-cafe – Closed Tuesday

Menu £ 18/22 – Carte £ 24/34 – *(booking advisable)*

Intimate neighbourhood eatery with an attractive terrace overlooking a duck pond. Have a cocktail in the bar before heading to the bistro-style restaurant. Italian-influenced menus change with the seasons and rely on island produce.

Godshill

Taverners

High St ✉ PO38 3HZ – ✆ (01983) 840 707 – www.thetavernersgodshill.co.uk – Closed first 3 weeks January

Carte £ 19/26

Passionately run roadside pub featuring its own deli selling homemade produce including bread, sauces and pies. Menus offer a mix of traditional and more adventurous dishes and use seasonal, local island ingredients.

Gurnard

Little Gloster with rm

31 Marsh Rd ✉ PO31 8JQ – ✆ (01983) 298 776 – www.thelittlegloster.com – Closed 1 January-early February

3 rm – £ 100/115 £ 145/165

Menu £ 24 (weekday lunch) – Carte £ 27/43 – *(closed Tuesday in low season, Sunday dinner and Monday)*

Set in a great spot among the beach huts, with lovely views over The Solent. Have a cocktail on the terrace beside the croquet lawn or head inside where you can sit at the large table looking into the kitchen or in the relaxed, shabby chic dining room. Unfussy, flavoursome cooking uses island produce. Bedrooms have a fresh nautical theme and come with Nespresso machines.

St Helens

Dans Kitchen

Lower Green Rd ✉ PO33 1TS – ✆ (01983) 872 303 – www.danskitcheniow.co.uk – Closed 3 weeks January, 1 week June, 1 week October, Sunday, Monday and Tuesday lunch

Menu £ 14 (lunch) – Carte £ 26/42

Old corner shop in a lovely location overlooking the village green. Simple wood furnishings, scatter cushions and nautical pictures feature. Traditional, hearty dishes showcase island produce; blackboard specials include the daily catch.

Seaview

Priory Bay

Priory Dr ✉ PO34 5BU – Southeast : 1.5 mi by B 3330 – ☎ (01983) 613 146 – www.priorybay.co.uk
20 rm – ♦£ 90/225 ♦♦£ 160/300 – 2 suites
Rest *Island Room* – Menu £ 50 – *(closed Sunday-Tuesday) (dinner only)*
Rest *Priory Oyster* – Menu £ 20 (lunch) – Carte £ 23/49
Peacefully located medieval priory with a romantic, shabby-chic interior and a relaxed vibe; wander down the woodland path and you arrive at their private beach. Bedrooms have good facilities and range in style from classical country house to nautical. The formal 'Island Room' boasts impressive 1810 murals, while bistro-style 'Priory Oyster' opens onto a terrace.

Seaview

High St ✉ PO34 5EX – ☎ (01983) 612 711 – www.seaviewhotel.co.uk – Closed 24-27 December
28 rm – ♦£ 105/160 ♦♦£ 135/190 – 3 suites
Rest *The Restaurant and Sunshine Room* – Menu £ 15 (dinner) – Carte £ 26/39 – *(dinner only and lunch in summer) (booking essential)*
Long-standing, bay-windowed hotel covered in foliage; its interesting nautical-themed interior filled with paintings and model ships. Comfortable bedrooms come in various styles; some are in annexes. There's a choice of two bars and two dining rooms where local fish features – the 'crab ramekin' is a hit.

Shalfleet

New Inn

Mill Rd ✉ PO30 4NS – ☎ (01983) 531 314 – www.thenew-inn.co.uk
Carte £ 17/39
Characterful pub on the main Newport to Yarmouth road, with inglenook fireplaces, slate floors and simple, scrubbed wood tables. Proper pub dishes are proudly made with island produce; lots of locally caught fish and seafood.

Shanklin

Newport 9 mi

Rylstone Manor

Rylstone Gdns ✉ PO37 6RG – ☎ (01983) 862 806 – www.rylstone-manor.co.uk – Closed 28 November-10 February
9 rm – ♦£ 73/110 ♦♦£ 135/165 **Rest** – Menu £ 33 – *(dinner only)*
This attractive part-Victorian house sits in the historic gardens and was originally a gift from the Queen to one of her physicians. The classical interior has a warm, cosy feel and combines antique furnishings with modern facilities. Carefully prepared dishes are served in the formally laid dining room.

Foxhills without rest

30 Victoria Ave ✉ PO37 6LS – ☎ (01983) 862 329 – www.foxhillsofshanklin.co.uk
8 rm – ♦£ 75/98 ♦♦£ 98
Large, honey-stone house on a tree-lined avenue into town, with a spacious Victorian-style lounge, a bright modern breakfast room and immaculately kept contemporary bedrooms. They also have a jacuzzi and a beauty treatment room.

Ventnor

Newport 10 mi

Royal

Belgrave Rd ✉ PO38 1JJ – ☎ (01983) 852 186 – www.royalhoteliow.co.uk – Closed 2 weeks January
53 rm – ♦£ 110/125 ♦♦£ 185/205
Rest – Menu £ 40 – *(closed Sunday lunch July-September) (dinner only and Sunday lunch)*
A sympathetically restored classic Victorian house with mature lawned gardens and a heated outdoor pool. The interior mixes bygone elegance with hints of modernity. Traditionally styled bedrooms have good facilities and some offer lovely sea views. A modern menu is served in the formal dining room.

Hillside 

✉ *PO38 1DR – ✆ (01983) 852 271 – www.hillsideventnor.co.uk*
12 rm – 🚹£ 80 🚹🚹£ 160
Rest – Carte £ 25/36 – *(closed Sunday) (dinner only) (booking essential)*
Set high above the town, this wonderful thatched Georgian house has a beautiful terrace and lovely sea views. The Danish owner has fused period furnishings with clean-lined Scandinavian styling, and displays over 350 pieces of CoBrA and Scandinavian art. Everything is immaculate and the linens are top quality. Frequently changing menus use local and garden produce.

Hambrough with rm — rest,

Hambrough Rd ✉ PO38 1SQ – ✆ (01983) 856 333 – www.thehambrough.com – Closed 3 weeks January, 2 weeks November, Sunday dinner, Monday and Tuesday lunch
7 rm – 🚹£ 150/250 🚹🚹£ 150/250
Menu £ 29/45 – Carte £ 39/48 – *(booking essential)*
Striking clifftop villa with a stylish dining room offering glorious coastal views; the most southern British sunsets can be admired from here. Top island ingredients feature in refined modern dishes, and service is polite and knowledgeable. Chic bedrooms come with good quality linens and espresso machines.

Yarmouth

Newport 10 mi

George — rm, rest,

Quay St ✉ PO41 0PE – ✆ (01983) 760 331 – www.thegeorge.co.uk
19 rm – 🚹£ 99/138 🚹🚹£ 120/288 – 1 suite
Rest *Isla's Conservatory* – see restaurant listing
Rest *Isla's* – Menu £ 70 – *(closed Sunday and Monday) (dinner only)*
Smart 17C townhouse that blends subtle modern touches with characterful period features. Bedrooms vary in shape and style: one has a large wet room and opens onto the garden; another has a sizeable balcony and excellent Solent views. Eat in the cool, elegant restaurant or modern conservatory.

Isla's Conservatory – George Hotel

Quay St ✉ PO41 0PE – ✆ (01983) 760 331 – www.thegeorge.co.uk
Carte £ 33/60
Hidden at the back of the George hotel is this modern conservatory with a lovely garden leading down to the water's edge. Flexible brasserie-style menus offer tasty nibbles and a choice of dish size; ingredients are local and organic.

Wootton Bridge

Lakeside Park

High St. ✉ PO33 4LJ – ✆ (01983) 882 266 – www.lakesideparkhotel.com
44 rm – 🚹£ 120/165 🚹🚹£ 130/175
Rest *Brasserie* – Menu £ 16 (lunch) – Carte £ 27/44
Unassuming, purpose-built hotel with a bright modern interior and a smart spa offering health and beauty treatments. Some of the stylish, well-equipped bedrooms have patios overlooking the lake. The airy multi-level brasserie and bar-lounge has a large decked terrace and lovely water views.

WIGHTON → See Wells-Next-The-Sea

Norfolk – Michelin Road map 504-W25

WILLIAN

Hertfordshire – Pop. 326 – See Regional map n°**12**-B2
London 38 mi – Croydon 48 mi – Barnet 24 mi – Ealing 37 mi
Michelin Road map 504-T28

Fox

✉ *SG6 2AE – ✆ (01462) 480 233 – www.foxatwillian.co.uk*
Carte £ 23/37
Set right in the heart of the village, a bright, airy pub that's always bustling. Dishes are modern with some Asian influences and there's a good choice of seafood and game in season; if you just can't decide, try 'The Fox Slate' for two.

WILMINGTON

Kent – See Regional map n°**8-B1**

London 17 mi – Maidstone 24 mi – Royal Tunbridge Wells 28 mi

Michelin Road map 504-U29

Rowhill Grange
rm, rest,

DA2 7QH Southwest : 2 mi on Hextable rd (B 258) – (01322) 615 136 – www.rowhillgrange.com

38 rm – £ 99/190 £ 109/450, £ 15 – 1 suite

Rest *RG'S Grill* – Menu £ 18 (weekday lunch) – Carte dinner £ 32/50

Early 19C house in 15 acres of pretty gardens, with smart modern bedrooms in dark, bold hues. The fantastic spa has 9 treatment rooms, a large gym and a superb swimming pool, along with a separate infinity pool with a waterfall. RG's Grill serves fresh seasonal dishes – try the mixed grill.

WIMBORNE MINSTER

Dorset – Pop. 15 174 – See Regional map n°**4-C3**

London 112 mi – Bournemouth 10 mi – Dorchester 23 mi – Salisbury 27 mi

Michelin Road map 503-O31 and 504 – Michelin Green Guide GREAT BRITAIN

Tickled Pig

26 West Borough BH21 1NF – (01202) 886 778 – www.thetickledpig.co.uk – Closed 25-26 December

Carte £ 24/43

Charmingly run shop conversion in the heart of a pretty market town. Modern, country style interior with a laid-back feel and a lovely rear terrace. Daily brown paper menus feature home-grown veg and home-reared pork; their mantra is 'taking food back to its roots'. Cooking is vibrant, flavourful and unfussy.

WINCHCOMBE

Gloucestershire – Pop. 4 538 – See Regional map n°**4-D1**

London 100 mi – Birmingham 43 mi – Gloucester 26 mi – Oxford 43 mi

Michelin Road map 503-O28 and 504

5 North St (Marcus Ashenford)

5 North St GL54 5LH – (01242) 604 566 – www.5northstreetrestaurant.co.uk – Closed 2 weeks January, 1 week August, Monday, Tuesday lunch and Sunday dinner

Menu £ 28/50

Long-standing neighbourhood restaurant that's very personally run by a husband and wife team. Characterful low-beamed ceilings and burgundy walls create an intimate feel. Menus change with the seasons and feature British ingredients in largely classical combinations. Dishes are precise, well-crafted and full of flavour.

→ Mackerel, crab & potato galette with pickled golden beetroot. Breast & stuffed leg of squab, truffle jus. Carrot & raisin cake, malted vanilla ice cream, tea syrup.

Wesley House with rm

High St GL54 5LJ – (01242) 602 366 – www.wesleyhouse.co.uk – Closed 26 December, Sunday dinner and Monday

5 rm – £ 65/80 £ 75/110 Menu £ 15/40 – Carte £ 27/55

Characterful 15C house with lots of beams, a cosy open-fired bar and a smart rear dining room and conservatory. Cooking is classical and flavourful, and service is relaxed and cheery; simpler meals are served in their next door wine bar. The cosy bedrooms have a comfortingly traditional feel.

Lion Inn with rm

North St GL54 5PS – (01242) 603 300 – www.thelionwinchcombe.co.uk

7 rm – £ 100/175 £ 100/175 Carte £ 22/40 – *(booking advisable)*

Located in the heart of this historic town, close to Sudeley Castle; a 15C Cotswold stone inn with chic, country style décor and a pleasant terrace and garden. Menus are guided by the latest seasonal produce available. Stylish, contemporary bedrooms come with biscuits and board games instead of TVs.

at Gretton Northwest: 2 mi by B4632 and B4078

Royal Oak 

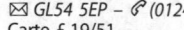

✉ *GL54 5EP* – ✆ *(01242) 604 999* – *www.royaloakgretton.co.uk*
Carte £ 19/51
In summer, head for the large garden, with its chickens, kids' play area, tennis court and passing steam trains; in winter, sit in one of two snug dining rooms or in the conservatory. Local produce features in honest, traditional dishes.

WINCHELSEA

East Sussex – See Regional map n°**9-C3**
London 64 mi – Brighton 46 mi – Folkestone 30 mi
Michelin Road map 504-W31 – Michelin Green Guide GREAT BRITAIN

Strand House

Tanyard's Ln. ✉ *TN36 4JT – East : 0.25 mi on A 259 –* ✆ *(01797) 226 276 – www.thestrandhouse.co.uk – Closed 1-14 January*
13 rm – †£ 55/165 ††£ 75/200
Rest – Menu £ 35 **s** – *(closed Sunday-Thursday) (dinner only)*
Part-timbered, low-beamed house dating from the 14 and 15C; mind your head! The cosy open-fired sitting room and bedrooms in the main house are hugely characterful – some have four-posters; three more spacious, modern rooms are found in the garden annexe. The elegant dining room offers simple home cooking.

ENGLAND

WINCHESTER

Hampshire – Pop. 45 184 – See Regional map n°**6-B2**
London 72 mi – Bristol 76 mi – Oxford 52 mi – Southampton 12 mi
Michelin Road map 503-P30 and 504 – Michelin Green Guide GREAT BRITAIN

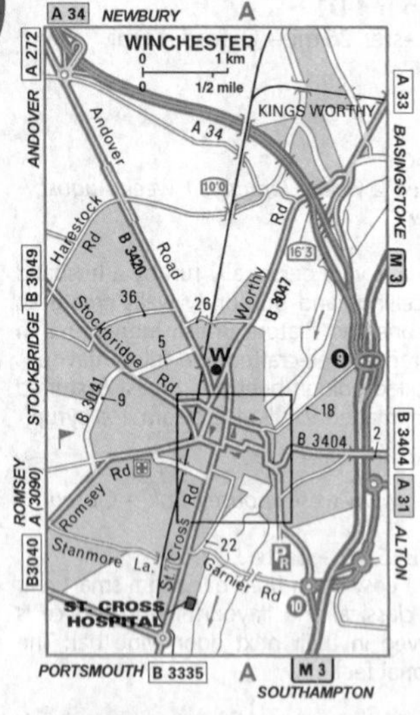

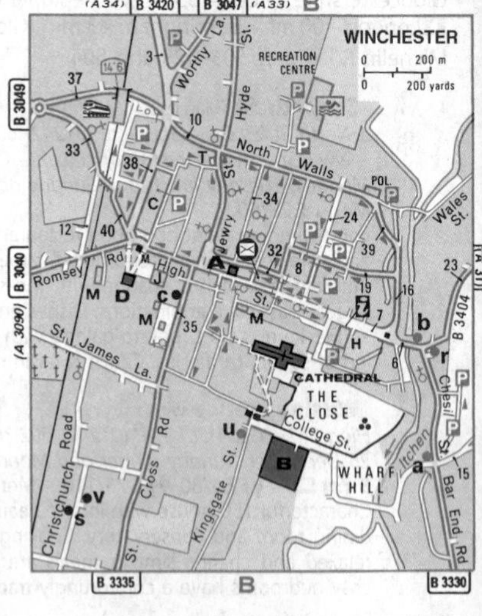

Alresford Rd	A 2	Eastgate St	B 16	St George's St	B 32
Andover Rd	B 3	Easton Lane	A 18	St Paul's Hill	B 33
Bereweeke Rd	A 5	East Hill	B 15	St Peter's St	B 34
Bridge St	B 6	Friarsgate	B 19	Southgate St	B 35
Broadway (The)	B 7	High St	B	Stockbridge Rd	B 37
Brooks Shopping Centre	B 8	Kingsgate Rd	A 22	Stoney Lane	A 36
Chilbolton Ave	A 9	Magdalen Hill	B 23	Sussex St	B 38
City Rd	B 10	Middle Brook St	B 24	Union St	B 39
Clifton Terrace	B 12	Park Rd	A 26	Upper High St	B 40

Winchester

Worthy Ln ✉ *SO23 7AB – (01962) 709 988* Town plan: A**w**
– www.thewinchesterhotel.co.uk
96 rm – £ 80/170 £ 80/170
Rest *Hutton's Brasserie* – Menu £ 18/25
Stylishly refurbished business hotel within walking distance of the town centre. Bright, fresh interior with modern bedrooms, a well-equipped gym and small pool. Open-plan foyer leads to the bar and restaurant, the latter serving a mix of grills and international favourites.

Hotel du Vin

rm, rest,

14 Southgate St ✉ *SO23 9EF – (01962) 841 414* Town plan: B**c**
– www.hotelduvin.com
24 rm – £ 119/190 £ 119/190, £ 15
Rest *Bistro* – Carte £ 25/48 – *(booking essential)*
Attractive Georgian house dating from 1715, and the first ever Hotel du Vin. Wine-themed bedrooms, split between the house and garden, are stylish and well-equipped; some have baths in the room. The characterful split-level bistro offers unfussy French cooking and – as hoped – an excellent wine selection.

Giffard House without rest

50 Christchurch Rd ✉ *SO23 9SU – (01962) 852 628* Town plan: B**s**
– www.giffardhotel.co.uk – Closed 24 December-2 January
13 rm – £ 76/128 £ 99/138
Imposing Victorian house in a quiet road. Spacious, classically styled guest areas include a comfy drawing room, modern bar and formal breakfast room. Individually styled bedrooms boast quality furnishings and good facilities.

29 Christchurch Road without rest

29 Christchurch Rd. ✉ *SO23 9SU – (01962) 868 661* Town plan: B**v**
– www.bedbreakfastwinchester.co.uk
3 rm – £ 65/80 £ 90/100
Spacious, Regency-style guesthouse with a pretty walled garden, set in an attractive residential area close to town. It's immaculately kept throughout, from the homely bedrooms to the fire-lit lounge and elegant breakfast room.

ENGLAND

XX

Chesil Rectory

Chesil St. ✉ *SO23 0HU – (01962) 851 555* Town plan: B**r**
– www.chesilrectory.co.uk – Closed 25-26 December and 1 January
Menu £ 20 (lunch and early dinner) – Carte £ 28/45
Timbered 15C house on edge of the town centre; its characterful interior taking in beamed ceilings and a large inglenook fireplace. Appealing menu of classically based dishes.

X

Black Rat

88 Chesil St. ✉ *SO23 0HX – (01962) 844 465* Town plan: B**a**
– www.theblackrat.co.uk – Closed 2 weeks December-January, 1 week spring and 1 week autumn
Menu £ 23 (lunch) – Carte £ 35/46 – *(dinner only and lunch Saturday-Sunday)*
This unassuming building conceals a quirky, bohemian-style interior with a small bar, a lounge and a two-roomed restaurant. Refined, classically based cooking displays Mediterranean influences and modern twists. The four wicker-roofed booths on the rear terrace are an unusual feature.
→ Grilled cuttlefish, jamon crust and crushed artichokes. Calf's sweetbread, beef heart bolognese and St. George's mushrooms. Burnt honey parfait, black olive praline, fennel ice cream.

Wykeham Arms with rm

75 Kingsgate St ✉ *SO23 9PE – (01962) 853 834* Town plan: B**u**
– www.wykehamarmswinchester.co.uk – Closed dinner 25 December
14 rm – £ 89/139 £ 139/190
Menu £ 18/22 (weekdays) – Carte £ 23/42 – *(booking essential)*
Red-brick pub decorated with all manner of bric-a-brac, including over a thousand tankards. Elaborate dishes showcase modern cooking techniques; for something a bit simpler, choose a dish from the 'home comforts' section. Individually styled bedrooms: some above the pub and some in an annexe over the road.

No.5 Bridge Street with rm

5 Bridge St ✉ SO23 0HN – ☎ (01962) 863 838 Town plan: B**b**
– www.no5bridgestreet.co.uk – Closed 25 December
6 rm – †£ 99/109 ††£ 110/124, ☕ £ 11 Carte £ 18/43
Roadside pub with a fashionable, modern feel; head to the dining room at the back for table service and a view of the open kitchen. Sections on the Mediterranean-influenced menu include 'small plates' and 'British charcuterie and cheese'. Simply styled, comfortable bedrooms – those at the front hear the traffic.

at Littleton Northwest: 2.5 mi by B3049 -(A)✉ Winchester

Running Horse Ⓝ with rm

88 Main Rd ✉ SO22 6QS – ☎ (01962) 880 218 – www.runninghorseinn.co.uk
– Closed dinner 25 December
9 rm ☕ – †£ 65/105 ††£ 75/105 Carte £ 22/36
A smart, grey-painted pub with a straw-roofed cabana at the front (heated, very cosy and it can be booked!) The menu is concise and constantly evolving and dishes are fuss-free and big on flavour. Service is pleasingly unpretentious and the simple bedrooms are arranged around the garden, motel-style.

at Sparsholt Northwest: 3.5 mi by B3049 -(A)✉ Winchester

Lainston House

Woodman Ln ✉ SO21 2LT – ☎ (01962) 776 088 – www.lainstonhouse.com
50 rm – †£ 190/225 ††£ 190/225, ☕ £ 21 – 3 suites
Rest *Avenue* – see restaurant listing
Impressive 17C William and Mary manor house with attractive gardens and a striking avenue of lime trees. Guest areas include a clubby wood-panelled bar and a modern drawing room; spacious bedrooms vary from classical to contemporary and boast good facilities. Relax over a game of tennis, croquet or boules.

Avenue – Lainston House Hotel

Woodman Ln ✉ SO21 2LT – ☎ (01962) 776 088 – www.lainstonhouse.com
Menu £ 33/55
Set within an impressive 17C country house and named after the mile-long avenue of lime trees it overlooks. Cooking is modern, innovative and complex, and features plenty of produce from the kitchen garden; opt for a tasting menu.

WINDERMERE

Cumbria – Pop. 5 243 – See Regional map n°**21**-A2
▶London 274 mi – Blackpool 55 mi – Carlisle 46 mi – Kendal 10 mi
Michelin Road map 502-L20 – Michelin Green Guide GREAT BRITAIN

Holbeck Ghyll

Holbeck Ln ✉ LA23 1LU – Northwest : 3.25 mi by A 591 – ☎ (015394) 32 375
– www.holbeckghyll.com – Closed first 2 weeks January
26 rm ☕ – †£ 150/250 ††£ 150/440 – 4 suites
Rest *Holbeck Ghyll* – see restaurant listing
Charming, stone-built Victorian hunting lodge, set in 15 acres and boasting stunning views over the lake and mountains. Traditional guest areas feature antiques and warming open fires. Well-equipped bedrooms range from classical to contemporary in style; Miss Potter, complete with a hot tub, is the best.

Miller Howe

Rayrigg Rd ✉ LA23 1EY – ☎ (015394) 42 536 Town plan: Y**s**
– www.millerhowe.com
15 rm ☕ – †£ 120/180 ††£ 200/260 – 2 suites
Rest – Menu £ 28/45 – Carte £ 32/53 – *(booking essential)*
Superbly situated Victorian villa in mature gardens, looking down the lake to the mountains. Arts and Crafts furnishings feature in the guest areas; take in the fabulous view from the conservatory. Comfy, classical bedrooms have a contemporary edge. Traditional menus are served in the split-level dining room.

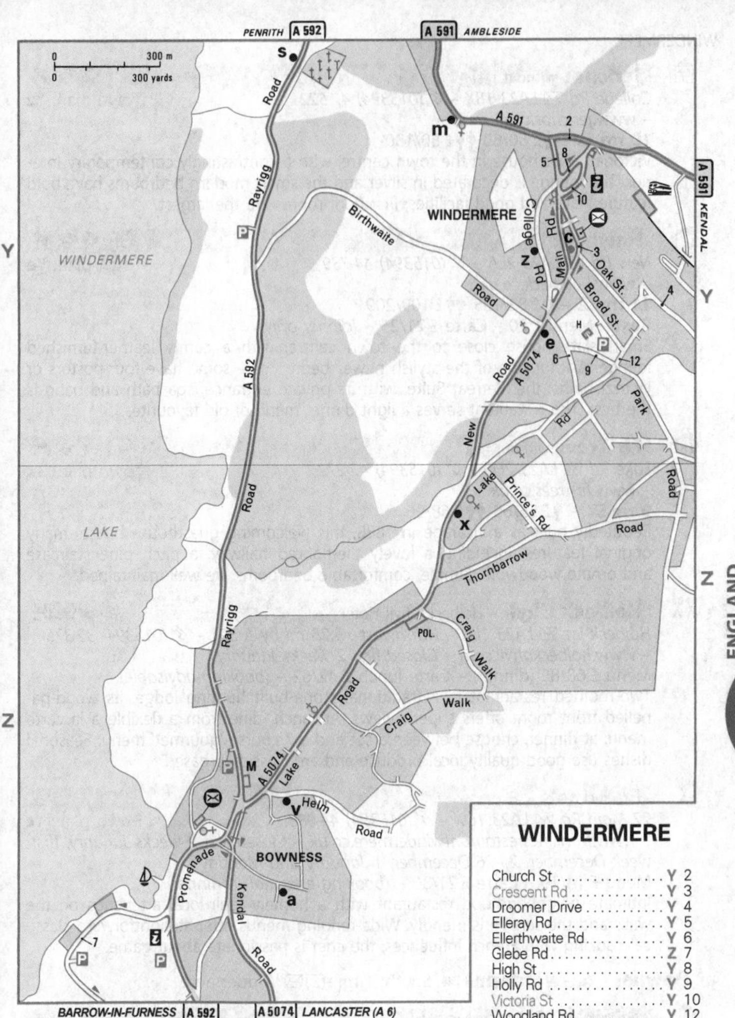

Windermere Suites without rest

New Rd ✉ *LA23 2LA – ✆ (015394) 47 672* Town plan: Y**e**
– www.windermeresuites.co.uk – Closed 24-25 December
8 rm ☕ – 🚹£ 180/295 🚹🚹£ 180/295
Spacious Edwardian house with a seductive interior. Funky, sexy bedrooms boast bold modern décor, iPod docks and walk-in wardrobes. Huge bathrooms feature TVs and colour-changing lights. Breakfast is served in your room.

Cedar Manor

Ambleside Rd ✉ *LA23 1AX – ✆ (015394) 43 192* Town plan: Y**m**
– www.cedarmanor.co.uk – Closed 4-22 January and 21-26 December
10 rm ☕ – 🚹£ 100/385 🚹🚹£ 125/435 **Rest** – Menu £ 40 – *(dinner only)*
Victorian house with ecclesiastical influences – built by a former minister, with a cedar tree in the garden. Contemporary country house bedrooms display locally made furniture; some have spa baths or views and the Coach House suite has a private terrace. Appealing menus of local produce.

Jerichos without rest

College Rd ✉ LA23 1BX – ✆ (015394) 42 522 Town plan: Y**z**
– www.jerichos.co.uk
10 rm – £ 50/60 £ 80/130
Victorian slate house in the town centre, with a contrastingly contemporary interior. The lounge is decorated in silver and the smart modern bedrooms have bold feature walls and good facilities; first floor rooms are the largest.

Howbeck

New Rd ✉ LA23 2LA – ✆ (015394) 44 739 Town plan: Y**e**
– www.howbeck.co.uk
11 rm – £ 82/105 £ 109/209
Rest – Menu £ 20 – Carte £ 21/25 – *(dinner only)*
Smart slate house close to the town centre, with a comfy leather-furnished lounge. Ask for one of the stylish newer bedrooms – some have four-posters or jacuzzi baths; the 'Retreat Suite' with its private entrance, spa bath and patio is the best. The restaurant serves a light dinner menu of old favourites.

Fir Trees without rest

Lake Rd ✉ LA23 2EQ – ✆ (015394) 42 272 Town plan: Z**x**
– www.fir-trees.co.uk
9 rm – £ 55/65 £ 68/96
Reputedly built as a vicarage in 1888, this welcoming guesthouse boasts many original features, including a lovely tile-floored hallway, a pitch pine staircase and ornate woodwork. Simple, comfortable bedrooms are well-maintained.

ENGLAND

Holbeck Ghyll – Holbeck Ghyll Hotel

Holbeck Ln ✉ LA23 1LU – Northwest : 3.25 mi by A 591 – ✆ (015394) 32 375
– www.holbeckghyll.com – Closed first 2 weeks January
Menu £ 68/85 (dinner) – Carte lunch £ 42/62 – *(booking advisable)*
Two-roomed restaurant in a traditional stone-built hunting lodge; its wood-panelled front room offers superb views. At lunch, dine from a flexible à la carte menu; at dinner, choose between a set and a 7 course 'gourmet' menu. Seasonal dishes use good quality local produce and are classically based.

Francine's

27 Main Rd ✉ LA23 1DX – ✆ (015394) 44 088 Town plan: Y**c**
– www.francinesrestaurantwindermere.co.uk – Closed last 2 weeks January, first week December, 25-26 December, 1 January and Monday
Menu £ 14/19 – Carte £ 21/36 – *(booking essential at dinner)*
Intimate neighbourhood restaurant with a homely feel; local art hangs on the walls and the service is friendly. Wide-ranging menus offer straightforward classical cooking with French influences; the chef is passionate about game.

at Bowness-on-Windermere South: 1 mi -(Z)✉ Windermere

Gilpin H. & Lake House

Crook Rd ✉ LA23 3NE – Southeast : 2.5 mi by A 5074 on B 5284 – ✆ (015394) 88 818 – www.thegilpin.co.uk
26 rm – £ 225/605 £ 335/605
Rest *Gilpin H. & Lake House* – see restaurant listing
Delightful country house hotel run by a charming, experienced family. Bedrooms range from contemporary country doubles to spacious garden suites with outdoor hot tubs. There are even more peaceful, luxurious suites a mile down the road beside a tarn – stay here for exclusive use of the smart spa.

Linthwaite House

Crook Rd ✉ LA23 3JA – South : 0.75 mi by A 5074 on B 5284 – ✆ (015394) 88 600 – www.linthwaite.com
30 rm – £ 95/530 £ 120/550
Rest *Linthwaite House* – see restaurant listing
Set in a peaceful spot overlooking the lake and fells, with stylish lounges and a funky bar with a fish tank in the wall. Smart bedrooms boast mood lighting, modern bathrooms and iPod docks; Room 31 has a telescope and a retractable window.

Lindeth Howe

Lindeth Dr. Longtail Hill ✉ LA23 3JF – South : 1.25 mi by A 5074 on B 5284 – ☎ (015394) 45 759 – www.lindeth-howe.co.uk – Closed 3-16 January
34 rm ☕ – 🚹£ 75/150 🚹🚹£ 140/190 – 2 suites
Rest *Dining Room* – Menu £ 13/47 – Carte £ 32/47
An attractive country house once bought by Beatrix Potter for her mother, with a clubby bar, a homely lounge and pleasant views from the drawing room. Bedrooms are traditional: the top floor rooms have the best views; the suites are more contemporary. The large, classical restaurant has menus to match.

Ryebeck (N)

Lyth Valley Rd ✉ LA23 3JP – South : 0.75 mi on A 5074 – ☎ (015394) 88 195 – www.ryebeck.com – Closed 1 week in January
26 rm – 🚹£ 69/199 🚹🚹£ 109/220
Rest – Menu £ 23/43 – *(dinner only and Sunday lunch)*
Have afternoon tea on the terrace, looking over the gardens and down to the famous lake. Some of the bright, airy bedrooms share the view and some come with patios or Juliet balconies. Kick-back in one of the cosy lounges then head to the dining room to sample fresh local meats and tasty Cumbrian produce.

Angel Inn

Helm Rd ✉ LA23 3BU – ☎ (015394) 44 080 Town plan: Z**v**
– www.theangelinnbowness.com – Closed 24-25 December
13 rm ☕ – 🚹£ 60/140 🚹🚹£ 70/180 **Rest** – Carte £ 22/43
A cosy creamwashed inn just off the main street, with a large open-fired lounge and comfortable, contemporary bedrooms – two are in an annexed 18C cottage with lake views. Dine on classic pub dishes or sharing plates in the welcoming bar or minimalistic dining room, or head for the terraced garden in summer.

Dome House without rest

Brantfell Rd ✉ LA23 3AE – ☎ (015394) 47 244 Town plan: Z**a**
– www.domehouselakedistrict.co.uk
5 rm ☕ – 🚹£ 145/290 🚹🚹£ 145/290
Futuristic-looking house with a grass-covered domed roof and superb lake views – the owner designed it himself and it was featured on 'Grand Designs'. Modern, minimalist bedrooms have balconies; one has a wooden bath in the room.

Fair Rigg without rest

Ferry View ✉ LA23 3JB – South : 0.5 mi on A 5074 – ☎ (015394) 43 941 – www.fairrigg.co.uk – Closed January-March
6 rm ☕ – 🚹£ 45/55 🚹🚹£ 60/90
Late 19C house run by cheery owners, set in a conservation area and affording distant lake and hill views. Spacious, immaculately kept bedrooms come with up-to-date facilities. Enjoy Cumbrian sausages and bacon at breakfast.

Gilpin H. & Lake House – Gilpin Hotel & Lake House

Crook Rd ✉ LA23 3NE – Southeast : 2.5 mi by A 5074 on B 5284 – ☎ (015394) 88 818 – www.thegilpin.co.uk
Menu £ 30/58 – Carte lunch £ 38/70 – *(booking essential)*
A series of intimate, individually styled dining rooms in a charming country house hotel; the Garden Room is perhaps the most pleasant. Start with an aperitif in the comfy lounge or the funky bar. Modern, very attractively presented dishes provide a fitting sense of occasion. Service is excellent.

Linthwaite House – Linthwaite House Hotel

Crook Rd ✉ LA23 3JA – South : 0.75 mi by A 5074 on B 5284 – ☎ (015394) 88 600 – www.linthwaite.com
Menu £ 20/62 – *(residents only Christmas and New Year)*
Contemporary restaurant in a traditional country house. Sit in the intimate Mirror Room with its romantic booths or in the airy, bay-windowed former billiard room. Daily menus showcase Lakeland produce; cooking is modern and flavoursome.

at Winster South: 4 mi on A5074 ✉ Windermere

Brown Horse Inn with rm

✉ *LA23 3NR On A 5074 – ✆ (015394) 43 443 – www.thebrownhorseinn.co.uk*
9 rm – †£ 55/100 ††£ 59/120 Carte £ 18/52
Shabby-chic coaching inn with a lovely split-level terrace. Seasonal menus feature unfussy, generous dishes and more adventurous specials. Much of the produce is from their fields out the back and they brew their own beers too. Bedrooms are a mix of classic and boutique styles; some have terraces.

WINDLESHAM

Surrey – Pop. 4 103 – See Regional map n°**7-C1**
London 40 mi – Reading 18 mi – Southampton 53 mi
Michelin Road map 504-S29

Brickmakers

Chertsey Rd ✉ GU20 6HT – East : 1 mi on B 386 – ✆ (01276) 472 267 – www.thebrickmakerswindlesham.co.uk
Carte £ 20/37
Beamed ceilings, wooden floors and open fires contribute to this 400 year old pub's charm and rusticity; its garden is the place to be in summer. Sandwiches, light bites and pub classics at lunch; more substantial dishes in the evening.

WINDSOR

Windsor and Maidenhead – Pop. 31 225 – See Regional map n°**11-D3**
London 28 mi – Reading 19 mi – Southampton 59 mi
Michelin Road map 504-S29 – Michelin Green Guide GREAT BRITAIN

ENGLAND

Macdonald Windsor rm, Town plan: Z**r**

23 High St. ✉ SL4 1LH – ✆ (01753) 483 100 – www.macdonald-hotels.co.uk/windsor
120 rm – †£ 145/265 ††£ 155/275, £ 18
Rest *Caleys* – Carte £ 18/46
Opened in 2010 in a former department store opposite the Guildhall. Pass by the attractive open-plan guest areas up to contemporary bedrooms with a high level of facilities and bold, masculine hues. Meeting rooms are small but state-of-the-art. The modern brasserie specialises in steaks from the Josper grill.

Sir Christopher Wren's House Town plan: Z**e**

Thames St ✉ SL4 1PX – ✆ (01753) 442 400 – www.sarova.com
99 rm – †£ 100/220 ††£ 120/400, £ 19 – 3 suites
Rest *Thames View* – Menu £ 26 **s** – Carte £ 28/47 **s**
Impressive house on the riverbank, built by Wren in 1676 as his family home. Characterful guest areas have high ceilings, panelled walls and bold modern furnishings. Some of the stylish bedrooms are beamed and some have balconies and river views. The modern restaurant has a lovely Thames outlook.

Royal Adelaide Town plan: Z**v**

46 Kings Rd ✉ SL4 2AG – ✆ (01753) 863 916 – www.theroyaladelaide.com
43 rm – †£ 69/115 ††£ 90/165 **Rest** – Menu £ 10/45 – Carte £ 25/55
Comprising three adjoining Georgian townhouses with a powder blue and white façade, set close to the 'Long Walk' and built for Queen Adelaide. It's bright and comfortable throughout; feel like royalty by choosing one of the four-poster bedrooms. The accessible brasserie menu also offers a few Moroccan dishes.

Christopher rm, rm, Town plan: Z**a**

110 High St, Eton ✉ SL4 6AN – ✆ (01753) 852 359 – www.thechristopher.co.uk
34 rm – †£ 99/148 ††£ 119/205, £ 14 **Rest** – Carte £ 18/32
18C brick-built coaching inn close to Eton College; cross the footbridge over the Thames to reach the castle. Contemporary bedrooms are spread about the main building and a mews; guest areas have an informal feel. The brightly coloured bistro offers international menus with subtle North African influences.

WINDSOR

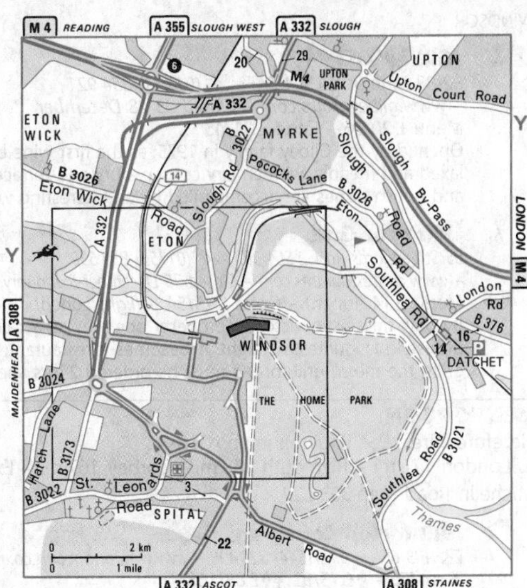

Bexley St . . . . Z 2
Bolton Rd . . . . Y 3
Castle Hill . . . . Z 4
Charles St. . . . . Z 5
Claremont Rd. . . . . Z 6
Clarence Crescent . . . . Z 7
Clewer Crescent Rd . . . . Z 8
Datchet Rd . . . . Z 9
Goswell Rd . . . . Z 10
Grove Rd . . . . Z 12
High St . . . . Z 13
High St DATCHET . . . . Y 14
Horton Rd . . . . Y 16
Keats Lane . . . . Z 17
King Edward Court
Centre . . . . Z
Peascod St. . . . . Z 19
Ragstone Rd . . . . Y 20
River St. . . . . Z 21
Sheet St Rd . . . . Y 22
Stovell Rd . . . . Z 23
Thames Ave. . . . . Z 24
Thames St . . . . Z 25
Trinity Pl. . . . . Z 27
Windsor Bridge . . . . Z 28
Windsor Rd . . . . Y 29

M 4 READING
A 355 SLOUGH WEST
A 332 SLOUGH
UPTON
UPTON PARK
M4
Upton Court Road
ETON WICK
A 332
MYRKE
B 3022
Slough
Slough By-Pass
Pocock's Lane
B 3026
Eton Wick
Slough Rd
Eton Road
LONDON
M 4
ETON
Southlea Rd
London Rd
B 376
DATCHET
WINDSOR
A 308
MAIDENHEAD
B 3024
THE HOME PARK
Hatch Lane
B 3173
B 3021
Southlea Road
B 3022
St. Leonards Road
SPITAL
Thames
Albert Road
2 km
1 mile
A 332 ASCOT
A 308 STAINES

A 332
Wick Road
B 3026
B 3022
ETON
ETON COLLEGE
THE HOME PARK
Windsor and Eton Relief Road
South Meadow Lane
High St.
Meadow Lane
King Edward VII Av.
RIVERSIDE
LEISURE CENTRE
Barry Avenue
Thames
CLEWER PARK
Mill Lane
CLEWER
Vansittart Road
CENTRAL
WINDSOR ROYAL STATION
CASTLE
Maidenhead Road
Arthur Rd
Oxford Rd
Parsonage Lane
KING EDWARD COURT CENTRE
Victoria St.
Sheet Street
Long Walk
Frogmore Drive
B 3024
Goslar Way
Alma Road
St. Leonards Road
Clarence Road
POL.
THE HOME PARK
CLEWER WITHIN
Alexandra Road
Frances Road
King's Road
FROGMORE
Osborne Rd
Springfield Road
Imperial Road
B 3173
Bolton Av.
The Long Walk
CENTRE
500 m
500 yards
A 308

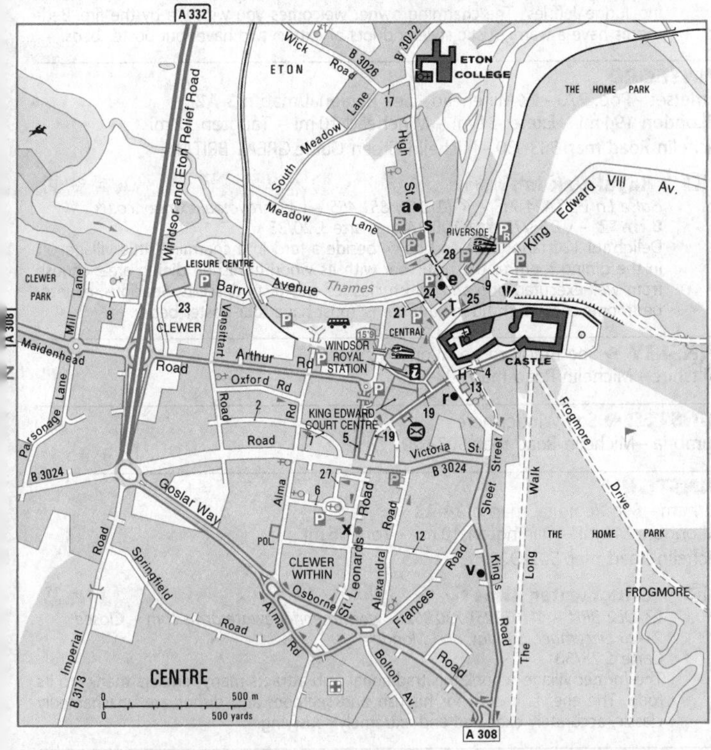

ENGLAND

X **Gilbey's** Ⓝ

82-83 High St ✉ SL4 6AF – ✆ (01753) 854 921 – www.gilbeygroup.com – Closed 23-28 December Town plan: Z**s**
Menu £ 20/26 – Carte £ 31/45
Opened by the Gilbey family in 1975, as the first wine bar outside London. It's relaxed and friendly, with an airy conservatory and terrace. Carefully cooked French and British dishes are accompanied by an interesting wine selection.

X **Windsor Grill**

65 St Leonards Rd ✉ SL4 3BX – ✆ (01753) 859 658 – www.awtrestaurants.com – Closed 25 December-5 January, Sunday and bank holidays Town plan: Z**x**
Menu £ 14 (lunch) – Carte £ 25/54 – *(light Lunch)*
By day, this rustic Victorian property operates as a café, offering light bites and pub-style favourites. At night, it becomes a restaurant, specialising in steaks and grills; the mixed grill for 3-4 must be ordered 24hrs ahead.

WINFORTON

Herefordshire – See Regional map n°**18**-A3
London 175 mi – Plymouth 188 mi – Torbay 167 mi – Exeter 151 mi
Michelin Road map 503-L27

Winforton Court without rest

✉ HR3 6EA – ✆ (01544) 328 498 – www.winfortoncourt.co.uk – Closed 23-27 December
3 rm – †£ 73/93 ††£ 88/108
Hugely characterful part-timbered house with 16C origins: once home to 'Hanging Judge Jeffries'. The charming owner welcomes you with tea by the fire. Bedrooms have a warm, rustic style and lots of extras; two have four-poster beds.

WINSFORD

Somerset – Pop. 270 – ✉ Minehead – See Regional map n°**3**-A2
London 194 mi – Exeter 31 mi – Minehead 10 mi – Taunton 32 mi
Michelin Road map 503-J30 – Michelin Green Guide GREAT BRITAIN

Royal Oak Inn with rm

Halse Ln ✉ TA24 7JE – ✆ (01643) 851 455 – www.royaloakexmoor.co.uk
8 rm – †£ 55/75 ††£ 100/140 Carte £ 20/33
Delightful 12C farmhouse and dairy, beside a ford in a charming little village. Sit in the dining room or the rustic bar with its wood-furnished dining area; choose from well-executed pub and British classics and tasty desserts. Spacious, country bedrooms come with huge bathrooms; most have four-poster beds.

WINSLEY → See Bradford-on-Avon

Wiltshire – Michelin Road map 503-N29

WINSTER → See Windermere

Cumbria – Michelin Road map 502-L20

WINSTON

Durham – See Regional map n°**24**-A3
London 244 mi – Darlington 10 mi – York 56 mi
Michelin Road map 502-O20

Bridgewater Arms Ⓝ

✉ DL2 3RN – ✆ (01325) 730 302 – www.thebridgewaterarms.com – Closed 25-26 December, Sunday and Monday
Carte £ 25/50
The former village school, this traditional pub attracts many regulars thanks to its food. The chef is known for his fish and seafood, and dishes are unashamedly classic, accurately executed and extremely satisfying.

WINTERBOURNE STEEPLETON → See Dorchester

Dorset – Michelin Road map 503-M31 and 504

ENGLAND

WINTERINGHAM

North Lincolnshire – Pop. 1 000 – ✉ Scunthorpe – See Regional map n°**23**-C3
▶London 176 mi – Kingston-upon-Hull 16 mi – Sheffield 67 mi
Michelin Road map 502-S22

XXX **Winteringham Fields** with rm

1 Silver St ✉ DN15 9ND – ✆ (01724) 733 096 – www.winteringhamfields.co.uk – Closed 1 week April, 3 weeks August, 2 weeks December-January, Sunday and Monday
11 rm – †£ 115/155 ††£ 180/220
Menu £ 45/89 – *(bookings essential for non-residents)*
Characterful 16C house in a remote rural location, featuring an elegant dining room and several private rooms. The chef adopts a complex modern approach to cooking, offering a set price or tasting menu at lunch and a daily 'Menu Surprise' of up to 11 courses at dinner; many of the ingredients come from their smallholding. Comfy bedrooms are furnished with antiques.

WISWELL

Lancashire – See Regional map n°**20**-B2
▶London 232 mi – Liverpool 49 mi – Manchester 28 mi
Michelin Road map 502-M22

Freemasons

8 Vicarage Fold ✉ BB7 9DF – ✆ (01254) 822 218 – www.freemasonsatwiswell.com – Closed 2-14 January and Monday-Tuesday except bank holidays
Menu £ 24 (lunch and early dinner) – Carte £ 37/67
A delightful pub, hidden away on a narrow lane, with flagged floors, low beams and open fires downstairs, and elegant, antique-furnished, country house style dining rooms upstairs. The interesting menu features modern versions of traditional pub dishes and cooking is refined and skilful. Charming service.

WIVETON → See Blakeney

Norfolk

WOBURN

– Pop. 1 534 – ✉ Milton Keynes – See Regional map n°**12**-A2
▶London 49 mi – Bedford 13 mi – Luton 13 mi – Northampton 24 mi
Michelin Road map 504-S28 – Michelin Green Guide GREAT BRITAIN

Inn at Woburn rm, rest,

George St ✉ MK17 9PX – ✆ (01525) 290 441 – www.thewoburnhotel.co.uk
55 rm – †£ 115/145 ††£ 145/175 – 1 suite
Rest *Olivier's* – ✆ (01525) 292 292 – Carte £ 27/38
18C coaching inn, part of Woburn Estate with its abbey and 3000 acre park. Pleasant modern furnishings and interior décor. Tastefully decorated rooms: book a Cottage suite. Classic dishes in contemporary Olivier's.

XXX **Paris House** (Phil Fanning)

Woburn Park ✉ MK17 9QP – Southeast : 2.25 mi on A 4012 – ✆ (01525) 290 692 – www.parishouse.co.uk – Closed dinner 24 December-6 January and Sunday dinner-Tuesday
Menu £ 39/75 – *(booking essential)*
Striking black & white timbered house; built in Paris and reassembled in this charming location, where deer wander freely. 5, 7 and 10 course tasting menus feature classic recipes given an imaginative modern makeover; dishes are boldly flavoured and artistically presented. Service is slick and unobtrusive.
→ Marinated hamachi with braised red dulse, miso sorbet and olive oil pearls. Hogget meze, hummus, walnuts, iced beetroot and mint oil. Thai green curry with marinated pineapple, coriander crisp and coconut sorbet.

Birch

20 Newport Rd ✉ MK17 9HX – North : 0.5 mi on A 5130 – ✆ (01525) 290 295 – www.birchwoburn.com – Closed 25-26 December, 1 January and Sunday dinner

Menu £ 13 (weekday lunch) – Carte £ 24/38 – *(booking essential)*

Long-standing former pub with a traditional façade and more modern interior. With its wood-panelled walls, the glass-roofed restaurant has a New England feel. The large menu offers a range of European dishes, along with grills by the ounce.

WOBURN SANDS

Milton Keynes – Pop. 5 959 – See Regional map n°**11**-D1

London 53 mi – Leeds 150 mi – Sheffield 120 mi – Manchester 163 mi

Michelin Road map 504-S27

Purple Goose

61 High St ✉ MK17 8QY – ✆ (01908) 584 385 – www.thepurplegoose.co.uk – Closed 2 weeks January, Sunday dinner and Monday

Menu £ 20 (lunch) – Carte £ 28/39 – *(dinner only and lunch Thursday-Sunday) (booking advisable)*

Simple, family-run restaurant split over two floors, with white walls and purple detailing. Menus mix classical and modern dishes and change every 6 weeks; some unusual flavour combinations feature. Most wines are available by the glass.

WOKING

Surrey – Pop. 105 367 – See Regional map n°**7**-C1

London 31 mi – Croydon 25 mi – Barnet 44 mi – Ealing 26 mi

Michelin Road map 504-S30

ENGLAND

London House

134 High St, Old Woking ✉ GU22 9JN – Southeast : 2 mi by A 320 on A 247 – ✆ (01483) 750 610 – www.londonhouseoldwoking.co.uk – Closed 3-18 August, 1-8 January, Sunday and Monday

Menu £ 37 – *(dinner only) (booking advisable)*

Friendly neighbourhood restaurant in a 17C red-brick former post office, where oil lamps create an element of intimacy. The classically trained French chef offers well-presented, satisfying dishes with interesting modern touches.

Red Lion

High St ✉ GU21 4SS – Northwest : 1.5 mi by A 324 – ✆ (01483) 768 497 – www.redlionhorsell.co.uk – Closed 26 December

Carte £ 22/41 – *(booking advisable)*

Sit on a sofa in the open-fired bar or amongst Brooklands racing memorabilia in the rustic beamed dining room; or head out to the terrace and landscaped garden. Dishes range from pub classics to some more unusual combinations.

WOLD NEWTON

East Riding of Yorkshire – See Regional map n°**23**-D2

London 229 mi – Bridlington 25 mi – Scarborough 13 mi

Wold Cottage

✉ YO25 3HL South : 0.5 mi on Thwing rd – ✆ (01262) 470 696 – www.woldcottage.com

6 rm – £ 75/90 £ 100/120 **Rest** – Menu £ 28

Fine Georgian manor house and an extensive collection of outbuildings, in 300 acres of peaceful farmland. Personal items abound in the homely, tastefully furnished interior. Sizeable bedrooms boast luxurious soft furnishings and antiques; some have four-posters – the courtyard rooms are simpler. Formal communal dining. Hearty British dishes showcase garden produce.

WOLVERHAMPTON

Staffordshire – Pop. 210 319 – See Regional map n°**19**-C2

London 132 mi – Birmingham 15 mi

Michelin Road map 502-N26 and 503

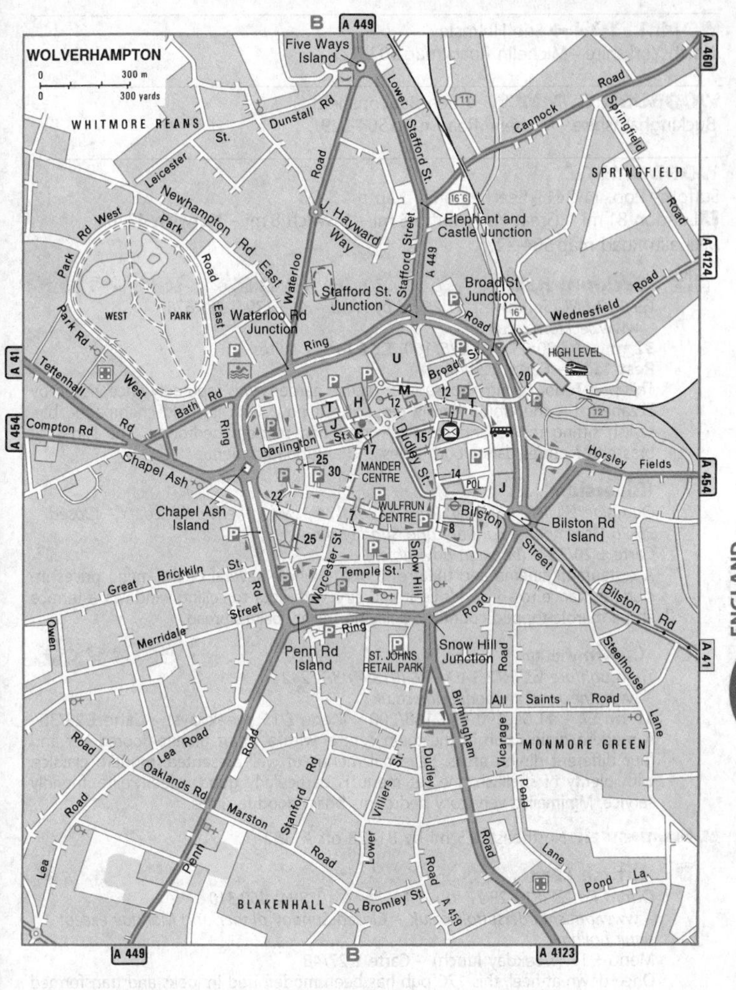

XX **Bilash** AC

No 2 Cheapside ✉ WV1 1TU – ☎ (01902) 427 762 Town plan: B**c**
– www.thebilash.co.uk – Closed 25-27 December and Sunday
Menu £ 10/45 – Carte £ 22/38
This smart contemporary restaurant is well-established and has several generations of the same family involved. Appealing, original menus offer South Indian and Bangladeshi dishes, crafted only from local and homemade produce.

WOMBLETON → See Helmsley

North Yorkshire – Michelin Road map 502-R21

WOOBURN COMMON → See Beaconsfield

Buckinghamshire – Michelin Road map 504-S29

WOODBRIDGE

Suffolk – Pop. 11 341 – See Regional map n°**15**-D3
London 81 mi – Great Yarmouth 45 mi – Ipswich 8 mi – Norwich 47 mi
Michelin Road map 504-X27

Seckford Hall

rm, rest,

IP13 6NU Southwest : 1.25 mi by A 12 – (01394) 385 678 – www.seckford.co.uk
32 rm – £ 90/95 £ 125/160, £ 14 – 7 suites
Rest *1530* – Carte £ 26/40
This part-Tudor country house in attractive gardens was reputedly once visited by Elizabeth I – she would hardly recognise it now, with its bold champagne bar, stylish sitting rooms and creatively designed modern bedrooms. The laid-back brasserie features dark wood tables and an updated menu.

Riverside

Quayside IP12 1BH – (01394) 382 174 – www.theriverside.co.uk – Closed 25-26 December, 1 January and Sunday dinner
Carte £ 20/33 – *(booking advisable)*
A restaurant, cinema and theatre in one – where several of the menu prices include entrance to a film. It's light and airy, with floor to ceiling windows, a terrace and a marble-topped counter displaying freshly baked bread.

ENGLAND

Crown with rm

Thoroughfare IP12 1AD – (01394) 384 242 – www.thecrownatwoodbridge.co.uk
10 rm – £ 90/190 £ 100/200 Menu £ 15 (weekdays) – Carte £ 23/38
A modern dining pub in the town centre, with a smart granite-floored bar and four different dining areas. Seasonal menus of well-presented, modern classics, with plenty of shellfish; the set menu is particularly good value. Polite, friendly service. Minimalist, very cosy bedrooms boast good facilities.

at Bromeswell Northeast: 2.5 mi by B1438 off A1152

British Larder

Orford Rd IP12 2PU – on A 1152 – (01394) 460 310 – www.britishlardersuffolk.co.uk – Closed Sunday dinner and Monday except bank holidays
Menu £ 17 (weekday lunch) – Carte £ 27/48
Once down-at-heel, this 17C pub has been modernised in looks and transformed into a beacon for local Suffolk produce, courtesy of its enthusiastic owners who have a passion for all things local. Skilled cooking uses ingredients thoughtfully; wine events and cookery classes are held regularly.

WOODSTOCK

Oxfordshire – Pop. 2 389 – See Regional map n°**10**-B2
London 65 mi – Gloucester 47 mi – Oxford 8 mi
Michelin Road map 503-P28 and 504 – Michelin Green Guide GREAT BRITAIN

Bear

rest,

Park St OX20 1SZ – (0844) 879 91 43 – www.macdonaldhotels.co.uk/bear
54 rm – £ 109/370 £ 109/390
Rest *Bear* – Menu £ 20/39
Characterful 13C coaching inn with exposed stone walls, charming oak beams, welcoming open fires and a cosy first floor lounge. Extremely comfy, well-equipped bedrooms are spread about the house and courtyard; pay the extra for an executive. The formal restaurant serves a menu of classically based dishes.

Feathers

Market St ✉ OX20 1SX – ✆ (01993) 812 291 – www.feathers.co.uk
21 rm – £ 199/319 £ 199/319 – 5 suites
Rest – Menu £ 20/55 – Carte £ 36/51 – *(booking essential)*
Stylish 17C house boasting individually styled bedrooms with boutique twists: some have feature walls; others, bold fabrics and modern art. The bar-lounge and walled terrace offer a casual menu and a fabulous gin selection. The formal dining room serves classically based dishes with a creative, original edge.

Kings Arms

19 Market St ✉ OX20 1SU – ✆ (01993) 813 636 – www.kingshotelwoodstock.co.uk
15 rm – £ 80 £ 150
Rest *Atrium* – Menu £ 17/30 – Carte £ 23/38
Keenly run, contemporary hotel in the heart of a busy market town. The immaculately kept interior shows a good eye for detail; the sleek, stylish bedrooms are named after English kings. Have a snack in the cosy open-fired bar or robust, flavoursome British dishes in the black and white tiled dining room.

WOOLER

Northumberland – Pop. 1 983 – See Regional map n°**24-A1**
London 330 mi – Alnwick 17 mi – Berwick-on-Tweed 17 mi
Michelin Road map 502-N17

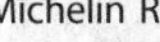

Firwood without rest

Middleton Hall ✉ NE71 6RD – South : 1.75 mi by Earle rd on Middleton Hall rd – ✆ (01668) 283 699 – www.firwoodhouse.co.uk – Closed 1 December-13 February
3 rm – £ 60 £ 90
Bay-windowed former hunting lodge in a peaceful setting with lovely countryside views. Beautiful original tiled hall; warm, comfy lounge. Spacious, simply furnished, period-style bedrooms. Friendly owners are a fount of local knowledge.

WOOLHOPE

Herefordshire – See Regional map n°**18-B3**
London 138 mi – Birmingham 70 mi

Butchers Arms

✉ HR1 4RF – ✆ (01432) 860 281 – www.butchersarmswoolhope.co.uk – Closed Sunday dinner in winter and Monday except bank holidays
Carte £ 23/35
Unfussy, classical cooking, with game in season, plenty of offal, tasty home-baked bread and hearty, reasonably priced dishes. The décor is traditional too, with a welcoming log fire, wattle walls and low-slung beams.

WOOTTON

Oxfordshire – See Regional map n°**10-B2**
London 61 mi – Birmingham 81 mi – Bristol 68 mi – Croydon 71 mi

Killingworth Castle

Glympton Rd ✉ OX20 1EJ – ✆ (01993) 811 401 – www.thekillingworthcastle.com
Carte £ 21/34
This 16C pub was rescued from dereliction by the Alexanders, who have set about returning it to its 'proper' pub status. Menus are interesting and provide good value – particularly the daily special – and ingredients are seasonal and locally sourced. You'll leave feeling suitably fortified.

WOOTTON BRIDGE

→ See Wight (Isle of)
– Michelin Road map 503-P31

WORCESTER

Worcestershire – Pop. 100 153 – See Regional map n°**18-B3**
London 124 mi – Birmingham 26 mi – Bristol 61 mi – Cardiff 74 mi
Michelin Road map 503-N27 and 504 – Michelin Green Guide GREAT BRITAIN

ENGLAND

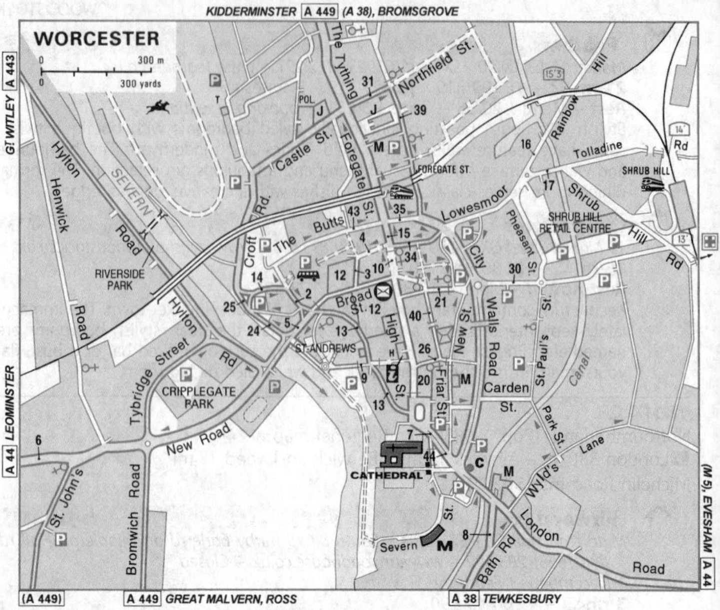

WORCESTER

KIDDERMINSTER A 449 (A 38), BROMSGROVE
G^T WITLEY A 443
A 44 LEOMINSTER
(M 5), EVESHAM A 44
(A 449) A 449 GREAT MALVERN, ROSS
A 38 TEWKESBURY

Street	No.	Street	No.	Street	No.
All Saints Rd	2	Deansway	13	Pump St	26
Angel Pl.	3	Dolday	14	St Martin's Gate	30
Angel St	4	Foregate (The)	15	St Mary's St	31
Bridge St	5	High St		St Nicholas St	34
Broad St		Lowesmoor Pl.	16	Sansome St	35
Bromyard Rd	6	Lowesmoor Terrace	17	Sansome Walk	39
College St	7	Lychgate Shopping Centre	20	Shambles (The)	40
Commandery Rd	8	Mealcheapen St	21	Shaw St	43
Copenhagen St	9	North Parade	24	Shrub Hill Retail Centre	
Cross (The)	10	North Quay	25	Sidbury	44
Crown Gate Centre	12				

Bindles

55 Sidbury ✉ WR1 2HU – ✆ (01905) 611 120 **Town plan:c**
– www.bindles.co.uk
Menu £ 16 (lunch and early dinner) – Carte £ 23/41
Modern, boldly decorated brasserie, set on a busy junction and run by a friendly team. The large menu offers everything from light bites and deli boards to pasta and steaks; the busy downstairs bar is well-known for its cocktails

WORKSOP

Nottinghamshire – Pop. 41 820 – See Regional map n°**16-B1**
London 160 mi – Sheffield 20 mi – Nottingham 37 mi – Rotherham 17 mi
Michelin Road map 502-Q24

Browns without rest

Old Orchard Cottage, Holbeck Ln, Holbeck. ✉ S80 3NF – Southwest : 4.5 mi by A 60 – ✆ (01909) 720 659 – www.brownsholbeck.co.uk
– Closed 24 December-2 January
3 rm – †£ 59/69 ††£ 85/95
Cross the ford to this keenly run, cosy cottage, which dates back to 1730. Lovely garden with mature fruit trees. Bedrooms are in the old cow shed; all have four-posters and open onto a large decked terrace. Appealing breakfast menu.

WORTH → See Deal

Kent – Michelin Road map 504-Y30

WREA GREEN

Lancashire – Pop. 1 373 – ✉ Kirkham – See Regional map n°**20-A2**
London 185 mi – Bristol 226 mi – Cardiff 246 mi – Plymouth 340 mi
Michelin Road map 502-L22

Spa
Ribby Hall Village, Ribby Rd ✉ PR4 2PR – East : 0.5 mi on B 5259 (Kirkham Rd) – ✆ (01772) 674 484 – www.ribbyhall.co.uk/spa-hotel
42 rm – †£ 198/400 ††£ 198/400 – 12 suites
Rest *Brasserie* – ✆ (01772) 674 477 – Carte £ 34/54 – *(light lunch)*
Holiday park and village with lodges, shops, bars, a swimming pool and an equestrian centre – all based around this superb spa hotel, which specialises in 'aqua thermal journeys'. Spacious, modern bedrooms; those on first floor have balconies. Light brasserie lunches and more formal evening meals.

WRINGTON

North Somerset – Pop. 1 918 – See Regional map n°**3-B2**
London 130 mi – Birmingham 99 mi – Bristol 12 mi – Leicester 130 mi
Michelin Road map 503-L29

The Ethicurean
Barley Wood Walled Garden, Long Ln ✉ BS40 5SA – East : 1.25 mi by School Rd on Redhill rd – ✆ (01934) 863 713 – www.theethicurean.com – Closed 2 weeks January and Monday
Carte £ 20/37 – *(lunch only and dinner Thursday-Saturday) (booking essential)*
Two converted glasshouses within a beautiful walled garden. It's rustic, informal and a break from the norm, and strives to be ethical and epicurean. The daily menu uses excellent ingredients – many, fresh from the garden; be sure to try the home-pressed apple juice. Service is friendly and knowledgeable.

WROTHAM

Kent – Pop. 1 767 – See Regional map n°**8-B1**
London 27 mi – Sevenoaks 9 mi – Maidstone 12 mi
Michelin Road map 504-U30

The Bull with rm
Bull Ln. ✉ TN15 7RF – ✆ (01732) 789 800 – www.thebullhotel.com
11 rm – †£ 69/139 ††£ 79/159 Carte £ 28/42
First impressions of this 14C inn might make you drive on past, but that would be a mistake. The interior is not the most characterful, but the food is mighty tasty: enjoy traditional British dishes as well as game in season, Spanish pork steak and USA hanger steaks. Bedrooms are smart and up-to-date.

WYMESWOLD

Leicestershire – See Regional map n°**16-B2**
London 120 mi – Birmingham 47 mi – Liverpool 109 mi – Leeds 91 mi
Michelin Road map 502-R25

hammer & pincers
5 East Rd ✉ LE12 6ST – ✆ (01509) 880 735 – www.hammerandpincers.co.uk – Closed 25 December, Sunday dinner and Monday
Menu £ 15/45 – Carte dinner £ 22/41
Formerly the village forge – the old water pump can still be seen at the back of the rustic restaurant. Classically based dishes in original combinations; the 7 course grazing menu is more modern and creative. Smooth, friendly service.

WYMONDHAM

Leicestershire – Pop. 600 – See Regional map n°**17-C2**
London 107 mi – Birmingham 70 mi – Liverpool 138 mi – Leeds 100 mi
Michelin Road map 504-R25

Berkeley Arms

59 Main St ✉ LE14 2AG – ✆ (01572) 787 587 – www.theberkeleyarms.co.uk – Closed first 2 weeks January, 2 weeks summer, Sunday dinner and Monday
Menu £ 15 (weekdays)/19 – Carte £ 21/44
Attractive 16C village pub run by an enthusiastic, experienced local couple. Turn left for the low-beamed bar or right for the slightly more formal dining room. Gutsy, satisfying dishes rely on local produce. Choose from daily changing bar snacks or a more adventurous à la carte. Relaxed, personable service.

WYNYARD

Stockton-on-Tees – See Regional map n°**24**-B3
London 250 mi – Leeds 72 mi – Bradford 74 mi – Sunderland 24 mi

Wynyard Hall

✉ TS22 5NF – ✆ (01740) 644 811 – www.wynyardhall.co.uk
25 rm – †£ 135/180 ††£ 135/240 – 2 suites
Rest *Wellington* – Menu £ 32/47
Impressive Georgian mansion built for the Marquis of Londonderry; its smart spa overlooks a lake. Traditional bedrooms in the main house and more modern lodges spread about the vast grounds. Classical guest areas feature stained glass, open fires and antiques. Formal dining room offers an ambitious menu.

YARM

Stockton-on-Tees – Pop. 19 184 – See Regional map n°**24**-B3
London 239 mi – Leeds 61 mi – Bradford 63 mi – Sunderland 34 mi
Michelin Road map 502-P20

ENGLAND

Judges Country House

Kirklevington Hall, Kirklevington ✉ TS15 9LW – South : 1.5 mi on A 67 – ✆ (01642) 789 000 – www.judgeshotel.co.uk
21 rm – †£ 99/200 ††£ 120/220, £ 19
Rest *Judges Country House* – see restaurant listing
Victorian former judge's house with wood panelling, antiques and ornaments, set in well-kept gardens. Traditional country house bedrooms offer a high level of facilities, bright modern bathrooms and extra touches such as fresh fruit, flowers and even a goldfish! Welcoming atmosphere; pleasant service.

Judges Country House – Judges Country House

Kirklevington Hall, Kirklevington ✉ TS15 9LW – South : 1.5 mi on A 67 – ✆ (01642) 789 000 – www.judgeshotel.co.uk
Menu £ 36/59
Formal, two-roomed restaurant on the ground floor of a traditional country house hotel; the conservatory extension has a lovely outlook over the lawns. Modern, well-prepared dishes are simple and straightforward, yet full of flavour.

Muse

104b High St ✉ TS15 9AU – ✆ (01642) 788 558 – www.museyarm.com – Closed 25 December, 1 January and Sunday dinner
Menu £ 14 (lunch and early dinner) – Carte £ 20/43 – *(booking advisable)*
Smart, modern continental café: bright and busy, with a pavement terrace in the summer. Extensive menu offers international brasserie dishes from lunchtime salads to pasta and grills; very good value set price menu of simpler dishes.

YARMOUTH → See Wight (Isle of)

Isle of Wight – Michelin Road map 503-P31 and 504

YATTENDON

West Berkshire – Pop. 288 – ✉ Newbury – See Regional map n°**10**-B3
London 54 mi – Bristol 68 mi – Newbury 9 mi
Michelin Road map 503-Q29 and 504

Royal Oak with rm

The Square ✉ RG18 0UF – ✆ (01635) 201 325 – www.royaloakyattendon.com
10 rm ☕ – †£ 90/130 ††£ 90/130
Menu £ 13 (weekday lunch) – Carte £ 25/42 – *(booking advisable)*
A red-brick pub bursting with country charm, in a picture postcard village close to the M4; you'll find a heavily beamed bar with a roaring fire at its hub. Menus offer honest British dishes and traditional puddings. Country house style bedrooms are named after guns; Heym is the most comfortable.

at Frilsham South: 1 mi by Frilsham rd on Bucklebury rd ✉ Yattendon

Pot Kiln

✉ RG18 0XX – ✆ (01635) 201 366 – www.potkiln.org – Closed 25 December and Tuesday
Menu £ 14 (weekday lunch) – Carte £ 28/35
A pretty pub in prime game country. Rustic, flavoursome British dishes arrive in unashamedly gutsy portions. The chef-owner stalks or gathers much of the produce himself and fish comes from local rivers.

YEOVIL

Somerset – Pop. 45 784 – See Regional map n°**3-B3**
London 130 mi – Bristol 42 mi – Cardiff 86 mi – Southampton 77 mi
Michelin Road map 503-M31 and 504 – Michelin Green Guide THE WEST COUNTRY

Lanes

West Coker ✉ BA22 9AJ – Southwest : 3 mi on A 30 – ✆ (01935) 862 555 – www.laneshotel.net
30 rm ☕ – †£ 90 ††£ 130/180 **Rest** – Menu £ 17 (lunch) – Carte £ 17/30
18C former rectory with modern extensions, set in pleasant walled grounds. Airy interior boasts modern meeting rooms, a laid-back lounge and a large bar. Relax in the smart leisure suite or on the croquet lawn. Stylish bedrooms come with up-to-date bathrooms. Modern bistro dishes in the striking dining room.

at Barwick South: 2 mi by A30 off A37 ✉ Yeovil

Little Barwick House with rm

rest,

✉ BA22 9TD – ✆ (01935) 423 902 – www.littlebarwickhouse.co.uk – Closed 26 December-27 January, dinner Sunday, Monday and lunch Tuesday
6 rm ☕ – †£ 75/95 ††£ 100/170 Menu £ 26/48 – *(booking essential)*
Attractive Georgian dower house on the outskirts of town, run by a hospitable husband and wife team. Relax on deep sofas before heading into the elegant dining room with its huge window and heavy drapes. Cooking is classical, satisfying and full of flavour – a carefully chosen wine list accompanies. Charming, comfortably furnished bedrooms, each with its own character.

ENGLAND

YORK

York – Pop. 198 900 – See Regional map n°**23-C2**
London 213 mi – Newcastle upon Tyne 90 mi – Scarborough 41 mi – Leeds 28 mi
Michelin Road map 502-Q22 – Michelin Green Guide GREAT BRITAIN

© Star Inn

ENGLAND

Hotels

 **Cedar Court Grand H. & Spa**  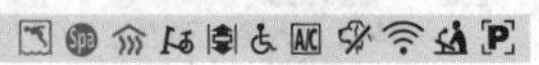

Station Rise ✉ *YO1 6HT* – ✆ *(01904) 380 038* – *www.cedarcourtgrand.co.uk* Town plan: CY**v**
107 rm – †£ 135/300 ††£ 135/300, ☕ £ 15 – 13 suites
Rest *Grill Room* – Carte £ 29/50
Rest *HQ* – Menu £ 55 – *(closed Sunday-Tuesday) (dinner only)*
Original features blend with contemporary décor in the former offices of the North Eastern Railway Company. Spacious, modern bedrooms are individually designed and well-equipped; and there's an impressive spa and leisure facility in the cellar. The Grill Room comes with views of the castle walls, while formal, intimate HQ serves more modern menus.

 **Middlethorpe Hall**

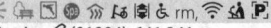

Bishopthorpe Rd ✉ *YO23 2GB – South : 1.75 mi* – ✆ *(01904) 641 241* – *www.middlethorpe.com*
29 rm ☕ – †£ 129/159 ††£ 199/279 – 9 suites
Rest – Menu £ 26 (weekday lunch) **s** – Carte £ 41/58 **s** – *(booking essential)*
A fine William and Mary House dating from 1699, set in 20 acres of impressive gardens and parkland. The elegant sitting room features French-style furnishings, oil paintings and fresh flower arrangements. Traditional, antique-furnished bedrooms are split between the house and courtyard. Classic cooking uses luxury ingredients, along with produce from the kitchen garden.

 **Grange** 

1 Clifton ✉ *YO30 6AA* – ✆ *(01904) 644 744* – *www.grangehotel.co.uk* Town plan: CX**u**
36 rm ☕ – †£ 89/360 ††£ 99/370 – 1 suite
Rest *Ivy* – see restaurant listing
Rest *Brasserie* – Carte £ 20/34 – *(dinner only)*
Well-run, classical, Grade II listed hotel; floral decorations, by the owner, and horse racing memorabilia abound. Choose between traditional bedrooms – some with four-posters – or more contemporary rooms with TVs in the bathrooms. Dine in the modern restaurant or informal brasserie.

 The symbol denotes a particularly interesting wine list.

YORK

Street	Grid	No.
Bishopgate St	CZ	3
Bishophill Senior	CZ	4
Blake St	CY	5
Campleshon Rd	AZ	7
Church St	DY	8
Clifford St	DY	10
Colliergate	DY	12
Coney St	CY	13
Cromwell Rd	CZ	15
Davygate	CY	16
Deangate	DY	18
Duncombe Pl	CY	20
Fawcett St	DZ	21
Fetter Lane	CY	22
Goodramgate	DY	25
High Ousegate	DY	26
High Petergate	CY	28
Knavesmire Rd	AZ	29
Leeman Rd	AY, CY	30
Lendal	CY	32
Lord Mayor's Walk	DX	33
Low Petergate	DY	35
Melrosegate	BY	36
Museum St	CY	39
Parliament St	DY	42
Pavement	DY	43
Peasholme Green	DY	45
Penley's Grove St	DX	46
Queen St	CZ	49
St Helen's Rd	AZ	50
St Leonard's Pl	CY	52
St Maurice's Rd	DXY	53
Shambles (The)	DY	54
Station Rd	CY	55
Stonebow (The)	DY	56
Stonegate	CY	58
Tower St	DZ	59
University Rd	BZ	60

ENGLAND

Hotel du Vin
rest,

89 The Mount ✉ YO24 1AX – ☎ (01904) 557 350 Town plan: CZ**a**
– www.hotelduvin.com
44 rm – †£ 105/225 ††£ 105/225, ☕ £ 15
Rest *Bistro* – ☎ (01904) 567 350 – Carte £ 23/43
Large Georgian manor house in a residential area just outside the city centre. Stylish interior with two snug lounges and a glass-roofed courtyard for afternoon tea. Well-equipped, contemporary bedrooms feature Nespresso machines. Chic champagne bar; imaginative wine list in the popular French bistro.

York Pavilion
45 Main St, Fulford ✉ YO10 4PJ – South : 1.5 mi on A 19 – ☎ (01904) 622 099 – www.yorkpavilionhotel.com
62 rm ☕ – †£ 79/140 ††£ 89/160
Rest *Langtons Brasserie* – Menu £ 16 (dinner) – Carte £ 22/36
This well-run Georgian property sits on the edge of the city and is a popular spot for weddings. Bedrooms in the main house are the most characterful; many of those in the extension have balconies. The French café style bar has a jazz theme and the informal brasserie serves steaks and grills.

Dean Court
rest,

Duncombe Pl ✉ YO1 7EF – ☎ (01904) 625 082 Town plan: CY**c**
– www.deancourt-york.co.uk
37 rm ☕ – †£ 85/150 ††£ 99/250
Rest *D.C.H* – Carte £ 28/44 – *(dinner only and lunch Saturday-Sunday)*
Built in 1865 next to York Minster, to house the visiting clerics. Bedrooms mix modern and classical styles; the smartest also have the best views. Guest areas include a contemporary lounge-bar serving all-day snacks and a restaurant with an ambitious modern menu; the rib of beef for two is popular.

ENGLAND

Hazelwood without rest
24-25 Portland St ✉ Y031 7EH – ☎ (01904) 626 548 Town plan: CX**c**
– www.thehazelwoodyork.com – Restricted opening in January
12 rm ☕ – †£ 75/125 ††£ 85/135
A pair of Victorian townhouses by the ancient city walls, in the Gillygate conservation area. It has a cosy basement lounge, a spacious Shaker-style breakfast room and well-kept, traditional bedrooms – some with four-poster beds.

Restaurants

Star Inn The City
Lendal Engine House, Museum St ✉ YO1 7DR Town plan: CY**s**
– ☎ (01904) 619 208 – www.starinnthecity.co.uk
Menu £ 22 (weekday lunch) – Carte £ 25/53
Busy, buzzy, all-day brasserie in an old brick engine house in Museum Gardens, affording views over the river. Well-judged dishes showcase top Yorkshire produce and are modern yet gutsy. The chargrilled meats are a highlight.

Ivy – Grange Hotel
1 Clifton ✉ YO30 6AA – ☎ (01904) 644 744 Town plan: CX**u**
– www.grangehotel.co.uk
Menu £ 15 (lunch) – Carte £ 29/39
Bright, three-roomed restaurant with bold artwork and colourful murals, set in a keenly run hotel. The classically based British menu relies on local produce and offers ambitious dishes with a modern edge; grills are a feature.

Melton's
7 Scarcroft Rd ✉ YO23 1ND – ☎ (01904) 634 341 Town plan: CZ**c**
– www.meltonsrestaurant.co.uk – Closed 3 weeks Christmas, Sunday and Monday
Menu £ 23 (lunch and early dinner) – Carte £ 28/38 – *(booking essential)*
Long-standing, split-level restaurant with simply laid tables and a large mural. Cooking is firmly rooted in the classics, with everything made to order and Yorkshire produce to the fore. Good value 'early bird' menu and speciality nights.

Le Langhe

Peasholme Grn ✉ YO1 7PW – ✆ (01904) 622 584 Town plan: DY**x**
– www.lelanghe.co.uk – Closed first 2 weeks January, 25-27 December, 31 March-1 April, Sunday and bank holidays
Menu £ 24 (lunch) – Carte dinner £ 24/33 – *(lunch only and dinner Friday-Saturday) (booking advisable)*
Well-established eatery consisting of an upmarket deli – selling imported Italian produce and a great array of wines – and a small dining room and terrace. They offer an extensive selection of fresh, unfussy Italian dishes and some well-priced fine wines. The formal upstairs dining room is open Fri and Sat.

Blue Bicycle with rm

34 Fossgate ✉ YO1 9TA – ✆ (01904) 673 990 Town plan: DY**e**
– www.thebluebicycle.com – Closed 24-28 December, 1-7 January and lunch 27 December
6 rm – £ 145/175 £ 145/175
Carte £ 30/47 – *(dinner only and lunch Thursday-Sunday and December) (booking essential)*
Characterful Mediterranean bistro overlooking the river, with a cosy bar and a spiral staircase leading down to intimate booths. It has a buzzy atmosphere and almost a burlesque feel. Menus offer modern classics. Smart, studio-style bedrooms are in a mews and breakfast ingredients are provided in the kitchen.

Melton's Too

25 Walmgate ✉ YO1 9TX – ✆ (01904) 629 222 Town plan: DY**a**
– www.meltonstoo.co.uk – Closed 25-26 December, 1 January and dinner 24 and 31 December
Menu £ 14 (lunch and early dinner) – Carte £ 21/31
This former saddlery has plenty of character courtesy of old oak timbers, exposed brick and crooked floors. There's a distinct Mediterranean flavour to the dishes, with a selection of tapas and plenty of vegetarian choices on offer.

at Newton-on-Ouse Northwest: 8 mi by A19 -(AY)

Dawnay Arms

✉ YO30 2BR – ✆ (01347) 848 345 – www.thedawnayatnewton.co.uk – Closed 1 January, Sunday dinner and Monday except bank holidays
Menu £ 19 (weekday lunch) – Carte £ 21/47
A handsome pub with stone floors, low beams, open fires and all manner of bric-a-brac; its delightful dining room has views over the terrace and garden to the river. Gutsy, well executed, British-inspired dishes, with plenty of local game.

ZENNOR

Cornwall – See Regional map n°**1-A3**
London 289 mi – Camborne 17 mi – Saint Austell 45 mi – Falmouth 33 mi
Michelin Road map 503-D33

Gurnard's Head with rm

Treen ✉ TR26 3DE – West : 1.5 mi on B 3306 – ✆ (01736) 796 928
– www.gurnardshead.co.uk – Closed 25 December and 4 days early December
7 rm – £ 85/130 £ 105/170
Menu £ 19 (weekday lunch) – Carte £ 25/33 – *(booking advisable)*
Remotely located, dog-friendly pub, with stone floors, shabby-chic décor, blazing fires and a relaxed, cosy feel. Menus rely on regional and foraged produce, and the wine list offers some interesting choices by the glass. Good value set lunch. Compact bedrooms feature good quality linen and colourful throws.

ABERDEEN

Aberdeen City – Pop. 195 021 – See Regional map n° [illegible]
■ Edinburgh 126 mi – London 522 mi – Dundee 65 mi – Dunfermline [illegible]
Michelin Road map 501 M12 – Michelin Green Guide SCOTLAND

[illegible]
39-43 Queens Rd [illegible] – ☎ (01224) 327 777 [illegible]
[illegible]
[illegible] rm – ♦ [illegible] 150/330 ♦♦ £ 150/350 – 2 suites
Rest [illegible] – Menu £30 [illegible]
This small, boutique townhouse fits perfectly in this wealthy residential area. Sleek, contemporary bedrooms come with the latest mod cons, including Apple [illegible] and show a keen eye for detail. The [illegible] restaurant are set over [illegible] and grills from the Josper oven are a highlight.

[illegible]
[illegible] Queens Rd [illegible] – ☎ (01224) 327 370 [illegible]
www.[illegible].com
[illegible] rm – [illegible] 119 ♦♦ £ 119/289 [illegible]
[illegible] Brasserie – Menu £25 (lunch) – Carte £ [illegible]
[illegible] in a smart [illegible] and built around a period property, now the height of [illegible]. Black [illegible]-floored [illegible] with [illegible] and [illegible] stylish [illegible] a whisky cellar [illegible], modern bedrooms have atmospheric lighting. [illegible] serves modern [illegible] with steaks a speciality.

[illegible]
52-59 Huntly [illegible] – ☎ (01224) 212 [illegible]
www.[illegible]
[illegible] rm – ♦ £ 65/[illegible] ♦♦ £ 85/210 – 1 suite
Rest – Carte £ 20/35 – (dinner only [illegible])
Modern hotel just off the main street. Its functional, minimalist style [illegible] with the Bauhaus school of design. Trendy lounge; stylish, colour-coded bedrooms with clean lines and uncluttered feel – [illegible] and [illegible] are the best. First floor restaurant offers a menu of modern classics.

[illegible]
[illegible] – ☎ (01224) 327 [illegible]
www.[illegible] – Closed [illegible]
[illegible] rm – ♦ £ [illegible] ♦♦ £ [illegible]
[illegible] style hotel [illegible] a good choice for the business traveller. Warm and friendly, with up-to-date interior. Bedrooms are well kept and bright; those on the top floor are the largest and some have cityscape views. [illegible] dining room [illegible]

[illegible] – ☎ [illegible]
[illegible]
[illegible] – Carte [illegible]
[illegible] granite townhouse [illegible] and a [illegible] grills served at lunch [illegible] in the bar in the evening [illegible] dinners in the restaurant.

[illegible]
Pocra Quay, North Pier ☑ AB11 5DQ – ☎ (01224 [illegible]
[illegible] – www.[illegible] – Closed 2 weeks [illegible]
Saturday lunch and Sunday
Menu £20 (weekday lunch) – Carte £ 35/56
Attractively set at the port entrance on the top floor of the castellated former customs house. Floor to ceiling windows make the most of the superb views. Well-presented, classical dishes; excellent quality seafood is a highlight.

Scotland

ABERDEEN

Aberdeen City – Pop. 195 021 – See Regional map n°**28**-D1

Edinburgh 126 mi – London 528 mi – Dundee 65 mi – Dunfermline 112 mi

Michelin Road map 501-N12 – Michelin Green Guide SCOTLAND

The Chester (N)

59-63 Queens Rd ✉ AB15 4YP – ☎ (01224) 327 777 – www.chester-hotel.com — Town plan: X**v**

54 rm – †£ 130/330 ††£ 150/350 – 2 suites

Rest ***IX*** – Menu £ 30 – Carte £ 32/80

This smart boutique townhouse fits perfectly in this wealthy residential area. Sleek, contemporary bedrooms come with the latest mod cons (including Apple TV), and show a keen eye for detail. The cocktail bar and restaurant are set over three levels; seafood and grills from the Josper oven are a highlight.

Malmaison

49-53 Queens Rd ✉ AB15 4YP – ☎ (01224) 327 370 – www.malmaison.com — Town plan: X**e**

79 rm – †£ 99/219 ††£ 119/289, £ 15

Rest ***Brasserie*** – Menu £ 25 (lunch) – Carte £ 27/48

In a smart city suburb and built around a period property; now the height of urban chic. Black, slate-floored reception adorned with bagpipes and kilts; stylish bar with a whisky cellar. Funky, modern bedrooms have atmospheric lighting. High-ceilinged brasserie serves modern dishes, with steaks a speciality.

bauhaus

52-60 Langstane Pl. ✉ AB11 6EN – ☎ (01224) 212 122 – www.thebauhaus.co.uk — Town plan: Z**r**

39 rm – †£ 65/115 ††£ 85/210 – 1 suite

Rest – Carte £ 20/35 – *(closed Sunday dinner)*

Modern hotel just off the main street, its functional, minimalist style in keeping with the Bauhaus school of design. Trendy lounge; stylish, colour-coded bedrooms with sharp, clean lines and uncluttered feel – 'Gropius' and 'Kandinsky' are the best. First-floor restaurant offers a menu of modern classics.

Atholl

54 King's Gate ✉ AB15 4YN – ☎ (01224) 323 505 – www.atholl-aberdeen.co.uk – Closed 1 January — Town plan: X**s**

34 rm – †£ 95/125 ††£ 125/150 **Rest** – Carte £ 21/40

Extended baronial-style hotel in a leafy suburb: a good choice for the business traveller. Warm and friendly, with an up-to-date interior. Bedrooms are well-kept and bright; those on the top floor are the largest and some have cityscape views. Comfortable dining room serves tried-and-tested Scottish classics.

Fusion

10 North Silver St ✉ AB10 1RL – ☎ (01224) 652 959 – www.fusionbarbistro.com – Closed 1-5 January, Sunday and Monday — Town plan: Z**c**

Menu £ 25 (dinner) – Carte £ 20/28

Modernised granite townhouse featuring an airy bar with striking lime green furniture and a more intimate mezzanine restaurant. Grazing and grills served at lunch and in the bar in the evening; concise set price dinners in the restaurant.

Silver Darling

Pocra Quay, North Pier ✉ AB11 5DQ – ☎ (01224) 576 229 – www.thesilverdarling.co.uk – Closed 2 weeks Christmas-New Year, Saturday lunch and Sunday — Town plan: X**a**

Menu £ 20 (weekday lunch) – Carte £ 35/66

Attractively set at the port entrance: on the top floor of the castellated former customs house. Floor to ceiling windows make the most of the superb views. Neatly presented, classical dishes; excellent quality seafood is a highlight.

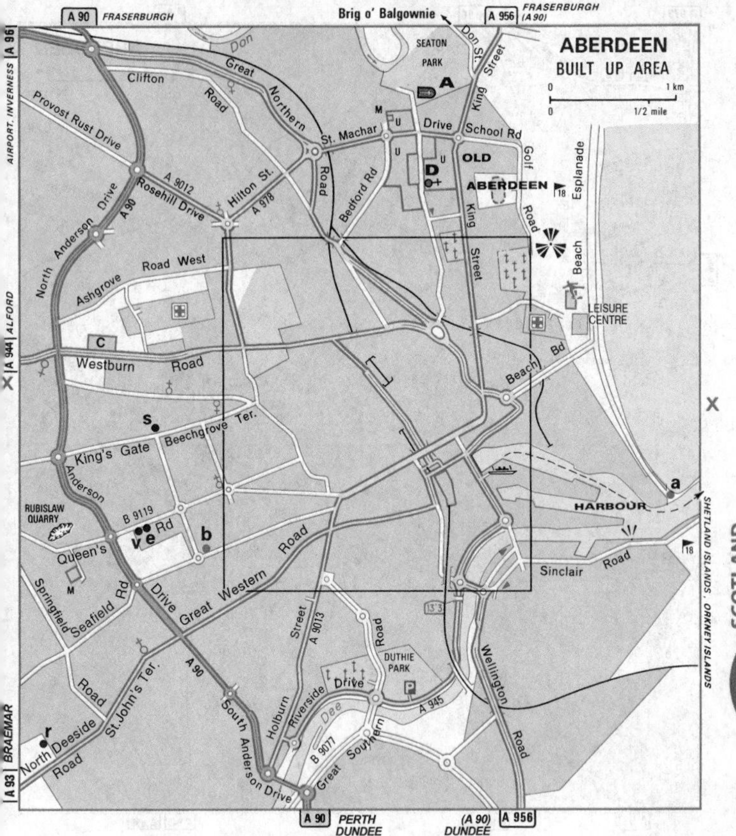

Rendezvous at Nargile

106-108 Forest Ave ✉ AB15 4UP – ✆ (01224) 323 700 Town plan: X**b**
– www.rendezvousatnargile.co.uk – Closed 25-26 December and 1-2 January
Carte £ 20/35

Bright, refreshing neighbourhood restaurant set opposite the Rendezvous Gallery. All-day menus offer plenty of choice, with cooking influenced by the Mediterranean and in particular, Turkey. Banquet meals are a highlight. Cheerful service.

Yatai

53 Langstane Pl ✉ AB11 6EN – ✆ (01224) 592 355 Town plan: Z**x**
– www.yatai.co.uk – Closed 25 December-5 January, Sunday and Monday
Carte £ 18/46 – *(booking advisable)*

Atmospheric Japanese restaurant in the style of a laid-back izakaya. The ground floor has a wooden counter and a robata grill; upstairs is airy and intimate. Menus offer tasty, authentic dishes – the sushi, sashimi and maki are highlights.

Yorokobi by CJ

51 Huntly St ✉ AB10 1TH – ✆ (01224) 566 002 Town plan: Z**a**
– www.yorokobibycj.co.uk – Closed 22 December-5 January, 14-27 July and Sunday
Carte £ 21/45 – *(dinner only and lunch Friday-Saturday) (booking advisable)*

Popular Japanese restaurant with a name meaning 'joyous bliss'; C is for chef and J is for Jang, who takes on that role. Flavourful, authentic, good value Japanese and Korean dishes; try one of the sizzling platters or a Korean pot dish.

ABERDEEN

Bon Accord Centre .... Y	Millburn St .... Z 23	Spring Garden .... Y 36
Broad St.................. Y 6	Rosemount Terrace .... Y 25	Trinity Centre............ Z
Castle St .... Y 7	Rosemount Viaduct .... Y 26	Trinity Quay .... Z 37
College St................ Z 9	St Andrew St............... Y 28	Union St.................. Z
Craigie Loanings .... Y 12	St Nicholas Centre .... Y 29	Union Terrace............. Z 39
Denburn Rd............... YZ 14	St Nicholas St .... YZ 30	Upperkirkgate .... Y 40
East North St............ Y 16	School Hill .... YZ 32	Victoria St .... Z 42
George St .... Y	South Esplanade West....... Z 33	Waverley Pl............... Z 43
Great Southern Rd .... Z 18	South Mount St............. Y 34	Wellington Pl............. Z 45
Guild St.................. Z 19	Springbank Terrace .... Z 35	Woolmanhill............... Y 48
Justice St................ Y 21		

ABOYNE

Aberdeenshire – Pop. 2 602 – See Regional map n°**28**-**D1**
▶Edinburgh 131 mi – Aberdeen 30 mi – Dundee 68 mi
Michelin Road map 501-L12 – Michelin Green Guide SCOTLAND

Boat Inn Ⓝ with rm — rm,

Charleston Rd ✉ AB34 5EL – ✆ (01339) 886 137 – www.theboatinnaboyne.co.uk – Closed 25 December and 1-2 January

8 rm – †£ 70/80 ††£ 80/105 Carte £ 18/27

Concise menu of traditional bar meals with the occasional international dish; portions are generous and there are freshly baked cakes for sale on the counter. Bright front room; cosy back bar and a smart private dining room called the Pine Loft. Spacious bedrooms come with their own kitchenette.

ABRIACHAN

Highland – Pop. 120 – See Regional map n°**30**-C2
Edinburgh 167 mi – London 567 mi – Dundee 148 mi – Dunfermline 153 mi
Michelin Road map 501-G11

Loch Ness Lodge without rest

Brachla ✉ IV3 8LA – on A 82 – ✆ (01456) 459 469 – www.loch-ness-lodge.com – Closed December-January

7 rm – †£ 95/260 ††£ 165/330

Passionately run modern country house, set in 18 acres of immaculately kept grounds overlooking Loch Ness. A classic-contemporary style features throughout. Spacious bedrooms have a high level of facilities and come with extras such as sherry and Penhaligan toiletries. Afternoon tea is served on arrival.

ACHILTIBUIE

Highland – See Regional map n°**30**-C1
Edinburgh 243 mi – Inverness 84 mi – Ullapool 25 mi
Michelin Road map 501-D9

Summer Isles

✉ IV26 2YG – ✆ (01854) 622 282 – www.summerisleshotel.com – Closed November-March

13 rm – †£ 125/170 ††£ 210/240 – 3 suites
Rest *Summer Isles (Bar)* – see restaurant listing
Rest – Menu £ 59 – *(booking essential) (set menu only)*

Remotely located hotel, with magnificent views over the eponymous islands. Individually styled, comfortable bedrooms are split between main house and various converted outbuildings. Pleasant restaurant, with polished, well-set tables offers a daily set menu of modern dishes, with the emphasis on seafood.

Summer Isles (Bar) – Summer Isles Hotel

✉ IV26 2YG – ✆ (01854) 622 282 – www.summerisleshotel.com – Closed November-March

Carte £ 20/38 – *(bookings not accepted)*

19C former crofters' bar with two snug rooms, a large garden and a small terrace with glorious views. Concise, daily menus have a strong seafood base. Baguettes, salads and platters are supplemented by blackboard specials in the evening.

ALTNAHARRA

Highland ✉ Lairg – See Regional map n°**30**-C1
Edinburgh 223 mi – London 627 mi – Inverness 68 mi
Michelin Road map 501-G9 – Michelin Green Guide SCOTLAND

Altnaharra

✉ IV27 4UE – ✆ (01549) 411 222 – www.altnaharra.com – Closed November-January

14 rm – †£ 65 ††£ 110/150 **Rest** – Menu £ 32 – *(bar lunch)*

Extended former drovers' inn dating back to the 1600s, with a cosy, homely interior and good-sized bedrooms with tartan décor. The small locals bar serves simple lunches; while the open-fired restaurant offers a classical menu. The nearby estate offers shooting, fishing and stalking.

ALYTH

Perth and Kinross – Pop. 2 403 – See Regional map n°**28**-C2
Edinburgh 63 mi – Aberdeen 69 mi – Dundee 16 mi – Perth 21 mi
Michelin Road map 501-J14

Tigh Na Leigh

22-24 Airlie St ✉ PH11 8AJ – ✆ (01828) 632 372 – www.tighnaleigh.co.uk – Closed 2 December-1 March

5 rm – †£ 55 ††£ 89/130
Rest – Carte £ 22/34 – *(dinner only) (residents only)*

Imposing Victorian house run in a professional yet relaxed manner. Surprisingly modern interior with spacious, inviting guest areas. Contemporary bedrooms boast feature beds and great bathrooms; some have spa baths. The superb kitchen garden informs the unfussy modern menu; lovely garden view while dining.

ANCRUM

The Scottish Borders – See Regional map n°**26**-**D2**
Edinburgh 44 mi – Glasgow 87 mi – Carlisle 55 mi – Perth 92 mi
Michelin Road map 501-M17

Ancrum Cross Keys

The Green ✉ TD8 6XH – ✆ (01835) 830 242 – www.ancrumcrosskeys.com – Closed Monday, Tuesday and lunch Wednesday
Carte £ 18/36
What sets this place apart is the food – this is not everyday pub grub but carefully crafted, tasty cooking with a refined edge. Sit in the larger of the dining rooms to watch the chef at work. Local ales and locals in the rustic bar.

ANNAN

Dumfries and Galloway – Pop. 8 960 – See Regional map n°**26**-**C3**
Edinburgh 79 mi – London 321 mi – Glasgow 84 mi – Liverpool 141 mi

Del Amitri

95a High St ✉ DG12 6DJ – ✆ (01461) 201 999 – www.del-amitri.co.uk – Closed 2-12 November, 16-26 February, Sunday dinner and Monday
Carte £ 24/32 – *(dinner only and Sunday lunch)*
Above a fish and chip shop on the main street. Dark walls provide an intimate feel and tables are elegantly laid. Interesting, intricate dishes are skilfully prepared and packed with local produce: the chef has close ties with his suppliers.

SCOTLAND

ANNBANK

South Ayrshire – Pop. 912 – See Regional map n°**25**-**B2**
Edinburgh 84 mi – Ayr 6 mi – Dumfries 54 mi – Paisley 34 mi
Michelin Road map 501-G17

Enterkine House

✉ KA6 5AL Southeast : 0.5 mi on B 742 (Coylton rd) – ✆ (01292) 520 580 – www.enterkine.com
15 rm – £ 80/120 £ 120/160 – 1 suite
Rest – Menu £ 17/38 – *(booking essential)*
Country house surrounded by 350 acres of countryside; originally built for the MacKay family in the 1930s and now a popular wedding venue. Spacious, individually furnished bedrooms; most with estate views. The Bothy is a honeymooners' cottage in the garden. Bright restaurant serves modern dishes.

ANSTRUTHER

Fife – Pop. 3 446 – See Regional map n°**28**-**D2**
Edinburgh 46 mi – Dundee 23 mi – Dunfermline 34 mi
Michelin Road map 501-L15 – Michelin Green Guide SCOTLAND

Spindrift

Pittenweem Rd ✉ KY10 3DT – ✆ (01333) 310 573 – www.thespindrift.co.uk – Closed January and 24-26 December
5 rm – £ 45/66 £ 70/100 **Rest** – Menu £ 25
Detached Victorian house on the edge of the village, originally owned by a tea clipper captain. Comfy lounge with an honesty bar. Cosy, individually furnished bedrooms, some with distant sea views; opt for the top floor Captain's Cabin. Cooking relies on local produce, with seafood from East Neuk to the fore.

APPLECROSS

Highland – See Regional map n°**29**-**B2**
Edinburgh 233 mi – London 607 mi – Glasgow 210 mi
Michelin Road map 501-C11

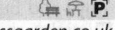

X **Applecross Walled Garden** 
✉ *IV54 8ND North : 0.5 mi – ✆ (01520) 744 440 – www.applecrossgarden.co.uk – Closed November-February*
Carte £ 25/37
Set in a former potting shed in a 17C walled garden; where much of the produce is grown. Simple interior with a small counter displaying homemade cakes. Light lunches and daily specials; original, North African influenced dishes at dinner.

Applecross Inn with rm 
Shore St ✉ IV54 8LR – ✆ (01520) 744 262 – www.applecross.uk.com – Closed 25 December and 1 January
7 rm ☕ – †£ 80/85 ††£ 120/130 Carte £ 19/40 – *(booking essential)*
Unpretentious inn with friendly service and a bustling atmosphere; take the scenic route over the hair-raising, single-track Bealach na Ba, with its stunning views and hairpin bends to reach it. Dine on the freshest of seafood, often caught within sight of the door. Simple bedrooms have marvellous sea views.

ARBROATH

Angus – Pop. 23 902 – See Regional map n°**28**-D2
▶Edinburgh 72 mi – Dundee 17 mi – Montrose 12 mi
Michelin Road map 501-M14

Old Vicarage without rest 
2 Seaton Rd ✉ DD11 5DX – Northeast : 0.75 mi by A 92 and Hayshead Rd – ✆ (01241) 430 475 – www.theoldvicaragebandb.co.uk
3 rm ☕ – †£ 65/75 ††£ 80/90
Detached 19C house with curios and antiques filling every room – look out for the lovely grandfather clock. Immaculately kept bedrooms have a Victorian feel; some have abbey views. Glorious buffet breakfasts include smokies from the quay.

ARCHIESTOWN

Moray – See Regional map n°**28**-C1
▶Edinburgh 194 mi – Aberdeen 62 mi – Inverness 49 mi
Michelin Road map 501-K11

Archiestown 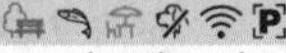
The Square ✉ AB38 7QL – ✆ (01340) 810 218 – www.archiestownhotel.co.uk – Closed 2 January-10 February and 23-29 December
11 rm ☕ – †£ 75/95 ††£ 160/200 **Rest** – Menu £ 15/26
Welcoming hotel overlooking the square in a planned Victorian village; ideal for fishermen and visitors to the Whisky Trail. Spacious, comfy sitting rooms with open fires. Classical bedrooms; many have country views. Intimate restaurant with a feature wall serves a traditional menu with Scottish touches.

ARDCHATTAN

Argyll and Bute – See Regional map n°**27**-B2
▶Edinburgh 123 mi – London 494 mi – Glasgow 98 mi – Belfast 146 mi

Blarcreen House 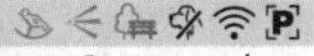
✉ PA37 1RG East : 1 mi past Ardchattan Priory and gardens on Bonawe rd – ✆ (01631) 750 272 – www.blarcreenhouse.com – Closed Christmas and New Year
3 rm ☕ – †£ 80/100 ††£ 100/120 **Rest** – Menu £ 30
Friendly Victorian former farmhouse set in a tranquil location down a single track and boasting superb views over Loch Etive. Homely lounge and comfy bedrooms: two with four-posters and double-aspects; all with robes, fridges and fresh milk. Lovely dining room offers a daily menu of home-cooked dishes.

ARDHASAIG → See Lewis and Harris (Isle of)

Western Isles – Michelin Road map 501-Z10

SCOTLAND

ARDUAINE

Argyll and Bute ✉ Oban – See Regional map n°**27**-B2
▶Edinburgh 141 mi – Glasgow 105 mi – Paisley 98 mi – Greenock 105 mi
Michelin Road map 501-D15 – Michelin Green Guide SCOTLAND

Loch Melfort

✉ *PA34 4XG – ☎ (01852) 200 233 – www.lochmelfort.co.uk – Closed December-January except Christmas-New Year and mid-week November-March*
25 rm – †£ 104/174 ††£ 148/268
Rest *Asknish Bay* – see restaurant listing
Rest *Chartroom II* – Carte £ 19/66
Large hotel next to the beautiful Arduaine Gardens, affording superb views out over the bay and Sound of Jura. Modern lounges with tartan/nautical themes. Bigger bedrooms in the main house; great outlook from private terraces in the wing. Simple, largely seafood menu in Chartroom II; more formal Asknish Bay.

XX

Asknish Bay – Loch Melfort Hotel

✉ *PA34 4XG – ☎ (01852) 200 233 – www.lochmelfort.co.uk – Closed December-January except Christmas-New Year and mid-week November-March*
Menu £ 40 – Carte £ 28/50 – *(dinner only)*
Formal hotel restaurant in a beautiful setting, with panoramic views of the bay. Menus focus on the freshest seafood available, with Loch Fyne langoustines, Islay scallops and Gigha halibut; carnivores are also well-catered for.

ARRAN (Isle of)

SCOTLAND

North Ayrshire – Pop. 4 629 – See Regional map n°**25**-A2
▶Edinburgh 83 mi – London 414 mi – Glasgow 37 mi – Liverpool 234 mi
Michelin Road map 501-E17 – Michelin Green Guide SCOTLAND

BRODICK

Auchrannie

✉ *KA27 8BZ Northwest : 0.75 mi by Shore Rd. – ☎ (01770) 302 234 – www.auchrannie.co.uk*
64 rm – †£ 65/140 ††£ 89/189 – 2 suites
Rest *Eighteen69* – Carte £ 14/33 – *(closed November-February and Tuesday-Wednesday) (dinner only)*
Rest *Brambles* – Menu £ 11 (lunch) – Carte £ 22/55
Rest *Cruize* – Carte £ 17/37
Mini resort hotel set in 96 acres and offering a good range of family orientated leisure facilities. Built in 1869, the old dower house boasts well-equipped, classical and contemporary bedrooms; family rooms are located in the resort house. Smart conservatory restaurant offers fine dining menu; Brambles serves seafood and grills; all-day Cruize is ideal for families.

Kilmichael Country House

Glen Cloy ✉ *KA27 8BY – West : 1 mi by Shore Rd, taking left turn opposite Golf Club – ☎ (01770) 302 219 – www.kilmichael.com – Closed November-Easter*
8 rm – †£ 95 ††£ 163/208
Rest – Menu £ 45 – *(closed Monday and Tuesday) (dinner only) (bookings essential for non-residents) (set menu only)*
Sympathetically restored 17C house – reputedly the oldest house on the Isle of Arran – delightfully located in a peaceful glen and surrounded by mountains. Comfy, antique-furnished bedrooms; those in the converted stable block offer a little more comfort and privacy. Daily changing 4 course menu of accomplished cooking served in the classically decorated dining room.

Douglas

✉ *KA27 8AW – ☎ (01770) 302 968 – www.thedouglashotel.co.uk*
22 rm – †£ 65/169 ††£ 85/224
Rest *Bistro* – Carte £ 22/38 – *(bar lunch)*
Stylish, modern hotel with attractive pink granite façade, set just past the ferry terminal. Spacious, light-filled bedrooms are decorated in a contemporary style; most have a sea view and room 202 has a large roof terrace. Informal, pubby bar. Smart bistro offers classical French dishes with a modern twist.

LAMLASH

Glenisle

Shore Rd. ⊠ *KA27 8LY – ✆ (01770) 600 559 – www.glenislehotel.com*
13 rm ☕ – 🚹£ 83/87 🚹🚹£ 119/203 **Rest** – Carte £ 18/37
Attractive whitewashed Victorian property, formerly an inn, boasting views over the bay to Holy Island. Open-plan bar-lounge and small snug. Bright, airy bedrooms come in natural hues; one covers the whole top floor and has a roll-top bath. Rustic dining room with terrace offers fresh, simple, homely cooking.

LOCHRANZA

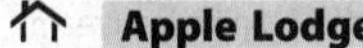

Apple Lodge

⊠ *KA27 8HJ – ✆ (01770) 830 229 – www.applelodgearran.co.uk*
– Closed 15 December-15 January
4 rm ☕ – 🚹£ 50 🚹🚹£ 78 **Rest** – Menu £ 25
Former manse with attractive gardens, in a quiet hamlet surrounded by mountains. Traditionally decorated, comfortable and personally run, with many regular guests. Bedrooms have pleasant views; Apple Cottage is a self-contained garden suite. 3 course menu of classic, home-cooked dishes served by candlelight.

AUCHENCAIRN

Dumfries and Galloway ⊠ Castle Douglas – See Regional map n°**25-B3**
▶ Edinburgh 94 mi – Dumfries 21 mi – Stranraer 60 mi
Michelin Road map 501-I19 and 502

Balcary Mews without rest

Balcary Bay ⊠ *DG7 1QZ – Southeast : 2 mi on Balcary rd – ✆ (01556) 640 276 – www.balcarymews.co.uk – Closed mid-December to mid-January*
3 rm ☕ – 🚹£ 65/80 🚹🚹£ 80
Former mews for the neighbouring country house, boasting superb views over Balcary Bay and the Solway Firth. Lovely garden with a gate down to the shore. Neat sun lounge and traditional bedrooms; all have views. Homemade bread and jam feature at breakfast.

AUCHTERARDER

Perth and Kinross – Pop. 4 206 – See Regional map n°**28-C2**
▶ Edinburgh 55 mi – London 438 mi – Aberdeen 102 mi – Glasgow 46 mi
Michelin Road map 501-I15 – Michelin Green Guide SCOTLAND

Gleneagles

rm, rest,

⊠ *PH3 1NF Southwest : 2 mi by A 824 on A 823 – ✆ (01764) 662 231 – www.gleneagles.com*
233 rm ☕ – 🚹£ 245/465 🚹🚹£ 245/465 – 16 suites
Rest *Andrew Fairlie at Gleneagles* ✿✿ – see restaurant listing
Rest *Strathearn* – ✆ (01764) 694 270 – Menu £ 60 – *(dinner only and Sunday lunch)*
Rest *Deseo* – ✆ (01764) 694 270 – Carte £ 23/83
World-famous resort hotel with a renowned championship golf course, majestic art deco styling, an elegant interior and luxurious bedrooms. Excellent leisure facilities include a state-of-the-art spa, a popular equestrian centre and a gun-dog school. Strathearn offers a classical menu and superb estate views. All-day Deseo serves Mediterranean-influenced dishes and tapas.

Cairn

Orchill Rd ⊠ *PH3 1LX – West : 0.5 mi by Townhead Rd and Western Rd – ✆ (01764) 662 634 – www.cairnlodge.co.uk*
14 rm ☕ – 🚹£ 99/350 🚹🚹£ 99/450
Rest *Grill Room* – see restaurant listing
Glitzy lodge with pleasant gardens and a monochrome theme; the younger sister to Gleneagles. Large bar with tub chairs and an inner hall with a piano. Bedrooms are modern and stylish, with black ash furnishings and Nespresso machines.

Andrew Fairlie at Gleneagles – Gleneagles Hotel 

✉ *PH3 1NF Southwest : 2 mi by A 824 on A 823 – ✆ (01764) 694 267 – www.andrewfairlie.co.uk – Closed 3 weeks January, 25-26 December and Sunday*

Menu £ 95/125 – *(dinner only)*

Elegant restaurant hung with portraits of its famous chef. The à la carte focuses on refined French classics, with a signature dish of home-smoked lobster. The 8 course dégustation menu showcases dishes 'en miniature' and the 'Menu du Marché', the latest seasonal produce. Accomplished, carefully balanced cooking is coupled with professional, good-humoured service.

→ Home-smoked lobster, lime and herb butter. Roast breast and confit leg of duck with citrus salsa and red wine jus. Hot rhubarb soufflé, vanilla ice cream.

XX

Grill Room – Cairn Hotel

Orchill Rd ✉ PH3 1LX – West : 0.5 mi by Townhead Rd and Western Rd – ✆ (01764) 662 634 – www.cairnlodge.co.uk

Carte £ 20/80

Chic hotel restaurant with an elegant bar and a large dining room with boldly papered and studded leather walls, twisty chandeliers and sumptuous leather seating. Wide ranging menu of burgers, grills and steaks, alongside a tapas selection.

AVIEMORE

Highland – Pop. 3 147 – See Regional map n°**30**-D3

Edinburgh 129 mi – Inverness 29 mi – Perth 85 mi

Michelin Road map 501-I12 – Michelin Green Guide SCOTLAND

SCOTLAND

Old Minister's Guest House 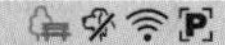

Rothiemurchus ✉ PH22 1QH – Southeast : 1 mi on B 970 – ✆ (01479) 812 181 – www.theoldministershouse.co.uk

5 rm – £ 100/115 £ 100/140 **Rest** – Menu £ 30

19C stone-built manse with unusual carved wood animals out the front and pretty gardens leading down to the river. The smart lounge has deep sofas and an honesty bar and the bedrooms are spacious and well-appointed. Home-cooked dinners use local produce and breakfast includes French toast and eggs Benedict.

AYR

South Ayrshire – Pop. 46 849 – See Regional map n°**25**-A2

Edinburgh 82 mi – London 395 mi – Glasgow 36 mi – Belfast 69 mi

Michelin Road map 501-G17 and 502 – Michelin Green Guide SCOTLAND

Western House

Ayr Racecourse, Craigie Rd ✉ KA8 0HA – ✆ (01292) 294 990 – www.westernhousehotel.co.uk Town plan: BZ**w**

48 rm – £ 80/190 £ 80/190 – 1 suite

Rest *The Jockey Club* – Carte £ 22/32

Attractive country house designed by Lutyens and set on the Ayr racecourse. Tastefully styled bedrooms are named after racecourses; those in the original house are the largest and most luxurious. Wood-panelled lounge-bar. Restaurant offers appealing menu of British classics based around Ayrshire ingredients.

No.26 The Crescent without rest

26 Bellevue Cres ✉ KA7 2DR – ✆ (01292) 287 329 – www.26crescent.co.uk – Closed 22-26 December Town plan: BZ**c**

5 rm – £ 53/60 £ 77/97

Well-run Victorian terraced house, displaying a pleasing mix of traditional features – such as original fireplaces – and smart, modern décor. Comfortable throughout, with individually furnished bedrooms; the best one has a four-poster. Cosy breakfast room; the smoked haddock with poached eggs is a speciality.

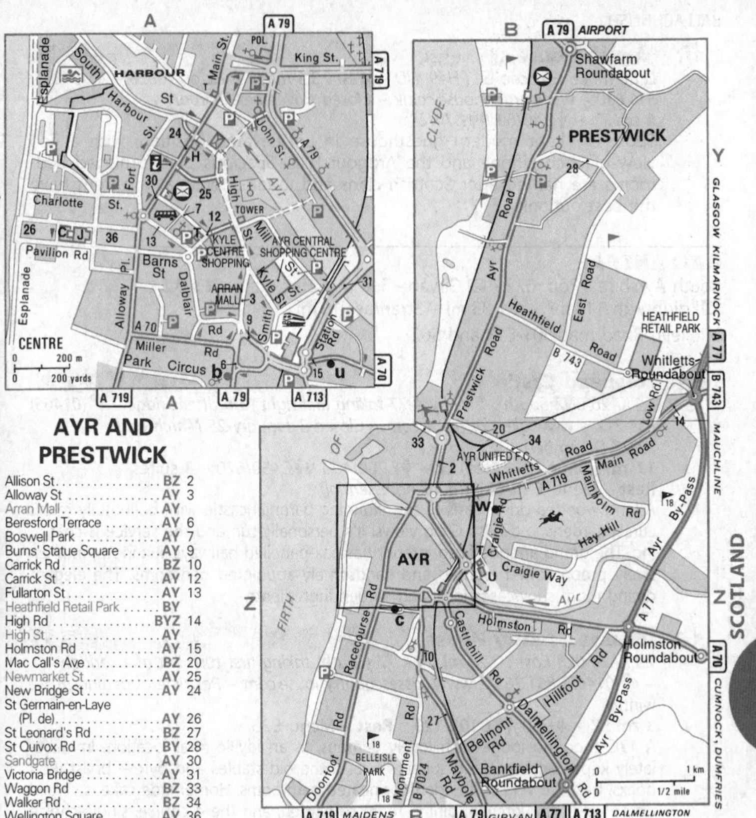

AYR AND PRESTWICK

Coila without rest

10 Holmston Rd ✉ *KA7 3BB – ✆ (01292) 262 642* Town plan: AY**u**
– www.coila.co.uk

4 rm – £ 45/65 £ 65/90

Comfortable, traditionally furnished Victorian house on the edge of town, proudly decorated with the owners' personal ornaments and family photos. Homely sitting room and well-kept bedrooms; those to the rear are quieter.

The Beresford

22 Beresford Terr. ✉ *KA7 2EG – ✆ (01292) 280 820* Town plan: AY**b**
– www.theberesfordayr.co.uk

Menu £ 10 (lunch) – Carte £ 20/39

Start with a cocktail in the downstairs bar, before tucking into the likes of pizza, pasta, seafood or steak, followed by pastries and ice cream sundaes in the spacious, buzzing brasserie. The first floor is an art gallery during the week.

BACK

→ See Lewis and Harris (Isle of)
Western Isles – Michelin Road map 501-B9

BALLACHULISH

Highland – Pop. 666 – See Regional map n°**30-C3**

Edinburgh 117 mi – Inverness 80 mi – Kyle of Lochalsh 90 mi – Oban 38 mi

Michelin Road map 501-E13 – Michelin Green Guide SCOTLAND

Ardno House without rest

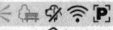

Lettermore, Glencoe ✉ PH49 4JD – West : 3.5 mi by A 82 on A 828 – ✆ (01855) 811 830 – www.ardnohouse.co.uk – Closed November-February

4 rm ☕ – †£ 40/68 ††£ 70/84

Spotlessly kept modern guesthouse in an elevated position, with a fine view of Loch Linnhe and the Ardgour Hills. Spacious pine-furnished bedrooms are named after Scottish clans and tartans; those at the front have the best outlooks.

BALLANTRAE

South Ayrshire – Pop. 672 – ✉ Girvan – See Regional map n°**25**-A2

Edinburgh 115 mi – Ayr 33 mi – Stranraer 18 mi

Michelin Road map 501-E18 and 502

Glenapp Castle

✉ KA26 0NZ South : 1 mi by A 77 taking first right turn after bridge – ✆ (01465) 831 212 – www.glenappcastle.com – Closed 3 January-25 March and 23-27 December

17 rm (dinner included) ☕ – †£ 280/490 ††£ 450/670 – 3 suites

Rest – Menu £ 40/65 – *(booking essential)*

A long wooded drive leads to this stunning baronial castle with beautifully manicured gardens and Ailsa Craig views; it's personally run and the service is charming. The grand antique-filled interior has oak-panelled hallways, luxurious, impressively proportioned lounges and handsomely appointed bedrooms. The elegant dining room showcases local and garden ingredients.

SCOTLAND

Cosses Country House

✉ KA26 0LR East : 2.25 mi by A 77 (South) taking first turn left after bridge – ✆ (01465) 831 363 – www.cossescountryhouse.com – Restricted opening in winter

3 rm ☕ – †£ 80 ††£ 100/120 **Rest** – Menu £ 35

A 17C shooting lodge with lovely gardens, in an idyllic rural location. Immaculately kept bedrooms and suites – two in the old stables and byre – boast iPod docks, fresh flowers and underfloor heated bathrooms. Homemade cake is served on arrival in the kitchen, dining room or garden, and the 4 course, single-choice set dinners showcase local and garden produce.

BALLATER

Aberdeenshire – Pop. 1 533 – See Regional map n°**28**-C1

Edinburgh 111 mi – Aberdeen 41 mi – Inverness 70 mi – Perth 67 mi

Michelin Road map 501-K12

Darroch Learg

Braemar Rd ✉ AB35 5UX – ✆ (013397) 55 443 – www.darrochlearg.co.uk – Closed last 3 weeks January and 20-27 December

12 rm ☕ – †£ 95/160 ††£ 140/250

Rest *Conservatory* – see restaurant listing

Victorian country house affording superb views over the Dee Valley and the Grampians. Personally run by the second family generation, it boasts comfy, open-fired, antique-furnished lounges and traditional, individually designed bedrooms.

Auld Kirk without rest

Braemar Rd ✉ AB35 5RQ – ✆ (013397) 55 762 – www.theauldkirk.com – Closed Christmas

7 rm ☕ – †£ 70/90 ††£ 100/120

Striking granite building – a church from 1870-1938; the bar-lounge still has the original stained glass windows. Bright, modern bedrooms with bold furnishings. Comprehensive breakfasts; the 'spirit of ecstasy' sculpture is a talking point!

Moorside House without rest
26 Braemar Rd ✉ AB35 5RL – ☎ (013397) 55 492 – www.moorsidehouse.co.uk – Closed October-Easter
9 rm – †£ 50 ††£ 60/70
Traditional 19C former manse with a large garden, simple, homely bedrooms and a comfortable lounge filled with books about the local area. Original Victorian features include ornate cornicing and an attractive pine staircase. Hearty breakfasts feature homemade bread, muffins, muesli and preserves.

Conservatory – Darroch Learg Hotel
Braemar Rd ✉ AB35 5UX – ☎ (013397) 55 443 – www.darrochlearg.co.uk – Closed last 3 weeks January and 20-27 December
Menu £ 45 – *(dinner only and Sunday lunch)*
Conservatory dining room in a Victorian country house, boasting attractive mountain views from the majority of its smartly laid tables. The concise menu showcases quality seasonal ingredients in carefully judged, well-crafted modern dishes.

BALLOCH

West Dunbartonshire ✉ Alexandria – See Regional map n°**25**-B1
Edinburgh 72 mi – Glasgow 20 mi – Stirling 30 mi
Michelin Road map 501-G15 – Michelin Green Guide SCOTLAND

Cameron House rm,
Loch Lomond ✉ G83 8QZ – Northwest : 1.5 mi by A 811 on A 82 – ☎ (01389) 755 565 – www.cameronhouse.co.uk
132 rm – †£ 140/345 ††£ 140/345 – 12 suites
Rest ***Martin Wishart at Loch Lomond*** ✿
Rest ***Camerons Grill***
Rest ***Boat House*** – see restaurant listing
Rest ***Claret Jug*** – Menu £ 20 (dinner) – Carte £ 16/34
Extensive Victorian house and lodges set in 250 acres on the shore of Loch Lomond. Excellent leisure facilities include a spa, a golf course, a launch and a seaplane. Bedrooms are modern and moody, while the suites are more traditional. There are several dining options; The Claret Jug serves British classics.

Martin Wishart at Loch Lomond – Cameron House Hotel
✿
Loch Lomond ✉ G83 8QZ – Northwest : 1.5 mi by A 811 on A 82 – ☎ (01389) 722 504 – www.mwlochlomond.co.uk – Closed 1-14 January, Monday and Tuesday
Menu £ 29/70 – *(dinner only and lunch Saturday-Sunday) (booking essential)*
Smart restaurant in a resort hotel on the banks of Loch Lomond, offering superb water and mountain views. Seasonal modern menus showcase Scottish ingredients in well-judged combinations; cooking is accomplished and dishes are attractively presented. There's a 6 course vegetarian tasting option available.
→ Torchon of foie gras and beetroot. Roast duck with turnip purée, chicory and bigarade orange sauce. Salt-baked pineapple, mango and passion fruit cremeux.

Camerons Grill – Cameron House Hotel
Loch Lomond ✉ G83 8QZ – Northwest : 1.5 mi by A 811 on A 82 – ☎ (01389) 722 582 – www.cameronhouse.co.uk – Closed 26 December
Menu £ 35 – Carte £ 35/85 – *(dinner only)*
Contemporary restaurant in a 19C house; dark leather furnishings and a large mural give it a moody, masculine feel. The menu is extensive – specialities include home-cured and home-smoked salmon, and steaks from the Josper grill.

Boat House – Cameron House Hotel
Loch Lomond ✉ G83 8QZ – Northwest : 1.5 mi by A 811 on A 82 – ☎ (01389) 722 585 – www.cameronhouse.co.uk
Carte £ 35/70
Set in the grounds of Cameron House, this casual restaurant has a New England feel and looks out to the jetty; bag a spot on the terrace if you can. The Mediterranean menu offers unfussy dishes, including fresh Loch Fyne seafood.

SCOTLAND

BALLYGRANT → See Islay (Isle of)

Argyll and Bute – Michelin Road map 501-B16

BALMACARA

Highland – See Regional map n°**29-B2**

Edinburgh 197 mi – London 573 mi – Glasgow 177 mi – Manchester 388 mi

Balmacara Mains without rest

Glaick ✉ IV40 8DN – West : 0.75 mi by A 87 – ☎ (01599) 566 240 – www.ontheloch.co.uk

8 rm – ✝£ 60/95 ✝✝£ 70/129

Old farmhouse in a superb lochside location between the castle and Skye Bridge. Modern lounge with a wood-burning stove; split-level breakfast room offers the likes of Skye smoked haddock. Light oak furnished bedrooms and marble bathrooms.

BALMEDIE

Aberdeenshire – Pop. 2 534 – See Regional map n°**28-D1**

Edinburgh 137 mi – Aberdeen 7 mi – Peterhead 24 mi

Michelin Road map 501-N12

Cock and Bull with rm

Ellon Rd, Blairton ✉ AB23 8XY – North : 1 mi on A 90 – ☎ (01358) 743 249 – www.thecockandbull.co.uk

4 rm – ✝£ 95/110 ✝✝£ 100/120, £ 10 Carte £ 22/36

Quirky pub with a profusion of knick-knacks; dine in the cosy, open-fired lounge, the formal dining room or the airy conservatory. Menus offer a mix of pub classics and well-presented, restaurant style dishes. Some of the contemporary bedrooms are in a nearby annexe; there's a complimentary shuttle service.

SCOTLAND

BALQUHIDDER

Stirling – See Regional map n°**27-B2**

Edinburgh 70 mi – Stirling 29 mi – Perth 42 mi

Michelin Road map 501-G14

Monachyle Mhor

✉ FK19 8PQ West : 4 mi – ☎ (01877) 384 622 – www.mhor.net – Closed 5-25 January

14 rm – ✝£ 185/256 ✝✝£ 185/265

Rest *Monachyle Mhor* – see restaurant listing

Eye-catching, pink former farmhouse, located in a beautiful, very remote valley. Contemporary furnishings blend with original features in the reception, lounge and bar. Smart, modern bedrooms boast slate-tiled bathrooms; those in the main house are smaller but afford great views over the Braes of Balquhidder.

Monachyle Mhor – Monachyle Mhor Hotel

✉ FK19 8PQ West : 4 mi – ☎ (01877) 384 622 – www.mhor.net – Closed 5-25 January

Menu £ 28/55 – *(booking essential)*

Rurally set restaurant in a pink-painted hotel; sit in the snug library or enjoy the valley view from the conservatory. Well-presented dishes champion Scottish produce and are strong on flavour with a modern edge.

Mhor 84 (N) with rm

Kingshouse ✉ FK19 8NY – East: 3 mi by Auchtubh rd – ☎ (01877) 384 646 – www.mhor.net

7 rm – ✝£ 45 ✝✝£ 70 Carte £ 12/25

Food is served all day, every day at this café-style restaurant, where shelves bursting with cakes and meringues from their bakery greet you. Fresh, regional ingredients feature in unfussy dishes; things step up a gear on the daily changing evening menu. Cosy, simply furnished bedrooms complete the picture.

BANCHORY

Aberdeenshire – Pop. 7 278 – See Regional map n°**28-D2**
Edinburgh 118 mi – Aberdeen 17 mi – Dundee 55 mi – Inverness 94 mi
Michelin Road map 501-M12 – Michelin Green Guide SCOTLAND

Raemoir House

AB31 4ED North : 2.5 mi by A 980 – (01330) 824 884 – www.raemoir.com
20 rm – £ 105/135 £ 160/300
Rest – Menu £ 45 – *(bar lunch Monday-Saturday)*
Impressive Scottish country house in an idyllic rural spot. Original features include an intricately carved counter in the bar and pitch pine panelling in the drawing room. Classical bedrooms have been subtly modernised. Elegant dining room serves a daily menu of classically based dishes with a modern twist.

Tor-Na-Coille

Inchmarlo Rd AB31 4AB – West : 0.5 mi on A 93 – (01330) 822 242 – www.tornacoille.com – Closed 5-18 January
25 rm – £ 120/145 £ 120/195
Rest – Carte £ 24/48 – *(bar lunch Monday-Saturday)*
Well-run mansion dating from 1873 and surrounded by mature grounds. The décor blends the modern with the classic and original cornicing, fireplaces and staircases feature. Bedrooms boast stylish wallpapers and bright, bold furnishings. The intimate restaurant showcases Scottish produce in modern dishes.

Cow Shed

Raemoir Rd AB31 5QB – North : 1.5 mi on A 980 – (01330) 820 813 – www.cowshedrestaurant.co.uk – Closed 1-7 January, Sunday dinner, Monday and Tuesday
Carte £ 24/41 – *(dinner only and lunch Saturday-Sunday) (booking advisable)*
Impressive modern building with a cavernous dining room and countryside views. Simple, good value lunches, followed by more ambitious evening menus; meat and game is from the surrounding estates. Cookery classes available.

SCOTLAND

BARCALDINE

Argyll and Bute – See Regional map n°**27-B2**
Edinburgh 124 mi – London 495 mi – Glasgow 98 mi – Leeds 317 mi
Michelin Road map 501-D14

Ardtorna without rest

Mill Farm PA37 1SE – Southwest : 1.5 mi on A 828 – (01631) 720 125 – www.ardtorna.co.uk
4 rm – £ 100/200 £ 160/200
Ultra-modern guesthouse in a stunning spot, with lovely views of the lochs and mountains, and amazing sunsets. Immaculate bedrooms have well-stocked fridges and plenty of space in which to relax; perhaps with a complimentary glass of Baileys or whisky. The charming owners offer archery lessons.

BARRA (Isle of)

Western Isles Castlebay – See Regional map n°**29-A3**
Edinburgh 126 mi – London 497 mi – Glasgow 101 mi – Liverpool 317 mi
Michelin Road map 501-X13

CASTLEBAY

Castlebay

rm,

HS9 5XD – (01871) 810 223 – www.castlebayhotel.com – Closed 21 December-6 January
15 rm – £ 59/150 £ 79/189 **Rest** – Carte £ 21/37 – *(bar lunch)*
Homely hotel boasting excellent castle and island views – the hub of the island community. Bedrooms mix styles: newer rooms feature subtle tartan fabrics; 'MacNeil' has harbour views. Cosy lounge and busy locals bar. Linen-clad dining room serves seafood specials.

Grianamul without rest 
✉ HS9 5XD – ✆ (01871) 810 416 – www.isleofbarraaccommodation.com – Closed October-March
3 rm – £ 45 £ 70
Set at the heart of a small hamlet; a homely guesthouse run by caring owners. Bright, clean, spacious bedrooms. Comfortable lounge and sunny breakfast room, where huge breakfasts are served.

North Bay

Heathbank 
✉ HS9 5YQ – ✆ (01871) 890 266 – www.barrahotel.co.uk – Closed November-March
5 rm – £ 64 £ 102 **Rest** – Carte £ 13/38 – *(booking essential) (bar lunch)*
Former Presbyterian Church, now a smart, modern hotel that's popular with locals and visitors alike. Fresh, up-to-date bedrooms. Bright, airy bar that forms the hotel's hub and, along with the dining room, serves straightforward, local seafood orientated menus.

BERNISDALE → See Skye (Isle of)

Highland – Michelin Road map 501-A/B11

BETTYHILL

Highland – See Regional map n°**30**-**C1**
Edinburgh 246 mi – London 647 mi – Glasgow 260 mi
Michelin Road map 501-H8

SCOTLAND

Côte du Nord
The School House, Kirtomy ✉ KW14 7TB – East : 4 mi by A 836 – ✆ (01641) 521 773 – www.cotedunord.co.uk – Closed October-March, Sunday-Tuesday and Thursday
Menu £ 39 – *(dinner only) (booking essential)*
Intimate restaurant of just 3 tables; converted from an old school house by a local doctor cum self-taught chef. Modern, innovative cooking; 12 course 'surprise' menu features local and foraged ingredients, and salt from reduced seawater.

BISHOPTON

Renfrewshire – See Regional map n°**25**-**B1**
Edinburgh 59 mi – Dumbarton 9 mi – Glasgow 13 mi
Michelin Road map 501-G16

Mar Hall rm, rest,
Earl of Mar Dr ✉ PA7 5NW – Northeast : 1 mi on B 815 – ✆ (0141) 812 99 99 – www.marhall.com
53 rm – £ 185/245 £ 185/245 – 2 suites
Rest *Cristal* – Carte £ 32/74
Rest *Il Posto* – Carte £ 21/41 – *(closed Tuesday and Wednesday)*
Impressive Gothic mansion – a former hospital – on the banks of the Clyde; popular for weddings and with good links to Glasgow city and the airport. Well-equipped spa and championship golf course. Spacious, contemporary bedrooms; 'Deluxe' have river views. Enjoy afternoon tea in the cavernous Grand Hall. Cristal offers a classic French menu; Italian fare in Il Posto.

BLAIRGOWRIE

Perth and Kinross – Pop. 8 954 – See Regional map n°**28**-**C2**
Edinburgh 60 mi – Dundee 19 mi – Perth 16 mi
Michelin Road map 501-J14 – Michelin Green Guide SCOTLAND

Kinloch House 
✉ PH10 6SG West : 3 mi on A 923 – ✆ (01250) 884 237 – www.kinlochhouse.com – Closed 12-29 December
15 rm – £ 100/225 £ 150/325 – 1 suite
Rest *Kinloch House* – see restaurant listing
Imposing ivy-clad country house in a tranquil, elevated setting, with beautiful walled gardens to the rear and 25 acres of grounds. Smart oak-panelled hall and a vast array of welcoming guest areas complete with log fires and antiques. Classical bedrooms are well-appointed and immaculately maintained.

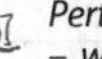

Gilmore House without rest

Perth Rd ✉ PH10 6EJ – Southwest : 0.5 mi on A 93 – ☎ (01250) 872 791 – www.gilmorehouse.co.uk

3 rm – †£ 45/50 ††£ 75/80

Proudly run, stone-built house with a pretty, flower-filled entrance. Antlers, deer heads and old lithographs fill the walls. The first floor lounge has a good outlook; complimentary sherry and whisky are left out for a traditional nightcap. Immaculately kept modern bedrooms and plentiful breakfasts.

Kinloch House – Kinloch House Hotel

✉ PH10 6SG West : 3 mi on A 923 – ☎ (01250) 884 237 – www.kinlochhouse.com – Closed 12-29 December

Menu £ 20/53

Formal hotel dining room with twinkling chandeliers and smartly dressed tables. Start with drinks in the clubby bar or cosy, open-fired sitting room. The latest local, seasonal produce informs the daily menu – maybe West Coast crab or Perthshire venison. Dishes are well-crafted, traditional and flavoursome.

Dalmore Inn

Perth Rd ✉ PH10 6QB – Southwest : 1.5 mi on A 93 – ☎ (01250) 871 088 – www.dalmoreinn.com – Closed 25 December and 1-2 January

Menu £ 10 (lunch) – Carte £ 21/40

Vivid yellow pub with a surprisingly stylish interior, where brightly coloured walls are juxtaposed with old stonework. Cooking is good value, unfussy and full of flavour, and everything is freshly prepared to order using Scottish produce.

BORVE → See Lewis and Harris (Isle of)

Western Isles – Michelin Road map 501-Y10

BOWMORE → See Islay (Isle of)

Argyll and Bute – Michelin Road map 501-B16

BRAEMAR

Aberdeenshire – Pop. 500 – See Regional map n°**28**-C2

Edinburgh 85 mi – Aberdeen 58 mi – Dundee 51 mi – Perth 51 mi

Michelin Road map 501-J12 – Michelin Green Guide SCOTLAND

Callater Lodge without rest

9 Glenshee Rd ✉ AB35 5YQ – ☎ (013397) 41 275 – www.callaterlodge.co.uk – Closed 1 week Christmas

6 rm – †£ 40/44 ††£ 80/84

A Victorian granite house on the village outskirts, with a classical interior featuring tartan carpets and stags' heads. There's a bright breakfast room and a comfy lounge with local info. Some of the bedrooms have valley views.

BROADFORD → See Skye (Isle of)

Highland – Michelin Road map 501-C12

BRODICK → See Arran (Isle of)

North Ayrshire – Michelin Road map 501-E17

BRORA

Highland – Pop. 1 282 – See Regional map n°**30**-D2

Edinburgh 234 mi – Inverness 78 mi – Wick 49 mi

Michelin Road map 501-I9

Royal Marine

Golf Rd ✉ KW9 6QS – ☎ (01408) 621 252 – www.royalmarinebrora.com

21 rm – †£ 105/145 ††£ 148/200

Rest *Lorimer's* – Carte £ 26/40 – *(bar lunch Monday-Saturday)*

Cream-washed Arts and Crafts house, set next to a top golf course. Leather-furnished lounges and a wood-floored bar. Smart, modern, country house bedrooms with warm fabrics and a good level of facilities. Formal linen-laid restaurant offers traditional Scottish menus.

SCOTLAND

BUNCHREW → See Inverness
Highland

BURRAY → See Orkney Islands (Mainland)
Orkney Islands – Michelin Road map 501-L7

CADBOLL → See Tain
Highland

CALLANDER
Stirling – Pop. 3 077 – See Regional map n°**28-C2**
Edinburgh 52 mi – Glasgow 43 mi – Oban 71 mi – Perth 41 mi
Michelin Road map 501-H15 – Michelin Green Guide SCOTLAND

Roman Camp
Main St ✉ FK17 8BG – ✆ (01877) 330 003 – www.romancamphotel.co.uk
15 rm – †£ 110/185 ††£ 160/250 – 3 suites
Rest *Roman Camp* – see restaurant listing
Pretty pink house – a former 17C hunting lodge – set by the river among well-tended gardens. Traditional bedrooms with a subtle contemporary edge and smart, marble-tiled bathrooms. Characterful panelled library and chapel. Charming service.

SCOTLAND

Westerton without rest

Leny Rd ✉ FK17 8AJ – ✆ (01877) 330 147 – www.westertonhouse.co.uk – Closed November-Easter
3 rm – †£ 90/130 ††£ 95/135
Sweet stone house run by delightful owners. Vast sweeping garden with mature trees and colourful azaleas. Open-plan lounge and breakfast room; tasty breakfasts feature fresh, local produce. Spotless bedrooms with DVD players and wi-fi.

Roman Camp – Roman Camp Hotel
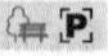
Main St ✉ FK17 8BG – ✆ (01877) 330 003 – www.romancamphotel.co.uk
Menu £ 28/55 – Carte £ 53/71
Enjoy drinks and canapés in the characterful lounge or library of this charming riverside hotel, before dinner in the formal restaurant. Ambitious, modern, well-presented cooking; choose the tasting menu for the best value.

Mhor Fish
75-77 Main St ✉ FK17 8DX – ✆ (01877) 330 213 – www.mhor.net – 25-26 December, 1 January and Monday except bank holidays
Carte £ 13/25
On one side, a classic take-away chippie; on the other, a funky, modern, all-day café with a fish counter displaying the day's catch. The tasty chips are cooked in beef dripping and the pies and bread are from their nearby bakery.

CARNOUSTIE
Angus – Pop. 11 394 – See Regional map n°**28-D2**
Edinburgh 46 mi – London 438 mi – Glasgow 46 mi – Aberdeen 102 mi
Michelin Road map 501-L14

Old Manor without rest
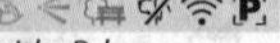
Panbride ✉ DD7 6JP – Northeast : 1.25 mi by A 930 on Panbride Rd – ✆ (01241) 854 804 – www.oldmanorcarnoustie.com – Closed 2 weeks Christmas-New Year
5 rm – †£ 65 ††£ 90
Sizeable house built in 1765 – formerly a manse – commanding great views over patchwork fields to the sea beyond. Comfortable lounge and a good-sized breakfast room. Spotlessly kept bedrooms come with quality bedding, biscuits and chocolates; 'Balmoral' and 'Dunotter' boast superb outlooks.

CARRADALE → See Kintyre (Peninsula)

Argyll and Bute – Michelin Road map 501-D17

CASTLE DOUGLAS

Dumfries and Galloway – Pop. 4 174 – See Regional map n°**25**-B3
▶ Edinburgh 98 mi – Ayr 49 mi – Dumfries 18 mi – Stranraer 57 mi
Michelin Road map 501-I19 and 502 – Michelin Green Guide SCOTLAND

Douglas House without rest

63 Queen St ✉ DG7 1HS – ✆ (01556) 503 262 – www.douglas-house.com – Closed Christmas

4 rm ☕ – †£ 38/40 ††£ 75/82

Attractive 19C stone-built house, set close to the high street. Open-plan lounge and breakfast room. Comfy, individually decorated bedrooms with contemporary feel. Extensive breakfast menu.

CASTLEBAY → See Barra (Isle of)

Western Isles – Michelin Road map 501-X12/1

CHIRNSIDE

The Scottish Borders – Pop. 1 459 – ✉ Duns – See Regional map n°**26**-D1
▶ Edinburgh 52 mi – Berwick-upon-Tweed 8 mi – Glasgow 95 mi – Newcastle upon Tyne 70 mi
Michelin Road map 501-N16

Chirnside Hall

✉ TD11 3LD East : 1.75 mi on A 6105 – ✆ (01890) 818 219 – www.chirnsidehallhotel.com – Closed March

10 rm ☕ – †£ 100/195 ††£ 150/195

Rest – Menu £ 25 – *(dinner only) (booking essential)*

Sizeable 1834 country house with a lovely revolving door and beautiful views over the Cheviots. Grand lounges have original cornicing and huge fireplaces. Bedrooms are cosy and classical; some have four-poster beds. Local, seasonal dishes in traditional dining room.

COLBOST → See Skye (Isle of)

Highland – Michelin Road map 501-A11

COMRIE

Perth and Kinross – Pop. 1 927 – See Regional map n°**28**-C2
▶ Edinburgh 66 mi – Glasgow 56 mi – Oban 70 mi – Perth 24 mi
Michelin Road map 501-I14

Royal

Melville Sq ✉ PH6 2DN – ✆ (01764) 679 200 – www.royalhotel.co.uk – Closed 25-26 December

11 rm ☕ – †£ 90/110 ††£ 150/190

Rest *Royal* – see restaurant listing

Charming coaching inn dating back to the 18C and set at the heart of a riverside town. Cosy bar and lovely open-fired library with squashy sofas. Well-appointed bedrooms; some with four-posters and antiques. Relaxed, personable service.

Royal – Royal Hotel

Melville Sq ✉ PH6 2DN – ✆ (01764) 679 200 – www.royalhotel.co.uk – Closed 25-26 December

Carte £ 26/41

Intimate dining room and a bright conservatory, set within a stylishly decorated coaching inn. Concise menu of classically based dishes with modern touches. Produce is seasonal and locally sourced; the mussels and steaks are superb.

CONNEL

Argyll and Bute ✉ Oban – See Regional map n°**27-B2**
▶ Edinburgh 118 mi – Glasgow 88 mi – Inverness 113 mi – Oban 5 mi
Michelin Road map 501-D14

Ards House without rest
✉ *PA37 1PT on A 85 – ✆ (01631) 710 255 – www.ardshouse.com – Closed Christmas-New Year*
4 rm – †£ 55/70 ††£ 88/100
Attractive house with an equally welcoming, hospitable owner. The large, homely lounge is packed with books and antiques. Cosy, personally decorated bedrooms show good attention to detail; small bathrooms boast locally made toiletries. Excellent breakfasts with fresh fruit and delicious roasted coffee.

CRIEFF

Perth and Kinross – Pop. 7 368 – See Regional map n°**28-C2**
▶ Edinburgh 60 mi – Glasgow 50 mi – Oban 76 mi – Perth 18 mi
Michelin Road map 501-I14 – Michelin Green Guide SCOTLAND

Merlindale without rest
Perth Rd ✉ PH7 3EQ – on A 85 – ✆ (01764) 655 205 – www.merlindale.co.uk – Closed mid-December-February
3 rm – †£ 70/90 ††£ 85/100
Spacious manor house with a comfy lounge, a well-stocked library and a dark wood furnished room for family-style breakfasts. Immaculate bedrooms have classic furnishings, floral drapes and large bathrooms; some boast roll-top baths.

SCOTLAND

Yann's at Glenearn House with rm
Perth Rd ✉ PH7 3EQ – on A 85 – ✆ (01764) 650 111 – www.yannsatglenearnhouse.com – Closed 1 week October and 25 December
4 rm – †£ 65/75 ††£ 90/100
Menu £ 15 (lunch) – Carte £ 22/37 – *(dinner only and lunch Thursday-Sunday)*
Busy restaurant in a Victorian house, with a delightful lounge and a large bistro-style dining room hung with French prints. Gallic cooking makes good use of Scottish produce and Savoyard sharing dishes are a speciality. Comfy, cosy bedrooms have good facilities and a relaxed, bohemian style. Pleasant team.

at Muthill South: 3 mi by A822

Barley Bree with rm
6 Willoughby St ✉ PH5 2AB – ✆ (01764) 681 451 – www.barleybree.com – Closed Christmas-New Year, Monday and Tuesday
6 rm – †£ 70/85 ††£ 110/150 Carte £ 32/47 **s** – *(booking advisable)*
Intimate converted coaching inn at the centre of a busy village, with a spacious fire-lit sitting room and a dining room hung with angling memorabilia. Rustic, classical cooking utilises local ingredients and arrives in generous portions. Service is friendly and bedrooms are comfortable and well-thought-out.

CRINAN

Argyll and Bute ✉ Lochgilphead – See Regional map n°**27-B2**
▶ Edinburgh 137 mi – Glasgow 91 mi – Oban 36 mi
Michelin Road map 501-D15 – Michelin Green Guide SCOTLAND

Crinan
✉ *PA31 8SR – ✆ (01546) 830 261 – www.crinanhotel.com – Closed January and Christmas*
20 rm – †£ 100/130 ††£ 190/260
Rest *Westward* – see restaurant listing
Rest *Seafood Bar* – Carte £ 21/34
Built in the 19C to accommodate the Laird of Jura's business associates and boasting lovely Sound views. Simply furnished bedrooms – some with balconies and views. Small coffee shop sells homemade cakes; superb 3rd floor bar with terrace. Larger, wood-panelled bar offers an appealing menu of seafood dishes.

XX **Westward** – Crinan Hotel
✉ *PA31 8SR – ✆ (01546) 830 261 – www.crinanhotel.com – Closed January and Christmas*
Menu £ 39 – *(dinner only)*
Set within a welcoming, family-run hotel and boasting lovely views over the loch and Sound of Jura. Concise seafood-based menus rely on local and island produce. Homemade chocolates to finish.

CULLODEN → See Inverness
Highland – Michelin Road map 501-H11

CULNAKNOCK → See Skye (Isle of)
Highland – Michelin Road map 501-B11

CUMNOCK
East Ayrshire – Pop. 9 039 – See Regional map n°**25**-B2
Edinburgh 85 mi – Glasgow 38 mi – Dumfries 44 mi – Carlisle 88 mi
Michelin Road map 501-H17

Dumfries House Lodge Ⓝ without rest
Dumfries House ✉ KA18 2NJ – West : 1.5 mi on A 70 – ✆ (01290) 429 920 – www.dumfrieshouselodge.co.uk – Closed 23-27 December and 31-December-3 January
22 rm – †£ 60/70 ††£ 60/145
This old factor's house and steading – at the entrance to the 2,000 acre Dumfries Estate – is now a stylish country house hotel. There are two cosy lounges and a billiard room; some of the furniture is from the original manor house.

SCOTLAND

CUPAR
Fife – Pop. 9 339 – See Regional map n°**28**-C2
Edinburgh 45 mi – Dundee 15 mi – Perth 23 mi
Michelin Road map 501-K15

XX **Ostler's Close**
25 Bonnygate ✉ KY15 4BU – ✆ (01334) 655 574 – www.ostlersclose.co.uk – Closed 2 weeks April, 25-26 December, 1-2 January, Sunday and Monday
Menu £ 29 (weekdays) – Carte £ 37/49 – *(dinner only and Saturday lunch)*
Long-standing, personally run restaurant down a narrow alley just off the main street. Three cosy rooms decorated in warm reds; friendly, chatty service. Concise, traditional menus with beef and seafood to the fore and a Mediterranean edge.

CURRIE → See Edinburgh
City of Edinburgh – Michelin Road map 501-K16

DALKEITH
Midlothian – Pop. 12 342 – See Regional map n°**26**-C1
Edinburgh 6 mi – London 374 mi – Glasgow 51 mi – Manchester 208 mi
Michelin Road map 501-K16

Sun Inn with rm
Lothian Bridge ✉ EH22 4TR – Southwest : 2 mi by A 6094 and B 6392 on A 7 – ✆ (0131) 663 24 56 – www.thesuninnedinburgh.co.uk – Closed 26 December and 1 January
5 rm – †£ 75 ††£ 95/150 Menu £ 14 (weekdays) – Carte £ 20/39
17C former blacksmith's with two large, open-fired rooms; their wood and stone-faced walls hung with modern black and white photos. Extensive menus feature good quality local produce; lunch keeps things simple but appealing. Smart bedrooms boast handmade furniture and Egyptian cotton linen.

DALRY

North Ayrshire – See Regional map n°**25-A1**
Edinburgh 70 mi – Ayr 21 mi – Glasgow 25 mi
Michelin Road map 501-F16 and 502

Lochwood Farm Steading without rest 
Saltcoats ✉ KA21 6NG – Southwest : 5 mi by A 737 and Saltcoats rd – ✆ (01294) 552 529 – www.lochwoodfarm.co.uk – Closed Christmas
4 rm – £ 120 £ 140
Remote farmhouse on a 100 acre working dairy farm, boasting impressive panoramic views. Luxuriously appointed bedrooms are split between an old barn and a rustic wood house – two have private hot tubs. Breakfast is served by candlelight!

XX

Braidwoods (Keith Braidwood)
Drumastle Mill Cottage ✉ KA24 4LN – Southwest : 1.5 mi by A 737 on Saltcoats rd – ✆ (01294) 833 544 – www.braidwoods.co.uk – Closed 25 December-29 January, 2 weeks September, Sunday dinner, Monday, Tuesday lunch and Sunday from May-mid September
Menu £ 25/50 – *(booking essential)*
Former crofter's cottage hidden away in the countryside; personally run by experienced owners. Cosy and charming, with just a handful of tables in each of its two rooms. Concise menu of confident, classical cooking uses quality seasonal ingredients; dishes have clear flavours. Great value lunch.
➜ Scallops on a leek and pea purée and mustard butter. Loin of deer with wild mushrooms and a celeriac and Jerusalem artichoke purée. Iced heather honey parfait with poached rhubarb, blood orange jelly and puff candy.

DEERNESS

➜ See Orkney Islands (Mainland)

DINGWALL

Highland – Pop. 5 491 – See Regional map n°**30-C2**
Edinburgh 172 mi – Inverness 14 mi – Glasgow 182 mi – Aberdeen 115 mi
Michelin Road map 501-G11

XX

Café India Brasserie
Lockhart House, Tulloch St ✉ IV15 9JZ – ✆ (01349) 862 552 – www.cafeindiadingwall.co.uk – Closed 25 December
Menu £ 9 (weekday lunch) – Carte £ 15/32
Well-run Indian restaurant close to the town centre. Small lounge and several dining areas separated by etched glass screens. Good range of authentic, regional dishes, with tasty Thalis, set menus for 2+ and good value two course lunches.

DINNET

Aberdeenshire – See Regional map n°**28-D1**
Edinburgh 114 mi – London 517 mi – Glasgow 134 mi – Bradford 325 mi
Michelin Road map 501-L12

Glendavan House without rest 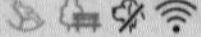
✉ AB34 5LU Northwest : 3 mi by A 97 on B 9119 – ✆ (01339) 881 610 – www.glendavanhouse.com
3 rm – £ 95/125 £ 120/160
Set in 9 lochside acres, this former shooting lodge is somewhere to 'get away from it all'. Two of the three bedrooms are very large suites; all are tastefully furnished with antiques and memorabilia. Delicious communal breakfasts.

DORNOCH

Highland – Pop. 1 208 – See Regional map n°**30-D2**
Edinburgh 219 mi – Inverness 63 mi – Wick 65 mi
Michelin Road map 501-H10 – Michelin Green Guide SCOTLAND

Links House

Golf Rd ✉ *IV25 3LW – (01862) 810 279 – www.linkshousedornoch.com – Closed 5 January-1 March*

8 rm – £ 270/360 £ 270/380

Rest *The Orangery* – Menu £ 60 – *(dinner only and Sunday lunch in winter) (bookings essential for non-residents) (set menu only)*

This restored 19C manse sits opposite the first tee of the Royal Dornoch Golf Club. Enjoy a dram from the honesty bar in the pine-panelled library or have tea and cake in the antique-furnished sitting room. Some of the beautifully furnished bedrooms feature bespoke tweed fabrics. The elegant orangery boasts an impressive stone fireplace and serves a modern set menu.

Highfield House without rest

Evelix Rd ✉ *IV25 3HR – (01862) 810 909 – www.highfieldhouse.co.uk – Closed January-February*

4 rm – £ 68 £ 90/95

Welcoming guesthouse with immaculately kept gardens and a pleasant summer house. Spacious guest areas consist of a conservatory style lounge and a smart breakfast room. Comfy bedrooms have good facilities.

DOUNBY → See Orkney Islands (Mainland)

– Michelin Road map 501-K16

DRUMBEG

Highland – See Regional map n°**30**-C1

Edinburgh 262 mi – Inverness 105 mi – Ullapool 48 mi

Michelin Road map 501-E9

Blar na Leisg at Drumbeg House

✉ *IV27 4NW Take first right on entering village from Kylesku direction – (01571) 833 325 – www.blarnaleisg.com*

5 rm – £ 75/150 £ 150/156 **Rest** – Menu £ 58

Remotely set Edwardian house affording lovely loch views. Large, open-fired sitting room filled with a vast array of books; spacious, luxuriously appointed bedrooms. Impressive modern art collection includes lots of Bauhaus works. Smart, contemporary dining room; Highland beef and game birds a speciality.

DRUMNADROCHIT

Highland – Pop. 1 101 – ✉ Milton – See Regional map n°**30**-C2

Edinburgh 172 mi – Inverness 16 mi – Kyle of Lochalsh 66 mi

Michelin Road map 501-G11 – Michelin Green Guide SCOTLAND

Drumbuie Farm without rest

Drumbuie ✉ *IV63 6XP – East : 0.75 mi by A 82 – (01456) 450 634 – www.loch-ness-farm.co.uk – Closed December-January*

3 rm – £ 44 £ 68/70

Friendly guesthouse above Loch Ness, on a 120 acre sheep and cattle farm. It's warm and welcoming, from the traditional lounge to the pine-furnished bedrooms; two of which have body jet showers. Take in the view from the breakfast room.

DUISDALEMORE → See Skye (Isle of)

Highland

DUMFRIES

Dumfries and Galloway – Pop. 32 914 – See Regional map n°**26**-C3

Edinburgh 80 mi – Ayr 59 mi – Carlisle 34 mi – Glasgow 79 mi

Michelin Road map 501-J18 and 502 – Michelin Green Guide SCOTLAND

DUMFRIES

Street	Grid	No.
Aldermanhill Rd	B	2
Bank St	A	3
Buccleuch St	A	4
Cardoness St	B	5
Cassalands	A	6
Castle Douglas Rd	A	8
Castle St	A	7
Catherine St	B	9
Corberry Ave	A	10
Cornwall Mount Rd	B	12
Cuckoo Bridge Retail Park	A	
Friars Vennel	A	13
Galloway St	A	14
Glebe St	B	15
Great King St	A	16
Hermitage Drive	A	17
High St	A	18
Loreburn Centre	A	20
Loreburn St	A	21
Nith St	AB	22
Queensberry St	A	24
Queen St	B	23
Rae St	B	26
St Mary's St	B	27
St Michael St	B	28
St Michael's Bridge Rd	A	30
Shakespeare St	B	31
Union St	A	32
Whitesands	A	34

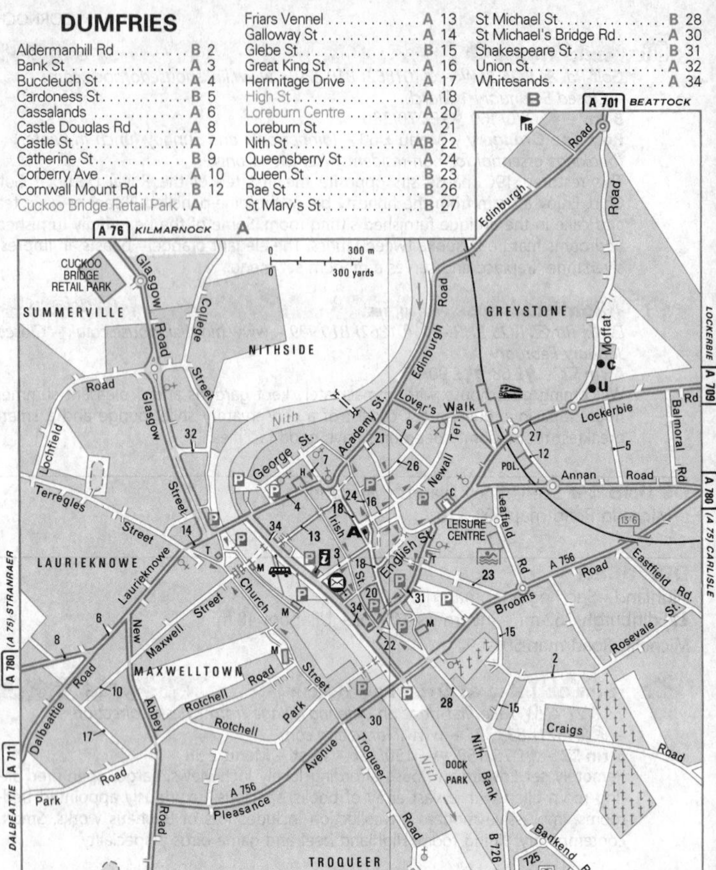

🏠 **Hazeldean House** without rest

4 Moffat Rd ✉ DG1 1NJ – ✆ (01387) 266 178 Town plan: B**u**

– www.hazeldeanhouse.com

6 rm ☕ – 🚹£ 37/45 🚹🚹£ 60/65

Victorian villa built in 1898, with a lovely garden, a curio-filled lounge and a conservatory breakfast room. Victorian-themed bedrooms – three with four-posters; the basement room has a nautical cabin style.

🏠 **Hamilton House** without rest

12 Moffat Rd ✉ DG1 1NJ – ✆ (01387) 266 606 Town plan: B**c**

– www.hamiltonhousedumfries.co.uk – Closed 24 December-3 January

7 rm ☕ – 🚹£ 40/50 🚹🚹£ 60/65

Converted Victorian townhouse next to the bowls club. Large conservatory lounge; neat breakfast tables overlook the tennis courts. Large bedrooms combine the classical and the contemporary.

DUNBAR

East Lothian – Pop. 8 486 – See Regional map n°**26**-D1
Edinburgh 30 mi – London 369 mi – Glasgow 76 mi – Leeds 190 mi
Michelin Road map 501-M15

Creel

The Harbour, 25 Lamer St ✉ EH42 1HG – ✆ (01368) 863 279 – www.creelrestaurant.co.uk – Closed Sunday dinner-Wednesday lunch
Menu £ 17/28 – *(booking essential)*
Unassuming former pub in a working harbour. Wood panelled walls and polished tables are brightened by a welcoming team. Experienced chef uses lesser known cuts from local suppliers and transforms them into good value, full-flavoured dishes.

DUNBLANE

Stirling – Pop. 8 811 – See Regional map n°**28**-C2
Edinburgh 42 mi – Glasgow 33 mi – Perth 29 mi
Michelin Road map 501-I15 – Michelin Green Guide SCOTLAND

Cromlix (N)

Kinbuck ✉ FK15 9JT – North : 3.5 mi on B 8033 – ✆ (01786) 822 125 – www.cromlix.com
16 rm – †£ 150/220 ††£ 220/400 – 5 suites
Rest *Chez Roux* – Menu £ 27/30 – Carte £ 35/55
This famous country house has had a top to toe makeover courtesy of new owner, Andy Murray. It boasts elegantly appointed sitting rooms, a whisky room and plush bedrooms with steam showers; along with a fabulous chapel and a smart tennis court in its 30 acre grounds. The modern brasserie serves French classics.

Doubletree by Hilton Dunblane Hydro

Perth Rd ✉ FK15 OHG – North : 0.75 mi on B 8033 – ✆ (01786) 826 600 – www.doubletreedunblane.com
200 rm – †£ 89/200 ††£ 99/250 – 6 suites
Rest *Kailyard by Nick Nairn* – see restaurant listing
A 'grand old lady' originally built in the 1800s; rejuvenated and given a modern, corporate style. Set in ten acres, it boasts extensive conference facilities, a family-orientated spa and smart, up-to-date bedrooms.

Kailyard by Nick Nairn – Doubletree by Hilton Dunblane Hydro Hotel

Perth Rd ✉ FK15 OHG – North : 0.75 mi on B 8033 – ✆ (01786) 822 551 – www.doubletreedunblane.com/the_kailyard
Menu £ 20/30
Large, contemporary restaurant set within a characterful, grand hotel; its name means 'small Scottish vegetable garden'. Menus focus on well-prepared modern classics with some Nick Nairn signature dishes.

Old Churches House (N) with rm

Cathedral Sq ✉ FK15 OAJ – ✆ (01786) 823 663 – www.oldchurcheshouse.com – Closed 25-26 December and 1 January
11 rm – †£ 55/95 ††£ 65/130 Carte £ 19/34
These sympathetically refurbished 18C cottages look out over the square towards the medieval cathedral. Exposed timbers are hung with twinkling lights in the first floor dining room. Traditional cooking uses Scottish ingredients in flavoursome dishes ranging from soup to steamed salmon. Bedrooms are cosy.

DUNDEE

Dundee City – Pop. 147 285 – See Regional map n°**28**-C2
Edinburgh 63 mi – London 458 mi – Glasgow 76 mi – Newcastle upon Tyne 163 mi
Michelin Road map 501-L14 – Michelin Green Guide SCOTLAND

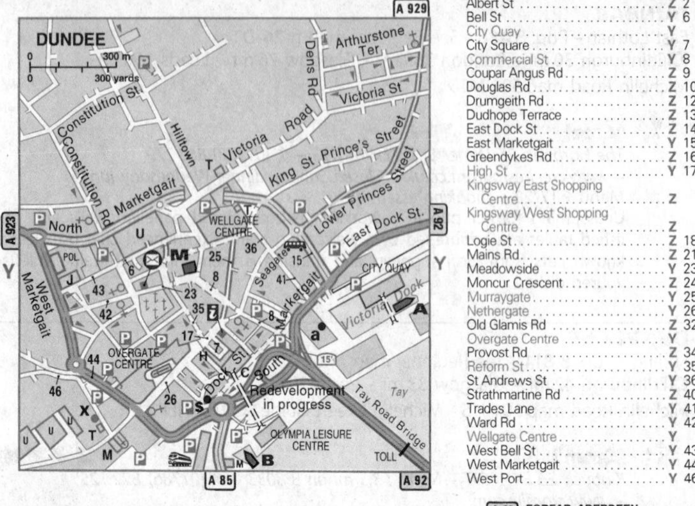

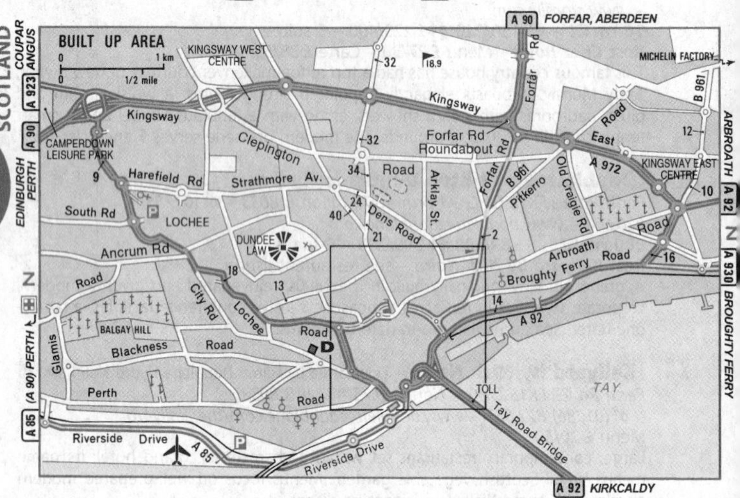

Apex City Quay

1 West Victoria Dock Rd ✉ *DD1 3JP – ✆ (01382) 202 404* Town plan: Y**a**
– www.apexhotels.co.uk

151 rm – †£ 72/235 ††£ 72/235, ☕ £ 10 – 2 suites
Rest *Metro Brasserie* – Menu £ 13/22 – Carte £ 22/43
Modern waterfront hotel with good business facilities and an atmospheric spa; located in an up-and-coming area. Well-proportioned, contemporary bedrooms boast king-sized beds and oversized windows that look out towards the city or the marina. Vast bar-lounge and spacious brasserie with an accessible menu.

Good food at moderate prices? Look for the Bib Gourmand ☺.

Malmaison (N)

44 Whitehall Cres ✉ DD1 4AY – ✆ (0844) 693 0661 – www.malmaison.com Town plan: Y**s**

91 rm – †£ 189 ††£ 189, ☕ £ 16

Rest *Brasserie* – Menu £ 20 – Carte £ 19/38

The best feature of this lovingly restored hotel is the wrought iron cantilevered staircase topped by a domed ceiling. Contemporary bedrooms come in striking bold colours and have a masculine feel. The all-day bar serves cocktails and nibbles and there's a DJ at weekends; the brasserie offers a grill menu.

Doubletree by Hilton Dundee

Kingsway West ✉ DD2 5JT – West : 4.5 mi by A 85 at junction with A 90 – ✆ (01382) 641 122 – www.doubletree3.hilton.com

92 rm – †£ 89/189 ††£ 99/199

Rest *Maze* – Carte £ 27/41

Charming granite country house – formerly a private residence – dating from 1870 and surrounded by smart landscaped gardens. Sizeable modern bedrooms have good facilities; there's also a small gym, and a 24hr business centre. The elegant L-shaped conservatory restaurant keeps Scottish ingredients to the fore.

XX **Playwright**

11 Tay Sq, South Tay St. ✉ DD1 1PB – ✆ (01382) 223 113 – www.theplaywright.co.uk – Closed 25-26 December, 1-3 January and Sunday Town plan: Y**x**

Menu £ 13/20 – Carte £ 32/48

Smart, modern bar and restaurant in an imposing 19C grey-stone building beside the Rep Theatre. Seasonal menus offer modern interpretations of classical dishes and everything from the bread to ice cream is made in-house. Great value lunch.

SCOTLAND

DUNKELD

Perth and Kinross – Pop. 1 005 – See Regional map n°**28**-C2

▶Edinburgh 58 mi – Aberdeen 88 mi – Inverness 98 mi – Perth 14 mi

Michelin Road map 501-J14 – Michelin Green Guide SCOTLAND

Letter Farm without rest

Loch of the Lowes ✉ PH8 0HH – Northeast : 3 mi by A 923 on Loch of Lowes rd – ✆ (01350) 724 254 – www.letter-farm.co.uk – Closed late November-early May

3 rm ☕ – †£ 46/50 ††£ 76/82

Traditional farmhouse on a family-run stock farm, nestled between Butterstone Loch and the Loch of Lowes Nature Reserve. Welcoming open-fired lounge and homely communal breakfast room. Comfy, immaculately kept bedrooms come with king-sized beds and nice extras touches; the only TV is in the lounge.

DUNOON

Argyll and Bute – Pop. 8 454 – See Regional map n°**27**-B3

▶Edinburgh 73 mi – Glasgow 27 mi – Oban 77 mi

Michelin Road map 501-F16 – Michelin Green Guide SCOTLAND

Dhailling Lodge

155 Alexandra Par ✉ PA23 8AW – North : 0.75 mi on A 815 – ✆ (01369) 701 253 – www.dhaillinglodge.com – Closed December-February

7 rm ☕ – †£ 40/70 ††£ 76/120 **Rest** – Menu £ 15

Proudly run Victorian villa set on the main seafront, with pleasant gardens and nice bay views from its guest areas. Snug, homely lounge and cosy, individually decorated bedrooms with good extras. The traditional dining room has a period fireplace and a classical daily menu of unfussy pies, roasts and fish.

DUNVEGAN

➜ See Skye (Isle of)

Highland – Michelin Road map 501-A11

DURNESS

Highland – See Regional map n°**30**-C1

Edinburgh 266 mi – Thurso 78 mi – Ullapool 71 mi

Michelin Road map 501-F8

Mackay's without rest

✉ IV27 4PN – ✆ (01971) 511 202 – *www.visitmackays.com* – *Closed October-April*

7 rm – †£ 110 ††£ 129/139

Smart grey house at the most north westerly point of the mainland; the family own a number of places in the village. Two nicely furnished, oak-clad lounges. Lovely bedrooms with exposed wood floors, plasma screen TVs and iPod docks.

DUROR

Highland – See Regional map n°**29**-B3

Edinburgh 131 mi – Ballachulish 7 mi – Oban 26 mi

Michelin Road map 501-E14

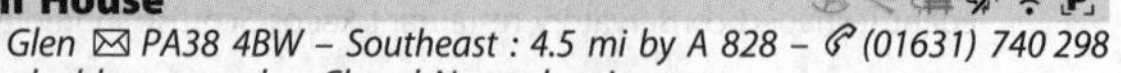

Bealach House

Salachan Glen ✉ *PA38 4BW – Southeast : 4.5 mi by A 828 –* ✆ *(01631) 740 298 – www.bealachhouse.co.uk – Closed November-January*

3 rm – †£ 65/75 ††£ 90/110 **Rest** – Menu £ 30

Superbly set, former crofter's house with an impressive 1.5 mile driveway lined with mature, deer-filled forest: the scenery is breathtaking. Snug conservatory and cosy bedrooms; homely guest areas are hung with Lowry tapestries. Classical, daily changing menu.

SCOTLAND

DYKE

Moray

Edinburgh 163 mi – London 564 mi – Aberdeen 81 mi – Glasgow 177 mi

Michelin Road map 501-J11

Old Kirk without rest

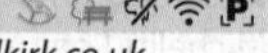

✉ *IV36 2TL Northeast : 0.5 mi –* ✆ *(01309) 641 414 – www.oldkirk.co.uk*

3 rm – †£ 70 ††£ 85

A peacefully set, converted 1856 church, surrounded by grain fields. Airy interior, with a cosy library and a comfortable, open-fired lounge displaying an original stained glass window. Charming, individually decorated bedrooms boast original stonework and arched windows; one has a carved four-poster.

EDDLESTON

→ See Peebles

The Scottish Borders – Michelin Road map 501-K16

EDINBANE

→ See Skye (Isle of)

Highland – Michelin Road map 501-A11

EDINBURGH

City of Edinburgh – Pop. 459 366 – See Regional map n°**26-C1**
London 397 mi – Glasgow 46 mi – Newcastle upon Tyne 120 mi – Aberdeen 126 mi
Michelin Road map 501-K16 – Michelin Green Guide SCOTLAND

© The Kitchin

Hotels

SCOTLAND

Balmoral rm, rm,

1 Princes St ✉ EH2 2EQ – ✆ (0131) 556 24 14 – www.roccofortehotels.com Town plan: EY**n**

188 rm – £ 180/540 £ 180/540 – 20 suites

Rest *Number One* – see restaurant listing

Rest *Hadrian's* – ✆ (0131) 557 50 00 – Menu £ 15/24 – Carte £ 25/51

Renowned Edwardian hotel which provides for the modern traveller whilst retaining its old-fashioned charm. Live harp music accompanies afternoon tea. Bedrooms are classically styled but have a subtle contemporary edge; JK Rowling completed the final Harry Potter book in one of the suites! Luxurious modern dining room or brasserie classics in delightful Hadrian's.

Sheraton Grand H. & Spa

1 Festival Sq ✉ EH3 9SR – ✆ (0131) 229 91 31 – www.sheratonedinburgh.co.uk Town plan: CDZ**v**

269 rm – £ 170/595 £ 170/595, £ 20 – 10 suites

Rest *One Square* – see restaurant listing

Spacious, modern hotel which has undergone a top-to-toe refurbishment. Sleek, stylish bedrooms boast strong comforts, the latest mod cons and smart bathrooms with mood lighting. An impressive four-storey glass cube houses the stunning spa.

Caledonian

Princes St ✉ EH1 2AB – ✆ (0131) 222 8888 – www.thecaledonianedinburgh.com Town plan: CZ**x**

241 rm – £ 175/599 £ 175/599, £ 21 – 7 suites

Rest *Galvin Brasserie De Luxe* **Rest *The Pompadour by Galvin*** – see restaurant listing

Smartly refurbished hotel in the old Princes Street railway terminus; the stylish cocktail bar is in the arrivals hall. Sumptuous modern bedrooms with excellent facilities; ask for a castle view. They have the first Guerlain spa in the UK.

Take note of the classification: you should not expect the same level of service in a X or as in a XXXXX or .

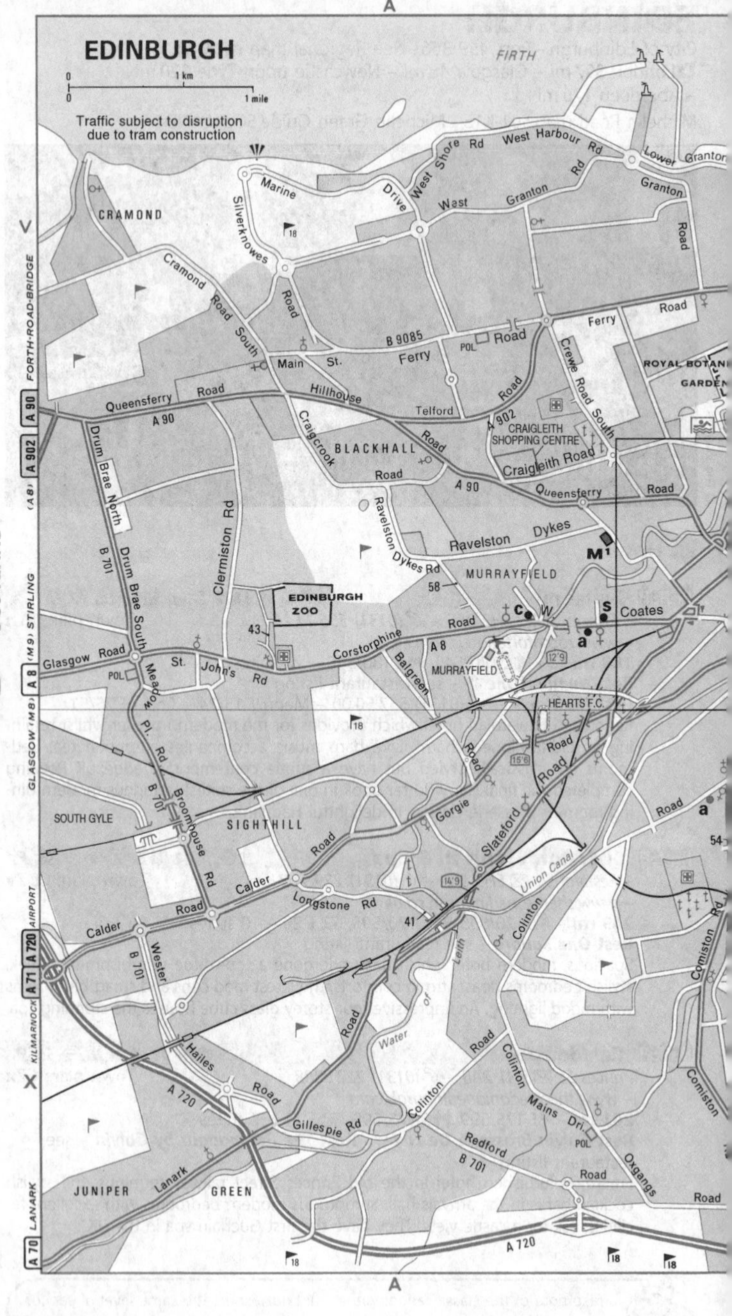
EDINBURGH
0 1 km
0 1 mile
Traffic subject to disruption
due to tram construction
FIRTH
CRAMOND
Marine
Drive
Silverknowes
Road
West Shore Rd
West Harbour Rd
West
Granton
Rd
Lower Granton
Granton
Road
Cramond
Road
South
B 9085
Main St.
Ferry
POL
Road
Crewe Road South
Ferry
Road
ROYAL BOTANIC
GARDEN
Queensferry
Road
A 90
Hillhouse
Road
Telford
Road
A 902
CRAIGLEITH
SHOPPING CENTRE
Craigleith Road
Craigcrook
BLACKHALL
Road
A 90
Queensferry
Road
Drum
Brae
North
B 701
Drum Brae South
Clermiston Rd
Ravelston
Dykes Rd
Ravelston
Dykes
M1
MURRAYFIELD
58
EDINBURGH
ZOO
43
C
W.
S
Coates
a
Road
Corstorphine
A 8
Glasgow Road
POL
St.
John's
Rd
Meadow
Pl.
Rd
Balgreen
Road
MURRAYFIELD
12'9
HEARTS F.C.
Road
15'6
Road
Gorgie
Road
a
54
B 701
Broomhouse
Rd
SOUTH GYLE
SIGHTHILL
Road
Calder
Slateford
Union Canal
14'9
Longstone Rd
Calder
Road
Road
41
Colinton
Comiston
Rd
B 701
Wester
Water
of
Leith
Road
Road
Colinton
Mains
Dri.
Comiston
Road
Hailes
Road
A 720
Colinton
Gillespie Rd
Redford
B 701
POL
Road
Oxgangs
Road
JUNIPER
Lanark
GREEN
A 720
A
V
X
FORTH-ROAD-BRIDGE
A 90
A 902
(A8) STIRLING (M9)
A 8
GLASGOW (M8)
AIRPORT
A 720
A 71
KILMARNOCK
LANARK
A 70
18

Street	Grid	No.
Bruntsfield Pl.	BX	8
Cameron Toll Centre	BX	
Commercial St	BV	15
Constitution St	BV	17
Craigleith Shopping Centre	AV	
Craigmillar Park	BX	20
Duddingston Park	BV	28
Gilmerton Dykes St	BX	34
Great Junction St	BV	36
Howden Hall Rd	BX	40
Inglis Green Rd	AX	41
Kaimes Rd	AV	43
Morningside Rd	AX	54
Murrayfield Rd	AV	58
Newtoft St	BX	60
North Junction St	BV	62
Ocean Terminal Shopping Centre	BV	
Portobello High St	BV	67
Salamander St	BV	76

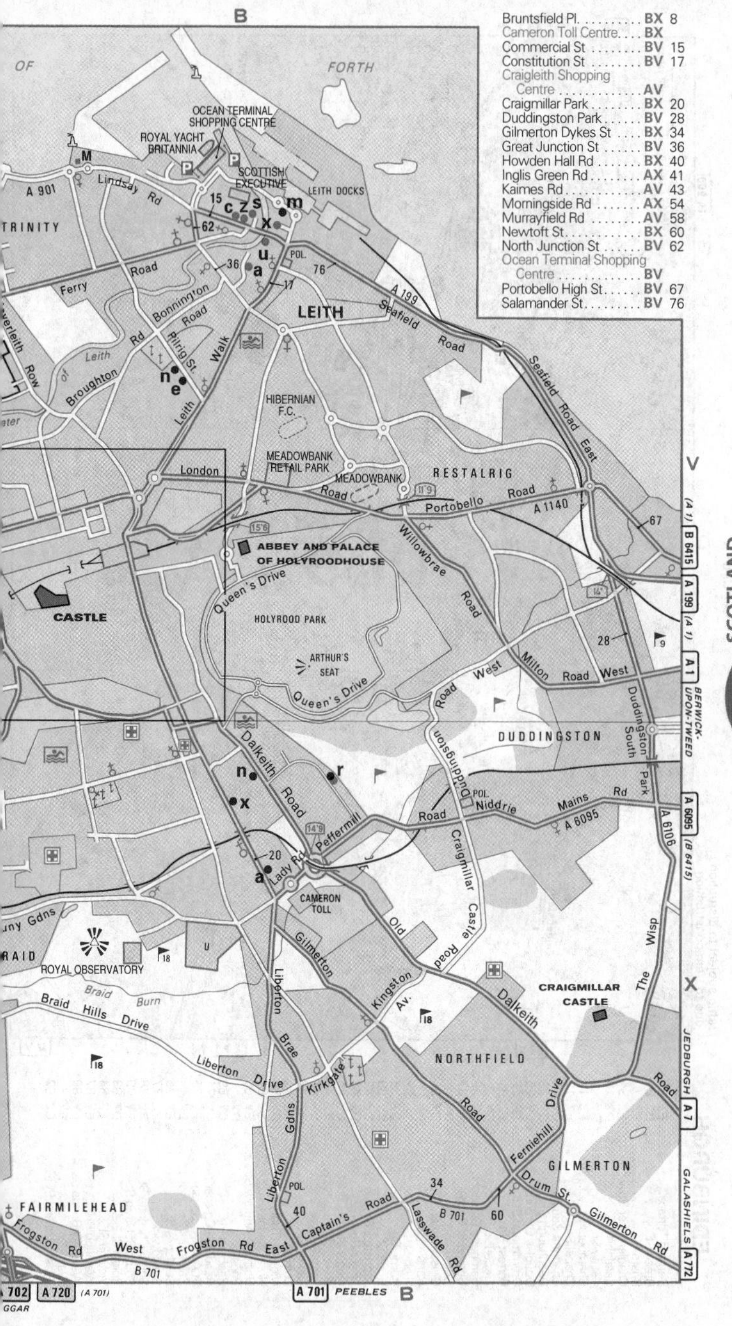

EDINBURGH

Street	Grid	No.
Bernard Terrace	EZ	3
Bread St	DZ	6
Bristo Pl.	EZ	7
Candlemaker Row	EZ	9
Castlehill	DZ	10
Castle St	DY	
Chambers St	EZ	12
Chapel St	EZ	13
Charlotte Square	CY	14
Deanhaugh St	CY	23
Douglas Gardens	CY	25
Drummond St	EZ	27
Forrest Rd	EZ	31
Frederick St	DY	
Gardner's Crescent	CZ	32
George IV Bridge	EZ	33
George St	DY	
Grassmarket	DZ	35
Hanover St	DY	
High St	EYZ	37
Home St	DZ	38
Hope St	CY	39
Johnston Terrace	DZ	42
King's Bridge	DZ	44
King's Stables Rd	DZ	45
Lawnmarket	EYZ	46
Leith St	EY	47
Leven St	DZ	48
Lothian St	EZ	51
Mound (The)	DY	55
North Bridge	EY	61
North St Andrew St	EY	66
Princes St	DY	
Raeburn Pl.	CY	69
Randolph Crescent	CY	71
St Andrew Square	EY	73
St James Centre	EY	
St Mary's St.	EY	75
Shandwick Pl.	CYZ	77
South Charlotte St	DY	78
South St David St	DEY	79
Spittal St	DZ	83
Victoria St.	EZ	84
Waterloo Pl.	EY	87
Waverley Bridge	EY	89
Waverley Market	EY	
West Maitland St	CZ	92

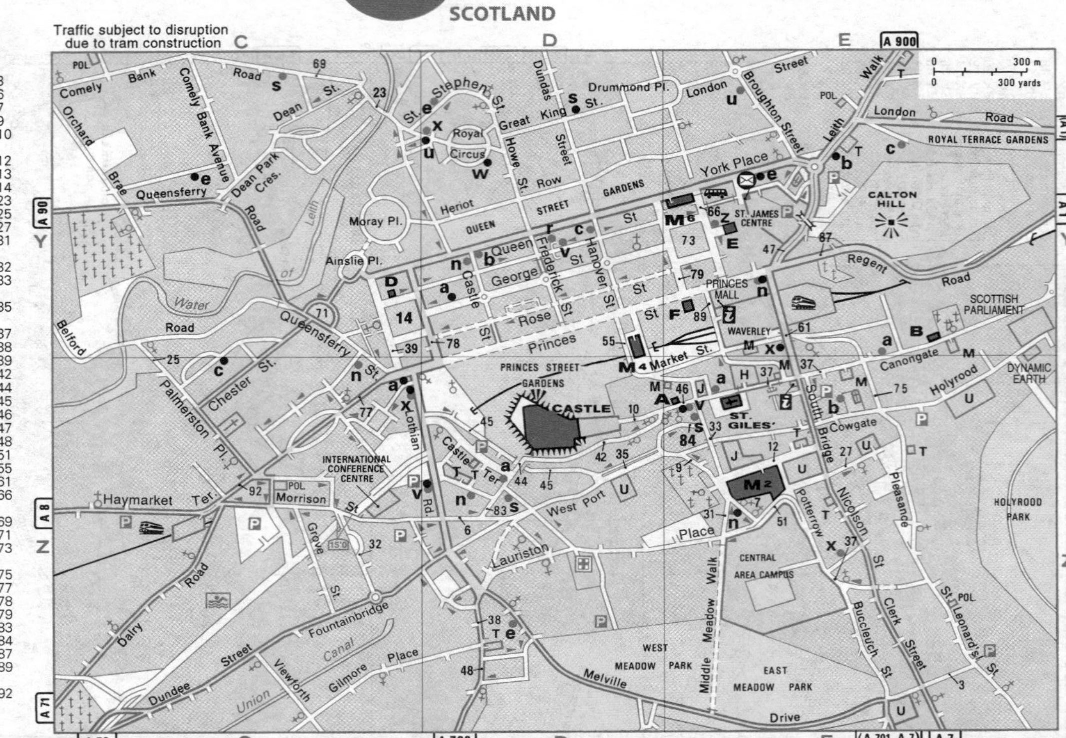

Prestonfield

Priestfield Rd ✉ *EH16 5UT* – *(0131) 225 78 00* Town plan: BX**r**
– *www.prestonfield.com*
28 rm – £ 295 £ 295 – 5 suites
Rest *Rhubarb* – see restaurant listing
17C country house in a pleasant rural spot, with an opulent, dimly lit interior displaying warm colours, fine furnishings and old tapestries; one of the most romantic hotels around. Various elegant lounges and a whisky room. Unique, luxurious bedrooms boast a high level of modern facilities. Excellent service.

Howard

34 Great King St ✉ *EH3 6QH* – *(0131) 557 35 00* Town plan: DY**s**
– *www.thehoward.com*
18 rm – £ 120/240 £ 140/280, £ 19 – 3 suites
Rest *Atholl* – Menu £ 35 – Carte £ 35/63 – *(booking essential)*
A series of three Georgian townhouses with comfortable period lounges and many characterful original features still in situ. Bedrooms vary in size and have classic furnishings and a contemporary edge; every room is assigned a butler. Formal dining from modern menus in the elegant restaurant.

G & V Royal Mile

1 George IV Bridge ✉ *EH1 1AD* – *(0131) 220 66 66* Town plan: EZ**v**
– *www.gandvhotel.com*
136 rm – £ 120/300 £ 180/450, £ 18 – 7 suites
Rest *Cucina* – see restaurant listing
Striking hotel in a great location on the historic Royal Mile. Bold colour schemes mix with modern furnishings and clever design features. Bedrooms come with Nespresso machines and are categorised 'Wee', 'Bonnie', 'Braw' or 'Muckle'.

SCOTLAND

Scotsman

20 North Bridge ✉ *EH3 1TR* – *(0131) 556 55 65* Town plan: EY**x**
– *www.thescotsmanhotel.co.uk*
69 rm – £ 125/325 £ 125/325, £ 17 – 2 suites
Rest *North Bridge Brasserie* – (0131) 622 29 00 – Menu £ 20 (lunch) – Carte dinner £ 26/49
Characterful Victorian hotel within the old Scotsman newspaper offices. Lovely period guest areas feature wood panelling and stained glass; traditional bedrooms are accessed via a marble staircase. Good business and leisure facilities. The stylish brasserie boasts a beautiful ceiling and a minstrels' gallery.

Channings

12-16 South Learmonth Gdns ✉ *EH4 1EZ* – *(0131) 315 2226* – *www.channings.co.uk* Town plan: CY**e**
42 rm – £ 79/260 £ 89/270 – 3 suites
Rest – Menu £ 32 – *(dinner only and lunch Friday-Sunday)*
Set over five adjoining Edwardian townhouses; a cosy, tastefully furnished property run by a friendly team. Traditionally styled drawing rooms and bedrooms; the newer ones are themed after Shackleton, who used to live in one of the houses. The formal basement restaurant serves appealing Gallic classics.

Hotel du Vin

11 Bristo Pl ✉ *EH1 1EZ* – *(0131) 247 49 00* Town plan: EZ**n**
– *www.hotelduvin.com/edinburgh*
47 rm – £ 95/160 £ 170/230, £ 16
Rest *Bistro* – Menu £ 17 – Carte £ 25/50
Boutique hotel featuring unique modern murals and dark wood, wine-themed bedrooms; located close to the Royal Mile. Guest areas include a whisky snug offering 300 spirits and a mezzanine bar with a wine tasting room and glass-fronted cellars. The classical bistro offers traditional European-based cooking.

Tigerlily
rm,

125 George St ✉ *EH2 4JN – ✆ (0131) 225 50 05* Town plan: DY**a**
– www.tigerlilyedinburgh.co.uk – Closed 25 December
33 rm ☕ – 👤£ 125/225 👥£ 125/225
Rest – Menu £ 15 (weekdays) – Carte £ 26/45
Classical Georgian townhouse concealing a funky, boutique interior. Large, individually designed bedrooms are luxurious, boasting seductive lighting, quality furnishings and superb wet rooms. The busy open-plan bar and dining room have similarly stylish modern décor and offer a worldwide menu.

Glasshouse without rest

2 Greenside Pl ✉ *EH1 3AA – ✆ (0131) 525 82 00* Town plan: EY**b**
– www.theetoncollection.co.uk – Closed 24-26 December
65 rm – 👤£ 115/475 👥£ 115/475, ☕ £ 19
A striking combination of a 150 year old church and sleek glass, topped by an impressive two acre roof garden. Stylish bedrooms feature floor to ceiling windows and lots of wood and leather; the suites open onto a sweeping balcony. Instead of a restaurant there's an honesty bar and 3 course room service.

Nira Caledonia

6 and 10 Gloucester Pl ✉ *EH3 6EF – ✆ (0131) 225 27 20* Town plan: DY**u**
– www.niracaledonia.com
28 rm ☕ – 👤£ 110/205 👥£ 129/450
Rest – Menu £ 25 – Carte £ 28/47 – *(dinner only)*
Two luxurious townhouses with romantic interiors and stunningly restored staircases. Bedrooms boast top class furnishings and are decorated in gold, black and silver colour schemes; some have jacuzzis in the rooms. The sleek, modern dining room - in the main house - offers meats cooked on the Josper grill.

SCOTLAND

Rutland
rm,

1-3 Rutland St ✉ *EH1 2AE – ✆ (0131) 229 34 02* Town plan: CZ**a**
– www.therutlandhotel.com – Closed 24-25 December
13 rm ☕ – 👤£ 145/325 👥£ 145/325 – 1 suite
Rest – Menu £ 12 (lunch) – Carte £ 24/48
Boutique hotel occupying a commanding position at the top of Princes Street. Stylish modern bedrooms have bold décor and large slate-floored shower rooms; ask for a castle view. A few doors down is the two-roomed suite. Muffins welcome you on arrival. The contemporary restaurant styles itself on a steakhouse.

Chester Residence without rest

9 Rothesay Pl ✉ *EH3 7SL – ✆ (0131) 226 2075* Town plan: CZ**c**
– www.chester-residence.com – Closed 23-26 December
23 suites – 👥£ 265/600, ☕ £ 9
Collection of townhouses boasting one and two bedroomed suites complete with fully equipped kitchens. State-of-the-art facilities include video entry and integrated sound systems. They can even arrange for a chef to cook in your room!

Hotel Indigo
rm,

51-59 York Pl ✉ *EH1 3JD – ✆ (0131) 556 5577* Town plan: EY**e**
– www.hiedinburgh.co.uk
60 rm ☕ – 👤£ 99/379 👥£ 99/379
Rest – Menu £ 19 (early dinner) – Carte £ 20/38
Five interconnecting Georgian townhouses; one was previously a famous tea and coffee merchant's. Contemporary décor throughout. Bedrooms have bold feature walls, good amenities and powerful showers – those at the front are larger. Simple bistro serves an accessible all-day menu; afternoon tea is popular.

The Dunstane

4 West Coates, Haymarket ✉ *EH12 5JQ – ✆ (0131)* Town plan: AV**s**
337 61 69 – www.thedunstane.co.uk – Closed 23-27 December
38 rm ☕ – 👤£ 75/135 👥£ 139/299
Rest *Skerries* – Carte £ 23/47 – *(dinner only)*
Grand house with well-tended gardens; once a training centre for the Royal Bank of Scotland. Guest areas retain original Victorian features and the smart modern bedrooms are warm and calming; some are located in the house opposite. The restaurant champions local produce, especially seafood.

Kingsburgh House without rest
2 Corstorphine Rd ✉ *EH12 6HN – ☎ (0131) 313 16 79* Town plan: AV**c**
– www.thekingsburgh.co.uk
6 rm ☕ – 🚹£ 110/140 🚹🚹£ 110/170
Attractive Victorian villa with keen, hands-on owners. Comfy lounge and formally laid breakfast room with ornate coving. Warm, classically styled bedrooms feature antiques, modern facilities and good extras; some have four-poster beds.

Kildonan Lodge
27 Craigmillar Pk. ✉ *EH16 5PE – ☎ (0131) 667 27 93* Town plan: BX**a**
– www.kildonanlodgehotel.co.uk – Closed 25-26 December
12 rm ☕ – 🚹£ 75/179 🚹🚹£ 79/210
Rest – Carte £ 22/39 – *(closed Sunday) (dinner only) (booking essential)*
Large detached Victorian house on the main road into the city. Cosy drawing room with an open fire and an honesty bar. Comfy, traditionally furnished bedrooms: some have four-posters or jacuzzis; those in the basement are more contemporary. Appealing, classical dishes feature plenty of Scottish produce.

One Royal Circus without rest
1 Royal Circus ✉ *EH3 6TL – ☎ (0131) 625 6669* Town plan: DY**w**
– www.oneroyalcircus.com
5 rm ☕ – 🚹£ 129/199 🚹🚹£ 138/258
Stunning house designed by William Playfair in 1823, with an elegant interior, a billiard room and two lounges – one featuring a marble bar and a grand piano. Bedrooms are stylish and understated; those to the rear are quietest.

94 DR without rest
94 Dalkeith Rd ✉ *EH16 5AF – ☎ (0131) 662 92 65* Town plan: BX**n**
– www.94dr.com – Closed 4-18 January and 25-26 December
6 rm ☕ – 🚹£ 75/145 🚹🚹£ 90/200
Victorian terraced house on the main road into the city. Brightly tiled hallway leads to a retro lounge with an honesty bar. Lovely breakfast conservatory opens onto a decked terrace. Stylish, well-equipped bedrooms have Scottish touches.

23 Mayfield without rest
23 Mayfield Gdns ✉ *EH9 2BX – ☎ (0131) 667 5806* Town plan: BX**x**
– www.23mayfield.co.uk
8 rm ☕ – 🚹£ 80/140 🚹🚹£ 90/185
Lovingly restored Victorian house with a very welcoming, helpful owner and an outdoor hot-tub. Spacious lounge has an honesty bar and a collection of old and rare books. Sumptuous bedrooms come with coordinated soft furnishings, some mahogany features and luxurious bathrooms. Extravagant breakfast choices.

Millers64 without rest
64 Pilrig St ✉ *EH6 5AS – ☎ (0131) 454 3666* Town plan: BV**e**
– www.millers64.co.uk
3 rm ☕ – 🚹£ 85/95 🚹🚹£ 95/150
Modernised Victorian terraced house, in an up and coming part of town. The smart, spacious bedrooms are all suites and boast good quality linens and extras. Communal breakfasts include a hot daily special and homemade pastries.

Kew House without rest
1 Kew Terr, Murrayfield ✉ *EH12 5JE – ☎ (0131)* Town plan: AV**a**
313 07 00 – www.kewhouse.com – Closed 4-31 January and 25-26 December
7 rm ☕ – 🚹£ 81/99 🚹🚹£ 99/179
Warm, welcoming stone-built house with a neat lounge and a wood-furnished breakfast room; set in a great location for Murrayfield Stadium. Modern, immaculately kept bedrooms come with chocolates, a decanter of sherry and fresh flowers.

Ardmor House without rest
74 Pilrig St ✉ *EH6 5AS – ☎ (0131) 554 4944* Town plan: BV**n**
– www.ardmorhouse.com
5 rm ☕ – 🚹£ 60/120 🚹🚹£ 85/155
Comfortable, laid-back guesthouse on a quiet residential street. Bedrooms range in size and boast bright décor, original plaster ceilings and granite fireplaces. Homemade preserves and cakes at breakfast. The owner has good local knowledge.

SCOTLAND

Restaurants

XXXX **Number One** – Balmoral Hotel

1 Princes St ✉ EH2 2EQ – ✆ (0131) 557 67 27 Town plan: EY**n**
– www.restaurantnumberone.com – Closed 2 weeks mid-January
Menu £ 64/75 – *(dinner only)*

A stylish, long-standing restaurant in the basement of a grand Edwardian hotel. Richly upholstered banquettes and red lacquered walls give it a plush, luxurious feel. Cooking is modern, intricate and very visually impressive, and prime Scottish ingredients are key. Service is professional and has personality.

➜ Scallops with white asparagus, pea and morel. Beef fillet with barley risotto and Bordelaise sauce. Gingerbread and banana soufflé, Madagascan vanilla ice cream.

XXX **21212** (Paul Kitching) with rm

3 Royal Terr ✉ EH7 5AB – ✆ (0131) 523 1030 Town plan: EY**c**
– www.21212restaurant.co.uk – Closed 10 days January and 10 days summer
4 rm – †£ 95/325 ††£ 95/325
Menu £ 22/69 **s** – *(closed Sunday and Monday)*

Stunningly refurbished Georgian townhouse designed by William Playfair. The glass-fronted kitchen is the focal point of the stylish, high-ceilinged dining room. '21212' reflects the number of dishes per course at lunch (dinner is '31313'); Cooking is skilful, innovative and features quirky combinations. Some of the luxurious bedrooms have views over the Firth of Forth.

➜ Chicken, duck and egg with smoked saffron ratatouille and egg custard. Beef olives, anchovy pasta, green olives and carrots. Chocolate, rice pudding, golden poached pears, hazelnuts and milk.

XXX **Castle Terrace** (Dominic Jack)

33-35 Castle Terr ✉ EH1 2EL – ✆ (0131) 229 12 22 Town plan: DZ**a**
– www.castleterracerestaurant.com – Closed Christmas, New Year, Sunday and Monday
Menu £ 29/75 – Carte £ 48/88

In the shadow of the castle, an understatedly stylish restaurant with a gilded ceiling and an attractive bar-lounge. Refined cooking showcases seasonal local produce in an assured, unfussy manner, following a 'nature to plate' philosophy.

➜ Tartare of salmon, sushi style. Seared 'Jacob's Ladder' served with foie gras and black truffle on a bed of organic spelt. Pistachio soufflé with a chocolate crumble.

XXX **The Pompadour by Galvin** – Caledonian Hotel

Princes St ✉ EH1 2AB – ✆ (0131) 222 8975 Town plan: CZ**x**
– www.galvinrestaurants.com – Closed first two weeks January, 26 December, dinner 25 December, Sunday and Monday
Menu £ 68 – *(dinner only)*

First floor hotel restaurant overlooking the castle, which opened in the 1920s and is modelled on a classic French salon. Gallic dishes showcase Scottish produce, using techniques introduced by Escoffier, executed with a lightness of touch.

XXX **Rhubarb** – Prestonfield Hotel

Priestfield Rd ✉ EH16 5UT – ✆ (0131) 225 13 33 Town plan: BX**r**
– www.prestonfield.com
Menu £ 20/35 – Carte £ 34/63

Sumptuous, richly decorated dining rooms set within a romantic 17C country house; so named as this was the first place in Scotland where rhubarb was grown. Concise menu of modern dishes with some innovative touches. Interesting wine list.

XX **Galvin Brasserie De Luxe** – Caledonian Hotel

Princes St ✉ EH1 2AB – (entrance on Rutland St) Town plan: CZ**x**
– ✆ (0131) 222 8988 – www.galvinrestaurants.com
Menu £ 17 (lunch and early dinner) – Carte £ 26/42

Accurately described by its name: a simply styled restaurant which looks like a brasserie of old but with the addition of a smart shellfish counter and fairly formal service. Appealing daily menu of French classics and a concise, good value set selection; dishes are refined, flavoursome and well-proportioned.

SCOTLAND

XX **The Honours**

58A North Castle St ✉ EH2 3LU – ✆ (0131) 220 2513 Town plan: DY**n**
– www.thehonours.co.uk – Closed 25-26 December, 1-3 January, Sunday and Monday
Menu £ 19/23 – Carte £ 28/61
Owned by a well-established chef; a bustling brasserie with a smart, stylish interior and a pleasingly informal atmosphere. Menus take their influences from across Europe but have a French leaning and always offer some Scottish dishes.

XX **Mark Greenaway**

69 North Castle St ✉ EH2 3LJ – ✆ (0131) 226 1155 Town plan: DY**p**
– www.markgreenaway.com – Closed 21-26 December, 1 January, Sunday and Monday
Menu £ 22 (lunch and early dinner) – Carte £ 35/55 – *(booking advisable)*
Set in an old bank on a corner site in the New Town; they store the wine in the old vault! The cosy dining room has a brasserie look and a formal feel. Menus range from 'set' to 'surprise'; the complex modern dishes have global influences.

XX **Ondine**

2 George IV Bridge (1st floor) ✉ EH1 1AD – ✆ (0131) 226 18 88 – www.ondinerestaurant.co.uk – Closed 1 week early January and 24-26 December Town plan: EZ**s**
Menu £ 23 (lunch and early dinner) – Carte £ 30/64
Smart, lively restaurant dominated by granite-topped bar and crustacean counter. Classic menus showcase prime Scottish seafood. Straightforward, tasty cooking. Well-structured service.

XX **Forth Floor at Harvey Nichols**

30-34 St Andrew Sq ✉ EH2 2AD – ✆ (0131) 524 83 50 Town plan: EY**z**
– www.harveynichols.com – Closed 25 December, 1 January and dinner Sunday-Monday
Menu £ 33 (lunch and early dinner) – Carte £ 33/47
Buzzy eatery with wonderful Firth of Forth views. Dine on ambitious dishes in the restaurant or old favourites in the all-day bistro. There's also a seafood bar, a tapas bar, a sushi counter and a conveyor belt of champagne and chocolates.

XX **Cucina** – G&V Royal Mile Hotel

1 George IV Bridge ✉ EH1 1AD – ✆ (0131) 220 66 66 Town plan: EZ**v**
– www.gandvhotel.com
Menu £ 19/21 – Carte £ 20/52
Set within a chic hotel, a buzzy mezzanine restaurant with bold black & white banquettes, smart red tables and striking kaleidoscope-effect blocks on the walls. Classic Italian dishes follow the seasons and dishes are nicely presented.

XX **Angels with Bagpipes**

343 High St, Royal Mile ✉ EH1 1PW – ✆ (0131) 220 1111 – www.angelswithbagpipes.co.uk – Closed 24-26 December Town plan: EZ**a**
Menu £ 15 (lunch) – Carte £ 26/42
Small, split-level restaurant, just across from St Giles Cathedral on the Royal Mile. Simple interior; some tables overlook a rear courtyard. Seasonal menus change every six weeks, offering a mix of unfussy classics and more modern dishes.

XX **One Square** – Sheraton Grand Hotel & Spa

1 Festival Sq ✉ EH3 9SR – ✆ (0131) 221 64 22 Town plan: CDZ**v**
– www.onesquareedinburgh.co.uk
Menu £ 16 (lunch and early dinner) – Carte £ 21/54
So named because it covers one side of the square, this smart hotel restaurant offers casual all-day dining and views towards Edinburgh Castle. The all-encompassing menu lists everything from a club sandwich to a grill selection.

SCOTLAND

Timberyard

10 Lady Lawson St ✉ EH3 9DS – ✆ (0131) 221 1222 Town plan: DZ**s**
– www.timberyard.co – Closed Christmas, 1 week April, 1 week October, Sunday and Monday
Menu £ 24 (lunch and early dinner) – Carte £ 33/41 – *(booking essential)*
Trendy warehouse restaurant; its spacious, rustic interior incorporating wooden floors and wood-burning stoves. Scandic-influenced menu offers 'bites', 'small' and 'large' sizes, with some home-smoked dishes and an emphasis on distinct, punchy flavours. Cocktails are made with vegetable purées and foraged herbs.

Bistro Moderne by Mark Greenaway

15 North West Circus Pl ✉ EH3 6SX – ✆ (0131) 225 4431 – www.bistromoderne.co.uk – Closed 25-26 December and 1-2 January Town plan: DY**x**
Menu £ 15 (lunch) – Carte £ 24/36
Updated bistro classics are the order of the day at this appealing former bank. Sit on the terrace, in the lively front room, or head to the rear for a more intimate experience. They open for breakfast Fri-Sun. Service is cheerful.

Passorn

23-23a Brougham Pl ✉ EH3 9JU – ✆ (0131) 229 1537 Town plan: DZ**e**
– www.passornthai.com – Closed 25-26 December, 1 January, Sunday and Monday lunch
Menu £ 11 (weekday lunch) – Carte £ 22/35 – *(booking essential)*
The staff are super-friendly at this extremely popular neighbourhood restaurant, whose name means 'Angel'. Authentic menus feature Thai classics and old family recipes; the seafood dishes are a highlight and presentation is first class. Spices and other ingredients are flown in from Thailand.

SCOTLAND

Edinburgh Larder Bistro

1a Alva St ✉ EH2 4PH – ✆ (0131) 225 4599 Town plan: CZ**n**
– www.edinburghlarder.co.uk – Closed Sunday and Monday January-February
Menu £ 15 – Carte £ 23/31
Sustainability and provenance are key here: the chef is a forager and fisherman, the tables are crafted from scaffold boards, old lobster creels act as lampshades, and the daily menu features carefully prepared seasonal dishes.

L'Escargot Bleu

56 Broughton St ✉ EH1 3SA – ✆ (0131) 557 16 00 Town plan: EY**u**
– www.lescargotbleu.co.uk – Closed Sunday except July and August
Menu £ 13 (lunch and early dinner) – Carte £ 25/37
Authentic French bistro offering boldly flavoured, regional French favourites; sit in the front room with its large windows and buzzy atmosphere. Dishes may be fiercely French but ingredients champion local produce from artisan producers.

Dogs

110 Hanover St (1st Floor) ✉ EH2 1DR – ✆ (0131) 220 1208 – www.thedogsonline.co.uk – Closed 25 December and 1 January Town plan: DY**c**
Carte £ 19/28
Cosy, slightly bohemian-style eatery on the first floor of a classic Georgian mid-terrace, with two high-ceilinged, shabby chic dining rooms and an appealing bar. Robust, good value comfort food is crafted from local, seasonal produce; sharing dishes and Scottish staples such as Arbroath Smokies feature.

Bon Vivant

55 Thistle St ✉ EH2 1DY – ✆ (0131) 225 3275 Town plan: DY**v**
– www.bonvivantedinburgh.co.uk – Closed 25-26 December and 1 January
Carte £ 14/35
Relaxed eatery in the city backstreets, with a dimly lit interior, tightly packed tables and a cheery, welcoming team. The appealing, twice daily menu has strong Mediterranean influences; start with some of the £ 1 bite-sized nibbles.

Blackfriars

57-61 Blackfriars St ✉ EH1 1NB – ✆ (0131) 558 8684 Town plan: EZ**b**
– www.blackfriarsedinburgh.co.uk – Closed 25-26 December, 1 January, Monday and Tuesday except August
Menu £ 19 (lunch) – Carte dinner £ 25/44
Hidden behind the castle is this intimate, nature-themed, neighbourhood restaurant, which is well run by its experienced owners. Produce is seasonal and dishes take their influences from around the world; the local game is a must-try.

Purslane

33a St Stephen St ✉ EH3 5AH – ✆ (0131) 226 3500 Town plan: DY**e**
– www.purslanerestaurant.co.uk – Closed 25-26 December, 1 January and Monday
Menu £ 15/28 – *(booking essential)*
Set in the basement of a Georgian house in a residential area; an intimate restaurant of just 9 tightly packed tables, with wallpaper featuring a pine tree motif. The chef prepares modern dishes using well-practiced techniques.

Field

41 West Nicholson St ✉ EH8 9DB – ✆ (0131) 667 7010 Town plan: EZ**x**
– www.fieldrestaurant.co.uk – Closed Sunday and Monday
Menu £ 15 (lunch and early dinner) – Carte £ 22/27
Small, rustic restaurant run by two young owners; the 8 tables are overlooked by a huge canvas of a prized cow. The appealing menu changes slightly each day, offering unfussy, traditional dishes with the focus firmly on the main ingredient.

Kanpai

8-10 Grindlay St ✉ EH3 9AS – ✆ (0131) 228 1602 Town plan: DZ**n**
– www.kanpaisushi.co.uk – Closed Monday
Carte £ 15/37
Uncluttered, modern Japanese restaurant with a smart sushi bar and cheerful service. Colourful, elaborate dishes have clean, well-defined flavours; the menu is designed to help novices feel confident and experts feel at home.

Bia Bistrot

19 Colinton Rd ✉ EH10 5DP – ✆ (0131) 452 84 53 Town plan: AX**a**
– www.biabistrot.co.uk – Closed first week January, 1 week July, Sunday and Monday
Menu £ 10 (lunch and early dinner) – Carte £ 19/34
Good value neighbourhood bistro with a buzzy vibe and a simple modern style; set in a smart residential area. Unfussy, flavoursome dishes range in their influences due to the friendly owners' Irish-Scottish and French-Spanish heritages.

Café St Honoré

34 North West Thistle Street Ln. ✉ EH2 1EA – ✆ (0131) 226 22 11 – www.cafesthonore.com – Closed 24-26 December and 1-2 January Town plan: DY**r**
Menu £ 16/24 – Carte £ 28/43 – *(booking essential)*
Long-standing French bistro, tucked away down a side street. The interior is cosy, with wooden marquetry, mirrors on the walls and tightly packed tables. Traditional Gallic menus use Scottish produce and they even smoke their own salmon.

Wedgwood

267 Canongate ✉ EH8 8BQ – ✆ (0131) 558 87 37 Town plan: EY**a**
– www.wedgwoodtherestaurant.co.uk – Closed 25-26 December and 2-23 January
Menu £ 13 (lunch) – Carte £ 29/46
Atmospheric, split-level bistro, hidden away at the bottom of the Royal Mile; it's personally run by a friendly team and a hit with the locals. Well-presented, seasonal dishes feature produce foraged from the surrounding countryside.

SCOTLAND

The Scran & Scallie

1 Comely Bank Rd, Stockbridge ✉ EH4 1DT – ✆ (0131) 332 6281 – www.scranandscallie.com – Closed 25 December Town plan: CY**s**

Menu £ 15 (weekday lunch) – Carte £ 19/54 – *(booking advisable)*

A more casual venture from Tom Kitchin and Dominic Jack, with a wood furnished bar and a dining room which blends rustic and contemporary décor. Extensive menus follow a 'Nature to Plate' philosophy and focus on the classical and the local.

at Leith

Malmaison

1 Tower Pl ✉ EH6 7BZ – ✆ (0844) 693 0652 – www.malmaison.com Town plan: BV**m**

100 rm – †£ 85/115 ††£ 145/215, ☕ £ 12

Rest *Brasserie* – Menu £ 16/20 – Carte £ 19/55

Impressive former seamen's mission located on the quayside; the first of the Malmaison hotels. The décor is a mix of bold stripes and contrasting black and white themes. Comfy, well-equipped bedrooms; one with a four-poster and a tartan roll-top bath. Intimate bar and a popular French brasserie and terrace.

Martin Wishart

54 The Shore ✉ EH6 6RA – ✆ (0131) 553 35 57 – www.martin-wishart.co.uk – Closed 31 December-18 January, 25-26 December, Sunday and Monday Town plan: BV**u**

Menu £ 29/75 – Carte approx. £ 70 – *(booking essential)*

Elegant modern restaurant with immaculately set tables and attentive, professional service. Three 6 course menus – Tasting, Seafood and Vegetarian – and a concise à la carte. Fine ingredients are used in well-judged, flavourful combinations. Dishes display a classical base and elaborate, original touches.

➜ Ravioli of squab pigeon, consommé, white radish and carrot. Roast turbot with bone marrow, artichoke and potato boulangère, truffle jus. Valrhona Manjari chocolate, exotic sorbet, mandarin curd and chocolate soil.

SCOTLAND

Kitchin (Tom Kitchin)

78 Commercial Quay ✉ EH6 6LX – ✆ (0131) 555 17 55 – www.thekitchin.com – Closed Christmas, New Year, Sunday and Monday Town plan: BV**z**

Menu £ 29/75 – Carte £ 60/88 – *(booking essential)*

'From nature to plate' is the motto of this passionate and focused chef, so expect refreshingly honest, seasonal cooking which shows great skill and clarity of flavours. The converted dockside warehouse has been given a plush, sumptuous feel – without over-formality – and service is confident and keen.

➜ Razor clams with diced vegetables, chorizo and wild herbs. Roe deer with a potato terrine, roasted vegetables and a red wine sauce. Baked crowdie cheesecake with poached rhubarb, jelly and sorbet.

Plumed Horse

50-54 Henderson St ✉ EH6 6DE – ✆ (0131) 554 55 56 – www.plumedhorse.co.uk – Closed 2 weeks summer, 1 week Easter, Christmas-early January, Sunday and Monday Town plan: BV**a**

Menu £ 24/69

Personally run restaurant with ornate ceiling, vivid paintings, an intimate feel and formal service. Well-crafted, classical cooking with strong, bold flavours and good use of Scottish ingredients.

Mithas

7 Dock Pl ✉ EH6 6LU – ✆ (0131) 554 0008 – www.mithas.co.uk – Closed Monday Town plan: BV**s**

Menu £ 16/75 – Carte £ 22/68

Smart, three-roomed Indian restaurant with booth seating. The large selection of menus centres on tasty kebabs and vibrant griddled dishes but there are also many vegetarian options; the set menus offer the best value. Attentive team.

XX **Bistro Provence** (N)

88 Commercial St ✉ EH6 6LX – ✆ (0131) 344 4295 Town plan: BV**c**
– www.bistroprovence.co.uk – Closed 1-12 January and Monday
Menu £ 13/26
This converted warehouse brings a taste of France to the cobbled quayside of Leith. It's very personally run by a gregarious owner and a welcoming team, and offers an appealing range of unfussy dishes with Provençal leanings.

Ship on the Shore

24-26 The Shore ✉ EH6 6QN – ✆ (0131) 555 04 09 Town plan: BV**x**
– www.theshipontheshore.co.uk – Closed 24-26 December
Carte £ 24/40
Smart period building on the quayside, modelled on the Royal Yacht Britannia and filled with nautical memorabilia. The seafood-orientated menu offers fresh, simply prepared, classic dishes and platters; try the smoked salmon at breakfast.

at Currie Southwest: 5 mi on A70✉ City Of Edinburgh

Violet Bank House without rest

167 Lanark Rd West ✉ EH14 5NZ – ✆ (0131) 451 51 03
– www.violetbankhouse.co.uk
3 rm – †£ 65/85 ††£ 100/140
200 year old cottage in a conservation zone, with attractive gardens running down to the river. Homely, individually decorated bedrooms have a host of thoughtful extras. Impressive breakfasts feature everything from pancakes to kedgeree.

at Kirknewton Southwest: 7 mi by A71 -(AX)✉ Edinburgh

Dalmahoy H. & Country Club rm, rest,

✉ EH27 8EB Northwest : 2 mi on A 71 – ✆ (0131) 333 18 45 – www.marriottdalmahoy.co.uk
215 rm – †£ 89/189 ††£ 89/189 – 2 suites
Rest *Pentland* – Carte £ 31/45 – *(closed 25 December) (dinner only and Sunday lunch)*
Rest *Zest* – Carte £ 20/39
Extended Georgian mansion boasting two championship golf courses and extensive leisure facilities. Country house style guest areas and well-equipped bedrooms; the best, in the main house, are a blend of the old and the new. Traditional, formal dining and good views over the 1,000 acre grounds in Pentland; laid-back all-day menus in bright, modern Zest.

at Ingliston West: 7 mi on A8

Norton House 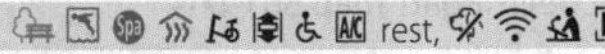

✉ EH28 8LX – ✆ (0131) 333 12 75 – www.handpicked.co.uk
83 rm – †£ 106/156 ††£ 116/366 – 5 suites
Rest *Ushers* – see restaurant listing
Rest *Brasserie* – Carte £ 25/55
19C country house in mature grounds, close to Edinburgh Airport. Classical bedrooms in the main house and stylish, modern executive rooms in the extension. The impressive oak staircase and country house lounges contrast with a state-of-the-art spa. Dine in the intimate restaurant or relaxed brasserie.

XX **Ushers** – Norton House Hotel

✉ EH28 8LX – ✆ (0131) 333 12 75 – www.handpicked.co.uk – Closed January-February and Sunday-Tuesday
Carte £ 41/59 – *(dinner only) (booking essential)*
Intimate hotel restaurant named after former owners of the house. Elaborate cooking uses top quality seasonal ingredients. Choose from the gourmet menu or concise weekly à la carte. Techniques are modern and combinations, original.

EDNAM → See Kelso
The Scottish Borders – and 502-M17

SCOTLAND

ELGIN

Moray – Pop. 23 128 – See Regional map n°**28**-C1
Edinburgh 198 mi – Aberdeen 68 mi – Fraserburgh 61 mi – Inverness 39 mi
Michelin Road map 501-K11 – Michelin Green Guide SCOTLAND

Mansion House

The Haugh ✉ IV30 1AW – via Haugh Rd – ✆ (01343) 548 811 – www.mansionhousehotel.co.uk – Closed 25 December
23 rm – †£ 97 ††£ 154/202 **Rest** – Menu £ 30
Grand Victorian country house in pleasant gardens. Beautiful Georgian-style drawing room with a grand piano, and a snooker table in the 'wee bar'. Luxurious bedrooms – some with sleigh beds, four-posters or river views. Classically furnished, formal dining room offers an eclectic mix of dishes.

Pines without rest

East Rd ✉ IV30 1XG – East : 0.5 mi on A 96 – ✆ (01343) 552 495 – www.thepinesguesthouse.com
6 rm – †£ 50/60 ††£ 66/70
Charming Victorian villa featuring original tiled floors and stained glass windows. Homely lounge and comfortable, traditionally styled bedrooms; Room 4 is the best with its antique four-poster bed. Highland products at breakfast.

ELIE

Fife – Pop. 942 – See Regional map n°**28**-D2
Edinburgh 44 mi – Dundee 24 mi – St Andrews 13 mi
Michelin Road map 501-L15

SCOTLAND

Sangster's (Bruce Sangster)

51 High St ✉ KY9 1BZ – ✆ (01333) 331 001 – www.sangsters.co.uk – Closed January-mid February, 1 week November, 25-26 December, Sunday dinner, Monday and Tuesday November-March
Menu £ 42 – *(dinner only and Sunday lunch) (booking essential)*
A sweet little restaurant in a sleepy coastal hamlet; slickly run by a husband and wife team. The well-respected chef uses Fife's natural larder and willingly embraces new ideas. Appealing, flavoursome dishes are well-proportioned and carefully executed: the simplest dishes are the best. Desserts are more modern.
→ Seared scallops with citrus foam, chilli and ginger caramel. Pork cheek and fillet, root vegetable purée and glazed apple. Iced mango and white chocolate parfait with tropical fruits.

ERISKA (Isle of)

Argyll and Bute✉ Oban – See Regional map n°**27**-B2
Edinburgh 127 mi – Glasgow 104 mi – Oban 12 mi
Michelin Road map 501-D14

Isle of Eriska

Benderloch ✉ PA37 1SD – ✆ (01631) 720 371 – www.eriska-hotel.co.uk – Closed 3-20 January
23 rm – †£ 260/420 ††£ 350/480 – 7 suites
Rest *Isle of Eriska* – see restaurant listing
19C baronial mansion in an idyllic spot on a private island, boasting fantastic views over Lismore and the mountains; unusually, it's family run. Open-fired guest areas display modern touches and the spa and leisure facilities are superb. Bedrooms are bright, stylish and well-equipped; some feature hot tubs.

Isle of Eriska – Isle of Eriska H.

Benderloch ✉ PA37 1SD – ✆ (01631) 720 371 – www.eriska-hotel.co.uk – Closed 3-20 January
Menu £ 50 – *(dinner only) (bookings essential for non-residents)*
Set in a country house on a private island, this modern dining room and conservatory offer enviable views. The concise daily menu has top Scottish produce to the fore and leaves plenty to the imagination; cooking is original and creative but still gives a nod to the classics. Textures and tastes are spot on.
→ Loch Creran salmon, brassica salad and caviar. Argyll venison with carrots, sprouts, oats and currants. Baked egg custard, buttermilk sponge and hibiscus.

EUROCENTRAL

North Lanarkshire – See Regional map n°**25**-**B1**

Edinburgh 34 mi – London 397 mi – Glasgow 12 mi – Paisley 20 mi

Dakota

rm,

1-3 Parklands Ave ✉ ML1 4WQ – ☎ (01698) 835 440 – www.dakotahotels.co.uk

92 rm – †£ 99/134 ††£ 99/134, ☕ £ 14

Rest *Grill* – Carte £ 25/51

Sleek black hotel visible from the M8: perfect for the image-conscious business traveller. Spacious bedrooms offer free wi-fi, king-sized beds and smart, modern shower rooms. Classic dishes served in the open-plan Grill restaurant, which is decorated with huge, blown-up pictures from 'The Eagle' comic.

FAIRLIE

North Ayrshire – Pop. 1 424 – See Regional map n°**25**-**A1**

Edinburgh 79 mi – London 434 mi – Douglas 199 mi – Belfast 78 mi

Michelin Road map 501-F16 and 502

Catch at Fins

Fencebay Fisheries, Fencefoot Farm ✉ KA29 0EG – South : 1.5 mi on A 78 – ☎ (01475) 568 989 – www.fencebay.co.uk – Closed 26 December, 1-2 January, Sunday dinner-Wednesday

Menu £ 30 – Carte £ 16/37 – *(booking essential)*

Eat in the cosy bothy or spacious conservatory at this long-standing, simply furnished restaurant, complete with smokery and farm shop. Menus offer unfussy dishes of fresh fish and shellfish, alongside their own beech-smoked products.

SCOTLAND

FIONNPHORT → See Mull (Isle of)

Argyll and Bute – Michelin Road map 501-A15

FLODIGARRY → See Skye (Isle of)

Highland – Michelin Road map 501-B11

FOCHABERS

Moray – Pop. 1 728 – See Regional map n°**28**-**C1**

Edinburgh 175 mi – London 580 mi – Aberdeen 56 mi – Inverness 48 mi

Michelin Road map 501-K11

Trochelhill Country House without rest

✉ *IV32 7LN West : 2.75 mi by A 96 off B 9015 – ☎ (01343) 821 267 – www.trochelhill.co.uk*

3 rm ☕ – †£ 70 ††£ 110

Whitewashed Victorian house; well-run by friendly owners who serve tea and cake on arrival. Spacious bedrooms feature modern bathrooms with walk-in showers; 2 have roll-top baths. Breakfast includes haggis, black pudding and homemade bread.

FORT AUGUSTUS

Highland – Pop. 621 – See Regional map n°**30**-**C3**

Edinburgh 158 mi – London 535 mi – Glasgow 138 mi – Manchester 350 mi

Michelin Road map 501-F12

The Lovat

✉ *PH32 4DU – ☎ (01456) 459 250 – www.thelovat.com*

28 rm ☕ – †£ 65/280 ††£ 80/295

Rest *Station Road* – Menu £ 50 – *(closed November-Easter and Sunday-Tuesday) (dinner only) (booking advisable)*

Rest *Brasserie* – Carte £ 24/43

Professionally run, Victorian house with well-tended, lawned gardens and a charming interior featuring old wood panelling and original fireplaces. Elegant drawing room and a comfy lounge complete with a piano. Contemporary bedrooms come with fruit and biscuits. Modern versions of classic dishes in the brasserie; ambitious, intricate set menu in the formal restaurant.

FORT WILLIAM

Highland – Pop. 5 883 – See Regional map n°**30**-C3
Edinburgh 133 mi – Glasgow 104 mi – Inverness 68 mi – Oban 50 mi
Michelin Road map 501-E13 – Michelin Green Guide SCOTLAND

Inverlochy Castle

Torlundy ✉ PH33 6SN – Northeast : 3 mi on A 82 – ✆ (01397) 702 177 – www.inverlochycastlehotel.com
18 rm – £ 395 £ 465/595 – 4 suites
Rest *Inverlochy Castle* – see restaurant listing
Striking castellated house in beautiful grounds, boasting stunning views over the loch to Glenfinnan. The classical country house interior comprises sumptuous open-fired lounges and a grand hall with an impressive ceiling mural. Elegant bedrooms offer the height of luxury; mod cons include mirrored TVs.

Grange without rest

Grange Rd. ✉ PH33 6JF – South : 0.75 mi by A 82 and Ashburn Lane – ✆ (01397) 705 516 – www.thegrange-scotland.co.uk – Closed November-mid March
3 rm – £ 130/140 £ 130/140
Delightful Victorian house with an attractive garden and immaculate interior, set in a quiet residential area. The beautiful lounge displays fine fabrics and the lovely breakfast room boasts Queen Anne style chairs. Bedrooms are extremely well appointed, with smart bathrooms.

Ashburn House without rest

18 Achintore Rd. ✉ PH33 6RQ – South : 0.5 mi on A 82 – ✆ (01397) 706 000 – www.highland5star.co.uk
6 rm – £ 55/60 £ 100/120
Attractive Victorian guesthouse overlooking the loch and mountains. Bedrooms are bright and modern; Room 1 is the largest and has the best views. On arrival, tea and homemade shortbread are served in the comfy conservatory lounge.

The Gantocks without rest

Achintore Rd. ✉ PE33 6RN – South : 1 mi on A 82 – ✆ (01397) 702 050 – www.fortwilliam5star.co.uk – Closed December and January
3 rm – £ 100/120 £ 120/140
Whitewashed bungalow with loch views; run by experienced owners. Spacious, modern bedrooms boast king-sized beds, large baths and nice toiletries. Unusual offerings and water views at breakfast.

Inverlochy Castle

Torlundy ✉ PH33 6SN – Northeast : 3 mi on A 82 – ✆ (01397) 702 177 – www.inverlochycastlehotel.com
Menu £ 38/87 – *(booking essential)*
Formal restaurant within a striking castle, set in the shadow of Ben Nevis and offering stunning loch views. Choose between three smart candlelit dining rooms filled with period sideboards and polished silver; the main room has the best views. Traditional dishes feature good quality Scottish produce.

Lime Tree An Ealdhain with rm

rest,

Achintore Rd ✉ PH33 6RQ – ✆ (01397) 701 806 – www.limetreefortwilliam.co.uk – Closed November and 24-26 December
9 rm – £ 60/120 £ 80/120 Carte £ 26/37 – *(dinner only)*
Attractive 19C manse – now an informally run restaurant and art gallery displaying the owner's landscape pieces. The appealingly rustic dining room has exposed beams and an open kitchen and cooking is fresh and modern. Bedrooms are simply furnished and well-priced – ask for one with a view of Loch Linnhe.

Crannog

Town Pier ✉ PH33 6DB – ✆ (01397) 705 589 – www.crannog.net – Closed 25-26 December and 1 January
Menu £ 15 (lunch) – Carte £ 28/39 – *(booking essential)*
Popular restaurant with a bright red roof and a colourful boat-like interior; set on the pier above Loch Linnhe – try to get a table by the window. Fresh local fish and shellfish are simply prepared. The 2 course lunch is good value.

FORTINGALL

Perth and Kinross – See Regional map n°**28**-C2
Edinburgh 84 mi – Perth 40 mi – Pitlochry 23 mi
Michelin Road map 501-H14

Fortingall

PH15 2NQ – (01887) 830 367 – www.fortingall.com
10 rm – £ 90/100 £ 180/220
Rest – Menu £ 40 – Carte £ 18/34 – *(bar lunch Monday-Saturday)*
Stylish Arts and Crafts house on a tranquil private estate, boasting lovely country views. Delightful interior with a snug, open-fired bar and two cosy sitting rooms filled with Scottish country knick-knacks. Bedrooms are modern but in keeping with the building's age. Traditional menu in the huge restaurant.

FORTROSE

Highland – Pop. 1 367 – See Regional map n°**30**-C2
Edinburgh 166 mi – London 571 mi – Inverness 12 mi – Elgin 48 mi
Michelin Road map 501-H11

Water's Edge without rest

Canonbury Ter IV10 8TT – on A 832 – (01381) 621 202 – www.watersedge.uk.com – Closed mid October-April
3 rm – £ 150/160 £ 150/160
Personally run guest house with attractive gardens and superb views over the Moray Firth. Immaculately kept guest areas. Three 1st floor rooms have French windows onto terrace.

GALSON → See Lewis and Harris (Isle of)

Western Isles – Michelin Road map 501-A8

GATTONSIDE → See Melrose

The Scottish Borders

GIGHA (Isle of)

Argyll and Bute – See Regional map n°**27**-A3
Edinburgh 168 mi – Oban 74 mi – Dunoon 100 mi
Michelin Road map 501-C16

The Boathouse N

Ardminish Bay PA41 7AA – (01583) 505 123 – www.boathousegigha.co.uk – Closed November-Easter
Carte £ 22/39
This 300 year old boathouse is set on a small community-owned island, overlooking the water. Whitewashed stone walls and beamed ceilings enhance the rustic feel. Menus cater for all, centring around fresh seafood and local meats.

SCOTLAND

GLASGOW

Glasgow City – Pop. 590 507 – See Regional map n°**25**-B1
Edinburgh 46 mi – London 399 mi
Michelin Road map 501-H16 and 502-H16 – Michelin Green Guide SCOTLAND

© Stravaigin

SCOTLAND

Hotels

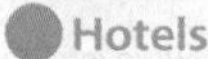

One Devonshire Gardens at Hotel du Vin

1 Devonshire Gdns G12 OUX – (0844) 736 42 56 Town plan: AV**a**
– www.hotelduvin.com
49 rm – £ 109/300 £ 109/300, £ 18 – 4 suites
Rest *Bistro* – see restaurant listing
Collection of adjoining townhouses boasting original 19C stained glass, wood panelling and a labyrinth of corridors. Furnished in dark, opulent shades but with a modern, country house air. Luxurious bedrooms; one with a small gym and sauna.

Blythswood Square

11 Blythswood Sq G2 4AD – (0141) 248 88 88 Town plan: CY**n**
– www.blythswoodsquare.com
100 rm – £ 100/280 £ 100/300 – 7 suites
Rest *Blythswood Square* – see restaurant listing
Stunning property on a delightful Georgian square; once the Scottish RAC HQ. Modern décor contrasts with original fittings. Dark, moody bedrooms with marble bathrooms; Penthouse Suite displays a bed adapted from a snooker table. Smart spa.

Radisson Blu

301 Argyle St. G2 8DL – (0141) 204 33 33 Town plan: DZ**d**
– www.radissonblu.co.uk/hotel-glasgow
247 rm – £ 99/305 £ 99/305 – 1 suite
Rest *Collage* – Menu £ 20 (lunch and early dinner) – Carte £ 27/54 – *(closed Sunday lunch)*
Stylish commercial hotel with an impressive glass atrium. Bedrooms come in three styles – Modern, City, and Gallery – all are spacious and contemporary, with a Scandinavian edge. The restaurant has a central buffet area and an all-encompassing menu; Peter Blake's artwork decorates the walls.

Malmaison

278 West George St G2 4LL – (0141) 572 10 00 Town plan: CY**c**
– www.malmaison.com
72 rm – £ 109/129 £ 119/155, £ 16 – 8 suites
Rest *Brasserie* – Menu £ 10/20 – Carte £ 23/39
Impressive-looking, former Episcopal church, with moody, masculine décor. Stylish, boldly coloured bedrooms offer good facilities; some are duplex. Named after Billy Connolly, the Big Yin Suite has a roll-top bath in the room. Characterful, intimate brasserie in the old vaults; French-influenced menus.

INDEX OF STREET NAMES IN GLASGOW

SCOTLAND

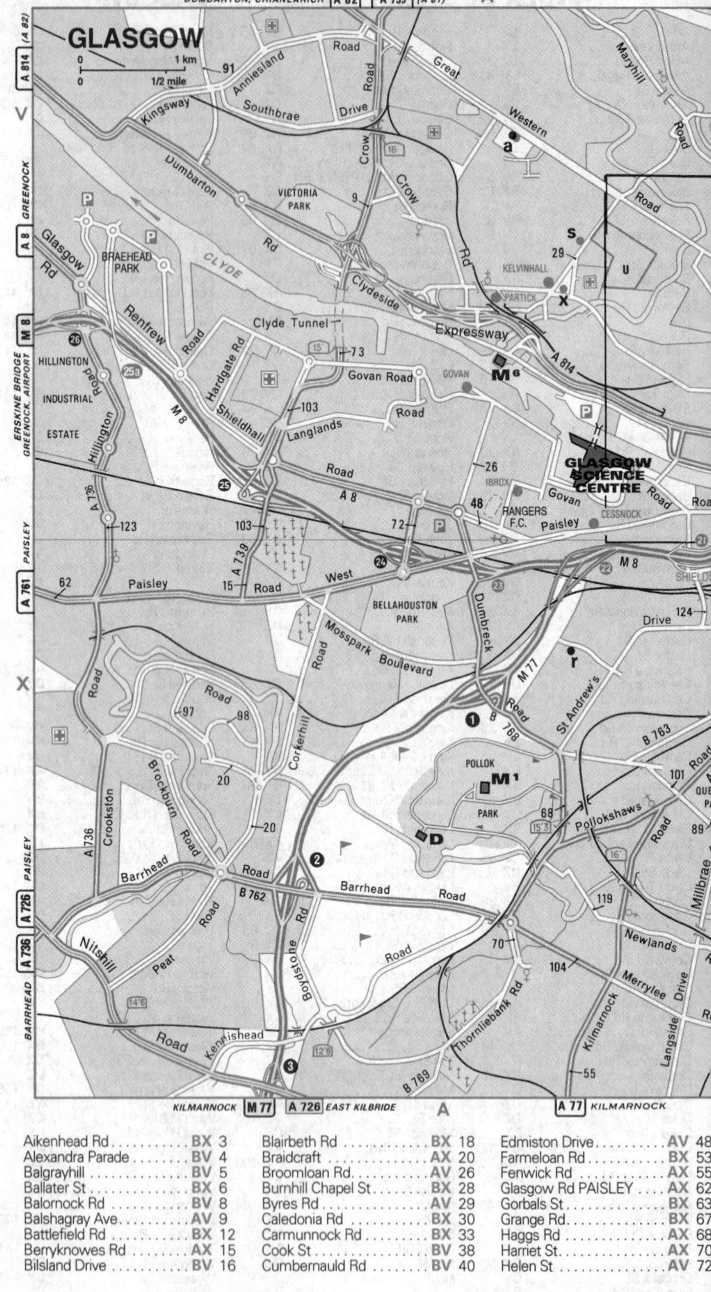

Aikenhead Rd	BX	3
Alexandra Parade	BV	4
Balgrayhill	BV	5
Ballater St	BX	6
Balornock Rd	BV	8
Balshagray Ave	AV	9
Battlefield Rd	BX	12
Berryknowes Rd	AX	15
Bilsland Drive	BV	16
Blairbeth Rd	BX	18
Braidcraft	AX	20
Broomloan Rd	AV	26
Burnhill Chapel St	BX	28
Byres Rd	AV	29
Caledonia Rd	BX	30
Carmunnock Rd	BX	33
Cook St	BV	38
Cumbernauld Rd	BV	40
Edmiston Drive	AV	48
Farmeloan Rd	BX	53
Fenwick Rd	AX	55
Glasgow Rd PAISLEY	AX	62
Gorbals St	BX	63
Grange Rd	BX	67
Haggs Rd	AX	68
Harriet St	AX	70
Helen St	AV	72

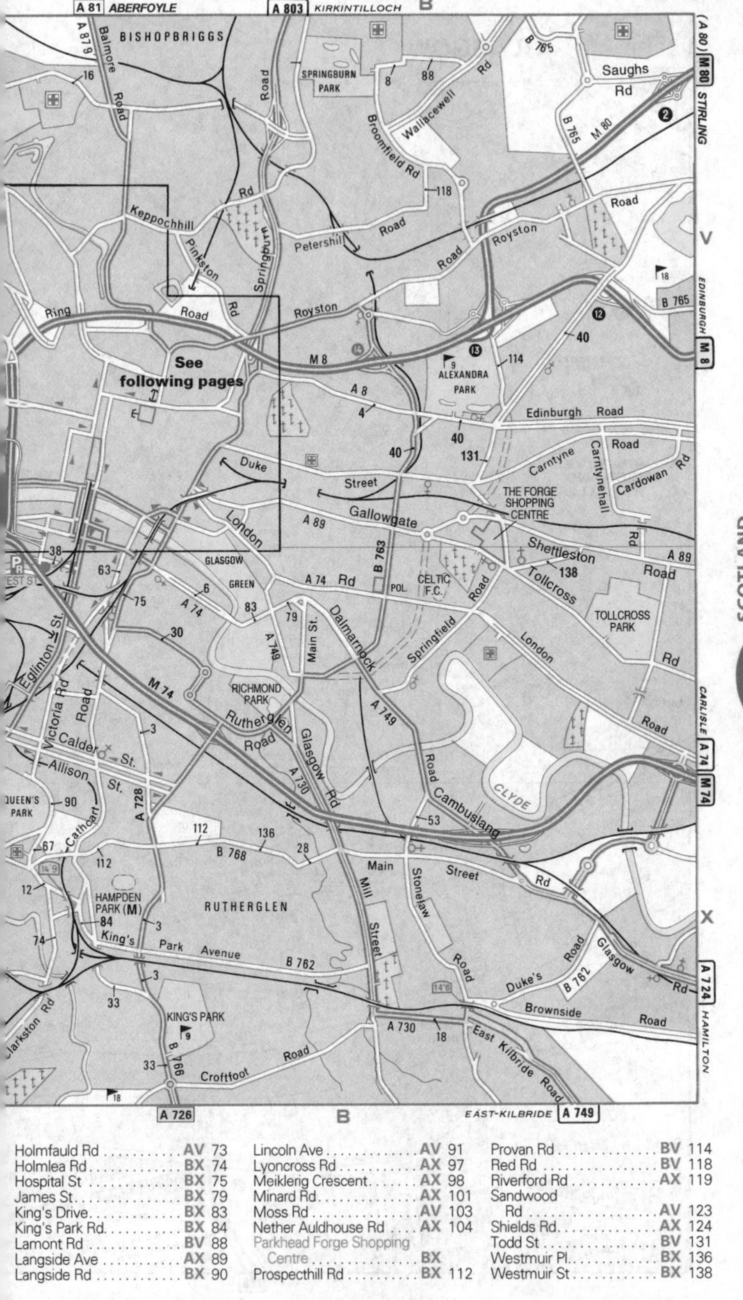

A 81 ABERFOYLE
A 803 KIRKINTILLOCH
B
(A 80) M 80 STIRLING
BISHOPBRIGGS
A 879
Balmore Road
16
SPRINGBURN PARK
8
88
B 765
Saughs Rd
Wallacewell Rd
Broomfield Rd
B 765
M 80
118
Keppochhill Rd
Pinkston Rd
Springburn Road
Petershill Road
Road
Royston Road
V
18
EDINBURGH
B 765
Ring Road
Royston
M 8
See following pages
14
13
12
40
9
ALEXANDRA PARK
114
A 8
4
40
40
Edinburgh Road
Road
131
Duke Street
Carntyne
Carntynehall Rd
Cardowan Rd
THE FORGE SHOPPING CENTRE
Gallowgate
A 89
London
B 763
38
Shettleston Road
A 89
GLASGOW GREEN
A 74 Rd
138
Tollcross
63
6
POL.
CELTIC F.C.
Road
TOLLCROSS PARK
75
A 74
83
79
Dalmarnock
London Rd
30
A 749
Main St.
Springfield
SCOTLAND
Eglinton St.
M 74
RICHMOND PARK
Victoria Rd
Road
Rutherglen Road
Glasgow Rd
A 749
Road
CARLISLE A 74
Calder St.
3
A 730
Road
Cambuslang
CLYDE
M 74
Allison St.
A 728
QUEEN'S PARK
90
53
112
136
67
Cathcart
112
B 768
28
Main Street
Rd
12
HAMPDEN PARK (M)
84
RUTHERGLEN
Mill Street
Stonelaw
X
74
3
King's Park Avenue
B 762
Road
Duke's Road
B 762
Glasgow Rd
A 724
3
33
Brownside Road
HAMILTON
Clarkston Rd
KING'S PARK
A 730
18
East Kilbride Road
B 766
33
Croftfoot Road
18
A 726
B
EAST-KILBRIDE A 749

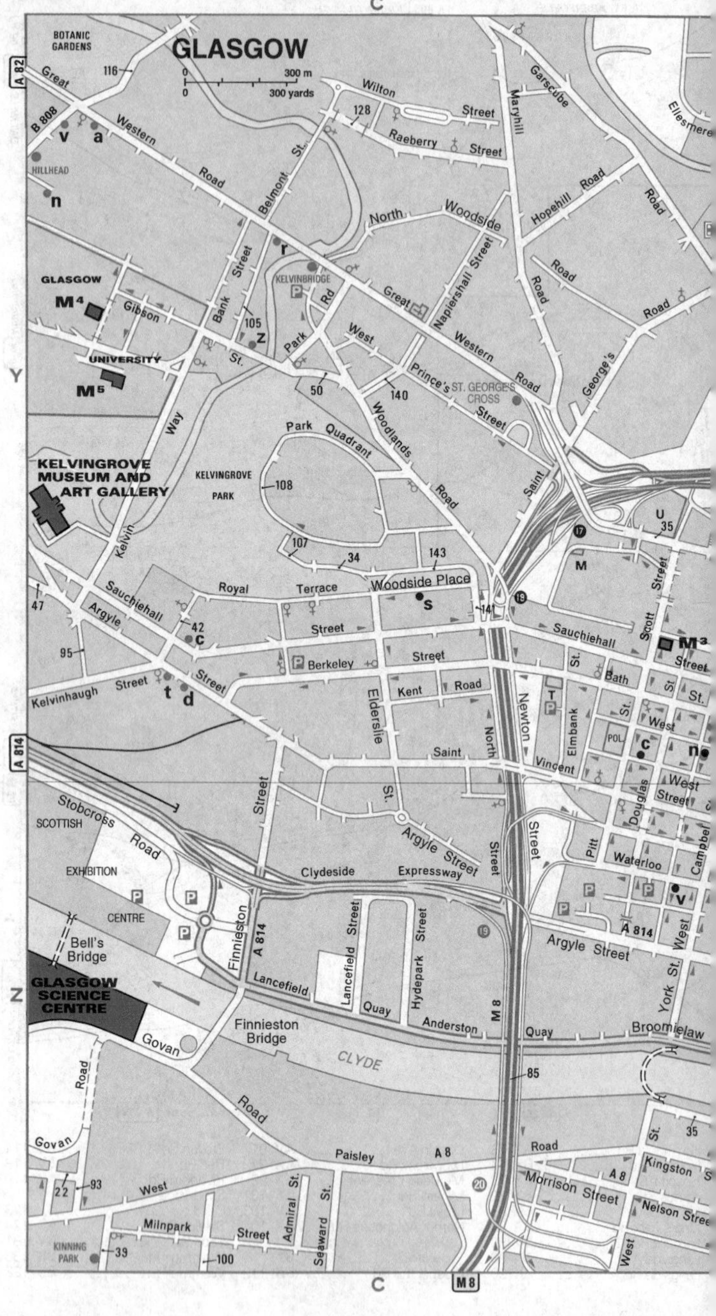
GLASGOW
0
300 m
0
300 yards
C
Y
Z
A 82
A 814
M 8
BOTANIC GARDENS
HILLHEAD
GLASGOW
M4
UNIVERSITY
M5
KELVINGROVE MUSEUM AND ART GALLERY
KELVINGROVE PARK
KELVINBRIDGE
ST. GEORGE'S CROSS
SCOTTISH EXHIBITION CENTRE
GLASGOW SCIENCE CENTRE
KINNING PARK
POL.
CLYDE
Great Western Road
B 808
Belmont St.
Bank Street
Gibson St.
Park Rd
Wilton Street
Raeberry Street
Maryhill Road
Garscube Road
Ellesmere
Hopehill Road
North Woodside Road
Napiershall Street
St. George's Road
West Prince's Street
Park Quadrant
Woodlands Road
Kelvin Way
Saint
Royal Terrace
Woodside Place
Sauchiehall Street
Argyle Street
Berkeley Street
Kent Road
Eldersile St.
Kelvinhaugh Street
North Street
Newton Street
Elmbank St.
Bath St.
Scott Street
West St.
Saint Vincent St.
West Regent St.
Douglas St.
Pitt St.
Waterloo St.
Campbell St.
Stobcross Road
Clydeside Expressway
Finnieston Street
A 814
Lancefield Street
Lancefield Quay
Hydepark Street
Anderston Quay
Broomielaw
Bell's Bridge
Finnieston Bridge
Govan Road
Paisley Road West
A 8
Morrison Street
Kingston St.
Nelson Street
West St.
York St.
West Campbell St.
Admiral St.
Seaward St.
Milnpark Street
v
a
n
r
z
c
t
d
s
U
M
T
P
c
n
v
M3
116
128
105
50
140
108
107
34
143
141
42
47
95
35
17
19
20
22
93
39
100
85

SCOTLAND

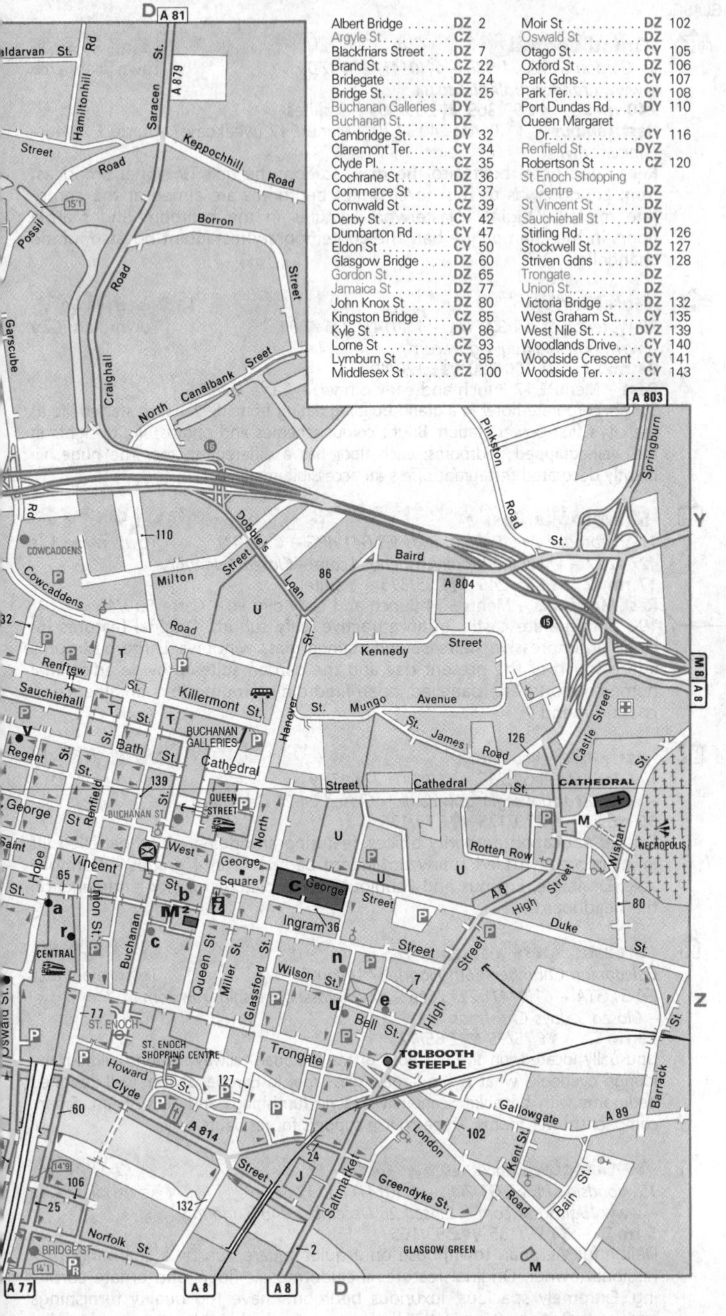

Street	Grid	No.
Albert Bridge	DZ	2
Argyle St	CZ	
Blackfriars Street	DZ	7
Brand St	CZ	22
Bridegate	DZ	24
Bridge St	CZ	25
Buchanan Galleries	DY	
Buchanan St	DZ	
Cambridge St	DY	32
Claremont Ter	CY	34
Clyde Pl	CZ	35
Cochrane St	DZ	36
Commerce St	DZ	37
Cornwald St	CZ	39
Derby St	CY	42
Dumbarton Rd	CY	47
Eldon St	CY	50
Glasgow Bridge	DZ	60
Gordon St	DZ	65
Jamaica St	DZ	77
John Knox St	DZ	80
Kingston Bridge	CZ	85
Kyle St	DY	86
Lorne St	CZ	93
Lymburn St	CY	95
Middlesex St	CZ	100
Moir St	DZ	102
Oswald St	DZ	
Otago St	CY	105
Oxford St	DZ	106
Park Gdns	CY	107
Park Ter	CY	108
Port Dundas Rd	DY	110
Queen Margaret Dr.	CY	116
Renfield St	DYZ	
Robertson St	CZ	120
St Enoch Shopping Centre	DZ	
St Vincent St	DZ	
Sauchiehall St	DY	
Stirling Rd	DY	126
Stockwell St	DZ	127
Striven Gdns	CY	128
Trongate	DZ	
Union St	DZ	
Victoria Bridge	DZ	132
West Graham St	CY	135
West Nile St	DYZ	139
Woodlands Drive	CY	140
Woodside Crescent	CY	141
Woodside Ter	CY	143

Grand Central

99 Gordon St ✉ G1 3SF – ✆ (0141) 240 37 00 – www.grandcentralhotel.co.uk Town plan: DZ**a**

240 rm – £ 99/369 £ 99/369 – 3 suites

Rest *Tempus* – ✆ (0141) 240 37 70 – Menu £ 17 (weekdays) – Carte £ 23/46 – *(dinner only)*

Renowned hotel built into the main station; the first TV signal broadcast from London was to this hotel. Smart bedrooms are aimed at the corporate market. Original plasterwork features in the ballroom and marble floors in the champagne bar. The contemporary restaurant boasts Murano chandeliers.

Hotel Indigo

75 Waterloo St ✉ G2 7DA – ✆ (0141) 226 77 00 – www.hotelindigoglasgow.com Town plan: CZ**v**

94 rm – £ 100/280 £ 120/400

Rest – Menu £ 17 (lunch and early dinner) – Carte £ 24/56

Stylish, corporate hotel in a grand building dating from 1892, which started life as the city's first power station. Bright colour schemes and photos of city sights in the well-equipped bedrooms; each floor has a different theme. The huge, vibrantly decorated restaurant offers an accessible menu.

Sherbrooke Castle

11 Sherbrooke Ave, Pollokshields ✉ G41 4PG – ✆ (0141) 427 42 27 – www.sherbrookecastlehotel.com – Closed 1 January Town plan: AX**r**

17 rm – £ 85/245 £ 95/375 – 1 suite

Rest *Morrisons* – Menu £ 14 (lunch and early dinner) – Carte £ 19/46

19C pink granite castle, in an attractive leafy suburb. Original features include an impressive staircase and stained glass windows. Large bedrooms add a touch of the present day and the garden suites provide additional home comforts. The panelled, open-fired dining room offers an all-encompassing menu.

Arthouse without rest

129 Bath St ✉ G2 2SZ – ✆ (0141) 221 67 89 – www.thearthouseglasgow.co.uk – Closed 24-26 December Town plan: DY**v**

59 rm – £ 79/175 £ 79/175

Former education authority offices, featuring an original wood-panelled lift in an impressive tiled stairwell. Modern bedrooms in 4 grades – Comfortable, Desirable, Envious and Fabulous – with pictures of city landmarks on the headboards.

Grasshoppers without rest

Caledonian Chambers (6th Floor), 87 Union St ✉ G1 3TA – ✆ (0141) 222 2666 – www.grasshoppersglasgow.com – Closed 3 days Christmas Town plan: DZ**r**

29 rm – £ 75/95 £ 85/125

Unusually located, on the 6th floor of the Victorian railway station building; the lounge overlooks what is the largest glass roof in Europe. Stylish, well-designed bedrooms with bespoke Scandinavian-style furnishings and Scottish art. Smart, compact shower rooms. Three course suppers for residents only.

15 Glasgow without rest

15 Woodside Pl. ✉ G3 7QL – ✆ (0141) 332 12 63 – www.15glasgow.com – Closed 25 December and 3 January Town plan: CY**s**

5 rm – £ 99/135 £ 99/165

Delightful Victorian townhouse on a quiet square, run by a charming, professional owner. Original features include mosaic floors and ornate cornicing. Extremely spacious, luxurious bedrooms have top quality furnishings and underfloor heating in the bathrooms. Cooked breakfast trays are delivered to your door.

Restaurants

XXX Brian Maule at Chardon d'Or

176 West Regent St. ✉ G2 4RL – ✆ (0141) 248 38 01 Town plan: CY**b**
– www.brianmaule.com – Closed 25 December, 1 January, Sunday and bank holidays
Menu £ 21 (lunch and early dinner) – Carte £ 43/56
Georgian townhouse in the city's heart, with original pillars, ornate carved ceilings and white walls hung with vibrant modern art. Classical cooking with a modern edge; luxurious ingredients and large portions. Friendly, efficient service.

XXX Bistro – One Devonshire Gardens at Hotel du Vin

1 Devonshire Gdns ✉ G12 OUX – ✆ (0844) 736 42 56 Town plan: AV**a**
– www.hotelduvin.com
Menu £ 22 (lunch and early dinner) – Carte £ 36/55
Elegant oak-panelled restaurant in a luxurious hotel. The three rooms are dark, moody and richly appointed, and there's a lovely lounge and whisky snug. Choose from well-prepared classics or more ambitious offerings on the degustation menu.

XXX Rogano

11 Exchange Pl. ✉ G1 3AN – ✆ (0141) 248 4055 Town plan: DZ**c**
– www.roganoglasgow.com – Closed 1 January
Menu £ 17 (lunch) – Carte £ 32/69
City institution established over 75 years ago. Charming art deco interior with marquetry reputedly from the craftsmen who fitted the Queen Mary. Formal service and a largely seafood-based menu. Keenly priced dishes in the basement café.

SCOTLAND

XX Gamba

225a West George St. ✉ G2 2ND – ✆ (0141) 572 08 99 Town plan: DZ**x**
– www.gamba.co.uk – Closed 25 December and first 2 weeks January
Menu £ 18 (lunch and early dinner) – Carte £ 31/56
Tucked away in a basement but well-known by the locals. Appealing seafood menu of unfussy, classical dishes with the odd Asian influence; lemon sole is a speciality. Cosy bar-lounge and contemporary dining room hung with fish prints.

XX Cail Bruich

725 Great Western Rd. ✉ G12 8QX – ✆ (0141) 334 62 65 Town plan: CY**a**
– www.cailbruich.co.uk – Closed 25-26 December, 1-2 January and Monday
Menu £ 18 (lunch and early dinner) – Carte £ 33/42
High ceilinged room with large pictures of produce. Run by two brothers; its name means 'to eat well'. Menus range from a good value market selection to tasting options. Mix of classic and modern dishes from a young, ambitious team.

XX Blythswood Square – Blythswood Square Hotel

11 Blythswood Sq ✉ G2 4AD – ✆ (0141) 248 88 88 Town plan: CY**n**
– www.blythswoodsquare.com
Menu £ 19 (lunch and early dinner) – Carte £ 21/70
Stylish hotel restaurant in the ballroom of the old RAC building; chic in black and white, with a zinc-topped bar and Harris Tweed banquettes. Classic menu with meats from the Josper grill. Desserts showcase the kitchen's ambitious side.

XX La Parmigiana

447 Great Western Rd, Kelvinbridge ✉ G12 8HH Town plan: CY**r**
– ✆ (0141) 334 06 86 – www.laparmigiana.co.uk – Closed 25-26 December, 1 January and Sunday dinner
Menu £ 17 (lunch) – Carte £ 26/52 – *(booking essential)*
Unashamedly classic in terms of its décor and its dishes, this well-regarded, professionally run Italian restaurant celebrated its 35th birthday in 2013. Red walls, white linen and efficient service. Refined cooking delivers bold flavours.

XX **Ubiquitous Chip**

12 Ashton Ln ✉ G12 8SJ – ✆ (0141) 334 5007 Town plan: CY**n**
– www.ubiquitouschip.co.uk – Closed 25 December and 1 January
Menu £ 20 (lunch and early dinner) – Carte £ 28/64 – *(bookings advisable at dinner)*
An iconic establishment on a cobbled street. The restaurant – with its ponds, fountains and greenery – offers modern classics which showcase local ingredients, while the mezzanine-level brasserie serves tasty Scottish favourites.

XX **Two Fat Ladies in the City**

118a Blythswood St ✉ G2 4EG – ✆ (0141) 847 00 88 Town plan: CY**e**
– www.twofatladiesrestaurant.com
Menu £ 16 (lunch and early dinner) – Carte £ 30/54
Intimate seafood restaurant which resembles an old-fashioned brasserie, with its wooden floor, banquettes and local art. Classic dishes are straightforward in style – but with fish this fresh, it doesn't need to be complicated.

XX **Urban**

23-25 St Vincent Pl. ✉ G1 2DT – ✆ (0141) 248 56 36 Town plan: DZ**b**
– www.urbanbrasserie.co.uk – Closed 25 December and 1 January
Menu £ 15 (early dinner) – Carte £ 20/50
Imposing 19C building; formerly home to the Bank of England. Sizeable bar and cosy wood-panelled lounge. Grand dining room with booths, vibrant artwork and an impressive illuminated glass and wrought iron ceiling. Classic British dishes.

SCOTLAND

X **The Gannet** N

1155 Argyle St ✉ G3 8TB – ✆ (0141) 204 20 81 Town plan: CY**t**
– www.thegannetglasgow.com – Closed first week January, first week July, 25 December and Monday
Menu £ 19 (lunch and early dinner) – Carte £ 22/33
You may well feel like a gannet after a visit to this appealingly rustic restaurant, where the tasty menus are constantly evolving. Classic dishes are presented in a modern style and are brought to the table by a charming team. Exposed stone, untreated wood and corrugated iron feature throughout.

X **Ox and Finch** N

920 Sauchiehall St ✉ G3 7TF – ✆ (0141) 339 8627 Town plan: CY**c**
– www.oxandfinch.com – Closed 25 December
Carte £ 20/28
A bright, breezy team run this appealingly rustic restaurant, with its tile-backed open kitchen and wines displayed in a huge metal cage. The Scottish and European small plates will tempt one and all: cooking centres around old favourites but with added modern twists, and the flavours really shine through.

X **Stravaigin**

28 Gibson St, ✉ G12 8NX – ✆ (0141) 334 26 65 Town plan: CY**z**
– www.stravaigin.co.uk – Closed 25 December and 1 January
Carte £ 18/40 – *(booking essential at dinner)*
Well-run, long-standing restaurant with a bustling bar, dining set over three levels and a relaxed, shabby-chic style. Interesting menus uphold the motto 'think global, eat local', with dishes ranging from carefully prepared Scottish favourites to tasty Asian-inspired fare. They hold monthly 'thali' nights.

X **Two Fat Ladies West End**

88 Dumbarton Rd ✉ G11 6NX – ✆ (0141) 339 1944 Town plan: AV**x**
– www.twofatladiesrestaurant.com – Closed 25-26 December and 1-2 January
Menu £ 16 (lunch and early dinner) – Carte £ 27/46
Quirky neighbourhood restaurant – the first in the Fat Ladies group – with red velour banquettes, bold blue and gold décor, and a semi open plan kitchen in the window. Cooking is simple and to the point, focusing on classical fish dishes.

Central Market

51 Bell St ✉ G1 1NX – ✆ (0141) 552 09 02 Town plan: DZ**e**
– www.centralmarketglasgow.com – Closed 2 January and 25 December
Carte £ 21/35
A trendy, informal 'café, restaurant and deli', with a huge plate glass façade, a horseshoe bar counter and an open kitchen. Appealing menu of tasty straightforward dishes, from jugged kippers or oysters to ox cheek stew or whole sea bream.

Dhabba

44 Candleriggs ✉ G1 1LE – ✆ (0141) 553 12 49 Town plan: DZ**u**
– www.thedhabba.com – Closed 25 December and 1 January
Menu £ 10 (weekday lunch) – Carte £ 16/38
Stylish, modern restaurant in the heart of the Merchant City; its walls decorated with huge photos of Indian street scenes. Menus focus on northern India, with interesting breads and lots of tandoor dishes – the speciality is 'dum pukht'.

Hanoi Bike Shop

8 Ruthven Ln ✉ G12 9BG – (off Byres Road) – ✆ (0141) Town plan: AV**s**
334 71 65 – www.thehanoibikeshop.co.uk – Closed 25 December and 1 January
Carte £ 15/24
Relaxed Vietnamese café; head to the lighter upstairs room with its fine array of lanterns. Simple menu of classic Vietnamese dishes including street food like rice paper summer rolls. Charming, knowledgeable staff offer recommendations.

La Vallée Blanche

360 Byres Rd ✉ G12 8AW – (1st floor) – ✆ (0141) Town plan: CY**v**
334 33 33 – www.lavalleeblanche.com – Closed 25-26 December, 1 January and Monday
Menu £ 13 (lunch and early dinner) – Carte £ 25/46
First floor restaurant with wood-clad walls, stag antler lights and simple wooden tables, giving it the feel of a ski chalet. Menus offer classic French dishes, from pork rillettes to coq au vin. Friendly service.

Dakhin

89 Candleriggs ✉ G1 1NP – ✆ (0141) 553 25 85 Town plan: DZ**n**
– www.dakhin.com – Closed 25 December and 1 January
Menu £ 10 (lunch) – Carte £ 16/38
It's all about the cooking at this modest, brightly decorated restaurant: authentic, southern Indian dishes might include seafood from Kerala, lamb curry from Tamil Nadu, and their speciality, dosas – available with a variety of fillings.

The Finnieston

1125 Argyle St ✉ G3 8ND – ✆ (0141) 222 28 84 Town plan: CY**d**
– www.thefinniestonbar.com – Closed 24-26 December
Carte £ 24/55
Small, cosy pub specialising in Scottish seafood and gin cocktails; with an intriguing ceiling, a welcoming fire and lots of booths. Dishes are light, tasty and neatly presented, relying on just a few ingredients so that flavours are clear.

GLENDEVON

Perth and Kinross – See Regional map n°**28**-C2
Edinburgh 37 mi – London 434 mi – Glasgow 43 mi – Aberdeen 109 mi
Michelin Road map 501-I/J15

Tormaukin Inn with rm

✉ FK14 7JY – ✆ (01259) 781 252 – www.tormaukinhotel.co.uk – Closed 25 December
13 rm – †£ 50/80 ††£ 50/80 Carte £ 20/39
Characterful inn run by a truly welcoming team. Eat in the dark beamed bar or the spacious, classical dining room. Well-priced, carefully executed dishes are traditionally based; try the tasty homemade bread and ice cream. Smart, tartan-floored bedrooms are spread between the inn, a stable block and a chalet.

SCOTLAND

GLENFINNAN

Highland ✉ Highland – See Regional map n°**29**-B3
▶ Edinburgh 150 mi – Inverness 85 mi – Oban 66 mi
Michelin Road map 501-D13

Prince's House

✉ PH37 4LT – ✆ (01397) 722 246 – www.glenfinnan.co.uk – Closed November-mid March except 27 December-2 January
9 rm – †£ 65/80 ††£ 130/160 **Rest** – Menu £ 45 – *(dinner only)*
This 17C coaching inn – named after Bonnie Prince Charlie – once served the 'Road to the Isles'. It's still fiercely traditional, with its pitch pine ceilinged lounge-bar and comfy, cosy bedrooms. Dine from a daily menu of classical dishes, surrounded by an eclectic array of the owner's art.

GLENROTHES

Fife – Pop. 39 277 – See Regional map n°**28**-C2
▶ Edinburgh 33 mi – Dundee 25 mi – Stirling 36 mi
Michelin Road map 501-K15 – Michelin Green Guide SCOTLAND

Balbirnie House

rest,

Balbirnie Park, Markinch ✉ KY7 6NE – Northeast : 1.75 mi by A 911 and A 92 on B 9130 – ✆ (01592) 610 066 – www.balbirnie.co.uk
31 rm – †£ 110 ††£ 180 – 1 suite
Rest *Orangery* – Menu £ 38 – *(dinner only and Sunday lunch)*
Rest *Bistro* – Menu £ 9 (lunch) – Carte £ 18/28
Stunning Palladian mansion with formal gardens and extensive parkland. Large, well-furnished, country house drawing rooms; period features abound. Luxurious, comfortable bedrooms come in varying sizes. Elegant glass-roofed Orangery serves classics with a twist. Basement Bistro offers French favourites.

SCOTLAND

GRANDTULLY

Perth and Kinross – Pop. 750 – See Regional map n°**28**-C2
▶ Edinburgh 70 mi – London 475 mi – Glasgow 84 mi – Dundee 51 mi

Inn on the Tay with rm

✉ PH9 0PL – ✆ (01887) 840 760 – www.theinnonthetay.co.uk
6 rm – †£ 75 ††£ 110 Carte £ 19/36
Smart, modern inn on the banks of the Tay; have coffee and homemade cake in the snug bar or head to the large dining room for superb views over the water. Choose from pub favourites on the bar menu or more ambitious dishes on the main menu. The owners are cheery and welcoming and the bedrooms, comfy and cosy.

GRANTOWN-ON-SPEY

Highland – Pop. 2 428 – See Regional map n°**30**-D2
▶ Edinburgh 143 mi – Inverness 34 mi – Perth 99 mi
Michelin Road map 501-J12

Culdearn House

Woodlands Terr ✉ PH26 3JU – ✆ (01479) 872 106 – www.culdearn.com
6 rm – †£ 72/82 ††£ 145/165
Rest – Menu £ 43 – *(dinner only) (booking essential)*
Granite house built in 1860 by Lord Seafield for one of his four daughters; its small garden is home to a family of red squirrels. The elegant, open-fired lounge and spacious bedrooms are furnished in a period style. Formal dining room offers a classical daily menu which features quality Scottish ingredients.

Dulaig without rest

Seafield Ave ✉ PH26 3JF – ✆ (01479) 872 065 – www.thedulaig.com – Closed 19 December-8 January
3 rm – †£ 115/135 ††£ 155/175
Small, detached, personally run guesthouse, built in 1910 and tastefully furnished with original Arts and Crafts pieces. Modern fabrics and an uncluttered feel in the comfortable bedrooms. Tea and homemade cake on arrival. Communal breakfasts include home-baked bread and muffins.

GULLANE

East Lothian – Pop. 2 568 – See Regional map n°**26**-C1
Edinburgh 20 mi – London 384 mi – Dundee 81 mi
Michelin Road map 501-L15 – Michelin Green Guide SCOTLAND

Greywalls

Duncur Rd, Muirfield ✉ EH31 2EG – Northeast : 0.75 mi by A 198 – ☎ (01620) 842 144 – www.greywalls.co.uk
23 rm – †£ 85/110 ††£ 275/335
Rest *Chez Roux* – see restaurant listing
Long-standing, classic Edwardian country house by Lutyens, in a superb location adjoining the famous Muirfield golf course. Constantly re-inventing itself and providing assured, professional service, it boasts spacious, antique-furnished bedrooms and delightful formal gardens designed by Jekyll.

Chez Roux – Greywalls Hotel

Duncur Rd, Muirfield ✉ EH31 2EG – Northeast : 0.75 mi by A 198 – ☎ (01620) 842 144 – www.greywalls.co.uk
Menu £ 27/30 – Carte £ 33/51 – *(bookings essential for non-residents)*
Set in a classic country house hotel but with a pleasant, modern feel; enjoy an aperitif in the lounge or in the delightful, Jekyll-designed gardens before dining with a superb view over the Muirfield golf course. Classical French menus have a Roux signature style and feature tried-and-tested classics.

La Potinière

Main St ✉ EH31 2AA – ☎ (01620) 843 214 – www.lapotiniere.co.uk – Closed January, 25-26 December, Sunday dinner October-April, Monday, Tuesday and bank holidays
Menu £ 20/45 – *(booking essential)*
Sweet little restaurant with white walls and striking red curtains. Concise, regularly changing menus of carefully prepared, classical dishes; lunch is good value and their homemade bread is renowned. The two owners share the cooking.

HARRAY → See Orkney Islands (Mainland)

– Michelin Road map 501-K6

HARRIS → See Lewis and Harris (Isle of)

Highland – Michelin Road map 501-Z10

INGLISTON → See Edinburgh

City of Edinburgh – Michelin Road map 501-J16

INNERLEITHEN

The Scottish Borders – Pop. 3 031 – See Regional map n°**26**-C2
Edinburgh 31 mi – Dumfries 57 mi – Glasgow 60 mi
Michelin Road map 501-K17 and 502

Caddon View

14 Pirn Rd. ✉ EH44 6HH – ☎ (01896) 830 208 – www.caddonview.co.uk – Closed 25-26 December
8 rm – †£ 53/55 ††£ 70/110
Rest – Menu £ 20 – *(closed Sunday and Monday) (dinner only)*
Substantial Victorian house run by a hospitable couple. Individually decorated bedrooms with modern touches; spacious 'Yarrow', and 'Moorfoot' with its view, are the best. Bright, airy dining room; regularly changing menu of local produce from the Tweed Valley.

INVERGARRY

Highland ✉ Inverness – See Regional map n°**30**-C3
Edinburgh 159 mi – Fort William 25 mi – Inverness 43 mi – Kyle of Lochalsh 50 mi
Michelin Road map 501-F12 – Michelin Green Guide SCOTLAND

Glengarry Castle

✉ *PH35 4HW South : 0.75 mi on A 82 – ✆ (01809) 501 254 – www.glengarry.net – Closed 3 November-19 March*

26 rm – †£ 77/180 ††£ 115/200 **Rest** – Menu £ 36 **s** – *(dinner only)*

Family-run Victorian house, named after the ruined castle in its 60 acre grounds. Two large, open-fired sitting rooms; stuffed wild animals abound. Classical, individually styled bedrooms, some with original art deco baths. Formal dining from 4 course Scottish menu.

Invergarry

✉ *PH35 4HJ On A 87 – ✆ (01809) 501 206 – www.invergarryhotel.co.uk*

12 rm – †£ 50/110 ††£ 80/140

Rest *The Brasserie* – Carte £ 24/39

Welcoming hotel in the style of a traditional inn. Small, quirky bedrooms in the eaves; the first floor 'Superior' rooms offer more space and luxury. Comfy lounge features shotguns, open fires and tartan carpets. Flavourful cooking focuses on fresh Highland produce.

INVERGORDON

Highland – See Regional map n°**30**-C2

Edinburgh 178 mi – Elgin 60 mi – Inverness 24 mi

Michelin Road map 501-H10

X **Birch Tree**

Delney Riding Centre ✉ IV18 0NP – Northeast : 3.75 mi on A 9 – ✆ (01349) 853 549 – www.the-birch-tree.com – Closed Sunday dinner, Monday and Tuesday

Menu £ 16/27 – Carte £ 24/33

Friendly little restaurant located within a rural riding school. The good value, set price lunch menu is followed by a more ambitious à la carte and a popular steak menu. Cooking is classically based and relies on Scottish ingredients.

SCOTLAND

INVERKEILOR

Angus – Pop. 902 – ✉ Arbroath – See Regional map n°**28**-D2

Edinburgh 85 mi – Aberdeen 32 mi – Dundee 22 mi

Michelin Road map 501-M14

XX **Gordon's** with rm

32 Main St ✉ DD11 5RN – ✆ (01241) 830 364 – www.gordonsrestaurant.co.uk – Closed 2 weeks January, lunch Tuesday and Saturday

5 rm – †£ 110 ††£ 110/150 Menu £ 34/55 – *(booking essential)*

Long-standing, passionately run restaurant; the wife oversees the service and the husband and son are in the kitchen. Charming stone walls, open fires and exposed beams. Concise menu of carefully prepared, classic dishes which use local seasonal produce. Well-kept bedrooms – the courtyard suite is the best.

INVERMORISTON

Highland – See Regional map n°**30**-C2

Edinburgh 164 mi – London 541 mi – Dundee 146 mi

Michelin Road map 501-G12

Tigh na Bruach without rest

✉ *IV63 7YE Southwest : 0.5 mi on A 82 – ✆ (01320) 351 349 – www.tighnabruach.com – Restricted opening in winter*

3 rm – †£ 90/105 ††£ 120/140

Superbly set on the lochside; its name meaning 'House on the Bank'. Traditional breakfast room. Comfy bedrooms with doors opening onto private terraces, which boast stunning views over neatly tended gardens to Loch Ness and the mountains.

INVERNESS

Highland – Pop. 48 201 – See Regional map n°**30**-C2

Edinburgh 156 mi – Aberdeen 107 mi – Dundee 134 mi

Michelin Road map 501-H11 – Michelin Green Guide SCOTLAND

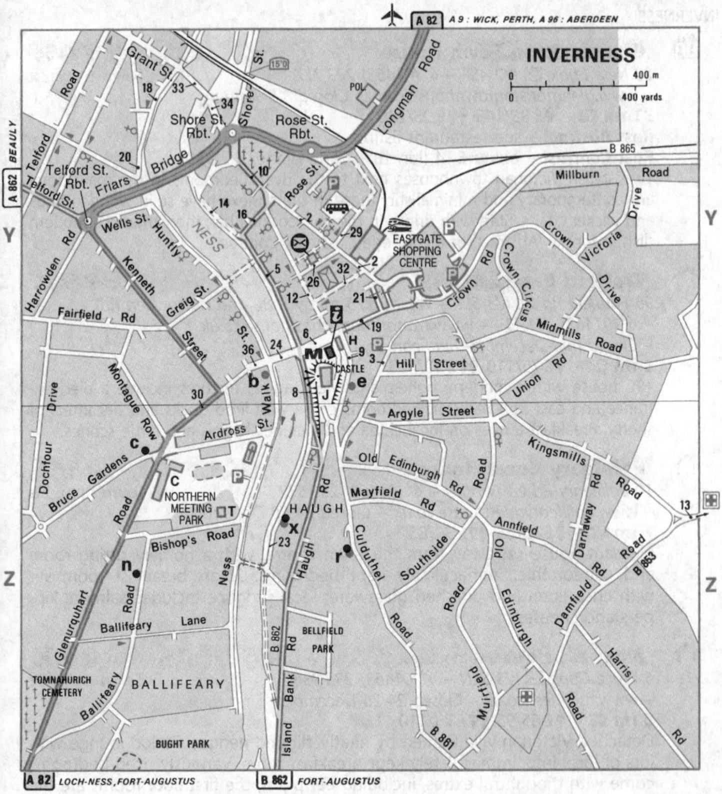

Academy St . . . . . Y 2
Ardconnel St . . . . . Y 3
Bank St . . . . . Y 5
Bridge St . . . . . Y 6
Castle Rd. . . . . YZ 8
Castle St . . . . . Y 9
Chapel St . . . . . Y 10
Church St. . . . . Y 12
Culcabock Rd. . . . . Z 13
Douglas Row . . . . . Y 14
Eastgate Shopping Centre . . . . . Y
Friars Lane . . . . . Y 16
Gilbert St . . . . . Y 18
High St. . . . . Y 19
Huntly Pl. . . . . Y 20
Inglis St . . . . . Y 21
Ness Bank . . . . . Z 23
Ness Bridge . . . . . Y 24
Queensgate . . . . . Y 26
Strothers Lane . . . . . Y 29
Tomnahurich St . . . . . YZ 30
Union St. . . . . Y 32
Waterloo Bridge . . . . . Y 33
Waterloo Pl. . . . . . Y 34
Young St. . . . . Y 36

Rocpool Reserve

14 Culduthel Rd ✉ *IV2 4AG* – ✆ *(01463) 240 089* – *www.rocpool.com*

Town plan: Z**r**

11 rm ☕ – 🚹£ 160/395 🚹🚹£ 195/395

Rest *Chez Roux* – see restaurant listing

Stylish boutique hotel with a chic lounge and a sexy split-level bar. Minimalist bedrooms come with emperor-sized beds and are graded 'Hip', 'Chic', 'Decadent' and 'Extra Decadent'; some have iPod docks, terraces, hot tubs or saunas.

Prices quoted after the symbol 🚹 refer to the lowest rate for a single room in low season, followed by the highest rate in high season.
The same principle applies to the symbol 🚹🚹 for a double room.

Glenmoriston Town House

20 Ness Bank ✉ IV2 4SF – ✆ (01463) 223 777 Town plan: Z**x**
– www.glenmoristontownhouse.com – Closed 8-9 January
31 rm ☕ – †£ 85/145 ††£ 95/240
Rest *Abstract* – see restaurant listing
Rest *Contrast* – Menu £ 14 (lunch) – Carte dinner £ 21/50
Two stylish Victorian townhouses next to the river. Bedrooms in the main hotel are contemporary and minimalistic; those in the annexe have solid wooden beds and wicker chairs. Start with drinks in the chic cocktail bar; then choose a modern dish in formal 'Abstract' or a brasserie classic in 'Contrast'.

Trafford Bank without rest

96 Fairfield Rd ✉ IV3 5LL – West : 0.75 mi by A 82 and Harrowden Rd – ✆ (01463) 241 414 – www.traffordbankguesthouse.co.uk – Closed mid-December-mid-February
5 rm ☕ – †£ 75/110 ††£ 90/128
19C house with a modern, bohemian style. Original features include a tiled entrance and cast iron banister. Bedrooms come with iPod docks and decanters of sherry. Breakfast arrives on local china and includes haggis and tattie scones.

Ballifeary Guest House without rest

10 Ballifeary Rd ✉ IV3 5PJ – ✆ (01463) 235 572 Town plan: Z**n**
– www.ballifearyguesthouse.co.uk – Closed 24-28 December
7 rm ☕ – †£ 45/65 ††£ 72/85
Pleasant house set away from the town centre, with a homely sitting room and comfortable, immaculately kept bedrooms. Smart breakfast room set with crisp linen and polished glassware; local produce includes salmon, kippers and cheeses.

Moyness House without rest

6 Bruce Gdns ✉ IV3 5EN – ✆ (01463) 233 836 Town plan: Z**c**
– www.moyness.co.uk – Closed 24-26 December
6 rm ☕ – †£ 65/95 ††£ 73/110
Detached Victorian villa framed by neatly clipped hedges. Period lounge with lots of local info; immaculately kept breakfast room. Variously sized bedrooms come with thoughtful extras, including ear plugs; the first floor rooms are the best.

Abstract – Glenmoriston Town House Hotel

20 Ness Bank ✉ IV2 4SF – ✆ (01463) 223 777 Town plan: Z**x**
– www.abstractrestaurant.com – Closed Sunday-Monday
Carte £ 40/63 – *(dinner only)*
Intimate hotel restaurant with abstract ink pictures hung on dark panelled walls and a contemporary, minimalistic style. Elaborate modern menus feature ambitious flavour combinations and there's a pianist Friday and Saturday nights.

Rocpool

1 Ness Walk ✉ IV3 5NE – ✆ (01463) 717 274 Town plan: Y**b**
– www.rocpoolrestaurant.com – Closed 25-26 December, 1-3 January and Sunday
Menu £ 15 (weekday lunch) – Carte £ 24/42
Well-run restaurant on the banks of the River Ness; close to town and popular with the locals. Modern, modish interior. Wide-ranging menus offer vibrant, colourful dishes that are full of flavour and have a distinct Mediterranean edge.

Chez Roux – Rocpool Reserve Hotel

14 Culduthel Rd ✉ IV2 4AG – ✆ (01463) 240 089 Town plan: Z**r**
– www.rocpool.com
Menu £ 28 (lunch and early dinner) – Carte £ 31/46
Smart modern restaurant consisting of three rooms; their walls hung with photos of the Roux brothers' early days. Polished tables are well-spaced and service is professional. The French-inspired menu offers robust, flavoursome dishes.

Café 1

Castle St ✉ IV2 3EA – ✆ (01463) 226 200 Town plan: Y**e**
– www.cafe1.net – Closed 25-26 December, 1-2 January and Sunday
Menu £ 13 (lunch and early dinner) – Carte £ 19/40
Bustling bistro opposite the castle. Small bar and two dining rooms with walnut veneer topped tables. Good value set lunch; more elaborate à la carte with an Asian and Mediterranean edge. Pork, beef and lamb comes from their own croft.

at Culloden East: 3 mi by A96 -(Y)✉ Inverness

Culloden House

✉ IV2 7BZ – ✆ (01463) 790 461 – www.cullodenhouse.co.uk – Closed 25-26 December
28 rm – 🛉£ 95/250 🛉🛉£ 140/395 – 3 suites
Rest *Adams Dining Room* – Menu £ 16/50 – Carte £ 34/59
Imposing Palladian mansion in 40 acres; requisitioned by Bonnie Prince Charlie as his HQ prior to the famous battle. Grand interior with high ceilings, chandeliers and Adam's plaster reliefs. Well-proportioned bedrooms; many with antiques and views of the grounds. Formal restaurant offers traditional menus.

at Bunchrew West: 3 mi on A862 -(Y)✉ Inverness

Bunchrew House

✉ IV3 8TA – ✆ (01463) 234 917 – www.bunchrewhousehotel.com
16 rm – 🛉£ 100/300 🛉🛉£ 120/400 **Rest** – Menu £ 24/43
Impressive 17C Scottish mansion, in a beautiful spot on the shore of Beauly Firth. Clubby, cosy, open-fired bar and intimate, wood-panelled drawing room. Good-sized, traditionally styled bedrooms; one with a four-poster, another with estuary views. Classical restaurant, with a menu to match and garden views.

SCOTLAND

ISLAY (Isle of)

Argyll and Bute – See Regional map n°**27-A3**
Edinburgh 164 mi – London 518 mi – Greenock 117 mi – Irvine 132 mi
Michelin Road map 501-B16

Ballygrant

Kilmeny Country House without rest

✉ PA45 7QW Southwest : 0.5 mi on A 846 – ✆ (01496) 840 668 – www.kilmeny.co.uk – Closed Christmas-New Year
5 rm – 🛉£ 90/120 🛉🛉£ 130/160
Delightful house in 350 acres of working farmland. Large lounge with a mock open fire and a fine array of books about Islay. Superb bedrooms have beautiful feature beds, lovely tartans, tweeds and woollens woven on the island, and thoughtful extras. Welcoming owner.

Bowmore

Harbour Inn with rm

The Square ✉ PA43 7JR – ✆ (01496) 810 330 – www.harbour-inn.com – Closed 21 December-12 January
7 rm – 🛉£ 85/130 🛉🛉£ 105/170 Menu £ 35 (dinner) – Carte £ 30/47
Traditional restaurant with a pleasant bar and chunky wooden tea tables covered in deep blue cloths. Classical cooking uses fresh local seafood and island meats. Bedrooms are brightly decorated. Two cosy residents' lounges afford fantastic bay and island views.

Port Charlotte

Port Charlotte

Main St ✉ PA48 7TU – ✆ (01496) 850 360 – www.portcharlottehotel.co.uk – Closed 24-26 December
10 rm – 🛉£ 125 🛉🛉£ 205 **Rest** – Carte £ 26/55 – *(bar lunch)*
Waterside hotel packed full of modern art. Large lounge with a wood burning stove and a cosy bar hung with old island photos. Bedrooms display traditional furniture and modern colour schemes; most have a sea view. Good mix of meat and fish dishes in the restaurant.

Port Ellen

Glenegedale House without rest 

✉ PA42 7AS Northwest : 4.75 mi on A 846 – ✆ (01496) 300 400 – www.glenegedalehouse.co.uk – Closed Christmas-New Year

6 rm ☕ – 👤£ 60/120 👥£ 90/140

Well-run hotel opposite the airport. Immaculately kept, individually styled bedrooms feature designer fabrics. Choice of two sitting rooms, both displaying leather sofas, coffee tables and an array of curios.

JEDBURGH

The Scottish Borders – Pop. 4 030 – See Regional map n°**26**-D2

▶Edinburgh 48 mi – Carlisle 54 mi – Newcastle upon Tyne 57 mi

Michelin Road map 501-M17 and 502 – Michelin Green Guide SCOTLAND

Willow Court without rest 

The Friars ✉ TD8 6BN – ✆ (01835) 863 702 – www.willowcourtjedburgh.co.uk

3 rm ☕ – 👤£ 75/80 👥£ 80/86

Contemporary guesthouse looking out over the town's rooftops. Comfortable ground floor bedrooms offer a light, stylish space and come with iPod docks, DVD players and smart modern bathrooms. Communal breakfasts feature eggs from their own hens. Take time for yourself in the conservatory or out on the patio.

SCOTLAND

KELSO

The Scottish Borders – Pop. 5 639 – See Regional map n°**26**-D2

▶Edinburgh 44 mi – Hawick 21 mi – Newcastle upon Tyne 68 mi

Michelin Road map 501-M17 and 502 – Michelin Green Guide SCOTLAND

Roxburghe 

Heiton ✉ TD5 8JZ – Southwest : 3.5 mi by A 698 – ✆ (01573) 450 331 – www.roxburghe-hotel.com

22 rm ☕ – 👤£ 105/260 👥£ 105/315 – 2 suites

Rest – Menu £ 18/32 – Carte £ 34/57 **s**

Characterful Jacobean-style mansion owned by the Duke of Roxburghe, set in extensive parkland and boasting a fly fishing school and golf course. Plush, cosy guest areas display antiques and heirlooms. Feature bedrooms are the most luxurious; courtyard rooms are more modern. Formal fine dining.

Ednam House 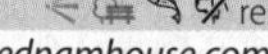 rest,

Bridge St ✉ TD5 7HT – ✆ (01573) 224 168 – www.ednamhouse.com

32 rm ☕ – 👤£ 80/115 👥£ 128/180 **Rest** – Menu £ 33 – Carte £ 29/43

Long-standing, fishing-orientated hotel on the banks of the Tweed; in the family since 1928 and now run by the 3rd generation. Grand drawing rooms and classically styled bedrooms boast a timeless elegance. The bar has a mural of the river, while the dining room overlooks it. Much of the produce is homemade.

at Ednam North: 2.25 mi on B6461✉ Kelso

Edenwater House 

✉ TD5 7QL Off Stichill rd – ✆ (01573) 224 070 – www.edenwaterhouse.co.uk – Closed 1 January-12 March

4 rm ☕ – 👤£ 70/75 👥£ 120

Rest – Menu £ 40 – *(closed Sunday-Tuesday) (dinner only)*

This delightful house is run by an equally charming couple. Relax in the lovely garden beside the stream or in one of the antique-filled lounges, then head up to the tastefully furnished, individually styled bedrooms. The pleasant dining room overlooks a meadow and offers a traditional menu Friday-Saturday, with wine-themed suppers in the cellar on a Wednesday.

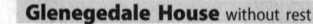

KENMORE

Perth and Kinross – Pop. 596 – See Regional map n°**28**-C2
Edinburgh 82 mi – London 469 mi – Glasgow 78 mi – Aberdeen 126 mi
Michelin Road map 501-I14 – Michelin Green Guide SCOTLAND

Kenmore

rest,

The Square ✉ PH15 2NU – ✆ (01887) 830 205 – www.kenmorehotel.com
39 rm – £ 79/129 £ 89/139
Rest *Grill Room* – Menu £ 16/25 – Carte £ 21/64
Smart hotel standing on the banks of the Tay; dating from 1572 and reputedly Scotland's oldest inn. The snug 'Poet's Parlour' bar displays Burns' original pencilled verse above its open fire. Bedrooms are cosy and well-kept. The Grill Room offers a large menu of juicy Scottish steaks and grills.

KILBERRY → See Kintyre (Peninsula)

Argyll and Bute – Michelin Road map 501-D16

KILCHRENAN

Argyll and Bute ✉ Taynuilt – See Regional map n°**27**-B2
Edinburgh 117 mi – Glasgow 87 mi – Oban 18 mi
Michelin Road map 501-E14 – Michelin Green Guide SCOTLAND

Ardanaiseig

✉ PA35 1HE Northeast : 4 mi – ✆ (01866) 833 333 – www.ardanaiseig.com
19 rm – £ 185/330 £ 185/330, £ 17 – 1 suite
Rest – Carte £ 25/41 – *(dinner only) (booking essential)*
Stunningly located, laid-back country house boasting a vast azalea-filled estate and lovely views down the loch. The large sitting room features impressive columns; bedrooms come in a mix of styles – the Boat Shed is the best. The elegant dining room offers modern dishes and water views.

Roineabhal without rest

✉ PA35 1HD – ✆ (01866) 833 207 – www.roineabhal.com – Closed Christmas-New Year
3 rm – £ 80 £ 110
Rustic stone and log house with a riverside garden – built by its charming owners, who provide tea and homemade biscuits on arrival. Relaxing lounge with an open fire. Immaculate bedrooms; two up a spiral staircase. The guest bathroom has a roll-top bath. Local produce is served in the homely breakfast room.

KILLIECRANKIE → See Pitlochry

Perth and Kinross – Michelin Road map 501-I13

KILMARNOCK

East Ayrshire – Pop. 46 159 – See Regional map n°**25**-B2
Edinburgh 64 mi – Ayr 13 mi – Glasgow 25 mi
Michelin Road map 501-G17 – Michelin Green Guide SCOTLAND

Hogarth's @ The Craigie Inn

5 Main St, Craigie ✉ KA1 5LY – Southwest : 6 mi by A 7038 and A 77 off B 730 – ✆ (01563) 860 286 – www.craigieinnhogarths.co.uk
Menu £ 13/19 – Carte £ 22/42
Former pub in a tiny Ayrshire hamlet; its décor a blend of the rustic and the more contemporary. Menus follow suit, with a mix of classics and more modern dishes; portions are large and flavours, pronounced.

KINCLAVEN

Perth and Kinross – Pop. 394 – ✉ Stanley – See Regional map n°**28**-C2
Edinburgh 55 mi – London 456 mi – Belfast 127 mi – Dundee 21 mi
Michelin Road map 501-J14

SCOTLAND

Ballathie House

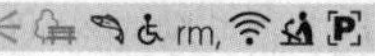

Stanley ✉ PH1 4QN – ✆ (01250) 883 268 – www.ballathiehousehotel.com
53 rm ☕ – 🚹£ 80/135 🚹🚹£ 150/190 – 3 suites **Rest** – Menu £ 25/50 **s**
Well-established, mid-19C former shooting lodge, set on a peaceful estate of several hundred acres, on the banks of the River Tay. Comfortable guest areas and individually furnished bedrooms: some with floral themes; some more contemporary. Concise country house menu showcases seasonal, regional produce.

KINGAIRLOCH

Highland – See Regional map n°**29**-B3
▶Edinburgh 139 mi – Fort William 25 mi – Oban 52 mi
Michelin Road map 501-D14

Boathouse

Ardgour ✉ PH33 7AE – ✆ (01967) 411 232 – www.kingairloch.co.uk – Closed November-March and Sunday dinner-Wednesday
Carte £ 22/36 – *(booking advisable)*
Smartly converted Victorian boathouse on the shore of Loch a'Choire, in the heart of the 14,000 acre Kingairloch Estate. Appealing dishes use venison from the estate and langoustines from Loch Linnhe, along with seasonal herbs and veg from the kitchen garden. Head straight for the terrace in warmer weather.

KINGUSSIE

Highland – Pop. 1 476 – See Regional map n°**30**-C3
▶Edinburgh 117 mi – Inverness 41 mi – Perth 73 mi
Michelin Road map 501-H12 – Michelin Green Guide SCOTLAND

SCOTLAND

Hermitage

Spey St ✉ PH21 1HN – ✆ (01540) 662 137 – www.thehermitage-scotland.com – Closed 20 December-4 January
5 rm ☕ – 🚹£ 45/90 🚹🚹£ 72/88 **Rest** – Menu £ 26 **s**
Traditional Victorian house built from stone and slate; formerly a doctor's surgery. Spacious garden affords great views of the Cairngorm Mountains and Ruthven Barracks. Warm, cosy lounge and comfy bedrooms; one has a super-king-sized bed and wet room. Simple dining room offers daily menu of home-cooked local produce.

Cross at Kingussie with rm

Tweed Mill Brae, Ardbroilach Rd ✉ PH21 1LB – ✆ (01540) 661 166 – www.thecross.co.uk – Closed January and Christmas
8 rm ☕ – 🚹£ 90/120 🚹🚹£ 100/190 Menu £ 25/55 – *(booking essential)*
19C tweed mill in four acres of wooded grounds. Enjoy drinks on the terrace or in the first floor lounge then head to the smart dining room with is low beams, antiques and ornaments. Cooking is modern British/Scottish and is attractively presented. Pleasant, pine-furnished bedrooms have thoughtful extras.

KINTILLO → See Perth

Perth and Kinross

KINTYRE (Peninsula)

Argyll and Bute – See Regional map n°**27**-B3
▶Edinburgh 165 mi – London 515 mi – Dundee 164 mi – Paisley 111 mi
Michelin Road map 501-D16 – Michelin Green Guide SCOTLAND

CARRADALE

Dunvalanree

Port Righ Bay ✉ PA28 6SE – ✆ (01583) 431 226 – www.dunvalanree.com – Closed Christmas
5 rm ☕ – 🚹£ 70 🚹🚹£ 100/135 **Rest** – Menu £ 24 – *(dinner only)*
1930s Arts and Crafts house with gardens and a terrace overlooking the beach and the Sound. Characterful interior with many original features. Unfussy, individually furnished bedrooms – one in Mackintosh style; some with views. Homely cooking has a traditional, seafood base.

KILBERRY

Kilberry Inn with rm

✉ PA29 6YD – ✆ (01880) 770 223 – www.kilberryinn.com – Closed January-mid March, Christmas and Monday

5 rm ☕ – †£ 125 ††£ 215

Carte £ 21/43 – *(dinner only and lunch Thursday-Sunday) (booking essential at dinner)*

Remotely set, rustic country inn with wooden beams, stone walls, open fires and mix of bare and linen-laid tables. Classical dishes are crafted from carefully sourced local produce; meat and fish are smoked in-house. Well-stocked bar. Comfy, modern bedrooms are named after nearby islands; one has an outdoor hot tub.

TARBERT

Anchor

Harbour St ✉ PA29 6UB – ✆ (01880) 820 577 – www.lochfyne-scotland.co.uk – Closed 5-12 January

12 rm ☕ – †£ 80/120 ††£ 80/120

Rest *Sea Bed* – Carte £ 20/45

Smart, blue, mid-terraced house; once a church and later, a cinema. Modern interior with bright bedrooms, king-sized beds and smart bathrooms; half of the rooms have views over the harbour. Informal, all-day bar-cum-restaurant offers good old favourites and tasty seafood specials.

KIRKBEAN

Dumfries and Galloway – See Regional map n°**26**-C3

▶Edinburgh 92 mi – Dumfries 13 mi – Kirkcudbright 29 mi

Michelin Road map 501-J19 – Michelin Green Guide SCOTLAND

Cavens

✉ DG2 8AA – ✆ (01387) 880 234 – www.cavens.com – Closed January-February

6 rm ☕ – †£ 70/150 ††£ 80/210

Rest – Menu £ 25 – Carte £ 27/42 – *(dinner only)*

Attractive 18C country house in 20 acres of mature grounds. Relax in the cosy, book-filled 'Green Room' or elegant drawing room with its grand piano. Luxurious 'Estate' bedrooms boast views over the Solway Firth, while the comfy 'Country' rooms have a simpler style. Linen-clad dining room offers an unfussy, daily menu of local produce; complimentary afternoon tea.

KIRKCUDBRIGHT

Dumfries and Galloway – Pop. 3 352 – See Regional map n°**25**-B3

▶Edinburgh 105 mi – London 369 mi – Glasgow 90 mi – Liverpool 185 mi

Michelin Road map 501-H19 and 502 – Michelin Green Guide SCOTLAND

Selkirk Arms

High St ✉ DG6 4JG – ✆ (01557) 330 402 – www.selkirkarmshotel.co.uk – Closed 24-26 December

16 rm ☕ – †£ 79/84 ††£ 98/110 – 2 suites

Rest *Artistas* – see restaurant listing

Well-run, 18C former coaching inn, where Robert Burns reputedly wrote the Selkirk Grace. Spacious, comfortable bedrooms; some recently refurbished. Light lunches in the cosy, busy bar, which displays paintings of local scenes.

Gladstone House

48 High St ✉ DG6 4JX – ✆ (01557) 331 734 – www.kirkcudbrightgladstone.com – Closed 2 weeks January-February and Christmas

3 rm ☕ – †£ 60 ††£ 78 **Rest** – Menu £ 28

Attractive 18C former merchant's house with friendly owners. Comfy, antique-furnished lounge. Simple, pastel-hued bedrooms with seating areas by the windows and views over the rooftops. 3 course dinner of local produce, tailored around guests' preferences.

SCOTLAND

Glenholme Country House

Tongland Rd ✉ DG6 4UU – Northeast : 1 mi on A 711 – ☎ (01557) 339 422 – www.glenholmecountryhouse.com – Closed Christmas-New Year

4 rm – †£ 95 ††£ 120 **Rest** – Menu £ 35

Take in mountain views from this stone house's spacious garden. Inside, it has a cosy, eye-catching style and there's a large book and music library in place of TVs. Bedrooms are themed around Victorian political figures. The dining room features Chinese furnishings and meals are tailored to guests' tastes.

Artistas – Selkirk Arms Hotel

High St ✉ DG6 4JG – ☎ (01557) 330 402 – www.selkirkarmshotel.co.uk – Closed 24-26 December except lunch 25 December

Carte £ 21/42

Formal restaurant in a traditional former coaching inn. Extensive menu offers regional ingredients in classic combinations; Galloway Beef and Kirkcudbright scallops feature. A carved copy of the Selkirk Grace hangs proudly on the wall.

KIRKNEWTON → See Edinburgh

West Lothian – Michelin Road map 501-J16

KYLESKU

Highland – See Regional map n°**30**-C1

Edinburgh 256 mi – Inverness 100 mi – Ullapool 34 mi

Michelin Road map 501-E9 – Michelin Green Guide SCOTLAND

Kylesku

✉ IV27 4HW – ☎ (01971) 502 231 – www.kyleskuhotel.co.uk – Closed November-February

8 rm – †£ 65/89 ††£ 97/120

Rest ***Kylesku (Bar)*** – see restaurant listing

Rest – Carte £ 16/43 – *(dinner only)*

Delightfully located 17C coaching inn, set beside 2 sea-lochs in a peaceful village. Take in the spectacular panoramic views from the cosy lounge, the restaurant and most of the homely bedrooms. Cooking centres around fresh Highland game and locally landed seafood.

Kylesku (Bar) – Kylesku Hotel

✉ IV27 4HW – ☎ (01971) 502 231 – www.kyleskuhotel.co.uk – Closed November-February

Carte £ 16/43

Cosy, homely bar with friendly staff, a relaxed atmosphere and breathtaking views of Loch Glendhu and the spectacular surrounding scenery. The menu focuses on fresh seafood, which is landed daily in front of the inn.

LAIRG

Highland – Pop. 857 – See Regional map n°**30**-C2

Edinburgh 218 mi – Inverness 61 mi – Wick 72 mi

Michelin Road map 501-G9

Park House without rest

✉ IV27 4AU – ☎ (01549) 402 208 – www.parkhousesporting.com – Closed Christmas-New Year

4 rm – †£ 65 ††£ 95

An old Victorian hunting lodge offering fishing and field sports and views over Loch Shin – its walls fittingly hung with rods and hunting prints. Relax in the cosy open-fired sitting room then retire to one of the homely bedrooms.

LEITH → See Edinburgh

City of Edinburgh – Michelin Road map 501-K16

LERWICK → See Shetland Islands (Mainland)

– Michelin Road map 501-Q3

LEWIS and HARRIS (Isle of)

Western Isles – See Regional map n°**29-A1**
Michelin Road map 501-A9 – Michelin Green Guide SCOTLAND

LEWIS

Western Isles – – See Regional map n°**29-A1**
Edinburgh 210 mi – London 611 mi – Dundee 192 mi

BACK

Broad Bay House

✉ *HS2 0LQ Northeast : 1 mi on B 895 – ✆ (01851) 820 990 – www.broadbayhouse.co.uk – Closed October-April*
4 rm – £ 139 £ 179 **Rest** – Menu £ 35
Delightful guesthouse with a decked terrace and a garden leading down to the beach. Luxurious interior features an open-plan, Scandinavian-style lounge and a dining area with panoramic views. Modern, oak-furnished bedrooms come with super king sized beds, sliding doors onto private terraces and great extras. Extensive hot and cold breakfasts and tasty 4 course dinners.

GALSON

Galson Farm 

South Galson ✉ HS2 0SH – ✆ (01851) 850 492 – www.galsonfarm.co.uk
4 rm – £ 52 £ 80/104 **Rest** – Menu £ 27
Welcoming guesthouse in a wonderfully remote location, boasting views out across the Atlantic. Traditional, homely guest areas and cosy bedrooms. The owner also operates the village post office from just inside the porch. Freshly prepared, home-cooked meals.

STORNOWAY

Braighe House without rest 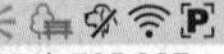

20 Braighe Rd ✉ HS2 0BQ – Southeast : 3 mi on A 866 – ✆ (01851) 705 287 – www.braighehouse.co.uk – Closed October-March
4 rm – £ 95/130 £ 110/149
Smart dormer bungalow with a neat garden and a relaxed, modern interior. Immaculately kept bedrooms come with mineral water and chocolates; 'Deluxe' rooms have sleigh beds and sea outlooks. Complimentary port. Diverse, appealing breakfasts.

UIG

XX **Auberge Carnish** with rm 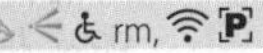

5 Carnish ✉ HS2 9EX – Southwest : 3.25 mi – ✆ (01851) 672 459 – www.aubergecarnish.co.uk – Closed December-mid February
4 rm – £ 95/129 £ 130/150
Menu £ 36 – *(dinner only) (booking essential)*
Modern, timber-clad building with decking all around, set in an idyllic position above the sweeping sands of Uig Bay. Lewis produce features in satisfying, classically based dishes with a twist; daily specials are usually seafood-based. Spacious, minimalist bedrooms have stylish bathrooms and stunning views.

HARRIS

Western Isles – – See Regional map n°**29-A1**
Edinburgh 261 mi – London 638 mi – Dundee 242 mi

ARDHASAIG

XX **Ardhasaig House** with rm

✉ *HS3 3AJ – ✆ (01859) 502 500 – www.ardhasaig.co.uk – Closed November*
6 rm – £ 55/80 £ 60/150 Menu £ 58 – *(dinner only) (booking essential)*
Purpose-built house that's been in the family for over 100 years. Modern, airy bar-lounge; flag-floored dining room with antique tables and dramatic bay and mountain views. Set menu offers local meats and seafood. Cosy bedrooms; the one in the stone lodge is the best.

BORVE

Pairc an t-Srath 

✉ HS3 3HT – ✆ (01859) 550 386 – www.paircant-srath.co.uk – Closed 2 weeks October-November

4 rm – †£ 52/82 ††£ 104 **Rest** – Menu £ 37

Welcoming guesthouse on a working croft, with views out over the Sound of Taransay. Comfy, open-fired lounge has a chaise longue; the intimate dining room offers delicious home-cooked meals and wonderful vistas. Extremely friendly owners serve tea and homemade cake on arrival. Immaculate bedrooms feature smart oak furniture and brightly coloured Harris Tweed fabrics.

SCALPAY

Hirta House without rest

✉ HS4 3XZ – ✆ (01859) 540 394 – www.hirtahouse.co.uk

3 rm – †£ 70/75 ††£ 70/75

Simple, characterful guesthouse in a small fishing village. Loch and mountain views from the lounge and conservatory. One traditional four-poster bedroom; two more modern rooms – one with a round bed. Nautically themed breakfast room.

SCARISTA

SCOTLAND

Scarista House

✉ HS3 3HX – ✆ (01859) 550 238 – www.scaristahouse.com – Closed 21 December-31 January and restricted opening in winter

6 rm – †£ 125/155 ††£ 210/240

Rest – Menu £ 43 – *(dinner only) (booking essential) (set menu only)*

19C former manse boasting amazing bay and mountain views. Caring owners; cosy, homely interior with open-fired library and drawing room. Traditional bedrooms, those at the rear are best. Classically inspired menu features garden produce.

TARBERT

Ceol na Mara without rest

7 Direcleit ✉ HS3 3DP – South : 1 mi by A 859 – ✆ (01859) 502 464 – www.ceolnamara.com

4 rm – †£ 90/120 ††£ 90/120

Former crofter's cottage – one of only three on the island with three storeys. Spacious, homely interior. Various well-kept lounges and good-sized, comfy bedrooms. Stunning lochside location.

LEWISTON

Highland – See Regional map n°**30**-C2

▶Edinburgh 172 mi – London 553 mi – Dundee 153 mi

Michelin Road map 501-G12 – Michelin Green Guide SCOTLAND

Loch Ness Inn with rm

✉ IV63 6UW – ✆ (01456) 450 991 – www.staylochness.co.uk

12 rm – †£ 65/85 ††£ 75/112 Carte £ 18/38

There are two parts to this pub: the small Brewery Bar, home to locals and walkers fresh from the Great Glen Way; and the open-plan Lewiston restaurant with its wood burning stove and bright timbered beams. Hearty, robust, flavoursome dishes champion Scottish produce. Bedrooms are spacious and comfortable.

LINLITHGOW

West Lothian – Pop. 13 462 – See Regional map n°**26**-C1

▶Edinburgh 19 mi – London 421 mi – Glasgow 35 mi – Aberdeen 125 mi

Michelin Road map 501-J16 – Michelin Green Guide SCOTLAND

Arden House without rest

Belsyde ✉ EH49 6QE – Southwest : 2.25 mi on A 706 – ✆ (01506) 670 172 – www.ardencountryhouse.com – Restricted opening in winter

3 rm – £ 60/100 £ 84/115

Purpose built guesthouse bordering a 105 acre sheep farm. Tea and cake on arrival. Spacious, tastefully styled bedrooms boast modern, slate-floored bathrooms and plenty of extras like fresh flowers and magazines. Tasty, wide-ranging breakfasts are a highlight. Welcoming owner pays great attention to detail.

Champany Inn with rm

rm,

✉ EH49 7LU Northeast : 2 mi on A 803 at junction with A 904 – ✆ (01506) 834 532 – www.champany.com – Closed 25-26 December, 1-2 January, Saturday lunch and Sunday

16 rm – £ 99/125 £ 109/135 Menu £ 26/43 – Carte £ 50/76

Set in a collection of whitewashed cottages; the traditional restaurant was once a flour mill, hence its unusual shape. The focus is on meat and wine – 21-day aged Aberdeen Angus beef is a speciality. There's also a well-stocked wine shop, a second, more laid-back restaurant and tartan-themed bedrooms.

Livingston's

52 High St ✉ EH49 7AE – ✆ (01506) 846 565 – www.livingstons-restaurant.co.uk – Closed 2 weeks January, 1 week June, 1 week October, Sunday and Monday

Menu £ 19/42

Long-standing, family-run restaurant tucked away off the high street. Conservatory-like dining room with large garden and terrace; friendly, efficient service. Modern cooking with some bold flavours and innovative touches.

LOANS

→ See Troon

South Ayrshire – Michelin Road map 501-G17 and 502

LOCHALINE

Highland – See Regional map n°**29-B3**

Edinburgh 162 mi – Craignure 6 mi – Oban 7 mi

Michelin Road map 501-C14

Whitehouse

✉ PA80 5XT – ✆ (01967) 421 777 – www.thewhitehouserestaurant.co.uk – Closed November-Easter, Sunday and Monday

Menu £ 18 (lunch) – Carte £ 27/48

Understated wood-panelled restaurant in a remote headland village, run by keen, hands-on owners. The constantly evolving blackboard menu showcases local seafood, game and garden produce. Cooking is pleasingly unfussy and flavoursome.

LOCHINVER

Highland – Pop. 470 – ✉ Lairg – See Regional map n°**30-C1**

Edinburgh 251 mi – Inverness 95 mi – Wick 105 mi

Michelin Road map 501-E9 – Michelin Green Guide SCOTLAND

Inver Lodge

Iolaire Rd ✉ IV27 4LU – ✆ (01571) 844 496 – www.inverlodge.com – Closed November-April

21 rm – £ 150 £ 225

Rest *Chez Roux* – see restaurant listing

Well-run hotel on the hillside, overlooking a quiet fishing village. Spacious open-fired lounge, elegant bar and billiard room. Smart bedrooms with good mod cons and great bay/island views.

Ruddyglow Park Country House without rest

Loch Assynt ✉ IV27 4HB – Northeast : 6.75 mi on A 837 – ✆ (01571) 822 216 – www.ruddyglowpark.com – Closed December-February

3 rm – £ 100/130 £ 130/200

Yellow-washed house in a superb location, boasting fantastic loch and mountain views. Spacious guest areas are filled with antiques, paintings and silverware. A high level of facilities and extras feature in the classically styled bedrooms; the room in the modern log cabin offers extra privacy.

XX **Albannach** (Colin Craig and Lesley Crosfield) with rm

Baddidarroch ✉ IV27 4LP – West : 1 mi by Baddidarroch rd – ☎ (01571) 844 407 – www.thealbannach.co.uk – Closed Christmas, Tuesday and Wednesday November to mid-March, except at New Year, and Monday

5 rm (dinner included) – £ 180/225 £ 260/380

Menu £ 69 – *(dinner only) (bookings essential for non-residents) (set menu only)*

Substantial 19C Scottish house in a remote location, boasting exceptional bay and mountain views from the conservatory, terrace and garden. Traditional 5 course dinners rely on top quality local produce, with seafood from the harbour below and Scottish beef the specialities. Contemporary bedrooms are spread about the building; one boasts a private terrace and a hot tub.

→ Wood pigeon with roast shallots and chocolate sauce. Wild turbot, croft black potatoes, charred fennel and red wine sauce. Caramelised pear tart, pear crisp and pear gelato.

XX **Chez Roux** – Inver Lodge Hotel

Iolaire Rd ✉ IV27 4LU – ☎ (01571) 844 496 – www.inverlodge.com – Closed November-April

Menu £ 43 – *(dinner only)*

Romantic restaurant hung with photos of the eponymous brothers and boasting well-spaced tables that take in fantastic bay and mountain views. Regularly changing, classical French menus.

LOCHRANZA → See Arran (Isle of)

North Ayrshire – Michelin Road map 501-E16 and 502

LUSS

Argyll and Bute – Pop. 402 – See Regional map n°**27**-B2

Edinburgh 89 mi – Glasgow 26 mi – Oban 65 mi

Michelin Road map 501-G15 – Michelin Green Guide SCOTLAND

 **Loch Lomond Arms** 

Main Rd ✉ G83 8NY – ☎ (01436) 860 420 – www.lochlomondarmshotel.com

14 rm – £ 90/110 £ 120/150 **Rest** – Carte £ 21/40

Retaining the warmth and character of an old inn, this hotel offers individual, contemporary bedrooms. 'Lomond' and 'Colquhoun' are the most luxurious: the former has a four-poster bed; the latter, superb views. Wide-ranging menu: dine in the open-fired bar, the relaxed dining room or the more formal library.

MELROSE

The Scottish Borders – Pop. 2 307 – See Regional map n°**26**-D2

Edinburgh 38 mi – London 347 mi – Glasgow 84 mi – Aberdeen 170 mi

Michelin Road map 501-L17 and 502 – Michelin Green Guide SCOTLAND

 **Burts**

Market Sq. ✉ TD6 9PL – ☎ (01896) 822 285 – www.burtshotel.co.uk – Closed 6-12 January and 26 December

20 rm – £ 74/95 £ 130/145 **Rest** – Carte £ 30/51

Characterful coaching inn on the main square; run by the same family for two generations. Appealing bedrooms blend contemporary furnishings with original features. Cosy bar serves old classics; formal dining room offers a mix of modern and traditional dishes.

Townhouse

Market Sq. ✉ TD6 9PQ – ☎ (01896) 822 645 – www.thetownhousemelrose.co.uk – Closed 12-20 January and 25-26 December

11 rm – £ 95/147 £ 130/147

Rest – Menu £ 15 (dinner) – Carte £ 22/38

Former home of Catherine Spence and contemporary sibling to nearby Burts. Stylish bedrooms are decorated in black and purple and display bold feature walls; some rooms come with a shower only. Trendy all day café-cum-bar or more formal dining room and courtyard offering top Border ingredients.

SCOTLAND

at Gattonside North: 2 mi by B6374 on B6360 ✉ Melrose

Fauhope House without rest 

✉ TD6 9LU East : 0.25 mi by B 6360 taking unmarked lane to the right of Monkswood Rd at edge of village – ✆ (01896) 823 184 – www.fauhopehouse.com

3 rm ☕ – ♦£ 60/90 ♦♦£ 100/120

Charming 19C house by the Tweed, overlooking Melrose – its delightful gardens stretching for 15 acres. Quirky interior displays an eclectic mix of art and antiques. Bedrooms are all very different; some boast stylish bold colour schemes.

MEMUS

Angus – See Regional map n°**28-D2**

▶Edinburgh 76 mi – London 478 mi – Dundee 21 mi

Drovers Inn

✉ DD8 3TY – ✆ (01307) 860 322 – www.the-drovers.com – Closed 25-26 December

Carte £ 24/39

Attractive Highland inn in an extremely remote spot, with a delightful beamed interior and an open-fired bar. The wide-ranging menu is good value for money and showcases local, seasonal produce; game and vegetables come from the estate.

MOFFAT

Dumfries and Galloway – Pop. 2 582 – See Regional map n°**26-C2**

▶Edinburgh 61 mi – Carlisle 43 mi – Dumfries 22 mi – Glasgow 60 mi

Michelin Road map 501-J17 and 502 – Michelin Green Guide SCOTLAND

Hartfell House 

Hartfell Cres. ✉ DG10 9AL – ✆ (01683) 220 153 – www.hartfellhouse.co.uk – Closed 1 week autumn, 1 week January and Christmas

7 rm ☕ – ♦£ 40/45 ♦♦£ 65/75

Rest *Lime Tree* – see restaurant listing

Keenly run Victorian house in a quiet crescent. Original features include parquet floors and ornate cornicing. The comfy lounge has a nice southerly aspect. Large, traditionally decorated bedrooms.

Bridge House 

Well Rd ✉ DG10 9JT – East : 0.75 mi by Selkirk rd (A 708) taking left hand turn before bridge – ✆ (01683) 220 558 – www.bridgehousemoffat.co.uk – Closed 25 December-February

7 rm ☕ – ♦£ 55 ♦♦£ 70/100 **Rest** – Menu £ 25

Large Victorian house on a quiet residential road, run by experienced owners and affording beautiful valley views. Relax in deep sofas in the comfortable lounge. Bedrooms are individually decorated; those to the front are the biggest. The dining room displays lovely cornicing and offers traditional fare.

Well View 

Ballplay Rd ✉ DG10 9JU – East : 0.75 mi by Selkirk rd (A 708) – ✆ (01683) 220 184 – Closed 1-14 May

3 rm ☕ – ♦£ 40/60 ♦♦£ 70/90 **Rest** – Menu £ 35

Substantial 19C house located in a peaceful suburb, boasting spacious, traditionally styled bedrooms and good comforts. It was formerly a restaurant, and dinner is still a key focus here. The daily changing 4 course set menu is taken at a communal table; wine is included.

XX **Brodies** AC

Altrive Pl ✉ DG10 9EB – ✆ (01683) 222 870 – www.brodiesofmoffat.co.uk – Closed 25-27 December

Menu £ 11 (early dinner) – Carte £ 20/37

Large, laid-back, modern eatery that caters for all appetites – serving snacks, light lunches, afternoon tea, more substantial dinners and all-day brunch on Sundays. Cooking has a traditional base and features fresh, local ingredients.

Lime Tree – Hartfell House Hotel 
Hartfell Cres. ✉ *DG10 9AL – ✆ (01683) 220 153 – www.hartfellhouse.co.uk – Closed 1 week autumn, 1 week October, Christmas, Sunday and Monday*
Menu £ 28 – *(dinner only) (booking essential)*
Small hotel restaurant with smartly laid tables, an open fire and attractive marquetry. Large bay window looks down the valley. Good value weekly menus feature tasty, well-presented classics.

MONTROSE

Angus – Pop. 11 955 – See Regional map n°**28**-D2
Edinburgh 92 mi – Aberdeen 39 mi – Dundee 29 mi
Michelin Road map 501-M13 – Michelin Green Guide SCOTLAND

36 The Mall without rest
36 The Mall ✉ DD10 8SS – North : 0.5 mi by A 92 at junction with North Esk Road – ✆ (01674) 673 646 – www.36themall.co.uk
3 rm – £ 55/65 £ 65/80
Large, immaculately kept former manse, run by warm, welcoming owners. Homely, characterful interior with tastefully styled, high-ceilinged bedrooms and a lovely conservatory overlooking the lawned garden. Good buffet selection and cooked choices in the communal breakfast room.

MUIR OF ORD

Highland – Pop. 2 555 – See Regional map n°**30**-C2
Edinburgh 173 mi – Inverness 10 mi – Wick 121 mi
Michelin Road map 501-G11

Dower House
Highfield ✉ IV6 7XN – North : 1 mi on A 862 – ✆ (01463) 870 090 – www.thedowerhouse.co.uk – Closed November-March
4 rm – £ 95/120 £ 140/160
Rest – Menu £ 38 – *(dinner only) (booking essential) (residents only)*
Personally run, part-17C house with charming mature gardens. Characterful guest areas include an antique-furnished dining room and a small, open-fired lounge with fresh flowers and shelves crammed with books. Comfy bedrooms; one with a bay window overlooking the garden. Traditional, daily set menu.

MULL (Isle of)

Argyll and Bute – Pop. 2 800 – See Regional map n°**27**-A2
Edinburgh 141 mi – London 512 mi – Belfast 163 mi – Dundee 136 mi
Michelin Road map 501-B/C14 – Michelin Green Guide SCOTLAND

FIONNPHORT

Ninth Wave
Bruach Mhor ✉ PA66 6BL – East : 0.75 mi by A 849 – ✆ (01681) 700 757 – www.ninthwaverestaurant.co.uk – Closed November-Easter and Monday
Menu £ 42/50 – *(dinner only) (booking essential)*
This stylish modern restaurant started life as a crofter's bothy, over 200 years ago. Local seafood plays a key role, with crab and lobster caught every day. The fruit, vegetables and herbs are from their organic kitchen garden.

TIRORAN

Tiroran House
✉ PA69 6ES – ✆ (01681) 705 232 – www.tiroran.com
10 rm – £ 110/170 £ 185/220 **Rest** – Menu £ 36 – *(light lunch)*
Stunning 19C whitewashed house with a welcoming owner, set in 17 acres of parkland that run down to the water's edge. Charming, antique-filled interior with two open-fired lounges and immaculate, highly individual bedrooms. The dining room is split into a conservatory and a darker, more clubby area, and offers concise, daily changing menus.

TOBERMORY

Tobermory without rest
53 Main St ✉ PA75 6NT – ☎ (01688) 302 091 – www.thetobermoryhotel.com – March-October
16 rm ☕ – 🛉£ 35/128 🛉🛉£ 40/128
Converted fishermen's cottages in a colourful quayside terrace, not far from the local distillery. Watch the sun go down over the sea while planning your next activity. Quirky bedrooms vary in size but most have pleasant harbour views.

Sonas House without rest
The Fairways ✉ PA75 6PS – North : 0.5 mi by Black Brae and Erray Rd following signs for the golf club – ☎ (01688) 302 304 – www.sonashouse.co.uk – Closed November-February
3 rm ☕ – 🛉£ 70/100 🛉🛉£ 90/125
Set in an elevated position above Tobermory, with views over the Sound of Mull. Choose a bedroom in the main house or in the annexe studio; all come with a host of extras and superb views. The lovely swimming pool is open year-round.

Brockville without rest
Raeric Rd ✉ PA75 6RS – by Back Brae and Erray Rd – ☎ (01688) 302 741 – www.brockville-tobermory.co.uk
3 rm ☕ – 🛉£ 75/95 🛉🛉£ 80/100
Welcoming guesthouse with a warm, homely feel; run by a friendly owner with plenty of local knowledge. Extremely spacious bedrooms offer good modern facilities and everything you could want. The communal breakfast room boasts pleasant sea views; menus change daily and feature plenty of fresh fruits.

Highland Cottage with rm
Breadalbane St ✉ PA75 6PD – via B 8073 – ☎ (01688) 302 030 – www.highlandcottage.co.uk – Closed 15 October-1 April
6 rm ☕ – 🛉£ 95/165 🛉🛉£ 135/165
Menu £ 40 – *(dinner only) (bookings essential for non-residents)*
Long-standing, personally run restaurant in an intimate cottage, where family antiques and knick-knacks abound. Classical linen-laid dining room and a homely lounge. Traditional daily menu with a seafood base features plenty of local produce. Bedrooms are snug and individually styled.

MUTHILL → See Crieff

Perth and Kinross – Michelin Road map 501-I15

NAIRN

Highland – Pop. 9 773 – See Regional map n°**30**-D2
▶Edinburgh 172 mi – Aberdeen 91 mi – Inverness 16 mi
Michelin Road map 501-I11 – Michelin Green Guide SCOTLAND

Golf View
63 Seabank Rd ✉ IV12 4HD – ☎ (01667) 452 301 – www.crerarhotels.com
42 rm ☕ – 🛉£ 110/140 🛉🛉£ 140/170 – 1 suite
Rest *Fairways* – Menu £ 13/33 – Carte £ 24/64
Rest *Links Brasserie* – Carte £ 24/46
Set on the coast, between two golf courses, with pleasant gardens and Moray Firth vistas. Large lounge, clubby bar and smart spa. Spacious bedrooms have Stag-style furnishings; one has a whirlpool bath and views from its four-poster bed. Traditional menus in the part-panelled dining room and airy brasserie.

Boath House
Auldearn ✉ IV12 5TE – East : 2 mi on A 96 – ☎ (01667) 454 896 – www.boath-house.com
8 rm ☕ – 🛉£ 190/260 🛉🛉£ 260/365
Rest *Boath House* ✿ – see restaurant listing
Owned by a charming couple, an elegant 1825 neo-classical mansion framed by Corinthian columns. Inside it cleverly blends contemporary furnishings and restored original features; most of the art is for sale. Elegant, intimate bedrooms – one has his and hers roll-top baths and some have views of the lake.

SCOTLAND

Cawdor House without rest

7 Cawdor St ✉ IV12 4QD – ✆ (01667) 455 855 – www.cawdorhousenairn.co.uk – Closed 21 December-14 January

7 rm – †£ 55/75 ††£ 76/96

Comfy 19C former manse whose original features blend with contemporary styling. Cosy lounge with a log fire; variously sized bedrooms are clean and uncluttered. The friendly owners are a font of local knowledge. Simple dining room with set menu dinners by arrangement.

Boath House – Boath House Hotel

Auldearn ✉ IV12 5TE – East : 2 mi on A 96 – ✆ (01667) 454 896 – www.boath-house.com

Menu £ 30/70 **s** – *(set menu at dinner) (booking essential)*

Elegant oval dining room in an early 19C mansion, with floor to ceiling windows affording lake views. Well-balanced modern menus showcase the chef's skill and understanding; cooking is accomplished, with vivid presentation and interesting flavours. Much of the produce is from their garden, orchard and bees.

→ Mackerel, carrot and capers. Roe deer with salsify and wild garlic. Rhubarb, almond and bergamot.

NEW CUMNOCK

East Ayrshire – Pop. 2 860 – See Regional map n°**25**-B2

Edinburgh 66 mi – London 378 mi – Glasgow 42 mi – Hamilton 36 mi

Michelin Road map 501-H17

Lochside House rest,

✉ KA18 4PN Northwest : 1.5 mi on A 76 – ✆ (01290) 333 000 – www.lochside-hotel.com

34 rm – †£ 90 ††£ 130 – 3 suites

Rest *Afton* – Carte £ 19/31

19C former shooting lodge for the Marquis of Bute, impressively located on the side of a small loch and surrounded by acres of countryside. Stylish, contemporary interior with an attractive spa, comfy bedrooms and luxurious suites. The restaurant offers a range of classic dishes and panoramic loch views.

NEWTON STEWART

Dumfries and Galloway – Pop. 4 092 – See Regional map n°**25**-B3

Edinburgh 131 mi – Dumfries 51 mi – Glasgow 87 mi – Stranraer 24 mi

Michelin Road map 501-G19 and 502 – Michelin Green Guide SCOTLAND

Kirroughtree House

✉ DG8 6AN Northeast : 1.5 mi by A 75 on A 712 – ✆ (01671) 402 141 – www.kirroughtreehouse.co.uk – Closed 2 January-1 February

17 rm – †£ 90/120 ††£ 160/230 – 2 suites

Rest – Menu £ 18/35 **s** – *(booking essential)*

Impressive 1719 mansion in landscaped gardens, overlooking the woods and bay. Grand interior with vast open-fired hall and impressive staircase. Traditionally styled bedrooms with plenty of extras. Concise 4 course menu of quality produce in classic combinations.

NIGG → See Tain

– Michelin Road map 501-H10

NORTH BAY → See Barra (Isle of)

Western Isles

NORTH BERWICK

East Lothian – Pop. 6 605 – See Regional map n°**26**-D1

Edinburgh 141 mi – London 512 mi – Belfast 163 mi – Dundee 136 mi

Michelin Road map 501-L15 – Michelin Green Guide SCOTLAND

Glebe House without rest
Law Rd ✉ EH39 4PL – ✆ (01620) 89 2608 – www.glebehouse-nb.co.uk
– Closed Christmas-New Year
3 rm – £ 85/95 £ 120/130
Spacious, welcoming Georgian house with walled gardens and views over the town and sea. Classical, country house drawing room and antique communal breakfast table. Comfortable, well-furnished bedrooms.

Canty Bay House without rest
Canty Bay ✉ EH39 5PL – West : 2.5 mi on A 198 – ✆ (01620) 248 216
– www.cantybayhouse.co.uk – Closed Christmas-New Year
4 rm – £ 130/170 £ 130/170
Small guesthouse perched on a clifftop, overlooking Tantallon Castle ruins, Bass Rock and the Firth of Forth. The smart interior has good quality furnishings and a snooker table. Two of the bedrooms open onto a small roof terrace.

NORTH QUEENSFERRY

Fife – Pop. 1 076 – See Regional map n°**28-C3**
Edinburgh 13 mi – London 416 mi – Glasgow 47 mi – Aberdeen 116 mi
Michelin Road map 501-J15

Wee Restaurant
17 Main St ✉ KY11 1JT – ✆ (01383) 616 263 – www.theweerestaurant.co.uk
– Closed 25-26 December, 1-2 January and Monday
Menu £ 20/34 **s**
Simple, quarry-floored restaurant in the shadow of the Forth Rail Bridge. Fresh Scottish ingredients are served in neatly presented, classical combinations. Lunch represents the best value.

SCOTLAND

NORTH UIST → See Uist (Isles of)

Western Isles – Michelin Road map 501-X/Y11

OBAN

Argyll and Bute – Pop. 8 574 – See Regional map n°**27-B2**
Edinburgh 123 mi – Dundee 116 mi – Glasgow 93 mi – Inverness 118 mi
Michelin Road map 501-D14 – Michelin Green Guide SCOTLAND

Manor House 
Gallanach Rd. ✉ PA34 4LS – ✆ (01631) 562 087 – www.manorhouseoban.com
– Closed 25 December
11 rm – £ 110/185 £ 120/235 **Rest** – Menu £ 43 – *(bar lunch)*
18C dower house; formerly part of the Argyll Estate. The country house style interior offers traditional comforts, and the spacious lounge and rustic bar boast delightful bay and harbour views. Individually styled bedrooms. Concise daily menu served in the formal dining room.

Glenburnie House without rest 
Corran Esplanade ✉ PA34 5AQ – ✆ (01631) 562 089 – www.glenburnie.co.uk
– Closed December-February
12 rm – £ 55/95 £ 90/120
Bay-windowed house on the main esplanade, affording great bay and island views. Period features include a delightful staircase and etched glass widows; antiques abound. Comfy, good-sized bedrooms.

Coast
104 George St ✉ PA34 5NT – ✆ (01631) 569 900 – www.coastoban.co.uk
– Closed 25-26 December, Sunday-Monday October-March and Sunday lunch April-September
Menu £ 15 (lunch and early dinner) – Carte £ 21/38
Busy high street restaurant in a former bank, with a high ceiling, a stripped wooden floor and khaki fabric strips on the walls. Unfussy, modern cooking with good seasoning; local produce is key. 'Light bite' lunches are a steal.

Ee-usk

The North Pier ✉ PA34 5QD – ✆ (01631) 565 666 – www.eeusk.com – Closed 2 weeks January and 25-26 December
Carte £ 23/52
Long-standing seafood restaurant run by experienced owners, located on the harbourfront and offering great views over the bay from its floor to ceiling windows. Extensive menus focus on simply prepared, fresh local fish and shellfish.

ONICH

Highland ✉ Fort William – See Regional map n°**29**-B3
Edinburgh 123 mi – Glasgow 93 mi – Inverness 79 mi – Oban 39 mi
Michelin Road map 501-E13

Lochleven Seafood Café

Lochleven ✉ PH33 6SA – Southeast : 6.5 mi by A 82 on B 863 – ✆ (01855) 821 048 – www.lochlevenseafoodcafe.co.uk – Closed November-March
Carte £ 24/63 **s** – *(bookings advisable at dinner)*
Simple little restaurant in a stunning lochside spot, looking towards the Glencoe Mountains. Fresh fish and shellfish come from the west coast of Scotland and the seafood platter is a speciality. In winter they host themed evenings.

ORKNEY ISLANDS

Orkney Islands – Pop. 21 349
Michelin Road map 501-K/L7 – Michelin Green Guide SCOTLAND

SCOTLAND

ISLE OF WESTRAY

Orkney Islands – – See Regional map n°**31**-A2
Edinburgh 289 mi – London 690 mi – Dundee 270 mi

PIEROWALL

No 1 Broughton without rest

✉ KW17 2DA – ✆ (01857) 677 726 – www.no1broughton.co.uk – Closed 24-25 December
3 rm – †£ 50/60 ††£ 60/80
19C pink-washed house on the waterside, with views over Pierowall Bay and out to Papa Westray. Comfortable lounge and conservatory; simple, homely bedrooms with modern bathrooms. Sauna on request. Dry stone walling courses also available!

MAINLAND

Orkney Islands – – See Regional map n°**31**-A3
Edinburgh 277 mi – London 677 mi – Dundee 258 mi

BURRAY

Sands

✉ KW17 2SS – ✆ (01856) 731 298 – www.thesandshotel.co.uk – Closed 1-3 January and 25-26 December
8 rm – †£ 50/90 ††£ 70/115 **Rest** – Carte £ 17/34
Converted 19C herring packing store in small hamlet overlooking Scapa Flow. Pleasant bedrooms boast smart bathrooms. Bar with pool table and dartboard offers traditional menu. Dining room serves more refined dishes, featuring island produce and lots of shellfish.

DEERNESS

Northfield without rest

✉ KW17 2QL West : 2 mi turning left by village shop – ✆ (01856) 741 353 – www.orkneybedandbreakfast.com
3 rm – †£ 60/80 ††£ 80
Set down a bumpy lane, right by the water's edge, with views across to some of the smaller islands. Horses, ducks and chickens can be found in the peaceful grounds. Cosy, homely, tastefully furnished bedrooms; one with views from the bed.

DOUNBY

Ashleigh without rest
Howaback Rd ✉ KW17 2JA – South : 0.75 mi by A 986 – ☎ (01856) 771 378 – www.ashleigh-orkney.com – Closed 20 December-20 January
4 rm – £ 40/43 £ 74/78
Purpose-built house in the heart of the island's countryside, boasting loch and mountain views. Large breakfast room and lounge filled with guidebooks. Good-sized bedrooms with modern facilities.

HARRAY

Merkister
✉ KW17 2LF Off A 986 – ☎ (01856) 771 366 – www.merkister.com – Closed 23 December-4 January
16 rm – £ 50/95 £ 70/218
Rest – Carte £ 21/40 **s** – *(bar lunch)*
Family-run, lochside hotel affording wonderful water and mountain views. Comfortable, well-kept bedrooms; those outside have their own terraces and gardens. Snug, open-fired bar serves snacks. Dining room offers strictly Orkney-based produce and a scenic backdrop.

Holland House without rest
✉ KW17 2LQ On St Michael's Church rd – ☎ (01856) 771 400 – www.hollandhouseorkney.co.uk – Closed 7 December-12 January and restricted opening in winter
3 rm – £ 52/60 £ 104
Converted manse run by a welcoming owner, with commanding views throughout. Open-fired lounge – packed with local art and handmade furniture – stone-floored breakfast room and conservatory. Spotless bedrooms with a host of extras and great attention to detail.

KIRKWALL

Michelin Green Guide SCOTLAND

Ayre
Ayre Rd. ✉ KW15 1QX – ☎ (01856) 873 001 – www.ayrehotel.co.uk – Closed 25 December and 1 January
51 rm – £ 80/95 £ 99/135
Rest – Carte £ 19/46 – *(bar lunch)*
Well-run hotel close to the harbour. Formerly 3 Victorian houses, now a traditionally styled hotel with comfortable bedrooms – the newer extension rooms are biggest and best. Spacious bar filled with locals. Dining room offers sizeable menu of Orcadian produce.

Lynnfield
Holm Rd ✉ KW15 1SU – ☎ (01856) 872 505 – www.lynnfieldhotel.com – Closed 1-7 January and 25-26 December
10 rm – £ 75/100 £ 100/155 – 3 suites
Rest – Carte £ 23/42 – *(bar lunch)*
Spacious hotel with cosy sitting rooms, Orcadian furniture and a fine range of Scotch whiskies. Supremely comfortable bedrooms; two with four-posters. Formal dining room with large conservatory affording great views of the countryside. Seasonal menus.

Avalon House without rest
Carness Rd ✉ KW15 1UE – Northeast : 1.5 mi by Shore St. – ☎ (01856) 876 665 – www.avalon-house.co.uk – Closed Christmas-New Year
5 rm – £ 45/50 £ 72
Modern, purpose-built guesthouse in a pleasant residential area. Lounge filled with maps and books about the islands. Good-sized bedrooms with simple, homely feel. Nice coastal outlook.

SCOTLAND

XX **Foveran** with rm

St Ola ✉ KW15 1SF – Southwest : 3 mi on A 964 – ✆ (01856) 872 389 – www.thefoveran.com – Restricted opening October-April
8 rm ☕ – 🚹£ 75/78 🚹🚹£ 110/116 Carte £ 22/41 – *(dinner only)*
Spacious restaurant boasting superb panoramic views over the Scapa Flow and the south islands. Traditional menu features local, seasonal produce, including Orcadian lamb and beef and plenty of fresh seafood. Homely, well-kept bedrooms have simple colour schemes.

St Margaret's Hope

XX **Creel** with rm

Front Rd ✉ KW17 2SL – ✆ (01856) 831 311 – www.thecreel.co.uk – Closed October-April, Sunday and Monday
3 rm ☕ – 🚹£ 75/85 🚹🚹£ 110/120 Menu £ 40 – *(dinner only)*
Long-standing, family-run restaurant in a seafront village. Spacious dining room is hung with local oils and prints. Daily changing menu displays a fresh, traditional seafood base. Comfortable, cosy bedrooms boast modern, co-ordinated furnishings and bay views.

Stromness

Michelin Green Guide SCOTLAND

X **Hamnavoe**

35 Graham Pl ✉ KW16 3BY – off Victoria St – ✆ (01856) 850 606 – Closed Monday and restricted opening in winter
Carte £ 27/43 – *(dinner only) (booking essential)*
Homely restaurant in a sleepy harbourside town; its name meaning 'Safe Haven'. Its plain walls are dotted with local oils and open fires. Unfussy home cooking utilises fresh market produce and dishes are hearty and full of flavour.

SCOTLAND

PEAT INN

Fife – See Regional map n°**28**-D2
Edinburgh 44 mi – London 447 mi – Belfast 134 mi – Dundee 16 mi

XXX ✿ **The Peat Inn** (Geoffrey Smeddle) with rm

✉ KY15 5LH – ✆ (01334) 840 206 – www.thepeatinn.co.uk – Closed 2 weeks January, Christmas, Sunday and Monday
8 rm ☕ – 🚹£ 175/205 🚹🚹£ 195/225
Menu £ 19/45 – Carte £ 46/53 – *(booking essential)*
Whitewashed former pub with a log fire in the lounge and a cosy, well-dressed restaurant – ask for a table overlooking the floodlit gardens. Accomplished, classical cooking has subtle modern touches and local ingredients to the fore. Stylish, split-level bedrooms in a separate stone building, with plenty of extras and breakfast served in-room. Charming, professional staff.
➜ Langoustine lasagne, chickpeas, almonds and preserved lemon. Seared pavé of beef, celeriac and horseradish purée and broad beans. Crème fraîche panna cotta with roast rhubarb and pistachio ice cream.

PEEBLES

The Scottish Borders – Pop. 8 376 – See Regional map n°**26**-C2
Edinburgh 24 mi – London 382 mi – Glasgow 53 mi – Aberdeen 151 mi
Michelin Road map 501-K17 and 502 – Michelin Green Guide SCOTLAND

Cringletie House

Edinburgh Rd ✉ EH45 8PL – North : 3 mi on A 703 – ✆ (01721) 722 510 – www.cringletie.com – Closed 2-22 January
15 rm ☕ – 🚹£ 110/250 🚹🚹£ 135/375 – 2 suites
Rest *The Sutherland* – Menu £ 38/23 **s** – *(dinner only and Sunday lunch)*
A handsome, early Victorian shooting lodge with a baronial feel, set in acres of gardens and parkland. Smart bedrooms – named after border towns – have views of the gardens. Dine under a stunning 1902 ceiling fresco; good quality local produce includes herbs and veg from the walled garden.

Rowanbrae without rest

103 Northgate ✉ EH45 8BU – ✆ (01721) 721 630 – www.aboutscotland.co./peebles/rowanbrae – Closed December-February

3 rm – £ 45 £ 70

Cosy Victorian villa close to town, with a pretty terrace and surprisingly spacious interior. Long-standing owners provide a warm welcome and a snug, homely atmosphere reigns. Pleasant, well-kept bedrooms have a modern edge, courtesy of their soft furnishings. Original cornices and pine woodwork feature.

Osso

Innerleithen Rd ✉ EH45 8BA – ✆ (01721) 724 477 – www.ossorestaurant.com – Closed 1 January, 25 December, dinner Tuesday and Wednesday in winter except December and dinner Sunday and Monday

Carte £ 19/38

By day, a bustling coffee shop serving a bewildering array of light snacks and daily specials. By night, a more sophisticated restaurant offering a great value, regularly changing menu of tasty, well-presented dishes, with the occasional Asian influence. Friendly, attentive service.

Restaurant at Kailzie Gardens

Kailzie Estate ✉ EH45 9HT – East : 2 mi on B 7062 – ✆ (01721) 722 807 – www.kailzie.com – Closed 1-14 January, Monday and Tuesday October-March

Carte £ 13/24 – *(lunch only) (booking advisable)*

Rustic eatery in the old stables of a large estate, surrounded by semi-formal gardens, a fishery and an osprey viewing centre. Brunch, homemade cakes and afternoon tea are accompanied by a concise selection of Scandic open sandwiches and classic dishes from 12pm. Seasonal dinners are served once a month.

at Eddleston North: 4.5 mi on A703

The Horseshoe with rm

rest, P

Edinburgh Rd ✉ EH45 8QP – ✆ (01721) 730 225 – www.horseshoeinn.co.uk – Closed first 2 weeks January, last 2 weeks September, Monday and Tuesday

8 rm – £ 90/120 £ 120/150 Menu £ 19 (lunch) – Carte £ 30/44

Once a roadside inn; now a smart, columned restaurant with elegant tableware and formal service. Sophisticated menus offer ambitious, well-presented dishes which take their influences from across Europe. Chic, modern bedrooms are located in the old village schoolhouse and come with pleasing extras.

PERTH

Perth and Kinross – Pop. 46 970 – See Regional map n°**28**-C2

Edinburgh 44 mi – Aberdeen 86 mi – Dundee 22 mi – Dunfermline 29 mi

Michelin Road map 501-J14 – Michelin Green Guide SCOTLAND

Parklands

2 St Leonard's Bank ✉ PH2 8EB – ✆ (01738) 622 451 – www.theparklandshotel.com – Closed 25 December-5 January Town plan: Z**n**

15 rm – £ 95/145 £ 109/189

Rest *63@Parklands* – see restaurant listing

Rest *No.1 The Bank* – Carte £ 26/46

Located close to the railway station, a personally run, extended Georgian house with a contemporary interior. Spacious modern bedrooms have good facilities and sizeable bathrooms; those to the front have pleasant views over the park. Modern menu in the intimate 63@Parklands; informal dining in No.1 The Bank.

Taythorpe without rest

Isla Rd ✉ PH2 7HQ – North : 1 mi on A 93 – ✆ (01738) 447 994 – www.taythorpe.co.uk – Closed 21 December-4 January Town plan: Y**a**

3 rm – £ 40/50 £ 75

Modern, stone-built house run by a bubbly owner; superbly located close to Scone Palace, the city and the racecourse. Large, cosy sitting room hung with homely pictures and salmon fishing maps; pleasant communal breakfast room where tasty Scottish dishes are served. Appealing, immaculately kept bedrooms.

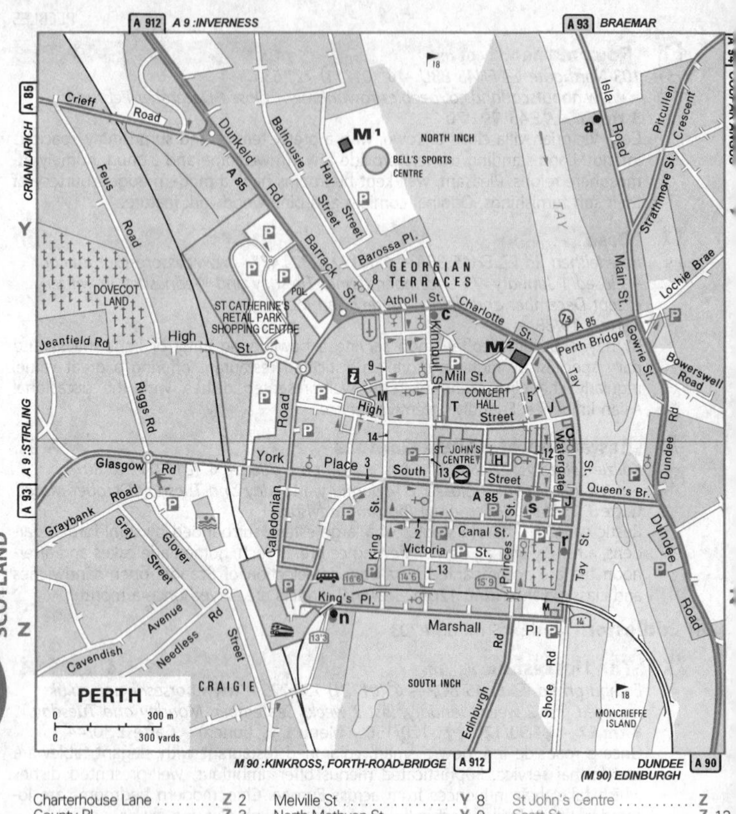

Charterhouse Lane	Z 2	Melville St	Y 8	St John's Centre	Z
County Pl.	Z 3	North Methven St.	Y 9	Scott St	Z 13
George St	Y 5	St Catherine's Retail Park	Y	South Methven St.	Y 14
High St	Y	St John St	Z 12	South St	Z

XX 63 Tay Street

63 Tay St ✉ *PH2 8NN – ✆ (01738) 441 451* Town plan: Z**r**
– www.63taystreet.co.uk – Closed 1-5 January, 7-13 July, 26-31 December, Sunday, Monday and lunch Tuesday-Wednesday
Menu £ 20/50 – Carte lunch £ 25/46
Well-established riverside restaurant with bold modern artwork and an attentive team. Good value lunches and a choice of grill or gourmet dinners; the latter where the cooking really comes into its own. The wine list has over 250 bins.

XX Deans @ Let's Eat

77-79 Kinnoull St ✉ *PH1 5EZ – ✆ (01738) 643 377* Town plan: Y**c**
– www.letseatperth.co.uk – Closed second and third weeks January, Sunday and Monday
Menu £ 17 (weekday lunch) – Carte £ 21/44
Bottle-green restaurant close to the theatre and the concert hall. Comfortable lounge and a friendly, chatty team. All-encompassing menus, with seasonal deals and special events; passionate, classically based cooking has an ambitious edge.

XX **63@Parklands** – Parklands Hotel

2 St Leonard's Bank ✉ PH2 8EB – ☎ (01738) 622 451 Town plan: Z**n**
– www.63atparklands.com – Closed 26 December-5 January, Tuesday and Wednesday
Menu £ 40 – *(dinner only)*
Intimate conservatory restaurant with a relaxed lounge, set within a privately run hotel. The gourmet-style 5 course menu offers one or two choices per course and changes weekly; cooking is modern and features some interesting combinations.

X **Pig Halle**

38 South St ✉ PH2 8PG – ☎ (01738) 248 784 Town plan: Z**s**
– www.pighalle.co.uk – Closed 26 December, 1 January and Monday
Menu £ 15/18 – Carte £ 19/34
Lively bistro; the square, marble-floored room tightly packed with tables and dominated by a mirror stencilled with a Paris Metro map. Menus list all the Gallic favourites. The adjoining deli serves wood-fired pizzas and tasty baguettes.

at Kintillo Southeast: 4.5 mi off A912

X **Roost**

Forgandenny Rd ✉ PH2 9AZ – ☎ (01738) 812 111
– www.theroostrestaurant.co.uk – Closed 1-16 January, 25-26 December, Monday and dinner Sunday, Tuesday and Wednesday
Menu £ 18 (lunch) – Carte £ 26/36
Converted hen house in the heart of the village, with a rustic modern interior. Well-crafted, classical dishes display Mediterranean touches and feature local meats and veg from the garden; desserts are a highlight. Run by a friendly team.

PIEROWALL → See Orkney Islands (Isle of Westray)

– Michelin Road map 501-K6

PITLOCHRY

Perth and Kinross – Pop. 2 776 – See Regional map n°**28**-**C2**
Edinburgh 71 mi – Inverness 85 mi – Perth 27 mi
Michelin Road map 501-I13 – Michelin Green Guide SCOTLAND

Fonab Castle Ⓝ

Foss Rd ✉ PH16 5ND – ☎ (01796) 470 140 Town plan: A**z**
– www.fonabcastlehotel.com
26 rm – †£ 140/250 ††£ 160/275 – 4 suites
Rest *Brasserie* – see restaurant listing
Rest *Sandemans* – Menu £ 75 – *(closed Sunday-Tuesday) (dinner only) (set menu only)*
This 19C baronial-style castle offers superb views over the loch to the hills beyond. Bedrooms have a subtle traditional feel and smart bathrooms; the 'Woodland' rooms are more modern and have terraces or balconies. Intimate Sandemans offer a 9 course tasting menu, while the Brasserie serves modern classics.

Green Park

Clunie Bridge Rd ✉ PH16 5JY – ☎ (01796) 473 248 Town plan: A**a**
– www.thegreenpark.co.uk – Closed 17-27 December
51 rm – †£ 80/115 ††£ 160/230
Rest – Menu £ 20/28 – *(booking essential at dinner) (bar lunch)*
Long-standing, family-run hotel on the shore of Loch Faskally; many of its guests return year after year. Well-appointed lounges offer stunning loch and countryside views. Bedrooms vary in style; the largest and most modern are in the newer wing. A traditional dinner is included in the price of the room.

East Haugh House

✉ PH16 5TE Southeast : 1.75 mi off A 924 (Perth Rd) – ☎ (01796) 473 121
– www.easthaugh.co.uk – Closed 1 week Christmas
13 rm – †£ 89/169 ††£ 99/179
Rest *Two Sisters* – see restaurant listing
17C turreted house in two acres of gardens; originally part of the Atholl Estate. Traditionally appointed bedrooms – named after fishing flies – are split between the house and two lodges. They also own fishing rights to Dalmarnock Beat.

SCOTLAND

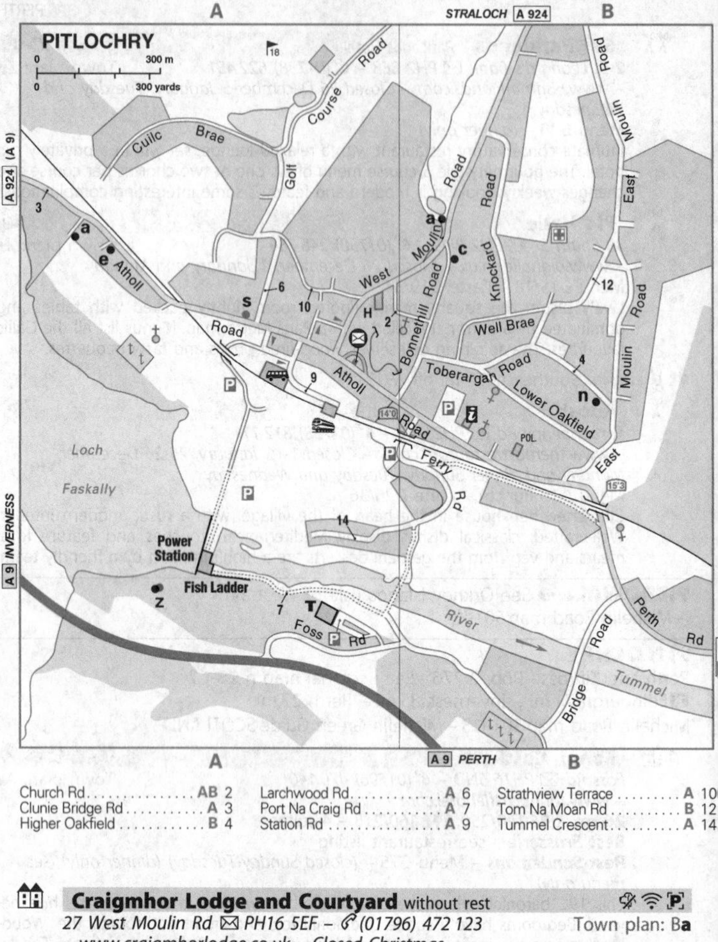

PITLOCHRY

Church Rd . . . . **AB** 2	Larchwood Rd . . . . **A** 6	Strathview Terrace . . . . **A** 10
Clunie Bridge Rd . . . . **A** 3	Port Na Craig Rd . . . . **A** 7	Tom Na Moan Rd . . . . **B** 12
Higher Oakfield . . . . **B** 4	Station Rd . . . . **A** 9	Tummel Crescent . . . . **A** 14

Craigmhor Lodge and Courtyard without rest

27 West Moulin Rd ✉ PH16 5EF – ✆ (01796) 472 123 Town plan: B**a**
– www.craigmhorlodge.co.uk – Closed Christmas
12 rm ☕ – 🚹£ 79/115 🚹🚹£ 79/150
Spacious, cosy house just out of town, with an airy breakfast room where local fruits, bacon and sausages are served. Well-kept modern bedrooms are set in the courtyard – some have balconies. Supper hampers can be delivered to your room.

Craigatin House and Courtyard without rest

165 Atholl Rd ✉ PH16 5QL – ✆ (01796) 472 478 Town plan: A**e**
– www.craigatinhouse.co.uk – Closed Christmas
14 rm ☕ – 🚹£ 75/122 🚹🚹£ 85/122
Built in 1822 as a doctor's house; now a stylish boutique hotel. The stunning open-plan lounge and breakfast room centres around a wood burning stove and overlooks the garden. Contemporary, minimalist bedrooms – some in the old stables.

Beinn Bhracaigh without rest

14 Higher Oakfield ✉ PH16 5HT – ✆ (01796) 470 355 Town plan: B**n**
– www.beinnbhracaigh.com – Closed 21-26 December
12 rm ☕ – 🚹£ 59/99 🚹🚹£ 65/119
Spacious stone house built in 1880 and run by passionate owners. Immaculately kept interior with good comforts; most rooms boast lovely views of the Tummel Valley. Breakfast includes French toast and pancakes with maple syrup and bacon.

Dunmurray Lodge without rest

72 Bonnethill Rd ✉ PH16 5ED – ✆ (01796) 473 624 Town plan: B**c**
– www.dunmurray.co.uk – Closed mid November-mid March

4 rm – †£ 55/65 ††£ 70/80

Imposing 19C former doctor's surgery, set close to the town and boasting views across to the mountains. Cosy, open-fired lounge and snug, well-equipped bedrooms with co-ordinating décor; the best outlooks are from the front. Bright, breakfast room – choose from a huge array of very locally sourced produce.

Two Sisters – East Haugh House Hotel

✉ PH16 5TE Southeast : 1.75 mi off A 924 (Perth Rd) – ✆ (01796) 473 121
– www.easthaugh.co.uk – Closed 1 week Christmas and lunch in winter

Carte £ 24/47

Charming fishermen's bar and a bright, laid-back restaurant, located in a lovely 17C stone house. The seasonal Scottish menu is served in both areas; cooking is clean and exact, with fish and game to the fore and tasty home-baked breads.

Brasserie (N) – Fonab Castle Hotel

Foss Rd ✉ PH16 5ND – ✆ (01796) 470 140 Town plan: A**z**
– www.fonabcastlehotel.com

Carte £ 25/50

Start with a cocktail on the upper floor 'Bar in the Air', then head down to the fashionable restaurant and terrace with their panoramic loch views. The concise menu offers modern classics and grills. Service is warm and friendly.

Auld Smiddy Inn

154 Atholl Rd ✉ PH16 5AG – ✆ (01796) 472 356 Town plan: A**s**
– www.auldsmiddyinn.co.uk – Closed last week January-first week February and 25-26 December

Carte £ 20/41

Old blacksmith's forge with a small, colourful garden and a large terrace and courtyard. It has a likeable simplicity, with polished slate floors and wood burning stoves. Summer menus feature fish and salads; winter menus, hearty classics.

at Killiecrankie Northwest: 4 mi by A924 -(A)- and B8019 on B8079 ✉ Pitlochry

Killiecrankie

✉ PH16 5LG – ✆ (01796) 473 220 – www.killiecrankiehotel.co.uk – Closed 3 January-15 March

11 rm – †£ 80/95 ††£ 160/190 **Rest** – Menu £ 42 – *(bar lunch)*

Whitewashed former vicarage built in 1840 and set in 4.5 acres of mature, rhododendron-filled grounds with a small kitchen garden to the rear. Charming open-fired lounge and a bar with a walnut-topped counter. Well-appointed bedrooms offer everything you might want. Choose from light suppers and more traditional dishes. Excellent levels of service.

PLOCKTON

Highland – See Regional map n°**29-B2**
Edinburgh 210 mi – Inverness 88 mi
Michelin Road map 501-D11 – Michelin Green Guide SCOTLAND

Plockton Hotel with rm

41 Harbour St ✉ IV52 8TN – ✆ (01599) 544 274 – www.plocktonhotel.co.uk

15 rm – †£ 45/95 ††£ 90/140 Carte £ 18/36

A one-time ships' chandlery with a distinctive black-tiled exterior and stunning views over Loch Carron to the mountains beyond. Cooking is honest and hearty with a strong Scottish influence, so expect haggis and whisky or herring in oatmeal – and don't miss the Plockton prawns. Simple, comfortable bedrooms.

POOLEWE

Highland – See Regional map n°**29**-B2
Edinburgh 230 mi – London 635 mi – Inverness 76 mi – Elgin 112 mi
Michelin Road map 501-D10

Pool House

✉ IV22 2LD – ✆ (01445) 781 272 – www.pool-house.co.uk – Closed mid March-mid November
4 rm – £ 190/225 £ 225/350
Rest – Menu £ 45 – *(closed Monday dinner) (dinner only) (booking essential) (residents only, set menu only)*
Unique, Victorian house by the water's edge; family-run, in a guesthouse rather than a hotel style. Bedrooms are all large suites – each individually themed with incredible attention to detail. Large billiards room, a country house lounge and a bar. The formal restaurant offers a classical, seasonal menu.

PORT APPIN

Argyll and Bute ✉ Appin – See Regional map n°**27**-B2
Edinburgh 136 mi – Ballachulish 20 mi – Oban 24 mi
Michelin Road map 501-D14

Airds

✉ PA38 4DF – ✆ (01631) 730 236 – www.airds-hotel.com – Closed 1-12 December and Monday-Tuesday November-February
11 rm – £ 175/405 £ 189/420
Rest – Menu £ 24/55 – *(booking essential)*
Characterful former ferryman's cottage fronted by colourful planters and offering lovely loch and mountain views. Two sumptuous, open-fired sitting rooms are furnished with antiques and bedrooms provide good comforts. The intimate dining room offers excellent water views and has a classical menu with a modern edge; a 7 course tasting menu is available at dinner.

PORT CHARLOTTE

→ See Islay (Isle of)
Argyll and Bute – Michelin Road map 501-A16

PORT ELLEN

→ See Islay (Isle of)
Argyll and Bute – Michelin Road map 501-B17

PORTMAHOMACK

Highland – See Regional map n°**30**-D2
Edinburgh 194 mi – Dornoch 21 mi – Tain 12 mi
Michelin Road map 501-I10

Oystercatcher with rm

Main St ✉ IV20 1YB – ✆ (01862) 871 560 – www.the-oystercatcher.co.uk – Closed November-February, Sunday dinner, Wednesday lunch, Monday and Tuesday
3 rm – £ 52 £ 82/108
Menu £ 37 (dinner) **s** – Carte lunch £ 20/42 **s** – *(booking essential)*
Set in a lovely spot in a tiny fishing village, with lobster pots hanging outside. One formal and one rustic room, with walls crammed with memorabilia. Menus offer fresh seafood in some unusual combinations; the boats that land the fish can be seen by the jetty. Modest bedrooms; nearly 20 choices at breakfast.

PORTPATRICK

Dumfries and Galloway – Pop. 534 – ✉ Stranraer – See Regional map n°**25**-A3
Edinburgh 141 mi – Ayr 60 mi – Dumfries 80 mi – Stranraer 9 mi
Michelin Road map 501-E19 and 502

Knockinaam Lodge

DG9 9AD Southeast : 5 mi by A 77 off B 7042 – (01776) 810 471 – www.knockinaamlodge.com
10 rm (dinner included) – £ 180/315 £ 290/440
Rest *Knockinaam Lodge* – see restaurant listing
Charming country house, superbly set in its own private cove, with the sea at the bottom of the garden. Classical guest areas include a wood-panelled bar and open-fired sitting rooms; a relaxed atmosphere pervades. Traditional, antique-furnished bedrooms; 'Churchill' boasts its original 100 year old bath.

Knockinaam Lodge – Knockinaam Lodge Hotel

DG9 9AD Southeast : 5 mi by A 77 off B 7042 – (01776) 810 471 – www.knockinaamlodge.com
Menu £ 30/65 – *(booking essential) (set menu only)*
Set in a charming Victorian house in its own private cove, a classically furnished, golden-hued dining room with crisp linen on the tables and lovely sea views. Carefully judged, daily 4 course menus; dishes showcase top quality seasonal ingredients in unfussy, well-balanced, classically based combinations.
→ Butter-poached lobster with a blood orange emulsion. Noisette of lamb, creamed spinach and rosemary scented jus. Hot rhubarb crumble soufflé.

PORTAVADIE

Argyll and Bute – See Regional map n°**27-B3**
Edinburgh 107 mi – Dunoon 28 mi – Oban 55 mi
Michelin Road map 501-E16

Portavadie

Portavadie Marina PA21 2DA – (01700) 811 075 – www.portavadiemarina.com
16 rm – £ 59/85 £ 85/99 **Rest *Marina*** – Carte £ 17/30
This peaceful lochside complex consists of a marina, self-catering apartments and a small hotel. Good-sized bedrooms have a modern Scandic style and pleasant views; some have balconies or kitchenettes. There's also an informal dining room with a leather-furnished lounge and a brasserie in another building.

PORTREE → See Skye (Isle of)

Highland – Michelin Road map 501-B11

RANNOCH STATION

Perth and Kinross – See Regional map n°**27-B2**
Edinburgh 108 mi – Kinloch Rannoch 17 mi – Pitlochry 36 mi
Michelin Road map 501-G13

Moor of Rannoch

PH17 2QA – (01882) 633 238 – www.moorofrannoch.co.uk – Closed November-mid February
5 rm – £ 80 £ 114 **Rest** – Menu £ 29 – *(dinner only)*
The ultimate in hiking getaways, this 19C hotel is perched high on the moor, in the middle of nowhere. The views are delightful, the whole place has a serene feel and wildlife is in abundance. Bedrooms are cosy and the open-fired guest areas have jigsaws, not TVs. Rustic cooking uses Scottish ingredients.

RATAGAN

Highland – See Regional map n°**29-B2**
Edinburgh 186 mi – London 563 mi – Belfast 214 mi – Dundee 168 mi

Grants at Craigellachie

IV40 8HP – (01599) 511 331 – www.housebytheloch.co.uk – Restricted opening October-Easter
4 rm – £ 70/123 £ 100/185
Rest – Carte £ 25/41 – *(closed Sunday and Monday)*
Set in an idyllic spot beside Loch Duich and named after the eponymous local gamekeeper. Compact, pine-furnished bedrooms in the main house; the larger annexe rooms are more comfortable but don't have water views. Small conservatory restaurant with a Mediterranean-influenced menu. Good malt whisky selection.

SCOTLAND

ST ANDREWS

Fife – Pop. 16 870 – See Regional map n°**28**-D2
Edinburgh 51 mi – Dundee 14 mi – Stirling 51 mi
Michelin Road map 501-L14 – Michelin Green Guide SCOTLAND

Old Course H. Golf Resort & Spa

Old Station Rd ✉ *KY16 9SP* – ✆ *(01334) 474 371*
– *www.oldcoursehotel.co.uk* Town plan: A**b**
144 rm – †£ 225/750 ††£ 255/780 – 15 suites
Rest ***Road Hole*** **Rest** ***Sands Grill*** – see restaurant listing
Vast resort hotel on a world-famous championship golf course, overlooking the bay. Spacious guest areas with stylish Scottish theme; superb spa, leisure and meeting facilities. Chic, comfortable bedrooms: some sumptuous, some contemporary.

Fairmont St Andrews

✉ *KY16 8PN Southeast : 3.5 mi on A 917* – ✆ *(01334) 837 000*
– *www.fairmont.com/standrews*
209 rm – †£ 189/279 ††£ 189/279
Rest ***La Cucina*** – Carte £ 19/40 – *(dinner only)*
Rest ***Clubhouse*** – Carte £ 23/43 – *(closed dinner 18 October-31 March)*
Modern, purpose-built property in 520 acres, with extensive conference and leisure facilities, including two golf courses, a superb spa and a wellness centre. Spacious guest areas have a subtle Scottish theme. Well-appointed bedrooms feature tartan and driftwood; 'Deluxe' are worth it for the view. La Cucina serves Italian fare; the Clubhouse offers steaks and seafood.

Hotel du Vin Ⓝ

40 The Scores ✉ *KY16 9AS* – ✆ *(0844) 748 92 69* Town plan: A**d**
– *www.hotelduvin.com*
36 rm – †£ 105/200 ††£ 140/450
Rest ***Bistro*** – Menu £ 17 (lunch and early dinner) – Carte £ 30/40
This stylish hotel sits overlooking West Sands beach, close to the famous 'Old Course'. Smart bedrooms come with monsoon showers and Egyptian cotton linen, and are named after wines and Scottish whisky houses. The elegant bistro serves French classics and steaks, and there's an impressive ballroom for events.

Rufflets Country House

Strathkinness Low Rd ✉ *KY16 9TX* – *West : 1.5 mi on B 939* – ✆ *(01334) 472 594*
– *www.rufflets.co.uk* – *Closed 4-20 January*
24 rm – †£ 120/200 ††£ 170/305 – 2 suites
Rest ***Terrace*** – Menu £ 40 – *(bar lunch Monday-Saturday)*
This modern country house hotel has been owned by the same family for over 60 years. Set in well-tended gardens, it features stylish, contemporary bedrooms. Modern interpretations of classic dishes are served in the restaurant at dinner, with a simpler, more traditional lunch menu offered in the bar and library.

Six Murray Park without rest

6 Murray Pk. ✉ *KY16 9AW* – ✆ *(01334) 473 319* Town plan: A**n**
– *www.sixmurraypark.co.uk* – *Closed 15 December-31 January*
9 rm – †£ 65/105 ††£ 110/170
Victorian terraced property with smart window boxes. Modern bedrooms boast bold feature walls and good facilities, including iPod docks. Hot daily specials are taken in the linen-laid, leather-furnished breakfast room.

Fairways without rest

8a Golf Pl. ✉ *KY16 9JA* – ✆ *(01334) 479 513* Town plan: A**z**
– *www.fairwaysofstandrews.co.uk*
3 rm – †£ 80/100 ††£ 100/150
The closest guesthouse in town to the famous 'Old Course'. Bedrooms are contemporary and offer good modern facilities; the top floor room boasts a balcony which overlooks the 18th hole.

ST ANDREWS

Abbey St . . . . . B 2
Abbey Walk . . . . . B 3
Alexandra Pl. . . . . . A 5
Alfred Pl. . . . . . A 6
Bridge St. . . . . . A 7
Butts Wynd . . . . . B 9
Castle St . . . . . B 10
Church St . . . . . AB 13
Ellice Pl. . . . . . A 15
Gibson Pl. . . . . . A 17
Gillespie Terrace . . . . . A 18
Greenside Pl. . . . . . B 20
Gregory Lane . . . . . B 21
Gregory Pl. . . . . . B 22
Greyfriars Garden . . . . . A 24
Hepburn Gardens . . . . . A 25
Link Crescent . . . . . A 27
Murray Park . . . . . A 28
Murray Pl. . . . . . A 29
Pilmour Links . . . . . A 31
Pilmour Pl. . . . . . A 32
Playfair Terrace . . . . . A 34
Queen's Gardens . . . . . A 35
Queen's Terrace . . . . . B 36
St Mary's Pl. . . . . . A 37
Union St . . . . . B 38

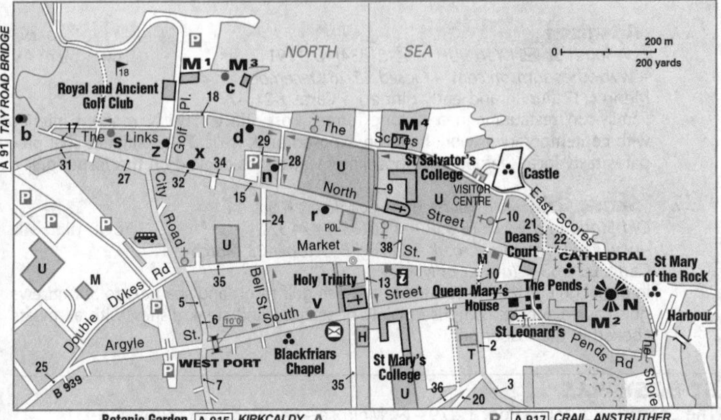

SCOTLAND

Five Pilmour Place without rest

5 Pilmour Pl. ✉ KY16 9HZ – ✆ (01334) 478 665 Town plan: A**x**
– www.5pilmourplace.com – Closed 18 December-31 January
7 rm ☕ – 👤£ 65/105 👥£ 90/170
Terraced Victorian house with neatly lawned rear garden. Flag-floored hall leads to bright lounge and communal breakfast room. Bedrooms range in size and come with boldly coloured feature walls and good facilities; one has a claw-foot bath.

Aslar House without rest

120 North St ✉ KY16 9AF – ✆ (01334) 473 460 Town plan: A**r**
– www.aslar.com – Closed January, February, December and first week July
6 rm ☕ – 👤£ 50/55 👥£ 90/110
Victorian terraced house in the town centre, run by a friendly, enthusiastic couple. Open-plan lounge and breakfast room. Neat, tidy bedrooms offer good facilities. The largest rooms are at the top; one has a lounge inside the turret.

Seafood

Bruce Embankment, The Scores ✉ KY16 9AB – ✆ (01334) 479 475 – www.theseafoodrestaurant.com – Closed 25-26 December and 1 January Town plan: A**c**
Carte £ 24/51 – *(booking essential)*
Unusual glass cube overhanging the beach, offering commanding bay views. Immaculate interior with black and white photos and an open kitchen. Dishes are seafood-based; try the daily special of 'fruits de mer' of local fish and shellfish.

Road Hole – Old Course Hotel Golf Resort & Spa

Old Station Rd ✉ KY16 9SP – ✆ (01334) 474 371 Town plan: A**b**
– www.oldcoursehotel.co.uk – Closed January, February, Monday, Tuesday and Wednesday lunch
Menu £ 55 (dinner) – Carte £ 27/59
Formally run restaurant within a smart golf resort and spa; dine with a full view of the 18th hole, the clubhouse and the beach. Modern versions of classic dishes use local produce; watch the chefs in the open kitchen while you eat.

XX **Rocca Bar & Grill**

Rusacks Hotel, The Links ✉ KY16 9JQ – ✆ (01334) 472 549 – www.roccagrill.com – Closed Sunday November-December Town plan: A**s**

Carte £ 31/59 – *(dinner only) (booking essential)*

Vibrant brasserie run by an experienced owner. Funky bar and vividly decorated dining room with views over the Old Course's 18th hole. Appealing menu of Scottish produce with 'classics', 'pasta' and 'steak' sections; interesting desserts.

XX **Adamson**

127 South St ✉ KY16 9UH – ✆ (01334) 479 191 – www.theadamson.com – Closed 25-26 December Town plan: A**v**

Menu £ 17 (lunch and early dinner) – Carte £ 21/47

Family-run restaurant in a historic former Post Office. Stylish, modern interior with contemporary artwork hung on exposed brick walls. The confident chef prepares tasty local seafood and appealing meat dishes cooked on the Josper grill.

XX **Sands Grill** – Old Course Hotel Golf Resort & Spa

Old Station Rd ✉ KY16 9SP – ✆ (01334) 474 371 – www.oldcoursehotel.co.uk – Closed 6 October-23 March Town plan: A**b**

Carte £ 24/63 – *(dinner only)*

Informal grill restaurant located in a stylish golf resort and spa next to St Andrews golf course. Menus comprise mainly of seafood and steak dishes, with all meats cooked in the Josper grill.

SCOTLAND

ST BOSWELLS

The Scottish Borders – Pop. 1 279 – ✉ Melrose – See Regional map n°**26**-D2

Edinburgh 39 mi – Glasgow 79 mi – Hawick 17 mi – Newcastle upon Tyne 66 mi

Michelin Road map 501-L17 and 502 – Michelin Green Guide SCOTLAND

Buccleuch Arms

The Green ✉ TD6 0EW – ✆ (01835) 822 243 – www.buccleucharms.com – Closed 24-25 December

19 rm – 🛉£ 75 🛉🛉£ 85/130 **Rest** – Carte £ 19/35

Long-standing, period coaching inn offering popular golfing, fishing and shooting breaks. Comfy, cosy bedrooms display co-ordinated headboards and soft furnishings. Semi-panelled, fire-lit bar and more formal dining room; choose from an extensive menu of classics, game and daily specials.

Whitehouse

✉ TD6 0ED Northeast : 3 mi on B 6404 – ✆ (01573) 460 343 – www.whitehousecountryhouse.com

3 rm – 🛉£ 85/90 🛉🛉£ 130/140 **Rest** – Menu £ 29/35

Former dower house built in 1872 by the Duke of Sutherland, with a cosy, country house feel. Traditionally furnished bedrooms boast excellent views across the estate. Many people come for the on-site shooting and fishing; wild salmon and local game – including venison – feature at dinner.

Clint Lodge

✉ TD6 0DZ North : 2.25 mi by B 6404 on B 6356 – ✆ (01835) 822 027 – www.clintlodge.co.uk

5 rm – 🛉£ 70/110 🛉🛉£ 120/130 **Rest** – Menu £ 35

Former shooting lodge with superb river and hill views. Characterful interior boasts antiques and fishing memorabilia. Traditionally decorated bedrooms; luxurious No. 4 and the south facing rooms are the best. Daily changing 5 course dinner served at a beautiful table.

ST FILLANS

Perth and Kinross – See Regional map n°**28**-C2

Edinburgh 65 mi – Lochearnhead 8 mi – Perth 29 mi

Michelin Road map 501-H14

Achray House
✉ PH6 2NF – ✆ (0560) 368 42 52 – www.achrayhouse.com – Closed January and December
8 rm – ♦£ 60/159 ♦♦£ 90/189
Rest – Menu £ 36 – *(closed Monday-Tuesday November-March) (dinner only)*
Superbly located Edwardian villa offering stunning views over Loch Earn. Bright breakfast room and an inviting lounge with open fires and a polished Douglas Fir floor. Modern bedrooms have bespoke pine furnishings and contemporary bathrooms. Simple restaurant offers global dishes crafted from local produce.

ST MARGARET'S HOPE → See Orkney Islands (Mainland)
– Michelin Road map 501-L7

ST MONANS
Fife – Pop. 1 265 – See Regional map n°**28**-D2
Edinburgh 47 mi – Dundee 26 mi – Perth 40 mi – Stirling 56 mi
Michelin Road map 501-L15

Craig Millar @ 16 West End
16 West End ✉ KY10 2BX – ✆ (01333) 730 327 – www.16westend.com – Closed Monday-Tuesday March-September and restricted opening October-March
Menu £ 18/60 – *(booking essential)*
Unassuming former pub with an attractive interior, run by a charming team. There's a characterful lounge and a smart restaurant with a small terrace and great harbour views. The experienced chef offers refined, flavoursome dishes.

SANQUHAR
Dumfries and Galloway – Pop. 2 021 – See Regional map n°**25**-B2
Edinburgh 57 mi – London 362 mi – Dundee 113 mi – Paisley 56 mi
Michelin Road map 501-I17

Blackaddie House with rm
Blackaddie Rd ✉ DG4 6JJ – ✆ (01659) 50 270 – www.blackaddiehotel.co.uk
8 rm – ♦£ 85/200 ♦♦£ 115/250
Menu £ 36/52 – *(booking essential at lunch)*
Former manse with 16C origins, set by the river. Lunch offers good value classics; dinner is more elaborate and features complex, original cooking. Ingredients are luxurious and dishes, well-presented. Bedrooms are named after game birds; ask for 'Grouse', which has a four-poster bed.

SCALPAY → See Lewis and Harris (Isle of)
Western Isles – Michelin Road map 501-A10

SCARISTA → See Lewis and Harris (Isle of)
Western Isles – Michelin Road map 501-Y10

SCOURIE
Highland ✉ Lairg – See Regional map n°**30**-C1
Edinburgh 245 mi – London 646 mi – Belfast 317 mi – Dundee 226 mi
Michelin Road map 501-E8 – Michelin Green Guide SCOTLAND

Eddrachilles
Badcall Bay ✉ IV27 4TH – South : 2.5 mi on A 894 – ✆ (01971) 502 080 – www.eddrachilles.com – Closed October-March
11 rm – ♦£ 80 ♦♦£ 110 **Rest** – Menu £ 28 – *(bar lunch)*
Remotely set, converted 18C manse, with views of the countryside, Badcall Bay and its islands. Snug bar and flag-floored breakfast room; cosy, well-kept bedrooms. Delightful outlook from the conservatory dining room, which offers a daily menu with a strong French slant. Meats are cured on-site.

SCRABSTER → See Thurso
Highland – Michelin Road map 501-J8

SCOTLAND

SHETLAND ISLANDS

Shetland Islands – Pop. 21 800 – See Regional map n°**31**-B2

Michelin Road map 501-P/Q3 – Michelin Green Guide SCOTLAND

MAINLAND

Shetland Islands – – See Regional map n°**31**-B2

Edinburgh 360 mi – London 543 mi – Belfast 224 mi – Dundee 86 mi

LERWICK

Michelin Green Guide SCOTLAND

 **Kveldsro House** 

Greenfield Pl ✉ ZE1 0AQ – ✆ (01595) 692 195 – www.shetlandhotels.com – Closed 25-26 December and 1-2 January

17 rm – †£ 115 ††£ 135

Rest – Carte £ 22/39 **s** – *(bar lunch Monday-Saturday)*

Spacious Georgian house hidden in the town centre; its name means 'evening peace'. Cosy sitting room with original ceiling mouldings, comfy bar with views of the islands and traditionally styled bedrooms. Menus offer mainly island produce; portions are hearty.

VEENSGARTH

 **Herrislea House** 

✉ ZE2 9SB – ✆ (01595) 840 208 – www.herrisleahouse.co.uk – Closed 10 December-10 January

9 rm – †£ 90/100 ††£ 130/150

Rest – Carte £ 21/38 – *(dinner only) (booking essential)*

Large, family-run hotel set just out of town. Unusual African hunting theme with mounted antlers, animal heads and skins on display. Cosy, individually designed bedrooms; some with valley views. Fresh cooking uses local produce and meats from the family crofts.

SCOTLAND

SHIELDAIG

Highland ✉ Strathcarron – See Regional map n°**29**-B2

Edinburgh 226 mi – London 627 mi – Perth 178 mi – Greenock 209 mi

Michelin Road map 501-D11 – Michelin Green Guide SCOTLAND

 **Tigh An Eilean** 

✉ IV54 8XN – ✆ (01520) 755 251 – www.tighaneilean.co.uk – Restricted opening in winter

11 rm – †£ 75/80 ††£ 150/160

Rest – Menu £ 45 (dinner) – Carte £ 17/32 – *(booking essential)*

Rest *Coastal Kitchen* – Carte £ 18/33 – *(closed 25 December)*

Personally run hotel in a charming lochside setting, with fine views over the Shieldaig Islands. Two small, cottagey lounges and well-kept, compact bedrooms – most with views. Linen-laid restaurant offers traditional, daily changing dishes; informal Coastal Kitchen serves a wide-ranging, all-day menu.

SKIRLING

The Scottish Borders ✉ Biggar – See Regional map n°**26**-C2

Edinburgh 29 mi – Glasgow 45 mi – Peebles 16 mi

Michelin Road map 501-J17 – Michelin Green Guide SCOTLAND

 **Skirling House** 

✉ ML12 6HD – ✆ (01899) 860 274 – www.skirlinghouse.com – Closed January, February and 1 week November-December

5 rm – †£ 80/105 ††£ 140/175 **Rest** – Menu £ 35

Delightful Arts and Crafts house set on the green in an attractive hamlet. Charming bedrooms come with good extras. The drawing room boasts a beautiful carved Florentine ceiling and an eclectic range of antiques and memorabilia. The 4 course daily menu is served in the conservatory or cosy dining room; accomplished cooking relies on home-grown produce.

SKYE (Isle of)

Highland – Pop. 10 008 – See Regional map n°**29**-B2

Michelin Road map 501-B11-/12 – Michelin Green Guide SCOTLAND

BERNISDALE

Spoons without rest

75 Aird Bernisdale ✉ IV51 9NU – ✆ (01470) 532 217
– www.thespoonsonskye.com – Closed mid-November-mid-March

3 rm – †£ 115/135 ††£ 140/160

Luxurious, purpose-built guesthouse in unspoilt hamlet, with an airy, wood-floored lounge and a breakfast room overlooking the loch. Bedrooms are individually decorated in a crisp, modern style and provide every conceivable extra. Superb 3 course breakfasts, with eggs from the charming owners' chickens.

BROADFORD

Tigh an Dochais

13 Harrapool ✉ IV49 9AQ – on A 87 – ✆ (01471) 820 022
– www.skyebedbreakfast.co.uk – Closed November-February

3 rm – †£ 70/75 ††£ 90 **Rest** – Menu £ 30

Striking house with award-winning architecture, overlooking Broadford Bay and the Applecross Peninsula. Comfy lounge has well-stocked bookshelves. Modern, minimalist bedrooms boast superb views and good facilities, including underfloor heating and plenty of extras. Communal, home-cooked meals by arrangement.

COLBOST

Hillstone Lodge (N)

✉ IV55 8ZT – ✆ (01470) 511 434 – www.hillstonelodge.com – Closed Christmas-New Year

3 rm – †£ 80/103 ††£ 115/138 **Rest** – Menu £ 29

With its superb outlook over Loch Dunvegan and plenty of stone, slate and wood on display, this striking modern house is at one with nature. Vibrant Scottish art covers the walls and stylish bedrooms have a minimalist feel. Local ingredients feature at breakfast and dinner (in winter only), often showcases island seafood. The owner is also qualified in 'sound massage'.

Three Chimneys & The House Over-By with rm — rest,

✉ IV55 8ZT – ✆ (01470) 511 258 – www.threechimneys.co.uk
– Closed December and January

6 rm – †£ 205/345 ††£ 205/345

Menu £ 37/90 – *(closed Sunday lunch in winter) (dinner only and lunch mid-March-October) (booking essential)*

Immaculately kept crofter's cottage in a stunning lochside setting. Three characterful, low-beamed dining rooms display contemporary artwork. Original, modern Scottish menus showcase superb local ingredients and seafood is a highlight; choose from a 5 or 8 course menu. Spacious, split-level bedrooms are stylishly understated; the residents' lounge has a great outlook.

➜ Bracadale brown crab parfait, apple and Mull cheddar. Blackface haggis pasty with asparagus and ramsons. Hot marmalade soufflé, Drambuie syrup and mealie ice cream.

CULNAKNOCK

Glenview with rm

✉ IV51 9JH – ✆ (01470) 562 248 – www.glenviewskye.co.uk – Closed January, December, Sunday and Monday

5 rm – †£ 60/75 ††£ 90/120 Menu £ 36 – *(dinner only) (booking essential)*

Simple little restaurant – formerly the village shop – with a cheerful host and an appealing vintage style. The daily dinner menu offers two choices per course, featuring local produce in unfussy, flavoursome dishes. Bedrooms have retro-style touches; breakfast is a highlight – try the blueberry pancakes.

SCOTLAND

DUISDALEMORE

Duisdale House

Sleat ✉ IV43 8QW – on A 851 – ✆ (01471) 833 202 – www.duisdale.com
19 rm ☕ – 👤£ 75/250 👥£ 79/310 – 1 suite
Rest – Menu £ 15/45 – Carte £ 18/45
Stylish, up-to-date hotel with lawned gardens, a hot tub and coastal views. Comfortable bedrooms boast bold décor, excellent bathrooms and a pleasing blend of contemporary and antique furniture. Modern cooking makes good use of local produce. Smart uniformed staff.

DUNVEGAN

Roskhill House without rest

Roskhill ✉ IV55 8ZD – Southeast : 2.5 mi by A 863 – ✆ (01470) 521 317 – www.roskhillhouse.co.uk – Closed 15 December-2 February
5 rm ☕ – 👤£ 54/63 👥£ 76/99
Welcoming 19C croft house with a small garden, set in peaceful location close to the water. Formerly the old post office, the lounge boasts exposed stone, wooden beams and an open fire. Fresh, bright bedrooms have a contemporary edge and smart, modern bathrooms.

EDINBANE

Greshornish House

✉ IV51 9PN North : 3.75 mi by A 850 in direction of Dunvegan – ✆ (01470) 582 266 – www.greshornishhouse.com – Restricted opening in winter
6 rm ☕ – 👤£ 90/135 👥£ 140/200
Rest – Menu £ 28/47 – *(closed Monday and Tuesday in winter) (booking essential)*
Early 18C lochside house. Relax in the comfy panelled drawing room or in the old billiard room with its snooker table, piano, books and games. Country house style bedrooms – some with four-posters or loch views. Breakfast is in the conservatory; seasonal, island dinners are taken in the candlelit dining room.

SCOTLAND

FLODIGARRY

Flodigarry Country House

✉ IV51 9HZ – ✆ (01470) 552 203 – www.flodigarry.co.uk – Restricted opening in winter
18 rm ☕ – 👤£ 130/250 👥£ 170/250
Rest – Carte £ 28/55 **s** – *(booking essential) (bar lunch Monday-Saturday)*
A Victorian house and cottage annexe, which was once Jacobite heroine Flora MacDonald's home. The comfortable, antique-filled interior has excellent island views and lawned garden leads down to the coast; bedrooms are cosy and homely. The characterful bar and dining room offer a modern Scottish menu.

PORTREE

Cuillin Hills

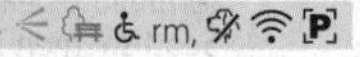

✉ IV51 9QU Northeast : 0.75 mi by A 855 – ✆ (01478) 612 003 – www.cuillinhills-hotel-skye.co.uk
26 rm ☕ – 👤£ 130/200 👥£ 200/320
Rest *View* – Carte £ 28/49
Yellow-washed 19C hunting lodge, in 15 acres of gardens and grounds which overlook the bay and hills. Comfortable lounge and stylish open-plan bar. Bedrooms offer good facilities; the best rooms are to the front. The relaxed brasserie and formal dining room offer a good outlook and modern menus.

Bosville

Bosville Terr ✉ IV51 9DG – ✆ (01478) 612 846 – www.bosvillehotel.co.uk
20 rm ☕ – 👤£ 79/128 👥£ 80/175
Rest *Bistro* – Carte £ 21/35
Boldly painted, purpose-built hotel in the town centre. Wood-furnished bar – formerly the village bank – and a small, traditionally decorated, first floor lounge. Modern bedrooms feature co-ordinated fabrics and have good facilities. Accessible menu served in the popular bistro.

Sleat

Kinloch Lodge

✉ *IV43 8QY* – ✆ *(01471) 833 214* – *www.kinloch-lodge.co.uk*
19 rm (dinner included) – £ 99/170 £ 198/380 – 3 suites
Rest *Kinloch Lodge* ✿ – see restaurant listing
With a loch in front and heather-strewn moorland behind, this 17C hunting lodge affords fantastic panoramic views. Inside, it has a traditional country house feel; comfy antique-filled lounges are hung with photos of the Macdonald clan and each of the contemporary bedrooms is themed around a different tartan.

Kinloch Lodge – Kinloch Lodge Hotel

✉ *IV43 8QY* – ✆ *(01471) 833 214* – *www.kinloch-lodge.co.uk*
Menu £ 33/80 **s** – *(booking essential)*
Traditional restaurant in a 17C hunting lodge, offering stunning views across the loch. Dine beneath portraits of the Macdonald clan or watch the kitchen action from the chef's table. Cooking is classically based but has clever modern touches. Good service and a well-written wine list complete the picture.
→ Warm crab mousse, seared scallop, Isle of Skye langoustine and seafood bisque. Black Isle lamb, with nutty herb crust, Jerusalem artichoke and beetroot dauphinoise. Warm dark chocolate melt, vanilla espuma and crème de menthe.

Struan

Ullinish Country Lodge

✉ *IV56 8FD West : 1.5 mi by A 863* – ✆ *(01470) 572 214*
– *www.theisleofskye.co.uk* – *Closed January, Christmas and New Year*
6 rm – £ 85/110 £ 110/160
Rest *Ullinish Country Lodge* – see restaurant listing
Personally run, 18C former hunting lodge in a windswept location, affording lovely loch and mountain views. Comfortable lounge filled with ornaments and books about the area. Warmly decorated bedrooms boast good facilities and extras.

Ullinish Country Lodge – Ullinish Country Lodge Hotel

✉ *IV56 8FD West : 1.5 mi by A 863* – ✆ *(01470) 572 214*
– *www.theisleofskye.co.uk* – *Closed January, Christmas and New Year*
Menu £ 50 – *(dinner only) (booking essential)*
Formal hotel dining room with traditional tartan fabrics, a masculine style and a house party atmosphere. The daily changing, 2-choice set menu uses quality local ingredients; dishes are modern and inventive, and combinations are ambitious.

Teangue

Toravaig House

Knock Bay ✉ *IV44 8RE* – *on A 851* – ✆ *(01471) 820 200* – *www.skyehotel.co.uk*
9 rm – £ 75/190 £ 79/260
Rest – Menu £ 48 (dinner) – Carte lunch £ 22/44 – *(booking essential)*
Stylish whitewashed house with neat gardens, set on the road to the Mallaig ferry. Cosy, open-fired lounge with baby grand piano and heavy fabrics. Individually designed bedrooms boast quality materials and furnishings. Good service with extras. Two-roomed restaurant offers concise, classical menu of island produce.

Waternish

Loch Bay Seafood

1 MacLeod Terr, Stein ✉ *IV55 8GA* – ✆ *(01470) 592 235*
– *www.lochbay-seafood-restaurant.co.uk* – *Closed November-Easter and Sunday-Tuesday*
Menu £ 33 – *(dinner only) (booking essential)*
Whitewashed cottage in a tiny hamlet overlooking the loch. Small room with low-backed chairs and benches. Concise menu of simply prepared seafood and blackboard specials. Friendly service.

SCOTLAND

Stein Inn with rm 
MacLeod Terr, Stein ✉ IV55 8GA – ✆ (01470) 592 362 – www.stein-inn.co.uk – Closed 1 January and 25 December
5 rm – †£ 45 ††£ 77/115 Carte £ 17/33
Family-run inn – the oldest on Skye; sit on the grassy terrace or in the cosy bar. Fresh, locally caught seafood dominates the menu; maybe sweet shrimps, rollmop herrings or half a lobster. Simple, comfy bedrooms have superb views to the Outer Hebrides instead of a TV, and the bar offers over 90 whiskies.

SLEAT → See Skye (Isle of)
Highland

SORN
East Ayrshire – See Regional map n°**25-B2**
Edinburgh 67 mi – Ayr 15 mi – Glasgow 35 mi
Michelin Road map 501-H17

Sorn Inn with rm
35 Main St ✉ KA5 6HU – ✆ (01290) 551 305 – www.sorninn.com – Closed 6-16 January and Monday
4 rm – †£ 50/60 ††£ 80/95 Carte £ 22/56
It's very much a family affair at this unassuming inn – the father checks you in and the son does the cooking. Sit in either the smart bar or larger dining room. The extensive menu includes a variety of British dishes plus some more elaborate international offerings. The neat, simple bedrooms are good value.

SPEAN BRIDGE
Highland – See Regional map n°**30-C3**
Edinburgh 143 mi – Fort William 10 mi – Glasgow 94 mi – Inverness 58 mi
Michelin Road map 501-F13

Corriegour Lodge 
Loch Lochy ✉ PH34 4EA – North : 8.75 mi on A 82 – ✆ (01397) 712 685 – www.corriegour-lodge-hotel.com – Closed November-22 March
11 rm – †£ 159/210 ††£ 159/210 **Rest** – Menu £ 50 – *(dinner only)*
19C hunting lodge with pretty gardens, set in a great lochside location – they even have their own private beach. Inside there's a homely curio-filled lounge and comfy bedrooms featuring top quality beds, linens and fabrics. Every dining table has a loch view; the classical 4 course menu features local meats.

Old Pines rm,
✉ PH34 4EG Northwest : 1.5 mi by A 82 on B 8004 – ✆ (01397) 712 324 – www.oldpines.co.uk – Closed November-January
7 rm – †£ 60/80 ††£ 90/120
Rest – Carte £ 25/37 – *(dinner only and light lunch in summer) (bookings essential for non-residents)*
A friendly couple run this log cabin style property, which blends well with the Highland scenery. Guest areas are comfy and homely. Feature walls add a splash of colour to the pine-furnished bedrooms and the slate-tiled bathrooms come with underfloor heating. Dining has a classic dinner party feel.

Distant Hills without rest 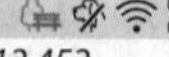
Roy Bridge Rd ✉ PH34 4EU – East : 0.5 mi on A86 – ✆ (01397) 712 452 – www.distanthillsspeanbridge.co.uk – Closed 10 November-26 February
7 rm – †£ 62/80 ††£ 80/95
Welcoming guesthouse with friendly owners, who suggest walks and provide packed lunches. The French windows in the large lounge lead to stream-side seating. Bedrooms are modern and the breakfasts are wide-ranging.

SCOTLAND

Corriechoille Lodge
rm,

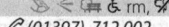

⊠ *PH34 4EY East : 2.75 mi on Corriechoille rd – ✆ (01397) 712 002 – www.corriechoille.com – Closed November-March*

4 rm – £ 47/52 £ 74/84 **Rest** – Menu £ 26

Charming, part-18C house in a remote location, boasting large gardens and views over the Grey Corries and Aonach Mor. Comfy lounge and spacious, pine-furnished bedrooms; two wooden bothy lodges provide more intimacy. Homely cooking; the fish is smoked on site.

Russell's at Smiddy House with rm
rest,

Roybridge Rd ⊠ PH34 4EU – ✆ (01397) 712 335 – www.smiddyhouse.com – Closed Monday to non residents

4 rm – £ 75/115 £ 80/115

Carte £ 33/49 – *(restricted opening in winter) (dinner only and Sunday lunch) (booking essential)*

Friendly, passionately run restaurant in an appealing Highland village, with a smart ornament-filled lounge and two intimate dining rooms. Tasty dishes use locally sourced ingredients and old Scottish recipes take on a modern style. Cosy, well-equipped bedrooms come with comfy beds and fine linens.

SPITTAL
Highland – See Regional map n°**30**-D1

Edinburgh 253 mi – London 654 mi – Belfast 325 mi – Dundee 234 mi

Michelin Road map 501-J8

Auld Post Office without rest

⊠ *KW1 5XR on A 9 – ✆ (01847) 841 391 – www.auldpostoffice.com*

3 rm – £ 55/60 £ 75/85

Greatly extended former post office, set in a remote spot on a road that cuts across the moors. Homely lounge with a wood-burning stove. Cosy, well-furnished bedrooms open onto a colourful garden and have compact, modern shower rooms.

SCOTLAND

SPITTAL OF GLENSHEE
Perth and Kinross ⊠ Blairgowrie – See Regional map n°**28**-C2

Edinburgh 79 mi – London 489 mi – Glasgow 98 mi – Livingston 81 mi

Michelin Road map 501-J13 – Michelin Green Guide SCOTLAND

Dalmunzie Castle

⊠ *PH10 7QG – ✆ (01250) 885 224 – www.dalmunzie.com – Closed November-23 December*

17 rm – £ 125/185 £ 135/215

Rest – Menu £ 25 (lunch)/55 – Carte £ 52/76

Edwardian hunting lodge on a stunning 6,500 acre estate, encircled by mountains and run by a keen team; the open hall has a large window looking towards the snow-capped peaks. Bedrooms and lounges have a traditional feel. The cosy bar stocks over 100 whiskies and the dining room offers pretty valley views.

STEVENSTON
North Ayrshire – Pop. 9 330 – See Regional map n°**25**-A2

Edinburgh 82 mi – Ayr 19 mi – Glasgow 36 mi

Michelin Road map 501-F17

Ardeer Farm Steading without rest

Ardeer Mains Farm ⊠ KA20 3DD – East : 0.75 mi by A 738 and B 752 taking fist left onto Kilwinning rd – ✆ (01294) 465 438 – www.ardeersteading.co.uk

6 rm – £ 38 £ 50

Converted, family-owned farm buildings on the edge of a 100 acre working farm. Large, leather-furnished lounge and breakfast room boast pleasant country views. Spacious, comfy, up-to-date bedrooms. Complimentary pick-up from the station.

STIRLING

Stirling – Pop. 36 142 – See Regional map n°**28**-**C2**

▶Edinburgh 37 mi – Dunfermline 23 mi – Falkirk 14 mi – Glasgow 28 mi

Michelin Road map 501-I15 – Michelin Green Guide SCOTLAND

Park Lodge

32 Park Terr ✉ FK8 2JS – ✆ (01786) 474 862 Town plan: B**a**
– www.parklodge.net – Closed Christmas and New Year
9 rm ☕ – 🚹£ 75/90 🚹🚹£ 95/110
Rest – Menu £ 16 (weekday lunch)/26 **s** – *(closed Sunday)*

Lovely part-Georgian, part-Victorian, creeper-clad house, with a mature garden and fruit trees to the rear. Warm, intimate bar and sitting room. Traditional, individually designed bedrooms; the four-poster room is particularly popular. Formal dining room has a beautiful ornate ceiling and traditional menu.

Number 10 without rest

10 Gladstone Pl ✉ FK8 2NN – ✆ (01786) 472 681 Town plan: B**v**
– www.cameron-10.co.uk
3 rm ☕ – 🚹£ 40/70 🚹🚹£ 50/75

Light-stone Victorian townhouse in a quiet street, with an attractive garden and a surprisingly spacious interior. Individually furnished bedrooms have good facilities. Linen-laid breakfast room features ornate coving; choose the porridge.

SCOTLAND

STIRLING

Street	Grid	No.
Barnton St	B	2
Borestone Crescent	A	3
Causewayhead Rd	A, B	4
Cornton Rd	A	7
Corn Exchange Rd	B	5
Coxithill Rd	A	8
Drummond Pl.	B	9
Dumbarton Rd	B	10
Goosecroft Rd	B	12
King St	B	13
Leisure Centre	B	
Murray Pl.	B	15
Newhouse	A	16
Park Pl.	A	18
Port St.	B	
Queen St	B	20
Randolph Terrace	A	22
St John St	B	23
St Mary's Wynd	B	24
Seaforth Pl.	B	25
Shirra's Brae Rd	A	26
Spittal St	B	27
Thistle Centre	B	
Union St	B	28
Upper Craigs	B	29
Weaver Row	A	31

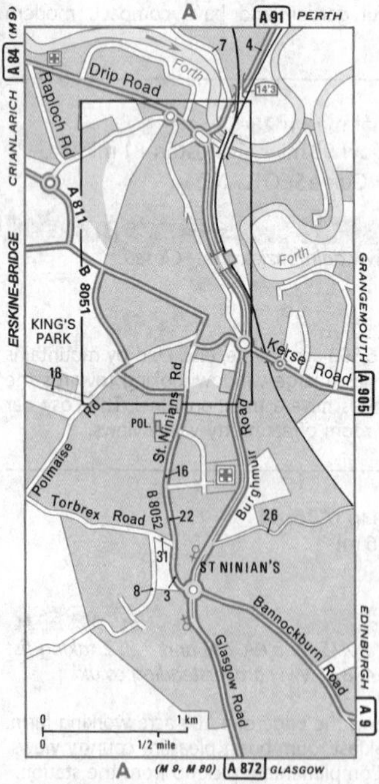

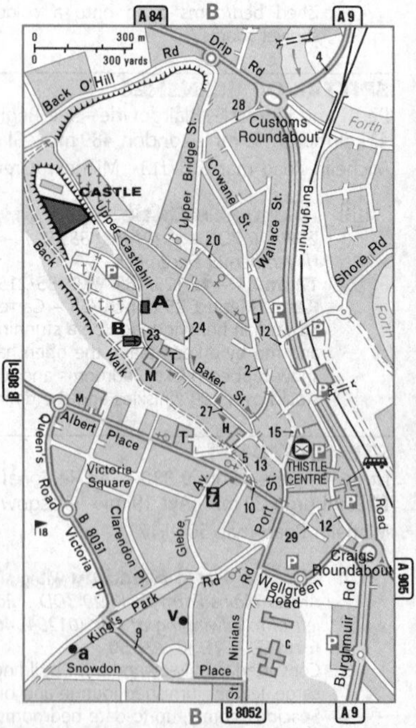

West Plean House without rest
✉ FK7 8HA South : 3.5 mi on A 872 (Denny rd) – ☎ (01786) 812 208
– *www.westpleanhouse.com – Closed 15 December-15 January*
4 rm ☕ – †£ 50/60 ††£ 80/90
Attractive house with a long history – its latest extensions added in 1803 – next to a working farm. Beautiful tiled hall, classic country house lounge and communal breakfast room. Warm, traditionally styled bedrooms. Pleasant walled garden.

STONEHAVEN

Aberdeenshire – Pop. 11 431 – See Regional map n°**28**-D2
▶Edinburgh 111 mi – Glasgow 130 mi – Dundee 50 mi – Aberdeen 15 mi
Michelin Road map 501-N13 – Michelin Green Guide SCOTLAND

Beachgate House without rest
Beachgate Ln ✉ AB39 2BD – ☎ (01569) 763 155 – www.beachgate.co.uk
5 rm ☕ – †£ 90/110 ††£ 95/115
Well-run guesthouse looking out over Stonehaven Bay. Super views from well-appointed, first floor lounge. Bedrooms are furnished in a luxurious, modern style. Breakfast includes fresh poached fish or a full Scottish with hen or duck eggs.

XX **Tolbooth**
Old Pier, Harbour ✉ AB39 2JU – ☎ (01569) 762 287
– www.tolbooth-restaurant.co.uk – Closed 3 weeks January, 1 week October, Sunday dinner, Monday and Tuesday
Menu £ 20 (weekday lunch) – Carte £ 29/47
Stonehaven's oldest building, located on the harbourside: formerly a store, sheriff's courthouse and prison. Classic dishes have modern touches; the emphasis being on local seafood, with langoustines and crab the highlights. Choose table 3.

SCOTLAND

STORNOWAY

→ See Lewis and Harris (Isle of)
Western Isles – Michelin Road map 501-A9

STRACHUR

Argyll and Bute – Pop. 628 – See Regional map n°**27**-B2
▶Edinburgh 112 mi – Glasgow 66 mi – Inverness 162 mi – Perth 101 mi
Michelin Road map 501-E15

Creggans Inn
✉ PA27 8BX – ☎ (01369) 860 279 – www.creggans-inn.co.uk – Closed 2 weeks January and Christmas
14 rm ☕ – †£ 75/95 ††£ 100/140 – 1 suite
Rest – Menu £ 37 – Carte £ 22/41 – *(dinner only)*
Rest *MacPhunn's* – Carte £ 21/40
Well-established inn on the shores of Loch Fyne; the conservatory is a popular spot for a taking in the enviable view. Spacious, well-kept bedrooms with traditional décor in keeping with the building's age. The vast restaurant serves classical dishes, while the pubby bar offers an accessible menu of local produce, along with drinks and a game of pool.

X **Inver Cottage**
Strathlaclan ✉ PA27 8BU – Southwest : 6.5 mi by A 886 on B 8000 – ☎ (01369) 860 537 – www.invercottage.com – Closed late December-March, Monday and Tuesday except July-August
Carte £ 24/42
Lochside former crofter's cottage boasting water and mountain views. Small bar and casual tables for drinks or afternoon tea; simple, airy restaurant. Constantly evolving menu uses only local produce.

STRATHPEFFER

Highland – Pop. 1 109 – See Regional map n°**30**-C2
Edinburgh 173 mi – London 573 mi – Belfast 245 mi – Dundee 154 mi
Michelin Road map 501-G11

Craigvar without rest
The Square ✉ IV14 9DL – ✆ (01997) 421 622 – www.craigvar.com – Closed 23 December-12 January
3 rm – †£ 60 ††£ 90/95
Proudly run by a charming owner, an attractive Georgian house overlooking the main square of a delightful spa village. Traditional guest areas include a comfy lounge and an antique-furnished breakfast room. Spacious bedrooms have a modern edge and plenty of personal touches. Good breakfast selection.

STRATHYRE

Stirling ✉ Callander – See Regional map n°**27**-B2
Edinburgh 62 mi – Glasgow 53 mi – Perth 42 mi
Michelin Road map 501-H15 – Michelin Green Guide SCOTLAND

Creagan House with rm
✉ FK18 8ND On A 84 – ✆ (01877) 384 638 – www.creaganhouse.co.uk – April-October
5 rm – †£ 90/100 ††£ 130/150
Menu £ 35 – *(closed Wednesday and Thursday) (dinner only)*
Long-standing, personally run restaurant in a 17C farmhouse. Snug sitting rooms lead to a baronial-style dining room with a vast fireplace and handmade local china. Traditional cooking uses Perthshire's natural larder; the 'Smokie in a Pokie' is a speciality. Watch red squirrels from the comfy, cosy bedrooms.

STROMNESS → See Orkney Islands (Mainland)

– Michelin Road map 501-K7

STRONTIAN

Highland – See Regional map n°**29**-B3
Edinburgh 139 mi – Fort William 23 mi – Oban 66 mi
Michelin Road map 501-D13

Kilcamb Lodge
On A 861 ✉ PH36 4HY – ✆ (01967) 402 257 – www.kilcamblodge.co.uk – Closed January and restricted opening in winter
11 rm (dinner included) – †£ 80/180 ††£ 95/190
Rest – Carte £ 26/46 – *(dinner only)*
Rest *Driftwood Brasserie* – Carte £ 28/46
Charming lochside hunting lodge with 19 acres of gardens and woodland running down to a private shore. The traditional interior has a modern edge but still boasts rich fabrics and log fires. Dine from classic menus in the laid-back brasserie; seafood and game feature highly in the more formal restaurant.

Rockpool House (N)
Acharacle ✉ PH36 4HX – West : 7.5 mi on A 861 – ✆ (01967) 431 335 – www.rockpoolhouse.co.uk – Closed 10 days Christmas
3 rm – †£ 75/90 ††£ 100 **Rest** – Menu £ 24/27
Be at one with nature in this comfy guesthouse on the Ardnamurchan Peninsula. Take in the views of the loch and the mountains from both the upstairs lounge and the modern, well-equipped bedrooms. Local meats and fish feature on the menu and you can buy local and homemade gifts from their craft shop.

STRUAN → See Skye (Isle of)

Highland

SWINTON

The Scottish Borders – Pop. 472 – ✉ Duns – See Regional map n°**26**-D2
Edinburgh 49 mi – London 351 mi – Newcastle upon Tyne 74 mi – Darlington 110 mi
Michelin Road map 501-N16 and 502

Wheatsheaf with rm
Main St ✉ TD11 3JJ – ✆ (01890) 860 257 – www.wheatsheaf-swinton.co.uk – Closed 24 and 26 December
14 rm ☕ – 🚹£ 89/109 🚹🚹£ 119/159
Carte £ 23/42 – *(closed Monday-Friday lunch January-March) (booking advisable)*
Substantial stone inn overlooking the village green. The extensive dinner menu offers ambitious dishes; specials feature seafood from Eyemouth, and meat comes from the surrounding border farms and is smoked on-site. Lunch is served only at weekends. Bedrooms are spacious, cosy and well-equipped.

TAIN
Highland – Pop. 3 655 – See Regional map n°**30-D2**
Edinburgh 191 mi – Inverness 35 mi – Wick 91 mi
Michelin Road map 501-H10

Golf View House without rest
13 Knockbreck Rd ✉ IV19 1BN – ✆ (01862) 892 856 – www.tainbedandbreakfast.co.uk
5 rm ☕ – 🚹£ 45/65 🚹🚹£ 70/85
Well-cared-for Victorian manse close to the golf course, boasting a neat lawned garden and views over the mountains and out to sea. The bright, fresh interior features modern, uncluttered bedrooms and a homely lounge and breakfast room.

at Nigg Southeast: 7 mi by A9, B9175 and Pitcalnie Rd

Wemyss House
Bayfield ✉ IV19 1QW – South : 1 mi past church – ✆ (01862) 851 212 – www.wemysshouse.com
3 rm ☕ – 🚹£ 110/115 🚹🚹£ 110/120 **Rest** – Menu £ 38
Remote, rurally set guesthouse with charming owners, well-maintained gardens and pleasant views. Cosy sitting room with grand piano. Spacious, immaculately kept bedrooms. Freshly prepared dishes use local ingredients. Excellent quality breakfasts.

at Cadboll Southeast: 8.5 mi by A9 and B9165 (Portmahomack rd) off Hilton rd ✉ Tain

Glenmorangie House
Fearn ✉ IV20 1XP – ✆ (01862) 871 671 – www.theglenmorangiehouse.com – Closed January
9 rm (dinner included) ☕ – 🚹£ 235 🚹🚹£ 370/400
Rest – Menu £ 60 – *(dinner only) (bookings essential for non-residents) (set menu only)*
Charming 17C house owned by the famous distillery. Antiques, hand-crafted local furnishings and open peat fires feature; there's even a small whisky tasting room. Luxuriously appointed bedrooms show good attention to detail; those in the courtyard cottages are suites. Communal dining from a classical Scottish menu.

TALMINE
Highland ✉ Lairg – See Regional map n°**30-C1**
Edinburgh 245 mi – London 651 mi – Inverness 92 mi – Elgin 128 mi
Michelin Road map 501-G8

Cloisters without rest
Church Holme ✉ IV27 4YP – ✆ (01847) 601 286 – www.cloistertal.demon.co.uk – Closed Christmas-New Year
3 rm ☕ – 🚹£ 38 🚹🚹£ 65
Converted church boasting great views over Tongue Bay and the Rabbit Islands. Homely interior packed with memorabilia. Leather-furnished lounge, snug breakfast area and simple, well-kept bedrooms.

TARBERT → See Kintyre (Peninsula)
Argyll and Bute – Michelin Road map 501-D16

TARBERT → See Lewis and Harris (Isle of)

Western Isles – Michelin Road map 501-Z10

TARBET

Argyll and Bute ✉ Arrochar – See Regional map n°**27**-B2

Edinburgh 88 mi – Glasgow 42 mi – Inverness 138 mi – Perth 78 mi

Michelin Road map 501-F15

Lomond View Country House without rest

✉ *G83 7DG On A 82 – ✆ (01301) 702 477 – www.lomondview.co.uk*

3 rm – †£ 50/70 ††£ 80/90

Purpose-built guesthouse which lives up to its name: there are stunning loch views. Spacious sitting room. Light and airy breakfast room. Sizeable, modern bedrooms.

TAYNUILT

Argyll and Bute – See Regional map n°**27**-B2

Edinburgh 114 mi – Oban 12 mi – Fort William 46 mi

Michelin Road map 501-E14

Taynuilt with rm

✉ *PA35 1JN – ✆ (01866) 822 437 – www.taynuilthotel.co.uk – Restricted opening in January*

10 rm – †£ 60/75 ††£ 75/195 Carte £ 22/46

Coleridge and Wordsworth enjoyed this inn's hospitality back in 1803; these days it is run with pride and passion by the McNulty family and cooking is the main focus. Menus offer tasty pub classics with a twist and they have their own bespoke lager on tap. Well-kept bedrooms are named after Scottish lochs.

SCOTLAND

TAYVALLICH

Argyll and Bute ✉ Lochgilphead – See Regional map n°**27**-B2

Edinburgh 148 mi – Glasgow 103 mi – Inverness 157 mi

Michelin Road map 501-D15

Tayvallich Inn

✉ *PA31 8PL – ✆ (01546) 870 282 – www.tayvallichinn.com – Closed Monday November-March*

Carte £ 18/38

Dine in the bar, the more formal dining room or on the decked terrace, with views over the bay. Menu focuses on locally caught fish and shellfish, but also lists classic pub dishes like steak and chips.

TEANGUE → See Skye (Isle of)

Highland – Michelin Road map 501-C12

THORNHILL

Dumfries and Galloway – Pop. 1 674 – See Regional map n°**25**-B2

Edinburgh 64 mi – Ayr 44 mi – Dumfries 15 mi – Glasgow 63 mi

Michelin Road map 501-I18 and 502 – Michelin Green Guide SCOTLAND

Buccleuch & Queensberry Arms

112 Drumlanrig St ✉ DG3 5LU – ✆ (01848) 323 101 – www.bqahotel.com

12 rm – †£ 70/130 ††£ 80/150 **Rest** – Carte £ 22/41

Smartly refurbished coaching inn, designed by the owner, who also runs an interiors shop. Boldly coloured bedrooms are named after various estates owned by the Duke of Buccleuch and come with eclectic artwork and superb bathrooms. Informal dining options range from bar snacks to a more adventurous à la carte

Gillbank House without rest

8 East Morton St ✉ DG3 5LZ – ✆ (01848) 330 597 – www.gillbank.co.uk

6 rm – †£ 60/80 ††£ 80

Red-stone house built in 1895; originally the Jenner family holiday home. Lovely stained glass front door, spacious, light-filled interior and airy breakfast room with distant hill views. Large, simply furnished bedrooms: two with feature beds; all with wet rooms.

THURSO

Highland – Pop. 7 933 – See Regional map n°**30**-D1
Edinburgh 289 mi – Inverness 133 mi – Wick 21 mi
Michelin Road map 501-J8 – Michelin Green Guide SCOTLAND

Forss House

Forss ✉ KW14 7XY – West : 5.5 mi on A 836 – ✆ (01847) 861 201 – www.forsshousehotel.co.uk – Closed 24 December-4 January

14 rm – †£ 99/135 ††£ 135/185 **Rest** – Carte £ 24/40 **s** – *(dinner only)*

Traditional Scottish hotel centred around fishing and offering timeshares on the river. Rods and mounted fish sit beside deer heads and open fires. Good-sized bedrooms – the annexe rooms are the most modern. Elegant dining room serves a classic menu; seafood is a speciality.

Pennyland House without rest

✉ KW14 7JU Northwest : 0.75 mi on A 9 – ✆ (01847) 891 194 – www.pennylandhouse.co.uk – Closed Christmas

6 rm – †£ 60 ††£ 80

Old farmhouse built in 1780; where the founder of the Boys' Brigade was born. Simple, stylishly furnished bedrooms with quality oak furnishings, golf course pictures and modern bathrooms. Open-plan lounge-cum-dining room with harbour views.

Murray House

1 Campbell St ✉ KW14 7HD – ✆ (01847) 895 759 – www.murrayhousebb.com – Closed Christmas-New Year

5 rm – †£ 30/50 ††£ 60/80 **Rest** – Menu £ 12

Family-run Victorian house in a great central location. Small lounge and breakfast room. Bright, compact bedrooms with modern shower rooms; two on the second floor are suitable for families. Home-cooked dinners must be pre-ordered; packed breakfasts and lunches available. Minimum two night stay.

SCOTLAND

at Scrabster Northwest: 2.25 mi on A9

Captain's Galley

The Harbour ✉ KW14 7UJ – ✆ (01847) 894 999 – www.captainsgalley.co.uk – Closed 25-26 December, 1-2 January, Sunday and Monday

Menu £ 49/65 – *(dinner only) (booking essential)*

Rustic seafood restaurant on the pier, with a vaulted stone dining room, a cosy lounge and an old chimney from its former ice house days. Classical daily menu; the owner was once a fisherman, so has excellent local contacts – he keeps some of his produce in creels in the harbour.

TIGHNABRUAICH

Argyll and Bute – See Regional map n°**27**-B3
Edinburgh 113 mi – Glasgow 63 mi – Oban 66 mi
Michelin Road map 501-E16

Royal An Lochan

Shore Rd ✉ PA21 2BE – ✆ (01700) 811 239 – www.theroyalanlochan.co.uk

11 rm – †£ 75/150 ††£ 75/150 **Rest** – Carte £ 27/41 **s**

Spacious 19C hotel located in a peaceful village, overlooking the Kyles of Bute. Comfortable bedrooms; some with excellent outlooks. The characterful bar with its nautical theme serves a snack menu, while the formal conservatory restaurant offers water views and seasonal seafood dishes.

TIRORAN → See Mull (Isle of)

Argyll and Bute – Michelin Road map 501-B14

TOBERMORY → See Mull (Isle of)

Argyll and Bute – Michelin Road map 501-B14

TORRIDON

Highland ✉ Achnasheen – See Regional map n°**29**-B2
Edinburgh 234 mi – Inverness 62 mi – Kyle of Lochalsh 44 mi
Michelin Road map 501-D11 – Michelin Green Guide SCOTLAND

Torridon

✉ *IV22 2EY South : 1.5 mi on A 896 – ✆ (01445) 791 242 – www.thetorridon.com – Closed January and Monday-Tuesday November-March*
18 rm – †£ 235/465 ††£ 235/465 – 2 suites
Rest – Menu £ 55 **s** – *(bar lunch) (booking essential) (set menu only)*
Family-run former hunting lodge built in 1887 by Lord Lovelace; set in 40 acres, with superb loch and mountain views. Delightful interior with wood-panelling, ornate ceilings and a peat fire. Mix of contemporary and a few classic bedrooms – all are spacious, with top quality furnishings and feature baths. Clubby bar and a smart dining room with a modern daily menu.

Torridon Inn with rm

rest,

✉ *IV22 2EY South : 1.5 mi on A 896 – ✆ (01445) 791 242 – www.thetorridon.com – Closed mid-December-January and Monday-Thursday November, February and March*
12 rm – †£ 110 ††£ 104/110 Carte £ 21/36 **s**
Tranquil inn geared towards those who enjoy outdoor pursuits. The timbered bar features stags' antlers and an ice axe; the restaurant overlooks the gardens and loch. Satisfying walkers' favourites mix with more elaborate dishes. Simply furnished, modern bedrooms; the larger ones are ideal for families.

SCOTLAND

TROON

South Ayrshire – Pop. 14 752 – See Regional map n°**25**-**A2**
Edinburgh 77 mi – Ayr 7 mi – Glasgow 31 mi
Michelin Road map 501-G17 and 502

Lochgreen House

Monktonhill Rd, Southwood ✉ KA10 7EN – Southeast : 2 mi on B 749 – ✆ (01292) 313 343 – www.costley-hotels.co.uk
31 rm – †£ 145/175 ††£ 170/210 – 1 suite
Rest *Tapestry* – see restaurant listing
Coastal Edwardian country house in neat, mature gardens. Sumptuous, classically furnished lounge with an extensive range of malt whiskies. Cosy, traditional bedrooms in main house; those in newer extension are larger and more luxurious.

Tapestry – Lochgreen House Hotel

Monktonhill Rd, Southwood ✉ KA10 7EN – Southeast : 2 mi on B 749 – ✆ (01292) 313 343 – www.costley-hotels.co.uk
Menu £ 18 (weekday lunch)/43
Cavernous room with rafters, mirrors and chandeliers, in an Edwardian country house hotel. Fixed price or 10 course tasting menus; tasty, original dishes have modern presentation and a strong Scottish base. Formal service.

at Loans East: 2 mi on A759✉ Troon

Highgrove House

Old Loans Rd ✉ KA10 7HL – East : 0.25 mi on Dundonald rd – ✆ (01292) 312 511 – www.costleyhotels.co.uk
9 rm – †£ 69 ††£ 110 **Rest** – Carte £ 22/38
Hillside property with a stunning panoramic view of the coastline and the Isle of Arran. Comfortable, contemporary bedrooms; Room 1 is the best. Clubby dining room with floor to ceiling windows and a smart, friendly team; sit in one of the plush booths at the top. Classic menus focus on seafood and grills.

TURNBERRY

South Ayrshire✉ Girvan – See Regional map n°**25**-**A2**
Edinburgh 97 mi – London 416 mi – Glasgow 51 mi – Carlisle 108 mi
Michelin Road map 501-F18 and 502 – Michelin Green Guide SCOTLAND

Turnberry rest,

✉ *KA26 9LT On A 719 – ✆ (01655) 331 000 – www.turnberryresort.co.uk*
149 rm – £ 155/305 £ 175/325 – 4 suites
Rest ***1906*** – see restaurant listing
Rest ***James Miller Room*** – Menu £ 75 – *(dinner only) (booking essential)*
Rest ***Tappie Toorie*** – Carte £ 24/44
Resort-style, Edwardian railway hotel boasting a smart spa and 3 championship golf courses. Spacious interior with a light, contemporary style. Luxurious bedrooms; suites have stunning coast and course views. Cocktails and snacks in Ailsa; French classics in 1906; ambitious, modern offerings in intimate James Miller and pub favourites in simpler Tappie Toorie.

XXX **1906** – Turnberry Hotel

✉ *KA26 9LT On A 719 – ✆ (01655) 331 000 – www.turnberryresort.co.uk*
Carte £ 33/89 – *(dinner only)*
Named after the year that the Turnberry opened, this smart hotel restaurant boasts lovely views across the sea. Classical French menus feature dishes true to the spirit of Auguste Escoffier.

UDNY GREEN

Aberdeenshire – See Regional map n°**28-D1**
Edinburgh 140 mi – London 543 mi – Belfast 218 mi – Dundee 80 mi

XX **Eat on the Green**

✉ *AB41 7RS – ✆ (01651) 842 337 – www.eatonthegreen.co.uk – Closed Monday, Tuesday and Saturday lunch*
Menu £ 22 (weekday lunch)/55 – Carte £ 30/49 – *(booking essential)*
Attractive former inn overlooking the village green, with a cosy lounge and two traditionally furnished dining rooms. Well-presented, classically based dishes change with the seasons. Professional, friendly service.

UIG → See Lewis and Harris (Isle of)

Western Isles – Michelin Road map 501-Y9

UIST (Isles of)

Western Isles – Pop. 3 510
Michelin Road map 501-X/Y11

NORTH UIST

Western Isles –

CARINISH

Western Isles – See Regional map n°**29-A2**

Temple View

✉ *HS6 5EJ – ✆ (01876) 580 676 – www.templeviewhotel.co.uk – Closed Christmas*
10 rm – £ 65/75 £ 105 **Rest** – Menu £ 24/28 **s** – Carte £ 17/35 **s**
Victorian house with an uncluttered interior and a homely style. Small bar, sitting room and sun lounge. Simple, comfortable bedrooms: those to the rear have moor views; those at the front overlook the sea or the 13C ruins of Trinity Temple. Cosy dining room offers popular seafood specials.

LANGASS

Western Isles – See Regional map n°**29-A2**

Langass Lodge rm,

✉ *HS6 5HA – ✆ (01876) 580 285 – www.langasslodge.co.uk – Closed 1 January, 24-25 and 31 December*
11 rm – £ 75/85 £ 95/145 **Rest** – Menu £ 36 – *(bar lunch)*
Victorian former shooting lodge nestled in heather-strewn hills and boasting distant loch views. Characterful bedrooms in the main house; more modern, spacious rooms with good views in the wing. Eat in the comfy bar or linen-clad dining room from simple, seafood based menus.

SCOTLAND

LOCHMADDY

Western Isles – See Regional map n°**29-A2**

Hamersay House

✉ HS6 5AE – ✆ (01876) 500 700 – www.hamersayhouse.co.uk
– Closed November-March
8 rm – †£ 75/95 ††£ 95/135
Rest – Carte £ 22/42 – *(booking essential) (bar lunch)*
Stylish hotel with a sleek, boutique style, a well-equipped gym, a sauna, a steam room and bikes for hire. Chic, modern bedrooms offer good facilities. The forward-thinking owner continually reinvests. Smart bar and dining room; menus display plenty of seafood.

ULLAPOOL

Highland – Pop. 1 541 – See Regional map n°**30-C2**
▶Edinburgh 215 mi – London 616 mi – Inverness 58 mi – Elgin 94 mi
Michelin Road map 501-E10 – Michelin Green Guide SCOTLAND

Point Cottage without rest

22 West Shore St ✉ IV26 2UR – ✆ (01854) 335 062
– www.pointcottagebandb.co.uk – Restricted opening in winter
3 rm – †£ 65/80 ††£ 65/80
18C former fisherman's cottage on the shore of Loch Broom; the Stornoway ferry passes in front. Compact, modern bedrooms with muted tweeds, contemporary art and good views. Small lounge and breakfast room; pre-order from a large selection.

SCOTLAND

Ardvreck without rest

Morefield Brae ✉ IV26 2TH – Northwest : 2 mi by A 835 – ✆ (01854) 613 000
– www.ardvreckhouse.com – Closed December-January
10 rm – †£ 50/75 ††£ 80/90
Modern house set away from the town centre, affording amazing views over Loch Broom to the mountains. Simply furnished bedrooms with tartan touches and local watercolours on the walls. The friendly owner is eager to please.

VEENSGARTH → See Shetland Islands (Mainland)

WALKERBURN

The Scottish Borders – Pop. 700 – See Regional map n°**26-C2**
▶Edinburgh 30 mi – London 362 mi – Aberdeen 161 mi – Hartlepool 120 mi

Windlestraw Lodge

✉ EH43 6AA On A 72 – ✆ (01896) 870 636 – www.windlestraw.co.uk
– Closed 24-26 December and 31 December- 2 January
6 rm – †£ 150/200 ††£ 180/220 **Rest** – Menu £ 50 – *(dinner only)*
Attractive Arts and Crafts property built in 1906, boasting original fireplaces, old plaster ceilings and great valley views. Stylish, tastefully modernised bedrooms. Comfy bar, plush lounge and an attractive, wood-panelled dining room offering a daily changing menu.

WATERNISH → See Skye (Isle of)

Highland – Michelin Road map 501-A11

WESTRAY (Isle of) → See Orkney Islands

– Michelin Road map 501-K/L6

WICK

Highland – Pop. 7 155 – See Regional map n°**30**-D1
Edinburgh 282 mi – Inverness 126 mi
Michelin Road map 501-K8 – Michelin Green Guide SCOTLAND

Clachan without rest
13 Randolph Pl, South Rd ✉ KW1 5NJ – South : 0.75 mi on A 99 – ☎ (01955) 605 384 – www.theclachan.co.uk – Closed 2 weeks Christmas-New Year
3 rm – †£ 60/65 ††£ 76/80
Smart detached house on the edge of town, a short drive from the Queen Mother's former holiday residence, the Castle of Mey. Stylish, well-kept bedrooms blend oak furnishings with tartan fabrics. Black and white photos of the town's herring fishing days decorate the cosy dining room. Extensive breakfasts.

Bord De L'Eau
2 Market St (Riverside) ✉ KW1 4AR – ☎ (01955) 604 400 – Closed 25-26 December, 1-2 January, Sunday lunch and Monday
Carte £ 25/40
Long-standing riverside bistro with a simple dining room and a conservatory. Framed Eiffel Tower prints and French posters adorn on the walls. Authentic, classic Gallic dishes feature plenty of local seafood.

WORMIT

Fife – See Regional map n°**28**-C2
Edinburgh 53 mi – London 455 mi – Aberdeen 70 mi – Gateshead 162 mi
Michelin Road map 501-L14

View
Naughton Rd ✉ DD6 8NE – ☎ (01382) 542 287 – www.view-restaurant.co.uk – Closed 25-26 December, 1-2 January and Monday
Menu £ 15 (lunch) – Carte £ 27/39
Unassuming former pub in a small village, boasting superb views over the Tay Bridge to Dundee. Extensive menu and daily specials board offer homemade small plates that can be served in succession or all at once; quality ingredients.

Wales

ABERAERON (Aber Aeron)

Ceredigion – Pop. 1 422 – See Regional map n°**33**-B3

London 231 mi – Cardiff 104 mi – Birmingham 138 mi – Liverpool 124 mi

Michelin Road map 503-H27

Ty Mawr Mansion Country House

Cilcennin ✉ SA48 8DB – East : 5 mi by A 482 – ✆ (01570) 470 033 – www.tymawrmansion.co.uk – Closed 27 December-20 January

9 rm – £ 90/180 £ 90/240 – 1 suite

Rest – Carte £ 32/45 – *(closed Sunday dinner) (dinner only)*

Grade II listed Georgian stone mansion in 12 acres of delightful grounds. Several well-appointed lounges with high ceilings; spacious bedrooms boast marble bathrooms and a good level of facilities. The small basement cinema offers dining packages and the smart restaurant offers bold, widely-influenced dishes.

3 Pen Cei without rest

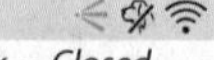

3 Quay Par ✉ SA46 0BT – ✆ (01545) 571 147 – www.pencei.co.uk – Closed 25-26 December

5 rm – £ 95 £ 105/150

Vibrant blue house on the harbourfront; formerly the Packet Steam Company HQ. Stylish modern bedrooms are named after local rivers: those to the front overlook the water; Aeron has a free-standing bath and large walk-in shower. Good choices at breakfast, from fruit salad to smoked salmon and scrambled eggs.

Llys Aeron without rest

Lampeter Rd ✉ SA46 0ED – on A 482 – ✆ (01545) 570 276 – www.llysaeron.co.uk – Closed 18 December-20 January

3 rm – £ 50/65 £ 80/105

Charmingly run Georgian guesthouse with a conservatory lounge and a breakfast room overlooking the pleasant walled garden. Bedrooms come in neutral colour schemes and have modern bathrooms. For breakfast, choose from extensive Aga-cooked options, as well as local honey and homemade granola and preserves.

Harbourmaster with rm

rest,

Quay Par ✉ SA46 0BA – ✆ (01545) 570 755 – www.harbour-master.com – Closed 25-26 December

13 rm – £ 65/240 £ 110/250 Carte £ 30/44

Vibrant blue inn with a New England style bar-lounge, a modern dining room and lovely harbour views. Choose between the bar menu, a more substantial evening à la carte and daily specials. Smart bedrooms, split between the house and a nearby cottage, are brightly decorated and well-equipped; some have terraces.

ABERDOVEY (Aberdyfi)

Gwynedd – Pop. 725 – See Regional map n°**32**-B2

London 230 mi – Dolgellau 25 mi – Shrewsbury 66 mi

Michelin Road map 503-H26 – Michelin Green Guide WALES

Llety Bodfor without rest

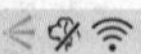

Bodfor Terr ✉ LL35 0EA – ✆ (01654) 767 475 – www.lletybodfor.co.uk – Closed 10-31 January

4 rm – £ 100/120 £ 120/150, £ 13

Two 19C seafront houses with a relaxed atmosphere and stylish interior design. Spacious, contemporary bedrooms come with bay views and kitchenettes; guests can also prepare snacks in the pantry. Breakfast is served three doors down.

ABERGAVENNY (Y-Fenni)

Monmouthshire – Pop. 13 423 – See Regional map n°**33**-C4

London 163 mi – Cardiff 31 mi – Gloucester 43 mi – Newport 19 mi

Michelin Road map 503-L28 – Michelin Green Guide WALES

Llansantffraed Court

Llanvihangel Gobion ✉ NP7 9BA – Southeast : 6.5 mi by A 40 and B 4598 off old Raglan rd – ☎ (01873) 840 678 – www.llch.co.uk
21 rm – †£ 100/120 ††£ 135/185
Rest *The Court* – see restaurant listing
Attractive William and Mary country house, with an ornamental lake and a chapel in its 20 acre grounds. Have afternoon tea in the traditional lounge. Bedrooms come in dark-hues – the corner rooms have both mountain and valley views.

Angel

rest,

15 Cross St ✉ NP7 5EN – ☎ (01873) 857 121 – www.angelabergavenny.com – Closed 25 December
34 rm – †£ 111/188 ††£ 111/188 – 2 suites
Rest *Oak Room* – Menu £ 25 (lunch and early dinner) – Carte £ 21/45 – *(closed dinner 24-31 December)*
Keenly run, family-owned, Georgian coaching inn and outbuildings. Characterful guest areas have a contemporary, shabby-chic feel. Mix of traditional and more contemporary bedrooms. Smart brasserie with oak furniture offers a classical menu with international influences. Afternoon tea in the Wedgewood Room.

The Court – Llansantffraed Court Hotel

Llanvihangel Gobion ✉ NP7 9BA – Southeast : 6.5 mi by A 40 and B 4598 off old Raglan rd – ☎ (01873) 840 678 – www.llch.co.uk
Menu £ 20 (lunch)/28 – Carte £ 27/41 – *(booking essential)*
Contemporary country house restaurant, hung with large photos of local scenes. Dishes have a classical British base but are given a modern twist; fruit, veg and herbs are from the walled garden. The wines provide plenty of interest.

WALES

at Llanddewi Skirrid Northeast: 3.25 mi on B4521 ✉ Abergavenny

Walnut Tree (Shaun Hill)

✉ NP7 8AW – ☎ (01873) 852 797 – www.thewalnuttreeinn.com – Closed 1 week Christmas, Sunday and Monday
Menu £ 25 (weekday lunch) – Carte £ 32/49 – *(booking essential)*
A reinvigorated, long-standing Welsh institution, set in a wooded valley and always bustling with regulars. Start with drinks in the flag-floored lounge-bar. Classic, seasonal dishes are well-priced and refreshingly simple, eschewing adornment and letting the ingredients speak for themselves.
→ Bourride of red mullet, turbot and scallop, braised in saffron stock. Loin of pork with its cheek and cromesqui. Dark chocolate and Grand Marnier torte.

at Cross Ash Northeast: 8.25 mi on B4521

1861

✉ NP7 8PB West : 0.5 mi on B 4521 – ☎ (01873) 821 297 – www.18-61.co.uk – Closed first 2 weeks January, Sunday dinner and Monday
Menu £ 22 (lunch)/35 – Carte £ 35/46
Part-timbered Victorian pub; now a cosy restaurant with a smart lounge, a red brick fireplace and contemporary furnishings. Choose from a set selection, a 7 course tasting menu or the à la carte. Classically based cooking has modern twists.

at Nant-Y-Derry Southeast: 6.5 mi by A40 off A4042 ✉ Abergavenny

Foxhunter

✉ NP7 9DN – ☎ (01873) 881 101 – www.thefoxhunter.com – Closed 25-26 December, 1 January, Sunday dinner and Monday
Menu £ 28 (lunch) – Carte £ 30/44
Attractive stone-built former station master's house with a small kitchen garden where they grow some of the produce. The characterful dining room features flagged floors and wood burning stoves. Cooking is hearty, unfussy and classical.

ABERSOCH

Gwynedd – Pop. 783 – ✉ Pwllheli – See Regional map n°**32**-B2
London 265 mi – Caernarfon 28 mi – Shrewsbury 101 mi
Michelin Road map 502-G25 and 503 – Michelin Green Guide WALES

Venetia with rm

Lon Sarn Bach ✉ LL53 7EB – ✆ (01758) 713 354 – www.venetiawales.com – Closed 4 January-12 February, 24-27 December, Sunday lunch July-August and Sunday dinner September-June
5 rm – £ 65/133 £ 80/148
Carte £ 23/44 – *(dinner only and Sunday lunch)*
Double-fronted house once owned by a sea captain, with a minimalist bar-lounge and a contemporary dining room with lime and aubergine seating. Classic Italian dishes are presented in a distinctly modern style. Friendly, efficient service. Chic, well-equipped bedrooms; one has a jacuzzi with a waterproof TV.

at Bwlchtocyn South: 2 mi ✉ Pwllheli

Porth Tocyn

✉ LL53 7BU – ✆ (01758) 713 303 – www.porthtocynhotel.co.uk – Easter-early November
17 rm – £ 78/185 £ 105/185
Rest – Menu £ 39/46 – Carte £ 21/38 – *(buffet lunch Sunday) (bar lunch Monday-Saturday)*
High on the headland overlooking Cardigan Bay, a traditional hotel that's been in the family for three generations. Relax in the cosy lounges or explore the many leisure and children's facilities. Homely, modernised bedrooms; some with balconies or sea views. Menus offer interesting, soundly executed dishes.

WALES

ABERYSTWYTH (Aberestuuth)

Ceredigion – Pop. 18 093 – See Regional map n°**32**-B2
London 238 mi – Chester 98 mi – Fishguard 58 mi – Shrewsbury 74 mi
Michelin Road map 503-H26 – Michelin Green Guide WALES

Nanteos rm,

Rhydyfelin ✉ SY23 4LU – Southeast : 4 mi by A 487 off A 4120 – ✆ (01970) 600 522 – www.nanteos.com
16 rm – £ 125/250 £ 180/300 – 2 suites
Rest *Nightingale* – Menu £ 40 (dinner) – Carte lunch £ 20/28 – *(closed Sunday dinner and Monday October-March)*
Impressive Georgian house in a peaceful wooded valley surrounded by mountains. Original flag flooring and ornate coving feature; breakfast is in the characterful old kitchen. Stylish, boldly coloured bedrooms come with antiques, modern facilities and super bathrooms. Classical menus feature Welsh produce.

Gwesty Cymru

19 Marine Terr ✉ SY23 2AZ – ✆ (01970) 612 252 – www.gwestycymru.com – Closed 23-31 December
8 rm – £ 67/80 £ 87/160
Rest – Menu £ 14 (weekday lunch)/20 – Carte £ 22/34 – *(booking essential)*
Grade II listed Georgian townhouse on the seafront, with a brightly painted exterior and a terrace overlooking the bay. Thoughtfully designed, modern bedrooms vary in size and décor – all are colour themed, with smart bathrooms. Small, stylish basement bar and dining room; ambitious, adventurous dishes.

ANGLESEY (Isle of) (Sir Ynys Môn)

Isle of Anglesey – Pop. 68 900 – See Regional map n°**32**-B1
London 270 mi – Cardiff 205 mi – Liverpool 92 mi – Birkenhead 86 mi
Michelin Road map 503-G/H24

BEAUMARIS

London 253 mi – Birkenhead 74 mi – Holyhead 25 mi
Michelin Green Guide WALES

Ye Olde Bull's Head Inn

Castle St ✉ LL58 8AP – ✆ (01248) 810 329 – www.bullsheadinn.co.uk – Closed 25-26 December and 1 January
26 rm – †£ 83/95 ††£ 105/175
Rest *Brasserie* Rest *Loft* – see restaurant listing
Characterful 1670s coaching inn. The traditional bedrooms in the main house are named after Dickens characters; those in the townhouse are more modern and colourful. Look out for the old water clock and ducking stool in the bar.

Cleifiog without rest

Townsend ✉ LL58 8BH – ✆ (01248) 811 507 – www.cleifiogbandb.co.uk – Closed Christmas-early January
3 rm – †£ 60/80 ††£ 90/110
Delightful seafront guesthouse overlooking the mountains and the Menai Strait; run by a welcoming owner. Watercolours hang on wood-panelled walls in the cosy, antique-furnished lounge. Comfortable bedrooms have fine linens and large bathrooms. Excellent communal breakfasts feature tasty fresh juices.

Churchbank without rest

28 Church St ✉ LL58 8AB – ✆ (01248) 810 353 – www.bedandbreakfastanglesey.com – Closed Christmas
3 rm – †£ 60/67 ††£ 75/90
Georgian guesthouse with a homely, antique-furnished interior and modern day comforts. Cosy bedrooms look out over the large walled garden and the church opposite; one has a private bathroom. Helpful, amiable owner and hearty breakfasts.

WALES

Loft – Ye Olde Bull's Head Inn

Castle St ✉ LL58 8AP – ✆ (01248) 810 329 – www.bullsheadinn.co.uk – Closed 25-26 December, 1 January, Sunday and Monday
Menu £ 45 – *(dinner only)*
Formal restaurant under the eaves of an old coaching inn, with a plush, open-fired lounge and an elegant candlelit dining room with exposed beams and immaculately laid tables. Ambitious dishes feature lots of different ingredients.

Cennin

13 Castle St ✉ LL58 8AP – ✆ (01248) 811 230 – www.restaurantcennin.com – Closed 25-26 December, Tuesday dinner in winter, Sunday dinner and Monday
Menu £ 20 (lunch) – Carte £ 32/43 – *(dinner only and Sunday lunch)*
First floor neighbourhood restaurant above a deli and café; its name is Welsh for 'leeks'. The chef is from the island and champions seasonal, local produce; meat comes from the owners' farms and includes the signature Welsh Black beef.

Brasserie – Ye Olde Bull's Head Inn

Castle St ✉ LL58 8AP – ✆ (01248) 810 329 – www.bullsheadinn.co.uk – Closed 25-26 December and 1 January
Carte £ 23/34 – *(bookings not accepted)*
Set overlooking a courtyard, a large brasserie in the old stables of a 17C coaching inn, with a Welsh slate floor, a fireplace built from local stone and a relaxed, modern feel. Wide ranging modern menus feature plenty of specials.

LLANERCHYMEDD

Michelin Green Guide WALES

Llwydiarth Fawr without rest 

✉ LL71 8DF North : 1 mi on B 5111 – ✆ (01248) 470 321 – www.llwydiarthfawr.com
4 rm – †£ 45/65 ††£ 85
Lovely Georgian house surrounded by 1,000 acres of farmland. Well-kept interior with an impressive hallway and an open-fired drawing room. Bedrooms are classically furnished, with smart wallpapers and colourful throws adding a modern edge.

LLANGAFFO

Outbuildings

Bodowyr Farmhouse ✉ LL60 6NH – Southeast : 1.5 mi by B 4419 turning left at crossroads and left again by post box. – ☎ (01248) 430 132 – www.theoutbuildings.co.uk

5 rm ☕ – 🛉£ 65/90 🛉🛉£ 90 **Rest** – Menu £ 20/30

Tastefully converted former granary, offering fantastic views over Snowdonia. Have afternoon tea in the cosy, open-fired lounge. Stylish, modern bedrooms come with local artwork and smart bathrooms; for a romantic hideaway, choose the Pink Hut. The large dining room offers simple three course dinners.

MENAI BRIDGE

Plas Rhianfa

Glyn Garth ✉ LL59 5NS – East : 1 mi on A 545 – ☎ (01248) 713 656 – www.chateaurhianfa.com

16 rm ☕ – 🛉£ 135/285 🛉🛉£ 149/299

Rest – Menu £ 45 – *(dinner only and lunch Saturday and Sunday)*

Built in 1849 and a smaller copy of the Château de Chenonceau. Formal gardens lead down to the Menai Strait and boast fantastic views over Snowdonia. The striking Victorian interior displays original wood panelling, stained glass and turrets, which contrast with bold modern colour schemes. Formal dining.

Sosban & The Old Butchers

Trinity House, 1A High St ✉ LL59 5EE – ☎ (01248) 208 131 – www.sosbanandtheoldbutchers.com – Closed January-mid February, Christmas-New Year and Sunday-Wednesday

Menu £ 44 – *(dinner only) (booking essential) (surprise menu only)*

Brightly painted restaurant with smart awnings; inside, one wall displays the Welsh slate and hand-painted tiles from its days as a butcher's shop. A well-balanced, four course surprise menu offers boldly flavoured, carefully cooked dishes.

Dylan's

St George's Rd ✉ LL59 5DE – ☎ (01248) 716 714 – www.dylansrestaurant.co.uk – Closed 25-26 December

Carte £ 17/57 – *(bookings advisable at dinner)*

An old boat yard timber store; now a smart, busy, two-storey eatery by the water's edge, overlooking Bangor. Extensive menus offer everything from home-made cakes and weekend brunch to sourdough pizzas. Find a spot on the terrace if you can.

RHOSCOLYN

White Eagle

✉ LL65 2NJ – ☎ (01407) 860 267 – www.white-eagle.co.uk – Closed 25 December

Menu £ 16 – Carte £ 20/39

Large pub with a cosy bar, a modern dining room, a decked terrace and stunning sea views. Monthly menus offer everything from sandwiches and pub classics to more sophisticated fare. Daily fish specials and regular themed weeks feature.

BALA

Gwynedd – Pop. 1 974 – ✉ Gwynedd – See Regional map n°**32**-B2

London 213 mi – Cardiff 160 mi – Chester 48 mi

Michelin Road map 503-J25

Bryniau Golau Ⓝ

Llangower ✉ LL23 7BT – South : 2 mi by A 494 and B 4931 off B 4403 – ☎ (01678) 521 782 – www.bryniau-golau.co.uk – Closed December-February

3 rm ☕ – 🛉£ 70/75 🛉🛉£ 100/110 **Rest** – Menu £ 25

Victorian tiling, plasterwork and fireplaces are proudly displayed in this elegant house. Spacious bedrooms overlook the lake and mountains: one has a four-poster bed; another, a bath which affords lake views. Their own honey features at breakfast, while dinner – served Fri and Sun – showcases local produce.

Abercelyn Country House without rest 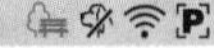
Llanycil ✉ LL23 7YF – Southwest : 1 mi on A 494 – ☎ (01678) 521 109 – www.abercelyn.co.uk – February-October
3 rm ☕ – 🚹£ 53/60 🚹🚹£ 70/90
Attractive former rectory with a brook running through the pleasant garden. Period charm blends with modern touches and up-to-date facilities; bedrooms are warmly decorated and the lounge is cosy. The owner knows the Fells well.

BEAUMARIS → See Anglesey (Isle of)
– Michelin Road map 504-H24

BEDDGELERT (Bedkelerd)
Gwynedd – Pop. 535 – See Regional map n°**32**-B1
▶London 249 mi – Caernarfon 13 mi – Chester 73 mi
Michelin Road map 502-H24 and 503 – Michelin Green Guide WALES

Sygun Fawr Country House
✉ LL55 4NE Northeast : 0.75 mi by A 498 – ☎ (01766) 890 258 – www.sygunfawr.co.uk – Closed 3 January-10 February and 3-29 December
12 rm ☕ – 🚹£ 60/64 🚹🚹£ 85/110
Rest – Carte £ 21/30 – *(closed Monday and Thursday to non-residents) (dinner only) (booking essential)*
Part-16C stone house, halfway up a mountain and boasting views over the valley. Charming open-fired interior with a snug sitting room and a spacious conservatory. Good-sized bedrooms have a cosy, homely feel. Traditional dining room serves hearty, regional dishes; Mon and Thurs they offer simpler suppers.

BETWS GARMON
Gwynedd – See Regional map n°**32**-B1
▶London 249 mi – Cardiff 168 mi – Birmingham 135 mi – Sheffield 154 mi

Betws Inn 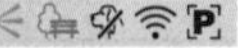
✉ LL54 7YY Northwest : 1 mi on A 4085 – ☎ (01286) 650 324 – www.betws-inn.co.uk
3 rm ☕ – 🚹£ 60/80 🚹🚹£ 65/85 **Rest** – Menu £ 30 **s**
Rustic former coaching inn surrounded by the towering mountains of Snowdonia. Superb inglenook fireplace on display in the cosy lounge; exposed stone walls and a pine dresser in the breakfast room. Warm, beamed bedrooms boast half-tester or four-poster beds and modern bathrooms – one is on two levels. Home-cooked meals showcase local produce and lamb features highly.

BETWS-Y-COED
Conwy – Pop. 255 – See Regional map n°**32**-B1
▶London 226 mi – Holyhead 44 mi – Shrewsbury 62 mi
Michelin Road map 502-I24 and 503 – Michelin Green Guide WALES

Tan-y-Foel Country House without rest
✉ LL26 0RE East : 2.5 mi by A 5, A 470 and Capel Garmon rd on Llanwrst rd – ☎ (01690) 710 507 – www.tyfhotel.co.uk – Closed December and January
6 rm ☕ – 🚹£ 100/145 🚹🚹£ 100/185
Personally run, part-16C country house in 4 acres of grounds, affording stunning views over the Vale of Conwy and Snowdonia. The snug lounge and breakfast room display traditional features. Modern, individually styled bedrooms have smart bathrooms; the spacious loft room has a vaulted ceiling.

Pengwern without rest
Allt Dinas ✉ LL24 0HF – Southeast : 1.5 mi on A 5 – ☎ (01690) 710 480 – www.snowdoniaaccommodation.co.uk – Closed 19 December-2 January
3 rm ☕ – 🚹£ 60/67 🚹🚹£ 70/82
Cosy Victorian house with stunning mountain and valley views. Warm, well-proportioned bedrooms are named after famous artists and retain charming original features like the old fireplaces. Comfy lounge. Communal breakfasts.

 **Bryn Bella** without rest

Lôn Muriau, Llanrwst Rd ✉ LL24 0HD – Northeast : 1 mi by A 5 on A 470 – ☎ (01690) 710 627 – www.bryn-bella.co.uk

5 rm ☕ – 🚹£ 75/80 🚹🚹£ 75/90

Comfy, well-kept guesthouse with a pleasant garden, valley views and every conceivable extra in the bedrooms. Keen, friendly owners provide reliable local info. Hearty cooked breakfasts feature fresh, tasty eggs from their rescued hens.

at Penmachno Southwest: 4.75 mi by A5 on B4406✉ Betws-Y-Coed

 **Penmachno Hall**

✉ LL24 0PU On Ty Mawr rd – ☎ (01690) 760 410 – www.penmachnohall.co.uk – Closed Christmas-New Year

3 rm ☕ – 🚹£ 75/100 🚹🚹£ 90/100 **Rest** – Menu £ 18/38

Former rectory built in 1862, set in a pleasant valley location and boasting delightful views. Breakfast-cum-sitting room filled with books; eclectic art collection and lovely mature gardens. Boldly coloured bedrooms, personally decorated by the friendly owners, contain a host of thoughtful extras. Traditional menus, with 2 courses on weekdays and 5 on Saturdays.

BETWS-YN-RHOS

Conwy – See Regional map n°**32**-**B1**

London 244 mi – Wrexham 41 mi – Bangor 27 mi

Michelin Road map 502-J24

 **Ffarm Country House** 

✉ LL22 8AR – ☎ (01492) 680 448 – www.ffarmcountryhouse.co.uk – Closed 25-26 December

8 rm ☕ – 🚹£ 75/118 🚹🚹£ 85/148

Rest – Carte £ 23/31 – *(closed Tuesday) (dinner only) (booking essential)*

A Gothic-style building which really stands out in this small village. Beautiful tiled hall and grand drawing room. Bedrooms, named after wine regions, have sleek bathrooms and a stylish, modern edge; Cape and Champagne are 2 of the largest.

WALES

BODUAN → See Pwllheli

Gwynedd

BRECHFA

Carmarthenshire – See Regional map n°**33**-**B3**

London 216 mi – Cardiff 71 mi – Birmingham 183 mi – Liverpool 164 mi

Michelin Road map 503-H28

Ty Mawr Country

✉ SA32 7RA – ☎ (01267) 202 332 – www.wales-country-hotel.co.uk

6 rm ☕ – 🚹£ 70/75 🚹🚹£ 115/130

Rest – Menu £ 25 – *(dinner only) (booking essential)*

16C stone-built farmhouse, set in the centre of the village next to the river. It's personally run and boasts charm and character aplenty, with exposed bricks, wooden beams, open fires, a comfy lounge and pine-furnished bedrooms. The modern menu has Welsh twists and produce is homemade or from the valley.

BRECON

Powys – Pop. 8 250 – See Regional map n°**33**-**C3**

London 171 mi – Cardiff 40 mi – Carmarthen 31 mi – Gloucester 65 mi

Michelin Road map 503-J28 – Michelin Green Guide WALES

 **Peterstone Court** rest,

Brecon Rd, Llanhamlach ✉ LD3 7YB – Southeast : 4 mi by B 4601 on A 40 – ☎ (01874) 665 387 – www.peterstone-court.com

12 rm ☕ – 🚹£ 105/200 🚹🚹£ 145/245 **Rest** – Menu £ 20 – Carte £ 26/38

Large Georgian house with a lovely mountain backdrop. Two comfy, characterful lounges. Sizeable, traditional bedrooms in the main house; those in the old stables are duplex-style. Two-roomed restaurant has lovely views and a terrace overlooking the swimming pool; extensive, classical menus of local produce.

Felin Glais

Aberyscir ✉ LD3 9NP – West : 4 mi by Cradoc rd turning right immediately after bridge – ☎ (01874) 623 107 – www.felinglais.co.uk – Closed 25 December
4 rm ☕ – 🚹£ 90 🚹🚹£ 90/100 **Rest** – Menu £ 40 **s**
17C stone barn and mill, set in a tranquil hamlet and run with pride. Spacious interior has a pleasant 'lived in' feel; cosy, homely bedrooms have toiletries and linen from Harrods. Large beamed lounge; dine here, at the communal table, or in the conservatory in summer. Lengthy menu – order two days ahead.

Felin Fach Griffin with rm

Felin Fach ✉ LD3 0UB – Northeast : 4.75 mi by B 4602 off A 470 – ☎ (01874) 620 111 – www.felinfachgriffin.co.uk – Closed 25 December and early January
7 rm ☕ – 🚹£ 100/125 🚹🚹£ 118/168
Menu £ 21 (weekday lunch)/29 – Carte £ 27/36
Set in picturesque countryside; a rather unique pub with bright paintwork, colourful art and an extremely laid back atmosphere. The young serving team are friendly and knowledgeable. Following the motto 'simple things, done well', the attractively presented dishes are straightforward, tasty and refined. Pleasant bedrooms come with comfy beds but no TVs.

BRIDGEND (Pen-y-Bont)

Bridgend – Pop. 46 757 – See Regional map n°**33**-**B4**
London 177 mi – Cardiff 20 mi – Swansea 23 mi
Michelin Road map 503-J29

Great House

High St, Laleston ✉ CF32 0HP – West : 2 mi on A 473 – ☎ (01656) 657 644 – www.great-house-laleston.co.uk – Closed 23-28 December
12 rm ☕ – 🚹£ 90/110 🚹🚹£ 135/165
Rest *Leicester's* – Menu £ 17 (lunch and early dinner) – Carte £ 22/44 – *(closed Sunday dinner and bank holidays)*
Welcoming 15C, Grade II listed property; the home of the Lord of the Manor of Laleston and reputedly a gift from Elizabeth I to the Earl of Leicester. Characterful bar and lounge. Individually styled bedrooms; those in the coach house are most modern. Restaurant offers a seasonal menu of regional produce.

BUILTH WELLS (Llanfair-ym-Muallt)

Powys – Pop. 2 829 – See Regional map n°**33**-**C3**
London 191 mi – Cardiff 63 mi – Brecon 20 mi – Swansea 58 mi
Michelin Road map 503-J27

Rhedyn

Cilmery ✉ LD2 3LH – West : 4 mi on A 483 – ☎ (01982) 551 944 – www.rhedynguesthouse.co.uk
3 rm ☕ – 🚹£ 80 🚹🚹£ 90 **Rest** – Menu £ 28
Former forester's cottage with a small garden and pleasant country views, run by very welcoming owners. Tiny lounge with a bookcase full of local info and DVDs; cosy communal dining room where home-cooked, local market produce is served. Good-sized, modern bedrooms feature heavy wood furnishings, good facilities and quirky touches. Tea and cake are served on arrival.

BWLCHTOCYN → See Abersoch

Gwynedd – Michelin Road map 502-G25 and 503

CAERNARFON

Gwynedd – Pop. 9 493 – See Regional map n°**32**-**B1**
London 249 mi – Birkenhead 76 mi – Chester 68 mi – Holyhead 30 mi
Michelin Road map 502-H24 and 503 – Michelin Green Guide WALES

WALES

Plas Dinas

✉ *LL54 7YF South : 2.5 mi on A 487 – ✆ (01286) 830 214 – www.plasdinas.co.uk – Closed Christmas and New Year*

9 rm ☕ – 👤£ 99/199 👥£ 99/249

Rest – Menu £ 26/35 – *(closed Sunday and Monday) (dinner only) (residents only)*

Former family home of Lord Snowdon, set in large gardens and filled with antiques, historical documents and family portraits. Spacious drawing room with an open fire and a piano. Smart bedrooms boast designer touches and immaculate bathrooms. Concise menu of unfussy, hearty dishes in the simple dining room.

at Seion Northeast: 5.5 mi by A4086 and B4366 on Seion rd ✉ Gwynedd

Ty'n Rhos Country House

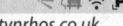

✉ *LL55 3AE Southwest : 0.75 mi – ✆ (01248) 670 489 – www.tynrhos.co.uk*

19 rm ☕ – 👤£ 70/85 👥£ 90/175

Rest – Menu £ 33/49 – *(dinner only and Sunday lunch)*

Personally run former farmhouse with a large conservatory and a cosy lounge with an inglenook fireplace. Comfortable, modern bedrooms; some have balconies or terraces and others, their own garden. The formal restaurant offers pleasant views over Anglesey; classically based dishes are presented in modern ways.

at Dolydd South: 3.5 mi by A487

Y Goeden Eirin

✉ *LL54 7EF – ✆ (01286) 830 942 – www.ygoedeneirin.co.uk – Closed Christmas-New Year*

3 rm ☕ – 👤£ 60/75 👥£ 80/90 **Rest** – Menu £ 28

Cosy stone cottage with interesting furniture, eclectic artwork and a slightly bohemian feel. The bedroom in the main house has views of both the mountains and the sea; bedrooms in the old outbuildings have slate floors, stable doors and small kitchen areas. Tasty home-cooked breakfasts.

at Llanrug East: 3 mi on A4086 ✉ Caernarfon

Seiont Manor

✉ *LL55 2AQ – ✆ (01286) 673 366 – www.handpickedhotels.co.uk*

28 rm ☕ – 👤£ 75/185 👥£ 95/265 **Rest** – Menu £ 25/37

Small manor house in a peaceful location; follow the nature trails or fish on the river in the 150 acre grounds. Spacious, modern country bedrooms – some with Juliet balconies or terraces. Have afternoon tea in one of the lounges, a light meal in the conservatory or modern classics in the formal restaurant.

WALES

CARDIFF

Cardiff – Pop. 346 090 – See Regional map n°**33**-C4

London 155 mi – Birmingham 110 mi – Bristol 46 mi – Coventry 124 mi

Michelin Road map 503-K29 – Michelin Green Guide WALES

© FoodCollection/Photononstop

Hotels

St David's H. & Spa

Havannah St, Cardiff Bay ✉ *CF10 5SD – ✆ (02920) 454 045 – www.principal-hayley.com/thestdavids* Town plan: CU**a**

142 rm – †£ 89/765 ††£ 89/765 – 12 suites

Rest *Tempus at Tides* – Carte £ 30/59

Modern, purpose-built hotel on the waterfront, affording lovely 360° views. Good-sized, minimalist bedrooms have a slightly funky feel; all boast balconies and bay outlooks. Smart spa features seawater pools and a dry floatation tank. Stylish restaurant with superb terrace views serves modern British dishes.

Hilton Cardiff

Kingsway ✉ *CF10 3HH – ✆ (029) 2064 6300 – www.placeshilton.com/cardiff* Town plan: BZ**x**

197 rm – †£ 119/149 ††£ 129/159 – 4 suites

Rest *Razzi* – Menu £ 15 – Carte dinner £ 18/48

Imposing former tax office in the city centre, with excellent views of the castle, law courts and city hall. Large atrium; well-equipped function rooms and leisure club. Spacious bedrooms are a touch functional – some have great outlooks. Conservatory-style restaurant offers a Mediterranean-influenced menu.

Park Plaza

Greyfriars Rd ✉ *CF10 3AL – ✆ (029) 20 111 111 – www.parkplazacardiff.com – Closed 25-26 December* Town plan: BY**s**

129 rm – †£ 80/340 ††£ 90/350, £ 13

Rest *Laguna Kitchen and Bar* – ✆ (029) 2011 1103 – Menu £ 16 (weekday lunch)/45 – Carte £ 23/48

Formerly municipal offices, now a light, airy hotel with a stylish lounge, extensive conference facilities and a vast leisure centre boasting a smart, stainless steel pool and 8 treatment rooms. Stark, modern bedrooms have laptop safes and slate bathrooms. Informal brasserie serves international dishes.

Radisson Blu Cardiff

rm,

Meridian Gate, Bute Terr. ✉ *CF10 2FL – ✆ (029) 2045 4777 – www.radissonblu.com/hotel-cardiff* Town plan: BZ**a**

215 rm – †£ 70/400 ††£ 80/410

Rest *Filini* – Menu £ 20 – Carte £ 19/31 – *(closed Sunday) (dinner only)*

Large glass building in great central location. Spacious, modern guest areas, excellent meeting facilities and smart bar. Modern, slightly minimalist bedrooms in three styles – Fresh, Fashion and Chic – all boast slate-tiled bathrooms and city views. Simply furnished restaurant offers accessible Italian menu.

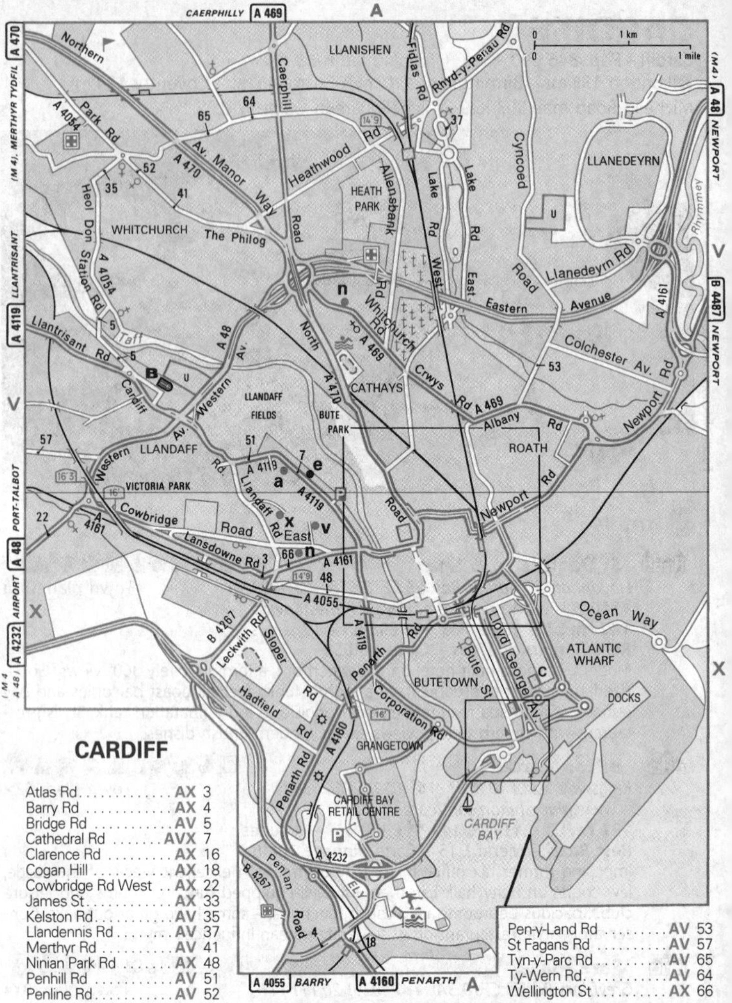

CARDIFF

Parc

Park Pl ✉ CF10 3UD – ✆ (0871) 376 9011 – www.thistle.com/theparchotel — Town plan: BZ**n**

140 rm – ♦£ 69/129 ♦♦£ 89/189 – 1 suite

Rest *Social* – ✆ (029) 2078 5593 – Menu £ 15/20 – Carte £ 19/36

Centrally located, commercial hotel with striking décor; hidden behind a classic Victorian façade. Marble-tiled lobby and fashionable bar. Stylish, contemporary bedrooms feature bright white décor and offer good facilities; those to the rear are quieter. Accessible menus in smart restaurant.

Lincoln House without rest

118-120 Cathedral Rd ✉ CF11 9LQ – ✆ (029) 2039 5558 – www.lincolnhotel.co.uk — Town plan: AV**e**

23 rm – ♦£ 70/125 ♦♦£ 90/150

Two lovingly restored Victorian houses on the main road into town: family owned and run, with a classic style and contemporary touches. Bedrooms offer a high level of facilities; some feature four-posters and those to the rear are quieter.

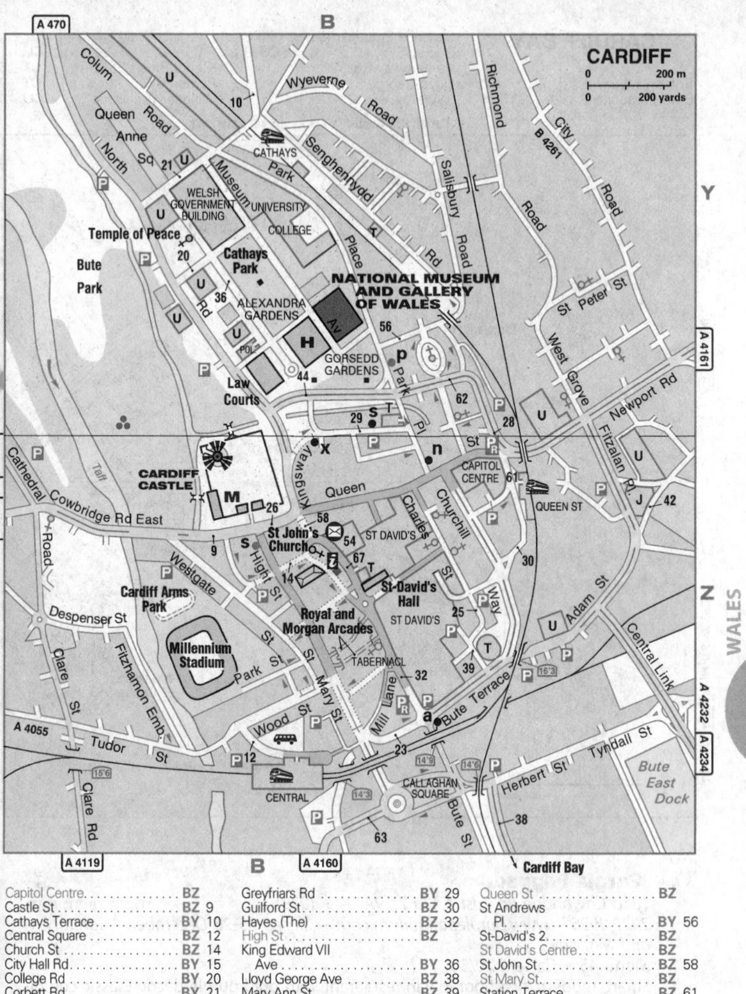

Restaurants

XXX Park House

20 Park Pl. ✉ CF10 3DQ – ✆ (029) 2022 4343 Town plan: BY**p**

– www.parkhouserestaurant.co.uk – Closed 24-25 December, 1 January, Monday and Tuesday

Menu £ 21 (weekday lunch)/25 – Carte approx. £ 48

Striking building designed by William Burgess in the late 1800s, overlooking Gorsedd Gardens. The oak-panelled dining room has a formal air. Menus are modern – each dish is matched with a wine from the impressive New World list.

CARDIFF BAY

Britannia Quay . . . . CU 2
Bute Crescent . . . . CT 4
Clarence Embankment . . . CT 8
Dudley St. . . . . CU 9
Hemingway Rd. . . . . CT 12
Lloyd George Ave . . . . CT 14
Mermaid Quay Shopping Centre. . . . . CU
Mount Stuart Square . . . . CT 15
Pomeroy St. . . . . CT 17
Windsor Esplanade . . . . . CU 19

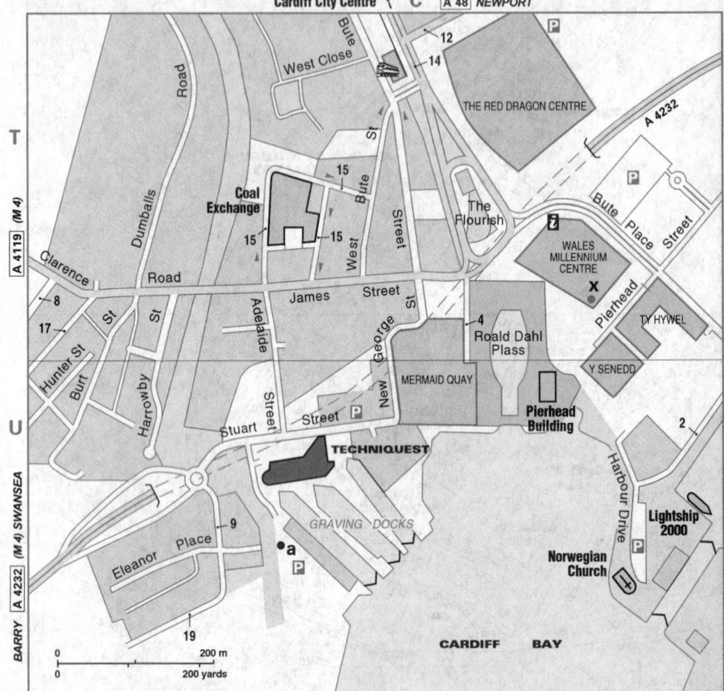

Purple Poppadom

185a Cowbridge Rd East ✉ CF11 9AJ – ✆ (029) 2022 0026 – www.purplepoppadom.com – Closed 25-26 December, 1 January and Monday — Town plan: AX**n**

Menu 45 – Carte £ 20/36

Smart, modern, first floor Indian restaurant with bold purple décor. Classic combinations are cooked in a modern style and given a personal twist; dishes are refined and flavoursome, with seafood being particularly popular.

'Bully's

5 Romilly Cres. ✉ CF11 9NP – ✆ (029) 2022 1905 – www.bullysrestaurant.co.uk – Closed Christmas and Sunday dinner — Town plan: AX**x**

Menu £ 10 (weekday lunch)/35 – Carte £ 26/45

Welcoming neighbourhood bistro run by a passionate, hands-on owner. Simply furnished interior boasts a fascinating array of memorabilia. Classical cooking displays a strong Gallic edge; carefully prepared dishes feature quality ingredients.

Potted Pig

27 High St ✉ CF10 1PU – ✆ (029) 2022 4817 – www.thepottedpig.com – Closed 23 December-3 January, Monday and Sunday dinner — Town plan: BZ**s**

Menu £ 18 (weekday lunch) – Carte £ 24/44

Atmospheric restaurant in a stripped back former bank vault, with brick walls, barrel ceilings and a utilitarian feel. Lesser-known products and cuts of meat are used in robust, tasty dishes. The gin cocktails are a speciality.

Mint & Mustard

134 Whitchurch Rd ✉ CF14 3LZ – ✆ (029) 2062 0333 Town plan: AV**n**
– www.mintandmustard.com – Closed 25-26 December and 1 January
Menu £ 38 – Carte £ 16/32 – *(booking essential at dinner)*
Well-run, welcoming neighbourhood restaurant with a modern, laid-back feel; ask for a table in the front room. The chef's training in Kerala is reflected in the extensive menu of original, authentic Indian dishes and well-balanced spicing.

La Cuina

11 Kings Rd ✉ CF11 9BZ – ✆ (029) 2019 0265 Town plan: AX**v**
– www.lacuina.co.uk – Closed 25-27 December, Sunday and Monday
Menu £ 10 (weekday lunch) – Carte £ 26/45
A smart, well-stocked ground floor deli sells top quality Spanish produce; the simple, rustic upstairs restaurant serves authentic, flavourful Spanish dishes with strong Catalonian influences. Tapas at lunch and on Tues/Weds evenings.

Ffresh

Wales Millennium Centre, Bute Plas, Cardiff Bay Town plan: CT**x**
✉ CF10 5AL – ✆ (029) 2063 6465 – www.ffresh.org.uk – Closed 25 December, Mondays in low season and Sunday dinner
Menu £ 17 (lunch and early dinner) – Carte £ 22/35
Located within the striking, modern 'Wales Millennium Centre', overlooking the piazza and frequented by theatregoers. Large, airy interior with a relaxed atmosphere. Simple, classical cooking is founded on fresh Welsh ingredients.

Fish at 85 (N)

85 Pontcanna St ✉ CF11 9HS – ✆ (029) 2023 5666 Town plan: AV**a**
– www.fishat85.co.uk – Closed Monday
Menu £ 10 (weekday lunch)/25 – Carte £ 25/70 – *(booking essential at dinner)*
Simplicity is key at this unpretentious, pared-down restaurant, where a large fish counter displays the latest catch from the day boats. Choose your fish, your cooking method and your accompaniments, and let the chef do the rest.

CARMARTHEN

Carmarthenshire – Pop. 15 854 – See Regional map n°**33**-B3
London 219 mi – Fishguard 47 mi – Haverfordwest 32 mi – Swansea 27 mi
Michelin Road map 503-H28 – Michelin Green Guide WALES

at Felingwm Uchaf Northeast: 8 mi by A40 on B4310✉ Carmarthen

Allt y Golau Uchaf without rest

✉ SA32 7BB North : 0.5 mi on B 4310 – ✆ (01267) 290 455
– www.alltygolau.com – Closed 20 December-2 January
3 rm – £ 45 ££ 70
Converted farmhouse dating from 1812, up a steep slope on a two acre smallholding. Well-kept, rustic interior; neat, pine-furnished bedrooms have a homely feel. Extensive breakfasts feature local meats and eggs from their own hens.

at Llanllawddog Northeast: 8 mi by A485

Glangwili Mansion without rest

✉ SA32 7JE – ✆ (01267) 253 735 – www.glangwilimansion.co.uk – Closed 24-25 December
4 rm – £ 100/110 ££ 115/135
Part-17C mansion rebuilt in a Georgian style, set in a great location on the edge of the forest. The spacious interior features sleek tiled floors, contemporary artwork and bright, bold bedrooms with modern oak furnishings.

at Nantgaredig East: 5 mi by A4300 on A4310✉ Carmarthen

Y Polyn

✉ SA32 7LH South : 1 mi on B 4310 – ✆ (01267) 290 000
– www.ypolynrestaurant.co.uk – Closed Sunday dinner and Monday
Menu £ 14 (weekday lunch)/35 – Carte lunch £ 27/34 – *(booking advisable)*
Small, rustic, unfussy pub on a busy country road; close to a stream and boasting pleasant views. Cooking is stout, filling and British at heart, offering satisfying soups, fresh salads, slow-cooked meats and classical puddings.

COLWYN BAY (Bae Colwyn)

Conwy – Pop. 29 405 – See Regional map n°**32**-B1

London 237 mi – Birkenhead 50 mi – Chester 42 mi – Holyhead 41 mi

Michelin Road map 502-I24 and 503 – Michelin Green Guide WALES

Pen-y-Bryn

Pen-y-Bryn Rd, Upper Colwyn Bay ✉ LL29 6DD – Southwest : 1 mi by B 5113 – ✆ (01492) 533 360 – www.penybryn-colwynbay.co.uk – Closed 25-26 December and 1 January

Carte £ 20/51

Unassuming pub with a spacious, open-plan interior, a laid-back feel and impressive panoramic views over Colwyn Bay, especially from the garden and terrace. The extensive all-day menu ranges from pub classics to more adventurous fare.

at Rhos-on-Sea Northwest: 1 mi✉ Colwyn Bay

Plas Rhos House without rest

53 Cayley Promenade ✉ LL28 4EP – ✆ (01492) 543 698 – www.plasrhos.co.uk – Mid March-October

5 rm – £ 60/75 £ 80/105

Smartly refurbished 19C house with a pleasant terrace, on a small street overlooking the sea. Cosy lounge and bright, cheery breakfast room. Bedrooms have modern bathrooms and thoughtful extras such as chocolates and a decanter of sherry.

CONWY

Conwy – Pop. 3 873 – See Regional map n°**32**-B1

London 241 mi – Caernarfon 22 mi – Chester 46 mi – Holyhead 37 mi

Michelin Road map 502-I24 and 503 – Michelin Green Guide WALES

Castle

High St ✉ LL32 8DB – ✆ (01492) 582 800 – www.castlewales.co.uk

27 rm – £ 85/99 £ 130/186 – 1 suite

Rest *Dawson's* – Carte £ 28/43

Friendly, family-run former coaching inn whose distinctive granite and red-brick façade, added in the late 19C, gives it a Victorian appearance. Bedrooms vary in style; some have a country house feel, while others are more modern. Wide-ranging menu available in both the restaurant and the cosy bar-lounge.

Signatures

Aberconwy Resort and Spa ✉ LL32 8GA – Northwest 1.5 mi by A 547 – ✆ (01492) 583 513 – www.signaturesrestaurant.co.uk – Closed Monday and Tuesday

Menu £ 22 (weekday dinner) – Carte £ 33/42 – *(dinner only) (booking advisable)*

Stylish, contemporary restaurant with elegantly laid tables and a well-versed team; unusually set in a holiday park close to the sea. Menus showcase classically based dishes with a modern edge; several are marked out as 'signature' dishes.

Groes Inn with rm

✉ LL32 8TN South : 3 mi on B 5106 – ✆ (01492) 650 545 – www.groesinn.com

14 rm – £ 100/200 £ 125/200 Carte £ 21/42

Characterful beamed inn, beautifully set overlooking the estuary, in the foothills of Snowdonia. British favourites arrive in neat, generous portions and everything is homemade; the specials are often a little more adventurous. Tastefully styled bedrooms have lovely views; some boast terraces or balconies.

at Rowen South: 3.5 mi by B5106

Tir Y Coed

✉ LL32 8TP – ✆ (01492) 650 219 – www.tirycoed.com

7 rm (dinner included) – £ 120/170 £ 135/185

Rest – Carte £ 32/40 – *(dinner only) (bookings essential for non-residents)*

Late 19C house in a secluded valley at the foothills of Snowdonia. With mature gardens which are a haven for wildlife, this is an ideal spot for those who have come away to unwind. Cosy bedrooms feature smart, modern bathrooms. The intimate dining room offers a daily menu of tried-and-tested classics.

CORWEN

Denbighshire – Pop. 477 – See Regional map n°**32**-C2
London 201 mi – Cardiff 148 mi – Liverpool 46 mi – Stoke-on-Trent 65 mi
Michelin Road map 502-J25

Bison Grill at Rhug Estate

Rhug Estate Farm Shop ✉ LL21 OEH – West : 1.5 mi on A 5 – ✆ (01490) 411 100 – www.rhug.co.uk – Closed 25-26 December
Menu £ 17 – Carte £ 22/32 – *(lunch only)*
State-of-the-art farm shop built using local materials and eco-friendly fixtures. The smart brasserie serves breakfast, snacks and Aberdeen Angus and bison steaks; they also sell organically reared estate meats and Welsh goodies.

COWBRIDGE (Y Bont Faen)

The Vale of Glamorgan – Pop. 3 616 – See Regional map n°**33**-B4
London 170 mi – Cardiff 15 mi – Swansea 30 mi
Michelin Road map 503-J29

Huddarts

69 High St ✉ CF71 7AF – ✆ (01446) 774 645 – Closed 1 week Christmas-New Year, 1 week summer, 1 week autumn, Sunday dinner and Monday
Menu £ 20 (lunch) – Carte £ 26/35
Honest restaurant in an ancient market town; the husband cooks and the wife looks after the friendly service. Traditional décor with a stone fireplace and colourful tapestries. Carefully executed, classic dishes with good presentation.

Arboreal (N)

68 Eastgate ✉ CF71 7AB – ✆ (01446) 775 093 – www.arboreal.uk.com – Closed last 2 weeks January, Monday and Tuesday in winter
Carte £ 20/42
There's a lively, Antipodean vibe at this all-day bar and café, where the Australian chef uses local produce in dishes with a Mediterranean, Asian and North African edge. The wooden oven features highly and folk music accompanies.

CRICCIETH

Gwynedd – Pop. 1 753 – See Regional map n°**32**-B2
London 249 mi – Caernarfon 17 mi – Shrewsbury 85 mi
Michelin Road map 502-H25 – Michelin Green Guide WALES

Bron Eifion

✉ LL52 OSA West : 1 mi on A 497 – ✆ (01766) 522 385 – www.broneifion.co.uk
18 rm – †£ 95 ††£ 145
Rest *Garden* – Menu £ 20 (weekday lunch)/30 – Carte £ 28/42
Characterful country house built in 1883 for a wealthy slate merchant; the feature staircase is constructed from Oregon pitch pine, which he brought back from the USA. Spacious modern bedrooms; some with carved wooden beds from the Middle East. Lovely garden views and an extensive menu in the restaurant.

CRICKHOWELL (Crucywel)

Powys – Pop. 2 063 – See Regional map n°**33**-C4
London 169 mi – Abergavenny 6 mi – Brecon 14 mi – Cardiff 40 mi
Michelin Road map 503-K28 – Michelin Green Guide WALES

Gliffaes Country House

✉ NP8 1RH West : 3.75 mi by A 40 – ✆ (01874) 730 371 – www.gliffaeshotel.com – Closed 4-28 January
23 rm – †£ 108/128 ††£ 115/275 **Rest** – Menu £ 18/44 **s**
Impressive country house built in 1886 in semi-Italianate style, set in 32 acres of delightful grounds that lead down to the river. Spacious, well-appointed lounges and great views from terrace. Smart, individually styled bedrooms; some with balconies. Victorian-style restaurant; menus showcase Welsh produce.

Bear 

High St ✉ NP8 1BW – ✆ (01873) 810 408 – www.bearhotel.co.uk
36 rm – £ 80/135 £ 99/169 – 1 suite
Rest ***Bear*** – see restaurant listing
Well-known, family-run coaching inn filled with various charming rooms and dating from the 15C. Bedrooms are modern; the most characterful are in the main house and feature beams, four-posters and fireplaces; some have jacuzzis.

Glangrwyney Court without rest

✉ NP8 1ES Southeast : 2 mi on A 40 – ✆ (01873) 811 288 – www.glancourt.co.uk
8 rm – £ 75/120 £ 110/150
Passionately run country house with Georgian origins, featuring a large lounge and a high-ceilinged breakfast room. Fresh flowers and objets d'art cover every surface. Bedrooms boast rich fabrics, good facilities and country views.

Ty Gwyn without rest

Brecon Rd ✉ NP8 1DG – ✆ (01873) 811 625 – www.tygwyn.com – March-October
3 rm – £ 40/50 £ 75/85
Proudly run whitewashed guesthouse with a stream running through the pretty garden; take it all in from the conservatory breakfast room. Simple, traditional bedrooms. The owners have good local knowledge – one is a certified guide!

Bear

High St ✉ NP8 1BW – ✆ (01873) 810 408 – www.bearhotel.co.uk – Closed 25 December
Carte £ 21/41 – *(bookings not accepted)*
Well-maintained 15C coaching inn adorned with hanging baskets and full of nooks and crannies. The menu offers honest pub classics alongside more elaborate specials. Sit in the hugely characterful lounge-bar or more formal restaurant.

WALES

CROSS ASH ➜ See Abergavenny
Monmouthshire

CROSSGATES ➜ See Llandrindod Wells
Powys – Michelin Road map 503-J27

DEGANWY ➜ See Llandudno
Conwy – Michelin Road map 502-I24 and 503

DENBIGH
Denbighshire – Pop. 8 514 – See Regional map n°**32**-**C1**
London 215 mi – Cardiff 162 mi – Swansea 151 mi – Telford 70 mi
Michelin Road map 502-J24

Castle House without rest

Bull Ln ✉ LL16 3LY – ✆ (01745) 816 860 – www.castlehousebandb.co.uk – Closed Christmas
4 rm – £ 85/170 £ 145/170
By the ruins of the 16C cathedral, overlooking the Vale of Clwyd; its gardens incorporate the ancient town walls. Spacious bedrooms retain period character and the décor blends the old and new. Afternoon tea by the fire or in the garden.

DINAS CROSS ➜ See Newport (Pembrokeshire)
Pembrokeshire

DOLFOR
Powys – See Regional map n°**32**-**C2**
London 199 mi – Cardiff 93 mi – Oswestry 34 mi – Ludlow 39 mi
Michelin Road map 503-K26

Old Vicarage

✉ SY16 4BN North : 1.5 mi by A 483 – ✆ (01686) 629 051 – www.theoldvicaragedolfor.co.uk – Closed Christmas-New Year
4 rm ☕ – 🚹£ 55/90 🚹🚹£ 75/120 **Rest** – Menu £ 28/35
Extended 19C red-brick house – formerly a vicarage – with large gardens where they grow the produce used in their home-cooked meals. Classical, country house style lounge and dining room. Cosy bedrooms – named after local rivers – mix period furnishings with bright modern colours. Chutney, preserves and soaps are for sale and afternoon tea is served on arrival.

DOLGELLAU

Gwynedd – Pop. 2 688 – See Regional map n°**32-B2**
London 221 mi – Birkenhead 72 mi – Chester 64 mi – Shrewsbury 57 mi
Michelin Road map 502-I25 and 503 – Michelin Green Guide WALES

Penmaenuchaf Hall

Penmaenpool ✉ LL40 1YB – West : 1.75 mi on A 493 (Tywyn Rd) – ✆ (01341) 422 129 – www.penhall.co.uk – Closed 12-22 December and 4-17 January
14 rm ☕ – 🚹£ 120/185 🚹🚹£ 180/270 **Rest** – Menu £ 21/28 – Carte £ 45/55
Personally run Victorian house with wood panelling, ornate ceilings and original stained glass windows. Bedrooms cleverly blend the traditional and the modern; some have balconies overlooking the beautiful grounds, mountains and estuary. Friendly staff and a family feel. Formal conservatory dining room.

Ffynnon without rest

Love Ln, off Calder Rd ✉ LL40 1RR – ✆ (01341) 421 774 – www.ffynnontownhouse.com – Closed Christmas
6 rm ☕ – 🚹£ 100/200 🚹🚹£ 150/200
Spacious Victorian house which once operated as a cottage hospital. Original features and period furnishings abound, offset by stylish modern designs which pay great attention to detail. Keep your wine and snacks in the pantry and dine on homemade crumpets in the morning. They even have an outdoor hot tub.

Y Meirionnydd

Smithfield Sq ✉ LL40 1ES – ✆ (01341) 422 544 – www.themeirionnydd.com – Closed Christmas and New Year
5 rm ☕ – 🚹£ 65/125 🚹🚹£ 85/125
Rest – Menu £ 27 – *(dinner only) (bookings essential for non-residents)*
Double-fronted house in the heart of a small town; Gwynedd was known as Meirionnydd up until the 1970s. Simple, modern, homely style with a small bar and a snug basement restaurant. Bedrooms are decorated in subtle hues and have very comfy beds. Hearty breakfasts and traditional dinners with a modern twist.

Tyddyn Mawr without rest

Islawdref, Cader Rd ✉ LL40 1TL – Southwest : 2.5 mi by Tywyn rd on Cader Idris rd – ✆ (01341) 422 331 – www.wales-guesthouse.co.uk – Closed December-January
3 rm ☕ – 🚹£ 65 🚹🚹£ 85
A peaceful haven on a secluded sheep farm; located at the foot of Cader Idris mountain and boasting stunning views. Immaculately kept bedrooms have handmade Welsh furnishings and plenty of extras; one has a balcony, another, a terrace. Great hospitality. 5 course breakfasts beside the impressive inglenook.

at Llanelltyd Northwest: 2.25 mi by A470 on A496

Mawddach

✉ LL40 2TA – ✆ (01341) 421 752 – www.mawddach.com – Closed 2 weeks November, 1 week January, 1 week spring, Sunday dinner, Monday,Tuesday and Wednesday dinner
Carte £ 28/39
Stylish barn conversion run by two brothers and set on the family farm. The terrace and airy first floor dining room offer superb views over the mountains and estuary. Unfussy cooking uses farm-bred meats and displays Italian influences.

DOLYDD → See Caernarfon

Gwynedd

WALES

FELINGWM UCHAF → See Carmarthen
Carmarthenshire

FISHGUARD
Pembrokeshire – Pop. 3 419 – See Regional map n°**33**-A3
London 265 mi – Cardiff 114 mi – Gloucester 176 mi – Holyhead 169 mi
Michelin Road map 503-F28 – Michelin Green Guide WALES

Manor Town House without rest
11 Main St ✉ SA65 9HG – ✆ (01348) 873 260 – www.manortownhouse.com – Closed 24-26 December
6 rm – †£ 65/85 ††£ 85/110
Well-run, listed Georgian townhouse, boasting fabulous harbour views. Stylish, elegant lounges and individually designed, antique-furnished bedrooms; some in art deco and some in Victorian styles. Tasty breakfasts; charming owners.

GLYNARTHEN
Ceredigion – See Regional map n°**33**-B3
London 231 mi – Birmingham 152 mi – Bristol 131 mi – Leicester 185 mi

Penbontbren without rest
Glynarthen ✉ SA44 6PE – North : 1 mi taking first left at crossroads then next left onto unmarked lane – ✆ (01239) 810 248 – www.penbontbren.com – Closed Christmas
5 rm – †£ 85/95 ††£ 99/110
Converted farm buildings surrounded by an attractive landscaped garden and 35 acres of rolling countryside. Spacious, stylish bedrooms; each has a sitting room, a mini bar, a coffee machine and a patio. The smart breakfast room features exposed stone, bold wallpaper, Portmeirion china and an extensive menu.

GRESFORD
Wrexham – Pop. 5 010 – See Regional map n°**32**-C1
London 199 mi – Rhyl 33 mi – Chester 10 mi
Michelin Road map 502-L24

Pant-yr-Ochain
Old Wrexham Rd ✉ LL12 8TY – South : 1 mi – ✆ (01978) 853 525 – www.pantyrochain-gresford.co.uk
Carte £ 21/60
A classic country manor house in disguise, with wattle and daub walls and mature gardens stretching down to a lake. The daily changing menu offers hearty, wholesome, all-day dishes, ranging from pub classics to more modern fare.

GROESLON → See Caernarfon
Gwynedd

HARLECH
Gwynedd – Pop. 1 762 – See Regional map n°**32**-B2
London 241 mi – Chester 72 mi – Dolgellau 21 mi
Michelin Road map 502-H25 and 503 – Michelin Green Guide WALES

Castle Cottage with rm
Pen Llech ✉ LL46 2YL – by B 4573 – ✆ (01766) 780 479 – www.castlecottageharlech.co.uk – Closed 3 weeks November
7 rm – †£ 85/125 ††£ 130/175
Menu £ 35/50 – *(dinner only) (booking essential)*
Sweet little cottage behind Harlech Castle, with a cosy yet surprisingly contemporary interior. Start with canapés and an aperitif in the lounge; the table is yours for the evening. Classical menus feature local produce and modern touches. Spacious bedrooms have smart bathrooms and stunning mountain views.

HAVERFORDWEST (Hwlffordd)
Pembrokeshire – Pop. 14 596 – See Regional map n°**33**-A3
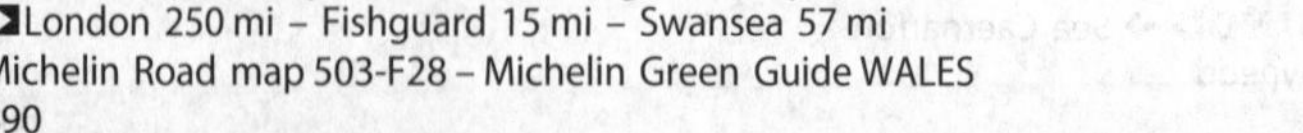
London 250 mi – Fishguard 15 mi – Swansea 57 mi
Michelin Road map 503-F28 – Michelin Green Guide WALES

Lower Haythog Farm without rest

Spittal ✉ SA62 5QL – Northeast : 5 mi on B 4329 – ✆ (01437) 731 279 – www.lowerhaythogfarm.co.uk

4 rm – £ 40/60 £ 75/85

Welcoming guesthouse with mature gardens, part-dating from the 14C and set on a working dairy farm. Cosy bedrooms feature bespoke cherry wood furniture and organic toiletries. Pleasant lounge and conservatory. Aga-cooked breakfasts.

Paddock

✉ SA62 5QL Northeast : 5 mi on B 4329 – ✆ (01437) 731 531 – www.thepaddockwales.co.uk

3 rm – £ 60/70 £ 80/90 **Rest** – Menu £ 24

Contemporary guesthouse on a working dairy farm. Comfy lounge with books, board games and a wood-burning stove. Modern bedrooms feature chunky wood furniture and sleigh beds made up with Egyptian cotton. Home-cooked meals rely on local and market produce; eggs are from their own hens.

HAWARDEN (Penarlâg)

Flintshire – Pop. 1 858 – See Regional map n°**32**-C1

London 205 mi – Chester 9 mi – Liverpool 17 mi – Shrewsbury 45 mi

Michelin Road map 502-K24

Glynne Arms

3 Glynne Way ✉ CH3 3NS – ✆ (01244) 569 988 – www.theglynnearms.co.uk

Menu £ 23 – Carte £ 19/40

200 year old coaching inn opposite Hawarden Castle; owned by the descendants of PM William Gladstone. Choose from 'Family Classics', steaks from the estate or more modern dishes with ambitious flavour combinations. Desserts are a highlight.

HOWEY → See Llandrindod Wells

Powys

KNIGHTON (Trefyclawdd)

Powys – Pop. 2 851 – See Regional map n°**33**-C3

London 162 mi – Birmingham 59 mi – Hereford 31 mi – Shrewsbury 35 mi

Michelin Road map 503-K26 – Michelin Green Guide WALES

Milebrook House

Ludlow Rd, Milebrook ✉ LD7 1LT – East : 2 mi on A 4113 – ✆ (01547) 528 632 – www.milebrookhouse.co.uk – Closed November-February Sunday and Monday

10 rm – £ 85/91 £ 144 **Rest** – Carte £ 29/40

Part-Georgian dower house surrounded by superb formal gardens filled with exotic plants; located in the Teme Valley and once home to explorer Wilfred Thesiger. Well-appointed lounges and spacious, comfortable bedrooms furnished in a country house style. Traditional restaurant showcases kitchen garden produce.

LLANARMON DYFFRYN CEIRIOG

Wrexham ✉ Llangollen (denbighshire) – See Regional map n°**32**-C2

London 196 mi – Chester 33 mi – Shrewsbury 32 mi

Michelin Road map 502-K25 and 503

Hand at Llanarmon with rm

✉ LL20 7LD – ✆ (01691) 600 666 – www.thehandhotel.co.uk – Closed 25 December

13 rm – £ 45/65 £ 90/128

Menu £ 15 (weekday lunch) – Carte £ 19/35

Rustic, personally run inn with stone walls, open fires and ancient beams, providing a warm welcome and wholesome meals to travellers through the lush Ceiriog Valley. Generous portions of fresh, flavoursome cooking. Cosy bedrooms offer hill views and modern bathrooms; most have a roll-top bath.

LLANDDERFEL

Gwynedd – Pop. 4 500 – See Regional map n°**32**-C2

London 210 mi – Cardiff 157 mi – Birmingham 97 mi – Liverpool 72 mi

Palé Hall

rm,

Palé Estate ⊠ LL23 7PS – ✆ (01678) 530 285 – www.palehall.co.uk

17 rm – £ 90/155 £ 125/210 – 2 suites **Rest** – Menu £ 25 (lunch)/35

Impressive Victorian house with lovely marquetry, fine oil paintings and a Scottish hunting lodge feel. Beautiful wood-panelled hall and traditional lounges; bedrooms boast period fireplaces and antique furniture. Classical menu in the elegant dining room. They even produce their own hydro-electricity here!

LLANDDEWI SKIRRID → See Abergavenny

Monmouthshire

LLANDEILO

Carmarthenshire – Pop. 1 731 – See Regional map n°**33**-B3

London 218 mi – Brecon 34 mi – Carmarthen 15 mi – Swansea 25 mi

Michelin Road map 503-I28 – Michelin Green Guide WALES

Plough Inn

rm,

Rhosmaen ⊠ SA19 6NP – Northeast : 1 mi on A 40 – ✆ (01558) 823 431 – www.ploughrhosmaen.com – Closed 26 December

23 rm – £ 75/85 £ 95/120

Rest – Menu £ 10 (lunch and early dinner)/29 – Carte £ 22/38

Powder blue inn with a contemporary interior and pleasant country views. Stylish, wood-furnished bedrooms feature good modern facilities; the best come with balconies and whirlpool baths. Small bar and gym. Various different rooms are used for informal lunches and more substantial dinners.

Fronlas without rest

7 Thomas St. ⊠ SA19 6LB – ✆ (01558) 824 733 – www.fronlas.com

4 rm – £ 55/100 £ 65/120

Old Edwardian house furnished in a contemporary style. Smart bedrooms display funky wallpapers, bold fabrics and stylish bathrooms. They operate an admirable sustainability ethos with solar panels, recycling bins and organic breakfasts.

LLANDENNY → See Usk

Monmouthshire – Michelin Road map 503-L28

LLANDOVERY

Carmarthenshire – Pop. 2 065 – See Regional map n°**33**-B3

London 207 mi – Cardiff 61 mi – Swansea 37 mi – Merthyr Tydfil 34 mi

Michelin Road map 503-I28

New White Lion

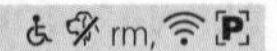

43 Stone St ⊠ SA20 0BZ – ✆ (01550) 720 685 – www.newwhitelion.com – Closed 25-27 December

6 rm – £ 100 £ 120/160 **Rest** – Menu £ 22/28 – *(dinner only)*

Laid-back, Grade II listed former pub, in a small town – now a stylish hotel. Comfortable lounge with an honesty bar. Smart, individually designed bedrooms are named after folklore characters and boast contemporary fabrics and furnishings. Cosy designer restaurant, where menus feature seasonal local produce.

LLANDRILLO

Denbighshire – Pop. 1 048 – ⊠ Corwen – See Regional map n°**32**-C2

London 210 mi – Chester 40 mi – Dolgellau 26 mi – Shrewsbury 46 mi

Michelin Road map 502-J25 and 503

Tyddyn Llan (Bryan Webb) with rm
LL21 0ST – (01490) 440 264 – *www.tyddynllan.co.uk* – *Closed last 2 weeks January*
13 rm – £ 110/150 £ 130/220
Menu £ 29/55 – Carte £ 42/55 – *(dinner only and lunch Friday-Sunday) (booking essential)*
Attractive former shooting lodge in a rural, valley location, surrounded by lovely gardens and run by a committed husband and wife team. Spacious country house lounge and two interconnecting dining rooms. Hearty, satisfying cooking is based around the classics, with daily menus providing extensive choice. Smart, luxurious bedrooms offer a good level of facilities.
→ Grilled lobster with coriander, lime and ginger butter. Rack of lamb with peas, artichokes, broad beans and mint. Panna cotta with blood orange and grappa.

LLANDRINDOD WELLS

Powys – Pop. 5 309 – See Regional map n°**33-C3**
London 204 mi – Brecon 29 mi – Carmarthen 60 mi – Shrewsbury 58 mi
Michelin Road map 503-J27 – Michelin Green Guide WALES

Metropole rm, rest,
Temple St LD1 5DY – (01597) 823 700 – *www.metropole.co.uk*
110 rm – £ 89/149 £ 99/159 – 10 suites
Rest – Carte £ 21/34 **s** – *(dinner only and Sunday lunch)*
Rest *Spencer's* – Carte £ 20/36 **s**
Large green hotel run for many years by the Baird-Murray family; popular with both leisure and business guests courtesy of its many lounges, conference rooms and leisure facilities. Spacious bedrooms offer good amenities; the tower rooms are popular. Smart brasserie with extensive classical menus; bright fine dining restaurant showcases local produce.

at Crossgates Northeast: 3.5 mi on A483 Llandrindod Wells

Guidfa House without rest
LD1 6RF – (01597) 851 241 – *www.guidfahouse.co.uk*
6 rm – £ 70/97 £ 90/117
Georgian gentleman's residence with a pleasant garden, smart breakfast room and period lounge displaying an original cast iron rose on the ceiling. Bright, airy bedrooms; the best is in the coach house. Friendly owners serve tea on arrival.

at Howey South: 1.5 mi by A483 Llandrindod Wells

Acorn Court without rest
Chapel Rd LD1 5PB – *Northeast : 0.5 mi* – (01597) 823 543 – *www.acorncourt.co.uk* – *Closed 24-27 December*
3 rm – £ 40/80 £ 75/85
Chalet-style house set in 40 acres, with views over rolling countryside towards a river and lake. Welcoming owner and a real family feel. Spacious, well-kept bedrooms come with good extras. Try the Welsh whisky porridge for breakfast.

LLANDUDNO

Conwy – Pop. 15 371 – See Regional map n°**32-B1**
London 243 mi – Birkenhead 55 mi – Chester 47 mi – Holyhead 43 mi
Michelin Road map 502-I24 and 503 – Michelin Green Guide WALES

Bodysgallen Hall rm,
Royal Welsh Way LL30 1RS – *Southeast : 2 mi on A 470* – (01492) 584 466 – *www.bodysgallen.com*
31 rm – £ 159/349 £ 179/425 – 21 suites
Rest *Dining Room* – see restaurant listing
Rest *1620* – Menu £ 17 (weekday dinner) – Carte £ 22/35 **s** – *(closed Sunday and Monday-Wednesday November-April)*
Stunning, National Trust owned country house with a 13C tower, 200 acres of delightful gardens and parkland, and a superb outlook to the mountains beyond. Welcoming, open-fired hall and characterful wood-panelled lounge. Antique-furnished bedrooms: some set in cottages and some affording splendid Snowdon views. Simple, traditional dishes served in the 1620 bistro.

WALES

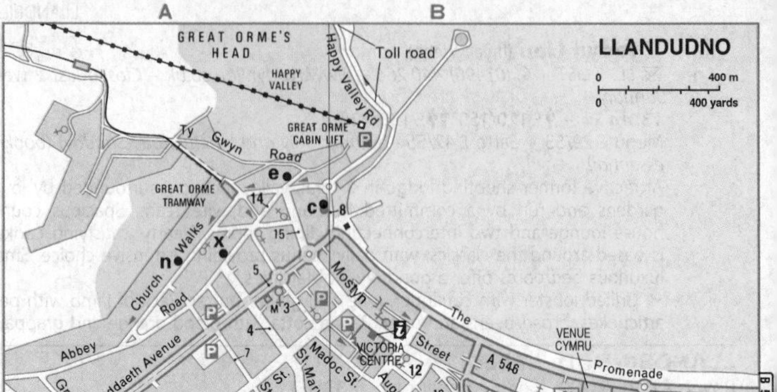

WALES

LLANDUDNO

- Chapel St . . . . **A** 3
- Deganwy Ave . . . . **A** 4
- Gloddaeth St . . . . **A** 5
- Maelgwyn Rd . . . . **A** 7
- Mostyn Champneys Retail Park . . . . **B**
- Mostyn St . . . . **B**
- North Parade . . . . **AB** 8
- Oxford Rd . . . . **B** 10
- Trinity Square . . . . **B** 12
- Tudno St . . . . **A** 14
- Tudor Crescent . . . . **B** 13
- Upper Mostyn St . . . . **A** 15
- Vaughan St . . . . **B** 16
- Victoria Centre . . . . **B**

Empire

rm,

73 Church Walks ✉ *LL30 2HE – (01492) 860 555* Town plan: A**e**
– www.empirehotel.co.uk – Closed 20-31 December
57 rm – £ 70/140 £ 110/170 – 1 suite
Rest *Watkins and Co.* – Menu £ 23 – *(dinner only and Sunday lunch)*
Family-run hotel – a former Victorian shopping arcade – with a grand columned façade, its interior hung with chandeliers and Russell Flint prints. Well-equipped gym and good-sized pool. Smartly dressed bedrooms with sleek, modern bathrooms; No. 72 is the most spacious. Set price menu in elegant Watkins.

Osborne House

17 North Par ✉ *LL30 2LP – (01492) 860 330* Town plan: A**c**
– www.osbornehouse.co.uk – Closed 20-31 December
6 rm – £ 130/185 £ 130/185
Rest *Osborne's Cafe and Grill* – see restaurant listing
Smart townhouse overlooking the bay. All of the bedrooms are large, luxurious suites and have stunning, almost whimsical styles; they boast canopied beds, spacious sitting rooms with Victorian fireplaces and marble bathrooms with double-ended, roll-top baths.

St Tudno
North Par ✉ LL30 2LP – ✆ (01492) 874 411 Town plan: A**c**
– www.st-tudno.co.uk
18 rm – †£ 80/95 ††£ 90/300 – 1 suite
Rest ***Terrace*** – see restaurant listing
Long-standing, personally run seaside hotel, set opposite the old Victorian pier. Classical sitting room and warm bar-lounge afford bay views. Well-kept, warmly furnished bedrooms with mini-bars; some have four-posters and whirlpool baths.

Escape Boutique B&B without rest
48 Church Walks ✉ LL30 2HL – ✆ (01492) 877 776 Town plan: A**n**
– www.escapebandb.co.uk – Closed 1 week Christmas
9 rm – †£ 74/125 ††£ 89/140
Attractive Arts and Crafts house with stained glass windows, parquet floors and a chic, modern interior that sets it apart. Stylish lounge and spacious, contemporary bedrooms; those on the top floor have a stunning view of the bay.

Lympley Lodge without rest
Colwyn Rd ✉ LL30 3AL – East : 2.5 mi on B 5115 – ✆ (01492) 549 304
– www.lympleylodge.co.uk – Closed mid December-February
3 rm – †£ 50/55 ††£ 80/85
Detached Victorian house close to the Little Orme headland; built in 1870 as a summer residence for a local family. Antique-filled lounge with views of the headland and bay. Individually themed bedrooms come with good extras and sea outlooks. Hearty breakfasts of local produce taken at antique tables.

Abbey Lodge without rest
14 Abbey Rd ✉ LL30 2EA – ✆ (01492) 878 042 Town plan: A**x**
– www.abbeylodgeuk.com – March- October
4 rm – †£ 45/50 ††£ 75/80
Welcoming terraced property – built in the early 1850s as a gentleman's residence and retaining its Victorian style. Individually decorated bedrooms with modern touches; all have baths. Cosy lounge and communal breakfasts from an extensive menu. Pleasant rear garden boasts views up to the Great Orme.

Sefton Court without rest
49 Church Walks ✉ LL30 2HL – ✆ (01492) 875 235 Town plan: A**n**
– www.seftoncourt-hotel.co.uk – Easter-October
10 rm – †£ 50/55 ††£ 74/80
Substantial Victorian house in an elevated position, affording good town views. Original features include pretty stained glass windows and interesting friezes. Contemporary bedrooms provide a pleasant contrast with their stylish wallpapers.

Dining Room – Bodysgallen Hall Hotel
Royal Welsh Way ✉ LL30 1RS – Southeast : 2 mi on A 470 – ✆ (01492) 584 466
– www.bodysgallen.com – Closed Tuesday November-March and Monday
Menu £ 20 (weekday lunch)/49 – *(booking essential)*
Located within a beautiful country house which part-dates from the 13C, and overlooking its delightful gardens, is this grand, formal dining room with clothed tables and an inglenook fireplace. Well-judged, modern interpretations of classically based dishes; simpler offerings at lunch. Smart dress required.

Terrace – St Tudno Hotel
North Par ✉ LL30 2LP – ✆ (01492) 874 411 Town plan: A**c**
– www.st-tudno.co.uk
Menu £ 20 – Carte £ 31/48 **s**
Smart, uniquely styled restaurant with murals of Lake Como running the length of the wall and chandeliers adorned with flowers. Set within a personally run seaside hotel and offering a modern, seasonal menu. Professional service.

WALES

XX **Osborne's Cafe and Grill** – Osborne House Hotel
17 North Par ✉ LL30 2LP – ☎ (01492) 860 330 Town plan: Ac
– www.osbornehouse.co.uk – Closed 20-31 December
Menu £ 13 (weekday lunch)/23 – Carte £ 22/43
Victorian-style, all-day hotel restaurant with an opulent lounge and an ornate dining room boasting Corinthian columns, gilded mirrors and chandeliers. All-encompassing menu ranges from tasty afternoon tea to flavourful British classics.

at Deganwy South: 2.75 mi on A546 -(A)✉ Llandudno

Quay H. & Spa
Deganwy Quay ✉ LL31 9DJ – ☎ (01492) 564 100 – www.quayhotel.co.uk
74 rm – †£ 95/350 ††£ 95/350 – 19 suites
Rest *Grill Room* – see restaurant listing
Smart hotel by the Conwy Estuary, in a modern marina development. Large guest areas have superb harbour and castle outlooks. Extensive meeting facilities; excellent pool and spa. Contemporary bedrooms and penthouses with balconies.

XX **Grill Room** – Quay Hotel & Spa
Deganwy Quay ✉ LL31 9DJ – ☎ (01492) 564 100 – www.quayhotel.co.uk
Menu £ 20/33 – Carte £ 34/55
Smart designer restaurant with a cosy bar, a large glass wine cave and a superb terrace looking over the estuary to Conwy Castle. Extensive menus offer locally sourced meat, seafood and grill dishes; good value set option at lunch.

WALES

LLANDYBIE

Carmarthenshire – Pop. 2 813 – See Regional map n°**33**-B4
London 204 mi – Birmingham 122 mi – Bristol 97 mi – Leicester 192 mi
Michelin Road map 503-I28

XX **Valans**
Primrose House, 29 High St ✉ SA18 3HX – ☎ (01269) 851 288
– www.valans.co.uk – Closed Sunday and Monday
Menu £ 12 (weekdays)/23 – Carte £ 17/41 – *(booking advisable)*
Simple little restaurant run by a local and his wife, with a bright red, white and black colour scheme. Fresh, unfussy dishes rely on local produce and offer classical flavour combinations. Good value light lunches; more elaborate dinners.

LLANDYRNOG

Denbighshire – See Regional map n°**32**-C1
London 211 mi – Cardiff 158 mi – Birmingham 98 mi – Liverpool 34 mi
Michelin Road map 503-J/K24

 **Pentre Mawr** 
✉ LL16 4LA North : 1.25 mi by B 5429 taking left hand fork after 0.75 mi
– ☎ (01824) 790 732 – www.pentremawrcountryhouse.co.uk – Closed Christmas, Monday and Tuesday
12 rm – †£ 120/150 ††£ 150/190 **Rest** – Menu £ 35
Unusual guesthouse on a 200 acre estate. Bedrooms in the Georgian house have a classical feel and boast jacuzzi baths – those in the outbuildings are more contemporary; there are also 6 luxurious African lodges with hot tubs. Characterful, antique-filled guest areas and modern conservatory. Classical cooking.

LLANELLI

Carmarthenshire – Pop. 43 878 – See Regional map n°**33**-B4
London 202 mi – Cardiff 54 mi – Swansea 12 mi
Michelin Road map 503-H28

XX **Sosban**

The Pump House, North Dock ✉ SA15 2LF – ✆ (01554) 270 020 – www.sosbanrestaurant.com – Closed 25 December, 1 January and Sunday dinner

Menu £ 20 – Carte £ 24/40

Built in 1872 to house a pumping engine for the adjacent docks. Impressively restored interior with a relaxed lounge-bar and airy dining room with exposed stone walls. Large à la carte offers tasty, well-prepared dishes; good value lunches.

LLANELLTYD → See Dolgellau

Gwynedd – Michelin Road map 503-I25

LLANERCHYMEDD → See Anglesey (Isle of)

– Michelin Road map 502-G24

LLANFAIRFECHAN

Conwy – Pop. 3 637 – ✉ Conwy – See Regional map n°**32**-**B1**

London 247 mi – Cardiff 200 mi – Swansea 166 mi – Telford 107 mi

Michelin Road map 502-I24

Grove without rest

Ffordd Aber ✉ LL33 OHR – West : 0.75 m on Bangor rd – ✆ (01248) 369 111 – www.thegrovenorthwales.co.uk

3 rm – £ 60/80 £ 65/90

Originally built for an Edwardian cockle merchant, this house has been tastefully modernised, retaining its period features and showcasing the owners' collection of books, antiques and Welsh porcelain. Cosy bedrooms are named after rivers.

LLAN FFESTINIOG

Gwynedd – See Regional map n°**32**-**B2**

London 234 mi – Bangor 35 mi – Wrexham 52 mi

Michelin Green Guide WALES

Cae'r Blaidd Country House

✉ LL41 4PH North : 0.75 mi by A 470 on Blaenau Rd – ✆ (01766) 762 765 – www.caerblaidd.com – Closed January

3 rm – £ 55 £ 85 **Rest** – Menu £ 20 **s** – *(dinner only)*

It's all about mountain pursuits at this alpine-themed guesthouse: the welcoming owners are mountain guides; ice axes, crampons and skis fill the walls; and there's a climbing wall, a drying room and even equipment for hire in the basement. Dine on local produce while taking in the stunning panoramic view.

LLANFIHANGEL → See Llanfyllin

Powys

LLANFIHANGEL-Y-CREUDDYN

Ceredigion – See Regional map n°**33**-**B3**

London 235 mi – Cardiff 109 mi – Birmingham 121 mi – Liverpool 123 mi

Michelin Road map 503-I26

Y Ffarmers

✉ SY23 4LA – ✆ (01974) 261 275 – www.yffarmers.co.uk – Closed first week January, Monday, Tuesday and Sunday dinner

Menu £ 12 (weekday lunch) – Carte £ 20/33

Life in this remote, picturesque valley revolves around the passionately run village pub. Sit in the locals bar or the homely restaurant which opens onto the garden. Regional and valley produce features in satisfying, original dishes.

LLANFYLLIN

Powys – Pop. 1 105 – See Regional map n°**32**-**C2**

London 188 mi – Chester 42 mi – Shrewsbury 24 mi – Welshpool 11 mi

Michelin Road map 502-K25 and 503 – Michelin Green Guide WALES

WALES

Seeds

5 Penybryn Cottages, High St ✉ SY22 5AP – ✆ (01691) 648 604 – Closed Wednesday in winter and Sunday-Tuesday
Menu £ 24 (weekday dinner) – Carte lunch £ 19/33
Converted 16C red-brick cottages in a sleepy village; run with pride by a friendly husband and wife team. Cosy, pine-furnished room with an old range and a country kitchen feel. Unfussy, classical dishes and comforting homemade desserts.

at Llanfihangel Southwest: 5 mi by A490 and B4393 on B4382 ✉ Llanfyllin

Cyfie Farm

✉ SY22 5JE South : 1.5 mi by B 4382 – ✆ (01691) 648 451 – www.cyfiefarm.co.uk – March- October
3 rm – †£ 100/125 ††£ 99/115 **Rest** – Menu £ 30
17C longhouse and barn conversions, set in a great spot and boasting far-reaching views across the valley. Mix of bedrooms and self-catering cottages; some with beams and wood-burning stoves. Spacious lounges and communal dining, with porridge cooked overnight on the Aga and Cordon Bleu dinners.

LLANGAFFO → See Anglesey (Isle of)

LLANGAMMARCH WELLS

Powys – See Regional map n°**33**-B3
London 200 mi – Brecon 17 mi – Builth Wells 8 mi – Cardiff 58 mi
Michelin Road map 503-J27

Lake Country House and Spa

rm,

✉ LD4 4BS East : 0.75 mi – ✆ (01591) 620 202 – www.lakecountryhouse.co.uk
31 rm – †£ 145/210 ††£ 195/260 – 8 suites
Rest – Menu £ 45 – *(booking essential)*
Extended, part-timbered 19C country house in 50 acres of mature gardens and parkland, with a pond, a lake and a river. Comfortable lounges and well-appointed bedrooms with antiques and extras; some are set in the lodge. The impressive spa overlooks the river. Breakfast is in the orangery; the elegant restaurant is perfect for a classical, candlelit dinner.

LLANGENNITH

Swansea – See Regional map n°**33**-B4
London 207 mi – Cardiff 61 mi – Swansea 17 mi – Newport 71 mi
Michelin Road map 503-H29

Blas Gŵyr

✉ SA3 1HU – ✆ (01792) 386 472 – www.blasgwyr.co.ok
4 rm – †£ 115 ††£ 125 **Rest** – Menu £ 25
Converted farm buildings on the Gower Peninsula. Smart, well-equipped bedrooms are set around a courtyard and feature local fabrics and slate bathrooms with underfloor heating. The small stone-walled coffee shop cum dining room serves simple, often Tuscan-based dinners; cockles are popular at breakfast.

LLANGOLLEN

Denbighshire – Pop. 3 466 – See Regional map n°**32**-C2
London 194 mi – Chester 23 mi – Holyhead 76 mi – Shrewsbury 30 mi
Michelin Road map 502-K25 – Michelin Green Guide WALES

Manorhaus Llangollen with rm

10 Hill St ✉ LL20 8EU – ✆ (01978) 860 775 – www.manorhaus.com
6 rm – †£ 83/125 ††£ 115/180 Menu £ 25/33 – *(dinner only)*
Stylish dining room in a double-fronted Victorian house in the centre of town. Weekly changing dinner menu of carefully cooked, classical dishes with some adventurous flavours; Welsh ingredients include the cheese platter. Funky, modern bar lounge. Smart, contemporary bedrooms and a hot tub with a view.

LLANGRANNOG

Ceredigion – See Regional map n°**33**-**B3**

London 241 mi – Caerdydd / Cardiff 96 mi – Aberystwyth / Aberyswyth 30 mi – Caerfyrddin / Carmarthen 28 mi

Michelin Road map 503-G27

Grange without rest

Pentregat ✉ SA44 6HW – Southeast : 3 mi by B 4321 on A 487 – ☎ (01239) 654 121 – www.grangecountryhouse.co.uk – Restricted opening in winter

4 rm – †£ 55/60 ††£ 80/90

Traditional Georgian manor house with a pretty breakfast room and individually decorated bedrooms which feature brass beds and cast iron slipper baths. On arrival, the hospitable owner welcomes you with a pot of tea beside the fire.

LLANGYBI → See Usk

Monmouthshire – Michelin Road map 503-L29

LLANLLAWDDOG → See Carmarthen

Carmarthenshire

LLANRHIDIAN

Swansea – Pop. 512 – See Regional map n°**32**-**B4**

London 198 mi – Birmingham 146 mi – Bristol 95 mi – Leicester 190 mi

Michelin Road map 503-H29

Fairyhill with rm

Reynoldston ✉ SA3 1BS – West : 2.5 mi by Llangennith Rd – ☎ (01792) 390 139 – www.fairyhill.net – Closed 3 weeks January, 25-26 December, Monday and Tuesday in winter

8 rm – †£ 170/270 ††£ 190/290

Menu £ 20 (weekday lunch)/45 – Carte £ 29/38

Attractive Georgian country house with a lake and well-manicured gardens; take it all in from the red and gold dining room or from the terrace. Modern menus rely on seasonal Gower produce. Spacious bedrooms blend the traditional and the contemporary and come with good facilities. Charming guest areas include a cosy bar and contemporary lounge with a piano.

LLANRUG → See Caernarfon

Gwynedd – Michelin Road map 502-H24

LLANRWST

Conwy – Pop. 3 323 – See Regional map n°**32**-**B1**

London 229 mi – Holyhead 51 mi – Chester 54 mi

Michelin Road map 502-I24

Ffin y Parc Country House & Gallery Ⓝ

Betwys Rd ✉ LL26 0PT – South : 1.75 mi on A 470 – ☎ (01492) 642 070 – www.ffinyparc.com – Closed January

6 rm – †£ 120/165 ††£ 135/180 **Rest** – Carte £ 18/40

This Victorian slate house is an impressive art gallery, a comfy café and an likeable guesthouse all in one. The elegant, well-proportioned interior mixes the classic and the contemporary and has a slightly bohemian feel; bedrooms are bold and bathrooms are modern. Dinner is served on Fridays and Saturdays.

LLANWRDA

Carmarthenshire – Pop. 287 – See Regional map n°**33**-**B3**

London 199 mi – Cardiff 65 mi – Swansea 33 mi – Newport 64 mi

Michelin Road map 503-I28

Tŷ Llwyd Hir without rest

✉ *SA19 8AS North : 2 mi by A 482 turning right at caravan park – ✆ (01550) 777 362 – www.bandbwestwales.co.uk – Closed 24-25 December*

3 rm – 🚹£ 65 🚹🚹£ 75/90

Follow the long track past the old farm buildings to reach this lovely slate guest-house on the hillside, which overlooks the Black Mountains in the Brecon Beacons National Park. Smart, modern rooms mix the old and the new. The friendly owners keep three donkeys and the brood of hens supply the breakfast eggs.

LLANWRTYD WELLS

Powys – Pop. 630 – See Regional map n°**33**-B3

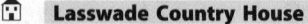

▶London 214 mi – Brecon 32 mi – Cardiff 68 mi – Carmarthen 39 mi

Michelin Road map 503-J27 – Michelin Green Guide WALES

Lasswade Country House

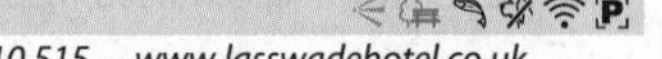

Station Rd ✉ LD5 4RW – ✆ (01591) 610 515 – www.lasswadehotel.co.uk

7 rm – 🚹£ 60/80 🚹🚹£ 90/120 **Rest** – Menu £ 34 – *(dinner only)*

Very proudly run Edwardian house, set on the edge of the town. Homely, book-filled lounge and conservatory breakfast room. Comfy, uncluttered bedrooms come in light hues and have pleasant country views. Smart dining room with polished wood tables; the traditional menu promotes local, sustainable produce.

Carlton Riverside with rm

Irfon Cres ✉ LD5 4SP – ✆ (01591) 610 248 – www.carltonriverside.com – Closed 23-30 December and Sunday

4 rm – 🚹£ 50 🚹🚹£ 65/100 Carte £ 27/47 – *(dinner only)*

Traditional stone building in the centre of the village, with two comfy lounges and a small bar filled with books and modern art. Well-spaced tables in the dining room, which overlooks the River Irfon. Concise menu utilises local produce; classic dishes have a modern touch. Neat, tidy, well-priced bedrooms.

WALES

LLECHRYD

Ceredigion – Pop. 875 – See Regional map n°**33**-A3

▶London 238 mi – Cardiff 93 mi – Swansea 53 mi – Newport 102 mi

Michelin Road map 503-G27

Hammet House

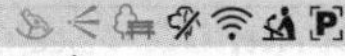

✉ *SA43 2QA – ✆ (01239) 682 382 – www.hammethouse.co.uk*

15 rm – 🚹£ 110/160 🚹🚹£ 145/220 **Rest** – Menu £ 40 – Carte £ 33/40

Attractive Georgian house built for a former Sheriff of London, Sir Benjamin Hammet. It has contemporary monochrome styling, quirky furnishings and a relaxed, bohemian feel. Bedrooms boast locally handmade beds, good facilities and views over the grounds. The smart restaurant offers appealing modern menus.

LLYSWEN

Powys ✉ Brecon – See Regional map n°**33**-C3

▶London 188 mi – Brecon 8 mi – Cardiff 48 mi – Worcester 53 mi

Michelin Road map 503-K27 – Michelin Green Guide WALES

Llangoed Hall

✉ *LD3 0YP Northwest : 1.25 mi on A 470 – ✆ (01874) 754 525 – www.llangoedhall.com*

23 rm – 🚹£ 175/250 🚹🚹£ 230/500

Rest *Llangoed Hall* – see restaurant listing

Homely country house beside the River Wye, redesigned by Sir Clough Williams-Ellis in 1910 and restored by the late Sir Bernard Ashley. Delightful lounges and sumptuous bedrooms feature rich fabrics, mullioned windows and antiques aplenty. The impressive art collection includes pieces by Whistler.

XXX **Llangoed Hall** N – Llangoed Hall Hotel
✉ LD3 0YP Northwest : 1.25 mi on A 470 – ✆ (01874) 754 525 – www.llangoedhall.com
Menu £ 85 **s** – Carte £ 57/79 – *(booking essential)*
A formal yet friendly team run this elegant country house restaurant in the Wye Valley. The décor and tableware are top quality, as are the ingredients – 65% of which are from within a 7 mile radius. Elaborate modern dishes use complex techniques; the 9 course tasting menu best represents the chef's skill.

MACHYNLLETH

Powys – Pop. 2 235 – See Regional map n°**32**-**B2**
London 220 mi – Shrewsbury 56 mi – Welshpool 37 mi
Michelin Road map 503-I26 – Michelin Green Guide WALES

Ynyshir Hall
Eglwysfach ✉ SY20 8TA – Southwest : 6 mi on A 487 – ✆ (01654) 781 209 – www.ynyshir-hall.co.uk – Closed January
10 rm – †£ 150/655 ††£ 205/710 – 3 suites
Rest *Ynyshir Hall* ✿ – see restaurant listing
Beautiful part-Georgian house set within a 1,000 acre RSPB reserve and run with pride and passion. Comfy lounges are decorated with the owner's eye-catching art. Sumptuous bedrooms have a chic, contemporary style yet retain their country house feel; the two most luxurious suites are situated in the grounds.

XXX ✿ **Ynyshir Hall** – Ynyshir Hall Hotel
Eglwysfach ✉ SY20 8TA – Southwest: 6 mi on A 487 – ✆ (01654) 781 209 – www.ynyshirhall.co.uk – Closed January
Menu £ 30/90 – *(booking essential)*
Set within a plush hotel, an opulent restaurant with azure blue walls, striking artwork and a summery vibe. The talented chef uses superb local and foraged ingredients to create original dishes with wonderfully balanced flavours; some are finished at the table, which adds a sense of theatre.
→ Mackerel sweet & sour. Salt-baked hogget. Yeast porridge with hazelnuts and raisins.

MENAI BRIDGE → See Anglesey (Isle of)

– Michelin Road map 502-H24

MOLD (Yr Wyddgrug)

Flintshire – Pop. 10 058 – See Regional map n°**32**-**C1**
London 211 mi – Chester 12 mi – Liverpool 22 mi – Shrewsbury 45 mi
Michelin Road map 502-K24 and 503 – Michelin Green Guide WALES

Glasfryn
Raikes Ln, Sychdyn ✉ CH7 6LR – North : 1 mi by A 5119 on Civic Centre rd (Theatr Clwyd) – ✆ (01352) 750 500 – www.glasfryn-mold.co.uk
Carte £ 21/31
Sizeable red-brick pub with Arts and Crafts styling and a terrace with a pleasant town outlook. Menus offer plenty of choice, from pub favourites to culinary classics. Portions are generous, prices are sensible and service is swift.

Tavern
Mold Rd, Alltami ✉ CH7 6LG – Northeast : 2.5 mi by A 5119 on A 494 – ✆ (01244) 550 485 – www.tavernrestaurant.co.uk
Carte £ 19/35
Modern-looking pub with heavy tables, leather chairs and a formal feel; in contrast, the cooking is hearty and comforting. Daily specials, particularly the market fish, prove popular; the 'Chef's Choice' and tasting menus are more refined.

MONMOUTH (Trefynwy)

Monmouthshire – Pop. 10 110 – See Regional map n°**33-C4**
London 135 mi – Abergavenny 19 mi – Cardiff 40 mi
Michelin Road map 503-L28 – Michelin Green Guide WALES

Stonemill

Rockfield ✉ NP25 5SW – West : 3.5 mi on B 4233 – ☎ (01600) 716 273 – www.thestonemill.co.uk – Closed 2 weeks January, 25-26 December, Sunday dinner and Monday
Menu £ 15 (lunch)/21 – Carte £ 30/40
Attractive 16C cider mill with exposed timbers and an old millstone at the centre of the characterful, rustic restaurant. Good value set menus are supplemented by a more ambitious evening à la carte. Dishes are hearty and classically based.

at Penallt South: 5 mi by B4293

The Inn at Penallt with rm

✉ NP25 4SE – ☎ (01600) 772 765 – www.theinnatpenallt.co.uk – Closed 5-22 January, Sunday dinner and Monday except bank holidays
4 rm – †£ 58 ††£ 80 Menu £ 16 (weekday lunch) – Carte £ 27/39
Proudly and personally run pub. Its neutrally hued rooms are furnished with heavy wood; for the best views, make for the conservatory. Menus offer good-sized dishes with classical roots. Bread is baked daily and the ice creams are homemade. Bedrooms are cosy, neat and tidy with modern facilities.

at Whitebrook South: 8.25 mi by A466✉ Monmouth

Crown at Whitebrook with rm

✉ NP25 4TX – ☎ (01600) 860 254 – www.crownatwhitebrook.co.uk – Closed 2 weeks January and Monday
8 rm – †£ 90/115 ††£ 115/140 Menu £ 24/65 – *(booking essential)*
Both the bedrooms and the cooking are modern and understated at this rustic house, where the atmosphere is intimate, relaxed and friendly. Menus showcase top quality local and foraged ingredients; descriptions are concise and the elegantly presented dishes are more complex than they first appear. You'll find this whitewashed property off the beaten track, in a wooded valley.
→ Scallops, chicory and blood orange. Roast duck breast, turnip and port purée. Poached pear with almond mousse, marzipan crumble and pear sorbet.

MONTGOMERY (Trefaldwyn)

Powys – Pop. 986 – See Regional map n°**32-C2**
London 194 mi – Birmingham 71 mi – Chester 53 mi – Shrewsbury 30 mi
Michelin Road map 503-K26 – Michelin Green Guide WALES

The Checkers (Stéphane Borie) with rm

Broad St ✉ SY15 6PN – ☎ (01686) 669 822 – www.thecheckersmontgomery.co.uk – Closed 2 weeks January, 1 week autumn, 25-26 December, Sunday, Monday and lunch Tuesday-Thursday
5 rm – †£ 100/150 ††£ 125/180 Carte £ 33/53 **s**
Charming 18C coaching inn on the main square of a hilltop town, with a characterful beamed lounge and a stylish restaurant split over two rooms. Monthly changing menus offer classical dishes that are executed with a deft touch, and flavours are sharply defined. Elegant bedrooms are furnished with antiques.
→ Salad of poached lobster with cucumber & lime jelly. Stuffed saddle of rabbit with confit shoulder & tarragon, butter beans and smoked bacon. Champagne rhubarb crumble soufflé.

MUMBLES (The) → See Swansea

Swansea – Michelin Road map 503-I29

NANTGAREDIG → See Carmarthen

Carmarthenshire – Michelin Road map 503-H28

NANT-Y-DERRY → See Abergavenny

Monmouthshire

NARBERTH

Pembrokeshire – Pop. 2 265 – See Regional map n°**33-A4**
London 234 mi – Cardiff 88 mi – Swansea 51 mi – Rhondda 79 mi
Michelin Road map 503-F28

Grove
Molleston ✉ SA67 8BX – South : 2 mi by A 478 on Herons Brook rd – ✆ (01834) 860 915 – www.thegrove-narberth.co.uk
20 rm – £ 170/310 £ 180/320 – 6 suites
Rest – Menu £ 28 (lunch)/49 **s**
Set in a charming rural location, the Grove comprises a 15C longhouse and an immaculately whitewashed property with Stuart and Victorian additions. Bedrooms blend boldly coloured walls and bright fabrics with more traditional furnishings; the spacious bathrooms boast every modern amenity. Seasonal menus offer creative, contemporary dishes with a classical base.

Canaston Oaks without rest
Canaston Bridge ✉ SA67 8DE – West : 3 mi by B 4314 and A 40 on A 4075 – ✆ (01437) 541 254 – www.canastonoaks.co.uk
7 rm – £ 85/140 £ 95/175
Converted longhouse and outbuildings in 35 acres of gardens and grasslands leading down to the river. Set around a courtyard water feature, the wood-furnished bedrooms boast fridges and DVD players; some have jacuzzis, others, patios.

NEWCASTLE EMLYN

Carmarthenshire – Pop. 1 883 – See Regional map n°**33-B3**
London 232 mi – Birmingham 156 mi – Bristol 121 mi – Leicester 189 mi
Michelin Road map 503-G27

Gwesty'r Emlyn
Bridge St ✉ SA38 9DU – ✆ (01239) 710 317 – www.gwestyremlynhotel.co.uk
29 rm – £ 80 £ 120 – 1 suite
Rest – Menu £ 11 (lunch)/29 – Carte £ 31/39
300 year old coaching inn set in the centre of town and concealing a surprisingly modern interior. Guest areas include a stylish lounge, a snug bar, a small fitness room and a sauna; bedrooms are contemporary and well-equipped. The smart restaurant offers a classic menu centred around local produce.

NEWPORT

Newport – Pop. 128 060 – See Regional map n°**33-C4**
London 145 mi – Bristol 31 mi – Cardiff 12 mi – Gloucester 48 mi
Michelin Road map 503-L29 – Michelin Green Guide WALES

Celtic Manor Resort
Coldra Woods ✉ NP18 1HQ – East : 3 mi on A 48 – ✆ (01633) 413 000 – www.celtic-manor.com
409 rm – £ 119/329 £ 142/366 – 19 suites
Rest *Terry M* – see restaurant listing
Rest *Rafters* – ✆ (01633) 410 262 – Menu £ 16 (lunch) – Carte dinner £ 25/63 **s**
Rest *Olive Tree* – ✆ (01633) 410 262 – Menu £ 33 **s** – *(dinner only and Sunday lunch)*
Rest *Le Patio* – ✆ (01633) 410 262 – Carte £ 28/52 **s** – *(dinner only)*
Vast resort hotel in 1,400 acres, boasting 3 golf courses, an impressive pool and spa, two floors of function rooms and even a shopping arcade. Mix of classical and modern bedrooms, which range from standard to presidential suites. Modern fine dining in Terry M; grills in Rafters, in the clubhouse; buffet and carvery in Olive Tree; and a French bistro menu in Le Patio.

Terry M – Celtic Manor Resort Hotel
Coldra Woods ✉ NP18 1HQ – East : 3 mi on A 48 – ✆ (01633) 413 000 – www.celtic-manor.com – Closed 6-28 January, Monday and Tuesday
Menu £ 23/50 **s**
Named after the owner of the huge hotel in which it's set. Comfy lounge for aperitifs and canapés; bright, contemporary dining room with well-spaced tables and cream leather chairs. Menus are modern and ambitious, and service is formal.

NEWPORT (Trefdraeth)

Pembrokeshire – Pop. 1 162 – See Regional map n°**33**-A3
London 258 mi – Fishguard 7 mi
Michelin Road map 503-F27 – Michelin Green Guide WALES

Cnapan

East St ✉ SA42 0SY – on A 487 – ☎ (01239) 820 575 – www.cnapan.co.uk – Closed January-mid-March and 25-26 December
5 rm – †£ 65 ††£ 95
Rest – Menu £ 26/32 – *(closed Tuesday) (dinner only) (booking essential)*
Keenly run, part-Georgian house in a busy coastal village. The bar and lounge have a homely feel. Well-maintained, compact bedrooms have a clean, modern style and smart shower rooms; a shared bath is available. The candlelit restaurant opens onto a large garden and offers an extensive menu of home cooking.

Llys Meddyg with rm

East St ✉ SA42 0SY – ☎ (01239) 820 008 – www.llysmeddyg.com – Closed Monday and Tuesday
8 rm – †£ 70/100 ††£ 100/160 Carte £ 29/43 – *(dinner only)*
Centrally located restaurant with a kitchen garden and a slightly bohemian style. Eat in the formal dining room or the characterful, laid-back cellar bar; the owner's father's art is displayed throughout. Cooking showcases local produce in ambitious, complex dishes. Modern bedrooms have a Scandinavian style.

at Dinas Cross West: 3.25 mi on A487

Y Garth without rest

Cae Tabor ✉ SA42 0XR – via un-named road opposite bus stop. – ☎ (01348) 811 777 – www.bedandbreakfast-pembrokeshire.co.uk – Closed 1 week Christmas
3 rm – †£ 90/110 ††£ 90/110
Welcoming pink-washed guesthouse in a small village. Comfy lounge with a conservatory extension where homemade cakes are served on arrival. Stylish bedrooms have bright, bold décor; 'Strumble Head' has views to the peninsula.

NEWTOWN

Powys – Pop. 11 357 – ✉ Blaenau Gwent – See Regional map n°**32**-C2
London 194 mi – Cardiff 98 mi – Birmingham 81 mi – Wolverhampton 69 mi
Michelin Road map 503-K26

Highgate without rest

Bettws Cedewain ✉ SY16 3LF – Northeast : 2.5 mi by B 4568 off B 4389 – ☎ (01686) 623 763 – www.highgatebandb.co.uk – Closed Christmas-New Year
4 rm – †£ 50/85 ††£ 80/100
Timbered farmhouse built in 1631, with stables, colourful gardens and superb views across rolling fields. Tastefully furnished, it boasts good-sized bedrooms and a warm, welcoming feel. Homemade breads and preserves feature at breakfast.

OLD RADNOR (Pencraig)

Powys – Pop. 400 – See Regional map n°**33**-C3
London 180 mi – Cardiff 81 mi – Birmingham 86 mi – Liverpool 121 mi
Michelin Road map 503-J27

Harp Inn with rm

✉ LD8 2RH – ☎ (01544) 350 655 – www.harpinnradnor.co.uk – Closed Monday except bank holidays and lunch Tuesday-Friday - Restricted opening in winter
5 rm – †£ 65/75 ††£ 95/105 Carte £ 20/34
This 15C stone inn welcomes drinkers and diners alike. The charming, flag-floored rooms boast open fires and beams hung with hop bines, and the terrace offers glorious views. 'Seasonality' and 'sustainability' are key, and menus are concise but original. Simple bedrooms come with wonderful views.

PEMBROKE (Penfro)

Pembrokeshire – Pop. 7 552 – See Regional map n°**33**-A4
London 252 mi – Carmarthen 32 mi – Fishguard 26 mi
Michelin Road map 503-F28 – Michelin Green Guide WALES

Lamphey Court

⊠ *SA71 5NT East : 1.75 mi by A 4139 – ✆ (01646) 672 273 – www.lampheycourt.co.uk*

39 rm ☕ – †£ 89/119 ††£ 109/179 **Rest** – Carte £ 19/42

Impressive Georgian mansion, fronted by columns and surrounded by mature parkland. Typical country house feel throughout, from the classical lounge to the well-kept bedrooms with mahogany furnishings. Smart modern spa and leisure facilities. Dine in the informal orangery or traditional dining room.

PENALLT → See Monmouth

Monmouthshire

PENARTH

The Vale of Glamorgan – Pop. 27 226 – See Regional map n°**32**-**C4**

London 152 mi – Birmingham 111 mi – Bristol 47 mi – Leicester 149 mi

Michelin Road map 503-K29

James Sommerin Ⓝ with rm

The Esplanade ⊠ CF64 3AU – ✆ (029) 2070 6559 – www.jamessommerinrestaurant.co.uk – Closed 25-26 December, 2-8 January and Monday

9 rm ☕ – †£ 100 ††£ 150/190 Menu £ 32/70 – *(set menu only)*

Smart restaurant on the esplanade, affording panoramic views over the Severn Estuary. Choose the 5 course 'Beach', 7 course 'Cliff' or 10 course surprise 'Clifftop' menu. Cooking is innovative and features unusual taste and texture combinations. Five of the comfy, relaxing bedrooms share the wonderful view.

Pier 64

Penarth Marina ⊠ CF64 1TT – ✆ (029) 2000 0064 – www.pier64.co.uk – Closed Christmas and Sunday dinner

Menu £ 13 (weekday lunch)/25 – Carte £ 25/59

Modern, wood-clad, all-day restaurant, set on stilts in an enviable harbour location. Light, airy interior with a smart bar and huge windows giving every table a view. Accessible menu features plenty of seafood and 28 day dry-aged steaks.

The Pilot

67 Queens Rd ⊠ CF64 1DJ – ✆ (029) 2071 0615 – www.knifeandforkfood.co.uk/pilot

Carte £ 19/32

A neat dining pub that's part of the local community. Regulars gather in the front room; diners head to the rear. A good-sized blackboard menu mixes hearty, honest pub dishes with more adventurous offerings. Ingredients are laudably local.

PENMACHNO → See Betws-y-Coed

Conwy – Michelin Road map 502-I24 and 503

PENNAL → See Aberdovey

Gwynedd – Michelin Road map 503-I26

Riverside

⊠ SY20 9DW – ✆ (01654) 791 285 – www.riversidehotel-pennal.co.uk

Menu £ 13 – Carte £ 18/34

Enter under the 'Glan Yr Afron' (Riverside) sign, then make for the 'Cwtch' with its wood-burning stove. Despite its Grade II listing, it has a bright modern feel. Hearty, no-nonsense pub classics are full of flavour and keenly priced.

PORTHCAWL

Bridgend – Pop. 15 672 – See Regional map n°**33**-**B4**

London 183 mi – Cardiff 28 mi – Swansea 18 mi

Michelin Road map 503-I29 – Michelin Green Guide WALES

Foam Edge without rest 
9 West Dr ✉ CF36 3LS – ✆ (01656) 782 866 – www.foam-edge.co.uk – Closed 25 December
3 rm ☕ – †£ 45/70 ††£ 70/100
A smart, modern, semi-detached house – a family home – set next to the promenade, with great views over the Bristol Channel. Spacious, stylish bedrooms offer good facilities. Comfortable lounge and communal breakfasts.

PORTMEIRION

Gwynedd – See Regional map n°**32**-B2
London 245 mi – Caernarfon 23 mi – Colwyn Bay 40 mi – Dolgellau 24 mi
Michelin Road map 502-H25 and 503 – Michelin Green Guide WALES

 **Portmeirion**
✉ LL48 6ER – ✆ (01766) 770 000 – www.portmerion-village.com – Closed 23 November-4 December
44 rm ☕ – †£ 104/194 ††£ 119/209 – 20 suites
Rest – Menu £ 24 (lunch)/38 – Carte £ 38/53 – *(booking essential)*
A unique, Italianate village built on a private peninsula and boasting wonderful estuary views – the life work of Sir Clough Williams-Ellis. There's an appealing 1930s hotel and snug, well-appointed bedrooms, which are spread about the village. The dining room has an art deco feel and a lovely parquet floor.

 **Castell Deudraeth** rest,
✉ LL48 6EN – ✆ (01766) 772 400 – www.portmeirion-village.com
11 rm ☕ – †£ 104/194 ††£ 119/209 – 3 suites
Rest *Grill* – Carte £ 24/37
Impressive crenellated manor house at the entrance to the Italianate village; its name means 'castle of two beaches'. Huge modern bedrooms have stylish bathrooms and kitchen areas. Have cocktails by the fire then head to the grill for brasserie classics and lovely views of the walled garden and the sea.

WALES

PWLLHELI

Gwynedd – Pop. 4 076 – See Regional map n°**32**-B2
London 261 mi – Aberystwyth 73 mi – Caernarfon 21 mi
Michelin Road map 502-G25 and 503 – Michelin Green Guide WALES

XX **Plas Bodegroes** with rm
✉ LL53 5TH Northwest : 1.75 mi on A 497 – ✆ (01758) 612 363 – www.bodegroes.co.uk – March-November
10 rm ☕ – †£ 90/160 ††£ 130/170
Menu £ 23 (lunch)/45 – *(closed Monday except bank holidays) (dinner only and Sunday lunch) (booking essential)*
Set in a charming location at the end of a winding drive; a delightful, Grade II listed Georgian house surrounded by colourful gardens. An eclectic collection of local art decorates the dining room. The friendly, long-standing team serve well-presented, modern dishes with clear flavours and the occasional innovative touch. Contemporary bedrooms have a Scandic style.

at Boduan Northwest: 3.75 mi on A497 ✉ Pwllheli

 **Old Rectory** without rest
✉ LL53 6DT – ✆ (01758) 721 519 – www.theoldrectory.net – Closed Christmas
3 rm ☕ – †£ 75/90 ††£ 95/105
Lovely part-Georgian family home with well-tended gardens and a paddock. Comfy lounge features a carved wood fireplace; communal breakfasts at a large table include plenty of fresh fruits. Tastefully decorated, homely bedrooms overlook the garden and come with complimentary chocolates and sherry or sloe gin.

RHOSCOLYN → See Anglesey (Isle of)

– Michelin Road map 503-G24

RHOS-ON-SEA → See Colwyn Bay

Conwy – Michelin Road map 502-I24 and 503

RHYL

Denbighshire – Pop. 25 149 – See Regional map n°**32-C1**
London 228 mi – Cardiff 181 mi – Birmingham 114 mi – Wolverhampton 108 mi
Michelin Road map 502-J24 and 503 – Michelin Green Guide WALES

XX **Barratt's at Ty'n Rhyl** with rm

167 Vale Rd. ✉ LL18 2PH – South : 0.5 mi on A 525 – ✆ (01745) 344 138 – www.barrattsattynrhyl.co.uk

3 rm – †£ 75 ††£ 95

Menu £ 40 – *(dinner only and Sunday lunch) (booking essential)*

Built in 1672 and retaining many original features, including a carved wooden fireplace reputed to have been the top of a bed owned by Catherine of Aragon! The characterful drawing rooms have a cosy, lived in feel; the dining room, by contrast, is light and airy. Classically based menus. Traditional bedrooms.

ROSSETT

Wrexham – Pop. 2 007 – ✉ Wrexham – See Regional map n°**32-C1**
London 200 mi – Holyhead 86 mi – Chester 9 mi
Michelin Road map 502-L24

X **Machine House** Ⓝ

Chester Rd ✉ LL12 0HW – ✆ (01244) 571 678 – www.machinehouse.co.uk – Closed 25-26 December, 1 January, Monday, Tuesday lunch and Sunday dinner

Menu £ 17 (lunch)/50 – Carte £ 19/58 – *(bookings advisable at dinner)*

Once an agricultural machinery repair shop, this whitewashed barn is more charming than its name implies, with its cosy, rustic interior and friendly service. Flavoursome cooking has a modern touch and uses the best of local produce.

ROWEN → See Conwy

Conwy

RUTHIN (Rhuthun)

Denbighshire – Pop. 5 461 – See Regional map n°**32-C1**
London 210 mi – Birkenhead 31 mi – Chester 23 mi – Liverpool 34 mi
Michelin Road map 502-K24 and 503 – Michelin Green Guide WALES

Firgrove

Llanfwrog ✉ LL15 2LL – West : 1.25 mi by A 494 on B 5105 – ✆ (01824) 702 677 – www.firgrovecountryhouse.co.uk – March- October

3 rm – †£ 60/90 ††£ 80/120 **Rest** – Menu £ 38

Attractive stone-built cottage set in stunning gardens. Sit in the snug by the cosy inglenook fireplace in winter or in the delightful, plant-filled glasshouse in summer. Two comfortable four-poster bedrooms and a self-contained cottage offer pleasant valley views. The owners join guests for hearty, home-cooked dinners which showcase locally sourced farm produce.

Eyarth Station without rest

Llanfair Dyffryn Clwyd ✉ LL15 2EE – South : 1.75 mi by A 525 – ✆ (01824) 703 643 – www.eyarthstation.co.uk – Closed January-February

6 rm – †£ 50 ††£ 75

Former railway station, with the old platform at heart of the house and the tracks running under the conservatory. Simple pine-furnished bedrooms feature railway memorabilia. Panoramic windows in the lounge offer great rural views.

XX **Manorhaus Ruthin** with rm

10 Well St ✉ LL15 1AH – ✆ (01824) 704 830 – www.manorhaus.com

8 rm – †£ 83/123 ††£ 115/170

Menu £ 25/33 – *(dinner only and lunch Saturday-Sunday by arrangement)*

Georgian townhouse which retains its period character whilst also boasting a stylish, 'of-the-moment' feel. Formally laid conservatory dining room serves classically based, seasonal dishes, presented in a modern style. Cocktail bar, basement cinema and regularly changing art. Cosy, cleverly designed bedrooms.

On the Hill
1 Upper Clwyd St ✉ LL15 1HY – ✆ (01824) 707 736 – www.onthehillrestaurant.co.uk – Closed 1-7 January, 25-26 December, 1 January and Monday
Menu £ 12 (lunch) – Carte £ 24/30 – *(booking essential)*
Immensely charming 16C house in a busy market town; a real family-run business. It has characterful sloping floors, exposed beams and a buzzy, bistro atmosphere. The accessible menu offers keenly priced, internationally influenced classics.

ST ASAPH
Denbighshire – Pop. 3 491 – See Regional map n°**32**-C1
London 223 mi – Cardiff 176 mi – Liverpool 46 mi – Manchester 69 mi
Michelin Road map 503-J24

Tan-yr-Onnen without rest
Waen ✉ LL17 0DU – East : 1.5 mi by A 55 and B 5429 on Trefnant rd – ✆ (01745) 583 821 – www.northwalesbreaks.co.uk – Closed 25-26 December
6 rm – †£ 75/95 ††£ 95/135
Extended modern building with pleasant gardens; its name means 'house under the tree'. Spacious, tastefully furnished bedrooms: ground floor rooms have French windows and terraces; first floor rooms come with their own sitting rooms.

ST CLEARS
Carmarthenshire – Pop. 1 989 – See Regional map n°**33**-B3
London 221 mi – Cardiff 76 mi – Swansea 37 mi – Llanelli 33 mi
Michelin Road map 503-G28

WALES

Coedllys Country House without rest
Llangynin ✉ SA33 4JY – Northwest : 3.5 mi by A 40 turning first left after 30 mph sign on entering village. – ✆ (01994) 231 455 – www.coedllyscountryhouse.co.uk – Closed 22-28 December
4 rm – †£ 70/80 ††£ 90/110
Lovely country house in a peaceful hillside location, complete with a sanctuary where they keep rescued animals – the hens provide the eggs at breakfast. Comfy, traditional guest areas and charming, antique-furnished bedrooms with good mod cons and binoculars for bird watchers. Welsh cakes served on arrival.

ST DAVIDS (Tyddewi)
Pembrokeshire – Pop. 1 959 – ✉ Haverfordwest – See Regional map n°**33**-A3
London 266 mi – Carmarthen 46 mi – Fishguard 16 mi
Michelin Road map 503-E28 – Michelin Green Guide WALES

Ramsey House

Lower Moor ✉ SA62 6RP – Southwest : 0.5 mi on Porth Clais rd – ✆ (01437) 720 321 – www.ramseyhouse.co.uk – Closed January, December and restricted opening November and February
6 rm – †£ 60/120 ††£ 105/120 **Rest** – Menu £ 40
Unassuming house on the edge of the UK's smallest city. Stylish modern bedrooms have coastal views, bold décor and a boutique style; the smart shower rooms feature aromatherapy toiletries. A comfy lounge leads through to the wood-furnished dining room, where tasty, attractively presented dishes are served.

Cwtch
22 High St ✉ SA62 6SD – ✆ (01437) 720 491 – www.cwtchrestaurant.co.uk – Closed 1 January-11 February, 25-26 December , Monday-Tuesday November-March
Menu £ 22/32 – *(dinner only) (booking advisable)*
Popular, laid-back restaurant; its name meaning 'hug'. The three rustic dining rooms boast stone walls, crammed bookshelves and log-filled alcoves. Classical British dishes arrive in generous portions and service is polite and friendly.

ST GEORGE (Llan Sain Siôr)

Conwy – See Regional map n°**32**-C1

London 227 mi – Cardiff 180 mi – Dublin 62 mi – Birmingham 113 mi

Kinmel Arms with rm

The Village ✉ LL22 9BP – ☎ (01745) 832 207 – www.thekinmelarms.co.uk – Closed Sunday and Monday

4 rm – †£ 115/155 ††£ 115/175 Carte £ 21/46

Early 17C stone inn, hidden away in a hamlet by the entrance to Kinmel Hall, with a delightful open-fired bar and two spacious dining areas. Lunch offers pub favourites, while dinner is more complex; home-grown herbs and fruit feature. Stylish, contemporary bedrooms boast large kitchenettes for breakfast.

SAUNDERSFOOT

Pembrokeshire – Pop. 2 767 – See Regional map n°**33**-A4

London 241 mi – Cardiff 90 mi – Pembroke 12 mi

Michelin Road map 503-F28

St Brides Spa

St Brides Hill ✉ SA69 9NH – ☎ (01834) 812 304 – www.stbridesspahotel.com

46 rm – †£ 130/205 ††£ 160/310 – 6 suites

Rest *Cliff* – see restaurant listing

Nautically styled hotel overlooking the harbour and bay, featuring wood panelling and contemporary Welsh art. The stylish spa boasts an outdoor infinity pool. Well-appointed bedrooms come in cream and blue hues and have smart bathrooms.

XX Cliff – St Brides Spa Hotel

St Brides Hill ✉ SA69 9NH – ☎ (01834) 812 304 – www.stbridesspahotel.com

Carte £ 29/44

Smart yet casual restaurant in a New England style hotel, boasting beautiful decked terraces and stunning views over the bay. Extensive lunch menu; dinner is more refined, offering modern British dishes with local produce to the fore.

X Coast (N)

Coppet Hall Beach ✉ SA69 9AJ – ☎ (01834) 810 800 – www.coastsaundersfoot.co.uk – Closed 25 December, Sunday dinner, Monday-Tuesday in winter

Carte £ 29/54

Start your day with brunch on the terrace of this striking restaurant, overlooking the stunning coastline. Seafood dominates the menu, which ranges from nibbles to a tasting selection. Local produce features in creative modern dishes.

SEION → See Caernarfon

Gwynedd

SKENFRITH

Monmouthshire – See Regional map n°**33**-C4

London 135 mi – Hereford 16 mi – Ross-on-Wye 11 mi

Michelin Road map 503-L28

Bell at Skenfrith with rm

✉ NP7 8UH – ☎ (01600) 750 235 – www.skenfrith.co.uk – Closed 2 weeks January

11 rm – †£ 70/120 ††£ 110/220 Carte £ 25/42 – *(booking essential)*

Well-run pub in a verdant valley, offering hearty, classical cooking with the occasional ambitious twist and using ingredients from the organic kitchen garden. There's an excellent choice of champagnes and cognacs, and service is warm and unobtrusive. Super-comfy bedrooms have an understated elegance.

SWANSEA

Swansea – Pop. 179 485 – See Regional map n°**33**-B4

London 191 mi – Birmingham 136 mi – Bristol 82 mi – Cardiff 40 mi

Michelin Road map 503-I29 – Michelin Green Guide WALES

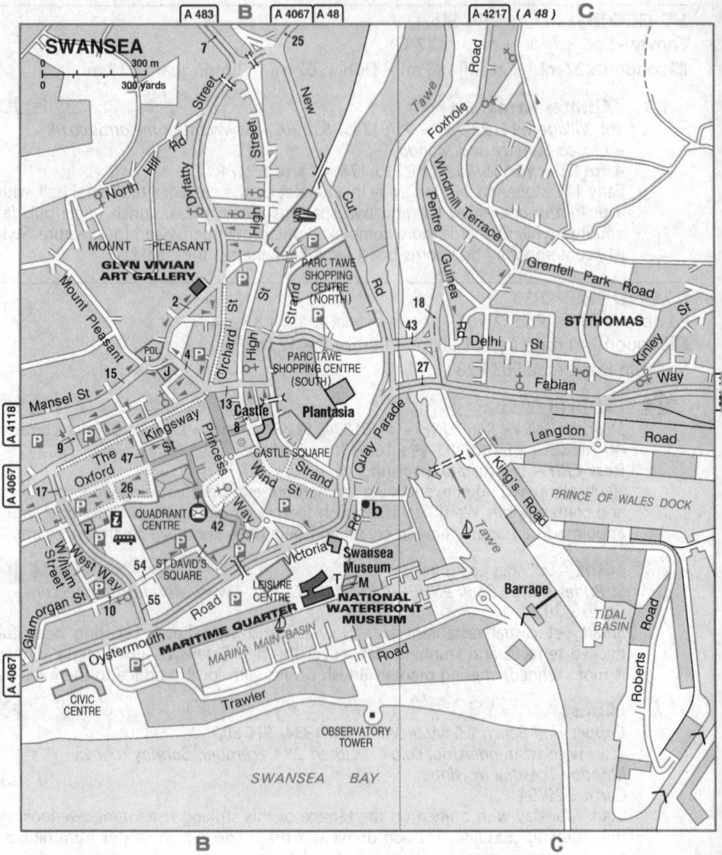

Street	Grid	No.
Alexandra Rd	B	2
Belle Vue Way	B	4
Carmarthen Rd	B	7
Castle St	B	8
Christina St	B	9
Clarence Terrace	B	10
College St	B	13
De la Beche St	B	15
Dillwyn St	B	17
East Bank Way	C	18
Grove Pl.	B	22
Kingsway (The)	B	
Nearth Rd	B	25
Nelson St	B	26
New Cut Bridge	C	27
Oxford St	B	
Parc Tawe Shopping Centre	B	
Princess Way	B	
Quadrant Centre	B	
St David's Square	B	
St Mary's Square	B	42
Tawe Bridge	C	43
Union St	B	47
Wellington St	B	54
West Way	B	55

Morgans

Somerset Pl ✉ SA1 1RR – ✆ (01792) 484 848 – www.morganshotel.co.uk

Town plan: B**b**

42 rm – †£ 65/250 ††£ 65/250 **Rest** – Carte £ 24/40

Impressive Edwardian building by the docks; once the harbour offices. Beautiful façade and charming interior with original plasterwork, stained glass and a soaring cupola. Modern bedrooms – those in the main house are the most spacious. The restaurant boasts an original hand-painted mural and a modern menu.

Symbols shown in red indicate particularly charming establishments.

SWANSEA

Clase Rd. . . . . A 12
Martin St . . . . A 24
Pen-y-Graig Rd. . . . . A 30
Plasmarl By-Pass. . . . . . . A 32
Ravenhill Rd. . . . . A 35
St Helen's Rd. . . . . A 40
Station Rd . . . . A 37
Terrace Rd . . . . A 45
Uplands Crescent . . . . . A 49
Walter Rd. . . . . A 52
Woodfield St . . . . A 60

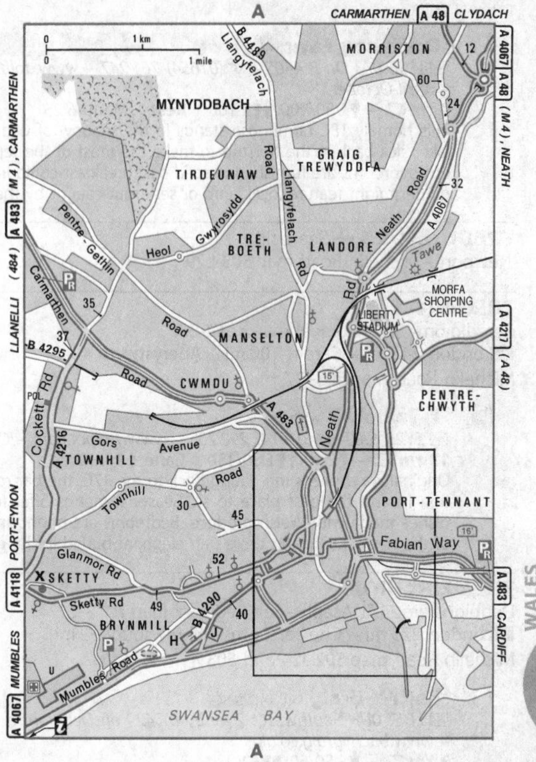

WALES

Slice

73-75 Eversley Rd, Sketty ✉ SA2 9DE – West : 2 mi by A 4118 – ☎ (01792) 290 929 – www.sliceswansea.co.uk – Closed 1 week autumn, 1 week Christmas, Monday and Tuesday — Town plan: Ax

Menu £ 17/35 – *(dinner only and Friday-Sunday lunch) (booking essential)*

Former haberdashery in a residential suburb; the name reflecting its tapered shape. Simple polished tables and unfussy, honest cooking. Concise menus feature homemade bread, home-grown veg and home-smoked meat. Chatty, friendly service.

at The Mumbles Southwest: 5 mi by A4067 -(A)✉ Swansea

Munch of Mumbles

650 Mumbles Rd ✉ SA3 4EA – ☎ (01792) 362 244 – www.munchofmumbles.com – Closed 1 week February, 1 week May, 3 weeks mid October, 25-26 December, 1 January, Monday, Tuesday and Sunday dinner

Menu £ 15 (lunch)/27 – *(booking advisable)*

It would be all too easy to walk past this simple bistro overlooking the bay – but you'd be missing out. Good value menus offer well-presented modern British dishes that are homemade and full of flavour. The BYO is only £ 1 a bottle!

TAL-Y-LLYN

Gwynedd ✉ Tywyn – See Regional map n°32-B2

London 224 mi – Dolgellau 9 mi – Shrewsbury 60 mi

Michelin Road map 502-I25 and 503 – Michelin Green Guide WALES

Dolffanog Fawr

LL36 9AJ On B 4405 – (01654) 761 247 – www.dolffanogfawr.co.uk – April-October

4 rm – £ 50/100 £ 100 **Rest** – Menu £ 25

This homely 18C farmhouse stands in the shadow of Cadair Idris, just up from a lake; kick-back in the hot tub to make the most of the terrific valley views. Modern bedrooms are furnished in solid oak. Breakfast could include Welsh cakes and dinner might feature local lamb or sea trout caught by the owner.

TREDUNNOCK → See Usk

Newport – Michelin Road map 503-L29

TREGARON

Ceredigion – See Regional map n°**33**-B3

London 245 mi – Cardiff 100 mi – Aberystwyth 18 mi

Michelin Road map 503-I27

Y Talbot with rm

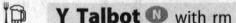

SY25 6JL – (01974) 298 208 – www.ytalbot.com – Closed 25 December

13 rm – £ 60 £ 80/130 Carte £ 17/30

Originally a drover's inn dating back to the 17C; the bar rooms are where the action is, and the best place to sit. Seasonal menus offer full-flavoured traditional dishes made with Welsh produce. Bedrooms are bright and modern: ask for one of the newest. Oh, and there's an elephant buried in the garden!

TREMEIRCHION

Denbighshire St Asaph – See Regional map n°**32**-C1

London 225 mi – Chester 29 mi – Shrewsbury 59 mi

Michelin Road map 502-J24 and 503

Bach-Y-Graig without rest

LL17 0UH Southwest : 2 mi by B 5429 off Denbigh rd – (01745) 730 627 – www.bachygraig.co.uk

3 rm – £ 50/60 £ 80

Welcoming 16C red-brick farmhouse, on a 200 acre working farm. The three decently sized bedrooms boast countryside views; antique furniture sits alongside mod cons like flat-screen TVs. Traditional lounges. Communal breakfasts.

USK

Monmouthshire – Pop. 2 834 – See Regional map n°**33**-C4

London 144 mi – Bristol 30 mi – Cardiff 26 mi – Gloucester 39 mi

Michelin Road map 503-L28 – Michelin Green Guide WALES

Glen-Yr-Afon House

rest,

Pontypool Rd NP15 1SY – (01291) 672 302 – www.glen-yr-afon.co.uk – Closed 24-26 December

28 rm – £ 99 £ 136

Rest *Clarkes* – Carte £ 22/40

Olive-green, extended Victorian villa just across the bridge from town. Comfortable, traditionally styled guest areas overlook the well-tended gardens. Mix of country house and more modern bedrooms; one is a four-poster. Wood-panelled, two-roomed restaurant serves traditional dishes made with Welsh produce.

at Llandenny Northeast: 4.25 mi by A472 off B4235 Usk

Raglan Arms

NP15 1DL – (01291) 690 800 – www.theraglanarms.co.uk – Closed 25-26 December, Sunday dinner and Monday

Carte £ 24/35

Cosy, stone-built village pub with fireside sofas, simply laid tables and vases of fresh flowers. Local produce features in unfussy, seasonal dishes with a good balance of flavours; the lunch menu offers particularly good value.

at Llangybi South: 2.5 mi on Llangybi rd ✉ Ceredigion

White Hart with rm

✉ NP15 1NP – ✆ (01633) 450 258 – www.thewhitehartvillageinn.com – Closed Monday except bank holidays and Sunday dinner

1 rm – £ 95 £ 95 Menu £ 20 (weekday dinner)/45 – Carte £ 25/42

Characterful pub with a priest's hole, 11 fireplaces from the 1600s and an interesting history. Choose from an adventurous à la carte of well-prepared, precisely presented dishes or a slightly simpler set menu; most produce is from within 10 miles. There's only one bedroom – a double with an adjoining single.

at Tredunnock South: 4.75 mi by Llangybi rd ✉ Newport

Newbridge on Usk with rm

rest,

✉ NP15 1LY East : 0.5 mi – ✆ (01633) 451 000 – www.celtic-manor.com

6 rm – £ 73/101 £ 79/132

Menu £ 20 (weekday lunch) – Carte £ 29/49

200 year old inn by a bridge over the River Usk; choose from several dining areas set over two levels or sit on the terrace to have the snack menu. Classic British cooking has a modern twist; sharing plates are popular and include a crumble dessert. The smart, comfortable bedrooms are in a separate block.

WHITEBROOK ➜ See Monmouth

Monmouthshire

WHITTON

Powys – Pop. 300 – See Regional map n°**33**-C3

London 185 mi – Cardiff 84 mi – Birmingham 84 mi – Liverpool 108 mi

Michelin Road map 503-J27

Pilleth Oaks without rest

✉ LD7 1NP Northwest : 1.25 mi on B 4356 – ✆ (01457) 560 272 – www.pillethoaks.co.uk – Closed 25-26 December

3 rm – £ 50 £ 75/85

Double-gabled country house set in 100 acres, overlooking two lakes and the surrounding hills. Traditional, antique-filled interior with an elegant lounge and comfortable bedrooms; one has a balcony and great views. The welcoming owner offers tea on arrival and communal breakfasts at a smart oak table.

WOLF'S CASTLE (Cas-Blaidd)

Pembrokeshire – Pop. 616 – ✉ Haverfordwest – See Regional map n°**33**-A3

London 258 mi – Fishguard 7 mi – Haverfordwest 8 mi

Michelin Road map 503-F28 – Michelin Green Guide WALES

Wolfscastle Country H.

rest,

✉ SA62 5LZ – ✆ (01437) 741 225 – www.wolfscastle.com – Closed 24-26 December

20 rm – £ 80/105 £ 120/145 **Rest** – Carte £ 23/39

Former manor house that's been greatly expanded over the years; a popular place for weddings and conferences. Bedrooms are modern, well-equipped and have very comfy beds – some are four-posters. Eat in the formal restaurant, in the bright and airy brasserie or on the terrace. Friendly, efficient service.

WALES

FoodCollection/Photononstop

Ireland

Northern Ireland

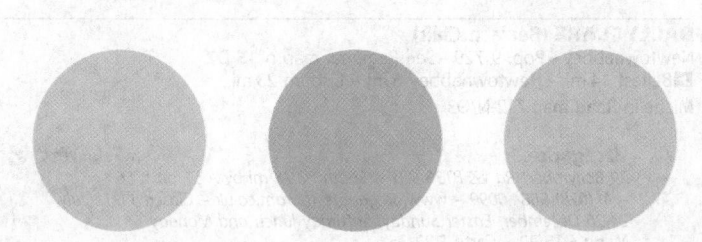

ANNAHILT = EANACH EILTE → See Hillsborough

Lisburn – Michelin Road map 712-N/O4

ARMAGH (Ard Mhacha)

Armagh – See Regional map n°**35**-C3

Belfast 39 mi – Dungannon 13 mi – Portadown 11 mi

Michelin Road map 712-M4

Moody Boar

Palace Stables, Palace Demense ✉ BT60 4EL – South : 0.5 mi off A 3 – ☎ (028) 3752 9678 – www.themoodyboar.com – Closed 25-26 December

Menu £ 13 (weekday lunch)/21 – Carte £ 24/37

Set in the stables of the former Primate of All Ireland's house and run by a young team. Characterful, rustic interior with a vaulted ceiling, a stone floor and booths in the old stalls. Wide choice of classic dishes with personal touches.

Uluru Bistro

16-18 Market St ✉ BT61 7BX – ☎ (028) 3751 8051 – www.ulurubistro.com – Closed 25-26 December, 1 January, Monday and Sunday lunch

Menu £ 17 (weekday dinner) – Carte £ 21/41 – *(booking essential)*

Modern, split-level bistro in the shadow of St Patrick's Cathedral. The Australian chef cooks tasty Mediterranean and Asian dishes, along with a few of his native meats such as crocodile, kangaroo and ostrich; veg is from their poly-tunnel.

BALLINTOY

Moyle – See Regional map n°**35**-C1

Belfast 59 mi – Ballycastle 8 mi – Londonderry 48 mi – Lisburn 67 mi

Michelin Road map 712-M2

Whitepark House without rest

150 Whitepark Rd ✉ BT54 6NH – West : 1.5 mi on A 2 – ☎ (028) 2073 1482 – www.whiteparkhouse.com – mid February-October

4 rm – †£ 80 ††£ 120

Charming 18C house near the Giant's Causeway, decorated with lovely wall hangings, framed silks and other artefacts from the personable owner's travels. Large, open-fired lounge where cakes are served on arrival. Bright, antique-furnished bedrooms have four-posters or half-testers and smart modern bathrooms.

BALLYCLARE (Bealach Cláir)

Newtownabbey – Pop. 9 729 – See Regional map n°**35**-D2

Belfast 14 mi – Newtownabbey 6 mi – Lisburn 23 mi

Michelin Road map 712-N/O3

Oregano

29 Ballyrobert Rd ✉ BT39 9RY – South : 3.25 mi by A 57 on B 56 – ☎ (028) 9084 0099 – www.oreganorestaurant.co.uk – Closed 11-12 July, 24-26 December, Easter Sunday, Saturday lunch and Monday

Menu £ 15/22 – Carte £ 22/35

Unassuming Victorian house in a countryside setting; the interior is a real contrast with its modern bar and dining room, featuring bold, colourful wallpaper and contemporary art. Local produce is used in unfussy, flavoursome brasserie dishes with some Mediterranean influences. Polite, well-organised service.

BALLYMENA (An Baile Meánach)

Ballymena – Pop. 29 782 – See Regional map n°**35**-C2

Belfast 27 mi – Dundalk 78 mi – Larne 21 mi – Londonderry 51 mi

Michelin Road map 712-N3 – Michelin Green Guide IRELAND

at Galgorm West: 3 mi on A42

Galgorm Resort and Spa

136 Fenaghy Rd ✉ BT42 1EA – West : 1.5 mi on Cullybacky rd – ✆ (028) 2588 1001 – www.galgorm.com
75 rm – £ 135/195 £ 135/275
Rest *River Room* – see restaurant listing
Rest *Gillies* – Menu £ 10 (weekday lunch) – Carte £ 20/41
Rest *Fratelli* – Carte £ 14/25 – *(closed Wednesday and Thursday) (dinner only)*
Victorian manor house with newer extensions, set in large grounds. Stylish interior with plenty of lounge space, a huge function capacity and an excellent leisure club with a superb outdoor spa pool. Modern bedrooms boast state-of-the-art facilities; some have balconies. Extensive all-day menus served in characterful Gillies; informal Fratelli offers Italian fare.

River Room – Galgorm Resort and Spa Hotel

136 Fenaghy Rd ✉ BT42 1EA – West : 1.5 mi on Cullybacky rd – ✆ (028) 2588 1001 – www.galgorm.com – Closed Monday and Tuesday
Carte £ 38/43 – *(dinner only and Sunday lunch)*
Formal, warmly decorated dining room set on the ground floor of a stylishly furnished, whitewashed Victorian manor house, with good views across the River Mein. Refined, classically based cooking and attentive service.

BANGOR (Beannchar)

North Down – Pop. 60 260 – See Regional map n°**35**-**D2**
Belfast 15 mi – Newtownards 5 mi
Michelin Road map 712-O/P4 – Michelin Green Guide IRELAND

Clandeboye Lodge

10 Estate Rd, Clandeboye ✉ BT19 1UR – Southwest : 3 mi by A 2 and Dundonald rd following signs for Blackwood Golf Centre – ✆ (028) 9185 2500 – www.clandeboyelodge.com – Closed 24-26 December
43 rm – £ 75/115 £ 85/135
Rest *Coq & Bull Brasserie* – Menu £ 18 (weekdays) – Carte £ 23/39 – *(dinner only and Sunday lunch)*
Well-run property on the site of a former estate school house. A popular wedding venue, it is surrounded by 4 acres of woodland and is well-placed for country and coast. Airy, open-plan guest areas and contemporary bedrooms with a high level of facilities. An accessible menu is served in the brasserie.

Salty Dog

10-12 Seacliff Rd ✉ BT20 5EY – ✆ (028) 9127 0696 – www.saltydogbangor.com
15 rm – £ 60/90 £ 80/110
Rest – Menu £ 16 – Carte £ 22/43 – *(booking advisable)*
Boutique hotel in a pair of bay-windowed, red-brick Victorian townhouses overlooking Bangor Marina and Belfast Lough. Contemporary bedrooms vary greatly in shape and size; go for one of the larger front rooms with a view. The bistro, with its terrace, serves a mix of classics and more ambitious dishes.

Cairn Bay Lodge without rest

278 Seacliffe Rd ✉ BT20 5HS – East : 1.25 mi by Quay St – ✆ (028) 9146 7636 – www.cairnbaylodge.com
8 rm – £ 50/60 £ 75/100
Large, whitewashed Edwardian house just out of the town centre, overlooking the bay. Comfy guest areas feature unusual objets d'art and ornaments; spacious, individually styled bedrooms boast plenty of extras. The friendly owners leave homemade cake on the landing. Small beauty and therapy facility.

Shelleven House without rest

59-61 Princetown Rd ✉ BT20 3TA – ✆ (028) 9127 1777 – www.shellevenhouse.com – Closed 23-28 December
10 rm – £ 50/80 £ 75/95
Double-fronted, three-storey, Victorian end terrace, in a smart residential area near the marina. Open-plan lounge and breakfast room; excellent breakfasts. Well-kept bedrooms vary in shape and size; front rooms boast great coastal views.

Boat House

Seacliff Rd ✉ BT20 5HA – ✆ (028) 9146 9253 – www.theboathouseni.co.uk – Closed 1 January, Monday and Tuesday

Menu £ 25 (lunch)/35

This delightful former lifeboat station is now home to an intimate dining room with a harbourside terrace. Ambitious modern menus have the occasional Dutch twist and the experienced owners – who are brothers – source top quality local produce. Be sure to try one of the specialist gins from around the world.

BELFAST

Belfast – Pop. 267 742 – See Regional map n°**35**-D2
Dublin 103 mi – Londonderry 70 mi
Michelin Road map 712-O4 – Michelin Green Guide IRELAND

Hotels

Merchant

16 Skipper St ✉ BT1 2DZ – ✆ (028) 9023 4888 – www.themerchanthotel.com Town plan: BX**x**

62 rm – †£ 140/220 ††£ 140/220, ☕ £ 14 – 2 suites

Rest *Great Room* – see restaurant listing

Rest *Berts* – Menu £ 17 (weekday dinner)/55 – Carte £ 23/40 – *(dinner only and lunch Saturday-Sunday)*

Former Ulster Bank HQ with an impressive Victorian façade. Bedrooms are plush and intimately styled; those in the annexe have an art deco theme. The rooftop gym comes with an outdoor hot tub and a skyline view; afterwards relax in the swish cocktail bar. Fine dining room and classic brasserie with live jazz.

Fitzwilliam

Great Victoria St ✉ BT2 7BQ – ✆ (028) 9044 2080 – www.fitzwilliamhotelbelfast.com Town plan: BY**e**

130 rm ☕ – †£ 130/180 ††£ 140/190 – 1 suite

Rest *Fitzwilliam* – see restaurant listing

Stylish hotel by the Grand Opera House. Smart modern bedrooms have striking colour schemes, contemporary furnishings and good facilities; the higher up you go, the better the grade. Informal dining in the bar and afternoon tea in the lobby.

Malmaison

rest,

34-38 Victoria St ✉ BT1 3GH – ✆ (0844) 693 06 50 – www.malmaison.com Town plan: BY**v**

64 rm – †£ 79/199 ††£ 99/269, ☕ £ 16 – 2 suites

Rest *Brasserie* – Menu £ 20 – Carte £ 24/52

Converted Victorian seed warehouse with an ornate exterior. Original features blend with modern furnishings. The dark-hued reception leads to a snug bar; stylish bedrooms offer good facilities – one boasts a 7' bed and a snooker table. French menus offered in the distressed wood, beach hut style brasserie.

Radisson Blu

3 Cromac Pl, Cromac Wood, Ormeau Rd ✉ BT7 2JB – ✆ (028) 9043 4065 – www.radissonblu.co.uk/hotel-belfast Town plan: BY**z**

120 rm ☕ – †£ 170/450 ††£ 170/450 – 1 suite

Rest *Filini* – Menu £ 20/42 – Carte £ 25/40 – *(closed Sunday dinner)*

Stylish hotel with spacious, open-plan guest areas; on the site of the former city gasworks. Smart, modern bedrooms come in Urban or Nordic styles and offer a high level of facilities, including underfloor heating in the bathrooms. Mediterranean-influenced menus in Filini, with its floor to ceiling windows.

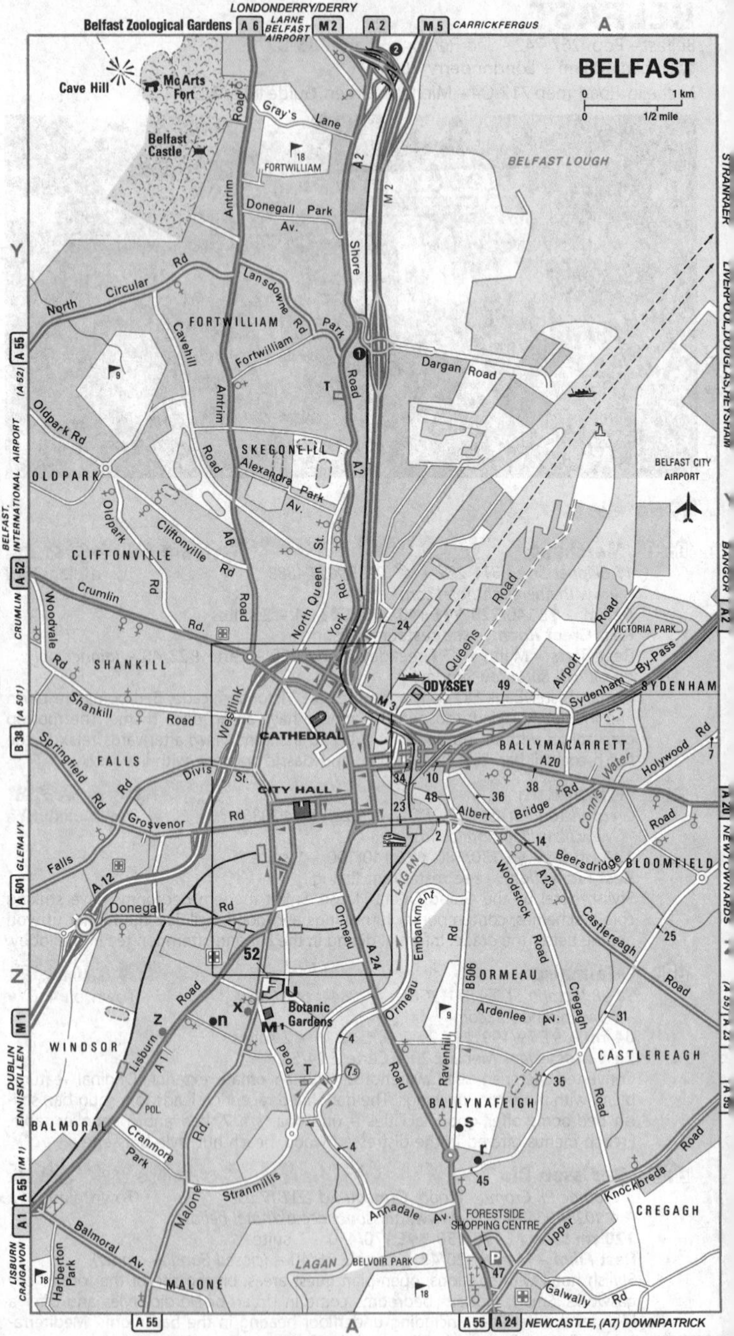

BELFAST

0 1 km
0 1/2 mile

LONDONDERRY/DERRY
Belfast Zoological Gardens A 6 LARNE BELFAST AIRPORT M 2 A 2 M 5 CARRICKFERGUS
A
Cave Hill
McArts Fort
Belfast Castle
Gray's Lane
FORTWILLIAM
BELFAST LOUGH
STRANRAER
LIVERPOOL, DOUGLAS, HEYSHAM
Antrim Road
Donegall Park Av.
Shore Road
North Circular Rd
Lansdowne Rd
Park
FORTWILLIAM
Fortwilliam
Cavehill
Dargan Road
Oldpark Rd
OLDPARK
SKEGONEILL
Alexandra Park Av.
BELFAST CITY AIRPORT
Oldpark Rd
Cliftonville Rd
CLIFTONVILLE
North Queen St.
York Rd.
Crumlin Rd.
Woodvale Rd
SHANKILL
Queens Road
Airport Road
VICTORIA PARK
Sydenham By-Pass
SYDENHAM
ODYSSEY
Shankill Road
Westlink
CATHEDRAL
Springfield Rd
FALLS
Divis St.
CITY HALL
BALLYMACARRETT
Holywood Rd
Conn's Water
Grosvenor Rd
Albert Bridge Rd
Falls
A 12
Beersbridge Road
BLOOMFIELD
LAGAN
Embankment
Woodstock Road
Castlereagh Road
Donegall Rd
Ormeau
52
ORMEAU
Ormeau Road
Botanic Gardens
Ardenlee Av.
Cregagh Road
WINDSOR
Lisburn Road
CASTLEREAGH
Ravenhill
BALLYNAFEIGH
BALMORAL
POL.
Cranmore Park
Malone Rd.
Stranmillis
Knockbreda Road
CREGAGH
Annadale Av.
FORESTSIDE SHOPPING CENTRE
Upper
Balmoral Av.
Harberton Park
LAGAN
BELVOIR PARK
Galwally Rd
MALONE
A 55 A A 55 A 24 NEWCASTLE, (A7) DOWNPATRICK

Y
Z
NORTHERN IRELAND
(A 52) A 55
BELFAST INTERNATIONAL AIRPORT
CRUMLIN A 52
(A 501)
B 38
GLENAVY A 501
DUBLIN ENNISKILLEN M 1
LISBURN CRAIGAVON A 1 A 55 (M 1)
BANGOR A 2
A 20 NEWTOWNARDS
(A 55) A 23
A 55

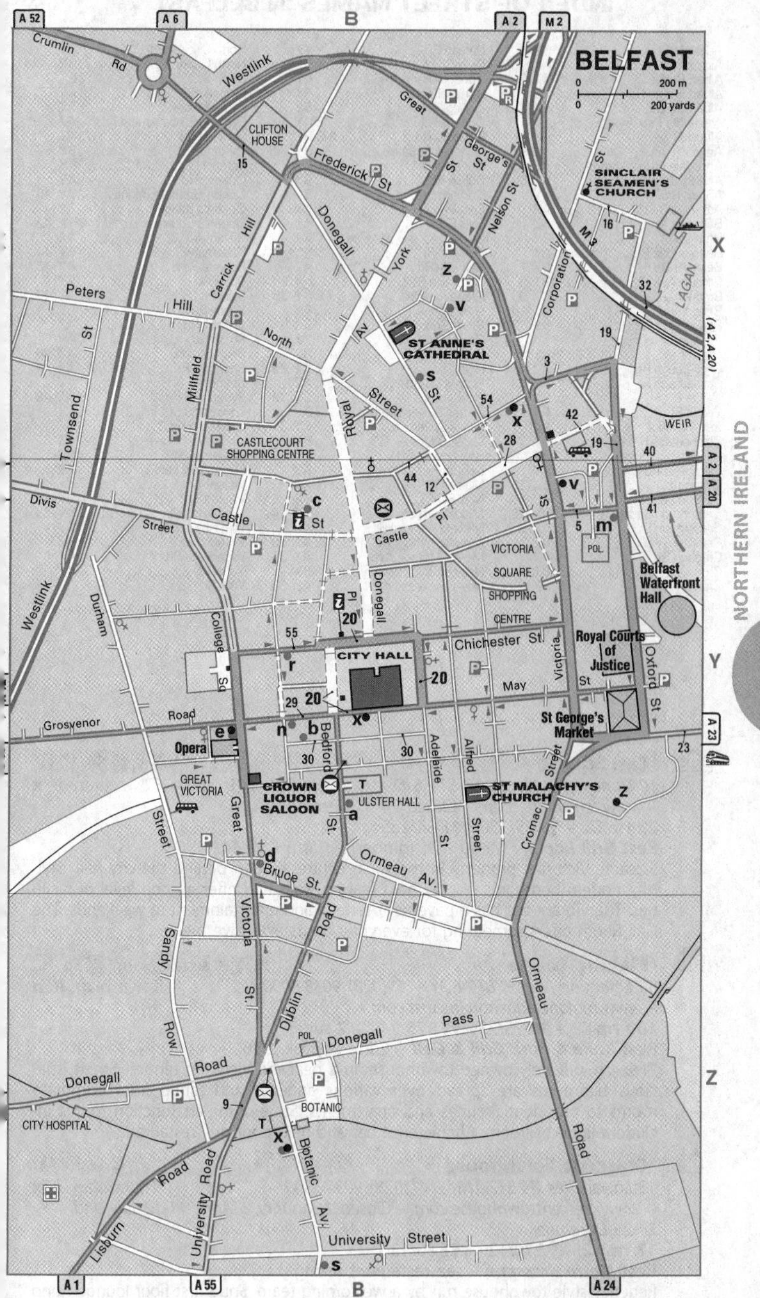
BELFAST
0 200 m
0 200 yards
NORTHERN IRELAND
CITY HALL
ST ANNE'S CATHEDRAL
SINCLAIR SEAMEN'S CHURCH
CLIFTON HOUSE
CASTLECOURT SHOPPING CENTRE
VICTORIA SQUARE SHOPPING CENTRE
Belfast Waterfront Hall
Royal Courts of Justice
St George's Market
ST MALACHY'S CHURCH
CROWN LIQUOR SALOON
ULSTER HALL
Opera
GREAT VICTORIA
BOTANIC
CITY HOSPITAL
WEIR
LAGAN
POL.
Crumlin Rd
Westlink
Frederick St
Great George's St
Donegall St
York St
Nelson St
Corporation St
Peters Hill
North Street
Royal Av
Carrick Hill
Millfield
Townsend St
Divis Street
Castle St
Castle Pl
Donegall Pl
Chichester St.
May St
Oxford St
Victoria St
Grosvenor Road
College Sq
Durham St
Great Victoria Street
Bedford St.
Adelaide St
Alfred Street
Cromac Street
Ormeau Av.
Bruce St.
Sandy Row
Dublin Road
Ormeau Road
Donegall Pass
Donegall Road
Lisburn Road
University Road
Botanic Av.
University Street
A 52
A 6
A 2
M 2
A 20
A 23
A 1
A 55
A 24
(A 2, A 20)
B
X
Y
Z

INDEX OF STREET NAMES IN BELFAST

NORTHERN IRELAND

Ten Square

10 Donegall Sq South ✉ BT1 5JD – ✆ (028) 9024 1001 – www.tensquare.co.uk – Closed 24-25 December Town plan: BY**x**

22 rm – †£ 85/150 ††£ 85/265

Rest *Grill Room* – Menu £ 26 (dinner) – Carte £ 19/44

Sizeable Victorian property in the town centre, hidden behind the city hall. Stylish, modern bedrooms display bold feature walls and offer a good level of facilities. The vibrant bar has a pavement terrace and entertainment at weekends. The Grill Room offers something for everyone on its extensive menu.

Malone Lodge

rest, rm,

60 Eglantine Ave ✉ BT9 6DY – ✆ (028) 9038 8000 – www.malonelodgehotelbelfast.com Town plan: AZ**n**

100 rm – †£ 75/239 ††£ 75/249 – 2 suites

Rest *Knife & Fork Grill & Deli* – Carte approx. £ 36

Well-run, privately owned townhouse, in a peaceful Victorian terrace. Smart, spacious bedrooms are spread over various annexes and range from corporate rooms to presidential suites and apartments. State-of-the-art function rooms include a large ballroom. Characterful bar and next door grill restaurant.

Crescent Townhouse

13 Lower Cres ✉ BT7 1NR – ✆ (028) 9032 3349 – www.crescenttownhouse.com – Closed 1 January, 5 April, 11-12 July and 24-26 December Town plan: BZ**x**

17 rm – †£ 70/120 ††£ 80/130

Rest *Metro Brasserie* – see restaurant listing

Regency-style townhouse run by a welcoming team. Snug first floor lounge hung with oils. Smart, spacious bedrooms are split between the old house and an extension; all are well-equipped and some boast four-posters and huge bathrooms.

Ravenhill House without rest
690 Ravenhill Rd ✉ BT6 0BZ – ✆ (028) 9020 7444 Town plan: AZ**s**
– www.ravenhillhouse.com – Closed 1-7 January, 7-15 July, 27 August-2 September and 20-31 December
5 rm – £ 55/75 £ 80/90
Red-brick Victorian house set in the city suburbs. Bright, homely lounge and wood-furnished breakfast room; colourful bedrooms boast good facilities. Organic breakfasts feature homemade muesli and the wheat for the bread is home-milled.

Roseleigh House without rest
19 Rosetta Park ✉ BT6 0DL – South : 1.5 mi by A 24 (Ormeau Rd) – ✆ (028) 9064 4414 – www.roseleighhouse.co.uk – Closed Easter, 2 weeks July and Christmas Town plan: AZ**r**
6 rm – £ 50 £ 75/80
Victorian bay-windowed house in a residential area by the Belvoir Park golf course; the friendly owner really makes guests feel welcome. Small lounge with lots of local info and a linen-laid breakfast room. Simple, well-kept bedrooms.

Restaurants

Eipic N
28-40 Howard St ✉ BT1 6PF – ✆ (028) 9033 1134 Town plan: BY**n**
– www.michaeldeane.co.uk – Closed 6-31 July, 25-26 December, 1 January and Sunday-Tuesday
Menu £ 40/70 – *(dinner only and Friday lunch) (booking essential)*
Elegant restaurant adjoined by a smart champagne bar. Top quality local ingredients feature on modern, seasonal menus and combinations are creative. Flavours are clearly defined and the occasional playful element features too.

Great Room – Merchant Hotel
16 Skipper St ✉ BT1 2DZ – ✆ (028) 9023 4888 Town plan: BX**x**
– www.themerchanthotel.com
Menu £ 19 (weekday dinner)/90 – Carte dinner £ 35/55
Grand old banking hall – set behind the impressive Victorian façade of the former Ulster Bank HQ – featuring ornate gold coving and plasterwork and original stained glass windows. Classic British dishes come with a Mediterranean edge.

OX N
1 Oxford St ✉ BT1 3LA – ✆ (028) 9031 4121 Town plan: BY**m**
– www.oxbelfast.com – Closed Christmas-January, 2 weeks July, Sunday and Monday
Menu £ 16 (lunch)/45 – Carte £ 22/38
The latest seasonal produce guides the menus at this buzzy, rustic restaurant. The welcoming minstrel's gallery is now a bar and the large windows offer views over the river. Cooking is modern and precise with Scandic influences.

Meat Locker N
28-40 Howard St ✉ BT1 6PF – ✆ (028) 9033 1134 Town plan: BY**n**
– www.michaeldeane.co.uk – Closed 12-14 July, 25-26 December, Easter Sunday-Monday, 1 January and Sunday
Menu £ 10/23 – Carte £ 25/58
Sit on smart banquettes and look through the large window into the meat fridge, where cubes of pink Himalayan salt gradually dry age the beef. Try the Carlingford rock oysters, followed by a prime Irish cut, cooked on the Asador grill.

James Street South
21 James St South ✉ BT2 7GA – ✆ (028) 9043 4310 Town plan: BY**b**
– www.jamesstreetsouth.co.uk – Closed Easter Monday, 12-17 July, 25-26 December, 1 January and Sunday
Menu £ 19/55 – Carte £ 24/44
Smart side-street restaurant with a Victorian façade, a bright dining room and a semi-open kitchen. Classical cooking relies on quality natural produce, prepared simply so that flavours shine through. Service is efficient and organised.

Shu

253 Lisburn Rd ✉ BT9 7EN – ✆ (028) 9038 1655 Town plan: AZ**z**
– www.shu-restaurant.com – Closed 1 January, 11-13 July, 24-26 December and Sunday
Menu £ 14 (weekday lunch)/31 – Carte £ 23/40
A well-established neighbourhood restaurant with a modern look and a lively, vibrant atmosphere. Menus are guided by seasonality and the ambitious, modern British dishes have international influences. Good value set price menu.

Fitzwilliam – Fitzwilliam Hotel

Great Victoria St ✉ BT2 7BQ – ✆ (028) 9044 2080 Town plan: BY**e**
– www.fitzwilliamhotelbelfast.com
Menu £ 16/55 – Carte £ 22/42 – *(dinner only) (booking essential)*
Bright, three-roomed restaurant on the first floor of a stylish hotel. If you're in a group choose one of the large communal tables; if you're a couple, opt for one of the intimate booths. Concise menus feature modern Irish dishes.

Bar + Grill at James Street South

21 James St South ✉ BT2 7GA – ✆ (028) 9560 0700 Town plan: BY**b**
– www.belfastbargrill.co.uk – Closed 1 January, 12 July and 25-26 December
Carte £ 19/39 – *(booking advisable)*
Vibrant modern bistro that's popular with one and all. It's a simple place with red brick walls, a high ceiling and warehouse-style windows. Menus are classic brasserie style. The grill dishes are a hit and the succulent steaks are cooked on the Josper grill, served on boards and come with a choice of sauces.

Deanes at Queens

1 College Gdns ✉ BT9 6BQ – ✆ (028) 9038 2111 Town plan: AZ**x**
– www.michaeldeane.co.uk – Closed 1 January, 5-6 April, 12 July, 25-26 December and Sunday dinner
Menu £ 30 – Carte £ 23/33
Bright, bustling brasserie with a pleasant terrace and a retro feel; large pictures of the owner and his suppliers hang on the walls. Cooking is simple and focuses on complementary flavour combinations – dishes have a classic brasserie base and modern twists. Service is polite and structured.

Deanes Deli

42-44 Bedford St ✉ BT2 7FF – ✆ (028) 9024 8800 Town plan: BY**a**
– www.michaeldeane.co.uk – Closed Easter, 1 January, 12 July, 25-26 December and Sunday
Menu £ 18 – Carte £ 21/38
Glass-fronted city centre eatery. One side is a smart restaurant offering an appealing menu of classical dishes with some Asian and Mediterranean influences; the other side acts as a coffee shop by day and a buzzy tapas bar by night.

Home

22 Wellington Pl ✉ BT1 6GE – ✆ (028) 9023 4946 Town plan: BY**r**
– www.homepopup.com – Closed Monday dinner
Menu £ 15 (weekday dinner) – Carte £ 20/32
A popular restaurant with a deli and café to the front – offering sandwiches and cakes – and a simple, rustic dining room to the rear. As its name suggests, cooking is straightforward, focusing on tasty, refined versions of dishes that are often prepared at home. Service is attentive and has personality.

Ginger Bistro

7-8 Hope St ✉ BT2 5EE – ✆ (028) 9024 4421 Town plan: BYZ**d**
– www.gingerbistro.com – Closed Christmas, New Year, Easter, 5 days mid-July, lunch Monday, Sunday and bank holidays
Carte £ 20/38
Rustic neighbourhood bistro close to the Grand Opera House. The two rooms feature bright modern artwork and bespoke fish-themed paintings. Good-sized menus feature simply cooked Irish ingredients and display some Asian influences.

Coppi

St Annes Sq ✉ BT1 2LD – ☎ (028) 9031 1959 Town plan: BX**z**
– www.coppi.co.uk – Closed 25 December
Carte £ 16/39

Set on the ground floor of a purpose built property in the Cathedral Quarter. It's big and buzzy, with rustic furnishings and leather booths, and staff are bright and friendly. The menu is Mediterranean with strong Italian influences and the home-made pastas are a must; start with a selection of cicchetti.

Love Fish

28-40 Howard St ✉ BT1 6PF – ☎ (028) 9033 1134 Town plan: BY**n**
– www.michaeldeane.co.uk – Closed 12-14 July, 25-26 December, Easter Sunday-Monday, 1 January and Sunday dinner
Carte £ 18/35

If it comes from the sea, they'll serve it here! A glass ceiling makes it light and airy and the décor has a maritime feel. The à la carte offers three sizes of platter and everything from cod croquettes to lobster. Lunch is good value.

Il Pirata

279-281 Upper Newtownards Rd ✉ BT4 3JF – East : 3 mi on A 2 – ☎ (028) 9067 3421 – www.ilpiratabelfast.com
Carte £ 16/26

Rustic restaurant with scrubbed wooden floors and an open kitchen. Mediterranean-influenced menus offer an extensive range of mainly Italian small plates; 3 or 4 dishes per person (plus dessert) should suffice. Bright, friendly service.

Hadskis

33 Donegall St ✉ BT1 2NB – ☎ (028) 9032 5444 Town plan: BX**s**
– www.hadskis.co.uk – Closed 25-26 December, 1 January and 12 July
Carte £ 15/35

This rustic conversion is in the up-and-coming Cathedral Quarter. The long, narrow room has an open kitchen, where you can watch the chefs use the latest market produce to prepare globally-influenced dishes and tasty small plates.

Mourne Seafood Bar

34-36 Bank St ✉ BT1 1HL – ☎ (02890) 248 544 Town plan: BY**c**
– www.mourneseafood.com – Closed 24-26 December, 1 January, 17 March, Easter Sunday-Monday and dinner Sunday
Carte £ 22/33 – *(booking essential at dinner)*

Popular, split-level seafood restaurant with a small shop, a large rear bar and a cookery school. Blackboard menus offer a huge array of freshly prepared dishes; go for the specials or the Carlingford oysters accompanied by a pint of stout.

Metro Brasserie – Crescent Townhouse Hotel

13 Lower Cres ✉ BT7 1NR – ☎ (028) 9032 3349 Town plan: BZ**x**
– www.crescenttownhouse.com – Closed 1 January, 5 April, 11-12 July and 24-26 December
Menu £ 11 – Carte £ 22/31 – *(dinner only)*

Smart, modern brasserie in a Regency-style townhouse hotel. Classic brasserie menus; contemporary cooking adds a modern twist. Trendy Metro Bar for light lunches, small plates and sharing platters; live music in the evenings.

Potted Hen Bistro

11 Edward St, St Anne's Sq ✉ BT1 2LR – ☎ (028) 9023 4554 – www.thepottedhen.co.uk – Closed 11-12 July and 24-27 December Town plan: BX**v**
Menu £ 18 (weekday dinner)/22 – Carte £ 24/38

Set in a redeveloped area of the city is this informal, two-floored bistro with exposed pipework, bright modern décor and a lively buzz. Extensive, classically based menus offer appealingly presented, unfussy dishes. Friendly service.

Molly's Yard

1 College Green Mews, Botanic Ave ✉ BT7 1LW Town plan: BZ**s**
– ✆ (028) 9032 2600 – www.mollysyard.co.uk – Closed 11-12 July, 24-26 December, 1 January and Sunday
Menu £ 16 (weekday dinner)/45 – Carte £ 24/45 – *(booking essential)*
Split-level bistro in a former coach house and stables, with exposed brickwork and a pleasant courtyard. Simple lunches and more ambitious dinners with classical combinations given a personal twist. Fine selection of ales and stouts.

BRYANSFORD → See Newcastle

Down – Michelin Road map 702-O5

BUSHMILLS (Muileann na Buaise)

Moyle – Pop. 1 343 – ✉ Bushmills – See Regional map n°**35**-C1
Belfast 57 mi – Ballycastle 12 mi – Coleraine 10 mi
Michelin Road map 712-M2 – Michelin Green Guide IRELAND

Bushmills Inn

9 Dunluce Rd ✉ BT57 8QG – ✆ (028) 2073 3000 – www.bushmillsinn.com
41 rm – £ 98/178 £ 128/398
Rest – Carte £ 25/43 – *(carvery lunch Sunday)*
Proudly run, part-17C whitewashed inn that successfully blends the old with the new. The conference room features a state-of-the-art cinema. Up-to-date bedrooms are split between the original house and an extension. Have a drink beside the peat fire in the old whiskey bar before dining on classic dishes.

Causeway Lodge without rest

52 Moycraig Rd, Dunseverick ✉ BT57 8TB – East : 5 mi by A 2 and Drumnagee Rd – ✆ (028) 2073 0333 – www.causewaylodge.com
5 rm – £ 80/100 £ 90/140
Set inland from the Giant's Causeway, in a peaceful location. Guest areas come with polished wood floors, leather furnishings and artwork of local scenes. Spacious, boutique bedrooms have bold feature walls and a high level of facilities.

COLERAINE (Cúil Raithin)

Coleraine – Pop. 24 455 – See Regional map n°**35**-C1
Belfast 53 mi – Ballymena 25 mi – Londonderry 31 mi – Omagh 65 mi
Michelin Road map 712-L2 – Michelin Green Guide IRELAND

Greenhill House without rest

24 Greenhill Rd, Aghadowey ✉ BT51 4EU – South : 9 mi by A 29 on B 66 – ✆ (028) 7086 8241 – www.greenhill-house.co.uk – March-October
4 rm – £ 45 £ 70
Long-standing guesthouse with mature gardens and a traditional country house style. Spacious open-fired lounge and linen-laid breakfast room; heavy drapes, antiques and ornaments feature. Simple, well-kept bedrooms. Chatty, welcoming owner.

COMBER (An Comar)

Ards – Pop. 8 933 – See Regional map n°**35**-D2
Belfast 10 mi – Newtownards 5 mi – Lisburn 17 mi
Michelin Road map 712-O4

Anna's House without rest

Tullynagee, 35 Lisbarnett Rd. ✉ BT23 6AW – Southeast : 4 mi by A 22 – ✆ (028) 9754 1566 – www.annashouse.com – Closed Christmas-New Year
4 rm – £ 60/70 £ 90/110
An extended farmhouse with welcoming owners, superb views, a cosy, contemporary lounge and good-sized bedrooms featuring modern bathrooms. Snug breakfast room with a wood burning stove: filling organic breakfasts use local produce.

NORTHERN IRELAND

Poacher's Pocket

181 Killinchy Rd, Lisbane ✉ BT23 5NE – Southeast : 3.5 mi on A 22 – ✆ (028) 9754 1589 – www.poacherspocketlisbane.com – Closed 25 December
Menu £ 10 (weekdays) – Carte £ 18/32
Neat, modern-looking building in the centre of a small village, with an adjoining off licence. Cooking is robust and satisfying and their ethos is 'local is best'; try one of the Irish Dexter beef dishes, which range from burgers to steaks.

CRUMLIN (Cromghlinn)

Antrim – Pop. 5 117 – See Regional map n°**35**-**C2**
Belfast 14 mi – Ballymena 20 mi
Michelin Road map 712-N4

Ballyrobin rm,

144-146 Ballyrobin Rd ✉ BT29 4EG – North : 7 mi by A 52 and A 26 on A 57 – ✆ (028) 9442 2211 – www.ballyrobincountrylodge.com – Closed 25 December
20 rm – £ 52/101 £ 52/101, £ 9
Rest – Menu £ 19 (weekday dinner)/21 – Carte £ 22/35
Smart, country style lodge – a former farmhouse – just a stone's throw from the airport and offering a week's free parking. Stylish, modern bedrooms. Dine on international dishes in one of the cosy rooms in the original pub building or in the conservatory-style extension.

Caldhame Lodge without rest

102 Moira Rd, Nutts Corner ✉ BT29 4HG – Southeast : 2 mi on A 26 – ✆ (028) 9442 3099 – www.caldhamelodge.co.uk
7 rm – £ 40/48 £ 70/78
Purpose-built guesthouse near the airport, with a pleasant mix of lawns and paved terracing. Comfy guest areas include a conservatory breakfast room and a lounge filled with family photos. Good-sized, individually decorated bedrooms are immaculately kept and feature warm fabrics and iPod docking stations.

DERRY/LONDONDERRY → See Londonderry

– Michelin Road map 712-K2/3

DONAGHADEE (Domhnach Daoi)

Ards – Pop. 6 856 – See Regional map n°**35**-**D2**
Belfast 18 mi – Ballymena 44 mi
Michelin Road map 712-P4 – Michelin Green Guide IRELAND

Grace Neill's

33 High St ✉ BT21 0AH – ✆ (02891) 884 595 – www.graceneills.com – Closed 25 December
Menu £ 12 (weekday lunch)/18 – Carte £ 18/39
Traditional beamed pub – reputedly the oldest in Ireland – dating from 1611 and decorated with antiques and pictures of old Donaghadee. The extensive, classical menu offers hearty, flavoursome cooking. Dishes are rustic yet refined.

Pier 36 with rm  rest,

36 The Parade ✉ BT21 0HE – ✆ (028) 9188 4466 – www.pier36.co.uk – Closed 25 December
6 rm – £ 50/79 £ 60/99 Menu £ 10/17 – Carte £ 18/41
Spacious family-run pub, set on the quayside, opposite a lighthouse, overlooking the picturesque harbour. Extensive menus feature a mix of classic, modern and international influences, with good weekday deals and plenty of fresh, local seafood. Bright, modern bedrooms; some with great sea and harbour views.

DUNDRUM (Dún Droma)

Down – Pop. 1 522 – See Regional map n°**35**-**D3**
Belfast 29 mi – Downpatrick 9 mi – Newcastle 4 mi
Michelin Road map 712-O5 – Michelin Green Guide IRELAND

NORTHERN IRELAND

Carriage House without rest

71 Main St ✉ BT33 0LU – ✆ (028) 4375 1635 – www.carriagehousedundrum.com
3 rm – £ 50/60 £ 80/90
Sweet, lilac-washed terraced house with colourful window boxes. Homely lounge with books and local info. Simple, antique-furnished bedrooms; some affording pleasant bay views. Breakfast in the conservatory, overlooking the pretty garden.

Buck's Head Inn

77-79 Main St ✉ BT33 0LU – ✆ (028) 4375 1868 – Closed 24-25 December and Monday from October-March
Menu £ 20 (weekday dinner)/30 – Carte lunch £ 21/32
Converted village pub. Have drinks in the lounge then head for the front room with its cosy booths and open fire, or the rear room which overlooks the garden. Unfussy, traditional lunches and more ambitious dinners; seafood is a strength.

Mourne Seafood Bar

10 Main St ✉ BT33 0LU – ✆ (028) 4375 1377 – www.mourneseafood.com – Closed dinner 24 December, 25 December and Monday-Wednesday in winter
Carte £ 16/31 – *(booking essential)*
Friendly, rustic restaurant on the main street of a busy coastal town. Simple, wood-furnished dining room with nautically themed artwork. Classic menus centre around seafood, with oysters and mussels from the owners' beds the specialities.

NORTHERN IRELAND

DUNGANNON (Dún Geanainn)

Dungannon – Pop. 14 380 – See Regional map n°**35**-C2
Belfast 42 mi – Ballymena 37 mi – Dundalk 47 mi – Londonderry 60 mi
Michelin Road map 712-L4 – Michelin Green Guide IRELAND

Grange Lodge

7 Grange Rd, Moy ✉ BT71 7EJ – Southeast : 3.5 mi by A 29 – ✆ (028) 8778 4212 – www.grangelodgecountryhouse.com – Closed 20 December-1 February
5 rm – £ 65/69 £ 80/89 **Rest** – Menu £ 39
Attractive Georgian country house surrounded by mature, well-kept gardens, ideal for afternoon tea. Antique-furnished guest areas display fine sketches and lithographs. Snug, well-appointed bedrooms are immaculately kept and have good extras. The flower-filled dining room serves classically based Irish dishes.

ENNISKILLEN (Inis Ceithleann)

Fermanagh – Pop. 13 757 – See Regional map n°**34**-A2
Belfast 84 mi – Londonderry 60 mi – Craigavon 62 mi – Portadown 59 mi
Michelin Road map 712-J4 – Michelin Green Guide IRELAND

Lough Erne Resort

rest, rm,

Belleek Rd ✉ BT93 7ED – Northwest : 4 mi by A 4 on A 46 – ✆ (028) 6632 3230 – www.locherneresort.com
120 rm – £ 110/150 £ 120/300 – 6 suites
Rest *Catalina* – Menu £ 20/75 – *(dinner only and Sunday lunch)*
Rest *Lochside Bar and Grill* – Menu £ 15 (lunch)/40
Vast, luxurious golf and leisure resort on a peninsula between two loughs. Bedrooms have a classical style and are extremely well-appointed; the suites and lodges are dotted about the grounds. Relax in the beautiful Thai spa or the huge pool with its stunning mosaic wall. Ambitious, contemporary dining and lough views in Catalina; steaks and grills in the clubhouse.

Manor House
Killadeas ✉ BT94 1NY – North : 7.5 mi by A 32 on B 82 – ☎ (028) 6862 2200 – www.manorhousecountryhotel.com
79 rm ☕ – †£ 70/125 ††£ 80/325 – 2 suites
Rest *Belleek* – Menu £ 20/35 – *(closed Monday-Friday lunch and Sunday dinner in winter)*
Rest *Cellar Door* – Carte £ 18/33
Impressive yellow-washed manor house overlooking Lough Erne and surrounded by mature grounds. Comfy, stylish guest areas mix the traditional and the contemporary. Bedrooms range from characterful in the main house to very smart and modern in the extensions. Formal dining room with ornate plasterwork and classical menus; more casual all-day dining in the old vaults.

GALGORM Antrim ➜ See Ballymena
Ballymena – Michelin Road map 712-N3

HILLSBOROUGH (Cromghlinn)
Lisburn – Pop. 3 738 – See Regional map n°**35**-C2
▶ Belfast 12 mi – London 358 mi – Lisburn 4 mi – Craigavon 21 mi
Michelin Road map 712-N4 – Michelin Green Guide IRELAND

Parson's Nose
48 Lisburn St ✉ BT26 6AB – ☎ (028) 9268 3009 – www.theparsonsnose.co.uk – Closed 25 December
Menu £ 10/23 – Carte £ 16/33 – *(booking advisable)*
Characterful Georgian property built by the first Marquis of Downshire. Rustic, open-fired bar; restaurant above overlooks a lake in the castle grounds. Unashamedly traditional menus and generous portions; the daily fish specials are a hit.

Plough Inn
3 The Square ✉ BT26 6AG – ☎ (028) 9268 2985 – www.theploughhillsbrough.co.uk – Closed 25-26 December
Menu £ 12/24 – Carte £ 16/33
Family-run, 18C coaching inn that's three establishments in one: a bar with an adjoining dining room; a café-cum-bistro; and a seafood restaurant. Dishes range from light snacks and pub classics to more modern, international offerings.

at Annahilt Southeast: 4 mi on B177 ✉ Hillsborough

Fortwilliam without rest
210 Ballynahinch Rd ✉ BT26 6BH – Northwest : 0.25 mi on B 177 – ☎ (028) 9268 2255 – www.fortwilliamcountryhouse.com – Closed 24-27 December
3 rm ☕ – †£ 50 ††£ 70
Attractive bay-windowed farmhouse with neat gardens, surrounded by 80 acres of land. Homely lounge and a country kitchen with an Aga. Traditional bedrooms have flowery fabrics, antiques and country views; two have private bathrooms.

Pheasant

410 Upper Ballynahinch Rd ✉ BT26 6NR – North : 1 mi on Lisburn rd – ☎ (028) 9263 8056 – www.thepheasantrestaurant.co.uk – Closed 12 July and 25 December
Menu £ 13 – Carte £ 16/32
Sizeable creamwashed pub with Gothic styling, Guinness-themed artwork and a typically Irish feel. Internationally influenced menus showcase local, seasonal produce, with seafood a speciality in summer and game featuring highly in winter.

HOLYWOOD (Ard Mhic Nasca)
North Down – Pop. 12 131 – See Regional map n°**35**-D2
▶ Belfast 7 mi – Bangor 6 mi
Michelin Road map 712-O4 – Michelin Green Guide IRELAND

Culloden

142 Bangor Rd ✉ BT18 0EX – East : 1.5 mi on A 2 – ✆ (028) 9042 1066 – www.hastingshotels.com

105 rm – †£ 145/180 ††£ 165/240 – 4 suites

Rest *Mitre* – Menu £ 45 (dinner) – Carte £ 30/48 – *(dinner only and Sunday lunch)*

Rest *Cultra Inn* – ✆ (028) 9042 5840 – Carte £ 19/39

An extended Gothic mansion overlooking Belfast Lough, with well-maintained gardens full of modern sculptures, and a smart spa. Charming, traditional, antique-furnished guest areas have open fires and fine ceiling frescoes. Characterful bedrooms offer good facilities. Classical menus and good views in formal Mitre; Cultra Inn is an informal grill restaurant.

Rayanne House

60 Demesne Rd ✉ BT18 9EX – by My Lady's Mile Rd – ✆ (028) 9042 5859 – www.rayannehouse.com

10 rm – †£ 77/87 ††£ 117/137

Rest – Menu £ 35/69 – *(closed 23-27 December) (dinner only) (residents only)*

Keenly run, part-Victorian house in a residential area. Homely, antique-filled guest areas. Smart, country house bedrooms with a modern edge; those to the front offer the best views. Ambitious, seasonal dishes in formal dining room; try the Titanic tasting menu – a version of the last meal served on the ship.

Beech Hill without rest

23 Ballymoney Rd, Craigantlet ✉ BT23 4TG – Southeast : 4.5 mi by A 2 on Craigantlet rd – ✆ (028) 9042 5892 – www.beech-hill.net

3 rm – †£ 55/60 ††£ 90/100

Antique-furnished guesthouse in a lovely countryside setting; personally run by the friendly owner – a local magistrate. Comfortable lounge and traditional, individually styled bedrooms with fresh flowers. Communal breakfasts.

Fontana

61A High St ✉ BT18 9AE – ✆ (028) 9080 9908 – www.restaurantfontana.com – Closed 25-26 December, 1-2 January, Saturday lunch, Sunday dinner and Monday

Menu £ 20 (weekday dinner)/23 – Carte £ 24/37

A favourite with the locals is this smart, modern, first floor restaurant; accessed down a narrow, town centre passageway and decorated with contemporary art. Menus offer British and Mediterranean dishes, with local seafood and steaks a speciality. Good value set menus are available at both lunch and dinner.

KILLINCHY

Ards – See Regional map n°**35**-D2

Belfast 16 mi – Newtownards 11 mi – Lisburn 17 mi – Bangor 16 mi

Michelin Road map 712-O4

Balloo House - Restaurant

1 Comber Rd, (1st floor) ✉ BT23 6PA – West : 0.75 mi on A 22 – ✆ (028) 9754 1210 – www.balloohouse.com – Closed 25 December, Sunday and Monday

Menu £ 28 (weekdays)/75 – Carte £ 35/43 – *(dinner only) (booking essential)*

Intimate, formally laid, first floor restaurant with high beamed ceilings and exposed stone walls; set in a rural location. Classically based menus see tried-and-tested combinations given a personal touch, with proud use of local produce.

LARNE (Latharna)

Larne – Pop. 18 323 – See Regional map n°**35**-D2

Belfast 23 mi – Ballymena 20 mi

Michelin Road map 712-O3 – Michelin Green Guide IRELAND

Manor House without rest

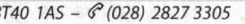

23 Olderfleet Rd, Harbour Highway ✉ BT40 1AS – ✆ (028) 2827 3305 – www.themanorguesthouse.com – Closed 25-26 December

8 rm ☕ – †£ 30/35 ††£ 55/60

Large Victorian house filled with antiques; the owner has been here nearly 50 years. Lounge boasts immense Chinese vase and gilded art; snug dining room has flocked walls. Cosy, immaculate bedrooms reached via original carved staircase.

LIMAVADY (Léim an Mhadaidh)

Limavady – Pop. 12 669 – See Regional map n°**34**-B1

Belfast 62 mi – Ballymena 39 mi – Coleraine 13 mi – Londonderry 17 mi

Michelin Road map 712-L2 – Michelin Green Guide IRELAND

Lime Tree

60 Catherine St ✉ BT49 9DB – ✆ (028) 7776 4300 – www.limetreerest.com – Closed 25-26 December, Sunday and Monday

Menu £ 20 (weekday lunch) – Carte £ 27/38 – *(dinner only and lunch Thursday-Friday)*

Keenly run neighbourhood restaurant; its traditional exterior concealing a modern room with purple velvet banquettes and colourful artwork. Unfussy, classical cooking features meats and veg from the village; try the homemade wheaten bread.

LISBANE

Ards – See Regional map n°**35**-D2

Belfast 451 mi – Dublin 113 mi

Michelin Road map 712-O4

Old Schoolhouse Inn with rm — rest,

100 Ballydrain Rd ✉ BT23 6EA – Northeast : 1.5 mi by Quarry Rd on Ballydrain Rd – ✆ (028) 9754 1182 – www.theoldschoolhouseinn.com – Closed Monday

8 rm ☕ – †£ 50/65 ††£ 75/85

Menu £ 15 (lunch) – Carte £ 23/40 – *(booking essential)*

Just a stone's throw from Strangford Lough is this stylish, sumptuous restaurant, which has been passed down from parents to son. Modern dishes are skilfully prepared, full of flavour and use top notch ingredients – including plenty of local seafood and game. Satisfyingly, the chef isn't afraid to prepare some simpler dishes too. Homely bedrooms complete the picture.

LISNASKEA

Fermanagh – Pop. 2 880 – See Regional map n°**34**-B3

Belfast 82 mi – Dublin 91 mi – Londonderry 67 mi – Omagh 33 mi

Michelin Road map 712-J5

Watermill Lodge with rm — rest,

Kilmore Quay ✉ BT92 0DT – Southwest: 3 mi by B 127 – ✆ (028) 6772 4369 – www.watermillrestaurantfermanagh.com – Closed January

7 rm ☕ – †£ 59 ††£ 79

Menu £ 16/24 – Carte £ 35/43 – *(dinner only and lunch Saturday and Sunday) (booking advisable)*

Charming red-brick cottage with a thatched roof, a delightful terrace and superb water gardens flowing down to Lough Erne – where you can hire one of their fishing boats. Characterful, rustic interior with smartly laid tables and a 25,000 litre aquarium; classical Gallic menu. Comfy, airy bedrooms have stone floors and heavy wood furnishings; some look over the water.

LONDONDERRY/DERRY

Derry – Pop. 85 016 – See Regional map n°**34**-B1

Belfast 70 mi – Dublin 146 mi

Michelin Road map 712-K2/3 – Michelin Green Guide IRELAND

City

Queens Quay ✉ BT48 7AS – ✆ (028) 7136 5800 – www.cityhotelderry.com – Closed 24-26 December

158 rm ☕ – 🚹£ 72/152 🚹🚹£ 79/159 – 8 suites

Rest *Thompson's* – Menu £ 18 (weekday dinner) **s** – Carte £ 21/33 **s** – *(bar lunch Monday-Saturday)*

Large, centrally located hotel overlooking the Peace Bridge on the River Foyle. Well-maintained, modern interior with a comfortable lounge and a well-equipped leisure centre. Smart bedrooms; those on the upper floors have great outlooks. Informal brasserie affords pleasant water views.

Beech Hill Country House

32 Ardmore Rd ✉ BT47 3QP – Southeast : 3.5 mi by A 6 – ✆ (028) 7134 9279 – www.beech-hill.com – Closed 24-25 December

32 rm ☕ – 🚹£ 75/95 🚹🚹£ 95/125 – 2 suites

Rest *Ardmore* – Menu £ 22 (lunch)/30 **s** – Carte £ 33/47 **s**

Once a US marine camp, this 18C house is now a welcoming hotel and popular wedding venue. Characterful guest areas feature ornate coving and antiques. Country house bedrooms in the original building; others are more modern and spacious. Dine from traditional menus overlooking the lake and water wheel.

Ramada H. Da Vinci's

15 Culmore Rd ✉ BT48 8JB – North : 1 mi on A 2 (Foyle Bridge rd) – ✆ (028) 7127 9111 – www.davincishotel.com – Closed 24-25 December

70 rm – 🚹£ 56/129 🚹🚹£ 65/170, ☕ £ 9

Rest *Grill Room* – Menu £ 22 – Carte £ 15/33 – *(dinner only and Sunday lunch)*

Set beside a characterful Irish pub – now the trendy hotel bar – at the northern edge of the city. Photos of stars who've stayed here fill one wall. Well-equipped, uniform bedrooms improve with grade. Charming brasserie displays rustic beams and exposed brickwork.

Browns In Town Ⓝ

Strand Rd ✉ BT48 7DJ – ✆ (028) 7136 2889 – www.brownsrestaurant.com – Closed Saturday lunch

Menu £ 20 (dinner) – Carte £ 22/39

Just across the river from the original 'Browns', is this stylish, modern bigger sister. A bewildering array of menus offer everything you could want, from light snacks to hearty main courses of Irish meats and local vegetables.

Browns

1 Bonds Hill, Waterside ✉ BT47 6DW – East : 1 mi by A 2 – ✆ (028) 7134 5180 – www.brownsrestaurant.com – Closed Monday, Saturday lunch and Sunday dinner

Menu £ 20/65 – Carte £ 17/41 – *(booking advisable)*

Smart neighbourhood restaurant with a plush lounge and an intimate dining room featuring monochrome photos and some banquette seating. Cooking is modern and technically adept, relying on local produce, home-baking and home-smoking.

MAGHERAFELT

Magherafelt – Pop. 8 881 – See Regional map n°**35**-C2

Belfast 76 mi – Dublin 117 mi – Londonderry 5 mi – Craigavon 75 mi

Church Street

23 Church St ✉ BT45 6AP – ✆ (028) 7932 8083 – www.churchstreetrestaurant.co.uk – Closed 7-17 January, 1 week July, Monday and Tuesday

Menu £ 12/14 – Carte £ 22/30 – *(dinner only and Sunday lunch)*

Located on the main street of a busy country town, a long, narrow restaurant with a mix of bistro, pew and high-backed seating, and a smart private dining room above. Unfussy, classically based dishes rely on good quality local produce.

MOUNTHILL

Antrim – Pop. 69 – See Regional map n°**35**-D2
Belfast 15 mi – Templepatrick 7 mi – Lar 5 mi
Michelin Road map 712-O3

Billy Andy's with rm

66 Browndod Rd ✉ BT40 3DX – Northeast : 0.5 mi on Browndod Rd – ☎ (028) 2827 0648 – www.billyandys.com – Closed 25-26 December and lunch Monday-Thursday
4 rm – £ 40/50 £ 60/80 Menu £ 16/19 – Carte £ 18/33
It used to be the village store as well as a pub, and although the groceries are gone, this place still seems to be all things to all people. Cooking is filling, with a strong Irish accent. They offer a fine selection of whiskies, there are four modern bedrooms and Saturday music sessions pack the place out.

NEWCASTLE (An Caisleán Nua)

Down – Pop. 7 723 – See Regional map n°**35**-D3
Belfast 32 mi – Londonderry 101 mi
Michelin Road map 712-O5 – Michelin Green Guide IRELAND

Slieve Donard

Downs Rd ✉ BT33 0AH – ☎ (028) 4372 1066 – www.hastingshotels.com
178 rm – £ 110/230 £ 130/280 – 4 suites
Rest *Oak* – Menu £ 42 – Carte £ 34/51 – *(dinner only and Sunday lunch)*
Rest *Percy French* – Carte £ 18/53
Rest *Lighthouse Lounge* – Carte £ 13/25
Grand railway hotel set right beside the beach and boasting its own museum, superb leisure facilities and excellent sea and mountain views. Spacious modern guest areas and stylish bedrooms with good mod cons. Smart spa with a pool overlooking the beach. Classical menu in formal Oak; accessible fare in informal Percy French; casual all-day dining in Lighthouse Lounge.

Burrendale H. & Country Club rest,

51 Castlewellan Rd ✉ BT33 0JY – North : 1 mi on A 50 – ☎ (028) 4372 2599 – www.burrendale.com
68 rm – £ 130/150 £ 180/220 – 1 suite
Rest – Menu £ 20/30 – Carte £ 16/32 **s**
Privately owned hotel between the Mourne Mountains and the Irish Sea, close to the Royal County Down golf course. Well-equipped modern bedrooms. Good leisure facilities and a vast spa offering a comprehensive range of treatments. Large, open-plan bar and lounge, with informal dining from extensive menus.

Vanilla

67 Main St ✉ BT33 0AE – ☎ (028) 4372 2268 – www.vanillarestaurant.co.uk – Closed 25-27 December and 1 January and Wednesday dinner in winter
Menu £ 20 – Carte £ 24/36
Contemporary restaurant; its black canopy standing out amongst the town centre shops. The long, narrow room is flanked by brushed velvet banquettes and polished tables. Attractively presented, internationally influenced, modern dishes.

at Bryansford Northwest: 2.75 mi on B180

Tollyrose Country House without rest

15 Hilltown Rd ✉ BT33 0PX – Southwest : 0.5 mi on B 180 – ☎ (028) 4372 6077 – www.tollyrose.com
6 rm – £ 45/55 £ 75/90
Purpose-built guesthouse beside the Tollymore Forest Park, at the foot of the Mourne Mountains. Simple, modern bedrooms come in neutral hues; those on the top floor have the best views. Lots of local info in the lounge. Friendly owners.

NEWTOWNABBEY

Newtownabbey – Pop. 61 713 – See Regional map n°**35**-D2
Belfast 7 mi – Templepatrick 12 mi – Carrickfurgus 13 mi
Michelin Road map 712-O4

Sleepy Hollow

15 Klin Rd ✉ BT36 4SU – Northwest : 1 mi by Ballyclare Rd and Ballycraig Rd – ✆ (028) 9083 8672 – www.sleepyhollowrestaurant.com – Closed 25-26 December

Menu £ 16/20 – Carte £ 20/35

This remote, passionately run restaurant is a real find, with its rustic rooms, large terrace, cosy hayloft bar and farm shop! Cooking is contrastingly modern, and the chef prides himself on using seasonal ingredients with a story.

NEWTOWNARDS (Baile Nua na hArda)

Ards – Pop. 28 437 – See Regional map n°**35**-D2

Belfast 10 mi – Bangor 144 mi – Downpatrick 22 mi

Michelin Road map 712-O4

Edenvale House without rest

130 Portaferry Rd ✉ BT22 2AH – Southeast : 2.75 mi on A 20 – ✆ (028) 9181 4881 – www.edenvalehouse.com – Closed Christmas-New Year

3 rm – £ 60 £ 100

Attractive Georgian farmhouse with a charming owner and pleasant lough and mountain views. It's traditionally decorated, with a comfy drawing room and a wicker-furnished sun room. Spacious, homely bedrooms boast good facilities.

PORTRUSH (Port Rois)

Coleraine – Pop. 6 640 – See Regional map n°**35**-C1

Belfast 58 mi – Coleraine 4 mi – Londonderry 35 mi

Michelin Road map 712-L2 – Michelin Green Guide IRELAND

Beulah without rest

16 Causeway St ✉ BT56 8AB – ✆ (028) 7082 2413 – www.beulahguesthouse.com – February-November

9 rm – £ 40/45 £ 65/70

Double-fronted terraced house in a seaside town, run by a charming, chatty owner with plenty of local knowledge. Comfy, spotlessly kept bedrooms have compact bathrooms. The house speciality at breakfast is pancakes with maple syrup.

PORTSTEWART (Port Stióbhaird)

Coleraine – See Regional map n°**35**-C1

Belfast 60 mi – Ballymena 32 mi – Coleraine 6 mi

Michelin Road map 712-L2

York

2 Station Rd ✉ BT55 7DA – On A2 – ✆ (028) 7083 3594 – www.theyorkportstewart.co.uk – Closed 25 December

8 rm – £ 59/120 £ 69/145 **Rest** – Carte £ 15/26

Smart hotel overlooking the North Coast. The marble-floored reception with its grand piano leads to a red-hued cocktail bar and a rustic locals bar which hosts live music events. Well-equipped modern bedrooms; those at the front are the largest, with terraces and excellent views. Busy, informal restaurant.

WARRENPOINT (An Pointe)

Newry and Mourne – Pop. 7 605 – See Regional map n°**35**-C3

Belfast 44 mi – Newry 7 mi – Lisburn 37 mi

Michelin Road map 712-N5

Restaurant 23

Balmoral Hotel (1st floor), 13 Seaview ✉ BT34 3NJ – ✆ (028) 4175 3222 – www.restaurant23warrenpoint.com – Closed 25 December

Menu £ 13 (lunch)/16 – Carte £ 26/39

Modern restaurant on the first floor of a seafront hotel, with a trendy bar and lounge, and views over Carlingford Lough. Precise, well-executed cooking has elaborate, sometimes flamboyant presentation. Service is professional.

NORTHERN IRELAND

Republic of Ireland

ABBEYLEIX (Mainistir Laoise)

Laois – Pop. 1 827 – See Regional map n°**39**-C2
Dublin 96 km – Kilkenny 35 km – Limerick 108 km
Michelin Road map 712-J9 – Michelin Green Guide IRELAND

Preston House with rm

Main St – (057) 873 14 32 – www.prestonhouse.ie – Closed 25 December and Monday
6 rm – € 105/120 € 120/180 Menu € 25 – Carte € 33/64
18C former school; very personally run by its two experienced owners. Have homemade cake or a light lunch in the cosy tearoom. The relaxed, informal restaurant offers set, à la carte and tasting menus – cooking is modern and features some original combinations. Simple, comfy bedrooms complete the picture.

ACHILL ISLAND (Acaill)

Mayo – See Regional map n°**36**-A2
Dublin 288 km – Castlebar 54 km – Galway 144 km
Michelin Road map 712-B5/6 – Michelin Green Guide IRELAND

DOOGORT (Dumha Goirt)

Gray's

– (098) 43 244 – www.grays-guesthouse.ie – April-September
14 rm – € 50 € 80 **Rest** – Menu € 26
Two adjoining whitewashed houses; one displaying an old clock face from its former life as a mission. Well-kept, modest bedrooms have small shower rooms and colourful throws and cushions. Striking artwork of local island scenes adorns the dining room walls. Simple dinners often feature the catch of the day.

REPUBLIC OF IRELAND

ADARE (Áth Dara)

Limerick – Pop. 1 106 – See Regional map n°**38**-B2
Dublin 210 km – Killarney 95 km – Limerick 16 km
Michelin Road map 712-F10 – Michelin Green Guide IRELAND

Adare Manor H. and Golf Resort

– (061) 605 200 – www.adaremanor.com – Closed 24-26 December
62 rm – € 200/600 € 200/600
Rest *Oakroom* – see restaurant listing
Rest *Carriage House* – Menu € 40 (weekdays) – Carte € 27/61
Part-19C Gothic mansion in 840 acres of riverside parkland: home to the Irish Open. Spacious, elaborately decorated guest areas. The most characterful bedrooms are in the main house and boast fireplaces, wood-panelling and ornate plasterwork. Dine in grand, formal Oakroom or more casual Carriage House.

Dunraven Arms

Main St – (061) 605 900 – www.dunravenhotel.com
86 rm – € 135/155 € 135/295
Rest *Maigue* – see restaurant listing
Greatly extended Irish coaching inn dating from 1792, with various small lounges, a busy bar and an annexed conference suite. Good-sized, classical bedrooms – some with four-posters and colourful garden outlooks. Lovely swimming pool.

Oakroom – Adare Manor Hotel and Golf Resort

– (061) 605 200 – www.adaremanor.com – Closed 24-26 December
Carte € 45/61 – *(dinner only)*
Grand hotel dining room with a beautiful drawing room and an intimate conservatory boasting an ornate ceiling and pleasant river views. Elegantly laid tables and formal service. Classically based menus showcase quality Irish ingredients.

Wild Geese

Rose Cottage – (061) 396 451 – www.thewild-geese.com – Closed 2 weeks January, 24-26 December, Sunday dinner and Monday
Menu € 25/37 – *(dinner only and Sunday lunch) (booking essential)*
Long-standing restaurant located in a delightful terrace of thatched cottages, on the main street of a pretty village. The atmosphere is intimate and cosy, and the service, friendly. Traditional menus make good use of local produce.

XX **Maigue** - Dunraven Arms Hotel
Main St – ✆ (061) 396 633 – www.dunravenhotel.com
Carte € 35/42 – *(bar lunch Monday-Saturday)*
Traditional hotel dining room with crystal chandeliers, a formal feel and professional service. Menus focus on Irish produce and are firmly rooted in tradition; a trolley features at every service, offering the likes of prime rib of beef.

ARAN ISLANDS (Oileáin Árann)

Galway – Pop. 1 280 – See Regional map n°**38**-B1
Dublin 260 km – Galway 43 km – Limerick 145 km – Ennis 111 km
Michelin Road map 712-C/D8 – Michelin Green Guide IRELAND

INISHMORE

Óstán Árann rm,
Kilronan – ✆ (099) 61 104 – www.aranislandshotel.com – mid February- October
22 rm – € 69/89 € 78/118 **Rest** – Carte € 24/50 **s** – *(bar lunch)*
Comfortable, family-owned hotel with a great view of the harbour. Bustling bar with live music most nights in high season. Spacious, up-to-date bedrooms are decorated in bright colours. Traditional dishes in the wood-floored restaurant.

Pier House
Kilronan – ✆ (099) 61 417 – www.pierhousearan.com – February- October
12 rm – € 50/80 € 70/100 **Rest** – Carte € 22/46
Brightly painted hotel in great location overlooking Kilronan pier, not far from the ferry point and the village centre; take advantage of the outlook from the comfy lounge. Cosy bedrooms come with good mod cons and some share the view. The intimate restaurant offers a concise, accessible menu.

Ard Einne Guesthouse
Killeany – ✆ (099) 61 126 – www.ardeinne.com – March-October
8 rm – € 60/90 € 80/120 **Rest** – Menu € 27
Close to the airport, an attractive chalet-style guesthouse set back on a hill and boasting superb views of Killeany Bay; relax in the comfy lounge while taking it all in. Uniformly decorated bedrooms have pine furnishings and afford great outlooks. Homely cooking with a menu featuring lots of island fish.

INISHMAAN

XX **Inis Meáin Restaurant & Suites** with rm
– ✆ (086) 826 60 26 – www.inismeain.com – April-September, 2 night minimum stay
5 rm – € 209/430 € 209/430
Menu € 65 – *(closed Sunday-Tuesday) (dinner only) (booking essential)*
Set on a beautiful island, this futuristic stone building is inspired by the surrounding landscapes and features limed walls, sage banquettes and panoramic views. Cooking is modern, tasty and satisfyingly straightforward, showcasing island ingredients, including seafood caught in currachs and hand-gathered urchins. Minimalist bedrooms feature natural furnishings.

INISHEER

South Aran House
– ✆ (099) 75 073 – www.southaran.com – Restricted opening in winter
4 rm – € 50/60 € 40/50 **Rest** – Carte € 24/37
Simple guesthouse on the smallest of the Aran Islands, where traditional living still reigns. With its whitewashed walls and tiled floors, it has a slight Mediterranean feel; bedrooms are homely, with wrought iron beds and modern amenities. Their next door restaurant serves breakfast, snacks and hearty meals.

ARDMORE (Aird Mhór)

Waterford – Pop. 435 – See Regional map n°**39**-C3
Dublin 240 km – Waterford 71 km – Cork 60 km – Kilkenny 123 km
Michelin Road map 712-I12

Cliff House

Middle Rd – ✆ (024) 87 800 – www.thecliffhousehotel.com – Closed 24-26 December
39 rm – € 150/170 € 180/495 – 3 suites
Rest *House* ✿ – see restaurant listing
Rest *Bar* – Menu € 40 – Carte € 25/57
Stylish cliffside hotel with a superb bay outlook and a lovely spa. Slate walls, Irish fabrics and bold colours feature throughout. Modern bedrooms have backlit glass artwork and smart bathrooms; some have balconies and all share the wonderful view. Choose from an extensive menu in the delightful bar and on the terrace; the restaurant serves more creative dishes.

House – Cliff House Hotel

– ✆ (024) 87 800 – www.thecliffhousehotel.com – Closed 24-26 December
Menu € 70/95 – Carte approx. € 68 – *(dinner only)*
Smart hotel restaurant where full length windows provide every table with an impressive coastal view. Local and garden produce features in concise menus; cooking is technically strong and complex. Creative, original dishes combine good flavours and textures; be sure to try the signature maple-smoked salmon.
→ Ballotine of cured salmon with pickled vegetables and horseradish. Rack of lamb, loin and sweetbreads with goat's cheese, garlic and broad beans. Dark chocolate, coffee, olive oil and sea salt.

ARTHURSTOWN (Colmán)

Wexford – Pop. 135 – See Regional map n°**39**-D2
Dublin 166 km – Cork 159 km – Limerick 162 km – Waterford 42 km
Michelin Road map 712-L11

Dunbrody Country House

– ✆ (051) 389 600 – www.dunbrodyhouse.com – Closed 21-27 December and Monday-Tuesday except July-August
16 rm – € 95/145 € 145/295 – 6 suites
Rest *Harvest Room* – see restaurant listing
Part-Georgian former hunting lodge; once owned by the Marquis of Donegal and now by celebrity chef, Kevin Dundon, who runs his cookery school here. Comfy lounge-bar with a marble-topped counter. Spacious bedrooms furnished in a period style.

Harvest Room – Dunbrody Country House Hotel

– ✆ (051) 389 600 – www.dunbrodyhouse.com – Closed 21-27 December
Menu € 35/65 – Carte € 40/65 – *(dinner only and Sunday lunch) (booking essential)*
Light, spacious, classically styled restaurant in keeping with the Georgian country house hotel in which it is sited; bright rugs and vividly coloured seats add a modern touch. Classic dishes feature produce from their own kitchen garden.

ASHFORD (Áth na Fuinseog)

Wicklow – Pop. 1 449 – See Regional map n°**39**-D2
Dublin 43 km – Rathdrum 17 km – Wicklow 6 km
Michelin Road map 712-N8

Ballyknocken House

Glenealy – South : 4.75 km on L 1096 – ✆ (0404) 44 627 – www.ballyknocken.com – March-November
7 rm – € 85/95 € 110/120 **Rest** – Menu € 46
Part-Victorian house with neat gardens and an adjoining cookery school, located next to the family farm. Traditional lounge and good-sized bedrooms with antique furnishings, modern feature walls and bright fabrics; some have claw-foot baths. Traditional dishes of local produce at gingham-clothed tables.

ATHLONE (Baile Átha Luain)

Westmeath – Pop. 15 558 – See Regional map n°**37**-C3
Dublin 120 km – Galway 92 km – Limerick 120 km – Roscommon 32 km
Michelin Road map 712-I7 – Michelin Green Guide IRELAND

Sheraton Athlone
Gleeson St – ✆ (090) 645 1000 – www.sheratonathlone.com – Closed 25-27 December
167 rm – € 79/230 € 95/240
Rest – Menu € 39 – Carte € 25/43 – *(dinner only)*
Modern hotel built around a smart shopping centre. The bedroom grade increases with the floor number – all have excellent mod cons and some offer super lough views – the best rooms are in the 11-storey glass tower. Very smart leisure, spa and aquatics area. Eat in the restaurant, laid-back café or chic bar.

Shelmalier House without rest
Retreat Rd., Cartrontroy – East : 2.5 km by Dublin rd (N 6) – ✆ (090) 647 22 45 – www.shelmalierhouse.com – March-November
7 rm – € 40 € 70
Well-run guesthouse with neat gardens, homely décor and strong green credentials. Clean, comfortable bedrooms – Room 1 is the best. Extensive breakfasts often include a daily special such as pancakes. Relax in the sauna or hot tub.

Left Bank Bistro
Fry Pl – ✆ (090) 649 44 46 – www.leftbankbistro.com – Closed 1 week Christmas, Sunday and Monday
Menu € 20 (weekday dinner) – Carte € 23/43
Keenly run bistro with an airy interior, rough floorboards, brick walls and an open-plan kitchen. Extensive menus offer an eclectic mix of dishes, from Irish beef and local fish specials right through to Asian-inspired fare.

Kin Khao
Abbey Ln. – ✆ (090) 649 88 05 – www.kinkhaothai.ie – Closed 24-25 December
Menu € 10 (weekday lunch)/20 – Carte € 24/52 – *(dinner only and lunch Wednesday-Friday and Sunday)*
Vivid yellow building with red window frames, hidden down a side street near the castle. Small downstairs bar; tapestries in the main room. Good choice of authentic Thai dishes and daily specials – try the owner's recommendations.

at Glasson Northeast: 8 km on N55 ✉ Athlone

Glasson Golf H. & Country Club
West : 2.75 km – ✆ (090) 648 51 20 – www.glassoncountryhouse.ie – Closed 24-25 December
65 rm – € 85/150 € 100/300
Rest – Menu € 26 (lunch)/55 **s** – Carte € 27/52 **s** – *(bar lunch)*
Greatly extended period house with views over the golf course and Lough Ree; the owner was born here and several family generations are now involved. Golfing memorabilia fills the walls. Bedrooms are spacious and modern; some have huge balconies and all have a view. Classical menu served in the dining room.

Wineport Lodge
Southwest : 1.5 km – ✆ (090) 643 90 10 – www.wineport.ie – Closed 24-26 December
30 rm – € 79/195 € 90/250
Rest – Menu € 25/49 – Carte € 45/56 – *(dinner only and Sunday lunch)*
Superbly set hotel, with the bedroom wing following the line of the lough shore and each luxurious room boasting a waterside terrace or balcony – it's worth paying extra for the Captain's Suite. Two treatment rooms and a rooftop hot tub for relaxation. Extensive menus utilise seasonal produce.

Glasson Stone Lodge without rest
– ✆ (090) 648 50 04 – www.glassonstonelodge.com – May-October
6 rm – € 55 € 78
Smart guesthouse with a baronial appearance, built from local Irish limestone. Pine features strongly throughout; bedrooms boast thoughtful extras and locally made furniture. Breakfast includes homemade bread and fruit from the garden.

Fatted Calf

– ✆ (090) 648 52 08 – www.thefattedcalf.ie – Closed Good Friday, 25 December and Monday except bank holidays
Menu € 25 (weekdays) – Carte € 30/55
Well-run pub with an attractive wood-panelled bar hung with original Guinness and Gilbey's signs, and a locals snug complete with a pool table. Dishes range from handmade sausages to local rabbit terrine, and tasty specials in the evening.

AUGHRIM (Eachroim)

Wicklow – Pop. 1 364 – See Regional map n°**39**-D2
Dublin 74 km – Waterford 124 km – Wexford 96 km
Michelin Road map 712-N9

Brooklodge H & Wells Spa

Macreddin Village – North : 3.25 km – ✆ (0402) 36 444 – www.brooklodge.com – Closed 24-25 December
86 rm – € 100/140 € 120/200 – 18 suites
Rest *Strawberry Tree* Rest *Armento* – see restaurant listing
Sprawling hotel in 180 peaceful acres in the Wicklow Valley. Flag-floored reception, comfy lounge, informal café and pub. Smart, modern bedrooms with large bathrooms; some in an annexe, along with the conference rooms. State-of-the-art spa.

Strawberry Tree – Brooklodge Hotel

Macreddin Village – North : 3.25 km – ✆ (0402) 36 444 – www.brooklodge.com – Closed 24-25 December
Menu € 65/85 – Carte approx. € 59 – *(dinner only)*
Ireland's only certified organic restaurant: formal, with an intimate, atmospheric feel, it is set on a village-style hotel estate. Menus feature wild and organic ingredients sourced from local artisan suppliers.

Armento – Brooklodge Hotel

Macreddin Village – North : 3.25 km – ✆ (0402) 36 444 – www.brooklodge.com – Closed 24-25 December
Menu € 35/35 – Carte approx. € 37 – *(dinner only)*
Informal Italian restaurant set in a smart hotel on a secluded 180 acre estate. Southern Italian menus feature artisan produce imported from Armento and pizzas cooked in the wood-fired oven.

BAGENALSTOWN (Muine Bheag)

Carlow – Pop. 2 775 – See Regional map n°**39**-D2
Dublin 101 km – Carlow 16 km – Kilkenny 21 km – Wexford 59 km
Michelin Road map 712-L9

Kilgraney Country House without rest

South : 6.5 km by R 705 (Borris Rd) – ✆ (059) 977 52 83 – www.kilgraneyhouse.com – Closed November-February and Monday-Wednesday
7 rm – € 120/135 € 170/240
Georgian country house which adopts a truly holistic approach. Period features blend with modern, minimalist furnishings and the mood is calm and peaceful. It boasts a small tea room, a craft gallery and a spa with a relaxation room, along with pleasant herb, vegetable, zodiac and monastic gardens.

BALLINA (Béal an Átha)

Mayo – Pop. 10 490 – See Regional map n°**36**-B2
Dublin 241 km – Galway 117 km – Roscommon 103 km – Sligo 59 km
Michelin Road map 712-E5 – Michelin Green Guide IRELAND

REPUBLIC OF IRELAND

Mount Falcon

Foxford Rd – South : 6.25 km on N 26 – ✆ (096) 74 472 – www.mountfalcon.com – Closed 24-26 December

32 rm – € 120/160 € 140/200 – 1 suite

Rest *Kitchen* – Menu € 32/54 – Carte € 37/52 – *(bar lunch Monday-Saturday)*

Classic country house built in 1872, with golf, cycling, fishing and archery available in its 100 acre grounds. Characterful bedrooms in the main house; spacious, contemporary rooms in the extension. Clubby bar. The restaurant is in the old kitchens and offers updated French classics. Relaxed service.

Ice House

The Quay Village – Northeast : 2.5 km by N 59 – ✆ (096) 23 500 – www.theicehouse.ie – Closed 24-26 December

32 rm – € 135/150 € 190

Rest – Carte € 33/47 – *(dinner only and Sunday lunch)*

A former ice vault for local fishermen; now a modern hotel offering great river and woodland views. Feature bedrooms have fireplaces and a traditional feel – the rest are modern and named after ice crystals; the spa suites are the largest. The restaurant opens onto a terrace with two hot tubs. Modern menus.

Crockets on the Quay

The Quay – Northeast : 2.5 km by N 59 – ✆ (096) 75 930 – www.crocketsonthequay.ie – Closed 24-26 December and Good Friday

Menu € 25 – Carte € 23/41 – *(dinner only and lunch Saturday-Sunday)*

Vibrant orange pub with a lively atmosphere. Generously proportioned dishes include tasty Irish steaks. They host regular poker, quiz and traditional Irish music nights and for sports fans, there are flat screen TVs in the garden.

BALLINASLOE (Béal Átha na Sluaighe)

Galway – Pop. 6 449 – See Regional map n°**36**-B3

Dublin 146 km – Galway 66 km – Limerick 106 km – Roscommon 58 km

Michelin Road map 712-H8 – Michelin Green Guide IRELAND

Moycarn Lodge and Marina

Shannonbridge Rd – Southeast : 2.5 km by N 6 off R 357 – ✆ (090) 964 50 50 – www.moycarnlodge.ie – Closed 25 December

15 rm – € 39/49 € 69/99 **Rest** – Menu € 10/30 – Carte € 17/30

Purpose-built hotel run by friendly owners; its pleasant gardens and terrace overlooking the river, where there's free berthing for guests. Light, airy bedrooms – five open onto a large shared balcony offering pleasant river views. Rustic bar and restaurant serve an accessible menu of traditional dishes.

BALLINGARRY (Baile an Gharraí)

Limerick – Pop. 527 – See Regional map n°**38**-B2

Dublin 227 km – Killarney 90 km – Limerick 29 km

Michelin Road map 712-F10 – Michelin Green Guide IRELAND

Mustard Seed at Echo Lodge

– ✆ (069) 68 508 – www.mustardseed.ie – Closed late January-mid February and 24-26 December

16 rm – € 110/165 € 130/320 – 2 suites

Rest – Menu € 45 (weekdays)/60 – *(dinner only)*

Brightly painted former convent with an exuberant owner, well-kept gardens and an interior filled with antique furnishings, paintings, books, magazines and fresh flowers. The main house bedrooms are furnished in a period style; those in the former school house are brighter and more modern. Dinner is an occasion – boldly flavoured cooking shows respect for the produce.

BALLSBRIDGE = DROICHEAD NA DOTHRA → See Dublin

Dublin – Michelin Road map 712-N8

BALLYBUNION (Baile an Bhuinneánaigh)

Kerry – Pop. 1 354 – See Regional map n°**38**-A2
Dublin 283 km – Limerick 90 km – Tralee 42 km
Michelin Road map 712-D10 – Michelin Green Guide IRELAND

Teach de Broc Country House
rest,

Link Rd – South : 2.5 km by Golf Club rd – (068) 27 581 – www.ballybuniongolf.com – Closed November-25 December and 7 January-February

14 rm – € 85/120 € 100/160

Rest *Strollers* – Menu € 28/40 – Carte € 31/49 – *(dinner only and Sunday lunch)*

Stylish house by the Ballybunion golf course. Spacious, modern interior boasts a nicely furnished bar-lounge with outdoor seating. Bedrooms are extremely comfortable and have smart bathrooms. Elegant dining room with smartly laid tables offers a wide-ranging menu.

19th Lodge without rest

Links Rd – South : 2.75 km by Golf Club rd – (068) 27 592 – www.ballybuniongolflodge.com – Closed Christmas and restricted opening in winter

14 rm – € 75/140 € 100/180

Set overlooking the fairways of the famed course and filled with golfing memorabilia. Comfy ground floor lounge; pleasant, classical décor throughout. 'Executive' bedrooms boast both showers and spa baths. Substantial breakfasts.

BALLYCASTLE (Baile an Chaisil)

Mayo – Pop. 215 – See Regional map n°**36**-B2
Dublin 267 km – Galway 140 km – Sligo 88 km
Michelin Road map 712-D5 – Michelin Green Guide IRELAND

Stella Maris Country House
rm,

Northwest : 3 km by R 314 – (096) 43 322 – www.stellamarisireland.com – 2 May-September

11 rm – € 149/177 € 192/240

Rest – Carte € 33/58 – *(dinner only) (booking essential)*

Former coastguard station and convent; now a homely hotel. Simple bedrooms display period furnishings and religious samplers that were left behind. The conservatory runs the length of the building and looks over the water. Snug, open-fired bar and a cosy dining room offering a daily menu of local ingredients.

BALLYCONNELL (Báal Atha Conaill)

Cavan – Pop. 1 061 – See Regional map n°**37**-C2
Dublin 143 km – Drogheda 122 km – Enniskillen 37 km
Michelin Road map 712-J5

Slieve Russell

Southeast : 2.75 km on N 87 – (049) 952 64 44 – www.slieverussell.ie

222 rm – € 93/141 € 125/221 – 2 suites

Rest *Conall Cearnach* – Menu € 29/40 **s** – Carte € 34/51 **s** – *(closed Sunday-Thursday September-July) (dinner only and Sunday lunch)*

Rest *Setanta* – Menu € 37 (dinner) **s** – Carte € 29/46 **s**

Well-run hotel with immaculate gardens, an impressive mock-Georgian façade and good facilities for families, golfers and businesspeople. Bedrooms overlook the grounds and are large and luxurious, with every mod con. The restaurants are named after Irish folk heroes – Conall Cearnach offers classical dishes and stylish Setanta serves a European menu.

BALLYCOTTON (Baile Choitín)

Cork – Pop. 476 – See Regional map n°**39**-C3
Dublin 265 km – Cork 43 km – Waterford 106 km
Michelin Road map 712-H12 – Michelin Green Guide IRELAND

Bayview

– ✆ (021) 464 67 46 – www.thebayviewhotel.com – April-October
35 rm ☕ – 🚹 € 70/96 👥 € 120/160 – 2 suites
Rest *Capricho* – Carte € 47/55 – *(bar lunch Monday-Saturday)*
A series of cottages in an elevated position, with superb views over the bay, the harbour and the island opposite. Two cosy lounges; one on each floor. Spacious bedrooms with floral fabrics and sea views – many have Juliet balconies. Ambitious modern menus; ask for a seat in one of the bay windows.

BALLYFARNAN (Béal Átha Fearnáin)

Roscommon – Pop. 205 – See Regional map n°**37**-**C2**
Dublin 111 km – Roscommon 42 km – Sligo 21 km – Longford 38 km
Michelin Road map 712-H5

Kilronan Castle

Southeast : 3.5 km on Keadew rd – ✆ (071) 961 80 00 – www.kilronancastle.ie
84 rm ☕ – 🚹 € 99/174 👥 € 99/249
Rest *Douglas Hyde* – Menu € 50 – *(dinner only and Sunday lunch)*
Impressively restored castle with characterful sitting rooms, a library and a palm court; wood panelling, antiques and oil paintings feature throughout. Smart leisure club and hydrotherapy centre. Opulent red and gold bedrooms offer a high level of comfort. The formal dining room offers a classical menu.

BALLYFIN

Laois – See Regional map n°**39**-**C1**
Dublin 69 km – Portlaoise 11 km – Cork 114 km – Limerick 67 km
Michelin Road map 712-J8

Ballyfin

– ✆ (057) 875 58 66 – www.ballyfin.com – Closed January-February
20 rm (dinner included) ☕ – 🚹 € 495/735 👥 € 840/1125 – 2 suites
Rest – – *(residents only)*
Immaculate Regency mansion built in 1820 and set in 600 acres. Stunning interior with a drawing room decorated in gold leaf, a library featuring 7,000 old books and elegant, antique-furnished bedrooms boasting marble bathrooms. The 4 course tasting menu is served in the State dining room. Excellent service.

BALLYLICKEY (Béal Átha Leice)

Cork ✉ Bantry – See Regional map n°**38**-**A3**
Dublin 347 km – Cork 88 km – Killarney 72 km
Michelin Road map 712-D12 – Michelin Green Guide IRELAND

Seaview House

– ✆ (027) 50 073 – www.seaviewhousehotel.com – mid March-mid November
25 rm ☕ – 🚹 € 70/95 👥 € 120/160
Rest – Menu € 25 – Carte € 36/43 – *(dinner only and Sunday lunch)*
Well-run Victorian house that upholds tradition in both its décor and its service. Pleasant drawing room, cosy bar and antique-furnished bedrooms; some with sea views. The attractive gardens lead down to the shore of the bay. A classical menu is served at elegant polished tables laid with silver tableware.

Ballylickey House without rest

– ✆ (027) 50 071 – www.ballylickeymanorhouse.com – May-September
6 rm ☕ – 🚹 € 90/100 👥 € 110/180
Pretty country house with an outdoor pool and beautiful gardens reaching down to the sea. Spacious, individually furnished bedrooms are split between the house and garden chalets. The period-style breakfast room displays attractive artwork.

BALLYLIFFIN (Baile Lifín)

Donegal – Pop. 461 – See Regional map n°**37-C1**
Dublin 174 km – Lifford 46 km – Letterkenny 39 km
Michelin Road map 712-J2

Ballyliffin Lodge
rest,

Shore Rd – (074) 937 82 00 – www.ballyliffinlodge.com – Closed 25 December
40 rm – € 95/120 € 110/190 **Rest** – Menu € 14/25 – Carte € 26/43
Remote hotel with well-kept gardens, affording a superb outlook over the countryside to the beach. Bedrooms offer good facilities; ask for one facing the front. Relax in the lovely spa and pool, or enjoy afternoon tea with a view in the lounge. Informal, bistro-style dining, with international menus.

BALLYMACARBRY (Baile Mhac Cairbre)

Waterford – Pop. 132 – Clonmel – See Regional map n°**39-C2**
Dublin 190 km – Cork 79 km – Waterford 63 km
Michelin Road map 712-I11 – Michelin Green Guide IRELAND

Hanora's Cottage

Nire Valley – East : 6.5 km by Nire Drive rd on Nire Valley Lakes rd – (052) 613 61 34 – www.hanorascottage.com – Closed 1 week Christmas
10 rm – € 99 € 110/130
Rest – Menu € 39 – *(closed Sunday and bank holiday Mondays) (dinner only and Sunday lunch) (booking essential)*
Dating back to 1891 and named after the owner's grandmother, to whom it once belonged. Relax on the terrace by the river or explore the nearby Comeragh Mountains. Spacious, brightly painted bedrooms have characterful furnishings and most boast whirlpool baths. The comfy dining room offers a classical menu.

Glasha Farmhouse

Northwest : 4 km by R 671 – (052) 613 61 08 – www.glashafarmhouse.com – Closed December
6 rm – € 60/70 € 100 **Rest** – Menu € 25
Large farmhouse between the Knockmealdown and Comeragh Mountains. Guest areas include a cosy lounge, an airy conservatory and a pleasant patio. Bedrooms are comfortable and immaculately kept; some have jacuzzis. The welcoming owner has good local knowledge. Home-cooked meals, with picnic lunches available.

BALLYMORE EUSTACE (An Baile Mór)

Kildare – Pop. 872 – See Regional map n°**39-D1**
Dublin 48 km – Naas 12 km – Drogheda 99 km
Michelin Road map 712-J2

Ballymore Inn

– (045) 864 585 – www.ballymoreinn.com
Menu € 23 (lunch)/35 – Carte € 29/46
Remote village pub with a spacious bar and a Parisian brasserie style dining area. The owner promotes small artisan producers, so you'll find organic veg, meat from quality assured farms and farmhouse cheeses. Portions are generous.

BALLYNAHINCH (Baile na hInse)

Galway Recess – See Regional map n°**36-A3**
Dublin 225 km – Galway 66 km – Westport 79 km
Michelin Road map 712-C7 – Michelin Green Guide IRELAND

Ballynahinch Castle

– (095) 31 006 – www.ballynahinch-castle.com – Closed February and Christmas
37 rm – € 160/360 € 170/450 – 3 suites
Rest *Owenmore* – Menu € 65 **s** – *(dinner only) (booking essential)*
Part-17C grey-stone castle and extensive grounds, set in an unrivalled riverside location. Log-fired entrance, well-appointed sitting rooms and modern country house style bedrooms with up-to-date facilities. The pub attracts the locals; the restaurant offers classical 4 course dinners and water views.

BALLYVAUGHAN (Baile Uí Bheacháin)

Clare – Pop. 258 – See Regional map n°**38**-B1
Dublin 240 km – Ennis 55 km – Galway 46 km
Michelin Road map 712-E8 – Michelin Green Guide IRELAND

Gregans Castle

Southwest : 6 km on N 67 – (065) 707 70 05 – www.gregans.ie – 14 February-1 November
21 rm – € 160/195 € 215/255 – 4 suites
Rest *Gregans Castle* – see restaurant listing
Well-run, part-18C country house with superb views of The Burren and Galway Bay. The open-fired hall leads to a cosy, rustic bar-lounge and an elegant sitting room. Bedrooms are furnished with antiques: two open onto the garden and one is in the old kitchen and features a panelled ceiling and a four-poster.

Drumcreehy House without rest

Northeast : 2 km on N 67 – (065) 707 73 77 – www.drumcreehyhouse.com – Closed 25-26 December and restricted opening in winter
12 rm – € 60/75 € 84/105
Brightly painted house overlooking Galway Bay. The interior is warm and welcoming, with rug-covered wood floors, peat fires and an honesty bar. The cosy bedrooms are named after flowers found on the Burren and feature bold colours and German stripped pine furnishings. Excellent continental buffet breakfasts.

Ballyvaughan Lodge without rest

– (065) 707 72 92 – www.ballyvaughanlodge.com – Closed 23-28 December
11 rm – € 45/60 € 75/90
Welcoming guesthouse with a colourful flower display and a decked terrace. The vaulted, light-filled lounge features a locally made flower chandelier; bedrooms boast co-ordinating fabrics. Breakfast uses quality farmers' market produce.

Gregans Castle – Gregans Castle Hotel

Southwest : 6 km on N 67 – (065) 707 70 05 – www.gregans.ie – 14 February-1 November
Menu € 55/69 **s** – *(bar lunch) (booking advisable)*
Have an aperitif in the drawing room of this country house hotel before heading through to the restaurant, where you can look across to Galway Bay. Interesting modern dishes have clean, clear flavours and showcase the latest local produce.

BALTIMORE (Dún na Séad)

Cork – Pop. 347 – See Regional map n°**38**-A3
Dublin 344 km – Cork 95 km – Killarney 124 km
Michelin Road map 712-D13 – Michelin Green Guide IRELAND

Casey's of Baltimore

rest,

East : 0.75 km on R 595 – (028) 20 197 – www.caseysofbaltimore.com – Closed 21-26 December
14 rm – € 70/120 € 90/150 **Rest** – Menu € 25 – Carte € 19/48 **s**
Extended 19C pub with a terracotta façade, well located near the seashore. Comfy lounge and simple pine-furnished bedrooms with good facilities. You're guaranteed a warm welcome from the family owners. The restaurant and beer garden overlook the bay; classical menus, and traditional music at the weekend.

Slipway without rest

The Cove – Southwest : 0.75 km – (028) 20 134 – www.theslipway.com – May-September
4 rm – € 55/68 € 70/80
Laid-back guesthouse in a lovely spot. The open-fired lounge is hung with tapestries made by the charming owner and the breakfast room leads onto a veranda with stunning views over the bay. Modest, well-kept bedrooms feature fresh flowers.

BANDON (Droichead na Bandan)

Cork – Pop. 1 917 – See Regional map n°**38**-B3
Dublin 181 km – Cork 20 km – Carrigaline 28 km – Cobh 33 km
Michelin Road map 712-F12

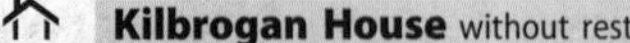

Kilbrogan House without rest

Kilbrogan Hill – North : 1 km on Macroom rd (R 589) – (023) 884 49 35 – www.kilbrogan.com – March-October
4 rm – € 50/60 € 80/90
Georgian house set above the town, boasting a stunning original staircase, fine cornicing and a conservatory overlooking the pleasant gardens. Simple bedrooms are furnished with antiques. Aga-cooked breakfasts feature homemade bread.

Poacher's Inn

Clonakilty Rd – Southwest : 1.5 km on N 71 – (023) 884 1159 – www.poachersinnbandon.com – Closed Monday-Tuesday
Menu € 25 (weekday dinner) – Carte € 25/45
Cosy neighbourhood pub that's popular with the locals. There's a wood-panelled bar, a cosy snug, and an upstairs restaurant which opens later in the week. Many dishes come in a choice of sizes and West Cork seafood takes centre stage.

BANSHA

South Tipperary – Pop. 349 – See Regional map n°**39**-C2
Dublin 121 km – Clonmel 21 km – Cork 59 km – Limerick 31 km
Michelin Road map 712-H10

Rathellen House without rest

Southeast : 3.5 km. by N 24 on Coopers Cottage rd – (062) 54 376 – www.facebook.com/rathellen
6 rm – € 60 € 90/110
Set in a peaceful location, a very comfortable Georgian-style property with a classic country house feel. Bedrooms feature antique furnishings and pleasant country or mountain outlooks; all the bathrooms boast heated floors and two come with whirlpool baths. Local ingredients are used at breakfast.

BANTRY (Beanntraí) Cork

Cork – See Regional map n°**38**-A3
Dublin 215 km – Cork 53 km – Killarney 49 km – Macroom 34 km
Michelin Road map 712-D12

O'Connors

Wolf Tone Sq – (027) 55 664 – www.oconnorsbantry.com – Closed Tuesday and Wednesday November-April
Menu € 20/25 – Carte € 25/45 – *(booking essential)*
Well-run harbourside restaurant, with a compact, bistro-style interior featuring model ships in the windows and modern art on the walls. The menu focuses on local seafood bought directly from the small fishing boats in the harbour.

BARNA (Bearna)

Galway – Pop. 1 878 – See Regional map n°**36**-B3
Dublin 227 km – Galway 9 km
Michelin Road map 712-E8

Twelve

Barna Crossroads – (091) 597 000 – www.thetwelvehotel.ie
48 rm – € 85/120 € 95/140 – 10 suites
Rest *Upstairs @ West* – see restaurant listing
Rest *The Pins* – Menu € 25 – Carte € 24/41 **s**
An unassuming exterior hides a keenly run boutique hotel complete with a bakery, a pizza kitchen and a deli. Stylish, modern bedrooms have large gilt mirrors, mood lighting and designer 'seaweed' toiletries; some even boast cocktail bars! Innovative menus in Upstairs @ West; modern European dishes in The Pins.

Upstairs @ West - Twelve Hotel

Barna Crossroads – ✆ (091) 597 000 – www.thetwelvehotel.ie – Closed Monday and Tuesday
Menu €25 (weekdays)/43 **s** – *(dinner only)*
Stylish first floor restaurant in a smart boutique hotel, with a chic champagne bar, booth seating and a moody, intimate feel. Seasonal menus offer ambitious, innovative dishes, showcasing meats and seafood from the 'West' of Ireland.

O'Grady's on the Pier

– ✆ (091) 592 223 – www.ogradysonthepier.com – Closed 24-26 December
Carte €32/62 – *(booking essential)*
Smartly painted white and powder blue building on the water's edge, with views across Co. Clare and a charming interior with real fires and fresh flowers. Fish is from Galway or Kinsale; go for the daily catch, which could be classically presented or may have a modern twist. Cheerful, attentive service.

BARRELLS CROSS → See Kinsale

Cork – Michelin Road map 712-G12

BEAUFORT = LIOS AN PHÚCA → See Killarney

Kerry – Michelin Road map 712-D11

BIRR (Biorra)

Offaly – Pop. 4 428 – See Regional map n°**39-C1**
Dublin 140 km – Athlone 45 km – Kilkenny 79 km – Limerick 79 km
Michelin Road map 712-I8 – Michelin Green Guide IRELAND

Maltings without rest

Castle St – ✆ (057) 912 13 45 – www.themaltingsbirr.com
6 rm – €45/50 €70/80
Characterful stone-built house, once used to store malt in the production of Guinness. Set over the river, its breakfast-room-cum-lounge overlooks the castle grounds. Simple, pine furnished bedrooms. Homemade soda bread, scones and jams.

BLACKLION (An Blaic)

Cavan – Pop. 229 – See Regional map n°**34-A3**
Dublin 194 km – Drogheda 170 km – Enniskillen 19 km
Michelin Road map 712-I5

MacNean House with rm

AC rest,

Main St – ✆ (071) 985 30 22 – www.macneanrestaurant.com – Closed January
19 rm – €67/96 €134/192
Menu €72/87 – *(closed Monday-Tuesday and Sunday dinner) (dinner only and Sunday lunch) (booking essential)*
Stylish restaurant in a smart townhouse, with a chic lounge and a plush dining room. Choose between a 6 or 9 course set menu – cooking is ambitious and uses complex techniques, and dishes are attractively presented. Charming, knowledgeable service team. Bedrooms are a mix of modern and country styles.

BLARNEY (An Bhlarna)

Cork – Pop. 2 437 – ✉ Cork – See Regional map n°**38-B3**
Dublin 268 km – Cork 9 km
Michelin Road map 712-G12 – Michelin Green Guide IRELAND

Killarney House without rest

Station Rd – Northeast : 1.5 km on Carrignavar rd. – ✆ (021) 438 18 41 – www.killarneyhouseblarney.com
6 rm – €40/45 €60/65
Well-kept, friendly guesthouse on the edge of town, with immaculate gardens, simple, spacious bedrooms, comfortable lounges and a wood-furnished breakfast room. Extensive breakfast menu includes the full Irish.

at Tower West: 3.25 km on R617 ✉ Cork

Ashlee Lodge without rest

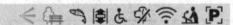

– ☎ (021) 438 53 46 – www.ashleelodge.com – April-October
10 rm ☕ – 👤 € 75/95 👥 € 99/140
Smart hotel with a cosy lounge featuring a wood burning stove, board games and an honesty bar. Comfortable bedrooms offer all you could want; some have whirlpool baths. Outdoor hot tub, sauna and in-room treatments. Extensive breakfasts.

BORRIS

Carlow – Pop. 646 – See Regional map n°**39**-D2
Dublin 121 km – Carlow 36 km – Waterford 66 km
Michelin Road map 712-L10

Step House

Main St – ☎ (059) 977 32 09 – www.stephousehotel.ie – Closed 15 August and 25 December
20 rm ☕ – 👤 € 75/95 👥 € 130/350 – 1 suite
Rest *Cellar* – see restaurant listing
Welcoming, family-run, Georgian townhouse in a small heritage village. Spacious, modern bedrooms; most have lovely mountain views and the penthouse boasts a terrace. Comfy bar, named after the year in which the hotel was originally built.

XX **Cellar** – Step House Hotel

Main St – ☎ (059) 977 32 09 – www.stephousehotel.ie – Closed 15 August and 25 December
Menu € 40 – *(closed Monday-Tuesday) (bar lunch)*
Atmospheric hotel restaurant with vaulted ceilings and archways; set in the kitchens of the old MacMurrough Kavanagh Estate dower house. Interesting modern menu of local and artisan ingredients.

XX **Clashganny House**

Clashganny – South : 5 km by R 702 and R 729 – ☎ (059) 977 10 03 – www.clashgannyhouse.com – Closed 1 week Christmas, Sunday dinner, Monday and Tuesday
Menu € 30 – *(dinner only and Sunday lunch)*
Hidden away in a lovely valley, this early Victorian house is the setting for the realisation of one couple's dream. The modern restaurant is split over three rooms; appealing menus balance light options with more gutsy dishes.

BOYLE (Mainistir na Búille)

Roscommon – Pop. 1 459 – See Regional map n°**36**-B2
Dublin 168 km – Roscommon 43 km – Galway 103 km
Michelin Road map 712-H6 – Michelin Green Guide IRELAND

Lough Key House without rest

Southeast : 3.75 km by R 294 on N 4 – ☎ (071) 966 21 61 – www.loughkeyhouse.com – Closed 2 January-16 March
5 rm ☕ – 👤 € 49/59 👥 € 85/98
Welcoming Georgian house in mature grounds, next to Lough Key Forest Park. Homely guest areas are filled with antiques and ornaments; bedrooms in the original house are the best, with their antique four-posters and warm fabrics.

Rosdarrig House without rest

Carrick Rd – East : 1.5 km on R 294 – ☎ (071) 966 20 40 – www.rosdarrig.com – Closed November-March
5 rm ☕ – 👤 € 40/45 👥 € 70/75
Neat house on the edge of town, close to the abbey, where friendly owners offer genuine Irish hospitality. Two comfy, homely lounges and a linen-laid breakfast room. Pleasant bedrooms with flowery fabrics overlook the garden.

REPUBLIC OF IRELAND

BRIDGE END

Donegal – Pop. 497 – See Regional map n°**37**-C1
Dublin 158 km – Lifford 25 km – Belfast 78 km – Londonderry 5 km
Michelin Road map 712-J2

XX **Harrys**
– ✆ *(074) 936 85 44 – www.harrys.ie – Closed 24-26 December*
Menu € 16/18 – Carte € 16/37
Long-standing, passionately run restaurant with open-plan interior and modern bistro feel. Menus evolve with the seasons, offering flavoursome, classically prepared dishes. Traceability is key, with much produce from their walled garden.

BUNDORAN (Bun Dobhráin)

Donegal – Pop. 1 781 – See Regional map n°**37**-C2
Dublin 259 km – Donegal 27 km – Sligo 37 km
Michelin Road map 712-H4 – Michelin Green Guide IRELAND

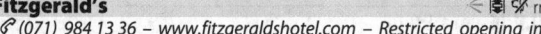

 **Fitzgerald's** rm,
– ✆ *(071) 984 13 36 – www.fitzgeraldshotel.com – Restricted opening in winter*
16 rm – € 55/80 € 80/140
Rest *Bistro* – Menu € 30 **s** – Carte € 28/40 **s** – *(closed Monday-Tuesday) (dinner only)*
Family-owned hotel in a popular seaside town overlooking Donegal Bay. Characterful guest areas feature tiled floors, stained glass windows and a wood burning stove. Bedrooms are pastel coloured; those facing the sea are the ones to choose. Informal, split-level bistro offers extensive menus of comfort dishes.

BUNRATTY (Bun Raite)

Clare – See Regional map n°**38**-B2
Dublin 207 km – Ennis 24 km – Limerick 13 km
Michelin Road map 712-F9 – Michelin Green Guide IRELAND

 **Bunratty Manor** rm,
– ✆ *(061) 707 984 – www.bunrattymanor.ie – Closed 23-28 December*
20 rm – € 79/89 € 99/109, € 10
Rest – Menu € 27/29 – Carte € 37/43 – *(dinner only and Sunday lunch)*
Smart hotel close to a castle and a folk park, in a busy tourist town. Comfy lounge has walls adorned with horse racing memorabilia. Good-sized, brightly decorated bedrooms display colourful fabrics. Traditional bar and restaurant with a courtyard offer a classical set menu and more imaginative à la carte.

CAHERLISTRANE (Cathair Loistreáin)

Galway – See Regional map n°**36**-B3
Dublin 256 km – Ballina 74 km – Galway 42 km
Michelin Road map 712-E7

 **Lisdonagh House** 
Northwest : 4 km by R 333 off Shrule rd – ✆ *(093) 31 163 – www.lisdonagh.com – May-October*
9 rm – € 98/120 € 120/180
Rest – Menu € 25/49 – *(dinner only) (residents only, set menu only)*
Ivy-clad Georgian house with pleasant lough views. The traditional country house interior boasts eye-catching murals and open-fired lounges. Antique-furnished bedrooms have marble bathrooms; the first floor rooms are larger and brighter. The grand dining room offers 5 course dinners and simpler suppers.

CAHERSIVEEN (Cathair Saidhbhín)

Kerry – Pop. 1 168 – See Regional map n°**38**-A2
Dublin 355 km – Killarney 64 km
Michelin Road map 712-B12 – Michelin Green Guide IRELAND

QC's with rm

3 Main St – ☏ (066) 947 22 44 – www.qcbar.com – Closed 2 weeks November, Monday-Wednesday in winter
6 rm ☕ – 🚹 € 65/85 🚹🚹 € 85/110
Menu € 21 (dinner) – Carte € 26/48 – *(booking advisable)*
Cosy little pub with characterful flagged floors, exposed stone walls and a strong nautical theme. Seafood-orientated menus offer fresh, unfussy classics and some more unusual daily specials; the family also own a local fish wholesalers. Spacious, well-equipped bedrooms are located just around the corner.

O'Neill's (The Point) Seafood Bar

Renard Point – Southwest : 4.5 km by N 70 – ☏ (066) 947 21 65 – Closed January-February
Carte € 34/42 – *(bookings not accepted)*
In a great location beside Valentia Island ferry terminal, and run by the O'Neill family for over 150 years. Generous portions of locally landed seafood; salmon comes from a nearby smokehouse. No chips, desserts or credit card payments.

CAMPILE (Ceann Poill)

Wexford – Pop. 411 – See Regional map n°**39**-**D2**
Dublin 154 km – Waterford 35 km – Wexford 37 km
Michelin Road map 712-L11 – Michelin Green Guide IRELAND

Kilmokea Country Manor

West : 8 km by R 733 and Great Island rd – ☏ (051) 388 109 – www.kilmokea.com – Closed January and December
6 rm ☕ – 🚹 € 75/95 🚹🚹 € 85/99
Rest – Menu € 20 (lunch) – Carte lunch € 20/28 – *(bookings essential for non-residents)*
Georgian rectory set in 20 acres, 7 of which are formal gardens open to the public. Small antique-furnished drawing room with oils and piano. Bedrooms, some in the old coach house, are more contemporary. Conservatory tea rooms and smart restaurant with daily changing classical menu of organic garden produce.

CAPPOQUIN (Ceapach Choinn)

Waterford – Pop. 759 – See Regional map n°**39**-**C2**
Dublin 219 km – Cork 56 km – Waterford 64 km
Michelin Road map 712-I11 – Michelin Green Guide IRELAND

Richmond House with rm

Southeast : 0.75 km on N 72 – ☏ (058) 54 278 – www.richmondhouse.net – Closed Christmas-New Year and Monday-Thursday January-February
9 rm ☕ – 🚹 € 60/80 🚹🚹 € 100/150
Menu € 25 (early dinner)/30 – *(dinner only)*
Imposing Georgian house built in 1704 for the Earl of Cork and Burlington, and filled with family curios. Have a drink in the cosy lounge before heading to the cove-ceilinged dining room. Cooking is classically based; be sure to try the delicious local lamb. Cosy bedrooms are decorated in period styles.

CARAGH LAKE (Loch Cárthaí)

Kerry – See Regional map n°**38**-**A2**
Dublin 341 km – Killarney 35 km – Tralee 40 km
Michelin Road map 712-C11 – Michelin Green Guide IRELAND

Ard-Na-Sidhe 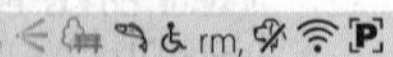

– ☏ (066) 976 91 05 – www.ardnasidhe.com – May- September
18 rm ☕ – 🚹 € 170/280 🚹🚹 € 190/300
Rest – Carte € 33/63 – *(dinner only) (booking essential)*
1913 Arts and Crafts house on the shores of Lough Caragh, surrounded by mountains. A subtle yet stylish modernisation has emphasised many original features, with oak-panelled walls, flag floors and smart, antique-furnished bedrooms. The restaurant offers classical dishes with subtle modern twists.

Carrig Country House

– ✆ *(066) 976 91 00* – *www.carrighouse.com* – *March-October*
17 rm – €125/175 €150/350 – 1 suite
Rest – Menu €48 – Carte €32/52 – *(dinner only) (booking essential)*
Victorian former hunting lodge set down a wooded drive, located on the lough shore and surrounded by mountains. Cosy, country house interior with traditionally furnished guest areas. Individually decorated bedrooms boast antique furnishings. Beautiful views from the dining room; fresh, country house cooking.

CARLINGFORD (Cairlinn)

Louth – Pop. 1 045 – See Regional map n°**37**-D2
Dublin 106 km – Dundalk 21 km
Michelin Road map 712-N5 – Michelin Green Guide IRELAND

Four Seasons

rest,

– ✆ *(042) 937 35 30* – *www.4seasonshotelcarlingford.ie*
58 rm – €65/150 €69/190
Rest – Menu €25 – Carte €23/36 – *(bar lunch)*
Purpose-built hotel on the edge of the village, with a lovely mountain backdrop. Large leisure centre; open-plan bar. Well-equipped bedrooms; 'Executives' are of a good size, with a separate bath and shower. Ask for a room with lough views. Informal bistro overlooks the garden with its wrought iron pergola.

Beaufort House without rest

– ✆ *(042) 937 38 79* – *www.beauforthouse.net*
6 rm – €65/120 €78/120
Modern house on the shores of the lough. Spacious lounge displays local art and old maritime charts; large, comfortable bedrooms boast water or mountain views. Welcoming owners also run a sailing school.

Carlingford House without rest

– ✆ *(042) 937 31 18* – *www.carlingfordhouse.com* – *Closed 3 January-6 February and Christmas*
5 rm – €60/65 €90/120
Early Victorian house close to the old ruined abbey; the owner was born and has always lived here. Smart, understated bedrooms have good mod cons and are immaculately kept. Pleasant breakfast room; tasty locally smoked salmon and bacon.

Bay Tree with rm

Newry St – ✆ *(042) 938 3848* – *www.belvederehouse.ie* – *Closed 24-26 December, Monday and Tuesday*
7 rm – €55/65 €80/90
Menu €25 (weekdays)/35 – Carte €31/49 – *(dinner only and Sunday lunch) (booking essential)*
Neighbourhood restaurant fronted by bay trees and decorated with wood, branches and hessian. Attractively presented, well-balanced modern dishes feature herbs and salad from the garden and seafood from nearby Carlingford Lough. Service is polite and organised. Simple bedrooms are located upstairs.

CARLOW (Ceatharlach)

Carlow – Pop. 13 698 – See Regional map n°**39**-D2
Dublin 80 km – Kilkenny 37 km – Wexford 75 km
Michelin Road map 712-L9

Barrowville Town House without rest

Kilkenny Rd – *South : 0.75 km on N 9* – ✆ *(059) 914 33 24* – *www.barrowville.com* – *Closed 24-26 December*
7 rm – €40/70 €70/90
Attractive Georgian house on the main road into town. Comfortable, characterful drawing room with heavy fabrics, period ornaments and a grand piano. Breakfast is in the conservatory, overlooking the pretty garden. Spacious, brightly decorated bedrooms offer a good level of comfort and modern facilities.

CARNAROSS (Carn na Ros)

Meath ✉ Kells – See Regional map n°**37**-D3
▶Dublin 69 km – Cavan 43 km – Drogheda 48 km
Michelin Road map 712-L6

Forge

Pottlereagh – Northwest : 7 km by R 147 and N 3 on L 7112 – ✆ (046) 924 50 03 – www.theforgerestaurant.ie – Closed 1 week February, 1 week July, 24-26 December, 1 January, Sunday dinner, Monday and Tuesday
Menu € 25/37 – Carte € 36/48 – *(dinner only and Sunday lunch)*
Stone-built former forge in rural Meath; its atmospheric interior features flagged flooring and warm red décor. Two fairly priced menus offer hearty dishes made from local produce, with pork and bacon from the pigs in the garden.

CARNE

Wexford – See Regional map n°**39**-D3
▶Dublin 169 km – Waterford 82 km – Wexford 21 km
Michelin Road map 712-M11

REPUBLIC OF IRELAND

Lobster Pot

Ballyfane – ✆ (053) 913 11 10 – www.lobsterpotwexford.ie – Closed 1 January-10 February, 24-26 December, Good Friday and Monday except bank holidays
Carte € 27/59
Popular pub filled with a characterful array of memorabilia. Large menus feature tasty, home-style cooking. Fresh seafood dishes are a must-try, with oysters and lobster cooked to order the specialities. No children after 6pm.

CARRICKMACROSS (Carraig Mhachaire Rois)

Monaghan – Pop. 1 978 – See Regional map n°**37**-D2
▶Dublin 92 km – Dundalk 22 km
Michelin Road map 712-L6 – Michelin Green Guide IRELAND

Nuremore

South : 2.25 km by R 178 on old N 2 – ✆ (042) 966 14 38 – www.nuremore.com
72 rm – † € 80/120 †† € 100/150
Rest *Nuremore* – see restaurant listing
Long-standing Victorian house with extensive gardens and golf course. Classical interior with formal bar and comfy lounge serving three-tiered afternoon tea. Good leisure facilities and smart pool. Peaceful bedrooms; many have rural views.

Nuremore – Nuremore Hotel

South : 2.25 km by R 178 on old N 2 – ✆ (042) 966 14 38 – www.nuremore.com
Menu € 30 – Carte € 27/48 – *(dinner only and lunch Saturday-Sunday)*
Traditional split-level dining room within a well-established Victorian hotel. Formally set, linen-laid tables are well-spaced and service is attentive. Menus showcase luxurious seasonal ingredients and dishes are stylishly presented.

Courthouse

1 Monaghan St – ✆ (042) 969 28 48 – www.courthouserestaurant.ie – Closed 1 week January, 25-26 December, Good Friday, Monday except bank holidays and Tuesday
Menu € 25 (weekday dinner) – Carte € 28/42 **s** – *(pre-book at weekends)*
Relaxed, rustic restaurant featuring wooden floors, exposed ceiling rafters and bare brick; ask for table 20, by the window. Great value menus offer carefully prepared, flavourful dishes which are a lesson in self-restraint – their simplicity being a key part of their appeal. Friendly, efficient service.

CARRICK-ON-SHANNON (Cora Droma Rúisc)

Leitrim – Pop. 3 980 – See Regional map n°**37**-C2

Dublin 156 km – Ballina 80 km – Galway 119 km – Roscommon 42 km

Michelin Road map 712-H6 – Michelin Green Guide IRELAND

Landmark

rest,

on N 4 – (071) 962 22 22 – www.thelandmarkhotel.com – Closed 25 December

49 rm – € 69/105 € 100/150

Rest *Boardwalk Café* – Carte € 25/46

Large, modern hotel next to the Shannon, with a water feature in reception and duck-themed pictures throughout; a popular venue for weddings. Bright, bold bedrooms with good facilities. Stylish cocktail lounge with a stunning contemporary design. Informal dining and pleasant river views in Boardwalk.

Oarsman

Bridge St – (071) 962 1733 – www.theoarsman.com – Closed 25-26 December, Good Friday and Monday

Menu € 17 (weekdays)/55 – Carte € 23/46

Traditional, family-run pub set close the river and filled with pottery, bygone artefacts and fishing tackle; it's a hit with the locals. Cooking is simple and produce, locally sourced. The upstairs restaurant opens later in the week.

CARRIGALINE (Carraig Uí Leighin)

Cork – Pop. 14 775 – See Regional map n°**38-B3**

Dublin 262 km – Cork 14 km

Michelin Road map 712-G12

Carrigaline Court

rest,

Cork Rd – (021) 485 21 00 – www.carrigcourt.com – Closed 22-26 December

91 rm – € 85/110 € 100/140 – 2 suites

Rest *The Bistro* – Carte € 27/47 **s** – *(closed Good Friday) (bar lunch)*

Purpose-built hotel in the heart of town. Excellent leisure centre boasting a 20m pool and well-equipped events facilities. Luxurious suites and spacious, modern bedrooms with queen-sized beds. Atmospheric bar for snacks and light meals; formal restaurant has eclectic décor and an international menu.

CARRIGANS (An Carraigain)

Donegal – Pop. 336 – See Regional map n°**37**-C1

Dublin 225 km – Donegal 66 km – Letterkenny 230 km – Sligo 124 km

Michelin Road map 712-J3

Mount Royd without rest

– (074) 914 01 63 – www.mountroyd.com – Closed 1 week Christmas and restricted opening in winter

4 rm – € 40 € 70

Remotely set, creeper-clad house with well-tended gardens, lovely rear terrace and fountain. Immaculately kept throughout with snug lounge and pleasant breakfast room. Cosy bedrooms; one leading to a terrace. Tasty, locally smoked salmon.

CASHEL (Caiseal)

South Tipperary – Pop. 2 275 – See Regional map n°**39**-C2

Dublin 162 km – Cork 96 km – Kilkenny 55 km – Limerick 58 km

Michelin Road map 712-I10 – Michelin Green Guide IRELAND

Cashel Palace

rm,

Main St – (062) 62 707 – www.cashel-palace.ie – Closed 24-27 December

20 rm – € 75/150 € 110/224

Rest – Menu € 27 (lunch) – Carte € 29/47 – *(bar lunch)*

Queen Anne house, once home to an archbishop, with pleasant gardens and path leading to the famous rock. Pillared entrance hall and high-ceilinged guest areas with ornate plasterwork and open fires. Traditional bedrooms; some in the old coach house. Characterful vaulted bar, buttery and elegant restaurant.

Baileys of Cashel
42 Main St – ✆ (062) 61 937 – www.baileyshotelcashel.com – Closed 23-28 December
20 rm – € 65/80 € 90/120
Rest – Menu € 20 (weekday lunch)/40 – Carte € 22/45
Extended Georgian townhouse, used as a grain store during the Irish famine. Small lounge with a library and spacious, contemporary bedrooms, furnished to a high standard. Popular cellar bar offers live music and traditional dishes. More contemporary restaurant serves modern European cooking.

Aulber House without rest
Deerpark, Golden Rd – West : 0.75 km on N 74 – ✆ (062) 63 713 – www.aulberhouse.com – March-October
11 rm – € 50/70 € 80/90
Within walking distance of the Rock of Cashel and the 13C Cistercian abbey ruins. Well-kept gardens with a wooden gazebo. Comfy, open-fired lounge. Bespoke mahogany staircase leads to an open-plan landing; many rooms have king-sized beds.

Chez Hans

Rockside, Moor Ln. – ✆ (062) 61 177 – www.chezhans.net – Closed last week January, 1 week Easter, 24-26 December, Sunday and Monday
Menu € 27 (weekday dinner) – Carte € 40/58 – *(dinner only) (booking essential)*
Imposing former Synod Hall built in 1861, with stained glass lancet windows and vast, high-ceilinged inner. Carefully prepared and creatively presented dishes rely on local produce.

REPUBLIC OF IRELAND

Cafe Hans

Rockside, Moore Lane St – ✆ (062) 63 660 – Closed 2 weeks late January, 1 week October, 25 December, Sunday and Monday
Menu € 23 – Carte € 23/35 – *(lunch only) (bookings not accepted)*
Just down the road from The Rock of Cashel, a vibrant, popular eatery set next to big sister 'Chez Hans' and run by the same family. Closely set tables and art-covered walls. Tasty, unfussy dishes crafted from local ingredients. Arrive early as you can't book.

CASHEL (An Caiseal)

Galway – See Regional map n°**36-A3**
Dublin 278 km – Galway 66 km
Michelin Road map 712-C7 – Michelin Green Guide IRELAND

Cashel House
– ✆ (095) 31 001 – www.cashel-house-hotel.com – Closed 1 January-mid February
30 rm – € 70/115 € 180/230
Rest – Menu € 32/58 – *(bar lunch Monday-Saturday) (booking essential)*
Whitewashed country house built in 1840, surrounded by delightful gardens (gardening courses are available). Plenty of peaceful little seating areas; china and knick-knacks abound. The rear bedrooms are biggest – those higher up have better views. Formal dining room and elegant conservatory. Classical menus.

CASTLEBALDWIN (Béal Átha na gCarraigíní)

Sligo Boyle (roscommon) – See Regional map n°**36-B2**
Dublin 190 km – Longford 67 km – Sligo 24 km
Michelin Road map 712-G5 – Michelin Green Guide IRELAND

Cromleach Lodge
Ballindoon – Southeast : 5.5 km – ✆ (071) 916 51 55 – www.cromleach.com
57 rm – € 70/140 € 80/200
Rest ***Moira's*** – see restaurant listing
Remotely located hotel with superb views over Lough Arrow and the Carrowkeel Cairns. Comfy split-level lounge and bar. Large, luxurious bedrooms in either a modern or classic style; some have balconies or terraces. Stylish, exclusive spa.

Moira's - Cromleach Lodge Hotel
Ballindoon - Southeast : 5.5 km - ✆ (071) 916 51 55 - www.cromleach.com
Menu € 30/55 - Carte € 39/58 - *(dinner only and Sunday lunch)*
Smart, modern hotel restaurant with a glass-fronted kitchen, brushed velvet booths, and lough and country views. Good-sized menus offer classically based dishes with personal twists; local growers and producers are credited on the menu.

CASTLEGREGORY (Caisleán Ghriaire)

Kerry - Pop. 243 - See Regional map n°**38**-**A2**
Dublin 330 km - Dingle 24 km - Killarney 54 km
Michelin Road map 712-B11

Shores Country House without rest
Conor Pass Rd, Cappateige - Southwest : 6 km on A 560 - ✆ (066) 713 91 95 - www.shorescountryhouse.com - Closed 2 December-10 January
6 rm - € 45/90 € 70/100
Modern guesthouse, beautifully set in an elevated position between Stradbally Mountain and a spectacular beach. The friendly owner has added a touch of fun to the place. Stylish bedrooms, some with antique beds; all with good attention to detail. Room 3 has a balcony. Plush breakfast room.

CASTLELYONS (Caisleán Ó Liatháin)

Cork - Pop. 292 - See Regional map n°**38**-**B2**
Dublin 219 km - Cork 30 km - Killarney 104 km - Limerick 64 km
Michelin Road map 712-H11

Ballyvolane House
Southeast : 5.5 km by Midleton rd on Britway rd - ✆ (025) 36 349 - www.ballyvolanehouse.ie - Closed 24 December-4 January and restricted opening in winter
6 rm - € 125/135 € 198/240 **Rest** - Menu € 60 - *(dinner only)*
Stately 18C Italianate mansion surrounded by lovely gardens, lakes and woodland; children can help feed the hens, collect the eggs, pet the donkeys or go on a tractor tour. Comfy guest areas and bedrooms match the period style of the house, and family antiques and memorabilia feature throughout. The walled garden and latest farm produce guide what's on the menu.

CASTLEMARTYR (Baile na Martra) Cork

Cork - Pop. 1 277 - See Regional map n°**39**-**C3**
Dublin 174 km - Cork 20 km - Ballincollig 25 km - Carrigaline 24 km
Michelin Road map 712-H12

Castlemartyr rm, rm,
- ✆ (021) 421 90 00 - www.castlemartyrresort.ie
103 rm - € 150/220 € 165/235 - 28 suites
Rest *Bell Tower* - see restaurant listing
Rest *Franchini's* - Carte € 26/41 - *(dinner only)*
Impressive 17C manor house in 220 acres of grounds, complete with castle ruins, lakes, a golf course and a stunning spa. Luxurious bedrooms have marble bathrooms and excellent mod cons. Look out for the superb old ceiling in the bar. Franchini's offers an extensive Italian menu; the Bell Tower is more formal.

Bell Tower - Castlemartyr Hotel
- ✆ (021) 421 90 00 - www.castlemartyrresort.ie
Menu € 45 **s** - Carte € 38/58 **s** - *(bookings essential for non-residents) (bar lunch)*
Formal dining room with crisply laid tables, set in a 17C manor house. The Garden Room is light and airy, while the Bell Tower has the best views over the grounds. Cooking is modern and sophisticated yet has a strong classical base.

REPUBLIC OF IRELAND

CASTLEPOLLARD (Baile na gCros)

Westmeath – Pop. 1 042 – See Regional map n°**37-C3**
Dublin 63 km – Mullingar 13 km – Tullamore 37 km – Édenderry 36 km
Michelin Road map 712-K6

Lough Bishop House

Derrynagarra, Collinstown – South : 6 km by R 394 taking L 5738 opposite church and school after 4 km – (044) 966 13 13 – www.loughbishophouse.com – Closed Christmas-New Year
3 rm – € 55/70 € 110 **Rest** – Menu € 30
Charming 18C farmhouse on a tranquil, south-facing hillside. The hospitable owners and their dogs greet you, and tea and cake are served on arrival in the cosy lounge. Simple bedrooms have neat shower rooms and no TVs. Communal dining – home-cooked dishes include meats and eggs from their own farm.

CASTLETOWNSHEND (Baile an Chaisleáin)

Cork – Pop. 187 – See Regional map n°**38-B3**
Dublin 346 km – Cork 95 km – Killarney 116 km
Michelin Road map 712-E13 – Michelin Green Guide IRELAND

Mary Ann's

Main St – (028) 36 146 – www.westcorkweek.com/maryanns – Closed 9 January-1 February, 24-26 December and Monday-Tuesday October-March
Carte € 26/52 – *(dinner only)*
Bold red pub set up a steep, narrow street in a sleepy village. Dine in the rustic bar, the linen-laid restaurant or the lovely garden; be sure to visit the art gallery. All-encompassing menus often feature seafood and several Asian dishes.

CAVAN (An Cabhán)

Cavan – Pop. 3 649 – See Regional map n°**37-C2**
Dublin 114 km – Drogheda 93 km – Enniskillen 64 km
Michelin Road map 712-J6 – Michelin Green Guide IRELAND

Radisson Blu Farnham Estate

Farnham Estate – Northwest : 3.75 km on R 198 rest,
– (049) 437 77 00 – www.farnhamestate.com
158 rm – € 99/170 € 109/210 – 4 suites
Rest *Botanica* – Menu € 45 – *(bar lunch Monday-Saturday)*
Set in extensive parkland, boasting every conceivable outdoor activity and an impressive spa. Original Georgian features are combined with contemporary furnishings. Luxury bedrooms offer superb views. Traditional menus feature local, seasonal ingredients.

Cavan Crystal

Dublin Rd – East : 2.5 km on R 212 – (049) 436 0600 – www.cavancrystalhotel.com – Closed 26-28 December
85 rm – € 75/130 € 99/160
Rest *Opus One* – see restaurant listing
Modern hotel next to – and owned by – the Cavan Crystal factory. Impressive atrium and spacious, stylish lounge-bar. Good meeting and leisure facilities. Up-to-date, red and black bedrooms in uniform designs.

Opus One – Cavan Crystal Hotel

Dublin Rd – East : 2.5 km on R 212 – (049) 436 0600 – www.cavancrystalhotel.com – Closed 26-28 December
Menu € 28/38 – Carte € 30/46 – *(light lunch)*
Contemporary first floor restaurant in a smart hotel. Fresh, unfussy dishes at lunch; more ambitious dishes with unusual combinations and textures in the evening. Quality ingredients used in modern techniques.

at Cloverhill North: 12 km by N3 on N54 ✉ Belturbet

XX **Olde Post Inn** with rm

– ✆ (047) 55 555 – www.theoldepostinn.com – Closed 24-27 December and Monday

6 rm – € 55/65 € 100/120

Menu € 33/58 – *(dinner only and Sunday lunch)*

Enjoy a fireside aperitif in the characterful, flag-floored bar or the wood-framed conservatory of this red-brick former post office. The well-established restaurant serves traditional cooking made with Irish produce, wherein classic flavour combinations are given a modern twist. Contemporary bedrooms.

CLAREMORRIS (Clár Chlainne Mhuiris)

Mayo – Pop. 3 412 – See Regional map n°**36-B2**

Dublin 149 km – Castlebar 18 km – Galway 39 km – Newbridge 41 km

Michelin Road map 712-E/F6

McWilliam Park

Knock Rd – East : 2 km on N 60 – ✆ (094) 937 80 00 – www.mcwilliampark.ie

103 rm – € 95/125 € 150/190 – 2 suites

Rest – Menu € 38 **s** – Carte € 29/64 **s** – *(carvery lunch Monday-Saturday)*

Popular, purpose-built hotel, named after an 18C landowner and located on the outskirts of town, close to the airport. Spacious, modern bedrooms; pay the extra for a VIP upgrade. Numerous meeting and events rooms. Carvery offered in the bar; wide-ranging menu in the restaurant. Breakfasts are cooked to order.

REPUBLIC OF IRELAND

CLIFDEN (An Clochán)

Galway – Pop. 2 056 – See Regional map n°**36-A3**

Dublin 291 km – Ballina 124 km – Galway 79 km

Michelin Road map 712-B7 – Michelin Green Guide IRELAND

Clifden Station House

– ✆ (095) 21 699 – www.clifedenstationhouse.com – Closed 25 December

78 rm – € 65/120 € 80/160 **Rest** – Menu € 20/30 – Carte € 19/33

Purpose-built hotel beside the old Galway-Clifden railway line, in a modern residential and leisure complex, with a residents-only kids club, gym and wellness centre. Spacious, uniform bedrooms have good facilities. Local seafood orientated menus in the restaurant. Classic pub dishes in the Signal Bar.

Ardagh

Ballyconneely Rd – South : 3 km. on R 341 – ✆ (095) 21 384 – www.ardaghhotel.com – Easter-October

19 rm – € 70/110 € 120/210

Rest – Menu € 43 – Carte € 36/55 – *(bar lunch)*

Neat, modern hotel overlooking a small bay. Choice of three lounges. Pleasant bedrooms; many with bold fabrics and colourful headboards designed by the owner - some with sofas and armchairs from which to admire the views. Bright restaurant affords an excellent outlook; seafood is a speciality.

Dolphin Beach Country House

Lower Sky Rd – West : 5.5 km. by Sky Rd – ✆ (095) 21 204 – www.dolphinbeachhouse.com – April-October

9 rm – € 55/85 € 100/150

Rest – Menu € 35 **s** – *(dinner only) (residents only)*

Terracotta-coloured former farmhouse in a peaceful hillside location. The interior is styled like a Mediterranean villa, with bright décor and red stone tiles. Good-sized bedrooms display artwork by the friendly owner. Traditional home-cooked meals and wonderful bay views from the dining room.

Quay House without rest
Beach Rd – ✆ (095) 21 369 – www.thequayhouse.com – mid March-October
14 rm – € 75/95 € 130/160
Creamwashed former harbourmaster's house and monastery, overlooking the bay. Relaxed, bohemian interior with antiques and wild animal memorabilia. Comfortable, spacious bedrooms; those in the wing have kitchenettes. Homemade bread and local cheese feature at breakfast.

Sea Mist House without rest
– ✆ (095) 21 441 – www.seamisthouse.com – April-October
4 rm – € 45/80 € 80/110
Centrally located, stone-built house with pleasant gardens, a homely lounge and a bright conservatory breakfast area. Spacious, modern bedrooms boast colourful co-ordinating fabrics and fresh flowers; no TVs. Eclectic Irish art collection.

Buttermilk Lodge without rest
Westport Rd – ✆ (095) 21 951 – www.buttermilklodge.com – Closed November-February
11 rm – € 50/65 € 80/100
Immaculate guesthouse filled with bovine memorabilia. Homely, colour co-ordinated bedrooms; games, hot drinks and a real turf fire in the lounge. Friendly owners offer local info, packed lunches and walking tours. Extensive breakfasts.

CLOGHEEN (An Chloichín)

South Tipperary – Pop. 491 – See Regional map n°**39**-C2
Dublin 122 km – Tipperary 23 km – Clonmel 21 km – Dungarvan 28 km
Michelin Road map 712-I11

Old Convent with rm
Mount Anglesby – Southeast : 0.5 km on R 668 (Lismore rd) – ✆ (052) 746 55 65 – www.theoldconvent.ie – Closed 24 December-31 January and Sunday-Wednesday except bank holidays
7 rm – € 80/120 € 120/190
Menu € 65 – *(dinner only) (booking essential) (set menu only)*
A substantial former convent on the edge of the village, featuring some delightful stained glass windows – dine in the vast, candlelit former chapel. Set 8 course daily menu with some unusual flavour combinations. Smart, comfortable bedrooms have good quality linens. Help yourself to goodies from the pantry.

CLONAKILTY (Cloich na Coillte)

Cork – Pop. 4 000 – See Regional map n°**38**-B3
Dublin 310 km – Cork 51 km
Michelin Road map 712-F13 – Michelin Green Guide IRELAND

Inchydoney Island Lodge and Spa rest,
South : 5.25 km by N 71 following signs for Inchydoney Beach – ✆ (023) 883 31 43 – www.inchydoneyisland.com – Closed 24-25 December
67 rm – € 110/195 € 158/250 – 4 suites
Rest *Gulfstream* – see restaurant listing
Rest *Dunes Bistro* – Carte € 27/55 **s**
Superbly located on a remote headland and boasting stunning views over the beach and out to sea. Contemporary bedrooms come with balconies or terraces and all you could ask for. The smart spa boasts a seawater pool. Dine in the formal restaurant or from an accessible menu in the nautically styled bistro-bar.

Gulfstream – Inchydoney Island Lodge and Spa Hotel
South : 5.25 km by N 71 following signs for Inchydoney Beach – ✆ (023) 883 31 43 – www.inchydoneyisland.com – Closed 24-25 December
Menu € 59 – *(dinner only and Sunday lunch)*
Formal, nautically styled restaurant set on the first floor of a vast hotel and offering superb views over the beach and out to sea. Modern menus highlight produce from West Cork and feature plenty of fresh local seafood. Smooth service.

Deasy's

Ring – Southeast : 3 km – ✆ (023) 883 57 41 – Closed 24-26 December, Good Friday, Sunday dinner, Monday and Tuesday dinner

Menu €26 (dinner)/32 – Carte €31/47

An appealing pub in a picturesque hamlet, offering lovely views out across the bay. Its gloriously dated maritime interior is decorated with framed fish prints and boat propellers. Menus are dictated by the seasons and the latest catch from the local boats; try the tasty Thai coconut fish soup.

An Súgán with rm

41 Wolfe Tone St – ✆ (023) 883 3719 – www.ansugan.com – Closed 25-26 December and Good Friday

7 rm – †€50/60 ††€80/100 Menu €24 (weekday dinner)/38 – Carte €24/49

Charming, personally run, salmon-pink pub with a characterful, memorabilia-filled interior. Traditional menus are based around the daily arrival of fresh local fish and shellfish; a few meat dishes also feature. Set in the old harbourmaster's house, bedrooms are spacious and have bold feature walls.

CLONEGALL (Cluain na nGall)

Carlow – Pop. 245 – See Regional map n°**39**-D2
Dublin 73 km – Carlow 20 km – Kilkenny 39 km – Wexford 30 km
Michelin Road map 712-M9

Sha-Roe Bistro

Main St – ✆ (053) 937 56 36 – Closed January, 1 week April, 1 week October, Sunday dinner, Monday and Tuesday

Menu €34 – Carte €32/43 – *(dinner only and Sunday lunch) (booking essential)*

Rurally located restaurant with a good reputation, set in a pretty little cottage and run by an keen, friendly couple. Rustic lounge and a small dining room with an enormous inglenook and a kitchen table. Flavoursome, classical cooking of local produce; the cheese comes from the weekly farmers' market.

CLONMEL (Cluain Meala)

South Tipperary – Pop. 15 793 – See Regional map n°**39**-C2
Dublin 174 km – Cork 95 km – Kilkenny 50 km – Limerick 77 km
Michelin Road map 712-I10 – Michelin Green Guide IRELAND

Stonehouse

29 Thomas St – ✆ (052) 612 88 77 – www.stonehouserestaurant.ie – Closed 25-26 December, 1 January, Sunday and Monday

Menu €18/27 – Carte €33/49

Smartly refurbished grain store with bright décor and a pianist on Friday and Saturday nights. Cooking is clean and fresh – focusing on the main ingredient of each dish by garnishing it simply and letting the flavours shine through.

CLONTARF = CLUAIN TARBH → See Dublin

Dublin – Michelin Road map 712-N7

CLOVERHILL = DROIM CAISIDE → See Cavan

Cavan – Michelin Road map 712-J5

COBH (An Cóbh)

Cork – Pop. 6 500 – See Regional map n°**38**-B3
Dublin 264 km – Cork 24 km – Waterford 104 km
Michelin Road map 712-H12 – Michelin Green Guide IRELAND

Knockeven House

Rushbrooke – West : 2 km by R 624 – ✆ (021) 481 17 78 – www.knockevenhouse.com – Closed 24-26 December

4 rm – †€65/75 ††€100 **Rest** – Menu €35

Double-fronted Victorian house with high ceilings and lovely cornicing; in the town that was the last port of call for the Titanic. Large period bedrooms come with antiques, feature beds and modern bathrooms. Communal breakfasts and dinners are taken at an antique table and afternoon tea is served from 2-5pm.

CONG (Conga)

Mayo – Pop. 178 – See Regional map n°**36**-A3
Dublin 257 km – Ballina 79 km – Galway 45 km
Michelin Road map 712-E7 – Michelin Green Guide IRELAND

Ashford Castle

– *(094) 954 60 03 – www.ashfordcastle.com*
82 rm – € 205/475 € 225/495 – 3 suites
Rest *Cullen's at the Cottage* – see restaurant listing
Rest *George V* – Menu €79/85 – Carte €55/68 – *(dinner only)*
Hugely impressive lochside castle surrounded by a moat and formal gardens; try your hand at archery, falconry and clay pigeon shooting in the large grounds. Handsome guest areas feature antiques and bedrooms are sumptuously appointed. Dine casually in Cullen's; elegant George V requires a jacket and tie.

The Lodge at Ashford Castle

The Quay – Southeast : 2.25 km by R 345 off R 346 – (094) 954 5400 – www.thelodgeac.com – Closed 23-27 December
50 rm – € 155/265 € 155/265 – 9 suites
Rest *Wilde's* – Menu €54 – Carte €29/44 – *(dinner only and Sunday lunch)*
This extended Georgian house is younger sister to Ashford Castle and offers lovely views down to Lough Corrib. Most of the stylish modern bedrooms overlook a courtyard and some are duplex. Unwind in the hot tub while the children are busy in the 'Wii' room. Modern menus feature in the four-roomed restaurant.

Ballywarren House

East : 3.5 km on R 346 – (094) 954 69 89 – www.ballywarrenhouse.com – Closed 1 week spring and 1 week autumn
3 rm – € 98/136 € 124/160 **Rest** – Menu €45 **s**
Passionately run guesthouse with a lovely oak staircase and a galleried landing. Open-fired guest areas feature chunky pine furnishings, squashy sofas and plenty to read. Bedrooms have luxurious linens and come with complimentary sherry and chocolates. Aga-cooked breakfasts and flavoursome homemade dinners. The charming owners ensure every guest's stay is special.

Michaeleen's Manor without rest

Quay Rd – Southeast : 1.5 km by R 346 – (094) 954 60 89 – www.quietman-cong.com
10 rm – € 50 € 70
'The Quiet Man' was filmed in the village over 60 years ago and this house pays homage – with black and white stills on the walls and rooms named after various characters. Homely lounges and brightly decorated bedrooms. Friendly owners.

Cullen's at the Cottage – Ashford Castle Hotel

– *(094) 954 53 32 – www.ashfordcastle.com*
Carte €39/56
Relaxed, all-day restaurant serving a modern bistro menu; located within the grounds of an imposing castle. In winter it operates from the vaulted basement and in summer, from a thatched cottage with a terrace and lovely views.

CORK (Corcaigh)

Cork – Pop. 119 230 – See Regional map n°**38**-B3
Dublin 253 km – Limerick 99 km
Michelin Road map 712-G12 – Michelin Green Guide IRELAND

Hayfield Manor

Perrott Ave, College Rd – (021) 484 59 00 Town plan: X**z**
– www.hayfieldmanor.ie
88 rm – € 159/269 € 159/289 – 4 suites
Rest *Orchids* Rest *Perrotts* – see restaurant listing
Luxurious country house with wood-panelled hall, impressive staircase and antique-furnished drawing rooms; the perfect spot for afternoon tea. Plush bedrooms have plenty of extras, including putting machines. Well-equipped residents spa.

REPUBLIC OF IRELAND

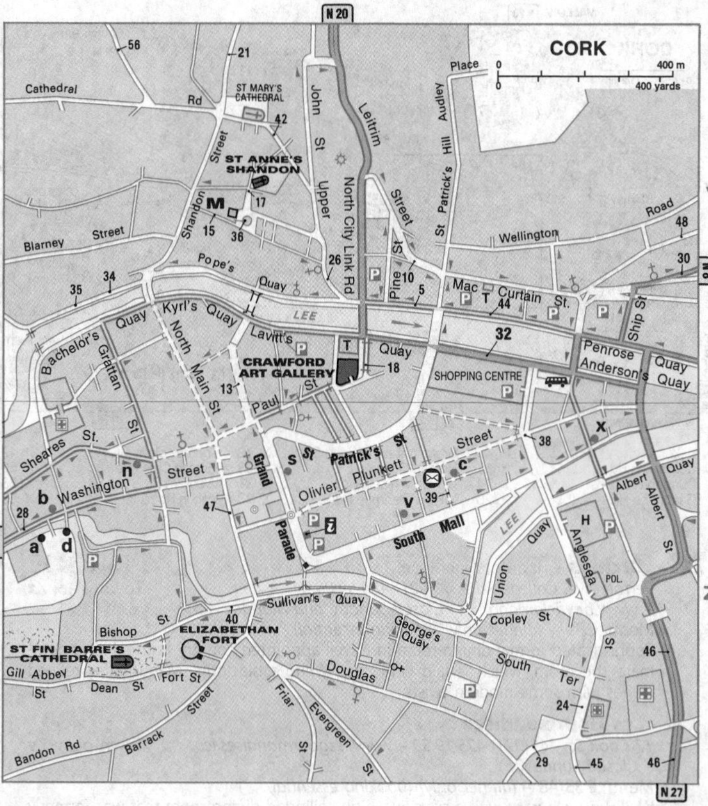

CORK

Street	Plan	No.	Street	Plan	No.	Street	Plan	No.
Buttermarket	Y	36	Langford Row	Z	29	Pembroke St	Z	39
Camden Pl.	Y	5	Lower Glanmire Rd.	Y	30	Proby's Quay	Z	40
Coburg St.	Y	10	Merchant Quay Shopping Centre	Y		Roman St.	Y	42
Corn Market St	Y	13	Merchant's Quay	Y	32	St Patrick's Quay	Y	44
Dominic St	Y	15	Newsom's Quay	Y	34	St Patrick's St.	Z	
Eason Hill	Y	17	North Main Street	YZ		Southern Rd.	Z	45
Emmet Pl.	Y	18	North Mall	Y	35	South City Link Rd.	Z	46
Gerald Griffin St	Y	21	Olivier Plunkett St	Z		South Main St	Z	47
Infirmary Rd	Z	24	Parnell Pl.	Z	38	Summer Hill	Y	48
John Redmond St	Y	26				Wolfe Tone St	Y	56
Lancaster Quay	Z	28						

River Lee

Western Rd. – *(021) 425 27 00* Town plan: Z**a**
– *www.doylecollection.com* – *Closed 23-26 December*
182 rm – € 165/225 € 195/245, €18
Rest *Weir Bistro* – Menu € 25/38 – Carte € 29/57
Modern, purpose-built hotel, 5min walk from the city centre. Large leisure centre with a gym, a 20m pool, and activity and treatment rooms. One whole floor consists of meeting rooms. Uniform bedrooms offer good facilities. Large bar and terrace, and a modern dining room with an unfussy menu and weir views.

Lancaster Lodge without rest

Lancaster Quay, Western Rd – *(021) 425 11 25* Town plan: Z**d**
– *www.lancasterlodge.com* – *Closed 23-28 December*
48 rm – € 79/139 € 79/139, €13
Purpose-built hotel next to the River Lee and within easy walking distance of the town centre. Spacious, bright bedrooms with bold fabrics and modern artwork; the executive suites have whirlpool baths. A good choice for the business traveller.

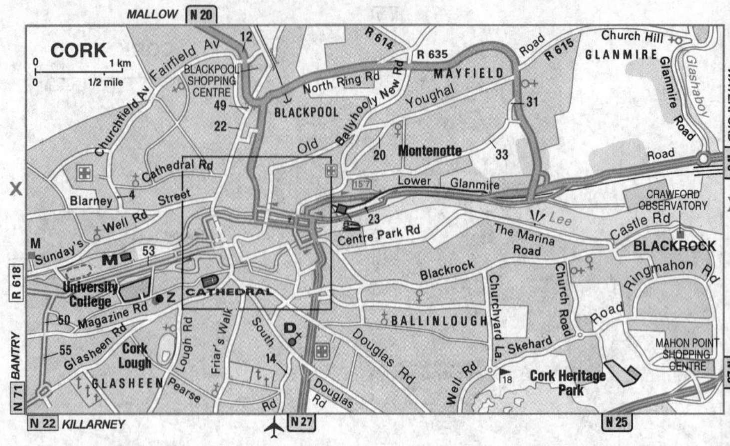

Baker's Rd . . . . . X 4	Great William O'Brien St . . . . X 22	Thomas Davis St. . . . . X 49
Commons Rd . . . . . X 12	Horgan Quay . . . . . X 23	Victoria Cross Rd. . . . . X 50
Curragh Rd . . . . . X 14	Lower Mayfield Rd . . . . . X 31	Western Rd. . . . . X 53
Gardiner's Hill . . . . . X 20	Middle Glanmire Rd . . . . . X 33	Wilton Rd. . . . . X 55

Orchids – Hayfield Manor Hotel

Perrott Ave, College Rd – (021) 484 59 00 Town plan: X**z**
– www.hayfieldmanor.ie – Closed Sunday and Monday
Menu €59 – *(dinner only) (booking essential)*
Sophisticated formal dining room in a well-appointed country house. Pillars dominate the room, which is laid with crisp white tablecloths. Menus offer refined dishes with some modern twists.

Les Gourmandises

17 Cook St – (021) 425 19 59 – www.lesgourmandises.ie Town plan: Z**v**
– Closed Sunday
Menu €33/48 – *(dinner only) (booking essential)*
Well-run restaurant with a spacious, high-ceilinged dining room that was formerly a Turkish bath. The experienced chef produces accomplished, detailed dishes with a classical French base and original touches.

Perrotts – Hayfield Manor Hotel

Perrott Ave, College Rd – (021) 484 59 00 Town plan: X**z**
– www.hayfieldmanor.ie – Closed 25 December
Menu €39/55 – Carte €32/55
Conservatory restaurant overlooking the gardens of a luxurious country house. Smart but comfortably furnished, with adjoining wood-panelled bar. Menu offers a modern take on brasserie classics.

Oysters

Clarion Hotel, Lapps Quay – (021) 427 3777 Town plan: Z**x**
– www.oysters.ie – Closed Sunday and Monday
Menu €24/27 – Carte €34/53 – *(dinner only)*
Set within the Clarion hotel and, surprisingly, Cork's only seafood restaurant! Modern room with a fish tank and central booths. Creative dishes use a classical base and add unusual modern twists. Presentation is bold and service, smooth.

Jacques

23 Oliver Plunket St – (021) 427 73 87 Town plan: Z**c**
– www.jacquesrestaurant.ie – Closed 25 December-3 January, Sunday, Monday dinner and bank holidays
Menu €32 – Carte €20/49
Personally run restaurant with a cosy, intimate feel; hidden away in the centre of town. Seasonal, Irish-inspired menu: honest regional cooking uses quality local ingredients and has clear, defined flavours. Friendly, helpful service.

Cafe Paradiso with rm

16 Lancaster Quay, Western Rd – (021) 427 79 39 Town plan: Z**b**
– www.cafeparadiso.ie – Closed 25-28 December and Sunday
2 rm – € 100/120 € 120
Menu € 29/40 – *(dinner only and lunch Saturday) (booking essential)*
Stylish little restaurant with a grey and green colour scheme, friendly service and intimate atmosphere. Extensive choice of interesting, original, vegetarian dishes which feature plenty of different flavours and textures. Spacious, modern bedrooms come in bright, bold colours.

Fenn's Quay

5 Sheares St – (021) 427 95 27 – www.fennsquay.net Town plan: Z**n**
– Closed 24-27 December, 1 January, Sunday and bank holidays
Menu € 23 (dinner)/35 – Carte € 22/46
Modest little bistro with whitewashed brick walls, closely set tables and a loyal following. Simple, flavoursome cooking offers light lunches and more substantial dishes at dinner; pop in for morning coffee or afternoon tea.

Farmgate Café

English Market (1st floor), Princes St – (021) 427 81 34 Town plan: Z**s**
– www.farmgate.ie – Closed 25-27 December, Sunday and bank holidays
Menu € 17/20 – Carte € 18/31 – *(lunch only)*
Popular, long-standing eatery above a bustling 200 year old market; turn right for self-service or left for the bistro. Daily menus use produce from the stalls below and are supplemented by the latest catch. Dishes are hearty and homemade.

at Cork Airport South: 6.5km by N27 -(X) Cork

Cork International Airport Hotel

rm,

Gate 2 – (021) 454 98 00 – www.corkinternationalairporthotel.com – Closed 24-25 December
145 rm – € 79/149 € 79/149, €15 – 4 suites
Rest *Strata* – Menu € 25 – Carte € 23/44 **s** – *(bar lunch Monday-Saturday)*
Quirky, modern, design-led hotel, with an aviation theme; a stone's throw from the airport terminal. Very spacious bedrooms offer good facilities for the modern business traveller. Strata contains the fuselage of a plane with authentic airline seating, and offers an appealing, international menu.

CORK AIRPORT = AERFORT CHORCAI Cork → See Cork

Cork – Michelin Road map 712-G12

CORROFIN (Cora Finne)

Clare – Pop. 689 – See Regional map n°**38-B1**
Dublin 228 km – Gort 24 km – Limerick 51 km
Michelin Road map 712-E9

Fergus View without rest

Kilnaboy – North : 3.25 km on R 476 – (065) 683 76 06 – www.fergusview.com – March-October
5 rm – € 45/50 € 72/76
Charming bay-windowed house – in the family for four generations; the delightful owners offer superb hospitality. Open-fired lounge, cosy breakfast room and country views. Bright, superbly kept bedrooms: smart but tiny bathrooms; no TVs.

CROMANE

Kerry – Pop. 115 – See Regional map n°**38-A2**
Dublin 201 km – Tralee 23 km – Cork 73 km – Limerick 78 km
Michelin Road map 712-C11

Jacks Coastguard

Cromane Lower – (066) 976 91 02 – www.jackscromane.com – Closed 7 January-9 February, Monday-Wednesday except June-October and Tuesday
Menu € 27/35 – Carte € 28/54
Remote coastguard station; now a bright, glitzy restaurant offering panoramic bay views. Seafood-orientated menus offer well-presented, classic combinations; concise selection at lunch. Smart bar-lounge features live piano at weekends.

CROOKHAVEN (An Cruachán)

Cork – Pop. 1 669 – See Regional map n°**38**-A3
Dublin 373 km – Bantry 40 km – Cork 120 km
Michelin Road map 712-C13

Galley Cove House without rest
West : 0.75 km on R 591 – (028) 35 137 – www.galleycovehouse.com – April-October
4 rm – € 40/50 € 70/85
Detached house just outside the town, affording superb southerly views over the sea towards Fastnet Rock. Conservatory breakfast room and simple, pine-furnished bedrooms with bright colour schemes; all have a sea outlook. Hospitable owners.

CROSSHAVEN

Cork – Pop. 2 093 – See Regional map n°**38**-B3
Dublin 170 km – Cork 15 km – Limerick 78 km – Galway 140 km
Michelin Road map 712-H12

Cronin's
– (021) 483 18 29 – www.croninspub.com – Closed 25 December and Good Friday
Carte € 18/40
In the family since 1970, a classic Irish pub now run by the 3rd generation. Interesting artefacts and boxing memorabilia. Unfussy seafood dishes feature local produce. Limited opening in restaurant, which offers more ambitious fare.

CROSSMOLINA (Crois Mhaoilíona)

Mayo – Pop. 1 061 – See Regional map n°**36**-B2
Dublin 252 km – Ballina 10 km
Michelin Road map 712-E5 – Michelin Green Guide IRELAND

Enniscoe House
Castlehill – South : 3.25 km on R 315 – (096) 31 112 – www.enniscoe.com – Closed 7 January-31 March and 1 November-27 December
6 rm – € 90/130 € 160/240
Rest – Menu € 50 **s** – *(dinner only) (booking essential)*
Classic Georgian manor, part-dating from 1740 and overlooking Lough Conn; the formal walled garden, heritage museum and tea shop are open to the public. Generously proportioned rooms are filled with antiques and family portraits. Traditional set menu of home-grown ingredients served in the formal dining room.

DINGLE (An Daingean)

Kerry – Pop. 1 965 – See Regional map n°**38**-A2
Dublin 347 km – Killarney 82 km – Limerick 153 km
Michelin Road map 712-B11 – Michelin Green Guide IRELAND

Castlewood House without rest
The Wood – (066) 915 27 88 Town plan: Y**w**
– www.castlewooddingle.com – Closed 6 January-13 February and 6-28 December
12 rm – € 65/110 € 95/195
Spacious house overlooking the harbour. Modern bedrooms; all with whirlpool baths – extras include robes, slippers and chocolates. Extensive breakfast buffet and wide range of cooked options; don't miss the bread and butter pudding.

Greenmount House without rest
Gortonora – (066) 915 14 14 Town plan: Z**c**
– www.greenmounthouse.ie – Closed 16-27 December
14 rm – € 60/130 € 80/150
Well-run hotel in an elevated position above the town, with views of the hills and harbour. Comfy lounges and spacious, modern bedrooms; some have balconies and others, small terraces. Excellent breakfasts with a view.

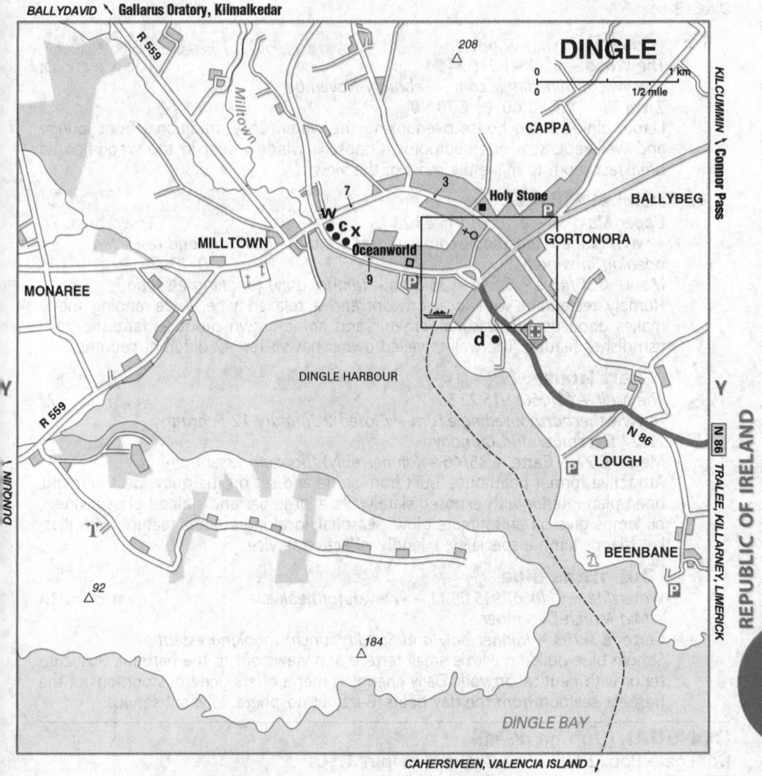

BALLYDAVID ↖ Gallarus Oratory, Kilmalkedar

DINGLE

0 1 km
0 1/2 mile

R 559
208
Milltown
CAPPA
KILCUMMIN ↖ Connor Pass
7
3
Holy Stone
BALLYBEG
W
c
x
MILLTOWN
Oceanworld
GORTONORA
9
MONAREE
d
DINGLE HARBOUR
Y
Y
R 559
N 86
N 86
TRALEE, KILLARNEY, LIMERICK
LOUGH
DUNQUIN ↖
BEENBANE
REPUBLIC OF IRELAND
92
184
DINGLE BAY
CAHERSIVEEN, VALENCIA ISLAND ↓

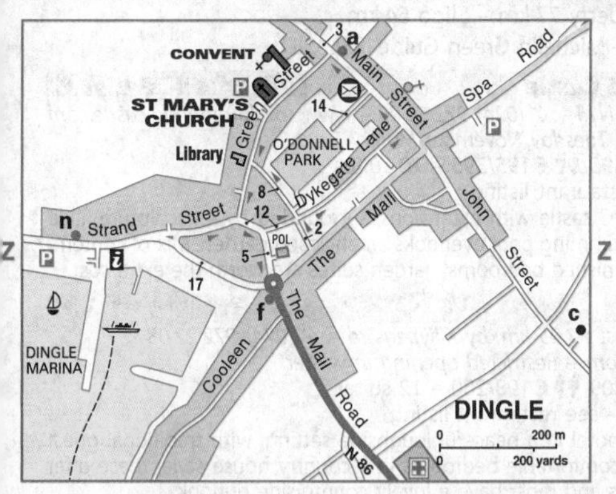

Avondale St	Z	2
Bridge St	Z	5
Goat St	Y, Z	3
Grey's Lane	Z	8
High Road (The)	Y	7
Holy Ground	Z	12
Orchard Lane	Z	14
Tracks (The)	Z	17
Wood (The)	Y	9

Heatons without rest

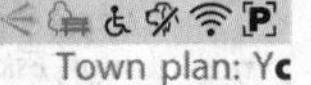

The Wood – ℘ (066) 915 22 88 – www.heatonsdingle.com Town plan: Y**c**
– Closed 2 January-1 February

16 rm ☕ – 🚹 € 55/90 🚹🚹 € 80/128

Large, family-run house, a short walk from town; a warm welcome guaranteed. Modern bedrooms; most have sea views and Room 8 has a balcony. Comprehensive breakfasts include homemade scones, pancakes, omelettes and Drambuie porridge.

Coastline without rest
The Wood – (066) 915 24 94 Town plan: Y**x**
– www.coastlinedingle.com – February-November
7 rm – € 50/60 € 70/90
Large, pink-painted house overlooking the water. Cosy, traditional front lounge and well-kept, spacious bedrooms. Choose a window seat in the wood-floored breakfast room to make the most of the view.

Global Village
Upper Main St – (066) 915 23 25 Town plan: Z**a**
– www.globalvillagedingle.com – Closed January- February and restricted opening in winter
Menu € 30/45 **s** – Carte € 33/50 **s** – *(dinner only) (booking essential)*
Homely restaurant with local artwork and a relaxed vibe. Wide-ranging menu makes good use of seasonal, organic and home-grown produce; fantastic fresh fish dishes feature. The well-travelled owner has visited 42 different countries!

Chart House
The Mall – (066) 915 22 55 Town plan: Z**f**
– www.thecharthousedingle.com – Closed 2 January-12 February, 22-27 December and Monday
Menu € 27 – Carte € 35/46 – *(dinner only) (booking essential)*
Attractive former boathouse, built from stone and set on the quayside. Charming, open-plan interior with exposed slate walls, a large bar and stained glass dividers; oil lamps give off an intimate glow. Seasonal, local ingredients feature, with Blasket Islands lamb a speciality. Friendly, effective service.

Out of the Blue
Waterside – (066) 915 08 11 – www.outoftheblue.ie Town plan: Z**n**
– Mid March-December
Carte € 38/53 – *(dinner only and Sunday lunch) (booking essential)*
Simple blue building with a small terrace and views out to the harbour. Rustic interior with nautical artwork. Daily changing menu offers generous portions of the freshest seafood from the day boats. Buzzy atmosphere. Efficient service.

DONEGAL (Dún na nGall)

Donegal – Pop. 2 607 – See Regional map n°**37**-C1
Dublin 264 km – Londonderry 77 km – Sligo 64 km
Michelin Road map 712-H4 – Michelin Green Guide IRELAND

Solis Lough Eske Castle
Northeast : 6.5 km by N15 – (074) 972 51 00 – www.solisloughheskecastle.com – Closed Monday and Tuesday November-March
96 rm – € 195/395 € 195/395 – 10 suites
Rest *Cedars* – see restaurant listing
Beautifully restored 17C castle with extensions, surrounded by 43 sculpture-filled acres. Fantastic spa; swimming pool overlooks an enclosed garden. Mix of contemporary and antique-furnished bedrooms, garden suites are worth the extra cost.

Harvey's Point
Lough Eske – Northeast : 7.25 km. by Killybegs rd – (074) 972 22 08 – www.harveyspoint.com – Restricted opening in winter
64 rm – € 149/209 € 198/280 – 12 suites
Rest *Harvey's Point* – see restaurant listing
Sprawling, family-run hotel in a peaceful loughside setting, with traditional guest areas and huge, very comfortable bedrooms in a country house style; these offer a high level of facilities and most have a lovely countryside outlook.

Ardeevin without rest
Lough Eske, Barnesmore – Northeast : 9 km by N 15 following signs for Lough Eske Drive – (074) 972 17 90 – www.ardeevin.tripod.com – 19 March-October
6 rm – € 48/52 € 70/80
Friendly, brightly painted house set in peaceful gardens and boasting beautiful views over Lough Eske; personally run by the friendly owner. Warm, pleasantly cluttered guest areas are filled with ornaments and curios. Individually designed bedrooms display quality furnishings and thoughtful extras.

XXX **Harvey's Point** – Harvey's Point Hotel
Lough Eske – Northeast : 7.25 km. by Killybegs rd – ✆ (074) 972 22 08 – www.harveyspoint.com – Closed Sunday-Tuesday November-April
Menu €49 – Carte €46/58 – *(dinner only)*
Formal, traditional restaurant set on the ground floor of a family-owned, country house hotel; its semi-circular windows affording delightful views of the lough. Classic dishes make use of local Donegal produce. Attentive service.

XX **Cedars** – Solis Lough Eske Castle Hotel
Northeast : 6.5 km by N15 – ✆ (074) 972 51 00 – www.solislougheskecastle.com – Closed Monday and Tuesday November-March
Menu €55 – *(dinner only and Sunday lunch)*
Stylish, modern restaurant in a 17C castle close to the lough, with romantic booths to the rear and a slate terrace boasting views over the lawns and woodland. Small menu with international influences, but Donegal produce to the fore.

DONNYBROOK = DOMHNACH BROC ➜ See Dublin

Dublin – Michelin Road map 712-N8

DOOGORT = DUMHA GOIRT ➜ See Achill Island

Mayo – Michelin Road map 712-B5/6

DOOLIN (Dúlainm)

Clare – See Regional map n°**38**-B1
Dublin 275 km – Galway 69 km – Limerick 80 km
Michelin Road map 712-D8 – Michelin Green Guide IRELAND

XX **Cullinan's** with rm
– ✆ (065) 707 41 83 – www.cullinansdoolin.com – Closed mid December-mid February, Sunday dinner and Wednesday
10 rm – € 40/80 €70/120
Menu €30 (early dinner) – Carte €33/47 – *(closed October-April) (dinner only) (booking essential)*
Run by a keen husband and wife team; an orange building in the middle of the Burren, with two walls of full length windows making the most of the view. Classical, comforting cooking uses Irish produce and portions are generous. Comfy, pine-furnished bedrooms; some overlook the River Aille.

DOONBEG

Clare – Pop. 272 – See Regional map n°**38**-B2
Dublin 286 km – Inis 45 km – Galway 115 km – Limerick 91 km
Michelin Road map 712-D9

Trump International H. and Golf Links
Northeast : 9 km on N 67 – ✆ (065) 905 5600 – www.trumphotelcollection.com
rm,
75 rm – €175/200 €175/245, €22
Rest *Ocean View* – Carte €38/64 – *(closed Monday-Thursday in winter) (dinner only)*
Rest *Trump's* – Carte €26/50
Smart resort complex now owned by Donald Trump. Stylish, sumptuous bedrooms and suites are spread about the grounds: some are duplex and feature fully fitted kitchens; all have spacious marble bathrooms and are extremely comfortable. Ocean View offers fine dining with a pleasant outlook over the sea; Trump's brasserie, in the golf clubhouse, serves a traditional menu.

Morrissey's with rm
rest,
– ✆ (065) 905 5304 – www.morrisseysdoonbeg.com – Closed January, February and Monday
6 rm – €50 €90 Carte €23/41 – *(dinner only and Sunday lunch)*
Smartly refurbished pub in a small coastal village; its terrace overlooking the river and the castle ruins. The menu may be simple but cooking is careful and shows respect for ingredients – locally caught fish and shellfish feature heavily. Bedrooms are modern and they have bikes and even a kayak for hire.

DROGHEDA (Droichead Átha)

Louth – Pop. 30 393 – See Regional map n°**37**-D3
Dublin 46 km – Dundalk 35 km
Michelin Road map 712-M6 – Michelin Green Guide IRELAND

The D

rest,

Scotch Hall, Marsh Rd. – (041) 987 77 00 – www.thedhotel.com – Closed Christmas

104 rm – € 70/280 € 80/300 **Rest** – Menu € 29/40 – Carte € 29/55

Smart, modern hotel, in an office and shopping complex on the south bank of the river. Spacious, open-plan guest areas are minimalist in style, with colourful furniture. Decently sized, slightly stark bedrooms; those overlooking the river are the most popular. Informal restaurant; characterful Irish pub.

Scholars Townhouse

King St – by West St and Lawrence St turning left at Lawrence's Gate – (041) 983 54 10 – www.scholarshotel.com – Closed 25-26 December

16 rm – € 75/109 € 89/139 **Rest** – Menu € 27/38 – Carte € 27/77

19C former priest's house: now a well-run, privately owned hotel with smart wood panelling and ornate coving featuring throughout. Appealing bar and cosy lounge; comfortable, well-kept bedrooms. Dine on classically based dishes under an impressive mural of the Battle of Boyne.

Eastern Seaboard Bar & Grill

1 Bryanstown Centre, Dublin Rd – Southeast : 2.5 km. by N 1 taking first right after railway bridge – (041) 980 25 70 – www.easternseaboard.ie – Closed Good Friday and 25 December

Carte € 18/43

A lively, buzzy bistro; its name a reference to its location within Ireland and also a nod to the East Coast of the USA, which influences its extensive menus. Open-plan, with concrete floors and exposed pipework giving an industrial feel.

The Kitchen

2 South Quay – (041) 983 4630 – www.kitchenrestaurant.ie – Closed 1-3 January, 25 August-9 September, 25-27 December and Monday-Tuesday

Carte € 28/42 – *(light lunch)*

Glass-fronted riverfront eatery. By day, a café serving homemade cakes, pastries, salads and sandwiches; by night, a more interesting, mainly Eastern Mediterranean menu is served, with influences from North Africa and the Middle East.

B. Sporrer/Bridge/Photononstop

DUBLIN

Dublin – Pop. 527 612 – See Regional map n°**39**-**D1**

▶ Belfast 166 km – Cork 248 km – Londonderry 235 km

Michelin Road map 712-N7 – Michelin Green Guide IRELAND

© S. Kuttig/imageBROKER/age fotostock

DUBLIN

Hotels

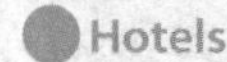 **Shelbourne**

27 St Stephen's Grn. ✉ *D2* – ✆ *(01) 663 45 00* Town plan: **6**JZ**c**
– *www.theshelbourne.ie*

262 rm – 🛉 € 190/850 🛉🛉 € 190/850, ☕ €29 – 12 suites

Rest *Saddle Room* – see restaurant listing

Famed hotel dating from 1824, overlooking an attractive green; this is where the 1922 Irish Constitution was signed. Elegant guest areas and classical architecture; it even has a tiny museum. The bar and lounge are THE places to go for drinks and afternoon tea. Chic spa and characterful, luxurious bedrooms.

Merrion

Upper Merrion St ✉ *D2* – ✆ *(01) 603 06 00* Town plan: **6**KZ**e**
– *www.merrionhotel.com*

142 rm – 🛉 € 495/635 🛉🛉 € 515/655, ☕ €29 – 10 suites

Rest *Cellar* – ✆ (01) 603 06 30
– Menu € 22 (lunch)/30 **s** – Carte dinner € 35/65 **s**

Rest *Cellar Bar* – Carte € 16/53 **s**

A classic Georgian façade conceals this luxury hotel; its opulent drawing rooms filled with antique furniture and fine artwork. Enjoy 'art afternoon tea' with a view of the formal parterre garden. Stylish bedrooms have an understated, classic feel and smart marble bathrooms. Compact spa with impressive pool. Accessible menu in the restaurant and barrel-ceilinged bar.

The Westbury

Grafton St ✉ *D2* – ✆ *(01) 679 1122* Town plan: **6**JY**x**
– *www.doylecollection.com/westbury*

205 rm – 🛉 € 190/535 🛉🛉 € 190/535, ☕ €25 – 8 suites

Rest *Wilde* – Carte € 37/65 – *(closed Sunday and Monday) (dinner only)*

Rest *Café Novo* – Carte € 27/45 – *(closed 25 December)*

Well-run hotel with a stylish bar, a comfy lounge (popular for afternoon tea) and state-of-the-art conference facilities; modern artwork features throughout. Well-equipped, elegant bedrooms come in browns and creams. Excellent service. Formal Wilde offers a modern Irish menu; Café Novo serves old favourites.

The symbol 🌙 guarantees a peaceful night's sleep.

DUBLIN

Adelaïde Rd	BT	3
Alfie Byrne Rd	CS	5
Bath Ave	CT	9
Benburb St	BS	15
Berkeley Rd	BS	16
Botanic Rd	BS	19
Canal Rd	BT	30
Clanbrassil St	BT	40
Conyngham Rd	AS	48
Denmark St	BS	52
Donnybrook Rd	CT	54
Dorset St	BS	55
Drimnagh Rd	AT	57
Eglinton Rd	CT	63
Grand Parade	BT	72
Inchicore Rd	AT	79
Infirmary Rd	AS	81
James St	BT	84
Leeson St Upper	BT	94
Macken St	BST	99
Morehampton Rd	BT	108
Mount St Upper	BT	112
Palmerston Park	BT	123
Phibsborough Rd	BS	132
Rathmines Rd Upper	BT	135
Ringsend Rd	CT	139
St Agnes Rd	AT	141
St Alphonsus Rd	BS	144
St John's Rd West	AS	147
Sandford Rd	BT	151
Shelbourne Rd	CT	157
Shrewsbury Rd	CT	159
South Circular Rd	AS	162
Suir Rd	AT	168
Terenure Rd East	BT	172
Thomas St West	BT	174
Victoria Quay	BS	178
Western Way	BS	184
Wolfe Tone Quay	BS	195

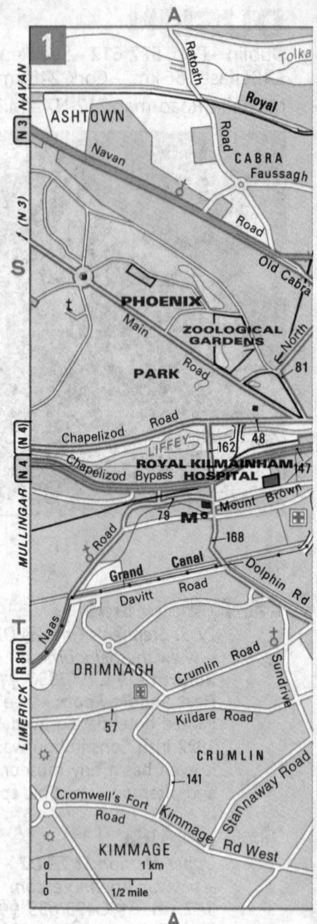

Westin

Westmoreland St ✉ *D2* – ✆ *(01) 645 10 00* Town plan: **6**JY**n**
– *www.thewestindublin.com*
163 rm – 🛉 € 150/500 🛉🛉 € 150/500, ☕ €22 – 13 suites
Rest *Mint* – Carte € 27/48
Built in 1860 as a bank; now a smart hotel set over 6 period buildings, with comfy lounges, impressive conference rooms and good facilities. Bedroom styles range from classic – with mahogany furniture – to contemporary, with leather furnishings and media hubs. The restaurant sits within the bank's old vaults.

Brooks

Drury St ✉ *D2* – ✆ *(01) 670 40 00* Town plan: **6**JY**r**
– *www.brookshotel.ie*
98 rm ☕ – 🛉 € 150/350 🛉🛉 € 160/360 – 1 suite
Rest *Francesca's* – Menu € 23/33 – Carte € 27/51 – *(bar lunch)*
Smart townhouse with a cosy basement lounge, good meeting facilities, including a screening room, and a stylish bar with a collection of whiskies. Bedrooms vary from traditional Classics to contemporary Executives with fresh flowers and thoughtful extras. Quality Irish ingredients feature in the restaurant.

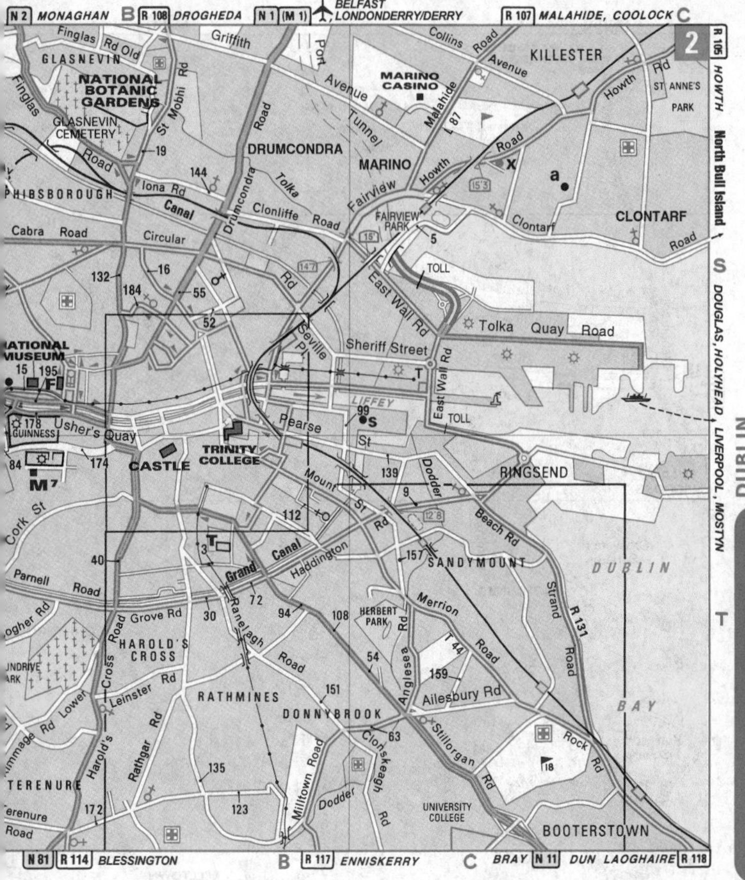

Clarence

6-8 Wellington Quay ✉ *D2* – ✆ *(01) 407 08 00* – *www.theclarence.ie*
Town plan: **5**HY**a**

51 rm – 🚹 € 139/449 🚹🚹 € 159/489, ☕ €15 – 5 suites

Rest *Cleaver East* – see restaurant listing

Stop for a drink in the famous domed cocktail bar of this old Customs House on the banks of the Liffey. Open fires and wood panelling feature throughout. Understated bedrooms combine Arts and Crafts styling with modern facilities.

Fitzwilliam

St Stephen's Grn ✉ *D2* – ✆ *(01) 478 70 00* – *www.fitzwilliamhotel.com*
Town plan: **6**JZ**d**

139 rm – 🚹 € 179/449 🚹🚹 € 179/449, ☕ €22 – 3 suites

Rest *Thornton's* ✿ – see restaurant listing

Rest *Citron* – Menu € 25/39 – Carte dinner € 38/50

Stylish, modern hotel set around an impressive roof garden. Contemporary bedrooms display striking bold colours and good facilities: most overlook the garden; the best overlook St Stephen's Green. Bright first floor brasserie, Citron, offers an original, international menu.

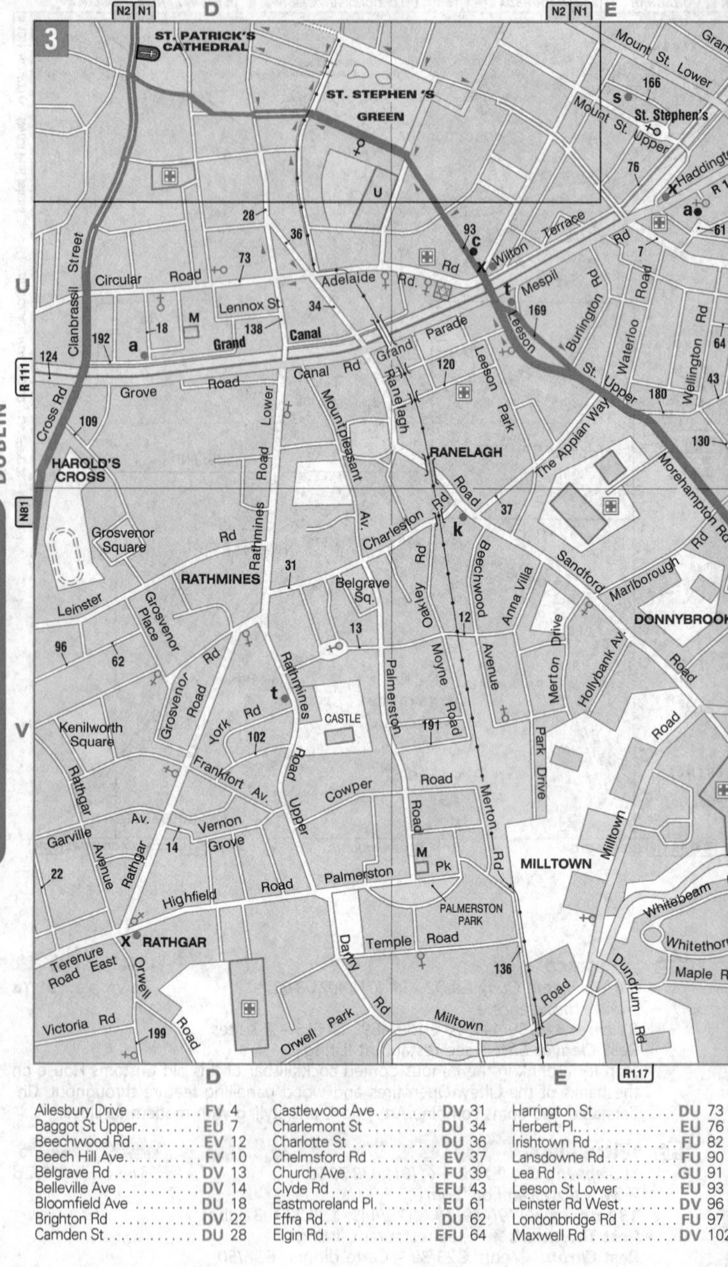

Ailesbury Drive . . . . FV 4		Castlewood Ave. . . . . DV 31		Harrington St . . . . DU 73			
Baggot St Upper. . . . . EU 7		Charlemont St . . . . DU 34		Herbert Pl. . . . . EU 76			
Beechwood Rd. . . . . EV 12		Charlotte St . . . . DU 36		Irishtown Rd . . . . FU 82			
Beech Hill Ave. . . . . FV 10		Chelmsford Rd . . . . EV 37		Lansdowne Rd . . . . FU 90			
Belgrave Rd . . . . DV 13		Church Ave . . . . FU 39		Lea Rd . . . . GU 91			
Belleville Ave . . . . DV 14		Clyde Rd . . . . EFU 43		Leeson St Lower . . . . EU 93			
Bloomfield Ave . . . . DU 18		Eastmoreland Pl. . . . . EU 61		Leinster Rd West. . . . . DV 96			
Brighton Rd . . . . DV 22		Effra Rd. . . . . DU 62		Londonbridge Rd . . . . FU 97			
Camden St . . . . DU 28		Elgin Rd. . . . . EFU 64		Maxwell Rd . . . . DV 102			

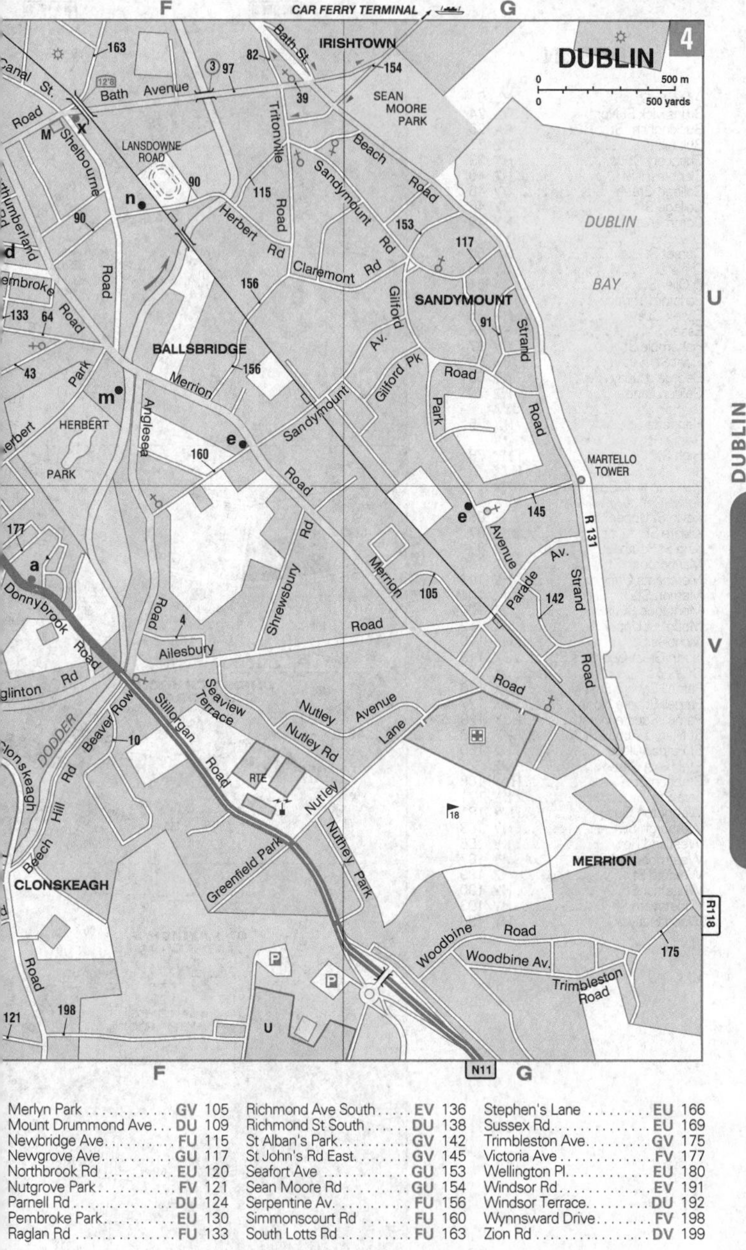

F
G
CAR FERRY TERMINAL
DUBLIN
4
0
500 m
0
500 yards
IRISHTOWN
SEAN MOORE PARK
DUBLIN BAY
Bath St.
Canal St.
Bath Avenue
Shelbourne Road
LANSDOWNE ROAD
Tritonville Road
Beach Road
Sandymount Rd
Herbert Rd
Claremont Rd
Gilford Av.
Gilford Pk
SANDYMOUNT
Strand Road
BALLSBRIDGE
Merrion Road
Sandymount Road
Park
Pembroke Road
Northumberland Rd
HERBERT PARK
Anglesea Road
MARTELLO TOWER
R 131
Avenue
Parade Av.
Strand Road
Shrewsbury Rd
Merrion Road
Ailesbury Road
Donnybrook Road
Eglinton Rd
DODDER
Beaver Row
Stillorgan Road
Seaview Terrace
Nutley Avenue
Nutley Rd
Nutley Lane
RTE
Clonskeagh Rd
Beech Hill Rd
CLONSKEAGH
Greenfield Park
Nuthey Park
MERRION
R118
Woodbine Road
Woodbine Av.
Trimbleston Road
N11
U
V
DUBLIN

DUBLIN

Street	Grid	No.
Anne St South	JYZ	6
Brunswick St North	HX	24
Buckingham St	KX	25
Bull Alley	HZ	27
Chancery St	HY	33
Clanbrassil St	HZ	40
College Green	JY	45
College St	JY	46
Cornmarket	HY	49
Dawson St	JYZ	
Dorset St	HX	55
Duke St	JY	58
D'Olier St	JY	51
Earlsford Terrace	JZ	60
Essex Quay	HY	65
Essex St	HY	66
Fishamble St	HY	67
Fleet St	JY	68
George's Quay	KY	69
Golden Lane	HZ	70
Grafton St	JYZ	
Henrietta St	HX	75
Henry St	JX	
High St	HY	78
Ilac Centre	HJX	
Irish Life Mall Centre	JKX	
Jervis Centre	HJX	
Kevin St Upper	HZ	85
Kildare St	JKZ	87
King St South	JZ	88
Marlborough St	JX	100
Merchants Quay	HY	103
Merrion St	KZ	104
Montague St	JZ	106
Mount St Upper	KZ	112
Nicholas St	HY	118
North Great George's St	JX	119
O'Connell St	JX	
Parnell Square East	JX	126
Parnell Square North	JX	127
Parnell Square West	HJX	129
St Mary's Abbey St	HY	148
St Patrick Close	HZ	150
Stephens Green	JZ	
Stephen St	HJY	165
Tara St	KY	171
Wellington Quay	HJY	181
Werburgh St	HY	183
Westland Row	KY	186
Westmoreland St	JY	187
Wexford St	HZ	189
Whitefriar St	HZ	190
Winetavern St	HY	193
Wood Quay	HY	196

DUBLIN

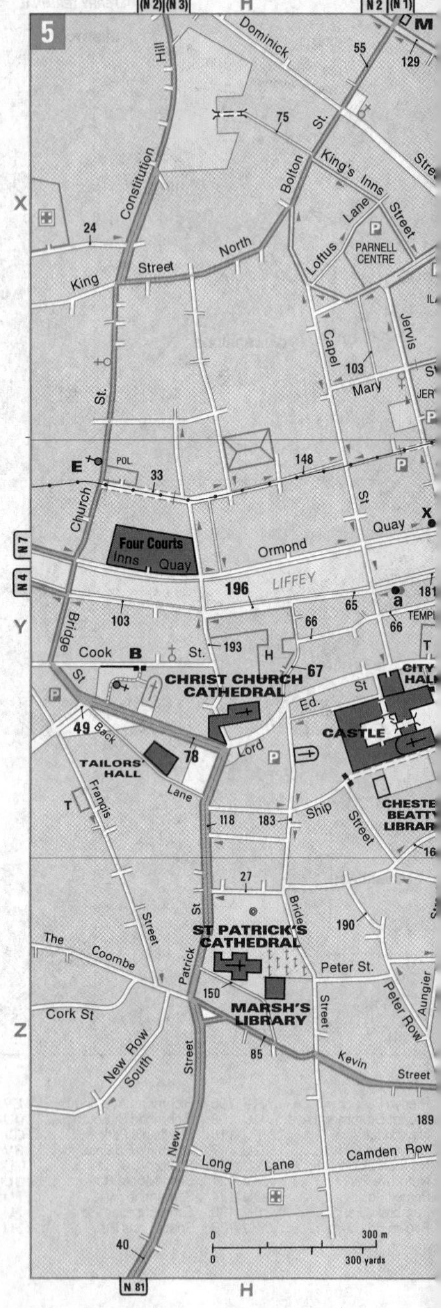

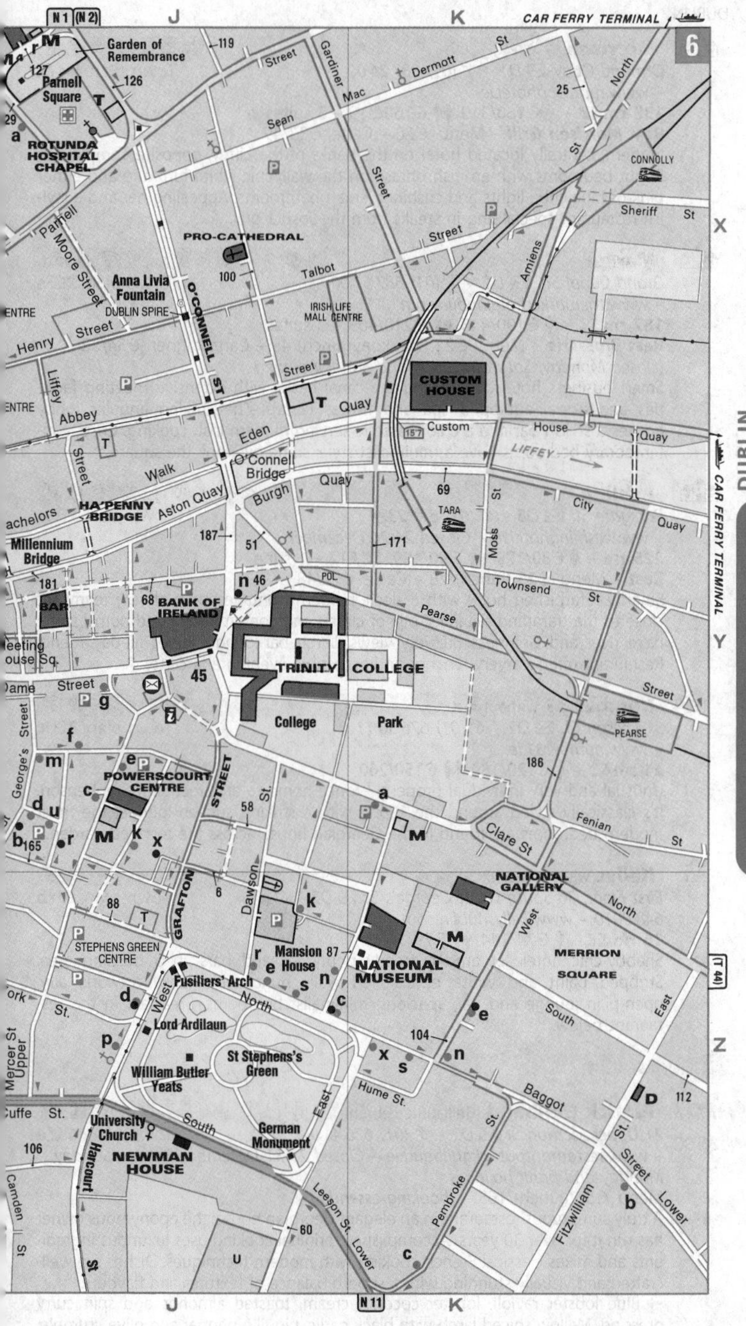

N 1
N 2
J
K
CAR FERRY TERMINAL
6
Garden of Remembrance
Parnell Square
ROTUNDA HOSPITAL CHAPEL
Sean
Mac
Dermott
St
Gardiner
Street
North
St
CONNOLLY
Sheriff
St
X
PRO-CATHEDRAL
Talbot
Street
Amiens
Parnell
Moore Street
Anna Livia Fountain
DUBLIN SPIRE
O'CONNELL ST
IRISH LIFE MALL CENTRE
Henry
Street
Liffey
Abbey
Street
CUSTOM HOUSE
Quay
Eden
Custom
House
Quay
LIFFEY
O'Connell Bridge
Walk
Aston Quay
Burgh
Quay
HA'PENNY BRIDGE
Bachelors
Millennium Bridge
TARA
City
Quay
Moss
St
Townsend
St
Pearse
Street
BAR
BANK OF IRELAND
Meeting House Sq.
TRINITY COLLEGE
College Park
Dame Street
PEARSE
George's Street
POWERSCOURT CENTRE
GRAFTON STREET
Dawson St.
Clare St
Fenian
St
NATIONAL GALLERY
North
West
MERRION SQUARE
STEPHENS GREEN CENTRE
Mansion House
NATIONAL MUSEUM
Fusiliers' Arch
York St.
North
Lord Ardilaun
St Stephens's Green
William Butler Yeats
Mercer St Upper
South
East
T 44
Z
Cuffe St.
Hume St.
Baggot
D
University Church
NEWMAN HOUSE
Harcourt St
German Monument
East
South
Camden St
Leeson St. Lower
Pembroke St.
Fitzwilliam St.
Street
Lower
N 11
DUBLIN

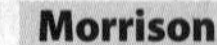

Morrison

Ormond Quay ✉ *D1* – ✆ *(01) 887 24 00* – *www.morrisonhotel.ie* — Town plan: **5**HY**x**

138 rm ☕ – 🚹 € 160/319 🚹🚹 € 160/319 – 3 suites

Rest *Morrison Grill* – Menu € 20 – Carte € 33/49

Modern, centrally located hotel on the banks of the Liffey, opposite Temple Bar. Bright bedrooms with an Irish phrase on the wall, chic white furniture and either pink or blue cube lights and cushions; smart bathrooms. Appealing bar and a stylish restaurant specialising in steaks from the Josper grill.

Marker

rm,

Grand Canal Sq. ✉ *D2* – ✆ *(01) 687 51 00* – *www.themarkerhoteldublin.com* — Town plan: **2**CS**s**

187 rm ☕ – 🚹 € 190/445 🚹🚹 € 210/465 – 3 suites

Rest *Brasserie* – Menu € 22 (weekday lunch)/45 – Carte dinner € 34/52 – *(closed Monday, Saturday lunch and Sunday dinner)*

Smart business hotel overlooking the canal basin, with extensive meeting facilities and a well-equipped spa and fitness centre. The striking angular lobby houses a stylish bar and a chic brasserie serving modern Irish cooking. Crisp, contemporary bedrooms have a minimalist style; some overlook the square.

Ashling

rm, rest,

Parkgate St. ✉ *D8* – ✆ *(01) 677 2324* – *www.ashlinghotel.ie* – *Closed 24-26 December* — Town plan: **2**BS**a**

225 rm – 🚹 € 80/179 🚹🚹 € 90/199, ☕ €12 – 1 suite

Rest – Menu € 25 (lunch)/28 – Carte € 22/48

Smartly refurbished hotel with a sleek, modern frontage and a cheery team; set close to the tram and rail links. Mix of classic and contemporary bedrooms; some have river and Guinness Brewery views. Large bar-lounge serves all-day menu. Restaurant offers carvery lunches and accessible evening à la carte.

Number 31 without rest

31 Leeson Cl. ✉ *D2* – ✆ *(01) 676 50 11* – *www.number31.ie* — Town plan: **3**EU**c**

21 rm ☕ – 🚹 € 120/180 🚹🚹 € 150/260

Unusual and very individual property – once home to architect Sam Stephenson. It's classically styled around the 1960s, with a striking sunken lounge; the most modern bedrooms are found in the Georgian house across the terraced garden.

Kellys without rest

First Floor, 36 South Great George's St ✉ *D2* – ✆ *(01) 648 0010* – *www.kellysdublin.com* — Town plan: **6**JY**b**

16 rm ☕ – 🚹 € 74/144 🚹🚹 € 79/149

Shabby-chic hotel set among trendy boutiques and bars, in a bustling area. Stripped paint and white emulsioned walls hung with funky artwork; airy, open-plan lounge and bar; spacious, minimalist bedrooms. Breakfast in the restaurant below.

Restaurants

Patrick Guilbaud (Guillaume Lebrun)

21 Upper Merrion St ✉ *D2* – ✆ *(01) 676 41 92* – *www.restaurantpatrickguilbaud.ie* – *Closed 25-31 December, 3 April, Sunday, Monday and bank holidays* — Town plan: **6**KZ**e**

Menu € 50 (lunch)/165 – *(booking essential)*

A truly sumptuous restaurant in an elegant Georgian house; the eponymous owner has run it for over 30 years. Accomplished, original cooking uses luxurious ingredients and mixes classical French cooking with modern techniques. Dishes are well-crafted and visually stunning with a superb balance of textures and flavours.

➜ Blue lobster ravioli, lobster coconut cream, toasted almonds and split curry dressing. Mellow spiced lamb with black garlic, piquillo pepper and olive crumble. Green apple parfait with pistachio ice cream and meringue.

Shanahan's on the Green

119 St Stephen's Grn ✉ D2 – ✆ (01) 407 09 39 Town plan: 6JZ**p**
– www.shanahans.ie – Closed 25-27 December, Good Friday and Sunday October-April
Menu €50 (weekdays)/80 – Carte €59/82 – *(dinner only and Friday lunch) (booking essential)*
Georgian townhouse overlooking the green; the basement 'Oval Office' bar features one of JFK's old rocking chairs. Very comfortable, formal dining beneath a fine rococo ceiling. Generous portions; aged Irish Angus beef is a speciality.

Chapter One (Ross Lewis)

The Dublin Writers Museum, 18-19 Parnell Sq ✉ D1 Town plan: 6JX**r**
– ✆ (01) 873 22 66 – www.chapteronerestaurant.com – Closed 2 weeks August, 2 weeks Christmas, Sunday, Monday and bank holidays
Menu €37/70 **s** – *(booking essential)*
Stylish basement restaurant under the Writers Museum, with a modern bar and several smart dining rooms hung with specially commissioned art. Various set and tasting menus offer flavoursome, classically based dishes prepared using modern techniques; the kitchen table has its own special menu. Service is slick.
→ Ceviche of turbot with crab mayonnaise, rope mussels and pickled Atlantic seaweed. Suckling pig cooked in milk with a pata negra crust and an oatmeal, turnip and pork dumpling. Set malted Irish milk with honeycomb, lemon purée, dried milk crisps and honey.

Thornton's (Kevin Thornton) – Fitzwilliam Hotel

128 St Stephen's Grn. ✉ D2 – ✆ (01) 478 70 08 Town plan: 6JZ**d**
– www.thorntonsrestaurant.com – Closed 2 weeks Christmas-New Year, Sunday, Monday and lunch Tuesday-Thursday
Menu €45/70
Elegant restaurant overlooking St Stephen's Green, on the first floor of the Fitzwilliam Hotel. Stylish, contemporary décor with eye-catching photographic montages. Concise, monthly changing à la carte menu; technically adept, modern cooking features classic combinations. 5 or 8 course tasting menu.
→ Dublin Bay prawns, duck egg sabayon and prawn bisque. Braised beef with pomme mousseline and shallot sauce. Rhubarb millefeuille, ginger and rhubarb sorbet.

L'Ecrivain (Derry Clarke)

109a Lower Baggot St ✉ D2 – ✆ (01) 661 19 19 Town plan: 6KZ**b**
– www.lecrivain.com – Closed Sunday and bank holidays
Menu €35/90 – Carte €64/80 – *(dinner only and lunch Thursday-Friday) (booking essential)*
A well-regarded and busy restaurant with a glitzy bar, a whiskey-themed private dining room and an attractive terrace. The refined, balanced menu has a classical foundation whilst also displaying touches of modernity; the ingredients used are superlative. Service is structured yet has personality.
→ Scallops with black olive gnocchi, basil emulsion and tomato. Beef fillet, garlic and herb purée, mushroom ketchup polenta and brisket. Salted caramel mousse, pickled apples and apple sorbet.

Forty One

41 St. Stephen's Grn. ✉ D2 – ✆ (01) 662 00 00 Town plan: 6KZ**x**
– www.restaurantfortyone.ie – Closed Good Friday, 25-30 December, Sunday and Monday
Menu €35 (lunch)/75 – Carte €59/77 – *(booking advisable)*
Intimate, richly furnished restaurant on the first floor of an attractive, creeper-clad townhouse, in a corner of St Stephen's Green. Accomplished, classical cooking features luxurious Irish ingredients and personal, modern touches.

XXX **Greenhouse**
Dawson St ✉ D2 – ✆ (01) 676 7015 Town plan: **6**JZ**r**
– www.thegreenhouserestaurant.ie – Closed 2 weeks July, 2 weeks Christmas, Sunday and Monday
Menu € 35 (weekday lunch)/86
Stylish restaurant with bold turquoise chairs and smooth service. Choose between three dinner menus – one is a 'Surprise' and two have suggested wine flights. Attractive, flavoursome dishes blend both classic and modern styles.

XXX **One Pico**
5-6 Molesworth Pl ✉ D2 – ✆ (01) 676 03 00 Town plan: **6**JZ**k**
– www.onepico.com – Closed bank holidays
Menu € 29/40 – Carte € 54/67
Stylish, modern restaurant tucked away on a back street; a well-regarded place that's a regular haunt for MPs. Muted colour scheme, mirrors and comfy banquettes; classic French cooking offers plenty of flavour.

XX **Hot Stove** (N)
38 Parnell Sq West ✉ D1 – ✆ (01) 874 7778 Town plan: **6**JX**a**
– www.thehotstove.ie – Closed 25 December- 9 January, Sunday and Monday
Menu € 20 (lunch and early dinner)/30 – Carte € 33/56
A popular pre-theatre spot, in the basement of a Georgian house; it takes its name from the range in one of the immaculate, elegant dining rooms. Flavoursome cooking showcases seasonal Irish produce in carefully prepared dishes.

XX **Bang**
11 Merrion Row ✉ D2 – ✆ (01) 400 42 29 Town plan: **6**KZ**a**
– www.bangrestaurant.com – Closed Sunday and bank holidays
Menu € 22 (weekday lunch)/69 – Carte € 42/58
Stylish, three floor restaurant with a pale blue colour scheme: the basement is intimate, the ground floor, light, and the top floor, elegant. Good value lunch and early evening menus; more luxurious, modern dishes on the à la carte.

XX **Saddle Room** – Shelbourne Hotel
27 St Stephen's Grn. ✉ D2 – ✆ (01) 663 45 00 Town plan: **6**JZ**c**
– www.theshelbourne.ie
Menu € 25 (weekday lunch)/42 – Carte € 35/108
Renowned restaurant with a history as long as that of the hotel in which it stands. The warm, inviting room features intimate gold booths and a crustacea counter. The menu offers classic dishes and grills; West Cork beef is a speciality.

XX **Pearl Brasserie**
20 Merrion St Upper ✉ D2 – ✆ (01) 661 35 72 Town plan: **6**KZ**n**
– www.pearl-brasserie.com – Closed 25 December and Sunday
Menu € 25 (weekdays)/48 – Carte € 38/63
Formal basement restaurant with a small bar-lounge and two surprisingly airy dining rooms; sit in a stylish booth in one of the old coal bunkers. Choose from modern menus of elaborate, stylishly presented dishes and a simpler market menu.

XX **Fade St. Social-Restaurant**
4-6 Fade St ✉ D2 – ✆ (01) 604 00 66 Town plan: **6**JY**u**
– www.fadestsocial.com – Closed 25-26 December, Good Friday and lunch Saturday and Sunday
Menu € 25/30 – Carte € 26/53
Have cocktails on the terrace then head for the big, modern brasserie with its raised open kitchen. Dishes use Irish ingredients but have a Mediterranean feel; they specialise in sharing dishes and large cuts of meat such as chateaubriand.

XX **Cliff Townhouse** with rm

22 St Stephen's Grn ✉ D2 – ✆ (01) 638 39 39 Town plan: **6**JZ**s**
– www.theclifftownhouse.com – Closed 17 March, 25-28 December and 1 January

9 rm – € 120/150 € 150/220

Menu € 28 (weekday lunch)/65 – Carte € 32/103 – *(booking advisable)*

Impressive Georgian townhouse overlooking the green. Large dining room with blue leather seating and a marble-topped oyster counter. Seafood-orientated menus offer plenty of choice, from fish and chips to seafood platters or market specials. Bedrooms display contemporary colour schemes and good comforts.

XX **Pichet**

14-15 Trinity St ✉ D2 – ✆ (01) 677 10 60 Town plan: **6**JY**g**
– www.pichetrestaurant.ie – Closed 25-26 December

Menu € 25 (lunch and early dinner) – Carte € 32/58 – *(booking essential)*

Popular brasserie with an open-plan kitchen, an enclosed terrace and a buzzy atmosphere; run by a friendly team. Neat, flavoursome, modern European cooking. Wines are available by the glass or in a 500ml 'pichet'. The front café-cum-bar offers light snacks and cocktails, and they open for breakfast too.

XX **Brasserie Le Pont**

25 Fitzwilliam Pl ✉ D2 – ✆ (01) 669 4600 Town plan: **3**EU**x**
– www.brasserielepont.ie – Closed 25-30 December, Saturday lunch and Monday dinner

Menu € 23 (lunch)/48 – Carte € 30/61 – *(bookings advisable at dinner)*

In the basement of a Georgian townhouse; enjoy lunch at the counter or grab one of the booths for more privacy. Gallic cooking has a classical base but is presented in a light, modern manner. Resident jazz band plays Friday and Saturday.

XX **Dax**

23 Pembroke St Upper ✉ D2 – ✆ (01) 676 14 94 Town plan: **6**KZ**c**
– www.dax.ie – Closed Easter, 10 days Christmas, Saturday lunch, Sunday and Monday

Menu € 22 (weekday lunch)/37 – Carte € 44/60 – *(booking essential)*

Simple, rustic restaurant, well-hidden in the old cellar of a Georgian terraced house near Fitzwilliam Square. Classical Gallic-inspired menus include a seven course 'surprise' selection; a few more modern twists are evident at dinner.

XX **Dobbin's**

15 Stephen's Ln ✉ D2 – (via Stephen's Pl off Lower Mount St) – ✆ (01) 661 95 36 – www.dobbins.ie – Closed 24 December-2 January, Saturday lunch, Sunday dinner, Mondays except December and bank holidays Town plan: **3**EU**s**

Menu € 25/40 – Carte € 36/54 – *(booking essential)*

Hidden away in a back alley. A small bar leads through to a long, narrow room with cosy leather booths, which opens into a spacious conservatory with a terrace. Good value lunch and early evening menus; cooking is in the classical vein.

XX **Peploe's**

16 St Stephen's Grn. ✉ D2 – ✆ (01) 676 31 44 Town plan: **6**JZ**e**
– www.peploes.com – Closed 25-26 December, Good Friday and lunch bank holidays

Menu € 23 (lunch)/50 – Carte € 38/60 – *(booking essential)*

Atmospheric cellar restaurant – formerly a bank vault – named after the artist. Comfy room with a warm, clubby feel and a large mural depicting the owner. The well-drilled team present Mediterranean dishes and an old world wine list.

X **Locks Brasserie**

1 Windsor Terr ✉ D8 – ✆ (01) 420 05 55 Town plan: **3**DU**a**
– www.locksbrasserie.com – Closed 25-28 December and bank holiday Mondays

Menu € 25/38 – Carte € 31/58 – *(dinner only and lunch Thursday-Sunday)*

Relaxed, neighbourhood restaurant on a quiet corner site. The pastel-hued room is full of natural light, with comfy banquette seating and a cocktail bar. The appealing menu features modern European dishes in some innovative combinations. Good value seasonal market menu. Professional, engaging service.

Pig's Ear

4 Nassau St ✉ D2 – ✆ (01) 670 38 65 Town plan: 6KY**a**
– www.thepigsear.ie – Closed first week January, Sunday and bank holidays
Menu € 27 – Carte € 33/49 – *(booking essential)*
Well-established restaurant in a Georgian townhouse, overlooking Trinity College. Floors one and two are bustling dining areas with porcine-themed memorabilia and hearty bistro dishes; floor three is a Scandinavian-style private room with a chef's counter and a more ambitious 12 course tasting menu.

Cleaver East – Clarence Hotel

6-8 Wellington Quay ✉ D2 – ✆ (01) 351 3500 Town plan: 5HY**a**
– www.cleavereast.ie – Closed Monday-Tuesday lunch
Carte € 21/35
Once the Clarence hotel's ballroom; now an industrial-style restaurant with large concrete slabs hanging from the ceiling and meat cleavers on the walls. Menus are made up of unfussy small plates, which are best enjoyed shared.

Fade St. Social-Gastro Bar

4-6 Fade St ✉ D2 – ✆ (01) 6040 066 Town plan: 6JY**u**
– www.fadestreetsocial.com – Closed 25-26 December and Good Friday
Carte € 21/38 – *(dinner only and lunch Saturday-Sunday) (booking essential)*
Buzzy restaurant with an almost frenzied feel. It's all about a diverse range of original, interesting small plates, from a bacon and cabbage burger to a lobster hot dog. Eat at the kitchen counter or on leather cushioned 'saddle' benches.

La Maison

15 Castlemarket ✉ D2 – ✆ (01) 672 7258 Town plan: 6JY**c**
– www.lamaisonrestaurant.ie – Closed 24 December-5 January
Menu € 22 (dinner) – Carte € 22/47
Sweet little French bistro with tables on the pavement and original posters advertising French products. The experienced, Breton-born chef-owner offers carefully prepared, seasonal Gallic classics, brought to the table by a personable team.

Rustic Stone

17 South Great George's St ✉ D2 – ✆ (01) 707 9596 Town plan: 6JY**m**
– www.rusticstone.ie – Closed 25-26 December and 1 January
Menu € 19 (lunch)/25 – Carte € 21/57
Split-level restaurant offering something a little different. Good quality ingredients are cooked simply to retain their natural flavours and menus focus on healthy and special dietary options; some meats and fish arrive on a sizzling stone.

Fallon & Byrne

11-17 Exchequer St ✉ D2 – ✆ (01) 472 10 00 Town plan: 6JY**f**
– www.fallonandbyrne.com – Closed 25-26 December, 1 January and Good Friday
Menu € 25/30 – Carte € 31/57
A former telephone exchange: now a large, busy, New York style food emporium with a basement wine shop. French-inspired, bistro-style first floor restaurant with banquettes and mirrors; seasonal menu of brasserie classics.

L'Gueuleton

1 Fade St ✉ D2 – ✆ (01) 675 37 08 Town plan: 6JY**d**
– www.lgueuleton.com – Closed 25-27 December, 1 January and Good Friday
Menu € 25 (dinner)/35 – Carte € 31/47 – *(bookings not accepted)*
Rustic restaurant with beamed ceilings, Gallic furnishings, a shabby-chic bistro feel and a large pavement terrace. Flavoursome cooking features good value, French country classics which rely on local, seasonal produce. Service is friendly.

Etto

18 Merrion Row ✉ D2 – ✆ (01) 678 8872 Town plan: 6KZ**s**
– www.etto.ie – Closed Sunday and Monday
Menu € 25 – Carte € 31/45 – *(booking essential)*
The name of this rustic restaurant means 'little' and it is totally apt! Blackboards announce the daily wines and the lunchtime 'soup and sandwich' special. Flavoursome dishes rely on good ingredients and have Italian influences; the chef understands natural flavours and follows the 'less is more' approach.

Camden Kitchen

3a Camden Mkt, Grantham St ✉ D8 – ✆ (01) 476 01 25 – www.camdenkitchen.ie – Closed 24-26 December, Sunday and Monday Town plan: 6JZ**x**

Menu €20 (lunch)/24 – Carte €30/49

Simple, modern, neighbourhood bistro set over two floors; watch the owner cooking in the open kitchen. Tasty dishes use good quality Irish ingredients prepared in classic combinations. Relaxed, friendly service from a young team.

Saba

26-28 Clarendon St ✉ D2 – ✆ (01) 679 2000 – www.sabadublin.com – Closed Good Friday and 25-26 December Town plan: 6JY**k**

Menu €14 (weekday lunch)/30 – Carte €24/47

Trendy, buzzy Thai restaurant and cocktail bar. Simple, stylish rooms with refectory tables, banquettes and amusing photos. Fresh, visual, authentic cooking from an all-Thai team, with a few Vietnamese dishes and some fusion cooking too.

Port House

64a South William St ✉ D2 – ✆ (01) 677 0298 – www.porthouse.ie – Closed 25 December Town plan: 6JY**e**

Menu €10 (weekday lunch) – Carte €11/29 – *(bookings not accepted)*

Characterful Spanish tapas bar serving a vast array of authentic, flavoursome dishes. The rustic candlelit interior features exposed bricks, a semi-vaulted ceiling and tightly packed tables. The tasty meats, cheeses and olives are imported.

at Ballsbridge

Four Seasons

Simmonscourt Rd. ✉ D4 – ✆ (01) 665 4000 – www.fourseasons.com/dublin Town plan: 4FU**e**

196 rm – †€205/435 ††€205/435, ☕ €20 – 40 suites

Rest – Menu €50/59 **s** – Carte €32/60 **s**

Imposing hotel on the edge of the RDS arena. Elegant guest areas, state-of-the-art meeting rooms and impressive ballrooms boast ornate décor, antiques and Irish art. Spacious, classical bedrooms have marble bathrooms and plenty of extras. A wide-ranging menu is served in the lounge and the Reading Room.

Dylan

Eastmoreland Pl ✉ D4 – ✆ (01) 660 30 00 – www.dylan.ie – Closed 24-26 December Town plan: 3EU**a**

44 rm – †€179/395 ††€179/395, ☕ €25

Rest – Menu €24 (lunch)/55 – Carte €32/54

Victorian nurses home with a sympathetically styled extension, set on a quiet side road; its funky, boutique interior makes vibrant use of colour. Tasteful, individually decorated bedrooms offer a host of extras; those in the original building are more spacious. Warm, stylish restaurant, with a zinc-topped bar and summer terrace, serves modern Irish dishes.

Herbert Park

✉ D4 – ✆ (01) 667 2200 – www.herbertparkhotel.ie Town plan: 4FU**m**

153 rm – †€115/400 ††€115/600, ☕ €20 – 2 suites

Rest *The Pavilion* – Menu €29 (lunch) – Carte €36/53

Striking modern building with a stark white, open plan, marble-floored lobby displaying eye-catching art. Comfortable bedrooms with plenty of natural light; choose an executive room for more luxury. Chic terrace lounge and bar. The Pavilion restaurant serves classic dishes and has park views.

Schoolhouse

2-8 Northumberland Rd ✉ D4 – ✆ (01) 667 5014 – www.schoolhousehotel.com – Closed 24-26 December Town plan: 3EU**e**

31 rm ☕ – †€99/269 ††€99/269

Rest – Menu €23 (dinner) – Carte €26/47

Dating back to 1861 and formerly the St Stephen's Parochial School. Spacious, well-kept bedrooms – most in the extension – boast William Morris designed fabrics and locally built Mackintosh-style furniture; some have half-tester beds. Busy bar with vaulted ceiling; formal restaurant serves classic dishes.

Ariel House without rest
50-54 Lansdowne Rd ✉ D4 – ☎ (01) 668 5512 Town plan: **4**FU**n**
– www.ariel-house.net – Closed 22-28 December
37 rm ☕ – 🚹 € 79/150 🚹🚹 € 89/220
Close to the Aviva Stadium and a DART station; a personally run Victorian townhouse with comfy, traditional guest areas and antique furnishings. Warmly decorated bedrooms have modern facilities and smart bathrooms; some feature four-posters.

Aberdeen Lodge without rest
53-55 Park Ave. ✉ D4 – ☎ (01) 283 8155 Town plan: **4**GV**e**
– www.aberdeen-lodge.com
16 rm ☕ – 🚹 € 90/109 🚹🚹 € 129/169
Two Edwardian townhouses knocked through into a hotel; in a smart suburban street, minutes' from the sea and a DART Station. Comfy lounge, warm, homely atmosphere and classically furnished, well-equipped bedrooms – some with garden views.

Pembroke Townhouse without rest
88 Pembroke Rd ✉ D4 – ☎ (01) 66 00 277 Town plan: **4**FU**d**
– www.pembroketownhouse.ie – Closed 1 week Christmas-New Year
48 rm – 🚹 € 70/320 🚹🚹 € 70/320, ☕ €15
Friendly, traditionally styled hotel set in 3 Georgian houses. Small lounge with honesty bar and pantry. Sunny breakfast room offering homemade bread, cakes and biscuits. Variously sized, neutrally hued bedrooms; go for a duplex room.

Asador
1 Victoria House, Haddington Rd ✉ D4 – ☎ (01) 254 5353 – www.asador.ie – Closed Monday Town plan: **3**EU**x**
Menu € 19 (dinner) – Carte € 22/56
Themed around the chargrill (or 'asador'); watch the chefs in the open-plan kitchen. Fresh, tasty cooking has South American and Spanish influences. On your own? Try the counter. In a group? Go for one of the curvaceous booths.

Chop House
2 Shelbourne Rd ✉ D4 – ☎ (01) 660 23 90 Town plan: **4**FU**x**
– www.thechophouse.ie
Menu € 27/32 – Carte € 30/49
Imposing pub close to the stadium, with a small side terrace, a dark bar and a bright, airy conservatory. The relaxed lunchtime menu is followed by more ambitious dishes in the evening, when the kitchen really comes into its own.

at Donnybrook

Mulberry Garden
Mulberry Ln ✉ D4 – off Donnybrook Rd – ☎ (01) 269 3300 – www.mulberrygarden.ie – Closed Sunday-Wednesday Town plan: **4**FV**a**
Menu € 35/60 – *(dinner only and Sunday lunch in summer) (booking essential)*
Delightful restaurant hidden away in the city suburbs; its interesting L-shaped dining room set around a small courtyard terrace. Choice of two dishes per course on the weekly menu; original modern cooking relies on tasty local produce.

at Ranelagh

Kinara Kitchen Ⓝ
17 Ranelagh Village ✉ D6 – ☎ (01) 406 0066 Town plan: **3**EV**k**
– www.kinarakitchen.ie – Closed 25-26 December and Good Friday
Menu € 17 (weekdays)/22 – Carte € 26/49
This smart restaurant has become a destination not just for its cooking but for its cocktails too. The friendly, professional team serve a menu of homely, well-spiced Pakistani classics, including a selection from the tandoor oven.

Forest Avenue

8 Sussex Ter ✉ D4 – ✆ (01) 667 8337 Town plan: **3**EU**t**
– www.forestavenuerestaurant.ie – Closed Monday and Tuesday dinner
Menu € 25 (weekday lunch)/48
An experienced couple run this intimate neighbourhood restaurant. It has a rustic feel, with stags' heads lining the walls and antler light fittings. Cooking is modern with the odd Asian twist; be sure to try the potato bread.

Brioche

51 Elmwood Ave Lower ✉ *D6 –* ✆ *(01) 497 91 63* Town plan: **3**EV**x**
– www.briocheranelagh.com – Closed 1-14 August , 25-27 December , 1 January, Sunday and Monday
Menu € 38/45 – Carte € 27/34 – *(dinner only)*
As the name suggests, it's all about France at this lovely bistro in the buzzy Ranelagh district. Choose from 13 attractively presented, modern French small plates; about three should suffice, followed by cheese or a dessert.

at Rathmines

Zen

89 Upper Rathmines Rd ✉ *D6 –* ✆ *(01) 497 94 28* Town plan: **3**DV**t**
– www.zenrestaurant.ie – Closed 25-27 December
Menu € 19 (weekday lunch)/24 – Carte € 23/34 – *(dinner only and Friday lunch)*
Long-standing, family-run restaurant, unusually set in an old church hall – at the centre of the elegant interior is a huge sun embellished with gold leaf. Imaginative Chinese cooking centres around Cantonese and spicy Sichuan cuisine.

at Dublin Airport North: 10.5 km by N1 -(BS)- and M1 ✉ Dublin

Carlton H. Dublin Airport

rest,

Old Airport Rd, Cloughran – South : 2 km on R 132 – ✆ *(01) 866 7500*
– www.carltondublinairport.com – Closed 24-26 December
100 rm – † € 79/199 †† € 79/249, ☕ €14 – 1 suite
Rest *Kittyhawks* – Menu € 22 (dinner)/26 – Carte € 21/50 – *(carvery lunch)*
Modern, purpose-built, business hotel with a spacious marbled reception and comfy guest areas. Up-to-date bedrooms have good facilities and smart bathrooms. Some rooms overlook the airfield; some have balconies. Informal all-day brasserie offers lunchtime carvery and a wide-ranging evening menu.

Bewleys

rest,

Baskin Ln – East : 4 km on N 32 – ✆ *(01) 871 1000 – www.bewleyshotels.com*
469 rm – † € 69/169 †† € 69/169, ☕ €10
Rest *The Brasserie* – Menu € 25 – Carte € 29/50 – *(carvery lunch)*
Eight-floor hotel with good conference facilities, plenty of parking and a free courtesy bus to and from the airport. Spacious, up-to-date bedrooms. All-day dining in the comfortable lobby bar and lounge. The Brasserie offers a buffet and carvery lunch, with a wide-ranging evening à la carte.

at Clontarf Northeast: 5.5km by R105 ✉ Dublin

Clontarf Castle

Castle Ave. ✉ *D3 –* ✆ *(01) 833 2321* Town plan: **2**CS**a**
– www.clontarfcastle.ie
111 rm – † € 119/440 †† € 119/650, ☕ €10
Rest *Fahrenheit Grill* – Menu € 24 – Carte € 28/44 – *(bar lunch Monday-Saturday)*
A historic castle, dating back to 1172, with modern extensions; well-located in a quiet residential area close to the city. Contemporary bedrooms are decorated with bold, warm colours. Fahrenheit offers grilled local meats and seafood in a medieval ambience.

DUBLIN

XX **Downstairs**
Hollybrook Park ✉ *D3 – ✆ (01) 833 8883* Town plan: **2**CS**x**
– www.downstairs.ie – Closed 25-26 December and Good Friday
Menu € 30 (lunch) – Carte € 32/45 – *(dinner only and Sunday lunch)*
Basement restaurant located beneath a bar, in a lovely neighbourhood close to the sea. It's spacious and contemporary in style, with an attractive tiled bar and a display of wooden wine cases. Menus offer an eclectic mix of dishes and the refined, balanced cooking shows respect for natural flavours.

at Dundrum Southeast: 8 km by N11 -(CT)✉ Dublin

XX **Ananda**
Sandyford Rd, Dundrum town centre ✉ *D14 – ✆ (01) 296 00 99*
– www.anandarestaurant.ie – Closed 25-26 December
Menu € 18 (lunch)/50 – Carte € 26/60 – *(dinner only and lunch Friday-Sunday)*
Meaning 'bliss' in ancient Sanskrit, and located in a shopping mall, is this stylish restaurant with a smart cocktail bar/lounge and attractive fretwork. Accomplished, original, modern Indian cooking. Attentive, professional service.

at Sandyford Southeast: 12 km by N11 and R112 off R133 -(CT)✉ Dublin

Beacon rest,
Beacon Court, Sandyford Business Region ✉ *D18 – ✆ (01) 291 5000*
– www.thebeacon.com – Closed 24-26 December
88 rm – € 90/180 € 120/250 – 1 suite
Rest *My Thai* – Menu € 20 (dinner)/35 – Carte € 29/39 **s**
Ultra-stylish hotel in a modern glass building; its stunning entrance lobby features mirrored walls and a bed for sitting on. Stark white bedrooms and luxurious, glass-walled bathrooms. Low-key meeting rooms. Modish Crystal bar. Funky, relaxed My Thai serves authentic Asian dishes.

XX **China Sichuan**
The Forum, Ballymoss Rd. ✉ *D18 – ✆ (01) 293 5100 – www.china-sichuan.ie*
– Closed 25-31 December, Good Friday, lunch Saturday and bank holidays
Menu € 15 (weekday lunch)/45 – Carte € 21/57
Established in 1979 and now run by the third generation of the family. Smart, modern interior matched by creative menus, where Irish produce is used in tasty Chinese dishes: largely Cantonese classics with some Sichuan specialities.

at Foxrock Southeast: 13 km by N11 -(CT)✉ Dublin

XX **Bistro One**
3 Brighton Rd ✉ *D18 – ✆ (01) 289 7711 – www.bistro-one.ie – Closed 25 December-3 January, Sunday and Monday*
Menu € 20 (weekdays) – Carte € 27/58 – *(booking essential)*
Long-standing neighbourhood bistro above a parade of shops; run by a father-daughter team and a real hit with the locals. Good value daily menus – dishes range from traditional Irish to Italian. They produce their own Tuscan olive oil.

at Rathgar South: 3.75 km by N81

X **Bijou**
46 Highfield Rd ✉ *D6 – ✆ (01) 496 1518* Town plan: **3**DV**x**
– www.bijourathgar.ie – Closed 25-26 December
Menu € 20/25 – Carte € 28/45
Friendly, two-floored restaurant with a heated terrace and a clubby feel; the experienced owners also run the nearby deli. Local ingredients feature in accomplished, full-flavoured, classically based dishes with modern touches.

DUBLIN AIRPORT = AERFORT BHAILE ÁTHA CLIATH → See Dublin
Fingal – Michelin Road map 712-N7

DUNBOYNE (Dún Búinne)
Meath – Pop. 6 959 – See Regional map n°**37**-D3
Dublin 17 km – Drogheda 45 km – Newbridge 54 km
Michelin Road map 712-M7

Dunboyne Castle

– (01) 801 35 00 – *www.dunboynecastlehotel.com*
145 rm – € 79/209 € 99/359 – 4 suites
Rest *The Ivy* – Menu € 22/27 – Carte € 31/52 – *(dinner only and Sunday lunch)*
Georgian house with vast, modern extensions and formal gardens, set in 20 acres. Large, relaxing spa has 18 treatment rooms and uses organic Irish seaweed products. Spacious bedrooms boast good mod cons; some have balconies. Informal dining in The Ivy, which offers classically based Irish dishes.

DUNCANNON (Dún Canann)

Wexford – Pop. 328 – See Regional map n°**39**-D2
Dublin 167 km – New Ross 26 km – Waterford 48 km
Michelin Road map 712-L11 – Michelin Green Guide IRELAND

Aldridge Lodge with rm

South : 2 km on Hook Head rd – (051) 389 116 – www.aldridgelodge.com – Closed 3 weeks January and 24-25 December
3 rm – € 45 € 90
Menu € 29/39 **s** – *(closed Monday and Tuesday) (dinner only and Sunday lunch) (booking essential)*
New-build house run by cheery owners. The constantly evolving menu offers tasty homemade bread and veg from the kitchen garden. The focus is on good value fish and shellfish – the owner's father is a local fisherman – with some Asian and fusion influences. Simply furnished bedrooms come with hot water bottles and home-baked cookies.

REPUBLIC OF IRELAND

DUNDALK (Dún Dealgan)

Louth – Pop. 31 149 – See Regional map n°**37**-D2
Dublin 82 km – Drogheda 35 km
Michelin Road map 712-M5/6 – Michelin Green Guide IRELAND

Crowne Plaza

Green Park – South : 2.75 km by R 132 – (042) 939 49 00 – www.cpdundalk.ie – Closed 24-25 December
129 rm – € 79/119 € 89/149 – 1 suite
Rest *Farenheit Grill* – Menu € 25 **s** – Carte € 23/47 **s** – *(closed Sunday-Wednesday) (bar lunch Monday-Saturday)*
Modern, 14-storey hotel tower block, close to the business park, with a stylish ground floor bar/lounge and good conference facilities. Uniform bedrooms boast a high level of facilities and countryside views; ask for one higher up. 13th floor restaurant offers a seasonal brasserie menu and a 360° vista.

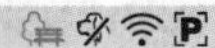

Rosemount without rest

Dublin Rd – South : 2.5 km on R 132 – (042) 933 58 78 – www.rosemountireland.com – Closed 22-27 December
10 rm – € 40/50 € 60/70
Attractive guesthouse fronted by a delightful flower-filled garden and run by a welcoming couple. Warmly decorated lounge. Snug, individually styled and spotlessly kept bedrooms feature Laura Ashley fabrics and have modern facilities. Tea and cake on arrival; freshly cooked breakfasts in the morning.

Left Bank

43-44 Park St – (042) 933 88 51 – www.leftbankdundalk.com – Closed 25-26 December, bank holidays, Monday and Tuesday
Menu € 14/25 – Carte € 28/43
Well-run bistro in a busy market town. Large bar and raised dining room with tightly packed tables and booth seating; chiller cabinet offers homemade pastries and cakes to take home. All-purpose menus offer carefully prepared, hearty dishes.

at Jenkinstown Northeast: 9 km by N52 on R173

Fitzpatricks

Rockmarshall – Southeast : 1 km – ☎ (042) 937 61 93 – www.fitzpatricks-restaurant.com – Closed Good Friday and 25 December

Menu € 28 (weekdays)/30 – Carte € 26/51

Hugely characterful pub on the coast road, at the foot of the mountains, with beautiful flower displays and a wealth of memorabilia. Extensive menu of hearty, flavoursome, traditional dishes; local steaks and seafood are a speciality.

DUNDRUM = DÚN DROMA → See Dublin

Dún Laoghaire-Rathdown – Michelin Road map 712-N8

DUNFANAGHY (Dún Fionnachaidh)

Donegal – Pop. 312 – ✉ Letterkenny – See Regional map n°**37**-C1

Dublin 277 km – Donegal 87 km – Londonderry 69 km

Michelin Road map 712-I2 – Michelin Green Guide IRELAND

Mill with rm

rest,

Southwest : 0.75 km on N 56 – ☎ (074) 913 69 85 – www.themillrestaurant.com – Mid March-December

6 rm – € 60 € 96 Menu € 38 – *(closed Monday) (dinner only)*

Converted flax mill on the waterside, with lovely garden edged by reeds and great view of Mount Muckish. Homely inner with conservatory lounge and knick-knacks on display throughout. Antique-furnished dining room has a classical Georgian feel. Traditional menus showcase seasonal ingredients and fish features highly. Cosy, welcoming bedrooms come in individual designs.

DUNGARVAN (Dún Garbhán)

Waterford – Pop. 7 991 – See Regional map n°**39**-C3

Dublin 190 km – Cork 71 km – Waterford 48 km

Michelin Road map 712-J11 – Michelin Green Guide IRELAND

Tannery with rm

rest,

10 Quay St – via Parnell St – ☎ (058) 45 420 – www.tannery.ie – Closed last 2 weeks January, 25-26 December and Good Friday

14 rm – € 60/70 € 100/110

Menu € 30 – Carte € 43/51 – *(dinner only and lunch Friday and Sunday)*

Characterful 19C tannery with a high ceiling, rustic girders and modern décor. Menus are concise and offer dishes ranging from the simple to the more imaginative (maybe crab crème brûlée). They also run a renowned cookery school. Stylish bedrooms come in contemporary, New England and French farmhouse styles.

DUNKINEELY (Dún Cionnaola)

Donegal – Pop. 375 – See Regional map n°**37**-C1

Dublin 156 km – Lifford 42 km – Sligo 53 km – Ballybofey 28 km

Michelin Road map 712-G4

Castle Murray House with rm

St John's Point – Southwest : 1.5 km by N 56 on St John's Point rd – ☎ (074) 973 70 22 – www.castlemurray.com – Closed January-mid February, 24-26 December, and Monday-Tuesday in winter

10 rm – € 65/85 € 55/70

Menu € 33/47 – *(dinner only and Sunday lunch light lunch in summer)*

Established restaurant in a delightful coastal location, offering great castle, sea and sunset views. Start in the snug bar with its seafaring memorabilia then move to the spacious dining room, large conservatory or vast decked terrace. The classical menu features mussels and oysters from the bay. Stylish bedrooms have gilt mirrors, plush fabrics and very comfy beds.

DUN LAOGHAIRE (Dún Laoghaire)

Dún Laoghaire-Rathdown – Pop. 23 857 – See Regional map n°**39-D1**
Dublin 12 km – Belfast 176 km – Cork 265 km – Lisburn 164 km
Michelin Road map 712-N8 – Michelin Green Guide IRELAND

XX **Rasam**

18-19 Glasthule Rd, 1st Floor (above Eagle House pub) **Town plan:e**
– (01) 230 0600 – www.rasam.ie – Closed 25-26 December and Good Friday
Menu €21 (weekday dinner)/45 – Carte €30/52 – *(dinner only)*

The perfume of rose petals greets you, as you head up to the plush lounge and contemporary restaurant. Fresh, authentic Indian dishes come in original combinations and are cooked from scratch; they even dry roast and blend their own spices.

X **Le Petit Cochon** (N)

57a Glasthule Rd – (01) 236 5971 **Town plan:x**
– www.lepetitcochon.com – Closed Good Friday and 24-26 December
Menu €26 – Carte €26/45 – *(dinner only and Sunday lunch)*

It might be run by the same team but that's all that's left of what was once 'Tribes'. As its name suggests, this bistro has a distinct Gallic feel. Start with onion soup, followed by entrecote frites, then finish with a crème brûlée.

X **Cavistons** AC

58-59 Glasthule Rd – ✆ (01) 280 9245 **Town plan:a**
– www.cavistons.com – Closed Sunday and Monday
Menu € 19 – Carte € 30/49 – *(lunch only and dinner Thursday-Saturday) (booking essential)*
A landmark in the town: a fresh fish shop, a well-stocked deli and a cosy bistro in one. Simple décor, with ten wooden tables and a mermaid mural. Fresh, carefully cooked fish and seafood. Swift, friendly service.

DUNLAVIN (Dún Luáin)

Wicklow – Pop. 830 – See Regional map n°**39**-D2
Dublin 50 km – Kilkenny 71 km – Wexford 98 km
Michelin Road map 712-L8

Rathsallagh House rest,

Southwest : 3.25 km on Grangecon rd – ✆ (045) 403 112 – www.rathsallagh.com – Closed mid week November-March
29 rm – € 145/175 € 145/200 – 1 suite
Rest – Menu € 29 – Carte € 32/54 – *(dinner only and Sunday lunch) (bookings essential for non-residents)*
Collection of converted 18C stables and farm buildings in a peaceful, rural location. Extensive grounds include a golf course and a working farm to the rear. Characterful, open-fired lounges and cottagey bar; spacious country house bedrooms with good facilities. Large formal restaurant serves classic dishes.

DUNMORE EAST (Dún Mór)

Waterford – Pop. 1 559 – ✉ Waterford – See Regional map n°**39**-C2
Dublin 186 km – Belfast 354 km – Cork 137 km – Lisburn 342 km
Michelin Road map 712-L11 – Michelin Green Guide IRELAND

Beach without rest

1 Lower Village – ✆ (051) 383 316 – www.dunmorebeachguesthouse.com – April-October
9 rm – € 50/70 € 70/90
Modern house overlooking a large cove, with the beach just metres away; take in the superb view from the conservatory lounge-cum-breakfast room. The place almost has a Mediterranean feel – bedrooms have whitewashed walls and ash furniture.

DURRUS (Dúras)

Cork – Pop. 334 – See Regional map n°**38**-A3
Dublin 338 km – Cork 90 km – Killarney 85 km
Michelin Road map 712-D13

XX **Blairscove House** with rm

Southwest : 1.5 km on R 591 – ✆ (027) 61 127 – www.blairscove.ie – 17 March-October
4 rm – € 105/160 € 150/260
Menu € 46/58 **s** – *(closed Sunday and Monday) (dinner only) (booking essential)*
Charming 18C barn and hayloft, just a stone's throw from the sea, with fantastic panoramic views, pretty gardens, a courtyard and a lily pond. Stylish bar and stone-walled, candlelit dining room. Starters and desserts are in buffet format, while the seasonal main courses are cooked on a wood-fired chargrill. Luxurious, modern bedrooms are dotted about the place.

ENNISCORTHY (Inis Córthaidh)

Wexford – Pop. 2 842 – See Regional map n°**39**-D2
Dublin 122 km – Kilkenny 74 km – Waterford 54 km – Wexford 24 km
Michelin Road map 712-M10 – Michelin Green Guide IRELAND

Monart rm, rest,

The Still – Northwest : 3 km by N 11 (Dublin rd) – (053) 923 8999 – www.monart.ie – Closed 20-27 December

68 rm – € 119/250 € 198/500 – 2 suites

Rest *The Restaurant* – Menu € 30/65 – Carte € 29/51 – *(dinner only and Sunday lunch)*

Rest *Garden Lounge* – Carte € 29/47

Comprehensively equipped destination spa in 100 acres of beautifully landscaped grounds; a haven of peace and tranquility. The Georgian house with its contemporary glass extension houses spacious, stylish bedrooms with a terrace or balcony. The Restaurant serves light, modern dishes; the minimalistic Garden Lounge offers global dishes in a more informal environment.

Ballinkeele House

Ballymurn – Southeast : 10 km by R 744 and Vinegar Hill rd on Curracloe rd – (053) 913 81 05 – www.ballinkeele.ie – March-November

5 rm – € 105/115 € 170/190 **Rest** – Menu € 35 **s**

Impressive Georgian house in 300 acres; family-run with traditional Irish hospitality. Grand, antique-filled sitting rooms. Bedrooms vary from cosy twins to luxurious doubles with four-posters. Four course, communal dinners feature produce from the garden. Homemade breads and fruit compotes for breakfast.

ENNISKERRY (Áth an Sceire)

Wicklow – Pop. 1 811 – See Regional map n°**39**-D1

Dublin 24 km – Belfast 204 km – Cork 273 km – Lisburn 192 km

Michelin Road map 712-N8 – Michelin Green Guide IRELAND

Powerscourt

Powerscourt Estate – West : 1.5 km by Powerscourt rd – (01) 274 88 88 – www.powerscourthotel.com

200 rm – € 190/290 € 220/350, €29 – 93 suites – € 260/600

Rest *Sika* – Carte € 48/62 – *(dinner only)*

Rest *Sugar Loaf lounge* – Carte € 30/36 – *(lunch only)*

Rest *McGills* – Carte € 32/47 – *(dinner only and lunch Saturday-Sunday)*

Impressive curved building overlooking Sugar Loaf Mountain, featuring stylish guest areas, luxurious bedrooms, state-of-the-art conference facilities and a superb spa; outdoor activities include archery and falconry. Sika offers modern, formal dining, while the plush lounge-bar serves a concise menu of classics. McGills is a traditional Irish pub with a menu to match.

Ferndale without rest

– (01) 286 35 18 – www.ferndalehouse.com – Closed 24-25, 31 December and 1 January

4 rm – € 50 € 80

Homely guesthouse filled with family artefacts; located in the centre of the village, close to Powerscourt House and Gardens. The simple bedrooms are fairly priced. The splendid 1 acre garden has lots of seating and a large water feature.

FANORE

Clare – See Regional map n°**38**-B1

Dublin 253 km – Inis 51 km – Galway 65 km – Limerick 92 km

Michelin Road map 712-E8

Vasco

Craggagh – West : 1 km on R 477 – (065) 707 60 20 – www.vasco.ie – Mid March-October, Monday and Wednesday dinner

Carte € 24/39

Remotely set restaurant opposite the seashore, with a minimalist interior and a glass-screened terrace. The keen owners collect the latest produce on their drive in; the daily menu ranges from sandwiches and cake to soup and light dishes.

REPUBLIC OF IRELAND

FENNOR

Waterford – See Regional map n°**39-C2**
Dublin 115 km – Waterford 12 km – Cork 75 km – Limerick 89 km
Michelin Road map 712-K11

Copper Hen

Mother McHugh's Pub – ✆ (051) 330 300 – www.thecopperhen.ie – Closed 1 week January, 25-26 December, Monday-Wednesday and Sunday dinner
Menu € 22 – *(dinner only and Sunday lunch) (booking advisable)*
Simple, likeable little restaurant above a pub, with rustic décor and a brightly coloured fireplace; set on the coast road from Tramore to Dungarvan. Keenly priced menus offer hearty, unfussy classics. The owners raise their own pigs.

FETHARD (Fiodh Ard)

South Tipperary – Pop. 1 541 – See Regional map n°**39-C2**
Dublin 161 km – Cashel 16 km – Clonmel 13 km
Michelin Road map 712-I10 – Michelin Green Guide IRELAND

Mobarnane House

North : 8 km. by Cashel rd on Ballinure rd – ✆ (052) 613 19 62 – www.mobarnanehouse.com – March-October
3 rm – € 105/125 € 150/190 **Rest** – Menu € 55 **s**
Lovingly restored house with a Georgian façade; set in 15 acres of grounds complete with a small lake and walks. Classically styled interior with period furnishings; the best bedrooms also have small sitting rooms. Formal set dinners are served around a large mahogany table in the beautiful dining room.

FOTA ISLAND (Oileán Fhóta)

Cork – See Regional map n°**38-B3**
Dublin 263 km – Cork 17 km – Limerick 118 km – Waterford 110 km
Michelin Road map 712-H12

Fota Island

– ✆ (021) 488 37 00 – www.fotaisland.ie – Closed 25 December
131 rm – € 139/189 € 153/219 – 8 suites
Rest *Fota* – Menu € 45 – Carte € 34/57 – *(bar lunch)*
A resort hotel set within Ireland's only wildlife park. Extensive business and leisure facilities include a golf course and a state-of-the-art spa. Bedrooms are spacious and well-appointed, and most have island views. The stylish restaurant offers modern takes on classical dishes.

FOXROCK = CARRAIG AN TSIONNAIGH → See Dublin

Dún Laoghaire-Rathdown – Michelin Road map 712-N7

FURBOGH/FURBO (Na Forbacha)

Galway – Pop. 1 236 – See Regional map n°**36-A3**
Dublin 219 km – Belfast 333 km – Cork 209 km – Lisburn 321 km
Michelin Road map 712-E8

Connemara Coast

– ✆ (091) 592 108 – www.connemaracoast.ie – Closed 15-27 December
141 rm – € 80/225 € 120/350 – 3 suites
Rest *The Gallery* – Menu € 43 **s** – Carte € 27/52 **s** – *(bar lunch)*
Over the years this has been transformed from a small house into an extensive hotel. Colonial-style lobby; smart bedrooms feature locally made furniture and offer superb views over the bay and The Burren. Dine in the bar or restaurant looking down the gardens to the water's edge; the latter is adults only.

GALWAY

Galway – Pop. 75 529 – See Regional map n°**36**-B3
Dublin 217 km – Limerick 103 km – Sligo 145 km
Michelin Road map 712-E8 – Michelin Green Guide IRELAND

© Aniar

REPUBLIC OF IRELAND

Hotels

Radisson Blu H. & Spa

Lough Atalia Rd – (091) 538 300 – www.radissonhotelgalway.com Town plan: D**a**

261 rm – € 110/400 € 120/400 – 2 suites

Rest *Marinas* – (091) 538 212 – Menu € 30 – Carte € 34/46 – *(dinner only and Sunday lunch)*

Rest *Raw* – (091) 538 212 – Menu € 35 – Carte € 23/33 – *(dinner only) (booking advisable)*

Corporate hotel overlooking a lough, with a striking atrium and vast meeting facilities. Spacious, modern bedrooms; those on the 5th floor have balconies and share a small business lounge. The spa has a thermal suite and a unique salt cave. Marinas offers international dishes, with a 'Food Market Buffet' at lunch; Raw serves sushi and raw meats.

G

Wellpark, Dublin Rd – (091) 865 200 – www.theghotel.ie – Closed 23-26 December Town plan: D**g**

101 rm – € 140/240 € 140/240 – 2 suites

Rest *Gigi's* – Menu € 21/55 – *(dinner only and Sunday lunch)*

Boutique hotel featuring boldly coloured walls hung with flamboyant mirrors designed by Irish milliner Philip Treacy. Bright, spacious bedrooms have a more calming feel. The spa has a thermal suite and a relaxation room overlooking a walled bamboo garden. The colourful restaurant serves modern Irish dishes.

Clayton

Ballybrit – East : 4 km on N 6 – (091) 721 900 – www.clayton.ie – Closed 20-27 December

195 rm – € 79/350 € 89/350, € 13

Rest – Menu € 35 – Carte € 25/48 – *(dinner only)*

Stylish hotel on the edge of the city, close to the famous racecourse. Modern guest areas and smart white bedrooms with sleek dark furnishings; go for a spacious 4th floor executive with a country or city view. The bar doubles as a lunchtime carvery and the restaurant offers a simple, traditional menu.

Take note of the classification: you should not expect the same level of service in a X or 🏠 as in a XXXXX or 🏨.

REPUBLIC OF IRELAND

GALWAY

Street	Grid	No.	Street	Grid	No.	Street	Grid	No.
Bothar Ui Eithir	BY	2	Main Guard St.	BY	9	Quay St	BZ	1
Claddagh Bridge	AZ	3	Market St	BY	10	St Francis St	BY	2
Corrib Shopping Centre	BY		Mary St	BY	11	St Vincent's Ave	BY	2
Courthouse St.	BZ	4	Newton Smith	BY	14	Shantalla Rd	AY	22
Father Griffin Ave	AZ	6	New Dock St.	BZ	13	Shop St	BY	24
Forster St	BY	7	O'Brien Bridge	AY	15	Upper Dominick St.	AZ	5
High St	BY	8	Presentation St	AY	17	William St	BY	2

Ardilaun

rest,

Taylor's Hill – ✆ (091) 521 433 – www.theardilaunhotel.ie **Town plan: Ca**
– Closed 22-26 December
123 rm – € 79/220 € 99/290 – 4 suites
Rest *Camilaun* – Menu € 40 – *(dinner only and Sunday lunch)*
Rest *Blazer's Bar and Bistro* – Menu € 28 – Carte € 18/36

Enlarged Georgian house with extensive leisure facilities, surrounded by 5 acres of colourful gardens. It's been family owned and run since 1962 and has a homely, traditional style. Bedrooms are spacious; ask for a newer room. Smart bar and restaurant with a sheltered terrace and classic seafood-based menus.

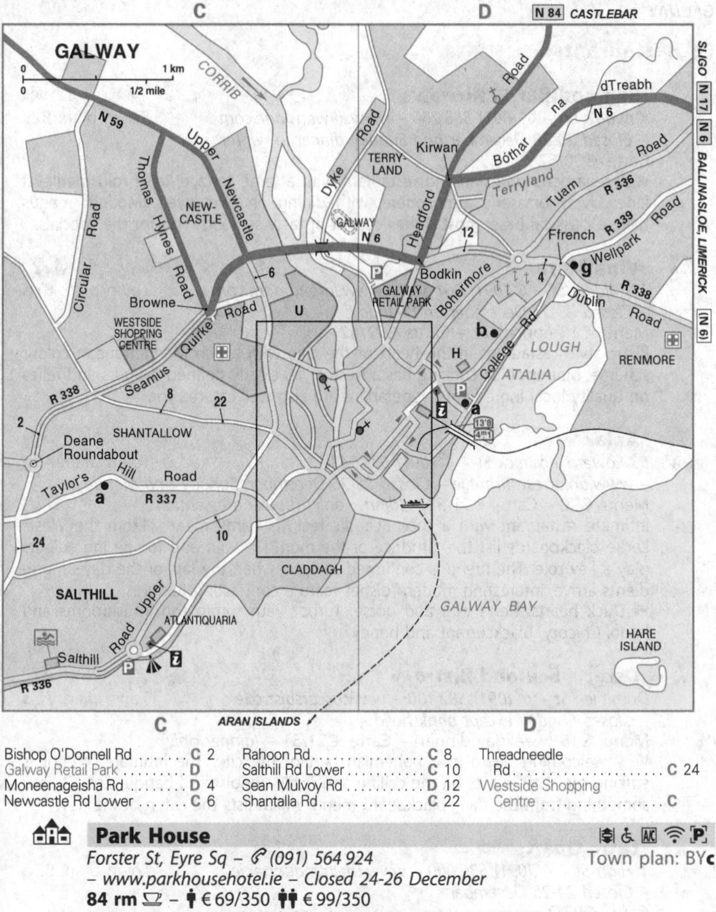

Bishop O'Donnell Rd .... **C** 2	Rahoon Rd .... **C** 8	Threadneedle Rd .... **C** 24
Galway Retail Park .... **D**	Salthill Rd Lower .... **C** 10	Westside Shopping Centre .... **C**
Moneenageisha Rd .... **D** 4	Sean Mulvoy Rd .... **D** 12	
Newcastle Rd Lower .... **C** 6	Shantalla Rd .... **C** 22	

Park House

Forster St, Eyre Sq – ✆ (091) 564 924 Town plan: BY**c**
– www.parkhousehotel.ie – Closed 24-26 December
84 rm ☕ – 🚹 € 69/350 🚹🚹 € 99/350
Rest – Menu € 33 (weekday dinner)/43 – Carte € 33/53
Popular grey-stone hotel in city centre. Marble reception and comfy seating areas. Boss Doyle's Bar is busy and spacious. Dark wood bedrooms with rich, soft fabrics. Strong international flavours define restaurant menus.

House

Lower Merchants Rd – ✆ (091) 538 900 Town plan: BZ**e**
– www.thehousehotel.ie – Closed 25-26 December
40 rm ☕ – 🚹 € 89/340 🚹🚹 € 99/350 – 1 suite
Rest – Menu € 22 (early dinner)/25 – Carte € 25/37 – *(bar lunch Monday-Saturday)*
Unassuming hotel with a surprisingly luxurious interior. Smart bedrooms are decorated with eye-catching Italian fabrics and feature quality linens. Service is professional yet friendly. Spacious guest areas include a laid-back lounge, and a bar and dining room serving modern day classics, coffee and cocktails.

Ardawn House without rest

College Rd. – ✆ (091) 568 833 – www.ardawnhouse.com Town plan: D**b**
– Closed 15-27 December
8 rm ☕ – 🚹 € 45/140 🚹🚹 € 75/160
Located next to the stadium and the greyhound track, with the city just a stroll away. Good-sized bedrooms are clean and fresh, with modern fabrics. A small lounge leads to a breakfast room laid with silver-plated cutlery. Friendly owners.

Restaurants

XX Seafood Bar @ Kirwan's

Kirwan's Ln – ✆ (091) 568 266 – www.kirwanslane.com Town plan: BZ**s**
– Closed 25-28 December and Sunday dinner in winter
Carte € 30/52
Well-regarded, long-standing restaurant with a large terrace, in an old medieval lane. Lively brasserie atmosphere, with dining on two levels. Modern menus have a classical base; most dishes consist of tasty seafood – go for the specials.

XX Vina Mara

19 Middle St – ✆ (091) 561 610 – www.infonamara.com Town plan: BY**n**
– Closed 25-27 December and Sunday
Menu € 18 (lunch)/24 – Carte € 27/42
Bistro-style restaurant in the heart of the city, with a rich Mediterranean colour scheme. Modern Irish cooking has a fresh style, clearly defined flavours and relies on quality local ingredients; vegetarians are also well-catered for.

X Aniar

✿ *53 Lower Dominick St – ✆ (091) 535 947* Town plan: AZ**a**
– www.aniarrestaurant.ie – Closed 25-26 December, Sunday and Monday
Menu € 70 – Carte € 51/58 – *(dinner only) (booking essential)*
Intimate restaurant with a cool, Scandic feel; its name means 'From the West'. Large blackboards list the 'produce of the month' – wild and forage ingredients play a key role. The menu is confirmed at 6pm, when the last of the day's ingredients arrive; interesting modern dishes feature contrasting textures.
→ Duck hearts, hen's egg and gorse. Turbot with turnip top, mushrooms and lardo. Chicory, blackcurrant and honey.

X Oscar's Seafood Bistro

Dominick St – ✆ (091) 582 180 – www.oscarsbistro.ie Town plan: AZ**s**
– Closed Sunday except bank holidays
Menu € 15 (weekday dinner) – Carte € 21/51 – *(dinner only)*
Very welcoming bistro in a bohemian part of the city. The intimate interior is striking red with fabrics on the ceiling and richly upholstered banquettes. Choose something from the daily blackboard menu, which lists the catch of the day.

X Latin Quarter (N)

1 High St – ✆ (091) 530 000 – www.thelatinquarter.ie Town plan: BZ**q**
– Closed 24-25 December
Carte € 27/32
The menu at this bright, two-floored restaurant alters as the day goes on. Lunch centres around one course – including a soup, a salad and maybe a pie of the day; while dinner is a more substantial. Cooking is honest and flavoursome.

X Cava Bodega (N)

1 Middle St – ✆ (091) 539 884 – www.cavarestaurant.ie Town plan: BZ**b**
– Closed 25-26 December and lunch Monday to Thursday
Carte € 25/45
This split-level tapas bar – with its reclaimed wood tables – has a rustic, neighbourhood feel; sit downstairs to watch the chefs in the open kitchen. It's all about sharing: choose around 3 dishes each and a Spanish beer or wine.

X Kai

22 Sea Rd – ✆ (091) 526 003 Town plan: AZ**x**
– www.kaicaferestaurant.com – Closed Sunday-Monday in winter and bank holidays
Carte € 33/45
Lovely, laid-back restaurant with a gloriously cluttered interior and old scrubbed floorboards on the walls. Morning cakes morph into fresh, simple lunches, then afternoon tea and tasty dinners. Produce is organic, free range and traceable.

Ard Bia at Nimmos

Spanish Arch – ✆ (091) 561 114 – www.ardbia.com Town plan: BZ**u**
– Closed 25-26 December
Carte € 30/43 – *(light lunch) (booking essential at dinner)*
Buzzy, bohemian restaurant where tables occupy every nook and cranny. They sell homemade cakes, bread and artisan products. Menus blend Irish, Mediterranean and Middle Eastern influences; the provenance of the ingredients takes precedence.

GARRYKENNEDY

North Tipperary – See Regional map n°**39**-C2
Dublin 176 km – Killaloe 14 km – Youghal 2 km
Michelin Road map 712-G9

Larkins

– ✆ (067) 23 232 – www.larkins.ie – Closed 25 December, Good Friday and Monday-Tuesday November-April
Menu € 20/35 – Carte € 23/41
Thatched pub in a charming loughside location. The traditional interior boasts old flag and timber floors, original fireplaces and plays host to folk music and Irish dancers. Choose from the unfussy bar menu or more ambitious à la carte.

GARRYVOE (Garraí Uí Bhuaigh)

Cork – Pop. 560 – ✉ Castlemartyr – See Regional map n°**39**-C3
Dublin 259 km – Cork 37 km – Waterford 100 km
Michelin Road map 712-H12

Garryvoe

rm,

– ✆ (021) 464 67 18 – www.garryvoehotel.com – Closed 25 December
82 rm – € 70/96 € 120/160 – 1 suite
Rest *Samphire* – Menu € 28/39 – Carte € 41/50 – *(dinner only and Sunday lunch)*
Rest *Lighthouse Bistro* – Menu € 39 (dinner) – Carte € 31/47
Modernised hotel with a well-equipped fitness centre, overlooking Ballycotton Bay. The contemporary interior features plenty of natural wood and slate. Bedrooms are spacious and comfortable; most boast balconies and sea views. Formal Samphire offers a modern menu of Irish produce. The relaxed Lighthouse Bistro serves simple pub classics.

GLASLOUGH (Glasloch)

Monaghan ✉ Monaghan – See Regional map n°**37**-D2
Dublin 133 km – Monaghan 11 km – Belfast 91 km – Lisburn 79 km
Michelin Road map 712-L5

Castle Leslie without rest

Castle Leslie Estate – ✆ (047) 88 100 – www.castleleslie.com – Closed 24-27 December
20 rm – € 150/350 € 150/360
Impressive castle set in 1,000 acres of parkland: home to the 4th generation of the Leslie family. Ornate, comfortable, antique-furnished guest areas and traditional, country house style bedrooms. Dine in Snaffles restaurant in the grounds.

Lodge at Castle Leslie Estate

– ✆ (047) 88 100 – www.castleleslie.com
29 rm – € 140/320 € 150/360 – 1 suite
Rest *Snaffles* – Carte € 40/70 – *(dinner only)*
Extended former hunting lodge to the main castle; set within 1,000 acres, in mature grounds and gardens. Estate horses for hire in the excellent equestrian centre. Stylish bedrooms; some with balconies. Charming, rustic bar and a mezzanine restaurant offering an extensive menu of modern Mediterranean dishes.

GLASSON → See Athlone

Westmeath – Michelin Road map 702-I7

REPUBLIC OF IRELAND

GOLEEN (An Góilín)

Cork – See Regional map n°**38-A3**
Dublin 230 km – Cork 74 km – Killarney 67 km
Michelin Road map 712-C13

Heron's Cove

The Harbour – (028) 35 225 – www.heronscove.com – Closed Christmas
5 rm – € 45/60 € 70/90 **Rest** – Menu € 28 – Carte € 30/50
Long-standing guesthouse hidden away in a pretty location, with views over a tiny harbour. Bedrooms are tidy and pleasantly furnished: all overlook the waterfront and most have a balcony – if you're lucky you might see herons at the water's edge. The busy restaurant offers seasonal menus of local produce.

GOREY (Guaire)

Wexford – Pop. 3 463 – See Regional map n°**39-D2**
Dublin 93 km – Waterford 88 km – Wexford 61 km
Michelin Road map 712-N9 – Michelin Green Guide IRELAND

Marlfield House

Courtown Rd – Southeast : 1.5 km on R 742 – (053) 942 11 24 – www.marlfieldhouse.com – Closed 3 January-February
19 rm – € 85/110 € 210/670
Rest – Menu € 35 (weekday dinner)/64 – *(closed Monday-Tuesday in November-December) (dinner only and Sunday lunch)*
Attractive Regency house surrounded by large informal gardens and woodland. Various stylish, classical lounges and drawing rooms with warm décor, heavy fabrics and antiques. Well-appointed bedrooms in period styles, with a good level of facilities and pleasant views over the grounds. Smart dining room and orangery offer refined, traditional dishes with a modern touch.

GRAIGUENAMANAGH (Gráig na Manach)

Kilkenny – Pop. 1 543 – See Regional map n°**39-D2**
Dublin 125 km – Kilkenny 34 km – Waterford 42 km – Wexford 26 km
Michelin Road map 712-L10 – Michelin Green Guide IRELAND

Waterside

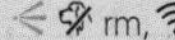

The Quay – (059) 972 42 46 – www.watersideguesthouse.com – Closed November-February
10 rm – € 49/59 € 78/90
Rest – Menu € 27 (dinner) – Carte € 23/36 – *(closed Monday-Thursday) (dinner only and Sunday lunch)*
This granite corn store stands at the foot of Brandon Hill and the Blackstairs Mountains and overlooks the River Barrow; hire one of their bikes to best explore the area. Homely bedrooms feature exposed beams and slate and have pleasant river views. The concise menu offers traditional Irish dishes.

GREYSTONES (Na Clocha Liatha)

Wicklow – Pop. 10 173 – See Regional map n°**39-D1**
Dublin 32 km – Wicklow 22 km – Rathmines 31 km – Dundalk 128 km
Michelin Road map 712-N8 – Michelin Green Guide IRELAND

Chakra by Jaipur

Meridian Point Centre (1st floor), Church Rd – (01) 201 72 22 – www.jaipur.ie – Closed 25 December
Menu € 17/31 – Carte € 24/51 – *(dinner only and Sunday lunch)*
Smart, spacious Indian restaurant with warm exotic hues and carved wooden statues, unusually set in a suburban shopping centre. Three themed set menus and an à la carte: accomplished, modern dishes feature original spicing and flavours.

A Caviston

1 Westview, Church Rd – ✆ (01) 287 7637 – www.acaviston.ie – Closed 26 December-7 January and bank holiday Mondays
Menu €20/30 – Carte €29/56 – *(lunch only and Friday-Saturday dinner) (booking essential)*
Through a superbly filled deli and past a comprehensive fish counter is this modestly furnished, family-run café and restaurant decorated with local art. Tasty fresh fish and shellfish are simply prepared in classical ways.

GWEEDORE (Gaoth Dobhair)

Donegal – See Regional map n°**37**-C1
Dublin 278 km – Donegal 72 km – Letterkenny 43 km – Sligo 135 km
Michelin Road map 712-H2

Gweedore Court

On N 56 – ✆ (074) 953 29 00 – www.gweedorecourthotel.ie – Closed January and 21-27 December
60 rm – €69/89 €99/150
Rest – Menu €20/30 – *(bar lunch Monday-Saturday)*
Privately owned, whitewashed hotel in a rural location, with spacious, comfortable lounges and a well-equipped leisure club. Bedrooms to the front have views over the River Clady to the forests and mountains; feature rooms boast four-posters. Traditional dining room with a menu to match.

HORSE AND JOCKEY (An Marcach)

North Tipperary – See Regional map n°**39**-C2
Dublin 146 km – Cashel 14 km – Thurles 9 km
Michelin Road map 712-I10

Horse and Jockey

– ✆ (0504) 44 192 – www.horseandjockeyhotel.com – Closed 24-26 December
69 rm – €80/100 €89/119 – 1 suite
Rest *Silks* – Menu €23 (lunch)/35 – Carte €23/41 **s**
Extended former pub in an area surrounded by racehorse trainers' stables and racecourses. Spacious, modern bedrooms and a superb spa; stylish, state-of-the-art lecture theatre and meeting rooms. The delightful coffee shop sells homemade cakes. The characterful bar and restaurant serve unfussy Irish dishes.

HOWTH (Binn Éadair)

Fingal – Pop. 8 186 – ✉ Dublin – See Regional map n°**39**-D1
Dublin 22 km – Swords 17 km – Belfast 172 km – Cork 276 km
Michelin Road map 712-N7 – Michelin Green Guide IRELAND

Aqua

1 West Pier – ✆ (01) 832 0690 – www.aqua.ie – Closed Good Friday, 25-26 December, and Monday-Tuesday in winter
Menu €29 (weekday lunch)/75 – Carte €34/62
Smart restaurant at the end of Howth's busy West Pier, with superb views across the Sound to Lambay Island. It has a cosy, open-fired bar-lounge with exposed brickwork, and a seafood-based menu which keeps things pleasingly traditional.

King Sitric with rm

rest,

East Pier – ✆ (01) 832 5235 – www.kingsitric.ie – Closed 25-26 December
8 rm – €110/145 €150/205
Menu €35/60 – Carte €33/63 – *(closed dinner Sunday, Tuesday and bank holidays) (dinner only and Sunday lunch)*
A long-standing establishment in a former harbourmaster's house, overlooking the water. Dine in the laid-back ground floor café or in the formal first floor restaurant. Seafood is the order of the day, with lobster a speciality. Bedrooms are named after lighthouses; those on the first floor have better views.

INISHMAAN = INIS MEÁIN → See Aran Islands

Galway – Michelin Road map 712-D8

REPUBLIC OF IRELAND

INISHMORE = ÁRAINN ➜ See Aran Islands

Galway – Michelin Road map 712-C/D8

JENKINSTOWN = BAILE SHEINICÍN ➜ See Dundalk

Louth

KANTURK (Ceann Toirc)

Cork – Pop. 2 263 – See Regional map n°**38**-B2
Dublin 259 km – Cork 53 km – Killarney 50 km – Limerick 71 km
Michelin Road map 712-F11 – Michelin Green Guide IRELAND

Glenlohane

Southeast : 4 km. by R 576 and R 580 on L1043 – (029) 50 014 – www.glenlohane.com

3 rm – € 90/100 € 180/200 **Rest** – Menu € 50

Grand Georgian country house set in 230 acres – which has been in the family for over 250 years. Traditional interior hung with portraits and paintings. Colour-themed bedrooms; 'Blue' has an antique four-poster and bathtub. Cosy library and drawing room. Open-fired dining room for home-cooked dinners.

KENMARE (Neidín)

Kerry – Pop. 2 175 – See Regional map n°**38**-A3
Dublin 338 km – Cork 93 km – Killarney 32 km
Michelin Road map 712-D12 – Michelin Green Guide IRELAND

Park

– (064) 664 12 00 – www.parkkenmare.com – Closed 2 January-17 April and 26 October-24 December Town plan: BY**k**

46 rm – € 211/264 € 336/410

Rest *Park* – see restaurant listing

Grand country house dating from 1897, offering superb views over the bay and the hills. Elegant interior with open fires, a cosy cocktail lounge and a charming drawing room filled with portraits and antiques. Tastefully furnished bedrooms have smart marble bathrooms. The stylish spa adds a modern touch.

Sheen Falls Lodge

Southeast : 2 km. by N 71 – (064) 664 16 00 – www.sheenfallslodge.ie – Closed January

66 rm – € 160/650 € 160/650 – 9 suites

Rest *La Cascade* – Carte € 54/69 – *(closed 1-18 December) (dinner only)*

Luxurious hotel in an idyllic spot, where the waterfalls drop away into the bay. Welcoming, wood-fired lobby, book-filled library and a lovely indoor pool; the well-appointed bedrooms overlook the falls. Light lunches in the cocktail bar and a classical menu with a modern touch in the formal restaurant.

Brook Lane

rm, rest,

Gortamullen – North : 1.5 km. by N 71 on N 70 – (064) 664 20 77 – www.brooklanehotel.com

21 rm – € 75/100 € 99/160

Rest *Casey's* – Menu € 23/35 – Carte € 24/53

Stylish, personally run hotel close to the town centre. Contemporary bedrooms offer a good level of comfort and range from 'Standard' to 'Luxury', the latter boasting impressive fabric headboards and designer touches. Informal bar and restaurant offer classic Irish and seafood dishes; regular live music.

Shelburne Lodge without rest

East : 0.75 km. on R 569 (Cork Rd) – (064) 664 10 13 – www.shelburnelodge.com – mid April- October

8 rm – € 75/100 € 100/160

Charming, wisteria-clad farmhouse with sweeping lawns, box hedges and a herb garden. Welcoming owners and an inviting open-fire. Home-baked breads and local meats at breakfast. Bedrooms mix antiques with modern colours; simple bathrooms.

KENMARE

Back Lane	BY	2
Cromwell's Bridge	AY	
Davitt's Place	AY	
Downing's Row	BY	5
East Park St	AY	7
Finnihy Bridge	AY	
Henry St	AY	
Henry's Lane	ABY	8
Killarney Rd	AY	
Main St	BY	
Market St	AY	
New St	AY	
Old Bridge St	AY	12
Railway Rd	BY	
Rock St	BY	14
Shelborne St	BY	
The Square	AY	

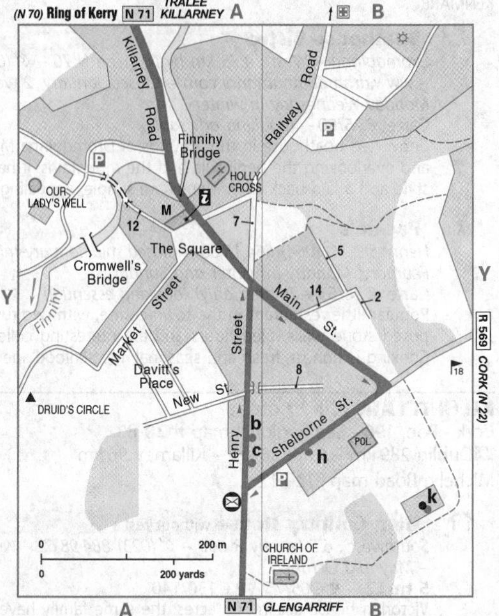

REPUBLIC OF IRELAND

Sallyport House without rest

South : 0.5 km. on N 71 – ✆ (064) 664 20 66 – www.sallyporthouse.com – April-October

5 rm – € 65/75 € 100/125

Unassuming 1930s house; its charming interior packed with antiques and Irish art. Pleasant lounge with local information. Breakfast is served from the characterful sideboard and features pancakes, stewed fruits and smoked salmon. Traditionally furnished bedrooms are immaculately kept and boast water views.

Park – Park Hotel

– ✆ (064) 664 12 00 – www.parkkenmare.com – Closed 2 January-17 April and 26 October-24 December Town plan: BY**k**

Menu € 55/70 – *(dinner only) (booking advisable)*

Elegant, candlelit dining room in a luxurious hotel, with good views over the grounds and a comforting style. Silver candelabras, cloches and gueridon trolleys feature; start with canapés in the lounge. Classically based dishes have a modern touch, with local ingredients to the fore. Highly professional team.

Mulcahys

36 Henry St – ✆ (064) 664 23 83 – Closed 24-26 December, Tuesday, and Monday and Wednesday October-April Town plan: AY**c**

Carte € 33/47 – *(dinner only)*

Intimately candlelit restaurant where vibrant contemporary art hangs on exposed stone walls. Seasonal ingredients are prepared with care and a modern touch. Combinations are well-judged and some sushi and Asian dishes feature.

Lime Tree

Shelbourne St. – ✆ (064) 664 12 25 Town plan: BY**h**

– www.limetreerestaurant.com – Easter-October and weekends in winter

Menu € 34/55 – Carte € 33/55 – *(dinner only)*

19C property that's taken on many guises over the years. The characterful, rustic interior features exposed stone walls, an open fire and even its own art gallery. Unfussy dishes feature quality local ingredients in generous portions.

X **Boathouse Bistro** 

Dromquinna – West : 4.75 km by N 71 on N 70 – ✆ (064) 664 2889 – www.dromquinnamanor.com – Closed January, 2 weeks December and Monday-Wednesday in winter

Carte € 25/50 – *(booking advisable)*

Converted boathouse in the grounds of Dromquinna Manor; set on the waterside and overlooking the peninsula and the mountains. It has a nautical, New England style and a laid-back vibe. Menus are simple, appealing and focus on seafood.

X **Packie's**

Henry St – ✆ (064) 664 15 08 – Closed mid January-mid February, Monday in winter and Sunday Town plan: AY**b**

Carte € 28/53 – *(dinner only) (booking essential)*

Popular little restaurant in the town centre, with two rustic, bistro-style rooms, exposed stone walls, tiled floors and an interesting collection of modern Irish art. Cooking is honest, fresh and seasonal; the seafood specials are a hit.

KILBRITTAIN (Cill Briotáin)

Cork – Pop. 196 – See Regional map n°**38**-B3

▶Dublin 289 km – Cork 38 km – Killarney 96 km

Michelin Road map 712-F12

Glen Country House without rest 

Southwest : 6.5 km. by R 600 – ✆ (023) 884 98 62 – www.glencountryhouse.com – May-mid October

5 rm – € 65/75 € 130/140

Victorian house set in 300 acres; the same family have farmed the land for over 350 years and are now in their 10th generation! Comfy open-fired lounge and breakfast room with antique furniture; smart bedrooms have distant sea views.

KILCOLGAN (Cill Cholgáin)

Galway ✉ Oranmore – See Regional map n°**36**-B3

▶Dublin 208 km – Belfast 322 km – Cork 179 km – Lisburn 310 km

Michelin Road map 712-F8

Moran's Oyster Cottage 

The Weir – Northwest : 2 km. by N 18 – ✆ (091) 796 113 – www.moransoystercottage.com – Closed Good Friday and 24-26 December

Carte € 28/46

Attractive whitewashed pub with golden thatch, hidden away in a tiny hamlet – a very popular place in summer. It's all about straightforward cooking and good hospitality. Dishes are largely seafood based and oysters are the speciality.

KILCULLEN

Kildare – Pop. 3 473 – See Regional map n°**39**-D1

▶Dublin 48 km – Naas 12 km – Rathmines 50 km – Navan 88 km

Michelin Road map 712-L8

Fallon's 

Main St – ✆ (045) 481 260 – www.fallonb.ie

Carte € 30/48

A 'proper' bar with a long wooden counter and a flagged floor; albeit one with a boutique colour scheme! The experienced chef offers a wide range of dishes, from pie of the day to grilled salmon, followed by tasty homemade puddings.

KILKENNY (Cill Chainnigh)

Kilkenny – Pop. 24 423 – See Regional map n°**39**-C2

▶Dublin 114 km – Cork 138 km – Killarney 185 km – Limerick 111 km

Michelin Road map 712-K10 – Michelin Green Guide IRELAND

Kilkenny rm, rest,
College Rd – Southwest : 1.25 km at junction with N 76 – (056) 776 20 00 – www.hotelkilkenny.ie
138 rm – € 40/105 € 80/210
Rest *Taste* – Menu € 18/35 **s** – *(bar lunch Monday-Saturday)*
Unassuming modern property just outside the city centre, with contrastingly stylish, contemporary interior. Well-equipped leisure centre and smart function rooms. Funky colour schemes feature throughout. Bright bedrooms have a slightly kitsch style. Mediterranean-influenced menus in pink-hued restaurant.

Pembroke
Patrick St – (056) 778 35 00 – www.pembrokekilkenny.com – Closed 24-25 December
74 rm – € 79/250 € 89/250
Rest *Stathams* – Menu € 27/20 – Carte € 28/42 – *(bar lunch Monday-Saturday)*
A usefully located business hotel with a stylish, contemporary look. Spacious, comfortable bedrooms; those at the back are a little quieter and offer views of the castle. Well-equipped business centre. Light lunches in the bar; traditional dinners in the modern restaurant with its appealing courtyard terrace.

Butler House without rest
15-16 Patrick St. – (056) 776 57 07 – www.butler.ie – Closed 23-29 December
13 rm – € 60/155 € 95/250
Beautifully restored Georgian house with some fine original features, a delightful formal garden and views of Kilkenny castle. Large, comfortable, up-to-date bedrooms. Breakfast is served in the adjacent Design Museum.

Rosquil House without rest
Castlecomer Rd – Northwest : 1 km – (056) 772 14 19 – www.rosquilhouse.com – Closed 5-18 January
7 rm – € 45/60 € 70/90
Modern, purpose-built guesthouse on the main road out of the city. Leather-furnished lounge filled with books and local information; spacious, comfortable bedrooms and a smart, linen-laid breakfast room. Extensive buffet breakfasts with a cooked daily special; omelettes feature. Experienced, welcoming owners.

Ristorante Rinuccini
1 The Parade – (056) 776 15 75 – www.rinuccini.com – Closed 26-27 December
Menu € 23 (dinner) – Carte € 30/51
Set in the basement of a townhouse and named after the 17C papal nuncio, this family-owned restaurant is well-known locally. Classic Italian cuisine with homemade ravioli a speciality. Some tables have views through to the wine cellar.

Campagne (Garrett Byrne)
5 The Arches, Gashouse Ln. – (056) 777 28 58 – www.campagne.ie – Closed 2 weeks January, Sunday dinner and Monday
Menu € 25/49 **s** – Carte € 46/54 **s** – *(dinner only and lunch Friday-Sunday) (booking advisable)*
Stylish, relaxed restaurant with vibrant, contemporary art and smart booths, hidden close to the railway arches, away from the city centre. Modern cooking has a classic base, and familiar combinations are delivered with an assured touch. Popular early bird menu. Well-run, with friendly, efficient service.
→ Roast quail, creamed peas and smoked bacon. Poached turbot, mussels, sprouting broccoli and saffron. Rhubarb jelly, glazed ginger cream and rhubarb ice cream.

Zuni with rm
26 Patrick St – (056) 772 39 99 – www.zuni.ie – Closed 25-26 December
13 rm – € 55/65 € 69/120 Menu € 24 – Carte € 30/45
Small wood-furnished café-bar opening out into a chic, light, modern restaurant with mirrored walls, leather panels and a heated terrace. Eclectic modern menus of Irish produce; desserts are a high point. Comfortable black and white bedrooms continue the smart, contemporary theme.

REPUBLIC OF IRELAND

X **Foodworks**

7 Parliament St – ✆ (056) 777 76 96 – www.foodworks.ie – Closed 11-21 January, Monday-Tuesday and Sunday dinner
Menu € 23 – Carte € 25/39 – *(dinner only)*
A former bank in the town centre: a high-ceilinged, airy space with a bright, fresh look which matches the style of the cooking. Unfussy dishes use quality local produce, including pork and vegetables from the experienced chef-owner's farm.

KILLALOE (Cill Dalua)

Clare – Pop. 1 292 – See Regional map n°**38-B2**
Dublin 175 km – Ennis 51 km – Limerick 21 km – Tullamore 93 km
Michelin Road map 712-G9 – Michelin Green Guide IRELAND

XX **Cherry Tree**

Lakeside, Ballina – follow signs for Lakeside Hotel – ✆ (061) 375 688 – www.cherrytreerestaurant.ie – Closed first week January, Good Friday, 25-26 December, Sunday dinner and Monday
Menu € 26/35 – Carte € 30/44 – *(dinner only)*
Modern restaurant with interesting local art hung on brightly coloured walls, and views across Lough Derg. Choose from an array of classical menus; dishes are well-balanced, seasonal and nicely presented. Service is cheery and welcoming.

REPUBLIC OF IRELAND

KILLARNEY (Cill Airne)

Kerry – Pop. 12 740 – See Regional map n°**38-A2**
Dublin 304 km – Cork 87 km – Limerick 111 km – Waterford 180 km
Michelin Road map 712-D11 – Michelin Green Guide IRELAND

Europe

Fossa – West : 4.75 km. by Port Rd on N 72 – ✆ (064) 667 13 00 – www.theeurope.com – Closed 14 December-6 February
187 rm – € 210/290 € 230/310 – 6 suites
Rest *Panorama* Rest *Brasserie* – see restaurant listing
Vast hotel in a superb lakeside location, boasting views over Lough Leane and Macgillycuddy's Reeks. Opulent guest areas, impressive events facilities and a sublime three-level spa. Bedrooms are lavishly appointed; some overlook the lake.

Killarney Park

– ✆ (064) 663 55 55 – www.killarneyparkhotel.ie – Closed 23-27 December Town plan: DX**k**
69 rm – € 250/350 € 250/350 – 4 suites
Rest *Park* – see restaurant listing
Large, luxurious hotel run by a well-versed team. Plush library and lavish drawing room; lunches in the clubby, wood-panelled bar. Bedrooms range in style, mixing modern furnishings with original features. Smart spa and leisure facilities.

Aghadoe Heights H. and Spa

Northwest : 4.5 km. by N 22 off L 2109 – ✆ (064) 663 17 66 – www.aghadoeheights.com – Weekends only November-April
74 rm – € 180/300 € 180/300 – 2 suites
Rest *Lake Room* – see restaurant listing
Striking, glass-fronted hotel looking out over lakes, mountains and countryside. Modern interior with an impressive spa and a stylish cocktail bar complete with an evening pianist. Bedrooms are spacious; many have balconies or terraces.

Ross

– ✆ (064) 663 18 55 – www.theross.ie – Weekends only November-March Town plan: DX**b**
29 rm – € 170/200 € 190/220
Rest *Cellar One* – Menu € 29 – Carte € 33/50
Striking, modern hotel in the centre of town, overlooking the famous 'Killarney Horse and Carriage Tours' HQ. Contemporary bar-lounge with multi-level design. Stylish, boldly coloured bedrooms are comfy and well-equipped. Vibrant basement restaurant features curved timbers, intimate lighting and global menu.

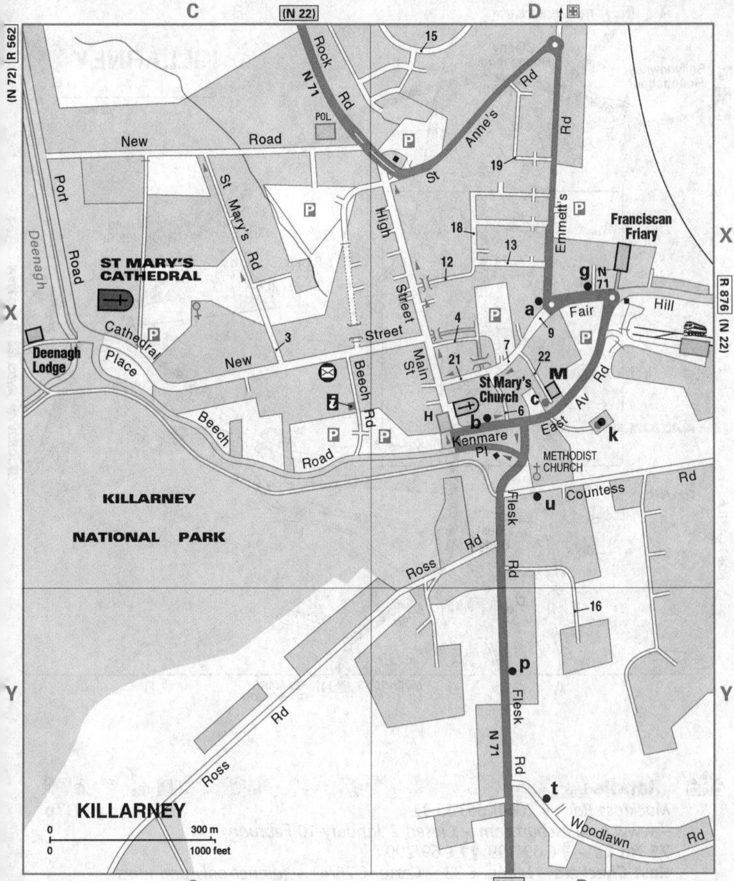

KILLARNEY

Street	Grid	No.
Bohereencael	DX	4
Bohereen Na Goun	CX	3
Brewery Lane	DX	6
College Square	DX	7
College St	DX	9
Green Lawn	CX	10
Hillard's Lane	DX	12
Mangerton	DX	13
Marian Terrace	DX	15
Muckross Drive	DXY	16
O'Connell's Terrace	DX	18
O'Sullivan's Pl.	DX	19
Plunkett St	DX	21
St Anthony's Pl.	DX	22

Cahernane House

Muckross Rd – *(064) 663 18 95* – *www.cahernane.com* Town plan: AZ**d**
– *March-November*

38 rm – € 95/145 € 150/190 – 1 suite

Rest *Herbert Room* – see restaurant listing

Fine Victorian house built in 1877, set in a peaceful location and affording westerly mountain views. Characterful open-fired library and drawing room with stags' heads, portraits and antiques. Bedrooms range from classical to contemporary.

Large towns and cities have detailed maps showing hotels and restaurants. Use the coordinates (eg.: **12**BM**e**) to find them.

Randles

Muckross Rd – ✆ (064) 663 53 33 — Town plan: DY**p**

– www.randlescourt.com – Closed 2 January-10 February

75 rm – € 69/199 € 69/299

Rest *Checkers* – Menu € 33 – Carte € 26/41 – *(dinner only and lunch Saturday-Sunday)*

Family-run hotel in a gabled Edwardian mansion; built as a rectory in 1906. Delightful, antique-furnished lounge with deep sofas and a coal fire. Comfy bedrooms with good facilities; those in newer wing are more modern. Characterful, checker-floored restaurant; traditional menu of local produce.

Killarney Royal

College St – ✆ (064) 663 1853 – www.killarneyroyal.ie — Town plan: DX**g**

– Closed Christmas, Easter and restricted opening in winter

32 rm – € 75/250 € 89/279

Rest *Candle Room* – Menu € 30 – Carte € 29/50 – *(closed Sunday) (bar lunch)*

Classically styled, centrally located hotel; in the family for four generations. Large, luxurious bedrooms boast air conditioning and putting machines. Take afternoon tea in the comfy, well-appointed lounge. Bistro-bar displays pleasing Parisian brasserie styling. Formal restaurant offers traditional menu.

Fairview without rest

College St. – ✆ (064) 663 41 64 — Town plan: DX**a**

– www.killarneyfairview.com – Closed 24-25 December

29 rm – € 50/150 € 70/250

Stylish townhouse in the centre of town, with a cosy, leather-furnished lounge and spacious, contemporary bedrooms with marble-tiled bathrooms. The Penthouse has a 4-poster, a whirlpool bath for two and mountain views from the balcony.

Earls Court House without rest
Woodlawn Rd. – ☎ (064) 663 40 09 Town plan: DY**t**
– www.killarney-earlscourt.ie – February-14 November
30 rm – € 65/90 € 90/140
Large, well-run hotel behind an unassuming façade. Afternoon tea is served on arrival, in one of two comfortable, antique-furnished lounges. Spacious bedrooms feature half-tester or four-poster beds; some have balconies and mountain views.

Kathleens Country House without rest
Madams Height, Tralee Rd. – North : 3.75 km on N 22 – ☎ (064) 663 28 10
– www.kathleens.net – May-September
17 rm – € 70/100 € 100/140
Personally run by a charming hostess: this is Irish hospitality at its best! Comfortable, well-kept and good value hotel, with spacious, pine-furnished bedrooms, an open-fired lounge and a cosy first floor library.

Killarney Lodge without rest
Countess Rd. – ☎ (064) 663 64 99 Town plan: DX**u**
– www.killarneylodge.net – 12 March-September
16 rm – € 60/100 € 90/140
Well-located on the edge of the town centre. Spacious, immaculately kept, well-furnished bedrooms; No. 12 boasts lovely mountain views. Bright and airy breakfast room where homemade bread and scones feature. Afternoon tea on arrival.

Panorama – Europe Hotel
Fossa – West : 4.75 km. by Port Rd on N 72 – ☎ (064) 667 13 00
– www.theeurope.com – Closed 14 December-6 February
Carte € 34/63 – *(closed Sunday dinner)*
Large, formal restaurant with a contemporary style, set in a luxurious hotel. Panoramic windows afford superb views across the lough towards the mountains. Creative modern menus follow the seasons and use the very best of Irish produce.

Park – Killarney Park Hotel
– ☎ (064) 663 55 55 – www.killarneyparkhotel.ie Town plan: DX**k**
– Closed 23-27 December
Menu € 55 – Carte € 39/55 – *(dinner only)*
Elegant restaurant boasting chandeliers, ornate cornicing and smartly laid tables, set in an impressive hotel. Classic menus with some modern combinations; Irish meats are a feature and the tasting menu a highlight. Nightly pianist in summer.

Lake Room – Aghadoe Heights Hotel and Spa
Northwest : 4.5 km. by N 22 off L 2109 – ☎ (064) 663 17 66
– www.aghadoeheights.com – Weekends only November-April
Menu € 55 – Carte € 34/69 – *(dinner only)*
Smart restaurant in a contemporary hotel; its two different levels making the most of the panoramic water and mountain view. Classical dishes showcase local produce and are executed with a modern touch; there's the odd French influence too.

Brasserie – Europe Hotel
Fossa – West : 4.75 km. by Port Rd on N 72 – ☎ (064) 667 13 00
– www.theeurope.com – Closed 14 December-6 February
Carte € 36/59 **s**
Set in a sumptuous lakeside hotel; a modern take on a classical brasserie, with lough and mountain views – head for the terrace in warmer weather. The accessible all-day menu ranges from soup and salads to steaks cooked on the open grill.

Herbert Room – Cahernane House Hotel
Muckross Rd – ☎ (064) 663 18 95 – www.cahernane.com Town plan: AZ**d**
– March-November
Menu € 12/48 – *(closed Sunday-Monday except in summer) (dinner only) (booking advisable)*
Set in a fine Victorian house; start with a drink in the atmospheric cellar bar then head for the traditional, two-roomed restaurant with its large fireplace and mountain views. Well-judged, classically based dishes display modern touches.

REPUBLIC OF IRELAND

Cucina Italiana
17 St Anthonys Pl – ✆ (064) 662 65 75 – Closed 10 January-28 February and Tuesday in winter Town plan: DX**c**
Carte € 43/69 – *(dinner only) (booking advisable)*
Charming, split-level restaurant tucked away in a side street, with frosted glass screens and a spiral staircase. Refined, tasty Italian dishes use top quality produce and are presented in an unfussy, modern style. Smooth, friendly service.

at Beaufort West: 9.75 km by N72 off Glencar rd ✉ Killarney

The Dunloe
Southeast : 2.5 km on Dunloe Golf Course rd – ✆ (064) 664 41 11 – www.thedunloe.com – 17 April-4 October
102 rm – € 170/220 € 190/260 – 2 suites
Rest *Oak* – Carte € 34/61 **s** – *(dinner only)*
Rest *Garden Café* – Carte € 25/57
Creeper-clad hotel in 65 acres, with a continental feel and superb views of the Gap of Dunloe and Macgillycuddy's Reeks. Several spacious lounges and bars. Classical bedrooms, most with balconies and views; the suites have steam rooms. Good-sized pool and stables. Formal dining room and all-day brasserie.

REPUBLIC OF IRELAND

KILLORGLIN (Cill Orglan)

Kerry – Pop. 2 082 – See Regional map n°**38**-A2
Dublin 333 km – Killarney 19 km – Tralee 26 km
Michelin Road map 712-C11 – Michelin Green Guide IRELAND

Giovannelli
Lower Bridge St – ✆ (087) 123 13 53
Carte € 28/57 – *(dinner only)*
Unassuming restaurant hidden in the town centre, with a traditional osteria-style interior. Concise, daily changing blackboard menu offers a mix of Italian and Irish dishes; the pastas are homemade and the herbs come from the owners' garden.

Sol y Sombra
Old Church of Ireland, Lower Bridge St – ✆ (066) 976 23 47 – www.solysombra.ie – Closed 9 January-9 February and Tuesday dinner in winter, Sunday and Monday
Menu € 19 – Carte € 27/41 – *(dinner only and Sunday lunch)*
Spanish restaurant in an imposing 19C former church, with a cavernous interior, stained glass windows and church pews. Fresh, vibrant cooking: go for the raciones, designed for sharing – 3 per person will suffice. Live music is a feature.

KILMALLOCK (Cill Mocheallóg)

Limerick – Pop. 1 635 – See Regional map n°**38**-B2
Dublin 212 km – Limerick 34 km – Tipperary 32 km
Michelin Road map 712-G10 – Michelin Green Guide IRELAND

Flemingstown House
Southeast : 4 km on R 512 – ✆ (063) 98 093 – www.flemingstown.com – February-October
5 rm – € 50/60 € 100/120 **Rest** – Menu € 45
Proudly run, creeper-clad house at the centre of a 200 acre working farm. The cosy, homely interior is filled with family knick-knacks and the scent of peat wafts from the open fires. Attractive, antique-furnished bedrooms have country views. Satisfying home-cooked dishes are served in the comfy dining room.

KINLOUGH (Cionn Locha)

Leitrim – Pop. 1 018 – See Regional map n°**37**-C2
Dublin 220 km – Ballyshannon 11 km – Sligo 34 km
Michelin Road map 712-H4

Courthouse with rm
Main St – ☎ (071) 984 23 91 – www.thecourthouserest.com – Closed Monday-Wednesday in winter and Tuesday
4 rm – € 35/40 € 70/75
Carte € 27/45 – *(dinner only and Sunday lunch) (booking essential)*
Boldly painted former courthouse with a pretty stained glass entrance. The Sardinian owner-chef creates extensive, seasonal menus of honest, authentic Italian dishes; some produce is imported and local seafood features. The atmosphere is informal and the service, friendly. Bedrooms are neat and good value.

KINSALE (Cionne tSáile)

Cork – Pop. 2 198 – See Regional map n°**38**-B3
Dublin 276 km – Belfast 444 km – Cork 25 km – Lisburn 432 km
Michelin Road map 712-G12 – Michelin Green Guide IRELAND

Perryville House without rest
Long Quay – ☎ (021) 477 27 31 – www.perryvillehouse.com – Closed November-15 April Town plan: Y**f**
22 rm – € 140/280 € 160/300
Luxuriously appointed house in the heart of town, overlooking the harbour and named after the family that built it in 1820. Two antique-furnished drawing rooms, a smart boutique and a tea shop. Tastefully styled bedrooms; 'Luxury' boast feature beds, chic bathrooms and harbour views. Comprehensive breakfasts.

Blue Haven rest, rest,
3-4 Pearse St – ☎ (021) 477 22 09 – www.bluehavenkinsale.com – Closed 25 December Town plan: Y**c**
17 rm – € 55/95 € 65/160
Rest *Fish Market* – Menu € 19/30 – Carte € 22/47
Rest *Bistro* – Menu € 19 (weekdays)/30 – Carte € 22/49
Small but well-established hotel right in the heart of town; its cosy, vibrant interior featuring interesting artwork. Chic, clubby lounge. Comfortable bedrooms are named after vineyards and have a subtle contemporary edge. The all-day bistro resembles the hull of an upturned boat and the restaurant specialises in seafood from local waters.

Old Bank Town House without rest
10-11 Pearse St. – ☎ (021) 477 40 75 – www.oldbankhousekinsale.com – Closed 23-26 December Town plan: Y**d**
17 rm – € 55/95 € 65/160
Substantial Georgian house in the heart of town. A food store and café, where breakfast is served, occupy the ground floor; above them is a cosy, classically furnished lounge. Bedrooms are traditional – No.17 has great harbour views.

Old Presbytery without rest
43 Cork St. – ☎ (021) 477 20 27 – www.oldpres.com – mid February-mid November Town plan: Y**a**
9 rm – € 60/80 € 90/125
18C building once housing priests from the nearby church; a few ecclesiastical pieces remain. Cosy lounge with a piano and gramophone; the breakfast room boasts some unusual chairs. Bedrooms feature brass or cast iron beds and Irish pine.

Desmond House without rest
42 Cork St. – ☎ (021) 477 35 35 – www.desmondhousekinsale.com – February-October Town plan: Y**x**
4 rm – € 50/70 € 100/140
Built by a Spanish merchant in 1780 and once belonging to the church – it still displays a tiny altar on the landing. Homemade bread and scones feature in the attractive, parquet-floored breakfast room. Comfortable bedrooms boast jacuzzis.

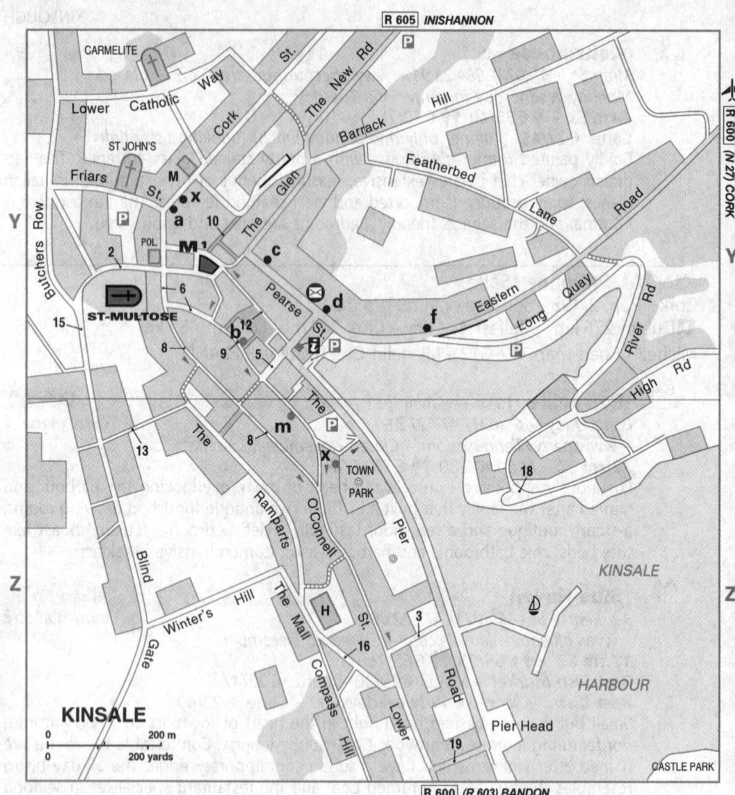

Church St	**Y** 2	Main St	**Y** 9	Rose Abbey	**Y** 15
Denis Quay	**Z** 3	Market Pl.	**Y** 10	St John's Hill	**Z** 16
Emmet St	**Y** 5	Market Quay	**Y** 12	Seilly Walk	**Z** 18
Guardwell	**Y** 6	Ramparts Lane	**Z** 13	World's End	**Z** 19
Higher O'Connel St	**YZ** 8				

XX Finns' Table

6 Main St – ✆ (021) 470 9636 – www.finnstable.com Town plan: Y**b**

– Closed November, Christmas, Sunday-Thursday January-mid March and Tuesday-Wednesday

Menu € 33 (early dinner) – Carte € 29/56 – *(dinner only)*

Behind the bright orange woodwork lie two attractive rooms – one with colourful banquettes, the other in powder blue with wine box panelling. Meat is from the owners' butchery and everything from the bread to the ice cream is homemade.

XX Max's

48 Main St. – ✆ (021) 477 24 43 – www.maxs.ie Town plan: Z**m**

– Closed December-March, Sunday-Monday except June-September and bank holidays

Menu € 25 – Carte € 33/49 – *(dinner only)*

Two-roomed restaurant on a quaint main street, with a simple yet smart rustic style; a spot well-known by the locals! The unfussy, classically based seafood menu offers good choice, try the tasty 'Fresh Catches'. Efficient, engaging team.

Fishy Fishy

Pier Rd – (021) 470 04 15 – www.fishyfishy.ie Town plan: Z**x**
– Closed Sunday and Monday except bank holidays
Carte € 29/49 **s**
Friendly, informal restaurant that's a local institution: dine at the bar and watch the kitchen shuck oysters; in the main room amongst 'fishy' memorabilia; or alfresco on the lovely terrace. Concise, all-day menus offer well-prepared seafood dishes and tasty specials. The owner collects the fish daily.

Toddies at The Bulman

Summercove – East : 2 km by R 600 and Charles Fort rd. – (021) 477 21 31 – www.thebulman.ie – Closed 25 December, Good Friday and Monday dinner
Carte € 34/51
Rustic pub with maritime décor and excellent views over Kinsale and the bay; look out for the Moby Dick mural and the carved Bulman Buoy. Lunch is taken in the bar and offers simple pub classics; dinner is served in the more formal restaurant and presents carefully prepared, globally influenced dishes.

at Barrells Cross Southwest: 5.75 km on R600 -(Z) Kinsale

Rivermount House without rest

North : 0.75 km on L 7302 – (021) 477 80 33 – www.rivermount.com – 14 November-9 March
6 rm – € 55/85 € 85/100
Spacious, purpose-built dormer bungalow overlooking the countryside and the river, yet not far from town. It has a distinctive modern style throughout, with attractive embossed wallpapers and quality furnishings. Bold, well-appointed bedrooms display high attention to detail and have immaculate bathrooms.

KNOCK (An Cnoc)

Mayo – Pop. 811 – See Regional map n°**36**-B2
Dublin 212 – Galway 74 – Westport 51
Michelin Road map 712-F6 – Michelin Green Guide IRELAND

*Hotels see : **Cong** SW : 58 km by N 17, R 331 R 334 and R 345*

LAHINCH (An Leacht)

Clare – Pop. 642 – See Regional map n°**38**-B1
Dublin 260 km – Galway 79 km – Limerick 66 km
Michelin Road map 712-D9 – Michelin Green Guide IRELAND

Vaughan Lodge

Ennistymon Rd – (065) 708 11 11 – www.vaughanlodge.ie – April-October
22 rm – € 110/160 € 130/230
Rest – Carte € 32/60 – *(closed Sunday and Monday) (dinner only)*
Stylish roadside hotel with a bright, modern interior, a leather-furnished lounge and a great selection of malts behind the bar. The smart, spacious bedrooms come in eye-catching colour schemes and offer good facilities. There are many golf courses nearby. The dining room serves a menu of modern classics.

Moy House

Southwest : 3 km on N 67 (Milltown Malbay rd) – (065) 708 28 00 – www.moyhouse.com – May-October
9 rm – € 140/220 € 185/360
Rest – Menu € 55 – *(dinner only) (set menu only)*
18C Italianate clifftop villa, overlooking the bay and run by a friendly, attentive team. Homely guest areas include a small library and an open-fired drawing room with an honesty bar; antiques, oil paintings and heavy fabrics feature throughout. Individually designed, classical bedrooms boast good extras and most have views. Formal dining is from a 5 course set menu.

LEENANE (An Líonán)

Galway ✉ Clifden – See Regional map n°**36**-A3
▶Dublin 278 km – Ballina 90 km – Galway 66 km
Michelin Road map 712-C7 – Michelin Green Guide IRELAND

Delphi Lodge

Northwest : 13.25 km by N 59 on Louisburgh rd – ✆ (095) 42 222 – www.delphilodge.ie – March-mid October
12 rm ☕ – 🚹 € 140/195 🚹🚹 € 230/320
Rest – Menu € 55 – *(dinner only) (set menu only)*
A former shooting lodge of the Marquis of Sligo, in a lovely loughside spot on a 1,000 acre estate. Bright, simple bedrooms with smart bathrooms. 'Special Experience' days, free bike hire and a large walkers' drying room. Communal dining from a set menu; guests are encouraged to mingle in the drawing room.

LEIGHLINBRIDGE (Leithghlinn an Droichid)

Carlow – Pop. 828 – See Regional map n°**39**-D2
▶Dublin 63 km – Carlow 8 km – Kilkenny 16 km – Athy 22 km
Michelin Road map 712-L9

Lord Bagenal

Main St – ✆ (059) 977 40 00 – www.lordbagenal.com – Closed 25-26 December
39 rm ☕ – 🚹 € 65/100 🚹🚹 € 90/160
Rest – Menu € 25/40 – Carte € 22/45 – *(carving lunch)*
Striking hotel on the banks of the River Barrow. It was originally just a tiny coaching inn – be sure to head to the characterful original bar for a comforting, classical dish and a pint of Guinness in front of the peat fire. Vast modern extensions house the rest of the guest areas and the modern bedrooms.

LETTERFRACK (Leitir Fraic)

Galway – See Regional map n°**36**-A3
▶Dublin 304 km – Ballina 111 km – Galway 91 km
Michelin Road map 712-C7 – Michelin Green Guide IRELAND

Rosleague Manor

West : 2.5 km. on N 59 – ✆ (095) 41 101 – www.rosleague.com – mid March- mid October
20 rm ☕ – 🚹 € 80/130 🚹🚹 € 130/190 **Rest** – Menu € 32/46 – *(dinner only)*
Creeper-clad country house in mature grounds, boasting excellent bay and mountain views. Large, classically styled bedrooms. Cosy, antique-filled drawing rooms with open fires; wicker-furnished conservatory for afternoon tea and evening drinks. The formal dining room overlooks the gardens.

LETTERKENNY (Leitir Ceanainn)

Donegal – Pop. 15 387 – See Regional map n°**37**-C1
▶Dublin 241 km – Londonderry 34 km – Sligo 116 km
Michelin Road map 712-I3 – Michelin Green Guide IRELAND

Radisson Blu

rest,

Paddy Harte Rd – ✆ (074) 919 44 44 – www.radissonblu.ie/hotel-letterkenny
114 rm ☕ – 🚹 € 84/180 🚹🚹 € 99/219
Rest *Brasserie Tribeca* – Menu € 20 **s** – Carte € 25/45 **s** – *(dinner only)*
Purpose-built hotel set on a shopping and retail park close to the city centre; its reception displays photos of the stars who have stayed here. Uniform bedrooms with modern bathrooms. Good leisure club. Spacious bar serves light meals and snacks; popular, brasserie-style dining room offers dishes to match.

LIMERICK (Luimneach)

Limerick – Pop. 57 106 – See Regional map n°**38**-B2
▶Dublin 195 km – Cork 99 km – Galway 102 km – Waterford 127 km
Michelin Road map 712-G9 – Michelin Green Guide IRELAND

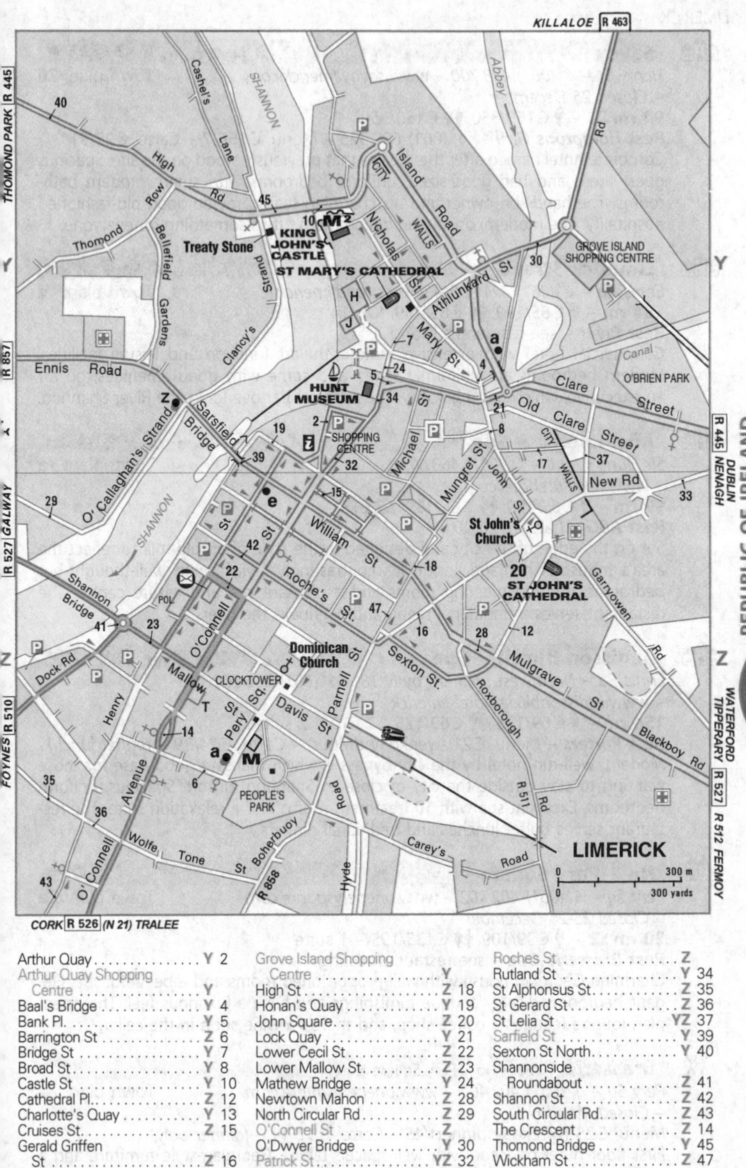

Arthur Quay . . . . Y 2
Arthur Quay Shopping Centre . . . . Y
Baal's Bridge . . . . Y 4
Bank Pl. . . . . Y 5
Barrington St . . . . Z 6
Bridge St . . . . Y 7
Broad St . . . . Y 8
Castle St . . . . Y 10
Cathedral Pl. . . . . Z 12
Charlotte's Quay . . . . Y 13
Cruises St. . . . . Z 15
Gerald Griffen St . . . . Z 16
Grattan St. . . . . Y 17
Grove Island Shopping Centre . . . . Y
High St . . . . Z 18
Honan's Quay . . . . Y 19
John Square . . . . Z 20
Lock Quay . . . . Y 21
Lower Cecil St . . . . Z 22
Lower Mallow St. . . . . Z 23
Mathew Bridge . . . . Y 24
Newtown Mahon . . . . Z 28
North Circular Rd . . . . Z 29
O'Connell St . . . . Z
O'Dwyer Bridge . . . . Y 30
Patrick St . . . . YZ 32
Penniwell Rd . . . . Z 33
Roches St . . . . Z
Rutland St . . . . Y 34
St Alphonsus St. . . . . Z 35
St Gerard St . . . . Z 36
St Lelia St . . . . YZ 37
Sarfield St . . . . Y 39
Sexton St North . . . . Y 40
Shannonside Roundabout . . . . Z 41
Shannon St . . . . Z 42
South Circular Rd. . . . . Z 43
The Crescent . . . . Z 14
Thomond Bridge . . . . Y 45
Wickham St . . . . Z 47
William St. . . . . Z

Savoy

Henry St – ✆ (061) 448 700 – www.savoylimerick.com Town plan: Z**e**
– Closed 25 December
94 rm – € 150/350 € 150/350
Rest *Hamptons Grill* – ✆ (061) 609 325 – Menu € 15/27 – Carte € 28/51
Corporate hotel named after the theatre that previously stood on the site. Spacious guest areas and bar; good-sized, uniform bedrooms with smart, modern bathrooms. The hands-on owner and his charming team provide good old-fashioned hospitality. The modern, open-plan dining room offers something for everyone.

Limerick Strand

Ennis Rd – ✆ (061) 421 800 – www.strandlimerick.ie Town plan: Y**z**
184 rm – € 85/199 € 85/199, €14
Rest *River* – see restaurant listing
Commercial hotel with extensive, state-of-the-art function and leisure facilities. Modern bedrooms are uniformly styled and come with good amenities; go for an executive, which has a balcony. The terraced bar overlooks the River Shannon.

Absolute H. & Spa

Sir Harry's Mall – ✆ (061) 463 600 Town plan: Y**a**
– www.absolutehotel.com
99 rm – € 65/199 € 65/199, €13
Rest *ABG* – Carte € 20/40
Set on the edge of the city and designed in the style of an old mill to reflect the area's industrial heritage. Inside it's contrastingly stylish, with well-thought-out bedrooms, modern meeting rooms and a pleasant spa and leisure centre. The restaurant serves a traditional menu and overlooks the river.

Radisson Blu H. & Spa

Ennis Rd – Northwest : 6.5 km by N 18 – ✆ (061) 456 200
– www.radissonblu.ie/hotel-limerick
154 rm – € 69/175 € 69/175, €10 – 2 suites
Rest *Porters* – Menu € 21 (weekday dinner) – Carte € 24/39 – *(buffet lunch)*
Modern, well-run hotel by the city bypass – which makes a good base for those wanting to stay outside the city or close to Shannon Airport. Spacious, uniform bedrooms. Excellent spa with 10 treatment rooms and a relaxation suite. The restaurant serves buffet lunches and traditional dinners.

No 1 Pery Square

Pery Sq – ✆ (061) 402 402 – www.oneperysquare.com Town plan: Z**a**
– Closed 25-26 December
20 rm – € 99/109 € 135/195 – 1 suite
Rest *Brasserie One* – see restaurant listing
Charming Georgian house with well-proportioned rooms and a beautiful spa. Elegant bedrooms display antique furnishings and have a luxurious feel. The open-plan lounge features a coffee shop, and there's a wine shop in the cellar.

Brasserie One – No 1 Pery Square Hotel

Pery Sq – ✆ (061) 402 402 – www.oneperysquare.com Town plan: Z**a**
– Closed Monday
Menu € 25 (weekday dinner)/45 – Carte € 32/49 – *(dinner only)*
First floor hotel brasserie with well-spaced tables, Georgian-style furniture and a semi-open kitchen. Modern, flavoursome bistro dishes showcase local and Irish produce; beef features highly. Well-versed service and a laid-back feel.

River – Limerick Strand Hotel

Ennis Rd – ✆ (061) 421 800 – www.strandlimerick.ie Town plan: Y**z**
Menu € 25 (weekdays) – Carte € 27/43 – *(dinner only)*
Stylish, modern hotel restaurant with smartly laid tables and river views. The experienced chef name-checks local producers on the menu; dishes are traditional and provide plenty of choice. There's also a good value early bird selection.

LISCANNOR (Lios Ceannúir)

Clare – Pop. 129 – See Regional map n°**38**-B1
Dublin 272 km – Ennistimmon 9 km – Limerick 72 km
Michelin Road map 712-D9 – Michelin Green Guide IRELAND

Vaughan's Anchor Inn with rm

rest,

Main St – (065) 708 15 48 – www.vaughans.ie – Closed 25 December
7 rm – € 50 € 70/80 Carte € 31/52
Family-run pub in a picturesque fishing village; the pleasantly cluttered bar comes complete with a small grocery shop. Dishes are a step above your normal pub fare and local seafood plays a big role; the seafood platter is a real hit. Smart bedrooms feature bright local art and colourful throws.

LISDOONVARNA (Lios Dúin Bhearna)

Clare – Pop. 739 – See Regional map n°**38**-B1
Dublin 268 km – Galway 63 km – Limerick 75 km
Michelin Road map 712-E8 – Michelin Green Guide IRELAND

Sheedy's Country House

rm,

– (065) 707 40 26 – www.sheedys.com – Easter-September
11 rm – € 80/110 € 99/170
Rest – Carte € 36/49 – *(dinner only) (booking essential)*
Mustard-yellow house in the village centre, with a kitchen garden in front. Relax in the comfy library, Lloyd Loom furnished sun lounge or traditional bar. Spacious, well-kept bedrooms feature flowery fabrics and have good facilities. A classical menu is offered in the dining room; service is exacting.

Wild Honey Inn with rm

South : 0.5 km on Ennistimon rd – (065) 707 43 00 – www.wildhoneyinn.com – Closed January-February, 24-26 December and restricted opening November-December and February-April
14 rm – € 55/65 € 90/110
Carte € 30/47 – *(closed lunch Monday-Wednesday) (bookings not accepted)*
Three-storey building at the end of a short terrace, located close to the limestone landscape of The Burren and the Cliffs of Moher. Menus stick with the classics and champion local produce, particularly seafood. Flavours are bold and presentation is modern. Bedrooms are simply furnished; two open onto the walled courtyard. Have breakfast overlooking the garden.

LISTOWEL (Lios Tuathail)

Kerry – Pop. 4 205 – See Regional map n°**38**-B2
Dublin 270 km – Killarney 54 km – Limerick 75 km – Tralee 27 km
Michelin Road map 712-D10 – Michelin Green Guide IRELAND

Allo's Bistro with rm

41-43 Church St – (068) 22 880 – www.allosbarbistro-townhouse.com – Closed Sunday and Monday except bank holidays
3 rm – € 50 € 50/80 Carte € 24/47 – *(booking essential)*
Former pub dating back to 1873; now a simple, well-run and characterful restaurant. Series of homely rooms and friendly, efficient service. Wide-ranging menus rely on regional produce, with theme nights on Thursdays and an adventurous gourmet menu at weekends. Individual, antique-furnished bedrooms.

LONGFORD (An Longfort)

Longford – Pop. 8 002 – See Regional map n°**37**-C3
Dublin 124 km – Drogheda 120 km – Galway 112 km – Limerick 175 km
Michelin Road map 712-I6

Viewmount House

Dublin Rd – Southeast : 1.5 km by R 393 – (043) 334 19 19 – www.viewmounthouse.com – Closed 25 October-4 November
12 rm – € 60/70 € 120/140
Rest *VM* – see restaurant listing
Georgian house in 4 acres of mature grounds, with a charming period style. Original features include an ornate vaulted ceiling in the breakfast room. Bedrooms are traditionally styled and furnished with antiques; opt for a duplex room.

XXX **VM** – Viewmount House Hotel
Dublin Rd – Southeast : 1.5 km by R 393 – ☎ (043) 334 19 19 – www.viewmounthouse.com – Closed 25 October-4 November
Menu € 30/55 – *(dinner only and Sunday lunch)*
Formal hotel restaurant in the old stables of a Georgian house, overlooking a Japanese garden. Classical lounge and a smart, rustic dining room with stone-faced walls. Interesting, original modern menus; orchard and garden produce features.

MALAHIDE (Mullach Íde)

Fingal – Pop. 15 846 – See Regional map n°**39**-D1
Dublin 19 km – Cork 274 km – Galway 224 km – Waterford 185 km
Michelin Road map 712-N7 – Michelin Green Guide IRELAND

XXX **bon appétit** (Oliver Dunne)
9 St James Terr – ☎ (01) 845 0314 – www.bonappetit.ie – Closed 24 December-7 January, Wednesday lunch and Sunday-Tuesday
Menu € 30 (lunch) – Carte dinner € 45/63 – *(booking essential)*
Set in a delightful Georgian terrace; ring the bell for entry. Have an aperitif in the subtly lit bar then head for the elegant first floor dining room with its ornate cornicing, crisp linen and detailed service. The concise menu offers well-judged, expertly executed classical dishes with distinct flavours.
→ Ham hock croquette, smoked saffron mayonnaise and salt-roast beetroot. Fillet of hake with smoked haddock brandade and lemon & spring onion dressing. Poached rhubarb, muscat jelly and goat's cheese cheesecake.

XX **Brasserie at bon appétit**
9 St James Terr – ☎ (01) 845 0314 – www.bonappetit.ie – Closed 25-26 December and Monday
Menu € 20 (early dinner) – Carte € 32/43 – *(dinner only and Sunday lunch) (booking essential)*
Buzzy basement brasserie below the more formal 'bon appétit'. Appealing, classical cooking with a French accent; dishes are prepared with care and precision and are very satisfying. Pleasant, efficient service and good value 'meal deals'. Selection of small plates in the trendy, dimly lit bar.

XX **Jaipur**
5 St James Terr – ☎ (01) 845 5455 – www.jaipur.ie – Closed 25 December
Menu € 16/22 – Carte € 25/48 – *(dinner only and Sunday lunch)*
Basement restaurant in terraced Georgian parade. Tasty, contemporary Indian cooking with Tandoori Jhinga (large prawns marinated in Indian spices) a speciality. Friendly, efficient service.

MALLOW (Mala)

Cork – Pop. 8 578 – See Regional map n°**38**-B2
Dublin 240 km – Cork 34 km – Killarney 64 km – Limerick 66 km
Michelin Road map 712-F11 – Michelin Green Guide IRELAND

Longueville House
West : 5.5 km by N 72 – ☎ (022) 47 156 – www.longuevillehouse.ie – Closed 24-27 December, Monday-Tuesday and restricted opening in winter
20 rm – † € 125/189 †† € 179/249
Rest *Presidents* – Menu € 38/75 – Carte € 36/61 – *(dinner only and Sunday lunch) (booking essential)*
Part-Georgian manor house built in William and Mary style, with pleasant views over Dromaneen Castle. Lovely stone-tiled hall, superb flying staircase and stunning drawing room. Well-appointed bedrooms boast antique furniture. Grand restaurant; traditional menus use produce from the kitchen garden and estate.

MIDLETON (Mainistir na Corann)

Cork – Pop. 3 733 – See Regional map n°**39**-C3
Dublin 259 km – Cork 19 km – Waterford 98 km
Michelin Road map 712-H12

REPUBLIC OF IRELAND

Farmgate Restaurant & Country Store
Coolbawn – ✆ (021) 463 27 71 – www.farmgate.ie – Closed 24 December-3 January, Sunday and Monday
Carte € 30/52 – *(bookings advisable at dinner)*
Friendly food store with a bakery, a rustic two-roomed restaurant and a courtyard terrace. Light lunches offer soups, sandwiches and tarts; dinner features regional fish and meats – the chargrilled steaks are popular. Cakes served all day.

Sage (N)
The Courtyard, 8 Main St – ✆ (021) 463 96 82 – www.sagerestaurant.ie – Closed 25-27 December, Good Friday and Monday
Menu € 29 (weekday dinner) – Carte € 28/46
Local produce is the focus at this homely restaurant and all of the ingredients come from within a 12 mile radius. Cooking has a classical base and showcases prime seafood and top quality meats – including some lesser-known cuts.

MOHILL (Maothail)

Leitrim – Pop. 928 – See Regional map n°**37**-**C2**
Dublin 98 km – Carrick-on-Shannon 11 km – Cavan 41 km – Castlerea 44 km
Michelin Road map 712-I6

Lough Rynn Castle rm,
Southeast : 4 km by R 201 off Drumlish rd – ✆ (071) 963 27 00 – www.loughrynn.ie
43 rm – € 80/155 € 99/195
Rest *Sandstone* – Menu € 20/44 – Carte € 39/105 – *(dinner only and Sunday lunch)*
18C country house with superb gardens and peaceful grounds; popular for weddings. Numerous lounges and a baronial hall with original parquet flooring and an impressive fireplace. Large, well-appointed bedrooms – those in the main house are the most characterful. Formal dining room; ambitious French cuisine.

Lough Rynn Country House without rest
Southeast : 3.5 km. by R 201 off Drumlish rd – ✆ (071) 963 2121 – www.loughrynnbandb.ie
5 rm – € 45 € 90
Stone house on a country road, boasting lovely views over Lough Rynn; three of the homely bedrooms share the view and one has a small balcony. Comfy lounge and cottagey breakfast room. Guests are welcomed with home-baked scones or muffins.

MULLINGAR (An Muileann gCearr)

Westmeath – Pop. 9 414 – See Regional map n°**37**-**C3**
Dublin 79 km – Cork 242 km – Galway 146 km – Waterford 177 km
Michelin Road map 712-J/K7 – Michelin Green Guide IRELAND

Mullingar Park rm, rest,
Dublin Rd – East : 2.5 km on Dublin Rd (N 4) – ✆ (044) 933 7500 – www.mullingarparkhotel.com – Closed 25-26 December
94 rm – € 80/120 € 120/200 – 1 suite
Rest – Carte € 30/48 **s** – *(dinner only and Sunday lunch)*
Large, contemporary hotel close to a business park and the main road to Dublin – a popular conference venue. Well-equipped, modern bedrooms in a uniform style. Comprehensive leisure facilities. Horseshoe bar-lounge and spacious formal dining room offering classical Irish cooking.

Marlinstown Court without rest
Dublin Rd – East : 2.5 km on Dublin Rd (N 4) – ✆ (044) 934 00 53 – www.marlinstowncourt.com – Closed 23-27 December
5 rm – € 40/50 € 70/75
Clean, tidy guesthouse close to the N4; a very homely, personal option for staying away. The light, airy lounge opens into a pleasant pine-furnished breakfast room overlooking the garden. Bedrooms are simply and brightly decorated.

REPUBLIC OF IRELAND

MULRANNY (An Mhala Raithní)

Mayo – See Regional map n°**36**-A2

Dublin 270 km – Castlebar 35 km – Westport 29 km

Michelin Road map 712-C6

Mulranny Park

On N 59 – (098) 36 000 – www.mulrannyparkhotel.ie – Closed 7-31 January and 25-26 December

61 rm – € 65/110 € 110/170 – 20 suites

Rest *Nephin* – Menu € 40 **s** – Carte € 25/59 **s** – *(dinner only and Sunday lunch)*

1897 railway hotel with stunning views of Clew Bay and Achill Island, and its own causeway to the beach. Modern, slightly minimalist bedrooms; the two-bedroomed suites are ideal for families. Impressive leisure and conference facilities. All-day snacks in the bar; modern menu in the restaurant. Charming team.

MURRISK

Mayo – Pop. 235 – See Regional map n°**36**-A2

Dublin 260 km – Castlebar 25 km – Galway 95 km

Michelin Road map 712-D6

Tavern

– (098) 64 060 – www.tavernmurrisk.com – Closed Good Friday and 25 December

Carte € 25/49

Vibrant pink pub with designer colours, leather banquettes and quirky basket lampshades. Wide-ranging dishes display a touch of refinement; the meats and seafood are local and the daily cheesecake is a must. Staff are smart and attentive.

NAAS (An Nás)

Kildare – Pop. 20 713 – See Regional map n°**39**-D1

Dublin 30 km – Kilkenny 83 km – Tullamore 85 km

Michelin Road map 712-L/M8 – Michelin Green Guide IRELAND

Killashee House H. & Villa Spa

Kilcullen Rd – South : 3 km on R 448 – (045) 879 277 – www.killasheehouse.com – Closed 25-26 December

141 rm – € 100/220 € 130/360 – 12 suites

Rest *Turners* – Menu € 50 – *(dinner only Friday-Saturday)*

Rest *Jack's* – Menu € 17 (lunch) – Carte € 29/48

Impressive part-1860s hunting lodge, surrounded by vast grounds and boasting spacious, traditionally styled guest areas, good event facilities and a superb leisure club and spa. Country house style bedrooms – those in the main building are the most characterful. Turners offers elegant fine dining overlooking the garden. Family-friendly brasserie menu in informal Jack's.

Vie de Châteaux

The Harbour – (045) 888 478 – www.viedechateaux.ie – Closed 24 December-2 January, lunch Saturday and bank holidays

Menu € 24 (weekday lunch)/29 – Carte € 33/47 – *(booking essential)*

Stylish, popular restaurant with a terrace, an open-plan kitchen and a brasserie feel; a stone's throw from the canal. Concise, keenly priced menu moves with the seasons; mainly French dishes but with some Mediterranean influences.

at Two Mile House Southwest: 6.5 km by R448

Brown Bear

– (045) 883 561 – www.thebrownbear.ie – Closed Monday, Tuesday and 24-27 December

Menu € 20 – Carte € 31/45 – *(dinner only and lunch Saturday-Sunday)*

Smart restaurant in a small village, boasting a pubby locals bar and leather-furnished dining room with a subtle brasserie feel. Decide between two menus: a two-choice set selection or a complex, ambitious à la carte with a Gallic twist.

NAVAN (An Uaimh)

Meath – Pop. 28 158 – See Regional map n°**37**-D3
Dublin 48 km – Drogheda 26 km – Dundalk 51 km
Michelin Road map 712-L7 – Michelin Green Guide IRELAND

Ma Dwyers without rest

Dublin Rd – South : 1.25 km on R 147 – (046) 907 79 92 – www.madwyers.com – Closed 24-27 December
26 rm – € 40 € 65
Surprisingly spacious detached house on the main road into town. Simple, brightly painted interior with a comfy lounge and large breakfast room. Good value bedrooms in an up-to-date, uniform style; bathrooms are shower only.

NEW QUAY (Bealaclugga)

Clare
Dublin 240 km – Ennis 55 km – Galway 46 km
Michelin Green Guide IRELAND

Mount Vernon

Flaggy Shore – North : 0.75 km on coast rd – (065) 707 8126 – www.mountvernon.ie – Closed November-March
5 rm – € 90/145 € 160/230 **Rest** – Menu € 50
Charming whitewashed house with a pretty walled garden, set close to the beach and affording lovely views. Antiques and eclectic curios fill the guest areas; spacious bedrooms have their own personalities – two open onto a terrace. Simply cooked dinners rely on fresh, local produce. Warm, welcoming owners.

Linnane's Lobster Bar

New Quay Pier – (065) 707 8120 – www.linnanesbar.com – Closed Good Friday, 25 December and Monday-Thursday October-Easter
Carte € 22/52
Simple but likeable place, with peat fires and full-length windows which open onto a terrace. They specialise in fresh, tasty fish and shellfish; watch the local boats unload their catch – some of which is brought straight to the kitchen.

NEWMARKET-ON-FERGUS (Cora Chaitlín)

Clare – Pop. 1 773 – See Regional map n°**38**-B2
Dublin 219 km – Ennis 13 km – Limerick 24 km
Michelin Road map 712-F7 – Michelin Green Guide IRELAND

Dromoland Castle

rm,

Northwest : 2.5 km on R 458 – (061) 368 144 – www.dromoland.ie
99 rm – € 257/662 € 257/662, €29 – 5 suites
Rest *Earl of Thomond* – Menu € 70 – Carte € 59/73 – *(dinner only)*
Rest *Fig Tree* – Carte € 28/50 – *(closed Sunday dinner)*
Impressive 16C castle in 450 acres, with a championship golf course and equestrian and falconry centres. Various richly appointed, antique-filled, country house lounges. Smart 'feature' bedrooms cleverly blend the old and new; the courtyard rooms are more traditional. Modern classics under crystal chandeliers in the formal restaurant; more casual dining in Fig Tree.

NEWPORT (Baile Uí Fhiacháin)

Mayo – Pop. 616 – See Regional map n°**36**-A2
Dublin 264 km – Ballina 59 km – Galway 96 km
Michelin Road map 712-D6 – Michelin Green Guide IRELAND

Newport House

– (098) 41 222 – www.newporthouse.ie – Closed November-18 March
14 rm – € 120/165 € 190/280 **Rest** – Menu € 65 – *(dinner only)*
Delightful creeper-clad mansion with lovely gardens and river views; they also own Lough Beltra, nearby. Large drawing room with family portraits; traditional, antique-filled bedrooms. The grand staircase is topped by a domed cupola. Dinner is a highlight, with salmon a speciality and a notable wine list.

REPUBLIC OF IRELAND

OUGHTERARD (Uachtar Ard)

Galway – Pop. 1 333 – See Regional map n°**36-A3**

Dublin 232 km – Cork 223 km – Galway 25 km – Waterford 253 km

Michelin Road map 712-E7 – Michelin Green Guide IRELAND

Currarevagh House

Northwest : 6.5 km on Glann rd – (091) 552 312 – www.currarevagh.com – April-October

12 rm – € 75/110 € 140/180 **Rest** – Menu € 48 – *(dinner only) (set menu only)*

Classically furnished Victorian manor house, in 180 acres bordering Lough Corrib. Run by the same family for over 100 years; it has a very 'lived-in' feel and offers a real 'country house' experience. Have afternoon tea by the fire or take a picnic out on the boat. Set dinners of unfussy, flavoursome dishes.

Ross Lake House

Rosscahill – Southeast : 7.25 km by N 59 – (091) 550 109 – www.rosslakehotel.com – 16 March-October

13 rm – € 97/105 € 134/250 – 2 suites

Rest – Menu € 43 – *(dinner only)*

Personally run Georgian country house with attractive gardens, set in a wooded estate. Traditionally styled bedrooms; Strefens suite and Killaguile are the best. Begin the evening in the cocktail bar before dining by candlelight at smartly set, cloth-clad tables.

REPUBLIC OF IRELAND

Railway Lodge without rest

West : 0.75 km by Costello rd taking first right onto unmarked road – (091) 552 945 – www.railwaylodge.net

4 rm – € 50/70 € 100/110

Stylish house in a remote farm setting, with views across the countryside and a beautifully kept, elegantly furnished interior. Bedrooms come with stripped pine furnishings and have a keen eye for detail. The charming owner offers good local recommendations. Homemade bread and scones; tea served on arrival.

Waterfall Lodge without rest

West : 0.75 km on N 59 – (091) 552 168 – www.waterfalllodge.net

6 rm – € 50 € 80

Heavily restored Victorian house run by an infectiously enthusiastic owner. A fishing river runs through the garden – look out for jumping salmon! Sympathetically styled bedrooms with rug-covered floors and modern bathrooms; some have four-posters. Pancakes, French toast and smoked salmon at breakfast.

PORTMAGEE (An Caladh)

Kerry – Pop. 109 – See Regional map n°**38-A2**

Dublin 365 km – Killarney 72 km – Tralee 82 km

Michelin Road map 712-A12 – Michelin Green Guide IRELAND

Moorings

rest,

– (066) 947 71 08 – www.moorings.ie – Closed 25 December

17 rm – € 60/100 € 90/140

Rest – Carte € 30/51 – *(closed Monday except bank holidays) (bar lunch)*

Cosy, personally run hotel overlooking the harbour and bridge, and made up a series of little cottages. First floor lounge offers great views, as do some of the pleasant bedrooms; 4 and 6 boast jacuzzis. Characterful bar with music nights. Nautically themed restaurant with seafood straight from local boats.

PORTLAOISE (Port Laoise)

Laois – Pop. 20 145 – See Regional map n°**39-C2**

Dublin 88 km – Carlow 40 km – Waterford 101 km

Michelin Road map 712-K8

Ivyleigh House without rest

Bank Pl, Church St – (057) 862 20 81 – www.ivyleigh.com – Closed 24-26 December

6 rm – € 55/85 € 90/160

Traditional listed Georgian property in the city centre, run by a welcoming owner. Comfy lounge and communal dining area, with antiques and ornaments displayed throughout. Good-sized bedrooms are decorated in a period style. Homemade breads, preserves, muesli and a Cashel blue cheesecake special at breakfast.

PORTMARNOCK (Port Mearnóg)

Fingal – Pop. 9 285 – See Regional map n°**39**-**D1**

Dublin 16 km – Belfast 165 km – Cork 271 km – Galway 221 km

Michelin Road map 712-N7 – Michelin Green Guide IRELAND

 **Portmarnock H. and Golf Links** rest,

Strand Rd – (01) 846 0611 – www.portmarnock.com – Closed 24-27 December

138 rm – € 99/215 € 115/230 – 3 suites

Rest *Osborne Brasserie* – Menu € 25 – *(bar lunch)*

Much-extended 19C house, previously owned by the Jameson family of whiskey fame, and set on its own championship golf course. Well-maintained, classically styled bedrooms; those in the newer wing are larger and more contemporary – ask for a sea view. Traditional menus served in the smart brasserie.

RAMELTON (Ráth Mealtain) /Rathmelton

Donegal – Pop. 1 212 – See Regional map n°**37**-**C1**

Dublin 248 km – Donegal 59 km – Londonerry 43 km – Sligo 122 km

Michelin Road map 712-J2 – Michelin Green Guide IRELAND

Moorfield Lodge without rest

Aughnagaddy Glebe, Moorfield – South : 3.25 km on R 245 – (074) 989 4043 – www.moorfieldlodge.com – April-October

3 rm – € 100/140 € 120/160

Striking, modern house run by a welcoming owner. Bright, stylish bedrooms with underfloor heating, floor to ceiling windows and Egyptian cotton sheets. Room 1 has its own terrace, a double jacuzzi bath and a TV built into the bathroom tiles. Communal breakfasts are served around an antique table.

Ardeen without rest

bear left at the fork in the village centre and left at T-junction – (074) 915 12 43 – www.ardeenhouse.com – Easter-September

5 rm – € 45 € 90

A Victorian house on the edge of the village, with peaceful gardens and a river nearby. Welcoming owner and homely, personally styled interior. Open-fired lounge with local info; communal breakfasts. Simple, well-kept bedrooms without TVs.

RANELAGH → See Dublin

Dublin – Michelin Road map 712-N7

RATHGAR → See Dublin

Dublin – Michelin Road map 712-N8

RATHMINES = RÁTH MAONAIS → See Dublin

Dublin – Michelin Road map 712-N8

RATHMULLAN (Ráth Maoláin)

Donegal – Pop. 518 – Letterkenny – See Regional map n°**37**-**C1**

Dublin 265 km – Londonderry 58 km – Sligo 140 km

Michelin Road map 712-J2 – Michelin Green Guide IRELAND

Rathmullan House rm,

North : 0.5 mi on R 247 – (074) 915 81 88 – www.rathmullanhouse.com – Closed 4 January-13 February and restricted opening in winter

34 rm – € 70/170 € 140/250

Rest *Cook & Gardener* – Carte € 35/57 – *(bar lunch)*

Family-run, part-19C house set by Lough Swilly. Country house style bedrooms in the original house; those in the extension are more modern and come with balconies or private terraces. The formal dining room has views over the grounds; traditional menus feature produce from the kitchen garden.

RATHNEW

Wicklow – Pop. 2 964 – ✉ Wicklow
▶Dublin 45 km – Gorey 44 km – Wexford 97 km
Michelin Road map 712-N8

Tinakilly House

On R 750 – ✆ (0404) 69 274 – www.tinakilly.ie – Closed 25 December
50 rm – € 80/160 € 100/280 – 1 suite
Rest *Brunel* – see restaurant listing
A substantial Victorian house in extensive grounds which stretch to the seashore: built for Captain Robert Halpin. Original features include an impressive staircase. Spacious, classically furnished bedrooms; some have four-posters.

Hunter's

Newrath Bridge – North : 1.25 km by Dublin rd on R 761 – ✆ (0404) 40 106 – www.hunters.ie – Closed Christmas
16 rm – € 75/95 € 130/180 **Rest** – Menu € 26/45
Late 17C former coaching inn run by the 5th generation of the same family. Traditionally styled throughout with homely lounges displaying flowery fabrics and drapes. Neat, country house style bedrooms boast sleigh beds and antique furnishings. Formal dining room offers menu of traditionally based dishes.

Brunel – Tinakilly House Hotel

On R 750 – ✆ (0404) 69 274 – www.tinakilly.ie – Closed 25 December
Menu € 25 – Carte € 42/56 – *(dinner only and Sunday lunch)*
Spacious, elegant restaurant in a hotel extension, overlooking the gardens: named after the builder of the Great Eastern ship on which Captain Halpin sailed. Light lunches; innovative, modern dinner dishes use the best Wicklow ingredients.

REPUBLIC OF IRELAND

RIVERSTOWN (Baile idir Dhá Abhainn)

Sligo – Pop. 374 – See Regional map n°**36**-B2
▶Dublin 189 km – Cork 309 km – Lisburn 193 km – Craigavon 170 km
Michelin Road map 712-G5

Coopershill

– ✆ (071) 916 51 08 – www.coopershill.com – April-October
8 rm – € 134/157 € 198/244
Rest – Menu € 54 – *(dinner only) (booking essential)*
Magnificent Georgian house run by the 7th generation of the same family; set on a working farm within a 500 acre estate. Spacious guest areas showcase original furnishings – now antiques – and family portraits adorn the walls. Warm, country house style bedrooms. Formal dining amongst polished silverware.

ROSCOMMON (Ros Comáin)

Roscommon – Pop. 5 693 – See Regional map n°**36**-B3
▶Dublin 151 km – Galway 92 km – Limerick 151 km
Michelin Road map 712-H7 – Michelin Green Guide IRELAND

Abbey

Galway Rd – On N 63 – ✆ (090) 662 62 40 – www.abbeyhotel.ie – Closed 24-26 December
50 rm – € 65/140 € 85/280 **Rest** – Menu € 30/45 – Carte € 27/41
Part-18C, family-run manor house with a castellated façade; overlooking the ruins of the 13C abbey. The most characterful bedrooms are in the original house; some boast feature beds and roll-top baths. Good function and leisure facilities. Dine from the carvery in the large bar, or in the formal restaurant.

ROSSLARE (Ros Láir)

Wexford – Pop. 1 547 – See Regional map n°**39**-D2
▶Dublin 167 km – Waterford 80 km – Wexford 19 km
Michelin Road map 712-M11 – Michelin Green Guide IRELAND

Kelly's Resort rest,

– (053) 913 21 14 – *www.kellys.ie – 17 February-November*
118 rm – € 88/110 € 176/220
Rest ***La Marine*** – see restaurant listing
Rest ***Beaches*** – Menu € 25 (lunch)/45 – Carte € 28/43
It started life in 1895 as a beachfront 'refreshment house'; now it's a sprawling leisure-orientated hotel run by the 4th generation of the Kelly family. Various lounges, large bar and sizeable spa. Well-appointed bedrooms; the newer rooms being the largest. Formal Beaches offers an exceptional wine list.

La Marine – Kelly's Resort Hotel

– *(053) 913 21 14 – www.kellys.ie – 17 February-October*
Menu € 22 – Carte € 29/43
Bistro-style restaurant located within a large beachfront hotel, boasting an open-kitchen and glass-fronted wine cellar. A large zinc-topped bar from France takes centre stage, while the menu offers a selection of tasty brasserie classics.

ROSSLARE HARBOUR (Calafort Ros Láir)

Wexford – Pop. 1 123 – See Regional map n°**39**-D2
Dublin 169 km – Waterford 82 km – Wexford 21 km
Michelin Road map 712-N11

Archways

Rosslare Rd, Tagoat – West : 6.25 km on N 25 – (053) 915 81 11
– www.thearchways.ie – Closed 20-27 December and 31 December-3 January
6 rm – € 52/65 € 75/85 **Rest** – Menu € 15
Spanish villa style bungalow, conveniently located for Rosslare harbour. Contemporary bedrooms feature coffee machines and smart bathrooms, with colour schemes themed around a single piece of art from a local artist. Daily changing set three course dinners use the best of seasonal, local produce.

ROUNDSTONE (Cloch na Rón)

Galway – Pop. 245 – See Regional map n°**36**-A3
Dublin 293 km – Galway 76 km – Ennis 144 km
Michelin Road map 712-C7 – Michelin Green Guide IRELAND

O'Dowds

– *(095) 35 809 – www.odowdsseafoodbar.com – Closed 25 December*
Menu € 22 – Carte € 22/48 – *(booking advisable)*
Busy pub in pretty harbourside town; popular with tourists and locals alike. Owned by the O'Dowd family for over 100 years, it specialises in fresh, simply cooked fish and shellfish. Sit in the cosy, fire-lit bar or wood-panelled restaurant.

ROUNDWOOD

Wicklow – Pop. 833 – See Regional map n°**39**-D2
Dublin 25 km – Wicklow 12 km – Belfast 137 km – Limerick 144 km
Michelin Road map 712-N9

Byrne & Woods

Main St – (01) 281 70 78 – www.byrneandwoods.com – Closed 25-26 December
Menu € 21 (weekday lunch)/26 – Carte € 24/45
Arguably the second highest pub in Ireland, set up in the Wicklow Mountains. 'Byrne' is a cosy bar with a wood-burning stove; dimly lit 'Woods' has leather and dark wood furnishings and a clubby feel. Cooking is fresh and straightforward.

SANDYFORD = ÁTH AN GHAINIMH → See Dublin

Dún Laoghaire-Rathdown – Michelin Road map 712-N8

SHANAGARRY (An Seangharraí)

Cork – Pop. 414 – ✉ Midleton – See Regional map n°**39**-C3
Dublin 262 km – Cork 40 km – Waterford 103 km
Michelin Road map 712-H12 – Michelin Green Guide IRELAND

Ballymaloe House 
Northwest : 2.5 km on R 629 – ☎ (021) 465 25 31 – www.ballymaloe.ie – Closed 2 weeks January and 24-26 December
29 rm – € 115/145 € 180/280
Rest – Menu € 40/70 – Carte € 36/49 – *(booking essential)*
With its pre-18C origins, this is the very essence of a country manor house. Family-run for 3 generations, it boasts numerous traditionally styled guest areas, comfortable, classical bedrooms and a famed cookery school. The 5 course daily menu offers local, seasonal produce.

SLANE

Meath – Pop. 1 349 – See Regional map n°**37-B3**
Dublin 34 km – Navan 8 km – City Centre 35 km – Craigavon 69 km
Michelin Road map 712-M6

 **Tankardstown** 
Northwest : 6 km by N 51 off R 163 – ☎ (041) 982 46 21 – www.tankardstown.ie – Closed 5-30 January and 25-25 December
12 rm – € 100/200 € 200/350 – 6 suites
Rest *Brabazon* – see restaurant listing
Fine Georgian manor house on a mature country estate; extensively restored to a luxurious level. Large, antique-furnished bedrooms in the main house – some with silk-lined walls. The smart, modern courtyard rooms have kitchens.

 **Conyngham Arms** 
– ☎ (041) 988 4444 – www.conynghamarms.ie – Closed 25-26 December
15 rm – € 80/120 € 109/159
Rest – Menu € 18 (weekday dinner) – Carte € 25/39
17C coaching inn close to a castle, in a small but busy town – set on the main street but with a hidden rear garden. Appealing, informal, French boutique styling. Bedrooms have good facilities; some boast sleigh beds or four-posters. Dine in the bar or restaurant, on produce sourced from within 25 miles.

XX **Brabazon** – Tankardstown Hotel 
Northwest : 6 km by N 51 off R 163 – ☎ (041) 982 46 21 – www.tankardstown.ie – Closed 5-30 January, 25-26 December and Monday-Tuesday
Carte € 37/62 – *(dinner only and Sunday lunch)*
Relaxed, rustic restaurant set in former piggery of the manor house, with modern interior, painted wooden tables and pleasant terrace overlooking the landscaped courtyard. Contemporary cooking makes use of good quality ingredients.

SLIGO (Sligeach)

Sligo – Pop. 17 568 – See Regional map n°**36-B2**
Dublin 214 km – Belfast 203 km – Dundalk 170 km – Londonderry 138 km
Michelin Road map 712-G5 – Michelin Green Guide IRELAND

 **Tree Tops** without rest 
Cleveragh Rd – South : 1.25 km by Dublin rd – ☎ (071) 916 23 01 – www.sligobandb.com – Closed Christmas-New Year
4 rm – € 40/45 € 72/76
Unassuming whitewashed house in a residential area, with immaculately kept bedrooms, a cosy lounge and a smart breakfast room overlooking the garden. The owners are chatty and welcoming, and they have an interesting Irish art collection.

XX **Montmartre**
Market Yard – ☎ (071) 916 99 01 – www.montmartrerestaurant.ie – Closed 11 January-4 February, Sunday and Monday
Menu € 24/37 – Carte € 27/47 – *(dinner only)*
Smart, modern restaurant in the shadow of the cathedral, with a tiled exterior and wooden blinds. The French chefs prepare classic Gallic menus which follow the seasons. The all-French wine list features interesting, lesser-known wines.

REPUBLIC OF IRELAND

Hargadons

4-5 O'Connell St – ✆ (071) 915 3709 – www.hargadons.com – Closed Sunday
Carte € 19/29 – *(bookings not accepted)*
Hugely characterful pub with sloping floors, narrow passageways, dimly lit anterooms and a lovely "Ladies' Room" complete with its own serving hatch. Cooking is warming and satisfying, offering the likes of Irish stew or bacon and cabbage.

at Strandhill West: 7 km on R292

Strandhill Lodge & Suites without rest

Top Hill – ✆ (071) 912 21 22 – www.strandhilllodgeandsuites.ie
22 rm – € 65/99 € 69/149
Modern guesthouse with a comfy lounge and a small breakfast room. Standard bedrooms look inland; go for one with a patio or a balcony overlooking the rooftops to the Atlantic. The suites have small kitchens and are ideal for longer stays.

SPANISH POINT (Rinn na Spáinneach)

Clare ✉ Milltown Malbay – See Regional map n°**38**-B2
Dublin 275 km – Galway 104 km – Limerick 83 km
Michelin Road map 712-D9

Red Cliff Lodge with rm

– ✆ (065) 708 57 56 – www.redclifflodge.ie – Easter-October
6 rm – € 80/150 € 110/200 Carte € 33/49 – *(dinner only)*
Thatched cottage in a superb spot on the headland; later extensions have created a U-shaped arrangement around a cobbled courtyard. The décor is bright and eye-catching, the tables are elegantly set and modern classics are served with flair. Smart, spacious bedrooms have kitchenettes and coffee machines.

STEPASIDE

Dún Laoghaire-Rathdown – See Regional map n°**39**-D1
Dublin 10 km – Dún Laoghaire 7 km – Belfast 121 km – Cork 164 km

Box Tree

Enniskerry Rd ✉ D18 – ✆ (01) 205 20 25 – www.theboxtree.ie – Closed 25-26 December and Good Friday
Menu € 25/29 – Carte € 38/53
Modern eatery beneath a small, new-build apartment block. The attractive restaurant serves good value menus of unfussy, classical dishes. On the other side of the bar is the Wild Boar, which serves slightly lighter offerings.

STRAFFAN (Teach Srafáin)

Kildare – Pop. 635 – See Regional map n°**39**-D1
Dublin 29 km – Belfast 192 km – Cork 238 km – Lisburn 180 km
Michelin Road map 712-M8 – Michelin Green Guide IRELAND

K Club

– ✆ (01) 601 72 00 – www.kclub.ie – Closed 8-22 January
69 rm – € 355/455 € 355/455 – 9 suites
Rest *Byerley Turk* – Menu € 89 – *(closed Monday-Wednesday) (dinner only)*
Rest *River Room* – Menu € 63 – *(dinner only)*
Rest *Legends* – Carte € 40/71
Rest *K Thai* – Carte € 38/41 – *(closed Monday and Tuesday) (dinner only)*
A golf resort with two championship courses, an extensive spa and beautiful formal gardens stretching down to the Liffey. The fine 19C house has elegant antique-filled guestrooms and luxurious bedrooms. Elegant Byerley Turk serves a 6 course tasting menu; grand River Room offers refined classics; Legends has a brasserie menu; and K Thai serves Thai and Malaysian fare.

Barberstown Castle

North : 0.75 km – (01) 628 81 57 – www.barberstowncastle.ie – Closed January and 24-26 December

55 rm – € 150/200 € 220/270

Rest *Barton Rooms* – Menu € 55 – *(closed Sunday-Thursday) (dinner only) (bookings essential for non-residents) (residents only)*

Rest *Tea Rooms* – Carte € 24/43

Set within 20 acres of grounds; a 13C castle with whitewashed Georgian and Victorian extensions – a popular venue for weddings. Large, luxurious country house bedrooms feature good facilities; many have four-poster beds and garden outlooks. Dine on traditional dishes in the informal, conservatory style bistro or from French menus in the Georgian house and stone keep.

STRANDHILL → See Sligo

Sligo

TERMONBARRY

Roscommon – Pop. 366 – See Regional map n°**37-C3**

Dublin 130 km – Galway 137 km – Roscommon 35 km – Sligo 100 km

Michelin Road map 712-I6 – Michelin Green Guide IRELAND

Keenan's

– (043) 332 60 52 – www.keenans.ie – Closed 25-26 December

12 rm – € 85/110 € 110/140

Rest – Menu € 35/45 – Carte € 29/47 – *(closed Sunday dinner)*

Modern extension to a characterful village pub; run by the 5th generation of the same family. Cosy residents lounge and breakfast room. Stylish black and white bedrooms with compact bathrooms; some have balconies overlooking the Shannon. Large restaurant offers classic menus; the bar serves pub favourites.

THOMASTOWN (Baile Mhic Andáin)

Kilkenny – Pop. 2 273 – See Regional map n°**39-C2**

Dublin 124 km – Kilkenny 17 km – Waterford 48 km – Wexford 61 km

Michelin Road map 712-K10 – Michelin Green Guide IRELAND

Mount Juliet rm, rm,

Southwest : 5.5 km by N 9 on R 4286 – (056) 777 3000 – www.mountjuliet.ie

58 rm – € 134/284 € 149/299 – 13 suites

Rest *Lady Helen* – see restaurant listing

Rest *Kendals Brasserie* – Menu € 25 – Carte € 27/46 – *(closed Monday and Wednesday) (bar lunch)*

Georgian gem situated in 1,500 acres, with a Jack Nicklaus designed golf course, a spa, an equestrian centre and even a stud farm. Bedrooms range from traditional in the main house to two-roomed garden lodges and smaller but equally comfy rooms in the former hunting stables. Grand restaurant; simple French dishes in the brasserie and light lunches in the clubhouse bar.

Abbey House without rest

Jerpoint Abbey – Southwest : 2 km on N 9 – (056) 772 41 66 – www.abbeyhousejerpoint.com – Closed 20-30 December

6 rm – € 50/90 € 75/100

Attractive whitewashed Victorian house with a neat, lawned garden and a friendly, hospitable owner; set opposite the ruins of Jerpoint Abbey. Traditionally styled lounge with plenty of local info. Simple bedrooms with antique furniture.

Lady Helen – Mount Juliet Hotel

Southwest : 5.5 km by N 9 on R 4286 – (056) 777 3000 – www.mountjuliet.ie – Closed Sunday and Tuesday

Menu € 65/75 – *(dinner only) (booking essential)*

Classical hotel restaurant consisting of two grand rooms with beautiful stuccowork, overlooking the River Nore. Accomplished cooking uses ingredients from the estate, the county and the nearest coast. Original, modern dishes are well-prepared, attractively presented and feature some stimulating combinations.

→ Scallops with celeriac, apple and dashi. Duck, bulgur wheat, ras el hanout and rhubarb. Coconut parfait, caramelised pineapple and muscovado sponge.

REPUBLIC OF IRELAND

TOORMORE (An Tuar Mór)

Cork – Pop. 207 – ✉ Goleen – See Regional map n°**38**-**A3**

Dublin 355 km – Cork 109 km – Killarney 104 km

Michelin Road map 712-D13

Fortview House without rest

Gurtyowen – Northeast : 2.5 km on R 591 (Durrus rd) – (028) 35 324 – www.fortviewhousegoleen.com – May-September

3 rm – € 50 € 100

Well-kept guesthouse on a 120 acre dairy farm, run by a very bubbly owner. It has a rustic, country feel courtesy of its stone walls, timbered ceilings, coir carpets and aged pine furniture. Breakfast is an event, with home-baked scones and bread, eggs from their hens and other local products all featuring.

TOWER → See Blarney

Cork – Michelin Road map 712-G12

TRALEE (Trá Lí)

Kerry – Pop. 20 814 – See Regional map n°**38**-**A2**

Dublin 297 km – Killarney 32 km – Limerick 103 km

Michelin Road map 712-C11 – Michelin Green Guide IRELAND

Grand rest,

Denny St – (066) 712 14 99 – www.grandhoteltralee.com – Closed 25 December

43 rm – € 55/95 € 70/170

Rest – Menu € 15 (dinner)/35 – Carte € 23/41

Opened in 1928 and located right in the heart of this bustling town. Small first floor lounge and comfy, contemporary bedrooms; those to the rear are quietest. Traditional bar, once the post office, is a popular spot, offering hearty all-day dishes. Global menu and Irish specialities in classical dining room.

Brook Manor Lodge without rest

Fenit Rd, Spa – Northwest : 3.5 km by R 551 on R 558 – (066) 712 04 06 – www.brookmanorlodge.com – April-October

8 rm – € 65/85 € 90/120

Spacious detached house with views to the Slieve Mish Mountains; good for those who like golf, hiking or fishing. Traditionally styled lounge and airy conservatory breakfast room. Immaculately kept bedrooms; those at the back have the view.

TRAMORE (Trá Mhór)

Waterford – Pop. 9 722 – See Regional map n°**39**-**C2**

Dublin 177 km – Belfast 345 km – Cork 123 km – Lisburn 333 km

Michelin Road map 712-K11 – Michelin Green Guide IRELAND

Glenorney without rest

Newtown – Southwest : 1.5 km by R 675 – (051) 381 056 – www.glenorney.com – March-November

6 rm – € 50/80 € 70/90

Smart yellow house with pretty gardens, set on the hillside, overlooking the bay. A homely lounge leads through to a dark wood furnished breakfast room where you can have pancakes, French toast and homemade preserves. Bedrooms are simply furnished, and the book-filled sun lounge is a pleasant place to relax.

TRIM (Baile Átha Troim)

Meath – Pop. 1 441 – See Regional map n°**37**-**D3**

Dublin 43 km – Drogheda 42 km – Tullamore 69 km

Michelin Road map 712-L7 – Michelin Green Guide IRELAND

Trim Castle rest,

Castle St – (046) 948 30 00 – www.trimcastlehotel.com – Closed 25 December

68 rm – € 75/130 € 95/145 **Rest** – Menu € 30 – Carte € 25/41

Modern family hotel opposite the castle, complete with a café, a homeware shop and a delightful roof garden with a great outlook. Good-sized bedrooms in contemporary hues – the front rooms share the view. Informal dining in the bar; traditional European dishes in the stylish first floor dining room.

Highfield House without rest 
Maudlins Rd. – ☎ (046) 943 63 86 – www.highfieldguesthouse.com – Closed 21 December-2 January
10 rm – € 55 € 86
Substantial 18C stone house close to the river and the oldest Norman castle in Europe. Well-appointed lounge and breakfast room, boldly coloured bedrooms and a delightful terraced courtyard. Comprehensive breakfasts; scones on arrival.

TULLAMORE (Tulach Mhór)

Offaly – Pop. 11 346 – See Regional map n°**39**-C1
Dublin 104 km – Kilkenny 83 km – Limerick 129 km
Michelin Road map 712-J8

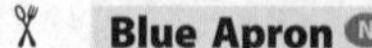

Blue Apron Ⓝ
Harbour St – ☎ (057) 936 0106 – www.theblueapronrestaurant.ie – Closed 24 January-7 February, 2 weeks August, 24-27 December, Monday-Tuesday and Sunday
Menu € 27 – Carte € 20/58 – *(dinner only and Sunday lunch)*
Friendly, engaging service sets the tone at this intimate restaurant, which is run by an enthusiastic husband and wife team. All-encompassing menus offer generous, flavoursome dishes that are prepared with care and understanding.

TWO MILE HOUSE → See Naas

VIRGINIA

Cavan – Pop. 2 282 – See Regional map n°**37**-C3
Dublin 89 km – Monaghan 76 km – Belfast 153 km – Craigavon 99 km
Michelin Road map 712-K6

St Kyrans 
Dublin Rd – South : 2.25 km. on N 3 – ☎ (049) 854 70 87 – www.stkyrans.com – Closed 5-29 January and 24-27 December
8 rm – € 60/70 € 90/100
Rest – Menu € 30 (weekday dinner) – Carte € 31/45 – *(closed Monday-Tuesday)*
Rurally set, off the main road, this hotel may be plain on the outside but it's a different story on the inside. There's a stylish lounge, modernised bedrooms – five with lough views – and a smart, linen-laid restaurant overlooking Lough Ramor. The menu offers classic dishes with an Irish heart.

WATERFORD (Port Láirge)

Waterford – Pop. 46 732 – See Regional map n°**39**-C2
Dublin 154 km – Cork 117 km – Limerick 124 km
Michelin Road map 712-K11 – Michelin Green Guide IRELAND

Waterford Castle H. and Golf Resort
The Island, Ballinakill – East : 4 km by R 683, Ballinakill Rd and private ferry – ☎ (051) 878 203 – www.waterfordcastle.com – Closed 24-26 December and weekends only 1 January-12 February
18 rm – € 95/195 € 180/280 – 5 suites
Rest *The Munster Room* – see restaurant listing
Attractive part-15C castle and lodges, set on a charming 320 acre private island in the river. The carved stone and wood-panelled hall displays antiques and old tapestries. Elegant, classical bedrooms boast characterful period bathrooms.

Athenaeum House
Christendom, Ferrybank – Northeast : 1.5 km by R 771 Town plan: Z**n**
– ☎ (051) 833 999 – www.athenaeumhousehotel.com – Closed 25-27 December
28 rm – € 66/140 € 80/150 – 3 suites
Rest *Zaks* – see restaurant listing
Bright yellow, part-Georgian house, hidden on the quieter side of the River Suir and well-run by a family team. Simple, open-fired lounge and smart, modern bedrooms. Relax on the long terrace or admire the river views from the gardens.

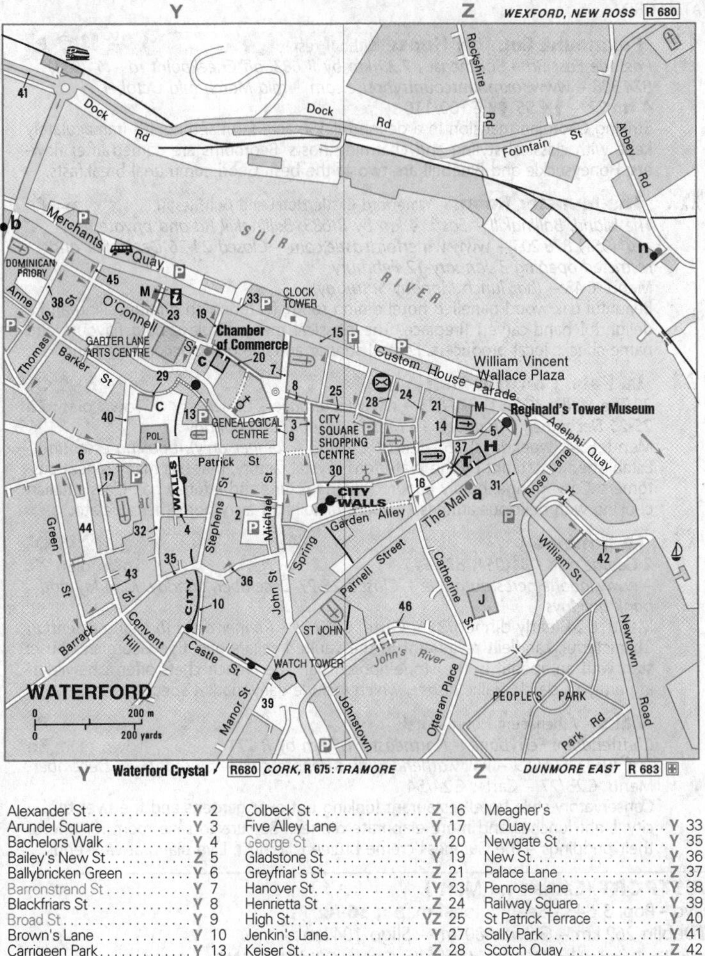

WATERFORD

Street		
Alexander St	Y	2
Arundel Square	Y	3
Bachelors Walk	Y	4
Bailey's New St	Z	5
Ballybricken Green	Y	6
Barronstrand St	Y	7
Blackfriars St	Y	8
Broad St	Y	9
Brown's Lane	Y	10
Carrigeen Park	Y	13
Cathedral Square	Z	14
City Square Shopping Centre	YZ	
Coal Quay	Y	15
Colbeck St	Z	16
Five Alley Lane	Y	17
George St	Y	20
Gladstone St	Y	19
Greyfriar's St	Z	21
Hanover St	Y	23
Henrietta St	Z	24
High St	YZ	25
Jenkin's Lane	Y	27
Keiser St	Z	28
King's Terrace	Y	29
Lady Lane	YZ	30
Lombard St	Z	31
Mayors Walk	Y	32
Meagher's Quay	Y	33
Newgate St	Y	35
New St	Y	36
Palace Lane	Z	37
Penrose Lane	Y	38
Railway Square	Y	39
St Patrick Terrace	Y	40
Sally Park	Y	41
Scotch Quay	Z	42
Shortcourse	Y	43
Trinity Square	Y	44
Vulcan St	Y	45
Water Side	Z	46

Fitzwilton

rm,

Bridge St – (051) 846 900 – www.fitzwiltonhotel.ie Town plan: Y**b**

– Closed 23-28 December

89 rm – € 58/129 € 58/189, € 12

Rest *Chez K's* – Menu € 19/25 – Carte € 26/32

Close to the Guinness brewery and the main bridge, with a modern glass façade and a chic bar. Bedrooms are spacious, good value and come with everything you might need, including an iron and ironing board; those at the back are the quietest. The restaurant offers international dishes made from Irish produce.

Foxmount Country House without rest

Passage East Rd – Southeast : 7.25 km by R 683, off Cheekpoint rd – ✆ (051) 874 308 – www.foxmountcountryhouse.com – mid March-mid October

4 rm – € 55 € 100/110

Striking Georgian mansion in a delightful 150 acre farm setting; it's immaculately kept, with classical styling and charming hosts. Bedrooms are named after flowers: Honeysuckle and Bluebell are two of the best. Good communal breakfasts.

The Munster Room – Waterford Castle Hotel and Golf Resort

The Island, Ballinakill – East : 4 km by R 683, Ballinakill Rd and private ferry – ✆ (051) 878 203 – www.waterfordcastle.com – Closed 24-26 December and restricted opening 3 January-12 February

Menu € 48 – *(bar lunch Monday-Saturday)*

Beautiful oak wood panelled hotel dining room, featuring an ornate ceiling and a delightful hand-carved fireplace. The classical menu displays bold flavours and name-checks local producers. Formal service and live piano accompaniment.

La Palma on The Mall

20 The Mall – ✆ (051) 879 823 – www.lapalma.ie – Closed 25-26 December, 1 January, 16 March, 18 April and Sunday Town plan: Z**a**

Menu € 24 (weekdays)/35 – Carte € 28/53 – *(dinner only) (booking essential)*

Established restaurant by the Waterford Crystal factory, that has many repeat customers. Cosy lounge, boldly papered dining rooms and a funky bar. Classic Italian cooking with delicious antipasti, superb ravioli and tasty homemade gelato.

La Bohème

2 George's St – ✆ (051) 875 645 – www.labohemerestaurant.ie – Closed 25-27 December, Sunday, Monday and bank holidays Town plan: Y**c**

Menu € 24 (early dinner)/35 – Carte € 35/53 – *(dinner only) (booking essential)*

Characterful, candlelit restaurant in the vaulted cellars of a fine Georgian house; start with an aperitif in the stone-floored bar. The French chefs offer a bewildering array of classic Gallic dishes, which include daily market specials.

Zaks – Athenaeum House Hotel

Christendom, Ferrybank – Northeast : 1.5 km by R 771 – ✆ (051) 833 999 – www.athenaeumhousehotel.com – Closed 25-27 December Town plan: Z**n**

Menu € 23/27 – Carte € 24/54

Conservatory-style hotel restaurant looking out over gardens and the river to the city. Light lunches and more elaborate dinners. Be sure to save room for one of their puddings – the Guinness crème brûlée is a must. Live piano at weekends.

WESTPORT (Cathair na Mart)

Mayo – Pop. 5 543 – See Regional map n°**36-A2**

Dublin 262 km – Galway 80 km – Sligo 104 km

Michelin Road map 712-D6 – Michelin Green Guide IRELAND

Knockranny House H. & Spa

Castlebar Rd, Knockranny – East : 1.25 km on N 5 – ✆ (098) 28 600 – www.knockrannyhousehotel.ie – Closed 24-27 December

97 rm – € 90/135 € 110/199 – 10 suites

Rest ***La Fougère*** – see restaurant listing

Modern hotel in an elevated position overlooking the town, mountains and bay, and furnished in contemporary yet classical style. Large, smart bedrooms offer excellent comforts; some have marble bathrooms or four-poster beds. Superb spa.

Ardmore Country House

The Quay – West : 2.5 km on R 335 – ✆ (098) 25 994 – www.ardmorecountryhouse.com – 15 March-October

13 rm – € 80/150 € 90/160

Rest – Carte € 35/46 – *(dinner only) (booking essential)*

Brightly painted hotel looking out over pretty gardens towards Clew Bay. Spacious, very well-kept bedrooms with good quality furnishings; some have sleigh beds or jacuzzi baths. Relax in the cosy lounge or piano bar. Classical set menu features plenty of local seafood. Service is personal yet professional.

Augusta Lodge without rest
Golf Links Rd – North : 0.75 km by N 59 – (098) 28 900 – www.augustalodge.ie – Closed 23-27 December
9 rm – € 40/65 € 30/100
Family run guesthouse with a small pitch and putt course on the front lawn and golfing memorabilia covering every surface inside. Simple, brightly coloured bedrooms have a homely feel. The welcoming owner has good local knowledge.

La Fougère – Knockranny House Hotel & Spa
Castlebar Rd, Knockranny – East : 1.25 km on N 5 – (098) 28 600 – www.knockrannyhousehotel.ie – Closed 24-27 December
Menu € 29/75 – Carte € 60/68 – *(dinner only) (booking advisable)*
Spacious hotel restaurant with a large bar, several different seating areas and huge windows offering views to Croagh Patrick Mountain. The three menus feature fresh, local produce, including langoustines from the bay below. Formal service.

An Port Mór
Brewery Pl, Bridge St – (098) 26 730 – www.anportmor.com – Closed 24-26 December
Menu € 22/29 – Carte € 25/47 – *(dinner only)*
Tucked away down a small alleyway and named after the chef's home village. Compact interior with shabby-chic, Mediterranean-style décor. Classically based menu showcases local produce in elaborate dishes; seafood specials on the blackboard.

Sheebeen
Rosbeg – West : 3 km on R 335 – (098) 26 528 – www.croninssheebeen.com – Closed Good Friday, 25 December and lunch weekdays November-mid March
Carte € 23/37
Pretty thatched pub with lovely bay and Croagh Patrick views. Hearty, unfussy dishes feature mussels, oysters and lobsters from the bay, and lamb and beef from the fields nearby. Sit outside, in the rustic bar or in the first floor dining room.

WEXFORD (Loch Garman)

Wexford – Pop. 19 913 – See Regional map n°**39**-D2
Dublin 141 km – Kilkenny 79 km – Waterford 61 km
Michelin Road map 712-M10 – Michelin Green Guide IRELAND

Whites rm,
Abbey St – (053) 912 23 11 – www.whitesofwexford.ie – Closed 24-27 December Town plan: Y**a**
157 rm – € 75/150 € 99/249 – 5 suites
Rest *Terrace* – Menu € 20 – Carte € 19/32 **s** – *(bar lunch)*
Striking angular hotel built around a paved central courtyard; its spacious lobby decorated with local art. Tranquility spa, coffee shop and library bar. Modern, minimalistic bedrooms; executives are larger with water views. Internationally influenced menu of traditional dishes in the contemporary restaurant.

Ferrycarrig rm, rest,
Ferrycarrig – Northwest : 4.25 km on N 11 – (053) 912 09 99 – www.ferrycarrighotel.ie Town plan: V**a**
102 rm – € 85/105 € 120/160 – 4 suites
Rest *Reeds* – Menu € 30 – Carte € 27/39 – *(bar lunch Monday-Saturday)*
Sitting pretty on the banks of the Slaney estuary and popular with families is this purpose built hotel with a busy leisure centre. The comfortable bedrooms have superb views and superior rooms have balconies. Waterside bar serves an all-day menu. Spacious Reeds offers traditional fare; ask for a window seat.

Rathaspeck Manor without rest
Rathaspeck – Southwest : 6.5 km by R 730 off Murntown rd – (053) 914 16 72 – www.rathaspeckmanor.ie – Closed November-December Town plan: X**k**
4 rm – € 110/160 € 110/160
Georgian house with its own 18 hole golf course. Comfortable first floor drawing room. Large, luxurious, individually furnished bedrooms with impressive bathrooms featuring underfloor heating; Father Albert's Room is the most comfortable.

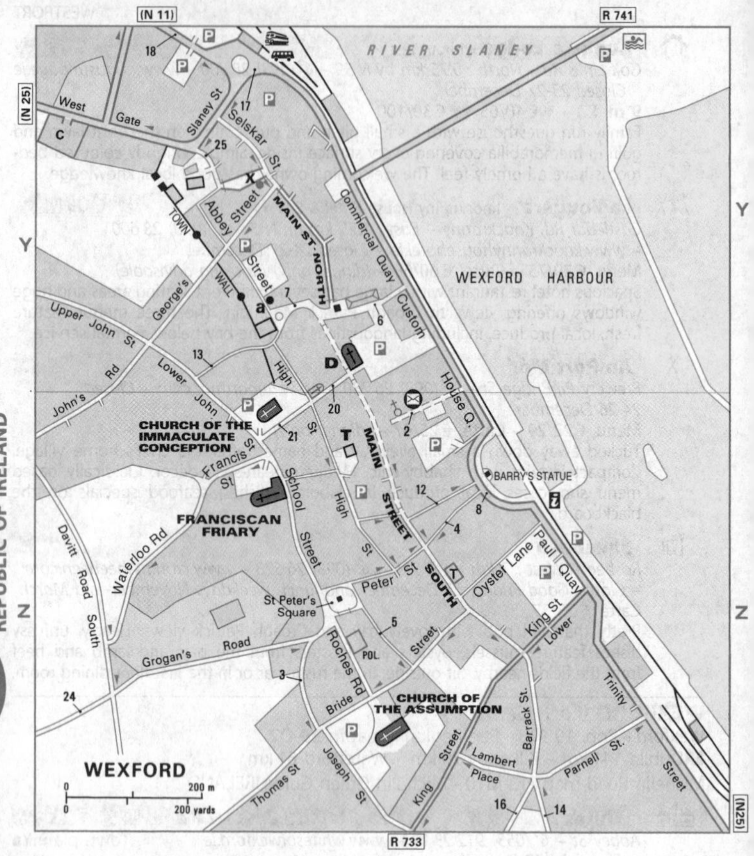

Anne St	Z 2	Henrietta St	Z 12	Redmond Rd	Y 18
Carrigeen St	Z 3	John's Gate St	Y 13	Rowe St Lower	YZ 20
Cinema Lane	Z 4	Kevin Barry St	Z 14	Rowe St Upper	Z 21
Clifford St	Z 5	Main St North	Y	Selskar St	Y
Common Quay St	Y 6	Main St South	Z	Summerhill Rd	Z 24
Cornmarket	Y 7	Michael St	Z 16	Temperance Row	Y 25
Crescent Quay	Z 8	Redmond Pl	Y 17		

Killiane Castle without rest

Drinagh – South : 5.5 km by R 730 off N 25 – ☎ (053) 915 88 85 – www.killianecastle.com – March-mid December

8 rm – € 65/80 €90/110

A 17C house and 12C castle on a family-owned dairy farm. Individually decorated, antique-furnished bedrooms look out over the surrounding farmland. Breakfast includes pork from their own pigs, home-laid eggs and homemade bread and yoghurt.

Greenacres

Selskar – ☎ (053) 91 22 975 – www.greenacres.ie – Closed 25-26 December and Good Friday Town plan: Y**x**

Menu € 25 (dinner)/59 – Carte € 31/51 – *(light lunch)*

Light, airy bistro with a deli and patisserie selling cheese, charcuterie, pastries and breads. Salads and platters at lunch; flavoursome modern dishes at dinner. Well-priced French wines fill the shelves: choose from over 1,300!

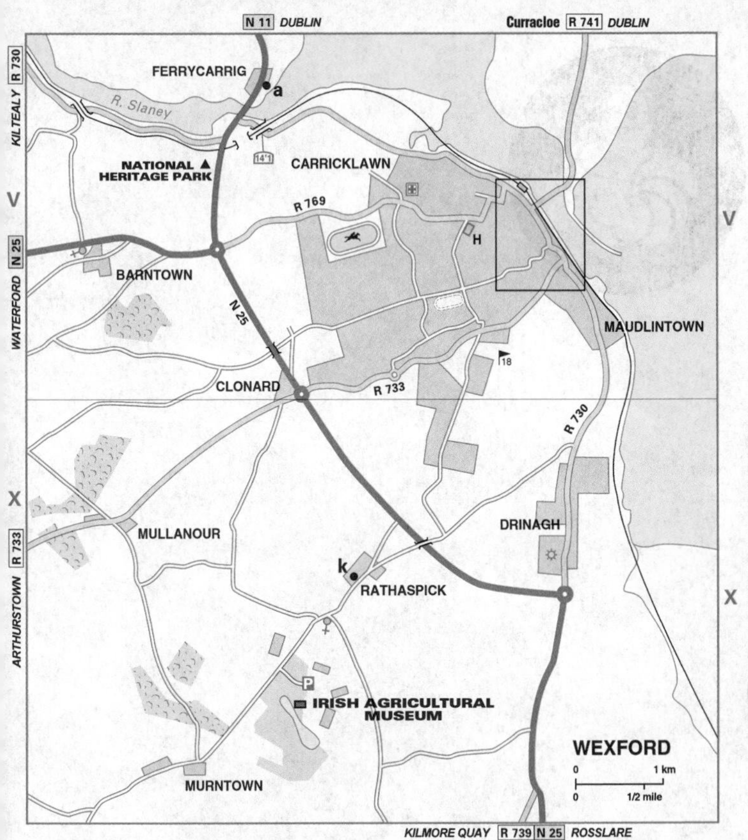

YOUGHAL (Eochaill)

Cork – Pop. 6 990 – See Regional map n°**39**-C3
Dublin 235 km – Cork 48 km – Waterford 75 km
Michelin Road map 712-I12 – Michelin Green Guide IRELAND

XX **Aherne's** with rm

163 North Main St – (024) 92 424 – www.ahernes.com – Closed 23-27 December
12 rm – €75/110 €110/180
Menu €24/60 – Carte €33/65 – *(bar lunch)*
Traditional seafood restaurant dating from 1910, passionately run by the third generation of the same family. Lunch in one of the bars; dinner in the restaurant. Fish and shellfish from local boats – hot buttered lobster a speciality. Antique-furnished bedrooms, some with balconies; comfy, open-fired lounge.

Index 2015

Starred establishments 2015

→ England

Ambleside The Samling ✿
Bagshot Michael Wignall at The Latymer ✿✿
Baslow Fischer's at Baslow Hall ✿
Bath Bath Priory ✿
Bath / Colerne The Park ✿
Beaulieu The Terrace ✿
Beverley / South Dalton Pipe and Glass Inn ✿
Biddenden West House ✿
Birkenhead Fraiche ✿
Birmingham Turners ✿
Birmingham adam's ✿
Birmingham Purnell's ✿
Birmingham Simpsons ✿
Blackburn / Langho Northcote ✿
Blakeney / Morston Morston Hall ✿
Bodiam Curlew ✿
Bourton-on-the-Water / Upper Slaughter Lords of the Manor ✿
Bray Hinds Head ✿
Bray Fat Duck ✿✿✿
Bray Royal Oak ✿
Bray Waterside Inn ✿✿✿
Bristol Casamia ✿
Bristol wilks ✿
Cambridge Alimentum ✿
Cambridge Midsummer House ✿✿
Castle Combe Bybrook ✿
Chagford Gidleigh Park ✿✿
Cheltenham Le Champignon Sauvage ✿✿
Chester Simon Radley at Chester Grosvenor ✿
Chew Magna Pony and Trap ✿
Chinnor / Sprigg's Alley Sir Charles Napier ✿
Cranbrook Apicius ✿
Cuckfield Ockenden Manor ✿
Darlington / Summerhouse Raby Hunt ✿
Dorchester Sienna ✿
East Chisenbury Red Lion Freehouse ✿
Eldersfield Butchers Arms ✿
Grange-over-Sands / Cartmel L' Enclume ✿✿
Helmsley / Harome Star Inn ✿ **N**
Horsham Restaurant Tristan ✿
Hunstanton The Neptune ✿
Ilkley Box Tree ✿
Jersey / La Pulente Ocean ✿
Jersey / St Helier Bohemia ✿
Jersey / St Helier Ormer by Shaun Rankin ✿
Jersey / St Helier Tassili ✿
Kenilworth Cross at Kenilworth ✿ **N**
Knowstone Masons Arms ✿

LONDON

Camden Dabbous ✿
Camden Hakkasan Hanway Place ✿
Camden Kitchen Table at Bubbledogs ✿ **N**
Camden Pied à Terre ✿
City of London City Social ✿ **N**
City of London Club Gascon ✿
City of Westminster Alain Ducasse at The Dorchester ✿✿✿
City of Westminster Alyn Williams at The Westbury ✿
City of Westminster Amaya ✿
City of Westminster Ametsa with Arzak Instruction ✿
City of Westminster Arbutus ✿
City of Westminster L'Atelier de Joël Robuchon ✿
City of Westminster L'Autre Pied ✿
City of Westminster Barrafina ✿ **N**
City of Westminster Benares ✿
City of Westminster Brasserie Chavot ✿
City of Westminster Dinner by Heston Blumenthal ✿✿
City of Westminster Fera at Claridge's ✿ **N**
City of Westminster Galvin at Windows ✿
City of Westminster Le Gavroche ✿✿
City of Westminster Greenhouse ✿✿
City of Westminster Gymkhana ✿ **N**
City of Westminster Hakkasan Mayfair ✿
City of Westminster Hibiscus ✿✿
City of Westminster Hélène Darroze at The Connaught ✿✿
City of Westminster Kai ✿
City of Westminster Lima ✿
City of Westminster Locanda Locatelli ✿
City of Westminster Marcus ✿✿
City of Westminster Maze ✿
City of Westminster Murano ✿
City of Westminster Pollen Street Social ✿
City of Westminster Pétrus ✿
City of Westminster Quilon ✿
City of Westminster Seven Park Place ✿
City of Westminster Sketch (The Lecture Room and Library) ✿✿
City of Westminster Social Eating House ✿

✿✿✿ Exceptional cuisine, worth a special journey
✿✿ Excellent cooking, worth a detour
✿ Very good cooking in its category

City of Westminster Square ✿✿
City of Westminster Tamarind ✿
City of Westminster Texture ✿
City of Westminster Trishna ✿
City of Westminster Umu ✿
City of Westminster Wild Honey ✿
City of Westminster Yauatcha ✿
Hackney (Borough of) Clove Club ✿ **N**
Hackney (Borough of) HKK ✿
Hammersmith and Fulham Harwood Arms ✿
Hammersmith and Fulham River Café ✿
Hounslow Hedone ✿
Hounslow La Trompette ✿
Islington (Borough of) Angler ✿
Islington (Borough of) St John ✿
Kensington and Chelsea Gordon Ramsay ✿✿✿
Kensington and Chelsea Kitchen W8 ✿
Kensington and Chelsea Launceston Place ✿
Kensington and Chelsea Ledbury ✿✿
Kensington and Chelsea Outlaw's at The Capital ✿
Kensington and Chelsea Rasoi ✿
Richmond-upon-Thames The Glasshouse ✿
Southwark (Borough of) Story ✿
Tower Hamlets Galvin La Chapelle ✿
Wandsworth (Borough of) Chez Bruce ✿
Lower Beeding The Pass ✿
Ludlow Mr Underhill's at Dinham Weir ✿
Malmesbury The Dining Room ✿✿
Marlborough / Little Bedwyn Harrow at Little Bedwyn ✿
Marlow Hand and Flowers ✿✿
Murcott Nut Tree ✿
Nottingham Restaurant Sat Bains ✿✿
Oakham / Hambleton Hambleton Hall ✿
Oldstead Black Swan ✿
Oxford / Great Milton Belmond Le Manoir aux Quat' Saisons ✿✿
Padstow Paul Ainsworth at No.6 ✿
Pateley Bridge Yorke Arms ✿
Petersfield JSW ✿
Port Isaac Outlaw's Fish Kitchen ✿ **N**
Portscatho Driftwood ✿
Reading / Shinfield L'Ortolan ✿
Ripley (Surrey) Drake's ✿
Rock Outlaw's at St Enodoc ✿✿
Royal Tunbridge Wells Thackeray's ✿
Sheffield Old Vicarage ✿
Sparkwell Treby Arms ✿ **N**
Titley Stagg Inn ✿
Torquay Room in the Elephant ✿
Whitstable / Seasalter The Sportsman ✿
Winchcombe 5 North St ✿
Winchester Black Rat ✿
Woburn Paris House ✿

→ Scotland

Auchterarder Andrew Fairlie at Gleneagles ✿✿
Balloch Martin Wishart at Loch Lomond ✿
Dalry Braidwoods ✿
Edinburgh Castle Terrace ✿
Edinburgh Number One ✿
Edinburgh 21212 ✿
Edinburgh / Leith Kitchin ✿
Edinburgh / Leith Martin Wishart ✿
Elie Sangster's ✿
Eriska (Isle of) Isle of Eriska ✿ **N**
Lochinver Albannach ✿
Nairn Boath House ✿
Peat Inn The Peat Inn ✿
Portpatrick Knockinaam Lodge ✿
Skye (Isle of) / Colbost Three Chimneys and The House Over-By ✿ **N**
Skye (Isle of) / Sleat Kinloch Lodge ✿

→ Wales

Abergavenny / Llanddewi Skirrid Walnut Tree ✿
Llandrillo Tyddyn Llan ✿
Machynlleth Ynyshir Hall ✿ **N**
Monmouth / Whitebrook Crown at Whitebrook ✿ **N**
Montgomery The Checkers ✿

→ Republic of Ireland

Ardmore House ✿
Dublin Chapter One ✿
Dublin L'Ecrivain ✿
Dublin Patrick Guilbaud ✿✿
Dublin Thornton's ✿
Galway Aniar ✿
Kilkenny Campagne ✿
Malahide bon appétit ✿
Thomastown Lady Helen ✿

Bib Gourmand 2015

➜ England

Aldeburgh	Lighthouse
Belbroughton	The Queens
Blackpool / Thornton	Twelve
Brighton	Chilli Pickle
Brighton	64° **N**
Bristol	Flinty Red
Bristol / Long Ashton	Bird in Hand
Britwell Salome	Red Lion
Bruntingthorpe	The Joiners
Bruton	At The Chapel
Bury	Waggon
Bury St Edmunds	Pea Porridge
Cheltenham	The Tavern
Chester	Joseph Benjamin
Christchurch	Kings Arms
Cirencester	Made by Bob **N**
Clyst Hydon	Five Bells Inn **N**
Cookham	White Oak
Darlington / Hurworth-on-Tees	Bay Horse
Derby	Ibérico World Tapas **N**
Donhead St Andrew	The Forester
Drighlington	Prashad
Droxford	Bakers Arms
Durham	Bistro 21
East Haddon	Red Lion
Exeter / Rockbeare	Jack in the Green
Gedney Dyke	Chequers
Gerrards Cross	Three Oaks **N**
Hastings and St. Leonards	St Clements
Hitchin	hermitage rd
Hunsdon	Fox and Hounds
Ingham	Ingham Swan
Jersey / Beaumont	Mark Jordan at the Beach
Kelvedon	George and Dragon
Keyston	Pheasant
Kibworth Beauchamp	Lighthouse

● LONDON

Brent	Sushi-Say
Bromley	Indian Essence **N**
Camden	Barnyard **N**
Camden	Barrica
Camden	Bradley's
Camden	Gail's Kitchen
Camden	Great Queen Street
Camden	Honey and Co
Camden	Made Bar and Kitchen
Camden	Market
Camden	Salt Yard
City of Westminster	A. Wong
City of Westminster	Bocca di Lupo
City of Westminster	Brasserie Zédel
City of Westminster	Copita
City of Westminster	Green Man and French Horn
City of Westminster	Hereford Road
City of Westminster	Kateh
City of Westminster	Koya
City of Westminster	Opera Tavern
City of Westminster	Palomar **N**
City of Westminster	Picture
City of Westminster	Polpetto **N**
City of Westminster	Polpo Covent Garden
City of Westminster	Polpo Soho
City of Westminster	Terroirs
Hackney (Borough of)	Empress
Hackney (Borough of)	Rotorino **N**
Hammersmith and Fulham	Azou
Islington (Borough of)	Comptoir Gascon
Islington (Borough of)	Drapers Arms
Islington (Borough of)	500
Islington (Borough of)	Medcalf
Islington (Borough of)	Morito
Islington (Borough of)	Polpo Smithfield
Islington (Borough of)	Roots at N1 **N**
Islington (Borough of)	Trullo
Islington (Borough of)	Yipin China **N**
Kings Cross St Pancras	Grain Store
Lambeth	Bistro Union
Lambeth	Canton Arms
Redbridge	Provender
Southwark (Borough of)	Anchor and Hope
Southwark (Borough of)	Del Mercato
Southwark (Borough of)	Elliot's
Southwark (Borough of)	José
Southwark (Borough of)	Zucca
Tower Hamlets	Brawn
Tower Hamlets	Cafe Spice Namaste
Tower Hamlets	Corner Room
Tower Hamlets	Galvin Café a Vin
Tower Hamlets	St John Bread and Wine
Wandsworth (Borough of)	Bibo **N**
Wandsworth (Borough of)	Earl Spencer **N**
Wandsworth (Borough of)	Soif

Longstock	Peat Spade Inn
Maidenhead	Crown **N**
Marazion / Perranuthnoe	Victoria Inn
Masham	Vennell's
Mells	Talbot Inn **N**
Moreton-in-Marsh / Bourton on the Hill	Horse and Groom
Newcastle upon Tyne	Broad Chare
Newlyn	Tolcarne Inn

Good food at moderate prices

North Shields	David Kennedy's River Cafe
Nottingham	Ibérico World Tapas
Oxford	Magdalen Arms
Oxford	Rickety Press
Padstow	Rick Stein's Café
Porthleven	Kota
Preston Candover	Purefoy Arms
Ramsbottom	Hearth of the Ram
Ramsgate	Age and Sons
Ripponden	El Gato Negro
Romsey	Three Tuns
St Ives	Black Rock
St Ives / Halsetown	Halsetown Inn **N**
Stamford	Jim's Yard
Stanton	Leaping Hare
Stathern	Red Lion Inn
Tavistock	Cornish Arms **N**
Tetbury	Gumstool Inn
Tewkesbury	Owens
Thorpe Market	Gunton Arms
Upper South Wraxall	Longs Arms
Wells	Old Spot
West Hoathly	Cat Inn
Wootton	Killingworth Castle
Wrington	The Ethicurean
Wymondham	Berkeley Arms
York	Le Langhe **N**

→ Scotland

Edinburgh	Dogs
Edinburgh	Galvin Brasserie De Luxe
Edinburgh	Passorn **N**
Glasgow	The Gannet **N**
Glasgow	Ox and Finch **N**
Glasgow	Stravaigin
Kintyre (Peninsula) / Kilberry	Kilberry Inn
Peebles	Osso
Peebles	Restaurant at Kailzie Gardens

→ Wales

Brecon	Felin Fach Griffin

→ Northern Ireland

Ballyclare	Oregano
Belfast	Bar + Grill at James Street South **N**
Belfast	Coppi
Belfast	Deanes at Queens **N**
Belfast	Home
Holywood	Fontana
Lisbane	Old Schoolhouse Inn **N**

→ République of Ireland

Carrickmacross	Courthouse
Clonakilty	Deasy's
Clonegall	Sha-Roe Bistro
Dingle	Chart House
Dublin	Etto **N**
Dublin	Pichet
Dublin	Pig's Ear
Dublin / Clontarf	Downstairs
Duncannon	Aldridge Lodge
Kinsale	Fishy Fishy
Lisdoonvarna	Wild Honey Inn
Malahide	Brasserie at bon appétit

Bib Hotel 2015

➜ England

Belper	Chevin Green Farm **N**
Bodmin	Bokiddick Farm
Boston Spa	Four Gables
Bourton-on-the-Water	Coombe House
Bungay / Earsham	Earsham Park Farm
Christchurch	Druid House
Deddington	Old Post House
Devizes	Blounts Court Farm
Earl Stonham	Bays Farm
Elton-on-the-Hill	The Grange **N**
Farningham	Beesfield Farm **N**
Filey	All Seasons **N**
Harrogate / Kettlesing	Knabbs Ash
Huccombe	Huccombe House
Leyburn	Clyde House
Morpeth / Longhorsley	Thistleyhaugh Farm
North Bovey	Gate House
Ouston	Low Urpeth Farm
Penrith	Brooklands
St Keverne	Old Temperance House
Salisbury / Little Langford	Little Langford Farmhouse
Scarborough	Alexander
Sheringham	Ashbourne House
Stow-on-the-Wold	Number Nine
Torquay	Kingston House **N**
Warwick	Charter House

➜ Scotland

Anstruther	Spindrift
Auchencairn	Balcary Mews
Ballater	Moorside House
Blairgowrie	Gilmore House
Carnoustie	Old Manor
Dunkeld	Letter Farm
Dyke	Old Kirk
Jedburgh	Willow Court
Kingussie	Hermitage
Montrose	36 The Mall
Mull (Isle of) / Tobermory	Brockville
Peebles	Rowanbrae
Perth	Taythorpe
Pitlochry	Dunmurray Lodge
Skye (Isle of) / Broadford	Tigh an Dochais
Strathpeffer	Craigvar
Thornhill	Gillbank House
Wick	Clachan

Good accommodation at moderate prices

Wales

Betws Garmon	Betws Inn
Builth Wells	Rhedyn
Dolgellau	Tyddyn Mawr
Llandudno	Abbey Lodge
Llandudno	Lympley Lodge
Llanwrda	Tŷ Llwyd Hir
Ruthin	Firgrove
Whitton	Pilleth Oaks

Northern Ireland

Bangor	Cairn Bay Lodge
Crumlin	Caldhame Lodge

Républic of Ireland

Ballyvaughan	Drumcreehy House
Bansha	Rathellen House
Carrigans	Mount Royd
Castlegregory	Shores Country House
Donegal	Ardeevin
Dundalk	Rosemount
Kilkenny	Rosquil House
Kinsale / Barrells Cross	Rivermount House
Oughterard	Railway Lodge
Oughterard	Waterfall Lodge
Toormore	Fortview House
Tramore	Glenorney

Particularly pleasant hotels & guesthouses 2015

England

LONDON

City of Westminster Berkeley
City of Westminster Claridge's
City of Westminster Connaught
City of Westminster Corinthia
City of Westminster Dorchester
City of Westminster Four Seasons
City of Westminster Mandarin Oriental Hyde Park
City of Westminster Ritz
City of Westminster Savoy

New Milton Chewton Glen
Oxford / Great Milton Belmond Le Manoir aux Quat' Saisons
Taplow Cliveden

England

Ascot Coworth Park
Aylesbury Hartwell House
Bath / Colerne Lucknam Park
Bourton-on-the-Water / Lower Slaughter Lower Slaughter Manor
Chagford Gidleigh Park
Cheltenham Ellenborough Park
Jersey / St Saviour (Jersey) Longueville Manor

LONDON

City of Westminster Bulgari
City of Westminster 45 Park Lane
City of Westminster Goring
City of Westminster One Aldwych
City of Westminster Soho

Lyndhurst Lime Wood
Malmesbury Whatley Manor
Newbury The Vineyard
Ston Easton Ston Easton Park

Scotland

Ballantrae Glenapp Castle
Eriska (Isle of) Isle of Eriska
Fort William Inverlochy Castle

Republic of Ireland

Ballyfin Ballyfin
Dublin Merrion
Kenmare Park

England

Amberley Amberley Castle
Bath Bath Priory
Beaulieu Montagu Arms
Bourton-on-the-Water / Upper Slaughter Lords of the Manor
Broadway Buckland Manor
Chaddesley Corbett Brockencote Hall
Dedham Maison Talbooth
East Grinstead Gravetye Manor
Egham Great Fosters
Evershot Summer Lodge
Frome Babington House

Guernsey / St Peter Port Old Government House H. and Spa
Hunstrete The Pig
Jersey / La Pulente Atlantic

LONDON

Camden Covent Garden
City of Westminster Charlotte Street
City of Westminster Chiltern Firehouse
City of Westminster Dukes
City of Westminster Halkin
City of Westminster Stafford
Islington (Borough of) South Place
Kensington and Chelsea Blakes
Kensington and Chelsea The Capital
Kensington and Chelsea The Milestone
Kensington and Chelsea The Pelham
Newcastle upon Tyne Jesmond Dene House
Oakham / Hambleton Hambleton Hall
Pooley Bridge Sharrow Bay Country House
Stamford George of Stamford
Tetbury Calcot Manor
Winchester / Sparsholt Lainston House
Windermere / Bowness-on-Windermere Gilpin H. and Lake House
Yarm Judges Country House
York Middlethorpe Hall

→ Scotland

Blairgowrie Kinloch House
Edinburgh Prestonfield
Gullane Greywalls
Torridon Torridon

→ Wales

Llandudno Bodysgallen Hall
Llangammarch Wells Lake Country House and Spa

→ Republic of Ireland

Ardmore Cliff House
Ballyvaughan Gregans Castle
Dublin / Ballsbridge Dylan
Gorey (Wexford) Marlfield House

→ England

Ambleside The Samling
Baslow Cavendish
Bath Queensberry
Bigbury-on-Sea Burgh Island
Blackburn / Langho Northcote
Blakeney / Morston Morston Hall
Blanchland Lord Crewe Arms
Brampton Farlam Hall
Brockenhurst The Pig
Cirencester / Barnsley Barnsley House
Gillingham Stock Hill Country House
Helmsley / Harome Pheasant
Lewdown Lewtrenchard Manor

LONDON

Kensington and Chelsea Egerton House
Kensington and Chelsea Knightsbridge
Kensington and Chelsea The Levin
Kensington and Chelsea Number Sixteen
North Walsham Beechwood
Orford Crown and Castle
Portscatho Driftwood
Rowsley Peacock
Rushlake Green Stone House
St Mawes Hotel Tresanton
Salcombe South Sands
Scilly (Isles of) Hell Bay
Southampton / Netley Marsh Hotel TerraVina
Stratford-upon-Avon Arden
Tavistock/Milton Abbot Hotel Endsleigh
Wareham Priory
Windermere Holbeck Ghyll

→ Scotland

Abriachan Loch Ness Lodge
Achiltibuie Summer Isles
Arran (Isle of) Kilmichael Country House
Balquhidder Monachyle Mhor
Dornoch Links House
Nairn Boath House
Port Appin Airds
Portpatrick Knockinaam Lodge
Skye (Isle of) / Sleat Kinloch Lodge

→ Wales

Llandudno	Osborne House
Machynlleth	Ynyshir Hall
Narberth	Grove

→ Republic of Ireland

Ballingarry	Mustard Seed at Echo Lodge
Kinsale	Perryville House

→ England

Cheltenham	No 38 The Park
Dartmouth / Kingswear	Nonsuch House
Durham	The Town House
Fivehead	Langford Fivehead
Fowey	Old Quay House
Helmsley / Harome	Cross House Lodge
Keswick / Portinscale	Swinside Lodge
Lynton	Hewitt's - Villa Spaldi
Lynton / Martinhoe	Old Rectory
Pershore / Eckington (Worcs)	Eckington Manor
Porlock	Oaks
St Ives	Tide House
Salisbury / Teffont Evias	Howard's House
Southampton	Pig-in the Wall

→ Scotland

Cumnock	Dumfries House Lodge
Kelso / Ednam	Edenwater House
Kirkbean	Cavens
Mull (Isle of) / Tiroran	Tiroran House
Pitlochry / Killiecrankie	Killiecrankie
Tain / Cadboll	Glenmorangie House
Walkerburn	Windlestraw Lodge

→ Wales

Betws-y-Coed	Tan-y-Foel Country House
Dolgellau	Ffynnon

→ Republic of Ireland

Bagenalstown	Kilgraney Country House
Castlelyons	Ballyvolane House
Lahinch	Moy House

→ England

Arnside	Number 43
Austwick	Austwick Hall
Benenden	Ramsden Farm
Blackpool	Number One St Lukes
Bridport / Burton Bradstock	Norburton Hall
Bristol	Number 38 Clifton
Broad Oak	Fairacres
Broadway	East House
Chipping Campden / Broad Campden	Malt House
Cranbrook	Cloth Hall Oast
Dartmouth / Strete	Strete Barton House
Doddington	Old Vicarage
East Hoathly	Old Whyly
Elton-on-the-Hill	The Grange
Ewhurst Green	Prawles Court
Hawkshead	West Vale
Herstmonceux / Wartling	Wartling Place
Lavenham	Lavenham Priory
Lizard	Landewednack House
Lurgashall	Barn at Roundhurst
Marazion / Perranuthnoe	Ednovean Farm
Moreton-in-Marsh	Old School
North Lopham	Church Farm House
Padstow	Treann House
Padstow	Treverbyn House
Pershore	Barn
Pickering	17 Burgate
Pickering / Levisham	Moorlands Country House
Ripon	Sharow Cross House
St Austell	Anchorage House

St Mellion	Pentillie Castle
Stow-on-the-Wold / Lower Swell	Rectory Farmhouse
Tavistock / Chillaton	Tor Cottage
Thursford Green	Holly Lodge
Warkworth	Roxbro House
Wells	Stoberry House
Wold Newton	Wold Cottage

→ Scotland

Ayr	No.26 The Crescent
Ballantrae	Cosses Country House
Barcaldine	Ardtorna
Connel	Ards House
Drumbeg	Blar na Leisg at Drumbeg House
Fort William	Grange
Fortrose	Water's Edge
Glasgow	15 Glasgow
Grantown-on-Spey	Dulaig
Harris (Isle of) / Borve	Pairc an t-Srath
Islay (Isle of) / Ballygrant	Kilmeny
Kilchrenan	Roineabhal
Lewis (Isle of) / Back	Broad Bay House
Linlithgow	Arden House
Lochinver	Ruddyglow Park Country House
Mainland (Orkney Islands) / Harray	Holland House
Skirling	Skirling House
Skye (Isle of) / Bernisdale	Spoons
Skye (Isle of) / Colbost	Hillstone Lodge
Strathpeffer	Craigvar
Tain / Nigg	Wemyss House

→ Wales

Aberaeron	3 Pen Cei
Anglesey (Isle of) / Beaumaris	Cleifiog
Betws-y-Coed / Penmachno	Penmachno Hall
Dolfor	Old Vicarage
Glynarthen	Penbontbren
Pwllheli / Boduan	Old Rectory
St Clears	Coedllys Country House

→ Northern Ireland

Ballintoy	Whitepark House

→ Republic of Ireland

Castlegregory	Shores Country House
Cong	Ballywarren House
Fethard	Mobarnane House
Kenmare	Sallyport House
Ramelton	Moorfield Lodge
Toormore	Fortview House

Particularly pleasant restaurants & pubs 2015

➜ England

London / City of Westminster	Alain Ducasse at The Dorchester
London / City of Westminster	Ritz Restaurant

➜ England

Bath / Colerne	The Park
Bray	Waterside Inn
Chagford	Gidleigh Park

LONDON

City of Westminster	Fera at Claridge's
City of Westminster	Hélène Darroze at The Connaught
City of Westminster	Marcus
City of Westminster	Sketch (The Lecture Room and Library)
Oxford / Great Milton	Belmond Le Manoir aux Quat' Saisons

➜ Republic of Ireland

Dublin	Patrick Guilbaud

➜ England

Baslow	Fischer's at Baslow Hall
Birmingham	Simpsons
Blackburn / Langho	Northcote
Bourton-on-the-Water / Upper Slaughter	Lords of the Manor
Cambridge	Midsummer House
Dedham	Le Talbooth
East Grinstead	Gravetye Manor
Faversham	Read's
Hetton	Angel Inn and Barn Lodgings
Ilkley	Box Tree
Jersey / La Pulente	Ocean
Jersey / St Saviour (Jersey)	Longueville Manor
Lavenham	Great House

LONDON

City of Westminster	Cut
City of Westminster	Delaunay

City of Westminster	Dining Room at The Goring
City of Westminster	Greenhouse
City of Westminster	Pétrus
City of Westminster	Quo Vadis
City of Westminster	The Wolseley
Hackney (Borough of)	Boundary
Hounslow	La Trompette
Kensington and Chelsea	Bibendum
Tower Hamlets	Galvin La Chapelle
New Milton	Vetiver
Oakham / Hambleton	Hambleton Hall
Padstow	Seafood
Pateley Bridge	Yorke Arms
Reading / Shinfield	L'Ortolan
Reading / Sonning	French Horn
Stamford	The Oak Panelled Restaurant
Ston Easton	Sorrel
Winchester / Sparsholt	Avenue
Windermere / Bowness-on-Windermere	Gilpin H. and Lake House
Winteringham	Winteringham Fields
Woburn	Paris House

→ Scotland

Edinburgh	21212
Nairn	Boath House
Peat Inn	The Peat Inn

→ Wales

Llandrillo	Tyddyn Llan
Llandudno	Dining Room
Llanrhidian	Fairyhill
Machynlleth	Ynyshir Hall

→ Republic of Ireland

Dublin	Chapter One
Kenmare	Park

→ England

Alkham	Marquis
Ambleside	The Samling
Ashwater	Blagdon Manor
Bath / Colerne	Brasserie
Blakeney / Morston	Morston Hall
Brockenhurst	The Pig
Bury St Edmunds	Maison Bleue

Cheltenham	Daffodil
Cirencester / Barnsley	The Potager
Cowan Bridge	Hipping Hall
Folkestone	Rocksalt
Grantham	Harry's Place
Helmsley / Harome	Pheasant
Hunstrete	The Pig
Kibworth Beauchamp	Lighthouse
● LONDON	
City of Westminster	Angelus
City of Westminster	Bar Boulud
City of Westminster	Brasserie Chavot
City of Westminster	Le Café Anglais
City of Westminster	Clos Maggiore
City of Westminster	Dinner by Heston Blumenthal
City of Westminster	Hawksmoor (Mayfair)
City of Westminster	J. Sheekey
City of Westminster	Momo
City of Westminster	Rules
City of Westminster	Wild Honey
Hackney (Borough of)	HKK
Hammersmith and Fulham	River Café
Islington (Borough of)	Angler
Kensington and Chelsea	Outlaw's at The Capital
Kings Cross St Pancras	Gilbert Scott
Ludlow	Mr Underhill's at Dinham Weir
Lyndhurst	Hartnett Holder and Co
Newquay / Watergate Bay	Fifteen Cornwall
Oldstead	Black Swan
Rowsley	Peacock
St Mawes	Restaurant Tresanton
Salcombe	Beachside
Sark	La Sablonnerie
Southampton / Netley Marsh	Restaurant TerraVina
Tavistock / Milton Abbot	Restaurant Endsleigh
Yeovil / Barwick	Little Barwick House

→ Scotland

Gullane	Chez Roux
Lochinver	Albannach
Portpatrick	Knockinaam Lodge
Skye (Isle of) / Colbost	Three Chimneys and The House Over-By

→ Wales

Pwllheli	Plas Bodegroes

→ Northern Ireland

Bangor	Boat House
Lisnaskea	Watermill Lodge

→ Republic of Ireland

Aran Islands / Inishmaan	Inis Meáin Restaurant and Suites
Ballyvaughan	Gregans Castle
Clogheen	Old Convent
Dunkineely	Castle Murray House
Durrus	Blairscove House

→ England

Abbey Dore	Toi et Moi
Blakeney	Wiveton Farm Café
Bruton	At The Chapel
Cheltenham	131 The Promenade
Emsworth	Fat Olives
Falmouth / Maenporth	Cove
Jersey / St Brelades Bay	Oyster Box
Jersey / St Helier	Banjo

LONDON

City of Westminster	Barrafina
City of Westminster	Bentley's (Oyster Bar)
City of Westminster	Bocca di Lupo
City of Westminster	Le Boudin Blanc
City of Westminster	Dehesa
City of Westminster	J. Sheekey Oyster Bar
City of Westminster	Nopi
Islington (Borough of)	Comptoir Gascon
Islington (Borough of)	Quality Chop House
Richmond-upon-Thames	Petersham Nurseries Café
Southwark (Borough of)	Oxo Tower Brasserie
Southwark (Borough of)	Zucca

Padstow	Paul Ainsworth at No.6
Padstow	St Petroc's
Plymouth	River Cottage Canteen and Deli
St Ives	Porthminster Beach Café
Shaldon	ODE
Stanton	Leaping Hare
Stowmarket	Buxhall Coach House
Stow-on-the-Wold / Daylesford	Café at Daylesford Organic

→ Scotland

Edinburgh	Timberyard

Kingairloch	Boathouse
Thurso / Scrabster	Captain's Galley

→ Wales

Abergavenny / Llanddewi Skirrid	Walnut Tree

→ Republic of Ireland

Barna	O'Grady's on the Pier
Clonegall	Sha-Roe Bistro
Dingle	Chart House
Kinsale	Fishy Fishy

→ England

Ambleside	Drunken Duck Inn
Barnard Castle / Romaldkirk	Rose and Crown
Bath / Combe Hay	Wheatsheaf
Baughurst	Wellington Arms
Beverley / South Dalton	Pipe and Glass Inn
Bolnhurst	Plough at Bolnhurst
Bray	Hinds Head
Burford / Swinbrook	Swan Inn
Cambridge / Little Wilbraham	Hole in the Wall
Cirencester / Barnsley	Village Pub
Clipsham	Olive Branch and Beech House
Helmsley / Harome	Star Inn
Hetton	Angel Inn
Kendal / Crosthwaite	Punch Bowl Inn
Keyston	Pheasant
Kingham	The Wild Rabbit
Kirkby Lonsdale / Lupton	Plough
Knowstone	Masons Arms
● **LONDON**	
Southwark (Borough of)	Garrison
Longstock	Peat Spade Inn
Lower Froyle	The Anchor Inn
Marlow	Hand and Flowers
Mells	Talbot Inn
Midhurst / Henley	Duke of Cumberland Arms
Northaw	Sun at Northaw
Northleach	Wheatsheaf Inn
Oxford / Fyfield (Oxford)	White Hart
Southrop	Swan
Stockbridge	Greyhound on the Test
Stoke-by-Nayland	Crown

Stow-on-the-Wold / Nether Westcote	Feathered Nest
Sutton-on-the-Forest	Rose and Crown
Thorpe Market	Gunton Arms
Tisbury	Beckford Arms
West Meon	Thomas Lord
Wiswell	Freemasons
Woodbridge / Bromeswell	British Larder
Wymondham	Berkeley Arms

→ Wales

Aberaeron	Harbourmaster
Brecon	Felin Fach Griffin
Skenfrith	Bell at Skenfrith

→ Republic of Ireland

Kinsale	Toddies at The Bulman

Hotels with Spas 2015

Extensive facility for relaxation & well-being

➜ England

Abberley	The Elms
Ascot	Coworth Park
Ashford (Kent)	Eastwell Manor
Aylesbury	Hartwell House
Bagshot	Pennyhill Park
Barnard Castle / Greta Bridge	Morritt
Bath	Bath Priory
Bath	Bath Spa
Bath	Homewood Park
Bath	Royal Crescent
Bath / Colerne	Lucknam Park
Birmingham	Hotel Du Vin
Birmingham	Hotel Indigo
Birmingham	Hyatt Regency
Birmingham	Malmaison
Blackburn / Mellor (Lancs)	Stanley House
Bolton Abbey	Devonshire Arms Country House
Bradford-on-Avon	Woolley Grange
Broadway	Dormy House
Broadway	Lygon Arms
Brockenhurst	New Park Manor
Calne	Bowood
Cambridge	Varsity
Cheltenham	Ellenborough Park
Cheltenham	Montpellier Chapter
Cheltenham / Shurdington	Greenway
Chester	Chester Grosvenor
Chester	DoubleTree by Hilton Chester
Chichester	Goodwood
Chipping Campden	Cotswold House H. and Spa
Christchurch	Captain's Club
Christchurch	Christchurch Harbour
Cirencester / Barnsley	Barnsley House
Cowley	Cowley Manor
Crewe	Crewe Hall
Cuckfield	Ockenden Manor
Darlington / Headlam	Headlam Hall
Darlington / Hurworth-on-Tees	Rockliffe Hall
Dartmouth	Dart Marina
Daventry	Fawsley Hall
Dogmersfield	Four Seasons
Eastbourne	Grand
Evershot	Summer Lodge
Exeter	Magdalen Chapter

Falmouth	St Michael's H and Spa
Forest Row	Ashdown Park
Frome	Babington House
Grasmere	Daffodil
Guernsey / St Martin	Bella Luce
Guernsey / St Peter Port	Old Government House H. and Spa
Guildford	Radisson Blu Edwardian
Harrogate	Hotel du Vin
Harrogate	Rudding Park
Helmsley	Feversham Arms
Hexham / Slaley	Slaley Hall
Hook	Tylney Hall
Jersey / St Brelades Bay	L'Horizon
Jersey / St Helier	Club Hotel and Spa
Jersey / St Helier	Grand Jersey
Jersey / St Helier	Royal Yacht
King's Lynn / Grimston	Congham Hall
Littlehampton	Bailiffscourt H. and Spa

LONDON

Camden	Rosewood London
City of Westminster	45 Park Lane
City of Westminster	Berkeley
City of Westminster	Bulgari
City of Westminster	Café Royal
City of Westminster	Connaught
City of Westminster	Corinthia
City of Westminster	Dorchester
City of Westminster	Four Seasons
City of Westminster	Grosvenor House
City of Westminster	Ham Yard
City of Westminster	InterContinental
City of Westminster	Jumeirah Lowndes
City of Westminster	Langham
City of Westminster	Mandarin Oriental Hyde Park
City of Westminster	Metropolitan
City of Westminster	Montcalm
City of Westminster	Sanderson
City of Westminster	Sofitel London St James
City of Westminster	The Landmark London
City of Westminster	W London
Heathrow Airport	Hilton London Heathrow Airport Terminal 5
Heathrow Airport	Sofitel
Hounslow	Hilton London Syon Park
Kensington and Chelsea	Chelsea Harbour
Kensington and Chelsea	Jumeirah Carlton Tower
Kings Cross St Pancras	St Pancras Renaissance
Lambeth	London Marriott H. County Hall
Wandsworth (Borough of)	Hotel Verta

London Stansted Airport	Radisson Blu H. London Stansted Airport
Luton	Luton Hoo
Lyndhurst	Lime Wood
Maidenhead	Fredrick's
Malmesbury	Whatley Manor
Manchester	Lowry
Manchester	Radisson Edwardian
Marlow	Danesfield House
Matfen	Matfen Hall
Melton Mowbray	Stapleford Park
Mere	Mere
Midhurst	Spread Eagle
Midhurst / Bepton	Park House
Nantwich	Rookery Hall
New Milton	Chewton Glen
Newbury	Donnington Valley H. and Spa
Newby Bridge	Lakeside
Newby Bridge	Swan
Newquay / Mawgan Porth	Bedruthan
Newquay / Mawgan Porth	Scarlet
Newquay / Watergate Bay	Watergate Bay
North Bovey	Bovey Castle
Oxford	Randolph
Rock / Trebetherick	St Moritz
Salcombe	Salcombe Harbour
Scarborough	Crown Spa
Seaham	Seaham Hall
Shepton Mallet	Charlton House
Sittingbourne	Hempstead House
Stoke Poges	Stoke Park
Stratford-upon-Avon	Welcombe H. Spa and Golf Club
Sutton Coldfield	New Hall
Sutton Coldfield	The Belfry
Taplow	Cliveden
Tetbury	Calcot Manor
Thornton Hough	Thornton Hall
Thurlestone	Thurlestone
Turners Hill	Alexander House
Warminster	Bishopstrow and Spa
Watford	Grove
Weybridge	Brooklands
Whitby	Raithwaite Hall
Wight (Isle of) / Wootton Bridge	Lakeside Park
Wilmington	Rowhill Grange
Winchester	Winchester
Wrea Green	Spa
Wynyard	Wynyard Hall
York	Cedar Court Grand H. and Spa
York	Middlethorpe Hall

➜ Scotland

Arran (Isle of)	Auchrannie
Auchterarder	Gleneagles
Balloch	Cameron House
Bishopton	Mar Hall
Dundee	Apex City Quay
Edinburgh	Balmoral
Edinburgh	Caledonian
Edinburgh	Scotsman
Edinburgh	Sheraton Grand H. and Spa
Edinburgh / Ingliston	Norton House
Eriska (Isle of)	Isle of Eriska
Glasgow	Blythswood Square
New Cumnock	Lochside House
St Andrews	Fairmont St Andrews
St Andrews	Old Course H. Golf Resort and Spa
Turnberry	Turnberry

➜ Wales

Cardiff	St David's H. and Spa
Llandudno	Bodysgallen Hall
Llandudno / Deganwy	Quay H. and Spa
Llangammarch Wells	Lake Country House and Spa
Newport (Newport)	Celtic Manor Resort
Pembroke	Lamphey Court
Saundersfoot	St Brides Spa

➜ Northern Ireland

Ballymena / Galgorm	Galgorm Resort and Spa
Enniskillen	Lough Erne Resort
Holywood	Culloden
Newcastle	Burrendale H. and Country Club
Newcastle	Slieve Donard

➜ Republic of Ireland

Ardmore	Cliff House
Arthurstown	Dunbrody Country House
Athlone	Sheraton Athlone
Aughrim	Brooklodge H and Wells Spa
Ballina	Ice House
Ballyconnell	Slieve Russell
Ballyfarnan	Kilronan Castle
Castlebaldwin	Cromleach Lodge
Castlemartyr	Castlemartyr
Cavan	Radisson Blu Farnham Estate
Clifden	Clifden Station House
Clonakilty	Inchydoney Island Lodge and Spa

Cork	Hayfield Manor
Donegal	Solis Lough Eske Castle
Doonbeg	Trump International H. and Golf Links
Dublin	Marker
Dublin	Shelbourne
Dublin / Ballsbridge	Four Seasons
Dunboyne	Dunboyne Castle
Enniscorthy	Monart
Enniskerry	Powerscourt
Fota Island	Fota Island
Galway	G
Galway	Radisson Blu H. and Spa
Glaslough	Lodge at Castle Leslie Estate
Gweedore	Gweedore Court
Horse and Jockey	Horse and Jockey
Kenmare	Park
Killarney	Aghadoe Heights H. and Spa
Killarney	Europe
Killarney	Killarney Park
Limerick	Absolute H. and Spa
Limerick	Radisson Blu H. and Spa
Naas	Killashee House H. and Villa Spa
Newmarket on Fergus	Dromoland Castle
Rosslare	Kelly's Resort
Straffan	K Club
Thomastown	Mount Juliet
Westport	Knockranny House H and Spa
Wexford	Whites

Index of towns

Index of towns

C

H

I

J

K

L

S

T

POPULATION - Source:
ONS / Office for National Statistics (www.statistics.gov.uk) [census 2011]
CSO / Central Statistics Office (www.cso.ie) [census 2011]

Michelin Travel Partner

Société par actions simplifiées au capital de 11 288 880 €
27 Cours de l'Ile Seguin - 92100 Boulogne Billancourt (France)
R.C.S. Nanterre 433 677 721

©Michelin, Propriétaires-Éditeurs
Dépôt légal September 2014

Printed in Italy - August 2014
Printed on paper from sustainably managed forests

Compogravure : JOUVE, Saran (France)

Impression et Finition : Lego (Italy)

Our editorial team has taken the greatest care in writing this guide and checking the information in it. However, practical information (prices, addresses, telephone numbers, internet addresses, etc) is subject to frequent change and such information should therefore be used for guidance only. It is possible that some of the information in this guide may not be accurate or exhaustive as at the date of publication.
We therefore accept no liability in regard to such information.